SECT___ _____ _
___ _____ _

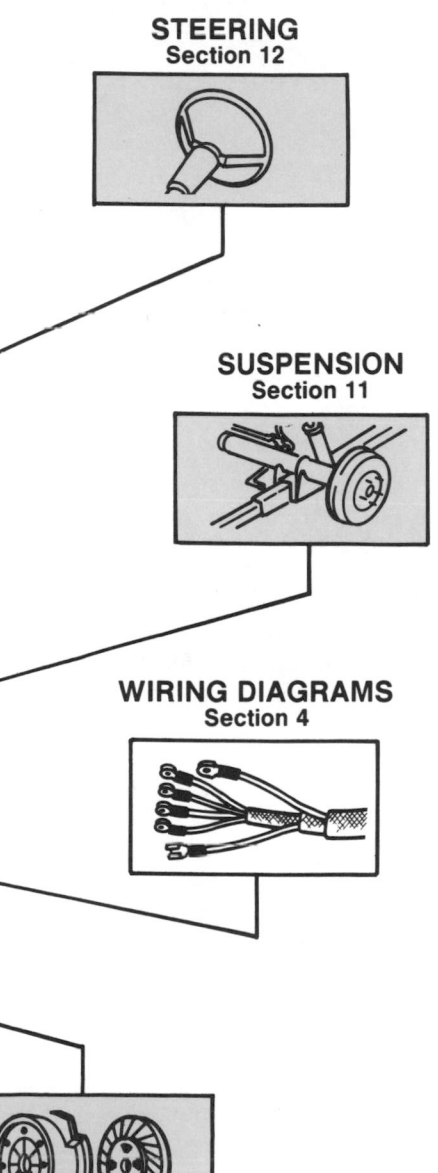

STEERING
Section 12

SUSPENSION
Section 11

WIRING DIAGRAMS
Section 4

CLUTCHES
Section 7

ENGINES
Section 6

ENGINE COOLING
Section 6a

CLUTCHES
Section 7

DRIVE AXLES
Section 8

BRAKES
Section 9

WHEEL ALIGNMENT
Section 10

SUSPENSION
Section 11

STEERING
Section 12

TRANSMISSION SERVICING
Section 13

LATEST CHANGES & CORRECTIONS

GENERAL INDEX

REFERENCE

PREFACE

This is the 1988 edition of Mitchell's
Domestic Car Service and Repair Manual, Volume II.
This manual, like the many Mitchell publications which have preceded it,
represents our commitment to professionalism
in the automotive service market.

The automotive industry advances every year,
and Mitchell pledges to advance and improve
its products as we maintain the quality and usefulness of all
our publications.

We cordially acknowledge the good will
and mutual goals that exist in the automotive business,
and it is in this spirit that we thank the automotive manufacturers,
distributors, dealers and the entire automotive industry
for their fine cooperation and assistance
which have made this manual possible.

The Standard in Professional Estimating and Repair Information.

1988 DOMESTIC CARS SERVICE & REPAIR

ENGINE CHASSIS

VOLUME II

Published by
MITCHELL INTERNATIONAL, INC.
P.O. BOX 26260
SAN DIEGO, CALIFORNIA 92126

ISBN 0-8470-0878-9

Mitchell International, Inc.

ACKNOWLEDGEMENT | Mitchell International, Inc. thanks the domestic manufacturers, distributors, and dealers for their generous cooperation and assistance which make this manual possible.

Chrysler Motors
Ford Motor Company
General Motors Corporation
Jeep/Eagle

EDITORIAL

Product Managers
Daniel M. Kelley
David R. Koontz
Daryl F. Visser

Art Director
Terry L. Blomquist
Graphics Supervisor
Judie LaPierre

Detroit Editors
Lynn D. Meeker
Andy Henry

Senior Editors
David L. Skora
Eddie Santangelo
Roger Leftridge
Chuck Vedra
Ronald E. Garrett

Technical Editors
Ramiro Gutierrez
Richard H. King
Scott A. Olsen
Bob Reel
Don Brudos
Brian Styve
David W. Himes
John M. Fisher
Christopher C. Chaney
Eddie L. Dorszynski, Jr.
Mark Zdeb
David R. Costantino
James A. Wafford
James A. Hawes
Tom L. Hall
Patrick G. San Nicolas
Alex A. Solis

ELECTRICAL

Senior Editor
Matthew Krimple

Electrical Editors
Leonard McVicker
Santiago Llano
Mike Debreceni
Harry Piper
Kelly Krueger
Michael Wertz
Lloyd Adams

Published By

MITCHELL INTERNATIONAL, INC.
9889 Willow Creek Road
P.O. Box 26260
San Diego, California 92126-0260

For Subscription Information:
CALL TOLL FREE 800–854-7030. In California CALL TOLL FREE 800–421-0159.
Or WRITE: P.O. Box 26260, San Diego, CA 92126-0260

ISBN 0-8470-0879-7

Introduction

You now have the most complete and up-to-date Service and Repair Manual available to the professional mechanic. Our staff of experts has spent thousands of hours gathering and processing service and repair information from sources throughout the automotive industry. More than 500 separate articles, providing step-by-step Testing, Adjusting and Repair procedures for 1988 Domestic Cars, are contained in this year's two-volume edition.

To use this manual in the most efficient and profitable way possible, please take the time to read the following instruction, "How To Find the Information". This will enable you to quickly locate the car model and the mechanical procedure you need, without wasting time thumbing through unnecessary pages.

HOW TO FIND THE INFORMATION

3 Quick Steps

(1) On the inside cover, you'll find the contents of this manual. Locate the section you want, and notice that it has a Black square next to it.

THUMB INDEX SPOT

ENGINES	
Section 6	

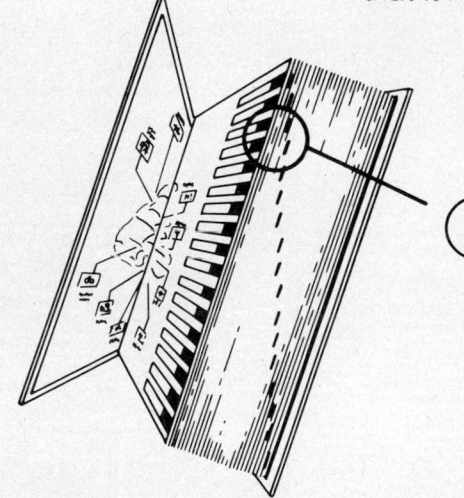

(2) Looking along the right edge of the book, you'll notice additional Black squares.

Match the Black square of the section listed on the cover with the Black square in line with it on the book's edge, then turn directly to that section.

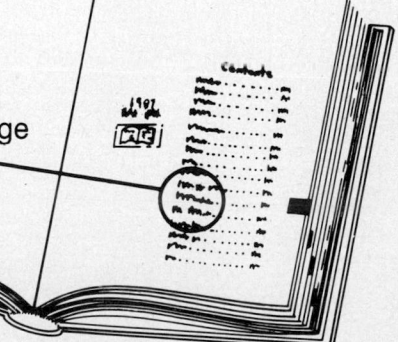

(3) Review the section contents page.

After locating the specific article and starting page needed, turn to the beginning of the article.

OR...

Determine, which volume you require...Volume I for Tune-Up and Electrical information, Volume II for Engine or Chassis information. Go directly to the expanded GENERAL INDEX located at the rear of that manual.
Go to the section covering the make of vehicle you are working on. Use the alphabetical guide as you would any type of reference index.

Section G

GENERAL INFORMATION

CONTENTS

NOTE: ALSO SEE GENERAL INDEX

VIN Code Explanation

ALL MANUFACTURERS

1G1AZ37AGJ5 100001

① ② ③ ④ ⑤ ⑥ ⑦ ⑧ ⑨ ⑩ ⑪ ⑫ ⑬ ⑭ ⑮ ⑯ ⑰

① Indicates Nation of Origin.
② Indicates Manufacturer.
③ Indicates Make and Type.
④ Indicates Restraint System (Engine Type for Eagle Premier).
⑤ Indicates Carline/Series. (Transmisson/Transaxle/Transfer Case for Eagle Premier).
⑥ Indicates Body Types.
⑦⑧ Indicates Engine Type and Make (Trim Package/Restraint System for Eagle Premier).
⑨ Indicates Check Digit.
⑩ Indicates Model Year.
⑪ Indicates Assembly Plant.
⑫⑬⑭⑮⑯⑰ Indicates Plant Sequential Number.

CHRYSLER MOTORS VIN ENGINE CODES

Code Digit	Engine
A	2.2L 4-Cyl. MPFI Turbo II
D	2.2L 4-Cyl. TBI
E	2.2L 4-Cyl. MPFI Turbo I
K	2.5L 4-Cyl. TBI
3	3.0L V6 MPFI
P	5.2L V8 2-Bbl. Std.
4	5.2L V8 2-Bbl. H.D.
S	5.2L V8 4-Bbl. Police

EAGLE PREMIER VIN ENGINE CODES

Code Digit	Engine
Z	2.5L 4-Cyl. TBI
J	3.0L V6 MPFI

FORD MOTOR CO. VIN ENGINE CODES

Code Digit	Engine
9	1.9L 4-Cyl. CFI
J	1.9L 4-Cyl. MPFI H.O.
A	2.3L 4-Cyl. MPFI
X	2.3L 4-Cyl. MPFI HSC
S	2.3L 4-Cyl. MPFI HSO
T	2.3L 4-Cyl. MPFI Turbo
D	2.5L 4-Cyl. CFI HSC
U	3.0L V6 MPFI
4	3.8L V6 MPFI
F	5.0L V8 SEFI
E	5.0L V8 SEFI H.O.
G	5.8L V8 2-Bbl. Police

GENERAL MOTORS VIN ENGINE CODES

Code Digit	Engine
4	1.6L 4-Cyl. 2-Bbl.
5	1.6L 4-Cyl. EFI DOHC
K	2.0L 4-Cyl. TBI
M	2.0L 4-Cyl. MFI Turbo
1	2.0L 4-Cyl. TBI H.O.
D	2.3L 4-Cyl. MFI DOHC
R	2.5L 4-Cyl. TBI
U	2.5L 4-Cyl. TBI
S	2.8L V6 MPFI
W	2.8L V6 MFI
9	2.8L V6 MFI
L	3.0L V6 MFI
3	3.8L V6 SFI
C	3.8L V6 "3800" SFI
7	3.8L V6 SFI Turbo
7	4.1L V8 PFI
Z	4.3L V6 TBI
5	4.5L V8 DFI
G	5.0L V8 4-Bbl. H.O.
H	5.0L V8 4-Bbl.
Y	5.0L V8 4-Bbl.
E	5.0L V8 TBI
F	5.0L V8 TPI
6	5.7L V8 4-Bbl. Police
8	5.7L V8 TPI

VIN DATE CODES ⑩

Code	Model Year
A	1980
B	1981
C	1982
D	1983
E	1984
F	1985
G	1986
H	1987
J	1988

ALL MANUFACTURERS

ENGINE SIZE CONVERSIONS

CHRYSLER MOTORS ENGINES

Liters	Cubic Inches
2.2 4-Cyl.	135
2.5 4-Cyl.	153
3.0 V6	181
5.2 V8	318

EAGLE PREMIER ENGINES

Liters	Cubic Inches
2.5 4-Cyl.	150
3.0 V6	180

FORD MOTOR CO. ENGINES

Liters	Cubic Inches
1.9 4-Cyl.	116
2.3 4-Cyl.	140
2.5 4-Cyl.	153
3.0 V6	182
3.8 V6	232
5.0 V8	302
5.8 V8	351

GENERAL MOTORS ENGINES

Liters	Cubic Inches
1.6 4-Cyl.	97
2.0 4-Cyl.	122
2.3 4-Cyl.	138
2.5 4-Cyl.	151
2.8 V6	173
3.0 V6	181
3.8 V6	231
4.1 V8	250
4.3 V6	262
4.5 V8	273
5.0 V8 (Chevrolet Built)	305
5.0 V8 (Oldsmobile Built)	307
5.7 V8	350

MODEL USAGE

Because many models produced by the domestic manufacturers share the same frame, powertrain and chassis components, Mitchell does not always list all the models in a given article. The following charts show the models as they are called out by Mitchell, and the complete model list for those same models according to the manufacturer.

1988 CHRYSLER MOTORS MODELS

Mitchell Application	Actual Models
Aries America	"LE" Coupe, Sedan & Wagon
Caravelle	Base, "SE" Sedans
Daytona	Base, Pacifica, Shelby "Z" Hatchbacks
Diplomat	Base, "SE" Sedans
Dynasty	Base, "LE" Sedans

1988 CHRYSLER MOTORS MODELS (Cont.)

Mitchell Application	Actual Models
Fifth Avenue	Sedan
Gran Fury	Sedan
Horizon America	Hatchback
Lancer	Base, "ES" Sedans
LeBaron	Base Coupe, Convertible, Sedan & Wagon
LaBaron GTS	Sedan
New Yorker	Sedan
New Yorker Landau	Sedan
New Yorker Turbo	Sedan
Omni America	Hatchback
Reliant America	Sedan & Wagon
Shadow	Base, "ES" Hatchbacks
Sundance	Hatchback
600	Base, "ES" Sedans

1988 EAGLE PREMIER MODELS

Mitchell Application	Actual Models
Eagle Premier	Sedan

1988 FORD MOTOR CO. MODELS

Mitchell Application	Actual Models
Continental	Base, Signature Sedans
Cougar	"LS", "XR7" Coupes
Escort	"GL", "GT", "EXP" Hatchbacks & "GL" Wagon
Grand Marquis	"GS", "LS" Sedans & Colony Park "GS", "LS" Wagons
Lincoln Town Car	Base, Signature, Cartier Sedans
LTD Crown Victoria	Base, "LX" Sedans & Wagons & LTD Country Squire, "LX" Wagons
Mark VII	"LSC", Bill Blass Coupes
Mustang	"LX", "GT" Hatchbacks & Convertibles & "LX" Sedan
Sable	"GS", "LS" Sedans & Wagons
Taurus	"GL", "L", "LX" Sedans & Wagons & "MT-5" Sedan
Tempo	"GL", "GLS", "LX", "ALL WHEEL DRIVE" Sedans
Thunderbird	Base, "LX", "SPORT", "TURBO" Coupes
Topaz	"GS", "LS", "LS SPORT", "XR5" Sedans

1988 GENERAL MOTORS – BUICK

Mitchell Application	Actual Models
Century	Custom Coupe, Sedan & Wagon, Limited Coupe & Sedan, & Estate Wagon
Electra	Limited, Park Ave., "T" Type Sedans
Electra Estate Wagon	Wagon
LeSabre	Base, Custom, Limited, "T" Type Coupes & Sedans
LeSabre Estate Wagon	Wagon
Regal (FWD)	Base, Custom, Limited Coupes
Regal (RWD)	Base, Limited Coupes
Riviera, Reatta	Base Coupe
Skyhawk	Custom Coupe, Sedan & Wagon & Sport Coupe
Skylark	Custom, Limited Coupes & Sedans

ALL MANUFACTURERS (Cont.)

1988 GENERAL MOTORS – CADILLAC

Mitchell Application	Actual Models
Allanté	Convertible
Brougham	Sedan
Cimarron	Sedan
DeVille	Coupe & Sedan
Eldorado	Coupe
Fleetwood	D'Elegance, Sixty Special Sedans
Seville	Sedan

1988 GENERAL MOTORS – CHEVROLET

Mitchell Application	Actual Models
Beretta	Base, "GT" Coupes
Camaro	Sport, "IROC-Z" Coupes & "IROC-Z" Convertible
Caprice	Base, "LS", Brougham Sedans & Classic Wagon
Cavalier	Base Coupe, Sedan & Wagon & "RS" Coupe & Sedan, & "Z24" Coupe & Convertible
Celebrity	Base, Eurosport Coupes, Sedans & Wagons
Corvette	Coupe & Convertible
Corsica	Base, "LT" Sedans
Monte Carlo	"LS", "SS" Coupes
Nova	Hatchback, Notchback Sedans & Twin Cam Notchback Sedan

1988 GENERAL MOTORS – OLDSMOBILE

Mitchell Application	Actual Models
Cutlass Calais	Base, "SL", International Coupes & Sedans
Cutlass Ciera	"LS", "SL", International Coupes & "LS", Brougham, International Sedans & "LS", Brougham, International Cruiser Wagons
Cutlass Supreme Classic	Base, Brougham Coupes
Cutlass Supreme	Base, "SL", International Coupes
Customer Cruiser	Base Wagon
Delta 88	Royale, Brougham Coupes & Sedans
Firenza	Base Coupe, Sedan & Wagon
Ninety-Eight	Brougham, Regency Sedans
Toronado	Base, Trofeo Coupes

1988 GENERAL MOTORS – PONTIAC

Mitchell Application	Actual Models
Bonneville	"LE", "SE", "SSE" Sedans
Fiero	Base, Sport, "GT" Coupes
Firebird	Base, Trans Am Coupes
Grand Am	Base, "LE", "SE" Coupes & Sedans
Grand Prix	"LE", "SE" Coupes
Safari	Wagon
Sunbird	Base, "GT" Sedans & "SE", "GT" Coupes & Convertibles & "SE","GT" Hatchbacks & Base Wagon
6000	Base, "LE", "SE" Sedans & Wagons, & "STE" Sedan

MODEL IDENTIFICATION

Repair procedures in these manuals are sometimes identified by body types. The following tables list body types, divisions (when applicable) and model names.

1988 CHRYSLER MOTORS MODEL IDENTIFICATION TABLE

Body Type	Model Name
"C" Body (FWD)	
Chrysler	New Yorker
Dodge	Dynasty
"E" Body (FWD)	
Chrysler	New Yorker Turbo
Dodge	600
Plymouth	Caravelle
"G" Body (FWD)	
Dodge	Daytona
"H" Body (FWD)	
Chrysler	LeBaron GTS
Dodge	Lancer
"J" Body (FWD)	
Chrysler	LeBaron Coupe & Convertible
"K" Body (FWD)	
Chrysler	LeBaron Sedan & Wagon
Dodge	Aries America
Plymouth	Reliant America
"L" Body (FWD)	
Dodge	Omni America
Plymouth	Horizon America
"M" Body (RWD)	
Chrysler	Fifth Avenue
Dodge	Diplomat
Plymouth	Grand Fury
"P" Body (FWD)	
Dodge	Shadow
Plymouth	Sundance

1988 EAGLE PREMIER MODEL IDENTIFICATION TABLE

Body Type	Model Name
"55" Body	Eagle Premier

1988 GENERAL MOTORS MODEL IDENTIFICATION TABLE

Body Type & Division	Model Name
"A" Body (FWD)	
Buick	Century
Chevrolet	Celebrity
Oldsmobile	Cutlass Ciera, Cutlass Cruiser
Pontiac	6000
"B" Body (RWD)	
Buick	LeSabre Wagon, Electra Wagon
Chevrolet	Caprice
Oldsmobile	Custom Cruiser
Pontiac	Safari
	Police models

1988 GENERAL MOTORS
MODEL IDENTIFICATION TABLE (Cont.)

Body Type & Division	Model Name
"C" Body (FWD)	
Buick	Electra
Cadillac	DeVille, Fleetwood
Oldsmobile	Ninety-Eight
"D" Body (RWD)	
Cadillac	Brougham
"E" Body (FWD)	
Buick	Riviera, Reatta
Cadillac	Eldorado
Oldsmobile	Toronado
"F" Body (RWD)	
Chevrolet	Camaro
Pontiac	Firebird
"G" Body (RWD)	
Buick	Regal GN
Chevrolet	Monte Carlo
Oldsmobile	Cutlass Supreme Classic
"H" Body (FWD)	
Buick	LeSabre
Oldsmobile	Delta 88
Pontiac	Bonneville
"J" Body (FWD)	
Buick	Skyhawk
Cadillac	Cimarron
Chevrolet	Cavalier
Oldsmobile	Firenza
Pontiac	Sunbird
"K" Body (FWD)	
Cadillac	Seville
"L" Body (FWD)	
Chevrolet	Beretta, Corsica
"N" Body (FWD)	
Buick	Skylark
Oldsmobile	Cutlass Calais
Pontiac	Grand Am
"P" Body (RWD)	
Pontiac	Fiero
"S" Body (FWD)	
Chevrolet	Nova
"V" Body (FWD)	
Cadillac	Allanté
"W" Body (FWD)	
Buick	Regal
Oldsmobile	Cutlass Supreme
Pontiac	Grand Prix
"Y" Body (RWD)	
Chevrolet	Corvette

Mitchell's Abbreviations

ABBREVIATIONS MOST OFTEN USED (Cont.)

EEC – Electronic Engine Control
EEC – Evaporative Emission Control
EFI – Electronic Fuel Injection
EFE – Early Fuel Evaporator
EGO – Exhaust Gas Oxygen
EGO Sens. Gnd. – EGO Sensor Ground
EGR – Exhaust Gas Recirculation
EGRC – EGR Control
EGRV – EGR Vent
EIS – Electronic Ignition System
ELC – Electronic Level (Load) Control
Elec. – Electric
Elect. – Electronic
Emis. or Emiss. – Emission
Eng. – Engine
EPA – Environmental Protection Agency
ESA – Electronic Spark Advance
ESC – Electronic Spark Control
EST – Electronic Spark Timing
Evap. – Evaporator or Evaporative
EVRV – Electronic Vacuum Regulator Valve
Exc. – Except or Excluding
Exch. – Exchange
Exh. – Exhaust
Ext. – Exterior

F

F or F° – Fahrenheit
F/B – Fuse Box or Block
F/B – Feedback
FBC – Feedback Carburetor
Fed. – Federal
FFOT – Ford Fixed Orifice Tube
FICD – Fuel Injection Control Device
Flshr. – Flasher
Freq. – Frequency
Fnt. – Front
Fnt. WD – Front Wheel Drive
F/Rly. Pnl. – Fuse/Relay Panel
Frwd. – Forward
Ft. Lbs. or ft. lbs. – Foot Pounds
Fus. – Fusible
4WD – Four-Wheel Drive
FWD – Front Wheel Drive

G

g – Grams
Ga. – Gauge
Gal. or Gals. – gallons
Gen. – Generator
Gnd. – Ground
Gov. – Governor

H

Harn. – Harness
Haz. – Hazard
HC – Hydrocarbons
H/D – Heavy Duty
Headlt. – Headlight
HEI – High Energy Ignition
Hg – Mercury
Hgt. – Height
Hi. – High
Hi. Alt. or High Alt. – High Altitude
Hi-Spd. – High Speed
Hndl. – Handle
HO – High Ouput
HP – Horsepower
HP – High Performance
Hrn. – Horn
Hsg. – Housing
Htr. – Heater

HTR – Heavy Truck
Hyd. – Hydraulic
Hz – Hertz (Cycles Per Second)

I

IAC – Idle Air Control
IAS – Idle Air Stepper
IC – Integrated Circuit
I.D. – Inside Diameter
Ign. – Ignition
Ign. Gnd. – Ignition Ground
Ign. Mod. Sens. – Ignition Module Sensor
IIA – Integrated Ignition Assembly
ILC – Idle Load Control
Illum. – Illumination
In. – Inch or Inches
Incand. – Incandescent
INCH Lbs. – Inch Pounds
Ind. – Indicator
Infl. – Inflate
Info. – Information
In. Hg – Inches of Mercury
Inhib. – Inhibitor
Inj. – Injector or Injection
IN. Lbs. – Inch Pounds
Inp. – Input
Inst. – Instrument
Int. – Interior
Interm. – Intermittent
Intrpt. – Interrupt
Invrtr. – Inverter
ISC – Idle Speed Control
ISS – Idle Stop Solenoid

J

J/B – Junction Box
Jmpr. – Jumper
Junc. – Junction

K

KAPWR – Keep Alive Power
kg – Kilograms
kg/cm² – Kilograms Per Square Centimeter
k/ohms – 1000 ohms
Key. – Keyless

L

L – Liter
Lat. – Latched
Lbs. – Pounds
LCD – Liquid Crystal Display
L/D – Light Duty Emissions
LED – Light Emitting Diode
L. Fnt. – Left Front
LFT – Left
Lftgte. – Liftgate
LH – Left-hand
Lic. – License
Lk. – Lock
Lo. – Low
Lps. – Lamps
LR – Left Rear
Lt. – Light
Lt. Duty – Light Duty
Ltr. – Lighter
Ltr. – Limiter
Lug. – Luggage
L4 – Straight 4-Cylinder
L6 – Straight 6-Cylinder

M

Ma – Milliamps
MAF – Mass Airflow
Mag. – Magnetic
Maint. – Maintenance
Man. – Manifold
Man. Trans. – Manual Transaxle or Transmission
Man. Stg. – Manual Steering
MAP – Manifold Absolute Pressure
MAT – Manifold Air Temperature
MCU – Microprocessor Control Unit
Mem. – Memory
Merc. – Mercury
Mess. – Message
Mfd. – Microfarads
Mir. – Mirror
Mixt. – Mixture
mkg – Meter Kilogram
Mm – Millimeters
Mod. – Module
MPC – Manifold Pressure Controlled
MPH – Miles Per Hour
MPI – Multi-Point Injection
Mtr. – Motor
M/T – Manual Transaxle or Transmission

N

"N" – Neutral Position
N.m – Newton Meter
NCA – No Color Available
Neut. – Neutral
No. or # – Number
Norm. – Normal
NOx – Oxides of Nitrogen

O

OBC – On-Board Computer
OC – Oxidation Catalyst
OL – Open Loop
Oper. – Operated
Opt. – Options or Optional
O/D – Overdrive
O₂ – Oxygen
Ozs. – Ounces

P

"P" – "PARK" Position
Pass. – Passenger
P/C – Printed Circuit
PCV – Positive Crankcase Ventilation
PFI – Port Fuel Injection
PGM-FI – Programmed Fuel Injection
PIP – Profile Ignition Pick-Up
Pkg. – Package
P/N – Park/Neutral
Pneu. – Pneumatic
Pnl. – Panel
Pos. – Positive
Postn. – Position
Pot. – Potentiometer
PPM – Parts Per Million
Pres. – Pressure
Prgmr. – Programmer
Pri. – Primary
PRNDL – Park, Reverse, Neutral, Drive, Low
Prom. – Programmable
P/S – Power Steering
psi – Pounds Per Square Inch
P/S Pres. Sw. – Power Steering Pressure Switch
PTO – Power Take Off
Pts. – Pints
Pwr. – Power

ABBREVIATIONS MOST OFTEN USED (Cont.)

Q

Qts. – Quarts

R

R – Rear
R/B – Relay Box
Rad. – Radiator
Recirc. – Recirculator
Ref. – Reference
Reg. – Regulator
Rel. – Release
Res. – Resistor
Resist. – Resistance
Retrac. – Retract or Retractor
Rev. – Revolution
Rheo. – Rheostat
Rly. – Relay
RPM – Revolutions Per Minute
Rsm. – Resume
Rt. – Right
Rtd. – Retard
Rt. Fnt. – Right Front
RH or RTH – Right-hand
Rtrn. – Return
RWD – Rear Wheel Drive

S

S/B – Seat Belt
SCC – Spark Control Computer
Sec. – Secondary
Sel. – Selector or Selection
Sen. or Sens. – Sensor
Send. – Sender or Sending
Sfty. – Safety
Sig. – Signal
Sol. – Solenoid

Sole-Vac. – Solenoid Vacuum
Spd. – Speed
Speedo. – Speedometer
SPFI – Sequential Port
 Fuel Injection
SRS – Supplementary Restraint
 System
SSI – Solid State Ignition
St. – Start
Sta. Wag. – Station Wagon
Stop Lt. – Stop Light
Strkr. – Striker
Strtr. – Starter
Std. – Standard
Strng. – Steering
Supp. – Supply
Susp. – Suspension
Sw. – Switch
Sys. – System

T

TAB – Thermactor Air By-Pass
TAC – Thermostatic Air
 Cleaner
Tach. – Tachometer
TAD – Thermactor Air Diverter
Taillt. – Taillight
TBI – Throttle Body Injection
TCC – Torque Converter Clutch
TDC – Top Dead Center
Temp. – Temperature
Term. – Terminal
TFI – Thick Film Integrated
Therm. – Thermostat
Throt. – Throttle
TPS or Th. Sens. – Throttle Position Sensor
T-Q – Thermo-Quad
Trans. – Transaxle/Transmission
Transis. – Transistor
Trnsmtr. – Transmitter
Tripmdr. – Tripminder

Turbo – Turbocharged
T.V. – Throttle Valve
TVS – Thermal Vacuum Switch
TWC – Three Way Catalytic
Twilt. – Twilight
2WD – 2-Wheel Drive
Typ. – Typical

U

Unlat. – Unlatched

V

V – Volts
V6 – V6 Engine
V8 – V8 Engine
Vac. – Vacuum
Var. – Variable
VATS – Vehicle Anti-Theft System
Vert. – Vertical
VIN – Vehicle Identification
 Number
Vlv. – Valve
Volt. – Voltage
V. Pwr. – Vehicle Power
VSS – Vehicle Speed Sensor

W

Warn. – Warning
Wshr. – Washer
W/B – Wheelbase
Wdo. – Window
Wip. – Wiper
W/Shield – Windshield
WOT – Wide Open Throttle
W/ – With
W/O – Without

Mitchell's Abbreviations

ABBREVIATIONS MOST OFTEN USED

NOTE: The following list of abbreviations, used most frequently in Mitchell's Service & Repair Manuals, is provided for your assistance. Although the majority of these abbreviations will be found in Mitchell's Wiring Diagrams, you may also find some of them used in articles dealing with Tune-Up, CEC, Emission, Fuel Systems, Electrical, Air Conditioning, Body Repair and other such subjects.

CAUTION: As some abbreviations may have more than one application, exercise caution that the definition provided here is logical for your vehicle's situation. For example, reason would help you determine whether "Alt." stands for Alternator, Altitude or for neither (an unlisted) definition.

A

A – Amperes
AAC – Auxiliary Air Control
ABDC – After Bottom Dead Center
ABS – Anti-Lock Brake System
Abs. – Absolute
AC – Alternating Current
ACT – Air Charge Temperature
A/C – Air Conditioning
A/C Cltch. – A/C Clutch
Accel. – Accelerator
Accum. – Accumulator
Accy. – Accessory
A/Cl. – Air Cleaner
Actu. – Actuator
Actv. – Active
ACV – Air Control Valve
Adj. – Adjust or Adjustable
Adv. – Advance
AFC – Airflow Controlled
A.I.R. – Air Injection Reactor
Air. Sel. – Air Selector
ALCL – Assembly Line Communication Link
ALDL – Assembly Line Data (Diagnostic) Link
Alt. – Alternator
Alt. or Alti. – High Altitude Emissions
Amb. – Ambient
AMC – American Motors Corporation
Amm. – Ammeter
Amp – Ampere
Amp. – Amplifier
Ant. – Antenna
Anti.-Dsl. – Anti-Diesel
Antic. – Anticipate
Assy. – Assembly (Wir. Diag. Only)
A/T – Automatic Transaxle or Transmission
ATDC – After Top Dead Center
ATC – Automatic Temperature Control
ATF – Automatic Transmission Fluid
Auto. – Automatic
Auto. Trans. – Automatic Transaxle or Transmission
Aux. – Auxiliary
AXOD – Automatic Overdrive Transaxle

B

Bap. Sens. – Barometric Absolute Pressure Sensor
Baro. – Barometric
Batt. – Battery
BBDC – Before Bottom Dead Center
Bbl. – Barrel
BCM – Body Control Module
Blst. – Ballast
Blwr. – Blower
Brkr. – Breaker
BTDC – Before Top Dead Center
Bulkhd. – Bulkhead
BTU – British Thermal Units

B/U – Back-Up
Buz. – Buzzer

C

C or C° – Celcius
C³I – Computer Controlled Coil Ignition
C4 – Computer Controlled Catalytic Converter
Calib. – Calibration
Calif. – California
Can. – Canada
Can. – Canister
Can. Prg. – Canister Purge
Canc. – Cancel
Cap. – Capacitor or Capacity
Carb. – Carburetor
CARB – California Air Resources Board
CB – Circuit Breaker
CC – Cruise Control
cc – Cubic Centimeters
CCC – Computer Command Control
CCOT – Cycling Clutch Orifice Tube
CCP – Controlled Canister Purge
CCW – Counterclockwise
CEC – Computerized Emission Control
CEC – Computerized Engine Control
CFI – Central Fuel Injection
Chng. – Change
Chg. – Charge or Charging
Chk. – Check
Chk. Eng. – Check Engine
CI – Cubic Inches
CID – Cubic Inch Displacement
Cig. – Cigarette
Cig. Ltr. – Cigarette Lighter
Circ. – Circuit
Circ. Brkr. – Circuit Breaker
CIS – Continuous Injection System
CIS-E – CIS-Electronic
Ckt. – Circuit
CL – Closed Loop
CLCC – Closed Loop Carburetor Control
Clch. – Clutch
Clmn. – Column
Clmt. – Climate
Clrnc. – Clearance
Clstr. – Cluster
CMH – Cold Mixture Heater
Cmpnstr. – Compensator
Cmptr. – Computer
Cntr. – Central or Center
Cnvnc. – Convenience
CO – Carbon Monoxide
CO₂ – Carbon Dioxide
Co-Ax. – Co-Axial
Colng. – Cooling
Colnt. – Coolant
Comb. – Combination
Comp. – Compressor
Compens – Compensation
Compt. – Compartment
Cond. – Condenser
Conn. – Connector or Connection

Cont. – Continued or Control
Conv. – Convertible or Converter
Convs. – Conversion
Count. – Counter
Crnr. – Corner
CRT – Cathode Ray Tube
CRTC – Cathode Ray Tube Controller
Ctrl. – Control
Ctrlld – Controlled
CTS – Coolant Temperature Switch
Ctsy. – Courtesy
Cu. In. – Cubic Inches
CV – Constant Velocity
CW – Clockwise
Cyl. – Cylinder

D

"D" – Drive
DC – Direct Current
Damp. – Damper
Decel. – Deceleration
Def. or Defog. – Defogger or Defroster
Deg. – Degree
De-Ice. – De-Icer
Del. – Delay
Desig. – Designation
Deton. – Detonation
Detec. – Detector
Detrnt. – Deterrent
DFI – Digital Fuel Injection
Dir. – Direction or Directional
Diag. – Diagnostic
Dig. – Digital
Dim. – Dimmer
Dist. or Distr. – Distributor
Disp. – Display
Dlx. – Deluxe
Dn. – Down
Dnshft. – Downshift
Dr. – Door
Drop. – Dropping
Drvr. – Driver
Dsl. – Diesel
Dstnc. – Distance

E

EAC – Electronic Air Control
EBCV – Electric Air Bleed Control Valve
ECA – Electronic Control Assembly
ECC – Electronic Chassis Control
ECC – Electronic Climate Control
ECC – Electronic Computer Control
ECCS – Electronic Concentrated Engine Control System
ECI – Electronically Controlled Injection
ECM – Electronic Control Module
Econ. – Economy
ECS – Emission Control System
ECT – Engine Coolant Temperature
ECU – Electronic Control Unit

Tool Applications

ALL MANUFACTURERS

DESCRIPTION

Tool applications used in this manual are noted in the text of all articles where applicable. These tools are usually specific tools that must be used to perform a specific function in Removal, Installation, Overhaul or Testing of a component.

For example; "Using Spline Adapter (J-28513) and Holding Wrench (J-28514), tighten pinion nut until end play is taken up." Although other tools could possibly be substituted, the tool references are those that are recommended by the vehicle manufacturer. These tools should be used whenever possible. Normally, in cases where a non-specific tool is called for, no tool number will be given.

For example; "Place bearing insert in rod and install guides on rod bolts. Compress piston rings using ring compressor." Since about any ring compressor that works and does not damage the components can be used, normally no specific tool number will be called out.

The following descriptions show an example of the reference in text, the maker of the tools recommended by the manufacturer and the tool maker's address. Further information on tools and local suppliers of the tools can be obtained from the tool maker. It is also possible, for example, that a Kent-Moore tool may be cross-referenced to another tool maker. In this case it is imperative that the tools be exactly the same in design, or the specific function of the tool may not be able to be performed.

CHRYSLER MOTORS

Chrysler Motors tool applications called out in this manual will appear as follows: "Assemble Pinion Locating Spacer (SP-6030) over body of main tool (SP-5385). Install Shaft Locating Sleeve (L-4507), Washer (C-4656) and Compression Nut (SP-533)."

The prefixes "C," "L" and "SP" mean that the tools are manufactured by Miller Special Tools. The number after the letter prefix is the basic tool part number. Any letters or numbers after the basic part number designate either a revised tool number or that the tool is part of a set.

CHRYSLER MOTORS TOOL MANUFACTURER

Miller Special Tools
Division of Utica Tool Co., Inc.
32615 Park Lane
Garden City, Mich. 48135
Telephone (313) 522-6717

FORD MOTOR CO.

Ford Motor Co. tool applications called out in this manual will appear as follows: "Remove pinion bearing with Slide Hammer (T50T-100A with Attachment T58L-101-A). Remove bearing with Puller (T81P-3504-S, T58L-101-A and T81P-3504-T)."

Ford Motor Co. tools are manufactured by Owatonna Tools. The prefix used with Ford tool numbers means that the tools are essential tools. The number after the prefix is the basic tool part number. Any letters or numbers after the basic part number designate either a revised tool number or that the tool is part of a set.

FORD MOTOR CO. TOOL MANUFACTURER

Owatonna Tool Co. Inc.
Owatonna, Minn. 55060
Telephone (507) 455-2626
Telex 29-0876

GENERAL MOTORS

General Motors tool applications called out in this manual will appear as follows; "Install Pivot Pin Remover (J-21854-1) and remove pins. Using Pin Punch (J-22635), drive out lever pin."

The "J" in front of the first set of numbers means that it is a Kent-Moore tool. The second set of numbers is the basic tool part number. Part numbers with no additional characters after the basic part number means that the tool listed is a complete tool. The last number means that it is either part of a set (-2,-3 etc.), or a revised tool number (-02,-03, or -B,-C etc,).

GENERAL MOTORS TOOL MANUFACTURER

Kent-Moore Tool Division
29784 Little Mack
Roseville, Mich., 48066-2298
Telephone (313) 774-9500
Telex 23-5377

JEEP/EAGLE

Eagle Premier tool applications called out in this manual will appear as follows: "Use Bearing Remover (J-21473-1) and Extension (J-21054-1) to drive out bearing." The "J" in front of the first set of numbers means that it is a Kent-Moore tool. The second set of numbers is the basic tool part number. Part numbers with no additional characters after the basic part number means that the tool listed is a complete tool. The last number means that it is either part of a set (-2,-3 etc.), or a revised tool number (-02,-03, or -B,-C etc,).

JEEP/EAGLE TOOL MANUFACTURER

Kent-Moore Tool Division
29784 Little Mack
Roseville, Mich., 48066-2298
Telephone (313) 774-9500
Telex 23-5377

Eagle Premier tool applications called out in this manual will appear as follows: "Install Spring Retainer (Sus.594-02). Adjust rocker arms using Adjuster (Mot.567)." The two or three letter code at the front of the number stands for the mechanical application, such as Mot. = Motor and Sus. = Suspension. The three digit number after the letters is the tool part number abbreviation. Any numbers after the three digit part number mean that there is more than one part to the tool.

RENAULT TOOL MANUFACTURER

Facom Tools Inc.
2177-0 Flintstone Dr.
Tucker, (Atlanta) Ga. 30084

Section 6

ENGINES

CONTENTS

NOTE: **ALSO SEE GENERAL INDEX**

Engine Trouble Shooting

GASOLINE ENGINE TROUBLE SHOOTING

CONDITION	POSSIBLE CAUSE	CORRECTION
Engine Lopes At Idle	Intake manifold-to-head leaks	Replace manifold gasket, see ENGINES
	Blown head gasket	Replace head gasket, see ENGINES
	Worn timing gears, chain or sprocket	Replace gears, chain or sprocket
	Worn camshaft lobes	Replace camshaft, see ENGINES
	Overheated engine	Check cooling system, see COOLING
	Blocked crankcase vent valve	Remove restriction
	Leaking EGR valve	Repair leak and/or replace valve
	Faulty fuel pump	Replace fuel pump
Engine Has Low Power	Leaking fuel pump	Repair leak and/or replace fuel pump
	Excessive piston-to-bore clearance	Install larger pistons, see ENGINES
	Sticking valves or weak valve springs	Check valve train components, see ENGINES
	Incorrect valve timing	Reset valve timing, see ENGINES
	Worn camshaft lobes	Replace camshaft, see ENGINES
	Blown head gasket	Replace head gasket, see ENGINES
	Clutch slipping	Adjust pedal and/or replace components, see CLUTCHES
	Engine overheating	Check cooling system, see COOLING
	Auto. trans. pressure regulator valve faulty	Replace pressure regulator valve
	Auto. trans. fluid level too low	Add fluid as necessary
	Improper vacuum diverter valve operation	Replace vacuum diverter valve
	Vacuum leaks	Inspect vacuum system and repair as required
	Leaking piston rings	Replace piston rings, see ENGINES
Faulty High Speed Operation	Low fuel pump volume	Replace fuel pump
	Leaking valves or worn valve springs	Replace valves and/or springs, see ENGINES
	Incorrect valve timing	Reset valve timing, see ENGINES
	Intake manifold restricted	Remove restriction
	Worn distributor shaft	Replace distributor
Faulty Acceleration	Improper fuel pump stroke	Remove pump and reset pump stroke
	Incorrect ignition timing	Reset ignition timing, see TUNE-UP
	Leaking valves	Replace valves, see ENGINES
	Worn fuel pump diaphragm or piston	Replace diaphragm or piston
Intake Backfire	Improper ignition timing	Reset ignition timing, see TUNE-UP
	Faulty accelerator pump discharge	Replace accelerator pump
	Improper choke operation	Check choke and adjust as required
	Defective EGR valve	Replace EGR valve
	Fuel mixture too lean	Reset air/fuel mixture, see TUNE-UP
	Choke valve initial clearance too large	Reset choke valve initial clearance
Exhaust Backfire	Vacuum leak	Inspect and repair vacuum system
	Faulty vacuum diverter valve	Replace vacuum diverter valve
	Faulty choke operation	Check choke and adjust as required
	Exhaust system leak	Repair exhaust system leak
Engine Detonation	Ignition timing too far advanced	Reset ignition timing, see TUNE-UP
	Faulty ignition system	Check ignition system, see ELECTRICAL
	Spark plugs loose or faulty	Retighten or replace plugs
	Fuel delivery system clogged	Inspect lines, pump and filter for clog
	EGR valve inoperative	Replace EGR valve
	PCV system inoperative	Inspect and/or replace hoses or valve
	Vacuum leaks	Check vacuum system and repair leaks
	Excessive combustion chamber deposits	Remove built-up deposits
	Leaking, sticking or broken valves	Inspect and/or replace valves
External Oil Leakage	Fuel pump improperly seated or worn gasket	Remove pump, replace gasket and seat properly
	Valve cover gasket broken	Replace valve cover gasket
	Oil filter gasket broken	Replace oil filter and gasket

GASOLINE ENGINE TROUBLE SHOOTING (Cont.)

CONDITION	POSSIBLE CAUSE	CORRECTION
External Oil Leakage (Cont.)	Oil pan gasket broken or pan bent	Straighten pan and replace gasket
	Timing chain cover gasket broken	Replace timing chain cover gasket
	Rear main oil seal worn	Replace rear main oil seal
	Oil pan drain plug not seated properly	Remove and reinstall drain plug
	Camshaft bearing drain hole blocked	Remove restriction
	Oil pressure sending switch leaking	Remove and reinstall sending switch
Excessive Oil Consumption	Worn valve stems or guides	Replace stems or guides, see ENGINES
	Valve "O" ring seals damaged	Replace "O" ring seals, see ENGINES
	Plugged oil drain back holes	Remove restrictions
	Improper PCV valve operation	Replace PCV valve
	Engine oil level too high	Remove excess oil
	Engine oil too thin	Replace with thicker oil
	Valve stem oil deflectors damaged	Replace oil defelctors
	Incorrect piston rings	Replace piston rings, see ENGINES
	Piston ring gaps not staggered	Reinstall piston rings, see ENGINES
	Insufficient piston ring tension	Replace rings, see ENGINES
	Piston ring grooves or oil return slots clogged	Replace piston rings, see ENGINES
	Piston rings sticking in grooves	Replace piston rings, see ENGINES
	Piston ring grooves excessively worn	Replace piston and rings, see ENGINES
	Compression rings installed upside down	Replace compression rings correctly, see ENGINES
	Worn or scored cylinder walls	Rebore cylinders or replace block
	Mismatched oil ring expander and rail	Replace oil ring expander and rail, see ENGINES
	Intake gasket dowels too long	Replace intake gasket dowels
	Excessive main or connecting rod bearing clearance	Replace main or connecting rod bearings, see ENGINES
No Oil Pressure	Low oil level	Add oil to proper level
	Oil pressure sender or gauge broken	Replace sender or gauge
	Oil pump malfunction	Remove and overhaul oil pump, see ENGINES
	Oil pressure relief valve sticking	Remove and reinstall valve
	Oil pump passages blocked	Overhaul oil pump, see ENGINES
	Oil pickup screen or tube blocked	Remove restriction
	Loose oil inlet tube	Tighten oil inlet tube
	Loose camshaft bearings	Replace camshaft bearings, see ENGINES
	Internal leakage at oil passages	Replace block or cylinder head
Low Oil Pressure	Low engine oil level	Add oil to proper level
	Engine oil too thin	Remove and replace with thicker oil
	Excessive oil pump clearance	Reduce oil pump clearance, see ENGINES
	Oil pickup tube or screen blocked	Remove restrictions
	Oil pressure relief spring weak or stuck	Eliminate binding or replace spring
	Main, rod or cam bearing clearance excessive	Replace bearing to reduce clearance, see ENGINES
High Oil Pressure	Improper grade of oil	Replace with proper oil
	Oil pressure relief valve stuck closed	Eliminate binding
	Oil pressure sender or gauge faulty	Replace sender or gauge
Noisy Main Bearings	Inadequate oil supply	Check oil delivery to main bearings
	Excessive main bearing clearance	Replace main bearings, see ENGINES
	Excessive crankshaft end play	Replace crankshaft, see ENGINES
	Loose flywheel or torque converter	Tighten attaching bolts
	Loose or damaged vibration damper	Tighten or replace vibration damper
	Crankshaft journals out-of-round	Re-grind crankshaft journals
	Excessive belt tension	Loosen belt tension

Engine Trouble Shooting

GASOLINE ENGINE TROUBLE SHOOTING (Cont.)

CONDITION	POSSIBLE CAUSE	CORRECTION
Noisy Connecting Rods	Excessive bearing clearance or missing bearing	Replace bearing, see ENGINES
	Crankshaft rod journal out-of-round	Re-grind crankshaft journal
	Misaligned connecting rod or cap	Remove rod or cap and realign
	Incorrectly tighten rod bolts	Remove and re-tighten rod bolts
Noisy Pistons and Rings	Excessive piston-to-bore clearance	Install larger pistons, see ENGINES
	Bore tapered or out-of-round	Rebore block
	Piston ring broken	Replace piston rings, see ENGINES
	Piston pin loose or seized	Replace piston pin, see ENGINES
	Connecting rods misaligned	Realign connecting rods
	Ring side clearance too loose or tight	Replace with larger or smaller rings
	Carbon build-up on piston	Remove carbon
Noisy Valve Train	Worn or bent push rods	Replace push rods, see ENGINES
	Worn rocker arms or bridged pivots	Replace rocker arms or pivots, see ENGINES
	Dirt or chips in valve lifters	Remove lifters and remove dirt/chips
	Excessive valve lifter leak-down	Replace valve lifters, see ENGINES
	Valve lifter face worn	Replace valve lifters, see ENGINES
	Broken or cocked valve springs	Replace or reposition springs
	Too much valve stem-to-guide clearance	Replace valve guides, see ENGINES
	Valve bent	Replace valve, see ENGINES
	Loose rocker arms	Retighten rocker arms, see ENGINES
	Excessive valve seat run-out	Reface valve seats, see ENGINES
	Missing valve lock	Install new valve lock
	Excessively worn camshaft lobes	Replace camshaft, see ENGINES
	Plugged valve lifter oil holes	Eliminate restriction or replace lifter
	Faulty valve lifter check ball	Replace lifter check ball, see ENGINES
	Rocker arm nut installed upside down	Remove and reinstall correctly
	Valve lifter incorrect for engine	Remove and replace valve lifters
	Faulty push rod seat or lifter plunger	Replace plunger or push rod
Noisy Valves	Improper valve lash	Re-adjust valve lash, see ENGINES
	Worn or dirty valve lifters	Clean and/or replace lifters
	Worn valve guides	Replace valve guides, see ENGINES
	Excessive valve seat or face run-out	Reface seats or valve face
	Worn camshaft lobes	Replace camshaft, see ENGINES
	Loose rocker arm studs	Re-tighten rocker arm studs, see ENGINES
	Bent push rods	Replace push rods, see ENGINES
	Broken valve springs	Replace valve springs, see ENGINES
Burned, Sticking or Broken Valves	Weak valve springs or warped valves	Replace valves and/or springs, see ENGINES
	Improper lifter clearance	Re-adjust clearance or replace lifters
	Worn guides or improper guide clearance	Replace valve guides, see ENGINES
	Out-of-round valve seats or improper seat width	Re-grind valve seats
	Gum deposits on valve stems, seats or guides	Remove deposits
	Improper spark timing	Re-adjust spark timing
Broken Pistons/Rings	Undersize pistons	Replace with larger pistons, see ENGINES
	Wrong piston rings	Replace with correct rings, see ENGINES
	Out-of-round cylinder bore	Re-bore cylinder bore
	Improper connecting rod alignment	Remove and realign connecting rods
	Excessively worn ring grooves	Replace pistons, see ENGINES
	Improperly assembled piston pins	Re-assemble pin-to-piston, see ENGINES
	Insufficient ring gap clearance	Install new rings, see ENGINES
	Engine overheating	Check cooling system
	Incorrect ignition timing	Re-adjust ignition timing, see TUNE-UP
Excessive Exhaust Noise	Leaks at manifold to head, or to pipe	Replace manifold or pipe gasket
	Exhaust manifold cracked or broken	Replace exhaust manifold, see ENGINES

ALL ENGINES

DESCRIPTION

Examples used in this article are general in nature and do not necessarily relate to a specific engine or system. Illustrations and procedures have been chosen to guide mechanic through engine overhaul process. Descriptions of cleaning, inspection, and assembly processes are included.

ENGINE IDENTIFICATION

Engine may be identified from Vehicle Identification Number (VIN) stamped on a metal tab. Metal tab may be located in different locations depending on manfacturer. Engine identification number or serial number is located on cylinder block. Location varies with manufacturer.

INSPECTION PROCEDURES

Engine components must be inspected to meet manufacturer's specifications and tolerances during overhaul. Proper dimensions and tolerances must be met to obtain proper performance and maximum engine life.

Micrometers, depth guages and dial indicator are used for checking tolerances during engine overhaul. Magnaflux, magnaglo, dye-check, ultrasonic and x-ray inspection procedures are used for parts inspection.

MAGNETIC PARTICLE INSPECTION
Magnaflux & Magnaglo

Magnaflux is an inspection technique used to locate material flaws and stress cracks. Component is subjected to a strong magnetic field. Entire component or a localized area can be magnetized. Component is coated with either a wet or dry material that contains fine magnetic particles.

Cracks which are outlined by the particles cause an interruption of magnetic field. Dry powder method of magnaflux can be used in normal lighting and crack appears as a bright line.

Florescent liquid is used along with a Blacklight in the Magnaglo magnaflux system. Darkened room is required for this procedure. The crack will appear as a glowing line. Complete demagnetizing of component upon completion is required on both procedures. Magnetic particle inspection applies to ferrous materials only.

PENETRANT INSPECTION
Zyglo

The Zyglo process coats material with a fluorescent dye penetrant. Component is often warmed to expand cracks that will be penetrated by the dye. Using darkened room and Blacklight, component is inspected for cracks. Crack will glow brightly.

Developing solution is often used to enhance results. Parts made of any material, such as aluminum cylinder heads or plastics, may be tested using this process.

Dye Check

Penetrating dye is sprayed on the previously cleaned component. Dye is left on component for 5-45 minutes, depending upon material density. Component is then wiped clean and sprayed with a developing solution. Surface cracks will show up as a bright line.

ULTRASONIC INSPECTION

If an expensive part is suspected of internal cracking, Ultrasonic testing is used. Sound waves are used for component inspection.

X-RAY INSPECTION

This form of inspection is used on highly stressed components. X-ray inspection may be used to detect internal and external flaws in any material.

PRESSURE TESTING

Cylinder heads can be tested for cracks using a pressure tester. Pressure testing is performed by plugging all but one of the holes of cylinder head and injecting air or water into the open passage.

Leaks are indicated by the appearance of wet or damp areas when using water. When air is used, it is necessary to spray the head surface with a soap solution. Bubbles will indicate a leak. Cylinder head may also be submerged in water heated to specified temperature to check for cracks created during heat expansion.

CLEANING PROCEDURES

All components of an engine do not have the same cleaning requirements. Physical methods include bead blasting and manual removal. Chemical methods include solvent blast, solvent tank, hot tank, cold tank and steam cleaning of components.

BEAD BLASTING

Manual removal of deposits may be required prior to bead blasting, followed by some other cleaning method. Carbon, paint and rust may be removed using bead blasting method. Components must be free of oil and grease prior to bead blasting. Beads will stick to grease or oil soaked areas causing area not to be cleaned.

Use air pressure to remove all trapped residual beads from component after cleaning. After cleaning internal engine parts made of aluminum, wash thoroughly with hot soapy water. Component must be thoroughly cleaned as glass beads will enter engine oil resulting in bearing damage.

CHEMICAL CLEANING

Solvent tank is used for cleaning oily residue from components. Solvent blasting sprays solvent through a syphon gun using compressed air.

The hot tank, using heated caustic solvents, is used for cleaning ferrous materials only. DO NOT clean aluminum parts such as cylinder heads, bearings or other soft metals using the hot tank. After cleaning, flush parts with hot water.

A non-ferrous part will be ruined and caustic solution will be diluted if placed in the hot tank. Always use eye protection and gloves when using the hot tank.

Use of a cold tank is for cleaning of aluminum cylinder heads, carburetors and other soft metals. A less caustic and unheated solution is used. Parts may be left in the tank for several hours without damage. After cleaning, flush parts with hot water.

Steam cleaning, with boiling hot water sprayed at high pressure, is recommended as the final cleaning process when using either hot or cold tank cleaning.

Engine Overhaul Procedures

ALL ENGINES (Cont.)

COMPONENT CLEANING

SHEET METAL PARTS

Examples of sheet metal parts are rocker covers, front and side covers, oil pan and bellhousing dust cover. Glass bead blasting or hot tank may be used for cleaning.

Ensure all mating surfaces are flat. Deformed surfaces should be straightened. Check all sheet metal parts for cracks and dents.

INTAKE & EXHAUST MANIFOLDS

Using solvent cleaning or bead blasting, clean manifolds for inspection. If intake manifold has an exhaust crossover, all carbon deposits must be removed. Inspect manifolds for cracks, burned or eroded areas, corrosion and damage to fasteners.

Exhaust heat and products of combustion, cause threads of fasteners to corrode. Replace studs and bolts as necessary. On "V" type intake manifolds, sheet metal oil shield must be removed for proper cleaning and inspection. Ensure all manifold parting surfaces are flat and free of burrs.

CYLINDER HEAD REPLACEMENT

REMOVAL

Remove intake and exhaust manifolds and valve cover. Cylinder head and camshaft carrier bolts (if equipped), should be removed only when engine is cold. On many aluminum cylinder heads, removal while hot will cause cylinder head warpage. Mark rocker arm or overhead cam components for location.

Remove rocker arm components or overhead cam components. Components must be installed in original location. Individual design rocker arms may utilize shafts, ball-type pedestal mounts or no rocker arms. For all design types, wire components together and identify according to corresponding valve. Remove cylinder head bolts. Note length and location. Some applications require cylinder head bolts be removed in proper sequence to prevent cylinder head damage. See Fig. 1. Remove cylinder head.

INSTALLATION

Ensure all surfaces and head bolts are clean. Check that head bolt holes of cylinder block are clean and dry to prevent block damage when bolts are tightened. Clean threads with tap to ensure accurate bolt torque.

Install head gasket on cylinder block. Some manufacturer's may recommend sealant be applied to head gasket prior to installation. Note that all holes are aligned. Some gasket applications may be marked so certain area faces upward. Install cylinder head using care not to damage head gasket. Ensure cylinder head is fully seated on cylinder block.

Some applications require head bolts be coated with sealant prior to installation. This is done if head bolts are exposed to water passages. Some applications require head bolts be coated with light coat of engine oil.

Install head bolts. Head bolts should be tightened in proper steps and sequence to specification.

See Fig. 1. Install remaining components. Tighten all bolts to specification. Adjust valves if required. See VALVE ADJUSTMENT in this article.

NOTE: Some manufacturers require that head bolts be retightened after specified amount of operation. This must be done to prevent head gasket failure.

Fig. 1: Typical Cylinder Head Tightening or Loosening Sequence

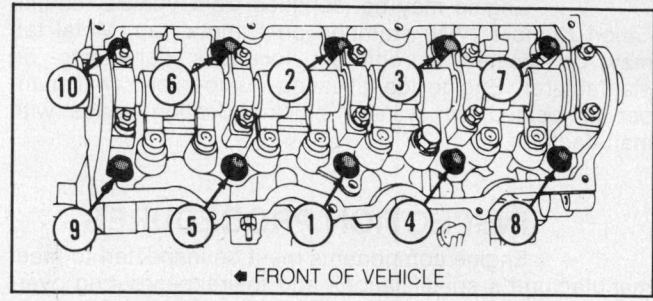

◄ FRONT OF VEHICLE

VALVE ADJUSTMENT

Engine specifications will indicate valve train clearance and temperature at which adjustment is to be made on most models. In most cases, adjustment will be made with a cold engine. In some cases, both a cold and a hot clearance will be given for maintenance convenience.

On some models, adjustment is not required. Rocker arms are tightened to specification and valve lash is automatically set. On some models with push rod actuated valve train, adjustment is made at push rod end of rocker arm while other models do not require adjustment.

Clearance will be checked between tip of rocker arm and tip of valve stem in proper sequence using a feeler gauge. Adjustment is made by rotating adjusting screw until proper clearance is obtained. Lock nut is then tightened. Engine will be rotated to obtain all valve adjustments to manufacturer's specifications.

Some models require hydraulic lifter to be bled down and clearance measured. Different length push rods can be used to obtain proper clearance. Clearance will be checked between tip of rocker arm and tip of valve stem in proper sequence using a feeler gauge.

On overhead cam engines designed without rocker arms actuate valves directly on a cam follower. A hardened, removable disc is installed between the cam lobe and lifter. Clearance will be checked between cam heel and adjusting disc in proper sequence using a feeler gauge. Engine will be rotated to obtain all valve adjustments.

On overhead cam engines designed with rocker arms, adjustment is made at push rod end of rocker arm. Ensure that the valve to be adjusted is riding on the heel of the cam on all engines. Clearance will be checked between tip of rocker arm and tip of valve stem in proper sequence using a feeler gauge. Adjustment is made by rotating adjusting screw until proper clearance is obtained. Lock nut is then tightened. Engine will be rotated to obtain all valve adjustments to manufacturer's specifications.

ALL ENGINES (Cont.)

CYLINDER HEAD OVERHAUL

DISASSEMBLY

Mark valves for location. Using valve spring compressor, compress valve springs. Remove valve locks. Carefully release spring compressor. Remove retainer or rotator, valve spring, spring seat and valve. See Fig. 2.

Fig. 2: Exploded View of Intake & Exhaust Valve Assemblies

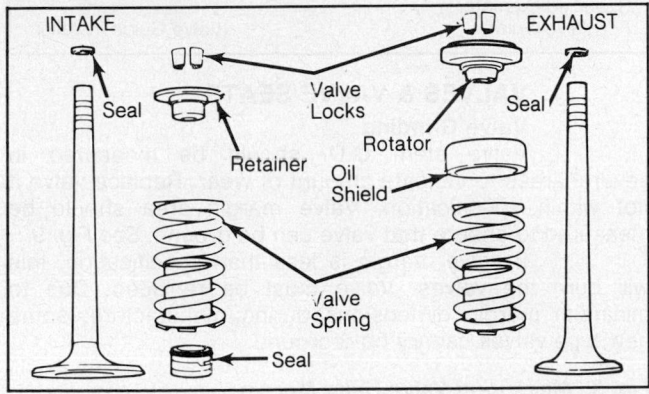

CLEANING & INSPECTION

Clean cylinder head and valve components using approved cleaning methods. Inspect cylinder head for cracks, damage or warped gasket surface. Place straightedge across gasket surface. Determine clearance at center of straightedge. Measure across both diagonals, longitudinal centerline and across the head at several points. See Fig. 3.

On cast cylinder heads, if warpage exceeds .003" (.08 mm) in a 6" span, or .006" (.15 mm) over total length, cylinder head must be resurfaced. On most aluminum cylinder heads, if warpage exceeds .002" (.05 mm) in any area, cylinder head must be resurfaced. Warpage specification may vary with manufacturer.

Cylinder head thickness should be measured to determine amount of material which can be removed before replacement is required. Cylinder head thickness must not be less than manufacturer's specifications.

If cylinder head required resurfacing, it may not align properly with intake manifold. On "V" type engines, misalignment is corrected by machining intake manifold surface that contacts cylinder head. Cylinder head may be machined on surface that contacts intake manifold.

Fig. 3: Checking Cylinder Head for Warpage

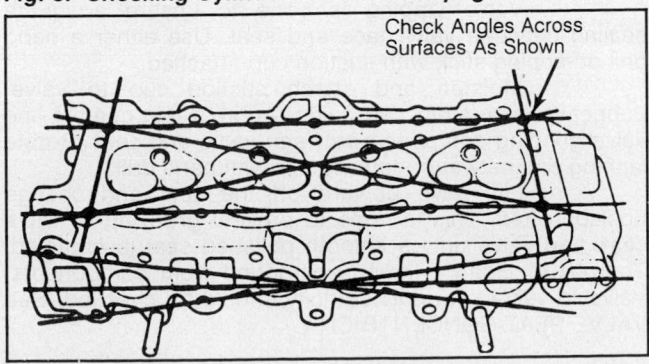

Check Angles Across Surfaces As Shown

Using oil stone, remove burrs or scratches from all sealing surfaces.

VALVE SPRINGS

Inspect valve springs for corroded or pitted valve spring surfaces which may lead to breakage. Polished spring ends caused by a rotating spring, indicates that spring surge has occurred. Replace springs showing evidence of these conditions.

Inspect valve springs for squareness using a 90 degree straightedge. See Fig. 4. Replace valve spring if out-of-square exceeds manufacturer's specification.

Fig. 4: Checking Valve Spring Squareness

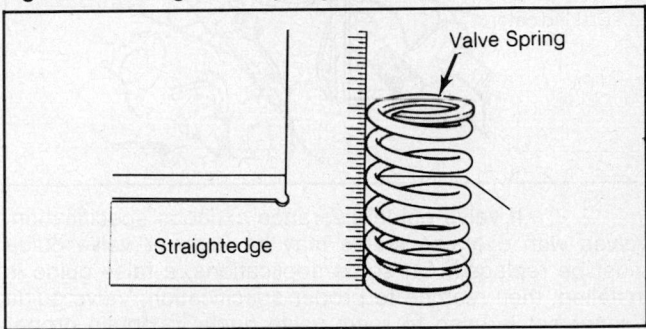

Using vernier caliper, measure free length of all valve springs. Replace springs if not within specification. Using valve spring tester, test valve spring pressure at installed and compressed heights. See Fig. 5.

Usually compressed height is installed height minus valve lift. Replace valve spring if not within specification. It is recommended to replace all valve springs when overhauling cylinder head.

Fig. 5: Checking Valve Spring Pressure

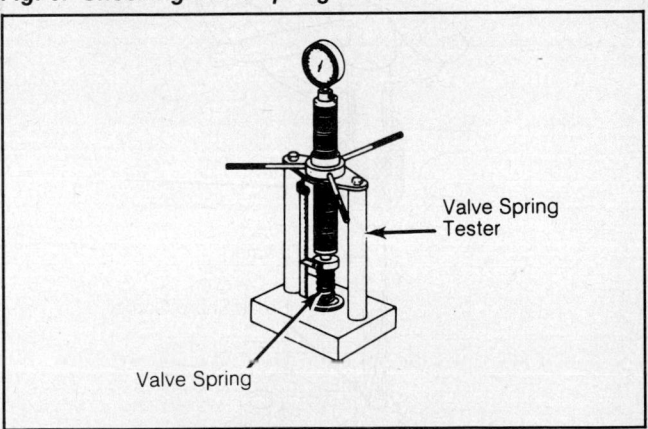

VALVE GUIDE

Measuring Valve Guide Clearance

Check valve stem-to-guide clearance. Ensure valve stem diameter is within specifications. Install valve in valve guide. Install dial indicator assembly on cylinder head with tip resting against valve stem just above valve guide. See Fig. 6.

Lower valve approximately 1/16" below valve seat. Push valve stem against valve guide as far as possible. Adjust dial indicator to zero. Push valve stem in opposite direction and note reading. Clearance must be within specification.

Engine Overhaul Procedures

ALL ENGINES (Cont.)

Fig. 6: Measuring Valve Stem-to-Guide Clearance

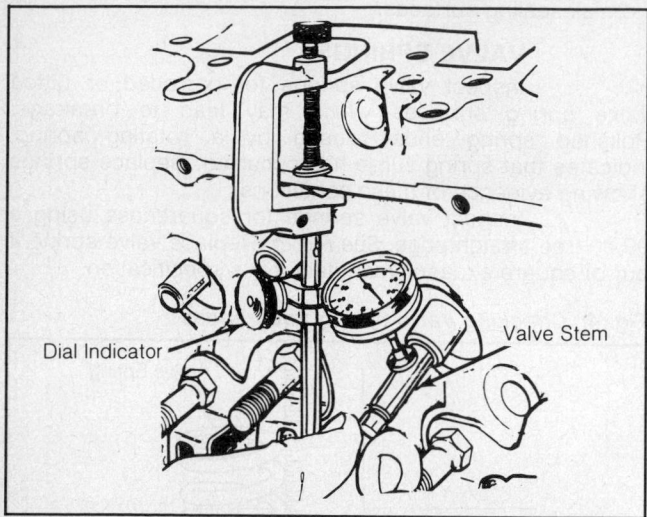

If valve guide clearance exceeds specification, valves with oversize stems may be used or valve guide must be replaced. On some applications, a false guide is installed, then reamed to proper specification. Valve guide reamer set is used to ream valve guide to obtain proper clearance for new valve.

Reaming Valve Guide

Select proper reamer for valve stem. Reamer must be of proper length to provide clean cut through entire length of valve guide. Install reamer in valve guide and rotate to cut valve guide. See Fig. 7.

Fig. 7: Reaming Valve Guides

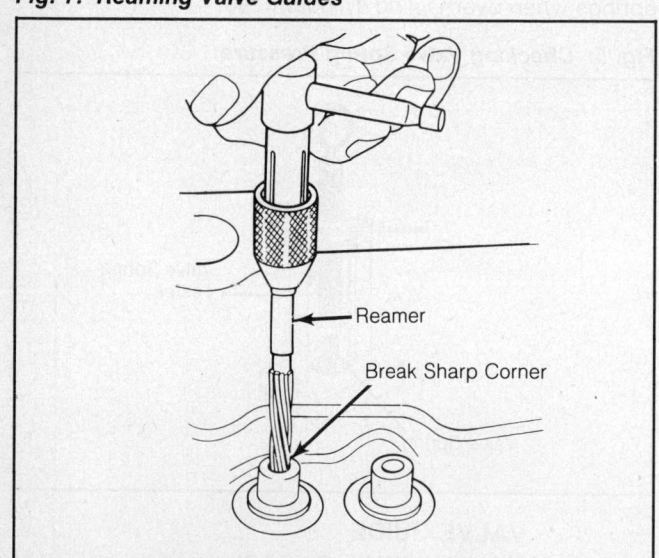

Replacing Valve Guide

Replace valve guide if clearance exceeds specification. Valve guides are either pressed, hammered or shrunk in place, depending upon cylinder head design and type of metal used.

Remove valve guide from cylinder head by pressing or tapping on a stepped drift. See Fig. 8. Once valve guide is installed, distance from cylinder head to top of valve guide must be checked. This distance must be within specification.

Aluminum heads are often heated before installing valve guide. Guide is sometimes chilled in dry ice before installation. Combination of a heated head and chilled guide insures a tight guide fit upon assembly. The new guide must be reamed to specification.

Fig. 8: Typical Valve Guide Remover & Installer

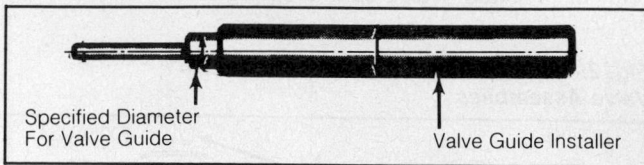

Specified Diameter For Valve Guide

Valve Guide Installer

VALVES & VALVE SEATS

Valve Grinding

Valve stem O.D. should be measured in several areas to indicate amount of wear. Replace valve if not within specification. Valve margin area should be measured to ensure that valve can be ground. See Fig. 9.

If valve margin is less than specification, this will burn the valves. Valve must be replaced. Due to minimum margin dimensions during manufacture, some new type valves cannot be reground.

Fig. 9: Measuring Valve Head Margin

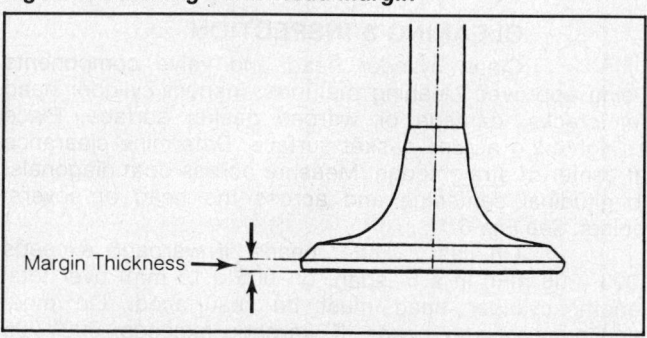

Margin Thickness

Resurface valve on proper angle specification using valve grinding machine. Follow manufacturer's instructions for valve grinding machine. Specifications may indicate a different valve face angle than seat angle.

Measure valve margin after grinding. Replace valve if not within specification. Valve stem tip can be refinished using valve grinding machine.

Valve Lapping

During valve lapping of recent designed valves, be sure to follow manufacturers recommendations. Surface hardening and materials used with some valves do not permit lapping. Lapping process will remove excessive amounts of the hardened surface.

Valve lapping is done to ensure adequate sealing between valve face and seat. Use either a hand drill or lapping stick with suction cup attached.

Moisten and attach suction cup to valve. Lubricate valve stem and guide. Apply a thin coat of fine valve grinding compound between valve and seat. Rotate lapping tool between the palms or with hand drill.

Lift valve upward off the seat and change position often. This is done to prevent grooving of valve seat. Lap valve until a smooth polished seat is obtained. Thoroughly clean grinding compound from components. Valve to valve seat concentricity should be checked. See VALVE SEAT CONCENTRICITY.

ALL ENGINES (Cont.)

CAUTION: Valve guides must be in good condition and free of carbon deposits prior to valve seat grinding. Some engines contain an induction hardened valve seat. Excessive material removal will damage valve seats.

Valve Seat Grinding

Select coarse stone of correct size and angle for seat to be ground. Ensure stone is true and has a smooth surface. Select correct size pilot for valve guide dimension. Install pilot in valve guide. Lightly lubricate pilot shaft. Install stone on pilot. Move stone off and on the seat approximately 2 times per second during grinding operation.

Select a fine stone to finish grinding operation. Grinding stones with 30 and 60 degree angles are used to center and narrow the valve seat as required. See Fig. 10.

Fig. 10: Adjusting Valve Seat Width

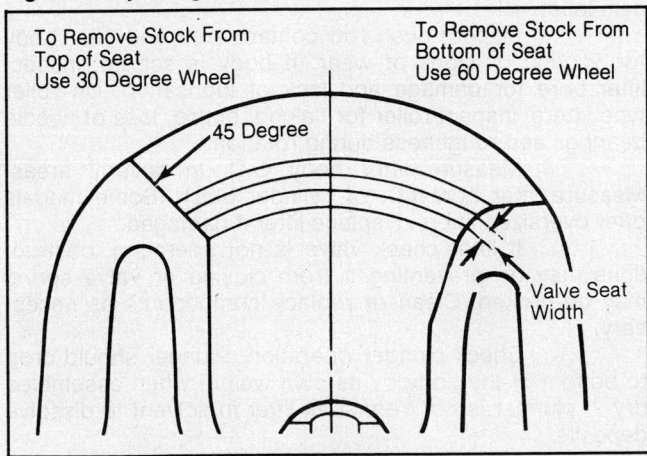

Valve Seat Replacement

Replacement of valve seat inserts is done by cutting out the old insert and machining an oversize insert bore. Replacement oversize insert is usually chilled and the cylinder head is sometimes warmed. Valve seat is pressed into the head. This operation requires specialized machine shop equipment.

Valve Seat Concentricity

Using dial gauge, install gauge pilot in valve guide. Position gauge arm on the valve seat. Adjust dial indicator to zero. Rotate arm 360 degrees and note reading. Runout should not exceed specification.

To check valve-to-valve seat concentricity, coat valve face lightly with Prusian Blue dye. Install valve and rotate it on valve seat. If pattern is even and entire seat is coated at valve contact point, valve is concentric with the seat.

REASSEMBLY

Valve Stem Installed Height

Valve stem installed height must be checked when new valves are installed or when valves or valve seats have been ground. Install valve in valve guide. Measure distance from tip of valve stem to spring seat. See Fig. 11. Distance must be within specifications.

Remove valve and grind valve stem tip if height exceeds specification. Valve tips are surface hardened. DO NOT remove more than .010" (.25 mm) from tip. Chamfer sharp edge of reground valve tip. Recheck valve stem installed height.

Fig. 11: Measuring Valve Stem Installed Height

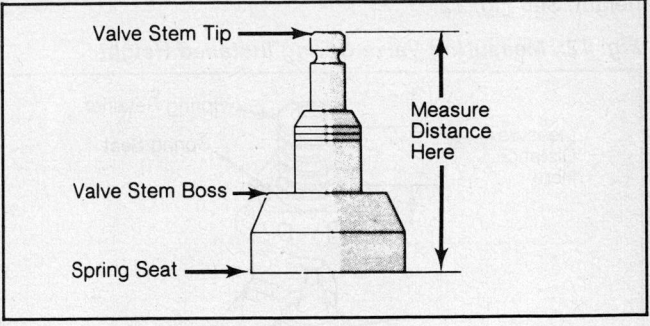

VALVE STEM OIL SEALS

Valve stem oil seals must be installed on valve stem. See Fig. 2. Seals are needed due to pressure differential at the ends of valve guides. Atmospheric pressure above intake guide, combined with manifold vacuum below guide, causes oil to be drawn into the cylinder.

Exhaust guides also have pressure differential created by exhaust gas flowing past the guide, creating a low pressure area. This low pressure area draws oil into the exhaust system.

Replacement (On Vehicle)

Mark rocker arm or overhead cam components for location. Remove rocker arm components or overhead cam components. Components must be installed in original location. Remove spark plugs. Valve stem oil seals may be replaced by holding valves against seats using air pressure.

Air pressure must be installed in cylinder using an adapter for spark plug hole. An adapter can be constructed by welding air hose connection to spark plug body with porcelain removed.

Rotate engine until piston is at top of stroke. Install adapter in spark plug hole. Apply a minimum of 140 psi (9.8 kg/cm²) line pressure to adapter. Air pressure should hold valve closed. If air pressure does not hold valve closed, check for damaged or bent valve. Cylinder head must be removed for service.

Using valve spring compressor, compress valve springs. Remove valve locks. Carefully release spring compressor. Remove retainer or rotator and valve spring. Remove valve stem oil seal.

If oversized valves have been installed, oversized oil seals must be used. Coat valve stem with engine oil. Install protective sleeve over end of valve stem. Install new oil seal over valve stem and seat on valve guide. Remove protective sleeve. Install spring seat, valve spring and retainer or rotator. Compress spring and install valve locks. Remove spring compressor. Ensure valve locks are fully seated.

Install rocker arms or overhead cam components. Tighten all bolts to specification. Adjust valves if required. Remove adapter. Install spark plugs, valve cover and gasket.

VALVE SPRING INSTALLED HEIGHT

Valve spring installed height should be checked during reassembly. Measure height from lower edge of valve spring to the upper edge. DO NOT include valve spring seat or retainer. Distance must be within specifications. If valves and/or seats have been ground, a

ALL ENGINES (Cont.)

valve spring shim may be required to correct spring height. *See Fig. 12.*

Fig. 12: Measuring Valve Spring Installed Height

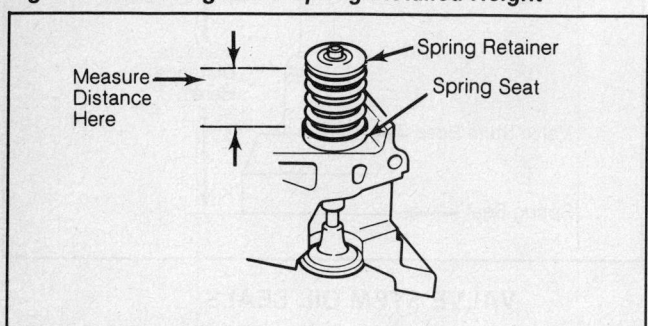

ROCKER ARMS & ASSEMBLIES

Rocker Studs

Rocker studs are either threaded or pressed in place. Threaded studs are removed by locking 2 nuts on the stud. Unscrew the stud by turning the jam nut. Coat new stud threads with Loctite and install. Tighten to specification.

Pressed in stud can be removed using a stud puller. Ream stud bore to proper specification and press in a new oversize stud. Pressed in studs are often replaced by cutting threads in the stud bore to accept a threaded stud.

Rocker Arms & Shafts

Mark rocker arms for location. Remove rocker arm retaining bolts. Remove rocker arms. Inspect rocker arms, shafts, bushings and pivot balls (if equipped) for excessive wear. Inspect rocker arms for wear in valve stem contact area. Measure rocker arm bushing I.D. Replace bushings if excessively worn.

The rocker arm valve stem contact point can be reground, using special fixture for valve grinding machine. Remove minimum amount of material as possible. Ensure all oil passages are clear. Install rocker arms in original locations. Ensure rocker arm is properly seated in push rod. Tighten bolts to specification. Adjust valves if required. See VALVE ADJUSTMENT in this article.

Push Rods

Remove rocker arms. Mark push rods for location. Remove push rods. Push rods can be steel or aluminum, solid or hollow. Hollow push rods must be internally cleaned to ensure oil passage to rocker arms is cleaned. Check push rods for damage, such as loose ends on steel tipped aluminum types.

Check push rod for straightness. Roll push rod on a flat surface. Using feeler gauge, check clearance at center. Replace push rod if bent. The push rod can also be supported at each end and rotated. A dial indicator is used to detect bends in the push rod.

Lubricate ends of push rod and install push rod in original location. Ensure push rod is properly seated in lifter. Install rocker arm. Tighten bolts to specification. Adjust valves if required. See VALVE ADJUSTMENT in this article.

LIFTERS

HYDRAULIC LIFTERS

Before replacing a hydraulic lifter for noisy operation, ensure noise is not caused by worn rocker arms or valve tips. Hydraulic lifter assemblies must be installed in original locations. Remove rocker arm assembly and push rod. Mark components for location. Some applications require intake manifold, or lifter cover removal. Remove lifter retainer plate (if used). To remove lifters, use a hydraulic lifter remover or magnet. Different type lifters are used. *See Fig. 13.*

On sticking lifters, disassemble and clean lifter. DO NOT mix lifter components or positions. Parts are select-fitted and are not interchangeable. Inspect all components for wear. Note amount of wear in lifter body-to-camshaft contact area. Surface must have smooth and convex contact face. If wear is apparent, carefully inspect cam lobe.

Inspect push rod contact area and lifter body for scoring or signs of wear. If body is scored, inspect lifter bore for damage and lack of lubrication. On roller type lifters, inspect roller for flaking, pitting, loss of needle bearings and roughness during rotation.

Measure lifter body O.D. in several areas. Measure lifter bore I.D. of cylinder block. Some models offer oversized lifters. Replace lifter if damaged.

If lifter check valve is not operating, obstructions may be preventing it from closing or valve spring may be broken. Clean or replace components as necessary.

Check plunger operation. Plunger should drop to bottom of the body by its own weight when assembled dry. If plunger is not free, soak lifter in solvent to dissolve deposits.

Lifter leak-down test can be performed on lifter. Lifter must be filled with special test oil. New lifters contain special test oil. Using lifter leak-down tester, perform leak-down test following manufacturer's instructions. If leak-down time is not within specifications, replace lifter assembly.

Lifters should be soaked in clean engine oil several hours prior to installation. Coat lifter base, roller (if equipped) and lifter body with ample amount of molykote or camshaft lubricant. *See Fig. 13.* Install lifter in original location. Install remaining components. Valve lash adjustment is not required on most hydraulic lifters. Preload of hydraulic lifter is automatic. Some models may require adjustment.

Mechanical Lifters

Lifter assemblies must be installed in original locations. Remove rocker arm assembly and push rod. Mark components for location. Some applications require intake manifold or lifter cover removal. Remove lifter retainer plate (if used). To remove lifters, use lifter remover or magnet.

Inspect push rod contact area and lifter body for scoring or signs of wear. If body is scored, inspect lifter bore for damage and lack of lubrication. Note amount of wear in lifter body-to-camshaft contact area. Surface must have smooth and convex contact face. If wear is apparent, carefully inspect cam lobe.

ALL ENGINES (Cont.)

Fig. 13: Typical Hydraulic Valve Lifter Assemblies

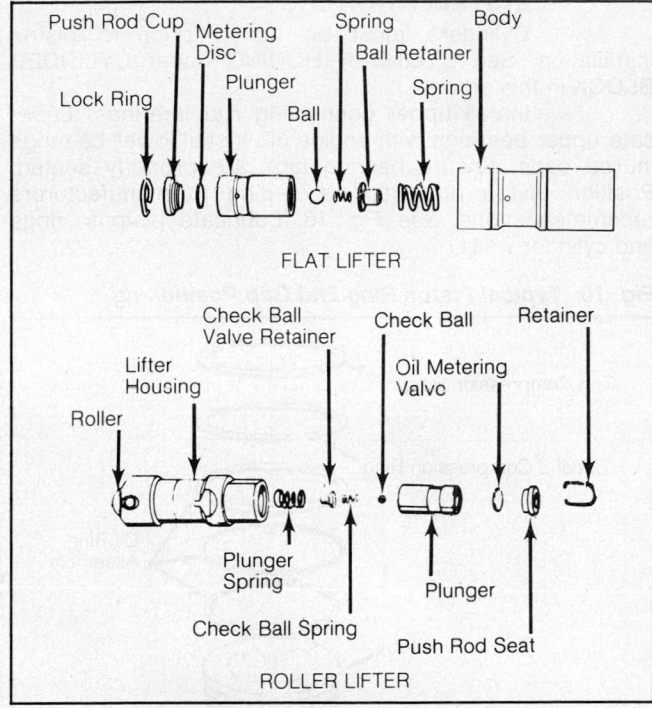

FLAT LIFTER

ROLLER LIFTER

Coat lifter base, roller (if equipped) and lifter body with ample amount of molykote or camshaft lubricant. Install lifter in original location. Install remaining components. Tighten bolts to specification. Adjust valves. See VALVE ADJUSTMENT in this article.

PISTONS, CONNECTING RODS & BEARINGS

RIDGE REMOVAL

Ridge in cylinder wall must be removed prior to piston removal. Failure to remove ridge prior to removing pistons will cause piston damage in piston ring locations.

With piston at bottom dead center, place rag in bore to trap metal chips. Install ridge reamer in cylinder bore. Adjust ridge reamer using manufacturer's instructions. Remove ridge using ridge reamer. DO NOT remove an excessive amount of material. Ensure ridge is completely removed.

PISTON & CONNECTING ROD REMOVAL

Note top of piston. Some pistons may contain a notch, arrow or be marked "FRONT". Piston must be installed in proper direction to prevent damage with valve operation.

Check that connecting rod and cap are numbered for cylinder location and which side of cylinder block the number faces. Proper cap and connecting rod must be installed together. Connecting rod cap must be installed on connecting rod in proper direction to ensure bearing lock procedure. Mark connecting rod and cap if necessary. Pistons must be installed in original location.

Remove cap retaining nuts or bolts. Remove bearing cap. Install stud protectors on connecting rod bolts. This protects cylinder walls from scoring during removal. Ensure proper removal of ridge. Push piston and

connecting rod from cylinder. Connecting rod boss can be tapped with a wooden dowel or hammer handle to aid in removal.

PISTON & CONNECTING ROD

Disassembly

Using ring expander, remove piston rings. Remove piston pin retaining rings (if equipped). On pressed type piston pins, special fixtures and procedures according to manufacturer must be used to remove piston pins. Follow manufacturer's recommendations to avoid piston distortion or breakage.

Cleaning

Remove all carbon and varnish from piston. Pistons and connecting rods may be cleaned in cold type chemical tank. Using ring groove cleaner, clean all deposits from ring grooves. Ensure all deposits are cleaned from ring grooves to prevent ring breakage or sticking. DO NOT attempt to clean pistons using wire brush.

Inspection

Inspect pistons for nicks, scoring, cracks or damage in ring areas. Connecting rod should be checked for cracks using Magnaflux procedure. Piston diameter must be measured in manufacturers specified area.

Using telescopic gauge and micrometer, measure piston pin bore of piston in 2 areas, 90 degrees apart. This is done to check diameter and out-of-round.

Install proper bearing cap on connecting rod. Ensure bearing cap is installed in proper location. Tighten bolts or nuts to specification. Using inside micrometer, measure inside diameter in 2 areas, 90 degrees apart.

Connecting rod I.D. and out-of-round must be within specification. Measure piston pin bore I.D. and piston pin O.D. All components must be within specification. Subtract piston pin diameter from piston pin bore in piston and connecting rod to determine proper fit.

Connecting rod length must be measured from center of crankshaft journal inside diameter to center of piston pin bushing using proper caliper. Connecting rods must be the same length. Connecting rods should be checked on an alignment fixture for bent or twisted condition. Replace all components which are damaged or not within specification.

PISTON & CYLINDER BORE FIT

Ensure cylinder is checked for taper, out-of-round and properly honed prior to checking piston and cylinder bore fit. See CYLINDER BLOCK in this article. Using dial bore gauge, measure cylinder bore. Measure piston at right angle to piston pin in center of piston skirt area. Subtract piston diameter from cylinder bore diameter. The difference is piston-to-cylinder clearance. Clearance must be within specification. Mark piston for proper cylinder location.

ASSEMBLING PISTON & CONNECTING ROD

Install proper fitted piston on connecting rod for proper cylinder. Ensure piston marking on top of piston marked is in correspondence with connecting rod and cap number. See Fig. 14.

Lubricate piston pin and install in connecting rod. Ensure piston pin retainers are fully seated (if equipped). On pressed type piston pins, follow manufacturer's recommended procedure to avoid distortion or breakage.

Fig. 14: Typical Piston Pin Installation

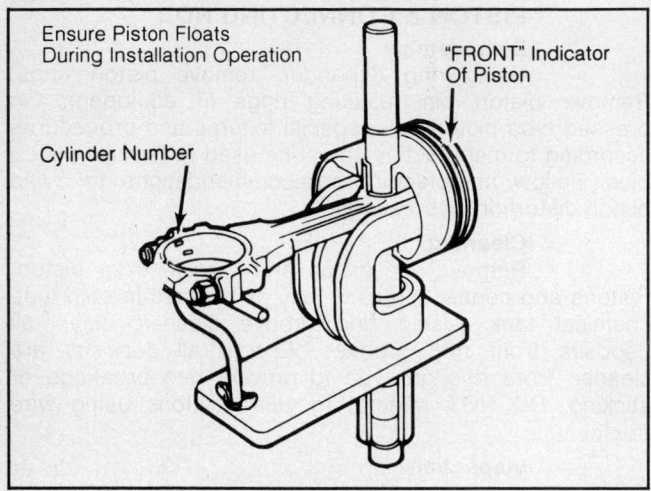

CHECKING PISTON RING CLEARANCES

Piston rings must be checked for side clearance and end gap. To check end gap, install piston ring in cylinder which it is to be installed. Using an inverted piston, push ring to bottom of cylinder in smallest cylinder diameter.

Using feeler gauge, check ring end gap. See Fig. 15. Piston ring end gap must be within specification. Ring breakage will occur with insufficient ring end gap.

On some manufacturers, insufficient ring end gap may be corrected by using a fine file while other manufacturers recommend using another ring set. Mark rings for proper cylinder installation after checking end gap.

Fig. 15: Checking Piston Ring End Gap

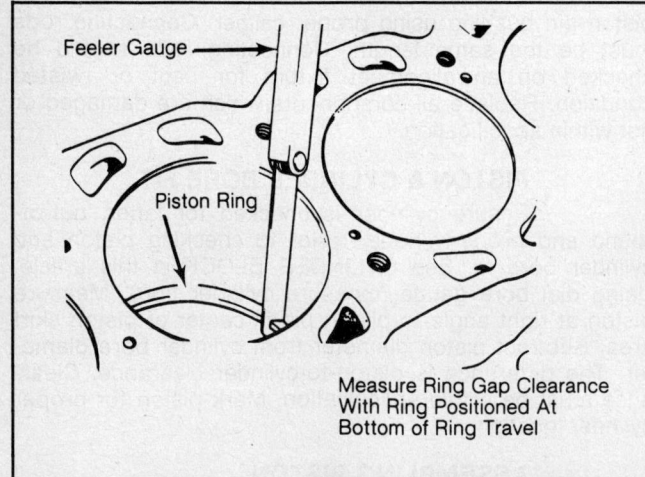

For checking side clearance, install rings on piston. Using feeler gauge, measure clearance between piston ring and piston ring land. Check side clearance in several areas around piston. Side clearance must be within specification.

If side clearance is excessive, piston ring grooves can be machined to accept oversized piston rings (if available). Normal practice is to replace piston.

PISTON & CONNECTING ROD INSTALLATION

Cylinders must be honed prior to piston installation. See CYLINDER HONING under CYLINDER BLOCK in this article.

Install upper connecting rod bearings. Lubricate upper bearings with engine oil. Install lower bearings in rod caps. Ensure bearing tabs are properly seated. Position piston ring gaps according to manufacturers recommendations. See Fig. 16. Lubricate pistons, rings and cylinder walls.

Fig. 16: Typical Piston Ring End Gap Positioning

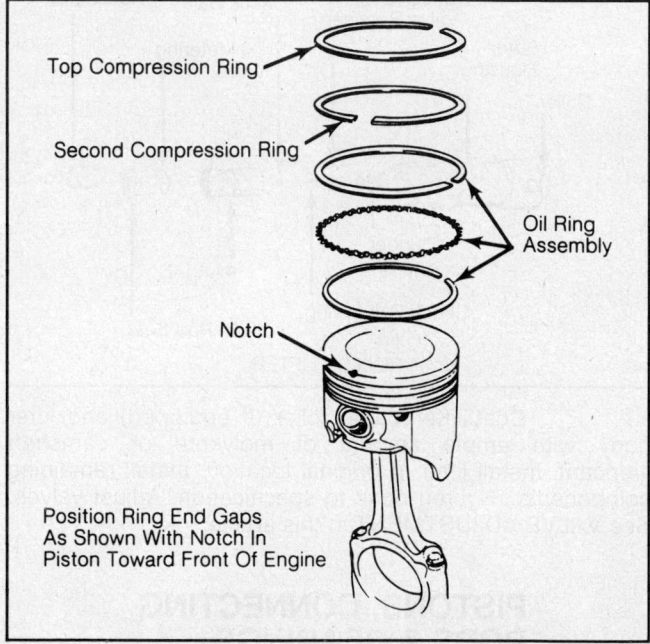

Install ring compressor. Use care not to rotate piston rings. Compress rings with ring compressor. Install plastic tubing protectors over connecting rod bolts. Install piston and connecting rod assembly. Ensure piston notch, arrow or "FRONT" mark is toward front of engine. See Fig. 17.

Fig. 17: Installing Piston & Connecting Rod Assembly

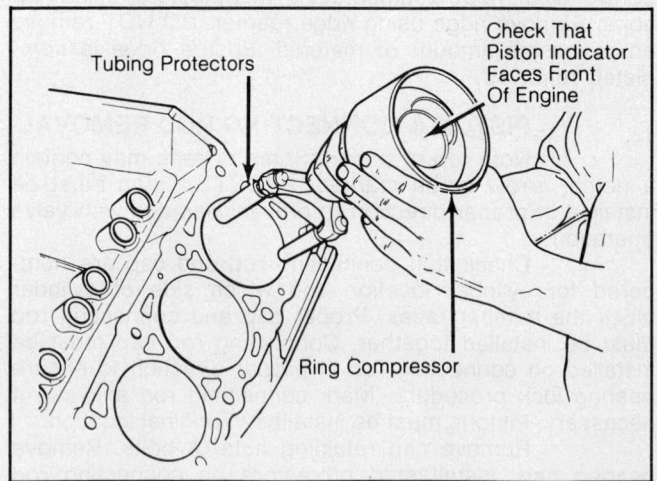

Carefully tap piston into cylinder until rod bearing is seated on crankshaft journal. Remove protec-

ALL ENGINES (Cont.)

tors. Install rod cap and bearing. Lightly tighten connecting rod bolts. Repeat procedure for remaining cylinders. Check bearing clearance. See MAIN & CONNECTING ROD BEARING CLEARANCE in this article.

Once clearance is checked, lubricate journals and bearings. Install bearing caps. Ensure marks are aligned on connecting rod and cap. Tighten rod nuts or bolts to specification. Ensure rod moves freely on crankshaft. Check connecting rod side clearance. See CONNECTING ROD SIDE CLEARANCE in this article.

CONNECTING ROD SIDE CLEARANCE

Position connecting rod toward one side of crankshaft as far as possible. Using feeler gauge, measure clearance between side of connecting rod and crankshaft. *See Fig. 18.* Clearance must be within specifications.

Check for improper bearing installation, wrong bearing cap or insufficient bearing clearance if side clearance is insufficient. Connecting rod may require machining to obtain proper clearance. Excessive clearance usually indicates excessive wear at crankshaft. Crankshaft must be repaired or replaced.

Fig. 18: Measuring Connecting Rod Side Clearance

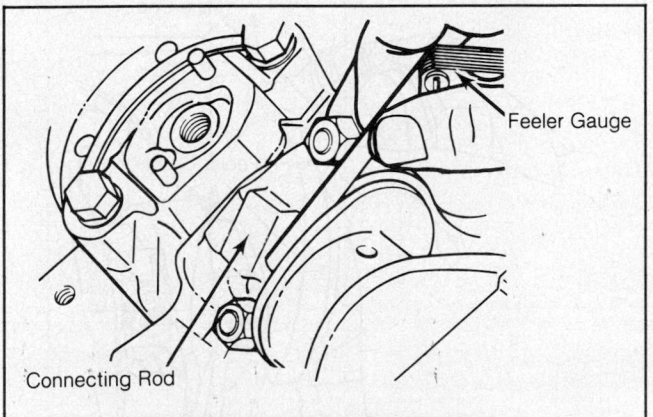

MAIN & CONNECTING ROD BEARING CLEARANCE
Plastigage Method

Plastigage method may be used to determine bearing clearance. Plastigage can be used with an engine in service or during reassembly. Plastigage material is oil soluble.

Ensure journals and bearings are free of oil or solvent. Oil or solvent will dissolve material and false reading will be obtained. Install small piece of Plastigage along full length of bearing journal. Install bearing cap in original location. Tighten bolts to specification.

CAUTION: DO NOT rotate crankshaft while Plastigage is installed. Bearing clearance will not be obtained if crankshaft is rotated.

Remove bearing cap. Compare Plastigage width with scale on Plastigage container to determine bearing clearance. *See Fig. 19.* Rotate crankshaft 90 degrees. Repeat procedure. This is done to check journal eccentricity. This procedure can be used to check oil clearance on both connecting rod and main bearings.

Fig. 19: Measuring Bearing Clearance

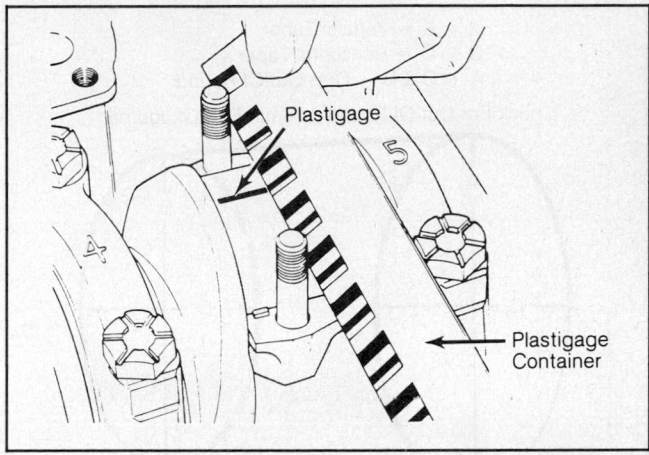

Micrometer & Telescopic Gauge Method

A micrometer is used to determine journal diameter, taper and out-of-round dimensions of the crankshaft. See INSPECTION under CRANKSHAFT & MAIN BEARINGS in this article.

With crankshaft removed, install bearings and caps in original location on cylinder block. Tighten bolts to specification. On connecting rods, install bearings and caps on connecting rods. Install proper connecting rod cap on corresponding rod. Ensure bearing cap is installed in original location. Tighten bolts to specification.

Using a telescopic gauge and micrometer or inside micrometer measure inside diameter of connecting rod and main bearings bores. Subtract each crankshaft journal diameter from the corresponding inside bore diameter. This is the bearing clearance.

CRANKSHAFT & MAIN BEARINGS

REMOVAL

Ensure all main bearing caps are marked for location on cylinder block. Some main bearing caps have an arrow stamped on it which must face front of engine. Remove main bearing cap bolts. Remove main bearing caps. Carefully remove crankshaft. Use care not to bind crankshaft in cylinder block during removal.

CLEANING & INSPECTION

Thoroughly clean crankshaft using solvent. Dry with compressed air. Ensure all oil passages are clear and free of sludge, rust, dirt, and metal chips.

Inspect crankshaft for scoring and nicks. Inspect crankshaft for cracks using Magnaflux procedure. Inspect rear seal area for grooving or damage. Inspect bolt hole threads for damage. If pilot bearing or bushing is used, check pilot bearing or bushing fit in crankshaft. Inspect crankshaft gear for damaged or cracked teeth. Replace gear if damaged. Check that oil passage plugs are tight (if equipped).

Using micrometer, measure all journals in 4 areas to determine journal taper, out-of-round and undersize. *See Fig. 20.* Some crankshafts can be reground to the next largest undersize, depending on the amount of wear or damage. Crankshafts with rolled fillet cannot be reground and must be replaced.

ALL ENGINES (Cont.)

Fig. 20: Measuring Crankshaft Journals

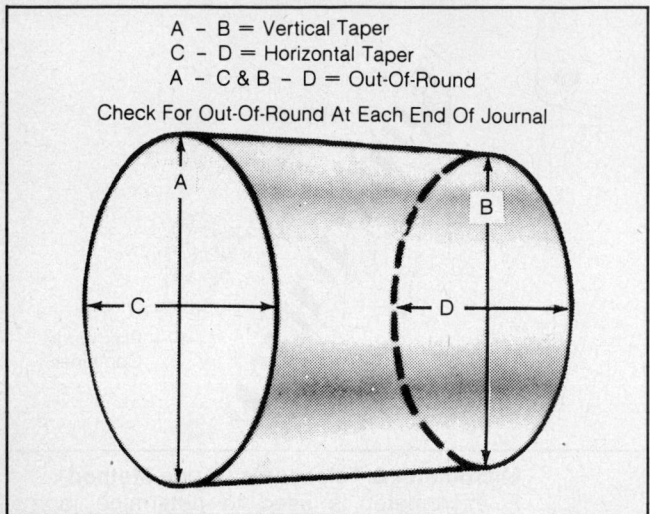

Crankshaft journal runout should be checked. Install crankshaft in "V" blocks or bench center. Position dial indicator with tip resting on the main bearing journal area. See Fig. 21. Rotate crankshaft and note reading. Journal runout must not exceed specification. Repeat procedure on all main bearing journals. Crankshaft must be replaced if runout exceeds specification.

Fig. 21: Measuring Crankshaft Main Bearing Journal Runout

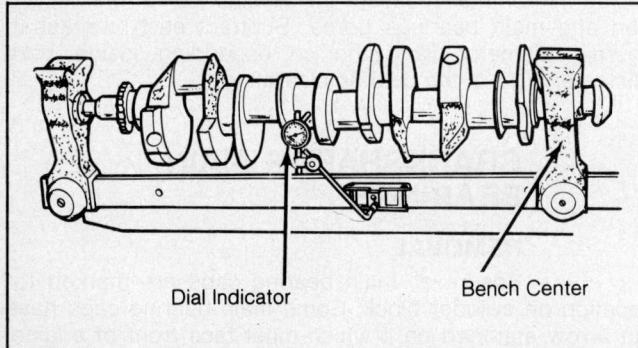

INSTALLATION

Install upper main bearing in cylinder block. Ensure lock tab is properly located in cylinder block. Install bearings in main bearing caps. Ensure all oil passages are aligned. Install rear seal (if removed).

Ensure crankshaft journals are clean. Lubricate upper main bearings with clean engine oil. Carefully install crankshaft. Check each main bearing clearance using Plastigage method. See MAIN & CONNECTING ROD BEARING CLEARANCE in this article.

Once clearance is checked, lubricate lower main bearing and journals. Install main bearing caps in original location. Install rear seal in rear main bearing cap (if removed). Some rear main bearing caps require sealant to be applied in corners to prevent oil leakage.

Install and tighten all bolts except thrust bearing cap to specification. Tighten thrust bearing cap bolts finger tight only. Thrust bearing must be aligned. On most applications, crankshaft must be moved rearward then forward. Procedure may vary with manufacturer. Thrust bearing cap is then tightened to specification.

Ensure crankshaft rotates freely. Crankshaft end play should be checked. See CRANKSHAFT END PLAY in this article.

CRANKSHAFT END PLAY

Dial Indicator Method

Crankshaft end play can be checked using dial indicator. Mount dial indicator on rear of cylinder block. Position dial indicator tip against rear of crankshaft. Ensure tip is resting against flat surface.

Pry crankshaft rearward. Adjust dial indicator to zero. Pry crankshaft forward and note reading. Crankshaft end play must be within specification. If end play is not within specification, check for faulty thrust bearing installation or worn crankshaft. Some applications offer oversized thrust bearings.

Feeler Gauge Method

Crankshaft end play can be checked using feeler gauge. Pry crankshaft rearward. Pry crankshaft forward. Using feeler gauge, measure clearance between crankshaft and thrust bearing surface. See Fig. 22.

Fig. 22: Checking Crankshaft End Play

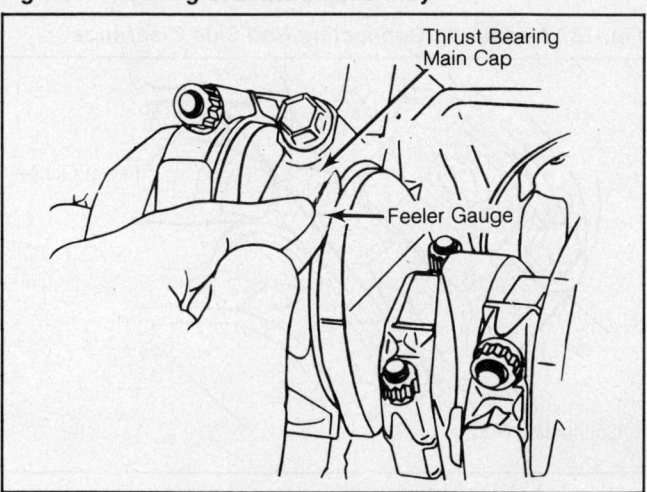

Crankshaft end play must be within specification. If end play is not within specification, check for faulty thrust bearing installation or worn crankshaft. Some applications offer oversized thrust bearings.

CYLINDER BLOCK

Block Cleaning

Only cast cylinder blocks should be hot tank cleaned. Aluminum cylinder blocks should be cleaned using cold tank method. Cylinder block is cleaned in order to remove carbon deposits, gasket residue and water jacket scale. Remove oil gallery plugs, freeze plugs and cam bearings prior to block cleaning.

Block Inspection

Visually inspect the block. Check suspected areas for cracks using the Dye Penetrant inspection method. Block may be checked for cracks using the magnaflux method.

Cracks are most commonly found at the bottom of cylinders, main bearing saddles, near expansion plugs and between cylinders and water jackets. Inspect lifter bores for damage. Inspect all head bolt holes for damaged threads. Threads should be cleaned using tap to ensure proper head bolt torque. Consult machine shop concerning possible welding and machining (if required).

ALL ENGINES (Cont.)

Cylinder Bore Inspection

Inspect bore for scoring or roughness. Cylinder bore is dimensionally checked for out-of-round and taper using dial bore gauge. For determining out-of-round, measure cylinder parallel and perpendicular to the block centerline. Difference in the 2 readings is the bore out-of-round. Cylinder bore must be checked at top, middle and bottom of piston travel area.

Bore taper is obtained by measuring bore at the top and bottom. If wear has exceeded allowable limits, block must be honed or bored to next available oversize piston dimension.

Cylinder Honing

Cylinder must be properly honed to allow new piston rings to properly seat. Cross-hatching at correct angle and depth is critical to lubrication of cylinder walls and pistons.

A flexible drive hone and power drill are commonly used. Drive hone must be lubricated during operation. Mix equal parts of kerosene and SAE 20W engine oil for lubrication.

Apply lubrication to cylinder wall. Operate cylinder hone from top to bottom of cylinder using even strokes to produce 45 degree cross-hatch pattern on the cylinder wall. DO NOT allow cylinder hone to extend below cylinder during operation.

Recheck bore dimension after final honing. Wash cylinder wall with hot soapy water to remove abrasive particles. Blow dry with compressed air. Coat cleaned cylinder walls with lubricating oil.

Deck Warpage

Check deck for damage or warped gasket surface. Place a straightedge across gasket surface of the deck. Using feeler gauge, measure clearance at center of straightedge. Measure across width and length of cylinder block at several points.

If warpage exceeds specifications, deck must be resurfaced. If warpage exceeds manufacturer's maximum tolerance for material removal, replace block.

Deck Height

Distance from crankshaft centerline to block deck is called the deck height. Measure and record front and rear main journals of crankshaft. To compute this distance, install crankshaft and retain with center main bearing and cap only. Measure distance from crankshaft journal to block deck, parallel to cylinder centerline.

Add one half of main bearing journal diameter to distance from crankshaft journal to block deck. This dimension should be checked at front and rear of cylinder block. Both readings should be the same.

If difference exceeds specifications, cylinder block must be repaired or replaced. Deck height and warpage should be corrected at the same time.

Main Bearing Bore & Alignment

For checking main bearing bore, remove all bearings from cylinder block and main bearing caps. Install main bearing caps in original location. Tighten bolts to specification. Using inside micrometer, measure main bearing bore in 2 areas 90 degrees apart. Determine bore size and out-of-round. If diameter is not within specification, block must be align-bored.

For checking alignment, place a straightedge along centerline of main bearing saddles. Check for clearance between straightedge and main bearing saddles. Block must be align-bored if clearance is present.

Expansion Plug Removal

Drill hole in center of expansion plug. Remove with screwdriver or punch. Use care not to damage sealing surface.

Expansion Plug Installation

Ensure sealing surface is free of burrs. Coat expansion plug with sealer. Using wooden dowel or pipe of slightly smaller diameter, install expansion plug. Ensure expansion plug is evenly located.

Oil Gallery Plug Removal

Remove threaded oil gallery plugs using appropriate wrench. Soft, press-in plugs are removed by drilling into plug and installing a sheet metal screw. Remove plug with slide hammer or pliers.

Oil Gallery Plug Installation

Ensure threads or sealing surface is clean. Coat threaded oil gallery plugs with sealer and install. Replacement soft press-in plugs are driven in place with a hammer and drift.

CAMSHAFT

CLEANING & INSPECTION

Clean camshaft with solvent. Ensure all oil passages are clear. Inspect cam lobes and bearing journals for pitting, flaking or scoring. Using micrometer, measure bearing journal O.D.

Support camshaft at each end with "V" blocks. Position dial indicator with tip resting on center bearing journal. Rotate camshaft and note reading. If reading exceeds specification, replace camshaft.

Check cam lobe lift by measuring base circle of camshaft using micrometer. Measure again at 90 degrees to tip of cam lobe. Cam lift can be determined by subtracting base circle diameter from tip of cam lobe measurement.

Different lift dimensions are given for intake and exhaust cam lobes. Reading must be within specifications. Replace camshaft if cam lobes or bearing journals are not within specifications.

Inspect camshaft gear for chipped, eroded or damaged teeth. Replace gear if damaged. On camshafts using thrust plate, measure distance between thrust plate and camshaft shoulder. Replace thrust plate if not within specification.

CAMSHAFT BEARINGS

Removal & Installation

Remove camshaft rear plug. Camshaft bearing remover is assembled with shoulder resting against bearing to be removed according to manufacturer's instructions. Tighten puller nut until bearing is removed. Remove remaining bearings, leaving front and rear bearings until last. These bearings act as guide for camshaft bearing remover.

To install new bearings, puller is rearranged to pull bearings toward the center of block. Ensure all lubrication passages of bearing are aligned with cylinder block. Coat new camshaft rear plug with sealant. Install camshaft rear plug. Ensure plug is even in cylinder block.

CAMSHAFT INSTALLATION

Lubricate bearing surfaces and cam lobes with ample amount of Molykote or camshaft lubricant. Carefully

Engine Overhaul Procedures

ALL ENGINES (Cont.)

install camshaft. Use care not to damage bearing journals during installation. Install thrust plate retaining bolts (if equipped). Tighten bolts to specification. On overhead camshafts, install bearing caps in original location. Tighten bolts to specification. Check end play.

CAMSHAFT END PLAY

Using dial indicator, check end play. Position dial indicator on front of engine block. Position indicator tip against camshaft. Push camshaft toward rear of engine and adjust indicator to zero.

Move camshaft forward and note reading. Camshaft end play must be within specification. End play may be adjusted by relocating gear, shimming thrust plate or replacing thrust plate depending on manufacturer.

TIMING CHAINS & BELTS

TIMING CHAINS

Timing chains will stretch during operation. Limits are placed upon amount of stretch before replacement is required. Timing chain stretch will alter ignition timing and valve timing.

To check timing chain stretch, rotate crankshaft to eliminate slack from one side of timing chain. Mark reference point on cylinder block. Rotate crankshaft in opposite direction to eliminate slack from remaining side of timing chain. Force other side of chain outward and measure distance between reference point and timing chain. See Fig. 23. Replace timing chain and gears if not within specification.

Fig. 23: Measuring Timing Chain Stretch

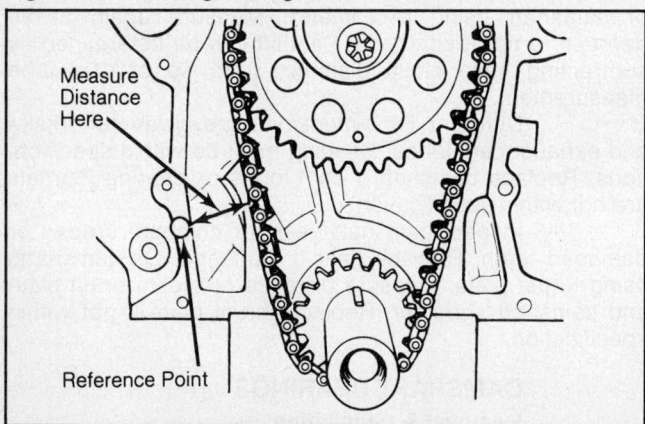

Timing chains must be installed so that timing marks on camshaft gear and crankshaft gear are aligned according to manufacturer. See Fig. 24.

TIMING BELTS

Cogged tooth belts are commonly used on overhead cam engines. Inspect belt teeth for rounded corners or cracking. Replace belt if cracked, damaged, missing teeth, or is oil soaked.

Used timing belt must be installed in original direction of rotation. Inspect all sprocket teeth for wear. Replace all worn sprockets. Sprockets are marked for

timing purposes. Engine is positioned so that crankshaft sprocket mark will be upward. Camshaft sprocket is aligned with reference mark on cylinder head and timing belt is installed. See Fig. 25.

Fig. 24: Typical Gear Timing Mark Alignment

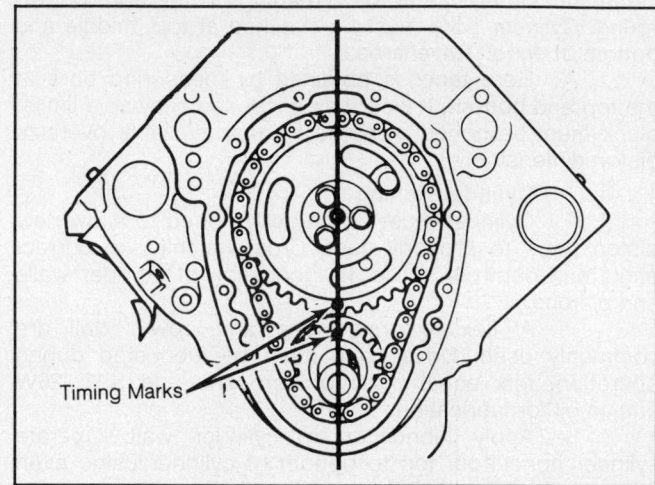

Fig. 25: Typical Camshaft Belt Sprocket Alignment

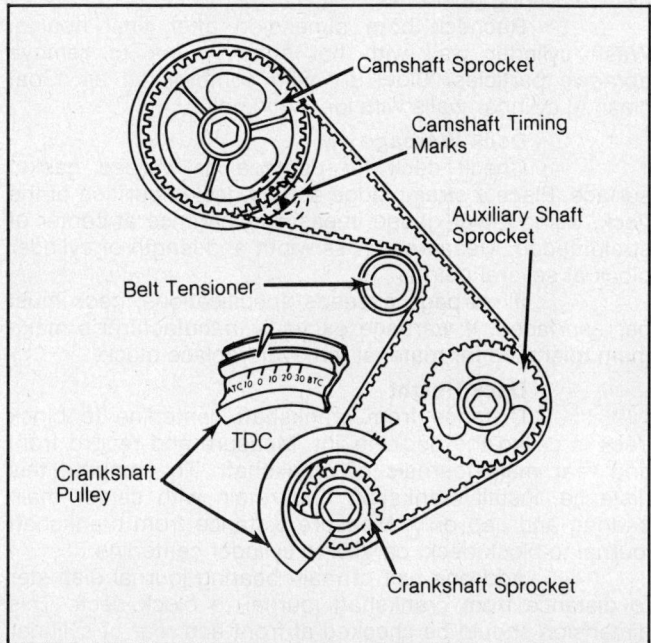

TENSION ADJUSTMENT

If guide rails are used with spring loaded tensioners, ensure at least half of original rail thickness remains. Spring loaded tensioner should be inspected for damage.

Ensure all timing marks are aligned. Adjust belt tension using manufacturer's recommendations. Belt tension may require checking using tension gauge. See Fig. 26.

ALL ENGINES (Cont.)

Fig. 26: Typical Timing Belt Tension Adjustment

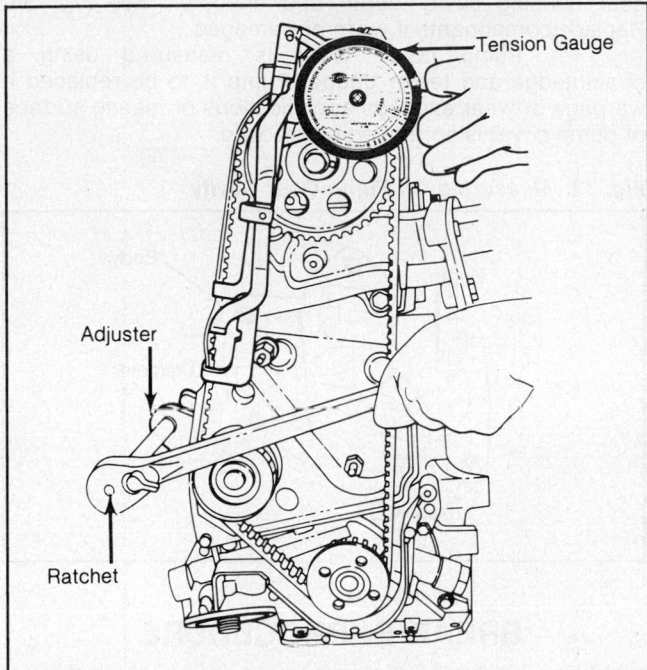

Fig. 27: Installing Typical One-Piece Oil Seal

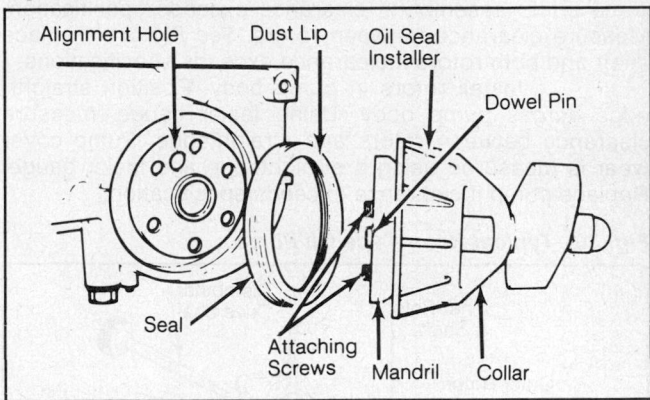

Fig. 28: Typical Rope Seal Installation

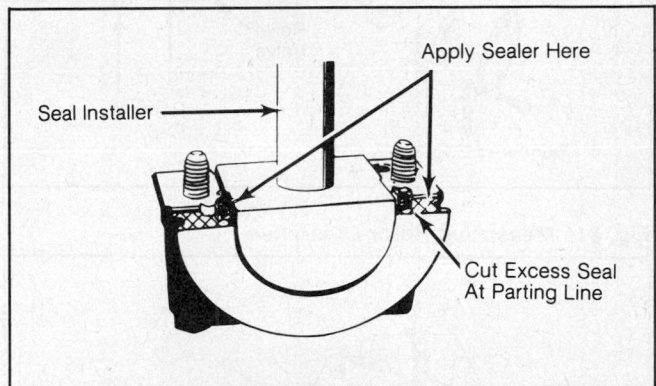

Fig. 29: Typical Split-Rubber Seal Installation

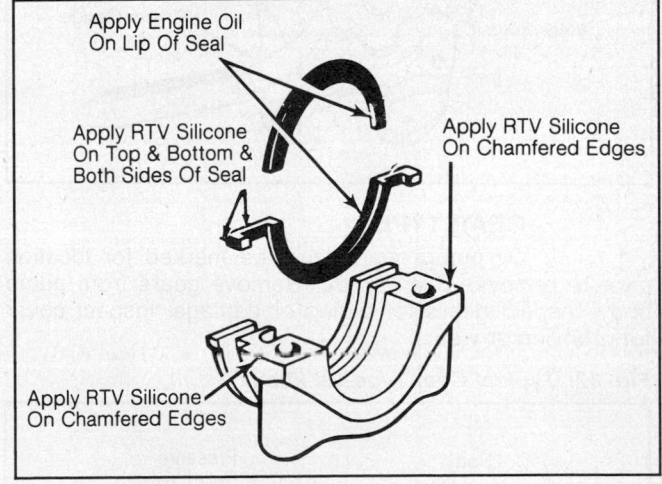

TIMING GEARS

TIMING GEAR BACKLASH & RUNOUT

On engines where camshaft gear operates directly on crankshaft gear, gear backlash and runout must be checked. To check backlash, install dial indicator with tip resting on tooth of camshaft gear. Rotate camshaft gear as far as possible. Adjust indicator to zero. Rotate camshaft gear in opposite direction as far as possible and note reading.

To determine timing gear runout, mount dial indicator with tip resting on face edge of camshaft gear. Adjust indicator to zero. Rotate camshaft gear 360 degrees and note reading. If backlash or runout exceed specifications, replace camshaft and/or crankshaft gear.

REAR MAIN OIL SEAL INSTALLATION

One-Piece Type Seal

For one-piece type oil seal installation, coat block contact surface of seal with sealer if seal is not factory coated. Ensure seal surface is free of burrs. Lubricate seal lip with engine oil and press seal into place using proper oil seal installer. *See Fig. 27.*

Rope Type Seal

For rope type rear main oil seal installation, press seal lightly into seat area. Using seal installer, fully seat seal in bearing cap or cylinder block.
Trim seal ends even with block parting surface. Some applications require sealer to be applied on main bearing cap prior to installation. *See Fig. 28.*

Split-Rubber Type Seal

Follow manufacturers procedures when installing split-rubber type rear main oil seals. Installation procedures vary with engine type. See appropriate ENGINE article in this section. *See Fig. 29.*

OIL PUMP

ROTOR TYPE

Oil pump rotors must be marked for location prior to removal. *See Fig. 30.* Remove outer rotor and measure thickness and diameter. Measure inner rotor thickness. Inspect shaft for scoring or wear. Inspect rotors for pitting or damage. Inspect cover for grooving or wear. Replace components if worn or damaged.

Engine Overhaul Procedures

ALL ENGINES (Cont.)

Measure outer rotor-to-body clearance. Replace pump assembly if clearance exceeds specification. Measure clearance between rotors. See Fig. 31. Replace shaft and both rotors if clearance exceeds specifications.

Install rotors in pump body. Position straightedge across pump body. Using feeler gauge, measure clearance between rotors and straightedge. Pump cover wear is measured using a straightedge and feeler gauge. Replace pump if clearance exceeds specification.

Fig. 30: Typical Rotor Type Oil Pump

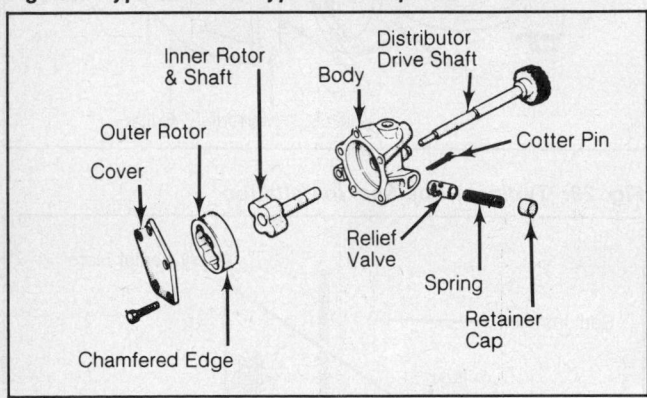

Fig. 31: Measuring Rotor Clearance

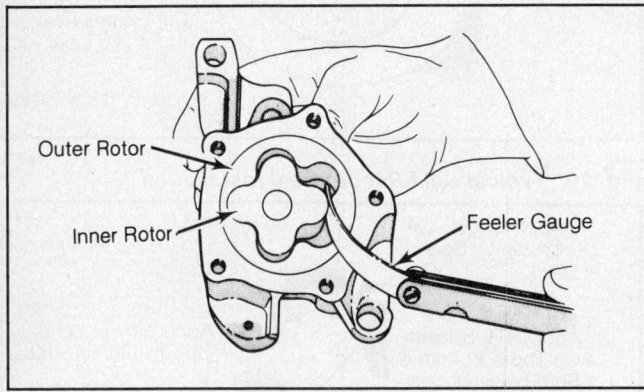

GEAR TYPE

Oil pump gears must be marked for location prior to removal. See Fig. 32. Remove gears from pump body. Inspect gears for pitting or damage. Inspect cover for grooving or wear.

Fig. 32: Typical Gear Type Oil Pump

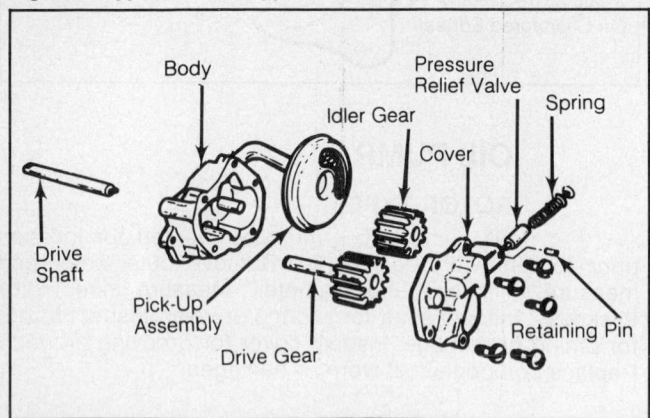

Measure gear diameter and length. Measure gear housing cavity depth and diameter. See Fig. 33. Replace components if worn or damaged.

Pump cover wear is measured using a straightedge and feeler gauge. Pump is to be replaced if warpage or wear exceeds specifications or mating surface of pump cover is scratched or grooved.

Fig. 33: Measuring Oil Pump Gear Cavity

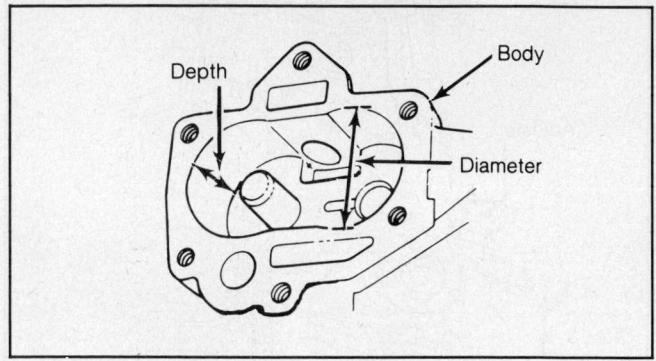

BREAK-IN-PROCEDURE

ENGINE PRE-OILING

Engine pre-oiling should be done prior to operation to prevent engine damage. Lightly oiled oil pump will cavitate unless oil pump cavities are filled with engine oil or petroleum jelly.

Engine pre-oiling can be done using pressure oiler (if available). Connect pressure oiler to cylinder block oil passage such as oil pressure sending unit. Operate pressure oiler long enough to ensure correct amount of oil has filled crankcase. Check oil level while pre-oiling.

If pressure oiler is not available, disconnect ignition system. Remove oil pressure sending unit and replace with oil pressure test gauge. Using starter motor, rotate engine starter until gauge shows normal oil pressure for several seconds. DO NOT crank engine for more than 30 seconds to avoid starter motor damage.

Ensure oil pressure has reached the most distant point from the oil pump. Reinstall oil pressure sending unit. Reconnect ignition system.

INITIAL START-UP

Start engine and operate engine at low speed while checking for coolant, fuel and oil leaks. Stop engine. Recheck coolant and oil level. Adjust if necessary.

CAMSHAFT

Break-in procedure is required when new or reground camshaft has been installed. Operate and maintain engine speed between 1500-2500 RPM for approximately 30 minutes. Procedure may vary due to manufacturers recommendations.

PISTON RINGS

Piston rings require a break-in procedure to ensure seating of rings to cylinder walls. Serious damage may occur to rings if correct procedures are not followed.

Extremely high piston ring temperatures are obtained during break-in process. If rings are exposed to excessively high RPM or high cylinder pressures, ring

ALL ENGINES (Cont.)

damage can occur. Follow piston ring manufacturers recommended break-in procedure.

FINAL ADJUSTMENTS

Check or adjust ignition timing and dwell (if applicable). Adjust valves (if necessary). Adjust carburetion or injection idle speed and mixture. Retighten cylinder heads (if required). If cylinder head or block is aluminum, retighten bolts when engine is cold. Follow the engine manufacturer's recommended break-in procedure and maintenance schedule for new engines.

NOTE: Some manufacturer's require that head bolts be retightened after specified amount of operation. This must be done to prevent head gasket failure.

ENGINE TROUBLE SHOOTING

See ENGINE TROUBLE SHOOTING at beginning of ENGINE section.

Chrysler Motors Engines
2.2 & 2.5L 4-CYLINDER

NOTE: For engine repair procedures not covered in this article, see ENGINE OVERHAUL PROCEDURES article at beginning of this section.

ENGINE CODING

ENGINE IDENTIFICATION

Engine may be identified using Vehicle Identification Number (VIN) stamped on metal tab located near lower left corner of windshield. The 8th character identifies the engine model.

Engine serial number must be used when ordering replacement components. On 2.2L, serial number is stamped on rear of cylinder block, directly below cylinder head. On 2.5L, serial number is located on right front of cylinder block, next to exhaust manifold stud.

ENGINE CODES

Engine	Code
2.2L	
TBI	D
Turbo I MPFI	E
Turbo II MPFI	A
2.5L	
TBI	K

ENGINE REMOVAL

See ENGINE REMOVAL & INSTALLATION at end of ENGINE section.

CYLINDER HEAD & MANIFOLDS

INTAKE & EXHAUST MANIFOLDS

NOTE: Exhaust and intake manifolds use a one-piece mounting gasket. Both manifolds must be removed to perform service to either manifold.

Removal (Non-Turbo)

1) Disconnect battery. Drain cooling system. Disconnect water crossover. Disconnect air cleaner hoses. Remove air cleaner.

2) Disconnect throttle cable and kickdown cable (if equipped). Disconnect and mark electrical connections from throttle body.

CAUTION: Fuel system is under pressure. Pressure must be released prior to disconnecting any fuel system component.

3) To release fuel pressure, loosen gas cap at tank. Remove wiring harness connector from injector. Ground one injector terminal. Connect a 12-volt jumper wire to remaining injector terminal. DO NOT apply voltage for longer than 10 seconds.

4) Disconnect and mark vacuum hoses to throttle body. Disconnect fuel lines from throttle body. Disconnect exhaust pipe from exhaust manifold. Remove intake and exhaust manifold bolts. Remove manifolds.

Removal (Turbo)

1) Disconnect battery. Drain cooling system. Disconnect intercooler hoses, air intake and outlet hoses from turbo. Disconnect air inlet hose at throttle body. Disconnect air intake hoses from air cleaner assembly. Remove air cleaner.

2) Disconnect throttle cable and kickdown cable (if equipped). Disconnect and mark electrical connections at throttle body. Disconnect PCV hose and brake booster vacuum hose.

3) Disconnect and mark vacuum hoses to throttle body. On Turbo II models, disconnect charge air temperature sensor located on intake manifold.

CAUTION: Fuel system is under pressure. Pressure must be released prior to disconnecting any fuel system component.

4) To release fuel pressure, loosen gas cap at tank. Remove wiring harness connector from injector. Ground one injector terminal. Connect a 12-volt jumper wire to remaining injector terminal. DO NOT apply voltage for longer than 10 seconds.

5) Remove throttle body-to-intake manifold nuts. Separate throttle body from intake manifold. Disconnect knock sensor and all fuel injector wiring connectors.

6) Remove fuel hose from fuel injector rail. Remove fuel return hose at fuel pressure regulator. See Fig. 1.

Fig. 1: Removing Fuel Injector Rail

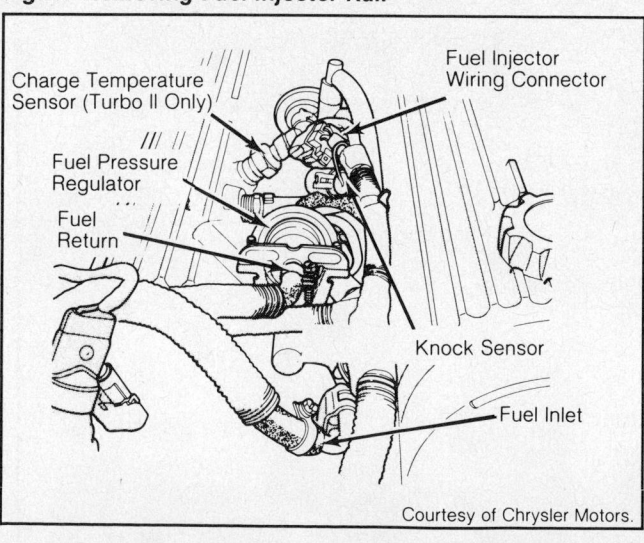

Courtesy of Chrysler Motors.

7) Disconnect vacuum hose from fuel pressure regulator. Remove fuel pressure regulator-to-fuel injector rail nuts. Separate fuel pressure regulator from fuel rail.

8) Remove fuel injector rail-to-valve cover bracket bolts. Remove fuel injector rail retaining bolts. Remove fuel injector rail and injectors from intake manifold. Cover fuel injector ports.

9) Remove front engine mount bolt. Rotate engine away from cowl. Disconnect exhaust pipe from turbine housing. Remove right front wheel. Remove right drive shaft. See FWD AXLE SHAFTS in DRIVE AXLES section.

10) Remove O_2 sensor electrical connector. Remove turbo-to-cylinder block bracket. Disconnect oil

2.2 & 2.5L 4-CYLINDER (Cont.)

lines from turbo. Disconnect wastegate rod-to-gate retaining clip.

11) Remove oil return line fitting. Remove turbo mounting nuts. Disconnect coolant lines from turbo. Remove turbo. Remove intake and exhaust manifold bolts. Remove manifolds.

Installation

1) Gasket surfaces must be flat within .006" (.15 mm) per 12" (305 mm). On non-turbo models, steel gasket must be coated with Sealant (3419115). If composition gasket is used, DO NOT use sealant. On turbo models, no sealant is to be used on gasket.

2) On all models, install gasket, exhaust manifold and intake manifold. Tighten bolts or nuts to specification, starting in center and working outward in both directions.

3) On turbo models, coat turbo mounting studs with anti-seize. Coat all line fittings with sealant. Coat injector and fuel pressure regulator "O" rings with clean engine oil.

4) Ensure fuel rail is drawn evenly into cylinder head. Reverse removal procedure for remaining components. Tighten bolts to specification.

5) Fill cooling system. Remove plug from top of thermostat housing. Allow air to bleed from cooling system. Install plug once coolant reaches thermostat housing level.

CYLINDER HEAD
Removal

1) Remove intake and exhaust manifolds as previously described. Remove timing belt. See TIMING BELT under CAMSHAFTS in this article. On vehicles using solid mounted air conditioning compressor bracket, bracket must be removed.

CAUTION: Solid mount air conditioning compressor bracket bolts must be removed in proper sequence.

2) Remove air conditioner compressor belt idler. Bolts must be removed in proper sequence. Remove side mounting bolts Nos. 1, 4, 5, 6 and 7. *See Fig. 2.* Remove front mounting nut No. 2, then loosen bolt No. 3.

Fig. 2: Removing & Installing Solid Mount Compressor Bracket

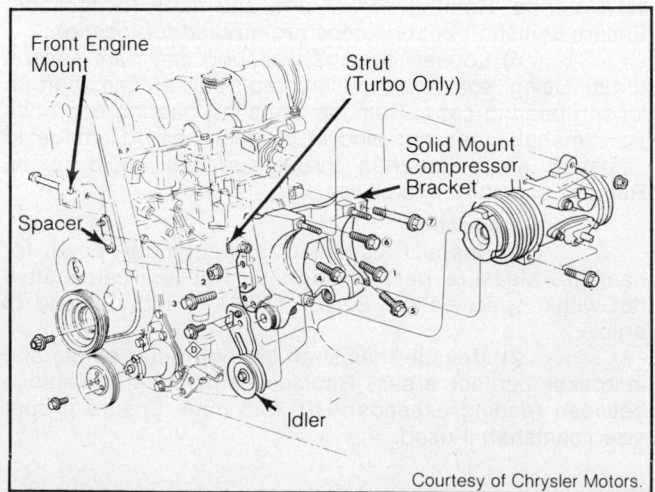

Courtesy of Chrysler Motors.

3) Bolt No. 3 will be removed with assembly. Rotate bracket and remove. Remove valve cover and oil baffle (if equipped).

4) Using Sprocket Holder (C-4687) for 2.2L or (C-4687-1) for 2.5L, hold camshaft sprocket. Remove sprocket bolt. Remove camshaft sprocket.

5) Disconnect dipstick tube from thermostat housing. Rotate dipstick tube bracket from stud. Remove cylinder head bolts in proper sequence. *See Fig. 3.* Bolts must be removed in sequence to prevent damage to cylinder head. Remove cylinder head and gasket.

Fig. 3: Cylinder Head Bolt Removal & Tightening Sequence

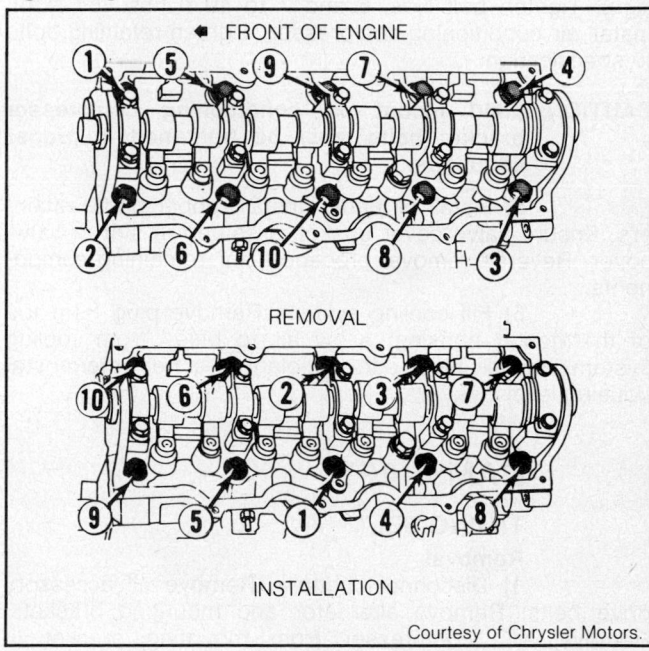

Courtesy of Chrysler Motors.

NOTE: Oversized camshaft may be used which requires cylinder head with oversized camshaft bores. Oversized camshaft is identified by Green painted barrel with letters "O/JS" stamped on air pump end of camshaft. Cylinder head is identified by Green painted bearing caps with letters "O/JS" stamped rearward of oil gallery plug on air pump end of cylinder head.

Inspection

Inspect cylinder head for cracks and warpage. Cylinder head must be resurfaced or replaced if warpage exceeds .004" (.10 mm). If cylinder head replacement is required, ensure proper size cylinder head is used.

Installation

1) Late model 11 mm head bolts are identified by the number 11 stamped on bolt head. Previous models used 10 mm bolts which will thread into hole. These bolts will strip cylinder block when tightened. Ensure proper bolts are used.

CAUTION: Turbo I models use a different head gasket than Turbo II models. Ensure proper gasket is used.

2) Install new gasket and cylinder head. Tighten bolts in sequence. *See Fig. 3.* Tighten to specification using proper steps. See TIGHTENING SPECIFICATIONS table at end of article.

CAUTION: Bolt torque should exceed 90 ft. lbs. (122 N.m) after final step. Replace bolt if torque is less than specification.

3) Install solid mount bracket and spacer over mounting stud. Loosely install bracket retaining bolts. Tighten bolt No. 1 to 30 INCH lbs. (3.39 N.m). *See Fig. 2.*

4) Tighten nut No. 2 and bolt No. 3 to 40 ft. lbs. (54 N.m). Tighten bolt Nos. 1, 4, and 5 to 40 ft. lbs. (54 N.m). Tighten bolt Nos. 6 and 7 to 40 ft. lbs. (54 N.m). Install air conditioning compressor. Tighten retaining bolts to specification.

CAUTION: Solid mount air conditioning compressor bracket bolts must be tightened in proper sequence.

5) Install oil baffle. Install rubber baffle retainers. Ensure valve cover gasket is seated in slot of valve cover. Reverse removal procedure for remaining components.

6) Fill cooling system. Remove plug from top of thermostat housing. Allow air to bleed from cooling system. Install plug once coolant reaches thermostat housing level.

CAMSHAFT

TIMING BELT
Removal
1) Disconnect battery. Remove all accessory drive belts. Remove alternator and mounting brackets. Remove A/C compressor from mounting bracket (if equipped). DO NOT disconnect refrigerant lines. Remove A/C belt idler.

2) Raise and support vehicle. Remove right inner splash shield. Remove water pump and crankshaft pulley. Remove upper and lower timing belt covers. Position jack under engine.

3) Remove front engine mount bolt. *See Fig. 2.* Raise engine slightly. Loosen timing belt tensioner retaining bolt. Rotate hex to release tension. Remove timing belt.

Installation
1) Remove spark plugs. Place No. 1 cylinder on TDC. Align timing marks on crankshaft and intermediate shaft sprockets. *See Fig. 4.* Rotate camshaft sprocket until the 2 holes align with camshaft cap-to-cylinder head line. Camshaft sprocket small hole must be at 12 o'clock position. *See Fig. 4.*

2) Install timing belt. Install Timing Belt Tensioner Adjuster (C-4703) horizontally on hex of belt tensioner pulley.

3) Reset belt tensioner to have axis within 15 degrees of horizontal (if necessary). Rotate engine clockwise 2 complete revolutions to TDC. Tighten tensioner retaining bolt while holding belt tensioner wrench in position. Ensure all timing marks are aligned.

Fig. 4: Engine Timing Marks

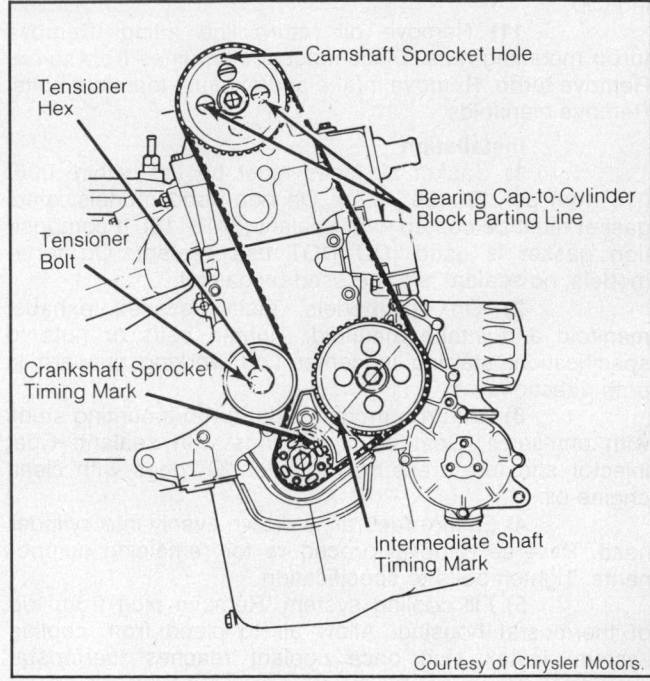

Courtesy of Chrysler Motors.

NOTE: DO NOT rotate crankshaft counterclockwise or rotate engine using camshaft or intermediate shaft sprocket bolt.

4) Reverse removal procedures for remaining components. Tighten bolts to specification.

CAMSHAFT
Removal
1) Remove timing belt as previously described. Remove valve cover and oil baffle (if equipped). Using Sprocket Holder (C-4687) for 2.2L or (C-4687-1) for 2.5L, hold camshaft sprocket. Remove sprocket bolt. Remove camshaft sprocket.

2) Using Seal Remover (C-4679), remove camshaft seals. Mark rocker arms for location. On each rocker arm, rotate camshaft until base circle contacts rocker arm.

3) Using Spring Compressor (4682), compress valve spring. Remove rocker arm and mark for location. Ensure camshaft bearing caps are marked for location.

4) Loosen camshaft bearing cap nuts several turns. Using soft-faced mallet, tap rear of camshaft to loosen bearing caps. Remove camshaft bearing cap bolts so camshaft does not bind in cylinder head. Damage to camshaft and/or bearing thrust surfaces could result. Remove camshaft and oil seals.

Inspection
1) Inspect camshaft and cylinder head for damage. Measure bearing journals. Replace camshaft if not within specification. See CAMSHAFT table at end of article.

2) Measure camshaft lobe on outer edges and in rocker contact areas. Replace camshaft if difference between reading exceeds .010" (.25 mm). Ensure proper sized camshaft if used.

2.2 & 2.5L 4-CYLINDER (Cont.)

NOTE: Oversized camshaft may be used which requires cylinder head with oversized camshaft bores. Oversized camshaft is identified by Green painted barrel with letters "O/JS" stamped on air pump end of camshaft. Cylinder head is identified by Green painted bearing caps with letters "O/JS" stamped rearward of oil gallery plug on air pump end of cylinder head.

Installation

1) Install camshaft on cylinder head. Arrows on bearing caps Nos. 1 thru 4 should point toward timing belt. Apply anaerobic sealer to Nos. 1 and 5 bearing caps at cap-to-cylinder head surfaces.

2) Install bearing caps with No. 1 bearing cap at timing belt end and bearing cap No. 5 at rear of cylinder head. Ensure arrows on bearing caps Nos. 1 thru 4 point toward timing belt. Install bearing cap bolts. Tighten to specification. See TIGHTENING SPECIFICATIONS table at end of article.

3) Using dial indicator, check camshaft end play. End play should be .005-.013" (.12-.33 mm). If end play exceeds specification, camshaft and/or cylinder head should be replaced.

4) Coat camshaft oil seal lips with oil. Using Seal Installer (C-4680), install camshaft oil seal even with camshaft bearing cap. Install rocker arms in original location.

CAUTION: Ensure valve spring retainer locks are fully seated after installing rocker arms.

5) If camshaft sprocket is replaced, ensure proper sprocket is installed. Camshaft sprocket on 2.2L contain a 4 hole pattern in sprocket hub, while the 2.5L contain a 6 hole pattern. The 2.5L sprockets contain an off-set hub for clearance.

6) Reverse removal procedure for remaining components. Tighten bolts to specification.

VALVES

VALVE ARRANGEMENT

All Engines
E-I-E-I-E-I-E-I (Front-to-rear).

VALVES

1) Measure valve stem O.D. Replace valve if not within specification. See VALVES table at end of article.

2) Measure valve margin. Replace valve if less than specification. See VALVE MARGIN SPECIFICATIONS table. Recheck valve margin after grinding valve.

VALVE MARGIN SPECIFICATIONS

Application	In. (mm)
Exhaust	.0468 (1.188)
Intake	.0312 (.79)

VALVE GUIDE

1) Check valve stem-to-guide clearance. Ensure valve stem O.D. is within specification. Valve guide must be reamed for valve with oversize valve stem if clearance exceeds specification. See VALVES table at end of article.

2) Valves are available with oversize valve stems of .006" (.15 mm), .016" (.40 mm) and .031" (.80 mm). Cylinder head must be replaced if guide cannot be cleaned up using .031" (.80 mm) reamer.

NOTE: DO NOT ream valve guides from standard to maximum oversize. Ream guides oversize in steps so guides are reamed true in relation to valve seat.

VALVE STEM OIL SEALS

Ensure oversize valve stem seals are used when oversize valves are installed.

VALVE SPRINGS

1) Remove valve springs. Measure free length of valve spring. Using Spring Tester (C-647), check spring tension. Replace springs if not within specifications. See VALVE SPRINGS table at end of article.

2) Check valve spring squareness. Replace valve spring if squareness exceeds .079" (2.01 mm).

VALVE STEM INSTALLED HEIGHT

Measure valve stem installed height after grinding valves or seats. Grind valve stem tip to obtain proper clearance. See VALVES SPECIFICATIONS table.

VALVE SPRING INSTALLED HEIGHT

Measure valve spring installed height from lower edge of valve spring to upper edge of spring retainer. DO NOT include valve spring seat or retainer. Additional spring seat may be required to maintain proper spring height. See VALVES SPECIFICATIONS table.

VALVE SPECIFICATIONS

Application	In. (mm)
Spring Installed Height	1.62-1.68 (41.20-42.70)
Stem Installed Height	1.960-2.009 (49.76-51.04)

ROCKER ARM ASSEMBLY

Install hydraulic valve lash adjusters and rocker arms in original location. Measure rocker arm-to-valve stem installed height between projecting ears of rocker arms and valve spring retainer. Clearance should be a minimum of .050" (1.27 mm). If insufficient clearance exists, grind rocker arm ears to obtain clearance.

HYDRAULIC VALVE LASH ADJUSTERS

1) No adjustment of lash adjusters is required. If disassembled for cleaning purposes, reassemble using new retainer caps.

2) Adjusters must be at least partially full of oil prior to installation. Little or no plunger travel should exist when adjuster is depressed.

NOTE: Service lash adjusters as complete assemblies. Parts are not interchangeable.

DRY LASH

1) Dry lash is amount of clearance between installed camshaft base circle and rocker arm pad. Valve lash adjuster must be completely collapsed and empty of oil to check clearance.

Chrysler Motors Engines

2.2 & 2.5L 4-CYLINDER (Cont.)

2) Remove retainer cap from valve lash adjuster. Disassemble and drain oil. Install adjuster completely collapsed. Using feeler gauge, measure clearance between camshaft base circle and rocker arm pad.

3) Clearance should be .024-.060" (.62-1.52 mm). If not within specifications, check wear on parts and replace as required. Fill adjusters with engine oil. Reassemble using new retainer cap. Allow 10 minutes for adjusters to bleed down before rotating camshaft.

CYLINDER BLOCK ASSEMBLY

CYLINDER BLOCK

Inspection

Using dial bore gauge, check cylinder bore out-of-round and taper. Repair or replace cylinder block as required if not within specification. See CYLINDER BLOCK SPECIFICATIONS table.

CYLINDER BLOCK SPECIFICATIONS

Application	In. (mm)
Cylinder Bore	
Out-of-Round	.002 (.05)
Taper	.005 (.13)

INTERMEDIATE SHAFT

Removal

1) Remove distributor assembly. Remove timing belt. See TIMING BELT under CAMSHAFT in this article. Using Sprocket Holder (C-4687) and Adapter (C-4786-1) for 2.5L, remove intermediate shaft sprocket retaining bolt. Remove sprocket.

2) Using Seal Remover (C-4679), remove intermediate shaft seal. Remove intermediate shaft retainer bolts. Remove retainer and intermediate shaft.

Inspection

Inspect bearing journals and bushings for damage. Measure bearing journal O.D. Measure intermediate shaft bushing I.D. Determine oil clearance. Replace shaft and/or bushing if not within specification. See INTERMEDIATE SHAFT SPECIFICATIONS table.

INTERMEDIATE SHAFT SPECIFICATIONS

Application	In. (mm)
Bearing Journal O.D.	
Large Journal	1.6799-1.6809 (42.670-42.695)
Small Journal	.7744-.7753 (19.670-19.695)
Bushing I.D.	
Large Journal	1.6822-1.6830 (42.730-42.750)
Small Journal	.7763-.7775 (19.720-19.750)

Installation

1) If bushings require replacement, remove intermediate shaft front bushing using Bushing Remover (C-4697-2), and (C-4686-2) for rear bushing.

2) Use Bushing Installer (C-4697-1) for front bushing and (C-4686-1) for rear bushing. Install bushings until bushing installer is even with cylinder block.

3) Coat distributor drive gear with oil. Install intermediate shaft. Apply .06" (1.5 mm) diameter bead of anaerobic gasket material to outer area of shaft retainer. Install retainer. Tighten bolts to specification.

4) Using Seal Installer (C-4680), install seal. Seal must be even with retainer surface. Install intermediate sprocket. Tighten bolt to specification. Align timing marks. *See Fig. 4.* Install timing belt.

5) Remove distributor cap, align rotor to No. 1 cylinder firing position. Install distributor. Tighten bolts to specification.

PISTONS, PINS & RINGS

OIL PAN

See OIL PAN REMOVAL at end of ENGINE section.

PISTON & ROD ASSEMBLY

Removal

1) Remove cylinder head. See CYLINDER HEAD under REMOVAL & INSTALLATION in this article. Remove oil pan.

2) Mark pistons, connecting rods and caps for cylinder location. Note direction of valve cuts or dished areas in top of piston. Remove rod cap nuts and rod cap. Remove piston assembly from cylinder block.

NOTE: Connecting rod bolt threads should be checked for "necking" by holding a straight-edge against threads. If threads do not fully touch straightedge, bolt should be replaced.

Installation

1) Ensure ring end gap and side clearance are within specification. Ensure "TOP" mark on Nos. 1 and 2 rings is toward top of piston.

2) Position rings gaps in proper location. Oil ring rail gaps are installed 180 degrees apart from each other. *See Fig. 5.*

Fig. 5: Piston Ring Locations

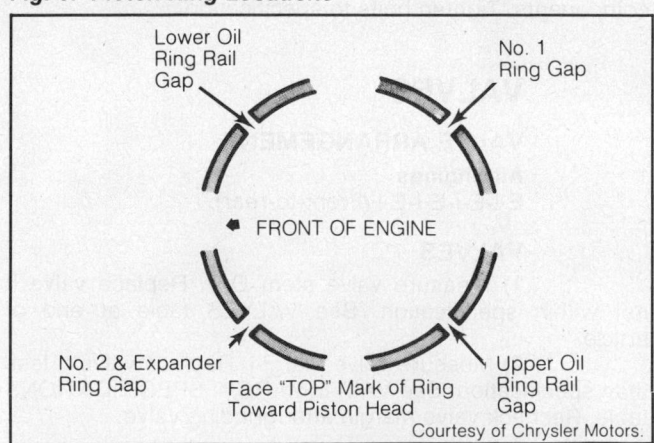

Courtesy of Chrysler Motors.

3) Install piston assembly in cylinder block. Ensure connecting rod oil hole and piston dished or cutout areas face front of engine. *See Fig. 6.*

4) Coat connecting rod bolt threads with oil. Rotate crankshaft so bearing journal to be checked starts moving toward top of engine. Install rod cap. Ensure marks on connecting rod and cap are aligned.

5) Check bearing clearance using Plastigage method. Lubricate bearings once clearance is checked. Tighten bolts to specification.

6) Ensure connecting rod moves freely on crankshaft. Check connecting rod side clearance. Clearance must be within specification. See CRANKSHAFT MAIN & CONNECTING ROD BEARINGS table at end of article.

Fig. 6: Piston & Connecting Rod Installation

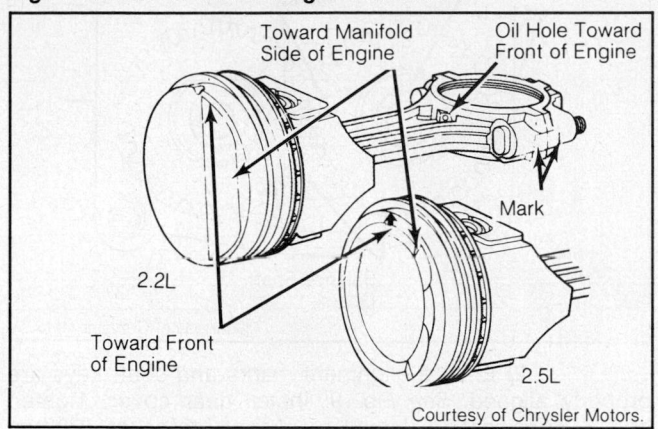

Courtesy of Chrysler Motors.

FITTING PISTONS

1) Measure piston diameter at point "B" using height "C". *See Fig. 7.* Measure diameter "A". Measurement "A" should less than "B" within specification. See PISTON DIMENSION SPECIFICATIONS table.

2) Measure piston at points "C" and "D". Measurement "D" should be larger than measurement "C" within specification. See PISTON DIMENSION SPECIFICATIONS table.

PISTON DIMENSION SPECIFICATIONS

Application	In. (mm)
"B" @ "C"	
Turbo	3.4416-3.4441 (87.416-87.480)
Non-Turbo	3.443-3.445 (87.452-87.503)
"A" Smaller Than "B"	
Turbo	.0074-.0106 (.188-.269)
Non-Turbo	.0118-.0138 (.299-.350)
"D" Larger Than "C"	
Turbo	.000-.0012 (.00-.030)
Non-Turbo	.000-.0020 (.00-.050)

3) Replace piston if not within specification. Measure cylinder bore. Determine piston-to-cylinder clearance. Clearance must be within specification. See PISTONS, PINS & RINGS table at end of article.

PISTON PIN REPLACEMENT

Information not available.

CRANKSHAFT

1) Check diameter of rod and main bearing journals. Repair or replace crankshaft if not within specification. See CRANKSHAFT MAIN & CONNECTING ROD BEARINGS table at end of article.

2) Check bearing journals for taper and out-of-round. Repair or replace crankshaft if not within specification. See CRANKSHAFT JOURNAL SPECIFICATIONS table.

Fig. 7: Piston Measurement Locations

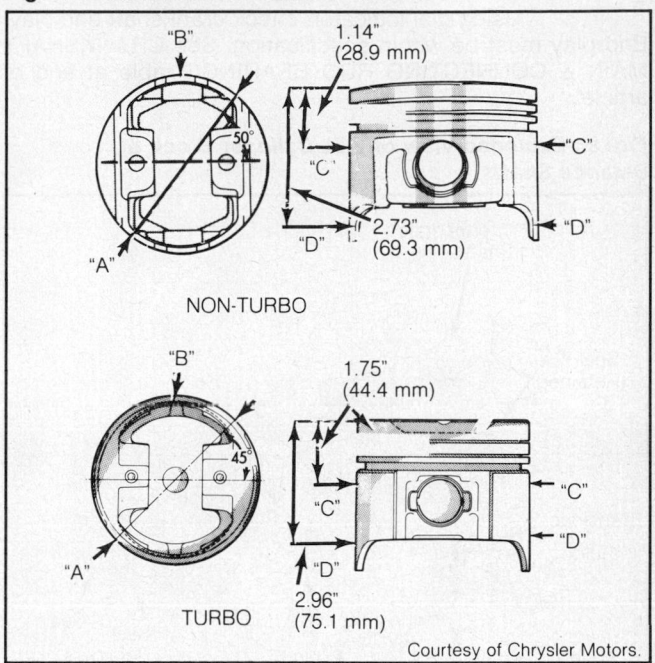

Courtesy of Chrysler Motors.

CRANKSHAFT JOURNAL SPECIFICATIONS

Application	In. (mm)
Out-of-Round	.0003-.005 (.007-.12)
Taper	.0003-.0004 (.007-.010)

CRANKSHAFT & ROD BEARINGS

NOTE: Connecting rod and main bearing bolt threads should be checked for "necking" by holding a straightedge against threads. If threads do not fully touch straightedge, bolt should be replaced.

MAIN BEARINGS

1) Main bearings Nos. 1, 2, 4 and 5 contain full oil groove and No. 3 contains half groove. Ensure bearing oil holes align. Apply light coat of oil to bearing cap bolts prior to installation.

2) Using Plastigage method, check bearing clearance. Tighten bolts to specification. Check crankshaft end play. See CRANKSHAFT END PLAY in this article.

CONNECTING ROD BEARINGS

1) Install bearings. Ensure bearings are fully seated. Coat connecting rod bolt threads with oil. Rotate crankshaft so bearing journal to be checked starts moving toward top of engine. Install rod cap. Ensure marks on connecting rod and cap are aligned.

2) Check bearing clearance using Plastigage method. Tighten bolts to specification. Ensure connecting rod moves freely on crankshaft. Check connecting rod side clearance. Clearance must be within specification. See CRANKSHAFT MAIN & CONNECTING ROD BEARINGS table at end of article.

2.2 & 2.5L 4-CYLINDER (Cont.)

CRANKSHAFT END PLAY

Using dial indicator, check crankshaft end play. End play must be within specification. See CRANKSHAFT MAIN & CONNECTING ROD BEARINGS table at end of article.

Fig. 8: Exploded View of 2.5L Cylinder Block & Balance Shafts

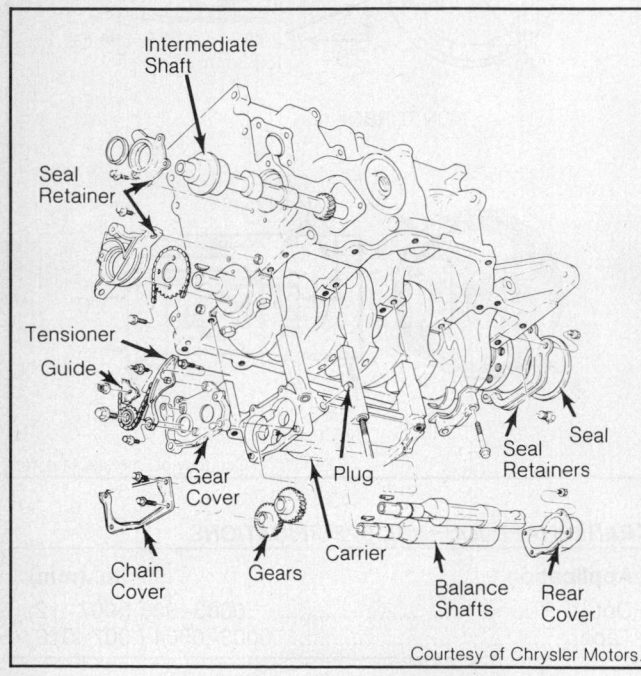

Courtesy of Chrysler Motors.

BALANCE SHAFT & CARRIER

Removal

1) Remove oil pan and oil pick-up. Remove timing belt. See TIMING BELT under CAMSHAFT in this article. Remove crankshaft sprocket and oil seal. See CRANKSHAFT SPROCKET OIL SEAL in this article.

2) Remove oil seal retainer. Remove chain cover and balance shaft chain sprocket bolt. See Fig. 8. Loosen tensioner retaining bolts. Position balance shaft through driven chain sprocket. Remove carrier-to-cylinder block bolts. Remove carrier assembly.

Installation

Reverse removal procedure. Check balance shaft timing. See BALANCE SHAFT GEAR TIMING in this article. Tighten bolts to specification.

BALANCE SHAFTS

Removal

1) Remove carrier assembly. Remove tensioner and guide. Remove balance shaft gear and chain sprocket retaining bolts.

2) Remove balance shaft gears and gear cover. Remove rear cover. Remove balance shafts.

Installation

Reverse removal procedure. Tighten bolts to specification. Set balance gear timing. See BALANCE SHAFT GEAR TIMING in this article.

BALANCE SHAFT GEAR TIMING

1) With balance shafts and carrier installed, rotate balance shafts until shaft keys are upward. See Fig.

9. Install short hub drive gear on sprocket driven shaft. Install long hub gear on gear driven shaft.

Fig. 9: Balance Gears Timing Marks

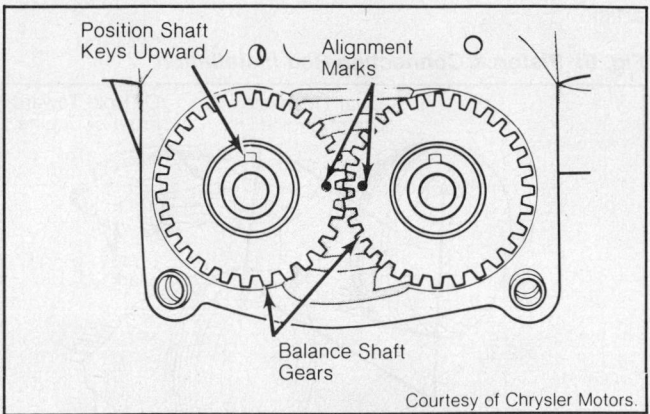

Courtesy of Chrysler Motors.

2) Ensure alignment marks and shaft keys are properly aligned. See Fig. 9. Install gear cover. Tighten bolt to specification. Install crankshaft sprocket. Tighten bolt to specification.

3) Rotate crankshaft to position No. 1 cylinder at TDC. Chain sprocket timing marks should align with parting line of No.1 main bearing cap. See Fig. 10.

4) Install chain on crankshaft sprocket. Position nickel plated link over crankshaft sprocket timing mark. See Fig. 10. Install balance shaft sprocket in timing chain.

5) The Yellow dot on balance shaft sprocket must align with the Yellow chain link. Install drive chain and balance shaft sprocket on balance shaft. Tighten balance shaft sprocket bolt to specification.

CAUTION: Ensure Yellow link, balance shaft sprocket timing mark and gear cover notch are aligned. See Fig. 10.

Fig. 10: Aligning Balance Shaft Timing Marks

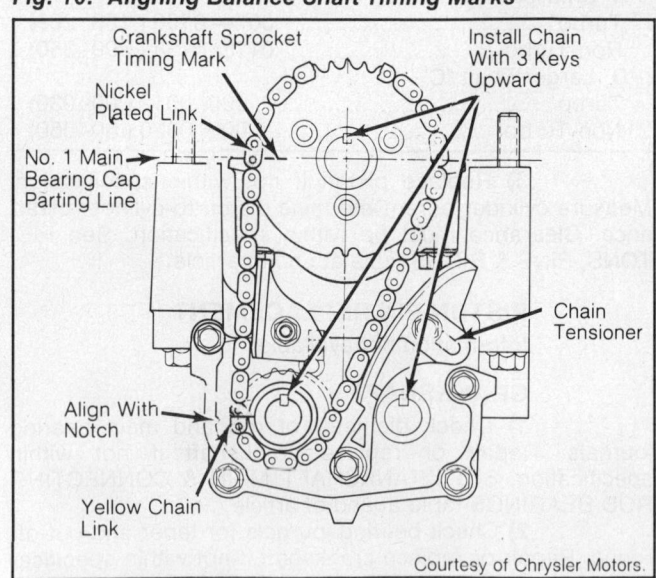

Courtesy of Chrysler Motors.

6) Install chain tensioner with mounting bolts loose. Install Tension Gauge (C-4916) between tensioner and chain. Shim stock with thickness of .039" (.99 mm)

2.2 & 2.5L 4-CYLINDER (Cont.)

and 2.57" (69.8 mm) long can be used in place of tension gauge.

7) Push tension gauge or shim stock and tensioner against chain. Apply firm pressure directly behind adjustment slot to tighten chain slack. Tighten top tensioner bolt, then bottom bolt to specification with pressure applied.

8) Remove tension gauge or shim stock. Install chain guide. Ensure chain guide aligns with gear cover slot. Install guide retaining bolt. Tighten to specification. Install carrier cover (if removed). Tighten bolts to specification.

CRANKSHAFT SPROCKET OIL SEAL

Removal
1) Remove timing belt. See TIMING BELT under CAMSHAFT in this article. Remove crankshaft sprocket retaining bolt.
2) Using Crankshaft Sprocket Puller (C-4685), remove crankshaft sprocket. Using Seal Remover (C-4679) for 2.2L or (C-4991) for 2.5L, remove oil seal.

Installation
Using Seal Installer (C-4680) for 2.2L or (C-4992) for 2.5L, install seal even with seal retainer surface. Install timing belt.

REAR MAIN BEARING OIL SEAL

Removal & Installation
Remove flywheel. Pry seal from crankshaft seal retainer. Coat outside diameter of seal with Loctite (4057987). Install seal and Oil Seal Installer (C-4681). Tap seal in until even with seal retainer surface.

ENGINE OILING

CRANKCASE CAPACITY
Crankcase capacity is 4 qts. (3.8L) with oil filter.

NORMAL OIL PRESSURE
Normal oil pressure is 4 psi (.28 kg/cm²) at curb idle or 25-90 psi (1.75-6.32 kg/cm²) at 3000 RPM with engine at normal operating temperature.

PRESSURE REGULATOR VALVE
Pressure regulator valve is located in oil pump cover.

OIL PUMP

Removal
Remove oil pan. Remove oil pick-up tube-to-oil pump bolt. Remove pick-up tube and "O" ring. Remove oil pump-to-cylinder block bolts. Remove oil pump.

Disassembly
Remove oil pump cover-to-pump housing bolts. Remove pump cover. Remove inner and outer rotors. See Fig. 12. Remove oil pressure relief valve pin, cup, spring and valve from oil pump housing.

Inspection
1) Install drive gear and rotor into pump housing. Place straightedge across pump housing. Using feeler gauge, check rotor end play clearance between rotors and straightedge.

Fig. 11: Engine Oiling System

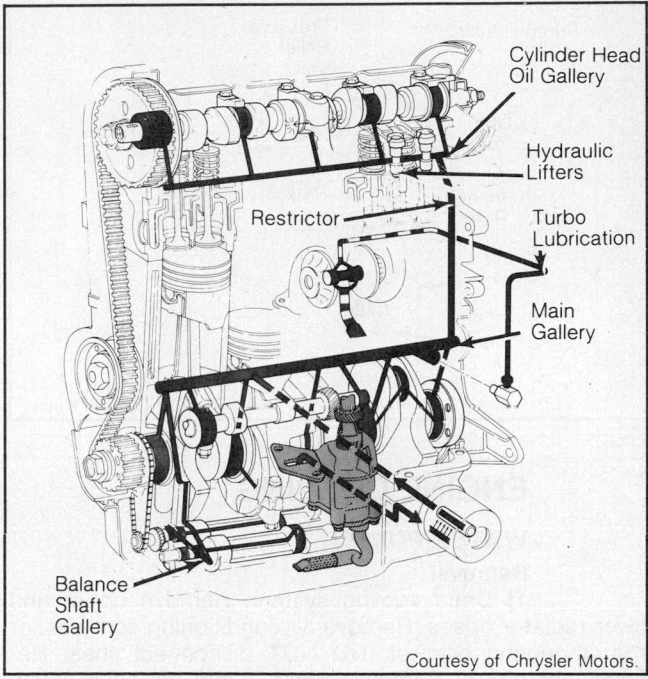

Cylinder Head Oil Gallery

Hydraulic Lifters

Turbo Lubrication

Restrictor

Main Gallery

Balance Shaft Gallery

Courtesy of Chrysler Motors.

2) Check clearance between rotor tips. Check clearance between outer rotor and housing. Remove outer rotor. Measure diameter and thickness of outer rotor. Check cover flatness.

3) Measure relief valve spring free length. Using spring pressure tester, check spring pressure. Spring pressure should be 20 lbs. at 1.34" (89 N at 34.0 mm). Replace oil pump assembly if not within all specifications. See OIL PUMP SPECIFICATIONS table.

OIL PUMP SPECIFICATIONS

Application	In. (mm)
Cover Flatness	.003 (.07)
Outer Rotor Diameter	2.469 (62.71)
Outer Rotor Thickness	.9435 (23.965)
Outer Rotor-to-Housing	.014 (.35)
Rotor End Play	.001-.0035 (.02-.088)
Rotor Tip Clearance	.008 (.20)
Valve Spring Free Length	1.95 (49.5)

Reassembly
Install outer rotor in pump housing with large chamfered edge toward pump housing. Lubricate inner rotor shaft and drive gear. Install inner rotor and drive gear. Install pump cover. Tighten bolts to specification. Install pressure relief valve in pump housing. Ensure relief valve slides freely in bore. Install spring, cup and pin.

Installation
1) Apply Loctite Sealer (515) to oil pump housing-to-cylinder block surface. Align slot in oil pump drive gear. Install oil pump. Rotate pump back and forth to ensure proper seating while tightening retaining bolts.
2) Tighten to specification. Install new "O" ring on pick-up tube. Reverse removal procedures. Tighten bolts to specification.

Fig. 12: *Exploded View of Oil Pump Assembly*

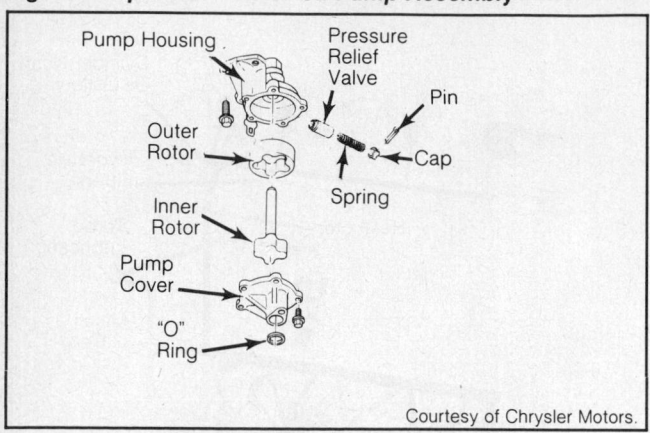

Courtesy of Chrysler Motors.

ENGINE COOLING

WATER PUMP

Removal

1) Drain cooling system. Remove upper and lower radiator hoses. Remove air conditioning compressor from mounting bracket. DO NOT disconnect lines. Remove alternator. Remove water pump by-pass hose. Remove water pump retaining bolts. Remove water pump from cylinder block.

2) Remove water pump pulley. Remove water pump-to-housing bolts. Separate water pump from housing. Remove "O" ring from housing groove.

Installation

1) Apply 1/8" bead of RTV sealant to housing. Install water pump on housing. Tighten retaining bolts to specification. Install new "O" ring in housing groove.

2) Install water pump pulley. Reverse removal procedures for remaining components. Tighten bolts to specification. Fill cooling system. Remove plug from top of thermostat housing. Allow air to bleed from cooling system. Install plug once coolant reaches thermostat housing level.

NOTE: For information on cooling system capacities and other cooling system components, see appropriate article in ENGINE COOLING section.

TIGHTENING SPECIFICATIONS

Application	Ft. Lbs. (N.m)
Air Pump Mounting Bolt	21 (29)
Balance Shaft Carrier-to-Cylinder Block Bolt	40 (54)
Balance Shaft Chain Sprocket Bolt	21 (29)
Balance Shaft Chain Sprocket-to-Crankshaft Bolt	11 (15)
Camshaft Bearing Cap Bolt	18 (24)
Camshaft Sprocket Bolt	65 (88)
Coolant Tube-to-Thermostat Housing	30 (41)
Connecting Rod Cap Nut	[1] 40 (54)
Crankshaft Belt Sprocket Bolt	50 (68)
Crankshaft Pulley Bolt	20 (27)
Cylinder Head Bolt	
Step 1	45 (61)
Step 2	65 (88)
Step 3	[1] 65 (88)
Exhaust Manifold Nut	17 (23)
Flywheel Bolt	70 (95)
Fuel Rail Bolt	21 (29)
Intake Manifold Bolt	17 (23)
Intermediate Shaft Sprocket Bolt	65 (88)
Main Bearing Cap Bolt	[1] 30 (41)
Oil Pick-Up Tube-to-Pump Bolt	21 (29)
Oil Pump-to-Block Bolt	17 (23)
Timing Belt Tensioner Bolt	45 (61)
Turbo Oil Feed Line	10 (14)
Turbo Support Bracket Bolt	
Lower	40 (54)
Upper	20 (27)
Turbo-to-Exhaust Manifold Nut	40 (54)
Water Pump Housing Mounting Bolt	
Lower	40 (54)
Upper	21 (29)

	INCH Lbs. (N.m)
Balance Shaft Chain Adjustment Bolt	105 (12)
Balance Shaft Chain Guide Nut	105 (12)
Balance Shaft Chain Tensioner Bolt	105 (12)
Balance Shaft Cover Bolt	105 (12)
Fuel Pressure Regulator Nut	65 (7.3)
Front Seal Retainer Bolt	105 (12)
Intermediate Shaft Retainer Bolt	105 (12)
Oil Pump Cover Bolt	105 (12)
Crankshaft Rear Seal Retainer Bolt	105 (12)
Timing Belt Cover Bolt	40 (4.5)
Valve Cover Bolt	105 (12)
Water Pump Pulley Bolt	105 (12)
Water Pump-to-Housing Bolt	105 (12)

[1] – Tighten an additional 1/4 turn.

2.2 & 2.5L 4-CYLINDER (Cont.)

ENGINE SPECIFICATIONS

GENERAL SPECIFICATIONS

Year	DISPLACEMENT		Fuel System	HP@RPM	Torque Ft. Lbs.@RPM	Compr. Ratio	BORE		STROKE	
	Cu. In.	Liters					In.	mm	In.	mm
1988 2.2L										
Base	135	2.2	TBI	93@4800	122@3200	9.5:1	3.44	87.5	3.62	92.0
Turbo I	135	2.2	MPFI	146@5200	170@2400	8.0:1	3.44	87.5	3.62	92.0
Turbo II	135	2.2	MPFI	174@5200	200@2400	8.0:1	3.44	87.5	3.62	92.0
2.5L	153	2.5	TBI	96@4400	133@2800	8.9:1	3.44	87.5	4.09	103.8

CRANKSHAFT MAIN & CONNECTING ROD BEARINGS

Engine	MAIN BEARINGS				CONNECTING ROD BEARINGS		
	Journal Diam. In. (mm)	Clearance In. (mm)	Thrust Bearing	Crankshaft End Play In. (mm)	Journal Diam. In. (mm)	Clearance In. (mm)	Side Play In. (mm)
2.2L & 2.5L	2.362-2.363 (59.987-60.013)	[1] .0004-.0028 (.010-.071)	No. 3	[2] .002-.007 (.05-.18)	1.968-1.969 (49.987-50.013)	[1] [3] .0008-.0034 (.020-.086)	.005-.013 (.13-.32)

[1] – Wear limit is .004" (.10 mm).
[2] – Wear limit is .014" (.35 mm).
[3] – Turbo model is .0008-.0031" (.020-.078 mm).

PISTONS, PINS & RINGS

Engine	PISTONS	PINS		RINGS		
	Clearance In. (mm)	Piston Fit In. (mm)	Rod Fit In. (mm)	Ring No.	End Gap In. (mm)	Side Clearance In. (mm)
2.2L & 2.5L Non-Turbo	.0005-.0015 (.013-.038)	....	....	No. 1	.011-.021 (.28-.53)	.0015-.0031 (.038-.078)
				No. 2	.011-.021 (.28-.53)	.0015-.0037 (.038-.093)
				No. 3	.015-.055 (.38-1.39)	.....
Turbo	.0015-.0026 (.038-.066)	....	....	No. 1	.010-.020 (.25-.51)	.0015-.0031 (.038-.078)
				No. 2	.009-.019 (.23-.48)	.0015-.0037 (.038-.093)
				No. 3	.015-.055 (.38-1.39)	.....

VALVES

Engine Size & Valve	Head Diam. In. (mm)	Face Angle	Seat Angle	Seat Width In. (mm)	Stem Diameter In. (mm)	Stem Clearance In. (mm)	Valve Lift In. (mm)
2.2L & 2.5L Intake [1]	1.60 (40.6)	45°	45°	.069-.088 (1.75-2.25)	.3124 (7.934)	.0009-.0026 (.022-.065)	.....
Exhaust [2]	1.39 (35.4)	45°	45°	.059-.078 (1.50-2.00)	.3103 (7.881)	.0030-.0047 (.076-.119)	.....

[1] – Intake valve length is 4.498" (114.25 mm) and exhaust valve is 4.522" (114.86 mm).

Chrysler Motors Engines

2.2 & 2.5L 4-CYLINDER (Cont.)

ENGINE SPECIFICATIONS (Cont.)

VALVE SPRINGS

Engine	Free Length In. (mm)	PRESSURE Lbs. @ In. (Kg @ mm)	
		Valve Closed	Valve Open
2.2L & 2.5L	[1] 2.39 (60.8)	108-120@1.65 (48-54@41.9)	195-215@1.22 (88-97@30.9)

[1] – Turbo models is 2.28" (57.9 mm).

CAMSHAFT

Engine	Journal Diam. In. (mm)	Clearance In. (mm)	Lobe Lift In. (mm)
2.2L & 2.5L	[1] 1.375-1.376 (34.93-34.96)	....	....

[1] – Oversize camshafts are 1.395-1.396" (35.44-35.46 mm).

3.0L V6

ENGINE CODING

ENGINE IDENTIFICATION

The engine can be identified by the 8th character of the Vehicle Identification Number (VIN). The VIN is located on a metal tag on upper left corner of dashboard and is visible through windshield. The engine can also be identified by the Engine Identification Number (EIN). The EIN is located on left side of engine block between the core plug and rear face of block.

ENGINE CODE

Engine	Code
3.0L (181")	3

ENGINE REMOVAL

See ENGINE REMOVAL & INSTALLATION article at end of ENGINE section.

ENGINE OVERHAUL

NOTE: For engine repair procedures not covered in this article, see ENGINE OVERHAUL PROCEDURES article at beginning of this section.

CYLINDER HEAD & MANIFOLDS

INTAKE MANIFOLD

CAUTION: Fuel system is under pressure. Fuel pressure must be released before disconnecting fuel lines.

Removal

1) Loosen gas cap to release fuel tank pressure. Remove wiring harness connector from any injector. Ground one injector terminal. Connect jumper wire to other terminal and touch battery positive terminal with jumper. DO NOT appply voltage to injector for longer than 10 seconds. Remove jumper wires.

2) Disconnect negative and positive battery cables. Drain cooling system. Remove air cleaner-to-throttle body hose. Disconnect accelerator cable and transaxle kickdown linkage. Disconnect Automatic Idle Speed (AIS) motor and Throttle Position Sensor (TPS) wiring harness connectors from throttle body. Remove vacuum hoses from throttle body.

3) Remove air cleaner-to-throttle body hose. Remove EGR tube flange from intake plenum. Disconnect wiring connectors from charge temperature sensor and coolant temperature sensor. Remove vacuum hoses from air intake plenum. Remove fuel hoses from fuel rail.

4) Remove 8 bolts and nuts retaining intake plenum to intake manifold. Remove air intake plenum. Cover intake manifold ports when servicing. Remove vacuum hoses from fuel rail and fuel pressure regulator. Disconnect fuel injector wiring harness from engine wiring harness.

5) Remove fuel pressure regulator from fuel rail. Remove fuel rail attaching bolts. Remove fuel rail assembly from intake manifold. Disconnect radiator and heater hoses from manifold. Remove 8 mounting nuts and washers. Remove intake manifold. See Fig. 1.

Fig. 1: Intake & Exhaust Manifolds

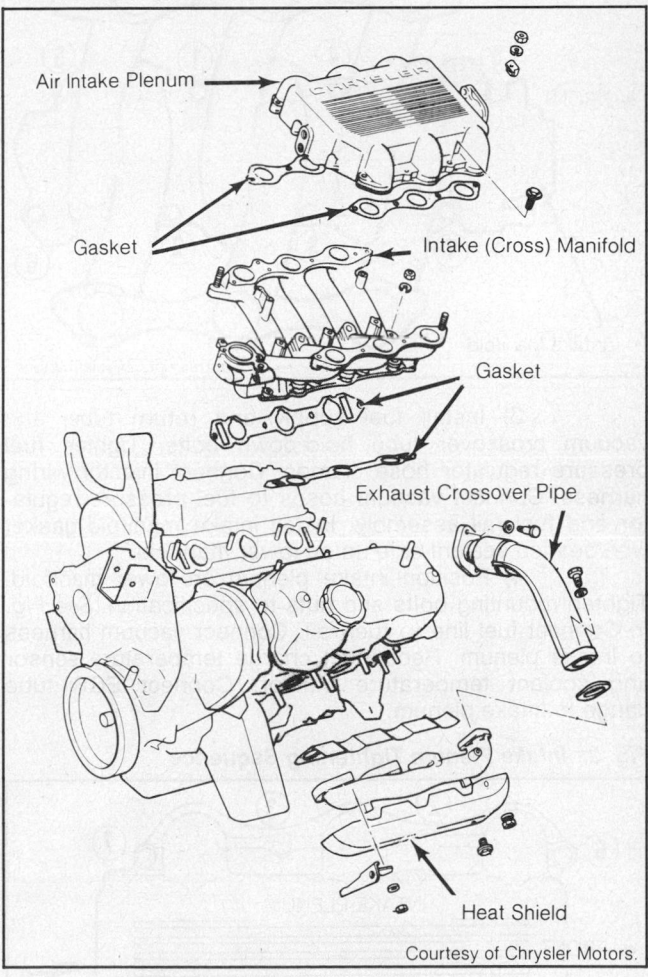

Courtesy of Chrysler Motors.

Inspection

Clean all gasket mating surfaces. Check for damage or cracks on all mounting surfaces. Check for clogged coolant and fuel passages in manifold. Check mounting surfaces for warpage.

INTAKE MANIFOLD WARPAGE

Application	In. (mm)
Intake Plenum Mounting Surface	
Standard	.004 (.15)
Maximum	.008 (.30)
Cylinder Head Mounting Surface	
Standard	.003 (.10)
Maximum	.005 (.20)

Installation

1) Position intake manifold gasket on cylinder head. Install intake manifold. Install 8 washers and nuts. Tighten nuts to specification in several steps.

2) Ensure injector holes are clean. Lubricate injector "O" rings. Install injector until firmly seated in port. Install fuel rail and tighten mounting bolts. Install fuel pressure regulator and hose assembly on fuel rail. Install manifold attaching bolts and tighten to specification. See Fig. 2.

Fig. 2: Intake Manifold Tightening Sequence

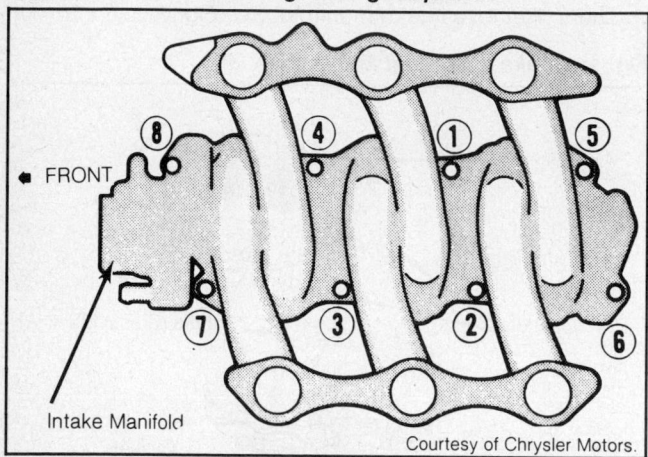

Courtesy of Chrysler Motors.

3) Install fuel supply and return tube, and vacuum crossover tube hold-down bolts. Tighten fuel pressure regulator hose clamps. Connect injector wiring harness. Connect vacuum hoses to fuel pressure regulator and fuel rail assembly. Install intake manifold gasket with beaded sealant side up on lower manifold.

4) Position intake plenum on lower manifold. Tighten mounting bolts and nuts to specification. *See Fig. 3.* Connect fuel line to fuel rail. Connect vacuum harness to intake plenum. Reconnect charge temperature sensor and coolant temperature sensor. Connect EGR tube flange to intake plenum.

Fig. 3: Intake Plenum Tightening Sequence

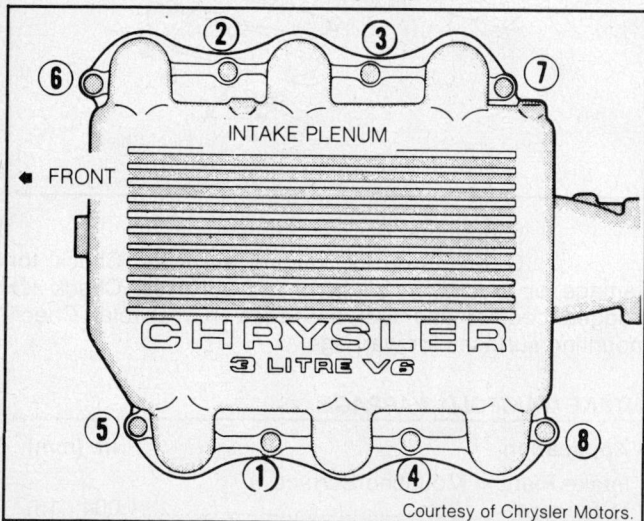

Courtesy of Chrysler Motors.

5) Tighten flange bolts to specification. Connect brake booster and PCV hoses to intake plenum. Connect AIS motor and TPS electrical connectors. Connect vacuum vapor harness to throttle body. Install throttle cable and transaxle kickdown linkage.

6) Install air inlet hose assembly. Install upper radiator hose and heater hose to intake manifold. Fill and bleed cooling system. Connect battery cable.

EXHAUST MANIFOLDS
Removal & Installation

1) Raise vehicle and disconnect exhaust pipe from rear exhaust manifold flange. Disconnect EGR tube from rear manifold. Disconnect O_2 sensor wiring. Remove crossover pipe mounting bolts. Remove nuts attaching rear manifold to cylinder head.

2) Lower vehicle. Remove screws attaching heat shield to front manifold. Remove bolts attaching crossover pipe to front manifold. Remove nuts attaching front manifold to cylinder head. Remove front exhaust manifold. Check manifolds for cracks and damage. Check mounting surfaces for warpage.

3) To install, reverse removal procedure. Install gasket with numbers 1-3-5 embossed on top, on rear exhaust manifold. Install gasket with numbers 2-4-6 embossed on top, on front exhaust manifold. Tighten mounting bolts and nuts to specification.

CYLINDER HEAD
Removal

1) Disconnect negative battery cable. Drain cooling system. Remove air cleaner assembly. Loosen accessory drive belts. Remove A/C compressor mounting bolts and set compressor aside. Remove A/C compressor mounting bracket and drive belt tensioner. Remove power steering/alternator belt tensioner. Remove power steering pump and set aside.

2) Raise vehicle and remove right inner fender shield. Remove crankshaft pulleys and vibration damper. Lower vehicle and support engine. Separate engine mount from engine bracket. Raise engine slightly. Remove engine mount bracket. Label and disconnect all wiring, hoses, lines and linkages from throttle body, distributor, manifolds and cylinder head.

3) Remove timing belt cover, noting length of bolts for reinstallation reference. Mark timing belt direction of rotation for reinstallation reference. Loosen timing belt tensioner. Remove timing belt. Using Camshaft Sprocket Holder (MB990775), hold camshaft sprocket and loosen camshaft sprocket retaining bolt. Remove retaining bolt and sprocket.

4) Remove spark plug wires. Remove valve covers. Check auto lash adjuster free play. Insert a small wire through air bleed hole in rocker arm and VERY LIGHTLY push the auto adjuster check ball down. While holding the check ball down, check rocker arm for free play. If there is no play, replace adjuster.

Fig. 4: Auto Lash Adjuster Retainers

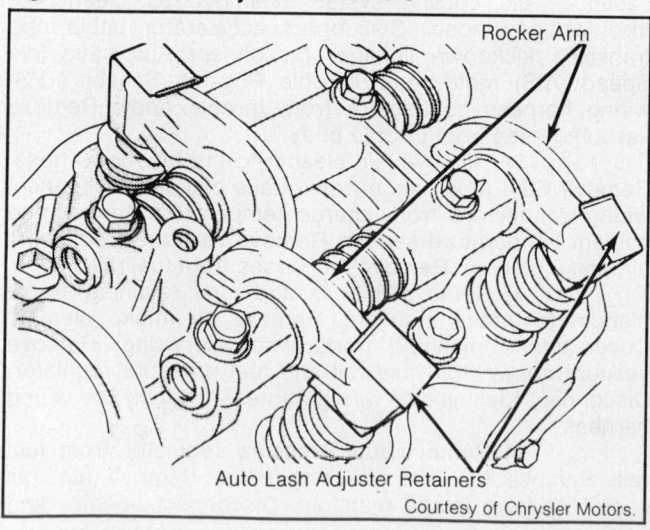

Courtesy of Chrysler Motors.

3.0L V6 (Cont.)

Fig. 5: Cylinder Head Removal & Installation Sequences

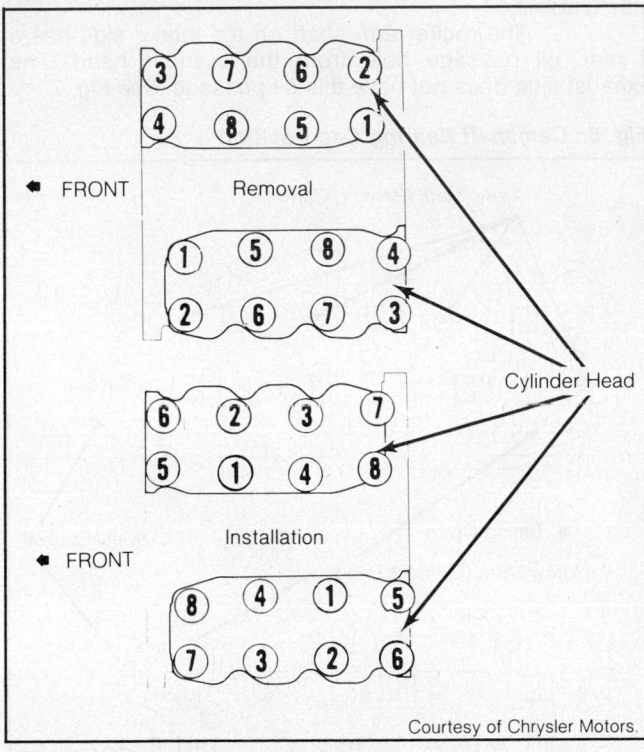

FRONT   Removal

Cylinder Head

FRONT   Installation

Courtesy of Chrysler Motors.

Tighten head bolts in 2-3 steps.

5) Install Auto Lash Adjuster Retainers (MD998443). *See Fig. 4.* Remove distributor adapter. Loosen, but DO NOT remove camshaft bearing cap bolts. Remove rocker arms, shafts and bearing shafts as an assembly. Remove camshafts. Remove cylinder head bolts in sequence and remove cylinder head. *See Fig. 5.*

Cleaning & Inspection

Clean gasket surfaces on block and cylinder head. Check cylinder head for cracks, damage or warpage. Resurface head if warped beyond .002" (.05 mm). DO NOT grind more than .008" (.2 mm) from surface of head or head surface on block. Replace head if not within specification.

Installation

1) To install, reverse removal procedure. Install new gasket over cylinder head dowels on block. Tighten cylinder head bolts in sequence using 2-3 steps. *See Fig. 5.* Lubricate and install camshaft.

2) Install rocker shaft assemblies, applying sealant to bearing cap mating surfaces at both ends of head. Ensure arrows on rocker shaft assemblies are pointing in same direction as arrows on cylinder heads.

3) Install new camshaft seals using Seal Installer (MD998713). Install end seal plug using Installer (MD998306). To complete installation, reverse removal procedure. Tighten all bolts to specification. See ENGINE TIGHTENING SPECIFICATIONS chart.

Fig. 6: Timing Mark & Sprocket Locations

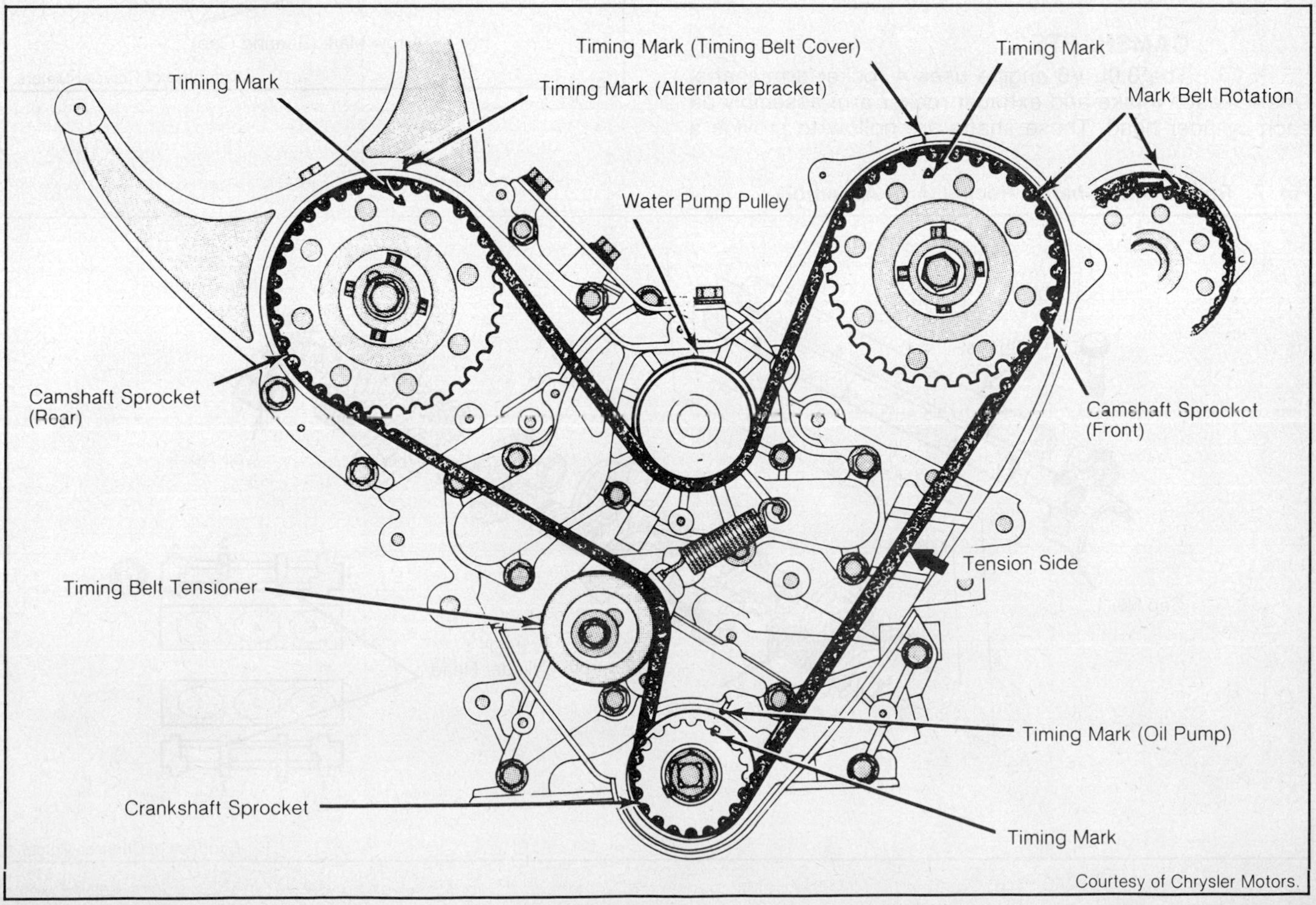

Timing Mark

Timing Mark (Timing Belt Cover)

Timing Mark (Alternator Bracket)

Timing Mark

Mark Belt Rotation

Water Pump Pulley

Camshaft Sprocket (Rear)

Camshaft Sprocket (Front)

Timing Belt Tensioner

Tension Side

Timing Mark (Oil Pump)

Crankshaft Sprocket

Timing Mark

Courtesy of Chrysler Motors.

Chrysler Motors Engines

3.0L V6 (Cont.)

CAMSHAFT

TIMING BELT
Removal

1) Support engine and transmission with floor jack. Remove front engine mount bracket. Remove upper (front outer) timing belt cover. Align timing marks on front and rear camshaft sprockets and timing mark on crankshaft sprocket. *See Fig. 6.*

2) Remove crankshaft pulleys and vibration damper. Loosen timing belt tensioner bolt and remove timing belt.

Inspection

Inspect timing belt for cracks, debris damage, missing teeth or loose cords.

Installation

1) Ensure all timing marks are aligned. Install timing belt on crankshaft sprocket first and while keeping belt tight on tension side, install belt on the front (radiator side) camshaft sprocket.

2) Install belt on water pump pulley and on the rear camshaft sprocket and finally on timing belt tensioner. Loosen tensioner bolt and allow spring to tension belt.

3) Turn crankshaft 2 full turns clockwise. Turn smoothly and in clockwise direction only. Recheck timing marks on sprockets and then tighten timing belt tensioner to 23 ft. lbs. (31 N.m). To complete installation, reverse removal procedure.

NOTE: Turn crankshaft smoothly and ONLY in clockwise direction.

CAMSHAFTS

The 3.0L V6 engine uses 4 rocker arm shafts. One for each intake and exhaust rocker arm assembly on each cylinder head. These shafts are hollow to provide a duct for oil flow from the cylinder head to the valve mechanisms.

The rocker arm shaft on the intake side has a 3 mm. oil passage hole from the cylinder head. The exhaust side does not have this oil passage. *See Fig. 7.*

Fig. 8: Camshaft Bearing Cap Position

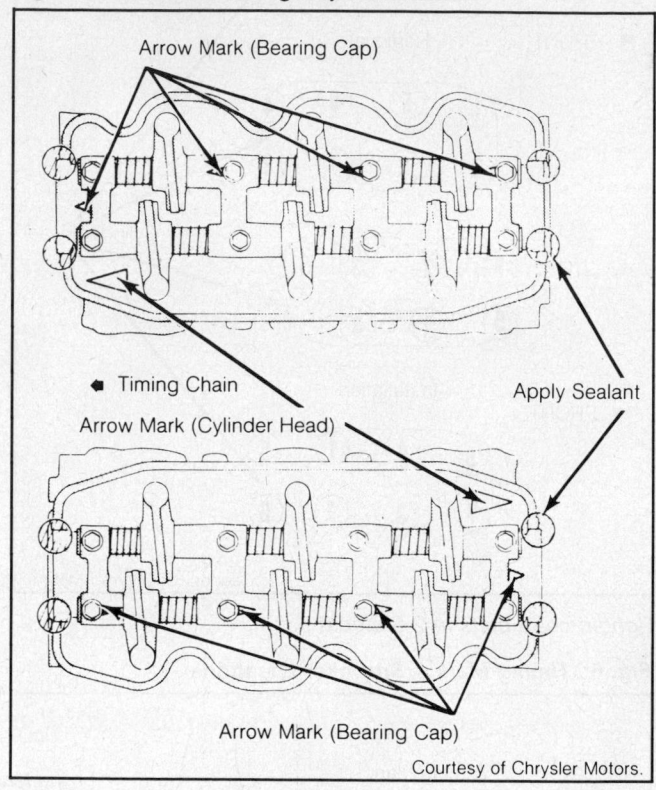

Courtesy of Chrysler Motors.

Fig. 7: Rocker Arm Shaft & Rocker Arm Assembly

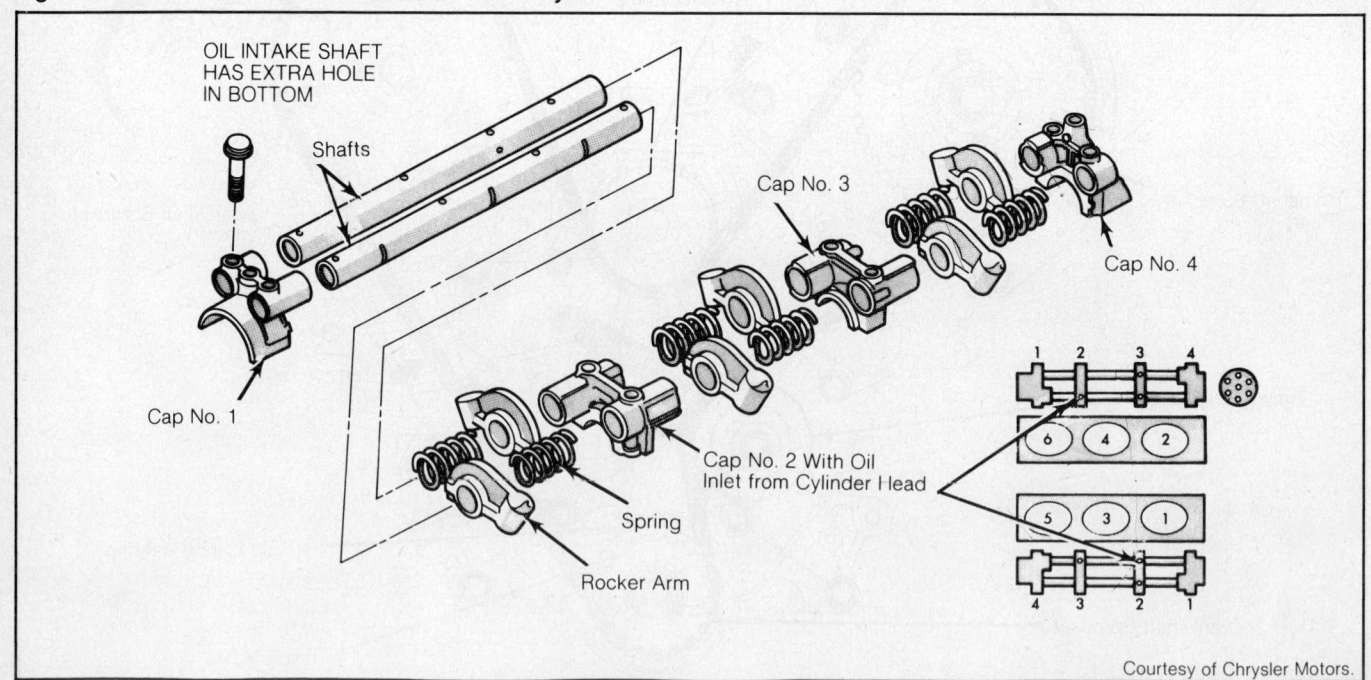

Courtesy of Chrysler Motors.

3.0L V6 (Cont.)

Removal & Installation

1) Install Auto Lash Adjuster Retainers (M0998443). Remove distributor extension.

2) When removing camshaft bearing caps, do not remove bolts from bearing caps. Remove rocker arm, rocker shafts and bearing cap as an assembly.

3) Inspect camshaft bearing journals for damage or binding. Check cylinder head oil passages for clogging. Check the cam surface for abnormal wear and damage and replace as necessary.

4) Measure cam height and replace if defective. Standard value is 1.615" (41 mm). Service limit is 1.595" (40.5 mm). Replace if out of limit. Reverse removal procedure to complete installation.

VALVES

VALVE ARRANGEMENT

Right Bank – I-E-I-E-I-E (Front-to-rear).
Left Side – E-I-E-I-E-I (Front-to-rear).

VALVE GUIDE SERVICING

1) Remove valve springs, retainers, locks and stem seals. Remove valves and keep in order for reinstallation in original location. Remove carbon and varnish from inside of valve guides.

2) Clean and inspect valves. If damaged or stem wear exceeds .004" (.10 mm) for intake and .006" (.15 mm) for exhaust, replace valve. Do not reuse valve stem seals.

VALVE STEM OIL SEALS

Do not reuse valve stem seals. Coat valve stems with oil and insert in cylinder heads. Press new shields or seals squarely over valve guide, using valve stem as a positioning aid. Do not force seal against top of guide.

VALVE SPRINGS

Removal

With cylinder head removed, compress valve springs using a valve spring compressor. Remove spring retainer locks, retainer, valve spring, spring seat and valve.

Installation

To install, reverse removal procedure. Install spring with enamelled ends facing the rocker arms. Compress spring only enough to install the locks. Check valve spring installed height.

VALVE SPRING INSTALLED HEIGHT

1) Valve spring must be square within 4 degrees maximum. Installed height of springs is measured from spring contact area on cylinder head to underside of spring retainer.

2) New spring free length is 1.99" (50.5 mm) with a service limit of 1.95" (49.5 mm).

VALVE SPRING HEIGHT

Application	In. (mm)
Free Height	1.99 (50.5)
Installed Height	1.59 (40.4)

AUTO LASH ADJUSTER

The automatic lash adjusters are precision units installed in machined openings in the valve actuating ends of the rocker arms. Do not disassemble auto lash adjusters.

Check auto lash adjusters for free play by inserting a small wire throught the air bleed hole in the rocker arm and very lightly push auto adjuster check ball down. Move rocker up and down to check free play. If there is no play, replace the adjuster.

Fig. 9: Checking Auto Lash Adjuster

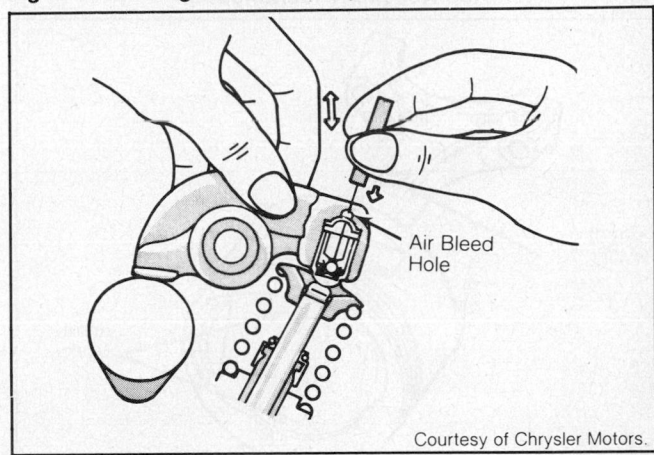

Air Bleed Hole

Courtesy of Chrysler Motors.

PISTONS, PINS & RINGS

OIL PAN

See OIL PAN REMOVAL at end of ENGINE section.

PISTON & ROD ASSEMBLY

Removal

1) With piston near bottom of stroke, cover with cloth or shop towels to collect the cuttings, remove ridge at top of cylinder bores using ridge reamer.

2) Rotate crankshaft and mark connecting rods and rod caps for cylinder identification. Push piston and rod assembly out top of cylinder bore.

Fig. 10: Piston Ring End Gap Position

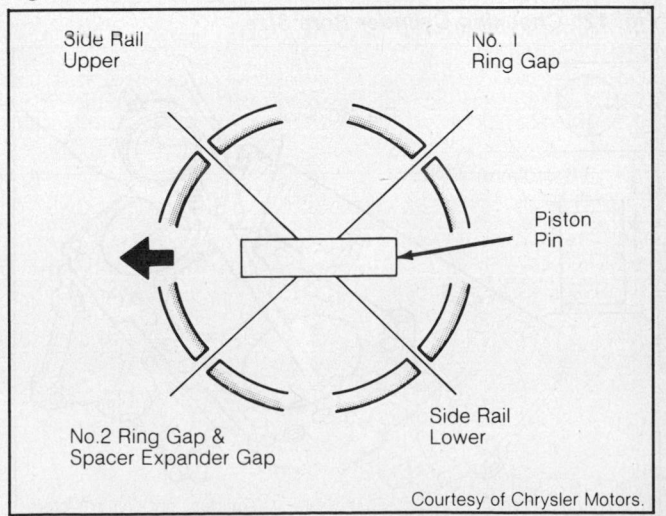

Side Rail Upper

No. 1 Ring Gap

Piston Pin

No.2 Ring Gap & Spacer Expander Gap

Side Rail Lower

Courtesy of Chrysler Motors.

Installation

Before installing piston and rod assemblies into cylinder block, follow ring arrangements and installation procedure. *See Fig. 10.*

1) For cylinders number 1, 3 and 5, install pistons with "R" marking towards front of engine (timing belt end), and for cylinders number 2, 4 and 6, install pistons with "L" marking towards the front of engine.

2) Connecting rod front mark "72" must always face towards front of engine (timing belt). *See Fig. 11.*

Fig. 11: Piston/Rod Assembly Identification

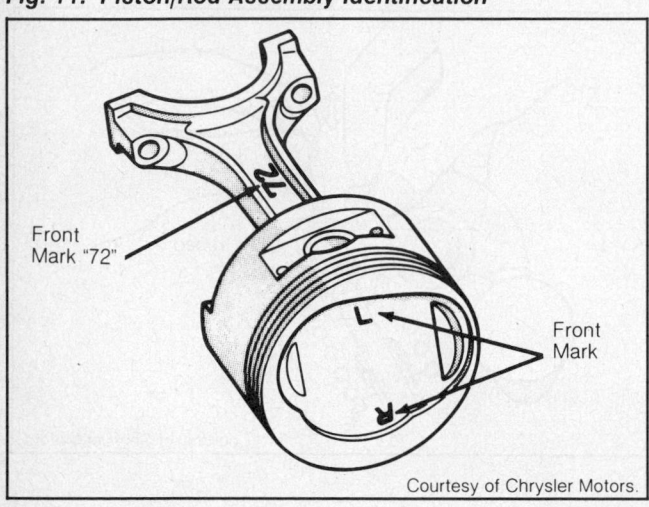

Front Mark "72"

L

R

Front Mark

Courtesy of Chrysler Motors.

3) Connecting rod side clearance is .004-.010" (0.10-0.25 mm). Maximum clearance is .015" (0.4 mm). Maximum allowable connecting rod twist is .0019" (.05 mm). To install, reverse removal procedure.

NOTE: **Do not allow position of rings to change during ring compressor installation and tightening.**

FITTING PISTONS

Pistons should be measured approximately .08" (2 mm) above the bottom of the piston skirt across the thrust face.

Measure cylinder bore at three levels. Top measurement should be .38" (10 mm) below the top

Fig. 12: Checking Cylinder Bore Size

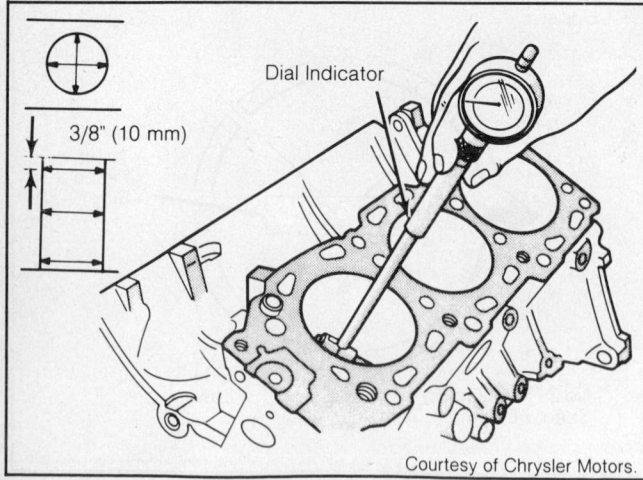

3/8" (10 mm)

Dial Indicator

Courtesy of Chrysler Motors.

surface of cylinder bore. Bottom measurement should be .38" (10 mm) from the bottom of cylinder bore. *See Fig. 12.*

Standard bore dimension is 3.59" (91.1 mm). Maximum out-of-round or taper is .0008" (.02 mm).

Oversize pistons are available in .25 mm increments. From .25 mm, .50 mm and 1.0 mm.

CRANKSHAFT & ROD BEARINGS

CONNECTING ROD BEARINGS

1) Ensure rod caps are marked for proper identification. Remove rod cap and use Plastigage method to check for proper bearing clearance. If clearance is not within specifications, replace with correct undersized bearing. Install rod cap with bearing insert and tighten nuts to 38 ft. lbs. (52 N.m).

2) Bearing clearance should be .0008-.0028" (.02-.67 mm). Side clearance limit is .015" (.4 mm).

MAIN BEARINGS
Removal & Installation

1) Use Plastigage method to check main bearing clearance. Measure clearance by installing main bearing cap and tightening bolts to specified torque. Remove bearing caps and measure Plastigage on scale.

2) All upper bearing shells in the crankcase have oil grooves. All lower bearing shells installed in the monoblock main bearing cap are plain. Crankshaft end play is controlled by thrust washers on number 3 main bearing journal.

3) Install upper main bearing shells. Ensure that they are aligned with oil holes and bearing tabs are seated in block tabs.

THRUST WASHER MAIN BEARING

Engine uses different types of thrust washer bearings. One type have positioning tabs, while the other type are plain. One SET of tab type thrust washer bearings are installed in the block and one SET of plain type thrust washer bearings are installed in the No. 3 main bearing cap. Install main bearing caps with arrows facing front of block.

CRANKSHAFT END PLAY

Crankshaft end play is controlled by the No. 3 thrust washer bearing. Crankshaft end play is .002-.010" (0.05-0.25 mm). For crankshaft end play checking procedure, see ENGINE OVERHAUL PROCEDURES article.

REAR MAIN BEARING OIL SEAL

NOTE: **Rear main bearing oil seal is a one-piece unit mounted on the oil seal housing.**

Removal & Installation

To remove rear main oil seal housing, remove 5 retaining bolts from housing. Carefully pry oil seal from housing.

Install rear crankshaft oil seal in housing with Tool (MD998718). Apply RTV gasket to oil seal housing. Apply light coating of engine oil to entire circumference of oil seal lip. Install seal assembly on cylinder block and tighten bolts to 104 ft. lbs. (12 N.m).

3.0L V6 (Cont.)

ENGINE OILING

ENGINE OILING SYSTEM

The engine lubrication system is a full flow filtration, pressure feed type. The oil pump is mounted on the front cover. The pump inner rotor is installed on and rotates with the crankshaft. The engine oil pan contains a baffle plate to control oil level fluctuation during engine operation.

CRANKCASE CAPACITY

Crankcase capacity is 4.5 qts. (4.3L) including oil filter.

OIL FILTER

A full-flow disposable cartridge type oil filter is used.

OIL PUMP

Removal & Installation

Oil pump is mounted on the timing belt end of the block with the inner pump rotor indexed and installed on the crankshaft nose. The oil pump case also retains the crankshaft front oil seal and provides front oil pan closure.

To remove oil pump, timing belt removal and installation procedures must be followed. Always install new gaskets and front oil seal whenever oil pump is removed.

NORMAL OIL PRESSURE

Normal oil pressure on a fully warmed up engine is 100 psi @ 3000 RPM.

Fig. 13: Exploded View of Oil Pump

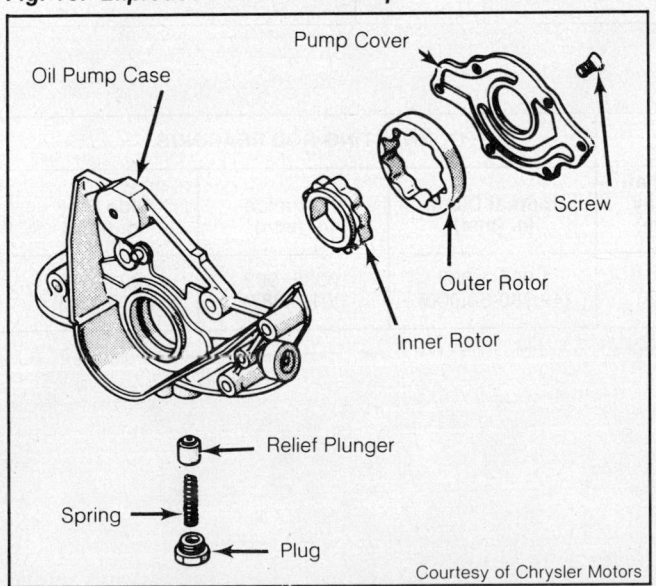

Pump Cover

Oil Pump Case

Screw

Outer Rotor

Inner Rotor

Relief Plunger

Spring

Plug

Courtesy of Chrysler Motors

OIL PUMP SPECIFICATIONS

Application	In. (mm)
Clearance Over Inner Rotor	.001-.002 (.03-.07)
Body Clearance	.004-.007 (.10-.18)
Side Clearance	.002-.004 (.03-.10)

ENGINE COOLING

WATER PUMP

Removal & Installation

Water pump is driven by the timing belt. Refer to TIMING BELT REMOVAL AND INSTALLATION section in this article for timing belt removal.

Drain cooling system. Remove mounting bolts. Separate water pump from coolant inlet pipe. Remove pump. To install, reverse removal procedure.

NOTE: For more information on cooling systems, see **ENGINE COOLING SYSTEMS** at end of ENGINE section.

TIGHTENING SPECIFICATIONS

Application	Ft. Lbs. (N.m)
Air Plenum Screws	11 (15)
Alternator Bracket	21 (29)
Camshaft Bearing Cap	15 (20)
Camshaft Sprocket Bolt	70 (95)
Connecting Rod Cap Nut	38 (52)
Crankshaft Pulley Bolt	150 (110)
Crankshaft Main Bearing Cap	60 (80)
Crossover Bolt	51 (69)
Cylinder Head Bolts	
Cold	70 (95)
Hot	75 (100)
Engine Support Bracket	35 (45)
Exhaust Manifold Nuts	16 (22)
Main Bearing Cap	60 (80)
Oil Drain Plug	30 (40)
Oil Pump Assembly-to-Block	11 (15)
Oil Pump Pick-Up Bolts	17 (23)
Rocker Arm Shaft Bolts	25 (34)
Timing Belt Tensioner	23 (31)
Water Pump Bolts	20 (27)

Application	INCH Lbs. (N.m)
Distributor Adaptor	120 (13)
Oil Pan Bolts	50 (6)
Oil Pump Cover	120 (13)
Rear Oil Seal Retainer	95 (11)
Rocker Cover	88 (10)
Thermostat Housing	113 (12)

Chrysler Motors Engines

3.0L V6 (Cont.)

ENGINE SPECIFICATIONS

GENERAL SPECIFICATIONS

| Year | DISPLACEMENT | | Fuel System | HP@RPM | Torque Ft. Lbs.@RPM | Compr. Ratio | BORE | | STROKE | |
	Cu. In.	Liters					In.	mm	In.	mm
1988	181	3.0	MPFI	140@4800	170@2800	8.8:1	3.59	91.1	2.99	76.0

VALVES

Engine Size & Valve	Head Diam. In. (mm)	Face Angle	Seat Angle	Seat Width In. (mm)	Stem Diameter In. (mm)	Stem Clearance In. (mm)	Valve Lift In. (mm)
3.0L							
Intake	1.69-1.70 (42.9-43.1)	45°	44°	.035-.051 (0.9-1.3)	.3130-.3140 (7.960-7.998)	.001-.002 (.03-.06)	.....
Exhaust	1.37-1.38 (34.9-35.1)	45°	44°	.035-.051 (0.9-1.3)	.312-.3125 (7.930-7.950)	.0019-.003 (.05-.09)	.....

PISTONS, PINS & RINGS

| Engine | PISTONS | PINS | | RINGS | | |
	Clearance In. (mm)	Piston Fit In. (mm)	Rod Fit In. (mm)	Ring No.	End Gap In. (mm)	Side Clearance In. (mm)
3.0L	.0008-.0015 (.02-.04)	.....	.....	1	.012-.018 (.30-.45)	.002-.0035 (.05-.09)
				2	.010-.016 (.25-.40)	.0008-.002 (.02-.06)
				3	.012-.035 (.30-.90)	.....

CRANKSHAFT MAIN & CONNECTING ROD BEARINGS

| Engine | MAIN BEARINGS | | | | CONNECTING ROD BEARINGS | | |
	Journal Diam. In. (mm)	Clearance In. (mm)	Thrust Bearing	Crankshaft End Play In. (mm)	Journal Diam. In. (mm)	Clearance In. (mm)	Side Play In. (mm)
3.0L	2.361-2.362 (59.980-60.000)	.0006-002 (.016-.046)	No. 3	.002-.010 (.05-.25)	1.968-1.969 (49.980-50.000)	.0006-.002 (.019-.087)	.004-.010 (.016-.046)

VALVE SPRINGS

| Engine | Free Length In. (mm) | PRESSURE Lbs. @ In. (Kg @ mm) | |
		Valve Closed	Valve Open
3.0L	1.988 (50.5)	....	73@1.59 (33@40.4)

5.2L V8

ENGINE CODING

ENGINE IDENTIFICATION

The 8th character of the Vehicle Identification Number (VIN) identifies engine cubic inch displacement and carburetor type. The VIN plate is attached to the upper left side of instrument panel and is visible through windshield. Cubic inch displacement may be found in the Engine Serial Number located on front left side of the block, below cylinder head. Engine Identification Number is located on right side of block. It is used to match the block number to the last 6 digits of the VIN and must be referenced when ordering parts.

ENGINE CODES

Engine	Code
5.2L (318")	
2-Bbl. Standard	P
4-Bbl. Standard	4
4-Bbl. Heavy Duty	S

SPECIAL ENGINE MARKS

Information identifying undersize crankshaft journals, oversize cylinder bores, tappets and valve stems is stamped in various locations on engine (depending on engine). Information and location is decoded as follows:

R or M – Numbers 1, 2, 3, or 4 following R or M indicates .001" undersize rod or main bearing journals and which journal is undersize. Stamp is on No. 8 crankshaft counterweight.

RX or MX – Indicates all rod or main bearing journals are .010" undersize. Stamped on the No. 8 crankshaft counterweight.

A – Indicates .020" oversize cylinder bore. Stamped after engine identification number.

♦ – Indicates .008" oversize tappets. Stamped on top pad at front of engine and on a flat surface at outside of each tappet bore.

X – Indicates .005" oversize valve stems. Stamped on milled pad adjacent to two .375" tapped holes on each end of cylinder head.

ENGINE REMOVAL

See ENGINE REMOVAL & INSTALLATION article at end of ENGINE section.

CYLINDER HEAD & MANIFOLDS

INTAKE MANIFOLD

Removal

1) Disconnect battery ground and drain cooling system. Remove air cleaner, alternator, and fuel line to carburetor. Disconnect upper radiator hose, by-pass hose and heater hoses.

2) Disconnect accelerator linkage. Label and disconnect all electrical wiring to intake manifold. Remove distributor cap, wires and vacuum hose. Remove evaporative control system and closed ventilation system. Remove valve covers. Remove intake manifold bolts. Remove intake manifold, coil and carburetor as an assembly.

Inspection

Clean gasket mating surfaces. Check intake manifold-to-cylinder head mounting surfaces for warpage. Gasket surfaces must not be warped more than .006" (.15 mm) per foot of manifold length. Check crossover passages for carbon deposits and clean as necessary.

Installation

1) Clean all gasket mating surfaces. Coat bottom of intake manifold side gaskets lightly with sealer and install on cylinder heads. Apply a thin even coat of quick drying cement to front and rear manifold gaskets and block surfaces.

CAUTION: On engines with 4-Bbl. carburetors, do not use any sealer on side intake manifold gaskets.

2) Install front and rear manifold gaskets on block, making sure that hole in gaskets engage dowels in block and end holes lock into tangs of head gaskets. Apply a bead of RTV sealer to each of 4 manifold-to-cylinder head gasket corners.

3) Lower intake manifold carefully into position and install bolts. Tighten bolts in proper sequence shown in *Fig. 1* using 3 steps to obtain specification.

Fig. 1: Engine Intake Manifold Tightening Sequence

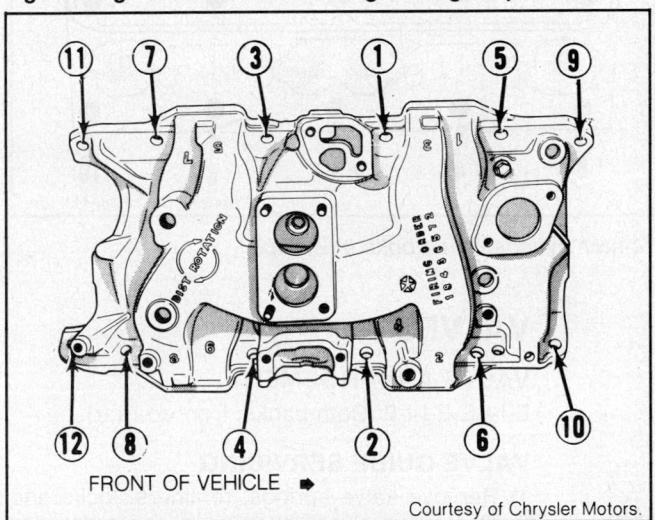

FRONT OF VEHICLE ➡

Courtesy of Chrysler Motors.

Tighten intake manifold bolts in 3 steps.

EXHAUST MANIFOLDS

Removal

Disconnect exhaust pipes from manifolds. Remove exhaust manifold bolts and nuts. If studs are removed with nuts, replace studs and install in head with sealer. Clean gasket from manifold and head.

Inspection

Check exhaust manifold-to-cylinder head mounting surface for warpage. Gasket surfaces must not be warped more than .006" (.15 mm) per foot of manifold length.

NOTE: Coolant leak may develop if sealer is not used on stud threads.

Chrysler Motors Engines

5.2L V8 (Cont.)

Installation

Install new gasket on studs. Install exhaust manifolds. Install conical washers on outboard arms of manifolds. Coat threads on bolts and studs with anti-seize compound and install. Tighten bolts and nuts from center outward. Install exhaust pipes and tighten.

CYLINDER HEAD

Removal

Remove intake and exhaust manifolds. Remove rocker shaft assemblies. Remove push rods and identify them to ensure installation in original locations. Remove cylinder head bolts, cylinder heads and gaskets.

Installation

With all gasket surfaces and bolt holes clean, place head gaskets on block and install heads. After cleaning threads on head bolts, coat threads with sealer. Install bolts in head and tighten in sequence. *See Fig. 2.* Use 2 steps to obtain specification.

Fig. 2: Cylinder Head Tightening Sequence

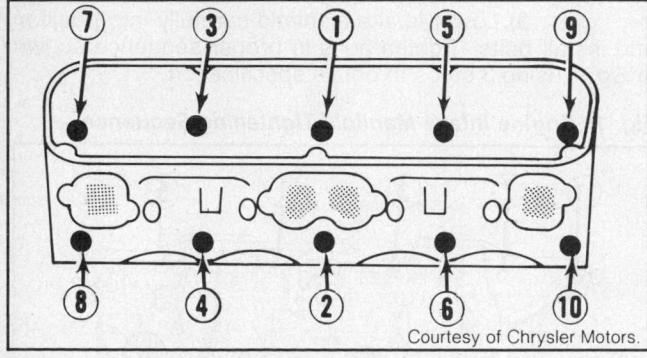

Courtesy of Chrysler Motors.

Tighten cylinder head bolts in 2 steps.

VALVES

VALVE ARRANGEMENT

E-I-I-E-E-I-I-E (Both banks, front-to-rear).

VALVE GUIDE SERVICING

1) Remove valve springs, retainers, locks and stem seals. Remove valves and keep in order for reinstallation in original location. Remove carbon and varnish from inside of valve guides.

2) Clean and inspect valves. If damaged or stem wear exceeds .002" (5 mm), replace valve. Install Sleeve (C-3973) over valve stem and install valve in guide.

3) Attach dial indicator to cylinder head and set it at right angle to valve stem being measured. *See Fig. 6.* Total side play should not exceed .017" (.43 mm).

4) If dial reading is excessive or stems are scuffed or scored, ream guides for installation of valves with oversize stems. Replacement valves with oversized stems are available in .005" (.013 mm), .015" (.038 mm) and .030" (.076 mm) sizes.

NOTE: Do not attempt to ream guides from standard diameter to .030" (.076 mm) oversize in one step. Gradually increase reamer size to obtain the required diameter.

Fig. 3: Identifying Rocker Arms

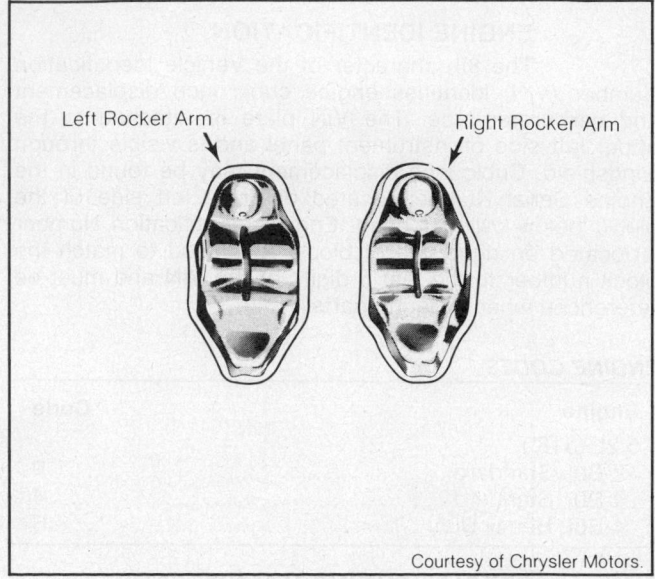

Left Rocker Arm   Right Rocker Arm

Courtesy of Chrysler Motors.

Note difference between right and left rocker arms.

VALVE STEM OIL SEALS

Cup type oil shields are used on all exhaust valves. Oil seals are used on intake valves. Coat valve stems with oil and insert in cylinder heads. Press new shields or seals squarely over valve guide, using valve stem as a positioning aid. Do not force seal against top of guide.

Fig. 4: Location of Rocker Arms

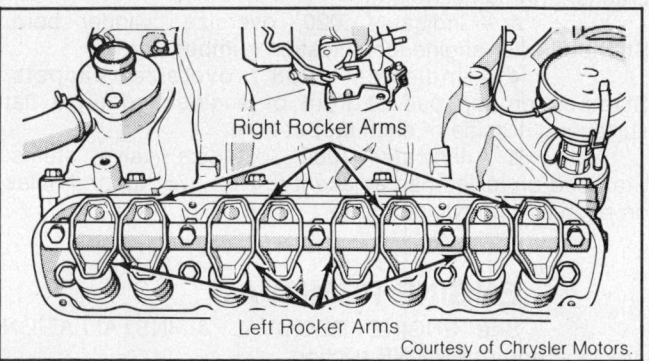

Right Rocker Arms

Left Rocker Arms

Courtesy of Chrysler Motors.

VALVE SPRINGS

Removal

With cylinder head removed, compress valve springs using a spring compressor. Remove valve retaining locks, retainers, valve springs and cup seals.

Installation

To install, reverse removal procedure. Compress spring only enough to install the locks. Check valve spring installed height.

VALVE SPRING INSTALLED HEIGHT

1) Valve springs must be square within .078" (1.98 mm). Installed height of springs is measured from spring contact area on cylinder head to underside of spring retainer.

5.2L V8 (Cont.)

Fig. 5: Measuring Valve Stem Length

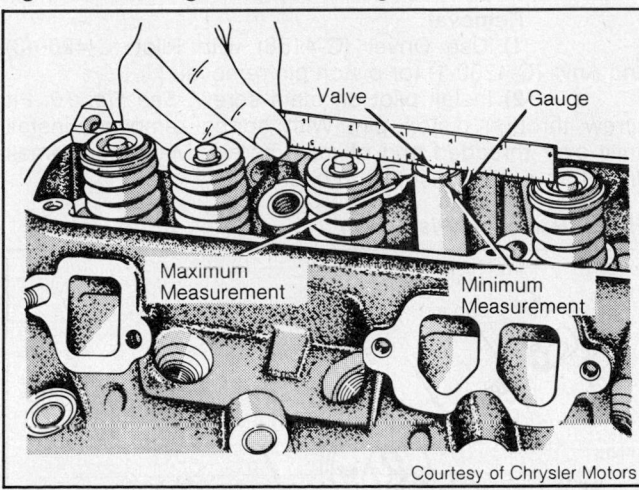

Courtesy of Chrysler Motors

2) If height is greater than maximum allowable, install a .063" (1.60 mm) spacer(s) in head counterbore to bring spring height back to normal. If spacers are installed, measure from top of spacer.

VALVE SPRING INSTALLED HEIGHT

Application	In. (mm)
Intake Valves	1.625-1.688 (41.27-42.86)
Exhaust Valves	1.453-1.516 (36.9-38.5)

ROCKER ARM SHAFT ASSEMBLY

Rocker arms are stamped steel type and identified as right or left. Design difference between rocker arms is in the outward position of the push rod cavity and valve contact pad. *See Fig. 3.*

Fig. 6: Measuring Valve Stem-to-Guide Clearance

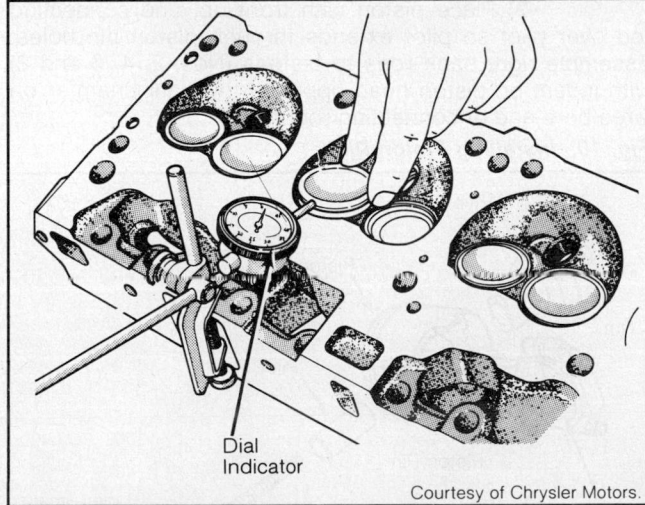

Courtesy of Chrysler Motors.

Total side play should not exceed .017" (.43 mm).

Removal & Installation

1) Remove 5 rocker shaft bolts with retainers and separate shaft assembly from cylinder head.

2) When rocker arm assemblies are being installed, tighten support bracket bolts slowly and evenly to allow lifters time to bleed down to operating length.

Fig. 7: Hydraulic Lifter Assembly

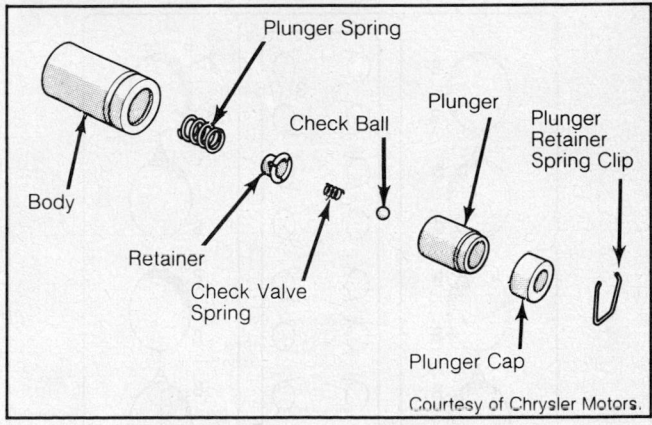

Courtesy of Chrysler Motors.

3) Notch on rocker shaft end must face center of engine and point to rear on right bank and to front on left bank. Long stamped steel retainers go in No. 2 and No. 4 positions. *See Fig. 4.*

HYDRAULIC ROLLER LIFTER ASSEMBLY

NOTE: **Lifters are serviced as complete assemblies only. Parts are not interchangeable between lifters. If any component of lifter is worn or damaged, complete lifter must be replaced.**

Removal

1) Remove valve cover, rocker arm assembly and push rods. If equipped with roller tappet, remove intake manifold, yoke retainer and aligning yokes.

2) Slide Tappet Remover (C-4129) through opening in cylinder head and seat tool firmly in head of tappet. With twisting motion pull tappet out of bore. Mark push rods and tappets for reassembly reference.

Disassembly, Cleaning & Reassembly

1) Remove plunger retainer clip and invert tappet body to remove plunger cap, plunger, check ball, check valve spring, retainer and plunger spring.

2) Clean all lifter parts in a solvent that will remove all varnish and carbon. Replace any lifters that are unfit for further service with new assemblies.

3) Assemble tappets in reverse order of disassembly. *See Fig. 7.*

PISTONS, PINS & RINGS

OIL PAN

See OIL PAN REMOVAL at end of ENGINE section.

PISTON & ROD ASSEMBLY

Removal

1) With piston near bottom of stroke and covered with cloth to collect the cuttings, remove ridge at top of cylinder bores using ridge reamer.

2) Rotate crankshaft and mark connecting rods and rod caps for cylinder identification. Remove rod cap and cover studs with rubber tubing to protect crankshaft journal. Push piston and rod assembly out top of cylinder bore. Remove tubing and install rod caps on mating rods.

Chrysler Motors Engines

5.2L V8 (Cont.)

Fig. 8: Positioning Oil Rings For Installation

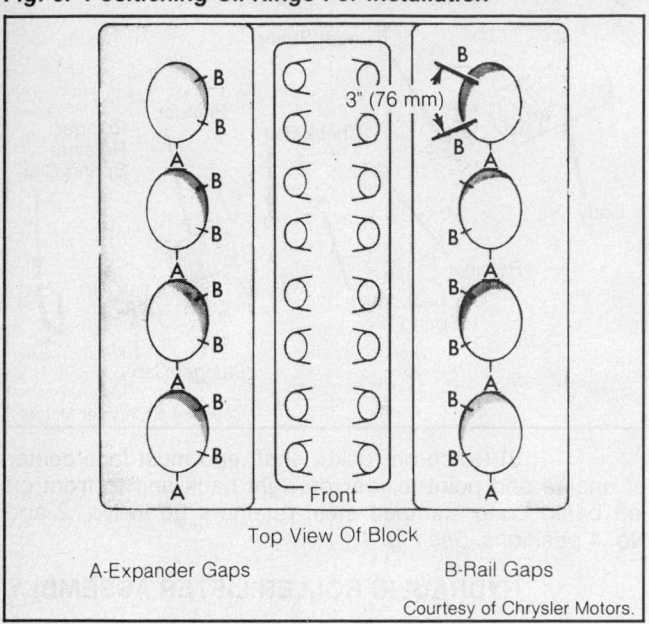

Top View Of Block

A-Expander Gaps   B-Rail Gaps

Courtesy of Chrysler Motors.

Do not allow ring gaps to change during installation.

Installation

Before installing piston and rod assemblies into cylinder block, note the following ring arrangements and installation procedure.

1) Make sure "ID" mark on each compression ring is facing upward toward top of piston and ring gaps are staggered so they do not line up with oil ring rail gaps.

2) Oil ring expander ends must be butted and in line with notch on top of piston and oil ring rail gaps must be facing toward middle of engine.

3) Lightly coat piston head and rings in clean engine oil. Slide ring compressor over piston and tighten. Install rubber tubing on rod bolt studs.

NOTE: **Do not allow position of rings to change during ring compressor installation and tightening.**

4) Rotate crankshaft so connecting rod journal is easily accessible. Tap piston into cylinder bore using wooden handle of a hammer and guide connecting rod into place on crankshaft journal.

5) Remove tubing, install rod cap and tighten nuts. Repeat procedure for each piston assembly.

NOTE: **Notch on top of piston must face front of engine and larger chamfer of connecting rod bore must be installed toward crankshaft journal fillet.**

FITTING PISTONS

Pistons should be measured 90 degrees to piston pin axis at top of skirt. Measure cylinder bore halfway down the bore, 90 degrees to crankshaft center line. Pistons and cylinder bores should be measured at normal room temperature, 70°F (21°C).

PISTON PINS

Removal

1) Use Driver (C-4158) with Pilot (C-4200-3) and Anvil (C-4200-1) for piston pin removal.

2) Install pilot on main screw. *See Fig. 10.* Fit screw through piston pin. With spring removed, install anvil over threaded end of main screw. Make sure small end of anvil is against piston boss.

Fig. 9: Removing Piston Pin

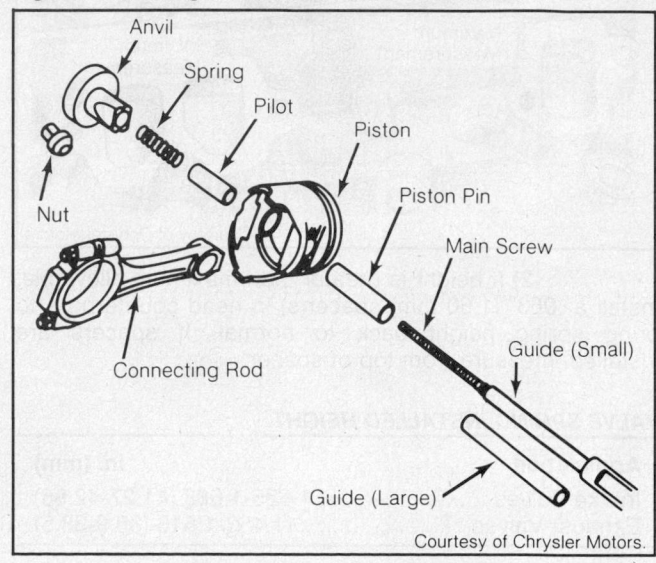

Courtesy of Chrysler Motors.

3) Install nut loosely on main screw and place assembly on press. Press pin from connecting rod. *See Fig. 9.*

Installation

1) Lubricate piston pin holes and connecting rod. With tools used for removal, install spring in pilot and pilot into anvil. Install piston over main screw.

2) Place piston with front up, and connecting rod over pilot so pilot extends through piston pin holes. Assemble right bank rods to pistons (Nos. 2, 4, 6 and 8) with indent on piston head opposite to larger chamfer on large bore end of connecting rod.

Fig. 10: Installing Piston Pin

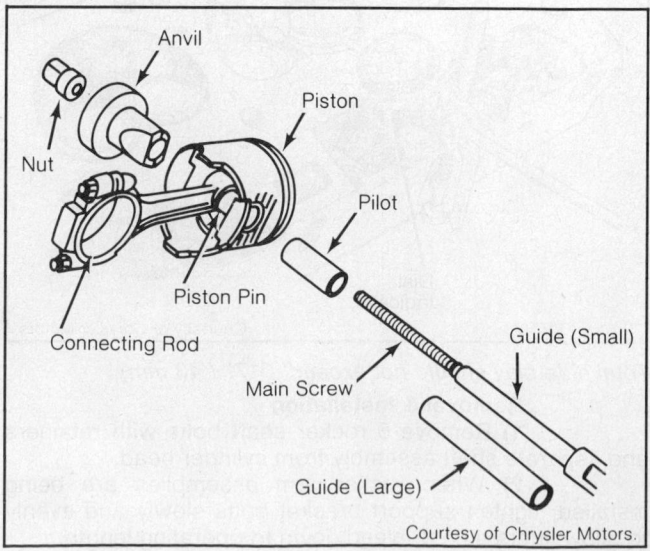

Courtesy of Chrysler Motors.

5.2L V8 (Cont.)

3) Assemble the left bank rods to pistons (Nos. 1, 3, 5 and 7) with indent on piston head on the same side as the large chamfer on the large bore end of connecting rod. *See Fig. 10*.

4) Install main screw and piston pin in piston and install nut on main screw to hold assembly together. Place assembly in a vise. Press piston pin in until piston pin bottoms on the pilot.

Checking Pin Fit

1) Assemble tool in the same manner as for piston pin removal and place assembly in a vise. Attach a torque wrench and test torque to 15 ft. lbs. (20 N.m).

2) If connecting rod moves downward on piston pin, reject the connecting rod and piston pin combination. Install a new connecting rod and recheck. If connecting rod does not move under 15 ft. lbs. (20 N.m) torque, piston pin fit is satisfactory.

CRANKSHAFT & ROD BEARINGS

CONNECTING ROD BEARINGS

1) Ensure rod caps are marked for proper identification. Remove rod cap and use Plastigage method to check for proper bearing clearance. If clearance is not within specifications, replace with correct undersized bearing. Install rod cap with bearing insert and tighten nuts.

2) New bearings inserts are available in standard and .001", .002", .003", .010" and .012" undersize. Always install bearings in pairs. Do not combine new bearing inserts with old or attempt to file rods or bearing caps to obtain proper clearance.

NOTE: When assembled to pistons correctly, rods are not interchangeable from bank to bank. Fit all rods on one bank until completed, before continuing to next bank.

MAIN BEARINGS

Removal & Installation

1) Use Plastigage method to check main bearing clearance. Measure clearance by loosening each bearing cap, one at a time, while all others remain tight. If clearance is not within specifications, replace bearing insert. New bearings inserts are available in standard and .001", .002", .003", .010" and .012" undersize.

NOTE: Main bearing caps are not interchangeable and should be marked to ensure proper installation.

2) With bearing cap removed, insert Roll-Out Pin (C-3059) in oil hole of journal. Rotate crankshaft clockwise to remove upper bearing half.

3) To install new upper bearing, slightly chamfer sharp edges from plain side of bearing and start bearing in place.

4) Install tool and slowly rotate crankshaft counterclockwise, sliding bearing into place. Remove tool. Install main bearing cap with new bearing installed and tighten. Check crankshaft end play. Replace the thrust bearing, main bearing No. 3, if not within specifications. Recheck crankshaft end play.

NOTE: Only main bearings No. 2 and No. 4 have interchangeable bearing halves. These bearing halves are only interchangeable with the bearing half of identical design. Do not interchange upper (grooved) with lower (plain) bearing halves.

REAR MAIN BEARING OIL SEAL

Removal (Upper & Lower)

With oil pan and oil pump removed, remove rear bearing cap. Remove upper seal by pressing on end of seal with screwdriver. *See Fig. 12*. Be careful not to damage crankshaft and seal contact surface. Remove lower seal using similiar procedure.

Fig. 11: Main Bearing Identification

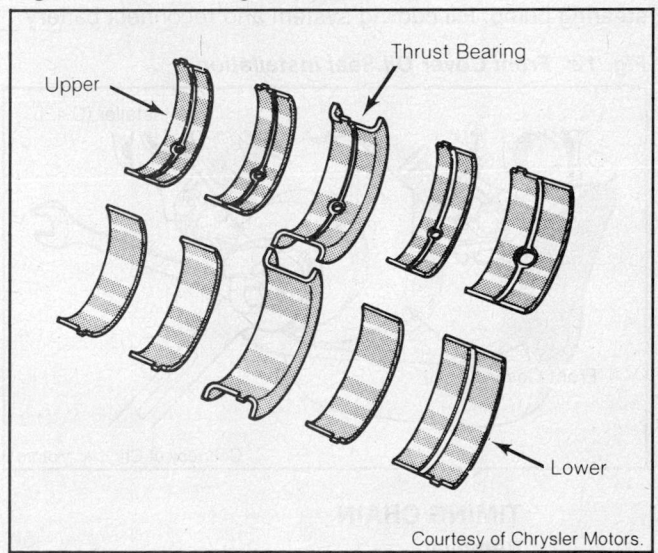

Courtesy of Chrysler Motors.

Installation

Insert cap seals into slots in bearing cap with seal edge toward inside of shoulder. Lightly oil crankshaft and lips of crankshaft seals. Rotate upper half seal into cylinder block with paint stripe toward the rear. Place other half seal in bearing cap with paint stripe toward rear. Assemble bearing cap to cylinder block and tighten.

CAUTION: Sharp edge of groove in block may shave or nick back of seal. Use care not to damage sealing lip.

CAMSHAFT

TIMING COVER & OIL SEAL

Removal

1) Disconnect battery ground and drain cooling system. Remove water pump assembly and power steering pump. Remove pulley from vibration damper. Remove damper bolt and using Puller Set (C-3688), remove damper assembly from end of crankshaft.

2) Remove fuel lines and fuel pump. Loosen oil pan bolts and remove the 2 front bolts at each side. Remove cover bolts and carefully remove timing cover without damaging oil pan gasket. Remove timing cover oil seal.

Chrysler Motors Engines

5.2L V8 (Cont.)

Installation

1) Check that mating surfaces of engine timing cover and cylinder block are clean and free from burrs. Apply 1/8" bead of sealer on oil pan gasket. Use a new gasket and install cover. Install cover bolts and tighten. Tighten cover bolts first, then oil pan bolts. Insert threaded shaft of Installer (C-4251) into threads of crankshaft.

2) Place seal with spring toward inside of engine. Place installation adapter with thrust bearing and nut on shaft. Tighten nut until tool is flush with cover. See Fig. 12.

NOTE: Timing cover oil seal may be installed in timing cover before installing on engine.

3) Install vibration damper, pulley and radiator shroud. Install belts and connect battery. Install fuel pump and fuel lines. Install water pump assembly and power steering pump. Fill cooling system and reconnect battery.

Fig. 12: Front Cover Oil Seal Installation

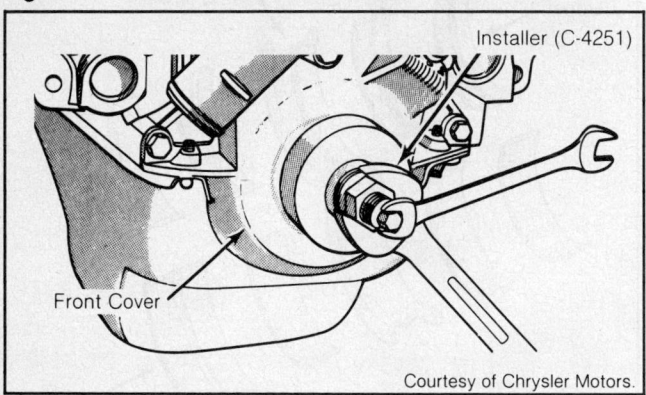

Courtesy of Chrysler Motors.

TIMING CHAIN

Removal

With front cover removed, align timing chain sprockets. See Fig. 13. Remove camshaft sprocket attaching bolt, with washer and fuel pump eccentric. Remove timing chain with crankshaft and camshaft sprockets.

Fig. 13: Timing Chain Sprocket Alignment

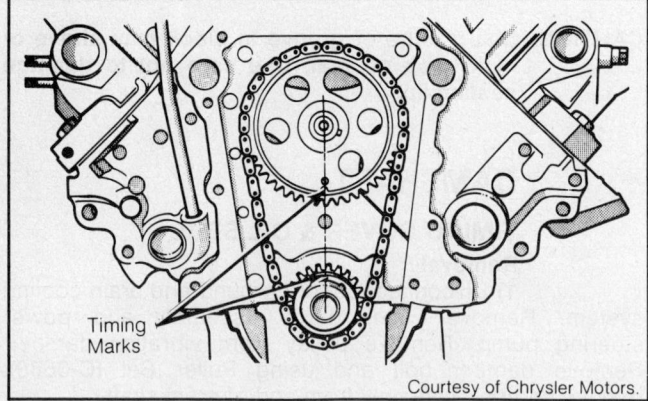

Courtesy of Chrysler Motors.

Align timing marks before removing old chain.

Installation

1) Place camshaft and crankshaft sprockets on bench with timing marks on imaginary centerline through bore of both sprockets. Place timing chain around both sprockets.

2) Turn crankshaft and camshaft to line up with keyway location in crankshaft sprocket and camshaft sprocket. Slide both sprockets evenly over their respective shafts, with new chain installed on sprockets.

3) Use a straightedge to measure alignment of timing marks. Install fuel pump eccentric, washer and camshaft sprocket bolt and tighten.

Chain Stretch Test

1) Place a torque wrench and socket over camshaft sprocket bolt and apply 30 ft. lbs. (41 N.m) torque in direction of rotation with cylinder heads installed, or 15 ft. lbs. (20 N.m) with heads removed.

Fig. 14: Measuring Timing Chain Stretch

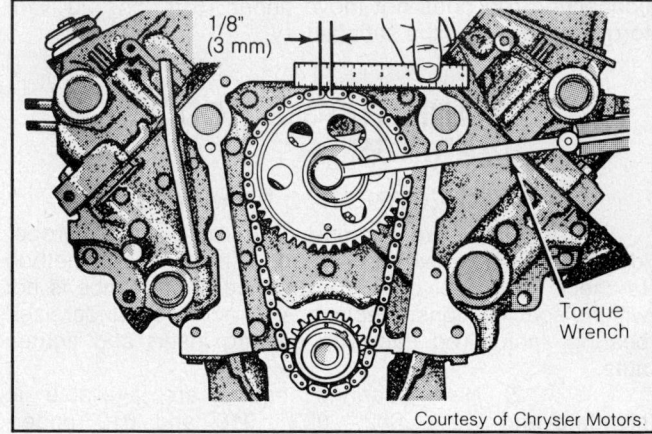

Courtesy of Chrysler Motors.

Do not allow crankshaft to rotate.

2) Block crankshaft to prevent rotation. Place scale next to chain link and apply 30 ft. lbs. (41 N.m) torque in reverse direction of rotation with heads installed, or 15 ft. lbs. (20 N.m) with heads removed. If more than 1/8" (3 mm) movement, replace chain.

CAMSHAFT

Removal

1) With engine removed from vehicle, remove rocker arm covers, intake manifold and front cover. Remove rocker arm assemblies, push rods, yoke retainer, lifter aligning yokes and lifters. Keep in order to ensure installation in original location.

Fig. 15: Exploded View of Camshaft Assembly

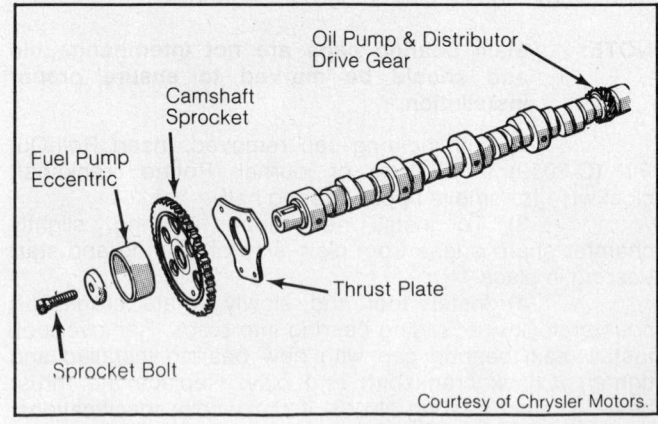

Courtesy of Chrysler Motors.

5.2L V8 (Cont.)

2) Remove the timing chain and sprockets, distributor with drive shaft, and thrust plate. Note location of oil tab. Install long bolt in front of camshaft to ease removal and carefully remove camshaft.

Installation

Lubricate camshaft lobes and bearing journals. Insert camshaft within 2" (50.8 mm) of final position in cylinder block. Install Camshaft Holder (C-3509) in distributor drive hole and hold in position using distributor retainer plate bolt. Install camshaft to proper position.

NOTE: **Tool will prevent camshaft from being pushed in too far and knocking out camshaft core plug. Leave tool installed until sprockets and chain are secured.**

CAMSHAFT BEARINGS

Removal & Installation

1) Drive out core plug at rear of block. Using Camshaft Bearing Driver (C-3132A), with proper adapter, drive out old bearings.

2) Slide new rear bearing over adapter and carefully drive bearing into place. Install the remaining bearings in same manner. Oil holes in new bearings must be aligned with oil passages from main bearings.

3) If oil holes are not in exact alignment, remove bearing and reinstall correctly. Coat core hole with sealer and install new core plug at rear of cylinder block.

CAMSHAFT END PLAY

End play is taken up by thrust plate behind camshaft sprocket. End play is .002-.006" (.05-.15 mm) with new thrust plate and up to .010" (.25 mm) with used thrust plate. If not within specifications, replace thrust plate.

VALVE TIMING

1) Turn crankshaft clockwise until No. 6 exhaust valve is closed and No. 6 intake valve is opening. Insert a .250" (6.35 mm) spacer between rocker arm pad and valve stem of No. 1 intake valve. Spring load will bleed lifter down giving in effect a solid lifter.

2) Install dial indicator so plunger contacts valve spring retainer in a perpendicular position. Zero indicator then turn crankshaft clockwise until valve has lifted .010" (.25 mm).

CAUTION: Do not turn crankshaft any further. Valve spring may bottom and result in damage to rocker arm or push rod.

3) Timing mark on crankshaft pulley should read from 10° BTDC to 2° ATDC. If reading is not correct, check sprocket index marks, inspect timing chain for wear and check accuracy of TDC mark on timing indicator.

ENGINE OILING

CRANKCASE CAPACITY

Crankcase capacity is 4 qts. (3.8L). Add 1 qt. (.9L) with filter change.

NORMAL OIL PRESSURE (HOT)

Normal oil pressure is 30-80 psi (2.1-5.6 kg/cm²) @ 3000 RPM.

PRESSURE REGULATOR VALVE

Pressure regulator valve is located in oil pump body and is not adjustable.

Fig. 16: Engine Oiling System

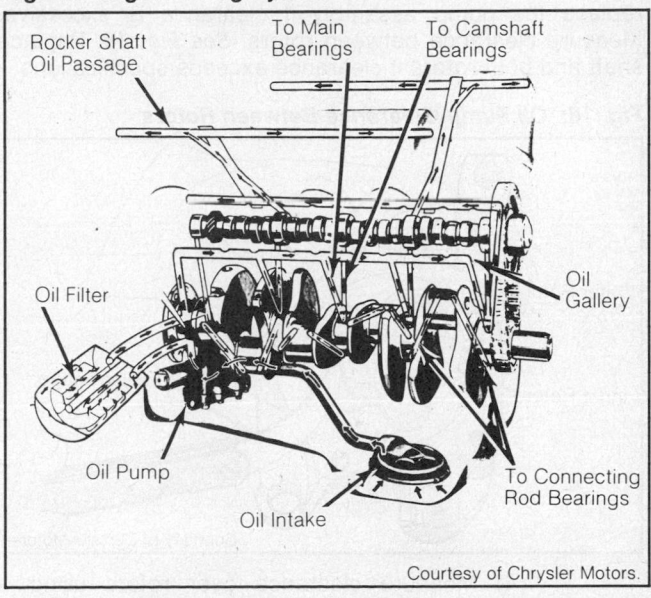

Courtesy of Chrysler Motors.

OIL PUMP

Removal & Disassembly

1) With the oil pan removed, remove pump retaining bolts and pump from main bearing cap. Remove cotter pin from pump housing. Drill a .125" (3.17 mm) hole into the relief valve retainer cap.

2) Insert a sheet metal screw into the cap. While holding pump, clamp the screw into a vise. Using a soft hammer, tap on pump body until retainer cap is pulled from pump body. Remove relief valve and spring from pump body.

3) Remove pump cover retaining bolts and cover. Remove the inner rotor, shaft and outer rotor. Wash all parts in solvent and inspect for wear or damage.

Fig. 17: Exploded View of Oil Pump

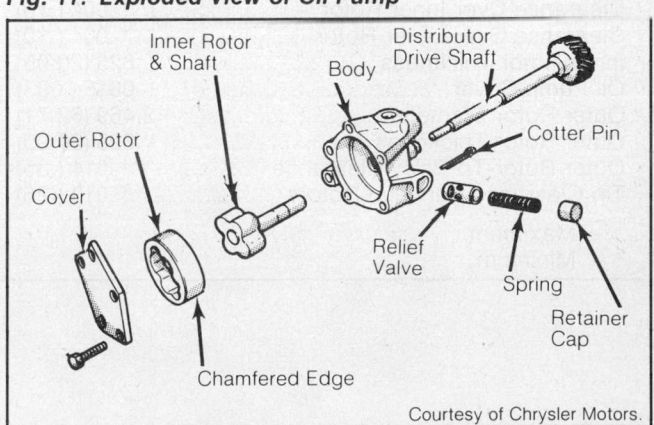

Courtesy of Chrysler Motors.

5.2L V8 (Cont.)

Inspection

1) Measure pump cover wear using a straightedge and feeler gauge. Replace pump if wear exceeds specifications or mating surface is scratched or grooved.

2) Measure outer rotor thickness and diameter. Replace rotor if either is less than specifications. Measure inner rotor thickness and replace rotor and shaft assembly if less than specifications.

3) Measure outer rotor-to-body clearance and replace the pump assembly if clearance is excessive. Measure clearance between rotors. See Fig. 18. Replace shaft and both rotors if clearance exceeds specifications.

Fig. 18: Oil Pump Clearance Between Rotors

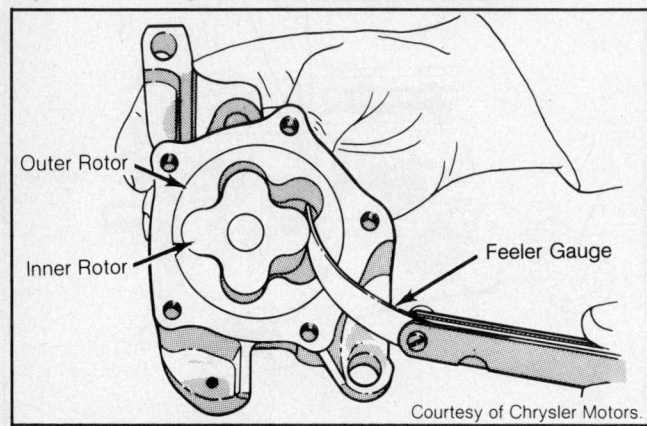

Courtesy of Chrysler Motors.

4) Measure clearance over rotors using a straightedge across face of pump body, between bolt holes, and inserting a feeler gauge between straightedge and rotors. Replace pump if clearance is excessive.

Reassembly & Installation

Reverse disassembly procedure to complete reassembly. Prime the pump by filling rotor cavity with oil while rotating pump shaft. Place pump on engine install retaining bolts and tighten to specification.

Pressure relief valve spring has free length of 2.031-2.047" (51.59-51.99 mm). Spring should test 16.2-17.2 lbs. (7.3-7.8 kg) when compressed to 1.344" (32.13 mm).

OIL PUMP SPECIFICATIONS

Application	In. (mm)
Clearance Over Inner Rotor	[1] .004 (.10)
Clearance Over Outer Rotor	[1] .004 (.10)
Inner Rotor Thickness	[2] .825 (20.95)
Oil Pump Cover	[1] .0015 (.003)
Outer Rotor Diameter	[2] 2.469 (62.71)
Outer Rotor Thickness	[2] .825 (20.95)
Outer Rotor-To-Body Clearance	[1] .014 (.35)
Tip Clearance Between Rotors	[1] .010 (.25)

[1] – Maximum.
[2] – Minimum.

ENGINE COOLING

WATER PUMP

Removal

1) Disconnect battery ground and drain cooling system. Disconnect upper radiator hose at radiator and secure out of the way. Remove alternator and power steering belts. Remove fan, fan assembly, water pump pulley and fan shroud. Disconnect alternator and mounting bracket and move aside.

2) Disconnect power steering pump and bracket and move aside. Disconnect air conditioning compressor and bracket (if equipped) and move aside. Disconnect lower radiator and by-pass hose at the water pump. Remove retaining bolts and remove water pump.

NOTE: To prevent loss of silicone fluid, store fan drive on flat surface with flange end up.

Installation

With mating surfaces clean use a new gasket and install water pump. After installation make sure pump rotates freely. Reverse removal procedure to complete installation. Adjust belts, fill cooling system and connect battery.

NOTE: For information on cooling system capacities and other cooling system components, see appropriate article in ENGINE COOLING SYSTEMS section.

TIGHTENING SPECIFICATIONS

Application	Ft. Lbs. (N.m)
Camshaft Sprocket Bolt	50 (68)
Camshaft Thrust Plate	18 (24)
Connecting Rod Cap Nut	45 (61)
Crankshaft Bolts	100 (136)
Cylinder Head Bolts	
Step 1	50 (68)
Step 2	105 (143)
Exhaust Manifold	
Bolts	20 (27)
Nut	15 (20)
Flex Plate-to-Converter Bolts	23 (31)
Flywheel-to-Crankshaft Bolts	55 (75)
Front Cover Bolts	35 (47)
Intake Manifold Bolts	
Step 1	25 (34)
Step 2	40 (54)
Step 3	45 (61)
Main Bearing Cap Bolts	85 (115)
Oil Pan Bolts	17 (23)
Oil Pump Attaching Bolts	30 (41)
Rocker Shaft Bracket Bolt	17 (23)
Vibration Damper Nut	100 (136)
Water Pump Bolts	30 (41)

	INCH Lbs. (N.m)
Oil Pump Cover Bolts	95 (11)
Rocker Arm Cover Bolts	95 (11)

5.2L V8 (Cont.)

ENGINE SPECIFICATIONS

GENERAL SPECIFICATIONS

Year	DISPLACEMENT		Fuel System	HP@RPM	Torque Ft. Lbs.@RPM	Compr. Ratio	BORE		STROKE	
	Cu. In.	Liters					In.	mm	In.	mm
1988	318	5.2	2-Bbl.	140@3600	265@2000	9.0:1	3.91	99.3	3.31	8.4
	318	5.2	4-Bbl.	175@4000	250@3200	8.4:1	3.91	99.3	3.31	8.4

VALVES

Engine Size & Valve	Head Diam. In. (mm)	Face Angle	Seat Angle	Seat Width In. (mm)	Stem Diameter In. (mm)	Stem Clearance In. (mm)	Valve Lift In. (mm)
5.2L Std. Intake	1.78 (45.2)	45°	45°	.065-.085 (1.65-2.15)	.372-.373 (9.44-9.47)	.0010-.0030 (.025-.076)	.373 (9.47)
Exhaust	1.50 (38.1)	45°	45°	.080-.100 (2.03-2.54)	.371-.372 (9.42-9.44)	.0020-.0040 (.051-.102)	.400 (10.16)
5.2L H.D. Intake	1.88 (47.7)	45°	45°	.065-.085 (1.65-2.15)	.3720-.3730 (9.449-9.474)	.0015-.0035 (.038-.089)	.373 (9.47)
Exhaust	1.60 (40.6)	45°	45°	.080-.100 (2.03-2.54)	.3705-.3715 (9.411-9.436)	.0025-.0045 (.064-.114)	.400 (10.16)

PISTONS, PINS & RINGS

Engine	PISTONS	PINS		RINGS		
	Clearance In. (mm)	Piston Fit In. (mm)	Rod Fit In. (mm)	Ring No.	End Gap In. (mm)	Side Clearance In. (mm)
5.2L	.0005-.0015 [1] (.012-.038)	.00025-.00075 (.0063-.0190)	Press Fit	1 & 2	.010-.020 (.25-.50)	.0015-.0030 (.038-.076)
				3	.015-.055 (.25-1.57)	.0002-.0050 (.005-.127)

[1] – 4-Bbl. H.D. .001-.002" (.025-.051 mm).

CRANKSHAFT MAIN & CONNECTING ROD BEARINGS

Engine	MAIN BEARINGS				CONNECTING ROD BEARINGS		
	Journal Diam. In. (mm)	Clearance In. (mm)	Thrust Bearing	Crankshaft End Play In. (mm)	Journal Diam. In. (mm)	Clearance In. (mm)	Side Play In. (mm)
5.2L	2.4995-2.5005 (63.487-63.627)	.0005-0015 [1] (.012-.038)	No. 3	.002-.009 (.05-.22)	2.124-2.125 (53.94-53.97)	.0005-.0025 (.012-.063)	.006-.014 (.15-.35)

[1] – Clearance for No. 1 only. Clearance for Nos. 2, 3, 4 & 5 is .0005-.0020" (.013-.051 mm). Limit .0025" (.063 mm).

Chrysler Motors Engines

5.2L V8 (Cont.)

ENGINE SPECIFICATIONS (Cont.)

VALVE SPRINGS

Engine	Free Length In. (mm)	PRESSURE Lbs. @ In. (Kg @ mm)	
		Valve Closed	Valve Open
5.2L Std.	2.00 (50.8)	77-88@1.687 (35-39@42.8)	170-184@1.313 (77-83@33.3)
5.2L H.D.	2.10 (53.3)	108-118@1.66 (.02-.07)	186-200@1.25
No. 2	1.982 (50.34)		.....
No. 3	1.967 (49.95)		.....
No. 4	1.953 (49.55)		.....
No. 5	1.561 (39.64)		.....

1.9L 4-CYLINDER

Escort, EXP

NOTE: For engine repair procedures not covered in this article, see ENGINE OVERHAUL PROCEDURES article at beginning of this section.

ENGINE CODING

ENGINE IDENTIFICATION

Engine may be identified from 8th character of Vehicle Identification Number (VIN). VIN is stamped on metal tab fastened to instrument panel on driver's side and is visible through windshield. VIN is also on Vehicle Certification label (VC label), located on left front door lock panel.

An engine identification label is attached to engine front cover. Symbol code on identification label identifies each engine for determining parts usage.

ENGINE CODES

Engine	Code
1.9L (116") CFI	9
1.9L HO (116") MPFI	J

SPECIAL ENGINE MARKS

Information identifying oversize tappets and oversize camshaft is stamped in various locations on engine. See Fig. 1. Information and location is decoded as follows:

.254 OT – This indicates that all lifters are oversize. This mark will appear on machined pad below rocker arm rail and above No. 1 exhaust port.

.38 O/C & .38 O/S – This indicates engine has oversize lifters and/or oversize camshaft. The mark .38 O/C will be located on cover rail tug on No. 4 exhaust port. The mark .38 O/S will appear on distributor drive end of camshaft.

Fig. 1: Oversize Identification

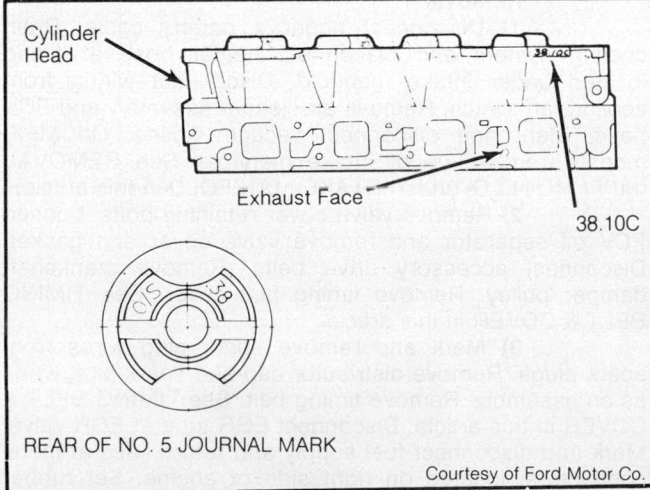

Cylinder Head

Exhaust Face

38.10C

REAR OF NO. 5 JOURNAL MARK

Courtesy of Ford Motor Co.

ENGINE REMOVAL

See ENGINE REMOVAL & INSTALLATION article at end of ENGINE section.

CYLINDER HEAD & MANIFOLDS

CAUTION: CFI and MPFI cylinder heads are different. Parts are not to be interchanged. Identify type being serviced before replacing or ordering parts.

INTAKE MANIFOLD

Removal (CFI Models)

1) Disconnect negative battery cable. Drain cooling system and disconnect heater hose at fitting located on side of intake manifold. Remove air cleaner assembly. Mark and remove vacuum hoses and wiring connectors at intake manifold. Remove EGR supply tube.

2) Raise vehicle. Remove Ported Vacuum Switch (PVS) hose connectors and label for reassembly reference. Remove 4 bottom intake manifold nuts. See Fig. 2. Lower vehicle. Remove fuel lines at throttle body. Disconnect throttle and speed control cables.

3) Disconnect throttle valve linkage at throttle body and remove cable bracket attaching bolts (ATX models). Remove 3 upper intake manifold nuts. Remove intake manifold and gasket. DO NOT lay intake manifold flat as gasket surface may be damaged. Clean gasket mating surfaces thoroughly.

Fig. 2: 1.9L CFI Intake Manifold Tightening Sequence

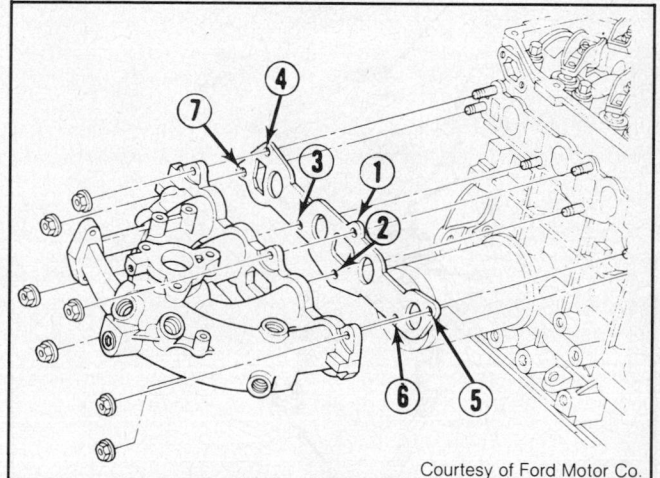

Courtesy of Ford Motor Co.

Installation

1) Install new intake manifold gasket on cylinder head. Position intake manifold on cylinder head and install nuts. Tighten nuts to specifications, in 2 steps and in sequence. See Fig. 2.

CAUTION: Tightening specifications are crucial. Compensate for extensions that are used.

2) To complete installation, reverse removal procedure. Tighten all bolts/nuts to specifications. Fill cooling system with specified coolant only. See ENGINE COOLING at end of this article.

Removal (MPFI Models)

1) Ensure ignition switch is off. Remove battery ground cable. Drain coolant. Remove fuel cap to release fuel tank pressure. Remove pressure relief valve cap. Attach pressure gauge and release pressure from fuel system at fuel pressure relief valve on fuel injector manifold assembly.

Ford Motor Co. Engines

1.9L 4-CYLINDER (Cont.)

2) Using Fuel Line Coupling Disconnect (D87L-9280-A or B), disconnect fuel supply line and return hoses. Disconnect Engine Coolant Temperature (ECT) sensor, in heater supply tube under lower intake manifold. Disconnect EEC harness. Disconnect air by-pass connector from EEC harness.

3) Remove air cleaner outlet tube from air intake throttle body and vane air meter. Remove throttle and speed control cables from mounting bracket and throttle lever. Mark and remove vacuum lines at intake manifold. Remove vacuum line from EGR valve. Disconnect EGR tube from upper intake manifold.

4) Remove upper support bracket bolt from upper intake manifold only. Remove bolts retaining upper intake manifold to lower intake manifold. Remove upper intake manifold. *See Fig. 3.*

5) Remove fuel supply and return lines. Remove nuts retaining lower intake manifold to cylinder head. Remove lower support bracket bolt from lower intake manifold and remove lower intake manifold with wiring harness.

Fig. 3: Exploded View of MPFI Intake Manifold

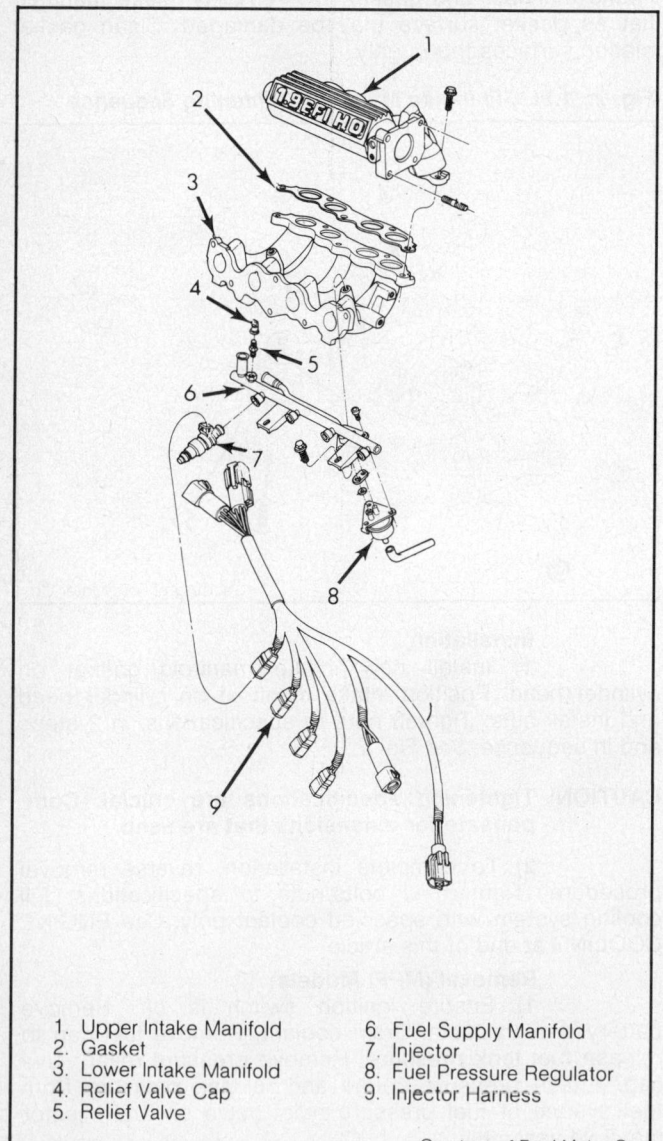

1. Upper Intake Manifold
2. Gasket
3. Lower Intake Manifold
4. Relief Valve Cap
5. Relief Valve
6. Fuel Supply Manifold
7. Injector
8. Fuel Pressure Regulator
9. Injector Harness

Courtesy of Ford Motor Co.

Installation
1) Remove all gaskets and clean gasket mating surfaces. Use care not to damage gasket mating surfaces. Clean and oil manifold studs, bolts and nuts. Ensure mating surfaces are flat. Maximum warpage is .003" (.08 mm) for every 6.0".

2) Install new gasket on cylinder head. Place lower intake manifold in position. Install top middle nut finger tight. Install 2 outside lower intake manifold nuts finger tight. Install remaining manifold mounting nuts. Tighten nuts in 2 steps and in sequence to specifications. *See Fig. 3.*

3) To complete installation, reverse removal procedure. Tighten all bolts/nuts to specifications. Fill cooling system with specified coolant. See ENGINE COOLING at end of this article. Check for leakage.

EXHAUST MANIFOLD
Removal
1) Disconnect negative battery cable. Remove air cleaner assembly. Disconnect electric fan wire. Remove radiator shroud. Disconnect EGR tube at exhaust manifold. Remove air conditioning hose bracket (if equipped). Remove oxygen sensor. Remove exhaust manifold heat shroud.

2) Remove exhaust manifold retaining nuts. Raise vehicle. Remove anti-roll brace. Disconnect water tube brackets. Disconnect exhaust pipe at catalytic converter. Remove exhaust manifold.

Installation
Clean gasket mating surfaces and check for flatness. Maximum warpage is .003" (.08 mm) every 6.0". Install new gaskets with "TOP UP" in proper position. To complete installation, reverse removal procedure. Tighten exhaust manifold nuts from center, working outward, toward both sides.

CYLINDER HEAD

NOTE: Do not remove cylinder head if hot. Allow engine to cool down first.

Removal
1) Disconnect negative battery cable. Drain cooling system and disconnect heater hose at fitting located under intake manifold. Disconnect wiring from cooling fan switch. Remove air cleaner assembly and PCV hose. Mark and disconnect vacuum hoses. On MPFI models, remove upper intake manifold. See REMOVAL (MPFI MODELS) under INTAKE MANIFOLD in this article.

2) Remove valve cover retaining bolts. Loosen PCV oil separator and remove valve cover and gasket. Disconnect accessory drive belts. Remove crankshaft damper pulley. Remove timing belt cover. See TIMING BELT & COVER in this article.

3) Mark and remove spark plug wires from spark plugs. Remove distributor cap and spark plug wires as an assembly. Remove timing belt. See TIMING BELT & COVER in this article. Disconnect EGR tube at EGR valve. Mark and disconnect fuel supply and return lines at metal connectors, located on right side of engine. Set rubber lines aside.

4) Disconnect throttle and speed control cable (if equipped). Disconnect alternator wiring harness. Remove alternator and mounting bracket. Raise vehicle. Disconnect exhaust pipe at exhaust manifold. Lower vehicle.

1.9L 4-CYLINDER (Cont.)

5) Remove and discard cylinder head bolts. Remove cylinder head with exhaust and intake manifold attached. Remove cylinder head gasket.

CAUTION: DO NOT lay cylinder head assembly flat. Damage to spark plugs, valves and gasket surface may result.

Inspection

1) Clean gasket mating surface on cylinder head and block. Check surfaces for flatness. Flatness should be .003" per 6" (.08 mm per 156.0 mm). Total allowable is .0059" (.150 mm). Check cylinder head for cracks between ports and cylinders. Replace cylinder head as necessary.

2) Check piston squish height every time cylinder head is removed. Piston squish height is the clearance of the piston dome to the cylinder head dome, at piston TDC. Place a small amount of SOFT lead solder on No. 1 piston spherical areas. *See Figs. 4 and 5.*

Fig. 4: Checking Piston Squish Height

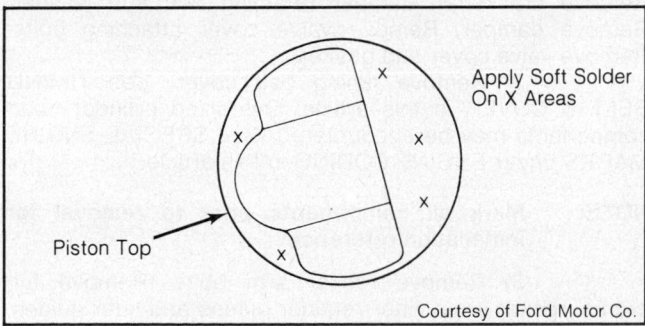

Apply Soft Solder On X Areas

Piston Top

Courtesy of Ford Motor Co.

Fig. 5: Sectional View of Piston Squish Height

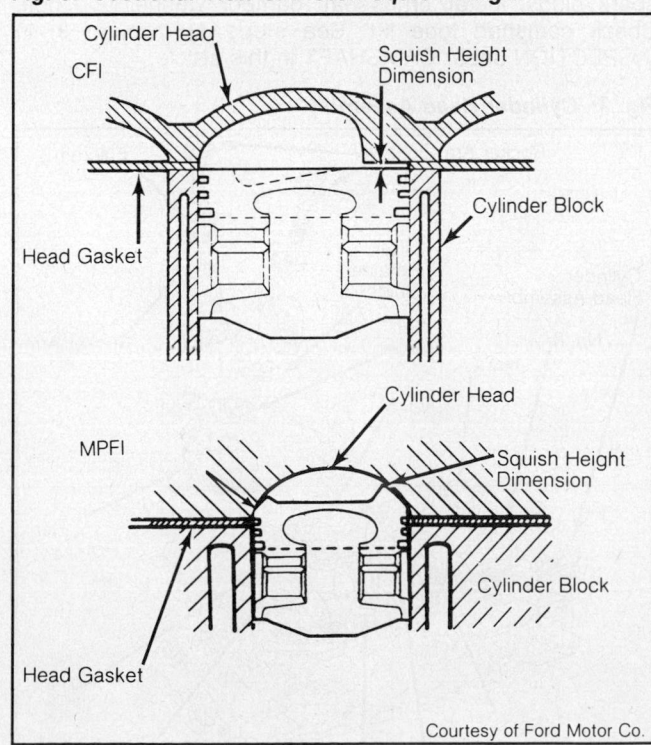

Cylinder Head

CFI

Squish Height Dimension

Head Gasket

Cylinder Block

Cylinder Head

MPFI

Squish Height Dimension

Cylinder Block

Head Gasket

Courtesy of Ford Motor Co.

3) Rotate crankshaft and lower piston in cylinder bore. Place a compressed (used) head gasket on engine block. Ensure camshaft sprocket timing mark is aligned with cylinder head mark. Install cylinder head. Install USED cylinder head bolts and tighten to 30-44 ft. lbs. (41-60 N.m), in sequence. *See Fig. 6.*

4) Rotate crankshaft and move piston through its TDC position. Remove cylinder head. Measure thickness of compressed solder to determine squish height at TDC. On CFI models, squish height must be .046-.060" (1.17-1.52 mm). On MPFI models, squish height must be .039-.070" (.99-1.78 mm).

5) If no parts other than head gasket are replaced, piston squish height should be within specifications. If parts other than head gasket are replaced and piston squish height is out of specifications, replace parts again. Recheck piston squish height. Clean and tap all cylinder head bolt threads in engine block.

CAUTION: DO NOT install cylinder head without performing piston squish height. See INSPECTION under CYLINDER HEAD in this article. DO NOT reuse cylinder head bolts under any circumstances.

Fig. 6: Cylinder Head Bolt Tightening Sequence

⑨ ③ ① ⑤ ⑦   Intake
○ ○ ○ ○ ○
○ ○ ○ ○ ○
⑧ ⑥ ② ④ ⑩   Exhaust

Courtesy of Ford Motor Co.

Tighten in 5 steps.

Installation

1) Ensure gasket mating surfaces are clean. Ensure camshaft timing mark is aligned with cylinder head mark and No. 1 piston is at TDC, before placing cylinder head on block. Position cylinder head gasket on engine block. Replace cylinder head bolts. Apply light coat of engine oil to new cylinder head bolts. Install NEW cylinder head bolts.

2) Tighten all cylinder head bolts in sequence to 44 ft. lbs. (60 N.m). *See Fig. 6.* Loosen all cylinder head bolts 2 turns. Retighten cylinder head bolts in sequence to 44 ft. lbs. (60 N.m). Again in sequence, tighten cylinder head bolts 90 degrees. To complete tightening, tighten cylinder head bolts in sequence a final 90 degrees.

3) To complete installation, reverse removal procedure. Tighten all bolts/nuts to specifications. Set ignition timing. Fill cooling system with specified coolant only. See ENGINE COOLING in this article. Check for vacuum, coolant, fuel and oil leaks.

CAMSHAFT

TIMING BELT & COVER

CAUTION: DO NOT rotate camshaft with timing belt removed, without rotating crankshaft 90 degrees BTDC first. Valves and pistons can be damaged.

Ford Motor Co. Engines

1.9L 4-CYLINDER (Cont.)

Removal

1) Disconnect negative battery cable. Remove accessory belts. Position No. 1 piston on TDC and align crankshaft damper mark with TDC mark on cover. Remove timing belt cover. Check camshaft sprocket timing mark to ensure alignment with mark on cylinder head.

2) If mark on camshaft sprocket and cylinder head do not align, rotate crankshaft until they are aligned. Position timing cover and ensure crankshaft damper mark align with TDC mark on cover. Remove timing cover if reinstalled. Remove crankshaft damper bolt. Remove crankshaft damper.

3) Ensure timing marks are in alignment. Loosen both belt tensioner attaching bolts. Pry tensioner away from belt and tighten one tensioner bolt. Remove timing belt from camshaft sprocket and water pump. Remove belt from crankshaft sprocket.

NOTE: **Engine must be at ambient temperature. DO NOT set torque on a hot engine.**

Installation

1) Ensure timing marks are all aligned. Position timing belt on crankshaft sprocket. Install timing belt over remaining sprockets in a counterclockwise direction. Keep belt on crankshaft sprocket-to-camshaft sprocket side tight during installation over remaining sprocket. Loosen tensioner bolt and allow tensioner to snap against timing belt.

2) Tighten one tensioner bolt. Install crankshaft damper. Using Damper Holding Wrench (YA-826), hold damper stationary and tighten damper bolt to specifications. Ensure camshaft timing marks are aligned. Position timing belt cover and check crankshaft timing mark alignment. Remove cover if aligned and proceed to next step. Repeat procedures if not aligned.

CAUTION: DO NOT crank engine if camshaft and crankshaft timing marks are not in proper alignment. Damage to engine may occur.

3) Seat timing belt in sprockets by connecting battery ground cable. Disconnect and ground coil wire to prevent engine from starting. Crank engine for 30 seconds. Disconnect battery ground cable. Install coil wire. Check and align camshaft timing marks.

4) Position timing belt cover on engine and check crankshaft timing mark alignment. Damper mark must align with TDC pointer on cover. If timing marks are not in alignment, remove timing belt and repeat complete procedure. If timing mark alignment is correct, remove timing belt cover and proceed to next step.

5) Set camshaft rotation torque by having an assistant hold crankshaft from rotating. Loosen tensioner bolt. A specified amount of torque will be applied to camshaft sprocket and crankshaft MUST NOT be allowed to move.

6) Using a torque wrench and Camshaft Holding Wrench (D81P-6256-A), evenly turn camshaft sprocket counterclockwise until torque wrench reaches specifications. See TIMING BELT TORQUE SPECIFICATIONS table in this article.

7) When specification is achieved, tighten both tensioner bolts to specifications. To complete installation, reverse removal procedure. Tighten all bolts/nuts to specifications.

TIMING BELT TORQUE SPECIFICATIONS

Application	Ft. Lbs. (N.m)
New Belt	27-32 (37-43)
Used Belt [1]	10 (14)

[1] – Belt in service for 30 days or more.

CAMSHAFT OIL SEAL

Removal & Installation

Remove timing belt. See TIMING BELT & COVER in this article. Remove camshaft sprocket. Pry camshaft seal out, using care not to damage surfaces. Lubricate new camshaft seal lip with SAE 30 motor oil. Use Camshaft Seal Replacer (T81P-6292-A) and install seal. To complete installation, reverse removal procedure.

CAMSHAFT

Removal

1) Disconnect negative battery cable. Remove air cleaner assembly, PCV hose and accessory drive belts. Remove crankshaft damper retaining bolt and washer. Remove damper. Remove valve cover attaching bolts. Remove valve cover and gasket.

2) Remove timing belt cover. See TIMING BELT & COVER in this article. Oversized cylinder head components may be encountered. See SPECIAL ENGINE MARKS under ENGINE CODING in this article.

NOTE: **Mark all components prior to removal for installation reference.**

3) Remove rocker arm bolts. Remove fulcrums, rocker arms, lifter retainer guides and lifter guides. *See Fig. 7.* Leave lifters in at this time. Mark spark plug wires and disconnect wires from spark plugs. Remove spark plugs. Install crankshaft damper washer and bolt. Check camshaft lobe lift. See steps **1)** through **3)** in INSPECTION under CAMSHAFT in this article.

Fig. 7: Cylinder Head Assembly

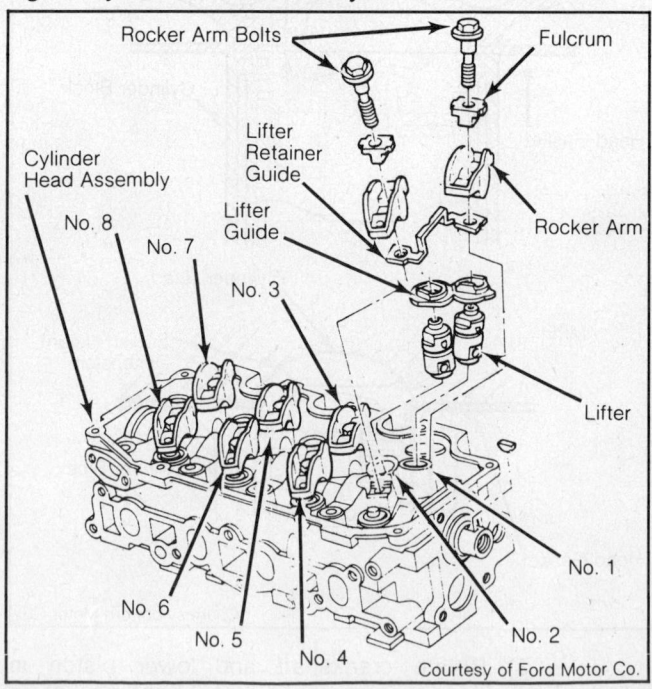

Courtesy of Ford Motor Co.

1.9L 4-CYLINDER (Cont.)

CAUTION: DO NOT rotate crankshaft with timing belt removed.

4) Remove lifters. Remove distributor cap. Note location of ignition rotor. Mark distributor-to-head location and remove distributor assembly. Remove timing belt from camshaft sprocket. See TIMING BELT & COVER in this article.

5) Remove camshaft sprocket and Woodruff key from camshaft. Remove camshaft thrust plate. Remove ignition coil and bracket. Carefully remove camshaft through rear of cylinder head (transaxle side). Check camshaft seal and replace if necessary.

Inspection
1) Check lift of each lobe in consecutive order and record each reading. Mount dial indicator on cylinder head with pointer on lifter top. Ensure bottom of lifter is seated on camshaft. *See Fig. 8.* Rotate crankshaft in normal operating direction only, until lifter is on lowest point of camshaft lobe.

Fig. 8: Checking Camshaft Lobe Lift

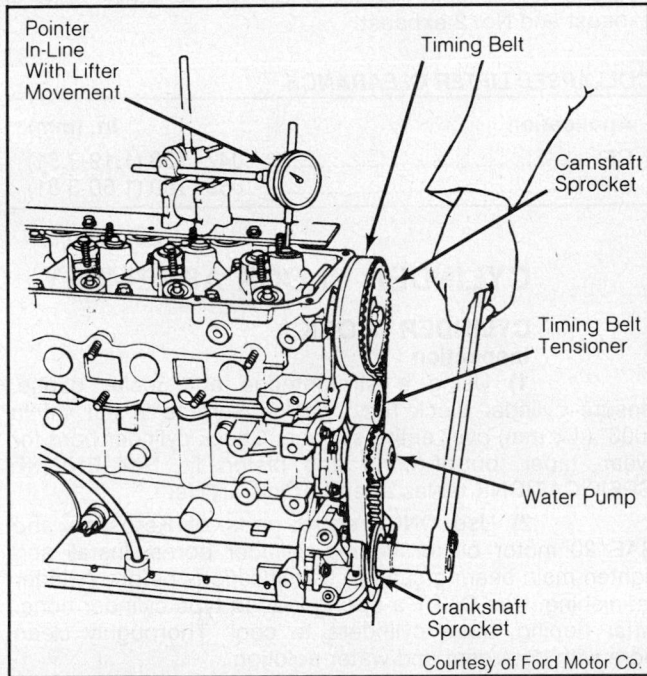

Courtesy of Ford Motor Co.

2) Zero dial indicator. Rotate crankshaft in same direction only, until lifter is on highest portion of camshaft lobe. Record reading. Recheck to ensure a proper dial indicator reading. Repeat complete procedure for remaining camshaft lobes. See ENGINE SPECIFICATIONS tables at end of this article.

3) If lift on any lobe is not within specifications, camshaft and lifters must be replaced. When installing rocker arms, always bleed down lifters BEFORE rotating crankshaft or serious damage may result.

4) Check lifters for wear, scoring, flat or concaved bottom surface. Bottom surface of lifters must be convex and smooth. Check lifter leak-down rate with hydraulic tester fluid only. Engine oil will not give accurate leak-down reading. Replace camshaft and lifters as necessary.

5) Check camshaft bores in cylinder head for size, taper, roundness, alignment and finish. Camshaft journals and bores in cylinder head may be machined

.015" (.38 mm), to accommodate undersize bearings. Camshaft replacement is suggested.

Installation
1) Thoroughly clean all bearing surfaces. Coat camshaft journals, lobes and thrust plate groove with heavy SF engine oil. Install camshaft seal (if removed), with Camshaft Seal Replacer (T81P-6292-A). Lubricate camshaft seal lip with SAE 30 engine oil.

2) Install camshaft through rear of cylinder head (transaxle side), with a rotating method. Use care not to damage bearing surfaces. Coat thrust plate bolts with Teflon sealer. Install camshaft thrust plate and tighten bolts to specifications. Install camshaft Woodruff key.

3) Align camshaft sprocket and Woodruff key. Install camshaft sprocket. Apply Teflon sealer to bolt. Install washer and bolt. Tighten to specifications. Check camshaft end play. End play should be .0018-.0060" (.046-.152 mm). Replace thrust plate as neccessary. Rotate camshaft until Woodruff key is in 12 o'clock position.

NOTE: **Ensure components are installed to position from which they were removed.**

4) Lubricate valve lifter bore with heavy SF engine oil. Install lifter, with hole in plunger facing upward. Position flats of lifters parallel with centerline of camshaft. Install lifter guides over lifter flats, with notch on guide toward exhaust side. *See Fig. 6.*

5) Lubricate top of lifter and valve tip with heavy SF engine oil. Position lifter retainer guides into slots in lifter guides, on both intake and exhaust sides. Ensure notch on lifter retainer guide is with exhaust lifter. *See Fig. 6.*

NOTE: **DO NOT rotate camshaft until lifters are bled down. Serious damage will result.**

6) Install rocker arms on lifter position Nos. 3, 6, 7 and 8. *See Fig. 6.* Lubricate rocker arm and fulcrum mating surfaces with heavy SF engine oil. Install fulcrums for Nos. 3, 6, 7 and 8. Ensure fulcrums are completely seated in slots and install bolts.

7) Position Woodruff key to 6 o'clock position. Repeat steps 4), 5) and 6) for Nos. 1, 2, 4 and 5. *See Fig. 6.* Tighten bolts to specifications. To complete installation, reverse removal. Tighten all bolts/nuts to specifications.

8) Ensure all timing marks are in alignment before starting engine. Fill all fluid levels. Fill cooling system with specified coolant only and bleed system. Check for leakage. Set ignition timing as necessary.

VALVES

VALVE ARRANGEMENT
Left Side - All Exhaust.
Right Side - All Intake.

NOTE: **"Right" and "Left" refer to right and left side of engine NOT the vehicle.**

CAMSHAFT BEARINGS
See step 5) in INSPECTION under CAMSHAFT in this article.

VALVE SEAT

NOTE: Valve seat replacement information not available at this time.

Refacing

On intake seats, use only a 77 degree angle grinding stone to remove stock from bottom of seat. On exhaust seats, use only a 70 degree angle grinding stone to remove stock from bottom of seat. Use an 18 degree grinding stone to remove stock from top of all seats. Valve and seat must be a true 45 degree angle with a seat width of .069-.091" (1.75-2.31 mm).

VALVES & VALVE GUIDES

Inspection

1) Mark all components prior to removal for installation reference. Thoroughly clean cylinder head and valves, using care not to damage surfaces. Check valve-to-guide clearance of each valve in its respective valve guide.

2) Install a valve and hold against seat. Install Valve Stem Clearance Tool (T65T-6505-H) on valve stem, until it is fully seated. Tighten tool set screw firmly. Allow valve to drop away from seat and tool to contact upper guide surface.

3) Install dial indicator with pointer against center portion of tool. *See Fig. 9.* Move clearance tool back and forth in-line with dial indicator pointer. Keep clearance tool on upper guide surface. Record dial indicator reading.

4) Divide dial indicator reading by 2. This total is the valve-to-guide clearance. If not within specifications, replace valve(s) with next available oversize valve. Ream valve guide until clearance with valve is within specification. See ENGINE SPECIFICATIONS tables at end of article.

Fig. 9: Valve-To-Guide Clearance

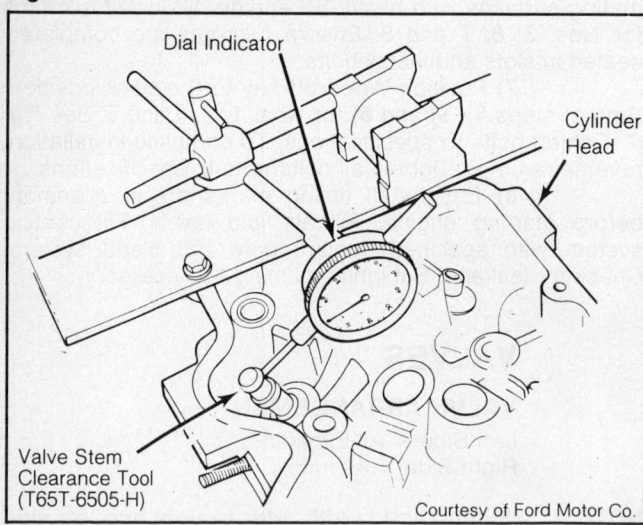

VALVE SPRINGS

Inspection

Inspect valve springs for cracks or damage. Measure installed height. Measure free length and out-of-square. Maximum out-of-square is .060" (1.52 mm). Check spring tension at a specified length. See ENGINE SPECIFICATIONS table at end of article.

HYDRAULIC LIFTER ASSEMBLY

Hydraulic Lifter Clearance

1) Valve stem-to-rocker arm clearance should meet specifications with lifter totally collapsed. Valve and/or valve seat refacing can diminish clearance and allow valve to be held open.

2) To determine rocker arm-to-lifter clearance, attach auxiliary starter switch to starting circuit. With ignition switch in "OFF" position, crank engine until No. 1 piston is on TDC of compression stroke. Install Lifter Collapser (T81P-6500-A) on No. 1 intake rocker arm.

3) Slowly apply pressure until lifter is completely bottomed. Hold lifter in this position and check clearance between rocker arm and valve stem tip. If not within specifications, replace components as necessary. See COLLAPSED LIFTER CLEARANCE table in this article.

4) With engine at TDC, check clearance on No. 1 intake, No. 1 exhaust and No. 2 intake. Rotate crankshaft 180 degrees. Check clearance on No. 3 intake and No. 3 exhaust. Rotate crankshaft another 180 degrees and check clearance on No. 4 intake, No. 4 exhaust and No. 2 exhaust.

COLLAPSED LIFTER CLEARANCE

Application	In. (mm)
CFI	.047-.138 (1.19-3.51)
MPFI	.059-.150 (1.50-3.81)

CYLINDER BLOCK ASSEMBLY

CYLINDER BLOCK

Inspection

1) Using a straightedge and feeler gauge, ensure cylinder block head gasket surface is flat within .003" (.08 mm) over entire surface. Check cylinder bore for wear, taper, out-of-round and piston fit. See ENGINE SPEIFICATIONS tables at end of this article.

2) Use ONLY equal parts of Kerosene and SAE 20 motor oil for honing cylinder bores. Install and tighten main bearing caps to specifications before cylinder refinishing. Use ONLY a spring-loaded type cylinder hone. After honing, allow cylinders to cool. Thoroughly clean bore with detergent and water solution.

3) Rinse solution in bore thoroughly with clean water. Wipe bores clean with lint free cloth. Lubricate cylinder bores with engine oil. Tap cylinder head bolt threads in cylinder block.

PISTONS, PINS & RINGS

OIL PAN

See appropriate OIL PAN REMOVAL article in this section.

PISTON & ROD ASSEMBLY

NOTE: Following procedures are with oil pan and oil pump removed. DO NOT position jack under crankshaft damper.

1.9L 4-CYLINDER (Cont.)

Inspection

Ensure pistons and rods are installed in cylinder from which they were removed. Ensure arrow on top of piston faces front of engine and oil squirt hole in rod faces intake manifold side of engine. Check piston pin fit. Replace as necessary. See ENGINE SPECIFICATIONS tables at end of article.

FITTING PISTONS

1) Check piston-to-bore clearance. See ENGINE SPECIFICATIONS tables at end of this article. Standard size pistons are color coded Red, Blue or Yellow on the piston dome.

2) If piston-to-bore clearance is in lower one-third of specified clearance, use a Red piston. If clearance is in middle of specified clearance, use Blue piston. The Yellow piston is .004" (.10 mm) oversize. Use proper piston to acquire specified clearance.

FITTING RINGS

1) Select proper rings for bore diameter. Place ring square in cylinder bore below normal ring wear area. Measure the ring end gap. If ring end gap is less than specifications, remove necessary amount from end of ring. If gap is greater than specifications, replace rings. Ensure rings are installed in cylinder in which they were measured.

2) Check side clearance of rings after installing on piston. Ensure clearance is within specifications around entire piston circumference. If lower lands of piston have high steps, replace piston. Replace piston and rings if not within specifications. See ENGINE SPECIFICATIONS tables at end of this article. Install rings on piston with ring ends 90 degrees apart.

CRANKSHAFT & ROD BEARINGS

Use Plastigage on main bearings and rod bearings. If clearance is not within specifications with standard bearings, use .002" (.050 mm) undersize and recheck clearance. Always replace rod or main bearings in pairs. When installing bearing, apply light coat of engine oil to journals and bearings. Tighten all bolts/nuts to specifications.

THRUST BEARING ALIGNMENT

Inspection

Install dial indicator on front of engine with pointer on end of crankshaft. Pry crankshaft fully rear and zero indicator. Pry crankshaft fully forward and note reading. If end play exceeds specifications, replace thrust bearing. If end play is less than specifications, remove thrust bearing and inspect surfaces. Replace as necessary.

REAR MAIN BEARING OIL SEAL

Removal

1) Remove transaxle. Remove clutch, pressure plate and flywheel/flexplate. For manual transaxle, see appropriate CLUTCHES article in this section. For automatic transaxle, see appropriate TRANSMISSION SERVICING article in this section.

2) Use an awl and punch a hole into metal surface of seal. Use care not to damage sealing surfaces. Install Jet Plug Remover (T77L-9533-B) and remove oil seal.

Installation

Check crankshaft seal surface for wear and replace as necessary. Coat crankshaft seal area and lip of seal with engine oil. Using Rear Crankshaft Seal Replacer (T81P-6701-A), install oil seal. Tighten bolts on seal replacer evenly to ensure seal is installed square. To complete installation, reverse removal procedure. *See Fig. 10.*

Fig. 10: Installing Crankshaft Rear Main Oil Seal

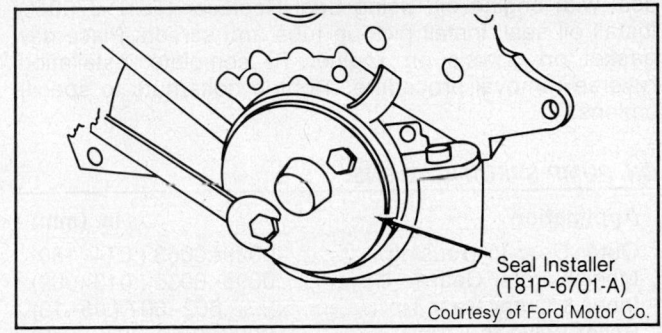

Seal Installer (T81P-6701-A)
Courtesy of Ford Motor Co.

FRONT CRANKSHAFT OIL SEAL

Removal & Installation

Remove timing belt, crankshaft damper and crankshaft sprocket. See TIMING BELT & COVER in this article. Pry out oil seal using care not damage sealing surfaces. Install oil seal with Seal Installer (T81P-6700-A). To complete installation, reverse removal.

ENGINE OILING

ENGINE OILING SYSTEM

Engine oiling is a full pressure system. Oil pump is bolted to front of cylinder block with pump drive gear positioned directly over crankshaft. Oil pump is driven directly by crankshaft.

CRANKCASE CAPACITY

Crankcase capacity is 4 quarts (3.8L) with filter change, 3.5 quarts (3.3L) without filter change.

NORMAL OIL PRESSURE

Normal oil pressure is 35-65 psi (2.40-4.50 kg/cm²) at 2000 RPM, with engine at normal operating temperature.

OIL PUMP

Removal

Disconnect negative battery cable. Remove timing belt, crankshaft damper and sprocket. Disconnect starter cable and remove starter. Drain engine oil and remove oil pan. See appropriate OIL PAN REMOVAL article in this section. Remove oil pump retaining bolts. Pull oil pump assembly from engine. Remove oil pump seal.

Disassembly & Reassembly

If oil pump is found to be defective, complete unit must be replaced.

Inspection

1) Wash parts in solvent and blow dry with compressed air. Inspect for wear or damage. Minor imperfections may be removed with oil stone. Measure

inner-to-outer rotor tip clearance. Use a straightedge and measure clearance between inner and outer rotor-to-housing.

2) Measure inner and outer-to-cover clearance. Check relief valve spring tension. Replace pump assembly if not within specifications. See OIL PUMP SPECIFICATIONS table in this article.

Installation

Lubricate outside diameter and lip of oil pump seal with engine oil. Using Seal Replacer (T81P-6700-A), install oil seal. Install pick-up tube and screen. Place new gasket on dowels on engine. To complete installation, reverse removal procedure. Tighten bolts/nuts to specifications.

OIL PUMP SPECIFICATIONS

Application	In. (mm)
Outer Gear-to-Housing	.0029-.0063 (.074-.160)
Inner & Outer Gear-to-Cover	.0005-.0035 (.013-.009)
Inner & Outer Gear Tip	.002-.007 (.05-.18)
Relief Valve-to-Bore [1]	.0008-.0031 (.020-.079)

[1] – Relief valve spring tension is 9.3-10.3 lbs. @ 1.11 in. (4.2-4.6 Kg @ 28.2 mm).

ENGINE COOLING

WATER PUMP

Removal

1) Disconnect negative battery cable. Drain the cooling system. Remove drive belts. Remove timing belt. See TIMING BELT & COVER in this article. Remove the rearward front timing cover stud. Remove the heater return tube hose connection at water pump inlet tube. See Fig. 11.

2) Remove alternator bracket, if necessary. Remove water pump inlet tube retainers. Remove water pump bolts. Remove water pump and gasket.

Fig. 11: Water Pump Inlet Tube-to-Water Pump

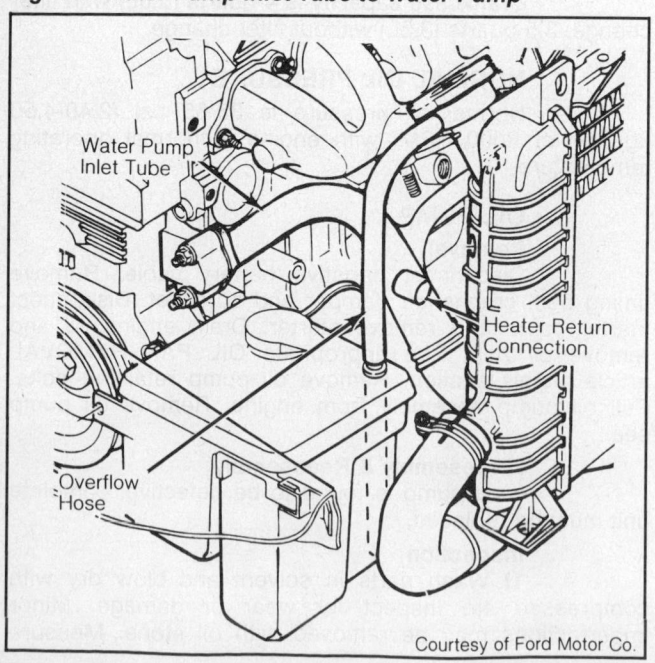

Courtesy of Ford Motor Co.

NOTE: Use only Ford Cooling System Fluid (E2FZ-19549-A) at a 50/50 ratio.

Installation

Clean all gasket mating surfaces. Hold water pump inlet tube gasket with mounting flange bolts. Apply pipe sealant with Teflon to water pump mounting bolts. Place water pump and new gasket on engine. Evenly tighten bolts to specifications. Ensure water pump impeller rotates freely. To complete installation, reverse removal procedure.

NOTE: For further information on cooling systems, see ENGINE COOLING section.

TIGHTENING SPECIFICATIONS

Application	Ft. Lbs. (N.m)
Belt Tensioner Bolts	17-20 (23-27)
Camshaft Sprocket Bolts	37-46 (50-63)
Connecting Rod Cap Nuts	19-25 (26-34)
Crankshaft Pulley Bolts	74-90 (101-122)
Cylinder Head Bolts [1]	
Step 1	44 (60)
Step 2	Loosen 2 Turns
Step 3	44 (60)
Step 4	90 Degrees
Step 5	90 Degrees
Exhaust Manifold Nuts	15-20 (20-27)
Flywheel Bolts	54-64 (73-87)
Intake Manifold-to-Head Nuts	12-15 (16-20)
Main Bearing Cap Bolts	67-80 (91-109)
Oil Pan-to-Block Bolts	15-22 (20-30)
Oil Pan-to-Transaxle Bolts	30-40 (41-54)
Oil Pump Relief Valve Plug	12-15 (16-20)
Rocker Arm Bolt	17-22 (23-30)

Application	INCH Lbs. (N.m)
Camshaft Thrust Plate Bolts	84-132 (10-15)
Crankshaft Rear Seal Retainer Bolts	72-96 (8-11)
Distributor-to-Block Bolt	72-96 (8-11)
Oil Pump	
Cover Bolts	72-108 (8-12)
Pick-Up Tube Bolt	72-108 (8-12)
Pump-to-Block Bolts	72-96 (8-11)
Valve Cover-to-Head Bolt	72-96 (8-11)

[1] – Tighten bolts in sequence. See Fig. 6.

Ford Motor Co. Engines

1.9L 4-CYLINDER (Cont.)

ENGINE SPECIFICATIONS

GENERAL SPECIFICATIONS

| Year | DISPLACEMENT | | Fuel System | HP@RPM | Torque Ft. Lbs.@RPM | Compr. Ratio | BORE | | STROKE | |
	Cu. In.	Liters					In.	mm	In.	mm
1988	232	3.8	MPFI	140 @ 3800	215 @ 2400	8.7:1	3.81	96.8	3.39	86

VALVES

Engine Size & Valve	Head Diam. In. (mm)	Face Angle	Seat Angle	Seat Width In. (mm)	Stem Diameter In. (mm)	Stem Clearance In. (mm)	Valve Lift In. (mm)
1.9L							
Intake	¹ 1.54 (39.1)	45°	45°	.069-.091 (1.75-2.32)	.3159-.3167 (8.025-8.043)	.0008-.0027 (.020-.069)	.468 ² (11.89)
Exhaust	¹ 1.34 (34.0)	45°	45°	.069-.091 (1.75-2.32)	.3149-.3156 (7.996-8.017)	.0018-.0037 (.046-.095)	² .468 (11.89)

¹ – On EFI HO models, intake diameter is 1.65" (41.9 mm) and exhaust diameter is 1.46" (37.1 mm).
² – On EFI HO models, intake and exhaust is .396" (10.06 mm).

CRANKSHAFT MAIN & CONNECTING ROD BEARINGS

| Engine | MAIN BEARINGS | | | | CONNECTING ROD BEARINGS | | |
	Journal Diam. In. (mm)	Clearance In. (mm)	Thrust Bearing	Crankshaft End Play In. (mm)	Journal Diam. In. (mm)	Clearance In. (mm)	Side Play In. (mm)
1.9L	2.2827-2.2835 (57.98-58.0)	.0011-.0022 (.028-.056)	No. 3	.004-.008 (.10-.20)	1.7279-1.7287 (43.89-43.91)	.0008-.0015 (.020-.038)	.004-.011 (.10-.28)

PISTONS, PINS & RINGS

| Engine | PISTONS | PINS | | | RINGS | | |
	Clearance In. (mm)	Piston Fit In. (mm)	Rod Fit In. (mm)	Ring No.	End Gap In. (mm)	Side Clearance In. (mm)
1.9L	.0016-.0024 (.040-.060)	.0003-.0005 (.007-.013)	Press Fit	1	.010-.020 (.25-.50)	.0015-.0032 (.04-.08)
				2	.010-.020 (.25-.50)	.0015-.0035 (.04-.09)
				3	.016-.055 (.40-1.40)	Snug Fit

VALVE SPRINGS

| Engine | Free Length In. (mm) | PRESSURE Lbs. @ In. (Kg @ mm) | |
		Valve Closed	Valve Open
1.9L			
CFI	1.86 (47.2)	95@1.46 (42@37.1)	200@1.09 (89@27.7)
EFI	1.90 (48.3)	94@1.46 (42@37.1)	216@1.02 (96@25.8)

CAMSHAFT

Engine	Journal Diam. In. (mm)	Clearance In. (mm)	Lobe Lift In. (mm)
1.9L	1.8007-1.8017 (45.738-45.763)	.0013-.0033 (.034-.084)	.240 (6.10)

Ford Motor Co.

2.3L OHC 4-CYLINDER

Mustang, Thunderbird

NOTE: For engine repair procedures not covered in this article, see ENGINE OVERHAUL PROCEDURES article at beginning of this section.

IDENTIFICATION CODING

ENGINE IDENTIFICATION

Engine is identified by the Vehicle Identification Number (VIN) at top of instrument panel on the left side near windshield and visible from outside. VIN number is also stamped on Vehicle Certification lable (VC lable), mounted on the left front door lock face panel. The VIN number contains 17 characters. The 8th character identifies engine and 10th character establishes model year.

ENGINE CODES

Engine	Code
2.3L (140") MPFI	A
2.3L (140") MPFI Turbo	T

ENGINE REMOVAL

See ENGINE REMOVAL at end of ENGINE section.

CYLINDER HEAD & MANIFOLDS

NOTE: Turbo charged engine components are not interchangable with non-turbo charged engines.

INTAKE MANIFOLD

Removal

1) Disconnect negative battery cable. Drain cooling system. Remove air cleaner assembly. On turbo engines, remove intercooler. Disconnect throttle linkage shield. Disconnect throttle linkage, cruise control and kick down cable and set aside. Mark and disconnect vacuum lines. Disconnect PCV hose from underside of upper intake manifold.

2) Disconnect water by-pass hose at loser intake manifold. Disconnect EGR tube at EGR valve. Remove nuts retaining dipstick tube to intake manifold. Remove 2 studs and 2 bolts from upper intake manifold. Remove upper intake manifold assembly and gasket.

3) Remove fuel cap to relieve fuel tank pressure. Using EFI Pressure Gauge (T80L-9974-B), release fuel pressure from relief valve. Relief valve is located on fuel line in right corner of engine compartment. Disconnect push connect fitting at manifold fuel supply and fuel return lines, with Quick Connect Remover (T87L-9280-A).

4) Disconnect electrical connectors at injectors and remove harness. Remove 2 fuel supply manifold retaining bolts. Remove fuel supply manifold. Mark and remove fuel injectors with a twisting/pulling motion. Remove 4 bottom bolts from lower intake manifold.

5) Remove 4 upper bolts from lower intake manifold. Remove lower intake manifold assembly and gasket.

Installation

1) Clean gasket mating surfaces. Check for flatness and machine or replace as necessary. Install new gasket. Install lower intake manifold. Install 4 top bolts finger tight. Install bottom 4 bolts. Tighten in sequence in 2 steps and to specifications. *See Fig. 1.*

Fig. 1: Upper & Lower Intake Manifold Tightening Sequence

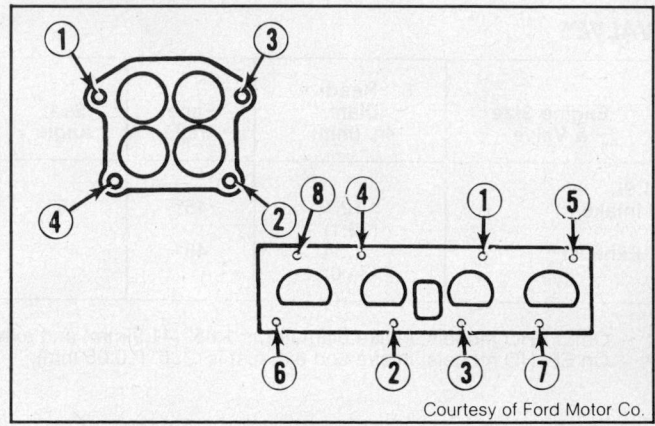

Courtesy of Ford Motor Co.

2) Replace fuel injector "O" rings. Lubricate "O" rings with Light Grade Oil (ESE-M2C39-F). Using a twisting/pushing motion, install injectors in fuel supply manifold. Carefully seat fuel supply manifold assembly and injectors into lower intake manifold. Install bolts and tighten to specifications.

3) Install injector harness. Clean upper and lower intake manifold gasket surfaces. Install new on lower intake manifold. Position upper intake manifold and install 4 bolts finger tight. Tighten bolts in sequence and to specifications. *See Fig. 1.* To complete installation, reverse removal procedure.

EXHAUST MANIFOLD

NOTE: For non-turbo engines begin with step 3).

Removal & Installation

1) Disconnect negative battery cable. Drain coolant from radiator. Remove intercooler. Mark and disconnect vacuum hoses and tubes. Disconnect PCV tube from turbo air inlet elbow. Disconnect air inlet tube from inlet elbow. Remove ground strap from inlet elbow and remove elbow with gasket. Remove coolant connection from turbo center housing.

2) Remove turbo oil supply line. Plug oil inlet hole. Raise vehicle. Remove exhaust pipe at turbo. Remove 2 bolts from oil return line, located below turbo. Remove lower turbo bracket-to-engine stud. Lower vehicle. Remove front lower turbo retaining bolt. Evenly remove 3 remaining nuts while sliding turbo off studs. Remove turbo assembly.

3) On non-turbo engines, disconnect exhaust pipe from exhaust manifold. Mark and disconnect tubes from exhaust manifold. On all models, remove manifold shield. Remove bolts retaining exhaust manifold to engine and remove exhaust manifold.

2.3L OHC 4-CYLINDER (Cont.)

4) To install, reverse removal procedure. Tighten bolts in sequence. *See Fig. 2.*

Fig. 2: Exhaust Manifold Tightening Sequence

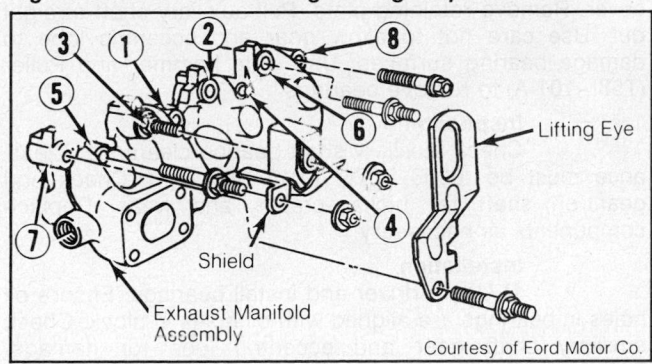

Courtesy of Ford Motor Co.

CYLINDER HEAD

Removal

1) Disconnect negative battery cable. Drain cooling system. Drain engine oil. Remove air cleaner or intercooler assembly. Remove heater hose from valve cover. Mark and remove spark plug wires from spark plugs. Remove distributor cap and set aside.

2) Remove spark plugs. Mark and disconnect vacuum hoses and tubes. Remove upper intake manifold assembly. Remove lower intake manifold assembly. See INTAKE MANIFOLD in this article. Remove valve cover bolts. Remove valve cover and gasket. Remove accessory belts. Remove alternator and bracket.

3) Remove upper radiator hose. Remove water pump fan and pulley. Remove timing belt cover. Remove timing belt. See TIMING BELT & COVER in this article. Remove timing belt tensioner assembly. Remove exhaust manifold-to-cylinder head bolts.

4) Disconnect wire from oil sending unit. Remove cylinder head bolts. Remove cylinder head assembly and gasket.

Inspection

1) Clean all gasket mating surfaces. Check flatness of cylinder head, cylinder block, intake manifold and exhaust manifold. Clean all carbon from ports. Use compressed air and clean cylinder head bolt threads in block. Tab head bolt thread holes.

2) On turbo engines, install valve cover gasket on valve cover with Contact Adhesive (D7AZ-19B508-A). Allow to set before installing. On all engines, position camshaft pin at 5:30 o'clock position to avoid damaging valves during installation. *See Fig. 3.*

Installation

1) Perform inspection prior to installation. Position new cylinder head gasket on block. Ensure marked side of gasket is properly positioned. Carefully install cylinder head. Install cylinder head bolts. Tighten bolts in 2 steps and in sequence. *See Fig. 3.*

2) To complete installation, reverse removal procedure. Tighten all bolts/nuts to specifications. Fill and bleed cooling system. Check for leakage.

Fig. 3: Cylinder Head Tightening Sequence

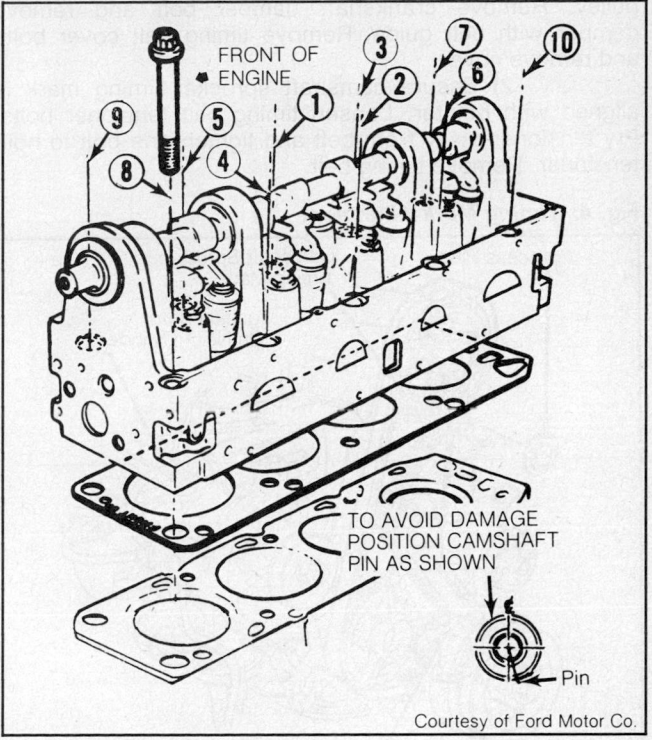

FRONT OF ENGINE

TO AVOID DAMAGE POSITION CAMSHAFT PIN AS SHOWN

Pin

Courtesy of Ford Motor Co.

CAMSHAFT

TIMING BELT & COVER

NOTE: Rotate crankshaft in direction of normal engine rotation only.

Checking Timing

Position No. 1 cylinder on TDC, compression stroke. Crankshaft damper timing mark should be aligned with mark on timing belt cover. Remove distributor cap. Ignition rotor should be at No. 1 cylinder. Remove plug from front of timing belt cover. Mark on camshaft gear should be aligned with pointer. *See Fig. 4.*

Timing Adjustment

1) If timing marks do not align, remove accessory belts and position alternator out of way. Align crankshaft damper timing mark with mark on timing belt cover. Remove timing belt cover. Loosen tensioner and secure away from timing belt. Remove belt from camshaft and auxiliary sprockets.

2) Align ignition rotor with No. 1 cylinder. Align camshaft sprocket timing mark with pointer. Reinstall timing belt counterclockwise and release tensioner against belt. Remove spark plugs. Rotate crankshaft 2 complete turns in direction of normal engine rotation only. Tighten tensioner bolts to specifications.

3) Recheck timing mark alignment. Ensure ignition rotor is on No. 1 cylinder. To complete, reverse procedures. Set final timing.

Removal

1) Position engine on No. 1 cylinder TDC, compression stroke. Align crankshaft damper timing mark. *See Fig. 4.* Remove spark plugs to ease engine rotation.

Remove accessory belts. Remove water pump fan and pulley. Remove crankshaft damper bolt and remove damper with belt guide. Remove timing belt cover bolts and remove cover.

2) Ensure camshaft sprocket timing mark is aligned with pointer. Loosen timing belt tensioner bolts. Pry tensioner away from belt and tighten one bolt to hold tensioner. Remove timing belt.

Fig. 4: Timing Mark Alignment

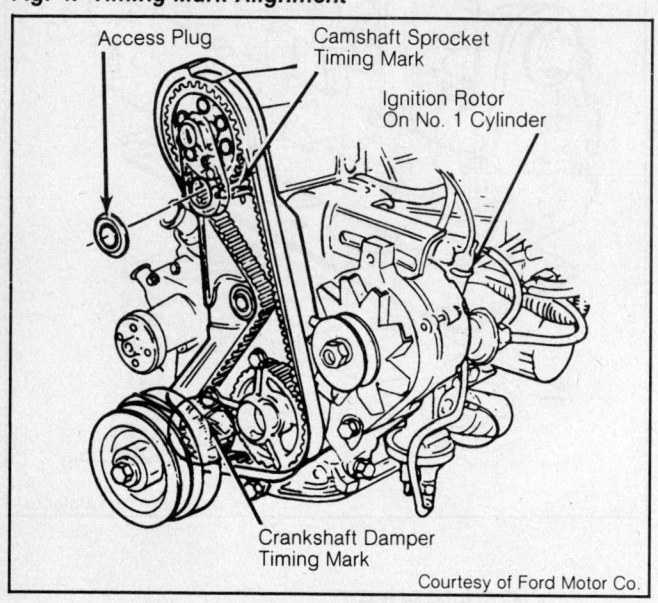

Access Plug

Camshaft Sprocket Timing Mark

Ignition Rotor On No. 1 Cylinder

Crankshaft Damper Timing Mark

Courtesy of Ford Motor Co.

Installation
1) Ensure crankshaft damper timing mark is at TDC, compression stroke. Align camshaft sprocket timing mark with pointer. Remove distributor cap. Position ignition rotor on No. 1 cylinder by rotating auxiliary sprocket.

2) Install timing belt over crankshaft sprocket. Install timing belt counterclockwise around auxiliary sprocket and camshaft sprocket. Keep tension on belt while installing on sprockets. Loosen tensioner and allow tensioner to move against belt.

3) Rotate engine 2 complete turns in normal operating direction. Tighten timing belt tensioner to specifications. Align timing marks and ensure proper alignment. To complete installation, reverse removal procedure.

FRONT COVER OIL SEAL

NOTE: If front cover is removed, install cover before installing oil seal.

Removal & Installation
Remove accessary drive belts. Remove crankshaft damper and belt guide. Remove timing belt cover and belt. See TIMING BELT & COVER in this article. Remove crankshaft sprocket. Do not remove front cover to replace oil seal. Using Front Cover Seal Remover (T74P-6700-B), remove oil seal. Use Front Seal Installer (T74P-6150-A) and install oil seal. To complete installation, reverse removal procedure.

NOTE: All front seals are replaced with the same tools. Procedures are the same.

AUXILIARY SHAFT & BEARINGS
Removal
Remove timing belt and cover. See TIMING BELT & COVER in this article. Remove auxiliary shaft cover. Remove retaining plate. Pull auxiliary shaft straight out. Use care not to allow gear and eccentric lobe to damage bearing surfaces. Use slide hammer and Puller (T58L-101-A) to remove bearings.

Inspection
Check auxiliary shaft bearing clearance. Clearance must be .0006-.0026" (.015-.066 mm). Check end gear on shaft for nicks, cracks and wear. Replace components as necessary.

Installation
1) Use a driver and install bearings. Ensure oil holes in bearings are aligned with oil holes in block. Check auxiliary shaft gear and eccentric lobe for damage. Replace as necessary. Completely submerge auxiliary shaft in engine oil.

2) Install auxiliary shaft using care not to damage bearings. Install retaining plate. Check end play. End play must be .001-.007" (.03-.18 mm). If not within specifications, replace retaining plate. To complete installation, reverse removal procedure.

CAMSHAFT & BEARINGS
Removal
1) Drain cooling system. Remove air cleaner or intercooler assembly. Mark and disconnect spark plug wires at spark plugs. Mark and disconnect vacuum hoses and tubes. Remove valve cover. Remove accessory belts. Remove alternator and set aside. Remove upper radiator hose.

2) Remove fan shroud. If equipped with electric fan, remove fan and shroud assembly. Disconnect lower radiator hose at radiator. Remove timing belt cover and belt. See TIMING BELT & COVER in this article. Remove 2 camshaft retaining plate screws from rear of camshaft.

3) Raise vehicle. Remove right and left engine mount through bolts. Remove right and left lower joint-to-bracket retaining bolts. Raise engine as far as possible and place wood blocks between engine mounts and crossmember. Lower vehicle.

4) Using Valve Spring Compressor (T74P-6565-A), depress valve springs and remove camshaft followers. Keep followers in order to ensure installation to original location. Remove camshaft sprocket. Remove camshaft oil seal with Front Cover Seal Remover (T74P-6700-B).

5) Remove camshaft out front of engine, using care not to damage bearings or camshaft. Using Camshaft Bearing Replacer (T71P-6250-A), remove bearings.

Inspection
Clean camshaft in solvent and wipe dry. Check camshaft lobes for scoring and abnormal wear. Check bearing journal for wear. Check camshaft end play and replace thrust plate if not within specifications. Check camshaft lobe lift. If not within specifications, replace camshaft and followers. See ENGINE SPECIFICATIONS tables at end of this article.

2.3L OHC 4-CYLINDER (Cont.)

CAUTION: Lifter must be collapsed after follower is installed. DO NOT rotate crankshaft or camshaft without collapsing lifters. Serious valve damage may result. See VALVES & LIFTERS in this article.

Installation

If replacing camshaft, ensure plug in rear of camshaft is installed. Coat camshaft lobes with Polyethylene Grease (DOAZ-19584-A). Lubricate camshaft journals and bearings with heavy SF engine oil. Install camshaft through front of engine. To complete installation, reverse removal procedure. Tighten all bolts/nuts to specifications.

VALVES

VALVE ARRANGEMENT

E-I-E-I-E-I-E-I (Front-to-Rear).

CAMSHAFT FOLLOWERS

Removal & Installation

1) Mark and remove vacuum hoses and tubes. Mark and remove spark plug wires. Remove spark plugs. Remove valve cover. Position engine on No. 1 cylinder TDC.

2) Using Valve Spring Compressor (T74P-6565-A), depress valve springs. Remove the camshaft followers which are on lowest point of camshaft lobe. Keep followers in order, to ensure installation to original location.

3) Rotate crankshaft 180 degrees in direction of normal engine rotation. Remove remaining followers. Reverse removal procedure for installation. After installing a follower, collapse lifter completely before rotating crankshaft.

CAMSHAFT OIL SEAL

See CAMSHAFT & BEARINGS in this article.

VALVE SEATS

Valve seats are replaceable. Valve seat replacement procedure is not available at this time.

VALVES & LIFTERS

Removal & Installation

1) Remove cylinder head. See CYLINDER HEAD in this article. Clean carbon from combustion chamber before disassembly. Remove camshaft followers with Valve Spring Compressor (T74P-6565-A). Keep followers in order for installation to original position. Remove camshaft.

2) Use a "C" type spring compressor and remove valve keepers. Keep all components in order of removal to ensure reassembly to original position. Remove retainer, valve spring assembly, valve seal and valve. Remove valve lifters. Reverse removal procedure for installation.

CAUTION: If followers are removed, DO NOT rotate crankshaft or camshaft without collapsing lifters first.

Inspection

1) Clean carbon from valves. Check valve clearance in valve guide. Ream valve guide and/or replace valve as necessary. Replace valves if bent or worn excessively. Reface valves to a true 45 degree angle. Replace valves if valve head thickness is less than .0313" (.794 mm), after grinding. Check valve stem-to-follower clearance after refacing valves and seats. Remove stock from stem as necessary.

2) Check bottom of lifter. Lifter must be convex and smooth. Check leak-down rate of lifter with hydraulic testing fluid only. Engine oil will not give accurate reading. Disassemble lifter and thoroughly clean prior to testing. Lifter should leak-down .125" (3.18 mm) in 2-8 seconds under a 50 lbs. load.

3) Install lifters in bore from which they were removed. Check lifter-to-bore clearance. Clearance should be .0007-.0027" (.018-.069 mm). Check lifter collapsed clearance. Reassemble cylinder head without installing followers. Install one follower and apply pressure to follower and lifter.

4) Maintain pressure on lifter until lifter is completely collapsed. Using a feeler gauge, measure clearance between lowest point on camshaft lobe and contact surface of follower. Clearance should be .040-.050" (1.02-1.27 mm). If not within specifications, repair or replace as necessary.

VALVE GUIDES

1) Mark all components prior to removal for installation reference. Thoroughly clean cylinder head and valves, using care not to damage surfaces. Check valve-to-guide clearance of each valve in its respective valve guide.

2) Install a valve and hold against seat. Install Valve Stem Clearance Tool (T65T-6505-H) on valve stem, until it is fully seated. Tighten tool set screw firmly. Allow valve to drop away from seat and tool to contact upper guide surface.

3) Install dial indicator with pointer against center portion of tool. *See Fig. 5.* Move clearance tool back and forth in-line with dial indicator pointer. Keep clearance tool on upper guide surface when moving back and forth. Record dial indicator reading.

4) Divide dial indicator reading by 2. This total is the valve-to-guide clearance. If not within specifications, replace valve(s) with next available oversize valve. Ream valve guide until clearance is within specifications. See ENGINE SPECIFICATIONS tables at end of this article.

Fig. 5: Checking Valve Stem-to-Guide Clearance

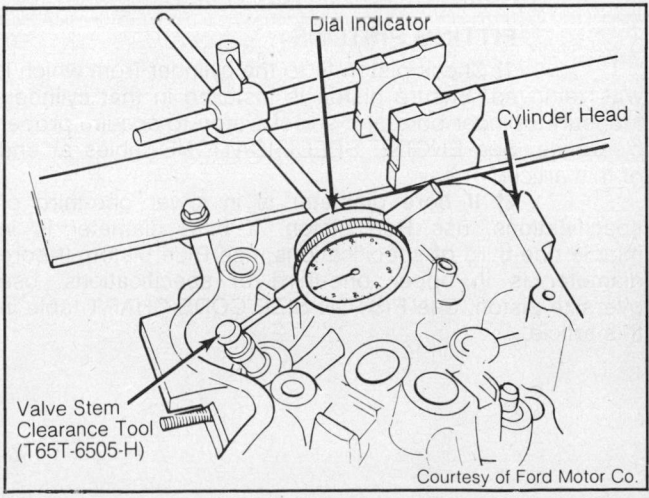

Courtesy of Ford Motor Co.

Ford Motor Co.

2.3L OHC 4-CYLINDER (Cont.)

VALVE SPRINGS

Inspection

Measure installed height, from bottom of spring assembly to top of retainer, without camshaft and followers installed. Inspect valve springs for cracks or damage. Measure free length and out-of-square. See ENGINE SPECIFICATIONS tables at end of this article. Replace valve springs as necessary.

CYLINDER BLOCK ASSEMBLY

Inspection

Using straightedge and feeler gauge, ensure cylinder block head gasket surface is flat within .003" (.08 mm) in any 6.0" area. Surface must be flat within .006" (.15 mm) overall. If not within specifications, surface may be machined. Check clyinder bore for wear, taper, out-of-round and piston fit. See PISTONS, PINS & RINGS in this article. See ENGINE SPECIFICATIONS tables at end of this article.

PISTONS, PINS & RINGS

OIL PAN

See OIL PAN REMOVAL at end of ENGINE section.

PISTON & ROD ASSEMBLY

Removal

Remove cylinder head. Remove oil pan. Check and remove carbon and ridge from top of cylinder bore. Ensure all rods and rod caps are marked with matching cylinder number. Remove rod nuts and remove rod caps with rod bearing. Cover rod bolts with hose. Tap rod and piston assembly out top of cylinder block. Remove piston rings. Clean piston assembly and ring grooves.

Installation

1) Fit pistons to cylinder bores. See FITTING PISTONS in this article. Check piston ring end gap and install piston rings. See FITTING RINGS in this article. Install upper rod bearing in rod. Position piston in correct cylinder bore as marked on rod and rod cap. Ensure notch on piston top is toward front of engine.

2) Use Plastigage method and check rod bearing clearance. See CRANKSHAFT & ROD BEARINGS in this article. To complete installation, reverse removal procedure.

FITTING PISTONS

1) Check piston fit to the cylinder from which it was removed. Ensure piston is installed in that cylinder. Measure cylinder bore and select piston to acquire proper clearance. See ENGINE SPECIFICATIONS tables at end of this article.

2) If bore diameter is in lower one-third of specifications, use Red piston. If bore diameter is in middle one-third of specifications, use Blue piston. If bore diameter is in upper one-third of specifications, use oversize piston. See PISTON SIZE CODE CHART table in this article.

PISTON SIZE CODE CHART

Code	Size In. (mm)
Red	3.7764-3.7770 (95.961-95.976)
Blue	3.7776-3.7782 (95.991-96.006)
.003" Oversize [1]	3.7788-3.7810 (96.022-96.037)

[1] – Piston may be color coded Yellow.

FITTING RINGS

1) Clean piston and ring grooves thoroughly. Select proper size rings for bore diameter. Install new ring (one at a time), squarely in cylinder bore. Push ring down into bore where normal ring wear is not encountered. Use feeler gauge and measure gap between ends. See ENGINE SPECIFICATIONS tables at end of this article.

2) If gap is less than specifications, remove enough stock from ring ends to acquire proper gap. If gap is greater than specifications, use a different set of rings. Repeat procedure and check all rings.

3) Install rings properly on piston. Use a feeler gauge and check piston ring side clearance of each ring. Ensure feeler gauge slides freely the entire circumference without binding. See ENGINE SPECIFICATIONS tables at end of this article. Replace piston and/or rings as necessary.

PISTON PIN REPLACEMENT

Removal

With piston removed and cleaned, mark piston-to-rod to ensure proper reassembly. Use Piston Pin Replacer (D81L-6135-A) and press pin out of piston and rod assembly. Light heat may be applied to ease in removal. Measure piston pin bore and rod pin bore to determine clearance. See ENGINE SPECIFICATIONS tables at end of this article.

Installation

Position rod in piston with oil hole on proper side of piston. *See Fig. 6.* Place pin in piston and lightly tap pin with plastic mallet to start pin in rod. Press pin into piston and rod assembly until rod is centered in piston. Protruding pin ends must be even on both ends. To complete installation, reverse removal procedure.

Fig. 6: Aligning Piston & Rod Assembly

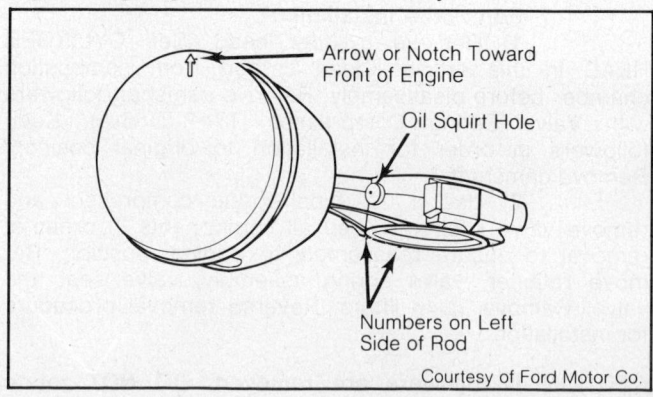

Arrow or Notch Toward Front of Engine

Oil Squirt Hole

Numbers on Left Side of Rod

Courtesy of Ford Motor Co.

2.3L OHC 4-CYLINDER (Cont.)

CRANKSHAFT & ROD BEARINGS

CRANKSHAFT MAIN BEARINGS

Removal

1) Drain oil and remove oil pan. Remove oil pump. Ensure main bearing caps are marked with sequence No. and direction of engine front. Remove main bearing cap bolts. Remove main bearing cap and lower bearing insert.

2) Use bearing remover or fabricated cotter key to remove upper bearings, if crankshaft is not being removed. Rotate crankshaft in direction of normal operation only. Repeat procedure for remaining bearings.

Inspection

Check bearings for abnormal wear. Check crankshaft for grooves, scratches and pitting. Check journals for out-of-round and diameter. Machine or replace as necessary. Check crankshaft end play. Replace thrust bearing as necessary. Use Plastigage method and check main bearing clearance. See ENGINE SPECIFICATIONS at end of this article.

Installation

Lubricate and install new bearing in cap and block. Ensure tangs on bearings are aligned with notch in cap and block. Place cap in proper location. Completely seat cap in block before installing and tightening bolts. Install and tighten bolts to specifications. To complete installation, reverse removal procedure.

CONNECTING ROD BEARINGS

Inspection

With piston removed, check rod bearing for abnormal wear. Check crankshaft journals for out-of-round and diameter. Check rod bearing clearance with Plastigage method. With piston and rod installed, check rod assembly side play. See ENGINE SPECIFICATIONS table at end of this article. Machine or replace as necessary.

REAR MAIN BEARING OIL SEAL

Removal

Remove transaxle. On manual transaxle, remove clutch and pressure plate. On all modles, remove flywheel or flexplate. Use an awl and punch a hole into oil seal metal surface, between lip and block. Use care not to damage sealing surfaces. Use a slide hammer with sheet metal screw and remove seal.

Installation

Coat seal with engine oil. Position seal on Seal Installer (T82L-6701-A). See Fig. 7. Position installer and seal to rear of engine. Tighten bolts evenly to ensure seal is installed squarely. To complete installation, reverse removal procedure.

ENGINE OILING

ENGINE OILING SYSTEM

Oiling system is force-feed type, using a full-flow oil filter. Oil is retrieved from oil pan by oil pump pick-up tube and distributed to oil filter. Oil is filtered and routed throughout the engine. See Fig. 8.

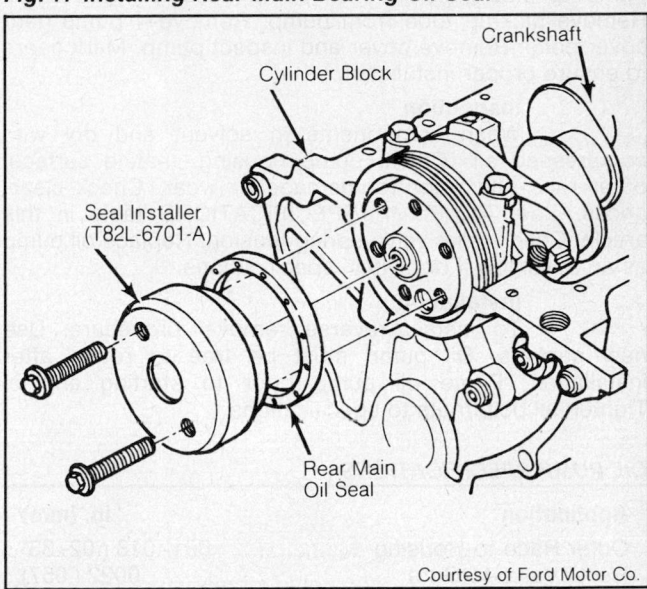

Fig. 7: Installing Rear Main Bearing Oil Seal

Crankshaft
Cylinder Block
Seal Installer (T82L-6701-A)
Rear Main Oil Seal
Courtesy of Ford Motor Co.

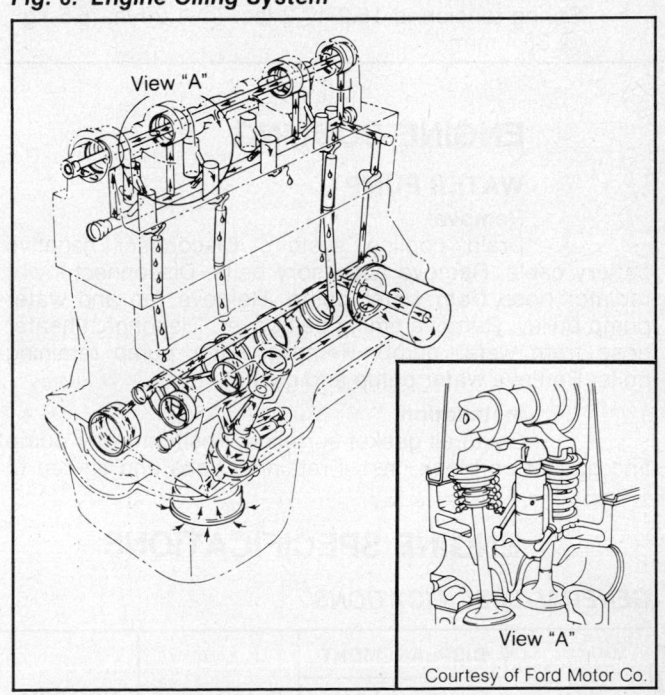

Fig. 8: Engine Oiling System

View "A"
View "A"
Courtesy of Ford Motor Co.

CRANKCASE CAPACITY

Crankcase capacity is 5 qts. (4.7L) with filter change. DO NOT change oil without changing oil filter.

NORMAL OIL PRESSURE (HOT)

Normal oil pressure is 40-60 psi (2.8-4.2 kg/cm²) at 2000 RPM, with engine at normal operating temperature.

OIL PUMP

Removal

Drain oil and remove oil pan. Remove pick-up tube-to-block mounting bolt. Remove 2 bolts retaining oil

Ford Motor Co.

2.3L OHC 4-CYLINDER (Cont.)

pump to block. Remove oil pump assembly and shaft. Remove pick-up tube from pump. Remove 4 pump gear cover bolts. Remove cover and inspect pump. Mark gears to ensure proper installation.

Inspection

Wash components in solvent and dry with compressed air. Check pump housing, mating surface, outer race and rotor for damage or wear. Check clearances. See OIL PUMP SPECIFICATIONS table in this article. Check relief valve spring tension. Replace oil pump as an assembly if not within specifications.

Installation

To install, reverse removal procedure. Use new gaskets. Oil pump must be free to rotate after installation. Prime oil pump prior to starting engine. Tighten all bolts/nuts to specifications.

OIL PUMP SPECIFICATIONS

Application	In. (mm)
Outer Race-to-Housing	.001-.013 (.02-.33)
Relief Valve-to-Bore	.0022 (.057)
Rotor Assembly End Clearance	.004 (.10)

[1] – Spring tension is 15.2-17.2 lbs. @ 1.20 in. (6.5 kg @ 30.4 mm).

ENGINE COOLING

WATER PUMP

Removal

Drain cooling system. Disconnect negative battery cable. Remove accessory belts. Disconnect lower radiator hose from water pump. Remove fan and water pump pulley. Remove timing belt cover. Disconnect heater hose from water pump. Remove water pump retaining bolts. Remove water pump and gasket.

Installation

Clean all gasket surfaces. Position water pump and gasket on block. Install retaining bolts and tighten to specifications. To complete installation, reverse removal procedure. Fill and bleed cooling system. Check for leaks.

NOTE: For further information on cooling systems, see ENGINE COOLING section.

TIGHTENING SPECIFICATIONS

Application	Ft. Lbs. (N.m)
Auxiliary Shaft Sprocket Bolt	28-40 (38-54)
Belt Tensioner Adjustment Bolt	14-21 (19-29)
Belt Tensioner Pivot Bolt	28-40 (38-54)
Camshaft Sprocket Bolt	50-71 (68-96)
Connecting Rod Nut	
Step 1	25-30 (34-41)
Step 2	30-36 (41-49)
Crankshaft Damper Bolt	103-133 (140-180)
Cylinder Head Bolt	
Step 1	50-60 (68-81)
Step 2	80-90 (108-122)
Exhaust Manifold-to-Head Bolt	
Step 1	15-17 (20-23)
Step 2	20-30 (27-41)
Flywheel Bolt	54-64 (73-87)
Intake Manifold-to-Head Bolt/Nut	20-29 (27-39)
Main Bearing Cap Bolt	
Step 1	50-60 (68-81)
Step 2	75-85 (102-115)
Oil Pan-to-Block	10-14 (14-19)
Oil Pump-to-Block Bolt	14-21 (19-29)
Oil Pump Pick-up Tube-to-Pump Bolt	14-21 (19-29)
Throttle Body-to-Upper Manifold Nut	12-15 (16-20)
Turbo-to-Manifold Nut	28-40 (38-54)
Upper-to-Lower Intake Manifold Bolt	15-22 (20-30)
	INCH Lbs. (N.m)
Auxiliary Shaft Cover Bolt	72-108 (8-12)
Auxiliary Shaft Thrust Plate Bolt	72-108 (8-12)
Camshaft Thrust Plate Bolt	72-108 (8-12)
Crankshaft Front Cover Bolt	72-108 (8-12)
Oil Pump Cover Bolt	90-130 (10-15)

ENGINE SPECIFICATIONS

GENERAL SPECIFICATIONS

Year	DISPLACEMENT		Fuel System	HP@RPM	Torque Ft. Lbs.@RPM	Compr. Ratio	BORE		STROKE	
	Cu. In.	Liters					In.	mm	In.	mm
1988 MPFI	140	2.3	EFI	90@3800	130@2800	9.5:1	3.78	96.0	3.126	79.40
Turbo										
Man. Trans.	140	2.3	EFI	190@4600	240@3400	8.0:1	3.78	96.0	3.126	79.40
Auto. Trans.	140	2.3	EFI	150@4400	200@3000	8.0:1	3.78	96.0	3.126	79.40

2.3L OHC 4-CYLINDER (Cont.)

ENGINE SPECIFICATIONS (Cont.)

VALVES

Engine Size & Valve	Head Diam. In. (mm)	Face Angle	Seat Angle	Seat Width In. (mm)	Stem Diameter In. (mm)	Stem Clearance In. (mm)	Valve Lift In. (mm)
2.3L Intake	1.730-1.740 (43.76-44.37)	44°	45°	.060-.080 (1.52-2.03)	.3416-.3423 (8.68-8.69)	.0010-.0027 (.025-.068)	.390 (9.91)
Exhaust	1.49-1.51 (37.8-38.3)	44°	45°	.070-.090 (1.77-2.28)	.3411-.3418 (8.66-8.68)	.0015-.0032 (.038-.081)	.390 (9.91)

PISTONS, PINS & RINGS

Engine	PISTONS Clearance In. (mm)	PINS Piston Fit In. (mm)	PINS Rod Fit In. (mm)	RINGS Ring No.	RINGS End Gap In. (mm)	RINGS Side Clearance In. (mm)
2.3L	.0030-.0038 (.076-.097)	.0003-.0005 (.007-.013)	Press Fit	1 & 2	.010-.020 (.25-.50)	.002-.004 (.05-.10)
				3	.010-.049 (.25-1.25)	Snug Fit

CRANKSHAFT MAIN & CONNECTING ROD BEARINGS

Engine	MAIN BEARINGS Journal Diam. In. (mm)	MAIN BEARINGS Clearance In. (mm)	MAIN BEARINGS Thrust Bearing	MAIN BEARINGS Crankshaft End Play In. (mm)	CONNECTING ROD BEARINGS Journal Diam. In. (mm)	CONNECTING ROD BEARINGS Clearance In. (mm)	CONNECTING ROD BEARINGS Side Play In. (mm)
2.3L	2.3982-2.3990 (60.914-60.934)	[1] .0008-.0015 (.020-.038)	No. 3	[2] 0.004-.008 (.10-.20)	2.0465-2.0472 (51.981-51.998)	[3] .0008-.0015 (.020-.038)	[4] .0035-.0105 (.088-.266)

[1] – Main bearing clearance service limit is .0008-.0026" (.020-.066 mm).
[2] – Crankshaft end play service limit is .012" (.30 mm).
[3] – Connecting rod bearing clearance service limit is .0008-.0026" (.020-.066 mm).
[4] – Connecting rod bearing side play limit is .014" (.355 mm).

VALVE SPRINGS

Engine	Free Length In. (mm)	PRESSURE Lbs. @ In. (Kg @ mm) Valve Closed	PRESSURE Lbs. @ In. (Kg @ mm) Valve Open
2.3L EFI	1.877 (47.68)	66-74@1.52 (30-34@38.6)	128-142@1.12 (58-64@28.12)
Turbo	1.877 (47.68)	71-79@1.52 (32-36@38.6)	152-166@1.12 (64-71@28.4)

CAMSHAFT

Engine	Journal Diam. In. (mm)	Clearance In. (mm)	Lobe Lift In. (mm)
2.3L	1.7713-1.7720 (44.991-45.008)	.001-.003 (.02-.07)	.400 (10.16)

Ford Motor Co. Engines

2.3L & 2.5L HSC & HSO 4-CYLINDER

Taurus, Tempo, Topaz

NOTE: For engine repair procedures not covered in this article, see ENGINE OVERHAUL PROCEDURES article at beginning of this section.

ENGINE CODING

ENGINE IDENTIFICATION

Engine may be identified by the Vehicle Identification Number (VIN) at top of instrument panel near windshield on left side of vehicle and visible from outside. VIN number is also stamped on Safety Certification Decal on left front door lock face panel and on Engine Identification Label on valve cover.

The VIN number contains 17 characters. The 8th character identifies the engine and the 10th character identifies the model year. To determine if the engine is High Swirl Combustion (HSC) or High Swirl Output (HSO), use the emission calibration number label located on the drivers door or pillar.

ENGINE CODES

Engine	Code
2.3L (140") HSC MPFI	X
2.3L (140") HSO MPFI	S
2.5L (153") HSC CFI	D

ENGINE REMOVAL

See ENGINE REMOVAL & INSTALLATION at end of ENGINE section.

CYLINDER HEAD & MANIFOLDS

INTAKE & EXHAUST MANIFOLDS
Removal
1) Disconnect negative battery cable. Drain cooling system. Remove air cleaner assembly. Remove heat stove tube at heat shield. Disconnect throttle cable. Mark and remove vacuum lines and electrical connectors.

2) Remove 3 nuts attaching exhaust manifold-to-inlet pipe. Remove exhaust manifold heat shield assembly. Disconnect oxygen sensor. Disconnect throttle linkage. Remove thermactor check valve hose at tube. Remove EGR and bracket. Disconnect coolant inlet tube at intake manifold.

3) On all models, mark and disconnect fuel lines to carburetor. Remove heater hose at fitting located under intake manifold. Remove intake manifold bolts and stud. Remove intake manifold. Remove exhaust manifold bolts. Remove exhaust manifold.

Inspection
Clean and check gasket mating surface. Check surfaces for warpage. Intake and exhaust manifold warpage should not exceed .005" (.12 mm) overall. Cylinder head mating surface should not exceed .007" (.18 mm) warpage overall.

Installation
1) Position exhaust manifold on cylinder head with Exhaust Manifold Alignment Studs (T84P-6065-B) in

holes No. 2 and 3. See Fig. 2. Install attaching bolts in remaining holes. Remove guide studs and install bolts. Tighten exhaust manifold bolts in 2 steps and sequence. See Fig. 2.

2) Coat new intake manifold gasket with sealer. Position intake manifold and gasket on cylinder head. Tighten bolts to specifications and in sequence. See Fig. 1. To complete installation, reverse removal procedure. Tighten all bolts/nuts to specifications.

Fig. 1: Intake Manifold Tightening Sequence

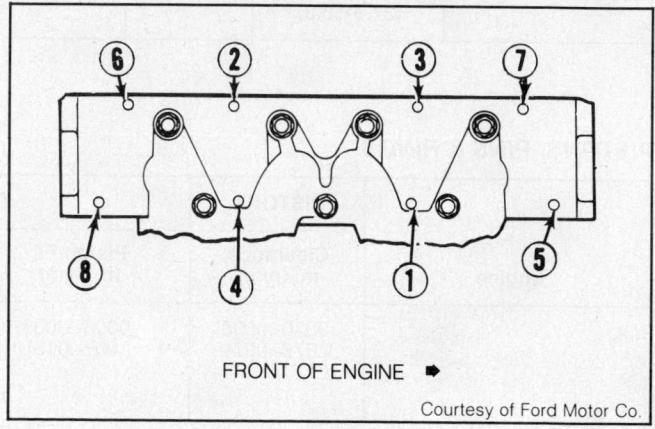

FRONT OF ENGINE ➡

Courtesy of Ford Motor Co.

Fig. 2: Exhaust Manifold Tightening Sequence

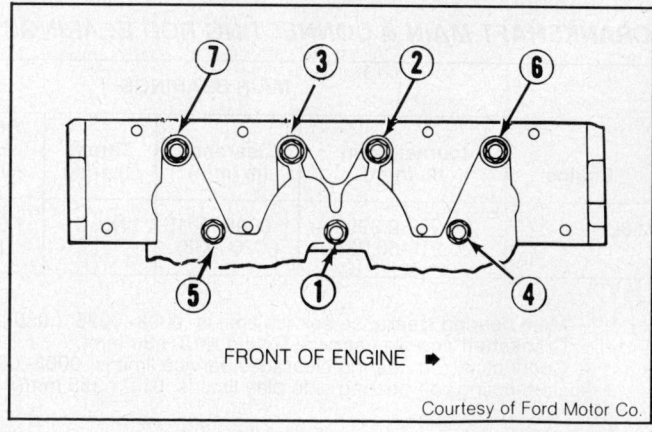

FRONT OF ENGINE ➡

Courtesy of Ford Motor Co.

CYLINDER HEAD
Removal
1) Remove negative battery cable. Drain cooling system at lower radiator hose. Disconnect heater hose at fitting located under intake manifold. Disconnect upper radiator hose at cylinder head. Remove air cleaner assembly.

2) Mark and disconnect vacuum lines. Disconnect electric cooling fan switch. Mark and disconnect spark plug wires at spark plugs. Remove distributor cap with wires. Remove accessory drive belts, alternator and mounting bracket from cylinder head.

3) Remove PCV hose. Remove valve cover. Disconnect fuel supply and return lines. Disconnect throttle cable. Disconnect EGR tube at EGR valve. Remove choke cap wire. Raise vehicle. Remove exhaust inlet pipe from exhaust manifold. Disconnect oxygen sensor. Lower vehicle.

2.3L & 2.5L HSC & HSO 4-CYLINDER (Cont.)

4) Remove rocker arm bolts. Keep all components in order to ensure installation to original location. Remove fulcrums and rocker arms. Remove push rods.

5) Remove cylinder head bolts. Remove cylinder head with intake and exhaust manifolds attached. Do not lay cylinder head flat. Damage to spark plugs and/or gasket surface may result.

Inspection

Clean combustion chambers before disassembly of cylinder head. Clean gasket mating surfaces. Check cylinder head for warpage. Warpage limit is .003" (.08 mm) in any 6". Overall cylinder head warpage is less than .007" (.18 mm). Clean and tap cylinder head bolt holes in cylinder block.

NOTE: **Cylinder head bolts on intake/exhaust side are longer than spark plug side of cylinder head.**

Installation

1) Use 2 old cylinder head bolts and cut the head off, to use as guide pins. Slot top of old bolts for screwdriver access. Install fabricated guide pins in Nos. 7 and 10 hole. See Fig. 3. Coat new head gasket with sealer and install gasket. Ensure marked side of gasket is in proper position.

2) Position cylinder head through guide pins and install cylinder head. Install cylinder head bolts until snug. Remove 2 guide pins and install 2 cylinder head bolts. Tighten cylinder head bolts in 2 steps and sequence. See Fig. 3.

3) Align crankshaft sprocket timing mark with camshaft sprocket timing mark. Install push rods, rocker arms and fulcrums on No. 1 intake and exhaust, No. 2 intake and No. 3 exhaust. Tighten rocker arm bolts to specifications. Completely collapse lifter by applying pressure on push rod before rotating engine.

4) Rotate crankshaft 180 degrees. Install push rods, rocker arms and fulcrums on No. 2 exhaust, No. 3 intake and No. 4 intake and exhuast. Tighten rocker arm bolts to specifications. Completely collapse lifters and rotate crankshaft 180 degrees.

5) To complete installation, reverse removal procedure. Tighten all bolts/nuts to specifications. Change oil and filter. Fill fluid levels. Start engine and check for leakage.

Fig. 3: Cylinder Head Tightening Sequence

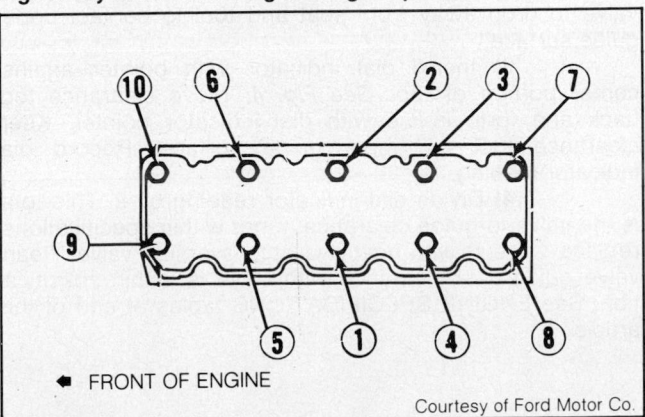

◀ FRONT OF ENGINE

Courtesy of Ford Motor Co.

CAMSHAFT

NOTE: **Front cover, front oil seal and camshaft procedures can only be performed with engine removed from vehicle.**

FRONT COVER & TIMING CHAIN

Removal

1) With engine and transaxle removed as an assembly, remove oil dipstick. Remove accessory drive belts. Remove crankshaft damper bolt and washer. Remove crankshaft damper with Remover (T77F-4220-B). Remove front cover oil seal using Seal Remover (T74P-6700-A). Remove bolts from front cover and necessary oil pan bolts.

2) Pry top of front cover away from cylinder block. Remove front cover and gasket. Check timing chain and components. See INSPECTION in this article. Align camshaft sprocket and crankshaft sprocket timing marks. Remove camshaft sprocket retaining bolt and washer. Slide camshaft sprocket, crankshaft sprocket and timing chain assembly forward. Remove as an assembly.

Inspection

1) Clean gasket mating surfaces. Check timing chain tensioner blade for wear. Check timing chain vibration damper for wear, located inside front cover. Check timing chain deflection by rotating crankshaft counterclockwise to take up slack on left side of chain. Mark a reference point on cylinder block and measure from this point to chain.

2) Move crankshaft in opposite direction to take up slack on right side of chain. Force left side of chain out with fingers. Measure distance between reference point and chain. The difference between the 2 measurements is the deflection. If not within specifications, replace necessary components. See TIMING CHAIN SPECIFICATIONS table in this article.

TIMING CHAIN SPECIFICATIONS

Application	In. (mm)
Timing Chain Deflection	.500 (12.70)
Tensioner Wear	.06 (1.5)

Installation

1) Clean and inspect components before installation. Align camshaft sprocket and crankshaft sprocket timing marks. Slide timing chain and sprockets into position. Install camshaft bolt and washer. Ensure flat side of washer faces camshaft sprocket.

2) Oil timing chain, sprockets and tensioner after installation. Apply Sealing Compound (B5A-19554-A) to new front cover gasket and position gasket on cover. DO NOT install front cover oil seal until cover is installed on block.

3) Install Front Cover Aligner (T84P-6019-C) on crankshaft. Install front cover and gasket. Install front cover bolts and tighten to specifications. Remove aligner.

4) Coat hub of crankshaft with Polyethylene Grease (DOAZ-19584-A). Using Pinion Seal Installer (T83T-4676-A), install new front cover seal. To complete installation, reverse removal procedure. Tighten bolts/nuts to specification. Fill fluid levels and check for leakage.

Ford Motor Co. Engines
2.3L & 2.5L HSC & HSO 4-CYLINDER (Cont.)

CAMSHAFT
Removal

1) Remove engine and transaxle. Drain engine oil. Remove accessory belts and pulleys. Remove cylinder head. See CYLINDER HEAD in this article. Position No. 1 cylinder on TDC. Mark spark plug wires and remove from spark plugs. Remove distributor cap and wires. Mark distributor-to-engine and remove distributor assembly.

2) Using a magnet, remove lifters. Keep in order of removal to ensure lifters are installed to original location. Remove front cover. See FRONT COVER & TIMING CHAIN in this article. Check camshaft end play. See CAMSHAFT END PLAY in this article.

3) Remove timing chain and sprockets as an assembly. See FRONT COVER & TIMING CHAIN in this article. Remove tensioners. Remove camshaft thrust plate. Pull camshaft out front of engine, using care not to damage journals or bearings.

Inspection

Clean all components and gasket mating surfaces. Check clearance of camshaft-to-bearings. Check lift of each lobe in consecutive order and record each reading. See CAMSHAFT LOBE LIFT in this article.

Installation

Coat camshaft lobes and journals with SAE 50 engine oil. Slide camshaft in through front of block. Install thrust plate. Ensure camshaft turns freely. To complete installation, reverse removal procedure. To install push rods and rocker arm assemblies, see step 3) in INSTALLATION under CYLINDER HEAD in this article. Tighten all bolts/nuts to specifications.

CAMSHAFT BEARINGS

NOTE: Camshaft bearings are prefinished to size. No reaming is required for standard or .015" undersize journal diameters.

Removal & Installation

Remove engine, camshaft, crankshaft, and rear bearing bore plug. Using Camshaft Bearing Replacer (T65L-5260-A) and instructions, remove camshaft bearings. Install camshaft bearings with replacer. Ensure oil holes in bearings and block are aligned. Install new rear bearing bore plug. To complete installation, reverse removal procedure.

CAMSHAFT END PLAY

Position dial indicator point on camshaft sprocket. Pry camshaft fully rear and zero indicator. Pry camshaft fully forward and note dial indicator reading. Replace thrust plate if not within specifications. Camshaft end play must be .009" (.23 mm).

CAMSHAFT LOBE LIFT

1) Camshaft lobe lift can be checked with camshaft installed or removed. Check camshaft lobe lift in consecutive order and record readings. With camshaft removed, measure distance between major and minor diameters of each lobe. The difference in reading is lobe lift.

2) With camshaft installed, remove valve cover. Remove rocker arm bolt. Remove fulcrum and rocker arm.

Install a dial indicator, with a cup shaped pointer, on top of cylinder head. Place push rod in cup shaped pointer in same plane as push rod movement.

3) Install remote starter and leave ignition switch off. Use remote starter and rotate crankshaft until push rod is in lowest position. Zero dial indicator. Rotate crankshaft slowly until push rod is in fully raised position. Record reading and repeat procedure for remaining lobes. Replace camshaft and lifters if not within specifications. See ENGINE SPECIFICATIONS tables at end of this article.

VALVES

VALVE ARRANGEMENT

I-E-I-E-E-I-E-I (Front-to-rear).

VALVE SEATS

NOTE: Valve seat replacement information not available at this time.

Refacing

1) On 2.3L models, intake seats, use only a 77 degree angle grinding stone to remove stock from bottom of seat. On exhaust seats, use only a 70 degree angle grinding stone to remove stock from bottom of seat. Use an 18 degree grinding stone to remove stock from top of all seats. Valve seat must be a true 45 degree finished angle with a seat width of .069-.091" (1.75-2.31 mm).

2) On 2.5L models, use only a 60 degree angle grinding stone to remove stock from bottom of all seats. Use a 30 degree angle grinding stone to remove stock from top of all seats. Valve seat must be a true 45 degree finished angle. Intake seat width should be .080" (2.03 mm) and exhaust seat width should be .090" (2.29 mm).

VALVES & VALVE GUIDES
Inspection

1) Mark all components prior to removal for installation reference. Thoroughly clean cylinder head and valves, using care not to damage surfaces. Remove valves. Check valve-to-guide clearance of each valve in its respective valve guide.

2) Install a valve and hold against seat. Install Valve Stem Clearance Tool (T65T-6505-H) on valve stem, until it is fully seated. Tighten tool set screw firmly. Allow valve to drop away from seat and tool to contact upper guide surface.

3) Install dial indicator with pointer against center portion of tool. See Fig. 4. Move clearance tool back and forth in-line with dial indicator pointer. Keep clearance tool on upper guide surface. Record dial indicator reading.

4) Divide dial indicator reading by 2. This total is the valve-to-guide clearance. If not within specifications, replace valve(s) with next available oversize valve. Ream valve guide until clearance with valve is within specification. See ENGINE SPECIFICATIONS tables at end of this article.

2.3L & 2.5L HSC & HSO 4-CYLINDER (Cont.)

Fig. 4: Valve-To-Guide Clearance

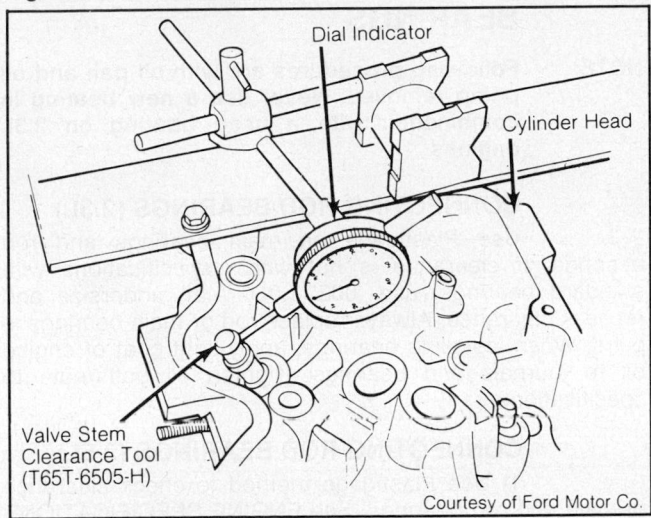

Courtesy of Ford Motor Co.

VALVE SPRINGS

Inspection

Inspect valve springs for cracks or damage. Measure installed height. Installed height should be 1.49" (37.9 mm). Measure free length and out-of-square. Maximum out-of-square is .060" (1.52 mm). Check spring tension at a specified length. See ENGINE SPECIFICATIONS tables at end of this article. Replace springs as necessary.

HYDRAULIC LIFTER ASSEMBLY

Hydraulic Lifter Clearance

1) Valve stem-to-rocker arm clearance should meet specifications with lifter totally collapsed. Valve and/or valve seat refacing can diminish clearance and allow valve to be held open.

2) To determine rocker arm-to-lifter clearance, attach auxiliary starter switch to starting circuit. With ignition switch in "OFF" position, crank engine until No. 1 piston is on TDC of compression stroke. Install Lifter Collapser (T81P-6500-A) on No. 1 intake rocker arm.

3) Slowly apply pressure until lifter is completely bottomed. Hold lifter in this position and check clearance between rocker arm and valve stem tip. If not within specifications, replace components as necessary. See COLLAPSED LIFTER CLEARANCE table in this article.

4) With engine at TDC, check clearance on No. 1 intake, No. 1 exhaust, No. 2 intake and No. 3 exhaust. Rotate crankshaft 180 degrees and check clearance on No. 2 exhaust, No. 3 intake, No. 4 intake and No. 4 exhaust.

COLLAPSED LIFTER CLEARANCE

Application	In. (mm)
2.3L & 2.5L	.072-.174 (1.83-4.42)

CYLINDER BLOCK ASSEMBLY

CYLINDER BLOCK

Inspection

1) Using a feeler gauge and straightedge, check cylinder block head surface for flatness. Surface should be flate within .003" (.08 mm) over entire surface. Check cylinder bore for wear, taper, out-of-round and piston fit. See ENGINE SPECIFICATIONS tables at end of this article.

2) Use only equal parts of kerosene and SAE 20 motor oil for honing cylinder bores. Install and tighten main bearing caps to specifications before cylinder refinishing. Use ONLY a spring-loaded type cylinder hone. After honing, allow cylinders to cool. Thoroughly clean bore with detergent and water solution.

3) Rinse solution in bore thoroughly with clean water. Wipe bores clean with lint free cloth. Lubricate cylinder bores with engine oil. Tap cylinder head bolt threads in cylinder block.

PISTONS, PINS & RINGS

OIL PAN

See appropriate OIL PAN REMOVAL article in this section.

PISTON & ROD ASSEMBLY

NOTE: The following procedures are with oil pan, oil pump and cylinder head removed. Ensure components are marked, to ensure installation to original position and location.

Inspection

1) Ensure pistons and rods are installed in cylinder from which they were removed. Ensure notch on piston faces front of engine. Ensure oil hole in rod and notch on piston are in proper position. *See Fig. 5.* Check piston fit before assembling piston on rod. See FITTING PISTONS in this article. Check rod bearing clearance.

2) Check piston pin fit. If not within specifications, remove pin and measure pin bore in piston and rod. Replace as necessary. If piston pin is to be replaced, replace piston and pin as an assembly. See ENGINE SPECIFICATIONS tables at end of this article.

Fig. 5: Piston & Rod Alignment

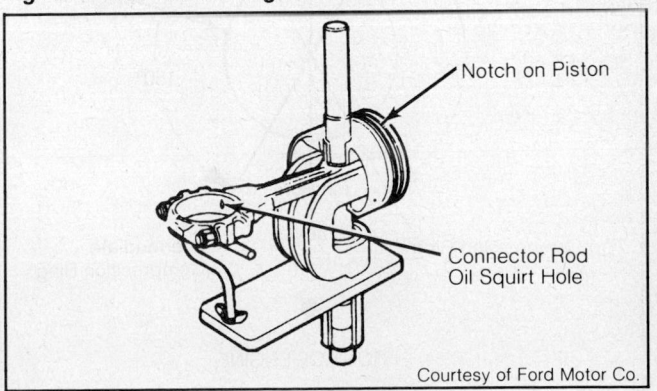

Courtesy of Ford Motor Co.

2.3L & 2.5L HSC & HSO 4-CYLINDER (Cont.)

FITTING PISTONS

1) Check piston-to-bore clearance. See ENGINE SPECIFICATIONS tables at end of this article. Standard size pistons are color coded Red, Blue or Yellow on the piston dome. See PISTON SIZE CODE table in this article.

2) If bore diameter is in lower one-third of specifications, use a Red coded piston. If bore diameter is in middle one-third of specifications, use a Blue coded piston. If bore diameter is in upper one-third of specifications, use Yellow coded piston. The Yellow coded piston is .004" (.10 mm) oversize. Use proper size piston to acquire specified clearance.

PISTON SIZE CODES

Code	In. (mm)
Red	3.6783-3.6789 (93.429-93.444)
Blue	3.6795-3.6801 (93.459-93.475)
Yellow	3.6807-3.6811 (93.490-93.500)

FITTING RINGS

1) Select proper rings for bore diameter. Place ring square in cylinder bore, below normal ring wear area. Measure the ring end gap. If ring end gap is less than specifications, remove necessary amount from end of ring. If ring gap is greater than specifications, use a different set of rings. Ensure rings are installed in cylinder bore in which they were measured.

2) Check side clearance of rings after installing on piston. Ensure clearance is within specifications around entire circumference. If lower lands of piston have high steps, replace piston. Replace piston and rings if side clearance is not within specifications. Properly set ring ends on piston before installing into cylinder. See Fig. 6. See ENGINE SPECIFICATIONS tables at end of this article.

Fig. 6: Piston Ring End Gap Spacing

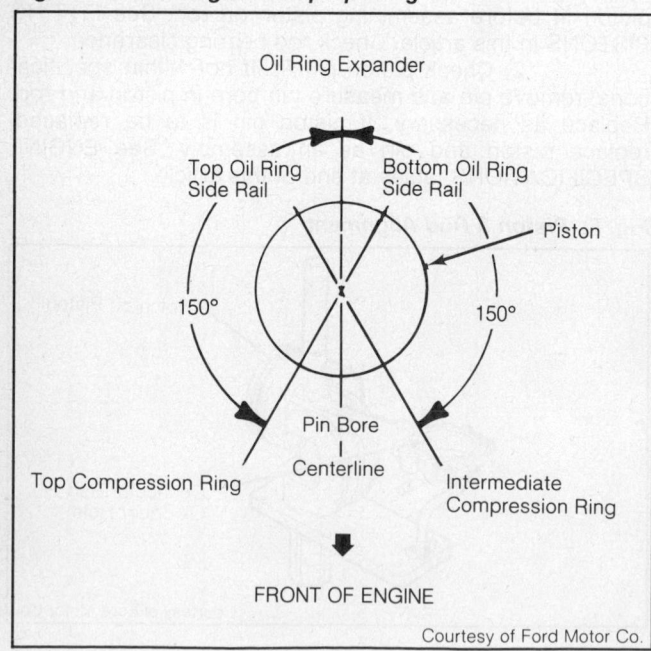

Oil Ring Expander

Top Oil Ring Side Rail

Bottom Oil Ring Side Rail

Piston

150°   150°

Top Compression Ring

Pin Bore Centerline

Intermediate Compression Ring

FRONT OF ENGINE

Courtesy of Ford Motor Co.

CRANKSHAFT & ROD BEARINGS

NOTE: Following procedures are with oil pan and oil pump removed. Never use a new bearing in combination with a used bearing on 2.3L engines.

CONNECTING ROD BEARINGS (2.3L)

Use Plastigage on main bearings and rod bearings. If clearance is not within specifications with standard bearings, use .002" (.050 mm) undersize and recheck clearance. Always replace rod or main bearings in pairs. When installing bearings, apply light coat of engine oil to journals and bearings. Tighten all bolts/nuts to specifications.

CONNECTING ROD BEARINGS (2.5L)

1) Use Plastigage method to check clearance of main and rod bearings. See ENGINE SPECIFICATIONS tables at end of this article. If replacing standard size bearings, use new bearings which fit with the minimum specified clearance.

2) If desired clearance cannot be obtained with standard bearing, try a standard bearing in combination with an undersize bearing. Standard bearings may be used with a .001" (.025 mm) or .002" (.050 mm) undersize bearing. Tighten all bolt/nuts to specifications.

THRUST BEARING ALIGNMENT

Inspection

Install dial indicator on front of engine with pointer on end of crankshaft. Pry crankshaft fully rear and zero indicator. Pry crankshaft fully forward and note reading. If end play exceeds specifications, replace thrust bearing. If end play is less than specifications, remove thrust bearing and inspect surfaces. Replace as necessary. See ENGINE SPECIFICATIONS tables at end of this article.

REAR CRANKSHAFT OIL SEAL

Removal

1) Remove transaxle. On manual transaxle models, remove clutch disc, pressure plate and flywheel. See appropriate CLUTCHES article in this section. On automatic transaxle models, remove flexplate. See appropriate TRANSMISSION SERVICING article in this section.

2) Use an awl and punch a hole into the metal surface of the seal. Use care not to damage sealing surfaces. Install Jet Plug Remover (T77L-9533-B) and remove oil seal.

Installtion

Check crankshaft seal surface for wear and replace as necessary. Coat crankshaft seal area and lip of oil seal with engine oil. Using Rear Crankshaft Seal Replacer (T81P--6701-A), install oil seal. Tighen bolts on seal replacer evenly, to ensure seal is installed squarely. To complete installation, reverse removal procedure.

FRONT CRANKSHAFT OIL SEAL

Removal & Installation

Remove accessory belts. Remove bolt and washer from crankshaft damper. Remove crankshaft damper with Differential Side Bearing Puller (T77F-4220-

2.3L & 2.5L HSC & HSO 4-CYLINDER (Cont.)

B1). Use Seal Remover (T74P-6700-A) and remove front oil seal. Coat new seal with Long-Life Lubricant C1AZ-19859-B). Use Pinion Oil Seal Installer (T83T-4676-A) and install new oil seal. To complete installation, reverse removal procedure.

ENGINE OILING

ENGINE OILING SYSTEM

Engine oiling is a full pressure system. Oil pump is bolted to bottom of engine block inside oil pan. An intermediate shaft attached to distributor drives the oil pump. *See Fig. 7.*

Fig. 7: Engine Oiling System

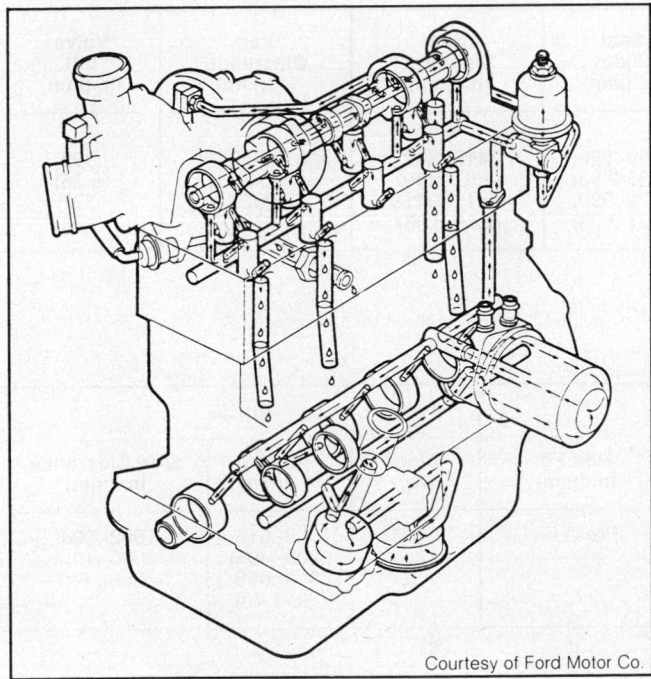

Courtesy of Ford Motor Co.

CRANKCASE CAPACITY

Crankcase capacity for the 2.3L engine is 4.5 qts. (4.3L) with filter change. The 2.5L engine is 5 qts. (4.7L) with filter change. DO NOT change oil without changing filter.

NORMAL OIL PRESSURE (HOT)

Normal oil pressure is 55-70 psi (3.9-4.9 kg/cm²) at 2000 RPM.

OIL PUMP

Removal & Installation

Remove oil pan. Remove oil pump and pick-up tube attaching bolts. Remove oil pump assembly. Remove pick-up tube from oil pump. To install, reverse removal procedure. Install new gaskets. Fill oil pump inlet port with engine oil. Rotate oil pump shaft until oil flows from outlet.

Inspection

Remove cover. Clean all components in solvent and dry with compressed air. Check inside of housing, outer race and rotor for wear and damage. Replace pump assembly if necessary. Measure inner rotor tip clearance. Measure rotor end play. Check relief valve

spring and replace pump assembly as necessary. See OIL PUMP SPECIFICATIONS table in this article.

OIL PUMP SPECIFICATIONS

Application	In. (mm)
Driveshaft-to-Housing Clearance	.0014-.0026 (.036-.066)
Outer Race-to-Housing Clearance	.001-.012 (.03-.31)
Relief Valve Spring Tension	[1]
Relief Valve-to-Bore Clearance	.0015-.0029 (.038-.074)
Inner Rotor Tip Clearance	.004 (.10)

[1] – Tension should be 16.5 lbs. @ 1.20" (7.5 kg @ 30.5 mm).

ENGINE COOLING

WATER PUMP

Removal & Installation

Disconnect negative battery cable and drain cooling system. Remove thermactor pump and bracket assembly. Remove accessory belts. Remove water pump inlet tube. Remove water pump retaining bolts. Remove water pump and gasket. Clean gasket mating surfaces. Coat new water pump gasket with Perfect Seal Sealing Compound (B5A-19554-A) and position on engine block. To complete installation, reverse removal procedure.

NOTE: For further information on cooling systems, see ENGINE COOLING section.

TIGHTENING SPECIFICATIONS

Application	Ft. Lbs. (N.m)
Camshaft Sprocket Bolt	41-56 (55-75)
Connecting Rod Cap Nut	21-26 (28-35)
Crankshaft Damper Bolt	140-170 (190-230)
Cylinder Head Bolt	
Step 1	51-59 (69-80)
Step 2	70-76 (95-103)
Distributor Hold-Down Bolt	17-25 (23-34)
Exhaust Manifold	
Step 1	5-7 (7-10)
Step 2	20-30 (27-41)
Flywheel Mount Bolt	54-64 (73-87)
Intake Manifold [1]	15-23 (20-30)
Intake Manifold Support Bracket	30-40 (41-54)
Main Bearing Cap Bolt	52-66 (71-90)
Oil Pump Mount Bolt	30-39 (41-50)
Rocker Arm Bolt	
Step 1	5-8 (7-11)
Step 2	20-27 (27-38)
Water Pump Mount Bolt	15-23 (20-30)
	INCH Lbs. (N.m)
Camshaft Tensioner Bolt	72-108 (8-12)
Camshaft Thrust Plate Bolt	72-108 (8-12)
Crankshaft Seal Retainer Bolt	72-108 (8-12)

[1] – Tighten intake manifold to specification in 2 steps.

Ford Motor Co. Engines

2.3L & 2.5L HSC & HSO 4-CYLINDER (Cont)

ENGINE SPECIFICATIONS

GENERAL SPECIFICATIONS

Year	DISPLACEMENT		Fuel System	HP@RPM	Torque Ft. Lbs.@RPM	Compr. Ratio	BORE		STROKE	
	Cu. In.	Liters					In.	mm	In.	mm
1988										
HSC	140	2.3	MPFI	86@3800	124@3200	9.0:1	3.68	93.53	3.30	84.0
HSO	140	2.3	MPFI	94@4000	126@3200	9.0:1	3.68	93.53	3.30	84.0
HSC	153	2.5	CFI	90@4400	130@2600	9.0:1	3.68	93.53	3.58	91.0

VALVES

Engine Size & Valve	Head Diam. In. (mm)	Face Angle	Seat Angle	Seat Width In. (mm)	Stem Diameter In. (mm)	Stem Clearance In. (mm)	Valve Lift In. (mm)
2.3L & 2.5L							
Intake	1.72-1.74 (43.76-44.37)	44°	45°	.060-.080 (1.53-2.03)	.3415-.3422 (8.67-8.69)	.0018 (.047)	.392 (9.96)
Exhaust	1.49-1.50 (37.98-38.3)	44°	45°	.070-.090 (1.77-2.28)	.3411-.3418 (8.66-8.68)	.0023 (.0595)	.377 (9.58)

PISTONS, PINS & RINGS

Engine	PISTONS Clearance In. (mm)	PINS Piston Fit In. (mm)	PINS Rod Fit In. (mm)	RINGS Ring No.	RINGS End Gap In. (mm)	RINGS Side Clearance In. (mm)
2.3L & 2.5L	.0012-.0022 (.036-.056)	.0002-.0005 (.005-.0013)	Press Fit	1 & 2	.008-.016 (.203-.406)	.002-.004 (.05-.10)
				3	.015-.055 (.38-1.40)	Snug Fit

CRANKSHAFT MAIN & CONNECTING ROD BEARINGS

Engine	MAIN BEARINGS Journal Diam. In. (mm)	MAIN BEARINGS Clearance In. (mm)	MAIN BEARINGS Thrust Bearing	MAIN BEARINGS Crankshaft End Play In. (mm)	CONNECTING ROD BEARINGS Journal Diam. In. (mm)	CONNECTING ROD BEARINGS Clearance In. (mm)	CONNECTING ROD BEARINGS Side Play In. (mm)
2.3L & 2.5L	2.2489-2.2490 (57.120-57.124)	.0008-.0015 (.020-.038)	No. 3	.004-.008 (.10-.20)	2.1232-2.1240 (53.92-53.94)	.0008-.0015 (.020-.038)	.0035-.0105 (.088-.266)

VALVE SPRINGS

Engine	Free Length In. (mm)	PRESSURE Lbs. @ In. (Kg @ mm) Valve Closed	PRESSURE Lbs. @ In. (Kg @ mm) Valve Open
2.3L & 2.5L	1.76 (44.93)	70-78@1.49 (32-35@38.1)	174-190@1.10 (79-86@28.13)

CAMSHAFT

Engine	Journal Diam. In. (mm)	Clearance In. (mm)	Lobe Lift In. (mm)
2.3L & 2.5L	2.0006-2.0008 (50.95-51.00)	.001-.003 (.02-.07)	[1] [2]

[1] - Intake .249" (6.35), Exhaust .239" (6.09).
[2] - 2.3L HO .2625" (6.67)

3.0L V6

Sable, Taurus

NOTE: For engine repair procedures not covered in this article, see ENGINE OVERHAUL PROCEDURES article at beginning of this section.

ENGINE CODING

ENGINE IDENTIFICATION

Engine may be identified by Vehicle Identification Number (VIN) at top of instrument panel, near windshield on left side of vehicle and is visible from outside. The 8th character of the VIN indicates engine type.

ENGINE CODE

Engine	Code
3.0L (182")	U

ENGINE REMOVAL

See ENGINE REMOVAL & INSTALLATION at end of ENGINE section.

CYLINDER HEAD & MANIFOLDS

CAUTION: Some engine components are aluminum. Use ONLY Ford Cooling System Fluid (E2FZ-19549-A) when refilling.

INTAKE MANIFOLD

Removal

1) Drain engine cooling system. Disconnect battery ground cable. Remove flex hose from throttle body and air cleaner. Remove throttle linkage shield. Mark and disconnect vacuum hoses from throttle body. Disconnect EGR valve. Disconnect throttle linkage. Mark and disconnect electrical connenctors.

2) Disconnect PCV hose. Remove alternator support brace. Remove 6 throttle body assembly bolts. Remove throttle body assembly and gasket. *See Fig. 1.* Remove fuel cap to relieve fuel tank pressure. Release fuel pressure at fuel pressure relief valve on fuel rail assembly.

3) Using Coupling Disconnect Tool (D87L-9974-B), disconnect fuel supply line and return line. Remove wiring harness from fuel injectors. Disconnect vacuum line from fuel pressure regulator valve. Remove upper radiator hose. Disconnect water outlet heater hose.

4) Mark and remove spark plug wires from spark plugs. Remove distributor cap and wires. Mark distributor-to-engine and remove distributor assembly. Remove intake manifold bolts. Remove intake mainfold and gaskets. *See Fig. 2.*

Installation

1) Cean gasket mating surfaces. Lightly oil attaching bolts and stud threads before installation. When using silicone rubber sealer, assembly must occur within 15 minutes after sealer is applied. Apply Silicone Rubber Sealer (D6AZ-19562-A) to intersection of cylinder block assembly and head assembly at all 4 corners.

Fig. 1: Throttle Body Assembly

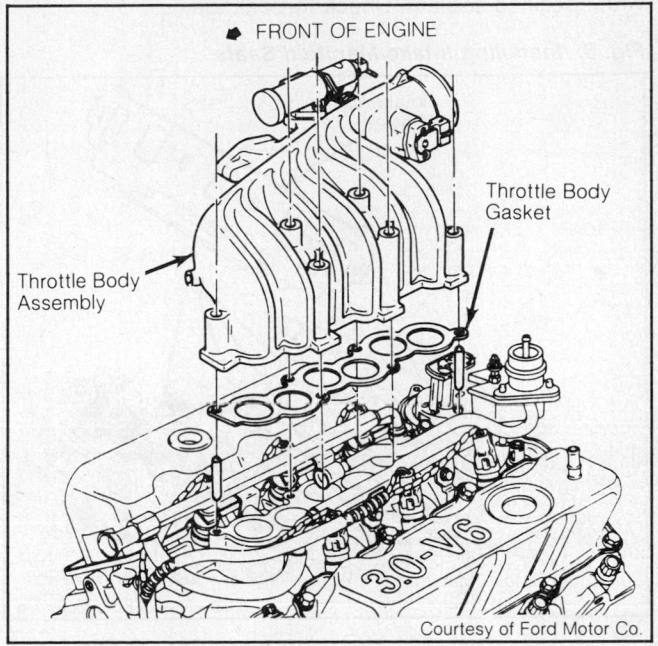

Courtesy of Ford Motor Co.

Fig. 2: Intake Manifold & Tightening Sequence

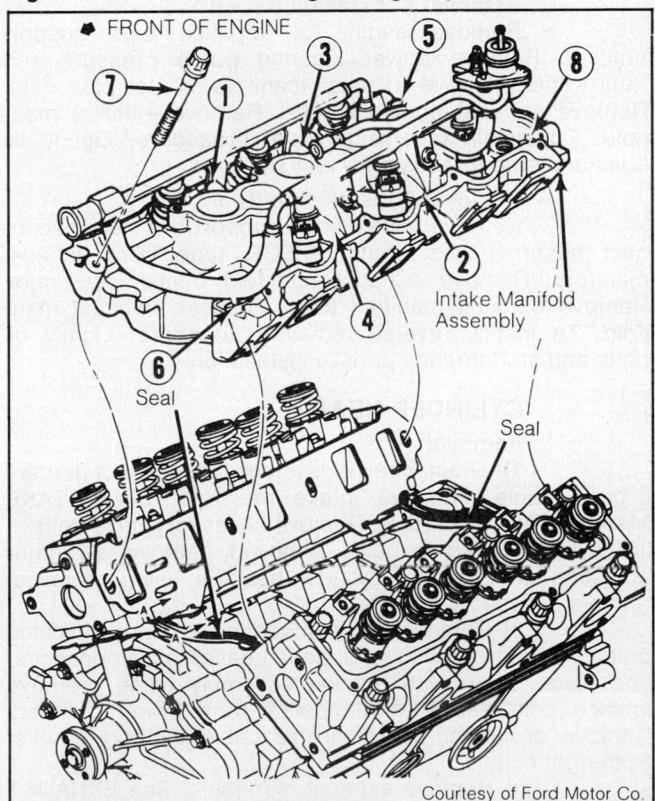

Courtesy of Ford Motor Co.

2) Install front and rear intake manifold seals. Position intake manifold gaskets in place with locking tabs over tabs on cylinder head gaskets. *See Fig. 3.* Carefully lower intake manifold into position on cylinder block and cylinder heads to prevent smearing silicone sealer.

3) Install intake manifold bolts and tighten in sequence and in 2 steps to specifications. To complete

3.0L V6 (Cont.)

installation, reverse removal procedure. Fill coolant level with specified coolant. Check for leakage.

Fig. 3: Installing Intake Manifold Seals

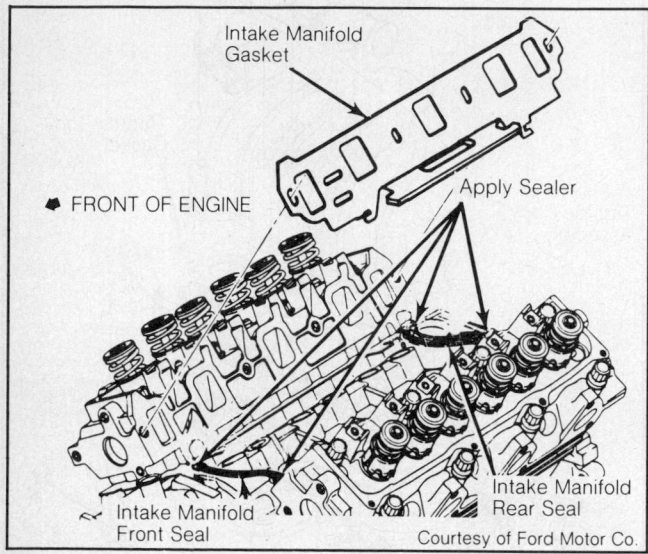

Courtesy of Ford Motor Co.

EXHAUST MANIFOLD

Removal & Installation (Left Side)

Remove engine oil dipstick tube support bracket. Remove power steering pump pressure and return line. Remove exhaust manifold-to-inlet pipe nuts. Remove exhaust manifold bolts. Remove exhaust manifold. To install, reverse removal procedure. Lightly oil bolts and stud threads prior to installation.

Removal & Installation (Right Side)

Remove heater hose support bracket. Disconnect heater hoses. Remove EGR tube from exhaust manifold. Remove exhaust manifold-to-inlet pipe nuts. Remove exhaust manifold bolts. Remove exhaust manifold. To install, reverse removal procedure. Lightly oil bolts and stud threads prior to installation.

CYLINDER HEAD

Removal

1) Drain cooling system. Disconnect battery ground cable. Remove intake manifold. See INTAKE MANIFOLD in this article. Remove accessory drive belts. If left cylinder head is being removed, remove alternator adjusting arm. If right cylinder head is being removed, remove accessory belt idler.

2) Remove pump mounting bracket attaching bolts (if power steering equipped). Leave hoses connected and place pump with bracket assembly aside. Remove ignition coil bracket and dipstick tube from left head. Remove grounding strap throttle cable support bracket from right head.

3) Remove exhaust manifolds. See EXHAUST MANIFOLD in this article. Remove PCV valve. Remove rocker arm covers. Loosen rocker arm bolts. Move rocker arm off push rod. Keep push rods in order, to ensure installation to original location and remove push rods. Remove cylinder head attaching bolts. Remove cylinder heads and gaskets.

Inspection

Clean head gasket mating surfaces. Clean carbon from combustion chambers. Use care not to damage surfaces. Check cylinder head for cracks and inspect gasket surface for burrs and nicks. Check cylinder heads for warpage. Warpage must not exceed .007" (.18 mm). Do not machine surface more than .010" (.25 mm). Replace cylinder head as necessary.

Installation

1) Replace dowels in cylinder block if damaged. Position new head gaskets on cylinder block using the dowels for alignment. Ensure marked side of gaskets are properly positioned. Install cylinder heads on block. Install cylinder head bolts. Tighten cylinder head bolts in sequence and in 2 steps. See Fig. 4.

Fig. 4: Cylinder Head Tightening Specifications

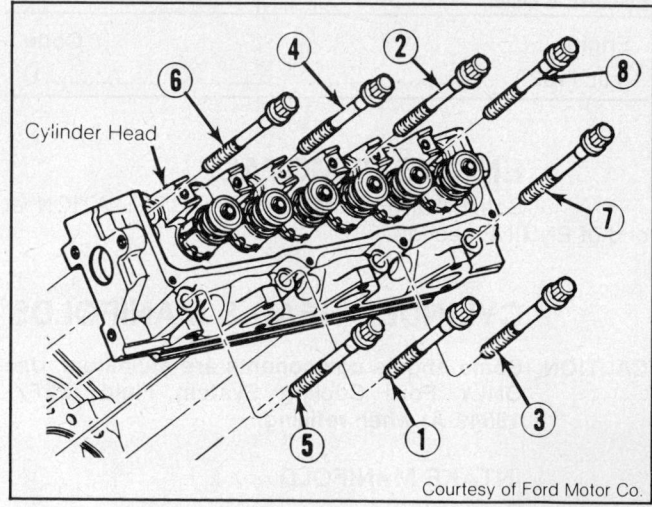

Courtesy of Ford Motor Co.

2) Dip each push rod end in Oil Conditioner (D9AZ-19579-C). Install push rods in position from which they were removed. For each valve, rotate crankshaft until lifter and push rod are at lowest point on camshaft. Position rocker arm over push rod. Collapse lifter and tighten rocker arm bolt to specifications.

NOTE: **Rocker arms must be fully seated in cylinder head and push rods must be seated in rocker arm sockets prior to final tightening.**

3) With all rocker arms installed, check clearance between rocker arm and valve stem tip. See HYDRAULIC LIFTER ASSEMBLY in this article. To complete installation, reverse removal procedure. Tighten all bolts/nuts to specifications. Fill cooling system with specified coolant only. Change oil and filter.

CAMSHAFT

TIMING COVER & FRONT SEAL

Removal

1) Remove fan shroud and fan clutch assembly. Drain cooling system. Remove negative battery cable. Remove accessory drive belts. Remove right front wheel. Remove water pump pulley. Remove crankshaft damper

pulley. Remove damper from crankshaft using Crankshaft Damper Remover (T58P-6316-D) and Vibration Damper Remover Adapter (T28L-6316-B).

2) Pry seal from timing cover. Use care to prevent damage to front cover and crankshaft. Remove lower radiator hose. Remove oil pan. Remove 10 bolts retaining front cover and water pump assembly to engine. See Fig. 5. Remove front cover and water pump as an assembly.

Fig. 5: Exploded View of Timing Cover

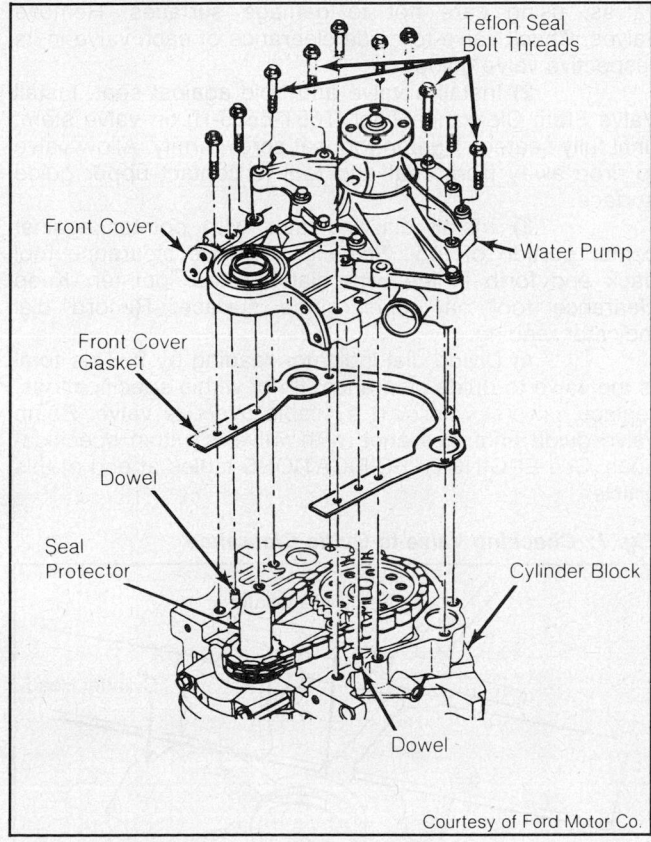

Courtesy of Ford Motor Co.

Installation
Clean gasket mating surfaces. Always install new gaskets. Use sealant for front cover bolts which thread into water jackets. To complete installation, reverse removal procedure. Tighen all bolts/nuts to specifications. Fill cooling system with specified coolant only. Change oil and filter.

FRONT COVER OIL SEAL
See TIMING COVER & FRONT SEAL in this article.

TIMING CHAIN
Removal
Remove timing cover. See TIMING COVER & FRONT SEAL in this article. Position No. 1 piston on TDC of compression stroke. Check alignment of camshaft and crankshaft sprocket timing marks. Check timing chain deflection. See INSPECTION in this article. Remove camshaft sprocket attaching bolts and washer. Slide sprockets and timing chain forward and remove as an assembly.

Inspection
1) Remove left side rocker arm cover. Loosen No. 5 exhaust rocker arm and rotate to one side. Install a dial indicator on end of push rod. Turn crankshaft clockwise until No. 1 piston is at TDC, to take up slack on right side of chain. The damper timing mark should point to TDC.

2) Zero dial indicator. Slowly turn crankshaft counterclockwise until slightest movement is seen on dial indicator. Note the number of degrees of travel from TDC. If reading exceeds 6 degrees, replace timing chain and sprockets.

CAUTION: DO NOT replace camshaft bolt with standard bolt. Bolt has a drilled oil passage.

Installation
Place timing chain on crankshaft and camshaft sprocket. Align timing marks on sprockets. See Fig. 6. Install camshaft bolt and washer. Tighten to specification. Ensure all timing marks are aligned. Apply oil to timing chain and sprockets after installation. To complete installation, reverse removal procedure. Tighten bolts/nuts to specifications.

Fig. 6: Location of Timing Sprocket Alignment Marks

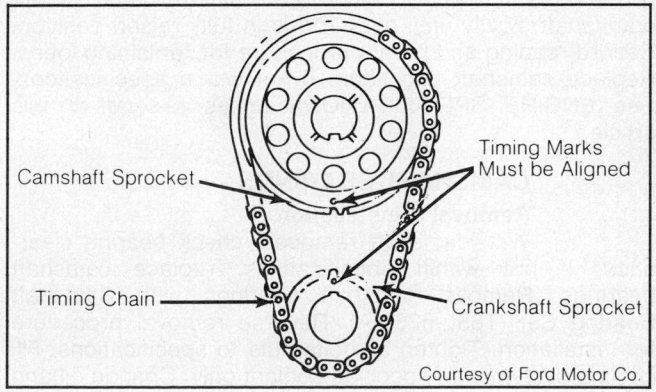

Courtesy of Ford Motor Co.

CAMSHAFT
Removal
1) Remove engine and transaxle. Remove timing cover. See TIMING COVER & FRONT SEAL in this article. Remove valve covers. Loosen rocker arms bolts. Move rocker arms off of push rods. Mark and remove push rods. Remove intake manifold. Mark and remove valve lifters. Check camshaft end play. See INSPECTION in this article.

2) Remove timing chain and sprockets as an assembly. Remove camshaft thrust plate. Remove camshaft by pulling out front of engine. Use care not to damage bearings, journals and lobes.

Inspection
Check camshaft end play with with dial indicator mounted to front of camshaft. Pry camshaft fully rear and zero indicator. Pry camshaft fully forward and not indicator reading. Replace thrust plate if not within specifications. Check camshaft lobe lift. See CAMSHAFT LOBE LIFT in this article. Replace camshaft and lifters as necessary. Clean and inspect all parts before installation.

Installation
1) Lubricate camshaft lobes and journals with heavy SAE 50W engine oil. Carefully slide camshaft

through bearings in cylinder block. Install thrust plate and recheck camshaft end play. Install timing chain and sprocket. See TIMING COVER & FRONT SEAL in this article.

2) Lubricate components with heavy SAE 50W engine oil during installation. To complete installation, reverse removal procedure. Ensure to collapse lifter before tightening rocker arm bolt. Tighten all bolts/nuts to specifications. Fill cooling system with specified coolant only. Check for leakage.

CAMSHAFT LOBE LIFT

1) Camshaft lobe lift can be checked with camshaft installed or removed. Check camshaft lobe lift in consecutive order and record readings. With camshaft removed, measure distance between major and minor diameters of each lobe. The difference in reading is lobe lift.

2) With camshaft installed, remove valve cover. Remove rocker arm bolt. Remove fulcrum and rocker arm. Install a dial indicator, with a cup shaped pointer, on top of cylinder head. Place push rod in cup shaped pointer in same plane as push rod movement.

3) Install remote starter and leave ignition switch off. Use remote starter and rotate crankshaft until push rod is in lowest position. Zero dial indicator. Rotate crankshaft slowly until push rod is in fully raised position. Record reading and repeat procedure for remaining lobes. Replace camshaft and lifters if not within specifications. See ENGINE SPECIFICATIONS tables at end of this article.

CAMSHAFT BEARINGS

Removal & Installation

With camshaft removed, check bearing clearance. If not within specifications, replace camshaft bearings. Remove camshaft bearings with Camshaft Bearing Set (T65L-6250-A). Reverse removal procedure for installation. Tighten all bolts/nuts to specifications. Fill cooling system with specified coolant only. Change oil and filter. Check for leakage.

CAMSHAFT CORE PLUG

Removal & Installation

Remove transaxle. Remove clutch disc, pressure plate and flywheel or flexplate. Punch a hole in the center of the plug and remove plug with slide hammer. Clean and remove burrs from core plug bore. Oversize plugs are available. Apply a light coat of Perfect-Seal Sealing Compound (D5AZ-19554-A) to sealing edge of plug and install plug squarely.

VALVES

VALVE ARRANGEMENT

Right Side – E-I-E-I-E-I.
Left Side – I-E-I-E-I-E.

NOTE: "Right" and "Left" refer to right and left side of the engine NOT the vehicle.

VALVE SEATS

NOTE: Valve seat replacement information not available at this time.

Refacing

Valve seat must be a true 45 degree finished angle. Use only a 60 degree angle grinding stone to remove stock from bottom of all seats. Use a 30 degree angle grinding stone to remove stock from top of all seats. Intake seat width should be .06-.08" (1.5-2.0 mm) and exhaust seat width should be .08-.10" (2.0-2.5 mm).

VALVES & VALVE GUIDE

1) Mark all components prior to removal for installation reference. Thoroughly clean cylinder head and valves, using care not to damage surfaces. Remove valves. Check valve-to-guide clearance of each valve in its respective valve guide.

2) Install a valve and hold against seat. Install Valve Stem Clearance Tool (T65T-6505-H) on valve stem, until fully seated. Tighten tool set screw firmly. Allow valve to drop away from seat and tool to contact upper guide surface.

3) Install dial indicator with pointer against center portion of tool. See Fig. 7. Move clearance tool back and forth in-line with dial indicator pointer. Keep clearance tool on upper guide surface. Record dial indicator reading.

4) Divide dial indicator reading by 2. This total is the valve-to-guide clearance. If not within specifications, replace valve(s) with next available oversize valve. Ream valve guide until clearance with valve is within specifications. See ENGINE SPECIFICATIONS tables at end of this article.

Fig. 7: Checking Valve-to-Guide Clearance

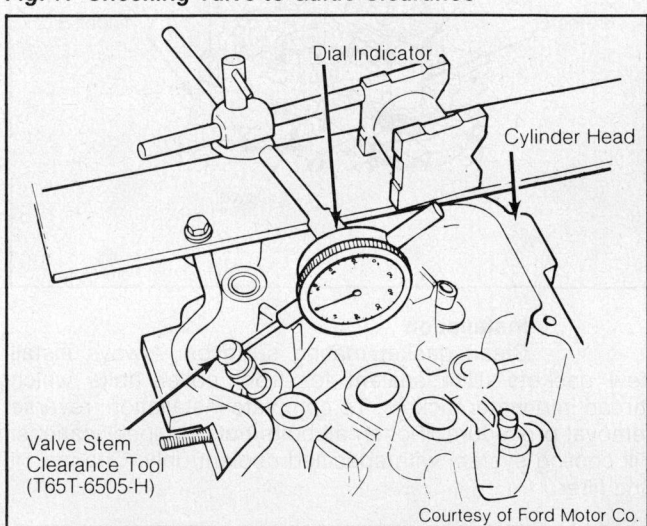

Dial Indicator

Cylinder Head

Valve Stem
Clearance Tool
(T65T-6505-H)

Courtesy of Ford Motor Co.

NOTE: Always reface valve seat after valve guide has been serviced.

5) Check valve face for pitting, cracks and runout. Reface or replace valve as necessary. Ensure valve face angle is a true 44 degrees. Ensure proper seat width is achieved. See ENGINE SPECIFICATIONS tables at end of this article.

VALVE SPRINGS

Inspection

Inspect valve springs for cracks or damage. Measure installed height. Install height should be 1.58"

3.0L V6 (Cont.)

(40.1 mm). Measure out-of-square. Maximum out-of-square is .060" (1.52 mm). Check free length. Check spring tension at specified length. See ENGINE SPECIFICATIONS tables at end of this article. Replace springs as necessary.

HYDRAULIC VALVE LIFTER ASSEMBLY

Inspection

With lifter removed, check bottom surface of lifter. Surface must be convex and smooth. Replace lifter assembly and check camshaft if surface is flat or concaved. Disassemble lifter and clean. Check leak-down rate of lifter with hydraulic tester fluid only. Leak-down should be 20-60 seconds, to travel .125" with 50 lbs. (3.18 mm with 23 kg) load. If not within specifications, replace lifter assembly. Always check camshaft and replace if necessary.

Hydraulic Lifter Clearance

1) Valve stem-to-rocker arm clearance should meet specifications with lifter totally collapsed. Valve and/or valve seat refacing can diminish clearance and allow valve to be held open.

2) To determine rocker arm-to-valve stem clearance, attach auxiliary starter switch to staring circuit. With ignition switch in "OFF" position, crank engine until No. 1 piston is on TDC of compression stroke. Completely collapse No. 1 intake valve lifter.

3) Measure clearance between rocker arm and tip of valve stem, holding lifter in collapsed position. Repeat procedure for No. 1 exhaust, No. 2 exhaust, No. 3 intake, No. 4 exhaust and No. 6 intake.

4) Rotate crankshaft 360 degrees (one revolution). Repeat procedure for No. 2 intake, No. 3 exhaust, No. 4 intake, No. 5 exhaust, No. 5 intake and No. 6 exhaust. If not within specifications, replace or grind valve stem as necessary. See COLLAPSED LIFTER CLEARANCE table in this article.

COLLAPSED LIFTER CLEARANCE

Application	In. (mm)
3.0L	.08-.18 (2.03-4.57)

CYLINDER BLOCK ASSEMBLY

CYLINDER BLOCK

Inspection

1) Using a feeler gauge and straightedge, check cylinder block head gasket surface for flatness. Surface should be flate within .003" (.08 mm) over 6" surface. Check cylinder bore for wear, taper, out-of-round and piston fit. See CYLINDER BORE SPECIFICATIONS table in this article.

2) Install all main bearing caps and tighten to specifications prior to cylinder bore honing. Use only equal parts of kerosene and SAE 20 motor oil for honing cylinder bores. Use ONLY a spring-loaded type cylinder hone. After honing, allow cylinders to cool. Thoroughly clean bore with detergent and water solution.

3) Rinse solution from bore thoroughly with clean water. Wipe bore clean with lint free cloth. Lubricate cylinder bores with engine oil. Tap cylinder head bolt threads in cylinder block.

CYLINDER BORE SPECIFICATIONS

Application	In. (mm)
Out-of-Round	.0006 (.015)
Taper	.002 (.05)

PISTONS, PINS & RINGS

OIL PAN

See appropriate OIL PAN REMOVAL article in this section.

PISTON & ROD ASSEMBLY

NOTE: The following procedure is with cylinder head, oil pan, oil pump, pick-up tube and baffle removed. Components must be marked, to ensure installation to original position and location.

Inspection

1) Ensure pistons and rods are installed in cylinder from which it was removed. Ensure notch on piston top and button on connecting rod faces front of engine. See Fig. 8. Check piston fit before assembling piston on rod. See FITTING PISTONS in this article.

2) Check piston pin fit. If not within specifications, remove pin and measure pin bore in piston and rod. Replace as necessary. If piston pin is to be replaced, replace piston and pin as an assembly. See ENGINE SPECIFICATIONS tables at end of this article.

Fig. 8: Piston & Rod Position

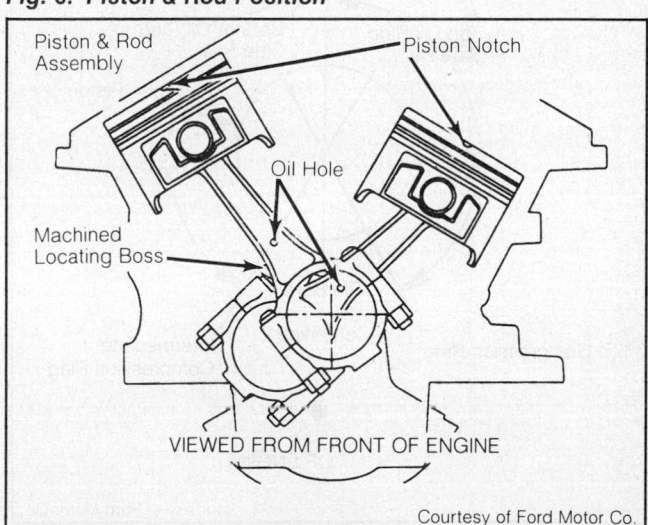

Courtesy of Ford Motor Co.

FITTING PISTONS

1) Check piston-to-bore clearance. See ENGINE SPECIFICATIONS tables at end of this article. Standard size pistons are color coded Red, Blue or Yellow on the piston dome. See PISTON SIZE CODE table in this article.

2) If bore diameter is in lower one-third of specifications, use a Red coded piston. If bore diameter is in middle one-third of specifications, use a Blue coded piston. If bore diameter is in upper one-third of specifications, use Yellow coded piston. The Yellow coded piston is .004" (.10 mm) oversize. Use proper size piston to acquire specified clearance.

PISTON SIZE CODES

Code	In. (mm)
Red	3.5024-3.5031 (88.961-88.979)
Blue	3.5035-3.5041 (88.989-89.004)
Yellow	3.5045-3.5051 (89.014-89.030)

FITTING PISTON RINGS

1) Select proper rings for bore diameter. Place ring square in cylinder bore, below normal ring wear area. Measure the ring end gap. If ring end gap is less than specifications, remove necessary amount from end of ring. If ring gap is greater than specifications, use a different set of rings. Ensure rings are installed in cylinder bore in which they were measured.

2) Check side clearance of rings after installing on piston. Ensure clearance is within specifications around entire circumference. If lower lands of piston have high steps, replace piston. Replace piston and rings if side clearance is not within specifications. Properly set ring ends on piston before installing pistons into cylinder. See Fig. 9. See ENGINE SPECIFICATIONS tables at end of this article.

Fig. 9: Piston Ring End Gap Spacing

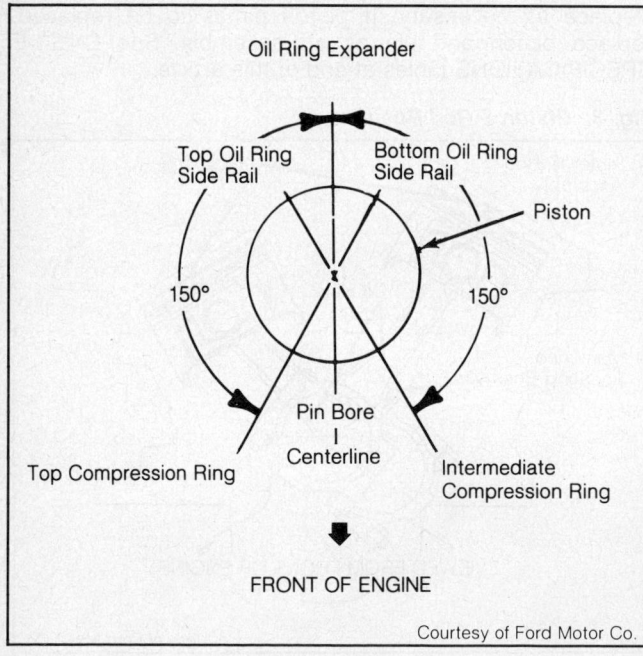

Courtesy of Ford Motor Co.

CRANKSHAFT & ROD BEARINGS

NOTE: Following procedures are with oil pan, oil pump, pick-up tube and baffle removed. Only one bearing at a time should be checked.

MAIN BEARING
Inspection

Use Plastigage method and check clearance between main bearing and crankshaft journal. Check crankshaft for nicks, scratches, scores and wear. If not within specifications, replace bearings. Machine or replace crankshaft as necessary. See ENGINE SPECIFICATIONS tables at end of this article. Check crankshaft end play. See THRUST BEARING ALIGNMENT in this article. Replace thrust bearing as necessary.

CONNECTING ROD BEARINGS

NOTE: Because 3.0L V6 engine crankshaft incorporates deep rolling of the main journal fillets, journal refinishing is limited to .010" (.25 mm) undersize of standard journal dimensions.

Inspection

Use Plastigage method and check clearance between rod bearing and crankshaft. If specified clearance cannot be obtained with standard bearings, try a standard bearing in combination with an undersize bearing. Standard bearings may be used with a .001" (.025 mm) or .002" (.050 mm) undersize bearing. Tighten all bolts/nuts to specifications. Desired clearance is minimum specified clearance. See ENGINE SPECIFICATIONS tables at end of this article.

THRUST BEARING ALIGNMENT
Inspection

Install dial indicator on front of engine with pointer on end of crankshaft. Pry crankshaft fully rear and zero indicator. Pry crankshaft fully forward and note reading. If end play exceeds specifications, replace thrust bearing. If end play is less than specifications, remove thrust bearing and inspect surfaces. Replace as necessary. See ENGINE SPECIFICATIONS tables at end of this article.

REAR CRANKSHAFT OIL SEAL
Removal

1) Remove transaxle. On manual transaxle models, remove clutch disc, pressure plate and flywheel. See appropriate CLUTCHES article in this section. On automatic transaxle models, remove flexplate. See appropriate TRANSMISSION SERVICING article in this section.

2) Use an awl and punch a hole into the metal surface of the seal. Use care not to damage sealing surfaces. Install Jet Plug Remover (T77L-9533-B) and remove oil seal.

Installtion

Check crankshaft seal surface for wear and replace as necessary. Coat crankshaft seal area and lip of oil seal with engine oil. Using Rear Crankshaft Seal Replacer (T81P--6701-A), install oil seal. Tighen bolts on seal replacer evenly, to ensure seal is installed squarely. To complete installation, reverse removal procedure.

FRONT CRANKSHAFT OIL SEAL
Removal & Installation

See TIMING COVER & FRONT SEAL in this article.

3.0L V6 (Cont.)

ENGINE OILING

ENGINE OILING SYSTEM

The lubrication is a force-feed type. The oil is supplied under full pressure to crankshaft, connecting rods, camshaft bearing and valve lifters. A controlled volume of oil is supplied to rocker arms and push rods. All other moving parts are lubricated by splash or gravity flow.

CRANKCASE CAPACITY

Crankcase capacity is 4 quarts (3.79L) without oil filter and 4.5 quarts (4.26L) with oil filter. It is not recommended to change oil without filter.

NORMAL OIL PRESSURE (HOT)

Normal oil pressure should be 40-60 psi (2.8-4.2 kg/cm²).

PRESSURE REGULATOR VALVE

Pressure regulator valve is located in oil pump and is not adjustable.

OIL PUMP

Removal & Installation

Remove oil pan. Remove oil pump pick-up tube retaining bolt. Remove oil pump retaining bolts. Remove oil pump and pick-up tube assembly. Remove and replace gasket. To install, reverse removal procedure. Tighten bolts/nuts to specifications.

Inspection

Remove pick-up tube from oil pump. Remove oil pump cover bolts. Remove oil pump cover and gasket. Check the inner-to-outer rotor clearance, gear backlash, drive shaft-to-housing clearance, gear height clearance, relief valve spring tension and relief valve to bore clearance. See OIL PUMP SPECIFICATIONS table in this article. Replace components as necessary.

OIL PUMP SPECIFICATIONS

Application	In. (mm)
Inner-To-Outer Rotor	.010 (.254)
Gear Backlash	.008-.012 (.20-.31)
Gear Height	.0005-.0055 (.013-.140)
Drive Shaft-to-Housing	.0005-.0019 (.013-.048)
Relief Valve-to-Bore Clearance	.0017-.0029 (.043-.074)
Relief Valve Spring Tension	1

1 – Spring tension should be 9.1-10.1 lbs. @ 1.11" (4.1-4.6 kg @ 28.2 mm).

ENGINE COOLING

WATER PUMP

Removal

Drain cooling system. Remove accessory drive belts. Remove idler bracket from engine. Disconnect heater hose at water pump. Remove water pump pulley bolts. Pulley will remain loose on hub due to insufficient clearance. Remove 11 water pump attaching bolts. See Fig. 10. Lift water pump assembly up and out.

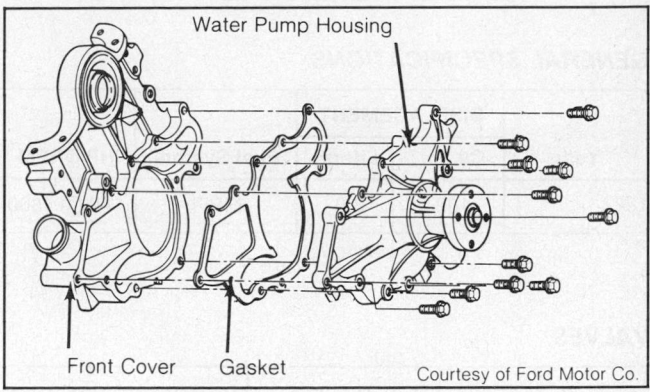

Fig. 10: Exploded View of Water Pump Assembly

Water Pump Housing

Front Cover   Gasket   Courtesy of Ford Motor Co.

Installation

Lightly oil bolt and stud threads before installation, except those specifying sealant. See Fig. 10. Apply Contact Adhesive (D7AZ-19B508-A) to new gasket and position on water pump. Install water pump and pulley as an assembly. To complete installation, reverse removal procedure. Tighten bolts/nuts to specifications. Fill cooling system with Ford Cooling System Fluid (E2FZ-19549-A) only. Check for leakage.

NOTE: For further information, see ENGINE COOLING SYSTEMS article at the end of this section.

TIGHTENING SPECIFICATIONS

Application	Ft. Lbs. (N.m)
Connecting Rod Nut	23-29 (31-39)
Crankshaft Pulley Bolt	20-28 (27-38)
Cylinder Head Bolt	
Step One	48-54 (65-75)
Step Two	63-80 (85-109)
Damper-to-Crankshaft Bolt	141-169 (190-230)
Exhaust Manifold Bolt	15-22 (20-30)
Front Cover-to-Block Bolt	15-22 (20-30)
Flywheel Bolt	54-64 (73-87)
Idler Pulley Bolt	30-40 (40-55)
Intake Manifold Bolt	
Step One	11 (15)
Step Two	18 (24)
Step Three	24 (33)
Main Bearing Cap Bolt	65-81 (88-110)
Oil Pump Bolt	30-40 (40-55)
Pulley-to-Damper Bolt	19-28 (26-38)
Rocker Arm Bolt	
Step One	5-11 (7-15)
Step Two	20-28 (27-38)
Water Pump Pulley Bolt	15-22 (20-30)

Application	INCH Lbs. (N.m)
Oil Pan Bolt	80-106 (9-12)
Spark Plug	60-132 (7-15)
Valve Cover Bolt	80-106 (9-12)
Water Pump Mounting Bolt	72-96 (8-11)

Ford Motor Co. Engines

3.0L V6 (Cont.)

ENGINE SPECIFICATIONS

GENERAL SPECIFICATIONS

| Year | DISPLACEMENT | | Fuel System | HP@RPM | Torque Ft. Lbs.@RPM | Compr. Ratio | BORE | | STROKE | |
	Cu. In.	Liters					In.	mm	In.	mm
1988	182	3.0	MPFI	140 @ 4800	160 @ 3000	9.25:1	3.50	89.00	3.20	80

VALVES

Engine Size & Valve	Head Diam. In. (mm)	Face Angle	Seat Angle	Seat Width In. (mm)	Stem Diameter In. (mm)	Stem Clearance In. (mm)	Valve Lift In. (mm)
3.0L Intake	1.57 (40.0)	44°	45°	.06-.08 (1.5-2.0)	.3126-.3134 (7.940-7.960)	.001-.0028 (.025-.071)	.419 (10.65)
Exhaust	1.30 (33.0)	44°	45°	.08-.10 (2.0-2.5)	.3121-.3129 (7.928-7.948)	.0015-.0033 (.038-.081)	.419 (10.65)

PISTONS, PINS & RINGS

| Engine | PISTONS | PINS | | RINGS | | |
	Clearance In. (mm)	Piston Fit In. (mm)	Rod Fit In. (mm)	Ring No.	End Gap In. (mm)	Side Clearance In. (mm)
3.0L	.0014.0022 (.036-.056)	.0002-.0005 (.005-.012)	Press Fit	1 & 2	.01-.02 (.25-.50)	.0012-.0031 (.031-.079)
				3	.010-.049 (.25-1.25)	Snug Fit

CRANKSHAFT MAIN & CONNECTING ROD BEARINGS

| Engine | MAIN BEARINGS | | | | CONNECTING ROD BEARINGS | | |
	Journal Diam. In. (mm)	Clearance In. (mm)	Thrust Bearing	Crankshaft End Play In. (mm)	Journal Diam. In. (mm)	Clearance In. (mm)	Side Play In. (mm)
3.0L	2.5190-2.5198 (63.98-64.00)	.0010-.0014 (.025-.036)	No. 3	.004-.008 (.10-.20)	2.1253-2.1261 (53.983-54.003)	.0010-.0014 (.025-.036)	.006-.014 (.15-.36)

CAMSHAFT

Engine	Journal Diam. In. (mm)	Clearance In. (mm)	Lobe Lift In. (mm)
3.0L	2.0074-2.0084 (50.988-51.013)	.001-.003 (.02-.07)	2.60 (66.0)

VALVE SPRINGS

| Engine | Free Length In. (mm) | PRESSURE Lbs. @ In. (Kg @ mm) | |
		Valve Closed	Valve Open
3.0L	1.84 (46.74)	65@1.58 (30@46.0)	180@1.16 (82@28.2)

3.8L V6

Continental, Cougar, Sable, Taurus, Thunderbird

NOTE: For engine repair procedures not covered in this article, see ENGINE OVERHAUL PROCEDURES article at beginning of this section.

ENGINE CODING

ENGINE IDENTIFICATION

The engine may be identified by the Vehicle Identification Number (VIN) stamped on a metal tab attached to the instrument panel near the windshield on driver's side of vehicle. The VIN number is also stamped on both Safety Certification Decals, mounted on the left front door lock panel and on the Engine Identification Label, mounted on the valve cover. The VIN number contains 17 characters. The 8th character identifies the engine and the 10th character establishes the model year.

ENGINE CODE

Engine	Code
3.8L (232") V6	4

ENGINE REMOVAL

See ENGINE REMOVAL & INSTALLATION at end of ENGINE section.

CYLINDER HEAD & MANIFOLDS

CAUTION: The 3.8L engine has aluminum cylinder heads and requires Ford Cooling System Fluid (E2FZ-19549-A) at 50/50 mixture.

INTAKE MANIFOLDS

NOTE: Some models may differ in removal and installation of some components, due to location and accessories.

Removal (Upper & Lower)

1) Disconnect negative battery cable. Remove fuel cap to release fuel tank pressure. Drain cooling system. Remove air cleaner assembly and heat tube. Remove alternator and set aside. Disconnect throttle cable and transmission linkage (auto. trans.) at throttle body. Remove throttle mounting bracket. Disconnect cruise control unit (if equipped) and set aside.

2) Disconnect thermactor air supply hose at check valve. Disconnect flexible fuel line from steel line over valve cover. Disconnect fuel lines at injector fuel rail assembly. Remove upper radiator hose from thermostat housing. Disconnect coolant by-pass hose and heater tube at intake manifold.

3) Remove heater tube support bracket nut. Remove heater hose at rear of heater tube. Loosen hose clamp at heater elbow and remove heater tube assembly with hose and fuel lines attached. Mark and disconnect vacuum lines from fuel rail and intake manifold. Mark and disconnect necessary electrical connectors.

4) Remove A/C compressor support bracket at manifold (if equipped). Remove one PCV line from upper intake manifold. Remove second PCV line from left valve cover and lower intake manifold. Remove EGR valve assembly from upper intake manifold.

5) Mark left cylinder head spark plug wires and remove wires from spark plugs. Remove spark plug wiring retainer bracket at left front of intake manifold and set spark plug wires aside. Remove upper intake manifold bolts/studs. Remove upper intake manifold and gasket. *See Fig. 1.*

Fig. 1: Exploded View of Intake Components

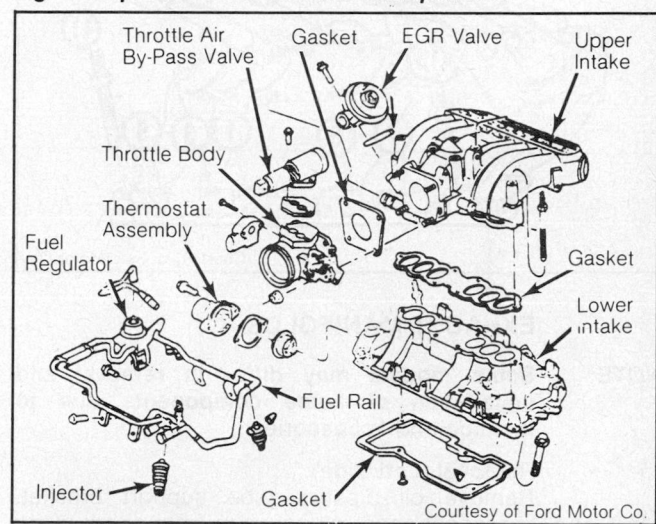

Courtesy of Ford Motor Co.

6) Remove fuel pressure from fuel rail through relief valve on fuel rail. Disconnect fuel injector wiring harness at fuel injectors and remove wiring harness. Using Spring Lock Coupling Remover (D87L-9280-A), disconnect crossover fuel hose from fuel rail.

NOTE: It may be easier to remove injectors with fuel rail assembly.

7) Remove 4 fuel rail retaining bolts. Using a side-to-side rocking motion, carefully disengage and remove fuel rail from injectors. Remove heater coolant outlet hose. Mark and remove lower intake manifold bolts. Remove lower intake manifold and gaskets.

CAUTION: If prying is required to remove lower intake manifold, use a flat screwdriver at front of manifold. Use care not to damage sealing surfaces.

Installation

1) Clean all gasket mating surfaces with a suitable solvent. Apply Contact Adhesive (D7AZ-19B508-A) on cylinder head intake gasket surfaces, to hold intake gaskets into place during installation. Position intake manifold gaskets on cylinder head.

NOTE: Assembly must occur within 15 minutes after silicone sealer is applied. Lightly coat all bolts and stud threads with oil prior to installation.

2) Apply a bead of Silicone Sealer (D6AZ-19562-B) at each corner where cylinder head joins cylinder

block. Install front and rear intake manifold end seals. Carefully lower intake manifold into position. Install intake manifold bolts in original location. Tighten to specifications in 3 steps. *See Fig. 2.* To complete installation, reverse removal procedure.

Fig. 2: Intake Manifold Tightening Sequence

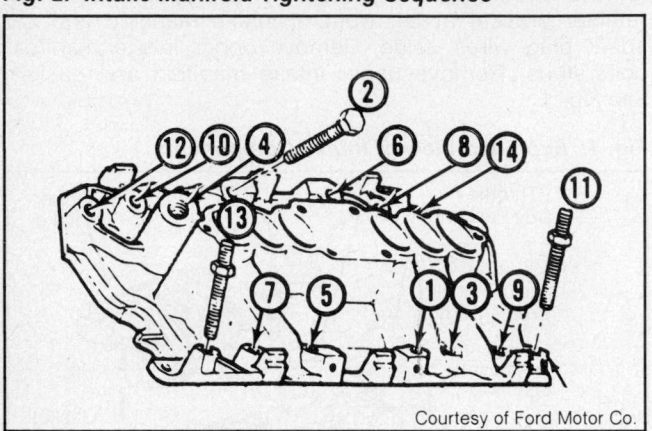

Courtesy of Ford Motor Co.

EXHAUST MANIFOLDS

NOTE: **Some models may differ in removal and installation of some components due to location and accessories.**

Removal (Left Side)

Remove oil dipstick tube support bracket. Mark and disconnect spark plugs wires from spark plugs on left side. Raise vehicle. Remove exhaust pipe from exhaust manifold. Lower vehicle. Remove exhaust manifold bolts/studs. Remove exhaust manifold and gasket.

NOTE: **Exhaust manifolds may warp slightly. Elongate necessary bolt holes, except for pilot hole.**

Installation

Clean mating surfaces on both cylinder head and exhaust manifold. Lightly oil bolt and stud threads. Position new gasket and manifold onto cylinder head. Install the lower front bolt of No. 5 cylinder for pilot. Install remaining bolts. Tighten bolts to specifications. To complete installation, reverse removal procedure.

Removal (Right Side)

1) Remove air cleaner assembly and heat tube. Disconnect thermactor hose from check valve. Mark and remove spark plug wires from spark plugs on right side. Remove spark plugs. Remove outer heat shield. Disconnect EGR tube. Raise vehicle. Remove transmission/transaxle dipstick tube. Remove thermactor downstream air tube.

2) Remove exhaust pipe from exhaust manifold. Lower vehicle. Remove exhaust manifold bolts/studs. Remove exhaust manifold and inner heat shield as an assembly. Remove gasket.

Installation

Clean mating surfaces on both cylinder head and exhaust manifold. Lightly oil bolt and stud threads. Position new gasket and manifold with inner heat shield onto cylinder head. Install the lower front bolt of No. 2 cylinder for pilot. Install remaining bolts. Tighten bolts to specifications. To complete installation, reverse removal procedure.

CYLINDER HEAD

NOTE: **Some models may differ in removal and installation of some components due to location and accessories.**

Removal

1) Disconnect negative battery. Drain cooling system. Remove air cleaner assembly with heat tube. Remove accessory drive belts. Remove oil filler cap, power steering pump/bracket assembly and A/C compressor/bracket assembly. Remove alternator assembly. Disconnect thermactor air valve from air pump. Remove accessory drive belt idler, thermactor pump assembly and PCV valve.

2) Remove upper and lower intake manifold. See INTAKE MANIFOLDS in this article. Remove valve covers. Remove exhaust manifolds. See EXHAUST MANIFOLDS in this article. Loosen rocker arm bolts enough to move rocker arm off push rod. Mark and remove pushrods. Remove cylinder head bolts, noting location of different size bolts for installation. Discard cylinder head bolts. Remove cylinder head and gasket.

Inspection

1) Thoroughly clean all gasket mating surfaces. A cleaning solvent for intake manifold gasket surfaces is required. Check dowels in cylinder block and replace if necessary. Check cylinder head(s) for cracks and warpage. Replace head if cracked.

2) Machine head if warpage exceeds .007" (.18 mm) overall. DO NOT machine more than .010" (.25 mm) from cylinder head. Clean and tap cylinder head bolt holes in cylinder block. Check cylinder block surface for warpage. See CYLINDER BLOCK ASSEMBLY in this article.

NOTE: **Always use NEW cylinder head bolts. The 3.8L engine has aluminum cylinder heads and requires Ford Cooling System Fluid (E2FZ-19549-A) at 50/50 mixture.**

Installation

1) Perform inspection before installing cylinder head(s). Place head gasket on cylinder block using dowels for guides. Install cylinder head on block. Apply a thin coat of Teflon Pipe Sealant (D8AZ-19554-A) to threads of NEW short cylinder head bolts. DO NOT apply sealant to long cylinder head bolts.

2) Install cylinder head bolts. Tighten cylinder head bolts to specifications and in sequence. See TIGHTENING SPECIFICATIONS table at end of this article. *See Fig. 3.* Dip each push rod in Oil Conditioner (D9AZ-19579-C) and install push rods in original position. Before each rocker arm is installed on push rod, rotate crankshaft until push rod is in full down position. Position rocker arm on push rod and tighten bolt to 43 INCH lbs. (5 N.m) maximum.

3.8L V6 (Cont.)

3) Repeat procedure for remaining push rods and rocker arms. Final tightening of rocker arms may be done with camshaft in any position. To complete installation, reverse removal procedure. Tighten all bolts/nuts to specifications. Change oil and filter. Fill cooling system with specified coolant. Check for leakage.

Fig. 3: Cylinder Head Tightening Sequence

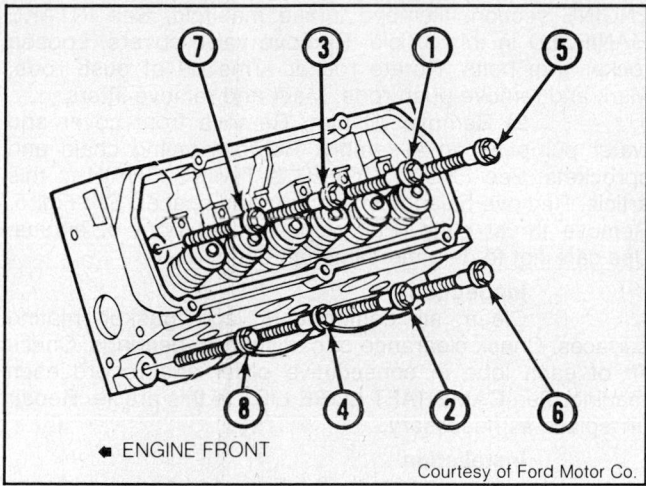

◄ ENGINE FRONT

Courtesy of Ford Motor Co.

CAMSHAFT

FRONT COVER & TIMING CHAIN

NOTE: Some models may differ in removal and installation of some components due to location and accessories.

Removal

1) Disconnect negative battery cable. Drain cooling system. Drain engine oil. Remove oil filter. Remove air cleaner assembly with heat tube. Remove accessory belts. Remove fan shroud, fan and clutch assembly. Remove water pump pulley. Leave hoses attached and remove power steering pump/bracket assembly. Leave hoses attached and remove A/C compressor/bracket assembly.

2) Disconnect coolant by-pass hose and heater hose at water pump. Remove radiator hose from thermostat housing. Mark and remove spark plug wires from spark plugs. Disconnect coil wire. Remove distributor cap and wires as an assembly. Position No. 1 cylinder at TDC on compression stroke. Ignition rotor should be at No. 1 cylinder.

CAUTION: Special care must be taken when removing crankshaft pulley and damper. They are initially balanced as a unit from the factory.

3) Mark distributor to engine and remove distributor. Raise vehicle. Mark crankshaft pulley-to-damper to ensure installation to original position. If sufficient room is available, DO NOT separate crankshaft pulley and damper. Using Crankshaft Damper Remover (T58P-6316-D) and Adapter (T82L-6316-B), remove crankshaft damper.

4) Remove lower radiator hose. Remove oil pan. See appropriate OIL PAN REMOVAL article in this

section. Lower vehicle. Remove front cover bolts. One front cover bolt is hid behind oil filter adapter. Remove front cover and water pump as an assembly. Remove gasket. Check timing chain deflection. See INSPECTION under FRONT COVER & TIMING CHAIN in this article.

5) Remove camshaft sprocket bolt and washer. Remove distributor drive gear. Remove camshaft sprocket, crankshaft sprocket and timing chain as an assembly. Pry evenly on crankshaft sprocket with 2 screwdrivers if necessary.

Inspection

1) Check timing chain deflection by removing right valve cover. Loosen No. 3 exhaust rocker arm and move off of push rod. Install dial indicator with pointer on tip of push rod. To eliminate slack on right side of timing chain, rotate crankshaft clockwise until No. 1 cylinder is on TDC. Zero dial indicator.

2) Slowly rotate crankshaft counterclockwise until initial dial indicator movement is noted. Note the number of degrees the crankshaft rotated. If the number of degrees exceeds 6 degrees replace timing chain and sprockets.

3) Clean and check all gasket mating surfaces thoroughly. Replace front cover oil seal before installing front cover. Place No. 1 cylinder on TDC before installing components.

Installation

1) Place crankshaft sprocket, camshaft sprocket and timing chain to engine block as an assembly. Timing marks on crankshaft and camshaft sprocket should be inline at closest point. *See Fig. 4.* If not aligned, rotate camshaft or crankshaft as necessary.

2) With timing chain assembly installed, install distributor drive gear. Install washer and bolt. Tighten to specifications. Thoroughly coat timing chain and sprockets with Oil Conditioner (D9AZ-19579-C). Lubricate front cover oil seal with engine oil. Apply Contact Adhesive (D7AZ-19B508-A) to engine side of front cover gasket and place gasket on engine.

3) Position front cover assembly to engine. Use dowels to help align if necessary. Install front cover bolts and tighten to specifications. To complete installation, reverse removal procedure. Tighten all bolts/nuts to specifications. Fill cooling system with specified coolant only. Check for leakage.

Fig. 4: Timing Chain Sprocket Alignment

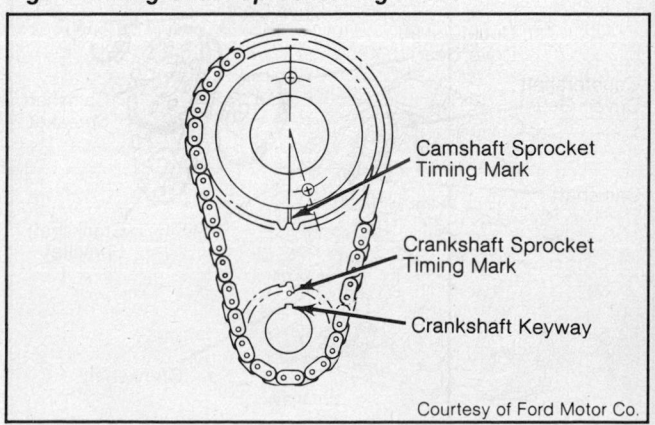

Camshaft Sprocket Timing Mark

Crankshaft Sprocket Timing Mark

Crankshaft Keyway

Courtesy of Ford Motor Co.

FRONT COVER OIL SEAL

Removal & Installation

1) Remove fan shroud and fan clutch assembly. Loosen accessory drive belt idler. Raise vehicle. Disengage accessory drive belt from crankshaft pulley. Mark crankshaft pulley-to-damper and remove pulley.

CAUTION: **Special care must be taken when removing crankshaft pulley and damper. They are initially balanced as a unit from the factory.**

2) Using Crankshaft Damper Remover (T58P-6316-D) and Adapter (T82L-6316-B), remove crankshaft damper. Pry oil seal out of front cover. Lubricate new oil seal with engine oil. Install seal with Seal Installer (T82L-6316-A and T70P-6B070-A). To complete installation, reverse removal procedure. Tighten all bolts/nuts to specifications.

CAMSHAFT

Removal (Cougar & Thunderbird)

1) Drain cooling system and remove radiator. Remove A/C condenser (if equipped). Remove grille. Remove accessory belts. Remove intake manifolds. See INTAKE MANIFOLDS in this article. Remove valve covers. Loosen rocker arm bolts. Rotate rocker arms off of push rods. Mark and remove push rods. Mark and remove lifters. Remove oil pan.

2) Remove front cover/water pump assembly. See FRONT COVER & TIMING CHAIN in this article. Remove balance shaft gear and spacer. See Fig. 5. Remove thrust plate. Pull camshaft out front of engine. Use care not to damage camshaft bearings.

Inspection

Clean all components and gasket mating surfaces. Check clearance of camshaft-to-bearings. Check lift of each lobe in consecutive order and record each reading. See CAMSHAFT LOBE LIFT in this article. Repair or replace as necessary.

Installation

Lubricate camshaft lobes and bearing surfaces with Oil Conditioner (D9AZ-19579-C). Install camshaft using care not to damage bearings and journal surfaces. To complete installation, reverse removal procedure.

Fig. 5: *Exploded View of Timing Chain Assembly*

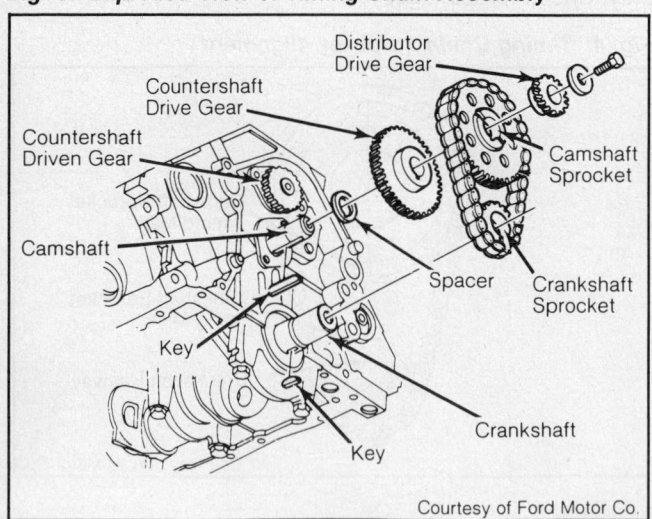

Distributor Drive Gear

Countershaft Drive Gear

Countershaft Driven Gear

Camshaft Sprocket

Camshaft

Spacer

Crankshaft Sprocket

Key

Crankshaft

Key

Courtesy of Ford Motor Co.

Ensure marked components are installed to original position. Change oil and filter. Fill cooling system with specified coolant only.

Removal & Installation (Continental, Sable & Taurus)

1) Remove engine and transaxle from vehicle. See ENGINE REMOVAL & INSTALLATION at end of ENGINE section. Remove intake manifold. See INTAKE MANIFOLD in this article. Remove valve covers. Loosen rocker arm bolts. Rotate rocker arms off of push rods. Mark and remove push rods. Mark and remove lifters.

2) Remove oil pan. Remove front cover and water pump as an assembly. Remove timing chain and sprockets. See FRONT COVER & TIMING CHAIN in this article. Remove balance shaft gear and spacer. See Fig. 5. Remove thrust plate. Pull camshaft out front of engine. Use care not to damage camshaft bearings.

Inspection

Clean all components and gasket mating surfaces. Check clearance of camshaft-to-bearings. Check lift of each lobe in consecutive order and record each reading. See CAMSHAFT LOBE LIFT in this article. Repair or replace as necessary.

Installation

Lubricate camshaft lobes and bearing surfaces with Oil Conditioner (D9AZ-19579-C). Install camshaft using care not to damage bearings and journal surfaces. To complete installation, reverse removal procedure. Ensure marked components are installed to original position. Change oil and filter. Fill cooling system with specified coolant only.

BALANCE SHAFT

Removal & Installation

1) Remove front cover and timing chain assembly. See FRONT COVER & TIMING CHAIN in this article. Mark balance shaft drive gear-to-driven gear. Remove balance shaft drive gear and spacer from camshaft. See Fig. 5.

2) Remove balance shaft thrust plate bolts. Slide balance shaft out front of engine. To install, reverse removal procedure. Ensure marks made at removal on drive and driven gears are aligned. Coat gears with Lubricant (ESE-M2C39-F).

CAMSHAFT BEARINGS

Removal

1) Remove engine and transaxle from vehicle. See ENGINE REMOVAL & INSTALLATION at end of ENGINE section. Remove transmission/transaxle. Remove clutch disc and pressure plate (if equipped). Remove flywheel/flexplate and rear cover plate. Remove camshaft. See CAMSHAFT in this article.

2) Remove crankshaft and push pistons to top of cylinder. Remove engine rear camshaft core plug. Using Camshaft Bearing Set (T65L-6250-A), remove camshaft bearings. Remove front camshaft bearing by install bearing set through rear of engine.

Installation

Camshaft bearings are available prefinished to size for standard and .015" (.38 mm) undersize journal diameters. Bearings are not interchangeable from one bore to another. Use Camshaft Bearing Set (T65L-6250-A)

3.8L V6 (Cont.)

to install camshaft bearings. Ensure bearing hole and cylinder block hole are aligned. To complete installation, reverse removal procedure.

BALANCE SHAFT BEARINGS
Removal & Installation
Remove balance shaft. See BALANCE SHAFT in this article. Use Camshaft Bearing Set (T65L-6250-A) to remove and install balance shaft bearings.

CAM LOBE LIFT
1) Loosen rocker arm bolt and rotate rocker arm off of push rod. Check lift of each lobe in consecutive order. Using a dial indicator, position point to end of push rod, in the same plane as push rod movement.
2) Rotate crankshaft until push rod is at lowest position. Zero indicator. Rotate crankshaft slowly until push rod is in fully raised position. Ensure that total lift recorded is within specifications. If any lobe is not within specifications, replace camshaft and lifters.

VALVES

VALVE ARRANGEMENT
Right Side – I-E-I-E-I-E.
Left Side – E-I-E-I-E-I.

NOTE: **"Right" and "Left" refer to right and left side of the engine NOT the vehicle.**

VALVE SEATS

NOTE: **Valve seat replacement information not available at this time. Repair valve guides if necessary, prior valve seat refacing.**

Refacing
Valve seat must be a true 44.5 degree finished angle. Use only a 60 degree angle grinding stone to remove stock from bottom of all seats. Use only a 30 degree angle grinding stone to remove stock from top of all seats. Intake and exhaust seat width should be .06-.08" (1.5-2.0 mm).

NOTE: **Lubricate valves and valve guides with heavy SF oil prior to installation. Apply Ford Poly-ethylene Grease (DOAZ-19584-A) to tip of valve stem prior to installation.**

VALVES & VALVE GUIDES
1) Mark all components prior to removal for installation reference. Clean carbon from cylinder head, using care not to damage surfaces. Remove valves. Check valve-to-guide clearance of each valve in its respective valve guide.
2) Install a valve and hold against seat. Install Valve Stem Clearance Tool (T65T-6505-H) on valve stem, until fully seated. Tighten tool set screw firmly. Allow valve to drop away from seat and tool to contact upper guide surface.
3) Install dial indicator with pointer against center portion of tool. *See Fig. 6.* Move clearance tool back and forth in-line with dial indicator pointer. Keep clearance tool on upper guide surface. Record dial indicator reading.

4) Divide dial indicator reading by 2. This total is the valve-to-guide clearance. If not within specifications, replace valve(s) with next available oversize valve. Ream valve guide until clearance with valve is within specifications. See ENGINE SPECIFICATIONS tables at end of this article.

Fig. 6: Checking Valve-to-Guide Clearance

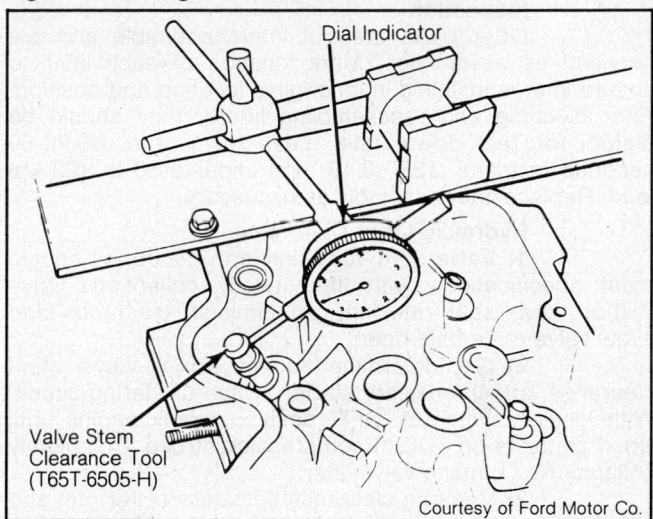

Courtesy of Ford Motor Co.

NOTE: **Always reface valve seat after valve guide has been serviced.**

5) Check valve face for pitting, cracks and runout. Reface or replace valve as necessary. Ensure valve face angle is a true 45.8 degrees. Ensure proper seat width is achieved. See ENGINE SPECIFICATIONS tables at end of this article.

VALVE SPRINGS
Inspection
1) Inspect valve springs for cracks or damage. Measure out-of-square. Maximum out-of-square is .060" (1.52 mm). Check free length. Check spring tension at specified length. See ENGINE SPECIFICATIONS tables at end of this article. Replace springs as necessary.

CAUTION: DO NOT install spacers unless necessary. Spacers used in excess of recommendations will cause premature failure.

Fig. 7: Measuring Valve Spring Installed Height

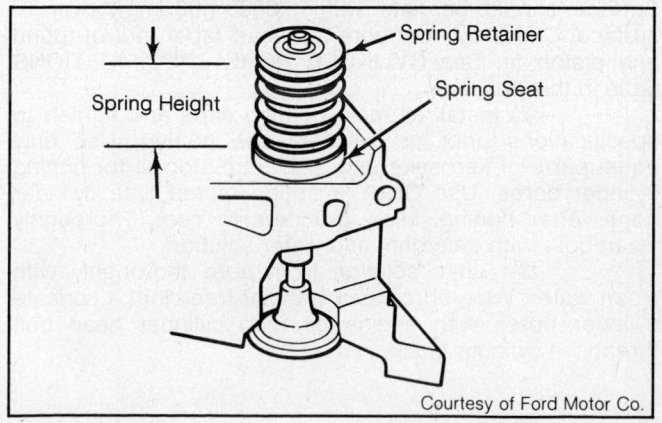

Courtesy of Ford Motor Co.

2) Measure installed height from top of spring seat to bottom of spring retainer. *See Fig. 7.* Install height should be 2.02" (51.3 mm). If assembled height is greater than specifications, install necessary .030" (.76 mm) thick spacer between cylinder head spring pad and spring seat.

HYDRAULIC LIFTER ASSEMBLY
Inspection
Lifter parts are not interchangeable and are serviced as assemblies. Mark location of each lifter to ensure lifter is installed in its original location and position. After cleaning and reassembling lifters, they should be tested for leak-down rate. Leak-down rate is 20-60 seconds to travel .125" (3.18 mm) under a 50 lb. (23 kg) load. Replace lifter assembly as necessary.

Hydraulic Lifter Clearance
1) Valve stem-to-rocker arm clearance should meet specifications with lifter totally collapsed. Valve and/or valve seat refacing can diminish clearance and allow valve to be held open.

2) To determine rocker arm-to-valve stem clearance, attach auxiliary starter switch to staring circuit. With ignition switch in "OFF" position, crank engine until No. 1 piston is on TDC of compression stroke. Completely collapse No. 1 intake valve lifter.

3) Measure clearance between rocker arm and tip of valve stem, holding lifter in collapsed position. Repeat procedure for No. 1 exhaust, No. 2 exhaust, No. 3 intake, No. 4 exhaust and No. 6 intake.

4) Rotate crankshaft 360 degrees (one revolution). Repeat procedure for No. 2 intake, No. 3 exhaust, No. 4 intake, No. 5 exhaust, No. 5 intake and No. 6 exhaust. If not within specifications, replace or grind valve stem as necessary. See COLLAPSED LIFTER CLEARANCE table in this article.

COLLAPSED LIFTER CLEARANCE

Application	In. (mm)
3.8L	.089-.189 (2.26-4.80)

CYLINDER BLOCK ASSEMBLY

CYLINDER BLOCK
Inspection
1) Using a feeler gauge and straightedge, check cylinder block head gasket surface for flatness. Surface should be flate within .003" (.08 mm) over 6" surface. Check cylinder bore for wear, taper, out-of-round and piston fit. See CYLINDER BORE SPECIFICATIONS table in this article.

2) Install all main bearing caps and tighten to specifications prior to cylinder bore honing. Use only equal parts of kerosene and SAE 20 motor oil for honing cylinder bores. Use ONLY a spring-loaded type cylinder hone. After honing, allow cylinders to cool. Thoroughly clean bore with detergent and water solution.

3) Rinse solution from bore thoroughly with clean water. Wipe bore clean with lint free cloth. Lubricate cylinder bores with engine oil. Tap cylinder head bolt threads in cylinder block.

CYLINDER BORE SPECIFICATIONS

Application	In. (mm)
Out-of-Round	.001 (.025)
Taper	.002 (.05)

PISTON PINS & RINGS

OIL PAN
See appropriate OIL PAN REMOVAL article in this section.

PISTON & ROD ASSEMBLY

NOTE: Following procedure is with cylinder head, oil pan and oil pump pick-up tube removed. Ensure components are marked for installation to original location and position.

Inspection
1) Ensure pistons and rods are measured and installed in cylinder from which it was removed. Ensure notch on piston top and hole hole on connecting rod faces front of engine. *See Fig. 8.* Check piston fit before assembling piston on rod. See FITTING PISTONS in this article.

2) Check piston pin fit. If not within specifications, remove pin and measure pin bore in piston and rod. Replace as necessary. If piston pin is to be replaced, replace piston and pin as an assembly. See ENGINE SPECIFICATIONS tables at end of this article.

Fig. 8: Piston & Rod Position

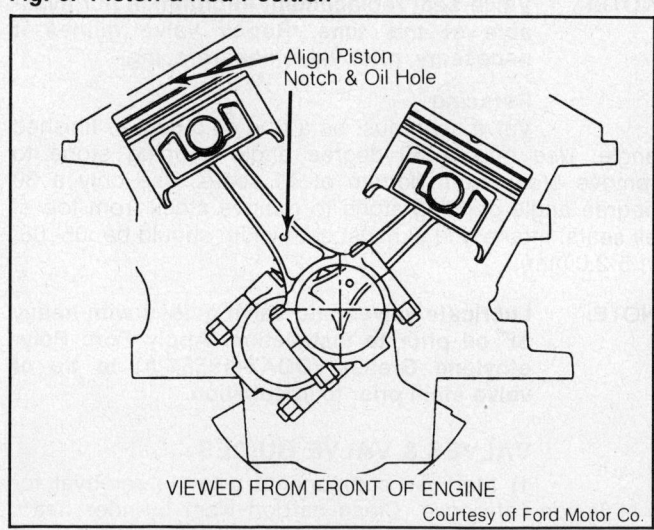

Align Piston Notch & Oil Hole

VIEWED FROM FRONT OF ENGINE

Courtesy of Ford Motor Co.

FITTING PISTONS
1) Check piston-to-bore clearance. See ENGINE SPECIFICATIONS tables at end of this article. Standard size pistons are color coded Red, Blue or Yellow on the piston dome. See PISTON SIZE CODE table in this article.

2) If bore diameter is in lower one-third of specifications, use a Red coded piston. If bore diameter is in middle one-third of specifications, use a Blue coded piston. If bore diameter is in upper one-third of specifica-

3.8L V6 (Cont.)

tions, use Yellow coded piston. The Yellow coded piston is .004" (.10 mm) oversize. Use proper size piston to acquire specified clearance. See PISTON SELECTION table in this article.

PISTON SIZE CODES

Code	In. (mm)
Red	3.8095-3.8101 (96.761-96.777)
Blue	3.8107-3.8113 (96.792-96.807)
Yellow	3.8119-3.8125 (96.822-96.836)

PISTON SELECTION

Bore Diameter In. (mm)	Piston Required Code
3.8110-3.8122 (96.799-96.830)	Red
3.8122-3.8134 (96.830-96.860)	Blue
3.8134-3.8146 (96.860-96.891)	Yellow

FITTING RINGS

1) Select proper rings for bore diameter. Place ring square in cylinder bore, below normal ring wear area. Measure the ring end gap. If ring end gap is less than specifications, remove necessary amount from end of ring. If ring gap is greater than specifications, use a different set of rings. Ensure rings are installed in cylinder bore in which they were measured.

2) Check side clearance of rings after installing on piston. Ensure clearance is within specifications around entire circumference. If lower lands of piston have high steps, replace piston. Replace piston and rings if side clearance is not within specifications. Properly set ring ends on piston before installing pistons into cylinder. *See Fig. 9.* See ENGINE SPECIFICATIONS tables at end of this article.

Fig. 9: Piston Ring End Gap Spacing

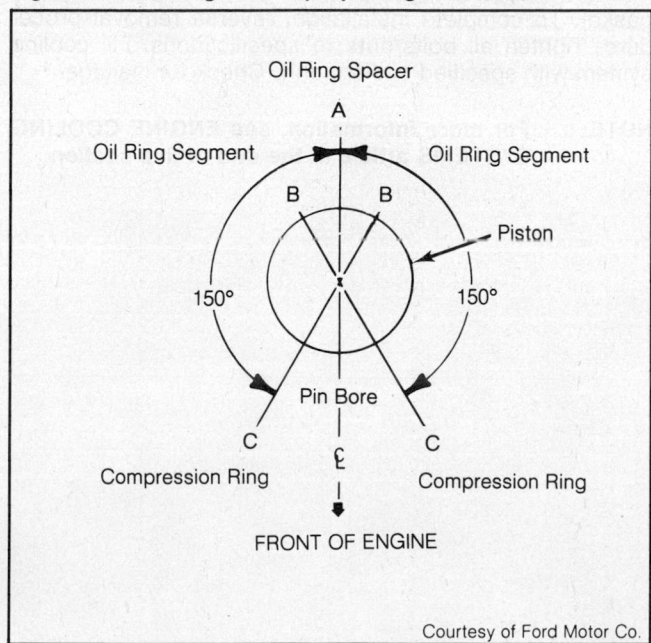

Oil Ring Spacer

A

Oil Ring Segment

Oil Ring Segment

B   B

Piston

150°   150°

Pin Bore

C   C

Compression Ring   Compression Ring

FRONT OF ENGINE

Courtesy of Ford Motor Co.

CRANKSHAFT & ROD BEARINGS

NOTE: Following procedures are with oil pan and oil pump pick-up tube removed. Only one bearing at a time should be checked or replaced.

MAIN BEARING

Inspection

Use Plastigage method and check clearance between main bearing and crankshaft journal. Check crankshaft for nicks, scratches, scores and wear. If not within specifications, replace bearings. Machine or replace crankshaft as necessary. See ENGINE SPECIFICATIONS tables at end of this article. Check crankshaft end play. See THRUST BEARING ALIGNMENT in this article. Replace thrust bearing as necessary.

CAUTION: The 3.8L V6 engine crankshaft has specially contoured journal fillets which are deep rolled for fatique strength improvement. They should not be machined.

CONNECTING ROD BEARINGS

Inspection

Use Plastigage method and check clearance between rod bearing and crankshaft. If specified clearance cannot be obtained with standard bearings, try a standard bearing in combination with an undersize bearing. Standard bearings may be used with a .001" (.025 mm) or .002" (.050 mm) undersize bearing. Tighten all bolts/nuts to specifications. Desired clearance is the minimum of the specified clearance. See ENGINE SPECIFICATIONS tables at end of this article.

THRUST BEARING ALIGNMENT

Inspection

Install dial indicator on front of engine with pointer on end of crankshaft. Pry crankshaft fully rear and zero indicator. Pry crankshaft fully forward and note reading. If end play exceeds specifications, replace thrust bearing. If end play is less than specifications, remove thrust bearing and inspect surfaces. Replace as necessary. See ENGINE SPECIFICATIONS tables at end of this article.

REAR CRANKSHAFT OIL SEAL

Removal

1) Remove transaxle. On manual transaxle models, remove clutch disc, pressure plate and flywheel. See appropriate CLUTCHES article in this section. On automatic transaxle models, remove flexplate. See appropriate TRANSMISSION SERVICING article in this section.

2) Use an awl and punch a hole into the metal surface of the seal. Use care not to damage sealing surfaces. Install Jet Plug Remover (T77L-9533-B) and remove oil seal.

Installation

Check crankshaft seal surface for wear and replace as necessary. Coat crankshaft seal area and lip of oil seal with engine oil. Using Rear Crankshaft Seal Replacer (T81P-6701-A), install oil seal. Tighen bolts on seal replacer evenly, to ensure seal is installed squarely. To complete installation, reverse removal procedure.

Ford Motor Co. Engines

3.8L V6 (Cont.)

FRONT CRANKSHAFT OIL SEAL

Removal & Installation

See FRONT COVER & TIMING CHAIN in this article.

ENGINE OILING

ENGINE OILING SYSTEM

The lubrication is a force-feed type. The oil is supplied under full pressure to crankshaft, connecting rods, camshaft bearing and valve lifters. A controlled volume of oil is supplied to rocker arms and push rods. All other moving parts are lubricated by splash or gravity flow.

CRANKCASE CAPACITY

Crankcase capacity is 4 qts. (3.8L) without filter and 4.5 qts. (4.3L) with filter change. DO NOT change oil without filter.

NORMAL OIL PRESSURE (HOT)

Normal oil pressure is 40-60 psi (2.8-4.2 kg/cm²) at 2500 RPM.

OIL PUMP

Removal & Installation

Remove oil filter. Remove oil pump-to-front cover bolts. Remove oil pump assembly. Replace "O" ring and lubricate with engine oil. Position oil pump to front cover. Install oil pump mounting bolts and tighten to specifications.

Inspection

With oil pump removed, place a straightedge across surface of housing. Use a feeler gauge and check clearance to the gears. Measure thickness of gear with micrometer. Measure depth of gear pocket in the housing. Measure diameter of gear with micrometer. Measure gear pocket diameter. Measure clearance between gear and pocket wall. If not within specifications, replace components as necessary. See OIL PUMP SPECIFICATIONS table in this article.

OIL PUMP SPECIFICATIONS

Application	In. (mm)
Inner-to-Outer Rotor	.010 (.254)
Gear Backlash	.008-.012 (.20-.31)
Gear Diameter	1.498-1.500 (38.05-38.10)
Gear Height	.0004-.0033 (.010-.084)
Gear Pocket Depth	1.200-1.202 (30.48-30.53)
Gear Pocket Diameter	1.5047-1.5079 (38.219-38.301)
Gear Thickness	1.199-1.200 (30.46-30.48)
Drive Shaft-to-Housing	.0015-.0030 (.038-.076)
Relief Valve-to-Bore	.0017-.0029 (.043-.074)
Relief Valve Spring Tension	1

1 – Spring tension should be 15.2-17.1 lbs. @ 1.20" (6.9-7.8 kg @ 30.5 mm).

ENGINE COOLING

CAUTION: The 3.8L engine has aluminum cylinder heads and requires Ford Cooling System Fluid (E2FZ-19549-A) at 50/50 mixture.

WATER PUMP

Removal & Installation (Cougar & Thunderbird)

1) Drain cooling system. Disconnect negative battery cable. Remove air cleaner and heater tube assembly. Remove fan clutch assembly and shroud. Loosen accessory drive belt idler. Remove accessory belts and water pump pulley. Remove power steering pump and bracket assembly with hoses attached (if equipped).

2) Remove A/C compressor front support bracket (if equipped). Leave A/C compressor in place. Disconnect coolant by-pass and heater hose from water pump. Remove water pump attaching bolts. Remove water pump assembly.

3) Clean gasket mating surfaces and replace gasket. To complete installation, reverse removal procedure. Tighten all bolts/nuts to specifications. Fill cooling system with specified coolant only. Check for leakage.

Removal & Installation (Continental, Sable & Taurus)

1) Drain cooling system. Disconnect negative battery cable. Remove lower nut on both right-hand engine mounts. Carefully raise engine. Loosen accessory belt idler. Remove accessory belts and and water pump pulley. Remove air suspension pump (if equipped).

2) Remove power steering pump and bracket assembly with hoses attached (if equipped). Remove A/C compressor front support bracket and leave compressor in place. Disconnect coolant by-pass and heater hose from water pump. Remove water pump attaching bolts. Remove water pump and gasket.

3) Clean gasket mating surfaces and replace gasket. To complete installation, reverse removal procedure. Tighten all bolts/nuts to specifications. Fill cooling system with specified coolant only. Check for leakage.

NOTE: For more information, see ENGINE COOLING SYSTEMS article at the end of this section.

3.8L V6 (Cont.)

TIGHTENING SPECIFICATIONS

Application	Ft. Lbs. (N.m)
Camshaft Sprocket Bolt	15-22 (20-30)
Continental	30-36 (41-49)
Cylinder Head Bolt	
Step 1	37 (50)
Step 2	45 (61)
Step 3	52 (70)
Step 4	59 (80)
Step 5	Back off 2-3 turns
Step 6	Repeat steps 1-4
Connecting Rod Nut	31-36 (42-49)
Exhaust Manifold Bolt	15-22 (20-30)
Flywheel-to-Crankshaft Bolt	54-64 (73-87)
Front Cover-to-Cylinder Block Bolt	15-22 (20-30)
Intake Manifold Bolt	
Step 1	7 (10)
Step 2	15 (20)
Step 3	24 (32)
Main Bearing Cap Bolt	65-74 (88-100)
Oil Pump-to-Front Cover	
Large 4 Bolts	17-23 (23-31)
Remaining Bolts	6-8 (8-11)

TIGHTENING SPECIFICATIONS (Cont.)

Application	Ft. Lbs. (N.m)
Pulley-to-Damper Bolt	[1] 20-28 (27-38)
Rocker Arm Bolt	
Step 1	5-11 (7-15)
Step 2	18-26 (25-35)
Damper-to-Crankshaft Bolt	93-121 (126-165)
Continental	104-132 (141-180)
Water Pump Bolt	15-22 (20-30)

Application	INCH Lbs.(N.m)
Fuel Rail Mount Bolt	71-104 (8-11.7)
Oil Pan-to-Cylinder Block Bolt	84-108 (10-12.2)
Spark Plug	60-132 (7-15)
Valve Cover Bolt	71-101 (8-11.4)
Water Pump Pulley Bolt	71-101 (8-11.4)

[1] – Damper and pulley are balanced as a unit at the factory and must be installed to original position.

ENGINE SPECIFICATIONS

GENERAL SPECIFICATIONS

Year	DISPLACEMENT		Fuel System	HP@RPM	Torque Ft. Lbs.@RPM	Compr. Ratio	BORE		STROKE	
	Cu. In.	Liters					In.	mm	In.	mm
1988	232	3.8	EFI	140 @ 3800	215 @ 2400	8.7:1	3.81	96.8	3.39	86

VALVES

Engine Size & Valve	Head Diam. In. (mm)	Face Angle	Seat Angle	Seat Width In. (mm)	Stem Diameter In. (mm)	Stem Clearance In. (mm)	Valve Lift In. (mm)
1.9L							
Intake	[1] 1.54 (39.1)	45°	45°	.069-.091 (1.75-2.32)	.3159-.3167 (8.025-8.043)	.0008-.0027 (.020-.069)	.468 [2] (11.89)
Exhaust	[1] 1.34 (34.0)	45°	45°	.069-.091 (1.75-2.32)	.3149-.3156 (7.996-8.017)	.0018-.0037 (.046-.095)	[2] .468 (11.89)

[1] – On EFI HO models, intake diameter is 1.65" (41.9 mm) and exhaust diameter is 1.46" (37.1 mm).
[2] – On EFI HO models, intake and exhaust is .396" (10.06 mm).

PISTONS, PINS & RINGS

Engine	PISTONS	PINS		RINGS		
	Clearance In. (mm)	Piston Fit In. (mm)	Rod Fit In. (mm)	Ring No.	End Gap In. (mm)	Side Clearance In. (mm)
3.8L	.0014-.0032 (.036-.081)	.0002-.0005 (.005-.012)	Press Fit	1 & 2	.01-.02 (.25-.50)	.0016-.0037 (.040-.094)
				3	.015-.058 (.38-1.48)	.....

Ford Motor Co. Engines
3.8L V6 (Cont.)

ENGINE SPECIFICATIONS (Cont.)

CRANKSHAFT MAIN & CONNECTING ROD BEARINGS

Engine	MAIN BEARINGS				CONNECTING ROD BEARINGS		
	Journal Diam. In. (mm)	Clearance In. (mm)	Thrust Bearing	Crankshaft End Play In. (mm)	Journal Diam. In. (mm)	Clearance In. (mm)	Side Play In. (mm)
3.8L	2.5190-2.5198 (63.98-64.00)	.0010-.0014 (.025-.035)	No. 3	.004-.008 (.10-.20)	2.3103-2.3111 (58.68-58.70)	.0010-.0014 (.025-.035)	.0047-.0114 (.12-.29)

CAMSHAFT

Engine	Journal Diam. In. (mm)	Clearance In. (mm)	Lobe Lift In. (mm)
3.8L	2.0505-2.0515 (52.082-52.108)	.001-.003 (.02-.07)	[1]

VALVE SPRINGS

Engine	Free Length In. (mm)	PRESSURE Lbs. @ In. (Kg @ mm)	
		Valve Closed	Valve Open
3.8L	2.02 (51.3)	73@1.70 (33@43.1)	190@1.28 (86@32.5)

[1] – Intake is 2.40" (60.1 mm), Exhaust is 2.41" (61.1 mm).

5.0L & 5.8L V8

**Cougar, Crown Victoria,
Grand Marquis, Mark VII LSC,
Mustang, Thunderbird, Town Car**

NOTE: For engine repair procedures not covered in this article, see ENGINE OVERHAUL PROCEDURES article at beginning of this section.

ENGINE CODING

ENGINE IDENTIFICATION

The engine may be identified by the Vehicle Identification Number (VIN) stamped on a metal tab attached to the instrument panel near the windshield on driver's side of vehicle. The VIN number is also stamped on both Safety Certification Decals, mounted on the left front door lock panel and on the Engine Identification Label, mounted on the valve cover. The VIN number contains 17 characters. The 8th character identifies the engine and the 10th character establishes the model year.

The 5.0L is available in standard output and High Output (HO). The 5.0L HO engine has unique throttle body assembly, intake manifold assembly, cylinder head assemblies, pistons, camshaft, valve assemblies and exhaust manifolds. The standard and HO components are not interchangeable. The 5.8L HO engine is available in Police models.

ENGINE CODES

Engine	Code
5.0L (302") SEFI	F
5.0L HO (302") SEFI	E
5.8L HO (351") 2-Bbl.	G

NOTE: The firing order on 5.0L and 5.0L HO engines are different. See Fig. 1.

Fig. 1: Firing Order

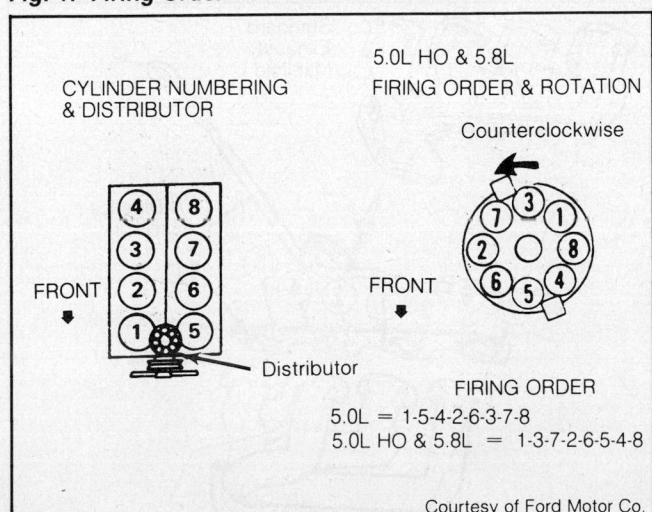

CYLINDER NUMBERING & DISTRIBUTOR

5.0L HO & 5.8L FIRING ORDER & ROTATION

Counterclockwise

FRONT

4 8
3 7
2 6
1 5

Distributor

FRONT

7 3 1
2 8
6 5 4

FIRING ORDER
5.0L = 1-5-4-2-6-3-7-8
5.0L HO & 5.8L = 1-3-7-2-6-5-4-8

Courtesy of Ford Motor Co.

ENGINE REMOVAL

See ENGINE REMOVAL & INSTALLATION at end of ENGINE section.

CYLINDER HEAD & MANIFOLDS

INTAKE MANIFOLD
Removal

1) Disconnect negative battery cable. Drain cooling system. Disconnect PCV system. Disconnect evaporative purge hoses. On 5.8L engines, remove air cleaner assembly and disconnect automatic choke heat tube. Disconnect throttle cable and speed control linkage. Mark and disconnect vacuum lines at intake manifold.

2) Remove automatic transmission kickdown linkage (if equipped). Mark and disconnect spark plug wires from spark plugs. Remove distributor cap and spark plug wires as an assembly.

3) On 5.0L engines, remove fuel tank cap to relieve tank pressure. Locate pressure relief valve on metal fuel line at left front corner of engine. Connect Pressure Gauge (T80L-9974-A) to relief valve and release fuel pressure. Thoroughly clean couplings before disconnecting. Disconnect fuel supply and return lines using Spring Lock Coupling Tool (D87L-9280-A or D87L-9280-B).

4) On 5.8L engines, remove fuel tank cap to relieve tank pressure. Remove fuel inlet line at carburetor. Disconnect vacuum hose at distributor.

5) On all engines, remove electrical connectors at distributor. Mark distributor-to-engine location and remove distributor assembly. Disconnect upper radiator hose from engine. Disconnect coolant temperature sending unit wire. Disconnect coolant by-pass hose from intake manifold.

6) On 5.0L engines, disconnect coolant hoses at throttle body. Mark and disconnect wires at solenoids

Fig. 2: 5.0L Intake Manifolds & Tightening Specifications

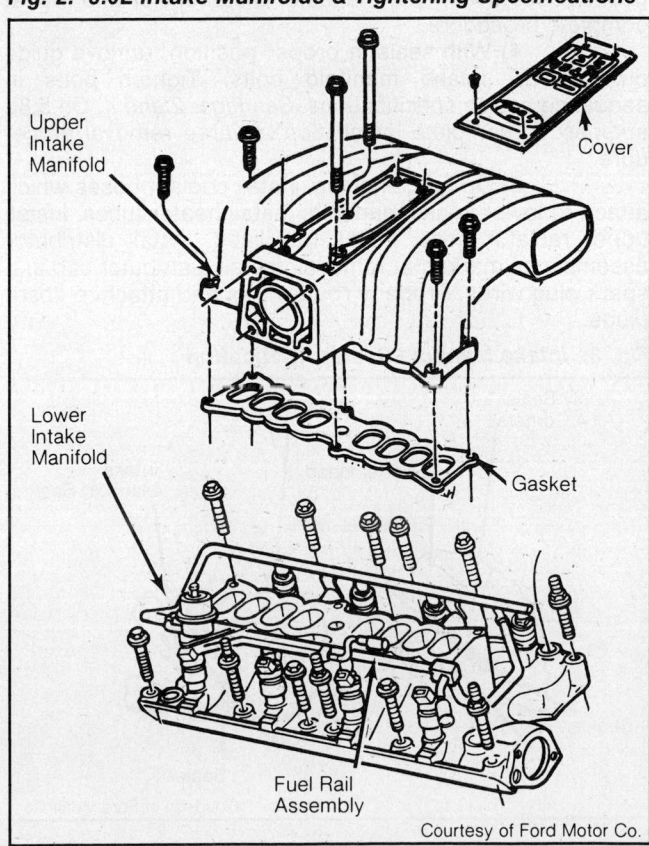

Upper Intake Manifold

Cover

Lower Intake Manifold

Gasket

Fuel Rail Assembly

Courtesy of Ford Motor Co.

Ford Motor Co. Engines

5.0L & 5.8L V8 (Cont.)

and EGR sensors. Disconnect injector wire connections, and fuel charging assembly wiring.

7) On 5.8L engines, disconnect EGR cooler T-fitting from heater return hose. Disconnect crankcase vent hose assembly at valve cover. Remove intake manifold retaining bolts. Remove intake manifold and carburetor as an assembly. Remove intake manifold gaskets and seals.

8) On 5.0L engines, disconnect crankcase vent hose assembly at rear of lower intake manifold. Disconnect purge hose. Remove upper intake manifold retaining bolts. *See Fig. 2.* Remove upper intake manifold and gasket. Remove lower intake manifold retaining bolts. Remove lower intake manifold, gaskets and seals.

Installation

1) Clean gasket mating surfaces using solvents such as lacquer thinner or chlorothane. Apply a .125" (3.18 mm) bead of Silicone Rubber Sealer (D6AZ-19562-A) to adjoining surfaces of cylinder head-to-cylinder block. *See Fig. 3.* Install front and rear seals. Install intake manifold gaskets. Ensure holes in gasket and cylinder block are properly aligned.

NOTE: Install components within 15 minutes after sealer is applied, as sealer will vulcanize within this time.

2) Apply a .063" (1.60 mm) bead of Silicone Rubber Sealer (D6AZ-19562-A) to outer ends of each intake manifold seal for the full width. *See Fig. 3.* Install 4 guide pins on front and rear of both cylinder heads. Carefully lower intake manifold into position (the lower intake manifold on 5.0L engines).

3) Check position of front and rear seals by running finger around seal area. If seals are not in position, remove intake manifold. Clean sealer and repeat complete procedure.

4) With seals in proper position, remove guide pins. Install intake manifold bolts. Tighten bolts in sequence and to specifications. *See Figs. 2 and 4.* On 5.8L engines, to complete installation, reverse removal procedure.

5) On 5.0L engines, install coolant hoses which attach to lower intake manifold. Install heater tubes. Install upper radiator hose. Install fuel lines. Install distributor assembly as marked at removal. Install distributor cap and spark plug wires. Properly route wires and attach to spark plugs.

Fig. 3: Intake Manifold Sealer Application

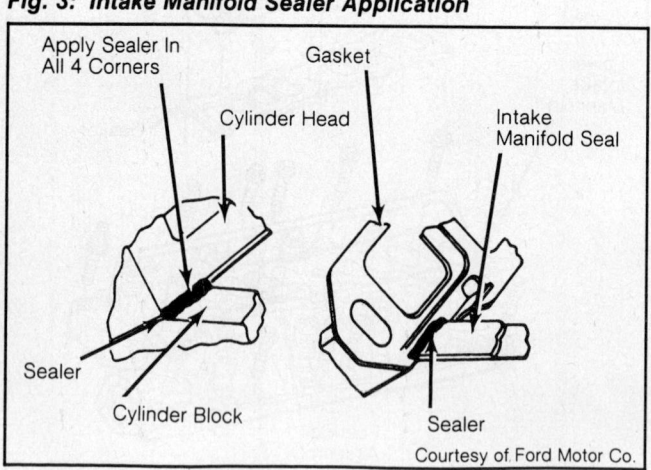

Apply Sealer In All 4 Corners — Gasket — Cylinder Head — Intake Manifold Seal — Sealer — Cylinder Block — Sealer

Courtesy of Ford Motor Co.

6) Clean upper and lower intake manifold gasket surfaces with solvents such as lacquer thinner or chlorothane. Position gasket on lower intake manifold surface. Install upper intake manifold assembly. Install bolts and tighten in sequence to specifications. To complete installation, reverse removal procedure. Fill cooling system with specified coolant. Check for leakage.

Fig. 4: 5.8L Intake Manifold Tightening Sequence

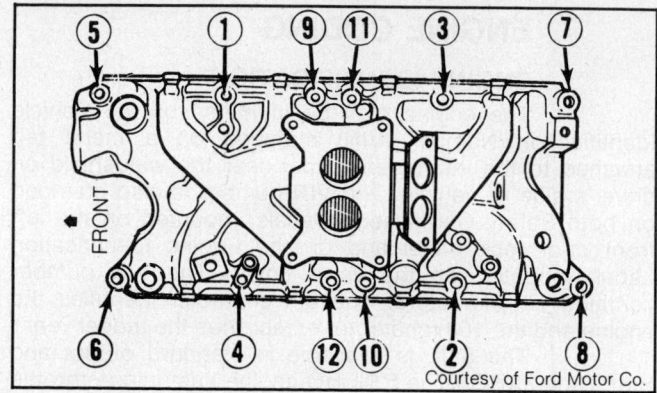

Courtesy of Ford Motor Co.

EXHAUST MANIFOLD

Removal

1) On right side exhaust manifold, remove the air cleaner-to-throttle body tube and thermactor hardware. Disconnect updraft reed valve hose. On left side manifold, remove the oil dipstick tube assembly and air cleaner assembly. On both sides, disconnect the exhaust manifold from inlet pipe.

2) Mark and remove spark plug wires and spark plugs. Disconnect the exhaust gas oxygen (EGO) sensor. On right side, remove nut retaining updraft pipe to exhaust manifold. Remove exhaust manifold attaching bolts and washers. Remove exhaust manifold assembly. On 5.0L HO engines, remove exhaust manifold gasket.

Fig. 5: Exhaust Manifold Tightening Sequence

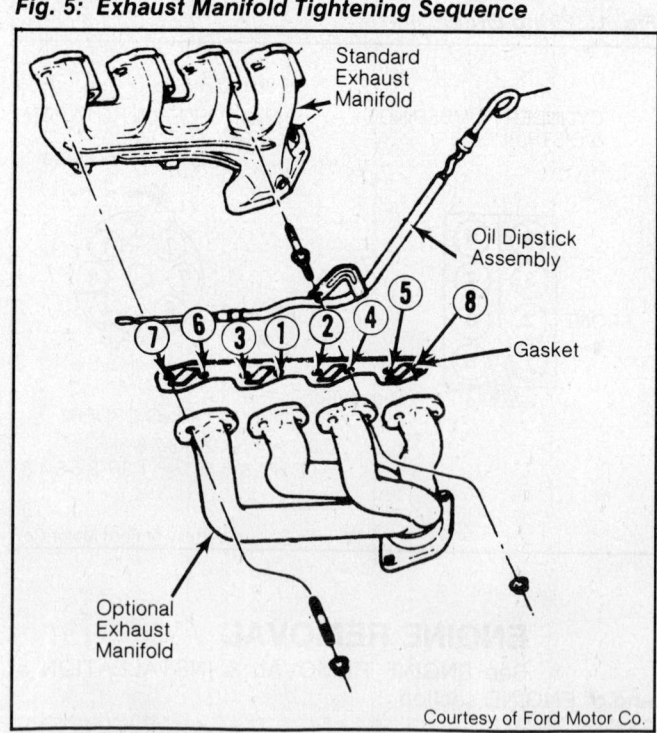

Standard Exhaust Manifold — Oil Dipstick Assembly — Gasket — Optional Exhaust Manifold

Courtesy of Ford Motor Co.

5.0L & 5.8L V8 (Cont.)

NOTE: The 5.0L HO engine is equipped with exhaust manifold gaskets and the 5.0L and 5.8L are not.

Installation

Clean mating surfaces of exhaust manifold and cylinder head thoroughly. Clean exhaust manifold flange and inlet pipe mating surface. On 5.0L HO engines, install exhaust manifold gasket. Install exhaust manifold and retaining bolts with washers. Tighten bolts in sequence and to specifications. See Fig. 5. To complete installation, reverse removal procedure.

CYLINDER HEAD

NOTE: Cylinder head should only be removed when engine is cold. Allow sufficient cool down time for hot engine before performing service.

Removal

1) Disconnect negative battery cable. Remove intake manifold(s). See INTAKE MANIFOLD in this article. Remove valve cover attaching bolts and remove valve covers. Remove accessory drive belts. Remove A/C compressor with hoses attached (if equipped). Remove power steering and bracket assembly with hoses attached (if equipped).

2) Remove thermactor crossover pipe from rear of cylinder heads. Remove alternator mounting bracket bolt and spacer. Remove fuel line from clip at right front cylinder head (if equipped). Disconnect exhaust manifold(s) from inlet pipe(s).

3) Loosen rocker arm bolts. Rotate rocker arms off push rods. Mark and remove push rods to ensure installation to original location. Mark and remove cylinder head retaining bolts. On some models, it may be necessary to remove exhaust manifold to gain access to lower cylinder head bolts. See EXHAUST MANIFOLD in this article.

4) Lift cylinder head off of engine block. If prying is necessary, use a flat tip screwdriver and pry between outer front boss on cylinder head and engine block. Use care not to damage gasket surfaces. Remove head gasket(s).

Inspection

Clean gasket mating surfaces using solvents such as lacquer thinner or chlorothane. Clean all carbon from cylinder head combustion chambers. Clean and tap cylinder head bolt threads in cylinder block. With cylinder head and block gasket surface thoroughly cleaned, check cylinder head and block for warpage. Cylinder head and block warpage should not exceed .0029" (.076 mm) in a 6" area or .006" (.152 mm) overall. DO NOT machine more than .010" (.254 mm) off of original cylinder head surface.

Installation

1) Perform inspection prior to installation. Position new head gasket over dowels on cylinder block. Install cylinder head assembly. Tighten head bolts in 2 or 3 steps and in sequence. See Fig. 6.

NOTE: When cylinder head bolts have been tightened, it is recommended to recheck for proper torque after extended operation.

2) Install exhaust manifolds (if removed). See EXHAUST MANIFOLD in this article. Apply Polyethylene

Grease (DOAZ-19584-A) to both ends of push rod and install as marked at removal. On roller type lifters, ensure collar on push rods are up. Apply Polyethylene Grease (DOAZ-19584-A) to tip of valve stem.

3) If valve train components are not replaced, complete installation by reversing removal procedure. If any valve train component is replaced, collapse lifters and check clearance. See HYDRAULIC LIFTERS in this article. To complete installation, reverse removal procedure. Tighten bolts/nuts to specifications. Change oil and filter. Fill cooling system with specified coolant. Check for leakage.

Fig. 6: Cylinder Head Tightening Sequence

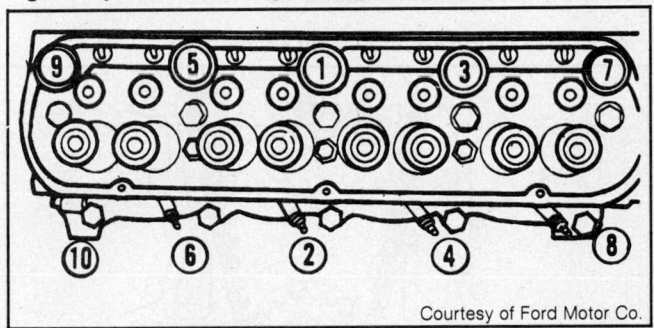

Courtesy of Ford Motor Co.

CAMSHAFT

FRONT COVER & TIMING CHAIN
Removal

1) Disconnect negative battery cable. Drain cooling system. Remove air inlet tube (if equipped). Remove fan shroud from radiator and position over cooling fan. Remove fan and clutch assembly. Remove A/C idler pulley and belt (if equipped). Remove remaining accessory belts. Remove accessory brackets which are attached to front cover and water pump.

2) Remove water pump pulley. Disconnect lower radiator hose, by-pass hose and heater hose from water pump. Drain engine oil. Remove crankshaft damper pulley. Remove damper retaining bolt and washer. Using Crankshaft Damper Remover (T58D-6316-D), remove damper from crankshaft. On 5.8L engines, remove fuel lines from fuel pump and remove fuel pump from front cover.

3) Remove bolts retaining oil pan to front cover. Loosen front cover bolts enough for a thin knife blade to cut oil pan gasket flush at engine block. This will allow front portion of oil pan gasket to be removed with front cover without damage to remaining oil pan gasket.

NOTE: Cover the oil pan cavity after front cover is removed to prevent foreign material from entering oil pan.

4) Remove front cover bolts. Remove front cover and water pump as an assembly. Remove front cover gasket. Mark and remove spark plug wires from spark plugs. Remove spark plugs. Check timing chain deflection. See TIMING CHAIN DEFLECTION in this article.

5) Rotate crankshaft and align timing marks on camshaft and crankshaft sprockets. See Fig. 8. Remove

bolt, washer and fuel pump eccentric (if equipped) from camshaft. Remove camshaft sprocket, crankshaft sprocket and timing chain assembly. Remove front cover oil seal.

Timing Chain Deflection

1) Rotate crankshaft counterclockwise (viewed from front), to take up slack on left side of timing chain. Use the block reference point and measure to the chain. See Fig. 7. Record the distance.

2) Rotate crankshat clockwise to take up slack on right side of timing chain. Force left side of timing chain out with fingers and measure distance between reference point and chain. The deflection is the difference between the 2 measurements. Replace timing chain and both sprockets if deflection exceeds .50" (12.7 mm).

Fig. 7: Measuring Timing Chain Deflection

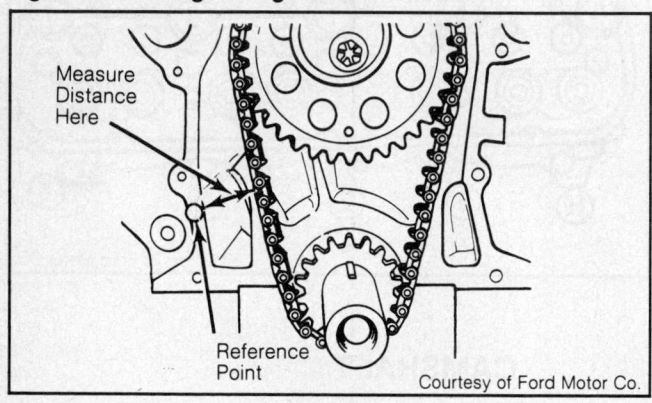

Courtesy of Ford Motor Co.

Fig. 8: Timing Mark Alignment

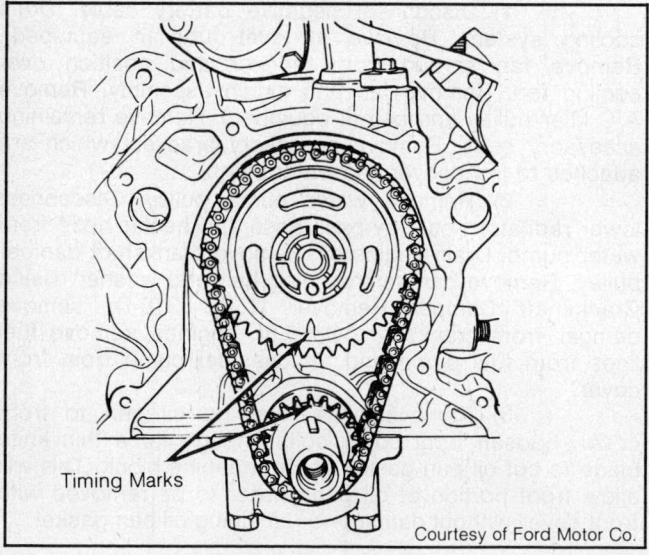

Courtesy of Ford Motor Co.

Installation

1) Clean all gasket mating surfaces. Position camshaft sprocket, crankshaft sprocket and timing chain assembly on engine. Align timing marks properly. See Fig. 8. Install fuel pump eccentric (if equipped). Install bolt and washer. Tighten to specifications. Lubricate timing chain assembly with new engine oil.

2) Install a new front cover oil seal. Apply Contact Adhesive (D7AZ-19508-A) to oil pan gasket and saddle seal surface to hold gasket and seal into position. Cut required sections of oil pan gasket and install on oil

pan. Intstall saddle seal on oil pan. Apply Silicone Sealer (D6AZ-19562-A) to adjoining surface of gasket-to-block.

3) Coat front cover and cylinder block gasket mating surfaces with Perfect Sealing Compound (B5A-19554-A) and position gasket on block. Using Front Cover Aligner (T61P-6019-B), install front cover. Coat threads of front cover bolts with Pipe Sealant Teflon (D8AZ-19554-A) and install bolts while pushing in on aligner. Tighten bolts to 9-11 ft. lbs. (12-15 N.m).

4) Retighten all front cover bolts to final specifications. To complete installation, reverse removal procedure. Use Crankshaft Damper Replacer (T52L-6306-AEE) to install damper. Fill and bleed cooling system. Add engine oil to proper level. Check for leakage. Check and adjust ignition timing.

FRONT COVER OIL SEAL

Removal & Installation

Remove fan shroud from radiator and place over cooling fan. Remove fan and shroud. Remove accessory drive belts. Remove crankshaft damper pulley. Remove damper attaching bolt and washer. Remove damper with Crankshaft Damper Remover (T58D-6316-D). Install Front Cover Seal Remover (T70P-6B070-B) and remove oil seal. Coat new seal with Lubriplate. Install seal with Front Cover Seal Installer (T70P-6B070-A). To complete installation, reverse removal procedure.

CAMSHAFT

NOTE: **On some engines the hydraulic lifters are a roller type. The roller type lifters must be installed so roller rotates on camshaft in the same direction as before they were removed.**

Removal

1) Drain cooling system and remove radiator, A/C condenser and necessary grille components. Remove intake manifold. See INTAKE MANIFOLD in this article. Remove timing chain assembly. See FRONT COVER & TIMING CHAIN in this article. Remove valve covers. Loosen rocker arm bolts enough to rotate rocker arms off of push rods.

2) Mark and remove push rods. Mark and remove lifters. Check camshaft end play with camshaft sprocket attached. See CAMSHAFT END PLAY table in this article. Remove camshaft thrust plate. Remove camshaft out front of vehicle.

CAMSHAFT END PLAY

Application	In. (mm)
5.0L & 5.0L HO	.0050-.0055 (.127-.140)
5.8L	.001-.007 (.025-.178)
Service Limit All	.009 (.229)

Inspection

Check camshaft lobe lift. See CAMSHAFT LOBE LIFT in this article. Check camshaft-to-camshaft bearing clearance. Clearance should be .001-.003" (.025-.076 mm). If not within specifications, replace bearings and/or camshaft as necessary. See CAMSHAFT BEARINGS in this article. Check lifter and replace as necessary. See HYDRAULIC LIFTERS in this article.

Installation

Oil camshaft journals with heavy SF engine oil. Apply Polyethylene Grease (DOAZ-19584-A) to camshaft

5.0L & 5.8L V8 (Cont.)

lobes. Install camshaft in reverse of removal. Install thrust plate. Install a new thrust plate if end play was not within specifications. Recheck end play. To complete installation, reverse removal procedure.

CAMSHAFT BEARINGS

Removal

Remove engine from vehicle. Remove camshaft. See CAMSHAFT in this article. Remove clutch disc, pressure plate and flywheel (if equipped). Remove flexplate (if equipped). Remove oil pan. Remove crankshaft. Push all piston assemblies to top of cylinders. Remove rear camshaft bore plug. Use Camshaft Bearing Set (T65L-6250-A) to remove and install camshaft bearings.

NOTE: **Camshaft bearings are available in standard and .015" (.38 mm) oversize. Bearings are not interchangeable from one bore to another.**

Installation

Use camshaft bearing set and install bearings. Align camshaft bearing oil hole with oil hole in block bore. Install front bearing .005-.020" (.13-.51 mm) below front face of block. *See Fig. 9.* To complete installation, reverse removal procedure.

Fig. 9: Installation of Front Camshaft Bearing

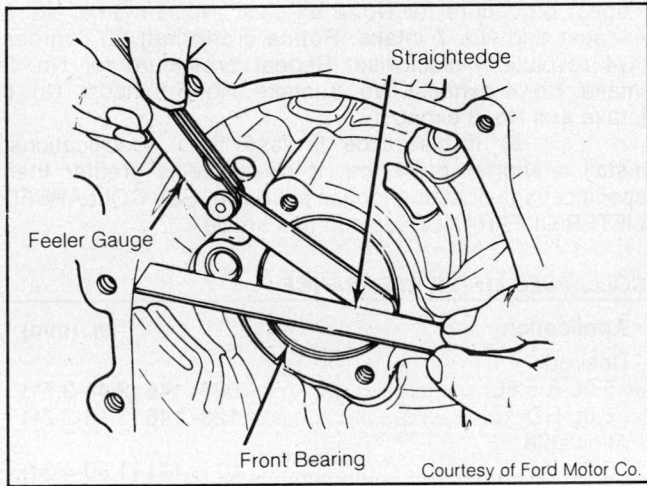

Courtesy of Ford Motor Co.

CAMSHAFT LOBE LIFT

With Camshaft Installed

1) Loosen rocker arm bolt and rotate rocker arm off of push rod. Check lift of each lobe in consecutive order. Using a dial indicator, position point on end of push rod, in the same plane as push rod movement.

2) Rotate crankshaft until push rod is at lowest position. Zero indicator. Rotate crankshaft slowly until push rod is in fully raised position. Record reading and proceed to remaining lobes. If any lobe is not within specifications, replace camshaft and lifters.

With Camshaft Removed

Measure distance from major point and minor point of each camshaft lobe with a Vernier caliper and record readings. The difference between readings on each lobe is the lobe lift. If readings do not meet specifications, replace camshaft and lifters.

VALVES

VALVE ARRANGEMENT

Right Side – I-E-I-E-I-E-I-E (front-to-rear).
Left Side – E-I-E-I-E-I-E-I (front-to-rear).

VALVE SEATS

NOTE: **Valve seat replacement information not available at this time. Service valve guides prior to valve seat refacing.**

Refacing

Valve seat must be a true 45 degree finished angle. Use only a 60 degree angle grinding stone to remove stock from bottom of all seats. Use only a 30 degree angle grinding stone to remove stock from top of all seats. Intake and exhaust seat width should be .06-.08" (1.5-2.0 mm).

NOTE: **Lubricate valves and valve guides with heavy SF oil prior to installation. Apply Ford Polyethylene Grease (DOAZ-19584-A) to tip of valve stem prior to installation.**

VALVES & VALVE GUIDES

1) Mark all components prior to removal for installation reference. Clean carbon from cylinder head, using care not to damage surfaces. Remove valves. Check valve-to-guide clearance of each valve in its respective valve guide.

2) Install a valve and hold against seat. Install Valve Stem Clearance Tool (T65T-6505-H) on valve stem, until fully seated. Tighten tool set screw firmly. Allow valve to drop away from seat and tool to contact upper guide surface.

3) Install dial indicator with pointer against center portion of tool. *See Fig. 10.* Move clearance tool back and forth in-line with dial indicator pointer. Keep clearance tool on upper guide surface. Record dial indicator reading.

4) Divide dial indicator reading by 2. This total is the valve-to-guide clearance. If not within specifications, replace valve(s) with next available oversize valve. Ream

Fig. 10: Checking Valve-to-Guide Clearance

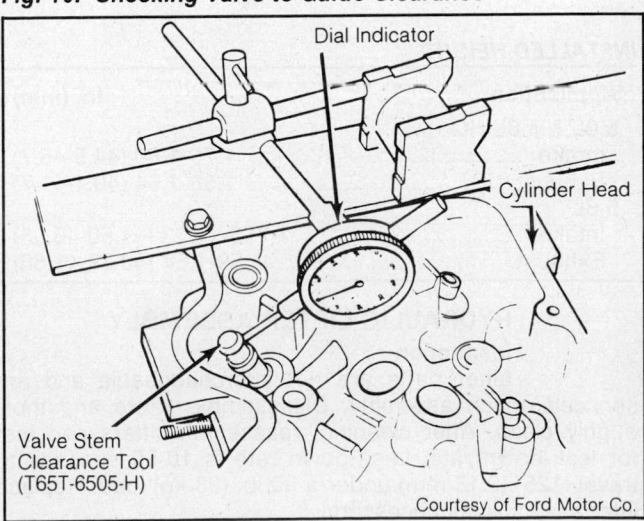

Courtesy of Ford Motor Co.

valve guide until clearance with valve is within specifications. See ENGINE SPECIFICATIONS tables at end of this article.

NOTE: **Always reface valve seat after valve guide has been serviced.**

5) Check valve face for pitting, cracks and runout. Reface or replace valve as necessary. Ensure valve face angle is a true 44 degrees. Ensure proper seat width is achieved. See ENGINE SPECIFICATIONS tables at end of this article.

VALVE SPRINGS

Inspection

1) Inspect valve springs for cracks or damage. Measure out-of-square. Maximum out-of-square is .078" (1.98 mm). Check free length. Check spring tension at specified length. See ENGINE SPECIFICATIONS tables at end of this article. Replace springs as necessary.

CAUTION: DO NOT install spacers unless necessary. Spacers used in excess of recommendations will cause premature failure.

2) Measure installed height from top of spring seat to bottom of spring retainer. *See Fig. 11.* If assembled height is greater than specifications, install .030" (.76 mm) thick spacer between cylinder head spring pad and spring seat. See INSTALLED HEIGHT table in this article.

Fig. 11: Measuring Valve Spring Installed Height

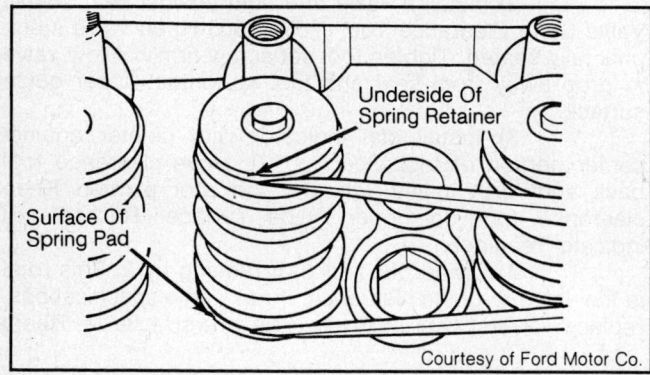

Courtesy of Ford Motor Co.

INSTALLED HEIGHT

Application	In. (mm)
5.0L & 5.0L HO	
Intake	1.75-1.80 (44.5-45.7)
Exhaust	1.58-1.64 (40.1-41.7)
5.8L	
Intake	1.750-1.813 (44.50-46.05)
Exhaust	1.59-1.64 (40.39-41.66)

HYDRAULIC LIFTER ASSEMBLY

Inspection

Lifter parts are not interchangeable and are serviced as an assembly. Disassemble lifters and thoroughly clean. After cleaning, reassemble lifters and test for leak-down rate. Leak-down rate is 10-50 seconds to travel .125" (3.18 mm) under a 50 lb. (23 kg) load. Replace lifter assembly as necessary.

NOTE: **Push rods are available in .060" (1.52 mm) undersize and .060" (1.52 mm) oversize.**

Hydraulic Lifter Clearance

1) Valve stem-to-rocker arm clearance should meet specifications with lifter totally collapsed. Valve and/or valve seat refacing can diminish clearance and cause improper valve operation.

2) To determine rocker arm-to-valve stem clearance, attach auxiliary starter switch to staring circuit. With ignition switch in "OFF" position, crank engine until No. 1 piston is on TDC of compression stroke. Completely collapse No. 1 intake valve lifter. Measure clearance between rocker arm and tip of valve stem, holding lifter in collapsed position.

3) On 5.0L standard engine, repeat procedure for No. 1 exhaust, No. 4 exhaust, No. 5 exhaust, No. 7 intake and No. 8 intake. Rotate crankshaft 360 degrees (one revolution) clockwise. Repeat procedure for No. 2 exhaust, No. 4 intake, No. 5 intake and No. 6 exhaust. Rotate crankshaft 90 degrees (1/4 revolution) clockwise. Repeate procedure for No. 2 intake, No. 3 intake, No. 3 exhaust, No. 6 intake, No. 7 exhaust and No. 8 exhaust.

4) On 5.0L HO and 5.8L engines, perform step 2). Repeat clearance check on No. 1 exhaust, No. 3 exhaust, No. 4 intake, No. 7 exhaust and No. 8 intake. Rotate crankshaft 360 degrees (one revolution) clockwise. Repeat procedure for No. 2 exhaust, No. 3 intake, No. 6 exhaust and No. 7 intake. Rotate crankshaft 90 degrees (1/4 revolution) clockwise. Repeat procedure for No. 2 intake, No. 4 exhaust, No. 5 intake, No. 5 exhaust, No. 6 intake and No. 8 exhaust.

5) If clearance is less than specifications, install a shorter push rod. If clearance is greater than specifications, install a longer push rod. See COLLAPSED LIFTER CLEARANCE table in this article.

COLLAPSED LIFTER CLEARANCE

Application	In. (mm)
Desired	
5.0L & 5.8L	.096-.146 (2.44-3.71)
5.0L HO	.123-.146 (3.12-3.71)
Allowable	
5.0L	.071-.171 (1.80-4.34)
5.0L HO & 5.8L	.098-.198 (2.49-5.03)

CYLINDER BLOCK ASSEMBLY

CYLINDER BLOCK

Inspection

1) Using a feeler gauge and straightedge, check cylinder block head gasket surface for flatness. Surface should be flate within .003" (.08 mm) over 6" surface and .006" (.15 mm) over entire surface. Check cylinder bore for wear, taper, out-of-round and piston fit. See CYLINDER BORE SPECIFICATIONS table in this article.

2) Install all main bearing caps and tighten to specifications prior to cylinder bore honing. Use only equal parts of kerosene and SAE 20 motor oil for honing cylinder bores. Use ONLY a spring-loaded type cylinder hone. After honing, allow cylinders to cool. Thoroughly clean bore with detergent and water solution.

5.0L & 5.8L V8 (Cont.)

3) Rinse solution from bore thoroughly with clean water. Wipe bore clean with lint free cloth. Lubricate cylinder bores with engine oil. Tap cylinder head bolt threads in cylinder block.

CYLINDER BORE SPECIFICATIONS

Application	In. (mm)
Out-of-Round	
Standard	.0015 (.038)
Service Limit	.005 (.13)
Taper	.010 (.25)

PISTONS, PINS & RINGS

OIL PAN

See appropriate OIL PAN REMOVAL article in this section.

PISTON & ROD ASSEMBLY

NOTE: **Following procedure is with cylinder heads, oil pan, oil pump and oil pump pick-up tube removed. Ensure components are marked for installation to original location and position.**

Inspection

1) Ensure pistons and rods are measured and installed in cylinder from which it was removed. Ensure notch or arrow on piston top faces front of engine. *See Fig. 12.* Check piston fit before assembling piston on rod. See FITTING PISTONS in this article.

2) Check piston pin fit. If not within specifications, remove pin and measure pin bore in piston and rod. See PISTON PIN SPECIFICATIONS table in this article. Replace as necessary. If piston pin is to be replaced, replace piston and pin as an assembly. See ENGINE SPECIFICATIONS tables at end of this article.

PISTON PIN SPECIFICATIONS

Application	In. (mm)
Length	3.010-3.040 (76.45-77.22)
Diameter	
Standard	.9119-.9124 (23.162-23.175)
.001 Oversize	.9130-.9133 (23.190-23.198)
.002 Oversize	.9140-.9143 (23.216-23.223)
Piston Bore	.9124-.9127 (23.174-23.182)

Fig. 12: Piston & Rod Position

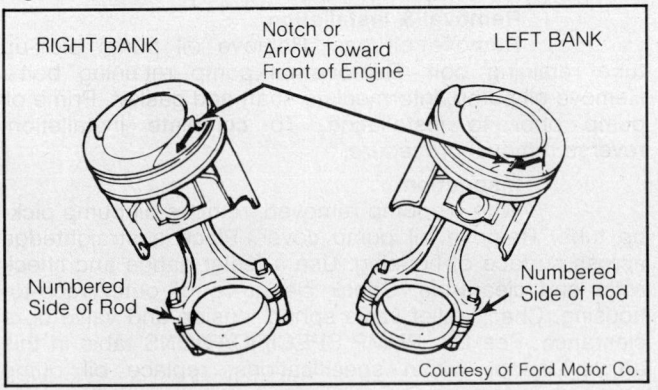

RIGHT BANK
Notch or Arrow Toward Front of Engine
LEFT BANK
Numbered Side of Rod
Numbered Side of Rod
Courtesy of Ford Motor Co.

FITTING PISTONS

1) Check piston-to-bore clearance. See ENGINE SPECIFICATIONS tables at end of this article. Standard size pistons are color coded Red, Blue or Yellow on the piston dome. An oversized piston is available.

2) If bore diameter is in lower one-third of specifications, use a Red coded piston. If bore diameter is in middle one-third of specifications, use a Blue coded piston. If bore diameter is in upper one-third of specifications, use Yellow coded piston. Use oversize piston if necessary. Use proper size piston to acquire specified clearance.

PISTON SIZE CODES

Code	In. (mm)
Red	
5.0L	3.9989-3.9995 (101.572-101.587)
5.0L HO	3.9972-3.9980 (101.529-101.549)
5.8L	3.9978-3.9984 (101.544-101.559)
Blue	
5.0L	4.0001-4.0007 (101.603-101.618)
5.0L HO	3.9984-3.9992 (101.559-101.580)
5.8L	3.9990-3.9996 (101.575-101.590)
Yellow	
5.0L	4.0013-4.0019 (101.633-101.648)
5.0L HO	3.9996-4.0004 (101.590-101.610)
5.8L	4.0014-4.0020 (101.636-101.651)
.003" (.076) Oversize	
5.8L	4.0002-4.0008 (101.605-101.620)

FITTING RINGS

1) Select proper rings for bore diameter. Place ring square in cylinder bore, below normal ring wear area. Measure the ring end gap. If ring end gap is less than specifications, remove necessary amount from end of ring. If ring gap is greater than specifications, use a different set of rings. Ensure rings are installed in cylinder bore in which they were measured.

Fig. 13: Piston Ring End Gap Spacing

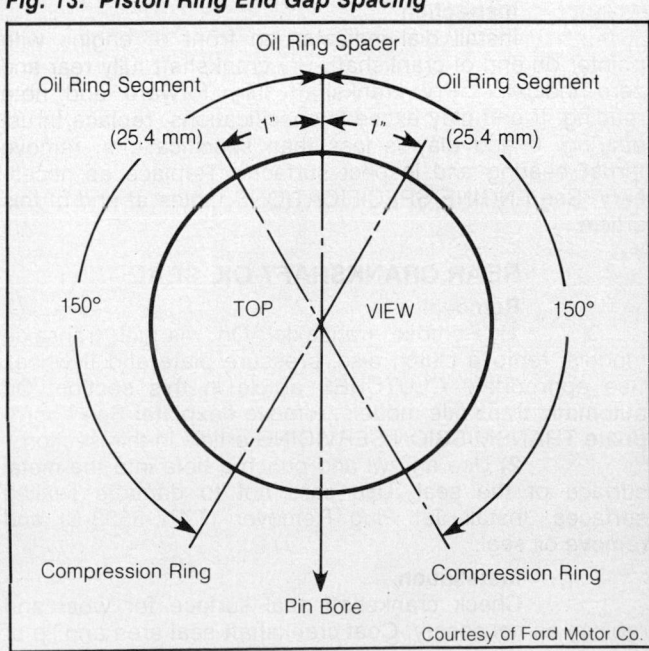

Oil Ring Spacer
Oil Ring Segment
Oil Ring Segment
(25.4 mm)
1"
1"
(25.4 mm)
150°
TOP
VIEW
150°
Compression Ring
Compression Ring
Pin Bore
Courtesy of Ford Motor Co.

2) Check side clearance of rings after installing on piston. Ensure clearance is within specifications around entire circumference. If lower lands of piston have high steps, replace piston. Replace piston and rings if side clearance is not within specifications. Properly set ring ends on piston before installing pistons into cylinder. *See Fig. 13.* See ENGINE SPECIFICATIONS tables at end of this article.

CRANKSHAFT & ROD BEARINGS

NOTE: Following procedures are with oil pan and oil pump pick-up tube removed. Only one bearing at a time should be checked or replaced.

MAIN BEARING

Inspection

Use Plastigage method and check clearance between main bearing and crankshaft journal. Check crankshaft for nicks, scratches, scores and wear. If not within specifications, replace bearings. Machine or replace crankshaft as necessary. See ENGINE SPECIFICATIONS tables at end of this article. Check crankshaft end play. See THRUST BEARING ALIGNMENT in this article.

CONNECTING ROD BEARINGS

Inspection

Use Plastigage method and check clearance between rod bearing and crankshaft. If specified clearance cannot be obtained with standard bearings, try a standard bearing in combination with an undersize bearing. Standard bearing may be used in combination with a .001" (.025 mm) or .002" (.050 mm) undersize bearing. Tighten all bolts/nuts to specifications. Desired clearance is the minimum of the specified clearance. See ENGINE SPECIFICATIONS tables at end of this article.

THRUST BEARING ALIGNMENT

Inspection

Install dial indicator on front of engine with pointer on end of crankshaft. Pry crankshaft fully rear and zero indicator. Pry crankshaft fully forward and note reading. If end play exceeds specifications, replace thrust bearing. If end play is less than specifications, remove thrust bearing and inspect surfaces. Replace as necessary. See ENGINE SPECIFICATIONS tables at end of this article.

REAR CRANKSHAFT OIL SEAL

Removal

1) Remove transaxle. On manual transaxle models, remove clutch disc, pressure plate and flywheel. See appropriate CLUTCHES article in this section. On automatic transaxle models, remove flexplate. See appropriate TRANSMISSION SERVICING article in this section.

2) Use an awl and punch a hole into the metal surface of the seal. Use care not to damage sealing surfaces. Install Jet Plug Remover (T77L-9533-B) and remove oil seal.

Installation

Check crankshaft seal surface for wear and replace as necessary. Coat crankshaft seal area and lip of oil seal with engine oil. Using Rear Crankshaft Seal Replacer (T81P-6701-A), install oil seal. Tighen bolts on seal replacer evenly, to ensure seal is installed squarely. To complete installation, reverse removal procedure.

ENGINE OILING

ENGINE OILING SYSTEM

System has force feed with rotor type oil pump. All oil from pump flows through full-flow oil filter before entering the engine. *See Fig. 14.* From oil filter, oil flows to main oil gallery located on right side of camshaft to lubricate engine components.

Fig. 14: Engine Oiling System

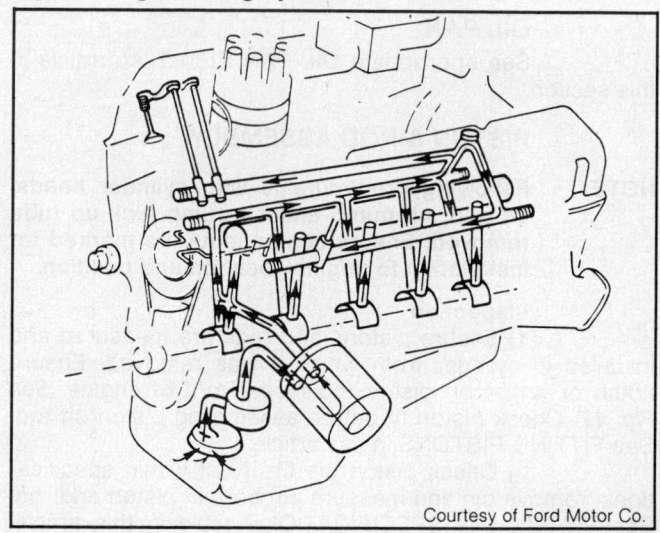

Courtesy of Ford Motor Co.

CRANKCASE CAPACITY

Crankcase capacity is 4 qts. (3.8L) without filter and 5 qts. (4.7L) with filter change. Do not change oil without filter change.

NORMAL OIL PRESSURE (HOT)

Normal oil pressure is 40-60 psi (2.8-4.2 kg/cm²) at 2000 RPM.

PRESSURE REGULATOR VALVE

Pressure regulator valve is located in oil pump body and is not adjustable.

OIL PUMP

Removal & Installation

Remove oil pan. Remove oil pump pick-up tube retaining bolt. Remove oil pump retaining bolts. Remove oil pump, intermediate shaft and gasket. Prime oil pump prior to installation. To complete installation, reverse removal procedure.

Inspection

With oil pump removed, remove oil pump pick-up tube. Remove oil pump cover. Place a straightedge across surface of housing. Use a feeler gauge and check rotor end clearance. Check clearance of outer race-to-housing. Check relief valve spring tension and valve bore clearance. See OIL PUMP SPECIFICATIONS table in this article. If not within specifications, replace oil pump assembly.

5.0L & 5.8L V8 (Cont.)

OIL PUMP SPECIFICATIONS

Application	In. (mm)
Outer Race-to-Housing	.0010-.0130 (.025-.330)
Max. Rotor End Clearance	.004 (.10)
Shaft-to-Housing Bearing	.0015-.0030 (.038-.076)
Relief Valve-to-Bore	.0015-.0030 (.038-.076)
Relief Valve Spring Tension	[1] [2]

[1] – All 5.0L engines, spring tension should be 10.6-12.2 lbs. @ 1.704" (4.8-5.5 kg @ 43.28 mm).

[2] – On 5.8L enignes, spring tension should be 18.2-20.2 lbs. @ 2.49" (8.3-9.2 kg @ 63.3 mm).

ENGINE COOLING

WATER PUMP

Removal

1) Disconnect negative battery cable and drain cooling system. Remove air inlet tube. Remove fan shroud and position shroud over fan. Remove fan and clutch assembly and shroud. Remove accessory drive belts. Remove alternator. Remove power steering pump (if equipped).

2) Remove accessory brackets attached to water pump. Remove water pump pulley. Disconnect lower radiator hose, heater hose and by-pass hose at water pump. Remove only the bolts that attach water pump to front cover. Remove water pump and gasket.

NOTE: Use only Ford Cooling System Fluid (E2FZ-19549-A) at 50/50 mixture.

Installation

Clean all gasket mating surfaces. Apply Perfect Sealing Compound (B5A-19554-A) to both sides of new water pump gasket. Install gasket on block. Install water pump. Install bolts and tighten to specifications. To complete installation, reverse removal procedure. Fill cooling system with specified coolant. Check for leakage.

NOTE: For more information, see ENGINE COOLING SYSTEMS article at the end of this section.

TIGHTENING SPECIFICATIONS

Application	Ft. Lbs. (N.m)
Camshaft Sprocket Bolt	40-45 (54-61)
Camshaft Thrust Plate Bolt	9-12 (12-16)
Connecting Rod Nut	19-24 (26-32)
Front Cover Bolt	12-18 (16-24)
Cylinder Head Bolt	
5.0L & 5.0L HO	
Step One	55-65 (76-88)
Step Two	65-72 (88-98)
Cylinder Head Bolt	
5.8L	
Step One	85 (115)
Step Two	95 (129)
Step Three	105-112 (142-152)
Damper-to-Crankshaft Bolt	70-90 (95-122)
Distributor Hold Down Bolt	18-26 (24-35)
Exhaust Manifold Bolt	18-24 (24-32)
Fan-to-Water Pump Bolt	
5.0L & 5.0L HO	15-22 (20-30)
5.8L	12-18 (16-24)
Flywheel Bolt	75-85 (102-115)
Fuel Pump Bolt	
5.8L	19-27 (26-37)
Intake Manifold	[1] 23-25 (31-34)
Main Bearing Cap Bolt	60-70 (81-95)
Oil Pump Mount Bolt	22-32 (30-43)
Oil Pan-to-Block Bolt	
5.8L	9-11 (12-15)
Pick-Up Tube-to-Pump Bolt	
5.0L & 5.0L HO	12-18 (16-24)
5.8L	10-15 (14-20)
Pick-Up Tube-to-Bearing Cap Nut	22-32 (30-43)
Pulley-to-Damper Bolt	35-50 (47-68)
Rocker Arm Bolt	18-25 (24-34)
Spark Plug	
5.8L	10-15 (14-20)
Water Pump Mount Bolt	12-18 (16-24)

Application	INCH Lbs. (N.m)
Fuel Filter-to-Carburetor	
5.8L	80-100 (9-11)
Oil Pan-to-Block Bolt	
5.0L & 5.0L HO	72-108 (8-12)
Spark Plug	
5.0L & 5.0L HO	60-120 (7-14)
Valve Cover Bolt	
5.0L & 5.0L HO	72-108 (8-12)
5.8L	36-60 (4-7)

[1] – After assembly, retighten with engine at operating temperature.

Ford Motor Co. Engines
5.0L & 5.8L V8 (Cont.)

ENGINE SPECIFICATIONS

GENERAL SPECIFICATIONS

| Year | DISPLACEMENT | | Fuel System | HP@RPM | Torque Ft. Lbs.@RPM | Compr. Ratio | BORE | | STROKE | |
	Cu. In.	Liters					In.	mm	In.	mm
1988 5.0L STD Except Thunderbird & Cougar	302	5.0	SEFI	[1] [2] 150@3200	[3] 270@2000	8.9:1	4.00	101.60	3.00	76.20
5.0L STD Thunderbird & Cougar	302	5.0	SEFI	155@3400	265@2200	8.9:1	4.00	101.60	3.00	76.20
5.0L HO	302	5.0	SEFI	225@4200	300@3200	9.2:1	4.00	101.60	3.00	76.20
5.8L	351	5.8	2-Bbl.	180@3600	285@2400	8.9:1	4.00	101.60	3.50	88.90

[1] – With dual exhaust, 160@3400.
[2] – With automatic transmission/transaxle, 160@3400.
[3] – With dual exhaust, 280@2200.

VALVES

Engine Size & Valve	Head Diam. In. (mm)	Face Angle	Seat Angle	Seat Width In. (mm)	Stem Diameter In. (mm)	Stem Clearance In. (mm)	Valve Lift In. (mm)
5.0L, 5.0L HO & 5.8L Intake	1.770-1.794 (44.96-45.57)	44°	45°	.060-.080 (1.52-2.03)	.3416-.3423 (8.67-8.69)	.0010-.0027 (.025-.069)	[1] .3776 (9.59)
Exhaust	1.453-1.468 (36.91-37.29)	44°	45°	.060-.080 (1.52-2.03)	.3411-.3418 (8.66-8.68)	.0015-.0032 (.038-.081)	[2] .3934 (9.99)

[1] – 5.0L HO is .442" (11.23 mm), 5.8L is .442" (11.23 mm).
[2] – 5.0L HO is .442" (11.23 mm), 5.8L is .450" (11.43 mm).

PISTONS, PINS & RINGS

Engine	PISTONS Clearance In. (mm)	PINS Piston Fit In. (mm)	Rod Fit In. (mm)	RINGS Ring No.	End Gap In. (mm)	Side Clearance In. (mm)
5.0L, 5.0L HO & 5.8L	[1] .0014-.0022 (.036-.056)	[2] .0002-.00045 (.005-.010)	Press Fit	1 & 2	.010-.020 (.25-.51)	.002-.004 (.05-.10)
				3	.015-.055 (.38-1.40)	Snug

[1] – On 5.0L HO and 5.8L engines, piston clearance is .0030-.0038" (.076-.097 mm).
[2] – On 5.0L and 5.8L piston pin fit is .0003-.0005" (.008-.013 mm).

CRANKSHAFT MAIN & CONNECTING ROD BEARINGS

Engine	MAIN BEARINGS Journal Diam. In. (mm)	Clearance In. (mm)	Thrust Bearing	Crankshaft End Play In. (mm)	CONNECTING ROD BEARINGS Journal Diam. In. (mm)	Clearance In. (mm)	Side Play In. (mm)
5.0L & 5.0L HO	2.2482-2.2490 (57.10-57.12)	.0004-.0015 (.01-.04)	No. 3	.004-.008 (.10-.20)	2.1228-2.1236 (53.92-53.94)	.0008-.0015 (.02-.04)	.010-.020 (.25-.51)
5.8L	2.9994-3.0002 (76.18-76.21)	.0008-.0015 (.02-.04)	No. 3	.004-.008 (.10-.20)	2.3103-2.3111 (58.68-58.70)	.0008-.0015 (.02-.04)	.010-.020 (.25-.51)

5.0L & 5.8L V8 (Cont.)

ENGINE SPECIFICATIONS (Cont.)

VALVE SPRINGS

Engine	Free Length In. (mm)	PRESSURE Lbs. @ In. (Kg @ mm)	
		Valve Closed	Valve Open
5.0L			
Intake	2.04 (51.82)	74-82@1.78 (35-38@45.21)	194-214@1.36 (88-97@34.54)
Exhaust	1.88 (47.75)	76-84@1.60 (35-38@40.60)	190-210@1.20 (86-95@30.48)
5.0L HO			
Intake	2.02 (51.31)	74-82@1.78 (34-37@45.21)	211-230@1.33 (96-104@33.78)
Exhaust	1.79 (45.47)	77-85@1.60 (35-39@40.64)	200-226@1.15 (91-103@29.21)
5.8L			
Intake	2.05 (52.07)	71-79@1.60 (32-36@40.64)	195-215@1.05 (89-98@26.67)
Exhaust	1.87 (45.47)	71-79@1.60 (32-36@40.64)	195-215@1.05 (89-98@26.67)

CAMSHAFT

Engine	Journal Diam. In. (mm)	Clearance In. (mm)	Lobe Lift In. (mm)
5.0L, 5.0L HO & 5.8L		.001-.003 (.025-.076)	Int. [1] .2375 (6.03)
No. 1	2.0805-2.0815 (52.84-52.87)		
No. 2	2.0655-2.0665 (52.46-52.49)		
No. 3	2.0505-2.0515 (52.08-52.11)		Exh. [2] .2474 (6.28)
No. 4	2.0355-2.0365 (51.70-51.73)		
No. 5	2.0205-2.0215 (51.32-51.35)		

[1] – 5.0L HO and 5.8L is .2780" (6.60 mm).
[2] – 5.0L HO is .2780" (7.06 mm), 5.8L is .2830" (7.19 mm).

General Motors Engines

1.6L 4-CYLINDER

NOTE: For engine repair procedures not covered in this article, see ENGINE OVERHAUL PROCEDURES article at beginning of this section.

ENGINE CODING

ENGINE IDENTIFICATION

The serial number and code are stamped on left rear side of engine block.

ENGINE CODES

Engine	Code
1.6L (96.8") 2-Bbl. (8-Valve)	4
1.6L (96.8") EFI (16-Valve)	5

ENGINE REMOVAL

See ENGINE REMOVAL & INSTALLATION at end of ENGINE section.

CYLINDER HEAD & MANIFOLDS

INTAKE & EXHAUST MANIFOLDS

NOTE: Intake and exhaust manifolds are removed and installed as an assembly.

Removal

1) Disconnect battery. Remove air cleaner assembly. Disconnect fuel and vacuum lines, choke and throttle linkage or cable at carburetor. On A/C equipped vehicles, remove vacuum idle-up hose.

2) Disconnect fuel, brake booster, emission control and heater inlet vacuum hoses. Remove heat insulator, PCV valve and PCV hose. Disconnect all hoses and wiring related to removal of manifolds.

3) Disconnect exhaust pipe at manifold. Remove manifold stay from exhaust manifold. Remove intake and exhaust manifold mounting nuts and bolts. Remove manifolds with carburetor as an assembly. Separate carburetor from manifolds as necessary.

Inspection

1) Inspect intake and exhaust manifold gasket surfaces for nicks or damage. Using straightedge and feeler gauge, check manifolds for warpage. *See Fig. 1.*

2) Warpage limit for intake manifold is .008" (.20 mm) on 8-valve engine, and .002" (.05 mm) on 16-valve. On all models, warpage limit for exhaust manifold is .012" (.30 mm). If warpage is beyond limits, resurface or replace manifolds as necessary.

Installation

Ensure mating surfaces are clean and new gaskets are used. Tighten 2 center bolts first. Tighten remainder in a front-to-rear, top-to-bottom pattern.

CYLINDER HEAD

Removal

1) Disconnect battery. Remove air cleaner assembly. Drain coolant and engine oil. Remove upper radiator hose. Disconnect heater inlet hose from cylinder head rear plate. Remove drive belts and water pump

pulley. Detach manifold stay from exhaust manifold. On A/C equipped vehicles, remove idle-up vacuum hose.

2) Remove A/C belt, compressor, condenser fan and power steering belt (if equipped). Remove power steering pump with bracket. Set assemblies aside. DO NOT discharge systems. Disconnect oxygen sensor wire. Remove remaining wiring, heater and vacuum hoses related to cylinder head. Remove intake and exhaust manifolds and carburetor as an assembly.

3) Remove spark plugs. Remove wires and distributor as an assembly. Remove valve cover with gasket and half circle plug, alternator upper bracket and water outlet. Remove fuel lines to fuel pump. Position No. 1 cylinder at TDC on compression stroke. Ensure rocker arms for No. 1 are loose. If not, rotate crankshaft one revolution.

4) Remove alternator as necessary. Using puller, remove crankshaft pulley. Remove air suction reed valve and components. Remove timing belt covers and gasket. Remove water pump. Mark position of camshaft timing sprocket and timing belt. Loosen idler pulley mount bolt and retighten pulley in far left position. Remove timing belt.

NOTE: DO NOT bend or twist timing belt. Keep belt free of oil, water or dust. Loosen head bolts in proper sequence or warpage and cracking may result.

5) Loosen cylinder head bolts, in 2 or 3 stages, in reverse sequence of tightening. See Fig. 1. Lift head from dowels on block. If difficult to remove, use a rubber mallet and lightly but firmly tap head loose.

Inspection

1) Clean all gasket material from top of block. Blow out carbon and oil from bolt holes. Using wire brush and gasket scraper, remove carbon and gasket material from combustion chambers, head and manifold surfaces. DO NOT scratch or damage gasket contact surfaces.

NOTE: DO NOT clean cylinder head in a "hot tank" or it may be damaged.

2) Using straightedge and feeler gauge, check head and block for warpage. Maximum warpage for block deck or for head is .002" (.05 mm). On 16 valve intake manifold surface, warpage limit is .002" (.05 mm). On all other manifold mounting surfaces, warpage limit is .004" (.10 mm). Maximum resurfacing limit is .004" (.10 mm). If warped beyond limits, resurface or replace cylinder head and/or block.

3) Using a dye penetrant, check combustion chambers, intake and exhaust ports, head surface and top of head for cracks. If crack is found, replace cylinder head.

Installation

1) Ensure mating surfaces are clean and camshaft caps and rocker arm assembly are tightened properly. Apply oil to all sliding and rotating surfaces. Install head gasket with sealer side facing up.

2) Install new head gasket and cylinder head. Tighten head bolts gradually, in sequence in 3 stages. *See Fig. 1.* Install timing belt. Check valve timing and timing belt tension. To complete installation, reverse removal procedure.

1.6L 4-CYLINDER (Cont.)

3) Set valve clearance. Fill cooling and oil system. Check ignition timing and idle speed. Run engine for several minutes, then let cool down and recheck head bolt torque.

Fig. 1: Cylinder Head Tightening Sequence

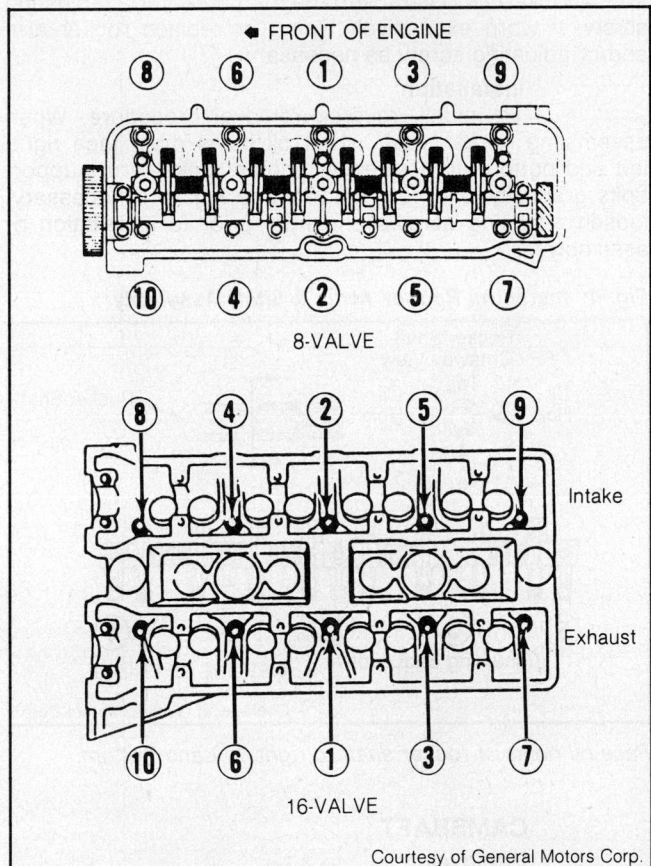

FRONT OF ENGINE

8-VALVE

Intake

Exhaust

16-VALVE

Courtesy of General Motors Corp.

CAMSHAFT

ENGINE FRONT COVERS

Removal
1) Drain cooling system. Remove radiator and air cleaner assembly. Remove alternator upper bracket and water outlet, if necessary. Remove A/C drive belt, idler pulley, fan shroud, fan and bracket.
2) Remove drive belts, water pump pulley and valve cover. Remove upper engine front cover mount bolts, cover and gasket. Set No. 1 piston at TDC on compression stroke.
3) Remove crankshaft pulley No. 2 (power steering only). Secure crankshaft and remove crankshaft pulley bolt. Using a gear puller, remove crankshaft pulley. Remove lower engine front cover.

Installation
Clean all gasket surfaces thoroughly. Install front covers and new gasket. Reverse removal procedure to complete installation.

TIMING BELT & SPROCKETS

NOTE: If reusing old timing belt, draw arrow on belt in direction of engine rotation. Place match marks on crankshaft, camshaft sprockets and belt. Ensure belt is not contaminated with water, oil or dust.

Removal
1) Drain cooling system. Remove fan shroud (A/C only). Remove radiator and air cleaner assembly. Remove drive belts, fan, water pump drive pulley and valve cover with gasket. Set No. 1 piston at TDC on compression stroke. Remove crankshaft pulley No. 2 (power steering only).
2) Using puller, remove crankshaft pulley. Remove upper and lower engine front cover mount bolts, gasket and covers. Mark timing belt location. Loosen idler pulley mount bolt, position pulley at far left and retighten mount bolt. Remove timing belt.

Inspection
1) Check belt for cracks or damage. If wear or cracks on flat belt face are found, check for nicks on one side of idler pulley lock.

Fig. 2: Timing Belt & Pulley Alignment

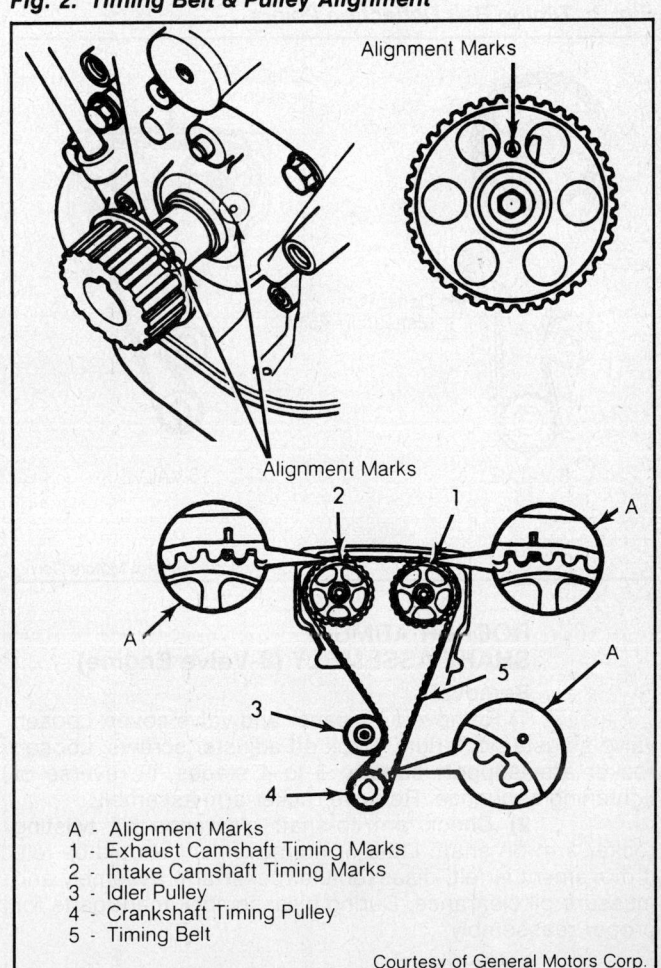

Alignment Marks

Alignment Marks

A - Alignment Marks
1 - Exhaust Camshaft Timing Marks
2 - Intake Camshaft Timing Marks
3 - Idler Pulley
4 - Crankshaft Timing Pulley
5 - Timing Belt

Courtesy of General Motors Corp.

General Motors 4 Engines

1.6L 4-CYLINDER (Cont.)

2) If wear or damage to only one side of belt is found, check belt guide and alignment of each pulley and sprocket. If noticeable wear is found on belt teeth, check timing cover gasket for damage and proper installation.

3) Ensure there is no foreign material on sprocket teeth. Check timing belt idler pulley for smooth rotation. Replace if roughness or noise is found.

Installation

1) Loosen timing belt idler pulley mount bolt, move pulley as far left as possible and retighten bolt. If reusing old belt, align marks made during removal. Install belt with arrow pointing in direction of rotation. DO NOT bend or twist belt. Release idler pulley and place tension on belt.

2) If installing new belt, align cramshaft(s) timing marks and crankshaft timing marks. See Fig. 2. Install timing belt. Release idler pulley and place tension on belt.

3) After installing new or used belt, slowly turn crankshaft 2 revolutions clockwise. Recheck timing marks. Adjust belt tension and deflection. See Fig. 3. Belt tension should be 4.4 lbs. (2 kg), with a deflection of .24-.28" (6-7 mm) on 8-valve engines and .16" (4 mm) on 16 valve engines.

Fig. 3: Timing Belt Deflection Points

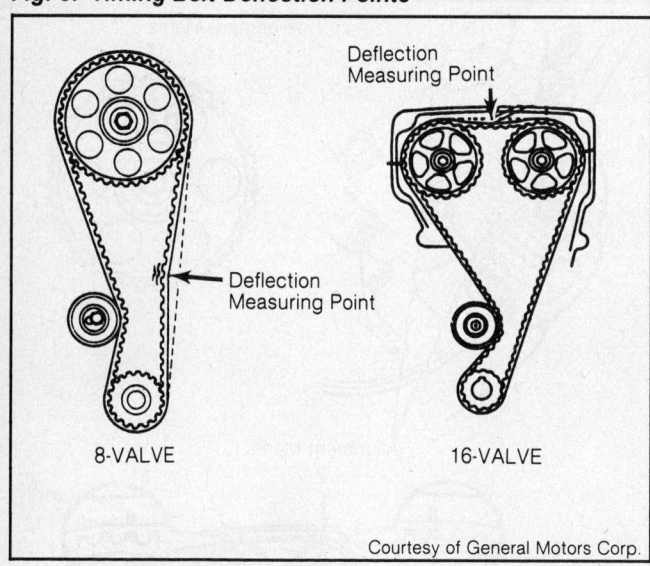

Courtesy of General Motors Corp.

ROCKER ARMS & SHAFT ASSEMBLY (8-Valve Engine)

Removal

1) Remove air cleaner and valve cover. Loosen valve adjuster lock nuts. Back off adjuster screws. Loosen rocker arm support bolts in 3 to 4 stages, in reverse of tightening sequence. Remove rocker arm assembly.

2) Check arm-to-shaft clearance by twisting rocker arm on shaft. Little or no movement should be felt. If movement is felt, disassemble rocker arm assembly and measure oil clearance. During disassembly, mark parts for proper reassembly.

Inspection

1) Measure inside diameter of rocker arm. Using a micrometer, measure outside diameter of rocker shaft. Subtract rocker diameter from shaft diameter.

2) Determine clearance. Standard rocker arm-to-shaft clearance is .0004-.0019" (.010-.048 mm). If clearance exceeds .0024" (.060 mm), replace rocker arm and/or shaft.

3) Check cam end contact surface of rocker arm and valve contact surface of rocker arm adjusting screw. If worn excessively, grind or replace rocker arm and/or adjusting screw as necessary.

Installation

To install, reverse removal procedure. When assembling rocker shaft, shaft oil holes must face right, left and bottom. In sequence, tighten rocker arm support bolts gradually, in 3 to 4 stages. See Fig. 4. If necessary, loosen adjusting screws and nuts prior to installation of assembly.

Fig. 4: Installing Rocker Arms & Shaft Assembly

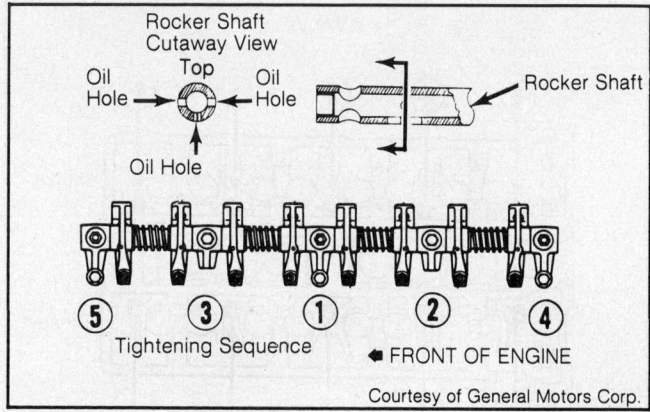

Courtesy of General Motors Corp.

Face oil holes of rocker shaft to right, left and bottom.

CAMSHAFT

Removal

1) Remove air cleaner assembly. Identify and remove all wiring and hoses interfering with valve cover removal. Remove valve cover and gasket. Remove engine front covers, gasket and timing belt.

2) On 8-valve engines, remove rocker arm assembly. On all engines, remove camshaft timing sprocket(s). Before removal of camshaft(s), measure camshaft end play. Remove camshaft bearing caps in reverse of installation sequence. See Fig. 6.

3) Keep bearing caps in order for assembly reference. Remove camshaft and oil seal. Detach distributor drive gear mount bolt from camshaft and remove drive gear.

NOTE: Camshaft rides directly on cylinder head bearing surface and caps. There are no replaceable cam bearings in head.

Inspection

1) Check for runout, on center journal. If beyond limit, replace camshaft. Inspect cam bearing caps for flaking or scoring. If caps are damaged or excessively worn, replace head and camshaft.

2) Tighten camshaft and bearing caps. Using Plastigauge method, check camshaft oil clearance. If clearance is beyond limit, replace camshaft and cylinder head.

1.6L 4-CYLINDER (Cont.)

Installation

1) Coat camshaft and bearing caps with oil. Apply grease to new oil seal lip and sealant to outside edge of seal. Install oil seal and camshaft.

2) On 8-valve engines, apply sealer to No. 1 bearing cap-to-head junction points and install. On all engines, install bearing caps with arrows on caps facing forward. On 16-valve engines, bearing caps are coded for reasembly reference. *See Fig. 5.*

3) Tighten bearing cap bolts in sequence, in 3 or 4 stages. *See Fig. 6* . To complete installation, reverse removal procedure.

Fig. 5: Camshaft Bearing Cap Code (16-Valve)

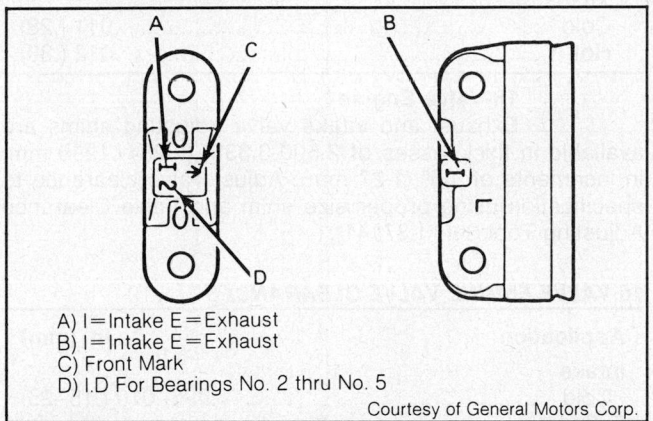

A) I=Intake E=Exhaust
B) I=Intake E=Exhaust
C) Front Mark
D) I.D For Bearings No. 2 thru No. 5

Courtesy of General Motors Corp.

Fig. 6: Camshaft Bearing Cap Installation

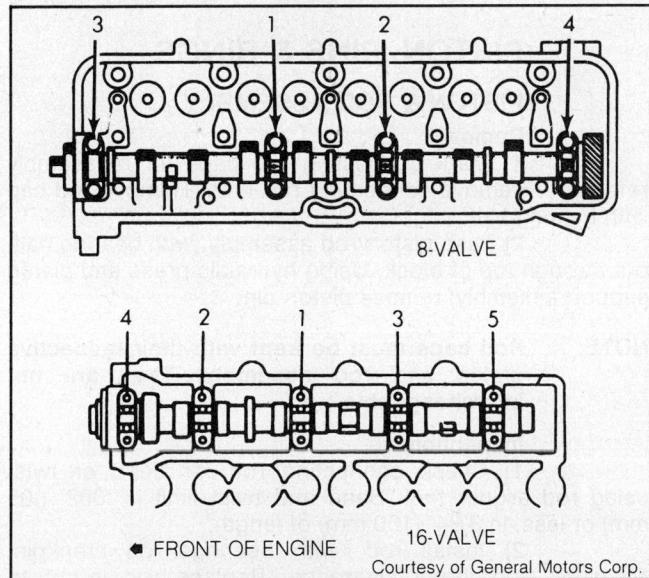

8-VALVE

◆ FRONT OF ENGINE   16-VALVE

Courtesy of General Motors Corp.

CAMSHAFT OIL SEAL

Removal & Installation

1) Remove air cleaner, valve cover, front covers and timing belt. On 8-valve engines, loosen rocker arm support bolts in reverse sequence of installation, in 3 to 4 stages. *See Fig. 4.* Remove rocker arm assembly.

2) On all engines, secure camshaft(s) and remove camshaft timing sprocket(s). Remove camshaft bearing caps following procedure given in CAMSHAFT REMOVAL.

3) Remove camshaft and oil seal. Inspect seal contact surface of camshaft for cracks or damage and replace as necessary. Apply grease to new oil seal lip and sealant to outside of seal.

4) Install oil seal. Ensure seal is installed squarely. Install bearing caps following procedure given in CAMSHAFT INSTALLATION.

VALVES

VALVE ARRANGEMENT

I-E-E-I-I-E-E-I (Front-to-rear).

VALVES

1) Using gasket scraper, chip carbon from valve head. Using wire brush, clean valve thoroughly. Inspect valves for worn, damaged or deformed head or stem. Check surface of valve stem tip for excessive wear.

2) Check valve head margin thickness. Check surface of valve stem tip for excessive wear. See VALVE LENGTH table for specifications.

VALVE LENGTH

Application	In. (mm)
8-Valve [1]	
Intake	4.188 (106.58)
Exhaust	4.184 (106.28)
16-Valve [1]	
Intake	3.9016 (99.101)
Exhaust	3.9075 (99.251)

[1] – Specifications are minimum demensions.

VALVE SPRINGS

Removal

With cylinder head, rocker arms and shaft assembly removed, remove cam bearing caps, seal and camshaft. Press valve spring down with Compressor (SST09202-43013). Remove valve keepers. Remove compressor, spring retainer, spring, valve, oil seal and valve spring seat.

NOTE: **Keep all valve train and camshaft components in order for reassembly reference.**

Inspection

1) Using steel square, check squareness of valve springs. Spring must be .08" (2 mm) or less out of square. Check free length of springs. Replace any springs not within limits.

2) Using spring tester, check tension of each spring at specified installed height. Replace spring if not to specification.

Installation

1) Before installing components, clean parts to be assembled. Apply oil to sliding and rotating surfaces. Install valve spring seats and new oil seals.

2) Install springs and retainers on valves. Using compressor, compress springs and install keepers. Tap stem lightly with plastic hammer to ensure keepers are seated properly.

VALVE GUIDE SERVICING
Clearance Check
1) Using valve guide brush and solvent, clean guides. Measure clearance between valve stem and guide with micrometer and telescope hole gauge. Check diameter of stem at top, center and bottom. Insert hole gauge in guide bore. Measure at center.

2) Subtract highest reading of stem diameter from guide bore to obtain clearance. If clearance is beyond limits and stem is not worn, replace guide.

NOTE: Replacement oversize valve guides are available.

Replacement
1) Using hammer and drift, tap guide firmly enough to break guide off flush with cylinder head surface. Remove snap ring. Gradually heat head to 195°F (90°C). Using Valve Guide Remover (J 35267 1) and a hammer, drive guide out from camshaft side.

2) Measure cylinder head valve guide hole. If hole-to-guide clearance is excessive, machine hole for oversized guide. With head at room temperature, ream guide hole to fit new guide. To install valve guide, reheat cylinder head.

3) Using Valve Guide Installer (J 35267 1), drive in new guide until snap ring contacts head. Using proper reamer, finish guide bore to specified clearance. After valve or guide repair or replacement, reface valve seat surface as needed. See Fig. 7.

Fig. 7: Installing Valve Guide

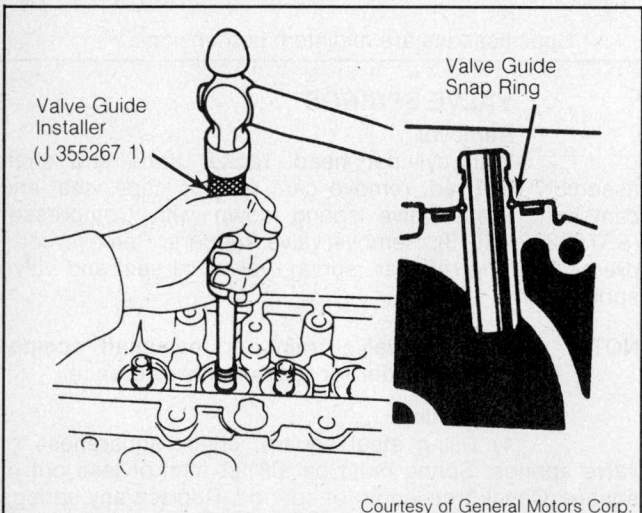

Courtesy of General Motors Corp.

VALVE CLEARANCE ADJUSTMENT
8-Valve Engine
NOTE: Valves should be adjusted with engine at normal operating temperature but not running. Cold specification are provided for initial settings after assembly.

1) With engine at normal operating temperature, stop engine and remove valve cover. Bring No. 1 piston to TDC of compression stroke. Ensure rockers on No. 1 cylinder are loose and No. 4 are tight.

2) If rockers are out of adjustment, rotate crankshaft one revolution. Realign cut-out on damper pulley with "O" timing mark on timing belt cover. Adjust No. 1 and 2 intake valves and No. 1 and 3 exhaust valves.

3) Rotate crankshaft one full turn (360 degrees) clockwise to realign timing mark on damper pulley with "O" mark on timing cover. Adjust No. 3 and 4 intake valves and No. 2 and 4 exhaust valves.

8-VALVE ENGINE VALVE CLEARANCES

Application	In. (mm)
Intake	
Cold	.007 (.18)
Hot	.008 (.20)
Exhaust	
Cold	.011 (.28)
Hot	.012 (.30)

16-Valve Engine
Exhaust and intake valve adjusting shims are available in thicknesses of 2.500-3.330" (.0984-.1299 mm) in incriments of .05" (1.27 mm). Adjust valve clearance to specification using proper size shim and Valve Clearance Adjusting Tool Set (J-37141).

16-VALVE ENGINE VALVE CLEARANCES

Application	In. (mm)
Intake	
Cold	.006-.010 (.15-.25)
Exhaust	
Cold	.008-.0012 (.28-.30)

PISTON, PINS & RINGS

PISTON & ROD ASSEMBLY
Removal
1) Mark connecting rod caps for reassembly reference. Remove connecting rod nuts. Remove rod cap with bearing half.

2) Push piston/rod assembly, with bearing half, out through top of block. Using hydraulic press and piston support assembly, remove piston pin.

NOTE: Rod caps must be kept with their respective piston and rod assembly. They are not interchangeable.

Inspection
1) Check connecting rod for bend or twist using rod aligner tool. Bend and twist limit is .002" (.05 mm) or less, in 3.94" (100 mm) of length.

2) Install rod, with bearings, on crankpin. Measure side thrust clearance. Replace rod if not to specifications.

Installation
For piston installation see FITTING PISTONS & RINGS in this article.

CRANKSHAFT BEARINGS
NOTE: There are 3 sizes of standard bearings, marked with a 1, 2 or 3. If replacing bearing, replace with one having the same number as marked on the cylinder block. See Fig. 8.

1.6L 4-CYLINDER (Cont.)

Fig. 8: Location of Main Bearing Marks on Cylinder Block

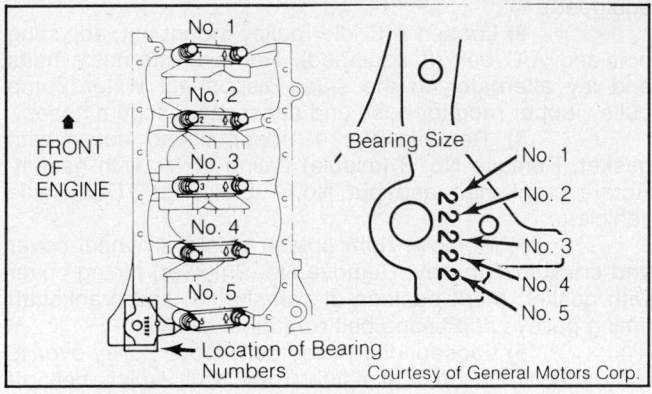

Courtesy of General Motors Corp.

Removal

With connecting rods disconnected, remove main bearing caps and lift out crankshaft. Remove upper main bearings from cylinder block. Clean main bearings and journals.

NOTE: **Since no undersize bearings are available, crankshaft cannot be machined. The pilot bearing in rear of crankshaft is permanently lubricated and requires no cleaning or lubrication.**

Installation

Inspect each bearing for pitting and radial scratches. Replace any damaged bearings. Measure clearances using Plastigage method. If clearance is greater than specified, replace main bearing.

CRANKSHAFT

Removal

1) With engine timing belt, timing pulley, oil pan, oil stainer and oil pump removed, mark rod caps and remove caps and bearings. Measure clearance at center bearing. If clearance is greater than specification, replace bearing as a set.

NOTE: **If replacing bearings, replace with those having same number as marked on cylinder block. There are 3 sizes of standard bearings, marked with a 1, 2 or 3.**

2) Remove main bearing caps. Lift out crankshaft. Remove upper main bearings from cylinder block and arrange caps and bearings in order.

Inspection & Installation

1) Measure crankshaft runout at center journal. If runout is greater than maximum, replace crankshaft. Check diameter of main and crankpin journal. Measure journals for out-of-round and taper. If journals are worn, replace crankshaft.

CRANKSHAFT IDENTIFICATION

Application	Main Journal Diameter In (mm)
No. 0	1.8895-1.8898 (47.994-48.000)
No. 1	1.8893-1.8895 (47.988-47.994)
No. 2	1.8891-1.8893 (47.983-47.988)
Undersize	1.8797-1.8801 (47.745-47.755)

2) Install main bearings. Place crankshaft in block and install upper thrust washers on center main bearing with oil grooves facing outward. Install thrust washers on bearing cap No. 3 with oil grooves facing outward.

3) Install bearing caps in numerical order with arrows facing forward. Tighten bolts to specified torque in 2 or 3 passes and in sequence. Make sure crankshaft turns.

4) Measure clearance at center bearing or crankshaft thrust. Install rear oil seal retainer. To complete installation, reverse removal procedure.

CYLINDER BLOCK

Clean & Inspect

1) Using a gasket scraper, remove all gasket material from cylinder block surface. Clean block using a soft brush and solvent. Using a precision straight edge and feeler gauge, check surface contacting cylinder head gasket for warpage.

2) If warpage is greater than maximum, replace cylinder block. Maximum warpage is .0020" (.05 mm). Visually inspect cylinders for vertical scratches. If deep scratches are present, rebore cylinder. If wear is less than .008" (.2 mm), use a ridge reamer to machine piston ring ridge at top of cylinder.

NOTE: **If cylinder block boring is necessary, bore all 4 cylinders for oversized piston outside diameter. Replace piston rings with ones matching pistons.**

3) Select oversized piston. Measure piston diameter at right angles to piston pin center line, .20" (5 mm) from lower edge of oil ring groove. Bore and hone cylinders to calculated dimensions. Amount of honing is .0008" (.02 mm) maximum. Excess honing will destroy finished roundness.

NOTE: **Before cylinder block machining operations, ensure main bearing caps are installed and tightened to specification. Bore cylinders in order of No. 2-4-1-3 to prevent distortion.**

FITTING PISTONS & RINGS

NOTE: **Pistons and rings are available in .01 mm and .02 mm oversize.**

1) Measure ring end gap. If not within specification, replace ring. DO NOT file ring end. Using a rod aligner, check connecting rod alignment. If rod is bent or twisted, replace connecting rod.

2) Align cavity on piston with protrusion on connecting rod. On 8-valve engines, coat piston pin and hole with engine oil. Press piston pin using hydraulic press and piston support assembly. On 16-valve engines, heat piston to 176°F (80°C) and press pin into piston using thumb pressure.

3) Install top 2 compression rings with code marks facing upward. Position rings so ring ends are 180 degrees from each other. DO NOT align end gaps. See Fig. 9.

4) Install bearings in connecting rods and rod caps. Lubricate face of bearings with clean engine oil. Lubricate cylinder bore and rod journals with clean engine oil.

General Motors 4 Engines

1.6L 4-CYLINDER (Cont.)

Fig. 9: Piston Ring Position

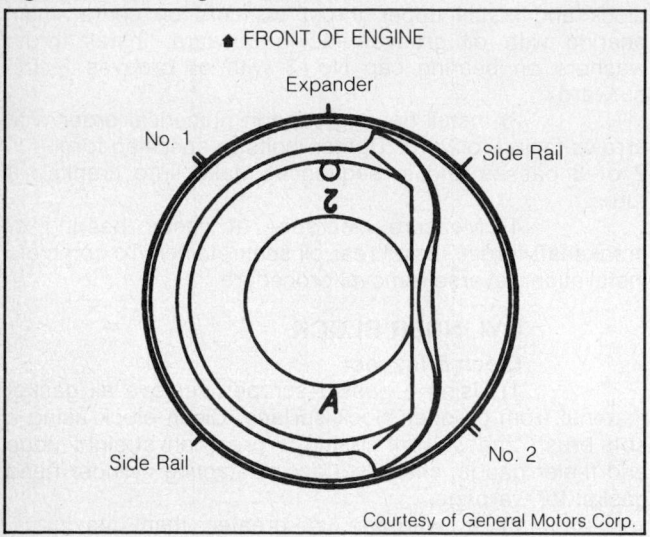

Courtesy of General Motors Corp.

5) Install correctly numbered piston and rod assembly into each cylinder. Make sure marks on connecting rod and piston are facing forward. Match numbered cap with numbered rod. Align marks punched on rod and cap and tighten cap nuts, alternately.

6) Measure connecting rod thrust clearance. After tightening caps, make sure crankshaft rotates smoothly. To complete installation, reverse removal procedure.

ENGINE OILING

CRANKCASE CAPACITY

Capacity is 4 qts. (3.8L) with filter change.

NORMAL OIL PRESSURE

On 8-valve engine, normal oil pressure at idle is 24 psi (1.7 kg/cm²) and oil pressure at 2000 rpm is 35 psi (2.5 kg/cm²).

On 16-valve engine, normal oil pressure at 600 rpm is 57 psi (4 kg/cm²).

ENGINE OILING SYSTEM

The oil pump is of an internal gear type and mounted on crankshaft at pulley side. Oil is drawn up through oil pump strainer and passed through pump to filter.

In one path, oil reaches crankshaft journal bearings. Oil from crankshaft journal bearings is supplied to connecting rod bearings by means of intersecting passages drilled in crankshaft, then injected from a small hole provided on big end of connecting rod to lubricate piston, rings and cylinder walls.

In another path, oil goes up to cylinder head and lubricates rocker arms, valves and camshaft. An oil pressure relief valve is provided on oil pump. The oil pressure relief valve starts relieving oil pressure when pressure goes over approximately 58 psi (4.0 kg/cm²). Relieved oil drains back to oil pan.

OIL PUMP

Removal

1) Remove oil pan. Drain cooling system. Remove oil strainer. Loosen water pump pulley bolts.

Remove alternator belt. Remove power steering belt (if equipped).

2) Loosen A/C idler pulley mount nut, adjusting bolt and A/C belt (if equipped). Remove alternator bolts and lay alternator to the side. Disconnect water pump pulley, upper radiator hose and necessary vacuum hoses.

3) Remove No. 1 upper timing cover with gasket. Remove No. 3 (middle) timing cover with gasket. Rotate crankshaft and put No. 1 piston at TDC. Raise vehicle.

4) Remove right splash shield, flywheel cover and crankshaft pulley. Remove No. 2 (lower) timing cover with gasket. Mark position of camshaft(s) and crankshaft timing pulleys and timing belt rotational direction.

5) Loosen idler pulley bolt, move pulley over to relieve belt tension and tighten bolt. Pull timing belt off crankshaft timing pulley. Remove crankshaft timing pulley.

6) Remove dipstick tube and timing belt idler pulley. Remove oil pump bolts and carefully tap off oil pump using plastic hammer.

Disassembly & Reassembly

Remove snap ring at relief valve and remove retainer, spring and relief valve piston. Remove oil pump cover. Remove drive and driven gears.

Inspection

1) Using a feeler gauge, measure clearance between driven gear and body. If clearance is greater than specified maximum, replace gear and/or body. Using feeler gauge, measure clearance between both gear tips and crescent.

2) If clearance is greater than specified maximum, replace gear and/or body. Using a feeler gauge and flat block, measure side clearance. If clearance is greater than specified maximum, replace gears and/or body. Carefully pry out oil seal.

Installation

1) Put new oil pump gasket against block and install oil pump to crankshaft with spline teeth of drive gear engaged with large teeth of crankshaft. Install timing belt idler pulley, dipstick tube, crankshaft timing pulley and timing belt.

2) Install No. 2 (lower) timing cover with gasket, crankshaft pulley, flywheel cover and splash shield. Lower vehicle. Install No. 3 (middle) timing cover with gasket and No. 1 (upper) timing cover with gasket.

3) Connect vacuum hoses, upper radiator hose at outlet and water pump pulley. Put alternator in position and tighten bolts. Install A/C adjusting bolt and idler pulley (if equipped).

4) Install A/C belt and tighten adjusting bolt and idler pulley mount nut (if equipped). Adjust belt. Install power steering and alternator belt and adjust.

5) Using new oil strainer gasket, install oil strainer. Refill cooling system. Install oil pan. Start engine and check for leaks.

OIL PUMP SPECIFICATIONS

Application	Specification
Oil Pump Gear-to-Body	
Max. Clearance	.008" (.2 mm)
Gear Tip-to-Cresent	
Max. Clearance	.0138" (.35 mm)
Oil Pump Side	
Max. Clearance	.004" (.1 mm)

1.6L 4-CYLINDER (Cont.)

ENGINE COOLING

WATER PUMP

Removal

1) Remove No. 1 (upper) timing cover. Remove inlet mount bolt. Remove 2 nuts at inlet pipe and pipe "O" ring. Disconnect inlet pipe at water inlet housing.

2) Remove inlet pipe from water pump. Remove oil level gauge guide. Remove right splash shield. Remove power steering adjusting bracket (if equipped). Remove water pump bolts, water pump pulley and water pump.

Installation

1) Install water pump and gasket. Install water pump pulley, power steering adjusting bracket and right splash shield. Install oil level gauge with new "O" ring. Coat "O" ring with a small amount of engine oil.

2) Connect inlet pipe at water inlet housing. Install 2 nuts at inlet pipe and water pump. Install inlet pipe mount bolt. Install No. 1 (upper) timing cover. Start engine and check for leaks.

NOTE: **For information on cooling system capacities and other cooling system components, see appropriate article in ENGINE COOLING SYSTEMS section.**

TIGHTENING SPECIFICATIONS

Application	Ft. Lbs. (N.m)
Camshaft Camshaft Sprocket Bolt	34 (46)
Connecting Rod Cap Nuts	
8-Valve	29 (39)
16-Valve	36 (48)
Crankshaft Pulley Bolt	
8-Valve	87 (117)
16-Valve	137 (186)
Cylinder Head Bolts	
8-Valve	43 (58)
16-Valve	[1]
Distributor Drive Gear Mount Bolt	20-23 (27-31)
Exhaust Pipe-to-Manifold Mount Bolts	26-32 (36-44)
Flywheel Bolts	55-61 (75-83)
Main Bearing Cap Bolts	43-44 (58-60)
Manifold Bolts	15-21 (20-29)
Oil Pump Mount Bolt	13-18 (18-24)
Rocker Shaft Support Bolts	17-19 (23-26)
Timing Belt Idler Mount Bolt	26-36 (36-49)

	INCH LBS. (N.m)
Camshaft Bearing Cap Bolts	108 (13)

[1] – Tighten bolts to 22 ft. lbs (29 N.m). After reaching specified torque, tighten bolts in sequence an additional 90 degrees. Again tighten bolts in sequence 90 degrees.

ENGINE SPECIFICATIONS

GENERAL SPECIFICATIONS

Year	DISPLACEMENT		Fuel System	HP@RPM	Torque Ft. Lbs.@RPM	Compr. Ratio	BORE		STROKE	
	Cu. In.	Liters					In.	mm	In.	mm
1988										
8-Valve	97	1.6	2-Bbl.	74@4800	86@2400	9.0:1	3.16	81	3.00	77
16-Valve	97	1.6	EFI	.....	.....	.....	3.16	81	3.00	77

VALVES

Engine Size & Valve	Head Diam. In. (mm)	Face Angle	Seat Angle	Seat Width In. (mm)	Stem Diameter In. (mm)	Stem Clearance In. (mm)	Valve Lift In. (mm)
1.6L 8-Valve							
Intake	[1] 1.42 (36.0)	44.5°	[3] 45°	.....	.....	.0031 Max (.078)	.....
Exhaust	[1] 1.37 (31.0)	44.5°	[3] 45°	.....	.....	.0039 Max (.099)	.....
16 Valve							
Intake	[2] 1.20 (30.5)	44.5°	[3] 45°	.....	.2350-.2356 (5.969-5.984)	.0010-.0024 (.025-.061)	.....
Exhaust	[2] 1.00 (25.5)	44.5°	[3] 45°	.....	.2348-.2354 (5.964-5.979)	.0012-.0026 (.030-.066)	.....

[1] – Minimum valve margin for intake is .02" (.5 mm) and .039" (.99 mm) for exhaust.
[2] – Valve margin is .031-.047" (.78-1.19 mm).
[3] – Upper correction angle is 30 degrees and lower correction angle is 60 degrees.

General Motors 4 Engines

1.6L 4-CYLINDER (Cont.)

ENGINE SPECIFICATIONS (Cont.)

PISTONS, PINS & RINGS

| Engine | PISTONS | PINS | | RINGS | | |
	Clearance In. (mm)	Piston Fit In. (mm)	Rod Fit In. (mm)	Ring No.	End Gap In. (mm)	Side Clearance In. (mm)
1.6L 8-Valve	.0035-.0043 (.089-.109)	Press	.....	1	.0098-.0185 (.248-.470)	.0016-.0031 (.041-.079)
				2	.0059-.0165 (.150-.420)	.0012-.0028 (.030-.071)
				Oil	.012-.040 (.30-1.02)	.....
16-Valve	.0039-.0047 (.10-.12)	[1]	.0016-.0003 (.004-.008)	1	.0098-.0138 (.249-.351)	.0016-.0031 (.041-.079)
				2	.0078-.0118 (.198-.300)	.0012-.0028 (.030-.711)
				Oil	.0059-.0157 (.150-.399)	.....

[1] – Heat piston to temperature of 176°F (80°C) and slide pin into piston using thumb pressure.

CRANKSHAFT MAIN & CONNECTING ROD BEARINGS

| Engine | MAIN BEARINGS | | | | CONNECTING ROD BEARINGS | | |
	Journal Diam. In. (mm)	Clearance In. (mm)	Thrust Bearing	Crankshaft End Play In. (mm)	Journal Diam. In. (mm)	Clearance In. (mm)	Side Play In. (mm)
1.6L [1] 8-Valve	[2] [3]	.0006-.0013 (.015-.033)	Center	.0008-.0073 (.020-.185)	[2]	.0008-.0020 (.020-.051)	.12 Max. (.3)
16-Valve	[2] [3]	.0006-.0013 (.015-.033)	Center	.0008-.0073 (.020-.185)	[2] [4] 1.6529-1.6535 (41.983-41.986)	.....	.12 Max. (.3)

[1] – Maximum runout is .0024" (.061 mm).
[2] – Maximum taper or out of round is .0008 (.020 mm).
[3] – See CRANKSHAFT IDENTIFICATION table in this article.
[4] – Also may be equipped with 1.6435-1.6439" (41.745-41.755 mm) diameter journals.

CAMSHAFT

Engine	Journal Diam. In. (mm)	Clearance In. (mm)	Lobe Lift In. (mm)
1.6L [1] [2] 8-Valve	1.1015-1.1022 (27.98-28.00)	.037-.073 (.0015-.0029)	[3]
16-Valve	1.0610-1.0616 (26.949-26.965)	.0014-.0028 (.035-.072)	[3]

[1] – Maximum Runout is .0024" (.060 mm).
[2] – End play should be .0031-.0071" (.078-.180 mm).
[3] – Lobe height is 1.5409" (39.139 mm) for 8-valve engine, and 1.3998-1.4002" (35.555-35.565 mm) for 16-valve engine.

VALVE SPRINGS

| Engine | Free Length In. (mm) | PRESSURE Lbs. @ In. (Kg @ mm) | |
		Valve Closed	Valve Open
1.6L [1] 8-Valve	1.756 (44.60)	46@1.52 (21@38.6)	.....
12-Valve	1.6177" (41.09)	35@1.366 (16@34.7)	.....

[1] – Spring out of square limit is .079" (2.01 mm) for 8-Valve engines, and .071" (1.80 mm) on 16-Valve engine.

2.0L OHC 4-CYLINDER

ENGINE CODING

ENGINE IDENTIFICATION

The 2.0L engine is available in standard or turbocharged versions. The engine may be identified from Vehicle Identification Number (VIN) stamped on metal tab located on top of instrument panel at lower left of windshield. VIN is also stamped on left side of engine, at transmission mounting flange. The VIN contains 17 characters. The 8th character identifies engine and 10th character establishes model year.

ENGINE CODES

Engine	Code
2.0L (122") TBI	K
2.0L (112") MFI (Turbo)	M

ENGINE REMOVAL

See ENGINE REMOVAL & INSTALLATION at end of ENGINE section.

CYLINDER HEAD & MANIFOLDS

INTAKE MANIFOLD

Removal (Non-Turbo Models)

1) Remove air cleaner, disconnect negative battery cable and drain cooling system. Remove power steering pump and bracket for accessibilty to work area. Remove alternator and bracket from camshaft carrier.

2) Remove ignition coil. Remove throttle cable from manifold bracket. Disconnect throttle and TV cables from fuel injection assembly. Detach wiring harness connectors from throttle body.

3) Remove brake vacuum hose at filter. Disconnect all fuel lines and inlet tube to water pump. Remove pre-heat hose from water pump and intake manifold.

4) Position ECM harness for accessibilty to lower manifold nuts. Remove intake manifold retaining nuts and washers. Remove intake manifold.

Installation

1) Clean all gasket mating surfaces. Install intake manifold with new gasket. Tighten bolts in sequence, starting in center and working outward.

2) Reverse removal procedure to complete installation. Refill cooling system and adjust all drive belts. Start engine and run until normal operating temperature is reached. Check for leaks.

Removal (Turbo Models)

1) Disconnect induction tube and negative battery cable. Detach MAT sensor, turbo boost switch, vacuum hoses and wiring to the throttle body. Remove throttle and cruise control cables from retainer.

2) Disconnect manifold bracket, ignition coil wiring and coolant reservoir. Remove alternator, power steering adjustment bracket and wiring to fuel injector.

3) Raise vehicle to disconnect fuel lines with bracket, regulator outlet from fuel regulator, lower end of manifold bracket and water pipe brace from fuel regulator. Disconnect knock sensor wiring, A/C compressor and harness retainer.

4) Lower vehicle to disconnect MAT sensor, coil ground wire and vacuum hoses from rear of manifold. Remove ECM harness clip and injector harness from manifold.

5) Disconnect wastegate vacuum hose and A/C connectors at thermostat housing. Remove intake manifold nuts with washers and lift manifold off engine.

Installation

1) Direct ECM harness through intake manifold. Connect ECM harness clip and injector harness. Install intake manifold and tighten nuts in sequence starting in center and working outward.

2) Reverse removal procedure to complete installation. Refill cooling system and adjust drive belts. Start engine and check for vacuum, fuel or cooling system leaks.

EXHAUST MANIFOLD

Removal

1) Remove air cleaner, spark plug wires and retainers. Remove oil dipstick tube and breather assembly. Disconnect oxygen sensor wire.

2) Separate exhaust inlet pipe from exhaust manifold. Remove exhaust manifold retaining nuts, manifold and gasket.

Installation

Clean gasket mating surfaces and install manifold with new gasket. Tighten bolts in sequence, starting in center and working outward. To complete installation, reverse removal procedure.

CYLINDER HEAD

NOTE: **Cylinder head bolts should be removed only when engine is cold. Check cylinder head for damage or warped gasket surface. DO NOT machine more than .015" (.39 mm) from original gasket surface. Remove burrs or scratches with an oil stone.**

Removal

1) Remove air cleaner and drain cooling system. Remove components related to intake and exhaust manifold removal. Remove upper radiator hose. Disconnect wiring harness and connectors from thermostat housing. Disconnect and remove spark plug and ignition coil wires.

2) Disconnect coil and Electronic Spark Control connectors. Remove distributor retaining nuts and distributor assembly. Disconnect ECM harness and connectors at intake manifold. Remove all water hoses from intake manifold. Remove front timing belt cover and timing probe holder.

3) Loosen water pump bolts and remove timing belt. Loosen and gradually remove camshaft carrier/cylinder head bolts in reverse of tightening sequence. See Fig. 1. Remove camshaft carrier assembly. Remove cylinder head, intake and exhaust manifolds as an assembly.

4) If cylinder head is to be serviced, remove carbon deposits from combustion chamber before removing valves. When disassembling, mark all valve components for proper reassembly.

CAUTION: **Turbo model fuel systems must be bled to relieve pressurized fuel lines prior to removal.**

General Motors Engines

2.0L OHC 4-CYLINDER (Cont.)

Installation

1) Clean all mating surfaces on cylinder head and camshaft carrier. Clean threads in cylinder head bolt holes. Install new head gasket and position cylinder head. Apply continuous bead of RTV sealer to camshaft carrier mating surface.

2) Install camshaft carrier and bolts. Gradually tighten cylinder head/camshaft carrier retaining bolts in sequence to 18 ft. lbs. (24 N.m). Then turn each bolt 60 degrees clockwise in proper sequence for 3 times until a 180 degree rotation is obtained.

NOTE: Cylinder head bolts and block threads must be clean prior to assembly. Dirt or other contamination will affect bolt torque.

3) Install distributor assembly. Install camshaft sprocket and timing belt. Connect PCV hose to camshaft carrier. To complete installation, reverse removal procedure. Start engine. Run until thermostat opens. Tighten cylinder head bolts an additional 30 degrees to 50 degrees in sequence. See Fig. 1.

Fig. 1: Cylinder Head Tightening Procedure

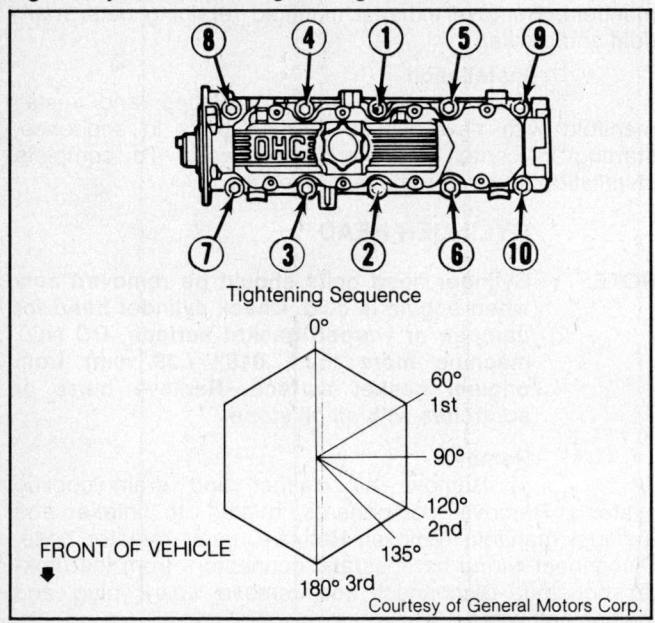

Tighten bolts in sequence using a 3-step process.

VALVES

NOTE: When reconditioning valves, ensure interference angles of valve and seat are not lapped out. Remove minor damage with an oil stone. DO NOT remove more than .010" (.254 mm) from end of valve stem.

VALVE ARRANGEMENT

E-I-E-I-E-I-E-I (Front-to-rear).

VALVE GUIDE SERVICING

1) Valve guides are integral with cylinder head. Check valve stem-to-guide clearance. If clearance exceeds service limits, recondition valve guide. To check valve guide wear, insert valve with head positioned .125" (2 mm) off seat and move it side to side measuring amount of movement with a dial indicator.

2) If dial indicator reading is excessive, oversize parts must be installed. See VALVES table for specifications. Use Valve Guide Reamer Set (J-5830) for servicing guides. When reconditioning, always use next oversize reamer and replacement valve.

3) Check valve seats for proper angle and seat width. Measure valve seat runout. Valve seat runout should be within .002" (.05 mm) for intake and exhaust.

NOTE: New valves must NOT be lapped. Lapping will destroy protective coating on valve face. Use old valve to lap in seat if necessary.

4) Valve seat must be refaced after guide has been reamed. Use scraper to break (lightly chamfer or bevel) sharp top inside edge of guide.

5) After valve guide repair, inspect valve stem end for wear before installation. Valve stem end may be reconditioned by grinding.

VALVE STEM OIL SEALS

Removal

1) Remove rocker arm components, keeping them in position for reinstallation in original location. Remove spark plugs. If valves or valve seats have not been damaged, valve springs, seals and retainers may be replaced by holding valves against seats using air pressure.

NOTE: To hold valves in place with head installed, an adapter can be constructed by welding an air hose connection to body of spark plug with porcelain removed.

2) Install Air Line Adapter (J-22794) in spark plug hole. A minimum of 140 psi (9.8 kg/cm²) line pressure is required. If air pressure does not hold valve shut, valve is damaged or burnt and cylinder head must be removed for service.

3) Remove rocker arms and guides. Using Valve Spring Compressor (J-33302), compress valve spring. Remove valve locks, retainer caps and valve spring. Remove valve stem oil seal and discard.

NOTE: If oversized valves have been installed, oversized oil seals must also be used.

Installation

1) Coat valve stem with engine oil. Install protective sleeve over end of valve. Slide new oil seal over valve stem and seat on valve guide. Remove protective sleeve.

2) Place valve spring seat or rotator, spring and retainer cap over valve stem. Compress spring and install valve locks. Install rocker guides and rocker arms. Remove spring compressor and air line adapter. Install spark plugs and cam carrier cover with new gasket.

VALVE SPRINGS

NOTE: Valve spring removal and installation is the same as REMOVAL & INSTALLATION procedures for VALVE STEM OIL SEALS.

1) Check valve springs for out of square with 90 degree straight edge. Valve spring out of square

2.0L OHC 4-CYLINDER (Cont.)

service limit is .0625" (1.587 mm). Install new valve stem oil seals. If necessary, install new valve springs and retainers.

2) Compress spring and install valve spring retainer locks. Apply Lubriplate to all rocker arm contact surfaces. Lubricate rocker arms before installing in position. Check valve spring for proper installed height.

VALVE SPRING & VALVE STEM INSTALLED HEIGHT

1) Measure installed height of valve spring from surface of spring pad to underside of spring retainer. If height is not within specifications, valve spring load loss may be excessive. Replace spring as necessary.

2) When new valves are installed or valves have been ground, valve stem height must be checked. Using Valve Stem Height Gauge (J-25289), check for .015" (.38 mm) clearance between valve stem tip and gauge.

3) If clearance is less than .015" (.38 mm), remove valve and grind tip to obtain proper clearance. Be certain to break (chamfer) sharp edge of reground valve tip. Recheck valve installed height.

4) If valve stem end is less than .005" (.127 mm) above rotator, valve is to short and must be replaced. Test valve spring pressure with Valve Spring Tester (J-8056). If not to specification, install new valve spring.

HYDRAULIC LIFTER ASSEMBLY

NOTE: Before replacing hydraulic lifter for noisy operation, be sure noise is not caused by worn rocker arms or valve tips.

1) Hydraulic lifter assemblies must be installed in original locations. Remove rocker arm assembly and identify for proper installation. Using Hydraulic Lifter Remover (J-3049) or magnet, remove lifters. Clean and inspect but do not mix components or positions. Parts are select-fitted and are not interchangeable.

2) If lifter is sticking, disassemble and clean dirt, metal chips or varnish from components. If lifter check valve is not functional, obstructions may be preventing it from closing or valve spring may be broken. Clean or replace components as necessary.

3) If plunger is not free in body of lifter, soak lifter in solvent to free plunger and dissolve deposits. Plunger should drop to bottom of body by its own weight when assembled dry. Assemble lifter and check free operation by pressing down on cap.

NOTE: When performing leak-down test (non-roller tappets only), use approved test fluid only. New lifters already contain test fluid. If new lifter is installed, remove sealer coating and check leak-down rate. If old lifter is disassembled and cleaned, fill with SAE 10 engine oil before installing.

4) Place lifter upright in Hydraulic Lifter Leakdown Tester (J-5790) and check leak-down rate. Leakdown rate should be within 12-90 seconds. If not within specifications, replace lifter assembly. Inspect lifter baseto-cam lobe contact area. Surface must be smooth and convex contact face.

5) Replace any lifter with flat or concave surface. Inspect related cam lobe for proper lobe lift. Replace camshaft (and lifters if necessary) if any lobe is worn beyond specification. Check lifter-to-bore clearance.

VALVE ADJUSTMENT

No hydraulic valve lifter lash adjustment is required. Preload of hydraulic lifter is automatic. Servicing of lifter requires only care and cleanliness when handling parts.

PISTONS, PINS & RINGS

OIL PAN

See OIL PAN REMOVAL at end of ENGINE section.

PISTON & ROD ASSEMBLY

NOTE: Before removing piston and connecting rod, mark rod caps for proper reassembly. DO NOT damage crankshaft journals or cylinder wall during removal.

Removal

1) With cylinder head and oil pan removed, inspect cylinder bores for ridges and/or deposits. Move piston to bottom of bore and cover with cloth to catch cuttings.

2) Remove ridge at top of cylinder bores (using ridge reamer) before removing pistons from block. Rotate crankshaft and mark connecting rods and rod caps for cylinder identification.

3) Remove rod cap and push each piston and rod assembly out top of cylinder bore. To protect crankshaft, place rubber tubing over rod bolts. Remove bearing inserts from rod and cap and inspect for size, wear and damage. Install rod caps on mating rods.

Installation

1) Check fit of new piston and/or rings in cylinder bore before assembling piston and pin to connecting rod. Check piston pin for clearance, etching or wear. New pistons must be installed in cylinder for which they were fitted. Install used pistons in cylinder from which they were removed.

2) Oil piston rings and cylinder walls with light coat of oil. Ensure ring gaps are properly spaced and install ring compressor on piston. See Fig. 2. Marked side of compression rings must be toward top of piston. Position piston so identification numbers on rod and cap are on same side and face water pump.

NOTE: Notch or arrow on piston top should be toward front of engine.

3) Install Connecting Rod Bolt Guide Set (J-6305-11) or rubber sleeves before installing piston and rod assembly in bore. Insert piston/rod assembly into cylinder bore.

4) After bearings have been inserted, apply engine oil to journals and bearings. Ensure oil hole in bearing insert aligns with oil hole in connecting rod. Turn crankshaft to bottom of throw. Guide piston/rod assembly over crankshaft journal until rod bearing seats.

5) Remove rod bolt protectors. Match rod cap to rod and install. Tighten cap nuts in two steps. Repeat procedure for each piston assembly. After piston/rod assembly is installed, check side clearance of connecting rod on each crankshaft journal.

Fig. 2: Oil Ring Gap Spacing

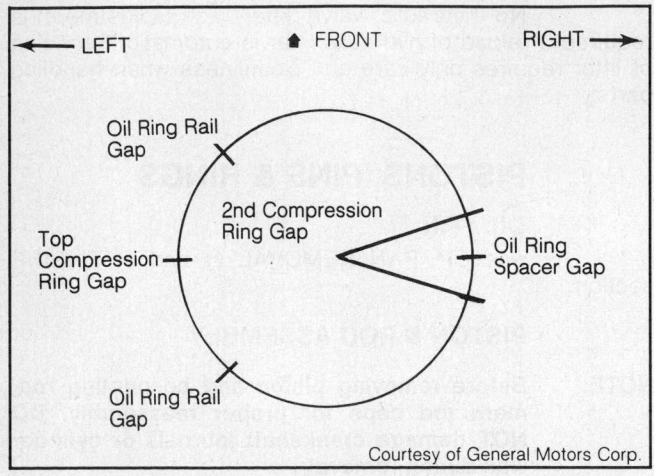

LEFT ← ♦ FRONT RIGHT →

Oil Ring Rail Gap

2nd Compression Ring Gap

Top Compression Ring Gap

Oil Ring Spacer Gap

Oil Ring Rail Gap

Courtesy of General Motors Corp.

FITTING PISTONS

1) Inspect pistons and replace any showing signs of excessive wear, wavy ring lands, or fractures. Replace piston if sponge-like or eroded surface is on edge of piston top (caused by detonation or pre-ignition).

2) Replace piston and/or rod as necessary. Inspect connecting rods for signs of fracture and bearing bores for out of round and taper.

3) Check pistons for fractures at ring lands, skirts and pin bosses. Check for scuffed, rough or scored skirts. Check piston-to-cylinder bore clearance by measuring piston and bore diameters.

4) Ensure piston and cylinder bore are clean, dry and at room temperature 70°F (21°C) during measurement. Measure diameter of cylinder bore at top, middle and bottom with gauge at right angle and parallel to centerline of engine.

5) Inspect cylinder walls for scoring, roughness or other signs of wear. Check bore for out-of-round and taper. Cylinder bore out-of-round and taper service limit is .005" (.127 mm).

6) Measure outer diameter of piston at centerline of pin bore and 90 degrees to pin bore axis. If cylinder wall is severely marred or worn beyond specifications, refinishing will be necessary. Pistons are available in oversize.

7) Before cylinder refinishing, ensure main bearing caps are in place and tightened to specification to avoid distortion during refinishing process. After refinishing, allow bore to cool, then clean bore with soap/water solution and oil cylinder walls.

FITTING PISTON RINGS

1) Clean ring grooves with ring groove cleaner or piece of broken ring. Ensure oil holes (or slots) in piston are clean. Measure piston ring side and end gap clearance.

2) Ring side clearance should be checked with feeler gauge between ring and piston lower ring land. Gauge should slide freely around entire circumference without binding. If step has formed around inner portion of lower ring land, piston must be replaced.

3) Using piston to position ring in cylinder bore, check ring end gap at least .63" (16 mm) from bottom of bore. Install rings on pistons with end gaps staggered at proper intervals. *See Fig. 2.* Ensure ring gap is not in line with thrust face of pin bore.

4) Be sure manufacturer's mark faces up when rings are installed. Install oil ring expander first, followed by lower oil ring side rail and upper side rail. DO NOT use ring expander on side rails. When installing lower side rail, place one end between piston ring groove and expander.

5) Hold end firmly and press down portion to be installed until side rail is in position. Install upper side rail. Using ring expander, install intermediate and upper rings. Ensure all components are within specifications.

6) If new piston rings are to be installed and no visible cross-hatch marks remain on cylinder walls, remove cylinder wall glaze using spring-type hone. After honing, clean bore and block with soap/water solution and oil cylinder walls.

FITTING PISTON PINS

NOTE: When removing or installing piston pin, connecting rod should be in firm contact with body of pin setting tool.

Removal

1) Remove bearing inserts from connecting rod and cap. Mark pistons, pins and inserts (if reusable) for reassembly reference. Press piston pin from piston and connecting rod using Piston Support (J-24086) and Piston Pin Remover/Replacer (J-24086-9).

2) Inspect and replace any piston pin showing signs of fracture, etching or wear. Check piston pin-to-rod bore fit. If necessary, replace rod and pin as an assembly.

Installation

1) Check piston to cylinder bore clearance before assembling piston and pin to connecting rod. Ensure oil hole in connecting rod aligns with oil hole in bearing and arrow or notch on top of piston is pointed toward front of engine. Start piston pin in piston and connecting rod.

2) Using guide bar and push rod, press pin through both piston and rod until pilot hub bottoms on support fixture and/or pin is centered in piston. DO NOT exceed 5000 lbs. (2275 kg) pressure with press. Make certain piston floats during pin installation operation.

CRANKSHAFT & ROD BEARINGS

NOTE: Following procedures are with oil pan and cylinder head removed. Main and rod bearing size is indicated by letter stamped into bearing tang or actual bearing size stamped opposite of tang. Undersize bearings are marked as follows: A = .0005", B = .0010", and C = .0015".

CONNECTING ROD BEARINGS

1) Remove connecting rod bearing caps and mark rods and caps for proper installation. Inspect each bearing for peeling, melting, seizure or improper contact. Replace defective bearings. Use Plastigage method for bearing clearance check.

2) Measure crankshaft connecting rod bearing journals for runout and taper. When checking connecting rod clearances, crankshaft does not have to be supported. Instead, turn crankshaft until connecting rod to be checked starts moving toward top of engine, thus unloading lower bearing.

2.0L OHC 4-CYLINDER (Cont.)

3) Cut Plastigage to same length as width of rod bearing. Place in bearing cap, parallel with crankshaft (not over oil hole or groove). Install rod bearings and cap, tightening in 2 steps to specifications. Always install caps with markings in original positions.

4) Do not turn crankshaft with Plastigage installed. Remove rod bearing cap from crankshaft and measure Plastigage at its widest part. If clearance exceeds specifications, replace bearing.

5) Selective fitting is required on each connecting rod. After inspection and/or replacement, coat bearing surfaces with heavy engine oil. Tighten connecting rod bearing caps in 2 steps.

NOTE: Connecting rod bearing cap and rod identification numbers must remain on same side and face toward water pump. Always replace bearings in pairs. Never use new bearing in combination with used bearing.

6) Check for shiny surface on either side of piston pin boss, indicating bent connecting rod. Twisted rods will not create identifiable wear patterns, but will disturb the action of entire crankshaft assembly and may cause excessive oil consumption.

7) Check connecting rod side clearance. If measurement is excessive, replace connecting rod and cap. If side clearance is less than specification, remove rod and cap. Check for scratches, burrs, nicks or dirt between crankshaft and rod. Dress minor imperfections with oil stone.

8) During assembly, oil hole in bearing must align with oil hole in connecting rod. Verify bearing tangs are seated to slots in rod and cap. Ensure connecting rod bolt heads are properly seated in connecting rod.

MAIN BEARINGS

NOTE: Selective fit main bearings are used in this engine. DO NOT scrape gum or varnish deposits from bearing shells. Clean inserts and caps thoroughly in solvent. DO NOT file or lap bearing caps or use bearing shims to obtain proper bearing clearance.

1) Inspect each bearing for peeling, melting, seizure or improper contact. Replace defective bearings. Measure crankshaft main bearing journals for runout or taper.

NOTE: Never use new bearing in combination with used bearing. Check location of high spots on main bearings. If high spots are not in line, crankshaft may be bent and should be checked.

2) Check clearances using Plastigage method. If standard and undersize bearing combination do not bring bearing clearance within specified limits, crankshaft must be refinished and undersize bearings installed. If journal will not clean up to maximum undersize bearing, replace crankshaft.

3) If journals are remachined, ensure same journal shoulder radius is reproduced. When journals are refinished, chamfer oil holes and polish journals with No. 320 grit polishing cloth and engine oil.

4) After chamfer and polish operations, clean crankshaft thoroughly in solvent and blow out oil passages with compressed air. When crankshaft main bearings are installed, ensure oil distributing grooves on bearings are installed on same side.

5) Oil new upper bearing and insert plain (unnotched) end between crankshaft and notched side of block. Rotate bearing into place. Install main bearing caps so bottom of number (cast on surface of main cap) faces rear of engine. Install main cap bolts and tighten. Fill rear main cap side grooves with G.M. Sealing Compound (No. 3997597). *See Fig. 3.*

Fig. 3: Sealing Rear Main Bearing Cap Side Grooves

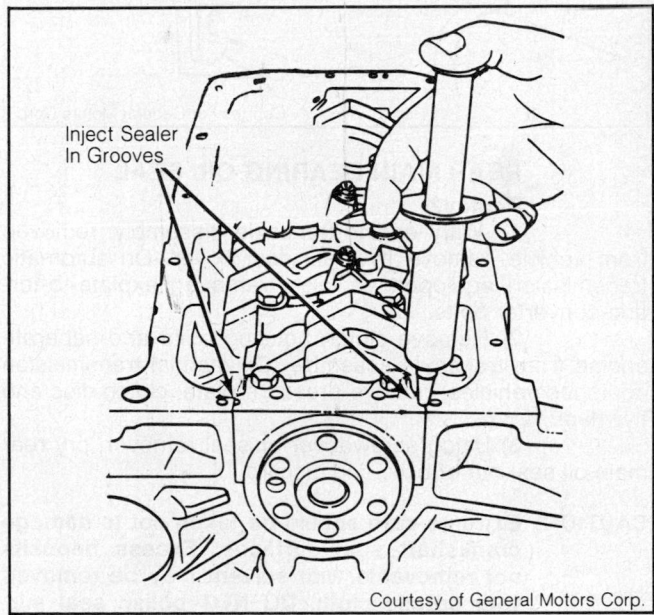

Inject Sealer In Grooves

Courtesy of General Motors Corp.

THRUST BEARING

1) Check crankshaft end play with crankshaft bearing caps installed. Replace center main thrust bearing if not to specification.

2) If end play is less than specification, inspect thrust bearing surfaces for scratches, burrs, nicks or dirt. Clean up minor imperfections with oil stone and recheck.

CRANKSHAFT FLANGE RUNOUT

1) With crankshaft installed, measure crankshaft flange runout. Mount dial indicator gauge plate flat against flange. Place dial indicator stem on lower left transmission mounting bolt boss (flat area around mounting bolt hole). Set indicator to zero.

2) Observe and record readings obtained on all mounting bolt hole bosses. Measurements should not vary more than .008" (.203 mm). If readings are over specification, remount dial gauge plate and recheck flange runout. If runout is excessive, replace crankshaft. Check threaded holes, clean and retap as necessary.

Fig. 4: Checking Crankshaft Flange Runout

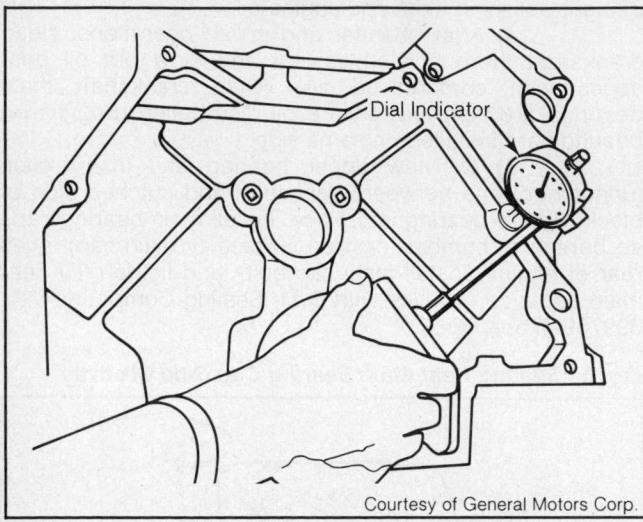

Courtesy of General Motors Corp.

REAR MAIN BEARING OIL SEAL
Removal

1) With engine/transaxle assembly removed from vehicle, remove flywheel dust cover. On automatic transmission equipped vehicles, remove flexplate-to-torque converter bolts.

2) Remove clutch housing bolts and separate engine from transaxle assembly. On manual transmission equipped vehicles, remove pressure plate, clutch disc and flywheel.

3) Using screwdriver or seal remover, pry rear main oil seal out of bore and discard.

CAUTION: Extreme care should be taken not to damage crankshaft seal surfaces. Excess deposits not removable with solvent may be removed with crocus cloth. DO NOT polish seal surface. A polished surface may produce poor sealing or cause premature seal wear.

Installation

1) Clean block and crankshaft sealing surface. Lubricate inside of seal with engine oil. Position seal on block and press into place with Seal Installer (J-33084).

2) If rear main seal bearing cap has been loosened, clean and reseal side grooves with G.M. Sealing Compound (No. 3997597). *See Fig. 3.* To complete installation, reverse removal procedure.

CAMSHAFT

TIMING BELT
Removal

1) Disconnect negative battery cable. Remove belts, brackets and shields necessary to gain access to crankshaft pulley. Remove timing belt front cover.

2) Rotate crankshaft so timing mark on crankshaft pulley lines up with 10 degree BTDC mark on indicator scale. Mark on camshaft sprocket must align with mark on camshaft carrier. Remove crankshaft pulley.

3) Remove timing probe holder. Verify timing marks are aligned and loosen water pump retaining bolts to remove timing belt.

Installation

1) Install new timing belt on sprockets. Install crankshaft pulley and check for alignment of timing marks. Using Cam Drive Belt Tension Adjusting Wrench (J-33039), rotate water pump clockwise until slack is removed from timing belt. Tighten water pump bolts. *See Fig. 5.*

Fig. 5: Timing Belt Tension Adjustment

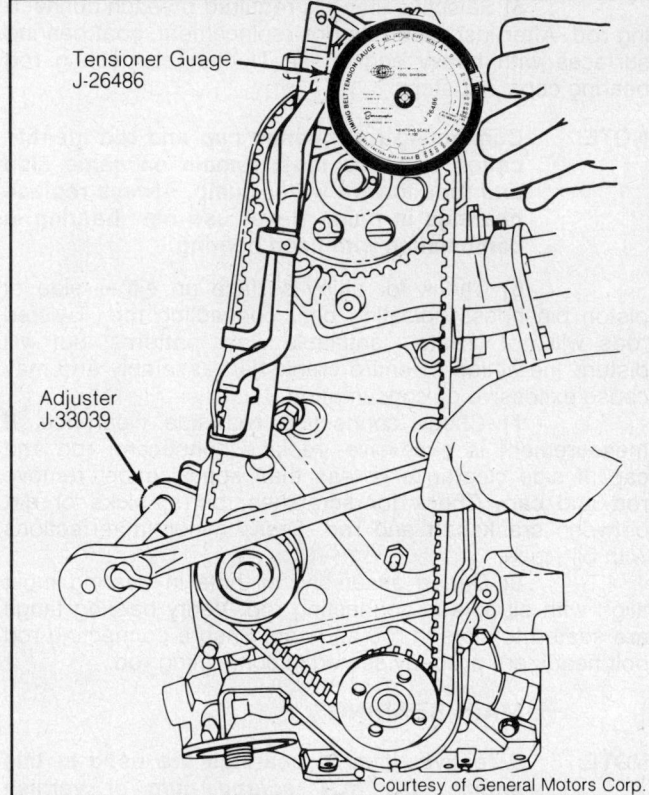

Courtesy of General Motors Corp.

NOTE: If new timing belt has been installed, check final tension with engine at operating temperature. If new head gasket is installed, cylinder head must be retightened AFTER initial warm up. Timing belt tension MUST then be rechecked.

2) Using Cam Drive Belt Tension Gauge (J-26486-A), check belt tension between water pump and camshaft sprocket. Initial new belt tension should be 38 lbs. (17 kg). Used belt tension should be 27-36 lbs. (12-16 kg).

3) Reassemble components and run engine to operating temperature (thermostat open). As new belt takes a set position, substantial tension loss will occur. After belt has been run, recheck tension with gauge on belt.

4) If belt tension is incorrect, loosen water pump bolts and rotate pump until correct tension is obtained. Hot timing belt tension specification is 30 lbs. (13 kg).

5) DO NOT leave tension gauge on belt during retightening or reading will be inaccurate. Tighten water pump bolts. Reverse removal procedure to complete installation.

2.0L OHC 4-CYLINDER (Cont.)

TIMING BELT REAR COVER
Removal & Installation

1) To remove timing belt rear cover, remove timing belt and related components. Remove rear cover mount bolts and rear cover. Remove gaskets and discard.

2) To install, clean gasket sealing surfaces and coat new. rear cover gaskets with sealer. Install gaskets, cover and mount bolts. Install timing belt and tighten to specification.

FRONT OIL SEAL
Removal

1) Remove timing belt front cover, crankshaft pulley, timing probe holder, timing belt, camshaft carrier cover, camshaft bolt and sprocket. Remove crankshaft sprocket bolt, washer and sprocket.

2) Remove key from crankshaft end. Remove rear thrust washer from crankshaft. Pry out crankshaft front oil seal and discard.

Installation

1) Install protective sleeve contained in Front Crankshaft Seal Installer Kit (J-33083), onto front of crankshaft.

2) Coat inside of new seal lip with oil and drive into place with seal installer. Remove sleeve from front of crankshaft.

3) Reinstall crankshaft sprocket. To complete installation, reverse removal procedure.

TIMING BELT SPROCKETS
Removal

1) Remove timing belt front cover and timing belt. Align mark on camshaft sprocket with mark on camshaft carrier. Remove timing probe holder.

2) Loosen water pump retaining bolts and remove timing belt from camshaft sprocket. Remove camshaft carrier cover. Hold camshaft with open-end wrench at hexagonal boss provided near rear of camshaft. See Fig. 6.

3) Remove camshaft sprocket retaining bolt, washer and camshaft sprocket. Remove crankshaft retaining bolt and thrust washer. Remove crankshaft sprocket.

Fig. 6: Removal & Installation of Camshaft Sprocket

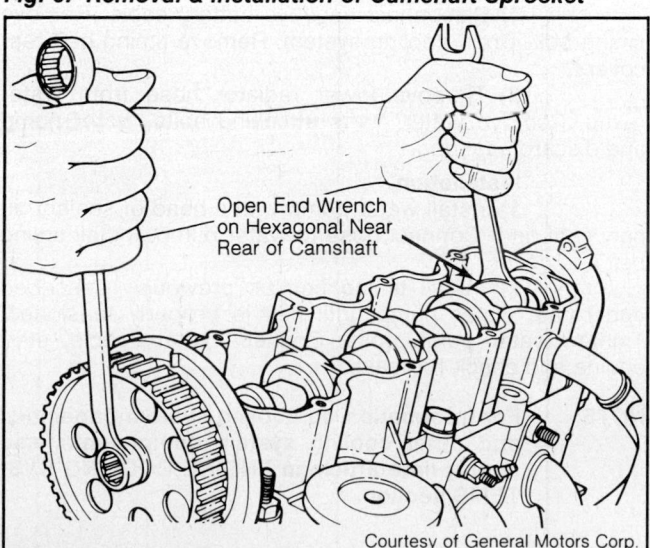

Open End Wrench on Hexagonal Near Rear of Camshaft

Courtesy of General Motors Corp.

Hold camshaft at hexagonal near rear of engine.

Installation

1) Install camshaft sprocket on camshaft. Align timing marks on camshaft sprocket and camshaft carrier. Hold camshaft, then install and tighten retaining bolt and washer.

2) Install camshaft carrier cover. Position crankshaft sprocket on end of crankshaft. Install thrust washer and retaining bolt.

CAMSHAFT
Removal

NOTE: Valves must be supported with compressed air using Air Line Adapter (J-22794).

1) Remove camshaft carrier cover. Using Valve Compressor (J-33302), compress valve springs and remove rocker arms. Remove timing belt front engine cover and remove timing belt.

2) Remove distributor assembly. Remove camshaft sprocket and camshaft thrust plate at rear of camshaft carrier. Slide camshaft rearward and remove from carrier.

Inspection

Check camshaft journals and camshaft lobe lift. If not to specification, replace camshaft.

Installation

1) Install new camshaft carrier front oil seal with Seal Installer (J-33085). Lubricate and place camshaft in carrier using care not to damage oil seal during installation. Install camshaft thrust plate retaining bolts and tighten.

2) Check camshaft end play. If not to specification, replace thrust plate. Recheck end play. If removed, apply sealer to camshaft carrier and install carrier on cylinder head. Tighten bolts in sequence. See Fig. 1.

3) Install distributor, camshaft sprocket and timing belt. Install camshaft carrier cover with new gasket. Reverse removal procedure to complete assembly.

CAMSHAFT CARRIER

NOTE: Camshaft carrier/cylinder head retaining bolts should be loosened only when engine is cold. Head gasket replacement is recommended whenever carrier/cylinder head retaining bolts are loosened.

Removal

1) Remove air cleaner and PCV hose. On turbo models, remove induction tube. Disconnect spark plug and ignition coil wires. Remove cam carrier cover, distributor and camshaft sprocket.

2) Remove camshaft carrier bolts in reverse of tightening sequence. See Fig. 1. Separate camshaft carrier from cylinder head and remove assembly from engine. Remove thrust plate from rear of carrier and slide camshaft out. Extract front oil seal and discard.

Installation

1) Inspect camshaft carrier bearing surfaces. If bearing surfaces are worn or damaged, camshaft carrier must be replaced. Install new camshaft carrier front oil seal. Place camshaft in carrier.

2) Install camshaft thrust plate retaining bolts and tighten. Check camshaft end play. Apply a continuous bead of sealer to camshaft carrier and install carrier on cylinder head.

3) Gradually tighten cylinder head/camshaft carrier retaining bolts in sequence to 18 ft. lbs. (24 N.m). Then turn each bolt 60 degrees clockwise in proper sequence three times until a 180 degree rotation (1/2 turn) is obtained. *See Fig. 1.*

4) Install distributor assembly, camshaft sprocket and timing belt. Connect PCV hose to camshaft carrier. After installation is complete, start engine and run until thermostat opens.

5) With engine at operating temperature, tighten all retaining bolts an additional 30-50 degrees in sequence. To complete installation, reverse removal procedure.

ENGINE OILING

CRANKCASE CAPACITY

Engine oil capacity is 4 qts. (3.8L) without filter change. Add .5 qt. (.47L) with new filter.

NORMAL OIL PRESSURE

Normal oil pressure is 65 psi (4.57 kg/cm²) at 2500 RPM, with engine at operating temperature.

PRESSURE REGULATOR VALVE

Pressure regulator valve is located in oil pump body and is not a serviceable component.

ENGINE OILING SYSTEM

Oil from the gear-type oil pump passes through a full flow oil filter to main oil galley on left side of block. Hydraulic lifters, connecting rod, main and camshaft journals are pressure lubricated. Full pressure lubrication is directed to connecting rods by drilled passages from adjacent main bearing journals.

Cylinder walls are spray lubricated from a drilled passage in connecting rods. Camshaft is lubricated from main oil gallery by way of passage to camshaft carrier at No. 3 journal. A pressure relief valve is located in left side cylinder head oil passage.

OIL PUMP

NOTE: DO NOT repair pump housing. If any component is not to specification, replace oil pump.

Removal & Disassembly

1) Remove crankshaft sprocket, timing belt and rear cover. Disconnect wire from oil pressure switch.

2) Remove oil pan and oil filter. Remove bolts attaching oil pick-up tube to block. Remove oil pump.

CAUTION: Pressure regulator valve spring is under pressure. Use caution during removal of cotter pin or when unscrewing plug.

3) Remove end cover and gasket from rear of pump. Remove pump gears. Remove plug (or cotter pin), spring and pressure regulator plunger.

4) Remove pick-up tube and "O" ring seal from oil pump body. Discard "O" ring seal. Check tube for looseness and screen for broken wire mesh.

Reassembly & Installation

1) Clean and inspect all parts for chipping or excessive wear. Check depth of wear pattern in end cover and replace if necessary. Install valve plunger and spring.

2) Coat valve plug with sealer and install. Prime pump as necessary and install pump gears with mark on outer gear surface facing front of engine. *See Fig. 7.*

Fig. 7: Exploded View of Oil Pump Assembly

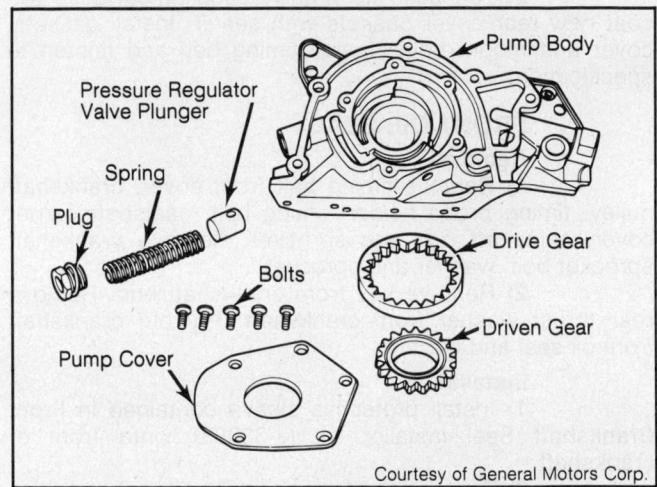

Courtesy of General Motors Corp.

3) Install oil pump cover with new gasket (using only original equipment). Gasket thickness is critical to proper function of oil pump. Using a new "O" ring, install pick-up tube. To complete installation, reverse removal procedure.

OIL PUMP SPECIFICATIONS

Application	In. (mm)
Drive Gear-to-Body Clearance	.014-.018 (.35-.45)
Idler Gear-to-Body Clearance	.004-.007 (.10-.19)
Gear-to-Cover End Clearance	
Below Pump Housing	.001-.004 (.03-.10)
Gear Lash	.004-.008 (.10-.20)

ENGINE COOLING

WATER PUMP

Removal

1) Disconnect negative battery cable. Remove timing belt. Drain cooling system. Remove timing belt rear covers.

2) Remove lower radiator hose from water pump. Remove water pump attaching bolts, water pump and discard seal ring.

Installation

1) Install water pump with a bead of sealant on new seal ring. Connect hose to water pump. Install timing belt and cover.

2) Install timing belt as previously described and rotate water pump until belt is properly tensioned. Tighten water pump bolts. Connect battery cable, start engine and check for leaks.

NOTE: For information on cooling system capacities and other cooling system components, see appropriate article in ENGINE COOLING SYSTEMS section.

2.0L OHC 4-CYLINDER (Cont.)

ENGINE SPECIFICATIONS

GENERAL SPECIFICATIONS

| Year | DISPLACEMENT | | Fuel System | HP@RPM | Torque Ft. Lbs.@RPM | Compr. Ratio | BORE | | STROKE | |
	Cu. In.	Liters					In.	mm	In.	mm
1988										
Turbo	122	2.0	MFI	.....	.....	8.0:1	3.38	86	3.38	86
Non-Turbo	122	2.0	TBI			8.8:1	3.38	86	3.38	86

VALVES

Engine Size & Valve	Head Diam. In. (mm)	Face Angle	Seat Angle	Seat Width In. (mm)	Stem Diameter In. (mm)	Stem Clearance In. (mm)	Valve Lift In. (mm)
2.0L							
Intake	1.69 43	46°	45°	[1][2]	[1]	.0006-.002 (.015-.050)	[1]
Exhaust	1.44 36.5	46°	45°			.0010-.0024 (.025-.061)	

[1] – Information not available.
[2] – Seat runout should not exceed .002" (.05 mm).

PISTONS, PINS & RINGS

| Engine | PISTONS | PINS | | RINGS | | |
	Clearance In. (mm)	Piston Fit In. (mm)	Rod Fit In. (mm)	Ring No.	End Gap In. (mm)	Side Clearance In. (mm)
2.0L	[1] .0004-.0012 (.010-.030)	.0004-.0006 (.010-.015)	Press Fit	1	.012-.020 (.30-.50)	.002-.003 (.05-.08)
				2	.012-.020 (.30-.50)	.001-.0024 (.025-.061)
				3	.016-.055 (.41-1.4)	.....

[1] - VIN K shown; VIN M is .0012-.0020" (.030-.050 mm).

CRANKSHAFT MAIN & CONNECTING ROD BEARINGS

| Engine | MAIN BEARINGS | | | | CONNECTING ROD BEARINGS | | |
	Journal Diam. In. (mm)	Clearance In. (mm)	Thrust Bearing	Crankshaft End Play In. (mm)	Journal Diam. In. (mm)	Clearance In. (mm)	Side Play In. (mm)
2.0L	[1][2] 2.2830-2.2833 (57.988-57.996)	.0006-.0016 (.015-.041)	No. 3	.003-.012 (.08-.30)	[2] 1.9278-1.9286 (48.97-48.98)	.0007-.0024 (.018-.061)	.0027-.0095 (.069-.241)

[1] – Brown coded crankshafts shown, Green coded crankshafts are 2.2827-2.2830" (57.981-57.988 mm).
[2] – Runout and taper must not exceed .0002 (.005 mm).

General Motors Engines

2.0L OHC 4-CYLINDER (Cont.)

ENGINE SPECIFICATIONS (Cont.)

VALVE SPRINGS

Engine	Free Length In. (mm)	PRESSURE Lbs. @ In. (Kg @ mm)	
		Valve Closed	Valve Open
2.0L	1	1	1

1 – Information not available.

CAMSHAFT

Engine	Journal Diam. In. (mm)	Clearance In. (mm)	Lobe Lift In. (mm)
2.0L 1			
No. 1	1.6714-1.6720 (42.45-42.47)	.0008 (.02)	Int. .241 (6.12)
No. 2	1.6812-1.6816 (42.70-42.71)	.0008 (.02)	2 Exh.
No. 3	1.6911-1.6917 (42.95-42.97)	.0008 (.02)	
No. 4	1.7009-1.7015 (43.20-43.22)	.0008 (.02)	
No. 5	1.7108-1.7144 (43.45-43.55)	.0008 (.02)	

1 – End play should be .016-.064" (.04-.16 mm).
2 – Information not available.

TIGHTENING SPECIFICATIONS

Application	Ft. Lbs. (N. m)
Camshaft Carrier & Cylinder Head Bolts	
Step 1	18 (24)
Step 2, 3 & 4	1
Step 5	2
Camshaft Sprocket Bolt	34 (45)
Connecting Rod Nuts	3 26 (35)
Crankshaft Pulley-to-Sprocket Bolt	20 (27)
Crankshaft Sprocket Retaining Bolt	34 (45)
Exhaust Manifold/Cylinder Head Bolts	16 (22)
Flywheel Bolts	48 (65)
Intake Manifold Bolts	16 (22)
Main Bearing Cap Bolts	4 44 (60)
Oil Pump Control Valve Plug	15 (20)
Water Pump Retaining Bolts	19 (25)

	INCH Lbs.
Camshaft Thrust Plate Bolt	72 (8)
Oil Pump Retaining Bolts	60 (7)
Oil Pickup Tube Bolts	60 (7)
Timing Belt Front Cover Bolt	60 (7)
Timing Belt Rear Cover Bolt	54 (6)

1 – Tighten an additional 180 degrees in 3 steps of 60 degrees each.
2 – Warm up engine, tighten bolts additional 30-50 degrees.
3 – Plus an additional 45 degree turn.
4 – Plus an additional 40-50 degree turn.

General Motors Engines

2.0L OHV 4-CYLINDER

NOTE: For engine repair procedures not covered in this article, see ENGINE OVERHAUL PROCEDURES article at beginning of this section.

ENGINE CODING

ENGINE IDENTIFICATION

Engine may be identified from Vehicle Identification Number (VIN) stamped on metal tab located on top of instrument panel at lower left of windshield. VIN number code also appears on pad at left rear of cylinder block (on transmission mounting flange). The VIN number contains 17 characters. The 8th character identifies engine.

ENGINE CODE

Engine	Code
2.0L (122") H.O. TBI	1

ENGINE REMOVAL

See ENGINE REMOVAL & INSTALLATION at end of ENGINE section.

CYLINDER HEAD & MANIFOLDS

INTAKE MANIFOLD

Removal

1) Disconnect battery negative cable. Drain cooling system. Remove air cleaner assembly. Disconnect necessary vacuum lines and electrical wires. Remove idler pulley.

2) If equipped, remove power steering drive belt and disconnect steering pump. Remove power steering adjusting bracket. Disconnect fuel lines. Disconnect TBI linkage and remove TBI assembly.

3) Remove distributor hold-down bracket bolt and distributor. Remove manifold attaching nuts and bolts. Remove intake manifold. Disconnect heater hose and condenser from bottom of intake manifold.

Fig. 1: Intake Manifold Tightening Sequence

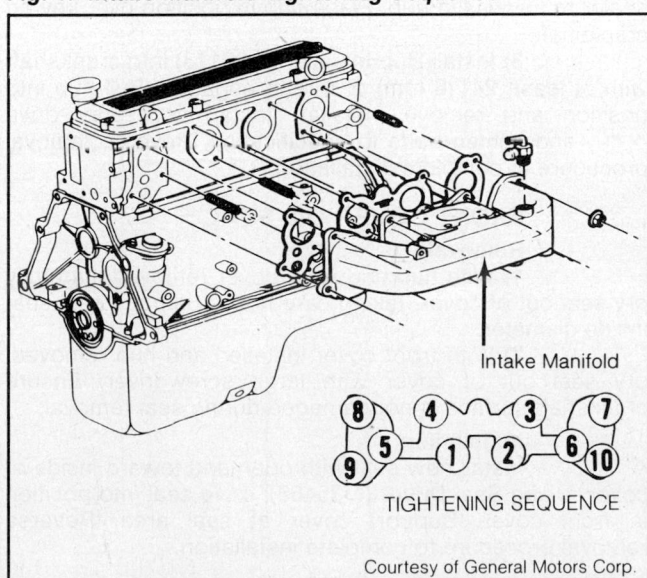

TIGHTENING SEQUENCE

Courtesy of General Motors Corp.

Installation

1) Clean mating surfaces of intake manifold and cylinder head. Position new manifold gasket on cylinder head. Install intake manifold.

2) Tighten manifold attaching nuts and bolts. *See Fig. 1.* Reverse removal procedure to complete installation. Adjust drive belts.

EXHAUST MANIFOLD

Removal

1) Disconnect battery negative cable. Remove air cleaner assembly. Remove oil dipstick and air cleaner hot air duct-to-shroud bolt.

2) Remove air cleaner hot air duct and hose. Remove dipstick tube bracket bolt. If equipped, remove A/C suction line bracket bolt. Disconnect oxygen sensor bracket.

3) Remove alternator belt, bracket bolts and spacer. Remove alternator support bracket. Remove pulsair pipe (if equipped). Raise vehicle and disconnect exhaust inlet pipe at manifold.

4) Lower vehicle and disconnect air management-to-check valve hose and bracket. If equipped with A/C, remove suction-line bracket. Remove exhaust manifold bolts. Remove manifold.

Installation

1) Clean all mating surfaces on exhaust manifold and cylinder head. Position manifold against head.

2) Install and tighten manifold bolts. *See Fig. 2.* Reverse removal procedure to complete installation.

Fig. 2: Exhaust Manifold Tightening Sequence

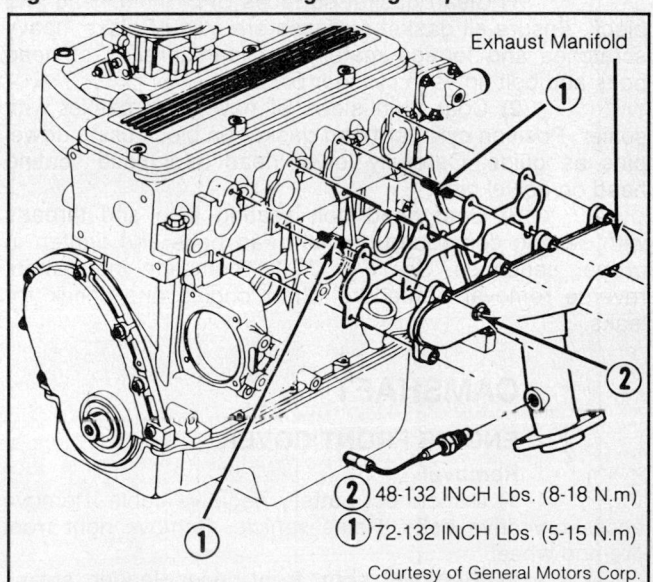

Exhaust Manifold

② 48-132 INCH Lbs. (8-18 N.m)
① 72-132 INCH Lbs. (5-15 N.m)

Courtesy of General Motors Corp.

CYLINDER HEAD

NOTE: Cylinder head should only be removed when engine is cold. Check cylinder head for warped gasket surface, nicks or damage. Replace head if cracked. Remove burrs or scratches with an oil stone.

2.0L OHV 4-CYLINDER (Cont.)

Removal

1) Disconnect battery negative cable and remove air cleaner. Drain cooling system. Raise vehicle. Remove exhaust manifold shield. Disconnect exhaust inlet pipe at manifold.

2) Remove heater hose from intake manifold. Lower vehicle. Remove engine lift bracket. Remove distributor. Disconnect vacuum manifold at alternator bracket. Disconnect remaining vacuum lines to intake manifold and thermostat.

3) If equipped, remove pulsair pipe assembly. Remove air management pipe at exhaust check valve. Disconnect accelerator linkage at TBI and remove linkage bracket. Disconnect necessary wiring. Remove upper radiator hose at thermostat housing. Remove dipstick tube and hot water bracket.

4) Remove idler pulley. Remove power steering drive belt (if equipped) and disconnect pump. Remove power steering adjusting bracket. Disconnect fuel line at TBI. Remove alternator with wiring. Remove alternator brace and upper bracket. Remove valve cover.

5) Remove rocker arms and push rods. Index mark these parts for reassembly reference. Remove cylinder head bolts. Remove cylinder head, TBI assembly, intake manifold and exhaust manifold as an assembly.

NOTE: **If cylinder head is to be serviced, remove carbon deposits from combustion chamber with scraper and wire brush before removing valves. When disassembling, index mark all valve components for reassembly reference.**

Installation

1) Clean gasket surfaces of cylinder head and block. Ensure all gasket surfaces are free of nicks, heavy scratches and foreign materials. Clean threads of head bolts and bolt holes in cylinder block.

2) Coat both sides of new head gasket with sealer. Position cylinder head gasket on block using dowel pins as guide. Carefully lower head into place seating head on dowel pins.

3) Coat head bolt seating face and threads with sealing compound. Install head bolts and tighten in proper sequence. *See Fig. 3.* To complete installation, reverse removal procedure. Start engine and check for leaks.

CAMSHAFT

ENGINE FRONT COVER

Removal

1) Disconnect battery negative cable. Remove accessory drive belts. Raise vehicle. Remove right front tire and wheel.

2) Remove right front inner fender splash shield. If equipped, remove A/C belt. Remove accessory drive pulley-to-hub retaining bolts. Remove pulley-to-crankshaft retaining bolt, washer and pulley.

3) Install Hub Puller (J-24420) on hub and remove hub. Remove front cover retaining bolts. Remove front cover.

Installation

1) Clean mating surfaces on block and front cover. Apply bead of RTV sealer to cover, using care to keep sealer out of cover bolt holes. At time of installation, flanges must be free of oil and sealer must be wet to touch. Install Front Cover Centerer (J-35468) in front cover seal. Coat front cover seal contact area with oil.

Fig. 3: Cylinder Head Tightening Sequence

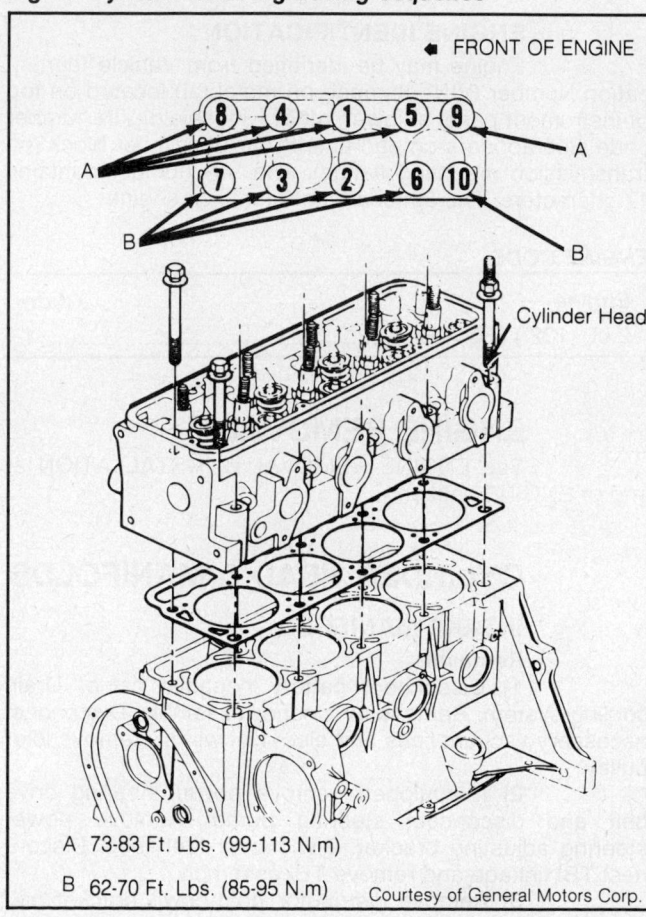

A 73-83 Ft. Lbs. (99-113 N.m)

B 62-70 Ft. Lbs. (85-95 N.m)   Courtesy of General Motors Corp.

2) Position front cover on block, install retaining bolts and tighten. Remove centering tool. Apply RTV sealer to keyway in hub. Place hub in position over key on crankshaft.

3) Install Hub Installer (J-29113) into crankshaft with at least .24" (6 mm) of thread engaged. Pull hub into position and remove installer. Install accessory drive pulley and tighten bolts to specification. Reverse removal procedure to complete installation.

FRONT COVER OIL SEAL

Removal

1) With hub and front cover removed, carefully pry seal out of cover, taking care not to damage seal seat inside diameter.

2) With front cover installed and hub removed, pry seal out of cover with large screwdriver. Ensure crankshaft surface is not damaged during seal removal.

Installation

Install new seal with open end toward inside of cover. Using Seal Driver (J-35468), drive seal into position in front cover. Support cover at seal area. Reverse removal procedure to complete installation.

2.0L OHV 4-CYLINDER (Cont.)

TIMING CHAIN & SPROCKETS

Removal

1) Remove crankcase front cover. Align marks on camshaft sprocket with marks on crankshaft sprocket. *See Fig. 4.* Remove attaching bolts, timing chain tensioner and damper.

Fig. 4: Timing Chain Sprocket Alignment

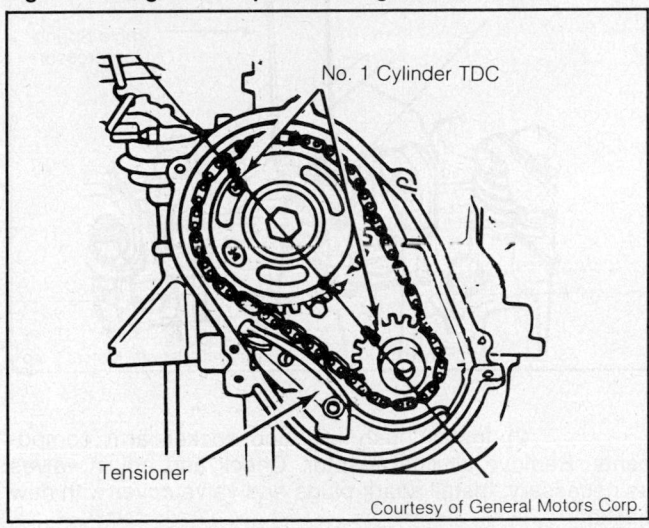

No. 1 Cylinder TDC

Tensioner

Courtesy of General Motors Corp.

2) Remove camshaft sprocket and timing chain. Using Sprocket Puller (J-22888), remove crankshaft sprocket.

Installation

1) If crankshaft sprocket was removed, install using Sprocket Installer (J-5590). Lubricate thrust surface of camshaft with Molykote.

2) Position chain over camshaft and crankshaft sprockets, making sure 2 marks on camshaft sprocket align with mark on crankshaft sprocket. Position camshaft sprocket on camshaft.

3) Ensure hole in camshaft sprocket aligns with dowel pin on camshaft. Draw camshaft sprocket onto camshaft using camshaft retaining bolts and tighten. Lubricate timing chain with oil.

CAUTION: Timing chain tensioner is spring-loaded and requires caution when reinstalling.

4) Using Timing Chain Tensioner (J-33875), position tangs of tool under sliding block and pull tool to compress spring. While compressing spring, insert fabricated holding tool (cotter pin or nail) into hole in tensioner to retain spring.

5) With spring compressed and held in place, remove Tensioner (J-33875). Install chain tensioner. Remove holding tool (cotter pin or nail). Install crankcase front cover. Reverse removal procedure to complete installation.

CAMSHAFT

Removal

1) With engine removed from vehicle, remove valve cover, rocker arm assembly, push rods and lifters. Remove engine front cover. Mark position of rotor and remove distributor.

NOTE: Use extreme care when removing camshaft, as all journals are same size and damage to bearings could result.

2) Remove fuel pump and push rod. Remove timing chain and camshaft sprocket. Remove thrust plate retaining bolts and remove thrust plate. Remove camshaft.

Inspection

1) Measure camshaft journals. Check camshaft end play. Replace thrust plate if clearance is excessive.

2) Check camshaft lobe lift. Attach dial gauge with Ball and Socket Attachment (J-8520) to camshaft carrier or "V" block. Measure lobe lift. If not to specification, replace camshaft.

Installation

1) Lubricate camshaft journals with engine oil and install camshaft. If new camshaft is installed, coat camshaft lobes with Molykote. Ensure new oil, filter and lifters are installed as necessary.

2) Apply RTV sealer to camshaft rear cover and on machined groove of engine block. Reverse removal procedure to complete installation.

CAMSHAFT BEARINGS

Removal

1) With camshaft and crankshaft removed, remove camshaft rear cover. Fasten connecting rods to side of engine to keep out of work area. Using Camshaft Bearing Remover (J-6098), fasten nut and thrust washer to end of threads.

2) Insert Camshaft Bearing Remover (J-6098) pilot in camshaft front bearing and install puller screw through pilot. Install Remover/Installer (J-6098) with shoulder toward bearing. Ensure a sufficient amount of threads are engaged.

3) Using an additional wrench to hold puller screw stationary, turn nut until bearing is pulled from block. Remove bearing from Remover/Installer (J-6098). Remove remaining bearings in same manner.

4) Insert pilot in camshaft rear bearing to remove rear intermediate bearing. Assemble Remover/Installer (J-6098) on driver handle and remove front and rear bearings by driving toward center of cylinder block.

Installation

1) Using Camshaft Bearing Remover (J-6098), fasten nut and thrust washer to end of threads. Insert pilot in camshaft bearing and install puller screw through pilot.

2) Insert bearing in bore with oil hole centered between 2 and 3 o'clock positions on rear and intermediate bearing. Front bearing has one oil hole at 11 o'clock, and the other centered between 2 and 3 o'clock positions.

3) Using additional wrench to hold puller screw stationary, turn nut until bearing is pulled into bore. Install remaining bearings in same manner. Ensure alignment holes are in proper positions.

4) Apply RTV sealer to groove in engine block and to camshaft rear cover. Position camshaft cover on block, install retaining bolts and tighten. Reverse removal procedure to complete installation.

VALVES

NOTE: When reconditioning valves, do not lap valves heavily. Do not remove more than .010" (.254 mm) from end of valve stem.

VALVE ARRANGEMENT

E-I-I-E-E-I-I-E (Front-to-rear).

VALVE GUIDE SERVICING

1) Valve guides are integral with cylinder head. Check valve stem-to-guide clearance. If clearance exceeds service limits, recondition valve guide. To check valve guide wear, insert valve with head positioned .08" (2 mm) away from valve seat.

2) Attach dial gauge to cylinder head. Position gauge indicator against valve stem at right angle and just above guide. Move valve side-to-side and measure guide wear shown on dial gauge.

3) Use Valve Guide Reamer Set (J-5330-1, 2 or 3) for reconditioning guides. For cleaning guides, use Valve Guide Cleaner (J-8101).

4) When reconditioning, always use next oversize reamer and oversize valve. Oversize valves are available in .0030" (.076 mm), .015" (.38 mm), and .030" (.076 mm) sizes. If valve face is reground, measure margin width. Minimum valve margin width is .030" (.076 mm).

5) Check valve seats for proper angle and seat width. Measure valve seat runout. Valve seat must be refaced if guide has been reamed. Measure valve seat widths.

6) Maximum valve seat runout is .002" (.05 mm). If necessary, use scraper to lightly chamfer or bevel sharp top inside edge of guide. Valve stem end may be reconditioned by grinding. Do not remove more than .010" (.254 mm) from end of valve stem.

VALVE STEM OIL SEALS

Removal

1) Remove valve cover. When removing rocker arm components, mark for reinstallation in original location. Remove spark plugs. If valve or valve seat have not been damaged, valve stem seals can be removed by holding valve against seat using air pressure.

2) Install Air Line Adapter (J-23590) in spark plug hole. A minimum of 140 psi (9.8 kg/cm²) line pressure is required. If air pressure does not hold valve shut, valve is damaged or burnt and cylinder head must be removed for service.

3) Compress valve spring using Spring Compressor (J-5892). See Fig. 5. Remove valve lock retainers and release spring compressor. Remove retainer cap, spring, valve stem oil seal, shim and push rod. Discard valve stem oil seal.

NOTE: If oversized valves have been installed, oversized oil seals must be used.

Installation

1) Coat valve stem with engine oil. Apply Lubriplate to all rocker arm contact surfaces. Install shim and new valve stem oil seal over valve stem and seat on valve guide. Place valve spring and retainer cap over valve stem. Compress spring and install retainer locks.

Fig. 5: Compressing Valve Springs

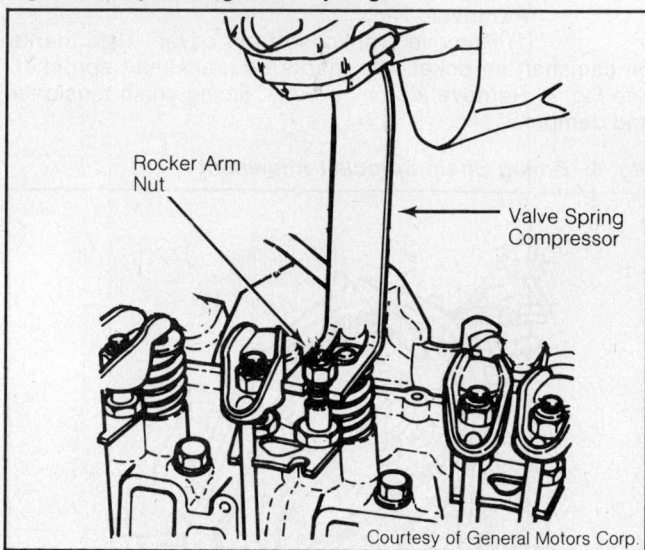

Rocker Arm Nut

Valve Spring Compressor

Courtesy of General Motors Corp.

2) Install push rod and rocker arm components. Remove air line adapter. Check and adjust valves as necessary. Install spark plugs and valve cover with new gasket.

VALVE SPRINGS

NOTE: For valve spring removal and installation procedures, refer to valve stem oil seal removal and installation.

1) Test valve spring pressure with Valve Spring Tester (J-8056). Springs must be within 10 lbs. (4.5 kg) of specified load (without dampers). Check valve spring squareness.

2) Valve spring out-of-square limit is .0625" (1.587 mm). Install new valve stem oil seals. If necessary, install new valve springs and retainers. Compress spring and install valve spring retainer locks.

3) Apply Lubriplate to all rocker arm contact surfaces. Dip rocker arms in engine oil before installing. Check valve spring for proper installed height.

VALVE SPRING INSTALLED HEIGHT

CAUTION: At no time should spring be shimmed to obtain spring height UNDER minimum specifications.

Measure from top of spring seat to bottom of retainer cap. If measurement exceeds specified height, install .03" (.7 mm) thick shim to correct spring height. See Fig. 6.

VALVE SPRING INSTALLED HEIGHT

Application	Installed Height In. (mm)
2.0L OHV	[1] 1.6 (40.6)

[1] – Including shim.

2.0L OHV 4-CYLINDER (Cont.)

Fig. 6: Measuring Valve Spring Installed Height

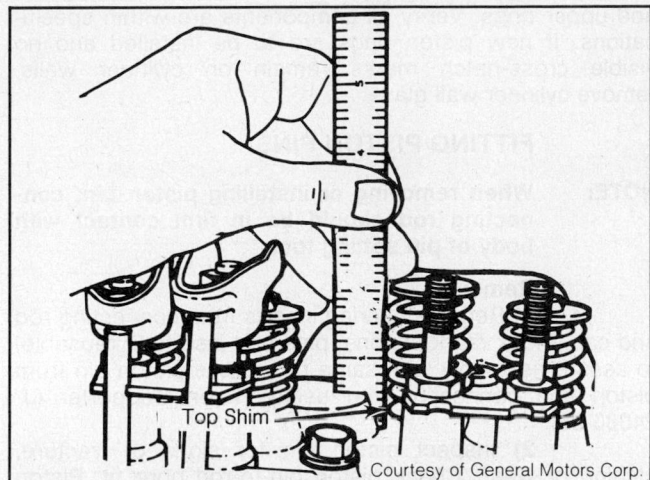

Top Shim

Courtesy of General Motors Corp.

*Check installed height from bottom of retainer cap
to top of spring seat.*

HYDRAULIC VALVE LIFTER ASSEMBLY

NOTE: Before replacing hydraulic lifter for noisy operation, check for worn rocker arms or valve tips. If lifter assembly sticks in bore, use hydraulic lifter puller tool or magnet to remove.

1) Hydraulic lifters are serviced as assemblies only. Parts are select-fit and are not interchangeable. Used lifter assemblies must be installed in original locations.

2) Using Lifter Remover (J-29834) or magnet, remove lifters. Clean and inspect but do not mix components or positions. If lifter is sticking, disassemble and clean lifter components.

3) If lifter check valve is not functional, obstructions may be preventing it from closing, or lifter or check valve spring may be broken. Clean and replace components as necessary.

4) If plunger does not move freely in body of lifter, soak lifter in solvent to free plunger and dissolve deposits if necessary. Plunger should drop to bottom of body easily when assembled dry. Assemble lifter and check unloaded operation by pressing down on cap.

NOTE: When performing leak-down test only calibrated test fluid can be used. If old lifter is disassembled and cleaned, fill with test fluid before installing and testing. New lifters contain test fluid. If new lifter is installed, remove sealer coating from inside of new lifter and check leak-down rate.

5) Place lifter upright in Leak-Down Tester (J-5790) and check leak-down rate. Leak-down rate should be 12-90 seconds. If not within specifications, replace lifter assembly. Inspect lifter base-to-cam lobe contact area. Surface must have smooth and convex contact face.

6) Inspect lifters for flattened or concave bottom surface. If lifter is replaced, inspect related cam lobe for proper lobe lift. If a lobe is worn beyond specification, replace camshaft (and lifters if necessary). Check lifter-to-bore clearance. Before installing lifters, coat bottom of lifter with Molykote.

HYDRAULIC VALVE LIFTER ADJUSTMENT

1) Rotate engine until No. 1 cylinder is at TDC of compression stroke. Ensure mark on crankshaft pulley lines up with "0" mark on timing plate. The following valves may be adjusted: No. 1 and 2 intake; No. 1 and 3 exhaust.

2) To adjust, back off adjusting nut until clearance is felt at push rod. Tighten adjusting nut until all clearance is removed. Turn adjusting nut an additional 1 1/2 turns to center lifter plunger in bore.

3) Rotate crankshaft 360 degrees and realign timing marks. Adjust No. 3 and 4 intake valves and No. 2 and 4 exhaust valves.

PISTONS, PINS & RINGS

OIL PAN

See OIL PAN REMOVAL at end of ENGINE section.

PISTON & ROD ASSEMBLY

NOTE: Before removing piston and connecting rod, ensure rod caps are marked for proper reassembly.

Removal

1) With cylinder head and oil pan removed, inspect cylinder bores for ridges and deposits. Remove ridge at top of cylinder bores. Rotate crankshaft and inspect connecting rods and rod caps for cylinder identification. Mark for reassembly reference.

2) Remove rod cap and place sleeve or hose over rod bolts. Push each piston and rod assembly out top of cylinder bore. Remove bearing inserts from rod and cap and inspect for size, wear and damage. Install rod caps on mating rods.

Installation

1) Check fit of new piston and rings in cylinder bore before assembling piston to connecting rod. Check piston pin for clearance, etching or wear. New pistons must be installed in cylinder for which they were fitted.

2) Install used pistons in the cylinder from which they were removed. Oil piston rings and cylinder walls with engine oil. Ensure ring gaps are properly spaced. *See Fig. 7.* Marked side of compression rings must be toward top of piston.

3) Install ring compressor on piston. Install piston and rod assembly with notch (or hole) on piston top facing front of engine and connecting rod bearing tang slots on side toward camshaft. Insert piston and rod assembly into cylinder bore.

4) After bearings have been inserted, apply engine oil to journals and bearings. Ensure oil hole in bearing insert aligns with oil hole in connecting rod. Turn crankshaft to bottom of stroke. Guide piston and rod assembly over crankshaft journal until rod bearing seats.

5) Match rod cap to rod and install. Tighten cap nuts in 2 steps. Repeat procedure for each piston assembly. After piston and rod assembly is installed, check side clearance of connecting rod on each crankshaft journal.

General Motors Engines

2.0L OHV 4-CYLINDER (Cont.)

Fig. 7: Piston Ring Gap Spacing

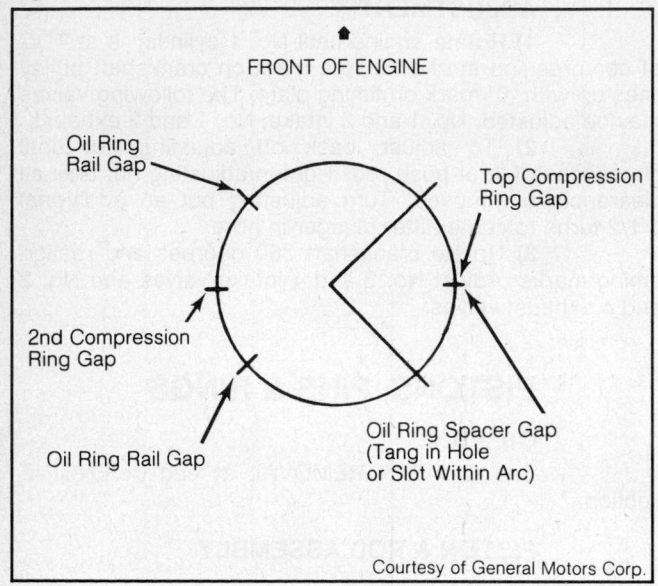

Courtesy of General Motors Corp.

FITTING PISTONS

1) Inspect pistons and replace any showing signs of excessive wear, wavy ring lands, or fractures. If shiny surface on thrust side of piston is found, check for bent connecting rod. Replace piston and/or rod as necessary. Inspect connecting rods for signs of fracture.

2) If rod is fractured, replace rod. Check pistons for fractures at ring lands, skirts and pin bosses. Check for scuffed, rough or scored skirts. Check piston-to-cylinder bore clearance by measuring piston and bore diameters.

3) Inspect cylinder walls for scoring, roughness or other signs of wear. Check bore for out-of-round and taper. Cylinder bore out-of-round and/or taper should not exceed .001" (.025 mm).

4) Measure outer diameter of piston at centerline of pin bore and 90 degrees to pin bore axis. If cylinder wall is severely marred and/or worn beyond specifications, refinishing will be necessary. Pistons are available in various oversizes. Measure new piston and hone cylinder to correct clearance.

5) Before cylinder refinishing, ensure main bearing caps are in place and tightened to specification to avoid distortion during refinishing operation. After refinishing operation, allow bore to cool, then clean bore with soap and water solution and oil cylinder walls.

FITTING PISTON RINGS

1) Clean ring grooves. Ensure oil holes (or slots) in piston are clean. Measure piston ring side and end gap clearance for all pistons. Ring side clearance should be checked. Gauge should slide freely around entire circumference without binding. If step has formed around inner portion of lower ring land, piston must be replaced.

2) Check ring end gap. Install rings on pistons with end gaps staggered at proper intervals. *See Fig. 7.* Ensure manufacturer's marks face up when rings are installed. Install oil ring expander first, followed by lower oil ring side rail and upper side rail.

3) Install upper side rail. Install intermediate and upper rings. Verify all components are within specifications. If new piston rings are to be installed and no visible cross-hatch marks remain on cylinder walls, remove cylinder wall glaze.

FITTING PISTON PINS

NOTE: **When removing or installing piston pin, connecting rod should be in firm contact with body of pin setting tool.**

Removal

1) Remove bearing inserts from connecting rod and cap. Index mark pistons, pins and inserts (if reusable) to assure assembly with same rod. Press piston pin from piston and connecting rod using Piston Supporter (J-24086-20).

2) Inspect piston pin for signs of fracture, etching or wear. Check piston pin-to-rod bore fit. Piston pins must fit into piston with light pressure. Repair or replace parts as necessary. Lubricate pin and small end of rod bore with engine oil.

Installation

1) Check piston-to-cylinder bore clearance before assembling piston and pin to connecting rod. Ensure oil hole in connecting rod aligns with oil hole in bearing. Be sure arrow or notch on top of piston is pointed toward front of engine. Start piston pin in piston and connecting rod.

2) Using guide bar and push rod, press pin through both piston and rod until pilot hub bottoms on support fixture and pin is centered in piston. After pilot hub bottoms, do not exceed 5000 lbs. (2275 kg) pressure with press. Make certain piston floats during pin installation operation.

CRANKSHAFT & ROD BEARINGS

NOTE: **Clean used inserts and caps thoroughly in solvent. Do not file or lap bearing caps or use shims to obtain proper clearance.**

CONNECTING ROD BEARINGS

1) Remove connecting rod bearing caps and mark rods and caps for proper installation. Inspect bearings for scoring, pitting or improper contact. Replace defective bearings.

2) Measure outside diameter of crankshaft connecting rod bearing journals to determine out-of-round and taper. Journal out-of-round and/or taper must not exceed .0002" (.005 mm). Use Plastigage to check bearing clearances.

3) If clearance is excessive, install undersize bearing. After inspection and/or replacement, coat bearing surfaces with heavy engine oil.

NOTE: **Connecting rod bearing cap and rod identification numbers must remain on same side. Replace bearings in pairs. Never use a new bearing in combination with a used bearing.**

2.0L OHV 4-CYLINDER (Cont.)

4) Check connecting rod side clearance with feeler gauge. If clearance is excessive, replace connecting rod and cap. If side clearance is less than specification, remove rod and cap and check for scratches, burrs, nicks or dirt between crankshaft and rod. Dress minor damage with oil stone.

5) During assembly, ensure oil hole in bearing aligns with oil hole in connecting rod. Be sure bearing tangs correctly seated in rod and cap. Tighten connecting rod bearing caps in 2 steps.

MAIN BEARINGS

NOTE: Install main bearing caps with arrow pointing toward front of engine.

1) Inspect each bearing for damage or improper contact. Replace defective bearings. Measure outside diameter of crankshaft main bearing journals. Journal out-of-round and/or taper must not exceed .0002" (.005 mm).

NOTE: Always replace bearings in pairs. Never use a new bearing in combination with a used bearing. Observe location of high spots on main bearings. If high spots are not in line, crankshaft may be bent and should be checked.

2) Using Plastigage method, main bearing clearance. If standard and undersize bearings do not bring bearing clearance within specified limits, crankshaft will have to be refinished and undersized bearings installed. If journal will not clean up to maximum undersize bearing, replace crankshaft.

3) If journals are remachined, ensure same journal shoulder radius is reproduced. Too small a radius will result in fatigue failure of crankshaft. Too large a radius will result in bearing failure due to radial ride of bearing.

4) When journals are refinished, chamfer oil holes and polish journals with No. 320 grit polishing cloth and engine oil. After chamfer and polish operations, clean crankshaft thoroughly in solvent, and blow out oil passages with compressed air.

5) Oil new bearings and install into place. Install main bearing cap so arrow faces front of engine. Install new rear main bearing seal in rear main bearing cap and cylinder block. Seal rear main bearing split-line surface with GM Sealing Compound (No. 1052357).

6) Very lightly tap main bearing caps to seated position. Hand tighten all main bearing caps. Tap end of crankshaft forward and back with lead or plastic hammer, thus lining up rear main bearing and crankshaft thrust surfaces. Tighten all main bearing caps to 63-77 ft. lbs. (85-105 N.m) in 2 steps.

THRUST BEARING ALIGNMENT

1) Measure end play at front end of No. 4 main bearing. Replace No. 4 main thrust bearing if not to specification. Standard crankshaft end play is .002-.008" (.05-.20 mm).

2) If end play is less than specification, inspect thrust bearing surfaces for scratches, burrs, nicks or dirt. Clean up minor imperfections with oil stone. Recheck end play. See Fig. 8.

Fig. 8: Measuring Crankshaft End Play

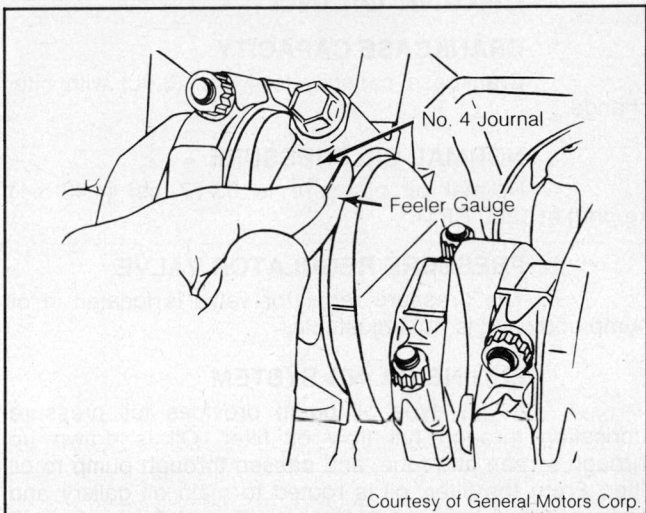

Courtesy of General Motors Corp.

Main bearing caps must be tight when checking end play.

REAR MAIN BEARING OIL SEAL

Removal

Support engine. Remove transmission and flywheel. Carefully remove seal by prying with screwdriver. Do not damage crankshaft. Carefully check crankshaft for any burrs or knicks, and correct.

Installation

1) Install new seal using Seal Installer (J-34686). See Fig. 9. Put seal over mandril and slide seal until dust lip bottoms against tool collar. Align dowel pin of tool with dowel pin hole in crankshaft and attach tool to crankshaft by hand.

Fig. 9: Installing Rear Main Oil Seal

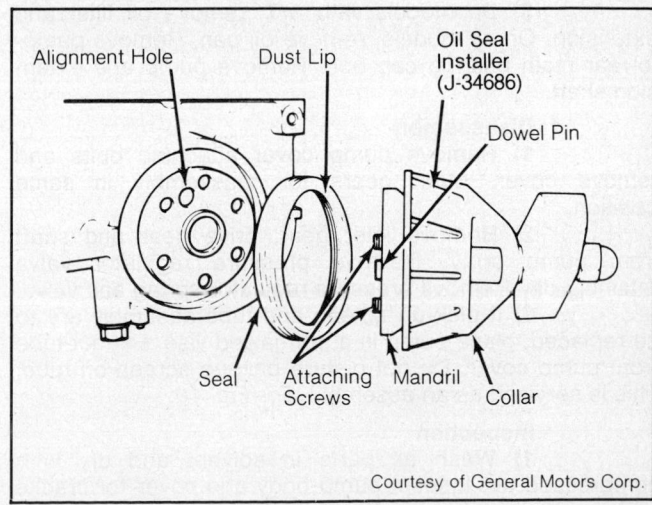

Courtesy of General Motors Corp.

2) Press seal into bore, turn "T" handle on installer until collar is tight in case. Loosen "T" handle and remove installer. Check seal. Install flywheel and transmission. Start engine and check for leaks.

General Motors Engines

2.0L OHV 4-CYLINDER (Cont.)

ENGINE OILING

CRANKCASE CAPACITY

Crankcase capacity is 4 qts. (3.8L) with filter change.

NORMAL OIL PRESSURE

Normal oil pressure is 63-77 psi (4.43-5.41 kg/cm²) at 1200 RPM.

PRESSURE REGULATOR VALVE

The pressure regulator valve is located in oil pump body and is not adjustable.

ENGINE OILING SYSTEM

A gear-type oil pump provides full pressure lubrication through full flow oil filter. Oil is drawn up through screen and tube, and passed through pump to oil filter. From the filter, oil is routed to main oil gallery and through drilled holes above camshaft (to left of camshaft centerline) and onto lifters.

Lifter pumps oil through push rods to rocker arms. Oil draining back from rocker arms is directed by cast dams (part of crankcase casting) to supply camshaft lobes with oil. Passages supplying oil to camshaft bearings also supply crankshaft bearings through passages drilled in crankshaft.

OIL PUMP

Removal

1) Disconnect battery negative cable. Remove exhaust pipe shield. Raise vehicle and drain crankcase. Disconnect exhaust inlet pipe. Disconnect A/C brace at starter and A/C bracket (if equipped).

2) Remove flywheel cover, starter bracket at block and starter. Raise and support vehicle. Remove right engine support bolts and lower support slightly.

3) On models with A/T, remove oil filter and extension. On all models, remove oil pan. Remove pump-to-rear main bearing cap bolt. Remove pump and extension shaft.

Disassembly

1) Remove pump cover attaching bolts and remove cover. Mark gears for reassembly in same position.

2) Remove idler gear, drive gear and shaft from pump body. Remove pressure regulator valve retaining pin. Remove pressure regulator spring and valve.

3) If pick-up screen and tube assembly are to be replaced, place pump in a soft-jawed vise. Extract tube from pump cover. Do not disturb pick-up screen on tube. This is serviced as an assembly. See Fig. 10.

Inspection

1) Wash all parts in solvent and dry with compressed air. Inspect pump body and cover for cracks or excessive wear.

2) Inspect gears for damage or excessive wear. Check for looseness of drive gear shaft in body.

NOTE: The pump gears and pump body cannot be serviced separately. If either gears or pump body is worn or damaged, replace entire oil pump assembly.

3) Inspect pump cover for wear that would allow oil to leak past ends of gears. Inspect pick-up

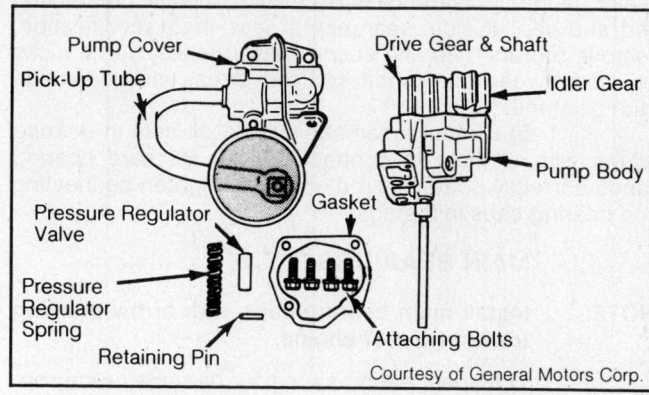

Fig. 10: Oil Pump Component Identification

Pump Cover
Pick-Up Tube
Drive Gear & Shaft
Idler Gear
Pump Body
Pressure Regulator Valve
Gasket
Pressure Regulator Spring
Retaining Pin
Attaching Bolts
Courtesy of General Motors Corp.

screen and tube assembly for damage. Check pressure regulator valve for fit in pump body.

Reassembly

1) If pick-up screen and tube assembly was removed, it should be replaced. Loss of press fit could cause an air leak, resulting in loss of oil pressure.

CAUTION: Use care not to twist, shear or collapse pipe when installing it in pump body.

2) Position pump in soft-jawed vise. Apply sealer to end of tube. Using Pick-up Tube Installer (J-8369) and soft-faced hammer, tap tube into place. Install pressure regulator valve and related parts.

3) Install drive gear, shaft and idler gear in pump body and align marks. Install new cover gasket. Reverse disassembly procedure to complete reassembly. Turn drive shaft by hand to check for smooth operation.

Installation

1) Assemble pump and extension shaft with retainer to rear main bearing cap. Align top end of hexagonal extension shaft with hexagonal lower end of distributor drive gear. Align pump with 2 dowel pins at bottom of cap.

2) Install pump to rear bearing cap retaining bolt and tighten. Install new oil pan gasket and oil pan. Reverse removal procedure to complete installation.

ENGINE COOLING

WATER PUMP

Removal

Disconnect battery negative terminal. Drain cooling system. Remove accessory drive belts. Remove alternator. Remove water pump pulley retaining bolts and remove pulley. Remove water pump retaining bolts and remove water pump.

Installation

1) Clean all gasket surfaces. Apply sealer to pump gasket and position gasket on pump. Position pump on engine, install retaining bolts and tighten.

2) Install water pump pulley and alternator. Install and adjust drive belts. Reverse removal procedure to complete installation.

NOTE: For information on cooling system capacities and other cooling system components, see appropriate article in ENGINE COOLING SYSTEMS section.

2.0L OHV 4-CYLINDER (Cont.)

ENGINE SPECIFICATIONS

GENERAL SPECIFICATIONS

| Year | DISPLACEMENT | | Fuel System | HP@RPM | Torque Ft. Lbs.@RPM | Compr. Ratio | BORE | | STROKE | |
	Cu. In.	Liters					In.	mm	In.	mm
1988	122	2.0	TBI	88@4800	110@2400	9.0:1	3.50	89	3.15	80

VALVES

Engine Size & Valve	Head Diam. In. (mm)	Face Angle	Seat Angle	Seat Width In. (mm)	Stem Diameter In. (mm)	Stem Clearance In. (mm)	Valve Lift In. (mm)
2.0L Intake	1.595-1.605 (40.51-40.77)	45°	46°	.049-.059 (1.25-1.50)		.0011-.0026 (.028-.066)	
Exhaust	1.373-1.383 (34.87-35.13)	45°	46°	.063-.075 (1.60-1.90)		.0014-.0031 (.035-.078)	

PISTONS, PINS & RINGS

| Engine | PISTONS | PINS | | RINGS | | |
	Clearance In. (mm)	Piston Fit In. (mm)	Rod Fit In. (mm)	Ring No.	End Gap In. (mm)	Side Clearance In. (mm)
2.0L	.0098-.0022 (.025-.055)	.0002-.0007 (.0051-.017)	.0008-.0020 (.021-.051)	1	.010-.020 (.25-.50)	.0010-.0030 (.025-.076)
				2	.010-.020 (.25-.50)	.0010-.0030 (.025-.076)
				3	.010-.05 (.25-1.3)	.0006-.009 (.015-.229)

CRANKSHAFT MAIN & CONNECTING ROD BEARINGS

| Engine | MAIN BEARINGS | | | | CONNECTING ROD BEARINGS | | |
	Journal Diam. In. (mm)	Clearance In. (mm)	Thrust Bearing	Crankshaft End Play In. (mm)	Journal Diam. In. (mm)	Clearance In. (mm)	Side Play In. (mm)
2.0L	2.4945-2.4954 (63.360-63.383)	.0006-.0019 (.015-.048)	No. 4	.002-.008 (.05-.20)	1.9983-1.9994 (50.757-50.784)	.0010-.0031 (.025-.079)	.004-.015 (.10-.38)

VALVE SPRINGS

| Engine | Free Length In. (mm) | PRESSURE Lbs. @ In. (Kg @ mm) | |
		Valve Closed	Valve Open
2.0L	1.91 (48.5)	73-81@1.60 (33-37@40.6)	176-188@1.33 (80-85@33.8)

CAMSHAFT

Engine	Journal Diam. In. (mm)	Clearance In. (mm)	Lobe Lift In. (mm)
2.0L	1.867-1.869 (47.42-47.47)	.0010-.0040 (.025-.102)	.26 (6.6)

TIGHTENING SPECIFICATIONS

Application	Ft. Lbs. (N.m)
Camshaft Sprocket	66-88 (90-120)
Connecting Rod Caps	34-43 (46-58)
Crankshaft Pulley Hub	66-88 (90-120)
Crankshaft Pulley	29-44 (40-60)
Cylinder Head Bolts	
Long	73-83 (99-113)
Short	62-70 (85-95)
Flywheel-to-Crankshaft	
Automatic Transmission	45-59 (61-80)
Manual Transmission	47-63 (65-85)
Intake Manifold	14-22 (20-30)
Main Bearing Caps	63-77 (85-105)
Oil Pump	26-38 (35-52)
Rocker Arm Stud	33-40 (45-55)
Water Pump	14-22 (20-30)
Water Pump Pulley	20-25 (27-34)

	INCH Lbs. (N.m)
Exhaust Manifold	72-156 (8-18)

General Motors Engines

2.3L "QUAD 4" 4-CYLINDER

ENGINE CODING

ENGINE IDENTIFICATION

The 2.3L "QUAD 4" engine may be identified from Vehicle Identification Number (VIN) stamped on metal tab located on top of instrument panel at lower left of windshield. VIN is also stamped on left side of engine, next to starter assembly. The VIN contains 17 characters. The 8th character identifies engine and 10th character establishes model year.

ENGINE CODE

Engine	Code
2.3L (138") MFI (DOHC)	D

ENGINE REMOVAL

See ENGINE REMOVAL and INSTALLATION at end of ENGINE section.

CYLINDER HEAD & MANIFOLDS

INTAKE MANIFOLD

Removal

1) Disconnect negative battery cable and drain cooling system. Disconect vacuum hose and electrical connector from MAP sensor. Remove coolant fan shroud. Remove throttle body to air cleaner duct and throttle cable bracket.

2) Disconnect power brake vacuum hose, retaining bracket to power steering bracket and position aside. Remove throttle body from intake manifold and position aside.

3) Remove oil/air separator bolts and hoses. Hoses should be left attached to separator. Disconnect oil/air separator from oil fill, chain housing and intake manifold. Remove as an assembly.

4) Remove oil fill cap, oil level indicator and oil fill tube upward to unseat from block. Disconnect injector connector. Remove intake manifold support bracket bolts and nut. Remove intake manifold retaining bolts, nuts and washers. Remove intake manifold.

Installation

1) Clean all gasket mating surfaces. Install intake manifold with new gasket. Tighten bolts in sequence, starting in center and working outward.

2) Reverse removal procedure to complete installation. Refill cooling system and adjust all drive belts. Start engine and run until normal operating temperature is reached. Check for leaks.

EXHAUST MANIFOLD

Removal

1) Remove oxygen sensor connector. Remove upper and lower exhaust manifold heat shields. Remove manifold to exhaust manifold brace bolt. Loosen exhaust pipe to manifold spring bolts.

2) Remove exhaust pipe spring bolts from manifold. Separate exhaust inlet pipe from exhaust manifold. Remove exhaust manifold to cylinder head retaining nuts. Remove exhaust manifold, seals and gasket.

Installation

Clean gasket mating surfaces and install manifold with new gasket. Tighten bolts in sequence, starting in center and working outward. To complete installation, reverse removal procedure.

CYLINDER HEAD

NOTE: Cylinder head bolts should be removed only when engine is cold. Check cylinder head for damage or warped gasket surface. DO NOT machine more than .015" (.39 mm) from original gasket surface. Remove burrs or scratches with an oil stone.

Removal

1) Disconnect negative battery cable and drain cooling system. Remove upper radiator hose, heater inlet and throttle body heater hoses from water outlet.

2) Remove exhaust manifold and intake and exhaust camshaft housings. Remove oil dipstick, dipstick tube and cap. Disconnect fuel injector connector. Remove throttle body to air cleaner duct and throttle body cable bracket.

3) Remove throttle body from intake manifold, with electrical harness, coolant hoses and throttle cable attached. Disconnect MAP sensor vacuum hose from intake manifold. Remove intake manifold to block bolt.

4) Disconnect coolant temperature sensor connectors. Remove cylinder head. If cylinder head is to be serviced, remove carbon deposits from combustion chamber before removing valves. When disassembling, mark all valve components for proper reassembly.

Installation

1) Clean all mating surfaces on cylinder head and camshaft carrier using a plastic or wood scrapper only. Clean threads in cylinder head bolt holes. Apply clean engine oil to cylinder head bolt threads and allow oil to drain.

2) Install cylinder head bolts. Gradually tighten cylinder head retaining bolts in sequence to 26 ft. lbs. (35 N.m). *See Fig. 1*. Turn shorter bolts 80 degrees, longer bolts 90 degrees clockwise in proper sequence for 3 times until a 180 degree rotation is obtained, or equivalent to 1/2 turn.

Fig. 1: Cylinder Head Tightening Procedure

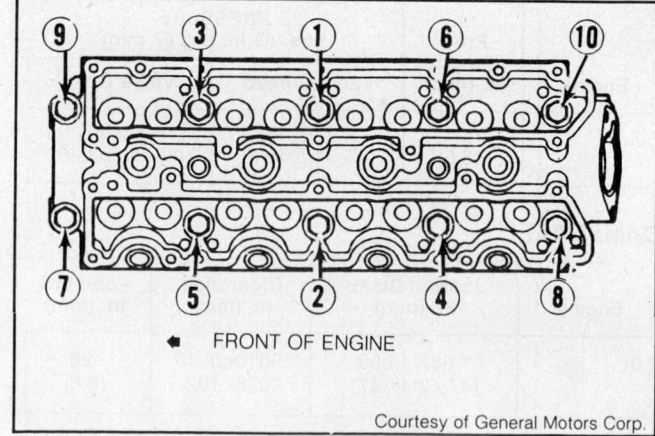

Courtesy of General Motors Corp.

Tighten bolts in sequence using a 3-step process.

2.3L "QUAD 4" 4-CYLINDER (Cont.)

NOTE: Cylinder head bolts and block threads must be clean prior to assembly. Dirt or other contamination will affect bolt torque.

3) To complete installation, reverse removal procedure. Start engine. Run until thermostat opens. Tighten cylinder head bolts an additional 30 degrees to 50 degrees in sequence. See Fig. 1.

CAMSHAFT

TIMING CHAIN

Removal

1) Disconnect negative battery cable. Remove belts, brackets and shields necessary to gain access to crankshaft pulley. Remove timing belt front cover.

2) Remove crankshaft oil slinger. Rotate crankshaft clockwise (as viewed from front of engine) until camshaft sprocket timing dowel pin holes align with timing chain housing holes.

3) Mark on crankshaft sprocket should line up with mark on cylinder block. Crankshaft sprocket keyway should be pointing upward and lined up with centerline of cylinder bores. Timing chain is now in "Timed" position. See Fig. 2.

Fig. 2: Timing Chain "Timed" Position

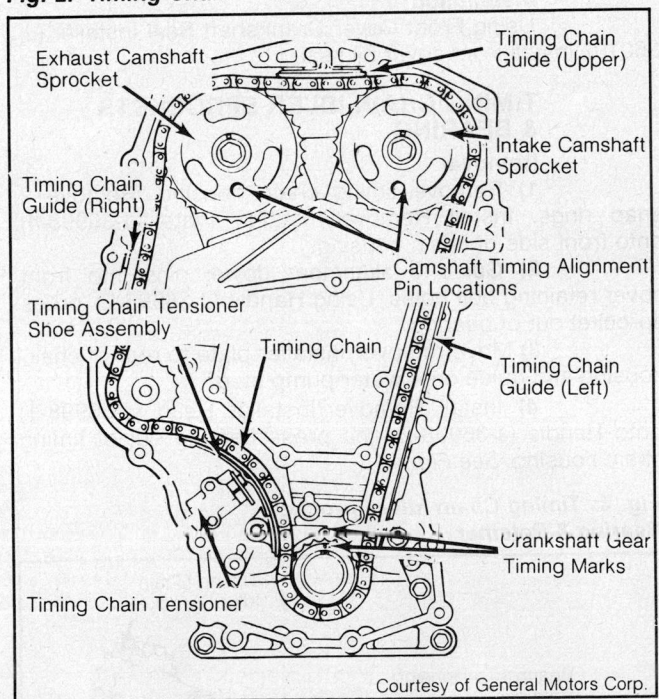

Courtesy of General Motors Corp.

CAUTION: Tensioner piston is spring loaded and could come out causing injury.

4) Remove 3 timing chain guides. Raise vehicle on hoist. Gently pry off timing chain tensioner spring retainer and remove spring. Remove timing chain tensioner shoe retainer.

5) Ensure all slack in timing chain is above tensioner. Remove chain tensioner shoe. Timing chain must be disengaged from wear grooves in tensioner shoe to remove shoe.

6) Slide screwdriver blade under timing chain while pulling shoe outward. If removing timing chain tensioner shoe is difficult, lower vehicle. Hold intake camshaft sprocket using Camshaft Sprocket Wrench (J-36013) and remove sprocket bolt and washer.

NOTE: DO NOT pry sprocket from camshaft or damage to sprocket or chain housing could occur.

7) Remove washer from bolt and reinstall bolt back into camshaft by hand. Remove intake cam sprocket using a 3 jaw puller into sprocket relief holes. Remove tensioner retaining bolts and tensioner. Remove housing to block stud and timing chain.

NOTE: Failure to follow the following installation procedure could result in severe engine damage.

Installation

1) Install new timing chain on sprockets. Install crankshaft pulley and check for alignment of timing marks. Install intake camshaft sprocket retaining bolt and washer.

2) Tighten bolt to specification while holding sprocket using Camshaft Sprocket Wrench (J-36013). Install camshaft sprocket alignment pins through camshaft sprocket holes into timing chain housing holes.

3) If camshafts are out of position and must be rotated more than 1/8 turn to install alignment dowel pins. Crankshaft MUST be rotated 90 degrees clockwise off TDC to give valves adequate clearance to open.

NOTE: DO NOT rotate crankshaft clockwise to TDC, valve or piston damage could occur.

4) When camshafts are in position and dowel is installed, rotate crankshaft counterclockwise back to TDC. Install timing chain over exhaust camshaft sprocket around idler sprocket and crankshaft sprocket.

5) Remove alignment dowel pin from intake camshaft. Using camshaft sprocket wrench, rotate intake camshaft sprocket counterclockwise enough to slide timing chain over intake cam sprocket.

6) Release camshaft sprocket wrench. Length of chain between 2 camshaft sprockets will tighten. If properly timed, intake cam alignment dowel pin should slide in easily.

7) If dowel pin does not slide in easily, camshafts are not timed correctly and procedure must be repeated. With alignment dowels pin installed, raise vehicle on hoist.

8) With slack removed from chain between intake cam sprocket, timing marks on crankshaft and cylinder block should be aligned. If marks are not aligned, move chain one tooth forward or rearward. Remove slack and recheck marks.

9) Install timing chain housing block stud and tighten to specification. Use the following to reload timing chain tensioner assembly to zero position. Assemble restraint cylinder, spring, and nylon plug into plunger. See Fig. 3.

10) Guide slot in restaint cylinder with peg in plunger. Rotating restaint cylinder clockwise, push restaint cylinder into plunger until it is at bottom. Continue rotating restaint cylinder clockwise and allow spring to push it out of plunger.

Fig. 3: Timing Chain Hydraulic Tensioner

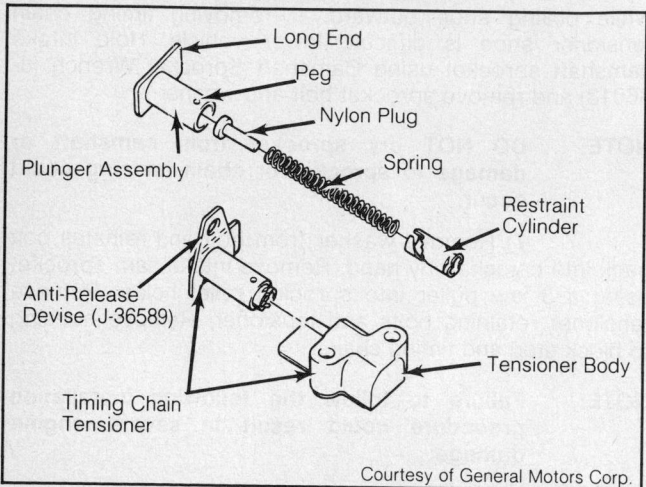

Courtesy of General Motors Corp.

11) Pin in plunger will lock the restaint in loaded position. Install Timing Chain Tensioner Spacer (J-36589) onto plunger assembly. Install plunger into tensioner body with long end toward crankshaft.

12) Install tensioner to chain housing. Recheck plunger installation, long end toward crankshaft is correct installation procedure. Install timing chain tensioner bolts and tighten to specifications.

13) Install tensioner shoe and shoe retainer. Remove timing chain tensioner spacer and squeeze plunger into tensioner body to unload plunger. Lower vehicle and remove alignment dowel pins.

14) Rotate crankshaft clockwise 2 full rotations. Align crankshaft timing mark with mark on cylinder block and reinstall alignment dowel pins. If engine is timed correctly, dowel pins will slide in easily.

15) Install 3 timing chain guides, crankshaft oil slinger and front engine cover. Start engine and inspect for any oil leaks.

TIMING CHAIN HOUSING
Removal

1) Disconnect negative battery cable. Remove coolant recovery reservoir and serpentine drive belt. Drain engine coolant. Disconnect oxygen sensor connector. Remove upper and lower exhaust shields.

2) Loosen manifold-to-exhaust pipe spring loaded bolts. Raise vehicle on hoist and remove right front wheel and lower splash shield. Using Crankshaft Balancer Holder (J-37086), remove balancer bolt.

3) Remove balancer using Crankshaft Balancer Puller (J-24420-B). Remove front cover lower bolts and nut. Remove manifold-to-exhaust pipe bolts. Lower vehicle. Remove exaust manifold-to-cylinder head retaining nuts.

4) Remove radiator outlet pipe inlet-to-water pump cover bolts. Remove water pump cover-to-cylinder block bolts and water pump cover. Remove water pump-to-timing chain housing nuts and water pump assembly.

5) Remove front cover upper bolts and nuts. Remove front cover and timing chain. Remove timing chain housing-to-belt tensioner bracket brace. Remove timing chain housing-to-block lower fasteners and 4 oil pan-to-front cover bolts.

6) Remove lowest front cover retaining stud from chain housing. Remove rear engine mount nut and lower vehicle. Remove front engine mount upper nut, reinstall nut and tighten 3 turns.

7) Remove oil/air separator hose from chain housing. Using camshaft sprocket wrench and holding sprockets, remove camshaft sprocket retaining bolts and washers.

8) Remove camshaft sprockets and 8 chain housing-to-camshaft housing bolts. Lift engine off front and rear mounts until front mount bracket contacts nut. Remove timing chain housing and gaskets.

Installation
Clean gasket surfaces. To complete installation, reverse removal procedure.

FRONT ENGINE COVER
Removal
Disconnect negative battery cable. Remove coolant recovery reservoir and serpentine drive belt. Remove upper and lower cover fasteners. Raise vehicle on hoist. Remove right front wheel and lower splash shield. Remove crankshaft balancer. Lower vehicle and remove front cover and gaskets.

Installation
To install, reverse removal procedure.

FRONT OIL SEAL
Removal
Remove engine front cover. Support front cover and drive out oil seal from back of cover.

Installation
Using Front Cover Crankshaft Seal Installer (J-36010), install front cover oil seal.

TIMING CHAIN IDLER SPROCKETS & BEARING
Removal

1) Remove timing chain housing. Remove 2 snap rings. Install Remover/Installer Plate (J-36998-4) onto front side of chain housing.

2) Guide 3 alignment dowel pins into front cover retaining bolt holes. Using Handle (J-36998-2), press sprocket out of bearing.

3) Move remover/installer plate to rear of chain housing and guide over water pump stud.

4) Install Remover/Installer Head (J-36998-1) onto Handle (J-36998-2) and press bearing out of timing chain housing. See Fig. 4.

Fig. 4: Timing Chain Idler Sprocket Bearing & Retainer

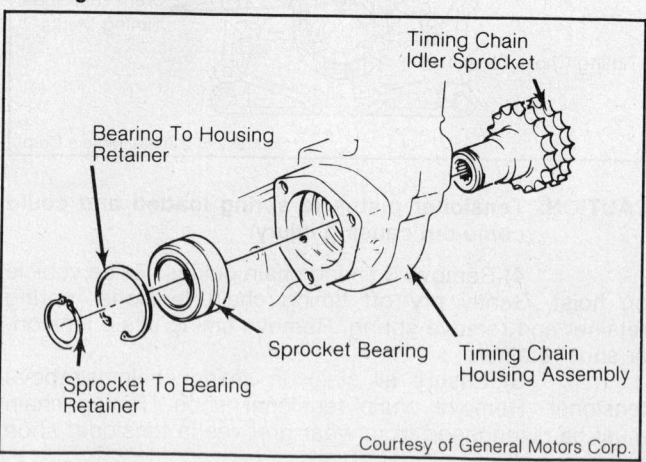

Courtesy of General Motors Corp.

2.3L "QUAD 4" 4-CYLINDER (Cont.)

Installation
Clean out chain housing groove and fill 2 injection holes with Black RTV. Coat bearing to chain housing mating surfaces with Locktite. To complete installation, reverse removal procedure.

INTAKE CAMSHAFT & HOUSING
Removal
1) Disconnect negative battery cable. Disconnect ignition coil and module assembly electrical connector. Remove 4 ignition coil and module-to-camshaft housing bolts and remove assembly by pulling straight up. See Fig. 5.

Fig. 5: Ignition Coil & Module

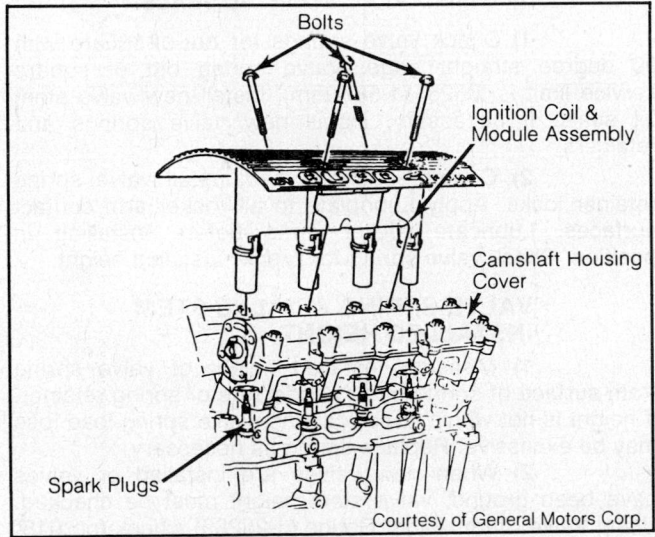

Courtesy of General Motors Corp.

2) Disconnect idle speed power steering pressure switch connector. Loosen power steering pump pivot bolts and remove drive belt. Remove rear power steering pump bracket-to-transaxle bolts.

3) Remove front power steering pump bracket-to-cylinder block bolt. Remove power steering pump assembly and carefully position pump aside. Using Power Steering Pulley and Camshaft Pulley Remover and Installer (J-29785-A and J-36015), remove power steering pump drive pulley from intake camshaft.

4) Remove oil/air separator bolts and hoses. Hoses should be left attached to separator. Disconnect separator from oil fill, chain housing and intake manifold. Remove as a complete assembly.

5) Disconnect fuel pressure regulator vacuum line and fuel injector harness connector. Remove fuel line retaining clamp from on top of intake cam housing. Remove fuel rail-to-camshaft housing retaining bolts and remove fuel rail from cylinder head.

6) Cover injector openings in cylinder head and injector nozzles. Leave fuel lines attached and place fuel rail on top of master cylinder. Disconnect timing chain housing (DO NOT remove from vehicle).

7) Remove intake cam housing cover-to-cam housing retaining bolts. Remove cam housing-to-cylinder head retaining bolts. Use reverse of tightening procedure when loosing camshaft housing-to-cylinder head bolts.

8) Leave 2 bolts loosely in place to hold cam housing while separating cam cover from housing. Install 4 housing-to-head retaining bolts into tapped holes in cam housing cover to remove housing cover.

9) Remove 2 loosely installed cam housing-to-head bolts and remove housing cover. Note the position of chain sprocket dowel pin for reassembly. Remove camshaft and camshaft seal.

Fig. 6: Camshaft Housing Bolt Tightening Sequence

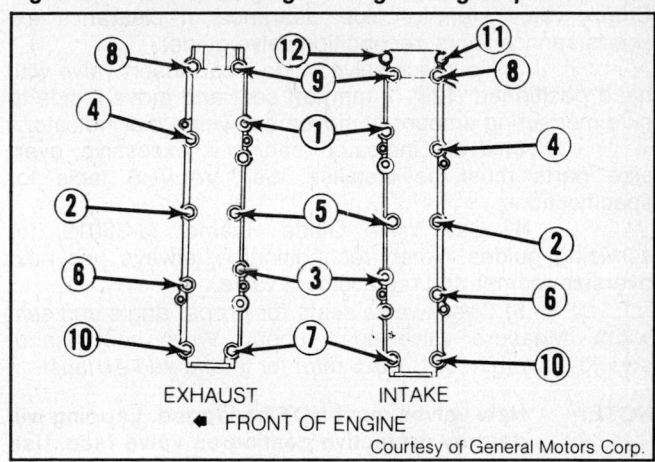

EXHAUST   INTAKE
◄ FRONT OF ENGINE

Courtesy of General Motors Corp.

Installation
To install, reverse removal procedure and tighten camshaft housing bolts. See Fig. 6.

EXHAUST CAMSHAFT & HOUSING
Removal
1) Disconnect negative battery cable. Disconnect ignition coil and module assembly electrical connector. Remove 4 ignition coil and module-to-camshaft housing bolts and remove assembly by pulling straight up. See Fig. 5.

2) Disconnect oil pressure switch connector. Remove transaxle fluid level indicator tube from exhaust camshaft cover and move tube aside. Remove camshaft cover and gasket.

3) Disconnect timing chain housing (DO NOT remove from vehicle). Remove exhaust camshaft housing-to-cylinder head bolts. Use reverse of tightening procedure when loosing camshaft housing-to-cylinder head bolts.

4) Leave 2 bolts loosely in place to hold cam housing while separating acm cover from housing. Install 4 housing-to-head retaining bolts into tapped holes in cam housing cover to remove housing cover.

5) Remove 2 loosely installed cam housing-to-head bolts and remove housing cover. Note the position of chain sprocket dowel pin for reassembly. Remove camshaft and camshaft seal.

Installation
To install, reverse removal procedure and tighten camshaft housing bolts. See Fig. 6.

VALVES

NOTE: The 2.3L "QUAD 4" engine has 16 valves, using 4 valves per cylinder. When reconditioning valves, ensure interference angles of valve and seat are not lapped out. Remove minor imperfections with an oil stone. DO NOT remove more than .010" (.254 mm) from end of valve stem.

General Motors Engines
2.3L "QUAD 4" 4-CYLINDER (Cont.)

VALVE ARRANGEMENT

Left Side - All Intake.

Right Side - All Exhaust.

VALVE GUIDE SERVICING

1) Valve guides are integral with cylinder head. Check valve stem-to-guide clearance. If clearance exceeds service limits, recondition valve guide.

2) To check valve guide wear, insert valve with head positioned .125" (2 mm) off seat and move it side to side measuring amount of movement with a dial indicator.

3) If dial indicator reading is excessive, oversize parts must be installed. See VALVES table for specifications.

4) Use Valve Guide Reamer (J-36019) for servicing guides. When reconditioning, always use next oversize reamer and replacement valve.

5) Check valve seats for proper angle and seat width. Measure valve seat runout. Valve seat runout should be within .001" (.025 mm) for intake and exhaust.

NOTE: New valves must NOT be lapped. Lapping will destroy protective coating on valve face. Use old valve to lap in seat if necessary.

6) Valve seat must be refaced after guide has been reamed. Use scraper to break (lightly chamfer or bevel) sharp top inside edge of guide.

7) After valve guide repair, inspect valve stem end for wear before installation. If valve stem end wear is not a circular pattern, rotator failure is indicated.

8) If rotator malfunctions, replacement is necessary. Valve stem end may be reconditioned by grinding.

VALVE STEM OIL SEALS
Removal

1) Remove rocker arm components, keeping them in position for reinstallation in original location. Remove spark plugs. If valves or valve seats have not been damaged, valve springs, seals and retainers may be replaced by holding valves against seats using air pressure.

NOTE: To hold valves in place with head installed, an adapter can be constructed by welding an air hose connection to body of spark plug with porcelain removed.

2) Install Air Line Adapter (J-22794) in spark plug hole. A minimum of 140 psi (9.8 kg/cm²) line pressure is required. If air pressure does not hold valve shut, valve is damaged or burnt and cylinder head must be removed for service.

3) Remove rocker arms and guides. Using Valve Spring Compressor T-Bolt (J-36588) and Valve Spring Compressor (J-5892-B), compress valve spring. Remove valve locks, retainer caps and valve spring. Remove valve stem oil seal and discard.

NOTE: If oversized valves have been installed, oversized oil seals must also be used.

Installation

1) Coat valve stem with engine oil. Install protective sleeve over end of valve. Slide new oil seal over valve stem and seat on valve guide. Remove protective sleeve.

2) Place valve spring seat or rotator, spring and retainer cap over valve stem. Compress spring and install valve locks. Install rocker guides and rocker arms. Remove spring compressor and air line adapter. Install spark plugs and cam carrier cover with new gasket.

VALVE SPRINGS

NOTE: Valve spring removal and installation is the same as REMOVAL & INSTALLATION procedures for VALVE STEM OIL SEALS.

1) Check valve springs for out-of-square with 90 degree straight edge. Valve spring out of square service limit is .0625" (1.587 mm). Install new valve stem oil seals. If necessary, install new valve springs and retainers.

2) Compress spring and install valve spring retainer locks. Apply Lubriplate to all rocker arm contact surfaces. Lubricate rocker arms before installing in position. Check valve spring for proper installed height.

VALVE SPRING & VALVE STEM INSTALLED HEIGHT

1) Measure installed height of valve spring from surface of spring pad to underside of spring retainer. If height is not within specifications, valve spring load loss may be excessive. Replace spring as necessary.

2) When new valves are installed or valves have been ground, valve stem height must be checked. Using Valve Stem Height Gauge (J-25289), check for .015" (.38 mm) clearance between valve stem tip and gauge.

3) If clearance is less than .015" (.38 mm), remove valve and grind tip to obtain proper clearance. Be certain to break (chamfer) sharp edge of reground valve tip. Recheck valve installed height.

4) If valve stem end is less than .005" (.127 mm) above rotator, valve is to short and must be replaced. Test valve spring pressure with Valve Spring Tester (J-8056). If not to specification, install new valve spring.

HYDRAULIC LIFTER ASSEMBLY

NOTE: Before replacing hydraulic lifter for noisy operation, be sure noise is not caused by worn rocker arms or valve tips.

1) Hydraulic lifter assemblies must be installed in original locations. Remove rocker arm assembly and identify for proper installation. Using Hydraulic Lifter Remover (J-3049) or magnet, remove lifters. Clean and inspect but do not mix components or positions. Parts are select-fitted and are not interchangeable.

2) If lifter is sticking, disassemble and clean dirt, metal chips or varnish from components. If lifter check valve is not functional, obstructions may be preventing it from closing or valve spring may be broken. Clean or replace components as necessary.

3) If plunger is not free in body of lifter, soak lifter in solvent to free plunger and dissolve deposits. Plunger should drop to bottom of body by its own weight when assembled dry. Assemble lifter and check free operation by pressing down on cap.

NOTE: New lifters already contain test fluid. If new lifter is installed, remove sealer coating and check leak-down rate. If old lifter is disassembled and cleaned, fill with SAE 10 engine oil before installing.

4) Place lifter upright in Hydraulic Lifter Leakdown Tester (J-5790) and check leak-down rate. If not within specifications, replace lifter assembly. Inspect lifter base-to-cam lobe contact area. Surface must have smooth and convex contact face.

5) Replace any lifter with flat or concave surface. Inspect related cam lobe for proper lobe lift. Replace camshaft (and lifters if necessary) if any lobe is worn beyond specification. Check lifter-to-bore clearance.

VALVE ADJUSTMENT

No hydraulic valve lifter lash adjustment is required. Preload of hydraulic lifter is automatic. Servicing of lifter requires only care and cleanliness when handling parts.

PISTONS, PINS & RINGS

OIL PAN

See OIL PAN REMOVAL at end of ENGINE section.

PISTON & ROD ASSEMBLY

NOTE: Before removing piston and connecting rod, mark rod caps for proper reassembly. DO NOT damage crankshaft journals or cylinder wall during removal.

Removal
1) With cylinder head and oil pan removed, inspect cylinder bores for ridges and/or deposits. Move piston to bottom of bore and cover with cloth to catch cuttings.

2) Remove ridge at top of cylinder bores (using ridge reamer) before removing pistons from block. Rotate crankshaft and mark connecting rods and rod caps for cylinder identification.

3) Remove rod cap and push each piston and rod assembly out top of cylinder bore. To protect crankshaft, place rubber tubing over rod bolts. Remove bearing inserts from rod and cap and inspect for size, wear and damage. Install rod caps on mating rods.

4) If No. 1 piston and rod assembly were removed, engine must be lifted prior to reinstallation to gain enough clearance for using torque angle meter. Lifting of engine is NOT necessary for reinstallation of Nos. 2, 3 and 4 piston and rod assemblies.

5) When lifting to reinstall No. 1 piston and rod assembly, hoist vehicle and remove rear engine mount nut. Lower vehicle and remove front engine mount nut. Reinstall mount nut and tighten nut 3 turns.

6) Install power steering pump front bracket to block bolt into block for use as lifting point. Install Engine

Support Fixture (J-28467), lift engine until front engine mount bracket contacts nut.

Installation
1) Check fit of new piston and/or rings in cylinder bore before assembling piston and pin to connecting rod. Check piston pin for clearance, etching or wear. New pistons must be installed in cylinder for which they were fitted. Install used pistons in cylinder from which they were removed.

2) Oil piston rings and cylinder walls with light coat of oil. Ensure ring gaps are properly spaced and install ring compressor on piston. Marked side of compression rings must be toward top of piston. Position piston so identification numbers on rod and cap are on same side and face water pump.

NOTE: Notch or arrow on piston top should be toward front of engine.

3) Install Connecting Rod Bolt Guide Set (J-6305-11) or rubber sleeves before installing piston and rod assembly in bore. Tap gently with wooden handle to insert piston/rod assembly into cylinder bore.

4) After bearings have been inserted, apply engine oil to journals and bearings. Ensure oil hole in bearing insert aligns with oil hole in connecting rod. Turn crankshaft to bottom of throw. Guide piston/rod assembly over crankshaft journal until rod bearing seats.

5) Remove rod bolt protectors. Match rod cap to rod and install. Tighten cap nuts in 2 steps. Repeat procedure for each piston assembly. After piston/rod assembly is installed, check side clearance of connecting rod on each crankshaft journal.

Fig. 7: Piston & Connecting Rod

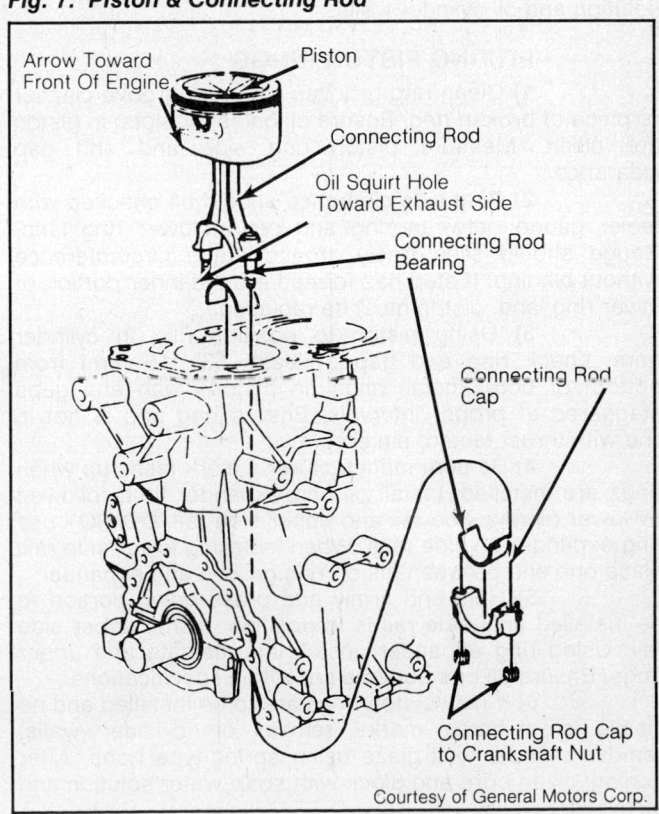

Courtesy of General Motors Corp.

FITTING PISTONS

1) Inspect pistons and replace any showing signs of excessive wear, wavy ring lands, or fractures. Replace piston if sponge-like or eroded surface is on edge of piston top (caused by detonation or pre-ignition).

2) If shiny surface on thrust side of piston is found, check for bent connecting rod. Replace piston and/or rod as necessary. Inspect connecting rods for signs of fracture and bearing bores for out of round and taper.

3) Check pistons for fractures at ring lands, skirts and pin bosses. Check for scuffed, rough or scored skirts. Check piston-to-cylinder bore clearance by measuring piston and bore diameters.

4) Ensure piston and cylinder bore are clean, dry and at room temperature 70°F (21°C) during measurement. Measure diameter of cylinder bore at top, middle and bottom with gauge at right angle and parallel to centerline of engine.

5) Inspect cylinder walls for scoring, roughness or other signs of wear. Check bore for out-of-round and taper. Cylinder bore out-of-round service limit is .004" (.10 mm). Cylinder bore taper should not be more than .003" (.08 mm).

6) Measure outer diameter of piston at centerline of pin bore and 90 degrees to pin bore axis. If cylinder wall is severely marred or worn beyond specifications, refinishing will be necessary. Pistons are available in standard and .010" oversize. Measure new piston and hone cylinder to correct clearance.

7) Before cylinder refinishing, ensure main bearing caps are in place and tightened to specification to avoid distortion during refinishing process. After refinishing, allow bore to cool, then clean bore with soap/water solution and oil cylinder walls.

FITTING PISTON RINGS

1) Clean ring grooves with ring groove cleaner or piece of broken ring. Ensure oil holes (or slots) in piston are clean. Measure piston ring side and end gap clearance.

2) Ring side clearance should be checked with feeler gauge between ring and piston lower ring land. Gauge should slide freely around entire circumference without binding. If step has formed around inner portion of lower ring land, piston must be replaced.

3) Using piston to position ring in cylinder bore, check ring end gap at least .63" (16 mm) from bottom of bore. Install rings on pistons with end gaps staggered at proper intervals. Ensure ring gap is not in line with thrust face of pin bore.

4) Be sure manufacturer's mark faces up when rings are installed. Install oil ring expander first, followed by lower oil ring side rail and upper side rail. DO NOT use ring expander on side rails. When installing lower side rail, place one end between piston ring groove and expander.

5) Hold end firmly and press down portion to be installed until side rail is in position. Install upper side rail. Using ring expander, install intermediate and upper rings. Ensure all components are within specifications.

6) If new piston rings are to be installed and no visible cross-hatch marks remain on cylinder walls, remove cylinder wall glaze using spring-type hone. After honing, clean bore and block with soap/water solution and oil cylinder walls.

FITTING PISTON PINS

NOTE: When removing or installing piston pin, connecting rod should be in firm contact with body of pin setting tool.

Removal

1) Remove bearing inserts from connecting rod and cap. Mark pistons, pins and inserts (if reusable) for reassembly reference. Remove 2 piston pin retainers and remove piston pin from piston and connecting rod.

2) Inspect and replace any piston pin showing signs of fracture, etching or wear. Check piston pin-to-rod bore fit. Check ID of connecting rod piston pin bore. If pin bore in rod is larger than specification, replace rod and pin as an assembly.

Installation

Check piston to cylinder bore clearance before assembling piston and pin to connecting rod. Ensure oil hole in connecting rod is facing exhaust side of block and arrow or notch on top of piston is pointed toward front of engine. Reinstall piston pin in piston and connecting rod. To complete installation, reverse removal procedure.

CRANKSHAFT & ROD BEARINGS

NOTE: Following procedures are with oil pan and cylinder head removed. Main and rod bearing size is indicated by letter stamped into bearing tang or actual bearing size stamped opposite of tang. Undersize bearings are not available.

CONNECTING ROD BEARINGS

1) Remove connecting rod bearing caps and mark rods and caps for proper installation. Inspect each bearing for peeling, melting, seizure or improper contact. Replace defective bearings. Use Plastigage method for bearing clearance check.

2) Measure outside diameter of crankshaft connecting rod bearing journals to check for journal runout or taper. Journal runout must not exceed .0002" (.005 mm). Journal taper must not exceed .0015" (.004 mm).

3) When checking connecting rod clearances, crankshaft does not have to be supported. Instead, turn crankshaft until connecting rod to be checked starts moving toward top of engine, thus unloading lower bearing.

4) Cut Plastigage to same length as width of rod bearing. Place in bearing cap, parallel with crankshaft (not over oil hole or groove). Install rod bearings and cap, tightening in 2 steps to specifications. Always install caps with markings in original positions.

5) Do not turn crankshaft with Plastigage installed. Remove rod bearing cap from crankshaft and measure Plastigage at its widest part. If clearance exceeds specifications, replace bearing.

6) Selective fitting is required on each connecting rod. After inspection and/or replacement, coat bearing surfaces with heavy engine oil. Tighten connecting rod bearing caps in 2 steps.

2.3L "QUAD 4" 4-CYLINDER (Cont.)

NOTE: Connecting rod bearing cap and rod identification numbers must remain on same side and face toward water pump. Always replace bearings in pairs. Never use new bearing in combination with used bearing.

7) Check for shiny surface on either side of piston pin boss, indicating bent connecting rod. Twisted rods will not create identifiable wear patterns, but will disturb the action of entire crankshaft assembly and may cause excessive oil consumption.

8) Check connecting rod side clearance with feeler gauge. Minimum clearance is .0059" (.150 mm) and should not exceed .0177" (.450 mm). If measurement is excessive, replace connecting rod and cap.

9) If side clearance is less than specification, remove rod and cap. Check for scratches, burrs, nicks or dirt between crankshaft and rod. Dress minor imperfections with oil stone.

10) During assembly, oil hole in bearing must align with oil hole in connecting rod. Verify bearing tangs are seated to slots in rod and cap. Ensure connecting rod bolt heads are properly seated in connecting rod.

MAIN BEARINGS

NOTE: Selective fit main bearings are used in this engine. DO NOT scrape gum or varnish deposits from bearing shells. Clean inserts and caps thoroughly in solvent. DO NOT file or lap bearing caps or use bearing shims to obtain proper bearing clearance.

1) Inspect each bearing for peeling, melting, seizure or improper contact. Replace defective bearings. If copper-lead bearing base is visible but not showing over 20% of total area, bearing is acceptable.

2) Measure outside diameter of crankshaft main bearing journals in at least 4 places to check for journal runout or taper. Journal runout must not exceed .0005" (.0127 mm). Journal taper must not exceed .0005" (.0127 mm).

NOTE: Never use new bearing in combination with used bearing. Check location of high spots on main bearings. If high spots are not in line, crankshaft may be bent and should be checked.

3) To check main bearings, shim adjacent main bearings to bearing being checked. Alternate method is to position jack under counterweight adjoining bearing being checked so weight of crankshaft will not compress Plastigage and provide an incorrect reading.

4) DO NOT position jack under crankshaft pulley as crankshaft damage can result. With all other bearing caps tight, check clearances using Plastigage method.

NOTE: If undersize bearings are used on more than one journal, position in cylinder block rather than bearing cap. DO NOT turn crankshaft with Plastigage installed.

5) If standard bearing does not bring bearing clearance within specified limits, crankshaft must be refinished and undersize bearings installed. If journal will not clean up to maximum undersize bearing, replace crankshaft.

6) If journals are remachined, ensure same journal shoulder radius is reproduced. Too small a radius will result in fatigue failure of crankshaft. Too large a radius will result in bearing failure due to radial ride of bearing. When journals are refinished, chamfer oil holes and polish journals with No. 320 grit polishing cloth and engine oil.

7) After chamfer and polish operations, clean crankshaft thoroughly in solvent and blow out oil passages with compressed air. When crankshaft main bearings are installed, ensure oil distributing grooves on bearings are installed on same side.

8) Oil new upper bearing and insert plain (unnotched) end between crankshaft and notched side of block. Rotate bearing into place. Install main bearing caps so bottom of number (cast on surface of main cap) faces rear of engine. Install main cap bolts and tighten.

THRUST BEARING

Information was not available from vehicle manufacturer.

CRANKSHAFT FLANGE RUNOUT

Information was not available from vehicle manufacturer.

REAR CRANKSHAFT OIL SEAL
Removal
1) With engine/transaxle assembly removed from vehicle, remove flywheel-to-crankshaft flange and flywheel bolts. Remove oil pan-to-crankshaft seal housing and seal housing to block bolts. Remove seal housing and gasket.

2) Using 2 wood blocks of equal thickness on a flat surface. Position seal housing and blocks so transaxle side of seal housing are supported across dowel pin and central bolt holes on both sides of seal opening.

3) Using small chisel in the relief grooves, drive crankshaft seal evenly out transaxle side of seal housing.

CAUTION: Extreme care should be taken not to damage crankshaft seal surfaces. Damaging of seal or seal surface will result in oil leaks.

Inspection
1) Inspect oil pan gasket inner silicone bead for cuts, deformation or separation from aluminum carrier. If any silicone bead damage is found, replace oil pan gasket.

2) Inspect silicone strips across top of aluminum carrier at oil pan, cylinder block, and seal housing 3-way joint. If silicone strips are damaged, repair using G.M. Silicone Sealer (No. 1052915).

Installation
1) Using Rear Crankshaft Seal Installer (J-36005), press new crankshaft seal into housing. Position seal housing to block gasket over alignment dowel pins. Using engine oil, lube lip of crankshaft seal.

2) Install seal housing assembly and bolts. Tighten bolts to specifications. *See Fig. 8.* To complete installation, reverse removal procedure.

Fig. 8: Rear Crankshaft Seal & Housing

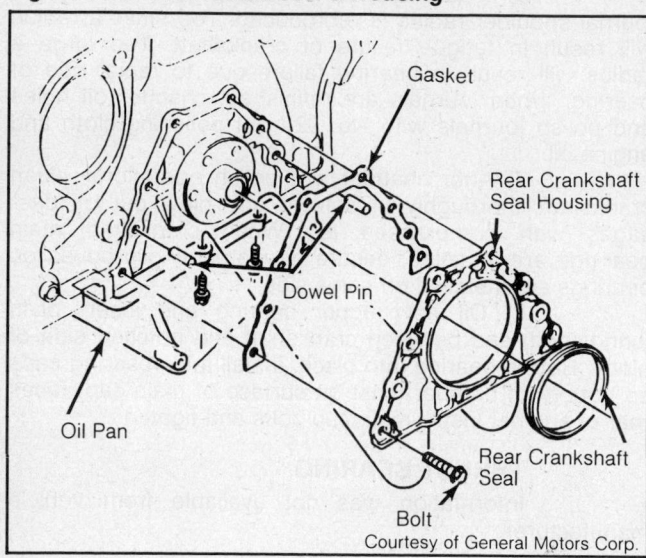

Courtesy of General Motors Corp.

Fig. 9: Exploded View of Oil Pump Assembly

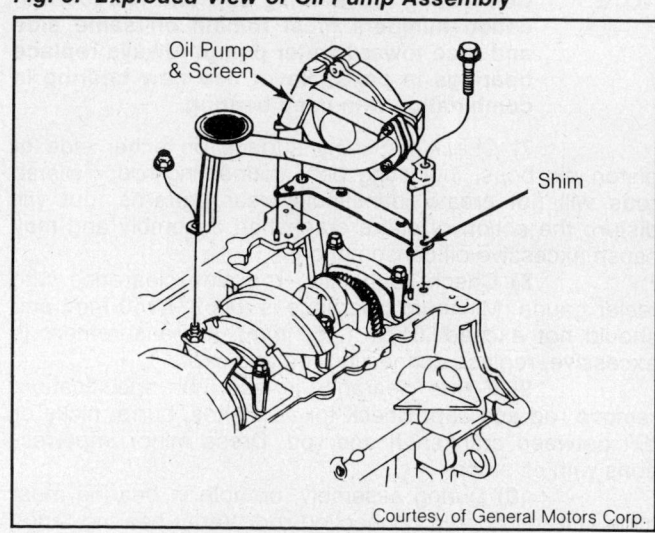

Courtesy of General Motors Corp.

ENGINE OILING

CRANKCASE CAPACITY

Engine oil capacity is 4 qts. (3.8L) without filter change. Add 1.0 qt. (1.0L) with new filter. Recommended oil change interval is 12 months or 7500 miles for all others. General Motors suggests 5W-30 oil for all outside temperatures. Oil rating should be SF/CC or SF/CD.

NORMAL OIL PRESSURE

Normal oil pressure is 25 psi (1.76 kg/cm²) at 2000 RPM, with engine at operating temperature.

PRESSURE REGULATOR VALVE

Pressure regulator valve is located in oil pump body and is not a serviceable component.

ENGINE OILING SYSTEM

Oil from the gear-type oil pump passes through a full flow oil filter to the main oil galley on the left side of the block. Hydraulic lifters, connecting rod, main and camshaft journals are pressure lubricated. Full pressure lubrication is directed to connecting rods by drilled passages from adjacent main bearing journals.

Cylinder walls are spray lubricated from a drilled passage in the connecting rods. Camshafts are lubricated from main oil gallery by way of passage to camshaft carrier journals.

OIL PUMP

Removal

Remove oil pan assembly. Remove oil pump assembly retainers, bolts and nut. Remove oil pump and shims (if shims are required). Check oil pump gear backlash when oil pump assembly or oil pump drive gear is replaced. See OIL PUMP DRIVE GEAR BACKLASH ADJUSTMENT.

Installation

Install oil pan baffle (if removed). Install oil pump assembly and (shims, if removed). Tighten oil pump-to-block bolts to specifications. Install oil pan and gasket. Start engine and check for leaks. See Fig. 9.

OIL PUMP DRIVE GEAR BACKLASH ADJUSTMENT

1) With oil pump removed from engine, remove 3 retaining bolts. Separate driven gear cover and screen assembly from oil pump.

2) Install oil pump on block using original shims (if shims are required) and tighten bolts to specifications. Install Dial Indicator Base and Dial Indicator (J-26900-13 and J-8001). See Fig. 10.

3) Measure oil pump drive-to-driven gear backlash clearance. Make sure crankshaft does not rotate. Oil pump drive-to-driven gear backlash clearance should be .010"-.014" (.254-.356 mm).

4) If clearance is not to specification, add or remove oil pump shims. Recheck backlash clearance. When proper clearance is obtained, rotate crankshaft 1/2 turn and recheck clearance.

5) Remove oil pump from block. Reinstall driven gear cover and screen assembly-to-pump and tighten to specification. Reinstall oil pump assembly on block and tighten bolts to specification.

Fig. 10: Measuring Oil Pump Driven Gear Backlash

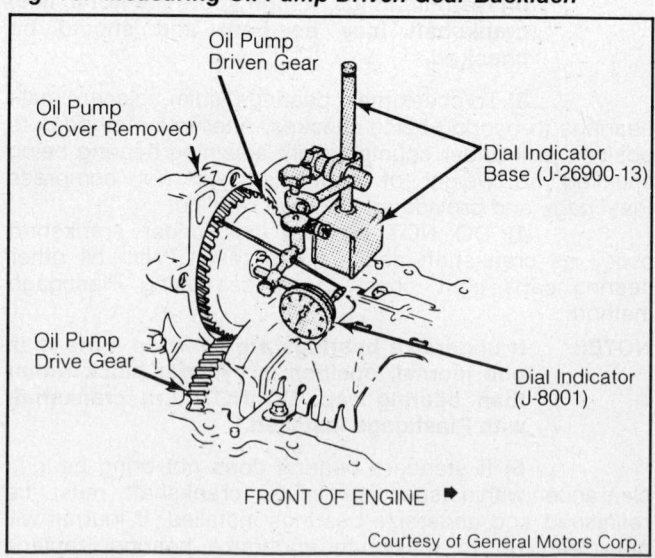

FRONT OF ENGINE ➡

Courtesy of General Motors Corp.

2.3L "QUAD 4" 4-CYLINDER (Cont.)

ENGINE COOLING

WATER PUMP

Removal

1) Disconnect negative battery cable. Drain cooling system. Remove exhaust manifold. Remove outlet pipe-to-water pump cover bolts. Remove water pump cover-to-cylinder block and water pump bolts.

2) Remove water pump cover. Remove water pump-to-timing chain housing nuts. Remove water pump assembly.

NOTE: It may be necessary to loosen and reposition rear engine mount and mount-to-engine block bracket to remove timing chain housing nuts.

Installation

To install, reverse removal procedure. Be sure water pump bolts and nuts are tightened to specification. Install water pump assembly-to-chain housing nuts, water pump cover-to-pump assembly bolts, water pump cover-to-block bolts, and radiator outlet pipe-to-water pump cover bolts in this order.

NOTE: For information on cooling system capacities and other cooling system components, see appropriate article in ENGINE COOLING SYSTEMS section.

TIGHTENING SPECIFICATIONS

Application	Ft. Lbs. (N.m)
Connecting Rod Nuts	[1] 15 (20)
Crankshaft Balancer-to-Crankshaft Bolts	[2] 74 (100)
Crankshaft Bearing Cap Bolts	15 (20)
Cylinder Head (Short Bolts)	[3] 26 (35)
Cylinder Head (Long Bolts)	[4] 26 (35)
Exhaust Manifold-to-Cylinder Head Bolts	27 (37)
Exhaust Manifold-to-Exhaust Pipe	22 (30)
Exhaust Manifold-to-Transaxle Brace	19 (26)
Flywheel-to-Converter Bolts	46 (63)
Fuel Rail-to-Camshaft Housing	19 (26)
Ignition Coil & Module-to-Housing	19 (26)
Intake Manifold-to-Cylinder Head Bolts	18 (25)
Oil Pump-to-Block	33 (45)
Oil Pump Screen-to-Block	19 (26)
Timing Chain Housing-to-Block Bolts	19 (26)
Throttle Body-to-Intake Manifold	19 (26)
Water Outlet-to-Cylinder Head	19 (26)
Water Pump Retaining Bolts	19 (26)

	INCH Lbs. (N.m)
Camshaft Housing & Cover-to-Cylinder Head Bolts	[5] 133 (15)
Camshaft Housing Cover (Exhaust) Bolts	124 (14)
Front Cover-to-Timing Chain Housing Bolts	106 (12)
Oil Pan Bolts	106 (12)
Oil Pump Cover-to-Oil Pump Body Bolts	106 (12)
Oil Pump Screen-to-Pump Bolts	106 (12)
Rear Crankshaft Seal Housing-to-Block Bolts	106 (12)
Timing Chain Tensioner-to-Housing & Block Bolts	124 (14)
Water Pump-to-Water Pump Cover Bolts	106 (12)

[1] – Tighten additional 75 degrees.
[2] – Tighten additional 90 degrees.
[3] – Tighten additional 80 degrees.
[4] – Tighten additional 90 degrees.
[5] – Tighten aaditional 75 degrees.

ENGINE SPECIFICATIONS

GENERAL SPECIFICATIONS

Year	DISPLACEMENT		Fuel System	HP@RPM	Torque Ft. Lbs.@RPM	Compr. Ratio	BORE		STROKE	
	Cu. In.	Liters					In.	mm	In.	mm
1988	138	2.3	MFI	.....	.....	9.5:0	3.35	85	3.62	92

VALVES

Engine Size & Valve	Head Diam. In. (mm)	Face Angle	Seat Angle	Seat Width In. (mm)	Stem Diameter In. (mm)	Stem Clearance In. (mm)	Valve Lift In. (mm)
2.3L Intake	140 (35.6)	46°	45°	.....	.....	.0009-.0027 (.025-.069)	.....
Exhaust	1.19 (30.1)	46°	45°			.0015-.0032 (.038-.081)	

General Motors Engines

2.3L "QUAD 4" 4-CYLINDER (Cont.)

ENGINE SPECIFICATIONS (Cont.)

PISTONS, PINS & RINGS

Engine	PISTONS	PINS		RINGS		
	Clearance In. (mm)	Piston Fit In. (mm)	Rod Fit In. (mm)	Ring No.	End Gap In. (mm)	Side Clearance In. (mm)
2.3L	.0007-.0020 (.019-.051)	.0004-.00035 (.001-.009)	....	1	.016-.025 (.40-.64)	.002-.0035 (.05-.09)
				2	.016-.025 (.40-.64)	.0016-.0031 (.040-.080)
				3	.016-.055 (.41-1.4)	.....

CRANKSHAFT MAIN & CONNECTING ROD BEARINGS

Engine	MAIN BEARINGS				CONNECTING ROD BEARINGS		
	Journal Diam. In. (mm)	Clearance In. (mm)	Thrust Bearing	Crankshaft End Play In. (mm)	Journal Diam. In. (mm)	Clearance In. (mm)	Side Play In. (mm)
2.3L	2.0470-2.0474 (51.994-52.006)	.0005-.0020 (.013-.053)	No. 3	.0034-.0095 (.087-.243)	1.8887-1.8897 (47.975-48.00)	.0005-.0025 (.013-.08)	....

VALVE SPRINGS

Engine	Free Length In. (mm)	PRESSURE Lbs. @ In. (Kg @ mm)	
		Valve Closed	Valve Open
2.3L	.....	64-70 @ 1.440 (29-32) @ 36.58	159-173 @ 1.04 (72-78) @ 26.42

CAMSHAFT

Engine	Journal Diam. In. (mm)	Clearance In. (mm)	Lobe Lift In. (mm)
2.3L All	1.3751-1.3760 (34.93-34.95)	[1] .0019-.0043 (.050-.110)	Int. .340 (8.640) Exh. .350 (8.890)

[1] – Camshaft end play is .006-.014" (.15-.35 mm).

2.5L 4-CYLINDER

ENGINE CODING

ENGINE IDENTIFICATION

Engine may be identified from Vehicle Identification Number (VIN) located on top of instrument panel at lower left of windshield. The VIN number contains 17 characters. The 8th character identifies engine. VIN number code is also stamped on left side of engine block below cylinder head and on transmission mounting flange. Engine unit and code number label is found on timing cover. Engine code stamping is found on pad at left rear of cylinder block below cylinder head.

ENGINE CODE

Engine	Code
2.5L (151") TBI	R or U

ENGINE REMOVAL

See ENGINE REMOVAL and INSTALLATION at end of ENGINE section.

CYLINDER HEAD & MANIFOLDS

INTAKE MANIFOLD

NOTE: Removal of aluminum intake manifold should be done only after engine has cooled.

Removal

1) Disconnect negative battery cable. Remove air cleaner, heat stove pipe, PCV valve and hose. Drain cooling system and separate all electrical connections, fuel lines and vacuum lines from TBI assembly.

Fig. 1: Intake Manifold Tightening Sequence

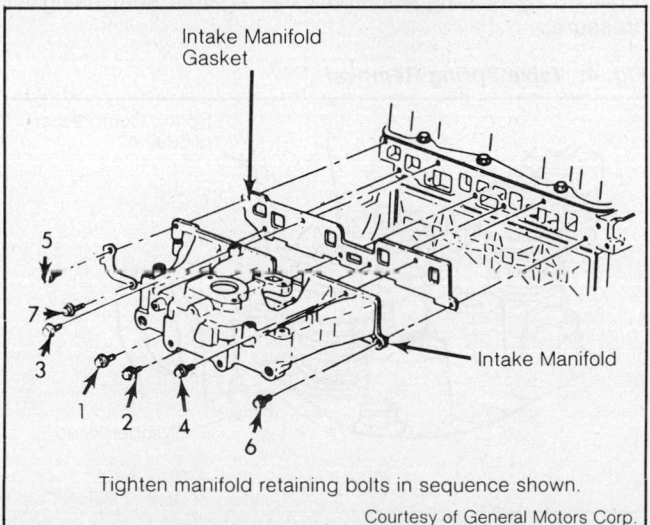

Tighten manifold retaining bolts in sequence shown.

Courtesy of General Motors Corp.

Tighten manifold retaining bolts in sequence shown.

2) Disconnect throttle linkage, transaxle downshift linkage and cruise control linkage (if equipped). Remove throttle and TV cables and support away from work area. Remove heater hose at intake manifold. Remove intake manifold retaining bolts and remove intake manifold.

Installation

1) Clean cylinder head and intake manifold gasket surfaces. Install manifold and new gasket on cylinder head. Start all bolts finger tight only.

2) Tighten manifold retaining bolts using sequence and specifications in *Fig. 1*. Reverse removal procedure to complete assembly.

EXHAUST MANIFOLD

Removal

Remove air cleaner and pre-heat tube. Remove alternator upper mounts. Raise vehicle to unbolt exhaust manifold from exhaust pipe. Lower vehicle to detach oxygen sensor lead wire. Remove exhaust manifold retaining bolts and lift manifold away from engine.

Installation

Clean gasket surface of exhaust manifold and cylinder head. Install manifold and new gasket on cylinder head. Tighten manifold retaining bolts using proper sequence. *See Fig. 2*. Reverse removal procedure to complete installation.

Fig. 2: Exhaust Manifold Tightening Sequence

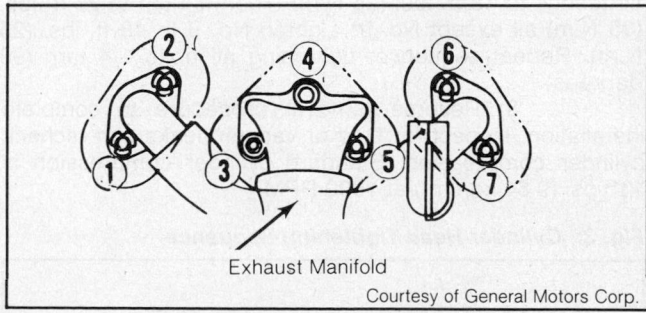

Exhaust Manifold

Courtesy of General Motors Corp.

CYLINDER HEAD

NOTE: Check cylinder compression before removing cylinder head. Check for damage or warped gasket surface. If cylinder head is to be refinished, DO NOT machine more than .010" (.25 mm) from gasket surface.

Removal

1) With engine cooled, remove air cleaner and drain cooling system. Disconnect negative battery cable and all electrical connections from TBI assembly. Remove oil dipstick tube and disconnect oxygen sensor connector.

2) Raise vehicle and disconnect exhaust pipe. Lower vehicle to remove throttle linkage and heater hose from intake manifold. Remove ignition coil and all wire connections from intake manifold and cylinder head.

3) Disconnect vacuum and fuel lines. Remove A/C compressor and position away from work area. Remove alternator, A/C, and upper power steering pump brackets. Remove radiator hoses and valve cover.

4) Remove rocker arms, push rods and cylinder head bolts. Separate cylinder head and lift away from engine. Remove intake and exhaust manifolds (if necessary).

Inspection

1) Check cylinder head and block for damage or warped surface. Gasket surface flatness is .003" (.08 mm) in any 6" length and .006" (.152 mm) overall. Replace

General Motors Engines

2.5L 4-CYLINDER (Cont.)

if either head or block must be machined more than .010" (.25 mm).

2) Clean push rods in solvent and blow out each oil passage with compressed air. Check ends of push rod for nicks, grooves or excessive wear. Ensure push rods are straight by checking with dial indicator and "V" block.

3) If runout exceeds .015" (.38 mm), replace push rod. DO NOT attempt to straighten push rod. Apply lubricant to rocker arm contact points and push rod ends. Cylinder head bolts and block threads must be clean as foreign material will affect torque readings.

NOTE: If cylinder head is to be serviced, remove carbon deposits from combustion chamber before removing valves. Mark valve components for reassembly.

Installation

1) Ensure gasket surfaces are clean and free of nicks. Install new gasket in position over dowel pins on cylinder block. Carefully install cylinder head over dowel pins and gasket.

2) Install all cylinder head bolts and tighten in sequence to 18 ft. lbs. (25 N.m). Then tighten to 26 ft. lbs. (35 N.m) all except No. 9. Tighten No. 9 to 18 ft. lbs. (25 N.m). Repeat sequence, tightening all bolts 1/4 turn (90 degrees).

3) Reverse removal procedure to complete installation. Inspect for fluid or vacuum leaks and recheck cylinder compression. Standard cylinder compression is 140 psi (9.84 kg/cm²) at 1600 RPM.

Fig. 3: Cylinder Head Tightening Sequence

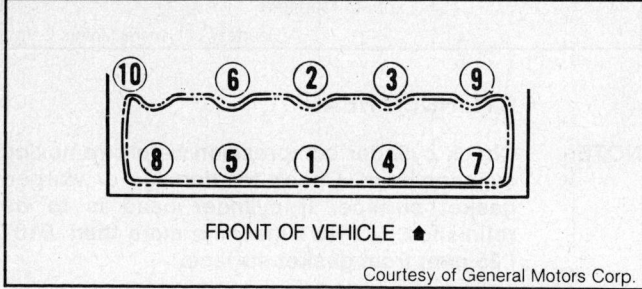

FRONT OF VEHICLE ⬆

Courtesy of General Motors Corp.

VALVES

NOTE: When servicing valves, ensure interference angles of valve and seat are not lapped out. New valves have protective coating and must not be lapped. Use old valve (with face in good condition) if lapping is necessary. Dress minor imperfections from end of valve stem with oil stone. DO NOT remove more than .010" (.25 mm) from valve stem end.

VALVE ARRANGEMENT
I-E-I-E-E-I-E-I (Front-to-rear).

VALVE GUIDE SERVICING

NOTE: Valve guides are integral with head. When measuring valve stem-to-guide clearance, check diameter of valve stem on top, center

and bottom. Exhaust valves have tapered stems and are .001" (.025 mm) larger at top of stem than at valve head end.

1) With cylinder head removed and disassembled, check valve stem-to-guide clearance. If clearance exceeds service limits, recondition valve guide. Service valves are available in standard, .003" (.076 mm) and .005" (.127 mm) oversize.

2) To check valve guide wear, insert valve with head positioned .079" (.020 mm) away from valve seat. Attach dial gauge to cylinder head. Position gauge indicator against valve stem at right angle and just above guide. Move valve in guide and note guide wear shown on dial gauge.

3) Maximum dial gauge reading for intake valve-to-guide clearance is shown in VALVES table at end of article. Use valve guide reamers in sequence to ream guides for installation of valves with oversize stems. Reface valve seat after valve guide is reamed.

4) If valve seat face is reground, check margin width dimension. Check valve seats for proper angle and seat width. Lightly chamfer or bevel sharp top inside edge of guide. Inspect valve stem end for wear before installation. Valve stem length may be adjusted by grinding.

VALVE STEM OIL SEALS

NOTE: An "O" ring type seal is installed on lower groove of all valve stems. An additional Teflon oil seal is installed on guide of intake valves only. A light coat of oil on stem will help prevent twisting of the "O" ring type seal during installation. Oversized valve stem oil seals are available for oversize valves.

1) If valve or valve seat have not been damaged, valve spring, seal, cap, and lock may be replaced by holding affected valve against seat using air pressure.

Fig. 4: Valve Spring Removal

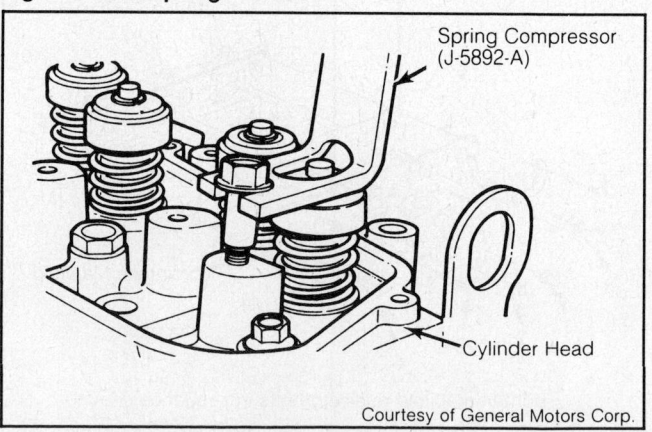

Courtesy of General Motors Corp.

2) Use Compressed Air Line Adapter (J-23590), installed in spark plug hole. A minimum of 140 psi (9.8 kg/cm²) line pressure is required. If air pressure does not hold valve shut, valve is damaged and cylinder head must be removed for service.

3) After removing rocker arm, reinstall rocker arm bolt. Insert slotted end of Spring Compressor (J-5892-A) under rocker bolt head. Compress valve spring and

2.5L 4-CYLINDER (Cont.)

remove valve retainer locks. Remove tool, retainer, cup shield, spring and oil seal.

4) With valve in head, install seal over end of valve stem. Oil protector cap and start stem seal carefully over cap. Push seal down until seal jacket touches top of valve guide. Using Valve Seal Installer/Tester (J-22330), bottom seal on valve guide.

VALVE SPRINGS

Removal

1) Remove valve cover and spark plug on cylinder to be serviced. Be sure piston is at top of stroke with both valves closed. Install Compressed Air Line Adapter (J-23590) in spark plug hole. Apply minimum of 140 psi (9.8 kg/cm²) line pressure.

NOTE: **If air pressure fails to hold valve closed, remove cylinder head for inspection.**

2) Remove required rocker arm and push rod. Use Spring Compressor (J-5892-A) to compress spring and remove retainer locks, spring retainer, cup shield and valve spring. Remove and discard valve stem seal(s). Do not remove air pressure as valve can drop in cylinder.

3) Check valve spring for out-of-square with 90 degree straightedge. Valve spring out-of-square service limit is .0625" (1.588 mm) for intake and exhaust springs. Check valve spring compression pressure (without dampers) and replace any spring not within specification.

4) Intake and exhaust valve spring compression pressure service limit is 71-78 lbs. at 1.44" (32-35 kg at 36.6 mm) closed. Valve spring service limit open is 158-170 lbs. at 1.04" (72-77 kg at 26.42 mm).

Installation

1) Lubricate valve stem with engine oil and install new valve stem seal. Place spring in position over valve and install cup shield and spring retainer. Compress valve spring and install locks. Check valve spring for proper installed height.

CAUTION: Install shim spacers only if necessary. Do not use more than 2 spacers, as this will overstress springs and overload camshaft lobes.

2) Remove air pressure and adapter to install spark plugs. Apply lubricant to ends of push rods and tip of valve stems. Install rocker arms and tighten.

VALVE SPRING INSTALLED HEIGHT

Installed height of valve spring should be 1.44" (36.58 mm). Measure spring height from surface of cylinder head pad to underside of spring retainer. If installed height exceeds specifications, install shim below spring to reduce height to specifications.

PUSH ROD SIDE COVER

Removal

1) Raise vehicle on hoist. Disconnect engine wiring harness clips. Remove 4 push rod cover attaching nuts. Reverse 2 nuts so washers face outward and install onto inner 2 studs.

2) Install 2 remaining nuts to same 2 inner studs with washers facing inward. Using a small wrench on inner nuts, jam 2 nuts tightly together. Using same wrench, unscrew studs with inner nut until cover breaks loose.

3) Remove jammed nuts from each stud. Remove cover from studs. Inspect stud and rubber washer assembly and replace if damaged.

NOTE: **Do not pry on cover or sealing surface damage may result.**

Installation

1) Clean side cover and cylinder block gasket surfaces. Apply continuous bead of RTV sealer to gasket surface of push rod cover.

2) Install cover with retaining bolts and tighten. Install wiring harness and clips. Lower vehicle. Start engine and check for leaks.

Fig. 5: Exploded View of Lifter Assembly

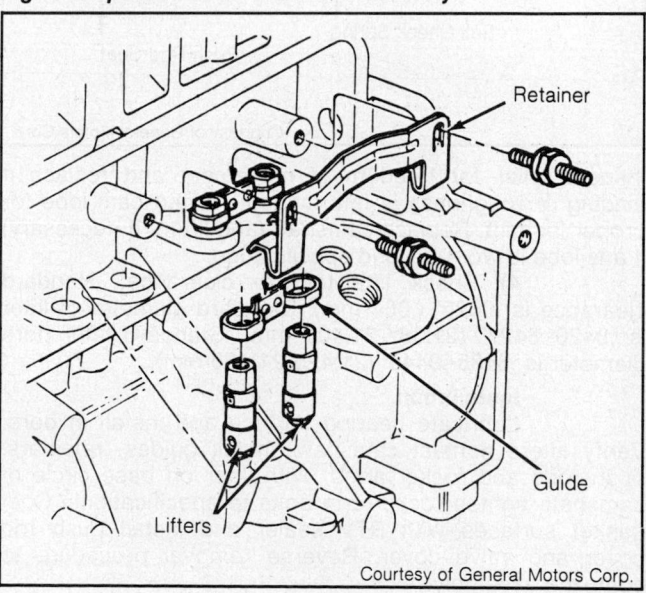

HYDRAULIC VALVE LIFTERS

NOTE: **Before replacing hydraulic lifter for noisy operation, Inspect lifter gap, rocker arms, push rods and valve tips. If lifter assembly is stuck in bore, use Hydraulic Lifter Puller (J-3049) or magnet.**

Removal

Remove valve cover, intake manifold and push rod cover. Loosen rocker arm and rotate for clearance from push rod. Remove push rod, lifter retainer and guide plates. Using lifter remover or magnet, remove lifters.

Inspection

1) Clean and inspect, but do not mix components as parts are select-fitted and not interchangeable. If lifter is sticking, disassemble and clean components. If lifter check valve is non-functional, check valve spring may be broken or dirt may be preventing it from closing when cam lobe activates lifter. See Fig. 6.

2) Clean or replace components as necessary. Plunger should drop to bottom of body by its own weight when assembled dry. If plunger is not free in body of lifter, replace entire assembly. Assemble lifter and check free operation by pressing down on cap.

3) Inspect lifter body for scuffing or wear and replace if worn. Inspect lifter roller-to-cam lobe contact area. Surface must be smooth with no pitts or flat spots.

Fig. 6: Exploded View of Hydraulic Roller Tappet

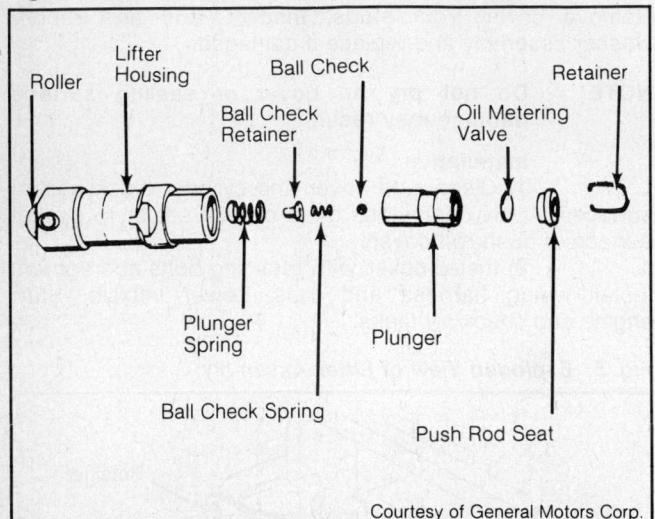

Courtesy of General Motors Corp.

Inspect roller for freedom of movement and replace it binding or roughness is felt. Inspect related cam lobe for proper lobe lift. Replace camshaft (and lifters if necessary) if any lobe is worn beyond specification.

4) Check lifter-to-bore clearance. Standard clearance is .0025" (.064 mm). Standard diameter of lifter is .8420-.8427" (21.387-21.405 mm). Standard lifter bore diameter is .8435-.8445" (21.425-21.450 mm).

Installation

Lubricate bearing surface and install in bore. Verify lifters contact camshaft. Install guides, retainers, push rods and rocker arms. With lifter on base circle of camshaft, tighten rocker arm bolts to specifications. Coat gasket surfaces with RTV sealer and install push rod cover and valve cover. Reverse removal procedure to complete assembly.

PISTONS, PINS & RINGS

OIL PAN

See OIL PAN REMOVAL at end of ENGINE section.

PISTON & ROD ASSEMBLY

NOTE: When removing ridge at top of cylinder bore, never cut into ring travel area more than .031" (.80 mm). Mark rod caps to their related rods for proper reassembly. DO NOT damage crankshaft journals or cylinder wall during removal.

Removal

1) Mark piston with number of cylinder from which piston is removed from. Mark connecting rod and rod cap for correct reassembly. Rotate crankshaft to bottom dead center (BDC).

2) With cylinder head and oil pan removed, inspect cylinder bores for ridges or deposits. Move piston to bottom of bore and cover with cloth to catch cuttings.

3) Remove ridge at top of cylinder bores (using ridge reamer) before removing pistons from block. Rotate crankshaft and inspect connecting rods and rod caps for cylinder identification.

4) Remove rod cap and push each piston with rod assembly out of cylinder bore. To protect crankshaft, place sleeve or rubber hose over rod bolts. Remove bearing inserts from rod and cap to inspect for size, wear and damage. Install rod caps on mating rods.

NOTE: Notch on top of piston faces front of engine.

Installation

1) Check fit of new piston and/or rings in cylinder bore before assembling piston and pin to connecting rod. Check piston pin for clearance, etching or wear. New pistons must be installed in cylinder for which they were fitted. Install used pistons in cylinder from which they were removed.

2) Lightly oil piston rings and cylinder walls. Verify ring gaps are properly spaced and install ring compressor on piston. Marked side of compression rings must be toward top of piston. Position piston so identification numbers on rod and cap are on same side. See Fig. 7.

Fig. 7: Ring Gap Spacing & Piston-to-Rod Location

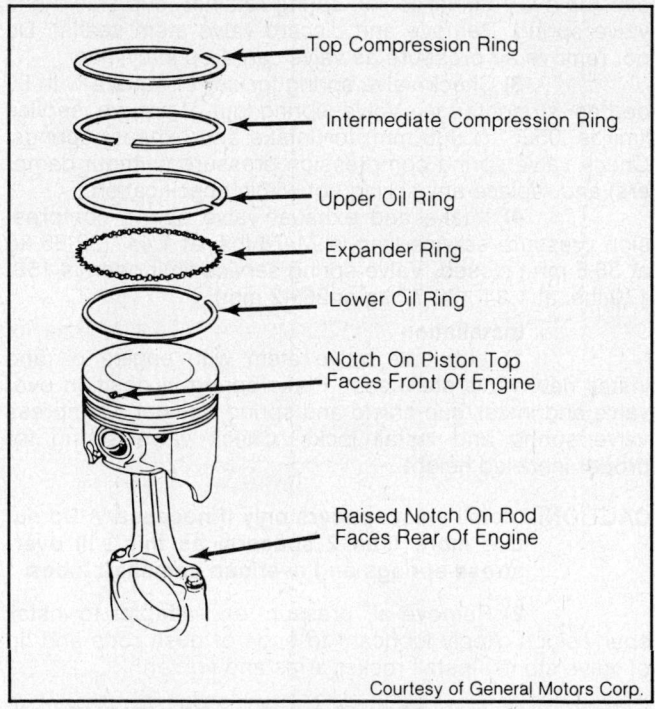

Courtesy of General Motors Corp.

3) Install Connecting Rod Bolt Guide Set (J-6305-11) or rubber sleeves before installing piston and rod assembly in bore. Tap gently with wooden handle to insert piston/rod assembly into cylinder bore.

4) After bearings have been inserted, apply engine oil to journals and bearings. Ensure oil hole in bearing insert aligns with oil hole in connecting rod. Turn crankshaft to bottom of stroke. Guide piston/rod assembly over crankshaft journal until rod bearing seats.

5) Remove rod bolt protectors. Match rod cap to rod and install. Tighten cap nuts in 2 steps. Repeat procedure for each piston assembly. After piston/rod assembly is installed, check side clearance of connecting rod on each crankshaft journal.

FITTING PISTONS

1) Inspect pistons and replace any showing signs of excessive wear, wavy ring lands, or fractures. If

2.5L 4-CYLINDER (Cont.)

piston has sponge-like or eroded surface edge (caused by detonation or pre-ignition) it must be replaced.

2) If shiny surface on thrust side of piston is found, check for bent connecting rod. Replace piston or rod as necessary. Inspect connecting rods for signs of fracture and bearing bores for out-of-round and taper.

3) If bore exceeds recommended limits or rod is fractured, replace rod. Check pistons for fractures at ring lands, skirts and pin bosses. Check for scuffed, rough or scored skirts. Check piston-to-cylinder bore clearance by measuring piston and bore diameters.

4) Piston and cylinder bore must be clean, dry and at approximately 70°F (21°C) during measurement. Measure cylinder bore diameter at top, middle and bottom with gauge at right angle parallel and to centerline of engine.

5) When measuring piston taper, measure at piston pin center and bottom of squirt. If measuring piston size, measure 3/4" below center line of piston pin hole.

6) Inspect cylinder walls for damage or signs of wear. Check bore for out-of-round and taper. *See Fig. 8.* Cylinder bore out-of-round should not be more than .0010" (.025 mm). Cylinder bore taper should not be more than .005" (.13 mm).

7) If cylinder wall is severely marred or worn beyond specifications, refinishing will be necessary. If cylinder bore measurements differ by .005" (.13 mm), bore cylinder block to next oversize.

8) Before cylinder refinishing, ensure main bearing caps are in place and tightened to specification to avoid distortion during refinishing operation. Pistons are available in standard size, .005", .010", .020" and .030" oversizes.

9) Measure new piston and hone cylinder to correct clearance. After refinishing operation, allow bore to cool, then clean bore with soap/water solution and oil cylinder walls.

Fig. 8: Measuring Cylinder Bore

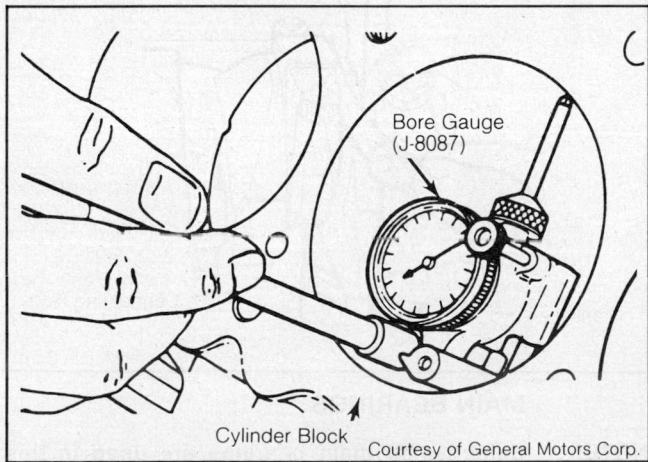

Bore Gauge (J-8087)

Cylinder Block

Courtesy of General Motors Corp.

FITTING PISTON RINGS

1) Clean ring grooves with ring groove cleaner or piece of broken ring. Ensure oil holes (or slots) in piston are clean. Measure piston ring side and end gap clearance for all pistons.

2) Ring side clearance should be checked with feeler gauge between top compression ring and top of ring groove. Gauge should slide freely around entire circumference without binding. *See Fig. 9.*

3) Using piston to position ring in cylinder bore, check ring end gap at least .63" (16 mm) from bottom of bore. Install rings on pistons with end gaps staggered at proper intervals. Ensure ring gap is not in line with thrust face of pin bore.

4) Be sure manufacturer's marks face up when rings are installed. Install oil ring expander first, followed by lower oil ring side rail and upper side rail. Do not use ring expander on side rails. When installing lower side rail, place one end between piston ring groove and expander.

5) Hold end firmly and press down portion to be installed until side rail is in position. Install upper side rail. Using ring expander, install intermediate and upper rings. Verify all components are within specifications.

6) If new piston rings are to be installed and no visible cross-hatch marks remain on cylinder walls, remove glaze using spring-type hone. After honing, clean bore and block with soap/water solution and oil cylinder walls.

Fig. 9: Measuring Piston Ring Side Clearance

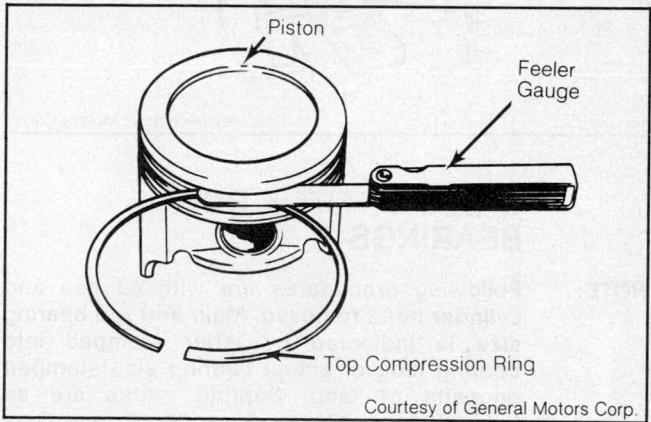

Piston

Feeler Gauge

Top Compression Ring

Courtesy of General Motors Corp.

FITTING PISTON PINS

NOTE: When removing or installing piston pin, connecting rod should be in firm contact with body of pin setting tool.

Removal

1) Remove bearing inserts from connecting rod and cap. Mark pistons, pins and inserts (if reusable) to assure assembly with same rod. Using Piston Pin Tool (J-24086), press piston pin from piston and connecting rod .

2) Inspect and replace any piston pin showing signs of fracture, etching or wear. Check piston pin-to-rod bore fit. Check ID of connecting rod piston pin bore. If pin bore in rod is larger than specification, install .0010" (.025 mm) oversize piston pin.

3) Ensure proper fit by honing or reaming piston pin bore to light slip fit. Standard piston pin diameter is .938-.942" (23.83-23.93 mm).

Installation

1) Check piston-to-cylinder bore clearance before assembling piston and pin to connecting rod. Ensure oil hole in connecting rod aligns with oil hole in bearing and arrow or notch on top of piston is pointed toward front of engine. Notch on rod big end near center of upper bearing insert must face rear of engine.

General Motors Engines

2.5L 4-CYLINDER (Cont.)

2) Start piston pin in piston and connecting rod. Using guide bar and push rod, press pin through both piston and rod until pilot hub bottoms on support fixture and pin is centered in piston. DO NOT exceed 5000 lbs. (2275 kg) pressure with press. Make certain piston floats during pin installation operation. *See Fig. 10.*

Fig. 10: Installing Piston Pin

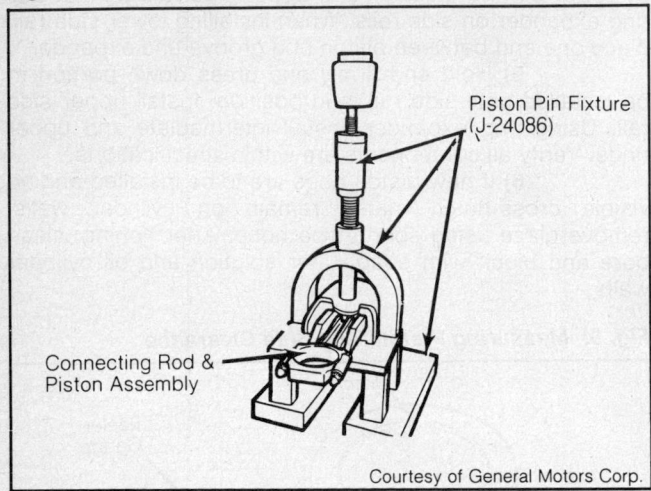

Courtesy of General Motors Corp.

CRANKSHAFT & ROD BEARINGS

NOTE: **Following procedures are with oil pan and cylinder head removed. Main and rod bearing size is indicated by letter stamped into bearing tang or actual bearing size stamped opposite of tang. Bearing marks are as follows: A = .0005", B = .0010", and C = .0015".**

CONNECTING ROD BEARINGS

1) Remove connecting rod cap and mark for proper installation. Inspect each bearing for peeling, melting, seizure or improper contact. Replace defective bearings. Use Plastigage method for bearing clearance check.

2) Measure outside diameter of crankshaft connecting rod bearing journals to determine if out-of-round or tapered. Journal out-of-round must not exceed .0005" (.013 mm) in a half turn. Journal runout (one turn) must not exceed .0005" (.013 mm). Journal taper must not exceed .0005" (.013 mm).

3) When checking connecting rod clearances, crankshaft does not have to be supported. Instead, turn crankshaft until connecting rod to be checked starts moving upward to unload lower bearing.

4) Cut Plastigage to same length as width of rod bearing. Place in bearing cap, parallel with crankshaft (not over oil hole or groove). Install rod bearings and cap. Tighten in 2 steps to specifications. Always install caps with markings in original positions.

5) Do not turn crankshaft with Plastigage installed. Remove rod bearing cap from crankshaft and measure Plastigage at its widest part (using scale on Plastigage package). If clearance exceeds specifications, replace bearing.

NOTE: **If clearance cannot be brought within specifications using service bearings, grind crankshaft to next undersize. If already ground to maximum undersize, replace crankshaft.**

6) Selective fitting is required on each connecting rod. Coat bearing surfaces with heavy engine oil. Tighten connecting rod bearing caps in 2 steps. Connecting rod bearing cap and rod identification numbers must remain on same side.

NOTE: **Precision bearings are used in this engine and shimming for clearance adjustment is not acceptable. Never use new bearing in combination with used bearing. Never file or grind connecting rods or caps when fitting bearings.**

7) Check for shiny surface on either side of piston pin boss, indicating bent connecting rod. Twisted rods will not create identifiable wear patterns, but will disturb the action of entire crankshaft assembly and may cause excessive oil consumption.

8) Check connecting rod side clearance with feeler gauge. Crankshaft to connecting rod side clearance is .006-.022" (.15-.56 mm). If clearance is excessive, replace connecting rod and cap. *See Fig. 11.*

9) If side clearance is below specification, remove rod and cap. Check for scratches, burrs, nicks or dirt between crankshaft and rod. Dress minor imperfections with oil stone.

10) During assembly, ensure oil hole in bearing aligns with oil hole in rod. Verify bearing tangs are seated in slots of rod and cap. Ensure connecting rod bolt heads are properly seated in connecting rod.

Fig. 11: Measuring Connecting Rod Side Clearance

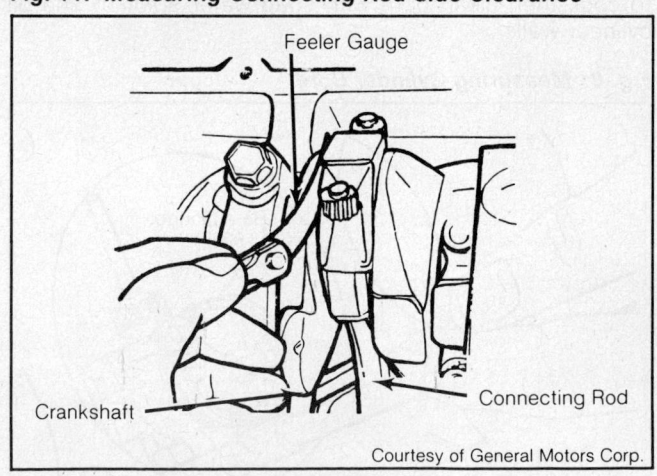

Courtesy of General Motors Corp.

MAIN BEARINGS

NOTE: **Selective fit main bearings are used in this engine. DO NOT scrape gum or varnish deposits from bearings. Clean inserts and caps in solvent. DO NOT file, lap or use shims to obtain proper bearing clearance.**

1) Inspect each bearing for peeling, melting, seizure or improper contact. Replace defective bearings. If copper-lead bearing base is visible but not showing over 20% of total area, bearing is reuseable.

2.5L 4-CYLINDER (Cont.)

2) Measure outside diameter of crankshaft main bearing journals in at least 4 places to determine if out-of-round or tapered. Journal out-of-round must not exceed .0005" (.013 mm) in a half turn. Journal runout (one turn) must not exceed .0005" (.013 mm). Journal taper must not exceed .0005" (.013 mm).

NOTE: Observe location of high spots on main bearings. If high spots are not in line, crankshaft may be bent and should be checked.

3) To check main bearings, shim adjacent main bearings to bearing being checked. Alternate method is to position jack under counterweight adjoining bearing so weight of crankshaft will not compress Plastigage and provide false reading.

4) DO NOT place jack under crankshaft pulley. Crankshaft damage may result. With all other bearing caps tight, check clearances using Plastigage method.

NOTE: If undersize bearings are used on more than one journal, position in cylinder block rather than bearing cap. Do not turn crankshaft with Plastigage installed.

5) If clearance cannot be brought within specified limits, crankshaft will have to be refinished and undersized bearings installed. If journal will not clean up to maximum undersize bearing, replace crankshaft.

6) If journals are remachined, ensure same journal shoulder radius is reproduced. Too small a radius will result in fatigue failure of crankshaft. Too large a radius will result in bearing failure due to radial ride of bearing.

7) When journals are refinished, chamfer oil holes and polish journals with No. 320 grit polishing cloth and engine oil. After chamfer and polish operations, clean crankshaft thoroughly in solvent and blow out oil passages with compressed air.

8) When main bearings are installed, oil distributing grooves must be installed on same side. Oil new upper bearing and insert plain (unnotched) end between crankshaft and notched side of block. Rotate bearing into place. Install main cap bolts and tighten.

THRUST BEARING ALIGNMENT

1) Check crankshaft end play with crankshaft bearing caps installed. Mount dial indicator to front of engine and locate probe on nose of crankshaft. Move crankshaft to rear of its travel. Zero dial indicator.

2) Move crankshaft forward and note end play reading on gauge. Replace No. 5 main thrust bearing (upper and lower) if not to specification. Standard crankshaft end play is .0035-.0085" (.09-.22 mm).

3) Rotate crankshaft to ensure there is no excessive drag. If end play is below specification, inspect thrust bearing surfaces for damage or dirt. Clean up minor imperfections with oil stone. Recheck end play.

CRANKSHAFT FLANGE RUNOUT

1) With engine removed and crankshaft installed, measure crankshaft flange runout. Mount dial indicator gauge plate flat against crankshaft flange. Place dial indicator stem on lower left transmission mounting

bolt boss (flat area around bolt hole). Set indicator to zero. See Fig. 12.

Fig. 12: Checking Crankshaft Flange Runout

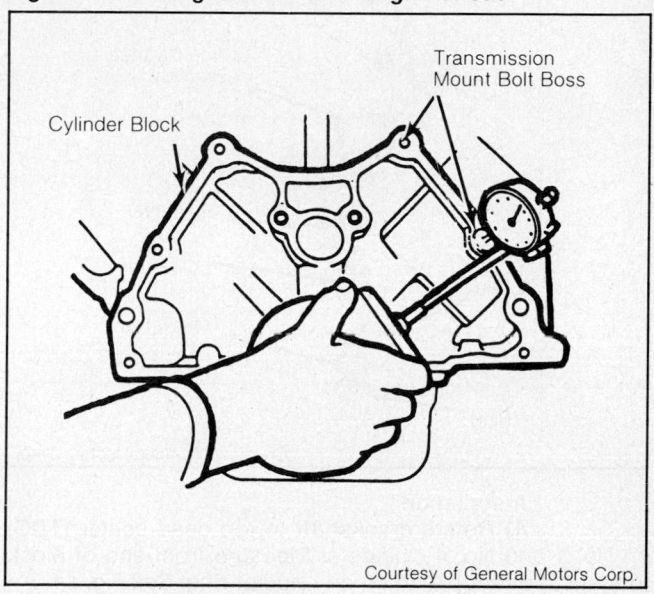

Courtesy of General Motors Corp.

2) Observe and record readings obtained on all mounting bolt hole bosses. Measurements should not vary more than .008" (.20 mm). If readings are more than specification, remount dial gauge plate and recheck flange runout. If runout is excessive, replace crankshaft. Check threaded holes, clean and re-tap as necessary.

REAR MAIN BEARING OIL SEAL

NOTE: Rear main bearing oil seal can be serviced without removal of oil pan or crankshaft.

Removal
1) Remove transaxle assembly. On manual transaxle, remove pressure plate and clutch disc. On all models, remove flywheel retaining bolts and flywheel.

2) Remove rear main bearing oil seal by prying out with screwdriver. Take care not to scratch crankshaft or seal surface. Clean block-to-seal mating surface.

Installation
1) Coat outside surface of new seal with engine oil and install with lip toward engine. Ensure seal is firmly in place.

2) Install flywheel. On manual transaxle, install pressure plate and clutch disc. Install transaxle assembly.

FORCE BALANCER ASSEMBLY

Removal
Oil pan must be drained and removed for access to balancer assembly. See OIL PAN REMOVAL at end of ENGINE section. Remove 2 short and 2 long balancer assembly bolts and remove balancer assembly. See Fig. 13.

General Motors Engines

2.5L 4-CYLINDER (Cont.)

Fig. 13: Balancer Assembly

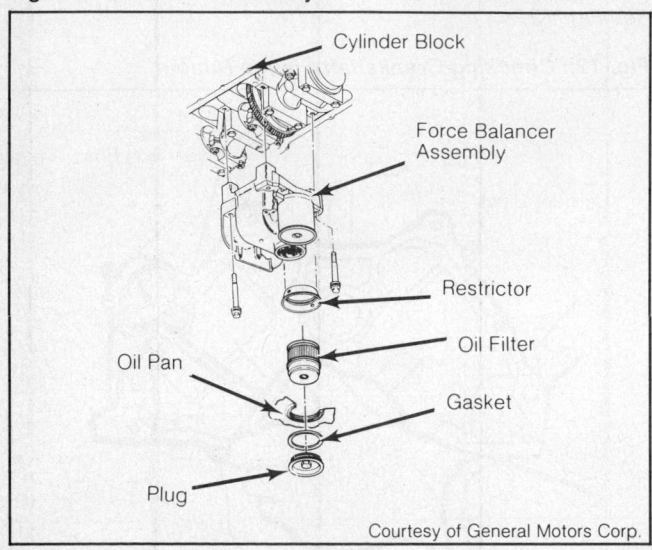

Courtesy of General Motors Corp.

Installation

1) Rotate crankshaft to top dead center (TDC) on No. 1 and No. 4 cylinders. Measure from end of block to first cut of double notch on reluctor ring. *See Fig. 14.*

2) Measurement should be 1 11/16" (42.8 mm). Mount balancer assembly with counterweights parallel and pointing away from crankshaft. *See Fig. 15.* DO NOT move crankshaft. Install balancer assembly. Install short and long bolts and tighten to specifications. Install oil pan.

Fig. 14: Crankshaft Positioning

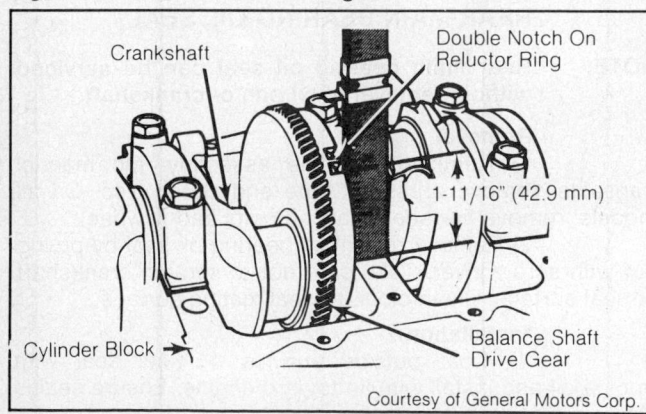

Courtesy of General Motors Corp.

Fig. 15: Counterweights Positioning

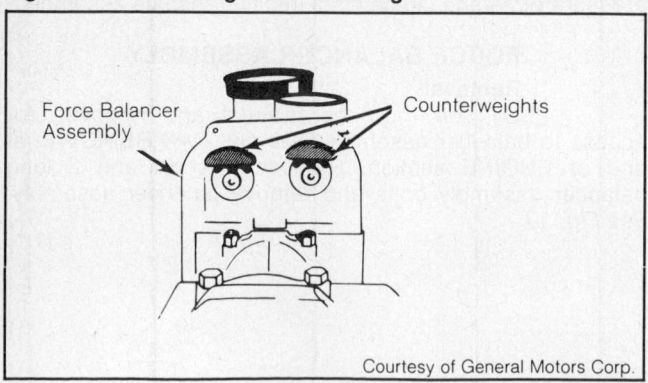

Courtesy of General Motors Corp.

CRANKSHAFT

Removal

1) With engine removed from vehicle. Mount engine on stand and drain engine oil. Remove spark plugs, crankshaft pulley and hub assembly, oil pan, force balancer, timing gear cover and crankshaft timing gear.

2) Remove connecting rod bearing caps with bearings and mark for reinstallation. Position connecting rod and piston assemblies away from crankshaft. Remove main bearing caps with bearings and mark for reinstallation. Remove crankshaft.

Installation

1) Install new upper bearings and position crankshaft in block. Install main bearing caps with new lower bearings. DO NOT tighten cap bolts. Oil upper and lower bearings before installing.

2) Install connecting rods and pistons into place. Install rod bearing caps, DO NOT tighten nuts. Using a rubber mallet, hit both ends of crankshaft to center thrust bearing rearward and then forward.

3) Tighten main bearing cap bolts to specifications. Check crankshaft end play. End play should be .0035-.0085" (.089-.216 mm). Tighten connecting rod bearing cap nuts to specifications.

4) Recheck bearing clearances. Install key from old crankshaft keyway in crankshaft. Install timing gear and align timing marks on timing gears by rotating crankshaft (if necessary).

5) Install timing gear cover with new seal. Install force balancer and oil pan, using new rear seal in rear main bearing cap and new front seal in timing gear cover.

6) Coat front cover oil seal contact area of pulley hub with engine oil and install seal. Install crankshaft pulley, hub and spark plugs. Reinstall engine into vehicle. Start engine and inspect for leaks.

Fig. 16: Crankshaft & Bearings

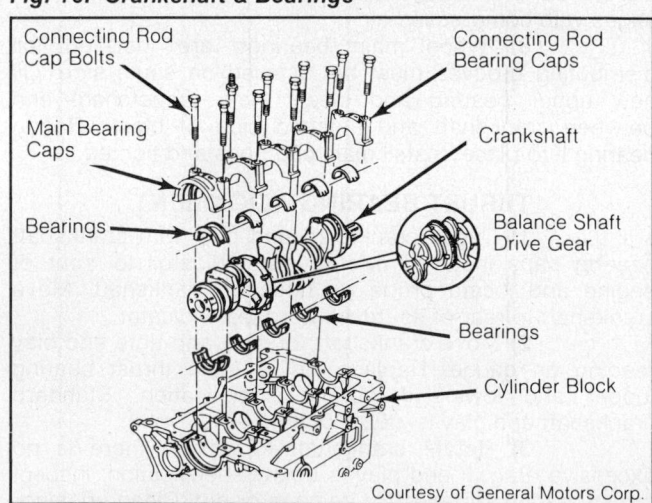

Courtesy of General Motors Corp.

CAMSHAFT

TIMING GEAR COVER

Removal

NOTE: **Engine or inner fender removal may be necessary depending on model applicaton.**

2.5L 4-CYLINDER (Cont.)

1) Disconnect negative battery cable. Remove engine drive belts. Remove center bolt to slide hub and pulley(s) from crankshaft. Remove alternator lower bracket. Remove front engine mount-to-cradle nuts. On Fiero model, remove starter, flywheel cover and right rear tire.

2) Install Engine Support Fixture (J28467) and raise engine. Unbolt engine mount to remove support bracket and mount as an assembly. Remove 2 oil pan-to-front cover bolts and all front cover-to-block bolts.

3) Pull front cover slightly forward to separate cover from oil pan gasket. If necessary, cut pan gasket flush with engine block on both sides. Remove front cover.

Installation

1) Clean mating surfaces of engine block and front cover. Cut tabs off new oil pan front gasket. *See Fig. 17.* Install gasket, coated with sealer, on front cover. Press tips into holes provided in cover.

Fig. 17: Oil Pan Sealer Application

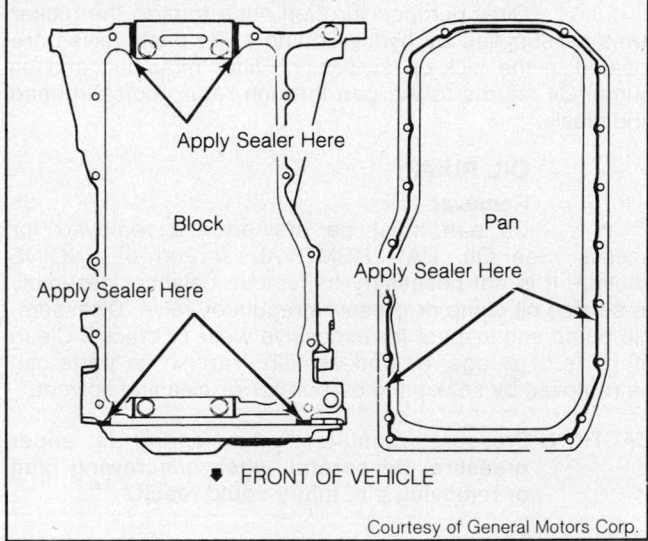

Courtesy of General Motors Corp.

2) Apply silicone sealer to joint at oil pan and engine block. Install Crankshaft Seal Centering Fixture (J-34995) in front cover seal. Install front cover to block.

3) Install and partially tighten 2 oil pan-to-front cover bolts. Install front cover-to-block bolts and tighten to 90 INCH lbs. (10 N.m). Remove centering tool. Reverse removal procedure to complete installation

FRONT COVER OIL SEAL

Removal

Remove engine drive belts or serpentine belt. Remove right front inner splash shield. Remove center hub bolt and slide hub and pulley(s) from crankshaft. Using large screwdriver, pry oil seal from front cover. DO NOT distort sheet metal timing chain cover.

Installation

1) Loosen front cover retaining bolts. Install new seal with lip toward rear of engine. Drive seal into place using Seal Driver (J34995). Coat oil seal contact area of balancer with engine oil.

2) Position hub on crankshaft and slide into position until it bottoms against crankshaft gear. Install center bolt and tighten. Install pulley-to-hub bolts using sealing compound and tighten.

3) Install belts and adjust tension. Reverse removal procedure to complete installation. Verify pulley alignment and check for oil leaks.

CAMSHAFT & TIMING GEAR

Removal

1) Remove engine and install on engine stand. On Fiero model, leave engine and transaxle attached to cradle. Remove valve cover, rocker arms and push rods. Remove intake manifold for accessibility. Remove push rod side cover and valve lifters.

2) Remove distributor and if necessary, fuel pump. Verify engine support is secure and remove front engine mount with bracket assembly. Remove front pulley, hub and timing gear cover.

3) Remove 2 camshaft thrust plate retaining bolts by working through holes in camshaft gear. *See Fig. 18.* Remove camshaft and gear by pulling it through front of block. Use care not to damage camshaft bearings.

Fig. 18: Thrust Plate Bolt Removal

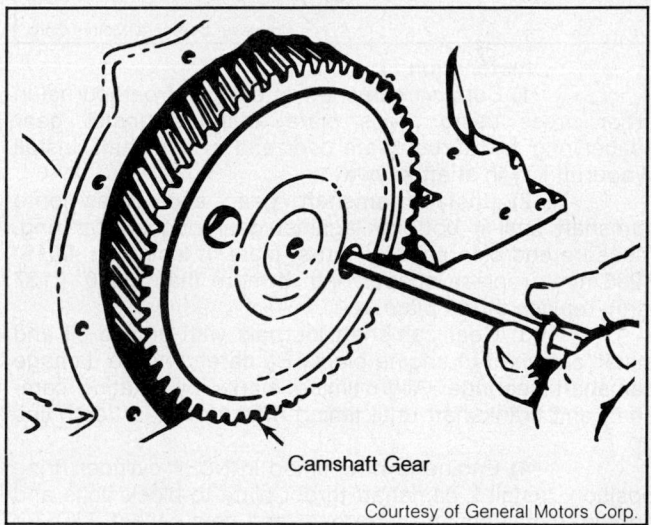

Camshaft Gear

Courtesy of General Motors Corp.

4) Use arbor press and adapter to remove timing gear from camshaft. Place camshaft through opening in tools on table of press and press camshaft out of timing gear. Position thrust plate so Woodruff key in camshaft does no damage during removal.

Inspection

1) Check camshaft journals for out-of-round condition. If journals exceed .0005" (.013 mm) out-of-round, replace camshaft. Check camshaft end play. *See Fig. 19.*

2) Standard end play is .0015-.0050" (.038-.127 mm). End play service limit is .009" (.229 mm). Replace thrust plate if clearance is more than .0050" (.127 mm). Replace spacer ring if clearance is less than .0015" (.038 mm).

3) Check camshaft journal runout. Runout limit is .005" (.013 mm). Check camshaft for alignment. Use "V" block and dial indicator. If dial gauge reads more than .0015" (.038 mm), replace camshaft. Check camshaft journal-to-bearing clearance.

NOTE: Camshaft lobes are ground and hardened. Front-to-rear taper is not present due to non-orbital characteristcs of roller lifters.

4) Check camshaft lobe lift. Attach dial indicator with a ball socket attachment to camshaft carrier or "V" block. Measure lobe lift. Allowable lobe lift loss is .005" (.013 mm). If not to specification, replace camshaft.

*Fig. 19: Camshaft Timing Gear/
Thrust Plate End Clearance*

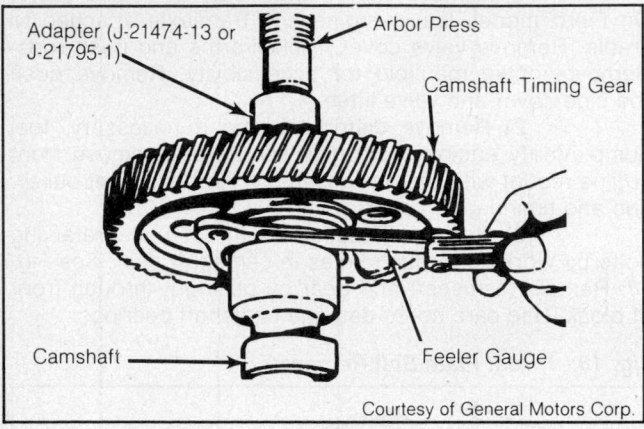

Courtesy of General Motors Corp.

Installation

1) Support camshaft at back of front journal in arbor press using press plate adaptors. Install gear spacer ring and thrust plate over end of camshaft. Install Woodruff key in shaft keyway.

2) Install camshaft gear and press onto camshaft until it bottoms against gear ring spacer ring. Measure end clearance of thrust plate. If less than .0015" (.038 mm), replace spacer ring. If more than .0050" (.127 mm), replace thrust plate.

3) Coat camshaft journals with engine oil and install camshaft in engine block. Be careful not to damage camshaft bearings. Align timing marks by rotating camshaft and crankshaft until timing marks on gear teeth line up.

4) Engine is now timed in No. 4 cylinder firing position. Install 2 camshaft thrust plate-to-block bolts and tighten. Install timing gear cover and new gasket. Line up hub keyway to crankshaft key, install hub and tighten bolt.

5) Install lifters, push rods, push rod cover, oil pump shaft and gear assembly and fuel pump. To install distributor, turn crankshaft 360 degrees to firing position of No. 1 cylinder (timing marks aligned on balancer and timing pad with valves closed).

6) Install distributor in original position and align shaft with rotor arm toward No. 1 plug contact. Pivot each rocker arm over push rod and tighten rocker arm bolt. To complete installation, reverse removal procedure.

CAMSHAFT BEARINGS

Removal

With engine, flywheel and camshaft removed, drive out expansion plug from rear camshaft bearing. Remove by driving out from inside. Using Camshaft Bearing Remover/Installer (J-33049), drive out front bearing toward rear of engine and rear bearing toward front. Drive center bearing out toward rear of engine.

Installation

Install each bearing on tool and replace by reversing removal procedure. Be sure oil hole in camshaft bearings and cylinder block line up. Install front camshaft bearing with bearing recessed about 1/8" into engine block. This uncovers oil hole to timing gear oil nozzle. Reverse removal procedure to complete installation.

ENGINE OILING

CRANKCASE CAPACITY

Engine oil capacity is 3 qts. (2.8L) without filter change. Add .5 qts. (.47L) with new filter.

NORMAL OIL PRESSURE

Normal oil pressure is 50 psi (3.51 kg/cm²) at 2000 RPM.

PRESSURE REGULATOR VALVE

The pressure regulator valve is located in oil pump body and is not serviceable.

ENGINE OILING SYSTEM

When engine is started, the oil pump draws oil from the pan, pumps it through the filter and into passage along right side of the block where it intersects lifter bosses. Oil is then routed to camshaft and crankshaft bearings through smaller drilled passages.

Oil is pumped through push rods to the rocker arms as supplied by hydraulic lifters. By-pass valves are located in the pick-up screen, oil filter mounting and oil pump. Oil returns to the pan through return holes in head and block.

OIL PUMP

Removal

Oil pan must be drained and removed for access. See OIL PAN REMOVAL at end of ENGINE section. It is not necessary to remove balancer assembly to service oil pump or pressure regulator valve. Disassemble pump and inspect for excessive wear or cracks. Clean all parts of sludge, oil and varnish. Varnish on parts can be removed by soaking in carburetor or cleaning solvent.

CAUTION: Pressure regulator valve spring is under pressure. Be careful when unscrewing plug or removing pin. Injury could result.

*Fig. 20: Exploded View of Balancer &
Oil Pump Assembly*

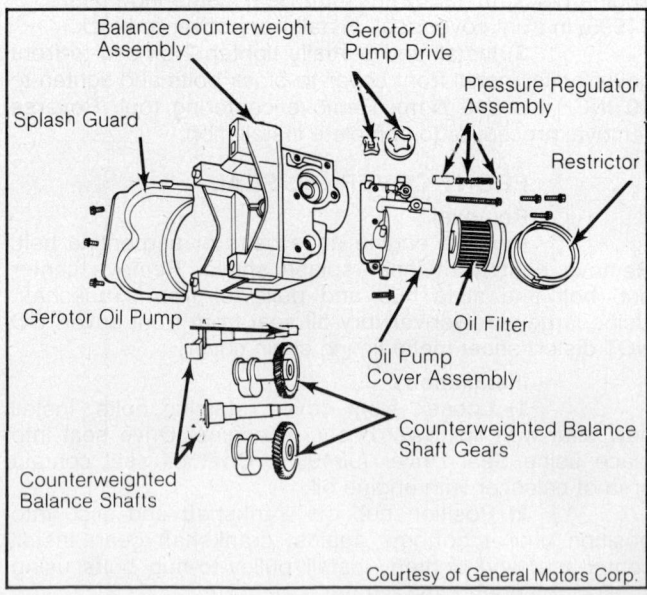

Courtesy of General Motors Corp.

2.5L 4-CYLINDER (Cont.)

OIL PUMP SPECIFICATIONS

Application	In. (mm)
Drive Gear-to-Body Clearance	.004 (.10) Maximum
Idler Gear-to-Body Clearance	.004 (.10) Maximum
Gear-to-Cover End Clearance	.002-.005 (.05-.13)
Gear Lash	.009-.015 (.23-.38)
Oil Pump Body	
Bore Depth	.995-.998 (25.27-25.35)
Bore Diameter	1.503-1.506 (38.18-38.25)
Oil Pump Gear	
Length	.999-1.002 (25.37-25.45)
Diameter	1.496-1.500 (38.05-38.10)

Installation

1) When assembling pump, lubricate all internal parts with engine oil. Fill oil pump cavaties with petroleum jelly to ensure immediate oil pressure. Install pump gears, oil pump cover assembly, pressure regulator valve and spring, and plug or pin.

2) If oil pressure does not build up almost immediately, remove oil pan and examine pump. Disassemble oil pump and repack all cavaties with petroleum jelly (if necessary). Running engine with out specified oil pressure will cause extensive damage.

ENGINE COOLING

WATER PUMP

Removal

Disconnect negative battery cable. Drain engine coolant. Remove fan and serpentine drive belt. Remove lower radiator hose at water pump. Remove water pump attaching bolts and remove water pump.

Installation

If installing new pump with old pulley, transfer pulley using Pulley Remover (J25034-B or J29785-A). Apply continuous bead of sealer to clean pump sealing surface and apply RTV sealer to water pump bolts. Install water pump while sealer is still wet and tighten attaching bolts to specifications. Install lower radiator hose and drive belts. Connect negative battery cable. Fill cooling system and check for leaks.

NOTE: For further information on cooling system, see article in ENGINE COOLING SYSTEMS section.

TIGHTENING SPECIFICATIONS

Application	Ft. Lbs. (N.m)
Connecting Rod Nuts	32 (44)
Cylinder Head Bolts	[1]
EGR Valve-to-Manifold Bolts	16 (22)
Exhaust Manifold Retaining Bolts	[2]
Flywheel-to-Crankshaft Bolts	
Automatic	55 (75)
Manual	69 (93)
Harmonic Balancer Bolts	162 (220)
Intake Manifold Retaining Bolts	25 (34)
Main Bearing Cap Bolts	70 (95)
Oil Filter Adapter Bolts	30 (41)
Oil Pan-to-Block Bolts	20 (27)
Rocker Arm Bolts	24 (32)
Thermostat Housing Bolts	20 (27)
Throttle Body-to-Manifold Bolts	15 (20)
Throttle Body-to-Manifold Nuts	15 (20)
Water Pump-to-Block Bolts	25 (34)

	INCH Lbs.
Camshaft Thrust Plate Bolts	90 (10)
Front Cover-to-Block Bolts	90 (10)
Force Balancer-to-Block Bolts	
Short Bolts	[3] 106 (12)
Long Bolts	[4] 106 (12)
Lifter Retainer-to-Block Bolts	90 (10)
Oil Pump Cover Bolts	97 (11)
Rocker Arm Cover Bolts	45 (5)

[1] – Tighten all cylinder head bolts in sequence to 18 ft. lbs. (25 N.m). Then tighten to 26 ft. lbs. (35 N.m) all except No. 9. Tighten No. 9 to 18 ft. lbs. (25 N.m). Repeat sequence, tightening all bolts 1/4 turn.

[2] – Tighten No. 1, 2, 6, and 7 bolts to 32 ft. lbs. (43 N.m).
Tighten No. 3, 4, 5 bolts to 37 ft. lbs. (50 N.m).

[3] – Tighten additional 75 degrees.

[4] – Tighten additional 90 degrees.

ENGINE SPECIFICATIONS

GENERAL SPECIFICATIONS

Year	DISPLACEMENT		Fuel System	HP@RPM	Torque Ft. Lbs.@RPM	Compr. Ratio	BORE		STROKE	
	Cu. In.	Liters					In.	mm	In.	mm
1988	151	2.5	TBI	.....	.....	8.3:1	4.00	101.6	3.00	76.2

General Motors Engines

2.5L 4-CYLINDER (Cont.)

ENGINE SPECIFICATIONS (Cont.)

VALVES

Engine Size & Valve	Head Diam. In. (mm)	Face Angle	Seat Angle	Seat Width In. (mm)	Stem Diameter In. (mm)	Stem Clearance In. (mm)	Valve Lift In. (mm)
2.5L Intake	1.72 (43.68)	45°	46°	.035-.075 (.889-1.90)	.313-.314 (7.95-7.98)	.....	.....
Exhaust	1.50 (38.10)	45°	46°	.058-.105 (1.47-2.667)	.312-.313 (7.92-7.95)	.....	.....

PISTONS, PINS & RINGS

Engine	PISTONS Clearance In. (mm)	PINS Piston Fit In. (mm)	PINS Rod Fit In. (mm)	RINGS Ring No.	RINGS End Gap In. (mm)	RINGS Side Clearance In. (mm)
2.5L	.0014-.0022 [1] (.036-.056)	.0002-.0004 (.005-.010)	Press Fit	1	.010-.020 (.254-.508)	.002-.003 (.051-.076)
				2	.010-.020 (.254-.508)	.001-.003 (.025-.076)
				3	.020-.060 (.508-1.52)	.015-.055 (.38-1.4)

[1] – Measure 1.8" (45.72 mm) below top of piston.

CRANKSHAFT MAIN & CONNECTING ROD BEARINGS

Engine	MAIN BEARINGS Journal Diam. In. (mm)	MAIN BEARINGS Clearance In. (mm)	MAIN BEARINGS Thrust Bearing	MAIN BEARINGS Crankshaft End Play In. (mm)	CONNECTING ROD BEARINGS Journal Diam. In. (mm)	CONNECTING ROD BEARINGS Clearance In. (mm)	CONNECTING ROD BEARINGS Side Play In. (mm)
2.5L	2.3 [1] (58.42)	.0005-.0022 (.013-.056)	No. 5	.0035-.0085 (.089-.216)	2.0 [1] (50.8)	.0005-.0026 (.013-.066)	.006-.022 (.15-.56)

[1] – Maximum out-of-round permissible is .0005" (.013 mm).

VALVE SPRINGS

Engine	Free Length In. (mm)	PRESSURE Lbs. @ In. (Kg @ mm) Valve Closed	PRESSURE Lbs. @ In. (Kg @ mm) Valve Open
2.5L	1.78 [1] (45.2)	71-78@1.440 (32-35@36.58)	158-170@1.04 (72-77@26.42)

[1] – Installed height for intake and exhaust is 1.44" (36.58 mm).

CAMSHAFT

Engine	Journal Diam. In. (mm)	Clearance In. (mm)	Lobe Lift In. (mm)
2.5L	1.869 (47.47)	.0007-.0027 [1] (.018-.069)	.398 (10.1)

[1] – Camshaft end play is .0015-.0050" (.038-.127 mm).

2.8L V6

NOTE: For engine repair procedures not covered in this article, see ENGINE OVERHAUL PROCEDURES article at beginning of this section.

ENGINE CODING

ENGINE IDENTIFICATION

Engine code is found in Vehicle Identification Number (VIN), stamped on metal tab, located on top of instrument panel at lower left corner of windshield. The VIN number contains 17 characters. The 8th character identifies engine type and the 10th establishes model year. The VIN number is also stamped on a pad located on left rear side of engine.

ENGINE CODES

Engine	Code
2.8L (173") V6 MPFI	S
2.8L (173") V6 MFI	W
2.8L (173") V6 MFI	9

ENGINE REMOVAL

See ENGINE REMOVAL & INSTALLATION at end of ENGINE section.

CYLINDER HEAD & MANIFOLDS

INTAKE MANIFOLD
Removal

CAUTION: Fuel system is under pressure. Before removing fuel rail, pressure regulator or injector, relieve system pressure.

NOTE: To relieve fuel system pressure, connect Fuel Gauge (J34730-1) to fuel pressure tap. To avoid spilling, wrap a shop towel around fitting while connecting. Install bleed hose into an approved gasoline container. Open valve to bleed system pressure.

1) Disconnect negative battery cable. Remove air cleaner. Drain cooling system. Disconnect spark plug wires. Mark distributor position and remove hold-down bracket. Remove distributor.

2) Disconnect vacuum lines. Remove EGR pipe-to-plenum bolts, throttle body bolts, and throttle cable bracket bolts. Remove plenum. Disconnect fuel lines at fuel rail. Remove rail retaining bolts, injector electrical connectors, and fuel rail assembly.

3) Remove air management hose and bracket (manual transmissions only). Disconnect emission canister hoses. Remove pipe bracket (front left valve cover). Remove valve covers. Remove accessory drive belt. Remove upper intake manifold.

4) Disconnect upper radiator hose and coolant sensor electrical connectors at thermostat housing. Remove intermediate manifold. Remove lower manifold bolts and manifold. Discard manifold gaskets and remove loose RTV sealer from front and rear ridges of cylinder case.

NOTE: Intake manifold gaskets are marked "Right Side" and "Left Side". Top of each gasket

will have to be cut to install behind push rods. See Fig. 1.

Fig. 1: Installing Intake Manifold Gasket

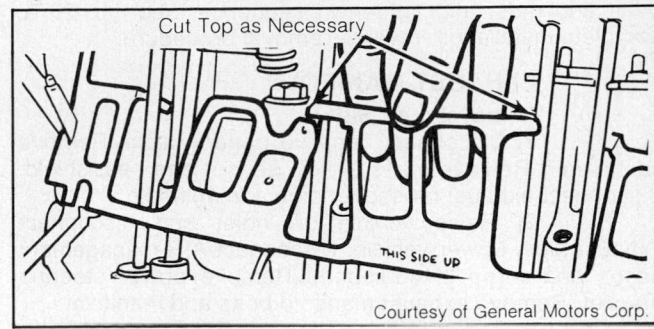

Courtesy of General Motors Corp.

Fig. 2: Intake Manifold Tightening Sequence

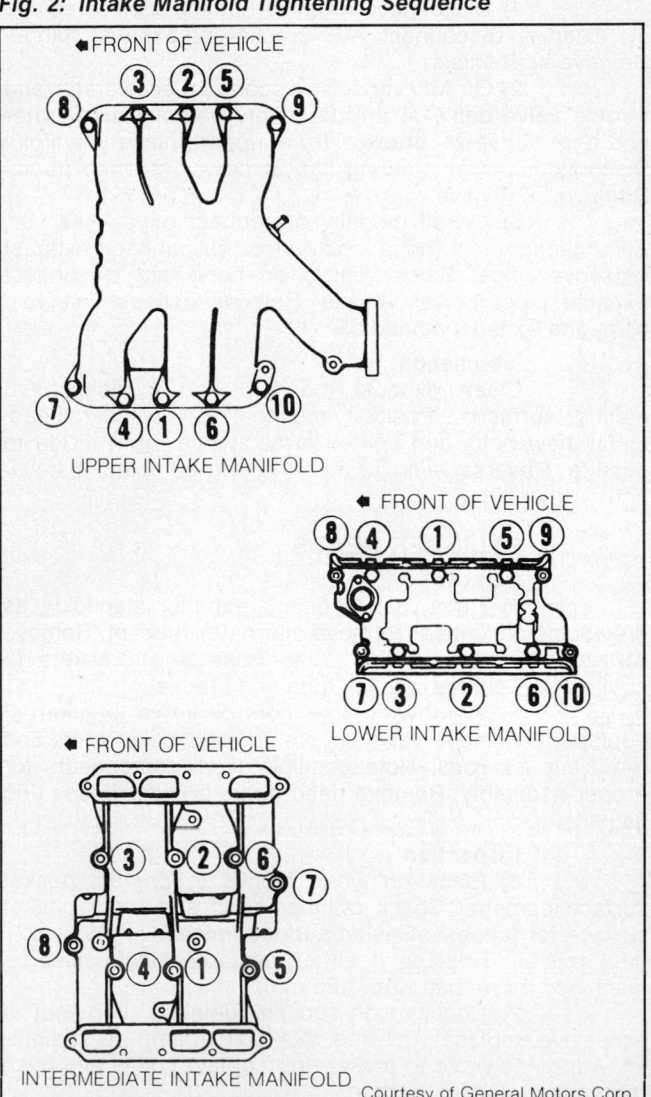

UPPER INTAKE MANIFOLD

LOWER INTAKE MANIFOLD

INTERMEDIATE INTAKE MANIFOLD

Courtesy of General Motors Corp.

Installation

1) Clean sealing surfaces on cylinder head, valve covers and intake manifold. Apply bead of RTV sealer on front and rear ridges of cylinder block. Install new intake manifold gaskets on cylinder heads. Hold in place by extending bead of RTV sealer onto gasket ends.

General Motors Engines

2.8L V6 (Cont.)

When applying sealer, keep out of bolt holes to prevent hydraulic lock of retaining bolts.

2) Install intake manifold and check area between ridges and manifold for complete seal. Install bolts and nuts, and tighten in sequence. *See Fig. 2.* To complete installation, reverse removal procedure.

EXHAUST MANIFOLD
Removal (Left Side)
1) Disconnect negative battery cable. Remove air cleaner. Remove mass airflow sensor and heat shield. Disconnect exhaust crossover pipe at manifold.

2) Raise vehicle on hoist and disconnect exhaust pipe. Lower vehicle. Disconnect AIR management hoses and wires (if equipped). Remove power steering bracket. Remove exhaust manifold bolts and manifold.

Removal (Right Side)
1) Disconnect negative battery cable. Remove air cleaner. Disconnect AIR bracket at exhaust flange. Remove heat shield.

2) On MFI models, disconnect accelerator and throttle valve cable at throttle lever. Remove accelerator and throttle valve bracket from upper intake manifold. Disconnect power steering line at power steering pump. Remove EGR valve.

3) On all models, disconnect oxygen sensor, AIR management hose and valve. Disconnect exhaust crossover pipe. Raise vehicle on hoist and disconnect exhaust pipe. Lower vehicle. Remove exhaust manifold bolts and exhaust manifold.

Installation
Clean exhaust manifold and cylinder head mating surfaces. Position manifold on cylinder head. Install new bolts and tighten in sequence, from inside to outside. Reverse removal procedure to complete installation.

CYLINDER HEADS
Removal
1) Remove intake and exhaust manifolds as previously described. Remove alternator bracket. Remove AIR management valve, pump, hose and brackets (if equipped). Remove dipstick tube and bracket.

2) Remove cruise control servo bracket (if equipped). Remove valve covers, loosen rocker arms and remove push rods. Note position of all components for proper assembly. Remove head bolts, cylinder heads and gaskets.

Inspection
1) Place on wood blocks to prevent gasket surface damage. Check cylinder head and block gasket surface for flatness. Gasket surface flatness is .005" (.127 mm) overall. Replace if either head or block must be machined more than .010" (.25 mm).

2) Check push rod straightness. If runout is excessive, replace push rod. DO NOT attempt to straighten. Apply Molykote to rocker arm contact points and push rod ends during installation.

Installation
1) Clean cylinder block and cylinder head mating surfaces. Ensure mating surfaces are free of any nicks or heavy scratches. Clean bolt hole threads in cylinder block to ensure proper bolt torque.

2) Install gaskets over dowel pins with note "THIS SIDE UP" showing. Install cylinder heads. Apply

sealing compound to head bolt threads and tighten in sequence. *See Fig. 3.*

3) Install push rods and rocker arms. Adjust valves. Ensure lower ends of push rods are in lifter seats. Reverse removal procedure to complete installation.

Fig. 3: Cylinder Head Tightening Sequence

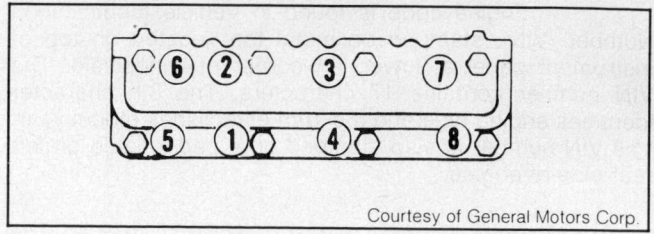

Courtesy of General Motors Corp.

CAMSHAFT

FRONT ENGINE COVER
Removal
1) Disconnect negative battery cable. Remove accessory drive belts and drain cooling system. Remove A/C compressor, AIR pump and bracket (if equipped).

2) Disconnect lower radiator hose at front cover and heater hose at water pump connection. Remove water pump. Raise vehicle. Remove torsional damper. Remove oil pan-to-front cover bolts.

3) Lower vehicle. Remove remaining front cover retaining bolts, front cover and gasket. Clean all gasket sealing surfaces of sealer and check for nicks, cracks or damage to components. *See Fig. 4.*

Fig. 4: Exploded View of Water Pump & Front Cover

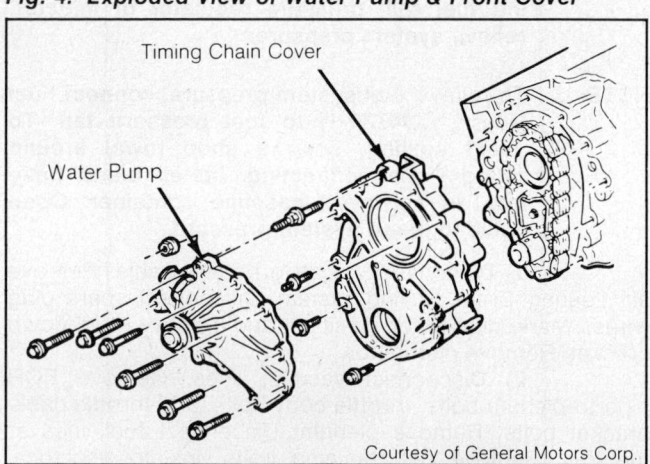

Timing Chain Cover

Water Pump

Courtesy of General Motors Corp.

Installation
1) When installing new gasket, be sure sealing surfaces are clean. Apply continuous bead of anaerobic sealant to front cover sealing surface. *See Fig. 5.* Apply continuous bead of RTV sealer to oil pan surface of front cover. Install components within 5 minutes of application.

2) Place front cover on engine and install stud bolt and remaining attaching bolts. Install water pump. Install water pump retaining bolts and tighten. Reverse removal procedure to complete installation. Run engine until thermostat opens. Check for leaks at all gasket junctions. Check coolant level and add coolant as necessary.

2.8L V6 (Cont.)

Fig. 5: Front Cover Sealant Placement

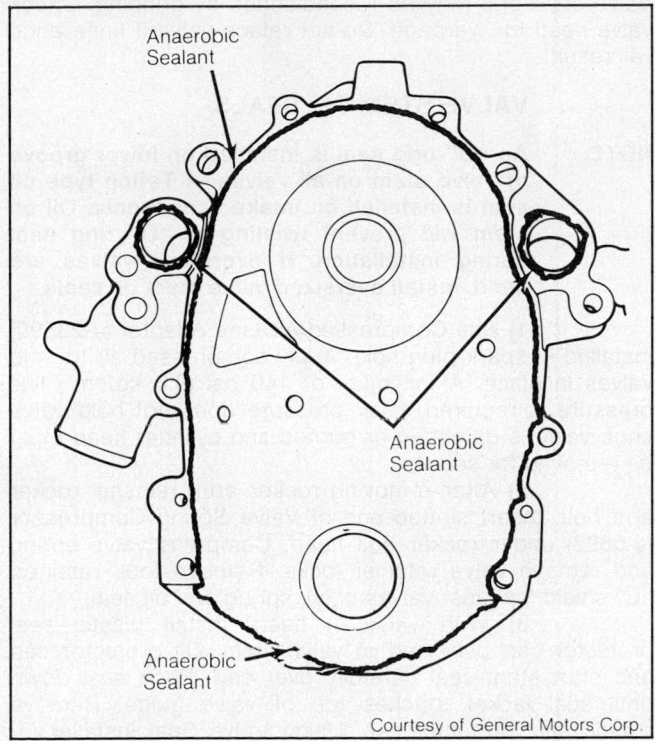

Anaerobic Sealant

Anaerobic Sealant

Anaerobic Sealant

Courtesy of General Motors Corp.

Fig. 6: Timing Chain Sprocket Alignment

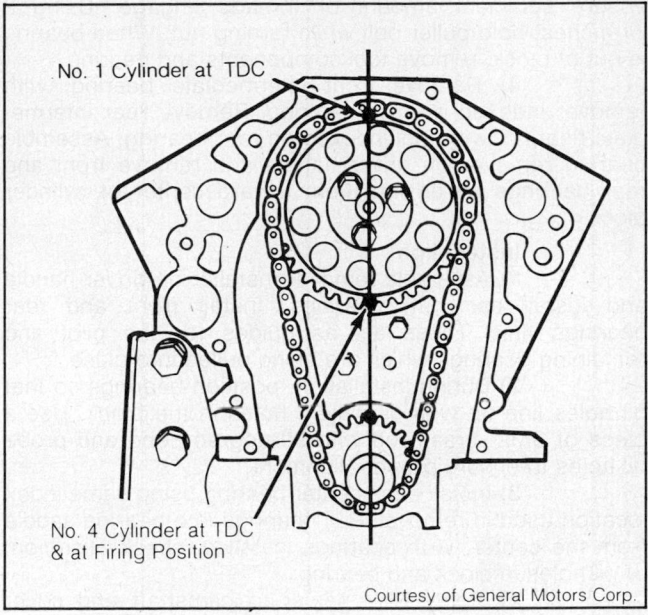

No. 1 Cylinder at TDC

No. 4 Cylinder at TDC & at Firing Position

Courtesy of General Motors Corp.

FRONT COVER OIL SEAL

Removal

The oil seal may be replaced without removing front cover. Raise vehicle. Remove torsional damper. Using large screwdriver, carefully wedge between crankshaft and seal. Pry seal out of cover. Use caution when removing seal to ensure crankshaft is not damaged.

Installation

Install new seal with open end of seal facing inside of front cover. Using Seal Aligner (J-23042), drive seal into position. To complete installation, reverse removal procedure.

TIMING CHAIN

Removal

Remove front engine cover and rotate No. 1 piston to TDC. Align timing marks on crankshaft and camshaft sprockets (No. 4 firing position). Remove camshaft sprocket bolts. Remove sprocket and chain. *See Fig. 6.*

Installation

1) Install timing chain over camshaft sprocket. Lube thrust surface with Molykote. Hold sprocket vertically with chain hanging down. Align marks on camshaft and crankshaft sprockets. *See Fig. 6.*

2) Align dowel on camshaft with dowel hole in camshaft sprocket. Install chain and sprocket on camshaft. Use mounting bolts to draw sprocket onto camshaft and tighten bolts to specifications.

3) Check sprocket alignment. Lubricate timing chain with engine oil. Install front engine cover (with new seal). To complete installation, reverse removal procedure.

CAMSHAFT

Removal

1) With engine removed from vehicle, remove front engine cover. Remove intake manifold, rocker arm assemblies, push rods and valve lifters. Remove mechanical fuel pump and fuel pump push rod (if equipped). Keep all components separate and in order of removal for proper installation.

2) Rotate No. 1 piston to TDC. Align timing marks on crankshaft and camshaft sprockets (No. 4 firing position). Remove camshaft sprocket retaining bolts. Remove timing chain and sprocket from end of camshaft. Remove camshaft.

NOTE: **All camshaft journals are same diameter. Use care during removal to avoid damage to camshaft bearings.**

Installation

Lubricate journals with engine oil and apply Molykote to camshaft lobes. If new camshaft is installed, ensure lifters, oil filter and oil are also replaced. Carefully install camshaft, and do not nick or damage camshaft lobes or journals. Reverse removal procedure to complete installation.

CAMSHAFT BEARINGS

Removal

1) With engine removed from vehicle, remove crankshaft and camshaft. Leave piston assemblies installed but move pistons up into bores and fasten connecting rods against sides of engine. Remove camshaft rear cover from cylinder block.

2) Use Camshaft Bearing Remover (J-6098) with nut and thrust washer installed to end of threads. Index pilot in camshaft front bearing and install puller bolt through pilot.

3) Install tool with shoulder toward bearing and ensure sufficient amount of threads engage. Using 2 wrenches, hold puller bolt while turning nut. When bearing is out of block, remove tool components and bearing.

4) Remove front intermediate bearing, with remover indexed on front bearing. Remove rear intermediate bearing, with tool indexed on rear bearing. Assemble bearing remover on driver handle and remove front and rear bearings by driving them toward center of cylinder block.

Installation

1) Assemble remover/installer on driver handle and install camshaft bearings. Install front and rear bearings first. These act as guides for the pilot and remaining bearings which are being pulled into place.

2) During installation, position bearings so that oil holes line up with oil gallery holes in the block. Use a piece of 3/32" brass rod with 90 degree bend and probe oil holes to ensure proper alignment.

3) Install each center bearing using same index location used in removal. Pull bearings into bearing saddle from the center. With bearings installed, check alignment of oil holes in block and bearing.

4) Apply RTV sealer to camshaft end cover and install. Apply RTV sealer onto engine block in machined groove. Sealant must be wet when installing. Tighten bolts. Reverse removal procedure to complete installation.

VALVES

NOTE: When reconditioning valves, ensure interference angles of valve and seat are not lapped out. Remove grooves and/or score marks from end of valve stem with oil stone. DO NOT remove excessive material from valve stem end.

VALVE ARRANGEMENT

E-I-I-E-I-E (Left bank, front-to-rear).
E-I-E-I-I-E (Right bank, front-to-rear).

VALVE GUIDE SERVICING

1) With cylinder head removed and disassembled, check valve stem-to-guide clearance. If valve stem-to-guide clearance exceeds specifications, ream valve guide to next size, using Valve Guide Reamer (J-5330-1, 2 or 3).

2) To check valve guide wear, insert valve with head positioned .079" (2 mm) away from valve seat. Attach dial gauge to cylinder head. Position gauge indicator directly against valve stem, just above guide. Move valve in guide and note guide wear shown on dial gauge.

3) Maximum dial gauge reading for valve-to-guide clearance is shown in specifications table. Use Valve Guide Cleaner (J-8101) to clean guides. Use valve guide reamers in sequence to ream guides for installation of valves with oversize stems.

4) Reface valve seat after valve guide is reamed. If valve seat face is reground, check margin width dimension. Check valve seats for proper angle and seat width. Measure valve seat runout.

5) Use scraper to break (lightly chamfer or bevel) sharp top inside edge of guide. After valve guide

repair, inspect valve stem end for wear before installation. Valve stem end may be reconditioned by grinding. Check valve head for warpage. Do not reface valve if knife edge will result.

VALVE STEM OIL SEALS

NOTE: An "O" ring seal is installed on lower groove of valve stem on all valves. A Teflon type oil seal is installed on intake valves only. Oil on stem will prevent twisting of "O" ring seal during installation. If oversized valves are used, install oversized valve stem oil seals.

1) Use Compressed Air Line Adapter (J-23590) installed in spark plug hole. Apply compressed air to hold valves in place. A minimum of 140 psi (9.8 kg/cm²) line pressure is required. If air pressure does not hold valve shut, valve is damaged or burned and cylinder head must be removed for service.

2) After removing rocker arm, reinstall rocker arm bolt. Insert slotted end of Valve Spring Compressor (J-5892) under rocker bolt head. Compress valve spring and remove valve retainer locks. Remove tool, retainer, cup shield (exhaust valves only), spring and oil seal.

3) With valve in head, install plastic seal protector cap over end of valve stem. Oil protector cap and start stem seal carefully over cap. Push seal down until seal jacket touches top of valve guide. Remove plastic seal protector cap. Using Valve Seal Installer (J-22330), bottom seal on valve guide. To ensure there are no air leaks, apply vacuum to valve cap with Valve Seal Tester (J-23994).

VALVE SPRINGS
Removal

1) Remove valve cover, spark plug, rocker arm and push rod on cylinder(s) to be serviced. Be sure piston is at top of stroke with both valves closed. Install air line adapter to spark plug port and apply compressed air to hold valves in place.

2) Compress valve spring using valve spring compressor. Remove valve locks, valve cap, oil shield (exhaust only), valve spring and damper. Remove and discard oil seals. *See Fig. 7.* DO NOT disconnect air pressure as valve can fall into cylinder.

Installation

1) Check valve spring for out of square with 90 degree straightedge. Valve spring out of square service limit is .0625" (1.588 mm) for intake and exhaust springs. Check valve spring compression pressure (without dampers) with valve spring tester. Springs should be replaced if not within 10 lbs. (4.5 kg) of specified load. Check valve spring free length.

2) Position valve spring, damper, oil seal (intake only), oil shield (exhaust only) and valve retainer cap in place. Compress spring and install "O" ring seals in lower groove of stems. Be sure seal is flat and not twisted. Lightly coat seal with oil, install valve locks and release compressor tool.

3) Ensure valve locks are properly seated in upper groove of valve stem. Remove air pressure and adapter. Install spark plugs. Apply Molykote to ends of push rods and tip of valve stems. Install rocker arms and tighten.

2.8L V6 (Cont.)

Fig. 7: Exploded View of Intake & Exhaust Valve Assemblies

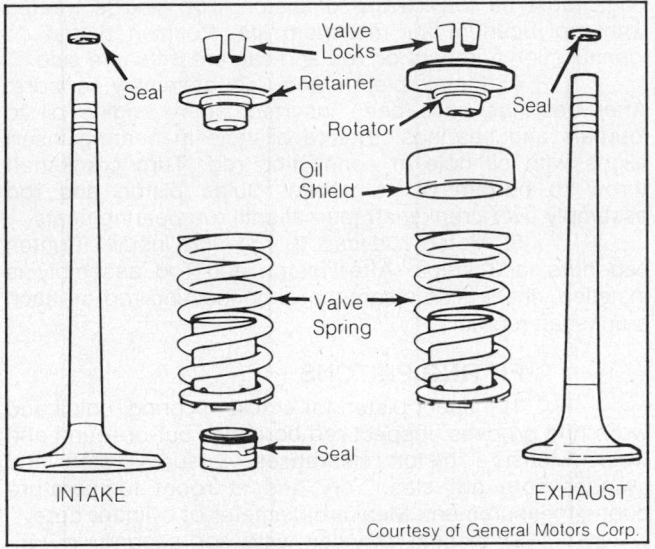

Courtesy of General Motors Corp.

VALVE SPRING INSTALLED HEIGHT

Installed height of valve spring should be within specifications. Measure from top of spring seat to top of oil shield (exhaust only) or retainer (intake only). If measurement exceeds specifications, install .030" (.75 mm) shim at spring seat. DO NOT install more than one shim. Ensure spring height with shim does not result in installed height under minimum specification. *See Fig. 8.*

Fig. 8: Checking Valve Spring Installed Height

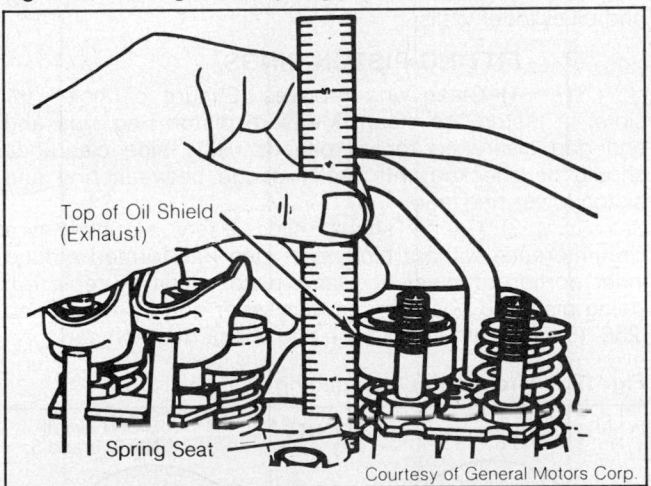

Courtesy of General Motors Corp.

VALVE ADJUSTMENT

1) Rotate crankshaft until mark on torsional damper lines up with "0" mark on timing tab. This should be firing position for piston No. 1.

2) While rotating, check by placing fingers on No. 1 rocker arms as mark on damper comes near "0" mark. If valves are not moving, engine is in No. 1 firing position. If valves move as mark comes up to timing tab, engine is in No. 4 firing position and should be rotated one revolution to reach No. 1 firing position.

3) Adjust intake valves in cylinders No. 1, 5, and 6, and exhaust valves No. 1, 2, and 3. Adjust valves

by backing off adjusting nut until lash is felt at push rod, then tighten until all lash is removed. Tighten adjusting nut an additional 1 1/2 turns. *See Fig. 9.*

Fig. 9: Adjusting Valve Lash

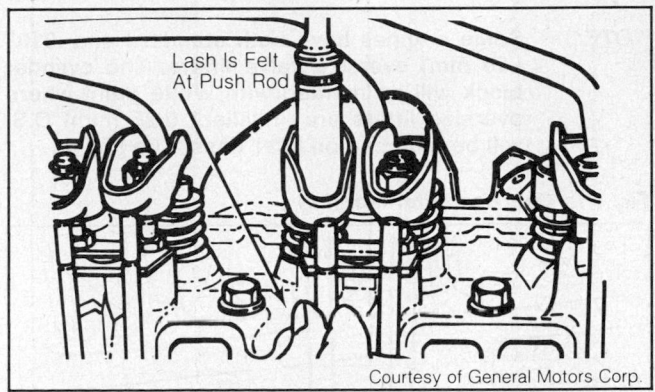

Courtesy of General Motors Corp.

4) Rotate crankshaft to No. 4 firing position and adjust intake valves in cylinders No. 2, 3 and 4, then exhaust valves in cylinders No. 4, 5 and 6.

ROCKER ARM STUDS

Cylinder heads use threaded rocker arm studs. Rocker arm studs having damaged threads should be replaced with new studs. If threads in head are damaged or stripped, head can be retapped and helical type insert installed. If helical insert is not available, replace cylinder head.

HYDRAULIC VALVE LIFTER ASSEMBLY

NOTE: Hydraulic lifter assemblies must be installed in original locations.

1) Remove rocker arm covers and intake manifold. Remove rocker arm nuts, rocker arm balls, rocker arms and push rods. Using lifter remover or magnet, remove lifters. Place components in a rack so they can be reinstalled in same location.

2) Clean and inspect lifters, but do not mix components or positions. Parts are select-fitted and not interchangeable. *See Fig. 10.*

Fig. 10: Exploded View of Hydraulic Lifter Assembly

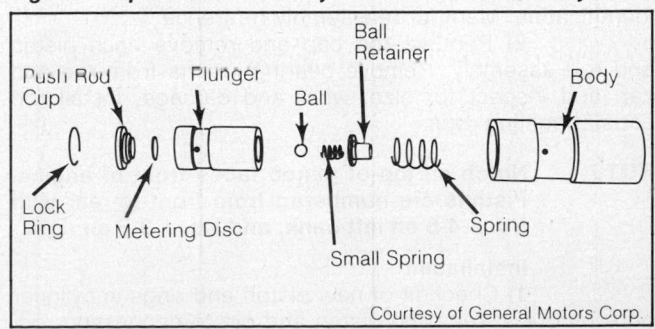

Courtesy of General Motors Corp.

3) Place lifter upright in Hydraulic Lifter Leak-Down Tester (J-5790) and check leak-down rate. Under a 50 lb. (22 kg) load, leak-down rate is 12-90 seconds measured from first line above set line to .0938" (2.38 mm) line on the tester.

2.8L V6 (Cont.)

4) Inspect lifter base-to-cam lobe contact area. Surface must have smooth and convex contact face. Inspect related cam lobe for proper lobe lift. If any lobe is worn beyond specification, replace camshaft (and lifters if necessary).

NOTE: Some engines have both standard and .010" (.25 mm) oversize valve lifters. The cylinder block will be marked with White paint where oversize lifters are installed; 0.25 (mm) O.S. will be stamped on lifter boss. See Fig. 11.

Fig. 11: Oversize Lifter Marking

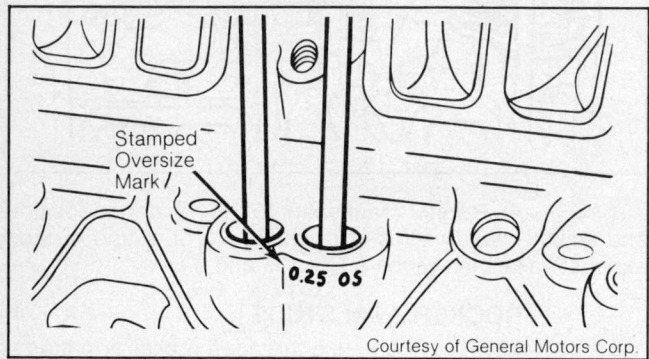

Courtesy of General Motors Corp.

5) Check lifter-to-bore clearance. Coat lifter base with Molykote. When installing, ensure lifter is on base circle of camshaft. Tighten rocker arm bolt. Coat gasket surfaces with RTV sealer and install valve covers and intake manifold.

PISTONS, PINS & RINGS

OIL PAN
See OIL PAN REMOVAL at end of ENGINE section.

PISTON & ROD ASSEMBLY
Removal
1) With cylinder head(s) and oil pan removed, inspect cylinder bores for ridges and/or deposits. Remove ridge at top of cylinder bores. Rotate crankshaft and inspect connecting rods and rod caps for cylinder identification. Mark for reassembly reference.

2) Remove rod cap and remove each piston and rod assembly. Remove bearing inserts from rod and cap and inspect for size, wear and damage. Install rod caps on mating rods.

NOTE: Notch on top of piston faces front of engine. Pistons are numbered from front-to-rear with No. 2-4-6 on left bank, and No. 1-3-5 on right.

Installation
1) Check fit of new piston and rings in cylinder bore before assembling piston and pin to connecting rod. Check piston pin for clearance, etching and wear. New pistons must be installed in cylinder they were fitted. Install used pistons in cylinder they were removed.

2) Measure cylinder bore diameter, piston diameter (with rod and pin removed) at skirt across centerline of piston pin. Oil piston rings and cylinder walls with light coat of oil.

3) Ensure ring gaps are properly spaced and install on piston. *See Fig. 12.* Marked side of compression rings must be toward top of piston. Top ring is treated with molybdenum for maximum life. Position piston so identification numbers on rod and cap are on same side.

4) Install piston and rod assembly in bore. After bearings have been inserted, apply engine oil to journals and bearings. Ensure oil hole in bearing insert aligns with oil hole in connecting rod. Turn crankshaft throw to bottom of its stroke. Guide piston and rod assembly over crankshaft journal until rod bearing seats.

5) Match rod cap to rod and install. Tighten cap nuts in 2 steps. After piston and rod assembly is installed, check side clearance of connecting rod on each crankshaft journal.

FITTING PISTONS
1) Inspect piston for cracks, scoring, holes and worn ring grooves. Inspect rod bores for out-of-round and wear. Measure piston clearances. Ensure piston and cylinder bore are clean, dry and at room temperature during measurement. Measure diameter of cylinder bore.

2) Inspect cylinder walls for scoring, roughness or other signs of wear. Measure outer diameter of piston at centerline of pin bore and 90 degrees to pin bore axis. If cylinder bore measurements differ by .0005" (.013 mm), bore cylinder block to next oversize.

3) Before cylinder refinishing, ensure main bearing caps are in place and tightened to avoid distortion during refinishing operation. Pistons are available in oversize.

4) Measure new piston. Bore and/or hone cylinder to correct clearance. After refinishing operation, allow bore to cool. Clean bore with soap and water, dry and oil cylinder walls.

FITTING PISTON RINGS
1) Clean ring grooves. Ensure oil holes (or slots) in piston are clean. Measure piston ring side and end gap clearance for all pistons. Ring side clearance should be checked with feeler gauge between ring and piston lower ring land.

2) Gauge should slide freely around entire circumference without binding. If step has formed around inner portion of lower ring land, piston must be replaced. Using piston to position ring in cylinder bore, position ring .236" (6 mm) from top of bore and check ring end gap.

Fig. 12: Piston Ring Gap Spacing

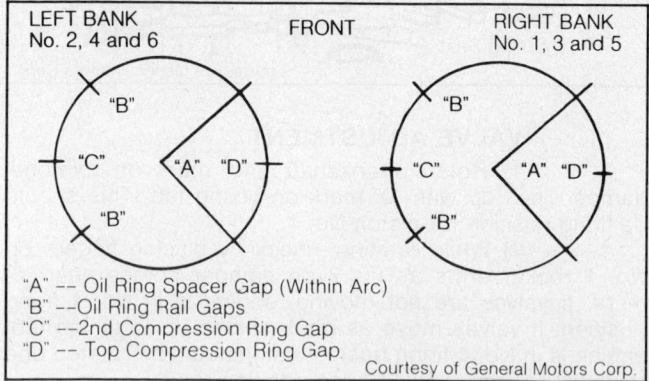

"A" -- Oil Ring Spacer Gap (Within Arc)
"B" --Oil Ring Rail Gaps
"C" -- 2nd Compression Ring Gap
"D" -- Top Compression Ring Gap

Courtesy of General Motors Corp.

3) Install rings on pistons with end gaps staggered at proper intervals. Ensure ring gap is not in line with thrust face of pin bore. *See Fig. 12.* Be sure manufacturer's mark faces upward when rings are installed.

4) Install oil ring expander first, followed by lower side rail. Do not use ring expander on side rails. When installing lower side rail, place one end between piston ring groove and expander.

5) Hold end firmly and press down portion to be installed until side rail is in position. Install upper side rail. Using ring expander, install intermediate and upper rings. Check that all components are within specifications.

6) If new piston rings are to be installed and no visible cross-hatch marks remain on cylinder walls, remove cylinder wall glaze using spring-type hone. After honing, clean bore and block with soap and water solution, dry, and oil cylinder walls.

FITTING PISTON PINS

NOTE: When removing or installing piston pin, connecting rod should be in firm contact with body of pin setting tool.

Removal

1) Remove bearing inserts from connecting rod and cap. Mark pistons, pins and inserts (if reusable) to assure assembly with same rod. Press piston pin from piston and connecting rod using Piston Support (J-24086).

2) Inspect and replace any piston pin showing signs of fracture, etching or wear. Check piston pin-to-rod bore fit and piston pin-to-piston fit. If pin bore in rod or piston is larger than specification, replace connecting rod or piston.

3) Ensure proper fit by honing or reaming piston pin bore. Standard piston pin diameter is .9052-.9055" (22.992-22.999 mm). Lubricate pin and small end of rod bore with engine oil.

Installation

1) Check piston-to-cylinder bore clearance before assembling piston and pin to connecting rod. Ensure oil hole in connecting rod aligns with oil hole in bearing and arrow or notch on top of piston is toward front of engine.

2) Start piston pin in piston and connecting rod. Using guide bar and push rod, press pin through both piston and rod until pilot-hub bottoms on support fixture and/or pin is centered in piston. After pilot-hub bottoms, DO NOT exceed 5000 lbs. (2275 kg) pressure with press. Remove piston assembly from tool and check piston pin for freedom of movement.

CRANKSHAFT & ROD BEARINGS

NOTE: Following procedures are with oil pan and cylinder head(s) removed. Main and rod bearing size is stamped on bearing insert, or indicated by letter stamped into bearing tang. Bearing letter codes are as follows: A = .0005", B = .0010", and C = .0015".

CONNECTING ROD BEARINGS

1) Remove connecting rod bearing caps and mark rods and caps for proper installation. Replace defective bearings. Use Plastigage method for checking bearing clearance.

2) Measure outside diameter of crankshaft connecting rod bearing journals to determine if out-of-round or tapered. Journal out-of-round and taper must not exceed .0002" (.005 mm).

3) Using Plastigage method, check connecting rod bearing clearance. If clearance exceeds specifications, replace bearing. If clearance cannot be brought within specifications with service bearings, grind crankshaft to next undersize. If already ground to maximum undersize, replace crankshaft.

4) Selective fitting is required on each connecting rod. After inspection and/or replacement, coat bearing surfaces with engine oil. Tighten connecting rod bearing cap nuts in 2 steps.

NOTE: Connecting rod bearing cap and rod identification numbers must remain on same side. Never file or grind connecting rods or caps when fitting bearings.

5) Tap each connecting rod lightly (parallel to crankshaft) to ensure clearance. Check connecting rod side clearance between connecting rod cap and crankshaft throw with feeler gauge. If clearance is excessive, replace connecting rod and cap.

6) During assembly, ensure oil hole in bearing aligns with oil hole in connecting rod. Ensure bearing tangs are seated in appropriate slots in rod and cap. Ensure connecting rod bolt heads are properly seated in connecting rod.

MAIN BEARINGS

1) Inspect each bearing for wear and replace if defective. Measure outside diameter of crankshaft main bearing journals in at least 4 places to determine if out-of-round or tapered. Journal out-of-round and taper must not exceed .0002" (.005 mm)

NOTE: Observe location of high spots on main bearings. If high spots are not in line, crankshaft may be bent and should be checked.

2) To check main bearings with engine in vehicle, crankshaft should be supported front and rear to remove clearance from upper bearing. DO NOT support under crankshaft pulley, otherwise crankshaft damage will result.

3) With all other bearing caps tight, check clearances using Plastigage method. When checking No. 1 main bearing, loosen accessory drive belts to prevent false reading.

4) If engine is out of vehicle and upside down, crankshaft will rest on upper bearings and clearance can be checked between lower bearing and journal using Plastigage method.

NOTE: New bearings are available in standard, .0006" (.016 mm), and .0012" (.032 mm) undersize for use with standard size crankshaft. Replace upper and lower inserts as a unit. If undersize bearings are used on more than one journal, position in cylinder block rather than on bearing cap.

5) If standard and undersize bearing combinations do not bring bearing clearance within specified limits, crankshaft will have to be refinished and undersized bearings installed. If journal will not clean up to maximum undersize bearing, replace crankshaft.

6) When journals are refinished, chamfer oil holes and polish journals with No. 320 grit polishing cloth and engine oil. After chamfer and polish operations, clean crankshaft thoroughly in solvent and blow out oil passages with compressed air.

7) When crankshaft main bearings are installed, ensure oil distributing grooves on bearings are installed on same side. Ensure main bearing caps are installed with arrows pointing toward front of engine. Install bearing cap and evenly tighten bolts.

THRUST BEARING ALIGNMENT

Check crankshaft end play with crankshaft bearing caps installed. Replace No. 3 main thrust bearing (upper and lower) if not to specification. Rotate crankshaft to ensure there is no excessive drag.

REAR MAIN BEARING OIL SEAL

Removal

Remove transaxle/transmission and flywheel. Remove old seal by prying dust lip with screwdriver. Care must be used not to damage surface of crankshaft. Check seal bore and crankshaft for nicks and burrs.

Installation

1) Apply light coat of engine oil to new seal. Place seal on Seal Installer (J-34686) until dust lip bottoms against collar of tool. Align dowel pin of tool with dowel pin hole in crankshaft. Attach tool to crankshaft by hand and tighten attaching screws to 24-60 INCH lbs. (2.7-3.7 N.m).

2) Turn "T" handle of tool so that collar pushes seal into bore. Turn handle until collar is tight against engine block. Loosen "T" handle. Remove attaching screws and installer.

3) Ensure seal is seated squarely into bore. Install flywheel. Install transaxle/transmission.

TORSIONAL DAMPER

NOTE: Inertia weight section of torsional damper is assembled to hub with rubber sleeve. Use proper tools for removal and installation or inertial movement of hub will upset engine timing reference.

Removal

Disconnect negative battery cable. Remove accessory drive belts. Raise vehicle. Remove inner fender splash shield. Remove accessory drive pulley and damper retaining bolt. Install Hub Puller (J-23523). Turn puller bolt and remove damper.

NOTE: The torsional damper has 3 timing notches on inertia ring. No. 1 cylinder timing reference is shown by White paint (in production). If new damper assembly is installed, mark in same location for reference. No. 1 cylinder refer-

ence is first clockwise mark from keyway when viewed from front of engine.

Installation

1) Coat front cover seal contact area on damper with oil. Clean and apply sealant to key and keyway. Place damper in position over key on crankshaft. Using Hub Installer (J-29113), pull damper in position on hub, leaving .24" (6 mm) of thread engagement. Remove installer.

2) Install accessory drive pulley and damper retaining bolts and tighten. Install inner fender splash shield. Lower vehicle and install belts. Tighten belts, nuts and bolts. Connect battery cable.

ENGINE OILING

CRANKCASE CAPACITY

Crankcase capacity is 4 quarts (3.8 L), with or without filter change.

NORMAL OIL PRESSURE

Normal oil pressure is 50-65 psi (3.5-4.5 kg/cm²) at 1200 RPM.

PRESSURE REGULATOR VALVE

The pressure regulator valve in oil pump body is not adjustable.

ENGINE OILING SYSTEM

Full pressure lubrication is supplied by gear-type oil pump. Pump is driven by distributor, which in turn is driven by helical gear on camshaft. An oil filter by-pass is used to ensure adequate oil supply should filter develop an excessive pressure drop. The by-pass is designed to open at 10-12 psi (.7-.8 kg/cm²).

The left main oil gallery (along upper left side of camshaft) supplies oil to left side hydraulic lifters. The left gallery also supplies oil to the camshaft bearings, crankshaft and right gallery.

The right oil gallery supplies oil to right side hydraulic lifters. The oil supplied to lifters lubricate rocker arms through hollow push rods. All other components are lubricated by splash or nozzle.

OIL PUMP

Removal

Disconnect negative battery cable and drain crankcase. Raise vehicle and remove starter. Remove flywheel dustcover. Disconnect exhaust pipe at manifold. Support engine and remove engine mount bracket. Remove oil pan bolts and remove oil pan. Clean gasket surfaces and bolt holes of old RTV sealer. Remove bolt attaching oil pump to rear main bearing cap. Remove pump and extension shaft.

Disassembly

1) Remove pump cover attaching bolts and pump cover. Mark teeth on both gears for reassembly with same teeth indexing. Remove idler gear, drive gear and shaft from pump body.

2) Remove pressure regulator valve retaining pin, valve and spring. If pick-up screen and pipe assembly need replacement, mount pump in soft-jawed vise and extract pipe from pump cover. DO NOT disturb pick-up screen on pipe. This is serviced as an assembly.

2.8L V6 (Cont.)

Fig. 13: Exploded View of Oil Pump

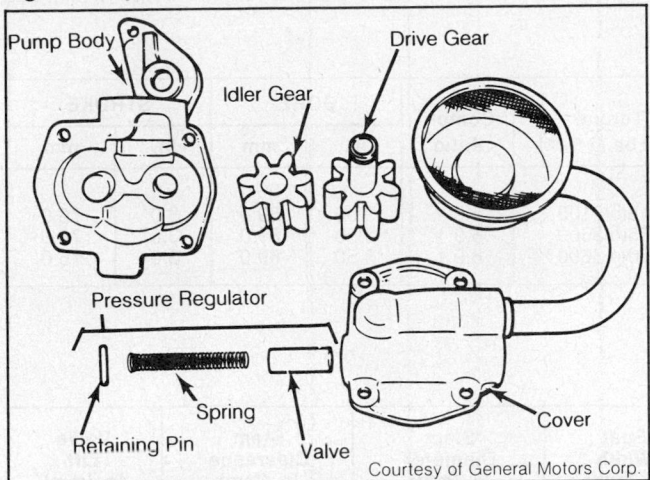

Courtesy of General Motors Corp.

Inspection

1) Check oil pump body for cracks or excessive wear. Inspect pump gears for cracks, excessive wear or damage. Check shaft for looseness in housing. Replace pump as a unit if necessary.

2) Check inside of cover for wear that would permit oil to leak past ends of gears. Check oil pick-up screen for damage to screen or relief grommet. Remove any debris from surface of screen.

OIL PUMP SPECIFICATIONS

Application	In. (mm)
Gear-to-Body Clearance	.003-.004 (.08-.10)
Gear-to-Cover End Clearance	.002-.005 (.05-.13)
Oil Pump Body	
Bore Depth	1.195-1.198 (30.35-30.43)
Bore Length	1.199-1.200 (30.45-30.48)
Oil Pump Gear	
Length	498-1.500 (38.05-38.10)

Reassembly

1) When assembling oil pump, fill pump cavities with petroleum jelly to ensure immediate oil pressure. If the pick-up screen and pipe assembly was removed, it should be replaced with a new part. Mount the pump in a soft-jawed vise, apply sealer to outside diameter of end of pipe, and using Installer (J-8369), tap the pipe in place with a plastic hammer.

2) Install pressure regulator valve, spring and retaining pin. Install idler gear, drive gear and shaft into pump body. Install pump cover gasket, cover, and check drive shaft for free operation.

Installation

Install oil pump in engine with top end of hexagonal extension shaft aligned with hexagonal socket in lower end of distributor drive gear. To complete installation, reverse removal procedure.

ENGINE COOLING

WATER PUMP

Removal

1) Disconnect negative battery cable. Drain cooling system by removing thermostat and replacing thermostat cap, open block drain plugs and drain plug on radiator. Remove accessory drive belts.

2) If equipped with MFI, remove air intake tube and mass airflow sensor. On all models, remove fan and pulley from water pump hub. Remove alternator brackets and power steering pump brackets if needed. Remove radiator hose and heater hose. Remove water pump bolts and nut. Remove water pump.

Installation

Clean water pump and engine block mating surfaces. Apply bead of RTV sealant to mating surfaces. Coat bolt threads with pipe sealant. Install water pump and reverse removal procedure to complete installation.

NOTE: For information on cooling system capacities and other cooling systems, see article in ENGINE COOLING SYSTEMS section.

TIGHTENING SPECIFICATIONS

Application	Ft. Lbs. (N.m)
Camshaft Sprocket Bolts	15-20 (20-27)
Clutch Pressure Plate Bolts	13-18 (18-24)
Connecting Rod Cap Nuts	34-45 (46-60)
Crankshaft Pulley Bolts	20-30 (27-41)
Crakshaft Pulley Hub Bolts	66-84 (90-114)
Cylinder Head Bolts	
VIN S	[1]
VIN W	[2]
VIN 9	65-90 (88-122)
Distributor Hold-Down Bolts	20-31 (27-42)
Engine Strut Bracket Bolts	30-40 (41-54)
Exhaust Manifold Bolts	22-18 (30-24)
Flex Plate-to-Torque Converter Bolts	25-35 (34-47)
Flywheel-to-Crankshaft Bolts	45-55 (61-75)
Front Cover Bolts	
8 mm	13-18 (18-24)
10 mm	20-30 (27-40)
Fuel Rail Bolts	15-20 (20-27)
Intake Manifold Bolts	
Intermediate-to-Lower	15 (20)
Lower-to-Cylinder Block	19 (26)
Main Bearing Cap Bolts	63-83 (85-112)
Oil Pan Bolts	
6 mm	6-9 (8-12)
8 mm	15-23 (20-30)
Oil Pump Bolts	26-35 (35-48)
Rocker Arm Nuts	10 25 (14-34)
Timing Chain Tensioner Bolts	13-18 (18-24)
Torsional Damper Bolts	66-85 (90-115)
Water Pump Bolts	
8 mm	13-22 (18-30)
10 mm	20-35 (27-48)
Water Pump Pulley Bolts	13-18 (18-24)

[1] – On VIN S, torque to 40 ft lbs. (54 N.m) and an additional 90 degree turn.

[2] – On VIN W, torque to 45 ft lbs. (60 N.m) and an additional 90 degree turn.

General Motors Engines
2.8L V6 (Cont.)

ENGINE SPECIFICATIONS

GENERAL SPECIFICATIONS

| Year | DISPLACEMENT | | Fuel System | HP@RPM | Torque Ft. Lbs.@RPM | Compr. Ratio | BORE | | STROKE | |
	Cu. In.	Liters					In.	mm	In.	mm
1988										
VIN W	173	2.8	MFI	130@4800	145@2100	8.9:1	3.50	89.0	3.0	76.0
VIN S	173	2.8	MFI	135@5100	165@3600	8.9:1	3.50	89.0	3.0	76.0
VIN 9	173	2.8	MFI	140@5200	170@3600	8.9:1	3.50	89.0	3.0	76.0

VALVES

Engine Size & Valve	Head Diam. In. (mm)	Face Angle	Seat Angle	Seat Width In. (mm)	Stem Diameter In. (mm)	Stem Clearance In. (mm)	Valve Lift In. (mm)
2.8L (VIN W)							
Intake	1.72 (43.7)	45°	46°	[1] .061-.073 (1.55-1.85)	.....	.001-.0027 (.026-.069)	.....
Exhaust	1.43 (36.0)	45°	46°	[1] .067-.079 (1.70-2.0)	.....	.001-.0027 (.026-.069)	
2.8L (VIN S & 9)							
Intake	.....	45°	46°	[2] .049-.059 (1.25-1.50)	.....	.001-.0027 (.026-.069)	.....
Exhaust	.....	45°	46°	[1] .063-.074 (1.60-1.90)	.....	.001-.0027 (.026-.069)	.....

[1] – Maximum valve seat runout is .001" (.025 mm).
[2] – Maximum valve seat runout is .05 degrees.

PISTONS, PINS & RINGS

| Engine | PISTONS | PINS | | RINGS | | |
	Clearance In. (mm)	Piston Fit In. (mm)	Rod Fit In. (mm)	Ring No.	End Gap In. (mm)	Side Clearance In. (mm)
2.8L	[1] .0020-.0028 (.051-.071)	.00025-.0036 (.0065-.0091)	[2] .0008-.0021 (.0198-.053)	1	.01-.020 (.25-.51)	.001-.003 (.025-.076)
				2	.01-.020 (.25-.51)	.001-.003 (.025-.076)
				3	.020-.055 (.51-1.40)	.008 Max (.2)

[1] – Specifications given are for VIN W engine. Specifications for VIN S and 9 engines are .0007-.0017" (.017-.043 mm).
[2] – Specifications given are a press fit for VIN W engine. Specifications for VIN S and 9 are .00074-.00202" (.0187-.0515 mm) press fit.

CRANKSHAFT MAIN & CONNECTING ROD BEARINGS

| Engine | MAIN BEARINGS | | | | CONNECTING ROD BEARINGS | | |
	Journal Diam. In. (mm)	Clearance In. (mm)	Thrust Bearing	Crankshaft End Play In. (mm)	Journal Diam. In. (mm)	Clearance In. (mm)	Side Play In. (mm)
2.8L	2.647-2.648 (67.23-67.26)	.0016-.003 (.041-.076)	No. 3	.0024-.0083 (.06-.21)	1.9994-1.9983 (50.784-50.757)	.0013-.0026 (.033-.066)	.0063-.0173 (.16-.44)

ENGINE SPECIFICATIONS (Cont.)

CAMSHAFT

Engine	Journal Diam. In. (mm)	Clearance In. (mm)	Lobe Lift In. (mm)
2.8L [1]	1.8678-1.8815 (47.42-47.790)	.001-.004 (.025-.10)	Int. .262 (6.67) Exh. .273 (6.93)

[1] – On VIN 9 engine it is possible to have a camshaft with a lobe lift of .231 (5.87 mm) intake, and .262 (6.67 mm) exhaust.

VALVE SPRINGS

Engine	Free Length In. (mm)	PRESSURE Lbs. @ In. (Kg @ mm)	
		Valve Closed	Valve Open
2.8L	1.91 (48.51)	90@1.70 (40.0@43)	215@1.30 (97.0@33)

General Motors Engines

3.0L, 3.8L & 3.8L "3800" V6

NOTE: For engine repair procedures not covered in this article, see ENGINE OVERHAUL PROCEDURES article at beginning of this section.

ENGINE CODING

ENGINE IDENTIFICATION

Engine may be identified from Vehicle Identification Number (VIN). VIN is stamped on metal tab located on top of instrument panel at lower left of windshield. The VIN number code also appears as part of production or unit number stamped on left rear of cylinder block on all models. The VIN number contains 17 characters. The 8th character identifies engine. The 10th character identifies model year.

ENGINE CODES

Engine	Code
3.0L (181") MFI	L
3.8L (231") SFI	3
3.8L (231") SFI Turbo	7
3.8L (231") SFI "3800"	C

ENGINE REMOVAL

See ENGINE REMOVAL & INSTALLATION at end of ENGINE section.

CYLINDER HEAD & MANIFOLDS

NOTE: On models without turbocharger, proceed to INTAKE MANIFOLD REMOVAL (NON-TURBO) in this article.

INTERCOOLER

Removal

Remove shroud from intercooler. Disconnect intercooler inlet pipe from turbocharger. Remove intercooler outlet pipe and throttle body. Remove intercooler mounting bracket bolts. Remove intercooler.

Installation

To install, reverse removal procedure.

TURBOCHARGER

NOTE: Before beginning removal procedure on a turbocharging system, clean area around turbocharger with non-caustic solution and use extreme care during removal to avoid damaging turbine blades.

Removal

1) Disconnect negative battery cable. Remove air inlet tube from compressor. Remove turbocharger and oil breather heat shields. Remove exhaust pipe from turbine outlet.

2) Remove oil breather vent from valve cover. Disconnect oil feed line and remove 2 nuts attaching turbocharger to bracket. Remove turbine inlet from exhaust manifold and disconnect oil return line from turbocharger.

3) Disconnect vacuum lines from wastegate actuator. Disconnect intercooler outlet from throttle body pipe and remove turbocharger from engine.

Installation

1) Position turbocharger on engine mount. Start bolts attaching turbocharger to exhaust manifold, but do not tighten. Start bolts attaching exhaust pipe to turbine outlet, but do not tighten.

2) Connect oil return line. Install turbocharger to mounting bracket. Tighten bolts attaching exhaust pipe to turbocharger, and bolts attaching exhaust pipe to turbine outlet. To complete installation, reverse removal procedure.

INTAKE MANIFOLD

Removal (Turbo)

1) Disconnect negative battery terminal and drain cooling system. Disconnect fuel line at fuel rail inlet and at pressure regulator (fuel rail outlet). Disconnect injector wiring harness connectors located behind coil.

2) Disconnect CTS (coolant temperature sensor) wire connectors located at front of manifold. Remove heater, by-pass and upper radiator hoses. Remove pressure regulator, EGR and PCV lines and/or hoses.

3) Disconnect throttle, cruise control and detent cables from throttle body. Remove EGR-VCV (vacuum control valve). Remove ignition wires from spark plugs. Remove intake manifold bolts. Remove intake manifold.

NOTE: Clean all gasket surfaces on intake mainfold and cylinder heads.

Installation

1) Install new intake manifold gaskets and end seals onto cylinder block. Ensure seal fits tightly and squarely against block and heads. Apply RTV sealer to seal ends.

2) Install and tighten intake manifold attaching bolts in sequence. See Fig. 1. Install lower, right side turbocharger mounting bracket to intake manifold, and install bracket support to plenum chamber. To complete installation, reverse removal procedure.

Removal (Non-Turbo)

1) Disconnect negative battery cable. Remove mass airflow sensor and air intake duct. Drain cooling system. Disconnect upper radiator hose and heater hose. Remove serpentine accessory drive belt, alternator and bracket.

2) Disconnect Computer Controlled Coil Ignition (C³I) module and wiring. Remove and label vacuum lines and wiring connectors as necessary. Remove throttle and cruise control cables from throttle body.

3) Remove fuel lines, fuel rail and injectors. Remove spark plug wires. Remove intake manifold bolts. Remove intake manifold and gasket.

NOTE: Clean gasket surfaces on intake manifold and cylinder heads.

Installation

Install new intake manifold gaskets and position new rubber seals on front and rear rails on cylinder block. Ensure pointed end of seal fits tightly against block and heads. Apply RTV sealer to ends of seals. Install intake manifold and tighten bolts in sequence. To complete installation, reverse removal procedure. See Fig. 1.

3.0L, 3.8L & 3.8L "3800" V6 (Cont.)

Fig. 1: Intake Manifold Tightening Sequence

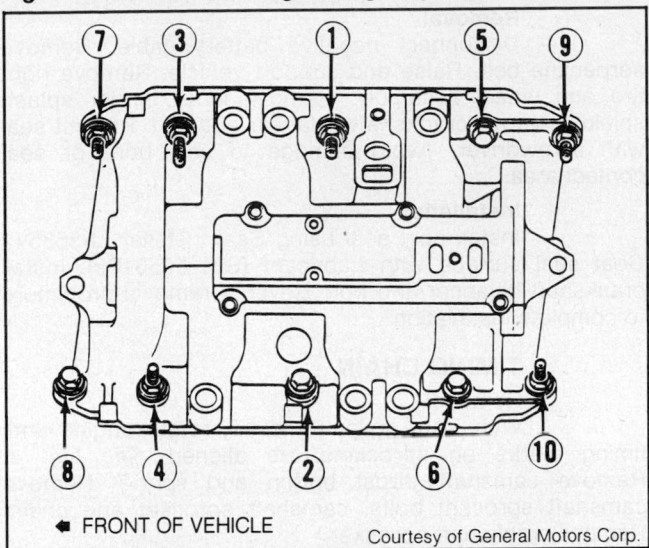

◄ FRONT OF VEHICLE

Courtesy of General Motors Corp.

EXHAUST MANIFOLD

Removal (Turbo)

1) Remove negative battery cable. Disconnect exhaust pipe from turbocharger. Disconnect oxygen sensor wire. Raise and support vehicle. Disconnect left and right side exhaust manifolds from crossover pipe.

2) Lower vehicle. Remove exhaust manifold bolts from both manifolds (6 on each side). Remove exhaust manifolds.

Installation

Clean mating surfaces of exhaust manifolds and cylinder heads. Check for cracks in manifolds. To complete installation, reverse removal procedure. Tighten exhaust manifold bolts to specification and check for exhaust leaks.

Removal (Century, Cutlass Ciera & Cutlass Cruiser)

1) Disconnect negative battery cable. On right side manifold, remove pinch bolt at intermediate shaft. Separate intermediate shaft from rack and pinion stub shaft.

CAUTION: Failure to separate intermediate shaft from rack and pinion stub shaft can result in damage to steering gear. A damaged steering gear can cause loss of steering control and can result in vehicle being unsafe to drive.

2) Raise and support vehicle. Remove 2 bolts attaching exhaust pipe to manifold. Lower vehicle. Disconnect upper engine support strut. Place a jack under front crossmember of cradle and raise jack until vehicle begins to rise.

3) Remove 2 front body mount bolts. Remove body mount bolt cushions and thread body mount bolts and retainers into cage bolts at least 3 turns. Release jack slowly. Remove power steering pump and bracket from cylinder head and exhaust manifold.

4) On left side of engine, remove upper engine support strut. Remove 2 nuts attaching crossover pipe to manifold. Remove exhaust manifold bolts and manifolds.

NOTE: If replacing exhaust manifold, transfer oxygen sensor and/or exhaust pipe seal to new manifold.

Installation

Clean sealing surfaces of exhaust manifolds and cylinder heads. Install manifolds by reversing removal procedure. Tighten exhaust manifold bolts and check for exhaust leaks.

Removal - Left Side (All Others)

1) Disconnect negative battery cable. On Riviera and Toronado, remove engine strut and engine cooling fan. On all models, remove 2 nuts attaching crossover pipe to manifold. Remove spark plug wires.

2) If necessary, remove oil level indicator and tube to provide additional clearance. Remove exhaust manifold bolts and manifolds.

Removal - Right Side (All Others)

1) Disconnect negative battery cable. Remove spark plug wires oxygen sensor lead and EGR pipe. Remove transaxle oil level indicator tube.

2) Remove 2 nuts attaching exhaust crossover pipe to manifold. Remove exhaust manifold heat shield upper bolts (if equipped). Remove manifold bolts and manifold.

NOTE: If replacing exhaust manifold, transfer oxygen sensor and exhaust pipe seal to new manifold.

Installation

Clean sealing surfaces of exhaust manifolds and cylinder heads. Install manifolds by reversing removal procedure. Tighten exhaust manifold bolts and check for exhaust leaks.

CYLINDER HEAD

Removal

1) Disconnect negative battery cable. Remove valve covers and intake manifold. Disconnect or remove exhaust manifolds. Remove ignition module, ignition wires, alternator bracket and A/C bracket.

2) Remove power steering pump, belt tensioner assembly and fuel line heat shield. Remove rocker arm assemblies, guide plate and pushrods. Remove or disconnect any remaining components interfering with head removal. Remove cylinder head bolts and cylinder head.

Inspection

Check cylinder head for damage. If more than .054" (.39 mm) must be removed from cylinder head to restore mounting surface flatness, replace cylinder head.

Installation

1) Clean cylinder block head bolt threads. Position new head gasket on block deck. Place head on head gasket. Coat new head bolts with sealer and install.

2) Tighten head bolts evenly in sequence to 25 ft. lbs. (81 N.m). *See Fig. 2.* Tighten bolts in sequence an additional 90 degrees without exceeding maximum torque specification. Again tighten bolts in sequence an additional 90 degrees without exceeding maximum torque specification.

CAUTION: Should you reach maximum torque, tightening procedure should be stopped. Replace or repair part(s) as necessary.

3) Reverse removal procedure to complete installation. Check for fluid leaks and verify fluid levels are correct.

Fig. 2: Cylinder Head Tightening Sequence

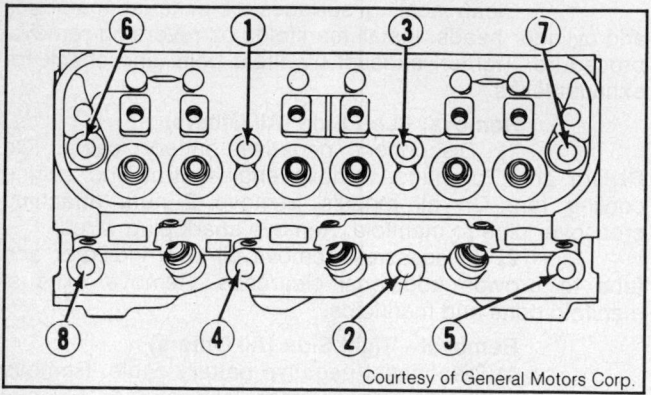

Courtesy of General Motors Corp.

CAMSHAFT

ENGINE FRONT COVER

Removal

1) Disconnect negative battery cable. Drain cooling system and disconnect radiator hoses and heater hose at water pump. Loosen water pump pulley and bolts. Remove serpentine drive belt. Remove water pump pulley. Raise and support vehicle. Remove right tire and wheel assembly.

2) Remove right inner fender splash shield. Drain engine oil. Remove crankshaft balancer and oil filter. Remove water pump and crankshaft sensor. Remove oil pan and front cover.

NOTE: **Whenever front cover is removed, oil pump may lose its prime. Remove oil pump cover and pack petroleum jelly tightly around oil pump gears.**

Installation

To install, reverse removal procedure. Ensure gasket surfaces are clean, and use a new gasket. Use sealer on bolt threads.

Fig. 3: Engine Front Cover Assembly

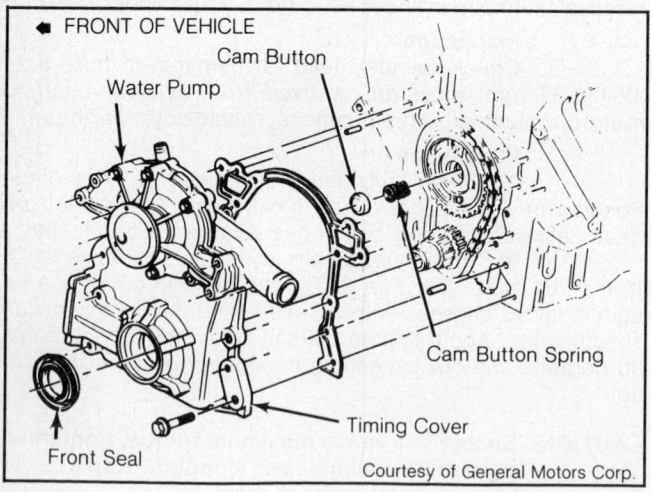

Courtesy of General Motors Corp.

FRONT COVER OIL SEAL

Removal

Disconnect negative battery cable. Remove serpentine belt. Raise and support vehicle. Remove right tire and wheel assembly. Remove inner fender splash shield. Remove crankshaft balancer and bolt. Pry out seal with screwdriver. Avoid damage to seal bore or seal contact area.

Installation

Install new seal using Seal Installer (J-35354). Coat seal surface with Lubricant (GM 1050169). Install crankshaft balancer and bolt. Reverse removal procedure to complete installation.

TIMING CHAIN

Removal

With front cover removed, rotate engine until timing marks on sprockets are aligned. *See Fig. 4.* Remove camshaft thrust button and spring. Remove camshaft sprocket bolts, camshaft sprocket and chain. Remove crankshaft sprocket.

Fig. 4: Timing Chain Sprocket Alignment

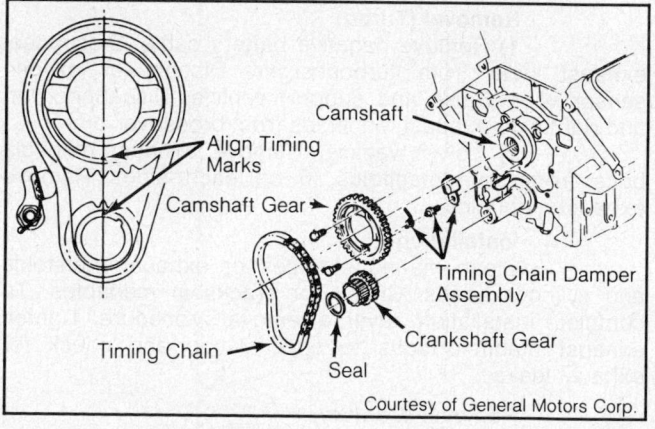

Courtesy of General Motors Corp.

Installation

1) Ensure No. 1 piston is at TDC and align camshaft timing marks. Carefully install timing chain and sprockets without disturbing alignment of marks.

2) Install camshaft sprocket bolts and tighten. Install camshaft thrust spring, button, and timing chain dampers. Install front cover and tighten bolts.

Balance Shaft ("3800")

Removal

1) Remove timing chain cover, balance shaft drive gear bolt, camshaft sprocket and timing chain. Remove balance shaft retainer bolts, retainer and balance shaft gear. Using Slide Hammer (J 6125-B), remove balance shaft.

2) Remove balance shaft rear plug. Using bearing driver (J 33049), drive balance shaft bearing out toward bellhousing side of engine. Inspect balance shaft rear bearing and journal for wear or scoring, replace parts as necessary.

NOTE: **Always replace front bearing whenever balance shaft is removed.**

Installation

1) Lubricate balance shaft rear bearing in clean engine oil. Using Installer (J 36995), install rear bearing. Install rear balance shaft plug. Using Driver (J 36996), install balance shaft. Install bearing shaft retainer and tighten bolts.

2) To complete installation, reverse removal procedure. Ensure balance shaft and camshaft marks are aligned properly. *See Fig. 5.*

Fig. 5: Aligning "3800" Balance Shaft & Camshaft Marks

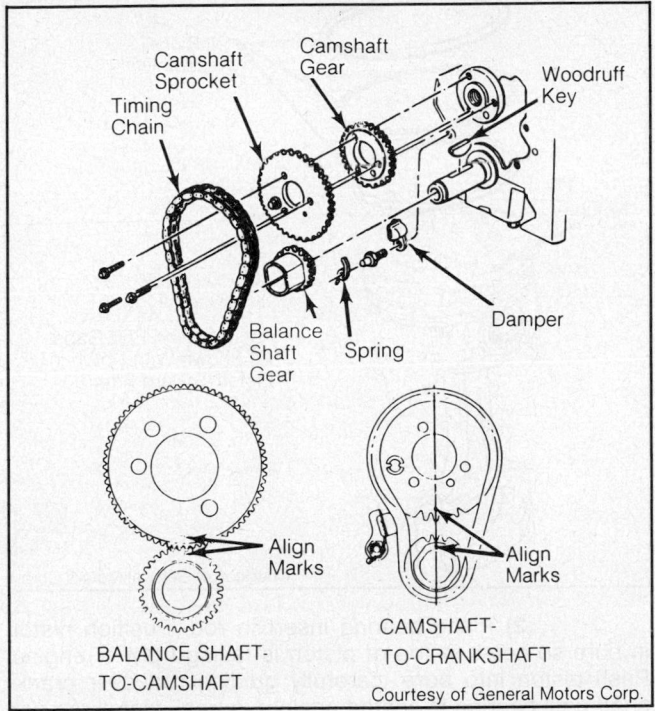

CAMSHAFT

Removal

Remove intake manifold, rocker arm assemblies, push rods, and lifters. Mark or identify push rods and lifters for installation in original position. Remove front engine cover and timing chain with sprockets. Remove camshaft gear and balance shaft gear (if equipped). Carefully slide camshaft out to avoid damaging camshaft bearings or lobes.

Installation

Thoroughly clean and inspect camshaft. Lubricate journals and camshaft lobes. Carefully insert camshaft taking care not to damage bearings or camshaft lobes. Reverse removal procedure to complete installation.

CAMSHAFT BEARINGS

Removal & Installation

1) Remove camshaft and rear cover plug. Using Camshaft Bearing Remover/Installer (J6098-01), remove inner bearings first. The front bearings are removed from rear by using a spacer between engine block and puller plate.

NOTE: Once camshaft bearings have been removed, they can NOT be reused.

2) Reverse removal procedure to install bearings and carefully pull them into place using Camshaft Bearing Remover/Installer (J6098-01). Be sure oil holes in bearings and journal are aligned. Apply RTV sealer to camshaft rear cover before installation.

VALVES

VALVE ARRANGEMENT

E-I-E-I-E (left side, front-to-rear).
E-I-I-E-I-E (right side, front-to-rear).

VALVE GUIDE SERVICING

If valve stem clearance is excessive, replace valve. Some valves with oversize stems are used in production and can be identified by stamped number on back side of valve head. Oversize valve guides and valve guide reamers are available in .003" (.08 mm), .006" (.15 mm), and .010" (.25 mm) oversize. When reconditioning, always use next oversize reamer and replacement valve.

VALVE STEM OIL SEALS

Valve stem oil seals are installed on intake valve guides. A new seal should be installed whenever valve spring is removed. To install new seals, carefully slide seal over valve stem and push down until it contacts valve guide. Push seal onto guide until seal bottoms against guide.

NOTE: If "UMBRELLA" type oil seals are used, seat them on valve guides. Use oversize seals with oversize valves. If "O" ring type oil seals are used, ensure they are properly seated and not twisted.

VALVE SPRINGS

Removal

With cylinder head removed, compress valve spring with spring compressor and remove valve keepers. Release spring compressor and remove spring retainer and spring. Remove valve stem oil seal from intake valves.

Inspection & Installation

Check valve springs in a valve spring tester and replace as necessary. Both intake and exhaust valve springs may be installed with either end up. Reverse removal procedure to complete installation.

ROCKER ARM ASSEMBLY

Removal

Remove valve cover, rocker arm retaining bolts, pedestal retainer, rocker arm and pedestal. Inspect rocker arms for wear, scoring, or damage. Replace components as necessary. *See Fig. 6.*

NOTE: Place rocker arm assemblies on a clean surface. Note component locations for correct reassembly.

Installation

Rocker arms must be installed in original locations. Reverse removal procedure to complete assembly.

General Motors Engines

3.0L, 3.8L & 3.8L "3800" V6 (Cont.)

Fig. 6: Rocker Arm Assemblies

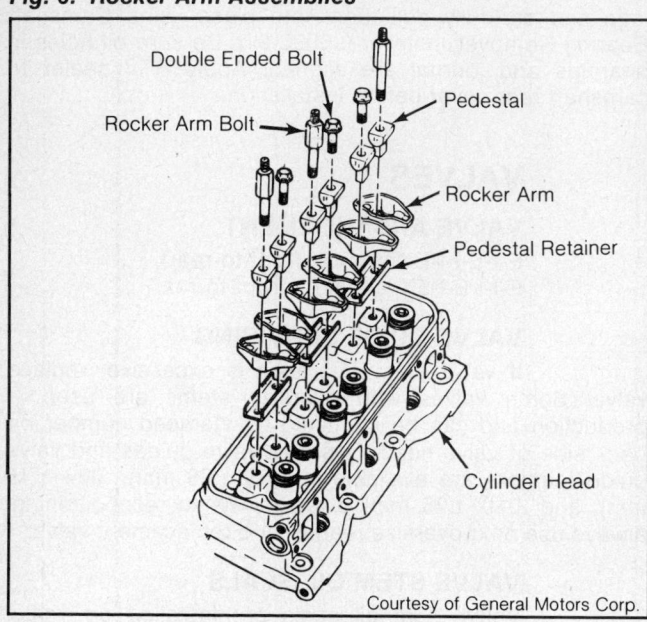

Courtesy of General Motors Corp.

HYDRAULIC VALVE LIFTER ASSEMBLY

If hydraulic valve lifters are being removed, mark or identify lifters to ensure they are installed in original position. Lifters are serviced as complete assemblies only. If lifter is damaged or worn, complete lifter must be replaced. If lifters are disassembled for cleaning and inspection, they should be tested using a leak-down rate tester after reassembly.

Fig. 7: Exploded View of Hydraulic Lifter Assembly

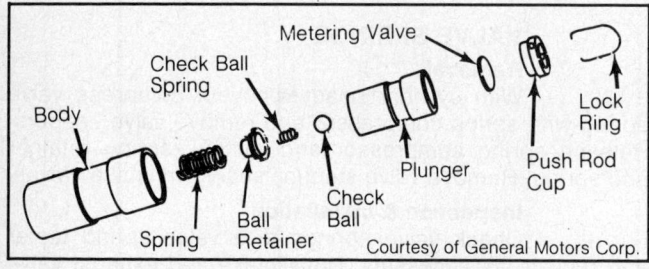

Courtesy of General Motors Corp.

PISTON, PINS & RINGS

OIL PAN

See OIL PAN REMOVAL at end of ENGINE section.

PISTON & ROD ASSEMBLY

Removal

1) With cylinder heads and oil pan removed, check top of cylinder bore for ridge. Remove ridge using a ridge reamer. Mark or identify pistons to ensure they are installed in original cylinders.

2) Remove rod nuts and cap. Remove piston and rod assemblies. Install rod caps on rods from which they were removed.

Installation

1) Position rings on piston. See Fig. 8. Clean cylinder bores, pistons, and bearing journals thoroughly.

Coat bearing surfaces, pistons, and cylinder bores with engine oil.

Fig. 8: Piston Ring Gap Positioning

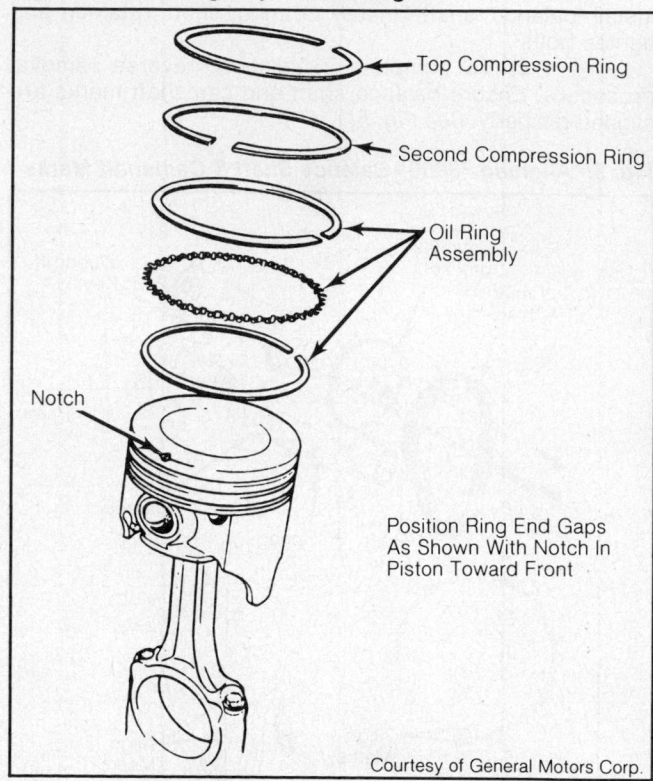

Courtesy of General Motors Corp.

2) Place bearing insert in rod. Position piston in bore so notch in top of piston is facing front of engine. Push piston into bore, carefully guiding rod over crankshaft until bearing is seated against journal. Install rod cap and bearing. Tighten rod cap nuts.

FITTING PISTONS

1) With piston and rod assembly removed, thoroughly clean cylinder bore. Inspect bore for taper or out-of-round. If cylinder taper is more than .004" (.01 mm), or is out-of-round more than .003" (.076 mm), cylinder must be bored and oversize piston and rings installed.

2) Measure piston diameter at 90 degree angle to piston pin and .25" (6.35 mm) below oil ring groove. If clearance between piston and cylinder is excessive, cylinder must be bored and oversize pistons and rings installed.

PISTON PINS

1) Piston pin is a press fit in connecting rod. Using a Piston Pin Remover/Installer (J-24086) and a press, remove piston pin and separate piston and rod.

2) Inspect pin for wear and/or scoring. Check clearance of pin in piston. If clearance is excessive, piston and pin assembly must be replaced.

3) Place connecting rod in correct position for bank in which piston and rod are being installed. Lubricate piston pin. Using Piston Pin Remover/Installer (J-24086) and press, install into piston and rod.

3.0L, 3.8L & 3.8L "3800" V6 (Cont.)

CRANKSHAFT & ROD BEARINGS

NOTE: Bearing ends must never be filed flush with parting surfaces of rod cap or cylinder block and cap.

CONNECTING ROD BEARINGS

1) With connecting rod cap removed, inspect bearings for flaking or wear. Check connecting rod journal for scoring or grooves. Measure rod journal check journal for out-of-round and taper.

2) Check bearing-to-journal clearance using Plastigage method. If clearance exceeds specification, undersize bearing may be installed to obtain correct clearance. If clearance is excessive, crankshaft must be replaced. Measure rod side clearance.

MAIN BEARINGS

1) The upper bearing halves are grooved to supply oil to connecting rod bearings. The lower cap bearing halves are not grooved. With main bearing cap removed, inspect bearing for flaking or scoring. Inspect main bearing journal for wear or grooves. Check journal for out-of-round and taper.

2) Check bearing-to-journal clearance using Plastigage method. If clearance exceeds specification, undersized bearing may be installed to obtain correct clearance. If clearance is excessive, crankshaft must be reconditioned or replaced.

REAR MAIN BEARING OIL SEAL

Removal & Installation (Crankshaft Installed)

1) Drain engine oil and remove oil pan. Remove rear main bearing cap and old seal. Using packing tool, drive new seal into groove in block until packed tight. Repeat on other end of seal in block.

2) Measure amount seal was driven up into cylinder block on one side, add 1/16", and cut this length from old seal removed from rear main bearing cap. Using 2 small screwdrivers, work pieces into block seal groove (one on each side).

3) Trim excess packing flush with block. Form new rope seal in main bearing cap. Apply a drop of sealer on each end of seal and cap. Install bolts and tighten. Reverse removal procedure to complete installation.

Removal & Installation (Crankshaft Removed)

1) Remove rope seal from rear main bearing cap and block. Clean bearing cap and seal grooves. Inspect for cracks. Apply Sealer (1052621) to cap seal contact surface. Wait one minute. Drive new rope seal into bearing cap with Seal Installer (J-25285A). Cut excess seal material flush with bearing cap.

2) Form new rope seal in rear seal groove in block. Push rope seal into block seal groove and trim excess. Apply sealant to mating surfaces. Lightly tap main bearing cap into place. Install main bearing cap bolts and tighten.

MAIN BEARING CAP SIDE SEALS

Neoprene seals are placed on sides of bearing cap. The seals are slightly undersize when newly installed (and may leak) since neoprene composition swells in presence of heat and oil. The seals are slightly longer than grooves in cap, but should not be cut off.

Soak seals in light oil or kerosene for 5 minutes before installation. After seals are installed, tap them into cap with hammer handle. Apply sealant to mating surface of main bearing cap before installing.

THRUST BEARING ALIGNMENT

With thrust bearing cap bolts finger tight, move crankshaft rearward, then forward. Tighten main bearing cap bolts and rotate crankshaft. Be sure there is no excessive drag. Check crankshaft end play.

ENGINE OILING

CRANKCASE CAPACITY

Crankcase capacity is 5 quarts (4.7L) with filter change; 4 quarts (3.8L) without.

NORMAL OIL PRESSURE

Normal oil pressure should be 37 psi (2.60 kg/cm²) at 2400 RPM.

PRESSURE REGULATOR VALVE

Pressure regulator valve is located in oil filter adapter and is nonadjustable.

ENGINE OILING SYSTEM

Engine lubrication is a force-feed type. The oil is supplied under full pressure to crankshaft, connecting rods, camshaft bearings, and valve lifters. A controlled volume of oil is supplied to rocker arms and push rods. All other moving parts are lubricated by splash or gravity flow.

Fig. 9: Engine Oiling System

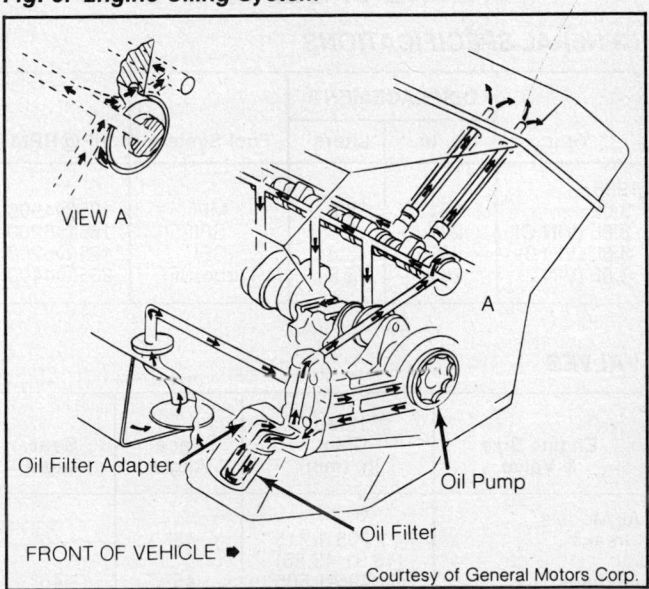

VIEW A

A

Oil Filter Adapter

Oil Pump

Oil Filter

FRONT OF VEHICLE ➡

Courtesy of General Motors Corp.

OIL PUMP

Removal

Remove engine front cover. Remove oil filter adapter, pressure regulator valve and valve spring. Remove oil pump cover attaching screws and cover. Remove pump gears.

General Motors Engines

3.0L, 3.8L & 3.8L "3800" V6 (Cont.)

Installation

Lubricate gears with oil. Assemble gears in housing. Pack pump cavity with petroleum jelly and install pump cover. Install pressure regulator valve spring and valve. Install oil filter adapter using new gasket. Tighten oil filter adapter bolts. Install front cover on engine.

Fig. 10: Oil Pump & Components

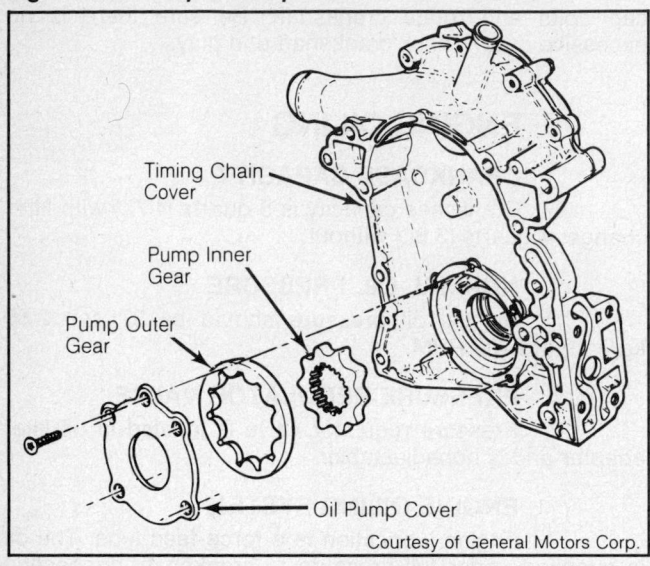

Timing Chain Cover

Pump Inner Gear

Pump Outer Gear

Oil Pump Cover

Courtesy of General Motors Corp.

OIL PUMP SPECIFICATIONS

Application	In. (mm)
Gear End Clearance	.001-.0035 (.025-.089)
Inner Gear Tip Clearance	.006 (.152)
Outer Gear Dia. Clearance	.008-.015 (.203-.381)

ENGINE COOLING

WATER PUMP

Removal

Disconnect negative battery cable. Loosen water pump pulley and bolts. Remove serpentine belt. Drain cooling system and remove hoses from water pump. Remove water pump attaching bolts and water pump.

Installation

If installing a new water pump, transfer pulley from old pump. Clean all sealing surfaces. Apply sealant to water pump sealing surface. While sealer is tacky, install water pump and tighten attaching bolts. To complete installation, reverse removal procedure.

NOTE: For information on cooling system capacities and other cooling system components, see appropriate article in ENGINE COOLING SYSTEMS section.

CAUTION: Following specifications apply only to 3.0L (VIN L), 3.8L (VIN 3) and 3.8"3800" (VIN C) engines.

ENGINE SPECIFICATIONS

GENERAL SPECIFICATIONS

Year	DISPLACEMENT Cu. In.	DISPLACEMENT Liters	Fuel System	HP@RPM	Torque Ft. Lbs.@RPM	Compr. Ratio	BORE In.	BORE mm	STROKE In.	STROKE mm
1988										
3.0L	181	3.0	MFI	125@4900	150@2400	9.0:1	3.80	96.52	2.66	67.56
3.8L (VIN C)	231	3.8	SFI	165@5200	210@2000	8.5:1	3.80	96.52	3.40	86.36
3.8L (VIN 3)	231	3.8	SFI	165@5200	210@2000	8.0:1	3.80	96.52	3.40	86.36
3.8L (VIN 7)	231	3.8	Turbo/SFI	235@4400	330@2800	8.0:1	3.80	96.52	3.40	86.36

VALVES

Engine Size & Valve	Head Diam. In. (mm)	Face Angle	Seat Angle	Seat Width In. (mm)	Stem Diameter In. (mm)	Stem Clearance In. (mm)	Valve Lift In. (mm)
All Models							
Intake	[1] 1.705-1.715 (43.31-43.56)	45°	[2] 46°	[3] .062 (1.57)	.....	.0015-.0035 (.038-.081)	.....
Exhaust	[1] 1.495-1.505 (37.97-38.23)	45°	[2] 46°	[3] .075-.104 (1.91-2.64)		.0015-.0032 (.038-.081)	.....

[1] – Minimum valve margin is .025" (.64 mm).
[2] – On VIN C engine, seat angle is 45 degrees.
[3] – Maximum seat runout is .002" (.05 mm).

3.0L, 3.8L & 3.8L "3800" V6 (Cont.)

ENGINE SPECIFICATIONS (Cont.)

CRANKSHAFT MAIN & CONNECTING ROD BEARINGS

Engine	MAIN BEARINGS				CONNECTING ROD BEARINGS		
	Journal Diam. In. (mm)	Clearance In. (mm)	Thrust Bearing	Crankshaft End Play In. (mm)	Journal Diam. In. (mm)	Clearance In. (mm)	Side Play In. (mm)
All Models	¹ 2.4988-2.4998 (63.469-63.494)	.0003-.0018 (.008-.005)	2	.003-.009 (.08-.23)	¹ 2.2487-2.2499 (57.117-57.147)	.0003-.0028 (.008-.071)	.003-.015 (.076-.38)

¹ – Maximum taper is .0003" (.008 mm).

PISTONS, PINS & RINGS

Engine	PISTONS	PINS		RINGS		
	Clearance In. (mm)	Piston Fit In. (mm)	Rod Fit In. (mm)	Ring No.	End Gap In. (mm)	Side Clearance In. (mm)
All Models	¹ .0013-.0035 (.033-.089)	.0004-.0007 (.010-.018)	.00075-.00125 (.019-.032)	1	.010-.020 (.254-.508)	.003-.005 (.08-.13)
				2	.010-.020 (.254-.508)	.003-.005 (.08-.13)
				3	.015-.035 (.381-.889)	.0035 (.09)

¹ – Measured at bottom of piston skirt. Clearance for 3.8L turbo is .001-.003" (.03-.08 mm).

VALVE SPRINGS

Engine	Free Length In. (mm)	PRESSURE Lbs. @ In. (Kg @ mm)	
		Valve Closed	Valve Open
3.8L (VIN C)	2.03 51.6	100-110@1.73 (45-49@44)	214-136@1.30 (97-61@33)
3.0L & 3.8L (VIN 3)	2.03 51.6	85-95@1.73 (39-42@44)	175-195@1.34 (79.1-88.2@34.04)
3.8L (VIN 7)	2.03 (51.6)	74-82@173 (33-37@44)	175-195@1.34 (79.1-88.2@34.04)

CAMSHAFT

Engine	Journal Diam. In. (mm)	Clearance In. (mm)	Lobe Lift In. (mm)
3.0L	1.785-1.786 (45.34-45.36)	.0005-.0025 (.013-.064)	Int. .210 (5.334) Exh. .240 (6.096)
3.8L (VIN C)	1.785-1.786 (45.34-45.36)	.0005-.0025 (.013-.064)	¹ .272 (6.909)
3.8L (VIN 3)	1.785-1.786 (45.34-45.36)	.0005-.0025 (.013-.064)	¹ .245 (6.223)
3.8L (VIN 7)	1.785-1.786 (45.34-45.36)	.0005-.0025 (.013-.064)	.....

¹ – Specification applies to both intake and exhaust.

CAUTION: Following specifications apply only to 3.0L (VIN L), 3.8L (VIN 3), 3.8L (VIN 7) and 3.8 "3800" (VIN C) engines.

TIGHTENING SPECIFICATIONS

Application	Ft. Lbs. (N.m)
Camshaft Sprocket Bolts	20 (27)
Balance Shaft Retainer Bolts	27 (37)
Balance Shaft Gear Bolt	45 (61)
Connecting Rod Bolts	45 (61)
Cylinder Head Bolts	¹ 60 (81)
Exhaust Manifold Bolts	37 (50)
Flywheel-to-Crankshaft Bolts	60 (81)
Front Engine Cover Bolts	22 (30)
Harmonic Balancer Bolt	219 (298)
Intake Manifold Bolts	²
Main Bearing Cap Bolts	100 (136)
Oil Pan Bolts	14 (19)
Outlet Exhaust Elbow-to-Turbo Housing	13 (17)
Pulley-to-Harmonic Balancer Bolts	20 (27)
Outlet Exhaust Right Side Exhaust Manifold-to-Turbo Housing	20 (27)
Rocker Arm Pedestal Bolts	37 (51)
Timing Chain Damper Bolt	14 (19)
Water Pump Bolts	13 (18)

¹ - Maximum torque is given. Follow specified procedure and sequence.

² - Tighten bolts to 80 INCH lbs. (9 N.m).

General Motors Engines

4.1L & 4.5L V8

ENGINE CODING

ENGINE IDENTIFICATION

Engine code is found in Vehicle Identification Number (VIN). The VIN is stamped on metal tab located on top of instrument panel at lower left, next to windshield. VIN number also appears on a pad attached to left rear corner of crankcase. The VIN number contains 17 characters. The 8th character identifies the engine, and 10th character identifies model year. The 4.1L and 4.5L engine is available only in Cadillac models.

ENGINE CODE

Engine	Code
4.1L (250") PFI	7
4.5L (273") DFI	5

SPECIAL ENGINE MARKS

Information identifying special components is stamped in following locations:

Oversize Valve Guides

Numeral "3", appearing on underside of cylinder head adjacent to valve seat, identifies oversize valves. A "3" indicates .003" oversize.

Swirl Port Heads

Large letter "S", cast in cylinder head and visible with rocker arm covers removed, identifies swirl port heads.

ENGINE REMOVAL

See ENGINE REMOVAL & INSTALLATION at end of ENGINE section.

CAUTION: The General Motors 4.1L and 4.5L V8 engine is constructed largely of aluminum. Special care must be exercised when cleaning gasket surfaces and tightening attaching bolts, as irrepairable damage to the engine can result.

CYLINDER HEAD & MANIFOLDS

INTAKE MANIFOLD

Removal

1) Disconnect negative battery cable. Remove air cleaner. Drain cooling system and remove accessory drive belt. Remove 2 upper power steering pump bracket bolts and loosen lower nuts.

2) On DeVille and Fleetwood models, remove heater hose at thermostat housing. On Seville and Eldorado models, remove right cross-car brace and coolant reservoir tank. On Allanté models, remove upper intake manifold and fuel rails.

3) Disconnect spark plug wires at plugs and distributor cap. Disconnect wire connectors at distributor, oil pressure switch, coolant sensor, and EGR solenoid.

4) Remove distributor. DO NOT rotate crankshaft with distributor removed. Disconnect cables from throttle lever, accelerator, cruise control module, transmission throttle valve, and move out of the way.

NOTE: Fuel system is under pressure. Carefully bleed fuel pressure at fuel line Schraeder valve using an appropriate tool and container.

5) Disconnect fuel lines at throttle body. Remove fuel line brackets at transmission and move lines out of the way. Remove upper radiator hose at thermostat housing, cruise control servo bracket at intake manifold, and vacuum line bracket at left rear engine lift bracket. Disconnect vacuum supply line at throttle body.

6) Disconnect transmission modulator vacuum line. Remove belt tensioner, power steering pump and bracket assembly. Remove air injection management valves and bracket assembly (if equipped). Remove EGR solenoid, bracket assembly, and MAP hose.

7) Remove alternator and bracket. Disconnect wire connectors at ISC motor, TPS, TBI base plate warmer, injectors, and MAT sensor.

8) Remove rocker arm covers, rocker arm support assemblies, and pushrods. Mark pushrods for reassembly reference. Remove idler pulley, brackets at front of right cylinder head, upper right front engine lift bracket bolt, oil filter and right rear engine lift bracket.

9) Remove intake manifold bolts, and intake manifold. Discard gaskets and seals.

Installation

1) Install new front and rear manifold seals. Apply RTV sealant to each corner of end seals where seals meet side gaskets. See Fig. 1. Install intake manifold gaskets with locating pins engaged with holes in cylinder head and apply RTV at 4 corners. Carefully lower intake manifold onto engine so dowel pins engage manifold.

Fig. 1: Intake Manifold Seals & Gaskets

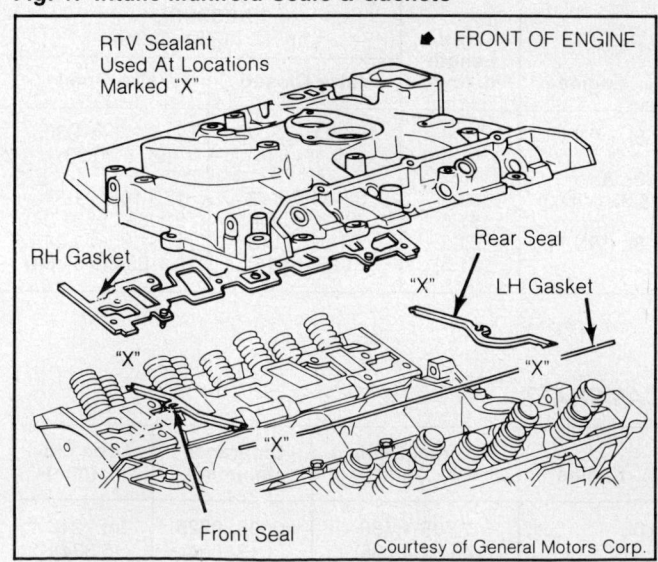

2) Loosely install 16 intake manifold bolts. See Fig. 2. Tighten intake manifold bolts in following sequence:
- Tighten bolts No. 1 through 4 in sequence to 15 ft. lbs. (20 N.m).
- Tighten bolts No. 5 through 16 in sequence to 22 ft. lbs. (30 N.m).
- Tighten all bolts in sequence to 22 ft. lbs. (30 N.m).

3) Install push rods in original positions and make sure push rods are seated in valve lifters. Assemble rocker arms and pivots to valve train support and install assembly over head bolts. Carefully position push rods

4.1L & 4.5L V8 (Cont.)

Fig. 2: Intake Manifold Tightening Sequence

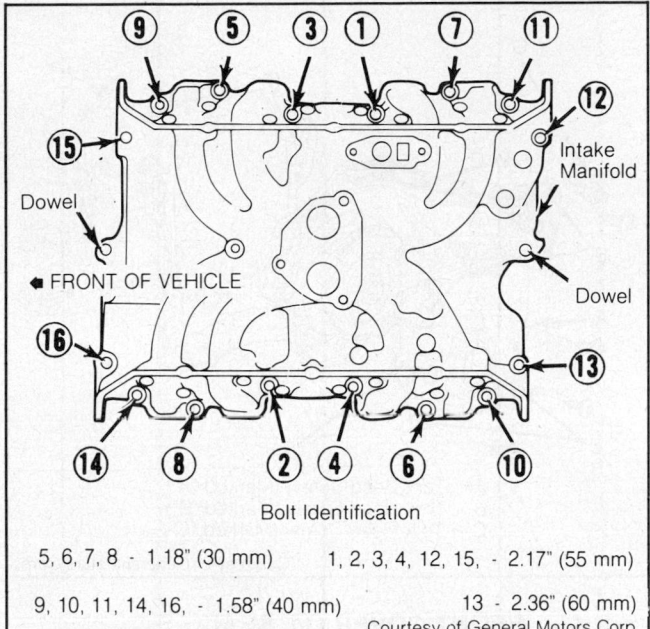

Bolt Identification

5, 6, 7, 8 - 1.18" (30 mm)   1, 2, 3, 4, 12, 15, - 2.17" (55 mm)

9, 10, 11, 14, 16, - 1.58" (40 mm)   13 - 2.36" (60 mm)

Courtesy of General Motors Corp.

into rocker arm seats and loosely install rocker arm assembly retaining nuts.

4) Recheck push rods for correct positioning and tighten retaining nuts alternately and evenly until seated. After seating retaining nuts, tighten nuts. To complete installation, reverse removal procedure.

EXHAUST MANIFOLD

Removal (Allanté, Right Side)

1) Remove negative battery cable, air cleaner assembly, and EGR pipe at manifold. Raise and support vehicle. Remove exhaust pipe.

2) Remove engine mount brace from front of manifold. Remove oxygen sensor wire, exhaust manifold bolts, and exhaust manifold.

Removal (Allanté, Left Side)

1) Disconnect negative battery cable. Remove air cleaner, air injection management pipe from air pump and oxygen sensor wire. Remove serpentine belt, power steering pump, tensioner, and air conditioning brackets. Remove 2 cooling fans and spark plug wires.

2) Raise vehicle and remove exhaust pipe, engine and air conditioning brace from manifold, exhaust manifold bolts, and exhaust manifold.

Removal (Fleetwood & DeVille, Right Side)

1) Disconnect negative battery cable. Remove air cleaner. Disconnect exhaust crossover pipe. Disconnect oxygen sensor and coolant temperature sensor connectors. Remove catalytic converter air pipe to air injection management pipe clip-bolt. Remove 2 upper forward exhaust manifold bolts.

2) Raise vehicle on a hoist and disconnect converter air pipe bracket from stud. Disconnect exhaust pipe from manifold. Lower vehicle and remove remaining exhaust manifold bolts. Remove air injection management pipe from manifold and remove exhaust manifold.

Removal (Fleetwood & DeVille, Left Side)

1) Disconnect negative battery cable. Remove left and right cooling fans. Disconnect exhaust crossover pipe. Remove accessory drive belt. Remove air injection management pump pivot bolt.

2) Remove belt tensioner and power steering pump brace. Remove exhaust manifold bolts. Remove air injection management pipe from manifold and remove exhaust manifold.

Removal (Eldorado & Seville, Right Side)

Disconnect negative battery cable. Remove air cleaner and 2 heat shield screws. Raise vehicle. Remove exhaust crossover pipe, engine brace from right side of manifold, oxygen sensor wire and heat shield. Remove exhaust manifold bolts and exhaust manifold.

Removal (Eldorado & Seville, Left Side)

1) Disconnect negative battery cable. Remove air cleaner, air injection management hose and pipe from air pump, and starter shield. Remove serpentine belt, power steering tensioner bracket covering manifold, A/C hose bracket and cooling fan.

2) Disconnect spark plug wires. Raise vehicle. Remove exhaust crossover pipe, engine and A/C brace from manifold, exhaust manifold bolts, and exhaust manifold.

Installation (All Models)

Apply a thin layer of graphite dry film lubricant to exhaust manifold sealing surfaces which contact cylinder head. Place exhaust manifold on cylinder head. Install manifold attaching bolts. Tighten attaching bolts to 16 ft. lbs. (21 N.m). Reverse removal procedure to complete installation.

CYLINDER HEADS

Removal

1) Disconnect negative battery cable. Drain cooling system and remove rocker arm covers and intake and exhaust manifolds. On Allanté, Eldorado and Seville, remove engine lift bracket, air injection management bracket, and dipstick tube. On Fleetwood and DeVille, remove cooling fans.

2) Remove cylinder head bolts. Remove head(s). Carefully remove all gasket material from cylinder head(s) and block, without damaging aluminum surfaces.

Installation

1) Inspect cylinder head(s) and block gasket surfaces to ensure they are clean. Blow out head bolt

Fig. 3: Cylinder Head Assembly & Torque Sequence

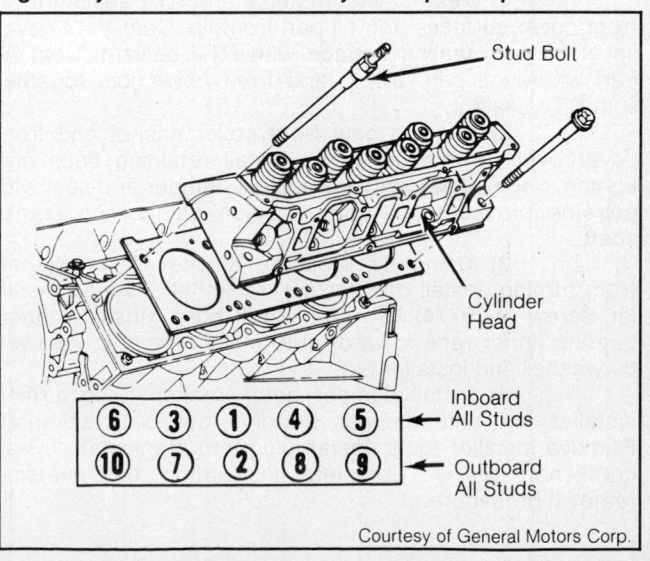

Courtesy of General Motors Corp.

General Motors Engines

4.1L & 4.5L V8 (Cont.)

holes with compressed air. Coat exhaust manifold surfaces of cylinder heads with graphite dry film lubricant. Install intake manifold gaskets with locating pins engaged with holes in cylinder head and apply RTV to 4 corners.

2) Install new head gaskets over dowels. Install cylinder head and tighten bolts finger tight. *See Fig. 3*. Tighten cylinder head bolts in sequence first to 38 ft. lbs (50 N.m), and then to 68 ft. lbs. (90 N.m). Finally tighten bolts 1, 3 and 4 to 90 ft. lbs. (120 N.m).

CAMSHAFT

ENGINE FRONT COVER

Removal

1) Disconnect negative battery cable. Drain cooling system. Remove air cleaner and accessory drive belt. On Fleetwood and DeVille, disconnect alternator and move out of the way.

2) Remove accumulator from bracket and lay aside. On Allanté, Eldorado and Seville, remove cross-car brace and coolant reservoir and air injection management filter and bracket.

3) Remove serpentine belt, idler pulley, water pump pulley and water pump. Remove crankshaft pulley.

4) Raise car on hoist. On all models except Allanté, remove right front tire and right front air deflector. Disconnect right side tie rod and ball joint. Support body of car and right side of engine cradle.

5) On all models except Allanté, remove right side engine cradle-to-body bolts. Lower right side of engine cradle out of the way. On all models, remove 4 crankshaft pulley-to-damper bolts and remove pulley. Remove spark plug and install Air Line Adapter (J-22794) finger tight. Apply air pressure to hold piston on compression stroke to prevent crankshaft rotation.

6) Remove plug from end of crankshaft. Install Puller Pilot (J-21052-4) in crankshaft bore. Install Puller (J-24420-B) on front of damper. Install 2 screws and washers and tighten finger tight.

7) Thread puller screw into tool until screw contacts pilot. Using wrench, remove damper from crankshaft by tightening screw. Remove front cover bolts and front cover.

Installation

1) Clean gasket material and RTV sealant from front cover surfaces and oil pan front lip. Coat front cover lip at oil pan sealing surface with RTV sealant. Coat oil pan where oil pan, block, and front cover join together with RTV sealant.

2) Position new front cover gasket and front cover over dowels on block. Install retaining bolts and tighten. *See Fig. 4*. Lubricate bore of damper and seal with extreme pressure lubricant. Position damper on crankshaft.

3) Using air pressure to prevent crankshaft from turning, install damper on crankshaft. Thread Installer Screw (J-29774) into crankshaft bore. Position thrust bearing (inner race foward) onto installer screw, followed by washer and installer nut.

4) Install damper onto crankshaft by turning installer nut until damper bottoms out on crankshaft. Remove installer tools. Install plug into crankshaft. Install crankshaft pulley. Complete installation by reversing removal procedure.

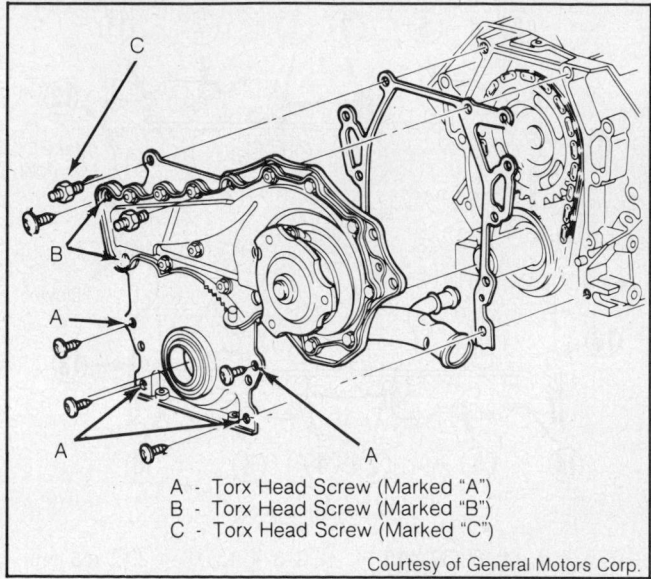

Fig. 4: Engine Front Cover Bolt Locations

A - Torx Head Screw (Marked "A")
B - Torx Head Screw (Marked "B")
C - Torx Head Screw (Marked "C")

Courtesy of General Motors Corp.

FRONT COVER OIL SEAL

Removal

With belts, crankshaft pulley, and hub removed, use front cover oil seal Puller Arms (J-23129) and front cover oil Seal Puller (J-1859-03) to remove oil seal from front cover.

Installation

To install, lubricate new oil seal lips with engine oil and position seal on end of crankshaft with garter spring side toward engine. Using Seal Installer (J-29662) and hammer, drive seal into front cover until installer bottoms against front cover. Install crankshaft hub, pulley and belts.

NOTE: **Seal Installer (J-29662) has been designed so that front cover seal can be pressed on using Installer Screw (J-29774), if it is inconvenient to hammer seal on.**

TIMING CHAIN

Removal

Remove front cover and oil slinger. Rotate crankshaft until timing marks are aligned, with No. 1

Fig. 5: Timing Chain Sprocket Alignment

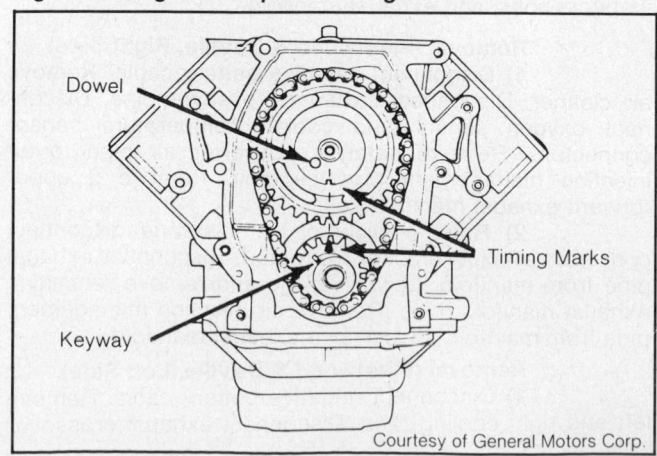

Dowel

Timing Marks

Keyway

Courtesy of General Motors Corp.

4.1L & 4.5L V8 (Cont.)

cylinder at TDC. *See Fig. 5.* Remove camshaft sprocket retaining screw. Remove timing chain and sprockets from crankshaft and camshaft at same time.

Installation

Install timing chain, crankshaft sprocket and camshaft sprocket so that timing marks are aligned. *See Fig. 5.* Ensure camshaft dowel aligns with camshaft sprocket hole. Install oil slinger and front cover.

CAMSHAFT

Removal

Remove engine from vehicle. See ENGINE REMOVAL at end of ENGINE section. Remove valve lifters and timing chain. Install long bolt, or reinstall camshaft sprocket, and carefully pull camshaft from engine.

NOTE: **If new camshaft is installed, new lifters and distributor driven gear must also be installed.**

Installation

To install, apply rear axle lubricant to all camshaft lobes, distributor gear teeth and bearing journals. Carefully guide camshaft into engine using care not to nick or scratch camshaft bearings. Reverse removal procedure to complete installation.

CAMSHAFT BEARINGS

NOTE: **Camshaft bearing diameters decrease in size from front to rear of engine. Universal Puller (J-33049) or 5 different bearing pushers must be used to replace bearings.**

Removal

1) Bearings must be replaced as a complete set. Using removal tools, remove bearings in order (No. 1 first, No. 2 second, etc.).

2) Do not remove lifter carrier to ease cam bearing replacement. Cam bearing bores are machined with this casting in place and correct alignment cannot be assured once removed.

NOTE: **If new camshaft is installed, new lifters and distributor driven gear must also be installed.**

Installation

1) It is not necessary to align cam bearing oil hole with corresponding oil hole in block. The block contains an oil groove around bearing. To install bearings, reverse removal procedure.

2) It is only necessary to align bearing oil hole in front and rear direction so it is aligned with groove. Side position of oil hole is not critical. When properly installed, cam bearing oil hole should be fully exposed to oil groove.

VALVES

VALVE ARRANGEMENT

I-E-I-E-E-I-E-I (Front-to-rear, both banks).

VALVE GUIDE SERVICING

Service valves are available with standard or .003" and .006" (.08 and .15 mm) oversize stems. If clearance is not within specifications, ream guide to next oversize using appropriate reamer. Install valve with corresponding oversize stem. When installing oversize

valves and guides, stamp oversize on cylinder head gasket surface.

VALVE STEM OIL SEALS

Oil seals are installed on all valve guides. A new seal should be installed whenever valve spring is removed. To install new seals, coat seal with engine oil, carefully slide seal over valve stem, and push down until it contacts valve guide. Using Seal Installer (J-29790), push seal onto guide until seal installer bottoms out.

VALVE SPRINGS

Removal (Cylinder Head Installed)

1) Remove rocker arm covers. Remove 5 nuts from valve train studs and remove valve train support assembly with rocker arms and pivots attached.

2) Remove spark plug from cylinder to be serviced. Install Air Line Adapter (J-22794) finger tight and apply compressed air to hold valves closed.

3) Using valve Spring Compressor (J-26513), compress spring until valve stem locks can be removed. Remove retainer and valve spring/damper assembly. Pry valve stem seal off guide with a small screwdriver and discard seal.

Removal (Cylinder Head Removed)

1) With rocker arm removed, compress valve spring using Spring Compressor (J-8062). Remove valve locks. Release compressor.

2) Remove retainer and valve spring/damper assembly. Pry oil seal off valve guide with small screwdriver and discard.

Installation

To install, reverse removal procedure and ensure ends of springs are installed against cylinder head in their original orientation.

ROCKER ARM ASSEMBLY

NOTE: **When removing rocker arm assembly, keep all components in order for proper installation. See Fig. 6.**

Removal

Remove rocker arm covers. Remove 4 rocker arm retaining bolts. Remove 5 nuts securing valve train support to stud bolts and remove valve train assembly

Fig. 6: Rocker Arm Assembly

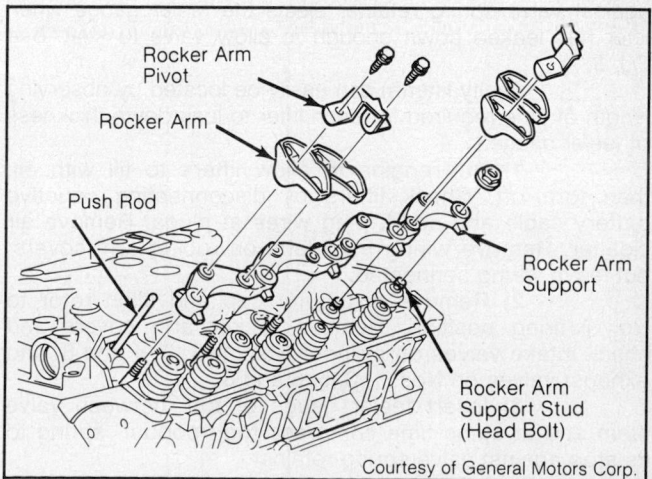

Courtesy of General Motors Corp.

with rocker arms and pivots attached. Secure support in vise and individually remove rocker arms and pivots.

Installation

Prior to assembly of rocker arms and pivots to valve train assembly, lubricate all parts with an extreme pressure lubricant such as Axle Lube (1052271). Assemble rocker arms and pivots to valve train and reverse removal procedure to install valve train assembly.

HYDRAULIC VALVE LIFTER ASSEMBLY

1) Remove lifters using valve Lifter Remover (J-29834). Keep lifters in sequence to ensure they are installed in original positions. Do not score aluminum lifter bores during removal or installation.

2) Valve lifter body and plunger assemblies are matched pairs and are not interchangeable. If valve lifters require replacement, ensure replacement lifters are specifically listed for 4.1L and 4.5L V8 engines. *See Fig. 7.*

Fig. 7: Hydraulic Valve Lifter Assembly

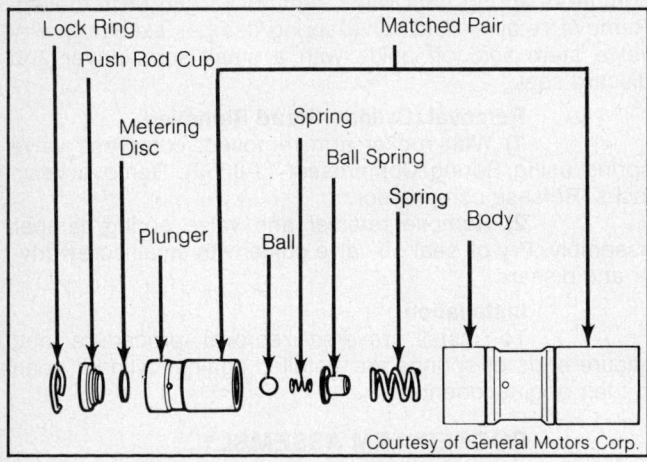

Courtesy of General Motors Corp.

HYDRAULIC VALVE LIFTER LEAK-DOWN TESTING

Use Valve Lifter Leak-Down Rate Tester (J-3074) to check for faulty lifters without removal from engine. This tool provides a feeler gauge of specific thickness which when placed between rocker arm and valve stem, causes valve spring pressure to force oil from lifter.

A spring attached to tool and compressed against valve spring retainer ejects the feeler gauge when lifter has leaked down enough to allow valve to seat. *See Fig. 8.*

Faulty lifter(s) can easily be located by observing length of time required for each lifter to leak down thickness of feeler gauge.

1) Run engine to allow lifters to fill with oil, then turn off. Check lifters by disconnecting negative battery cable and spark plug wires at plugs. Remove air cleaner. Remove wiring from tabs on rocker arm covers, but leave wiring connected.

2) Remove distributor cap and align rotor to No. 1 firing position. Remove rocker arm covers and check intake valves on cylinder Nos. 1, 2, 3, 4 and 8, and exhaust valves on Nos. 1, 3, 5, 6 and 8.

3) Insert feeler gauge of tool between valve stem and at same time compress tool "popout" spring to its stop against valve spring retainer.

4) Install tool as quickly as possible to avoid unnecessary lifter leak-down. Note interval tool is held in place by valve spring pressure. Noisy lifter(s) will have shortest leak-down time.

5) Install components previously removed and start engine to fill lifters with oil. Repeat removal of components in step 2).

6) Rotate engine so distributor rotor is now in No. 6 firing position. Check intake valves on cylinder Nos. 3, 4 and 6, and exhaust valves on Nos. 5, 6 and 7. Note leak-down interval. Install components by reversing removal procedure.

Fig. 8: Checking Valve Lifter Leak-Down Rate

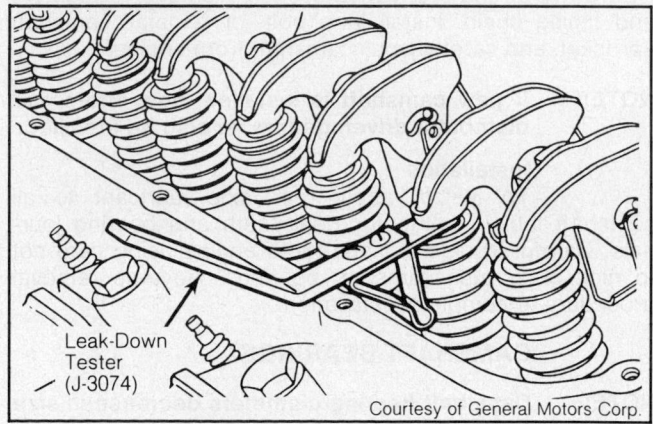

Courtesy of General Motors Corp.

PISTONS, PINS & RINGS

OIL PAN

See OIL PAN REMOVAL at end of ENGINE section.

PISTON & ROD ASSEMBLY

Removal

1) Remove cylinder head(s) and oil pan. Install Cylinder Liner Holder (J-29775) along top of cylinder liners.

2) Mark connecting rods and caps for cylinder identification. Remove rod cap and push rubber hose onto connecting rod bolts to protect crankshaft and cylinder liner bore. Push piston and rod assembly out top of cylinder liner. Install cap on mating rod.

Installation

1) When installing piston rings, make sure markings on top of compression rings face up. Lightly coat pistons, rings and cylinder liner bores with oil. Compress piston rings using ring compressor.

2) Install piston and rod assembly in cylinder liner bore, making sure notch in top of piston faces front of engine. Lubricate bearing and install rod cap with bearing lock tangs aligned on same side of rod. Install rod cap nuts and tighten. Remove cylinder liner holder.

CYLINDER LINERS

NOTE: **Cylinder liners match their corresponding piston only. Ink mark assemblies for identification. Reused liners must be replaced in original location within cylinder block.**

4.1L & 4.5L V8 (Cont.)

Removal

Mark cylinder liners for reassembly reference. After removing piston assemblies, remove cylinder liner holder and pull liners from cylinder block. Discard "O" ring from bottom of cylinder liner. Minor nicks or burrs on mating surfaces of cylinder block and cylinder liner can be polished out with crocus cloth.

Installation (Original Liners)

If liners are reused, install new "O" ring on bottom of cylinder liner. Position liner in original position, aligning with marks made during disassembly. Seat liners and install cylinder liner holder. Install pistons in corresponding liner.

Installation (New Liners)

1) Position new liner in block without "O" ring installed on liner. Place Cylinder Liner Gauge (J-29776) on a flat surface. Using moderate pressure, zero gauge indicator. See Fig. 9.

Fig. 9: Zeroing Dial Indicator

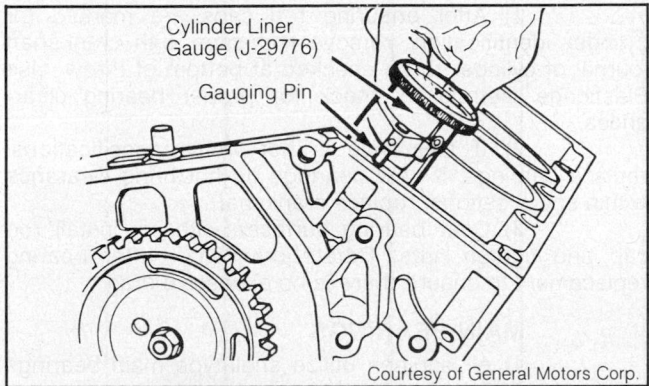

2) Measure liner height by inserting spring loaded guide pins of gauge into liner. Ensure machined

Fig. 10: Measuring Height of New Cylinder Liners

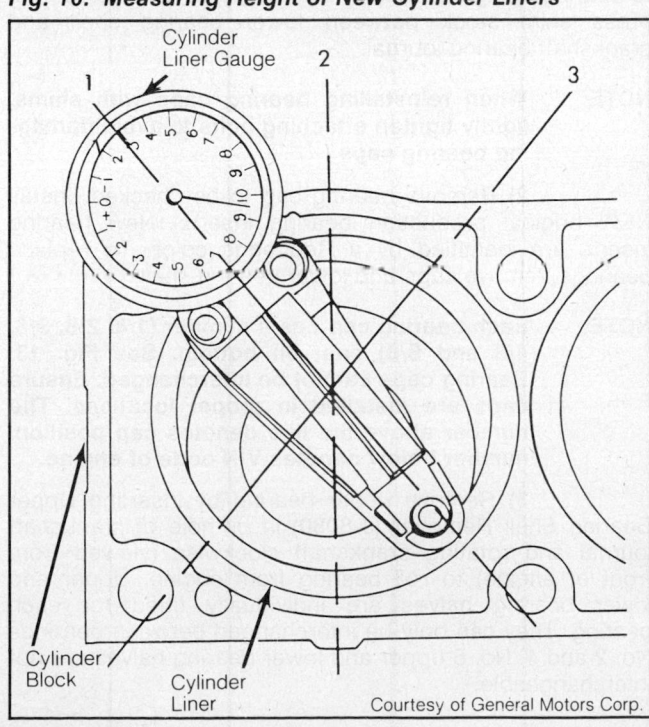

pads rest on edge of liner and indicator pointer of gauge touches cylinder head mating surface of cylinder block. See Fig. 10. Apply moderate pressure to gauge until pointer stops moving.

3) Read and record liner gauge reading. If reading is a positive value, liner is higher than cylinder head mounting surface of block. If reading is a negative value, liner is lower than cylinder head mounting surface.

NOTE: The indicator readings are graduated in millimeters (+1=.01 mm, -3=-.03 mm).

4) Repeat steps 2) and 3) at locations shown. See Fig. 10. Record readings. Determine actual liner height by calculating average of all 3 readings (add readings and divide sum by 3).

5) Correct liner height is .00-.0031" (.0-.08 mm) above cylinder head mounting surface of block. Any liner below or above specification must be replaced with new liner. After establishing liner height within specifications, liner-to-liner dimension must be measured.

NOTE: Liners may be rotated within cylinder block. After determining final position of liner, mark location of liner in block.

6) To determine liner-to-liner height, install adjacent liner in its original position and orientation without "O" ring installed. Using cylinder liner gauge, place indicator pointer on upper surface of adjacent liner and hold second liner in position. See Fig. 11.

7) Liner-to-liner reading must be within ±.002" (±.05 mm). After setting liner-to-liner height, mark liner location for final reassembly and complete measurement process on all other liners.

8) After measurement is completed, remove liner. Install "O" ring, liner holder and piston assemblies.

Fig. 11: Measuring Liner-to-Liner Height

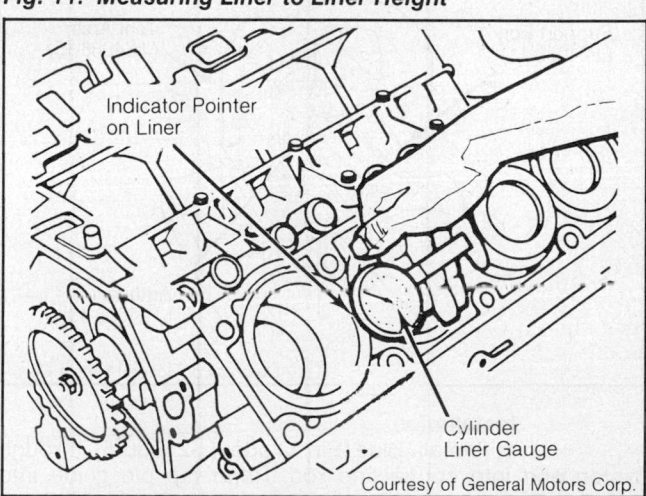

Height may be checked without "O" rings installed.

FITTING PISTONS

1) With piston and rod assembly removed, thoroughly clean cylinder liner bore. Inspect bore for scoring or grooves. Measure liner bore for out-of-round. If liner out-of-round exceeds .0008" (.020 mm), new piston and liner must be installed.

2) Measure piston diameter at right angle to piston pin, 3/8" below oil ring groove, and at piston skirt. If piston taper exceeds .0005-.0020" (.013-.050 mm), piston and liner must be replaced.

NOTE: Do not attempt to hone or rebore cylinder liners.

PISTON PINS

NOTE: If piston will be discarded, use "V" block to support piston instead of using piston pin remover/installer assembly.

Removal

1) Place Adapter (J-24086-50) on support assembly at piston boss. Support fork of Holder (J-24086-11) between connecting rod and piston. See Fig. 12.

2) Install Removal Arbor (J-24086-8) through alignment hole in base of remover/installer assembly. Center piston assembly with removal arbor and press piston pin out of connecting rod.

Fig. 12: Piston Pin Installation Tools

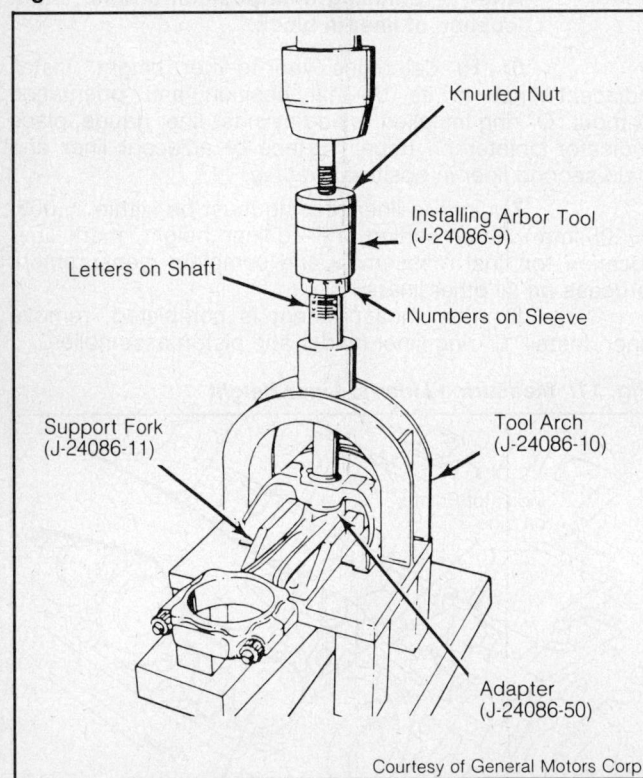

Knurled Nut

Installing Arbor Tool
(J-24086-9)

Letters on Shaft

Numbers on Sleeve

Support Fork
(J-24086-11)

Tool Arch
(J-24086-10)

Adapter
(J-24086-50)

Courtesy of General Motors Corp.

Installation

1) Install Blue Pin Guide (J-24086-5) through piston and into connecting rod. Hand tap pin guide into position for proper retention. Adapter (J-24086-50) must be positioned between connecting rod and piston pin boss.

NOTE: Pin guide centers connecting rod in piston. When piston and components are positioned on fork of tool, pin guide will center assembly in tool. Using too small a pin guide will not center piston assembly in tool and damage may occur.

2) Install piston assembly into fork assembly of tool. Tool will support connecting rod at piston pin. Piston assembly must slide onto fork until pin guide contacts fork.

3) Adjust Installing Arbor (J-24086-9) to "12" by turning numbered sleeve on lettered shaft. Turn knurled nut to lock numbered sleeve. See Fig. 12.

4) Insert installing arbor through hole in tool arch. Press piston pin into connecting rod until sleeve on installing arbor contacts top of tool arch. Pin guide will fall out of connecting rod as piston pin is pressed in.

NOTE: Do not exceed 5000 lbs. (2268 kg) of force when seating arbor sleeve against arch.

CRANKSHAFT & ROD BEARINGS

CONNECTING ROD BEARINGS

1) After ensuring rod caps are marked for cylinder identification, remove rod caps with crankshaft journal of cylinder to be checked at bottom of throw. Use Plastigage method to check for proper bearing clearances.

2) If clearance is not within specifications, replace bearings. If new bearings do not bring clearance within specifications, replace crankshaft.

3) Coat bearing surfaces with oil, install rod cap and tighten nuts. Rotate crankshaft after bearing replacement to ensure there is no excessive drag.

MAIN BEARINGS

1) All engines utilize shell-type main bearings of steel-backed aluminum. If bearings are being measured with engine in vehicle, crankshaft must be supported in order to take up clearance between upper bearing shell and crankshaft. To do this, remove bearing caps adjacent to bearing being checked. Place a strip of .005" (0.13 mm) brass shim stock between lower bearing shell and crankshaft bearing journal.

NOTE: When reinstalling bearing caps with shims, lightly tighten attaching bolts to avoid damaging bearing caps.

2) Remove bearing cap to be checked. Install NEW original production bearing inserts. New bearing inserts are identified by a Red edge color. To replace bearings, remove caps and lower bearing shell.

NOTE: Each bearing cap has a number (1/8, 2/8, 3/8, 4/8 and 5/8) cast on bottom. See Fig. 13. Bearing caps cannot be interchanged. Ensure caps are installed in proper locations. The number above the line denotes cap position, number below denotes VIN code of engine.

3) Remove upper bearing by inserting Upper Bearing Shell Remover (J-8080) in oil hole of crankshaft journal and rotating crankshaft clockwise (viewed from front of engine) to roll bearing from engine. Upper and lower bearing halves are individually fitted for each bearing. They can only be interchanged between bearings No. 2 and 4. No. 5 upper and lower bearing halves are not interchangeable.

4.1L & 4.5L V8 (Cont.)

4) Oil new upper bearing and insert in place as far as possible by hand with locating tang in correct position. Rotate crankshaft counterclockwise to roll bearing in place. Install lower bearing in cap so indentation in bearing and cap coincide. Install bearing cap and tighten bolts. Check main bearing clearances one at a time using Plastigage method.

NOTE: Bearing clearance measurements must always be performed with new bearings.

5) If No. 1 main bearing clearance is greater than .002" (.050 mm), install new oversize service bearing with Blue edge color. If bearing clearance is less than .002" (.050 mm), leave Red bearing in engine.

6) If No. 2, 3 or 4 main bearing clearance is greater than .004" (.10 mm), bearing should be replaced. If No. 5 main bearing clearance is .004" (.10 mm) or more with original production bearing with Pink edge color, install oversized, Blue-edged color service bearing. If new bearings cannot bring clearance within specifications, replace crankshaft.

Fig. 13: Main Bearing Cap Location

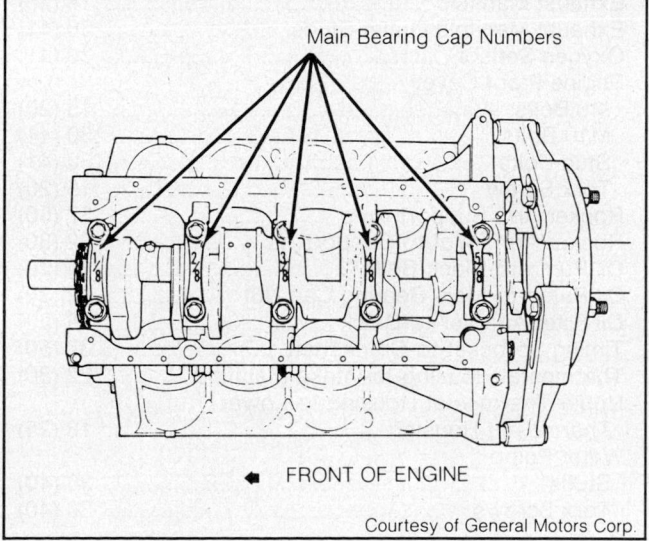

Main Bearing Cap Numbers

FRONT OF ENGINE

Courtesy of General Motors Corp.

THRUST BEARING ALIGNMENT

1) With all main bearing cap bolts finger tight, tap crankshaft forward, then rearward several times to align thrust bearings. Tighten all main bearing cap bolts. Rotate crankshaft to ensure there is no excessive drag.

2) Measure crankshaft end play by forcing crankshaft to extreme forward position. Using feeler gauge, measure at front end of No. 3 bearing. End play should be within specification.

REAR MAIN BEARING OIL SEAL

Removal

Remove transaxle assembly from vehicle. Remove flexplate from crankshaft. Use Seal Remover (J-26868) and remove rear main oil seal.

Installation

1) Remove any foreign material from crankshaft and seal bore with a clean rag. Lubricate lip of seal with chassis grease. Position seal on crankshaft with spring facing toward inside of engine. Using Seal Installer (J-34604), press seal into position.

Fig. 14: Rear Main Bearing Oil Seal Removal Tool

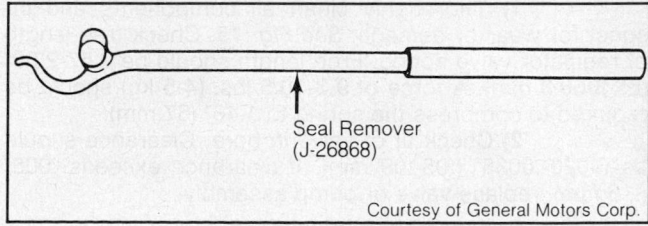

Seal Remover
(J-26868)

Courtesy of General Motors Corp.

2) Seal should be installed flush with block or slightly recessed into block .039" (1 mm). Seal must be installed square to crankshaft or an oil leak could result.

ENGINE OILING

CRANKCASE CAPACITY

Capacity is 5 quarts (4.7L) for all models, with or without filter change.

NORMAL OIL PRESSURE

Normal oil pressure is 30-45 psi (2.1-3.2 kg/cm²) at 1500 RPM.

PRESSURE REGULATOR VALVE

The pressure regulator valve is located in oil pump and is nonadjustable.

ENGINE OILING SYSTEM

Lubrication is force-feed type. Oil is supplied under full pressure to crankshaft, connecting rods, camshaft bearings and valve lifters. Controlled volume of oil is supplied to rocker arms and push rods. All other parts are lubricated by splash or gravity flow. An oil cooler is used to cool oil.

OIL COOLER

A partial by-pass oil cooler is mounted in right side of radiator (left side on Fleetwood and DeVille). A by-pass valve, located in oil filter adapter, forces all oil supplied by oil pump to flow out the cooler inlet port when oil pressure is below a specified value. Above this value, some of the oil is forced to by-pass the cooler and flow directly to cooler outlet (filter inlet) port.

OIL PUMP

NOTE: Oil pan must be removed to gain access to oil pump. See OIL PAN REMOVAL at end of ENGINE section.

Removal

Raise vehicle on hoist, drain oil and remove oil pan. Remove oil pump mounting hardware and oil pump assembly. Remove and discard oil pump outlet pipe "O" ring. Oil pick-up tube is affixed to pump housing and cannot be removed.

Disassembly

To disassemble, remove 4 oil pump cover-to-housing screws. Remove cover and discard gasket. Slide drive shaft, drive gear and driven gear out of pump housing. Remove oil pressure regulator valve and spring from housing bore.

4.1L & 4.5L V8 (Cont.)

Inspection

1) Thoroughly clean all components and inspect for wear or damage. *See Fig. 15.* Check free length of regulator valve spring. Free length should be 2.57-2.69" (65.3-68.3 mm). A force of 9.3-10.5 lbs. (4-5 kg) should be required to compress the spring to 1.46" (37 mm).

2) Check fit of valve in bore. Clearance should be .0020-.0035" (.05-.09 mm). If clearance exceeds .005" (.13 mm), replace valve or pump assembly.

Reassembly & Installation

1) Position drive gear over shaft nearest regulator bore. Slide driven gear into position, meshing driven gear with drive gear. Rotate gears to be sure they turn freely.

2) Install oil pressure regulator spring and valve into bore of pump housing. Install new gasket. Position cover on pump and tighten cover retaining screws. Install new outlet pipe "O" ring and position pump on block by engaging drive shaft with distributor gear.

Fig. 15: Oil Pump & Components

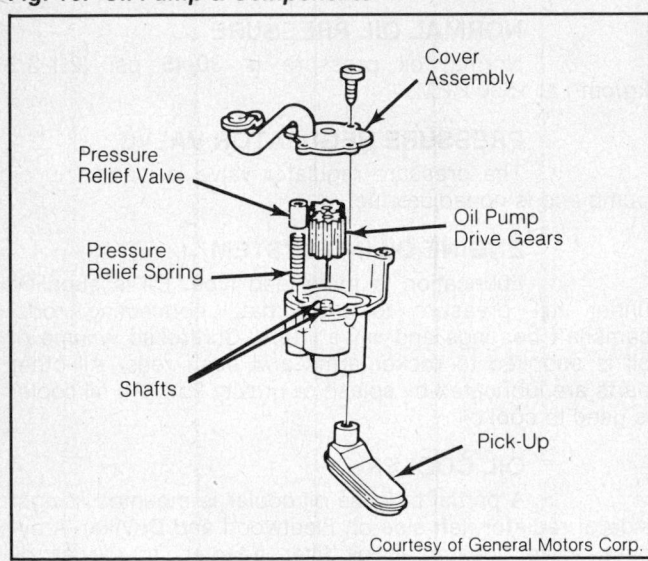

Cover Assembly

Pressure Relief Valve

Pressure Relief Spring

Oil Pump Drive Gears

Shafts

Pick-Up

Courtesy of General Motors Corp.

ENGINE COOLING

WATER PUMP

Removal

1) Disconnect negative battery cable. Drain cooling system. On Fleetwood and DeVille, disconnect A/C accumulator from bracket and move out of the way. Remove A/C accumulator bracket. On Eldorado and Seville, remove air injection management filter assembly and coolant recovery tank.

2) Remove right cross-car brace. Remove accessory drive belt. Remove drive belt, idler pulley and bracket. Remove water pump pulley and water pump. Discard gasket and clean gasket surfaces.

Installation

To install, mount new gasket on water pump flange and reverse removal procedure.

NOTE: For information on cooling system capacities and other cooling system components, see appropriate article in ENGINE COOLING SYSTEMS section.

TIGHTENING SPECIFICATIONS

Application	[1] Ft. Lbs. (N.m)
Cylinder Head Bolts	
1st Step	38 (50)
2nd Step	68 (90)
3rd Step	[2]
Air Pipe-to-Cylinder Head (Nut or Screw)	22 (30)
Connecting Rod Bolts	22 (30)
Main Bearing Caps	85 (116)
Crankshaft Pulley-to-Harmonic Hub Bolt	18 (25)
Flywheel-to-Crankshaft Bolts	
16 mm Head	37 (50)
Intake Manifold	[3]
Exhaust Manifold	18 (25)
Exhaust Manifold Outlet Studs	30 (41)
Oxygen Sensor	30 (41)
Engine Front Cover	
M8 Bolts	15 (20)
M10 Bolts	30 (41)
Stud Bolts	30 (41)
Torx Screw	15 (20)
Rocker Arm Support Nuts	37 (50)
Rocker Arm Pivot-to-Support	22 (30)
Oil Pump-to-Block Bolts	15 (20)
Oil Pump-to-Main Bearing Cap Nut	22 (30)
Oil Filter Adapter-to-Block	15 (20)
Timing Sprocket-to-Crankshaft	37 (50)
Thermostat Housing-to-Intake Manifold	22 (30)
Upper Thermostat Housing-to-Lower	
Thermostat Housing	18 (25)
Water Pump	
Studs	30 (40)
Torx Screws	30 (40)

	INCH Lbs. (N.m)
Oil Pump Cover Bolts	60 (7)
Water Pump	
Hex Head Screws	60 (7)
Nuts	60 (7)

[1] – When servicing 4.1L and 4.5L V8 engine, which is constructed largely of aluminum, care must be exercised in following tightening specifications so as not to strain characteristics of this material.

[2] – Tighten bolts 1, 3, and 4 to 90 ft. lbs. (120 N.m). *See Fig. 3.*

[3] – See INTAKE MANIFOLD section. Final torque must not exceed 22 ft. lbs. (30 N.m).

4.1L & 4.5L V8 (Cont.)

ENGINE SPECIFICATIONS

GENERAL SPECIFICATIONS

| Year | DISPLACEMENT | | Fuel System | HP@RPM | Torque Ft. Lbs.@RPM | Compr. Ratio | BORE | | STROKE | |
	Cu. In.	Liters					In.	mm	In.	mm
1988										
4.1L	250	4.1L	PFI	[1] 125 @ 4200	[2] 190 @2000	9.0:1	3.47	88	3.31	84
4.5L	273	4.5L	DFI				3.62	92	3.31	84

[1] – HP varies with model (125-135).
[2] – Torque varies with model (190-200).

CRANKSHAFT MAIN & CONNECTING ROD BEARINGS

| Engine | MAIN BEARINGS | | | | CONNECTING ROD BEARINGS | | |
	Journal Diam. In. (mm)	Clearance In. (mm)	Thrust Bearing	Crankshaft End Play In. (mm)	Journal Diam. In. (mm)	Clearance In. (mm)	Side Play In. (mm)
4.1L & 4.5L	2.64 (67)	[1] .0008-.0039 (.020-.100)	No. 3	[2] .001-.007 (.025-.178)	1.93 (49)	[3] .0005-.0028 (.013-.071)	.008-.020 (.20-.51)

[1] – Wear limit .0045" (.115 mm).
[2] – Wear limit .015" (.38 mm).
[3] – Wear limit .0035" (.090 mm).

VALVES

Engine Size & Valve	Head Diam. In. (mm)	Face Angle	Seat Angle	Seat Width In. (mm)	Stem Diameter In. (mm)	Stem Clearance In. (mm)	Valve Lift In. (mm)
4.1L & 4.5L							
Intake	1.54 (39)	44°	45°	.....	.3413-.3420 (8.67-8.69)	.001-.003 (.025-.076)	.384 (9.75)
Exhaust	1.30 (33)	44°	45°	.....	.3413-.3420 (8.67-8.69)	.001-.003 (.025-.076)	.396 (10.06)

PISTONS, PINS & RINGS

| Engine | PISTONS | PINS | | RINGS | | |
	Clearance In. (mm)	Piston Fit In. (mm)	Rod Fit In. (mm)	Ring No.	End Gap In. (mm)	Side Clearance In. (mm)
4.1L & 4.5L	[1] .0010-.0018 (.025-.045)	.0002-.0004 (.005-.010)	Press Fit	1	.015-.025 (.38-.64)	.002-.004 (.05-.10)
				2	.015-.025 (.38-.64)	.002-.004 (.05-.10)
				3	.010-050 (.25-1.27)	None

[1] – Measured at top of piston skirt.

General Motors Engines
4.1L & 4.5L V8 (Cont.)

ENGINE SPECIFICATIONS (Cont.)

CAMSHAFT

Engine	Journal Diam. In. (mm)	Clearance In. (mm)	Lobe Lift In. (mm)
4.1L & 4.5L	....	[1] .002-.004 (.05-.10)	Int. .384 (9.75) Exh. .396 (10.06)

[1] – Out-of-round, not over .002" (.05 mm).

VALVE SPRINGS

Engine	Free Length In. (mm)	PRESSURE Lbs. @ In. (Kg @ mm)	
		Valve Closed	Valve Open
4.1L & 4.5L Int.	2.31 (59)	94-104 @ 1.73 (42-47 @ 44)	209-216 @ 1.28 (95-98 @ 32.5)
Exh.	2.12 (54)	93-104 @ 1.73 (43-47 @ 44)	204-221 @ 128 (93-100 @ 32.5)

VALVE TIMING

Engine	INTAKE		EXHAUST	
	Open (BTDC)	Close (ABDC)	Open (BBDC)	Close (ATDC)
4.1L & 4.5L	20°	77°	64°	29°

4.3L V6, 5.0L (VIN F, G & H) & 5.7L V8

NOTE: For engine repair procedures not covered in this article, see ENGINE OVERHAUL PROCEDURES article at beginning of this section.

ENGINE CODING

ENGINE IDENTIFICATION

Engine may be identified from Vehicle Identification Number (VIN) The VIN is stamped on a metal tab located on top of instrument panel at lower left corner of windshield. The VIN number contains 18 characters. The 9th character identifies engine and 11th character establishes model year. Stick on labels attached to engine indicate engine unit number and code.

ENGINE CODE

Engine	Code
4.3L (262") TBI V6	Z
5.0L (305") TBI V8	E
5.0L (305") TPI V8	F
5.0L (305") 4-Bbl. V8 (High Output)	G
5.0L (305") 4-Bbl. V8	H
5.7L (350") 4-Bbl. V8 (Police)	6
5.7L (350") TPI V8	8

ENGINE REMOVAL

See ENGINE REMOVAL & INSTALLATION at end of ENGINE section.

CYLINDER HEAD & MANIFOLDS

INTAKE MANIFOLD

CAUTION: Before servicing any fuel related component on fuel injected vehicles, relieve fuel pressure. Connect Fuel Gauge (J 34730-1) to fuel pressure valve. Wrap shop towel around fitting during installation to avoid spillage. Install bleed hose. Turn valve and drain fuel into a container.

Removal (V6 & V8 Carbureted Models)

1) Disconnect negative battery cable. Drain cooling system. Remove air cleaner. Remove heater and upper radiator hoses and upper alternator bracket. Remove cruise control servo and bracket (if equipped). Disconnect fuel line clips and lines at throttle body (V6).

2) Disconnect carburetor linkage, throttle valve linkage (A/T), fuel line, vacuum lines and electrical wiring at manifold. Disconnect right bank spark plug wires at plugs (V8). On V8 engines, remove carburetor. On V6 engines, remove coil.

3) Remove distributor cap and wires. Mark position of rotor and remove distributor. Remove A/C compressor and bracket (if equipped). Remove EGR solenoids and bracket. Remove dipstick tube and alternator adjusting brace.

4) On V8 engines, disconnect Computer Command Control (CCC) wiring harness and lay aside. Disconnect fuel lines at air injection control valve bracket. Remove manifold bolts and intake manifold.

Removal (V8 Fuel Injected Models)

1) Disconnect negative battery cable and drain cooling system. Remove air intake duct. Disconnect accelerator, throttle valve and cruise control cables (if equipped).

2) Remove air intake duct, mass airflow sensor (MAF), and air intake tube. Disconnect coolant hoses at throttle body. Disconnect wiring, vacuum lines, and breather hoses from throttle body. Relieve fuel system pressure. Disconnect fuel inlet and return lines. Remove throttle body from plenum. Remove distributor shield.

3) Disconnect cable retaining bracket. Remove throttle body retaining bolts. Disconnect throttle position sensor (TPS) and idle air control (IAC) valve connectors. Disconnect vacuum lines and brake vacuum lines at plenum. Disconnect canister control valve fresh air pipe.

4) Remove right runners. Remove plenum retaining bolts and lift off plenum. Disconnect cold start valve and fuel line. Disconnect fuel lines and injector harness connectors. Loosen fuel rail retaining bolts and raise rail. Remove runners, fuel rail, and injectors as an assembly.

NOTE: When servicing fuel rail assembly, ensure no dirt or contaminants enter fuel passages. Cap fittings and plug holes during servicing. Replace "O" rings before reinstalling fuel rail.

5) Remove distributor cap and mark rotor position. Remove cold start valve retaining bolts, fuel supply line, and cold start valve. Remove distributor and disconnect EGR solenoid.

6) Disconnect heater hose at rear of intake manifold. Remove drive belt. Remove air injection pump bracket bolts and air injection pump. Disconnect coolant temperature sensor. Remove intake manifold bolts and intake manifold.

Installation (All Models)

1) Clean mating surfaces. Install gaskets on cylinder heads. On Corvette, position blocked openings in gaskets rearward. Bend tab flush with rear face of cylinder head.

2) On all models, apply 3/16" (5 mm) bead of RTV sealant along front and rear ridge of block. On all models except Corvette, place sealant around water passages and about 1/2" (13 mm) up each head to seal and retain manifold side gaskets.

3) On Corvette, apply Loctite to manifold bolts. On all models, install manifold and bolts. Tighten bolts in sequence. See Fig. 1. On all fuel injected engines, snug bolts first, then tighten to final value. On all models, reverse removal procedure to complete installation. Adjust idle, timing and check for leaks.

EXHAUST MANIFOLD

Removal (Right Side – V6)

1) Disconnect battery. Remove air cleaner and raise vehicle. Remove exhaust pipe bolts at manifold and suspend exhaust pipe with wire. Disconnect air injection pipe at left side of block (if equipped). Lower vehicle. Disconnect fuel pipes at air injection control valve bracket (if equipped).

2) Disconnect air injection control valve bracket. Disconnect catalytic converter air injection pipe at exhaust manifold. Disconnect spark plug wires. Remove air injection pipe at heads and at manifold. Disconnect air injection hoses at catalytic converter and manifold check valve.

3) Remove air injection check valve (if equipped). Remove exhaust manifold bolts and exhaust manifold.

4.3L V6, 5.0L (VIN F, G & H) & 5.7L V8 (Cont.)

Fig. 1: Intake Manifold Tightening Sequence

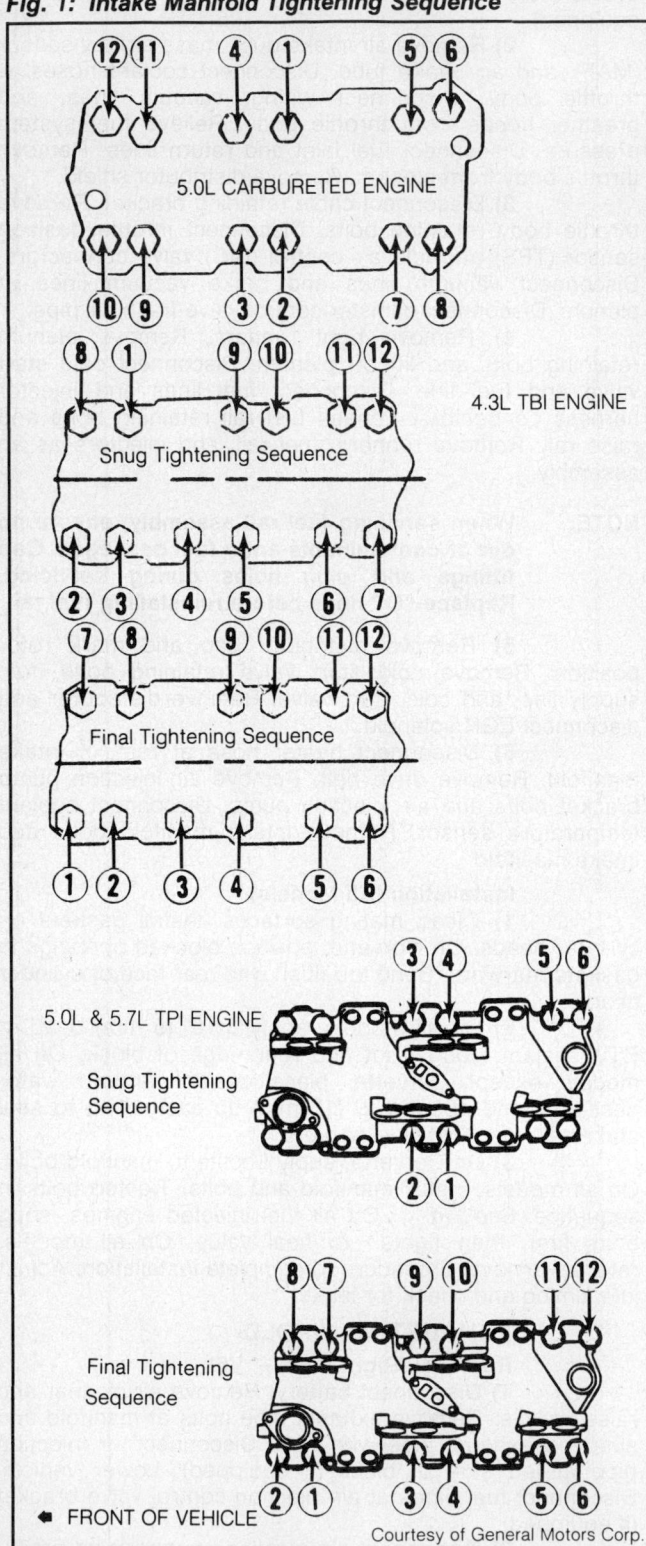

5.0L CARBURETED ENGINE

4.3L TBI ENGINE

Snug Tightening Sequence

Final Tightening Sequence

5.0L & 5.7L TPI ENGINE

Snug Tightening Sequence

Final Tightening Sequence

◄ FRONT OF VEHICLE

Courtesy of General Motors Corp.

Removal (Left Side – V6)
Disconnect negative battery cable. Raise vehicle. Remove exhaust pipe bolts. Remove A/C compressor and power steering pump (if equipped). Remove A/C and lower rear power steering adjusting braces (if equipped). Disconnect spark plug wires at plugs. Remove manifold bolts and manifold.

Removal (Right Side – Carbureted V8)
1) Disconnect battery. Raise vehicle. Disconnect exhaust pipe at manifold. Lower vehicle. Remove air cleaner. Disconnect spark plug wires. Disconnect vacuum hoses at early fuel evaporative valve. Disconnect air injection hose.

2) Loosen alternator drive belt. Remove lower alternator bracket and air injection valve. Disconnect air injection pipe at rear of manifold. Remove manifold bolts and manifold.

Removal (Left Side – Carbureted V8)
1) Disconnect battery. Raise vehicle. Remove exhaust pipe at manifold. Disconnect oxygen sensor connector. Lower vehicle. Disconnect air injection hose. Remove power steering pump (if equipped).

2) If equipped with A/C, loosen bracket at front of head. Remove rear bracket and remove compressor. Remove lower power steering pump adjusting bracket (if equipped). Remove manifold bolts. Disconnect wiring harness connector at valve cover and remove exhaust manifold.

Removal (Right Side – Camaro & Firebird EFI)
Disconnect negative battery cable. Disconnect spark plug wires. Disconnect air injection hoses. Remove air management valve. Raise vehicle. Remove exhaust pipe nuts at manifold and suspend exhaust pipe with wire. Lower vehicle. Remove dipstick tube. Remove manifold bolts and manifold.

Removal (Left Side – Camaro & Firebird EFI)
1) Disconnect negative battery cable. Disconnect spark plug wires. Disconnect air injection hoses. If equipped with A/C, remove compressor and lay aside without disconnecting hoses. Remove power steering pump and lay aside without disconnecting hoses (if equipped).

2) Loosen brackets. Remove rear A/C and power steering adjusting bracket (if equipped). Remove lower power steering adjusting bracket. Raise vehicle and remove exhaust pipe nuts. Lower vehicle. Remove manifold bolts and manifold.

Removal (Right Side – Corvette)
1) Disconnect negative battery cable. Remove plenum extension. Disconnect EGR wire and remove EGR pipe bolts at intake manifold. Remove rear A/C compressor brace and allow to hang at compressor. Remove dipstick tube.

2) Remove air injection check valve at manifold. Disconnect air injection hose at catalytic converter air pipe. Disconnect wire at temperature sending unit. Disconnect spark plug wires at plugs, head, and valve cover. Remove spark plugs. Raise vehicle.

3) Remove catalytic converter air injection pipe clamp at manifold. Disconnect exhaust crossover pipe at both manifolds. Remove bolts from catalytic converter front hanger. Remove catalytic converter air injection pipe. Lower vehicle.

4) Remove manifold bolts and manifold with EGR pipe attached. Remove EGR pipe clamp and pipe if manifold is being replaced.

Removal (Left Side – Corvette)
1) Disconnect negative battery cable. Remove air cleaner. Disconnect PCV hose from intake and rocker cover. Disconnect air injection hose at exhaust check valve.

2) Disconnect rear alternator brace at manifold and allow to hang from alternator. Raise vehicle and

4.3L V6, 5.0L (VIN F, G & H) & 5.7L V8 (Cont.)

disconnect exhaust pipe at manifold. Lower vehicle. Remove manifold bolts and manifold.

Installation (All Models)

Clean mating surfaces of manifolds and heads. Position manifold and install bolts finger tight. Reverse removal procedure to complete installation. Tighten bolts to specification.

CYLINDER HEAD

NOTE: **Check compression before removal of cylinder head. Remove when cold. Check for warped gasket surface, nicks or damage. If cylinder head refinishing is needed, DO NOT machine more than .006" (.15 mm) from gasket surface. Replace head if cracked. Remove burrs or scratches with oil stone.**

Removal (Except Corvette)

1) Remove intake and exhaust manifolds as previously described. Remove lower alternator mounting bolt and position alternator aside.

NOTE: **When removing valve covers, DO NOT distort sealing flange.**

2) Remove valve covers and rocker arm assemblies. Drain coolant. Remove diverter valve, head bolts and cylinder heads. Remove gaskets.

Removal (Right Side – Corvette)

1) Remove intake manifold as previously outlined. Disconnect air injection hose from exhaust check valve. Remove 2 rear A/C compressor braces and mounting bolt. Remove A/C compressor bracket nuts at water pump. Slide A/C compressor mounting bracket forward and disconnect wires.

2) Remove upper A/C compressor mounting bolt and remove compressor. Remove valve cover bolts. Bend bracket at rear of head and remove valve cover. Disconnect air injection hose at catalytic converter pipe check valve.

3) Remove spark plugs. Remove temperature sending unit. Disconnect air injection hose at exhaust manifold. Raise vehicle. Remove 2 rear exhaust manifold bolts. Disconnect exhaust pipe at manifold. Remove dipstick tube at manifold. Lower vehicle.

4) Remove remaining manifold bolts and manifold. Disconnect plug wire holder at rear of head. Loosen rocker arm nuts and remove push rods. Remove head bolts and cylinder head.

Removal (Left Side – Corvette)

1) Remove intake manifold as previously outlined. Remove alternator bolts and lay alternator aside. Remove valve cover bolts. Disconnect spark plug wires at spark plugs. Bend bracket at rear of head and remove valve cover. Disconnect air injection hose at exhaust check valve.

2) Raise vehicle. Disconnect exhaust pipe at manifold. Lower vehicle. Remove exhaust manifold and upper air injection pump bracket with power steering reservoir.

3) Disconnect plug wire holder and ground wire at rear of head. Disconnect temperature sending unit connector. Remove push rods, head bolts and cylinder head.

NOTE: **When servicing head, remove carbon deposits from combustion chamber with scraper**

and wire brush before removing valves. When disassembling, mark valve components for proper reassembly.

Installation (All Models)

1) Clean cylinder block and head mating surfaces of gasket material, carbon and dirt. Ensure mating surfaces are free of nicks or scratches.

2) Clean bolt hole threads in cylinder block to ensure proper bolt torque. If steel gaskets are used, apply thin, even coat of sealer to both sides of gasket.

3) On composition steel asbestos gaskets, DO NOT use sealer. Install gaskets over dowel pins with "bead" side up. Install cylinder heads.

NOTE: **Use ONLY composition head gaskets without sealer on Corvette models.**

4) Apply sealing compound to head bolt threads. Install and gradually tighten in sequence to specification. *See Fig. 2.* Reverse removal procedure to complete installation.

Fig. 2: Cylinder Head Tightening Sequence

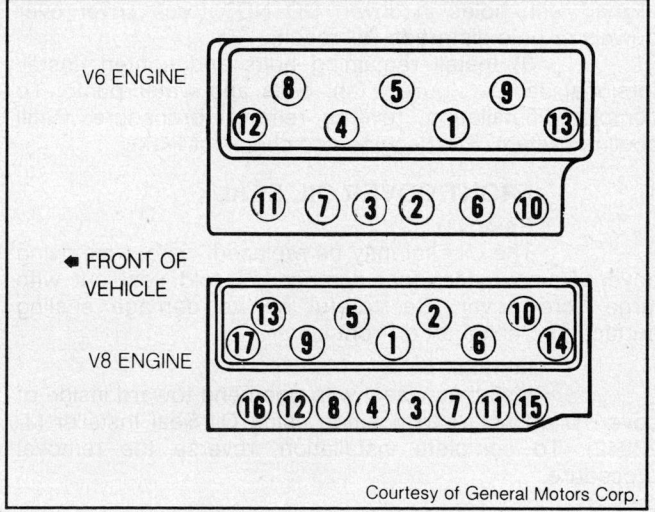

Courtesy of General Motors Corp.

CAMSHAFT

FRONT ENGINE COVER

Removal (Corvette)

1) Remove torsional damper as previously outlined. Remove air injection pump pulley and air management valve adapter. Remove air injection pump bolts and pump. Disconnect fuel inlet and return lines.

2) If equipped, remove rear A/C compressor braces and lower A/C mount bolts. Remove compressor bracket nuts at water pump. Slide mounting bracket forward and remove compressor mount bolt. Disconnect wires at compressor and lay unit aside.

3) Disconnect air injection hose at right exhaust manifold. Remove compressor mount bracket. Remove upper air injection pump bracket with power steering reservoir. Remove lower air injection pump bracket.

4) Drain cooling system. Disconnect radiator and heater hoses. Remove water pump. Remove front cover retaining bolts, cover and gasket.

Removal (All Other Models)

1) Remove torsional damper as previously outlined. Drain cooling system. Remove fan shroud or radiator upper support, as applicable. Remove fan and pulley from water pump hub.

2) Remove alternator upper and lower brackets, air brace and bracket. Remove power steering pump lower bracket (if equipped) from water pump and swing aside.

3) Remove radiator lower hose and heater hose from water pump. Remove water pump-to-block attaching bolts. Remove water pump. Remove front cover attaching screws, front cover, and gasket. Discard gasket.

Installation

1) Clean gasket surfaces. Apply gasket sealer to new gasket. Apply RTV sealer to joint formed where oil pan meets cylinder block (trim excess gasket material that protrudes at junction). Place gasket on cover. Install cover-to-oil pan seal. Place light coat of engine oil on bottom of seal.

2) Place cover over end of crankshaft and loosely install upper cover-to-block bolts. Tighten bolts alternately while pressing down on cover so dowels are aligned with holes in cover. DO NOT force cover over dowels or hole distortion will result.

3) Install remaining bolts and tighten. Install torsional damper, pulley, fan, belts and water pump. To complete installation, reverse removal procedure. Refill cooling system. Start engine and check for leaks.

FRONT COVER OIL SEAL

Removal

The oil seal may be replaced without removing cover. Remove torsional damper. Pry old seal out with large screwdriver. Be careful not to damage sealing surface of crankshaft or front cover.

Installation

Install new seal with open end toward inside of cover. Drive seal into position using Oil Seal Installer (J-23042). To complete installation, reverse the removal procedure.

TIMING CHAIN

Removal

Remove front cover. Using torsional damper retaining bolt to rotate crankshaft, align timing marks. Remove camshaft sprocket bolts. Use 2 large screwdrivers to alternately pry camshaft sprocket forward until free.

Installation

1) With camshaft installed, place timing chain over camshaft sprocket so it hangs below sprocket. Align marks on camshaft and crankshaft sprockets. See Fig. 3.

2) Align dowel in camshaft with dowel hole in camshaft sprocket and install sprocket. Use mounting bolts to draw sprocket onto camshaft. Tighten bolts. Check sprocket alignment, lubricate chain and install remaining components.

CAMSHAFT

Removal

1) Remove intake manifold and torsional damper as previously outlined. Remove front engine cover and water pump as previously described. Disconnect upper and lower transmission cooler lines (if equipped). Remove fan shroud, radiator (and grille, if necessary).

Fig. 3: Timing Chain Sprocket Alignment

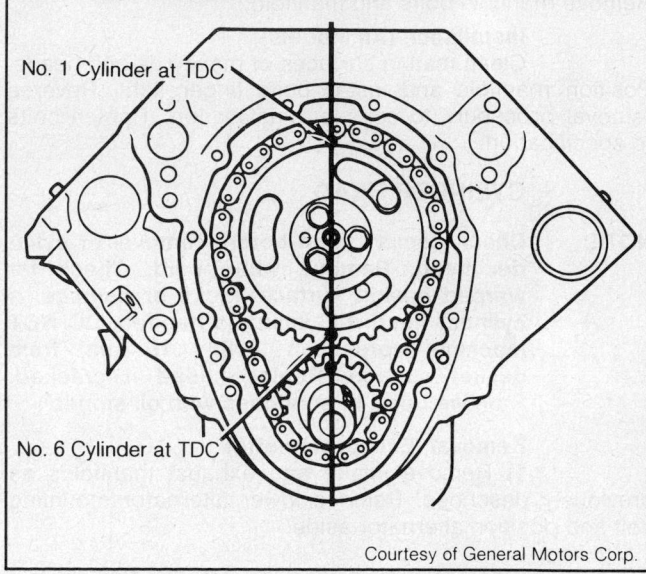

No. 1 Cylinder at TDC

No. 6 Cylinder at TDC

Courtesy of General Motors Corp.

2) Remove cooling fan. Remove power steering pump (if equipped). Remove drive belts, crankshaft pulley and torsional damper. If equipped, remove A/C compressor mount bolts, brackets, accumulator and compressor. Set unit aside. Remove air injection pump and brackets.

3) Remove water pump and front engine cover. Remove fuel pump (mechanical) push rod. Rotate crankshaft and align timing marks. Remove camshaft bolts, gear and chain. Install two 5/16"-18 x 4" bolts in camshaft bolt holes and carefully remove camshaft.

NOTE: All camshaft journals are same diameter. Use care when removing camshaft to prevent damage to lobes or journals.

Inspection

1) Check camshaft journals for out-of-round condition. If journals exceed .001" (.025 mm) out-of-round, replace camshaft and lifters. Check camshaft end play. Standard end play is .0040-.0012" (.102-.030 mm). If not to specification, check camshaft end cover for grooves or wear. Replace as necessary.

2) Check camshaft lobe lift. Attach dial indicator with a ball/socket attachment to camshaft carrier or "V" block. Measure lobe lift. If lobe lift loss is more than .002" (.05 mm), replace camshaft.

NOTE: Camshaft lobes are ground, hardened and tapered with high side of lobe toward rear of engine. This causes valve lifters to rotate.

Installation

Lubricate journals with engine oil and, on new camshafts, apply Molykote to camshaft lobes. Carefully install camshaft. Complete installation by reversing removal procedure.

CAMSHAFT BEARINGS

Removal

1) With crankshaft and camshaft removed, fasten rods against side of engine, out of the way. Drive rear camshaft plug out of block. Using Camshaft Bearing

4.3L V6, 5.0L (VIN F, G & H) & 5.7L V8 (Cont.)

Remover (J-6098), index pilot in front bearing and install puller screw through pilot.

2) Install tool with shoulder toward No. 2 bearing. Ensure enough threads are engaged. With 2 wrenches, hold puller screw while turning nut. With bearing pulled from bore, remove tool and bearing from screw. Remove No. 3 bearing in same manner.

3) Index pilot in rear bearing to pull rear intermediate (No. 4) bearing. Assemble remover on driver handle and remove front and rear bearings by driving toward center of block.

Installation
1) Install front and rear bearings first. These bearings act as guides for pilot and center remaining bearings being pulled into place. Assemble tool on driver handle. Align oil holes. Install camshaft front and rear bearings by driving toward center of block.

NOTE: **No. 1 bearing should be installed so oil holes are equal distance from 6 o'clock position; No. 2 through No. 4 bearings should be installed with oil holes at 5 o'clock position; No. 5 at 12 o'clock position.**

2) Using camshaft bearing remover, install 2 center bearings with oil holes aligned with holes in block. Coat camshaft plug with sealer. Plug should be installed flush to 1/32" (.79 mm) deep and parallel with block surface. Reverse removal procedure to complete installation.

VALVES

NOTE: **When reconditioning valves, ensure interference angles of valve and seat are not lapped out. Remove grooves and/or score marks from end of valve stem with oil stone. DO NOT remove more than .010" (.25 mm) from valve stem end.**

VALVE ARRANGEMENT
V6 Engines
E-I-E-I-I-E (Left bank, Front-to-rear).
E-I-I-E-I-E (Right bank, Front-to-rear).

V8 Engines
E-I-I-E-E-I-I-E (Both banks, Front-to-rear).

VALVE & VALVE GUIDE SERVICING
1) To check valve guide wear, insert valve with head positioned 1/16" above seat. Attach dial indicator to cylinder head. Position dial indicator stem against valve stem just above guide.

2) Move valve in guide and measure wear shown on indicator. If guide wear is excessive, ream to next oversize. Service valves are available in standard, .003", .015" and .030" oversize.

3) Clean valve guides. Reface valve seat if guide is reamed. If valve seat face is reground, check margin width dimension.

4) Check seats for proper angle and width. Measure valve seat runout. Runout should be within .002" (.05 mm) for intake and exhaust.

5) Use scraper to break (lightly chamfer or bevel) sharp top inside edge of guide. After guide repair, inspect valve stem end for wear. Valve stem end may be reconditioned by grinding to proper dimension at 90 degree angle.

6) Check valve head for warpage. DO NOT reface if knife edge will result. Knife edges lead to breakage, burning or preignition due to heat localizing on edge. Replace if edge of valve head is less than .031" (.79 mm) thick after grinding.

7) When new valves are installed or after grinding, measure valve stem height. Ensure there is at least .015" (.381 mm) minimum clearance between Gauge (BT-6428 or J-25289) surface and end of valve stem. Ensure distance between gauge surface and spring retainer is .005" (.13 mm) minimum.

8) If gauge-to-stem clearance is less than specification, remove valve and grind tip of stem at 90 degree angle for clearance.

VALVE SPRINGS
Removal (Cylinder Head Installed)
1) Rotate engine to TDC of compression stroke. Remove valve cover, spark plug, rocker arms and push rods on cylinder(s) to be serviced.

2) Install Air Line Adapter (J-23590) to spark plug port. Apply minimum of 140 psi (9.8 kg/cm²) line pressure to hold valves in place.

NOTE: **If air pressure fails to hold valve closed, remove cylinder head for inspection.**

3) Using Spring Compressor (J-5892), compress valve spring and remove valve locks, retainer cap (or rotator), spring and damper. Remove valve stem oil seal.

Removal (Cylinder Head Removed)
1) With rocker arm removed, compress valve spring using Spring Compressor (J-8062). Remove valve locks. Release compressor.

2) Remove valve retainer (or rotator), spring and damper, oil seals and shim(s). Keep components in order for installation in original location.

Inspection
1) Check valve spring for out of square with 90 degree straightedge. Out of square service limit is .0625" (1.588 mm) for intake and exhaust springs.

2) Check valve spring tension using Valve Spring Tester (J-8056). Springs must be within 10 lbs. of specified load at required height (without dampers).

CAUTION: Install shims only if necessary. DO NOT use more than 2 shims.

3) Check valve springs for proper installed height of 1.688-1.750" (42.88-44.45 mm). On Corvette, valve spring installed height is 1.72" (43.66 mm) intake and 1.59" (40.48 mm) exhaust.

4) Measure from top of valve seat to top of valve spring or bottom of valve retainer. If height is excessive, install .0625" (1.587 mm) valve spring seat shim. Ensure spring height with shim does not result in installed height under minimum specification.

Installation
To install, reverse removal procedure.

VALVE STEM OIL SEALS
Installation
1) Oil seals are installed on all valve stems and must be replaced when valve service is performed. To remove oil seals, see VALVE SPRING REMOVAL for disassembly procedure.

2) To reassemble, coat seals with oil. Install valve stem oil seal over stem and seat against cylinder head. Set shim, spring, damper, oil shedder and valve cap (or rotator) in place and compress spring.

3) Install oil seal on lower groove of stem. Ensure seal is flat and not twisted. Install retainer locks. Release valve spring compressor and remove air line adapter. After assembly, use Vacuum Applier (J-23994) to apply vacuum to valve cap. Ensure no air leaks past seal. To complete installation, reverse removal procedure.

ROCKER ARM STUDS

NOTE: Cylinder heads use pressed-in rocker arm studs. Replace studs with damaged threads or loose fit in head. Studs are available in standard, .003" and .013" oversize.

Removal

Remove valve cover and rocker arm assembly for stud needing repair. Place Rocker Arm Stud Puller (J-5802-1) over stud. Install flat washer and nut. Tighten nut until stud is removed.

Installation

1) Using Reamer (J-5715 for .003" and J-6036 for .013" oversize studs), ream stud hole for oversize stud, as necessary. DO NOT install oversize stud without reaming stud hole, as damage to head may occur.

2) Coat press fit area of stud with hypoid gear oil. Drive stud into place using Stud Guide (J-6880) and hammer. When stud guide bottoms on head, stud is at correct height.

VALVE ADJUSTMENT

1) To adjust valves, rotate crankshaft to No. 1 firing position and adjust following valves:

- V6 – Intake No. 1, 2 and 3.
  Exhaust No. 1, 5 and 6.
- V8 – Intake No. 1, 2, 5 and 7.
  Exhaust No. 1, 3, 4 and 8.

2) Adjust valves by backing off adjusting nut until lash is felt at push rod, then tighten until lash is removed. Tighten adjusting nut an additional one full turn.

3) Rotate crankshaft to No. 4 firing position on V6 engines or No. 6 firing position on V8 engines. Adjust following valves:

- V6 – Intake No. 4, 5 and 6.
  Exhaust No. 2, 3 and 4.
- V8 – Intake No. 3, 4, 6 and 8.
  Exhaust No. 2, 5, 6 and 7.

4) When adjustment is complete, install valve covers. Start engine and check timing and idle speed.

HYDRAULIC VALVE LIFTER ASSEMBLY

NOTE: Before replacing lifter for noisy operation, ensure noise is not caused by improper collapsed lifter gap, worn rocker arms, push rods or valve tips. If lifter assembly is stuck in bore, use lifter puller or magnet.

1) Hydraulic lifter assemblies must be installed in original locations. Remove valve cover and intake manifold. Loosen rocker arm and rotate for clearance from push rod. Remove push rod. On roller lifter equipped models, remove lifter restrictor retainer and lifter restrictor. On all models, using Hydraulic Lifter Puller (BT-6407 or J-3049) or magnet, remove lifters.

2) Clean and inspect but DO NOT mix components or positions. Parts are select-fitted and not interchangeable. If lifter is sticking, disassemble and clean dirt, metal chips or varnish from components. If lifter check valve is not functional, obstructions may prevent it from closing when cam lobe is moving lifter or check valve spring may be broken. *See Fig. 4.*

Fig. 4: Exploded View of Hydraulic Lifter Assembly

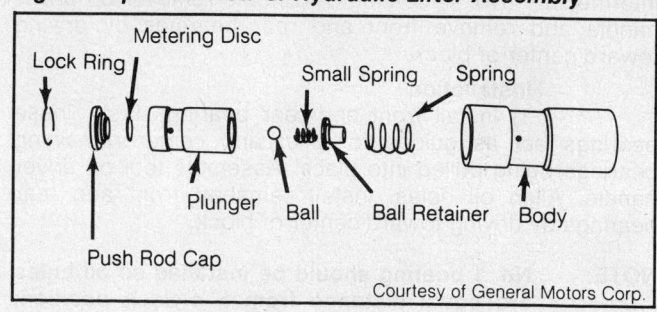

Courtesy of General Motors Corp.

3) Clean or replace components as necessary. If plunger is not free in body of lifter, replace entire assembly. Plunger should drop to bottom of body by its own weight when assembled dry. Assemble lifter and check free operation by pressing down on cap.

NOTE: Camshaft lobes are ground, hardened and tapered with high side of lobe toward rear of engine. This causes lifters to rotate.

4) Inspect lifter base-to-cam lobe contact area. Surface must have smooth and convex contact face. Replace any lifter with flat or concave surface. Inspect related cam lobe for proper lobe lift. Replace camshaft (and lifters) if any lobe is worn beyond specification.

5) Coat lifter base with Molykote. When installing, ensure lifter is on base circle of camshaft. Reverse removal procedure to complete installation. Coat gasket surfaces with RTV sealer.

PISTONS, PINS & RINGS

OIL PAN

See OIL PAN REMOVAL at end of ENGINE section.

PISTON & ROD ASSEMBLY

NOTE: When removing ridge at top of cylinder bore, never cut into ring travel area more than .03125" (.794 mm). Before removing piston and connecting rod, ensure rod caps are marked to their related rods for proper reassembly. DO NOT damage crankshaft journals or cylinder wall during removal.

Removal

1) With cylinder heads, oil pan, and oil pump removed, inspect cylinder bores for ridges and/or deposits. Move piston to be removed to bottom of bore and cover with cloth to catch cuttings.

2) Remove ridge at top of cylinder bores before removing pistons from block. Rotate crankshaft and inspect rods and caps for identification. Mark if necessary.

4.3L V6, 5.0L (VIN F, G & H) & 5.7L V8 (Cont.)

3) Remove rod cap and push each piston and rod assembly out top of cylinder bore. Remove bearing inserts from rod and cap. Inspect for size, wear and damage. Install rod caps on mating rods.

NOTE: Notch on piston top faces front of engine. V8 pistons are numbered from front-to-rear with No. 2-4-6-8 on right bank and No. 1-3-5-7 on left bank. V6 pistons are numbered from front-to-rear with No. 1-3-5 on left bank and No. 2-4-6 on right bank.

Installation

1) Check fit of new piston and/or rings in cylinder bore before assembling piston and pin to connecting rod. Install piston on connecting rod. Check piston pin for clearance, etching or wear. New pistons must be installed in cylinder for which they were fitted, used pistons in cylinders from which they were removed.

2) Measure cylinder bore diameter. Measure piston diameter (at skirt, across centerline of piston pin). Oil piston rings and cylinder walls. Ensure ring gaps are properly spaced. Install ring compressor on piston. Marked side of rings must be toward top of piston.

3) Position piston with identification marks on rod and cap on same side. Install rod bolt guide set or rubber sleeves before installing piston and rod assembly in bore. Insert piston/rod assembly into cylinder bore.

4) After bearings have been inserted, oil journals and bearings. Ensure oil hole in bearing aligns with oil hole in rod. Turn crankshaft throw to bottom of stroke. Guide piston/rod assembly over crankshaft journal until rod bearing seats.

5) Remove rod bolt protectors. Match rod cap to rod and install. Tighten cap nuts in two steps. Repeat for each piston assembly. After piston/rod assembly is installed, check side clearance of rod on each crankshaft journal.

FITTING PISTONS

1) Inspect pistons. Replace any showing signs of excessive wear, wavy ring lands, or fractures. Replace if sponge-like or eroded surface is on edge of piston top (caused by detonation or pre-ignition).

2) If shiny surface on thrust side of piston is found, check for bent connecting rod. DO NOT straighten rod, replace as necessary. Inspect rods for signs of fracture and bearing bores for out-of-round and taper. If bore exceeds limits and/or rod is fractured, replace rod.

3) Check pistons for fractures at ring lands, skirts and pin bosses. Check for scuffed, rough or scored skirts. When measuring piston for side clearance or taper, measurement must be made at centerline of pin bore and 90 degrees from piston pin hole.

4) Check piston-to-cylinder bore clearance. Inspect cylinder walls for scoring, roughness or wear. Check bore for out-of-round and taper. Standard bore out-of-round is .0010" (.025 mm). Maximum out-of-round is .0020" (.051 mm).

5) Cylinder bore taper should not be more than .0005" (.013 mm) for thrust side and .0010" (.025 mm) for relief side. If cylinder wall is severely marred and/or worn, refinishing is needed.

6) Before cylinder refinishing, ensure main bearing caps are in place and tightened to specification to avoid distortion during refinishing operation. Pistons are available in standard, standard high limit and .010" oversize.

FITTING RINGS

1) Clean ring grooves with ring groove cleaner or piece of broken ring. Ensure oil holes (or slots) in piston are clean. Measure piston ring side and end gap clearance for all pistons.

2) Ring side clearance should be checked with feeler gauge between ring and piston lower ring land. Gauge should slide freely around entire circumference without binding. If step has formed around inner portion of lower ring land, piston must be replaced.

3) Using piston to position ring in cylinder bore, check ring end gap at least .63" (16 mm) from bottom of bore. Install rings on pistons with end gaps staggered at proper intervals. Ensure ring gap is not in line with thrust face of pin bore. *See Fig. 5.*

Fig. 5: Piston Ring Gap Spacing

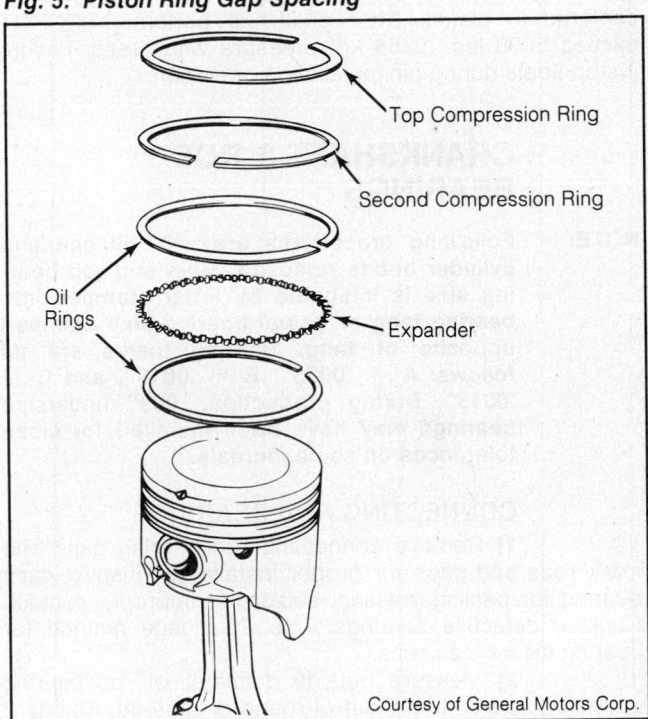

Top Compression Ring

Second Compression Ring

Oil Rings

Expander

Courtesy of General Motors Corp.

4) Be sure manufacturer's marks face up when rings are installed. Install oil ring expander first, followed by lower side rail and upper side rail. DO NOT use ring expander on side rails, use only on middle and top rings.

5) If new piston rings are to be installed and no cross-hatch marks remain on cylinder walls, remove cylinder glaze using spring-type hone. After honing, clean bore and block with soap/water solution and oil cylinder walls.

PISTON PINS

NOTE: When removing or installing piston pin, connecting rod should be in firm contact with body of pin setting tool.

Removal

1) Remove inserts from connecting rod and cap. Mark pistons, pins and inserts (if reusable) to assure assembly with same rod. Press pin from piston and rod using arbor press and Piston Pin Remover/Installer (J-24086-8 and 9).

General Motors Engines

4.3L V6, 5.0L (VIN F, G & H) & 5.7L V8 (Cont.)

2) Inspect and replace any piston pin showing signs of fracture, etching or wear. Check pin-to-rod bore fit. Check ID of rod pin bore. If pin bore in rod is larger than specification, replace rod.

3) Ensure proper fit by honing or reaming piston pin bore to light slip fit. If clearance exceeds .0010" (.025 mm), replace piston and pin assembly. Standard piston pin diameter is .9270-.9273" (23.54-23.55 mm). Lubricate pin and small end of rod bore with engine oil.

Installation

1) Check piston-to-cylinder bore clearance before assembling piston and pin to rod. Ensure oil hole in rod aligns with oil hole in bearing and arrow on top of piston is pointed toward front of engine.

2) Start piston pin in piston and rod. Using guide bar and push rod, press pin through both piston and rod until pilot hub bottoms on support fixture and/or pin is centered in piston. After pilot hub bottoms, DO NOT exceed 5000 lbs. (2268 kg) pressure with press. Ensure piston floats during pin installation operation.

CRANKSHAFT & ROD BEARINGS

NOTE: Following procedures are with oil pan and cylinder heads removed. Main and rod bearing size is indicated by letter stamped into bearing tang or actual bearing size stamped opposite of tang. Bearing marks are as follows: A = .0005", B = .0010", and C = .0015". During production, .009" undersize bearings may have been installed for close tolerances on some journals.

CONNECTING ROD BEARINGS

1) Remove connecting rod bearing caps and mark rods and caps for proper installation. Inspect each bearing for peeling, melting, seizure or improper contact. Replace defective bearings. Use Plastigage method for bearing clearance check.

2) Measure outside diameter of rod bearing journals to determine if out-of-round or tapered. Standard journal out-of-round and taper is .0005" (.013 mm). If journals are more than .0010" (.025 mm) out-of-round or tapered, crankshaft must be reconditioned or replaced.

NOTE: On Corvette models, the standard rod journal out-of-round is .0002" (.005 mm) and must not exceed .0010" (.025 mm). Standard rod journal taper is .0003" (.008 mm) and must not exceed .0010" (.025 mm).

3) When checking connecting rod clearances, do not support crankshaft. Instead, turn crankshaft until rod to be checked starts moving up, thus unloading lower bearing.

4) Cut Plastigage to same length as width of rod bearing. Place in bearing cap, parallel with crankshaft (not over oil hole or groove). Install rod bearings and cap and tighten. Always install caps with markings in original positions.

5) DO NOT turn crankshaft with Plastigage installed. Remove rod bearing cap from crankshaft and measure Plastigage at its widest part (using scale on Plastigage package). If clearance exceeds specifications, replace bearing.

NOTE: If clearance cannot be brought within specifications with service bearings, grind crankshaft to next undersize. If already ground to maximum undersize, replace crankshaft.

6) Selective fitting is required on each connecting rod. Service bearings are available in standard size, .001" and .002" undersize for new or used crankshaft. Bearings of .010" and .020" undersize are for use with reconditioned crankshafts. After inspection and/or replacement, coat bearing surfaces with oil. Tighten connecting rod bearing caps in two steps.

NOTE: Connecting rod bearing cap and rod identification numbers must remain on same side. Always replace bearings in pairs. Never use new bearing in combination with used bearing. Never file or grind connecting rods or caps when fitting bearings.

7) Check for shiny surface on either side of piston pin boss, indicating bent connecting rod. Twisted rods will not create identifiable wear patterns, but will disturb the action of entire crankshaft assembly and may cause excessive oil consumption.

8) Check connecting rod side clearance with dial gauge indicator resting against rod cap. Pull cap toward front of engine and zero gauge. Push cap toward rear of engine and compare readings. If excessive, replace rod and cap.

9) Standard connecting rod side clearance is .006-.014" (.15-.36 mm). If side clearance is less than specification, remove rod and cap. Check for scratches, burrs, nicks or dirt between crankshaft and rod. Dress minor imperfections with oil stone.

10) During assembly, ensure oil hole in bearing aligns with oil hole in connecting rod. Check bearing tangs are seated in appropriate slots in rod and cap. Ensure rod bolt heads are properly seated in rod.

MAIN BEARINGS

NOTE: Selective fit main bearings are used. If a .009" undersize and a .010" undersize bearings were used for precision fitting during production, the main bearing cap is painted Light Green on each side of affected journal. The crankshaft throw will also be stamped with a "9" on one side of undersize journal, and have a large spot of Light Green paint.

1) Inspect each bearing for peeling, melting, seizure or improper contact. Replace defective bearings.

NOTE: DO NOT scrape gum or varnish deposits, clean inserts and caps in solvent. DO NOT file or lap caps to obtain proper bearing clearance. If main bearing caps are replaced, shimming may be needed. Laminated shims are available in various sizes.

2) Measure outside diameter of crankshaft main bearing journals. Standard journal out-of-round and taper is .0002" (.005 mm). If journals are more than .0010" (.025 mm) out-of-round or tapered, crankshaft must be reconditioned or replaced.

NOTE: Observe location of high spots on main bearings. If high spots are not in line, crankshaft may be bent and should be checked.

4.3L V6, 5.0L (VIN F, G & H) & 5.7L V8 (Cont.)

3) To check main bearing clearance, shim adjacent main bearings to bearing being checked. Alternate method is to position jack under counterweight adjoining bearing being checked so weight of crankshaft will not compress Plastigage and provide incorrect reading.

4) DO NOT position jack under crankshaft pulley. Crankshaft post damage will result. With all bearing caps tight (other than one being checked), check clearances using Plastigage method. DO NOT turn crankshaft with Plastigage installed.

NOTE: New bearings are available in standard size and .0010", .0020", .0090", .010" and .020" undersize. Replace both upper and lower inserts together. If undersize bearings are used on more than one journal, position in cylinder block rather than bearing cap.

5) If standard and undersize bearing combination do not bring clearance within specified limits, crankshaft will have to be refinished and undersized bearings installed. If journal will not clean up to maximum undersize bearing, replace crankshaft. Remove and replace crankshaft sprocket as necessary.

NOTE: Crankshaft sprocket removal will require Sprocket Remover (J-5825). Sprocket installation will require Sprocket Installer (J-5590).

6) If journals are remachined, ensure same journal shoulder radius is reproduced. Too small a radius results in fatigue failure of crankshaft. Too large a radius results in bearing failure due to radial ride of bearing.

7) When journals are refinished, chamfer oil holes and polish journals with No. 320 grit polishing cloth and engine oil. After chamfer and polish operations, clean crankshaft in solvent and blow out oil passages with compressed air.

8) When main bearings are installed, ensure oil grooves on bearings are installed on same side. Oil new upper bearing and insert plain (unnotched) end between crankshaft and notched side of block. Rotate bearing into place. Ensure main bearing caps are installed with arrows pointing toward front of engine. Install main cap bolts and tighten.

NOTE: Some production engines may have rear main bearings where the distance between thrust faces is .008" wider than standard. Crankshaft will have .008" stamped on rear counterweight. Ensure proper distance between thrust faces is maintained if rear main bearings are replaced.

THRUST BEARING ALIGNMENT

1) Tighten main bearing cap bolts (except rear main) to specification. Tighten rear main bolts to 11 ft. lbs. (15 N.m). Tap end of crankshaft rearward and forward to line up main bearing thrust surfaces with crankshaft thrust face.

2) Tighten all main bearing cap bolts to specification. Rotate crankshaft to ensure there is no excessive drag. Measure end play at front end of rear main bearing using feeler gauge. Standard end play is .002-.006" (.05-.15 mm).

REAR MAIN BEARING OIL SEAL

NOTE: Always replace upper and lower seals as a unit. Lip of seals should face front of engine.

Removal

Remove oil pan and oil pump. Using notches provided in seal retainer, pry out seal with a screwdriver. DO NOT nick crankshaft sealing surface with screwdriver during removal.

Installation

Lubricate inside and outside diameters of seal with engine oil. Place seal on Seal Installer (J-35621). Thread screws of seal installer guide into rear of crankshaft. Using a screwdriver, tighten guide snugly. Tighten seal installer until it bottoms. Remove installer and guide. See Fig. 6.

Fig. 6: Installing Rear Main Bearing Oil Seal

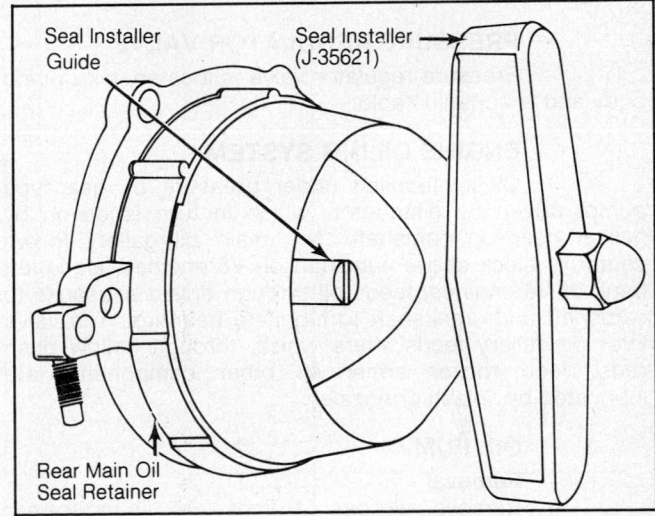

Seal Installer Guide

Seal Installer (J-35621)

Rear Main Oil Seal Retainer

TORSIONAL DAMPER

NOTE: The inertia weight section of torsional damper is assembled to hub with rubber sleeve. Removal and installation procedures (using proper tools) must be followed or movement of inertia weight section on hub will destroy tuning of damper and engine timing reference.

Removal

Disconnect negative battery cable. Remove accessory drive belt(s). Raise vehicle, if necessary, and remove crankshaft pulley and damper retaining nut. On Corvette, check clearance of power steering line and remove as necessary to mount Hub Puller/Installer (J-23523). Install puller/installer. Turn puller bolt and remove damper.

Installation

1) Coat front cover seal contact area on damper with oil. Place damper in position over key on crankshaft. Using hub puller/installer, position threaded end of tool on crankshaft, ensuring .50" (13 mm) of thread engagement.

2) Install remaining tool components and pull damper into position. Remove installer tool. Install crankshaft pulley. Install and tighten damper retaining bolts. Install accessory drive belt(s) and related components. Tighten belts, nuts and bolts.

ENGINE OILING

CRANKCASE CAPACITY

On 4.3L V6 engines, crankcase capacity with or without filter change is 4 qts. (3.8L).

On all V8 engines, crankcase capacity without filter change is 4 qts. (3.8L). Crankcase capacity with filter change is 5.0 qts. (4.7L).

NORMAL OIL PRESSURE

On all engines, oil pressure is 50-65 psi (3.5-4.6 kg/cm²) at 2000 RPM.

PRESSURE REGULATOR VALVE

Pressure regulator valve is located in oil pump body and is nonadjustable.

ENGINE OILING SYSTEM

Oil is supplied under pressure by gear-type pump, driven by distributor, which in turn is driven by helical gear on camshaft. The main oil gallery (down center of block above camshaft on V8 engines, along left bank of V6 engines) feeds oil through drilled passages to camshaft and crankshaft to lubricate bearings. The valve lifter oil gallery feeds lifters which, through hollow push rods, feed rocker arms. All other components are lubricated by splash or nozzle.

OIL PUMP

Removal

Remove oil pan. Remove oil pump-to-rear main bearing cap bolt. Remove oil pump and extension shaft.

Disassembly

1) Remove pump cover and mark gear teeth so they may be reassembled with same teeth indexing. Remove idler gear, drive gear and shaft from pump body. Remove pressure regulator valve retaining pin, valve and related parts. *See Fig. 7.*

Fig. 7: Exploded View of Oil Pump Assembly

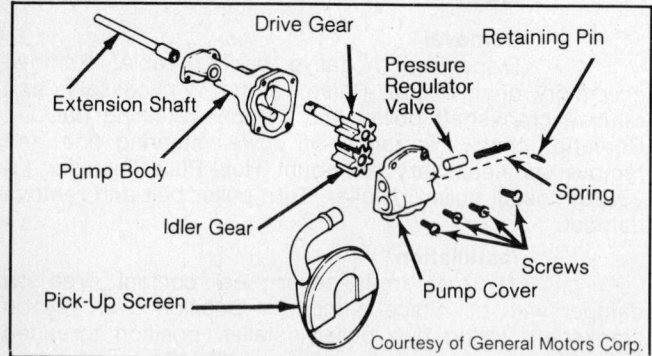

Courtesy of General Motors Corp.

2) If replacement is necessary, mount pump in soft-jawed vise and pull pick-up screen and pipe assembly from pump body. DO NOT disturb pick-up screen on pipe. This is serviced as an assembly.

Inspection

1) Check oil pump body for cracks or wear. Inspect pump gears for cracks, wear or damage. Check shaft for looseness in housing. Replace pump as a unit if any parts are not to specification.

2) Check inside of cover for wear which would permit oil to leak past ends of gears. Check oil pick-up screen for damage to screen or relief grommet. Remove debris from surface of screen.

3) When assembling oil pump, fill cavities with petroleum jelly to ensure immediate oil pressure. Install cover, tighten bolts and ensure shaft turns freely. Install regulator valve plunger, spring, retainer and pin.

Reassembly

1) If pick-up screen and pipe assembly was removed, replacement with new part is necessary. Loss of press fit could result in air leak and loss of oil pressure.

NOTE: **When installing new oil pump pipe assembly, be careful of twisting, shearing or collapsing pipe.**

2) Apply sealer to end of replacement pick-up tube. Using Oil Pump Pipe Installer (J-8369), tap tube in place with plastic hammer. Install pressure regulator valve and related parts.

3) Install drive gear and shaft in pump body. Install idler gear in pump body with smooth side of gear toward opening. Install pump cover. Turn drive shaft to ensure smooth operation.

Installation

Install pump and extension shaft to rear main bearing cap. Align slot on top end of extension shaft with drive tang on lower end of distributor drive shaft. Install pump to rear main bearing cap bolt and tighten.

ENGINE COOLING

WATER PUMP

Removal

1) Disconnect battery. Drain cooling system. Remove fan shroud or upper radiator support, if necessary. Remove drive belt(s). Remove fan and pulley. Remove upper and lower alternator brackets and power steering pump lower bracket from water pump (if equipped) and swing aside.

2) On Corvette, remove air injection pump pulley, brackets, air management valve adapter, and air injection pump. Disconnect fuel inlet and return lines. Remove A/C compressor brackets, wires, mount bolts and compressor. Remove right and left air injection hoses at check valve.

3) Remove air injection pipe at intake and power steering reservoir bracket. On all models, remove lower radiator hose and heater hose from water pump. Remove water pump-to-block attaching bolts and pump.

Installation

To install, reverse removal procedure. If using a new pump, transfer pulley and heater hose fitting from old pump. Use new gasket.

NOTE: **For further information on cooling systems, see ENGINE COOLING section.**

4.3L V6, 5.0L (VIN F, G & H) & 5.7L V8 (Cont.)

ENGINE SPECIFICATIONS

GENERAL SPECIFICATIONS

| Year | DISPLACEMENT | | Fuel System | HP@RPM | Torque Ft. Lbs.@RPM | Compr. Ratio | BORE | | STROKE | |
	Cu. In.	Liters					In.	mm	In.	mm
1988	262	4.3	TBI	140@4000	225@2000	9.3:1	4.00	101.6	3.48	88.4
	305	5.0	4-Bbl.	150@4000	240@2000	8.6:1	3.74	95.0	3.48	88.4
	305	5.0	4-Bbl.	190@4800	240@3200	9.5:1	3.74	95.0	3.48	88.4
	305	5.0	TBI	210@4400	270@3200	9.5:1	3.74	95.0	3.48	88.4
	350	5.7	4-Bbl.	.....	.....	8.2:1	4.00	101.6	3.48	88.4
	350	5.7	TPI	230@4000	330@3200	9.0:1	4.00	101.6	3.48	88.4

VALVES

Engine Size & Valve	Head Diam. In. (mm)	Face Angle	Seat Angle	Seat Width In. (mm)	Stem Diameter In. (mm)	Stem Clearance In. (mm)	Valve Lift In. (mm)
4.3L & 5.7L							
Intake	1.94 (49.28)	45°	46°	.031-.063 (.79-1.60)	.3410-.3417 (8.661-8.679)	.0010-.0027 (.025-.069)	.....
Exhaust	1.50 (38.1)	45°	46°	.063-.094 (1.60-2.39)	.3410-.3417 (8.661-8.679)	.0010-.0027 (.025-.069)	.....
5.0L							
Intake	1.84 (46.73)	45°	46°	.031-.063 (.79-1.60)	.3410-.3417 (8.661-8.679)	.0010-.0027 (.025-.069)	.....
Exhaust	1.50 (38.1)	45°	46°	.063-.094 (1.60-2.39)	.3410-.3417 (8.661-8.679)	.0010-.0027 (.025-.069)	.....

PISTONS, PINS & RINGS

Engine	PISTONS Clearance In. (mm)	PINS Piston Fit In. (mm)	PINS Rod Fit In. (mm)	RINGS Ring No.	RINGS End Gap In. (mm)	RINGS Side Clearance In. (mm)
4.3L, 5.0L & 5.7L	.0007-.0017 (.018-.043)	.00025-.00035 (.0064-.0089)	.0008-.0016 (.020-.040) Press Fit	1	.010-.020 (.25-.51)	.0012-.0032 (.030-.081)
				2	.010-.025 (.25-.64)	.0012-.0032 (.030-.081)
				3	.015-.055 (.38-1.40)	.002-.007 (.051-.178)

CRANKSHAFT MAIN & CONNECTING ROD BEARINGS

Engine	MAIN BEARINGS Journal Diam. In. (mm)	MAIN BEARINGS Clearance In. (mm)	MAIN BEARINGS Thrust Bearing	MAIN BEARINGS Crankshaft End Play In. (mm)	CONNECTING ROD BEARINGS Journal Diam. In. (mm)	CONNECTING ROD BEARINGS Clearance In. (mm)	CONNECTING ROD BEARINGS Side Play In. (mm)
4.3L, 5.0L & 5.7L	[1] 2.4484-2.4493 (62.189-62.212)	[2] .0008-.0020 (.020-.050)	.....	.002-.006 (.05-.15)	[4] 2.0986-2.0998 (53.304-53.335)	.0013-.0035 (.033-.089)	.006-.014 (.15-.36)

[1] – Front is given; rear 2.4479-2.4488" (62.177-62.199 mm), Intermediate 2.4481-2.4490" (62.182-62.205 mm).
[2] – Front is given; rear .0017-.0032" (.043-.081 mm), Intermediate .0011-.0023" (.028-.058 mm).
[3] – 4.3L is No. 4; 5.0L & 5.7L are No. 5.
[4] – V8 is given; V6 is 2.2487-2.2498" (57.117-57.125 mm).

General Motors Engines

4.3L V6, 5.0L (VIN F, G & H) & 5.7L V8 (Cont.)

ENGINE SPECIFICATIONS (Cont.)

CAUTION: The following specifications apply only to 5.7L engines and 5.0L engines with a engine VIN code of F, G or H.

CAMSHAFT

Engine	Journal Diam. In. (mm)	Clearance In. (mm)	Lobe Lift In. (mm)
4.3L	1.8682-1.8692 (47.452-47.478)	.....	Int. .234 (5.94) Exh. .257 (6.53)
5.0L 4-Bbl.	1.8682-1.8692 (47.452-47.478)	.....	Int. .234 (5.94) Exh. .257 (6.53)
5.0L HO, TBI & TPI	1.8682-1.8692 (47.452-47.478)	.....	Int. .269 (6.83) Exh. .276 (7.01)
5.7L 4-Bbl.	1.8682-1.8692 (47.452-47.478)	.....	Int. .257 (6.53) Exh. .269 (6.83)
5.7L TPI	1.8682-1.8692 (47.452-47.478)	.....	Int. .273 (6.93) Exh. .282 (7.16)

TIGHTENING SPECIFICATIONS (VIN F, G & H)

Application	Ft. Lbs. (N.m)
Camshaft Sprocket Bolts	20 (27)
Clutch Pressure Plate Bolts	30 (41)
Connecting Rod Cap Nuts	45 (61)
Cylinder Head Bolts	67 (91)
Exhaust Manifold Bolts	20 (27)
Flywheel-to-Crankshaft Bolts	60 (81)
Intake Manifold Bolts	35 (47)
Main Bearing Cap Bolts	80 (108)
Oil Pump Bolts	65 (88)
Torsional Damper Bolt	70 (94)
Water Pump Bolts	30 (41)

	INCH Lbs. (N.m)
Crankcase Front Cover Nuts	80 (9)

VALVE SPRINGS

Engine	Free Length In. (mm)	PRESSURE Lbs. @ In. (Kg @ mm)	
		Valve Closed	Valve Open
4.3L, 5.0L & 5.7L	[1] 2.03 (51.56)	[2] 76-84 @ 1.70 (34-38 @ 43.2)	[3] 194-206 @ 1.25 (88-93 @ 31.8)

[1] – Damper spring free length for all engines is 1.86" (47.2 mm).

[2] – 5.7L TPI Intake is given. Exhaust is 76-84 @ 1.61 (34-38 @ 40.9).

[3] – 5.7L TPI Intake is given. Exhaust is 194-206 @ 1.16 (88-93 @ 29.5).

5.0L (VIN Y) V8

NOTE: For engine repair procedures not covered in this article, see ENGINE OVERHAUL PROCEDURES article at beginning of this section.

ENGINE CODING

ENGINE IDENTIFICATION

Engine may be identified from Vehicle Identification Number (VIN). The VIN is on a plate on top of instrument panel, at lower left corner of windshield. VIN number also appears as part of production or unit number on pad fastened to front of block, just below left cylinder head. The VIN number contains 18 characters. The 9th character identifies engine. The 11th character identifies model year. Stick on labels attached to engine identifies engine unit number and code.

ENGINE CODE

Engine	Code
5.0L (307") 4-Bbl.	Y

ENGINE REMOVAL

See ENGINE REMOVAL & INSTALLATION at end of ENGINE section.

CYLINDER HEAD & MANIFOLDS

INTAKE MANIFOLD

Removal

1) Disconnect battery negative cable and drain coolant. Remove air cleaner assembly. Remove AIR crossover tube. Disconnect upper radiator hose and thermostat by-pass hose. Disconnect coolant hoses at manifold. Disconnect fuel and vacuum lines.

2) Disconnect throttle and detent cables from carburetor. Remove temperature sensor and wires. Remove alternator, A/C compressor and brackets. DO NOT discharge A/C. Remove cruise control servo and bracket (if equipped). Remove carburetor solenoid or idle control unit. Remove EGR valve. Remove intake manifold bolts and manifold.

Installation

1) Clean sealing surfaces of manifold, block and cylinder heads. Coat new intake manifold gasket with

Fig. 1: Intake Manifold Tightening Sequence

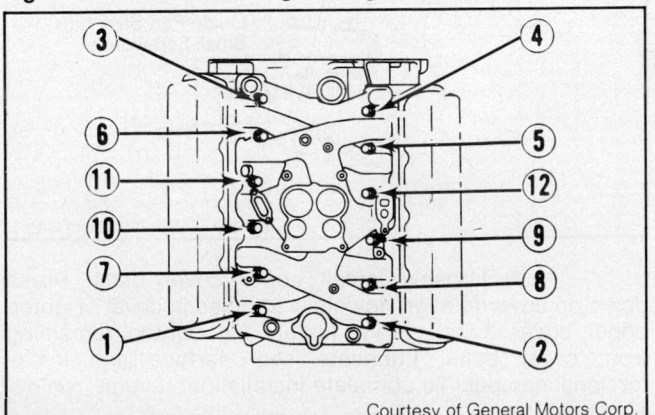

Courtesy of General Motors Corp.

RTV sealer. Apply bead of sealer on front and rear sealing surfaces of cylinder block.

2) Extend bead of sealer 1/2" up each cylinder head to seal and retain manifold side gaskets. Use sealer at water passages. Install gasket and end seals. Ensure end of seals are positioned under edges of heads.

3) Install manifold. Coat bolts threads with oil and install. Tighten bolts in sequence using 2 steps. See Fig. 1. Reverse removal procedure to complete installation.

EXHAUST MANIFOLD

Removal (Left Side)

1) Disconnect battery negative cable and spark plug wires. Remove air cleaner. Bend exhaust manifold locking tabs back.

Fig. 2: Exhaust Manifold Hot Air Shrouds

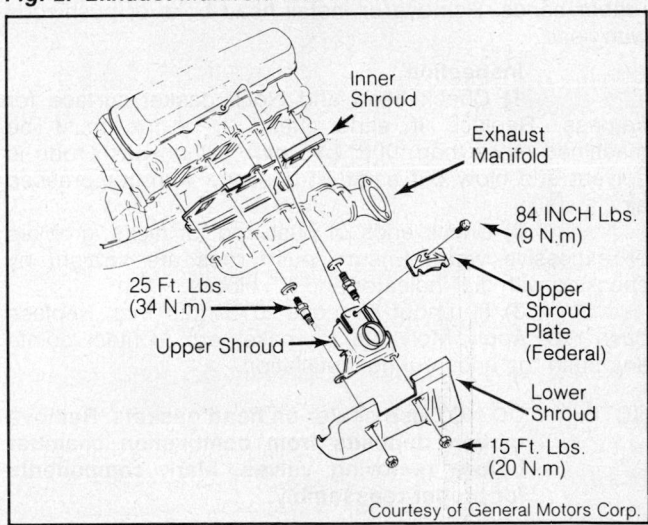

Courtesy of General Motors Corp.

2) Remove exhaust heat shroud(s). See Fig. 2. If necessary, remove lower power steering and/or alternator adjusting brackets. Raise and support vehicle. Disconnect exhaust pipe.

3) Lower vehicle. Disconnect intermediate steering column shaft. Remove lower alternator bracket. Loosen manifold retaining bolts from outside-to-inside (with engine cold). Remove exhaust manifold.

Removal (Right Side)

Disconnect battery negative cable and spark plug wires. Remove exhaust heat shrouds (if equipped). Remove oxygen sensor lead. Raise and support vehicle. Disconnect exhaust crossover pipe and exhaust inlet pipe. Remove oil filter adapter. Remove right front tire. Remove exhaust manifold. Lower vehicle.

Installation

Clean mating surfaces of exhaust manifold and cylinder head. Position manifold and install retaining bolts finger tight. Tighten bolts in 2 steps. To complete installation, reverse removal procedure.

CYLINDER HEAD

NOTE: Check compression before removal. Check for warped gasket surface, nicks or damage. If refinishing is needed, DO NOT machine more than .006" (.152 mm) from gasket surface.

5.0L (VIN Y) V8 (Cont.)

Removal

1) Disconnect battery negative cable and drain coolant. Remove intake and exhaust manifolds. Remove valve covers, rocker arm bolts, rocker arm pivots, rocker arms and push rods. Note component locations for reassembly reference.

NOTE: When removing valve covers, DO NOT distort sealing flange.

2) Remove accessory brackets as necessary. Remove diverter valve (if equipped). Disconnect ground strap. Remove head bolts, head and gasket. Place assembly on wood blocks to prevent gasket surface damage.

3) If clearance problem is found when removing No. 7 or No. 8 head bolts or push rods, pull components out enough to clear block and secure with rubber bands. Remove or install head bolts or push rods with head.

Inspection

1) Check head and block gasket surface for flatness. Replace if either head or block must be machined more than .006" (.15 mm). Clean push rods in solvent and blow out each oil passage with compressed air.

2) Check ends of push rod for nicks, grooves or excessive wear. Ensure push rods are straight by checking with dial indicator and "V" blocks.

3) If runout exceeds .015" (.38 mm), replace push rod. Apply Molykote to rocker arm contact points and push rod ends during installation.

NOTE: DO NOT use sealer on head gaskets. Remove carbon deposits from combustion chamber before removing valves. Mark components for proper reassembly.

Installation

1) Clean gasket surfaces. Install head gasket onto dowel pins. Install cylinder head over dowel pins and gasket. Dip head bolt threads in oil and install.

2) Tighten bolts before installing rocker arms and pivots if clearance problem is encountered. Tighten head bolts in correct sequence, in 2 steps. See Fig. 3. To complete installation, reverse removal procedure.

Fig. 3: Cylinder Head Tightening Sequence

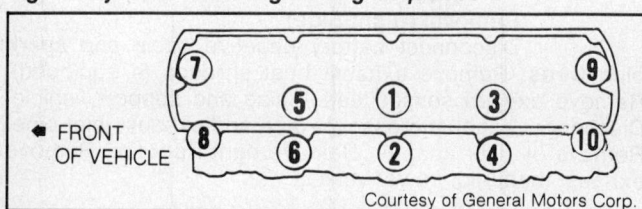

Courtesy of General Motors Corp.

CAMSHAFT

ENGINE FRONT COVER
Removal

1) Drain coolant. Disconnect transmission oil cooler lines and radiator hoses. Remove fan shroud and radiator. Remove power steering pump with hoses attached and lay aside. Remove belts, fan, fan pulley and crankshaft pulley.

2) Remove engine damper. Remove water pump. Remove front cover attaching bolts. Remove front cover and timing indicator. Remove 2 dowel pins.

Installation

1) Clean gasket surfaces of block and front cover. Lightly grind chamfer in one end of each dowel pin. On each side of block, cut excess gasket material from end of oil pan gasket. See Fig. 4. Apply RTV sealant to joint at oil pan and cylinder block.

Fig. 4: Oil Pan-to-Front Cover Gasket & Seal

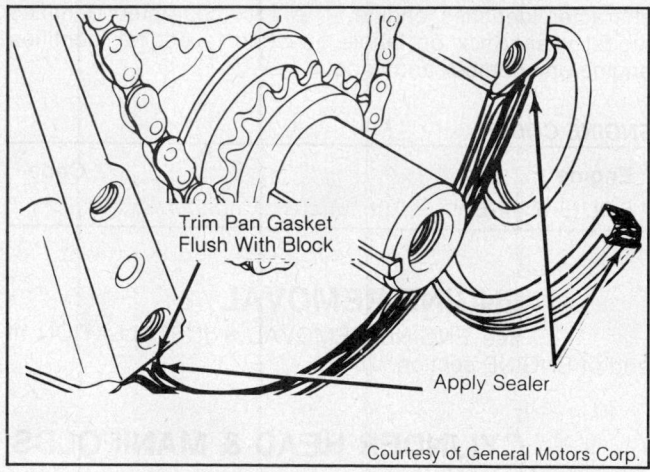

Courtesy of General Motors Corp.

2) Coat new front cover gasket with sealer and place in position. Install new cover-to-oil pan gasket (coat lightly with oil). Position cover over crankshaft end. Rotate cover left and right while guiding seal into cavity with small screwdriver. See Fig. 5.

Fig. 5: Installing Front Cover

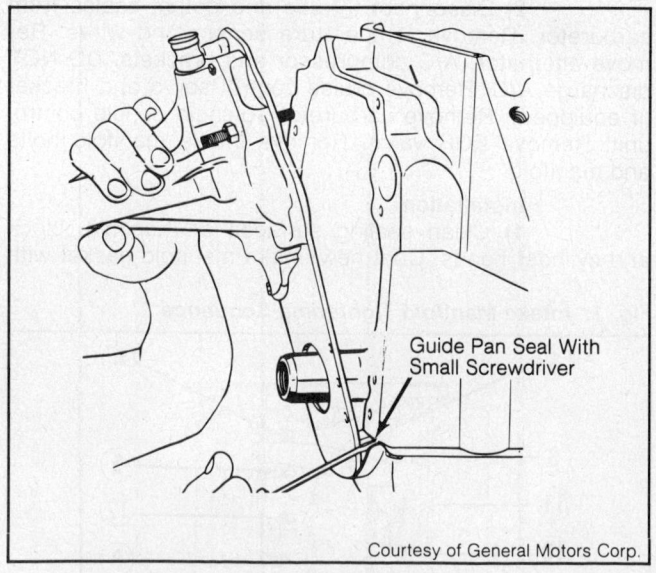

Courtesy of General Motors Corp.

3) Loosely install upper cover bolts. Press down on cover to align dowels with holes in cover. Tighten upper cover bolts evenly. Install and tighten remaining front cover bolts. Lubricate seal surface and install torsional damper. To complete installation, reverse removal procedure.

5.0L (VIN Y) V8 (Cont.)

FRONT COVER OIL SEAL

Removal

Remove crankshaft pulley and engine damper. Remove oil seal using Seal Remover (J-25264). Use caution to avoid damaging seal surface or front cover.

Installation

Apply sealant to outside diameter of seal. Lightly coat inner diameter of seal with engine oil. Install seal partway into front cover (open side in). Use Seal Installer (J-25264) to drive seal in completely. Use care not to

TIMING CHAIN

Removal

Remove front cover, fuel pump eccentric and oil slinger. Remove camshaft sprocket and timing chain. Remove camshaft sprocket key. Use Sprocket Remover (J-25287) to remove crankshaft sprocket.

NOTE: **Always remove camshaft sprocket key before using sprocket remover.**

Installation

1) Slide camshaft gear, crankshaft gear and timing shain on to shafts as an assembly. The crankshaft gear timing mark should be pointing up. The crankshaft keyway should be in about the 2 o'clock position. See Fig. 6.

Fig. 6: Timing Chain Sprocket Alignment

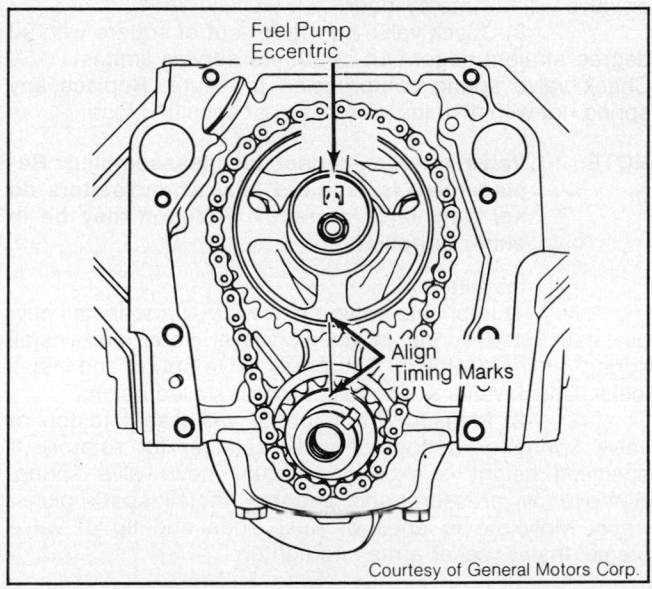

Fuel Pump Eccentric

Align Timing Marks

Courtesy of General Motors Corp.

NOTE: **When timing marks are aligned, No. 6 piston is at TDC. To obtain TDC for cylinder No. 1, rotate crankshaft one revolution. Verify camshaft and crankshaft sprocket timing marks are pointing up.**

2) Install fuel pump eccentric. Drive crankshaft sprocket key fully into place. Install oil slinger, front cover and related components.

CAMSHAFT

Removal

1) Disconnect negative battery cable and drain coolant. Remove radiator, radiator hoses and support clamp. Disconnect wiring as necessary. Remove distributor cap and wires. Drain engine oil.

2) Remove crankshaft pulley, engine damper and front pulley. Remove valve covers, intake manifold and manifold gaskets/seals. Remove rocker arms, push rods and lifters.

3) Discharge A/C system (if equipped) and remove condenser. Remove air pump, power steering pump, fan, fan clutch, and water pump. Remove alternator bracket and move alternator aside. Remove timing chain cover. Remove fuel pump eccentric, oil slinger and timing chain. Carefully slide camshaft out of engine.

Inspection

1) Measure camshaft journals. Check camshaft end play. If camshaft end play exceeds specification, check end plate for wear or grooves. Replace if necessary.

2) Check camshaft journal clearance. Compare camshaft lobe lift. If lobe lift less than specification, replace camshaft and lifters.

NOTE: **Before installation, coat camshaft lobes with Molycote lubricant. Install new lifters when installing a new camshaft.**

Installation

Carefully slide camshaft into engine. To complete installation, reverse removal procedure.

CAMSHAFT BEARINGS

Removal

Remove oil pan, camshaft and related components. Use Bearing Remover/Installer (J-33049) to remove camshaft bearings.

Installation

NOTE: **Bearing installation order is critical because each bearing is a different size. All bearings must be removed and discarded before a new bearing can be installed.**

1) Place camshaft bearing on bearing installer. Position bearing on installer so oil hole in bearing lines up with oil hole in journal and install. Repeat procedure with remaining bearings. Make a final check to verify all bearing oil holes line up with journal oil holes.

2) Coat outside diameter of rear plug with sealant. Install plug .15-.19" (3.8-4.8 mm) deep in bore. Coat camshaft lobes and journals with Molykote and carefully install. To complete installation, reverse removal procedure.

VALVES

CAUTION: **DO NOT lap new valves. Protective coating on valve face will be destroyed. If valve stem end refinishing is necessary, do not remove more than .010" (.25 mm) from valve end.**

5.0L (VIN Y) V8 (Cont.)

VALVE ARRANGEMENT

I-E-I-E-E-I-E-I (Front-to-rear, both banks).

VALVE & VALVE GUIDE SERVICING

1) Guides are integral with head. Valves are available in oversizes. With head removed and disassembled, check valve stem-to-guide clearance. If clearance exceeds specification, ream guide to next oversize.

2) Inspect valve stem end for wear. Valve stem end may be reconditioned by grinding to proper dimension at 90 degree angle. If valve seat face is reground, check margin width dimension. Check seats for proper angle and width.

3) Measure valve seat runout. Maximum runout is .002" (.05 mm) for intake valves and .004" (.10 mm) for exhaust valves. Intake seat width is .037-.075" (.94-1.90 mm). Exhaust seat width is .050-.100" (1.27-2.54 mm). Use scraper to break (lightly chamfer or bevel) sharp top inside edge of guide.

4) Check valve head for warpage. Do not reface valve if warped. Valve must be replaced if knife edge will result after refacing. Whenever new valves are installed or after grinding valves or seats, measure valve stem height.

5) Using Valve Stem Height Gauge (J-25289 or BT-6428), check for .015" (.38 mm) minimum clearance between gauge surface and end of valve stem.

6) If gauge-to-stem clearance is less than specified, remove valve and grind tip of valve stem at 90 degree angle to gain proper clearance. If valve stem end is less than .005" (.13 mm) above spring retainer, replace valve.

VALVE STEM OIL SEALS

1) "Umbrella" type seals are used on all valves. If valve or valve seat has not been damaged, valve springs, seals and retainers may be removed by holding affected valve against seat using air pressure. Install air line with adapter in spark plug hole. Apply a minimum of 140 psi (9.8 kg/cm²) line pressure.

2) After removing rocker arm, install rocker arm bolt. Insert slotted end of Valve Spring Compressor

Fig. 7: Rocker Arm & Valve Assembly

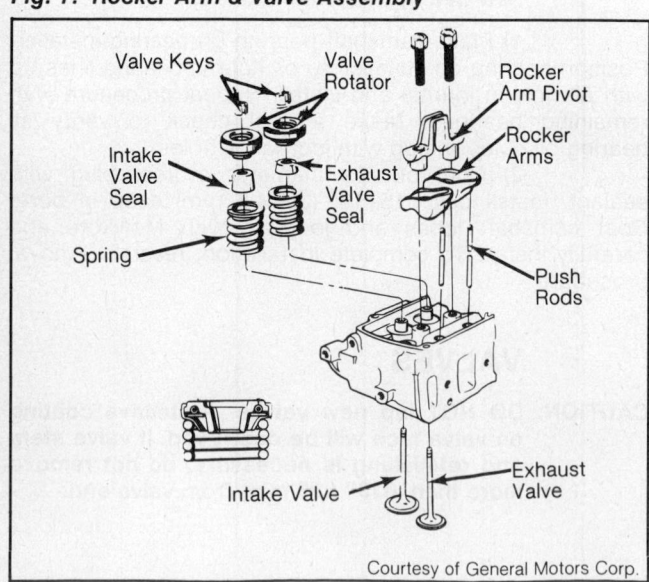

Intake Valve
Exhaust Valve

Valve Keys
Valve Rotator
Rocker Arm Pivot
Rocker Arms
Intake Valve Seal
Exhaust Valve Seal
Spring
Push Rods

Courtesy of General Motors Corp.

(J-25892-1) under rocker bolt head. Compress valve spring. Remove valve retainer locks. Remove tool, retainer, spring and oil seal.

3) To install, reverse removal procedure. Install oil seal protector cap over end of valve stem and start stem seal carefully over cap. Push seal down until seal jacket touches top of valve guide. Remove plastic seal protector cap. Using Valve Seal Installer (J-26251), bottom seal on valve guide.

4) Friction surfaces of rocker arms and pivots must be coated with lubricant upon reassembly and installed in original locations. *See Fig. 7.* Tighten hardened flanged bolts alternately to prevent breaking pivots.

VALVE SPRINGS

Removal

1) Remove valve cover and spark plug for cylinder to be serviced. Ensure piston is at top of stroke with both valves closed. Install air line with adapter in spark plug hole. Apply minimum of 140 psi (9.8 kg/cm²) line pressure.

NOTE: If air pressure fails to hold valve closed, remove cylinder head for inspection.

2) Remove required rocker arm and push rod. Use spring compressor to compress valve and remove retainer locks, spring retainer (or rotator) and valve spring. Remove and discard oil seal. Do not remove air pressure or valve will fall into cylinder.

3) Check valve spring for out of square with 90 degree straight edge. Out of square service limit is 1/16". Check valve spring compression pressure. Replace any spring not within 10 lbs. (0.454 kg) of specified load.

NOTE: Valve rotators cannot be disassembled. Replacement is required only when rotators do not turn valve correctly. Rotation may be in either direction.

Installation

1) Lubricate valve stem with oil and install new oil seal. Place spring in position over valve and install spring retainer (rotator). Compress valve spring and install locks. Check valve spring for proper installed height.

2) Measure from top of valve seat to top of valve spring or bottom of valve retainer (or rotator). If specified height is exceeded, install new valve spring. Remove air pressure and adapter. Install spark plugs. Apply Molykote to ends of push rods and tip of valve stems. Install rocker arms and tighten.

HYDRAULIC ROLLER LIFTER ASSEMBLY

NOTE: The 5.0L engine uses hydraulic roller lifters for reduced fiction on camshaft lobes. An "O" stamped in side of lifter bore indicates .010" oversize lifters.

1) Clean and inspect components. DO NOT mix component positions. Parts are select-fit and not interchangeable. If lifter is sticking, disassemble and clean dirt, metal chips or varnish from components.

2) If plunger is not free in lifter body, replace lifter. Plunger should drop to bottom of body easily when assembled dry. Assemble lifter and check operation by pressing down on cap.

5.0L (VIN Y) V8 (Cont.)

3) Inspect lifter roller lobe contact area. Surface must be free of pits and must roll freely with no binding. Replace any lifter with scored or worn body surface. Inspect related cam lobe(s) for proper lobe lift. Replace camshaft and lifters if worn.

4) Check lifter-to-bore clearance. Standard clearance is .0005-.0022" (.013-.056 mm). Check lifter leak-down rate. With 50 lbs. of pressure, leak down should take 12-87 seconds. Replace any lifter not within specification. *See Fig. 8.*

Fig. 8: Exploded View of Hydraulic Lifter Assembly

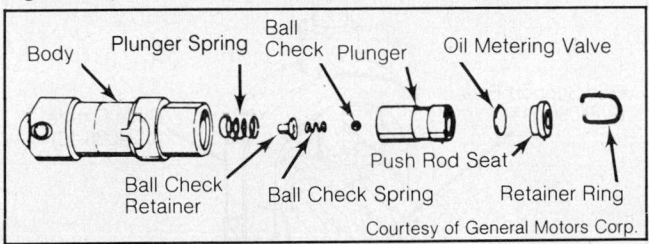

Courtesy of General Motors Corp.

5) Coat lifter base with Molykote. When installing, ensure lifter is on base circle of camshaft and straight (in relation to lobe). Tighten lifter guide and retainer. *See Fig. 9.* Tighten rocker arm bolts. Coat gasket surfaces with RTV sealer and install valve covers and intake manifold.

Fig. 9: Exploded View of Valve Lifter & Retainer

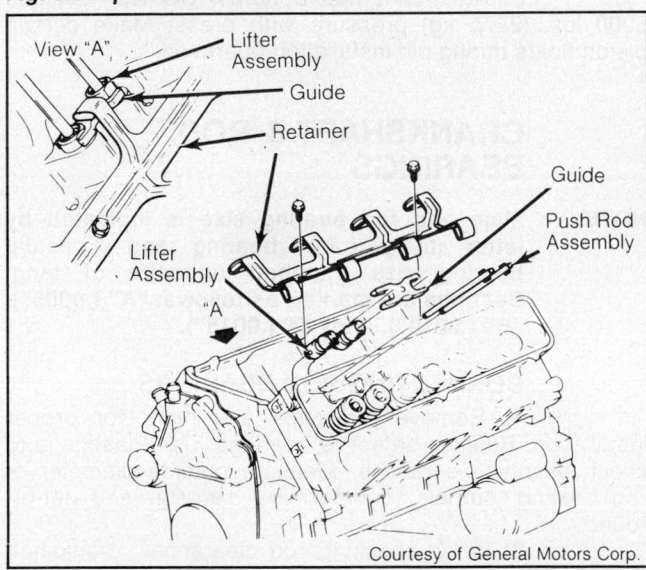

Courtesy of General Motors Corp.

PISTONS, PINS & RINGS

OIL PAN

See OIL PAN REMOVAL at end of ENGINE section.

PISTON & ROD ASSEMBLY

Removal

1) With cylinder head(s) and oil pan removed, inspect cylinder bores for ridges and/or deposits. Move piston to be removed to bottom of bore and cover with cloth to catch cuttings.

2) Remove any ridge at top of cylinder bores before removing pistons from block. Rotate crankshaft and inspect rods and caps for cylinder identification. Mark for reassembly reference.

3) Remove rod cap and push each piston and rod assembly out top of bore. Place sleeve or rubber hose over rod bolts. Remove bearings from rod and cap and inspect. Install rod caps on mating rods.

Installation

1) Check fit of new piston and/or rings in cylinder bore before assembling piston and pin to rod. Check piston pin for clearance, etching or wear. New pistons must be installed in cylinder for which they were fitted. Install used pistons in cylinder from which they were removed.

2) Measure cylinder bore diameter, then measure piston diameter (with rod and pin removed) at skirt across centerline of piston pin. Calculate piston-to-cylinder clearance. Replace and/or repair parts as necessary.

3) Oil piston rings and cylinder walls. Ensure ring gaps are properly spaced. Install ring compressor on piston. Marked side of compression rings must be toward top of piston. Position piston so identification numbers on rod and cap are on same side. Insert piston/rod assembly into cylinder bore.

NOTE: **Notch on top of piston must face front of engine.**

4) After bearings have been inserted, oil journals and bearings. Ensure oil hole in bearing aligns with oil hole in rod. Turn crankshaft throw to bottom of stroke. Guide piston/rod assembly over crankshaft journal until rod bearing seats.

5) Match rod cap to rod and install. Tighten cap nuts in 2 steps. Repeat procedure for each piston assembly. After piston/rod assembly is installed, check side clearance of connecting rod on each crankshaft journal.

FITTING PISTONS

1) Inspect pistons and replace any which show signs of excessive wear, wavy ring lands, or fractures. Measure piston.

2) Standard piston taper is .0003-.0017" (.007-.043 mm). Check clearance between piston and bore. Ensure piston and cylinder bore are clean, dry and at room temperature 70°F (21°C) during measurement.

3) Check bore for out of round. Cylinder bore out-of-round should not exceed .0015" (.038 mm). If cylinder wall is severely marred or worn, refinishing will be needed.

4) Before refinishing, ensure main bearing caps are in place and tightened to avoid distortion during boring operation. Pistons are available in .010" oversize.

FITTING PISTON RINGS

1) Clean ring grooves. Ensure oil holes (or slots) in piston are clean. Measure piston ring side and end gap clearance for all pistons.

2) Ring side clearance should be checked with feeler gauge between ring and upper piston ring land. Gauge should slide freely around entire circumference without binding. If step has formed around inner portion of lower ring land, piston must be replaced.

3) Using piston to position ring in cylinder bore, check end gap at least 5/8" (16 mm) from bottom of bore. Install rings on pistons with end gaps staggered. *See Fig. 10.*

Fig. 10: Piston Ring Gap Spacing

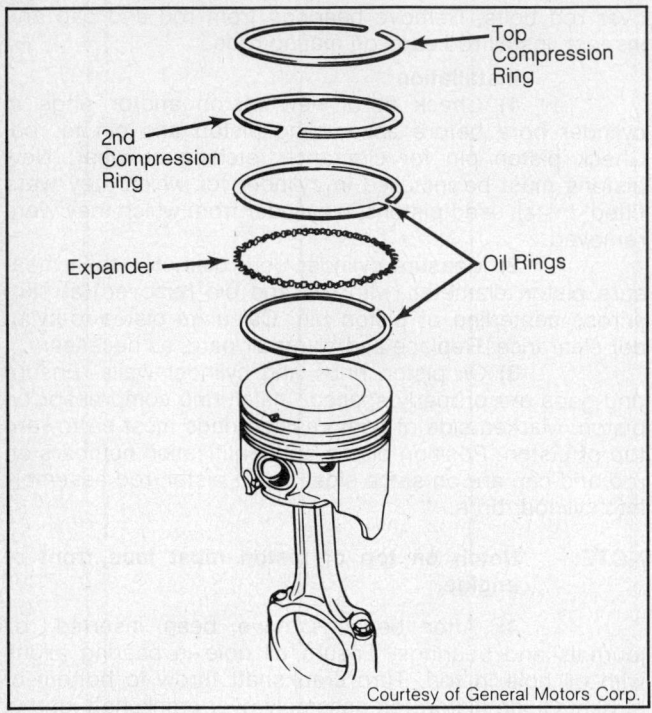

Courtesy of General Motors Corp.

4) If new rings are to be installed and no visible cross-hatch marks remain on cylinder walls, remove cylinder wall glaze using spring-type hone. After honing, clean bore and block with soap/water solution and apply oil to cylinder walls.

FITTING PISTON PINS

NOTE: When removing or installing piston pin, connecting rod should be in firm contact with body of pin setting tool.

Removal

1) Remove bearings from connecting rod and cap. Mark pistons, pins and inserts (if reusable) to assure assembly with same rod. Press pin from piston and rod using arbor press and Piston Pin Remover/Installer (J-24086). *See Fig. 11.*

2) Replace piston pins showing fractures, etching or wear. Measure piston pin diameter. Check I.D. of rod pin bore and replace if bore is too large. Calculate pin-to-rod bore fit. Ensure proper fit by honing or reaming piston pin bore to light slip fit. Lubricate pin and small end of rod bore with oil.

Installation

1) Ensure oil hole in rod aligns with oil hole in bearing and arrow or notch on top of piston is pointed toward front of engine.

2) Start pin in piston and rod. Using guide bar and push rod, press pin through piston and rod until pilot hub bottoms on support fixture and/or pin is centered in piston.

Fig. 11: Piston Pin Removal & Installation

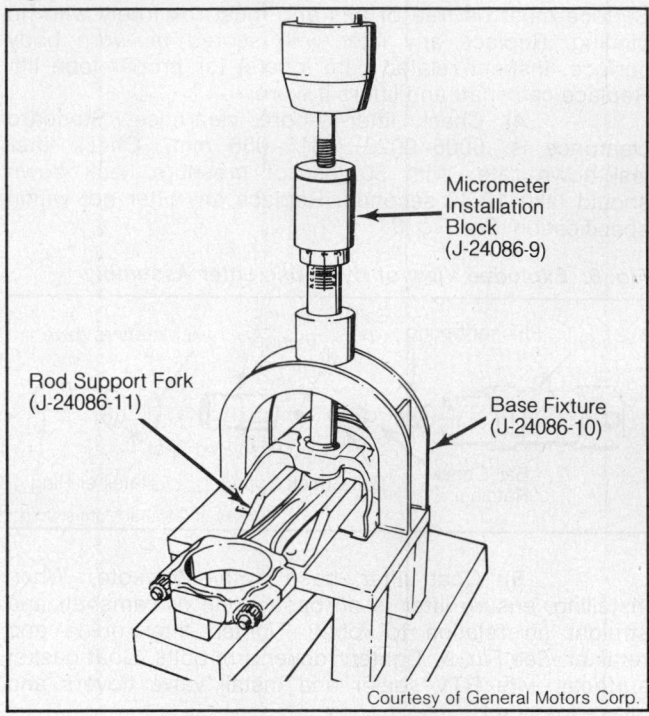

Courtesy of General Motors Corp.

3) After pilot hub bottoms, DO NOT exceed 5000 lbs. (2275 kg) pressure with press. Make certain piston floats during pin installation operation.

CRANKSHAFT & ROD BEARINGS

NOTE: Main and rod bearing size is indicated by letter stamped into bearing tang or actual bearing size stamped opposite of tang. Bearings are marked as follows: "A" (.0005"), "B" (.0010"), and "C" (.0015").

CONNECTING ROD BEARINGS

1) Remove rod caps and mark for proper installation. Replace defective bearings. Use Plastigage to check bearing clearances. Measure outside diameter of rod bearing journals to determine diameter and out-of-round.

2) When checking rod clearances, crankshaft does not have to be supported. Instead, turn crankshaft until rod to be checked starts moving toward top of engine, thus unloading lower bearing.

3) Use Plastigage method to determine clearances. Always install caps with markings in original positions. If clearance exceeds specification, replace bearing. Bearings are available in standard and various undersizes. After inspection and/or replacement, coat bearings with oil. Install rod caps and tighten in 2 steps.

NOTE: Connecting rod bearing cap and rod identification numbers must remain on same side.

4) Check rod side play. If clearance is less than specification, remove rod and cap. Check for

5.0L (VIN Y) V8 (Cont.)

scratches, burrs, or dirt between crankshaft and rod. Dress minor imperfections with oil stone. If clearance is more than specification, replace parts as necessary.

5) During assembly, ensure oil hole in bearing aligns with oil hole in connecting rod. Ensure bearing tangs are seated in appropriate slots in rod and cap. Ensure connecting rod bolt heads are properly seated in rod.

MAIN BEARINGS

1) Measure diameter of main bearing journals. Standard journal out-of-round is .0002" (.005 mm) maximum. To check main bearing clearance, position jack under counterweight adjoining bearing being checked so weight of crankshaft will not compress Plastigage and provide incorrect reading.

2) DO NOT position jack under crankshaft pulley. Crankshaft post damage will result. Check clearances using Plastigage method. New bearings are available in standard, .0010", .0020", .010" and .020" undersize. If undersize bearings will not bring bearing clearance within limits, crankshaft must be replaced.

3) When journals are refinished, chamfer oil holes. Polish journals with No. 320 grit polishing cloth and oil. After chamfer and polish operations, clean crankshaft in solvent and blow out oil passages with compressed air.

4) Ensure oil distributing grooves on main bearings are installed on same side. Oil new upper bearing and insert plain (unnotched) end between crankshaft and notched side of block. Rotate bearing into place. Ensure main bearing caps are installed with arrows pointing toward front of engine. Install main cap bolts and tighten.

THRUST BEARING ALIGNMENT

Check crankshaft end play with crankshaft bearing caps installed. Crankshaft end play specification is .0035-.0135" (.089-.343 mm). Replace main thrust bearing (No. 3) if crankshaft end play is incorrect. Rotate crankshaft and check for excessive drag.

REAR MAIN BEARING OIL SEAL

Removal & Installation (Crankshaft Installed)

1) Drain engine oil and remove oil pan. Remove rear main bearing cap and old seal. Using packing tool, drive new seal into groove in block until packed tight. Repeat on other end of seal in block.

2) Measure amount seal was driven up into cylinder block on one side, add 1/16", and cut this length from old seal removed from rear main bearing cap.

3) Using 2 small screwdrivers, work pieces into block seal groove (one on each side). Trim excess packing flush with block. Form new rope seal in main bearing cap. Apply a drop of sealer on each end of seal and cap. Install bolts and tighten. Reverse removal procedure to complete installation.

Removal & Installation (Crankshaft Removed)

1) Remove rope seal from rear main bearing cap and block. Clean bearing cap and seal grooves. Inspect for cracks. Apply Sealer (1052621) to cap seal contact surface. Wait one minute. Drive new rope seal into bearing cap with Seal Installer (J-25285A). Cut excess seal material flush with bearing cap.

2) Form new rope seal in rear seal groove in block. Complete crankshaft repair and install. Push rope seal into block seal groove and trim excess. Apply sealant to mating surfaces. Lightly tap main bearing cap into place. Install main bearing cap bolts and tighten. To complete installation, reverse removal procedure.

TORSIONAL DAMPER

Removal

Disconnect negative battery cable. Remove accessory drive belts and pulley. Raise vehicle. Remove crankshaft pulley and damper retaining bolt. Use Hub Puller (J-8614-3) to remove damper.

Installation

1) Coat front cover seal contact area on damper with oil. Clean and apply sealant to key and keyway. Place damper in position over key on crankshaft. Using Hub Installer (J-25288), pull damper in position on hub leaving .50" (13 mm) of thread engagement. Remove hub installer.

2) Install accessory drive pulley and tighten damper retaining bolts. Lower vehicle. Install accessory drive belts and related components.

ENGINE OILING

CRANKCASE CAPACITY

Crankcase capacity is 5 qts. (4.7L) with filter change.

NORMAL OIL PRESSURE

Normal oil pressure is 30-45 psi (2.10-3.16 kg/cm²) at 1500 RPM.

PRESSURE REGULATOR VALVE (PRV)

Pressure regulator valve is located in oil pump body and is nonadjustable.

ENGINE OILING SYSTEM

A gear-type oil pump provides full pressure lubrication through full flow oil filter. Oil is drawn up through screen and tube, and passed through pump to oil filter. From the filter, oil is routed to main oil gallery and through drilled holes above camshaft (to left of camshaft centerline) and on to lifters.

Lifter pumps oil through push rods to rocker arms. Oil draining back from rocker arms is directed by cast dams (part of crankcase casting) to supply camshaft lobes with oil. Passages supplying oil to camshaft bearings also supply crankshaft bearings through passages drilled in crankshaft.

OIL PUMP

Removal & Installation

Remove oil pan. Remove pump mounting bolts. Remove pump and drive shaft extention. To install, reverse removal procedure. Turn drive shaft by hand to verify smooth operation.

Disassembly

CAUTION: Use caution when removing cotter pin. Pressure regulator valve spring is under pressure.

Remove oil pump drive shaft extension but DO NOT remove washers from shaft. Place thumb over

5.0L (VIN Y) V8 (Cont.)

pressure regulator (PRV) valve bore. Remove cotter pin, spring and PRV. Remove oil pump cover screws, cover and gasket. Remove drive and idler gears from pump body. *See Fig. 12.*

Fig. 12: Exploded View of Oil Pump Assembly

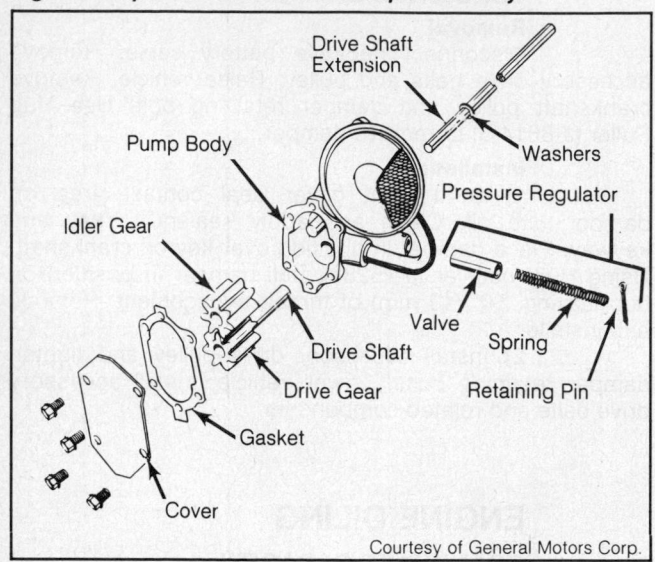

Courtesy of General Motors Corp.

OIL PUMP SPECIFICATIONS

Application	Specifications In. (mm)
Gear-to-Body Clearance	.0015-.0045" (.04-.11 mm)
Gear-to-Cover	
End Clearance	.0025-.0065" (.063-.165 mm)
Oil Pump Body	
Bore Depth	1.500-1.509" (38.10-38.33 mm)
Bore Diameter	1.534-1.539" (38.96-39.09 mm)
Oil Pump Gear	
Length	1.5075-1.5095" (38.29-38.34 mm)
Diameter	1.529-1.531" (38.84-39.89 mm)
Regulator Valve-to-Bore	
Clearance	.0025-.0050" (.063-.13 mm)

NOTE: When installing drive shaft extention to drive shaft, ensure extention shaft washer is 1 $^{11}/_{32}$" from end of shaft.

Reassembly

1) Install idler and drive gears in pump body. Check gear end clearance by placing straightedge over gears and measuring clearance between straightedge and gasket surface.

2) If clearance is at or near upper limit, check for scoring in cover which would make total clearance go over specification. Check regulator valve-to-bore clearance. Replace valve and/or bore if necessary. To complete installation, reverse removal procedure.

ENGINE COOLING

WATER PUMP

Removal

1) Disconnect battery and drain cooling system. Disconnect radiator and heater hoses. Disconnect by-pass hose (if equipped). Remove fan assembly and pulley bolts. Remove pulley.

2) Disconnect alternator, A/C compressor and power steering brackets. Remove water pump attaching bolts and remove pump. Clean pump and engine block mating surfaces.

Installation

Transfer pulley from old to new pump (if necessary). Apply sealant to water pump mating surface. Install pump and tighten attaching bolts while sealant is tacky. To complete installation, reverse removal procedure.

NOTE: For information on cooling system capacities and other cooling system components, see appropriate article in ENGINE COOLING SYSTEMS section.

CAUTION: The following specifications apply only to 5.0L engines with an engine VIN code of "Y".

TIGHTENING SPECIFICATIONS (VIN Y)

Application	Ft. Lbs. (N.m)
Camshaft Sprocket Bolts	65 (88)
Connecting Rod Cap Nuts	[1] 18 (24)
Cylinder Head Bolts	[2] 130 (176)
EGR Valve-to-Manifold	20 (27)
Exhaust Manifold Bolts	25 (34)
Fan-to-Water Pump	20 (27)
Flexplate-to-Converter	46 (63)
Flexplate-to-Crankshaft Bolts	60 (82)
Front Engine Cover Bolts	35 (48)
Harmonic Balancer Bolt	200-310 (271-420)
Intake Manifold Bolts	[2] 40 (54)
Main Bearing Cap Bolts	
No. 1-4	80 (108)
No. 5	120 (163)
Oil Filter Adapter	35 (48)
Oil Pan Bolts	10 (14)
Oil Pan Nuts	17 (23)
Oil Pump-to-Main Cap Bolt	35 (48)
Rocker Arm Pivot Bolts	22 (30)
Water Pump	11 (15)

[1] – Rotate Nut an additional 70 degrees after reaching specified torque.
[2] – Clean and dip in engine oil.

5.0L (VIN Y) V8 (Cont.)

ENGINE SPECIFICATIONS

GENERAL SPECIFICATIONS

Year	DISPLACEMENT		Fuel System	HP@RPM	Torque Ft. Lbs.@RPM	Compr. Ratio	BORE		STROKE	
	Cu. In.	Liters					In.	mm	In.	mm
1988	307	5.0	4-Bbl.	140@3600	240@1600	8.0:1	3.80	96.5	3.39	85.9

VALVES

Engine Size & Valve	Head Diam. In. (mm)	Face Angle	Seat Angle	Seat Width In. (mm)	Stem Diameter In. (mm)	Stem Clearance In. (mm)	Valve Lift In. (mm)
5.0L & 5.0L HO Intake	1.745-1.755 (44.32-44.57)	44°	45°	.037-.075 (.94-1.91)	.3425-.3432 (8.699-8.717)	.0010-.0027 (.025-.069)	
Exhaust	1.497-1.507 (38.02-38.28)	30°	31°	.050-.100 (1.27-2.54)	.3420-.3427 (8.687-8.705)	.0015-.0032 (.038-.081)	(10.16)

PISTONS, PINS & RINGS

Engine	PISTONS	PINS		RINGS		
	Clearance In. (mm)	Piston Fit In. (mm)	Rod Fit In. (mm)	Ring No.	End Gap In. (mm)	Side Clearance In. (mm)
5.0L	.00075-.00175 (.0191-.0445)	¹ .0003-.0005 (.0076-.013)	.00015-.00095 (.0038-.0241)	No.1	.009-.019 (.23-.48)	.0018-.0038 (.05-.10)
				No. 2	.009-.019 (.23-.48)	.0018-.0038 (.046-.10)
				No. 3	.015-.055 (.38-1.40)	.001-.005 (.025-.127)

¹ – Piston pin diameter is .98035-.98055" (24.900-24.906 mm).

CRANKSHAFT MAIN & CONNECTING ROD BEARINGS

Engine	MAIN BEARINGS				CONNECTING ROD BEARINGS		
	Journal Diam. In. (mm)	Clearance In. (mm)	Thrust Bearing	Crankshaft End Play In. (mm)	Journal Diam. In. (mm)	Clearance In. (mm)	Side Play In. (mm)
5.0L	¹ 2.4985-2.4994 (63.461-63.487)	² .0005-.0021 (.013-.053)	No. 3	.0035-.0135 (.089-.343)	2.1238-2.1248 (53.94-53.97)	.0004-.0033 (.010-.084)	.006-.020 (.152-.508)

¹ – No. 2-5 journals shown, No. 1 journal is 2.4988-2.4948" (63.466-63.495 mm).
² – No. 1-4 journals shown, No. 5 clearance is .0015-.0031" (.038-.081 mm).

VALVE SPRINGS

Engine	Free Length In. (mm)	PRESSURE Lbs. @ In. (Kg @ mm)	
		Valve Closed	Valve Open
5.0L	1.96 (49.8)	76-84@1.67 (34-38@42.4)	180-194@1.27 (81-88@32.3)

CAMSHAFT

Engine	Journal Diam. In. (mm)	Clearance In. (mm)	Lobe Lift In. (mm)
5.0L ¹	² 2.0365-2.0352 (51.727-51.694)	.0020-.0058 (.051-.147)	³ .247 (6.27)

¹ – End play is .006-.022 (.15-.56 mm).
² – No. 1 journal. Moving toward rear of engine, each succeeding journal is .020" (.51 mm) smaller than preceding journal.
³ – Intake shown; exhaust lobe lift is .251" (6.38).

Engine Removal & Installation

CHRYSLER MOTORS

4-CYLINDER MODELS

2.2L (135") & 2.5L (153")

1) Disconnect battery cables. Mark hinge position on hood for reinstallation. Remove hood. Drain cooling system. Remove radiator and heater hoses. On automatic transaxle models, remove oil cooler lines from radiator. On all models, remove radiator and shroud assembly.

2) Remove air cleaner with hoses attached. Remove A/C compressor and power steering pump from mounting brackets and position aside (if equipped). Leave refrigerant lines and power steering hoses connected. Remove oil filter. Disconnect electrical wiring, vacuum lines and accelerator cable at engine.

3) Remove gas cap to relieve fuel tank pressure. Remove wiring harness from any injector. Connect one injector terminal to battery negative terminal and other terminal to battery positive terminal. DO NOT leave injector connected for longer than 10 seconds. Remove jumper wires. Remove fuel line.

4) Remove alternator mounting bolts and position alternator aside. On manual transaxle models, disconnect clutch cable. Remove transaxle housing inspection cover. On all models, disconnect exhaust pipe at manifold. Disconnect starter motor and position aside. Support transaxle.

5) On automatic transaxle models, remove converter housing inspection cover. Mark converter-to-flex plate position. Remove converter-to-flex plate bolts. Attach "C" clamp to bottom of transaxle housing to prevent converter movement. Support transaxle.

6) Install engine lift. Remove right side inner fender splash shield. Remove ground strap. Remove right engine mount through bolt. Remove bolts attaching engine to transaxle.

7) Mark front engine mount location for reinstallation. Remove front engine mount bolt and nut.

Remove anti-roll strut/damper from manual transaxle. Remove insulator bracket-to-transaxle screws or insulator through bolt (from inside wheelwell). Lift engine and remove from vehicle.

8) To install, reverse removal procedure. Align engine mounts and install. DO NOT tighten mounting bolts until all mounting brackets and bolts have been installed. Check drive axle shaft length, with damper weight removed, and adjust as necessary. See Fig. 1.

9) If drive axle shaft length requires adjustment, support engine/transaxle assembly with a floor jack. Loosen right engine mount verticle fasteners, front engine mount bracket and front crossmember fasteners. Pry engine right or left as required to obtain correct drive axle shaft length. See DRIVE AXLE SHAFT LENGTH SPECIFICATIONS table.

10) Tighten mounting bolts and nuts to specification. Recheck drive axle shaft length. Install damper weight and tighten to specification. Fill cooling system. Bleed air from cooling system by removing plug above thermostat housing. Reinstall plug when coolant level reaches plug opening. Tighten plug to specification.

Fig. 1: Measuring Axle Shaft Length

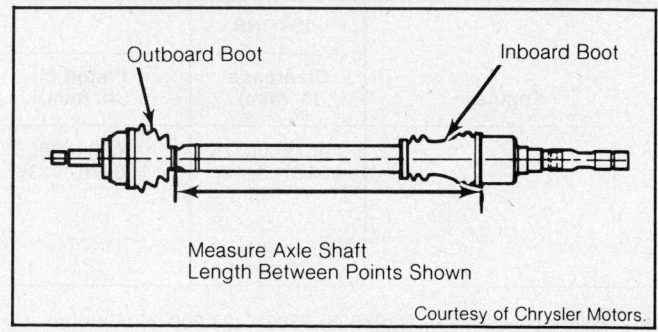

Courtesy of Chrysler Motors.

AXLE SHAFT LENGTH SPECIFICATIONS

Application	Engine	Shaft Type	Side of Vehicle	Transaxle	Length In. (mm)
Dynasty, New Yorker	3.0L	G.K.N. (82-98)	Right	All	18.9-19.2 (481-489)
			Left	All	8.5-8.8 (216-224)
Horizon, Omni	2.2L	G.K.N. (69-92)	Right	Auto	19.6-19.8 (498-504)
			Left	Auto	8.2-8.7 (208-221)
		G.K.N. (69-92)	Right	Manual	19.6-19.8 (498-504)
			Left	Manual	9.4-10.0 (240-253)
All Other Models	2.2L	G.K.N. (69-92)	Right	All	19.9-20.3 (505-515)
			Left	All	8.9-9.6 (227-245)
		G.K.N. (82-98)	Right	All	19.3-19.6 (490-498)
			Left	All	8.9-9.2 (227-234)
		A.C.I.	Right	All	18.8-19.1 (477-485)
			Left	All	7.8-8.3 (197-212)
		S.S.G.	Right	All	18.0-18.5 (457-469)
			Left	All	7.2-7.9 (184-200)
	2.2L Turbo I	G.K.N. (82-98)	Right	All	8.9-9.2 (227-234)
			Left	All	8.9-9.2 (227-234)
		S.S.G.	Right	All	7.4-7.7 (187-196)
			Left	All	7.4-7.7 (187-196)
	2.2L Turbo II [1]	G.K.N.	Right	All	8.9-9.2 (227-234)
			Left	All	8.9-9.2 (227-234)

[1] – Available in Daytona Shelby Z and Lancer Shelby models with man. trans. only.

CHRYSLER MOTORS (Cont.)

V6 MODELS

3.0L (181")

1) Disconnect negative and positive battery cables. Mark hood hinge location on hood and remove hood. Drain cooling system. Label and disconnect all electrical connections. Remove upper and lower radiator hoses. Disconnect heater hoses. Remove radiator and fan assembly.

2) Loosen gas cap to release fuel tank pressure. Remove wiring harness connector from any injector. Connect one injector terminal to battery negative terminal and other terminal to battery positive terminal. DO NOT appply voltage to injector for longer than 10 seconds. Remove jumper wires.

3) Disconnect fuel lines and accelerator cable. Remove air cleaner assembly. Raise vehicle and drain engine oil. Remove air conditioning compressor mounting bolts and set compressor aside. Disconnect exhaust pipe at manifolds. Remove transaxle inspection cover.

4) Mark flex plate-to-torque converter position. Remove torque converter mounting bolts. Attach "C" clamp to torque converter housing to keep torque converter from coming out. Remove power steering pump and set aside. Remove 2 lower transaxle-to-block mounting bolts. Remove starter.

5) Lower vehicle. Label and disconnect vacuum hoses. Disconnect ground strap. Support transaxle. Attach engine hoist to engine. Remove upper transaxle-to-block mounting bolts. Mark right engine mount position on right rail support. Remove mount-to-rail mounting bolts.

6) Remove front engine mount through bolt. Remove left engine mount through bolt from inside wheelwell or insulator bracket-to-transaxle bolts. Remove engine.

7) To install, reverse removal procedure. Align engine mounts and install. DO NOT tighten mounting bolts until all mounting brackets and bolts have been installed. Check drive axle shaft length with damper weight removed, and adjust as necessary. *See Fig. 1.* If drive axle shaft length requires adjustment, support engine/transaxle assembly with a floor jack.

8) Loosen right engine mount verticle fasteners, front engine mount bracket and front crossmember fasteners. Pry engine right or left as required to obtain correct drive axle shaft length. See DRIVE AXLE SHAFT LENGTH SPECIFICATIONS table. Tighten mounting bolts and nuts to specification. Recheck drive axle shaft length. Install damper weight and tighten to specification.

V8 MODELS

5.2L (318")

1) Mark hood hinges for reinstallation. Remove hood. Drain cooling system. Remove battery. Remove air cleaner assembly. Remove radiator hoses, heater hoses, fan shroud and transmission cooler lines from radiator. Remove radiator. Remove fan shroud. Disconnect fuel lines at fuel pump and filter.

2) Remove A/C compressor from engine with refrigerant lines connected and position aside (if equipped). Remove vacuum hoses, distributor cap and wiring. Remove carburetor and linkage. Remove starter and oil pressure sending unit wiring. Disconnect engine harness wiring and set aside.

3) Remove power steering pump and set aside (if equipped). Remove alternator, charcoal canister, starter motor and horns. Disconnect exhaust pipe at manifolds. Remove bellhousing bolts and inspection plate. Mark torque converter and flex plate for reinstallation.

4) Remove torque converter-to-flex plate bolts. Support the transmission with Support Stand (C-3201A). Attach a "C" clamp to bottom front of torque converter housing to retain converter. Using eyebolt fixture, attach engine hoist to engine. Remove front motor mount bolts. Remove engine.

5) To install, reverse removal procedure.

CHRYSLER MOTORS TIGHTENING SPECIFICATIONS

Application	Ft. Lbs. (N.m)
4-Cylinder Engines	
Anti-Roll Strut Mounting Nut	
Manual Transaxle	40 (54)
Coolant Air Bleed Plug	15 (20)
Drive Axle Shaft Damper Weight Bolt	
A.C.I.	8 (11)
G.K.N.	23 (30)
S.S.G.	21 (28)
Engine-to-Transaxle Bolts	70 (95)
Flex Plate-to-Torque Converter Bolts	55 (74)
Front Engine Mount-to-Bracket Nut	40 (54)
Front Engine Mount-to-Engine Bolt	75 (102)
Front Engine Mount-to-Frame Nuts	40 (54)
Left Engine Mount-to-Engine Bolt	40 (54)
Left Engine Mount-to-Frame Bolt	50 (68)
Right Engine Mount Bolt & Nut	75 (102)
Right Engine Mount-to-Frame Bolt	21 (28)
Turbocharger Damper	
Mount-to-Engine Nuts	21 (28)
Turbocharger Damper-to-Mount Nut	16 (22)
V6 Engines	
Drive Axle Shaft Damper Weight Bolt	23 (30)
Engine Mounts	
Front Insulator-to-Block Bolts & Nut	75 (102)
Front Insulator-to-Frame Rail Bolts & Nuts	40 (54)
Left Insulator Through Bolt	50 (68)
Left Mount Damper Weight Bolt	17 (23)
Right Mount Nut [1]	75 (102)
Right Mount Through Bolt	75 (102)
Right Mount-to-Frame Rail Bolt	21 (28)
Engine-to-Transaxle Bolts	75 (102)
Flex Plate-to-Converter Bolts	55 (75)
V8 Engines	
Engine Mount-to-Engine Bolts	65 (88)
Engine Mount-to-Frame Bolts	75 (102)
Flex Plate-to-Converter Bolts	23 (31)
Engine-to-Transmission Bolts	30 (41)

[1] – Tighten nut before tightening through bolt.

Engine Removal & Installation

EAGLE PREMIER

4-CYLINDER MODELS

NOTE: This procedure must be performed with a side mount hoist.

2.5L (150")

1) Disconnect negative and positive battery cables. Remove battery. Drain cooling system. Remove air bonnet and air intake duct. Remove crankcase ventilation and charcoal canister hoses at air cleaner. Disconnect throttle cable and cruise control cable (if equipped). Compress mounting tabs and remove throttle and cruise control cables from mounting bracket.

2) Disconnect hot air tube at air cleaner. Label and disconnect all vacuum hoses as necessary. Disconnect air supply tube at air cleaner. Remove air cleaner assembly. Remove fuel tank filler cap to relieve fuel tank pressure. Reinstall filler cap.

3) Disconnect fuel supply hose (Black) and fuel return hose (Grey) from throttle body by squeezing retaining tabs and pulling tabs out. The retainers will remain on fuel hoses. Disconnect crankcase ventilation hose at valve cover. Open clamp and remove molded vacuum manifold assembly.

4) Remove bulkhead connector screw and bulkhead connector. Lay connector on top of engine. Disconnect electrical connector at dash panel. Remove vacuum hose from brake booster. Disconnect heater hoses from heater core and lay hoses on top of engine. Remove hose from coolant expansion bottle. Disconnect upper radiator hose.

5) Disconnect coil secondary wire. Disconnect lower hose from bottom of coolant expansion bottle. Loosen power steering pump and remove belt. Remove power steering pump. Remove lower radiator hose. Remove wiring from starter. Disconnect ground wire from starter mounting bolt. Disconect A/C compressor wiring.

6) Remove 4 A/C compressor mounting bolts and relocate compressor to passenger side of engine compartment. Label and disconnect wiring from alternator and oil pressure sending unit. Disconnect TPS connector. Position hoist under vehicle. *See Fig. 1.* Raise vehicle halfway.

Fig. 1: Positioning Hoist for Raising Vehicle

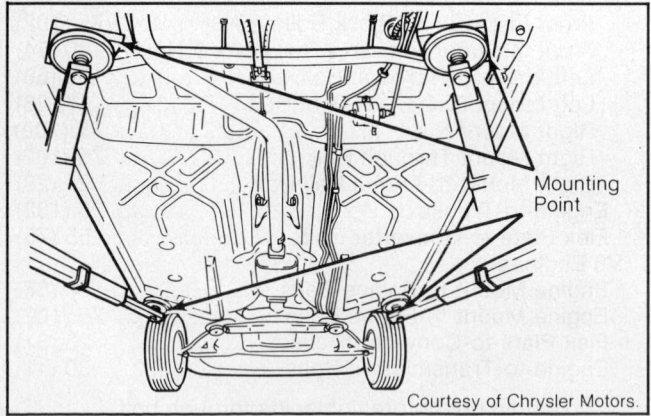

Mounting Point

Courtesy of Chrysler Motors.

Position mounting pads as shown.

7) Remove front tires. Disconnect front brake calipers and pads. Wire calipers to springs. Do not disconnect brake hose or hang caliper by hose. Hold hub in place using Spanner Wrench (Rou. 604.01). Loosen hub

nuts. Remove nuts attaching steering knuckles to front struts. Do not turn the bolts, as they are splined into steering knuckle.

8) Tap upper bolt from steering knuckle using a brass hammer. Pull strut out, pivoting steering knuckle on lower bolt. Tap lower bolt from knuckle. Separate knuckle from strut. Raise vehicle fully. Remove 4 bolts and transaxle shield. Disconnect transaxle shift cable from linkage arm by prying cable up with a screwdriver.

9) Remove transaxle shifter cable bracket mounting bolts. Allow cable and bracket to hang freely. Disconnect exhaust system at catalytic converter. Pull pipe hook out of hanger. Allow converter and pipe assembly to hang. Remove splash shield. Disconnect oil level sensor connector. Disconnect pitch restrictor from bracket on body front lower crossmember.

10) Drain fluid from transaxle. Remove solenoid from transaxle. Remove wiring harness clips from transaxle dipstick tube. Place solenoid and harness aside. Disconnect Transmission Control Unit (TCU) wiring harness connector at transaxle by squeezing tabs and pulling it out.

11) Remove multifunction switch from transaxle. Remove sensor mounting bolt and clip from side of transaxle. Disconnect wiring harness clip and ground wire. Place multifunction switch, TCU harness, sensor and wiring harness in engine compartment. Install special attaching bolts into engine cradle. Put large end of bolt channel iron into hole, followed by threaded portion of bolt.

12) Ensure channel portion of bolt lays flat in cradle. Install Subframe Dolly (Mot. 1040.99) to the engine cradle with wheels toward rear of vehicle and arms of dolly pointing up toward cradle. Install and tighten nuts on special attaching bolts. Lower hoist until dolly is resting on floor. Remove 4 cradle mounting bolts from below vehicle.

13) Ensure all hoses and wiring are disconnected and positioned away from engine/transaxle assembly. Slowly raise vehicle from engine. Mark position of dolly wheels and legs on floor for realignment during installation. Position floor jack under center of front crossbar of dolly. Raise front of dolly and remove assembly from below vehicle.

14) To install, reverse removal procedure. Align dolly legs and wheels with marks on floor made during removal. Lower vehicle onto engine assembly. Stop when vehicle just touches cradle bolt pads. Position cradle with spacer between body and washer.

V6 MODELS

NOTE: This procedure must be performed with a side mount hoist.

3.0L (180")

1) Disconnect negative and positive battery cables. Remove battery. Drain cooling system. Remove hose from idle speed regulator. Remove throttle body bonnet and air intake duct. Remove crankcase ventilation and charcoal canister hoses at air cleaner. Disconnect air sensor vacuum hose at air cleaner. Disconnect coil secondary wire.

2) Disconnect throttle cable and cruise control cable (if equipped) from throttle arm. Compress mounting tabs and remove throttle and cruise control cables from

EAGLE PREMIER (Cont.)

mounting bracket. Disconnect hot air tube at air cleaner. Remove air cleaner assembly. Remove fuel tank filler cap to relieve fuel tank pressure. Reinstall filler cap.

3) Disconnect fuel supply hose (Black) from fuel rail and fuel return hose (Grey) from pressure regulator. Squeeze retaining tabs and pull connectors apart. Label and disconnect all vacuum hoses as necessary. Remove bulkhead connector screw and bulkhead connector.

4) Lay connector on top of engine. Disconnect electrical connector at dash panel. Remove vacuum hose from brake booster. Disconnect heater hoses at firewall. Remove lower hose from coolant expansion bottle. Disconnect radiator hoses from water pump. Disconnect front engine shock absorber from engine bracket.

5) Push shock absorber up against cooling fan. Open driver's side door and remove bottom instrument panel section from below steering wheel. Disconnect shifter cable from arm on steering column. Depress tabs on side of cable housing and pull cable through mounting bracket.

6) Position hoist and raise vehicle. *See Fig. 1.* Remove splash shield from below alternator. Disconnect knock sensor, oil level sensor, oil pressure sending unit and alternator connectors. Disconnect wiring harness clip from back of alternator. Loosen alternator pivot bolt, locking bolt and adjusting bolt. Remove accessory drive belt.

7) Loosen power steering pump nuts and bolts until front bracket drops down. Remove bolt from behind bracket. Remove rear power steering pump bolts. Remove power steering pump and set it aside. Remove power steering reservoir. Lower vehicle. Remove 4 A/C compressor mounting bolts and relocate compressor to passenger side of engine compartment (if equipped). Raise vehicle halfway.

8) Remove front tires. Disconnect front brake calipers and pads. Wire calipers to springs. Do not disconnect brake hose or hang caliper by hose. Hold hub in place using Spanner Wrench (Rou. 604.01). Loosen hub nuts. Remove nuts attaching steering knuckles to front struts. Do not turn the bolts, as they are splined into steering knuckle.

9) Tap upper bolt from steering knuckle using a brass hammer. Pull strut out, pivoting steering knuckle on lower bolt. Tap lower bolt from knuckle. Separate knuckle from strut. Raise vehicle fully. Disconnect wiring from starter. Remove middle starter mounting bolt and disconnect ground cable.

10) Remove 4 bolts and subframe shield. Disconnect O$_2$ sensor connector at "Y" pipe. Pull grommet surrounding shifter cable down. Grasp cable and pull it through hole in body. Disconnect catalytic converter from "Y" pipe. Install special attaching bolts into engine cradle. Put large end of bolt channel iron into hole, followed by threaded portion of bolt. Ensure channel portion of bolt lays flat in cradle.

11) Install Subframe Dolly (Mot. 1040.99) to the engine cradle with wheels toward rear of vehicle and arms of dolly pointing up toward cradle. Install and tighten nuts on special attaching bolts. Lower hoist until dolly is resting on floor. Remove 4 cradle mounting bolts from below vehicle. Ensure all hoses and wiring are disconnected and positioned away from engine/transaxle assembly.

12) Slowly raise vehicle from engine. Mark position of dolly wheels and legs on floor for realignment during installation. Position floor jack under center of dolly front crossbar. Raise front of dolly and remove assembly from below vehicle. If engine is to be separated from transaxle, use Support Brackets (Mot. 1040.97 and 1040.98) to support transaxle.

13) To install, reverse removal procedure. Align dolly legs and wheels with marks on floor made during removal. Lower vehicle onto engine assembly. Stop when vehicle just touches cradle bolt pads. Position cradle with spacer between body and washer.

EAGLE PREMIER TIGHTENING SPECIFICATIONS

Application	Ft. Lbs. (N.m)
A/C Compressor Mounting Bolts	20 (27)
Alternator Lock Bolt	20 (27)
Alternator Pivot Bolt	37 (50)
Differential Cover Bolts	20 (27)
Engine Cradle Mounting Bolts	92 (125)
Engine Mount Nuts	30 (40)
Front Engine Support Bracket-to-Lower Body Crossmember Bolts (4-Cyl.)	32 (43)
Front Engine Support-to-Support Bracket Nut (4-Cyl.)	75 (102)
Hub Nuts	181 (245)
Power Steering Pump 4-Cylinder Mounting Bolts & Nuts	20 (27)
V6 Front Bolts	30 (40)
Mounting Nut	30 (40)
Mounting Stud	30 (40)
Rear Bolts	20 (27)
Starter Mounting Bolts	31 (42)
Strut-to-Knuckle Nuts	123 (167)
Torque Converter-to-Drive Plate Bolts	24 (33)
Wheel Lug Nuts	63 (85)

FORD MOTOR CO.

4-CYLINDER MODELS

1.9L (114")

Removal

1) Mark hinges for reinstallation and remove hood. Remove air cleaner, hot air tube, alternator air tube, and airflow sensor (if equipped). Disconnect negative battery cable at both ends. Remove secondary wire from ignition coil. Drain cooling system.

2) Remove all drive belts. Remove alternator mounting bolts and position alternator aside. Disconnect thermactor pump hoses and remove pump (if equipped). Disconnect upper and lower radiator hoses at engine. Disconnect transaxle oil cooler lines at radiator (if equipped).

Engine Removal & Installation

FORD MOTOR CO. (Cont.)

3) Disconnect heater return hose at engine. Disconnect all electrical wiring and vacuum hoses at engine. Disconnect fuel lines at pump or intake manifold. Remove fan motor and shroud assembly.

4) On automatic transaxles, remove transaxle cooler line routing clip. On all models, remove radiator. Disconnect heater hose at steel tube. Remove power steering pump filter tube and plug pump opening (if equipped).

5) Disconnect throttle kickdown linkage (if equipped), accelerator cable and bracket at engine. Disconnect vacuum hose from thermactor valve. Disconnect accelerator cable and remove cable routing bracket screws. Disconnect vapor hose at carbon canister tube.

6) Raise vehicle on hoist. Remove clamp from heater supply and return tubes. Disconnect battery cable from starter motor. Remove brace at front of starter motor. On manual transaxles, remove roll restrictor.

7) On all models, remove starter motor, and brace rear section. Disconnect exhaust pipe at manifold. Remove converter/flywheel cover and brackets.

8) On all models, remove crankshaft pulley. On manual transaxles, remove lower timing belt cover bolts. Remove lower clutch housing bolts. On automatic transaxles, remove torque converter-to-drive plate nuts. Remove lower converter/flywheel housing bolts.

9) On all models, remove coolant by-pass hose at intake manifold. Remove lower right side engine mount bolt and nut. Lower vehicle. Attach engine lift to brackets. Remove right side engine mount through-bolt and remove engine mount.

10) On manual transaxles, remove timing belt cover. Remove insulator attaching bracket from engine. Position floor jack under transaxle and support transaxle. Remove upper converter/flywheel housing attaching bolts. Remove engine, making sure converter studs clear drive plate.

Installation

1) To install, reverse removal procedure. Ensure half-shaft alignment is proper by adjusting following clearances. Crankshaft damper-to-frame rail should be .63" (16.0 mm).

2) Manual transaxle case-to-frame rail should be .98" (25.0 mm). On automatic transaxle models, transaxle oil pump housing-to-frame rail should be .98" (25.0 mm). Check fluid levels. Start engine and check for leaks.

2.3L (141") OHC
Removal
1) Raise hood and secure in vertical position. Disconnect ground cable. Drain cooling system. Drain crankcase. Remove air cleaner or turbocharger.

2) Remove upper and lower radiator hoses. Disconnect transmission oil cooler lines (if equipped). Remove radiator and fan. On vehicles equipped with an electric cooling fan, disconnect power lead to fan motor, then remove fan and shroud assembly.

3) Disconnect heater hose from water pump and carburetor choke fitting. Disconnect all wiring, vacuum hoses and linkages from engine. Remove A/C compressor from mounting bracket (if equipped). Position compressor aside with lines connected.

4) Disconnect flexible fuel line at fuel pump or at fuel rail (EFI) and plug. Remove starter. Raise vehicle on hoist. Remove upper bellhousing bolts. Disconnect

exhaust pipe from exhaust manifold or turbocharger outlet.

5) Disconnect right and left motor mounts at crossmember pedestal. Remove bellhousing cover. On automatic transmission equipped vehicles, remove bolts attaching converter to flex plate.

6) Disconnect oil cooler lines from engine. On all models, Remove remaining bolts attaching bellhousing to engine. Lower vehicle. Support transmission with a jack. Attach engine hoist and remove engine.

Installation
To install, reverse removal procedure. Check fluid levels. Start engine and check for leaks.

2.3L (141")
HIGH SWIRL COMBUSTION (HSC) &
HIGH SWIRL OUTPUT (HSO)

NOTE: Engine/transaxle is removed as an assembly.

Removal
1) Mark hinges for reinstallation. Remove hood. Disconnect ground cable. Remove air cleaner assembly. Drain cooling system. Remove upper and lower radiator hoses. Disconnect transaxle cooler lines at hoses below radiator (if equipped).

2) Remove coil assembly. Disconnect cooling fan. Remove radiator shroud and fan as assembly. Remove radiator. Discharge A/C system and disconnect hoses at compressor (if equipped). Disconnect all electrical and vacuum lines.

3) On automatic transaxle, disconnect TV linkage. Disconnect clutch cable on manual transaxle. Disconnect accelerator linkage, fuel lines at engine, and thermactor discharge hose at pump.

4) Disconnect power steering hoses at pump (if equipped). Remove hose bracket at cylinder head. Attach engine support tool to lifting eye. Raise vehicle.

5) Remove starter cable, hose from catalytic converter, exhaust pipe bracket bolt at oil pan, and exhaust pipe-to-manifold nuts. Remove exhaust system from grommets and set aside. Disconnect speedometer cable at transaxle.

6) Disconnect heater hoses at engine. Remove water pump inlet tube and clamps. Disconnect control arms at body. Remove stabilizer bar brackets. Remove half-shaft assemblies and install alignment plugs in differential side gears. See FWD AXLE SHAFTS article in DRIVE AXLE section.

7) On manual transaxle, remove roll restrictor, shift stabilizer bar-to-transaxle bolts, and shift mechanism-to-shift shaft bolt. On automatic transaxle, disconnect manual shift cable clip and remove manual shift linkage bracket.

8) Remove left rear insulator mount bracket. Remove left front insulator-to-transaxle mount bolts. Lower vehicle. Attach engine hoist to lifting eyes. Remove engine support tool.

CAUTION: Do not allow front wheels to touch floor.

9) Remove right-hand insulator intermediate bracket from engine bracket and insulator. Lower engine/transaxle assembly to floor.

Installation
To install, reverse removal procedure. Check fluid levels. Start engine and check for leaks.

FORD MOTOR CO. (Cont.)

2.5L (153")
Removal
1) Relieve fuel system pressure by disconnecting electrical connector at inertia switch, then cranking engine for 15 seconds. On ATX automatic transaxle equipped models, remove timing window cover at transaxle and rotate engine until flywheel timing marker is aligned with timing pointer. Mark crankshaft pulley at 12 o'clock position (TDC). Rotate crankshaft pulley mark to 6 o'clock position.

2) On all models, disconnect battery negative cable. Mark hood hinge position and remove hood. Remove air cleaner assembly. Drain cooling system. Remove upper radiator hose at engine. Remove all wiring and vacuum lines as necessary.

3) Disconnect crankcase ventilation hose at valve cover and intake manifold. Remove fuel lines at throttle body. Disconnect ground wire at engine. Remove accelerator cable and throttle valve control cable at throttle body. Discharge air conditioning system and remove pressure and suction lines from compressor (if equipped).

4) On manual transaxle equipped models, remove engine damper brace. On all models, remove drive belt, water pump pulley, and air cleaner-to-canister hose. Raise and support vehicle. Drain engine oil and remove oil filter. Disconnect starter cable and remove starter motor.

5) On automatic transaxle equipped models only, remove converter nuts and position mark previously made on crankshaft pulley as close to 6 o'clock position (BDC) as possible with converter stud visible.

NOTE: **Flywheel timing marker must be in 6 o'clock (BDC) position for proper engine removal.**

6) Remove engine insulator nuts. Disconnect exhaust pipe from manifold. Remove cansiter bracket and halfshaft bracket from engine. Remove lower engine-to-transmission attaching bolts. Remove engine from vehicle.

Installation
To install, reverse removal procedure. Check fluid levels. Start engine and check for leaks.

V6 MODELS

3.0L (183")
Removal
1) Disconnect battery cables. Mark hinges for reinstallation and remove hood. Drain cooling system and discharge A/C (if equipped). Remove air cleaner assembly, battery and tray, integrated relay controller, cooling fan, radiator and shroud. Remove bounce damper bracket on shock tower.

2) Disconnect evaporative emission line, upper radiator hose, starter brace, lower radiator hose, and exhaust manifold at pipe. Remove power steering pump lines, fuel lines, vacuum lines, ground strap, and heater hoses. Disconnect accelerator cable linkage, throttle valve linkage, and speed control cable.

3) Disconnect following connections: alternator, A/C compressor, EGO sensor, ignition coil, radio frequency suppressor, cooling fan voltage resistor, coolant temperature sensor, and TFI module.

4) Remove following components of injector wiring harness: 6 injectors, ACT sensor, ISC, and throttle position sensor. Remove oil pressure sending switch, ground wire, block heater (if equipped), knock sensor, EGR sensor and oil level sensor. Install engine lifting bolts and chains.

5) Remove lower damper bolt from right side of engine. Raise and support vehicle. Place jack and wood block under engine block. Remove nuts attaching right front and right rear insulators to frame. Raise engine with jack. Remove 2 through bolts and remove insulator from engine bracket.

6) Remove left tire and wheel. With jack and wood block still under engine, remove nut and bolt attaching hydraulic engine damper to transmission support assembly. Push damper shaft up out of way. Remove 2 nuts attaching insulator to support assembly.

7) Remove 2 through bolts attaching insulator to frame. Raise transmission with jack. Remove bolts attaching support assembly to transmission. Remove the insulator and/or transmission support assembly.

8) Remove bolt attaching lower end of right engine damper to engine bracket. Remove bolts attaching upper damper bracket to shock tower bracket. Remove engine damper. Remove speed control servo and bracket assembly.

9) Remove bolt and nut attaching lower end of left engine damper to engine mount attaching bracket. Remove bolts attaching upper damper bracket to side rail bracket. Remove left engine damper. Remove engine.

Installation
To install, reverse removal procedure. Check fluid levels. Start engine and check for leaks.

3.8L (232")
Removal (All Except Continental)

NOTE: **Information for Continental not available from manufacturer.**

1) Drain cooling system. Disconnect negative battery cable. Disconnect under hood wiring connector retaining engine compartment light. Mark hinges for reinstallation and remove hood.

2) Remove air cleaner assembly, air intake duct and heat tube. Remove oil level indicator tube and fan shroud attaching screws. Remove fan/clutch assembly and shroud. Loosen accessory drive belt idler. Remove drive belt. Remove water pump pulley.

3) Disconnect upper and lower radiator hoses at radiator. Disconnect thermactor hose from downstream air tube check valve. Remove downstream air tube bracket bolt from rear of right cylinder head.

4) Remove coil secondary wire from coil. Remove power steering pump attaching bolts (if equipped). Place pump aside with hoses connected.

5) Remove A/C compressor attaching bolts (if equipped). Position compressor aside leaving refrigerant lines connected. Disconnect and remove alternator. Disconnect heater hoses from heater tube and water pump.

6) Remove cruise control servo and bracket (if equipped). Disconnect all vacuum hoses, electrical wiring and linkages from engine. Disconnect engine ground strap at dash panel. Disconnect transmission linkage at fuel charging assembly.

7) Remove crankshaft pulley assembly. Disconnect fuel lines connecting engine to vehicle body. Plug the hoses to prevent leakage.

8) Raise vehicle. Drain crankcase. Remove dust shield from converter housing. Remove flex plate-to-

Engine Removal
FORD MOTOR CO. (Cont.)

torque converter bolts. Disconnect battery cable from starter motor. Remove starter motor.

9) Remove transmission oil cooler line routing clip. Remove exhaust inlet pipe at exhaust manifold. Disconnect exhaust heat control valve vacuum line (if equipped). Remove valve from exhaust manifold studs.

10) Remove transmission-to-engine lower attaching bolts. Remove engine mount bolts. Lower vehicle. Support transmission with a jack.

11) Remove remaining bolts connecting transmission to engine. Slightly raise engine. Carefully pull engine away from transmission. Remove engine from engine compartment.

Installation

To install, reverse removal procedure. Check fluid levels. Start engine and check for leaks.

V8 MODELS

5.0L (302")
Removal

1) Mark hinges for reinstallation and remove hood. Drain crankcase and cooling system. Disconnect battery and alternator ground cables from engine. Remove air cleaner and intake duct assembly.

2) Disconnect upper and lower radiator hoses. Disconnect transmission oil cooler lines from radiator. Remove bolts attaching fan shroud to radiator. Remove radiator.

3) Remove fan, spacer, belt, pulley and shroud. Remove alternator bolts and position alternator aside. Disconnect oil pressure sending unit wire from sending unit.

4) Disconnect flexible fuel line at fuel tank line. On EFI equipped vehicles, relieve pressure in fuel lines before disconnecting. Plug fuel tank line. Disconnect accelerator cable from carburetor. Disconnect speed control cable (if equipped).

5) Disconnect throttle valve vacuum line from intake manifold (if equipped). Disconnect transmission filler tube bracket from engine block. On vehicles equipped with A/C, remove A/C compressor and set aside.

6) If power steering equipped, disconnect power steering pump bracket from cylinder head. Remove drive belt. Position pump aside. If power brake equipped, disconnect brake vacuum line from intake manifold.

7) Disconnect heater hoses from water pump and intake manifold. Disconnect coolant temperature sending unit wire from sending unit. Remove flywheel/converter housing-to-engine upper bolts.

8) Disconnect primary wiring connector from ignition coil. Remove wire harness and position aside. Disconnect ground strap from block.

9) Raise front of vehicle. Disconnect starter cable from starter. Remove starter. Disconnect exhaust pipes from exhaust manifolds. Disconnect engine support insulators.

10) On automatic transmission equipped models, disconnect transmission cooler lines from retainer and remove converter housing inspection cover. Disconnect converter from flex plate. Secure converter assembly in housing. On all models, remove remaining converter housing-to-engine bolts.

11) Lower vehicle and support transmission. Attach engine hoist and carefully separate engine from transmission. Remove engine.

Installation

To install, reverse removal procedure. Check fluid levels. Start engine and check for leaks.

5.8L (351")
Removal

1) Drain cooling system and crankcase. Mark hinges for reinstallation and remove hood. Disconnect battery cables from engine block. Remove air cleaner and intake duct assembly. Remove upper and lower radiator hoses.

2) Disconnect transmission oil cooler lines from radiator. Remove fan shroud attaching bolts. Remove radiator, fan, spacer, belt pulley and shroud. Remove alternator bolts and position out of way.

3) Disconnect oil pressure sending unit wire from sending unit. Disconnect low oil level sensor wire (if equipped). Remove flexible fuel line at fuel tank and plug fuel tank line. Disconnect accelerator cable from carburetor. Disconnect TV rod on automatic overdrive transmissions. Disconnect speed control cable (if equipped).

4) Remove throttle valve vacuum line from intake manifold (if equipped). Disconnect transmission filler tube bracket from cylinder block. On air conditioning equipped vehicles, remove compressor. On power steering equipped models, remove power steering pump bracket from cylinder head. Remove drive belt. Position power steering pump out of way.

5) On all models, disconnect brake vacuum line from intake manifold. Remove heater hoses from water pump and intake manifold. Remove coolant temperature sending unit. Remove bolts connecting bellhousing to upper engine.

6) Disconnect primary wiring connector from ignition coil. Disconnect wiring-to-solenoid on left rocker arm cover. Remove wire harness from left rocker arm cover and position wires out of way. Remove ground strap from block.

7) Raise front of vehicle. Disconnect starter cable from starter. Remove starter. Remove exhaust pipes from exhaust manifolds. Disconnect engine support insulators from chassis. Disconnect downstream thermactor tubing and check valve from right exhaust manifold stud (if equipped).

8) On automatic transmission equipped models, remove transmission cooler lines from retainer and remove converter housing inspection cover. Disconnect flex plate from converter. Secure converter assembly in housing. On all models, remove remaining bolts connecting bellhousing to engine.

9) Lower vehicle and support transmission. Attach engine lift sling to lifting brackets on intake manifold. Raise engine slightly and pull from transmission. Remove engine.

Installation

To install, reverse removal procedure. Check fluid levels. Start engine and check for leaks.

FORD MOTOR CO. (Cont.)

FORD MOTOR CO. TIGHTENING SPECIFICATIONS

Application	Ft. Lbs. (N.m)
4-Cylinder Engines	
1.9L (114")	
Left Side Front	
Bracket-to-Crossmember Bolts	30-42 (41-57)
Motor Mount Bracket-to-Transaxle Bolts	25-35 (34-47)
Motor Mount Through Bolts	55-75 (75-102)
Left Side Rear	
Motor Mount-to-Transaxle Bolts	55-75 (75-102)
Motor Mount Through Bolts	25-35 (34-47)
Right Side	
Motor Mount-to-Bracket Bolts	65-70 (88-95)
Motor Mount-to-Engine Bolts	35-40 (47-54)
Motor Mount Through Bolts	65-70 (88-95)
2.3L (140") OHC	
Converter-to-Flex Plate Bolts	27-49 (37-66)
Crossmember-to-Frame Bolts	50-70 (68-95)
Motor Mount Bracket-to-Engine Bolts	33-45 (45-61)
Motor Mount Bracket-to-Frame Bolts	70-90 (95-122)
Rear Mount-to-Crossmember Bolts	25-35 (34-47)
Rear Mount-to-Transmission Bolts	50-70 (68-95)
2.3L (140") HSC	
CV Hub Nut	180-200 (244-271)
Intermediate Bracket-to-Engine Bracket Bolts	75-100 (102-136)
Insulator Bracket-to-Body Bracket Bolts	75-100 (102-136)
Roll Restrictor-to-Transaxle Bolts	25-45 (35-61)
Shift Stabilizer-to-Transaxle Bolts	23-35 (31-47)
Shifter-to-Input Shaft Bolts	7-10 (10-14)
2.5L (153") [1]	
Left Front Insulator-to-Bracket Nut	75-100 (100-135)
Left Front Insulator-to-Transaxle Bolts	25-37 (35-50)
Left Rear Insulator-to-Body Bolts	75-100 (100-135)
Left Rear Insulator-to-Transaxle Bolts	35-50 (50-68)
Right Insulator Nuts	75-100 (100-135)
Right Intermediate Bracket Bolt	55-75 (75-100)

FORD MOTOR CO. TIGHTENING SPECIFICATIONS (Cont.)

Application	Ft. Lbs. (N.m)
V6 Engine	
3.0L (183") [1]	
A/C Bracket Bolt	40-55 (54-75)
Engine Mount Bolt	40-55 (54-75)
Left Engine Damper	
Bolt	21-30 (28-41)
Nut	21-30 (28-41)
Left Insulator/Support Nut & Bolt	70-96 (95-130)
Right Engine Damper	
Bolt	40-55 (54-75)
Nut	21-30 (28-41)
Rt. Front/Rt. Rear Insulator-to-Frame Bolt	55-75 (75-102)
3.8L (232")	
Crossmember-to-Frame Bolts	35-50 (47-68)
Fan/Clutch Assembly Bolts	12-18 (16-24)
Motor Mount-to-Engine Bolts	35-50 (47-68)
Motor Mount-to-Frame Bolts	70-100 (95-122)
Rear Mount-to-Trans. Bolts	50-70 (68-95)
V8 Engines	
5.0L (302") [1]	
Crossmember-to-Frame Bolts	35-50 (47-68)
Motor Mount Through Bolts	35-50 (47-68)
Motor Mount-to-Crossmember Bolts	57-65 (77-88)
Motor Mount-to-Engine Bolts	35-60 (47-81)
Rear Mount-to-Trans. Bolts	50-70 (68-95)
5.8L (351") [1]	
Insulator Bracket Bolt	35-60 (48-81)
Motor Mount Bolts	26-38 (35-52)
Motor Mount Stud	35-60 (48-81)
Motor Mount Through Bolt	40-46 (54-62)
Rear Engine Mount Bolts	50-70 (68-95)
Rear Engine Mount Nuts	35-50 (48-68)

[1] – Always replace self-locking fasteners.

GENERAL MOTORS – BUICK

4-CYLINDER MODELS

2.0L (122") VIN K

Removal

1) Disconnect battery cables. Drain cooling system and remove radiator hoses. Remove air cleaner. Disconnect electrical harness at firewall. Disconnect electrical connector at brake cylinder.

2) Disconnect wiring at Electronic Control Module (ECM), temperature switch at thermostat housing, and A/C relay cluster switches. Disconnect vacuum hoses at Manifold Absolute Pressure (MAP) sensor, canister, and Electronic Fuel Injection (EFI).

3) Remove power steering hoses at pump return port and cut-off switch. Disconnect accelerator cable at bracket and EFI. Disconnect shifter cable at transmission. Raise and support vehicle.

4) Remove speedometer cable and bracket. Disconnect exhaust pipe at manifold and converter. Remove heater hoses and fuel lines. Remove transaxle cooler lines.

5) Remove both front wheels. Remove right spoiler section and splash shield. Remove front brake

GENERAL MOTORS — BUICK (Cont.)

calipers and support with wire. Remove right and left tie rod ends.

6) Disconnect electrical connections at A/C compressor. Remove A/C compressor and mounting brackets. Support A/C compressor with wire in wheel opening. Remove front suspension attaching bolts.

CAUTION: Be sure to support vehicle and transaxle weight during following steps.

7) Lower vehicle. Support front of vehicle by placing 2 jack stands under radiator core support. Position jack at rear of cowl with 4" x 4" x 6' timber spanning vehicle width. Raise and support vehicle enough to remove jack stands.

8) Position 4-wheel dolly under transaxle assembly with three 4" x 4" x 12" blocks as support. Let support rails hang free.

9) Slightly lower vehicle onto 4-wheel dolly. Remove rear transaxle mounting bolts. Remove left front engine mounting bolts. Remove 2 engine support-to-body mounting bolts behind right-hand inner axle universal joint.

10) Remove one mounting bolt and nut from right-hand chassis side rail-to-engine mount bracket. Remove 6 strut attaching nuts. Disconnect stabilizer bar from lower control arms. Raise and support vehicle, letting engine, transaxle, and suspension rest on 4-wheel dolly.

Installation
To install, reverse removal procedure.

2.0L (122") VIN 1
Removal

1) Disconnect battery cables. Drain cooling system and disconnect radiator hoses. Remove air cleaner. Disconnect accelerator and TV cables at throttle body. Disconnect ECM harness at engine.

2) Disconnect all vacuum hoses and heater hoses at engine. Remove exhaust heat shield, A/C adjustment bolt at motor mount, windshield washer bottle, and engine wiring harness at bulkhead.

3) Remove all drive belts. Disconnect fuel hoses. Raise and support vehicle. Remove A/C compressor brace (if equipped). Remove inner fender and flywheel splash shield. Remove A/C compressor from engine and position aside. Remove starter wires, front starter brace, and starter. Remove torque converter bolts (if equipped).

4) Remove crankshaft pulley, hub and oil filter. Disconnect engine-to-transmission support bracket. Disconnect exhaust pipe at manifold and center hanger. Loosen muffler hanger. Remove TV/shift cable bracket.

5) Remove 2 lower bellhousing bolts. Lower vehicle. Remove right front motor mount nuts. Remove alternator and adjusting brace. Remove master cylinder from booster and support out of the way. Attach lifting device. Remove right front motor mount bracket.

6) Disconnect upper bellhousing bolts. Remove power steering pump while lifting engine. Remove engine.

Installation
To install, reverse removal procedure.

2.3L (138")
Removal

1) Disconnect negative battery cable. Drain coolant. Remove air cleaner duct, fan shroud, upper radiator support and cooling fan. Remove oil filter.

2) On A/C equipped models, discharge A/C system. Remove coupled hose assembly at A/C compressor and discard "O" rings. On all models, disconnect and label all linkage, hoses, vacuum lines and electrical wiring that will interfere with engine removal.

3) Remove power steering pivot bolt, pump, and drive belt. Position power steering pump aside. Disconnect exhaust manifold and front engine mount. Install Engine Support (J 28467). Raise vehicle.

4) Remove front right wheel assembly. Remove right lower splash shield and radiator air deflector. Separate ball joints from steering knuckles. Support suspension crossmember and stabilizer shaft. Remove suspension support retaining bolts.

5) Remove suspension supports, crossmember and stabilizer shaft as an assembly. Install Drive Axle Seal Protector (J 34754) on drive axle boots. Remove axle shafts from transaxle and position aside.

6) Remove nut from transaxle mount through bolt and rear engine mount through bolt. Remove engine mount body bracket. Position suitable support below engine and lower car onto support.

7) Remove transaxle through bolt. Mark support fixture hooks so that positioning can be duplicated when reinstalling engine. Remove engine support fixture. Raise vehicle off engine and transaxle assembly. Separate engine from transaxle.

Installation
To install, reverse removal procedure. When tightening transaxle mount through bolt, ensure all related gaps are within .08" (2 mm) of each other. Check all fluid levels.

2.5L (151")
Removal (Automatic Transaxle)

1) Disconnect battery cables. Drain cooling system and disconnect radiator hoses. Remove air cleaner. Disconnect engine wiring harness connector. Disconnect vacuum and heater hoses. Remove A/C compressor with hoses attached and place aside.

2) Remove front reaction rod/strut. Disconnect throttle and transaxle linkage. Remove transaxle-to-engine bolts, except 2 upper bolts. Remove front mount-to-cradle nuts. Remove forward exhaust pipe. Remove converter housing cover. Remove converter-to-drive plate bolts. Remove starter motor.

3) Remove power steering pump with hoses attached and position aside (if equipped). Remove 2 rear transaxle support bracket bolts. Disconnect fuel line at fuel filter.

4) Position jack with wood block under transaxle and raise engine and transaxle until front engine mount studs clear cradle. Support engine weight with lift equipment. Remove 2 upper transaxle-to-engine bolts. Remove engine.

Installation
To install, reverse removal procedure.

Removal (Manual Transaxle)

1) Disconnect battery cables. Remove air cleaner. Raise and support vehicle. Remove front engine mount-to-cradle nuts. Remove forward exhaust pipe. Remove starter motor with wires attached and position to side.

2) Remove flywheel inspection cover and lower bellhousing bolts. Lower vehicle. Remove forward torque

rod/strut from engine. Remove A/C compressor and position aside with refrigerant lines connected (if equipped). Remove heater blower motor.

3) Disconnect emission hoses at canister. Disconnect power steering hoses (if equipped). Remove all vacuum hoses. Drain coolant. Disconnect radiator and heater hoses. Disconnect wiring at solenoid. Disconnect engine harness at firewall.

4) Disconnect throttle cable. Disconnect fuel line. Attach lifting device and remove engine.

Installation
To install, reverse removal procedure.

V6 MODELS

2.8L (173")
Removal
1) Disconnect battery cables. Remove air cleaner. Drain cooling system. Remove engine strut bracket from radiator support and position to rear. Remove A/C compressor from mounting bracket and lay aside (if equipped).

2) Disconnect vacuum hoses. Disconnect accelerator cable and TV cable (if equipped). Disconnect engine harness from ECM and pull connector through front of dash. Disconnect engine harness from junction block at left side of dash panel.

3) Disconnect radiator and heater hoses from engine. Remove power steering pump and bracket from engine (if equipped). Disconnect fuel lines at rubber hose connections on left side of engine compartment.

4) Raise and support vehicle. Remove engine front mount-to-cradle retaining nuts on right side of vehicle. Disconnect battery cables from engine. Remove starter.

5) Remove transaxle inspection cover. On automatic transaxle equipped vehicles, disconnect torque converter from drive plate. On all vehicles, remove crankshaft pulley and all belts. Disconnect exhaust pipe.

6) Remove lower transaxle-to-engine bolt from rear of engine. Disconnect power steering cut-off switch (if equipped).

7) Lower vehicle. Remove exhaust crossover pipe. Remove remaining transaxle-to-engine bolts. Make note of ground stud location for reassembly.

8) Place support under transaxle rear extension. Attach engine lift and remove engine.

Installation
To install, reverse removal procedure.

3.8L (231")
Removal (Century)
1) Disconnect negative battery cable. Remove air cleaner. Drain cooling system. Disconnect vacuum lines. Disconnect TV cable and accelerator linkage at carburetor.

2) Remove alternator. Disconnect engine wiring harness connector. Disconnect ground strap from engine at engine forward strut. Disconnect radiator hoses from radiator. Remove heater hoses from engine.

3) Remove fan blower motor. Remove fuel line. Remove gas piston at hood and support hood in full open position. Remove AIR pump and mounting bracket. Raise and support vehicle. Remove power steering lines at

steering gear. Disconnect exhaust pipe at manifold. Remove front engine mount-to-cradle nuts.

4) Disconnect battery cables at starter and transaxle housing. Remove converter inspection cover. After marking converter/drive plate position, remove converter-to-drive plate bolts. Remove transaxle-to-engine block support bracket bolts. Lower vehicle. Position support under transaxle rear extension.

5) Remove engine strut bracket from radiator support and swing rearward. Remove transaxle-to-engine bolts, noting location of ground stud.

6) Remove A/C compressor from mounting bracket and position aside, leaving refrigerant lines connected (if equipped). Attach engine lift and remove engine.

Installation
To install, reverse removal procedure.

Removal (Electra)
1) Raise hood and cover fenders. Remove negative battery cable. Remove airflow sensor wiring. Disconnect air intake duct. Drain cooling system. Raise and support vehicle.

2) Disconnect exhaust pipe. Disconnect engine mount bolts. Remove driveline vibration absorber. Remove starter wiring and starter. Disconnect A/C compressor and set aside (if equipped).

3) Remove lower transaxle-to-engine bolts. One bolt is located between transaxle case and engine block and is installed in opposite direction. Remove drive plate cover. Use a scribe to mark drive plate-to-torque converter relationship to assure proper reassembly. Remove drive plate-to-torque converter bolts.

4) Disconnect engine support bracket at transaxle. Lower vehicle. Remove radiator hoses. Disconnect heater hoses at engine. Remove alternator. Disconnect engine wiring harness. Remove remaining transaxle-to-engine bolts. Remove engine.

Installation
To install, reverse removal procedure.

Removal (LeSabre, Regal & Riviera)
1) Mark hinges for reinstallation and remove hood. Remove negative battery cable. Drain cooling system. Remove air cleaner. Remove cooling fan, pulleys and belts.

2) Disconnect A/C compressor and set aside (if equipped). Remove radiator and heater hoses from engine. Remove fan shroud assembly. On Riviera, remove cooler lines from radiator and then remove radiator.

3) Disconnect power steering pump and set aside. Disconnect fuel line and vacuum hoses. Disconnect battery ground cable from engine. Disconnect accelerator cable at carburetor.

4) Disconnect engine wiring harness connector, alternator and engine-to-ground straps. Raise and support vehicle. Disconnect crossover pipe from exhaust manifolds.

5) Use a scribe to mark relationship of torque converter to drive plate to assure proper reassembly. Remove transmission converter cover and torque converter bolts. Disconnect wiring at starter motor.

6) Remove right output shaft support bolts. Install final drive support chain. Disconnect final drive-to-engine support bracket.

7) Remove transmission-to-cylinder block attaching bolts. Remove front motor mount-to-frame bracket

attaching bolts. Lower vehicle and support transmission. Install engine lift. Remove engine.

Installation
To install, reverse removal procedure.

Removal (Skylark)
1) Raise hood and cover fenders. Scribe marks around hood hinges and remove hood. Remove negative battery cable. Raise and support vehicle. Disconnect starter wiring and remove starter.

2) Remove drive plate cover. Use a scribe to mark drive plate-to-torque converter relationship to assure proper reassembly. Remove drive plate-to-torque converter bolts.

3) Disconnect A/C compressor and wiring connector and set aside. Drain cooling system and remove lower radiator hose. Remove right front motor mount bolts. Remove right inner fender splash shield.

4) Remove transaxle-to-engine mount bolt located between transaxle and cylinder block. Remove rear motor mount nuts. Disconnect exhaust pipe from manifold. Remove all heater hoses.

5) Lower vehicle. Remove serpentine drive belt, alternator and power steering pump. Remove mass airflow sensor and intake duct. Disconnect electrical connector and remove cooling fan.

6) Remove upper radiator hose and radiator. Position engine lift. Remove left upper transaxle mount. Remove master cylinder. Remove fuel lines and fuel rail. Remove TV and cruise control cable at throttle body. Remove all remaining engine-to-transaxle mounting bolts. Remove engine.

Installation
To install, reverse removal procedure.

V8 MODELS

5.0L (307")
Removal
1) Drain cooling system. Remove air cleaner and hot air pipe. Mark hinges for reinstallation and remove hood. Disconnect negative battery cable. Remove engine ground strap from right cylinder head to cowl.

2) Remove radiator hoses. Remove automatic transmission cooler lines from radiator. Remove all heater hoses and vacuum hoses connected to engine.

3) Disconnect power steering pump with hoses attached. Remove power steering hose bracket from engine. Remove A/C compressor and position aside with hoses and brackets attached (if equipped).

4) Disconnect fuel hose from fuel line. Disconnect all wiring from engine. Disconnect accelerator cable. Remove radiator. Raise and support vehicle. Disconnect exhaust and crossover pipes at manifolds.

5) Remove torque converter cover and bolts attaching converter to drive plate. Remove engine mount bolts or nuts. Remove 3 transmission-to-engine bolts on right side. Remove starter and secure to frame with wires attached.

6) Lower vehicle. Install engine lift. Place a wood block on top of a jack and slightly raise transmission. Remove transmission-to-engine bolts on left side. Remove engine. If vehicle is to be moved, install converter holding tool and transmission support chain.

Installation
To install, reverse removal procedure.

BUICK TIGHTENING SPECIFICATIONS

Application	Ft. Lbs. (N.m)
4-Cylinder Engines	
2.0L (122") VIN K	
Drive Plate-to-Converter Bolts	31 (42)
Left Front Motor Mount Bolts	18 (24)
Right Rear Motor Mount Bolts	38 (52)
Right Rear Mount-to-Frame Bolts	38 (52)
Transaxle-to-Engine Bolts	42 (57)
2.0L (122") VIN 1	
Drive Plate-to-Converter Bolts	31 (42)
Front Motor Mount-to-Engine Bolts	25-35 (34-47)
Lower Motor Mount-to-Engine Bolts	15-20 (20-27)
Motor Mount-to-Frame Bolts	35-45 (47-61)
Starter-to-Engine Bolts	26-37 (35-50)
Transaxle-to-Engine Bolts	48-63 (65-85)
2.3L (138")	
Motor Mounts-to-Engine Bolts	55 (76)
Drive Plate-to-Converter Bolts	46 (61)
2.5L (151")	
Drive Plate-to-Converter Bolts	31 (42)
Motor Mount-to-Engine Bolts	35 (47)
Motor Mount-to-Frame Bolts	35 (47)
Starter-to-Engine Bolts	31 (42)
Transaxle-to-Engine Bolts	55 (75)
V6 Engines	
2.8L (173")	
Eng. Mntg. Brkt.-to-Engine Bolts	70-92 (95-125)
Eng. Mntg. Torque Strut Brkt. Bolts	30-40 (41-54)
Drive Plate-to-Converter Bolts	25-35 (34-47)
Starter-to-Engine Bolts	26-37 (35-50)
Transaxle-to-Engine Bolts	55 (75)
3.8L (231")	
All Models	
Drive Plate-to-Converter Bolts	35 (47)
Starter-to-Engine Bolts	35 (47)
Transmission-to-Engine Bolts	35 (47)
FWD Models	
Motor Mount-to-Engine Bolts	66 (89)
Motor Mount-to-Frame Bolts	66 (89)
Final Drive-to-Engine Bolts	66 (89)
Output Shaft-to-Engine Support Bolts	
Front	80 (108)
Rear	55 (75)
RWD	
Motor Mount-to-Engine Bolts	59 (80)
Motor Mount-to-Frame Bolts	33 (45)
Motor Mount-to-Bracket Bolts	48 (65)
V8 Engines	
5.0L (307")	
Drive Plate-to-Converter Bolts	35 (47)
Motor Mount-to-Engine Bolts	75 (102)
Motor Mount-to-Frame Bolts	35 (47)
Motor Mount Through Bolts	55 (75)
Starter-to-Engine Bolts	30 (41)
Transmission-to-Engine Bolts	35 (47)

GENERAL MOTORS – CADILLAC

V6 MODELS

2.8L (173")
Removal

1) Disconnect battery cables. Drain cooling system. Remove air cleaner. Remove mass airflow sensor. Remove exhaust crossover heat shield. Remove exhaust crossover pipe.

2) Remove serpentine belt and tensioner. Remove power steering pump mounting bracket. Disconnect heater pipe at power steering pump mounting bracket. Disconnect radiator hose at engine. Disconnect accelerator and TV cable at throttle valve.

3) Remove alternator. Disconnect wiring harness at engine. Disconnect fuel lines. Disconnect coolant by-pass and overflow hoses at engine. Disconnect canister purge hose at canister. Remove vacuum hoses. Raise and support vehicle.

4) Remove right inner fender splash shield. Remove harmonic balancer. Remove flywheel cover. Remove wires at starter and remove starter. Disconnect wires at oil sending unit.

5) Remove A/C compressor and bracket. Disconnect exhaust pipe at rear of manifold. Remove drive plate-to-torque converter bolts. Remove transaxle-to-engine brace bolts. Remove engine rear mount-to-frame nuts.

6) Disconnect shift cable bracket at transaxle. Remove lower bellhousing bolts. Lower vehicle. Disconnect heater hoses at engine. Install engine lift. Support transaxle with jack.

7) Remove upper bellhousing and front mount bolts. Remove master cylinder. Remove engine.

Installation
To install, reverse removal procedure.

V8 MODELS

4.1L (250")
Removal

1) Disconnect negative battery cable. Drain cooling system. Remove air cleaner. Mark hinges for reassembly reference and remove hood. Remove cooling fans and accessory drive belt. Remove upper intake manifold. Remove radiator and heater hoses from intake manifold.

2) Remove following wire connectors and reposition out of way: oil pressure switches, coolant temperature sensor, distributor, engine temperature switch, injectors at injector harness connector, oxygen sensors, alternator, and ground wires at alternator bracket.

3) Remove cruise control diaphram with bracket and move out of way. Remove oil and transmission cooler lines from radiator and remove radiator. Remove oil cooler lines. Remove air cleaner mounting bracket and oil filter adapter.

4) Remove AIR tubes from diverter valve. Remove cross-car brace, right front heater hose, coolant reservoir, and AIR filter and bracket. Remove P/S line brace on right cylinder head. Remove P/S pump and tensioner assembly and position out of way. Discharge A/C system. Remove A/C lines to accumulator and condenser.

NOTE: Carefully bleed fuel pressure at fuel line Schrader valve. Use a container to catch fuel.

5) Remove fuel line bracket and move fuel lines out of way. Raise and support vehicle. Remove electrical connectors from starter and ground wires from block. Remove oil level sensor and oxygen sensor(s). Remove exhaust "Y" pipe, starter, and drive plate cover. Remove drive plate-to-converter bolts, A/C compressor lower dust shield, right front tire and wheel assembly, and outer wheelhouse plastic shield.

6) Remove right rear transmission/engine mounting bolt, front engine mount nuts and right rear transmission mount bolts. Remove alternator, oxygen sensor wires and heater by-pass bracket from right of vehicle. Remove right engine brace.

7) Lower vehicle. Remove 5 top engine/transmission mounting bolts. Install engine lift chain and remove engine.

Installation
To install, reverse removal procedure.

4.5L (273")
Removal (DeVille & Fleetwood)

1) Disconnect battery cables. Drain cooling system. Remove air cleaner. Mark hinges for reassembly reference and remove hood. Disconnect A/C hose strap from right strut tower. Disconnect A/C accumulator from bracket and move aside.

2) Disconnect canister hose and ground wire from A/C accumulator bracket. Disconnect A/C accumulator bracket from wheel housing. Remove cooling fan. Remove accessory drive belt and heater hose. Remove upper radiator hose.

3) Disconnect all engine wiring. Disconnect cables from throttle lever. Disconnect cruise control diaphram with bracket and move out of way. Disconnect vacuum hoses. Disconnect exhaust crossover pipe.

4) Disconnect oil cooler lines from oil filter adapter. Disconnect oil cooler line bracket at transmission and move lines aside. Remove air cleaner bracket.

NOTE: Carefully bleed fuel pressure at fuel line Schrader valve. Use a container to catch fuel.

5) Disconnect fuel lines at throttle body. Disconnect fuel line bracket at transmission and move fuel lines aside. Remove AIR valve with bracket. Remove pulley idler.

6) Remove power steering hose strap from stud bolt. Remove stud bolt. Remove AIR pipe clip. Remove power steering pump and belt tensioner with bracket and move aside. Raise and support vehicle.

7) Remove drive plate covers. Disconnect starter wires and remove starter. Remove 3 drive plate-to-converter bolts. Remove A/C compressor lower dust shield. Remove right front tire and wheel assembly. Remove outer wheelhouse plastic shield.

8) Remove A/C compressor mounting bolts and lower compressor aside. Remove lower radiator hose. Remove driveline vibration damper with brackets from lower right front of engine and cradle. Pull alternator wire with plastic cover down, out of way. Remove 3 right front engine-to-transmission bracket bolts.

9) Remove 2 exhaust pipe-to-manifold bolts and springs. Remove the AIR pipe-to-converter bracket

Engine Removal & Installation

GENERAL MOTORS – CADILLAC (Cont.)

from the exhaust manifold stud. Remove lower right transaxle-to-engine bolt. Support engine.

10) Remove upper 5 transaxle-to-engine bolts. Remove 3 left front engine mount bracket-to-engine bolts. Remove engine.

Installation
To install, reverse removal procedure.

Removal (All Other Models)
1) Disconnect battery cables. Drain cooling system. On RWD models, remove 2 screws attaching radiator cover to strut support rods at radiator cover. Remove one screw from each side at strut. Move support rods aside.

2) On all models, remove 2 screws attaching top radiator shroud to radiator support. Remove rivets securing upper fan shroud to lower fan shroud.

3) Remove screws and washers attaching radiator cover to radiator support and remove cover. Remove 2 screws attaching power steering reservoir to upper fan shroud. Position reservoir aside and remove shroud.

4) After marking hinge location, remove hood. Remove air cleaner and inlet duct. Disconnect upper radiator hose from thermostat housing. Disconnect all wires at engine. Disconnect all vacuum hoses to engine. Disconnect accelerator linkage.

5) Disconnect vapor canister hose. Remove clutch fan assembly. Disconnect lower radiator hose at water pump. Disconnect A/C compressor from engine and position aside with hoses attached. Remove hose from water nipple, located in rear of intake manifold. Disconnect fuel inlet and return lines.

6) Raise and support vehicle. Disconnect engine oil cooler lines at radiator on RWD models or at junction on right side of engine compartment on FWD models. Remove 6 transmission-to-engine bolts. Remove front engine mount-to-frame crossmember nuts on FWD models and motor mount through bolts on RWD models.

7) On RWD models, disconnect strut rods connecting engine mounts to bellhousing. Remove drive

plate cover. Remove drive plate-to-converter bolts. Disconnect starter motor wiring, engine ground wire, and oil pressure switch wiring. Support exhaust system. Disconnect exhaust system at manifolds.

8) Lower vehicle. Support transmission. Attach engine lift, using chain with spreader bar. Raise engine slowly to disengage from transmission and remove engine.

Installation
To install, reverse removal procedure.

CADILLAC TIGHTENING SPECIFICATIONS

Application	Ft. Lbs. (N.m)
V6 Engine	
Engine Mounting	
Bracket-to-Engine Bolts	70-92 (95-125)
Engine Mounting	
Torque Strut Bracket Bolts	30-40 (41-54)
Drive Plate-to-Converter Bolts	25-35 (34-47)
Starter-to-Engine Bolts	26-37 (35-50)
Transaxle-to-Engine Bolts	55 (75)
V8 Engines	
All Models	
Drive Plate-to-Converter Bolts	46-48 (62-65)
Starter-to-Engine Bolts	30 (41)
FWD Models	
Transmission-to-Engine Bolts	55 (74)
Motor Mount-to-Engine Bolts	33 (45)
Motor Mount-to-Frame Bolts	65 (88)
Transaxle-to-Engine Bracket Bolts	33 (45)
Output Shaft Support Bracket Bolts	
Front	80 (108)
Rear	55 (75)
RWD Models	
Transmission-to-Engine Bolts	35 (47)
Motor Mount-to-Engine Bolts	33 (45)
Motor Mount-to-Frame Bolts	33 (45)
Motor Mount Through Bolts	44 (60)

GENERAL MOTORS – CHEVROLET

4-CYLINDER MODELS

Removal (Nova)
1) Mark hinges for reinstallation and remove hood. Disconnect negative battery cable. Drain cooling system, engine oil and transmission fluid or gear oil.

2) Remove air cleaner assembly. Disconnect upper radiator hose at outlet. Disconnect overflow hose. Disconnect coolant hose at cylinder head rear of coolant pipe.

3) Disconnect coolant hose at thermostat housing. Disconnect fuel hoses at fuel pump. Remove alternator, power steering belt and A/C belt (if equipped). Disconnect necessary wires at engine and vacuum hoses.

4) Disconnect wires at transaxle. Disconnect speedometer cable at transaxle. Raise and support vehicle. Disconnect exhaust pipe at manifold. Disconnect air hose at converter pipe (Federal vehicles). Disconnect

transaxle cooler lines at radiator and remove right and left under covers.

5) Disconnect power steering pump and A/C compressor and lay aside (if equipped). Disconnect speedometer cable and bracket at transaxle. Disconnect steering knuckles at lower control arms.

6) Disconnect drive shafts at transaxle. Remove flywheel cover. Remove flexplate-to-torque converter bolts. Disconnect front and rear mounting at center member. Disconnect cable and remove center member.

7) Lower vehicle. Remove radiator with fan. Install engine lifting device. Remove right motor mount through bolt. Remove left transaxle mount bolt and mount. Remove engine and transaxle.

Installation
To install, reverse removal procedure.

GENERAL MOTORS – CHEVROLET (Cont.)

2.0L (122")

Removal

1) Disconnect battery cable. Drain cooling system. Remove air cleaner. Remove window washer bottle.

2) Disconnect accelerator and TV cables. Disconnect ECM harness at engine. Disconnect radiator and heater hoses at engine. Disconnect all vacuum hoses at engine. Disconnect engine harness at bulkhead connector.

3) Remove exhaust heat shield. Remove A/C adjustment bolt at motor mount (if equipped). Remove alternator and power steering belts. Disconnect fuel lines. Raise and support vehicle.

4) Remove inner fender splash shield. Remove A/C brace and compressor (if equipped). Remove flywheel shield. Remove starter wires, front brace, and starter. Remove drive plate-to-converter bolts.

5) Remove crankshaft pulley and hub. Remove oil filter. Disconnect engine-to-transmission bracket. Disconnect right rear motor mount. Disconnect exhaust pipe at manifold and center hanger. Loosen muffler hanger.

6) Disconnect TV/shift cable bracket. Remove 2 lower bellhousing bolts. Lower vehicle. Disconnect right front motor mount. Remove alternator and adjusting brace. Disconnect master cylinder and move aside. Attach engine lift.

7) Remove right front motor mount bracket. Remove upper bellhousing bolts. Remove power steering pump while lifting engine. Remove engine.

Installation

To install, reverse removal procedure.

2.5L (151")

FWD Man. Trans. Models

1) Disconnect battery cables. Drain coolant system. Raise and support vehicle. Remove front engine mount-to-cradle nuts. Remove forward exhaust pipe. Remove starter motor with wiring attached and position aside.

2) Remove flywheel inspection cover. Lower vehicle. Remove air cleaner. Remove all bellhousing-to-engine bolts.

3) Remove forward torque reaction rod from engine and radiator core support. Remove A/C compressor and position aside with hoses attached (if equipped).

4) Remove vacuum hoses at canister. Remove power steering hose (if equipped). Remove all vacuum hoses and electrical connectors at solenoid. Remove heater blower motor. Disconnect accelerator cable. Drain cooling system.

5) Disconnect heater and radiator hoses. Disconnect engine wiring harness at bulkhead connector.

6) Install engine lift and lift engine slightly. Remove heater hose and fuel line from intake manifold. Remove engine.

Installation

To install, reverse removal procedure.

FWD Auto. Trans. Models

Removal

1) Disconnect battery cables. Drain cooling system. Remove air cleaner and heat tube. Disconnect engine wiring harness connector. Disconnect all vacuum hoses. Remove throttle and transaxle linkage at EFI assembly and intake manifold.

2) Remove upper radiator hose. Remove A/C compressor from brackets and position aside with hoses connected (if equipped). Remove front engine strut assembly. Disconnect heater hose at intake manifold. Remove transaxle-to-engine bolts, leaving top 2 bolts in place.

3) Remove front mount-to-cradle nuts. Remove forward exhaust pipe. Remove flywheel cover and starter. Remove drive plate-to-converter bolts. Remove power steering pump with bracket and position aside. Remove remaining heater hose and lower radiator hose.

4) Remove 2 rear transaxle support bracket bolts. Remove fuel line at fuel filter. With floor jack and block of wood under transaxle, raise engine until front mount studs clear cradle.

5) Attach engine lift to engine and tension slightly. Remove 2 remaining transaxle-to-engine bolts. Remove engine.

Installation

To install, reverse removal procedure.

V6 MODELS

2.8L (173")

Removal (Beretta & Corsica)

1) Disconnect battery cables. Remove air cleaner, inlet hose and mass airflow sensor. Drain cooling system. Remove exhaust manifold/crossover assembly. Remove serpentine belt tensioner and belt. Disconnect power steering pump and lay aside. Remove idler pulley (if equipped).

2) Remove radiator hose at engine. Remove accelerator and T.V. cable at throttle valve bracket at plenum. Remove alternator and lay aside. Disconnect wiring harness, fuel hoses, coolant by-pass and overflow hoses at engine. Remove canister purge at canister. Remove all attaching vacuum hoses.

3) Support engine with Engine Holding Fixture (J-28467). Raise and support vehicle. Remove right inner fender splash shield, harmonic dampener, and flywheel cover. Remove starter bolts, wires and starter. Remove wires at oil sending unit. Remove A/C compressor and brackets (if equipped).

4) Remove exhaust pipe, flywheel-to-torque converter bolts, front and rear motor mount bolts and brackets. Remove intermediate shaft bracket-to-engine. Disconnect shift cable bracket at transaxle. Remove lower bellhousing bolts and lower vehicle.

5) Remove heater hoses at engine. Install lifting devise. Remove holding fixture. Support transaxle with jack. Remove upper bellhousing bolts and front mount bolts. Remove transaxle mount bracket and engine.

Installation

To install, reverse removal procedure.

Removal (Camaro)

1) Disconnect battery cables. Remove air cleaner. Mark hinges for reassembly and remove hood. Drain cooling system. Remove lower radiator hose. Remove upper fan shroud. Remove upper radiator hose and coolant recovery hose.

2) Disconnect transmission cooler lines at radiator. Remove radiator. Remove fan assembly. Remove heater hoses.

GENERAL MOTORS – CHEVROLET (Cont.)

3) Disconnect throttle and cruise control detent linkages from carburetor. Disconnect all vacuum lines and wiring to engine. Remove distributor cap.

4) Remove power steering pump and position aside with hoses connected. Raise and support vehicle. Remove exhaust pipes at manifolds. Remove converter cover. Remove drive plate-to-converter bolts. Disconnect starter wires.

5) Remove transmission-to-engine bolts. Remove motor mount through bolts. Disconnect fuel lines at fuel pump.

6) Lower vehicle. Remove bracket holding Air Injection (AIR)-to-converter pipes. Support transmission with jack. Install engine lift. Remove engine, disconnecting wire from bracket at left rear of engine.

Installation
To install, reverse removal procedure.

Removal (Cavalier)
1) Disconnect battery ground cable. Drain cooling system. Remove air cleaner. Remove mass airflow sensor. Remove exhaust crossover heat shield. Remove exhaust crossover pipe.

2) Remove serpentine belt and tensioner. Remove power steering pump mounting bracket. Disconnect heater pipe at power steering pump mounting bracket. Disconnect radiator hose at engine. Disconnect accelerator and TV cable at throttle valve.

3) Remove alternator. Disconnect wiring harness at engine. Disconnect fuel lines. Disconnect coolant by-pass and overflow hoses at engine. Disconnect canister purge hose at canister. Remove vacuum hoses. Raise and support vehicle.

4) Remove right inner fender splash shield. Remove harmonic balancer. Remove flywheel cover. Remove wires at starter and remove starter. Disconnect wires at oil sending unit.

5) Remove A/C compressor and bracket. Disconnect exhaust pipe at rear of manifold. Remove drive plate torque bolts at converter. Remove the transaxle-to-engine brace bolts. Remove the engine rear mount-to-frame nuts.

6) Disconnect shift cable bracket at transaxle. Remove lower bellhousing bolts. Lower vehicle. Disconnect heater hoses at engine. Install engine lift. Support transaxle with jack.

7) Remove upper bellhousing bolts and front mount bolts. Remove master cylinder. Remove engine.

Installation
To install, reverse removal procedure.

Removal (Celebrity)
1) Disconnect battery cables. Remove air cleaner. Drain cooling system. Remove engine strut bracket from radiator support and swing rearward. Remove Air Injection Reaction (AIR) pump and bracket.

2) Remove A/C compressor from bracket and set aside (if equipped). Disconnect vacuum hoses from all non-engine mounted components. Disconnect accelerator cable and detent cable (if equipped). Disconnect engine harness from Electronic Control Module (ECM) and pull connector through front of dash.

3) Disconnect radiator and heater hoses from engine. Remove power steering pump and bracket from engine (if equipped).

4) Disconnect fuel lines at rubber hose connections at left side of engine compartment. Raise and support vehicle.

5) Remove engine front mount-to-cradle and mount-to-engine bracket retaining nuts at right side of vehicle. Disconnect battery cables from engine at starter and transaxle housing bolt.

6) Remove starter. Remove transaxle cover plate and drive plate-to-converter bolts. Remove crankshaft lower pulley and all belts. Disconnect exhaust pipe.

7) Remove one lower transaxle-to-engine bolt from rear of engine. Disconnect power steering cut-off switch (if equipped).

8) Lower vehicle. Remove exhaust crossover pipe. Remove remaining transaxle-to-engine bolts. Make note of ground stud location. Place support under transaxle rear extension. Install engine lift and remove engine.

Installation
To install, reverse removal procedure.

4.3L (262")
Removal
1) Mark hinges for reinstallation and remove hood. Disconnect battery cables. Drain cooling system. Raise and support vehicle.

2) Disconnect exhaust at manifold. Remove flywheel cover. Disconnect transmission oil cooler lines at oil pan. Remove left motor mount through bolt and right bolt.

3) Remove flywheel-to-torque converter bolts. Remove bell housing bolts. Disconnect Computer Command Control (CCC) harness at transmission. Disconnect knock sensor.

4) Disconnect fuel hoses at frame. Remove lower fan shroud. On Monte Carlo, disconnect starter wires and remove starter. Lower vehicle.

5) On all models, disconnect Electronic Control Module (ECM) harness at engine. Disconnect necessary wires and vacuum hoses. Remove upper fan shroud. Remove accelerator and TV cables. Disconnect heater hoses. Disconnect radiator hoses. Remove A/C compressor and lay aside.

6) Remove power steering pump and lay aside. Disconnect transmission cooler lines at radiator. On Caprice, remove radiator, disconnect overflow tube and A/C hose at alternator. Remove alternator adjusting brace.

7) Disconnect heater hose at bracket on intake manifold. Disconnect ground strap at rear of cylinder head. On Monte Carlo, remove fan and pulley, and disconnect ground straps at both cylinder heads.

8) On all models, disconnect battery cables at frame. Disconnect converter Air Injection Reaction (AIR) pipe at exhaust manifold. Disconnect AIR hose at converter AIR pipe. Support transmission with jack and remove engine.

Installation
To install, reverse removal procedure.

GENERAL MOTORS – CHEVROLET (Cont.)

V8 MODELS

5.0L (305") & 5.7L (350")

(Except Corvette)

1) Disconnect battery and remove air cleaner. Drain radiator. Disconnect radiator hoses and remove upper fan shroud. Remove fan assembly. Disconnect heater hoses at engine.

2) Remove power steering pump and lay aside. Remove A/C compressor and lay aside. Disconnect accelerator and TV cable. Disconnect cooler lines at radiator. Remove radiator.

3) Disconnect vacuum hoses. Disconnect Computer Command Control (CCC) wiring harness. Disconnect Air Injection Reaction (AIR) hose at pipe from converter. Remove washer bottle. Disconnect engine wiring harness at bulkhead. Disconnect necessary wires. Remove hood.

4) Remove distributor cap. Disconnect cruise control cable. Disconnect battery positive cable to battery and frame. Disconnect battery negative cable at A/C hose bracket and alternator bracket. Raise and support vehicle.

5) Remove crossover pipe and catalytic converter as an assembly. Remove flywheel cover. Remove torque converter bolts. Remove motor mount bolts. Disconnect fuel hose at fuel pump. Disconnect torque converter clutch wiring at transmission.

6) Disconnect transmission cooler lines at clip on engine pan. Remove transmission-to-engine bolts. Lower vehicle. Support transmission. Install lifting device and remove engine.

Installation

To install, reverse removal procedure.

5.7L (350")

Removal (Corvette)

1) Disconnect negative battery cable. Drain coolant. Remove air cleaner. Remove serpentine belt. Remove braces at back of A/C compressor. Disconnect wires at A/C compressor.

2) Disconnect fuel lines. Remove A/C compressor mounting bracket nuts and bolts. Disconnect heater hoses. Disconnect fuel line clip at fuel pump cover plate. Disconnect upper radiator hose at thermostat outlet.

3) Remove A/C compressor-to-mounting bracket bolt and move compressor aside. Remove mounting bracket. Disconnect Port Fuel Injection (PFI) harness at engine. Disconnect cruise, detent and accelerator cables.

4) Remove distributor shield and cap. Disconnect detent cable bracket at intake. Remove distributor. Disconnect wires at oil pressure sending unit. Remove oil pressure sending unit. Disconnect vacuum hoses.

5) Disconnect power steering hoses at rack and pinion. Remove crankshaft pulley. Disconnect bulkhead connector and necessary connectors. Disconnect AIR hose at converter check valve. Move fuel lines out of way.

6) Disconnect radiator hose at water pump. Disconnect upper radiator hose at power steering reservoir bracket. Raise and support vehicle. Disconnect Air Injection Reaction (AIR) pipe at exhaust manifold. Remove AIR converter pipe.

7) Disconnect "Y" pipe hanger. Disconnect heat shields at "Y" pipe and converter. Disconnect oxygen sensor wire. Remove "Y" pipe. Remove flywheel cover.

Remove torque converter bolts. Loosen motor mount through bolts.

8) Remove motor mount-to-engine block bolts. Remove bellhousing bolts and lower vehicle. Disconnect knock sensor wire. Disconnect ground cable at engine. Disconnect positive battery cable at battery and harness.

9) Remove right rear intake manifold bolt and install lift hook. Support transmission with floor jack. Install engine lift. Remove engine, disconnecting wire from bracket at left rear of engine.

Installation

To install, reverse removal procedure.

CHEVROLET TIGHTENING SPECIFICATIONS

Application	Ft. Lbs. (N.m)
4-Cylinder Engines	
1.6L (98")	
Drive Plate-to-Converter Bolts	20 (27)
Engine Mount Nuts	48 (65)
Transmission-to-Engine Bolts	47 (64)
2.0L (122")	
Drive Plate-to-Converter Bolts	31 (42)
Front Motor Mount-to-Engine Bolts	25-35 (34-47)
Lower Motor Mount-to-Engine Bolts	15-20 (20-27)
Motor Mount-to-Frame Bolts	35-45 (47-61)
Starter-to-Engine Bolts	26-37 (35-50)
Transaxle-to-Engine Bolts	48-63 (65-85)
2.5L (151")	
Drive Plate-to-Converter Bolts	30 (41)
Motor Mount-to-Engine Bolts	35 (47)
Motor Mount-to-Frame Bolts	35 (47)
Starter-to-Engine Bolts	32 (43)
Transmission-to-Engine Bolts	48-63 (65-85)
V6 Engines	
2.8L (173")	
Drive Plate-to-Converter Bolts	25-35 (34-47)
Motor Mount-to-Engine Bolts	35 (47)
Motor Strut Through Bolts	35 (47)
Starter-to-Engine Bolts	32 (43)
Transmission-to-Engine Bolts	48-63 (65-85)
4.3L (262")	
Drive Plate-to-Converter Bolts	35 (47)
Motor Mount-to-Engine Bolts	59 (80)
Motor Mount-to-Frame Bolts	33 (45)
Motor Mount Through Bolts	47 (64)
Starter-to-Engine Bolts	35 (47)
Transmission-to-Engine Bolts	35 (47)
V8 Engines	
5.0L (305")	
Drive Plate-to-Converter Bolts	35 (47)
Motor Mount-to-Engine Bolts	75 (102)
Motor Mount-to-Frame Bolts	35 (47)
Motor Mount Through Bolts	55 (75)
Starter-to-Engine Bolts	30 (41)
Transmission-to-Engine Bolts	35 (47)
5.7L (350")	
Crankshaft Pulley Bolts	26-37 (35-50)
Drive Plate-to-Converter Bolts	35 (47)
Intake Bolts	35 (47)
Motor Mount-to-Engine Bolts	33-49 (45-66)
Motor Mount Through Bolts	70-85 (95-115)
Transmission-to-Engine Bolts	30 (41)

Engine Removal & Installation
GENERAL MOTORS – OLDSMOBILE

4-CYLINDER MODELS

2.0L (122") VIN K
Removal

1) Disconnect battery cables. Drain cooling system. Remove air cleaner. Disconnect electrical harness at bulkhead. Disconnect electrical connector at brake cylinder.

2) Remove accelerator cable and vacuum hoses from carburetor. Remove power steering hose at cut-off switch. Remove vacuum hoses at MAP sensor and canister. Disconnect A/C relay switches.

3) Remove power steering return hose at pump. Disconnect ECM wire connections. Remove upper and lower radiator hoses. Remove electrical connections from temperature switch at thermostat housing.

4) Disconnect transaxle shift cable at transaxle. Raise and support vehicle. Remove speedometer cable. Disconnect exhaust pipe at manifold and remove from converter. Remove heater hoses and fuel lines. Remove transaxle cooler lines.

5) Remove both front wheels. Remove right spoiler section and splash shield. Remove brake calipers and support with wire. Remove tie rod ends.

6) Disconnect electrical connections at A/C compressor. Remove A/C compressor and mounting brackets. Support A/C compressor with wire in wheel opening. Remove front suspension attaching bolts.

CAUTION: Be sure to support vehicle and transaxle weight during following steps.

7) Lower vehicle. Support front of vehicle by placing 2 jack stands under core support. Position jack at rear of cowl with 4" x 4" x 6' timber spanning vehicle width. Raise vehicle enough to remove jack stands.

8) Position 4-wheel dolly under transaxle assembly with three 4" x 4" x 12" wood blocks as support. Allow support rails to hang free.

9) Slightly lower vehicle onto 4-wheel dolly. Remove rear transaxle mounting bolts. Remove 2 engine support-to-body mounting bolts behind right inner axle universal joint.

10) Remove one mounting bolt and nut from right chassis side rail-to-engine mount bracket. Remove 6 strut attaching nuts. Raise vehicle. Allow engine, transaxle and suspension to rest on 4-wheel dolly.

Installation
To install, reverse removal procedure.

2.0L (122") VIN 1
Removal

1) Disconnect battery cables. Drain cooling system. Remove air cleaner. Remove power steering pump (if equipped). Remove window washer bottle. Remove A/C relay bracket at bulkhead connector (if equipped). Remove bulkhead connector.

2) Remove cruise control servo bracket (if equipped). Disconnect all vacuum hoses and wiring to engine. Remove bolts attaching vacuum booster to master cylinder. Lay vacuum booster aside. Remove heater hose at hot water pipe. Remove fan assembly. Remove horn. Remove fuel injection linkage.

3) Raise and support vehicle. Remove heater hose and fuel line at intake manifold. Remove A/C

compressor brace (if equipped). Remove exhaust shield. Remove starter. Remove exhaust pipe at manifold. Remove front wheels.

4) Remove stabilizer bar at lower control arms. Remove ball joints from steering knuckle. Remove drive axles at transaxle. Remove transaxle strut. Remove inner fender shield, A/C drive belt and compressor (if equipped).

5) Remove front motor mount nuts. On manual transaxle equipped vehicles, remove clutch cable at transaxle. On automatic transaxle equipped vehicles, remove detent cable at transaxle. On all models, install engine lift. Remove transaxle mount and bracket. Remove engine.

Installation
To install, reverse removal procedure.

2.3L (138")
Removal

1) Disconnect negative battery cable. Drain coolant. Remove air cleaner duct, fan shroud, upper radiator support and cooling fan. Remove oil filter.

2) On A/C equipped models, discharge A/C system. Remove coupled hose assembly at A/C compressor and discard "O" rings. On all models, disconnect and label all linkage, hoses, vacuum lines and electrical wiring that will interfere with engine removal.

3) Remove power steering pivot bolt, pump, and drive belt. Position power steering pump aside. Disconnect exhaust manifold and front engine mount. Install Engine Support (J 28467). Raise vehicle.

4) Remove front right wheel assembly. Remove right lower splash shield and radiator air deflector. Separate ball joints from steering knuckles. Support suspension crossmember and stabilizer shaft. Remove suspension support retaining bolts.

5) Remove suspension supports, crossmember and stabilizer shaft as an assembly. Install Drive Axle Seal Protector (J 34754) on drive axle boots. Remove axle shafts from transaxle and position aside.

6) Remove nut from transaxle mount through bolt and rear engine mount through bolt. Remove engine mount body bracket. Position suitable support below engine and lower car onto support.

7) Remove transaxle through bolt. Mark support fixture hooks so that positioning can be duplicated when reinstalling engine. Remove engine support fixture. Raise vehicle off engine and transaxle assembly. Separate engine from transaxle.

Installation
To install, reverse removal procedure. When tightening transaxle mount through bolt, ensure all related gaps are within .08" (2 mm) of each other. Check all fluid levels.

2.5L (151")
Removal
(Cutlass Calais – Automatic Transaxle)

1) Disconnect battery cables. Drain engine coolant. Remove air cleaner. Disconnect ECM connections and feed harness through bulkhead. Disconnect engine wiring harness. Disconnect vacuum hoses. Disconnect radiator and heater hoses.

2) Disconnect A/C compressor, leaving hoses attached and move aside. Disconnect transaxle strut (front). Disconnect fuel lines at TBI. Disconnect cooler lines and shifter linkage.

3) Disconnect downshift cable. Disconnect throttle cable at TBI. Disconnect engine grounds. Remove multi-relay bracket. Raise and support vehicle. Remove power steering line bracket from engine.

4) Remove front wheels. Disconnect brake calipers and tie to springs. Remove brake rotors. Remove knuckle-to-strut bolts, 2 per side. Disconnect exhaust pipe at manifold and hangers, and swing aside.

5) Loosen remaining 8 body-to-cradle bolts at ends. Remove one bolt at each end of each cradle side, leaving one bolt per corner. Place jack stands under front of body. Move hoist back to body pan with 4" x 4" x 6' timber between hoist and vehicle.

6) Lift hoist and remove jack stands. Place dolly under engine transaxle assembly with 4" x 4" blocks to maintain position on dolly. Lower vehicle, allowing engine/transaxle assembly to rest on dolly.

7) Remove engine mount bolts and right front bracket. Remove remaining 4 cradle-to-body bolts. Lift vehicle off engine/transaxle assembly. Separate engine and transaxle.

Installation
To install, reverse removal procedure.

Removal (Cutlass Ciera)
1) Disconnect battery cables. Drain cooling system. Remove air cleaner and heat tube. Disconnect engine wiring harness connector. Disconnect all vacuum lines. Remove throttle and transaxle linkage at fuel injection assembly.

2) Remove upper radiator hose. Remove A/C compressor from brackets and position aside with hoses attached (if equipped). Remove front engine strut assembly. Disconnect heater hose at intake manifold. Remove transaxle-to-engine bolts, leaving top 2 bolts in place.

3) Remove front mount-to-cradle nuts. Remove forward exhaust pipe. Remove flywheel inspection cover. Remove starter. Remove drive plate-to-converter bolts. Remove power steering pump and position aside. Remove remaining heater hose and lower radiator hose.

4) Remove rear transaxle support bracket bolts. Remove fuel line at fuel filter. With floor jack and block of wood under transaxle, raise engine until front mount studs clear cradle.

5) Attach engine lift to engine. Remove 2 remaining transaxle-to-engine bolts. Remove engine.

Installation
To install, reverse removal procedure.

V6 MODELS

2.8L (173")
Removal (Cutlass Ciera)
1) Disconnect battery cables. Remove air cleaner. Drain cooling system. Remove engine strut bracket from radiator support and swing rearward.

2) Remove A/C compressor from bracket and set aside. Disconnect vacuum hoses. Disconnect accelerator cable and detent cable (if equipped). Disconnect engine harness from ECM and pull connector through front of dash.

3) Disconnect radiator and heater hoses from engine. Remove power steering pump and bracket from engine (if equipped).

4) Disconnect fuel lines at rubber hose connections at left side of engine compartment. Raise and support vehicle.

5) Remove engine front mount-to-cradle and mount-to-engine bracket retaining nuts from right side of vehicle. Disconnect battery cables from engine at starter and transaxle housing bolt.

6) Remove starter. Remove transaxle inspection cover plate and disconnect drive plate-to-converter bolts. Remove crankshaft lower pulley and remove all belts. Disconnect exhaust pipe.

7) Remove lower transaxle-to-engine bolt from rear of engine. Disconnect power steering cut-off switch (if equipped).

8) Lower vehicle. Remove exhaust crossover pipe. Remove remaining transaxle-to-engine bolts. Make note of ground stud location. Place support under transaxle rear extension. Install engine lift and remove engine.

Installation
To install, reverse removal procedure.

Removal (Cutlass Supreme)
1) Disconnect negative battery cable. Remove hood. Remove airflow tube at air cleaner and throttle valve. Remove A.I.R. belt and serpentine belt cover.

2) Disconnect and label all linkage, hoses, vacuum lines and electrical wiring that will interfere with engine removal. Remove A/C mounting bolts from mounting bracket. Remove power steering pump and set aside. Remove EGR from exhaust.

3) Raise vehicle. Remove A/C from engine. Remove drive plate cover. Remove starter, torque converter bolts and transaxle bracket. Remove engine front mount retaining nuts. Disconnect exhaust pipe at crossover.

4) Lower vehicle. Disconnect engine torque struts. Remove coolant recovery bottle. Disconnect left crossover pipe to manifold clamp. Pull engine assembly forward and support. Disconnect right crossover pipe to manifold clamp.

5) Remove engine support and allow engine to move to normal position. Support transaxle. Remove bolts attaching transaxle to engine. Attach lifting device to engine and remove engine.

Installation
To install, reverse removal procedure.

3.0L (181")
Removal (Cutlass Calais)
1) Raise hood and cover fenders. Scribe marks around hood hinges and remove hood. Remove negative battery cable. Raise and support vehicle. Disconnect starter wiring and remove starter.

2) Remove drive plate cover. Use a scribe to mark drive plate-to-torque converter relationship to assure proper reassembly. Remove drive plate-to-torque converter bolts.

3) Disconnect A/C compressor and wiring connector and set aside. Drain cooling system and remove lower radiator hose. Remove right front motor mount bolts. Remove right inner fender splash shield.

4) Remove transaxle-to-engine mount bolt located between transaxle and cylinder block. Remove rear motor mount nuts. Disconnect exhaust pipe from manifold. Remove all heater hoses.

Engine Removal & Installation

GENERAL MOTORS – OLDSMOBILE (Cont.)

5) Lower vehicle. Remove serpentine drive belt, alternator and power steering pump. Remove mass airflow sensor and intake duct. Disconnect electrical connector and remove cooling fan.

6) Remove upper radiator hose and radiator. Position engine lift. Remove left upper transaxle mount. Remove master cylinder. Remove fuel lines at fuel rail. Remove TV and cruise control cable at throttle body. Remove all remaining engine-to-transaxle mounting bolts. Remove engine.

Installation
To install, reverse removal procedure.

3.8L (231")
Removal (Cutlass Ciera)

1) Disconnect negative battery cable. Remove air cleaner. Drain cooling system. Disconnect vacuum lines. Disconnect T.V cable and accelerator linkage at carburetor.

2) Remove alternator. Disconnect engine wiring harness connector. Disconnect ground strap from engine at engine forward strut. Disconnect radiator hoses from radiator. Remove heater hoses from engine.

3) Remove fan blower motor. Remove fuel line. Remove damper at hood and support hood in full open position. Remove A.I.R. pump and mounting bracket. Raise and support vehicle. Remove power steering lines at steering gear. Disconnect exhaust pipe at manifold. Remove front engine mount-to-cradle nuts.

4) Disconnect battery cables at starter and transaxle housing. Remove converter inspection cover. After marking torque converter-to-drive plate position, remove torque converter-to-drive plate bolts. Remove transaxle-to-engine block support bracket bolts. Lower vehicle. Position support under transaxle rear extension.

5) Remove engine strut bracket from radiator support and swing rearward. Remove transaxle-to-engine bolts, noting location of ground stud.

6) Remove A/C compressor from mounting bracket and position aside, leaving refrigerant lines connected. Attach engine lift and remove engine.

Installation
To install, reverse removal procedure.

Removal (Delta 88, Ninety-Eight & Toronado)
1) Mark hinges for reinstallation and remove hood. Remove negative battery cable. Drain cooling system. Remove air cleaner. Remove cooling fan, pulleys and belts. Disconnect mass airflow sensor wiring and air intake duct.

2) Disconnect A/C compressor and set aside (if equipped). Raise and support vehicle. Remove exhaust pipe. Remove engine mount bolts. Remove drive line vibration absorber. Disconnect starter wiring and starter.

3) Remove power steering hoses at steering gear assembly. Remove lower transaxle-to-engine bolts. One bolt is located between transaxle case and engine block. Remove flywheel cover. Remove flywheel-to-torque converter bolts. Use a scribe to mark flywheel-to-torque converter to assure proper reassembly.

4) Remove engine support bracket at transaxle. Lower vehicle. Remove radiator and heater hoses at engine. Remove alternator and rotate to cowl. Disconnect engine wiring harness. Remove remaining transaxle-to-engine bolts. Remove engine assembly.

Installation
To install, reverse removal procedure.

V8 MODELS

5.0L (307")
Removal

1) Drain cooling system. Remove air cleaner and hot air pipe. Mark hinges for reassembly and remove hood. Disconnect negative battery cable. Remove engine ground strap from right cylinder head to cowl.

2) Remove radiator hoses. Remove automatic transmission cooler lines from radiator. Remove all heater hoses and vacuum hoses connected to engine.

3) Disconnect power steering pump with hoses attached. Remove A/C compressor and position aside with hoses and brackets attached (if equipped).

4) Disconnect fuel hose from fuel line. Disconnect all wiring from engine. Disconnect accelerator cable. Remove radiator. Raise and support vehicle. Disconnect exhaust and crossover pipes at manifold.

5) Remove torque converter cover and drive plate-to-converter bolts. Remove engine mount bolts or nuts. Remove 3 transmission-to-engine bolts on right side. Remove starter and secure to frame with wires attached.

6) Lower vehicle. Install engine lift. Place a wood block on top of a jack and slightly raise transmission. Remove 3 transmission-to-engine bolts on left side. Remove engine.

Installation
To install, reverse removal procedure.

OLDSMOBILE TIGHTENING SPECIFICATIONS

Application	Ft. Lbs. (N.m)
4-Cylinder Engines	
2.0L (122") VIN K	
Drive Plate-to-Converter Bolts	31 (42)
Left Front Motor Mount-to-Engine Bolts	18 (24)
Right Rear Motor Mount-to-Engine Bolts	38 (52)
Right Rear Mount-to-Frame Bolts	38 (52)
Transaxle-to-Engine Bolts	42 (57)
2.0L (122") VIN 1	
Drive Plate-to-Converter Bolts	31 (42)
Front Motor Mount-to-Engine Bolts	25-35 (34-47)
Lower Motor Mount-to-Engine Bolts	15-20 (20-27)
Motor Mount-to-Frame Bolts	35-45 (47-61)
Starter-to-Engine Bolts	26-37 (35-50)
Transaxle-to-Engine Bolts	48-63 (65-85)
2.3L (138")	
Motor Mounts-to-Engine Bolts	55 (76)
Drive Plate-to-Converter Bolts	46 (61)
2.5L (151")	
Drive Plate-to-Converter Bolts	31 (42)
Motor Mount-to-Engine Bolts	35 (47)
Motor Mount-to-Frame Bolts	35 (47)
Starter-to-Engine Bolts	31 (42)
Transaxle-to-Engine Bolts	48-63 (65-86)

GENERAL MOTORS – OLDSMOBILE (Cont.)

OLDSMOBILE TIGHTENING SPECIFICATIONS (Cont.)

Application	Ft. Lbs. (N.m)
V6 Engines	
2.8L (173")	
Drive Plate-to-Converter Bolts	44 (60)
Eng. Mntg. Brkt.-to-Engine Bolts	70-92 (95-125)
Eng. Mntg. Torque Strut	
Bracket Bolts	30-40 (41-54)
Starter-to-Engine Bolts	26-37 (35-50)
Transaxle-to-Engine Bolts	55 (75)
3.0L (181")	
Drive Plate-to-Converter Bolts	35 (47)
Motor Mount-to-Engine Bolts	55 (75)
Starter-to-Engine Bolts	35 (47)
Transaxle-to-Engine Brace Bolts	37 (50)
Transmission-to-Engine Bolts	35 (47)
3.8L (231")	
All Models	
Drive Plate-to-Converter Bolts	35 (47)
Starter-to-Engine Bolts	35 (47)
Transmission-to-Engine Bolts	35 (47)
FWD Models	
Final Drive-to-Engine Bolts	66 (89)
Motor Mount-to-Engine Bolts	66 (89)
Motor Mount-to-Frame Bolts	66 (89)
Output Shaft-to-Engine Support Bolts	
Front	80 (108)
Rear	55 (75)
RWD Models	
Motor Mount-to-Bracket Bolts	48 (65)
Motor Mount-to-Engine Bolts	59 (80)
Motor Mount-to-Frame Bolts	33 (45)

OLDSMOBILE TIGHTENING SPECIFICATIONS (Cont.)

Application	Ft. Lbs. (N.m)
V8 Engines	
5.0L (307")	
Drive Plate-to-Converter Bolts	35 (47)
Starter-to-Engine Bolts	30 (41)
Transmission-to-Engine Bolts	35 (47)
Motor Mount-to-Engine Bolts	75 (102)
Motor Mount-to-Frame Bolts	35 (47)
Motor Mount Through Bolt	55 (75)

GENERAL MOTORS – PONTIAC

4-CYLINDER MODELS

2.0L (122") VIN K & M

Removal

1) Disconnect battery cables. Drain cooling system. Remove air cleaner. Disconnect engine harness at bulkhead. Disconnect electrical connectors at brake cylinder, A/C relay cluster switches, and temperature switch at thermostat housing.

2) Disconnect wiring at ECM and pull harness through bulkhead. Remove accelerator cable from EFI and bracket. Remove power steering hoses at cut-off switch and return hose at pump. Remove vacuum hoses at MAP sensor, canister, and EFI.

3) Remove upper and lower radiator hoses. Disconnect shift cable at transaxle. Raise and support vehicle.

4) Remove speedometer cable and bracket. Disconnect exhaust pipe at manifold and converter. Remove heater hoses and fuel lines. Remove transaxle cooler lines.

5) Remove both front wheels. Remove right spoiler section and splash shield. Remove brake calipers and support with wire. Remove tie rod ends.

6) Disconnect electrical connections at A/C compressor. Remove A/C compressor and mounting brackets. Support A/C compressor with wire in wheel opening. Remove front suspension attaching bolts.

CAUTION: Support vehicle and transaxle weight properly during following steps.

7) Lower vehicle. Support front of vehicle by placing 2 jack stands under core support. Position jack at rear of cowl with 4" x 4" x 6' timber spanning vehicle width. Raise vehicle enough to remove jack stands.

8) Position 4-wheel dolly under transaxle assembly with three (3) 4" x 4" x 12" wood blocks as support. Allow support rails to hang free.

9) Slightly lower vehicle weight onto 4-wheel dolly. Remove rear transaxle mount. Remove left front engine mount. Remove engine support-to-body mounting bolts behind right inner axle universal joint.

10) Remove one mounting bolt and nut from right-hand chassis side rail-to-engine mount bracket. Remove 6 strut attaching nuts. Disconnect torque rod attachment. Raise vehicle. Allow engine, transaxle and suspension to rest on 4-wheel dolly.

Installation

To install, reverse removal procedure.

Engine Removal & Installation

GENERAL MOTORS – PONTIAC (Cont.)

2.3L (138")

Removal

1) Disconnect negative battery cable. Drain coolant. Remove air cleaner duct, fan shroud, upper radiator support and cooling fan. Remove oil filter.

2) On A/C equipped models, discharge A/C system. Remove coupled hose assembly at A/C compressor and discard "O" rings. On all models, disconnect and label all linkage, hoses, vacuum lines and electrical wiring that will interfere with engine removal.

3) Remove power steering pivot bolt, pump, and drive belt. Position power steering pump aside. Disconnect exhaust manifold and front engine mount. Install Engine Support (J 28467). Raise vehicle.

4) Remove front right wheel assembly. Remove right lower splash shield and radiator air deflector. Separate ball joints from steering knuckles. Support suspension crossmember and stabilizer shaft. Remove suspension support retaining bolts.

5) Remove suspension supports, crossmember and stabilizer shaft as an assembly. Install Drive Axle Seal Protector (J 34754) on drive axle boots. Remove axle shafts from transaxle and position aside.

6) Remove nut from transaxle mount through bolt and rear engine mount through bolt. Remove engine mount body bracket. Position suitable support below engine and lower car onto support.

7) Remove transaxle through bolt. Mark support fixture hooks so that positioning can be duplicated when reinstalling engine. Remove engine support fixture. Raise vehicle off engine and transaxle assembly. Separate engine from transaxle.

Installation

To install, reverse removal procedure. When tightening transaxle mount through bolt, ensure all related gaps are within .08" (2 mm) of each other.

2.5L (151")

Removal (Grand Am)

1) Disconnect battery cables. Drain engine coolant. Remove air cleaner. Disconnect ECM connections and feed harness through bulkhead. Disconnect engine wiring harness. Disconnect vacuum hoses. Disconnect radiator and heater hoses.

2) Disconnect A/C compressor. Leave hoses attached and move compressor aside. Disconnect front transaxle strut. Disconnect fuel lines at TBI. On automatic transaxle equipped models, disconnect cooler lines and shifter linkage. On manual transaxle equipped models, disconnect clutch and shifter linkage.

3) On automatic transaxle equipped models, disconnect downshift cable. On all models, disconnect throttle cable at TBI. Disconnect engine grounds. Remove multi-relay bracket. Raise and support vehicle. Remove power steering line bracket from engine.

4) Remove front wheels. Disconnect brake calipers and secure to springs. Remove brake rotors. Remove 2 knuckle-to-strut bolts per side. Disconnect exhaust pipe at manifold and hangers and swing aside.

5) Loosen remaining 8 body-to-cradle bolts at ends. Remove one bolt at each end of each cradle side, leaving one bolt per corner. Place jack stands under front of body. Move hoist back to body pan with 4" x 4" x 6' timber between hoist and vehicle.

6) Lift hoist and remove jack stands. Place dolly under engine/transaxle assembly with 4" x 4" blocks to maintain position on dolly. Lower vehicle, allowing engine/transaxle assembly to rest on dolly.

7) Remove engine mount bolts and right front bracket. Remove remaining 4 cradle-to-body bolts. Lift engine/transaxle assembly. Separate engine and transaxle.

Installation

To install, reverse removal procedure.

Removal (6000 Auto. Trans.)

1) Disconnect battery cables. Drain cooling system. Remove air cleaner. Disconnect engine wiring harness connector. Disconnect all vacuum lines. Remove throttle and transaxle linkage at fuel injection assembly.

2) Remove radiator and heater hoses. Remove A/C compressor from brackets and position aside with hoses connected (if equipped). Remove front engine strut assembly. Remove transaxle-to-engine bolts, leaving 2 upper bolts in place.

3) Remove front mount-to-cradle nuts. Remove forward exhaust pipe. Remove flywheel inspection cover. Remove starter. Remove drive plate-to-converter bolts. Remove power steering pump and position aside. Disconnect fuel line at filter.

4) Remove 2 rear transaxle support bracket bolts. With floor jack and block of wood under transaxle, raise engine until front mount studs clear cradle.

5) Attach engine lift to engine. Remove 2 remaining transaxle-to-engine bolts. Remove engine.

Installation

To install, reverse removal procedure.

Removal (6000 Man. Trans.)

1) Disconnect battery cables. Remove air cleaner. Drain coolant. Raise and support vehicle. Remove front engine mount-to-cradle nuts. Remove forward exhaust pipe. Remove starter motor and position aside with wiring attached.

2) Remove flywheel housing inspection cover and lower bellhousing bolts. Lower vehicle. Remove all bellhousing-to-engine bolts.

3) Remove forward torque reaction rod from engine and radiator core support. Remove A/C compressor and position aside with refrigerant lines connected (if equipped).

4) Remove emission hoses at canister. Remove power steering hoses (if equipped). Remove all vacuum hoses. Disconnect wiring at solenoid and engine harness at bulkhead. Remove heater blower motor. Disconnect heater and radiator hoses.

5) Disconnect throttle cable. Disconnect fuel line. Attach engine lift and remove engine.

Installation

To install, reverse removal procedure.

Removal (Fiero)

1) Disconnect battery cables. Drain coolant. Remove rear compartment lid. Do not remove torsion rod retaining bolts.

2) Remove air cleaner. Disconnect throttle and shift cables. Disconnect heater hose at intake manifold. Remove vacuum hoses. Disconnect fuel lines and filter.

3) Disconnect fuel pump relay and oxygen sensor. On automatic transaxle models, disconnect transaxle cooler lines. On manual transaxle models, disconnect clutch slave cylinder. Disconnect engine-to-chassis ground strap.

GENERAL MOTORS — PONTIAC (Cont.)

4) Disconnect radiator and heater hoses. Disconnect engine harness at bulkhead. Discharge A/C system (if equipped). Disconnect and plug refrigerant hoses at compressor. Remove rear console.

5) Remove ECM harness through bulkhead panel. Attach engine support fixture. Mark bolt and bracket for reassembly and disconnect engine strut. Raise and support vehicle. Remove rear wheels.

6) On automatic transaxle models, remove drive plate-to-converter bolts. Disconnect parking brake cable. Remove calipers with hoses attached and wire out of way. Mark strut-to-knuckle relationship for reassembly reference and remove strut-to-knuckle bolts. Check rear camber and toe adjustments upon reassembly.

7) Disconnect A/C wiring (if equipped). Remove cradle bolts. Disconnect parking brake cable at cradle, using Brake Tool (J-34065). Lower vehicle.

CAUTION: Support engine/transaxle and cradle assembly on dolly. Be sure to support outboard ends of lower control arms.

8) Disconnect engine support fixture. Raise and support vehicle. Leave engine/transaxle and cradle assembly on dolly.

Installation
To install, reverse removal procedure.

V6 MODELS

2.8L (173")
Removal (6000)
1) Disconnect battery cables. Remove air cleaner. Drain cooling system. Remove engine strut bracket from radiator support and swing rearward. Remove AIR pump and bracket.

2) Remove A/C compressor from bracket and set aside. Disconnect all vacuum hoses. Disconnect accelerator and TV cables. Disconnect engine harness from ECM and pull connector through front of dash.

3) Disconnect radiator hoses from radiator. Disconnect heater hoses from engine. Remove power steering pump and bracket (if equipped).

4) Disconnect fuel lines at rubber hose connections at left side of engine. Raise and support vehicle. Disconnect engine front mount-to-cradle nuts on right side. Disconnect battery cables from engine at starter and transaxle housing bolt.

5) Remove starter. Remove transaxle inspection cover plate and remove drive plate-to-converter bolts on automatic transaxle models. Remove crankshaft pulley and remove all belts. Disconnect exhaust pipe.

6) Remove lower transaxle-to-engine bolt at rear of engine. Disconnect power steering cut-off switch (if equipped).

7) Lower vehicle. Remove exhaust crossover pipe. Remove remaining transaxle-to-engine bolts. Make note of ground stud location. Place support under transaxle rear extension. Attach engine lift and remove engine.

Installation
To install, reverse removal procedure.

Removal (Fiero)
1) Disconnect battery cables. Drain coolant. Remove rear compartment lid. Do not remove torsion rod retaining bolts.

2) Remove intake flex duct. Disconnect throttle and shift cables. Disconnect heater hose at intake manifold. Remove vacuum hoses. Disconnect fuel lines and filter.

3) Disconnect fuel pump relay and oxygen sensor. On automatic transaxle models, disconnect transaxle cooler lines. On manual transaxle models, disconnect clutch slave cylinder. Disconnect engine-to-chassis ground strap.

4) Disconnect radiator and heater hoses. Disconnect engine harness at bulkhead. Discharge A/C system (if equipped). Disconnect and plug refrigerant hoses at compressor. Remove rear console.

5) Remove ECM harness through bulkhead panel. Attach engine support fixture. Disconnect engine strut bracket, after marking bolt and bracket for reassembly. Raise and support vehicle. Remove rear wheels.

6) On automatic transaxle models, remove drive plate-to-converter bolts. Disconnect parking brake cable. Remove calipers with hoses attached and wire out of way. Mark strut-to-knuckle relationship for reassembly reference and remove strut-to-knuckle bolts. Check rear camber and toe adjustments upon reassembly.

7) Disconnect A/C wiring (if equipped). Remove cradle bolts. Disconnect parking brake cable at cradle, using Brake Tool (J-34065). Lower vehicle.

CAUTION: Support engine/transaxle and cradle assembly on dolly. Be sure to support outboard ends of lower control arms.

8) Disconnect engine support fixture. Raise and support vehicle. Leave engine/transaxle and cradle assembly on dolly.

Installation
To install, reverse removal procedure.

Removal (Firebird)
1) Disconnect battery cables. Remove air cleaner. Mark hinges for reassembly and remove hood. Drain cooling system. Remove lower radiator hose. Remove upper fan shroud. Remove upper radiator hose and coolant recovery hose.

2) Disconnect transmission cooler lines at radiator. Remove radiator, fan assembly and heater hoses. Disconnect wiring and vacuum lines at engine.

3) Disconnect throttle, cruise control, and detent linkages from carburetor. Remove power steering pump from engine and position aside with hoses connected.

4) Raise and support vehicle. Remove exhaust pipes at manifolds. Remove converter inspection cover. Disconnect drive plate-to-converter bolts. Disconnect starter wires.

5) Remove transmission-to-engine bolts. Remove motor mount through bolts. Disconnect fuel lines at fuel pump.

6) Lower vehicle. Remove bracket attaching air injection pipe to converter. Support transmission with jack. Attach engine lift. Remove engine, disconnecting wire from bracket at left rear of engine.

Engine Removal & Installation

GENERAL MOTORS — PONTIAC (Cont.)

Installation
To install, reverse removal procedure.

3.8L (231")
Removal

1) Mark hinges for reinstallation and remove hood. Remove negative battery cable. Drain cooling system. Remove air cleaner. Remove cooling fan, pulleys and belts.

2) Disconnect A/C compressor and set aside (if equipped). Remove radiator and heater hoses from engine. Remove fan shroud assembly.

3) Disconnect power steering pump and set aside. Disconnect fuel line and vacuum hoses. Disconnect battery ground cable from engine. Disconnect accelerator cable at carburetor.

4) Disconnect engine wiring harness connector, alternator and engine-to-ground straps. Raise and support vehicle. Disconnect crossover pipe from exhaust manifolds.

5) Use a scribe to mark relationship of torque converter-to-drive plate to assure proper reassembly. Remove transaxle converter cover and torque converter bolts. Disconnect wiring at starter motor.

6) Remove transaxle-to-cylinder block attaching bolts. Remove front motor mount-to-frame bracket attaching bolts. Lower car and support transaxle. Install engine lift. Remove engine.

Installation
To install, reverse removal procedure.

V8 MODELS

5.0L (305") & 5.7L (350")
Removal

1) Mark hinges for reassembly and remove hood. Disconnect battery cables. Remove air cleaner. Drain cooling system. Disconnect radiator hoses and heater hoses. Remove radiator and fan shroud.

2) Disconnect all wiring to engine. Disconnect accelerator linkage at intake manifold. Disconnect all fuel lines from engine. Disconnect all vacuum hoses to engine. Remove power steering pump and position aside with hoses connected (if equipped).

3) Raise and support vehicle. Drain crankcase. Disconnect exhaust pipes at manifold. Remove starter. Remove flywheel or converter housing inspection cover.

4) Remove drive plate-to-converter bolts on automatic transmission equipped models. Remove motor mount through bolts.

5) Remove transmission-to-engine bolts. Lower vehicle. Raise transmission using a floor jack. Attach engine lift to engine. Raise engine slightly. Remove motor mount-to-engine brackets. Remove engine.

Installation
To install, reverse removal procedure.

PONTIAC TIGHTENING SPECIFICATIONS

Application	Ft. Lbs. (N.m)
4-Cylinder Engines	
2.0L (122") VIN K & M	
Drive Plate-to-Converter Bolts	31 (42)
Front Motor Mount-to-Engine Bolts	38 (52)
Front Mounting Bracket-to-Frame Bolts	23 (31)
Rear Mounting Bracket-to-Frame Bolts	38 (52)
Rear Mount-to-Engine Bolts	41 (56)
2.3L (138")	
Motor Mounts-to-Engine Bolts	55 (76)
Drive Plate-to-Converter Bolts	46 (61)
2.5L (151")	
Drive Plate-to-Converter Bolts	30 (41)
Motor Mount-to-Engine Bolts	35 (47)
Motor Mount-to-Frame Bolts	35 (47)
Starter-to-Engine Bolts	32 (43)
Transaxle-to-Engine Bolts	48-63 (65-85)
Fiero Cradle Bolts	
Front	66 (90)
Rear	76 (103)
V6 Engines	
2.8L (173")	
Drive Plate-to-Converter Bolts	25-35 (34-47)
Motor Mount-to-Engine Bolts	70-92 (95-125)
Motor Mount Strut Bracket Bolts	30-40 (41-54)
Starter-to-Engine Bolts	26-37 (35-50)
Transaxle-to-Engine Bolts	55 (75)
Transmission-to-Engine Bolts	48-63 (65-85)
Fiero Cradle Bolts	
Front	66 (89)
Rear	76 (103)
3.8L (231")	
Drive Plate-to-Converter Bolts	35 (47)
Starter-to-Engine Bolts	35 (47)
Transaxle-to-Engine Bolts	35 (47)
Final Drive-to-Engine Bolts	66 (89)
Motor Mount-to-Engine Bolts	66 (89)
Motor Mount-to-Frame Bolts	66 (89)
Output Shaft-to-Engine Support Bolts	
Front	80 (108)
Rear	55 (75)
V-8 Engines	
5.0L (305")	
Drive Plate-to-Converter Bolts	35 (47)
Transmission-to-Engine Bolts	35 (47)
Starter-to-Engine Bolts	30 (41)
Motor Mount-to-Engine Bolts	55 (75)
Motor Mount-to-Frame Bolts	35 (47)
Motor Mount Through Bolts	75 (102)

Oil Pan Removal

CHRYSLER MOTORS

4-CYLINDER MODELS

2.2L (135") & 2.5L (153")

Disconnect negative battery cable and remove engine oil dipstick. Drain crankcase, remove oil pan bolts and oil pan.

V6 Models

3.0L

Drain crankcase, remove oil pan bolts and oil pan. When installing oil pan tighten bolts in a criss-cross pattern working from the center outward.

V8 MODELS

5.2L (318")

Disconnect negative battery cable and remove engine oil dipstick. Raise and support vehicle. Drain crankcase. Remove steering and idler arm ball joints from steering linkage center link and remove center link. Remove exhaust crossover pipe, starter and starter mounting stud. Remove flywheel access cover, oil pan bolts and oil pan.

CHRYSLER MOTORS TIGHTENING SPECIFICATIONS

Application	INCH Lbs. (N.m)
Oil Pan	
4-Cylinder	
2.2L (135")	204 (23)
2.5L (153")	53 (6)
V6	
3.0L (183")	53 (6)
V8	
5.2L (318")	204 (23)

EAGLE PREMIER

4-CYLINDER

2.5L (153")

Information not available from manufacture.

V6

3.0L (183")

NOTE: **To remove oil pan, it is necessary to remove front anti-sway bar and engine cradle.**

1) With vehicle weight on front wheels, remove anti-sway bar retainers. Place nut on one sway bar retainer bolt lower control arm and tighten to retain ball joint positions.

2) Raise vehicle on side arm type hoist. Drain engine oil. Loosen engine mount stud and nut assemblies to obtain clearance for engine cradle removal. Remove front tires. Remove lower ball joint retaining bolts and seperate lower control arms from steering knuckles.

3) Remove bolts retaining rear of transaxle to crossmember. Lower vehicle. Install Engine Support Bar (MS 1900) and raise engine as far as possible. Place dolly under engine cradle. Remove cradle mounting bolts. Raise vehicle off engine cradle. Remove oil pan.

EAGLE PREMIER TIGHTENING SPECIFICATIONS

Application	Ft. Lbs. (N.m)
V6	
Oil Pan	[1]
Engine Cradle Mounting Bolts	92 (125)
Steering Knuckle-to-Ball Joint	77 (105)
Transaxle-to-Crossmember Nuts	20 (27)

[1] – Tighten to 108 INCH lbs. (12 N.m).

FORD MOTOR CO.

4-CYLINDER MODELS

1.9L (114")
Escort & EXP

1) Disconnect negative battery cable. Raise and support vehicle. Drain crankcase. Disconnect lower radiator hose. Remove roll restictor (if equipped). Disconnect cable at starter. Remove starter.

2) Disconnect interfering exhaust pipe. Remove oil pan retaining bolts and oil pan. Remove oil pan gasket.

2.3L (140") OHC
Mustang

1) Disconnect negative battery cable and remove fan shroud. If equipped with electric fan, disconnect power lead and remove fan and shroud assembly.

Oil Pan Removal

FORD MOTOR CO. (Cont.)

Drain cooling system and disconnect upper and lower hoses at radiator.

2) Raise and support vehicle. Drain crankcase. Remove right and left engine support through bolts. Using a jack, raise engine as far as possible and place support blocks between the mounts and crossmember pedestals. Remove jack.

3) Remove shake brace, sway bar retaining bolts and lower sway bar. Remove steering gear retaining bolts and lower gear. Disconnect starter wiring, remove starter. Remove oil pan bolts, lower pan to crossmember and remove pan.

NOTE: The No. 4 piston must be up so rear of oil pan clears crankshaft.

Thunderbird

1) Disconnect negative battery cable. Raise and support vehicle. Drain crankcase and cooling system. Remove right and left engine support through bolts. Using a jack, raise engine as far as possible.

2) Place support blocks between the mounts and crossmember pedestals. Remove jack. Remove steering gear retaining nuts and bolts. Remove bolt retaining steering flex coupling to steering gear. Move steering gear forward and down.

3) Remove shake brace, disconnect starter wiring and remove starter. Remove engine rear support-to-crossmember nuts. Using a jack, raise transmission. Remove oil pan bolts. On turbocharged models, remove oil pump and lay in oil pan. On all models, remove oil pan.

2.3L (140") HSC & HSO
Tempo & Topaz

1) Disconnect negative battery cable. Raise and support vehicle. Drain crankcase. Remove lower radiator hose to drain coolant. On manual transaxle models, remove roll resistor. On all models, remove starter wiring and starter.

2) Disconnect exhaust pipe bracket from oil pan. Remove heater return hose at lower radiator and water pump inlet tube locations. Remove tube support tabs and position air conditioning line aside. Remove oil pan bolts and oil pan.

2.5L (153")
Sable & Taurus

1) Disconnect negative battery cable. Raise and support vehicle. Drain crankcase. Drain coolant by removing lower radiator hose. Remove roll restrictor (MTX only). Disconnect starter cable.

2) Remove starter. Disconnect exhaust pipe from oil pan. Remove engine coolant tube located at lower radiator hose, at water pump and at tabs on oil pan. Position air conditioner line off to side. Remove oil pan.

V6 MODELS

3.0L (183")
Sable & Taurus

1) Disconnect negative battery cable and remove oil level dipstick. Raise and support vehicle. Remove electrical connector and retainer clip at low oil level sensor (if equipped).

2) Drain oil from crankcase. Remove starter motor. Disconnect EGO sensor. Remove exhaust pipe

assembly and lower engine/flywheel dust cover from converter housing. Remove oil pan attaching bolts and oil pan.

3.8L (232")

Disconnect negative battery cable. Raise and support vehicle. Drain crankcase. Remove oil filter. Remove converter assembly. Remove starter motor. Remove converter housing cover. Remove bolts retaining oil pan assembly. Remove oil pan assembly.

V8 MODELS

5.0L (302") & 5.8L (351")
Mark VII, Thunderbird,
Cougar & Mustang

1) Disconnect negative battery cable. Remove fan shroud bolts and position shroud over fan. Remove oil level indicator from left-hand side of cylinder block. Remove air cleaner tube.

2) Raise and support vehicle. Drain engine oil. Remove starter motor wires and starter. Remove catalytic converter and muffler inlet pipes. Remove engine mount-to-No. 2 crossmember bolts.

3) Remove No. 3 crossmember and support assemblies. Remove steering gear attaching bolts and position steering gear forward out of work area. Raise and support engine for clearance of oil pan removal.

4) Remove oil pan attaching bolts and lower oil pan. Remove oil pump and pick-up tube assembly to drop into oil pan. Remove oil pan.

Crown Victoria,
Grand Marquis, Town Car & Wagon

1) Remove air cleaner, disconnect accelerator and kickdown rods at carburetor and remove accelerator mounting bracket. Remove fan shroud bolts and position shroud over fan. Disconnect wiring from harness and remove wiper motor.

2) Disconnect windshield washer hose and remove wiper motor mounting cover. Remove dipstick and dipstick tube retaining bolt at exhaust manifold. Remove thermactor air dump tube retaining clamp and thermactor crossover tube at rear of engine.

3) Raise vehicle and drain crankcase. Remove filler tube and drain crankcase. Disconnect starter wiring, remove starter. Relieve fuel pressure and disconnect fuel line. Disconnect inlet pipes from exhaust manifold.

4) Remove exhaust gas oxygen sensor from exhaust manifold and thermactor secondary air tube-to-converter housing clamps. Disconnect exhaust pipes to catalytic converter outlet. Remove catalytic converter secondary air tube and inlet pipes to exhaust manifold.

5) Remove rear engine mount through bolts and shift crossover bolts at transmission. Disconnect transmission kickdown rod. Remove flywheel access cover. Remove brake line retainer from front crossmember. Using a jack, raise engine as far as possible.

6) Place support blocks between engine mounts and chassis brackets. Remove jack. Disconnect low oil sensor from oil pan. Remove oil pan bolts and lower pan. Remove oil pump pickup tube assembly and place in oil pan. Remove oil pan.

FORD MOTOR CO. (Cont.)

FORD MOTOR CO. TIGHTENING SPECIFICATIONS

Application	INCH Lbs. (N.m)
Oil Pan	
4-Cylinder	
1.9L (114")	71-97 (8-11)
2.3L (140")	
6 mm Bolts	62-97 (7-11)
8 mm Bolts	97-115 (11-13)
2.3L (140") HSC	71-106 (8-12)
2.5L (153")	[1]
V6	
3.0L (183")	71-106 (8-12)
3.8L (232")	80-106 (9-12)
V8	
5.0L (302")	106-133 (12-15)

[1] – Tighten to 15 23 ft. lbs. (20-30 N.m).

GENERAL MOTORS – BUICK

4-CYLINDER MODELS

2.0L (122") VIN K

1) Disconnect negative battery cable. Raise and support vehicle. Remove right front wheel and front splash shield. Position jack stands at jack points.

2) Drain crankcase. Remove exhaust pipe from exhaust manifold or waste gate. Remove 4 flywheel cover bolts. Remove oil pan and bolts.

2.0L (122") VIN 1

1) Disconnect negative battery cable. Disconnect exhaust pipe shield and remove. Raise and support vehicle. Drain crankcase. Remove A/C brace at starter and at A/C bracket.

2) Remove starter bracket at block. Remove starter and lay aside. Remove flywheel cover and A/C brace. Remove 4 right support bolts. Lower support slightly to gain clearance for oil pan removal. Remove oil filler and extension on automatic transaxles. Remove oil pan bolts and oil pan.

2.3L (141")

Drain engine oil. Remove transaxle drive plate cover. Remove splash shield-to-suspension support bolt. Disconnect exhaust manifold brace. Remove radiator outlet pipe-to-oil pan bolt, transaxle-to-oil pan bolt and stud. Pry spacer from between oil pan and transaxle. Remove bolt connecting oil pan to transaxle. Remove oil pan and gasket.

2.5L (151")

1) Disconnect negative battery cable. Raise and support vehicle. Drain crankcase. Remove front engine mount nuts. Disconnect exhaust pipe at manifold and at converter. Remove starter and flywheel access cover.

2) Remove splash shield, power steering pump and bracket. Install Engine Support Fixture (J-28467), and raise engine. Remove power steering pump and bracket (if equipped). Remove engine strut. Remove lower alternator and engine support brackets. Remove oil pan bolts and oil pan.

V6 MODELS

2.8L (173")

Disconnect negative battery cable. Raise and support vehicle. Drain crankcase. Remove flywheel access cover and starter. Support engine and remove engine mount bolts. Remove oil pan bolts. Raise engine and remove oil pan.

3.0L (181") & 3.8L (231")
Century Models

Disconnect negative battery cable. Raise and support vehicle. Drain crankcase and remove flywheel access cover. Remove oil pan bolts and oil pan.

Electra, LeSabre, Regal & Skylark

Disconnect negative battery cable. Raise and support vehicle. Drain crankcase. Remove flywheel access cover and crossover pipe. Disconnect engine mounts. Raise and support engine. Remove oil pan bolts and oil pan.

Riviera

1) Disconnect negative battery cable. Remove upper final drive bolt and support engine. Raise and support vehicle. Disconnect idler arm at frame.

2) Lock steering against left-turn stop. Remove final drive unit, splash shield, starter and flywheel access cover. Drain crankcase, remove oil pan bolts and oil pan.

Oil Pan Removal

GENERAL MOTORS — BUICK (Cont.)

V8 MODELS

5.0L (307")

1) Disconnect negative battery cable and oil dipstick. Remove fan shroud screws. Raise and support vehicle. Drain crankcase and remove flywheel access cover. Disconnect exhaust and crossover pipes.

2) Remove starter and disconnect engine mounts at cylinder block. Install Engine Support Fixture (BT-6501) with Adapters (BT-7109 & BT-7203). Raise engine and remove pan bolts and oil pan.

BUICK TIGHTENING SPECIFICATIONS

Application	INCH Lbs. (N.m)
Oil Pan	
4-Cylinder	
2.0L (122")	
Front	88-159 (10-18)
Rear	133-212 (15-24)
Studs	162-89 (7-10)
All Other Bolts	53-106 (6-12)
2.3L (138")	
Stud Nut	[1]
Bolts	106 (12)
2.5L (151")	54 (6)
V6 Engines	
2.8L (173")	
6 mm Bolts	71-106 (8-12)
8 mm Bolts	168-266 (19-30)
3.0L (181") & 3.8L (231")	159 (18)
V8 Engines	
5.0L (307")	71 (8)

[1] – Tighten nut to 41 ft. lbs. (56 N.m).

GENERAL MOTORS — CADILLAC

V6 MODELS

2.8L (173")

Disconnect negative battery cable. Raise and support vehicle. Drain crankcase and remove flywheel dust cover. Remove starter. Remove oil pan bolts and oil pan.

V8 MODELS

4.1L (250")

Disconnect negative battery cable, raise vehicle and drain crankcase. Disconnect oil level sensor, flywheel cover, and exhaust "Y" pipe. Remove oil pan bolts and 2 nuts from studs. Remove oil pan.

4.5L (273")

Disconnect negative battery cable, raise vehicle and drain crankcase. Remove 2 flywheel access covers, disconnect exhaust "Y" pipe at manifolds, remove bolts from converter and lower exhaust. Remove oil pan bolts, and remove pan.

5.0L (307")

Disconnect negative battery cable. Remove oil dipstick. Remove fan shroud attaching screws. Raise vehicle. Drain oil pan. Remove drive plate cover. Disconnect crossover pipe. Remove starter. Disconnect engine mounts at cylinder block. Raise front of engine as far as possible. Remove oil pan.

CADILLAC TIGHTENING SPECIFICATIONS

Application	INCH Lbs. (N.m)
Oil Pan	
4-Cylinder	
2.0L (122")	
Front	89-159 (10-18)
Rear	133-212 (15-24)
All Other Bolts	53-106 (6-12)
V6	
2.8L (173")	
6 mm	71-106 (8-12)
8 mm	168-266 (19-30)
V8	
4.1L (250")	132 (15)

GENERAL MOTORS — CHEVROLET

4-CYLINDER MODELS

1.6L (98")

Disconnect negative battery cable. Drain engine oil. Remove right engine undercover. Remove front exhaust pipe. Remove oil pan.

2.0L (122")

1) Disconnect negative battery cable. Raise vehicle, drain crankcase and disconnect exhaust pipe at manifold. Remove A/C brace at starter and A/C bracket (if equipped). Remove flywheel access cover, starter bracket and starter.

2) Remove A/C brace (if equipped). Support vehicle, remove right support bolts and lower support to facilitate pan removal. Remove automatic transaxle oil filter and extension (if equipped). Remove oil pan bolts and oil pan.

2.5L (151")

1) Disconnect negative battery cable, raise vehicle and drain crankcase. On Camaro models, disconnect exhaust pipe at manifold and loosen hanger. Remove engine mount through bolts and raise engine. Remove oil pan bolts and remove pan.

2) On all other models, remove cradle-to-front engine mount nuts. Disconnect exhaust pipe at manifold and rear transaxle mount. Disconnect starter and remove flywheel access cover.

3) Remove upper alternator bracket. Install Engine Support (J-28467) and raise engine. Remove lower alternator and engine support bracket. Remove oil pan bolts and pan.

V6 MODELS

2.8L (173")

Except Camaro

Disconnect negative battery cable and raise vehicle. Drain crankcase, remove flywheel access cover and starter. Support engine and remove engine mount bolts. Raise engine, remove oil pan bolts and remove pan.

NOTE: Upon reinstallation of oil pan, timing gear cover bolts should be installed last. Cover bolts are installed at an angle and holes align after other pan bolts are snugged.

Camaro

1) Disconnect negative battery cable. Remove air cleaner and distributor cap. Remove upper half of fan shroud. Raise vehicle and drain crankcase.

2) Remove flywheel access cover, starter, converter dust cover. Disconnect exhaust pipe at manifold. Remove engine mount through bolts and raise engine. Remove oil pan bolts and pan.

4.3L (262")

1) Disconnect negative battery cable and remove air cleaner and fan shroud. Raise vehicle and support vehicle. Drain crankcase. Remove exhaust crossover pipe at manifold and converter.

2) Remove starter. Remove flywheel cover. Disconnect transmission oil cooler lines at oil pan. Loosen engine mount bolts and remove mounts. Remove oil pan bolts and lower oil pan.

3) Check that forward crankshaft throw and/or counter balance weight are not extended downward so as to block oil pan removal. Turn crankshaft, as necessary, to put throw on horizontal plane. Raise engine and remove oil pan.

V8 MODELS

5.0L (305")

Except Camaro

1) Disconnect negative battery cable and remove air cleaner and fan shroud. Remove upper fan shroud. Raise vehicle and drain crankcase. Remove cruise control servo bracket (if equipped).

2) Remove Air Injection Reaction (AIR) hose-to-converter pipe. Remove AIR pipe-to-exhaust manifold. Remove the exhaust crossover pipe at manifold and converter. Remove starter and flywheel access cover. Disconnect transmission lines at oil pan. Remove engine mount through bolts.

3) Remove oil pan bolts and lower pan. Position front crankshaft throw and/or counterweight on horizontal plane so it does not interfere with oil pan removal. Raise engine, reinstall through bolts and remove oil pan.

Camaro

1) Disconnect negative battery cable. Remove air cleaner, fan shroud, and distributor cap. Raise vehicle and drain crankcase. Disconnect exhaust pipe at manifold, AIR pipe clamp, and converter hanger bolts.

2) Remove front starter brace, starter and flywheel access cover. On models with manual transmission, it may be necessary to remove oil filter, to remove flywheel cover bolts.

3) Remove engine mount through bolts and oil pan bolts. Raise engine and lower pan. Position front crankshaft throw and/or counterweights as to clear oil pan, and remove pan.

5.7L (350")

Corvette

Disconnect negative battery cable. Raise the vehicle and drain crankcase. Remove starter, flywheel access cover, oil pan bolts and oil pan.

Oil Pan Removal

GENERAL MOTORS – CHEVROLET (Cont.)

CHEVROLET TIGHTENING SPECIFICATIONS

Application	INCH Lbs. (N.m)
Oil Pan	
4-Cylinder	
1.6L (98")	53 (6)
2.0L (122")	
Rear	133-212 (15-24)
Studs	62-89 (7-10)
Oil Pan-to-Front Cover	89-159 (10-18)
All Other Bolts	53-106 (6-12)
2.5L (151")	53 (6)
V6 Engines	
2.8L (173")	
6 mm Bolts	71-106 (8-12)
8 mm Bolts	168-266 (19-30)
4.3L (262")	124 (14)
V8 Engines	
5.0L (305") & 5.7L (350")	
1/4" Bolts & Studs	80 (9)
5/16" Bolts & Nuts	168 (19)
5.7L (350")	124 (14)
1/4" Bolts & Studs	150 (17)
5/16" Bolts & Studs	88 (10)

GENERAL MOTORS – OLDSMOBILE

4-CYLINDER MODELS

2.0L (122") VIN K

Disconnect negative battery cable. Raise and support vehicle at lift points. Remove right front wheel and right front splash shield. Drain crankcase, remove exhaust pipe from manifold. Remove flywheel access cover. Remove oil pan bolts and oil pan.

2.0L (122") VIN 1

1) Disconnect negative battery cable. Remove exhaust pipe shield. Raise and support vehicle. Drain crankcase, remove A/C brace at starter and at A/C bracket (if equipped). Remove flywheel access cover and starter. Remove A/C brace (if equipped).

2) Remove 4 right support bolts and lower support enough to aid oil pan removal. Remove automatic transaxle oil filter and extension (if equipped). Remove oil pan bolts and oil pan.

2.3L (141")

Drain engine oil. Remove transaxle drive plate cover. Remove splash shield-to-suspension support bolt. Disconnect exhaust manifold brace. Remove radiator outlet pipe-to-oil pan bolt, transaxle-to-oil pan bolt and stud. Pry spacer from between oil pan and transaxle. Remove bolt connecting oil pan to transaxle. Remove oil pan and gasket.

2.5L (151")
Cutlass Calais

Disconnect negative battery cable. Raise and support vehicle. Drain crankcase and disconnect exhaust pipe at manifold and hangers and move out of way.

Disconnect starter and remove flywheel access cover. Remove oil pan bolts and oil pan.

Cutlass Ciera

Disconnect negative battery cable. Raise and support vehicle. Remove nuts from front engine-to-cradle. Disconnect exhaust pipe at manifold and converter. Remove flywheel access cover and starter. Remove splash shield, power steering pump and bracket. Using Engine Support Fixture (J-28467), raise engine and remove engine front support bracket. Remove oil pan bolts and oil pan.

V6 MODELS

2.8L (173")

Disconnect negative battery cable. Raise and support vehicle. Drain crankcase, remove flywheel access cover and starter. Remove oil pan bolts, and oil pan.

3.0L (181") & 3.8L (231")

Disconnect negative battery cable. Raise and support vehicle. Drain crankcase and remove oil filter. Remove starter if necessary. Remove flywheel access cover, oil pan bolts, oil pan tensioner spring and oil pan.

V8 MODELS

5.0L (307")

1) Disconnect negative battery cable and remove engine oil dipstick. Remove upper fan shroud screws. Raise and support vehicle, drain crankcase. Remove flywheel access cover.

GENERAL MOTORS – OLDSMOBILE (Cont.)

2) Disconnect exhaust and crossover pipes. Remove oil cooler lines at filter base and remove starter. Install Engine Support Fixture (BT-6501) and raise front of engine. Remove engine mount attaching bolt. Remove oil pan bolts and oil pan.

OLDSMOBILE TIGHTENING SPECIFICATIONS

Application	INCH Lbs. (N.m)
Oil Pan	
4-Cylinder	
2.0L (122") VIN K	44 (5)
2.0L (122") VIN 1	72 (8)
2.3L (141") VIN D	18 (25)
2.5L (151")	89 (10)
V6	
2.8L (173")	
6 mm Bolts	71-106 (8-12)
8 mm Bolts	168-266 (19-30)
3.0L (181")	89 (10)
3.8L (231")	168 (19)
V8	
5.0L (307")	
Bolts	124 (14)
Nuts	212 (24)

GENERAL MOTORS – PONTIAC

4-CYLINDER MODELS

2.0L (122")

1) Disconnect negative battery cable. Remove right front wheel and splash sheld. Raise vehicle, drain crankcase and disconnect exhaust pipe at manifold or waste gate (if equipped).

2) Remove A/C brace at starter and bracket (if equipped). Remove flywheel access cover, starter bracket and starter.

3) Remove automatic transaxle oil filter and extension (if equipped). Remove oil pan bolts and oil pan.

2.3L (138")

1) Drain engine oil. Remove flywheel access cover and splash shield-to-suspension support bolt (if equipped). Remove radiator outlet pipe-to-oil pan bolt.

2) Remove transaxle-to-oil pan nut and stud. Gently pry spacer out from between oil pan and transaxle. Remove oil pan-to-transaxle bolt, oil pan bolts, oil pan and gasket.

2.5L (151")

Except Fiero & Grand Am

1) Raise vehicle and drain crankcase. Remove cradle-to-front engine mount nuts. Disconnect exhaust pipe at exhaust manifold and rear transaxle mount.

2) Remove starter, flywheel access cover and upper alternator bracket. Install Engine Support Fixture (J-22825-40). Remove lower alternator and engine support brackets. Remove oil pan bolts and oil pan.

Fiero

1) Install Engine Support Fixture (J-28467) with one leg attached to left strut mounting nuts and other resting on inner side rail above battery. Raise engine enough to relieve tension on cradle mounts.

2) Raise vehicle and support at lift points. Disconnect exhaust pipe at manifold and remove spring hangers. Remove both rear wheels and disconnect both lower control arms and toe-link rods at knuckle.

3) Disconnect emergency brake cable at cradle. Remove engine and transmission mount nuts. Remove cradle bolts and cradle assembly. Drain crankcase and remove front engine mount-to-support bracket nuts.

4) Remove flywheel access cover, starter and upper alternator bracket. Raise engine. Remove lower alternator and engine support brackets. Remove oil pan bolts and oil pan.

Grand Am

Disconnect negative battery cable. Raise vehicle. Remove exhaust pipe at manifold and move out of way. Remove flywheel access cover and starter. Remove oil pan bolts and oil pan.

NOTE: When reinstalling oil pan on all 2.5L models, install timing gear cover bolts after oil pan bolts are tightened.

V6 MODELS

2.8L (173")

1) Disconnect negative battery cable. On Firebird models, remove air cleaner, distributor cap and upper fan shroud. On all models, raise vehicle, drain crankcase and remove flywheel access cover.

2) On Firebird models, disconnect exhaust pipe at manifold. On all models, remove starter, support engine and remove engine mount bracket-to-engine bolts. Remove oil pan bolts. Raise engine and remove oil pan.

3.8L (231")

Disconnect negative battery cable. Raise and support vehicle. Drain crankcase. Remove flywheel access cover, exhaust crossover pipe and engine mount

Oil Pan Removal

GENERAL MOTORS — PONTIAC (Cont.)

bolts. Raise and support engine. Remove oil pan bolts and oil pan.

V8 MODELS

5.0L (305")

1) Disconnect negative battery cable. Remove air cleaner and fan shroud. Remove cruise control screw bracket (if equipped). Raise vehicle and drain crankcase. Disconnect exhaust pipe at manifold and converter.

2) Remove starter, flywheel access cover and engine mount through bolts. Remove oil pan bolts, lower oil pan and position forward crankshaft throw and/or counterweight horizontally. Raise engine, loosely reinstall through bolts and remove oil pan.

PONTIAC TIGHTENING SPECIFICATIONS

Application	INCH Lbs. (N.m)
Oil Pan	
4-Cylinder	
2.0L (122")	44 (5)
2.3L (138")	
Bolts	106 (12)
Stud Nut	[1]
2.5L (151")	53 (6)
V6 Engines	
2.8L (173")	
6 mm Bolts	71-106 (8-12)
8 mm Bolts	168-266 (19-30)
3.8L (231")	156 (18)
V8 Engines	
5.0L (305")	80 (9)

[1] – Tighten nut to 41 ft. lbs. (56 N.m).

Section 6a

ENGINE COOLING

CONTENTS

NOTE: **ALSO SEE GENERAL INDEX.**

Engine Cooling

COOLING SYSTEM TROUBLE SHOOTING

CONDITION	POSSIBLE CAUSE	CORRECTION
Engine Overheats With or Without Coolant Loss	Low coolant level	Add coolant, see ENGINE COOLING
	Thermostat stuck closed	Replace thermostat, see ENGINE COOLING
	Faulty fan clutch	Replace fan clutch, see ENGINE COOLING
	Faulty electric fan motor	Replace motor
	Faulty thermal relay switches	Check switches and connections
	Water distribution tube clogged	Flush system, see ENGINE COOLING
	Radiator air flow passages blocked	Clean or replace radiator
	Incorrect coolant concentration	Refill with proper amount of coolant
	Incorrect ignition timing	Reset ignition timing
	Faulty ignition advance	Check and/or replace
	Exhaust system restricted	Correct restriction
	Broken or slipping fan belt	Replace fan belt
	Water pump shaft broken	Replace water pump, see ENGINES
	Leaking freeze plug(s)	Replace freeze plug(s)
	Faulty radiator pressure cap	Replace pressure cap, see ENGINE COOLING
Engine Overheats With Internal Coolant Leakage	Warped or cracked intake manifold	Replace intake manifold, see ENGINES
	Blown cylinder head gasket	Replace head gasket, see ENGINES
	Warped/cracked cylinder head/block	Resurface or replace head or block
Engine Fails to Reach Normal Temperature	Thermostat stuck in open position	Replace thermostat, see ENGINE COOLING
	Temperature gauge or light defective	Inspect gauge, light or sending unit
	Faulty temperature sending unit	Replace sending unit
	Faulty thermal relay switches	Replace switches
	Incorrect thermostat	Replace thermostat, see ENGINE COOLING
	Improper coolant level	Add coolant to proper level
Poor Coolant Flow	Plugged or restricted radiator	Flush or replace radiator
	Restricted cylinder head or block	Flush entire cooling system
	Collapsed lower radiator hose	Replace lower hose
	Faulty water pump	Replace water pump, see ENGINES
Radiator Foaming	Incorrect coolant concentration	Flush system, add proper amount of coolant
Coolant Loss	Radiator, reservoir or heater core leaks	Repair radiator, reservoir or heater
	Water pump seal or gasket leaking	Replace seal or gasket, see ENGINES
	Cylinder head gasket leaking	Replace head gasket, see ENGINES
	Incorrect cylinder head bolt torque	Retighten bolts, see ENGINES
	Air in system	Bleed cooling system, see ENGINE COOLING
	Faulty water control valve	Replace control valve
Recovery System Inoperative	Low coolant level	Add coolant as required
	Leak in system	Inspect system, see ENGINE COOLING
	Radiator cap loose or defective	Inspect and/or replace as required
	Overflow tube clogged or leaking	Remove tube restriction
	Recovery bottle vent restricted	Remove vent restriction
No Coolant Flow Through Heater Core	Plugged return pipe in water pump	Inspect or replace water pump, see ENGINES
	Heater hose collapsed or plugged	Remove restriction and/or replace hose
	Plugged heater core and/or thermostat	Remove blockage in core or housing
	Plugged cylinder head heater flow hole	Flush system, see ENGINE COOLING
	Faulty water valve	Replace water valve
Cooling System Noise	Fan contacting shroud	Reposition fan and/or shroud
	Loose water pump impeller	Replace water pump, see ENGINES
	Dry fan belt	Replace fan belt
	Rough surface on drive pulley	Smooth surface or replace pulley
	Water pump bearing worn	Replace water pump, see ENGINES
	Improper alignment of fan belts	Reposition and/or replace belts

GENERAL COOLING SYSTEM SERVICING

DESCRIPTION

The basic liquid cooling system consists of a radiator, water pump, thermostat, cooling fan, pressure cap, heater (if equipped), various connecting hoses and cooling passages in the block and cylinder head. In addition, many cars use a fan clutch (incorporating a thermostatic control) or flexible fan blade. These reduce noise and power requirements at higher engine speeds.

Some models may use a thermostatic vacuum switch to advance ignition timing in the event of overheating. Most models use a coolant recovery system to prevent loss of anti-freeze.

MAINTENANCE

DRAINING

Remove radiator cap and open heater control valve to maximum heat position. Open drain cocks or remove plugs in bottom of radiator and in engine block. In-line engines usually have one plug or cock, while "V" type engines will have two, one in each bank of cylinders.

CLEANING

A good cleaning compound removes most rust and scale. Follow manufacturers instructions in the use of cleaner. If considerable rust and scale has to be removed, flushing should be used. Clean radiator air passages by blowing with compressed air from back to front of radiator.

FLUSHING

CAUTION: Some manufacturers use an aluminum/plastic radiator on some models (identified by a note below the filler neck). Material used for cleaning and flushing must be compatible with aluminum, according to manufacturers recommendations.

1) Back flushing is a very effective means of removing rust and scale from a cooling system. For best results, radiator, engine and heater core should be flushed separately.

2) To flush radiator, connect flushing gun to water outlet of radiator and disconnect water inlet hose. Use a leadaway hose, connected to radiator inlet, to prevent flooding engine. Use air in short bursts only, this will prevent damage to radiator. Continue flushing until water runs clear.

3) To flush engine, first remove thermostat and replace housing. Connect flushing gun to water outlet of engine. Disconnect heater hoses from engine. Flush using short air bursts until water runs clean. Flush heater core as described for radiator. Make sure heater valve is set to maximum heat position before flushing heater.

REFILLING

Engine should be running while refilling cooling system to prevent air from being trapped in engine block. After system is full, continue running engine until thermostat is open, then recheck fill level. Do not overfill system.

THERMOSTAT

1) Visually inspect thermostat for corrosion and proper sealing of valve and seat. If satisfactory, suspend thermostat and a thermometer in a container with a 50/50 mixture of anti-freeze and water. *See Fig. 1.*

2) Do not allow either thermostat or thermometer to touch bottom of container as this concentration of heat could cause an incorrect reading. Heat water until thermostat just begins to open.

Fig. 1: Testing Thermostat in Anti-Freeze/Water Solution

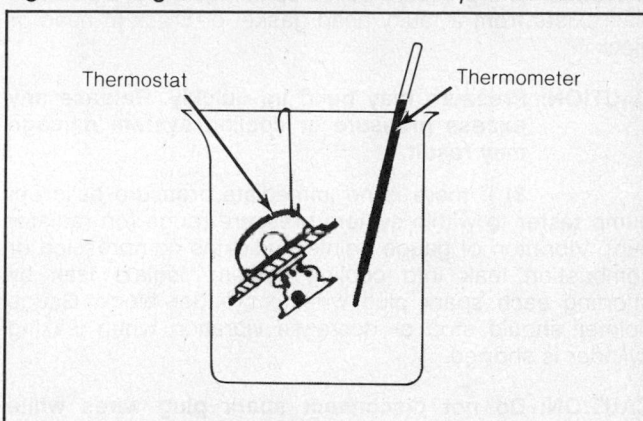

Thermometer should not touch bottom of container.

3) Read temperature on thermometer. This is the initial opening temperature and should be within specifications. Continue heating water until thermostat is fully open and note temperature. This is the fully opened temperature. If either reading is outside of specifications, replace thermostat, as it is not adjustable.

NOTE: **General Motors Corp. recommends hanging thermostat in 33% glycol solution at 25°F (4°C) above temperature stamped on thermostat. Valve should open. Remove thermostat from solution and place in similar solution at 10°F (-12°C) below stamped temperature. Valve should close.**

PRESSURE TESTING

A pressure testing tool is used to test both radiator cap and complete cooling system. Test as follows, following tool manufacturer's instructions.

Radiator Cap

Visually inspect radiator cap, then dip cap in water and connect to tester. Pump tester to bring pressure to upper limit of cap specifications. If cap fails to hold pressure within specifications, replace cap.

Fig. 2: Testing Radiator Pressure Cap

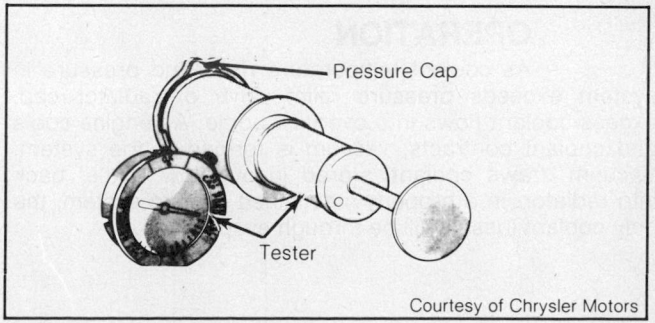

Courtesy of Chrysler Motors

Wet cap gasket before testing.

Engine Cooling Systems

GENERAL COOLING SYSTEM SERVICING (Cont.)

Cooling System

1) With engine off, wipe radiator filler neck seat clean. Fill radiator to correct level. Attach tester to radiator and pump until pressure is at upper limit of radiator rating.

2) If pressure drops, inspect for external leaks. If no leaks are apparent, detach tester and run engine until normal operating temperature is obtained. Reattach tester and observe. If pressure builds up immediately, a possible leak exists from a faulty head gasket or crack in head or block.

CAUTION: Pressure may build up quickly. Release any excess pressure or cooling system damage may result.

3) If there is no immediate pressure build up, pump tester to within system pressure range (on radiator cap). Vibration of gauge pointer indicates compression or combustion leak into cooling system. Isolate leak by shorting each spark plug wire to cylinder block. Gauge pointer should stop or decrease vibration when leaking cylinder is shorted.

CAUTION: Do not disconnect spark plug wires while engine is operating, or operate engine with spark plug shorted for more than 1 minute as catalytic converter may be damaged.

4) Remove engine and transmission (automatic only) oil dipsticks and check if water drops appear in oil. If so, a serious internal leak is indicated. If all checks are negative and system holds pressure for 2 minutes, there are no serious leaks in system.

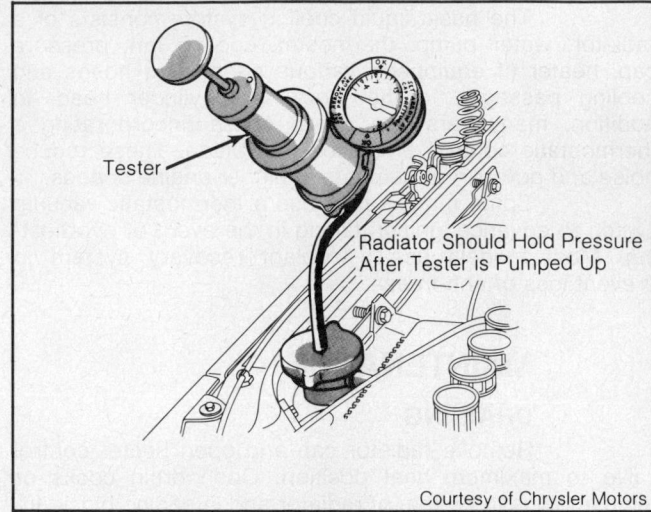

Fig. 3: Pressure Testing Cooling System

Tester

Radiator Should Hold Pressure After Tester is Pumped Up

Courtesy of Chrysler Motors

Pump up to specified pressure.

ANTI-FREEZE CONCENTRATION

NOTE: **On models using aluminum engines or cooling system components, refer to Owners Manual for anti-freeze requirements and recommendations. Aluminum components require a different formulation of anti-freeze to prevent corrosion.**

On all cooling systems, test anti-freeze concentration using anti-freeze tester. Tester should have a temperature-compensating feature, as failing to take temperature into consideration could cause an error as large as 30°F (-1°C). Follow tester manufacturer's instructions for correct use of tester.

COOLANT RECOVERY SYSTEMS

DESCRIPTION

A coolant recovery system differs from other cooling systems in that an overflow bottle is connected to the radiator overflow hose. Overflow bottle is transparent or translucent to permit checking of coolant level without removing radiator cap. No adjustment or test is required except keeping vent hole or hose clean and checking pressure relief of radiator cap.

OPERATION

As coolant temperature rises and pressure in system exceeds pressure relief valve of radiator cap, excess coolant flows into overflow bottle. As engine cools and coolant contracts, vacuum is formed in the system. Vacuum draws coolant, stored in overflow bottle, back into radiator. In a properly maintained cooling system, the only coolant losses will be through evaporation.

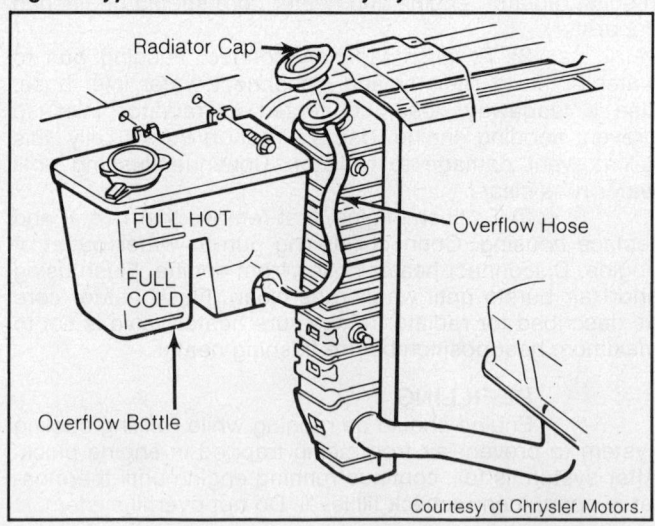

Fig. 1: Typical Coolant Recovery System

Radiator Cap

FULL HOT

FULL COLD

Overflow Hose

Overflow Bottle

Courtesy of Chrysler Motors.

THERMOSTATICALLY CONTROLLED ELECTRIC COOLING FANS
CHRYSLER MOTORS

CHRYSLER MOTORS
ELECTRIC COOLING FAN APPLICATIONS

Application	Engine
Dynasty	2.5L & 3.0L
New Yorker	2.5L & 3.0L
Caravelle	2.2L & 2.5L
600	2.2L & 2.5L
Daytona	2.2L & 2.5L
Lancer	2.2L & 2.5L
LeBaron	2.2L & 2.5L
Reliant	2.2L & 2.5L
Aries	2.2L & 2.5L
Sundance	2.2L & 2.5L
Shadow	2.2L & 2.5L

DESCRIPTION

All FWD models use electric motor driven cooling system fans. The fan modules include a motor support which may (depending on model) include a shroud. The module is fastened to the radiator by clips or bolts. There are a number of combinations of fan motor sizes and RPM, as well as fan sizes.

CAUTION: All fan motors have one speed. Attempts to reduce high temperature gauge reading by increasing engine speed, at the same vehicle speed, will only increase temperature.

NOTE: There are no repairs to be made to the fan. If the fan is warped, cracked, or otherwise damaged, it must be replaced with only the recommended part for adequate strength, performance and safety.

OPERATION

Fan control is accomplished 2 ways. The fan always runs when the A/C compressor clutch is engaged. In addition to this control, the fan is turned on by the temperature of the coolant which is sensed by the coolant temperature sensor which sends the message to the on-board computer. The computer turns on the fan through the fan relay.

Switching through the on-board computer provides for fan control. The fan should not run during cranking until the engine starts, no matter what the coolant temperature is. Fan should always run when the A/C clutch is engaged.

On non-A/C vehicles or with A/C off, the fan should run at vehicle speeds above about 40 MPH only if coolant temperature reaches 230°F (110°C) and will turn off when the temperature drops to 220°F (104°C).

At speeds below 40 MPH the fan switches on at 210°F (99°C) and off at 200°F (93°C). The fan will run only below 60°F (16°C) ambient, from 100°F (38°C) to 195°F (97°C) coolant temperature, only at idle, and zero car speed and then only for 3 minutes.

NOTE: At idle with A/C off, temperature gauge will rise slowly to about 5/8 gauge travel, the fan will come on and the gauge will quickly drop to about 1/2 gauge travel. This is normal.

DIAGNOSIS

ELECTRIC FAN MOTOR

To check the electric fan motor, disconnect fan motor wire connector. Observing correct polarity, connect a 12-volt battery source and ground to the fan motor connector. Positive side of connector is male and negative side is female. If the fan runs normally, the motor is functioning properly. If not, replace motor.

NOTE: If the motor is noticeably overheated, system voltage may be too high. Check charging system.

FAN RELAY & SINGLE
MODULE ENGINE CONTROLLER (SMEC)

1) Bring engine to normal running temperature. Check fan motor wiring harness connector for proper engagement. Check the computer for fault codes. If fault codes 88, 12, 35 and 55 are detected, proceed to step **3)**.

2) Code 88 indicates start of diagnostic mode. This code must appear first in the diagnostic mode or fault codes will be inaccurate. Code 55 indicates end of diagositic mode. Code 12 will be present if the SMEC has been cleared within the last 50-100 engine starts. Code 35 is a fault in the radiator fan relay circuit.

3) With ignition switch in run position, test for battery voltage at single pin connector at fan relay. If voltage reading is okay, proceed to step **4)**. Voltage at 0-1 volt, proceed to step **5)**

4) With ignition off, disconnect 60-pin connector from SMEC and return ignition to run position. Test for battery voltage at cavity No. 57 of connector. If voltage reading is okay and female terminal is not damaged, replace the SMEC. With a zero voltage reading, repair open or short in the circuit.

Fig. 1: SMEC 60-Pin Connector

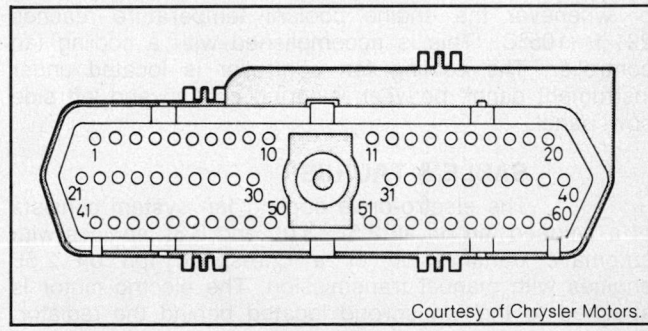

Courtesy of Chrysler Motors.

5) With ignition off, disconnect 60-pin connector from SMEC and return ignition to run position. Test for battery voltage at single pin connector at fan relay. If voltage reading is okay, replace the SMEC. With a voltage reading of 0-1 volt, proceed to step **6)**.

6) With ignition in run position, test for battery voltage at Blue wire in 3-way connector of fan relay. If voltage is okay, replace fan relay. If voltage reading is zero, repair open or short in circuit. Turn ignition off, connect 60-pin connector to SMEC and test system.

Engine Cooling Systems

THERMOSTATICALLY CONTROLLED ELECTRIC COOLING FANS
FORD MOTOR CO.

FORD MOTOR CO.
ELECTRIC COOLING FAN APPLICATIONS

Application	Engine
Continental	3.8L
Escort	1.9L
Mustang	2.3L
Sable	2.5L, 3.0L & 3.8L
Taurus	2.5L, 3.0L & 3.8L
Tempo	2.3L
Thunderbird	2.3L EFI Turbo
Topaz	2.3L

DESCRIPTION

CONTINENTAL

The electro-drive cooling fan system consists of a fan and 2-speed electric motor attached to a fan shroud located behind the radiator. The electro-drive cooling fan is wired to operate only when the ignition switch is in the "RUN" position, thereby preventing cooling fan operation after the ignition switch is turned to the "OFF" position.

ESCORT, TEMPO & TOPAZ

The electro-drive cooling fan system consists of a fan and electric motor attached to a fan shroud located behind the radiator. The system utilizes a coolant temperature switch mounted in the thermostat housing. Vehicles equipped with air conditioning have a cooling fan controller and cooling fan relay for the cooling fan system. On vehicles with a standard heater, the engine cooling fan is powered through the cooling fan relay.

MUSTANG

The system is designed to have engine cooling fan operation, whenever the A/C compressor is operating or whenever the engine coolant temperature reaches 221°F (105°C). This is accomplished with a cooling fan controller. The cooling fan controller is located under instrument panel, between steering column and left side cowl panel.

SABLE & TAURUS

The electro-drive cooling fan system consists of a 2-speed fan on all 2.5L, 3.0L and 3.8L engines with automatic transmission or a one-speed fan on 2.5L engines with manual transmission. The electric motor is attached to the fan shroud located behind the radiator. The electro-drive cooling fan is wired to operate only when the ignition switch is in the "RUN" position, thereby preventing cooling fan operation after the ignition switch is turned to the "OFF" position.

THUNDERBIRD

The electro-drive cooling fan system consists of 2 fans attached to a fan shroud that is located behind the radiator. Each fan is driven by a one-speed electric motor. The electro-drive cooling system is wired to operate only when the ignition switch is in the "RUN" position, there by preventing cooling fan operation after the ignition is turned to the "OFF" position. The cooling fan controller is located under instrument panel, between steering column and left side cowl panel.

OPERATION

CAUTION: Disconnect the cooling fan prior to performing any underhood service. The fan could cycle if the ignition switch is left in the "ON" position, even though the engine is not running.

CONTINENTAL

The cooling fan is controlled during vehicle operation by the integrated relay control assembly and EEC-IV module, which will energize the cooling fan under the following conditions:

- Engine temperature is higher than normal. Fan comes on at 215°F (102°C), and goes off at 210°F (99°C).
- A/C is on and vehicle speed does not provide enough natural air flow. Fan comes on at speeds at or below 43 MPH and goes off at 48 MPH.
- Cooling fan is turned on high speed if engine temperature is higher than desirable and fan has been operating at a low speed. The cooling fan operates at high speed when 230°F (110°C) is reached, and turns off at 224°F (107°C). During idle, the cooling fan operates at 236°F (113°C).
- Cooling fan will turn off (providing engine coolant temperature is not too high) if driver demand is Wide Open Throttle (WOT) or A/C is not operating.

When there is low refrigerant suction pressure, the clutch cycling pressure switch cuts off power to the Electronic Control Assembly (ECA), this interrupts the compressor and engine cooling fan operation.

The Wide Open Throttle (WOT) A/C cutout is used on all applications. During hard acceleration, a signal is sent to the ECA. The ECA then signals the integrated relay control assembly to cut off power to the A/C clutch field coil. This keeps the engine from being overloaded.

ESCORT, TEMPO & TOPAZ

The electro-drive cooling fan is wired to operate only when the ignition switch is in the "RUN" position on Tempo and Topaz vehicles. The cooling fan will operate whenever the cooling fan temperature switch is closed on Escort.

If the vehicle is equipped with A/C, the cooling fan will then be controlled by the cooling fan controller and a fan relay. The cooling fan motor will be energized whenever the A/C cycling pressure switch closes with the select lever in "A/C" or "DEFROST" position. The A/C clutch coil will be energized once voltage is available at the fan motor. The A/C clutch will cycle with the A/C clutch cycling pressure switch.

The fan motor will stay energized as the clutch cycles if the cycling pressure switch open intervals are less than 2-3 minutes in duration. If the coolant temperature switch closes in the A/C mode at 210°F (55°C) on Escort, the fan motor will run continuously until the coolant temperature drops below 193°F (75°C). Fully depressing the throttle will also de-energize the A/C clutch coil.

Two different fan controllers are used, depending on the vehicle. Proper operation of the cooling system cannot be obtained unless the proper fan controller is used. Each controller is identified with a color code and part number.

THERMOSTATICALLY CONTROLLED ELECTRIC COOLING FANS
FORD MOTOR CO. (Cont.)

The function control lever controls system vacuum and electrical operation. Vacuum motors operate doors to direct air flow. The electrical switches attached to the function control lever connect power to the blower motor, the clutch cycling pressure switch, and the A/C fan controller.

The cooling fan motor will be energized when the A/C select lever is moved to the "A/C" or "DEFROST" position. The fan will be energized first, then the A/C clutch will be powered if voltage is available at the cooling fan. The fan has limited cycling (2-3 minutes intervals) while the A/C clutch cycles with the A/C cycling pressure switch.

The cooling fan operates when the engine coolant temperature goes above 210°F (85°C) or when the A/C is operated. When there is low refrigerant suction pressure, the clutch cycling pressure switch signals the A/C fan controller to cut off power to the A/C clutch field coil, fan motor and throttle solenoid kicker.

The cooling fan controller on Escort is located under the instrument panel, forward of the evaporator mounting bracket. On Tempo and Topaz, the controller is mounted on the right cowl panel under the instrument panel. The controller can be serviced through the glove compartment opening.

MUSTANG

The cooling fan controller consists of 2 relays mounted on a printed circuit board. One relay powers the fan motor and the other relay powers the A/C compressor coil. Solid-state circuitry on the printed circuit board provides timing and control for the 2 relays.

When the engine coolant temperature reaches 221°F (105°C), the cooling fan temperature switch (located in the heater hose tube) will close to complete the ground circuit to the fan relay coil in the cooling fan controller. When the relay is energized, the contacts close to complete the circuit for engine cooling fan motor operation. The fan will continue to operate until the engine coolant temperature drops to approximately 201°F (94°C).

During A/C operation, the A/C clutch cycling pressure switch controls evaporator temperature by controlling compressor operation. The pressure switch will cause the fan relay to operate first (withing 2-4 seconds of start-up), then the A/C relay will operate if voltage is available at the fan motor terminal. The A/C compressor will cycle together with the A/C pressure switch, however, the cooling fan motor will remain on for A/C pressure switch open intervals less than 2 minutes.

The fan motor will de-energize if the A/C pressure remains open for more than 2 minutes or if the ignition switch is turned to the "OFF" position. Under WOT conditions, the A/C compressor will de-energize, but the cooling fan motor will continue operating. Turning A/C or defrost demand switch to "OFF" position, will not disengage the fan motor for 2-3 minutes, unless the ignition switch is turned to the "OFF" position.

SABLE & TAURUS

The cooling fan is controlled during vehicle operation by the integrated relay control assembly and EEC-IV module. The cooling fan will energize under the following conditions:

• Engine temperature is higher than normal. Fan comes on at 215°F (102°C), and goes off at 210°F (99°C).

• A/C is on and vehicle speed does not provide enough natural air flow. Fan comes on at speeds at or below 43 MPH and goes off at 48 MPH. Low speed cooling fan motor operation is achieved by using a dropping resistor in series with the motor.

• Cooling fan is turned on high if engine temperature is higher than desirable and fan has been operating at a low speed. Fan comes on at 230°F (110°C), and goes off at 224°F (107°C).

• Cooling fan will turn off (providing engine coolant temperature is not too high) if driver demand is Wide Open Throttle (WOT) or A/C clutch is not cycling rapidly.

Several different controllers are available depending on application. Proper operation of the system cannot be obtained unless the correct controller is used.

THUNDERBIRD

The cooling fans are controlled during vehicle operation by the integrated relay assembly and the ECC-IV module. The 4-blade passenger side fan will energize when the engine temperature, measured by Engine Coolant Temperature (ECT) sensor, is higher than normal. Fan turns on at 200°F (93°C) and off at 190°F (87°C). It also turns on when the A/C is on.

The 7-blade fan turns on when engine temperature is at 220°F (105°C). It turns off at 210°F (99°C) and when the 4-blade fan has been running for at least 10 seconds. Also, the fan comes on when A/C head pressure rises to 310 psi and cuts off at 265 psi. This function is independent of the EEC-IV system and engine block temperature. Both fans will be off when the A/C clutch has been de-energized for more than 2 seconds and the engine coolant temperature is below the predetermined fan off temperature.

TROUBLE SHOOTING

ESCORT, TEMPO & TOPAZ
Cooling Fan Controller

A cooling fan controller is used with all models equipped with A/C, to control engine cooling fan operation. The system components consist of a cooling fan and electric motor connected to the fan shroud, coolant temperature sensor mounted in the thermostat housing, cooling fan controller and relay. Whenever the coolant temperature is above 210°F (117°C) and the ignition switch in the "RUN" position (Tempo and Topaz only), the cooling fan controller signals the cooling fan motor to operate. The engine cooling fan will operate during A/C compressor operation and will cycle on and off with the compressor clutch.

The cooling fan controller is located below the instrument panel forward of the evaportor mounting bracket on Escort models. On Tempo and Topaz models the controller is located on the right side cowl panel under the instument panel and can be serviced through the glove box opening. Each cooling fan controller has the part number stamped on the housing. It is important that the correct controller be installed for proper operation.

If the cooling fan controller is suspected of not operating properly, diagnosis can be performed by taking voltage and/or continuity readings at the controller connector with controller plugged in. These readings are

Engine Cooling Systems

THERMOSTATICALLY CONTROLLED ELECTRIC COOLING FANS
FORD MOTOR CO. (Cont.)

Fig. 1: Escort, Tempo & Topaz Cooling Fan Controller Testing Specifications

TEMPO/TOPAZ
TEST 1 — IGNITION SWITCH OFF

Connector Pin Number	Voltmeter should read
1	0-volts
2	(not used)
3	0-volts
4	Battery voltage
5	0-volts
6	0-volts
7	0-volts
8	0-volts
9	0-volts
10	0-volts

ESCORT
TEST 1: IGNITION SWITCH OFF

Connector Pin Number	Voltmeter should read
1	12-volts with coolant temperature switch open.
2	(not used)
3	0 voltage (with coolant temperature switch open)
4	Battery voltage
5	0-volts
6	0-volts
7	0-volts
8	0-volts
9	0-volts
10	0-volts

TEMPO/TOPAZ
TEST 2 — IGNITION SWITCH IN RUN — ENGINE AND A/C OR DEFROST OFF

Connector Pin Number	Voltmeter should read
1	Battery voltage with coolant temperature switch open.
2	(not used)
3	0-volts with coolant temperature switch open — Battery voltage with coolant temperature switch closed.
4	Battery voltage
5	0-volts — continuity with ground
6	6-volts
7	0-volts
8	0-volts
9	Battery voltage
10	0-volts

ESCORT
TEST 2: IGNITION SWITCH IN RUN, ENGINE RUNNING AND A/C/DEFROST OFF

Connector Pin Number	Voltmeter should read
1	Battery voltage with coolant temperature switch open — Less than 1-volt with coolant temperature switch closed.
2	(not used)
3	0-volts with coolant temperature switch open — Battery voltage with coolant temperature switch closed.
4	Battery voltage
5	0-volts
6	6-volts
7	0-volts
8	0-volts
9	Battery voltage
10	0-volts

TEMPO/TOPAZ
TEST 3: IGNITION SWITCH IN RUN — ENGINE RUNNING AND A/C OR DEFROST ON

Connector Pin Number	Voltmeter should read
1 (c)	0-volts with clutch cycling pressure switch closed/or coolant temperature switch closed.
2	(not used)
3 (c)	Battery voltage with coolant temperature switch closed and/or clutch cycling pressure switch closed (a) — 0-volts otherwise.
4	Battery voltage
5	0-volts
6	6-volts during normal operation — 0-volts during wide-open throttle operation (b).
7	Battery voltage
8 (a)	Battery voltage when A/C clutch cycling pressure switch is closed and throttle is normal (c) — 0-volts with cycling switch open or throttle closed.
9	Battery voltage
10	Battery voltage when A/C clutch cycling pressure switch and high pressure cut-out switch closed — 0-volts if switch is open.

(a) When Pin 6 is grounded, Pin 8 will have 0 volts.

(b) High pressure cutout switch (if used) must also be closed.

(c) On fan controllers with prefix E53Z or later the fan motor will stay energized when the WOT switch is open. The fan motor will stay energized if the A/C cycling pressure switch opens for less than 2-3 minutes.

NOTE: Indicated voltages in the 50 states and Canada procedures can vary, depending on the type of meter used.

ESCORT
TEST 3: IGNITION SWITCH IN RUN, ENGINE RUNNING AND A/C/DEFROST ON

Connector Pin Number	Voltmeter should read
1	Less than 1.0-volt with coolant temperature switch closed.
2	(not used)
3	Battery voltage with temperature switch and/or clutch cycling pressure cut-out switch closed — 0-volts if both switches are open. ①
4	Battery voltage
5	0-volts
6	Wide-open throttle: 0-volts. Not wide-open throttle: 6-volts.
7	Battery voltage
8	Battery voltage with clutch cycling, switch closed or not wide-open throttle 0-volts if A/C cycling switch open or wide-open throttle.
9	Battery voltage
10	Battery voltage with clutch cycling pressure switch closed.

① On fan controllers with prefix E5EZ or later, the fan motor will stay energized when the WOT switch is open. The fan motor will stay energized if the A/C cycling pressure switch opens for less than 2-3 minutes.

Courtesy of Ford Motor Co.

taken under the following 3 conditions: ignition switch off, ignition switch in "RUN" position while engine and A/C are off and ignition switch in "RUN" position with engine running and A/C on. The readings should be obtained at the indicated connector pins. See Figs. 1, 3 and 8. If indicated voltage and/or continuity readings are not present, refer to wiring diagrams and COOLING FAN SYSTEM DAIGNOSIS WITH A/C.

COOLING FAN SYSTEM DIAGNOSIS WITHOUT A/C

ESCORT
Without A/C

1) Disconnect fan motor connector. Install a jumper wire between negative lead and body ground. Apply battery voltage to positive lead. If fan motor does not run, replace motor. If fan motor does run, reconnect fan motor lead and go to next step.

2) Disconnect electrical connector at cooling fan temperature switch. With ignition off, check for battery voltage at circuit No. 197. See Fig. 2. If voltage is present go to next step. If voltage is not present, check for an open or short in circuit No. 197 and/or circuit breaker. Repair as necessary and recheck.

3) Install a jumper wire between terminals of cooling fan temperature switch connector. With ignition off, cooling fan should run. If so, replace cooling fan temperature switch and recheck operation. If not, leave jumper wire intact and go to next step.

4) Disconnect fan motor connector. With ignition off, check circuit No. 228 for battery voltage. If battery voltage is present, go to next step. If not, check circuit No. 228 and No. 182 for an open. See Fig. 2. Repair or replace as necessary and recheck operation.

5) Check ground circuit No. 57 for continuity to ground. If continuity is present, replace cooling fan motor, connect cooling fan temperature switch connector and recheck. If no continuity is present, repair open in circuit No. 57. Connect cooling fan motor connector and temperature switch connector and recheck operation.

THERMOSTATICALLY CONTROLLED ELECTRIC COOLING FANS
FORD MOTOR CO. (Cont.)

WIRING DIAGRAMS

Fig. 2: Escort Without A/C Electric Cooling Fan

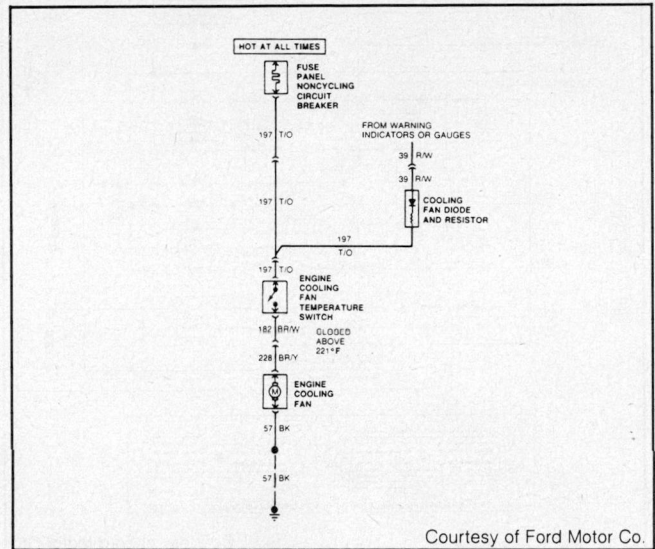

Courtesy of Ford Motor Co.

Fig. 3: Escort with A/C Electric Cooling Fan

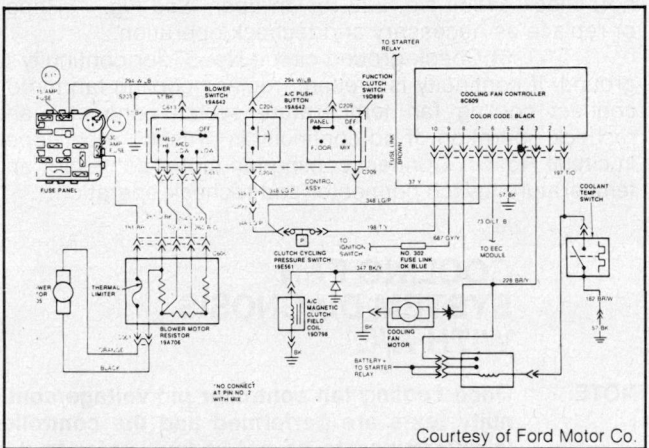

Courtesy of Ford Motor Co.

Fig. 4: Mustang (2.3L) Electric Cooling Fan

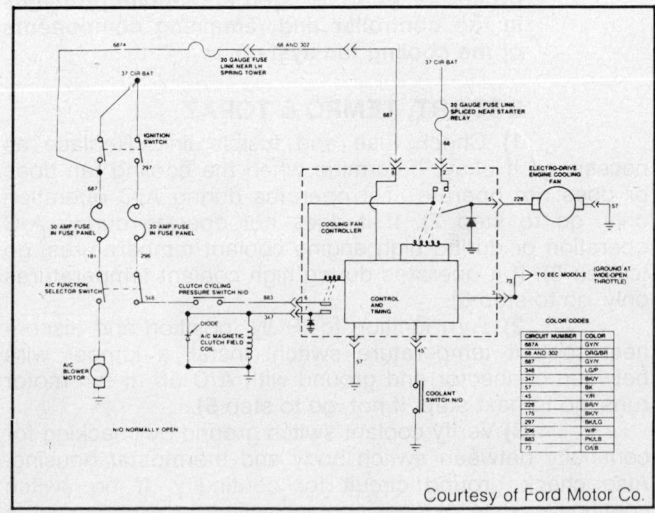

Courtesy of Ford Motor Co.

Fig. 5: Sable & Taurus (2.5L CFI Manual Transaxle) Electric Cooling Fan

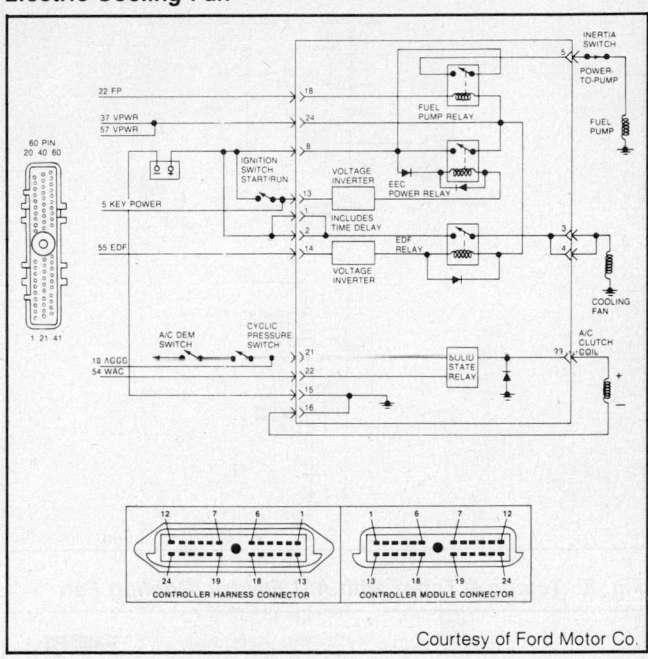

Courtesy of Ford Motor Co.

Fig. 6: Sable, Taurus (2.5L CFI) & (3.0L EFI Automatic Transaxle w/OD) & Continental (3.8L EFI Manual Transaxle w/OD) Electric Cooling Fan

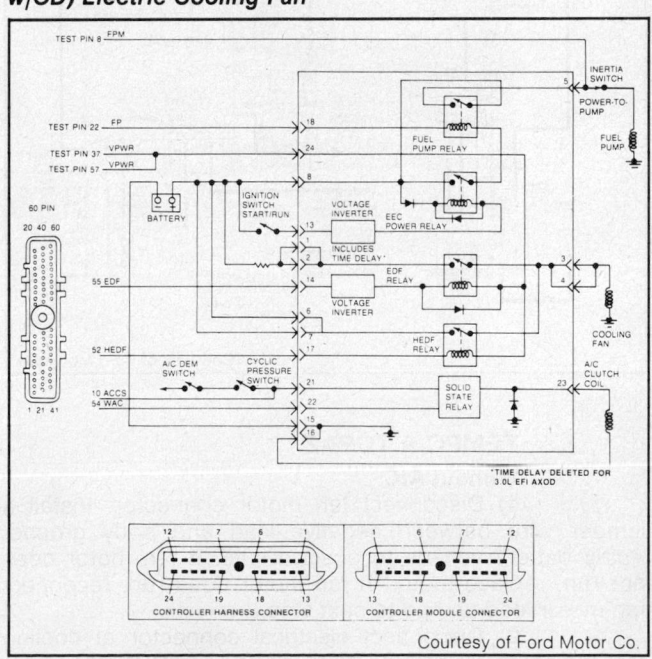

Courtesy of Ford Motor Co.

Engine Cooling Systems

THERMOSTATICALLY CONTROLLED ELECTRIC COOLING FANS
FORD MOTOR CO. (Cont.)

Fig. 7: Tempo & Topaz without A/C Electric Cooling Fan

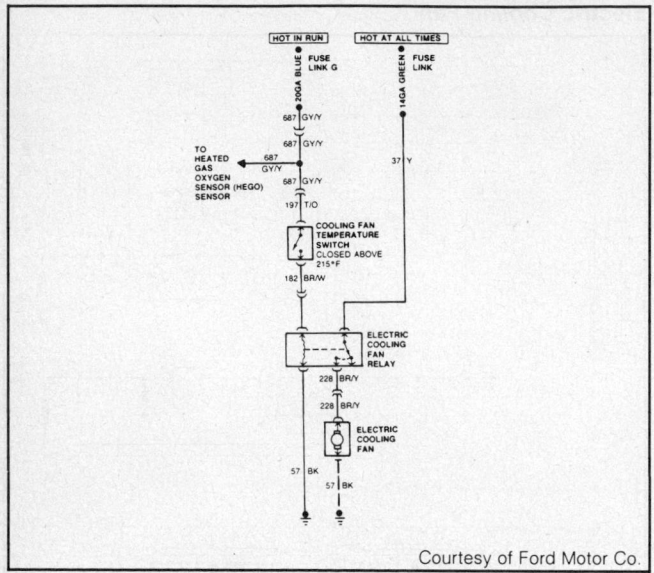

Courtesy of Ford Motor Co.

Fig. 8: Tempo & Topaz with A/C Electric Cooling Fan

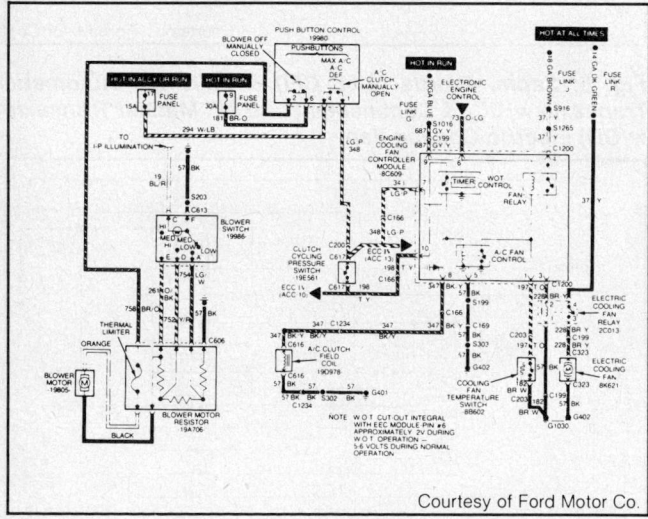

Courtesy of Ford Motor Co.

TEMPO & TOPAZ

Without A/C

1) Disconnect fan motor connector. Install a jumper wire between negative lead and body ground. Apply battery voltage to positive lead. If fan motor does not run, replace motor. If fan motor does run, reconnect fan motor lead and go to next step.

2) Disconnect electrical connector at cooling fan temperature switch. With ignition in "RUN" position, check for battery voltage at circuit No. 197. If voltage is present, go to next step. If voltage is not present, check for an open or short in circuit No. 197. *See Fig. 7*. Repair as necessary and recheck operation.

3) Install a jumper wire between terminals of cooling fan temperature switch connector. With ignition in "RUN" position, cooling fan should run. If so, replace cooling fan temperature switch and recheck operation. If not, leave jumper wire intact and go to next step.

4) Disconnect fan motor connector. With ignition in "RUN" position, check circuit No. 228 for battery

Fig. 9: Thunderbird (2.3L Turbo) Electric Cooling Fan

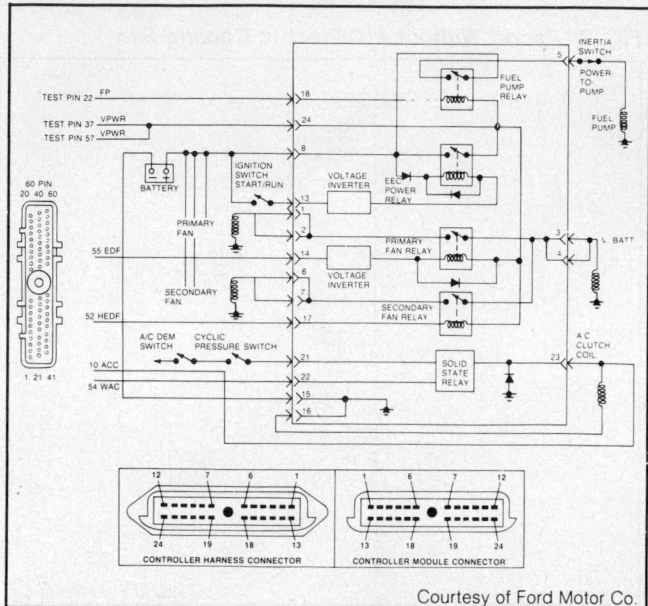

Courtesy of Ford Motor Co.

voltage. If battery voltage is present, go to next step. If not, check circuit No. 228 for an open. *See Fig. 7*. Repair or replace as necessary and recheck operation.

5) Check ground circuit No. 57 for continuity to ground. If continuity is present, replace cooling fan motor, connect cooling fan temperature switch connector and recheck operation. If no continuity is present, repair open in circuit No. 57. Connect cooling fan motor connector and temperature switch connector and recheck operation.

COOLING FAN SYSTEM DIAGNOSIS WITH A/C

NOTE: Once cooling fan controller pin voltage/continuity tests are performed and the controller is determined to be not at fault, refer to this section for diagnosis information. These procedures can be used to pinpoint problems in the controller and remaining components of the cooling fan system.

ESCORT, TEMPO & TOPAZ

1) Check fuse and fusible link. Replace as necessary. If okay, determine when the cooling fan does or does not operate. If it operates during A/C operation only, go to step **2)**. If it does not operate during A/C operation or during high engine coolant temperatures, go to step **8)**. If it operates during high coolant temperatures only, go to step **6)**.

2) Turn ignition to "RUN" position and disconnect coolant temperature switch. Install a jumper wire between connector and ground with A/C off. If fan motor runs, go to next step. If not, go to step **5)**.

3) Verify coolant switch ground by checking for continuity between switch body and thermostat housing. Also check ground circuit for continuity. If no switch continuity exists, tighten coolant switch until continuity is achieved.

THERMOSTATICALLY CONTROLLED ELECTRIC COOLING FANS
FORD MOTOR CO. (Cont.)

4) Verify coolant temperature has exceeded 210°F (84.7°C) by idling vehicle for about 25 minutes. If cooling fan motor operates, cooling fan system is okay. If not, replace coolant temperature switch.

5) Unplug connector from cooling fan controller and check for continuity of circuit No. 197 from controller coolant temperature switch. If continuity exists, replace cooling fan controller. If not service open circuit.

6) Check fan controller system ground at terminal No. 5 of fan controller. If ground is okay, go to next step. If not, repair ground circuit.

7) Remove connector from cooling fan controller. Check for voltage at circuits No. 198 and No. 348 *See Fig. 3 and 8.* If no voltage at one or both circuits, go to next step. If voltage is present, replace fan controller.

8) Remove connector from clutch cycling pressure switch and install a jumper wire between connector terminals. If fan motor engages, go to next step. If not, go to step **10)**.

9) Check A/C system for refrigerant charge pressure of 50 psi (3.5 kg/cm²) with ambient temperature of about 50°F (10°C). If no refrigerant pressure is present, leak test, service and recharge system. If refrigerant pressure is above 50 psi, replace clutch cycling pressure switch.

10) Remove connector from A/C control assembly. Install jumper wire in between circuits No. 348 and No. 294. Check for voltage at circuit No. 198. *See Fig. 3 and 8.* If voltage is present, replace A/C button switch and return to step **7)**. If no voltage is present, service open circuit.

11) Unplug connector at cooling fan motor. Apply battery voltage and ground to fan motor. If fan motor runs, go to next step. If not, replace cooling fan motor.

12) Remove jumper wire and reconnect connector to fan motor. Disconnect connector from cooling fan controller and turn ignition switch to run. Check for voltage at circuits No. 37, 687, 175, 198 and 348. Check for good ground at circuit No. 57. If voltage and grounds are okay, go to next step. If not, service circuits without voltage.

13) Install a jumper wire between circuit No. 37 and No. 228A at the cooling fan controller. If fan motor runs, replace fan controller. If not, go to next step.

14) On Escort models, check continuity between circuit No. 37 of the fan controller. Check for continuity between terminal No. 3 and of fan motor relay and circuit No. 228A. *See Fig. 3 and 8.* Check circuit No. 197 between coolant switch and fan motor relay.

NOTE: Steps 15), 16) and 17) apply to Tempo and Topaz only.

15) Install a jumper wire between circuit No. 37 and No. 228 at the cooling fan controller. If fan motor runs, replace fan relay. If not, go to next step.

16) Unplug 5-way connector of the engine compartment mounted fan relay. Jumper circuit No. 37 to circuit No. 228A. If fan motor runs, go to next step. If not, service fan motor ground.

17) Install a jumper wire between circuit No. 57 and terminal No. one of the fan motor relay. Also install a jumper wire between circuit No. 37 and circuit No. 228. If fan motor runs, service faulty circuits. If not, replace fan relay.

MUSTANG (2.3L OHC)
Cooling Fan Inoperative

1) Disconnect fan motor lead and install a jumper wire between negative lead and ground. Install jumper lead between positive lead and battery voltage. If fan motor runs, replace fan motor. If not, reconnect fan motor lead and go to next step

2) Disconnect coolant temperature switch connector and install a jumper wire between connector and ground on circuit No. 45 (Yellow/Red wire). Turn ignition switch on. If fan motor runs, check coolant temperature switch ground circuit No. 45. *See Fig. 4.* If okay, replace coolant temperature switch. If fan motor does not run, go to next step.

3) With ignition off, remove jumper wire. Check continuity of circuit No. 45 from cooling fan controller (terminal No. 1) to coolant temperature switch. If no continuity is present, fix open in circuit No. 45. If continuity is present, install jumper wire between coolant temperature switch and ground and go to next step.

4) Install a jumper wire between circuit No. 687 of cooling fan controller connector (terminal No. 8) and battery voltage. If motor runs, check ignition feed circuits No. 68 and No. 687 for an open. *See Fig. 4.* If motor does not run, remove jumper wire and go to next step.

5) Disconnect cooling fan controller connector. Jumper circuit No. 228 (terminal No. 5) to battery voltage. If motor runs, remove jumper wire and go to next step. If not, check for open in circuit No. 228.

6) Install a jumper wire between circuits No. 68 (terminal No. 2) and No. 228 (terminal No. 5) at the cooling fan controller connector. If motor does not run, check circuit No. 68 for an open. If fan motor does run, replace cooling fan controller and remove jumper from coolant temperature switch.

Cooling Fan Works,
But Does Not Operate In A/C Mode

1) Turn A/C switch to "ON" position. Wait for 4 seconds. If fan motor does not operate, go to next step. If fan motor goes off and on repeatedly, go to step **7**.

2) Check 20-amp fuse in fuse panel. If fuse is blown, replace it. If not, disconnect A/C clutch cycle pressure switch connector and install a jumper wire between terminals of connector. If fan motor runs, go to next step. If not, go to step **6)**.

3) Check A/C system for loss of refrigerant charge. If refrigerant level is low, add refrigerant. If refrigerant pressure is above 50 psi (3.5 cm/kg²), go to next step.

4) Check for continuity between terminals of A/C clutch cycling pressure switch with connector removed. If continity is present, go to next step. If not, replace A/C clutch cycling pressure switch.

5) Check for voltage of circuit No. 348 at A/C clutch cycling pressure switch connector. *See Fig. 4.* If voltage is present, go to step **7)**. If no voltage is present, go to next step.

6) Check for voltage at circuits No. 296 and No. 348 at function selector switch in instrument panel. If voltage is present on circuit No. 296, but not on circuit No. 348, A/C control assembly needs service. If no voltage is present at circuit No. 296, check for short on circuits No. 296 and 297 to the ignition switch.

7) Check for voltage on circuit No. 883 (pin No. 6) of cooling fan controller. *See Fig. 4.* If voltage is

Engine Cooling Systems

THERMOSTATICALLY CONTROLLED ELECTRIC COOLING FANS
FORD MOTOR CO. (Cont.)

present, go to next step. If voltage is not present, repair open in circuit No. 883 to the controller.

8) With fan controller connected, ground circuit No. 57 (pin No. 4) of the controller. If fan runs, repair ground circuit No. 57. If not, replace fan controller.

CONTINENTAL, SABLE, TAURUS & THUNDERBIRD (2.3L Turbo)
A/C Integrated Relay Controller

The Integrated Relay Controller Module (IRCM) interfaces with the EEC-IV system to provide control of the cooling fan, A/C clutch, and fuel pump. The module incorporates the ECC power relay which supplies current to the EEC-IV system. *See Figs. 5, 6 and 9.*

The location of the IRCM for all models (except Thunderbird), is on the radiator support bracket. The Thunderbird models IRCM is located on the right side fender apron at the shock tower. The operating voltage of the IRCM is between 7 and 17 volts.

For diagnostic information concerning A/C components controlled the IRCM and/or for the IRCM itself, see the following A/C INTREGRATED RELAY CONTROLLER trouble shooting charts.

A/C INTEGRATED RELAY CONTROLLER

The Integrated Relay Controller Module (IRCM) interfaces with the EEC-IV system to provide control of the cooling fan, A/C clutch, and fuel pump. The module incorporates the ECC power relay which supplies current to the EEC-IV system.

The location of the IRCM for all models except Thunderbird, is on the radiator support bracket. The Thunderbird models IRCM is located on the right side fender apron at the shock tower.

The operating temperature parameters for the IRCM are -20°F to 240°F (-30°C to 100°C). The storage parameters are -40°F to 315°F (-40°C to 125°C). The operating voltage of the IRCM is between 7 and 17 volts.

NOTE: This test should be performed only after obtaining service codes 72, 78, 82, 83, 87, 88, 95 and/or 96 or if you are following a diagnosis by symptom procedure. A Break Out box is required for this series of testing.

NOTE: All tests in the following procedures do not apply solely to the A/C system, many are combination tests for other circuits as well as the A/C system. All tests are not numbered in sequential order. Be aware that the following components of non-EEC areas may be at fault in the A/C system and should be checked prior to replacing any components: A/C clutch, A/C demand switch, cooling fan motor, battery cables and ground straps.

The following tests apply to these models: Continental (3.8L AXOD), Cougar (3.8L AXOD), Sable (All), Taurus (All) and Thunderbird (2.3L Turbo & 3.8L AXOD).

NOTE: Refer to MITCHELL'S COMPUTERIZED ENGINE CONTROLS DIAGNOSIS & TESTING for instructions on performing additional testing procedures and/or explaination of terms not covered in this section.

TEST STEP	RESULT	▶	ACTION TO TAKE
VEHICLE BATTERY			
X1 CHECK BATTERY VOLTAGE			
• Key on, engine off.	Yes	▶	GO to X2.
• DVOM on 20 volt scale.			
• Measure voltage across battery terminals.	No	▶	SERVICE discharged battery.
• Is voltage greater than 10.5 volts?			
X2 CHECK BATTERY GROUND			
• Key on, engine off.	Yes	▶	GO to X3.
• Processor connected.			
• DVOM on 20 volt range.	No	▶	GO to X6.
• Measure voltage between battery negative post and SIGNAL RETURN circuit in the Self-Test connector.			
• Is voltage greater than 0.5 volts?			
X3 GROUND FAULT ISOLATION			
• Key off.	Yes	▶	GO to X4.
• Disconnect processor 60 pin connector. Inspect for damaged pins, corrosion, loose wires etc. Service as necessary.	No	▶	Circuit(s) with greater than 0.5 volts has high resistance or open. SERVICE open ground circuit. RERUN Quick Test.
• Install breakout box.			
• Key on, engine off.			
• Processor connected.			
• DVOM on 20 volt scale.			
• Measure voltage between battery negative post and Test Pins 40 and 60 at the breakout box.			
• Are both voltages less than 0.5 volts?			
X4 PROCESSOR GROUND FAULT ISOLATION			
• Breakout box installed.	Yes	▶	GO to X5.
• Key off, wait 10 seconds.			
• Processor connected.	No	▶	REMOVE breakout box. REPLACE processor. RERUN Quick Test.
• DVOM on 200 ohm scale.			
• Measure resistance between Test Pin 46 and Test Pin 40 and between Test Pin 46 and Test Pin 60 at the breakout box.			
• Are both resistances less than 5 ohms?			

TEST STEP	RESULT	▶	ACTION TO TAKE
X5 CHECK CONTINUITY OF SIGNAL RETURN CIRCUIT			
• Breakout box installed.	Yes	▶	System OK. RUN Quick Test.
• Key off, wait 10 seconds.			
• Processor connected.	No	▶	REMOVE breakout box. RECONNECT processor. SERVICE open circuit. RERUN Quick Test.
• DVOM on 200 ohm scale.			
• Measure resistance between Test Pin 46 at the breakout box and SIGNAL RETURN circuit at Self-Test connector.			
• Is resistance less than 5.0 ohms?			
X6 MEASURE VOLTAGE AND GROUND TO INTEGRATED CONTROLLER			
• Key off.	Yes	▶	GO to X7.
• Disconnect Integrated Controller Module.	No	▶	GO to X9.
• DVOM on 20 volt scale.			
• Measure voltage between Test Pin 8 and Test Pin 15 at the Integrated Controller vehicle harness connector.			
• Is voltage greater than 10.5 volts?			
X7 KEY POWER TO INTEGRATED CONTROLLER			
• Integrated Controller disconnected.	Yes	▶	GO to X8.
• DVOM on 20 volt scale.			
• Key on.	No	▶	SERVICE open between Pin 13 and ignition switch. RECONNECT Integrated Controller. RERUN Quick Test.
• Measure voltage between Pin 13 and Pin 15 at the Integrated Controller vehicle harness connector.			
• Refer to schematic			
• Is voltage greater than 10.5 volts?			

THERMOSTATICALLY CONTROLLED ELECTRIC COOLING FANS
FORD MOTOR CO. (Cont.)

A/C INTEGRATED RELAY CONTROLLER (Cont.)

TEST STEP	RESULT	▶	ACTION TO TAKE
X8 MEASURE CONTINUITY OF VPWR			
• Key off. • Integrated Controller disconnected. • Disconnect processor 60 pin connector. Inspect for damaged pins, corrosion, loose wires, etc. Service as necessary. • Install breakout box, leave processor disconnected. • DVOM on 200 ohm scale. • Measure resistance between Test Pin 37 and 57 at the breakout box and Test Pin 24 at the Integrated Controller harness. • Is resistance greater than 5.0 ohms?	Yes No	▶ ▶	REMOVE breakout box. RECONNECT processor. SERVICE open in VPWR circuit. RECONNECT Integrated Controller. RERUN Quick Test. REMOVE breakout box. RECONNECT processor. REPLACE Integrated Controller. RERUN Quick Test.
X9 MEASURE CONTINUITY OF POWER GROUND TO INTEGRATED CONTROLLER			
• Key off. • Integrated Controller disconnected. • DVOM on 200 ohm scale. • Measure resistance between battery negative post and at Test Pin 15 at the Integrated Controller connector. • Is resistance greater than 5.0 ohms?	Yes No	▶ ▶	RECONNECT Integrated Controller. SERVICE open in battery ground to Pin 15 (Integrated Controller harness connector). RERUN Quick Test. RECONNECT Integrated Controller. SERVICE open in battery positive to Pin 8 (Integrated Controller harness connector). RERUN Quick Test.

TEST STEP	RESULT	▶	ACTION TO TAKE
X12 CHECK RESISTANCE OF FUEL PUMP INERTIA SWITCH			
• Key off, wait 10 seconds. • Fuel pump(s) disconnected. • Locate and disconnect fuel pump inertia switch. • DVOM on 200 ohm scale. • Measure the resistance of the fuel pump inertia switch. • Is resistance less than 5.0 ohms?	Yes No	▶ ▶	GO to **X13**. REPLACE fuel pump inertia switch. RERUN Quick Test.
X13 POWER-TO-PUMP CIRCUIT CONTINUITY CHECK			
• Key off. • DVOM on 200 ohm scale. • Disconnect Integrated Controller. • Fuel pump(s) disconnected. • Measure resistance between Pin 5 at the integrated controller vehicle harness connector and POWER-TO-PUMP(S) circuit at the fuel pump vehicle harness connector. • Is resistance less than 5.0 ohms?	Yes No	▶ ▶	REPLACE Integrated Controller. RECONNECT all components. RERUN Quick Test. SERVICE open in POWER-TO-PUMP(S) circuit. RECONNECT Integrated Controller. RERUN Quick Test.
X14 CHECK POWER-TO-PUMP(S) FOR SHORTS TO POWER			
• Key off. • Disconnect Integrated Controller. • Disconnect fuel pumps. • DVOM on 200,000 ohm scale. • Measure resistance between Pin 5 and Pin 24 at the Integrated Controller vehicle harness connector. • Measure resistance between Pin 5 at the Integrated Controller vehicle harness connector and battery positive post. • Is either resistance less than 10,000 ohms?	Yes No	▶ ▶	SERVICE short circuit. RECONNECT all components. ATTEMPT to start vehicle. If vehicle runs, RERUN Quick Test. If vehicle will not run, REPLACE Integrated Controller. RERUN Quick Test. RECONNECT fuel pump. REPLACE Integrated Controller. RERUN Quick Test.

TEST STEP	RESULT	▶	ACTION TO TAKE
X10 CODE 72 OR 78: INTERMITTENT OPEN IN VPWR CIRCUIT			
NOTE: Code 72 or 78 indicates that while key power was present, VPWR had an interrupt, or interference from electrical noises caused the processor to reset, resulting in possible stalls, high idle rpm, lack of power on acceleration or other drive symptoms. Possible Causes: • Intermittent open in VPWR circuit from integrated controller to processor. • EEC power relay intermittent malfunction. • Intermittent open in VBATT circuit to integrated controller. • Intermittent open in KEY POWER circuit to integrated controller. • EEC harness to close to the distributor spark plug wires and other vehicle harnesses. • Using Continuous Monitor Mode Observe VOM or STAR LED for indication of a fault while performing the following: • Shake, bend and twist harness from integrated controller to the processor, to the ignition switch and to battery positive. • Is a fault indicated or does Code 72 or 78 reappear in continuous memory if Quick Test is rerun?	Yes No	▶ ▶	CHECK for proper routing of EEC harness. SERVICE as necessary. If OK SERVICE intermittent VPWR circuit. RERUN Quick Test. INSPECT component and harness connectors of integrated controller and processor, for loose or damaged pins, corrosion, etc. SERVICE as necessary. If OK, ROAD TEST vehicle through a variety of drive modes to verify if symptom exists. REPLACE integrated controller, otherwise testing complete. RERUN Quick Test.
X11 CHECK POWER-TO-PUMP(S) CIRCUIT			
• Key on, engine off. • Locate and disconnect fuel pump(s). • DVOM on 20 volt scale. • Measure voltage between CHASSIS GROUND and POWER-TO-PUMP(S) circuit at fuel pump during crank mode. • Is voltage greater than 8.0 volts during crank?	Yes No	▶ ▶	Electric Fuel Pump Faulty GO to **X12**.

TEST STEP	RESULT	▶	ACTION TO TAKE
SERVICE CODE: 87			
X15 CHECK CONTINUITY OF FUEL PUMP CIRCUIT			
• Key off. • Disconnect processor 60 pin connector. Inspect for damaged pins, corrosion, loose wires, etc. Service as necessary. • Install breakout box, leave processor disconnected. • Disconnect Integrated Controller. • DVOM on 200 ohm scale. • Measure resistance between Test Pin 22 at the breakout box and Pin 18 at the Integrated Controller vehicle harness connector. • Is resistance less than 5.0 ohms?	Yes No	▶ ▶	GO to **X16**. SERVICE open in fuel pump circuit. REMOVE breakout box. RECONNECT processor and controller. RERUN Quick Test.

Engine Cooling Systems

THERMOSTATICALLY CONTROLLED ELECTRIC COOLING FANS
FORD MOTOR CO. (Cont.)

A/C INTEGRATED RELAY CONTROLLER (Cont.)

TEST STEP	RESULT	▶	ACTION TO TAKE
X16 CHECK FUEL PUMP CIRCUIT FOR SHORTS TO POWER AND GROUND			
• Key off. • Breakout box installed. • Processor disconnected. • Integrated Controller disconnected. • DVOM on 200,000 ohm scale. • Measure resistance between Test Pin 22 and Test Pins 37, 57 and battery positive post and between Test Pin 22 and Test Pins 40, 60 and battery negative. • Are all resistances greater than 10,000 ohms?	Yes No	▶ ▶	GO to X17 REMOVE breakout box. SERVICE fuel pump circuit shorts to power or ground. RECONNECT all components. RERUN Quick Test. If code 87 is still present, GO to X17.
X17 CHECK RESISTANCE OF FUEL PUMP RELAY COIL			
• Key off. • Breakout box installed. • Processor disconnected. • Integrated Controller disconnected. • DVOM on 200 ohm scale. • Measure resistance of Integrated Controller from Pin 18 to 24. • Is resistance between 65 and 100 ohms?	Yes No	▶ ▶	REMOVE breakout box. REPLACE processor. RECONNECT Integrated Controller. RERUN Quick Test. REMOVE breakout box. RECONNECT processor. REPLACE Integrated Controller. RERUN Quick Test.
X20 NO FAN, HIGH OR LOW WITH NO CODE 83			
• Key off. • Disconnect Integrated Controller. • DVOM on 20 volt scale. • Measure voltage between battery negative post and Pins 1, 2, 6 and 7, respectively at the Integrated Controller vehicle harness connector. • Is voltage greater than 10.5 volts?	Yes No	▶ ▶	GO to X21 RECONNECT Integrated Controller. SERVICE open in battery power circuit. RE-EVALUATE symptom.
X21 CHECK FAN MOTOR			
• Key off. • Integrated Controller disconnected. • Jumper Pin 3 to Pin 6 at Integrated Controller harness. • Does fan run?	Yes No	▶ ▶	GO to X22 GO to X23

TEST STEP	RESULT	▶	ACTION TO TAKE
X22 CHECK FAN RUNNING MODE (LOW)			
• Key off. • Disconnect processor. • Reconnect Integrated Controller. • Key on. • Does fan run at low speed?	Yes No	▶ ▶	GO to X25. CHANGE Integrated Controller. RECONNECT processor and controller. RE-EVALUATE symptom.
X23 MEASURE BATTERY VOLTAGE SUPPLY AT FAN — BYPASSING INTEGRATED CONTROLLER			
• Key Off. • Disconnect cooling fan. • Integrated Controller disconnected. • Jumper Pin 3 to Pin 6 at Integrated Controller vehicle harness connector. • DVOM on 20 volt scale. • Measure voltage at cooling fan vehicle harness connector. • Is voltage greater than 8.0 volts?	Yes No	▶ ▶	RECONNECT Integrated Controller. CHANGE fan motor. RE-EVALUATE symptom. GO to X24.
X24 COOLING FAN GROUND VERIFICATION			
• Key off. • Cooling fan disconnected. • Integrated Controller disconnected. • Jumper Pin 3 to Pin 6 at Integrated Controller vehicle harness connector. • DVOM on 20 volt scale. • Measure voltage between voltage positive at cooling fan harness connector and negative battery post. • Is voltage greater than 8.0 volts?	Yes No	▶ ▶	SERVICE Open in ground circuit to fan. RECONNECT Integrated Controller and cooling fan. RE-EVALUATE symptom. SERVICE open in power-to-fan circuit from 3 and 4 of Integrated Controller harness connector to cooling fan connector. RECONNECT cooling fan and controller, RE-EVALUATE symptom.

TEST STEP	RESULT	▶	ACTION TO TAKE
X25 JUMPER HIGH ELECTRIC-DRIVE SIGNAL (HEDF) TO GROUND			
• Key off. • Inspect processor 60 pin connector for damaged pins, corrosion, loose wires, etc. Service as necessary. • Install breakout box, leave processor disconnected. • Integrated Controller connected. • Key on. • Jumper Test Pin 52 to Test Pin 40 at breakout box. • Does fan speed change from low to high?	Yes No	▶ ▶	GO to X26. REMOVE breakout box. REPLACE Integrated Controller. RECONNECT processor. RE-EVALUATE symptom.
X26 CHECK ECT SENSOR			
• Key off, wait 10 seconds. • Connect processor to breakout box. • Check engine coolant level. • Warm engine to operating temperature before taking ECT resistance measurement. • Key off, wait 10 seconds. • Disconnect harness from ECT sensor. • DVOM on 200,000 ohm scale. • Measure resistance of the ECT sensor. • Is the resistance between 1500 ohms and 2000 ohms?	Yes No	▶ ▶	REMOVE breakout box. REPLACE processor. RECONNECT harness to ECT sensor. RECONNECT Integrated Controllers. RE-EVALUATE symptom. REMOVE breakout box. REPLACE ECT sensor. RECONNECT all components. RE-EVALUATE symptom.
X30 SERVICE CODE 83: CHECK RESISTANCE OF HEDF CONTROLLER CIRCUIT			
• Key off. • Disconnect Integrated Controller. • DVOM on 200 ohm scale. • Measure resistance between Pin 17 and Pin 24 at the Integrated Controller. • Is the resistance reading between 50 ohms and 100 ohms?	Yes No	▶ ▶	GO to X31. REPLACE controller. RERUN Quick Test.

TEST STEP	RESULT	▶	ACTION TO TAKE
X31 CHECK HEDF PROCESSOR SIGNAL TO INTEGRATED CONTROLLER FOR OPEN			
• Key off. • Disconnect processor 60 pin connector. Inspect for damaged pins, corrosion, loose wires, etc. Service as necessary. • Install breakout box, leave processor disconnected. • Integrated Controller disconnected. • DVOM On 200 ohms scale. • Measure resistance between Test Pin 52 at breakout box and Pin 17 of Integrated Controller vehicle harness connector. • Is resistance less than 5 ohms?	Yes No	▶ ▶	GO to X32. REMOVE breakout box. SERVICE open in HEDF circuit. RECONNECT all components. RERUN Quick Test.
X32 CHECK FOR SHORTS TO GROUND IN THE HEDF CIRCUIT			
• Key off. • Breakout box installed. • Processor and Integrated Controller disconnected. • DVOM on 200,000 ohm scale. • Measure resistance between Test Pin 52 and Test Pin 40. • Is resistance less than 10,000 ohms?	No Yes	▶ ▶	GO to X33. REMOVE breakout box. RECONNECT processor and Integrated Controller. SERVICE short to ground in HEDF circuit. RERUN Quick Test.
X33 CHECK FOR SHORTS TO POWER IN THE HEDF CIRCUIT			
• Key off. • Breakout box installed. • Processor and Integrated Controller disconnected. • DVOM on 200,000 ohms scale. • Measure resistance between Test Pin 52 and Test Pin 37. • Is resistance less than 10,000 ohms?	No Yes	▶ ▶	REMOVE breakout box. REPLACE Processor. RECONNECT all components. RERUN Quick Test. REMOVE breakout box. SERVICE short to power. RECONNECT all components. RERUN Quick Test. If code 83 is still present, REPLACE controller. RERUN Quick Test.

Courtesy of Ford Motor Co.

THERMOSTATICALLY CONTROLLED ELECTRIC COOLING FANS
FORD MOTOR CO. (Cont.)

A/C INTEGRATED RELAY CONTROLLER (Cont.)

TEST STEP	RESULT	▶	ACTION TO TAKE
X35 LOW SPEED OR HIGH SPEED FAN ALWAYS "ON", NO SERVICE CODE 83 OR 67			
• Key off. • Disconnect processor 60 pin connector. Inspect for damaged pins, corrosion, loose wires. Service as necessary. • Install breakout box, leave processor disconnected. • Disconnect the Integrated Controller. • DVOM on 200 ohm scale. • Measure the resistance between Test Pin 55 and controller vehicle harness Pin 14. • Is resistance less than 5 ohms?	Yes No	▶ ▶	GO to **X36** . REMOVE breakout box. SERVICE open in EDF circuit. RECONNECT all components. RE-EVALUATE symptom.
X36 CHECK EDF CIRCUIT FOR SHORTS TO POWER			
• Key off. • Breakout box installed. • Processor and Integrated Controller disconnected. • DVOM on 200,000 ohm scale. • Measure resistance between Test Pin 55 and Test Pin 37 and between Test Pin 55 and battery positive post. • Is resistance less than 10,000 ohms?	Yes No	▶ ▶	SERVICE short to power in EDF circuit. GO to **X37** . GO to **X37** .
X37 CHECK EDF FOR SHORT TO GROUND			
• Key on. • Breakout box installed. • Processor disconnected. • Connect Integrated Controller. • Jumper Test Pin 55 to Test Pin 40 or 60. • Does fan continue to run?	Yes No	▶ ▶	REMOVE breakout box. RECONNECT processor. REPLACE controller. RE-EVALUATE symptom. REMOVE breakout box. RECONNECT controller. REPLACE processor. RE-EVALUATE symptom.

TEST STEP	RESULT	▶	ACTION TO TAKE
X44 CHECK EDF CIRCUIT FOR SHORT TO GROUND			
• Key off. • Processor and controller disconnected. • DVOM on 200,000 ohm scale. • Measure resistance from Pin 14 to Pin 15 at Integrated Controller vehicle harness connector. • Is resistance greater than 10,000 ohms?	Yes No	▶ ▶	REPLACE Integrated Controller. RECONNECT processor and controller. RE-EVALUATE symptom. SERVICE short to ground in EDF circuit. RECONNECT processor and Integrated Controller. RE-EVALUATE symptom.
X45 COOLING FAN GROUND VERIFICATION			
• Key off. • Cooling fan disconnected. • Integrated Controller disconnected. • Jumper Pin 1 to Pin 3 at Integrated Controller vehicle harness connector. • DVOM on 20 volt scale. • Measure voltage between voltage positive at cooling fan harness connector and negative battery post. • Is voltage greater than 8.0 volts?	Yes No	▶ ▶	SERVICE open in ground circuit to fan. RECONNECT Integrated Controller, RE-EVALUATE symptom. SERVICE open in power-to-fan circuit from 3 and 4 of Integrated Controller harness connector to cooling fan connector. RECONNECT controller. RE-EVALUATE symptom.
X46 ECT SENSOR CHECK			
• Reconnect processor. • Check engine coolant level. • Warm engine to operating temperature before taking ECT resistance measurement. • Key off, wait 10 seconds. • Harness disconnected from ECT sensor. • DVOM on 200,000 ohm scale. • Measure resistance of the ECT sensor. • Is the resistance reading between 1500 ohms and 2000 ohms?	Yes No	▶ ▶	REPLACE processor. RECONNECT harness to ECT sensor. RECONNECT Integrated Controller. RE-EVALUATE symptom. REPLACE ECT sensor. RECONNECT all components. RE-EVALUATE symptom.

TEST STEP	RESULT	▶	ACTION TO TAKE
X40 NO FAN			
• Key off. • Disconnect Integrated Controller. • DVOM on 20 volt scale. • Measure voltage between battery negative post and Pin 1 and Pin 2, respectively at the Integrated Controller vehicle harness connector. • Is voltage greater than 10.5 volts?	Yes No	▶ ▶	GO to **X41** . RECONNECT controller. SERVICE open in battery power circuit. RE-EVALUATE symptom.
X41 CHECK FAN MOTOR			
• Key off. • Integrated Controller disconnected. • Jumper Pin 1 to Pin 3 at Integrated Controller harness. • Does fan run?	Yes No	▶ ▶	GO to **X42** . GO to **X43** .
X42 CHECK FAN RUNNING MODE			
• Key off. • Disconnect processor. • Connect Integrated Controller. • Key on. • Does fan run?	Yes No	▶ ▶	GO to **X46** . GO to **X44** .
X43 MEASURE BATTERY VOLTAGE SUPPLY AT FAN — BYPASSING INTEGRATED CONTROLLER			
• Key off. • Disconnect cooling fan. • Integrated Controller disconnected. • Jumper Pin 1 to Pin 3 at Integrated Controller vehicle harness connector. • DVOM on 20 volt scale. • Measure voltage at cooling fan vehicle harness connector. • Is voltage greater than 8.0 volts?	Yes No	▶ ▶	RECONNECT all components. CHANGE fan. RE-EVALUATE symptom. GO to **X45** .

TEST STEP	RESULT	▶	ACTION TO TAKE
X50 CHECK FOR VOLTAGE AT A/C CLUTCH			
• Key on, engine off. • A/C demand switch to A/C ON position. • DVOM on 20 volt scale. • Check voltage at A/C clutch harness connector. • Is voltage greater than 10.5 volts?	Yes No	▶ ▶	Check A/C System For Proper Operation. GO to **X51** .
X51 CHECK FOR CONTINUITY FROM INTEGRATED CONTROLLER TO A/C CLUTCH			
• Key off. • Disconnect Integrated Controller. • DVOM on 200 ohm scale. • Measure resistance between Pin 23 of the controller harness and power side of the A/C clutch harness connector and between Pin 16 of the controller harness and ground side of the A/C clutch harness connector. • Are both resistances less than 5 ohms?	Yes No	▶ ▶	GO to **X61** . SERVICE open in power to A/C clutch or ground to A/C clutch. RE-EVALUATE symptom.
X52 ENTER OUTPUT STATE CHECK			
NOTE: Do not use STAR tester for this Step, use VOM/DVOM. • Key off, wait 10 seconds. • Disconnect processor 60 pin connector. Inspect for damaged pins, corrosion, loose wires, etc. Service as necessary. • Install breakout box. Connect processor to breakout box. • DVOM on 20 volt scale. • Connect DVOM negative test lead to STO and positive test lead to battery positive. • Jumper STI to SIGNAL RETURN. • Perform Key On Engine Off Self-Test until the completion of the Continuous Test Codes. • DVOM will indicate zero volts. • Depress and release the throttle. • Did DVOM reading change to a high voltage reading?	Yes No	▶ ▶	REMAIN in Output State Check. GO to **X53** . DEPRESS throttle to WOT and RELEASE. If STO voltage does not go high, Check Throttle Linkage LEAVE equipment hooked up.

Engine Cooling Systems

THERMOSTATICALLY CONTROLLED ELECTRIC COOLING FANS
FORD MOTOR CO. (Cont.)

A/C INTEGRATED RELAY CONTROLLER (Cont.)

TEST STEP	RESULT	▶	ACTION TO TAKE
X53 CHECK WAC OUTPUT FOR PROPER ELECTRICAL OPERATION			
• Key on, engine off. • A/C demand switch to A/C on position. • Breakout box installed, processor connected. • DVOM on 20 volt scale. • Connect DVOM positive test lead to Test Pin 37 and negative test lead to Test Pin 54. • While observing DVOM, depress and release the throttle several times (to cycle output on and off). • Does voltage output cycle high and low?	Yes No	▶ ▶	2.3L EFI T/C only, GO to X61. All others, GO to X54. GO to X57.
X54 CHECK FOR VOLTAGE AT A/C CLUTCH SWITCH			
• Key on, engine off. • A/C demand switch to A/C on position. • DVOM on 20 volt scale. • Breakout box installed. • Processor and Integrated Controller connected. • Measure voltage between Test Pin 10 and Test Pin 40 at breakout box. • Is voltage greater than 10.5 volts?	Yes No	▶ ▶	GO to X55. GO to X56.
X55 CHECK CONTINUITY OF ACCS TO INTEGRATED CONTROLLER			
• Key off, wait 10 seconds. • Breakout box installed. • Processor disconnected. • Integrated Controller disconnected. • DVOM on 200 ohm scale. • Measure resistance between Test Pin 10 at breakout box and Pin 21 at controller harness connector. • Is resistance less than 5 ohms?	Yes No	▶ ▶	REMOVE breakout box. RECONNECT processor. REPLACE Integrated Controller. RE-EVALUATE symptom. REMOVE breakout box. RECONNECT all components. SERVICE open in ACCS circuit. RE-EVALUATE symptom.

TEST STEP	RESULT	▶	ACTION TO TAKE
X56 CHECK CONTINUITY OF ACCS CIRCUIT			
• Key off, wait 10 seconds. • Breakout box installed. • A/C demand switch to A/C ON position. • Processor and Integrated Controller connected. • DVOM on 200 ohm scale. • Measure resistance between Test Pin 10 and A/C demand switch. • Is resistance less than 5 ohms?	No Yes	▶ ▶	SERVICE open in circuit. RERUN Quick Test. REMOVE breakout box. RECONNECT all components. EEC-IV system OK. REMOVE breakout box. RECONNECT all components. Check A/C System For Proper Operation
X57 CHECK CONTINUITY IN WAC TO INTEGRATED CONTROLLER CIRCUIT			
• Key off, wait 10 seconds. • Breakout box installed. • Disconnect processor and Integrated Controller. • DVOM on 200 ohm scale. • Measure resistance between Test Pin 54 and Pin 22 at Integrated Controller harness. • Is resistance less than 50 ohms?	No Yes	▶ ▶	REMOVE breakout box. RECONNECT all components. SERVICE open in WAC circuit. RE-EVALUATE symptom. GO to X58.
X58 CHECK WAC CIRCUIT FOR SHORTS TO GROUND			
• Key off, wait 10 seconds. • Leave breakout box installed and processor disconnected. • Integrated Controller disconnected. • DVOM on 200,000 ohm scale. • Measure resistance between Test Pin 54 and Test Pin 40 and between Test Pin 54 and Test Pin 46 and between Test Pin 54 and battery negative post. • Are all resistances greater than 10,000 ohms?	Yes No	▶ ▶	GO to X59. REMOVE breakout box. RECONNECT all components. SERVICE shorts to ground in WAC circuit. RE-EVALUATE symptom.

TEST STEP	RESULT	▶	ACTION TO TAKE
X59 CHECK WAC CIRCUIT FOR SHORTS TO POWER			
• Key off, wait 10 seconds. • Leave Breakout box installed and processor disconnected. • Integrated Controller disconnected. • DVOM on 200,000 ohm scale. • Measure resistance between Test Pin 54 and Test Pin 37 and between Test Pin 54 and battery positive. • Are both resistances greater than 10,000 ohms?	Yes No	▶ ▶	GO to X60. REMOVE breakout box. RECONNECT all components. SERVICE short to power in WAC circuit. GO to X60.
X60 CHECK FOR VOLTAGE AT A/C CLUTCH			
• Key off, wait 10 seconds. • Leave breakout box installed. • Processor disconnected. • Connect Integrated Controller. • A/C clutch disconnected. • A/C demand switch to A/C ON position. • Key on, engine off. • DVOM on 20 volt scale. • Measure voltage at A/C clutch harness connection. • Is voltage greater than 10.5 volts?	Yes No	▶ ▶	REMOVE breakout box. RECONNECT all components. REPLACE processor. RE-EVALUATE symptom. REMOVE breakout box. RECONNECT all components. REPLACE Integrated Controller. RE-EVALUATE symptom.
X61 CHECK FOR VOLTAGE AT A/C INPUT TO CONTROLLER			
• Key off, wait 10 seconds. • Leave breakout box installed. • Processor connected. • Integrated controller disconnected. • Key on, engine off. • A/C demand switch to A/C ON position. • DVOM on 20 volt scale. • Measure voltage between Pin 21 at controller harness connector and test Pin 40. • Is voltage greater than 10.5 volts?	Yes No	▶ ▶	REMOVE breakout box. RECONNECT all components. REPLACE Integrated Controller. RE-EVALUATE symptom. REMOVE breakout box. RECONNECT all components. SERVICE open in A/C input circuit to controller. RE-EVALUATE symptom.

TEST STEP	RESULT	▶	ACTION TO TAKE
X70 NO FAN PRIMARY OR SECONDARY WITH NO CODE 82 OR 88			
• Key off, wait 10 seconds. • Disconnect Integrated controller. • DVOM on 20 volt scale. • Measure voltage between battery negative post and Pins 3 and 4 respectively at controller harness connector. • Are all voltages greater than 10.5 volts?	Yes No	▶ ▶	GO to X71. RECONNECT Integrated Controller. SERVICE open in battery power circuit. RE-EVALUATE symptom.
X71 FAN MOTORS CHECK			
• Key off. • Integrated controller disconnected. • Jumper Pin 3 to Pin 1 (for primary fan) and Pin 3 to Pin 6 (for secondary fan) at integrated controller harness connector. • Do both fans run?	Yes No	▶ ▶	GO to X72. GO to X73.
X72 CHECK FAN RUNNING MODE (LOW)			
• Key off. • Disconnect processor. • Connect Integrated controller. • Key on, engine off. • Does primary fan run?	Yes No	▶ ▶	GO to X75. REPLACE Integrated Controller. RECONNECT all components. RE-EVALUATE symptom.
X73 MEASURE BATTERY VOLTAGE SUPPLY AT FANS — BYPASSING INTEGRATED CONTROLLER			
• Key off. • Disconnect cooling fans. • Integrated controller disconnected. • Jumper Pin 3 to Pin 1 (for primary fan) and Pin 3 to Pin 6 if equipped (for secondary fan) at integrated controller harness connector. • DVOM on 20 volt scale. • Measure voltage at one or both cooling fan harness connectors as equipped. • Is either voltage greater than 8.0 volts?	Yes No	▶ ▶	CHANGE fan(s). RE-EVALUATE symptom. GO to X74.

THERMOSTATICALLY CONTROLLED ELECTRIC COOLING FANS
FORD MOTOR CO. (Cont.)

A/C INTEGRATED RELAY CONTROLLER (Cont.)

TEST STEP	RESULT	▶	ACTION TO TAKE
X74 COOLING FAN GROUND VERIFICATION			
• Key off. • Cooling fan disconnected. • Integrated controller disconnected. • Jumper Pin 3 to Pin 1 (for primary fan) and Pin 3 to Pin 6 if equipped (for secondary fan) at integrated controller harness connector. • DVOM on 20 volt scale. • Measure voltage between voltage positive at one or both cooling fan harness connectors and negative battery post as equipped. • Is voltage greater than 8.0 volts?	Yes	▶	SERVICE open in ground circuit to fan(s). RECONNECT all components. RE-EVALUATE symptom.
	No	▶	SERVICE open in power circuit to fan(s). RECONNECT all components. RE-EVALUATE symptom.
X75 JUMPER SECONDARY ELECTRIC DRIVE SIGNAL (HEDF) TO GROUND			
• Key off. • Disconnect processor 60 pin connector. Inspect for damaged pins, corrosion, loose wires, etc. Service as necessary. • Install breakout box, leave processor disconnected. • Integrated controller connected. • Jumper Test Pin 52 to Test Pin 40 at breakout box. • Key on. • Does secondary fan run?	Yes	▶	GO to X76.
	No	▶	REMOVE breakout box. REPLACE Integrated Controller. RECONNECT processor. RE-EVALUATE symptom.
X76 ECT SENSOR CHECK			
• Connect processor. • Check engine coolant level. • Warm engine to operating temperature before taking ECT resistance measurement. • Key off, wait 10 seconds. • Disconnect harness from ECT sensor. • DVOM on 200,000 ohm scale. • Measure resistance of ECT sensor. • Is resistance between 1500 and 2000 ohms?	Yes	▶	REMOVE breakout box. REPLACE processor. RECONNECT all components. RE-EVALUATE symptom.
	No	▶	REMOVE breakout box. REPLACE ECT sensor. RECONNECT all components. RE-EVALUATE symptom.

TEST STEP	RESULT	▶	ACTION TO TAKE
X82 FAN ALWAYS ON WITH CODE 82 OR 88: CHECK EDF PROCESSOR SIGNAL TO INTEGRATED CONTROLLER FOR OPEN CIRCUIT			
• Key off. • Disconnect processor 60 pin connector. Inspect for damaged pins, corrosion, and loose wires, etc. Service as necessary. • Install breakout box. • Processor and integrated controller disconnected. • DVOM on 200 ohm scale. • Measure resistance between Test Pin 55 and Integrated Controller harness Pin 14. • Is resistance less than 5 ohms?	Yes	▶	GO to X83.
	No	▶	REMOVE breakout box. SERVICE open in EDF circuit. RECONNECT all components. RERUN Quick Test.
X83 CHECK EDF CIRCUIT FOR SHORTS TO POWER			
• Key off. • Breakout box installed. • Processor and integrated controller disconnected. • DVOM on 200,000 ohm scale. • Measure resistance between Test Pin 55 and Test Pin 37, and between Test Pin 55 and battery positive. • Is resistance less than 10,000 ohms?	Yes	▶	REMOVE breakout box. RECONNECT all components. SERVICE short to power in EDF circuit. GO to X84.
	No	▶	GO to X84.
X84 CHECK EDF SHORT TO GROUND			
• Key off. • Breakout box installed. • Processor disconnected. • Integrated controller connected. • Key on, engine off. • Jumper test Pin 55 to Test Pin 40 or 60. • Does fan continue to run?	Yes	▶	REMOVE breakout box. REPLACE Integrated Controller. RECONNECT all components. RERUN Quick Test.
	No	▶	REMOVE breakout box. REPLACE processor. RECONNECT all components. RERUN Quick Test.

TEST STEP	RESULT	▶	ACTION TO TAKE
X80 SERVICE CODE 82 OR 88: CHECK EDF PROCESSOR SIGNAL TO INTEGRATED CONTROLLER FOR SHORTS TO GROUND			
NOTE: If fan is always on with Code 82 or 88, GO to X82. • Key off. • Disconnect processor 60 pin connector. Inspect for damaged pins, corrosion, and loose wires, etc. Service as necessary. • Install breakout box, leave processor disconnected. • Disconnect Integrated controller. • DVOM on 200,000 ohm scale. • Measure resistance between Test Pin 55 and Test Pin 40. • Is resistance less than 10,000 ohms?	Yes	▶	SERVICE short to ground in EDF circuit. RECONNECT all components. RERUN Quick Test.
	No	▶	GO to X81.
X81 CHECK FAN RUNNING MODE			
• Key off. • Breakout box installed. • Processor disconnected. • Connect integrated controller. • Key on, engine off. For 2.5L MTX 〉 Does fan run? For 2.5L, 3.0L and 3.8L AXOD 〉 Does fan run at low speed? For 2.3L EFI TC 〉 Does primary fan run?	Yes	▶	REMOVE breakout box. REPLACE processor. RECONNECT all components. RERUN Quick Test.
	No	▶	REMOVE breakout box. REPLACE Integrated Controller. RECONNECT all components. RERUN Quick Test.

TEST STEP	RESULT	▶	ACTION TO TAKE
X90 SERVICE CODE 95: CHECK INERTIA SWITCH			
NOTE: Key On Engine Off Service Code 95 indicates that one of the following has occured: — Open circuit in/or between the fuel pump and Test Pin 8 (see schematic) — Poor fuel pump ground — FUEL PUMP circuit short to power — Fuel pump relay contacts always closed • Key off, wait 10 seconds. • Locate and disconnect fuel pump inertia switch. • DVOM on 200 ohm scale. • Measure resistance of the fuel pump inertia switch. • Is resistance less than 5.0 ohms?	Yes	▶	RECONNECT inertia switch. GO to X91.
	No	▶	REPLACE or RESET inertia switch. RERUN Quick Test.
X91 VERIFY THAT FUEL PUMP IS OFF			
• Key off. • Listen for motor noise from fuel pump. • Is fuel pump off?	Yes	▶	GO to X93.
	No	▶	GO to X92.
X92 CHECK FOR FUEL PUMP RELAY ALWAYS CLOSED			
• Key off. • Locate and disconnect integrated controller. • Does fuel pump shut off when controller is disconnected?	Yes	▶	REPLACE Integrated Controller. RERUN Quick Test
	No	▶	SERVICE short to power in POWER-TO-PUMP/FPM circuit. RECONNECT integrated controller. RERUN Quick Test.

Engine Cooling Systems

THERMOSTATICALLY CONTROLLED ELECTRIC COOLING FANS
FORD MOTOR CO. (Cont.)

A/C INTEGRATED RELAY CONTROLLER (Cont.)

TEST STEP	RESULT ▶	ACTION TO TAKE
X93 CHECK CONTINUITY OF FPM CIRCUIT • Key off. • Disconnect processor 60 pin connector. Inspect for damaged pins, corrosion, loose wires, etc. Service as necessary. • Install breakout box, leave processor disconnected. • Disconnect integrated controller. • DVOM on 200 ohm scale. • Measure resistance between Test Pin 8 at the breakout box and integrated controller harness connector pin 5. • Is resistance less than 5.0 ohms?	Yes ▶ No ▶	GO to X94 . REMOVE breakout box. RECONNECT processor and integrated controller. SERVICE open circuit. RERUN Quick Test.
X94 CHECK FOR CONTINUITY BETWEEN FPM CIRCUIT AND GROUND • Key off. • Breakout box installed, processor disconnected. • Integrated controller disconnected. • DVOM on 200 ohm scale. • Measure resistance between Test Pin 8 at the breakout box and battery negative post. • Is resistance less than 5.0 ohms?	Yes ▶ No ▶	REMOVE breakout box. RECONNECT integrated controller. REPLACE processor. RERUN Quick Test. REMOVE breakout box. RECONNECT processor and integrated controller. Electric Fuel Pump for open in POWER-TO-PUMP circuit, poor fuel pump ground, open in fuel pump, etc. Electric Fuel Pump Faulty.

TEST STEP	RESULT ▶	ACTION TO TAKE

X100   CONTINUOUS MEMORY CODE 95: CHECK EEC-IV HARNESS
 	
A Continuous Memory Code 95 indicates that one of the following intermittent conditions has occurred:
  — Open circuit in or between the fuel pump and Pin 8 in the processor (see schematic
  — Poor fuel pump ground.
• Start engine.
• Check for engine stall/stumble while performing the following (also, if possible, listen for fuel pump turning off).
  — Shake, wiggle, bend the power-to-pump circuit between the Integrated Controller pin 5 and the fuel pump.
  — Shake, wiggle, bend the fuel pump ground circuit from the fuel pump to ground.
  — Lightly tap the inertia switch and the fuel pump to simulate road shock.
• Key off.
• Inspect the fuel pump electrical connector and the fuel pump ground for corrosion, damaged pins, etc.
• Is fault indicated/found?
	Yes ▶
	
	No ▶
		ISOLATE fault and SERVICE as necessary. CLEAR Continuous Memory Code 95.
		
		RERUN Quick Test.
		
		GO to X101 .

X101 CHECK FPM CIRCUIT • Key off. • Disconnect processor 60 pin connector. Inspect for damaged pins, corrosion, loose wires, etc. Service as necessary. • Install breakout box, leave processor disconnected. • Key on, engine off. • Connect a test lamp between Test Pin 8 and Test Pin 37. • Observe test lamp for an indication of a fault while performing the following (The light will go out when a fault is found indicating an open): — Shake, wiggle, bend the fuel pump monitor circuit (Pin 8) between the processor and splice into the POWER-TO-PUMP circuit. • Is fault found/indicated?	Yes ▶ No ▶	ISOLATE fault and SERVICE as necessary. REMOVE breakout box. CLEAR Continuous Memory Code 95. RERUN Quick Test. Unable to duplicate fault at this time. CLEAR Continuous Memory Code 95.

TEST STEP	RESULT ▶	ACTION TO TAKE
X95 SERVICE CODE 96: CHECK CONTINUITY OF POWER-TO-PUMP CIRCUIT **NOTE: Service Code 96 indicates that when the fuel pump is being activated, power is not being supplied to the fuel pump.** • Key off, wait 10 seconds. • Disconnect processor 60 pin connector. Inspect for damaged pins, corrosion, loose wires, etc. Service as necessary. • Install breakout box, leave processor disconnected. • Disconnect integrated relay controller. • DVOM on 200 ohm scale. • Measure resistance between Test Pin 8 at the breakout box and integrated controller harness connector pin 5. • Is resistance less than 5.0 ohms?	Yes ▶ No ▶	GO to X96 . REMOVE breakout box. RECONNECT processor and integrated controller. SERVICE open in POWER-TO-PUMP circuit between FPM splice and the integrated controller. RERUN Quick Test.
X96 VERIFY FUEL PUMP OPERATION • Key off. • Breakout box installed. • Reconnect processor and integrated controller. • DVOM on 20 volt scale. • Connect DVOM between Test Pin 8 and Test Pin 40 at the breakout box. • While observing DVOM, turn key to on. • Does voltage increase to greater than 10.5 volts for about 1 second after key is turned to on?	Yes ▶ No ▶	REMOVE breakout box. REPLACE processor. RERUN Quick Test. REMOVE breakout box. RECONNECT processor. REPLACE integrated controller. RERUN Quick Test.

TEST STEP	RESULT ▶	ACTION TO TAKE
X102 CONTINUOUS MEMORY CODE 96 CHECK FOR CONTINUOUS MEMORY CODE 87 • Is Continuous Memory Code 87 also present?	Yes ▶ No ▶	GO to X104 . GO to X103 .

X103   CHECK EEC-IV HARNESS
 	
A Continuous Memory Code 96, without the presence of a Continuous Memory Code 87, indicates that during vehicle operation, one of the following has occurred:
  — Fuel pump relay contacts opened.
  — Open in the POWER-TO-PUMP circuit from the integrated relay controller pin 5 to the FPM splice. (See schematic
• Start engine.
• Check for engine stall/stumble while performing the following (also, if possible, listen for fuel pump turning off):
  — Shake, wiggle, bend the POWER-TO-PUMP circuit from the integrated relay controller to the FPM splice.
  — Lightly tap the integrated relay controller (to simulate road shock).
• Key off.
• Inspect the integrated relay controller 24 pin connectors for corrosion, damaged pins, etc.
• Is fault indicated/found?
	Yes ▶
	
	No ▶
		ISOLATE fault and SERVICE as necessary. CLEAR Continuous Memory Code.
		
		RERUN Quick Test.
		
		Unable to duplicate fault at this time. CLEAR Continuous Memory Code 96.
		
		Continuous Memory Code 96 testing complete.

THERMOSTATICALLY CONTROLLED ELECTRIC COOLING FANS
FORD MOTOR CO. (Cont.)

A/C INTEGRATED RELAY CONTROLLER (Cont.)

TEST STEP	RESULT ▶	ACTION TO TAKE
X104 CONTINUOUS MEMORY SERVICE CODE 87: CHECK EEC-IV HARNESS		
A Continuous Memory Code 87 indicates that one of the following intermittent conditions has occurred: — Open VPWP circuit in the integrated relay controller. — Open coil in fuel pump relay. — Open in fuel pump primary circuit. • Start engine. • Check for engine stall/stumble while performing the following (also, if possible, listen for fuel pump turning off): — Shake, wiggle, bend the EEC-IV Harness fuel pump circuit (pin 22) between the processor and the Integrated Controller (pin 18). — Lightly tap the Integrated Controller (to simulate road shock). • Key off. • Inspect the processor 60 pin connectors and the integrated relay controller 24 pin connectors for corrosion, damaged pins, etc. • Is fault indicated/found?	**Yes** ▶ **No** ▶	ISOLATE fault and SERVICE as necessary. CLEAR Continuous Memory Service Code(s). RERUN Quick Test. Unable to duplicate fault at this time. CLEAR Continuous Memory Code(s).

Courtesy of Ford Motor Co.

THERMOSTATICALLY CONTROLLED ELECTRIC COOLING FANS
GENERAL MOTORS

NOTE: In following diagnostic charts, illustrations and flow-charts are supplied courtesy of General Motors Corp.

NOTE: This article contains test charts that are part of General Motors Computerized Engine Controls. Only those charts required to test electric cooling fans are included. Other diagnostic codes may appear while performing electric cooling fan diagnosis. For complete information, see GENERAL MOTORS COMPUTER COMMAND CONTROL article in the COMPUTERIZED ENGINE CONTROLS section.

NOTE: This article contains test charts that are part of General Motors Computerized Engine Controls. Only those charts required to test electric cooling fans are included. Other diagnostic codes may appear while performing electric cooling fan diagnosis. For complete information, see GENERAL MOTORS COMPUTER COMMAND CONTROL article in the COMPUTERIZED ENGINE CONTROLS manual or appropriate article in the TUNE-UP SERVICE & REPAIR DOMESTIC CARS 1988 SUPPLEMENT manual.

GENERAL MOTORS
ELECTRIC COOLING FAN APPLICATIONS

Application	Engine
"A" Body	2.5L, 2.8L, 3.1L & 3.8L
"C" Body	3.8L & 4.5L
"E" Body	3.8L & 4.5L
"H" Body	3.8L
"J" Body	2.0L & 2.8L
"K" Body	4.5L
"L" Body	2.0L & 2.8L
"N" Body	2.0L, 2.3L, 2.5L & 3.0L
"P" Body	2.5 & 2.8L
"S" Body	1.6L
"W" Body	2.8L
"Y" Body	5.7L

Engine Cooling Systems

THERMOSTATICALLY CONTROLLED ELECTRIC COOLING FANS GENERAL MOTORS (Cont.)

GENERAL MOTORS BODY IDENTIFICATION

Body	Models
"A" Body	Celebrity, Century, Cutlass Ciera, Cutlass Cruiser & 6000
"C" Body	Electra, DeVille, Fleetwood & Ninety-Eight
"E" Body	Eldorado, Riviera & Toronado
"H" Body	Bonneville, Delta 88 & LeSabre
"J" Body	Cavalier, Cimarron & Firenza, Skyhawk & Sunbird
"K" Body	Seville
"L" Body	Beretta & Corsica
"N" Body	Calais, Grand Am & Skylark
"P" Body	Fiero
"S" Body	Nova
"W" Body	Cutlass Supreme, Grand Prix & Regal
"Y" Body	Corvette

DESCRIPTION

All FWD, and some other vehicles, use an electric cooling fan. This fan is used for engine and A/C condenser cooling but fan only operates under certain conditions.

OPERATION

All electric cooling fans operate when engine coolant temperature exceeds a certain value. On all models except "S" Body, the ECM completes ground path for the winding of coolant fan relay. Relay contacts then close and complete circuit between fusible link and fan motor. When the engine cools, the switch opens and fan stops. If coolant sensor fails, the ECM will command constant fan.

A/C equipped vehicles have a separate signal line to the ECM for fan control. When A/C control switch is "ON", and the low pressure switch closed, the ECM receives a signal on this line and turns on the fan. The compressor clutch does not have to engage for ECM to turn fan on.

On some models, when engine is shutdown, ECM may turn on the fan relay and run fan for up to 7 minutes. This occurs if hot conditions were present while engine was running. Hot conditions are based on Manifold Air Temperature sensor (MAT), coolant temperature and time from start.

On "S" Body, temperature sensor switch closes when a certain temperature has been reached. Relay contacts then close and complete the circuit to the fan motor.

DIAGNOSIS & TESTING

1.6L 2-BBL. & 1.6L EFI ("S" BODY)

Low Temperature – Below 181°F (83°C)
1) With engine temperature below 181°F (83°C), turn ignition on to confirm that fan does not operate. If fan does operate, check fan relay and temperature switch. Also check for a separated connector or a broken wire between relay and temperature switch.

2) Disconnect temperature switch wire and confirm fan rotation. If fan fails to rotate, check fan relay, fan motor, ignition relay and fuse. Also check for a short between fan relay and temperature switch. Reconnect temperature switch wire.

High Temperature – Above 194°F (90°)
Start engine and raise coolant temperature to above 194°F (90° C). Confirm fan rotation. If fan fails to rotate, replace temperature switch.

Temperature Switch
Using an ohmmeter, ensure that there is no continuity when coolant temperature is above 194°F (90°C). Ensure that there is continuity when coolant is below 181°F (83°C).

Ignition Relay
1) Using an ohmmeter, measure resistance between terminals No. 1 and 2. Resistance should be 50-80 ohms. See Fig. 1.

Fig. 1: Testing "S" Body Ignition Relay

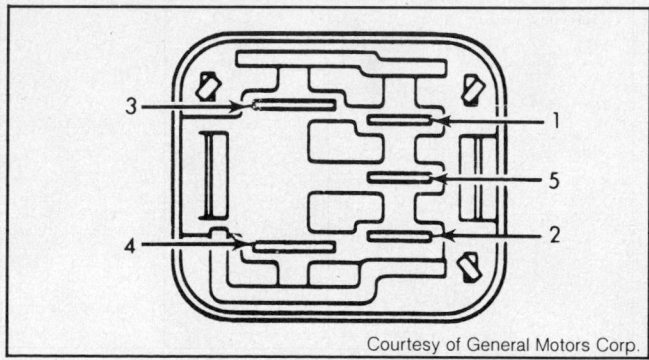

Courtesy of General Motors Corp.

2) Connect battery voltage between terminals No. 1 and 2. Using an ohmmeter, ensure there is continuity between terminals No. 3 and 4. Also, make sure that there is no continuity between terminals. No. 4 and 5. See Fig. 1.

Fan Motor Relay
1) Using an ohmmeter, measure resistance between terminals No. 1 and 2. Resistance should be 50-80 ohms. See Fig. 2.

Fig. 2: Testing "S" Body Fan Relay

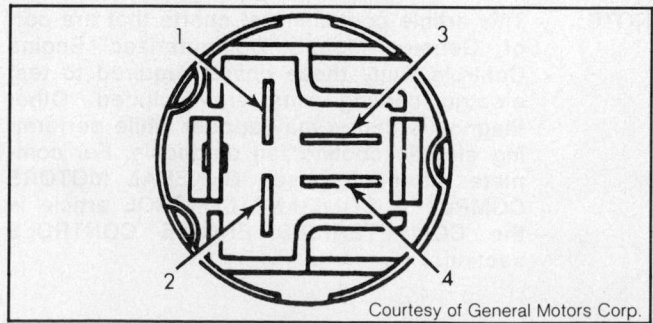

Courtesy of General Motors Corp.

2) Connect battery voltage between terminals No. 1 and 2. Using an ohmmeter, ensure there is continuity between terminals No. 3 and 4.

Fan Motor
Connect battery voltage and ammeter to fan motor connector. Ensure that motor rotates smoothly and current draw is 3.4-5.0 amps.

Engine Cooling Systems

THERMOSTATICALLY CONTROLLED ELECTRIC COOLING FANS
GENERAL MOTORS (Cont.)

TROUBLE SHOOTING

NOTE: Refer to GENERAL MOTORS COMPUTER COMMAND CONTROL article in the COMPUTERIZED ENGINE CONTROLS section for more information.

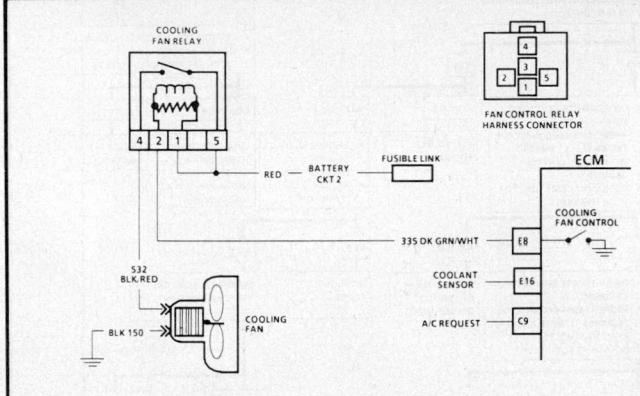

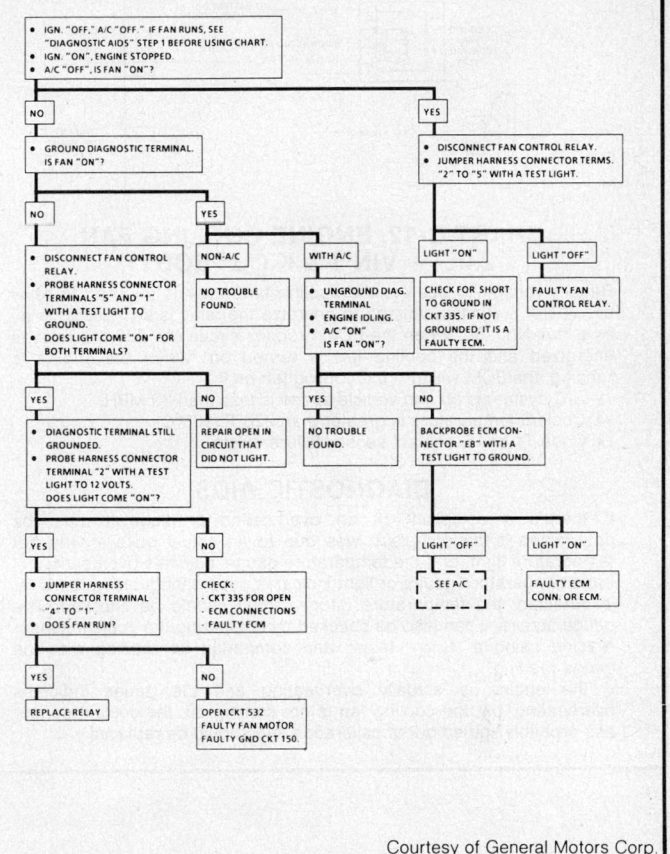

CHART C-12, ENGINE COOLING FAN 2.0L MFI TURBO ("J" & "N" BODIES)

Battery voltage is supplied to fan relay terminal No. 1 and from ignition to terminal No. 5. Grounding relay terminal No. 2 will close relay, supplying battery voltage to fan motor. Above 30 MPH, ECM will remove ground from circuit No. 335. If coolant temperature is normal and A/C pressure switches are open, fan will stop. Cooling fan will also run continuously if a Code 14 or 15 (CTS failure) is set.

DIAGNOSTIC AIDS

If an overheating condition is suspected, verify if this is due to actual boilover. If gauge or light indicates an overheat condition, and no boilover is in evidence, inspect the gauge/light circuit for malfunction.

If the vehicle is overheating and the gauge or light indicates the same, but the cooling fan is not coming on, check the coolant sensor temperature using a "Scan" tester. The sensor may have shifted calibration and should be replaced. If the engine is overheating and the cooling fan is on, the cooling system should be checked.

Engine Cooling Systems

THERMOSTATICALLY CONTROLLED ELECTRIC COOLING FANS
GENERAL MOTORS (Cont.)

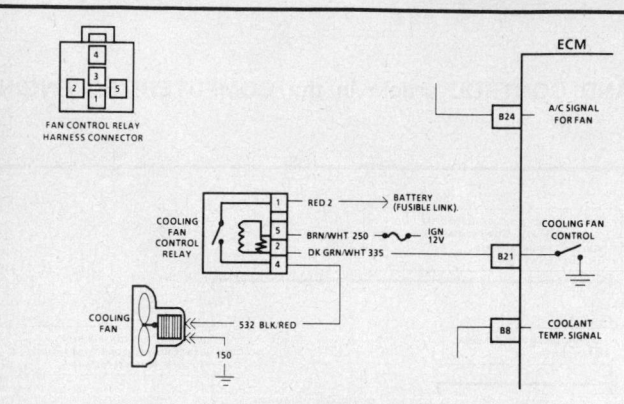

FAN CONTROL RELAY
HARNESS CONNECTOR

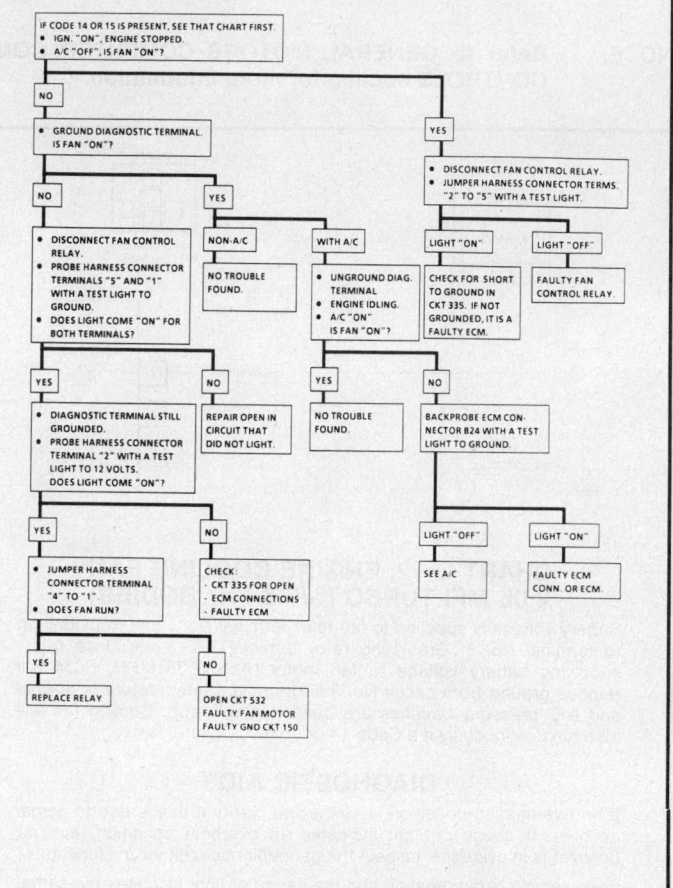

CHART C-12, ENGINE COOLING FAN
2.0L – VIN 1 & K ("J" BODY)

Battery voltage to operate the cooling fan motor is supplied to relay circuit No. 2. Ignition voltage to energize the relay is supplied to relay by circuit No. 250. When the ECM grounds circuit No. 335, the relay is energized and the cooling fan is turned on. When the engine is running, the ECM will turn the cooling fan on if:

- A/C system is on and vehicle speed is less than 30 MPH.
- Coolant temperature is greater than 226°F (108°C).
- Code 14 or 15, coolant sensor failure exists.

DIAGNOSTIC AIDS

If there's a complaint of an overheating problem, it must be determined if the complaint was due to an actual boilover, the hot temperature light, or if the temperature gauge indicates overheating.

If the temperature gauge or light indicates overheating, but no boilover is detected, the temperature gauge circuit should be checked. The gauge accuracy can also be checked by comparing the coolant sensor reading using a "Scan" tester and comparing its reading with the gauge reading.

If the engine is actually overheating and the gauge indicates overheating, but the cooling fan is not coming on, the coolant sensor has probably shifted out of calibration and should be replaced.

Courtesy of General Motors Corp.

THERMOSTATICALLY CONTROLLED ELECTRIC COOLING FANS
GENERAL MOTORS (Cont.)

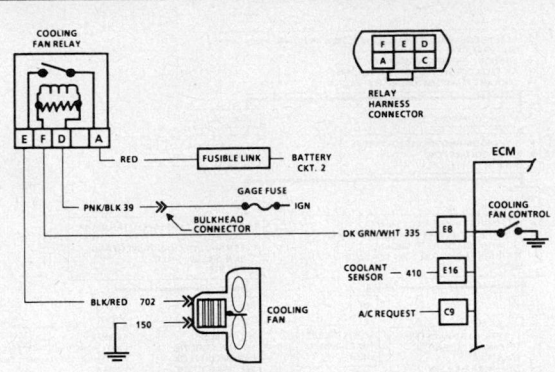

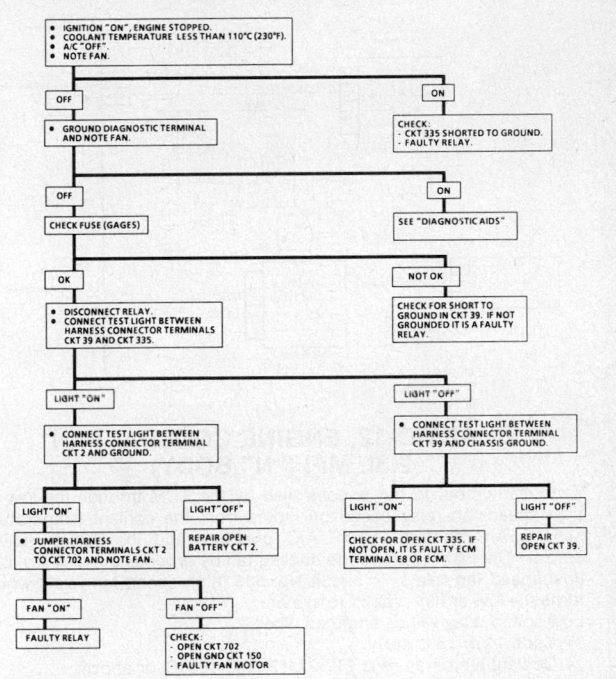

CHART C-12, ENGINE COOLING FAN
2.0L – VIN 1 ("L" BODY)

Battery voltage to operate the cooling fan motor is supplied to relay circuit No. 2. Ignition voltage to energize the relay is supplied to relay by circuit No. 250. When the ECM grounds circuit No. 335, the relay is energized and the cooling fan is turned on. When the engine is running, the ECM will turn the cooling fan on if:
• A/C system is on and vehicle speed is less than 30 MPH.
• Coolant temperature is greater than 226°F (108°C).
• Code 14 or 15, coolant sensor failure exists.

DIAGNOSTIC AIDS

If there's a complaint of an overheating problem, it must be determined if the complaint was due to an actual boilover, the hot temperature light, or if the temperature gauge indicates overheating.

If the temperature gauge or light indicates overheating, but no boilover is detected, the temperature gauge circuit should be checked. The gauge accuracy can also be checked by comparing the coolant sensor reading using a "Scan" tester and comparing its reading with the gauge reading.

If the engine is actually overheating and the gauge indicates overheating, but the cooling fan is not coming on, the coolant sensor has probably shifted out of calibration and should be replaced.

Courtesy of General Motors Corp.

Engine Cooling Systems

THERMOSTATICALLY CONTROLLED ELECTRIC COOLING FANS
GENERAL MOTORS (Cont.)

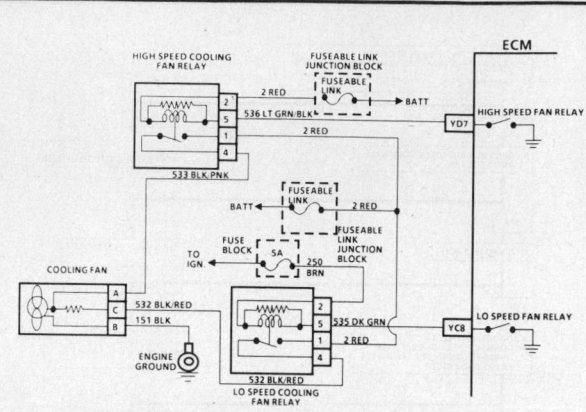

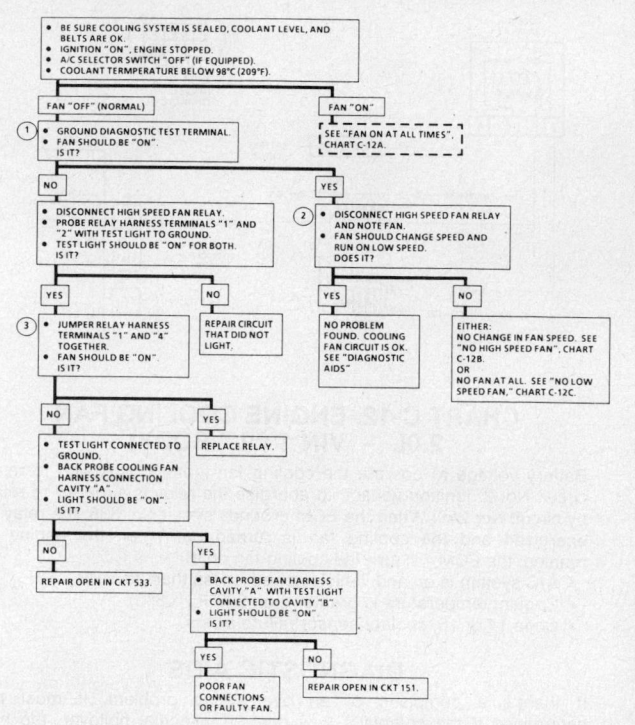

CHART C-12, ENGINE COOLING FAN 2.3L MFI ("N" BODY)

The electric cooling fan is controlled by the ECM through the low or high speed fan relay based on inputs from the coolant temperature sensor, A/C control switch, A/C pressure and the vehicle speed sensor. The ECM controls the cooling fan by grounding circuit No. 535 (low speed fan relay), or circuit No. 536 (high speed fan relay) which turns the low or high speed relays on.

Low speed relay will be engaged when:
- Code 14 or 15 is set.
- Coolant temperature is 217-221°F (103-105°C) or above.
- A/C clutch is engaged and vehicle speed is less than 35 MPH.

High speed fan relay will engage regardless of engine speed when:
- No code 14 or 15 is set.
- Coolant temperature is 239-244°F (115-118°C) or more.
- A/C pressure is high.

The cooling fan will be commanded on high speed when engine is not running and coolant temperature is above 239°F (115°C) or more. Fan will run for about 7 minutes immediately after ignition is turned off.

NOTE: Test numbers refer to test numbers on diagnostic charts.

1) Grounding diagnostic connector should cause ECM to ground circuits No. 535 and No. 536 and the fan should run.
2) Removing high speed relay tests for high and low speed cooling fan. Grounded test terminal should turn both fans on.
3) Test to see if fault is in wiring to fan or connections.

DIAGNOSTIC AIDS

If there's a complaint of an overheating problem, it must be determined if the complaint was due to an actual boilover, the hot temperature light, or if the temperature gauge indicates over heating.

If the temperature gauge or light indicates overheating, but no boilover is detected, the temperature gauge circuit should be checked. The gauge accuracy can also be checked by comparing the coolant sensor reading using a "Scan" tester and comparing its reading with the gauge reading.

If the engine is actually overheating and the gauge indicates overheating, but the cooling fan is not coming on, the coolant sensor has probably shifted out of calibration and should be replaced.

THERMOSTATICALLY CONTROLLED ELECTRIC COOLING FANS
GENERAL MOTORS (Cont.)

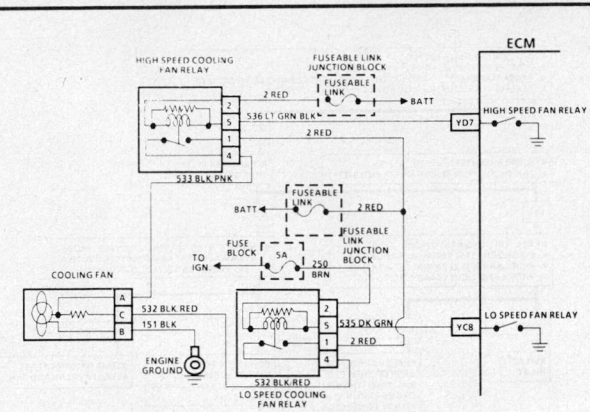

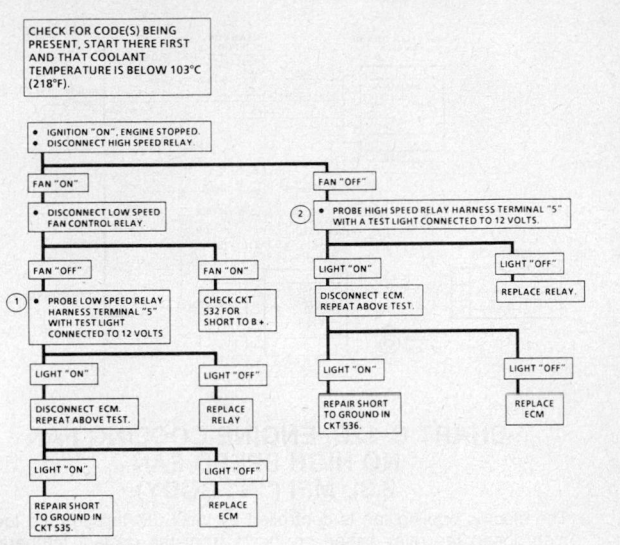

CHART C-12A, ENGINE COOLING FAN
FAN ON AT ALL TIMES
2.3L MFI ("N" BODY)

The electric cooling fan is controlled by the ECM through the low or high speed fan relay based on inputs from the coolant temperature sensor, A/C control switch, A/C pressure and the vehicle speed sensor. The ECM controls the cooling fan by grounding circuit No. 535 (low speed fan relay), or circuit No. 536 (high speed fan relay) which turns the low or high speed relays on.

Low speed relay will be engaged when:
- Code 14 or 15 is set.
- Coolant temperature is 217-221°F (103-105°C) or above.
- A/C clutch is engaged and vehicle speed is less than 35 MPH.

High speed fan relay will engage regardless of engine speed when:
- No code 14 or 15 is set.
- Coolant temperature is 239-244°F (115-118°C) or more.
- A/C pressure is high.

The cooling fan will be commanded on high speed when engine is not running and coolant temperature is above 239°F (115°C) or more. Fan will run for about 7 minutes immediately after ignition is turned off.

NOTE: **Test numbers refer to test numbers on diagnostic charts.**

1) Checks to see if circuit No. 535 is shorted to ground, which would keep relay grounded at all times.
2) Checks to see if circuit No. 536 is shorted to ground. If light indicates wire shorted to ground, the following steps will isolate short.
3) If test light is off, after disconnecting, ECM is shorted internally. Before replacing ECM, check resistance value of low speed side of fan control relay. Replace relay if resistance is less than 20 ohms. Check that circuit No. 535 is not shorted to battery voltage. Check canister purge solenoid resistance and replace if under 20 ohms.

Engine Cooling Systems

THERMOSTATICALLY CONTROLLED ELECTRIC COOLING FANS GENERAL MOTORS (Cont.)

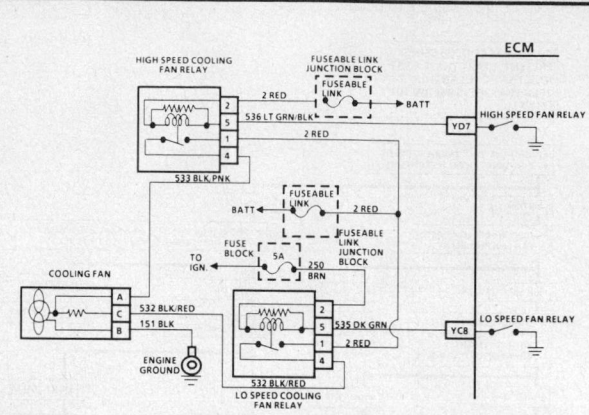

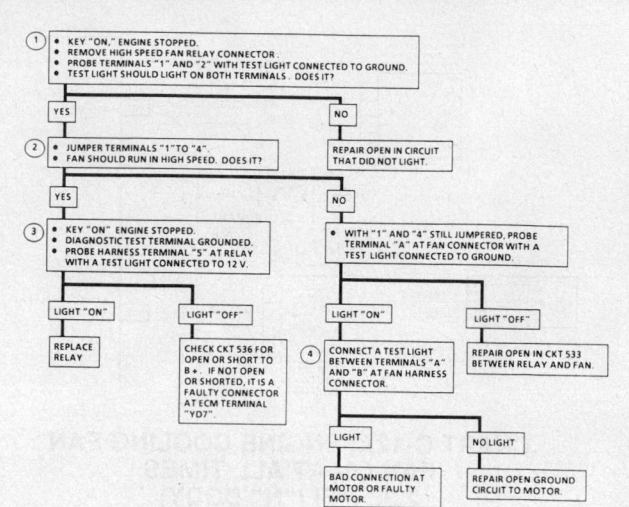

CHART C-12B, ENGINE COOLING FAN NO HIGH SPEED FAN 2.3L MFI ("N" BODY)

The electric cooling fan is controlled by the ECM through the low or high speed fan relay based on inputs from the coolant temperature sensor, A/C control switch, A/C pressure and the vehicle speed sensor. The ECM controls the cooling fan by grounding circuit No. 535 (low speed fan relay), or circuit No. 536 (high speed fan relay) which turns the low or high speed relays on.

Low speed relay will be engaged when:
- Code 14 or 15 is set.
- Coolant temperature is 217-221°F (103-105°C) or above.
- A/C clutch is engaged and vehicle speed is less than 35 MPH.

High speed fan relay will engage regardless of engine speed when:
- No code 14 or 15 is set.
- Coolant temperature is 239-244°F (115-118°C) or more.
- A/C pressure is high.

The cooling fan will be commanded on high speed when engine is not running and coolant temperature is above 239°F (115°C) or more. Fan will run for about 7 minutes immediately after ignition is turned off.

NOTE: **Test numbers refer to test numbers on diagnostic charts.**

1) Checks for battery voltage at relay harness connector.
2) Jumpering terminals No. "B" to "D" by-passes relay, which should cause fan to run, if fan motor and wiring are good.
3) Grounding test terminal should cause ECM to ground circuit No. 536. Test light should light at this point, if ECM is good and circuit No. 536 isn't open.
4) Checks for battery voltage and ground to fan motor. Test light on at this point indicates a faulty fan motor connection, or fan motor.

THERMOSTATICALLY CONTROLLED ELECTRIC COOLING FANS
GENERAL MOTORS (Cont.)

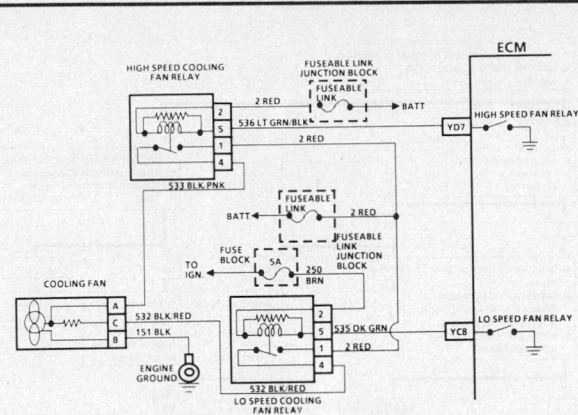

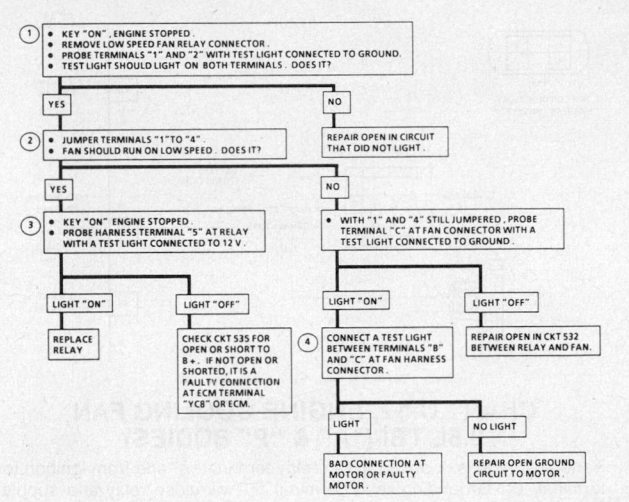

CHART C-12C, ENGINE COOLING FAN
NO LOW SPEED FAN
2.3L MFI ("N" BODY)

The electric cooling fan is controlled by the ECM through the low or high speed fan relay based on inputs from the coolant temperature sensor, A/C control switch, A/C pressure and the vehicle speed sensor. The ECM controls the cooling fan by grounding circuit No. 535 (low speed fan relay), or circuit No. 536 (high speed fan relay) which turns the low or high speed relays on.

Low speed relay will be engaged when:
- Code 14 or 15 is set.
- Coolant temperature is 217-221°F (103-105°C) or above.
- A/C clutch is engaged and vehicle speed is less than 35 MPH.

High speed fan relay will engage regardless of engine speed when:
- No code 14 or 15 is set.
- Coolant temperature is 239-244°F (115-118°C) or more.
- A/C pressure is high.

The cooling fan will be commanded on high speed when engine is not running and coolant temperature is above 239°F (115°C) or more. Fan will run for about 7 minutes immediately after ignition is turned off.

NOTE: Test numbers refer to test numbers on diagnostic charts.

1) Checks for battery voltage at relay harness connector.
2) Jumpering terminals No. "1" to "4" by-passes the relay, which should cause fan motor to run, if fan motor and wiring are good.
3) Grounding test terminal should cause ECM to ground circuit No. 535. At this point, test light should light, if ECM is good and circuit No. 535 isn't open.
4) This checks for battery voltage and ground to fan motor. Test light on at this point indicates a faulty fan motor connection, or motor.

Courtesy of General Motors Corp.

Engine Cooling Systems

THERMOSTATICALLY CONTROLLED ELECTRIC COOLING FANS
GENERAL MOTORS (Cont.)

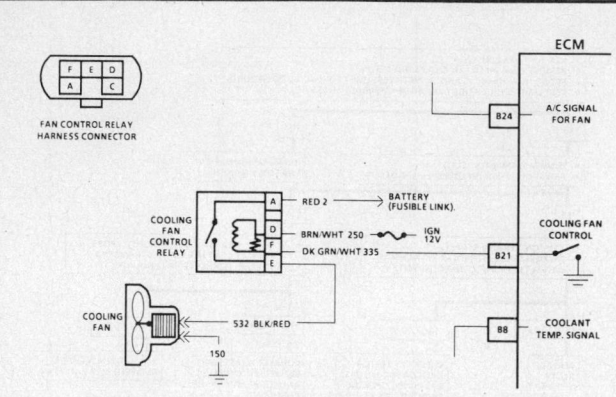

CHART C-12, ENGINE COOLING FAN
2.5L TBI ("A" & "P" BODIES)

Battery voltage is supplied to fan relay terminal "A" and from ignition to terminal "D". Grounding relay terminal "F" will close relay and supply battery voltage to fan motor. Above 30 MPH, the ECM will remove ground from circuit No. 335. If coolant temperature and A/C pressure switches are open, fan will stop. Fan is energized when:
- A/C is "on" and vehicle speed is less than 30 MPH.
- Coolant temperature is greater than 226°F (108°C).
- Code 14 or 15 is set.

DIAGNOSTIC AIDS

If an overheating condition is suspected, verify if this is due to actual boilover. If gauge or light indicates an overheat condition, and no boilover is in evidence, inspect the gauge/light circuit for malfunction.

If the vehicle is overheating and the gauge or light indicates the same, but the cooling fan is not coming on, check the coolant sensor temperature using a "scan" tester. The sensor may have shifted calibration. If the engine is overheating and the cooling fan is on, the cooling system should be checked.

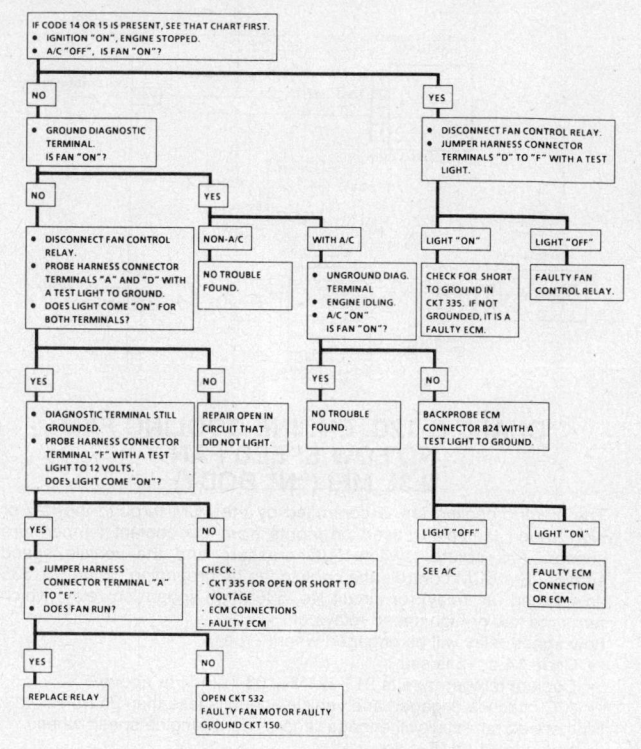

Courtesy of General Motors Corp.

THERMOSTATICALLY CONTROLLED ELECTRIC COOLING FANS
GENERAL MOTORS (Cont.)

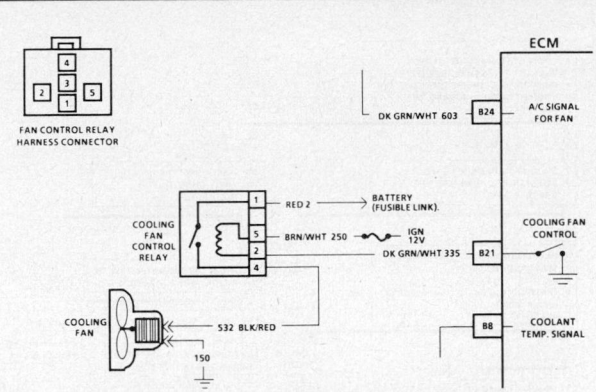

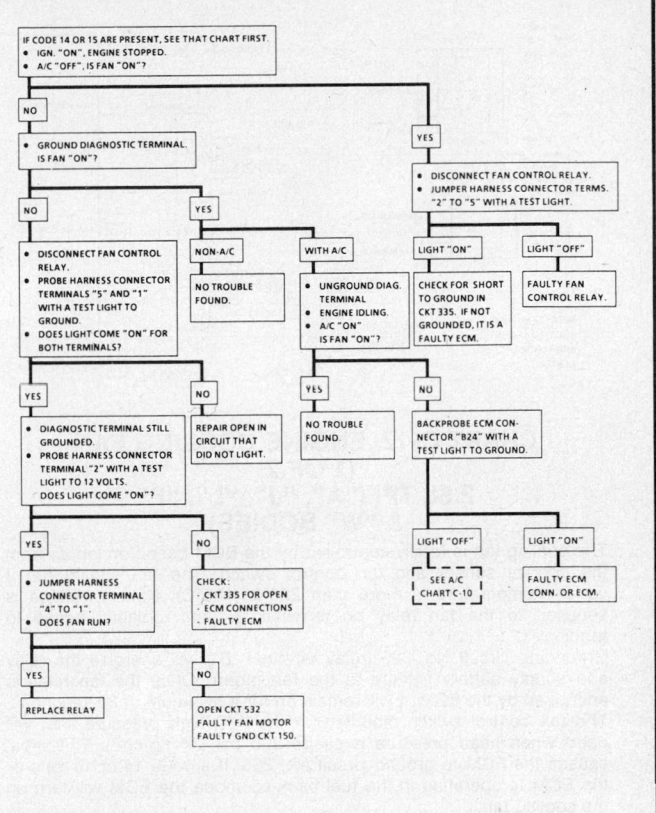

CHART C-12, ENGINE COOLING FAN
2.5L TBI ("N" BODIES)

Battery voltage is supplied to fan relay terminal No. 1 and from ignition to terminal No. 5. Grounding relay terminal No. 2 will close relay and supply battery voltage to fan motor. Above 30 MPH, the ECM will remove ground from circuit No. 335. If coolant temperature and A/C pressure switches are open, fan will stop. Fan is energized when:

- A/C is "on" and vehicle speed is less than 30 MPH.
- Coolant temperature is greater than 226°F (108°C).
- Code 14 or 15 is set.

DIAGNOSTIC AIDS

If an overheating condition is suspected, verify if this is due to actual boilover. If gauge or light indicates an overheat condition, and no boilover is in evidence, inspect the gauge/light circuit for malfunction.

If the vehicle is overheating and the gauge or light indicates the same, but the cooling fan is not coming on, check the coolant sensor temperature using a "Scan" tester. The sensor may have shifted calibration.

Courtesy of General Motors Corp.

Engine Cooling Systems

THERMOSTATICALLY CONTROLLED ELECTRIC COOLING FANS
GENERAL MOTORS (Cont.)

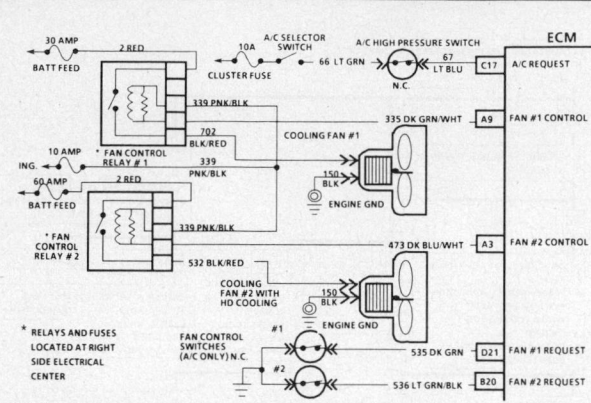

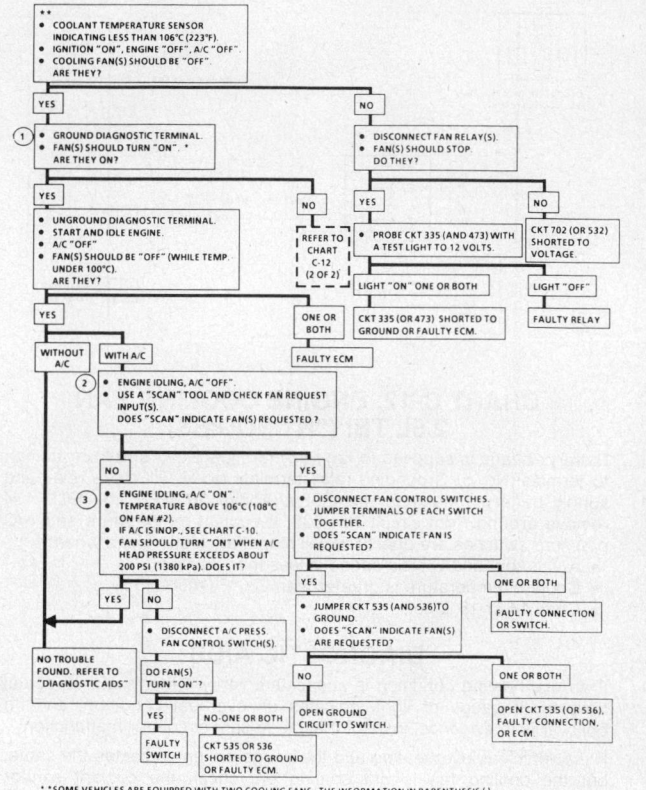

CHART C-12, ENGINE COOLING FAN
(1 OF 2)
2.8L TPI ("A", "J", "L", "P"
& "W" BODIES)

The cooling fan is totally controlled by the ECM based on inputs from the coolant sensor and fan control switch. The fan should run if cooant temperature is more than 226°F (108°C). Battery voltage is supplied to the fan relay on terminal "E" and ignition voltage to terminal "C".

Grounding circuit No. 335 (relay terminal "B") will energize the relay and supply battery voltage to the fan motor. Once the fan relay is energized by the ECM, it will remain on for a minimum of 30 seconds. The fan control switch mounted, in the A/C high pressure line, will open when head pressure exceeds 200 psi (14 kg/cm²). This input causes the ECM to ground circuit No. 335. If a code 14 or 15 sets or the ECM is operating in the fuel back-up mode the ECM will turn on the cooling fan.

NOTE: Test numbers refer to test numbers on diagnostic charts.

1) With diagnostic terminal grounded, cooling fan control driver will close, which should energize fan control relay.
2) If A/C fan control switch or circuit is open, the fan would run whenever A/C is requested.
3) With A/C clutch engaged, A/C fan control switch should open, when A/C pressure exceeds 200 psi (14 kg/cm²).

DIAGNOSTIC AIDS

If an overheating condition is suspected, verify if this is due to actual boilover. If gauge or light indicates an overheat condition, and no boilover is in evidence, inspect the gauge/light circuit for malfunction.

If the vehicle is overheating and the gauge or light indicates the same, but the cooling fan is not coming on, check the coolant sensor temperature using a "Scan" tester. The sensor may have shifted calibration and should be replaced. If the engine is overheating and the cooling fan is on, the cooling system should be checked.

Engine Cooling Systems

THERMOSTATICALLY CONTROLLED ELECTRIC COOLING FANS GENERAL MOTORS (Cont.)

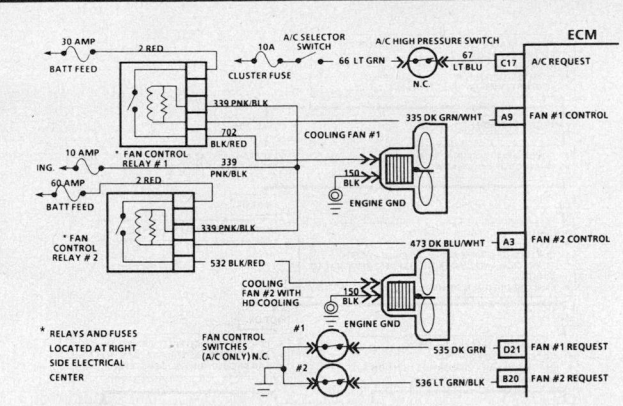

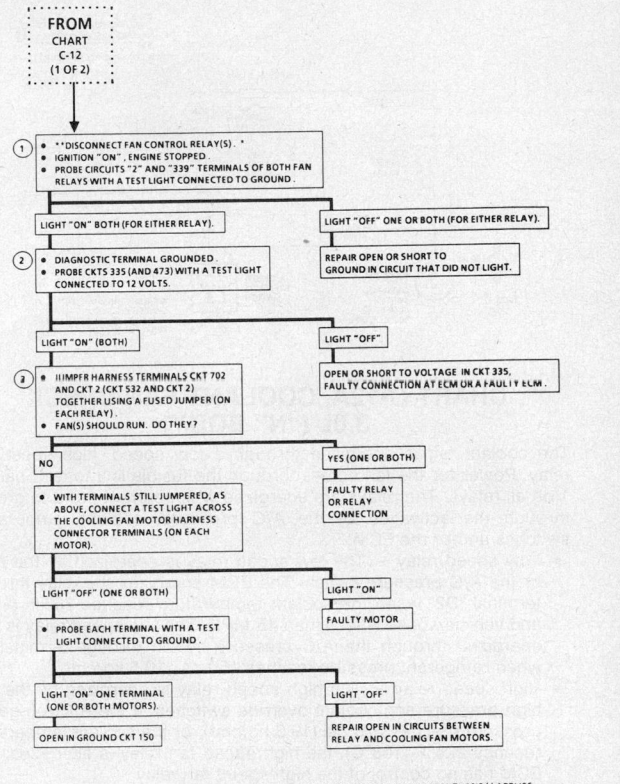

CHART C-12, ENGINE COOLING FAN (Cont.) (2 OF 2) 2.8L TPI ("A", "J", "L", "P" & "W" BODIES)

The cooling fan is totally controlled by the ECM based on inputs from the coolant sensor and fan control switch. The fan should run if coolant temperature is more than 226°F (108°C). Battery voltage is supplied to the fan relay on terminal "E" and ignition voltage to terminal "C".

Grounding circuit No. 335 (relay terminal "B") will energize the relay and supply battery voltage to the fan motor. Once the fan relay is energized by the ECM, it will remain on for a minimum of 30 seconds.

The fan control switch mounted, in the A/C high pressure line, will open when head pressure exceeds 200 psi (14 kg/cm²). This input causes the ECM to ground circuit No. 335. If a code 14 or 15 sets or the ECM is operating in the fuel back-up mode the ECM will turn on the cooling fan.

NOTE: Test numbers refer to test numbers on diagnostic charts.

1) Battery voltage should be available to both terminals "E" and "C" when ignition is on.

2) This test checks ability of the ECM to ground circuit No. 335. "Service Engine Soon" light should also be flashing at this point. If it isn't flashing, CEC system should be checked.

3) If fan does not turn on at this point, circuit No. 702 or circuit No. 150 is open, or cooling fan motor is faulty.

Courtesy of General Motors Corp.

Engine Cooling Systems

THERMOSTATICALLY CONTROLLED ELECTRIC COOLING FANS
GENERAL MOTORS (Cont.)

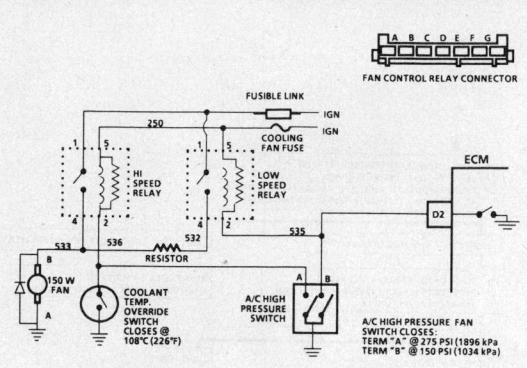

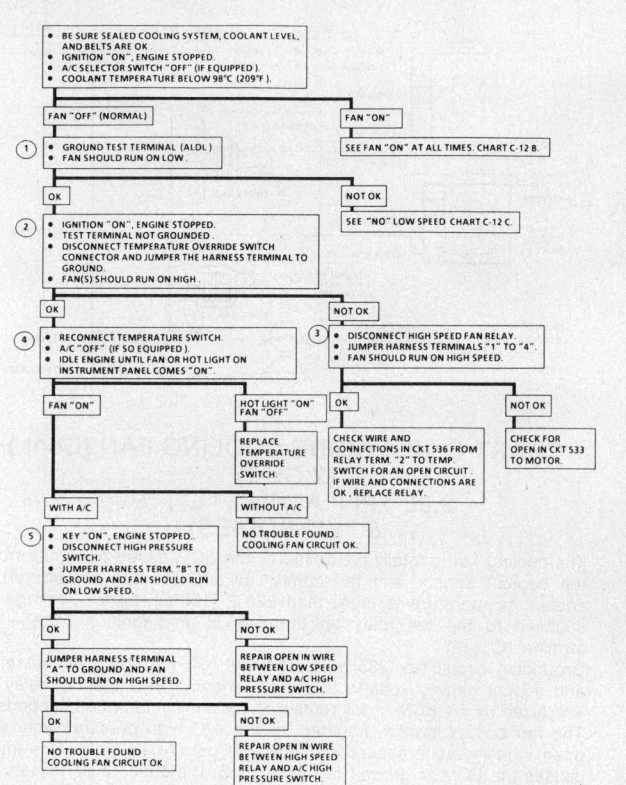

CHART C-12A, COOLANT FAN CHECK 3.0L ("N" BODY)

The coolant fan is energized through a low speed, high speed fan relay. Power for the fan comes through the fusible link to terminal No. 1 on all relays. The relays are energized when current flows to ground through the activation of the A/C pressure, coolant temperature switches and/or the ECM.

- Low speed relay – The low speed relay is energized by the ECM or the A/C pressure switch. The ECM energizes the relay through terminal "D2" when the coolant temperature reaches 208°F (98°C) and vehicle speed is less than 45 MPH. The low speed relay is also energized through the A/C pressure switch through terminal "B" when refrigerant pressure reaches 150 psi (10.5 kg/cm²).
- High speed relay – The high speed relay is energized by the A/C high pressure and coolant override switches. If the A/C refrigerant pressure reaches 275 psi (19.3 kg/cm²), or the coolant temperature reaches 226°F (108°C), the high speed fan relay is energized. The ECM has no control of the high speed fan relay.

NOTE: Test numbers refer to test numbers on diagnostic charts.

1) Grounding the diagnostic test terminal should cause the ECM to ground circuit No. 535 and the fan to run at low speed.

2) Grounding the temperature switch harness terminal will check circuit No. 536 and will also check the high speed fan and if equipped, pusher fan (VO8) relay.

3) This test checks circuit No. 533 between the fan control relay terminal No. 4 and the motor. If the fan does not operate, circuit No. 533 is open.

4) This test checks to see if the temperature switch is grounding and is grounded when the light comes on. The switch should close at 226°F (108°C).

5) If the vehicle is equipped with A/C, the following test will check the high pressure switch and related wiring from the switch to the fan control relay. The low speed fan should come on if high pressure exceeds 150 psi (10.5 kg/cm²).

Engine Cooling Systems

THERMOSTATICALLY CONTROLLED ELECTRIC COOLING FANS
GENERAL MOTORS (Cont.)

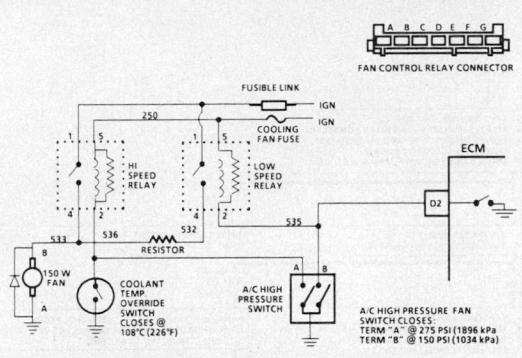

CHART C-12B, COOLANT FAN CHECK
FAN ON AT ALL TIMES
3.0L ("N" BODY)

The coolant fan is energized through a low speed, high speed fan relay. Power of the fan comes through the fusible link to terminal No. 1 on all relays. The relays are energized when current flows to ground through the fusible link to terminal No. 1 on all relays. The relays are energized when current flows to ground through the activation of the A/C pressure, coolant temperature switches, and/or the ECM.

- Low speed relay – The low speed relay is energized by the ECM or the A/C pressure switch. The ECM energizes the relay through terminal "D2" when the coolant temperature reaches 208°F (98°C) and vehicle speed is less than 45 MPH. The low speed relay is also energized through the A/C pressure switch through terminal "B" when refrigerant pressure reaches 150 psi (10.5 kg/cm²).
- High speed relay – The high speed relay is energized by the A/C high pressure and coolant override switches. If the A/C refrigerant pressure reaches 275 psi (19.3 kg/cm²) or the coolant temperature reaches 226°F (108°C) the high speed fan relay is energized. The ECM has no control of the high speed relay.

NOTE: Test numbers refer to test numbers on diagnostic charts.

1) Check to see if circuit No. 535 is shorted to ground which would keep the relay grounded at all times.
2) Check to see if circuit No. 536 is shorted to ground. A light indicates the wire is shorted to ground and the following tests will isolate the short.
3) If the test light is off after disconnecting, the ECM is shorted internally. Before replacing the ECM, be sure to check the resistance value of low speed side of the fan control relay. Replace if resistance is less than 20 ohms. Also be sure that circuit No. 535 is not shorted to battery voltage, and check the resistance of the canister purge solenoid. Replace solenoid if under 20 ohms.

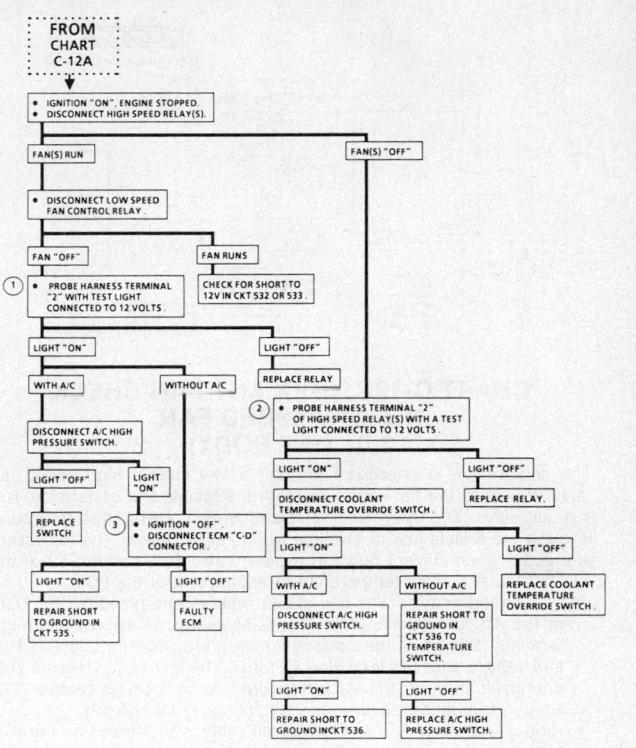

Engine Cooling Systems

THERMOSTATICALLY CONTROLLED ELECTRIC COOLING FANS GENERAL MOTORS (Cont.)

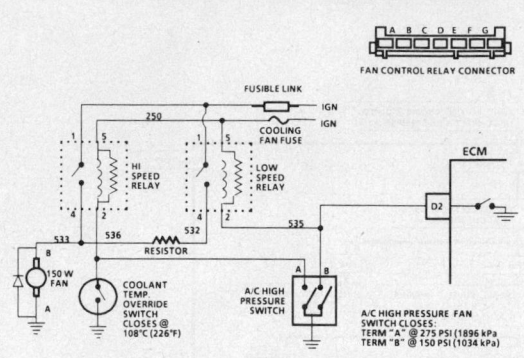

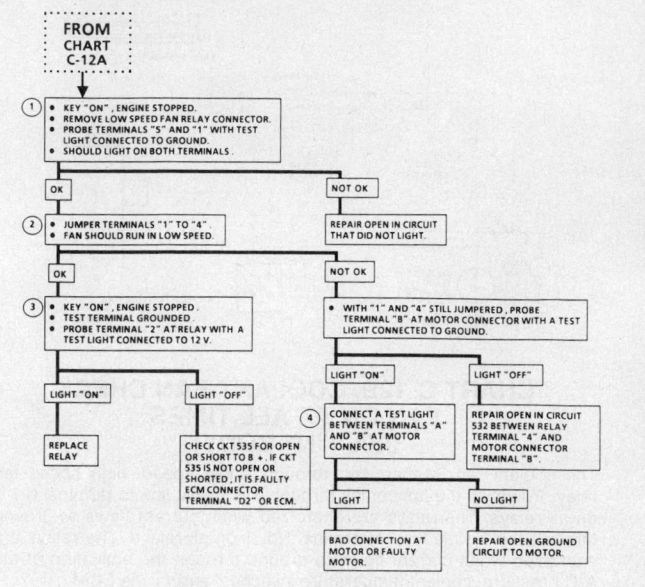

CHART C-12C, COOLANT FAN CHECK NO LOW SPEED FAN 3.0L ("N" BODY)

The coolant fan is energized through a low speed, high speed fan relay. Power to the fan comes through the fusible link on terminal No. 1 of all relays. The relays ar engergized when current flows to ground through the fusible link to terminal No. 1 on all relays. The relays are energized when current flows to ground through the activation of the A/C pressure, coolant temperature switches, and/or the ECM.

- Low speed relay – The low speed relay is energized by the ECM or the A/C pressure switch. The ECM energizes the relay through terminal "D2" when the coolant temperature reaches 208°F (98°C) and vehicle speed is less than 45 MPH. The low speed relay is also energized through the A/C pressure switch through terminal "B" when refrigerant pressure reaches 150 psi (10.5 kg/cm²).

- High speed relay – The high speed relay is energized by the A/C high pressure and coolant override switches. If the A/C refrigerant pressure reaches 275 psi (19.3 kg/cm²), or the coolant temperature reaches 226°F (108°C), the high speed fan relay is energized. The ECM has no control of the high speed relay.

NOTE: Test numbers refer to test numbers on diagnostic charts.

1) Checks for battery voltage at relay harness connector.
2) Jumpering terminals No. 1 and 4 by-passes the relay which should cause the fan to run if fan motor and wiring to the motor are good.
3) Grounding the test terminal should cause the ECM to ground circuit No. 535. At this point, the test light should light if the ECM is good and circuit No. 535 isn't open.
4) This checks for battery voltage and ground to the fan motor. A test light on at this point indicates a faulty fan motor connection or motor.

THERMOSTATICALLY CONTROLLED ELECTRIC COOLING FANS
GENERAL MOTORS (Cont.)

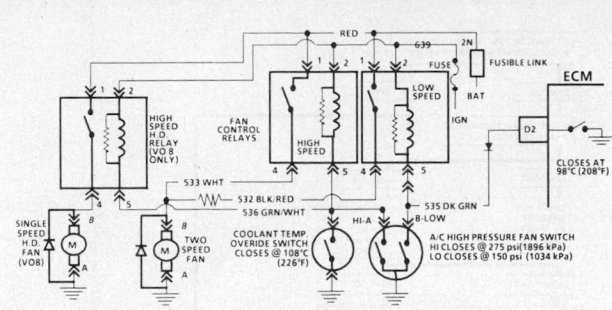

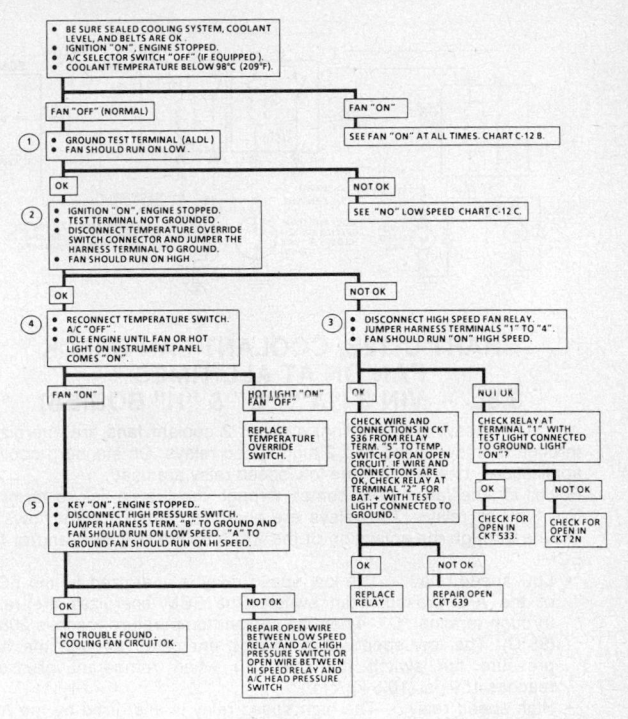

CHART C-12A, COOLANT FAN CHECK
3.8L – VIN 3 ("A", "C" & "H" BODIES)

On "VO8" (heavy duty cooling) system, 2 coolant fans are energized through one low speed and 2 high speed relays. On standard cooling applications, one fan and one low speed relay are used.

Power for the fan motors comes through the fusible link to terminal No. 1 on all relays. The relays are energized when current flows to ground through the activation of the A/C, coolant switches, and/or the ECM.

- Low speed relay – The low speed relay is energized by the ECM or the A/C pressure fan switch. The ECM energizes the relay through terminal "D2" when the coolant temperature reaches 208°F (98°C) The low speed relay is also energized through the A/C pressure fan switch (terminal "B") when refrigerant pressure reaches 150 psi (10.5 kg/cm²).
- High speed relay – The high speed relay is energized by the A/C high pressure fan switch and coolant temperature override switches. If the A/C refrigerant pressure reaches 275 psi (19 kg/cm²), or the coolant temperature reaches 226°F (108°C), the high speed fan relay is energized. The ECM has no control of the high speed fan relay.

Optional high speed relay – The optional high speed relay is energized by the A/C high pressure fan switch and coolant temperature override switch and/or the temperature switch. Relay is energized any time the standard high speed relay is energized. The ECM has no control of the optional high speed relay.

NOTE: Test numbers refer to test numbers on diagnostic charts.

1) Grounding the diagnostic test terminal should cause the ECM to ground circuit No. 535 and the fan should run in low speed.

2) Grounding the temperature switch harness terminal will check circuit No. 536 and the high side portion of the fan control relay.

3) This test separates and checks relay driver circuit and relay to fan circuit for open circuit or faulty relay.

4) This test checks to see if the temperature switch is grounding and is also grounded when the test light is on. The switch should close at 226°F (108°C).

5) The following steps will check the high pressure switches and related wiring from the switch to the fan control relay. If poor A/C performance is noted, the A/C pressure switches should be checked. The low speed fan should come on if high pressure exceeds 260 psi (18.3 kg/cm²).

Engine Cooling Systems

THERMOSTATICALLY CONTROLLED ELECTRIC COOLING FANS
GENERAL MOTORS (Cont.)

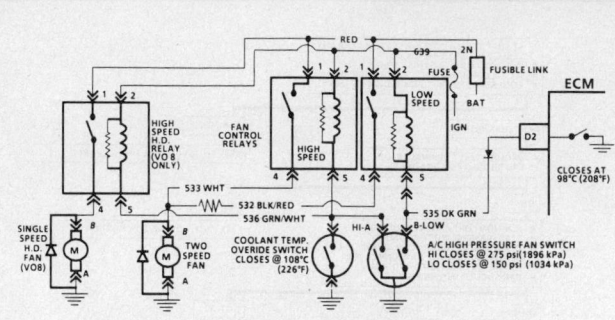

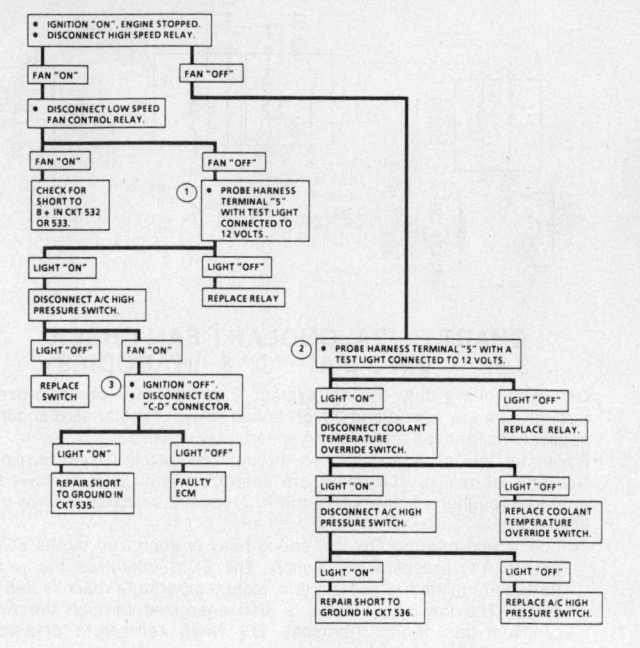

CHART C-12B, COOLANT FAN CHECK
FAN ON AT ALL TIMES
3.8L – VIN 3 ("A", "C" & "H" BODIES)

On "VO8" (heavy duty cooling) system, 2 coolant fans are energized through one low speed and 2 high speed relays. On standard cooling applications, one fan and one low speed relay are used.

Power for the fan motors comes through the fusible link to terminal No. 1 on all relays. The relays are energized when current flows to ground through the activation of the A/C, coolant switches, and/or the ECM.

- Low speed relay – The low speed relay is energized by the ECM or the A/C pressure fan switch. The ECM energizes the relay through terminal "D2" when the coolant temperature reaches 208°F (98°C). The low speed relay is also energized through the A/C pressure fan switch (terminal "B") when refrigerant pressure reaches 150 psi (10.5 kg/cm²).

- High speed relay – The high speed relay is energized by the A/C high pressure fan switch and coolant temperature override switches. If the A/C refrigerant pressure reaches 275 psi (19 kg/cm²), or the coolant temperature reaches 226°F (108°C), the high speed fan relay is energized. The ECM has no control of the high speed fan relay.

Optional high speed relay – The optional high speed relay is energized by the A/C high pressure fan switch and coolant temperature override switch and/or the temperature switch. Relay is energized any time the standard high speed relay is energized. The ECM has no control of the optional high speed relay.

NOTE: Test numbers refer to test numbers on diagnostic charts.

1) Checks to see if circuit No. 535 is shorted to ground. This would keep the relay grounded at all times.

2) Checks to see if circuit No. 536 is shorted to ground. A light indicates the wire is shorted to ground. The following tests will isolate the short.

3) If the test light is off after disconnecting ECM C-D connector, the ECM is shorted internally. Before replacing the ECM, be sure and check the resistance value of low speed side of the fan control relay. Replace if resistance is less than 20 ohms. Also, be sure the circuit No. 535 is not shorted to battery voltage. Check the resistance of the canister purge solenoid, and replace if under 20 ohms.

THERMOSTATICALLY CONTROLLED ELECTRIC COOLING FANS
GENERAL MOTORS (Cont.)

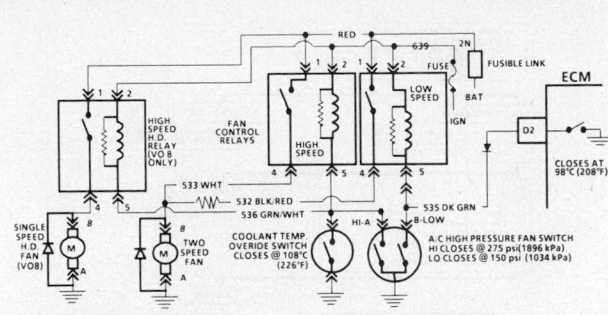

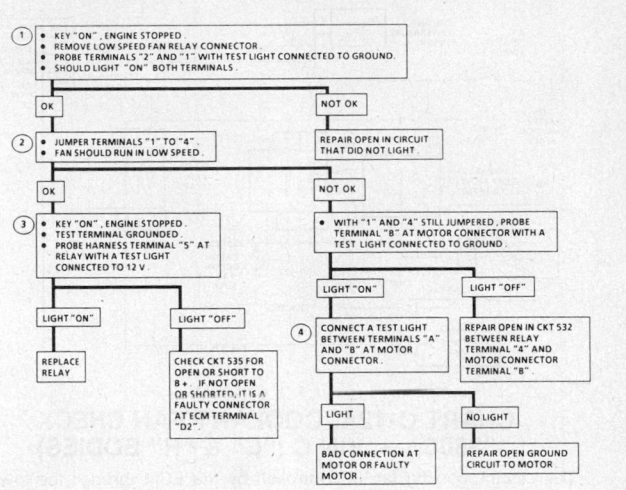

CHART C-12C, COOLANT FAN CHECK
NO LOW SPEED FAN
3.8L – VIN 3 ("A", "C" & "H" BODIES)

On "VO8" (heavy duty cooling) system, 2 coolant fans are energized through one low speed and 2 high speed relays. On standard cooling applications, one fan and one low speed relay are used.

Power for the fan motors comes through the fusible link to terminal No. 1 on all relays. The relays are energized when current flows to ground through the activation of the A/C, coolant switches, and/or the ECM.

- Low speed relay – The low speed relay is energized by the ECM or the A/C pressure fan switch. The ECM energizes the relay through terminal "D2" when the coolant temperature reaches 208°F (98°C). The low speed relay is also energized through the A/C pressure fan switch (terminal "B") when refrigerant pressure reaches 150 psi (10.5 kg/cm²).

- High speed relay – The high speed relay is energized by the A/C high pressure fan switch and coolant temperature override switches. If the A/C refrigerant pressure reaches 275 psi (19 kg/cm²), or the coolant temperature reaches 226°F (108°C), the high speed fan relay is energized. The ECM has no control of the high speed fan relay.

Optional high speed relay – The optional high speed relay is energized by the A/C high pressure fan switch and coolant temperature override switch and/or the temperature switch. Relay is energized any time the standard high speed relay is energized. The ECM has no control of the optional high speed relay.

NOTE: Test numbers refer to test numbers on diagnostic charts.

1) Check for battery voltage at relay harness connector.

2) Jumpering terminals No. 1 and 4 by-passes the relay. This should cause the fan to run, if fan motor and wiring to the motor are okay.

3) Grounding the test terminal should cause the ECM to ground circuit No. 535. At this point, the test light should light, if the ECM is okay and circuit No. 535 isn't open.

4) This checks for battery voltage and ground to the fan motor. If test light is on at this point, it indicates a faulty fan motor connection, motor connection or motor.

Engine Cooling Systems

THERMOSTATICALLY CONTROLLED ELECTRIC COOLING FANS
GENERAL MOTORS (Cont.)

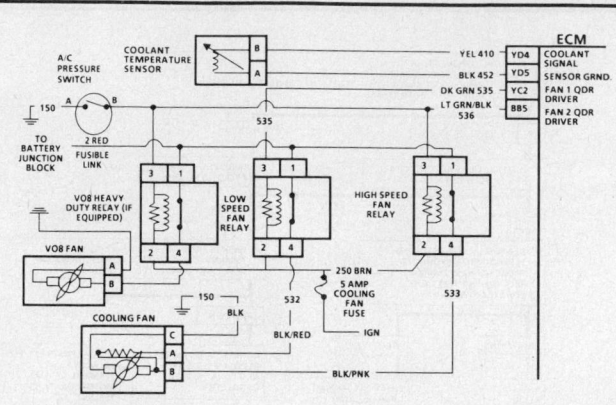

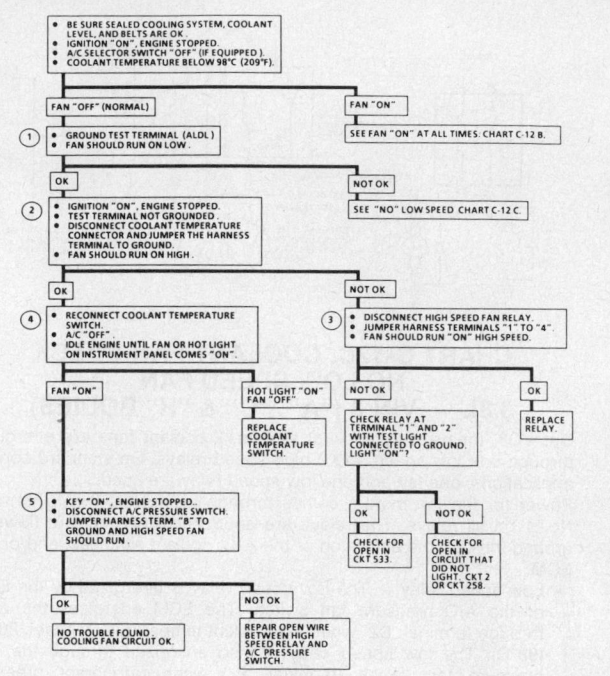

CHART C-12A, COOLANT FAN CHECK
"3800" – VIN C ("C" & "H" BODIES)

The electric cooling fan is controlled by the ECM through the low or high speed fan relay based on inputs from the coolant temperature sensor, A/C control switch, A/C pressure and the vehicle speed sensor. The ECM controls the cooling fan by grounding circuit No. 535 (low speed fan relay), or circuit No. 536 (high speed fan relay) which turns the low or high speed relays on.

Low speed relay will be engaged when coolant temperature reaches 208°F (101°C). High speed fan relay will be engage when coolant temperature reaches 226°F (108°C) or A/C refrigerant pressure reaches 275 psi (19 kg/cm²).

NOTE: **Test numbers refer to test numbers on diagnostic charts.**

1) Grounding diagnostic test terminal should cause to ECM to ground circuit 535 and fan should run on low speed.
2) Grounding coolant temperature switch harness terminal will check circuit 536 and will also check high speed fan control relay.
3) This test separates and checks ECM driver circuit and relay to fan circuit for open circuit or faulty relay.
4) This step checks to see if coolant temperature switch is grounded when light comes on. Switch should close at 226°F (108°C).
5) This will check the A/C pressure switch and related wiring from switch to fan control relay. Low speed fan should come on if high pressure exceeds 260 psi (18 kg/cm²).

Engine Cooling Systems

THERMOSTATICALLY CONTROLLED ELECTRIC COOLING FANS
GENERAL MOTORS (Cont.)

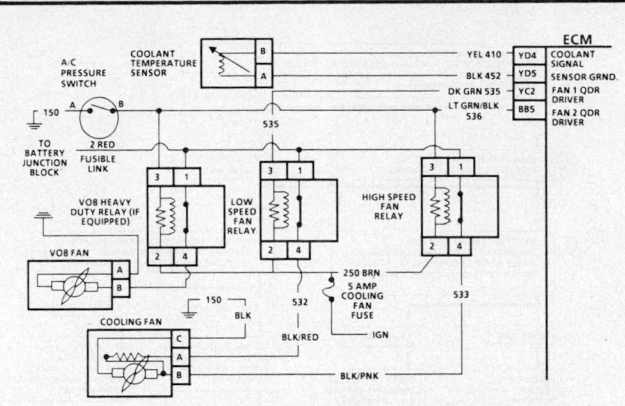

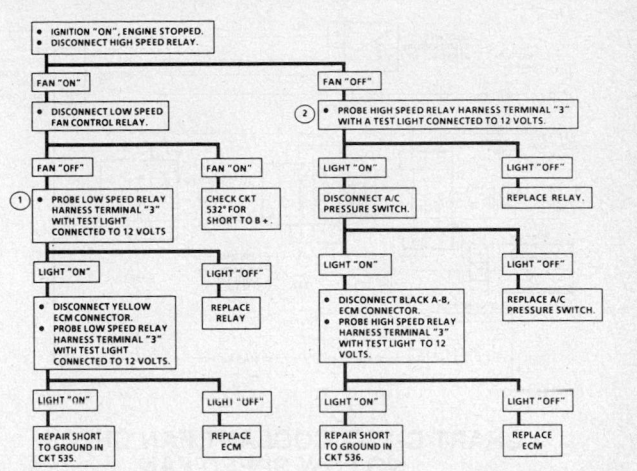

CHART C-12B, COOLANT FAN CHECK
FAN ON AT ALL TIMES
"3800" – VIN C ("C" & "H" BODIES)

The electric cooling fan is controlled by the ECM through the low or high speed fan relay based on inputs from the coolant temperature sensor, A/C control switch, A/C pressure and the vehicle speed sensor. The ECM controls the cooling fan by grounding circuit No. 535 (low speed fan relay), or circuit No. 536 (high speed fan relay) which turns the low or high speed relays on.

Low speed relay will be engaged when coolant temperature reaches 208°F (101°C). High speed fan relay will engage when coolant temperature reaches 226°F (108°C) or A/C refrigerant pressure reaches 275 psi (19 kg/cm²).

NOTE: Test numbers refer to test numbers on diagnostic charts.

1) Checks to see if circuit No. 535 is shorted to ground, which would keep relay grounded ar all times.

2) Checks to see if circuit No. 536 is shorted to ground. A light indicates wire is shorted to ground. The following steps will isolate the short.

3) If test light is off after disconnecting, ECM is shorted internally. Before replacing ECM, check resistance value of low speed side of fan control relay. Replace relay if resistance is less than 20 ohms. Check that circuit No. 535 is not shorted to battery voltage. Check canister purge solenoid resistance and replace if under 20 ohms.

Engine Cooling Systems

THERMOSTATICALLY CONTROLLED ELECTRIC COOLING FANS
GENERAL MOTORS (Cont.)

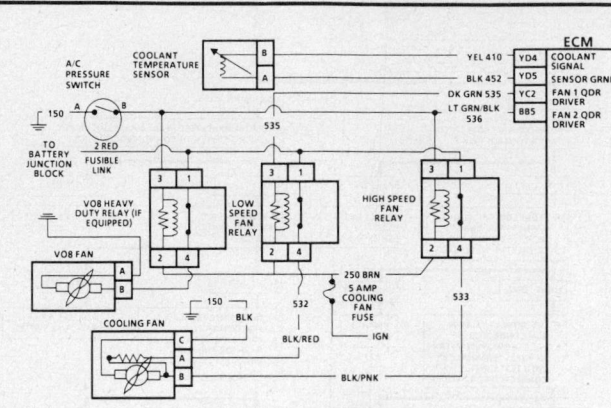

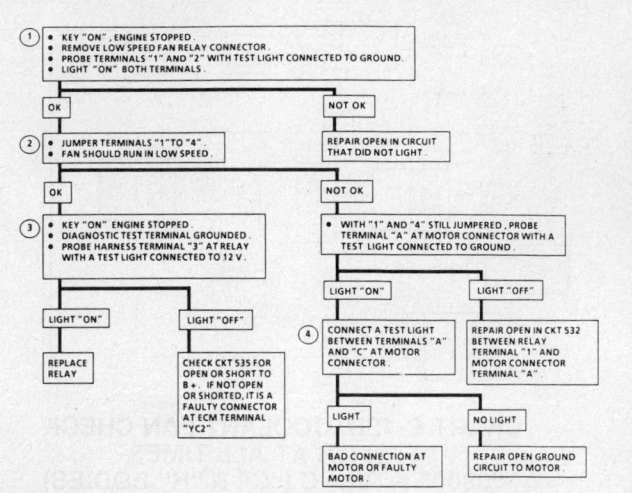

CHART C-12C, COOLANT FAN CHECK
NO LOW SPEED FAN
"3800" – VIN C ("C" & "H" BODIES)

The electric cooling fan is controlled by the ECM through the low or high speed fan relay based on inputs from the coolant temperature sensor, A/C control switch, A/C pressure and the vehicle speed sensor. The ECM controls the cooling fan by grounding circuit No. 535 (low speed fan relay), or circuit No. 536 (high speed fan relay) which turns the low or high speed relays on.

Low speed relay will be engaged when coolant temperature reaches 208°F (101°C). High speed fan relay will engage when coolant temperature reaches 226°F (108°C) or A/C refrigerant pressure reaches 275 psi (19 kg/cm²).

NOTE: Test numbers refer to test numbers on diagnostic charts.

1) Checks for battery voltage at relay harness connector.
2) Jumpering terminals "B" and "D" by-passes the relay. This should cause the fan to run, if fan motor and wiring to the motor are good.
3) Grounding the test terminal should cause the ECM to ground circuit No. 535. At this point, the test light should light, if the ECM is okay and circuit No. 535 isn't open.
4) This checks for battery voltage and ground to the fan motor. A test light on, at this point, indicates a faulty fan motor connection, motor connection or motor.

THERMOSTATICALLY CONTROLLED ELECTRIC COOLING FANS
GENERAL MOTORS (Cont.)

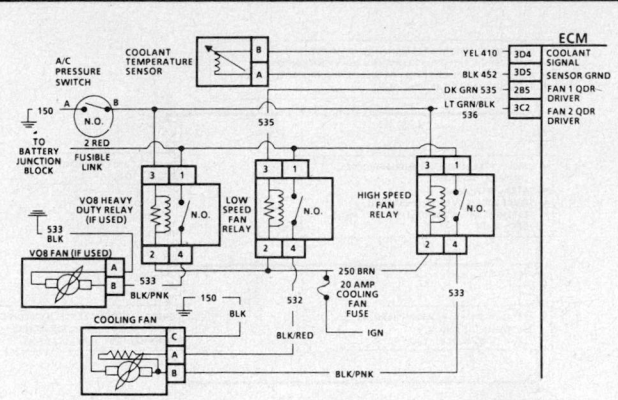

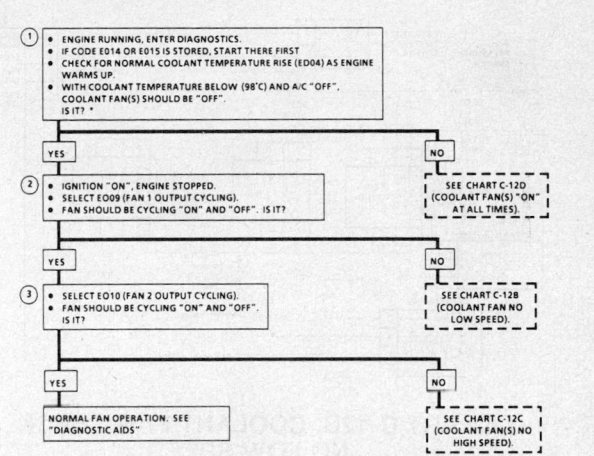

* WITH HEAVY DUTY COOLING (V08), TWO FAN MOTORS ARE USED. DURING HIGH SPEED OPERATION, BOTH FANS SHOULD BE "ON". IF ONLY ONE OR NONE OPERATES, SEE "NO HIGH SPEED CHECK".

CHART C-12A, COOLANT FAN CHECK
"3800" – VIN C ("E" BODY)

On standard duty applications, one electric cooling fan is used. It is controlled by the ECM through one low and one high speed fan relays. On heavy duty cooling systems, 2 cooling fans are used. The 2 cooling fans are controlled by one low speed and 2 high speed relays. Relay control is based on inputs from the coolant temperature sensor and A/C pressure.

The ECM controls the cooling fan by grounding circuit No. 535 (low speed fan relay), or circuit No. 536 (high speed fan relay) which turns the low or high speed relays on.

Low speed relay will be engaged when coolant temperature reaches 208°F (98°C). High speed fan relay will be engage when coolant temperature reaches 226°F (108°C) or A/C refrigerant pressure reaches 275 psi (19 kg/cm²). Pusher fan relay is installed as part of of the heavy duty cooling package. Pusher fan relay is on anytime high speed fan is running.

NOTE: Test numbers refer to test numbers on diagnostic charts.

1) Codes E014 or E015 could mean coolant system or sensor operation is not normal. If these codes appear, cooling fan operation can't be checked correctly.
2) ECM output EO09 grounds low speed relay through ECM for 3 seconds on and 3 seconds off. Low speed fan should be on for 3 seconds and off for 3 seconds.
3) Grounding A/C pressure switch harness terminal "B" should energize high speed relay and fan should run at high speed.

Engine Cooling Systems

THERMOSTATICALLY CONTROLLED ELECTRIC COOLING FANS
GENERAL MOTORS (Cont.)

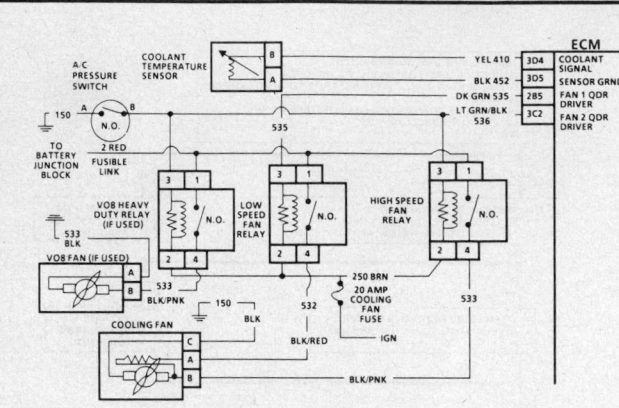

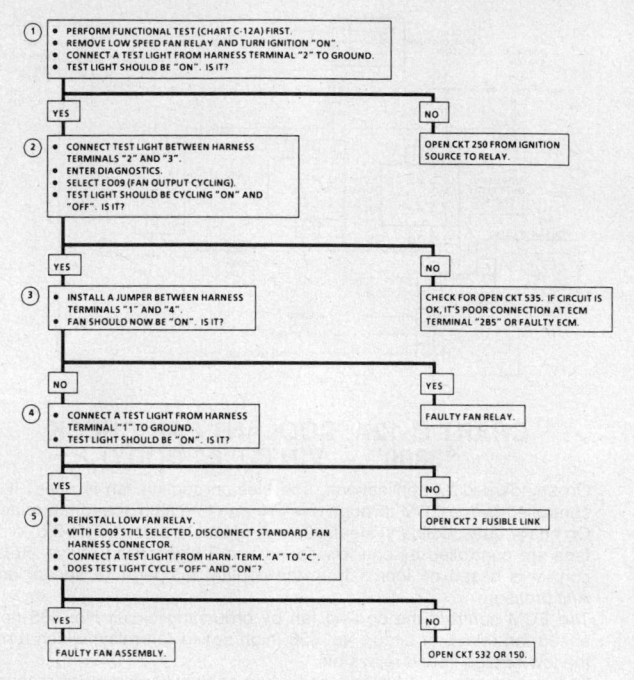

CHART C-12B, COOLANT FAN CHECK
NO LOW SPEED
"3800" – VIN C ("E" BODY)

On standard duty applications, one electric cooling fan is used. It is controlled by the ECM through one low and one high speed fan relays. On heavy duty cooling systems, 2 cooling fans are used. The 2 cooling fans are controlled by one low speed and 2 high speed relays. Relay control is based on inputs from the coolant temperature sensor and A/C pressure.

The ECM controls the cooling fan by grounding circuit No. 535 (low speed fan relay), or circuit No. 536 (high speed fan relay) which turns the low or high speed relays on.

Low speed relay will be engaged when coolant temperature reaches 208°F (98°C). High speed fan relay will be engage when coolant temperature reaches 226°F (108°C) or A/C refrigerant pressure reaches 275 psi (19 kg/cm²). Pusher fan relay is installed as part of of the heavy duty cooling package. Pusher fan relay is on anytime high speed fan is running.

NOTE: Test numbers refer to test numbers on diagnostic charts.

1) Test light should be on because harness terminal No. 2 has battery voltage with ignition on.

2) Test light should be on for 3 seconds and off for 3 seconds as EO09 cycles fan on/off at 3 second intervals.

3) Jumpering harness terminals No. 1 and No. 4 by-passes relay. If fan runs, relay is faulty.

4) If circuit No. 2 was open, test light would be off.

5) Cycling of test light proves circuits No. 532 and No. 150 are good and fan motor is faulty.

THERMOSTATICALLY CONTROLLED ELECTRIC COOLING FANS
GENERAL MOTORS (Cont.)

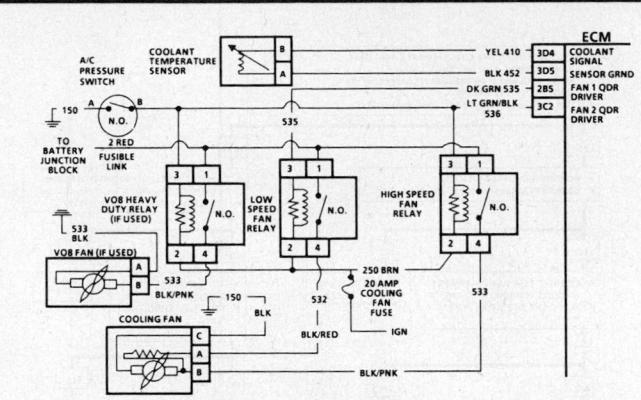

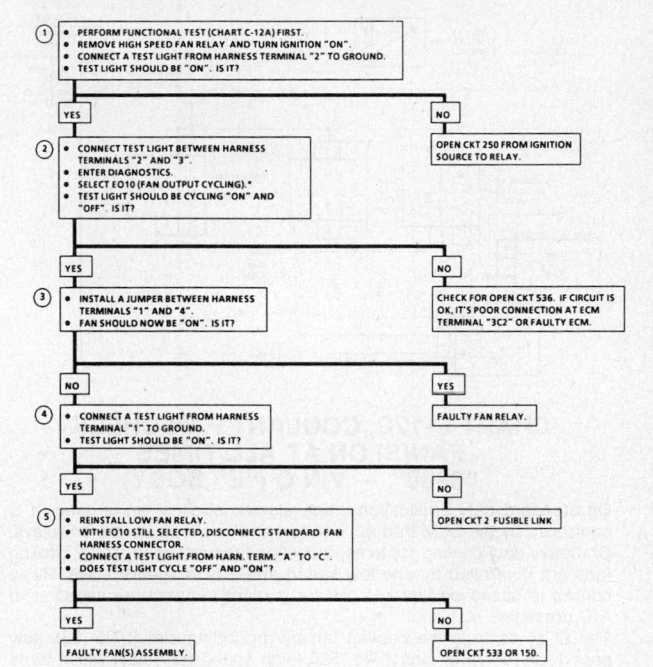

CHART C-12C, COOLANT FAN CHECK
NO HIGH SPEED
"3800" – VIN C ("E" BODY)

On standard duty applications, one electric cooling fan is used. It is controlled by the ECM through one low and one high speed fan relays. On heavy duty cooling systems, 2 cooling fans are used. The 2 cooling fans are controlled by one low speed and 2 high speed relays. Relay control is based on inputs from the coolant temperature sensor and A/C pressure.

The ECM controls the cooling fan by grounding circuit No. 535 (low speed fan relay), or circuit No. 536 (high speed fan relay) which turns the low or high speed relays on.

Low speed relay will be engaged when coolant temperature reaches 208°F (98°C) High speed fan relay will be engage when coolant temperature reaches 226°F (108°C) or A/C refrigerant pressure reaches 275 psi (19 kg/cm²). Pusher fan relay is installed as part of of the heavy duty cooling package. Pusher fan relay is on anytime high speed fan is running.

NOTE: Test numbers refer to test numbers on diagnostic charts.

1) Test light should be on. Harness terminal No. 2 has battery voltage with ignition switch on.
2) Test light should be on for 3 seconds and off for 3 seconds as EO09 cycles fan on/off at 3 second intervals.
3) Jumpering harness terminals No. 1 and No. 4 by-passes relay. If fan runs, relay is faulty.
4) If circuit No. 2 was open, test light would be off.
5) Cycling of test light proves circuits No. 533 and No. 150 are good and fan motor is faulty.

Engine Cooling Systems

THERMOSTATICALLY CONTROLLED ELECTRIC COOLING FANS
GENERAL MOTORS (Cont.)

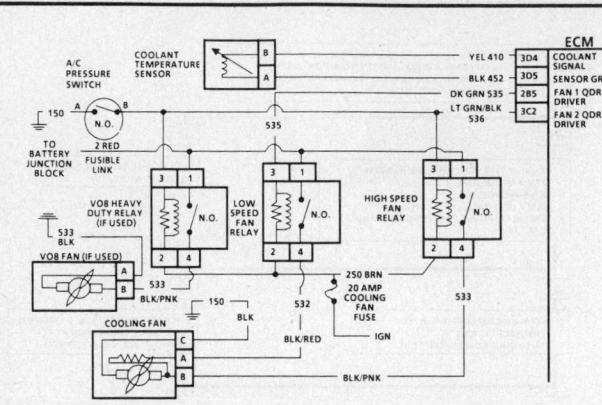

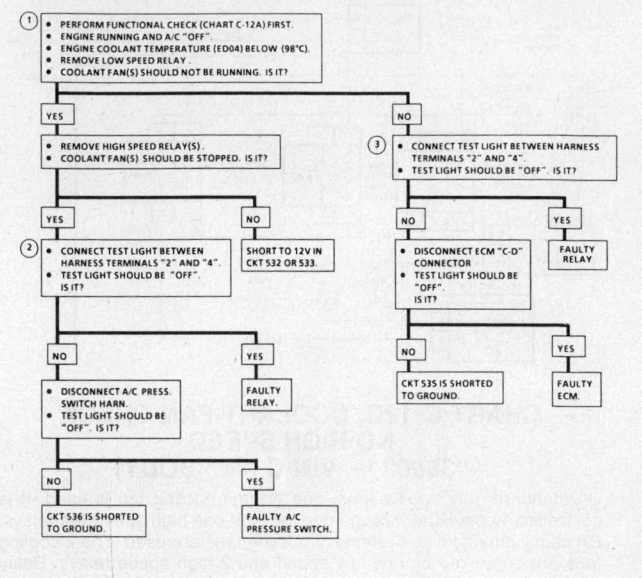

CHART C-12D, COOLANT FAN CHECK
FAN(S) ON AT ALL TIMES
"3800" – VIN C ("E" BODY)

On standard duty applications, one electric cooling fan is used. It is controlled by the ECM through one low and one high speed fan relays. On heavy duty cooling systems, 2 cooling fans are used. The 2 cooling fans are controlled by one low speed and 2 high speed relays. Relay control is based on inputs from the coolant temperature sensor and A/C pressure.

The ECM controls the cooling fan by grounding circuit No. 535 (low speed fan relay), or circuit No. 536 (high speed fan relay) which turns the low or high speed relays on.

Low speed relay will be engaged when coolant temperature reaches 208°F (98°C) High speed fan relay will be engage when coolant temperature reaches 226°F (108°C) or A/C refrigerant pressure reaches 275 psi (19 kg/cm²). Pusher fan relay is installed as part of of the heavy duty cooling package. Pusher fan relay is on anytime high speed fan is running.

NOTE: Test numbers refer to test numbers on diagnostic charts.

1) Checks to see if circuit No. 535 is shorted to ground which would energize low speed relay at all times.

2) If relay is faulty test light will be off. If test light is on, temperature sensor, A/C high pressure switch or circuit No. 536 is shorted to ground.

3) If test light is off relay is faulty. If test light is on, A/C high pressure switch, ECM or circuit No. 535 is shorted to ground.

THERMOSTATICALLY CONTROLLED ELECTRIC COOLING FANS
GENERAL MOTORS (Cont.)

CHART, ENGINE COOLING FAN
4.5L DFI ("C" "E" & "K" BODIES)

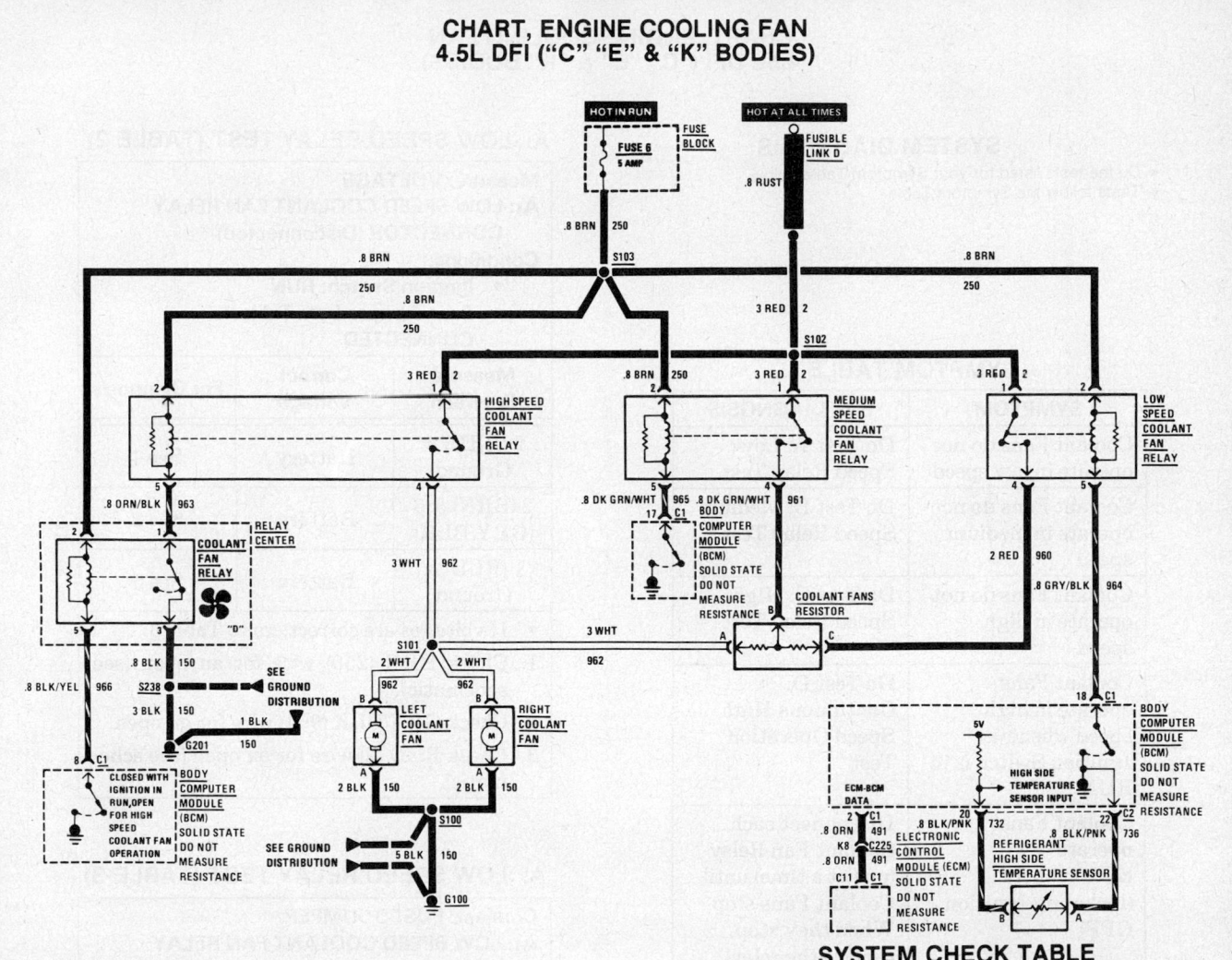

TROUBLE SHOOTING HINTS

Try the following checks before performing System Check

1) If coolant fans do not operate, check fuse No. 6 and fusible link "D".

2) If only one coolant fan does not operate, check the electrical wires to that coolant fan. If the wiring is okay, replace coolant fan.

3) If coolant fan only operates in high speed, check the WHT (962) wire from the coolant fan resistor. If the wire is good, replace coolant fans resistor.

SYSTEM CHECK

• Use System Check Table as a guide to normal operation. Refer to System Diagnosis for a list of symptoms and diagnostic steps.

SYSTEM CHECK TABLE

ACTION	NORMAL RESULT
Enter diagnostics and select COOLING FANS OVERRIDE. Press (and hold) the LO button on the Climate Control Panel	Coolant Fans should be off. If on, their speed decreases until they turn off
Release the LO button. Press (and hold) the HI button on the Climate Control Panel	Coolant Fans begin at low speed, increase to medium speed, and then increase to high speed
Release the HI button	Coolant Fans remain at high speed for approximately 4½ minutes. They then return to BCM control

Courtesy of General Motors Corp.

Engine Cooling Systems

THERMOSTATICALLY CONTROLLED ELECTRIC COOLING FANS
GENERAL MOTORS (Cont.)

CHART, ENGINE COOLING FAN
4.5L DFI ("C" "E" & "K" BODIES)

SYSTEM DIAGNOSIS

- Do the tests listed for your Symptom Table below.
- Tests follow the Symptom Table

SYMPTOM TABLE

SYMPTOM	FOR DIAGNOSIS
Coolant Fans do not operate in low speed	Do Test A: Low Speed Relay Test
Coolant Fans do not operate in medium speed	Do Test B: Medium Speed Relay Test
Coolant Fans do not operate in high speed	Do Test C: High Speed Relay Test
Coolant Fans operate in high speed whenever Ignition Switch is in RUN	Do Test D: Continuous High Speed Operation Test
Coolant Fans operate continuously (including Ignition OFF)	Disconnect each Coolant Fan Relay (one at a time) until Coolant Fans stop. When they stop, replace the relay that was just disconnected.

A: LOW SPEED RELAY TEST (TABLE 1)

Connect: FUSED JUMPER
At: BCM CONNECTOR C1 (Connected)
Condition:
- **Ignition Switch: RUN**

Connect Between	Correct Result	For Diagnosis
18 (GRY/ BLK) & Ground	Coolant Fans run at low speed	See 1

- If result is correct, replace the Body Computer Module (BCM).
1. Go to Table 2.

A: LOW SPEED RELAY TEST (TABLE 2)

Measure: VOLTAGE
At: LOW SPEED COOLANT FAN RELAY
    CONNECTOR (Disconnected)
Conditions:
- **Ignition Switch: RUN**
- **Fuse Jumper from Table 1: CONNECTED**

Measure Between	Correct Voltage	For Diagnosis
2 (BRN) & Ground	Battery	See 1
2 (BRN) & 5 (GRY/BLK)	Battery	See 2
1 (RED) & Ground	Battery	See 3

- If voltages are correct, go to Table 3.
1. Check BRN (250) wire for an open (see schematic).
2. Check GRY/BLK (964) wire for an open.
3. Check RED (2) wire for an open (see schematic).

A: LOW SPEED RELAY TEST (TABLE 3)

Connect: FUSED JUMPER
At: LOW SPEED COOLANT FAN RELAY
    CONNECTOR (Disconnected)

Connect Between	Correct Result	For Diagnosis
1 (RED) & 4 (RED)	Coolant Fans run at low speed	See 1

- If result is correct, replace Low Speed Coolant Fan Relay.
1. Check RED (960) wire for an open. If wire is good, replace Coolant Fans Resistor.

THERMOSTATICALLY CONTROLLED ELECTRIC COOLING FANS
GENERAL MOTORS (Cont.)

CHART, ENGINE COOLING FAN
4.5L DFI ("C" "E" & "K" BODIES)

B: MEDIUM SPEED RELAY TEST (TABLE 1)

Connect: FUSED JUMPER
At: BCM CONNECTOR C1 (Connected)
Condition:
- Ignition Switch: RUN

Connect Between	Correct Result	For Diagnosis
17 (DK GRN/ WHT) & Ground	Coolant Fans run at medium speed	See 1

- If result is correct, replace the Body Computer Module (BCM).
1. Go To Table 2.

B: MEDIUM SPEED RELAY TEST (TABLE 2)

Measure: VOLTAGE
At: MEDIUM SPEED COOLANT FAN RELAY
    CONNECTOR (Disconnected)
Conditions:
- Ignition Switch: RUN
- Fused Jumper from Table 1: CONNECTED

Measure Between	Correct Voltage	For Diagnosis
2 (BRN) & Ground	Battery	See 1
2 (BRN) & 5 (DK GRN/ WHT)	Battery	See 2
1 (RED) & Ground	Battery	See 3

- If voltages are correct, go to Table 3.
1. Check BRN (250) wire for an open

2. Check DK GRN/WHT (965) wire for an open.
3. Check RED (2) wire for an open

B: MEDIUM SPEED RELAY TEST (TABLE 3)

Connect: FUSED JUMPER
At: MEDIUM SPEED COOLANT FAN RELAY
    CONNECTOR (Disconnected)

Connect Between	Correct Result	For Diagnosis
1 (RED) & 4 (DK GRN/ WHT)	Coolant Fans run at medium speed	See 1

- If result is correct, replace Medium Speed Coolant Fan Relay.
1. Check DK GRN/WHT (961) wire for an open. If wire is good, replace Coolant Fans Resistor.

C: HIGH SPEED RELAY TEST (TABLE 1)

Connect: FUSED JUMPER
At: RELAY CENTER, RELAY "D"
Conditions:
- Coolant Fan Relay: REMOVED
- Ignition Switch: RUN

Connect Between	Correct Result	For Diagnosis
1 (ORN/BLK) & Ground	Coolant Fans run at high speed	See 1

- If result is correct, go to Table 4.
1. Go to Table 2.

Engine Cooling Systems

THERMOSTATICALLY CONTROLLED ELECTRIC COOLING FANS
GENERAL MOTORS (Cont.)

CHART, ENGINE COOLING FAN
4.5L DFI ("C" "E" & "K" BODIES)

C: HIGH SPEED RELAY TEST (TABLE 2)

Measure: VOLTAGE
At: HIGH SPEED COOLANT FAN RELAY
    CONNECTOR (Disconnected)
Conditions:
- Ignition Switch: RUN
- Fused Jumper from Table 1: CONNECTED

Measure Between	Correct Voltage	For Diagnosis
2 (BRN) & Ground	Battery	See 1
2 (BRN) & 5 (ORN/BLK)	Battery	See 2
1 (RED) & Ground	Battery	See 3

- If voltages are correct, go to Table 3.
1. Check BRN (250) wire for an open (see schematic).
2. Check ORN/BLK (963) wire for an open (see schematic).
3. Check RED (2) wire for an open (see schematic).

C: HIGH SPEED RELAY TEST (TABLE 3)

Connect: FUSED JUMPER
At: HIGH SPEED COOLANT FAN RELAY
    CONNECTOR (Disconnected)

Connect Between	Correct Result	For Diagnosis
1 (RED) & 4 (WHT)	Coolant Fans run at high speed	See 1

- If result is correct, replace High Speed Coolant Fan Relay.
1. Check WHT (962) wire for an open.

C: HIGH SPEED RELAY TEST (TABLE 4)

Separate: CONNECTOR C1
At: BODY COMPUTER MODULE (BCM)
Condition:
- Ignition Switch: RUN

Action	Correct Result	For Diagnosis
Disconnect BCM connector C1	Coolant Fans run at high speed	See 1

- If result is correct, replace Body Computer Module (BCM).
1. Go to Table 5.

C: HIGH SPEED RELAY TEST (TABLE 5)

Measure: VOLTAGE
At: RELAY CENTER
Conditions:
- Coolant Fan Relay: REMOVED
- Ignition Switch: RUN
- BCM Connector C1: DISCONNECTED

Measure Between	Correct Voltage	For Diagnosis
2 (BRN) & 5 (BLK/YEL)	0	See 1
2 (BRN) & 3 (BLK)	Battery	See 2

- If voltages are correct, replace High Speed Coolant Fan Relay.
1. Check BLK/YEL (966) wire for a short to ground.
2. Check BLK (150) wire for an open.

Engine Cooling Systems

THERMOSTATICALLY CONTROLLED ELECTRIC COOLING FANS GENERAL MOTORS (Cont.)

**CHART, ENGINE COOLING FAN
4.5L DFI ("C" "E" & "K" BODIES)**

D: CONTINUOUS HIGH SPEED OPERATION TEST (TABLE 1)

Connect: FUSED JUMPER
At: BCM CONNECTOR C1 (Connected)
Condition:
- Ignition Switch: RUN

Connect Between	Correct Result	For Diagnosis
8 (BLK/YEL) & Ground	Coolant Fans turn off	See 1

- If result is correct, replace Body Computer Module (BCM).
1. Go to Table 2.

D: CONTINUOUS HIGH SPEED OPERATION TEST (TABLE 2)

Measure: VOLTAGE
At: RELAY CENTER
Conditions:
- Coolant Fan Relay: REMOVED
- Ignition Switch: RUN
- Fuse Jumper from Table 1: CONNECTED

Measure Between	Correct Voltage	For Diagnosis
2 (BRN) & Ground	Battery	See 1
2 (BRN) & 5 (BLK/YEL)	Battery	See 2

- If voltages are correct, check ORN/BLK (963) wire for a short to ground. If wire is good, replace Coolant Fan Relay.
1. Check BRN (250) wire for an open (see schematic).
2. Check BLK/YEL (966) wire for an open.

Courtesy of General Motors Corp.

Engine Cooling Systems

THERMOSTATICALLY CONTROLLED ELECTRIC COOLING FANS GENERAL MOTORS (Cont.)

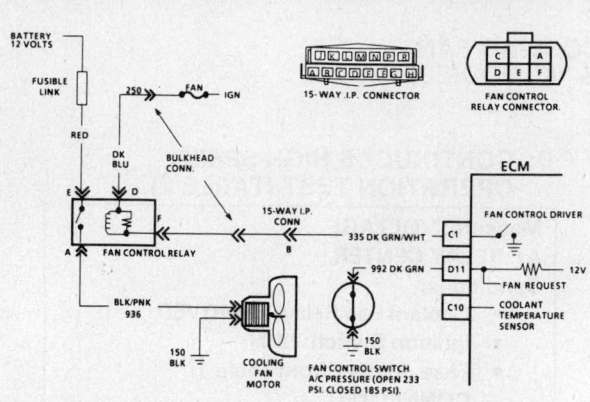

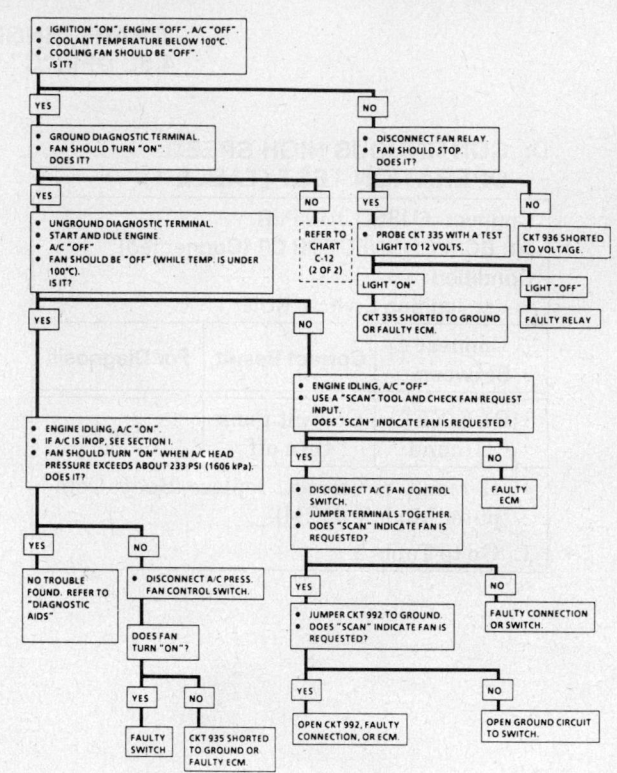

CHART C-12, ENGINE COOLING FAN (1 OF 2)
5.7L TPI ("Y" BODY)

The cooling fan is totally controlled by the ECM based on inputs from the coolant sensor and fan control switch. The fan should run if coolant temperature is more than 226°F (108°C). Battery voltage is supplied to the fan relay on terminal "E" and ignition voltage to terminal "D".

Grounding circuit No. 335 (relay terminal "F") will energize the relay and supply battery voltage to the fan motor. Once the fan relay is energized by the ECM, it will remain on for a minimum of 30 seconds. The ECM will remove the ground to circuit No. 335, if vehicle speed is over 40 MPH (unless engine is overheating).

The fan control switch (mounted in the A/C high pressure line) will open when head pressure exceeds 233 psi (16 kg/cm²). This input causes the ECM to ground circuit No. 335. If a code 14 or 15 sets, or the ECM is operating in the fuel back-up mode, the ECM will turn on the cooling fan.

DIAGNOSTIC AIDS

If an overheating condition is suspected, verify if this is due to actual boilover. If gauge or light indicates an overheat condition, and no boilover is in evidence, inspect the gauge/light circuit for malfunction.

If the vehicle is overheating and the gauge or light indicates the same, but the cooling fan is not coming on, check the coolant sensor temperature using a "Scan" tester. The sensor may have shifted calibration and should be replaced. If the engine is overheating and the cooling fan is on, the cooling system should be checked.

THERMOSTATICALLY CONTROLLED ELECTRIC COOLING FANS
GENERAL MOTORS (Cont.)

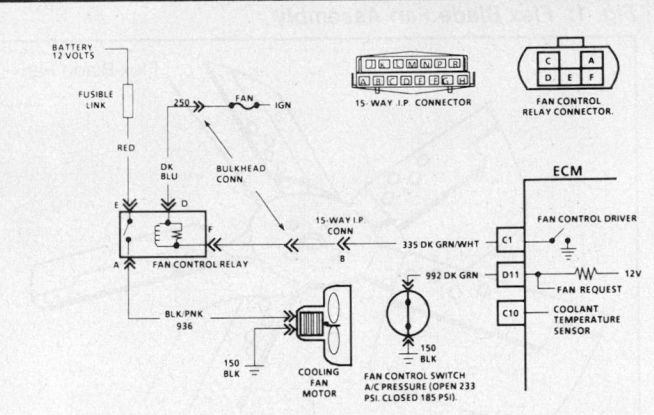

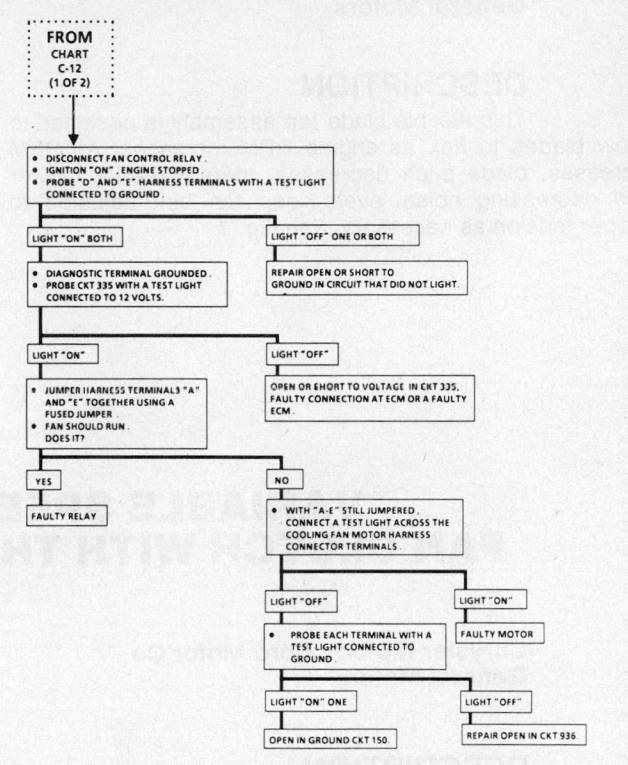

CHART C-12, ENGINE COOLING FAN (Cont.)
(2 OF 2)
5.7L TPI ("Y" BODY)

The cooling fan is totally controlled by the ECM based on inputs from the coolant sensor and fan control switch. The fan should run if coolant temperature is more than 226°F (108°C). Battery voltage is supplied to the fan relay on terminal "E" and ignition voltage to terminal "D".

Grounding circuit No. 335 (relay terminal "F") will energize the relay and supply battery voltage to the fan motor. Once the fan relay is energized by the ECM, it will remain on for a minimum of 30 seconds. The ECM will remove the ground to circuit No. 335, if vehicle speed is over 40 MPH (unless engine is overheating).

The fan control switch (mounted in the A/C high pressure line) will open when head pressure exceeds 233 psi (16 kg/cm²). This input causes the ECM to ground circuit No. 335. If a code 14 or 15 sets, or the ECM is operating in the fuel back-up mode, the ECM will turn on the cooling fan.

DIAGNOSTIC AIDS

If an overheating condition is suspected, verify if this is due to actual boilover. If gauge or light indicates an overheat condition, and no boilover is in evidence, inspect the gauge/light circuit for malfunction.

If the vehicle is overheating and the gauge or light indicates the same, but the cooling fan is not coming on, check the coolant sensor temperature using a "Scan" tester. The sensor may have shifted calibration and should be replaced. If the engine is overheating and the cooling fan is on, the cooling system should be checked.

Courtesy of General Motors Corp.

Engine Cooling Systems
VARIABLE SPEED COOLING FANS
FLEX-BLADE FANS

**Chrysler Motors, Ford Motor Co.,
General Motors**

DESCRIPTION

This flexible blade fan assembly is designed to allow blades to flex as engine RPM increases. As RPM increases, blade pitch decreases, thereby saving power and decreasing noise level. Keep fan belt adjusted to proper tension as necessary. *See Fig. 1.*

Fig. 1: Flex Blade Fan Assembly

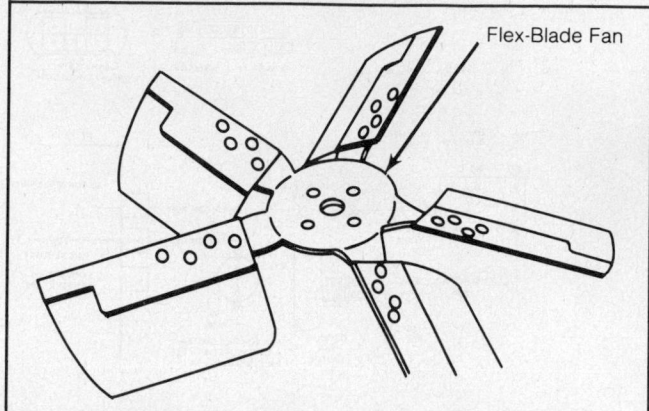

Flex-Blade Fan

VARIABLE SPEED COOLING FANS
FAN CLUTCH WITH THERMOSTATIC CONTROL

**Chrysler Motors, Ford Motor Co.,
General Motors**

DESCRIPTION

Most air conditioned models use a thermostatically controlled fluid fan and torque control clutch. Thermal control drive is a silicone-filled coupling connecting fan to a fan pulley, and is operated by an internal control valve. The control valve is operated by a temperature sensitive bi-metallic coil (or strip) and controls flow of silicone through the clutch.

Fig. 1: Thermostatically Controlled Fan Assembly

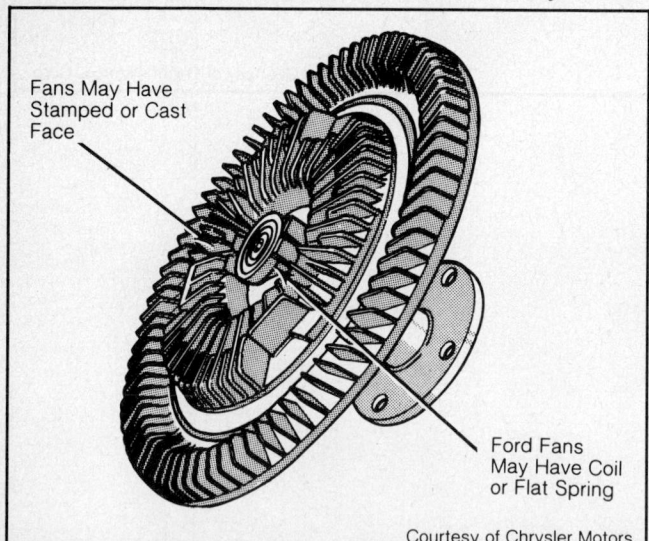

Fans May Have Stamped or Cast Face

Ford Fans May Have Coil or Flat Spring

Courtesy of Chrysler Motors.

Shown with stamped face and bi-metal coil spring.

During periods of operation when radiator discharge air temperature is low, fan clutch speeds are slowed, decreasing fan speed and increasing engine warm-up. High radiator discharge air temperature causes bi-metallic coil or strip to allow a greater flow of silicone to enter clutch. This increases drag between driven member and driving member resulting in a higher fan speed and increased cooling.

TESTING

1) In cases of engine overheating or insufficient air conditioning start with a cool engine to ensure complete fan clutch disengagement. Cover radiator grille sufficiently to induce high engine temperature.

2) Start engine and operate at 2000 RPM. On all models except Chrysler Motors, turn on air conditioning (if equipped). A fan roar will be noticed when fan clutch engages.

NOTE: **It takes approximately 5-10 minutes for temperature to become hot enough to allow engagement of fan clutch. While operating engine under this condition, observe temperature light or gauge to prevent overheating. If car overheats, remove cover from radiator grille.**

3) When clutch engages, remove radiator grille cover and turn A/C off to assist in engine cooling. After several minutes fan clutch should disengage. This can be determined by a reduction in fan speed and roar. If fan clutch fails to function as described, it should be replaced.

Engine Cooling Systems

SERPENTINE DRIVE BELTS

**Chrysler Motors, Eagle Premier,
Ford Motor Co., General Motors**

DESCRIPTION

Many manufactures are converting to single ("serpentine" or "V" ribbed) belt systems to drive components which normally have required multiple "V" belts. The serpentine belt system incorporates a tensioner which makes it possible to rigidly mount belt-driven components which previously required individual adjustment. Manufacturers claim a belt life of 100,000 miles and little, if any, adjustment is necessary.

The serpentine belt tensioner controls belt tension over a wide range of belt lengths. The tensioner cannot compensate for extreme belt lengths. Poor tension control or possible tensioner damage can result from excessive length belts.

INSPECTION

Check belt for fraying. If fraying is noticed, be sure both belt and tensioner are aligned properly. *See Fig. 1.* If tensioner reaches limit of travel, belt is stretched and should be replaced. If a whining or grinding noise can be heard around tensioner or idler, check for possible bearing failure.

Fig. 1: Serpentine Belt Alignment

Proper Alignment

Improper Alignment

Courtesy of Ford Motor Co.

INSTALLATION

SERPENTINE BELT ROUTING

Install belt on crankshaft and belt-driven components as shown. Adjust tensioner. *See Figs. 2-24.*

Fig. 2: Chrysler Motors 3.0L Engine Serpentine Belt Routing With Air Conditioning

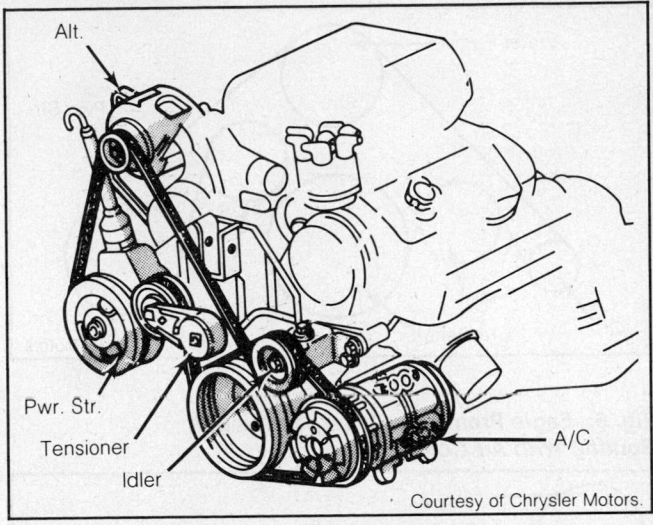

Alt.

Pwr. Str.

Tensioner

Idler

A/C

Courtesy of Chrysler Motors.

Fig. 3: Eagle Premier 2.5L Engine Serpentine Belt Routing Without Air Conditioning

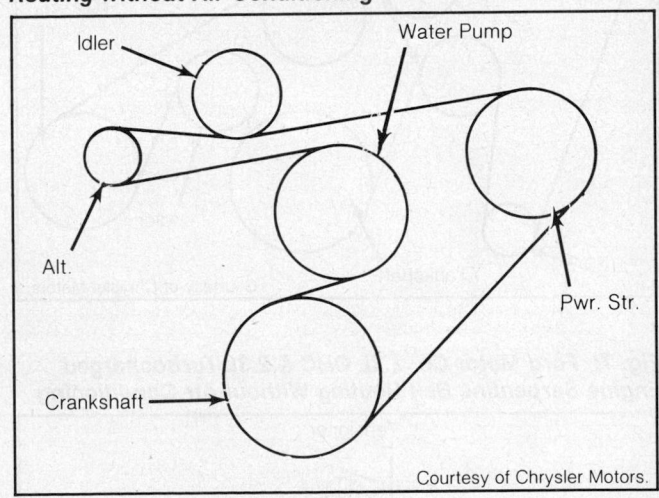

Idler

Water Pump

Alt.

Pwr. Str.

Crankshaft

Courtesy of Chrysler Motors.

Fig. 4: Eagle Premier 2.5L Engine Serpentine Belt Routing With Air Conditioning

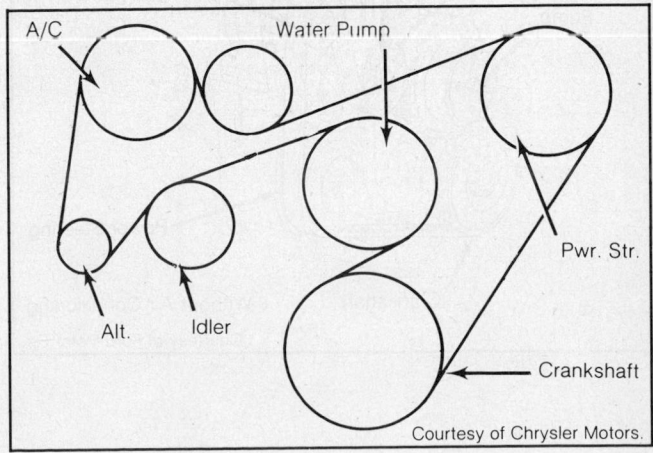

A/C

Water Pump

Pwr. Str.

Alt.

Idler

Crankshaft

Courtesy of Chrysler Motors.

Engine Cooling Systems

SERPENTINE DRIVE BELTS (Cont.)

Fig. 5: Eagle Premier 3.0L Serpentine Belt Routing Without Air Conditioning

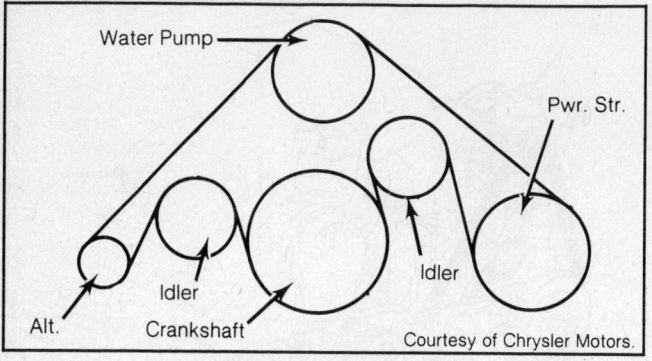

Fig. 6: Eagle Premier 3.0L Serpentine Belt Routing With Air Conditioning

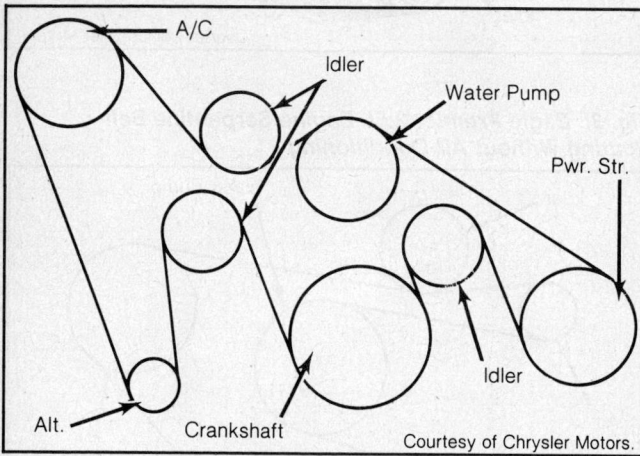

Fig. 7: Ford Motor Co. 2.3L OHC & 2.3L Turbocharged Engine Serpentine Belt Routing Without Air Conditioning

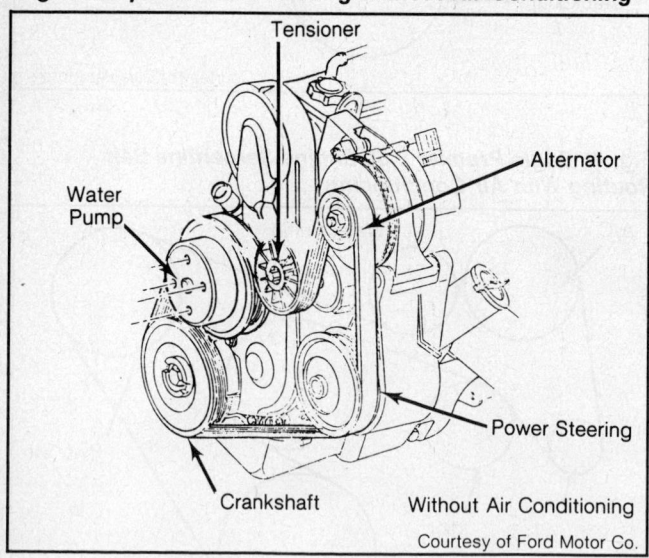

Fig. 8: Ford Motor Co. 2.3L OHC & 2.3L Turbocharged Engine Serpentine Belt Routing With Air Conditioning

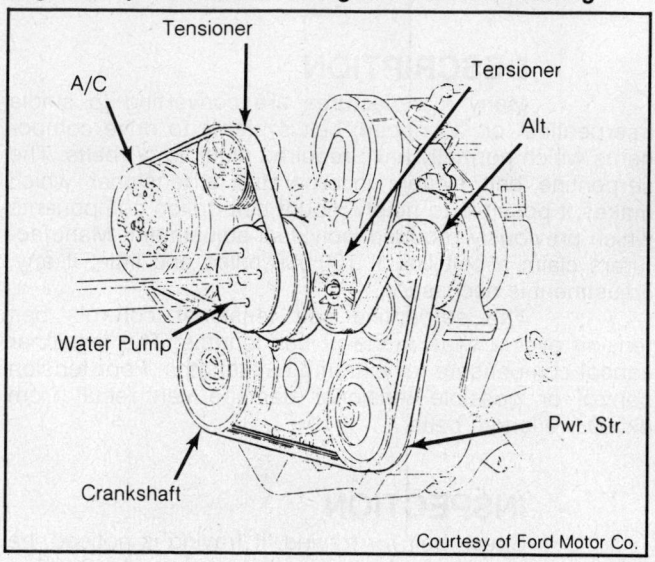

Fig. 9: Ford Motor Co. 2.5L Engine Serpentine Belt Routing With Air Conditioning

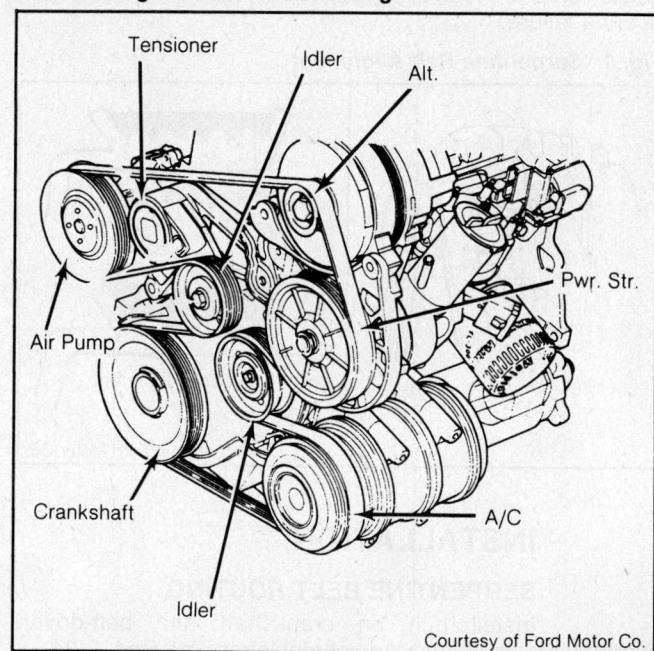

SERPENTINE DRIVE BELTS (Cont.)

Fig. 10: Ford Motor Co. 3.0L Engine Serpentine Belt Routing With Air Conditioning

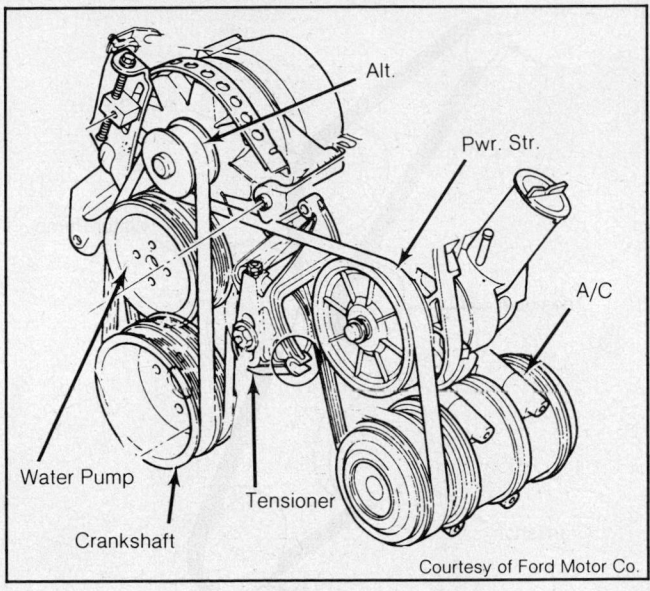

Alt.

Pwr. Str.

A/C

Water Pump

Tensioner

Crankshaft

Courtesy of Ford Motor Co.

Fig. 11: Ford Motor Co. 3.8L Engine Serpentine Belt Routing With Air Conditioning

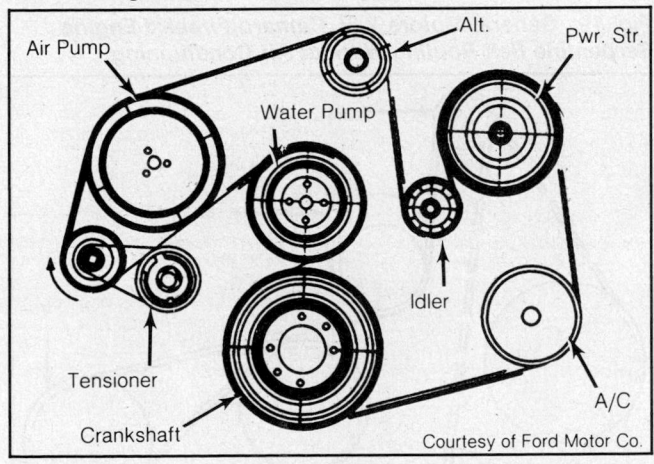

Air Pump

Alt.

Pwr. Str.

Water Pump

Idler

Tensioner

Crankshaft

A/C

Courtesy of Ford Motor Co.

Fig. 12: Ford Motor Co. 3.8L Engine Dual Tensioner Serpentine Belt Routing With Air Conditioning

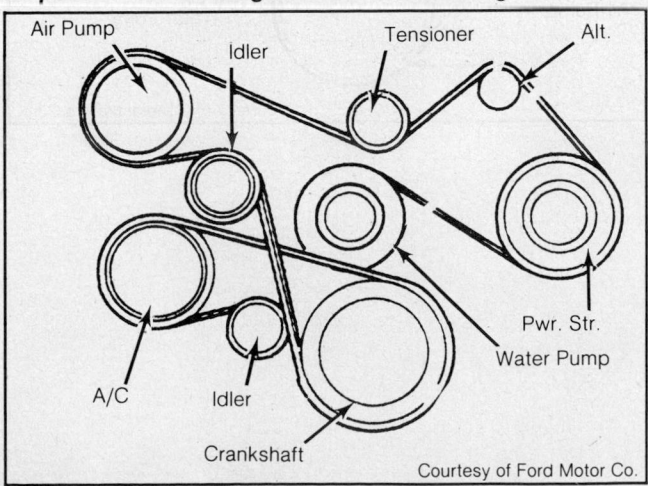

Air Pump

Idler

Tensioner

Alt.

Pwr. Str.

Water Pump

A/C

Idler

Crankshaft

Courtesy of Ford Motor Co.

Fig. 13: Ford Motor Co. 5.0L Engine Serpentine Belt Routing Without Air Conditioning

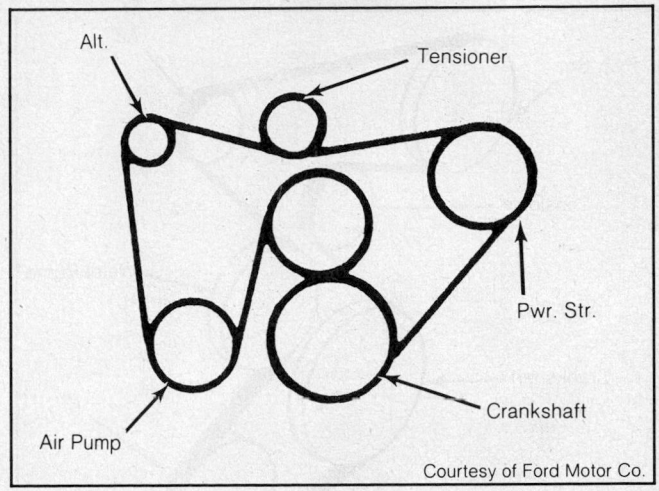

Alt.

Tensioner

Pwr. Str.

Crankshaft

Air Pump

Courtesy of Ford Motor Co.

Fig. 14: Ford Motor Co. 5.0L Engine Serpentine Belt Routing With Air Conditioning

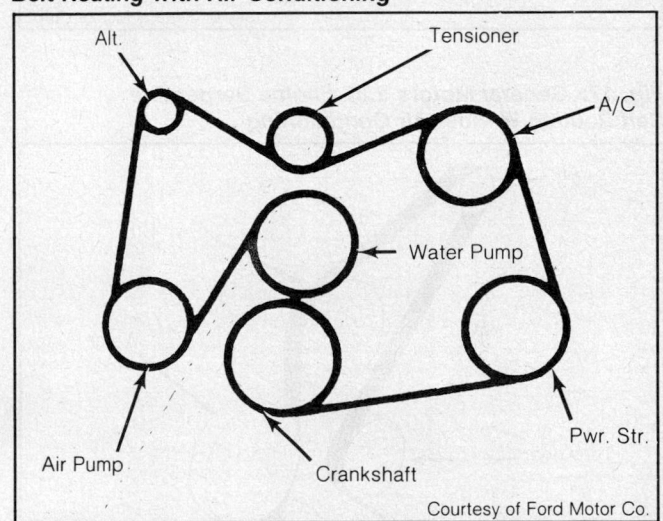

Alt.

Tensioner

A/C

Water Pump

Air Pump

Crankshaft

Pwr. Str.

Courtesy of Ford Motor Co.

Fig. 15: General Motors 2.0L & 2.5L Engine Serpentine Belt Routing Without Air Conditioning

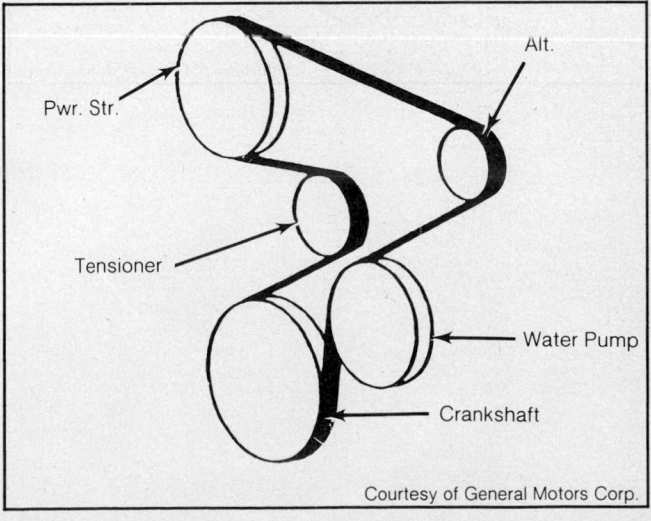

Pwr. Str.

Alt.

Tensioner

Water Pump

Crankshaft

Courtesy of General Motors Corp.

Engine Cooling Systems

SERPENTINE DRIVE BELTS (Cont.)

Fig. 16: *General Motors 2.0L & 2.5L Engine Serpentine Belt Routing With Air Conditioning*

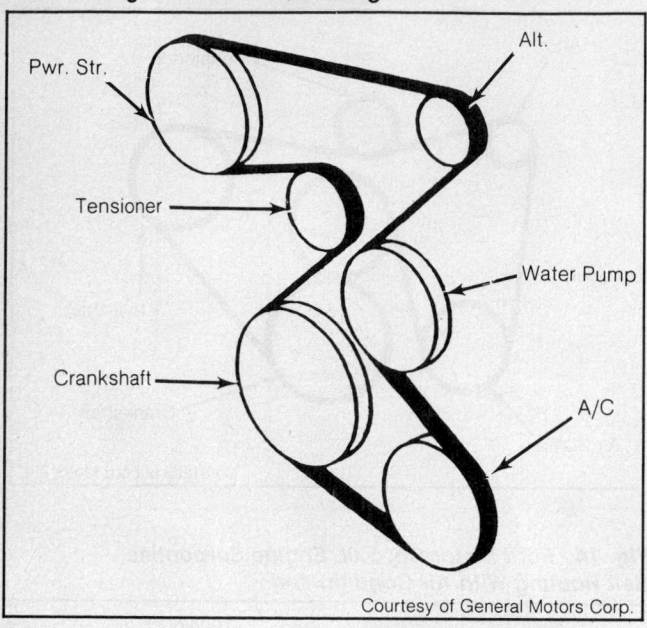

Courtesy of General Motors Corp.

Fig. 18: *General Motors 2.8L Engine Serpentine Belt Routing With Air Conditioning*

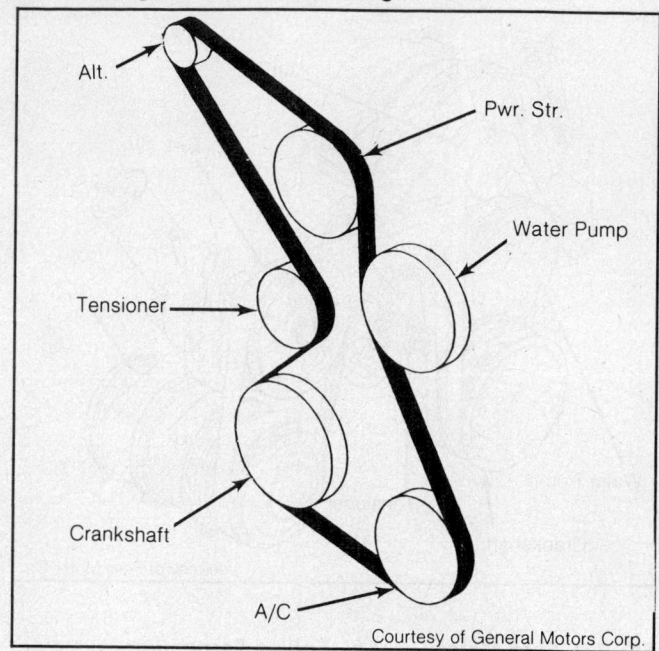

Courtesy of General Motors Corp.

Fig. 17: *General Motors 2.8L Engine Serpentine Belt Routing Without Air Conditioning*

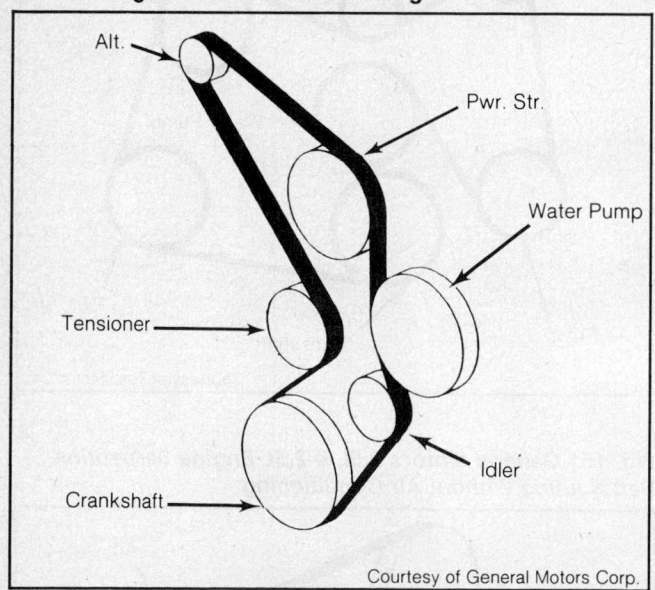

Courtesy of General Motors Corp.

Fig. 19: *General Motors 2.8L Camaro/Firebird Engine Serpentine Belt Routing Without Air Conditioning*

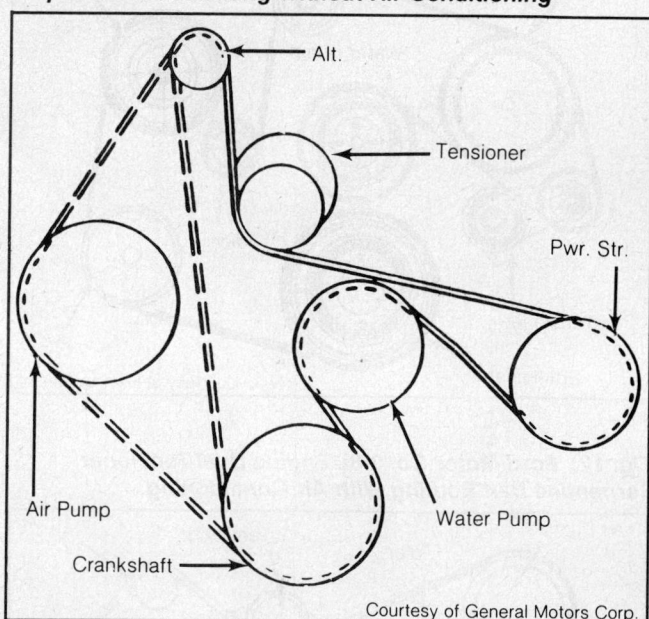

Courtesy of General Motors Corp.

SERPENTINE DRIVE BELTS (Cont.)

Fig. 20: General Motors 2.8L Camaro/Firebird Engine Serpentine Belt Routing With Air Conditioning

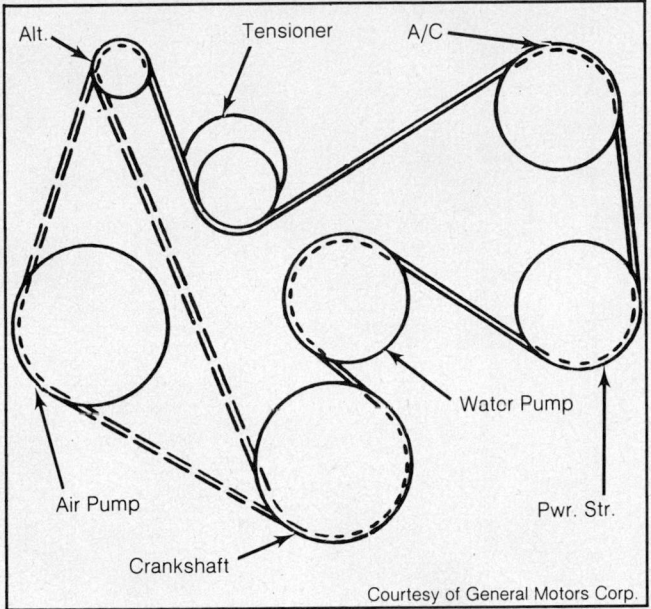

Fig. 22: General Motors 4.5L Engine Serpentine Belt Routing With Air Conditioning

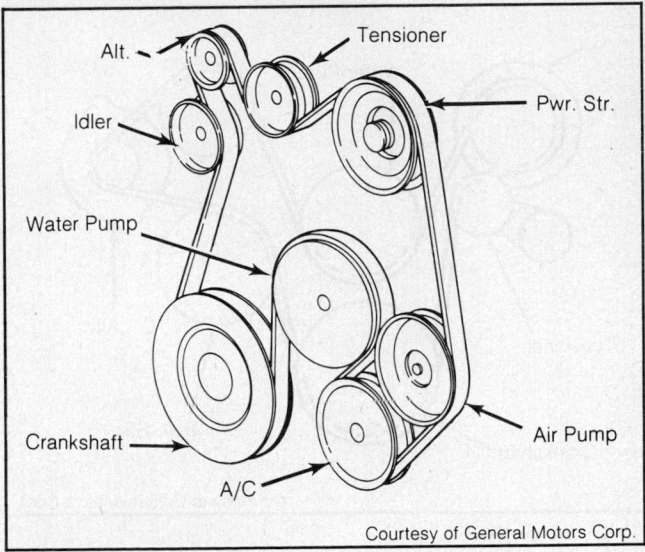

Fig. 21: General Motors 3.8L Engine Serpentine Belt Routing With Air Conditioning

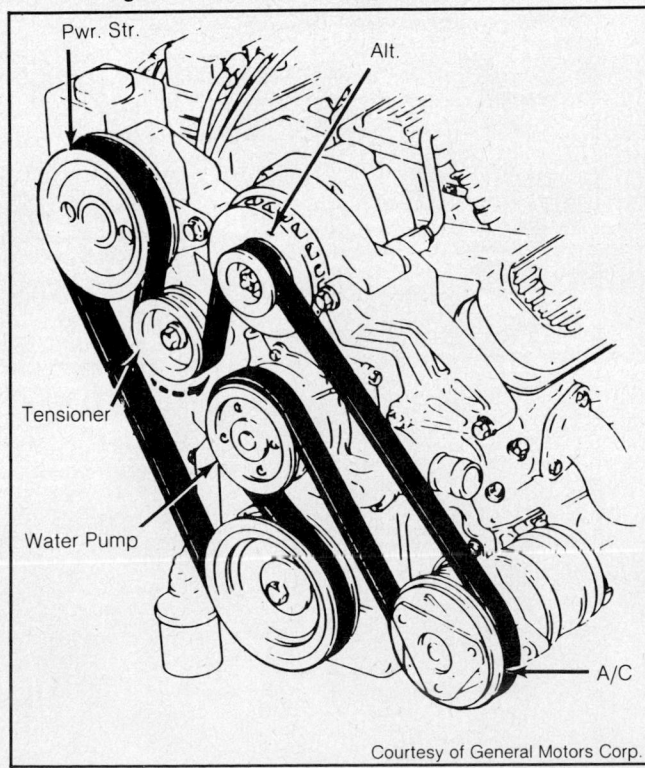

Fig. 23: General Motors 5.0L & 5.7L Engine Serpentine Belt Routing With Air Conditioning

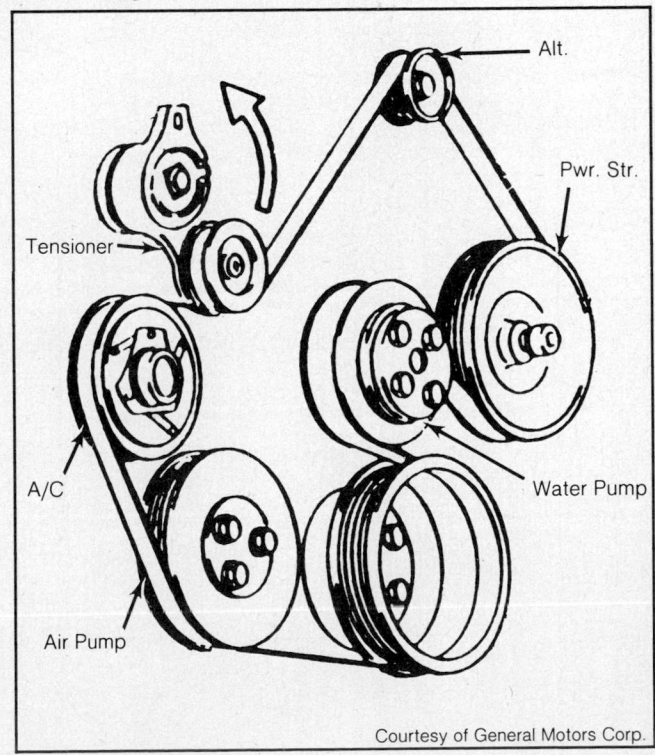

Engine Cooling Systems

SERPENTINE DRIVE BELTS (Cont.)

Fig. 24: *General Motors 5.7L Corvette Engine Serpentine Belt Routing With Air Conditioning*

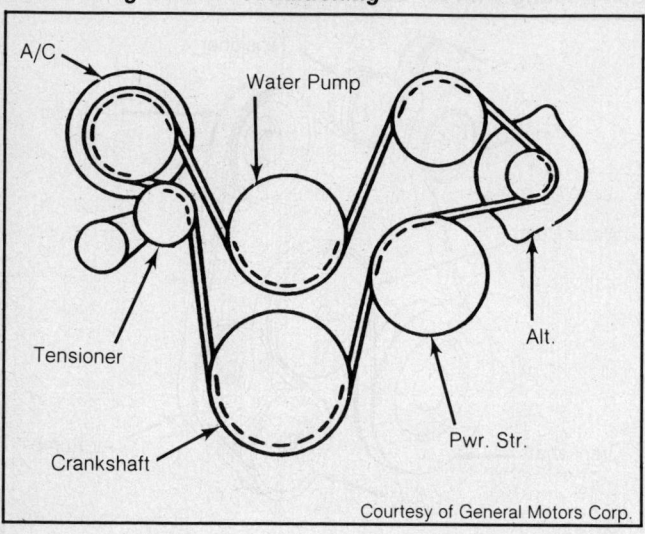

Courtesy of General Motors Corp.

ENGINE COOLANT SPECIFICATIONS

**Chrysler Motors, Eagle Premier,
Ford Motor Co., General Motors**

DESCRIPTION

THERMOSTAT

Most thermostats are thermal wax pellet type. As coolant temperatures rise the wax begins to expand. This expansion over comes spring tension allowing the thermostat to open. Some thermostats also incorporate an additional bleed hole to allow a small amount of circulation and helps eliminate air locks.

PRESSURE CAP

Modern cooling systems use a closed system type cap. This system allows for coolant expansion during engine operation. As coolant expands and builds pressure, some coolant is permitted to bleed past the cap into the over flow tank. When the engine cools and coolant contracts, the cap allows the coolant in the over flow tank to siphon back into the system.

The pressure cap also increases pressure in the cooling system. The increased pressure raises the boiling point, one pound of pressure raises the boiling point approximately 10° F (12.2° C).

COOLANT MIXTURE

Engine coolant must be mixed with water to a specific percent. A 100% coolant mixture could cause system over heating or premature system failure. Coolants are designed to function best when mixed with water. The percentage of coolant to water can vary depending on climate condition, but a 50/50 mixture is a standard percentage.

Engine coolant should also include an aluminum protection additive. This will help protect against metal deterioration.

MAINTENANCE

Periodic maintenance is necessary for extended cooling system and engine life. Because engine and cooling sytems are made of different metals, electrolysis begins to destroy the metals. Changing the coolant at scheduled maintenance periods reduces electrolysis and removes sediment. See COOLANT REPLACEMENT SCHEDULE in this article.

NOTE: Approximate capacity figures are shown. Capacities may vary 15% due to system variations.

COOLING SYSTEM SPECIFICATION

Application	Therm. F° (C°)	Pres. Cap PSI	Coolant Cap. Qts. (L)
CHRYSLER MOTORS			
"P" Body			
2.2L	195 (91)	16	8.5 (8.1)
2.2L Turbo	195 (91)	16	8.5 (8.1)
"C" Body			
2.5L	195 (91)	16	8.0 (7.6)
3.0L	195 (91)	16	9.5 (9.0)

COOLING SYSTEM SPECIFICATION (Cont.)

Application	Therm. F° (C°)	Pres. Cap PSI	Coolant Cap. Qts. (L)
CHRYSLER MOTORS (Cont.)			
All Other FWD	195 (91)	16	9.0 (8.5)
All RWD	195 (91)	16	16.0 (15.1)
EAGLE PREMIER			
2.5L	195 (91)	18	9.6 (9.1)
3.0L	195 (91)	18	9.6 (9.1)
FORD MOTOR CO.			
Continental			
3.8L	197 (91)	16	12.1 (11.5)
Cougar, Thunderbird			
2.3L Turbo	195 (91)	16	8.9 (8.4)
3.8L	195 (91)	16	10.8 (10.2)
5.0L	195 (91)	16	13.4 (12.7)
Escort			
1.9L	192 (89)	16	7.9 (7.5)
1.9L [2]	192 (89)	16	7.9 (7.5)
Victoria, Marquis, Town Car, Wagon			
5.0L	195 (91)	16	14.4 (13.6)
Mark VII			
5.0L [2]	195 (91)	16	14.1 (13.3)
Mustang			
2.3L	192 (89)	16	9.2 (8.7)
5.0L [2]	195 (91)	16	14.1 (13.3)
Sable, Taurus			
2.5L	192 (89)	16	12.1 (11,5)
3.0L	192 (89)	16	12.1 (11.5)
3.8L	195 (91)	16	12.1 (11.5)
Tempo, Topaz			
2.3L HSC	192 (89)	16	8.1 (7.6)
2.3L HSO	192 (89)	16	8.1 (7.6)
GENERAL MOTORS			
"A" Body			
2.5L	195 (91)	15	9.8 (9.2)
2.8L	195 (91)	15	12.6 (12.0)
3.8L	195 (91)	15	13.2 (12.5)
"B" Body			
4.3L	195 (91)	15	12.3 (11.6)
5.0L (H) [1]	195 (91)	15	17.0 (16.1)
5.0L (Y) [1]	195 (91)	15	15.6 (14.8)
5.7L (6) [1]	195 (91)	15	7.0 (16.1)
"C" Body			
3.8L	195 (91)	15	12.4 (11.7)
4.5L	195 (91)	15	10.6 (10.0)
"D" Body			
5.0L	195 (91)	15	15.3 (14.5)
"E" Body			
3.8L	180 (82)	15	12.0 (11.3)
4.5L	195 (91)	15	12.0 (11.3)

[1] – Refers to VIN engine code.
[2] – Refers to H.O. engine.

Engine Cooling Systems

ENGINE COOLANT SPECIFICATIONS (Cont.)

COOLING SYSTEM SPECIFICATION (Cont.)

Application	Therm. F° (C°)	Pres. Cap PSI	Coolant Cap. Qts. (L)
GENERAL MOTORS (Cont.)			
"F" Body			
2.8L	195 (91)	15	12.8 (12.0)
5.0L (E) [1]	195 (91)	15	16.8 (15.9)
5.0L (F) [1]	195 (91)	15	17.2 (16.3)
5.7L (8) [1]	195 (91)	15	17.2 (16.3)
"G" Body			
3.8L	195 (91)	15	13.0 (12.3)
4.3L	195 (91)	15	13.1 (12.4)
5.0L (G) [1][2]	195 (91)	15	16.7 (15.8)
5.0L (H) [1]	195 (91)	15	16.5 (15.6)
5.0L (Y) [1]	195 (91)	15	16.4 (15.5)
"H" Body			
3.8L (3) [1]	195 (91)	15	13.4 (12.6)
3.8L (C) [1]	195 (91)	15	12.4 (11.7)
"J" Body			
2.0L (K) [1]	195 (91)	15	7.9 (7.5)
2.0L (M) [1]	195 (91)	15	7.9 (7.5)
2.0L (1) [1][2]	195 (91)	15	7.9 (7.5)
2.8L	195 (91)	15	11.1 (10.5)
"K" Body			
4.5L	195 (91)	15	12.0 (11.3)
"L" Body			
2.0L [2]	195 (91)	15	14.1 (13.4)
2.8L	195 (91)	15	11.1 (10.5)
"N" Body			
2.0L	195 (91)	15	7.8 (7.4)
2.3L DOHC	192 (89)	15	7.6 (7.2)
2.5L	195 (91)	15	7.8 (7.4)
3.0L	195 (91)	15	10.3 (9.8)
"P" Body			
2.5L	195 (91)	15	13.8 (13.0)
2.8L	195 (91)	15	13.8 (13.0)
"S" Body			
1.6L	180 (82)	13	6.3 (6.0)
1.6L DOHC	180 (82)	13	6.3 (6.0)
"W" Body			
2.8L	195 (91)	15	12.4 (11.7)
"Y" Body			
5.7L	195 (91)	15	14.0 (13.3)

[1] – Refers to VIN engine code.
[2] – Refers to H.O. engine.

COOLANT REPLACEMENT SCHEDULE

Application	Months (Miles)
Chrysler Motors	[1] 36 (52,500)
Eagle Premier – Information not available.	
Ford Motor Co.	36 (30,000)
General Motors	24 (30,000)

[1] – All additional replacement should be 24 months and 30,000 miles.

CHRYSLER MOTORS

HEATER ONLY

RWD MODELS
Removal & Installation

1) Disconnect battery and drain coolant. Disconnect hoses from heater core and plug tubes to prevent leakage to vehicle interior. Disconnect vacuum lines from heater control valve and manifold "T". Push rubber grommet and vacuum lines through instrument panel. Remove 4 nuts holding heater to instrument panel.

2) From passenger compartment, slide seat rearward as far as possible and remove console, if equipped. Remove cluster bezel assembly, instrument panel upper cover and steering column cover. Remove right intermediate side cowl trim panel.

3) Remove lower instrument panel. Remove reinforcement between lower and center instrument panel. If vehicle is equipped with a floor console, remove it. Remove right center air distribution duct. Disconnect locking tab on defroster duct. Disconnect blower motor feed and ground wires.

4) Disconnect vacuum lines from engine compartment heater control valve and vacuum source "T". Remove heat distribution housing. Depress tab on temperature control cable flag and remove cable from receiver on heater housing. Support heater assembly and remove plenum mounting brace.

5) Pull heater assembly back, rotate to the right and remove from under instrument panel. With heater assembly on workbench, remove top cover from heater. Remove screw holding core to housing and lift out core. To install, reverse removal procedure.

NOTE: RWD vehicles use 1/2" (13 mm) and 5/8" (16 mm) heater hoses.

FWD MODELS EXCEPT HORIZON & OMNI
Removal & Installation

1) Disconnect battery negative cable and drain radiator. Disconnect blower motor wiring connector. From under heater assembly, depress tab on mode door and temperature control cables, pull flags from receivers and remove self-adjusting clip from door crank arms.

2) Remove glove box assembly. Disconnect heater hoses on engine side of firewall. Plug hoses and heater core pipes. Remove hanger strap to heater assembly screw by reaching through glove box opening. Remove 2 heater assembly attaching nuts from engine compartment.

NOTE: Blower motor resistor block is located under the upper right side of instrument panel.

3) On Daytona models, remove 2 screws attaching demister adapter to the top of heater assembly. On all models, pull instrument panel outward just enough to allow heater assembly to slide out. Remove heater assembly. To install heater assembly, reverse removal procedure.

HORIZON & OMNI
Removal & Installation

1) Disconnect battery negative cable and drain radiator. Disconnect blower motor wiring connector. Remove ashtray and holder assembly. Depress tab on temperature control cable flag and pull temperature control cable out of receiver on heater assembly.

2) Remove glove box and door assembly. Disconnect heater hoses and plug hoses and heater core pipes. From engine compartment, remove 2 nuts attaching heater assembly to firewall. Remove wire connector from blower motor and resistor block. Disconnect heater assembly brace.

NOTE: Blower motor resistor block is located on right side of heater housing.

3) Remove heater support bracket nut. Disconnect strap from plenum stud. From under instrument panel, lower heater assembly just enough to reach mode control cable. Depress tab on flag and pull mode door control cable out of receiver on heater assembly.

4) Move heater assembly toward right side of vehicle and then lower out from under instrument panel. To install heater assembly, reverse removal procedure.

NOTE: FWD vehicles use 1/2" (13 mm) heater hose.

MANUAL A/C-HEATER

NOTE: Manual A/C-heater systems are only available on FWD vehicles. RWD vehicles have automatic A/C-heater systems.

FWD MODELS EXCEPT HORIZON, OMNI & LEBARON CONVERTIBLE
Removal & Installation

1) Discharge system. Drain engine coolant. Disconnect battery fusible link. Disconnect heater hoses at heater core. Plug heater core tube openings.

2) Disconnect vacuum lines at engine intake manifold and heater control valve. Remove right scuff plate and cowl side trim panel. Remove condensate drain tube.

3) On "J" and "C" bodies, remove right upper and lower underpanel silencers. On "E" bodies and LeBaron with passive restraint, remove right underpanel lower trim. On "P", "H" and "C" bodies, remove steering wheel column cover.

4) On "G" bodies and LeBaron with passive restraint, remove outer steering column cover as well as hood release and parking brake release handles from inner steering column cover. Remove inner steering column cover and position right front seat to the full back position.

5) On LeBaron with passive restraint and "C" bodies, remove left underpanel silencer. On "P" bodies, remove right A-pillar trim and right cowl side trim. On "J" bodies, pull back right A pillar trim to remove right side cowl trim.

6) On all models, remove glove box. On "G" bodies, LeBaron with passive restraint, "H" and "C" bodies, remove instrument panel reinforcement. On "P", "K" and "E" bodies, remove right instrument panel roll-up screw.

7) On "G" and "J" bodies, remove forward console bezel, side trim and lower carpet panels. Loosen floor console and move rearward. Remove forward console. On LeBaron with passive restraint only, remove instrument panel to floor reinforcement.

Heater Core Replacement

CHRYSLER MOTORS (Cont.)

8) On "P" bodies, remove center bezel and lower center module cover. Remove floor console. Remove instrument panel support brace between steering column opening and right lower side of instrument panel. Remove instrument panel support panel below glove box. Remove ashtray and radio. Remove instrument panel top cover. Remove 3 right side (below windshield) panel attaching screws.

9) On "E" bodies, remove forward console and mounting bracket. On "K" bodies, remove floor console. On "H" bodies, remove front and rear consoles. On "C" bodies, remove ashtray.

10) On "P", "K" and "E" bodies, pull right lower side of instrument panel rearward. Remove center distribution and defroster adapter duct. On "P", "C" and "H" bodies, disconnect relay module. On "P" bodies, remove instrument panel to A/C unit bracket. Remove lower air distribution duct.

11) On "K" and "E" bodies, remove audible message center and right side cowl to plenum brace. Disconnect blower motor wire connector and demister hose from top of unit. On "K" and "E" bodies, with Automatic Climate Control (ATC), remove temperature control cable from control unit and move out of way. Disconnect vacuum lines at control unit.

12) On "K" and "E" bodies with ATC, disconnect instrument panel wiring from rear face of ATC unit. On "C" and "H" bodies, disconnect 25-way connector bracket and fuse block from instrument panel. On "H" bodies, remove cable from retaining clip on top of unit. On "G" and "J" bodies, remove cable from retaining clip on rear face of unit.

13) On all bodies except "C" and "H", fold back right side carpet and remove 4 unit mounting nuts. Remove unit strap lower mounting screw and rotate strap out of way. Move heater-A/C unit rearward to clear studs and lower unit.

14) On "P" bodies, remove demister adapter from top of unit. While pulling back on lower right side of instrument panel, slide unit upright and out from under instrument panel. On all bodies except "P", rotate unit while pulling out from under dash.

15) To remove heater and evaporator cores, remove unit top cover. Remove heater core to dash panel seal from heater core tubes, and remove heater core. Remove expansion valve sealing plate seal retaining screw. Remove evaporator core. To install, reverse removal procedures.

LEBARON CONVERTIBLE
Removal & Installation

NOTE: To remove A/C-Heater unit from LeBaron Convertibles, follow the steps outlined above, in addition to the following steps.

1) Remove floor distribution duct from housing. Remove upper instrument panel pad. Remove instrument panel mounting screws along windshield. Using 2 people, lift up on instrument panel while pulling evaporator/heater unit backward and rolling it out from under instrument panel.

2) To remove heater and evaporator cores, remove unit top cover. Remove heater core to dash panel seal from heater core tubes, and remove heater core. Remove expansion valve sealing plate seal retaining screw. Remove evaporator core. To install, reverse removal procedures.

HORIZON & OMNI
Removal & Installation

1) Discharge refrigerant from system. Drain engine coolant. Disconnect negative battery cable. Disconnect blend air door cable and disengage from retaining clip on air duct. Remove glove box. Disconnect center distribution duct.

2) Remove defroster duct adapter. Disconnect heater hoses and A/C lines at dash panel. Plug openings of all lines and hoses. Disconnect vacuum lines at engine and water valve. From engine compartment, remove 4 mounting nuts that attach unit to firewall.

3) Remove right side cowl trim. Remove right side instrument panel pivot bracket screw. Remove 2 screws securing lower instrument panel at steering column. Remove panel top cover. Remove all but left panel fenceline (along windshield) attaching screws. Pull back carpet from under A/C unit as far back as possible.

4) Remove support strap nut and blower motor ground cable. While supporting unit with hands, remove support strap from its mounting stud. Using 2 people lift up on unit and and pull it as far rearward as possible, to clear dash panel and liner. Also at this time panel will need to be pulled rearward to allow unit removal clearance.

5) Slowly lower unit taking care to prevent dash attachment studs from catching in dash liner. Continue lowering unit until it reaches floorboard and then slide entire unit out.

NOTE: When reinstalling A/C-heater unit, be careful that vacuum lines to engine compartment do not get hung up on the accelerator or become trapped between the unit and the dash. Proper routing of these lines during installation, may require 2 people. Also the portion of the vacuum harness that is routed through steering column must be positioned before the distribution housing is reinstalled. Vacuum harness is routed above the temperature control cable.

6) To remove heater and evaporator cores, remove unit top cover. Remove heater core to dash panel seal from heater core tubes, and remove heater core. Remove expansion valve sealing plate seal retaining screw. Remove evaporator core. To install, reverse removal procedures.

SEMI-AUTOMATIC A/C-HEATER (TEMPERATURE CONTROL)

RWD MODELS

NOTE: Evaporator-heater housing assembly must be removed from vehicle to service evaporator coil or heater core.

Removal & Installation

1) Discharge refrigerant and disconnect battery. Drain cooling system and remove air cleaner. Disconnect heater hoses, and plug heater core tubes. Remove "H" valve, and cap all refrigerant openings. Slide front seat to rear as far as possible.

2) Remove instrument cluster and instrument panel upper cover. Remove steering column cover, right intermediate side cowl trim panel, and lower instrument

CHRYSLER MOTORS (Cont.)

panel. Remove center instrument panel, lower reinforcement and floor console (if equipped).

3) Remove right center air distribution duct, and disconnect locking tab on defroster duct. Disconnect blower motor resistor block wiring.

4) Disconnect vacuum lines from water valve and vacuum source. Remove wiring from evaporator housing. Remove vacuum lines from inlet air housing and vacuum harness coupling.

5) Remove drain tube and housing mounting nuts. Remove hanger strap from plenum stud. Roll evaporator assembly back to clear dash panel, and remove assembly from vehicle.

6) With evaporator-heater housing assembly on bench, remove servomotor from shaft. Remove screw from top cover and lift off cover.

7) Remove mounting flange screw located behind core seal. Lift heater core or evaporator coil out of housing. To install, reverse removal procedure.

ELECTRONIC AUTOMATIC TEMPERATURE CONTROL

FWD MODELS

Removal & Installation

1) Disconnect negative battery cable. Discharge refrigerant from A/C system using a manifold gauge set. Drain coolant from radiator. Remove heater hoses from heater core. Plug heater core tubes to prevent spillage during removal. Disconnect vacuum lines from intake manifold and water valve.

2) Remove right scuff plate from upper quarter trim panel. Remove right cowl side trim panel. Remove glove box assembly. Remove automatic temperature control panel. Remove upper instrument panel pad.

3) Remove instrument panel mounting screws along windshield. If equipped, remove console assembly and mounting bracket. Remove 2 center duct assembly mounting screws. Remove center duct assembly. Remove floor air duct from A/C-heater housing.

4) Remove defroster adapter duct. Remove drain tube from evaporator. Disconnect electrical connectors. Remove right side cowl-to-plenum brace. Pull carpet away from A/C-heater housing. Remove hanger-to-housing mounting screws.

5) Remove 4 A/C-heater mounting nuts from inside engine compartment. Lift up on dash assembly and pull A/C-heater housing out until mounting studs clear dash liner. Remove A/C-heater housing from vehicle. Remove heater core from housing. Reverse procedure for installation.

EAGLE PREMIER

HEATER ONLY

EAGLE PREMIER

Removal & Installation

1) Disconnect battery negative cable. Remove 3 screws attaching instrument panel lower trim cover. Remove 2 screws attaching instument panel support rod. Remove screw attaching steering column wiring harness bulkhead connector.

2) Using screwdriver, disconnect automatic transaxle shift cable from lever. Compress shift cable retainer tangs with pliers and slide cable out of column mounting bracket. Remove cable anchoring bracket. Remove shift indicator cable from pulley on shift lever.

3) Pull plastic sleeve at base of steering column down, exposing steering column universal joint. Make a reference mark on the steering column shaft and intermediate shaft. Remove bolt from intermediate shaft universal joint.

4) Remove bolts and nuts that attach steering column to instrument panel. Carefully lower column assembly to vehicle floor. Separate steering shaft from intermediate shaft. Remove steering column.

5) Remove defroster grille. Remove 4 bolts visible through defroster grille opening. Loosen 2 nuts attaching instrument panel to kick panels. Remove screws attaching parking brake release handle and then lower handle. Remove ashtray and cigarette lighter.

6) Remove screw in ashtray cavity. Remove bolt from brake master cylinder mounting bracket. Disconnect all electrical connections. Remove 2 bolts attaching instrument panel to center floor bracket. Carefully lift up

and rearward to disengage and remove instrument panel. remove rear floor duct extension.

7) Drain cooling system. Squeeze and slide heater hose clamps and remove hoses.

NOTE: **Heater core spouts are made of plastic and may break if too much pressure is applied.**

8) Disconnect coolant reservoir level switch connector. Remove coolant reservoir retaining strap and move reservoir aside. remove coolant reservoir mounting bracket bolts and remove bracket.

9) Disconnect blower motor connector. Disconnect vacuum hose. Remove 4 exterior and 2 interior nuts attaching blower housing to firewall. Carefully pull heater housing rearward to remove it from vehicle.

10) To install, reverse removal procedure. Fill cooling system. Ensure that shift indicator aligns with proper gear. If not, adjust shift control cable at anchor bracket.

AUTOMATIC A/C-HEATER

EAGLE PREMIER

Removal & Installation

1) Disconnect negative battery cable. Remove screw attaching instrument panel lower trim cover. Remove 2 screws that attach instrument panel support rod and remove rod. Remove 5 screws attaching steering column wiring harness bulkhead connector.

2) Disconnect automatic transaxle shift cable from lever and remove. Compress cable retaining tangs

Heater Core Replacement

EAGLE PREMIER (Cont.)

and slide cable out of column mounting bracket. Loosen screw retaining cable mounting bracket, slide and remove. Lift indicator wire off pulley and remove.

3) Pull plastic steering column sleeve down to expose column "U" joint. Mark shaft and remove retaining bolt to remove steering column at "U" joint. Remove column support nuts and bolts that hold steering column to instrument panel/brake sled.

4) Carefully lower steering column assembly to vehicle floor. Separate steering column shaft from intermediate shaft. Remove column assembly from vehicle. Remove defroster grille. Remove bolts at base of windshield. Loosen but do not remove nut located on parking brake release handle. Remove retaining nut located on passenger side kick panel.

5) Remove screw retaining lower parking brake release lever handle. Remove ashtray. Disconnect cigarette lighter connector. Remove screw from ashtray cavity. Remove bolt from brake sled. Disconnect all electrical harnesses.

6) Remove bolts that hold instrument panel to center floor bracket. Disconnect interior temperature sensor. Carefully lift up and rearward to remove instrument panel. Remove floor duct extentsion. Drain cooling system and discharge A/C system.

CAUTION: Do not apply excessive pressure to the plastic heater core outlet tubes, or damage may occur.

7) Remove heater hoses from heater core outlet tubes. Disconnect coolant level switch connector. Remove coolant reservoir retaining strap. Remove reservoir mounting bracket. Disconnect blower motor connector.

8) Disconnect vacuum hose. Disconnect refrigerant lines at dash panel. Remove unit mounting nuts from firewall. From inside vehicle, remove A/C-Heater housing mounting nuts and carefully pull rearward to remove.

9) Remove heating and A/C housing. Remove plastic tabs and lift out heater core. To remove evaporator core, remove A/C-heater housing. Disconnect harness from Air Control Module (ACM).

10) Remove mounting screws and ACM from vehicle. While unlocking retaining tabs, remove motor arm from door pivot arm. Remove spring "L" and clear vacuum line from motor. Lift up and pull hose out of its hole in housing. Disengage tabs that retain heater core and remove core.

11) Remove foam gasket "M" and "N". Pry off retaining clip and disconnect wires from blower motor. Remove blower motor mounting screws and blower motor. Remove retaining screws from upper and lower halves of evaporator case.

12) Remove clips and separate halves. Remove evaporator core. To install, reverse removal procedure. Add 3 ounces (88.7 mm) of refrigerant oil to evaporator. Evacuate, recharge, and leak test system. Check system for proper operation.

FORD MOTOR CO.

HEATER ONLY

ESCORT

Removal & Installation

1) Drain cooling system. Disconnect heater hoses and plug openings. Remove glove box liner.

2) Move temperature control lever to "WARM" position. Remove heater core cover screws. Remove cover through glove box opening. From inside engine compartment, remove heater case mounting stud nuts.

3) Push heater core tubes and seal toward passenger compartment to loosen core from case. Pull heater core out through glove box area. To install, reverse removal procedure.

TEMPO & TOPAZ

Removal & Installation

1) Drain cooling system. Disconnect heater hoses and plug openings. From inside of vehicle, remove 2 screws retaining floor duct to plenum. Remove 2 screws retaining floor duct to instrument panel. Remove floor duct.

2) Remove 4 screws attaching heater core cover to heater case. Remove heater core cover and heater core from plenum. To install, reverse removal procedure.

MUSTANG

Removal

1) Disconnect negative battery cable. Drain coolant from radiator. Disconnect heater hoses from heater core. Plug heater core tubes. Disconnect vacuum

supply hose from inside engine compartment. Remove instrument panel. See REMOVAL & INSTALLATION – INSTRUMENT PANEL in this article.

2) Remove bracket screw connecting air inlet duct and blower housing bracket to cowl top panel. Disconnect vacuum line and blower electrical connector. Remove 2 underhood nuts attaching heater assembly to dash panel. Remove one upper and one lower heater case bracket mounting screws. Carefully remove heater case from vehicle.

Disassembly

Remove 4 access cover screws from heater case. Remove heater core from heater case.

Installation

Install heater core. Install access cover. Reverse removal procedure for installation. Fill radiator with coolant and start engine. Check system operation.

SABLE

Removal & Installation

1) Disconnect negative battery cable. Remove 4 retaining screws at bottom of steering column. Remove steering column trim. Disconnect all electrical connectors from steering column. Remove bolt and nut from "U" joint pillar. Remove 4 steering column bracket retaining screws.

2) Remove lower trim panel. Remove 5 instrument panel retaining screws. Rock upper edge of panel toward driver and remove panel. Depress side of glove box and remove. Disconnect electrical connectors, vacu-

FORD MOTOR CO. (Cont.)

um hoses, A/C-heater control cables and radio antenna cable.

3) Disconnect underhood electrical connectors from main wire loom. Remove rubber grommets from instrument panel. Feed underhood electrical connectors into instrument panel area. Remove bolt attaching instrument panel to floor brace.

4) Remove 2 bolts retaining lower instrument panel to side cowl. Remove both speaker covers and defroster grilles. Remove 3 upper instrument panel mounting screws. Remove instrument panel.

5) Reverse procedure for installation. Connect all electrical and vacuum connections before installing instrument panel.

6) Remove bracket screw connecting instrument panel to heater case. Remove 2 screws mounting floor outlet to heater case. Remove floor outlet. Remove 3 heater case mounting nuts. Remove 2 upper heater case bracket mounting screws.

7) Carefully remove heater case from vehicle. Remove 4 access cover screws from heater case. Remove heater core from heater case.

TAURUS
Removal & Installation

1) Disconnect negative battery cable. Remove 4 steering column cover screws. Remove cover. Remove sound insulator from cowl area. Remove steering column trim cover. Disconnect all electrical connectors from steering column.

2) Remove 4 steering column bracket mounting bolts. Lower steering column. Remove 2 lower trim screws. Unsnap left and right lower trim and remove. Remove 7 instrument panel trim retaining screws. Remove jam nut from behind headlight switch knob.

3) Remove screws from behind clock or clock cover. Release panel by rocking upper edge of panel toward driver position. Swing fuse panel downward and disconnect speedometer cable. Disconnect all electrical, vacuum hoses, radio antenna cable and control cables from instrument panel.

4) Disconnect underhood connections from wire harness. Disconnect main wire harness from instrument panel. Feed engine compartment connectors through grommet hole into instrument panel area. Remove 2 screws retaining lower instrument panel to side cowl.

5) Remove 2 instrument panel retaining screws from under radio. Snap out both radio speaker covers from instrument panel. Remove 3 upper instrument panel retaining screws. Remove instrument panel.

6) Remove bracket screw connecting instrument panel to heater case. Remove 2 screws mounting floor outlet to heater case. Remove floor outlet. Remove 3 heater case mounting nuts. Remove 2 upper heater case bracket mounting screws.

7) Carefully remove heater case from vehicle. Remove 4 access cover screws from heater case. Remove heater core from heater case.

8) Reverse procedure for installation. Connect all electrical and vacuum connections before installing instrument panel.

MANUAL A/C-HEATER
COUGAR & THUNDERBIRD
Removal

1) Disconnect ground cable from battery. Disconnect all underhood wiring connectors from main wiring harnesses. Disengage rubber grommet seat from dash panel and push wiring harness and connectors through into passenger compartment. Remove 3 screws attaching steering column opening cover to instrument panel. Remove 2 screws retaining both right and left lower finish panels.

2) Pull panel rearward to disengage clips and remove both right and left side sound insulator covers. Remove 2 nuts retaining hood latch release handle mounting bracket to brake pedal support below steering column. Remove both right and left side cowl side trim covers. Disconnect emergency brake cable from instrument panel.

3) Remove 10 screws attaching cluster opening finish panel. If NOT equipped with a center console, open ashtray and remove 2 screws. Remove 4 center finish panel retaining screws. If equipped with console, remove both front finish panels from console. Remove steering brace assemblies and disconnect all wiring harness connectors from steering column.

4) If equipped with column mounted shift, disconnect shift indicator cable from steering column by unhooking cable from shifting lever. Remove 4 mounting bracket-to-brake pedal support nuts below steering column. Allow steering column to rest on front seat. Remove radio speaker grilles and center access cover.

5) Remove 3 upper cowl retaining screws. Remove push nuts attaching glove box straps to glove box. Allow glove box and door to hang by hinge. Remove nut attaching instrument panel brace to instrument panel through glove box opening. Remove 2 side cowl retaining screws. Lift instrument panel away from cowl and remove or disconnect remaining A/C control and/or wire connectors.

6) Lay instrument panel on front seat. Drain cooling system. Discharge refrigerant from system using a manifold gauge set. Disconnect high and low pressure hoses from evaporator core tube fittings. Cap evaporator tube openings.

7) Remove heater hoses from heater core. Plug hoses and core. Remove screw attaching air inlet duct and housing assembly support brace to top cowl panel. Disconnect vacuum supply hose (black) from in-line vacuum check valve in engine compartment). Disconnect blower motor wiring and wiring harness from resistor.

8) Remove 2 nuts retaining evaporator case to dash panel, located inside rear engine compartment. Remove screws located under dash attaching evaporator case support to cowl top panel. Remove screws or nuts retaining the bracket below evaporator case to the dash panel. Carefully pull evaporator case away from dash panel and remove evaporator case assembly from vehicle.

9) To remove evaporator core, remove air inlet duct and blower housing from evaporator case. Drill a 3/16" hole in both upright tabs on top of evaporator case. Using a small blade saw, cut top of evaporator case. Remove evaporator core.

10) To remove heater core, remove 5 screws attaching heater core cover to top of evaporator case.

Remove heater core cover. Lift heater core and seals from evaporator case. Remove 2 seals from heater core tubes.

Installation
To install, reverse removal procedure. Install spring nuts to evaporator case, if evaporator was removed. Evacuate, leak test and recharge system. Check system for proper operation.

CROWN VICTORIA & GRAND MARQUIS
Removal
1) Disconnect ground cable from battery. Drain coolant from radiator. Disconnect heater hoses from heater core. Cap heater hoses.

2) Remove bolt attaching left end of plenum to dash panel. Remove nut retaining upper left corner of evaporator case to dash panel.

3) Disconnect control system vacuum supply hose from vacuum source and push grommet and vacuum supply hose into passenger compartment. Remove glove box.

4) Loosen right door sill plate and remove right side cowl trim panel. Remove bolt attaching lower right end of instrument panel to side cowl.

5) Remove 2 screws attaching instrument panel pad to instrument panel at each defroster opening. Remove screw attaching each outboard end of pad to instrument panel.

6) On Crown Victoria models, remove pad attaching screw near upper right corner of glove box. Remove 5 screws attaching lower edge of pad to instrument panel. Remove pad.

7) Disengage temperature control cable housing from bracket on top of plenum. Disconnect cable from temperature blend door crank arm.

8) Disconnect vacuum harness at multiple vacuum connector near floor air distribution duct. Disconnect White vacuum hose from outside-recirculation door vacuum motor.

9) Remove 2 screws attaching passenger side of floor air distribution duct to plenum. It may be necessary to remove 2 screws attaching lower panel door vacuum motor to mounting bracket to gain access to right screw.

10) Remove one plastic push fastener retaining floor air distribution duct to left end of plenum. Remove floor air distribution duct.

11) Remove 2 nuts from 2 studs along lower edge of plenum. Remove plenum assembly. Remove 4 retaining screws from heater core cover. Remove cover.

12) Remove retaining screw from heater core inlet and outlet tube bracket. Remove heater core and seal assembly from plenum assembly.

Installation
To install, reverse removal procedure.

MUSTANG
Removal
1) Disconnect negative battery cable. Discharge refrigerant from A/C system using a manifold gauge set. Remove instrument pad. Remove steering column lower cover. Remove steering column trim panel. Remove 4 steering column to brake pedal support bracket attaching nuts.

2) Lower steering column. On models with automatic transmission, remove shift selector cable from shift selector lever. Remove cable clamp from steering column tube. On all models, remove lower instrument panel mounting screws. Disconnect temperature control cable from evaporator case and temperature blend door. Disconnect 7-port vacuum connector from evaporator case.

3) Disconnect blower motor and resistor electrical connectors. Remove instrument panel to side cowl mounting screws. Pull instrument panel toward passenger compartment. Disconnect electrical connectors and speedometer cable from instrument panel. Remove instrument panel. Disconnect A/C lines from evaporator core. Plug A/C lines.

4) Disconnect heater hoses from heater core. Plug heater hoses and heater core tubes. Remove blower housing support brace mounting screw. Disconnect Black vacuum supply hose from in-line check valve, inside engine compartment. Remove 2 evaporator case mounting nuts. Remove 2 evaporator case to upper cowl mounting screws. Remove evaporator case.

5) To remove evaporator core, remove 4 air inlet duct to evaporator case attaching screws. Drill a 3/16" hole in both upright tabs on top of evaporator case. Remove blower motor resistor. Using a small blade saw, cut top of evaporator case. Remove evaporator core.

6) To remove heater core, remove evaporator case using steps 1) thru 4). Remove 5 heater core cover attaching screws. Remove heater core.

Installation
To install, reverse removal procedure. Install spring nuts to evaporator case, if evaporator core was removed. Evacuate, leak test and recharge system.

TAURUS
Removal
1) Disconnect negative battery cable. Remove 4 steering column cover screws. Remove cover. Remove sound insulator from cowl area. Remove steering column trim cover. Disconnect all electrical connectors from steering column.

2) Remove 4 steering column bracket mounting bolts. Lower steering column. Remove 2 lower trim screws. Unsnap left and right lower trim and remove. Remove 7 instrument panel trim retaining screws. Remove jam nut from behind headlamp switch knob.

3) Remove screws from behind clock or clock cover. Release panel by rocking upper edge of panel toward driver position. Swing fuse panel downward and disconnect speedometer cable. Disconnect all electrical, vacuum hoses, radio antenna cable and control cable from instrument panel.

4) Disconnect underhood connections from wire harness. Disconnect main wire harness from instrument panel. Feed engine compartment connectors through grommet hole into instrument panel area. Remove 2 lower instrument panel to side cowl retaining screws from both sides.

5) Remove 2 instrument panel retaining screws from underneath radio. Snap out both radio speaker covers from instrument panel. Remove 3 upper instrument panel retaining screws. Remove instrument panel.

6) Remove vacuum source line from heater core tube seal. Remove heater core tube seal. Remove 4 heater core access cover mounting screws. Remove heater core access cover. Remove heater core from evaporator case.

FORD MOTOR CO. (Cont.)

Installation

Reverse procedure for installation. Connect all electrical and vacuum connections before installing instrument panel.

SABLE

Removal

1) Disconnect negative battery cable. Remove 4 retaining screws at bottom of steering column. Remove steering column trim. Disconnect all electrical connections from steering column. Remove bolt and nut from U-joint pillar. Remove 4 steering column bracket retaining screws.

2) Remove lower trim panel. Remove 5 instrument panel retaining screws. Rock upper edge of panel toward driver and remove panel. Depress side of glove box and remove. Disconnect electrical connections, vacuum hoses, A/C-heater control cables and radio antenna cable.

3) Disconnect underhood electrical connectors from main wire loom. Remove rubber grommets from dash panel. Feed underhood electrical connectors into instrument panel area. Remove instrument panel to floor brace attaching bolt.

4) Remove 2 lower instrument panel to side cowl bolts. Remove both speaker covers and defroster grilles. Remove 3 upper instrument panel mounting screws. Remove instrument panel.

5) Remove vacuum source line from heater core tube seal. Remove heater core tube seal. Remove 4 heater core access cover mounting screws. Remove heater core access cover. Remove heater core from evaporator case.

Installation

Reverse procedure for installation. Connect all electrical and vacuum connections before installing instrument panel.

AUTOMATIC A/C-HEATER

CROWN VICTORIA, GRAND MARQUIS & TOWN CAR

Removal & Installation

1) Disconnect ground cable from battery. Drain coolant from radiator. Disconnect heater hoses from heater core. Cap heater hoses.

2) Remove bolt, located below windshield wiper motor attaching left end of plenum to dash panel. Remove nut retaining upper left corner of evaporator case to dash panel.

3) Disconnect control system vacuum supply hose from vacuum source and push grommet and vacuum supply into passenger compartment. Remove glove box.

4) Loosen right door sill plate and remove right side cowl trim panel. Remove bolt attaching lower right end of instrument panel to side cowl.

5) Remove 2 screws attaching instrument panel pad to instrument panel at each defroster opening. Remove screw attaching each outboard end of pad to instrument panel.

6) On Crown Victoria models, remove pad attaching screw near upper right corner of glove box. Remove 5 screws attaching lower edge of pad to instrument panel. Remove pad.

7) Disengage temperature control cable housing from ATC sensor. Disconnect vacuum connector from ATC sensor. Disconnect eletrical plug from ATC servo plug.

8) Disconnect ATC sensor tube from sensor and evaporator case connector. Disconnect vacuum harness at multiple vacuum connector near floor air distribution duct.

9) Disconnect White vacuum hose from outside-recirculation door vacuum motor. Remove 2 screws attaching passenger side of floor air distribution duct to plenum. It may be necessary to remove 2 screws attaching lower panel door vacuum motor to mounting bracket to gain access to right screw.

10) Remove plastic push fastener retaining floor air distribution duct to left end of plenum. Remove floor air distribution duct.

11) Remove 2 nuts from 2 studs along lower edge of plenum. Remove plenum assembly. Remove 4 retaining screws from heater core cover. Remove cover.

12) Remove retaining screw from heater core inlet and outlet tube bracket. Remove heater core and seal assembly from plenum assembly. To install, reverse removal procedure.

ELECTRONIC AUTOMATIC TEMPERATURE CONTROL

COUGAR & THUNDERBIRD

Removal & Installation

1) Discharge A/C system. Disconnect negative battery cable and remove air cleaner. Disconnect heater hoses from heater core. Plug heater hoses. Disconnect wiring harness from pressure switch on receiver-drier.

2) Disconnect refrigerant lines at evaporator core. Cap all openings. Remove receiver-drier and set liquid lines aside. Remove 2 evaporator case retaining nuts (on engine compartment side of firewall).

3) Remove steering column cover from instrument panel. Remove left/right instrument panel sound insulators. Remove left/right cowl trim panels. Remove ashtray. Remove 2 screws securing instrument panel to floor brace.

4) Remove steering column shroud. Disconnect transmission indicator cable from steering column. Remove instrument panel. Unplug blower motor connectors. Disconnect in-vehicle temperature sensor hose from elbow evaporator case.

5) Unplug connectors from control panel. Disconnect radio antenna cable from radio. Cut carpeting along top of transmission tunnel (stop at instrument panel attaching bracket).

6) Fold carpet back to expose rear seat heater duct. Cut top and side from rear seat heater duct. Remove top from floor duct. Remove 3 screws and evaporator case.

7) Remove steering column opening cover. Remove screws from lower left/right instrument panel finish panels. Carefully pull on upper portion of finish panels to disengage panels from instrument panel.

8) Remove parking brake and hood release cables. Remove left/right insulator and cowl trim panels. Remove 10 screws attaching instrument cluster finish panel.

Heater Core Replacement

FORD MOTOR CO. (Cont.)

9) If vehicle is NOT equipped with center console, open ashtray and remove 2 outboard screws inside ashtray opening. On all models, remove 4 center finish panel screws.

10) Remove steering column braces and disconnect wiring from steering column. Disconnect transmission shift indicator lever cable and plastic adjustment ring clamp from steering column (if equipped).

11) Remove 4 nuts attaching steering column to brake pedal support. Lower and rest steering column on front seat. Remove radio speaker grilles and center access cover by disengaging them from clips.

12) Remove 3 cowl top retaining screws. Open glove box, disengage stops, and allow glove box door to hang by hinge. Working through glove box opening, remove nut attaching brace to center reinforcement.

13) Remove side cowl attaching screws. Pull instrument panel away from cowl. Disconnect wiring harness and control cables as required to remove instrument panel and evaporator case.

14) Remove 5 screws attaching heater core cover to top of evaporator case. Remove heater core cover. Lift heater core and seals from evaporator case. Remove 2 seals from heater core tubes. To install, reverse removal procedure.

MARK VII
Removal & Installation

1) Discharge A/C system. Disconnect negative battery cable and remove air cleaner. Drain radiator coolant. Remove heater hoses from heater core. Plug hoses and heater core tubes. Disconnect wiring from pressure switch on top of receiver-drier.

2) Disconnect refrigerant lines at evaporator core. Cap all openings. Remove receiver-drier and set liquid lines aside. Remove 2 evaporator case retaining nuts (on engine compartment side of firewall).

3) Disconnect main wiring harness on engine compartment side. Disengage rubber grommet from firewall. Feed main wiring harness and connectors through opening and into instrument panel area.

4) Remove steering column opening trim cover. Remove left/right sound insulators from under instrument panel. From driver's side floor duct outlet, locate and remove demister feed "Y" connector.

5) Remove hood release handle. Remove left/right cowl trim panels. Remove 5 screws and steering column trim shrouds. Disconnect wiring from steering column.

6) Remove 4 nuts attaching steering column to brake pedal support. Lower and rest steering column on front seat. Remove defroster grille from top of instrument panel. Grille is held in position by 3 tabs.

7) Remove glove compartment door lock bezel from center console. Pull rear of front finish panel up and rearward to disengage from front clips. Disconnect cigarette lighter and light connectors. Remove front finish panel from console.

8) Remove nuts attaching front console bracket to instrument panel. Remove 2 screws attaching front console bracket to floor. Pull carpet back at front edges of console.

9) Detach Velcro fasteners to gain access to 2 screws securing console to instrument panel. Remove screws. Remove 4 screws securing switch plate to console base.

10) Disconnect wiring and shift cable (if equipped) from center console. Open console door and remove cover in bottom of tray (snaps out) to gain access to rear console screws. Remove screws and slide console back.

11) Remove screw attaching instrument panel to floor. Remove 2 screws attaching panel to cowl. Remove nut attaching panel to steering column support bracket. Disconnect wiring harness from behind instrument panel, steering column support, blower motor, and right cowl area.

12) Disconnect radio antenna and vacuum hoses attached to instrument panel. Remove 3 screws and instrument panel from firewall. To install, reverse removal procedure.

CONTINENTAL
Removal & Installation

1) Disconnect negative battery cable. Drain cooling system and discharge A/C system. Disconnect hoses from heater core. Plug heater core tubes and blow out coolant from core.

2) Disconnect vacuum supply hose from in-line vacuum check valve in engine compartment. Disconnect liquid line and accumulator from evaporator core. Plug all openings.

3) Remove 4 screws and lower steering column cover. Remove 3 screws and upper steering column shroud. Remove screw and tilt-wheel lever.

4) Insert a small Allen wrench into groove located beneath lock cylinder. Place key into ignition and gently wiggle lock cylinder free. Pull out lower steering column shroud.

5) Remove screws securing steering wheel horn pad and disconnect wiring. Remove 15 mm bolt and steering wheel. Remove bolt retaining shift indicator cable to steering column.

6) Unplug electrical connectors under instrument panel. Disconnect hood and brake release cables. Remove 3 plastic retainers, from each side, holding right/left close-out panels in place. Remove close-out panels. Disconnect ignition switch wiring.

7) Remove lower "U" joint retention nuts and pull shaft away from steering column. Remove 4 nuts and lower steering column. Remove screw and clip retaining shift cable. Unplug vacuum and electrical connectors and remove steering column from vehicle.

8) Remove center finish panel molding by releasing from 5 clips. Remove left finish panel retaining screws and panel. Unplug light sockets and electrical connectors.

9) Remove 5 screws retaining instrument cluster finish panel and snap out to release. Unplug light socket and electrical connectors. Remove right finish panel retaining screws and panel. Unplug electrical connectors.

10) Remove 4 screws securing radio and storage bin. Unplug electrical connectors. Remove 4 screws securing A/C control panel. Unplug vacuum and electrical connectors.

11) Remove screws and instrument cluster reinforcement brace. Remove 4 screws retaining instrument cluster. Unplug electrical connectors at cluster. Remove 3 screws, 2 plastic clips, and glove box assembly.

FORD MOTOR CO. (Cont.)

12) Snap out and remove speaker grilles. Unplug electrical connectors at right grille. Remove screws seated in plastic clips and center defrost grille. Disconnect main wiring harness on engine compartment side.

13) Disengage rubber grommet from firewall. Feed main wiring harness and connectors through opening and into instrument panel area. Remove 3 screws (2 on sill plate) from right/left cowl trim panels. Remove trim panels.

14) Remove 3 lower instrument panel screws. Remove 3 upper instrument panel screws and carefully lower panel. Unplug vacuum and electrical connectors. Remove instrument panel.

15) Remove instrument panel shake brace from evaporator case. Remove 2 screws attaching floor register or rear seat adapter to bottom of evaporator case.

16) Remove 3 nuts (in engine compartment) attaching evaporator case to firewall. Remove 2 screws attaching support brackets to cowl top panel. Carefully pull evaporator case away from firewall. To install, reverse removal procedure.

SABLE

Removal & Installation

1) Disconnect negative battery cable. Remove 4 steering column cover screws and cover. Remove sound insulator by removing nuts from studs on evaporator case. Remove steering column trim shrouds. Unplug connectors from steering column switches.

2) Remove bolt and nut from steering shaft "U" joint. Remove 4 screws and steering column. Remove lower left and radio trim panels. Remove 5 instrument cluster retaining screws.

3) Release instrument cluster trim panel by rocking upper edge of panel toward driver's seat. Disconnect speedometer cable. Release glove box assembly by pressing side of glove box bin and swinging assembly downward.

4) Disconnect vacuum hoses, wiring harness, radio antenna cable, and A/C-heater control cable by reaching through steering column, instrument cluster, and glove box openings.

5) Disconnect wiring harness on engine compartment side. Disengage rubber grommet from firewall. Feed main wiring harness and connectors through opening and into instrument panel area.

6) Snap out right/left speaker covers and defroster grille. Remove 3 upper and lower instrument panel retaining screws (one screw is located above left side of transmission tunnel). Remove instrument panel.

7) Remove evaporator case. Remove vacuum line from heater core tube seal. Remove seal from heater core tubes. Remove 3 screws attaching blend door actuator to evaporator case.

8) Remove actuator and cold engine lock-out switch from case. Remove 4 heater core access cover mounting screw, access cover, seal, and heater core from evaporator case. To install, reverse removal procedure.

TAURUS

Removal & Installation

1) Disconnect negative battery cable. Remove 4 steering column cover screws and cover. Remove sound insulator by removing nuts from studs on evaporator case. Remove steering column trim shrouds. Unplug connectors from steering column switches.

2) Remove 4 steering column bracket mounting bolts. Lower steering column. Remove lower left and radio trim panels. Remove 7 instrument cluster trim panel retaining screws. Remove jam nut from behind headlamp switch knob.

3) Remove screws from behind clock or clock cover. Release trim panel by rocking upper edge of panel toward driver's seat. Disconnect speedometer cable. Release glove box assembly by pressing side of glove box bin and swinging assembly downward.

4) Disconnect vacuum hoses, wiring harness, radio antenna cable, and A/C-heater control cable by reaching through steering column, instrument cluster, and glove box openings.

5) Disconnect wiring harness on engine compartment side. Disengage rubber grommet from firewall. Feed main wiring harness and connectors through opening and into instrument panel area.

6) Snap out right/left speaker covers. Remove 3 upper and lower instrument panel retaining screws (one screw is located under radio). Remove instrument panel.

7) Remove instrument panel shake brace from evaporator case. Remove 2 screws attaching floor register or rear seat adapter to bottom of evaporator case.

8) Remove 3 nuts (in engine compartment) attaching evaporator case to firewall. Remove 2 screws attaching support brackets to cowl top panel. Carefully pull evaporator case away from firewall. Remove heater core from case. To install, reverse removal procedure.

Heater Core Replacement

GENERAL MOTORS

MODEL IDENTIFICATION

Repair procedures in this article are identified by body type. The following table lists GM division, model name and body type.

**1988 GENERAL MOTORS
MODEL IDENTIFICATION TABLE**

Body Type & Division	Model Name
"A" Body (FWD)	
Buick	Century
Chevrolet	Celebrity
Oldsmobile	Cutlass Ciera, Cutlass Cruiser
Pontiac	6000
"B" Body (RWD)	
Buick	LeSabre Wagon, Electra Wagon
Chevrolet	Caprice
Oldsmobile	Custom Cruiser
Pontiac	Safari
	Police models
"C" Body (FWD)	
Buick	Electra
Cadillac	DeVille, Fleetwood
Oldsmobile	Ninety-Eight
"D" Body (RWD)	
Cadillac	Brougham
"E" Body (FWD)	
Buick	Riviera, Reatta
Cadillac	Eldorado
Oldsmobile	Toronado
"F" Body (RWD)	
Chevrolet	Camaro
Pontiac	Firebird
"G" Body (RWD)	
Buick	Regal GN
Chevrolet	Monte Carlo
Oldsmobile	Cutlass Supreme Classic
"H" Body (FWD)	
Buick	LeSabre
Oldsmobile	Delta 88
Pontiac	Bonneville
"J" Body (FWD)	
Buick	Skyhawk
Cadillac	Cimarron
Chevrolet	Cavalier
Oldsmobile	Firenza
Pontiac	Sunbird
"K" Body (FWD)	
Cadillac	Seville
"L" Body (FWD)	
Chevrolet	Beretta, Corsica
"N" Body (FWD)	
Buick	Skylark
Oldsmobile	Cutlass Calais
Pontiac	Grand Am
"P" Body (RWD)	
Pontiac	Fiero
"S" Body (FWD)	
Chevrolet	Nova
"V" Body (FWD)	
Cadillac	Allanté
"W" Body (FWD)	
Buick	Regal
Oldsmobile	Cutlass Supreme
Pontiac	Grand Prix
"Y" Body (RWD)	
Chevrolet	Corvette

HEATER ONLY

"A" & "W" BODIES
Removal & Installation

1) Drain cooling system. Remove instrument panel lower sound absorber. On all models, disconnect coolant hoses at heater core. Remove heater duct and heater case side cover.

2) Remove heater lower outlet. Remove 2 housing cover to air valve housing clips. Remove core retaining straps. Remove core tubing retainers and remove core. To install, reverse removal procedure and refill cooling system.

"B" BODY
Removal & Installation

1) Disconnect battery ground. Disconnect electrical wires from blower motor and resistor. Disconnect heater core ground strap from dash. Drain radiator. Disconnect heater hoses and plug hoses and heater core tubes.

2) Remove heater core shroud screws. Remove shroud with heater core, then remove screws attaching shroud to heater core. To install, reverse removal procedure.

"F" BODY
Removal & Installation

1) Disconnect battery negative cable. Drain radiator. Disconnect heater hoses and plug hoses and heater core tubes. Remove lower right sound panel and lower right instrument trim panel.

2) On vehicles equipped with 5.0L engine, remove the ESC control module. Remove screw from lower right instrument panel carrier to cowl. Remove heater case cover screws and remove cover.

3) Remove screws from support plate and heater core. Remove heater core with support plate. To install, reverse removal procedure.

"J" BODY
Removal & Installation

1) Disconnect battery negative cable. Drain cooling system. Disconnect heater hoses, plug heater core tubes and heater hoses. Remove radio noise suppression strap, heater core bracket and shroud strap or heater outlet deflector (if equipped).

2) Remove heater core cover retaining screws and remove cover. Remove heater core. To install, reverse removal procedure making sure seals are not damaged.

"L" BODY
Removal & Installation

1) Drain cooling system. Remove heater inlet and outlet hoses from heater core. Remove heater outlet deflector.

2) Remove heater core cover. Remove heater core retaining straps and remove heater core. To install, reverse removal procedures.

"P" BODY
Removal & Installation

1) Disconnect battery negative cable. Drain cooling system. Disconnect wires at heater relay, heater blower resistor, blower switch connection, heater ground

GENERAL MOTORS (Cont.)

strap and forward courtesy light socket (if equipped). Remove windshield washer reservoir.

2) Disconnect heater hose from heater core and plug hose and core openings. Remove heater core opening grommets. Remove attaching screws and remove heater case cover. Remove heater core retainer. Remove heater core. To install, reverse removal procedure.

"S" BODY
Removal & Installation

Disconnect heater hoses from heater core. Remove 6 clips connecting lower case to upper case. Remove lower case. Remove heater core from case. To install, reverse removal procedure.

MANUAL A/C-HEATER

"A" BODY
Removal & Installation

1) Drain cooling system. Disconnect heater hoses from heater core. Remove heater duct and heater case side covers. Remove heater lower outlet.

2) Remove 2 housing cover-to-air valve housing clips. Remove cover, core straps, tubing retainers and heater core. Reverse removal procedure to install.

BUICK "B" & "G" BODIES
Removal & Installation

1) Disconnect negative battery cable. Disconnect electrical connections from blower motor, resistor, pressure cycling switch and hi-blower relay. Disconnect heater core ground strap.

2) Discharge A/C system and disconnect evaporator inlet and outlet lines (if evaporator core is to be removed). Remove right side hood seal and 7 air inlet screen screws.

3) Remove 5 top case-to-dash bolts. Remove 9 upper-to-lower case screws from flange and 2 upper-to-lower case screws from inside air intake plenum. Lift upper case straight up and off.

4) Remove accumulator pipe bracket-to-case screws and lift evaporator core straight up and out of case. Disconnect heater hoses from core and lift out heater core. Reverse removal procedure to install, using new sealer as needed to prevent air and water leaks.

CHEVROLET & PONTIAC "B" BODY
Removal & Installation

1) Drain coolant and disconnect heater hoses at core. Discharge A/C system. Remove heater core retaining bracket and ground strap. Remove weather seal and leaf screen. Remove right side windshield wiper.

2) Remove diagnostic connector, hi-blower relay and thermostatic switch mounting screws. Disconnect all electrical connections. Remove housing top cover. Remove heater core.

3) Remove accumulator mounting bracket screws. Disconnect accumulator input and output lines. Remove evaporator core. Reverse removal procedure to install. Use new sealer as needed to prevent air and water leaks.

CHEVROLET & PONTIAC "G" BODY
Removal & Installation

1) Disconnect negative battery cable. Discharge A/C system and drain cooling system. Remove

both windshield wipers and stops. Remove windshield molding, leaf screen and lower windshield molding brackets.

2) Remove module top cover screws and bolts, disconnect electrical connections, remove top cover and lift out evaporator core. Remove heater core clamp bolt and remove heater core. Reverse removal procedure to install.

"C" & "H" BODIES
Removal & Installation

1) Disconnect negative battery cable. Drain cooling system. Remove spalsh cover around heater hoses. Disconnect heater hoses from heater core.

2) Remove right side insulator. Remove lower instrument panel trim panels. Remove heater core cover. Remove heater core. To install, reverse removal procedure.

"F" BODY
Removal & Installation

1) Drain cooling system. Remove heater hoses from heater core. Remove right side lower hush panel and right-hand lower trim of instrument panel. Remove lower right side instrument carrier-to-cowl screw.

2) Remove 4 heater case cover screws. Upper left side screw is reached using a long socket extension through panel opening. Lift corner of instrument panel slightly to align socket. Remove heater case cover.

3) Remove core support plate and baffle screws. Remove heater core, support plate and baffle. Reverse removal procedure to install. Seal any air leaks and check for coolant leakage.

"J" BODY
Removal & Installation

1) Disconnect negative battery cable. Discharge A/C system. Drain cooling system. Raise vehicle. Disconnect rear lateral transaxle strut (if equipped).

2) Disconnect heater hoses from heater core. Disconnect A/C lines from evaporator core. Remove drain tube. Lower vehicle. Remove sound insulators, steering column trim, heater outlet and instrument panel.

3) Remove heater core cover. Remove heater core. Remove evaporator cover and evaporator. To install, reverse removal procedure.

"L" BODY
Removal & Installation

1) Disconnect negative battery cable and drain cooling system. Hoist vehicle and remove drain tube from heater case. Remove heater hoses from heater core.

2) Lower vehicle and remove right and left hush panels, steering column trim cover, heater outlet duct and glove box. Remove heater core cover. Carefully pull straight rearward when removing cover to avoid breaking drain tube. Remove heater core clamps and remove heater core. To install, reverse removal procedures.

"N" BODY
Removal & Installation

1) Disconnect negative battery cable. Discharge A/C system. Drain cooling system. Raise vehicle. Disconnect heater hoses from heater core. Remove drain tube.

2) Remove block fitting at evaporator. Lower vehicle. Remove lower portion of instrument panel. Remove lower heater duct hoses. Remove heater core cover. Remove heater core. Remove evaporator cover and core. To install, reverse removal procedure.

OLDSMOBILE "B" & "G" BODIES
Removal & Installation

1) Disconnect battery ground. If removing evaporator, discharge refrigerant. Drain cooling system, if removing heater core. Disconnect all electrical connections from blower motor, resistor, sensing switch and relay. Remove right side windshield washer arm.

2) Remove rubber seal and module air intake screen. Remove top cover screws and bolts. Remove cover. To remove heater core, lift out of case. To remove evaporator core, remove accumulator bracket screws. Disconnect refrigerant lines, and remove core from case.

3) Reverse removal procedure to install. Add 3 oz. new refrigerant oil to compressor, if evaporator core is replaced. Apply new sealant along edges of module cover to prevent water leaks. Evacuate and charge system.

"P" BODY
Removal & Installation

Open hood and disconnect heater hoses from core. Remove grille and speaker. Remove heater core cover, retainers and heater core. Reverse removal procedures to install.

"W" BODY
Removal & Installation

1) Disconnect battery ground cable and discharge system. Drain cooling system. Remove upper firewall weatherstrip.

2) Remove upper secondary front of dash. Disconnect evaporator core block connection at firewall. Remove heater hoses from heater core. Remove electrical module and bracket from rear sear heater duct adapter. Remove hush panels. Remove rear sear heater duct adapter.

3) Remove heater core cover and heater core. Remove evaporator core cove and evaporator core. Reverse removal procedure to install. Always use new "O" rings lubricated with clean refrigerant oil. DO NOT soak "O" rings as this will cause them to expand.

"Y" BODY
Removal & Installation

1) Disconnect negative battery cable. Remove the instrument cluster bezel including the tilt wheel lever and instrument panel pad. Remove A/C distributor duct and disconnect the flex hose. Remove the right side hush panel.

2) Remove the side window defroster to heater cover screws and disconnect the extension. Remove the temperature control cable and bracket assembly at heater cover. Disconnect heater door control shaft. Remove ECM and disconnect electrical connectors.

3) Remove the tubular support brace from the door pillar to aluminum instrument panel reinforcement brace. Remove heater core cover attaching screws. Remove heater pipe and heater control valve bracket attaching screws.

4) Cut heater hoses at heater core pipes. Remove heater core. Reverse removal procedure to install. Replace heater hoses.

AUTOMATIC A/C-HEATER

ALLANTÉ, ELDORADO, SEVILLE & TORONADO
Removal & Installation

1) Disconnect negative battery cable. Partially drain coolant. Remove glove box and lower sound insulator. Remove programmer, electronic control module and bracket.

2) Remove module assembly heater core cover. Remove inlet and outlet hoses to heater core. Remove heater core retaining screws. Remove heater core. To install, reverse removal procedure.

CORVETTE
Removal & Installation

1) Disconnect negative battery cable. Remove instrument cluster bezel including tilt wheel lever and instrument panel pad. Remove A/C distribution duct and disconnect flex hose. Remove right side hush panel.

2) Remove side window defroster flex hose. Remove side window defroster to heater cover screws and disconnect extension. Remove temperature control cable and bracket assembly at heater cover and disconnect heater door control shaft.

3) Remove ECM and disconnect wiring harness. Remove tubular support brace from door pillar to aluminum instrument panel reinforcement brace. Remove heater core cover attaching screws.

4) Remove heater pipe and heater control valve bracket attaching screws. Cut heater hose at heater core pipes. Remove heater core. To install, reverse removal procedure. Fill cooling system and check for leaks.

CUSTOM CRUISER, DELTA 88, ELECTRA, LESABRE, NINETY-EIGHT, REGAL & SKYHAWK

NOTE: See Manual A/C-Heater Systems HEATER CORE removal in this article.

DEVILLE & FLEETWOOD
Removal & Installation

1) Remove juntion block cover nut and cover. Drain radiator and remove heater hoses from heater core. Plug heater core tube openings. Remove glove box and lower sound insulator.

2) Remove 2 screws aatching BCM bracket to A/C-heater case. Disconnect air-mix door link at programmer. Disconnect wiring harnees and vacuum hoses from programmer.

3) Remove module assembly and heater core cover with programmer attached. Remove screws and heater core. To install, reverse removal procedure. Adjust air-mix door.

Heater Core Replacement

GENERAL MOTORS (Cont.)

RIVIERA

Removal & Installation

1) Remove negative battery cable. Drain cooling system. Remove right sound insulator. Remove center and lower instrument panel trim plates. Remove right speaker grille and speaker.

2) Remove wires and hoses from programmer. Remove programmer linkage cover and linkage. Remove programmer. Remove heater core cover. Remove splash cover to access heater hoses. Remove heater hoses. Remove heater core. To install, reverse removal procedure.

Section 7

CLUTCHES

CONTENTS

NOTE: **ALSO SEE GENERAL INDEX**

Clutches
CLUTCH TROUBLE SHOOTING

CONDITION	POSSIBLE CAUSE	CORRECTION
Chattering or Grabbing	Incorrect clutch adjustment	Adjust clutch
	Oil, grease or glaze on facings	Disassemble and clean or replace
	Loose "U" joint flange	See DRIVE AXLES
	Worn input shaft spline	Replace input shaft
	Binding pressure plate	Replace pressure plate
	Binding release lever	See CLUTCHES
	Binding clutch disc hub	Replace clutch disc
	Unequal pressure plate contact	Replace worn/misaligned components
	Loose/bent clutch disc	Replace clutch disc
	Incorrect transmission alignment	Realign transmission
	Worn pressure plate, disc or flywheel	Replace damaged components
	Broken or weak pressure springs	Replace pressure plate
	Sticking clutch pedal	Lubricate clutch pedal & linkage
	Incorrect clutch disc facing	Replace clutch disc
	Engine loose in chassis	Tighten all mounting bolts
Failure To Release	Oil or grease on clutch facings	Clean or replace clutch disc
	Incorrect release lever or pedal adjustment	See CLUTCHES
	Dust or dirt on clutch disc	Clean or replace
	Worn or broken clutch facings	Replace clutch disc
	Bent clutch disc or pressure plate	Replace damaged components
	Clutch disc hub binding on input shaft	Clean or replace clutch disc and/or input shaft
	Binding pilot bearing	Replace pilot bearing
	Sticking release bearing sleeve	Replace release bearing and/or sleeve
	Binding clutch cable	See CLUTCHES
	Defective clutch master cylinder	Replace master cylinder
	Defective clutch slave cylinder	Replace slave cylinder
	Air in hydraulic system	Bleed hydraulic system
Rattling	Weak or broken release lever spring	Replace spring and check alignment
	Damaged pressure plate	Replace pressure plate
	Broken clutch return spring	Replace return spring
	Worn splines on clutch disc or input shaft	Replace clutch disc and/or input shaft
	Worn clutch release bearing	Replace release bearing
	Dry or worn pilot bearing	Lubricate or replace pilot bearing
	Unequal release lever contact	Align or replace release lever
	Incorrect pedal free play	Adjust free play
	Warped or damaged clutch disc	Replace damaged components
Slipping	Pressure springs worn or broken	Replace pressure plate
	Oily, greasy or worn clutch facings,	Clean or replace clutch disc
	Incorrect clutch alignment	Realign clutch assembly
	Warped clutch disc or pressure plate	Replace damaged components
	Binding release levers or clutch pedal	Lubricate and/or replace release components
Squeaking	Worn or damaged release bearing	Replace release bearing
	Dry or worn pilot or release bearing	Lubricate or replace bearing assembly
	Pilot bearing turning in crankshaft	Replace pilot bearing and/or crankshaft
	Worn input shaft bearing	Replace bearing and seal
	Incorrect transmission alignment	Realign transmission
	Dry release fork between pivot	Lubricate release fork and pivot
Heavy and/or Stiff Pedal	Sticking release bearing sleeve	Replace release bearing and/or sleeve
	Dry or binding clutch pedal hub	Lubricate and align components
	Floor mat interference with pedal	Lay mat flat in proper area
	Dry or binding ball/fork pivots	Lubricate and align components
	Faulty clutch cable	Replace clutch cable
Noisy clutch pedal	Faulty interlock switch	Replace interlock switch
	Self-adjuster ratchet noise	Lubricate or replace self-adjuster
	Speed control interlock switch	Lubricate or replace interlock switch

Clutches

CLUTCH TROUBLE SHOOTING (Cont.)

CONDITION	POSSIBLE CAUSE	CORRECTION
Clutch pedal sticks down	Binding clutch cable	See CLUTCHES
	Springs weak in pressure plate	Replace pressure plate
	Binding in clutch linkage	Lubricate and free linkage
Noisy	Dry release bearing	Lubricate or replace release bearing
	Dry or worn pilot bearing	Lubricate or replace bearing
	Worn input shaft bearing	Replace bearing
Transmission click	Weak springs in pressure plate	Replace pressure plate
	Release fork loose on ball stud	Replace release fork and/or ball stud
	Oil on clutch disc damper	Replace clutch disc
	Broken spring in slave cylinder	Replace slave cylinder

Clutches

CHRYSLER MOTORS

FWD Models

DESCRIPTION

Clutches used in all models are a single plate, dry disc-type with a self-adjusting clutch cable release mechanism. A constant-running clutch release bearing is used on all models. The clutch pedal is connected to a torque shaft which actuates a cable and lever. Upper end of the clutch pedal pivots on the pedal bracket using 2 nylon bushings, which require no periodic lubrication.

ADJUSTMENT

Clutch release cable cannot be adjusted. When cable is properly installed, spring on clutch pedal will hold release cable in proper position, regardless of clutch disc wear. See Fig. 1.

Fig. 1: Self-Adjusting Clutch Release Mechanism

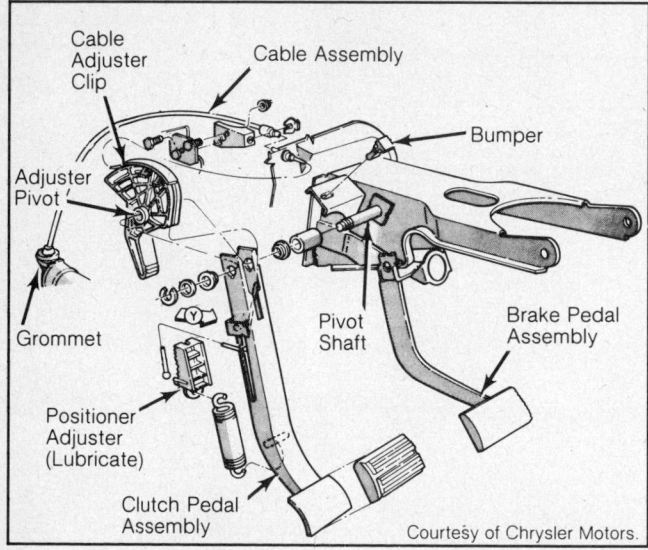

Courtesy of Chrysler Motors.

REMOVAL & INSTALLATION

CLUTCH

CAUTION: **When servicing clutch assembly or components, do not create dust by sanding or cleaning clutch parts with dry brush or compressed air.**

Removal

1) Disconnect negative battery cable. Disconnect speedometer cable and clutch cable. Disconnect backup light harness and starter motor wiring. Remove starter motor.

2) Disconnect gearshift operating lever from selector shaft. Install "lifting eye" on battery ground strap bolt (on left side of engine) and support engine with engine support fixture. Disconnect gear select cables and brackets at transaxle.

3) Raise and support vehicle. Remove front wheel assemblies and left front splash shield. Drain transaxle oil. Remove left engine mount from transaxle. Remove anti-rotational link from crossmember bracket (do not remove bracket from transaxle).

4) Remove left and right side drive axle shafts and support out of the way. Secure transaxle jack under transaxle and remove transaxle-to-engine bolts. Ensure

that all cables, mounts and wires have been disconnected and do not interfere when lowering transaxle.

5) Index mark pressure plate to flywheel for installation reference. Install Clutch Aligner (C-4676) and gradually loosen pressure plate cover bolts in succession to avoid distortion of cover flange. See Fig. 2.

Fig. 2: Installed Clutch Aligner

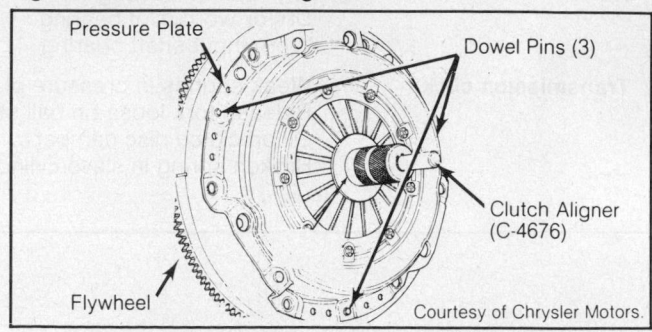

Courtesy of Chrysler Motors.

6) Remove clutch disc and pressure plate from flywheel. Remove clutch release shaft from transaxle and slide release bearing assembly off input shaft bearing retainer. Remove fork from release bearing thrust plate.

NOTE: **Prior to installing clutch disc, ensure that flywheel mating surface, pilot bearing/bushing and release bearing are all in satisfactory condition. Repair and/or replace as necessary.**

Installation

1) Align index marks previously made and position pressure plate and clutch disc on flywheel. Using Clutch Aligner (C-4676), center clutch disc and apply pressure to sliding cone. Install pressure plate-to-flywheel bolts sufficiently enough to hold disc in position. Alternately tighten 1 or 2 turns at a time until torqued to specifications. See Fig. 2.

2) Remove aligning tool. To complete installation reverse removal procedure. Use locating pins in place of top 2 transaxle-to-engine bolts for alignment purposes. Lubricate inside of release bearing where it contacts input shaft bearing retainer and release fork-to-bearing surface. Install new gearshift operating lever nut when assembling.

CLUTCH CABLE

1) Remove clip from shock tower mount and remove cable from bracket. Remove retainer from clutch release lever at transaxle.

2) Pry out ball end of cable from positioner adjuster and remove cable. To install, reverse removal procedure. After installation, push clutch pedal 2 or 3 times to adjust cable.

TIGHTENING SPECIFICATIONS

Application	Ft. Lbs. (N.m)
Flywheel-to-Crankshaft Bolts	70 (95)
Gearshift Lever Nut	21 (28)
Pressure Plate-to-Flywheel Bolts	21 (28)
Transaxle Case-to-Engine Block Bolts	70 (95)

	INCH Lbs. (N.m)
Transaxle Covers-to-Case Bolts	108 (12)

FORD MOTOR CO.

Cougar, Escort, EXP, Mustang, Sable Taurus, Tempo, Thunderbird, Topaz

DESCRIPTION

Clutch is a single dry disc design with a Belleville spring type pressure plate. All models except Cougar and Thunderbird use a self-adjusting cable operated clutch system. Cougar and Thunderbird models use a hydraulically controlled clutch release system.

ADJUSTMENT

SELF-ADJUSTING CLUTCH

On cable controlled models, clutch cable is adjusted automatically by a self-adjusting mechanism attached to clutch pedal. On hydraulically controlled clutch systems, clutch pedal is automatically located and requires no adjustment.

REMOVAL & INSTALLATION

CLUTCH

Removal (FWD)

1) Disconnect negative battery cable. Wedge a wood block (approximately 7") between clutch pedal and floor to hold clutch pedal up beyond its normal position. Disconnect clutch cable at release fork.

2) Remove clutch cable casing from rib on transaxle case. Remove 2 upper transaxle-to-engine bolts. Remove top bolt that secures air management valve bracket to transaxle (if necessary). Raise and support vehicle.

3) Remove nut and bolt securing lower control arm ball joint to steering knuckle assembly. Discard nut and bolt. Repeat procedure on other side. Using Half-Shaft Remover (D83P-4026-A) or equivalent, pry lower control arm away from knuckle. Repeat on other side.

CAUTION: Use care when using pry bar to remove CV joint. Damage to oil seal may result.

4) Using large pry bar, pry left side inboard CV joint assembly from transaxle. Install Transaxle Plugs (T81P-1177-B) or equivalent to prevent transaxle from draining.

5) Swing steering knuckle and half-shaft outward from transaxle. Secure half-shaft (using wire) in a near level position to prevent damage. Repeat on other side.

6) Disconnect backup light switch on top of transaxle. Remove 3 starter bolts and remove starter. Remove shift mechanism-to-shift shaft attaching nut and bolt. Disconnect mechanism from shift shaft.

7) Remove shift mechanism stabilizer bar from transaxle and remove control selector indicator switch arm from shaft. Remove 2 stiffener braces from front of bellhousing and remove speedometer cable.

8) Secure transaxle jack under transaxle and remove 2 bolts attaching rear support mount to floorpan brace. Loosen nut on bottom of front support mount. Remove 3 bolts securing front mount to transaxle.

9) Lower transaxle until it clears rear mount. Support engine block with a screw jack stand and wood block under oil pan. Remove 4 engine-to-transaxle bolts and lower transaxle from vehicle.

10) If same pressure plate cover is to be installed, index mark pressure plate cover to flywheel. Loosen 6 pressure plate cover attaching bolts evenly to avoid distorting cover. Remove pressure plate and clutch disc from flywheel.

11) Remove pin attaching release bearing to clutch release fork. Remove set bolt attaching clutch release fork to clutch release shaft on transaxle. Slide clutch release shaft assembly out from transaxle.

Installation

1) Clutch disc must be installed with flatter side toward flywheel as marked. Position clutch disc and align dowel pins of pressure plate onto flywheel. Start pressure plate cover bolts but do not tighten to flywheel. Install

Fig. 1: Exploded View of Ford FWD Clutch Assembly

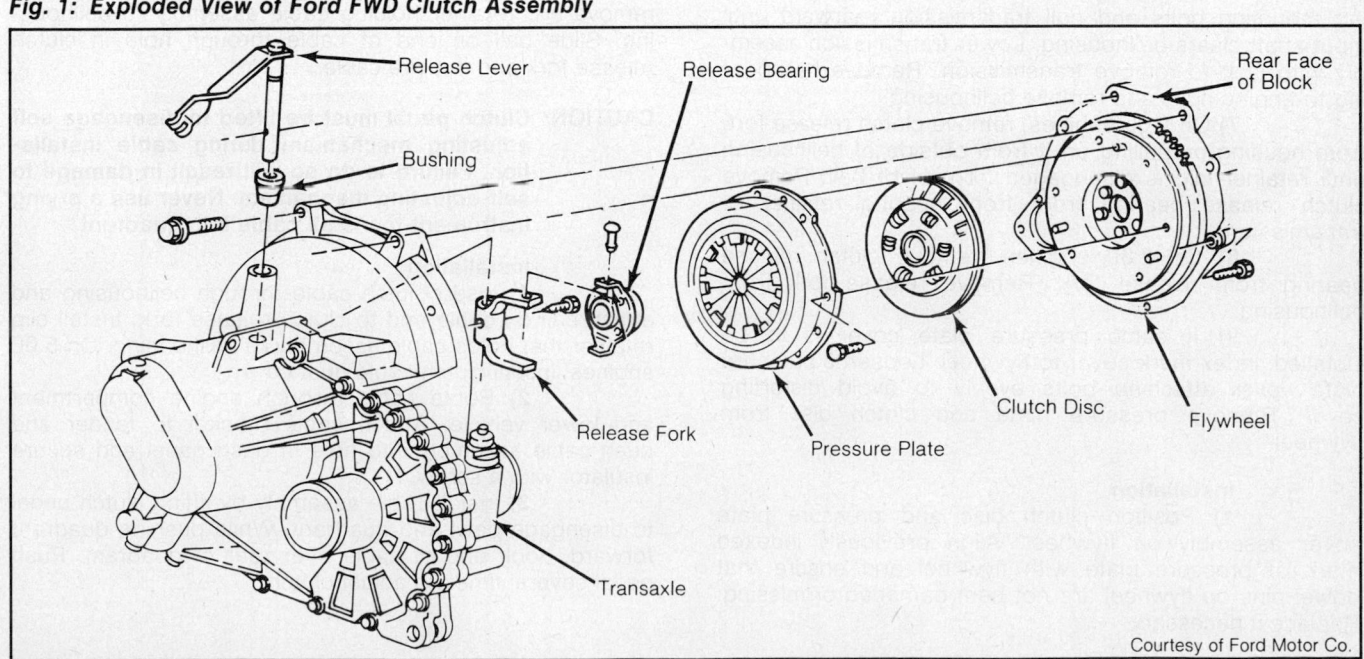

Release Lever

Release Bearing

Rear Face of Block

Bushing

Release Fork

Pressure Plate

Clutch Disc

Flywheel

Transaxle

Courtesy of Ford Motor Co.

Clutches

FORD MOTOR CO. (Cont.)

Clutch Plate Aligner (T81P-7550-A) or equivalent into crankshaft pilot bearing.

2) With clutch aligned, alternately tighten pressure plate cover bolts until they are fully seated. Torque cover bolts to specifications and remove clutch aligner.

3) Before installation of transaxle, lubricate: outside diameter of transaxle front bearing retainer, inside of release bearing, clutch release fork fingers and contact surface of release shaft.

4) To complete installation of transaxle, reverse removal procedure. Use new nut and bolt when attaching lower control arm ball joint to steering knuckle.

Removal (RWD)

1) On 5.0L engines, lift clutch pedal to disengage pawl from quadrant (located above pedal). Unhook clutch cable from quadrant and allow it to slowly swing rearward.

2) All models disconnect negative battery cable and raise and support vehicle. Remove cable dust shield. Disconnect clutch cable from release fork and remove cable from bellhousing (if applicable). Remove clutch slave cylinder if hydraulically controlled.

3) Disconnect wiring for starter motor and remove starter. Remove bolts attaching rear engine plate to bellhousing. Index mark rear propeller shaft flange to differential and remove propeller shaft. Install transmission rear seal plug.

4) Remove bolts attaching catalytic converter to exhaust system and remove catalytic converter. On Thunderbird 2.3L turbo engines, remove catalytic converter and inlet pipe. Remove nuts attaching transmission mount to crossmember.

5) Secure transmission jack under transmission and relieve weight from crossmember. Remove crossmember and transmission mount. Lower transmission enough to expose 2 bolts securing shift handle to transmission shift tower. Remove bolts and disconnect shift handle from transmission.

6) Disconnect all external electrical connectors and wiring harnesses from transmission and disconnect speedometer cable. Remove 4 transmission-to-bellhousing mounting bolts and pull transmission rearward until input shaft clears bellhousing. Lower transmission assembly with jack to remove transmission. Remove bellhousing-to-engine bolts and remove bellhousing.

7) On 5.0L engines, remove clutch release fork from housing by pulling on it from outside of bellhousing until retainer clip is disengaged from pivot ball. Remove clutch release bearing from front bearing retainer of transmission.

8) On 2.3L engines, remove clutch release bearing from release fork. Remove release fork from bellhousing.

9) If same pressure plate cover is to be installed, index mark cover to flywheel. Loosen 6 pressure plate cover attaching bolts evenly to avoid distorting cover. Remove pressure plate and clutch disc from flywheel.

Installation

1) Position clutch disc and pressure plate cover assembly on flywheel. Align previously indexed mark of pressure plate with flywheel and ensure that dowel pins on flywheel are not bent damaged or missing. Replace if necessary.

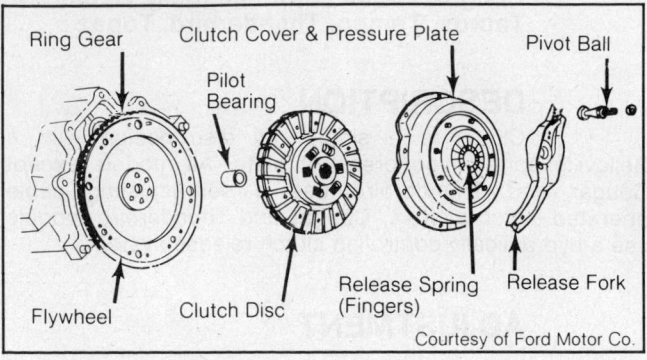

Fig. 2: View of Ford RWD Clutch Assembly

Ring Gear — Clutch Cover & Pressure Plate — Pivot Ball — Pilot Bearing — Flywheel — Clutch Disc — Release Spring (Fingers) — Release Fork

Courtesy of Ford Motor Co.

2) Start cover attaching bolts but do not tighten. Align clutch disc using proper Clutch Aligner (T81P-7550-A) or equivalent. Alternately tighten bolts a few turns at a time until they are all torqued to specifications.

3) Before installation of transmission, lubricate: outside diameter of transmission front bearing retainer, inside groove of release bearing, clutch release fork fingers, release fork pivot ball and mating release fork pocket.

4) To complete installation of transmission, reverse removal procedure.

CLUTCH CABLE

Removal

1) Lift clutch pedal to its upward most position to disengage pawl and quadrant. Push quadrant forward and unhook cable from quadrant and allow it to slowly swing rearward.

2) Remove screw (from engine side) that holds cable assembly insulator to dash panel. Pull cable through dash panel and into engine compartment. Remove cable bracket screw from fender apron.

3) Raise vehicle on a hoist. On 5.0L engines, remove clutch cable dust cover from bellhousing and remove clip retainer holding cable assembly to bellhousing. Slide ball on end of cable through hole in clutch release fork and remove cable.

CAUTION: Clutch pedal must be lifted to disengage self adjusting mechanism during cable installation. Failure to do so will result in damage to self-adjusting mechanism. Never use a prying instrument to install cable into quadrant.

Installation

1) Insert clutch cable through bellhousing and attach ball on cable end to clutch release fork. Install clip retainer that holds cable assembly to bellhousing. On 5.0L engines, install clutch cable dust cover.

2) Route cable through engine compartment and lower vehicle. Attach cable bracket to fender and push cable assembly into hole in dash panel and secure insulator with a screw.

3) Install cable assembly by lifting clutch pedal to disengage pawl and quadrant. While pushing quadrant forward, hook end of cable over rear of quadrant. Push pedal several times to adjust clutch.

FORD MOTOR CO. (Cont.)

SELF-ADJUSTING ASSEMBLY

Removal

1) Disconnect negative battery cable. Remove steering wheel using Steering Wheel Puller (T67L-3600-A) or equivalent. Remove lower dash panel section to the left of steering column.

2) Remove shrouds from steering column. Disconnect brake light switch and master cylinder push rod from brake pedal. Rotate clutch quadrant forward and unhook clutch cable. Allow quadrant to slowly swing rearward.

3) Remove bolt holding brake pedal support bracket (lateral brace) to left side of vehicle. Disconnect all electrical connectors leading to steering column. Remove 4 nuts holding steering column to brake pedal support bracket and lower steering column to the floor.

4) Remove 4 booster nuts that hold brake pedal support bracket to dash panel. Remove bolt that holds bracket to underside of instrument panel. Remove bracket assembly from vehicle.

5) Remove clutch pedal shaft nut and clutch pedal. Slide self-adjusting mechanism out of brake pedal support bracket. Remove self-adjusting mechanism shaft bushings from both sides of brake pedal support bracket and replace if worn.

Fig. 3: Self Adjusting Quadrant Assembly

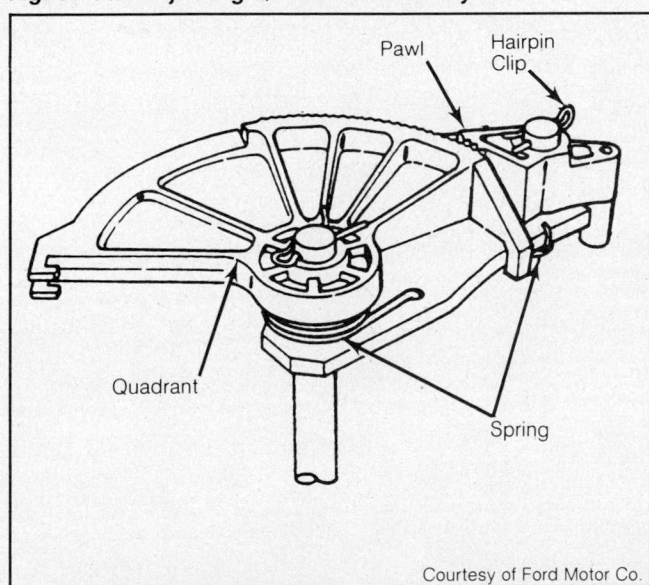

Pawl

Hairpin Clip

Quadrant

Spring

Courtesy of Ford Motor Co.

Installation

1) Lubricate self-adjusting mechanism shaft with motor oil. Install mechanism into brake pedal support bracket. Position quadrant in an upward position. Align flats on shaft with flats in clutch pedal assembly and install retaining nut.

2) Position brake pedal support bracket assembly beneath instrument panel aligning 4 holes with studs in dash panel. Install 4 nuts loosely. Install bolt through support bracket into instrument panel and tighten.

3) Tighten 4 booster nuts that hold brake pedal support bracket to dash panel. Connect brake light switch and master cylinder push rod to brake pedal. Attach clutch cable to quadrant. Position steering column onto 4 studs in support bracket and start 4 nuts.

4) Connect steering column electrical connectors and install steering column shrouds. Install brake pedal support (lateral brace). Tighten steering column attaching nuts. Install lower dash panel section.

5) Install steering wheel assembly and connect negative battery cable. Check steering column for proper operation. Depress clutch pedal several times to adjust cable.

SLAVE CYLINDER

Removal & Installation

Remove slave cylinder dust cover by removing self tapping screw. Unlatch slave cylinder from transmission housing bracket. Remove pressure line (if necessary) by removing roll pin. To install, reverse removal procedure. Use new "O" ring and roll pin when installing pressure line.

MASTER CYLINDER

Removal & Installation

1) Remove slave cylinder. Remove 2 nuts attaching master cylinder reservoir to vacuum bracket. Disengage push rod from clutch pedal.

2) Turn master cylinder 45 degrees clockwise and gently pull master cylinder out. Remove pressure line (if necessary) by removing roll pin. To install, reverse removal procedure. Use new "O" ring and roll pin when installing pressure line.

CLUTCH PILOT BEARING

Removal

Remove transmission, pressure plate and clutch disc. Pull bearing from crankshaft using Slide Hammer (T50T-100A, T59L-100B) and Puller Attachment (T58L-101-A).

Fig. 4: Servicing Pilot Bearings

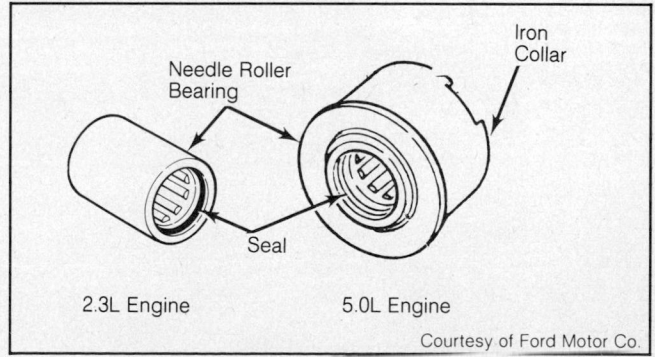

Iron Collar

Needle Roller Bearing

Seal

2.3L Engine

5.0L Engine

Courtesy of Ford Motor Co.

5.0L bearings with iron collar are serviced only as a unit.

Installation

1) Ensure that crankshaft pilot bore is clean and free from nicks or burrs. Lightly coat pilot bearing bore of crankshaft with Lubricant (C1AZ-19590-B).

2) On 2.3L, install pilot bearing (with seal end toward transmission) using Clutch Aligner (T71P-7137-H) and Pilot Bearing Installer (T71P-7137-C). Carefully tap pilot bearing squarely into bore until flush with flywheel.

3) On 5.0L, install pilot bearing using Pilot Bearing Installer (T81P-7120-B). Carefully tap pilot bearing squarely into bore until flush with flywheel. Check that needle bearings are not damaged or repositioned in collar.

NOTE: Care must be taken when installing transmission, so that input shaft does not damage bearing.

Clutches

FORD MOTOR CO. (Cont.)

TIGHTENING SPECIFICATIONS

Application	Ft. Lbs. (N.m)
Front Wheel Drive Models	
Bellhousing-to-Engine Bolts	28-38 (38-52)
Bracket-to-Clutch Pedal Bolts	25-30 (34-40)
Flywheel-to-Crankshaft Bolts	59-69 (80-94)
Pedal-to-Support Bracket Nuts	15-25 (20-34)
Pressure Plate-to-Flywheel Bolts	12-24 (16-33)
Release Fork Bolt	30-40 (40-55)
Rear Wheel Drive Models	
2.3L	
Bellhousing-to-Engine Bolts	28-38 (38-52)
Flywheel-to-Crankshaft Bolts	56-64 (76-87)
Pressure Plate-to-Flywheel Bolts	12-24 (16-33)
5.0L	
Bellhousing-to-Engine Bolts	38-55 (52-75)
Clutch Pedal Attaching Nuts	17-26 (23-36)
Flywheel-to-Crankshaft Bolts	75-85 (102-116)
Pressure Plate-to-Flywheel Bolts	12-24 (16-33)
Steering Column Attaching Nut	20-37 (27-50)
Support Bracket-to-Dash Panel Bolt ..	13-25 (18-34)

GENERAL MOTORS

All Models

DESCRIPTION

All models use a single plate clutch disc, a diaphragm spring-type pressure plate and a permanently lubricated clutch release bearing. Clutch release system is hydraulically operated and consists of a clutch pedal, clutch master cylinder, clutch slave cylinder and clutch release fork.

The hydraulic clutch system locates the clutch pedal height and provides automatic clutch adjustment. No adjustment is ever required of clutch linkage or pedal position. See Fig. 1.

Fig. 1: Clutch Hydraulic System Components

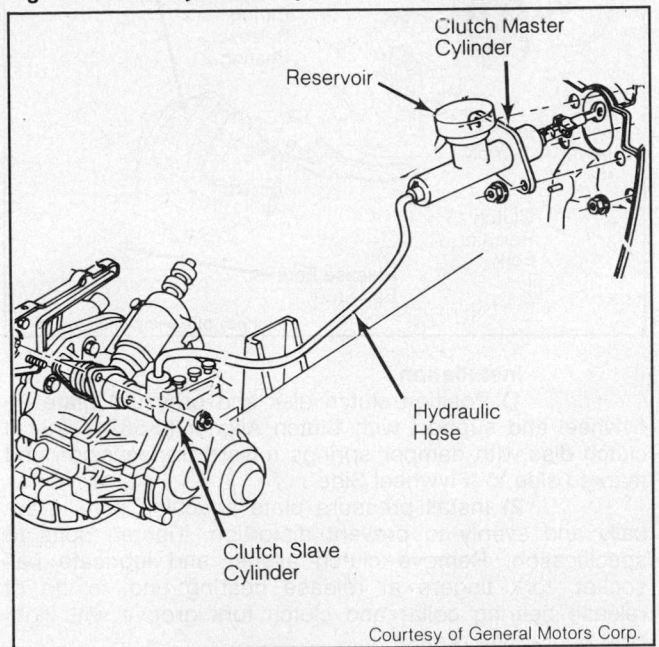

Courtesy of General Motors Corp.

ADJUSTMENTS

NOTE: Do not use mineral or parafin base oil in clutch hydraulic system. The use of these fluids will result in damage to rubber parts in cylinders.

SLAVE CYLINDER PUSH ROD TRAVEL

1) Raise and secure vehicle. Measure slave cylinder push rod travel as clutch pedal is depressed. See SLAVE CYLINDER PUSH ROD TRAVEL SPECIFICATIONS chart for minimum travel allowed.

NOTE: Never under any circumstances reintroduce used hydraulic fluid into system.

2) If push rod travel distance is not correct, check master cylinder fluid reservoir level. If fluid level is low, check hydraulic system components for leakage. It is recommended to replace both master cylinder and slave cylinder if excessive leakage is evident.

PEDAL FREE PLAY

Pedal free play adjustment is fully automatic. No manual adjustment is required.

SLAVE CYLINDER PUSH ROD TRAVEL SPECIFICATIONS

Application Model	Minimum Travel In. (mm)
Camaro & Firebird	.57 (14.53)
Celebrity	.37 (9.50)
Corvette	.70 (17.78)
All Other Models	.43 (11.00)

REMOVAL & INSTALLATION

CAUTION: On all models, clutch master cylinder push rod must be removed from clutch pedal prior to service requiring slave cylinder removal. If push rod is not removed, permanent slave cylinder damage will result.

CLUTCH

Removal (All FWD Models Except Nova)

1) Disconnect negative cable at battery. Remove sound insulator from inside vehicle. Disconnect clutch master cylinder push rod from clutch pedal. Install Engine Holding Fixture (J-28467). Attach fixture hook to engine and raise engine enough to take pressure off motor mounts. See Fig. 2.

Fig. 2: Engine Support Fixture

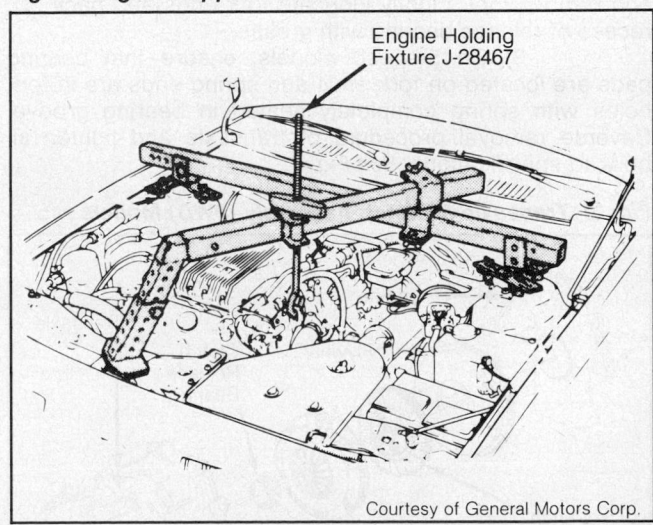

Courtesy of General Motors Corp.

NOTE: On some models, when removing transaxle mount, an alignment bolt (M6.0 x 1 x 65) must be installed in right front engine mount to prevent powertrain misalignment.

2) On some Buick models, remove air intake duct, left fender brace, battery, manifold sensor lead at air cleaner, PCV pipe clamp, air cleaner, heat shield at crossover pipe and exhaust crossover pipe.

3) On all models, disconnect clutch slave cylinder from transaxle support bracket and lay aside. Remove transaxle mount attaching bolts and mount bracket bolts and nuts. Disconnect shift cables and retaining clips at transaxle.

4) Disconnect ground cables at transaxle mounting stud. Remove air management valve attaching bolts. Raise vehicle and drain transaxle. Remove left front tire and remove left front inner splash shield. Remove transaxle strut.

Clutches

GENERAL MOTORS (Cont.)

5) Remove transaxle strut bracket. Remove clutch housing cover bolts. Disconnect speedometer cable or sensor at transaxle. Disconnect stabilizer bar at left suspension support and control arm. Disconnect ball joint from steering knuckle.

6) Remove left suspension support attaching bolts and remove support and control arm as an assembly. Install boot protectors and disengage drive axles at transaxle. Remove left side drive axle. Secure transaxle to jack.

7) Remove transaxle-to-engine mounting bolts and carefully lower jack while guiding right drive axle out of transaxle. Index mark pressure plate to flywheel for reassembly reference.

8) Loosen attaching bolts one turn at a time until pressure plate spring tension is relieved. Remove clutch disc and pressure plate.

Installation

NOTE: Clutch lever must not move toward flywheel until transxale is mounted to engine or damage to transaxle will occur.

1) Position clutch disc and pressure plate onto flywheel. Install clutch disc with damper springs offset toward transaxle. Stamped letters identify "Flywheel Side".

2) Install pressure plate to flywheel attaching bolts evenly and gradually. Tighten bolts to specification and remove tool. Lightly lubricate fork ends and pack I.D. recess of release bearing with grease.

3) On 5-speed models, ensure that bearing pads are located on fork ends and spring ends are in fork holes with spring completely seated in bearing groove. Reverse removal procedure of transaxle and tighten all bolts to specifications. See Fig. 3.

Fig. 3: Transaxle & Clutch Assembly (FWD) Models

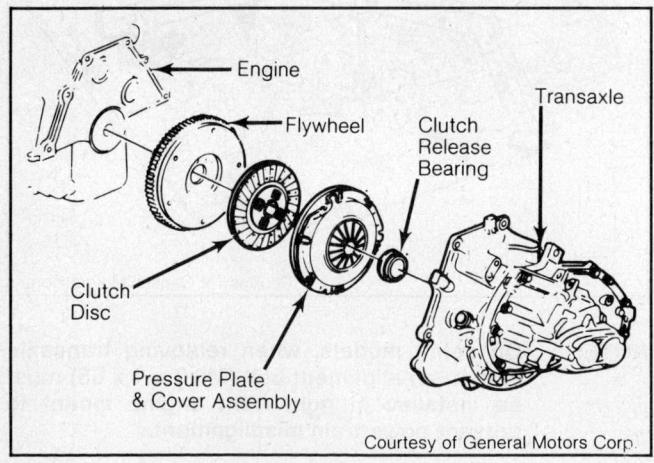

Courtesy of General Motors Corp.

Removal (Corvette)

1) Remove negative cable from battery. Remove distributor cap and raise vehicle. Remove complete exhaust system as an assembly. Remove exhaust hanger from transmission. Remove upper and lower underbody braces on vehicles equipped with convertible top.

2) Support transmission with jack. Remove driveline beam bolts and remove driveline beam. Mark propeller shaft to axle companion flange. Remove trunnion bearing straps and disengage rear universal joint from axle. Slide propeller shaft slip yoke from overdrive unit and remove.

3) Disconnect cooler lines at overdrive unit. Disconnect shift linkage at cover side. Disconnect all electrical connections. Support engine and lower transmission. Remove 4 transmission-to-bellhousing bolts. Remove transmission.

4) Remove slave cylinder attaching bolts and remove bellhousing. Mark pressure plate and flywheel for reassembly reference. Loosen pressure plate attaching bolts one turn at a time until spring pressure is released. Remove pressure plate and clutch disc. See Fig. 4.

Fig. 4: Clutch Assembly on RWD Models

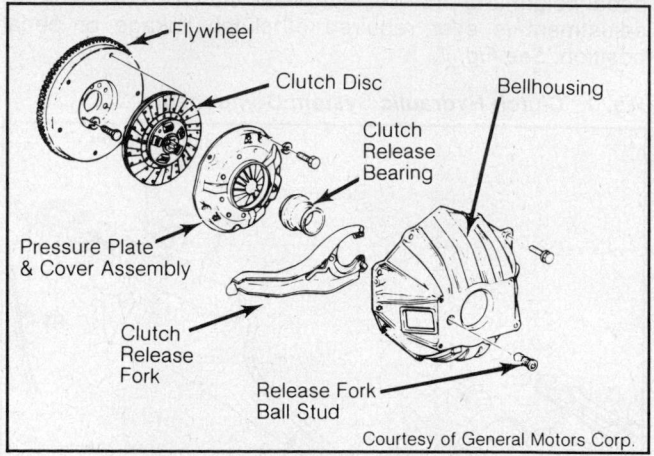

Courtesy of General Motors Corp.

Installation

1) Position clutch disc and pressure plate on flywheel and support with Clutch Aligner (J-5824). Install clutch disc with damper springs toward transmission and marked side to "Flywheel Side".

2) Install pressure plate attaching bolts gradually and evenly to prevent distortion. Tighten bolts to specification. Remove clutch aligner and lubricate ball socket, fork fingers at release bearing end, inside of release bearing collar and clutch fork groove with light coat of graphite grease.

3) Reverse removal procedure and tighten all bolts to specified torque. Check system for proper operation.

CAUTION: DO NOT overtighten the bolts attaching the driveline beam to transmission. Over tightening can damage bushing and seal in the overdrive unit and result in fluid leakage. Inadequate fluid level will damage transmission.

Removal (Camaro & Firebird)

1) Disconnect negative cable at battery and remove shift lever boot attaching screws. Slide boot up lever and remove lever from transmission. Raise and support vehicle.

2) Remove rear suspension torque arm. Index mark and remove propeller shaft from vehicle. Disconnect speedometer cable and remove transmission mount attaching bolts. Remove catalytic converter hanger. Remove crossmember attaching bolts and remove crossmember.

3) Remove dust cover. Remove 4 transmission-to-bellhousing bolts and remove transmission. Remove slave cylinder heat shield and slave cylinder. Remove bellhousing from engine and index mark pressure plate and flywheel for reassembly reference.

Clutches

GENERAL MOTORS (Cont.)

4) Loosen attaching bolts one turn at a time until pressure plate spring pressure is relieved. Remove clutch disc and pressure plate.

Installation

1) Position clutch disc and pressure plate onto flywheel and insert Clutch Aligner (J-33169). Install clutch disc with damper springs toward transmission. Stamped letters identify "Flywheel Side".

2) Align marks made during removal and tighten attaching bolts gradually and evenly. Tighten to specification. Remove clutch aligner and lubricate fork fingers, ball socket, inside of release bearing collar and clutch fork groove with graphite grease.

3) Reverse removal procedure and tighten all bolts to specifications. Check system for proper operation.

Removal (Fiero)

1) Remove negative battery cable, deck lid, louvered panels and upper rear engine support bolt. Install Engine Support Fixture (J-28467). Raise vehicle and remove both rear tires. Disconnect slave cylinder and shift cables.

2) Remove EGR outlet pipe from exhaust manifold. Disconnect parking brake cable from calipers and body. Disconnect lower ball joints and tie rods. Disconnect drive axle shafts from transaxle and remove left axle shaft.

3) Remove rubber skirts from splash shields. Remove rear transaxle bracket bolts. Remove engine mount nuts from front engine mount cradle. Remove crossover pipe to converter bolts. Disconnect sensor wire.

4) Remove cradle bolts and cradle from engine. Support cradle on adjustable stand. Remove crossover pipe heat shield and crossover pipe. Secure transaxle jack under transaxle and remove engine-to-transaxle bolts. Remove clutch inspection plate cover.

5) Remove lower engine bolt studs. Remove coolant pipe from stud. Lower transaxle. Remove right axle driveshaft while lowering transaxle from vehicle. Index mark pressure plate to flywheel for installation reference.

6) Remove pressure plate attaching bolts one turn at a time until spring pressure is relieved. Remove pressure plate and clutch disc.

Installation

NOTE: Clutch lever must not move toward flywheel until transxale is mounted to engine or damage to transaxle will occur.

1) Position pressure plate and clutch disc on flywheel and hand tighten bolts. Insert Clutch Aligner (J-29074). Tighten attaching bolts evenly and gradually. Tighten to specified torque and remove aligner. Lightly lubricate both outer groove on release bearing and I.D. recess of bearing with grease.

2) Install right side drive axle into transaxle while transaxle is being positioned to engine. Reverse removal procedure to complete installation.

Removal (Nova)

1) Disconnect negative battery cable. Remove air inlet tube. Disconnect speedometer cable and thermostat housing at transaxle. Disconnect ground wire at transaxle.

2) Disconnect slave cylinder and lay aside. Disconnect all electrical connections. Install engine support fixture. Remove upper bellhousing bolts and transaxle mount upper bolt.

3) Raise vehicle. Remove left front wheel, left splash shield, right splash shield, center splash shield, center beam and inspection cover. Disconnect left and right lower control arm at spindle.

4) Disconnect both axle shafts at transaxle. Disconnect starter bolts and support transaxle. Remove transaxle mount bolts. Separate transaxle from engine and lower.

5) Mark pressure plate and flywheel for reassembly reference. Loosen pressure plate mounting bolts one turn at a time until spring pressure is released. Remove clutch disc and pressure plate.

Installation

NOTE: Clutch lever must not move toward flywheel until transxale is mounted to engine or damage to transaxle will occur.

1) Install clutch disc and pressure plate onto flywheel. Insert Clutch Aligner (J-35757). Tighten pressure plate attaching bolts evenly and gradually to specified torque.

2) Lubricate release fork and hub contact point, clutch spline, fork pivot point, fork and push rod contact point and release bearing inside groove. To complete installation, reverse removal procedure. Tigthen bolts to specification. Check system for proper operation.

TIGHTENING SPECIFICATIONS

Application	Ft. Lbs. (N.m)
Flywheel-to-Crankshaft Bolts	
Camaro & Firebird	
V6	50 (68)
V8	74 (100)
Corvette	74 (100)
Fiero	50 (68)
Nova	58 (78)
All Other Models	52 (70)
Pressure Plate-to-Flywheel Bolts	
Corvette	30 (40)
Nova	14 (19)
All Other Models	16 (21)
Transaxle/Transmission-to-Engine Block Bolts	
	55 (75)
Transmission-to-Bellhousing Bolts	15 (20)

Section 8

DRIVE AXLES

CONTENTS

NOTE: **ALSO SEE GENERAL INDEX**

Drive Axles

TROUBLE SHOOTING RWD VEHICLES

CONDITION	POSSIBLE CAUSE	CORRECTION
General Knocking or Clunking	Excessive differential side gear clearance	See OVERHAUL in DRIVE AXLES
	Worn rear axle pinion shaft	See OVERHAUL in DRIVE AXLES
	Worn case or differential cross shaft in case	See OVERHAUL in DRIVE AXLES
	Excessive end play of axle shafts-to-differential cross shaft	See OVERHAUL in DRIVE AXLES
	Gear teeth mutilated	See OVERHAUL in DRIVE AXLES
	Improper axle shaft spline fit	See OVERHAUL in DRIVE AXLES
	Total axle backlash too great	See OVERHAUL in DRIVE AXLES
	Incorrect driveline angle	See ADJUSTMENT in PROPELLER SHAFT ALIGNMENT
Clunking During Initial Engagement	Excessive differential side gear clearance	See OVERHAUL in DRIVE AXLES
	Excessive ring and pinion backlash	See OVERHAUL in DRIVE AXLES
	Worn or loose pinion shaft	See OVERHAUL in DRIVE AXLES
Gear Howl or Whine	Improper pinion depth	See OVERHAUL in DRIVE AXLES
	Improper ring gear backlash adjustment	See OVERHAUL in DRIVE AXLES
	Improper ring gear runout	See OVERHAUL in DRIVE AXLES
	Improper bearing preload	See OVERHAUL in DRIVE AXLES
	Excessive pinion bearing wear	See OVERHAUL in DRIVE AXLES
Clicking or Chatter on Turns	Wrong lubricant in differential	Drain and fill with proper lubricant
	Clutch plates worn	See LUBRICATION in POSITIVE TRACTION DIFFERENTIALS
	Differential side gears or pinion worn	See OVERHAUL in DRIVE AXLES
Knock or Click Approximately Every Second Revolution	Flat spot on rear wheel bearing	See OVERHAUL in DRIVE AXLES
Grunt Noise on Stops	Lack of lubricant in propeller shaft slip yoke	See UNIVERSAL JOINTS in PROPELLER SHAFTS
Groan in Forward or Reverse	Wrong lubricant in differential	Drain and fill with proper lubricant
Knock in Drive Line in High Gear at 10 MPH	Worn or damaged universal joints	See UNIVERSAL JOINTS in PROPELLER SHAFTS
	Side gear hub counterbore in differential worn oversize	See OVERHAUL in DRIVE AXLES
Ping, Snap or Click in Drive Line	Loose upper or lower control arm bushing bolts	See REPLACEMENT in REAR SUSPENSION
	Loose companion flange	See OVERHAUL in DRIVE AXLES
Scraping Noise	Slinger, companion flange or end yoke rubbing on rear axle carrier	See OVERHAUL in DRIVE AXLES
Car Will Not Move	Broken axle shaft	See OVERHAUL in DRIVE AXLES
	Broken pinion stem	See OVERHAUL in DRIVE AXLES
	Axle lock-up	See OVERHAUL in DRIVE AXLES
	Broken gear teeth	See OVERHAUL in DRIVE AXLES
	Broken wheel bearing	See OVERHAUL in DRIVE AXLES
Axle Backlash	Excessive ring and pinion clearance	See OVERHAUL in DRIVE AXLES
	Loose fitting differential pinion shaft	See OVERHAUL in DRIVE AXLES
	Excessive side gear-to-case clearance	See OVERHAUL in DRIVE AXLES
Leakage at Differential or Driveshaft	Rough outside surface on splined yoke	See OVERHAUL in DRIVE AXLES
	Drive pinion seal or nut	See OVERHAUL in DRIVE AXLES
	Axle cover gasket, or axle shaft seal	See OVERHAUL in DRIVE AXLES

Drive Axles

TROUBLE SHOOTING RWD VEHICLES (Cont.)

CONDITION	POSSIBLE CAUSE	CORRECTION
Roughness, Shudder or Vibration Upon Heavy Acceleration	Double cardan joint ball seats worn, and ball set spring may be broken	See UNIVERSAL JOINTS in PROPELLER SHAFTS
	Excessive joint angle	See PROPELLER SHAFTS
	Sticking inboard joint assembly	See UNIVERSAL JOINTS in PROPELLER SHAFTS
	Worn or damaged inboard or outboard joints	See UNIVERSAL JOINTS in PROPELLER SHAFTS
Roughness, Vibration or Body Boom Experienced at Any Speed	Rough rear wheel bearings	See OVERHAUL in DRIVE AXLES
	Unbalanced or damaged propeller shaft	Check and/or balance propeller shaft
	Unbalanced or damaged tires	Check and/or balance tires
	Worn or damaged universal joints	See UNIVERSAL JOINTS in PROPELLER SHAFTS
	Bent or damaged drive shaft, or undercoating on drive shaft	Check drive shaft balance
	Tight universal joints	Lubricate or replace as necessary
	Burrs or gouges on companion flange	Resurface or replace flange
	Drive shaft or companion shaft runout too great	Repair or replace as necessary
	Excessive looseness at slip yoke spline	See OVERHAUL in DRIVE AXLES

TROUBLE SHOOTING FWD VEHICLES

CONDITION	POSSIBLE CAUSE	CORRECTION
Grease Leaks	Joint boot torn, split or cracked	See DISASSEMBLY in FWD AXLES SHAFTS
Clicking Noise on Cornering	Damaged or worn outboard joint	See DISASSEMBLY in FWD AXLES SHAFTS
Clunk Noise on Acceleration	Damaged or worn inboard joints	See DISASSEMBLY in FWD AXLES SHAFTS
	Transaxle gears or bearings	
Vibration or Shudder on Acceleration	Sticking, damaged or worn joints	See DISASSEMBLY in FWD AXLES SHAFTS
	Excessive alignment or spring height	
Squealing or Humming	Insufficient or Improper Joint Lubrication	See DISASSEMBLY in FWD AXLES SHAFTS
	Wheel Bearing Problem	See HUB & BEARING ASSEMBLY in FWD AXLES SHAFTS

Drive Axle

DRIVE AXLE GEAR TOOTH PATTERNS

INSPECTION

Clean lubricant from internal parts for visual inspection. Rotate ring gear and inspect for noise, wear or damage. Mount a dial indicator to housing and check backlash at several points around ring gear. Backlash must be within specifications at all points. If no defects are found, check gear tooth contact patterns.

GEAR TOOTH CONTACT PATTERN

1) Drive pattern should be well centered on ring gear teeth. Coast pattern should be centered but may be slightly toward toe end of ring gear teeth. Apply marking compound to several ring gear teeth. Apply some form of load to differential case to resist rotation. Rotate pinion gear until ring gear has made one full revolution.

2) Turn pinion gear in opposite direction to complete one full revolution of ring gear. Examine ring gear teeth for contact pattern. Correct as necessary by removing or adding appropriate shims.

ADJUSTMENTS

GEAR BACKLASH & PINION SHIM CHANGES

NOTE: **Change in tooth pattern is directly related to change in shim and/or backlash adjustment.**

1) With no change in backlash, moving pinion further from ring gear moves drive pattern toward heel and top of tooth, and moves coast pattern toward toe and top of tooth.

2) With no change in backlash, moving pinion closer to ring gear moves drive pattern toward toe and bottom of tooth, and moves coast pattern toward heel and bottom of tooth.

3) With no change in pinion shim thickness, an increase in backlash moves ring gear further from pinion. Drive pattern moves toward heel and top of tooth, and coast pattern moves toward heel and top of tooth.

4) With no change in pinion shim thickness, a decrease in backlash moves ring gear closer to pinion gear. Drive pattern moves toward toe and bottom of tooth, and coast pattern moves toward toe and bottom of tooth.

Fig. 1: Drive Axle Gear Tooth Patterns Showing Necessary Corrections

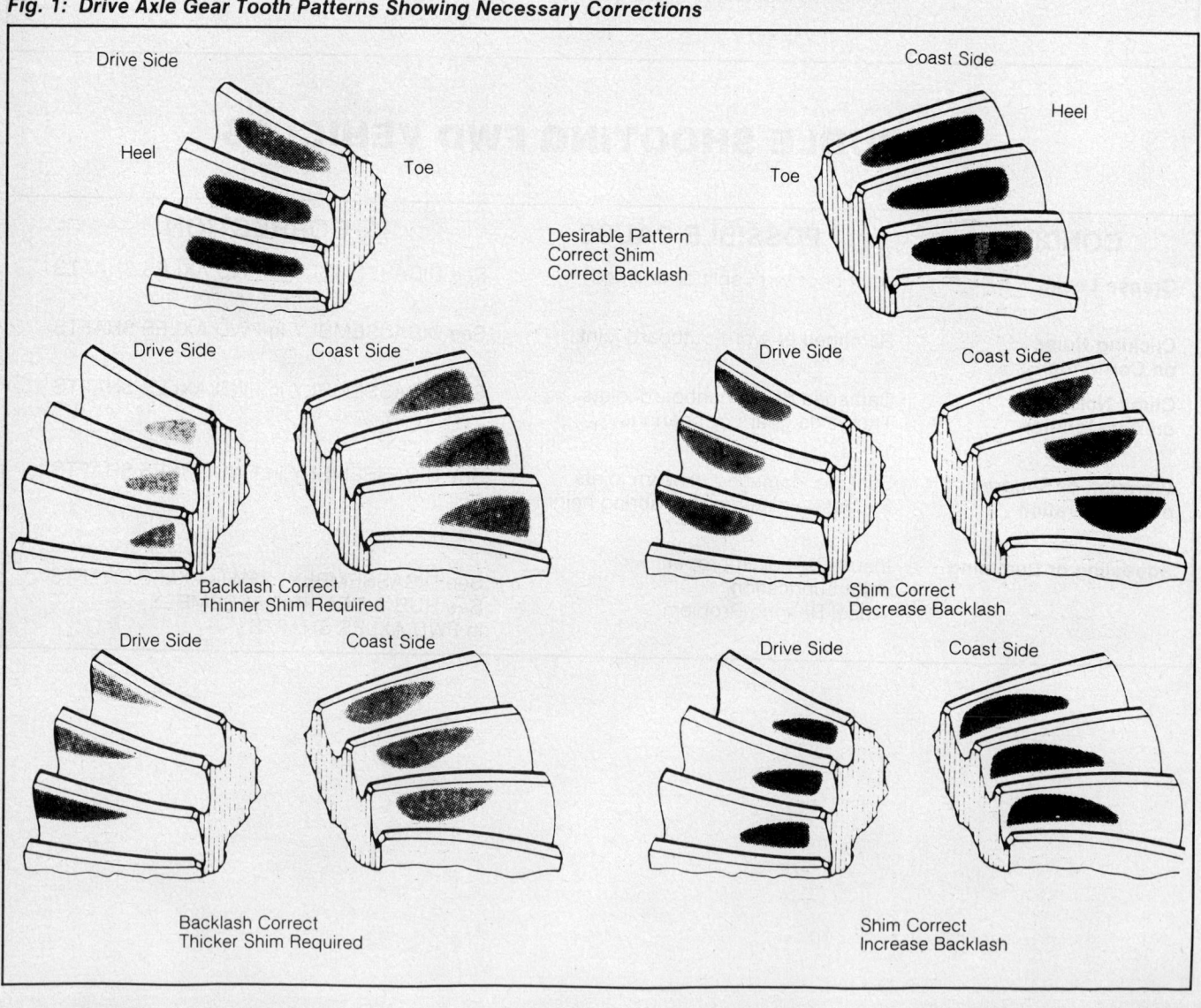

Drive Side — Coast Side

Heel — Toe — Toe — Heel

Desirable Pattern
Correct Shim
Correct Backlash

Drive Side — Coast Side — Drive Side — Coast Side

Backlash Correct
Thinner Shim Required

Shim Correct
Decrease Backlash

Drive Side — Coast Side — Drive Side — Coast Side

Backlash Correct
Thicker Shim Required

Shim Correct
Increase Backlash

CHRYSLER MOTORS – 7 1/4" & 8 1/4" RING GEAR

RWD Models

DESCRIPTION

The rear axle is a semi-floating, hypoid gear type with a differential carrier integral within rear axle housing. All of components can be inspected, removed, and serviced without removing complete axle assembly from vehicle.

The "C" type lock washers on inboard ends of each axle shaft retain shafts in position. When axle shafts and "C" washers are properly installed, outer portion of "C" washer is positioned in machined recess of side gear. When differential pinion shaft is properly installed and retained in place by its lock screw, axle shafts are locked in position and cannot slide out. This method of locking axle shafts, eliminates need for axle shaft bearing end play adjustment.

CAUTION: If rear axle becomes submerged in water, lubricant must be changed to avoid possibility of early axle failure resulting from contamination of lubricant by water.

AXLE RATIO & IDENTIFICATION

The 7 1/4" drive axle is available in one gear ratio and 8 1/4" is available in 2 gear ratios. Gear ratio is stamped on a small metal tag attached to one cover bolt. Ring gear diameter can be identified by observing number of cover bolts and housing tube diameter.

All axles have a 10 bolt cover and axle housing tube diameters of 3.0" (76.2 mm). The 7 1/4" axle tube inner ends are 2.5" (63.5 mm) in diameter. The 7 1/4" axle vent is located on left side and 8 1/4" axle vent is located on right side.

AXLE RATIO IDENTIFICATION

Axle Dia.	Axle Ratio	No. of Teeth Pinion/Ring Gear
7 1/4"	2.26:1	19/43
8 1/4"	2.24:1	21/47
8 1/4"	2.94:1	16/47

REMOVAL & INSTALLATION

AXLE SHAFTS & BEARINGS

Removal

1) Raise and support vehicle. Remove wheels and brake drums. Loosen housing cover screws to drain lubricant. Remove housing cover.

NOTE: Remove all dirt and foreign material from housing cover area.

2) Turn differential case for access to lock screw. Remove lock screw and pinion shaft. Push axle shafts toward center of vehicle. Remove "C" locks from groove in axle shafts. Remove shafts from housing.

3) Do not damage roller bearings which remain in axle housing. Remove shaft seal from housing bore. Dents caused by axle shaft splines should be polished

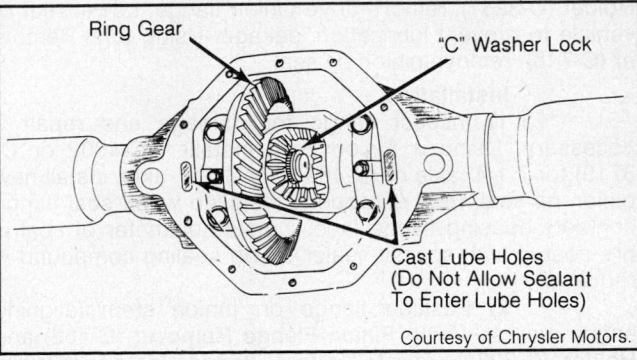

Fig. 1: 7 1/4" Direct-On Roller Differential

Ring Gear

"C" Washer Lock

Cast Lube Holes (Do Not Allow Sealant To Enter Lube Holes)

Courtesy of Chrysler Motors.

smooth or rubber on outside diameter of seal will be torn and seal leakage will result.

4) To remove axle bearing, use Bearing Separator (C-4167) and Slide Hammer (C-637). If axle shaft and bearing are not damaged, they may be reused. DO NOT reuse axle shaft seal after removal.

NOTE: Any time axle assembly is serviced and axle shaft is loosened or removed, both brake support plate gaskets and inner axle shaft oil seals must be replaced.

Installation

When installing axle shaft bearing, use Bearing Installer (C-4198) and Bearing Installer Handle (C-4171). To install axle shaft seal, use Seal Installer (C-4203). To complete installation, reverse removal procedure.

REAR AXLE ASSEMBLY

Removal

1) Raise vehicle and support body at front of rear springs. Block brake pedal in UP position. Remove wheel and drum assemblies. Remove brake hose and junction block from axle housing. Remove axle shaft and bearing assemblies.

2) Remove brake backing plate retainer nuts. Remove backing plates, with shoes and parking brake cables attached, and wire to frame. Place alignment marks on propeller shaft and companion flange for installation reference. See PROPELLER SHAFT ALIGNMENT in this section.

3) Disconnect and support propeller shaft out of the way. Remove shock absorbers and spring "U" bolts. Remove rear axle assembly from vehicle.

Installation

To install, reverse removal procedure.

PINION FLANGE & OIL SEAL

Removal

1) Raise and support vehicle. Place alignment marks on propeller shaft, companion flange, and end of pinion stem for installation reference. Disconnect propeller shaft and support out of the way. Remove wheels and brake drums to prevent any drag or false preload readings.

2) Measure pinion bearing preload by rotating pinion with an INCH lb. torque wrench. Rotate pinion through several revolutions and record torque while pinion is being rotated. Hold companion flange and remove drive pinion nut and Belleville washer.

Drive Axles

CHRYSLER MOTORS — 7 1/4" & 8 1/4" RING GEAR (Cont.)

3) Using Pinion Flange Remover (C-452) and Holder (C-3281), remove drive pinion flange. Lower rear of vehicle to prevent lubrication leakage. Using Seal Remover (C-748), remove pinion oil seal.

Installation

1) Inspect flange for damage and repair if necessary. Using a Pinion Seal Installer (C-4002 or C-3719) for 7 1/4" axle or (C-4076) for 8 1/4" axle, install new pinion oil seal. Seal is properly installed when seal flange contacts housing flange face. Outside diameter of seal is pre-coated with special sealer so no sealing compound is required.

2) Position flange on pinion stem (aligning scribe marks). Using Pinion Flange Remover (C-452) and Holder (C-3281), reinstall pinion flange. Install Belleville washer (convex side of washer out) and pinion nut. Make sure bearing rollers are properly seated. Using a torque wrench, measure pinion bearing preload.

3) Continue tightening pinion nut and checking preload until preload is at original setting. At a minimum pinion nut torque of 210 ft. lbs. (285 N.m), pinion bearing preload should be 15-30 INCH lbs. (1.7-3.4 N.m) for 7 1/4" axle or 20-35 INCH lbs. (2-4 N.m) for 8 1/4" axles with new bearings and not exceed 10 INCH lbs. (1.1 N.m) over original setting for used bearings.

CAUTION: If desired preload is exceeded, a new collapsible spacer must be installed and nut retightened until proper preload is obtained.

OVERHAUL

NOTE: **Overhaul may be accomplished without removing complete axle assembly from vehicle. Axle shafts must be removed as previously outlined.**

DISASSEMBLY

NOTE: **Side play and runout checks should be made during disassembly for use at reassembly.**

1) Block brake pedal in UP position. Drain fluid from housing, remove cover, and clean interior of differential. Position screwdriver between left side of housing and differential case flange.

2) Using a prying motion, determine if side play is present. No side play should be present. Side play resulting from bearing cones becoming loose on differential case hubs requires replacement of case. Otherwise, tighten threaded adjusting nut to remove side play.

3) Mount a dial indicator on Pilot Stud (C-3288-B) and load indicator stem slightly when plunger is at right angles to back face of ring gear. Measure ring gear runout by turning ring gear several complete revolutions. Mark ring gear and differential case at point of maximum runout. Runout should not exceed .005" (.13 mm).

4) Mark axle housing and differential bearing caps for installation in original positions during reassembly. Remove adjuster lock from each bearing cap. Loosen but DO NOT remove bearing caps. Insert Hex Adjuster (C-4164) through each axle tube and loosen hex adjusters.

Fig. 2: Chrysler Motors Rear Axle Assembly

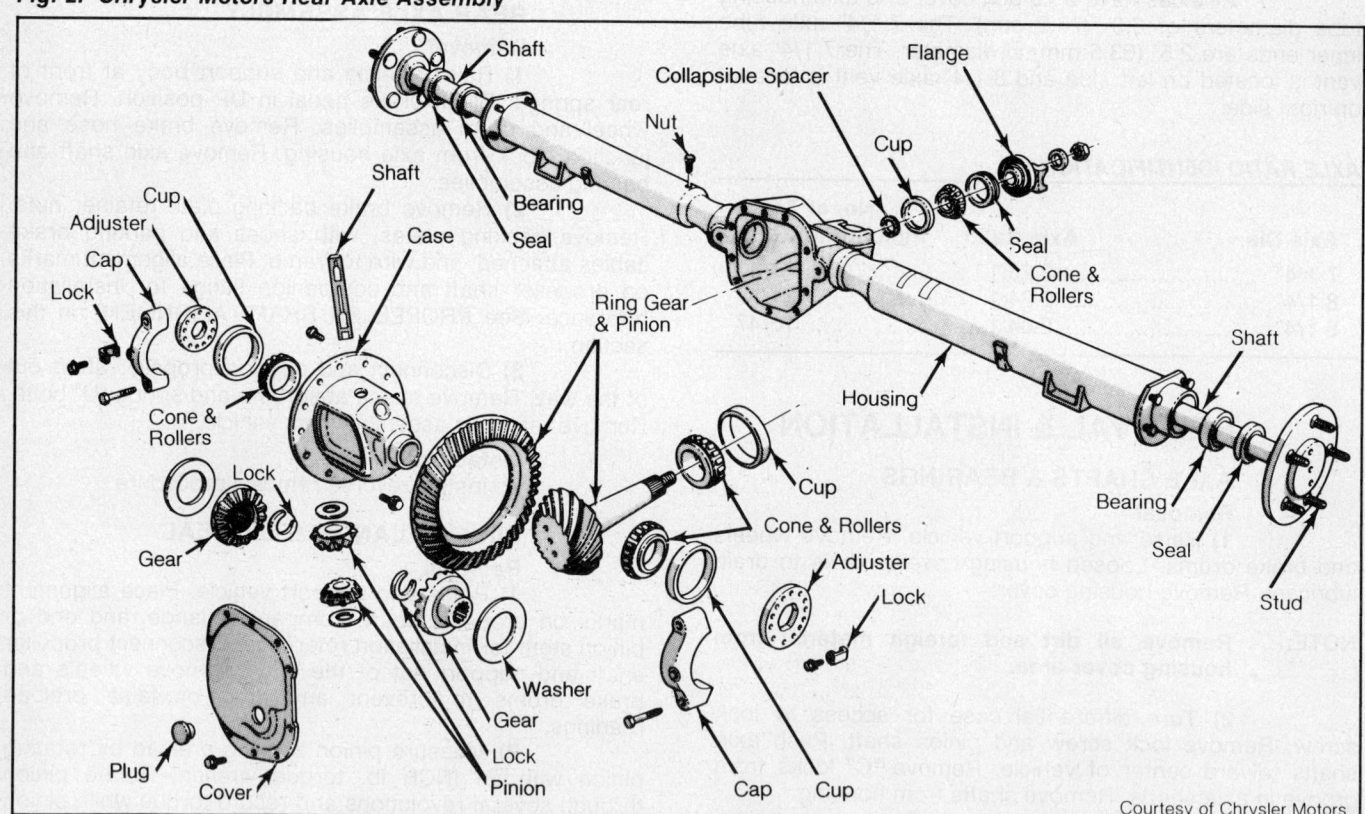

Courtesy of Chrysler Motors.

CHRYSLER MOTORS – 7 1/4" & 8 1/4" RING GEAR (Cont.)

5) Hold differential in position. Using caution, remove bearing caps and differential assembly. Keep bearing caps and cups with their respective bearings. On 8 1/4" axle, threaded adjusters must be kept with respective bearings. On 7 1/4" axle, adjusters remain in housing.

NOTE: DO NOT remove ring gear from case unless either case or gear set is to be replaced or if runout exceeds .005" (.13 mm).

6) Mount differential case and ring gear assembly in soft-jawed vise. Remove and discard ring gear bolts. Using a brass drift or plastic mallet, tap ring gear loose from differential case and remove ring gear. Ring gear bolts have left-hand threads. If ring gear runout exceeded .005" (.13 mm), proceed to step **7)**. If not, proceed to step **10)**.

7) Install differential case (without ring gear installed) and respective bearing cups in housing. Install bearing caps and tighten bearing cap bolts lightly. Using Hex Adjuster (C-4164), tighten both hex adjusters to remove all side play.

8) Mount a dial indicator to housing and position plunger so it contacts ring gear side of differential case flange. Rotate differential case several complete revolutions and note total indicator reading. Runout must NOT exceed .003" (.08 mm).

9) If runout exceeds .003" (.08 mm), replace differential case. Remove dial indicator, bearing cap bolts, bearing caps, and differential. If runout does not exceed .003" (.08 mm), runout may be reduced by positioning ring gear 180 degrees from point of maximum runout during reassembly.

10) Check side gear axial clearance by using two .005" (.13 mm) feeler gauges. Attempt to insert one feeler gauge at top and other feeler gauge at bottom of side gear thrust surfaces. Feeler gauges should not fit.

11) With differential mounted in soft-jawed vise, drive out pinion shaft lock pin with hammer and drift. Using a brass drift, remove pinion shaft. Rotate side gears until pinion gears appear at case window. Remove pinion gears, side gears, and thrust washers. Using Bearing Remover/Installer (C-293-PA), Adapter (C-293-44) for 7 1/4" axle or (C-293-48) for 8 1/4" axle, and Plug (SP-3289), remove differential side bearings.

12) Using an INCH lb. torque wrench, measure pinion bearing preload and record reading. Remove pinion nut and washer. Remove pinion flange and pinion oil seal. Remove pinion and front bearing cup.

NOTE: To remove drive pinion or front pinion bearing cone, pinion stem must be driven rearward out of bearing. This will damage bearing rollers and cup, so new cone and cup assembly must be installed.

13) Discard collapsible spacer. Using Bearing Remover/Installer and Handle (C-4306 and C-4171), remove front and rear bearing cups from housing. Using Bearing Remover/Installer and Adapter (C-293-PA and C-293-40) on 7 1/4" axles and (C-293-PA and C-293-42) on 8 1/4" axles, remove rear pinion bearing from pinion stem. Remove shim from drive pinion and record thickness.

REASSEMBLY
Differential Case
1) Lubricate all parts when assembling and adjusting. If .005" (.13 mm) feeler gauges could be inserted behind side gears during disassembly, replace thrust washers with thickest pair that will permit assembly. Install thrust washers on differential side gears and position gears in case. Place thrust washers on both differential pinion gears. Mesh pinion gears with side gears, placing pinion gears 180 degrees apart.

2) Rotate side gears to align pinion gears and washers with pinion shaft hole in case. Install differential pinion shaft and align lock pin hole in differential case. Install lock pin from ring gear side of case. Recheck side gear clearance. If .005" (.13 mm) feeler gauges can be inserted with thickest service thrust washers installed, replace differential assembly.

3) Using a whetstone, relieve sharp edge of chamfer on inside diameter of ring gear. Heat ring gear with heat lamp or by immersing in hot water or oil. Temperature should not exceed 300°F (148°C). Do not use a torch to heat ring gear. Using pilot studs to align gear to case, install new ring gear bolts (left-hand threads) through case flange and into ring gear.

Fig. 3: Locating Ring Gear to Case

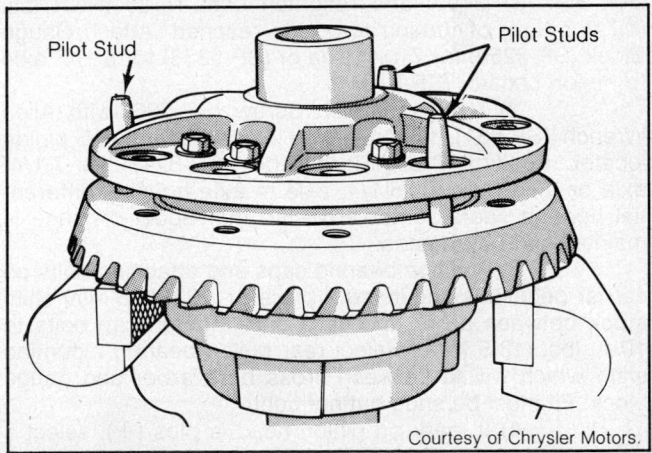

Pilot Stud

Pilot Studs

Courtesy of Chrysler Motors.

4) Place unit in soft-jawed vise and alternately tighten bolts. Using an arbor press and Bearing Installer (C-3716-A) for 7 1/4" axle or (C-4340) for 8 1/4" axle with Handle (C-4171), install differential bearing cones. Do not exert pressure against bearing cage as damage will result.

Pinion Bearing Cup
1) Place Pinion Locator (SP-3244) for 7 1/4" axle or (SP-6030) for 8 1/4" axle over Pinion Locator (SP-3191 or SP-5385) for 7 1/4" axle or (SP-5385) for 8 1/4" axle followed by rear bearing cone.

2) After positioning tool assembly in rear axle housing, install Pinion Shaft Locating Sleeve (SP-3245) for 7 1/4" axle or (SP-5382) for 8 1/4" axle, front bearing cone, Washer (SP-6022) for 8 1/4" axle, Compression Sleeve (SP-3194-B), Centralizing Washer (SP-534), and Compression Nut (SP-3193).

3) While holding Compression Sleeve (SP-3194-B) with Handle (C-3281), tighten Compression Nut (SP-3193) to draw pinion bearing cups into axle housing cup bores.

4) Permit tool to turn several revolutions during tightening operation to align bearing rollers. Position of the drive pinion with respect to the drive gear (depth of mesh) is determined by the location of the bearing cup shoulders in the carrier and the portion of the pinion in back of the rear bearing. A shim is located between the rear pinion bearing cone and the head of the pinion.

Drive Axles

CHRYSLER MOTORS — 7 1/4" & 8 1/4" RING GEAR (Cont.)

Fig. 4: Chrysler Motors Pinion Gauge Tool Set

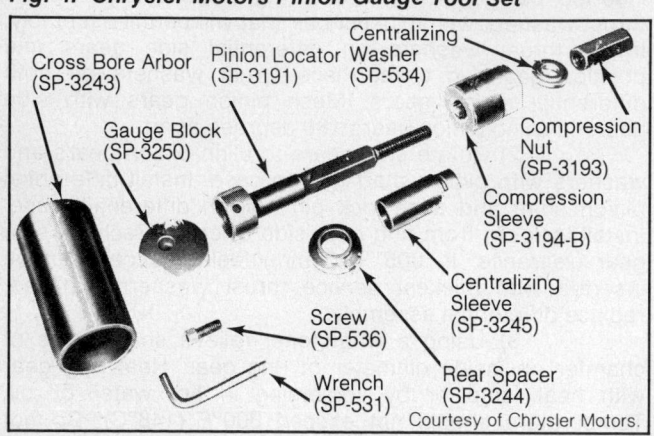

Cross Bore Arbor (SP-3243)
Pinion Locator (SP-3191)
Centralizing Washer (SP-534)
Gauge Block (SP-3250)
Compression Nut (SP-3193)
Compression Sleeve (SP-3194-B)
Centralizing Sleeve (SP-3245)
Screw (SP-536)
Rear Spacer (SP-3244)
Wrench (SP-531)
Courtesy of Chrysler Motors.

These tools required for 7 1/4" rear axle.

Pinion Shim Thickness

1) With bearing installation tool left in housing after installing drive pinion bearing cups, loosen Compression Nut (SP-3193) and retighten until 15-25 INCH lbs. (1.7-2.8 N.m) of turning torque is reached. Attach Gauge Block (SP-3250) for 7 1/4" axle or (SP-5383) for 8 1/4" axle to Pinion Locator (SP-5385).

2) Using an Allen Screw (SP-536) with Allen Wrench (SP-531), fasten gauge block securely to pinion locator. Position Cross Bore Arbor (SP-3243) for 7 1/4" axle or (SP-6029) for 8 1/4" axle to axle housing differential bearing seat. Center arbor so that equal distance is maintained at both ends.

3) Position bearing caps and attaching bolts on carrier pedestals and insert a piece of .002" (.05 mm) shim stock between arbor and each cap. Tighten cap bolts to 10 ft. lbs. (13.5 N.m). Select rear pinion bearing mounting shim which will fit between cross bore arbor and gauge block. Fit must be snug but not tight.

4) If mark on pinion head is plus (+), select a shim that many thousandths thinner for installation. If mark on pinion has a minus (−), select a shim that many thousandths thicker for installation. Treat other pinion markings in a similar manner. Spacers are available in .001" (.025 mm) increments from .020-.038" (.50-.96 mm).

Pinion Installation & Bearing Preload

1) Place shim and rear bearing cone on pinion stem. Press bearing on pinion shaft using an arbor press and Bearing Installer (C-3717) for 7 1/4" axle or (C-4040) for 8 1/4" axle. Lubricate bearing cones with rear axle lubricant and insert pinion and bearing assembly up through axle casting.

2) Install new collapsible spacer followed by front bearing onto pinion shaft. Install companion flange using Companion Flange Remover/Installer (C-3718) and Holder (C-3281).

NOTE: During installation of drive pinion shaft, DO NOT collapse spacer.

3) Remove tool and companion flange from pinion shaft. Install drive pinion oil seal, using Oil Seal Installer (C-4002 or C-3719) for 7 1/4" axle or (C-4076) for 8 1/4" axle, until seal flange contacts housing flange face. While supporting pinion in carrier, reinstall companion flange. Remove tools and install Belleville washer (convex side up) and pinion nut.

4) Hold companion flange with Holder (C-3281) and tighten nut until no end play can be detected. Continue tightening nut and checking preload with an INCH lb. torque wrench until pinion bearing preload is 15-30 INCH lbs. (1.7-3.4 N.m) for 7 1/4" axle or 20-35 INCH lbs. (2-3 N.m) for 8 1/4" axle. Final nut torque must be at least 210 ft. lbs. (285 N.m).

5) If installing NEW front pinion bearing and original rear bearing, correct preload is 10 INCH lbs. (1.2 N.m) greater than tear down reading. Under no circumstances should pinion nut be backed off. If desired preload is exceeded, a new spacer will be required and pinion nut tightened until proper preload is reached.

Differential Bearing Preload & Ring & Pinion Backlash Adjustment

1) Coat differential bearings, cups, and adjusters with axle lubricant. Carefully position differential case (with bearing cups installed) into axle housing. Install bearing caps in original position. Tighten top bearing cap bolts to 10 ft. lbs. (13.6 N.m) and tighten lower bolts finger tight, until head is just seated on bearing cap.

2) Using Hex Adjuster (C-4164), turn each hex adjuster in until bearing free play is eliminated with approximately .01" (.25 mm) backlash existing between ring gear and pinion. Seat bearings by rotating pinion 1/2 turn in each direction 5-10 times each time adjusters are moved.

3) Install dial indicator and position plunger against drive side of a ring gear tooth. Find point of minimum backlash by checking at 4 positions approximately 90 degrees apart around ring gear. Rotate gear to position of least backlash and mark index so all backlash readings will be taken with same teeth in mesh.

4) Loosen right adjuster and tighten left adjuster until backlash is .003-.004" (.08-.10 mm), with each adjuster tightened to 10 ft. lbs. (13.6 N.m). Seat bearings and tighten bearing cap screws to 45 ft. lbs. (61 N.m) for 7 1/4" axle or 100 ft. lbs. (136 N.m) for 8 1/4" axle. Tighten right adjuster to 70 ft. lbs. (95 N.m) and seat bearings at same time until torque remains constant at 70 ft. lbs. (95 N.m).

5) Measure backlash. Backlash should be .003-.006" (.08-.15 mm) for 7 1/4" axle or .005-.008" (.13-.20 mm) for 8 1/4" axle. If backlash does not meet specification, increase torque on right adjuster and seat bearing until correct backlash is obtained. Tighten left adjuster to 70 ft. lbs. (95 N.m) and seat bearings at same time until torque remains constant.

6) If all steps were performed correctly, initial reading on left adjuster should be about 70 ft. lbs. (95 N.m). If it is substantially less, complete procedure must be repeated.

7) After adjustments are completed, install adjuster locks. Lock teeth must be engaged in adjuster threads (for 7 1/4" axle) or lock finger engaged in adjuster hole (for 8 1/4" axle). Tighten lock screws to 90 INCH lbs. (10 N.m).

Differential Side Gear Clearance Checking & Adjustment

1) With axle shaft and "C" lock in place, measure clearance behind each side gear by inserting equal thickness feeler gauges on opposite sides of hub. If measurement is .005" or less, check to see if axle shaft on that side is contacting pinion shaft. Check while feeler gauges are still in place. If axle shaft is not contacting

CHRYSLER MOTORS – 7 1/4" & 8 1/4" RING GEAR (Cont.)

pinion shaft, side gear fit is okay on that side. Check opposite side. *See Fig. 5.*

Fig. 5: Measuring Side Gear Clearance

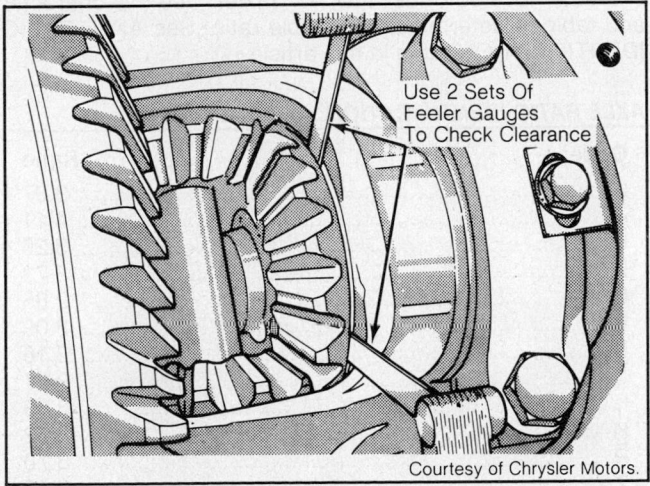

Use 2 Sets Of Feeler Gauges To Check Clearance

Courtesy of Chrysler Motors.

2) If clearance was greater than .005" and axle shaft does not contact pinion shaft, then record side gear clearance. Remove thrust washer and measure its thickness with a micrometer. Add thrust washer thickness to side clearance. Install new thrust washer that is closest to, but does not exceed, this total thickness.

3) If axle shaft contacted pinion shaft with feeler gauges in place, "C" lock prevents side gear from moving inward any farther. Measure clearance with "C" lock in place. Remove "C" lock and remeasure clearance.

4) Remove and measure thrust washer thickness. If clearance changes less than .012" (.30 mm) with "C" lock removed, add side gear clearance recorded with "C" lock in place to thrust washer thickness. Install new thrust washer that is closest to, but does not exceed, this total thickness.

5) If clearance increased more than .012" (.30 mm) with "C" lock removed, replace both side gears and repeat measurement test. If side gear clearance still exceeds .012" (.30 mm) when using new side gears and the thickest thrust washers, differential case must be replaced.

AXLE ASSEMBLY SPECIFICATIONS

Application	Specification
Capacity	
7 1/4" Gear	2.5 pts. (1.2L)
8 1/4" Gear	4.4 pts. (2.1L)
Pinion Bearing Preload [1]	
Used	10-25 INCH lbs. (1.1-2.8 N.m)
New	
7 1/4" Gear	15-30 INCH lbs. (1.7-3.4 N.m)
8 1/4" Gear	20-35 INCH lbs. (2.3-4.0 N.m)
Ring Gear & Case Runout [2]	.005" (.13 mm) Max.
Ring & Pinion Backlash [3]	
7 1/4" Gear	.003-.006" (.08-.15 mm)
8 1/4" Gear	.005-.008" (.13-.20 mm)

[1] – Turning torque.
[2] – See text for more information.
[3] – At point of minimum backlash.

TIGHTENING SPECIFICATIONS

Application	Ft. Lbs. (N.m)
Brake Support Plate Retainer Nuts	35 (47)
Carrier Cover Bolts (7 1/4" Gear)	35 (47)
Differential Bearing Cap Bolts	
7 1/4" Gear	45 (61)
8 1/4" Gear	100 (136)
Drive Pinion Flange Nut	210 (285) Min.
Ring Gear-to-Case Bolts	70 (95)
Shock Absorber Stud Nuts (Lower)	50 (68)
Spring "U" Bolt Nuts	45 (61) Max.
Wheel Stud Nuts	85 (115)

Application	INCH Lbs. (N.m)
Carrier Cover Bolts (8 1/4" Gear)	250 (28)
Prop. Shaft Bolts (Rear)	170-200 (19-23)

Drive Axles

FORD MOTOR CO. ALL-WHEEL DRIVE REAR AXLE

Tempo, Topaz

DESCRIPTION & OPERATION

Rear axle assembly is an intergal-type housing, hypoid gear design. The center line of the drive pinion is below the center line of the ring gear. The ring gear diameter is 4.75" (120.7 mm) and is bolted to differential assembly. The drive pinion is supported by 2 opposed bearing assemblies.

The differential assembly consists of a 1-piece case with 2 openings to allow for service and lubricant flow. The axles are splined into side gears and retained with snap rings. Differential is equipped with Traction-Lok consisting of disc and plate assemblies located on the axle side of each side gear.

Rear axle receives power from engine through transaxle transfer case and drive shaft. Drive shaft is a 2 piece with a unique center yoke phasing that MUST be maintained. With all-wheel drive disengaged, the rear wheels drive the axle shafts, rear differential, and driveshaft.

IDENTIFICATION

The vehicle certification label is located on the left front door lock panel. The axle ratio is identified by the character located under the "AX" (axle). Use this character and table to determine the vehicle ratio. See AXLE RATIO IDENTIFICATION table in this article.

AXLE RATIO IDENTIFICATION

Code	Ratio
0	3.07
4	4.11
6	3.26
7	3.73
8	2.85
9	3.09
B	3.16
C	3.37
F	3.63
H	3.52
P	3.70
Z	3.19

Fig. 1: Exploded View of Rear Differential

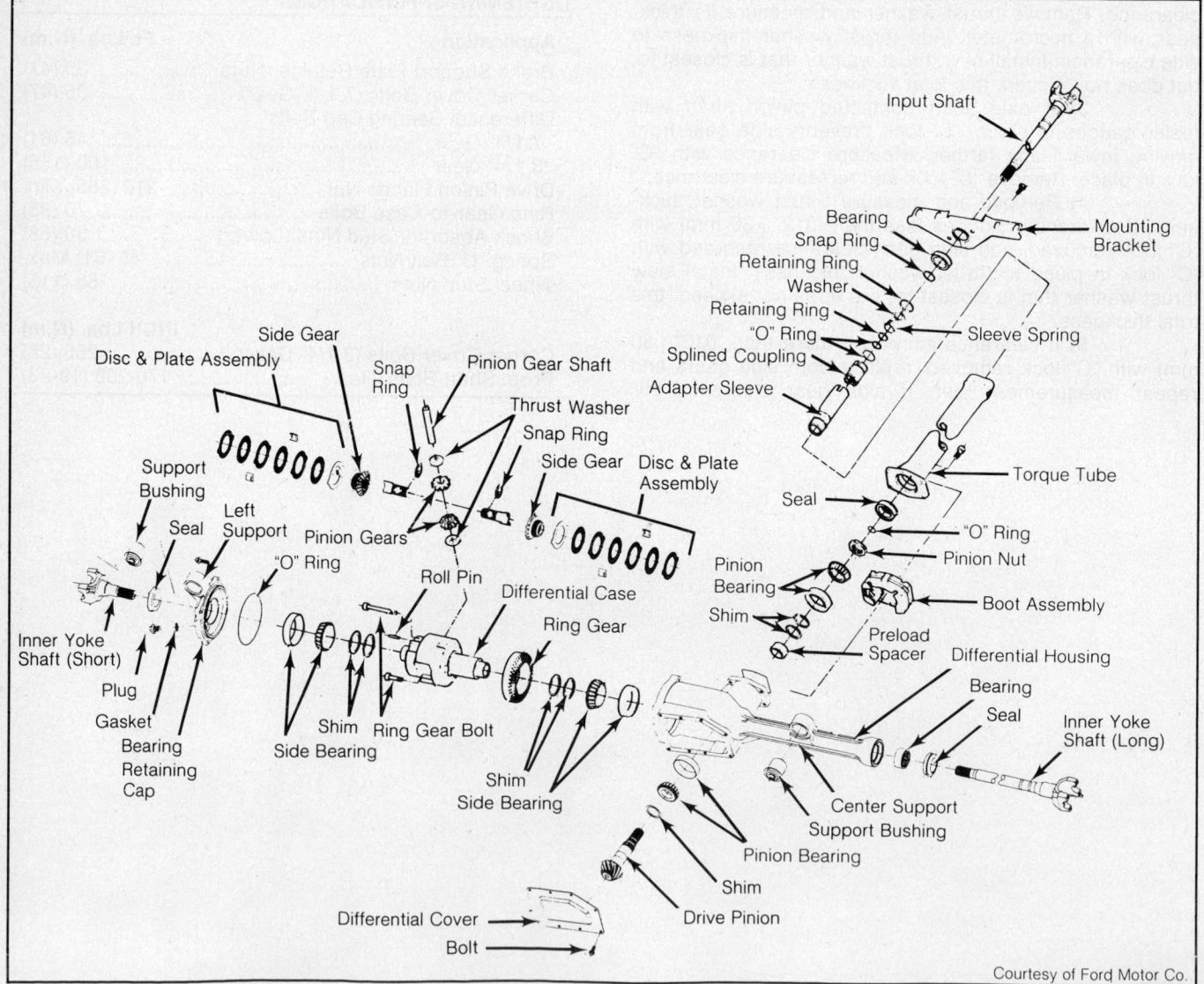

Courtesy of Ford Motor Co.

FORD MOTOR CO. ALL-WHEEL DRIVE REAR AXLE (Cont.)

LUBRICATION

The rear axle assembly uses 20.5 ozs. (581 g) of Hypoid Gear Lubricant (C6AZ-1958-E) and 1.5 ozs. (43 g) of Friction Modifier (C8AZ-19B546-A).

REMOVAL & INSTALLATION

REAR DIFFERENTIAL ASSEMBLY

NOTE: **Remove rear axle assembly and place on work bench to perform all repairs.**

Removal

1) Raise and support vehicle. Position a jack under axle assembly. Remove exhaust system from catalytic converter back. Index drive shaft-to-yoke flanges. Remove rear "U" joint bolts retaining drive shaft. Lower drive shaft. Remove torque tube support bracket mounting bolts. Remove damper and position drive shaft out of way.

CAUTION: **Any time a "U" joint retaining bolt is removed, Loctite 242 (Ford specification E0AZ-14554-A) must be applied to threads.**

2) Remove left and center axle support mounting bolts. Index axle shaft-to-yoke mounting. Lower differential assembly enough to remove bolts retaining inner axle shafts. Remove both axle shafts from differential and support with wire. Lower and remove differential.

CAUTION: **Apply Loctite 242 (Ford specification E0AZ-14554-A) to all removed "U" joint bolts.**

Installation

Position differential under vehicle and raise enough to connect axle shafts. Align marks made durning removal and attach axle shafts. To complete installation, reverse removal procedure. Tighten all bolts/nuts to specifications. Fill differential with specified lubricant.

AXLE SHAFTS

Removal & Installation

Remove rear suspension control arm bolt. Index inner and outer axle shaft-to-yoke. Remove "U" joint bolts. Slide axle shaft together and remove axle shaft. To install, reverse removal procedure. Tighten bolts/nuts to specification.

OVERHAUL

AXLE SHAFTS

Disassembly

1) Remove axle shaft to be repaired and place on work bench. See AXLE SHAFTS under REMOVAL & INSTALLATION in this article. Index axle shaft at splined joint before separating. Cut and remove boot clamps. Separate axle shaft.

2) Remove and discard "U" joint snap rings. Using "U" Joint Remover (T74P-4635-C), remove bearings from yoke.

Reassembly

1) Fill boot with approximately 10 grams of Multipurpose Long-Life Lubricant (C1AZ-19590-B). Coat splines with same lubricant. Install original equipment clamps and boot on shaft with external splines. Align index marks and carefully install axle shafts. Ensure splines are properly aligned. Do not force shafts together.

2) Remove excess grease and air pressure from boot and slip yoke. Install clamps on boot and retain with Clamp Pliers (T63P-9171-A). To complete installation, reverse disassembly procedure.

REAR DIFFERENTIAL ASSEMBLY

Disassembly

1) Remove differential. See REAR DIFFERENTIAL ASSEMBLY under REMOVAL & INSTALLATION in this article. Place differential assembly on work bench. Remove protective shield from torque tube-to-differential. Remove bolts retaining torque tube to differential and remove torque tube.

2) Remove 2 mounting bolts retaining support bracket to torque tube. Pull input shaft from torque tube and place shaft horizontally in a vise with protected jaws. Remove adapter sleeve snap ring. Position shaft vertically in vise. Remove adapter sleeve.

3) Use a 2 jaw-type puller and remove splined coupling from shaft. Remove splined coupling "O" ring. Remove sleeve spring snap ring. Remove sleeve spring, flatwasher and adapter sleeve retaining ring. See Fig. 1.

4) Place yoke side of input shaft in vise. Remove snap ring retaining bearing-to-shaft. Use a press and remove bearing and bracket from shaft. Replace bracket if it is bent or damaged. Remove seal from torque tube with a 3 jaw-type puller and discard seal.

5) Remove differential housing cover bolts. Remove cover and drain lubricant. Remove both side gear snap rings and remove both inner yoke shafts. Use a 3 jaw-type puller and slide hammer to remove side bearings and seals from left and right yoke bore.

6) Remove 4 bearing retaining cap bolts from left side of differential. Remove bearing retaining cap and discard "O" ring. Remove differential case assembly from differential housing. Use a 2 jaw-type puller and remove side bearings. Mark bearings for reassembly.

7) Remove ring gear retaining bolts. Alternately tap ring gear off of case. Place differential case on short axle shaft and mount axle shaft yoke vise. Remove roll pin retaining pinion shaft to case. Remove pinion shaft out roll pin end.

8) Remove differential case from short axle shaft and place on bench with short axle shaft side down. Install Step Plate (D80L-630-1) between side gears. Install forcing screw through long yoke shaft bore. Place Threaded Adapter (T87P-4205-A) between step plate and side gear. See Fig. 2. Thread forcing screw into adapter.

9) Place differential case on short yoke shaft. Tighten forcing screw until pinion gears become loose. Use an appropriate feeler gauge and push pinion gear thrust washers from differential case. Do not mix thrust washers and pinion gears. Rotate differential case until pinion gears can be removed and remove pinion gears.

10) Remove differential case from short yoke shaft. Remove tooling. Remove one side gear at a time using care not to drop clutch pack. DO NOT mix components.

11) Remove and discard pinion adapter "O" ring at pinion. Remove staked portion on pinion nut and remove nut. Tap pinion with soft hammer amd remove pinion. Retain preload spacer and shim(s) for reassembly. Remove outer pinion bearing. Press inner bearing from pinion and retain any shim(s).

FORD MOTOR CO. ALL-WHEEL DRIVE REAR AXLE (Cont.)

Fig. 2: Disassembling Differential Case Assembly

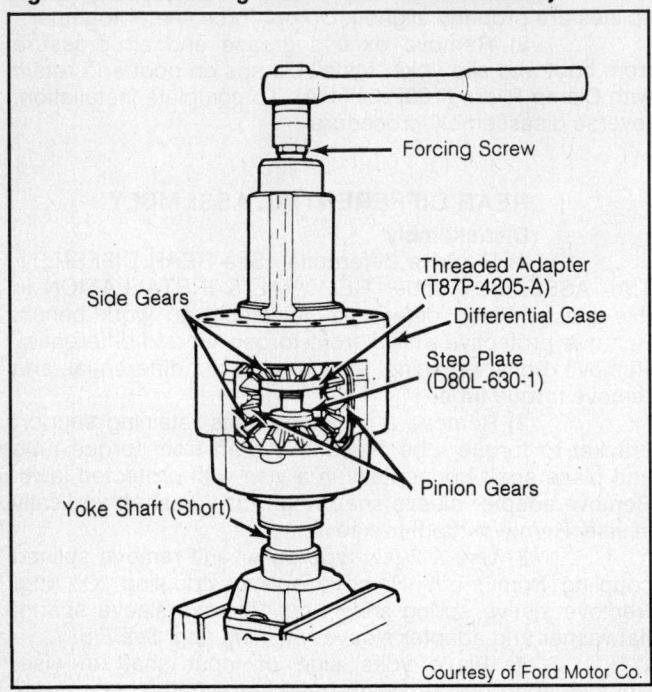

Courtesy of Ford Motor Co.

12) Remove inner and outer pinion bearing races and side bearing races with 3 jaw-type puller and slide hammer. Remove left and center support bushing from axle housing (if replacing), with a "C" clamp and appropriate adapter.

Inspection

1) Thoroughly clean componets with clean solvent (except clutch pack). Inspect all bearings and races for pitting, scoring and damage. Inspect ring gear and drive pinion for tooth contact pattern, cracks or damage. Replace ring and pinion as a set only.

2) Check differential case for cracks and damage. Ensure pinion gear thrust washer surface of case is not damaged. Inspect pinion gears, side gears and pinion gear shaft for wear or damage. Inspect clutch pack for wear or burnt surfaces.

3) Inspect axle housing for cracks and damage. Check for metal or contamination in bottom of axle housing. Inspect axle shaft for wear and damage. Check boots for cracks or splits. Replace defective components as necessary.

Reassembly

1) Lubricate clutch pack with Friction Modifier Additive (C8AZ-19B546-A). Reassemble left side gear and clutch pack. With short shaft of differential case facing up, install left side gear assembly with retainers aligned with differential case.

2) Hold left hand side gear in place and turn differential case over. Reassemble and install right side gear as stated in step **1)**. Ensure retainers are aligned with differential case. Install tooling used at disassembly. *See Fig. 2.* Place differential case on short yoke shaft and tighten, forcing-screw slightly.

3) Place differential pinion gears and thrust washers in position in opening of case. Ensure gears are 180 degrees apart with shaft bore of gears aligned. Ensure pinion gears are in proper mesh with side gears. Rotate differential case until pinion gears are aligned with shaft bore.

4) With differential pinion gears installed, remove tooling. Install pinion shaft and roll pin. DO NOT install ring gear at this time. Set differential case aside.

5) Install inner and outer pinion bearing race in differential housing, with an appropriate size driver. Install Handle (T76P-4020-A11), Screw (T80T-4020-F43), Dummy Pinion Aligning Adapter (T76P-4020-A14) and Gauge Block and Disc Kit (T87P-4020-A) into inner pinion bearing bore. Slide Gauge Bar (T87P-4020-A1) through left side of case. *See Fig. 3.*

Fig. 3: Drive Pinion Setting

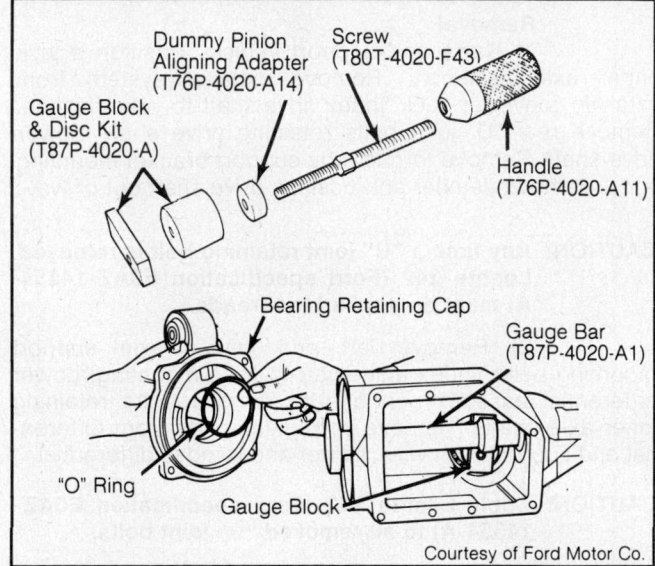

Courtesy of Ford Motor Co.

6) Install bearing retaining cap with "O" ring from block and disc kit. Tighten retaining cap screws snug. Use a feeler gauge or shim and determine distance between gauge bar and block. A slight drag should be felt. Check pinion gear for an etched reading.

7) If pinion gear is marked with a (+) amount, this amount must be subtracted from obtained feeler gauge or shim thickness amount found in step **6)**. If pinion gear is marked with a (-) amount, this must be added to amount found in step **6)**. Add or subtract for proper shim to be used.

8) Press inner pinion bearing and proper shim on pinion. Install disassembled preload spacer, shim(s) and new "O" ring on pinion. Place pinion assembly in differential housing. Install outer pinion bearing race. Install and tighten pinion nut, but do not stake at this time.

9) Use an INCH lb. torque wrench and measure pinion rotation torque. Rotation torque should be 15-35 INCH lb. (1.7-4 N.m). If not within specifications, add or remove shims as necessary. Install Gauge Bar (PS85-167-1-1A) and Dummy Pinion (PS85-167-1-3). *See Fig. 4.* Use a feeler gauge or shim and measure clearance. A slight drag should be felt.

10) Drive pinions are machined and fitted at factory. An etched value is located on the drive pinion gear in either a plus (+) or a minus (-). Note the etched value and use for setting drive pinion height.

11) If drive pinion is not etched with a value the pinion is zero. The standard pinion height is .020" (.051 mm) with a tolerance of plus (+) or minus (-) .002" (.051 mm). Use the example in step **12)** for etched value specifications.

FORD MOTOR CO. ALL-WHEEL DRIVE REAR AXLE (Cont.)

Fig. 4: Measuring Drive Pinion Height

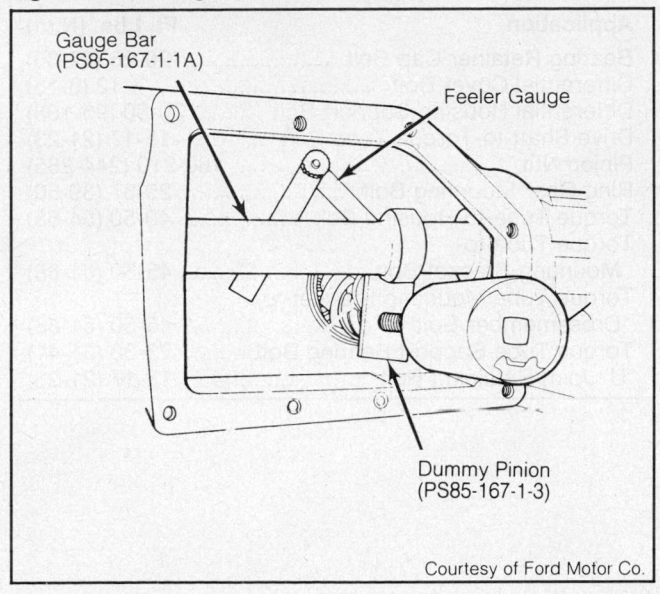

Courtesy of Ford Motor Co.

Fig. 6: Checking End Play

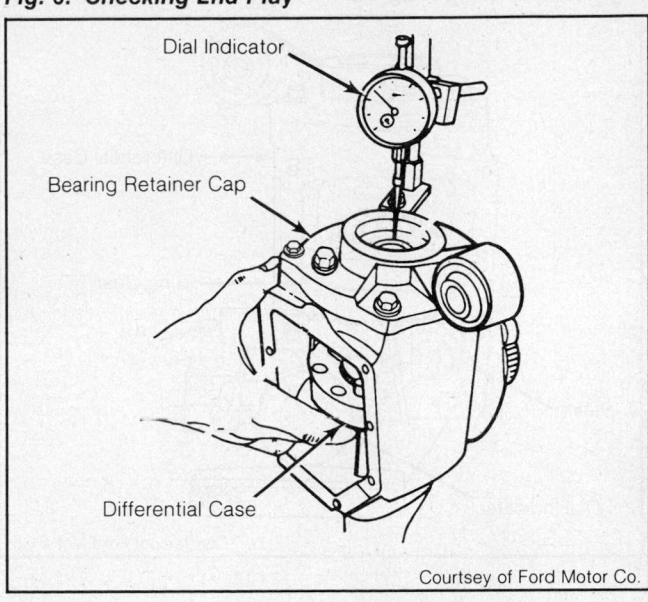

Courtsey of Ford Motor Co.

12) For example, a drive pinion with etched value of -2 would have an .18" (.46 mm) distance with a tolerance of .002" (.051 mm). The shim requirement amount would be .016-.020" (.40-.50 mm).

13) To adjust the distance, remove or increase shim (s) located beneath inner pinion bearing cone. Use thinner shim(s) to increase or thicker shim(s) to decrease the distance. With pinion set to specifications, recheck rotation torque. With rotation torque at specifications, stake pinion nut.

14) Install Master Bearings (T87P-4222-A) on differential case. *See Fig. 5.* Place differential housing in a vise with bearing retainer cap upward. Install differential case in housing. Install bearing retainer cap. Mount a dial indicator to bearing retainer cap. Tighten bearing retainer cap to 20-26 ft. lbs. (27-35 N.m).

15) Adjust dial indicator so tip touches machined end of differential case trunnion. Zero dial indicator. *See Fig. 6.* Lift differential case upward and record reading on dial indicator. Repeat procedure and use the consistent reading for shim selection.

Fig. 5: Installing Master Bearings

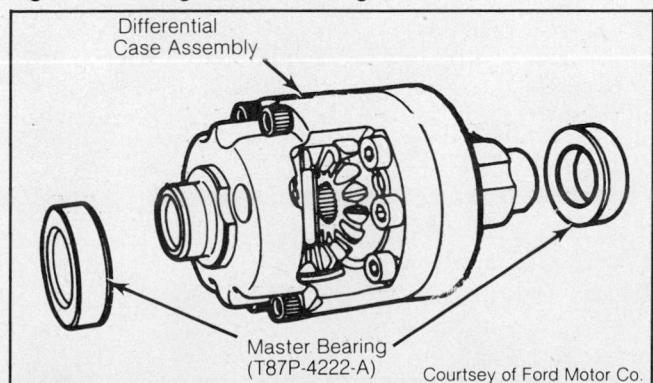

Courtesy of Ford Motor Co.

16) Remove dial indicator and differential case from housing. Install ring gear and tighten to specifications. Reinstall differential case in housing with master bearings still installed on case. Reinstall bearing retainer cap and dial indicator as in step **14)** and **15)**. *See Fig. 6.*

17) Lift differential case upward and record reading. Repeat procedure and use the consistent reading for shim selection. Using the consistent reading, subtract reading with ring gear installed from reading without ring gear installed. Use this total for shim thickness on pinion side of case.

NOTE: **Pinion side of case is the tooth side of mounted ring gear. Ring gear side of case is the backside of mounted ring gear.**

18) For ring gear side of case, use the consistent reading and subtract reading with ring gear from reading without ring gear. Subtract and additional .008" (.20 mm) from the total. Use this total for shim thickness on ring gear side.

19) Remove differential case. Remove master bearings. Install proper selected shim(s) to proper side and install side bearings with an appropriate size driver. Install side bearing race in bearing retainer cap with appropriate size driver. Thoroughly lubricate bearings and races.

20) Install differential case assembly in housing. Install and tighten bearing retainer cap. Mount a dial indicator and measure ring gear backlash in 3 equally spaced points. *See Fig. 7.* Backlash should be .004-.006" (.10-.15 mm). If backlash is excessive, change side bearing shim(s) from pinion side to ring gear side. This will move ring gear closer to pinion.

21) If backlash is less than specifications, change shim(s) from ring gear side to pinion side. This will move ring gear away from pinion. With backlash within specifications, check total pinion rotating torque. Pinion rotating torque with case assembly installed should be 4-7 INCH lb. (50-80 N.m).

22) With backlash and pinion rotating torque within specification, complete reassembly by reversing disassembly procedure. Install axle shaft bearings in differential housing with name on bearing facing axle shaft (outboard side). Ensure to align all matching marks made at disassembly. Tighten all bolts/nuts to specifications. Fill differential assembly with specified grease.

FORD MOTOR CO. ALL-WHEEL DRIVE REAR AXLE (Cont.)

Fig. 7: Measuring Ring Gear Backlash

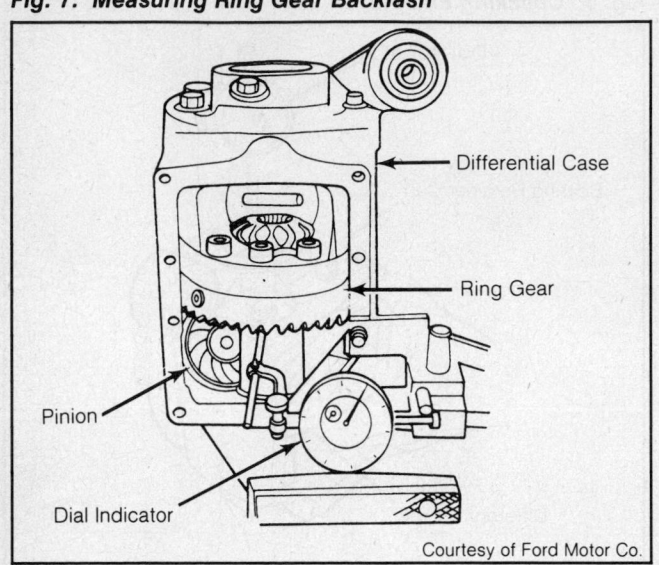

Differential Case

Ring Gear

Pinion

Dial Indicator

Courtesy of Ford Motor Co.

TIGHTENING SPECIFICATION

Application	Ft. Lbs. (N.m)
Bearing Retainer Cap Bolt	20-26 (27-35)
Differential Cover Bolt	7-12 (9-16)
Differential Housing Support Bolt	70-80 (95-108)
Drive Shaft-to-Torque Tube Bolt	15-17 (21-23)
Pinion Nut	180-210 (244-285)
Ring Gear Mounting Bolt	29-37 (39-50)
Torque Tube-to-Housing Bolt	40-50 (54-68)
Torque Tube-to-Mounting Bracket Bolt	45-50 (61-68)
Torque Tube Mounting Bracket-to-Crossmember Bolt	45-50 (61-68)
Torque Tube Support Bearing Bolt	23-30 (31-41)
"U" Joint Retaining Bolt	15-17 (21-23)

FORD MOTOR CO. — 7 1/2" & 8 3/4" RING GEAR

RWD Models

DESCRIPTION

The rear axle is a hypoid design ring and pinion gear encased in an integral cast iron housing. Differential case assembly and pinion are mounted in axle housing using tapered bearings assemblies. A 1-piece differential case contains a conventional 2-pinion differential assembly. Semi-floating axle shafts are retained by "C" washer locks at splined end of axle shafts.

AXLE RATIO & IDENTIFICATION

On Ford Motor Co. vehicles Vehicle Certification Label attached to left front door lock panel or pillar post contains axle identification code. *See Fig. 1.* Using axle identification code, axle ratio maybe determined.

Fig. 1: Vehicle Identification Label

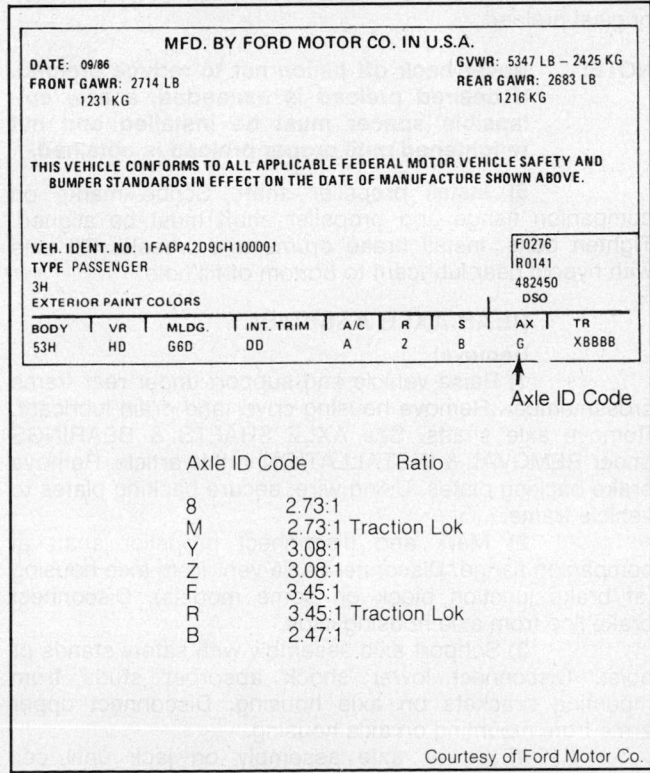

Axle ID Code	Ratio
8	2.73:1
M	2.73:1 Traction Lok
Y	3.08:1
Z	3.08:1
F	3.45:1
R	3.45:1 Traction Lok
B	2.47:1

Courtesy of Ford Motor Co.

Fig. 2: Rear Axle Identification Tag

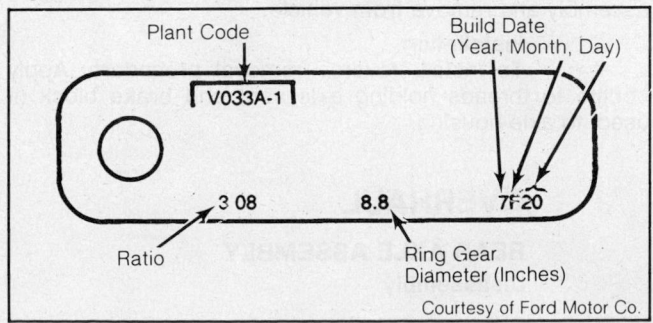

Courtesy of Ford Motor Co.

A metal tag stamped with axle model, date of manufacture, ratio, ring gear diameter and assembly plant is mounted under housing cover-to-carrier cap screw. *See Fig. 2.* Using axle model code, gear ratio may be determined. See AXLE RATIO IDENTIFICATION table.

AXLE RATIO IDENTIFICATION

Ratio	Code
7 1/2" Axle	
2.73:1	272-F, 478-B & 912-A
3.08:1	462-B & 495-B
3.27:1	277-F, 282-D & 496-B
3.45:1	281-D
3.73:1	266-D
8 3/4" Axle	
2.73:1	030-A, 012-A
3.08:1	014-A, 014-P, 422-E 446-C & 033-A
3.27:1	016-A, 016-P, 424-E & 038-A

REMOVAL & INSTALLATION

AXLE SHAFTS & BEARINGS

Removal

1) Raise and support vehicle. Remove wheels and brake drums. Remove housing cover and drain lubricant. Remove differential pinion shaft lock bolt and pinion shaft.

2) Remove wheel speed sensor (if equipped). Wheel speed sensor must be removed to prevent damage during axle shaft removal. Push axle toward center and remove "C" locks. Remove axles, using care not to damage axle seal. Using a slide hammer and puller, remove bearing and seal as a unit.

Installation

1) Lubricate bearing with rear axle lubricant. Install wheel bearing and seal into axle housing using proper sized driver. Check that seal was not damaged during installation. Lubricate seal lips with multi-purpose lubricant. If seal becomes cocked during installation, remove and replace with a new one.

2) On 8 3/4" ring gears, install "O" ring on splined end of axle shaft. Install axle shaft in axle housing, using care not to damage oil seal. Install "C" locks on axle shafts. Push shafts outboard to seat locks in counterbore of differential side gears.

3) Coat pinion shaft with gear lubricant. Install pinion shaft and lock bolt. See TIGHTENING SPECIFICATIONS table at end of article. Check that housing cover sealing surfaces are clean and free of burrs. Apply 1/8-3/16" bead of silicone sealant to face of axle housing.

4) Install housing cover, identification tag and retaining bolts. Tighten retaining bolts in crosswise pattern. Install wheel speed sensor (if equipped).

NOTE: No gasket, other than silicone sealant, is used. Cover assembly must be installed within 15 minutes of application of sealant.

5) Refill axle with hypoid gear lubricant to bottom of fill hole. Install and tighten fill plug. On Mark VII, Continental and Mustang vehicles, remove axle housing vent. Pour 4-8 ozs. (.12-.23L) of hypoid gear lubricant through vent hole. Install vent and tighten.

FORD MOTOR CO. — 7 1/2" & 8 3/4" RING GEAR (Cont.)

Fig. 3: Ford Motor Co. 7 1/2" & 8 3/4"
Integral Housing Axle Assembly

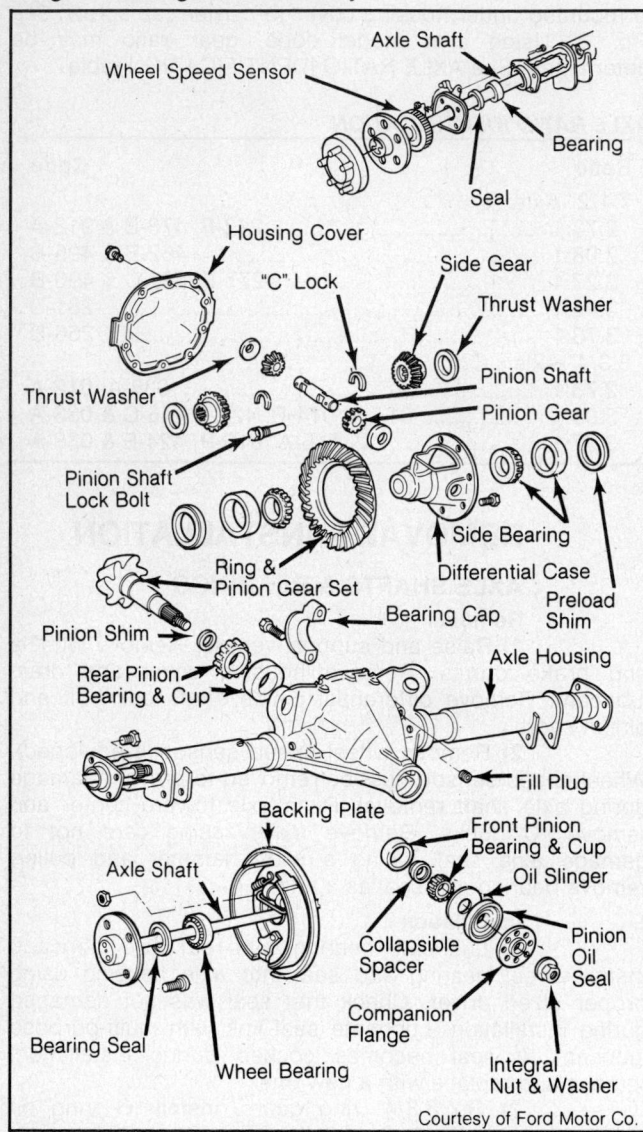

Courtesy of Ford Motor Co.

PINION FLANGE & OIL SEAL

CAUTION: Pinion flange and oil seal replacement affects bearing preload. Preload must be carefully reset during reassembly.

Removal

1) Raise and support vehicle. Remove wheels and brake drums. Scribe alignment marks on companion flange and propeller shaft for installation reference. Remove propeller shaft. Install seal installer in transmission extension housing to prevent oil leakage.

2) Using an INCH lb. torque wrench, measure and record torque required to rotate pinion through several revolutions. Mark companion flange in relation to pinion shaft. Hold companion flange and remove pinion nut. Using Companion Flange Remover (T65L-4851-B), remove companion flange. Pry oil seal from axle housing using small pry bar. DO NOT damage sealing surface of axle housing.

Installation

1) Check that all sealing surfaces are clean and free of burrs. Using Seal Installer (T79P-4676-A), install oil seal. If oil seal becomes cocked during installation, remove and replace oil seal. Lubricate oil seal lips with multi-purpose lubricant.

2) Check pinion and companion flange splines for burrs. Coat companion flange splines with small amount of gear lubricant. Align marks on companion flange and pinion. Install companion flange on pinion. Coat washer side of nut with gear lubricant. Install new nut and washer.

3) Using Companion Flange Holder (T78P-4851-A), hold companion flange and gradually tighten nut. DO NOT hammer on companion flange, or install with power tools. Rotate pinion and check pinion bearing preload often, until original preload is obtained.

4) If original preload is less than specification, tighten to obtain proper specification. See AXLE ASSEMBLY SPECIFICATIONS table at end of article. If original preload was higher than specification, tighten nut to reach original preload.

NOTE: **Never back off pinion nut to reduce preload. If desired preload is exceeded, a new collapsible spacer must be installed and nut retightened until proper preload is obtained.**

5) Install propeller shaft. Scribe marks on companion flange and propeller shaft must be aligned. Tighten bolts. Install brake drums and wheels. Fill axle with hypoid gear lubricant to bottom of fill hole.

REAR AXLE ASSEMBLY
Removal

1) Raise vehicle and support under rear frame crossmember. Remove housing cover and drain lubricant. Remove axle shafts. See AXLE SHAFTS & BEARINGS under REMOVAL & INSTALLATION in this article. Remove brake backing plates. Using wire, secure backing plates to vehicle frame.

2) Mark and disconnect propeller shaft at companion flange. Disconnect axle vent from axle housing (at brake junction block on some models). Disconnect brake line from axle housing clips.

3) Support axle assembly with safety stands or hoist. Disconnect lower shock absorber studs from mounting brackets on axle housing. Disconnect upper arms from mounting on axle housing.

4) Lower axle assembly on jack until coil springs are released. Remove coil springs. Disconnect and remove lower arms from axle housing. Lower axle assembly and remove from vehicle.

Installation

To install, reverse removal procedure. Apply Loctite to threads holding axle vent and brake block (if used) to axle housing.

OVERHAUL

REAR AXLE ASSEMBLY
Disassembly

NOTE: **Differential case and drive pinion may be serviced with housing installed in vehicle.**

FORD MOTOR CO. — 7 1/2" & 8 3/4" RING GEAR (Cont.)

1) Raise vehicle and support under rear frame crossmember. Lower hoist until axle drops down far enough for working ease. Remove housing cover and drain lubricant.

2) Mount a dial indicator on axle housing and measure ring gear backlash and runout. *See Fig. 7.* Record readings for reassembly purposes. Check that ring gear runout and backlash variation between teeth is within specification. See AXLE ASSEMBLY SPECIFICATIONS table at end of article. Replace ring gear and pinion if backlash variation is excessive.

3) Remove rear wheels and brake drums. Remove axle shafts. See AXLE SHAFTS & BEARINGS under REMOVAL & INSTALLATION in this article. Place alignment marks on propeller shaft and companion flange for reassembly reference. Remove propeller shaft.

4) Mark one bearing cap for reassembly reference. Note arrow position on bearing cap for reassembly reference. Loosen bearing cap bolts and bearing caps. Pry differential case, bearing cups and shims out until they are loose in bearing caps. Remove bearing caps and differential. Mark all components location for reassembly.

NOTE: Bearing cups, caps and shims must be installed in original positions.

5) Remove pinion nut and companion flange. See PINION FLANGE & OIL SEAL under REMOVAL & INSTALLATION in this article. Drive pinion from front bearing with soft-faced hammer. Remove pinion from rear of axle housing. Pry oil seal from axle housing.

6) Remove front bearing. Remove pinion bearings if damaged. Mount bearing puller on pinion and press pinion from bearing. Remove, measure and record thickness of shim located behind bearing.

NOTE: Do not remove pinion bearing cups unless damaged. If bearing cups are replaced, bearings must also be replaced.

7) Bearing cups in axle housing may be removed using brass drift and hammer. Tap alternately on each side of bearing cup during removal to prevent bearing cup from binding in axle housing.

8) If ring gear runout was beyond specification, install differential assembly with bearings and cups in axle housing without pinion assembly. Install a .265" (6.73 mm) shim on the left side of differential assembly. Install left bearing cap and bolts finger tight.

9) Apply pressure on ring gear toward left side to ensure bearing has seated in cup. Install largest shim possible on right side until slight drag is felt. Install bearing cap and bolts. Tighten bolts to 70-85 ft. lbs. (95-115 N.m). Rotate differential assembly to ensure free rotation.

10) Install dial indicator and check ring gear runout. If runout is within specification, excessive runout was caused by improper bearing preload. If runout is still excessive, remove differential assembly.

11) Mark ring gear and differential assembly for reassembly reference. Remove ring gear bolts. Tap ring gear from differential case. Install differential assembly in axle housing as previously described.

12) Recheck runout on differential carrier case flange. If runout is within specification, install new ring gear and pinion. See AXLE ASSEMBLY SPECIFICATIONS table at end of article. If runout is not within specification, inspect differential case or bearings for damage. If bearings are not damaged, replace differential case and bearings.

13) Remove differential side bearings with a puller. Mark differential case and ring gear for reassembly reference. Remove pinion gears, side gears and thrust washers.

Cleaning & Inspection

1) Clean all parts thoroughly in cleaning solvent. Dry components with compressed air. DO NOT spin dry bearings. Coat all bearings with light coat of gear lubricant to prevent corrosion.

2) Inspect all bearings and cups for pitting or flaking. Check all bearings for smooth rotation while installed in cups. Inspect all gears and thrust washers for chipping or flaking. Inspect differential case bearing shoulders for damage during bearing removal.

3) Using micrometer, measure thickness of all thrust washers. Replace thrust washers that are not within specifications. See AXLE ASSEMBLY SPECIFICATIONS table.

4) Inspect companion flange for seal and bearing contact area for wear or damage. Replace all worn or damaged components. When replacing ring gear and pinion, note original factory shim thickness to adjust for variations in both carrier casting and original gear set dimension.

NOTE: Ring and pinion gear set must be replaced in matched sets.

Reassembly

1) If new components have been installed, proper gear set assembly must be checked using a Pinion Depth Gauge (T79P-4020-A) to determine correct pinion shim thickness. See PINION DEPTH under ADJUSTMENTS in this article.

2) Install new bearing cups in axle housing if necessary. Bearing cups must be seated in bores so that a .0015" (.038 mm) feeler gauge will not fit between bearing cup and bottom of bore.

3) Install proper shims on pinion used to position pinion depth. Press inner bearing on pinion shaft. Check that bearing is seated against shims. Lubricate pinion bearings with gear lubricant. Install pinion in axle housing. Install new collapsible spacer and outer pinion bearing.

4) Check that all sealing surfaces are clean and free of burrs. Using Seal Installer (T79P-4676-A), install oil seal. If oil seal becomes cocked during installation, remove and replace. Lubricate oil seal lips with multi-purpose lubricant.

5) Check pinion and companion flange splines for burrs. Coat companion flange splines with small amount of gear lubricant. Align marks on companion flange and pinion on used pinion only. Install companion flange on pinion. Coat washer side of nut with gear lubricant. Install new nut and washer.

6) Using Companion Flange Holder (T78P-4851-A), hold companion flange and gradually tighten nut. See TIGHTENING SPECIFICATIONS table at end of article. DO NOT hammer on companion flange, or install with power tools. Rotate pinion and check pinion bearing preload often until correct preload is obtained. See AXLE ASSEMBLY SPECIFICATIONS table at end of article.

FORD MOTOR CO. — 7 1/2" & 8 3/4" RING GEAR (Cont.)

NOTE: Never back off pinion nut to reduce preload. If desired preload is exceeded, a new collapsible spacer must be installed and nut retightened until proper preload is obtained.

7) Lubricate all parts with gear axle lubricant. Place side gears and thrust washers into differential case. Place pinion gears and thrust washers exactly opposite each other in differential case openings and mesh with side gears.

8) Install ring gear with new mounting bolts. Apply Loctite to bolt threads and tighten bolts. See TIGHTENING SPECIFICATIONS table at end of article. Press new bearings on differential cases using proper sized sleeve. Check that bearings are fully seated on differential cases.

9) Once proper shims have been chosen to obtain proper ring gear backlash and bearing preload, differential assembly may be installed. See DIFFERENTIAL BEARING PRELOAD & RING GEAR BACKLASH under ADJUSTMENTS in this article.

10) Install differential assembly and bearing cups in axle housing. Install bearing caps and bolts. Tighten bearing cap bolts. See TIGHTENING SPECIFICATIONS table at end of article.

11) Check ring gear backlash and gear tooth contact pattern. See GEAR TOOTH CONTACT PATTERN in this section. Gear tooth contact pattern does not need to be checked if pinion depth gauge is used and backlash is correct. Pinion depth and ring gear backlash may be adjusted to obtain proper gear tooth contact pattern.

12) Once all adjustments are correct, install axle shafts, housing cover, brake drums and rear wheels. Install propeller shaft. Check that reference mark is aligned. Fill axle housing with hypoid gear lubricant.

ADJUSTMENTS

PINION DEPTH

1) Assemble Pinion Depth Gauge (T79P-4020-A). Install aligning adapter, gauge disc, .89" (23 mm) thick for 7 1/2" ring gear and 1.19" (30 mm) thick for 8 3/4" ring gear, and screw. *See Fig. 4.* Place rear pinion bearing over aligning disc and into bearing cup of carrier housing.

Fig. 4: Pinion Depth Gauge

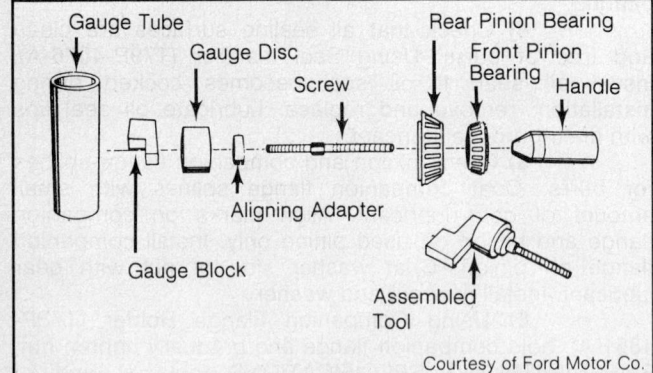

Courtesy of Ford Motor Co.

2) Install front pinion bearing into front bearing cup. Place tool handle onto screw and tighten to 20 INCH lbs. (2.25 N.m). *See Fig. 5.* Make sure pinion depth measuring tool is properly installed and tightened.

Fig. 5: Installing Pinion Depth Gauge

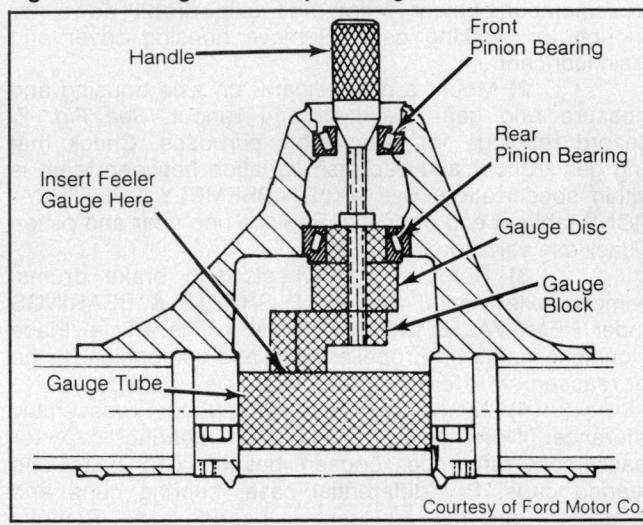

Courtesy of Ford Motor Co.

3) Apply a light film of oil to pinion bearings. Rotate gauge block several times to seat bearings. Rotational torque on gauge block assembly should be 20 INCH lbs. (2.25 N.m) with new bearings. Final position of gauge block should be 45 degrees above axle shaft centerline.

4) Clean differential bearing bores thoroughly and install gauge tube. Tighten bearing cap bolts. Using flat pinion shims as a gauge for shim selection, hold gauge block in proper position and measure clearance between gauge block and tube.

5) Correct shim selection is accomplished when a slight drag is felt as shim is drawn between gauge block and tube. Various thicknesses of shims are available. Install proper shim on pinion for reassembly. Pinion bearings must be installed in same location they were during pinion depth measurement.

PINION BEARING PRELOAD

1) Place preselected shim on pinion. Press bearing onto pinion until bearing and shim are firmly seated against shoulder of pinion. Install new collapsible spacer on pinion.

2) Lubricate bearings with axle lubricant. Install front pinion bearing in housing. Install new pinion oil seal. Lubricate pinion oil seal.

3) Insert companion flange into seal and hold firmly in place. From rear of axle housing, install pinion shaft into flange.

4) Start a new pinion nut on pinion and gradually tighten pinion nut while holding companion flange. Checking pinion bearing preload often. As soon as preload is measured, turn pinion shaft in both directions several times to seat bearings.

5) Tighten pinion nut and continue to measure pinion bearing preload until specified pinion torque is obtained. See TIGHTENING SPECIFICATIONS table at end of article.

6) If bearing preload is exceeded before torque specification is reached, replace collapsible spacer. See AXLE ASSEMBLY SPECIFICATIONS table at end of article for proper specification. Install new pinion nut and repeat procedure. DO NOT loosen pinion nut to reduce pinion bearing preload.

FORD MOTOR CO. – 7 1/2" & 8 3/4" RING GEAR (Cont.)

DIFFERENTIAL BEARING PRELOAD & RING GEAR BACKLASH

1) With pinion depth set and pinion installed, place differential case and gear assembly, with bearings and cups, into axle housing. Install a .265" (6.3 mm) shim on left (ring gear side) side of differential. Install left bearing cap finger tight.

2) Choose largest shim that will fit with a slight drag and install it on right (pinion gear side) side of differential. Install right bearing cap and tighten all cap bolts to specification. Rotate gear assembly to ensure free operation.

3) Check ring and pinion backlash. If backlash is within specifications, go to step **7)**. If backlash is not within specifications, go to step **5)**. If zero backlash was recorded, go to next step.

4) If zero backlash was recorded, add .020" (.51 mm) to shim size on right side and subtract .020" (.51 mm) from shim size on left side. Check ring and pinion backlash.

5) If backlash is not within specifications, increase shim thickness on one side and decrease shim thickness on opposite side by same amount. See BACK-LASH-TO-SHIM THICKNESS CONVERSION chart for approximate shim change. *See Fig. 6.*

6) Install shim and bearing caps. Tighten bearing cap bolts. Rotate gear assembly several times.

Recheck backlash. If backlash is within specification, go to next step. If not, repeat step **5)**.

7) Increase both left and right shim sizes .006" (.15 mm) and reinstall for correct bearing preload. Make sure shims are fully seated and gear assembly turns freely. Using marking compound, check gear tooth contact pattern.

BACKLASH-TO-SHIM THICKNESS CONVERSION

Required Change In Backlash In. (mm)	Required Change In Shim Thickness In. (mm)
.001" (.025 mm)	.002" (.05 mm)
.002" (.051 mm)	.002" (.05 mm)
.003" (.076 mm)	.004" (.10 mm)
.004" (.10 mm)	.006" (.15 mm)
.005" (.13 mm)	.006" (.15 mm)
.006" (.15 mm)	.008" (.20 mm)
.007" (.18 mm)	.010" (.25 mm)
.008" (.20 mm)	.010" (.25 mm)
.009" (.23 mm)	.012" (.30 mm)
.010" (.25 mm)	.014" (.35 mm)
.011" (.28 mm)	.014" (.35 mm)
.012" (.30 mm)	.016" (.41 mm)
.013" (.33 mm)	.018" (.46 mm)
.014" (.36 mm)	.018" (.46 mm)
.015" (.38 mm)	.020" (.51 mm)

AXLE ASSEMBLY SPECIFICATIONS

Application	Specifications
Capacity	
7 1/2" Ring Gear	3.5 pts. (1.7L)
8 3/4" Ring Gear	4.0 pts. (1.9L)
Differential Case Runout	.003 (.08)
Ring Gear Backface Runout	.004" (.10 mm) MAX.
Differential Side Gear	
Thrust Washer Thickness	.030-.032" (.76-.81 mm)
Pinion Gear Thrust Washer	
Thickness	.030-.032" (.76-.81 mm)
Nominal Pinion Shim Thickness	.030" (.76 mm)
Ring Gear Backlash	.008-.015" (.20-.38 mm)
Maximum Backlash Variation	
Between Teeth	.004" (.10 mm)
Pinion Bearing Preload (With Oil Seal)	
Original Bearings	8-14 INCH lbs. (.9-1.6 N.m)
New Bearings	16-29 INCH lbs. (1.8-3.3 N.m)

TIGHTENING SPECIFICATIONS

Application	Ft. Lbs. (N.m)
Axle Vent	11-19 (15-26)
Bearing Cap Bolts	70-85 (95-115)
Brake Backing Plate Bolts	20-40 (27-54)
Oil Filler Plug	15-30 (20-41)
Pinion Shaft Lock Bolt	15-30 (20-41)
Propeller Shaft-to-Companion	
Flange Bolts	70-95 (95-130)
Ring Gear Attaching Bolts [1]	70-85 (95-115)
Rear Cover Bolts	25-35 (34-47)
Pinion Nut	
7 1/2" Ring Gear	170 (230) MIN.
8 3/4" Ring Gear	140 (190) MIN.

[1] – Using Loctite.

Fig. 6: Backlash Adjustment

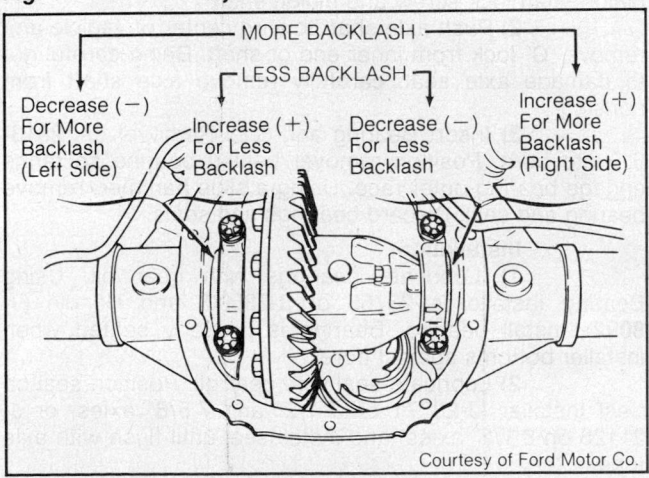

Courtesy of Ford Motor Co.

Fig. 7: Measuring Ring Gear Backlash

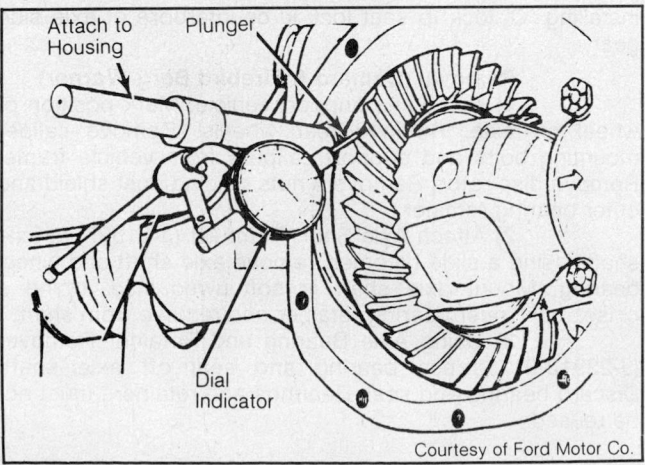

Courtesy of Ford Motor Co.

Drive Axles

GENERAL MOTORS INTEGRAL HOUSING

RWD Models Except Corvette, Fiero

NOTE: Fiero drive axles are included in GENERAL MOTORS FWD AXLE SHAFTS article in this section. Corvette drive axles are included in GENERAL MOTORS DRIVE AXLE SHAFT article in this section.

DESCRIPTION

Drive axle is a semi-floating hypoid gear type axle with integral housing. Centerline of pinion is set below centerline of ring gear. A removable steel cover, bolted to rear of housing, permits servicing differential case without removing complete axle assembly from vehicle.

NOTE: Some models are equipped with Borg-Warner, Dana, Eaton or General Motors design positive traction differentials. For testing and overhaul procedures for these units, see POSITIVE TRACTION DIFFERENTIAL articles in this section.

AXLE RATIO & IDENTIFICATION

Rear axle identification information is stamped on forward side of left or right axle tube on all models except Cadillac. On Cadillac, 3 different locations are used. An identification code is stamped on rear of right axle tube approximately 3" (76 mm) from differential housing and on outside of right brake drum or backside of right caliper support plate.

Fig. 1: Axle Ratio Code Locations

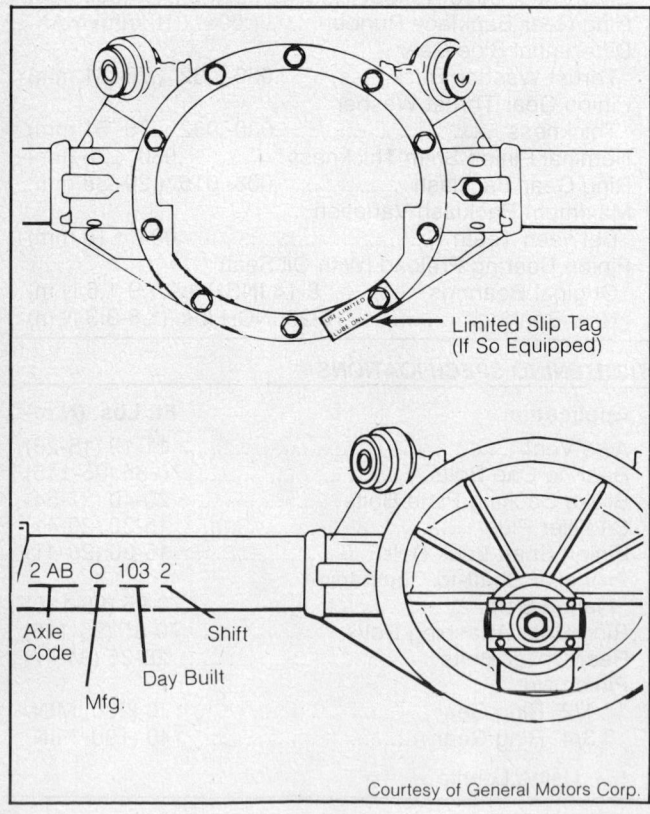

2 AB O 103 2
Axle Code — Mfg. — Day Built — Shift

Limited Slip Tag
(If So Equipped)

Courtesy of General Motors Corp.

AXLE RATIO IDENTIFICATION

Ratio	Code
2.41:1	2AJ, *2BJ
2.56:1	*6GA, 6GM, 6GS
2.73:1	*6GB, 6GT, 6GN, *6HE, 6HP, *6HT
2.77:1	¹ 4ET
2.93:1	6YC, 6TC
3.08:1	2AC, *2BC, *6HB, *6HF, 6HK, 6LG, 6LJ, 6YY, 6ZE, *6ZV
3.23:1	6LH, 6MC, 6YE
3.27:1	¹ 4EU
3.45:1	¹ 4EW
3.73:1	2TF, 2TH

* – Indicates Positive Traction.
¹ – Borg Warner Axle.

REMOVAL & INSTALLATION

AXLE SHAFTS & BEARINGS

Removal
(Except Camaro & Firebird Borg-Warner)

1) Raise and support vehicle. Remove rear wheels and brake drums (or disc calipers and rotors). Support calipers from vehicle frame (if equipped). Drain lubricant from differential by removing cover. Remove pinion shaft lock screw and pinion shaft.

2) Push axle shaft toward center of vehicle and remove "C" lock from inner end of shaft. Being careful not to damage axle seal, carefully remove axle shaft from housing.

3) Insert Bearing and Seal Remover (J-22813-01) into bore. Position remover behind bearing so tangs engage bearing outer race. Using a slide hammer, remove bearing and seal. Discard bearings and seals.

Installation

1) Lubricate bearings with gear oil. Using Bearing Installer (J-23765 or J-23690) and Handle (J-8092), install bearing. Bearing is properly seated when installer bottoms against bore.

2) Lubricate seal with gear oil. Position seal on Seal Installer (J-23771 on 7 1/2" and 7 5/8" axles, or J-21128 on 8 1/2" axles) and install seal until flush with axle tube.

3) To complete installation, reverse removal procedure. Axle shaft must be pushed outward after installing "C" lock to seat lock in counterbore of axle side gear.

Removal (Camaro & Firebird Borg-Warner)

1) Raise and support vehicle. Mark position of wheel on axle. Remove rear wheels. Remove caliper mounting bolts and support calipers from vehicle frame. Remove disc rotor. Remove 4 nuts holding dust shield and outer bearing retainer.

2) Attach Axle Shaft Remover (J-21597) to axle shaft. Using a slide hammer, remove axle shaft and wheel bearing. Mount axle shaft in soft-jawed vise. Using a chisel, split inner bearing retainer and remove from shaft.

3) Using Axle Bearing and Retainer Remover (J-22912-01), press bearing and seal off axle shaft. Discard bearing and seal. Bearings and retainers must not be reused.

GENERAL MOTORS INTEGRAL HOUSING (Cont.)

Fig. 2: General Motors Integral Rear Axle Assembly (Except Corvette, Firebird & Camaro With Borg-Warner Axle)

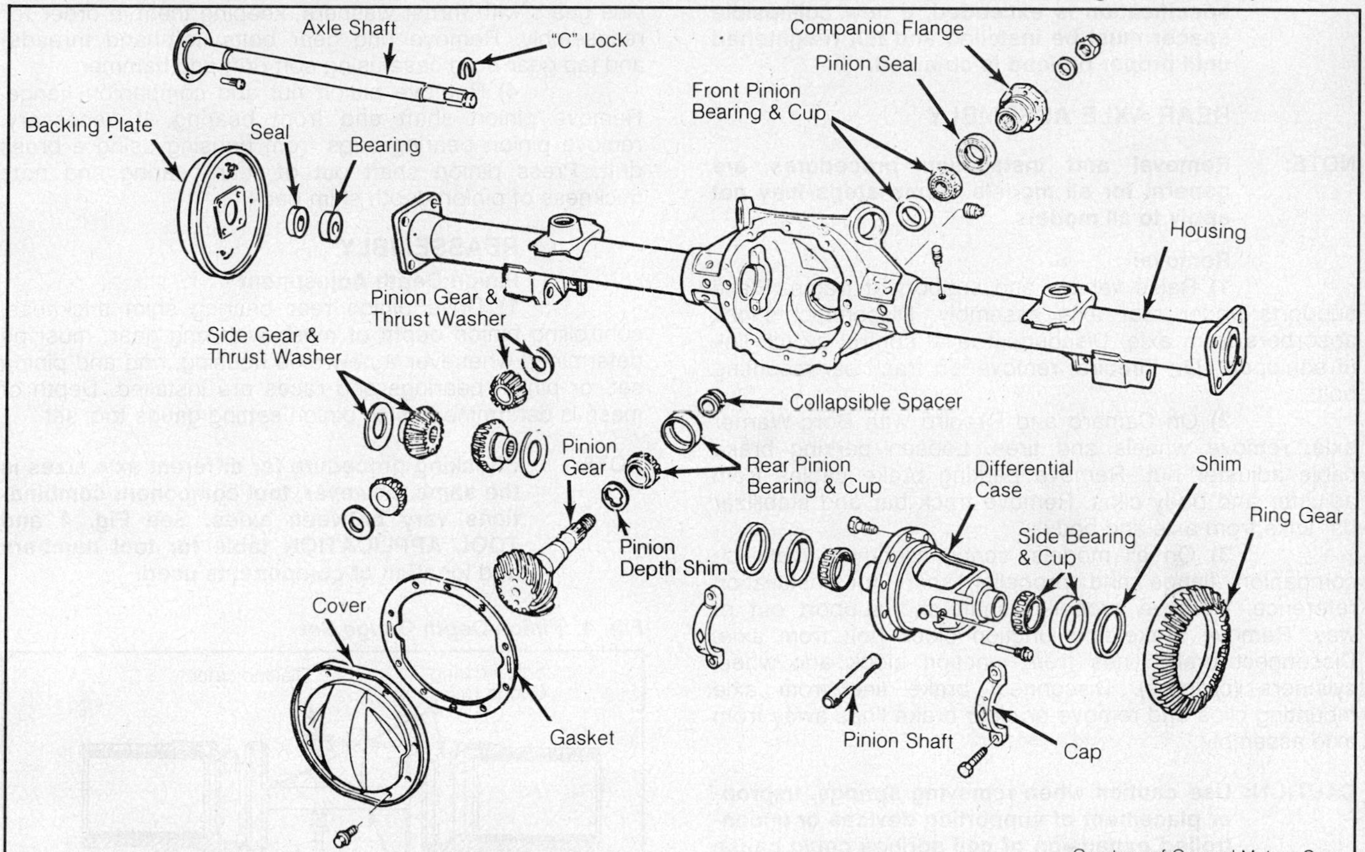

Axle Shaft
"C" Lock
Companion Flange
Pinion Seal
Front Pinion Bearing & Cup
Backing Plate
Seal
Bearing
Housing
Pinion Gear & Thrust Washer
Side Gear & Thrust Washer
Collapsible Spacer
Pinion Gear
Rear Pinion Bearing & Cup
Differential Case
Shim
Ring Gear
Pinion Depth Shim
Side Bearing & Cup
Cover
Gasket
Pinion Shaft
Cap

Courtesy of General Motors Corp.

Installation

1) Place outer bearing retainer on axle shaft. Position oil seal on shaft with spring side facing center of axle. Lightly coat seal lips with grease. Excessive amount of grease can damage seal.

NOTE: **Right axle shaft seal has Black band, and left axle shaft seal has Gold band. Seals must not be interchanged.**

2) Position bearing and inner retainer on shaft with outer chamfer of retainer facing bearing. Using Axle Bearing/Retainer Installer (J-8853), press bearing and retainer on shaft until completely seated.

3) To complete installation, reverse removal procedure. Ensure both axle shaft splines are fully engaged before rotating axle shafts to ensure proper spline alignment.

COMPANION FLANGE & OIL SEAL

Removal

1) Raise and support vehicle. Remove propeller shaft, marking parts for reassembly reference. Scribe an alignment mark on companion flange, pinion and pinion nut for reassembly. Using an INCH lb. torque wrench, measure and record pinion bearing preload.

2) Remove pinion nut and washer. Using a puller, remove companion flange. *See Fig. 3.* Pry seal out of housing.

Installation

1) Pack seal lip of new seal with lithium based extreme pressure grease. Install seal into housing until it

seats against shoulder. On Camaro and Firebird models with Borg-Warner axle, install seal flush, or recess up to .010" (.25 mm) from edge of housing. Install companion flange, washer and pinion nut.

Fig. 3: Companion Flange Removal

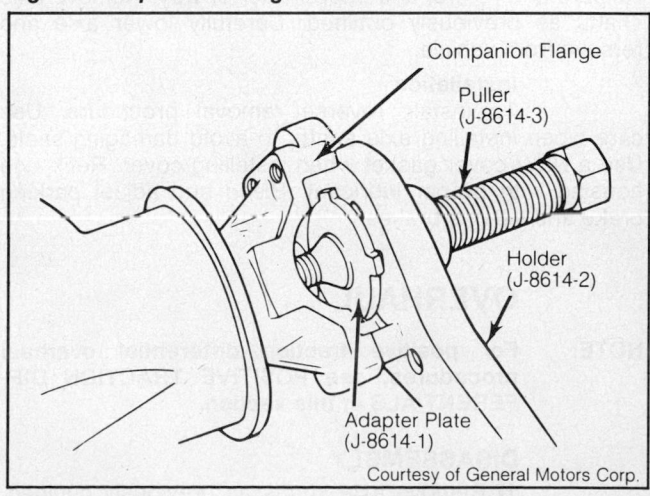

Companion Flange
Puller (J-8614-3)
Holder (J-8614-2)
Adapter Plate (J-8614-1)

Courtesy of General Motors Corp.

2) Tighten pinion nut until all end play is removed. Continue tightening nut up to 1/16 turn beyond alignment mark made at disassembly, checking to make sure original preload is not exceeded by more than 3-5 INCH lbs. (.3-.6 N.m). Install propeller shaft.

GENERAL MOTORS INTEGRAL HOUSING (Cont.)

NOTE: If pinion nut is overtightened, or preload specification is exceeded, a new collapsible spacer must be installed and nut retightened until proper preload is obtained.

REAR AXLE ASSEMBLY

NOTE: Removal and installation procedures are general for all models. Some steps may not apply to all models.

Removal

1) Raise vehicle and support at frame. Place supports under rear axle assembly. Disconnect shock absorbers from axle. Disconnect level control switch link (if equipped). On Firebird, remove left track bar mounting bolt.

2) On Camaro and Firebird with Borg-Warner axle, remove wheels and tires. Loosen parking brake cable adjuster nut. Remove parking brake cables from adjuster and body clips. Remove track bar and stabilizer bar links from axle and body.

3) On all models, scribe alignment mark on companion flange and propeller shaft for installation reference. Remove propeller shaft and support out of way. Remove brake line junction block bolt from axle. Disconnect brake lines from junction block and wheel cylinders (calipers). Disconnect brake line from axle mounting clips and remove or clear brake lines away from axle assembly.

CAUTION: Use caution when removing springs. Improper placement of supporting devices or uncontrolled expansion of coil springs could cause bodily injury or damage to vehicle.

4) Disconnect upper control arms from axle assembly. Lower axle and remove springs. Disconnect lower control arms and torque arm from axle (if equipped). Remove wheels and tires.

5) Remove brake drums and backing plates, or calipers and rotors, and support out of way. Remove axle shafts as previously outlined. Carefully lower axle and remove from vehicle.

Installation

To install, reverse removal procedure. Use care when installing axle shafts to avoid damaging seals. Use a NEW cover gasket when installing cover. Refill axle housing with proper lubricant. Bleed and adjust parking brake and service brakes.

OVERHAUL

NOTE: For positive traction differential overhaul procedures, see POSITIVE TRACTION DIFFERENTIALS in this section.

DISASSEMBLY

1) Remove axle shafts as previously outlined. Check ring and pinion gear backlash and pinion bearing preload. This will indicate gear or bearing wear or an error in backlash or preload setting.

2) Mark differential bearing caps and housing for reassembly reference. Remove caps and pry differential case from housing. Remove bearing cups and shims. Keep each set with proper bearing cap for reassembly.

3) Remove differential pinion shaft, gears, and side gears with thrust washers, keeping them in order for reassembly. Remove ring gear bolts (left-hand threads) and tap gear from case using soft drift and hammer.

4) Remove pinion nut and companion flange. Remove pinion shaft and front bearing. If necessary, remove pinion bearing cups from housing using a brass drift. Press pinion shaft out of rear bearing and note thickness of pinion depth shim pack.

REASSEMBLY

Pinion Depth Adjustment

1) Drive pinion rear bearing shim thickness, controlling pinion depth of mesh with ring gear, must be determined whenever a new axle housing, ring and pinion set, or pinion bearings and races are installed. Depth of mesh is determined using pinion setting gauge tool set.

NOTE: Checking procedure for different axle sizes is the same, however, tool component combinations vary between axles. See Fig. 4 and TOOL APPLICATION table for tool numbers and location of components used.

Fig. 4: Pinion Depth Gauge Set

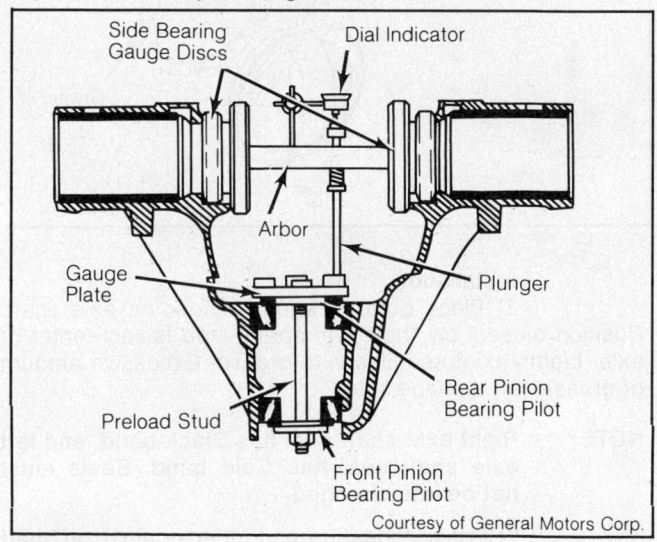

Courtesy of General Motors Corp.

2) If removed, install pinion bearing races. Install lubricated pinion bearings. Position gauge plate and rear pinion bearing pilot on preload stud. Then install assembly through rear pinion bearing, front pinion bearing and front pinion bearing pilot. *See Fig. 4.*

3) Install hex nut until snug. Rotate bearings to ensure proper seating. Hold preload stud stationary with a wrench on flats. Tighten hex nut until 20 INCH lbs. (2.3 N.m) is required to rotate bearings.

4) Mount side bearing gauging discs on ends of arbor. Place arbor into carrier making sure discs are properly seated. Install side bearing caps and bolts. Tighten bolts to avoid movement.

5) Position dial indicator on mounting post of arbor, with contact button resting on top surface of plunger. Preload dial indicator one-half revolution and tighten.

6) Place plunger onto gauging area of gauge plate. Rock plunger rod slowly back and forth across

GENERAL MOTORS INTEGRAL HOUSING (Cont.)

gauging area until dial indicator reads greatest deflection. Set indicator to zero. Repeat rocking action several times to verify setting.

TOOL APPLICATION

Tool Name	Tool Number
Front Pinion Bearing Pilot	
6 1/2" Ring Gear	J-23597-21
All Others	J-21777-42
Preload Stud (All)	J-21777-43
Rear Pinion Bearing Pilot	
6 1/2" Ring Gear	J-23597-21
8 1/2" Ring Gear	J-21777-35
All Others	J-21777-40
Gauge Plate	
6 1/2" Ring Gear	J-23597-20 or J-23597-30
8 1/2" Ring Gear	J-21777-21 or J-23597-29
All Others	J-21777-11
Arbor	
6 1/2" Ring Gear	J-23597-6
8 1/2" Ring Gear	J-21777-1
All Others	J-23597-1
Side Bearing Gauge Discs	
6 1/2" Ring Gear	J-23597-4
All Others	J-21777-45

7) Once zero reading is obtained, swing plunger until it is removed from gauging area. Dial indicator will now read required pinion shim thickness for a "nominal pinion". Record this reading.

8) Check drive pinion for painted or stamped markings on pinion stem, or a stamped code number on small end of pinion gear. *See Fig. 5.* If marking is found to be a plus or minus number (for instance +2 or −5), add or subtract that many thousandths from indicator reading. This will then be thickness of rear pinion bearing shim pack. If no markings are found on pinion, use dial indicator reading as shim thickness.

9) Remove bearing caps and gauging tools from housing. Place selected shim pack on drive pinion. Using a press, install lubricated pinion bearing on pinion shaft.

Fig. 5: Pinion Marking Locations

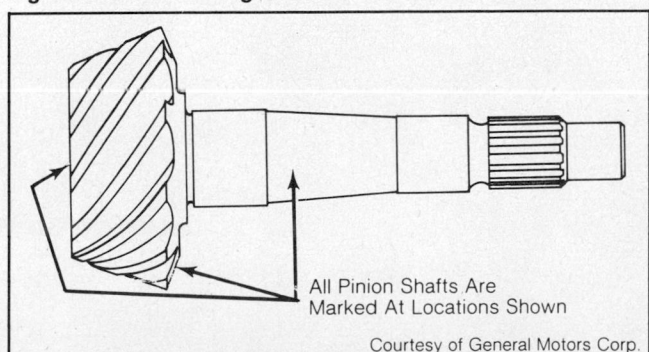

All Pinion Shafts Are Marked At Locations Shown

Courtesy of General Motors Corp.

Case Reassembly

1) Install ring gear on case with NEW bolts. Alternately tighten bolts to pull ring gear into position on case. Place side gear thrust washers over side gear hubs. Install assemblies into case in their original position.

2) Install pinions and thrust washers into case. Install pinion shaft and lock bolt. Using installing tools, install side bearings onto differential case.

Differential Shim Selection

1) Measure thickness of original side bearing preload shims. Select a service spacer, .16" (4.1 mm) for 6 1/2" ring gear and .17" (4.3 mm) for all others, and service shims with a total thickness slightly less than original shims.

NOTE: Standard service shims are steel and are available in .002" (.05 mm) increments from .040-.082" (1.02-2.08 mm). Production shims are cast iron and are available in .002" (.05 mm) increments from .210-.272" (5.33-6.91 mm). Do not attempt to reuse production shims because they may break when tapped into position.

2) Install differential case in housing. Install spacer between each bearing cup and housing with chamfered edge of spacer against housing. Install left bearing cap loosely so that differential case is free to move.

3) With left bearing race and spacer against housing, install both left and right service shims previously selected between right bearing race and service spacer.

4) Insert progressively larger feeler gauges between right service spacer and shim pack until a slight drag is felt. Total thickness of required shim pack is equal to feeler gauge thickness plus shim thickness used in step **1)**. Remove differential case, shims and spacers from axle housing.

Pinion Installation & Preload Adjustment

1) Install a NEW collapsible spacer over pinion stem, then position pinion in housing. While holding pinion forward, carefully drive front pinion bearing onto pinion shaft until a few threads are exposed.

NOTE: There are 2 types of collapsible spacers. Conventional spacer is used on 7 1/2" and 8 1/2" axles. New inverted type is used on 7 5/8" axle.

2) Install new oil seal, then install companion flange, and washer and nut. Tighten nut until end play is removed.

3) Rotate pinion several times to seat bearings, then check preload using an INCH lb. torque wrench. Continue tightening nut and checking preload until proper preload is obtained. DO NOT overtighten.

CAUTION: DO NOT back off nut to lessen preload. If preload is exceeded, a new collapsible spacer must be installed and nut retightened until proper preload is obtained.

Ring & Pinion Gear Backlash

1) With pinion depth set and pinion installed, place differential case and ring gear assembly into axle housing. Select 2 shims with a combined thickness equal to that of service shims and feeler gauge used in shim selection procedure. Install shims and spacers between bearing cups and housing. Install differential bearing caps and tighten cap bolts.

2) Rotate differential case several times to seat bearings and then check backlash using a dial indicator. Increase or decrease shim size where necessary to correct backlash reading. *See Fig. 6.* Recheck backlash at 4 points, equally spaced around ring gear. Ensure that variation between points does not exceed .002" (.05 mm).

Drive Axles

GENERAL MOTORS INTEGRAL HOUSING (Cont.)

Fig. 6: Backlash Adjustment

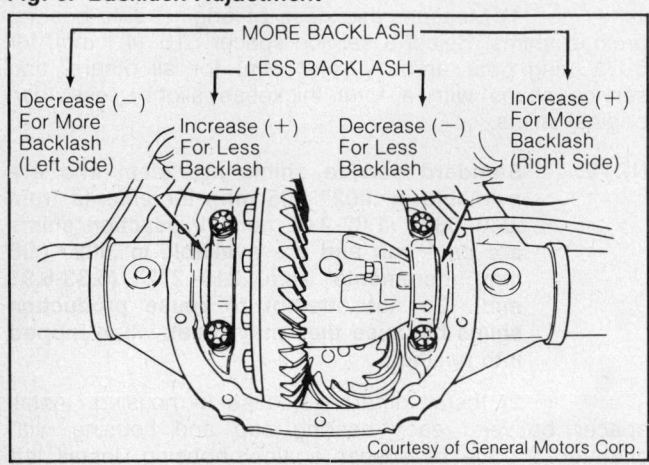

Courtesy of General Motors Corp.

Differential Bearing Preload

1) Remove differential bearing caps and increase left and right shim sizes .004" (.10 mm). Gentle tapping may be necessary to install second shim. Make sure shims are seated and differential turns freely.

2) Using gear marking compound, check gear tooth contact pattern to verify proper assembly and adjustment. Install axle shafts. After all settings have been made, install differential cover and fill with lubricant.

DRIVE AXLE CAPACITIES

Application	Capacity Pts. (L)
6 1/2" Ring Gear	1.7 (.8)
7 1/2", 7 3/4" & 7 5/8" Ring Gears	3.5 (1.7)
8 1/2" Ring Gear	4.25 (2.0)

AXLE ASSEMBLY SPECIFICATIONS

Application	Specification
Pinion Bearing Preload [1]	
Cadillac	
New Bearings	20-25 INCH lbs. (2.3-2.8 N.m)
Used Bearings	10-15 INCH lbs. (1.1-1.7 N.m)
All Others	
New Bearings	24-32 INCH lbs. (2.7-3.6 N.m)
Used Bearings	8-12 INCH lbs. (1.0-1.4 N.m)
Ring Gear Backlash	.005-.009" (.13-.23 mm)
Side Bearing Preload	[2] Slip Fit Plus .008" (.20 mm)

[1] – Measured with new seal without ring gear installed.

[2] – Add .004" (.10 mm) to each side to preload bearings.

TIGHTENING SPECIFICATIONS

Application	Ft. Lbs. (N.m)
Bearing Cap Bolt	45-65 (61-88)
Housing Cover Bolts	20-30 (27-41)
Ring Gear-to-Case Bolt	
Borg Warner Axle Equipped	101(137)
7 1/2" & 7 5/8"	80-95 (108-129)
8 1/2"	70-90 (95-122)
Rear Universal Joint Retainer Nut	65-75 (88-102)

Drive Axles

CORVETTE

DESCRIPTION

The Corvette uses 2 rear axle carriers, a Dana Model 36 (7 7/8" ring gear) and a Dana Model 44 (8 1/2" ring gear). The Model 36 is used in vehicles with automatic transmissions and Model 44 is used in vehicles with manual transmissions. Both of these differential carrier housings and the cover beam are constructed of aluminum.

The axle is a semi-floating type. Differential carrier housing encloses the differential case and hypoid gears. Internal components of carrier are of conventional design, incorporating hypoid gear set with a pinion supported on 2 preloaded, tapered roller bearing assemblies, and a 2-pinion differential assembly supported on tapered roller bearings.

Pinion mounting distance adjustments are made through the use of shims, as are differential bearing preload and backlash adjustments. Differential side gears drive 2 splined yokes which are retained laterally by snap rings located on yoke splined end. Yokes are supported on caged needle bearings pressed into carrier. A lip seal, pressed in outboard of the bearings, prevents oil leakage and dirt entry.

AXLE RATIO & IDENTIFICATION

Axle identification number is stamped on back of carrier.

AXLE RATIO IDENTIFICATION

Axle Dia.	Axle Ratio	No. of Teeth Pinion/Ring Gear
Model 36 (7 7/8")	2.59:1	17/44
Model 36 (7 7/8")	3.07:1	14/43
Model 44 (8 1/2")	3.07:1	14/43

REMOVAL & INSTALLATION

AXLE SHAFTS

Removal

1) Raise and support vehicle. Disconnect leaf spring and tie rod end from knuckle. Scribe an alignment mark on camber adjusting cam and mounting bracket. Remove cam bolt and separate spindle support rod from mounting bracket at carrier.

2) Remove axle shaft trunnion straps at spindle and at side gear yoke. Push out on wheel and tire assembly and remove axle shaft.

Installation

To install, reverse removal procedure. Realign scribe mark on cam bolt with scribe mark on bracket. Tighten all bolts to specification. Check and adjust rear suspension alignment as necessary.

AXLE BEARINGS

Carrier assembly must be removed to remove axle bearings and seals. See OVERHAUL in this article.

Fig. 1: Exploded View of Corvette Rear Axle Assembly

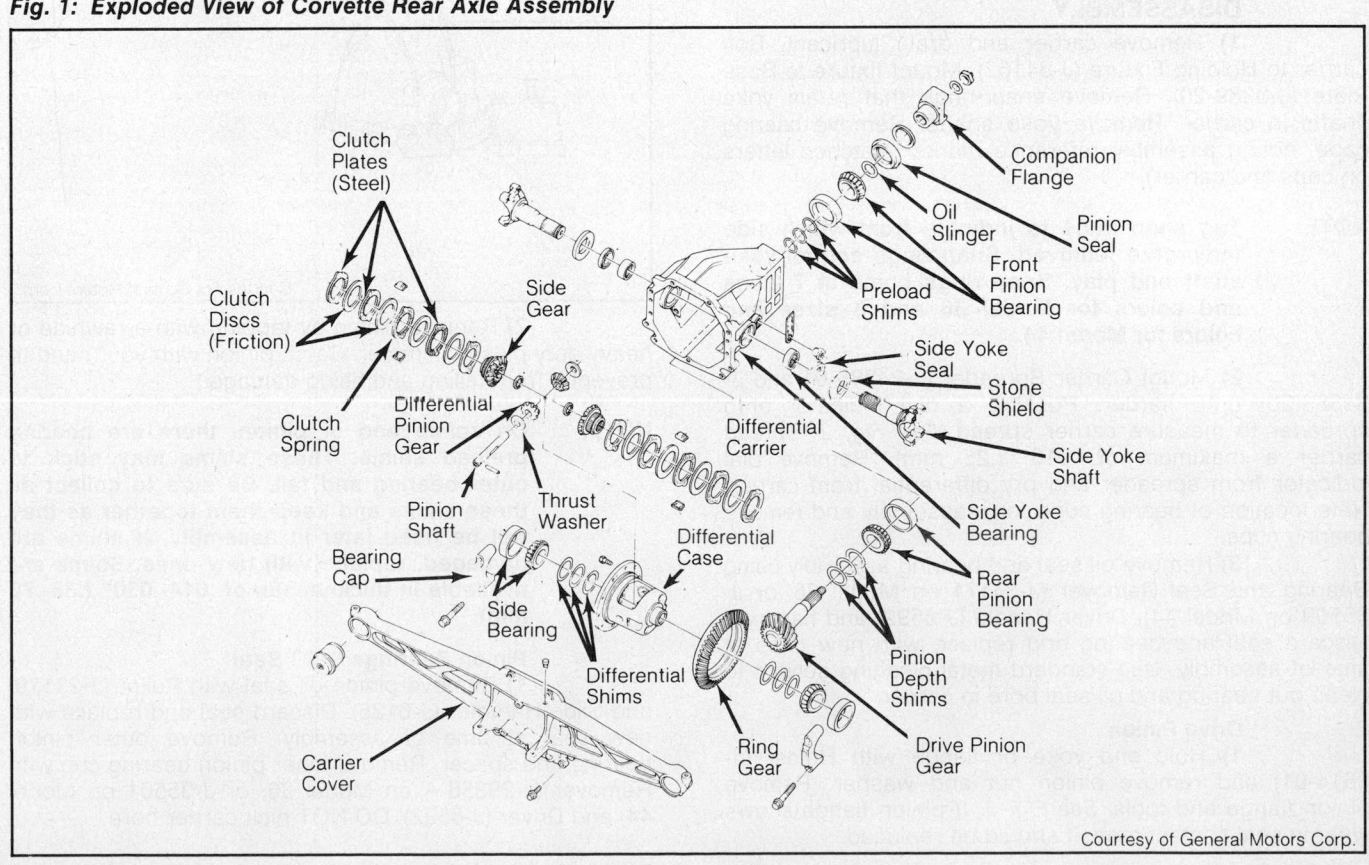

Courtesy of General Motors Corp.

Drive Axles

CORVETTE (Cont.)

REAR AXLE ASSEMBLY

Removal

1) Remove air cleaner. Disconnect distributor cap from distributor. Raise and support vehicle. Remove spare tire and spare tire cover. Remove upper and lower underbody braces. Remove exhaust system assembly.

2) Disconnect leaf spring at knuckles and remove attaching bolts at cover. Remove leaf spring from vehicle.

3) Scribe an alignment mark on camber adjusting cam and mounting bracket. Remove cam bolts. Remove mounting bracket from carrier. Disconnect tie rod ends from knuckles.

4) Remove axle shaft trunnion straps from side gear yokes. Push wheel and tire assemblies outboard to disengage trunnions from side gear yokes. Mark relationship of prop shaft to companion flange. Remove propeller shaft trunnion straps at pinion flange. Push propeller shaft forward into transmission and tie shaft to support beam. Support transmission.

5) Remove differential cover/beam attaching bolts at frame brackets. Remove support beam attaching bolts at front of differential carrier. Remove differential carrier assembly from vehicle.

Installation

To install, reverse removal procedure. Torque all bolts. Apply sealant to support beam and differential carrier. Fill carrier with lubricant. Check and adjust rear suspension alignment as required.

OVERHAUL

DISASSEMBLY

1) Remove carrier and drain lubricant. Bolt carrier to Holding Fixture (J-34162). Mount fixture to Base Plate (J-3389-20). Remove snap rings that retain yoke shafts in carrier. Remove yoke shafts. Remove bearing caps, noting assembly reference marks (matched letters on caps and carrier).

NOTE: Tag snap rings to indicate from which side they were removed. Snap rings control yoke shaft end play. Snap rings come in 7 sizes and colors for Model 36 and 8 sizes and colors for Model 44.

2) Mount Carrier Spreader (J-24385-01 and J-24385-20) onto carrier. Position a dial indicator onto spreader to measure carrier spread. See Fig. 2. Spread carrier a maximum of .010" (.25 mm). Remove dial indicator from spreader and pry differential from carrier. Note location of bearing cups for reassembly and remove bearing cups.

3) Remove oil seal and bearing assembly using Bearing and Seal Remover (J-34171 on Model 36, or J-35509 on Model 44), Driver Handle (J-8592) and hammer. Discard seal and bearing and replace with new ones at time of assembly. Use standard metal cleaning solvent to clean out bearing and oil seal bore in carrier.

Drive Pinion

1) Hold end yoke or flange with Holder (J-8614-01) and remove pinion nut and washer. Remove pinion flange and tools. See Fig. 3. If pinion flange shows wear in seal contact area, it should be replaced.

Fig. 2: Spreading Carrier

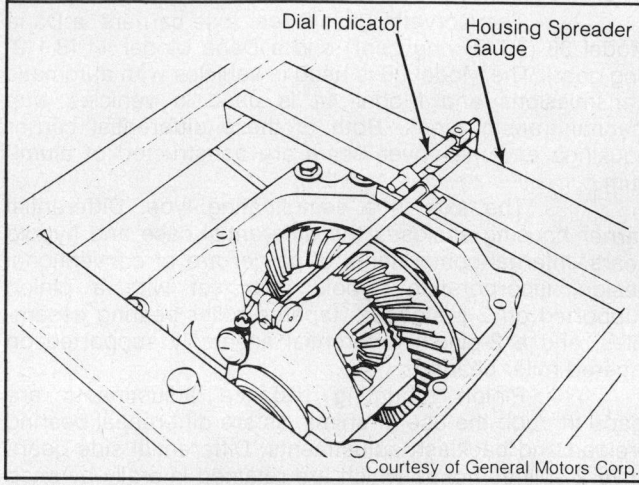

DO NOT spread carrier more than .010" (.25 mm).

Fig. 3: Removing Pinion Flange

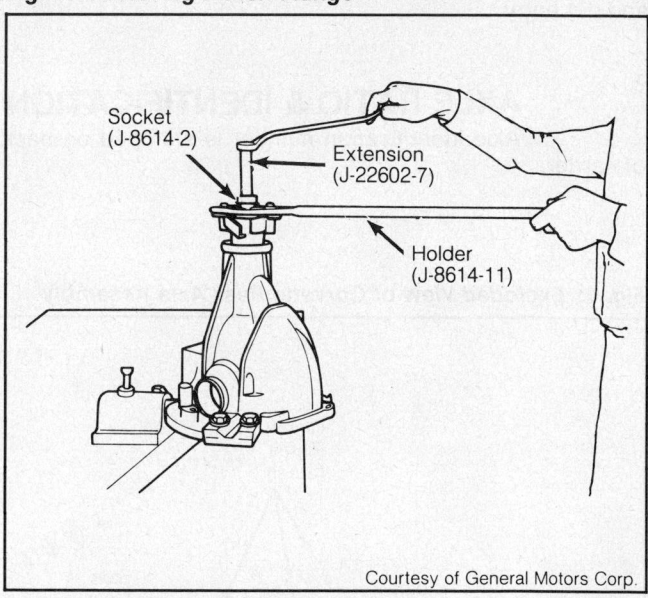

2) Remove pinion by tapping with a rawhide or heavy duty plastic hammer. Catch pinion with your hand to prevent it from falling and being damaged.

NOTE: On spline end of pinion, there are bearing preload shims. These shims may stick to outer bearing and fall. Be sure to collect all these shims and keep them together as they will be used later in assembly. If shims are damaged, replace with new ones. Shims are available in thicknesses of .014-.030" (.36-.76 mm).

Pinion Bearings & Oil Seal

1) Remove pinion oil seal with Puller (J-23129) and Slide Hammer (J-6125). Discard seal and replace with new seal at time of assembly. Remove outer pinion bearing and spacer. Remove inner pinion bearing cup with Remover (J-29358-A on Model 36, or J-35501 on Model 44) and Driver (J-8592). DO NOT nick carrier bore.

CORVETTE (Cont.)

NOTE: Shims are located between inner bearing cup and carrier bore. If shims are bent or nicked, replace at time of assembly. Measure each shim individually and wire shim stack together. If stack has to be replaced, replace with stack of same thickness.

2) Turn nose of carrier down. Remove outer pinion bearing cup using Remover (J-29359 on Model 36, or J-35502 on Model 44) and Driver (J-8592). Do not nick carrier bore. Remove inner pinion bearing with Remover (J-34165 on Model 36, or J-8612-B on Model 44). See Fig. 4.

Fig. 4: Removing Inner Pinion Bearing

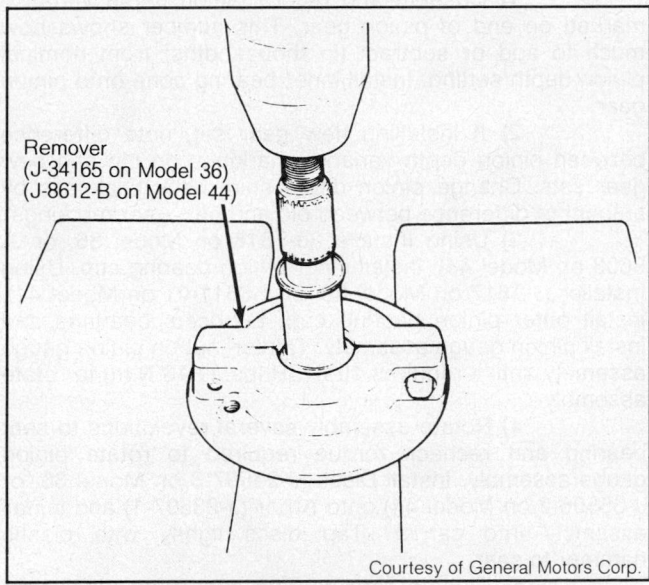

Remover
(J-34165 on Model 36)
(J-8612-B on Model 44)

Courtesy of General Motors Corp.

Differential Side Bearing
1) Remove differential bearings with Remover (J-34168 on Model 36, or J-34108-A on Model 44) and Adapter Plug (J-8107-2). See Fig. 5.

Fig. 5: Removing Differential Side Bearings

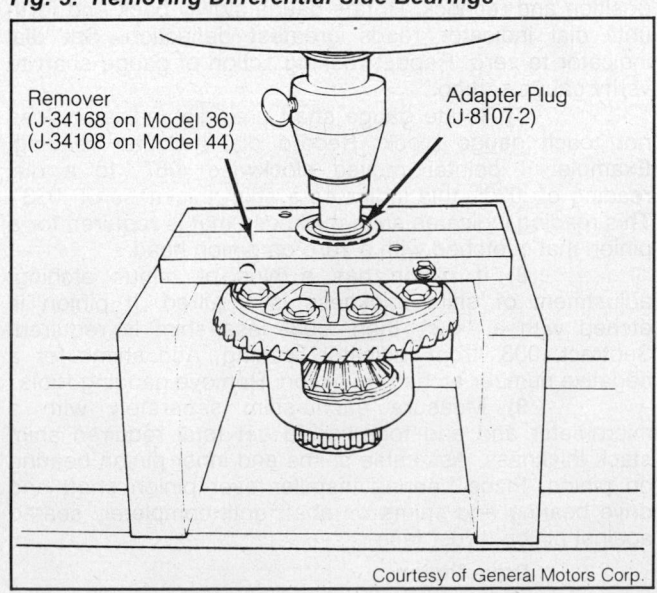

Remover
(J-34168 on Model 36)
(J-34108 on Model 44)

Adapter Plug
(J-8107-2)

Courtesy of General Motors Corp.

2) Wire shims, bearing cup and bearing cone together, and identify from which side they were removed (ring gear side or opposite side). If shims are damaged,

replace with new ones at time of assembly. Shims are available in thicknesses of .003" (.08 mm), .005" (.13 mm), .010" (.25 mm), and .030" (.76 mm).

NOTE: Install new bearings when bearings are removed, regardless of mileage.

Ring Gear
1) Place one of the axle shafts, which was removed from assembly, into a vise. Spline end of shaft is not to exceed 2.75" (69.85 mm) above top of vise. This will prevent shaft from fully entering into side gear and causing interference with step plate during disassembly of pinion gears. Caution should be used so that vise jaws do not locate on axle splines or any machined surfaces.

2) Place shop towels over vise to prevent any damage during removal of ring gear. Place differential on axle shaft with ring gear bolt heads up. Remove ring gear bolts. Remove ring gear.

NOTE: Whenever ring gear bolts are removed, replace with new ones.

Differential Case
1) Position differential case onto axle shaft. Remove retaining pin from cross pin with a punch. Use hammer and punch to remove cross pin from case.

2) Assemble adapter plate into bottom side gear. Install threaded adapter plate into top side gear. Thread forcing screws into threaded adapter until it becomes centered in bottom adapter plate.

3) Tighten forcing screw until it becomes slightly tight. This will collapse dished spacers and allow a loose condition between side gears and pinion gears. Remove both pinion gear spherical washers. Use .020" (.51 mm) thick shim to push out spherical washers.

4) Relieve tension of dished spacers by loosening forcing screw. It might be necessary to adjust forcing screw slightly to allow case to rotate. Assemble Turning Adapter (J-34501) onto Handle (J-8592). Insert small O.D. end of adapter into cross pin hole of case. Pull on handle and rotate case until pinion gears can be removed. Remove gears. See Fig. 6.

Fig. 6: Removing Gears From Differential Case

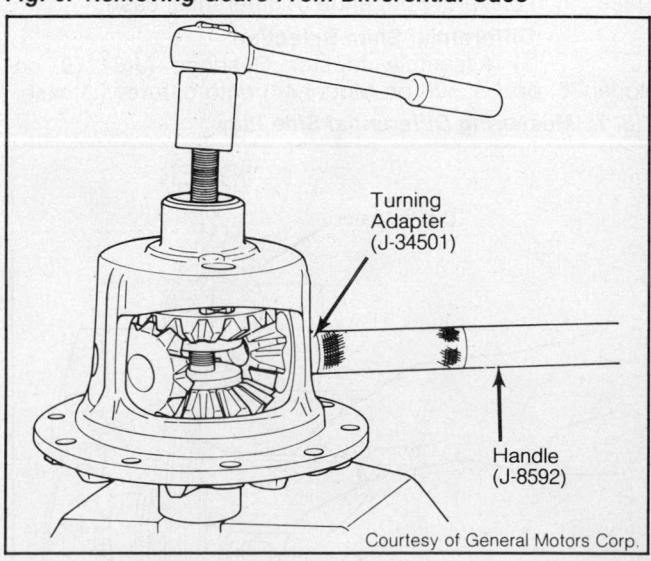

Turning
Adapter
(J-34501)

Handle
(J-8592)

Courtesy of General Motors Corp.

5) Hold top clutch pack with one hand and remove tools. Remove top side gear and clutch pack.

Drive Axles

CORVETTE (Cont.)

Keep stack of plates and discs intact in exactly same position while being removed.

6) Remove case from axle shaft. Turn case with flange or ring gear side up and allow adapter plate, side gear and clutch pack to be removed from case. Remove retainer clips from both clutch packs to allow separation of plates and discs. Keep stack of plates and discs exactly as they were removed.

REASSEMBLY
Differential Case
1) Prelube thrust face of side gears, plates and discs with limited slip rear axle lube. Assemble plates and discs in the same position as they were removed. Assemble retainer clips to ears of plates. Make sure both clips are completely assembled onto ears of plates.

2) Assemble clutch pack and side gear into top side gear bore. Make sure clutch pack stays assembled to side gear splines, and retainer clips are completely seated in case pockets. To prevent pack from falling out of case, hold them in place by hand while repositioning case on bench.

3) Position Adapter Plate (J-34174) onto side gear. Assemble other clutch pack and side gear. Hold clutch pack in position and insert Forcing Screw (J-34174). Tighten forcing screw into bottom adapter. This will hold both clutch packs in position. Position case onto axle shaft by aligning splines of side gear with splines of shaft.

4) Tighten forcing screw to compress clutch packs in order to provide clearance for pinion gears. Insert pinion gears. While holding gears in place, insert Turning Adapter (J-34501) with Handle (J-8592) in cross pin hole of case. Pull on handle and rotate case, allowing gears to turn.

5) Make sure holes of pinion gears are aligned with those in case. It may be necessary to adjust tension of forcing screw to rotate case. Prelube spherical washers and assemble into case. Use a small screwdriver to push washers into place. Remove tools.

6) Position cross pin shaft in case and drive in with a hammer. Be sure retaining pin hole of cross pin shaft is properly aligned to allow installation of retaining pin. Using a punch, install retaining pin to proper depth. Stake pin in place at both ends of differential case.

Differential Shim Selection
1) Assemble Master Bearings (J-34170 on Model 36, or J-35505 on Model 44) onto differential case.

Fig. 7: Measuring Differential Side Play

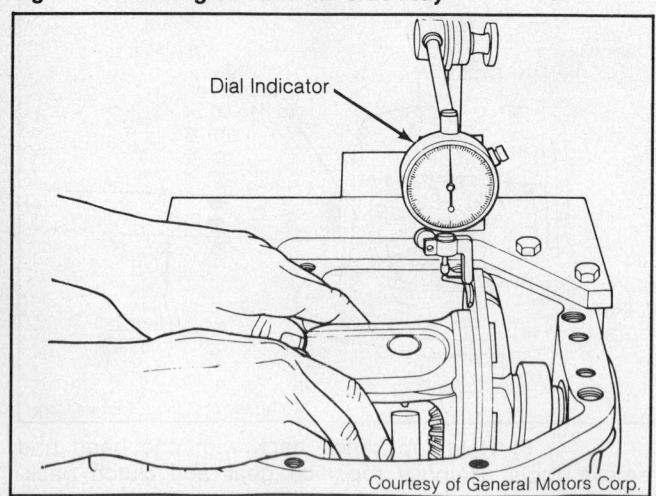

Dial Indicator

Courtesy of General Motors Corp.

Install differential case into carrier, less pinion gear. Mount a dial indicator on supporting fixture to read differential side play at ring gear flange. Force differential toward indicator. See Fig. 7.

2) With pressure applied, set dial indicator at zero. Force differential in opposite direction and check indicator reading. Repeat procedure until consistent reading is obtained and record final reading. This thickness of shims will be used in final assembly shim stacks to establish differential bearing preload and ring gear backlash. Remove dial indicator and differential case from carrier.

Pinion Depth & Preload
1) Observe and record pinion depth variance marked on end of pinion gear. This number shows how much to add or subtract (in thousandths) from nominal pinion depth setting. Install inner bearing cone onto pinion gear.

2) If installing new gear set, note difference between pinion depth variance markings on old and new gear sets. Change pinion depth shim pack thickness by amount of difference between old and new gear markings.

3) Using Installer (J-7818 on Model 36, or J-8608 on Model 44), install inner pinion bearing cup. Using Installer (J-7817 on Model 36, or J-8611-01 on Model 44), install outer pinion bearing cup. Lubricate bearings and install pinion gauge assembly. Tighten nut on pinion gauge assembly until it requires 10 INCH lbs. (1.13 N.m) to rotate assembly.

4) Rotate assembly several revolutions to seat bearing and recheck torque required to rotate pinion gauge assembly. Install Discs (J-23597-8 on Model 36, or J-35506-2 on Model 44) onto Arbor (J-23597-1) and install assembly into carrier. Tap discs lightly with plastic hammer to seat.

5) Tighten side bearing caps onto discs until slight resistance is felt when rotating arbor. Position gauge plunger onto proper gauging step of gauge block for axle being serviced. Install dial indicator on arbor post.

6) Push dial indicator downward until needle rotates 3/4 turn clockwise. Tighten dial indicator in this position and recheck. Rotate gauge slowly back and forth until dial indicator reads greatest deflection. Set dial indicator to zero. Repeat rocking action of gauge shaft to verify gauge setting.

7) Rotate gauge shaft until dial indicator does not touch gauge block. Record dial indicator reading. Example: If pointer moved clockwise .067" to a dial reading of .033", this indicates a shim thickness of .033". This reading indicates shim thickness that is required for a pinion that is etched with a zero on pinion head.

8) If pinion has a plus or minus etching, adjustment of shim thickness is required. If pinion is etched with a "+3", then .003" less shim is required. Subtract .003" from indicator reading. Add shims for a negative number etched on pinion. Remove gauging tools.

9) Measure each shim separately with a micrometer and add together to get total required shim stack thickness. Assemble shims and inner pinion bearing on pinion. Place bearing installer over pinion shaft and drive bearing and shims on shaft until completely seated against pinion thrust face.

Drive Pinion
1) Lubricate inner and outer bearings. Install outer bearing and spacer in carrier. Lubricate lip of new pinion seal. Using Seal Installer (J-34163 on Model 36, or J-35503 on Model 44), install seal in carrier. Assemble

CORVETTE (Cont.)

original thickness of preload shims onto pinion. Insert pinion into carrier.

2) Assemble pinion flange, washer, and NEW pinion nut onto pinion. Hold flange with Holder (J-34179) and tighten pinion nut to specification. Using an INCH lb. torque wrench, rotate pinion. Pinion rotating torque, with new bearings installed, should be 15-35 INCH lbs. (1.7-4.0 N.m) on Model 36 or 20-40 INCH lbs. (2.3-4.5 N.m) on Model 44.

3) To increase preload, remove shims. To decrease preload, add shims. After pinion, bearings and seal have been installed, preloaded and tightened to specifications with measured shim stack, pinion position can be checked. Reinstall Discs (J-23597-8 on Model 36, or J-35506-2 on Model 44) and Arbor (J-23597-1) into carrier. *See Fig. 8.*

Fig. 8: Installing Pinion Depth Gauge Assembly

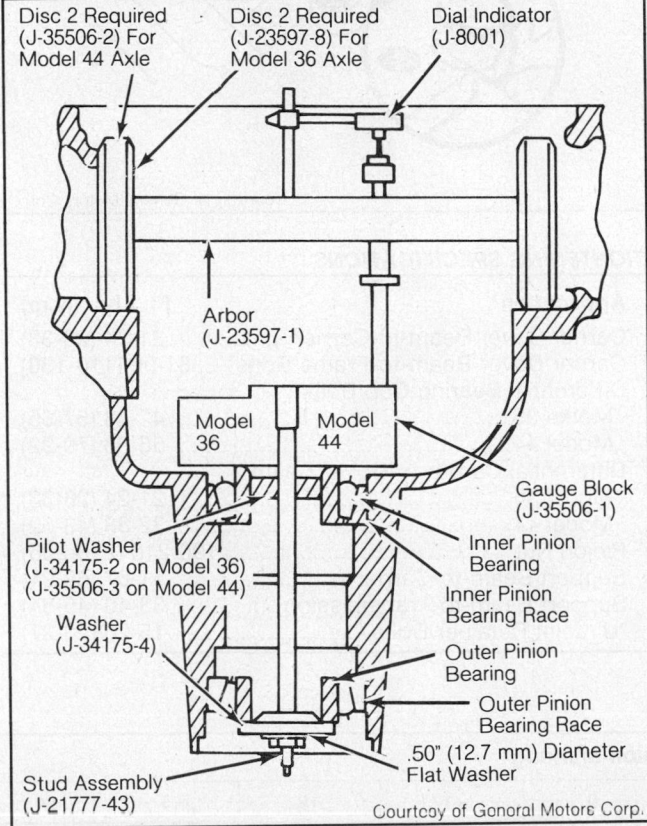

Disc 2 Required (J-35506-2) For Model 44 Axle
Disc 2 Required (J-23597-8) For Model 36 Axle
Dial Indicator (J-8001)
Arbor (J-23597-1)
Model 36
Model 44
Gauge Block (J-35506-1)
Inner Pinion Bearing
Inner Pinion Bearing Race
Outer Pinion Bearing
Outer Pinion Bearing Race
Pilot Washer (J-34175-2 on Model 36) (J-35506-3 on Model 44)
Washer (J-34175-4)
Stud Assembly (J-21777-43)
.50" (12.7 mm) Diameter Flat Washer
Courtesy of General Motors Corp.

4) Tighten all side bearing caps equally, using a torque wrench, onto discs until slight resistance is felt when rotating arbor. Place Gauge Block (J-35506-4) on top of pinion button. Position gauge plunger onto proper gauging step of gauge plate for the drive gear being serviced. *See Fig. 9.*

5) Install dial indicator to arbor post. Push dial indicator downward until needle rotates about 3/4 turn clockwise. Tighten dial indicator in this position and recheck. While pushing gauge block down on top of pinion, rotate gauge shaft slowly back and forth until dial indicator reads greatest deflection. At this point, set dial indicator to zero.

6) Repeat rocking action of gauge shaft to verify gauge setting. After zero setting is obtained, rotate

gauge shaft until dial indicator plunger does not touch gauge block. Remove gauge block from top of pinion and place the groove onto proper side of block (for ring gear being serviced) around indicator plunger between arbor and plunger head. Do not disturb dial indicator.

7) Read dial indicator. This reading indicates pinion position. An indicator reading within .002" (.05 mm) of etching on pinion is acceptable. If not within .002" (.05 mm), shim stack thickness is incorrect and must be adjusted. Add or subtract shims as necessary to correct depth. Recheck pinion depth to confirm correct adjustment. *See Fig. 9.*

Differential Preload & Backlash

1) Install ring gear using new bolts. Install Master Bearings (J-34170 on Model 36, or J-35505 on Model 44) or original bearings, without shims, onto differential case. Place differential case in carrier and assemble bearing caps finger tight. Install dial indicator to read differential side play at back side of ring gear flange.

2) Force differential away from pinion gear until seated against cross bore face of carrier. With force still applied to differential case, place dial indicator tip on flat machined surface of differential case, or on head of ring gear bolt. Zero dial indicator.

3) Force differential into pinion gear, rocking gear to make sure teeth are meshed. Read dial indicator and repeat procedure to obtain a consistent reading. Make sure dial indicator reads zero each time differential is pressed away from pinion gear.

4) This reading, minus .006" (.15 mm), will be thickness of shims to be installed on ring gear side of differential. Remove dial indicator and differential case from carrier. Remove bearings from differential. From shim pack selected in differential shim selection procedure, assemble amount of shims selected in step **2)**.

5) Install shim pack from step **2)** and bearing cone onto ring gear side of differential. For proper backlash and preload, add .015-020" (.38-.51 mm) of shims for Model 36 and .008-.012" (.20-.30 mm) for Model 44 to remaining shim pack and install onto differential with bearing.

Differential Case & Carrier Assembly

1) Install carrier spreader and dial indicator as previously outlined. Spread carrier to a maximum of .010" (.25 mm) and remove dial indicator. Assemble differential bearing cups onto differential. Install differential case into housing (gentle tapping may be necessary to seat assembly in carrier cross bore). Take care to avoid nicking gear teeth when installing differential.

2) Install bearing caps and bolts, aligning assembly reference marks. Check backlash at 3 equally spaced points around ring gear. To increase backlash, move shims from ring gear side to pinion gear side of differential. To decrease backlash, move shims from pinion gear side of differential to ring gear side.

3) Install side yoke bearings, seals and shafts. Retain side yoke shafts with snap rings. End play should be .0005-.0085" (.013-.216 mm). Adjust with different thickness snap ring. Apply a 1/4" bead of sealer on mating surface. Position cover on carrier and install attaching bolts. Tighten cover bolts alternately.

Drive Axles

CORVETTE (Cont.)

Fig. 9: Measuring Pinion Depth

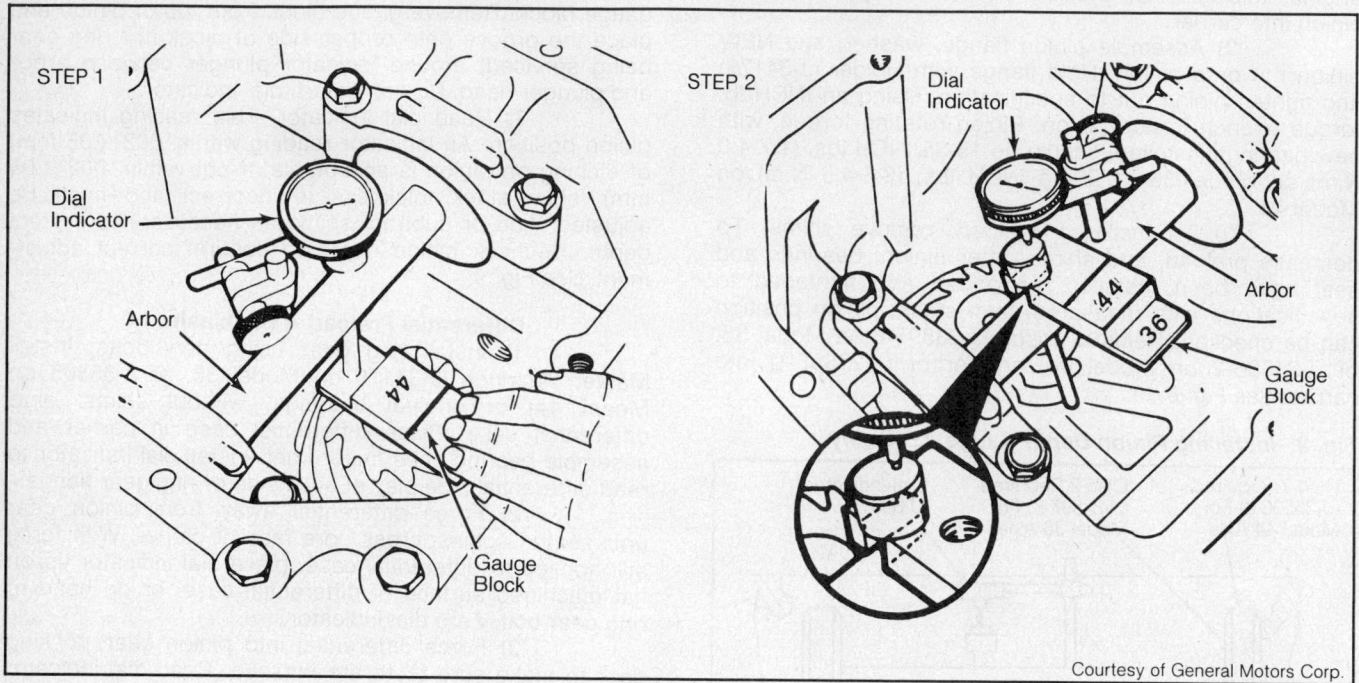

Courtesy of General Motors Corp.

AXLE ASSEMBLY SPECIFICATIONS

Application	Specification
Pinion Bearing Preload	
Model 36	15-35 INCH lbs. (1.7-4.0 N.m)
Differential Bearing Preload	.006" (.15 mm)
Model 44	20-40 INCH lbs. (2.3-4.5 N.m)
Ring & Pinion Gear Backlash	.006-.009" (.15-.23 mm)
Max. Backlash Variation	.001-.0015" (.03-.04 mm)

TIGHTENING SPECIFICATIONS

Application	Ft. Lbs. (N.m)
Carrier Cover Beam-to-Carrier	21-24 (28-33)
Carrier Cover Beam-to-Frame Bolts	81-96 (110-130)
Differential Bearing Cap Bolts	
Model 36	42-48 (57-65)
Model 44	58-68 (79-92)
Differential Carrier-to-Cover Beam	
Model 36	21-24 (28-33)
Model 44	32-38 (43-52)
Pinion Nut	190-210 (258-285)
Support Beam-to-Carrier	51-67 (69-91)
Support Beam-to-Transmission	33-40 (45-54)
"U" Joint Retainer Bolts	15-20 (20-27)

PINION VARIANCE CHART

Old Pinion Marking	New Pinion Marking								
	−4	−3	−2	−1	0	+1	+2	+3	+4
+4	+0.008	+0.007	+0.006	+0.005	+0.004	+0.003	+0.002	+0.001	0
+3	+0.007	+0.006	+0.005	+0.004	+0.003	+0.002	+0.001	0	−0.001
+2	+0.006	+0.005	+0.004	+0.003	+0.002	+0.001	0	−0.001	−0.002
+1	+0.005	+0.004	+0.003	+0.002	+0.001	0	−0.001	−0.002	−0.003
0	+0.004	+0.003	+0.002	+0.001	0	−0.001	−0.002	−0.003	−0.004
−1	+0.003	+0.002	+0.001	0	−0.001	−0.002	−0.003	−0.004	−0.005
−2	+0.002	+0.001	0	−0.001	−0.002	−0.003	−0.004	−0.005	−0.006
−3	+0.001	0	−0.001	−0.002	−0.003	−0.004	−0.005	−0.006	−0.007
−4	0	−0.001	−0.002	−0.003	−0.004	−0.005	−0.006	−0.007	−0.008

CLUTCH PACK TYPE

Ford Motor Co., General Motors

DESCRIPTION

Positive traction type differentials direct major driving force to wheel with greatest amount of traction. This is accomplished by a spring-loaded multiple disc clutch pack behind each side gear. Each clutch pack uses friction surfaced clutch discs splined to the side gear and steel clutch plates held by the differential case. The only major difference in designs is the type of preload spring used.

The General Motors limited slip differential uses 4 coil springs held by a spring retainer plate located between side gears. Ford Motor Co. design employs a single "S" shaped spring located between side gears to provide outward pressure on side gears and clutch pack.

In operation, preload spring pressure is accompanied by side gear thrust load to compress clutch packs, providing resistance to normal differential action. Preload spring pressure is calibrated to allow some slippage of clutch packs under variable torque conditions (turning corners, etc.).

IDENTIFICATION

Differential can be identified as a positive traction unit by raising vehicle and turning one rear wheel. Place transmission in Neutral. Rotate wheels. If both wheels rotate in same direction, differential is a positive traction differential.

Fig. 1: Axle Code Locations

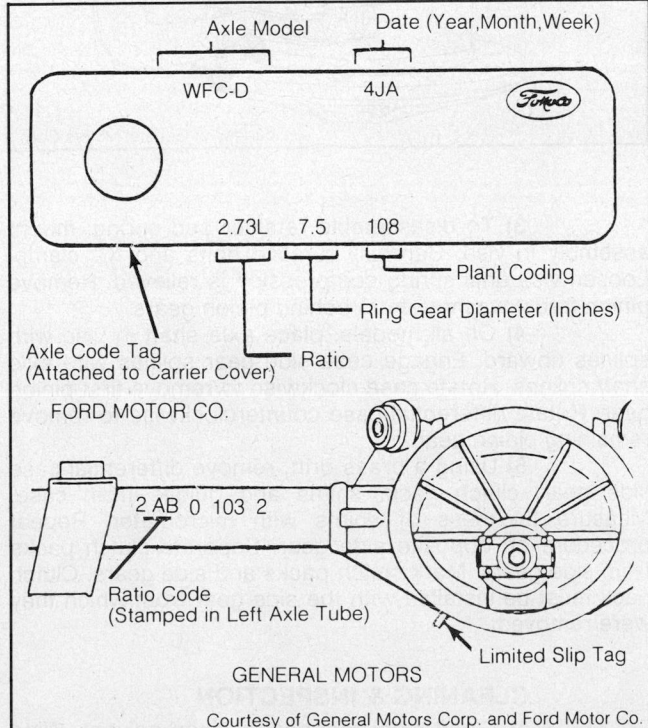

Courtesy of General Motors Corp. and Ford Motor Co.

General Motors differentials may be identified as a positive traction unit by axle code stamped on axle housing. Disassembly may be required to determine type of positive traction unit used. Both Ford and General Motors differentials have an identification tag attached to housing cover bolt. *See Fig. 1.*

Axle ratio, ring gear diameter and differential type is contained in axle code. Using axle model code, gear ratio may be determined. See AXLE RATIO IDENTIFICATION table.

AXLE RATIO IDENTIFICATION

Axle Ratio	Axle Code
Ford Motor Co.	
7 1/2" Ring Gear	
3.08:1	462 B & 479 B
3.45:1	281 D
3.73:1	266 D
8 3/4" Ring Gear	
2.73:1	013 A, 031 A & 201 A
3.08:1	015 A, 034 A, 445 C, 447 C, 203 F, 423 F, & 015 P
3.27:1	017 A, 039 A, 407 E, 205 F & 017 P
3.55:1	037 A, 431 B & 037 P
3.73:1	433 B
General Motors	
7 1/2" Ring Gear	
2.41:1	2 BJ
2.56:1	6 GA
2.71:1	4 ET
2.73:1	6 GB
3.08:1	2 BC
7 5/8" Ring Gear	
2.73:1	6 HE & 6 HT
3.08:1	6 HF & 6 HB
3.73:1	2 TH
7 3/4" Ring Gear	
2.77:1	4 ET
3.27:1	4 EU
3.45:1	4 EW
8 1/2" Ring Gear	
3.08:1	6 ZV
3.23:1	6 YE

LUBRICATION

FORD MOTOR CO.

Proper lubrication must be installed in all clutch type axles. Fill axle with Ford Hypoid Gear Lubricant (ESP-M2C154-A) with 4 ounces (.12L) of Ford Friction Modifier (C8AZ-19B546-A). See LUBRICATION CAPACITIES table for approximate capacity.

GENERAL MOTORS

Clutch type axles should be filled with proper lubrication to ensure correct operation. Fill axles with 80W or 80W-90 GL-5 gear lubricant General Motors Corp. (1052271). Some models require special gear lubricant and additive to be used along with gear lubricant. See LUBRICATION CAPACITIES table for approximate capacity.

Positive Traction Differentials

CLUTCH PACK TYPE (Cont.)

LUBRICATION CAPACITIES

Application	Pts. (L)
Ford Motor Co. [1]	
7 1/2" Ring Gear	3.75 (1.7)
8 3/4" Ring Gear	3.75 (1.7)
General Motors [2]	
7 1/2 & 7 5/8" Ring Gears	3.50 (1.6)
7 3/4" Ring Gear	3.75 (1.7)
8 1/2" Ring Gear	4.25 (2.0)

[1] – Does not include additive used in all models.
[2] – Does not include additive used in some models.

TESTING

FORD MOTOR CO.

1) Test positive traction differential by raising one rear wheel. Place transmission in Neutral. Attach a Traction-Lok Torque Adapter (T59L-4204-A) to wheel studs. *See Fig. 2.* Using a 200 ft. lb. (271 N.m) torque wrench, rotate axle shaft through one revolution and note torque reading.

2) Rotating torque should be at least 20 ft. lbs. (27 N.m). Initial break-away torque may be higher, but this is normal. If rotating torque is less than specified, check differential for proper assembly.

Fig. 2: *Testing Ford Motor Co. Differential In Vehicle*

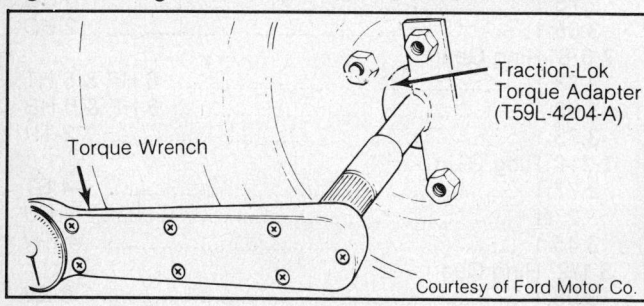

Torque Wrench
Traction-Lok Torque Adapter (T59L-4204-A)
Courtesy of Ford Motor Co.

GENERAL MOTORS

1) Place transmission in Park and release parking brake. Raise both rear wheels off ground. Attach Axle Shaft Puller (J-21579) and Adapter (J-2619-1) to axle shaft flange.

2) Using a torque wrench, measure torque required to rotate one wheel. Rotating torque should be at least 35 ft. lbs. (47 N.m). If torque reading is less than specified, disassemble and repair differential. *See Fig. 3.*

Fig. 3: *Testing General Motors Differential In Vehicle*

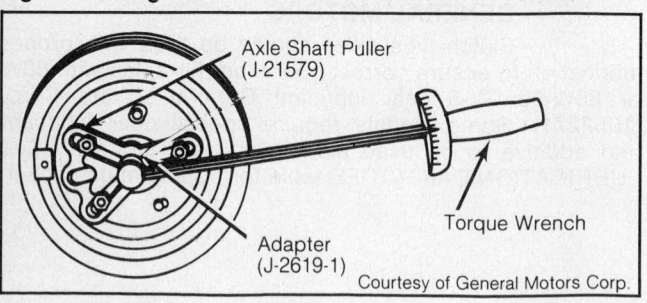

Axle Shaft Puller (J-21579)
Torque Wrench
Adapter (J-2619-1)
Courtesy of General Motors Corp.

REMOVAL & INSTALLATION

DIFFERENTIAL ASSEMBLY

See appropriate DRIVE AXLE article in this section for individual manufacturer's removal and installation procedures.

OVERHAUL

DISASSEMBLY

1) With ring gear removed, remove pinion shaft lock bolt. Use a punch to drive pinion shaft from differential case. On Ford models, carefully drive out "S" shaped preload spring with hammer and drift. Use caution, as preload spring is under pressure.

2) On General Motors differentials, drive preload spring retainer and springs through differential case hole only far enough to install a "C" clamp. Insert two 1/4" bolts through spring retainers and tighten enough to remove retainer and spring assembly. *See Fig. 4.*

Fig. 4: *General Motors Preload Spring Assembly*

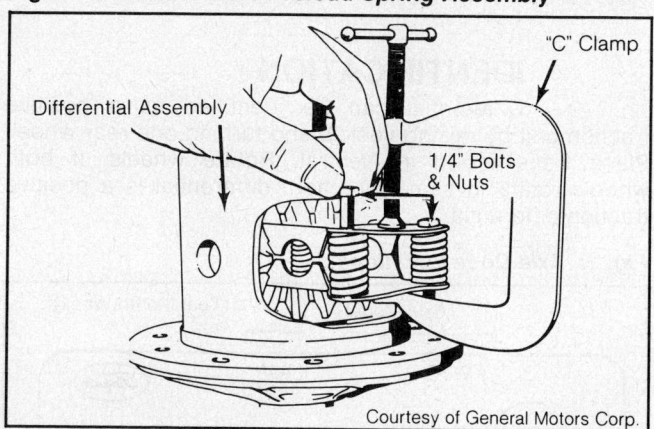

"C" Clamp
Differential Assembly
1/4" Bolts & Nuts
Courtesy of General Motors Corp.

3) To disassemble retainer and spring, mount assembly in vise. Carefully remove bolts and "C" clamp. Loosen vise until spring compression is relieved. Remove pinion thrust washers from behind pinion gears.

4) On all models, place axle shaft in vise with splines upward. Engage case side gear splines with axle shaft splines. Rotate case clockwise to remove first pinion gear. Rotate differential case counterclockwise to remove remaining pinion gear.

5) Using a brass drift, remove differential case side gear, clutch pack, shims and guides from case. Measure thickness of shims with micrometer. Repeat procedure on opposite side gear. Separate clutch packs from side gears. Mark clutch packs and side gears. Clutch pack must be installed with the side gear from which they were removed.

CLEANING & INSPECTION

1) Clean side bearings in clean solvent. Wipe friction plates with clean rag. DO NOT use solvent. Inspect pinion shaft, pinion gears, and side gears for excessive wear, cracks or scoring. Replace worn or damaged components.

CLUTCH PACK TYPE (Cont.)

Fig. 5: General Motors Positive Traction Differential

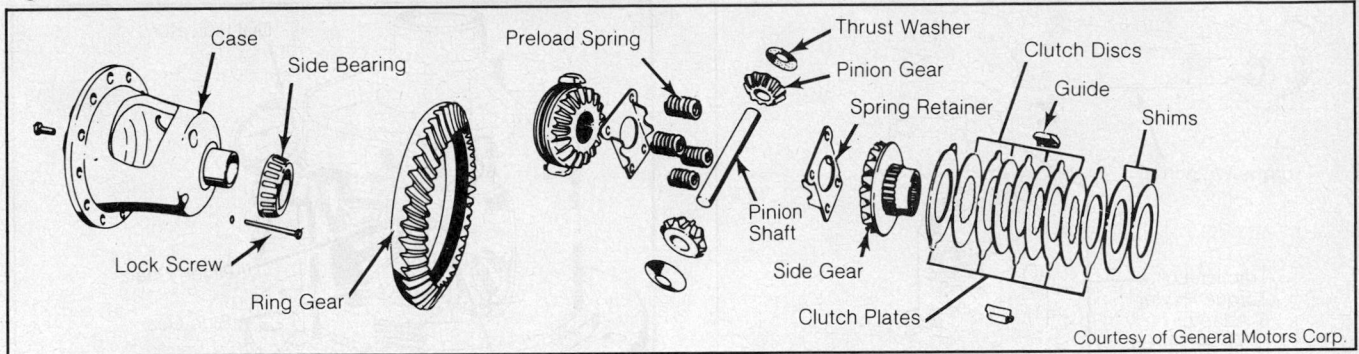

Case, Side Bearing, Preload Spring, Thrust Washer, Pinion Gear, Clutch Discs, Guide, Spring Retainer, Shims, Lock Screw, Ring Gear, Pinion Shaft, Side Gear, Clutch Plates

Courtesy of General Motors Corp.

2) Check side bearing inner races on differential case for tight fit. Replace side bearings or differential case if not a tight press fit. Inspect clutch plates for scoring, wear, cracks, distortion or signs of excessive heat. Replace if damaged.

REASSEMBLY
Ford Motor Co.
1) Lubricate clutch plates and discs with proper gear lubricant. Install side gear and clutch pack on Differential Clutch Gauge (T84P-4946-A). Tighten nut to 60 INCH lbs. (7 N.m). Checking with a feeler gauge, select thickest blade that will fit between gauge and clutch pack. This will be required shim thickness for this side gear. *See Fig. 7.* Repeat procedure for remaining side gear.

2) Remove pinion shaft, gears and thrust washers. Install remaining side gear, clutch pack assembly, and shims in differential case. Install pinion gears and thrust washers and rotate into position. Use a soft-faced hammer to drive "S" spring into case. Install pinion shaft and lock bolt. DO NOT tighten at this time.

3) Mount Traction-Lok Torque Holder (T59L-4204-A) in vise. Position case over holder. Using Traction-Lok Torque Adapter (T59L-4204-A) and 200 ft. lb. (271 N.m) torque wrench, measure torque required to rotate one side gear while other side gear is held stationary. *See Fig. 8.*

Fig. 7: Clutch Pack Shim Measurement

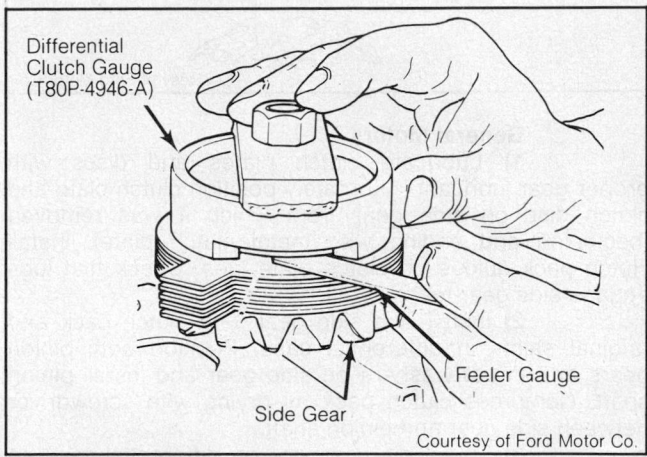

Differential Clutch Gauge (T80P-4946-A), Feeler Gauge, Side Gear

Courtesy of Ford Motor Co.

4) Initial break-away torque for original clutch pack should not be less than 20 ft. lbs. (27 N.m). For new clutch packs, break-away torque should be 80-200 ft. lbs. (108-271 N.m). If less than specified, check differential for proper assembly. Tighten pinion shaft lock bolt. Install ring gear using new bolts.

Fig. 6: Ford Motor Co. Clutch Pack Type Positive Traction Differential

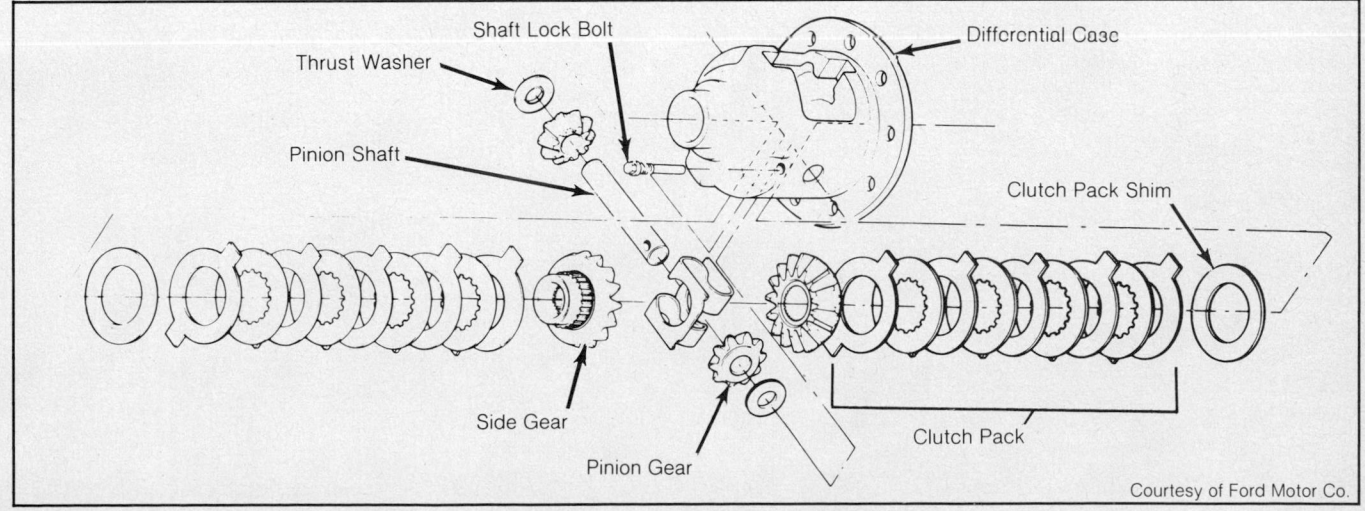

Thrust Washer, Shaft Lock Bolt, Differential Case, Pinion Shaft, Clutch Pack Shim, Side Gear, Pinion Gear, Clutch Pack

Courtesy of Ford Motor Co.

Positive Traction Differentials

CLUTCH PACK TYPE (Cont.)

Fig. 8: Bench Testing Ford Motor Co. Differential

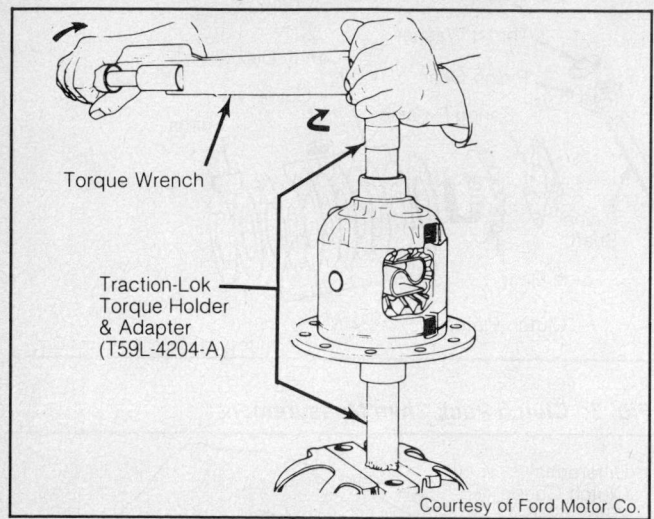

Torque Wrench

Traction-Lok Torque Holder & Adapter (T59L-4204-A)

Courtesy of Ford Motor Co.

Fig. 9: Measuring Pinion Clearance

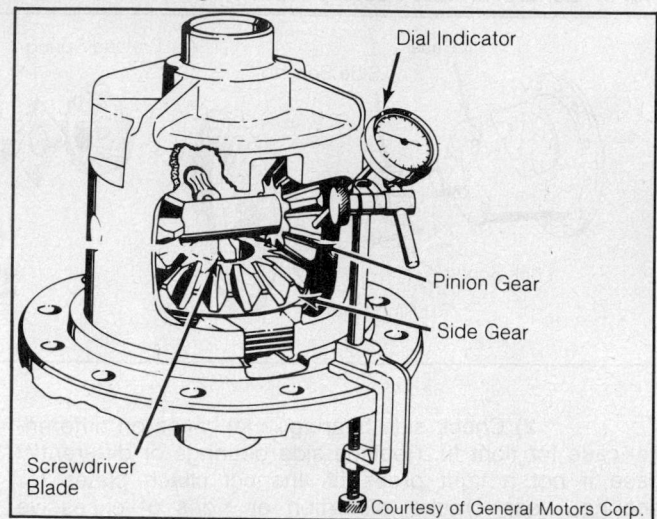

Dial Indicator

Pinion Gear

Side Gear

Screwdriver Blade

Courtesy of General Motors Corp.

General Motors

1) Lubricate clutch plates and discs with proper gear lubricant. Alternately position clutch plate and clutch disc on side gear from which it was removed (beginning and ending with metal clutch plate). Install clutch pack guides on clutch plate lugs. Check that lugs engage side gear teeth.

2) Install one side gear with clutch pack and original shims in differential case. Position both pinion gears and thrust washers on side gear and install pinion shaft. Compress clutch pack by prying with screwdriver between side gear and pinion shaft.

3) Mount dial indicator on differential case so tip rests against pinion gear. See Fig. 9. Rotate pinion gear and note pinion clearance. Pinion clearance should be .001-.006" (.03-.15 mm).

4) If pinion clearance is more than .006" (.15 mm), add shims between clutch pack and differential case. If clearance is less than .001" (.03 mm), remove shims. A shim thickness of .002" (.05 mm) will change clearance approximately .001" (.03 mm). Remove side gear assembly and repeat procedure for remaining side gear.

5) Remove pinion shaft, gears and thrust washers. Install remaining side gear, clutch pack assembly, and shims in differential case. Install pinion gears and thrust washers and rotate into position.

6) Mount springs in spring retainer and clamp spring assembly in vise. Install "C" clamp and shim stock on retainer to hold assembly together. Install 1/4" bolt and nut in each front spring.

7) Install spring assembly between side gears. Remove shim stock and "C" clamp. Drive spring pack into side gear enough to retain front springs and remove bolts. Drive spring assembly into position, checking alignment of spring retainer with side gears. Spring assembly can be moved slightly, if required.

TIGHTENING SPECIFICATIONS

Application	Ft. Lbs. (N.m)
Bearing Pinion Shaft Lock Bolt	20 (27)
Ring Gear Bolts	
7 1/2 & 7 5/8"	80-95 (108-129)
8 1/2"	70-90 (95-122)

CONE BRAKE TYPE

Chrysler Motors, General Motors

DESCRIPTION

Positive traction type differential directs major driving force to the wheel with greatest amount of traction. This is accomplished by 2 spring-loaded thrust plates pressing against the differential side gears which are seated into tapered brake cones.

The brake cones fit into a tapered recess in each end of differential cases where outward pressure of thrust plate assembly forces brake cones against recesses, providing resistance to normal differential action. Thrust plate spring load is calibrated to permit some slippage under variable torque conditions.

Chrysler Motors uses the Sure-Grip unit which is not serviceable. General Motors uses both Borg-Warner and Auburn cone brake type units. The Borg-Warner unit is serviceable while Auburn unit is not. The Auburn and Sure-Grip must be replaced as a complete unit.

IDENTIFICATION

The differential can be identified as a positive traction unit by raising vehicle and rotating one rear wheel. With transmission in Neutral, both rear wheels rotate in same direction if vehicle is equipped with a positive traction differential.

The axle may be identified by axle code on General Motors vehicles. The axle code is stamped on front of right rear axle tube. *See Fig. 1.*

The axle ratio, ring gear diameter and differential type is contained in axle code. Using axle model code, gear ratio may be determined. See AXLE RATIO IDENTIFICATION table. Disassembly may be required to determine type of positive traction unit used.

Chrysler Motors does not use axle codes. Axle ratio is located on a tag bolted to differential cover. Positive traction unit may be identified by removing oil fill plug and noting type of differential case used.

Fig. 1: General Motors Axle Identification

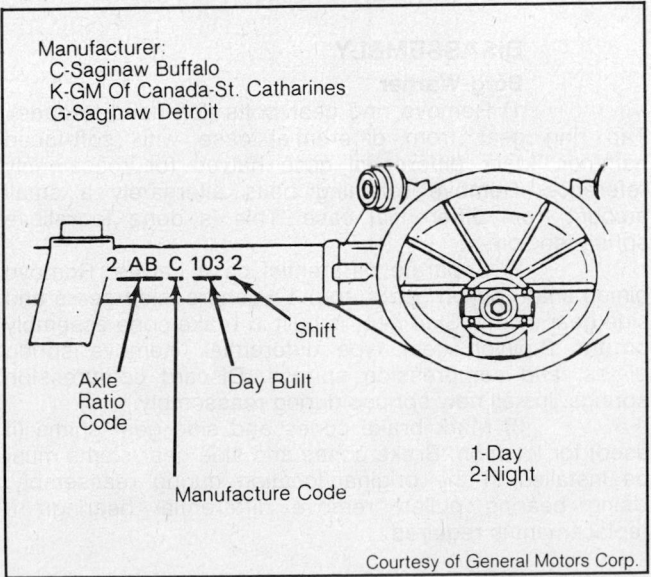

Manufacturer:
C-Saginaw Buffalo
K-GM Of Canada-St. Catharines
G-Saginaw Detroit

2 AB C 103 2

Shift

Axle Ratio Code

Day Built

Manufacture Code

1-Day
2-Night

Courtesy of General Motors Corp.

AXLE RATIO IDENTIFICATION

Axle Ratio	Axle Code
General Motors	
7 1/2" Ring Gear	
2.41:1	2 BJ
2.56:1	6 GA
2.71:1	4 ET
2.73:1	6 GB
3.08:1	2 BC
7 5/8" Ring Gear	
2.73:1	6 HE & 6 HT
3.08:1	6 HF & 6 HB
3.73:1	2 TH
7 3/4" Ring Gear	
2.77:1	4 ET
3.27:1	4 EU
3.45:1	4 EW
8 1/2" Ring Gear	
3.08:1	6 ZV
3.23:1	6 YE

LUBRICATION

CHRYSLER MOTORS

Proper lubrication must be installed in all cone type axles. Fill axle with Mopar Hypoid Gear Lubricant (4318058) or equivalent and 4 ounces (.12L) of Mopar Hypoid Gear Oil Additive (4318060) or equivalent. See LUBRICATION CAPACITIES table for approximate refill capacity.

GENERAL MOTORS

Clutch type axles should be filled with proper lubrication to ensure correct operation. Fill axles with 80W or 80W-90 GL-5 gear lubricant General Motors (1052271). Some models require special gear lubricant and additive to be used along with special gear lubricant. See LUBRICATION CAPACITIES table for approximate capacity.

LUBRICATION CAPACITIES

Application	Pts. (L)
Chrysler Motors [1]	
8 1/4" Ring Gear	4.4 (2.1)
General Motors [2]	
7 1/2 & 7 5/8" Ring Gears	3.50 (1.6)
7 3/4" Ring Gear	3.75 (1.7)
8 1/2" Ring Gear	4.25 (2.0)

[1] – Does not include additive used in all models.
[2] – Does not include additive used in some models.

TESTING

CHRYSLER MOTORS

1) Differential can be tested externally by raising both rear wheels from ground. Place transmission in Park on automatic transmissions, or Low gear on manual transmissions.

Positive Traction Differentials

CONE BRAKE TYPE (Cont.)

2) Attempt to turn one wheel by hand. Wheel assembly must be very difficult to turn. If wheel can be turned easily, differential assembly should be replaced as a complete unit.

GENERAL MOTORS

Borg-Warner Differential

1) Place transmission in Park. Raise rear of vehicle until both wheels are free from ground. Remove wheel and tire. Attach Axle Shaft Puller (J-21579) and Adapter (J-2619-1) to axle shaft flange. Install 1/2" x 13 bolt into adapter. *See Fig. 2.*

2) With opposite wheel held from turning, attach torque wrench to adapter and measure torque required to rotate opposite wheel assembly. If torque reading is less than 35 ft. lbs. (48 N.m), disassemble and repair differential case.

Fig. 2: Testing Differential in Vehicle

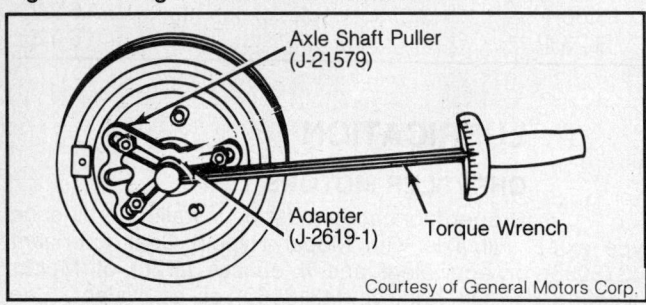

Axle Shaft Puller
(J-21579)

Adapter
(J-2619-1)

Torque Wrench

Courtesy of General Motors Corp.

Auburn Differential

1) Place transmission in Park. Raise rear of vehicle until both wheels are free from ground. Remove wheel and tire. Attach Adapter (J-2619-1) to axle shaft flange. Install 1/2" x 13 bolt into adapter. *See Fig. 2.*

2) Rotate one wheel and note torque required for rotation. The reading should be within 125-225 ft. lbs. (169-305 N.m). Lower vehicle so that one wheel is on ground. Place transmission in Neutral.

3) Check torque to rotate remaining wheel. Reading should be 45-100 ft. lbs. (61-136 N.m). Replace differential assembly if not within specifications.

Fig. 3: Auburn Differential Assembly

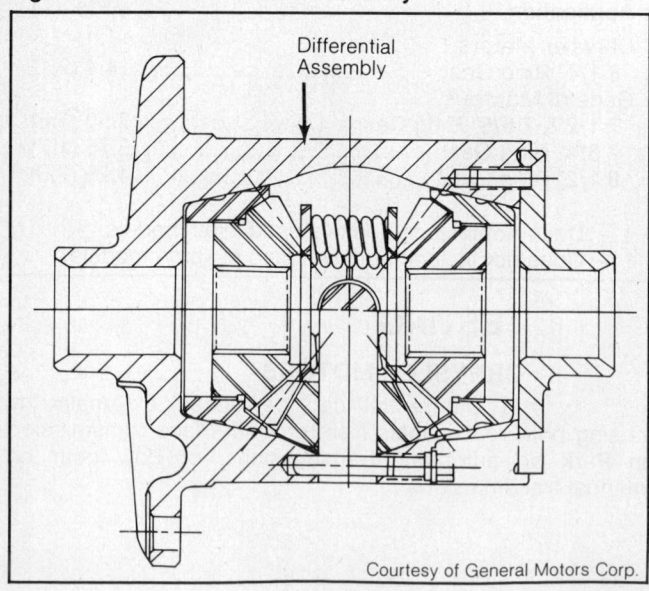

Differential
Assembly

Courtesy of General Motors Corp.

Fig. 4: Sure-Grip Differential Assembly

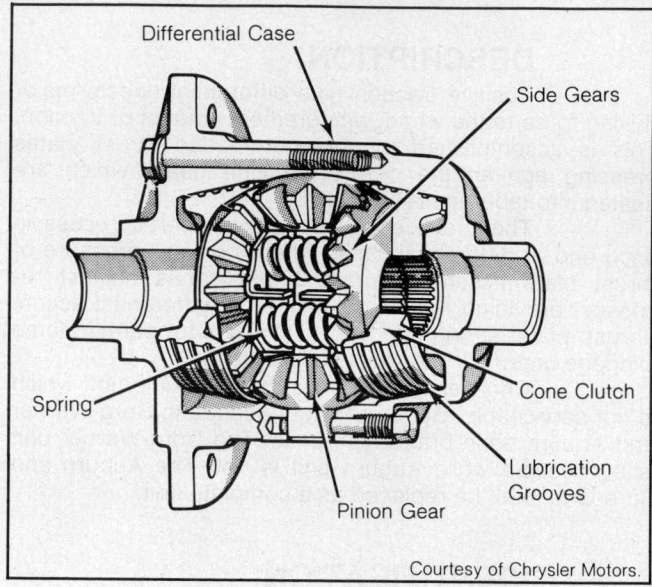

Differential Case

Side Gears

Cone Clutch

Lubrication
Grooves

Pinion Gear

Spring

Courtesy of Chrysler Motors.

REMOVAL & INSTALLATION

DIFFERENTIAL ASSEMBLY

See appropriate DRIVE AXLE article in this section for individual manufacturer's removal and installation procedures.

NOTE: Once differential and first axle shaft have been installed in axle housing, DO NOT rotate axle. This will prevent misalignment of splines in opposite cone and gear assembly.

OVERHAUL

NOTE: Chrysler Motors Sure-Grip and the Auburn differential units are serviced as a complete assembly only.

DISASSEMBLY

Borg-Warner

1) Remove ring gear bolts (left-hand threads). Tap ring gear from differential case with soft-faced hammer. Mark differential case halves for reassembly reference. Remove retaining bolts alternately a small amount from differential case. This is done to relieve spring tension.

2) Separate differential case halves. Remove pinion shaft, pinion gears, thrust washers, side gears and side gear shims. Side gear is built in brake cone assembly on the 2-pinion gear type differential. Remove spring plates, and compression springs. Discard compression springs. Install new springs during reassembly.

3) Mark brake cones and side gear shims (if used) for location. Brake cones and side gear shims must be installed in the original location during reassembly. Using bearing puller, remove differential bearings if replacement is required.

INSPECTION

Inspect all gears for cracks, flaking or damaged teeth. Check that the brake cone seats are smooth

CONE BRAKE TYPE (Cont.)

Fig. 5: Exploded View of 4-Pinion Gear Borg-Warner Differential

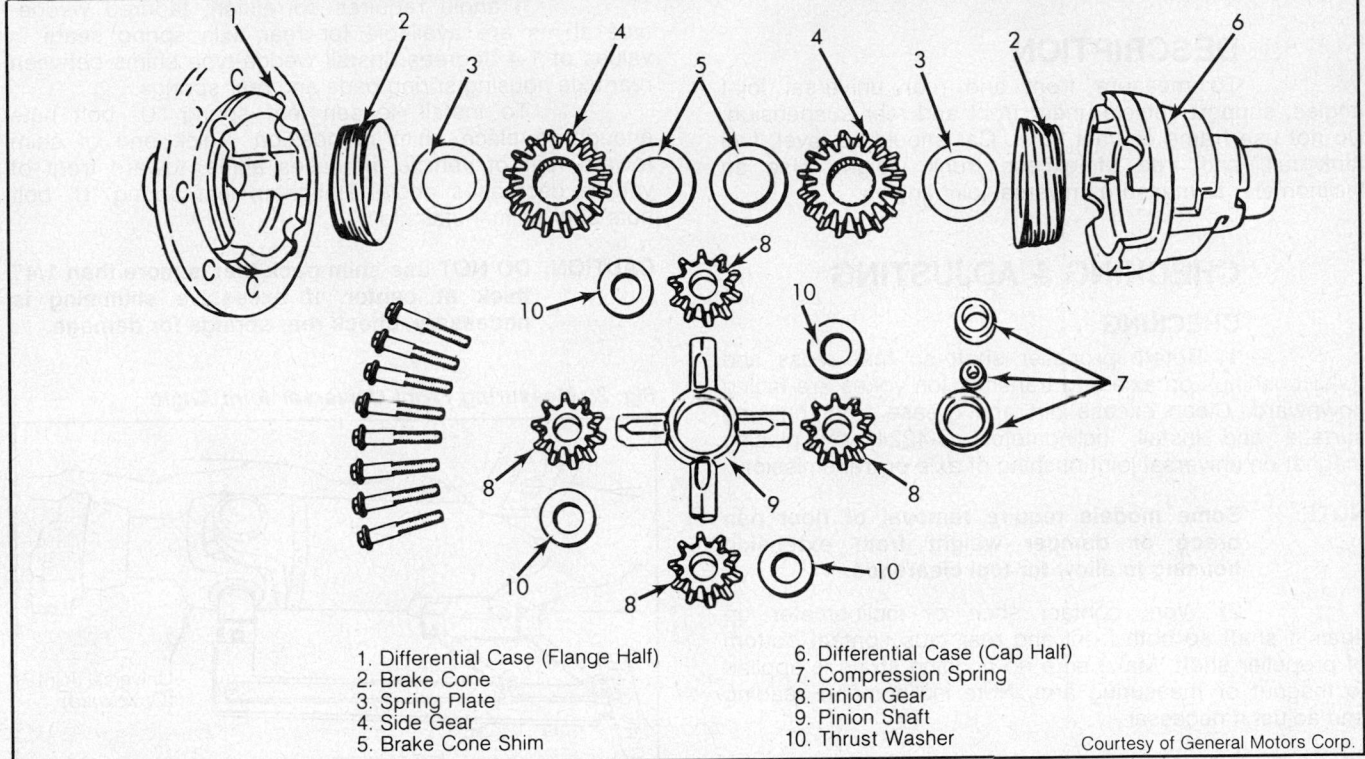

1. Differential Case (Flange Half)
2. Brake Cone
3. Spring Plate
4. Side Gear
5. Brake Cone Shim
6. Differential Case (Cap Half)
7. Compression Spring
8. Pinion Gear
9. Pinion Shaft
10. Thrust Washer

Courtesy of General Motors Corp.

and free of excessive scoring. Inspect brake cones for scoring or damage. If the brake cone or differential case is damaged, replace brake cones and differential case as a unit.

REASSEMBLY

Borg-Warner

1) Install brake cones in the differential case. Measure the distance from differential case mating surface to flat surface on brake cone when it is fully seated. This is done to determine the size brake cone shim required. See REQUIRED BRAKE CONE SHIM CHART.

REQUIRED BRAKE CONE SHIM CHART

Distance Measured In. (mm)	Shim Size In. (mm)
1.155-1.162 (29.34-29.51)	No shim required.
1.163-1.167 (29.54-29.64)	.005 (.13)
1.168-1.172 (29.67-29.77)	.010 (.25)

2) Using rear axle lubricant, lubricate pinion thrust washers, pinion bores and differential pinion shaft. Install the pinions and thrust washers on the pinion shaft.

3) Install proper brake cone shim and side gear in the cap half of the differential case. Brake cone must be installed in proper location. Apply mixture of molybdenum disulphide and rear axle lubricant to the face of both side gears.

4) Install spring plate on the side gear. Convex side must face the flange half of differential case. Install pinion shaft, pinion gears and thrust washers into cap half of the differential case. Ensure pinions mesh with side gear.

5) Install 3 new concentric thrust springs through center of pinion shaft. Install remaining spring plate and springs. Convex side must face the springs. Install side gear shim (if required).

6) Install remaining brake cone on spring plate. Install flange half of differential case while aligning oil channels. Install 2 bolts 180 degrees apart and finger tighten.

7) Use axle shaft to align side gear and brake cone splines. Place "C" clamp on axle shaft so 3" (76 mm) extends beyond "C" clamp. Install differential assembly onto axle shaft splines, flanged half first.

8) Install another axle shaft through cap side of differential case aligning the side gear and brake cone splines. Install remaining bolts. Tighten to specification. See TIGHTENING SPECIFICATIONS table at end of article. Install side bearings and ring gear (if removed).

TIGHTENING SPECIFICATIONS

Application	Ft. Lbs. (N.m)
Borg Warner	
Differential Case Bolt	29 (38)
Ring Gear Bolt [1]	101 (137)

[1] – Always use new ring gear bolts.

Propeller Shaft Alignment

CHRYSLER MOTORS

RWD Models

DESCRIPTION

To measure front and rear universal joint angles, support vehicle under front and rear suspension. Do not use frame contact hoist. Car should be level, fuel tank full, and free of excess trunk weight. Use an inclinometer to measure universal joint angles.

CHECKING & ADJUSTING

CHECKING

1) Rotate propeller shaft so that cross and roller bushings on axle and transmission yokes are facing downward. Clean excess dirt and grease from bushing surface and install Inclinometer (C-4224) by placing magnet on universal joint bushing of axle or transmission.

NOTE: **Some models require removal of floor pan brace or damper weight from extension housing to allow for tool clearance.**

2) Work contact shoe of inclinometer up against shaft so both front and rear tabs contact bottom of propeller shaft. Make sure no bending strain is applied to magnet or measuring arm. Note inclinometer reading and adjust if necessary.

ADJUSTING

Front

To reduce high readings, place shims between extension housing of transmission and rear engine mount. Install shims by removing rear engine mount bolts and raising transmission extension housing enough to allow installation of shims. Each 1/8" shim will reduce angle 1/4 degree. After shims are in place, reinstall rear engine mount bolts and tighten to specification. If angle reads low or negative, no correction is required.

Fig. 1: Measuring Rear Universal Joint Angle Using Inclinometer

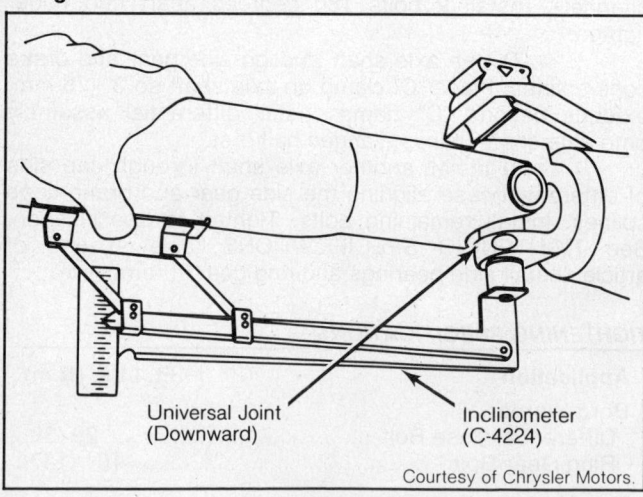

Courtesy of Chrysler Motors.

Rear

If angle requires correction, tapered wedge-type shims are available for rear axle spring seats in values of 1-4 degrees. Install wedge-type shims between rear axle housing spring pads and rear springs.

To install, loosen leaf spring "U" bolt nuts enough to place shim in position. Thick end of shim toward rear of vehicle increases angle, toward front of vehicle decreases angle. Retighten leaf spring "U" bolt nuts after shim installation.

CAUTION: **DO NOT use shim pack that is more than 1/4" thick at center. If excessive shimming is necessary, check rear springs for damage.**

Fig. 2: Measuring Front Universal Joint Angle

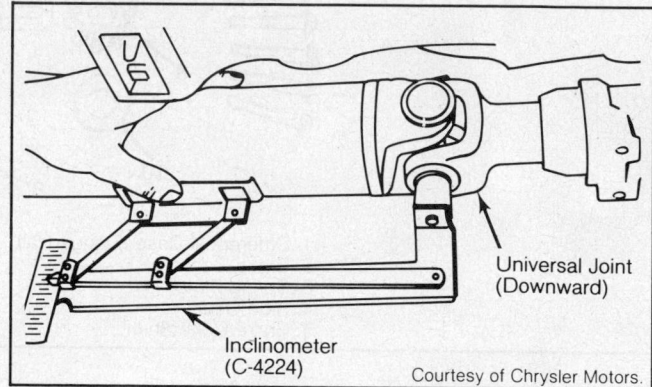

Courtesy of Chrysler Motors.

REAR AXLE IDENTIFICATION

Application	Housing Diameter IN. (mm)
7 1/4" Axle	2.5 (63.5) & 3 (76.2)
8 1/4" Axle	3 (76.2)

UNIVERSAL JOINT ANGLE SPECIFICATIONS

Application	[1] Front Angle (Degrees)	[1] Rear Angle (Degrees)
7 1/4" Axle	0	+2 1/4
8 1/4" Axle	0	+3

[1] – Angles may be ± 1/2 degrees.

TIGHTENING SPECIFICATION

Application	Ft. Lbs. (N.m)
Rear Engine Mount Bolt	50 (68)
7 1/4" Axle Leaf Spring "U" Bolt	40 (54)
8 1/4" Axle Leaf Spring "U" Bolt	45 (61)

FORD MOTOR CO.

RWD Models

DESCRIPTION

The propeller shaft universal joint angle is controlled by rear axle upper control arms on both coil spring and air suspension models. Whenever upper control arms are removed, universal joint angle must be checked and adjusted if necessary.

Fig. 1: Universal Joint Angle Adjustment

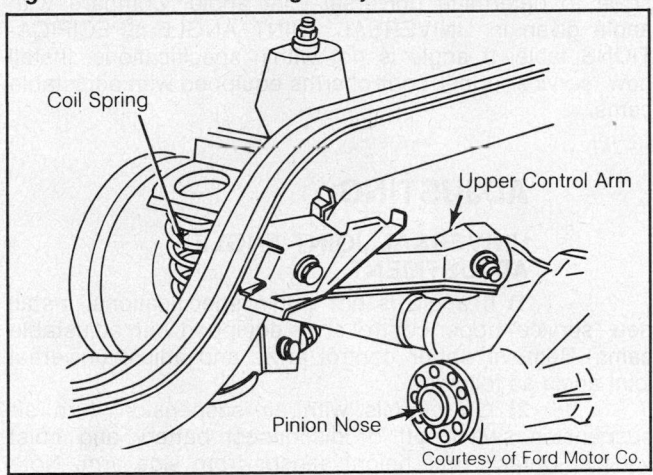

Courtesy of Ford Motor Co.

CHECKING

COIL SPRING SUSPENSION

Before checking universal joint angle, measure and adjust vehicle curb height. *See Fig. 2.* Measure curb height from top of axle housing tube to axle bumper bracket on bottom of side rail (outer edge of side rail on Crown Victoria, Grand Marquis and Town Car).

Adjust vehicle curb height to dimension given in UNIVERSAL JOINT ANGLE SPECIFICATIONS table by loading or unloading weight in vehicle. After setting proper curb height, proceed to UNIVERSAL JOINT ANGLE CHECK.

Fig. 2: Measuring Coil Spring Suspension Curb Height

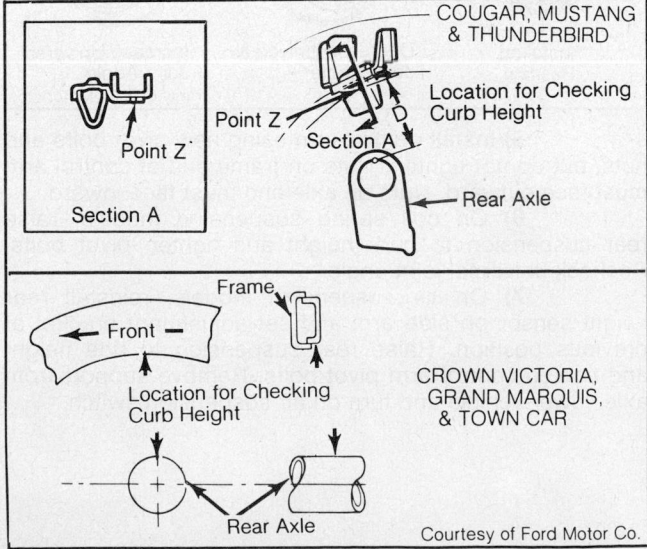

Courtesy of Ford Motor Co.

AIR SUSPENSION

Before checking universal joint angle on models with air suspension, set vehicle trim. In addition, check front and rear suspension ride height, and adjust if necessary.

CAUTION: The electrical power supply to the air suspension system must be shut off prior to hoisting, jacking or towing vehicle. Turn off air suspension switch located on left hand side of vehicle trunk or disconnect battery.

CAUTION: The following hoist restrictions must be observed: use only a "body hoist" and lift vehicle using standard procedures. Place jack stands at each corner as a safety precaution. If "body hoist" is not available, use standard hydraulic floor jack. Raise front of vehicle at No. 2 crossmember. Place jack stands at front corners of body. For rear, use same procedures, but use rear jacking location.

Vehicle Trim Setting Procedure

NOTE: If vehicle temperature differs 20°F (11°C) or more from shop area, allow enough time for temperature of vehicle to adjust.

Position vehicle on alignment rack. Turn ignition off and exit vehicle. Level rack as required. Re-enter vehicle and turn ignition to "RUN" position (DO NOT START). After 1 minute, push trunk release, turn ignition off, and exit vehicle. Allow vehicle 20 seconds to settle to trim height (doors closed), then turn air suspension switch off (in trunk on left side).

Fig. 3: Checking Air Suspension Ride Height

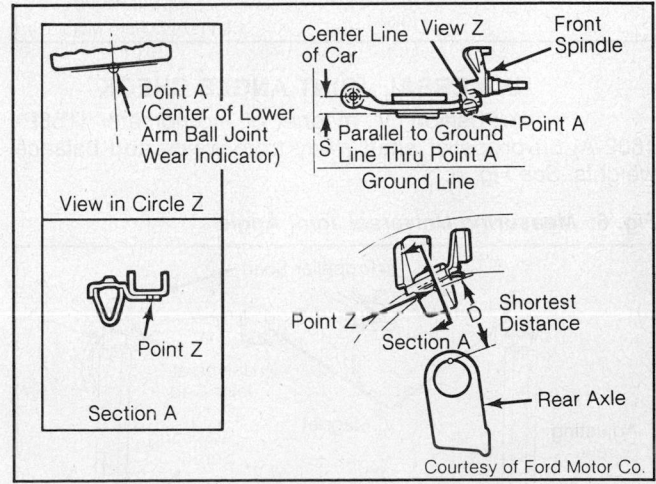

Courtesy of Ford Motor Co.

Front Suspension Ride Height Check

1) Measure distance between lower ball joint and centerline of lower control arm inner bushing. *See Fig. 3.* If dimension "S" is not 1/4" (6 mm), loosen front left and/or right lower air suspension sensor bracket stud and screw. *See Fig. 4.*

2) There are 3 adjustment positions provided. Moving 1 position will change "S" dimension 1/2" (12.7 mm). Move sensor up or down until centerline of lower control arm bushing is .24" (6.1 mm) above lower ball joint (Point "A" in *Fig. 3*).

Propeller Shaft Alignment

FORD MOTOR CO. (Cont.)

Fig. 4: Adjusting Front Air Suspension Ride Height

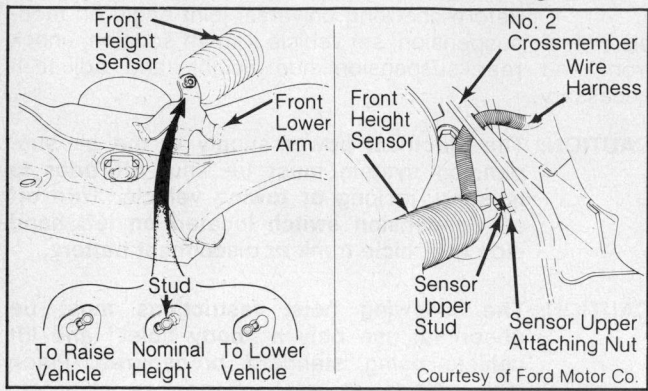

Courtesy of Ford Motor Co.

Rear Suspension Ride Height Check

Measure distance between top of axle housing tube and axle bumper bracket on bottom of side rail. *See Fig. 3.* If dimension "D" is not 5.06" (128.5 mm), loosen rear air suspension sensor bracket nut and move up or down. *See Fig. 5.* Moving the bracket 1 index mark will change dimension "D" 1/4" (6.4 mm).

Fig. 5: Adjusting Rear Air Suspension Ride Height

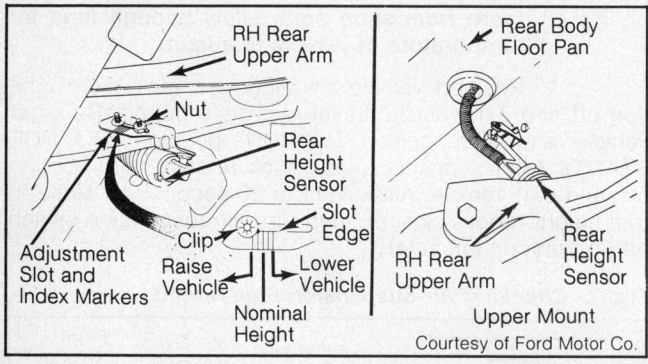

Courtesy of Ford Motor Co.

UNIVERSAL JOINT ANGLE CHECK

1) Position "V" magnet of Inclinometer (T68P-4602-A) on propeller shaft away from welds and balance weights. *See Fig. 6.*

Fig. 6: Measuring Universal Joint Angle

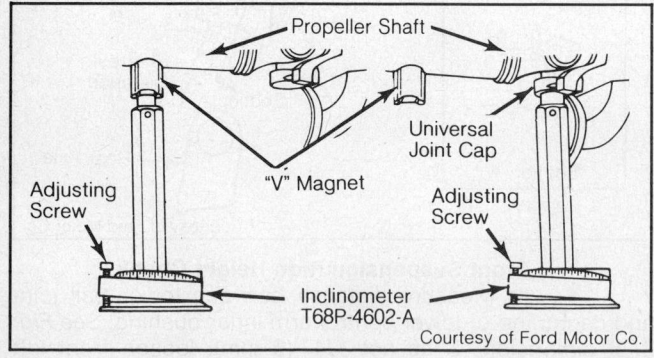

Courtesy of Ford Motor Co.

2) From left side of vehicle, position inclinometer on "V" magnet with adjusting screw to left. Adjust dial until left side of bubble is on zero line.

3) Remove inclinometer from "V" magnet. Install it on universal joint bearing cap in same relative position as it was on "V" magnet. Crown Victoria, Grand Marquis, and Town Car models require placing inclinometer on bearing cap of circular flange.

NOTE: Circular flange bearing cap snap ring must be removed and reinstalled after reading is completed.

4) Read position of bubble's left hand edge on scale to determine universal joint angle. Compare with angle given in UNIVERSAL JOINT ANGLE SPECIFICATIONS table. If angle is not within specifications, install new "service" upper control arms equipped with adjustable cams.

ADJUSTING

UNIVERSAL JOINT ANGLE ADJUSTMENT

1) If angle is not within specifications, install new "service" upper control arms equipped with adjustable cams. Remove upper control arms and adjust universal joint angle as follows:

2) On models with air suspension, turn air suspension switch off or disconnect battery and hoist vehicle. Detach rear height sensor from side arm. Note sensor bracket position for reassembly.

3) On all models, raise vehicle on hoist and support rear axle and pinion nose. Remove upper control arm-to-axle pivot bolt and arm-to-frame pivot bolt. Remove control arm.

4) Insert wide flat screwdriver in eccentric inner sleeve (accessible through attaching bolt hole). *See Fig. 7.* Rotate cams an equal amount clockwise to raise or counterclockwise to lower pinion angle. Ensure that both upper arms have same cam setting.

Fig. 7: Adjusting Cams on "Service" Control Arms

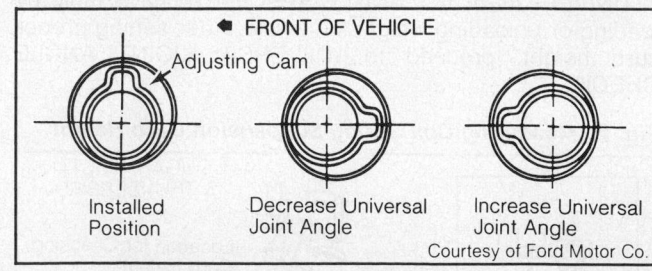

Courtesy of Ford Motor Co.

5) Install control arm using new pivot bolts and nuts, but do not tighten. Nuts on frame end of control arm must face outward. Nuts on axle end must face inward.

6) On coil spring suspension models, raise rear suspension to curb height and tighten pivot bolts. Recheck universal joint angle.

7) On air suspension models, reinstall rear height sensor on side arm and set adjustment bracket at previous position. Raise rear suspension to ride height and tighten control arm pivot bolts. Remove support from axle, lower vehicle and turn on air suspension switch.

FORD MOTOR CO. (Cont.)

UNIVERSAL JOINT ANGLE SPECIFICATIONS

Application	Universal Joints (Front & Rear) [1] (Degrees)	Curb Height Inches (mm)
6 3/4" Axle		
Mustang	2 1/6	5.29 (134.3)
7 1/2" Axle		
Mustang	2 1/2	5.07 (128.8)
Continental & Mark VII Air Suspension		
Front	3 3/4	.24 (6.0)
Rear	3 3/4	5.06 (128.6)
Cougar & T-Bird	2 2/3	5.77 (146.5)
8 3/4" Axle		
Crown Victoria & Grand Marquis		
Sedan	2 1/3	6.02 (152.9)
Wagon	3	6.47 (164.3)
Town Car	2 1/3	5.58 (141.8)

[1] – Angles may be ± 1/2 degrees.

TIGHTENING SPECIFICATIONS

Application	Ft. Lbs. (N.m)
Upper Control Arm-to-Frame	
Exc. Crown Victoria, Grand Marquis & Town Car	80-105 (108-142)
Crown Victoria, Grand Marquis & Town Car	120-150 (162-203)
Upper Control Arm-to-Axle	
Exc. Crown Victoria, Grand Marquis & Town Car	70-100 (95-135)
Crown Victoria, Grand Marquis & Town Car	103-133 (140-180)

Propeller Shaft Alignment

BUICK

RWD Models

DESCRIPTION

Measure front and rear universal joint angles with vehicle at proper trim height (distance from top of axle tube to bottom of frame). If necessary, add weight to set trim height specification.

Use an inclinometer to measure universal joint angles. Adjust by loosening rear suspension control arm bolts and repositioning the pinion nose by shimming transmission mount, or by changing control arms.

CHECKING & ADJUSTING

CHECKING

Front Universal Joint Angle

1) Place the Inclinometer (J-23498) on front propeller shaft bearing cap. Cap must be straight up and down and clean. Center bubble in sight glass and record measurement.

2) Rotate propeller shaft 90 degrees. Place the inclinometer on front slip spline yoke bearing cap. Center bubble in sight glass and record measurement. Subtract smaller reading from larger reading for existing front joint angle.

Fig. 1: Measuring Front Universal Joint Angle

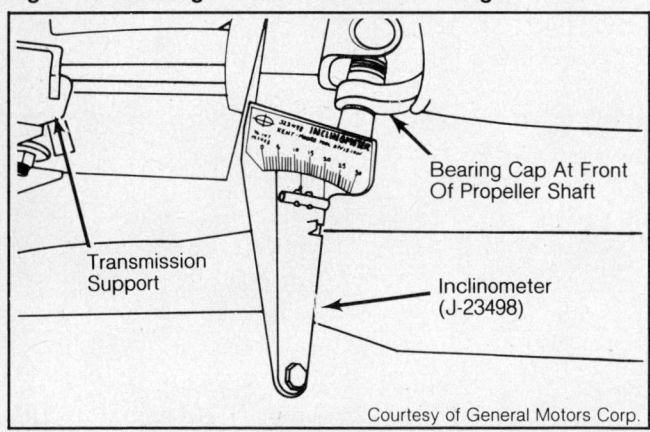

Courtesy of General Motors Corp.

Rear Universal Joint Angle

1) Place inclinometer on rear propeller shaft bearing cap. Cap must be straight up and down and clean. Center bubble in sight glass and record measurement.

2) Rotate propeller shaft 90 degrees and place inclinometer on rear drive yoke bearing cap. Center bubble in sight glass and record measurement. Subtract smaller reading from larger reading to obtain existing rear joint angle.

ADJUSTING

Transmission Shimming

Adding 1 shim at transmission mount will decrease front universal joint angle by 1/2 degree and increase rear angle by 1/4 degree. Removing 1 shim will increase front angle 1/2 degree and decrease rear angle 1/4 degree.

NOTE: Production bolt is 10-1.5 x 35 mm. When using 2 or more shims, a 10-1.5 x 50 mm bolt must be used.

Fig. 2: Measuring Rear Universal Joint Angle

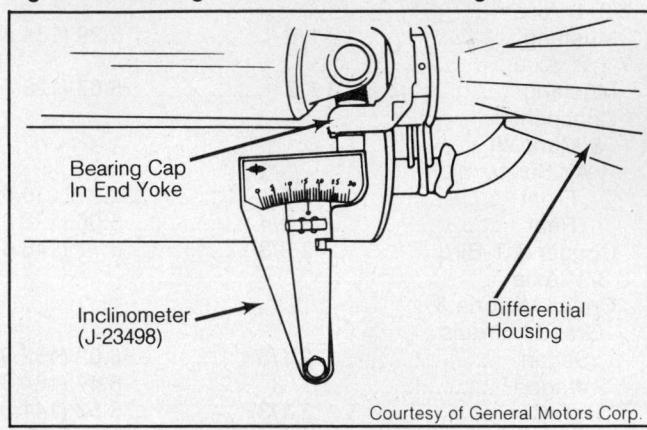

Courtesy of General Motors Corp.

Repositioning Pinion Nose

Suspension bracket bolt holes will permit a 1 degree adjustment of rear joint angle. Loosen all rear suspension control arm bolts and reposition pinion nose up or down.

Control Arm Change

Shorter or longer rear control arms may be used to change propeller shaft angles at transmission and differential.

REAR UPPER CONTROL ARM CHANGE

Appliction	Front Angle Change (Degrees)	Rear Angle Change (Degrees)
Estate Wagon		
Short Arm	+1/3	+2
Long Arm	-1/3	-2

UNIVERSAL JOINT ANGLE

Application	[1] Height Inches (mm)	[2] Front Joint (Degs.)	[2] Rear Joint (Degs.)
Estate Wagon			
8 1/2" Axle	6 1/8 (155)	1 3/4	2

[1] – Axle tube-to-frame height ± 1/4" (6mm).
[2] – The angles may be ± 1/2 degree.

Propeller Shaft Alignment

CADILLAC

RWD Models

DESCRIPTION

To properly measure front and rear universal joint angles, vehicle must be at proper trim height (distance from top of axle tube to bottom of frame). If necessary, add weight to meet trim height of 5 1/4" (133 mm). With vehicle level and supported at axles, measure universal joint angles using an inclinometer.

Adjustment may be made by shimming rear transmission mount. Rear universal joint angle may be adjusted by loosening all rear suspension control arm bolts and repositioning pinion nose.

CHECKING & ADJUSTING

CHECKING

1) Clean all bearing caps and place Inclinometer (J-23498) on rear propeller shaft bearing cap. Bearing cap must be straight up and down. Center bubble in sight glass and record reading. Remove inclinometer, rotate propeller shaft 90 degrees and install inclinometer on drive yoke bearing cap. Measure angle and subtract smaller reading from larger reading to determine rear universal joint angle.

2) Attach Inclinometer Adapter (J-23498-20) to front propeller shaft bearing cap. Attach inclinometer to adapter and repeat procedure used on rear universal joint to obtain front universal joint angle.

Fig. 1: Measuring Front Universal Joint Angle

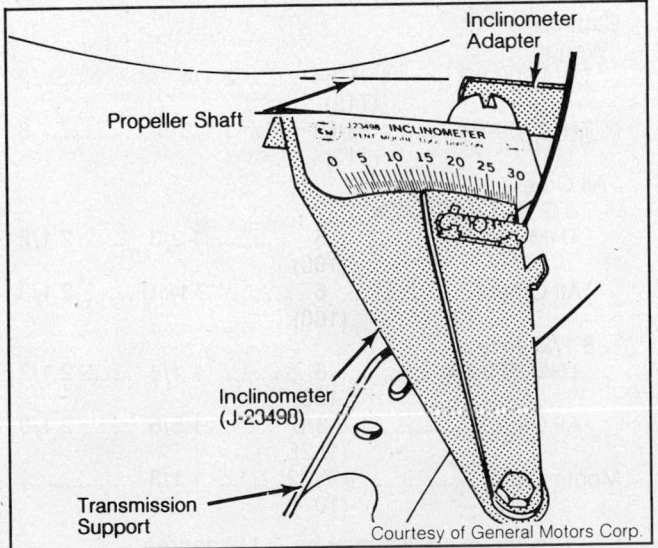

Courtesy of General Motors Corp.

ADJUSTING
Transmission Shimming

Adding 1 shim at transmission mount will decrease front universal joint angle 1/2 degrees and increase rear angle 1/4 degrees. Removing 1 shim will increase front angle 1/2 degrees and decrease rear angle 1/4 degrees.

NOTE: Production bolt is 10-1.5 x 35 mm. When using 2 or more shims, a 10-1.5 x 50 mm bolt must be used.

Fig. 2: Measuring Rear Universal Joint Angle

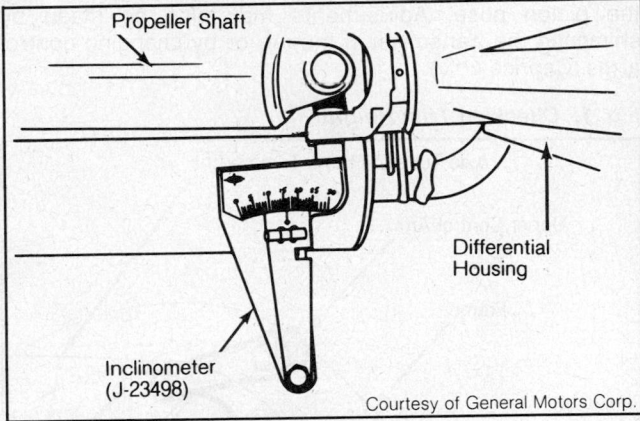

Courtesy of General Motors Corp.

Repositioning Pinion Nose

Suspension bracket bolt hole tolerances will permit adjustment of rear universal joint angle. Loosen all rear suspension control arm bolts and reposition pinion nose up or down. Tighten all bolts.

UNIVERSAL JOINT ANGLE

Application	Front Joint	Rear Joint
5.0L Engine	2°	2°

Propeller Shaft Alignment
CHEVROLET

RWD Models (Except Corvette)

DESCRIPTION

To properly measure front and rear universal joint angles, vehicle must be at proper trim height (distance from top of axle tube to bottom of frame). If necessary, add weight to meet this distance. With vehicle level and supported at axles, measure universal joint angles using an inclinometer.

Adjustment may be made by loosening all of the rear suspension control arm bolts and repositioning the pinion nose. Adjustments may also be made by shimming the transmission mount, or by changing control arms (Caprice only).

Fig. 1: Checking Trim Height

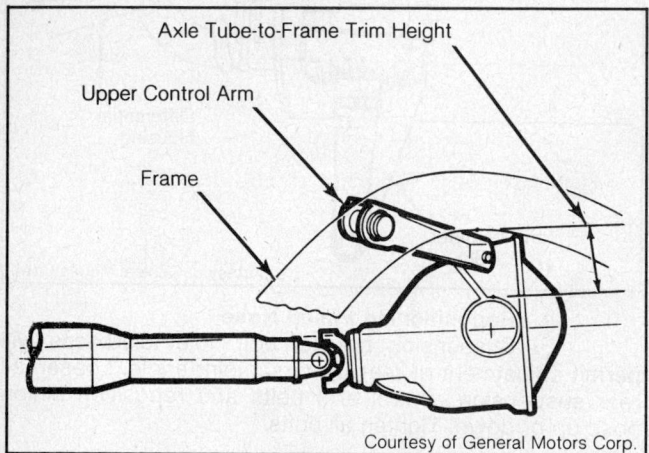

Courtesy of General Motors Corp.

CHECKING & ADJUSTING

CHECKING

1) Clean all bearing caps and place Inclinometer (J-23498) on rear propeller shaft bearing cap. Bearing cap must be straight up and down. Center sight glass bubble and record reading.

Fig. 2: Measuring Rear Universal Joint Angle

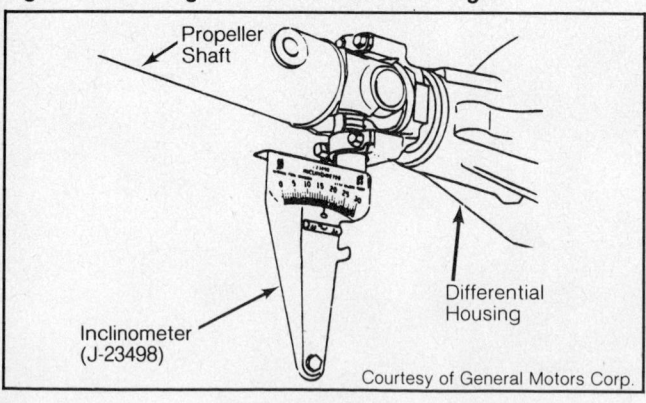

Courtesy of General Motors Corp.

2) Rotate propeller shaft 90 degrees and place inclinometer on rear drive yoke bearing cap. Measure angle and subtract smaller reading from larger reading to determine rear universal joint angle. Repeat procedure on front universal joint to determine front universal joint angle.

ADJUSTING
Transmission Shimming

Adding 1 shim to transmission mount will decrease front angle 1/2 degree and will increase rear angle 1/4 degree. Removing 1 shim will increase front angle 1/2 degree and decrease rear angle 1/4 degree.

NOTE: Production bolt is 10-1.5 x 35 mm. When using 2 or more shims, a 10-1.5 x 50 mm bolt must be used.

Repositioning Pinion Nose

Suspension bracket bolt hole tolerances will permit a 1 degree adjustment of rear universal joint angle. Loosen all rear suspension control arm bolts and reposition pinion nose up or down. Tighten all bolts.

Upper Control Arm Change (Caprice)

Shorter or longer arms may be used to change universal joint angle ± 2 degrees.

UNIVERSAL JOINT ANGLE [1]

Application	Height [2] Inches (mm)	Front Joint (Degrees)	Rear Joint (Degrees)
Camaro	4 11/16 (119)	1 1/10	1 1/2
Caprice Wagon			
THM 200-4R	4 25/64 (112)	2 1/4	3
THM 700-R4	4 25/64 (112)	1 1/3	3
All Others 7 1/2" & 7 5/8" Axles			
THM 700-R4	6 (160)	1 2/3	2 1/2
All Others	6 (160)	2 1/10	2 1/3
8 1/2" Axle			
THM 700-R4	6 (160)	1 1/4	2 1/2
All Others	6 3/8 (162)	1 5/6	2 1/6
Monte Carlo	4 7/32 (107)	1 1/3	1

[1] – The above angles may be ± 1/2 degree.
[2] – Axle tube-to-frame height is ± 1/4" (6 mm).

Propeller Shaft Alignment

OLDSMOBILE

RWD Models

DESCRIPTION

To properly measure front and rear universal joint angles, vehicle must be at proper trim height (distance from top of axle tube to bottom of frame). If necessary, add weight to meet this distance. With vehicle level and supported at axles, measure universal joint angles using an inclinometer.

Adjustment may be made by loosening all of the rear suspension control arm bolts and repositioning the pinion nose. Adjustments may also be made by shimming the transmission mount or by changing control arms.

Fig. 1: Checking Trim Height

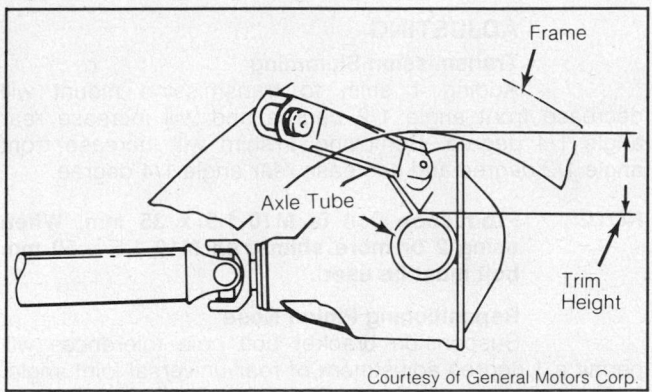

Courtesy of General Motors Corp.

CHECKING & ADJUSTING

CHECKING

1) Clean all bearing caps and place Inclinometer (J-23498) on rear propeller shaft bearing cap. Bearing cap must be straight up and down. Center sight glass bubble and record reading.

2) Rotate propeller shaft 90 degrees and place inclinometer on rear drive yoke bearing cap. Measure angle and subtract smaller reading from larger reading to determine rear universal joint angle. Repeat procedure on front universal joint to determine front universal joint angle.

Fig. 2: Measuring Rear Universal Joint Angle

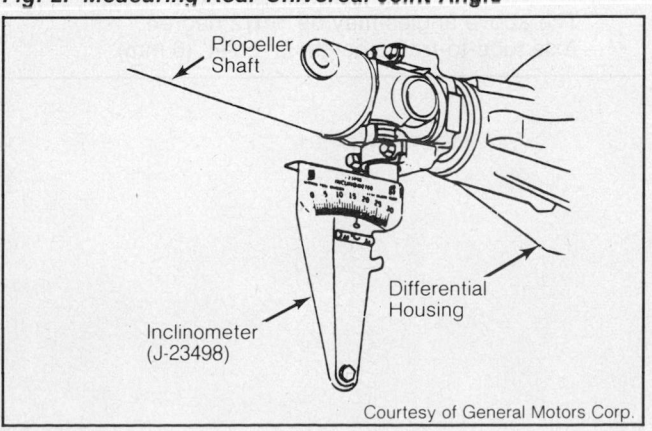

Courtesy of General Motors Corp.

ADJUSTING

Transmission Shimming

Adding 1 shim to transmission mount will decrease front angle 1/2 degree and will increase rear angle 1/4 degree. Removing 1 shim will increase front angle 1/2 degree and decrease rear angle 1/4 degree.

NOTE: **Production bolt is 10-1.5 x 35 mm. When using 2 or more shims, a 10-1.5 x 50 mm bolt must be used.**

Repositioning Pinion Nose

Suspension bracket bolt hole tolerances will permit a 1 degree adjustment of rear universal joint angle. Loosen all rear suspension control arm bolts and reposition pinion nose up or down. Tighten all bolts.

Upper Control Arm Change

Shorter or longer arms may be used to change universal joint angle ± 2 degrees on Custom Cruiser, or ± 1.5 degrees on Cutlass at differential.

REAR UPPER CONTROL ARM

Application	Front Angle Change (Degrees)	Rear Angle Change (Degrees)
Cutlass		
Short Arm	+1/3	+1 3/4
Long Arm	−1/10	−1 1/4
Custom Cruiser		
Short Arm	+1/3	+2
Long Arm	−1/3	−2

UNIVERSAL JOINT ANGLE

Application	[1] Trim Height Inches (mm)	[2] Front Joint (Deg.)	[2] Rear Joint (Deg.)
Cutlass	5 (127)	1/2	1
Custom Cruiser	6 1/8 (156)	1 3/4	2

[1] – Axle tube-to-frame height may be ± 1/4" (6 mm).
[2] – The angles may be ± 1/2 degree.

Propeller Shaft Alignment
PONTIAC

RWD Models (Except Fiero)

DESCRIPTION

To properly measure front and rear universal joint angles, vehicle must be at proper trim height (distance from top of axle tube to bottom of frame) and curb weight with a full tank of gasoline. If necessary, add weight to meet this distance. With vehicle level and supported at axles, an inclinometer is used to determine driveline angles.

Adjustment may be made by shimming the transmission mount. Adjustments may also be made by loosening all the rear suspension control arm bolts and repositioning the pinion nose, or by changing control arms (except Firebird).

Fig. 1: Measuring Vehicle Trim Height

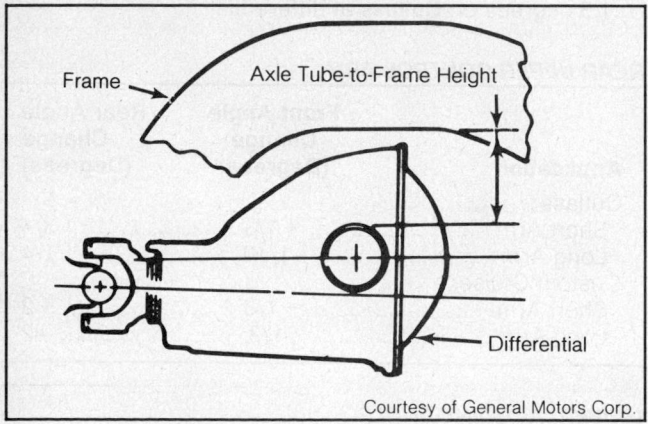

Frame

Axle Tube-to-Frame Height

Differential

Courtesy of General Motors Corp.

CHECKING & ADJUSTING

CHECKING

1) Lift and support vehicle at axle tubes. Check trim height and adjust as necessary to meet specifications.

2) Clean all bearing caps and place Inclinometer (J-23498A) on rear propeller shaft bearing cap. Bearing cap must be straight up and down. Center sight glass bubble and record reading.

3) Remove inclinometer, rotate propeller shaft 90 degrees, and place inclinometer on rear drive yoke bearing cap. Measure angle and subtract smaller reading from larger reading to determine rear universal joint angle. Repeat procedure on front universal joint to determine front universal joint angle.

Fig. 2: Measuring Front Universal Joint Angle

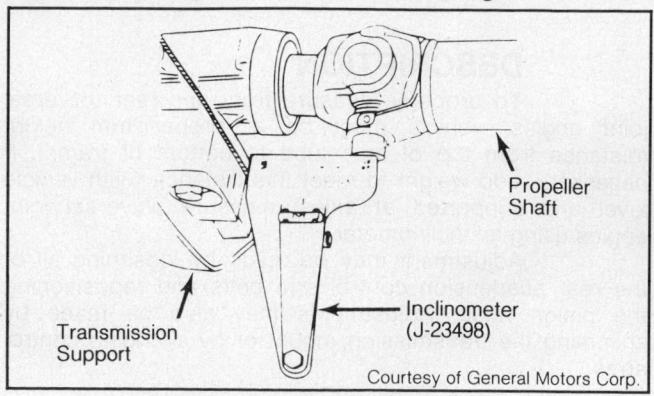

Propeller Shaft

Inclinometer (J-23498)

Transmission Support

Courtesy of General Motors Corp.

ADJUSTING

Transmission Shimming

Adding 1 shim to transmission mount will decrease front angle 1/2 degree and will increase rear angle 1/4 degree. Removing 1 shim will increase front angle 1/2 degree and decrease rear angle 1/4 degree.

NOTE: Production bolt is M10-1.5 x 35 mm. When using 2 or more shims, an M10-1.5 x 50 mm bolt must be used.

Repositioning Pinion Nose

Suspension bracket bolt hole tolerances will permit a 1 degree adjustment of rear universal joint angle. Loosen all rear suspension control arm bolts and reposition pinion nose up or down. Tighten all bolts. Changes to universal joint angles cannot be made on Firebird by repositioning pinion nose.

**Upper Control Arm Change
(Safri Wagon only)**

Shorter or longer arms may be used to change universal joint angle ± 2 degrees.

UNIVERSAL JOINT ANGLE [1]

Application	[2] Height Inches (mm)	Front Joint (Degrees)	Rear Joint (Degrees)
Firebird	4 11/16 (119)	1 1/10	1 1/2
Safari Wagon	4 2/5 (112)	2 1/4	3

[1] – The above angles may be ± 1/2 degree.
[2] – Axle tube-to-frame height is ± 1/4" (6 mm).

ALL MODELS

REMOVAL & INSTALLATION

PROPELLER SHAFT

Removal

Raise vehicle and support with stands, with front end slightly lower to prevent loss of transmission fluid. Index shaft and differential yoke for reassembly to orginal location. Remove trunnion bearing straps or flange bolts. Slide propeller shaft with slip yoke from transmission output shaft.

NOTE: **Do not use pry bar or heavy tool to hold propeller shaft while removing strap bolts or flange bolts, as damage to bearing seals may result. In addition, do not allow one end of shaft to hang free or bend at a sharp angle.**

Installation

1) Clean sliding yoke splines and outside diameter. Check machined surface for nicks, scratches or foreign material and apply lubricant to splines and outside surface of yoke.

2) Install yoke onto transmission output shaft and align shaft with companion flange. Connect exposed bearing cups to companion flange with straps and bolts (single joint), or connect propeller shaft flange to companion flange with bolts (constant velocity joint).

OVERHAUL

CROSS & ROLLER TYPE JOINT

NOTE: **Some vehicles use an injected nylon ring in place of snap rings or "C" locks. Replacement universal joints use "C" lock rings. Remains of sheared nylon rings must be completely removed in order for new lock rings to seat properly.**

Disassembly

Remove bearing cup retainers. Press out bearing cups using arbor press or vise and supporting tools. Remove cross assembly from yoke. Do not remove seal retainers from cross.

Reassembly

Hold cross between ears of propeller shaft flange. Partially install 2 bearing cups. Align cross with cups. Using arbor press or vise, press cups into yoke until locks can be inserted. Install locks or snap rings.

CONSTANT VELOCITY TYPE JOINT

CAUTION: **Care must be taken when moving shaft horizontally. Shaft must be supported at both ends or damage could result to center ball. Shaft may be carried in vertical position without resulting damage.**

Disassembly

Scribe alignment marks on all yokes to maintain proper order and balance upon reassembly. Press bearing cups from coupling (link) yoke and continue disassembly as for single cross and roller joint.

Centering Ball Replacement

1) Using ball remover, place inner part of tool under ball. Place outer cylinder of tool over ball, thread nut on tool and draw off ball. Place replacement ball on stud. Using tool, drive ball onto stud until ball seats firmly against shoulder at base of stud.

Fig. 1: Single Cross & Roller Type Joint

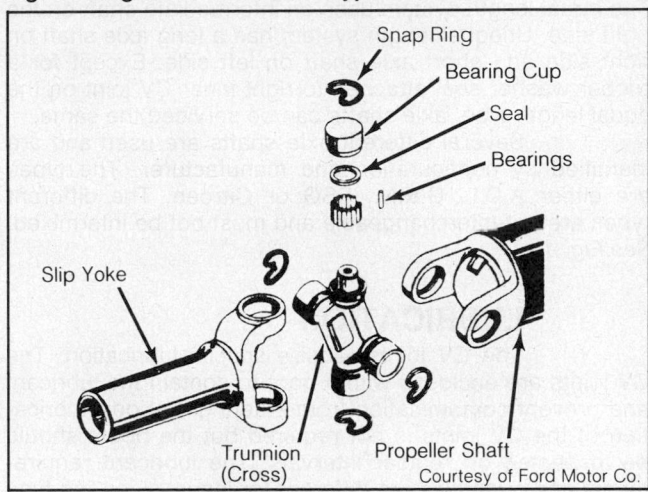

Courtesy of Ford Motor Co.

2) Lubricate all parts and insert into ball seat cavity in following order: spring, washer (smallest OD), ball seats (with largest opening outward to receive ball), washer (largest OD), and seal. Lubricate seal lip and press seal flush with seal installer. Fill cavity with grease, then install flange yoke to centering ball, aligning marks. Install cross and bearing cups.

Reassembly

Pack all bearing cups with grease and reverse disassembly procedure, ensuring crosses and yokes are in original positions. Check for free movement of joint. If binding exists, use brass hammer and seat bearings with sharp rap on yoke. DO NOT hammer on bearing cups as damage may occur.

Fig. 2: Constant Velocity Type Joint (Typical)

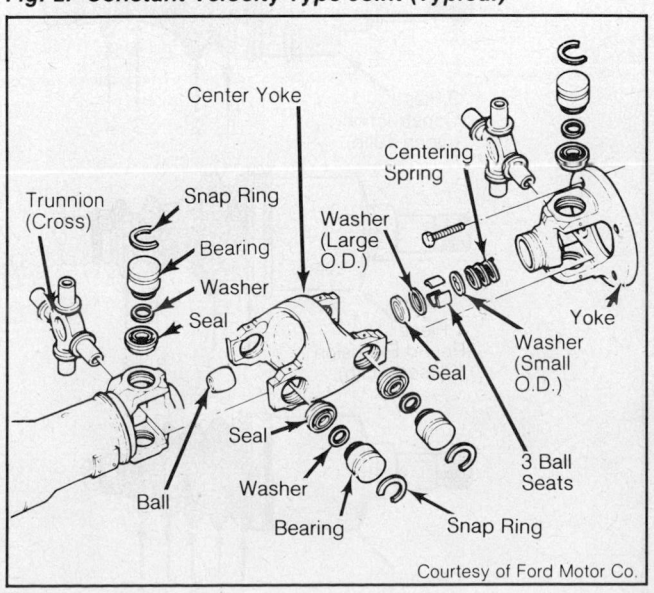

Courtesy of Ford Motor Co.

FWD Axle Shafts

CHRYSLER MOTORS

FWD Models

DESCRIPTION & IDENTIFICATION

Only 2.2L turbo models use axle shafts of equal length. All others use unequal length axle shafts. The equal length system uses an intermediate shaft on the right side. Unequal length system has a long axle shaft on right side and short axle shaft on left side. Except for a rubber washer seal attached to right inner CV joint on the equal length type, axle shafts can be serviced the same.

Several different axle shafts are used and are identified by configuration and manufacturer. The types are either A.C.I., G.K.N., SSG or Citroen. The different types are not interchangeable and must not be intermixed. *See Fig. 1.*

LUBRICATION

The CV joints require special lubrication. The CV joints are enclosed with a boot to contain the lubricant and prevent contamination from entering. Periodic lubrication of the CV joints is not required but the boots should be inspected on regular intervals. The lubricant requirements and quantities are different for inner, outer and type of CV joints being serviced. Use only the specified lubricant.

If necessary to refill transaxle with fluid, use SAE, SF or SF/CC rated 5W-30 engine oil for manual transaxles. For automatic transaxles, use Mopar ATF Plus (7176). If Mopar ATF is not available, Dexron II should be used.

SERVICE (IN-VEHICLE)

HUB BEARINGS

NOTE: **Hub and axle shaft are splined together through knuckle hub bearing and retained by hub nut. New bearings MUST be installed whenever hub is removed.**

Removal

1) Remove dust cap, cotter pin, nut lock and spring washer. With vehicle on ground, apply brakes and loosen wheel nuts and hub nut. Raise and support vehicle. Remove wheel. Remove hub nut and washer. Tap end of axle shaft lightly (if necessary), with brass hammer to free axle shaft from hub splines.

2) Disconnect brake hose retainer from strut damper. Remove lower ball joint clamp bolt. Remove

Fig. 1: Axle Shaft Identification

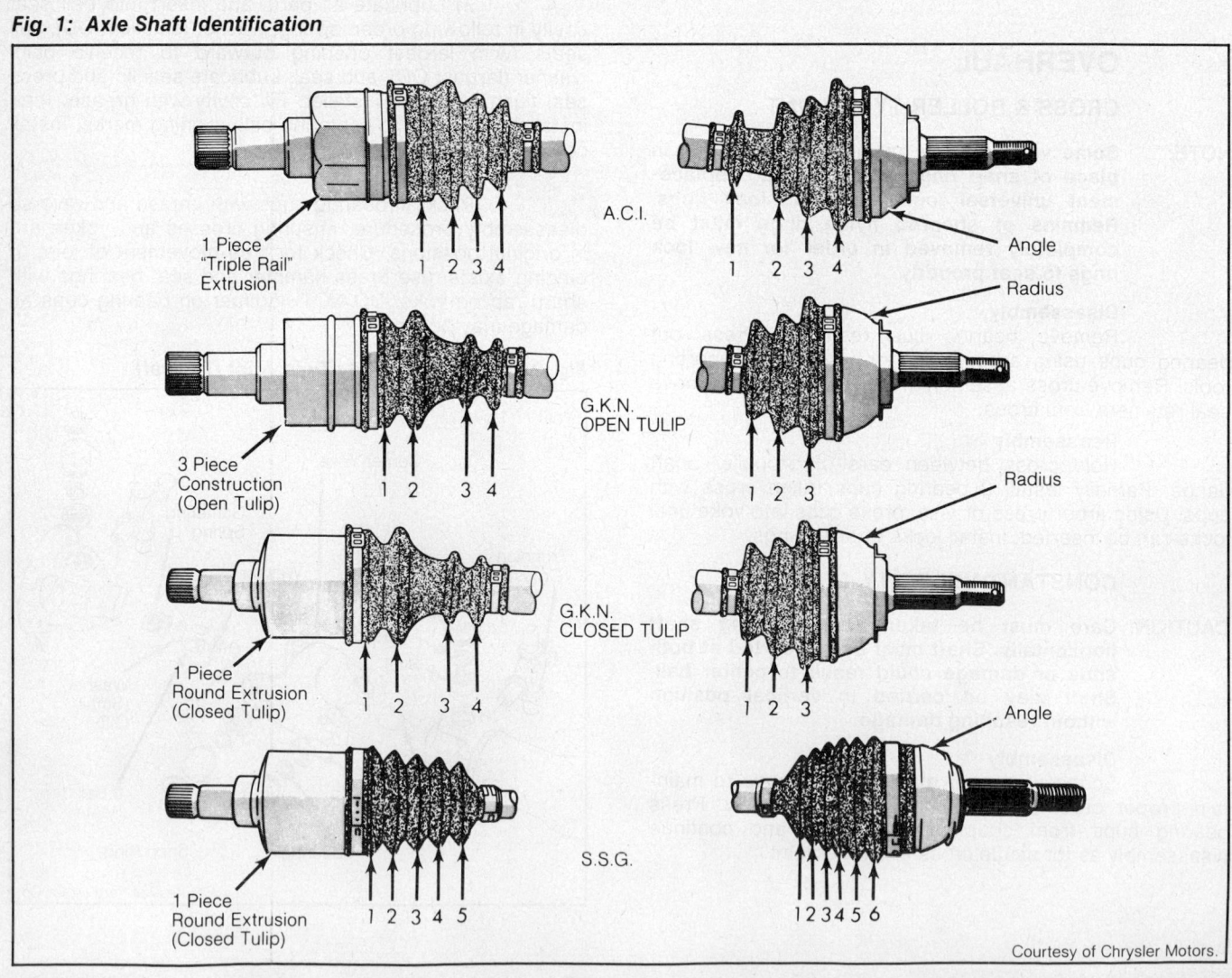

1 Piece "Triple Rail" Extrusion — 1 2 3 4 — A.C.I. — Angle

Radius

3 Piece Construction (Open Tulip) — 1 2 3 4 — G.K.N. OPEN TULIP — 1 2 3

Radius

1 Piece Round Extrusion (Closed Tulip) — 1 2 3 4 — G.K.N. CLOSED TULIP — 1 2 3

Angle

1 Piece Round Extrusion (Closed Tulip) — 1 2 3 4 5 — S.S.G. — 1 2 3 4 5 6

Courtesy of Chrysler Motors.

CHRYSLER MOTORS (Cont.)

brake caliper and support caliper to vehicle frame. Remove brake rotor. Separate lower ball joint from steering knuckle. Pull steering knuckle out and away from axle shaft.

Fig. 2: Installing Hub Tool

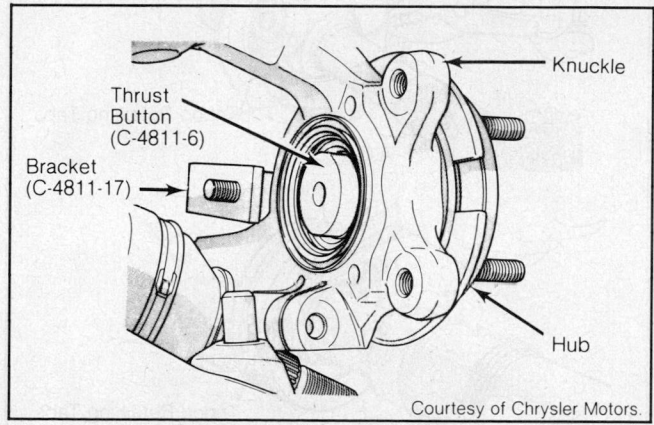

Courtesy of Chrysler Motors.

3) Install Bracket (C-4811-17) to steering knuckle. Install Thrust Button (C-4811-6) inside hub bore. *See Fig. 2.* Install Puller (C-4811-14) and remove hub. *See Fig. 4.* Use a universal puller and remove outer bearing race from hub. Remove bearing retainer from steering knuckle.

4) Pry out bearing seal from machined recess in steering knuckle and thoroughly clean recess. Install Puller Kit (C-4811) and remove bearing from steering knuckle. *See Fig. 5.*

Installation

1) Reverse Puller (C-4811) and press new bearing in steering knuckle. Install bearing with Red seal portion of bearing facing bearing retainer. Install new seal and bearing retainer. Tighten retainer bolts to specifica-

Fig. 4: Removing Hub From Steering Knuckle

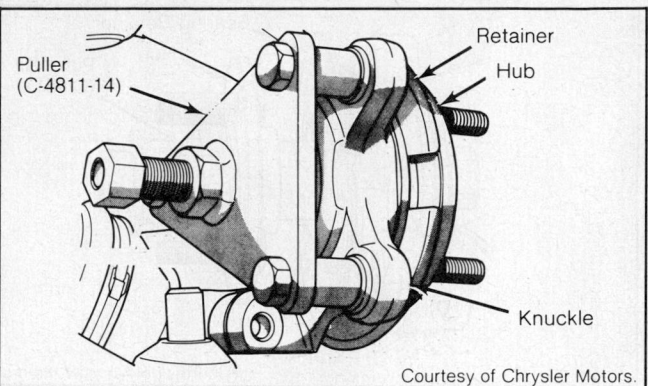

Courtesy of Chrysler Motors.

tions. Press hub into steering knuckle with Puller Kit (C-4811). *See Fig. 6.*

2) Using Mopar Multi-Purpose Grease (4318063), lubricate complete circumference of seal and wear sleeve. To complete installation, reverse removal procedure. Tighten all bolts/nuts to specifications.

Fig. 5: Removing Bearing

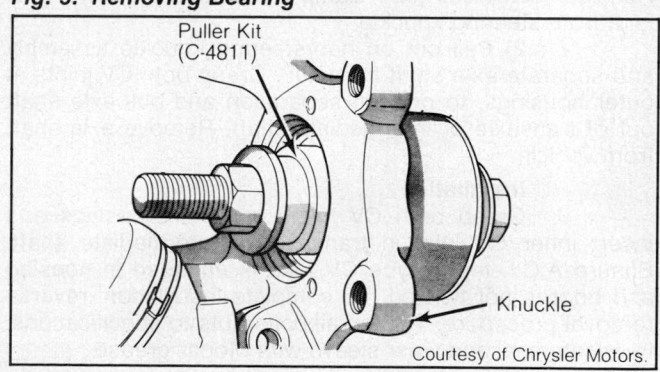

Courtesy of Chrysler Motors.

Fig. 3: Exploded View of Typical Axle Shaft

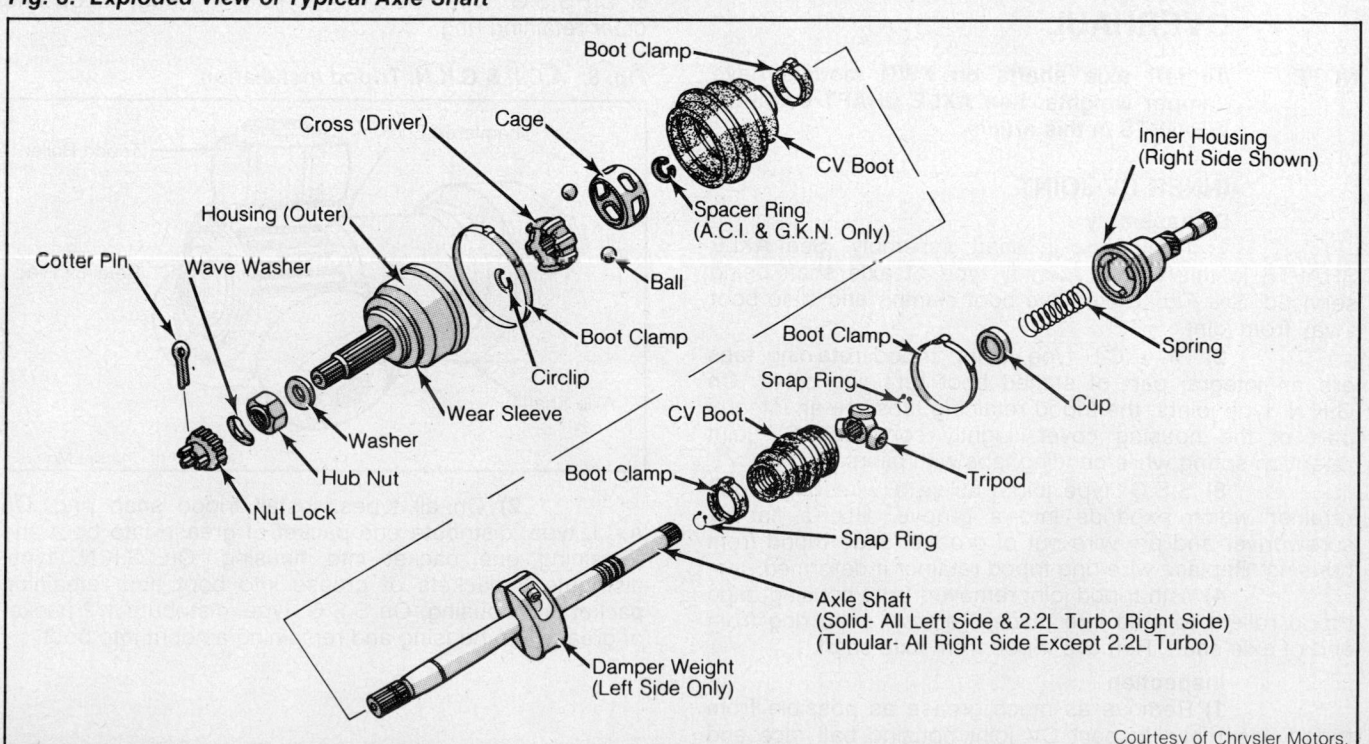

Courtesy of Chrysler Motors.

Fig. 6: Installing Hub

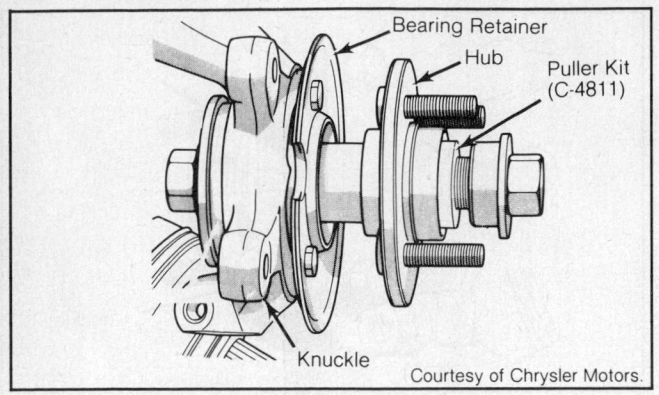

Courtesy of Chrysler Motors.

Fig. 7: Separating A.C.I. & G.K.N. Joints

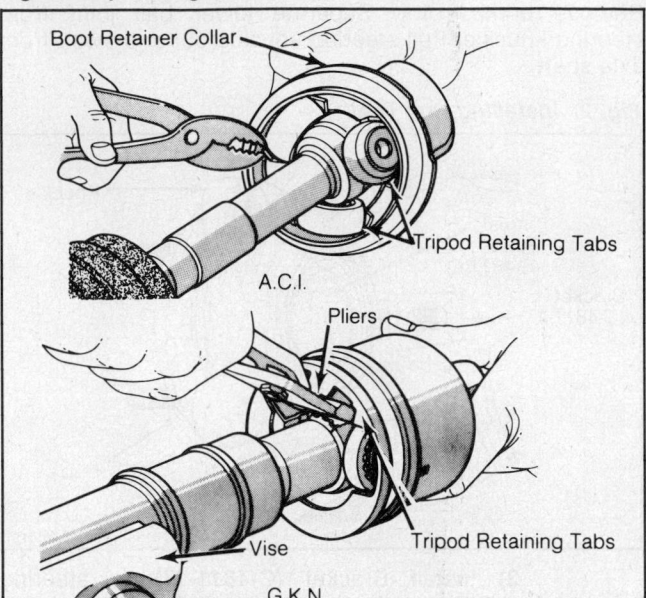

Courtesy of Chrysler Motors.

AXLE SHAFTS
Removal
1) Remove spindle nut. Raise and support vehicle. If removing right axle shaft, remove speedometer pinion assembly from transaxle. Tap axle shaft end lightly with brass hammer to free axle shaft from hub splines. Remove lower ball joint clamp bolt. Separate lower ball joint from steering knuckle.

2) Pull out on hub/steering knuckle assembly and separate axle shaft from hub. Grasp both CV joints at outer housings, to prevent separation and pull axle shaft out of transaxle or intermediate shaft. Remove axle shaft from vehicle.

Installation
Grasp both CV joints at outer housings and insert inner CV joint in transaxle or intermediate shaft. Ensure A.C.I. tripod type CV joint is engaged in housing and boot is not twisted. To complete installation, reverse removal procedure. Tighten all bolts/nuts to specifications. Lubricate seal and wear sleeve with Mopar grease.

OVERHAUL

NOTE: **All left axle shafts on FWD models have damper weights. See AXLE SHAFT DAMPER WEIGHTS in this article.**

INNER CV JOINT
Disassembly
1) Remove axle shaft assembly. See AXLE SHAFTS in this article. Identify type of axle shaft being serviced. See Fig. 1. Remove boot clamps and slide boot away from joint.

2) On A.C.I. type joints, tripod retaining tabs are an integral part of staked boot retaining collar. On G.K.N. type joints, the tripod retaining tabs are an integral part of the housing cover. Lightly compress CV joint retention spring while bending tabs with pliers. See Fig. 7.

3) S.S.G. type joints utilize a wire ring tripod retainer which expands into a groove. Use a flat tip screwdriver and pry wire out of groove. Slide tripod from housing. Replace wire ring tripod retainer if deformed.

4) With tripod joint removed from housing, tape tripod rollers to hold into place. Remove snap ring from end of axle shaft. Remove tripod from axle shaft.

Inspection
1) Remove as much grease as possible from tripod assembly. Inspect CV joint housing ball race and tripod components for excessive wear. Inspect spring, spring cup and spherical end of connecting shaft for damage or excessive wear.

2) Clean and check CV joint boot for cracks, tears and/or scuffed areas on interior surfaces. Replace components as necessary.

Reassembly
1) On Turbo models install rubber washer seal over right inner stub shaft and seat in groove. Lubricate boot and slide boot on axle shaft (if removed). On A.C.I. and G.K.N. type, install tripod with chamfered end toward long length of axle shaft and install retaining ring. See Fig. 8. On S.S.G. type, install inner retaining ring, tripod and outer retaining ring.

Fig. 8: A.C.I. & G.K.N. Tripod Installation

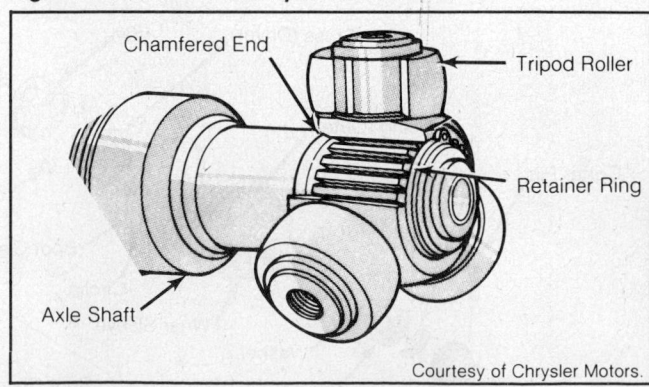

Courtesy of Chrysler Motors.

2) On all types, install tripod snap ring. On A.C.I. type, distribute one packet of grease into boot and remaining one packet into housing. On G.K.N. type, distribute 2 packets of grease into boot and remaining packet into housing. On S.S.G. type, distribute 1/2 packet of grease into housing and remaining amount into boot.

CHRYSLER MOTORS (Cont.)

CAUTION: On retaining tab type joints, DO NOT bend retaining tabs to original position. Instead, reattach boot to hold housing onto axle shaft. Tripod must be reengaged in housing when axle shaft is installed in vehicle.

3) Position spring in housing and install spring cup. Place a small amount of grease on concave surface of spring cup. To complete reassembly, reverse disassembly procedure. Ensure spring in housing is centered in housing.

OUTER CV JOINT
Disassembly

1) Remove axle shaft from vehicle. See AXLE SHAFTS in this article. Remove boot clamps. On A.C.I. and G.K.N. type, support axle shaft in vise with protected jaws. Tap top of CV joint housing to dislodge joint from internal circlip. On S.S.G. type, loosen damper weight bolts and slide it and boot towards inner joint. Expand circlip and slide joint off axle shaft. Reinstall damper weights.

2) On A.C.I. and G.K.N. type, do not remove heavy spacer ring from axle shaft unless replacing shaft. If replacing boot only, do not disassemble further. If CV joint is defective, replace complete unit. If lubricating CV joint proceed to next step.

Fig. 9: Disassembling Outer CV Joint

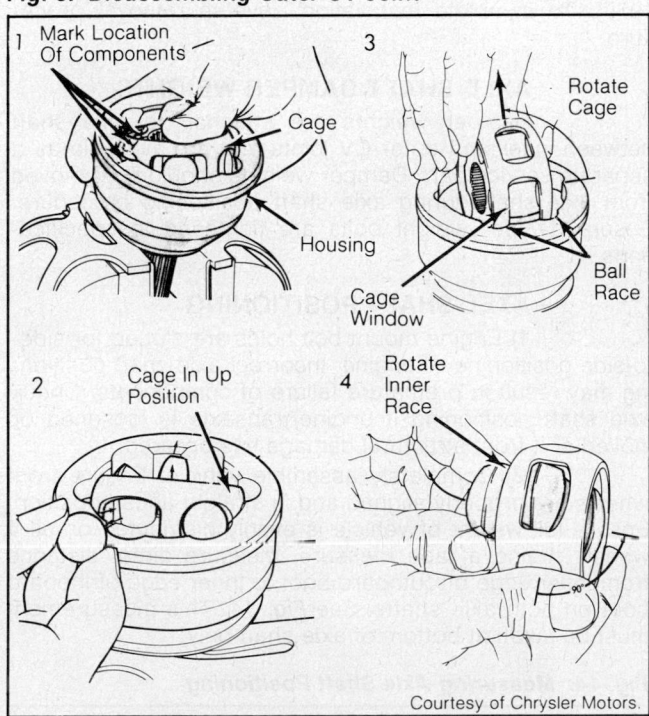

Courtesy of Chrysler Motors.

3) Wipe surplus grease and mark position of inner cross, cage and housing. Clamp splined end of shaft in vise with protected jaws (joint vertical). Press down on one side of inner race to tilt cage and remove ball. See Fig. 9. If joint is tight, a hammer and brass drift may be used to tilt cage. DO NOT hit cage. Repeat procedure for remaining balls.

4) Tilt cage and inner race assembly vertically and position 2 opposing cage windows in area between ball grooves. Remove cage and inner race assembly. Turn inner cross 90 degrees to cage and align one of the race

spherical lands with cage window. Raise land into cage window and remove inner race. See Fig. 9.

Inspection

1) Check grease for contamination. Wash all parts in solvent and dry with compressed air. Inspect housing ball races for defects, excessive wear and scoring. Check splined shaft and nut threads for damage. Inspect all 6 balls for pitting, cracks, scoring and wear.

2) Inspect cage for excessive wear on inside and outside spherical surfaces, heavy brinelling of cage windows, cracks and chipping. Inspect inner race for excessive wear or scoring of ball races. If any of the conditions are found, replace complete CV joint assembly.

Reassembly

Install a new wear sleeve on CV joint housing. Lightly oil all components prior to reassembly. Align marks made at disassembly. To complete reassembly, reverse disassembly procedure. Use new circlips. Tighten all bolts/nuts to specifications.

INTERMEDIATE SHAFT ASSEMBLY
Removal & Installation

Remove right axle shaft. See AXLE SHAFTS in this article. Remove 2 bolts from bearing bracket-to-engine. Remove assembly from transaxle extension by pulling outward on yoke. To install, reverse removal procedure.

Disassembly

1) Mark relationship of stub axle shaft to intermediate shaft to ensure proper reassembly. Apply penetrating oil to bearing caps and remove snap rings. Place yoke and "U" joint in vise. Use a suitable socket and hammer and remove one "U" joint cap at a time. With all caps removed, remove cross section of "U" joint.

2) Using arbor press, press stub axle out of bearing assembly and outer slinger. Use care not to dent or damage slinger or end of stub shaft. If replacing slinger, carefully press shaft out through slinger.

Reassembly

Place a new slinger on stub shaft and drive it on until it bottoms. Use care not to damage slinger at installation. Press bearing assembly into position. There should be a minimum clearance of .0313" (.795 mm) between slinger and bearing assembly. To install "U" joint, reverse disassembly procedure. Tighten all bolts/nuts to specifications.

CV JOINT BOOTS
Removal

Cut boot clamps. Disassemble CV joint. See DISASSEMBLY under INNER CV JOINT or OUTER CV JOINT in this article. Remove boot from axle shaft.

Installation (A.C.I. & G.K.N.)

1) Use strap and buckle type clamp with Strap Installer (C-4653) only. Slide small end of boot over shaft. Position boot to edge of locating mark or groove. See Fig. 10. Slide large diameter of boot into position. Wrap strap around boot twice. Add 2.50" (63.5 mm) and cut strap.

2) Remove strap from CV joint. Install buckle on strap and fold strap back about 1.125" (28.58 mm), on inside of buckle. Wrap strap around CV joint once and pass through buckle. Wrap strap around a second time and pass through buckle again. See Fig. 11. Using Strap Installer (C-4653), tighten strap. Do not pull installer downward to tighten strap as this can break strap.

3) Disconnect installer and retighten strap if necessary. With strap tight enough, remove installer sideways and cut off strap .125" (3.18 mm). Complete job by folding strap neatly into buckle.

Fig. 10: CV Joint Boot Positioning

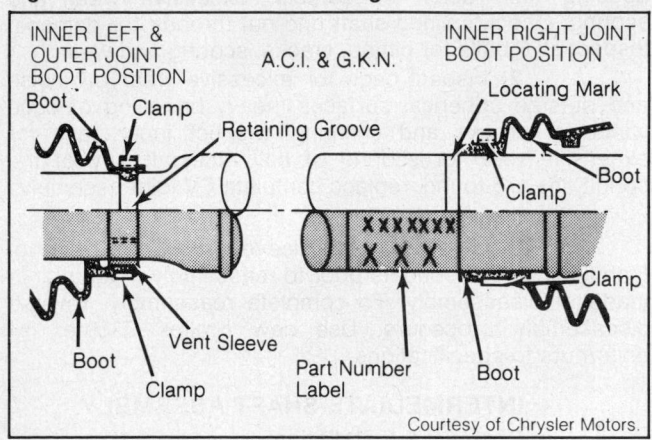

Courtesy of Chrysler Motors.

Fig. 11: Installing Strap

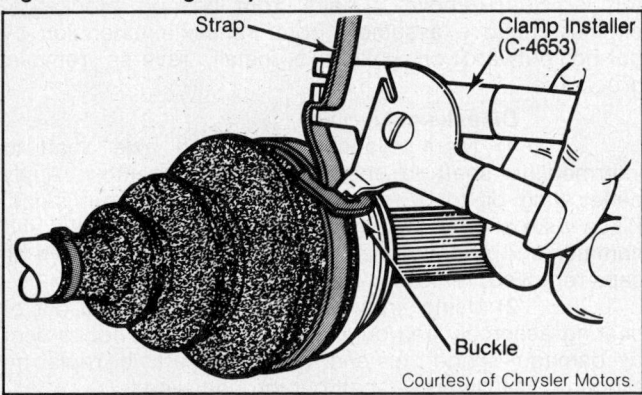

Courtesy of Chrysler Motors.

Installation (S.S.G., Right Inner)

1) Slide small boot clamp onto axle shaft. Install boot onto shaft and position on flat between locating shoulders. *See Fig. 12.* Position clamp on boot and crimp bridge of clamp with Crimper (C-4124).

2) Install CV joint. See INSTALLATION under INNER CV JOINT or OUTER CV JOINT in this article. Position large end of boot on housing and install clamp. Crimp bridge of clamp with Crimper Tool (C-3250). Lubricate wear sleeve and seal with Mopar Multi-Purpose Grease (4318063). To complete installation, reverse removal procedure.

Fig. 12: Right Inner S.S.G. Boot Installation

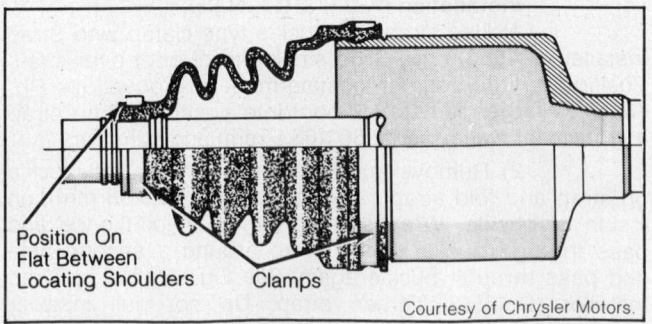

Courtesy of Chrysler Motors.

Installation
(S.S.G., Left Inner & All Outer)

1) Install small clamp on axle shaft. Position small end of boot over axle shaft with lip of boot in third groove, toward center of axle shaft. *See Fig. 13.* Install boot clamp evenly over boot. Crimp bridge of clamp with Clamp Installer (C-4975).

Fig. 13: S.S.G. Boot Positioning

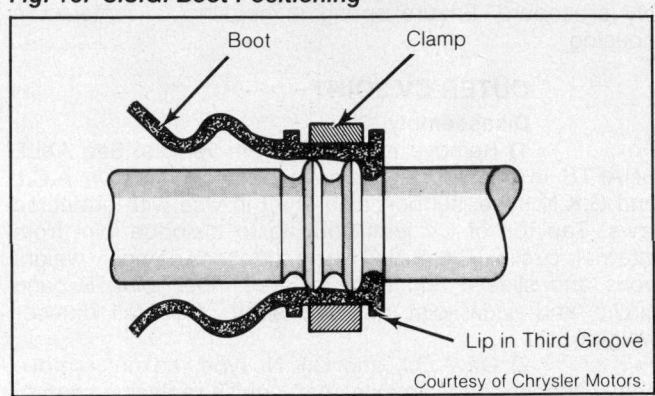

Courtesy of Chrysler Motors.

2) Install CV joint. See INSTALLATION under INNER CV JOINT or OUTER CV JOINT in this article. Position large end of boot over housing and install boot clamp. Crimp bridge of clamp with Clamp Installer (C-4975). To complete installation, reverse removal procedure.

AXLE SHAFT DAMPER WEIGHTS

Damper weights are attached to axle shaft between inner and outer CV joints and are available as a separate service part. Damper weights should be removed from axle shaft during axle shaft positioning procedure. Ensure damper weight bolts are tightened to specifications.

AXEL SHAFT POSITIONING

1) Engine mount bolt holes are slotted for side-to-side positioning of engine. Incorrect axle shaft positioning may result in premature failure of components. Check axle shaft positioning if engine/transaxle is loosened or moved or if front structural damage has occured.

2) Completely assemble vehicle. Ensure front wheels are properly aligned and in straight ahead position. Ensure full weight of vehicle is evenly distributed on all 4 wheels. Using a tape measure, measure direct distance from inner edge of outboard boot to inner edge of inboard boot on both axle shafts. *See Fig. 14.* This measurement must be taken at bottom of axle shaft only.

Fig. 14: Measuring Axle Shaft Positioning

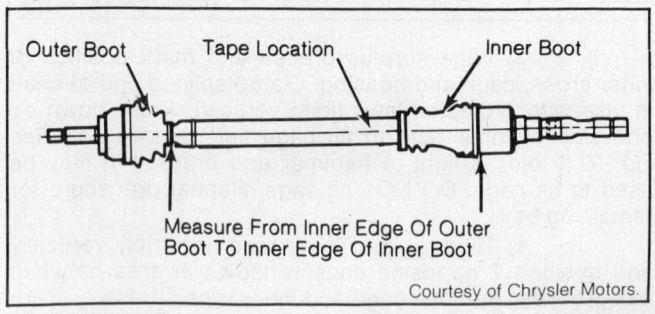

Courtesy of Chrysler Motors.

CHRYSLER MOTORS (Cont.)

AXLE SHAFT POSITIONING SPECIFICATIONS

Application	Engine	Shaft Type	Side of Vehicle	Transaxle	Length In. (mm)
Dynasty, New Yorker	3.0L	G.K.N. (82-98)	Right	All	18.9-19.2 (481-489)
			Left	All	8.5-8.8 (216-224)
Horizon, Omni	2.2L	G.K.N. (69-92)	Right	Auto	19.6-19.8 (498-504)
			Left	Auto	8.2-8.7 (208-221)
		G.K.N. (69-92)	Right	Manual	19.6-19.8 (498-504)
			Left	Manual	9.4-10.0 (240-253)
All Other Models	2.2L	G.K.N. (69-92)	Right	All	19.9-20.3 (505-515)
			Left	All	8.9-9.6 (227-245)
		G.K.N. (82-98)	Right	All	19.3-19.6 (490-498)
			Left	All	8.9-9.2 (227-234)
		A.C.I.	Right	All	18.8-19.1 (477-485)
			Left	All	7.8-8.3 (197-212)
		S.S.G.	Right	All	18.0-18.5 (457-469)
			Left	All	7.2-7.9 (184-200)
	2.2L Turbo I	G.K.N. (82-98)	Right	All	8.9-9.2 (227-234)
			Left	All	8.9-9.2 (227-234)
		S.S.G.	Right	All	7.4-7.7 (187-196)
			Left	All	7.4-7.7 (187-196)
	2.2L Turbo II [1]	G.K.N.	Right	All	8.9-9.2 (227-234)
			Left	All	8.9-9.2 (227-234)

[1] – Available in Daytona Shelby Z and Lancer Shelby models with man. trans. only.

3) If both axle shafts are within specifications, no further service is necessary. If either left or right axle shaft is not within specifications, proceed to next step.

4) Support engine/transaxle assembly with a floor jack. Loosen right engine mount verticle fasteners, front engine mount bracket and front crossmember fasteners. Pry engine right or left as required to obtain correct axle shaft length. See AXLE SHAFT POSITIONING SPECIFICATIONS table in this article.

5) Tighten mounting bolts/nuts to specifications. Recheck axle shaft length. Install damper weights and tighten to specifications.

TIGHTENING SPECIFICATIONS

Application	Ft. Lbs. (N.m)
Ball Joint Clamp Bolt	70 (95)
Brake Caliper Bolt	160 (217)
Brake Hose Retainer Bolt	10 (14)
Damper Weight Bolt	
S.S.G.	21 (28)
G.K.N.	23 (31)
Hub Bearing Retainer Bolt	20 (27)
Inner CV Joint Flange	36 (49)
Intermediate Shaft	
Bracket-to-Bearing Bolt	21 (28)
Bracket-to-Engine Bolt	40 (54)
Spindle Nut	180 (244)
Tie Rod Nut	35 (47)
Wheel Nut	95 (129)

	INCH Lbs. (N.m)
Damper Weight Bolt	
A.C.I.	96 (11)
Speedometer Gear Bolt	60 (7)

EAGLE PREMIER

Eagle Premier

DESCRIPTION

Axle shafts transfer power from transaxle to the front driving wheels. The axle shafts are splined to the wheel hub and secured by a spindle nut. The axle shafts are splined into the transaxle and retained by a roll pin.

LUBRICATION

The transaxle and differential are integral. The transaxle must use ONLY Mercon automatic transmission fluid. The differential uses synthetic 75W-140 hypoid gear lubricant.

CAUTION: Vehicle must be raised on a drive-on or side mounted swing arm hoist and in special areas of vehicle. See ENGINE REMOVAL & INSTALLATION at end of ENGINE section.

SERVICE (IN-VEHICLE)

HUB & WHEEL BEARINGS
Removal
1) Raise and support vehicle. Remove front wheel. Remove caliper and and support out of way. Hold hub secure and remove spindle nut. Push axle shaft out of hub. If necessary, use Hub Puller (T.AV. 1050) to push axle shaft out.

CAUTION: DO NOT strike end of axle shaft as damage to axle threads may occur.

2) Leave brake rotor attached. Install Hub Puller (T.AV. 1050) on hub. Attach a slide hammer to hub puller. Remove hub. *See Fig. 1.* Using a press and bearing puller, remove bearing race from back side of hub. Remove brake rotor. Remove bolts retaining bearing assembly to steering knuckle. Remove bearing assembly.

Fig. 1: Removing Front Hub

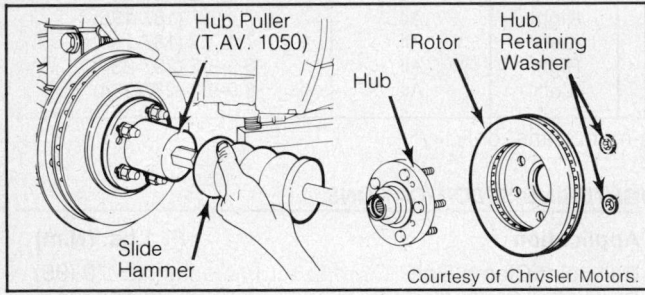

Courtesy of Chrysler Motors.

Installation
1) Pack bearing with the grease supplied with replacement kit. If not replacing, pack old bearing with EP bearing lubricant. Install one bearing race on back side of bearing assembly. Press remaining bearing race on wheel hub.

2) Install bearing and race assembly on steering knuckle. Install and tighten bearing assembly bolts to specifications. Install brake rotor. Use a brass hammer and tap hub into position. Install drive axle. To complete installation, reverse removal procedure. Tighten bolts/nuts to specifications.

AXLE SHAFTS
Removal
1) Remove front hub, rotor and bearing. See HUB & WHEEL BEARINGS in this article. Remove axle shaft roll pin, attaching axle shaft to transaxle. *See Fig. 2.* Remove nut from lower ball joint and leave bolt installed.

Fig. 2: Axle Shaft Roll Pin

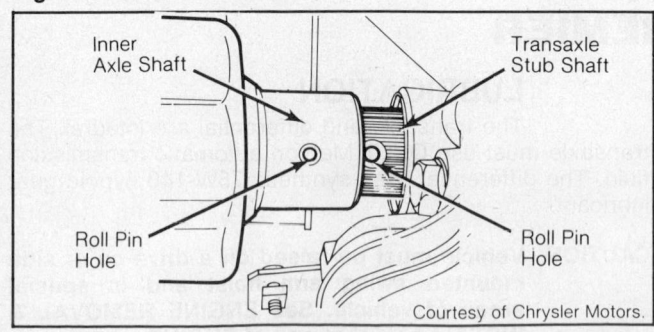

Courtesy of Chrysler Motors.

Loosen 2 upper steering knuckle nuts until they are at end of bolts. The bolts are splined at the head end.

2) Tap nuts with brass hammer to loosen bolts. Remove nuts and bolts. Place a drain pan under transaxle end of axle shaft. Wrap shop rags around CV joint boots to protect boots. Tilt upper steering knuckle away from strut. Remove axle shaft from hub. Slide axle shaft out of transaxle and remove from vehicle.

Installation
Tape shop rags around CV joint boots to protect boots during installation. Align axle shaft roll pin hole with output shaft hole and slide axle shaft on output shaft. *See Fig. 2.* Install a new roll pin. To complete installation, reverse removal procedure. Tighten bolts/nuts to specifications. Check and fill fluid levels.

OVERHAUL

AXLE SHAFTS

NOTE: **Inner CV joint can be disassembled and repaired. The outer CV joint must be replaced as an assembly. Both boots can be serviced.**

Disassembly (Outer CV Joint)
Remove axle shaft from vehicle. See AXLE SHAFTS in this article. Cut and remove boot clamps using care not to damage boot. Slide boot rearward enough to gain access to plastic retaining ring. Use snap ring pliers and spread the plastic retaining ring. Tap outer CV joint with plastic mallet and remove from axle shaft. Remove boot (if replacing). *See Fig. 3.*

Fig. 3: Removing Outer CV Joint

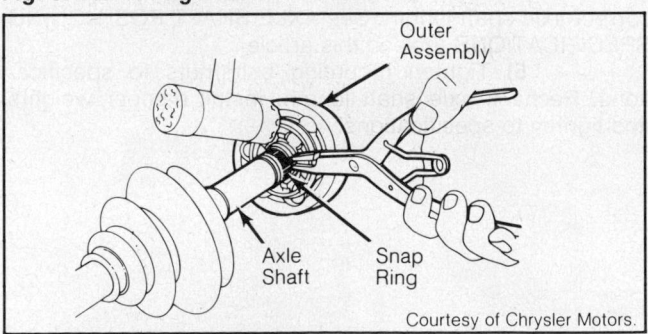

Courtesy of Chrysler Motors.

Reassembly
Replace plastic retaining ring. Ensure tapered end goes into CV joint and segmented end toward axle shaft. Slide CV joint boot onto axle shaft (if removed). Thoroughly lubricate CV joint with grease supplied in kit. Tap CV joint onto axle shaft until retaining ring clicks. To complete installation, reverse removal procedure. Ensure boot is properly positioned before clamping.

Disassembly (Inner CV Joint)
Remove axle shaft. See AXLE SHAFTS in this article. Cut and remove boot clamps using care not to damage boot. Slide boot off CV joint yoke. Slide yoke straight off tripod joint. Remove tripod joint plastic retaining ring with snap ring pliers. Tap tripod joint off axle shaft with plastic mallet. Remove boot (if replacing).

Reassembly
1) Install a new plastic retaining ring in tripod joint with tapered end towards axle shaft and segmented

EAGLE PREMIER (Cont.)

Fig. 4: Reassembly of Inner CV Joint

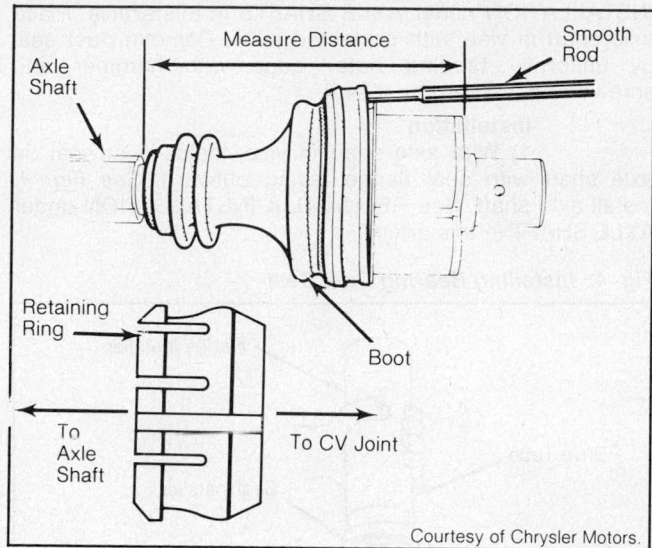

Courtesy of Chrysler Motors.

end towards tripod joint. *See Fig. 4.* Install boot (if removed). Tap tripod joint onto axle shaft until fully seated in groove on axle shaft. Thoroughly lubricate yoke and tripod joint with grease supplied in kit.

2) Slide yoke onto tripod joint. Position boot on yoke and axle shaft. Bleed air from boot using a smooth rod between boot and yoke. Lift up on boot and allow trapped air to escape. Extend and retract CV joint until distance is 6.10-6.18" (155-157 mm). *See Fig. 4.* To complete installation, reverse removal procedure. Ensure boot is properly seated before installing clamps.

TIGHTENING SPECIFICATIONS

Application	Ft. Lbs. (N.m)
Axle Spindle Nut	181 (245)
Lower Ball Joint Bolt/Nut	77 (104)
Steering Knuckle-to-Strut	123 (167)
Wheel Bearing Bolt	11 (15)
Wheel-to-Hub Bolt	63 (85)

FORD MOTOR CO.

Continental, Escort, Sable,
Taurus, Tempo, Topaz

DESCRIPTION

Power from transaxle is transferred to driving wheels by 2 unequal length axle shafts. Both axle shafts use CV joints at inner and outer ends. CV joints are enclosed in CV joint boots and connected by and interconnecting shaft. Interconnecting shaft is splined on both ends.

Circlips retain the interconnecting shaft in the inner and outer CV joints. A circlip retains the inner CV joint stub shaft in the differential side gear. Outer CV joint stub shaft is splined into the wheel hub and secured by a spindle nut. On some automatic transaxle models, the right axle shaft must be removed to remove left axle shaft.

LUBRICATION

Front hub bearings are a cartridge design and require no scheduled maintenance. Inner and outer joints utilize 2 different grease specifications. The inner CV joint requires High Temperature Grease (E43Z-19590-A). The outer CV joint requires CV Joint Grease (E2FZ-19590-A). Transaxle lubricant must be filled with Mercon (ESP-M2C185-A).

SERVICE (IN-VEHICLE)

HUB BEARINGS

NOTE: **Bearings are preset and cannot be adjusted. If bearing is disassembled, complete bearing unit must be replaced.**

Removal

1) Loosen wheel lug nuts. Remove hub nut retainer by turning nut counterclockwise and breaking locking tab. Do not use screwdriver or chisel to remove locking tabs. Continue turning nut until nut retainer is removed. Remove washer. Raise and support vehicle on safety stands. Remove tire/wheel assembly.

NOTE: **DO NOT reuse nut retainer.**

2) Remove brake caliper by loosening locating pins and rotating caliper off rotor from lower end and lifting upward. Do not remove caliper pins from caliper assembly. Support caliper out of way with wire.

3) Pull rotor from hub. If rotor is restricted, apply rust penetrator to rotor and hub mating surfaces. Install 3-jaw type puller and remove rotor by pulling on outside diameter of rotor and pushing on center of hub. If excessive removal force is used, check rotor for lateral runout.

Fig. 1: Separating CV Joint & Knuckle Assembly

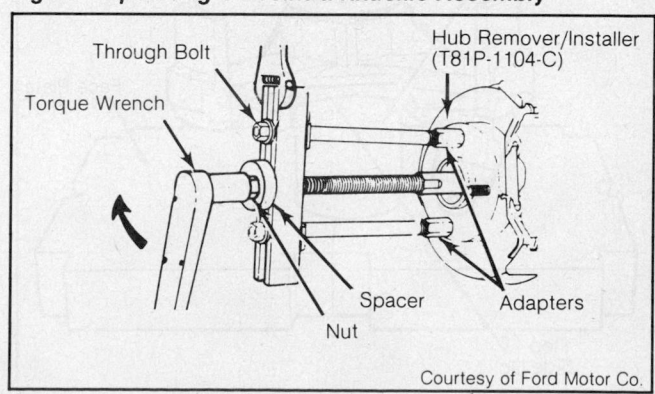

Courtesy of Ford Motor Co.

4) Disconnect lower control arm and tie rod from steering knuckle (leave strut attached). Loosen 2 nuts at top of strut mount in engine compartment. Install Hub Remover/Installer (T81P-1104-C) assembly and push CV joint out of hub assembly. *See Fig. 1.*

5) Hold knuckle assembly with wire and remove strut bolt-to-knuckle. Slide knuckle assembly off stut. Remove wire and place knuckle assembly on bench. Install 2-jaw type puller and remove hub from knuckle. Ensure a shaft protector is used, clears bearing I.D. and is centered. *See Fig. 2.*

Fig. 2: Removing Hub From Knuckle

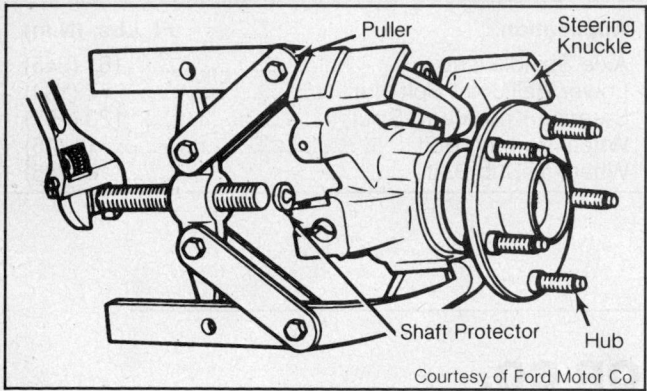

Courtesy of Ford Motor Co.

6) Using a screwdriver, remove and discard snap ring, which retains bearing in knuckle. Using Bearing Remover/Installer Kit (T83P-1104-AH), place appropriate spacer on inboard side of knuckle, with step side of spacer up. Place spacer and knuckle on press plate. Install bearing remover on inner bearing race. Press bearing out of knuckle and discard. *See Fig. 3.*

Fig. 3: Removing Hub Bearing From Knuckle

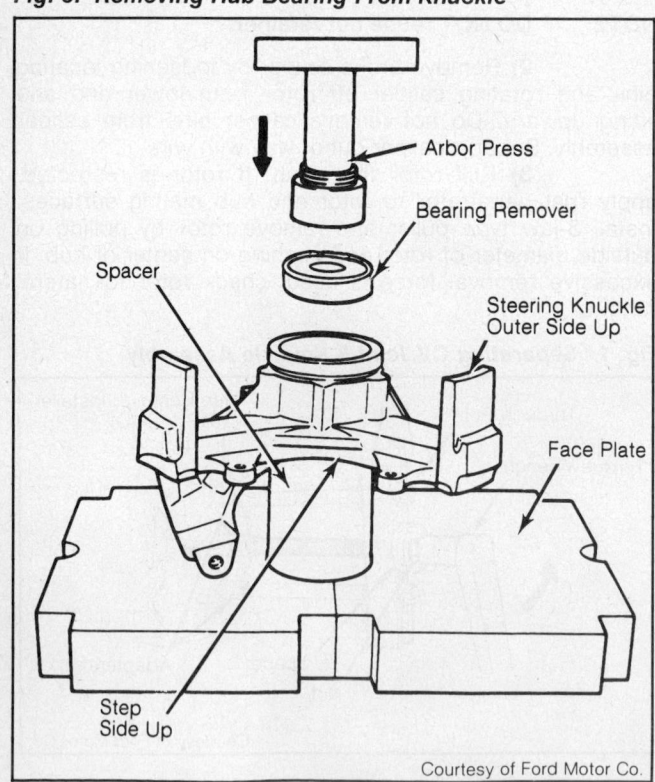

Courtesy of Ford Motor Co.

7) Remove axle shaft. See REMOVAL & INSTALLATION under AXLE SHAFTS in this article. Place axle shaft in vise with protected jaws. Remove dust seal by uniformly tapping outer edge with hammer and screwdriver. Discard dust seal.

Installation

1) With axle shaft in vise, install dust seal on axle shaft with seal flange facing outward. *See Fig. 4.* Install axle shaft. See REMOVAL & INSTALLATION under AXLE SHAFT in this article.

Fig. 4: Installing Bearing Dust Seal

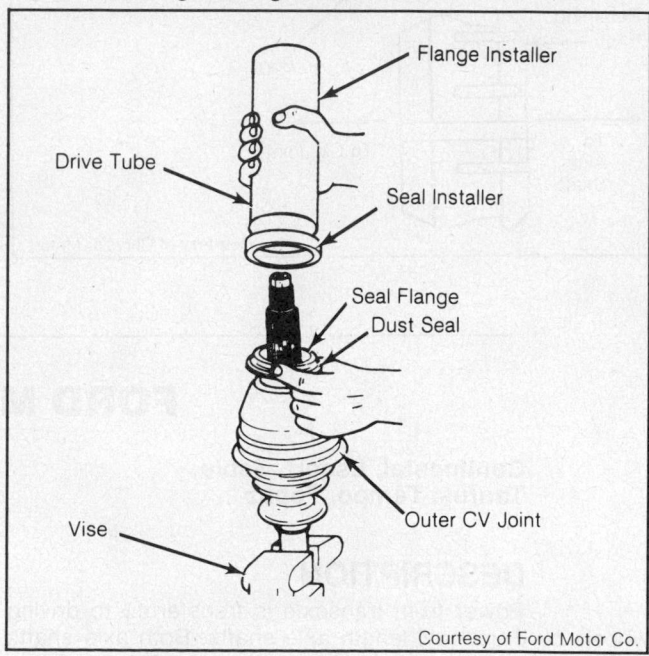

Courtesy of Ford Motor Co.

2) Remove all foreign material from knuckle bearing bore and hub bearing journal. If hub bearing journal is scored or damaged, replace hub assembly. Using bearing remover/installer kit, place knuckle (inboard of knuckle facing up), on appropriate spacer (with step side down). *See Fig. 5.*

NOTE: Bearing installers must be positioned as indicated to prevent bearing damage during installation.

3) Install appropriate bearing installer on bearing outer race face, with undercut side of installer facing bearing. *See Fig. 5.* Press bearing in knuckle until it seats completely against knuckle bore shoulder. Install a new snap ring in knuckle groove. Ensure snap ring is seated properly.

4) Position spacer on press plate with step side down. Position hub on spacer. Position knuckle assembly on hub with outboard side of knuckle down. Poistion appropriate bearing remover on bearing with flat side down and centered. *See Fig. 6.*

NOTE: Do not use power tools to tighten hub nut retainer. Do not move vehicle without tightening hub nut retainer.

5) Press remover until bearing is fully seated on hub. Ensure hub rotates freely on knuckle. To complete installation, reverse removal procedure. Lubricate CV joint splines with SAE 30W oil prior to installing in hub.

FWD Axle Shafts

FORD MOTOR CO. (Cont.)

Fig. 5: Installing Hub Bearing in Knuckle

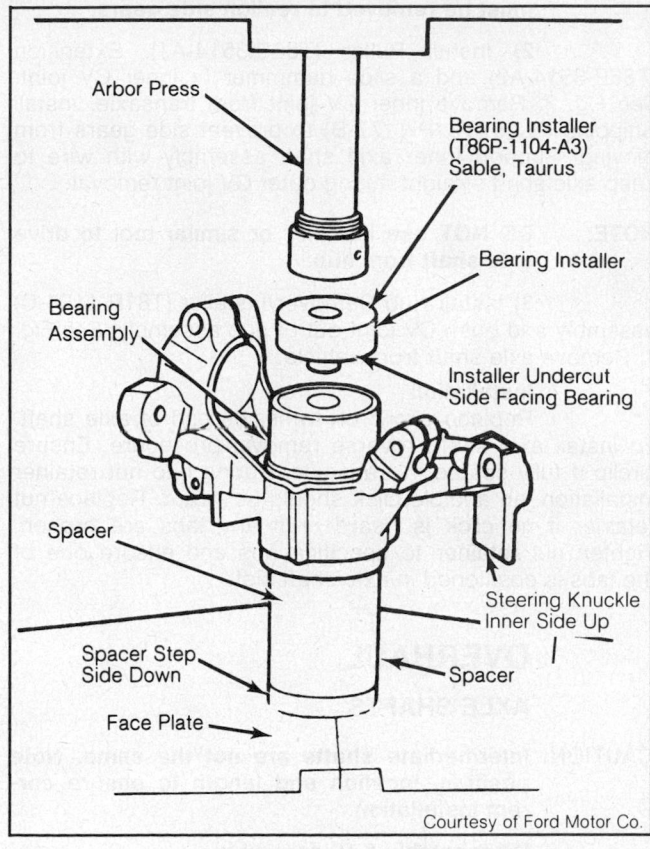

Arbor Press

Bearing Installer
(T86P-1104-A3)
Sable, Taurus

Bearing Installer

Bearing
Assembly

Installer Undercut
Side Facing Bearing

Spacer

Steering Knuckle
Inner Side Up

Spacer Step
Side Down

Spacer

Face Plate

Courtesy of Ford Motor Co.

Fig. 6: Installing Hub & Knuckle

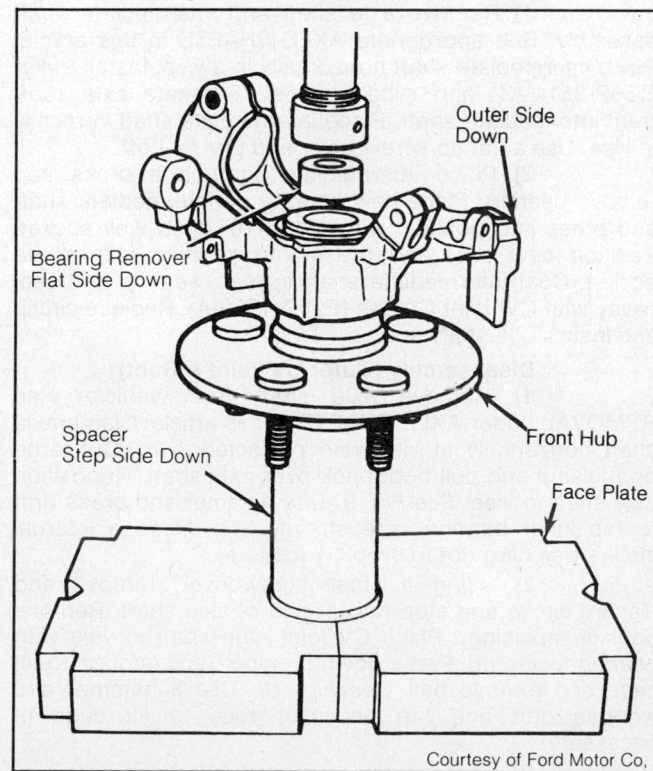

Outer Side
Down

Bearing Remover
Flat Side Down

Spacer
Step Side Down

Front Hub

Face Plate

Courtesy of Ford Motor Co,

6) During hub nut retainer installation, an audible click should be heard. Replace nut retainer if no click is heard or if any tabs are broken. Tighten nut

retainer to specifications and ensure one of the tabs is positioned in axle shaft slot.

AXLE SHAFTS

CAUTION: DO NOT reuse hub nut retainers, circlips, snap rings or lower ball joint pinch bolt and nut.

On some transaxles models, the right axle shaft must be removed from transaxle to remove the left axle shaft. Differential Rotator (T81P-4026-A) must then be inserted to drive left inner CV joint out of differential.

Removal (Continental, Escort, Tempo & Topaz)

1) Remove wheel/tire assembly and hub nut retainer. See step **1)** in REMOVAL under HUB BEARINGS in this article. Remove bolt attaching brake hose to strut. Remove and discard bolt and nut retaining lower ball joint to steering knuckle. On Continental models, remove anti-lock brake sensor, height sensor link and stabilizer bar link.

2) On all models, move brake rotor shield out of way and pry down on control arm assembly to separate ball joint from steering knuckle.

NOTE: **If differential side gears move, transaxle must be removed to realign side gears.**

3) On Escort, Tempo and Topaz models, pry axle shaft out of transaxle. Use care not to damage differential oil seal, case or CV joint boot. Install Shipping Plugs (T81P-1177-B) to prevent side gears from moving. Support inner axle shaft assembly with wire to keep axle shaft straight during outer CV joint removal.

4) On Continental models, install Puller (T86P-3514-A1), Extension (T86P-3514-A2) and a slide hammmer to inner CV joint. See Fig. 7. Remove inner CV joint from transaxle. Install Shipping Plugs (T81P-1177-B) to prevent side gears from moving. Support inner axle shaft assembly with wire to keep axle shaft straight during outer CV joint removal.

NOTE: **DO NOT use hammer or similar tool to drive axle shaft from hub.**

5) On all models, install Hub Remover/Installer (T81P-1104-C) assembly and push CV joint out of hub assembly. See Fig. 1. Remove axle shaft from vehicle.

Installation

Replace inner CV joint circlip. To install axle shaft, reverse removal procedure. Ensure circlip if fully seated in transaxle. During hub nut retainer installation, an audible click should be heard. Replace nut retainer if no click is heard or if any tabs are broken. Tighten nut retainer to specifications and ensure one of the tabs is positioned in axle shaft slot.

Removal (Sable & Taurus, Right Axle Shaft With MTX Transaxle & Right & Left Axle Shaft With FLC Transaxle)

1) Remove wheel/tire assembly and hub nut retainer. See step **1)** in REMOVAL under HUB BEARINGS in this article. Remove bolt attaching brake hose to strut. Remove and discard bolt and nut retaining lower ball joint to steering knuckle. Move brake rotor shield out of way and pry down on control arm assembly to separate ball joint from steering knuckle.

FORD MOTOR CO. (Cont.)

NOTE: If differential side gears move, transaxle must be removed to realign side gears.

2) Remove 2 bolts attaching intermediate shaft bearing to bracket. Pull intermediate shaft from transaxle. Install Shipping Plugs (T81P-1177-B) to prevent side gears from moving. Support axle shaft assembly at transaxle with wire, to keep axle shaft straight during outer CV joint removal.

NOTE: On FLC transaxle models, remove right axle shaft to remove left axle shaft.

3) On FLC transaxle models, install Differential Rotator (T81P-4026-A) and drive out left axle shaft from transaxle. To complete left axle shaft removal, proceed with next step.

NOTE: DO NOT use hammer or similar tool to drive axle shaft from hub.

4) Install Hub Remover/Installer (T81P-1104-C) assembly and push CV joint out of hub assembly. *See Fig. 1.* Remove axle shaft and/or axle shaft/intermediate shaft as an assembly. To separate intermediate shaft from axle shaft, see INTERMEDIATE SHAFT under OVERHAUL in this article.

Installation
Replace circlip on intermediate shaft. To install axle shaft, reverse removal procedure. Ensure circlip is fully seated in transaxle. During hub nut retainer installation, an audible click should be heard. Replace nut retainer if no click is heard or if any tabs are broken. Tighten nut retainer to specifications and ensure one of the tabs is positioned in axle shaft slot.

Fig. 7: Removing Inner CV Joint

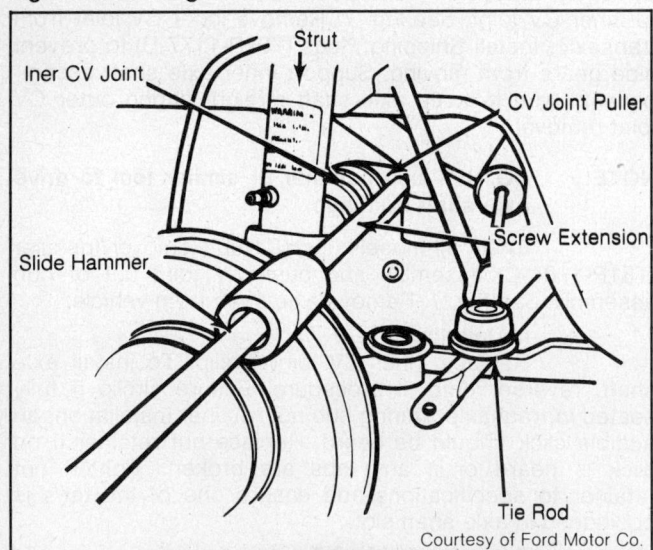

Courtesy of Ford Motor Co.

Removal (Sable & Taurus, Right & Left Axle Shaft With AXOD Transaxle & Left Axle Shaft With MTX Transaxle)
1) Remove wheel/tire assembly and hub nut retainer. See step 1) in REMOVAL under HUB BEARINGS in this article. Remove bolt attaching brake hose to strut. Remove and discard bolt and nut retaining lower ball joint to steering knuckle. Move brake rotor shield out of way and pry down on control arm assembly to separate ball joint from steering knuckle.

NOTE: If differential side gears move, transaxle must be removed to realign side gears.

2) Install Puller (T86P-3514-A1), Extension (T86P-3514-A2) and a slide hammmer to inner CV joint. *See Fig. 7.* Remove inner CV joint from transaxle. Install Shipping Plugs (T81P-1177-B) to prevent side gears from moving. Support inner axle shaft assembly with wire to keep axle shaft straight during outer CV joint removal.

NOTE: DO NOT use hammer or similar tool to drive axle shaft from hub.

3) Install Hub Remover/Installer (T81P-1104-C) assembly and push CV joint out of hub assembly. *See Fig. 1.* Remove axle shaft from vehicle.

Installation
Replace circlip on transaxle end of axle shaft. To install axle shaft, reverse removal procedure. Ensure circlip if fully seated in transaxle. During hub nut retainer installation, an audible click should be heard. Replace nut retainer if no click is heard or if any tabs are broken. Tighten nut retainer to specifications and ensure one of the tabs is positioned in axle shaft slot.

OVERHAUL

AXLE SHAFTS

CAUTION: Intermediate shafts are not the same. Note position, location and length to ensure correct installation.

Disassembly & Reassembly (Intermediate Shaft)
1) Remove axle shaft and intermediate shaft assembly. See appropriate AXLE SHAFTS in this article. Place intermediate shaft horizontally in a vise. Install Puller (T86P-3514-A1) and slide hammer. Separate axle shaft from intermediate shaft. Place intermediate shaft vertically in vise. Use a flat tip screwdriver and pry seal off.

2) Place intermediate shaft in a press and remove bearing. Place new bearing on intermediate shaft and press into position with a 1 3/16" deep well socket. Position new seal and press into position with same socket. Coat intermediate shaft splines, seal lip and seal cavity with CV Joint Grease (E2FZ-1950-A). Replace circlip and install axle shaft.

Disassembly (Outer CV Joint & Boot)
1) Remove axle shaft from vehicle. See REMOVAL under AXLE SHAFTS in this article. Clamp axle shaft horizontally in vise with protected jaws. Cut large boot clamp and pull boot back over axle shaft. Reposition axle shaft in vise. *See Fig. 9.* Use hammer and brass drift to tap inner bearing race sharply and dislodge internal circlip. Use care not to drop CV joint.

2) Using a small screwdriver, remove and discard circlip and stop ring at end of axle shaft. Remove boot (if replacing). Place CV joint stub shaft in vise with bearing facing up. Press down on inner race enough to tilt cage and remove ball. *See Fig. 10.* Use a hammer and wooden drift and tap on inner race to tilt cage (if necessary).

3) Use a screwdriver without sharp edges to remove balls (if necessary). Repeat procedure for remaining balls. Pivot cage and inner race assembly until it is straight up and down in outer race. Align cage windows

FWD Axle Shafts

FORD MOTOR CO. (Cont.)

Fig. 8: Exploded View of Axle Shaft & CV Joint Assembly

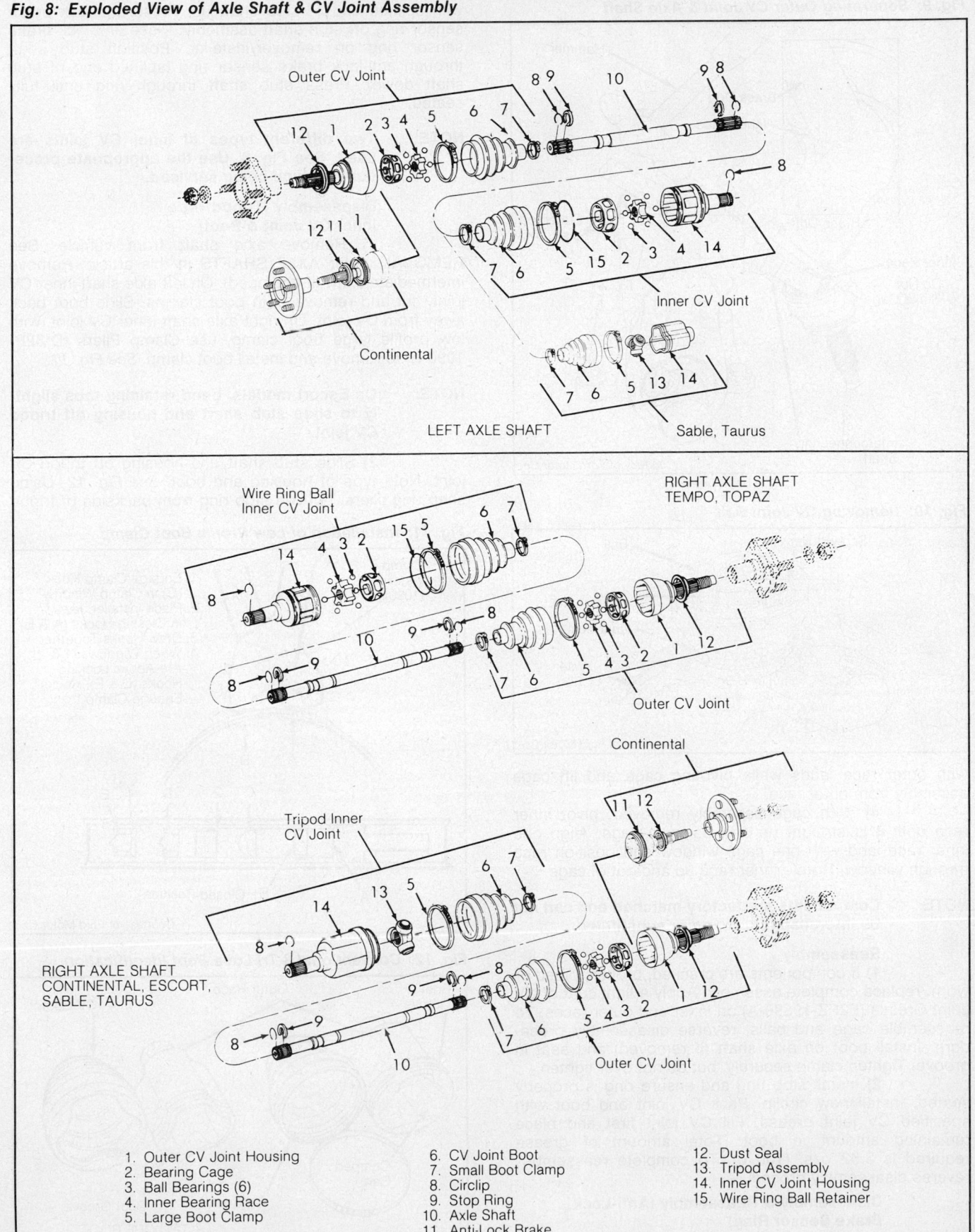

1. Outer CV Joint Housing
2. Bearing Cage
3. Ball Bearings (6)
4. Inner Bearing Race
5. Large Boot Clamp
6. CV Joint Boot
7. Small Boot Clamp
8. Circlip
9. Stop Ring
10. Axle Shaft
11. Anti-Lock Brake Sensor Ring
12. Dust Seal
13. Tripod Assembly
14. Inner CV Joint Housing
15. Wire Ring Ball Retainer

Courtesy of Ford Motor Co.

FWD Axle Shafts

FORD MOTOR CO. (Cont.)

Fig. 9: Separating Outer CV Joint & Axle Shaft

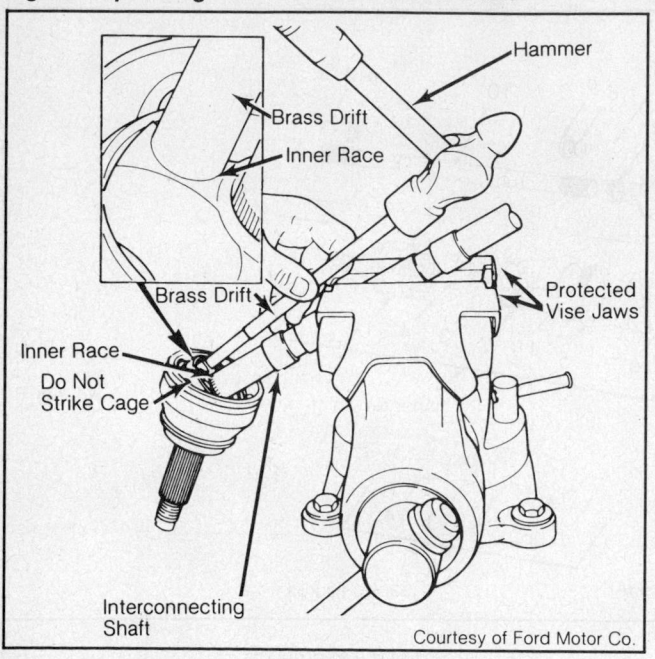

Courtesy of Ford Motor Co.

Fig. 10: Removing CV Joint Ball

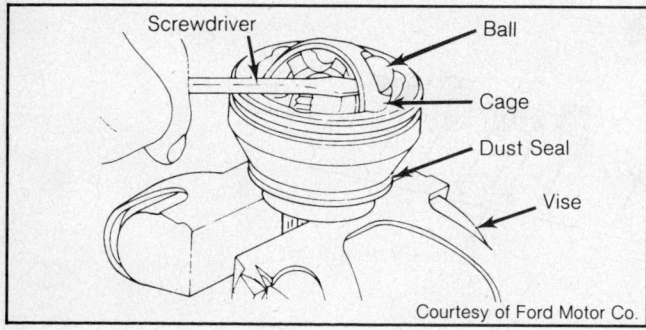

Courtesy of Ford Motor Co.

with outer race lands while pivoting cage and lift cage assembly from outer race.

4) With cage assembly removed, pivot inner race until it is straight up and down in cage. Align one inner race land with one cage window and position race through window. Rotate inner race up and out of cage.

NOTE: Components are factory matched and can not be interchanged, mixed or substituted.

Reassembly

1) If components are cracked, broken, pitted or worn, replace complete assembly. Apply a light coat of CV Joint Grease (E2FZ-19590-A) on inner and outer races. To reassemble cage and balls, reverse disassembly procedure. Install boot on axle shaft (if removed) and seat in groove. Tighten clamp securely, but do not over tighten.

2) Install stop ring and ensure ring is properly seated. Install new circlip. Pack CV joint and boot with specified CV joint grease. Fill CV joint first and place remaining amount in boot. Total amount of grease required is 3.52 ozs. (100 g). To complete reassembly, reverse disassembly procedure.

Disassembly & Reassembly (Anti-Lock Brake Sensor Ring)

Separate outer CV joint from axle shaft. Place stub shaft assembly on Remover/Installer (T88P-20202-A)

with splined end of stub shaft up. Press anti-lock brake sensor ring off stub shaft assmebly. Place anti-lock brake sensor ring on remover/installer. Position stub shaft through anti-lock brake sensor ring (splined end of stub shaft down). Press stub shaft through ring until fully seated.

NOTE: Two different types of inner CV joints are used. See Fig. 8. Use the appropriate procedure for type being serviced.

Disassembly (Tripod Type Inner CV Joint & Boot)

1) Remove axle shaft from vehicle. See REMOVAL under AXLE SHAFTS in this article. Remove intermediate shaft (if equipped). On left axle shaft inner CV joint, cut and remove both boot clamps. Slide boot back away from CV joint. On right axle shaft inner CV joint, with low profile large boot clamp, use Clamp Pliers (D-82P-1090-A) to remove and install boot clamp. See Fig. 11.

NOTE: On Escort models, bend retaining tabs slightly to slide stub shaft and housing off tripod CV joint.

2) Slide stub shaft and housing off tripod CV joint. Note type of housing and boot. See Fig. 12. Using snap ring pliers, remove stop ring from backside of tripod

Fig. 11: Installation of Low Profile Boot Clamp

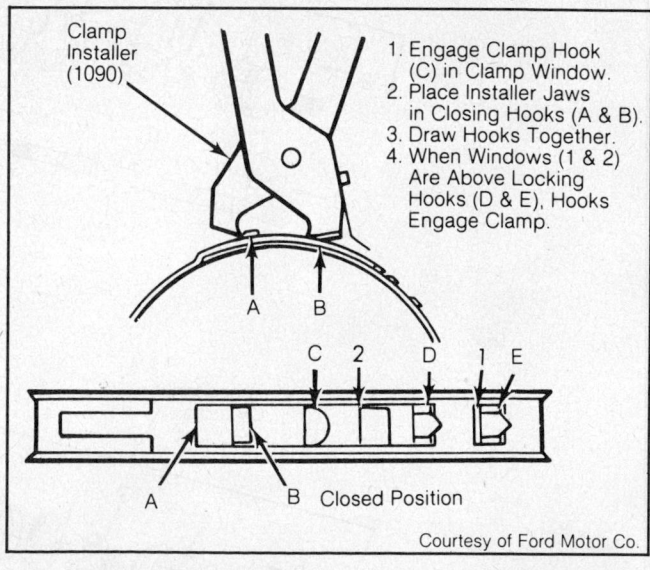

1. Engage Clamp Hook (C) in Clamp Window.
2. Place Installer Jaws in Closing Hooks (A & B).
3. Draw Hooks Together.
4. When Windows (1 & 2) Are Above Locking Hooks (D & E), Hooks Engage Clamp.

Courtesy of Ford Motor Co.

Fig. 12: Conventional & Tri-Lobe Boot Identification

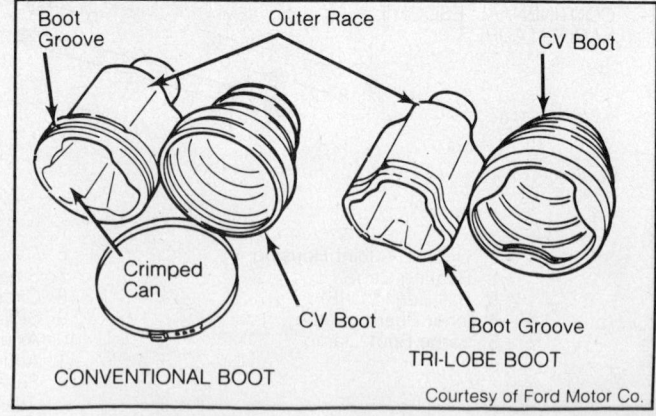

Courtesy of Ford Motor Co.

Fig. 13: Axle Shaft Assembled Lengths

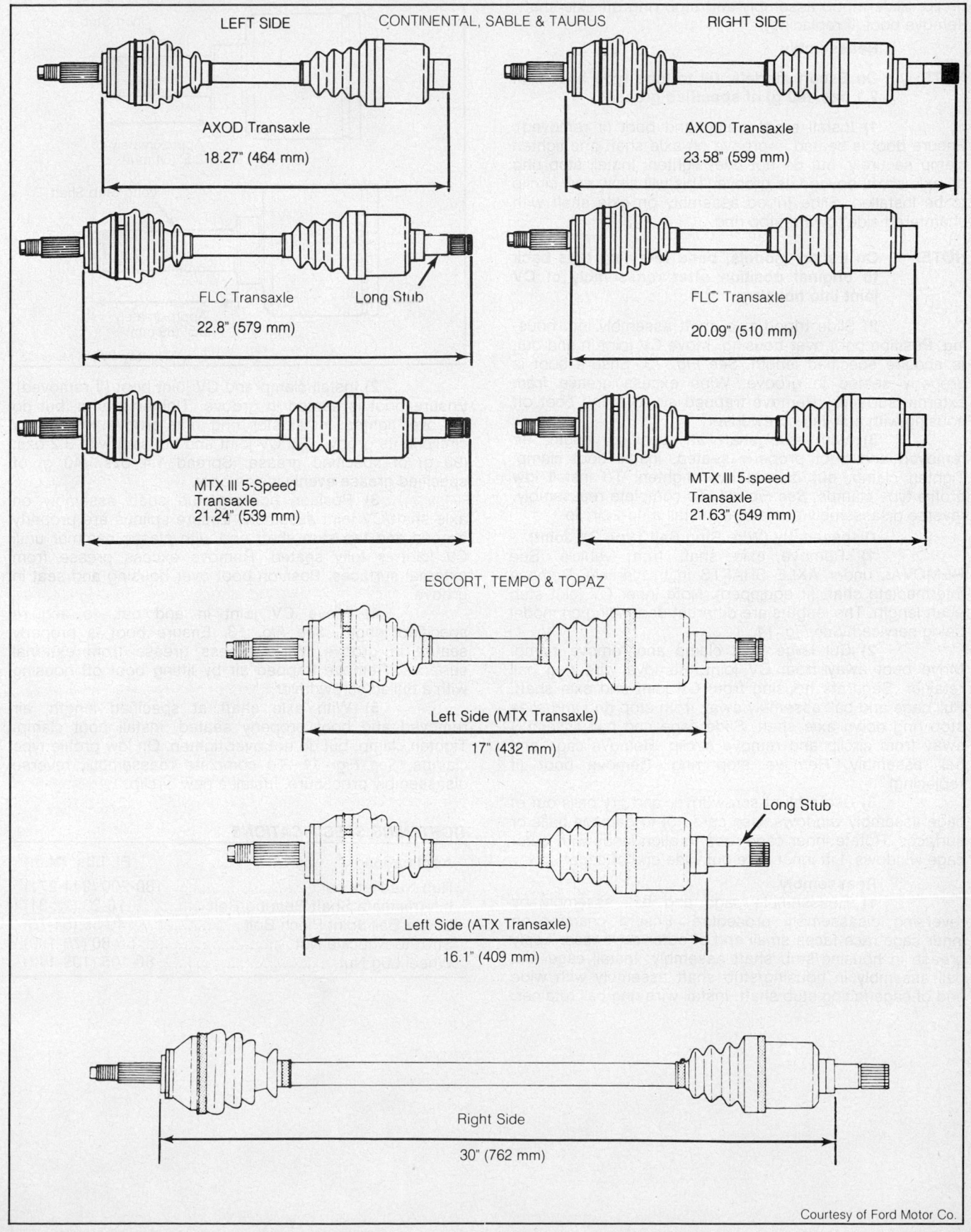

LEFT SIDE   CONTINENTAL, SABLE & TAURUS   RIGHT SIDE

AXOD Transaxle
18.27" (464 mm)

AXOD Transaxle
23.58" (599 mm)

FLC Transaxle
22.8" (579 mm)

Long Stub

FLC Transaxle
20.09" (510 mm)

MTX III 5-speed
Transaxle
21.24" (539 mm)

MTX III 5-speed
Transaxle
21.63" (549 mm)

ESCORT, TEMPO & TOPAZ

Left Side (MTX Transaxle)
17" (432 mm)

Long Stub

Left Side (ATX Transaxle)
16.1" (409 mm)

Right Side
30" (762 mm)

Courtesy of Ford Motor Co.

FWD Axle Shafts

FORD MOTOR CO. (Cont.)

assembly. Moved tripod assembly back and remove circlip. Slide tripod assembly and stop ring off axle shaft. Remove boot (if replacing).

Reassembly

NOTE: On Escort models, fill tri-lobe type boot with **2.1 ozs. (60 g) of specified grease.**

1) Install small clamp and boot (if removed). Ensure boot is seated in groove on axle shaft and tighten clamp securely, but do not over tighten. Install stop ring on axle shaft, beyond its groove. This will allow new circlip to be installed. Slide tripod assembly on axle shaft with chamfered side toward stop ring.

NOTE: On Escort models, bend retaining tabs back to original position after reassembly of CV joint into housing.

2) Slide tripod/axle shaft assembly into housing. Position boot over housing. Move CV joint in and out, to acquire specified length. *See Fig. 13.* Ensure boot is properly seated in groove. Wipe excess grease from external surfaces. Remove trapped air by lifting boot off housing with a dulled screwdriver.

3) With axle shaft at specified length, air removed and boot properly seated, install boot clamp. Tighten clamp, but do not over tighten. To install low profile type clamps, *See Fig. 11.* To complete reassembly, reverse disassembly procedure. Install a new circlip.

Disassembly (Wire Ring Ball Type CV Joint)

1) Remove axle shaft from vehicle. See REMOVAL under AXLE SHAFTS in this article. Remove intermediate shaft (if equipped). Note inner CV joint stub shaft length. The lengths are different depending on model being serviced. *See Fig. 14.*

2) Cut large boot clamp and remove clamp. Move boot away from CV joint. Remove wire ring ball retainer. Separate housing from CV joint and axle shaft. Pull cage and ball assembly away from stop ring and slide stop ring down axle shaft. Slide cage and ball assembly away from circlip and remove circlip. Remove cage and ball assembly. Remove stop ring. Remove boot (if replacing).

3) Use a blunt screwdriver and pry balls out of cage assembly windows. Use care not to damage balls or surfaces. Rotate inner cage race to align lands with outer cage windows. Lift inner race out wide end of cage.

Reassembly

1) Reassemble cage and ball assembly by reversing disassembly procedure. Ensure chamfer on inner cage race faces small end of outer cage race. Apply grease in housing/stub shaft assembly. Install cage and ball assembly in housing/stub shaft assembly with wide end of cage facing stub shaft. Install wire ring ball retainer.

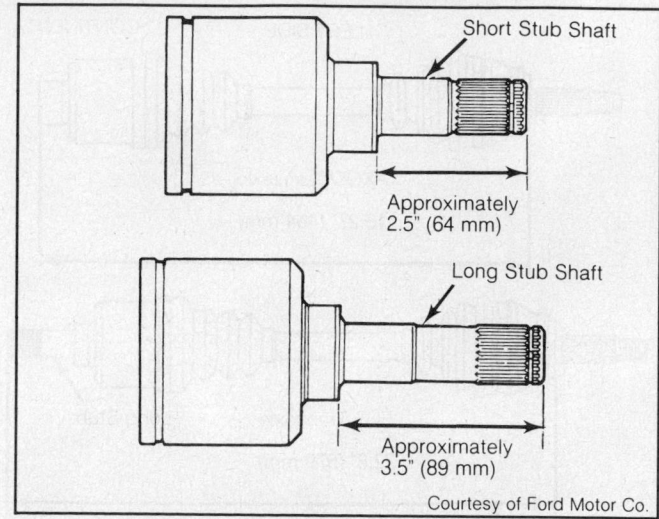

Fig. 14: Inner CV Joint Stub Shaft Identification

Short Stub Shaft

Approximately 2.5" (64 mm)

Long Stub Shaft

Approximately 3.5" (89 mm)

Courtesy of Ford Motor Co.

2) Install clamp and CV joint boot (if removed). Ensure boot is seated in groove. Tighten clamp, but do not over tighten. Install stop ring in its groove. Install new circlip in its groove. Fill CV joint and housing with 3.2 ozs. (90 g) of specified grease. Spread 1.4 ozs. (40 g) of specified grease evenly inside boot.

3) Position housing/stub shaft assembly on axle shaft/CV joint assembly. Ensure splines are properly aligned and tap stub shaft end with plastic hammer until CV joint is fully seated. Remove excess grease from external surfaces. Position boot over housing and seat in groove.

4) Move CV joint in and out, to acquire specified length. *See Fig. 13.* Ensure boot is properly seated in groove. Wipe excess grease from external surfaces. Remove trapped air by lifting boot off housing with a dulled screwdriver.

5) With axle shaft at specified length, air removed and boot properly seated, install boot clamp. Tighten clamp, but do not over tighten. On low profile type clamps, *See Fig. 11.* To complete reassembly, reverse disassembly procedure. Install a new circlip.

TIGHTENING SPECIFICATIONS

Application	Ft. Lbs. (N.m)
Hub Nut Retainer	180-200 (244-271)
Intermediate Shaft Bearing Bolt	16-23 (22-31)
Lower Ball Joint Pinch Bolt	40-55 (54-75)
Strut-to-Knuckle Nut	55-80 (75-109)
Wheel Lug Nut	80-105 (109-142)

FWD Axle Shafts

GENERAL MOTORS

"A" Body – Celebrity, Century,
Cutlass Ciera, Cutlass Cruiser, 6000
"C" Body – DeVille, Electra,
Fleetwood, Ninety-Eight
"E" Body – Eldorado, Riviera, Toronado
"H" Body – Bonneville,
Delta 88, LeSabre
"J" Body – Cavalier, Cimarron,
Firenza, Skyhawk, Sunbird
"K" Body – Seville
"L" Body – Beretta, Corsica
"N" Body – Cutlass Calais,
Grand Am, Skylark
"P" Body – Fiero
"S" Body – Nova
"V" Body – Allanté
"W" Body – Cutlass Supreme,
Grand Prix, Regal

DESCRIPTION

Power is transferred from transaxle to drive wheels by axle shafts. Axle shafts are completely flexible assemblies consisting of an inner and outer CV joint. Inner CV joints have the capability of in and out movement. Axle shafts, except left inner of automatic transaxles, use a male splined end and interlock with transaxle gears by a snap ring. Left inner with automatic transaxles uses a female splined end and interlocks with protruding stub shaft.

Vehicles with a 5-speed manual transaxle, RPO MG2, will use the cross-groove type axle shaft. Some models use an intermediate shaft to connect to transaxle. Some models use dampers on the right side axle shafts. See Fig. 1 and 2. On "S" body with 4A-GE engines, the inner CV joints are attached to transaxle by bolts/nuts.

Fig. 1: Exploded View of Tripod Type Axle Shaft

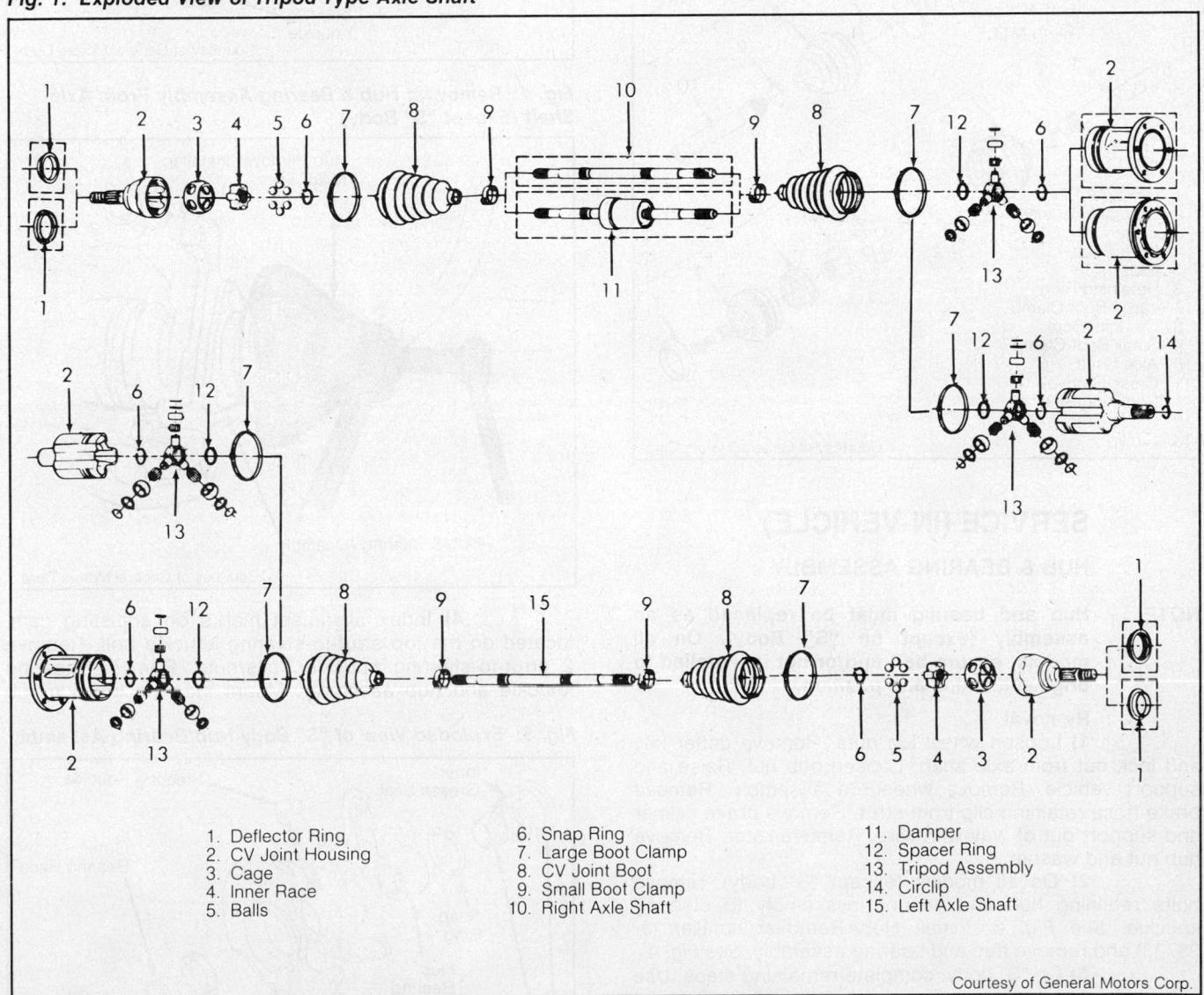

1. Deflector Ring	6. Snap Ring	11. Damper
2. CV Joint Housing	7. Large Boot Clamp	12. Spacer Ring
3. Cage	8. CV Joint Boot	13. Tripod Assembly
4. Inner Race	9. Small Boot Clamp	14. Circlip
5. Balls	10. Right Axle Shaft	15. Left Axle Shaft

Fig. 2: Exploded View of Cross-Groove Type Axle Shaft

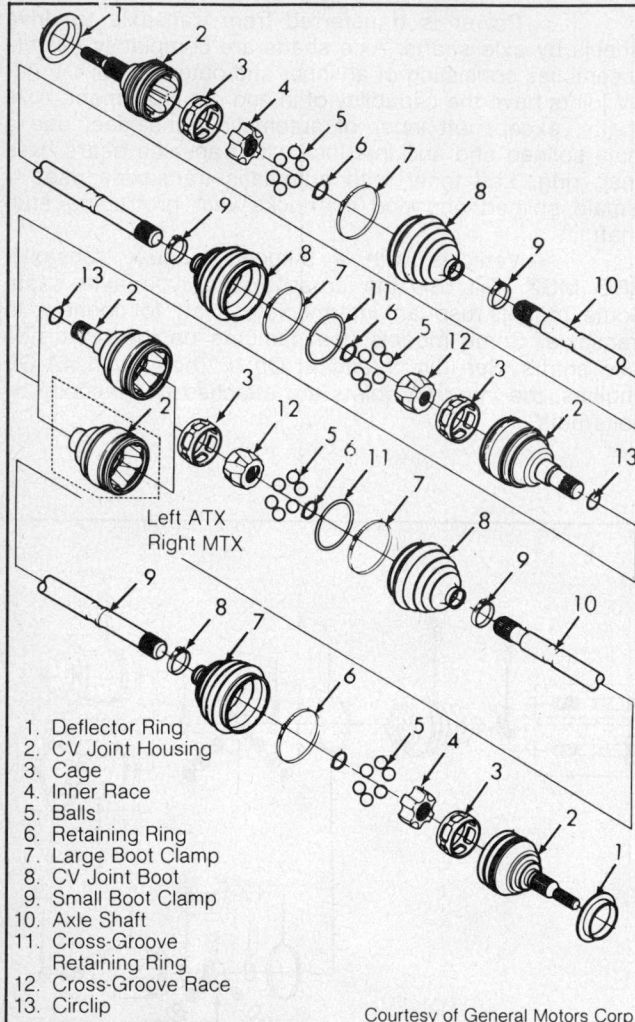

1. Deflector Ring
2. CV Joint Housing
3. Cage
4. Inner Race
5. Balls
6. Retaining Ring
7. Large Boot Clamp
8. CV Joint Boot
9. Small Boot Clamp
10. Axle Shaft
11. Cross-Groove
    Retaining Ring
12. Cross-Groove Race
13. Circlip

Left ATX
Right MTX

Courtesy of General Motors Corp.

SERVICE (IN-VEHICLE)

HUB & BEARING ASSEMBLY

NOTE: Hub and bearing must be replaced as an assembly (except on "S" Body). On all models, ensure bolt and/or nut is installed to original location and position.

Removal

1) Loosen wheel lug nuts. Remove cotter key and lock nut from axle shaft. Loosen hub nut. Raise and support vehicle. Remove wheel/tire assembly. Remove brake hose retaining clip from strut. Remove brake caliper and support out of way with wire. Remove rotor. Remove hub nut and washer.

2) On all models (except "S" body), remove bolts retaining hub and bearing asssembly to steering knuckle. See Fig. 3. Install Hub Remover/Installer (J-28733) and remove hub and bearing assembly. See Fig. 4.

3) On "S" body, complete remaining steps. Use a 2 jaw-type puller and push axle shaft from hub. Support outer end of axle shaft to keep it straight during removal. Separate tie rod from steering knuckle. Remove lower ball joint-to-control arm bolt and nuts.

Fig. 3: Exploded View of Hub & Bearing Assembly (Except "S" Body)

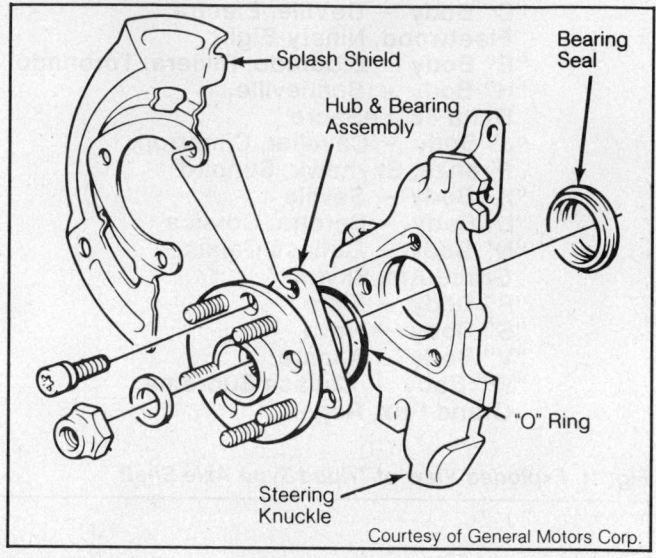

Splash Shield

Bearing Seal

Hub & Bearing Assembly

"O" Ring

Steering Knuckle

Courtesy of General Motors Corp.

Fig. 4: Removing Hub & Bearing Assembly From Axle Shaft (Except "S" Body)

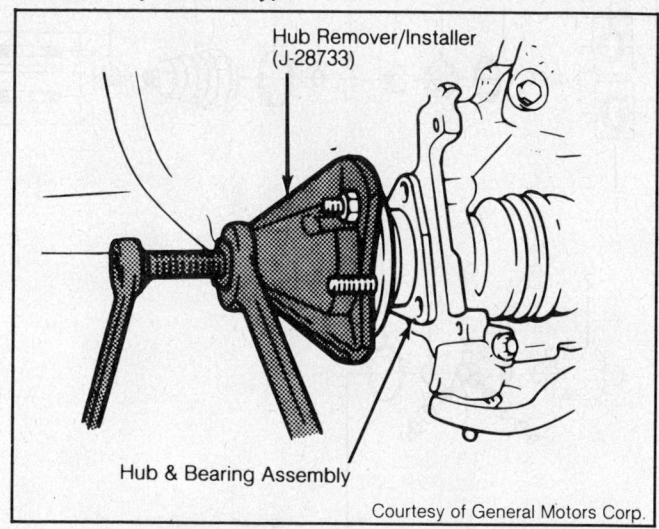

Hub Remover/Installer (J-28733)

Hub & Bearing Assembly

Courtesy of General Motors Corp.

4) Index alignment marks on adjusting cam, located on the top strut-to-steering knuckle bolt. Remove 2 strut-to-steering knuckle bolts/nuts. Remove steering knuckle and hub assembly. Mount steering knuckle/hub

Fig. 5: Exploded View of "S" Body Hub/Bearing Assembly

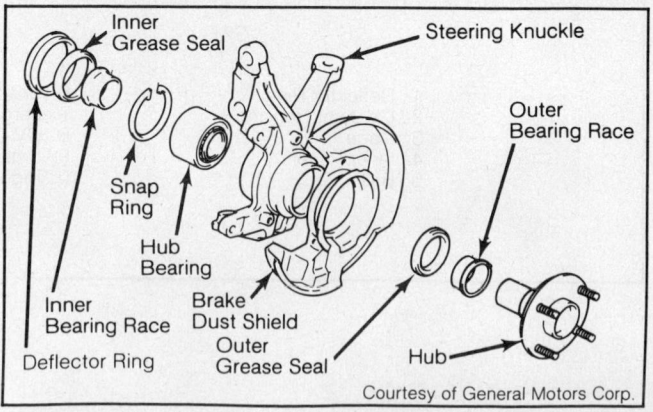

Inner Grease Seal

Steering Knuckle

Snap Ring

Outer Bearing Race

Hub Bearing

Inner Bearing Race

Brake Dust Shield

Outer Grease Seal

Hub

Deflector Ring

Courtesy of General Motors Corp.

GENERAL MOTORS (Cont.)

assembly in vise. Remove lower ball joint from steering knuckle.

5) Pry dust reflector seal from rear of knuckle. Using Seal Remover (J-26941) and slide hammer, remove inner grease seal. Remove bearing snap ring. Remove brake rotor dust shield. *See Fig. 5.* Use a 2 jaw-type puller and push hub out of knuckle.

6) Use a 2 jaw-type puller and remove inner bearing race from hub. Remove outer grease seal from hub with seal remover and slide hammer. Place knuckle assembly (inboard side down) on a spacer and drive hub bearing out of knuckle.

Inspection

Clean and inspect bearing mating surfaces and knuckle bore for dirt, knicks and burrs. If hub and bearing assembly is being replaced, lubricate new seal and knuckle bore with grease.

NOTE: **DO NOT reuse self-locking nuts or hub nut. Ensure all bolts and nuts are installed to original location and position.**

Installation (Except "S" Body)

1) Install new "O" ring on hub and bearing assembly. Install new seal in steering knuckle with driver. Position hub and bearing assembly in steering knuckle bore. Install NEW hub nut until bearing and hub assembly is seated, aproximately 74 ft. lbs. (100 N.m). Install hub-to-steering knuckle bolts and tighten evenly to specifications.

2) To complete installation, reverse removal procedure. On models with bracket stops on upper and lower ends of brake calipers, check clearance. Clearance should be .005-.012" (.13-.31 mm) at each end. Replace or grind stops as necessary. This will ensure caliper slides freely. Tighten bolts/nuts to specifications.

Installation ("S" Body)

1) Reverse removal procedure to install seals, bearing and inner bearing race. Apply sealer to brake rotor dust shield and install shield. Apply Multi-Purpose grease to seal lip, seal and bearing. Drive hub into steering knuckle. Install snap ring.

2) Install inner grease seal. Install dust reflector seal with open end down. Install lower ball joint in control arm and tighten to specifications. Place knuckle-/hub assembly onto lower ball joint.

3) Reinstall the OLD lower ball joint nut and tighten to 14 ft. lbs. (19 N.m). Remove old nut and install a NEW nut. To complete installation, reverse removal procedure. Ensure cam on strut is installed to position marked at removal. Tighten bolts/nuts to specifications. Check and adjust alignment as necessary.

AXLE SHAFTS

CAUTION: Avoid damage by protecting CV joint boots and keeping axle shaft straight during removal and installation.

Removal (Except "S" Body)

Disconnect negative battery cable. Remove hub from steering knuckle. See HUB & BEARING ASSEMBLY in this article. Place drain pan under transaxle. On right axle shaft, use slide hammer and Remover (J-33008) to remove axle shaft from transaxle or intermediate shaft. *See Fig. 6.* On left axle shaft, pry axle shaft from transaxle with groove provided at inner CV joint. Remove all axle shafts through steering knuckle.

Installation

1) Slide axle shaft through steering knuckle and into transaxle. Install hub/bearing assembly in steering knuckle. Loosely tighten hub/bearing assembly-to-knuckle bolts/nuts. Ensure axle shaft snap ring is engaged by prying on inner CV joint groove. Pry against frame cradle or lower control arm.

2) Grip inner CV joint housing and pull outboard. DO NOT pull on axle shaft. If snap ring is seated, axle shaft will remain intact. To complete installation, reverse removal procedure.

Removal ("S" Body)

1) Disconnect negative battery cable. Loosen lug nuts. Remove cotter key and lock nut from axle shaft. Loosen hub nut. Raise and support vehicle. Remove wheel/tire assembly. Remove hub nut and washer. Remove lower ball joint-to-control arm bolt and nuts. Remove tie rod from steering knuckle. Remove brake hose retained to strut.

Fig. 6: *Removing Axle Shaft From Transaxle*

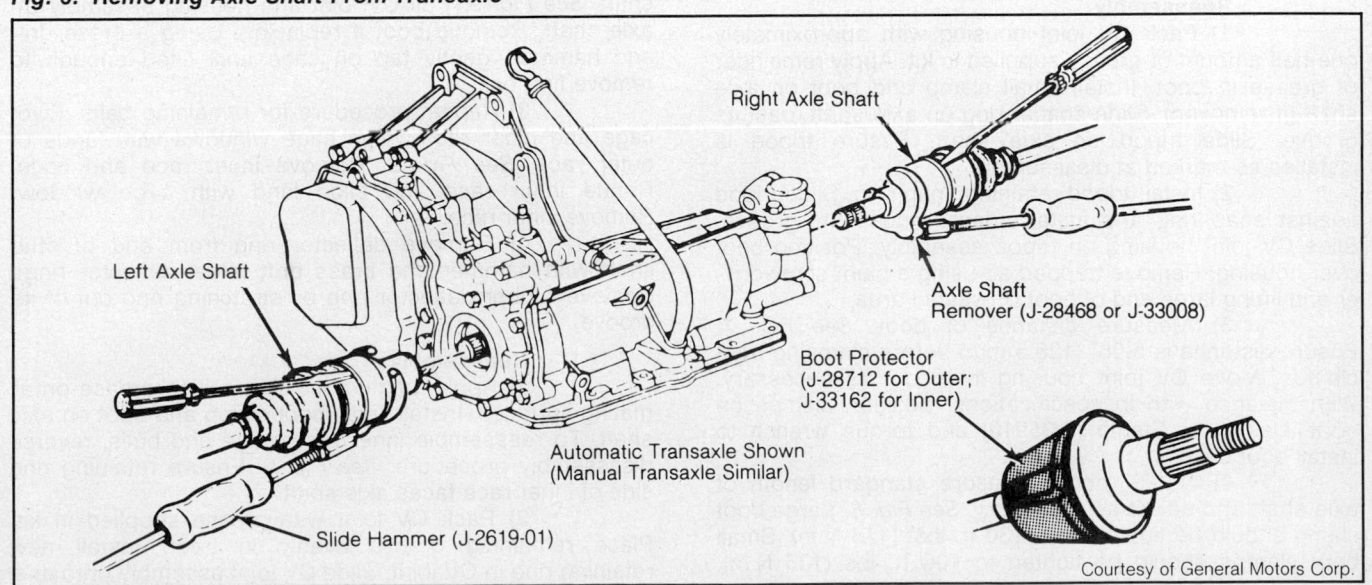

Left Axle Shaft
Right Axle Shaft
Axle Shaft Remover (J-28468 or J-33008)
Boot Protector (J-28712 for Outer; J-33162 for Inner)
Automatic Transaxle Shown (Manual Transaxle Similar)
Slide Hammer (J-2619-01)

Courtesy of General Motors Corp.

2) Remove and support brake caliper. Remove brake rotor. Using a 2 jaw-type puller, push axle shaft from hub. On models without 4A-GE engine, use slide hammer and Remover (J-35762) and remove axle shaft from transaxle. See Fig. 6. On models with 4A-GE engine, remove nuts retaining axle shaft to transaxle. Remove axle shaft from vehicle.

Installation

Check inner grease seal and replace if necessary. Slide axle shaft into transaxle or install nuts (depending on engine type). Install axle through hub assembly. To complete installation, reverse removal procedure. Tighten bolts/nuts to specifications.

OVERHAUL

AXLE SHAFTS

NOTE: Models equipped with Anti-Lock Braking System have a speed sensor ring. Speed senor ring and joint must be replaced as a unit. Speed sensor ring adjustment must be checked and adjusted as necessary.

Disassembly (Inner Tripod Type)

1) Remove axle shaft from vehicle. See REMOVAL under AXLE SHAFTS in this article. Place axle shaft in vise with protected jaws. Cut boot clamps and remove clamps. Slide boot away from CV joint. Mark CV joint to housing for reassembly reference. Pull CV joint housing off tripod/axle assembly.

2) Slide spacer ring back away from tripod joint and slide tripod away from retaining ring. Remove tripod retaining ring. Mark tripod-to-axle shaft for installation reference. Slide tripod off axle shaft. Remove spacer ring. Remove boot (if replacing).

Inspection

Wash all parts (except boots) in solvent and dry with compressed air. Wash boots with soap and water. Inspect races for excessive wear and scoring. Inspect splined areas of shafts for wear, cracks and twists. Inspect balls for pitting, cracking or scoring. Check for cracks, chips or heavy brinelling of cage windows.

Reassembly

1) Pack CV joint housing with approximately one-half amount of grease supplied in kit. Apply remainder of grease in boot. Install small clamp and boot on axle shaft (if removed). Slide spacer ring on axle shaft, past its groove. Slide tripod on axle shaft. Ensure tripod is installed as marked at disassembly.

2) Install tripod retaining snap ring. Slide tripod against snap ring and install spacer ring in its groove. Slide CV joint housing on tripod assembly. Position boot over housing. Remove trapped air using a blunt screwdriver and lifting large end of boot off sealed area.

3) Measure distance of boot. See Fig. 7. Ensure distance is 5.06" (128.5 mm) before clamping boot clamps. Move CV joint housing in or out as necessary. With distance with in specifications, position clamps on boot. Use Boot Clamp (J-35910) and torque wrench to install boot clamps.

4) On "S" body, measure standard length of axle shaft and adjust as necessary. See Fig. 8. Large boot clamp should be tightened to 130 ft. lbs. (176 N.m). Small boot clamps should be tighten to 100 ft. lbs (136 N.m).

Recheck boot length. To complete installation, reverse disassembly procedure.

Fig. 7: Measuring CV Boot Lengths

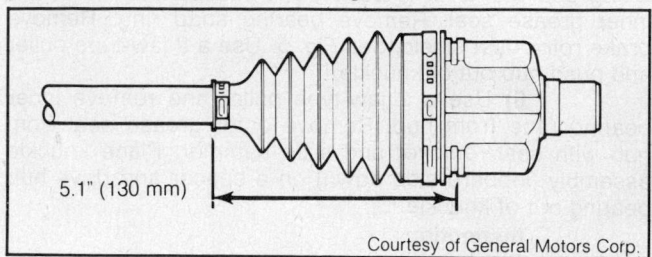

5.1" (130 mm)

Courtesy of General Motors Corp.

Fig. 8: "S" Body Axle Shaft Standard Length

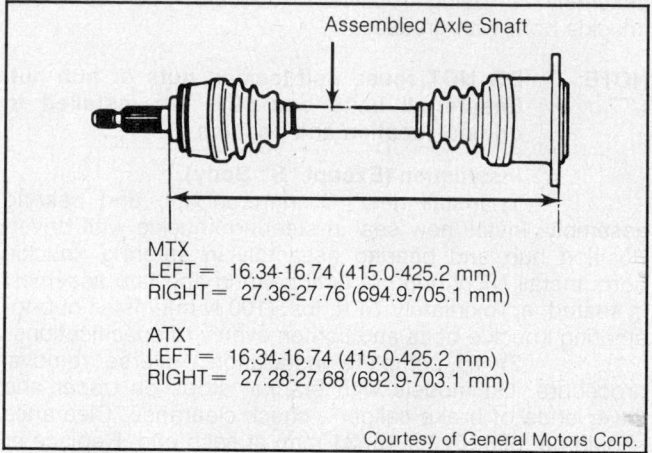

Assembled Axle Shaft

MTX
LEFT = 16.34-16.74 (415.0-425.2 mm)
RIGHT = 27.36-27.76 (694.9-705.1 mm)

ATX
LEFT = 16.34-16.74 (415.0-425.2 mm)
RIGHT = 27.28-27.68 (692.9-703.1 mm)

Courtesy of General Motors Corp.

NOTE: On cross-groove type axle shaft CV joints, the inner CV joints are not to be disassembled. Replace as a complete assembly.

Disassembly (Cross-Groove Type Drive Axle Outer CV Joints)

1) Remove axle shaft from vehicle. See REMOVAL under AXLE SHAFTS in this article. Place axle shaft in vise with protected jaws. Cut boot clamps and remove clamps. Slide boot away from CV joint assembly.

2) Remove snap ring retaining CV joint to axle shaft. See Fig. 9. Pull CV joint and housing assembly off axle shaft. Remove boot if replacing. Using a brass drift and hammer, gently tap on cage until tilted enough to remove first ball.

3) Repeat procedure for remaining balls. Pivot cage and inner race. Align cage windows with lands of outer race. See Fig. 9. Remove inner race and cage. Rotate inner race and align land with cage window. Remove inner race.

4) Remove deflector ring from end of stub shaft with hammer and brass drift (steel deflector ring). Remove rubber deflector ring by stretching ring out of its groove.

Reassembly

1) Apply a light coat of specified grease on all mating surfaces. Install small boot clamp and boot on axle shaft. To reassemble inner race, cage and balls, reverse disassembly procedure. See Fig. 9. Ensure retaining ring side of inner race faces axle shaft.

2) Pack CV joint with grease supplied in kit. Place remaining grease evenly in boot. Install new retaining ring in CV joint. Slide CV joint assembly onto axle

GENERAL MOTORS (Cont.)

Fig. 9: Disassembly of Outer CV Joint

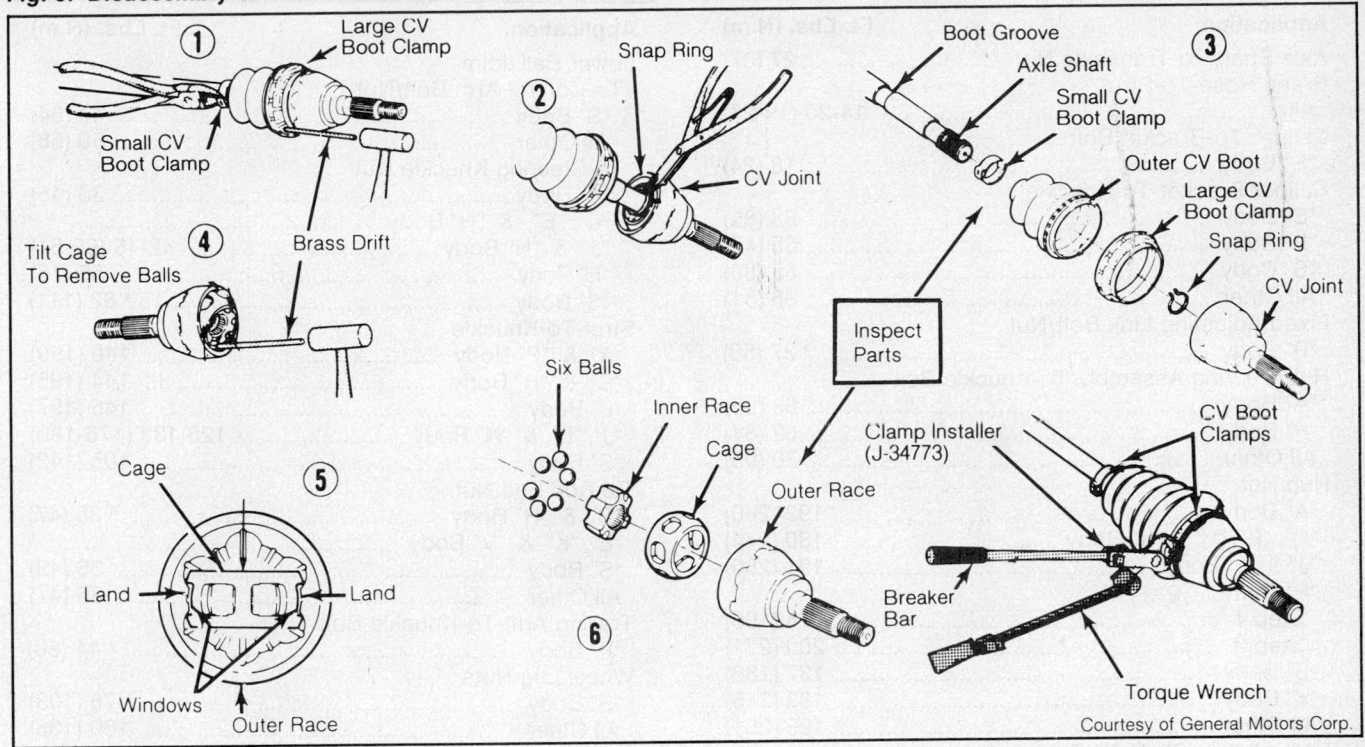

Courtesy of General Motors Corp.

shaft. Ensure retaining ring seats in groove on axle shaft. Position large end of boot over housing and install boot clamp.

3) Use clamp installer and torque wrench and install small boot clamp. Tighten small boot clamp to 100 ft. lbs. (130 N.m). Use clamp installer and torque wrench and tighten large boot clamp to 130 ft. lbs. (176 N.m).

4) Install new steel deflector ring with flange towards CV joint (if equipped). *See Fig. 10.* On rubber deflector rings, flange is toward hub assembly. Install rubber deflector ring by stretching ring over housing and seating in groove. To complete reassembly, reverse removal procedure.

Intermediate Shaft
1) Remove axle shaft from vehicle. See REMOVAL under AXLE SHAFTS in this article. Remove intermediate shaft bracket retaining bolts/nuts. On some models, the bracket may be removed from intermediate shaft. On other models, the bracket is removed with intermediate shaft assembly.

2) On some models the intermediate shaft is bolted to transaxle. On other models, the intermediate shaft is retainined in transaxle by the bracket near axle

Fig. 10: Installing Steel Deflector Ring

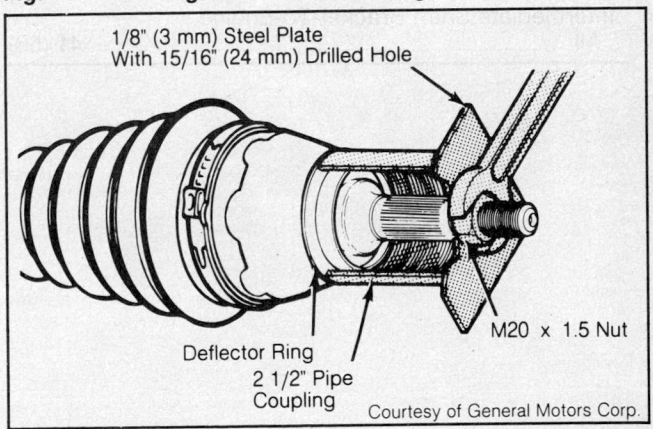

Courtesy of General Motors Corp.

shaft. Remove bolts retaining intermediate shaft to transaxle (if equipped) On all models, pull intermediate shaft out of transaxle.

NOTE: Further information on intermediate shaft is not available from factory.

TIGHTENING SPECIFICATIONS

Application	Ft. Lbs. (N.m)
Axle Shaft-To-Transaxle Nut	27 (37)
Brake Hose-To-Strut	
All	14-20 (19-27)
Caliper-To-Bracket Bolt	
"S" Body	18 (24)
Caliper Bracket-To-Knuckle	
"E" Body	63 (85)
"P" Body	35 (47)
"S" Body	65 (88)
All Other	38 (51)
Fixed Adjusting Link Bolt/Nut	
"P" Body	[1] 37 (50)
Hub/Bearing Assembly-To-Knuckle Bolt	
"A" Body	63 (85)
"P" Body	62 (84)
All Other	70 (95)
Hub Nut	
"A" Body	192 (260)
"C", "E", "H" & "K" Body	180 (244)
"J" & "L" Body	191 (260)
"P" Body	
Step 1	74 (100)
Step 2	200 (271)
"S" Body	137 (186)
"V" Body	183 (245)
All Other	185 (251)
Intermediate Shaft-To-Transaxle	
All	18 (24)
Intermediate Shaft Bracket-To-Engine	
All	41 (56)

TIGHTENING SPECIFICATIONS (Cont.)

Application	Ft. Lbs. (N.m)
Lower Ball Joint-	
To-Control Arm Bolt/Nut	
"S" Body	47 (64)
All Other	50 (68)
To-Steering Knuckle Nut	
"A" Body	33 (45)
"C", "E", & "H" Body	[2] [3]
"J" & "N" Body	42-45 (60-61)
"L" Body	55 (75)
"S" Body	[4] 82 (111)
Strut-To-Knuckle	
"A" & "P" Body	140 (190)
"C" & "H" Body	144 (195)
"E" Body	145 (197)
"J", "L" & "N" Body	129-133 (175-180)
"S" Body	105 (142)
Tie Rod End Nut	
"C" & "H" Body	[5] 35 (47)
"E", "K" & "V" Body	[6]
"S" Body	36 (49)
All Other	35 (47)
Trailing Arm-To-Knuckle Bolt	
"P" Body	[1] 44 (60)
Wheel Lug Nuts	
"S" Body	76 (103)
All Other	100 (136)

[1] – Tighten an additional 90 degrees.

[2] – Tighten to 88 INCH lbs. (10 N.m), then turn nut additional 120 degrees. Minumum torque of 37 ft. lbs. (50 N.m) must be obtained.

[3] – On replacement ball joint, tighten nut to 81 ft. lbs. (110 N.m) at initial installation only.

[4] – Install OLD nut and tighten to 14 ft. lbs. (19 N.m). Remove old nut and install a NEW nut. Tighten nut to specifications.

[5] – Maximum 52 ft. lbs. (71 N.m) to align cotter key.

[6] – Tighten to 88 INCH lbs. (10 N.m), then turn nut an additional 1/3 turn. Minimum torque of 33 ft. lbs. (45 N.m) must be obtained.

Section 9

BRAKES

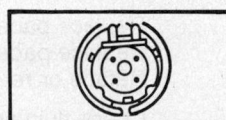

CONTENTS

NOTE: **ALSO SEE GENERAL INDEX.**

Brakes

BRAKE SYSTEM TROUBLE SHOOTING

CONDITION	POSSIBLE CAUSE	CORRECTION
Brakes Pull Left or Right	Incorrect tire pressure	Inflate tires to proper pressure
	Front end out of alignment	See WHEEL ALIGNMENT
	Mismatched tires	Check tires sizes
	Restricted brake lines or hoses	Check hose routing
	Loose or malfunctioning caliper	See DISC BRAKES
	Bent shoe or oily linings	See DRUM BRAKES
	Malfunctioning rear brakes	See DRUM or DISC BRAKES
	Loose suspension parts	See SUSPENSION
Noises Without Brakes Applied	Front linings worn out	Replace linings
	Dust or oil on drums or rotors	See DRUM or DISC BRAKES
Noises with Brakes Applied	Insulator on outboard shoe damaged	See DISC BRAKES
	Incorrect pads or linings	Replace pads or linings
Brake Rough, Chatters or Pulsates	Excessive lateral runout	Check rotor runout
	Parallelism not to specifications	Reface or replace rotor
	Wheel bearings not adjusted	See SUSPENSION
	Rear drums out-of-round	Reface or replace drums
	Disc pad reversed, steel against rotor	Remove and reinstall pad
Excessive Pedal Effort	Malfunctioning power unit	See POWER BRAKES
	Partial system failure	Check fluid and pipes
	Worn disc pad or lining	Replace pad or lining
	Caliper piston stuck or sluggish	See DISC BRAKES
	Master cylinder piston stuck	See MASTER CYLINDERS
	Brake fade due to incorrect pads or linings	Replace pads or linings
	Linings or pads glazed	Replace pads or linings
	Worn drums	Reface or replace drums
Excessive Pedal Travel	Partial brake system failure	Check fluid and pipes
	Insufficient fluid in master cylinder	See MASTER CYLINDERS
	Air trapped in system	See BLEEDING
	Rear brakes not adjusted	See Adjustment in DRUM BRAKES
	Bent shoe or lining	See DRUM BRAKES
	Plugged master cylinder cap	See MASTER CYLINDER
	Improper brake fluid	Replace brake fluid
Pedal Travel Decreasing	Compensating port plugged	See MASTER CYLINDERS
	Swollen cup in master cylinder	See MASTER CYLINDERS
	Master cylinder piston not returning	See MASTER CYLINDERS
	Weak shoe retracting springs	See DRUM BRAKES
	Wheel cylinder piston sticking	See DRUM BRAKES
Dragging Brakes	Master cylinder pistons not returning	See MASTER CYLINDERS
	Restricted brake lines or hoses	Check line routing
	Incorrect parking brake adjustment	See DRUM BRAKES
	Parking brake cables frozen	See DRUM BRAKES
	Incorrect installation of inboard disc pad	Remove and replace correctly
	Power booster output rod too long	See POWER BRAKE UNITS
	Brake pedal not returning freely	See DISC or DRUM BRAKES
Brakes Grab or Uneven Braking Action	Malfunction of combination valve	See CONTROL VALVES
	Malfunction of power brake unit	See POWER BRAKE UNITS
	Binding brake pedal	See DISC or DRUM BRAKES
Pulsation or Roughness	Uneven pad wear caused by caliper	See DISC BRAKES
	Uneven rotor wear	See DISC BRAKES
	Drums out-of-round	Reface or replace drums

Brake Servicing

HYDRAULIC BRAKE BLEEDING

DESCRIPTION

Hydraulic system bleeding is necessary any time air has been introduced into system. Bleed brakes at all 4 wheels if master cylinder lines have been disconnected or master cylinder has run dry. Bleeding can be accomplished by using pressure bleeding equipment or by manually pumping brake pedal and using a clear bleeder hose.

SERVICING

METERING VALVE

1) On disc brake equipped vehicles, the metering section of combination valve must be held open before pressure bleeding.

2) Hold metering valve open while pressure bleeding front brakes. To loosen front mounting bolt and install pressure bleeding tool on combination valve, valve stem should be fully extended or depressed.

NOTE: Never reintroduce brake fluid that has been drained from hydraulic brake system or that has been allowed to stand in an open container for an extended period of time. Also, do not use fluid that contains a petroleum base. Petroleum based fluids will cause swelling and distortion of rubber parts in hydraulic system.

Fig. 1: Combination Valve (Manual Override)

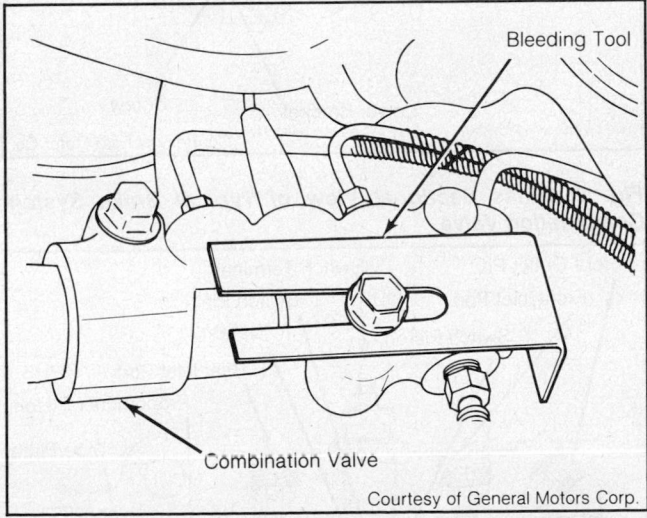

Bleeding Tool

Combination Valve

Courtesy of General Motors Corp.

BENCH BLEEDING MASTER CYLINDER

NOTE: Bleed tubes must have a residual pressure check valve installed to keep tubes from siphoning brake fluid.

1) Clamp master cylinder in vise by mounting flange. Install and tighten threaded end of bleed tubes in outlet ports of master cylinder with oposite end of bleeder tube in reservoirs. Fill reservoirs with clean brake fluid so that bleed tube ends are submerged in brake fluid.

2) Slowly compress and release piston assemblies until bubbles cease to appear in brake fluid. Remove tubes and plug master cylinder outlets to keep fluid from draining.

MANUAL BLEEDING

NOTE: Ensure that fluid level in master cylinder is adequate at all times during bleeding procedure.

1) Fill master cylinder with clean brake fluid. Install bleeder hose to wheel assembly being serviced. Submerge other end of hose in clean glass jar partially filled with clean brake fluid.

2) Depress brake pedal slowly through its full travel and hold. Open bleed screw 3/4-1 turn. Close bleed screw. Release brake pedal. Repeat procedure until brake fluid shows no signs of air bubbles.

PRESSURE BLEEDING

1) To prevent dirt from falling into reservoir, clean master cylinder and cover/diaphram assembly, With pressure tank at least 1/3 full, connect to master cylinder using adapters.

2) Install bleeder hose to wheel assembly being serviced. Submerge other end of hose in clean glass jar partially filled with clean brake fluid.

3) Open release valve on pressure bleeder. Open bleed screw 3/4-1 turn. Close bleed screw when brake fluid is clear and free of bubbles. Bleed remaining wheel assemblies in sequence and in same manner. Remove pressure bleeding tool.

BLEEDING SEQUENCE

If vehicle is equipped with power brakes, exhaust vacuum reserve from power unit by depressing brake pedal several times. Bleed master cylinder before bleeding wheel assemblies. Generally, system is bled starting with wheel assembly furthest from master cylinder and working to wheel assembly closest to master cylinder.

BLEEDING PRESSURES

Application	Psi (kg/cm²)
Chrysler Motors	35 (2.46)
Eagle Premier	15-20 (1.05-1.40)
Ford Motor Co.	10-30 (.70-2.10)
General Motors	20-25 (1.40-1.75)

Brake Systems

HYDRAULIC SYSTEM CONTROL VALVES

DESCRIPTION

All vehicles have some type of hydraulic system control valve or switch incorporated in the brake system. Unit is usually mounted on left front fender splash shield or frame side rail beneath master cylinder.

Valve is connected in-line with master cylinder, wheel cylinders and calipers. Combination disc/drum systems use valves combining warning switch with metering valve and proportioning valve. Vehicles that use 4-wheel disc brakes use a proportioning valve and differential warning switch.

DIFFERENTIAL WARNING SWITCH

Warning switch is used to alert vehicle operator that one of the hydraulic systems has failed. When hydraulic pressure is equal in both front and rear systems, switch piston remains centered and does not contact terminal in switch cylinder bore.

Switch includes a centering spring on each side of piston to hold piston in centered position. If pressure falls in one of the systems, hydraulic pressure moves piston toward inoperative side. Shoulder of piston then contacts switch terminal to provide a ground from warning lamp circuit and lights warning lamp.

PROPORTIONING VALVE

Valve operates by restricting, at a given ratio, hydraulic pressure to rear brakes when system pressure reaches a certain point. This improves front-to-rear brake balance at high deceleration, when a percentage of rear weight is transferred to front wheels. Valve reduces rear brake pressure, and delays rear wheel skid. On light pedal applicatons, valve allows full hydraulic pressure to rear brakes.

HEIGHT SENSING PROPORTIONING VALVE

Sable/Taurus Sedan

To provide improved brake performance for the Sable/Taurus sedan, a height sensing brake proportioning valve is incorporated into the brake system. This valve takes the place of fixed ratio brake proportioning valves used on Station Wagon models. This valve provides more brake pressure to rear brakes with increased rear vehicle weight and less brake pressure with decreased rear weight. This is accomplished by reaction of the valve to any rear suspension variations as a result of changing vehicle load.

METERING VALVE

Valve holds off hydraulic pressure to front disc brakes to allow rear drum brake shoes to overcome return spring pressure and begin to contact drums.

This feature helps prevent locking front brakes on slippery or icy surfaces under light braking conditions. Valve has no effect on front brake pressure during hard braking conditions.

TESTING

ELECTRICAL CIRCUIT

Disconnect wire from switch terminal and ground wire. Turn ignition switch to "ON" position. Warning light should come on. If lamp does not light, bulb is defective, or wiring circuit is defective. Replace bulb or wiring as necessary. When light comes on, turn off ignition and reconnect wire to switch.

Fig. 1: Cross Sectional View of Height Sensing Brake Proportioning Valve Assembly

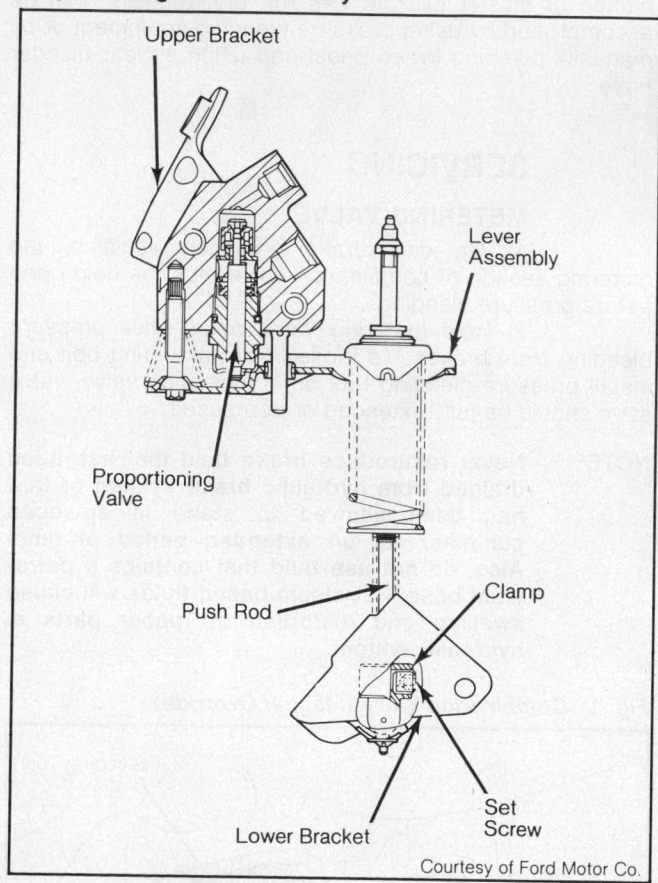

Upper Bracket

Lever Assembly

Proportioning Valve

Push Rod

Clamp

Set Screw

Lower Bracket

Courtesy of Ford Motor Co.

Fig. 2: Cross Sectional View of Typical Brake System Combination Valve

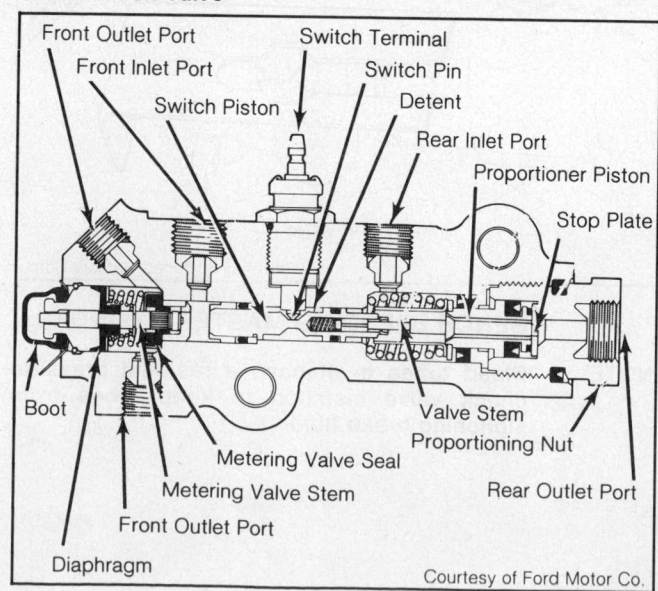

Front Outlet Port

Front Inlet Port

Switch Piston

Switch Terminal

Switch Pin

Detent

Rear Inlet Port

Proportioner Piston

Stop Plate

Valve Stem

Proportioning Nut

Rear Outlet Port

Metering Valve Seal

Metering Valve Stem

Front Outlet Port

Boot

Diaphragm

Courtesy of Ford Motor Co.

HYDRAULIC SYSTEM CONTROL VALVES (Cont.)

WARNING LIGHT SWITCH SELECTION

Attach bleeder hose to either rear brake and immerse other end of hose in container with brake fluid. Turn ignition switch to "ON" position, open bleeder screw while pressure is applied to brake pedal. Warning lamp should light. Close bleeder screw before pressure is released from pedal. Reapply pedal pressure (moderate to heavy).

Light should go out. Repeat test on front system. Results should be same. Turn ignition off. If lamp does not light on either system, but electrical system checked good, warning light switch part of valve is defective.

ADJUSTMENTS

Most hydraulic system switches and valves are non-adjustable and non-serviceable with the exception of Sable/Taurus Sedan. On non-serviceable systems, if any part of the valve is found to be defective, entire unit must be replaced.

HEIGHT SENSING BRAKE PROPORTIONING VALVE

Sable/Taurus Sedan

1) Place vehicle on a drive-on type hoist or alignment machine so that vehicle is supported on its wheels at curb height. Measure distance "A" between operating rod upper nut and retainer valve lever. *See Fig. 3.*

2) The distance for a normal setting should be .64 ± .012 (16.3 mm ± .3 mm). If distance is outside these settings, the rear height sensor brake proportioning valve should be adjusted. Proceed to step **3)**.

3) Ensure that suspension is at curb height. To decrease pressure at rear brakes, loosen set screw in adjusting sleeve.

NOTE: Do not change positon of upper nut on valve operating rod.

4) Move adjusting sleeve UP toward valve body on operating rod .04" (1 mm) for each 60 psi (4.2 kg/cm²) pressure decrease. Tighten set screw in adjusting sleeve in desired position.

5) To increase pressure at rear brakes, loosen set screw in adjusting sleeve. Move adjusting sleeve DOWN away from valve body on operating rod .04" (1 mm) for each 60 psi (4.2 kg/cm²) pressure increase. Tighten set screw in desired position.

Fig. 3: Brake Pressure Control Valve Adjustment

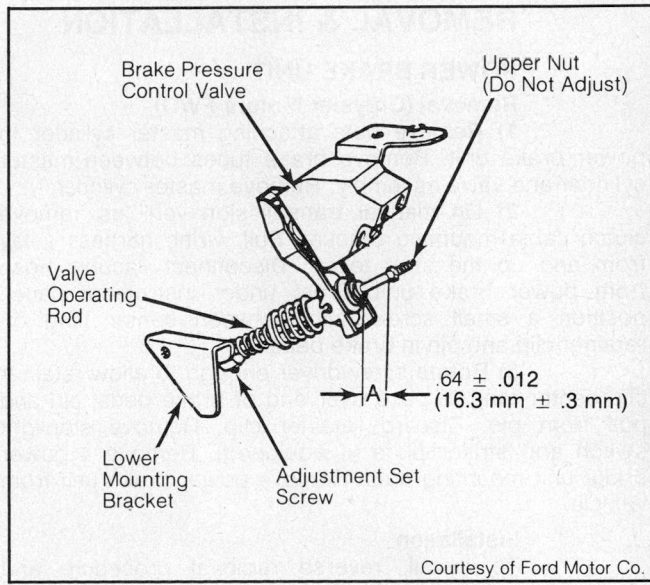

Courtesy of Ford Motor Co.

Power Brake Units
CHRYSLER MOTORS & FORD MOTOR CO.
SINGLE DIAPHRAGM

Chrysler Motors, Ford Motor Co.

DESCRIPTION

The power brake booster uses intake manifold vacuum and atmospheric pressure to provide its power. Vacuum power unit contains power piston assembly, which houses control valve, reaction mechanism and return spring. Control valve consists of air valve, floating control valve assembly and push rod. Reaction mechanism consists of reaction plate and levers. A vacuum check valve is mounted in front housing for connection to vacuum source.

REMOVAL & INSTALLATION

POWER BRAKE UNIT

Removal (Chrysler Motors FWD)

1) Remove nuts attaching master cylinder to power brake unit. Remove brake tubes between master cylinder and valve assembly. Remove master cylinder.

2) On manual transmission vehicles, remove clutch cable mounting bracket. Pull wiring harness away from and up the strut tower. Disconnect vacuum hose from power brake unit. From under instrument panel, position a small screwdriver between center tang on retainer clip and pin in brake pedal.

3) Rotate screwdriver enough to allow retainer clip center tang to pass over end of brake pedal pin and pull from pin. Discard retainer clip. Remove stoplight switch and striker plate (if equipped). Remove 4 power brake unit mounting nuts. Remove power brake unit from vehicle.

Installation

To install, reverse removal procedure and bleed brakes. See HYDRAULIC BRAKE BLEEDING in this section.

Removal (Chrysler Motors RWD)

1) Remove nuts attaching master cylinder to power brake unit. Carefully slide master cylinder off mounting studs and allow to rest against fender shield. Disconnect vacuum hose from power brake.

2) From under dash panel, position a small screwdriver between center tang on retainer clip and pin in brake pedal. Rotate screwdriver enough to allow retainer clip center tang to pass over end of brake pedal pin and pull retainer clip from pin. Discard retainer clip.

3) Remove lower pivot retaining bolt and nut. Remove 4 power brake unit attaching nuts. Rotate linkage as necessary and remove power brake unit from vehicle. Remove pivot bushing and sleeve for reuse.

Installation

To install, reverse removal procedure.

Removal (Ford Motor Co. Escort, Tempo & Topaz)

1) Disconnect battery and remove tubes from primary and secondary outlet ports of master cylinder. Remove 2 nuts attaching master cylinder to brake booster assembly and remove master cylinder.

2) Under dash, remove stoplight switch connector from switch. Remove push rod retainer and outer nylon washer from pedal pin. Slide stoplight switch along brake pedal pin just far enough for outer hole to clear pin. Remove switch by sliding it upward. Avoid damaging switch during removal.

3) Remove booster-to-dash panel attaching nuts. Slide booster push rod and push rod bushing off brake pedal pin. Inside engine compartment, disconnect manifold vacuum hose from booster check valve. Move booster forward until booster studs clear dash panel and remove booster.

Installation

To install, reverse removal procedure and bleed brakes. See HYDRAULIC BRAKE BLEEDING in this section.

Removal (Ford Motor Co. Taurus & Sable)

1) Disconnect battery ground cable and remove brake tubes from primary and secondary outlet ports of master cylinder. Disconnect vacuum hose from booster. Disconnect warning light.

2) Remove master cylinder attaching nuts and remove master cylinder.

3) Under dash, remove stoplight switch connector and push rod retaining clip. Slide stoplight switch and push rod off brake pedal pin.

4) Remove booster-to-firewall nuts and cowl intrusion bolt. Slide booster forward.

5) Under hood, remove manifold vacuum fitting at cowl. Remove transmission shift cable and bracket. Remove booster.

Installation

To install, reverse removal procedure and bleed brakes. See HYDRAULIC BRAKE BLEEDING in this section.

Removal (Ford Motor Co. Crown Victoria, Grand Marquis & Town Car)

1) Disconnect battery and remove master cylinder from booster. Set it aside without disturbing hydraulic lines. It is not necessary to disconnect brake lines, but use care to avoid kinking them. Disconnect manifold vacuum hose from booster check valve.

2) Under dash, remove stoplight switch connector. Remove switch retaining pin. Slide stoplight switch off brake pedal pin just far enough for outer plate of stoplight switch to clear pin, then remove switch from pin. Avoid damaging switch during removal.

3) Remove booster-to-dash panel attaching nuts. Slide booster push rod, nylon washers, and bushing off brake pedal pin. Remove booster assembly from dash panel by sliding push rod out through engine side of dash panel.

Installation

To install, reverse removal procedure.

Removal (Ford Motor Co. Cougar, Mustang & Thunderbird with 3.8L or 5.0L Engine)

1) Disconnect battery and remove air cleaner. Disconnect manifold vacuum hose from booster check valve. Remove brake lines from primary and secondary outlet ports of master cylinder. Remove 2 nuts attaching master cylinder to brake booster assembly. Remove master cylinder.

2) Under dash, remove stoplight switch wiring connector from switch. Remove hairpin retainer and outer nylon washer from pedal pin. Slide stoplight switch off brake pedal pin just far enough for outer arm to clear pin. Remove switch. Avoid damaging switch during removal.

3) Remove booster-to-dash panel attaching nuts. On vehicles equipped with speed control, remove and set aside control amplifier which is mounted to lower outboard booster stud. Slide booster push rod, bushing, and inner nylon washer off brake pedal pin.

CHRYSLER MOTORS & FORD MOTOR CO.
SINGLE DIAPHRAGM (Cont.)

4) Under hood, move booster forward until booster studs clear dash panel. Rotate front of booster inward (toward engine) and remove booster by raising up until clear.

Installation

To install, reverse removal procedure and bleed brakes. See HYDRAULIC BRAKE BLEEDING in this section.

Removal (Ford Motor Co. Cougar, Mustang & Thunderbird with 2.3L Engine)

1) Disconnect battery and remove air cleaner. Disconnect accelerator cable from throttle body. Remove screw that secures accelerator cable to accelerator shaft bracket, and remove cable from bracket.

2) Remove 2 screws that secure accelerator shaft bracket to manifold, and rotate bracket toward engine. Remove RPO horn on all models except Cougar and Thunderbird. Disconnect 2 manifold injector connectors located near oil dipstick retaining bracket.

CAUTION: The fuel system is under pressure and must be bled prior to disconnecting quick connect fittings.

Fig. 1: Ford Motor Co. Brake Push Rod Gauge

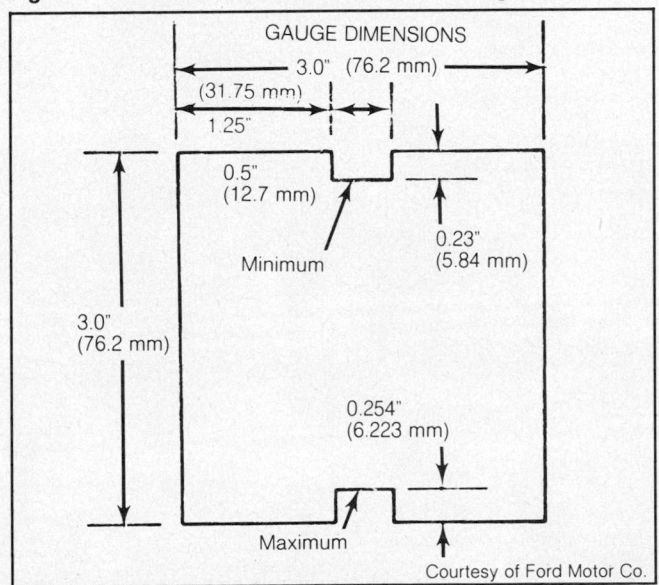

Use this gauge for Escort, Sable, Taurus, Tempo and Topaz.

3) Disconnect 2 fuel hoses to fuel supply manifold assembly. Remove 3 bolts holding oil dipstick bracket to upper intake manifold. Remove dipstick and bracket. Remove windshield wiper motor.

4) Remove vacuum hoses directly over brake booster at dash panel vacuum "T". Remove bolt holding clutch cable stand and move bracket to side rail at fender inner panel. If equipped with speed control, move speed control cable aside to clear booster.

5) Disconnect manifold vacuum hose from booster check valve. Remove brake lines from primary and secondary outlet ports of master cylinder. Remove 2 nuts attaching master cylinder to brake booster assembly, and remove master cylinder.

6) Under dash, remove stoplight switch wiring connector from switch. Remove hairpin retainer and outer nylon washer from pedal pin. Slide stoplight switch off

Fig. 2: Ford Motor Co. Brake Push Rod Gauge

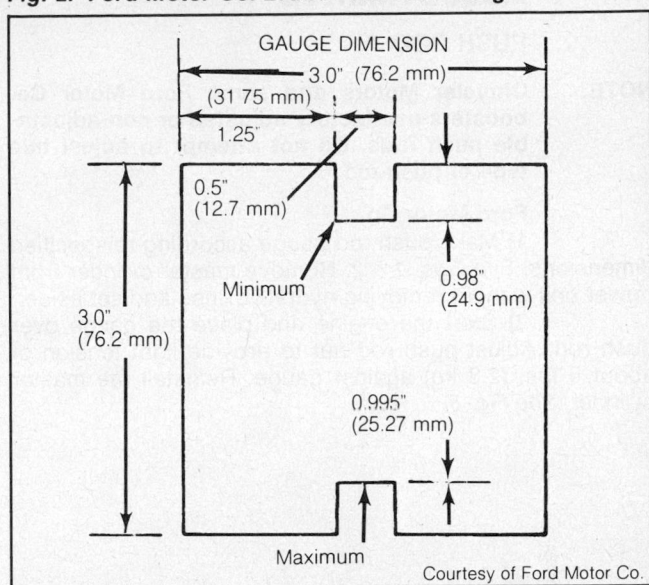

Use this gauge for Thunderbird/Cougar, Mustang, Town Car, Crown Victoria and Grand Marquis.

Fig. 3: Measuring Brake Push Rod Height

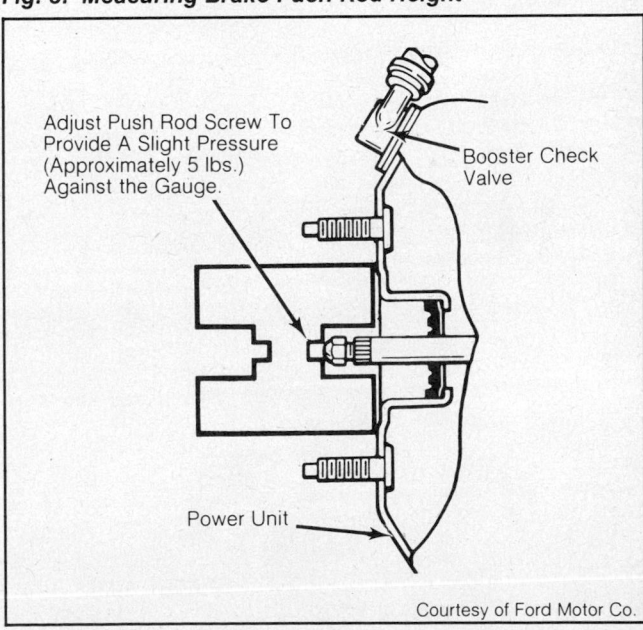

brake pedal pin just far enough for outer arm to clear pin. Remove switch. Be careful not to damage switch during removal. Remove booster-to-dash panel attaching nuts.

7) On vehicles equipped with speed control, remove and set aside control amplifier which is mounted to lower outboard booster stud. Slide booster push rod, bushing, and inner nylon washer off brake pedal pin.

8) Under hood, move booster forward until booster studs clear dash panel. Rotate front of booster inward (toward engine) and remove booster by raising it up until clear.

Installation

To install, bleed brakes and reverse removal procedure. See HYDRAULIC BRAKE BLEEDING in this section.

Power Brake Units
CHRYSLER MOTORS & FORD MOTOR CO.
SINGLE DIAPHRAGM (Cont.)

ADJUSTMENTS

PUSH ROD

NOTE: **Chrysler Motors and some Ford Motor Co. boosters use factory adjusted or non-adjustable push rods. Do not attempt to adjust this type of push rod.**

Ford Motor Co.

1) Make push rod gauge according to specified dimensions. *See Figs. 1 & 2.* Remove master cylinder from power unit without removing hydraulic lines and set aside.

2) Start the engine and place the gauge over push rod. Adjust push rod nut to provide light tension of about 5 lbs. (2.3 kg) against gauge. Reinstall the master cylinder. *See Fig. 3.*

3) With engine idling and master cylinder reservoir cover removed, observe fluid surface when brake pedal is applied rapidly. Movement of fluid surface in forward reservoir indicates properly adjusted push rod. If fluid surface movement did not occur, push rod is adjusted too long and procedure must be repeated to prevent brake drag.

TIGHTENING SPECIFICATION

Application	Ft. Lbs. (N.m)
All Models	
Booster-to-Dash	12-26 (16-35)
Master Cylinder-to-Booster	13-25 (18-34)
Brake Tube-to-Master Cylinder	10-19 (14-26)
Cowl Intrusion Bolt	13-25 (18-34)

Power Brake Units

CORVETTE SINGLE DIAPHRAGM

DESCRIPTION

This booster is a single diaphragm vacuum suspended unit. In a normal operating mode, with the service brakes in the released position, the booster has vacuum on both sides of its diaphragm.

When the brakes are applied, air at atmospheric pressure is admitted to the back side of the diaphragm to provide power assist. Tie rods extend through the booster and are attached to the cowl on one end and the master cylinder on the other.

REMOVAL & INSTALLATION

POWER BRAKE UNIT

Removal

1) Remove nuts attaching master cylinder to booster tie rods and remove master cylinder. Disconnect vacuum hose from vacuum check valve.

2) Disconnect push rod (part of valve assembly) from brake pedal. Remove nuts from booster tie rods and remove booster.

Installation

1) Attach booster to cowl and torque nuts on booster tie rods to 15 ft. lbs. (21 N.m). Attach push rod (part of valve assembly) to brake pedal.

2) Connect vacuum hose to vacuum check valve. Attach master cylinder and torque nuts to booster tie rods to 13 ft. lbs. (18 N.m).

OVERHAUL

POWER BRAKE UNIT

CAUTION: Failure to hold 2 shell halves together during overhaul will result in a shell half flying off due to high spring pressure.

Disassembly

1) Remove vacuum check valve. Unscrew nuts approximately 1/2" back on tie rods, but do not remove. If shell halves stick together, pry them apart with a thin blade screwdriver using extreme care not to chip or otherwise damage either shell.

2) When bond between shells is broken, return spring will force front shell out against nuts. Then, holding shells together, completely remove nuts and coned springs. Remove front shell and return spring.

3) Remove grommet and front seal from front shell. Remove boot, tie rods and gasket from rear shell. Loosen bead of diaphragm from rear shell. Remove ends of tie rod boots from posts in rear shell and remove vacuum piston.

4) Remove diaphragm and tie rod boots from vacuum piston. Remove rear seal and washers on tie rod posts from rear shell. Remove output rod retainer and reaction disc.

5) Remove stop plate from vacuum piston by pressing on open end of stop plate and pulling on closed end. Remove valve assembly from vacuum piston.

NOTE: Use all components included in repair kits to service this booster. Lubricate parts, where indicated, with silicone grease. The torque values specified are for dry, unlubricated fasteners. If any hydraulic component is removed or brake line disconnected, bleed all air from the brake system.

Reassembly

1) Lubricate outside diameter of new valve assembly and fit it into vacuum piston. Retain valve assembly by installing stop plate. Make sure stop plate is fully installed to locked position. Lubricate reaction disc and install in vacuum piston.

2) Fit new tie rod boots into holes in vacuum piston. Liberally coat insides of these boots with silicone grease. Lubricate outside diameter lip on diaphragm and fit diaphragm into vacuum piston.

Fig. 1: Proper Installation of Coned Spring

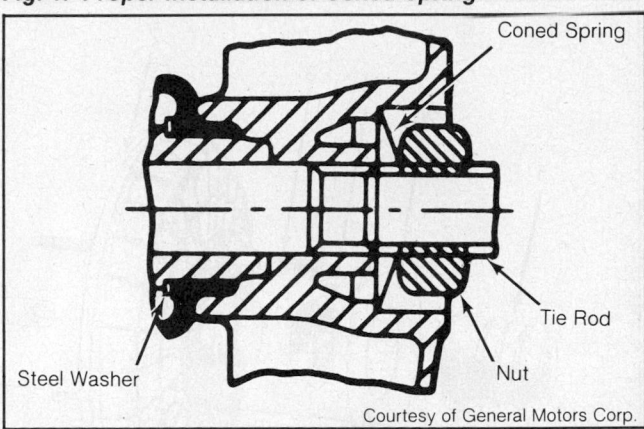

Coned Spring
Tie Rod
Nut
Steel Washer

Courtesy of General Motors Corp.

3) Press new rear seal into rear shell and place washers on tie rod posts. Lubricate inside diameter of rear seal. Install vacuum piston assembly into rear shell. Push tie rod boots over rear shell posts and locate diaphragm bead around rear shell.

Fig. 2: Assembling Shell Halves

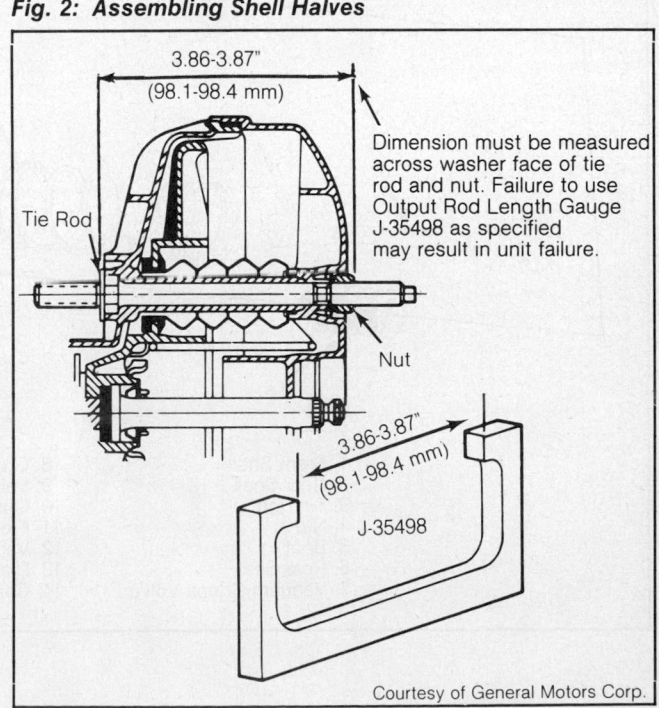

3.86-3.87"
(98.1-98.4 mm)

Dimension must be measured across washer face of tie rod and nut. Failure to use Output Rod Length Gauge J-35498 as specified may result in unit failure.

Tie Rod

Nut

3.86-3.87"
(98.1-98.4 mm)

J-35498

Courtesy of General Motors Corp.

Power Brake Units

CORVETTE SINGLE DIAPHRAGM (Cont.)

4) Install tie rods in rear shell. Position rear shell with parts assembled thus far in fixture (J-23456-51A). Install output rod and new retainer in vacuum piston. Lubricate output rod.

CAUTION: Do not attempt to adjust domed screw on output rod. This has been correctly set at the factory and should not be disturbed.

5) Fit new front seal in front shell, with metal face of seal facing out. Push seal into bottom. Locate return spring in mouth of vacuum piston. Install front shell on rear shell and other assembled parts using care not to unseat bead of diaphragm.

6) Press shells together by hand and install coned springs and nuts. Make sure coned springs are positioned correctly. *See Fig. 1.* Uniformly tighten nuts until shells are .20" (5 mm) apart. Check that diaphragm is properly seated over rim of rear shell.

7) Tighten nuts to obtain correct dimension using Output Rod Length Gauge (J-35498). *See Fig. 2.* This dimension is measured across washer face on tie rod and nut, not across shell surfaces.

8) Lubricate grommet and vacuum check valve and install in front shell. Install gasket and boot onto rear shell. Be sure boot locates over flange on rear seal.

Fig. 3: *Exploded View of Corvette Single Diaphragm Power Brake Unit*

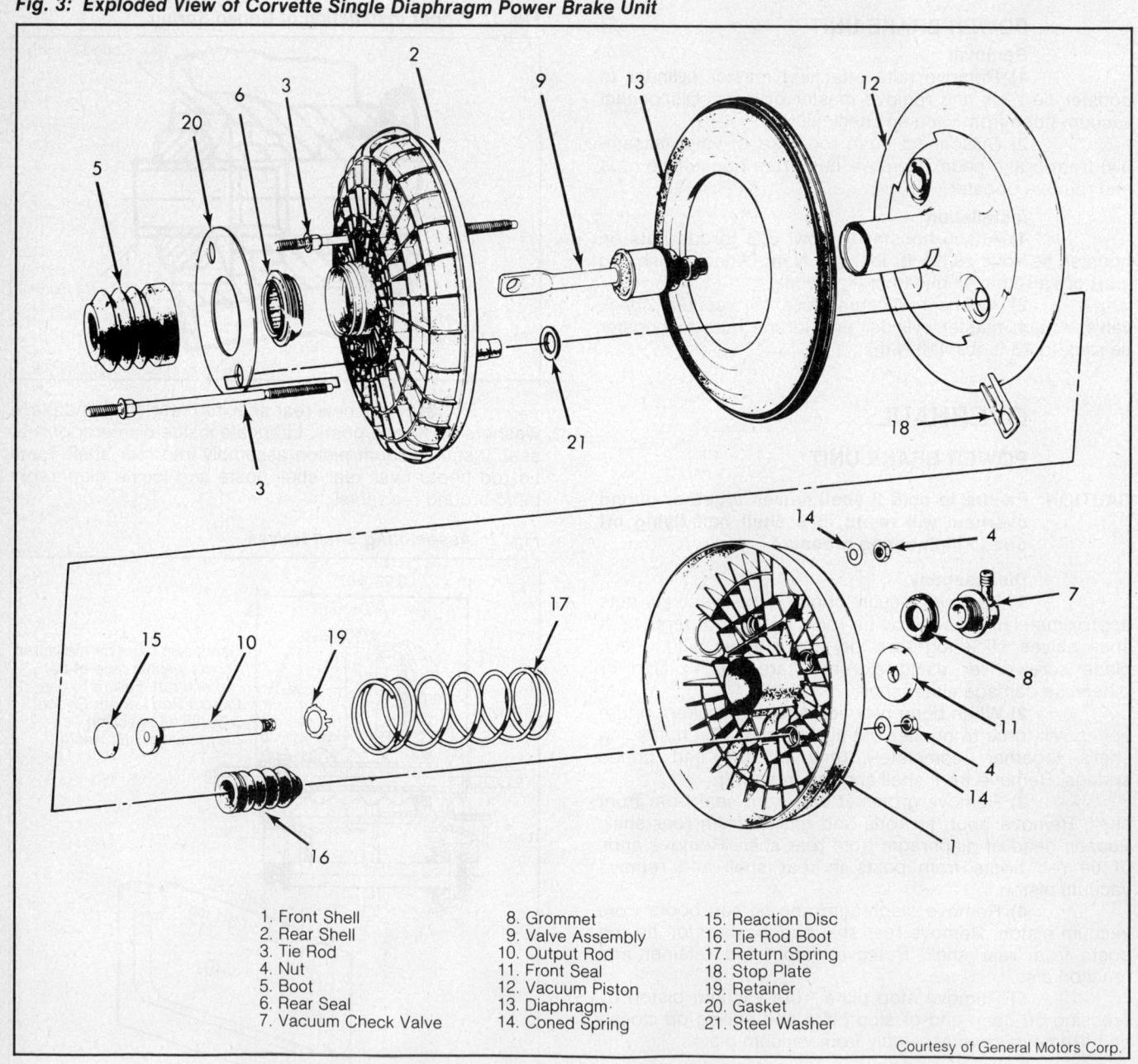

1. Front Shell	8. Grommet	15. Reaction Disc
2. Rear Shell	9. Valve Assembly	16. Tie Rod Boot
3. Tie Rod	10. Output Rod	17. Return Spring
4. Nut	11. Front Seal	18. Stop Plate
5. Boot	12. Vacuum Piston	19. Retainer
6. Rear Seal	13. Diaphragm	20. Gasket
7. Vacuum Check Valve	14. Coned Spring	21. Steel Washer

Power Brake Units

DELCO-MORAINE TANDEM DIAPHRAGM

**Buick, Cadillac, Chevrolet,
Oldsmobile, Pontiac**

DESCRIPTION

Unit is mounted on firewall and connected directly to brake pedal. A combination of vacuum and atmospheric pressure is used to provide power assist. Power cylinder houses power piston assembly, which contains primary and secondary diaphragms, pistons, floating control valve, reaction piston and disc.

REMOVAL & INSTALLATION

POWER BRAKE UNIT

Removal

1) Without disconnecting hydraulic lines, remove master cylinder from power unit and position to one side. On models equipped with pipe distribution and switch mounting bolt, remove bolt before moving master cylinder away from power unit.

CAUTION: Do not bend or kink hydraulic lines. DO NOT force push rod to the side when disconnecting.

2) Disconnect vacuum hose from check valve on front of power unit. Disconnect push rod from brake pedal. Remove nuts mounting power unit to firewall. Remove power unit.

Installation

To install, reverse removal procedure. Check stoplight and cruise control (if equipped) switch adjustments.

OVERHAUL

POWER BRAKE UNIT

Disassembly

1) Remove push rod boot, silencer, front housing seal, grommet and vacuum check valve.

2) Scribe a mark on front and rear housings for reassembly reference. Attach front housing to Holding Fixture (J-23456). Press down on holding tool and turn counterclockwise to unlock housings.

3) Remove power piston group, power piston return spring, and power piston bearing. Remove piston rod, reaction retainer and power head silencer.

4) Grasp assembly at outside edge of divider and diaphragms. Hold with push rod down against a hard surface. Use a slight force or impact to dislodge diaphragm retainer.

5) Remove primary diaphragm, primary support plate, secondary power piston bearing, housing divider, secondary support plate and diaphragm, and power piston assembly.

6) Remove reaction body retaining snap ring. Remove reaction body. Remove reaction disc and piston from reaction body. Remove air valve spring and reaction bumper from air valve push rod.

7) Remove snap ring from air valve push rod. Insert a screwdriver through push rod eyelet. Remove air valve push rod. Remove filter, retainer and "O" ring.

Cleaning & Inspection

Clean all plastic, metal and rubber parts in denatured alcohol. Blow out all passages, orifices and valve holes. Air dry all parts. Slight rust on housing may

---

Fig. 1: Exploded View of Delco-Moraine Tandem Diaphragm Power Brake Unit

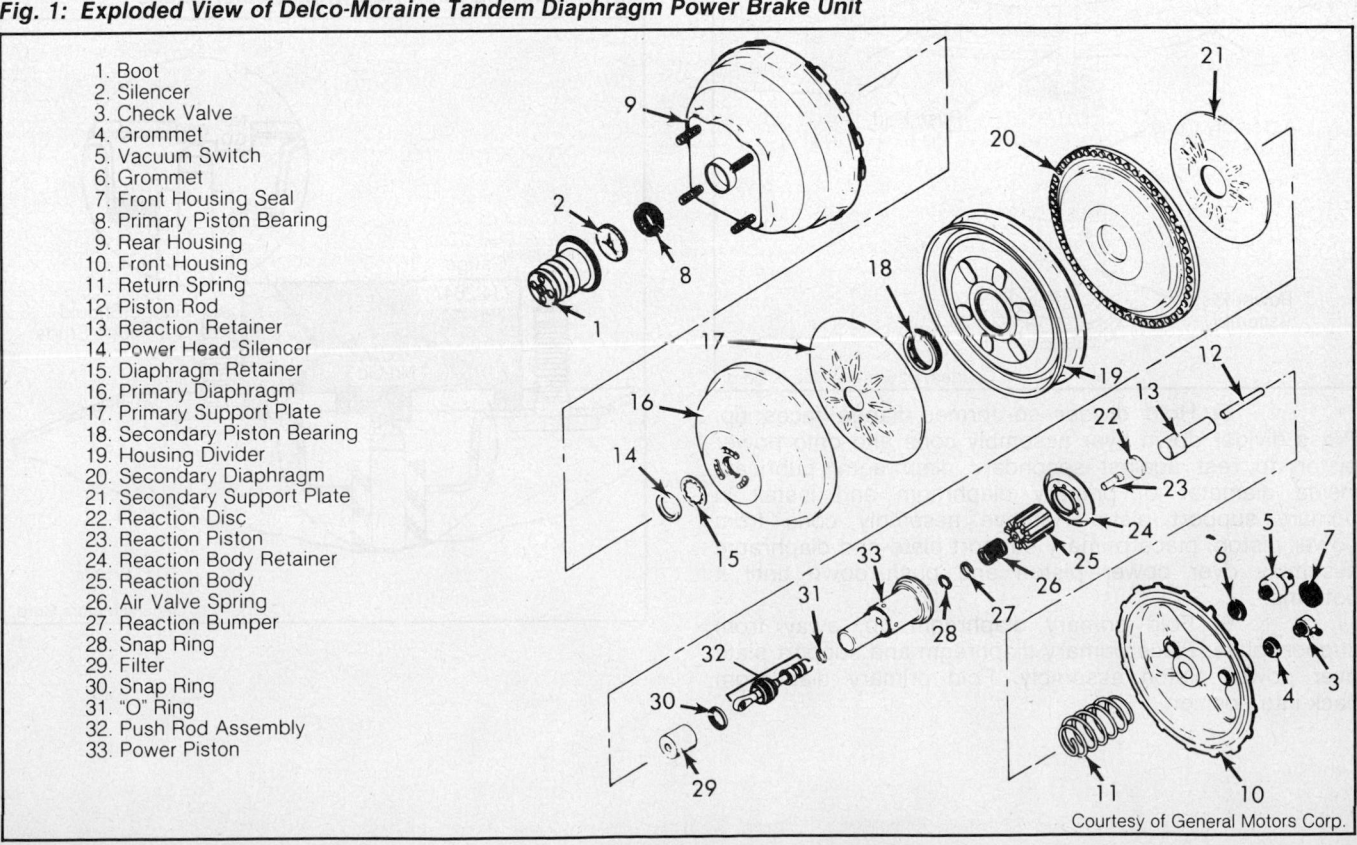

1. Boot
2. Silencer
3. Check Valve
4. Grommet
5. Vacuum Switch
6. Grommet
7. Front Housing Seal
8. Primary Piston Bearing
9. Rear Housing
10. Front Housing
11. Return Spring
12. Piston Rod
13. Reaction Retainer
14. Power Head Silencer
15. Diaphragm Retainer
16. Primary Diaphragm
17. Primary Support Plate
18. Secondary Piston Bearing
19. Housing Divider
20. Secondary Diaphragm
21. Secondary Support Plate
22. Reaction Disc
23. Reaction Piston
24. Reaction Body Retainer
25. Reaction Body
26. Air Valve Spring
27. Reaction Bumper
28. Snap Ring
29. Filter
30. Snap Ring
31. "O" Ring
32. Push Rod Assembly
33. Power Piston

Courtesy of General Motors Corp.

Power Brake Units

DELCO-MORAINE TANDEM DIAPHRAGM (Cont.)

be cleaned with crocus or emery cloth. Do not reinstall any rubber parts with cuts, nicks or distortion. If in doubt, replace the part.

NOTE: **Prior to installation of rubber, plastic, and metal friction parts, lubricate with silicone lube.**

Reassembly

1) Install "O" ring onto air valve push rod. Install push rod in power piston. Using Push Rod Retainer Installer (J-29282), install retainer and seat. Install filter and snap ring. Install reaction bumper and air valve spring.

2) Install reaction piston and reaction disc into reaction body. Install reaction body and snap ring Place power piston on bench with push rod end up. Install Assembly Cone (J-28458) over push rod end of piston.

3) Lubricate inside diameter of secondary diaphragm with silicone lubricant and fit in secondary support plate. Install secondary diaphragm and support plate over power piston and push down until it bottoms.

4) Lubricate inside diameter of secondary power piston bearing. Install bearing in housing divider with flat surface of bearing on the same side as 6 raised lugs on divider.

Fig. 2: Installing Secondary Diaphragm & Support Plate

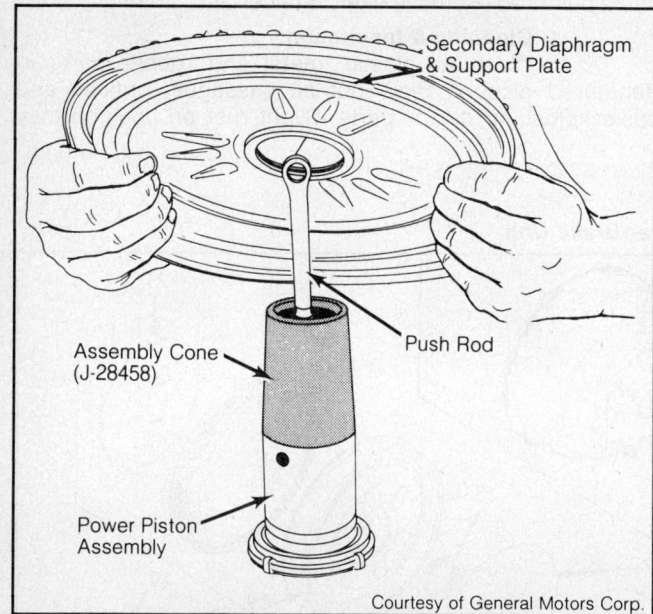

Secondary Diaphragm & Support Plate

Assembly Cone (J-28458)

Push Rod

Power Piston Assembly

Courtesy of General Motors Corp.

5) Hold divider so formed flange faces up. Press divider down over assembly cone and onto power piston to rest against secondary diaphragm. Lubricate inside diameter of primary diaphragm and install in primary support plate. Remove assembly cone from power piston, place primary support plate and diaphragm assembly over power piston and push down until it bottoms.

6) Fold primary diaphragm up, away from support plate. Place primary diaphragm and support plate over power piston assembly. Fold primary diaphragm back into position.

7) Pull diaphragm over formed flange of honing divider. Ensure diaphragm beads are seated properly. Using Assembly Cone (J-28458), install diaphragm retainer and seat. Install silencer, reaction retainer and piston rod.

8) Place primary power piston bearing in rear housing center hole. Lubricate with silicone lubricant on inner diameter. Attach power piston assembly to rear housing.

9) Install power piston return spring over reaction retainer and lower rear housing onto front housing. Align scribe marks and press down with holding fixture handle and turn clockwise to lock 2 housings.

10) Stake 2 housing tabs into sockets at 2 new locations 180 degrees apart. Lubricate inside and outside diameters of grommet and front housing seal. Install seal, grommet, vacuum check valve, silencer and push rod boot.

ADJUSTMENTS

PUSH ROD

1) Place power unit in padded vise with front housing up. Do not clamp tight. Insert master cylinder push rod, flat end first, into piston rod retainer. Ensure rod is properly seated. Remove front housing seal to assure no vacuum is in unit.

2) Place Gauge (J-22647) over push rod, in a position which will allow gauge to be moved right or left without contacting studs. Push rod must contact shorter section gauge. Rod is non-adjustable, and if out of limits, must be replaced with adjustable service rod. With service rod, adjust self-locking screw to meet gauging specifications.

Fig. 3: Gauging Push Rod with Special Gauge

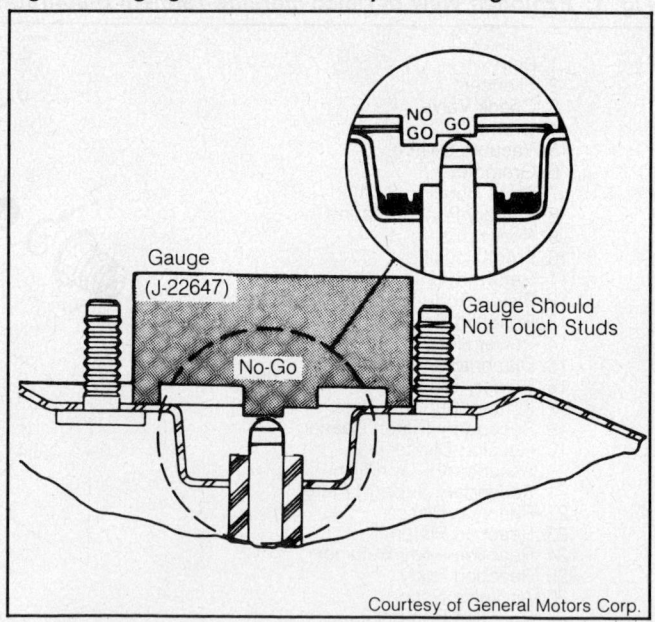

NO GO   GO

Gauge (J-22647)

No-Go

Gauge Should Not Touch Studs

Courtesy of General Motors Corp.

Power Brake Units

NOVA SINGLE DIAPHRAGM

DESCRIPTION

The power brake booster is mounted on the firewall and is directly connected to brake pedal. The self-contained unit uses engine manifold vacuum with atmospheric pressure to provide its power. Reserve vacuum supply provides additional power assisted brake application after engine has stopped.

Although power brake units often differ in structure and internal component arangement, all function basically the same. A vacuum suspended, rolling diaphragm is mounted between the front and rear body of the unit. As the brake pedal is applied, atmospheric pressure enters the rear chamber. The resulting interaction with engine vacuum in the front chamber overwhelms the diaphragm spring and applies thrust to the master cylinder pushrod.

REMOVAL & INSTALLATION

POWER BRAKE UNIT

Removal

1) Remove the master cylinder and 3-way brake line "Tee". Remove vacuum hose.

2) Remove lower panel and air duct for accessibility to rear operating rod. Remove brake pedal return spring and clevis pin. Remove 4 booster unit mounting nuts.

3) Carefully break gasket seal and slide power unit out of firewall. Removal of clevis will be necessary if it interferes with disassembly.

Fig. 1: Exploded View of Nova Power Brake Booster

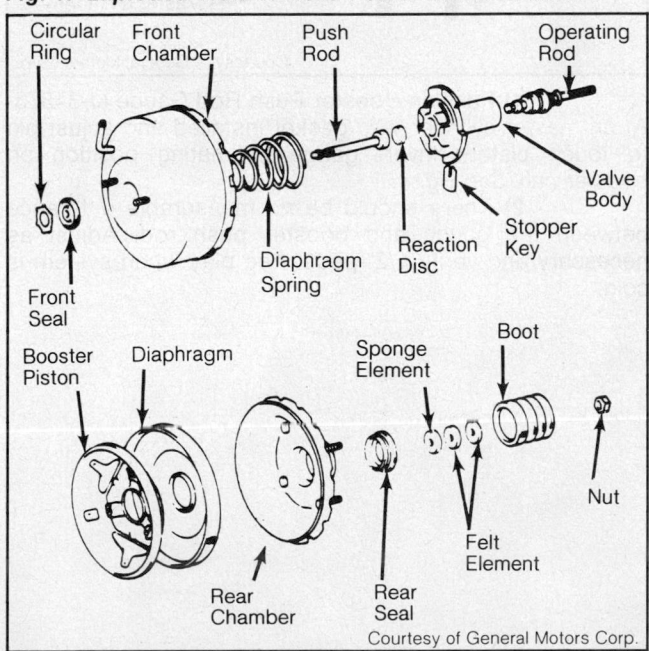

Courtesy of General Motors Corp.

Installation

NOTE: Whenever booster or master cylinder have been removed, check and adjust booster push rod length. See ADJUSTMENTS this section.

Install booster assembly and clevis. Torque mounting nuts to 9 ft. lbs. (13 N.m) and install brake pedal assembly. Install air duct and lower panel. Torque master cylinder nuts to 9 ft. lbs. (13 N.m). Reverse removal procedure to complete installation. Check for fluid leaks and bleed all air from system.

OVERHAUL

POWER BRAKE UNIT

Disassembly

1) Bolt Adapter (J-22805-01) to front chamber and secure in vise. Scribe a reference line across power booster for reassembly. Remove nut and boot from operating rod.

NOTE: Adapter (J-22805-01) may have to be modified by enlarging mount holes to adapt to booster assembly.

2) Attach Spanner Wrench (J-9504-01) to rear chamber with 2 nuts and separate chamber halves. Remove push rod, diaphragm and spring from chambers.

3) With Adapter (J-24435-4), support rear body and remove seal with Driver (J-34874). *See Fig. 2.* Rotate valve body and diaphragm clockwise to separate from booster piston. While pushing operating rod in valve body, remove stopper key.

4) Remove operating rod to extract 2 felt elements and sponge. Detach reaction disc from valve body. Take booster out of vise and remove adapters. Pry the circular ring and seal out of the front chamber.

Fig. 2: Rear Booster Seal Removal

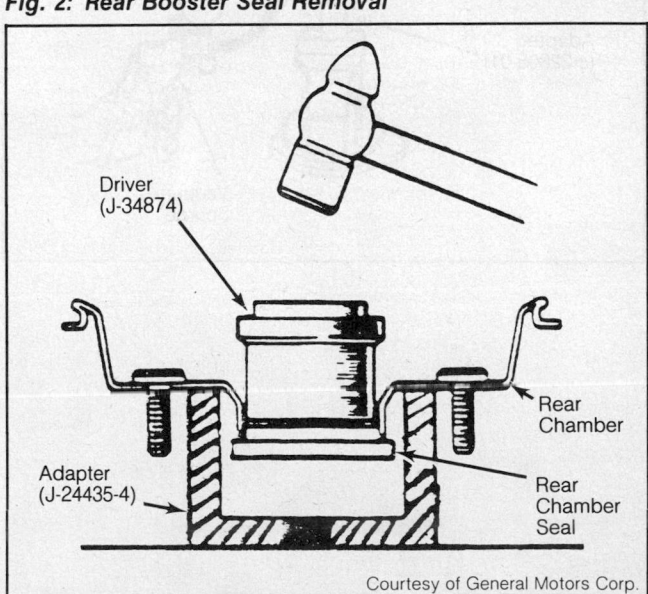

Courtesy of General Motors Corp.

Invert chamber for seal installation.

Cleaning & Inspection

1) Gaskets and seals are often damaged during disassembly. It is therefore advisable to use all components supplied in the repair kit. Clean all parts using denatured alcohol. Remove light rust with crocus or emery cloth. If any rubber parts are damaged and serviceabilty is doubted, replace the part.

Power Brake Units

NOVA SINGLE DIAPHRAGM (Cont.)

2) Silicone grease must be applied to the reaction disc and the contact surfaces of the diaphragm to booster body. Lubricate sliding surfaces of push rod, operating rod, valve body and both body seals.

Reassembly

1) Position seal in front chamber and secure with circular ring. Bolt Adapter (J-22805-1) to chamber and mount unit in vise. Seat operating rod in valve body and install stopper key.

2) Assemble 2 felt and one sponge element with reaction disc to valve body. Assemble diaphragm and valve body to booster piston and rotate counterclockwise into position. Use Adapter (J-24435-4) and Driver (J-34874) to install rear chamber seal. See Fig. 2.

3) Assemble diaphragm assembly to rear chamber and push rod with spring to front chamber. Prepare to assemble halves by attaching vacuum pump to vacuum port and spanner wrench to rear chamber. See Fig. 3.

4) Seat chamber halves together and apply vacuum. Adjust unit to line up with scribe mark. If resistance is excessive, add more silicone grease to contact area. Remove special tools. Install boot and nut to operating rod. Adjust rod to length. Install booster.

Fig. 3: Assembling Power Booster

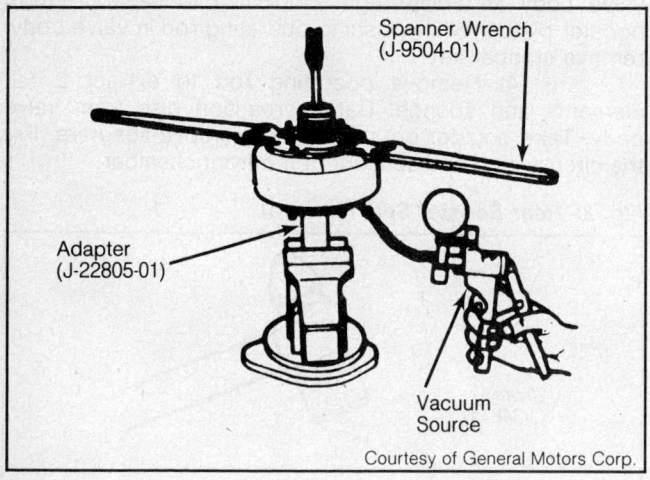

Courtesy of General Motors Corp.

ADJUSTMENTS

PUSH ROD

NOTE: Adjustment of the booster push rod is required whenever servicing assemblies or a push rod end play problem exists. General Motors recommends using Booster Push Rod Gauge (J-34873-A) and the following procedure for this adjustment.

Fig. 4: Power Booster Push Rod Adjustment

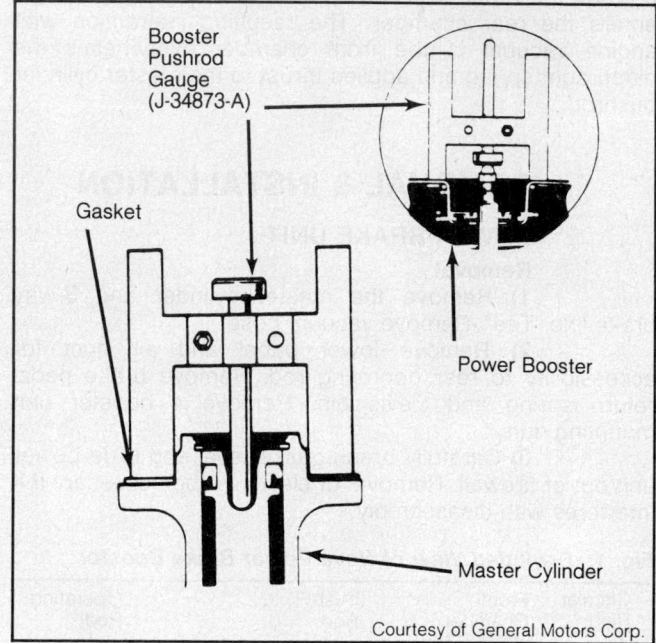

Courtesy of General Motors Corp.

1) Position Booster Push Rod Gauge (J-34873-A) on master cylinder with gasket installed and adjust pin to touch piston. Invert gauge to mating position on booster unit. See Fig. 4.

2) There should be no measurable difference between the gauge and booster push rod. Adjust as necessary and verify 1/2" pedal free play when system is cold.

BOSCH ANTI-LOCK BRAKE SYSTEM (ABS) CHRYSLER MOTORS

Chrysler Motors: Dynasty, New Yorker

DESCRIPTION

Bosch Anti-Lock Brake System (ABS-3) is designed to prevent wheel lock-up during heavy braking. This allows operator to maintain steering control, while stopping vehicle in shortest distance possible. Major components consist of hydraulic assembly, 4 wheel sensors, Brake Control Module (BCM), 2 warning lights (Red "BRAKE" and Yellow "ABS"), and pump/motor assembly. *See Fig. 1.* ABS has a self-diagnostic system to inform of system malfunction and trouble shooting.

OPERATION

Each wheel sensor sends an AC signal to the BCM. The BCM translates this information as wheel speed. When decelerating wheel speed rate is determined to be excessive, the BCM cycles hydraulic brake pressure to each wheel, through hydraulic assembly each wheel. *See Fig. 2.* ABS turns itself off at 3-5 MPH. Minor lock-up may occur at this point.

Red "BRAKE" warning light will come on when ignition switch is in "START" position. Light should go off when ignition is released. If not, light indicates the following problems: parking brake not fully released, low brake fluid, low accumulator pressure or low hydraulic pressure.

Yellow "ABS" warning light will come on for 1-30 seconds after ignition is turned on. This indicates system is performing a self-diagnosis test. If light does not go off after indicated time, system has found a fault. ABS is deactivated during this period. Normal braking is unaffected. Testing should be done to find and correct fault. See TESTING in this article.

Fig. 1: ABS Component Locations

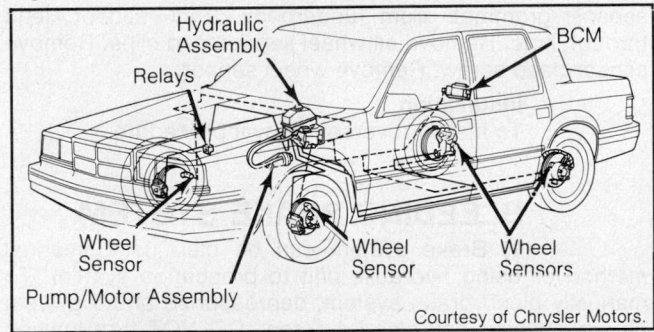

Courtesy of Chrysler Motors.

TESTING

NOTE: An ABS Tester (MST-6100) is necessary to test and diagnose system.

SYSTEM PRECAUTIONS

1) DO NOT unplug or plug in BCM connector with ignition on. Depressurize hydraulic assembly, by depressing brake pedal 25 times or more with ignition switch in "OFF" position, before disconnecting any hydraulic brake component (including brake lines).

2) Unplug BCM connector before using an arc welder on vehicle. when painting vehicle, BCM and sensor block should be insulated or removed before placing vehicle in oven.

Fig. 2: Exploded View of Hydraulic Assembly Components

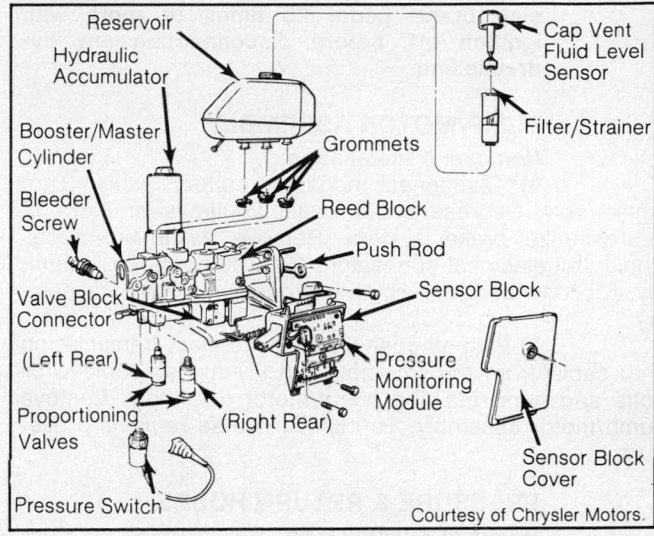

Courtesy of Chrysler Motors.

3) Visually inspect ABS system before performing any test. Ensure hydraulic system, normal brake system, charging system and battery is okay. Low battery voltage can cause faulty reading. If necessary, connect a battery charger and apply slow charge. DO NOT fast charge battery.

ACCESSING TROUBLE CODES

Trouble codes are erased when ignition is turned off. It may be necessary to drive vehicle to obtain and store codes. Connect a battery charger to battery and apply slow charge while testing system (if necessary).

1) Fully release parking brake. Turn ignition on. Check if Red or Yellow warning light comes on. If not, it may be necessary to drive vehicle. Once a fault is indicated (Red or Yellow light is on), stop vehicle if driving. DO NOT turn ignition off.

2) Depress brake pedal firmly. After about 5 seconds, Red "BRAKE" light should begin to blink. Count number of blinks to obtain stored code. If light blinks, stays on continuously or does not come on at all, see FAULT CODES table and appropriate trouble shooting chart.

FAULT CODES

Code	Problem
1	LF Wheel Circuit Valve
2	RF Wheel Circuit Valve
3	RR Wheel Circuit Valve
4	LR Wheel Circuit Valve
5	LF Wheel Speed Sensor
6	RF Wheel Speed Sensor
7	RR Wheel Speed Sensor
8	LR Wheel Speed Sensor
9	LF/RR Wheel Speed Sensor
10	RF/LR Wheel Speed Sensor
11	Replenishing Valve
12	Valve Relay
13	Circuit Failure
14	Piston Travel Switches
15	Stoplight Switch
16	BCM Error

Brake Systems
BOSCH ANTI-LOCK BRAKE SYSTEM (ABS)
CHRYSLER MOTORS (Cont.)

REMOVAL & INSTALLATION

NOTE: Depressurize hydraulic system, by depressing brake pedal 25 times or more with ignition off, before disconnecting any hydraulic line.

PUMP/MOTOR ASSEMBLY
Removal & Installation
1) Disconnect negative battery cable. Turn ignition off. Depress brake pedal 25 times or more to depressurize brake system. Remove air intake ducts. Unplug all electrical connectors from pump/motor assembly. Disconnect hydraulic lines from pump/motor assembly.

2) Plug all open lines. Disconnect transmission shift cable from transmission and lay aside. Remove all bolts and nuts retaining pump/motor assembly. Remove pump/motor assembly. To install, reverse removal procedure.

PRESSURE & RETURN HOSES
Removal & Installation
Remove pump/motor assembly. Remove pressure and return hoses. To install, reverse removal procedure. Install rubber "O" rings on return hoses. Install steel "O" rings on pressure hoses.

SENSOR BLOCK
Removal
1) Depressurize brake system. Unplug all electrical connectors from hydraulic assembly. From under instrument panel, remove clip retaining brake pedal and discard. Remove insulator sound panel from driver's side. Remove nuts retaining hydraulic assembly.

2) From engine compartment, pull hydraulic assembly outward enough to gain access to sensor block. DO NOT disconnect brake lines from hydraulic assembly. Remove sensor block cover.

3) Unplug 12-pin connector from sensor block. Remove 3 bolts retaining sensor block. Carefully remove sensor block. DO NOT damage "O" ring at pressure port.

Installation
To install, reverse removal procedure. Tighten sensor block retaining bolts to 11 ft. lbs. (15 N.m).

HYDRAULIC ASSEMBLY
Removal
1) Disconnect negative battery cable. Turn ignition off. Depress brake pedal 25 times or more to depressurize brake system. Remove air intake ducts. Unplug all electrical connectors from hydraulic assembly.

2) Remove fluid from reservoir. Disconnect pressure and return hoses from hydraulic assembly. Plug all openings. Disconnect all brake lines from hydraulic assembly.

3) From under instrument panel, remove clip and brake pedal pin. Discard clip. Remove driver's side insulator panel. Remove hydraulic assembly. To install, reverse removal procedure. Install new clip. Bleed brake system. See BRAKE BLEEDING in this article.

OVER-VOLTAGE & PUMP/MOTOR RELAYS
Removal & Installation
Remove radiator overflow bottle. Remove relay bracket retaining screw. Remove relay. See Fig. 3. To install, reverse removal procedure.

Fig. 3: Over-Voltage & Pump/Motor Relay Locations

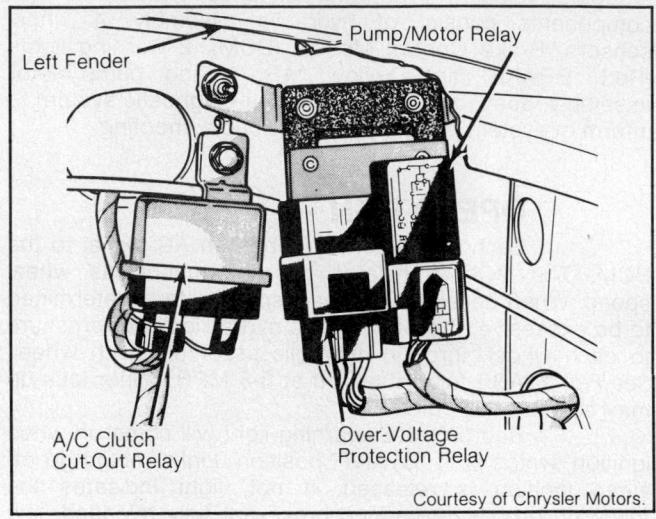

Courtesy of Chrysler Motors.

WHEEL SENSORS

NOTE: DO NOT use pliers to remove wheel sensor.

Removal (Front)
Raise front of vehicle and support. Remove wheel. Remove clip retaining sensor wire to fender sheild and strut. Remove sensor head screw. Carefully remove sensor.

Removal (Rear)
Raise and support rear of vehicle. Remove sensor grommet from underbody. Pull sensor lead through hole. Remove all wheel sensor lead clips. Remove sensor head screw. Remove wheel sensor.

Installation
To install, reverse removal procedure.

BLEEDING BRAKE SYSTEM
1) Brake system can be bled using manual method or using hydraulic unit to pressurize system. To manually bleed brake system, depressurize brake system before opening any bleeder screw. DO NOT turn ignition on any time system is being manually bled.

2) To bleed system using hydraulic unit, depressurize brake system. Ensure reservoir is full. Open bleeder screw. Turn ignition on. Allow pump/motor assembly to run until brake fluid from bleeder screw contains no air.

3) Close bleeder screw. Turn ignition off. Depressurize brake system. Fill reservoir with brake fluid. Perform same procedure as prevouisly described for each wheel.

NOTE: The following charts and diagrams are courtesy of Chrysler Motors.

BOSCH ANTI-LOCK BRAKE SYSTEM (ABS)
CHRYSLER MOTORS (Cont.)

TROUBLE SHOOTING CHARTS

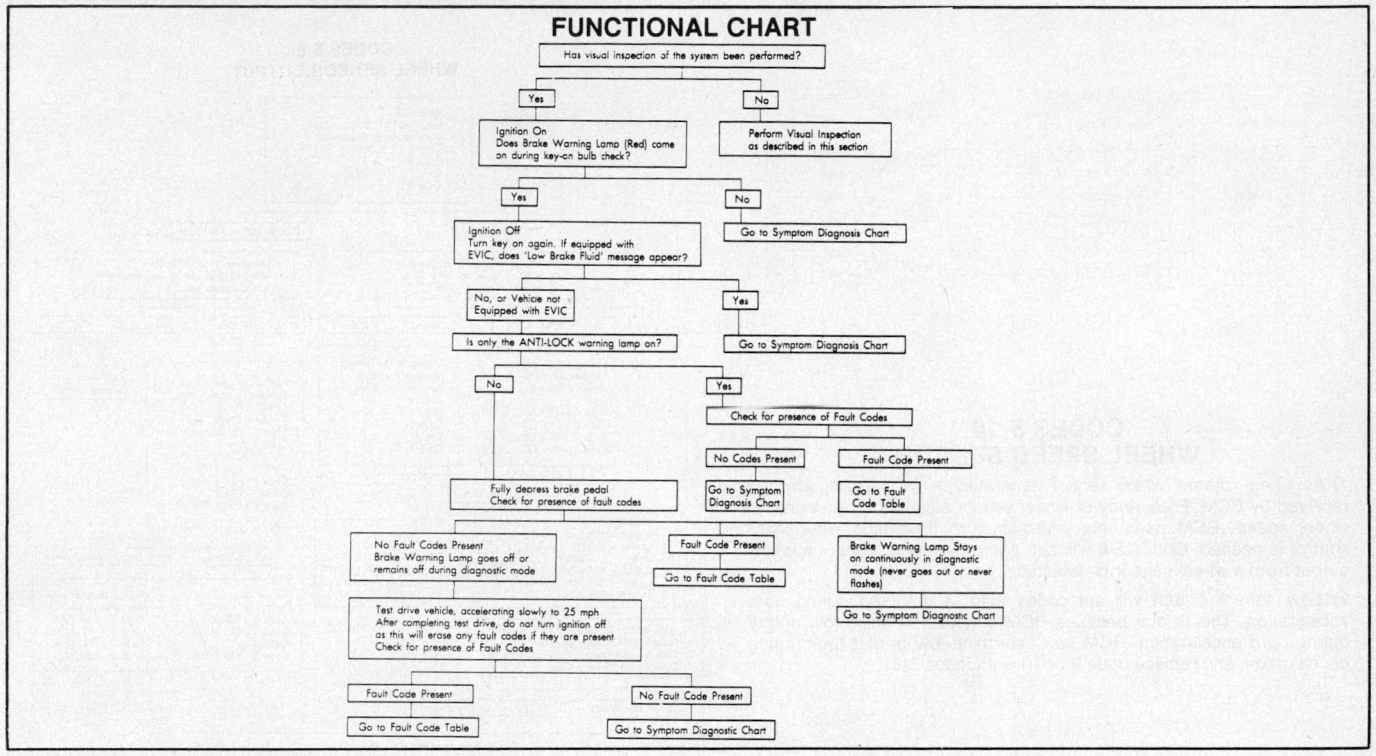

FUNCTIONAL CHART

Has visual inspection of the system been performed?
- Yes → Ignition On. Does Brake Warning Lamp (Red) come on during key-on bulb check?
- No → Perform Visual Inspection as described in this section

Ignition On. Does Brake Warning Lamp (Red) come on during key-on bulb check?
- Yes → Ignition Off. Turn key on again. If equipped with EVIC, does 'Low Brake Fluid' message appear?
- No → Go to Symptom Diagnosis Chart

Ignition Off. Turn key on again. If equipped with EVIC, does 'Low Brake Fluid' message appear?
- No, or Vehicle not Equipped with EVIC → Is only the ANTI-LOCK warning lamp on?
- Yes → Go to Symptom Diagnosis Chart

Is only the ANTI-LOCK warning lamp on?
- No → Fully depress brake pedal. Check for presence of fault codes
- Yes → Check for presence of Fault Codes

Check for presence of Fault Codes
- No Codes Present → Go to Symptom Diagnosis Chart
- Fault Code Present → Go to Fault Code Table

Fully depress brake pedal. Check for presence of fault codes
- No Fault Codes Present. Brake Warning Lamp goes off or remains off during diagnostic mode
- Fault Code Present → Go to Fault Code Table
- Brake Warning Lamp Stays on continuously in diagnostic mode (never goes out or never flashes) → Go to Symptom Diagnostic Chart

Test drive vehicle, accelerating slowly to 25 mph. After completing test drive, do not turn ignition off as this will erase any fault codes if they are present. Check for presence of Fault Codes
- Fault Code Present → Go to Fault Code Table
- No Fault Code Present → Go to Symptom Diagnostic Chart

FAULT CODES 1-4: WHEEL CIRCUIT VALVE PROBLEM

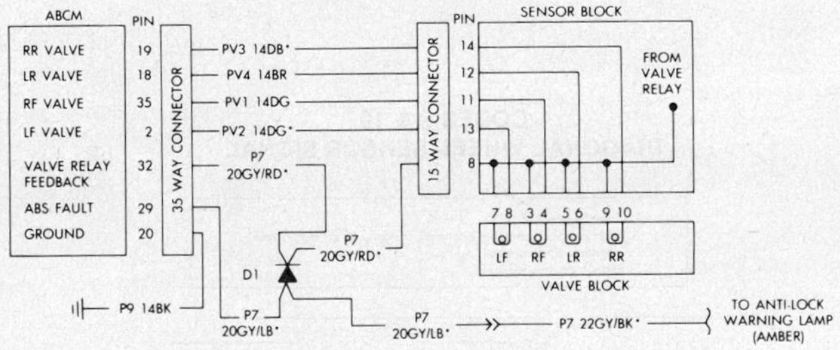

ABCM	PIN
RR VALVE	19
LR VALVE	18
RF VALVE	35
LF VALVE	2
VALVE RELAY FEEDBACK	32
ABS FAULT	29
GROUND	20

PV3 14DB*
PV4 14BR
PV1 14DG
PV2 14DG*
P7 20GY/RD*
P7 20GY/RD*
D1
P7 20GY/LB*
P9 14BK
P7 20GY/LB*   P7 20GY/LB*   P7 22GY/BK*
TO ANTI-LOCK WARNING LAMP (AMBER)

SENSOR BLOCK / PIN 14 11 12 13 8 / FROM VALVE RELAY

7 8 3 4 5 6 9 10
LF RF LR RR
VALVE BLOCK

CODES 1-4
WHEEL CIRCUIT VALVE

Valve block, attached to bottom of booster/master cylinder, controls hydraulic fluid pressure to each wheel by amount of ground circuit allowed. This is controlled by BCM. Power to each circuit is received through valve relay, inside sensor block. BCM power the valve relay when ignition is turned on.

CODE 1 – LF VALVE
CODE 2 – RR VALVE
CODE 3 – RF VALVE
CODE 4 – LR VALVE

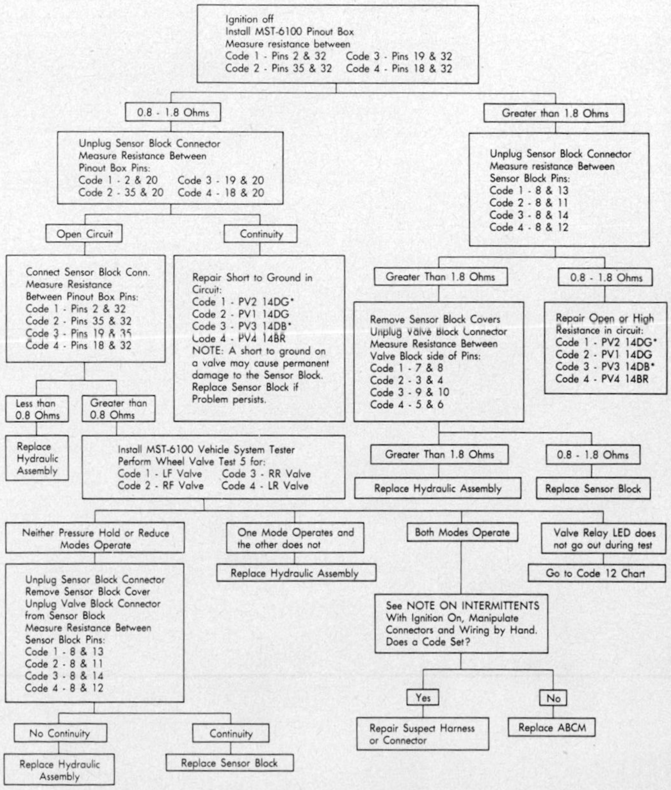

Ignition off. Install MST-6100 Pinout Box. Measure resistance between
Code 1 - Pins 2 & 32   Code 3 - Pins 19 & 32
Code 2 - Pins 35 & 32   Code 4 - Pins 18 & 32

- 0.8 - 1.8 Ohms
- Greater than 1.8 Ohms

0.8 - 1.8 Ohms branch:
Unplug Sensor Block Connector. Measure Resistance Between Pinout Box Pins:
Code 1 - 2 & 20   Code 3 - 19 & 20
Code 2 - 35 & 20   Code 4 - 18 & 20
- Open Circuit → Connect Sensor Block Conn. Measure Resistance Between Pinout Box Pins: Code 1 - Pins 2 & 32, Code 2 - Pins 35 & 32, Code 3 - Pins 19 & 35, Code 4 - Pins 18 & 32
  - Less than 0.8 Ohms → Replace Hydraulic Assembly
  - Greater than 0.8 Ohms → Install MST-6100 Vehicle System Tester. Perform Wheel Valve Test 5 for: Code 1 - LF Valve, Code 2 - RF Valve, Code 3 - RR Valve, Code 4 - LR Valve
- Continuity → Repair Short to Ground in Circuit: Code 1 - PV2 14DG*, Code 2 - PV1 14DG, Code 3 - PV3 14DB*, Code 4 - PV4 14BR. NOTE: A short to ground on a valve may cause permanent damage to the Sensor Block. Replace Sensor Block if Problem persists.

Greater than 1.8 Ohms branch:
Unplug Sensor Block Connector. Measure resistance Between Sensor Block Pins:
Code 1 - 8 & 13
Code 2 - 8 & 11
Code 3 - 8 & 14
Code 4 - 8 & 12
- Greater Than 1.8 Ohms → Remove Sensor Block Covers. Unplug Valve Block Connector. Measure Resistance Between Valve Block side of Pins: Code 1 - 7 & 8, Code 2 - 3 & 4, Code 3 - 9 & 10, Code 4 - 5 & 6
  - Greater than 1.8 Ohms → Replace Hydraulic Assembly
  - 0.8 - 1.8 Ohms → Replace Sensor Block
- 0.8 - 1.8 Ohms → Repair Open or High Resistance in circuit: Code 1 - PV2 14DG*, Code 2 - PV1 14DG, Code 3 - PV3 14DB*, Code 4 - PV4 14BR

Wheel Valve Test 5 results:
- Neither Pressure Hold or Reduce Modes Operate → Unplug Sensor Block Connector. Remove Sensor Block Cover. Unplug Valve Block Connector from Sensor Block. Measure Resistance Between Sensor Block Pins: Code 1 - 8 & 13, Code 2 - 8 & 11, Code 3 - 8 & 14, Code 4 - 8 & 12
  - No Continuity → Replace Hydraulic Assembly
  - Continuity → Replace Sensor Block
- One Mode Operates and the other does not → Replace Hydraulic Assembly
- Both Modes Operate → See NOTE ON INTERMITTENTS. With Ignition On, Manipulate Connectors and Wiring by Hand. Does a Code Set?
  - Yes → Repair Suspect Harness or Connector
  - No → Replace ABCM
- Valve Relay LED does not go out during test → Go to Code 12 Chart

Brake Systems

BOSCH ANTI-LOCK BRAKE SYSTEM (ABS)
CHRYSLER MOTORS (Cont.)

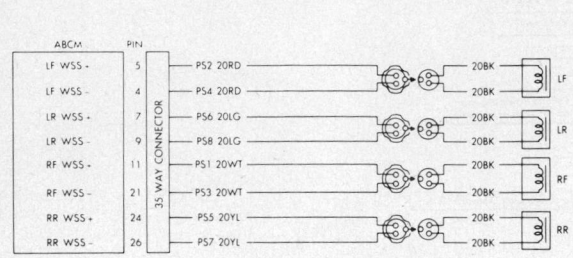

CODES 5-10
WHEEL SPEED SENSOR

1) As wheel rotates, wheel sensor generates an AC current, which is received by BCM. Frequency of wheel sensor signal is proportional to wheel speed. BCM uses this information to determine when ABS control is needed. Codes 5-8 will set, if intermittent or continuous low output from a wheel sensor is detected.

2) Low sensor output will set codes 9-10, if detected during hard acceleration. This is due because BCM cannot determine low output during hard acceleration. BCM can determine low output fault during deceleration, and replace code 9 or 10 with codes 5-8.

CODES 5-8
WHEEL SENSOR OUTPUT

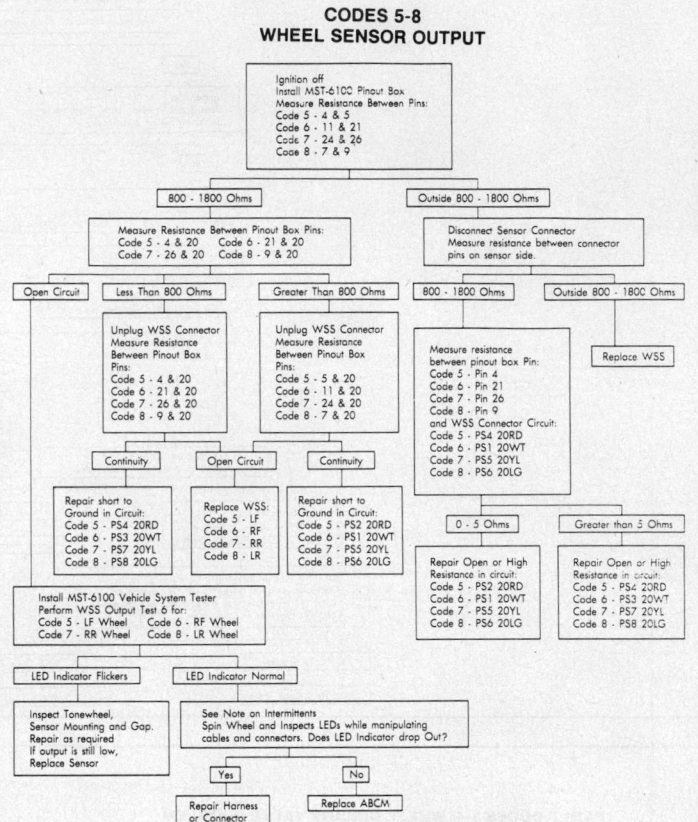

CODES 9 & 10
DIAGONAL WHEEL SENSOR SIGNAL

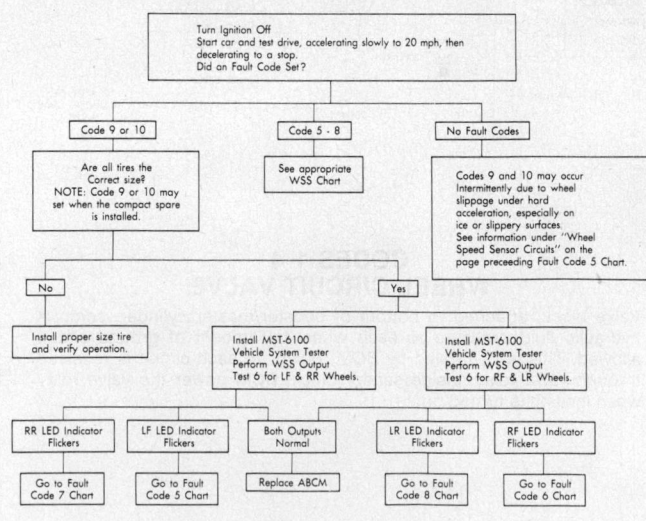

BOSCH ANTI-LOCK BRAKE SYSTEM (ABS)
CHRYSLER MOTORS (Cont.)

FAULT CODE 11: REPLENISHING VALVE PROBLEM

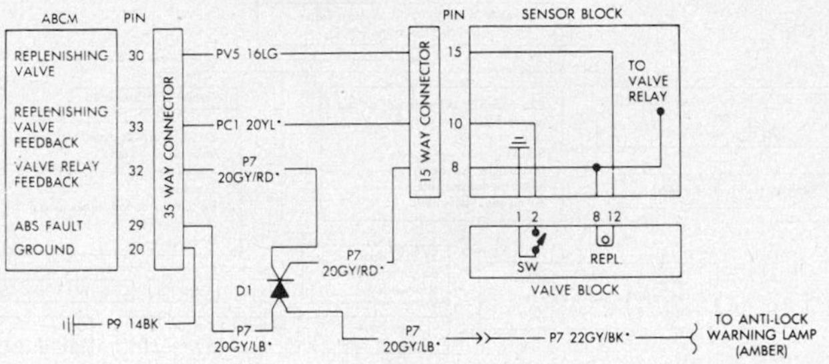

ABCM	PIN		PIN	SENSOR BLOCK
REPLENISHING VALVE	30	PV5 16LG	15	
REPLENISHING VALVE FEEDBACK	33	PC1 20YL*	10	TO VALVE RELAY
VALVE RELAY FEEDBACK	32	P7 20GY/RD*	8	
ABS FAULT	29			
GROUND	20			

35 WAY CONNECTOR / 15 WAY CONNECTOR

D1

P9 14BK

P7 20GY/RD*

P7 20GY/LB*   P7 20GY/LB*   P7 22GY/BK*   TO ANTI-LOCK WARNING LAMP (AMBER)

1 2   8 12   SW   REPL.   VALVE BLOCK

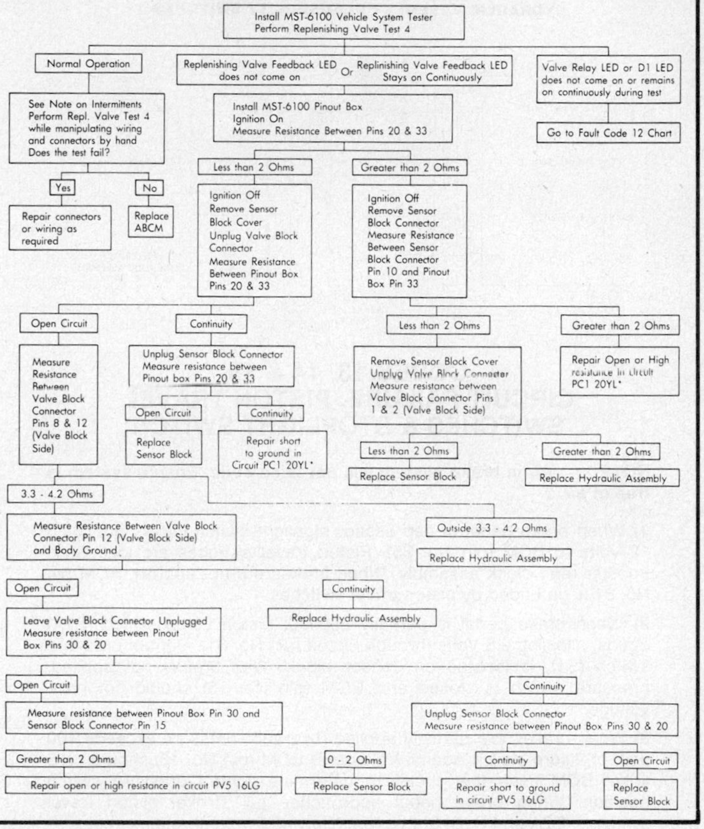

CODE 11
REPLENISHING VALVE

1) Replenishing valve, located inside valve block, prevents excessive brake pedal travel during ABS operation and hard braking without ABS operating. It directs pressurized brake fluid from booster servo to master cylinder. It prevents low or soft brake pedal if air is in system.

2) Replenishing valve receives power from valve relay. Battery voltage should be present with ignition on. When replenishing valve is activated, feedback switch attached to valve (pin No. 33 at controller), is open allowing 5 volts through feedback wire.

3) This is done by pin No. 30 at controller grounding. When system is deactivated, feedback wire is grounded. Code 11 will be detected if commanded replenshing valve position and valve position, indicated by feedback wire, do not match.

FAULT CODE 11
REPLENISHING VALVE PROBLEM

Install MST-6100 Vehicle System Tester
Perform Replenishing Valve Test 4

- Normal Operation
- Replenishing Valve Feedback LED does not come on **Or** Replenishing Valve Feedback LED Stays on Continuously
- Valve Relay LED or D1 LED does not come on or remains on continuously during test → Go to Fault Code 12 Chart

Normal Operation branch:
See Note on Intermitents Perform Repl. Valve Test 4 while manipulating wiring and connectors by hand Does the test fail?
- Yes → Repair connectors or wiring as required
- No → Replace ABCM

Replenishing Valve Feedback LED branch:
Install MST-6100 Pinout Box Ignition On Measure Resistance Between Pins 20 & 33
- Less than 2 Ohms → Ignition Off Remove Sensor Block Cover Unplug Valve Block Connector Measure Resistance Between Pinout Box Pins 20 & 33
  - Open Circuit → Measure Resistance Between Valve Block Connector Pins 8 & 12 (Valve Block Side)
    - Open Circuit → Replace Sensor Block
    - Continuity → Repair short to ground in Circuit PC1 20YL*
    - 3.3 - 4.2 Ohms → Measure Resistance Between Valve Block Connector Pin 12 (Valve Block Side) and Body Ground
      - Open Circuit → Leave Valve Block Connector Unplugged Measure resistance between Pinout Box Pins 30 & 20
        - Open Circuit → Measure resistance between Pinout Box Pin 30 and Sensor Block Connector Pin 15
          - Greater than 2 Ohms → Repair open or high resistance in circuit PV5 16LG
          - 0 - 2 Ohms → Replace Sensor Block
        - Continuity → Unplug Sensor Block Connector Measure resistance between Pinout Box Pins 30 & 20
          - Continuity → Repair short to ground in circuit PV5 16LG
          - Open Circuit → Replace Sensor Block
      - Continuity → Replace Hydraulic Assembly
  - Continuity → Unplug Sensor Block Connector Measure resistance between Pinout box Pins 20 & 33
    - Open Circuit → Replace Sensor Block
    - Continuity → Repair short to ground in Circuit PC1 20YL*
- Greater than 2 Ohms → Ignition Off Remove Sensor Block Connector Measure Resistance Between Sensor Block Connector Pin 10 and Pinout Box Pin 33
  - Less than 2 Ohms → Remove Sensor Block Cover Unplug Valve Block Connector Measure resistance between Valve Block Connector Pins 1 & 2 (Valve Block Side)
    - Less than 2 Ohms → Replace Sensor Block
    - Greater than 2 Ohms → Replace Hydraulic Assembly
    - Outside 3.3 - 4.2 Ohms → Replace Hydraulic Assembly
  - Greater than 2 Ohms → Repair Open or High resistance in circuit PC1 20YL*

FAULT CODE 12: VALVE RELAY CIRCUIT ERROR

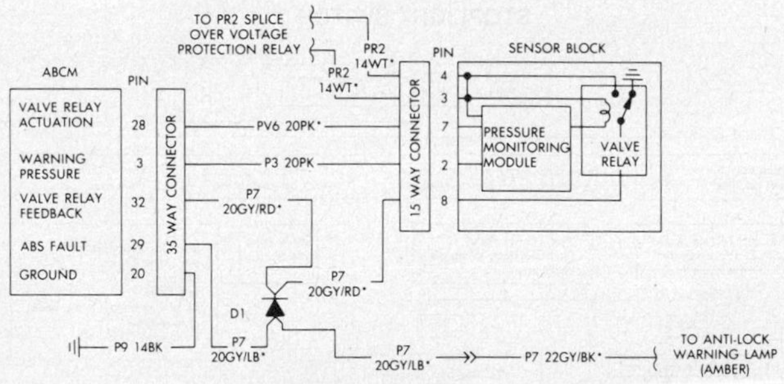

ABCM	PIN		PIN	SENSOR BLOCK
VALVE RELAY ACTUATION	28	PV6 20PK*	4	
WARNING PRESSURE	3	P3 20PK	3	PRESSURE MONITORING MODULE / VALVE RELAY
VALVE RELAY FEEDBACK	32	P7 20GY/RD*	2	
ABS FAULT	29			
GROUND	20			

TO PR2 SPLICE OVER VOLTAGE PROTECTION RELAY
PR2 14WT*   PR2 14WT*

35 WAY CONNECTOR / 15 WAY CONNECTOR

D1

P9 14BK   P7 20GY/RD*

P7 20GY/LB*   P7 20GY/LB*   P7 22GY/BK*   TO ANTI-LOCK WARNING LAMP (AMBER)

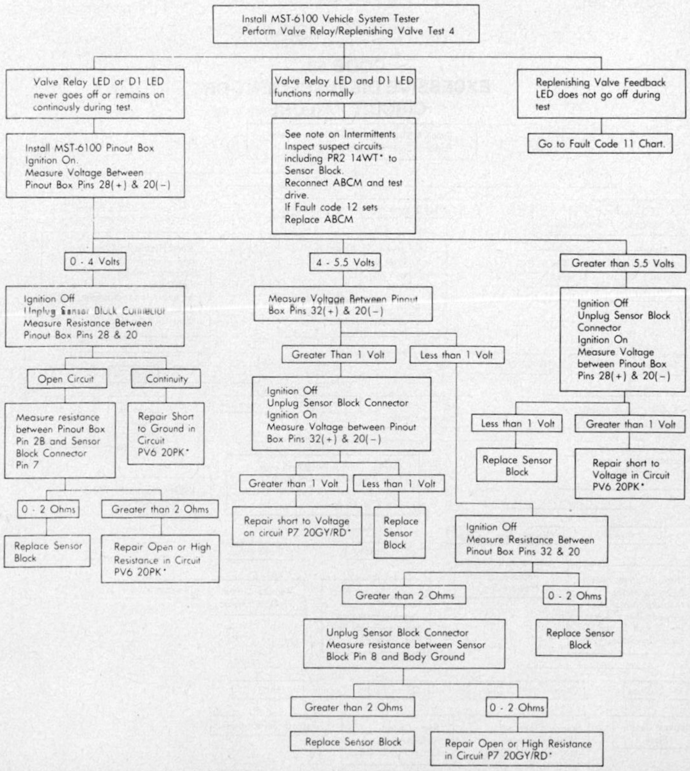

CODE 12
VALVE RELAY

1) Valve relay, located in sensor block, provides power to wheel circuit valves and replenishing valve. Current flow through the valve relay coil is controlled by pressure monitoring module, located in sensor block.

2) Pressure monitor module energizes and de-engerizes pump/motor circuit to maintain proper accumulator pressure. It also turns on Red "BRAKE" light on if accumulator pressure (hydraulic pressure) drops below proper amount.

3) In case of malfunction, module can disable valve relay due to low hydraulic pressure, without being commanded by BCM. Valve relay is activated when BCM grounds valve relay actuation wire (pin No. 28).

4) When valve relay is energized, valve relay feedback line (pin No. 32), should have battery voltage. When de-energized, valve relay feedback line (pin No. 32) should be grounded. Code 12 will appear if pressure monitor or valve relay fail, or incorrect voltage condition.

FAULT CODE 12
VALVE RELAY

Install MST-6100 Vehicle System Tester
Perform Valve Relay/Replenishing Valve Test 4

- Valve Relay LED or D1 LED never goes off or remains on continously during test
- Valve Relay LED and D1 LED functions normally
- Replenishing Valve Feedback LED does not go off during test → Go to Fault Code 11 Chart.

Valve Relay LED and D1 LED functions normally branch:
See note on Intermitents Inspect suspect circuits including PR2 14WT* to Sensor Block. Reconnect ABCM and test drive. If Fault code 12 sets Replace ABCM

Valve Relay LED or D1 LED never goes off branch:
Install MST-6100 Pinout Box Ignition On Measure Voltage Between Pinout Box Pins 28(+) & 20(-)

- 0 - 4 Volts → Ignition Off Unplug Sensor Block Connector Measure Resistance Between Pinout Box Pins 28 & 20
  - Open Circuit → Measure resistance between Pinout Box Pin 2B and Sensor Block Connector Pin 7
    - 0 - 2 Ohms → Replace Sensor Block
    - Greater than 2 Ohms → Repair Open or High Resistance in Circuit PV6 20PK*
  - Continuity → Repair Short to Ground in Circuit PV6 20PK*

- 4 - 5.5 Volts → Measure Voltage Between Pinout Box Pins 32(+) & 20(-)
  - Greater Than 1 Volt → Ignition Off Unplug Sensor Block Connector Ignition On Measure Voltage between Pinout Box Pins 32(+) & 20(-)
    - Greater than 1 Volt → Repair short to Voltage on circuit P7 20GY/RD*
    - Less than 1 Volt → Replace Sensor Block
  - Less than 1 Volt → Unplug Sensor Block Connector Measure resistance between Sensor Block Pin 8 and Body Ground
    - Greater than 2 Ohms → Replace Sensor Block
    - 0 - 2 Ohms → Repair Open or High Resistance in Circuit P7 20GY/RD*

- Greater than 5.5 Volts → Ignition Off Unplug Sensor Block Connector Ignition On Measure Voltage between Pinout Box Pins 28(+) & 20(-)
  - Less than 1 Volt → Replace Sensor Block
  - Greater than 1 Volt → Repair short to Voltage in Circuit PV6 20PK*
    - Ignition Off Measure Resistance Between Pinout Box Pins 32 & 20
      - Greater than 2 Ohms → Replace Sensor Block
      - 0 - 2 Ohms → Replace Sensor Block

Brake Systems

BOSCH ANTI-LOCK BRAKE SYSTEM (ABS)
CHRYSLER MOTORS (Cont.)

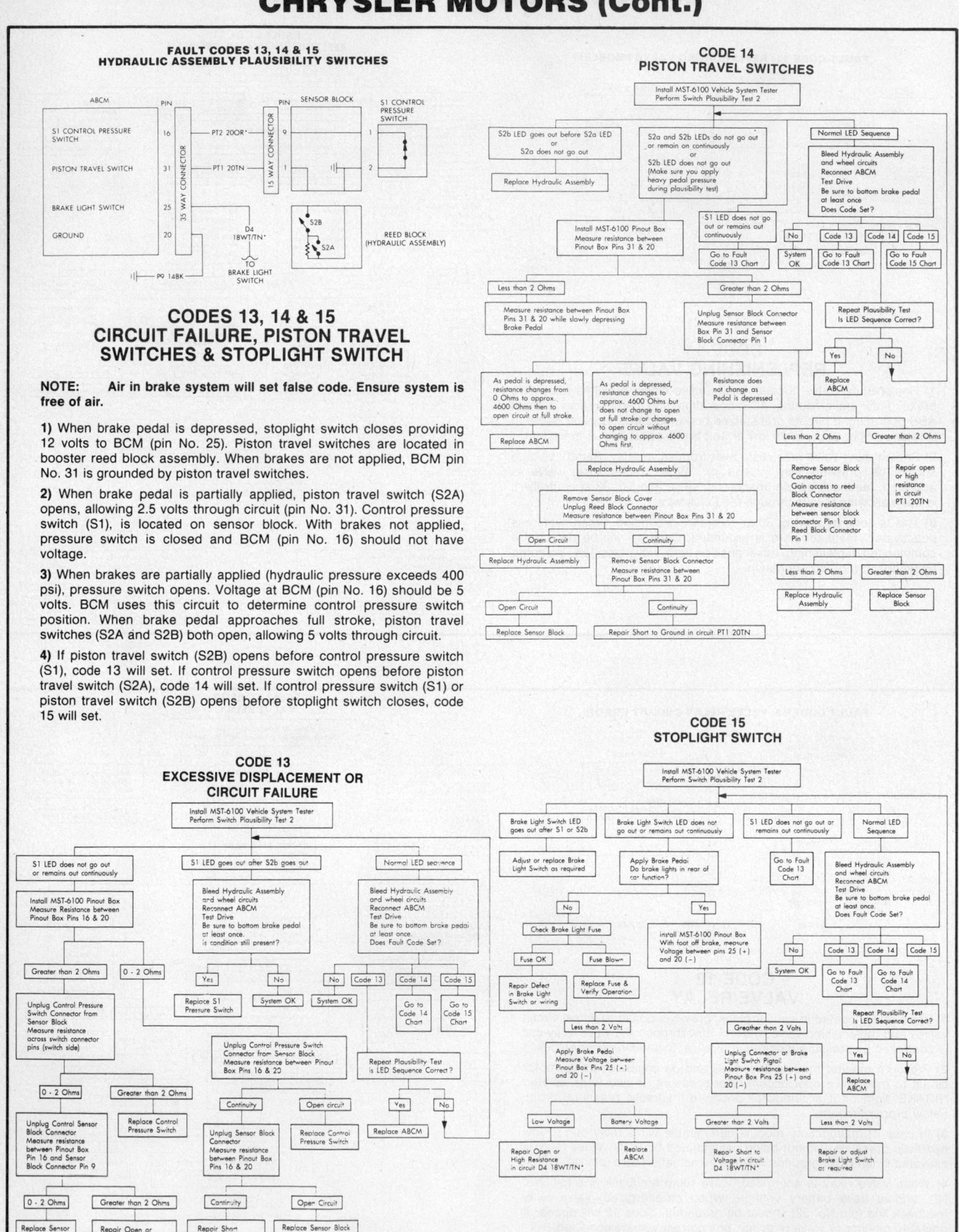

CODES 13, 14 & 15
CIRCUIT FAILURE, PISTON TRAVEL
SWITCHES & STOPLIGHT SWITCH

NOTE: Air in brake system will set false code. Ensure system is free of air.

1) When brake pedal is depressed, stoplight switch closes providing 12 volts to BCM (pin No. 25). Piston travel switches are located in booster reed block assembly. When brakes are not applied, BCM pin No. 31 is grounded by piston travel switches.

2) When brake pedal is partially applied, piston travel switch (S2A) opens, allowing 2.5 volts through circuit (pin No. 31). Control pressure switch (S1), is located on sensor block. With brakes not applied, pressure switch is closed and BCM (pin No. 16) should not have voltage.

3) When brakes are partially applied (hydraulic pressure exceeds 400 psi), pressure switch opens. Voltage at BCM (pin No. 16) should be 5 volts. BCM uses this circuit to determine control pressure switch position. When brake pedal approaches full stroke, piston travel switches (S2A and S2B) both open, allowing 5 volts through circuit.

4) If piston travel switch (S2B) opens before control pressure switch (S1), code 13 will set. If control pressure switch opens before piston travel switch (S2A), code 14 will set. If control pressure switch (S1) or piston travel switch (S2B) opens before stoplight switch closes, code 15 will set.

Brake Systems

BOSCH ANTI-LOCK BRAKE SYSTEM (ABS) CHRYSLER MOTORS (Cont.)

CODE 16
BCM ERROR

Code 16 will set if internal BCM failure is detected. Perform FUNCTION CHECK. Always test drive vehicle again and see if code 16 resets.

FAULT CODE 16
ABCM ERRORS

```
IGNITION OFF
TEST DRIVE CAR AGAIN, ACCELERATING SLOWLY
  TO 25 MPH
REPEAT ACCELERATION AND STOP 2 TIMES
DID FAULT CODE SET?
```

NO	CODE 16	OTHER CODES
SEE INTERMITTENT FAULTS	REPLACE ABCM	GO TO APPROPRIATE ABS CODE CHART

SYMPTOM DIAGNOSIS CHART

Perform FUNCTION CHECK before using this chart.

SYMPTOM	REFER TO
No power assist (with or without BRAKE warning lamp on) High pedal effort (with or without BRAKE warning lamp on) Pump does not run Pumps runs for extended periods of time Pump runs every brake apply BRAKE warning lamp stays on for more than 20 seconds after key-on BRAKE warning lamp comes on while braking BRAKE warning lamp on continuously Brake boost system will not hold pressure (excessive pressure leakdown)	Chart C
BRAKE warning lamp inoperative	Chart D
LOW BRAKE FLUID message displayed and BRAKE warning lamp on continuously (EVID equipped cars only)	Chart E
BRAKE warning lamp on and power assist available	Chart F
No system power	Chart G
ANTI-LOCK warning lamp on (BRAKE warning lamp off) and no Fault Codes set	Chart H
Low or spongy pedal	Chart J

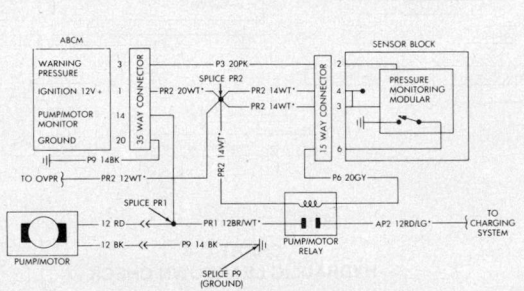

CHARTS C, C-1, C-2, C-3 & C-4 PUMP/MOTOR CIRCUIT

NOTE: Pump/Motor is not controlled by BCM.

1) Pump/motor operation is controlled by pressure monitoring module, located in sensor block. Inside module, a pressure switch with 2 redundant sensors, monitors accumulator pressure.

2) If each sensor output do not match the other one, ABS is disabled and Red "BRAKE" light is turned on. Pressure monitoring module is calibrated to activate pump/motor when accumulator pressure reaches 2100 psi (14,500 kPa). It deactivates pump/motor when pressure reaches 2600 psi (18,000 kPa).

3) Pressure monitoring module grounds wire at pin No. 6 of 15-way connector. This grounds coil inside pump/motor relay to activate pump/motor. A monitoring wire from pump/motor to BCM (pin No. 14), is used for testing purposes only.

CHART C
HYDRAULIC SYSTEM
PERFORMANCE CHECK

```
Depressurize Accumulator by pumping pedal 25 times with key off
Ignition on
Does Pump/Motor run?
```

Yes / No → To to Chart C-1

```
Ignition off
Depressurize accumulator
Install Pressure Gauge and adapter to Hydraulic Assembly Bleeder Port
```

```
Ignition on
Observe pressure gauge and Brake Warning lamp in instrument cluster
Brake Warning Lamp should turn off when pressure reaches 1700-2450 PSI
Brake Warning Lamp should turn off within 25 seconds
```

Normal Operation	Pressure does not reach lamp shut-off pressure (1700-2450 psi) within 25 seconds	Brake Warning Lamp turns off at pressure other than 1700-2450 psi
	Go to Chart C-2	Replace Sensor Block

```
OBSERVE PUMP PERFORMANCE

Ignition off
Depressurize accumulator
Ignition on
Observe pump and pressure gauge
Pump should stop when pressure reaches 2400-2900 psi
```

Normal Operation	Does not reach pump shut off pressure within 30 seconds	Reaches 2900 psi but pump continues to run	Pump Stops at pressure other than 2400-2900 psi
	Go to Chart C-2	Does pump stop within 45 seconds?	Replace Sensor Block

Yes / No

| Replace Sensor Block | Go to Chart C-3 |

```
Allow pump to stop
While watching pressure gauge, slowly pump brake pedal
Pump should start when pressure reaches 1750-2450 psi
```

Normal Operation	Pump starts at pressure other than 1750-2350 psi	Pressure immediately Drops below 1700 Psi and pump starts
	Replace Sensor Block	Go to Chart C-4

```
Allow pump to stop
Unplug Pump/Motor electrical connector
While watching Brake Warning Lamp and pressure gauge,
slowly pump brake pedal
Lamp should turn ON when pressure reaches 1100-1800 psi
```

Normal Operation	Brake Warning Lamp turns on at pressure other than 1100-1800 psi
Install Pump/Motor Connector Go to Chart C-4	Replace Sensor Block

Brake Systems

BOSCH ANTI-LOCK BRAKE SYSTEM (ABS) CHRYSLER MOTORS (Cont.)

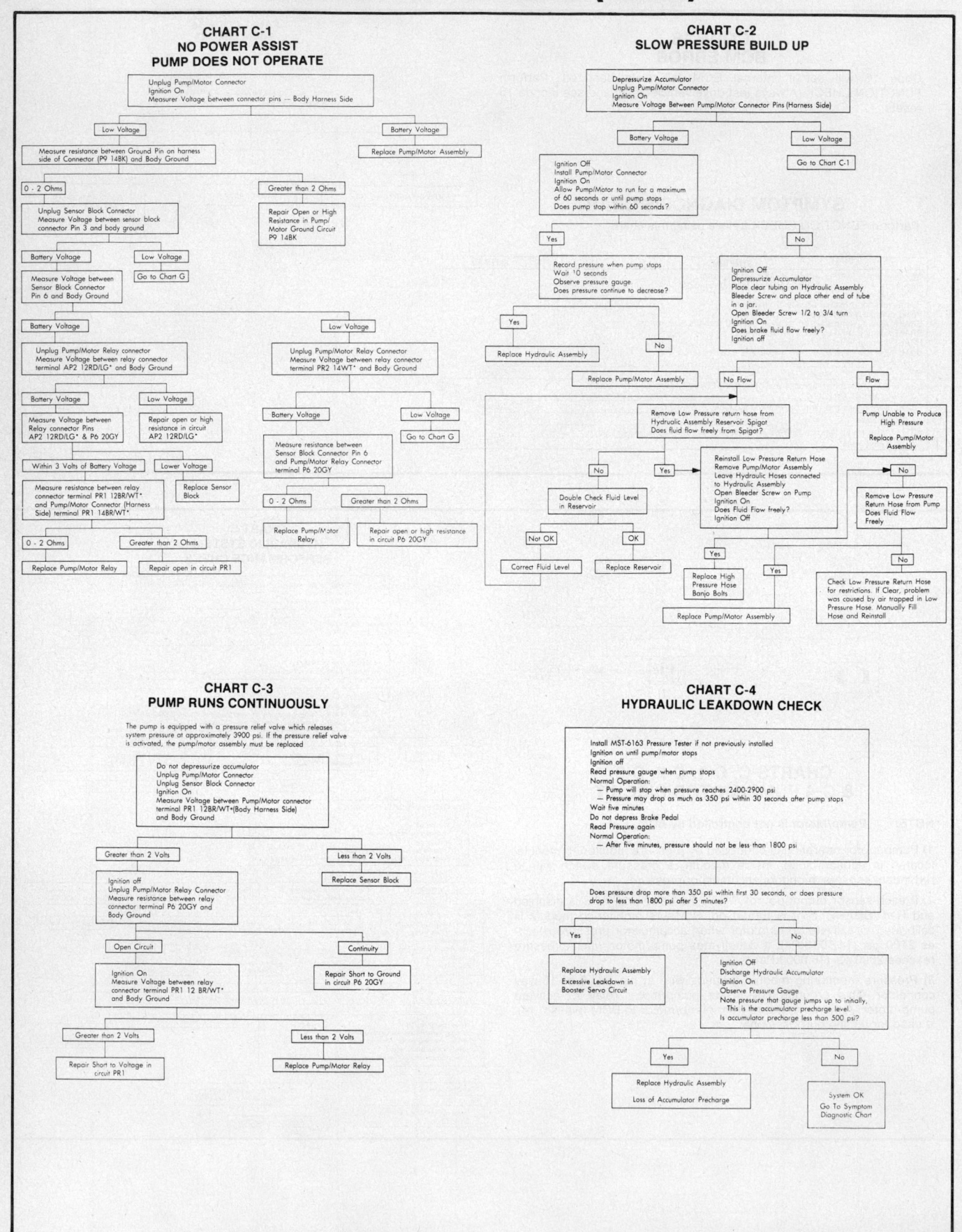

CHART C-1
NO POWER ASSIST PUMP DOES NOT OPERATE

CHART C-2
SLOW PRESSURE BUILD UP

CHART C-3
PUMP RUNS CONTINUOUSLY

CHART C-4
HYDRAULIC LEAKDOWN CHECK

BOSCH ANTI-LOCK BRAKE SYSTEM (ABS)
CHRYSLER MOTORS (Cont.)

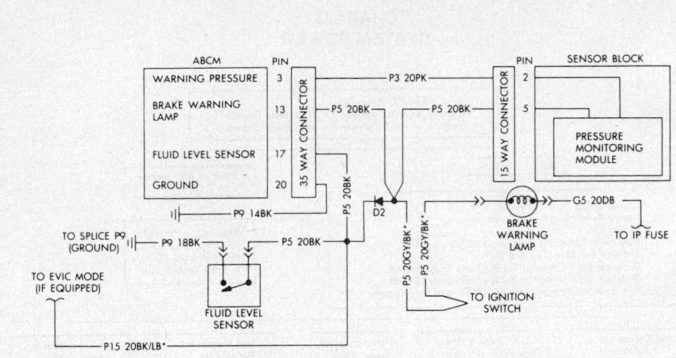

CHARTS D, E & F
RED "BRAKE" LIGHT CIRCUIT

1) Red "BRAKE" light is powered through instrument panel fuse. If failure in system is indicated, circuit is grounded and light will come on. Source that ground this circuit is BCM pin No. 13, when code is set.

2) Pressure monitoring module pin No. 5 (sensor block), if hydraulic pressure is 1400 psi (9660 kPa) or below. Light should automatically go off when pressure reaches 2100 psi (14,500 kPa).

3) If pressure monitoring module turned Red "BRAKE" light on, light will not go out or flash during ABS diagnostic mode. Parking brake switch will turn light on, if not fully released.

CHART D
STOPLIGHT LIGHT OFF
WITH KEY ON

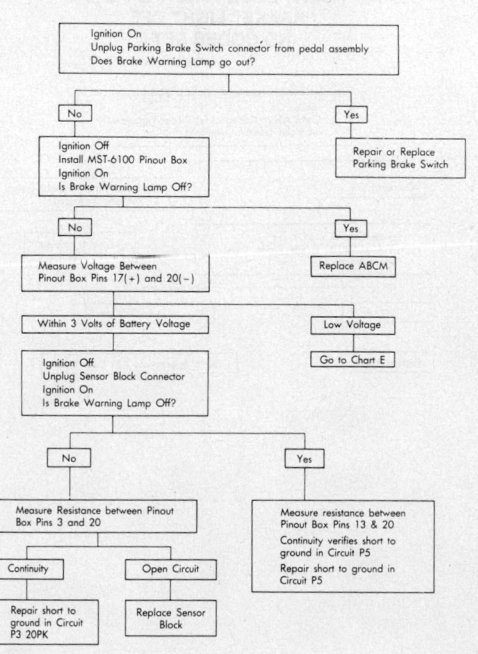

CHART E
"LOW BRAKE FLUID" DISPLAYED
WITH KEY ON OR "BRAKE" LIGHT ON

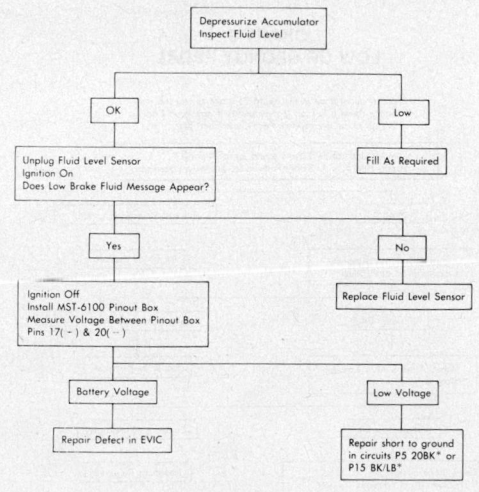

CHART F
"BRAKE" LIGHT ON CONSTANTLY
& POWER ASSIST AVAILABLE

Brake Systems

BOSCH ANTI-LOCK BRAKE SYSTEM (ABS)
CHRYSLER MOTORS (Cont.)

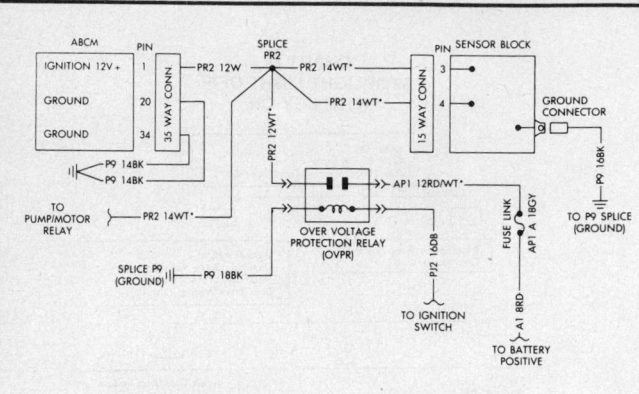

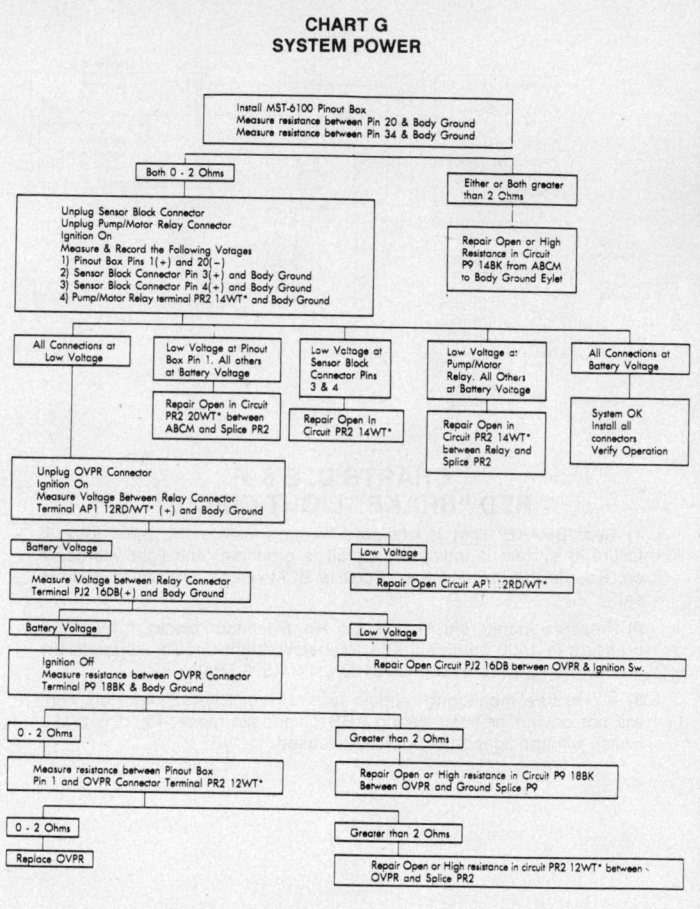

CHART G
SYSTEM POWER

CHARTS G, H & J
SYSTEM POWER CIRCUIT

ABS power is provided through over-voltage protection relay, located inside engine compartment, on left fender. Relay incorpates a special diode arrangement to propect system in case of excessively high system voltage. Over-protection relay powers: BCM pin No. 1, sensor block pins No. 3 and 4 and pump/motor relay.

CHART H
"ANTI-LOCK" LIGHT ON &
"BRAKE" LIGHT OFF
NO CODES SET

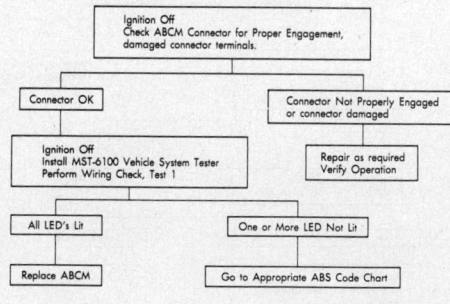

CHART J
LOW OR SPONGY PEDAL

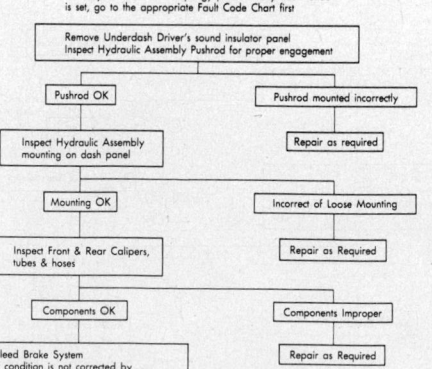

BOSCH ANTI-LOCK BRAKE SYSTEM (ABS) CHRYSLER MOTORS (Cont.)

Fig. 4: *Bosch Anti-Lock Brake System Wiring Diagram (Dynasty & New Yorker)*

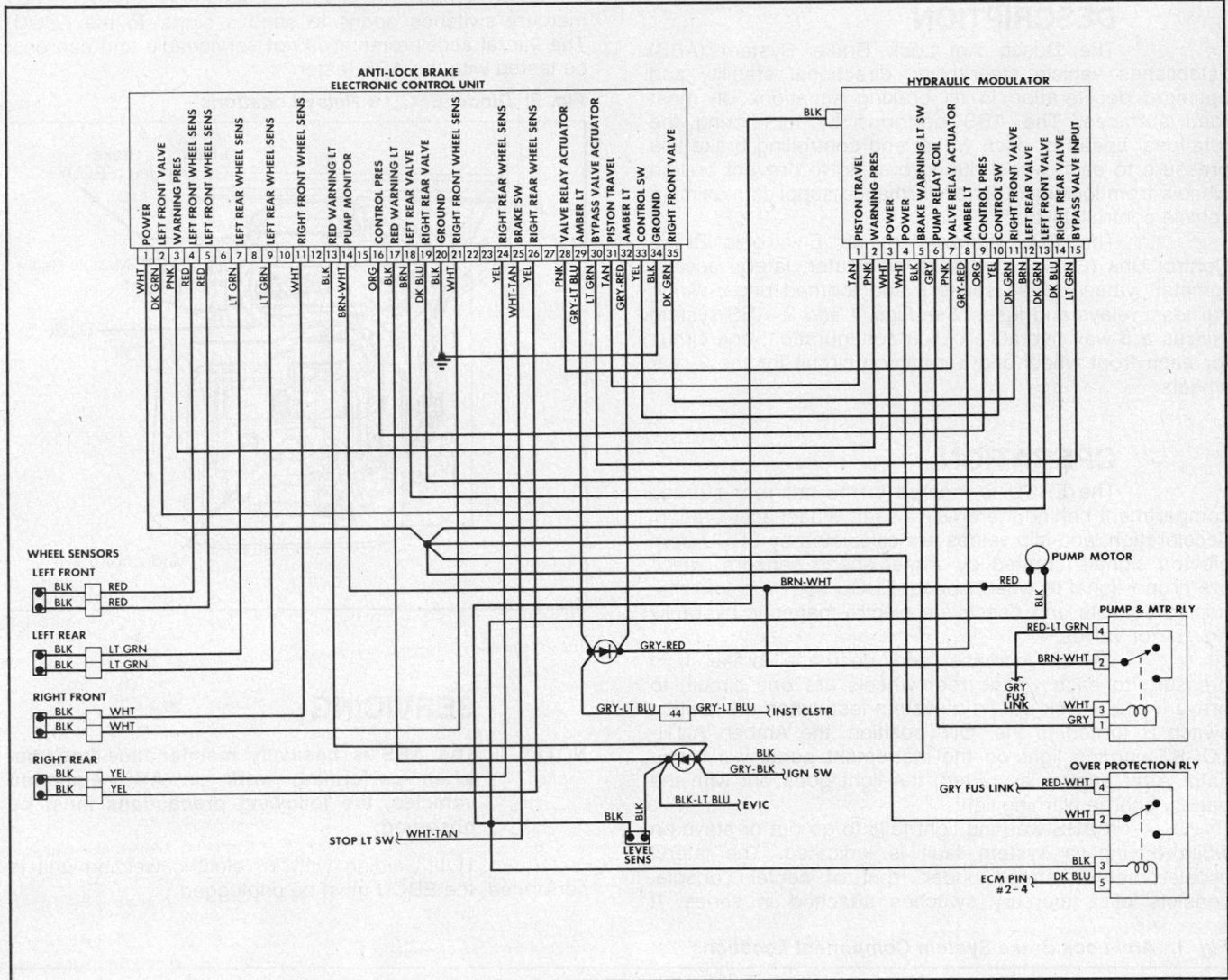

Brake Systems

BOSCH ANTI-LOCK BRAKE SYSTEMS (ABS) GENERAL MOTORS

Corvette

DESCRIPTION

The Bosch Anti-Lock Brake System (ABS) establishes vehicle steerability, directional stability and optimum deceleration in all braking situations on most road surfaces. The ABS performs by monitoring the rotational speed of each wheel and controlling brake line pressure to each wheel during braking to prevent braked wheels from locking. This performance supplies maximum vehicle controllability.

The ABS consists of an Electronic Brake Control Unit (EBCU), hydraulic modulator, lateral accelerometer, wheel speed sensors and toothed rings, wiring harness, relays and fuses. *See Figs. 1 and 2.* ABS system utilizes a 3-way hydraulic circuit configuration; one circuit for each front wheel and a common circuit for the 2 rear wheels.

OPERATION

The EBCU is located in the left rear storage compartment behind the driver's seat. Wheel acceleration, deceleration, and slip values are calculated by EBCU from electric signals created by wheel speed sensors, which are proportional to wheel speed. EBCU uses this information to activate and deactivate electro-magnetic hydraulic modulator valves.

Valves increase and decrease brake fluid pressure to each wheel (rear wheels are one circuit) to prevent wheel lock-up. As a system test, when the ignition switch is turned to the "ON" position, the Amber "ANTI-LOCK" warning light on the instrument panel will illuminate. After engine is started, the light goes out with the battery charge warning light.

If ABS warning light fails to go out or stays on while driving, a system fault is indicated. The lateral accelerometer, located under front of center console, consists of 2 mercury switches attached in series. It determines if vehicle is going around a corner faster than a given curve speed.

When this speed is exceeded, one of two mercury switches opens to send a signal to the EBCU. The lateral accelerometer is not serviceable and can only be tested with the ABS tester.

Fig. 2: Diode, EBCU & Relay Locations

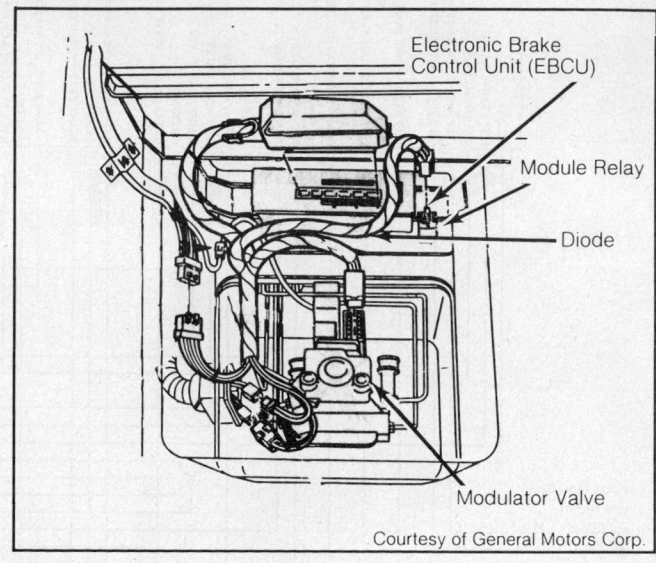

Electronic Brake Control Unit (EBCU)

Module Relay

Diode

Modulator Valve

Courtesy of General Motors Corp.

SERVICING

NOTE: **The ABS is basically maintenance-free, but when performing work on ABS equipped vehicles, the following precautions must be observed:**

1) If welding with an electric welding unit is performed, the EBCU must be unplugged.

Fig. 1: Anti-Lock Brake System Component Locations

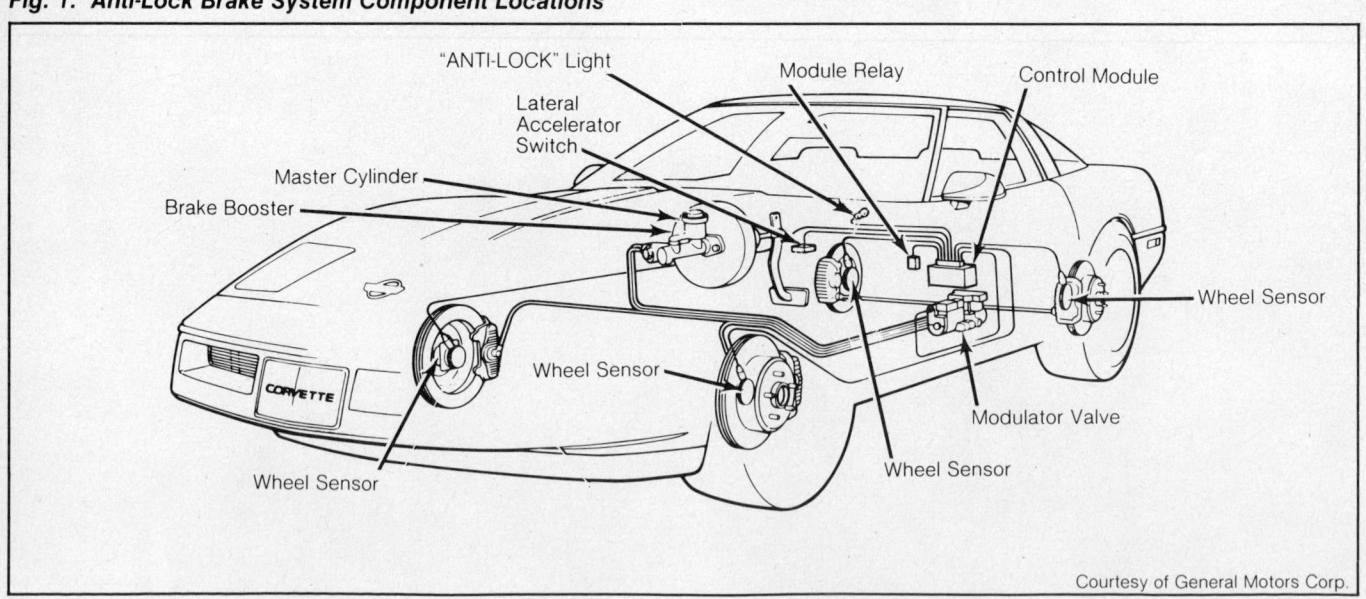

"ANTI-LOCK" Light

Lateral Accelerator Switch

Master Cylinder

Brake Booster

Module Relay

Control Module

Wheel Sensor

Wheel Sensor

Wheel Sensor

Modulator Valve

Wheel Sensor

Courtesy of General Motors Corp.

BOSCH ANTI-LOCK BRAKE SYSTEMS (ABS)
GENERAL MOTORS (Cont.)

2) During painting procedures, the EBCU may be subjected to a maximum of 203°F (95°C) for brief periods and a maximum of 185°F (85°C) for periods up to 2 hours.

3) After replacing hydraulic modulator, EBCU, wheel speed sensors or wiring harness as well as work involving ABS assemblies (i.e., work performed after accidents), the entire ABS system should be checked with the ABS Diagnostic Tester (J-35890). Ensure that brake lines are properly routed.

NOTE: **If brake lines are reversed (inlet vs. outlet), it can be detected in one of two ways, using ABS diagnosic tester or by doing an anti-stop, at which time wheels will do the opposite, lock-up.**

4) Do not use a fast charger to start the engine. Disconnect battery from vehicle electrical system when fast charging.

5) Never disconnect battery from vehicle electrical system with engine running. Ensure that all connectors of wiring harness are securely connected.

6) Never connect or disconnect wiring harness plug of EBCU with ignition switched on.

7) For safety reasons, hydraulic modulator must not be repaired, but complete unit must be replaced. Exceptions to this are return-pump relay and valve relay which are replaceable.

8) Do not loosen any screws on hydraulic modulator other than brake line connections. After loosening, it is no longer possible to get brake circuits leak tight.

9) When replacing hydraulic modulator, it must be removed through access in rear storage compartment. Protect vehicle interior/exterior to avoid damage from brake fluid spillage. Do not attempt to remove bottom of rear storage compartment to replace hydraulic modulator.

10) Be sure to wipe out bottom of rear storage compartment when replacing hydraulic modulator. Do not support suspension components by wheel speed sensor wires.

11) The wheel speed sensors are a tight fit into knuckle and are to be pushed in by hand. Do not hammer sensors into position.

Fig. 3: Exploded View of ABS Electrical Circuit & Testing Points

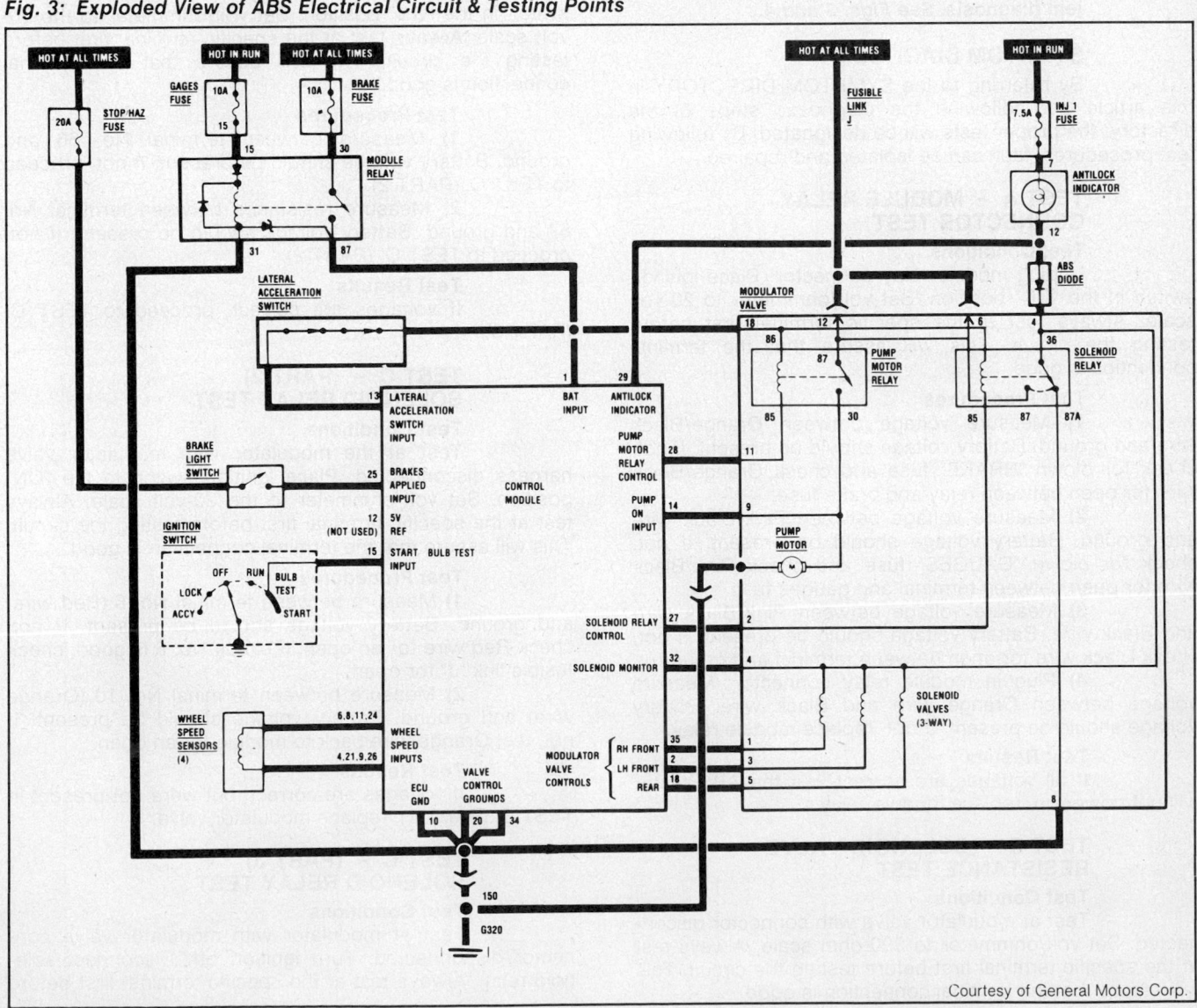

Courtesy of General Motors Corp.

Brake Systems

BOSCH ANTI-LOCK BRAKE SYSTEMS (ABS) GENERAL MOTORS (Cont.)

12) The 4 wheel speed sensors must be installed in their respective locations. Each is identified with a White tag, located 20 mm from sensor neck, labeled L (left) and R (right).

13) Remove tire and wheel assemblies when replacing sensors. Coat sensors with wax before installation. Do not use grease. The use of silicone brake fluid is prohibited.

14) Always note routing, position, mounting, and locations of all components, wiring, connectors, clips, brackets, brake lines, etc., when performing ABS system service. Proper system operation is only possible if system is restored to original equipment condition.

DIAGNOSIS & TESTING

NOTE: Diagnosis and testing requires use of ABS Diagnostic Tester (J-35890). Tester connects to vehicle through a removable wiring harness. Tester performs 6 seperate ABS tests and can be used to pinpoint ABS faults. Message on tester display will indicate proper lettered test to be followed for problem diagnosis. *See Figs. 3 and 4.*

SYMPTOM DIAGNOSIS

By referring to the SYMPTOM DIRECTORY in this article and following the diagnostic steps of the directory, the proper tests will be designated. By following test procedures, fault can be isolated and repaired.

TEST A – MODULE RELAY CONNECTOR TEST

Test Conditions

Unplug module relay connector. Place ignition switch in the "ON" position. Set volt/ohmmeter to 20-volt scale. Always test at the specific terminal first before testing the circuit. This will assure that the terminal connection is good.

Test Procedures

1) Measure voltage between Orange/Black wire and ground. Battery voltage should be present. If not, check for blown "BRAKE" fuse and check Orange/Black wire for open between relay and brake fuse.

2) Measure voltage between Pink/Black wire and ground. Battery voltage should be present. If not, check for blown "GAUGES" fuse and check Pink/Black wire for open between terminal and gauges fuse.

3) Measure voltage between Pink/Black wire and Black wire. Battery voltage should be present. If not, check Black wire for open between terminal and ground.

4) Plug in module relay connector. Measure voltage between Orange wire and Black wire. Battery voltage should be present. If not, replace module relay.

Test Results

If all voltages are correct, but the ABS tester will not power-up, replace module relay.

TEST B – SOLENOID VALVE RESISTANCE TEST

Test Conditions

Test at modulator valve with connector disconnected. Set volt/ohmmeter to 200-ohm scale. Always test at the specific terminal first before testing the circuit. This will assure that the terminal connection is good.

Test Procedures

1) Measure resistance between terminal No. 1 (Black/Red wire) and terminal No. 4 (Dark Green/White wire). Resistance should be between .8-1.5 ohms. If not, replace modulator valve.

2) Measure resistance between terminal No. 3 (Black/Yellow wire) and terminal No. 4 (Dark Green/White wire). Resistance should be between .8-1.5 ohms. If not, replace modulator valve.

3) Measure resistance between terminal No. 5 (Dark Blue/White wire) and terminal No. 4 (Dark Green/White wire). Resistance should be between .8-1.5 ohms. If not, replace modulator valve.

Test Results

If the actual measured values of resistance differ by more than 0.1 ohm from one solenoid valve to another, replace modulator valve. If measured resistance values are correct, return to SYMPTOM DIRECTORY.

TEST C – (PART 1) SOLENOID RELAY TEST

Test Conditions

Unplug solenoid relay connector. Place ignition switch in the "ON" position. Set volt/ohmmeter to the 20-volt scale. Always test at the specific terminal first before testing the circuit. This will assure that the terminal connection is good.

Test Procedures

1) Measure between terminal No. 86 and ground. Battery voltage should be present, If not, proceed to TEST C, (PART 2).

2) Measure resistance between terminal No. 87 and ground. Battery voltage should be present, If not, proceed to TEST C, (PART 2).

Test Results

If voltages are correct, proceed to TEST C, (PART 3).

TEST C – (PART 2) SOLENOID RELAY TEST

Test Conditions

Test at the modulator with modulator valve harness disconnected. Place ignition switch in the "ON" position. Set volt/ohmmeter to the 20-volt scale. Always test at the specific terminal first before testing the circuit. This will assure that the terminal connection is good.

Test Procedures

1) Measure between terminal No. 6 (Red wire) and ground. Battery voltage should be present. If not, check Red wire for an open. If circuit No. 6 is good, check fusible link "J" for open.

2) Measure between terminal No. 10 (Orange wire) and ground. Battery voltage should be present. If not, test Orange wire back to module for an open.

Test Results

If voltages are correct, but were not present in TEST C, (PART 1), replace modulator valve.

TEST C – (PART 3) SOLENOID RELAY TEST

Test Conditions

Test at modulator with modulator valve connector disconnected. Turn ignition off. Disconnect solenoid relay. Always test at the specific terminal first before

BOSCH ANTI-LOCK BRAKE SYSTEMS (ABS)
GENERAL MOTORS (Cont.)

testing the circuit. This will assure that the terminal connection is good.

Test Procedures

1) Measure resistance between solenoid relay connector terminal No. 85 and modulator valve connector terminal No. 2 (Light Green/Black wire). No resistance should be measured. If resistance is measured, replace modulator valve.

2) Measure resistance between solenoid relay connector terminal No. 30 and modulator valve connector terminal No. 4 (Dark Green/White wire). No resistance should be measured. If resistance is measured, replace modulator valve.

3) Measure resistance between solenoid relay connector terminal No. 87A and modulator valve connector terminal No. 8 (Black wire). No resistance should be measured. If resistance is measured, replace modulator valve.

Test Results

If voltage readings in TEST C, (PART 1) and resistance readings in this test are correct but ABS tester indicates that solenoid valves are open, replace solenoid valves.

TEST D – ANTI-LOCK BRAKE DIODE TEST

Test Conditions

Disconnect ABS diode. Using Digital Multimeter (J-34029), set for diode continuity, measure diode continuity.

Test Procedures

1) Measure between terminals No. 1 and 2. Correct reading should be between 0.4-0.6 ohms. If not, replace ABS diode.

2) Reverse probes and measure between same terminals again. Correct reading should be an open condition (infinity). If not, replace ABS diode.

Test Results

If results are correct, diode is good. If incorrect, replace diode.

TEST E – LATERAL ACCELERATION SWITCH TEST

Test Conditions

Turn ignition off. Disconnect lateral acceleration switch and remove from vehicle. Hold switch in approximate position and angle in which it was mounted in vehicle.

Test Procedures

1) Measure resistance between terminals No. 1 and 2. Correct reading shoud be zero ohms. If not, replace lateral acceleration switch.

2) Tilt switch and measure same terminals again. Correct reading should be an open condition (infinity). If not, replace lateral acceleration switch.

Test Results

If both measurements are correct, lateral acceleration switch is good. Return to SYMPTOM DIRECTORY for further diagnosis.

TEST F – WHEEL SPEED SENSOR TEST

Test Conditions

Turn ignition off. Disconnect EBCU connector. Attach Pin-Out Box (J-35592) to EBCU connector. Using a digital volt/ohmmeter set on the 2000-ohm scale, measure resistance between specific pins.

Test Procedures

1) Measure resistance between pin No. 4 (Yellow wire) and pin No. 6 (Light Blue wire). Resistance should be between 900-1500 ohms. If not, check left front wheel sensor connector for proper connection. Check connector, under LH side of cargo compartment, behind seat, for damage. Check sensor wires for opens. If all wiring is good and sensor resistance is incorrect, replace sensor.

2) Measure resistance between pin No. 11 (Dark Green wire) and pin No. 21 (Tan wire). Resistance should be between 900-1500 ohms. If not, check right front wheel sensor connector for proper connection. Check connector, under LH side of cargo compartment, behind seat, for damage. Check sensor wires for opens. If all wiring is good and sensor resistance is incorrect, replace sensor.

3) Measure resistance between pin No. 9 (Black wire) and pin No. 8 (Red wire). Resistance should be between 900-1500 ohms. If not, check left rear wheel sensor connector for proper connection. Check connector, under LH side of cargo compartment, behind seat, for damage. Check sensor wires for opens. If all wiring is good and sensor resistance is incorrect, replace sensor.

4) Measure resistance between pin No. 24 (Brown wire) and pin No. 26 (Light Blue wire). Resistance should be between 900-1500 ohms. If not, check right rear wheel sensor connector for proper connection. Check connector, under LH side of cargo compartment, behind seat, for damage. Check sensor wires for opens. If all wiring is good and sensor resistance is incorrect, replace sensor.

Test Results

Check that all sensors have a resistance value within 100 ohms of one another. If any sensor's resistance varies by more than 100 ohms from any others, replace sensor.

TEST G – (PART 1) PUMP MOTOR RELAY TEST

Test Conditions

Turn ignition switch to the "ON" position. Disconnect pump motor relay connector at the pump motor relay. Set volt/ohmmeter to the 20-volt scale. Always test at the specific terminal first before testing the circuit. This will assure that the terminal connection is good.

Test Procedures

1) Measure voltage between terminal No. 86 and ground. Battery voltage should be present. If not, proceed to TEST G (PART 2).

2) Measure voltage between terminal No. 87 and ground. Battery voltage should be present. If not, proceed to TEST G (PART 2).

Test Results

If voltages are correct, proceed to TEST G, (PART 3).

Brake Systems
BOSCH ANTI-LOCK BRAKE SYSTEMS (ABS)
GENERAL MOTORS (Cont.)

TEST G – (PART 2)
PUMP MOTOR RELAY TEST

Test Conditions
Turn ignition switch to the "ON" position. Disconnect modulator valve harness connector. Set volt/ohmmeter to the 20-volt scale. Always test at the specific terminal first before testing the circuit. This will assure that the terminal connection is good.

Test Procedures
1) Measure voltage between terminal No. 10 (Gray/Black wire) and ground. Battery voltage should be present. If not, check Gary/Black wire for an open back to the module relay.

2) Measure voltage between terminal No. 12 (Red wire) and ground. Battery voltage should be present. If not, check Red wire for an open between terminal No. 12 of the modulator relay and splice, located in ABS harness, under LH side of cargo compartment.

Test Results
If voltages are correct but were not present in TEST G, (PART 1), replace modulator valve.

TEST G – (PART 3)
PUMP MOTOR RELAY TEST

Test Conditions
Turn ignition off. Disconnect modulator valve connector. Set volt/ohmmeter to the 200-ohm scale. Always test at the specific terminal first before testing the circuit. This will assure that the terminal connection is good.

Test Procedures
1) With the pump motor relay connected, measure resistance between terminal No. 10 (Gray/Black wire) and terminal No. 11 (Black/Light Green wire). Approximately 50 ohms resistance should be read. If not, check pump motor relay for an open. If relay coil is good, replace modulator valve.

2) Remove pump motor relay. Measure resistance between terminal No. 30 (on pump motor relay plug-in) and terminal No. 9 (Black/Light Blue wire). Resistance measured should be less than 0.1 ohm. If not, replae modulator valve.

3) Measure resistance between terminal No. 9 (Black/Light Blue wire) and ground. Approximately 0.3 ohms should be present.

Test Results
If all measurements are correct but pump motor relay does not operate, replace pump motor.

REMOVAL & INSTALLATION

CAUTION: Before removal of any components which contain high pressure, it is mandatory that the hydraulic pressure in the system be reduced to managable levels. This can be accomplished by turning the ignition switch to the "OFF" position and pumping the brake pedal a minimum of 25 times until an increase in pedal force is clearly felt.

ELECTRONIC BRAKE
CONTROL UNIT (EBCU)

Removal & Installation
1) Remove negative battery cable. Remove storage tray and insulation from behind driver's seat. Disconnect control module connector by depressing spring clip under neck of connector. Remove 2 screws holding EBCU to bracket and remove EBCU.

2) To install EBCU, reverse removal procedure.

HYDRAULIC MODULATOR

Removal
1) Disconnect negative battery cable. Remove storage tray and insulation from behind driver's seat.

2) Disconnect and remove entire ABS wiring harness from storage compartment. See WIRING HARNESS REMOVAL in this section.

3) Disconnect hydraulic modulator ground from body harness. Place shop rags under hydraulic modulator fittings to catch and fluid which might spill.

4) Disconnect 5 brake lines from the modulator. Note locations for reassembly.

5) Remove 3 nuts holding modulator to bracket. Remove Modulator from storage compartment.

CAUTION: When removing hydraulic modulator from storage compartment, be careful not to spill brake fluid in interior of vehicle. Wipe fluid spillage from bottom of storage compartment.

Installation
To install hydraulic modulator, reverse removal procedure. Torque brake lines to 13 ft. lbs. (18 N.m). After completing installation, bleed brakes in the conventional manner in the following order: right front, right rear, left rear and left front.

LATERAL ACCELERATION
SWITCH

Removal & Installation
1) Disconnect negative battery cable. Remove screws holding trim plate to instrument cluster. Remove screws retaining instrument panel accessory trim plate. Remove trim plate.

2) Remove screws retaining console trim plate. Remove trimplate. Disconnect cigarette lighter.

3) Remove A/C control head. Remove lateral acceleration switch retaining bolts. Disconnect switch wiring harness. Remove switch.

4) To install switch, reverse removal procedure.

FRONT & REAR
SPEED SENSORS

Removal
1) Raise vehicle with floor jack and support on safety stands. Remove wheel assembly. Unclip sensor connector from bracket and disconnect.

2) Remove sensor wire grommets from brackets. Note wire routing for installation.

BOSCH ANTI-LOCK BRAKE SYSTEMS (ABS)
GENERAL MOTORS (Cont.)

3) Remove sensor hold-down bolts from steering knuckle. Remove sensor.

Installation

1) Coat new sensor with anti-corrosion compound. Install sensor in steering knuckle. DO NOT pound sensor into knuckle.

2) Install sensor hold-down bolts. To complete installation, reverse removal procedure. There are no adjustments required for speed sensors.

WIRING HARNESS
Removal & Installation

1) Disconnect negative battery cable. Remove storage tray and insulation from behind driver's seat.

2) Disconnect wiring harness connectors as follows:

- **Control module** - depress spring clip located under neck of connector and remove connector.

- **Modulator valve** - remove 2 screws from harness retainer. Remove connector.
- **Battery feed** - disconnect 12-gauge Red wire.
- **Wheel speed sensor** - disconnect.
- **Body harness** - disconnect.
- **Module relay** - remove module relay from control module bracket and disconnect.

3) To install harness, reverse removal procedure.

OVERHAUL

Component overhaul procedures are not available. If components test defective, entire component must be replaced.

Brake Systems
BOSCH ANTI-LOCK BRAKE SYSTEMS (ABS)
GENERAL MOTORS (Cont.)

MESSAGE	POSSIBLE CAUSE	CORRECTION
No Power-Up Messages	No battery voltage to ABS tester Open ABS ground circuit	Perform test "A" Repair ground circuit (Black wire from EBCU Pin No. 20)
LOW BATTERY	Battery not fully charged	Charge battery
LF VALVE OPEN (Left Front Solenoid Valve Open)	Open circuit in left front solenoid valve Open in wire between valve and EBCU	Perform test "B" Check for open in circuit No. 921
RF VALVE OPEN (Right Front Solenoid Valve Open)	Open circuit in right front wheel solenoid valve Open in wire between valve and EBCU	Perform test "B" Check for open in circuit No. 914
REAR VALVE OPEN	Open in rear wheels solenoid valve Open in wire between valve and EBCU	Perform test "B" Check for open in circuit No. 916
LF VALVE OPEN, RF VALVE OPEN, REAR VALVE OPEN	Open solenoid relay contacts Open between terminal No. 8 of modulator valve and grounding point (terminal No. G320)	Perform test "C" Part 3 Check for open in circuit No. 150
CHK ABS DIODE (Check ABS Diode)	Open or shorted ABS diode Open in circuits No. 915 or 922	Perform test "D" Check for opens in circuit No. 915 between ABS diode and terminal No. 29 of EBCU or circuit No. 922 between ABS diode and terminal No. 32 of EBCU
CHK CONT MOD GND (Check Control Module Ground)	Open in circuit No. 150 between EBCU and ground point (terminal No. G320)	Check for open in circuit No. 150 between EBCU terminal No. 20 and terminal "B" of connector No. C400 Check for open in circuit No. 150 between EBCU terminal No. 10 and terminal "B" of connector No. C400
CHK SYSTEM GND (Check System Ground)	Open circuit No. 150 between EBCU and ground point (terminal No. G320)	Check open in circuit No. 150 between terminal No. 34 of EBCU and terminal "B" of connector No. C400
LAT ACCEL SW OPEN (Lateral Acceleration Switch (LAS) Open)	Open lateral acceleration switch Open circuits No. 911, 919 or 920	Perform test "E" Check for loose connector Check circuits No. 911 and 919 between terminal No. 1 of EBCU and LAS Check circuit No. 920 between terminal No. 13 of EBCU and LAS
CHK BRK LIGHT SW (Check Brake Light Switch)	Blown "STOP/HAZ" fuse Misadjusted, permanently closed or inoperative brake light switch Open in circuit No. 20 between EBCU and brake light switch	Operate hazard flashers to test fuse Check for proper stop light operation If stop lights inoperative, replace Check that connectors No. C209 and C400 are firmly mated Check for open in circuit No. 20

Brake Systems

BOSCH ANTI-LOCK BRAKE SYSTEMS (ABS) GENERAL MOTORS (Cont.)

MESSAGE	POSSIBLE CAUSE	CORRECTION
CHK IGNITION SWITCH (Check Ignition Switch)	Ignition switch not grounded to terminal No. 15 of EBCU in "BULB TEST" and "START" mode Open in circuit No. 917 between EBCU and ignition switch	Check for proper operation of Ignition switch in "BULB TEST" and "START" conditions Check that connectors No. C210 and C400 are properly mated Check for an open in circuit No. 917
CHK LF SPD SENS (Check Left Front Speed Sensor)	Open in left front speed sensor	Perform test "F"
CHK RF SPD SENS (Check Right Front Speed Sensor)	Open in Right front speed sensor	Perform test "F"
CHK LR SPD SENS (Check Left Rear Speed Sensor)	Open in left Rear speed sensor	Perform test "F"
CHK RR SPD SENS (Check Right Rear Speed Sensor)	Open in Right Rear speed sensor	Perform test "F"
CHK ANTILOCK LT (Check Anti-Lock Light)	Anti-lock lamp burned-out Connector pin improperly mated Open in circuits No. 915 or 639 between INJ 1 fuse and EBCU	Replace lamp Check that connectors No. C210 and C400 are firmly mated Check for opens in circuits No. 639 and 915
CHK MOTOR RELAY (Check Motor Relay)	Pump motor relay not closing Open circuit to pump motor relay coil or pump "ON" circuit	Perform test "G" Check for open in circuit No. 913 Check for open in circuit No. 912
CHK SPD SENS CKT (Check Speed Sensor Circuit)	Damaged wheel speed sensor	Check sensor for damage
CHK TOOTHED WHL (Check Toothed Wheel)	Missing teeth in toothed wheel	Check for missing or damaged teeth Check sensor for damage
CHK VALVE RELAY (Check Valve Relay)	Solenoid relay inoperative Open circuit to solenoid relay or solenoid monitor input	Perform test "C" Check for open in circuit No. 918 Check for open in circuit No. 922 between modulator valve terminal No. 4 and EBCU terminal No. 32
CHK HYDRAULICS (Check Hydraulics)	Faulty hydraulic fluid connection	Inspect all brake fluid connections for signs of leaking
CHK HYDRA WIRING (Check Hydraulics Wiring)	Wiring to or inside modulator valve	Check modulator valve harness connector for tight fit Check that the solenoid and pump motor relays are properly seated

Brake Systems
BOSCH ANTI-LOCK BRAKE SYSTEMS (ABS) GENERAL MOTORS (Cont.)

Fig. 4: Bosch Anti-Lock Brake System Wiring Diagram (Corvette)

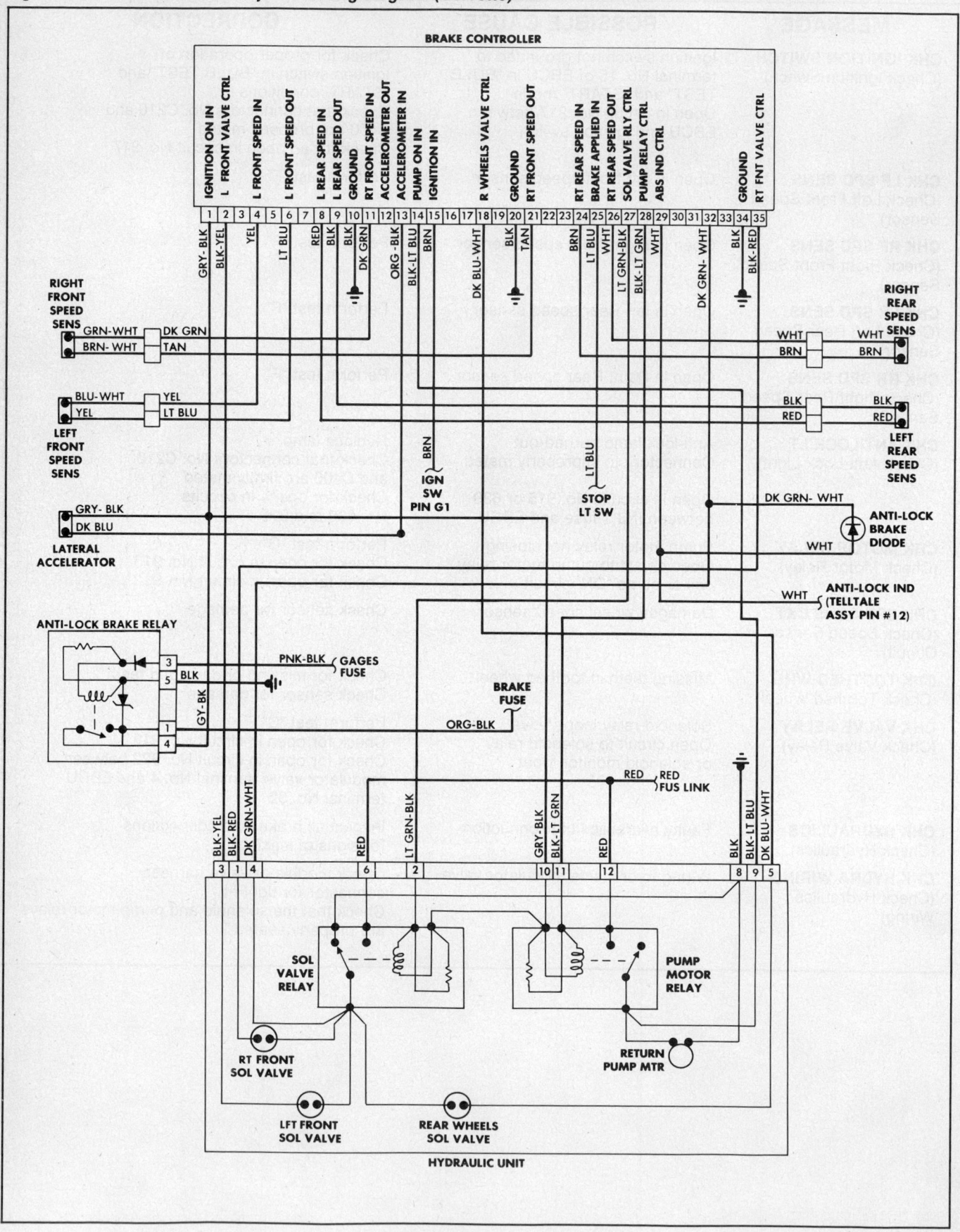

TEVES ANTI-LOCK BRAKE SYSTEMS (ABS) FORD MOTOR CO.

Ford: Thunderbird
Lincoln: Continental, Mark VII

DESCRIPTION

Teves Anti-Lock Brake System (ABS) is design to allow driver to stop vehicle in shortest distance while maintaining steering control. System consists of a master cylinder/booster assembly, electric pump/motor, solenoid valve block assembly, Electric Brake Control Module (EBCM), 4 wheel sensors and toothed rings, 2 warning lights ("ANTI-LOCK" and "BRAKE"), and various relays and switches. *See Fig. 1.*

OPERATION

EBCM receives an AC signal from each wheel sensor. This information is translated into calculated wheel speed. When EBCM determines that wheel lock-up is about to occur, solenoid valves are activated and deactivated to vary hydraulic pressure to each front wheel (separate circuits) and both rear wheels (one circuit) to prevent wheel lock-up.

Electric pump/motor assembly provides constant hydraulic pressure to actuation assembly. ABS does not operate during normal braking conditions. ABS has a self-diagnosis system to obtain trouble codes for testing purposes. See TESTING in this article.

Fig. 1: Anti-Lock Brake System Component Locations

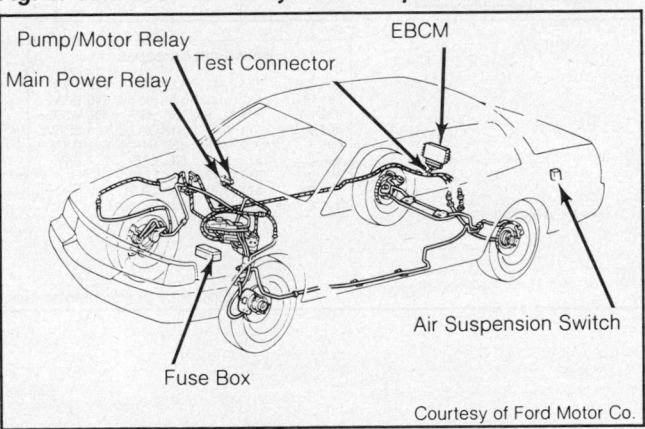

Pump/Motor Relay
Main Power Relay
Test Connector
EBCM
Fuse Box
Air Suspension Switch

Courtesy of Ford Motor Co.

DEPRESSURIZING BRAKE SYSTEM

CAUTION: **Failure to depressurize ABS before disconnecting any hydraulic component may lead top personnel injury.**

Turn ignition off. Pump brake pedal minimum of 20 times. Pedal force should increase. If not, continue until increased force is felt.

TESTING

NOTE: **Before hoisting vehicle off ground, turn air suspension switch, located in luggage compartment off. Failure to do so can damage air suspension.**

TESTING EQUIPMENT

There are 2 ways of testing ABS system: system check or quick check. Quick check will not find intermittent faults. System check requires Star Tester (007-00017) or Super Star Tester (007-00019), Break-Out Box (T83L-50-EEC-IV), Adapter (T87P-50-ALA) and a digital multimeter. Quick check requires break-out box and adapter.

TESTING PROCEDURE & PRECAUTIONS

Testing should be done in the following sequence: On-Board Self-Test Codes, Manual Quick Check, Warning Light Symptom Chart, and Trouble Shooting Charts. If Star Tester is not available, On-Board Self-Test Codes step may be eliminated.

Failure to test system in sequence will result in misdiagnosis of ABS and unnecessary replacement of components. EBCM cannot store trouble code with same first digit (25 and 26). Lowest number code (25) will be stored first.

Solenoid valve service code will override all other codes stored. If no codes are stored, system has passed self-test. If code appears, refer to PIN POINT TEST chart. If "BRAKE" warning light is on or intermittently comes on, use diagnostic light symptom chart. *See Fig. 3.*

TESTING STAR TESTER OR SUPER START TESTER

1) Turn ignition off. Open luggage compartment. On Thunderbird, lower RH module panel. On Continental FWD, remove panel from rear seat. On all models, connect Star Tester or Super Star Tester to test plug. Turn tester power switch on. "00" should appear on tester.

2) This indicates tester is ready to receive test codes. If "LO BAT" appears, replace tester battery. Push "SELF-TEST" button. A colon should appear. Press button again to deactivate tester. Tester is ready to obtain codes.

OBTAINING TROUBLE CODES

1) Connect start tester. Turn tester on. Latch button down in "TEST" position. Turn ignition on. First code should appear on tester. Push button on tester to hold code. Place button in "TEST" position again. Record second code. Continue this procdure until all codes are received. See TROUBLE CODE INDEX table.

NOTE: **Super Start Tester will only display codes in tenths (10, 20, etc.). To identify code, disregard last beep or flash. All codes in the 20's must be serviced before any other code can be obtained.**

2) After code has been serviced, it can be ignored. If code 61 is received with any other code, disregard it. If code 61 appears with no other code, service code 61. If no code or code 10 appears, diagnosis problem. *See Fig. 4.*

CLEARING TROUBLE CODES

After all stored trouble codes have been received and serviced, operate vehicle above 25 MPH. Memory should be cleared. If not, check for more codes stored. All codes must be received before memory can be cleared.

Brake Systems

TEVES ANTI-LOCK BRAKE SYSTEMS (ABS) FORD MOTOR CO. (Cont.)

Fig. 2: Anti-Lock Brake System Testing Circuits

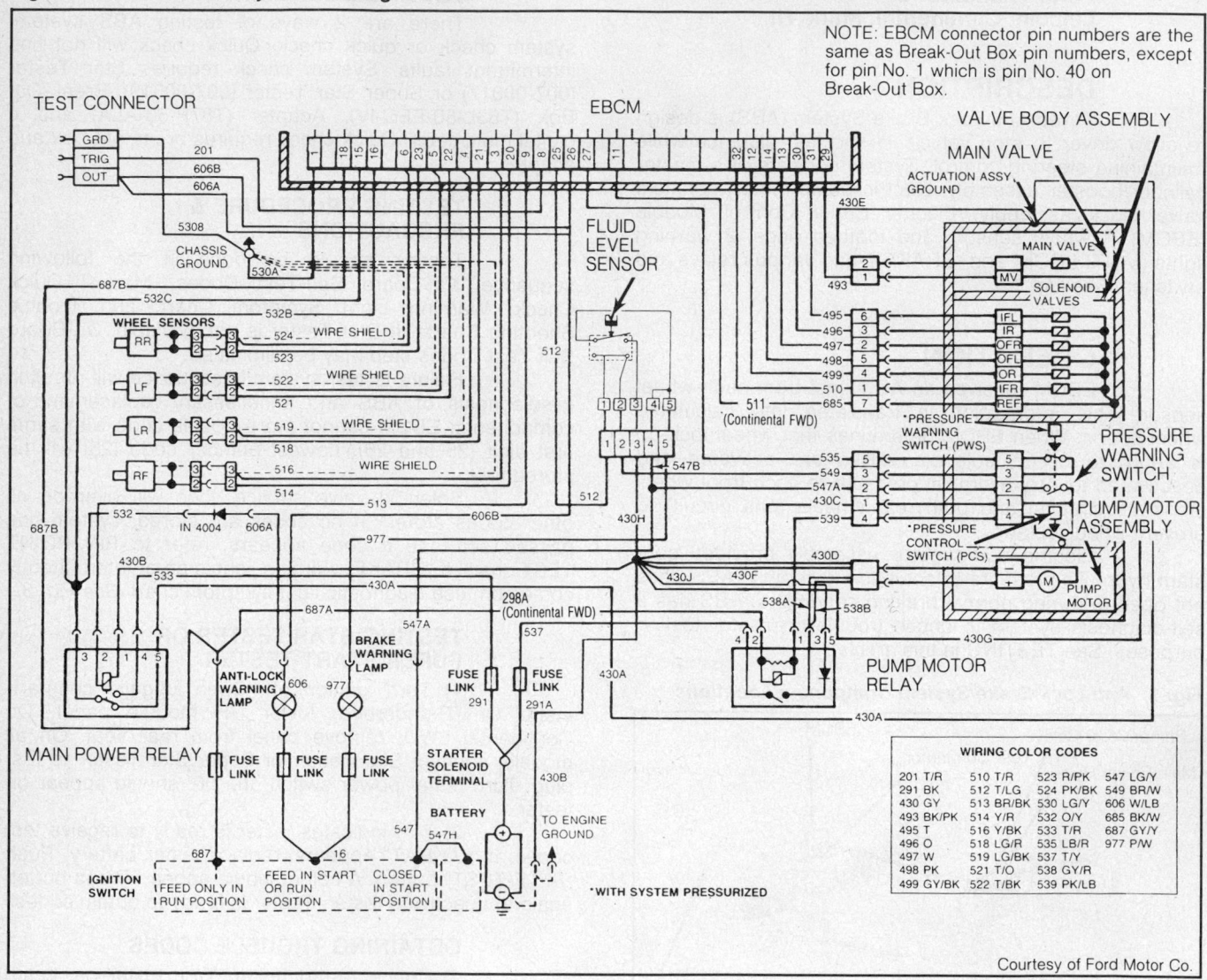

Courtesy of Ford Motor Co.

Brake Systems

TEVES ANTI-LOCK BRAKE SYSTEMS (ABS) FORD MOTOR CO. (Cont.)

Fig. 3: Diagnostic Light Symptom Sequence

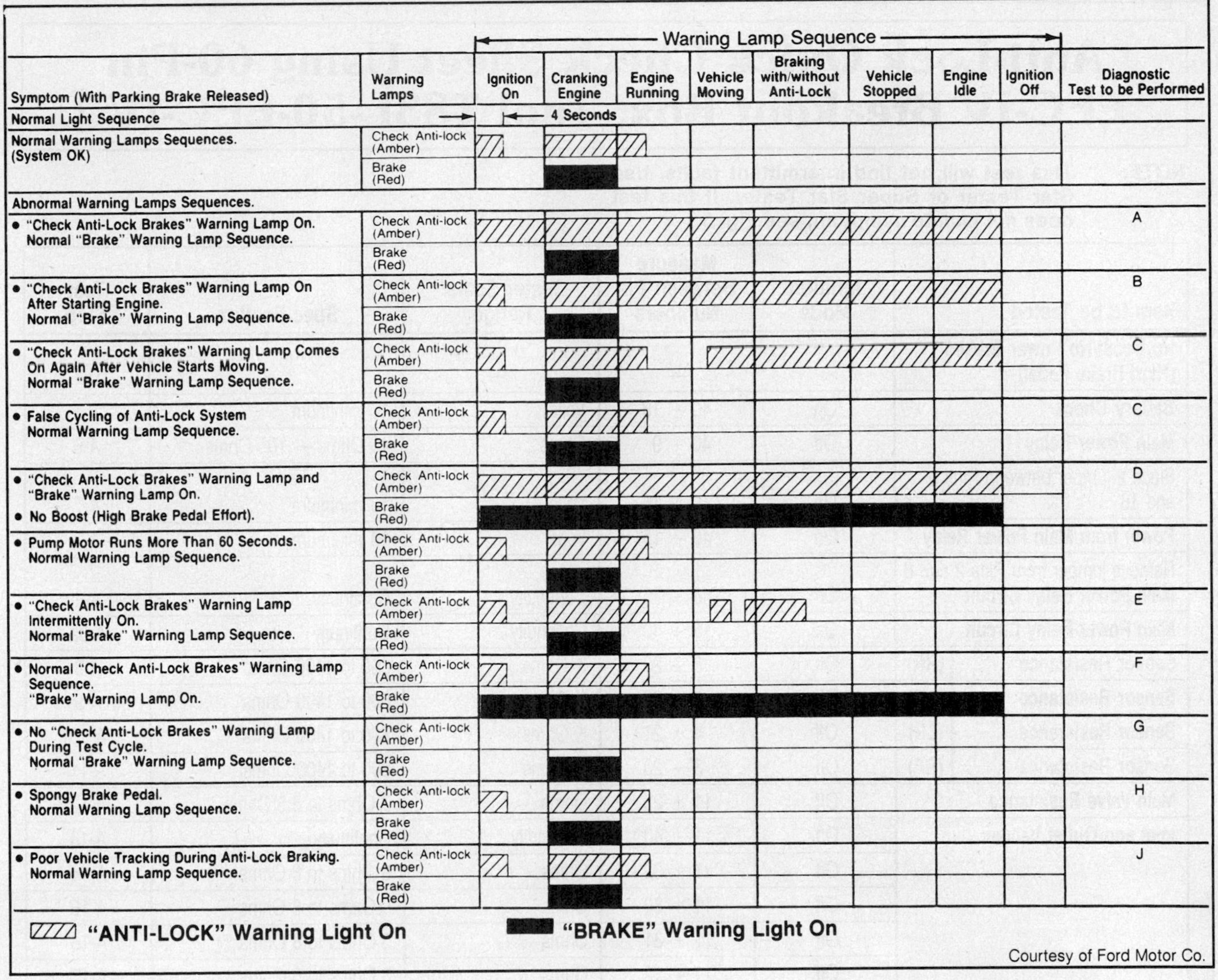

Symptom (With Parking Brake Released)	Warning Lamps	Ignition On	Cranking Engine	Engine Running	Vehicle Moving	Braking with/without Anti-Lock	Vehicle Stopped	Engine Idle	Ignition Off	Diagnostic Test to be Performed
Normal Light Sequence (←4 Seconds→)										
Normal Warning Lamps Sequences. (System OK)	Check Anti-lock (Amber)	▨	▨							
	Brake (Red)		████							
Abnormal Warning Lamps Sequences.										
• "Check Anti-Lock Brakes" Warning Lamp On. Normal "Brake" Warning Lamp Sequence.	Check Anti-lock (Amber)	▨	▨	▨	▨	▨	▨	▨		A
	Brake (Red)		████							
• "Check Anti-Lock Brakes" Warning Lamp On After Starting Engine. Normal "Brake" Warning Lamp Sequence.	Check Anti-lock (Amber)	▨		▨	▨	▨	▨	▨		B
	Brake (Red)		████							
• "Check Anti-Lock Brakes" Warning Lamp Comes On Again After Vehicle Starts Moving. Normal "Brake" Warning Lamp Sequence.	Check Anti-lock (Amber)	▨	▨		▨	▨	▨	▨		C
	Brake (Red)		████							
• False Cycling of Anti-Lock System Normal Warning Lamp Sequence.	Check Anti-lock (Amber)	▨	▨							C
	Brake (Red)		████							
• "Check Anti-Lock Brakes" Warning Lamp and "Brake" Warning Lamp On. • No Boost (High Brake Pedal Effort).	Check Anti-lock (Amber)	▨	▨	▨	▨	▨	▨	▨		D
	Brake (Red)	████	████	████	████	████	████	████		
• Pump Motor Runs More Than 60 Seconds. Normal Warning Lamp Sequence.	Check Anti-lock (Amber)	▨	▨							D
	Brake (Red)		████							
• "Check Anti-Lock Brakes" Warning Lamp Intermittently On. Normal "Brake" Warning Lamp Sequence.	Check Anti-lock (Amber)	▨	▨		▨ ▨					E
	Brake (Red)		████							
• Normal "Check Anti-Lock Brakes" Warning Lamp Sequence. "Brake" Warning Lamp On.	Check Anti-lock (Amber)	▨	▨							F
	Brake (Red)	████	████	████	████	████	████	████		
• No "Check Anti-Lock Brakes" Warning Lamp During Test Cycle. Normal "Brake" Warning Lamp Sequence.	Check Anti-lock (Amber)									G
	Brake (Red)		████							
• Spongy Brake Pedal. Normal Warning Lamp Sequence.	Check Anti-lock (Amber)	▨	▨							H
	Brake (Red)		████							
• Poor Vehicle Tracking During Anti-Lock Braking. Normal Warning Lamp Sequence.	Check Anti-lock (Amber)	▨	▨							J
	Brake (Red)		████							

▨ "ANTI-LOCK" Warning Light On   ████ "BRAKE" Warning Light On

Courtesy of Ford Motor Co.

Brake Systems

TEVES ANTI-LOCK BRAKE SYSTEMS (ABS) FORD MOTOR CO. (Cont.)

Fig. 4: Anti-Lock Brake System Check Quick Chart Using Break-Out Box (T83L-50-EEC-IV)

Anti-Lock Quick Check Sheet Using 60-Pin EEC-IV Breakout Box, Tool T83L-50-EEC-IV ①

NOTE: This test will not find intermittent faults. Use Star Tester or Super Star Tester. If this test does not isolate symptom, see Fig. 3.

Item to be Tested		Ignition Mode	Measure Between Pin Numbers	Tester Scale/ Range	Specification	Test Step
No Boost/No Power Brakes (Hard Brake Pedal)		—	—	—	—	D-1
Battery Check		On	40 + 18	Volts	10 minimum	A-1
Main Power Relay		Off	40 + 9	Ohms	45 Ohms — 105 Ohms	A-6
Place a jumper between Pins 9 and 18		On	40 + 16	Volts	10 minimum	A-7
Power from Main Power Relay		On	40 + 15	Volts	10 minimum	A-3
Remove jumper from Pins 2 and 8 Main Power Relay Circuit		Off	40 + 16	Continuity	Continuity	A-2
Main Power Relay Circuit		Off	15 + 40	Continuity	Continuity	A-3a
Sensor Resistance	(RR)	Off	6 + 23	K Ohms	800 to 1400 Ohms	A-8
Sensor Resistance	(LF)	Off	5 + 22	K Ohms	800 to 1400 Ohms	A-9
Sensor Resistance	(LR)	Off	4 + 21	K Ohms	800 to 1400 Ohms	A-10
Sensor Resistance	(RF)	Off	3 + 20	K Ohms	800 to 1400 Ohms	A-11
Main Valve Resistance		Off	11 + 29	Ohms	2 Ohms to 5.5 Ohms	A-12
Inlet and Outlet Valves		Off	11 + 40	Continuity	Continuity	A-13
		Off	11 + 32	Ohms	5 Ohms to 8 Ohms	A-14
		Off	11 + 30	Ohms	5 Ohms to 8 Ohms	A-15
		Off	11 + 31	Ohms	5 Ohms to 8 Ohms	A-16
		Off	11 + 12	Ohms	3 Ohms to 6 Ohms	A-17
		Off	11 + 14	Ohms	3 Ohms to 6 Ohms	A-18
		Off	11 + 13	Ohms	3 Ohms to 6 Ohms	A-19
Reservoir Warning		On	25 + 27	Ohms	Less than 5 Ohms	A-4a
Remove Reservoir Cap. With a Non-Magnetic Probe, Push the Float Down Until Bottoming		Off	25 + 27	Ohms	Infinite (Open Circuit)	A-5a
Sensor Cable Continuity Shielding to Ground	(RR)	Off	40 + 6	Continuity	No Continuity	B-1a
	(LF)	Off	40 + 5	Continuity	No Continuity	B-2a
	(LR)	Off	40 + 4	Continuity	No Continuity	B-3a
	(RF)	Off	40 + 3	Continuity	No Continuity	B-4a
Sensor Voltage (Rotate wheels at 1 revolution per second minimum) (Shut off air suspension switch in luggage compartment with vehicle on hoist if so equipped).	(RR)	Off	6 + 23	AC Millivolts	50-700 Millivolts	C-5
	(LF)	Off	5 + 22	AC Millivolts	50-700 Millivolts	C-6
	(LR)	Off	4 + 21	AC Millivolts	50-700 Millivolts	C-7
	(RF)	Off	3 + 20	AC Millivolts	50-700 Millivolts	C-8

① If Quick Test does not isolate symptom, refer to Diagnostic Lamp Symptom Chart.

Courtesy of Ford Motor Co.

TEVES ANTI-LOCK BRAKE SYSTEMS (ABS)
FORD MOTOR CO. (Cont.)

Fig. 5: Connector Testing Points

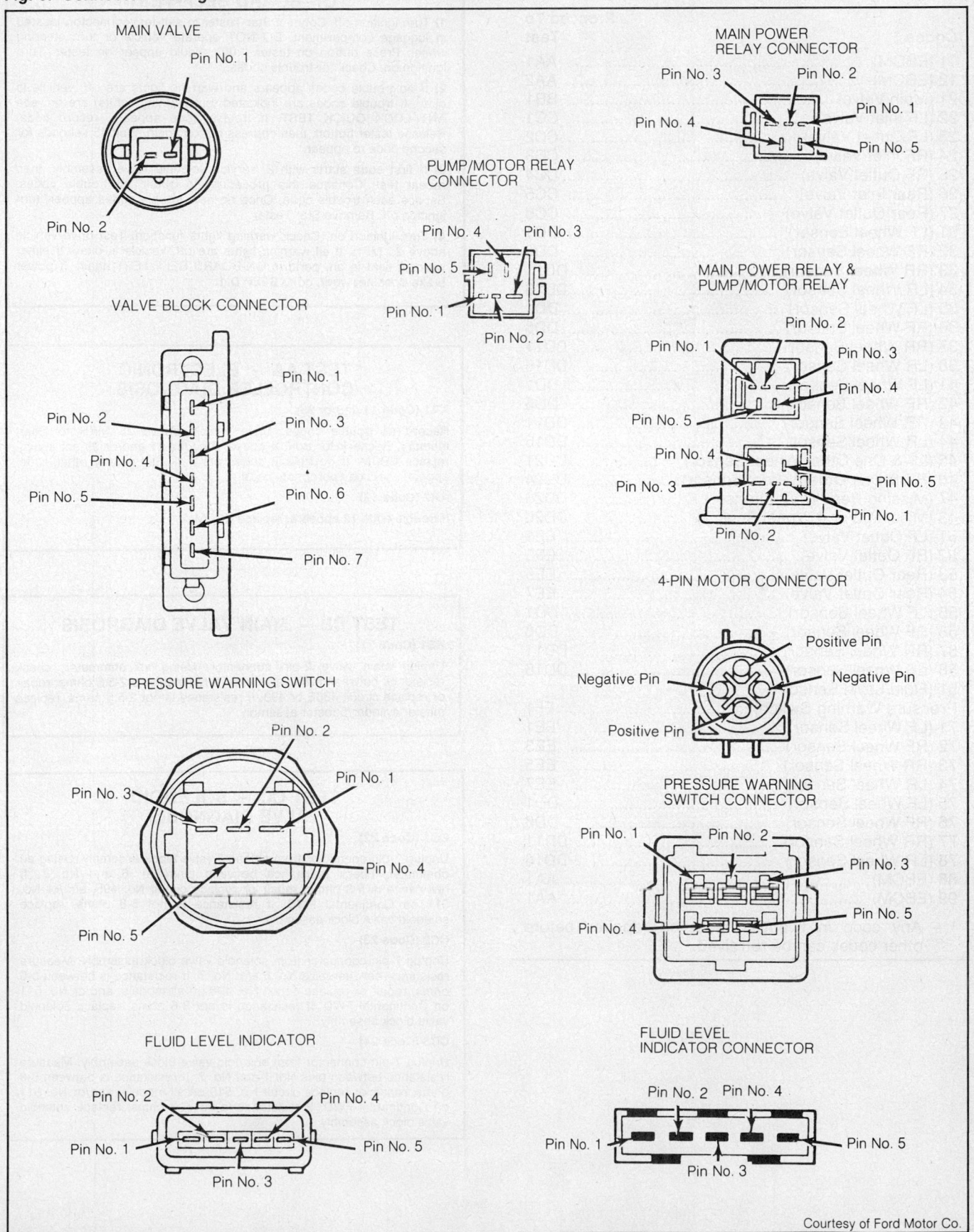

Brake Systems

TEVES ANTI-LOCK BRAKE SYSTEMS (ABS) FORD MOTOR CO. (Cont.)

TROUBLE CODE INDEX

Codes [1]	Procced To Test
11 (EBCM)	AA1
12 (EBCM)	AA2
21 (Main Valve)	BB1
22 (LF Inlet Valve)	CC1
23 (LF Outlet Valve)	CC2
24 (RF Inlet Valve)	CC3
25 (RF Outlet Valve)	CC4
26 (Rear Inlet Valve)	CC5
27 (Rear Outlet Valve)	CC6
31 (LF Wheel Sensor)	DD1
32 (RF Wheel Sensor)	DD6
33 (RR Wheel Sensor)	DD11
34 (LR Wheel Sensor)	DD16
35 (LF Wheel Sensor)	DD1
36 (RF Wheel Sensor)	DD6
37 (RR Wheel Sensor)	DD11
38 (LR Wheel Sensor)	DD16
41 (LF Wheel Sensor)	DD1
42 (RF Wheel Sensor)	DD6
43 (RR Wheel Sensor)	DD11
44 (LR Wheel Sensor)	DD16
45 (LF & One Other Wheel Sensor)	DD21
46 (RF & One Other Wheel Sensor)	DD24
47 (Missing Rear Wheel Sensor)	DD25
48 (Missing 3 or 4 Wheel Sensor)	DD26
51 (LF Outlet Valve)	EE1
52 (RF Outlet Valve)	EE3
53 (Rear Outlet Valve)	EE5
54 (Rear Outlet Valve)	EE7
55 (LF Wheel Sensor)	DD1
56 (RF Wheel Sensor)	DD6
57 (RR Wheel Sensor)	DD11
58 (LR Wheel Sensor)	DD16
61 (Fluid Level Sensor & Pressure Warning Switch)	FF1
71 (LF Wheel Sensor)	EE1
72 (RF Wheel Sensor)	EE3
73 (RR Wheel Sensor)	EE5
74 (LR Wheel Sensor)	EE7
75 (LF Wheel Sensor)	DD1
76 (RF Wheel Sensor)	DD6
77 (RR Wheel Sensor)	DD11
78 (LR Wheel Sensor)	DD16
88 (EBCM)	AA1
99 (EBCM)	AA1

[1] – Any code in twenties must be repaired before other codes can be retreived.

ON-BOARD SELF-TEST

1) Turn ignition off. Connect Star Tester to self-test connector, located in luggage compartment. DO NOT operate vehicle or turn steering wheel. Press button on tester. ":00" should appear on tester. Turn ignition on. Check for trouble codes.

2) If no trouble codes appears and warning lights are off, vehicle is okay. If trouble codes are indicated, but warning light(s) are on, see ANTI-LOCK QUICK TEST. If trouble code appears, record code. Release tester button, then depress button again. Wait 45 seconds for second code to appear.

3) If first code starts with 2, service solenoid valve assembly, then repeat test. Continue this procedure to obtain all trouble codes. Service each trouble code. Once no new trouble codes appear, turn ignition off. Remove Star Tester.

4) Turn ignition on. Check warning lights function. Test drive vehicle above 25 MPH. If all warning lights are off, vehicle is okay. If either warning light is on, perform ON-BOARD SELF-TEST again. If power brake does not work, go to **STEP D-1**.

TEST AA – ELECTRONIC CONTROLLER DIAGNOSIS

AA1 (Code 11 and/or 99)

Record all trouble codes. Drive vehicle above 25 MPH to clear memory. Recheck for trouble codes. If codes 11 and/or 99 set again, replace EBCM. If no trouble codes are indicated or any other code appears, service appropriate code.

AA2 (Code 12)

If trouble code 12 appears, replace EBCM.

TEST BB – MAIN VALVE DIAGNOSIS

BB1 (Code 21)

Unplug main valve 2-pin connector. Using an ohmmeter, check resistance between main valve pins. If resistance is 2-5.5 ohms, repair or replace circuit 430E or 493. If resistance is not 2-5.5 ohms, replace master cylinder/booster assembly.

TEST CC – SOLENOID VALVE DIAGNOSIS

CC1 (Code 22)

Unplug 7-pin connector from solenoid valve block assembly. Using an ohmmeter, check resistance between pins No. 6 and No. 7. If resistance is 5-8 ohms, repair or replace circuit No. 495, and/or No. 511 on Continental FWD. If resistance is not 5-8 ohms, replace solenoid valve block assembly.

CC2 (Code 23)

Unplug 7-pin connector from solenoid valve block assembly. Measure resistance between pins No. 5 and No. 7. If resistance is between 3-6 ohms, repair or replace circuit No. 498, and/or No. 511 on Continental FWD. If resistance is not 3-6 ohms, replace solenoid valve block assembly.

CC3 (Code 24)

Unplug 7-pin connector from solenoid valve block assembly. Measure resistance between pins No. 1 and No. 7. If resistance is between 5-8 ohms, repair or replace circuit No. 510 on all models, and/or No. 511 on Continental FWD. If resistance is not 5-8 ohms, replace solenoid valve block assembly.

TEVES ANTI-LOCK BRAKE SYSTEMS (ABS)
FORD MOTOR CO.

TEST CC – SOLENOID VALVE DIAGNOSIS (Cont.)

CC4 (Code 25)

Unplug 7-pin connector from solenoid valve block assembly. Measure resistance between pins No. 2 and No. 7. If resistance is between 3-6 ohms, repair or replace circuit No. 497 on all models, and/or No. 511 on Continental FWD. If resistance is not 3-6 ohms, replace solenoid valve block assembly.

CC5 (Code 26)

Unplug 7-pin connector from solenoid valve block assembly. Measure resistance between pins No. 5 and No. 7. If resistance is between 3-6 ohms, repair or replace circuit No. 498 on all models, and/or No. 511 on Continental FWD. If resistance is not 3-6 ohms, replace solenoid valve block assembly.

CC6 (Code 27)

1) Turn ignition off. Unplug 32-pin connector from EBCM. Connect Break-Out Box (T83L-50-EEC-IV) and Adapter (T87P-50-ALA) to connector. Measure resistance between pin No. 11 and No. 12 on break-out box. If resistance is 3-6 ohms, go to **CC7**. If resistance is not 3-6 ohms, go to next step.

2) Unplug 7-pin connector from solenoid valve block assembly. Measure resistance between pins No. 4 and No. 7. If resistance is 3-6 ohms, repair or replace circuit No. 499 on all models, and/or No. 511 on Continental FWD. If resistance is not 3-6 ohms, replace solenoid valve block assembly.

CC7 (Solenoid Valve Ground)

1) Measure resistance between pins No. 11 and No. 40 on break-out box. If resistance less than 2 ohms, reverify symptom. If resistance is 2 ohms or more, go to next step.

2) Check resistance between pin No. 7 on solenoid valve 7-pin connector and solenoid valve block assembly body. If resistance is less than 2 ohms, repair or replace circuit No. 685. If resistance is 2 ohms or more, disconnect negative battery cable.

3) Check for continuity between between solenoid valve body and body ground. If there is continuity, replace solenoid valve body assembly. If there is no or poor continuity, repair or replace circuit 430G.

TEST DD – WHEEL SENSOR DIAGNOSIS

DD1 (Codes 31, 35, 41, 55 or 75)

1) Turn ignition off. Unplug 32-pin connector from EBCM. Connect break-out box and adapter. Measure resistance at pins No. 5 and No. 22 on break-out box. If resistance is 800-1400 ohms, go to **DD2**.

2) If resistance is not 800-1400 ohms, unplug LF wheel sensor connector. If resistance is 800-1400 ohms, repair or replace circuit No. 521 or No. 522. If resistance is not 800-1400 ohms, replace wheel sensor.

DD2 (LF Wheel Sensor Voltage)

1) Turn ignition off. Open luggage compartment and turn air suspension switch off (if equipped). Raise vehicle and support. Place multimeter on "2V" in AC range. Rotating LF wheel at one revolution per second, measure voltage at break-out box pins No. 5 and No. 22.

2) If voltage is .05-.70 volt, go to **DD3**. If voltage is not .05-.70 volt, check sensor mounting, sensor air gap or toothed ring for damage, wear or misalignment.

DD3 (LF Wheel Sensor Continuity – Continental FWD)

Check for continuity between break-out box pin No. 40 and body ground. If there is continuity, go to **DD5**. If there is no continuity, repair or replace circuit No. 530.

DD3 (LF Wheel Sensor Continuity – All Others)

1) Check for continuity between break-out box pins No. 5 and No. 40. If there is no continuity, go to **DD4**. If there is continuity, unplug LF wheel sensor connector.

2) Check for continuity between each wheel sensor terminal and body ground. If there is continuity at either terminal, replace wheel sensor. If there is no continuity at either terminal, Repair or replace wheel sensor cable.

TEST DD – WHEEL SENSOR DIAGNOSIS (Cont.)

DD4 (EBCM Ground Circuit)

Check for continuity between break-out box pin No. 40 and body ground. If there is continuity, go to **DD5**. If continuity is not present, repair or replace circuit No. 530A.

DD5 (LF Wheel Bearing)

Check front wheel bearing adjustment. See appropriate FRONT SUSPENSION article in SUSPENSION section. Check toothed sensor ring for damage. Adjust wheel bearings or replace toothed sensor ring. If no problem is found, reverify symptom.

DD6 (Codes 32, 36, 42, 56 or 76)

1) Turn ignition off. Unplug 32-pin connector from EBCM. Connect break-out box and adapter. Measure resistance at pins No. 3 and No. 20 on break-out box. If resistance is 800-1400 ohms, go to **DD7**.

2) If resistance is not 800-1400 ohms, unplug RF wheel sensor connector. If resistance is 800-1400 ohms, repair or replace circuit No. 514 or No. 516. If resistance is not 800-1400 ohms, replace wheel sensor.

DD7 (RF Wheel Sensor Voltage)

1) Turn ignition off. Open luggage compartment and turn air suspension switch off (if equipped). Raise vehicle and support. Place multimeter on "2V" in AC range. Rotating RF wheel at one revolution per second, measure voltage at break-out box pins No. 3 and No. 20.

2) If voltage is .05-.70 volt, go to **DD8**. If voltage is not .05-.70 volt, check sensor mounting, sensor air gap or toothed ring for damage, wear or misalignment.

DD8 (RF Wheel Sensor Continuity – Continental FWD)

Check for continuity between break-out box pin No. 40 and body ground. If there is continuity, go to **DD10**. If there is no continuity, repair or replace circuit No. 530.

DD8 (RF Wheel Sensor Continuity – All Others)

1) Check for continuity between break-out box pins No. 3 and 40. If there is no continuity, go to **DD9**. If there is continuity, unplug RF wheel sensor connector.

2) Check for continuity between each wheel sensor terminal and body ground. If there is continuity at either terminal, replace wheel sensor. If there is no continuity at either terminal, Repair or replace wheel sensor cable.

DD9 (EBCM Ground Circuit)

Check for continuity between break-out box pin No. 40 and body ground. If there is continuity, go to **DD10**. If continuity is not present, repair or replace circuit No. 530A.

DD10 (RF Wheel Bearing)

Check front wheel bearing adjustment. See appropriate FRONT SUSPENSION article in SUSPENSION section. Check toothed sensor ring for damage. Adjust wheel bearings or replace toothed sensor ring. If no problem is found, reverify symptom.

DD11 (Codes 33, 37, 43, 57 or 77)

1) Turn ignition off. Unplug 32-pin connector from EBCM. Connect break-out box and adapter. Measure resistance at pins No. 6 and No. 23 on break-out box. If resistance is 800-1400 ohms, go to **DD12**.

2) If resistance is not 800-1400 ohms, unplug RR wheel sensor connector. If resistance is 800-1400 ohms, repair or replace circuit No. 523 or No. 524. If resistance is not 800-1400 ohms, replace wheel sensor.

DD12 (RR Wheel Sensor Voltage)

1) Turn ignition off. Open luggage compartment and turn air suspension switch off (if equipped). Raise vehicle and support. Place multimeter on "2V" in AC range. Rotating RR wheel at one revolution per second, measure voltage at break-out box pins No. 6 and No. 23.

2) If voltage is .05-.70 volt, go to **DD13**. If voltage is not .05-.70 volt, check sensor mounting, sensor air gap or toothed ring for damage, wear or misalignment.

DD13 (RR Wheel Sensor Continuity – Continental FWD)

Check for continuity between break-out box pin No. 40 and body ground. If there is continuity, go to **DD15**. If there is no continuity, repair or replace circuit No. 530.

TEVES ANTI-LOCK BRAKE SYSTEMS (ABS)
FORD MOTOR CO. (Cont.)

TEST DD – WHEEL SENSOR DIAGNOSIS (Cont.)

DD13 (RR Wheel Sensor Continuity – All Others)

1) Check for continuity between break-out box pins No. 6 and No. 40. If there is no continuity, go to DD14. If there is continuity, unplug LF wheel sensor connector.

2) Check for continuity between each wheel sensor terminal and body ground. If there is continuity at either terminal, replace wheel sensor. If there is no continuity at either terminal, Repair or replace wheel sensor cable.

DD14 (EBCM Ground Circuit)

Check for continuity between break-out box pin No. 40 and body ground. If there is continuity, go to DD15. If continuity is not present, repair or replace circuit No. 530A.

DD15 (Excessive Axle Vibration)

Check rear axle and housing for excessive play. Check toothed sensor ring for damage. Replace toothed sensor ring (if necessary). If no problem is found, reverify symptom.

DD16 (Codes 34, 38, 44, 58 or 78)

1) Turn ignition off. Unplug 32-pin connector from EBCM. Connect break-out box and adapter. Measure resistance at pins No. 4 and No. 21 on break-out box. If resistance is 800-1400 ohms, go to DD17.

2) If resistance is not 800-1400 ohms, unplug LR wheel sensor connector. If resistance is 800-1400 ohms, repair or replace circuit No. 518 or No. 519. If resistance is not 800-1400 ohms, replace wheel sensor.

DD17 (LR Wheel Sensor Voltage)

1) Turn ignition off. Open luggage compartment and turn air suspension switch off (if equipped). Raise vehicle and support. Place multimeter on "2V" in AC range. Rotating LR wheel at one revolution per second, measure voltage at break-out box pins No. 4 and No. 21.

2) If voltage is .05-.70 volt, go to DD18. If voltage is not .05-.70 volt, check sensor mounting, sensor air gap or toothed ring for damage, wear or misalignment.

DD18 (LR Wheel Sensor Continuity – Continental FWD)

Check for continuity between break-out box pin No. 40 and body ground. If there is continuity, go to DD20. If there is no continuity, repair or replace circuit No. 530.

DD18 (LR Wheel Sensor Continuity – All Others)

1) Check for continuity between break-out box pins No. 4 and No. 40. If there is no continuity, go to DD19. If there is continuity, unplug LR wheel sensor connector.

2) Check for continuity between each wheel sensor terminal and body ground. If there is continuity at either terminal, replace wheel sensor. If there is no continuity at either terminal, Repair or replace wheel sensor cable.

DD19 (EBCM Ground Circuit)

Check for continuity between break-out box pin No. 40 and body ground. If there is continuity, go to DD20. If continuity is not present, repair or replace circuit No. 530A.

DD20 (Excessive Axle Vibration)

Check rear axle and housing for excessive play. Check toothed sensor ring for damage. Replace toothed sensor ring (if necessary). If no problem is found, reverify symptom.

DD21 (Code 45 – 2 Missing Wheel Sensor Signals; One Being LF)

1) Turn ignition off. Install break-out box and adapter. Turn air suspension switch off, located inside luggage compartment. Raise and support vehicle. Measure voltage between break-out box pins No. 5 and No. 22, while rotating LF wheel one revolution per second.

2) If voltage is .05-.70 volt AC, go to DD22. If voltage is not .05-.70 volt AC, check wheel sensor air gap or incorrect or damaged toothed ring. Perform same check at the following wheels and pins: RF – pins No. 3 and No. 20, RR – pins No. 6 and No. 23, LR – pins No. 4 and No. 21.

DD22 (EBCM Ground Circuit)

Check for continuity between break-out box pin No. 40 and body ground. If there is continuity, go to DD20. If continuity is not present, repair or replace circuit No. 530A.

TEST DD – WHEEL SENSOR DIAGNOSIS (Cont.)

DD23 (Excessive Wheel Bearing End Play)

Check for excessive wheel bearing end play, on all wheels. Check toothed sensor ring for damage. Replace toothed sensor ring (if necessary). If no problem is found, reverify symptom.

DD24 (Code 46 – 2 Missing Wheel Sensor Signals; One Being RF)

1) Turn ignition off. Install break-out box and adapter. Turn air suspension switch off, located inside luggage compartment. Raise and support vehicle. Measure voltage between break-out box pins No. 3 and No. 20, while rotating RF wheel one revolution per second.

2) If voltage is .05-.70 volt AC, go to DD22. If voltage is not .05-.70 volt AC, check wheel sensor air gap or incorrect or damaged toothed ring. Perform same check at the following wheels and pins: RR – pins No. 6 and No. 23, LR – pins No. 4 and No. 21.

DD25 (Code 47 – Missing Rear Wheel Sensor Signals)

1) Turn ignition off. Install break-out box and adapter. Turn air suspension switch off, located inside luggage compartment. Raise and support vehicle. Measure voltage between break-out box pins No. 6 and No. 23, while rotating RR wheel one revolution per second.

2) If voltage is .05-.70 volt AC, go to DD22. If voltage is not .05-.70 volt AC, check wheel sensor air gap or incorrect or damaged toothed ring. Perform same check between pins No. 4 and No. 21 for LR wheel.

DD26 (Code 48 – Missing 3-4 Wheel Sensor Signals)

1) Turn ignition off. Install break-out box and adapter. Turn air suspension switch off, located inside luggage compartment. Raise and support vehicle. Measure voltage between break-out box pins No. 5 and No. 22, while rotating LF wheel one revolution per second.

2) If voltage is .05-.70 volt AC, go to DD22. If voltage is not .05-.70 volt AC, check wheel sensor air gap or incorrect or damaged toothed ring. Perform same check at the following wheels and pins: RF – pins No. 3 and No. 20, RR – pins No. 6 and No. 23, LR – pins No. 4 and No. 21.

TEST EE – OUTLET VALVE DIAGNOSIS

EE1 (Code 51 and/or 71)

1) Turn ignition off. Unplug 32-pin connector from EBCM. Connect break-out box and adapter. Check for continuity between break-out box pins No. 5 and No. 40. If there is no continuity, go to EE2.

2) If there is continuity, unplug LF wheel sensor connector. Check for continuity between each sensor terminal and body ground. If there is continuity at either terminal, replace wheel sensor. If there is no continuity, repair or replace wheel sensor cable.

EE2 (LF Anti-Lock Operation)

1) Open luggage compartment and turn air suspension switch off (if equipped). Raise and support vehicle. Ensure all wheels rotate freely. Short break-out box pins Nos. 14, 18 and 31 together.

2) Apply moderate brake pedal effort. Check that LF wheel will not rotate. Turn ignition on. LF wheel should rotate. If wheel rotates, reverify symptom. If wheel does not rotate, drags or brake pedal drops, replace solenoid valve block assembly.

NOTE: DO NOT leave ignition on for more than 60 seconds or damage to solenoid valve block assembly may occur.

EE3 (Code 52 and/or 72)

1) Turn ignition off. Unplug 32-pin connector from EBCM. Connect break-out box and adapter. Check for continuity between break-out box pins No. 5 and No. 40. If there is no continuity, go to EE4.

2) If there is continuity, unplug RF wheel sensor connector. Check for continuity between each sensor terminal and body ground. If there is continuity at either terminal, replace wheel sensor. If there is no continuity, repair or replace wheel sensor cable.

EE4 (RF Anti-Lock Operation)

1) Open luggage compartment and turn air suspension switch off (if equipped). Raise and support vehicle. Ensure all wheels rotate freely. Short break-out box pins No. 13, 18 and 32 together.

TEVES ANTI-LOCK BRAKE SYSTEMS (ABS) FORD MOTOR CO. (Cont.)

TEST EE – OUTLET VALVE DIAGNOSIS (Cont.)

2) Apply moderate brake pedal effort. Check that RF wheel will not rotate. Turn ignition on. RF wheel should rotate. If wheel rotates, reverify symptom. If wheel does not rotate, drags or brake pedal drops, replace solenoid valve block assembly.

NOTE: DO NOT leave ignition on for more than 60 seconds or damage to solenoid valve block assembly may occur.

EE5 (Code 53 and/or 73)

1) Turn ignition off. Unplug 32-pin connector from EBCM. Connect break-out box and adapter. Check for continuity between break-out box pins No. 6 and No. 40. If there is no continuity, go to **EE6**.

2) If there is continuity, unplug RR wheel sensor connector. Check for continuity between each sensor terminal and body ground. If there is continuity at either terminal, replace wheel sensor. It there is no continuity, repair or replace wheel sensor cable.

EE6 (RR Anti-Lock Operation)

1) Open luggage compartment and turn air suspension switch off (if equipped). Raise and support vehicle. Ensure all wheels rotate freely. Short break-out box pins No. 12, 18 and 30 together.

2) Apply moderate brake pedal effort. Check that RR wheel will not rotate. Turn ignition on. RR wheel should rotate. If wheel rotates, reverify symptom. If wheel does not rotate, drags or brake pedal drops, replace solenoid valve block assembly.

NOTE: DO NOT leave ignition on for more than 60 seconds or damage to solenoid valve block assembly may occur.

EE7 (Code 54 and/or 74)

1) Turn ignition off. Unplug 32-pin connector from EBCM. Connect break-out box and adapter. Check for continuity between break-out box pins No. 4 and No. 40 (pins No. 6 and No. 40 on Continental FWD). If there is no continuity, go to **EE8**.

2) If there is continuity, unplug LR wheel sensor connector. Check for continuity between each sensor terminal and body ground. If there is continuity at either terminal, replace wheel sensor. If there is no continuity, repair or replace wheel sensor cable.

EE8 (LR Anti-Lock Operation)

1) Open luggage compartment and turn air suspension switch off (if equipped). Raise and support vehicle. Ensure all wheels rotate freely. Short break-out box pins No. 12, 18 and 30 together.

2) Apply moderate brake pedal effort. Check that LR wheel will not rotate. Turn ignition on. LR wheel should rotate. If wheel rotates, reverify symptom. If wheel does not rotate, drags or brake pedal drops, replace solenoid valve block assembly.

NOTE: DO NOT leave ignition on for more than 60 seconds or damage to solenoid valve block assembly may occur.

TEST FF – WIRING CIRCUIT DIAGNOSIS

FF1 (Code 61 – Continental FWD)

1) Turn ignition off. Unplug 32-pin connector from EBCM. Connect break-out box and adapter. Check resistance between break-out box pins No. 25 and No. 27. If resistance is less than 5 ohms, go to **FF2**.

2) If resistance is 5 ohms or more, check DC voltage at fluid level sensor connector pin No. 1. If there is volatge, repair or replace circuit No. 512. If there is no voltage, check for voltage at fluid level sensor pin No. 2 and pressure warning switch connector pin No. 3.

3) If there is voltage at either pin, repair or replace circuit No. 549. If there is no voltage, check for voltage at pressure warning switch connector pin No. 5. If there is voltage, repair or replace circuit No. 535. If there is no voltage, turn ignition off. Reconnect system and reverify symptom.

FF1 (Code 61 – All Others)

1) Turn ignition off. Unplug 32-pin connector from EBCM. Connect break-out box and adapter. Check resistance between break-out box pins No. 25 and No. 27. If resistance is less than 5 ohms, go to **FF2**.

TEST FF – WIRING CIRCUIT DIAGNOSIS (Cont.)

2) If resistance is 5 ohms or more, unplug fluid level sensor 5-pin connector. Ensure fluid level is at maximum mark on reservoir. Check resistance between fuid level sensor pins No. 1 and No. 2. If resistance is 2 ohms or more, replace sensor.

3) If resistance is less than 2 ohms, unplug pressure warning switch 5-pin connector. Ensure system is pressurized. Check for continuity between pressure warning switch pins No. 3 and No. 5. If there is no continuity, replace pressure warning switch and pump/motor relay.

4) If there is continuity, Check for continuity between break-out box pin No. 25 and fluid level sensor connector pin No. 1. If there is no continuity, repair or replace circuit No. 512. If there is continuity, check for continuity between fluid level sensor connector pin No. 2 and pressure warning switch connector pin No. 3.

5) If there is no continuity, repair or replace circuit No. 549. If there is continuity, check for continuity between pressure warning switch connector pin No. 5 and break-out box pin No. 27. If there is no continuity, repair or replace circuit No. 535. If there is continuity, plug in all connectors and reverify symptom.

FF2 (Fluid Level Sensor & Pressure Warning Switch Isolation Test)

1) Check for continuity between break-out box pin No. 25 and body ground, and pin No. 27 and body ground. If there is no continuity, reverify symptom. If there is continuity, check for continuity between fluid level sensor connector pin No. 1 and body ground.

2) If there is continuity, repair or replace circuit No. 512. If there is no continuity, unplug pressure warning switch connector. Check for continuity between fluid level sensor connector pin No. 2 and body ground. If there is continuity, repair or replace circuit No. 549.

3) If there is no continuity, check between pressure warning switch connector pin No. 3 and body ground, and pin No. 5 and body ground. If there is continuity at either pin, replace pressure warning switch and pump-/motor relay.

4) If no continuity is present at either pin, check for continuity between pressure warning switch connector pin No. 5 and body ground. If there is continuity, repair or replace circuit No 535. If there is no continuity, reconnect all connectors. Reverify symptom.

NOTE: The following charts A through J are for use with Break-Out Box on all models with ABS.

TEST A – ANTI-LOCK WARNING LIGHT ON WITH BRAKE WARNING LIGHT OFF

TEST A-1 (32-Pin Plug Testing)

1) Turn ignition off. Unplug 32-pin plug from EBCM. Connect Break-Out Box (T83L-50-EEC-IV) and Adapter (T87P-50-ALA) to 32-pin harness.

2) Set multimeter to DC volts setting. Turn ignition on with engine off. Measure voltage between break-out box pins No. 40 and No. 18. If more than 10 volts present, go to **TEST A2**. If less than 10 volts is present, go to **TEST A1a**.

TEST A1a (EBCM Ground Wire)

1) Check battery and fusible link to anit-lock warning light. Remove positive battery cable. Check continuity between break-out box pin No. 40 and ground.

2) If continuity is present, go to TEST A1b. If no continuity is present, repair or replace circuit No. 530A.

TEST A1b (Ignition-to-EBCM Wire)

1) Check continuity between break-out box pin No. 18 and ignition switch wire (circuit No. 298C on Continental FWD, No. 687A on all other models).

2) If continuity is okay, reconnect positive batter cable. Check power at ignition switch pin with switch "ON". If okay, connect EBCM and recheck symptom. If no continuity, repair or replace circuit No. 687B or No. 298C.

Brake Systems

TEVES ANTI-LOCK BRAKE SYSTEMS (ABS) FORD MOTOR CO. (Cont.)

TEST A – ANTI-LOCK WARNING LIGHT ON WITH BRAKE WARNING LIGHT OFF

TEST A2 (Main Power Relay Secondary Circuit (Normal)

Turn ignition off. Check continuity between break-out box pins No. 40 and No. 16. If continuity is present, go to **TEST A3**. If no continuity present, go to **TEST A2a**.

TEST A2a (Main Power Relay Secondary Circuit – Normal)

1) Disconnect main relay from socket. Check for continuity between main power relay socket pins No. 3 and No. 5.

2) If continuity present, go to **TEST A2b**. If no continuity present, replace main power relay.

TEST A2b (Main Power Relay Secondary Circuit Wiring Harness)

1) Disconnect positive battery cable. Check continuity between main power relay socket pin No. 3 and break-out box pin No. 16.

2) If continuity present, go to **TEST A2c**. If no continuity present, repair or replace circuit No. 532A or No. 532B.

TEST A2c (Main Power Relay Secondary Circuit Wiring Harness)

Check for continuity between main power relay socket pin No. 5 and body ground. If continuity present, reconnect main power relay, EBCM and battery cable. Recheck symptom. If no continuity present, repair or replace circuit No. 430A.

TEST A3 (Main Power Relay Secondary Circuit – Normal)

Check continuity between break-out box pins No. 40 and No. 15. If continuity present, go to **TEST A4**. If no continuity present, go to **TEST A3a**.

TEST A3a (Main Power Relay Secondary Circuit Wiring Harness)

Remove main power relay. Check for continuity between main power relay socket pin No. 3 and break-out box pin No. 15. If continuity present, connect main power relay and EBCM. Recheck symptom. If no continuity present, repair or replace circuit No. 532A or No. 532C.

TEST A4 (Fluid Level Sensor & Pressure Warning Switch Circuit)

Turn ignition on with engine off. Measure resistance between break-out box pins No. 25 and No. 27. If resistance is less than 5 ohms, go to **TEST A5**. If resistance greater than 5 ohms, go to **TEST A4a**.

TEST A4a (Fluid Level Sensor Anti-Lock Warning Circuit)

Disconnect 5-pin plug on fluid level sensor. Ensure fluid level is at maximum level, marked on reservoir. Measure resistance between sensor pins No. 1 and 2. If less than 2 ohms, go to **TEST A4b**. If greater than 2 ohms, replace fluid level sensor.

TEST A4b (Pressure Warning Switch Anti-Lock Warning Circuit)

Ensure system is pressurized. Unplug 5-pin connector at pressure warning switch. Check continuity between pressure warning switch pins No. 3 and No. 5. If continuity present, go to **TEST A4c**. If no continuity present, replace pressure warning switch and pump/motor relay.

TEST A4c (EBCM-to-Fluid Level Sensor Circuit)

Check for continuity between break-out box pin No. 25 and fluid level sensor connector pin No. 1. If continuity is present, go to **TEST A4d**. If no continuity present, repair or replace circuit No. 512.

TEST A4d (Fluid Level Sensor-to-Pressure Warning Switch Circuit)

Check for continuity between pin No. 2 of 5-pin fluid level sensor connector and pressure warning switch connector pin No. 3. If continuity present, go to **TEST A4e**. If continuity present, repair or replace circuit No. 549.

TEST A4e (Pressure Warning Switch-to-EBCM Circuit)

Check continuity between pressure warning switch connector pin No. 5 and break-out box pin No. 27. If continuity present, turn ignition off. Connect all electrical connections. Recheck symptom. If no continuity present, repair or replace circuit No. 535.

TEST A5 (Fluid Level Sensor & Pressure Warning Switch Isolation Test)

Check continuity between break-out box pin No. 25 and body ground. If continuity present, go to **TEST A5a**. If no continuity present, go to **TEST A6**.

TEST A – ANTI-LOCK WARNING LIGHT ON WITH BRAKE WARNING LIGHT OFF (Cont.)

TEST A5a (Fluid Level Sensor Pin No. 2 Check)

Ensure fluid level is even with maximum mark on reservoir. Disconnect FLI 5-pin plug. Check for continuity between fluid level sensor pin No. 2 and body ground. Also check for continuity between pin No. 1 and body ground. If continuity is present, replace fluid level sensor. If no continuity, go to **TEST A5b**.

TEST A5b (Fluid Level Sensor Pin No. 1 Check)

Check continuity between fluid level sensor connector pin No. 1 and body ground. If continuity present, repair or replace circuit No. 512. If no continuity present, go to **TEST A5c**.

TEST A5c (Fluid Level Sensor Pin No. 2 Check)

Unplug 5-pin plug from pressure warning switch. Check continuity between fluid level sensor connector pin No. 2 and body ground. If continuity present, repair or replace circuit No. 549. If no continuity present, go to **TEST A5d**.

TEST A5d (Continuity Between Pressure Warning Switch Pins No. 3 & No. 5 & Body Ground)

Depressurize brake system for this test. Check for continuity between pressure warning switch pin No. 3 and body ground, and No. 5 and body ground. If continuity is present, replace pressure warning switch and pump/motor relay. If no continuity present, go to **TEST A5e**.

TEST A5e (Pressure Warning Switch Connector Pin No. 5 & Ground)

Check continuity between pressure warning switch connector pin No. 5 and body ground. If continuity present, repair or replace circuit No. 535. If no continuity present, connect all plugs and recheck symptom.

TEST A6 (Main Relay Primary Circuit Resistance)

Turn ignition off. Measure resistance between breakout box pins No. 40 and No. 9. If resistance is between 45-105 ohms, go to **TEST A7**. If any other value, go to **TEST A6a**.

TEST A6a (Main Power Relay Primary Coil Resistance)

Disconnect main power relay plug. Measure resistance between main power relay pins No. 1 and 2. If resistance is between 45-105 ohms, go to **TEST A6b**. If any other value, replace main power relay.

TEST A6b (Main Power Relay Primary-to-EBCM Wire)

Check continuity between main power relay connector pin No. 2 and break-out box pin No. 9. If continuity present, go to **TEST A6c**. If no continuity present, repair or replace circuit No. 513.

TEST A6c (Main Power Relay Primary-to-Ground Wire)

Check continuity between main power relay socket pin No. 1 and ground. If continuity present, reconnect all electrical connections. Recheck symptom. If no continuity present, repair or replace circuit No. 430B.

TEST A7 (Main Power Relay Secondary – Activated)

1) Place jumper wire between break-out box pins No. 18 and 9. Turn ignition on with engine off. Measure voltage between break-out box pins No. 40 and No. 16.

2) If more than 10 volts is present, go to **TEST A8**. If under 10 volts present, check fuse F5. Remove jumper wire and go to **TEST A7a**.

TEST A7a (Main Power Relay Secondary Circuit – Active)

1) Turn ignition off. Unplug main power relay from socket. Apply battery power to main relay pin No. 1 and ground pin No. 2. Check for continuity between main power relay pins No. 3 and No. 4.

2) If continuity is present, go to **TEST A7b**. If no continuity is present, replace main power relay.

TEST A7b (Main Power Relay Secondary Circuit Power Wire)

Check continuity between main power relay connector pin No. 4 and positive battery terminal. If continuity is present, plug in main power relay. Recheck symptom. If no continuity is present, repair or replace circuit No. 533 or fuse link in circuit No. 291.

TEST A8 (RR Wheel Sensor Circuit Resistance)

Turn ignition off. Measure resistance between break-out box pins No. 6 and No. 23. If resistance is 800-1400 ohms, go to **TEST A9**. If resistance is any other value, go to **TEST A8a**.

TEVES ANTI-LOCK BRAKE SYSTEMS (ABS)
FORD MOTOR CO. (Cont.)

TEST A – ANTI-LOCK WARNING LIGHT ON WITH BRAKE WARNING LIGHT OFF (Cont.)

TEST A8a (RR Wheel Sensor Resistance)

Unplug right rear sensor plug. Measure resistance between sensor pins. If reading is 800-1400 ohms, repair or replace circuit No. 523 or No. 524. If any other value, replace RR wheel sensor.

TEST A9 (LF Wheel Sensor Circuit Resistance)

Measure resistance between break-out box pins No. 5 and No. 22. If resistance is 800-1400 ohms, go to **TEST A10**. If any other value, go to **TEST A9a**.

TEST A9a (LF Wheel Sensor Resistance)

Disconnect LF wheel sensor plug. Measure resistance between sensor pins. If resistance is 800-1400 ohms, repair or replace circuit No. 521 or No. 522. If any other value, replace LF wheel sensor.

TEST A10 (LR Wheel Sensor Circuit Resistance)

Measure resistance between break-out box pins No. 4 and No. 21. If reading is 800-1400 ohms, go to **TEST A11**. If any other value, go to **TEST A10a**.

TEST A10a (LR Wheel Sensor Resistance)

Disconnect LR wheel sensor plug. Measure sensor resistance between sensor pins. If reading is 800-1400 ohms, repair or replace circuit No. 518 and 519. If any other value, replace LR wheel sensor.

TEST A11 (RF Wheel Sensor Circuit Resistance)

Measure resistance between break-out box pins No. 3 and 20. If reading is 800-1400 ohms, go to **TEST A12**. If any other value, go to **TEST A11a**.

TEST A11a (RF Wheel Sensor Resistance)

Disconnect RF sensor plug. Measure resistance between sensor pins. If reading is 800-1400 ohms, repair or replace circuit No. 514 or No. 516. If any other value, replace RF wheel sensor.

TEST A12 (Main Valve Circuit Resistance)

Turn ignition off. Measure resistance between break-out box pins No. 11 and No. 29. If resistance is 2-5 ohms, go to **TEST A13**. If any other value, go to **TEST A12a**.

TEST A12a (Main Valve Resistance)

Disconnect main valve 2-pin plug. Measure resistance between main valve pins No. 1 and 2. If reading is 2-5.5 ohms, repair or replace circuit No. 430E or No. 493. If any other value, replace master cylinder/booster assembly.

TEST A13 (Solenoid Valve Block Ground Circuit)

Measure resistance between break-out box pins No. 11 and No. 40. If reading is less than 2 ohms, go to **TEST A14**. If resistance is greater than 2 ohms, go to **TEST A13a**.

TEST A13a (Solenoid Valve Block Plug Pin No. 7)

Unplug solenoid valve block 7-pin plug. Measure resistance between solenoid valve block connector pin No. 7 and body ground. If reading is less than 2 ohms, repair or replace circuit No. 685. If reading is greater than 2 ohms, go to **TEST A13b**.

TEST A13b (Solenoid Valve Block Ground Wire)

Disconnect battery negative cable. Check for continuity between solenoid valve block and body ground. If continuity is present, replace solenoid valve block unit (internal ground problem). If no or poor continuity, repair or replace circuit No. 430G.

TEST A14 (RF Inlet Valve Circuit Resistance)

Measure resistance between break-out box pins No. 11 and No. 32. If resistance is 5-8 ohms, go to **TEST A15**. If any other value, go to **TEST A14a**.

TEST A14a (RF Inlet Valve Resistance)

Disconnect solenoid valve block 7-pin plug. Measure resistance between solenoid valve block connector pins No. 7 and No. 1. If 5-8 ohms, repair or replace circuit No. 510. If any other value, replace solenoid valve block.

TEST A15 (Rear Inlet Valve Circuit Resistance)

Measure resistance between break-out box pins No. 11 and No. 30. If resistance is 5-8 ohms, go to **TEST A16**. If any other value, go to **TEST A15a**.

TEST A15a (Rear Inlet Valve Resistance)

Disconnect solenoid valve block 7-pin plug. Measure resistance between solenoid valve block connector pins No. 7 and No. 3. If resistance is 5-8 ohms, repair or replace circuit No. 496. If any other value, replace solenoid valve block.

TEST A16 (LF Inlet Valve Circuit Resistance)

Measure resistance between break-out box pins No. 11 and No. 31. If resistance is 5-8 ohms, go to **TEST A17**. If any other value, go to **TEST A16a**.

TEST A16a (LF Inlet Valve Resistance)

Disconnect solenoid valve block 7-pin plug. Measure resistance between solenoid valve block connector pins No. 6 and No. 7. If resistance is 5-8 ohms, repair or replace circuit No. 495. If any other reading, replace solenoid valve block.

TEST A17 (Rear Outlet Valve Circuit Resistance)

Measure resistance between break-out box pins No. 11 and No. 12. If resistance is 3-6 ohms, go to **TEST A18**. If any other value, go to **TEST A17a**.

TEST A17a (Rear Outlet Valve Resistance)

Unplug solenoid valve block 7-pin plug. Measure resistance between solenoid valve block connector pins No. 7 and No. 4. If resistance is 3-6 ohms, repair or replace circuit No. 499. If any other value, replace solenoid valve block.

TEST A18 (LF Outlet Valve Circuit Resistance)

Measure resistance between break-out box pins No. 11 and No. 14. If reading is 3-6 ohms, go to **TEST A19**. If any other reading, go to **TEST A18a**.

TEST A18a (LF Outlet Valve Resistance)

Disconnect solenoid valve block 7-pin plug. Measure resistance between solenoid valve block connector pins No. 5 and No. 7. If resistance is 3-6 ohms, repair or replace circuit No. 498. If any other value, replace solenoid valve block.

TEST A19 (RF Outlet Valve Circuit Resistance)

Measure resistance between break-out box pins No. 11 and No. 13. If resistance is 3-6 ohms, go to **TEST A20**. If any other reading, go to **TEST A19a**.

TEST A19a (RF Outlet Valve Resistance)

Disconnect solenoid valve block 7-pin plug. Measure resistance between solenoid valve block connector pins No. 7 and No. 2. If resistance is 3-6 ohms, repair or replace circuit No. 497 harness. If any other value, replace solenoid valve block.

TEST A20 (Check Pressure Warning Switch Brake Light Circuit – No System Pressure)

1) Vehicle must be at room temperature. Discharge brake system turning ignition off and pumping brake pedal at least 20 times until pedal becomes hard.

2) Unplug pressure warning switch 5-pin plug. Check continuity between pressure warning switch pins No. 1 and No. 2. If there is continuity, to go **TEST A21**. If there is no continuity, replace pressure warning switch and pump/motor relay.

TEST A21 (Check Pressure Warning Switch Brake Light Circuit – With System Pressurized)

1) Reconnect pressure warning switch 5-pin plug. Turn ignition on with engine off. When pump motor stops, turn ignition off. Disconnect presure warning switch 5-pin plug again.

2) Check for continuity between pressure warning switch pins No. 1 and No. 2. If continuity present, replace pressure warning switch. If no continuity present, go to **TEST A22** and pump/motor relay.

TEST A22 (Check Pressure Warning Switch Brake Light Circuit Threshold)

1) Discharge the brake system by turning ignition off. Pump brake pedal at least 20 times until pedal feel becomes hard.

2) Remove high pressure banjo bolt below brake fluid reservoir on brake booster. Disconnect quick-connect nipple from Anti-Lock High Pressure Gauge (T85P-20215-A). Install nipple in place of high pressure banjo bolt. Ensure "O" rings are installed correctly.

Brake Systems

TEVES ANTI-LOCK BRAKE SYSTEMS (ABS) FORD MOTOR CO. (Cont.)

TEST A – ANTI-LOCK WARNING LIGHT ON WITH BRAKE WARNING LIGHT OFF (Cont.)

CAUTION: DO NOT disconnect pressure gauge while system is under pressure.

3) Connnect anti-lock pressure gauge to gauge nipple. Reconnect pressure warning switch 5-pin connector.

4) Turn ignition on with engine off. When pump motor stops, disconnect pressure warning switch 5-pin plug.

5) Lower hydraulic accumulator pressure by slowly pumping brake pedal until there is continuity between pressure warning switch pins No. 1 and No. 2. Observe hydraulic pressure gauge when continuity is reached.

6) Pressure gauge should read 1450-1595 psi (100-110 Bar). If pressure is okay, go to **TEST A23**. If any other value, replace pressure warning switch and pump/motor relay.

7) If you want to verify reading, reconnect 5-pin plug. Turn ignition on until pump stops. Disconnect 5-pin plug and recheck readings.

TEST A23 (Pressure Warning Switch Harness Ground)

Check continuity between pressure warning switch connector pin No. 1 and body ground. If continuity present, go to **TEST A24**. If no continuity present, repair or replace circuit No. 430C.

TEST A24 (Reverify System Symptom)

1) Plug in all electrical connectors. Install high pressure banjo bolt. Discharge brake system pressure by turning ignition off. Pump brake pedal at least 20 times until pedal feels hard. Check for system symptom.

2) If symptom not present, fault may have been loose electrical connection. If symptom still present, replace EBCM.

TEST B ("ANTI-LOCK" LIGHT ON AFTER ENGINE STARTS BUT "BRAKE" WARNING LIGHT OFF)

TEST B1 (Continuity of RR Wheel Sensor Circuit)

Turn ignition off. Disconnect 32-pin plug from EBCM. Connect break-out box with adapter to 32-pin connector. Check for continuity between break-out box pins No. 6 and 40. If continuity exists, go to **TEST B1a**. If no continuity is present, go to **TEST B2**.

TEST B1a (Continuity of RR Wheel Sensor Harness)

1) Disconnect RR wheel sensor plug. Check for continuity between each RR wheel sensor pin and vehicle ground.

2) If continuity exists, replace RR wheel sensor. If no continuity present, repair or replace circuit No. 523 or No. 524.

TEST B2 (Continuity of LF Wheel Sensor Harness)

Check continuity between break-out box pins No. 40 and No. 5. If continuity exists, go to **TEST B2a**. If no continuity exists, go to **TEST B3**.

TEST B2a (Continuity of LF Wheel Sensor)

Disconnect LF wheel sensor plug. Check continuity between each LF wheel sensor pin and vehicle ground. If continuity exists, replace LF wheel sensor. If no continuity exists, repair or replace circuit No. 521 or No. 522.

TEST B3 (Continuity of LR Wheel Sensor Harness)

Check for continuity between break-out box pins No. 4 and No. 40. If continuity exists, to **TEST B3a**. If no continuity exists, go to **TEST B4**.

TEST B3a (Continuity of LR Wheel Sensor)

Disconnect LR wheel sensor plug. Check for continuity between each LR wheel sensor pin and vehicle ground. If continuity exists, replace LR wheel sensor. If no continuity exists, repair or replace circuit No. 518 or No. 519.

TEST B4 (Continuity of RF Wheel Sensor Harness)

Check continuity between break-out box pins No. 3 and No. 40. If continuity exists, go to **TEST B4a**. If no continuity exists, test is complete. If anti-lock light pattern remains, repeat **TEST B**.

TEST B – "ANTI-LOCK" LIGHT ON AFTER ENGINE STARTS BUT "BRAKE" LIGHT OFF

TEST B4a (Continuity of RF Wheel Sensor)

Disconnect RF wheel sensor plug. Check continuity between each wheel sensor pin and vehicle ground. If continuity exists, replace RF wheel sensor. If no continuity exists, repair or replace circuit No. 514 or No. 516.

TEST C ("ANTI-LOCK" WARNING LIGHT ON AFTER VEHICLE STARTS TO MOVE OR FALSE CYCLING OF ANTI-LOCK SYSTEM)

TEST C1 (RR Wheel Sensor Circuit Resistance)

1) Turn ignition off. Disconnect 32-pin plug from EBCM. Connect break-out box and adapter to 32-pin plug.

2) Measure resistance between break-out box pins No. 4 and No. 23. If resistance is 800-1400 ohms, go to **TEST C2**. If resistance is any other value, go to **TEST C1a**.

TEST C1a (RR Wheel Sensor Resistance)

Turn ignition off. Disconnect RR wheel sensor plug. Measure resistance between wheel sensor pins. If resistance is 800-1400 ohms, repair or replace circuit No. 523 or No. 524. If resistance is any other value, replace RR wheel sensor.

TEST C2 (LF Wheel Sensor Circuit Resistance)

Measure resistance between break-out box pins No. 5 and No. 22. If resistance is 800-1400 ohms, go to **TEST C3**. If any other value, go to **TEST C2a**.

TEST C2a (LF Wheel Sensor Harness Resistance)

Disconnect LF wheel sensor plug. Measure resistance between wheel sensor pins. If resistance is 800-1400 ohms, repair or replace circuit No. 521 or No. 522. If resistance is any other value, replace LF wheel sensor.

TEST C3 (LR Wheel Sensor Circuit Resistance)

Measure resistance between break-out box pins No. 4 and No. 21. If resistance is 800-1400 ohms, go to **TEST C4**. If any other value, go to **TEST C3a**.

TEST C3a (LR Wheel Sensor Resistance)

Disconnect LR wheel sensor plug. Measure resistance between wheel sensor pins. If resistance is 800-1400 ohms, repair or replace circuit No. 518 and No. 519. If resistance is any other value, replace LR wheel sensor.

TEST C4 (RF Wheel Sensor Circuit Resistance)

Measure resistance between break-out box pins No. 3 and No. 20. If resistance is 800-1400 ohms, go to **TEST C5**. If any other value, go to **TEST C4a**.

TEST C4a (RF Wheel Sensor Resistance)

Disconnect RF wheel sensor plug. Measure resistance between wheel sensor pins. If resistance is 800-1400 ohms, repair or replace circuit No. 514 or No. 516. If resistance is any other value, replace RF wheel sensor.

TEST C5 (RR Wheel Sensor Check)

1) Turn ignition off. Turn off air suspension switch, located inside luggage compartment (if equipped). Raise and support vehicle. Set multimeter to "2V" AC. Measure voltage between break-out box pins No. 6 and No. 23 while spinning right rear wheel at one revolution per second.

2) If reading is between .05-.70 volts AC, go to **TEST C6**. If less than .05 or more than .70 volts AC, check sensor mounting, air gap or toothed wheel mounting. Repair as necessary.

TEST C6 (LF Wheel Sensor Check)

Measure voltage between break-out box pins No. 5 and No. 22 while spinning left front wheel at one revolution per second. If reading is between .05-.70 volts AC, go to **TEST C7**. If less than .05 or more than .70 volts AC, check sensor mounting, air gap or toothed wheel mounting. Repair as necessary.

TEVES ANTI-LOCK BRAKE SYSTEMS (ABS)
FORD MOTOR CO. (Cont.)

TEST C – "ANTI-LOCK" LIGHT ON AFTER VEHICLE STARTS TO MOVE OR FALSE CYCLING OF ANTI-LOCK SYSTEM

TEST C7 (LR Wheel Sensor Check)

Measure voltage between break-out box pins No. 4 and No. 21 while spinning left rear wheel at one revolution per second. If reading is between .05-.70 volts AC, go to **TEST C8**. If less than .05 or more than .70 volts AC, check sensor mounting, air gap or toothed wheel mounting. Repair as necessary.

TEST C8 RF Wheel Sensor Check)

Measure voltage between break-out box pins No. 3 and No. 20 while spinning right front wheel at one revolution per second. If reading is between .05-.70 volts AC, go to **TEST C9**. If less than .05 or more than .70 volts AC, check sensor mounting, air gap or toothed wheel mounting. Repair as necessary.

TEST C9 (Front Wheel Bearing Check)

1) Check front wheel bearing end play. Inspect each toothed sensor ring visually for damaged teeth. Turn air suspension switch "ON" when vehicle is off hoist.

2) If there are loose or damaged parts, repair as necessary. If no loose or damaged parts, recheck symptom.

TEST D (ANTI-LOCK WARNING LIGHT & BRAKE WARNING LIGHT ON OR PUMP MOTOR RUNS MORE THAN 60 SECONDS)

TEST D1 (Check Pump Motor Operation)

Turn ignition off. Pump brake pedal 20 times or until it becomes hard. Turn ignition on. Pump motor should operate. If okay, go to **TEST D2**. If not okay, go to **TEST D1a**.

NOTE: Pump motor will shut off if continuously ran for more than 20 minutes. A 2-10 minute cool-down period will be necessary before motor will reactivate.

TEST D1a (Pump/Motor Unit)

Unplug 4-pin connector from pump/motor unit. Turn ignition on. Place multimeter on 20-volt DC scale. Check voltage at 4-pin connector. Note there is 2 positive and negative terminals. Only use one of each when testing. If is 10 volts or more, go to **TEST D2**. If voltage is less than 10 volts, go to **TEST D1b**.

TEST D1b (Checking For Continuity Between Pump/Motor Relay & Motor)

Unplug pump/motor relay connector. Using an ohmmeter, check for continuity between pump/motor relay connector pin No. 3 and each positive pin of 4-pin motor connector. If there is no continuity, repair circuits No. 538a and No. 538b. If there is continuity, go to **TEST D1c**.

TEST D1c (Checking For Continuity Between Motor Connector & Ground)

Using an ohmmeter, check for continuity between each negative pin of 4-pin motor connector and ground. If there is no continuity, repair circuit No. 430D or No. 430F. If there is continuity, go to **TEST D1d**.

TEST D1d (Checking For Continuity Between Battery & Pump/Motor Relay)

1) Turn ignition off. Disconnect positive battery cable from battery. Unplug pump/motor relay connector. Using an ohmmeter, check for continuity between positive battery cable and pump/motor relay connector pin No. 4.

2) If there is no continuity, repair or replace fusible link and/or circuits No. 537 and No. 291A. If there is continuity, reconnect positive battery cable and go to **TEST D1e**.

TEST D1e (Checking Continuity Between Ignition Switch & Pump-/Motor Relay)

Using an ohmmeter, check for continuity between ignition switch "ON" pin and pump/motor relay connector pin No. 2. If there is no continuity, repair or replace fusible link or circuit No. 687A. If there is continuity, go to **TEST D1f**.

TEST D1f (Checking Pressure Warning Switch Ground)

Unplug pressure warning switch 5-pin connector. Using an ohmmeter, check between connector pin No. 1 and ground. If there is continuity, go to **TEST D1g**. If there is no continuity, repair circuit No. 430C.

TEST D – "ANTI-LOCK" LIGHT & BRAKE LIGHT ON OR PUMP MOTOR RUNS MORE THAN 60 SECONDS

TEST D4 (Checking Hydraulic Unit)

Turn ignition on. After pump motor stops, wait 3 more minutes. This allows pressure to stabilize. Read pressure gauge. Wait 5 more minutes and recheck pressure gauge. If pressure gauge drops less than 140 psi (10 bar) after 5 minutes, go to **TEST D5**. If pressure drops more than specified, check for external leaks. If no leaks can be found, go to **TEST D4a**.

TEST D1g (Checking Continuity Between Pressure Warning Switch & Pump/Motor Relay)

Using an ohmmeter, check for continuity between pressure warning switch connector pin No. 4 and pump/motor relay connector pin No. 1. If there is no continuity, repair circuit No. 539. If there is continuity, go to **TEST D1h**

TEST D1h (Checking Pressure Warning Switch)

Using an ohmmeter, check for continuity between pins No. 1 and No. 4 on pressure warning switch. System MUST be depressurized. If there is no continuity, replace pressure warning switch and pump/motor relay. If there is continuity, go to **TEST D1j**.

TEST D1j (Checking Pump/Motor Relay)

1) Place multimeter on 200 ohm scale. Check resistance between pins No. 1 and No. 2 on pump motor relay. If resistance is 45-105 ohms, check for continuity between pins No. 3 and No. 4.

2) If resistance is not as specified and there is continuity between pins No. 3 and No. 4, replace pump/motor relay and pressure warning switch. If there is no continuity, connect battery to pump/motor relay terminals No. 1 and No. 2. Using an ohmmeter, check for continuity between terminals No. 3 and No. 4.

3) If there is no continuity, replace pump/motor relay and pressure warning switch. If there is continuity, check for continuity between pump/motor relay pins No. 3 and No. 5. If there is no continuity, replace pump/motor relay.

4) If there is continuity, apply 12 volts to pump motor connector (one positive pin and one negative pin). Pump motor should operate. If motor runs, recheck symptom. If motor does not run, replace motor and pump/motor relay.

TEST D2 (Checking Pump Motor)

Turn ignition off. Pump brake pedal 20 times to depressurize brake system. Connect an ammeter between battery positive terminal and positive cable. Turn all accessories off. Ensure 4-pin pump motor connector is plugged in. Turn ignition on. If ammeter reading is 25 amps or more, replace pump motor. If ammeter reading is less than 25 amps, go to **TEST D2a**.

TEST D2a (Checking Pump Motor)

1) Turn ignition off. Pump brake pedal 20 times or until brake pedal becomes hard. Turn ignition on. Measure time pump takes to shut off. If pump shuts off in less than 60 seconds, go to **TEST D2b**.

2) If pump takes 60 seconds or more, check for corroded connections in the following locations: Pump motor 4-pin connector, ground circuits (Nos. 430D and No. 430F, pump/motor relay pin No. 4 or battery to pin No. 4 wire. When corroded connection have been repaired, go to **TEST D2b**.

TEST D2b (Check Low Pressure Flow)

Turn ignition off. Disconnect low pressure hose from pump. Allow fluid to drain into a container. If there is no fluid or restricted fluid flow from hose, repair or replace reservoir or hose. If there is free fluid flow, reconnect hose. Fill reservoir and go to **TEST D2c**.

TEST D2c (Checking Voltage to Pump Motor)

1) Turn ignition off. Pump brake pedal 20 times to discharge pressure from system. Set multimeter to 20-volt DC scale. Connect multimeter in parallel at pump motor 4-pin connector. Turn ignition on. Pump motor should be running.

2) If voltage is 8 volts or less, check wiring from battery to pin No. 4. Also, check pump motor relay pins No. 3 and No. 4 for voltage drop. If voltage is over 8 volts, go to **TEST D3**.

Brake Systems

TEVES ANTI-LOCK BRAKE SYSTEMS (ABS)
FORD MOTOR CO. (Cont.)

TEST D – "ANTI-LOCK" LIGHT & BRAKE LIGHT ON OR PUMP MOTOR RUNS MORE THAN 60 SECONDS (Cont.)

TEST D3 (Checking Accumulator Pre-Charge – Continental FWD)

Cool vehicle to room temperature. Depressurize brake system Remove hydraulic accumulator. Install Pressure Gauge (D88M-20215-A). Reinstall hydraulic accumulator. Turn ignition on. Record hydraulic accumulator pre-charge pressure when ignition was turned on. If pressure is 600-1325 psi (4137-9135 kPa), go to **TEST D4**. If pressure is not as specified, replace hydraulic accumulator.

TEST D3 (Checking Accumulator Pre-Charge – All Others)

Cool vehicle to room temperature. Depressurize brake system. Remove high pressure banjo bolt below brake fluid reservoir, located on brake booster. Install Anti-Lock Pressure Gauge (T85P-20215A). Turn ignition on. Record pressure gauge reading. If reading is 600-1325 psi (4137-9135 kPa), go to **TEST D4**. If reading is not as specified, replace hydraulic accumulator.

TEST D4a (Checking For Hydraulic Leaks)

Check for external leak around brake lines, calipers, pressure hoses, reservoir seals and hydraulic accumulator. A small amount of leakage around pressure warning switch is normal. If no leakage is found, go to **TEST D5**. If leakage is found repair or replace leaking component.

TEST D5 (Checking Pump Pressure)

With pressure gauge attached, turn ignition on. Pump brake pedal until motor starts operating. Check pressure gauge reading when motor starts to operate. If reading is 1900-2200 psi (13,100-15,169 kPa) when motor starts, go to TEST D6. If reading is not as specified, replace pressure warning switch and pump/motor relay.

TEST D6 (Checking Pressure Warning Switch)

With ignition on, check pressure gauge reading when pump motor stops running. If pressure is 2350-2800 psi (16,203-19,305 kPa), and pump takes more than 60 seconds to obtain specified pressure, replace pump/motor assembly. If pressure is reached under 60 seconds, reverify symptom. If pressure is not as specified, replace pressure warning switch and pump/motor relay.

TEST E (ANTI-LOCK WARNING LIGHT INTERMITTENTLY ON)

TEST E1 (Fluid Level Sensor & Pressure Warning Switch Circuit)

1) Unplug 32-pin connector from EBCM. Connect EEC-IV Break-Out Box (T83L-50-ECC-IV) and Adapter (T87P-50-ALA) to connector. Turn ignition on.

2) Using an ohmmeter, check resistance between break-out box pins No. 25 and 27. If resistance is less than 5 ohms, go to **TEST E2**. If resistance is more than 5 ohms, go to **TEST E1a**.

TEST E1a (Checking Fluid Level Sensor Anti-Lock Warning Circuit)

Unplug 5-pin connector from fluid level sensor. Using an ohmmeter, measure resistance between fluid level sensor connector pins No. 1 and No. 2 with brake fluid at maximum level. If resistance is more than 2 ohms, replace fluid level sensor. If resistance is less than 2 ohms, go to **TEST E1b**.

TEST E1b (Checking PWS Anti-Lock Warning Circuit – No Pressure)

1) Turn ignition off. Depressuize brake system. Unplug 5-pin connector from pressure warning switch. Using an ohmmeter, check continuity between pressure warning switch pins No. 3 and No. 5.

2) If there is continuity, replace pressure warning switch and pump/motor relay. If there is no continuity, go to **TEST E1c**.

TEST E1c (Checking Fluid Level Sensor-to-EBCM Circuit)

Using an ohmmeter, check for continuity between break-out box pin No. 25 and fluid level sensor connector pin No. 1. If there is no continuity, repair circuit No. 512. If there is continuity, go to **TEST E1d**.

TEST E1d (Checking Fluid Level Sensor-to-Pressure Warning Switch Circuit)

Using an ohmmeter, check for continuity between fluid level sensor connector pin No. 2 and pressure warning switch connector pin No. 3. If there is no continuity, repair circuit No. 549. If there is continuity, go to **TEST E1e**.

TEST E – "ANTI-LOCK" LIGHT INTERMITTENTLY ON (Cont.)

TEST E1e (Checking Pressure Warning Switch-to-EBCM Circuit)

Using an ohmmeter, check for continuity between pressure warning switch connector pin No. 5 and break-out box pin No. 27. If there is no continuity, repair circuit No. 535. If there is continuity, turn ignition off. Reconnect all connections. Reverify symptom.

TEST E2 (Fluid Level Sensor & Pressure Warning Switch Isolation Test)

Check for continuity between break-out box pin No. 25 and ground. If there is no continuity, reverify symptom. If there is continuity, go to **TEST E2a**.

TEST E2a (Checking Fluid Level Sensor Continuity)

Unplug fluid level sensor connector. Using an ohmmeter, check for continuity between sensor pin No. 1 and pins No. 3, No. 4, and No. 5. Also check between pin No. 2 and pins No. 3, No. 4, and No. 5. If there is continuity, replace fluid level sensor. If there is no continuity, go to **TEST E2b**.

TEST E2b (Continuity of Fluid Level Sensor Pin No. 1 Circuit)

Using an ohmmeter, check continuity between fluid level sensor connector pin No. 1 and ground. If there is continuity, repair circuit No. 512. If there is no continuity, go to **TEST E2c**.

TEST E2c (Checking Continiuty Between Pressure Warning Switch & Fluid Level Sensor)

Unplug pressure warning sensor 5-pin connector. Using an ohmmeter, check for continuity between fluid level sensor connector pin No. 2 and ground. If there is continuity, repair circuit No. 549. If there is no continuity, go to **TEST E2d**.

TEST E2d (Checking Pressure Warning Switch Continuity)

Using an ohmmeter, check for continuity between pressure warning switch pin No. 3 and ground, and pin No. 5 to ground. If there is continuity, replace pressure warning switch and pump/motor relay. If there is no continuity, go to **TEST E2e**.

TEST E2e (Checking Continuity Between Pressure Warning Switch & EBCM)

Using an ohmmeter, check for continuity between pressure warning switch connector pin No. 5 and ground. If there is continuity, repair circuit No. 535. If there is no continuity, plug in all connectors and reverify symptom.

TEST F ("BRAKE" WARNING LIGHT ON, "ANTI-LOCK" WARNING LIGHT OFF; PARKING BRAKE RELEASE & BRAKE LINING WEAR CHECKED)

TEST F1 (Check Brake Fluid Level)

Turn ignition on. Pump brake pedal until motor starts to operate. When motor stops operating, check brake fluid level. If brake fluid level is low, check for external leaks. Repair leak. If brake fluid level is okay, go to **TEST F2**.

TEST F2 (Checking Fluid Level Sensor Continuity)

Unplug 5-pin connector from fluid level sensor. Set ohmmeter on 200 ohm scale. Check resistance between fluid level sensor pins No. 3 and No. 4. If resistance is less than 10 ohms, replace fluid level sensor. If resistance is 10 ohms or above, go to **TEST F3**.

TEST F3 (Checking Pressure Warning Switch Continuity)

Turn ignition on and wait until motor stops running. Unplug pressure warning switch 5-pin connector. Using an ohmmeter, check for continuity between pressure warning switch pins No. 1 and No. 2. If there is continuity, replace pressure warning switch and pump/motor relay. If there is no continuity, go to **TEST F4**.

TEST F4 (Checking Wiring Continuity)

Check all wiring circuits from fluid level sensor. If okay, check parking brake electrical circuit. If not okay, repair wiring.

TEVES ANTI-LOCK BRAKE SYSTEMS (ABS) FORD MOTOR CO. (Cont.)

TEST G ("ANTI-LOCK" WARNING LIGHT NOT ON WHEN IGNITION IS TURNED ON)

TEST G1 (Checking Fuse & Fuse Links)

Ensure fuses and fuse links are okay. If not, repair as necessary. If okay, go to **TEST G2**.

TEST G2 (Check "ANTI-LOCK" Warning Light Bulb)

Check warning light bulb. Replace, if necessary. If okay, go to **TEST G3**.

TEST G3 (Check "ANTI-LOCK" Warning Light Operation)

Unplug 32-pin connector from control module. Turn ignition on. If warning light goes on, repair circuit No. 606. If light does not come on, repair or replace connector to main wiring harness.

TEST H (SPONGY BRAKE PEDAL WITH/WITHOUT ANTI-LOCK FUNCTION; NO WARNING LIGHT)

TEST H1 (Check Component Mounting)

Check brake pedal and hydraulic unit for proper mounting. Bleed brakes. If brakes are spongy, go to **TEST H2**.

TEST H2 (Bleed Brake System)

Turn off air suspension switch, located in luggage compartment. Rebleed brake system. Turn air suspension on when vehicle is off hoist. If brake pedal is still spongy, replace master cylinder/booster assembly.

TEST J (POOR VEHICLE TRACKING DURING ANTI-LOCK FUNCTION; WARNING LIGHT OFF)

TEST J1 (Verify Condition)

Verify condition exists. Turn air suspension off. Bleed brake system. Turn air suspension on when vehicle is off hoist. If vehicle still does not track proper, go to **TEST J2**.

TEST J2 (Check Anti-Lock Operation – LF Wheel)

1) Turn air suspension off. Raise vehicle. Ensure wheels rotate freely. Turn ignition off. Unplug 32-pin connector from EBCM. Connect Break-Out Box (T83L-50-EEC-IV) and Adapter (T87P-50-ALA) to EBCM connector.

2) Short break-out box pins No. 14, No. 18 and No. 31 together. Apply moderate brake pedal effort. Check that LF wheel will not rotate. Turn ignition on. DO NOT leave ignition on for more than one minute.

3) LF wheel should rotate freely with ignition on. If wheel rotates freely, turn ignition off. Disconnect wire leads and go to **TEST J3**. If wheel does not rotate freely or brake pedal drops, replace solenoid valve block assembly. Turn air suspension on when vehicle is off hoist.

TEST J3 (Check Anti-Lock Operation – RF Wheel)

1) Turn air suspension off. Short break-out box pins No. 13, No. 18 and No. 32 together. Apply moderate brake pedal effort. Check that RF wheel will not rotate. Turn ignition on. DO NOT leave ignition on for more than one minute.

2) RF wheel should rotate freely with ignition on. If wheel rotates freely, turn ignition off. Disconnect wire leads and go to **TEST J4**. If wheel does not rotate freely or brake pedal drops, replace solenoid valve block assembly. Turn air suspension on when vehicle is off hoist.

TEST J4 (Check Anti-Lock Operation – Rear Wheels)

1) Turn air suspension off. Short break-out box pins No. 12, No. 18 and No. 30 together. Apply moderate brake pedal effort. Check that rear wheels will not rotate. Turn ignition on. DO NOT leave ignition on for more than one minute.

2) Rear wheels should rotate freely with ignition on. If wheels rotate freely, turn ignition off. Disconnect wire leads and break-out box.

3) Lower vehicle. reverify symptom. If wheels do not rotate freely or brake pedal drops, replace solenoid valve block assembly. Turn air suspension on when vehicle is off hoist.

REMOVAL & INSTALLATION

NOTE: Before hoisting vehicle off ground, turn air suspension switch off. Switch is located in luggage compartment. Failure to do so can damage air suspension.

MASTER CYLINDER/BOOSTER ASSEMBLY

Removal & Installation

1) Depressuize brake system. Disconnect negative battery cable. On Continental FWD, remove air

Fig. 6: Exploded View of Master Cylinder/Booster Assembly (Continental FWD)

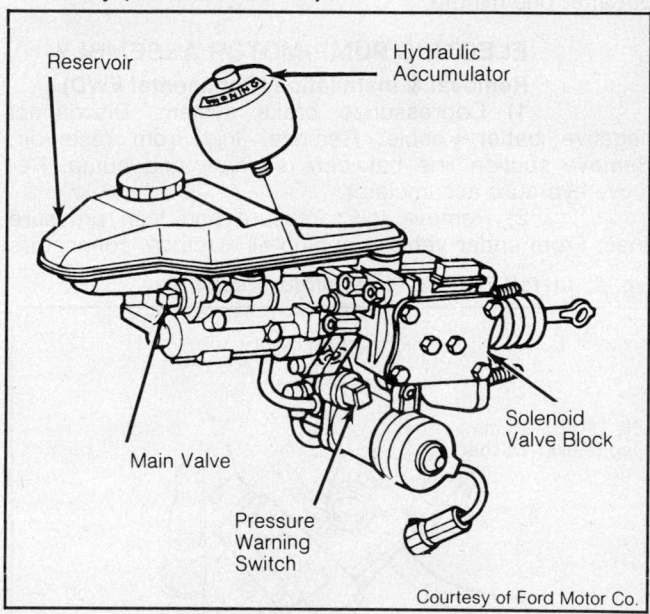

Reservoir
Hydraulic Accumulator
Main Valve
Solenoid Valve Block
Pressure Warning Switch

Courtesy of Ford Motor Co.

Fig. 7: Exploded View of Master Cylinder/Booster Assembly (Continental FWD)

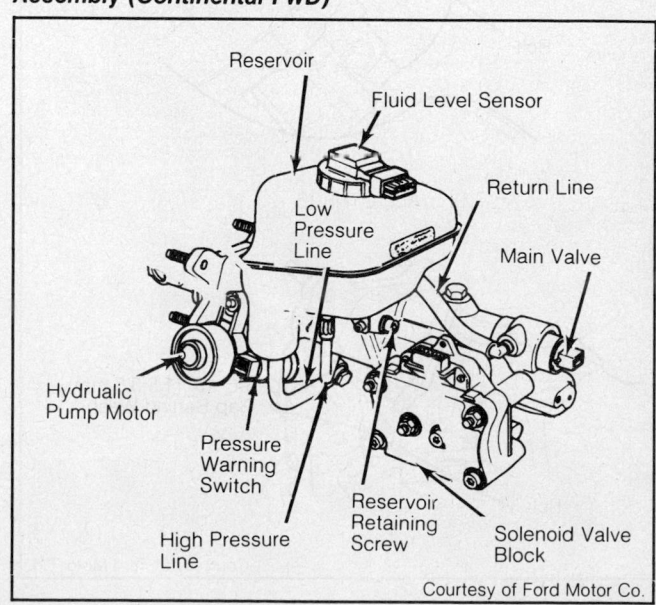

Reservoir
Fluid Level Sensor
Low Pressure Line
Return Line
Main Valve
Hydrualic Pump Motor
Pressure Warning Switch
High Pressure Line
Reservoir Retaining Screw
Solenoid Valve Block

Courtesy of Ford Motor Co.

Brake Systems

TEVES ANTI-LOCK BRAKE SYSTEMS (ABS) FORD MOTOR CO. (Cont.)

cleaner. On all models, unplug all electrical connectors from master cylinder/booster attaching components. Disconnect brake lines from valve block and mark. Plug all line openings. *See Figs. 6 and 7.*

2) Remove accumulator. Ensure no dirt falls into open port. On Continental FWD, remove trim panel from under steering column. On all models, remove stoplight switch. Remove 4 mounting nuts. From engine compartment, remove master cylinder/booster assembly. To install, reverse removal procedure.

HYDRAULIC ACCUMULATOR

Removal & Installation

Depressurize brake system. Remove hydraulic accumulator. To install, reverse removal procedure. Install new "O" ring. Turn ignition on. Ensure warning lights go out after one minute.

ELECTRIC PUMP/MOTOR ASSEMBLY

Removal & Installation (Continental FWD)

1) Depressurize brake system. Disconnect negative battery cable. Remove fluid from reservoir. Remove suction line between reservoir and pump. Remove hydraulic accumulator.

2) Remove low pressure and high pressure lines. From under vehicle, unplug all electrical connectors

Fig. 8: Install Electric Pump/Motor Assembly

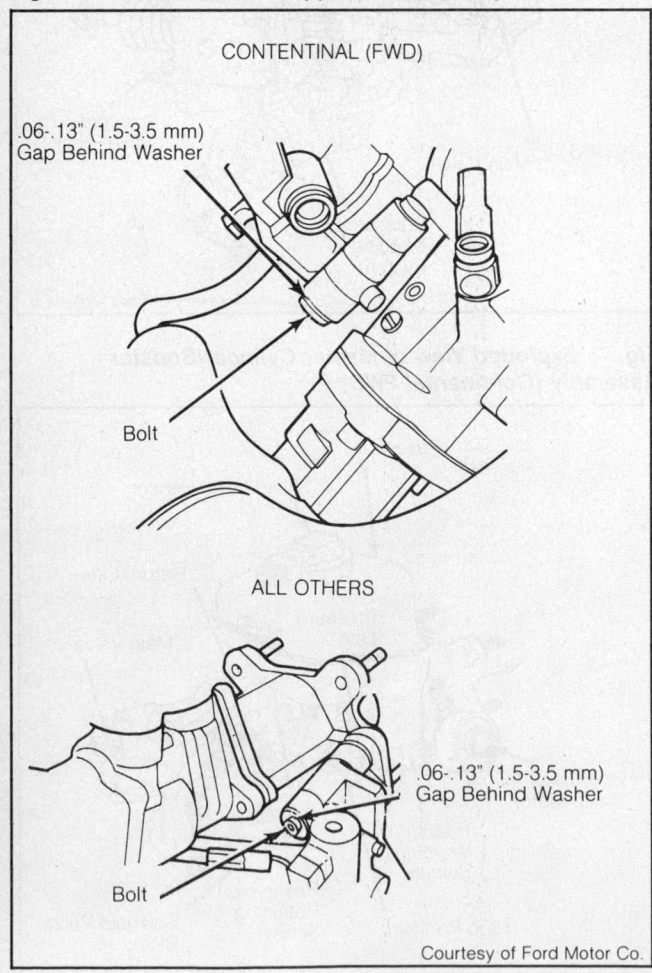

CONTENTINAL (FWD)

.06-.13" (1.5-3.5 mm) Gap Behind Washer

Bolt

ALL OTHERS

.06-.13" (1.5-3.5 mm) Gap Behind Washer

Bolt

Courtesy of Ford Motor Co.

from assembly. Remove Allen head bolt retaining pump-/motor assembly to master cylinder/booster assembly. Remove pump/motor assembly.

3) To install, reverse removal procedure. Ensure gap behind washer on retaining bolt is .06-.13" (1.5-3.5 mm). *See Fig. 8.* If gap is incorrect, noisy operation or vibration will occur.

Removal & Installation (All Others)

1) Depressurize brake system. Disconnect negative battery cable. Unplug all electrical connectors from attached components. Remove fluid from reservoir. Remove suction and return hoses.

2) Remove reservoir. Remove pressure hose banjo bolt. DO NOT lose "O" rings. Remove hydraulic accumulator. Using a long extension and "U" joint socket, remove assembly retaining bolt.

3) Retain spacer between extension housing and shock mount. Move assembly toward engine. Remove assembly from retainer pin. To install, reverse removal procedure. Ensure gap behind washer on retaining bolt is .06-.13" (1.5-3.5 mm). If gap is incorrect, noisy operation or vibration will occur.

SOLENOID VALVE BLOCK ASSEMBLY

Removal & Installation

1) Depressurize brake system. Disconnect negative battery cable. Remove master cylinder/booster assembly. Gently clamp off reservoir-to-master cylinder hose.

2) Remove 3 nuts retaining solenoid valve block assembly. Remove assembly. To install, reverse removal procedure. Install 4 new "O" rings in solenoid valve block assembly. Lubricate "O" rings with clean brake fluid.

RESERVOIR

Removal & Installation

1) Depressurize brake system. Disconnect negative battery cable. Remove brake fluid from reservoir. Remove suction and return hoses. Remove reservoir mounting bolt.

2) Place a screwdriver between reservoir-to-master cylinder nipples and gently pry upward. Remove sleeve and "O" ring. To install, reverse removal procedure. Ensure sleeve and "O" ring are positioned correctly.

PRESSURE SWITCH

NOTE: **Manufacturer recommends replacement of pump/motor relay anytime pressure switch is replaced.**

Removal & Installation

Depressurize brake system. Disconnect negative battery cable. Unplug electrical connectors from solenoid valve block assembly and pressure switch. Using Socket (T85P-20215-B), remove pressure switch. To install, reverse removal procedure.

WHEEL SENSORS

Removal & Installation (Front)

1) Unplug wheel sensor connector from inside engine compartment. Raise front of vehicle and support. Remove tire and wheel. Remove sensor wiring from retaining clips. Loosen sensor set screw. Remove wheel sensor.

TEVES ANTI-LOCK BRAKE SYSTEMS (ABS)
FORD MOTOR CO. (Cont.)

2) To install, reverse removal procedure. On all models except Continental FWD, if old sensor is being used, scrape sensor face with a dull knife, to ensure sensor slide freely on post. Glue new paper spacer (marked "F") on pole face.

3) Spacer thickness should be .051" (1.3 mm). Position wheel sensor until paper spacer contacts toothed ring. Tighten set screw to 21-26 INCH lbs. (2.4-3.0 N.m). Ensure wiring is secured in retaining clips.

Removal & Installation
(Rear – Thunderbird)

1) From inside luggage compartment, unplug sensor connector. Raise rear of vehicle and support. Remove tire and wheel. Remove sensor wiring from retaining clips. Remove sensor retaining bolt. Remove wheel sensor.

2) On Continental FWD, install Spring Replacement Arm (T88P-5310-A) on front suspension arm. Using a 3/4" breaker bar, lower arm to allow wheel sensor wire to be removed.

3) To install, reverse removal procedure. Wheel sensor is nonadjustable. Ensure wiring is secured in retaining clips.

Removal & Installation
(Rear – Mark VII)

1) From inside luggage compartment, unplug sensor connector. Raise rear of vehicle and support. Remove tire and wheel. Remove sensor wiring from retaining clips. Remove rear brake caliper and rotor. Remove sensor retaining bolt.

2) Remove wheel sensor bracket. Loosen set screw. Remove wheel sensor. If old sensor is being used, scrape sensor face with a dull knife, to ensure sensor slide freely on post. Glue new paper spacer (marked "R") on pole face. Spacer thickness should be .043" (1.1 mm).

3) Install wheel sensor bracket. Position wheel sensor until paper spacer contacts toothed ring. Tighten set screw to 21-26 INCH lbs. (2.4-3.0 N.m). Secure wiring in retaining clips. To complete installation, reverse removal procedure.

TIGHTENING SPECIFICATIONS

Application	Ft. Lbs. (N.m)
Banjo Bolts	
High Pressure	12-15 (16-20)
Low Pressure	19-24 (26-33)
Hydraulic Accumulator	30-34 (41-46)
Pressure Switch	15-25 (20-34)
Valve Block Nut	15-21 (20-29)
Wheel Sensor Bracket Bolt	10-15 (14-20)

	INCH Lbs. (N.m)
Reservoir Mounting Bolt	35-53 (4.0-6.0)
Wheel Sensor Bracket Post Bolt	40-60 (4.5-6.8)
Wheel Sensor Set Screw	21-26 (2.4-3.0)

Brake Systems

TEVES ANTI-LOCK BRAKE SYSTEMS (ABS) FORD MOTOR CO. (Cont.)

Fig. 9: *Teves Anti-Lock Brake System Wiring Diagram (Continental)*

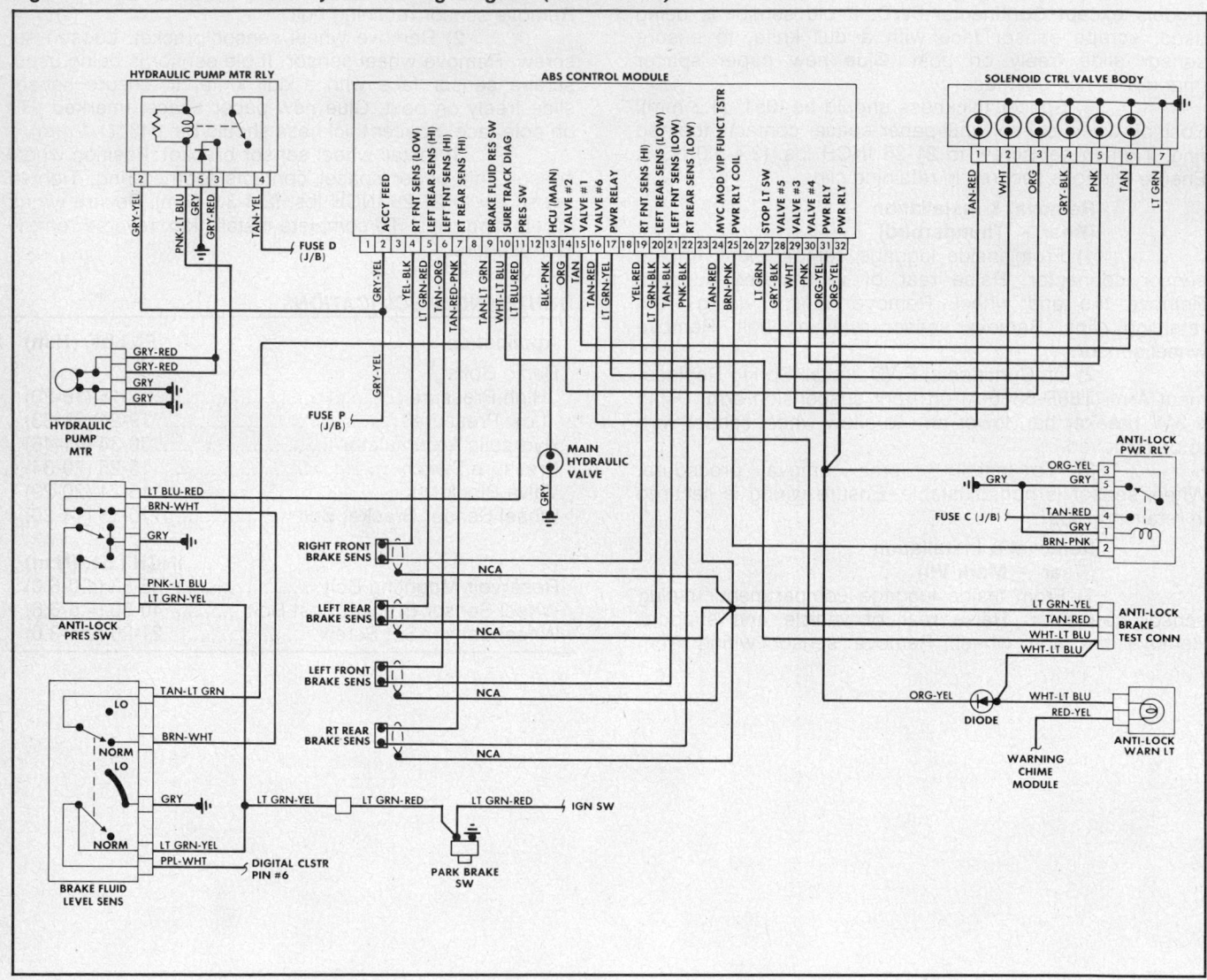

TEVES ANTI-LOCK BRAKE SYSTEMS (ABS)
FORD MOTOR CO. (Cont.)

Fig. 10: Teves Anti-Lock Brake System Wiring Diagram (Mark VII)

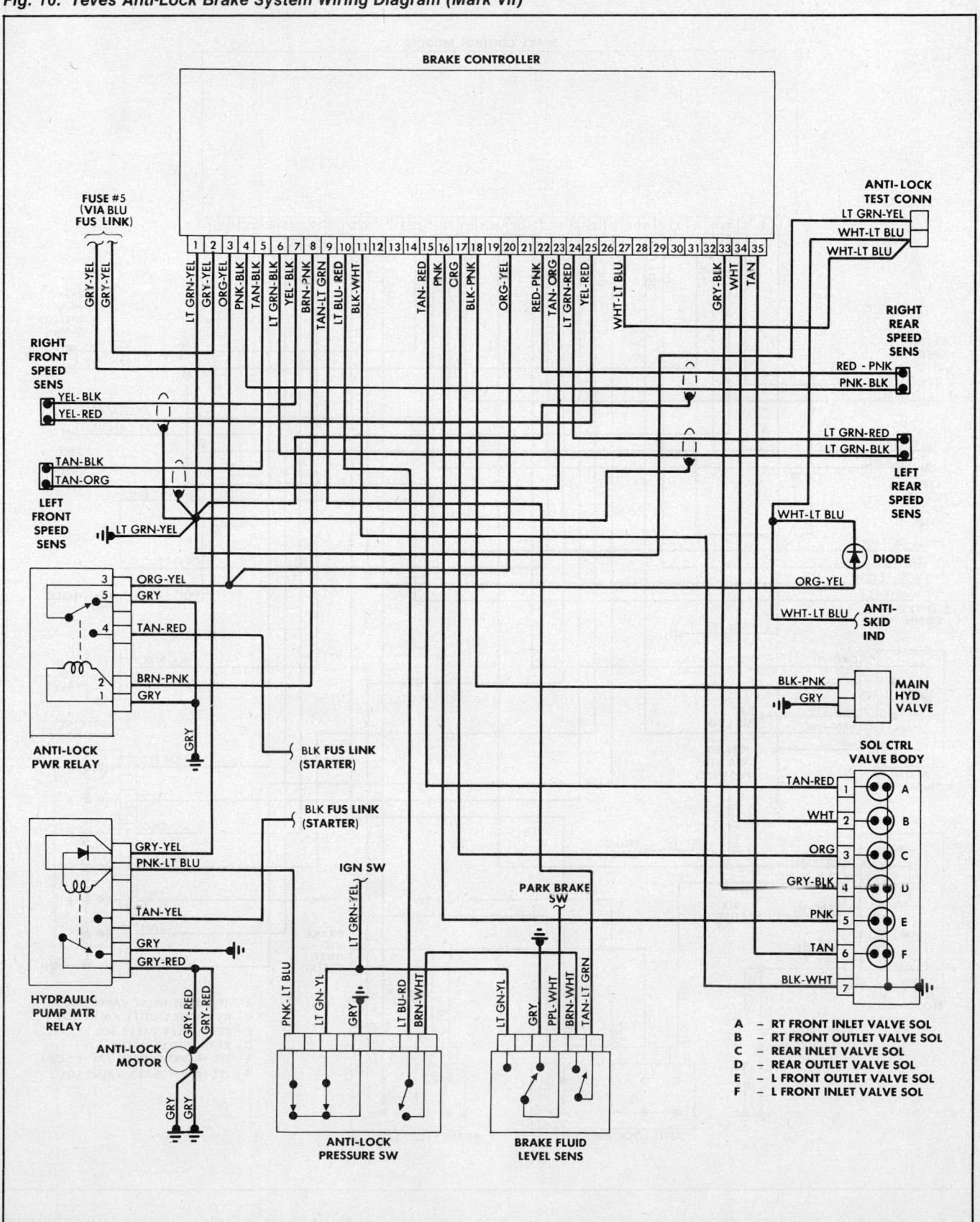

Brake Systems

TEVES ANTI-LOCK BRAKE SYSTEMS (ABS) FORD MOTOR CO. (Cont.)

Fig. 11: Teves Anti-Lock Brake System Wiring Diagram (Thunderbird)

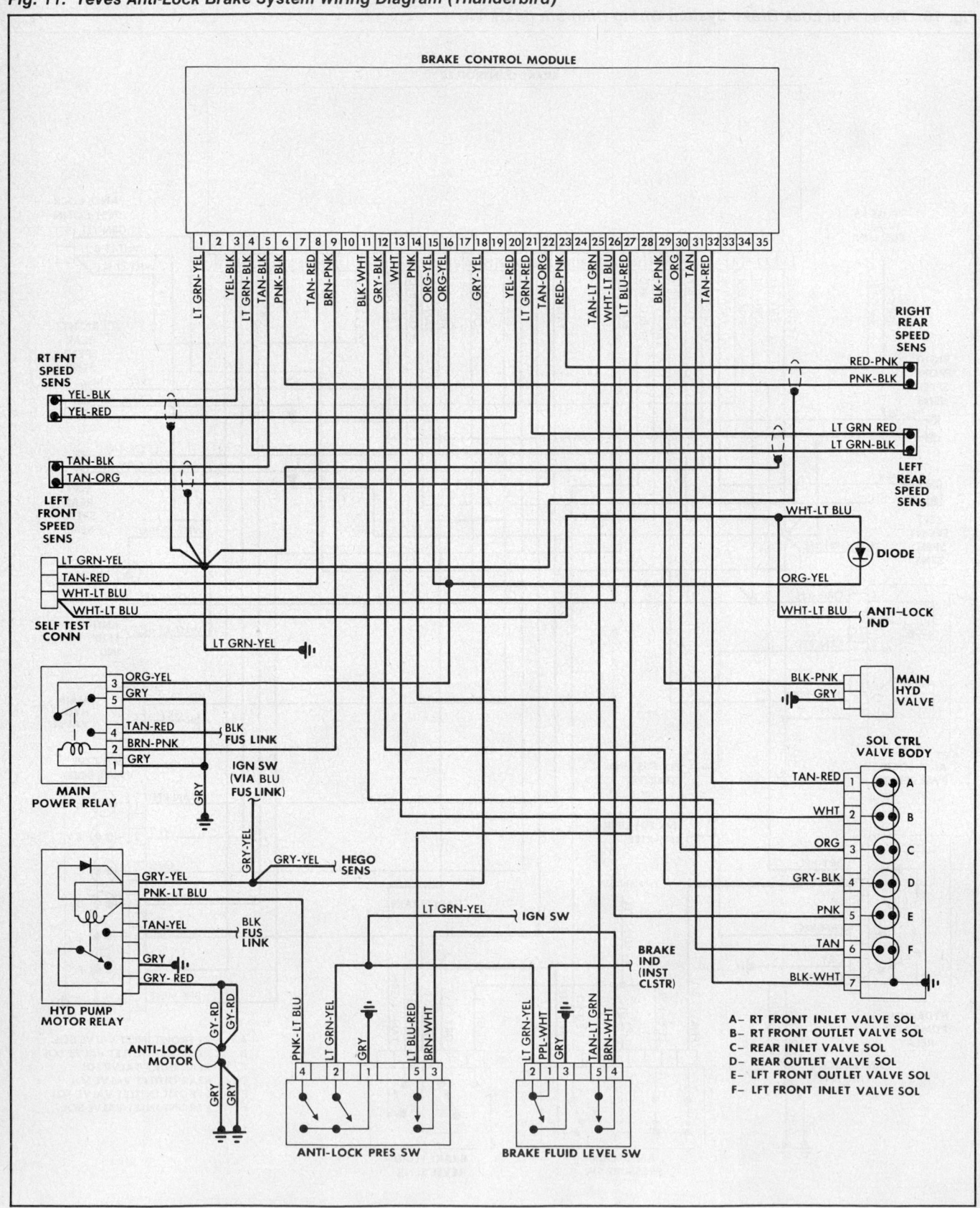

TEVES ANTI-LOCK BRAKE SYSTEMS (ABS)
EXCEPT GM WITH BCM & ELDORADO, SEVILLE & 6000

Buick: Electra, LeSabre
Cadillac: DeVille, Fleetwood
Oldsmobile: Delta 88, Ninety-Eight
Pontiac: Bonneville

NOTE: General Motors, (except Corvette) use Teves designed anti-lock system. See appropriate TEVES ANTI-LOCK BRAKE SYSTEM article. Corvette uses a Bosch designed anti-lock system. For Corvette, see BOSCH (GENERAL MOTORS) ANTI-LOCK BRAKE SYSTEM.

DESCRIPTION

The Teves 4-wheel Anti-Lock Brake System is desgined to prevent wheel lock-up during heavy braking. This allows driver to maintain steering control while stopping vehicle to stop in shortest distance.

Major component parts of system include: pump motor assembly, hydraulic accumulator, pressure switch, fluid reservoir with integral filter, 4 wheel speed sensors, valve block assembly, fluid level sensor, Electronic Brake Control Module (EBCM), hydraulic booster/master cylinder assembly, and "BRAKE" and "ANTI-LOCK" warning lights. See Fig. 1.

OPERATION

ANTI-LOCK BRAKE SYSTEM

During normal driving and braking operations, ABS acts like a conventional braking system. Each wheel sensors constantly sends an AC signal to EBCM. This information is translated to wheel rotation speed. When EBCM determines that wheel lock-up is about to occur, it activates electro-magnetic valves, located inside valve block to increase or decrease hydraulic pressure to each wheel.

A slight pulsation should be felt through brake pedal. Warning lights should come on when key is turned on and vehicle is started. If either light stays on after approximately 30 seconds after vehicle is started, system malfunction is indicated. See TESTING in this article.

DIAGNOSIS & TESTING

NOTE: Break-Out Box (J-35592) and a pressure gauge must be used to diagnose ABS.

Diagnosis of the ABS malfunction involves 3 basic steps which must be followed in order to isolate fault, accurately determine its cause and repair the condition with the least amount of diagnostic time. The proper diagnostic procedure consists of the following steps: PRE-DIAGNOSIS INSPECTION, LIGHT SEQUENCE DETERMINATION and TROUBLE SHOOTING CHARTS.

PRE-DIAGNOSIS INSPECTION

The Pre-Diagnosis Inspection consists of a quick visual check of specific system components which could create an apparent anti-lock system malfunction.

LIGHT SEQUENCE DETERMINATION

1) The second step in diagnosis of any anti-lock brake system condition is determination of the warning light behavior. The system uses 2 warning lights, the Red "BRAKE" warning light and an Amber "ANTI-LOCK" light.

2) By observing when these lights come on, specific components and sub-systems of the brake system may be isolated as likely causes of a system malfunction.

3) Each light sequence illustration is divided into 7 areas which represent vehicle status, with behavior

Fig. 1: Anti-Lock Brake System Component Locations

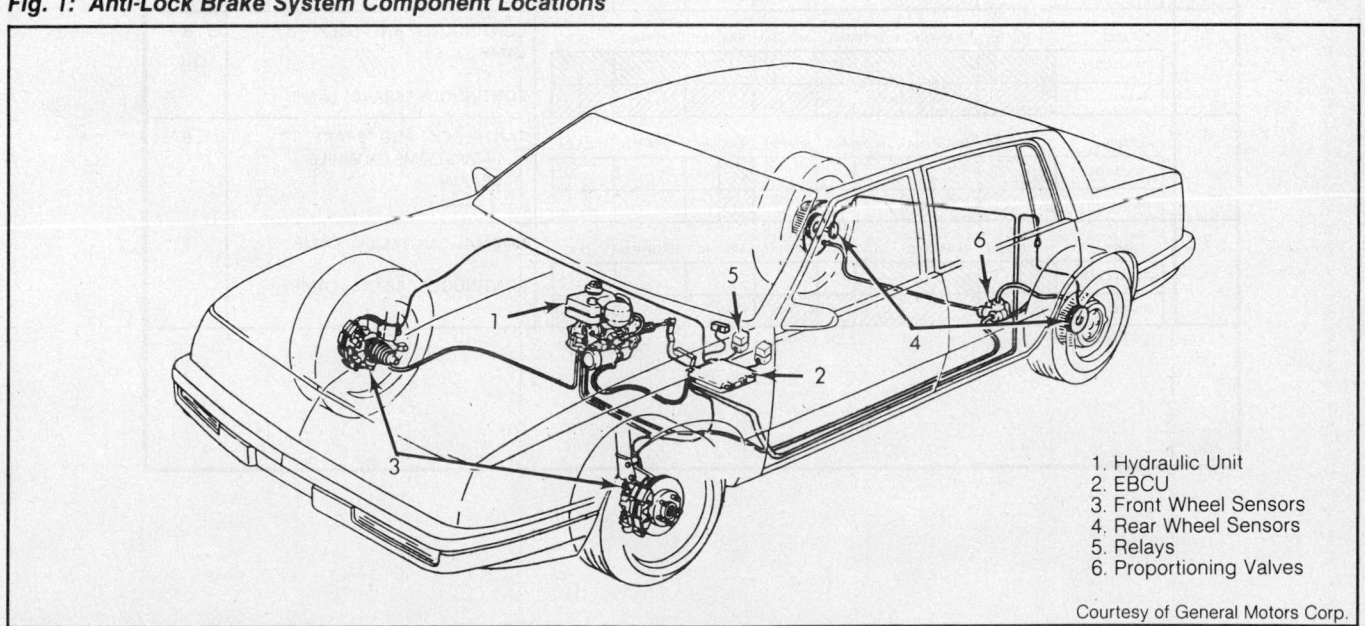

1. Hydraulic Unit
2. EBCU
3. Front Wheel Sensors
4. Rear Wheel Sensors
5. Relays
6. Proportioning Valves

Brake Systems

TEVES ANTI-LOCK BRAKE SYSTEMS (ABS) EXCEPT GM WITH BCM & ELDORADO, SEVILLE & 6000 (Cont.)

Fig. 2: Light Sequence Chart

LIGHT SEQUENCE CHART

SEE LAMP SEQUENCE DETERMINATION PROCEDURE
IN THIS SECTION BEFORE USING THIS CHART

SEQ. NO.	LAMP SEQUENCE	SYMPTOM DESCRIPTION	PERF TEST
1	LAMPS — IGN ON, CRANKING, RUNNING, MOVING, BRAKING, STOPPED, IDLE; "ANTI-LOCK"; BRAKE	NORMAL LAMP SEQUENCE WITH - EXCESSIVE PEDAL TRAVEL OR SPONGY PEDAL - ANTI-LOCK BRAKING OPERATION OR VALVE CYCLING DURING NORMAL STOP ON DRY PAVEMENT - POOR VEHICLE TRACKING DURING ANTI-LOCK BRAKING	G C D
2	LAMPS — IGN ON, CRANKING, RUNNING, MOVING, BRAKING, STOPPED, IDLE; "ANTI-LOCK"; BRAKE	CONTINUOUS "ANTI-LOCK" LAMP NORMAL "BRAKE" LAMP	A
3	LAMPS — IGN ON, CRANKING, RUNNING, MOVING, BRAKING, STOPPED, IDLE; "ANTI-LOCK"; BRAKE	"ANTI-LOCK" LAMP COMES ON AFTER VEHICLE STARTS MOVING NORMAL BRAKE LIGHT	C
4	LAMPS — IGN ON, CRANKING, RUNNING, MOVING, BRAKING, STOPPED, IDLE; "ANTI-LOCK"; BRAKE	NO "ANTI-LOCK" LAMP WHILE CRANKING NORMAL "BRAKE" LAMP	A-19
5	LAMPS — IGN ON, CRANKING, RUNNING, MOVING, BRAKING, STOPPED, IDLE; "ANTI-LOCK"; BRAKE	NO "ANTI-LOCK" LAMP NORMAL "BRAKE" LAMP	E
6	LAMPS — IGN ON, CRANKING, RUNNING, MOVING, BRAKING, STOPPED, IDLE; "ANTI-LOCK"; BRAKE	INTERMITTANT "ANTI-LOCK" WHILE DRIVING NORMAL "BRAKE" LAMP	F
7	LAMPS — IGN ON, CRANKING, RUNNING, MOVING, BRAKING, STOPPED, IDLE; "ANTI-LOCK"; BRAKE	CONTINUOUS "ANTI-LOCK" LAMP CONTINUOUS "BRAKE" LAMP	B
8	LAMPS — IGN ON, CRANKING, RUNNING, MOVING, BRAKING, STOPPED, IDLE; "ANTI-LOCK"; BRAKE	"ANTI-LOCK" AND "BRAKE" LAMPS COME ON WHILE BRAKING	B
9	LAMPS — IGN ON, CRANKING, RUNNING, MOVING, BRAKING, STOPPED, IDLE; "ANTI-LOCK"; BRAKE	NORMAL "ANTI-LOCK" LAMP CONTINUOUS "BRAKE" LAMP	B

TEVES ANTI-LOCK BRAKE SYSTEMS (ABS)
EXCEPT GM WITH BCM & ELDORADO, SEVILLE & 6000 (Cont.)

of "BRAKE" and "ANTI-LOCK" lights represented in horizontal rows below vehicle status headers. See Fig. 2.

4) "BRAKE" and "ANTI-LOCK" light status is indicated by shaded areas in horizontal rows below each vehicle status header. A vehicle status block which is not entirely shaded means that light is on only for part of the test period.

LIGHT SEQUENCE TEST PROCEDURE

1) Determine customer complaint as accurately as possible. If reduced braking ability is described, use caution in evaluating vehicle.

2) Turn ignition off for a minimum of 15 seconds. Turn ignition on and observe "BRAKE" and "ANTI-LOCK" lights. If accumulator has been discharged, both lights may remain on for approximately 30 seconds. If this occurs, allow lights to turn off and turn ignition off for another 15 seconds. If lights do not go out within 30 seconds, proceed to step 5).

3) Turn ignition on and observe warning lights. At this time, "BRAKE" light should remain off. "ANTI-LOCK" light should come on for 3 to 6 seconds and then go out.

4) Turn ignition switch to "START" position and observe warning lights. Both warning lights should illuminate while ignition switch is in "START" position.

5) When engine starts, release key to "RUN" position and observe warning lights. "BRAKE" light should turn off immediately. "ANTI-LOCK" light should remain on for 3 to 6 seconds and then go off.

6) Drive vehicle at a minimum speed of 20 mph for a short period of time and observe warning lights. Both lights should remain off for this step and remainder of test. Note as accurately as possible the conditions under which either light comes on.

7) Stop vehicle using a normal brake application. Both lights should remain off. Place transaxle in Park and allow vehicle to idle for a few seconds. Observe warning lights. Both should remain off.

8) From information obtained in test above, determine light sequence and/or symptom which most closely matches behavior of complaint and perform indicated tests.

NOTE ON INTERMITTENTS

The diagnostic procedures in this section may or may not be helpful in determining cause of intermittent problems in anti-lock brake system electrical components. Fault must be present to locate problem effectively using TEST "A" PIN-OUT CHECKS and trouble charts.

A light sequence description from vehicle owner can be helpful in locating a likely component or circuit in case of an intermittent failure. Use LIGHT SEQUENCE CHART if a good description of light behavior can be obtained. See Fig. 2.

On all models, most intermittent problems are caused by faulty electical connections or wiring. When an intermittent failure is encountered, check suspect circuits for:

- Poor mating or connector halves or terminals not fully seated in connector body (backed out).
- Improperly formed or damaged terminals. All connector terminals in a problem circuit should be carefully reformed to increase contact tension.
- Poor terminal-to-wire connection. Requires removing terminal and wire from connector body to inspect.

If visual check does not find cause of problem, operate vehicle with EBCM connected in an attempt to duplicate condition.

Circuits which could possibly cause intemittent operation of "ANTI-LOCK" light include:

- Wheel speed sensor circuits – low or intermittent output.
- Ignition enable circuit – interruption of 12 volt input.
- EBCM switch loop circuit (low fluid/low pressure sensors) – intermittent open.
- Main relay – interruption in coil or switched battery power.

INSTALLING PRESSURE GAUGE

NOTE: **Before connecting pressure gauge, hydraulic accumulator must be depressurized. With ignition off, pump brake pedal a MINIMUM of 20 times using full pedal strokes. When a definite increase in pedal effort is felt, pump pedal 2 more times.**

Some diagnostic procedures require that a pressure gauge be connected to the energy unit to read accumlator pressure. Use the following procedure:

1) Depressurize accumulator. Remove pressure hose fitting (banjo bolt) from pump body. Take care not to drop the 2 "O" ring seals when removing fitting.

2) Install one of the 2 "O" ring seals on pressure gauge fitting and insert gauge fitting into pressure hose coupling.

3) Install second "O" ring seal on gauge fitting on the underside of pressure hose coupling and thread gauge fitting into pump body. Tighten fitting to 15 ft. lbs. (20 N.m).

4) When removing gauge and installing pressure fitting, inspect "O" ring seals for cuts or damage. Replace any cut or damaged "O" ring seals.

REMOVAL & INSTALLATION

CAUTION: **Before servicing any component which contains high pressure, it is mandatory that hydraulic pressure in the system be discharged. With ignition off, pump brake pedal a MINIMUM of 20 times using full pedal strokes. When a definite increase in pedal effort is felt, pump pedal 2 more times.**

HYDRAULIC UNIT

Removal & Installation

1) Disconnect negative battery cable. Depressurize brake system. Unplug all electrical connectors from hydraulic unit. Remove pump bolt. Move hydraulic unit aside to gain access to brake pipes. Disconnect brake lines. DO NOT allow brake fluid to come in contact with any electrical connectors.

2) From inside passenger compartment, disconnect hydraulic booster push rod from brake pedal. Push dust boot forward past hex on push rod. Separate push rod halves by unthreading the 2 pieces. Remove 2 bolts attaching unit to push rod bracket.

3) Remove unit. Front half of push rod will remain in hydraulic unit. See Fig. 3. To install, reverse removal procedure. Bleed brake system after installation

Brake Systems

TEVES ANTI-LOCK BRAKE SYSTEMS (ABS)
EXCEPT GM WITH BCM & ELDORADO, SEVILLE & 6000 (Cont.)

of hydraulic unit. See BLEEDING BRAKE SYSTEM in this article.

HYDRAULIC ACCUMULATOR

Removal

Turn ignition off. Discharge brake system pressure. Remove hydraulic accumulator and "O" ring by turning accumulator. See Fig. 3. Ensure no dirt particles fall into open port.

Installation

1) Before installing accumulator inspect "O" ring for damage and replace if necessary. Be sure "O" ring is in position on accumulator and is wet with brake fluid. Screw in accumulator. Wipe off any excess fluid.

2) Turn ignition on. Check that "BRAKE" light goes out after one minute. Top off fluid reservoir up to "MAX" mark with a fully charged accumulator.

Fig. 3: Exploded View of Hydraulic Unit

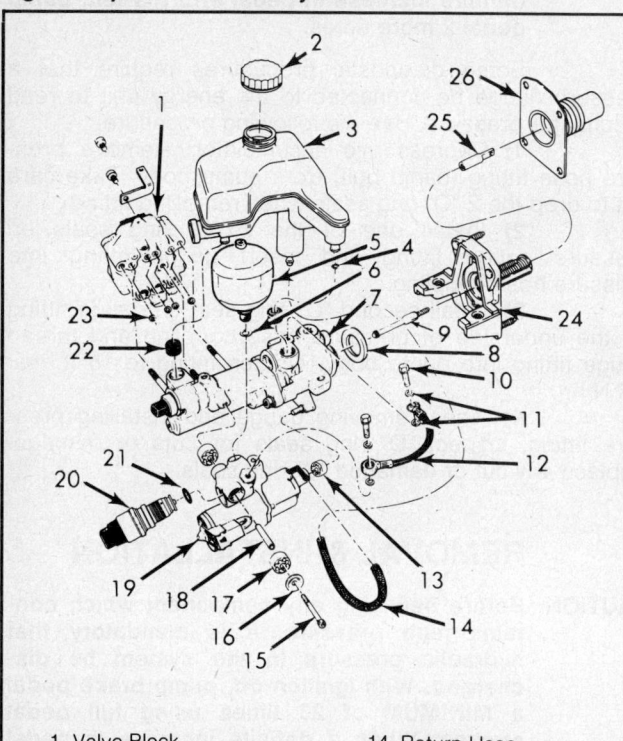

1. Valve Block
2. Reservoir Cap
3. Reservoir
4. "O" Ring
5. Hydraulic Accumulator
6. "O" Ring
7. Booster & Master Cylinder
8. Seal
9. Push Rod (Front)
10. Banjo Bolt
11. "O" Rings
12. Pressure Hose
13. Insulator
14. Return Hose
15. Bolt
16. Washer
17. Insulator
18. Sleeve
19. Pump/Motor Assembly
20. Pressure Switch
21. "O" Ring
22. Grommet
23. "O" Ring
24. Push Rod Assembly
25. Push Rod (Rear)
26. Dust Boot

Courtesy of General Motors Corp.

PUMP/MOTOR ASSEMBLY

Removal & Installation

1) Disconnect negative battery cable. Discharge system pressure. Unplug electrical connections at hydraulic pump motor and pressure warning switch. Remove fluid from reservoir. Unscrew hydraulic accumulator. Ensure no dirt particles fall into open port.

2) Remove pressure line fitting at pump. Remove pressure line and "O" rings. Wire clip and pull return hose fitting out of pump body. See Fig. 3. Remove bolt attaching pump motor to hydraulic booster/master cylinder assembly.

3) Remove pump/motor assembly by sliding off of locating pin. To install, reverse removal procedure. Inspect "O" rings and replace if damaged. Install new grommets. Fill reservoir to "MAX" level.

RESERVOIR ASSEMBLY

Removal & Installation

1) Discharge system pressure. Disconnect negative battery cable. Remove return hose. Drain reservoir. Unplug electrical connector from fluid level sensor. Remove reservoir to valve block mounting bracket bolt.

2) Carefully pry reservoir from booster housing. To install, reverse removal procedure. Inspect "O" rings and replace if necessary. Install new grommets. See BLEEDING BRAKE SYSTEM in this article.

VALVE BLOCK ASSEMBLY

Removal & Installation

Disconnect negative battery cable. Depressurize brake system. Remove fluid from reservoir. Remove hydraulic unit. Remove 3 nuts and washers. Remove valve block assembly and "O" rings. To install, reverse removal procedure. Inspect "O" rings and replace if necessary. See BLEEDING BRAKE SYSTEM in this article.

PRESSURE SWITCH

Removal & Installation

1) Turn ignition off. Discharge system pressure. Disconnect negative battery cable. Disconnect electrical connector from switch.

CAUTION: **Failure to remove connector can result in damage to connector if pressure switch wrench handle should slip and strike connector.**

2) Remove pressure switch using Pressure Switch Remover (J-35804). To install, reverse removal procedure. Turn ignition on. "BRAKE" light should go out within one minute.

WHEEL SENSORS

Removal & Installation

1) On rear sensors, disconnect sensor connector in trunk area. Raise and support vehicle. Remove wheel and tire assembly. Remove sensor retaining screws. Remove sensor.

2) On front sensors, disconnect sensor connector located near shock tower. Remove sensor retaining screw. Remove sensor. To install front or rear sensor, reverse removal procedure.

3) Adjust sensor air gap to specification. See WHEEL SENSOR AIR GAP table in this article. Ensure

TEVES ANTI-LOCK BRAKE SYSTEMS (ABS)
EXCEPT GM WITH BCM & ELDORADO, SEVILLE & 6000 (Cont.)

sensor wiring is routed correctly as to avoid contact with suspension components.

WHEEL SENSOR AIR GAP

Application	In. (mm)
All Models	.040 (1.0)

BLEEDING BRAKE SYSTEM

NOTE: Use only Dot 3 brake fluid. Use of Dot 5 silicone fluid is NOT recommended. Internal damage to pump components may result.

FRONT BRAKES

The front brakes can be bled in conventional manner or by pressure bleeding. The manufacturer recommends pressure bleeding front brakes with a minimum of 20 psi (1.4 kg/cm²).

Bleeding Front Brakes With Pressure Bleeder

1) Bleed front brakes only when rear brakes have been bled first. Remove reservoir cap. Attach Bleeder Adapter (J-35798) to reservoir. Attach bleeding equipment and pressurize system to 20 psi (1.4 kg/cm²).

2) Attach a bleeder hose to one front bleeder valve and submerge other end of hose in a container of clean brake fluid. Open bleeder valve.

3) Allow fluid to flow until no air is seen coming out end of hose. Close bleeder valve. Repeat procedure for other front brake. Fill reservoir to maximum level with a fully charged accumulator.

REAR BRAKES

Bleeding the rear brakes requires a fully charged accumulator. The manufacturer does NOT recommend bleeding rear brakes by using a pressure bleeder.

CAUTION: Care must be exercised when opening rear caliper bleeder screws, due to extremely high pressure available from a fully charged accumulator at bleeder screws.

Bleeding Rear Brakes With
Fully Charged Accumulator

1) Turn ignition on. Allow system to become fully charged. Pump motor will stop when system is fully charged. Attach a bleeder hose to one rear bleeder valve and submerge other end of hose in a container of clean brake fluid. Open bleeder valve.

2) With ignition on, slightly depress brake pedal for at least 10 seconds. Continue procedure until there is no more air coming out of hose. Repeat procedure for other rear brake. Fill reservoir to maximum level with a fully charged accumulator.

Fig. 4: Teves Anti-Lock Brake System Testing Points

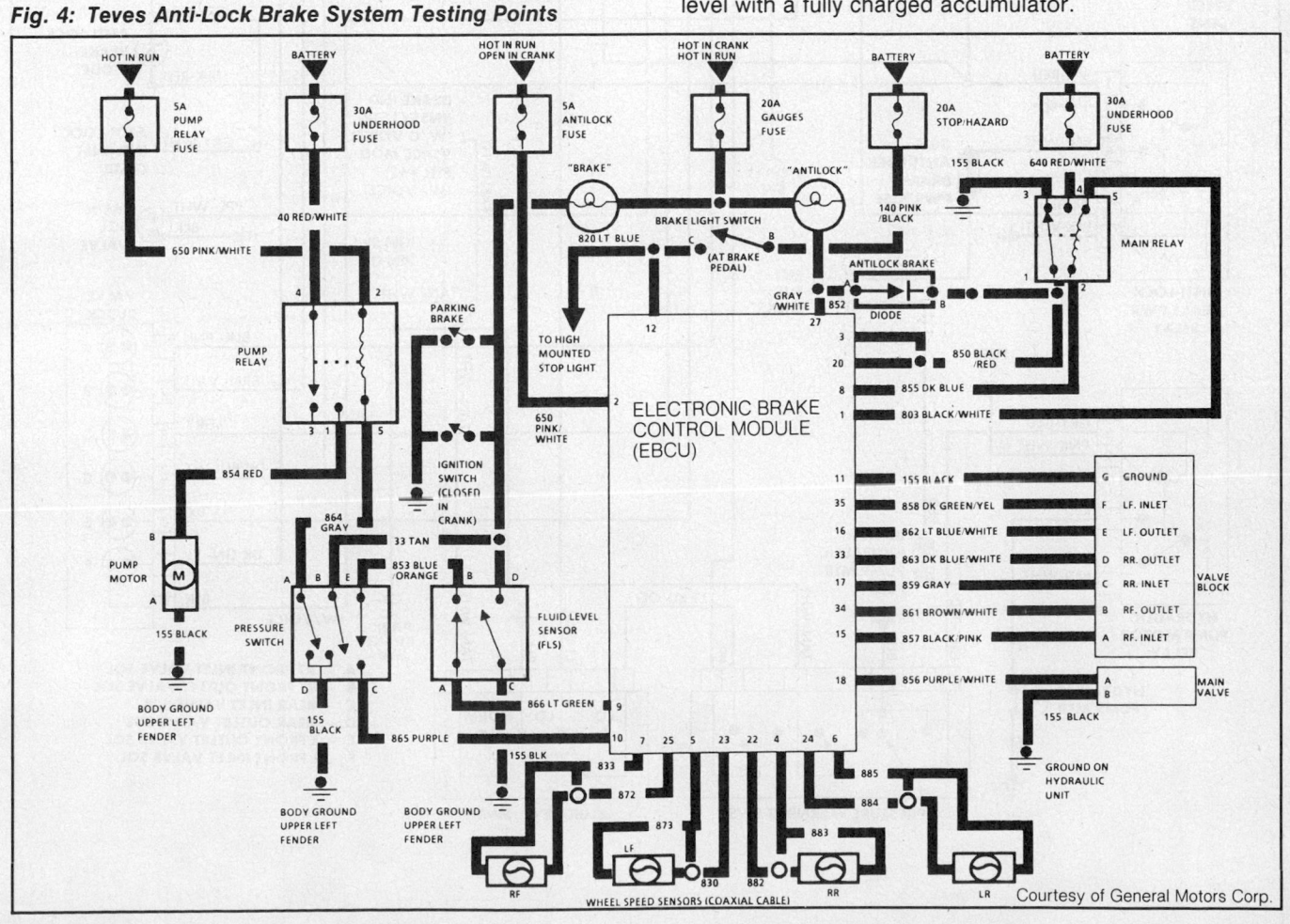

Courtesy of General Motors Corp.

Brake Systems
TEVES ANTI-LOCK BRAKE SYSTEMS (ABS) EXCEPT GM WITH BCM & ELDORADO, SEVILLE & 6000 (Cont.)

Fig. 5: Teves Anti-Lock Brake System Wiring Diagram (Bonneville, Electra & LeSabre)

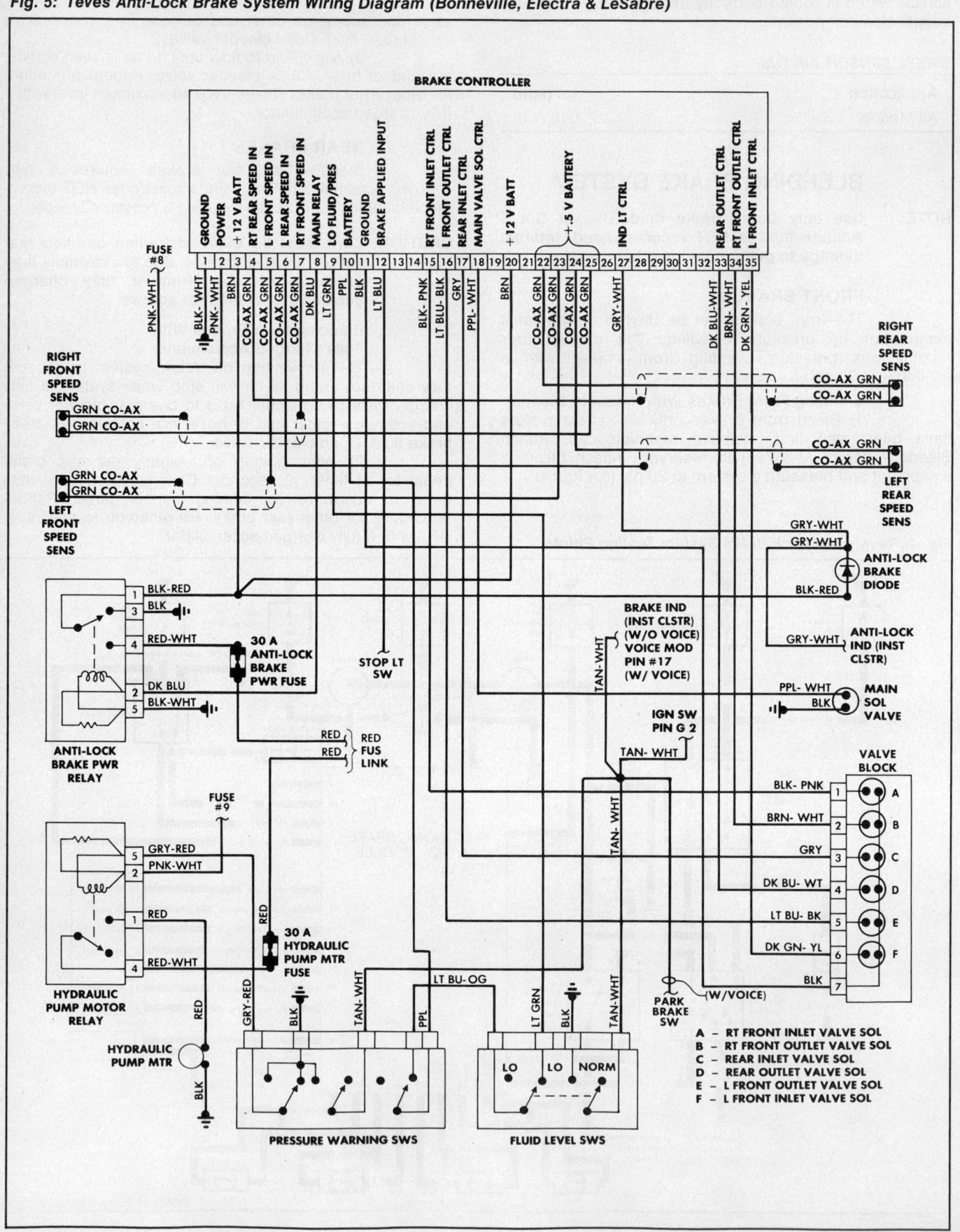

TEVES ANTI-LOCK BRAKE SYSTEMS (ABS)
EXCEPT GM WITH BCM & ELDORADO, SEVILLE & 6000 (Cont.)

TEST A
PIN-OUT CHECKS

- CONNECT BREAK-OUT BOX J 35592 TO 35-PIN EBCM HARNESS CONNECTOR AS DESCRIBED IN THIS SECTION
- PERFORM CHECKS WITH HIGH IMPEDANCE DIGITAL MULTIMETER J 34029-A OR EQUIVALENT
- ALL CHECKS ARE MADE WITH ENGINE STOPPED

CIRCUIT TO BE TESTED	IGNITION SWITCH POSITION	MULTIMETER SCALE/RANGE	MEASURE BETWEEN PIN NUMBERS	SPECIFICATION	IF RESULT NOT WITHIN SPECIFICATION, SEE CHART
IGNITION ENABLE	RUN	20 DCV	2(+)* .1(-)*	10 V MINIMUM	A-1
MAIN RELAY GROUND	OFF	200 Ω	1, 3	CONTINUITY	A-2
	OFF	200 Ω	1, 20	CONTINUITY	
MAIN RELAY COIL	OFF	200 Ω	1, 8	45-105 Ω	A-3

BEFORE PERFORMING THIS TEST:
- REMOVE GAGE FUSE FROM FUSE PANEL
- PLACE FUSED JUMPER BETWEEN BREAK-OUT BOX PINS 2 & 8

MAIN RELAY POWER	ON	20 DCV	3 (+) .1(-)	10 V MINIMUM	A-4
	ON	20 DCV	20 (+) .1(-)	10 V MINIMUM	

BEFORE PROCEEDING:
- REMOVE JUMPER FROM PINS 2 & 8
- INSTALL GAGE FUSE

EBCM SWITCH LOOP	OFF	200 Ω	9, 10	LESS THAN 5 Ω	A-5
	OFF	200 Ω	1, 9	NO CONTINUITY	A-6
RR SENSOR RESISTANCE	OFF	2k Ω	4, 22	800-1400 Ω	A-7
LF SENSOR RESISTANCE	OFF	2k Ω	5, 23	800-1400 Ω	A-8
LR SENSOR RESISTANCE	OFF	2k Ω	6, 24	800-1400 Ω	A-9
RF SENSOR RESISTANCE	OFF	2k Ω	7, 25	800-1400 Ω	A-10
MAIN VALVE SOLENOID	OFF	200 Ω	11, 18	2-5 Ω	A-11
VALVE BLOCK GROUND	OFF	200 Ω	1, 11	LESS THAN 2 Ω	A-12
RF INLET VALVE	OFF	200 Ω	11, 15	5-7 Ω	A-13
LF INLET VALVE	OFF	200 Ω	11, 35	5-7 Ω	A-14
REAR INLET VALVE	OFF	200 Ω	11, 17	5-7 Ω	A-15
RF OUTLET VALVE	OFF	200 Ω	11, 34	3-5 Ω	A-16
LF OUTLET VALVE	OFF	200 Ω	11, 16	3-5 Ω	A-17
REAR OUTLET VALVE	OFF	200 Ω	11, 33	3-5 Ω	A-18

BEFORE PERFORMING THIS TEST:
- REMOVE MAIN RELAY FROM CONNECTOR ON RELAY BRACKET (5 WIRES ATTACHED)

DIODE	OFF	DIODE ⊣◄−	27 (+), 3(-)	CONTINUITY	A-19
	OFF	DIODE ⊣◄−	3 (+), 27(-)	NO CONTINUITY	

BEFORE PROCEEDING:
- INSTALL MAIN RELAY

- WITH BRAKE PEDAL RELEASED

	ON	20 DCV	12 (+), 1(-)	0 V	A-20
BRAKE LIGHT SWITCH		• WITH BRAKE PEDAL APPLIED			
	ON	20 DCV	12 (+), 1(-)	10 V MINIMUM	A-20

*(+) OR (-) INDICATES MULTIMETER POLARITY

IF ALL TEST RESULTS ARE WITHIN SPECIFICATION, RECONNECT EBCM AND VERIFY CONTINUOUS "ANTILOCK" LAMP OPERATION
- IF NORMAL OPERATION RESUMES, SEE NOTE ON INTERMITTENTS
- IF LAMP REMAINS ON, SEE CHART A-21

Brake Systems
TEVES ANTI-LOCK BRAKE SYSTEMS (ABS)
EXCEPT GM WITH BCM & ELDORADO, SEVILLE & 6000 (Cont.)

CHART A-1
IGNITION ENABLE CIRCUIT

Ignition enable circuit energizes ECBM to perform self-diagnosis and initialize system. Battery volatge is supplied through 5-amp brake fuse to ECBM pin No. 2. Ground circuit is at ABS ground junction, located on left fender rail, at ECBM pin No. 1. "ANTI-LOCK" warning light will stay on if EBCM does not receive ignition enable input.

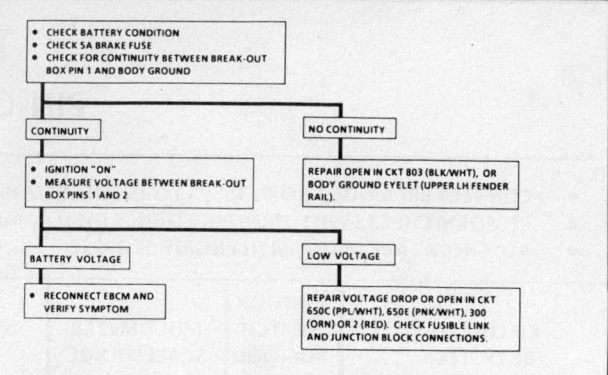

CHARTS A-2, A-3 & A-4
MAIN RELAY CIRCUIT

1) Main relay circuit provides battery voltage to ECBM to power main valve, solenoid valves, logic circuit and some self-diagnosis circuits. Main relay coil receives power from ECBM pin No. 8.

2) ECBM does not applied power to main relay coil until after ECBM receives ignition enable circuit information. Relay is grounded at ABS ground junction, located on left fender rail. Power for main relay comes through a fuseable link from battery junction box.

CHART A-3
MAIN RELAY COIL CIRCUIT

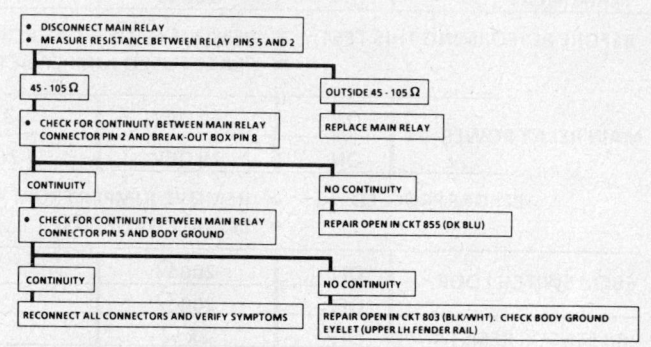

CHART A-2
MAIN RELAY GROUND CIRCUIT

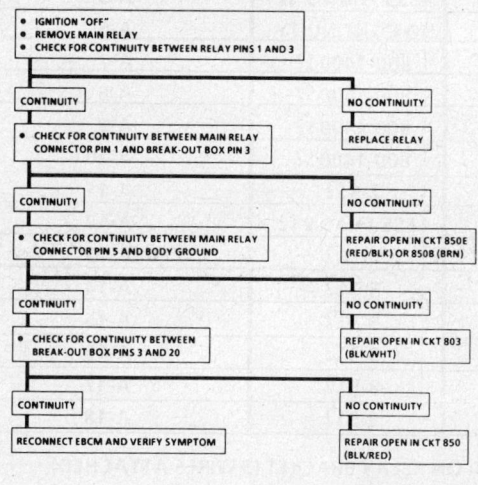

CHART A-4
MAIN RELAY POWER CIRCUIT

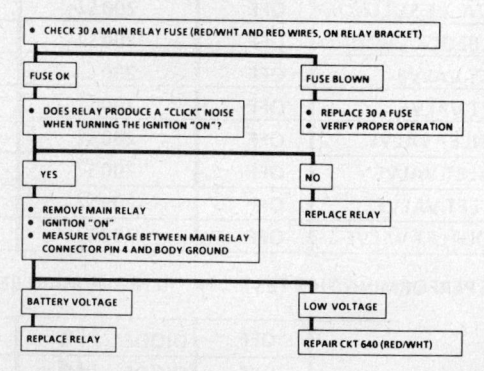

Brake Systems
TEVES ANTI-LOCK BRAKE SYSTEMS (ABS)
EXCEPT GM WITH BCM & ELDORADO, SEVILLE & 6000 (Cont.)

CHARTS A-5 & A-6
EBCM LOOP CIRCUIT

1) EBCM loop circuit consists of pressure switch and fluid level switch. Switches are normally closed. If fault is indicated by either switch, loop is opened, and "ANTI-LOCK" warning light will come on. ABS will deactivate front wheels.

2) Pressure switch detects low accumulator pressure. Pressure switch will open when pressure is below 1500 psi (10,350 kPa). Switch will close when pressure reaches 1900 psi (13,100 kPa). When fluid level is low, fluid level switch float opens circuit, turning warning light on.

CHART A-5
EBCM LOOP OPEN

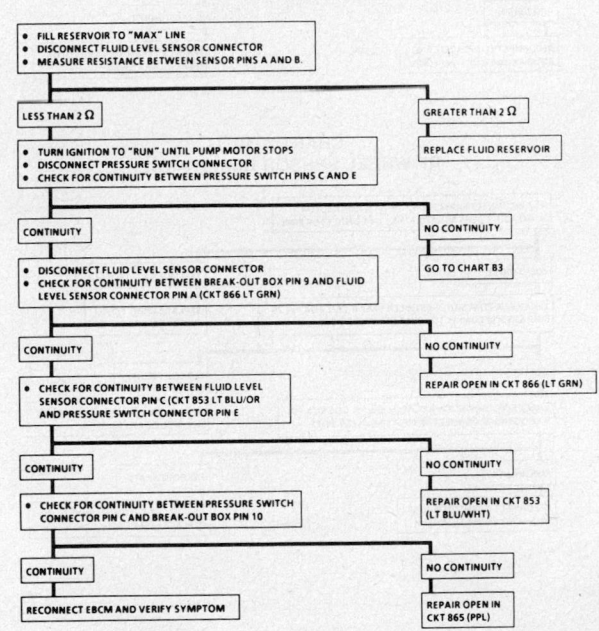

CHART A-6
EBCM LOOP SHORT

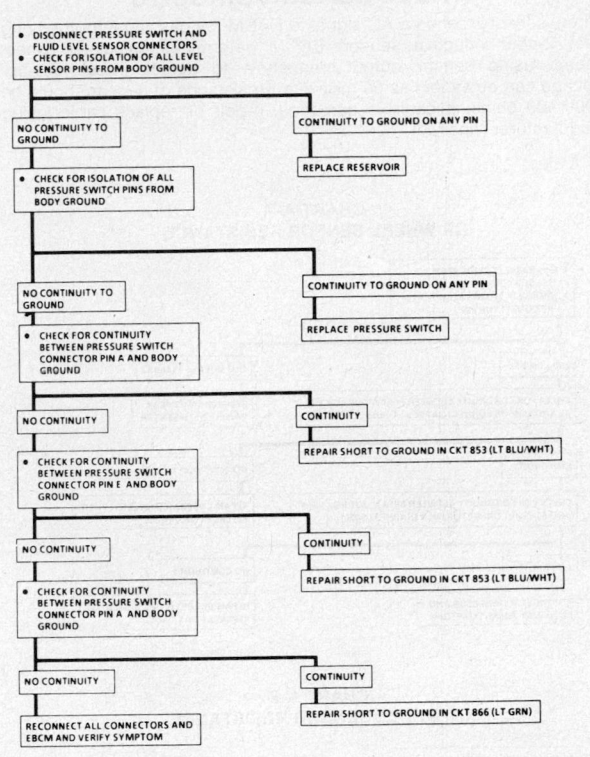

Brake Systems
TEVES ANTI-LOCK BRAKE SYSTEMS (ABS) EXCEPT GM WITH BCM & ELDORADO, SEVILLE & 6000 (Cont.)

CHARTS A-7 THROUGH A-10 WHEEL SENSOR CIRCUITS

Wheel sensors, sends a AC signal to EBCM, by passing a toothed ring past 2-pole inductive sensor. EBCM determines calculated wheel speed, using sensor output frequency, to detect wheel lock-up. Voltage can be as low as 50 millivolts. Resistance of sensor should be 800-1400 ohms. If cable is damaged, repair or replace cable, using manufacturer repair kit.

CHART A-7 RR WHEEL SENSOR RESISTANCE

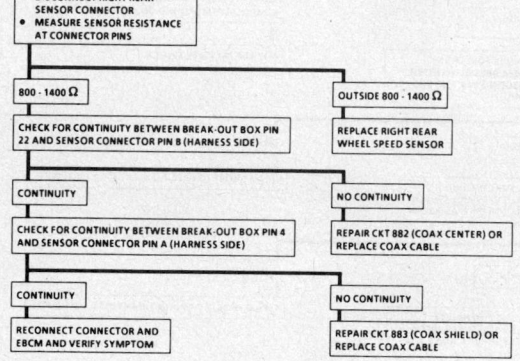

CHART A-8 LF WHEEL SENSOR RESISTANCE

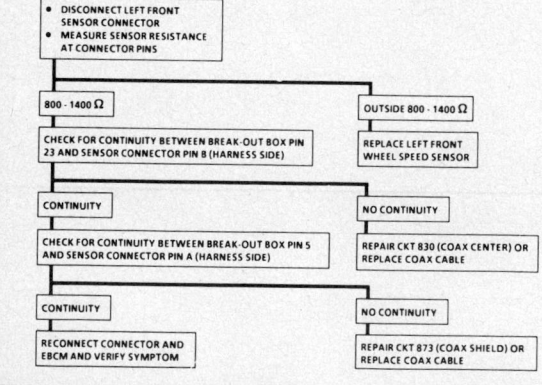

CHART A-9 LR WHEEL SENSOR RESISTANCE

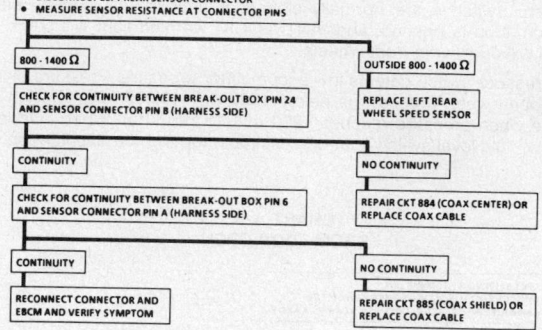

CHART A-10 RF WHEEL SENSOR RESISTANCE

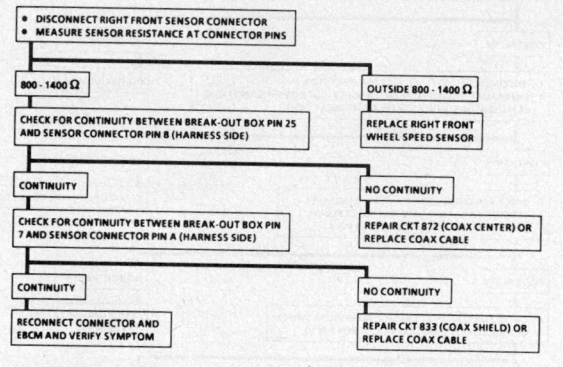

Brake Systems
TEVES ANTI-LOCK BRAKE SYSTEMS (ABS)
EXCEPT GM WITH BCM & ELDORADO, SEVILLE & 6000 (Cont.)

CHARTS A-11 THROUGH A-18
VALVE BLOCK & MAIN VALVE CIRCUITS

NOTE: Manually activating inlet or outlet valves can be done by jumpering pins on break-out box. DO NOT activate valves for more than 30 seconds. NEVER manually activate main valve.

1) Main valve, located inside hydraulic unit, is energized when system is in ABS mode. EBCM applies 12 volts to main valve solenoid from pin No. 18. Valve is grounded through hydraulic unit. Normal resistance is 2-5 ohms.

2) Valve block ground comes from EBCM pin No. 11. Inlet and outlet valves are grounded by hydraulic unit. Resistance between valve block ground (EBCM pin No. 11) and body ground should never exceed 2 ohms. Inlet valves are normally open.

3) When EBCM applies 12 volts at pins No. 15, 17 or 35, inlet valves close. Valves are closed for short period of time to hold pressure or pressure reduction is desired. Resistance for inlet valve should be 5-7 ohms. Outlet valves operate the same as inlet valve. EBCM applies voltage at pins No. 34, 33 and 16. Resistance should be 3-5 ohms.

CHART A-11
MAIN VALVE SOLENOID RESISTANCE

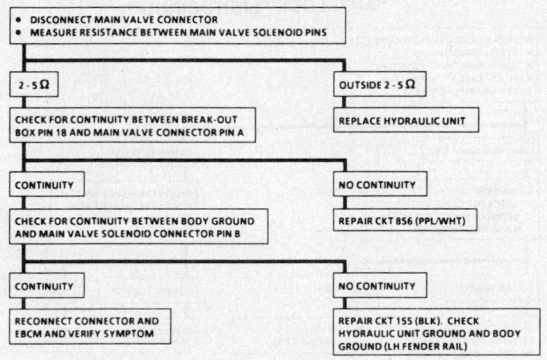

CHART A-12
VALVE BLOCK GROUND REFERENCE CIRCUIT

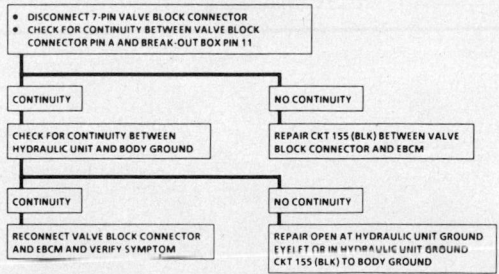

CHART A-13
RF INLET VALVE RESISTANCE

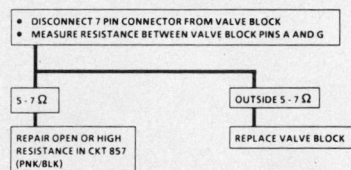

CHART A-14
LF INLET VALVE RESISTANCE

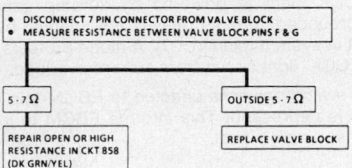

CHART A-15
REAR INLET VALVE RESISTANCE

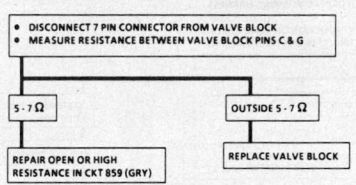

CHART A-16
RF OUTLET VALVE RESISTANCE

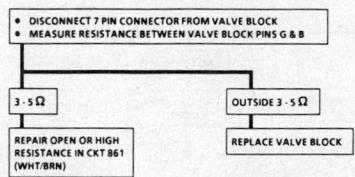

CHART A-17
LF OUTLET VALVE RESISTANCE

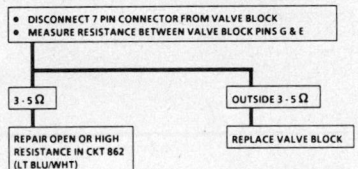

CHART A-18
REAR OUTLET VALVE RESISTANCE

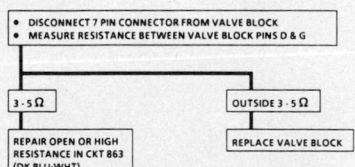

Brake Systems
TEVES ANTI-LOCK BRAKE SYSTEMS (ABS)
EXCEPT GM WITH BCM & ELDORADO, SEVILLE & 6000 (Cont.)

CHARTS A-19 THROUGH A-21
"ANTI-LOCK" LIGHT & STOPLIGHT CIRCUIT

1) "ANTI-LOCK" light is powered by 20-amp gauge fuse. Light is turned on (grounded), if main relay is not enabled by EBCM or EBCM detects fault in system (pin No. 27). A diode protects EBCM pin No. 27 and "ANTI-LOCK" light circuit from current overload.

2) Stoplight switch power is directed to EBCM (pin No. 12) whenever brake pedal is depressed. This informs EBCM to increase sensitivity to wheel sensor input signal.

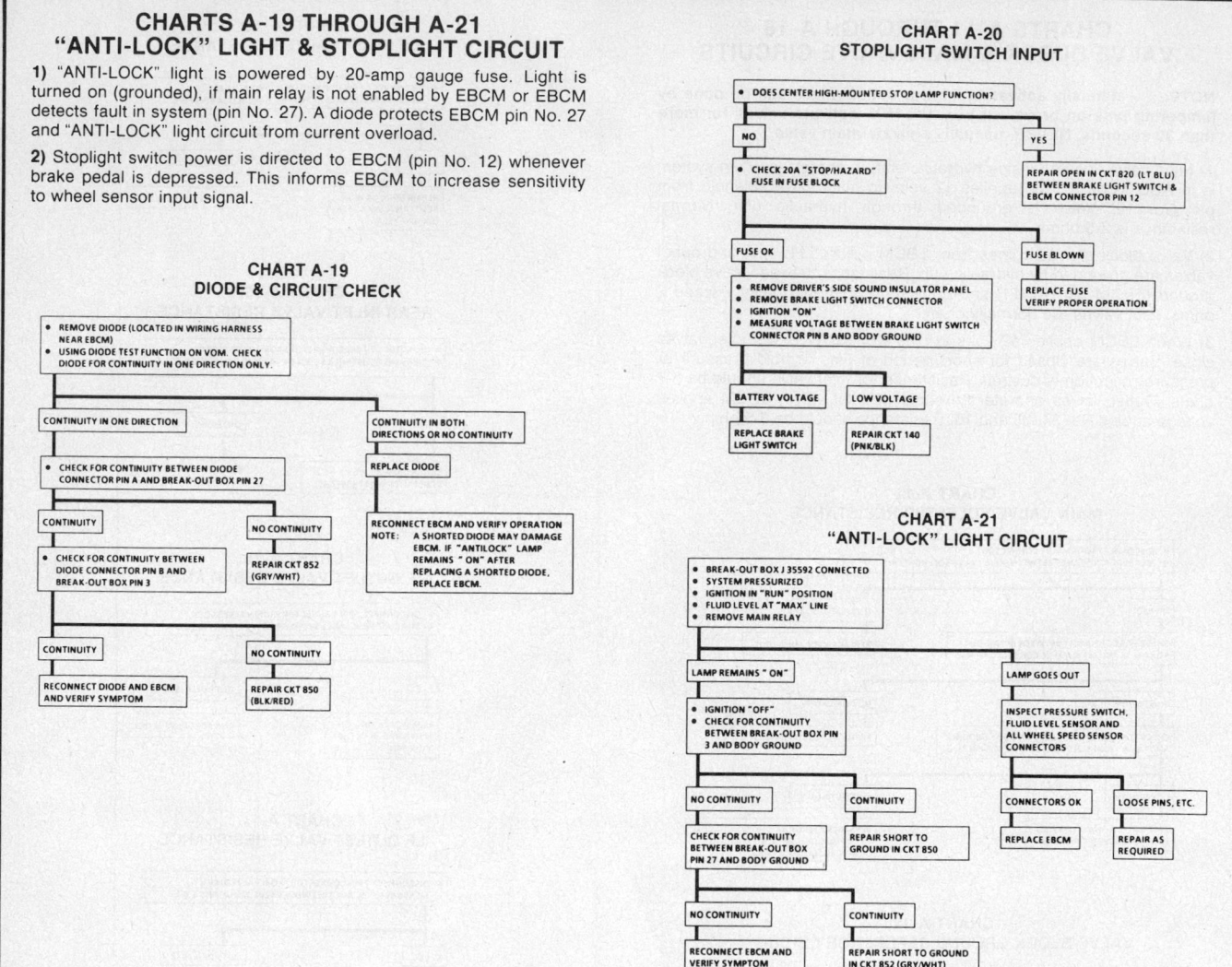

CHART A-19
DIODE & CIRCUIT CHECK

CHART A-20
STOPLIGHT SWITCH INPUT

CHART A-21
"ANTI-LOCK" LIGHT CIRCUIT

Brake Systems
TEVES ANTI-LOCK BRAKE SYSTEMS (ABS)
EXCEPT GM WITH BCM & ELDORADO, SEVILLE & 6000 (Cont.)

CHART B THROUGH B-5
PUMP/MOTOR & "BRAKE" LIGHT CIRCUIT

1) Pump/motor assembly is designed to provide hydraulic accumulator with specified pressure. Pump/motor is controlled by pressure switch. Pressure switch closes, which activates pump/motor. This circuit grounds relay coil.

2) Positive circuit for relay coil comes from 5-amp pump relay fuse. Power for relay comes from 30-amp fuse, located in engine compartment. When pressure drops to 2030 psi (14,000 kPa), pressure switch circuit closes, grounding relay coil.

3) This activates relay allowing pump/motor to operate. When pressure reaches 2610 psi (18,000 kPa), pressure switch circuit opens, deactivating pump/motor. "BRAKE" light curcuit is powered by 20-amp gauge fuse. Circuit is grounded if parking brake is applied, fluid level is low or pressure is low.

4) Pressure switch will open when pressure is below 1500 psi (10,350 kPa). Switch will close when pressure reaches 1900 psi (13,100 kPa). When fluid level is low, fluid level switch float opens circuit, turning warning light on

CHART B
HYDRAULIC UNIT FUNCTIONAL CHECK

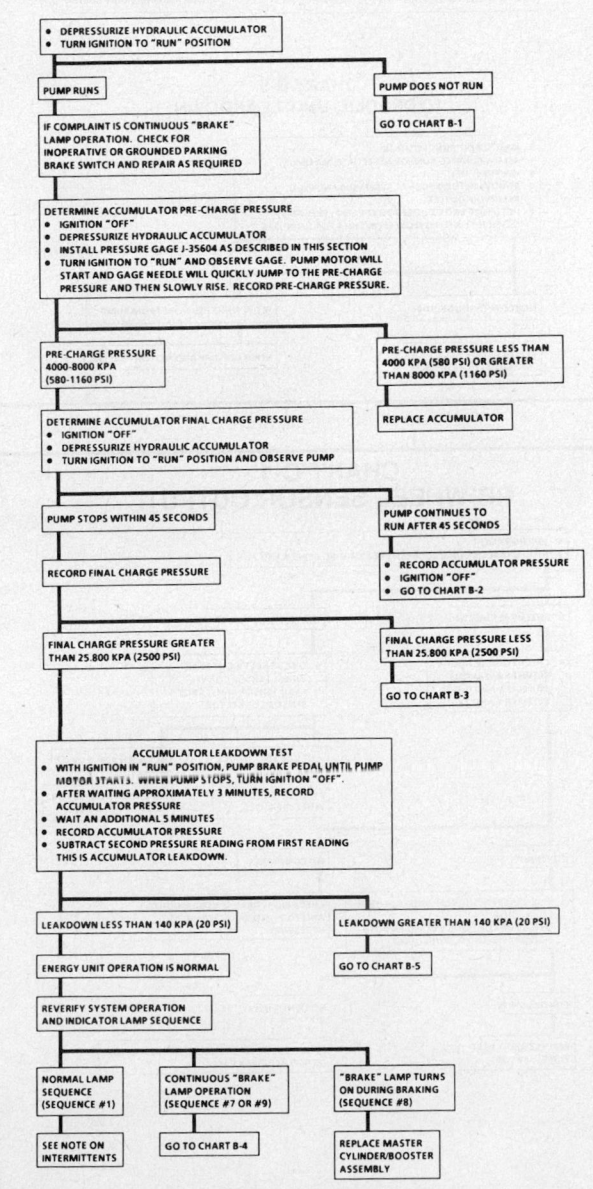

CHART B-1
PUMP DOES NOT RUN

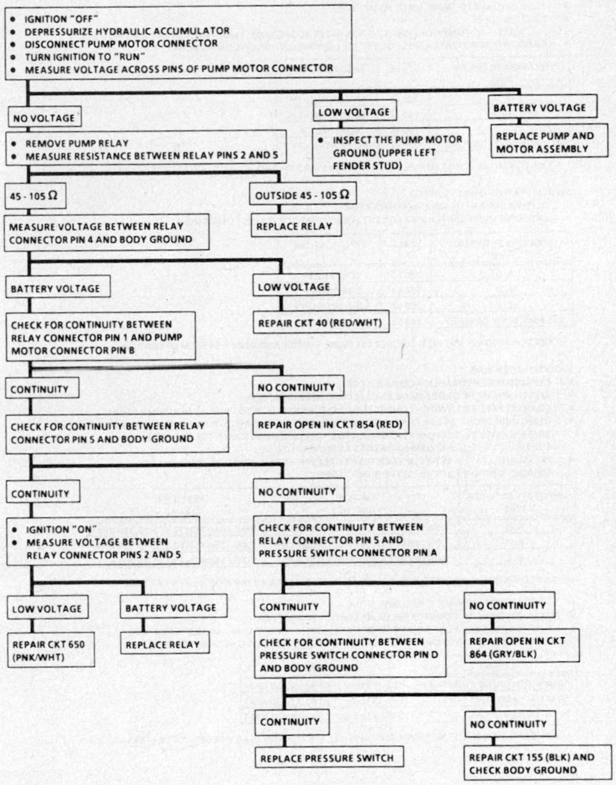

- IGNITION "OFF"
- DEPRESSURIZE HYDRAULIC ACCUMULATOR
- DISCONNECT PUMP MOTOR CONNECTOR
- TURN IGNITION TO "RUN"
- MEASURE VOLTAGE ACROSS PINS OF PUMP MOTOR CONNECTOR

NO VOLTAGE
- REMOVE PUMP RELAY
- MEASURE RESISTANCE BETWEEN RELAY PINS 2 AND 5

45 - 105 Ω → MEASURE VOLTAGE BETWEEN RELAY CONNECTOR PIN 4 AND BODY GROUND

OUTSIDE 45 - 105 Ω → REPLACE RELAY

BATTERY VOLTAGE → CHECK FOR CONTINUITY BETWEEN RELAY CONNECTOR PIN 1 AND PUMP MOTOR CONNECTOR PIN B

LOW VOLTAGE → REPAIR CKT 40 (RED/WHT)

CONTINUITY → CHECK FOR CONTINUITY BETWEEN RELAY CONNECTOR PIN 5 AND BODY GROUND

NO CONTINUITY → REPAIR OPEN IN CKT 854 (RED)

CONTINUITY →
- IGNITION "ON"
- MEASURE VOLTAGE BETWEEN RELAY CONNECTOR PINS 2 AND 5

NO CONTINUITY → CHECK FOR CONTINUITY BETWEEN RELAY CONNECTOR PIN 5 AND PRESSURE SWITCH CONNECTOR PIN A

LOW VOLTAGE → REPAIR CKT 650 (PNK/WHT)

BATTERY VOLTAGE → REPLACE RELAY

CONTINUITY → CHECK FOR CONTINUITY BETWEEN PRESSURE SWITCH CONNECTOR PIN D AND BODY GROUND

NO CONTINUITY → REPAIR OPEN IN CKT 864 (GRY/BLK)

CONTINUITY → REPLACE PRESSURE SWITCH

NO CONTINUITY → REPAIR CKT 155 (BLK) AND CHECK BODY GROUND

LOW VOLTAGE → INSPECT THE PUMP MOTOR GROUND (UPPER LEFT FENDER STUD)

BATTERY VOLTAGE → REPLACE PUMP AND MOTOR ASSEMBLY

CHART B-2
PUMP RUNS LONGER THAN 45 SECONDS

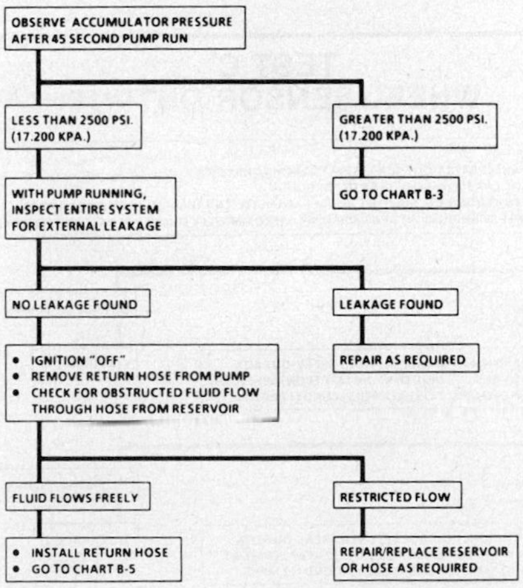

OBSERVE ACCUMULATOR PRESSURE AFTER 45 SECOND PUMP RUN

LESS THAN 2500 PSI. (17.200 KPA.) → WITH PUMP RUNNING, INSPECT ENTIRE SYSTEM FOR EXTERNAL LEAKAGE

GREATER THAN 2500 PSI. (17.200 KPA.) → GO TO CHART B-3

NO LEAKAGE FOUND →
- IGNITION "OFF"
- REMOVE RETURN HOSE FROM PUMP
- CHECK FOR OBSTRUCTED FLUID FLOW THROUGH HOSE FROM RESERVOIR

LEAKAGE FOUND → REPAIR AS REQUIRED

FLUID FLOWS FREELY →
- INSTALL RETURN HOSE
- GO TO CHART B-5

RESTRICTED FLOW → REPAIR/REPLACE RESERVOIR OR HOSE AS REQUIRED

Brake Systems
TEVES ANTI-LOCK BRAKE SYSTEMS (ABS)
EXCEPT GM WITH BCM & ELDORADO, SEVILLE & 6000 (Cont.)

CHART B-3
PRESSURE SWITCH PERFORMANCE

I. SWITCH STATUS - PRESSURIZED
- TURN IGNITION TO "RUN" UNTIL PUMP STOPS
- IGNITION "OFF"
  - NOTE: IF PUMP CONTINUES TO RUN AFTER 45 SECONDS, TURN IGNITION OFF AND PROCEDE
- CHECK PRESSURE SWITCH PINS FOR THE FOLLOWING CONDITIONS USING VOM

MEASURE BETWEEN PINS	SCALE	SPECIFICATION
B, D	200 Ω	NO CONTINUITY
A, D	200 Ω	NO CONTINUITY
C, E	200 Ω	CONTINUITY
ALL PINS, BODY GROUND	200 Ω	NO CONTINUITY

IF ANY CONDITION IS NOT MET, REPLACE PRESSURE SWITCH AND VERIFY SYSTEM OPERATION

II. SWITCH STATUS - DEPRESSURIZED
- DEPRESSURIZE HYDRAULIC ACCUMULATOR
- CHECK PRESSURE SWITCH PINS FOR THE FOLLOWING CONDITIONS USING VOM

MEASURE BETWEEN PINS	SCALE	SPECIFICATION
B, D	200 Ω	CONTINUITY
A, D	200 Ω	CONTINUITY
C, E	200 Ω	NO CONTINUITY
ALL PINS, BODY GROUND	200 Ω	NO CONTINUITY

IF ANY CONDITION IS NOT MET, REPLACE PRESSURE SWITCH AND VERIFY SYSTEM OPERATION

III. SWITCH THRESHOLDS
- DEPRESSURIZE HYDRAULIC ACCUMULATOR
- INSTALL PRESSURE GAGE J 35604 AS DESCRIBED IN THIS SECTION
- CONNECT PRESSURE SWITCH CONNECTOR AND TURN IGNITION TO "RUN" UNTIL PUMP STOPS
- USING VOM, MONITOR FOR CONTINUITY BETWEEN PRESSURE SWITCH PINS AS SHOWN BELOW WHILE SLOWLY BLEEDING OFF ACCUMULATOR PRESSURE BY PUMPING THE BRAKE PEDAL. CONTINUITY SHOULD BE GAINED OR LOST AS INDICATED.
- PRESSURIZE SYSTEM BETWEEN EACH TEST BY RECONNECTING PRESSURE SWITCH AND TURNING IGNITION TO "RUN" UNTIL PUMP STOPS

MEASURE BETWEEN PINS	SWITCH STATUS	PRESSURE RANGE
A, D	CONTINUITY SHOULD BE GAINED AT:	1980-2080 PSI (13.650-14.350 KPA)
B, D	CONTINUITY SHOULD BE GAINED AT:	1500-1550 PSI (10.350-10.700 KPA)
C, E	CONTINUITY SHOULD BE LOST AT:	1550-1550 PSI (10.350-10.700 KPA)

IF ANY CONDITION IS NOT MET, REPLACE PRESSURE SWITCH AND VERIFY PROPER OPERATION

- DEPRESSURIZE HYDRAULIC ACCUMULATOR
- WITH IGNITION OFF, CONNECT PRESSURE SWITCH CONNECTOR
- TURN IGNITION TO "RUN" AND OBSERVE GAGE, "ANTI-LOCK" LAMP, "BRAKE" LAMP AND PUMP MOTOR. EVENTS SHOULD OCCUR AT PRESSURES INDICATED IN CHART BELOW

EVENT	PRESSURE
"ANTI-LOCK" LAMP TURNS OFF	1900-1975 PSI (13.100-13.600 KPA)
"BRAKE" LAMP TURNS OFF	1900-1975 PSI (13.100-13.600 KPA)
PUMP MOTOR STOPS	2550-2670 PSI (17.580-18.400 KPA)

IF ANY CONDITION IS NOT MET, REPLACE PRESSURE SWITCH AND VERIFY PROPER OPERATION

CHART B-4
"BRAKE" LIGHT CIRCUIT

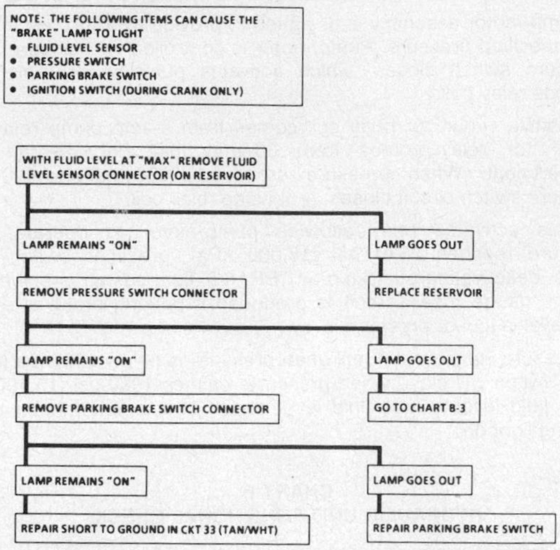

NOTE: THE FOLLOWING ITEMS CAN CAUSE THE "BRAKE" LAMP TO LIGHT
- FLUID LEVEL SENSOR
- PRESSURE SWITCH
- PARKING BRAKE SWITCH
- IGNITION SWITCH (DURING CRANK ONLY)

WITH FLUID LEVEL AT "MAX" REMOVE FLUID LEVEL SENSOR CONNECTOR (ON RESERVOIR)

- LAMP REMAINS "ON" → REMOVE PRESSURE SWITCH CONNECTOR
- LAMP GOES OUT → REPLACE RESERVOIR

- LAMP REMAINS "ON" → REMOVE PARKING BRAKE SWITCH CONNECTOR
- LAMP GOES OUT → GO TO CHART B-3

- LAMP REMAINS "ON" → REPAIR SHORT TO GROUND IN CKT 33 (TAN/WHT)
- LAMP GOES OUT → REPAIR PARKING BRAKE SWITCH

CHART B-5
HYDRAULIC UNIT LEAKDOWN

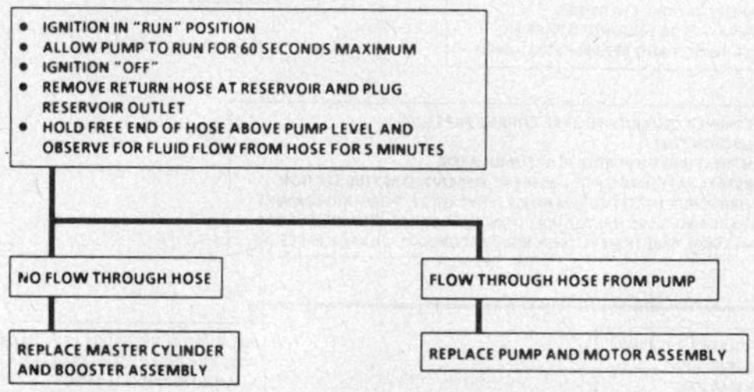

- IGNITION IN "RUN" POSITION
- ALLOW PUMP TO RUN FOR 60 SECONDS MAXIMUM
- IGNITION "OFF"
- REMOVE RETURN HOSE AT RESERVOIR AND PLUG RESERVOIR OUTLET
- HOLD FREE END OF HOSE ABOVE PUMP LEVEL AND OBSERVE FOR FLUID FLOW FROM HOSE FOR 5 MINUTES

- NO FLOW THROUGH HOSE → REPLACE MASTER CYLINDER AND BOOSTER ASSEMBLY
- FLOW THROUGH HOSE FROM PUMP → REPLACE PUMP AND MOTOR ASSEMBLY

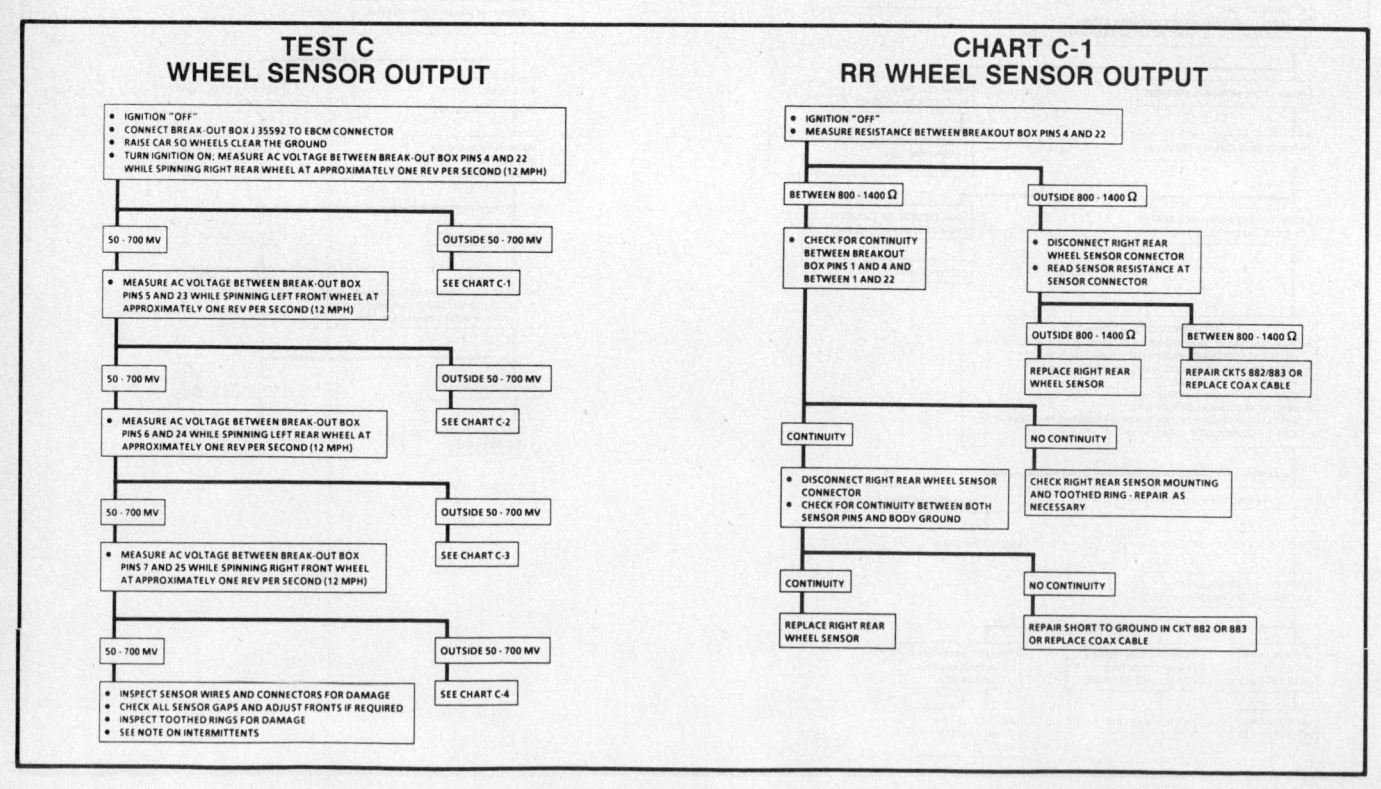

TEST C
WHEEL SENSOR OUTPUT

- IGNITION "OFF"
- CONNECT BREAK-OUT BOX J 35592 TO EBCM CONNECTOR
- RAISE CAR SO WHEELS CLEAR THE GROUND
- TURN IGNITION ON; MEASURE AC VOLTAGE BETWEEN BREAK-OUT BOX PINS 4 AND 22 WHILE SPINNING RIGHT REAR WHEEL AT APPROXIMATELY ONE REV PER SECOND (12 MPH)

- 50 - 700 MV / OUTSIDE 50 - 700 MV → SEE CHART C-1
- MEASURE AC VOLTAGE BETWEEN BREAK-OUT BOX PINS 5 AND 23 WHILE SPINNING LEFT FRONT WHEEL AT APPROXIMATELY ONE REV PER SECOND (12 MPH)
- 50 - 700 MV / OUTSIDE 50 - 700 MV → SEE CHART C-2
- MEASURE AC VOLTAGE BETWEEN BREAK-OUT BOX PINS 6 AND 24 WHILE SPINNING LEFT REAR WHEEL AT APPROXIMATELY ONE REV PER SECOND (12 MPH)
- 50 - 700 MV / OUTSIDE 50 - 700 MV → SEE CHART C-3
- MEASURE AC VOLTAGE BETWEEN BREAK-OUT BOX PINS 7 AND 25 WHILE SPINNING RIGHT FRONT WHEEL AT APPROXIMATELY ONE REV PER SECOND (12 MPH)
- 50 - 700 MV / OUTSIDE 50 - 700 MV → SEE CHART C-4
- INSPECT SENSOR WIRES AND CONNECTORS FOR DAMAGE
- CHECK ALL SENSOR GAPS AND ADJUST FRONTS IF REQUIRED
- INSPECT TOOTHED RINGS FOR DAMAGE
- SEE NOTE ON INTERMITTENTS

CHART C-1
RR WHEEL SENSOR OUTPUT

- IGNITION "OFF"
- MEASURE RESISTANCE BETWEEN BREAKOUT BOX PINS 4 AND 22

- BETWEEN 800 - 1400 Ω → CHECK FOR CONTINUITY BETWEEN BREAKOUT BOX PINS 1 AND 4 AND BETWEEN 1 AND 22
- OUTSIDE 800 - 1400 Ω → DISCONNECT RIGHT REAR WHEEL SENSOR CONNECTOR; READ SENSOR RESISTANCE AT SENSOR CONNECTOR
  - OUTSIDE 800 - 1400 Ω → REPLACE RIGHT REAR WHEEL SENSOR
  - BETWEEN 800 - 1400 Ω → REPAIR CKTS 882/883 OR REPLACE COAX CABLE

- CONTINUITY → DISCONNECT RIGHT REAR WHEEL SENSOR CONNECTOR; CHECK FOR CONTINUITY BETWEEN BOTH SENSOR PINS AND BODY GROUND
- NO CONTINUITY → CHECK RIGHT REAR SENSOR MOUNTING AND TOOTHED RING - REPAIR AS NECESSARY

- CONTINUITY → REPLACE RIGHT REAR WHEEL SENSOR
- NO CONTINUITY → REPAIR SHORT TO GROUND IN CKT 882 OR 883 OR REPLACE COAX CABLE

Brake Systems
TEVES ANTI-LOCK BRAKE SYSTEMS (ABS)
EXCEPT GM WITH BCM & ELDORADO, SEVILLE & 6000 (Cont.)

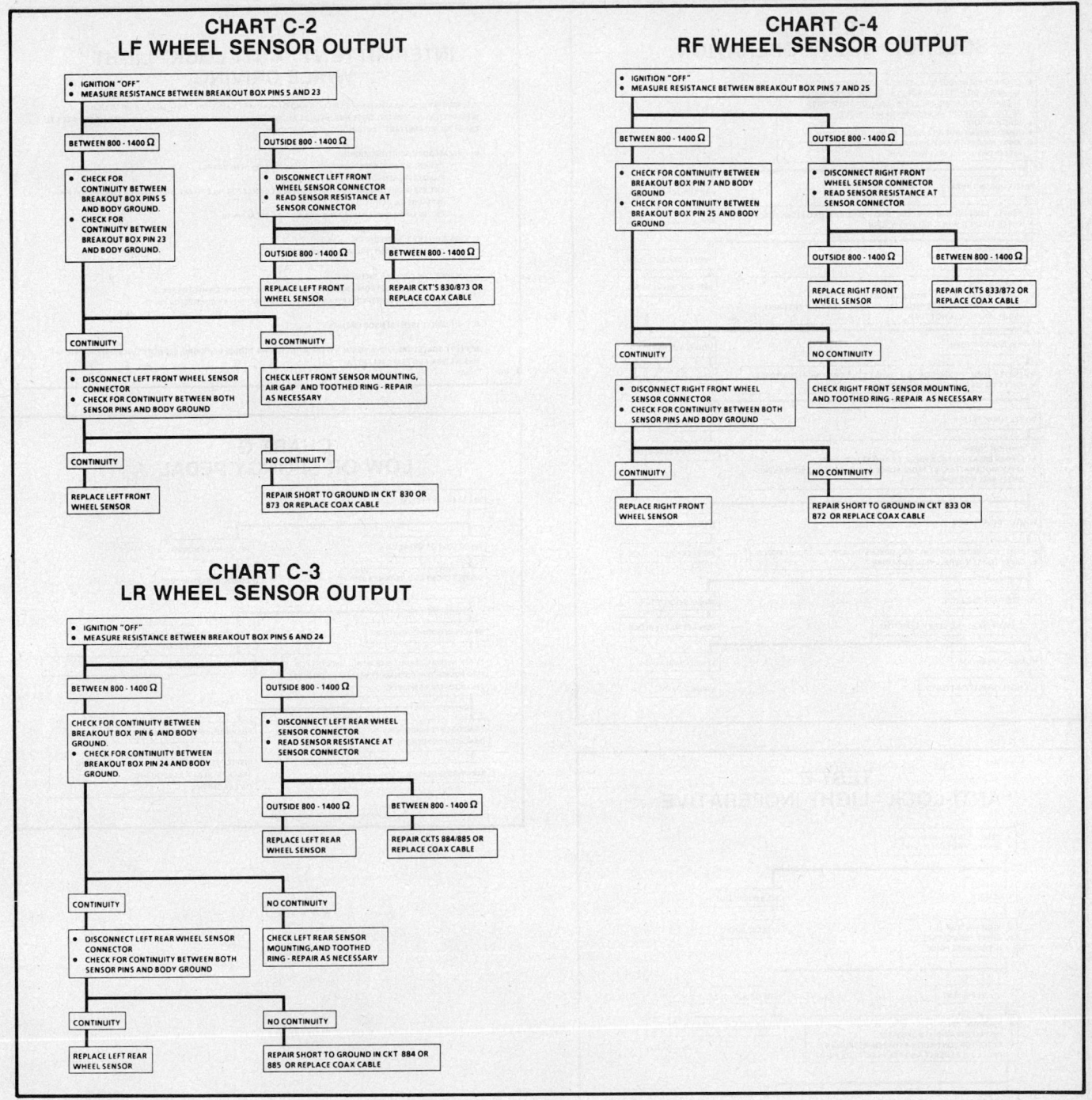

CHART C-2
LF WHEEL SENSOR OUTPUT

- IGNITION "OFF"
- MEASURE RESISTANCE BETWEEN BREAKOUT BOX PINS 5 AND 23

BETWEEN 800 - 1400 Ω
- CHECK FOR CONTINUITY BETWEEN BREAKOUT BOX PINS 5 AND BODY GROUND.
- CHECK FOR CONTINUITY BETWEEN BREAKOUT BOX PIN 23 AND BODY GROUND.

OUTSIDE 800 - 1400 Ω
- DISCONNECT LEFT FRONT WHEEL SENSOR CONNECTOR
- READ SENSOR RESISTANCE AT SENSOR CONNECTOR

OUTSIDE 800 - 1400 Ω
REPLACE LEFT FRONT WHEEL SENSOR

BETWEEN 800 - 1400 Ω
REPAIR CKT'S 830/873 OR REPLACE COAX CABLE

CONTINUITY
- DISCONNECT LEFT FRONT WHEEL SENSOR CONNECTOR
- CHECK FOR CONTINUITY BETWEEN BOTH SENSOR PINS AND BODY GROUND

NO CONTINUITY
CHECK LEFT FRONT SENSOR MOUNTING, AIR GAP AND TOOTHED RING - REPAIR AS NECESSARY

CONTINUITY
REPLACE LEFT FRONT WHEEL SENSOR

NO CONTINUITY
REPAIR SHORT TO GROUND IN CKT 830 OR 873 OR REPLACE COAX CABLE

CHART C-4
RF WHEEL SENSOR OUTPUT

- IGNITION "OFF"
- MEASURE RESISTANCE BETWEEN BREAKOUT BOX PINS 7 AND 25

BETWEEN 800 - 1400 Ω
- CHECK FOR CONTINUITY BETWEEN BREAKOUT BOX PINS 7 AND BODY GROUND
- CHECK FOR CONTINUITY BETWEEN BREAKOUT BOX PIN 25 AND BODY GROUND

OUTSIDE 800 - 1400 Ω
- DISCONNECT RIGHT FRONT WHEEL SENSOR CONNECTOR
- READ SENSOR RESISTANCE AT SENSOR CONNECTOR

OUTSIDE 800 - 1400 Ω
REPLACE RIGHT FRONT WHEEL SENSOR

BETWEEN 800 - 1400 Ω
REPAIR CKTS 833/872 OR REPLACE COAX CABLE

CONTINUITY
- DISCONNECT RIGHT FRONT WHEEL SENSOR CONNECTOR
- CHECK FOR CONTINUITY BETWEEN BOTH SENSOR PINS AND BODY GROUND

NO CONTINUITY
CHECK RIGHT FRONT SENSOR MOUNTING, AND TOOTHED RING - REPAIR AS NECESSARY

CONTINUITY
REPLACE RIGHT FRONT WHEEL SENSOR

NO CONTINUITY
REPAIR SHORT TO GROUND IN CKT 833 OR 872 OR REPLACE COAX CABLE

CHART C-3
LR WHEEL SENSOR OUTPUT

- IGNITION "OFF"
- MEASURE RESISTANCE BETWEEN BREAKOUT BOX PINS 6 AND 24

BETWEEN 800 - 1400 Ω
CHECK FOR CONTINUITY BETWEEN BREAKOUT BOX PIN 6 AND BODY GROUND.
- CHECK FOR CONTINUITY BETWEEN BREAKOUT BOX PIN 24 AND BODY GROUND.

OUTSIDE 800 - 1400 Ω
- DISCONNECT LEFT REAR WHEEL SENSOR CONNECTOR
- READ SENSOR RESISTANCE AT SENSOR CONNECTOR

OUTSIDE 800 - 1400 Ω
REPLACE LEFT REAR WHEEL SENSOR

BETWEEN 800 - 1400 Ω
REPAIR CKTS 884/885 OR REPLACE COAX CABLE

CONTINUITY
- DISCONNECT LEFT REAR WHEEL SENSOR CONNECTOR
- CHECK FOR CONTINUITY BETWEEN BOTH SENSOR PINS AND BODY GROUND

NO CONTINUITY
CHECK LEFT REAR SENSOR MOUNTING, AND TOOTHED RING - REPAIR AS NECESSARY

CONTINUITY
REPLACE LEFT REAR WHEEL SENSOR

NO CONTINUITY
REPAIR SHORT TO GROUND IN CKT 884 OR 885 OR REPLACE COAX CABLE

Brake Systems
TEVES ANTI-LOCK BRAKE SYSTEMS (ABS)
EXCEPT GM WITH BCM & ELDORADO, SEVILLE & 6000 (Cont.)

TEST D
SOLENOID VALVE OPERATION

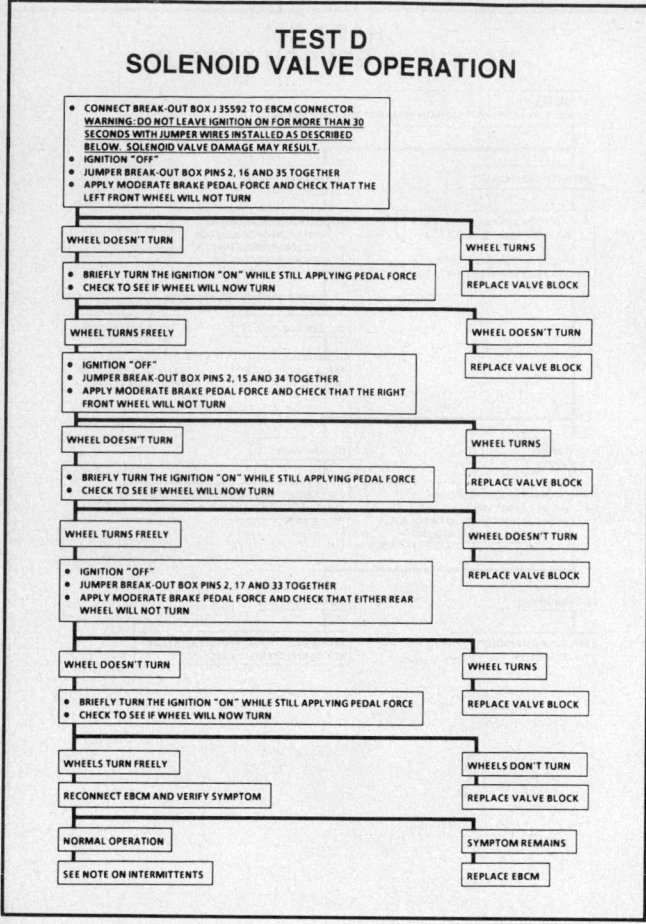

- CONNECT BREAK-OUT BOX J 35592 TO EBCM CONNECTOR
  WARNING: DO NOT LEAVE IGNITION ON FOR MORE THAN 30 SECONDS WITH JUMPER WIRES INSTALLED AS DESCRIBED BELOW. SOLENOID VALVE DAMAGE MAY RESULT.
- IGNITION "OFF"
- JUMPER BREAK-OUT BOX PINS 2, 16 AND 35 TOGETHER
- APPLY MODERATE BRAKE PEDAL FORCE AND CHECK THAT THE LEFT FRONT WHEEL WILL NOT TURN

WHEEL DOESN'T TURN	WHEEL TURNS

- BRIEFLY TURN THE IGNITION "ON" WHILE STILL APPLYING PEDAL FORCE
- CHECK TO SEE IF WHEEL WILL NOW TURN | REPLACE VALVE BLOCK

| WHEEL TURNS FREELY | WHEEL DOESN'T TURN |

REPLACE VALVE BLOCK

- IGNITION "OFF"
- JUMPER BREAK-OUT BOX PINS 2, 15 AND 34 TOGETHER
- APPLY MODERATE BRAKE PEDAL FORCE AND CHECK THAT THE RIGHT FRONT WHEEL WILL NOT TURN

| WHEEL DOESN'T TURN | WHEEL TURNS |

- BRIEFLY TURN THE IGNITION "ON" WHILE STILL APPLYING PEDAL FORCE
- CHECK TO SEE IF WHEEL WILL NOW TURN | REPLACE VALVE BLOCK

| WHEEL TURNS FREELY | WHEEL DOESN'T TURN |

REPLACE VALVE BLOCK

- IGNITION "OFF"
- JUMPER BREAK-OUT BOX PINS 2, 17 AND 33 TOGETHER
- APPLY MODERATE BRAKE PEDAL FORCE AND CHECK THAT EITHER REAR WHEEL WILL NOT TURN

| WHEEL DOESN'T TURN | WHEEL TURNS |

- BRIEFLY TURN THE IGNITION "ON" WHILE STILL APPLYING PEDAL FORCE
- CHECK TO SEE IF WHEEL WILL NOW TURN | REPLACE VALVE BLOCK

| WHEELS TURN FREELY | WHEELS DON'T TURN |

| RECONNECT EBCM AND VERIFY SYMPTOM | REPLACE VALVE BLOCK |

| NORMAL OPERATION | SYMPTOM REMAINS |

| SEE NOTE ON INTERMITTENTS | REPLACE EBCM |

TEST E
"ANTI-LOCK" LIGHT INOPERATIVE

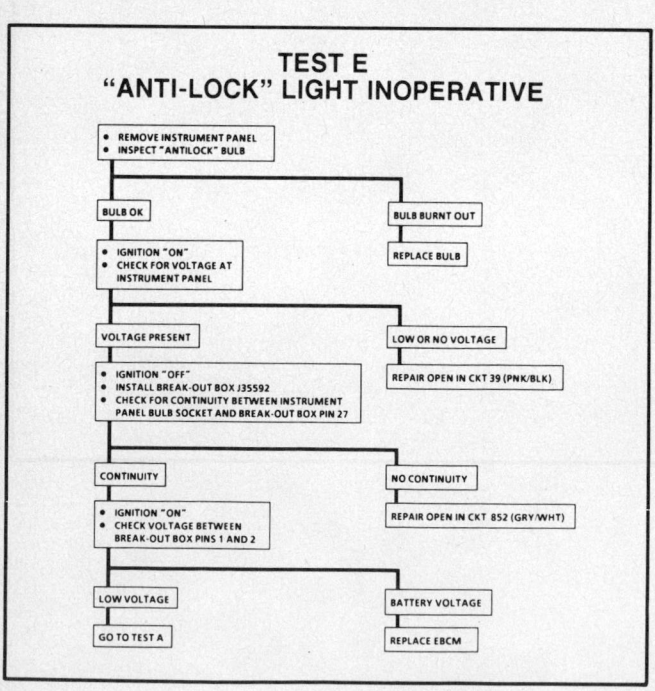

- REMOVE INSTRUMENT PANEL
- INSPECT "ANTILOCK" BULB

BULB OK	BULB BURNT OUT
	REPLACE BULB

- IGNITION "ON"
- CHECK FOR VOLTAGE AT INSTRUMENT PANEL

| VOLTAGE PRESENT | LOW OR NO VOLTAGE |
| | REPAIR OPEN IN CKT 39 (PNK/BLK) |

- IGNITION "OFF"
- INSTALL BREAK-OUT BOX J35592
- CHECK FOR CONTINUITY BETWEEN INSTRUMENT PANEL BULB SOCKET AND BREAK-OUT BOX PIN 27

| CONTINUITY | NO CONTINUITY |
| | REPAIR OPEN IN CKT 852 (GRY/WHT) |

- IGNITION "ON"
- CHECK VOLTAGE BETWEEN BREAK-OUT BOX PINS 1 AND 2

| LOW VOLTAGE | BATTERY VOLTAGE |
| GO TO TEST A | REPLACE EBCM |

TEST F
INTERMITTENT "ANTI-LOCK" LIGHT
WHILE DRIVING

INTERRUPTIONS IN THE FOLLOWING CIRCUITS AND OTHERS MAY CAUSE THE "ANTILOCK" LAMP TO LIGHT INTERMITTENTLY. THIS LIST DOES NOT INCLUDE ALL POSSIBILITIES. BUT INCLUDES THOSE CIRCUITS MOST LIKELY TO CAUSE AN INTERMITTENT "ANTILOCK" LAMP CONDITION.

- EBCM LOOP CIRCUIT, INCLUDING:
  - CKT 866 (LT GRN) FROM EBCM PIN 9 TO FLUID LEVEL SENSOR PIN A
  - FLUID LEVEL SENSOR SWITCH
  - CKT 853 (LT BLU) FROM FLUID LEVEL SENSOR CONNECTOR PIN C TO PRESSURE SWITCH CONNECTOR PIN E
  - PRESSURE SWITCH
  - CKT 865 (PPL) FROM PRESSURE SWITCH PIN TO EBCM PIN 10

- IGNITION ENABLE CIRCUIT, INCLUDING:
  - CKT 650 (PNK/WHT) FROM FUSE TO EBCM

- MAIN RELAY CIRCUITS, INCLUDING:
  - CKT 855 (DK BLU) FROM EBCM PIN 8 TO RELAY COIL (RELAY CONNECTOR PIN 2)
  - CKT 803 (BLK/WHT) FROM RELAY COIL TO EBCM PIN 1 (RELAY CONNECTOR PIN T)

- ALL WHEEL SPEED SENSOR CIRCUITS

INSPECT CONNECTORS AND WIRES IN THESE CIRCUITS. IF NO TROUBLE IS FOUND, SEE NOTE ON INTERMITTENTS IN THIS SECTION AND PERFORM TEST A.

CHART G
LOW OR SPONGY PEDAL

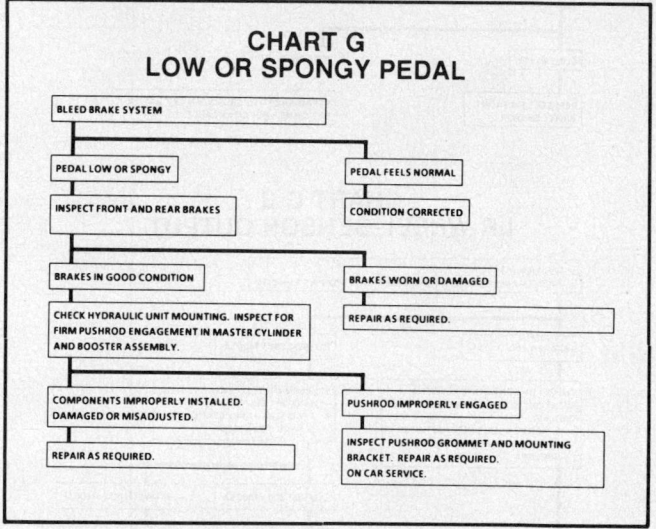

BLEED BRAKE SYSTEM

PEDAL LOW OR SPONGY	PEDAL FEELS NORMAL
INSPECT FRONT AND REAR BRAKES	CONDITION CORRECTED

| BRAKES IN GOOD CONDITION | BRAKES WORN OR DAMAGED |
| CHECK HYDRAULIC UNIT MOUNTING. INSPECT FOR FIRM PUSHROD ENGAGEMENT IN MASTER CYLINDER AND BOOSTER ASSEMBLY. | REPAIR AS REQUIRED. |

| COMPONENTS IMPROPERLY INSTALLED. DAMAGED OR MISADJUSTED. | PUSHROD IMPROPERLY ENGAGED |
| REPAIR AS REQUIRED. | INSPECT PUSHROD GROMMET AND MOUNTING BRACKET. REPAIR AS REQUIRED. ON CAR SERVICE. |

Brake Systems
TEVES ANTI-LOCK BRAKE SYSTEMS (ABS)
EXCEPT GM WITH BCM & ELDORADO, SEVILLE & 6000 (Cont.)

Fig. 6: Teves Anti-Lock Brake System Wiring Diagram (Delta 88 & Ninety-Eight)

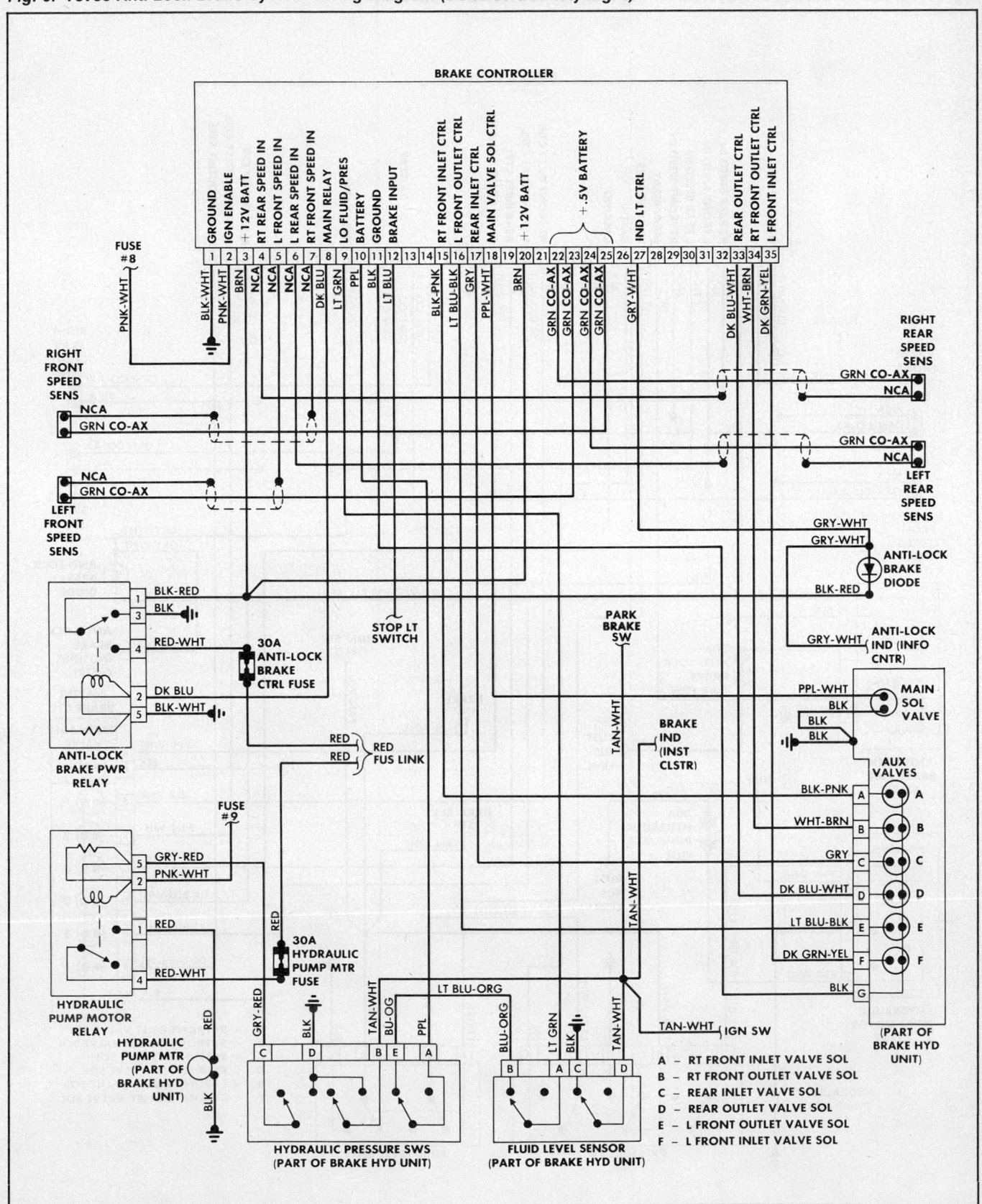

Brake Systems
TEVES ANTI-LOCK BRAKE SYSTEMS (ABS)
EXCEPT GM WITH BCM & ELDORADO, SEVILLE & 6000 (Cont.)

Fig. 7: Teves Anti-Lock Brake System Wiring Diagram (DeVille & Fleetwood)

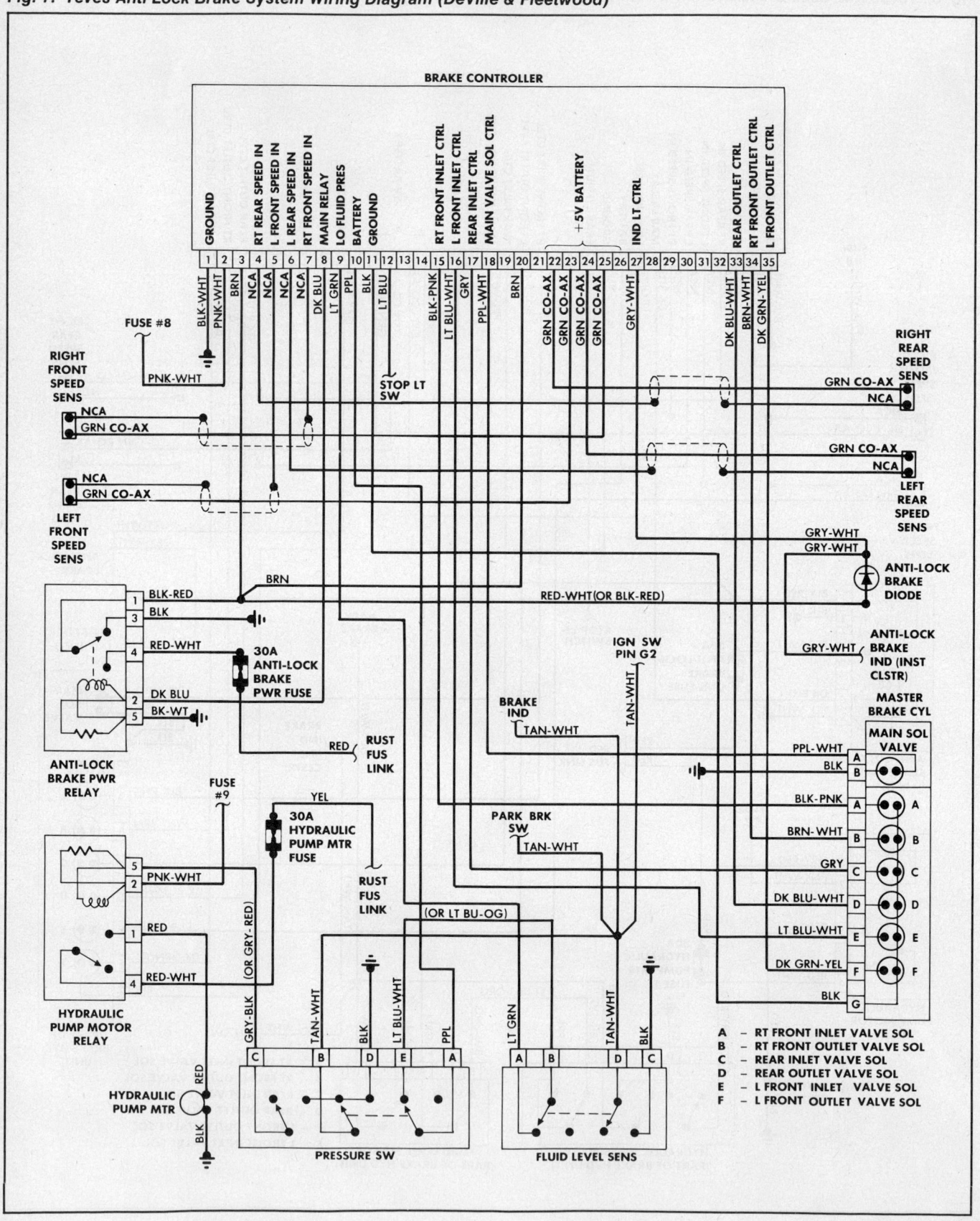

TEVES ANTI-LOCK BRAKE SYSTEMS (ABS)
GM WITH BCM & ELDORADO & SEVILLE

Buick: Riviera
Cadillac: Eldorado, Seville
Oldsmobile: Toronado

DESCRIPTION

The Teves 4-wheel Anti-Lock Brake System is designed to prevent wheel lock-up during heavy braking. This allows driver to maintain steering control and vehicle to stop in shortest distance.

Major component parts of system include: pump motor assembly, hydraulic accumulator, pressure switch, fluid reservoir with integral filter, 4 wheel speed sensors, valve block assembly, fluid level sensor, Electronic Brake Control Module (EBCM), 2 relays, hydraulic booster/master cylinder assembly, and "BRAKE" and "ANTI-LOCK" warning lights. *See Fig. 1.*

Messages can also appear on Driver Information Center (DIC) on Toronado or Graphic Control Center (GCC) to indicate problem.

Fig. 1: Anti-Lock Brake System Component Locations

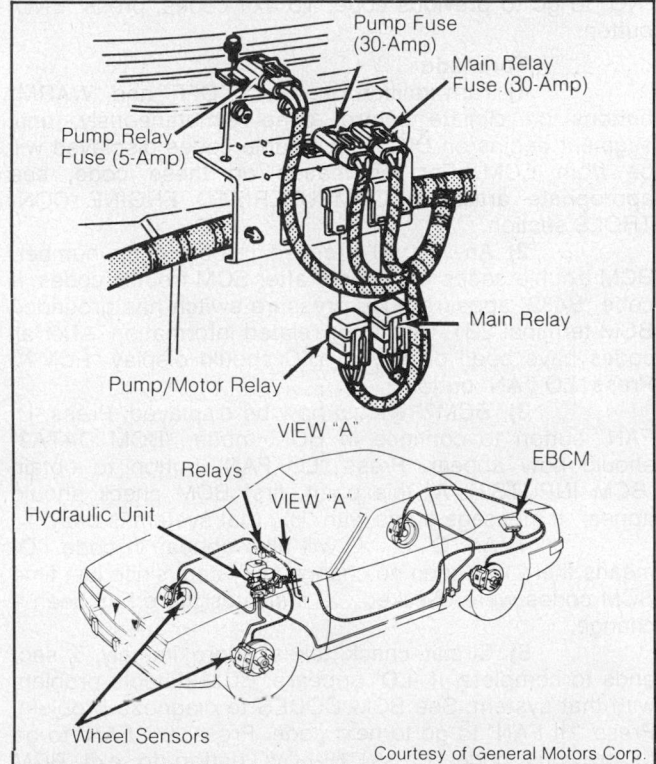

Courtesy of General Motors Corp.

OPERATION

ANTI-LOCK BRAKE SYSTEM

During normal driving and braking opertions, ABS acts like a conventional braking system. Each wheel sensors constantly sends an AC signal to EBCM. This information is translated to wheel rotation speed. When EBCM determines that wheel lock-up is about to occur, it activates electro-magnetic valves, located inside valve block to increase or decrease hydraulic pressure to each wheel. A slight pulsation should be felt through brake pedal.

Warning lights should come on when key is turned on and vehicle is started. If either light stays on after approximately 30 seconds after vehicle is started, system malfunction is indicated. See TESTING in this article.

On Riviera and Toronado, "BRAKE" warning light is controlled by Body Computer Module (BCM). Light will come on, if parking brake is applied, low brake fluid or low accumulator pressure. Light will be on when key is turn on. Light should go out after engine is started. "ANTI-LOCK" warning light is controlled by EBCM. Light will come on if EBCM detects problem with system. When light is on, ABS is partially or totally disabled.

Driver's Information Center (DIC) on Toronado or Graphic Control Center (GCC) on Riviera, will inform driver with message about certain problems. On Toronado, "BRAKE FLUID IS LOW" or "LOW BRAKE PRESSURE" will be displayed on DIC when BCM detects problem. On Riviera message will be similar. On all models, if parking brake is not fully released, DIC or GCC will display "PARK BRAKE IS ON". Message will be displayed only when vehicle is shifted from Park or Neutral to Reverse or Drive. Chime will sound for 30 seconds unless "System Monitor" button is depressed.

DIAGNOSIS & TESTING

NOTE: **Break-Out Box (J-35592) and a pressure gauge must be used to diagnose ABS.**

Diagnosis of the ABS malfunction involves 3 basic steps which must be followed in order to isolate fault, accurately determine its cause and repair the condition with the least amount of diagnostic time. The proper diagnostic procedure consists of the following steps: VISUAL INSPECTION, FUNCTIONAL CHECK and any additional test prescribed by functional check.

CAUTION: ABS must be depressurized before disconnecting any hydraulic component.

GENERAL PRECAUTIONS

Depressurize brake system before disconnecting any hydraulic component. Unplug EBCM before arc welding any part of vehicle. DO NOT unplug or plug in EBCM or valve block connector with ignition on. Low battery voltage can lead to false voltage readings. Connect a battery charger and apply slow charge, if necessary, during testing.

VISUAL INSPECTION

Check brake fluid level. Ensure parking brake is released. Check all fuses. Check all electrical connectors for corrosion or improper mating.

ACCESSING ABS TROUBLE CODES
Eldorado & Seville

1) To obtain and determine light sequence code, turn ignition on and check if "ANTI-LOCK" light stays on after 30 seconds. If so, turn ignition off. Place a jumper wire between ALDL terminals "A" and "G". *See Fig. 2.* ALDL connector is located next to parking brake lever.

2) Turn ignition on. After a 4 second delay, "ANTI-LOCK" light should start blinking first digit of code.

Brake Systems
TEVES ANTI-LOCK BRAKE SYSTEMS (ABS) GM WITH BCM & ELDORADO & SEVILLE (Cont.)

After first digit is shown, a 3 second delay will occur before light links second digit.

3) After code has been obtained, light will stay on solid. DO NOT count last time light comes on as a digit. With ignition still on, unplug jumper wire from ALDL connector and the reinstall jumper wire. This procedure will check for additional code.

4) Repeat this procedure until all codes are obtained. Codes cannot be cleared until all codes have been displayed. Up to 7 codes can be stored by EBCM.

Riviera & Toronado

1) Turn ignition on. Both warning lights should stay on for 30 seconds maximum. If "ANTI-LOCK" light stay on after 30 seconds, turn ignition off. Remove cover and place a jumper wire between ALDL terminals "A" and "G". ALDL connector is located just right of parking brake pedal. *See Fig. 2.*

2) Turn ignition on. Count flash sequence of "ANTI-LOCK" light. A 4 second delay should occur before light sequence begins. If light is on for 4 seconds, then goes out, go to FUNCTIONAL CHECK.

3) There is a 3 second pause between first and second digit code. After second digit code, light will continuously be on. DO NOT count last pause (when light is continuously on), as digit of code. With ignition still on, disconnect jumper wire.

4) Reconnect jumper wire. Check flashes again. If more than one code was set, second code will flash. Continue to perform this procedure until no more trouble codes are set. EBCM is able to store up to 7 trouble codes. When all trouble codes have been displayed, disconnect jumper wire. Record all trouble codes and proceed to FUNCTIONAL CHECK.

NOTE: Trouble codes cannot be cleared unless all trouble codes have been displayed.

Fig. 2: ALDL Connector Location

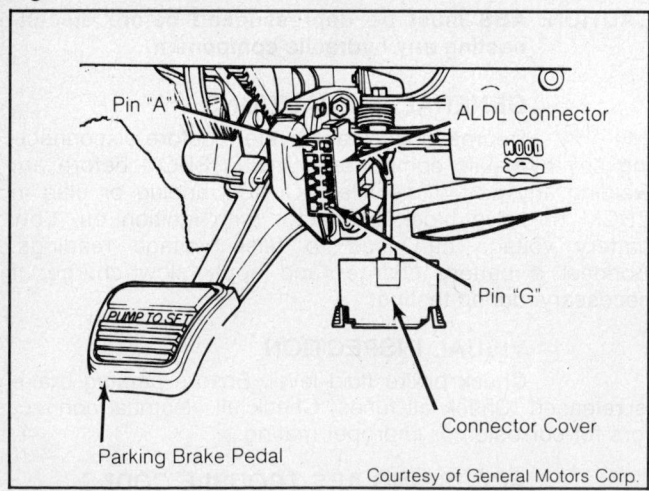

Courtesy of General Motors Corp.

CLEARING TROUBLE CODES

Drive vehicle more than 18 MPH. Trouble codes will automatically clear. Try to access trouble codes. If trouble codes did not clear, attempt to clear codes again. If trouble codes do not clear, check for additional repairs.

ACCESSING BCM TROUBLE CODES
Riviera

1) Turn ignition on. Select "Climate" screen by pressing button in upper right-hand corner of GCC. Press "OFF" and "WARM" buttons simultaneously until "SERVICE MODE" appears on screen. "ECM?" should appear on screen. If you want any ECM code, press "YES" button.

2) ECM codes will appear with "E" preceeding test number code. If ECM codes are not wanted, press "NO". "BCM?" should then appear on screen. Press "YES" button. If no BCM codes are present, "NO BCM CODES" will appear. If there are BCM codes, "BCM INPUTS?" will appear.

3) Press "YES" button. BCM codes should appear. BCM codes will appear with "B" preceeding test number code. "HI" or "LO" will appear. "HI" refers to 12 volts on input circuit. "LO" refers to zero volts on input circuit.

4) An "O" or "X" will also appear in code. "O" means there has been no change in system since last time BCM codes were checked. "X" indicates there has been a change. Press "YES" again to check next code. Press "NO" to go to previous code. To exit codes, press "END" button.

Toronado

1) Turn ignition on. Press "OFF" and "WARM" buttons on climate control panel simutaneously, until segment begins on DIC. First trouble codes displayed will be from ECM. For information on these code, see appropriate article in COMPUTERIZED ENGINE CONTROLS section.

2) An "E" will preceed trouble code number. BCM trouble codes will appear after ECM trouble codes. If code "B482" appears, ABS pressure switch has grounded BCM terminal 2B1. Check for related information. After all codes have been displayed, DIC should display "ECM?". Press "LO FAN" button.

3) "BCM?" should now be displayed. Press "HI FAN" button to continue in BCM mode. "BCM DATA?" should now appear. Press "LO FAN" button to obtain "BCM INPUTS?". At this point, first BCM check should appear. If message starts with "HI", that system is okay.

4) An "O" or "X" will also appear in code. "O" means there has been no change in system since last time BCM codes were checked. "X" indicates there has been a change.

5) Circuit check takes approximately 5 seconds to complete. If "LO" appears, BCM detects problem with that system. See BCM CODES to diagnose problem. Press "HI FAN" to go to next code. Press "LO FAN" to go to previous code. Press "BI-LEV" button to exit BCM check.

BCM CODES
"B482" – Low Brake Pressure

Code will set if, hydraulic accumulator pressure is low. Check ABS trouble code(s). "LOW BRAKE PRESSURE" should display on DIC.

"BI18" – Brake Pressure

Check for low hydraulic brake pressure.

"BI21" – Brake Fluid

Code is used to check brake fluid level and brake fluid level circuit.

Brake Systems
TEVES ANTI-LOCK BRAKE SYSTEMS (ABS) GM WITH BCM & ELDORADO & SEVILLE (Cont.)

NOTE ON INTERMITTENTS

Intermittent failures may be difficult to accurately diagnose. To help isolate intermittent failure, display and clear all EBCM codes. Test drive vehicle. Ensure vehicle has exceeded 20 MPH. Attempt to repeat circumstances which lead to orginial problem.

Attempt to display trouble code. If no trouble code is displayed, perform symptom diagnosis. Most intermittent problems are due to poor electrical connections. Most common intermittent problem areas are low system voltage, low brake fluid or low accumulator pressure.

DEPRESSURIZING BRAKE SYSTEM

Disconnect negative battery cable. Pump brake pedal 25 times or more. A noticeable change in pedal feel should be felt. After change in pedal is felt, pump brake pedal a few more times.

REMOVAL & INSTALLATION

CAUTION: Depressurize brake system before disconnecting any hydraulic component. See DEPRESSURIZING BRAKE SYSTEM in this article.

Fig. 3: Exploded View of Hydraulic Unit

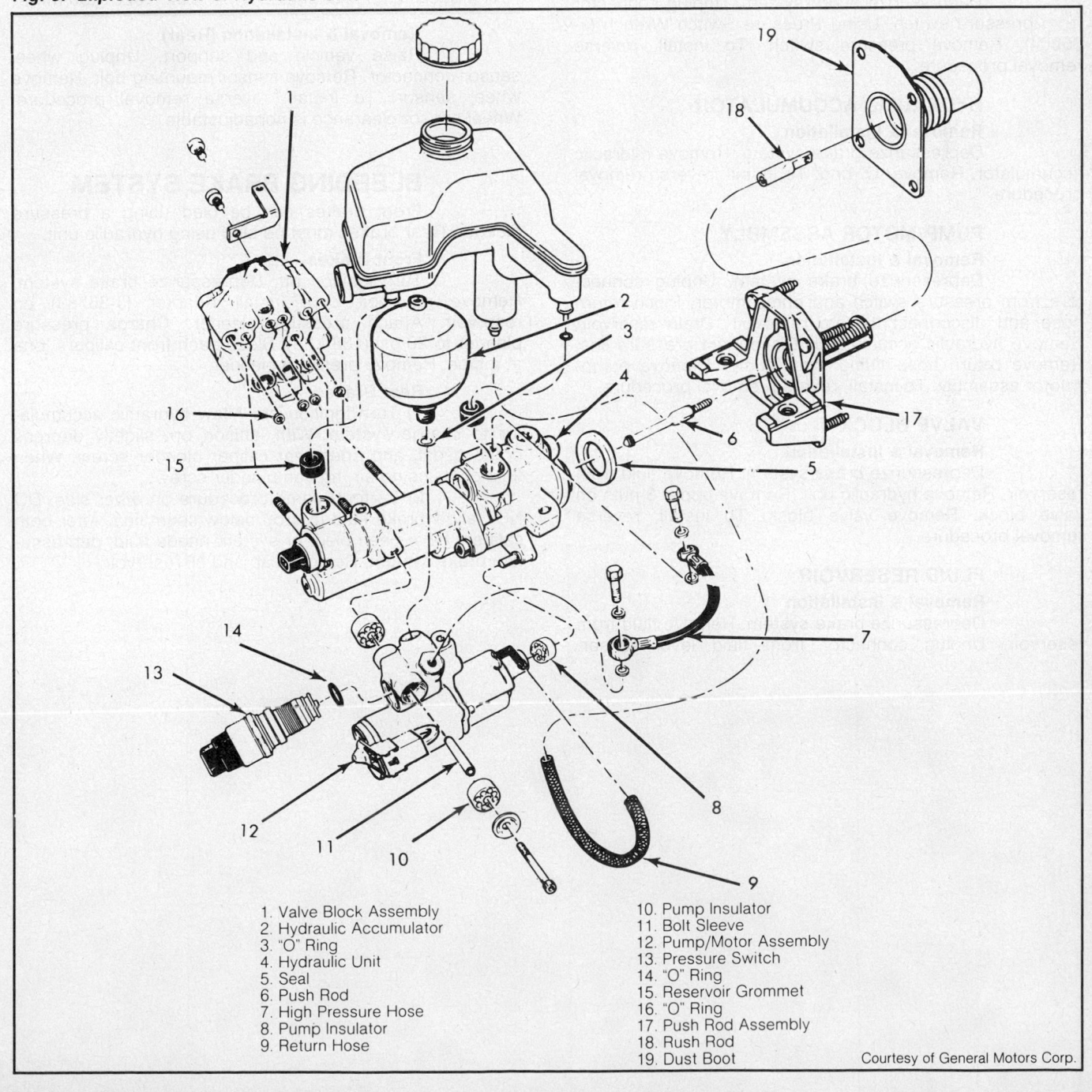

1. Valve Block Assembly
2. Hydraulic Accumulator
3. "O" Ring
4. Hydraulic Unit
5. Seal
6. Push Rod
7. High Pressure Hose
8. Pump Insulator
9. Return Hose
10. Pump Insulator
11. Bolt Sleeve
12. Pump/Motor Assembly
13. Pressure Switch
14. "O" Ring
15. Reservoir Grommet
16. "O" Ring
17. Push Rod Assembly
18. Rush Rod
19. Dust Boot

Courtesy of General Motors Corp.

Brake Systems
TEVES ANTI-LOCK BRAKE SYSTEMS (ABS) GM WITH BCM & ELDORADO & SEVILLE (Cont.)

HYDRAULIC UNIT
Removal & Installation

1) Depressurize brake system. Unplug all electrical connectors from hydraulic unit. Remove cross brace from engine compartment. Remove pump bolt. Disconnect 3 brake lines from hydraulic unit. Plug all line openings.

2) From inside vehicle, disconnect push rod from brake pedal. Push dust boot forward. Separate push rod halves. From engine compartment, remove hydraulic unit. *See Fig. 3*. To install, reverse removal procedure.

PRESSURE SWITCH
Removal & Installation

Depressurize brake system. Unplug connector from pressure switch. Using Pressure Switch Wrench (J-35804), Remove pressure switch. To install, reverse removal procedure.

HYDRAULIC ACCUMULATOR
Removal & Installation

Depressurize brake system. Remove hydraulic accumulator. Remove "O" ring. To install, reverse removal procedure.

PUMP/MOTOR ASSEMBLY
Removal & Installation

Depressurize brake system. Unplug connectors from pressure switch and pump motor. Pinch return hose and disconnect it from reservoir. Drain reservoir. Remove hydraulic accumulator. Disconnect pressure line. Remove return hose fitting from pump. Remove pump-/motor assembly. To install, reverse removal procedure.

VALVE BLOCK
Removal & Installation

Depressurize brake system. Remove fluid from reservoir. Remove hydraulic unit. Remove upper 3 nuts on valve block. Remove valve block. To install, reverse removal procedure.

FLUID RESERVOIR
Removal & Installation

Depressurize brake system. Remove fluid from reservoir. Unplug connector from fluid level sensor. Remove reservoir mounting bolt. Prying between master cylinder and reservoir, carefully remove reservoir.

WHEEL SENSORS
Removal & Installation (Front)

Unplug sensor connector located near strut tower. Raise and support vehicle. Remove sensor retaining screw. Remove sensor. To install, reverse removal procedure. Adjust sensor air gap to specification. See WHEEL SENSOR CLEARANCE table in this article.

WHEEL SENSOR CLEARANCE

Application	Air Gap
All Models	.020" (.50 mm)

Removal & Installation (Rear)

Raise vehicle and support. Unplug wheel sensor connector. Remove sensor mounting bolt. Remove wheel sensor. To install, reverse removal procedure. Wheel sensor clearance is nonadjustable.

BLEEDING BRAKE SYSTEM

Front brakes can be bled using a pressure bleeder. Rear brakes must be bled using hydraulic unit.

Front Brakes

Turn ignition off. Depressurize brake system. Remove reservoir cap. Install Adapter (J-35789) on reservoir. Attach pressure bleeder. Charge pressure bleeder to 20 psi (138 kPa). Bleed each front calipers, one at a time. Remove pressure bleeder.

Rear Brakes

1) Turn ignition on. Allow hydraulic accumulator to charge system. With ignition on, slightly depress brake pedal, and open rear caliper bleeder screw. When fluid contains no air, tighten bleeder screw.

2) Perform same procedure on other side. DO NOT allow brake fluid to drop below seam line. After both calipers have been bled, or system needs fluid, depressurize brake system. Remove cap and fill reservoir.

TEVES ANTI-LOCK BRAKE SYSTEMS (ABS)
GM WITH BCM & ELDORADO & SEVILLE (Cont.)

FUNCTIONAL CHECK

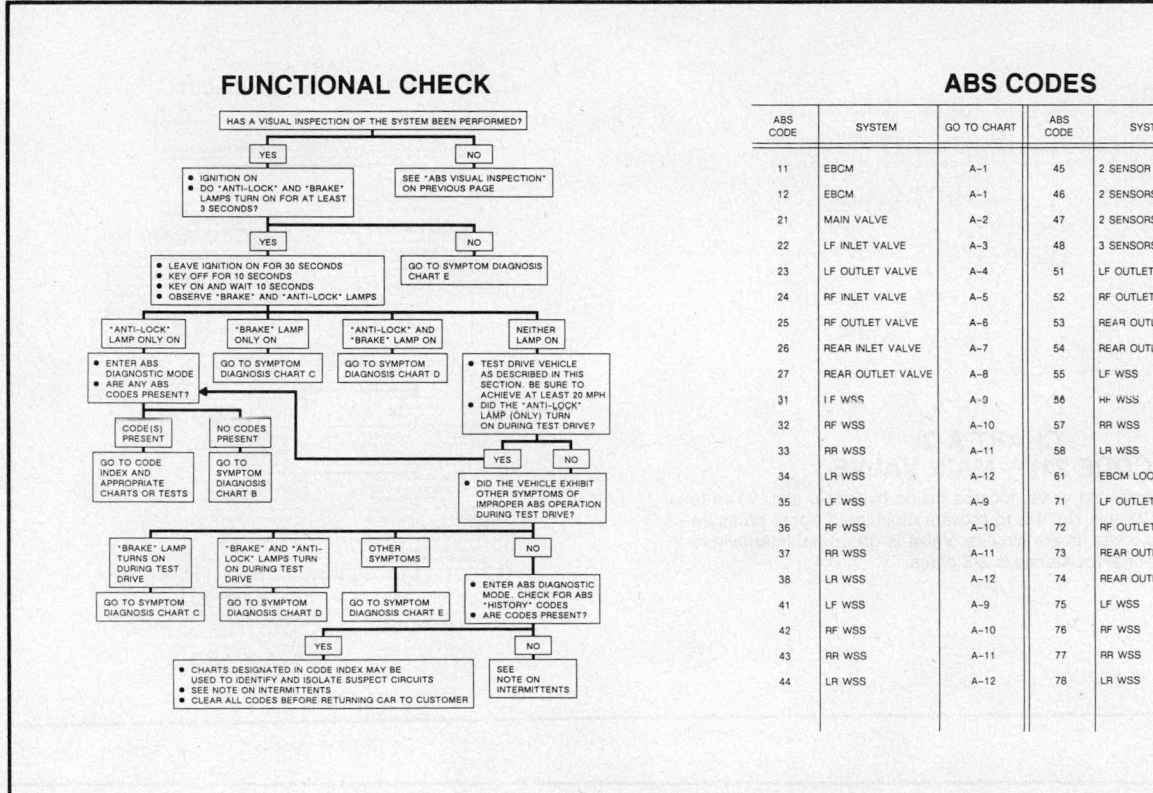

ABS CODES

ABS CODE	SYSTEM	GO TO CHART	ABS CODE	SYSTEM	GO TO CHART
11	EBCM	A-1	45	2 SENSOR (LF)	A-13
12	EBCM	A-1	46	2 SENSORS (RF)	A-13
21	MAIN VALVE	A-2	47	2 SENSORS (REAR)	A-13
22	LF INLET VALVE	A-3	48	3 SENSORS	A-13
23	LF OUTLET VALVE	A-4	51	LF OUTLET VALVE	A-14
24	RF INLET VALVE	A-5	52	RF OUTLET VALVE	A-14
25	RF OUTLET VALVE	A-6	53	REAR OUTLET VALVE	A-14
26	REAR INLET VALVE	A-7	54	REAR OUTLET VALVE	A-14
27	REAR OUTLET VALVE	A-8	55	LF WSS	A-9
31	LF WSS	A-9	56	HF WSS	A-10
32	RF WSS	A-10	57	RR WSS	A-11
33	RR WSS	A-11	58	LR WSS	A-12
34	LR WSS	A-12	61	EBCM LOOP CKT	A-15
35	LF WSS	A-9	71	LF OUTLET VALVE	A-14
36	RF WSS	A-10	72	RF OUTLET VALVE	A-14
37	RR WSS	A-11	73	REAR OUTLET VALVE	A-14
38	LR WSS	A-12	74	REAR OUTLET VALVE	A-14
41	LF WSS	A-9	75	LF WSS	A-9
42	RF WSS	A-10	76	RF WSS	A-10
43	RR WSS	A-11	77	RR WSS	A-11
44	LR WSS	A-12	78	LR WSS	A-12

CHART A-1
CODES 11 & 12 – EBCM PROBLEM

Codes 11 and 12 indicates problem with EBCM. In most cases, either code indicates replacement of EBCM. Ensure ground circuit is okay. False code can be set due to external electromagnetic disturbances.

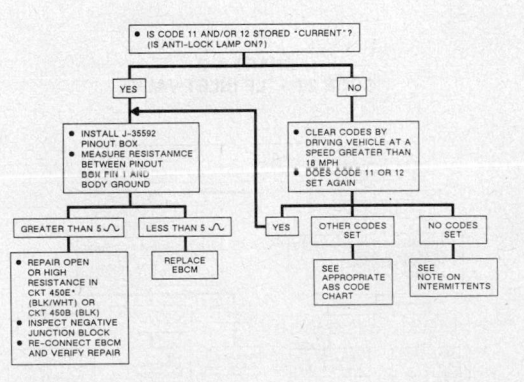

*CKT 450E IS BLK ON VEHICLES WITH COLUMN SHIFT

Brake Systems
TEVES ANTI-LOCK BRAKE SYSTEMS (ABS)
GM WITH BCM & ELDORADO & SEVILLE (Cont.)

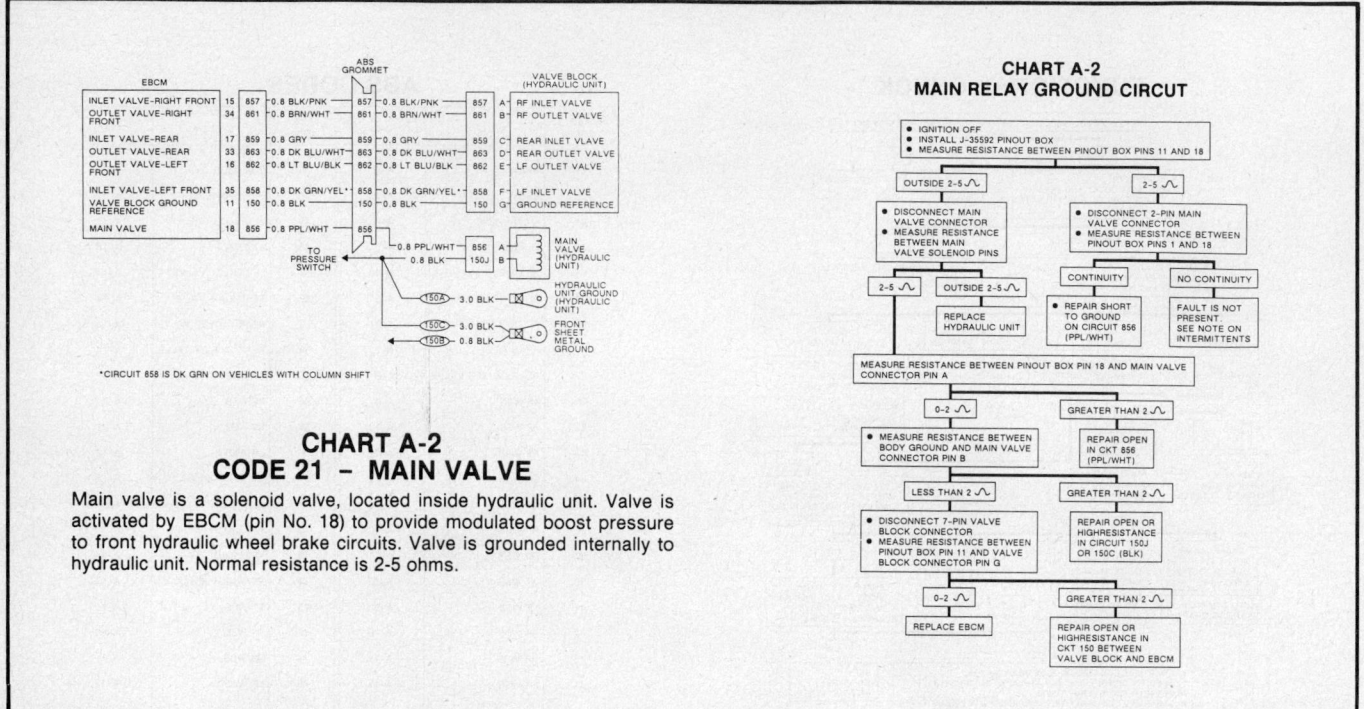

CHART A-2
CODE 21 – MAIN VALVE

Main valve is a solenoid valve, located inside hydraulic unit. Valve is activated by EBCM (pin No. 18) to provide modulated boost pressure to front hydraulic wheel brake circuits. Valve is grounded internally to hydraulic unit. Normal resistance is 2-5 ohms.

CHART A-3 & A-4
CODES 22 & 23 – LF INLET & OUTLET VALVE

1) Inlet valve is normally open. EBCM applies 12 volts (pin No. 35) to inlet valve to close it. Valve is closed for short periods to increase or decrease hydraulic pressure. Normal resistance is 5-7 ohms.

2) Outlet valve is normally closed. EBCM opens valve by applying 12 volts (EBCM pin No. 16) to outlet valve. Valve is open for short period of time to increase or decrease pressure. Normal resistance is 3-5 ohms.

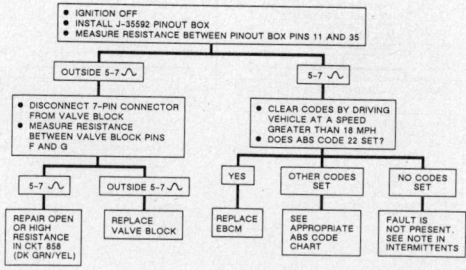

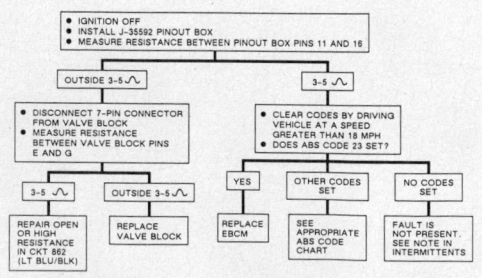

Brake Systems

TEVES ANTI-LOCK BRAKE SYSTEMS (ABS)
GM WITH BCM & ELDORADO & SEVILLE (Cont.)

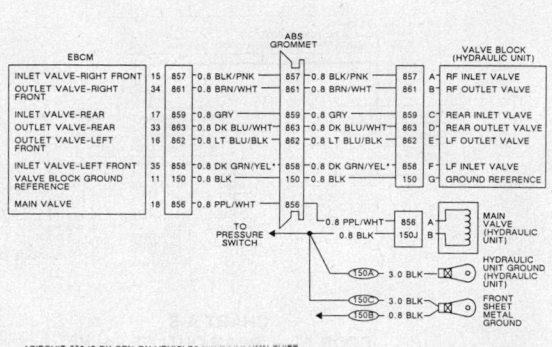

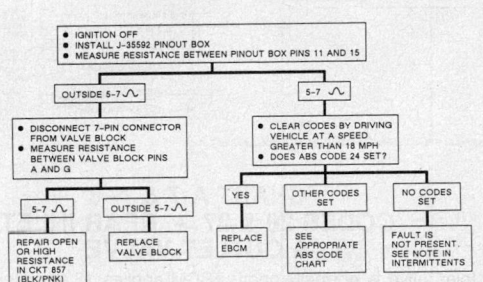

CHART A-5
CODE 24 – RF INLET VALVE

CHART A-5 & A-6
CODES 24 & 25 – RF INLET & OUTLET VALVE

1) Inlet valve is normally open. EBCM applies 12 volts (pin No. 15) to inlet valve to close it. Valve is closed for short periods to increase or decrease hydraulic pressure. Normal resistance is 5-7 ohms.

2) Outlet valve is normally closed. EBCM opens valve by applying 12 volts (EBCM pin No. 34) to outlet valve. Valve is open for short period of time to increase or decrease pressure. Normal resistance is 3-5 ohms.

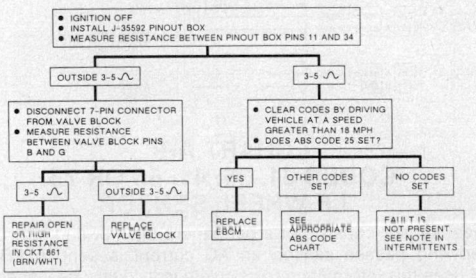

CHART A-6
CODE 25 – RF OUTLET VALVE

Brake Systems
TEVES ANTI-LOCK BRAKE SYSTEMS (ABS)
GM WITH BCM & ELDORADO & SEVILLE (Cont.)

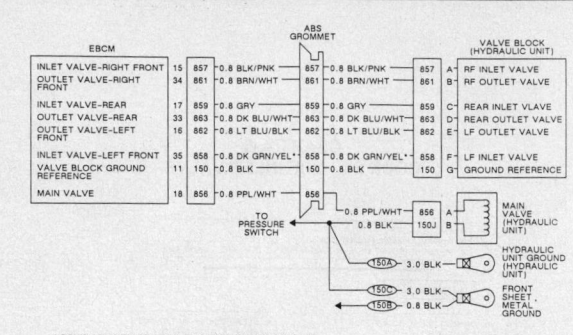

*CIRCUIT 858 IS DK GRN ON VEHICLES WITH COLUMN SHIFT

CHART A-7 & A-8
CODES 26 & 27 – REAR INLET & OUTLET VALVE

1) Inlet valve is normally open. EBCM applies 12 volts (pin No. 17) to inlet valve to close it. Valve is closed for short periods to increase or decrease hydraulic pressure. Normal resistance is 5-7 ohms.

2) Outlet valve is normally closed. EBCM opens valve by applying 12 volts (EBCM pin No. 33) to outlet valve. Valve is open for short period of time to increase or decrease pressure. Normal resistance is 3-5 ohms.

CHART A-7
CODE 26 – REAR INLET VALVE

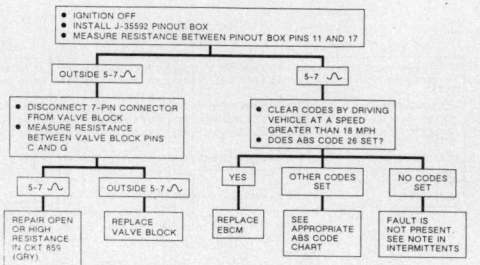

CHART A-8
CODE 27 – REAR OUTLET VALVE

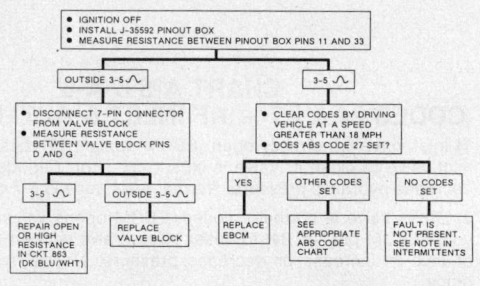

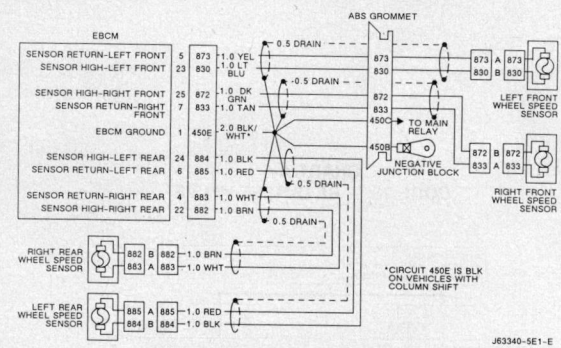

J63340-5E1-E

*CIRCUIT 450E IS BLK ON VEHICLES WITH COLUMN SHIFT

CHART A-9
CODES 31, 35, 41, 55 OR 75
LF WHEEL SENSOR

1) Wheel sensor consists of a permanent magnet and coil. Each time toothed ring passes sensor, an AC current is sent to EBCM. The EBCM uses this information to calculate individual wheel speed.

2) Two checks can be made on wheel sensor: continuity and output. At low speeds, wheel sensor can set code, then clear itself. At high speeds, code will be set and remain set. Intermittent open in sensor cable can lead to code being set, then clearing itself.

CHART A-10
CODES 32, 36, 42, 56 OR 76
RF WHEEL SENSOR

1) Wheel sensor consists of a permanent magnet and coil. Each time toothed ring passes sensor, an AC current is sent to EBCM. The EBCM uses this information to calculate individual wheel speed.

2) Two checks can be made on wheel sensor: continuity and output. At low speeds, wheel sensor can set code, then clear itself. At high speeds, code will be set and remain set. Intermittent open in sensor cable can lead to code being set, then clearing itself.

CHART A-9
LR WHEEL SENSOR RESISTANCE

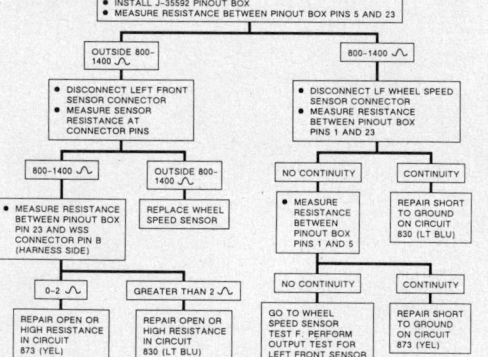

CHART A-10
RF WHEEL SENSOR RESISTANCE

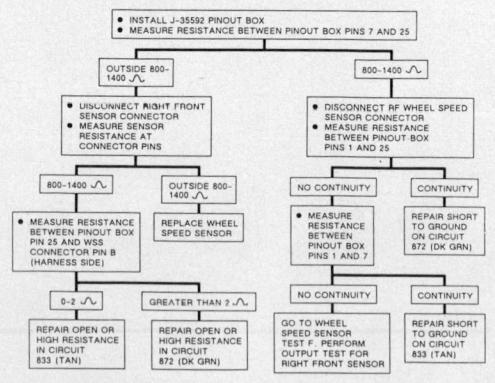

TEVES ANTI-LOCK BRAKE SYSTEMS (ABS)
GM WITH BCM & ELDORADO & SEVILLE (Cont.)

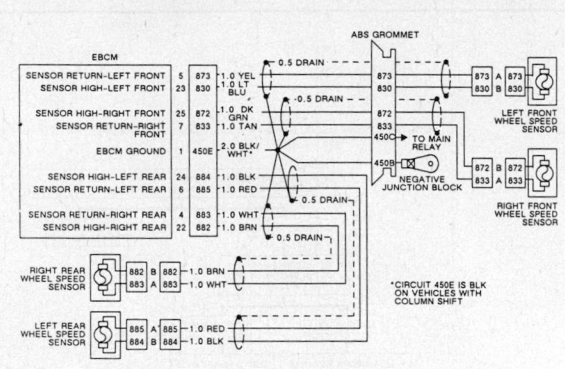

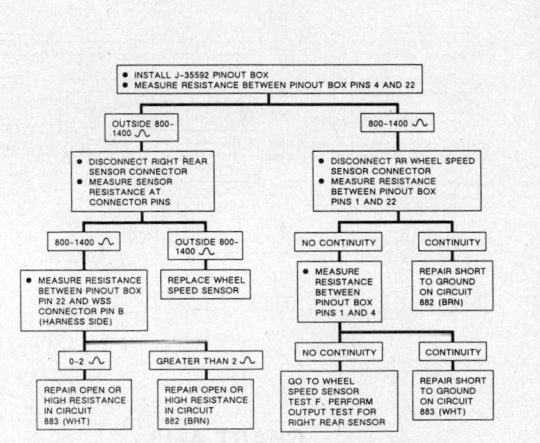

CHART A-11
CODES 33, 37, 43, 57 OR 77
RR WHEEL SENSOR

1) Wheel sensor consists of a permanent magnet and coil. Each time toothed ring passes sensor, an AC current is sent to EBCM. The EBCM uses this information to calculate individual wheel speed.

2) Two checks can be made on wheel sensor: continuity and output. At low speeds, wheel sensor can set code, then clear itself. At high speeds, code will be set and remain set. Intermittent open in sensor cable can lead to code being set, then clearing itself.

CHART A-12
CODES 34, 38, 44, 58 OR 78
LR WHEEL SENSOR

1) Wheel sensor consists of a permanent magnet and coil. Each time toothed ring passes sensor, an AC current is sent to EBCM. The EBCM uses this information to calculate individual wheel speed.

2) Two checks can be made on wheel sensor: continuity and output. At low speeds, wheel sensor can set code, then clear itself. At high speeds, code will be set and remain set. Intermittent open in sensor cable can lead to code being set, then clearing itself.

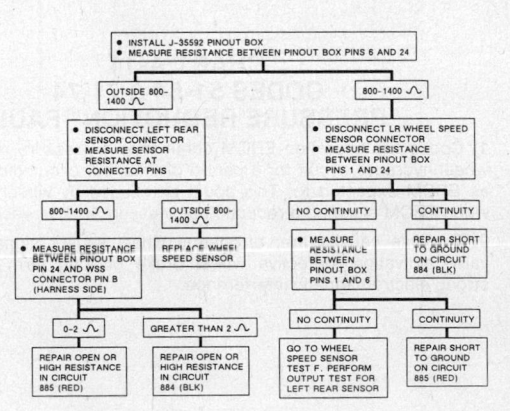

Brake Systems

TEVES ANTI-LOCK BRAKE SYSTEMS (ABS)
GM WITH BCM & ELDORADO & SEVILLE (Cont.)

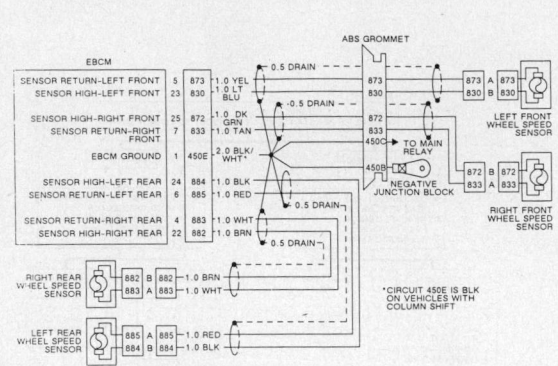

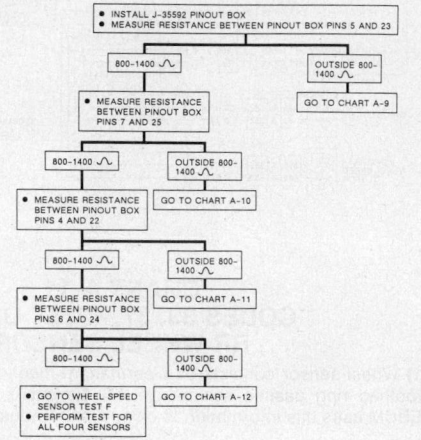

NOTE: THESE CODES (45, 46, 47 AND 48) INDICATE MORE THAN ONE WHEEL SPEED SENSOR WITH A MISSING SIGNAL

CHART A-13
CODES 45, 46, 47 OR 48
MISSING WHEEL SENSOR SIGNAL

1) EBCM checks wheel sensor output and continuity checks. It also checks output signal with expected valve and compares each output signal with other ones. If EBCM detects wheel sensor reading that is missing, code will be set. Code 45 will be set if reading from left front wheel sensor is missing.

2) Code 46 is for right front reading missing. Code 47 will be set if either rear sensor reading is missing. It is impossible to determine which rear sensor signal is missing. Code 48 will set if any 3 readings are missing.

3) At low speeds, wheel sensor can set code, then clear itself. At high speeds, code will be set and remain set. Intermittent open in sensor cable can lead to code being set, then clearing itself.

CHART A-14
CODES 51-54 & 71-74
"PRESSURE REDUCTION" FAULT

1) Codes will set when EBCM commands a pressure reduction to a wheel hydraulic circuit for a period of time, but circuit did not respond as EBCM expected to. This could be caused by wheel speeding up when EBCM signaled a reduction of pressure to that wheel.

2) Possible causes are: erroneous wheel sensor signals, improper valve activation, defective wheel brake or long term exposure to strong electromagnetic interference.

NOTE: CODES 51-54 AND 71-74 INDICATE A CONDITION WHICH MAY BE ATTRIBUTABLE TO EITHER THE WHEEL SPEED SENSOR CIRCUIT OR THE OUTLET VALVE

FOR THESE CODES:	PERFORM THESE TESTS:
51 AND/OR 71	• GO TO CHART A-9 IF NO TROUBLE IS FOUND WHILE PERFORMING TESTS ON CHART A-9, DO NOT GO TO TEST F. INSTEAD, GO TO SOLENOID VALVE TEST G • PERFORM SOLENOID VALVE TEST FOR LEFT FRONT VALVES • IF NO TROUBLE IS FOUND, REPLACE EBCM
52 AND/OR 72	• GO TO CHART A-10 IF NO TROUBLE IS FOUND WHILE PERFORMING TESTS ON CHART A-10, DO NOT GO TO TEST F. INSTEAD, GO TO SOLENOID VALVE TEST G • PERFORM SOLENOID VALVE TEST FOR RIGHT FRONT VALVES • IF NO TROUBLE IS FOUND, REPLACE EBCM
53 AND/OR 73	• GO TO CHART A-11 IF NO TROUBLE IS FOUND WHILE PERFORMING TESTS ON CHART A-11, DO NOT GO TO TEST F. INSTEAD, GO TO SOLENOID VALVE TEST G • PERFORM SOLENOID VALVE TEST FOR REAR VALVES • IF NO TROUBLE IS FOUND, REPLACE EBCM
54 AND/OR 74	• GO TO CHART A-12 IF NO TROUBLE IS FOUND WHILE PERFORMING TESTS ON CHART A-12, DO NOT GO TO TEST F. INSTEAD, GO TO SOLENOID VALVE TEST G • PERFORM SOLENOID VALVE TEST FOR REAR VALVES • IF NO TROUBLE IS FOUND, REPLACE EBCM

TEVES ANTI-LOCK BRAKE SYSTEMS (ABS)
GM WITH BCM & ELDORADO & SEVILLE (Cont.)

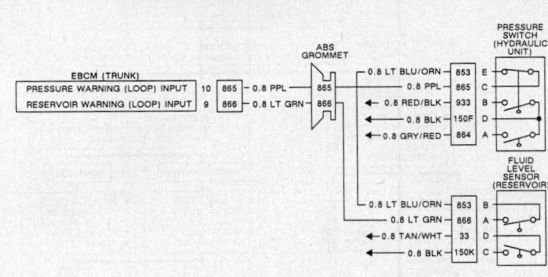

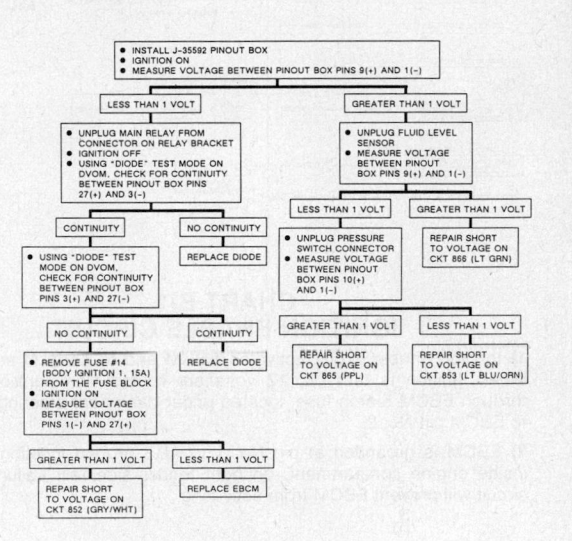

CHART A-15
CODE 61 – LOW FLUID/PRESSURE LOOP
INPUT NOT PROCESSABLE

1) EBCM has a normally closed loop from pin No. 9 through fluid level sensor, located on fluid reservoir, and pressure switch, located on hydraulic unit back to EBCM pin No. 10. Voltage at pin No. 9 is normally at 12 volts.

2) If pin No. 10 detects drop in voltage, EBCM partially disables ABS. If accumulator pressure drops below 1500 psi (10,350 kPa), pressure switch opens, dropping voltage to pin No. 10. Pressure switch will automatically reset when pressure reaches 1900 psi (13,100 kPa).

3) A reed switch and float, inside reservoir, activate and deactivate fluid level sensor. When code 61 is set, a shorted circuit, in pressure switch or fluid level switch, is indicated. Code will not set is fluid level or fluid pressure is low. A shorted ABS diode, located under dash just left of steering column, can cause this code.

CHART B
"ANTI-LOCK" LIGHT ON
NO CODES SET

Use this chart as indicated by FUNCTIONAL CHECK chart. Areas this chart will check are: EBCM power source, EBCM grounds and low fluid/pressure loop.

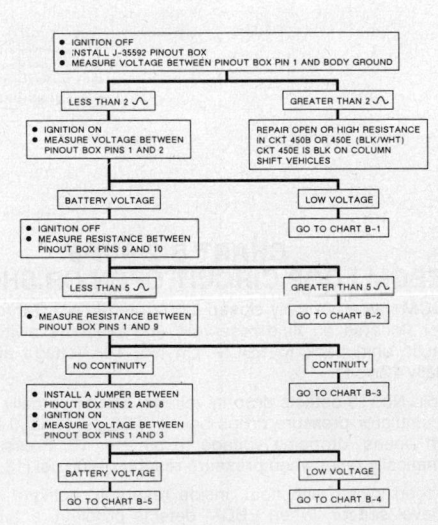

Brake Systems
TEVES ANTI-LOCK BRAKE SYSTEMS (ABS)
GM WITH BCM & ELDORADO & SEVILLE (Cont.)

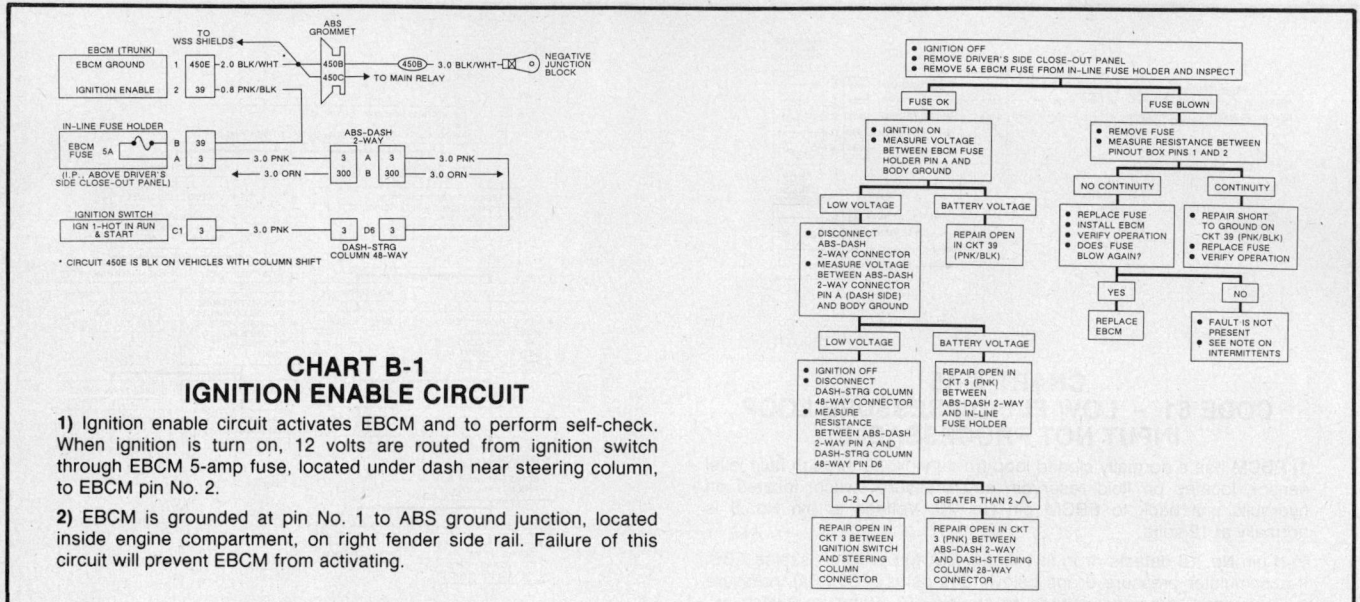

CHART B-1
IGNITION ENABLE CIRCUIT

1) Ignition enable circuit activates EBCM and to perform self-check. When ignition is turn on, 12 volts are routed from ignition switch through EBCM 5-amp fuse, located under dash near steering column, to EBCM pin No. 2.

2) EBCM is grounded at pin No. 1 to ABS ground junction, located inside engine compartment, on right fender side rail. Failure of this circuit will prevent EBCM from activating.

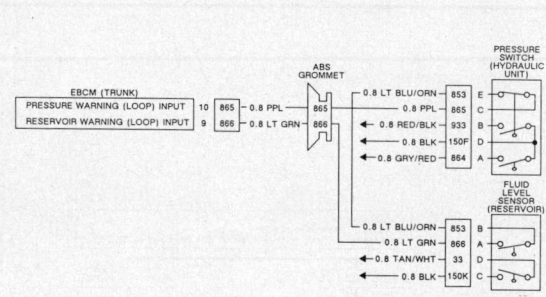

CHART B-2 & B-3
EBCM LOOP CIRCUIT OPEN OR SHORTED

1) EBCM has a normally closed loop from pin No. 9 through fluid level sensor (located on fluid reservoir) and pressure switch (located on hydraulic unit) back to EBCM pin No. 10. Voltage at pin No. 9 is normally 12 volts.

2) If pin No. 10 detects drop in voltage, EBCM partially disables ABS. If accumulator pressure drops below 1500 psi (10,350 kPa), pressure switch opens, dropping voltage to pin No. 10. Pressure switch will automatically reset when pressure reaches 1900 psi (13,100 kPa).

3) A reed switch and float, inside reservoir, activate and deactivate fluid level sensor. When EBCM detects problem, anti-lock control to front wheels is disabled. Rear anti-lock function will still operate.

CHART B-2
EBCM LOOP CIRCUIT OPEN

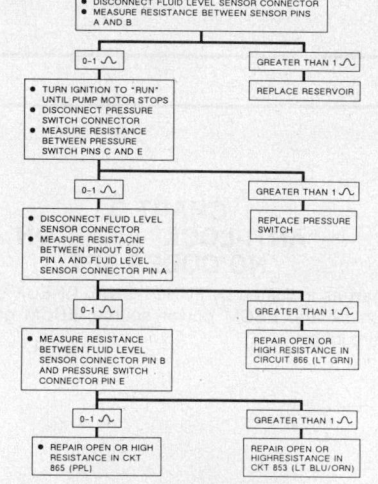

CHART B-3
EBCM LOOP CIRCUIT SHORTED

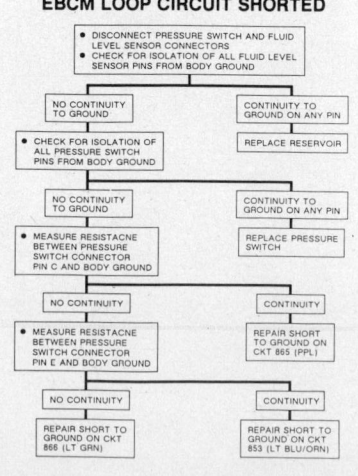

TEVES ANTI-LOCK BRAKE SYSTEMS (ABS)
GM WITH BCM & ELDORADO & SEVILLE (Cont.)

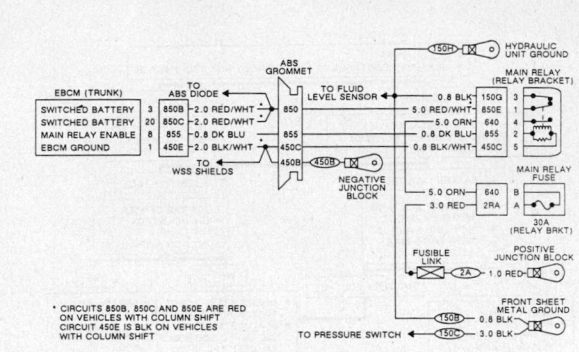

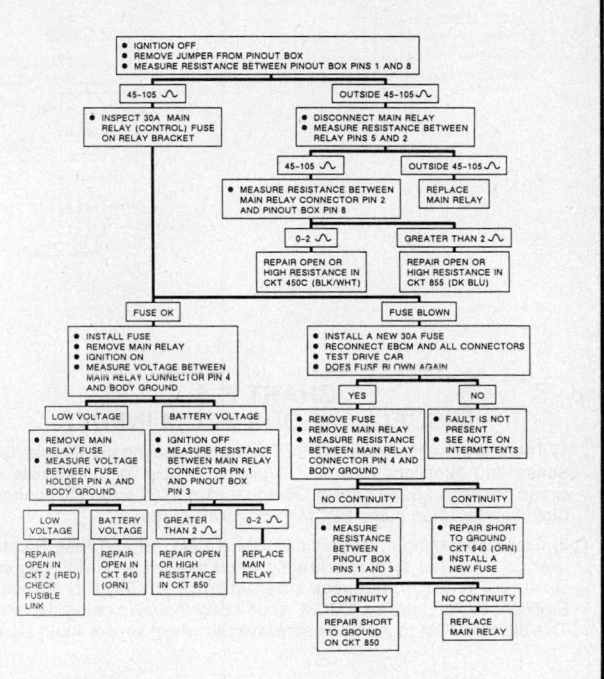

CHART B-4
MAIN RELAY CIRCUITS

1) Main relay supplies 12 volts to EBCM, through pins No. 3 and 20, to operate main valve, solenoid valves, logic circuit and self-checks. After EBCM receives Ignition Enable Circuit, it provides 12 volts through pin No. 8 to power main relay coil.

2) When main relay coil receives this power, 12 volts is provided to EBCM pins No. 3 and 20. Main relay power comes from a 30-amp fuse, located at relay bracket.

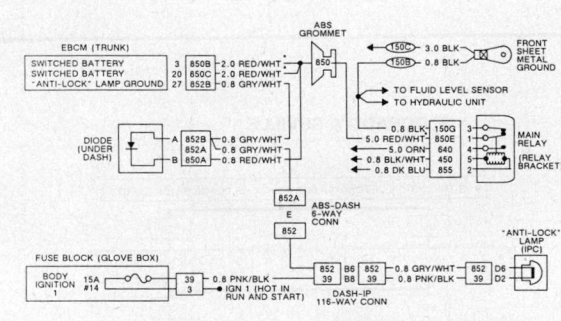

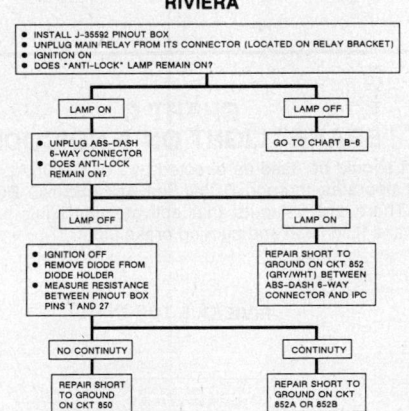

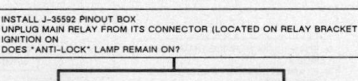

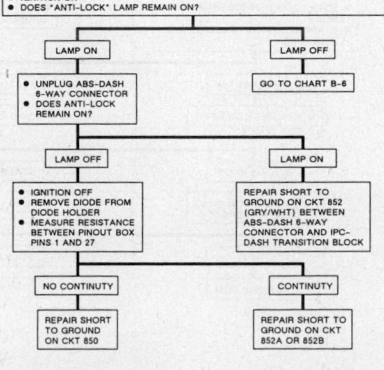

CHART B-5
"ANTI-LOCK" LIGHT CIRCUIT

"ANTI-LOCK" light is powered by fuse (15-amp) No. 14. If main relay is not activated by EBCM, light is grounded through ABS diode, at main relay. Light is also grounded if main relay is activated or not by EBCM at pin No. 27. Diode prevents over-voltage from light. If diode shorts, code 61 should be found.

Brake Systems
TEVES ANTI-LOCK BRAKE SYSTEMS (ABS)
GM WITH BCM & ELDORADO & SEVILLE (Cont.)

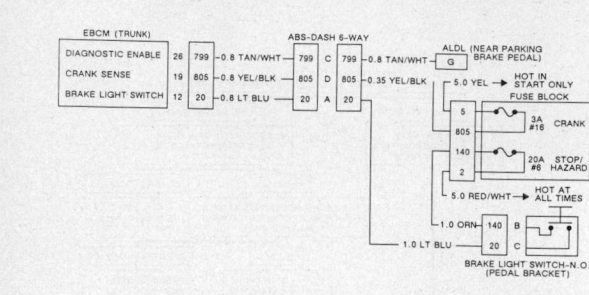

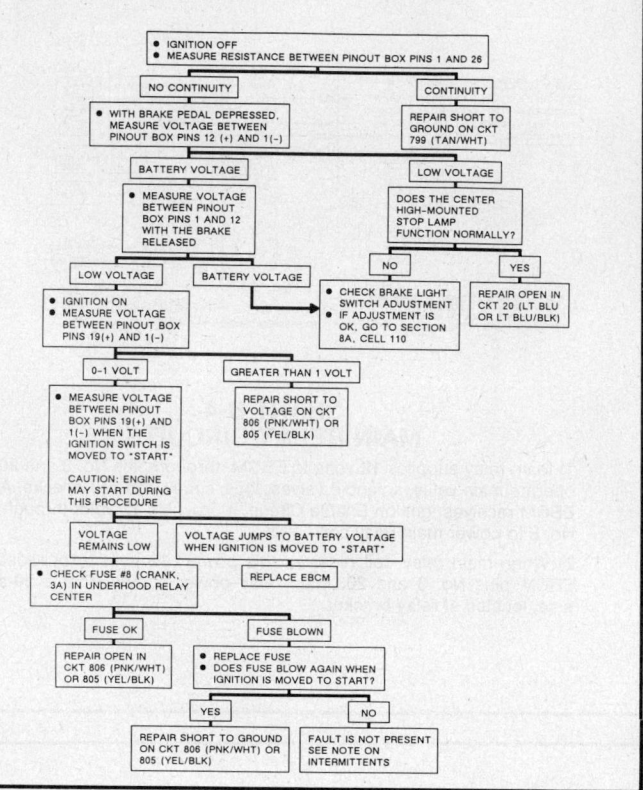

CHART B-6
MISCELLANEOUS EBCM INPUTS

1) There are 3 miscellaneous EBCM inputs: Diagnostic Enable, Crank Sense and Stoplight Switch. Diagnostic enable input consists of a circuit between EBCM pin No. 26 and terminal "G" on ALDL connector. Circuit is design to place EBCM in diagostic mode.

2) Crank sense input, between EBCM pin No. 19 and fuse No. 16, is used to initialized system correctly when ignition is on. Missing crank sense will result in improper initialization of EBCM with ignition on. Stoplight switch informs EBCM when brake pedal is being depressed. This alerts EBCM to increase sensitivity to wheel sensor input signals.

CHART C
"BRAKE" LIGHT ON & NO CODES

This chart should be used as directed by FUNCTIONAL CHECK chart. This light operates through BCM. See ACCESSING BCM TROUBLE CODES. There are 3 inputs that activate this light: brake pressure switch, brake fluid level and parking brake input.

RIVIERA & TORONADO

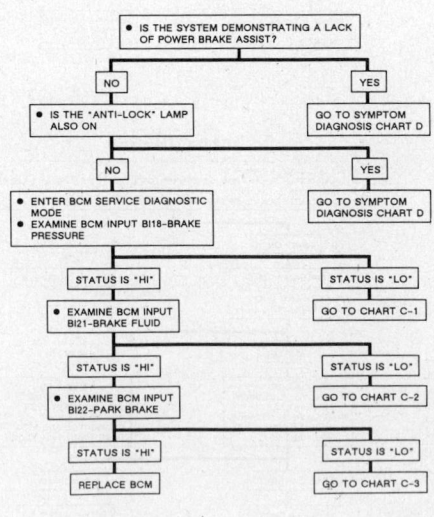

ELDORADO & SEVILLE

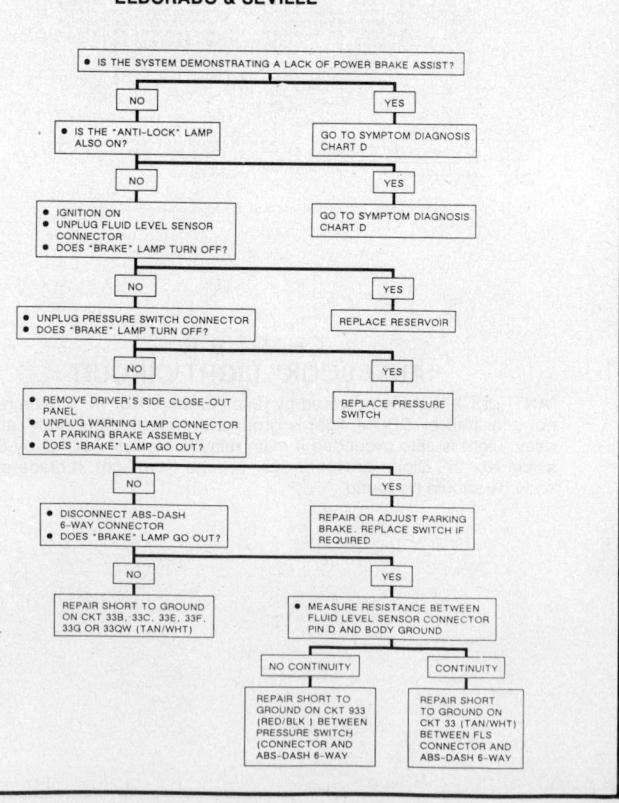

TEVES ANTI-LOCK BRAKE SYSTEMS (ABS)
GM WITH BCM & ELDORADO & SEVILLE (Cont.)

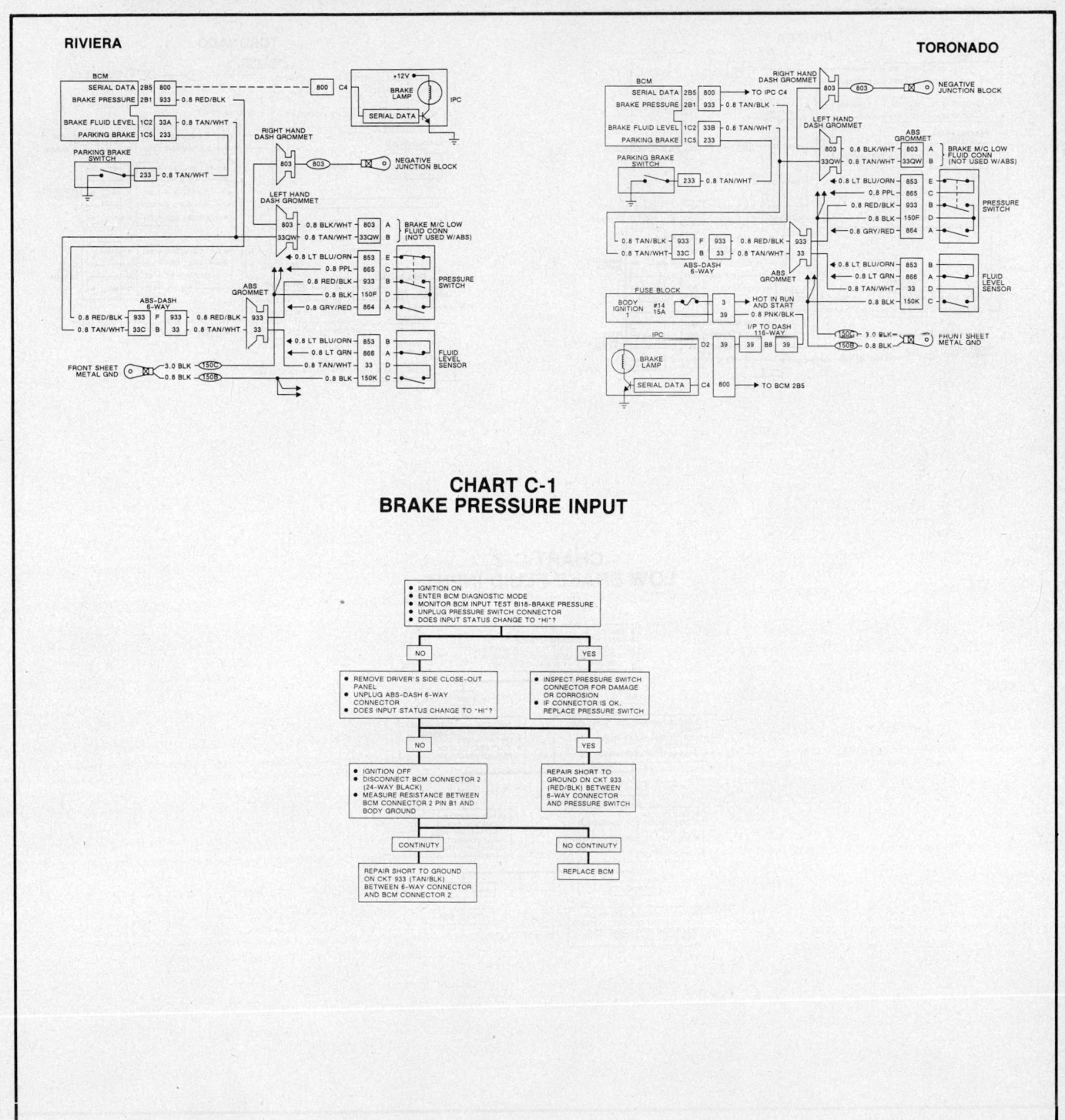

CHART C-1
BRAKE PRESSURE INPUT

Brake Systems
TEVES ANTI-LOCK BRAKE SYSTEMS (ABS)
GM WITH BCM & ELDORADO & SEVILLE (Cont.)

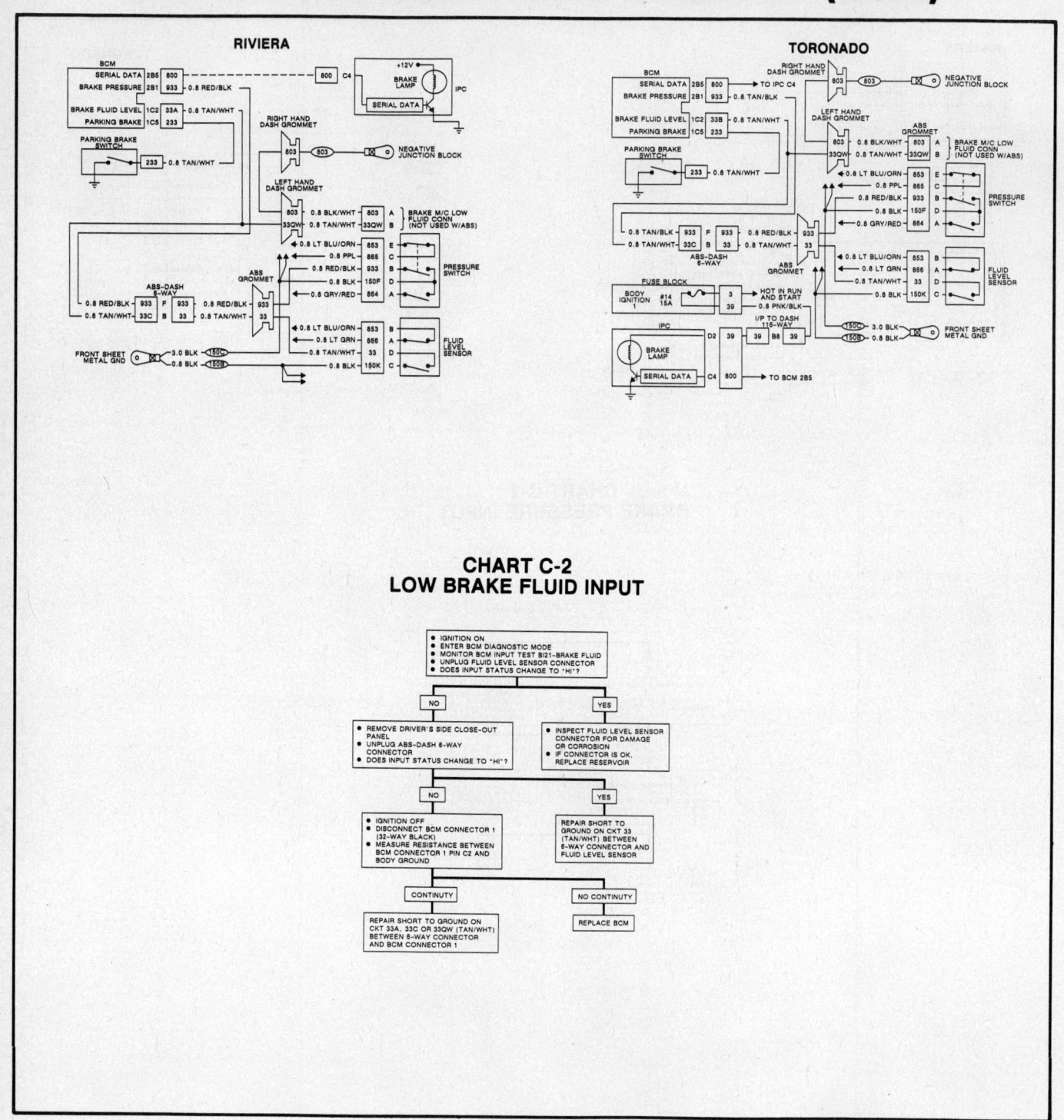

CHART C-2
LOW BRAKE FLUID INPUT

Brake Systems
TEVES ANTI-LOCK BRAKE SYSTEMS (ABS)
GM WITH BCM & ELDORADO & SEVILLE (Cont.)

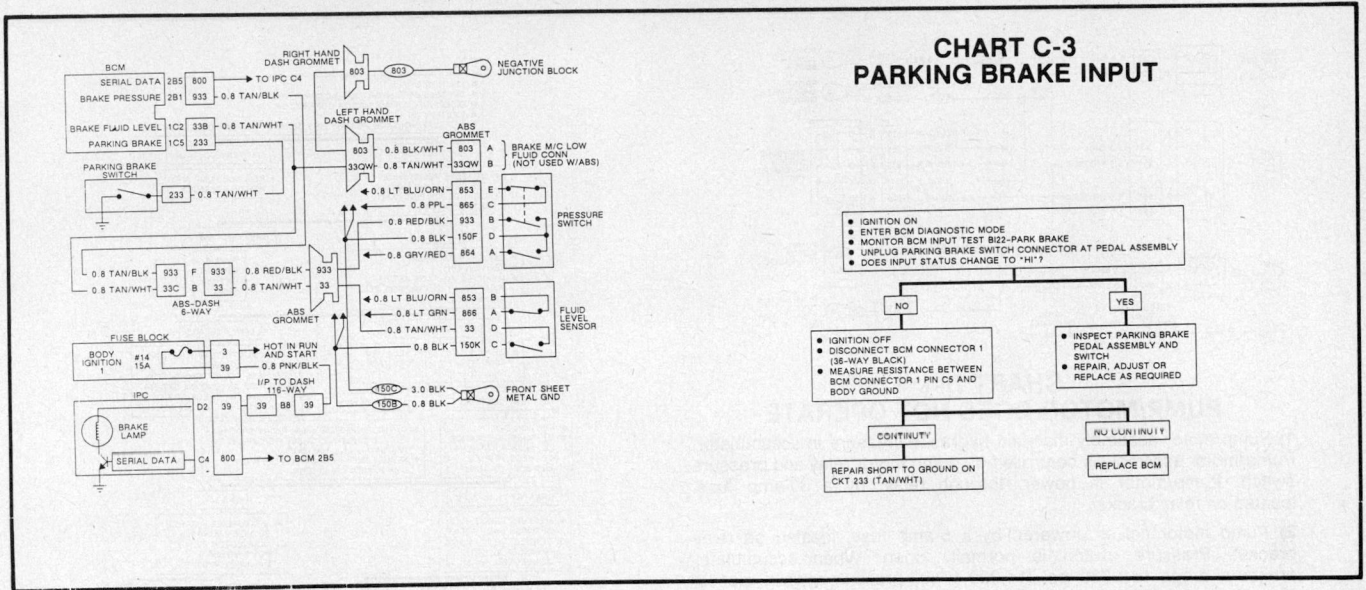

CHART C-3
PARKING BRAKE INPUT

CHART D
"BRAKE" & "ANTI-LOCK" LIGHTS ON

This chart should be used as indicated in FUNCTIONAL CHECK chart. Leading problems to this condition are: low brake fluid level in hydraulic unit, false low fluid sensor reading, low accumulator pressure or false pressure switch reading.

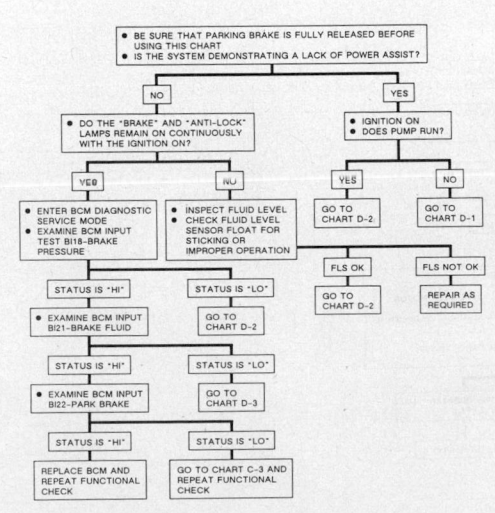

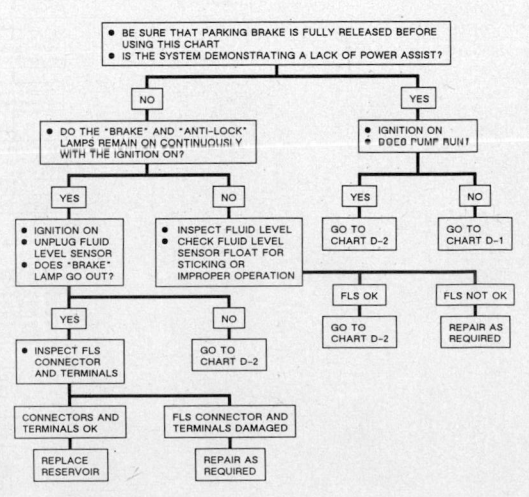

Brake Systems
TEVES ANTI-LOCK BRAKE SYSTEMS (ABS) GM WITH BCM & ELDORADO & SEVILLE (Cont.)

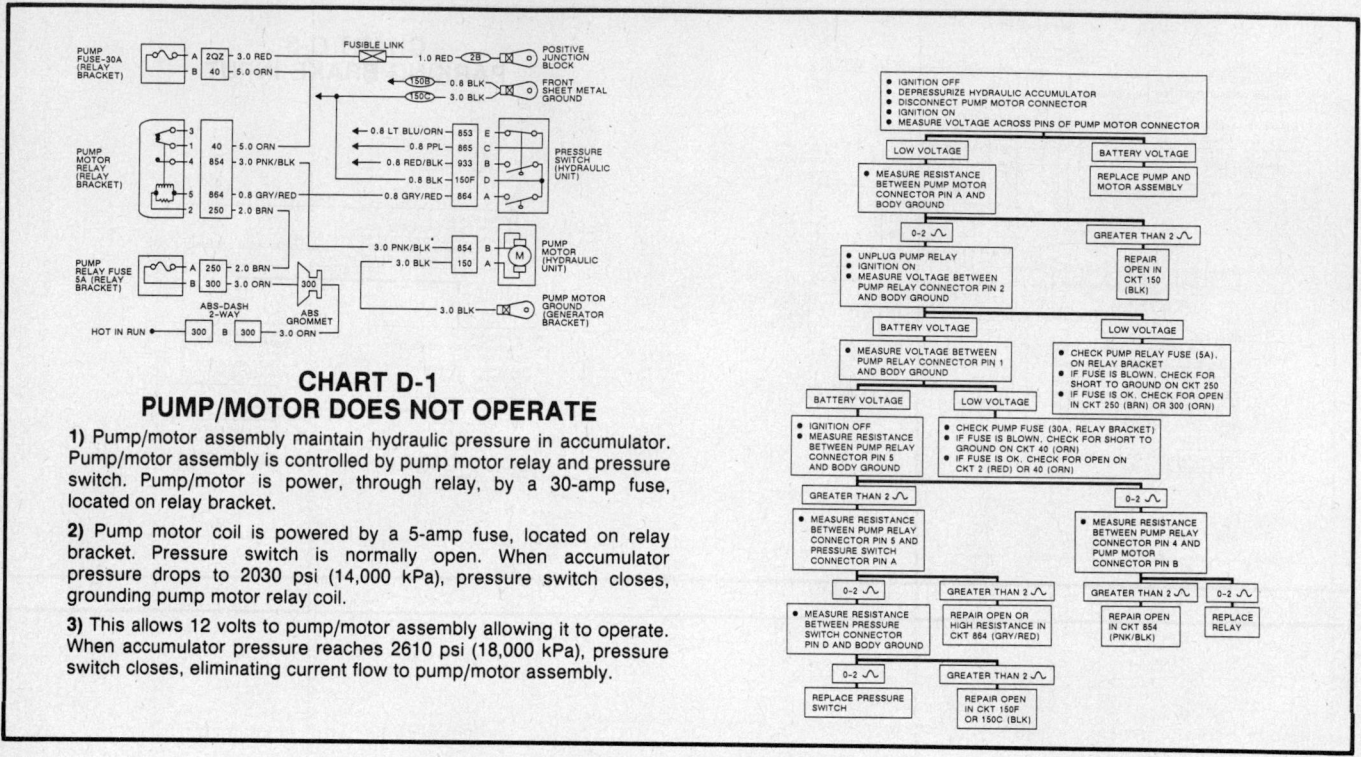

CHART D-1
PUMP/MOTOR DOES NOT OPERATE

1) Pump/motor assembly maintain hydraulic pressure in accumulator. Pump/motor assembly is controlled by pump motor relay and pressure switch. Pump/motor is power, through relay, by a 30-amp fuse, located on relay bracket.

2) Pump motor coil is powered by a 5-amp fuse, located on relay bracket. Pressure switch is normally open. When accumulator pressure drops to 2030 psi (14,000 kPa), pressure switch closes, grounding pump motor relay coil.

3) This allows 12 volts to pump/motor assembly allowing it to operate. When accumulator pressure reaches 2610 psi (18,000 kPa), pressure switch closes, eliminating current flow to pump/motor assembly.

CHART D-2
HYDRAULIC UNIT FUNCTIONAL CHECK

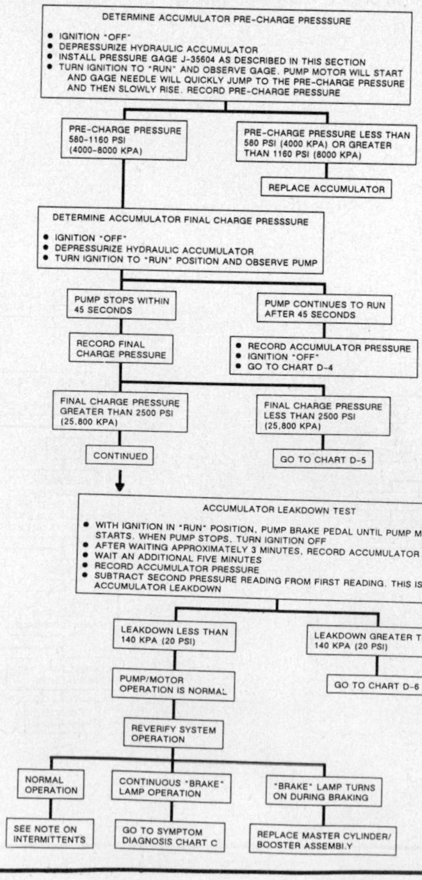

DETERMINE ACCUMULATOR PRE-CHARGE PRESSSURE
- IGNITION "OFF"
- DEPRESSURIZE HYDRAULIC ACCUMULATOR
- INSTALL PRESSURE GAGE J-35604 AS DESCRIBED IN THIS SECTION
- TURN IGNITION TO "RUN" AND OBSERVE GAGE. PUMP MOTOR WILL START AND GAGE NEEDLE WILL QUICKLY JUMP TO THE PRE-CHARGE PRESSURE AND THEN SLOWLY RISE. RECORD PRE-CHARGE PRESSURE

- PRE-CHARGE PRESSURE 580-1160 PSI (4000-8000 KPA)
- PRE-CHARGE PRESSURE LESS THAN 580 PSI (4000 KPA) OR GREATER THAN 1160 PSI (8000 KPA) → REPLACE ACCUMULATOR

DETERMINE ACCUMULATOR FINAL CHARGE PRESSSURE
- IGNITION "OFF"
- DEPRESSURIZE HYDRAULIC ACCUMULATOR
- TURN IGNITION TO "RUN" POSITION AND OBSERVE PUMP

- PUMP STOPS WITHIN 45 SECONDS → RECORD FINAL CHARGE PRESSURE
- PUMP CONTINUES TO RUN AFTER 45 SECONDS → RECORD ACCUMULATOR PRESSURE / IGNITION "OFF" / GO TO CHART D-4

- FINAL CHARGE PRESSURE GREATER THAN 2500 PSI (25.800 KPA) → CONTINUED
- FINAL CHARGE PRESSURE LESS THAN 2500 PSI (25.800 KPA) → GO TO CHART D-5

ACCUMULATOR LEAKDOWN TEST
- WITH IGNITION IN "RUN" POSITION, PUMP BRAKE PEDAL UNTIL PUMP MOTOR STARTS. WHEN PUMP STOPS, TURN IGNITION OFF
- AFTER WAITING APPROXIMATELY 3 MINUTES, RECORD ACCUMULATOR PRESSURE
- WAIT AN ADDITIONAL FIVE MINUTES
- RECORD ACCUMULATOR PRESSURE
- SUBTRACT SECOND PRESSURE READING FROM FIRST READING. THIS IS ACCUMULATOR LEAKDOWN

- LEAKDOWN LESS THAN 140 KPA (20 PSI) → PUMP/MOTOR OPERATION IS NORMAL
- LEAKDOWN GREATER THAN 140 KPA (20 PSI) → GO TO CHART D-6

REVERIFY SYSTEM OPERATION
- NORMAL OPERATION → SEE NOTE ON INTERMITTENTS
- CONTINUOUS "BRAKE" LAMP OPERATION → GO TO SYMPTOM DIAGNOSIS CHART C
- "BRAKE" LAMP TURNS ON DURING BRAKING → REPLACE MASTER CYLINDER/BOOSTER ASSEMBLY

Brake Systems
TEVES ANTI-LOCK BRAKE SYSTEMS (ABS)
GM WITH BCM & ELDORADO & SEVILLE (Cont.)

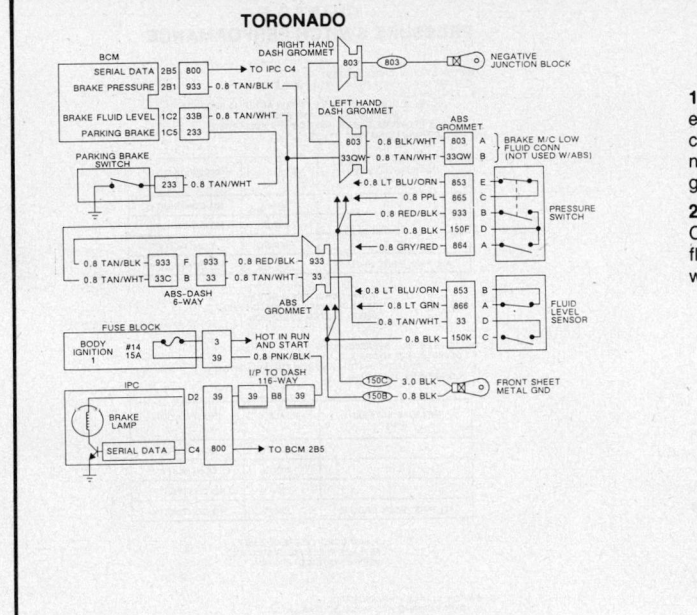

TORONADO

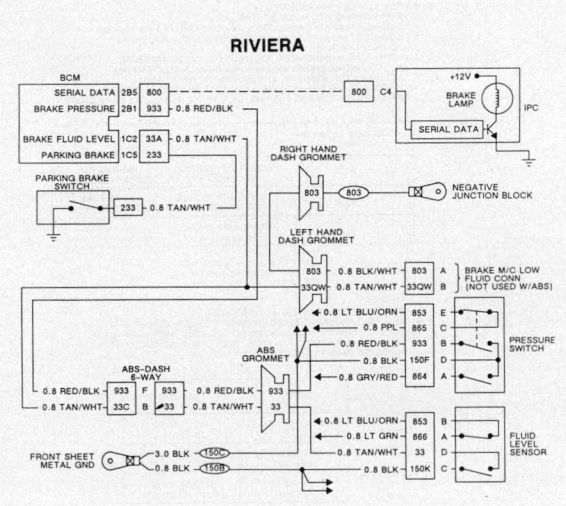

RIVIERA

CHART D-3
FLUID LEVEL SENSOR

1) Fluid level sensor consists of reed switch and float. There are 2 electrically independent switches inside sensor. Fluid level sensor can cause "BRAKE" or "ANTI-LOCK" light to come on. One switch is normally open. When fluid level is low, switch closes and circuit is grounded.

2) BCM receives this grounded signal and activates "BRAKE" light. Other switch, for EBCM, is normally closed and is part of low fluid/pressure loop. When fluid level is low, switch opens, sending a warning input to EBCM. EBCM then will turn on "ANTI-LOCK" light.

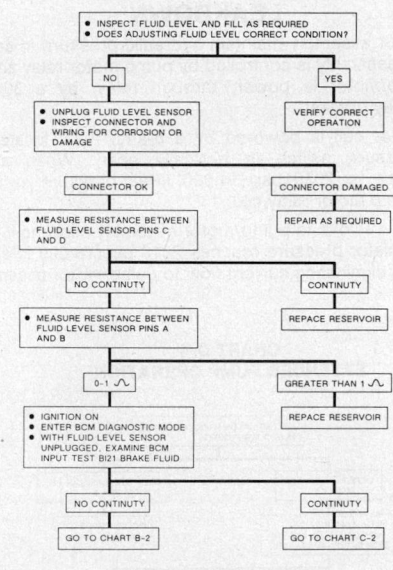

Brake Systems

TEVES ANTI-LOCK BRAKE SYSTEMS (ABS) GM WITH BCM & ELDORADO & SEVILLE (Cont.)

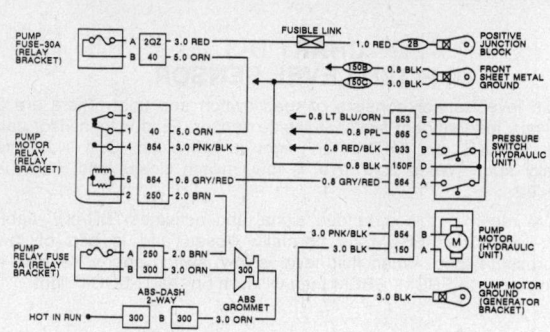

CHARTS D-4, D-5 & D-6
EXTENDED PUMP OPERATION & HYDRAULIC LEAKDOWN

1) Pump/motor assembly maintain hydraulic pressure in accumulator. Pump/motor assembly is controlled by pump motor relay and pressure switch. Pump/motor is power, through relay, by a 30-amp fuse, located on relay bracket.

2) Pump motor coil is powered by a 5-amp fuse, located on relay bracket. Pressure switch is normally open. When accumulator pressure drops to 2030 psi (14,000 kPa), pressure switch closes, grounding pump motor relay coil.

3) This allows 12 volts to pump/motor assembly allowing it to operate. When accumulator pressure reaches 2610 psi (18,000 kPa), pressure switch closes, eliminating current flow to pump/motor assembly.

CHART D-4
EXTENDED PUMP OPERATION

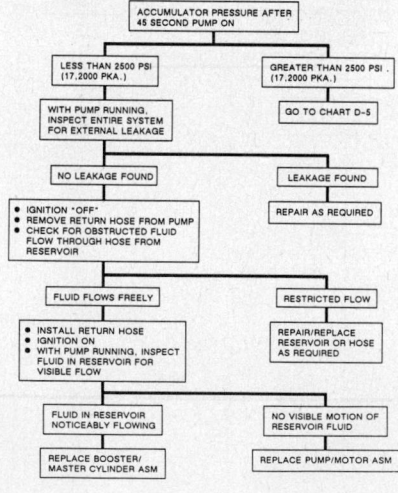

CHART D-5
PRESSURE SWITCH PERFORMANCE

I. SWITCH STATUS - PRESSURIZED
- TURN IGNITION TO "RUN" UNTIL PUMP STOPS
- IGNITION "OFF"
  NOTE: IF PUMP CONTINUES TO RUN AFTER 45 SECONDS, TURN IGNITION OFF AND PROCEDE
- CHECK PRESSURE SWITCH PINS FOR THE FOLLOWING CONDITIONS USING VOM

MEASURE BETWEEN PINS	SCALE	SPECIFICATION
B, D	200 Ω	NO CONTINUITY
A, D	200 Ω	NO CONTINUITY
C, E	200 Ω	CONTINUITY
ALL PINS, BODY GROUND	200 Ω	NO CONTINUITY

IF ANY CONDITION IS NOT MET, REPLACE PRESSURE SWITCH AND VERIFY SYSTEM OPERATION

II. SWITCH STATUS - DEPRESSURIZED
- DEPRESSURIZE HYDRAULIC ACCUMULATOR
- CHECK PRESSURE SWITCH PINS FOR THE FOLLOWING CONDITIONS USING VOM

MEASURE BETWEEN PINS	SCALE	SPECIFICATION
B, D	200 Ω	CONTINUITY
A, D	200 Ω	CONTINUITY
C, E	200 Ω	NO CONTINUITY
ALL PINS, BODY GROUND	200 Ω	NO CONTINUITY

IF ANY CONDITION IS NOT MET, REPLACE PRESSURE SWITCH AND VERIFY SYSTEM OPERATION

III. SWITCH STATUS - PRESSURIZED
- DEPRESSURIZE HYDRAULIC ACCUMULATOR
- INSTALL PRESSURE GAGE J-35604 AS DESCRIBED IN THIS SECTION
- CONNECT PRESSURE SWITCH CONNECTOR AND TURN IGNITION TO "RUN" UNTIL PUMP STOPS
- USING VOM, MONITOR FOR CONTINUITY BETWEEN PRESSURE SWITCH PINS AS SHOWN BELOW WHILE SLOWLY BLEEDING OFF ACCUMULATOR PRESSURE BY PUMPING THE BRAKE PEDAL.
- PRESSURIZE SYSTEM BETWEEN EACH TEST BY RECONNECTING PRESSURE SWITCH AND TURNING IGNITION TO "RUN" UNTIL PUMP STOPS

MEASURE BETWEEN PINS	SCALE	SPECIFICATION
A, D	CONTINUITY SHOULD BE GAINED AT:	1980-2080 PSI (13,650-14,350 KPA)
B, D	CONTINUITY SHOULD BE GAINED AT:	1500-1550 PSI (10,350-10,700 KPA)
C, E	CONTINUITY SHOULD BE GAINED AT:	1500-1550 PSI (10,350-10,700 KPA)

IF ANY CONDITION IS NOT MET, REPLACE PRESSURE SWITCH AND VERIFY SYSTEM OPERATION

- DEPRESSURIZE HYDRAULIC ACCUMULATOR
- WITH IGNITION OFF, CONNECT PRESSURE SWITCH CONNECTOR
- TURN IGNITION TO "RUN" AND OBSERVE GAGE, "ANTI-LOCK" LAMP, "BRAKE" LAMP AND PUMP MOTOR. EVENTS SHOULD OCCUR AT PRESSURES INDICATED IN CHART BELOW

EVENT	PRESSURE
"ANTI-LOCK" LAMP TURN OFF	1850-1950 PSI (12,750-13,450 KPA)
"BRAKE" LAMP TURN OFF	1850-1950 PSI (12,750-13,450 KPA)
PUMP MOTOR STOPS	2550-2670 PSI (17,580-18,400 KPA)

IF ANY CONDITION IS NOT MET, REPLACE PRESSURE SWITCH AND VERIFY SYSTEM OPERATION

CHART D-6
HYDRAULIC LEAKDOWN

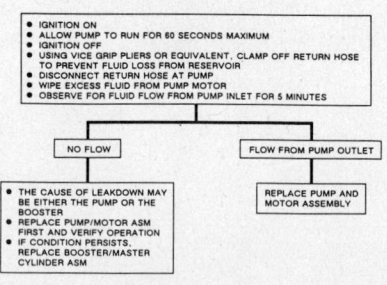

Brake Systems

TEVES ANTI-LOCK BRAKE SYSTEMS (ABS)
GM WITH BCM & ELDORADO & SEVILLE (Cont.)

CHART E
SYMPTOM DIAGNOSIS

RIVIERA

- ABS FUNCTIONAL CHECK MUST BE PERFORMED BEFORE USING THIS CHART
- IF ANY ABS TROUBLE CODES ARE SET, SEE APPROPRIATE TROUBLE CODE CHART

SYMPTOM:	GO TO:
• "ANTI-LOCK" LAMP INOPERATIVE AT KEY-ON	CHART E-1
• "BRAKE" LAMP INOPERATIVE AT KEY-ON	
• VALVE CYCLING (CHATTER) DURING NORMAL STOPS	CHART E-3
• LOW OR SPONGY BRAKE PEDAL	CHART E-4
• POOR VEHICLE TRACKING DURING ANTI-LOCK STOPS	CHART E-5

ALL OTHERS

- ABS FUNCTIONAL CHECK MUST BE PERFORMED BEFORE USING THIS CHART
- IF ANY ABS TROUBLE CODES ARE SET, SEE APPROPRIATE TROUBLE CODE CHART

SYMPTOM:	GO TO:
• "ANTI-LOCK" LAMP INOPERATIVE AT KEY-ON	CHART E-1
• "ANTI-LOCK" LAMP DIM OR INOPERATIVE DURING START	CHART E-2
• "BRAKE" LAMP INOPERATIVE AT KEY-ON	
• VALVE CYCLING (CHATTER) DURING NORMAL STOPS	CHART E-3
• LOW OR SPONGY BRAKE PEDAL	CHART E-4
• POOR VEHICLE TRACKING DURING ANTI-LOCK STOPS	CHART E-5

Brake Systems

TEVES ANTI-LOCK BRAKE SYSTEMS (ABS) GM WITH BCM & ELDORADO & SEVILLE (Cont.)

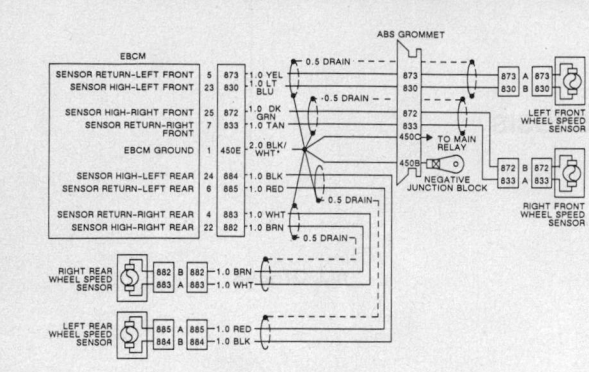

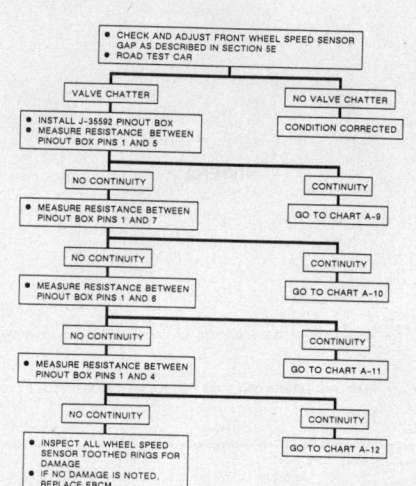

CHART E-3
VALVE CYCLING DURING NORMAL STOPS

1) This chart should be used as indicated by FUNCTIONING CHECK chart. If valve is heard cycling during normal braking, possible cause is an erroneous wheel sensor signal.

2) Low wheel sensor signal can be mistaken by EBCM, as wheel lock-up. EBCM will then engage ABS and signal valve to reduce pressure to wheels. This condition can occur without EBCM setting a trouble code.

CHART E-4
LOW OR SPONGY PEDAL

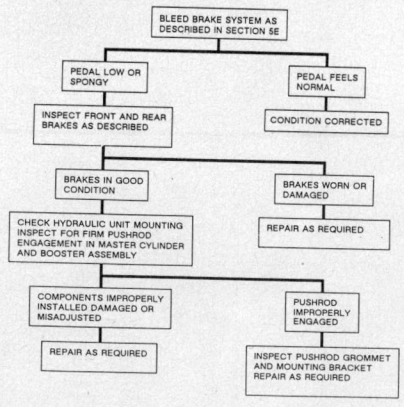

CHART E-5
POOR VEHICLE TRACKING DURING ABS OPERATION

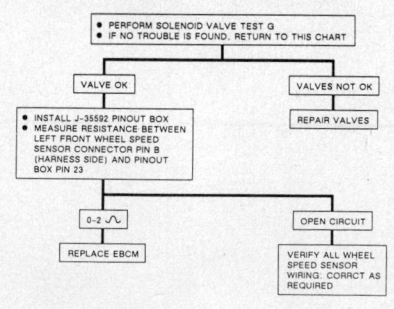

• IF CONDITION IS STILL NOT CORRECTED, REPLACE BOOSTER/MASTER CYLINDER ASM

Brake Systems

TEVES ANTI-LOCK BRAKE SYSTEMS (ABS) GM WITH BCM & ELDORADO & SEVILLE (Cont.)

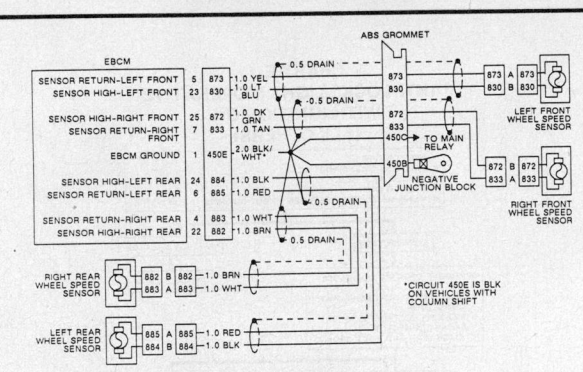

CHARTS F THROUGH F-4 WHEEL SENSOR OUTPUT

1) Wheel sensor consists of a permanent magnet and coil. Each time toothed sensor ring passes sensor, an AC current is sent to EBCM. The EBCM uses this information to calculate individual wheel speed.

2) Low wheel sensor output is normally caused by improper gap or mounting. If wheel sensor output drops lower than 50 mV, ABS can no longer function properly.

CHART F
WHEEL SENSOR OUTPUT

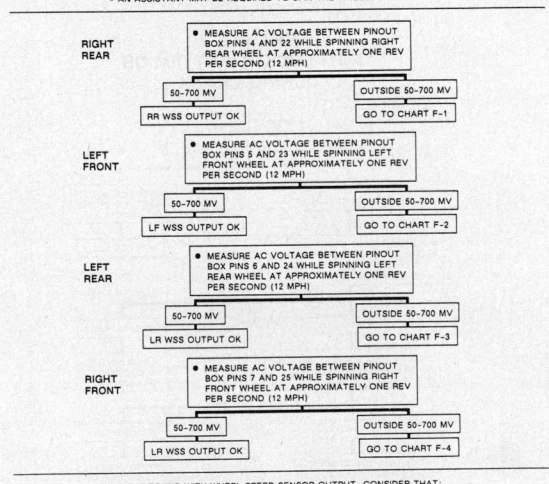

IF NO TROUBLE IS FOUND WITH WHEEL SPEED SENSOR OUTPUT, CONSIDER THAT:
- OUTPUT SHOULD NOT BE SIGNIFICANTLY DIFFERENT FROM LF TO RF AND LR TO RR
- FRONT WSS OUTPUT SHOULD BE SLIGHTLY HIGHER THAN REAR WSS OUTPUT
- IMPROPER OUTPUT MAY BE CAUSD BY MIS-ADJUSTED FRONT SENSOR
- WHEEL SPEED SENSOR CABLES SOMETIMES CAN INTERMITTENTLY GO OPEN, PARTICULARLY IN THE WHEELHOUSE AREA. MANIPULATE THE CABLES BY HAND WHEN INSPECTING FOR AN OPEN CIRCUIT
- TOOTHED SENSOR RINGS SHOULD ALSO BE INSPECTED FOR DAMAGE OR MISSING TEETH

CHART F-1
RR WHEEL SENSOR OUTPUT

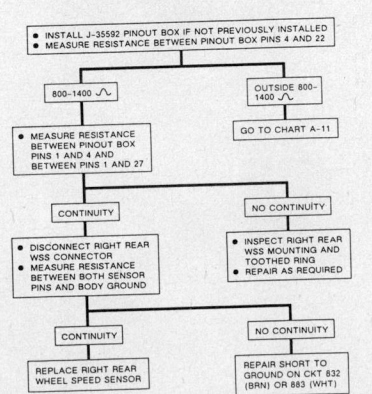

CHART F-2
LF WHEEL SENSOR OUTPUT

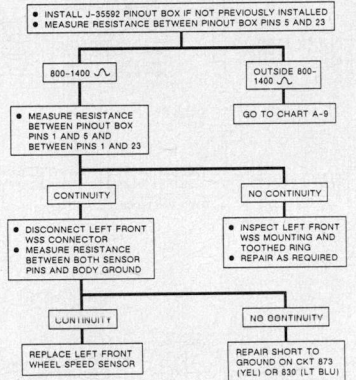

CHART F-3
LR WHEEL SENSOR OUTPUT

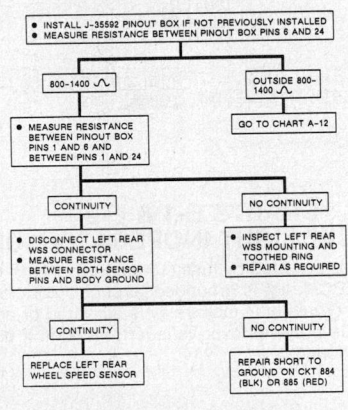

CHART F-4
RF WHEEL SENSOR OUTPUT

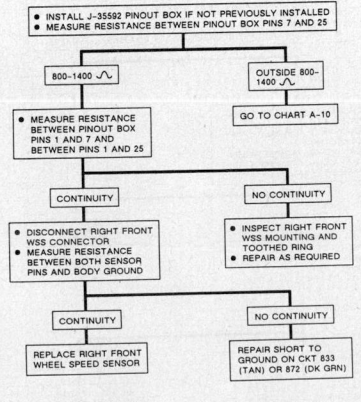

Brake Systems
TEVES ANTI-LOCK BRAKE SYSTEMS (ABS)
GM WITH BCM & ELDORADO & SEVILLE (Cont.)

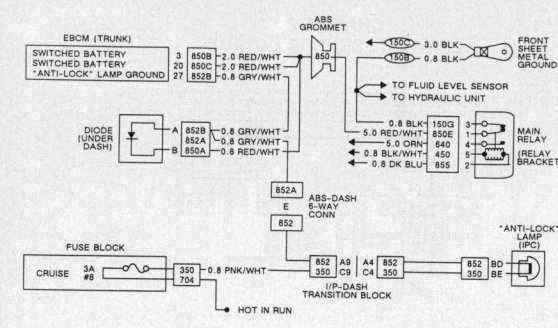

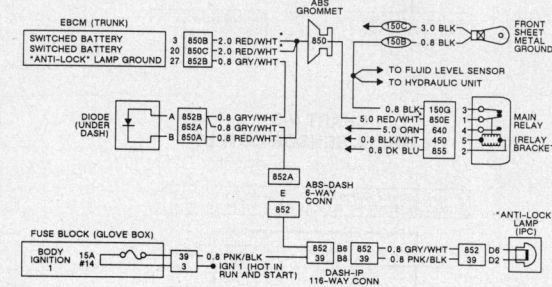

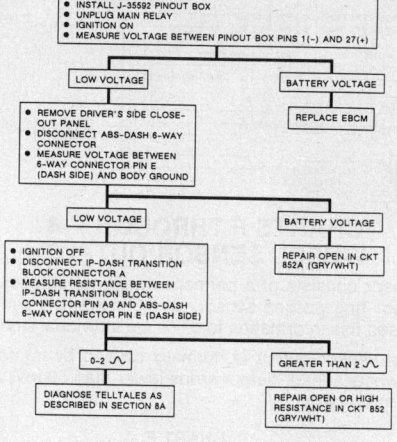

CHARTS E-1 & E-2
"ANTI-LOCK" LIGHT INOPERATIVE OR DIM

"ANTI-LOCK" light is powered by fuse (15-amp) No. 14. If main relay is not activated by EBCM, ligt is grounded through ABS diode, at main relay. Light is also grounded if main relay is activated or not by EBCM at pin No. 27. Diode prevents over-voltage from light. If diode shorts, code 61 should be found.

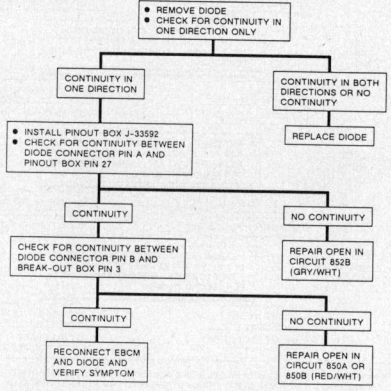

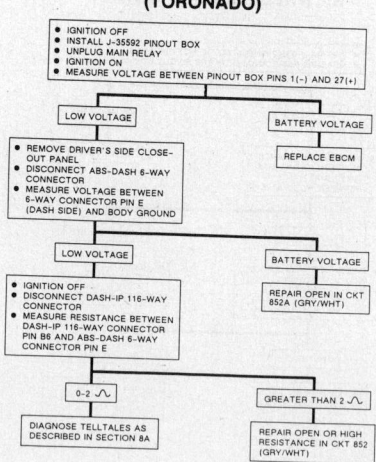

TEVES ANTI-LOCK BRAKE SYSTEMS (ABS)
GM WITH BCM & ELDORADO & SEVILLE (Cont.)

CHART G
SOLENOID VALVES

1) Inlet valves is normally open. EBCM applies 12 volts, through pins No. 15 (RF), No. 17 (Rear) and No. 35 (LF) to close each valve. Valves are closed for short periods to increase or decrease hydraulic pressure. Outlet valves are normally closed.

2) EBCM opens valve by applying 12 volts to pins No. 34 (RF), No. 33 (Rear) and No. 16 (LF) to open valves. Valves are open for a short period of time to increase or decrease pressure.

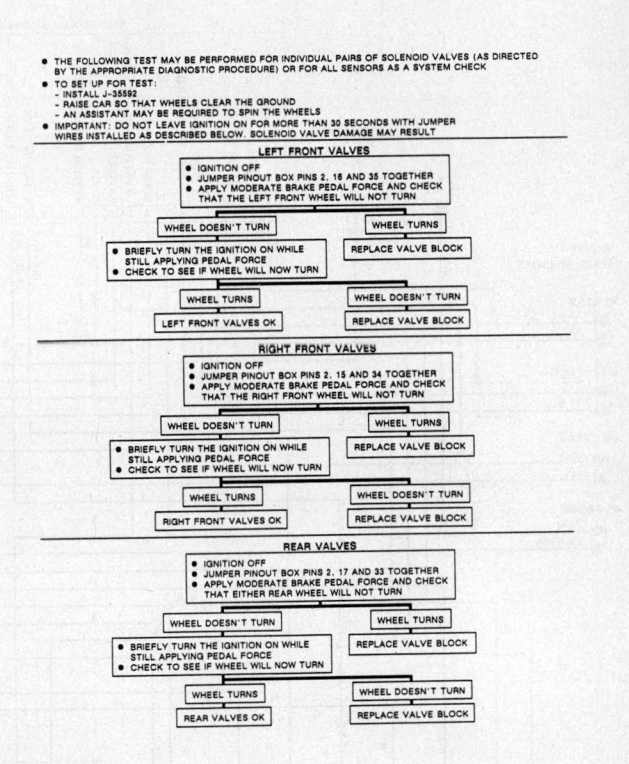

Brake Systems
TEVES ANTI-LOCK BRAKE SYSTEMS (ABS) GM WITH BCM & ELDORADO & SEVILLE (Cont.)

Fig. 4: *Teves Anti-Lock Brake System Wiring Diagram (Eldorado & Seville)*

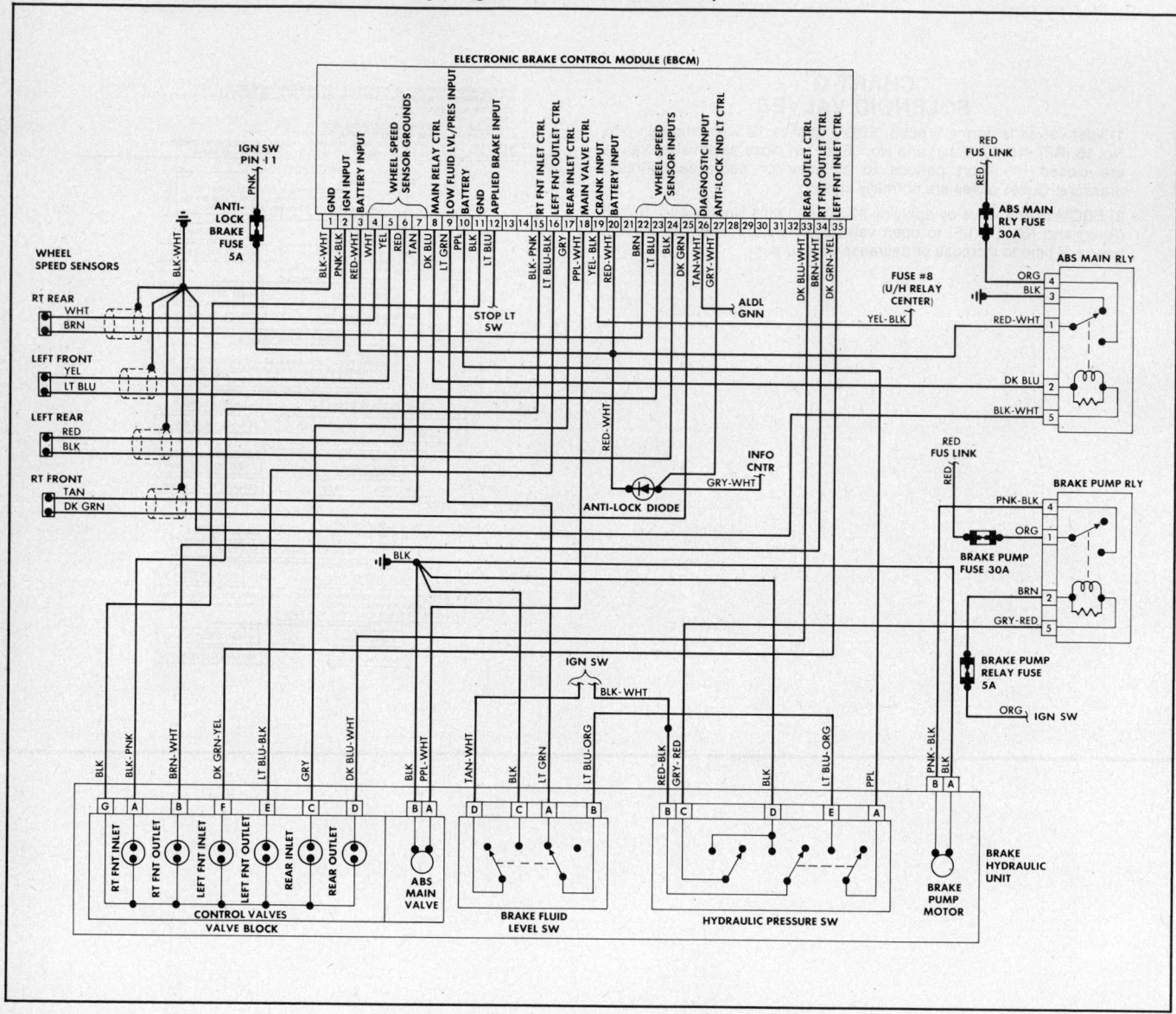

TEVES ANTI-LOCK BRAKE SYSTEMS (ABS) GM WITH BCM & ELDORADO & SEVILLE (Cont.)

Fig. 5: Teves Anti-Lock Brake System Wiring Diagram (Riviera & Toronado)

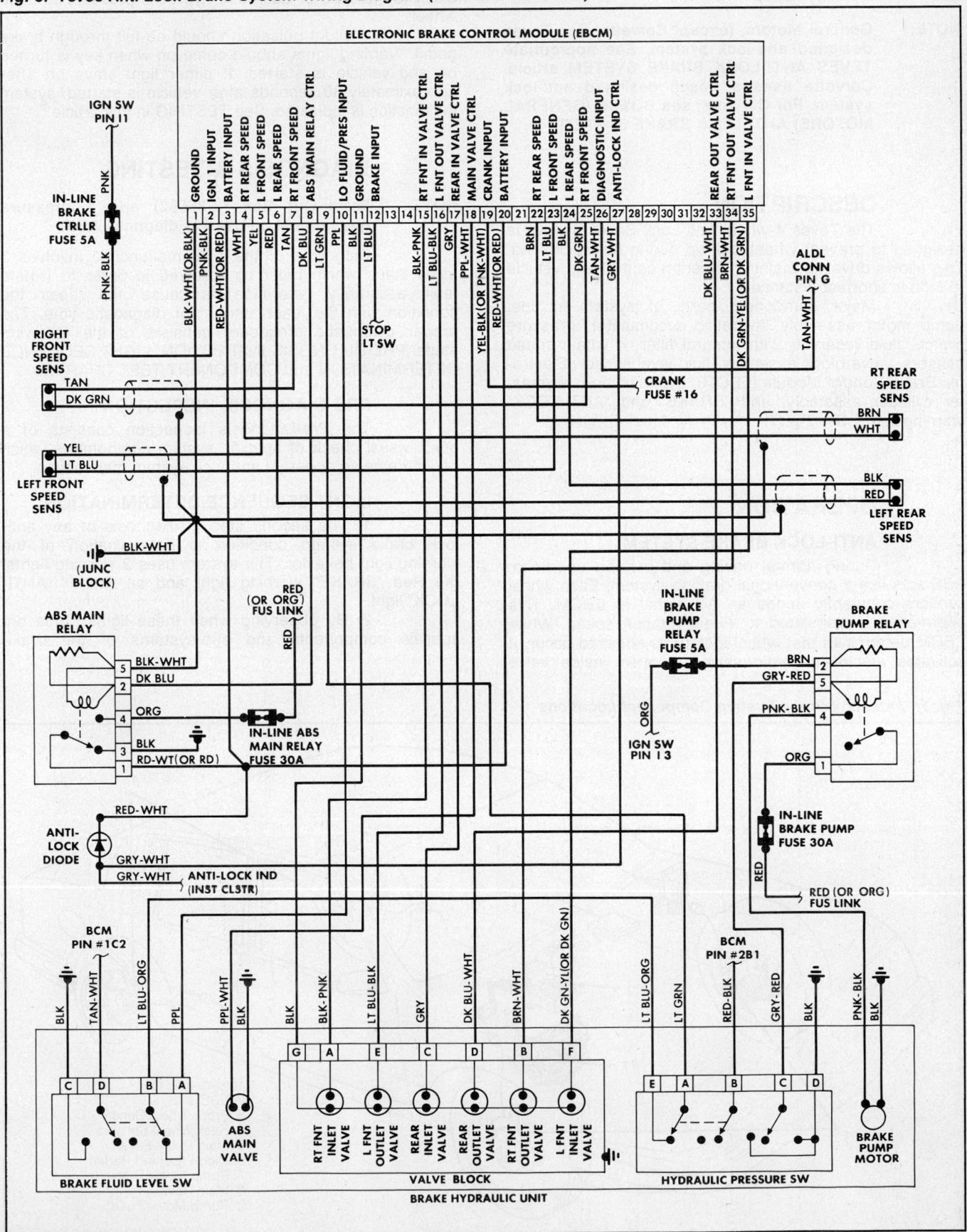

Brake Systems

TEVES ANTI-LOCK BRAKE SYSTEMS (ABS)
GENERAL MOTORS – PONTIAC 6000

Pontiac: 6000

NOTE: General Motors, (except Corvette) use Teves designed anti-lock system. See appropriate TEVES ANTI-LOCK BRAKE SYSTEM article. Corvette uses a Bosch designed anti-lock system. For Corvette, see BOSCH (GENERAL MOTORS) ANTI-LOCK BRAKE SYSTEM.

DESCRIPTION

The Teves 4-wheel Anti-Lock Brake System is designed to prevent wheel lock-up during heavy braking. This allows driver to maintain steering control and vehicle to stop in shortest distance.

Major component parts of system include: pump motor assembly, hydraulic accumulator, pressure switch, fluid reservoir with integral filter, 4 wheel speed sensors, valve block assembly, fluid level sensor, Electronic Brake Control Module (EBCM), hydraulic booster/master cylinder assembly, and "BRAKE" and "ANTI-LOCK" warning lights. *See Fig. 1.*

OPERATION

ANTI-LOCK BRAKE SYSTEM

During normal driving and braking opertions, ABS acts like a conventional braking system. Each wheel sensors constantly sends an AC signal to EBCM. This information is translated to wheel rotation speed. When EBCM determines that wheel lock-up is about to occur, it activates electro-magnetic valves, located inside valve block to increase or decrease hydraulic pressure to each wheel.

A slight pulsation should be felt through brake pedal. Warning lights should come on when key is turned on and vehicle is started. If either light stays on after approximately 30 seconds after vehicle is started, system malfunction is indicated. See TESTING in this article.

DIAGNOSIS & TESTING

NOTE: Break-Out Box (J-35592) and a pressure gauge must be used to diagnose ABS.

Diagnosis of the ABS malfunction involves 3 basic steps which must be followed in order to isolate fault, accurately determine its cause and repair the condition with the least amount of diagnostic time. The proper diagnostic procedure consists of the following steps: PRE-DIAGNOSIS INSPECTION, LIGHT SEQUENCE DETERMINATION and COMPONENT TEST CHARTS.

PRE-DIAGNOSIS INSPECTION

The Pre-Diagnosis Inspection consists of a quick visual check of specific system components which could create an apparent anti-lock system malfunction.

LIGHT SEQUENCE DETERMINATION

1) The second step in diagnosis of any anti-lock brake system condition is determination of the warning light behavior. The system uses 2 warning lights, the Red "BRAKE" warning light and an Amber "ANTI-LOCK" light.

2) By observing when these lights come on, specific components and sub-systems of the brake

Fig. 1: *Anti-Lock Brake System Component Locations*

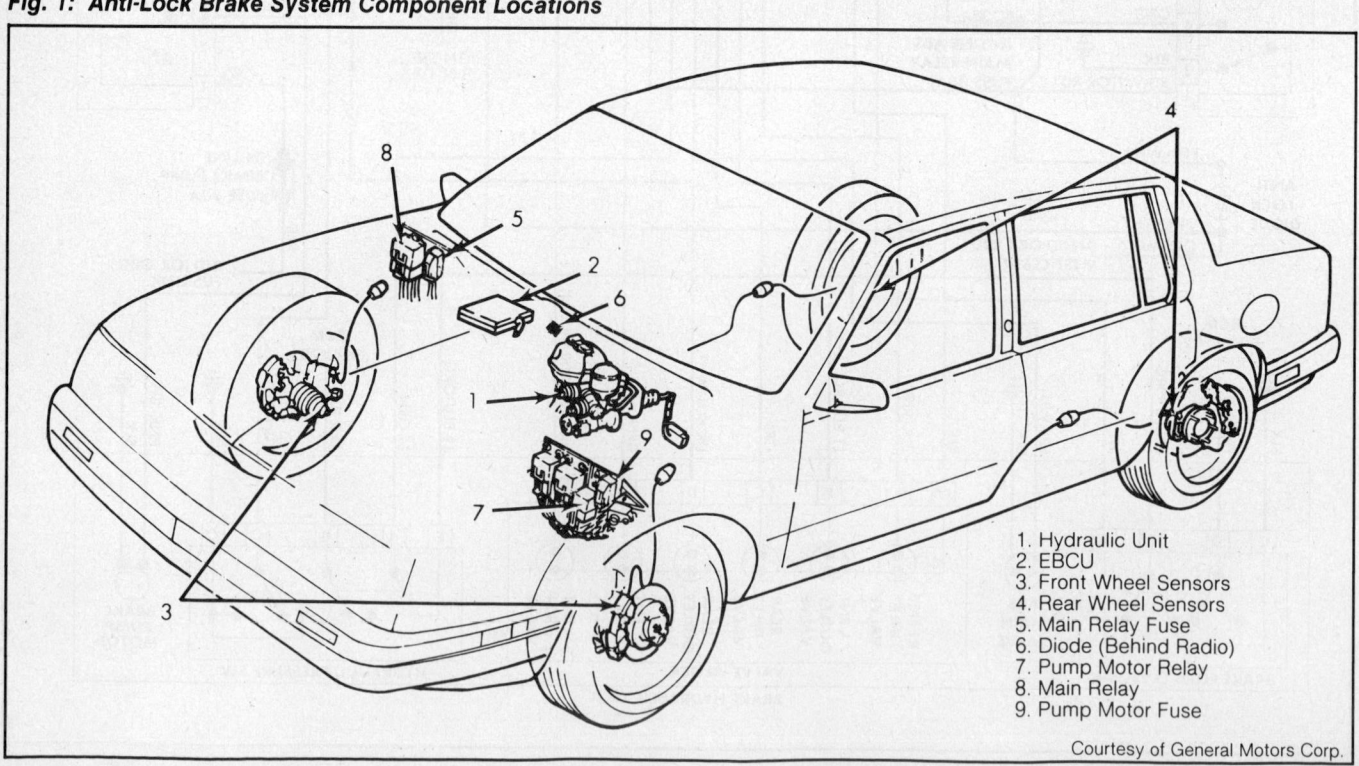

1. Hydraulic Unit
2. EBCU
3. Front Wheel Sensors
4. Rear Wheel Sensors
5. Main Relay Fuse
6. Diode (Behind Radio)
7. Pump Motor Relay
8. Main Relay
9. Pump Motor Fuse

Courtesy of General Motors Corp.

TEVES ANTI-LOCK BRAKE SYSTEMS (ABS)
GENERAL MOTORS — PONTIAC 6000 (Cont.)

system may be isolated as likely causes of a system malfunction.

3) Each light sequence illustration is divided into 7 areas which represent vehicle status. Behavior of "BRAKE" and "ANTI-LOCK" lights represented in horizontal rows below vehicle status headers. *See Fig. 2.*

4) "BRAKE" and "ANTI-LOCK" light status is indicated by shaded areas in horizontal rows below each vehicle status header. A vehicle status block which is not entirely shaded means that light is on only for part of the test period.

LIGHT SEQUENCE TEST PROCEDURE

1) Determine customer complaint as accurately as possible. If reduced braking ability is described, use caution in evaluating vehicle.

2) Turn ignition off for a minimum of 15 seconds. Turn ignition on and observe "BRAKE" and "ANTI-LOCK" lights. If accumulator has been discharged, both lights may remain on for approximately 30 seconds. If this occurs, allow lights to turn off and turn ignition off for another 15 seconds. If lights do not go out within 30 seconds, proceed to step **5)**.

3) Turn ignition on and observe warning lights. At this time, "BRAKE" light should remain off. "ANTI-LOCK" light should come on for 3 to 6 seconds and then go out.

4) Turn ignition switch to "START" position and observe warning lights. Both warning lights should illuminate while ignition switch is in "START" position.

5) When engine starts, release key to "RUN" position and observe warning lights. "BRAKE" light should turn off immediately. "ANTI-LOCK" light should remain on for 3 to 6 seconds and then go off.

6) Drive vehicle at a minimum speed of 20 mph for a short period of time and observe warning lights. Both lights should remain off for this step and remainder of test. Note as accurately as possible the conditions under which either light comes on.

7) Stop vehicle using a normal brake application. Both lights should remain off. Place transaxle in Park and allow vehicle to idle for a few seconds. Observe warning lights. Both should remain off.

8) From information obtained in test above, determine light sequence and/or symptom which most closely matches behavior of complaint and perform indicated tests.

NOTE ON INTERMITTENTS

The diagnostic procedures in this section may or may not be helpful in determining cause of intermittent problems in anti-lock brake system electrical components. Fault must be present to locate problem effectively using TEST "A" PIN-OUT CHECKS and trouble charts.

A light sequence description from vehicle owner can be helpful in locating a likely component or circuit in case of an intermittent failure. Use LIGHT SEQUENCE CHART if a good description of light behavior can be obtained. *See Fig. 2.*

On all models, most intermittent problems are caused by faulty electical connections or wiring. When an intermittent failure is encountered, check suspect circuits for:
- Poor mating or connector halves or terminals not fully seated in connector body (backed out).

- Improperly formed or damaged terminals. All connector terminals in a problem circuit should be carefully reformed to increase contact tension.
- Poor terminal-to-wire connection. Requires removing terminal and wire from connector body to inspect.

If visual check does not find cause of problem, operate vehicle with EBCM connected in an attempt to duplicate condition.

Circuits which could possibly cause intermittent operation of "ANTI-LOCK" light include:
- Wheel speed sensor circuits – low or intermittent output.
- Ignition enable circuit – interruption of 12-volt input.
- EBCM switch loop circuit (low fluid/low pressure sensors) – intermittent open.
- Main relay – interruption in coil or switched battery power.

INSTALLING PRESSURE GAUGE

NOTE: Before connecting pressure gauge, hydraulic accumulator must be depressurized. With ignition off, pump brake pedal a MINIMUM of 20 times using full pedal strokes. When a definite increase in pedal effort is felt, pump pedal 2 more times.

Some diagnostic procedures require that a pressure gauge be connected to the energy unit to read accumlator pressure. Use the following procedure:

1) Depressurize accumulator. Remove pressure hose fitting (banjo bolt) from pump body. Take care not to drop the 2 "O" ring seals when removing fitting.

2) Install one of the 2 "O" ring seals on pressure gauge fitting and insert gauge fitting into pressure hose coupling.

3) Install second "O" ring seal on gauge fitting on the underside of pressure hose coupling and thread gauge fitting into pump body. Tighten fitting to 15 ft. lbs. (20 N.m).

4) When removing gauge and installing pressure fitting, inspect "O" ring seals for cuts or damage. Replace any cut or damaged "O" ring seals.

REMOVAL & INSTALLATION

CAUTION: Before servicing any component which contains high pressure, It Is mandatory that hydraulic pressure in the system be discharged. With ignition off, pump brake pedal a MINIMUM of 20 times using full pedal strokes. When a definite increase in pedal effort is felt, pump pedal 2 more times.

HYDRAULIC UNIT
Removal & Installation

1) Disconnect negative battery cable. Depressurize brake system. Unplug all electrical connectors from hydraulic unit. Remove pump bolt. Move hydraulic unit aside to gain access to brake pipes. Disconnect brake lines. DO NOT allow brake fluid to come in contact with any electrical connectors.

2) From inside passenger compartment, disconnect hydraulic booster push rod from brake pedal.

Brake Systems

TEVES ANTI-LOCK BRAKE SYSTEMS (ABS)
GENERAL MOTORS — PONTIAC 6000 (Cont.)

Fig. 2: Lamp Sequence Chart

LAMP SEQUENCE CHART

WARNING LAMP SEQUENCE	SYMPTOM DESCRIPTION	SEE FIGURE

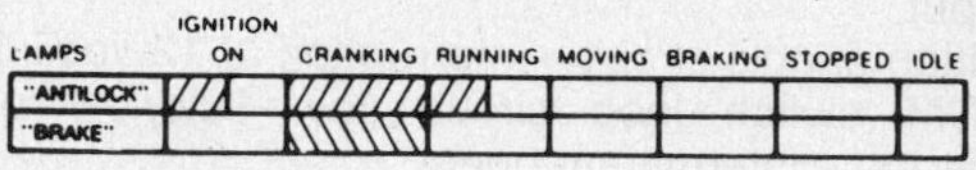	NORMAL WARNING LAMP SEQUENCE WITH
	– EXCESSIVE PEDAL TRAVEL OR SPONGY PEDAL
	– ANTI-LOCK BRAKING OPERATION OR
	   VALVE CYCLING DURING NORMAL STOPS
	   ON DRY PAVEMENT
	– POOR VEHICLE TRACKING DURING
	   ANTI-LOCK BRAKING
		21
		45
		
		59

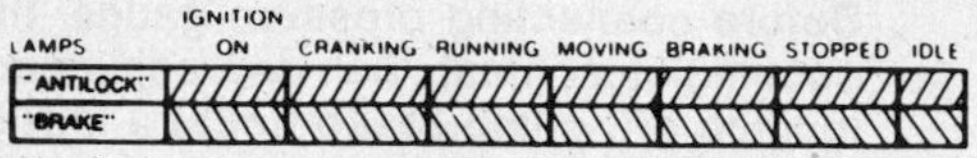	CONTINUOUS "ANTILOCK" WARNING LAMP CONTINUOUS "BRAKE" WARNING LAMP	22
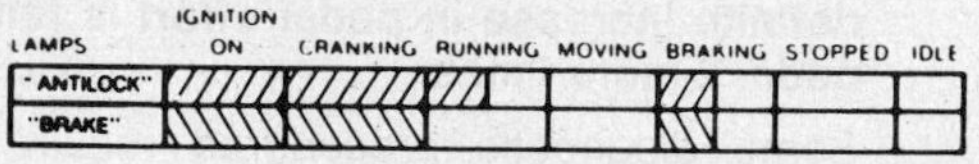	"ANTILOCK" AND "BRAKE" WARNING LAMPS COME ON WHILE BRAKING	22
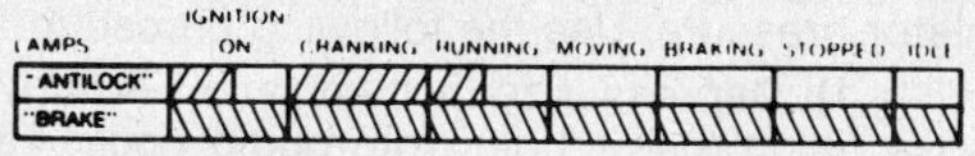	NORMAL "ANTILOCK" WARNING LAMP CONTINUOUS "BRAKE" WARNING LAMP	22
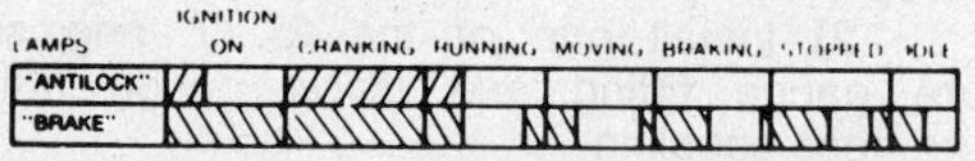	NORMAL OR CONTINUOUS "ANTILOCK" WARNING LAMP FLASHING "BRAKE" WARNING LAMP	22
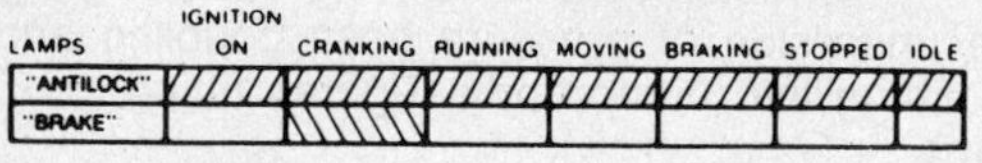	CONTINUOUS "ANTILOCK" WARNING LAMP NORMAL "BRAKE" WARNING LAMP	26
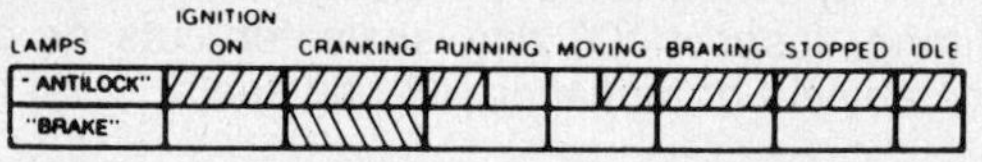	"ANTILOCK" WARNING LAMP COMES ON AFTER VEHICLE STARTS MOVING NORMAL "BRAKE" WARNING LAMP	45
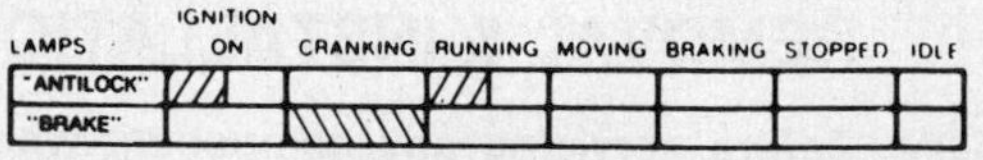	NO "ANTILOCK" WARNING LAMP WHILE CRANKING NORMAL "BRAKE" WARNING LAMP	64
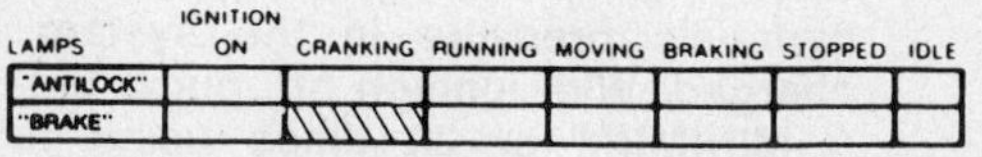	NO "ANTILOCK" WARNING LAMP NORMAL "BRAKE" WARNING LAMP	65
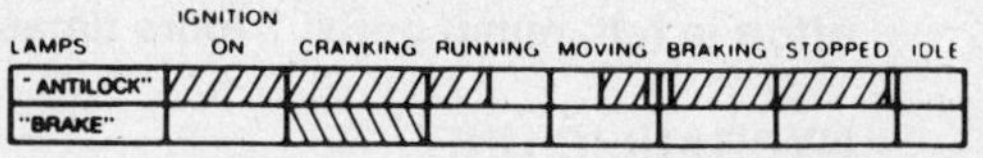	INTERMITTENT "ANTILOCK" WARNING LAMP WHILE DRIVING NORMAL "BRAKE" WARNING LAMP	66

LAMP STATUS
- SHADED AREAS: LAMP ON
- BLANK AREAS (NO SHADING): LAMP OFF
- PARTIALLY SHADED AREAS: LAMP ON FOR PART OF TEST PERIOD

Courtesy of General Motors Corp.

Brake Systems

TEVES ANTI-LOCK BRAKE SYSTEMS (ABS)
GENERAL MOTORS — PONTIAC 6000 (Cont.)

Push dust boot forward past hex on push rod. Separate push rod halves by unthreading the 2 pieces. Remove 2 bolts attaching unit to push rod bracket.

3) Remove unit. Front half of push rod will remain in hydraulic unit. *See Fig. 3*. To install, reverse removal procedure. Bleed brake system after installation of hydraulic unit. See BLEEDING BRAKE SYSTEM in this article.

HYDRAULIC ACCUMULATOR

Removal

Turn ignition off. Discharge brake system pressure. Remove hydraulic accumulator and "O" ring by turning accumulator. *See Fig. 3*. Make sure that no dirt particles fall into open port.

Installation

1) Before installing accumulator inspect "O" ring for damage and replace if necessary. Be sure "O" ring is in position on accumulator and is wet with brake fluid. Screw in accumulator. Wipe off any excess fluid.

2) Turn ignition on. Check that "BRAKE" light goes out after a maximum of one minute. Top off fluid reservoir up to "MAX" mark with a fully charged accumulator.

Fig. 3: Exploded View of Hydraulic Unit

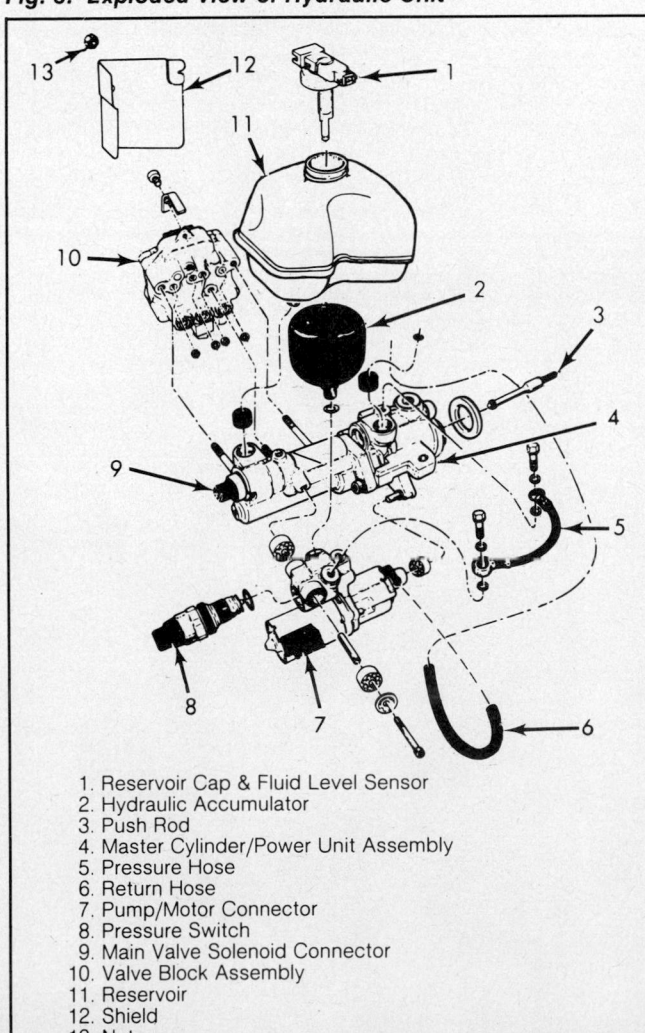

1. Reservoir Cap & Fluid Level Sensor
2. Hydraulic Accumulator
3. Push Rod
4. Master Cylinder/Power Unit Assembly
5. Pressure Hose
6. Return Hose
7. Pump/Motor Connector
8. Pressure Switch
9. Main Valve Solenoid Connector
10. Valve Block Assembly
11. Reservoir
12. Shield
13. Nut

Courtesy of General Motors Corp.

PUMP/MOTOR ASSEMBLY

Removal & Installation

1) Disconnect negative battery cable. Discharge system pressure. Unplug electrical connections at hydraulic pump motor and pressure warning switch. Remove fluid from reservoir. Unscrew hydraulic accumulator. Make sure that no dirt particles fall into open port.

2) Remove pressure line fitting at pump. Remove pressure line and "O" rings. Wire clip and pull return hose fitting out of pump body. *See Fig. 3*. Remove bolt attaching pump motor to hydraulic booster/master cylinder assembly.

3) Remove pump/motor assembly by sliding off of locating pin. To install, reverse removal procedure. Inspect "O" rings and replace if damaged. Install new grommets. Fill reservoir to "MAX" level.

VALVE BLOCK ASSEMBLY

Removal & Installation

1) Disconnect negative battery cable. Depressurize brake system. Remove fluid from reservoir. Remove hydraulic unit. Remove 3 nuts and washers.

2) Remove valve block assembly and "O" rings. To install, reverse removal procedure. Inspect "O" rings and replace if necessary. See BLEEDING BRAKE SYSTEM in this article.

PRESSURE SWITCH

Removal & Installation

1) Turn ignition off. Discharge system pressure. Disconnect negative battery cable. Disconnect electrical connector from switch.

CAUTION: **Failure to remove connector can result in damage to connector if pressure switch wrench handle should slip and strike connector.**

2) Remove pressure switch using Pressure Switch Remover (J-35804). To install, reverse removal procedure. Turn ignition on. "BRAKE" light should go out within one minute.

WHEEL SENSORS

Removal & Installation

1) On rear sensors, disconnect sensor connector in trunk area. Raise and support vehicle. Remove wheel and tire assembly. Remove sensor retaining screws. Remove sensor.

2) On front sensors, disconnect sensor connector located near shock tower. Remove sensor retaining screw. Remove sensor. To install front or rear sensor, reverse removal procedure.

3) Adjust sensor air gap to specification. See WHEEL SENSOR AIR GAP table in this article. Ensure sensor wiring is routed correctly as to avoid contact with suspension components.

WHEEL SENSOR AIR GAP

Application	In. (mm)
6000	.028 (.71)

Brake Systems

TEVES ANTI-LOCK BRAKE SYSTEMS (ABS)
GENERAL MOTORS — PONTIAC 6000 (Cont.)

BLEEDING BRAKE SYSTEM

NOTE: Use only Dot 3 brake fluid. Use of Dot 5 silicone fluid is NOT recommended. Internal damage to pump components may result.

FRONT BRAKES

The front brakes can be bled in conventional manner or by pressure bleeding. The manufacturer recommends pressure bleeding front brakes with a minimum of 20 psi (1.4 kg/cm²).

Bleeding Front Brakes With Pressure Bleeder

1) Bleed front brakes only when rear brakes have been bled first. Remove reservoir cap. Attach Bleeder Adapter (J-35798) to reservoir. Attach bleeding equipment and pressurize system to 20 psi (1.4 kg/cm²).

2) Attach a bleeder hose to one front bleeder valve and submerge other end of hose in a container of clean brake fluid. Open bleeder valve. Allow fluid to flow until no air is seen coming out end of hose. Close bleeder valve. Repeat procedure for other front brake. Fill reservoir to maximum level with a fully charged accumulator.

REAR BRAKES

Bleeding the rear brakes requires a fully charged accumulator. The manufacturer does NOT recommend bleeding rear brakes by using a pressure bleeder.

CAUTION: Care must be exercised when opening rear caliper bleeder screws, due to extremely high pressure available from a fully charged accumulator at bleeder screws.

Bleeding Rear Brakes With Fully Charged Accumulator

1) Turn ignition on. Allow system to become fully charged. Pump motor will stop when system is fully charged. Attach a bleeder hose to one rear bleeder valve and submerge other end of hose in a container of clean brake fluid. Open bleeder valve.

2) With ignition on, slightly depress brake pedal for at least 10 seconds. Continue procedure until there is no more air coming out of hose. Repeat procedure for other rear brake. Fill reservoir to maximum level with a fully charged accumulator.

Brake Systems

TEVES ANTI-LOCK BRAKE SYSTEMS (ABS)
GENERAL MOTORS — PONTIAC 6000 (Cont.)

Fig. 4: Anti-Lock Brake System Testing Circuit

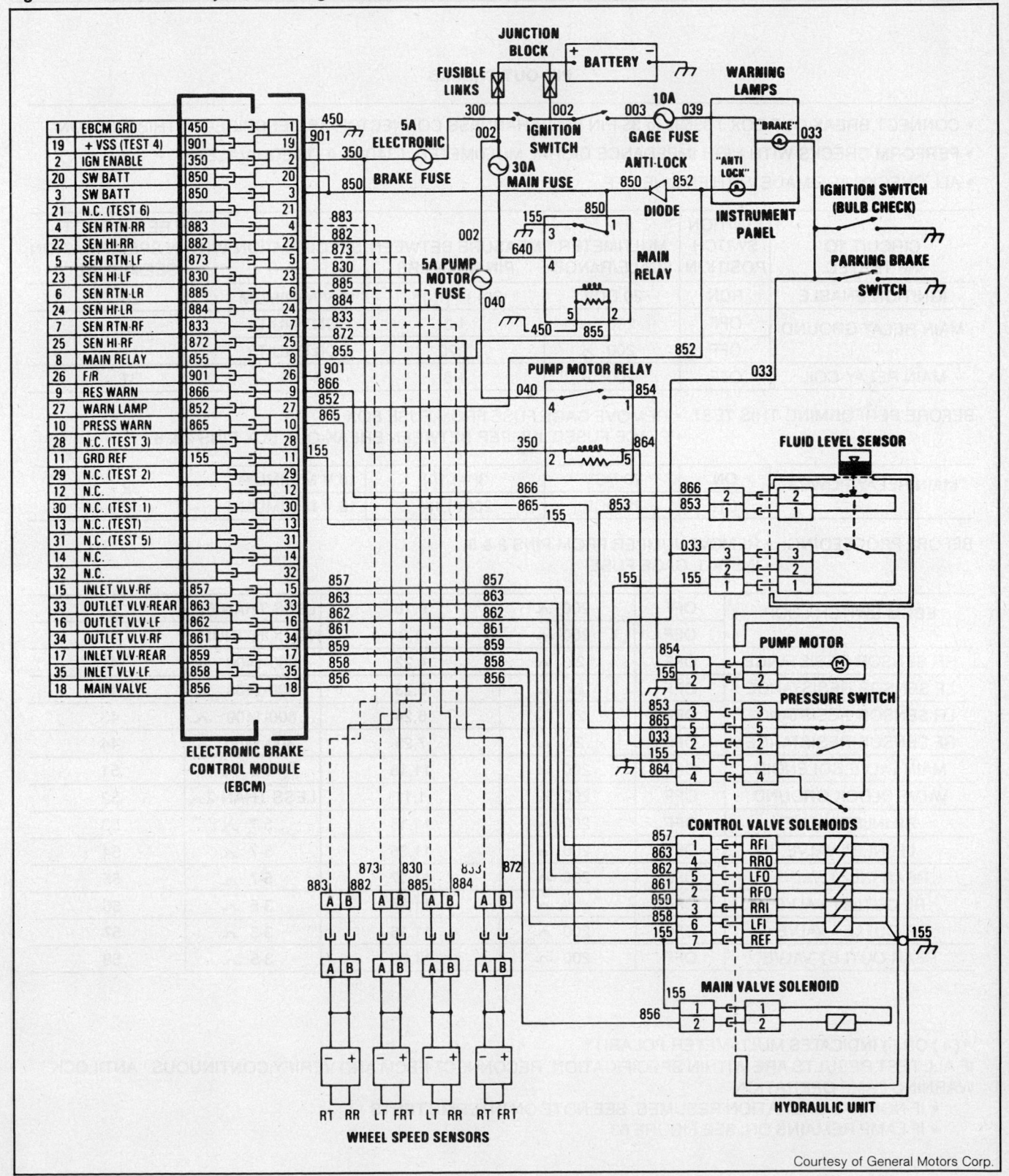

Courtesy of General Motors Corp.

Brake Systems

TEVES ANTI-LOCK BRAKE SYSTEMS (ABS)
GENERAL MOTORS – PONTIAC 6000 (Cont.)

Fig. 5: *Teves Anti-Lock Brake System Pin-Out Check*

PIN-OUT CHECKS

- CONNECT BREAK-OUT BOX J 35592 to 35-PIN EBCM HARNESS CONNECTOR AS DESCRIBED IN THIS SECTION
- PERFORM CHECKS WITH HIGH IMPEDANCE DIGITAL MULTIMETER J 34029-A OR EQUIVALENT
- ALL CHECKS ARE MADE WITH ENGINE OFF

CIRCUIT TO BE TESTED	IGNITION SWITCH POSITION	MULTIMETER SCALE/RANGE	MEASURE BETWEEN PIN NUMBERS	SPECIFICATION	IF RESULT NOT WITHIN SPECIFICATION, SEE FIGURE
IGNITION ENABLE	RUN	20 DCV	2(+)*,1(-)*	10 V MINIMUM	28
MAIN RELAY GROUND	OFF	200 ᴧ	1,3	CONTINUITY	30
	OFF	200 ᴧ	1,20	CONTINUITY	
MAIN RELAY COIL	OFF	200 ᴧ	1,8	45-105 ᴧ	31

BEFORE PERFORMING THIS TEST: • REMOVE GAGE FUSE FROM FUSE BOX
• PLACE FUSED JUMPER BETWEEN BREAK-OUT BOX PINS 2 & 8

MAIN RELAY POWER	ON	20 DCV	3(+),1(-)	10 V MINIMUM	32
	ON	20 DCV	20(+),1(-)	10 V MINIMUM	

BEFORE PROCEEDING: • REMOVE JUMPER FROM PINS 2 & 8
• INSTALL GAGE FUSE

EBCM SWITCH LOOP	OFF	200 ᴧ	9,10	LESS THAN 5 ᴧ	38
	OFF	200 ᴧ	1,9	NO CONTINUITY	39
RR SENSOR RESISTANCE	OFF	2k ᴧ	4,22	800-1400 ᴧ	41
LF SENSOR RESISTANCE	OFF	2k ᴧ	5,23	800-1400 ᴧ	42
LR SENSOR RESISTANCE	OFF	2k ᴧ	6,24	800-1400 ᴧ	43
RF SENSOR RESISTANCE	OFF	2k ᴧ	7,25	800-1400 ᴧ	44
MAIN VALVE SOLENOID	OFF	200 ᴧ	11,18	2-5 ᴧ	51
VALVE BLOCK GROUND	OFF	200 ᴧ	1,11	LESS THAN 2 ᴧ	52
RF INLET VALVE	OFF	200 ᴧ	11,15	5-7 ᴧ	53
LF INLET VALVE	OFF	200 ᴧ	11,35	5-7 ᴧ	54
REAR INLET VALVE	OFF	200 ᴧ	11,17	5-7 ᴧ	55
RF OUTLET VALVE	OFF	200 ᴧ	11,34	3-5 ᴧ	56
LF OUTLET VALVE	OFF	200 ᴧ	11,16	3-5 ᴧ	57
REAR OUTLET VALVE	OFF	200 ᴧ	11,33	3-5 ᴧ	58

*(+) OR (-) INDICATES MULTI-METER POLARITY
IF ALL TEST RESULTS ARE WITHIN SPECIFICATION, RECONNECT EBCM AND VERIFY CONTINUOUS "ANTILOCK" WARNING LAMP OPERATION
- IF NORMAL OPERATION RESUMES, SEE NOTE ON INTERMITTENTS
- IF LAMP REMAINS ON, SEE FIGURE 63

TEVES ANTI-LOCK BRAKE SYSTEMS (ABS)
GENERAL MOTORS – PONTIAC 6000 (Cont.)

CHART A-1
IGNITION ENABLE CIRCUIT

Ignition enable circuit engergizes EBCM to perform self-daignosis and initialize system. Battery volatge is supplied through 5-amp brake fuse to EBCM pin No. 2. Ground circuit is at ABS ground junction, located on left fender rail, at EBCM pin No. 1. "ANTI-LOCK" warning light will stay on if EBCM does not receive ignition enable input.

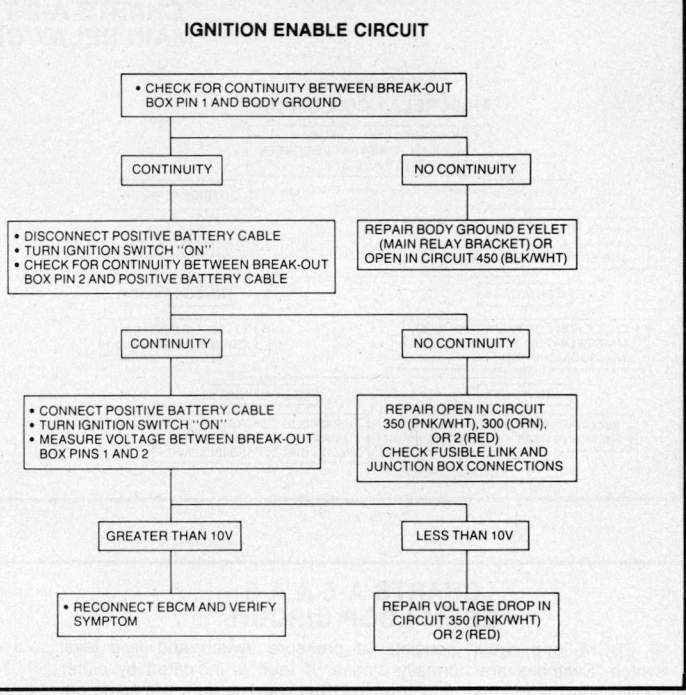

CHARTS A-2 THROUGH A-4
MAIN RELAY CIRCUIT

1) Main relay circuit provides battery voltage to EBCM to power main valve, solenoid valves, logic circuit and some self-diagnosis circuits. Main relay coil receives power from EBCM pin No. 8.

2) EBCM does not applied power to main relay coil until after ECBM receives ignition enable circuit information. Relay is grounded at ABS ground junction, located on left fender rail. Power for main relay comes through a fusable link from battery junction box.

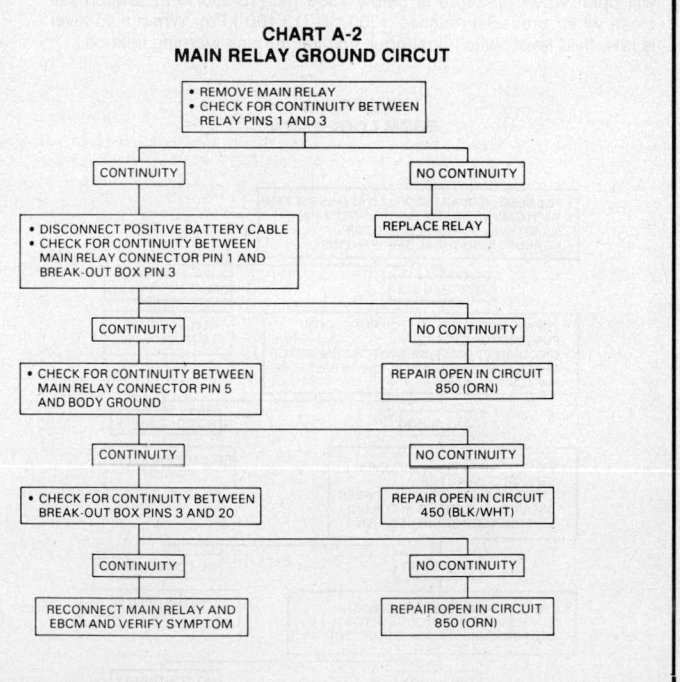

Brake Systems

TEVES ANTI-LOCK BRAKE SYSTEMS (ABS)
GENERAL MOTORS – PONTIAC 6000 (Cont.)

CHARTS A-2 THROUGH A-4
MAIN RELAY CIRCUIT (Cont.)

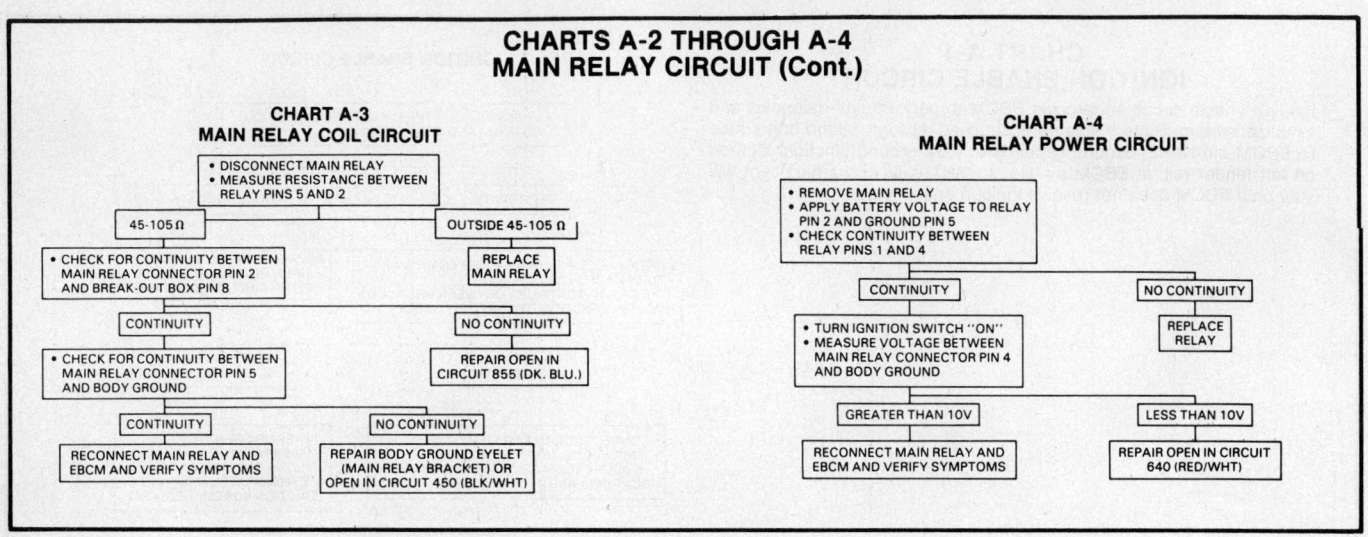

CHART A-3
MAIN RELAY COIL CIRCUIT

- DISCONNECT MAIN RELAY
- MEASURE RESISTANCE BETWEEN RELAY PINS 5 AND 2

45-105 Ω / OUTSIDE 45-105 Ω

- CHECK FOR CONTINUITY BETWEEN MAIN RELAY CONNECTOR PIN 2 AND BREAK-OUT BOX PIN 8

REPLACE MAIN RELAY

CONTINUITY / NO CONTINUITY

- CHECK FOR CONTINUITY BETWEEN MAIN RELAY CONNECTOR PIN 5 AND BODY GROUND

REPAIR OPEN IN CIRCUIT 855 (DK. BLU.)

CONTINUITY / NO CONTINUITY

RECONNECT MAIN RELAY AND EBCM AND VERIFY SYMPTOMS

REPAIR BODY GROUND EYELET (MAIN RELAY BRACKET) OR OPEN IN CIRCUIT 450 (BLK/WHT)

CHART A-4
MAIN RELAY POWER CIRCUIT

- REMOVE MAIN RELAY
- APPLY BATTERY VOLTAGE TO RELAY PIN 2 AND GROUND PIN 5
- CHECK CONTINUITY BETWEEN RELAY PINS 1 AND 4

CONTINUITY / NO CONTINUITY

- TURN IGNITION SWITCH "ON"
- MEASURE VOLTAGE BETWEEN MAIN RELAY CONNECTOR PIN 4 AND BODY GROUND

REPLACE RELAY

GREATER THAN 10V / LESS THAN 10V

RECONNECT MAIN RELAY AND EBCM AND VERIFY SYMPTOMS

REPAIR OPEN IN CIRCUIT 640 (RED/WHT)

CHARTS A-5 & A-6
EBCM LOOP CIRCUIT

1) EBCM loop circuit consists of pressure switch and fluid level switch. Switches are normally closed. If fault is indicated by either switch, loop is opened, and "ANTI-LOCK" warning light will come on. ABS will deactivate front wheels.

2) Pressure switch detects low accumulator pressure. Pressure switch will open when pressure is below 1500 psi (10,350 kPa). Switch will close when pressure reaches 1900 psi (13,100 kPa). When fluid level is low, fluid level switch float opens circuit, turning warning light on.

CHART A-6
EBCM LOOP SHORT

- DISCONNECT PRESSURE SWITCH AND 2-PIN FLUID LEVEL SENSOR CONNECTORS
- CHECK FOR CONTINUITY BETWEEN FLUID LEVEL SENSOR PINS AND BODY GROUND

NO CONTINUITY / CONTINUITY

- CHECK FOR CONTINUITY BETWEEN ALL PRESSURE SWITCH PINS AND BODY GROUND

REPLACE FLUID LEVEL SENSOR

NO CONTINUITY / CONTINUITY

- CHECK FOR CONTINUITY BETWEEN PRESSURE SWITCH CONNECTOR PIN 5 AND BODY GROUND

REPLACE PRESSURE SWITCH

NO CONTINUITY / CONTINUITY

- CHECK FOR CONTINUITY BETWEEN PRESSURE SWITCH CONNECTOR PIN 3 AND BODY GROUND

REPAIR SHORT TO GROUND IN CIRCUIT 865 (PPL)

NO CONTINUITY / CONTINUITY

- CHECK FOR CONTINUITY BETWEEN 2-PIN FLUID LEVEL SENSOR CONNECTOR PIN 2 AND BODY GROUND

REPAIR SHORT TO GROUND IN CIRCUIT 853 (LT. BLU/ORN)

NO CONTINUITY / CONTINUITY

- RECONNECT ALL CONNECTORS AND EBCM AND VERIFY SYMPTOM

REPAIR SHORT TO GROUND IN CIRCUIT 866 (LT. GRN)

CHART A-5
EBCM LOOP OPEN

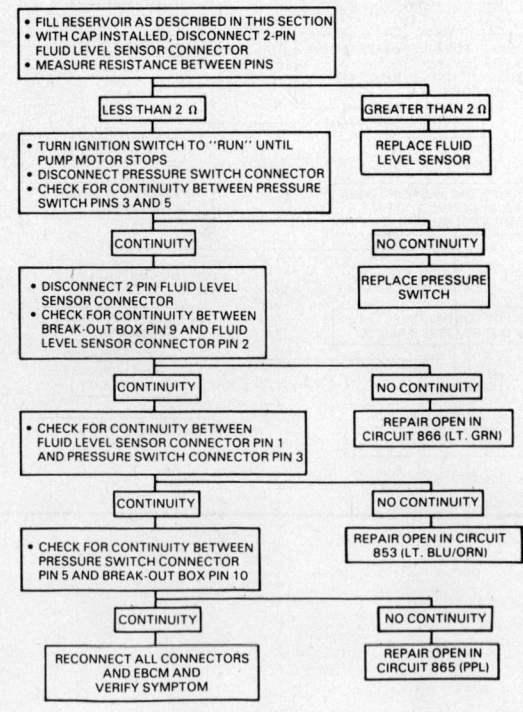

- FILL RESERVOIR AS DESCRIBED IN THIS SECTION
- WITH CAP INSTALLED, DISCONNECT 2-PIN FLUID LEVEL SENSOR CONNECTOR
- MEASURE RESISTANCE BETWEEN PINS

LESS THAN 2 Ω / GREATER THAN 2 Ω

- TURN IGNITION SWITCH TO "RUN" UNTIL PUMP MOTOR STOPS
- DISCONNECT PRESSURE SWITCH CONNECTOR
- CHECK FOR CONTINUITY BETWEEN PRESSURE SWITCH PINS 3 AND 5

REPLACE FLUID LEVEL SENSOR

CONTINUITY / NO CONTINUITY

- DISCONNECT 2 PIN FLUID LEVEL SENSOR CONNECTOR
- CHECK FOR CONTINUITY BETWEEN BREAK-OUT BOX PIN 9 AND FLUID LEVEL SENSOR CONNECTOR PIN 2

REPLACE PRESSURE SWITCH

CONTINUITY / NO CONTINUITY

- CHECK FOR CONTINUITY BETWEEN FLUID LEVEL SENSOR CONNECTOR PIN 1 AND PRESSURE SWITCH CONNECTOR PIN 3

REPAIR OPEN IN CIRCUIT 866 (LT. GRN)

CONTINUITY / NO CONTINUITY

- CHECK FOR CONTINUITY BETWEEN PRESSURE SWITCH CONNECTOR PIN 5 AND BREAK-OUT BOX PIN 10

REPAIR OPEN IN CIRCUIT 853 (LT. BLU/ORN)

CONTINUITY / NO CONTINUITY

RECONNECT ALL CONNECTORS AND EBCM AND VERIFY SYMPTOM

REPAIR OPEN IN CIRCUIT 865 (PPL)

TEVES ANTI-LOCK BRAKE SYSTEMS (ABS)
GENERAL MOTORS — PONTIAC 6000 (Cont.)

CHARTS A-7 THROUGH A-16
WHEEL SENSOR CIRCUITS

Wheel sensors send a AC signal to EBCM by passing a toothed ring past 2-pole inductive sensor. EBCM determines calculated wheel speed, using sensor output frequency, to detect wheel lock-up. Voltage can be as low as 50 millivolts. Resistance of sensor should be 800-1400 ohms. If cable is damaged, repair or replace cable, using manufacturer repair kit.

CHART A-8
LF WHEEL SENSOR RESISTANCE

- DISCONNECT LEFT FRONT SENSOR CONNECTOR
- MEASURE SENSOR RESISTANCE AT CONNECTOR PINS

| 800-1400 Ω | OUTSIDE 800-1400 Ω |

| CHECK FOR CONTINUITY BETWEEN BREAK-OUT BOX PIN 23 AND SENSOR CONNECTOR PIN B (HARNESS SIDE) | REPLACE LEFT FRONT WHEEL SENSOR |

| CONTINUITY | NO CONTINUITY |

| CHECK FOR CONTINUITY BETWEEN BREAK-OUT BOX PIN 5 AND SENSOR CONNECTOR PIN A (HARNESS SIDE) | REPAIR CIRCUIT 830 (COAX CENTER) |

| CONTINUITY | NO CONTINUITY |

| RECONNECT CONNECTOR AND EBCM AND VERIFY SYMPTOM | REPAIR CIRCUIT 873 (COAX SHIELD) |

CHART A-7
RR WHEEL SENSOR RESISTANCE

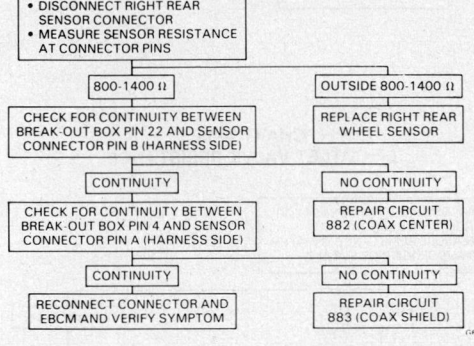

- DISCONNECT RIGHT REAR SENSOR CONNECTOR
- MEASURE SENSOR RESISTANCE AT CONNECTOR PINS

| 800-1400 Ω | OUTSIDE 800-1400 Ω |

| CHECK FOR CONTINUITY BETWEEN BREAK-OUT BOX PIN 22 AND SENSOR CONNECTOR PIN B (HARNESS SIDE) | REPLACE RIGHT REAR WHEEL SENSOR |

| CONTINUITY | NO CONTINUITY |

| CHECK FOR CONTINUITY BETWEEN BREAK-OUT BOX PIN 4 AND SENSOR CONNECTOR PIN A (HARNESS SIDE) | REPAIR CIRCUIT 882 (COAX CENTER) |

| CONTINUITY | NO CONTINUITY |

| RECONNECT CONNECTOR AND EBCM AND VERIFY SYMPTOM | REPAIR CIRCUIT 883 (COAX SHIELD) |

CHART A-9
LR WHEEL SENSOR RESISTANCE

- DISCONNECT LEFT REAR SENSOR CONNECTOR
- MEASURE SENSOR RESISTANCE AT CONNECTOR PINS

| 800-1400 Ω | OUTSIDE 800-1400 Ω |

| CHECK FOR CONTINUITY BETWEEN BREAK-OUT BOX PIN 24 AND SENSOR CONNECTOR PIN B (HARNESS SIDE) | REPLACE LEFT REAR WHEEL SENSOR |

| CONTINUITY | NO CONTINUITY |

| CHECK FOR CONTINUITY BETWEEN BREAK-OUT BOX PIN 6 AND SENSOR CONNECTOR PIN A (HARNESS SIDE) | REPAIR CIRCUIT 884 (COAX CENTER) |

| CONTINUITY | NO CONTINUITY |

| RECONNECT CONNECTOR AND EBCM AND VERIFY SYMPTOM | REPAIR CIRCUIT 885 (COAX SHIELD) |

Brake Systems

TEVES ANTI-LOCK BRAKE SYSTEMS (ABS) GENERAL MOTORS – PONTIAC 6000 (Cont.)

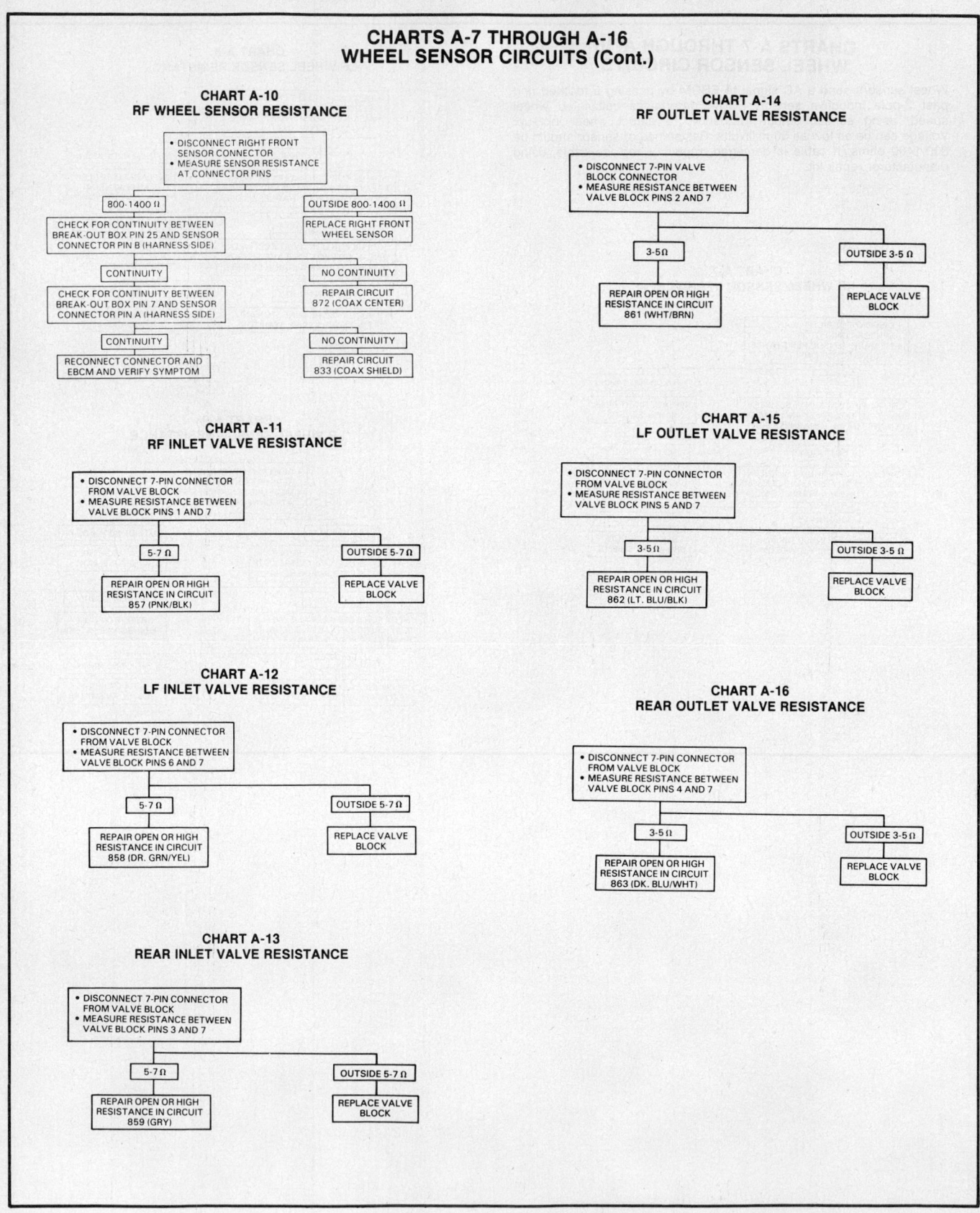

CHARTS A-7 THROUGH A-16
WHEEL SENSOR CIRCUITS (Cont.)

CHART A-10
RF WHEEL SENSOR RESISTANCE

- DISCONNECT RIGHT FRONT SENSOR CONNECTOR
- MEASURE SENSOR RESISTANCE AT CONNECTOR PINS

800-1400 Ω → CHECK FOR CONTINUITY BETWEEN BREAK-OUT BOX PIN 25 AND SENSOR CONNECTOR PIN B (HARNESS SIDE)

OUTSIDE 800-1400 Ω → REPLACE RIGHT FRONT WHEEL SENSOR

CONTINUITY → CHECK FOR CONTINUITY BETWEEN BREAK-OUT BOX PIN 7 AND SENSOR CONNECTOR PIN A (HARNESS SIDE)

NO CONTINUITY → REPAIR CIRCUIT 872 (COAX CENTER)

CONTINUITY → RECONNECT CONNECTOR AND EBCM AND VERIFY SYMPTOM

NO CONTINUITY → REPAIR CIRCUIT 833 (COAX SHIELD)

CHART A-11
RF INLET VALVE RESISTANCE

- DISCONNECT 7-PIN CONNECTOR FROM VALVE BLOCK
- MEASURE RESISTANCE BETWEEN VALVE BLOCK PINS 1 AND 7

5-7 Ω → REPAIR OPEN OR HIGH RESISTANCE IN CIRCUIT 857 (PNK/BLK)

OUTSIDE 5-7 Ω → REPLACE VALVE BLOCK

CHART A-12
LF INLET VALVE RESISTANCE

- DISCONNECT 7-PIN CONNECTOR FROM VALVE BLOCK
- MEASURE RESISTANCE BETWEEN VALVE BLOCK PINS 6 AND 7

5-7 Ω → REPAIR OPEN OR HIGH RESISTANCE IN CIRCUIT 858 (DR. GRN/YEL)

OUTSIDE 5-7 Ω → REPLACE VALVE BLOCK

CHART A-13
REAR INLET VALVE RESISTANCE

- DISCONNECT 7-PIN CONNECTOR FROM VALVE BLOCK
- MEASURE RESISTANCE BETWEEN VALVE BLOCK PINS 3 AND 7

5-7 Ω → REPAIR OPEN OR HIGH RESISTANCE IN CIRCUIT 859 (GRY)

OUTSIDE 5-7 Ω → REPLACE VALVE BLOCK

CHART A-14
RF OUTLET VALVE RESISTANCE

- DISCONNECT 7-PIN VALVE BLOCK CONNECTOR
- MEASURE RESISTANCE BETWEEN VALVE BLOCK PINS 2 AND 7

3-5 Ω → REPAIR OPEN OR HIGH RESISTANCE IN CIRCUIT 861 (WHT/BRN)

OUTSIDE 3-5 Ω → REPLACE VALVE BLOCK

CHART A-15
LF OUTLET VALVE RESISTANCE

- DISCONNECT 7-PIN CONNECTOR FROM VALVE BLOCK
- MEASURE RESISTANCE BETWEEN VALVE BLOCK PINS 5 AND 7

3-5 Ω → REPAIR OPEN OR HIGH RESISTANCE IN CIRCUIT 862 (LT. BLU/BLK)

OUTSIDE 3-5 Ω → REPLACE VALVE BLOCK

CHART A-16
REAR OUTLET VALVE RESISTANCE

- DISCONNECT 7-PIN CONNECTOR FROM VALVE BLOCK
- MEASURE RESISTANCE BETWEEN VALVE BLOCK PINS 4 AND 7

3-5 Ω → REPAIR OPEN OR HIGH RESISTANCE IN CIRCUIT 863 (DK. BLU/WHT)

OUTSIDE 3-5 Ω → REPLACE VALVE BLOCK

Brake Systems

TEVES ANTI-LOCK BRAKE SYSTEMS (ABS)
GENERAL MOTORS – PONTIAC 6000 (Cont.)

CHARTS A-17 & A-18
VALVE BLOCK & MAIN VALVE CIRCUITS

NOTE: Manually activating inlet or outlet valves can be done by jumpering pins on break-out box. DO NOT activate valves for more than 30 seconds. NEVER manually activate main valve.

1) Main valve, located inside hydraulic unit, is energized when system is in ABS mode. EBCM applies 12 volts to main valve solenoid from pin No. 18. Valve is grounded through hydraulic unit. Normal resistance is 2-5 ohms.

2) Valve block ground comes from EBCM pin No. 11. Inlet and outlet valves are grounded by hydraulic unit. Resistance between valve block ground (EBCM pin No. 11) and body ground should never exceed 2 ohms. Inlet valves are normally open.

3) When EBCM applies 12 volts at pins No. 15, 17 or 35, inlet valves close. Valves are closed for short period of time to hold pressure or pressure reduction is desired. Resistance for inlet valve should be 5-7 ohms. Outlet valves operate the same as inlet valve. EBCM applies voltage at pins No. 34, 33 and 16. Resistance should be 3-5 ohms.

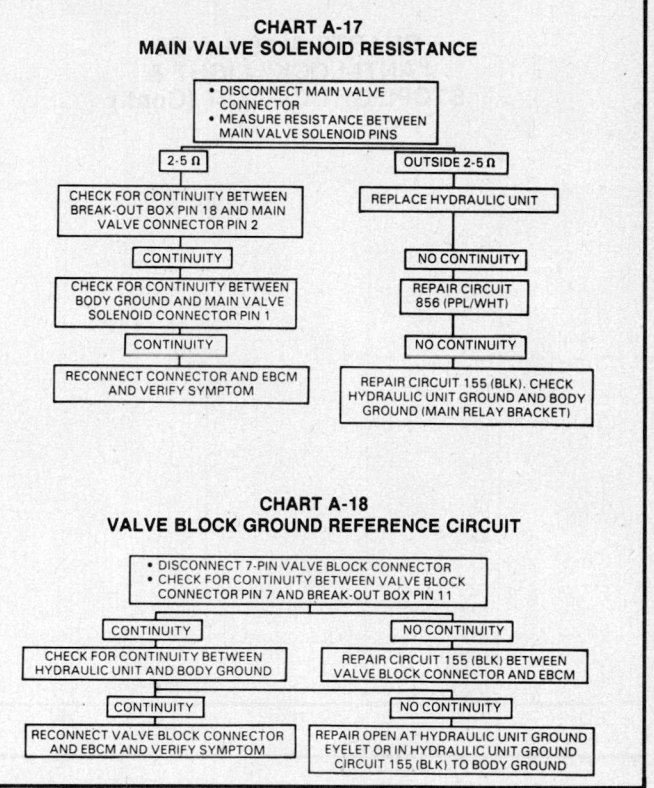

CHART A-17
MAIN VALVE SOLENOID RESISTANCE

CHART A-18
VALVE BLOCK GROUND REFERENCE CIRCUIT

CHARTS A-19 & A-20
"ANTI-LOCK" LIGHT & STOPLIGHT CIRCUIT

1) "ANTI-LOCK" light is powered by 20-amp gauge fuse. Light is turned on (grounded) if, main relay is not enabled by EBCM or EBCM detects fault in system (pin No. 27). A diode protects EBCM pin No. 27 and "ANTI-LOCK" light circuit from current overload.

2) Stoplight switch power is directed to EBCM (pin No. 12) whenever brake pedal is depressed. This informs EBCM to increase sensitivity to wheel sensor input signal.

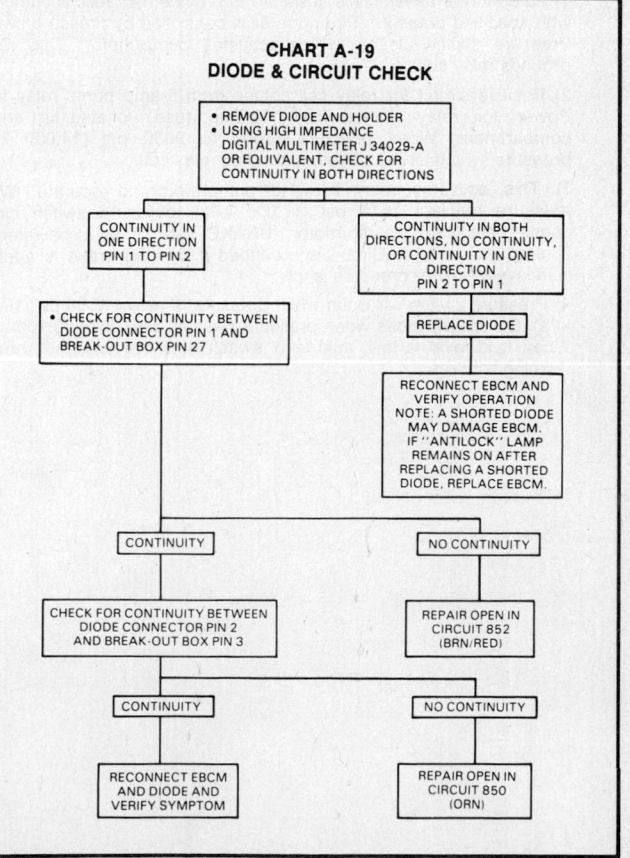

CHART A-19
DIODE & CIRCUIT CHECK

TEVES ANTI-LOCK BRAKE SYSTEMS (ABS)
GENERAL MOTORS – PONTIAC 6000 (Cont.)

CHARTS A-19 & A-20
"ANTI-LOCK" LIGHT & STOPLIGHT CIRCUIT (Cont.)

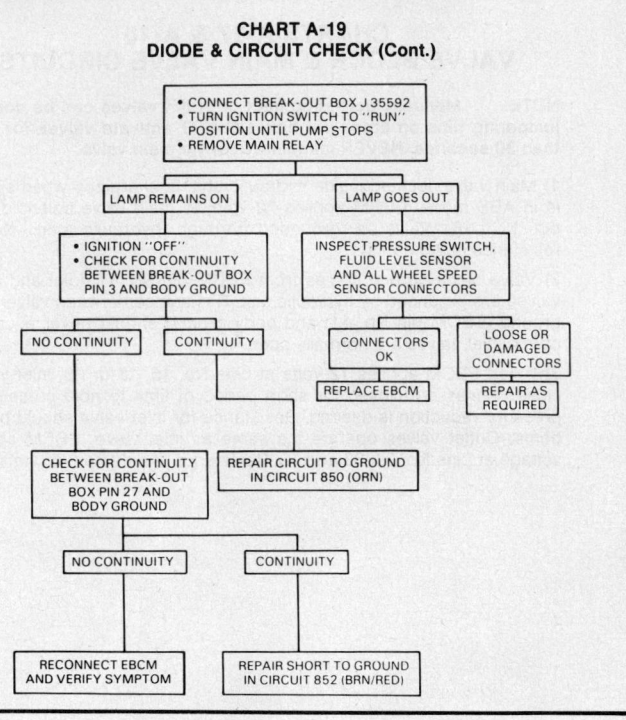

CHART A-19
DIODE & CIRCUIT CHECK (Cont.)

CHART B THROUGH B-5
PUMP/MOTOR & "BRAKE" LIGHT CIRCUIT

1) Pump/motor assembly is designed to provide hydraulic accumulator with specified pressure. Pump/motor is controlled by pressure switch. Pressure switch closes, which activates pump/motor. This circuit grounds relay coil.

2) Positive circuit for relay coil comes from 5-amp pump relay fuse. Power for relay comes from 30-amp fuse, located in engine compartment. When pressure drops to 2030 psi (14,000 kPa), pressure switch circuit closes, grounding relay coil.

3) This activates relay allowing pump/motor to operate. When pressure reaches 2610 psi (18,000 kPa), pressure switch circuit opens, deactivating pump/motor. "BRAKE" light circuit is powered by 20-amp gauge fuse. Circuit is grounded if parking brake is applied, fluid level is low or pressure is low.

4) Pressure switch will open when pressure is below 1500 psi (10,350 kPa). Switch will close when pressure reaches 1900 psi (13,100 kPa). When fluid level is low, fluid level switch float opens circuit, turning warning light on.

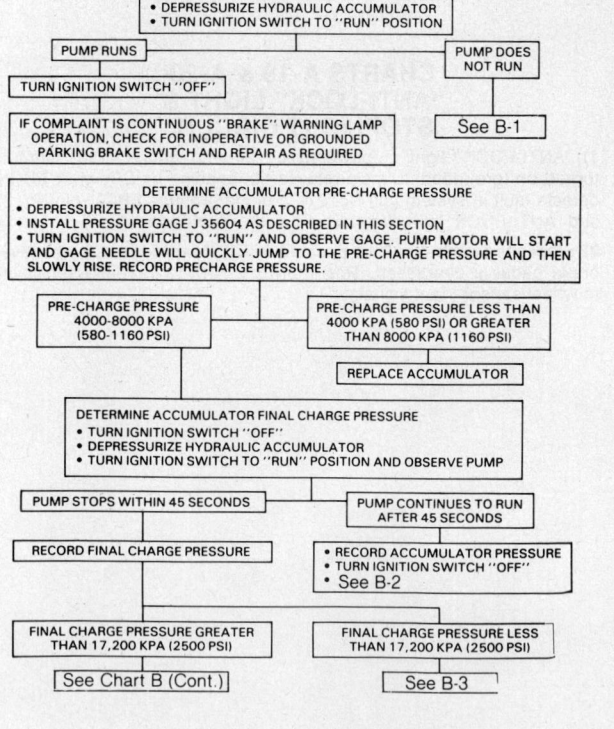

CHART B
HYDRAULIC UNIT FUNCTIONAL CHECK

Brake Systems

TEVES ANTI-LOCK BRAKE SYSTEMS (ABS)
GENERAL MOTORS — PONTIAC 6000 (Cont.)

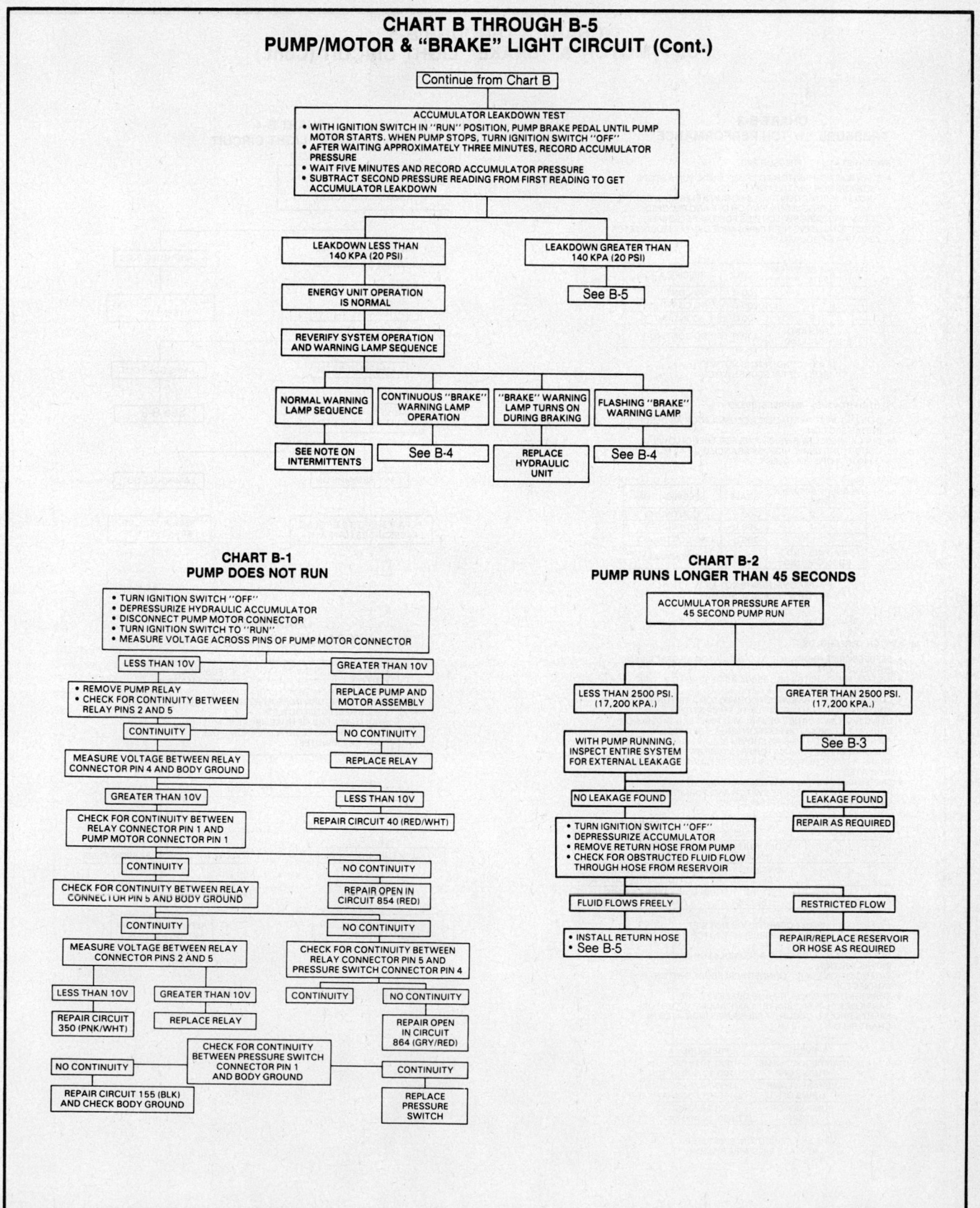

CHART B THROUGH B-5
PUMP/MOTOR & "BRAKE" LIGHT CIRCUIT (Cont.)

Continue from Chart B

ACCUMULATOR LEAKDOWN TEST
- WITH IGNITION SWITCH IN "RUN" POSITION, PUMP BRAKE PEDAL UNTIL PUMP MOTOR STARTS. WHEN PUMP STOPS, TURN IGNITION SWITCH "OFF"
- AFTER WAITING APPROXIMATELY THREE MINUTES, RECORD ACCUMULATOR PRESSURE
- WAIT FIVE MINUTES AND RECORD ACCUMULATOR PRESSURE
- SUBTRACT SECOND PRESSURE READING FROM FIRST READING TO GET ACCUMULATOR LEAKDOWN

LEAKDOWN LESS THAN 140 KPA (20 PSI)

LEAKDOWN GREATER THAN 140 KPA (20 PSI)

ENERGY UNIT OPERATION IS NORMAL

See B-5

REVERIFY SYSTEM OPERATION AND WARNING LAMP SEQUENCE

NORMAL WARNING LAMP SEQUENCE

CONTINUOUS "BRAKE" WARNING LAMP OPERATION

"BRAKE" WARNING LAMP TURNS ON DURING BRAKING

FLASHING "BRAKE" WARNING LAMP

SEE NOTE ON INTERMITTENTS

See B-4

REPLACE HYDRAULIC UNIT

See B-4

CHART B-1
PUMP DOES NOT RUN

- TURN IGNITION SWITCH "OFF"
- DEPRESSURIZE HYDRAULIC ACCUMULATOR
- DISCONNECT PUMP MOTOR CONNECTOR
- TURN IGNITION SWITCH TO "RUN"
- MEASURE VOLTAGE ACROSS PINS OF PUMP MOTOR CONNECTOR

LESS THAN 10V

GREATER THAN 10V

- REMOVE PUMP RELAY
- CHECK FOR CONTINUITY BETWEEN RELAY PINS 2 AND 5

REPLACE PUMP AND MOTOR ASSEMBLY

CONTINUITY

NO CONTINUITY

MEASURE VOLTAGE BETWEEN RELAY CONNECTOR PIN 4 AND BODY GROUND

REPLACE RELAY

GREATER THAN 10V

LESS THAN 10V

CHECK FOR CONTINUITY BETWEEN RELAY CONNECTOR PIN 1 AND PUMP MOTOR CONNECTOR PIN 1

REPAIR CIRCUIT 40 (RED/WHT)

CONTINUITY

NO CONTINUITY

CHECK FOR CONTINUITY BETWEEN RELAY CONNECTOR PIN 5 AND BODY GROUND

REPAIR OPEN IN CIRCUIT 854 (RED)

CONTINUITY

NO CONTINUITY

MEASURE VOLTAGE BETWEEN RELAY CONNECTOR PINS 2 AND 5

CHECK FOR CONTINUITY BETWEEN RELAY CONNECTOR PIN 5 AND PRESSURE SWITCH CONNECTOR PIN 4

LESS THAN 10V

GREATER THAN 10V

CONTINUITY

NO CONTINUITY

REPAIR CIRCUIT 350 (PNK/WHT)

REPLACE RELAY

REPAIR OPEN IN CIRCUIT 864 (GRY/RED)

CHECK FOR CONTINUITY BETWEEN PRESSURE SWITCH CONNECTOR PIN 1 AND BODY GROUND

NO CONTINUITY

CONTINUITY

REPAIR CIRCUIT 155 (BLK) AND CHECK BODY GROUND

REPLACE PRESSURE SWITCH

CHART B-2
PUMP RUNS LONGER THAN 45 SECONDS

ACCUMULATOR PRESSURE AFTER 45 SECOND PUMP RUN

LESS THAN 2500 PSI. (17,200 KPA.)

GREATER THAN 2500 PSI. (17,200 KPA.)

WITH PUMP RUNNING, INSPECT ENTIRE SYSTEM FOR EXTERNAL LEAKAGE

See B-3

NO LEAKAGE FOUND

LEAKAGE FOUND

- TURN IGNITION SWITCH "OFF"
- DEPRESSURIZE ACCUMULATOR
- REMOVE RETURN HOSE FROM PUMP
- CHECK FOR OBSTRUCTED FLUID FLOW THROUGH HOSE FROM RESERVOIR

REPAIR AS REQUIRED

FLUID FLOWS FREELY

RESTRICTED FLOW

- INSTALL RETURN HOSE
- See B-5

REPAIR/REPLACE RESERVOIR OR HOSE AS REQUIRED

Brake Systems

TEVES ANTI-LOCK BRAKE SYSTEMS (ABS) GENERAL MOTORS — PONTIAC 6000 (Cont.)

CHART B THROUGH B-5
PUMP/MOTOR & "BRAKE" LIGHT CIRCUIT (Cont.)

CHART B-3
PRESSURE SWITCH PERFORMANCE

I. SWITCH STATUS — PRESSURIZED

- TURN IGNITION SWITCH TO "RUN" UNTIL PUMP STOPS
- TURN IGNITION SWITCH "OFF"
  - NOTE: IF PUMP CONTINUES TO RUN AFTER 45 SECONDS, TURN IGNITION SWITCH OFF AND PROCEED
- CHECK PRESSURE SWITCH PINS FOR THE FOLLOWING CONDITIONS USING HIGH IMPEDANCE DIGITAL MULTIMETER J 34029-A OR EQUIVALENT

MEASURE BETWEEN PINS	SCALE	SPECIFICATION
1, 2	200 Ω	NO CONTINUITY
1, 4	200 Ω	NO CONTINUITY
3, 5	200 Ω	CONTINUITY
ALL PINS AND BODY GROUND	200 Ω	NO CONTINUITY

IF ANY CONDITION IS NOT MET,
REPLACE PRESSURE SWITCH

II. SWITCH STATUS — DEPRESSURIZED

- DEPRESSURIZE HYDRAULIC ACCUMULATOR AS DESCRIBED IN THIS SECTION
- CHECK PRESSURE SWITCH PINS FOR THE FOLLOWING CONDITIONS USING HIGH IMPEDANCE DIGITAL MULTIMETER J 34029-A OR EQUIVALENT

MEASURE BETWEEN PINS	SCALE	SPECIFICATION
1, 2	200 Ω	CONTINUITY
1, 4	200 Ω	CONTINUITY
3, 5	200 Ω	NO CONTINUITY
ALL PINS AND BODY GROUND	200 Ω	NO CONTINUITY

IF ANY CONDITION IS NOT MET,
REPLACE PRESSURE SWITCH

III. SWITCH THRESHOLDS

- DEPRESSURIZE HYDRAULIC ACCUMULATOR AS DESCRIBED IN THIS SECTION
- INSTALL PRESSURE GAGE J 35604 AS DESCRIBED IN THIS SECTION
- CONNECT PRESSURE SWITCH CONNECTOR AND TURN IGNITION SWITCH TO "RUN" UNTIL PUMP STOPS
- USING HIGH IMPEDANCE DIGITAL MULTIMETER J 34029-A OR EQUIVALENT, MONITOR FOR CONTINUITY BETWEEN PRESSURE SWITCH PINS AS SHOWN BELOW WHILE SLOWLY BLEEDING OFF ACCUMULATOR PRESSURE BY PUMPING THE BRAKE PEDAL. CONTINUITY SHOULD BE GAINED OR LOST AS INDICATED.
- PRESSURIZE SYSTEM BETWEEN EACH TEST BY RECONNECTING PRESSURE SWITCH AND TURNING IGNITION SWITCH TO "RUN" UNTIL PUMP STOPS

MEASURE BETWEEN PINS	SWITCH STATUS	PRESSURE RANGE
1, 4	CONTINUITY SHOULD BE GAINED AT:	1980-2080 PSI (13,650-14,350 KPA)
1, 2	CONTINUITY SHOULD BE GAINED AT:	1500-1550 PSI (10,350-10,700 KPA)
3, 5	CONTINUITY SHOULD BE LOST AT:	1500-1550 PSI (10,350-10,700 KPA)

IF ANY CONDITION IS NOT MET,
REPLACE PRESSURE SWITCH

- DEPRESSURIZE HYDRAULIC ACCUMULATOR AS DESCRIBED IN THIS SECTION
- WITH IGNITION "OFF," CONNECT PRESSURE SWITCH CONNECTOR
- TURN IGNITION TO "RUN" AND OBSERVE GAGE, "ANTILOCK" LAMP, "BRAKE" LAMP AND PUMP MOTOR. EVENTS SHOULD OCCUR AT PRESSURES INDICATED IN CHART BELOW

EVENT	PRESSURE
"ANTILOCK" LAMP TURNS OFF	1900-1975 PSI (13,100-13,600 KPA)
"BRAKE" LAMP TURNS OFF	1900-1975 PSI (13,100-13,600 KPA)
PUMP MOTOR STOPS	2550-2670 PSI (17,580-18,400 KPA)

IF ANY CONDITION IS NOT MET,
REPLACE PRESSURE SWITCH

CHART B-4
"BRAKE" LIGHT CIRCUIT

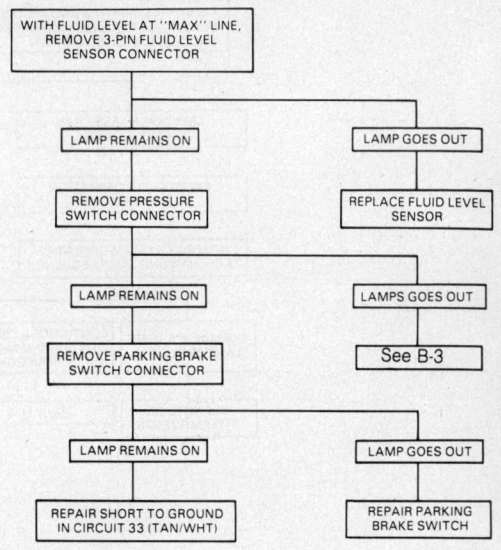

CHART B-5
HYDRAULIC UNIT LEAKDOWN

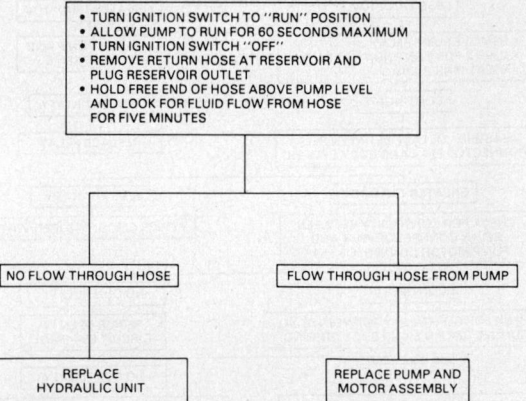

TEVES ANTI-LOCK BRAKE SYSTEMS (ABS)
GENERAL MOTORS — PONTIAC 6000 (Cont.)

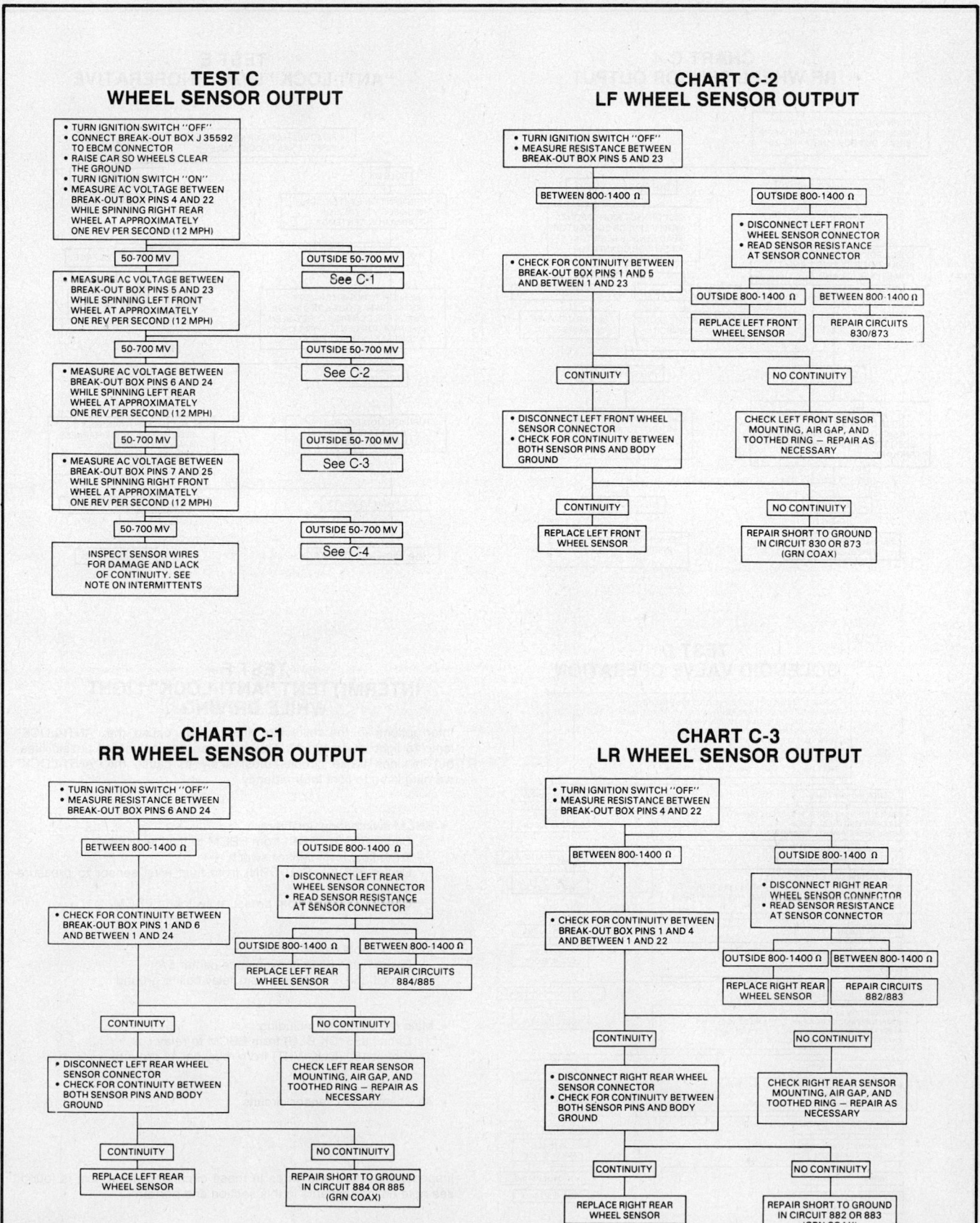

TEST C
WHEEL SENSOR OUTPUT

- TURN IGNITION SWITCH "OFF"
- CONNECT BREAK-OUT BOX J 35592 TO EBCM CONNECTOR
- RAISE CAR SO WHEELS CLEAR THE GROUND
- TURN IGNITION SWITCH "ON"
- MEASURE AC VOLTAGE BETWEEN BREAK-OUT BOX PINS 4 AND 22 WHILE SPINNING RIGHT REAR WHEEL AT APPROXIMATELY ONE REV PER SECOND (12 MPH)

50-700 MV → MEASURE AC VOLTAGE BETWEEN BREAK-OUT BOX PINS 5 AND 23 WHILE SPINNING LEFT FRONT WHEEL AT APPROXIMATELY ONE REV PER SECOND (12 MPH)

OUTSIDE 50-700 MV → See C-1

50-700 MV → MEASURE AC VOLTAGE BETWEEN BREAK-OUT BOX PINS 6 AND 24 WHILE SPINNING LEFT REAR WHEEL AT APPROXIMATELY ONE REV PER SECOND (12 MPH)

OUTSIDE 50-700 MV → See C-2

50-700 MV → MEASURE AC VOLTAGE BETWEEN BREAK-OUT BOX PINS 7 AND 25 WHILE SPINNING RIGHT FRONT WHEEL AT APPROXIMATELY ONE REV PER SECOND (12 MPH)

OUTSIDE 50-700 MV → See C-3

50-700 MV → INSPECT SENSOR WIRES FOR DAMAGE AND LACK OF CONTINUITY. SEE NOTE ON INTERMITTENTS

OUTSIDE 50-700 MV → See C-4

CHART C-2
LF WHEEL SENSOR OUTPUT

- TURN IGNITION SWITCH "OFF"
- MEASURE RESISTANCE BETWEEN BREAK-OUT BOX PINS 5 AND 23

BETWEEN 800-1400 Ω → CHECK FOR CONTINUITY BETWEEN BREAK-OUT BOX PINS 1 AND 5 AND BETWEEN 1 AND 23

OUTSIDE 800-1400 Ω → DISCONNECT LEFT FRONT WHEEL SENSOR CONNECTOR / READ SENSOR RESISTANCE AT SENSOR CONNECTOR

OUTSIDE 800-1400 Ω → REPLACE LEFT FRONT WHEEL SENSOR

BETWEEN 800-1400 Ω → REPAIR CIRCUITS 830/873

CONTINUITY → DISCONNECT LEFT FRONT WHEEL SENSOR CONNECTOR / CHECK FOR CONTINUITY BETWEEN BOTH SENSOR PINS AND BODY GROUND

NO CONTINUITY → CHECK LEFT FRONT SENSOR MOUNTING, AIR GAP, AND TOOTHED RING — REPAIR AS NECESSARY

CONTINUITY → REPLACE LEFT FRONT WHEEL SENSOR

NO CONTINUITY → REPAIR SHORT TO GROUND IN CIRCUIT 830 OR 873 (GRN COAX)

CHART C-1
RR WHEEL SENSOR OUTPUT

- TURN IGNITION SWITCH "OFF"
- MEASURE RESISTANCE BETWEEN BREAK-OUT BOX PINS 6 AND 24

BETWEEN 800-1400 Ω → CHECK FOR CONTINUITY BETWEEN BREAK-OUT BOX PINS 1 AND 6 AND BETWEEN 1 AND 24

OUTSIDE 800-1400 Ω → DISCONNECT LEFT REAR WHEEL SENSOR CONNECTOR / READ SENSOR RESISTANCE AT SENSOR CONNECTOR

OUTSIDE 800-1400 Ω → REPLACE LEFT REAR WHEEL SENSOR

BETWEEN 800-1400 Ω → REPAIR CIRCUITS 884/885

CONTINUITY → DISCONNECT LEFT REAR WHEEL SENSOR CONNECTOR / CHECK FOR CONTINUITY BETWEEN BOTH SENSOR PINS AND BODY GROUND

NO CONTINUITY → CHECK LEFT REAR SENSOR MOUNTING, AIR GAP, AND TOOTHED RING — REPAIR AS NECESSARY

CONTINUITY → REPLACE LEFT REAR WHEEL SENSOR

NO CONTINUITY → REPAIR SHORT TO GROUND IN CIRCUIT 884 OR 885 (GRN COAX)

CHART C-3
LR WHEEL SENSOR OUTPUT

- TURN IGNITION SWITCH "OFF"
- MEASURE RESISTANCE BETWEEN BREAK-OUT BOX PINS 4 AND 22

BETWEEN 800-1400 Ω → CHECK FOR CONTINUITY BETWEEN BREAK-OUT BOX PINS 1 AND 4 AND BETWEEN 1 AND 22

OUTSIDE 800-1400 Ω → DISCONNECT RIGHT REAR WHEEL SENSOR CONNECTOR / READ SENSOR RESISTANCE AT SENSOR CONNECTOR

OUTSIDE 800-1400 Ω → REPLACE RIGHT REAR WHEEL SENSOR

BETWEEN 800-1400 Ω → REPAIR CIRCUITS 882/883

CONTINUITY → DISCONNECT RIGHT REAR WHEEL SENSOR CONNECTOR / CHECK FOR CONTINUITY BETWEEN BOTH SENSOR PINS AND BODY GROUND

NO CONTINUITY → CHECK RIGHT REAR SENSOR MOUNTING, AIR GAP, AND TOOTHED RING — REPAIR AS NECESSARY

CONTINUITY → REPLACE RIGHT REAR WHEEL SENSOR

NO CONTINUITY → REPAIR SHORT TO GROUND IN CIRCUIT 882 OR 883 (GRN COAX)

Brake Systems

TEVES ANTI-LOCK BRAKE SYSTEMS (ABS)
GENERAL MOTORS – PONTIAC 6000 (Cont.)

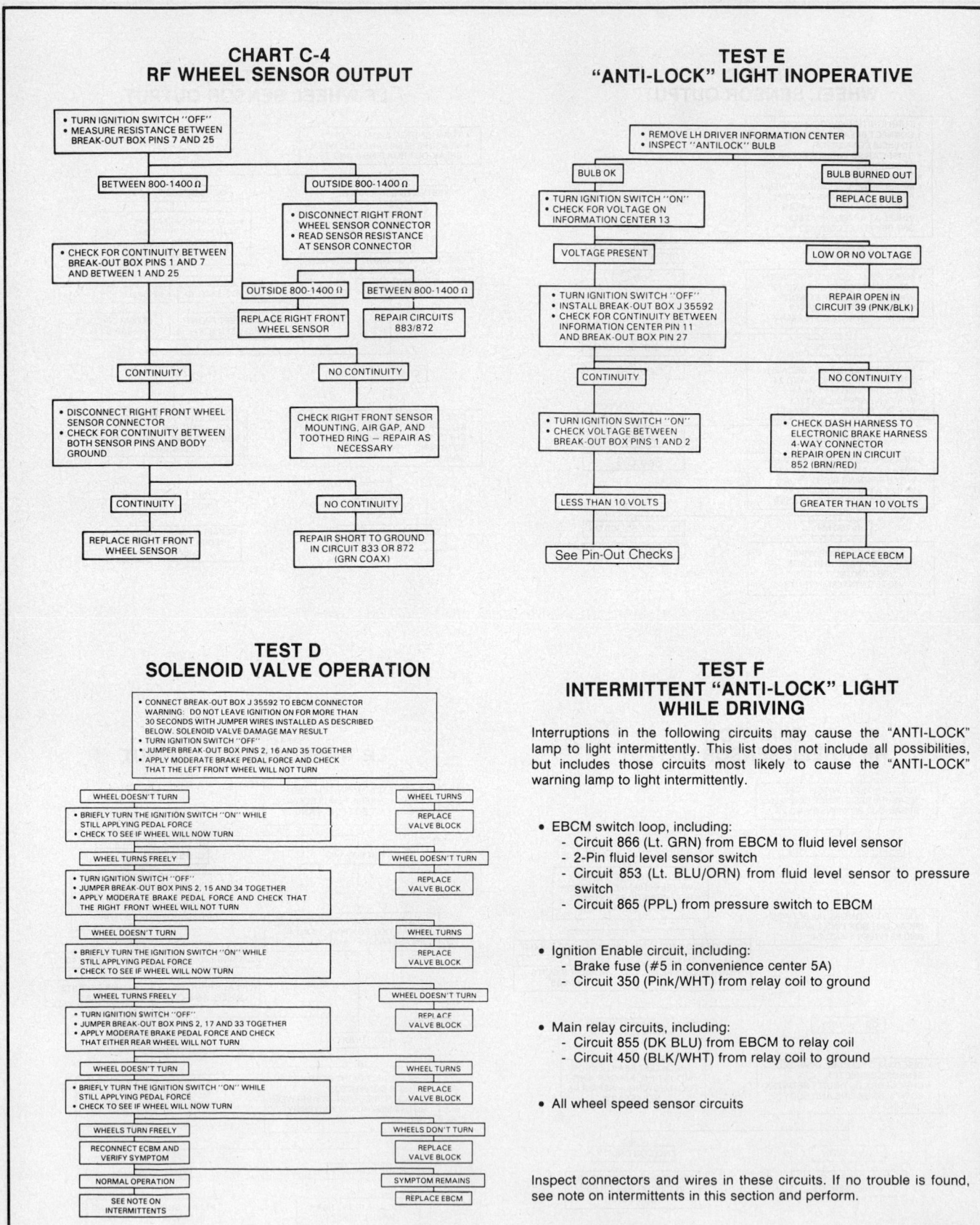

CHART C-4
RF WHEEL SENSOR OUTPUT

- TURN IGNITION SWITCH "OFF"
- MEASURE RESISTANCE BETWEEN BREAK-OUT BOX PINS 7 AND 25

BETWEEN 800-1400 Ω

- CHECK FOR CONTINUITY BETWEEN BREAK-OUT BOX PINS 1 AND 7 AND BETWEEN 1 AND 25

OUTSIDE 800-1400 Ω

- DISCONNECT RIGHT FRONT WHEEL SENSOR CONNECTOR
- READ SENSOR RESISTANCE AT SENSOR CONNECTOR

OUTSIDE 800-1400 Ω → REPLACE RIGHT FRONT WHEEL SENSOR

BETWEEN 800-1400 Ω → REPAIR CIRCUITS 883/872

CONTINUITY

- DISCONNECT RIGHT FRONT WHEEL SENSOR CONNECTOR
- CHECK FOR CONTINUITY BETWEEN BOTH SENSOR PINS AND BODY GROUND

NO CONTINUITY → CHECK RIGHT FRONT SENSOR MOUNTING, AIR GAP, AND TOOTHED RING — REPAIR AS NECESSARY

CONTINUITY → REPLACE RIGHT FRONT WHEEL SENSOR

NO CONTINUITY → REPAIR SHORT TO GROUND IN CIRCUIT 833 OR 872 (GRN COAX)

TEST E
"ANTI-LOCK" LIGHT INOPERATIVE

- REMOVE LH DRIVER INFORMATION CENTER
- INSPECT "ANTILOCK" BULB

BULB OK

- TURN IGNITION SWITCH "ON"
- CHECK FOR VOLTAGE ON INFORMATION CENTER 13

BULB BURNED OUT → REPLACE BULB

VOLTAGE PRESENT

- TURN IGNITION SWITCH "OFF"
- INSTALL BREAK-OUT BOX J 35592
- CHECK FOR CONTINUITY BETWEEN INFORMATION CENTER PIN 11 AND BREAK-OUT BOX PIN 27

LOW OR NO VOLTAGE → REPAIR OPEN IN CIRCUIT 39 (PNK/BLK)

CONTINUITY

- TURN IGNITION SWITCH "ON"
- CHECK VOLTAGE BETWEEN BREAK-OUT BOX PINS 1 AND 2

NO CONTINUITY

- CHECK DASH HARNESS TO ELECTRONIC BRAKE HARNESS 4-WAY CONNECTOR
- REPAIR OPEN IN CIRCUIT 852 (BRN/RED)

LESS THAN 10 VOLTS → See Pin-Out Checks

GREATER THAN 10 VOLTS → REPLACE EBCM

TEST D
SOLENOID VALVE OPERATION

- CONNECT BREAK-OUT BOX J 35592 TO EBCM CONNECTOR WARNING: DO NOT LEAVE IGNITION ON FOR MORE THAN 30 SECONDS WITH JUMPER WIRES INSTALLED AS DESCRIBED BELOW. SOLENOID VALVE DAMAGE MAY RESULT
- TURN IGNITION SWITCH "OFF"
- JUMPER BREAK-OUT BOX PINS 2, 16 AND 35 TOGETHER
- APPLY MODERATE BRAKE PEDAL FORCE AND CHECK THAT THE LEFT FRONT WHEEL WILL NOT TURN

WHEEL DOESN'T TURN

- BRIEFLY TURN THE IGNITION SWITCH "ON" WHILE STILL APPLYING PEDAL FORCE
- CHECK TO SEE IF WHEEL WILL NOW TURN

WHEEL TURNS → REPLACE VALVE BLOCK

WHEEL TURNS FREELY

- TURN IGNITION SWITCH "OFF"
- JUMPER BREAK-OUT BOX PINS 2, 15 AND 34 TOGETHER
- APPLY MODERATE BRAKE PEDAL FORCE AND CHECK THAT THE RIGHT FRONT WHEEL WILL NOT TURN

WHEEL DOESN'T TURN → REPLACE VALVE BLOCK

WHEEL DOESN'T TURN

- BRIEFLY TURN THE IGNITION SWITCH "ON" WHILE STILL APPLYING PEDAL FORCE
- CHECK TO SEE IF WHEEL WILL NOW TURN

WHEEL TURNS → REPLACE VALVE BLOCK

WHEEL TURNS FREELY

- TURN IGNITION SWITCH "OFF"
- JUMPER BREAK-OUT BOX PINS 2, 17 AND 33 TOGETHER
- APPLY MODERATE BRAKE PEDAL FORCE AND CHECK THAT EITHER REAR WHEEL WILL NOT TURN

WHEEL DOESN'T TURN → REPLACE VALVE BLOCK

WHEEL DOESN'T TURN

- BRIEFLY TURN THE IGNITION SWITCH "ON" WHILE STILL APPLYING PEDAL FORCE
- CHECK TO SEE IF WHEEL WILL NOW TURN

WHEEL TURNS → REPLACE VALVE BLOCK

WHEELS TURN FREELY

RECONNECT ECBM AND VERIFY SYMPTOM

WHEELS DON'T TURN → REPLACE VALVE BLOCK

NORMAL OPERATION → SEE NOTE ON INTERMITTENTS

SYMPTOM REMAINS → REPLACE EBCM

TEST F
INTERMITTENT "ANTI-LOCK" LIGHT WHILE DRIVING

Interruptions in the following circuits may cause the "ANTI-LOCK" lamp to light intermittently. This list does not include all possibilities, but includes those circuits most likely to cause the "ANTI-LOCK" warning lamp to light intermittently.

- EBCM switch loop, including:
  - Circuit 866 (Lt. GRN) from EBCM to fluid level sensor
  - 2-Pin fluid level sensor switch
  - Circuit 853 (Lt. BLU/ORN) from fluid level sensor to pressure switch
  - Circuit 865 (PPL) from pressure switch to EBCM

- Ignition Enable circuit, including:
  - Brake fuse (#5 in convenience center 5A)
  - Circuit 350 (Pink/WHT) from relay coil to ground

- Main relay circuits, including:
  - Circuit 855 (DK BLU) from EBCM to relay coil
  - Circuit 450 (BLK/WHT) from relay coil to ground

- All wheel speed sensor circuits

Inspect connectors and wires in these circuits. If no trouble is found, see note on intermittents in this section and perform.

Brake Systems

TEVES ANTI-LOCK BRAKE SYSTEMS (ABS)
GENERAL MOTORS — PONTIAC 6000 (Cont.)

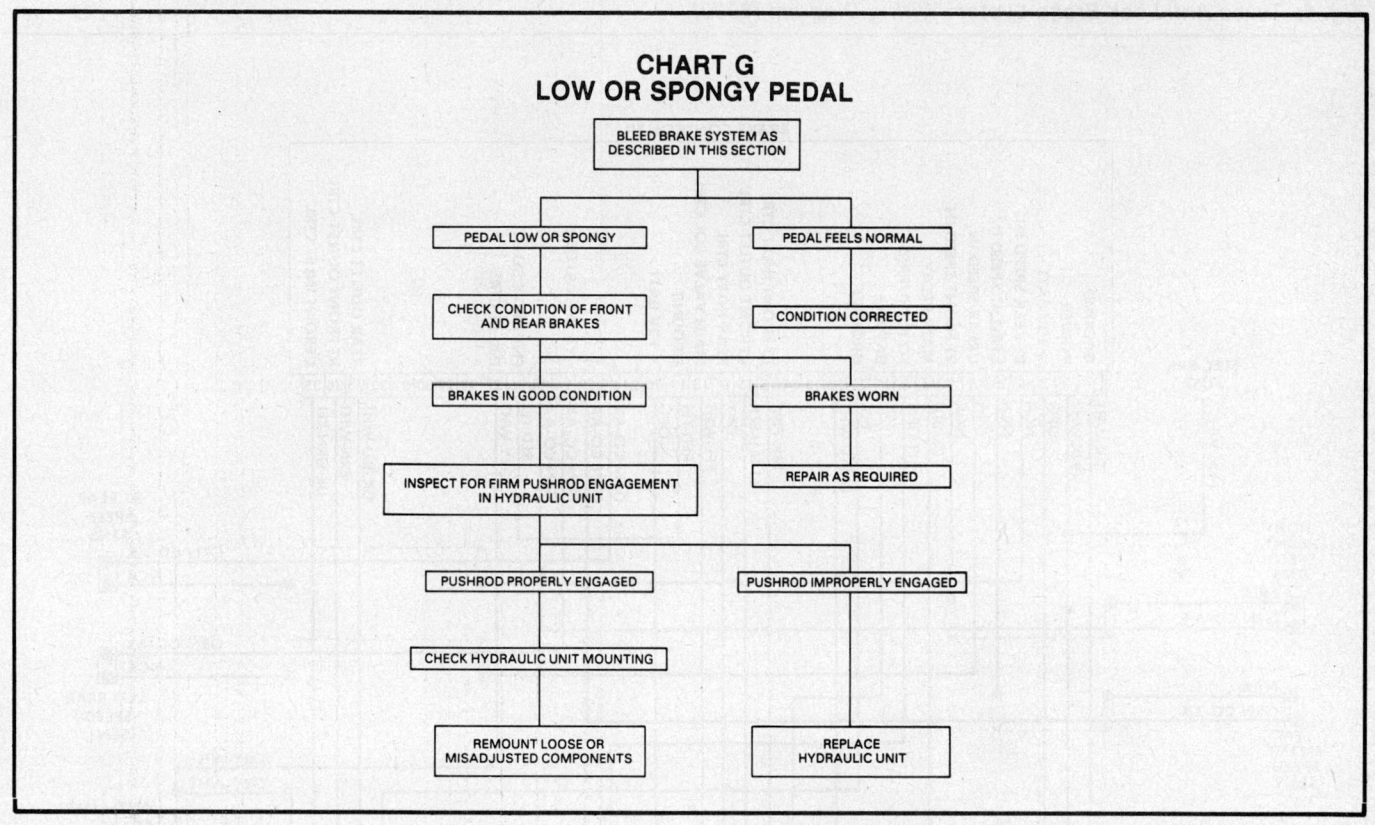

CHART G
LOW OR SPONGY PEDAL

BLEED BRAKE SYSTEM AS DESCRIBED IN THIS SECTION

PEDAL LOW OR SPONGY — PEDAL FEELS NORMAL

CHECK CONDITION OF FRONT AND REAR BRAKES — CONDITION CORRECTED

BRAKES IN GOOD CONDITION — BRAKES WORN

INSPECT FOR FIRM PUSHROD ENGAGEMENT IN HYDRAULIC UNIT — REPAIR AS REQUIRED

PUSHROD PROPERLY ENGAGED — PUSHROD IMPROPERLY ENGAGED

CHECK HYDRAULIC UNIT MOUNTING

REMOUNT LOOSE OR MISADJUSTED COMPONENTS — REPLACE HYDRAULIC UNIT

Brake Systems

TEVES ANTI-LOCK BRAKE SYSTEMS (ABS) GENERAL MOTORS — PONTIAC 6000 (Cont.)

Fig. 6: Teves Anti-Lock Brake System Wiring Diagram (6000)

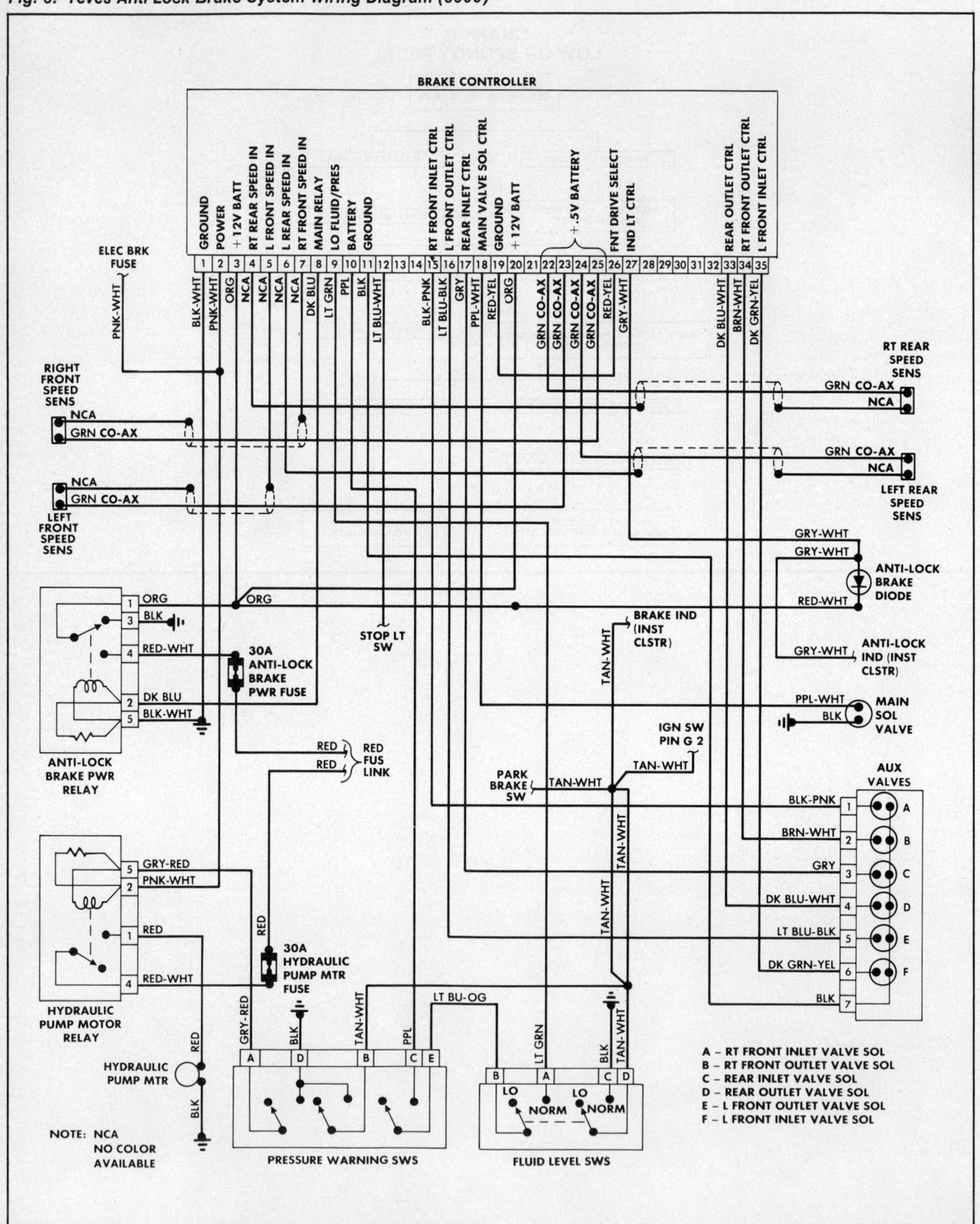

CHRYSLER MOTORS SINGLE PISTON – FRONT

DESCRIPTION

A single piston sliding caliper assembly is used on all models. The disc brake assembly consists of a caliper, disc pads, adapter and rotor. A splash shield is used on all RWD models.

FWD models use one of 3 types of calipers. A Kelsey-Hayes single pin, a Kelsey-Hays double pin and a A.T.E. double pin calipers are used. The single pin Kelsey-Hays and A.T.E. use bolt-on adapters. The double pin Kelsey-Hays mounts to rails on steering knuckle.

On RWD models, a Chrysler Motors caliper is used. The caliper is mounted on 2 machined pads on steering knuckle adapter and held in position by 2 retaining clips. The adapters position and align the calipers from front-to-rear and side-to-side.

ADJUSTMENTS

STOP LIGHT SWITCH

**Except Horizon, Omni &
All RWD Models**

1) Install switch in retaining bracket and push it forward as far as possible. Brake pedal will move slightly forward.

2) Gently pull back on pedal, bringing striker back toward switch until pedal will go no further. This will cause switch to ratchet backward to correct position.

**Horizon, Omni &
All RWD Models**

Loosen switch assembly screw. Press brake pedal down and release. Place a .130" (3.3 mm) spacer gauge against pedal-to-switch surface. Do not pull brake pedal back at any time. Press switch against spacer until plunger is fully depressed. Tighten switch mounting screw, remove spacer and check switch operation.

SERVICE BRAKES

Disc brakes are self-adjusting. Caliper piston seals are designed to retract pistons just enough to allow brake lining to lightly brush disc without any drag.

SERVICING

BLEEDING SYSTEM

See HYDRAULIC BRAKE BLEEDING in this section.

**Fig. 1: Exploded View of A.T.E. Caliper Assembly
(Kelsey-Hayes Caliper Similar)**

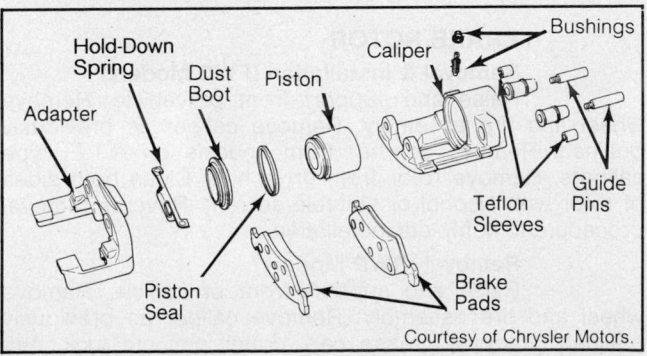

Hold-Down Spring · Adapter · Dust Boot · Piston · Caliper · Bushings · Teflon Sleeves · Guide Pins · Piston Seal · Brake Pads

Courtesy of Chrysler Motors.

DISC PAD INSPECTION

Inspect condition of disc pads any time wheels are removed. When disc pad assembly is worn to a thickness of approximately 5/16" (7.94 mm) it should be replaced. Some vehicles are equipped with an electronic brake lining wear sensor in the disc brake pads.

REMOVAL & INSTALLATION

CALIPER & PADS

NOTE: **Both disc pad assemblies should be replaced at the same time.**

Removal (FWD Models)

1) Raise and support front of vehicle. Remove wheel and tire assembly. On A.T.E. calipers, remove hold-down spring from caliper by pushing in at center of spring and pushing it outward. Loosen but do not remove caliper guide pins until caliper is free. Remove guide pins only if bushings or sleeves are to be replaced.

2) On Kelsey-Hayes calipers, remove caliper guide pin. After pin removal, use a screwdriver to pry the caliper away from rotor.

3) Remove either caliper by slowly sliding it out and away from rotor. Suspend caliper with wire to prevent damage to brake hose. Remove inner pad from caliper piston and outer pad from adapter on A.T.E. calipers. Remove outer pad, rotor and inner pad from Kelsey-Hayes calipers.

Installation

NOTE: **Before compressing caliper piston back into bore, remove a small amount of brake fluid from master cylinder, or an overfill condition will occur.**

1) Slowly push pistons back into caliper bores until bottomed. Clean machined ways and lubricate adapter and guides with multipurpose lubricant. Remove protective paper from noise suppression gasket on pads.

2) On A.T.E. calipers, install inner pad on caliper while pushing retainer into bore of piston. Install outer pad on adapter and carefully lower caliper over outer pad and rotor.

3) On Kelsey-Hayes calipers, install inner pad on adapter and install rotor on drive hub. Install outer pad on adapter and carefully lower caliper over pads and rotor.

4) Install caliper guide pins, using care not to cross threads. Tighten to specification. Install hold-down spring on A.T.E. calipers. Pump brake pedal several times until a firm pedal is obtained. Refill master cylinder and bleed brake system if necessary.

5) Install wheel and tire assembly. Tighten lug nuts to specification. Skip every other nut while going around. Repeat sequence to full torque. Road test vehicle.

Removal (RWD Models)

Raise and support front of vehicle. Remove wheel and tire assembly. Remove retaining screws, clips and anti-rattle springs. Slowly slide caliper out and away from rotor. Remove outer pad by prying between pad and caliper fingers. Suspend caliper with wire to prevent damage to brake hose. Remove inner pad.

Disc Brake Systems

CHRYSLER MOTORS SINGLE PISTON — FRONT (Cont.)

Fig. 2: Chrysler Motors Caliper Assembly

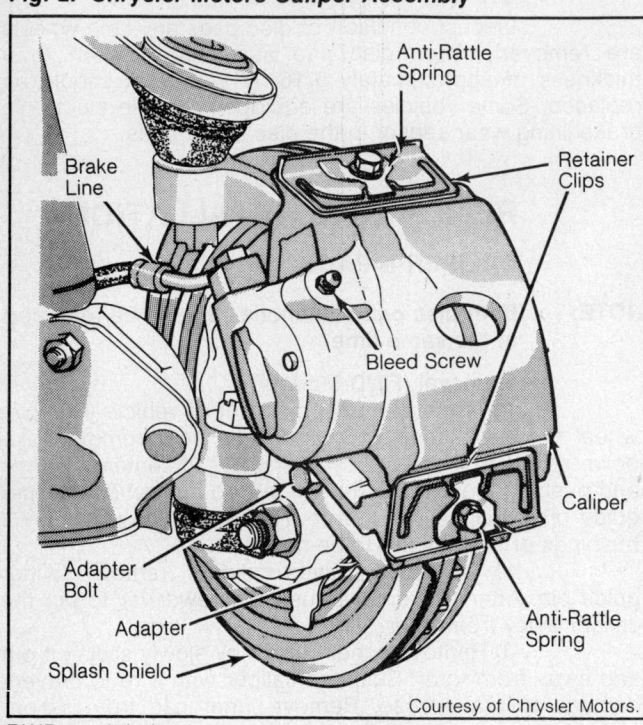

RWD model shown.

Courtesy of Chrysler Motors.

Installation

1) Remove a small amount of brake fluid at master cylinder to prevent overflow as piston is pushed back into caliper. Slowly and carefully push piston into bore of caliper until bottomed. Install outer pad into recess of caliper. No free play between outer pad flanges and caliper fingers should exist.

2) If free play is evident by vertical pad movement after installation, remove pad and bend flanges to eliminate free play. Install pad after modification, using a "C" clamp if necessary. Install inner pad with flanges in machined guides of adapter. Slowly slide caliper assembly into adapter and over rotor. Align caliper on machined guides of adapter.

CAUTION: Be careful not to pull dust boot from its groove as piston and boot slide over inner pad.

3) Install anti-rattle springs and retaining clips and tighten retaining screws. Make sure inner anti-rattle spring is installed on top of retaining spring plate.

4) Pump brake pedal several times until a firm brake pedal is obtained. Refill master cylinder and bleed brake system if necessary. Install wheel and tire assembly and lower vehicle.

BRAKE CALIPER

Caliper removal and installation procedures are the same as for disc pad assembly replacement, except that it will be necessary to disconnect brake hose from caliper.

ROTOR SERVICING

Lateral Runout

1) To check lateral runout on FWD models, install and tighten lug nuts to hold rotor on hub. Attach dial indicator to suspension so that dial pointer contacts rotor face approximately one inch from outer edge.

2) Rotate rotor and record measurement. If runout exceeds specifications, check hub lateral runout as shown. *See Fig. 3.*

3) Before removing rotor, chalk mark rotor and one wheel stud on high side of runout. Remove rotor and check hub runout. Runout should not exceed .003" (.08 mm).

4) If runout exceeds specifications, hub must be replaced. If hub runout does not exceed specifications, install the rotor on hub 180 degrees from original position. Recheck lateral runout. If runout exceeds specification, refinish or replace rotor as required.

5) On RWD models, tighten wheel bearings until all end play is eliminated. Attach dial indicator to suspension so that dial pointer contacts rotor surface approximately one inch from outer edge. Rotate and record measurement. If runout exceeds .004" (.10 mm) refinish or replace rotor/hub assembly as required. Readjust wheel bearing after lateral runout check.

Fig. 3: Checking Hub Runout

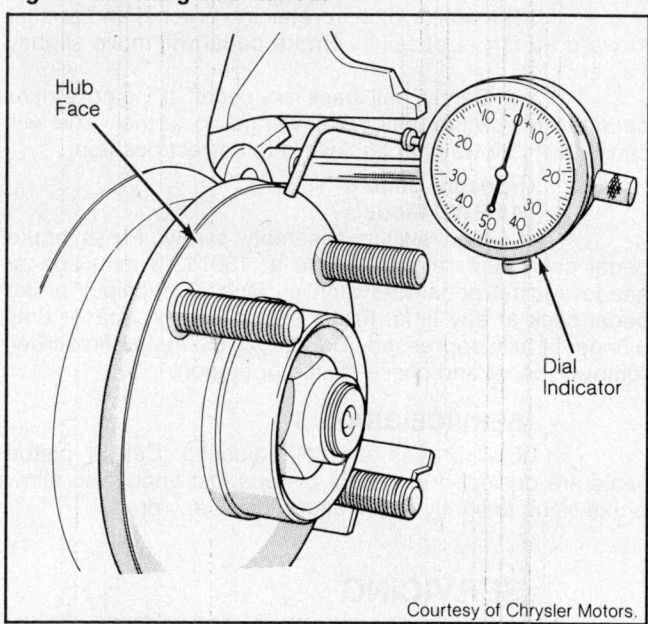

Courtesy of Chrysler Motors.

Parallelism

To check parallelism on both FWD and RWD models, measure thickness of rotor at 12 points around rotor. Make all measurements one inch from edge of rotor. If rotor exceeds specifications, refinish or replace rotor/hub assembly as required.

BRAKE ROTOR

Removal & Installation (FWD Models)

Raise and support front of vehicle. Remove wheel and tire assembly. Remove caliper as previously outlined. Remove adapter from knuckle on A.T.E. type calipers. Remove rotor from drive hub. Clean both sides of rotor with alcohol or suitable solvent. Reverse removal procedure to complete installation.

Removal (RWD Models)

Raise and support front of vehicle. Remove wheel and tire assembly. Remove caliper as previously outlined. Remove grease cap, cotter pin, nut lock, nut,

CHRYSLER MOTORS SINGLE PISTON — FRONT (Cont.)

thrust washer, and outer wheel bearing. Remove rotor-/hub assembly from spindle. Install rotor/hub assembly after servicing rotor.

Installation

Clean both sides of rotor with alcohol or suitable solvent. Install rotor/hub assembly on spindle. Install outer wheel bearing, thrust washer and nut. Tighten wheel bearing adjusting nut to specification while rotating rotor. Back off adjusting nut to release preload. Retighten adjusting nut finger tight. Install nut lock, cotter pin and grease cup. Reverse removal procedure to complete installation.

OVERHAUL

CALIPER

Disassembly

CAUTION: Chrysler Motors recommends that compressed air not be used to remove piston from caliper.

1) With caliper removed from rotor and brake hose still attached, carefully depress brake pedal to hydraulically force piston out of bore. If both pistons are to be removed, disconnect flexible brake line at frame bracket after removing first piston. Plug brake tube and repeat procedure.

2) Disconnect brake hose from caliper. Place caliper in vise and remove dust boot. Using a small wooden or plastic stick, pry piston seal from caliper bore groove. Remove bushings from A.T.E. and Kelsey-Hayes calipers. Discard bushings and Teflon sleeves on A.T.E. calipers.

Cleaning & Inspection

Clean all components (including bleeder screw) using alcohol or suitable solvent. Blow out all passages and bores with compressed air. Inspect piston and bore for scoring or pitting. Clean light scoring or corrosion with crocus cloth. Bores with deep scoring may be honed, providing diameter of bore is not increased more than .001" (.025 mm). If specification is exceeded, replace caliper.

Reassembly

1) Dip new piston seal in clean brake fluid and gently work seal into groove until seated. Coat new piston boot with clean brake fluid, leaving a generous amount inside boot.

2) Position dust boot over piston. Install piston, pushing it past seal, until it bottoms in bore. Position boot in counterbore. Using a hammer and dust boot installer, drive boot into counterbore.

3) Remove Teflon sleeves from bushings before installing bushings into A.T.E. caliper. Install new bushings on either caliper by pressing in on bushings until seated. Be sure that bushing flanges extend evenly over caliper casting. After bushings are installed, reinstall Teflon sleeves. Clean machined ways of caliper to remove rust and corrision before lubricating or reinstalling.

TIGHTENING SPECIFICATIONS

Application	Ft. Lbs. (N.m)
Adapter Mounting Bolts	
FWD Models	130-190 (176-258)
RWD Models	95-125 (129-169)
Guide Pins	
A.T.E.	18-26 (24-35)
Kelsey-Hayes	
Single Pin	25-35 (34-47)
Double Pin	18-25 (24-34)
Lug Nuts	
FWD Models	95 (129)
RWD Models	85 (115)
Brake Hose to Caliper	19-29 (26-39)

DISC BRAKE ROTOR SPECIFICATIONS

Application	Disc Diameter In. (mm)	Lateral Runout In. (mm)	Parallelism In. (mm)	Original Thickness In. (mm)	Min. Refinish Thickness In. (mm)	Discard Thickness In. (mm)
RWD	11.0 (279.4)	.004 (.10)	.0005 (.013)	1.000-1.010 (25.4-25.7)	.970 (24.6)	.940 (23.9)
FWD						
Horizon, Omni	8.98 (228.0)	.005 (.13)	.0005 (.013)	.490-.505 (12.5-12.8)	.461 (11.71)	.431 (10.95)
All Other Models	¹ 9.45 (240.0)	.005 (.13)	.0005 (.013)	.930-.940 (23.6-23.9)	.912 (23.2)	.882 (22.4)

¹ — Heavy Duty Disc is 10.24" (260.0 mm).

Disc Brake Systems

CHRYSLER MOTORS SINGLE PISTON — REAR

Daytona, Dynasty, New Yorker (Except Turbo)

DESCRIPTION

The single piston, floating caliper rear disc brake assembly consists of a hub assembly, caliper, disc pads, adapter, rotor, and a mechanically operated parking brake.

"C" body vehicles use a caliper with a 1.42" (36 mm) piston and a mechanical parking brake. The caliper assembly rides on rubber bushings with metal sleeves on 2 bolts which mount assembly to an adapter.

"G" body vehicles use a caliper with a 1.30" (33 mm) piston. Inside the piston assembly is an automatic brake adjuster and self adjusting parking brake mechanism. The caliper assembly rides on rubber bushings, with teflon sleeves on 2 guide pins that attach to the adapter.

ADJUSTMENTS

SERVICE BRAKES

Disc brakes are self-adjusting, except "G" body. See CALIPER & PADS INSTALLATION in this article. Caliper seals are designed to retract piston enough to allow only very light brake contact without any drag.

PARKING BRAKE

NOTE: **Service brakes must be properly adjusted before adjusting parking brake.**

1) Raise and support vehicle. Release parking brake and loosen parking brake adjusting nut until cables are slack.

2) Begin tightening adjusting nut. Stop tightening nut, when slight drag is felt while rotating rear wheels.

3) Loosen adjusting nut until rear wheels turn freely. Loosen nut an additional 2 full turns.

4) Apply and release parking brake several times to ensure proper operation.

SERVICING

BLEEDING SYSTEM

CAUTION: **Vehicles equipped with ABS brake systems MUST follow brake bleeding procedure. See BOSCH ANTI-LOCK BRAKE SYSTEM (ABS) CHRYSLER MOTORS in this section.**

See HYDRAULIC BRAKE BLEEDING in this section for vehicles without ABS brake systems.

DISC PAD INSPECTION

Inspect condition of disc pads any time wheels are removed. When a disc pad assembly is worn to a thickness of approximately 9/32" (7.14 mm), it should be replaced.

DISC PAD REPLACEMENT

See REMOVAL & INSTALLATION in this section.

BRAKE ROTOR

Lateral Runout

1) To check lateral runout, install and tighten lug nuts to hold rotor on hub, tighen wheel bearings until all end play is eliminated. Attach dial indicator to suspension so that dial pointer contacts rotor face approximately one inch from outer edge. See Fig. 1.

2) Rotate rotor and record measurement. If runout exceeds specifications, check hub lateral runout as shown.

3) Before removing rotor, chalk mark rotor and one wheel stud on high side of runout. Remove rotor and check hub runout. Runout should not exceed .003" (.08 mm).

4) If runout exceeds specifications, hub must be replaced. If hub runout does not exceed specifications, install the rotor on hub 180 degrees from original position. Recheck lateral runout. If runout exceeds specification, refinish or replace rotor as required. Readjust wheel bearings.

Fig. 1: Checking Hub Runout

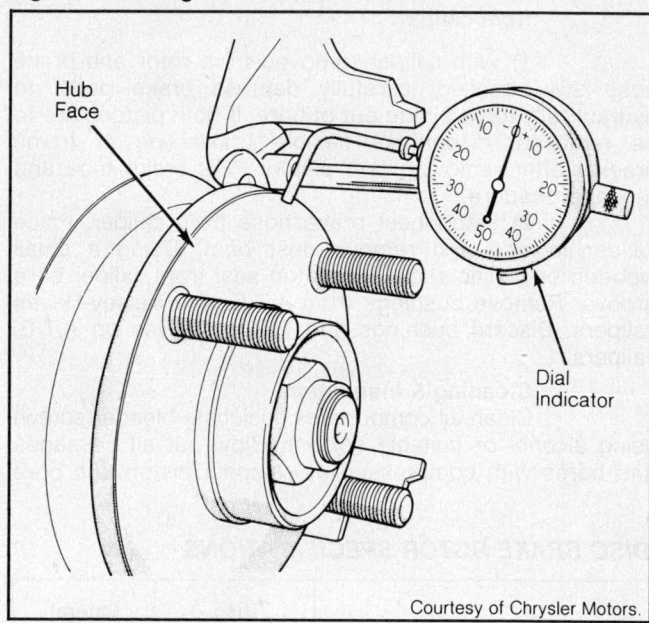

Courtesy of Chrysler Motors.

Parallelism

To check parallelism, measure thickness of rotor at 12 points around rotor. Make all measurements one inch from edge of rotor. If rotor exceeds specifications, refinish or replace rotor.

REMOVAL & INSTALLATION

CALIPER & PADS

NOTE: **Rear calipers are not servicable. If fluid leaks are detected around caliper piston, calipers must be replaced as an assembly.**

Removal ("C" Body)

1) Raise and support vehicle. Remove wheel and tire assembly. Drive out disc pad retainer pin and remove 2 caliper mounting bolts. See Fig. 2.

2) Lift caliper up and away from disc. Suspend caliper on wire hook to prevent damage to brake hose. Remove disc pads.

Disc Brake Systems

CHRYSLER MOTORS SINGLE PISTON — REAR (Cont.)

Fig. 2: "C" Body Rear Brake Assembly

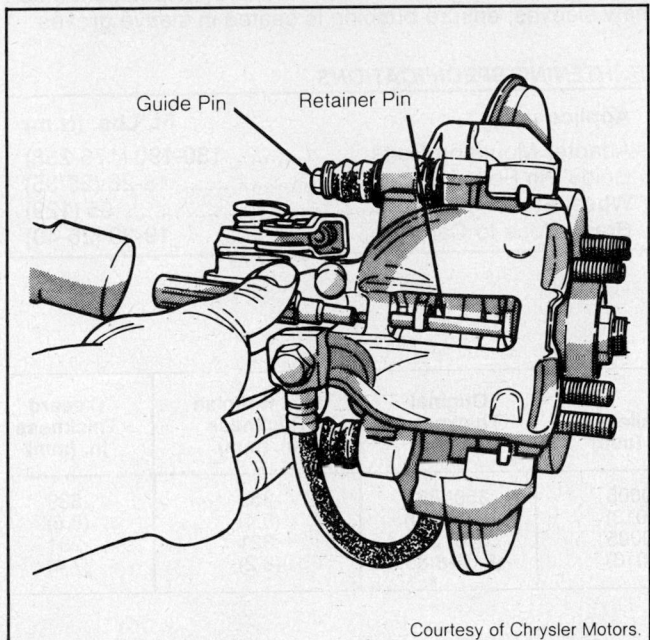

Courtesy of Chrysler Motors.

Fig. 3: "G" Body Rear Brake Assembly

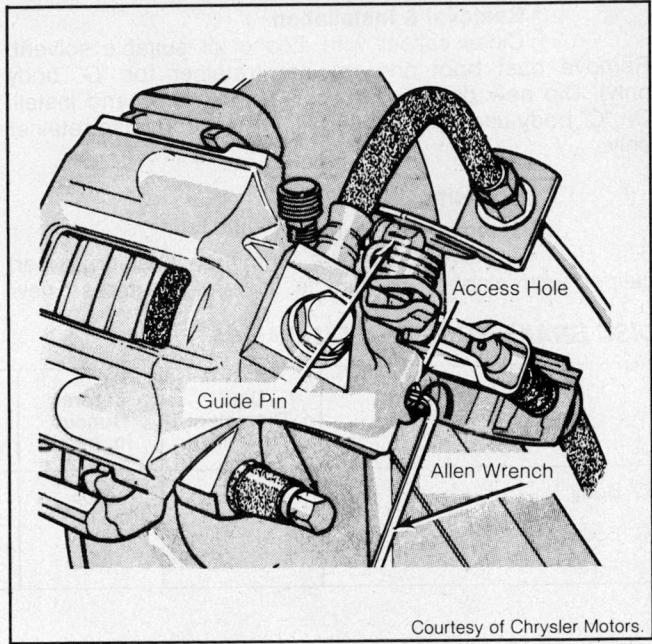

Courtesy of Chrysler Motors.

Installation

NOTE: Before compressing caliper piston back into bore, remove a small amount of brake fluid from master, or overfill condition will occur.

1) Slowly push piston back into caliper bores until bottomed. Clean and lubricate machined ways. Install new disc pads.

2) Carefully, place caliper over disc and pads. Lower end must be installed first. Install anti-rattle clip through top opening in caliper.

3) Drive disc pad retainer pin through caliper and disc pads. Push down caliper assembly and torque upper and then lower caliper mounting bolts. Install wheels and tires. Pump brakes and ensure pedal is firm. Road test and check for leaks.

Removal ("G" Body)

1) Raise and support vehicle. Remove wheel and tire assembly. Clean area around access plug and remove plug. *See Fig. 3.*

2) Insert 4 mm Allen wrench through access hole and turn retraction shaft counterclockwise a few turns. This will increase disc pad clearance. Remove anti-rattle spring. Do not bend spring.

3) Back out guide pins enough to remove caliper assembly. Lift caliper up and away from disc. Suspend caliper on wire hook to prevent damage to brake hose. Remove disc pads.

Installation

NOTE: Rear calipers are not servicable. If fluid leaks are detected around caliper piston, calipers must be replaced as an assembly.

1) Installation of new disc pads will require retacting caliper piston further. Insert Allen wrench through access hole. Apply pressure to face of piston and turn Allen wrench counterclockwise until slight increase in pressure is felt.

2) Install inboard disc pad into caliper piston. Install outboard pad on adapter. Be sure to note outboard pad markings, "R" or "L".

3) Carefully lower caliper over disc and outboard pad. Install guide pins and torque to specification.

4) Initial pad clearance must be adjusted. Insert Allen wrench through access hole and turn clockwise until pads are snug (no clearance between disc and pad). Turn Allen wrench back 1/3 turn and install access plug. Pump brakes to ensure pedal is firm. Road test and check for leaks.

OVERHAUL

CALIPER

NOTE: Rear calipers are not servicable. If fluid leaks are detected around caliper piston, calipers must be replaced as an assembly.

Disc Brake Systems

CHRYSLER MOTORS SINGLE PISTON — REAR (Cont.)

DUST BOOT
Removal & Installation
Clean caliper with alcohol or suitable solvent. Remove dust boot and retainer (retainer for "G" body only). Dip new dust boot in clean brake fluid and install. On "C" body use Tool (C-4383-7). On "G" body use retainer only.

BUSHING & SLEEVE
Removal & Installation
Remove old sleeve, and then bushing. Clean caliper with alcohol or suitable solvent. Compress new

bushings with fingers and work into proper position. Insert new sleeves, ensure bushing is seated in sleeve groves.

TIGHTENING SPECIFICATIONS

Application	Ft. Lbs. (N.m)
Adapter Mounting Bolts	130-190 (176-258)
Guide Pin Bolts	18-26 (25-35)
Wheel Studs	95 (129)
Brake Hose to Caliper	19-29 (26-40)

DISC BRAKE ROTOR SPECIFICATIONS

Application	Disc Diameter In. (mm)	Lateral Runout In. (mm)	Parallelism In. (mm)	Original Thickness In. (mm)	Min. Refinish Thickness In. (mm)	Discard Thickness In. (mm)
"C" Body	10.8 (275)	.005 (.13)	.0005 (.013)	.350-.358 (8.9-9.10)	.369 (9.4)	.339 (8.6)
"G" Body	10.8 (275)	.005 (.13)	.0005 (.013)	.340-.348 (8.65-8.85)	.321 (8.2)	.291 (7.4)

CORVETTE 4-WHEEL DISC

DESCRIPTION

The Corvette features a 4-wheel disc brake system. The system incorporates finned aluminum, double piston front caliper and a single piston rear. Hydraulic pressure is converted into friction through a clamping action on rotor by caliper and friction pads.

Parking brake is incorporated into rear caliper and is seperate from hydralic system. When parking brake is applied, lever on caliper causes pushrod, actuating collar and clamp rod assembly to be moved outward causing caliper to slide inward, mechanically forcing linings against rotor.

ADJUSTMENTS

STOPLIGHT SWITCH

1) With brake pedal depressed, insert switch assembly into tubular clip until switch body seats on tube clip. Note that audible "clicks" can be heard as threaded portion of switch and valve are pushed through clip toward brake pedal.

2) Pull brake pedal fully rearward against pedal stop, until audible "click" sounds can no longer be heard. Switch assembly will be moved in tubular clip providing proper adjustment.

NOTE: Use of excessive force while adjusting stoplight switch may damage power booster.

3) Release brake pedal and repeat step **3)** to ensure no audible "click" sounds remain.

SERVICE BRAKES

Disc brakes are self-adjusting. Caliper piston seals are designed to retract pistons just enough to allow brake lining to lightly brush rotor without any drag. Sliding caliper design compensates for any lining wear.

PARKING BRAKE

Disabling Automatic Parking Brake Adjuster

1) Remove drivers seat cushion, parking brake lever cover and screws. Fabricate a hook on end of a .08" (2 mm) diameter solid wire.

2) Using wire hook, hold drive pawl so it is disengaged from drive sector. Insert a nail through hole in anchor plate to retain drive pawl in disengaged position.

3) Move lever until it aligns with lock pawl. Depress button on lever and move lever to down position. Visually inspect to see that anchor plate is against stud. If anchor plate is not against stud, repeat procedure as needed.

Cable Free Play

NOTE: Brake pads must be new or within .006" (0.15 mm) thickness of each other. Parking brake adjustment will not be acurate with heavily tapered pads. Parking brake free play should only be made if caliper has been disassemble. Free play adjustment will not correct a condition such as levers not returning to their stops.

1) With parking brake automatic adjuster disabled, have an assistant apply a light brake pedal load

(enough to stop rotor from turning by hand). Apply pressure to caliper lever *See Fig. 1*. Free play between caliper lever and housing must be .024"-.027" (.61-.69 mm).

2) If free play is incorrect, remove adjustment screw and clean threads. Coat threads with adhesive. Screw in adjusting screw far enough to obtain proper free play between caliper lever and caliper housing. Have assistant release brake pedal, apply brake pedal firmly three times. Recheck free play and adjust if necessary.

Fig. 1: Rear Caliper

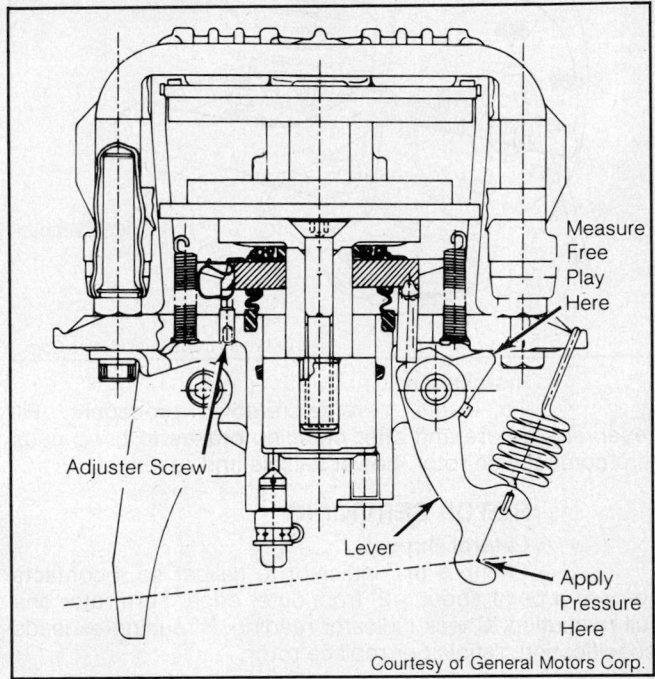

Measure Free Play Here

Adjuster Screw

Lever

Apply Pressure Here

Courtesy of General Motors Corp.

SERVICING

BLEEDING

See HYDRAULIC BRAKE BLEEDING in this section.

BRAKE LINING INSPECTION

Inspect linings every 6000 miles or whenever wheels are removed. Replace, in complete sets only, any linings that are worn to within .031" (.79 mm) of the shoe.

DISC LINING REPLACEMENT
Removal

1) Remove 2/3 of brake fluid from reservoirs. Lift and support vehicle. Mark relationship of wheel to axle. Remove wheel. Reinstall 2 lug nuts to hold rotor in position.

2) On rear brakes, position "C" clamp over caliper and tighten clamp until piston bottoms in bore. *See Fig. 2*. Remove upper caliper mounting bolt. Rotate caliper on lower bolt and guide pin to expose pads. Remove pads.

3) On front brakes, remove caliper guide pins and caliper. Using adjustable pliers, bottom pistons in caliper. Remove brake pads.

Disc Brake Systems

CORVETTE 4-WHEEL DISC (Cont).

4) On all brakes, clean mounting bracket and caliper housing outer legs of all residue. If guide pins or dust boots are damaged, replace them with new ones.

Fig. 2: Backing Piston into Bore

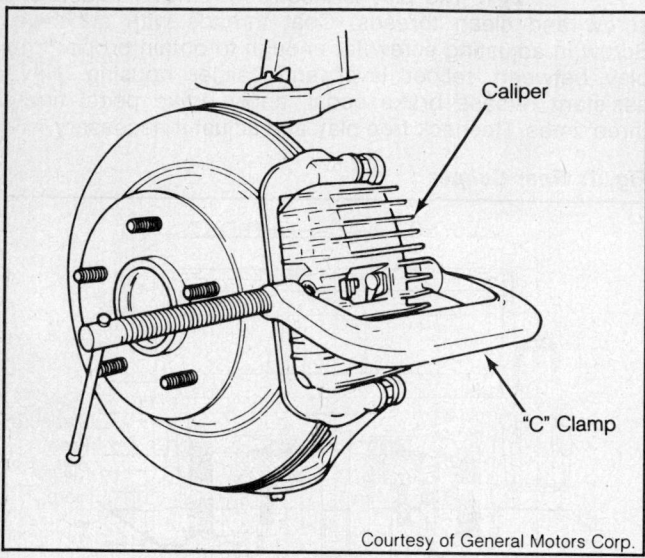

Courtesy of General Motors Corp.

Installation

To install, reverse removal procedure. Fill reservoirs before and after pumping brakes to bring pads into contact with rotor. Lower vehicle and road test.

ROTOR SERVICING

Lateral Runout

Clamp a dial indicator to caliper so it contacts rotor at a point about 1/2" from outer edge. Turn rotor one full revolution. Check indicator reading. If reading exceeds specification, refinish or replace rotor.

Parallelism

Check thickness of rotor at 4 or more points around edge of rotor. Make all measurements the same distance from edge. If thickness varies from specification, refinish or replace rotor.

REMOVAL & INSTALLATION

CALIPER

Removal & Installation

1) To remove caliper, remove brake line attached to caliper and plug. On front brakes, remove retaining pin circlip, pin and caliper.

2) On rear brakes, disable automatic parking brake adjuster. See DISABLING AUTOMATIC PARKING BRAKE ADJUSTER in this article. Remove caliper lever return spring. Replace return spring if damaged.

3) Disconnect parking brake cable from caliper lever and caliper bracket. Remove caliper guide pin bolts and caliper. To install, reverse removal procedure and bleed brakes.

ROTOR

Removal & Installation (Front)

Remove caliper and caliper mounting bracket. Remove rotor. To install, reverse removal procedure

Removal & Installation (Rear)

Remove caliper and caliper mounting bracket. Remove spindle nut and spindle lock nut, bearing washer

and outer wheel bearing. Slide rotor from spindle. To install rotor, reverse removal procedure. Bleed brakes if brake line was removed from caliper.

OVERHAUL

CALIPER

Disassembly (Front)

1) With caliper assembly removed from vehicle, pad interior of caliper with shop cloths. To remove pistons, direct compressed air into brake hose port. Always use eye protection when performing this step.

2) Inspect pistons for scoring, nicks, corrosion and worn or damaged chrome plating. Replace piston(s) if any of these defects are found. Remove piston boot from housing by hand and discard.

3) Remove piston seals from groove in caliper bore with a piece of wood or plastic. Do not use a metal tool of any type, as damage to bore may result. Remove bleeder screw. Clean and inspect bleeder screw. Replace as necessary. Inspect guide pins. Clean or replace as necessary. Inspect caliper bores. If badly scored or corroded around seal area, replace with a new housing.

Reassembly

1) Clean all parts not included in repair kit in denatured alcohol. Dry parts with non-lubricated dry compressed air. Check piston to bore fit by sliding piston into bore. Install cap and bleeder screw.

2) Lubricate a new piston seal with clean brake fluid. Install in caliper bore seal groove. Make sure seal is not twisted. Lubricate bore with clean brake fluid.

3) Install boot over end of piston so that fold in boot will face outward. Position piston over caliper bore and seat boot into groove in caliper bore by hand.

4) Insert pistons into caliper bore. By hand, push pistons to bottom of bore. Make sure boot is properly seated in groove around pistons and groove in caliper bores. Reinstall pads and caliper. Bleed brakes and road test.

Dissasembly (Rear)

1) Remove caliper assembly. Disconnect collar return springs from actuating collar. Pull actuating collar with assembled parts out of caliper housing by pulling on both ends of actuating collar. See Fig. 3.

2) Remove clamp rod and compliance bushing from actuating collar. Remove boot retainers and boots pushrod from actuating collar. Remove preload spring from retainer.

3) Pad interior of caliper with shop cloths. To remove piston, direct compressed air into brake hose port. Always use eye protection when performing this step.

4) Inspect piston for scoring, nicks, corrosion and worn or damaged chrome plating. Replace piston if any of these defects are found. Remove piston boot from housing by hand and discard.

5) Remove piston seal from groove in caliper bore with a piece of wood or plastic. Do not use a metal tool of any type, as damage to bore may result. Remove bleeder screw. Clean and inspect bleeder screw. Replace as necessary.

6) Inspect guide pins. Clean or replace as necessary. Inspect caliper bores. If badly scored or corroded around seal area, replace with a new housing.

CORVETTE 4-WHEEL DISC (Cont).

Fig. 3: Exploded View of Rear Caliper

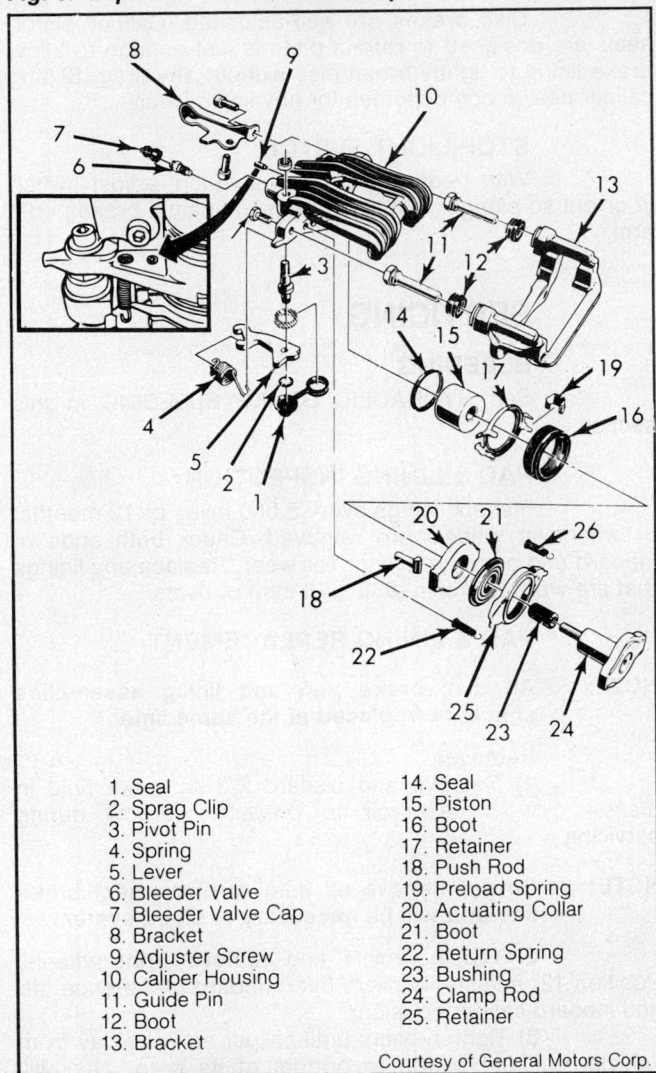

1. Seal
2. Sprag Clip
3. Pivot Pin
4. Spring
5. Lever
6. Bleeder Valve
7. Bleeder Valve Cap
8. Bracket
9. Adjuster Screw
10. Caliper Housing
11. Guide Pin
12. Boot
13. Bracket
14. Seal
15. Piston
16. Boot
17. Retainer
18. Push Rod
19. Preload Spring
20. Actuating Collar
21. Boot
22. Return Spring
23. Bushing
24. Clamp Rod
25. Retainer

Courtesy of General Motors Corp.

Reassembly

1) Clean all parts not included in repair kit in denatured alcohol. Dry parts with non-lubricated dry compressed air. Inspect all parts for damage, replace if necessary. Check piston to bore fit by sliding piston into bore. Install cap and bleeder screw.

2) Lubricate a new piston seal with clean brake fluid and install in caliper bore seal groove. Make sure seal is not twisted. Lubricate bore with clean brake fluid. Insert pistons into caliper bore. Using hand pressure, push piston to bottom of bore.

3) Install pushrod, new boots and new retainer to actuating collar by lightly coating actuating collar with lubricant provided in repair kit, clamping retainers firmly against actuating collar and bending tabs on retainer to hold assembly together.

4) Install spring into boot retainer. Lightly coat clamp rod with lubricant in repair kit. Slide clamp rod through holes in boot and actuating collar. Ensure boot is against reaction plate on clamp rod. Lubricate new compliance bushing with provided lubricant and install to clamp rod.

5) Lubricate grooved bead of inner boot and boot groove in caliper housing with provided lubricant. Use remainder of lubricant to coat actuating collar, paying particular attention to center hole. Push clamp rod firmly to bottom of mating hole into piston.

6) Pull on actuating collar and seat inner boot into boot groove in caliper housing, ensure pushrod enters hole in caliper housing. Install new bleeder valve cap and bleeder valve in caliper housing.

7) Tighten bleeder valve. Install pivot pin and new nut to caliper housing. Tighten pivot pin nut. Lubricate caliper parking brake lever and pivot pin with provided grease. Install pivot pin seal. Install caliper parking brake lever and new sprag clip with teeth facing away from lever. Snap pivot pin seal over pivot pin.

8) Install 2 collar return springs to retainer (retainer must enter springs at end of second coil). Install adjustment screw into caliper housing until actuating collar is about parallel to piston bore face of caliper housing.

9) Lubricate 2 guide pins with grease provided in repair kit. Slide new boots on guide pins. Fill boots with provided grease. Assemble to mounting bracket. Make sure boots fit into grooves of guide pins and mounting bracket. Install caliper.

TIGHTENING SPECIFICATIONS

Application	Ft. Lbs. (N.m)
Mounting Bracket Bolt	
Front	133 (180)
Rear	70 (95)
Brake Hose-to-Caliper	32 (44)
Self-Locking Bolt	24 (32)
	INCH lbs. (N.m)
Bleeder Screw	84 (9)

DISC BRAKE ROTOR SPECIFICATIONS

Application	Disc Diameter In. (mm)	Lateral Runout In. (mm)	Parallelism In. (mm)	Original Thickness In. (mm)	Min. Refinish Thickness In. (mm)	Discard Thickness In. (mm)
Corvette						
Front						
Standard	11.5 (292)	.006 (.15)	.0005 (.013)	.780 (19.9)	.744 (18.9)	.724 (18.4)
Heavy Duty	13 (330)	.006 (15)	.0005 (.013)	1.110 (28.2)	1.059 (18.9)	1.039 (18.4)
Rear	11.5 (292)	.006 (.15)	.0005 (.013)	.780 (19.9)	.744 (18.9)	.724 (18.4)

Disc Brake Systems

DELCO-MORAINE SINGLE PISTON – FRONT

Buick, Cadillac, Chevrolet (Exc. Corvette, Nova), Oldsmobile, Pontiac

DESCRIPTION & OPERATION

Caliper has a single bore and is mounted to a support bracket with 2 mounting bolts. Hydraulic force, created by applying pressure to the brake pedal, is converted by the caliper to friction through 2 friction pads. Pads are made of stamped steel with riveted linings.

The caliper forms a clamping action on a rotor. Rotor is made of cast iron, with ventilation fins separating the 2 braking surfaces. Some models use a groove machined in the braking surfaces to help control brake noise. Pads incorporate a wear sensor made from a piece of spring steel, riveted to rear edge of the inner friction pad. The sensor produces a high pitched squeal when lining needs replacement.

Fig. 1: Exploded View of Caliper Assembly (All Except Allanté)

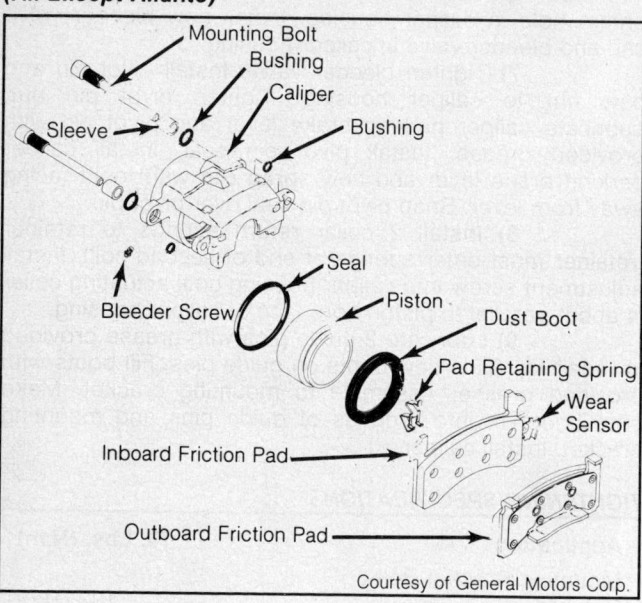

Courtesy of General Motors Corp.

Fig. 2: Exploded View of Allanté Caliper Assembly

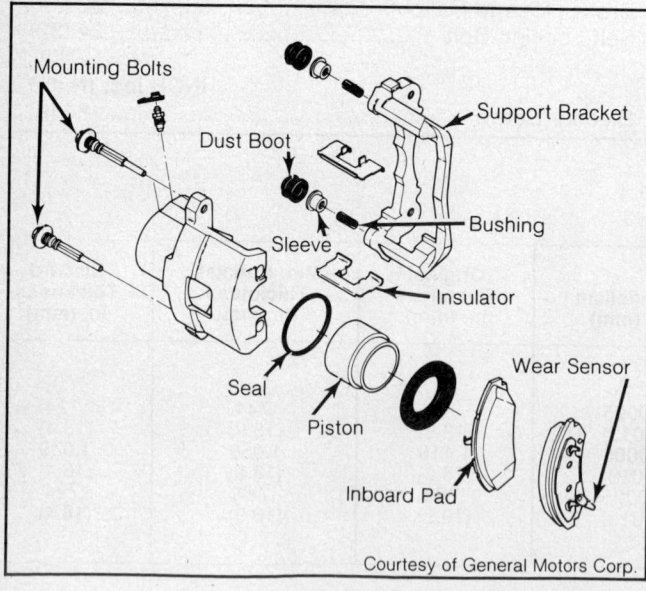

Courtesy of General Motors Corp.

ADJUSTMENTS

Disc brakes are self-adjusting. Caliper piston seals are designed to retract pistons just enough to allow brake lining to lightly brush disc without any drag. Sliding caliper design compensates for any lining wear.

STOP LIGHT SWITCH

With pedal in released position, adjust switch in or out so plunger is fully depressed against brake pedal arm.

SERVICING

BLEEDING

See HYDRAULIC BRAKE BLEEDING in this section.

PAD & LINING INSPECTION

Inspect linings every 6,000 miles or 12 months, or whenever wheels are removed. Check both ends of inboard and outboard linings for wear. Replace any linings that are worn to within .030" (.76 mm) of rivets.

PAD & LINING REPLACEMENT

NOTE: All disc brake pad and lining assemblies should be replaced at the same time.

Removal

1) Remove and discard 2/3 of brake fluid in master cylinder reservoir to prevent overflow during servicing.

NOTE: Do not remove all fluid or disconnect brake line or it will be necessary to bleed system.

2) Raise vehicle and remove front wheels. Position 12" adjustable pliers over inboard brake shoe tab and inboard caliper housing.

3) Tighten pliers until caliper moves away from vehicle, pushing piston to bottom of its bore. This will allow pads to back off from rotor surface. Remove pliers. Unbolt caliper from support bracket.

4) Lift caliper off rotor and support with a wire so brake hose will not be damaged. Remove pads and pad support spring from cavity in piston. Remove sleeves from inboard ears of caliper and rubber bushings from all caliper ears.

Installation (Allanté)

1) With piston retracted into caliper cylinder. Lubricate new bushings and install into mounting bolt holes in caliper mounting bracket.

Fig. 3: Installing Allanté Outboard Pad

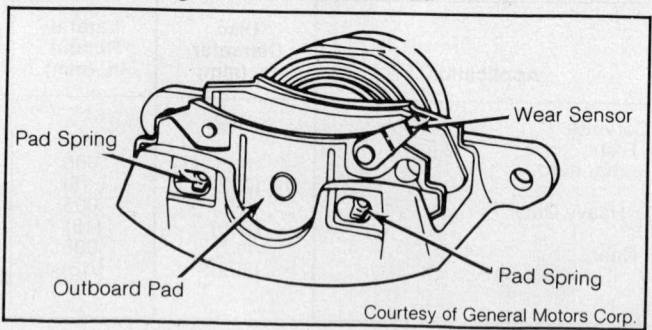

Courtesy of General Motors Corp.

DELCO-MORAINE SINGLE PISTON – FRONT (Cont.)

2) Install inboard pad by snapping shoe retainer spring into piston, ensure pad lays flat against piston. Install outboard pad by snapping pad rings into holes in caliper housing. *See Fig. 3.* Wear indicator should be at rear of vehicle.

3) Add brake fluid to fill master cylinder to within 1/8" of top. Pump brake pedal to seat pads against rotor.

Installation (All Except Allanté)

1) Using silicone lubricant, coat and install new sleeves and rubber bushings in caliper ears. Attach pad support spring to inboard pad. Ensure pad is installed in caliper with wear indictor toward rear of vehicle.

2) Position outboard pad in caliper. Engage tab at bottom of pad with caliper cut-out and pad ears with caliper ears at top of pad. Place caliper over rotor, aligning caliper ears with mounting holes.

3) Start bolts through inboard caliper ears and mounting bracket. Make sure bolts pass under retaining ears of inboard pad. Push bolts through caliper to engage holes in outboard pad and ears of caliper. Thread bolts into mounting bracket and tighten.

Fig. 4: Clinching Tabs on Outboard Pad

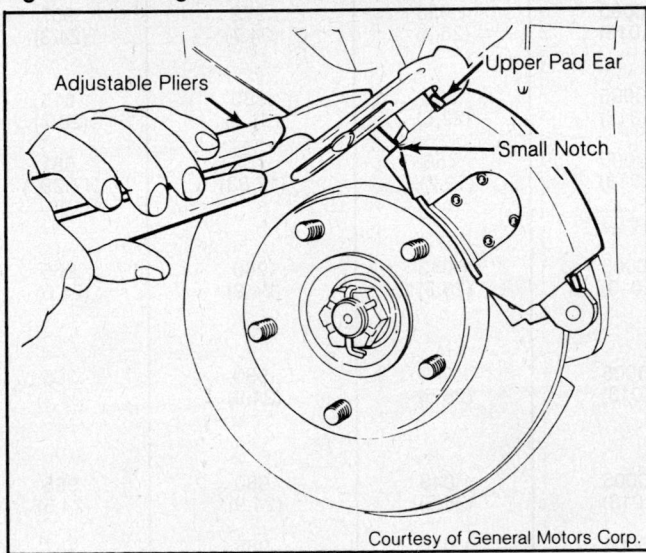

Courtesy of General Motors Corp.

4) Add brake fluid to fill master cylinder to within 1/8" of top. Pump brake pedal to seat pads against rotor.

5) Use pliers to clinch upper ears of outboard pad against caliper. Make sure ears are flat against caliper with no clearance. *See Fig. 4.* Recheck fluid level. Replace wheels and lower vehicle.

ROTOR SERVICING

Lateral Runout

Adjust wheel bearings until all end play is eliminated. Attach a dial indicator to front suspension so pointer contacts face of rotor about one inch from edge. Set gauge to zero. Turn rotor through one complete revolution. Check gauge reading with specifications for maximum lateral runout.

Parallelism

Check thickness of rotor at 4 or more points around edge of rotor. Make all measurements same distance from edge. If thickness varies more than specified, refinish or replace rotor.

REMOVAL & INSTALLATION

BRAKE CALIPER

Removal & Installation

1) Remove and discard 2/3 of brake fluid in master cylinder reservoir to prevent overflow during servicing. Raise vehicle and remove front wheels. Position 12" adjustable pliers over inboard brake shoe tab and inboard caliper housing.

2) Tighten pliers until caliper moves away from vehicle, pushing piston to bottom of its bore. This will allow pads to back off from rotor surface. Remove pliers. Unbolt caliper from support bracket. Lift caliper off rotor and support with a wire so brake hose will not be damaged.

BRAKE ROTOR

Removal & Installation (FWD Models)

Raise and support vehicle. Remove front wheel and reinstall one wheel nut to retain rotor during caliper removal. Remove cotter pin and nut securing brake hose to upper control arm. Remove caliper and wire up out of way. Mark rotor and hub for reassembly and remove rotor. To install brake rotor, reverse procedure.

Removal & Installation (RWD Models)

Raise and support vehicle. Remove wheel. Remove and support caliper. Remove grease cup, cotter pin and nut. Remove rotor. To install brake rotor, reverse removal procedure.

OVERHAUL

BRAKE CALIPER

Disassembly

1) Clean exterior of caliper with denatured alcohol and place on a clean work surface. Remove brake pads and discard copper gasket. Drain fluid from caliper.

2) Using clean shop towels to pad interior of caliper, apply just enough clean compressed air to caliper inlet so piston will ease out of bore.

CAUTION: While applying compressed air to caliper to remove piston, do not attempt to catch or protect piston with fingers. Always use eye protection while performing this step.

3) Using a screwdriver, pry boot out of caliper. Remove seal from caliper using a seal pick, being carefull not to score inside bore of caliper. Remove bleeder valve from caliper.

Cleaning & Inspection

1) Clean all parts in denatured alcohol. Dry parts using clean dry compressed air. Lubricated shop air will ruin rubber parts upon contact at reassembly.

2) Check mounting bolts for corrosion, breaks in plating or other damage. Replace bolts if damaged in any way. DO NOT attempt to wire brush or clean bolts.

3) Check outside diameter of piston for scoring, nicks, corrosion, or worn and damaged plating. If surface defects are visible, replace piston. DO NOT attempt to refinish with abrasives.

4) Check piston bore in caliper for scratches or other damage. Minor scratches or corrosion may be polished clean with crocus or emery cloth. Thoroughly

Disc Brake Systems

DELCO-MORAINE SINGLE PISTON — FRONT (Cont.)

clean bore after polishing. Replace caliper if corrosion is not easily cleaned.

Reassembly

1) Replace boot, piston seal, rubber bushings and sleeves each time caliper is overhauled.

2) Lubricate caliper bore and new piston seal with clean brake fluid. Position seal in caliper bore groove. Lubricate piston with clean brake fluid. Install new boot into groove in piston.

3) Insert piston into caliper bore using care not to unseat seal. Do not force piston to bottom of bore. Position outer diameter of boot in caliper counterbore. Seat boot using dust boot installer.

4) Check boot installation to make sure retaining ring molded into boot is not bent and that boot is installed completely below caliper face. Install brake hose, using a new copper gasket.

NOTE: **After caliper has been overhauled and installed, bleed brakes.**

TIGHTENING SPECIFICATIONS

Application	Ft. Lbs. (N.m)
Brake Hose-to-Caliper	
Fiero	39 (53)
All Others	32 (43)
Caliper-to-Mounting Bracket Bolts	
Fiero	35 (48)
All Others	38 (51)

DISC BRAKE ROTOR SPECIFICATIONS

Application	Disc Diameter In. (mm)	Lateral Runout In. (mm)	Parallelism In. (mm)	Original Thickness In. (mm)	Min. Refinish Thickness In. (mm)	Discard Thickness In. (mm)
Allanté, Bonneville, [1] Delta 88 & LeSabre	10.24 (260)	.004 (.10)	.0005 (.013)	1.035 (26.3)	.972 (24.7)	.957 (24.3)
Beretta, Cavalier, Cimarron, [2] Corsica, Cutlass Calais, Firenza, Grand Am & Skylark	9.72 (247)	.004 (.10)	.0005 (.013)	.885 (22.5)	.830 (21.1)	.815 (20.7)
Fiero	10.43 (265)	.003 (.076)	.0005 (.013)	.756 (19.2).	.702 (17.83)	.681 (17.297)
Camaro, Cutlass Supreme, Cutlass Supreme Classic, Firebird, Grand Prix, Monte Carlo & Regal GN	10.50 (267)	.004 (.13)	.0005 (.013)	1.043 (26.5)	.980 (24.9)	.965 (24.5)
Standard Caprice, Custom Cruiser, Electra Wagon, LeSabre-Wagon & Safari	11.00 (279)	.004 (.10)	.0005 (.013)	1.043 (26.5)	.980 (24.9)	.965 (24.5)
Heavy Duty Caprice, Custom Cruiser, Electra Wagon, LeSabre-Wagon & Safari	12.00 (305)	.004 (.10)	.0005 (.013)	1.043 (26.5)	.980 (24.9)	.965 (24.5)
Eldorado, Riviera, Seville & Toronado	10.50 (267)	.004 (.10)	.0005 (.013)	1.035 (26.3)	.965 (24.5)	.957 (24.3)

[1] – Also includes heavy duty brakes for DeVille, Electra, Fleetwood & Ninety-Eight.
[2] – Also includes light duty brakes for DeVille, Electra, Fleetwood & Ninety-Eight.

DELCO-MORAINE SINGLE PISTON – REAR

Allanté, Camaro, Eldorado, Fiero,
Firebird, Riviera, Seville, Toronado,
6000

DESCRIPTION

The brake caliper has a single bore and is mounted to a support bracket with 2 mounting bolts. During normal braking, hydraulic force, created by applying pressure to brake pedal, is converted by the caliper to friction.

The hydraulic force acts equally against piston and bottom of caliper bore to move piston outward and to move (slide) caliper inward, resulting in a clamping action on rotor. This clamping action forces linings against rotor, creating friction to stop vehicle.

When parking brake is applied, lever turns actuator screw which is threaded into a nut in piston assembly. This causes plston to move outward and caliper to slide inward, forcing linings against rotor. Piston assembly contains a self-adjusting mechanism for parking brake.

ADJUSTMENTS

SERVICE BRAKES

Caliper design automatically compensates for wear. No brake adjustment is required.

PARKING BRAKE

Allanté

1) Depress brake pedal 3 times with a force of about 175 lbs. (79 kg). Apply and release parking brake 3 times. Raise and support vehicle. Inspect parking brake assembly for full release. Turn ignition on. Brake warning light should be off. If light is on, operate manual brake release and pull down on front parking brake cable to remove slack from pedal assembly.

2) The 2 parking brake levers should be against lever stops on caliper housings. If not, check for binding in rear cables and/or loosen cables at adjuster until both left and right levers are against stops. Tighten parking brake cable at adjuster until either left or right lever begins to move off stop. Loosen adjustment until lever moves back, slightly touching stop.

3) Operate parking brake to ensure adjustment is correct. Firm pedal feel should be obtained by pumping pedal less than 3 1/2 strokes. Rear wheels should not rotate when parking brake is applied. Lower vehicle.

All Other Models

1) With parking brake pedal fully released and rear wheels raised, hold brake cable stud from turning and tighten equalizer nut until cable slack is removed. Make sure levers are on caliper housing stops. If not, loosen equalizer nut until levers return against stops.

2) After adjustment, pedal travel with about 125 lbs. (57 kg) force should be 4-5 1/2" (101.6-139.7 mm) on Eldorado, Seville, Toronado and Riviera. With 150 lbs. (68 kg) force on brake lever, adjustment on Camaro and Firebird should give about 14 clicks, Fiero should give about 8 clicks.

SERVICING

BLEEDING

See HYDRAULIC BRAKE BLEEDING in this section.

SHOE & LINING INSPECTION

Inspect lining every 6000 miles or anytime wheels are removed. Check both ends of inner and outer pads for wear. Replace all linings if any one wears to about shoe thickness.

SHOE & LINING REPLACEMENT

Removal

1) Remove and discard 2/3 of brake fluid from master cylinder reservoir. Raise vehicle, mark relationship of wheel to axle and remove wheel. Replace 2 lug nuts (flat side toward rotor) to retain rotor when caliper is removed.

2) Loosen tension on parking brake cable at equalizer. Disconnect cable and return spring from parking brake lever. Hold lever and remove lock nut. Remove lever, lever seal and anti-friction washer. Using a large "C" clamp, compress caliper piston until it bottoms in bore. Remove "C" clamp.

NOTE: Do not position "C" clamp on actuator screw.

3) Clean and lubricate caliper housing surface under lever seal with silicone brake lubricant. Install new anti-friction washer. Lubricate new lever seal with silicone and install with sealing bead against housing. Install lever on actuator screw with lever pointing down.

4) Remove brake line from caliper. Plug opening to prevent fluid loss and keep dirt out of system. Remove caliper mounting bolts. Remove caliper and brake pads. Inspect caliper for damage. Replace or repair as needed. Remove and discard 2 caliper mounting sleeves and 4 bushings. Remove and discard piston check valve.

Fig. 1: Clinching Outer Shoe Ears

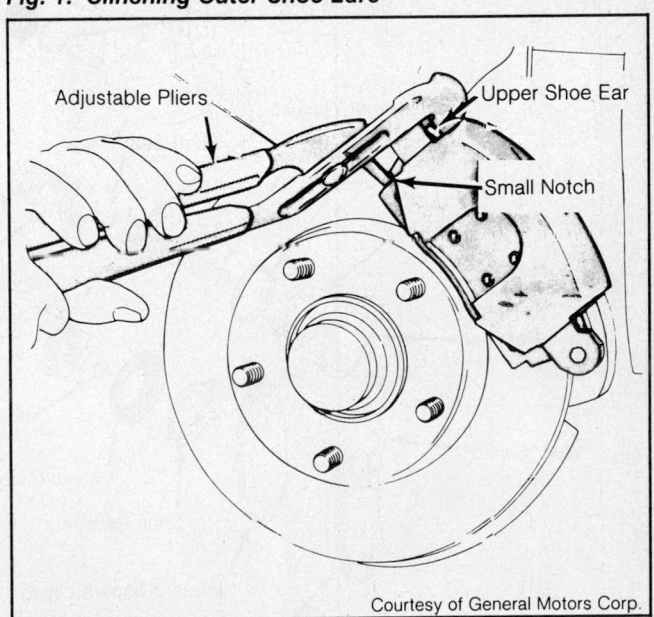

Adjustable Pliers

Upper Shoe Ear

Small Notch

Courtesy of General Motors Corp.

Disc Brake Systems

DELCO-MORAINE SINGLE PISTON — REAR (Cont.)

Installation

1) Install new piston check valve. Using silicone grease, install new bushings and sleeves. Place new inner shoe on piston with "D" shaped tab fitting into piston notch. If tab does not line up with notch, turn piston with a Spanner Wrench (J-7624). Install outer shoe and lining.

2) Slide caliper over rotor and install mounting bolts under inner shoe ears. Using new washers, install brake line. Pump brake pedal to seat lining against caliper. Using adjustable lock pliers, clinch upper ears of outer shoe against caliper, making sure all ears are flat against caliper with no clearance.

3) Rotate lever toward front of vehicle and tighten nut. Rotate lever back against caliper stop and install spring. Connect and adjust parking brake cable. Bleed brake system. Remove 2 lug nuts used to retain rotor and install wheel.

ROTOR SERVICING

Lateral Runout

Mount a dial indicator so that pointer contacts rotor face about 1" from rotor edge. Set gauge to zero. Turn rotor one revolution while checking gauge. Refinish or replace rotor if runout is excessive.

Parallelism

Check rotor thickness at 4 or more points around rotor circumference. Make all measurements at same distance from rotor edge. If thickness variation is excessive, refinish or replace rotor.

REMOVAL & INSTALLATION

CALIPER, SHOES & LININGS

See SHOE & LINING REPLACEMENT for caliper, shoe and lining removal and installation.

ROTOR

Removal & Installation

With caliper removed as previously described, remove lug nuts attaching rotor, and remove rotor. To install, place rotor on axle and hold in place with 2 lug nuts. To complete installation, see SHOE & LINING REPLACEMENT.

REAR AXLE SEAL & BEARING REPLACEMENT

Removal (Camaro & Firebird)

1) Raise vehicle and remove wheel, caliper and rotor as previously outlined. Clean and remove carrier cover to drain lubricant.

Fig. 2: Exploded View of Delco-Moraine Single Piston Rear Caliper

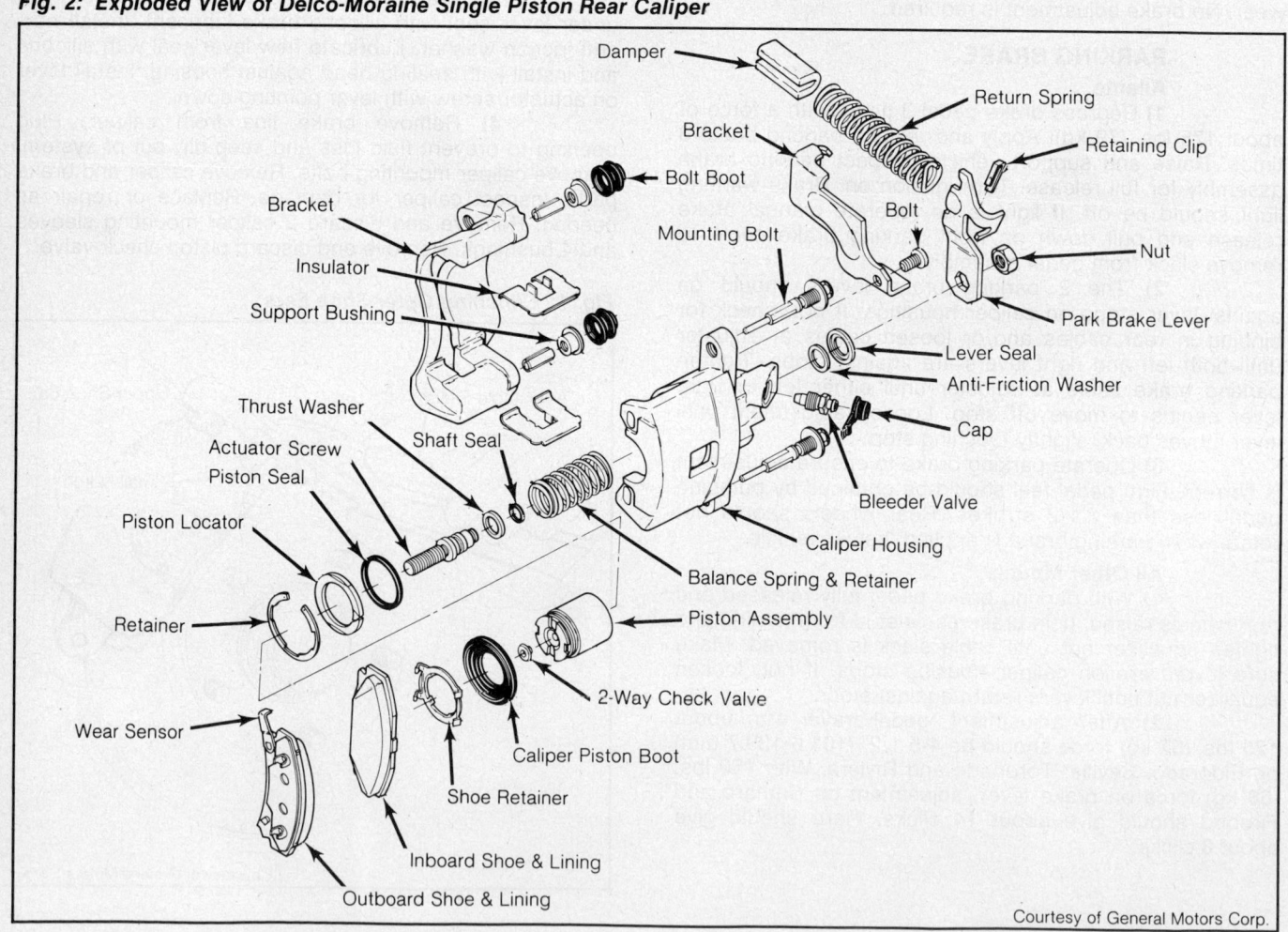

Damper
Return Spring
Bracket
Retaining Clip
Bolt Boot
Bolt
Bracket
Nut
Mounting Bolt
Insulator
Park Brake Lever
Support Bushing
Lever Seal
Anti-Friction Washer
Thrust Washer
Shaft Seal
Cap
Actuator Screw
Piston Seal
Bleeder Valve
Piston Locator
Caliper Housing
Balance Spring & Retainer
Retainer
Piston Assembly
Wear Sensor
2-Way Check Valve
Caliper Piston Boot
Shoe Retainer
Inboard Shoe & Lining
Outboard Shoe & Lining

Courtesy of General Motors Corp.

Allanté, Eldorado, Riviera, Seville and Toronado caliper is shown. Camaro, Fiero, Firebird and 6000 are similar.

DELCO-MORAINE SINGLE PISTON — REAR (Cont.)

2) Remove pinion shaft lock screw and pinion shaft. Push flanged axle shaft end toward center of vehicle. Remove "C" lock from shaft button end. Remove axle shaft and pry seal from housing. Remove bearing with a slide hammer.

Installation

1) Lubricate new bearing and install with Bearing Installer (J-23690). Lubricate seal lips and install seal with Seal Installer (J-23771). Tap seal until flush with axle housing.

2) Slide axle shaft in housing, making sure splines engage without damaging oil seal. To complete installation, reverse removal procedure. Use new carrier cover gasket and fill axle with gear oil.

OVERHAUL

BRAKE CALIPER

Disassembly

1) With caliper held in a vise, remove 2 mounting sleeves and 4 bushings from caliper and discard. Remove brake pads and lever return spring. Using a shop towel to catch piston and brake fluid, rotate lever back and forth to move piston out of caliper.

NOTE: **If piston will not release from caliper, remove lock nut, lever, seal and anti-friction washer. Turn actuator screw until piston releases from caliper.**

2) Remove piston seal and balance spring. Remove lock nut, lever, seal and anti-friction washer (if not already removed). Push screw from caliper and remove shaft seal, thrust washer, boot and piston seal.

3) Clean all parts with denatured alcohol. Inspect caliper bore for scoring, nicks, corrosion or wear.

Use crocus cloth to polish any light corrosion. Replace caliper if needed. Check piston outer diameter for nicks, scoring or damage and replace if needed.

Reassembly

1) Install bleeder screw, fitting and bolt (use new copper washers). Lubricate new piston seal with brake fluid and install in caliper bore groove.

2) Fit boot on piston with inside boot lip in piston groove and boot fold toward inner brake shoe end of piston. Install new thrust washer and seal on actuator screw.

3) Lubricate actuator screw with brake fluid and install in piston. Fit balance spring in piston and start piston assembly in caliper housing.

NOTE: **Caliper housing and activator screws must be installed on same side of vehicle from which they were removed.**

4) Using Piston Installer (J-23072), push piston to bottom of bore. Ensure piston is straight or screw may damage seal as it passes through. Before removing tool, install lever away from stop, rotate forward and hold while tightening nut.

5) Remove piston installer and rotate lever back to stop. Using Boot Installer (J-28678), seat boot in housing. Install dampening spring on piston end groove. Install lining and caliper. See SHOE & LINING REPLACEMENT.

TIGHTENING SPECIFICATIONS

Application	Ft. Lbs. (N.m)
Brake Hose-to-Caliper	15 (20)
Caliper Mounting Bolts	38 (52)
Brake Lever Actuator Screw	35 (47)

DISC BRAKE ROTOR SPECIFICATIONS

Application	Disc Diameter In. (mm)	Lateral Runout In. (mm)	Parallelism In. (mm)	Original Thickness In. (mm)	Min. Refinish Thickness In. (mm)	Discard Thickness In. (mm)
Buick						
Riviera	10.50 (267)	.004 (.10)	.0005 (.013)	1.035 (26.3)	.980 (24.9)	.965 (24.5)
Cadillac						
Allante	10.00 (254.5)	.003 (.076)	.0005 (.013)	.494 (12.55)	.444 (11.28)	.429 (10.90)
Eldorado & Seville	10.50 (267)	.004 (.10)	.0005 (.013)	1.035 (26.3)	.980 (24.9)	.965 (24.5)
Chevrolet						
Camaro	10.50 (267)	.005 (.13)	.0005 (.013)	1.042 (26.5)	.986 (25.0)	.965 (24.5)
Oldsmobile						
Toronado	10.50 (267)	.004 (.10)	.0005 (.013)	1.043 (26.5)	.971 (24.7)	.965 (24.5)
Pontiac						
Fiero	10.43 (265)	.003 (.08)	.0005 (.013)	.756 (19.2)	.702 (17.8)	.681 (17.29)
Firebird	10.50 (267)	.005 (.13)	.0005 (.013)	1.042 (26.5)	.986 (25.0)	.965 (24.5)
6000	10.24 (260)	.004 (.10)	.0005 (.013)	.494 (12.55)	.439 (11.15)	.425 (10.8)

Disc Brake Systems

EAGLE PREMIER & FORD MOTOR CO. SINGLE PISTON

Eagle Premier, Ford Motor Co.

DESCRIPTION

The disc brake assembly consists of a rotor, a single-piston caliper, 2 shoe and lining assemblies, a splash shield and an anchor plate. The cast iron rotor has cooling fins between the 2 braking surfaces. Brake linings are riveted to brake shoes and insulator gaskets are bonded to back of each brake shoe.

All models use a sliding caliper that slides on 2 locating pins. Locating pins on Ford Motor Co. models attach caliper, combination anchor plate and spindle. Continental, Mark VII and Thunderbird Turbo have single-piston calipers at all 4 wheels.

ADJUSTMENTS

STOP LIGHT SWITCH

Stop light switch is mechanically actuated by brake pedal and is mounted on master cylinder push rod. Switch is not adjustable. If switch remains on, check for binding linkage.

SERVICE BRAKES

Disc brakes are self-adjusting. Caliper piston seal retracts caliper piston and lining from rotor. Parking brake is also self-adjusting.

SERVICING

BLEEDING SYSTEM

See HYDRAULIC BRAKE BLEEDING in this section.

SHOE & LINING INSPECTION

Inspect condition of lining anytime wheel is removed. On Premier, replace lining if worn to less than a .236" (6.0 mm) thickness (including backing plate). On Ford Motor Co. vehicles, replace lining if worn to less than a .125" (3.18 mm) thickness (not including backing plate).

SHOE & LINING REPLACEMENT

NOTE: Replace shoes and linings on both sides of vehicle to maintain equal braking action.

Removal

1) Remove enough brake fluid from master cylinder to prevent overflow when piston is pushed into caliper. Raise and support front of vehicle. Remove front wheels.

2) On Eagle Premier models, press caliper piston into bore using a screwdriver or "C" clamp. On Ford Motor Co. models, be careful not to pry directly against plastic caliper piston.

3) Disconnect parking brake cable on rear caliper models. On Mark VII rear calipers, loosen caliper end retainer 1/2 turn only. Press piston into bore.

NOTE: If caliper end retainer is loosened more than 1/2 turn, brake fluid may leak into parking brake mechanism chamber. If this happens, remove end retainer and clean parking brake mechanism chamber.

4) On all models, remove caliper mounting bolts lift caliper assembly from anchor plate and rotor. Support caliper assembly with wire to prevent damage to brake hose. Remove outer shoe. Remove inner shoe and anti-rattle clip or spring.

5) On Ford Motor Co. models, remove and discard locating pin insulators and plastic sleeves (if equipped). DO NOT reuse these parts.

Installation (Eagle Premier)

Install anti-rattle clip with split end facing toward rotor on bottom of shoe. Install inner and outer shoes while holding clip. Install caliper and caliper mounting pins. Install wheels, lower vehicle and fill master cylinder with fluid. Pump pedal several times to seat shoes and check brake operation.

Installation (Ford Motor Co. – Rear)

1) On Mark VII models, tighten caliper end retainer. Install new locating pin insulators and plastic sleeves. Lubricate insulators with silicone grease and ensure they straddle housing holes. On all models, install parking brake lever. Seat piston in caliper and install caliper into position.

2) On Mark VII models, install anti-rattle spring on inner shoe anchor plate and install shoes in caliper. Pull caliper so outboard shoe is held against rotor. Hold inboard shoe against rotor and measure gap between caliper and inboard shoe. If gap is greater than .094 (2.4 mm) remove caliper and adjust caliper piston out.

3) On Continental and Thunderbird models, install shoes and anti-rattle springs in proper position. See Fig. 3. On all models, ensure one of 2 round torque buttons on shoes are seated in piston hole. With locking compound on retaining bolts, install and tighten.

4) Install wheels, lower vehicle and fill master cylinder with fluid. Pump pedal several times to seat shoes and check brake operation.

Installation (Ford Motor Co. – Front)

Seat piston in caliper bore. Install inner shoe in caliper without bending shoe clips. Install correct outer shoe and seat clips. Install caliper over rotor. Install wheels, lower vehicle and fill master cylinder with fluid. Pump pedal several times to seat shoes and check brake operation.

ROTOR SERVICING

Lateral Runout

1) With rotor mounted on lath, mount a dial indicator with indicator pointer contacting center of braking surface.

2) Turn rotor one revolution, checking indicator reading as rotor moves. If runout is excessive, replace or resurface rotor as needed.

Parallelism

Measure rotor thickness at 4 or more points, at equal distances from edge of rotor. If rotor does not meet specifications, replace or resurface rotor as needed.

Disc Brake Systems

EAGLE PREMIER & FORD MOTOR CO.
SINGLE PISTON (Cont.)

**Fig. 1: Exploded View of Eagle Premier
Front Sliding Caliper Assembly**

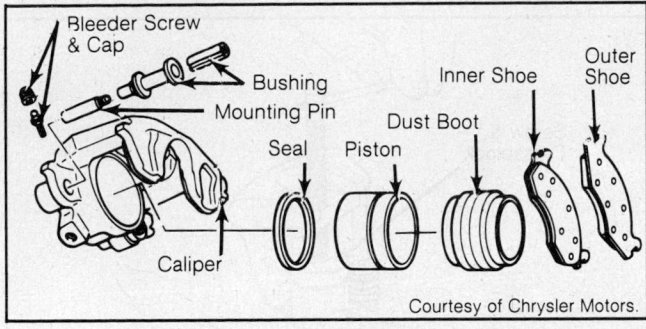

Courtesy of Chrysler Motors.

REMOVAL & INSTALLATION

BRAKE CALIPER

Remove brake caliper as previously described. See SHOE & LINING REPLACEMENT in this article. Disconnect brake hose from caliper and plug openings. To install, reverse removal procedure. Refill and bleed air from system.

ROTOR
Removal

1) Raise and support front of vehicle and remove front wheel. Remove caliper assembly and support out of way to avoid damaging brake hose.

2) On Ford Motor Co. RWD models, remove grease cap from hub. Remove cotter key, nut lock, adjusting nut and thrust washer from spindle. Remove outer wheel bearing, pull hub and rotor assembly from spindle.

3) On Ford Motor Co. FWD models and Eagle Premier models, rotor can be pulled from hub after caliper is removed.

Installation

To install, reverse removal procedure and adjust wheel bearings. See WHEEL BEARING ADJUSTMENT in SUSPENSION section.

**Fig. 2: Exploded View of Ford Motor Co.
Front Sliding Caliper Assembly (RWD)**

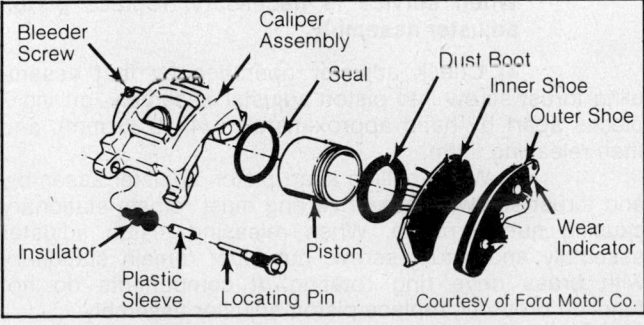

Courtesy of Ford Motor Co.

OVERHAUL

BRAKE CALIPER
Disassembly (Front)

With caliper assembly removed from vehicle, pad interior of caliper with shop cloths. Apply compressed air to caliper inlet port to remove piston. If piston is seized, lightly tap around piston while applying air pressure. Remove dust boot from caliper. Using a plastic or wooden tool to prevent scratching caliper bore, remove piston seal from caliper groove.

Cleaning & Inspection

Clean all parts with denatured alcohol or clean brake fluid and dry with compressed air. Clean out and dry all grooves and passages with compressed air. Inspect piston and caliper bore for wear, pitting, scoring, nicks or corrosion. Replace components as necessary.

Reassembly

Apply a film of clean brake fluid to new piston seal and dust boot and install into caliper bore. Coat piston with clean brake fluid and install into caliper bore. Seat dust boot in piston groove. Spread dust boot over piston.

Disassembly
(Continental & Thunderbird – Rear)

1) Mount caliper in vise. Using Piston Turning Tool (T75P-2588-B), rotate piston counterclockwise and remove piston from caliper. Remove and discard piston dust boot seal and piston seal from caliper bore. Using snap ring pliers, remove snap ring retaining push rod assembly from caliper.

CAUTION: Snap ring and spring cover are under spring load. Care should be taken when removing snap ring.

2) Remove spring cover, spring washer, key plate and pull out push rod and strut pin. Remove and discard "O" ring seal from push rod. Remove parking brake lever return spring. Unscrew parking brake lever stop bolt and pull parking brake lever out of caliper housing.

Inspection

Clean all metal parts with isopropyl alcohol. Use clean dry compressed air to clean out grooves and passages. Ensure caliper bore and component parts are completely free of any foreign material. Inspect caliper bores for damage or excessive wear. If piston is pitted, scored or plating is worn off, replace piston assembly.

Reassembly

1) Lightly grease parking brake lever bore and lever shaft seal with Silicone Dielectric Compound (D7AZ-19A331-A). Press parking brake lever shaft seal into caliper bore. Grease parking brake shaft recess and parking brake lever shaft. Insert shaft into bore in caliper housing.

2) Screw lever stop bolt into caliper housing. Tighten to 54-84 INCH lbs. (6-9.5 N.m). Attach parking brake lever return spring to stop bolt and insert free end into parking brake lever slot. Install new "O" ring in groove of push rod. Grease recess at push rod end with Silicone Dielectric Compound (D7AZ-19A331-A).

3) Position strut pin into caliper housing on recess of parking brake lever shaft. Insert push rod into push rod bore of caliper housing. Ensure pin is positioned correctly between shaft recess and recess at end of pusrod.

4) Place key plate over push rod so locating recess fits into drilled locating hole in caliper housing. Install flat washer, push rod, spring and spring cover in

Disc Brake Systems

EAGLE PREMIER & FORD MOTOR CO. SINGLE PISTON (Cont.)

order. Insert outer spacer and inner spacer into piston bore.

5) Place snap ring inside of inner spacer. Position spring compressor and screw crossblock on pushrod. *See Fig. 4.* Lightly compress spring until snap ring clicks into position, DO NOT over compress spring.

6) Lubricating new piston seal with brake fluid and install in groove in piston bore. Coat piston and piston dust boot with clean brake fluid and install into piston bore.

7) Spread dust boot over piston and seat in piston groove. Using Piston Turning Tool (T75P-2588-B), rotate piston clockwise until piston is fully seated. Ensure one slot in piston face is positioned so it will engage with alignment protrusion on brake pad shoe. Install caliper assembly.

Fig. 3: Exploded View of Ford Motor Co. Rear Sliding Caliper Assembly

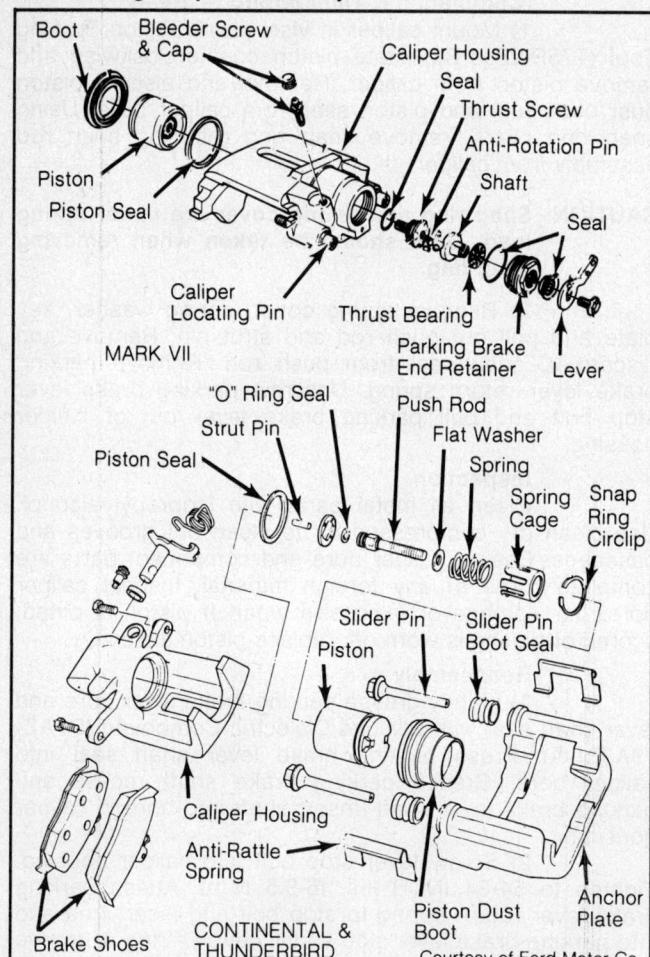

MARK VII

CONTINENTAL & THUNDERBIRD

Courtesy of Ford Motor Co.

Disassembly (Mark VII – Rear)

1) With caliper removed, remove parking brake cable bracket and caliper end retainer. Lift out operating shaft, thrust bearing and balls. Using magnet or tweezers, remove thrust screw anti-rotation pin.

2) Remove thrust screw by rotating counterclockwise with a 1/4" Allen wrench. Remove piston adjuster assembly by installing Piston Turning Tool (T75P-2588-B) through back of caliper housing and push piston out.

Fig. 4: Installing Continental & Thunderbird Rear Caliper Snap Ring

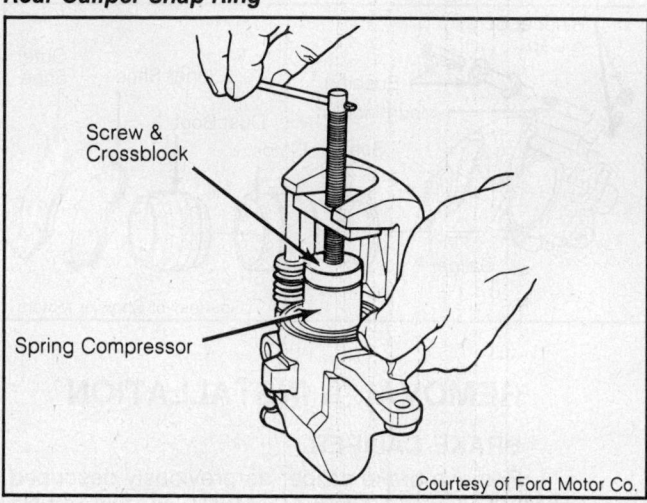

Screw & Crossblock

Spring Compressor

Courtesy of Ford Motor Co.

CAUTION: Use care not to damage polished surface in thrust screw bore, do not press or attempt to move adjuster can, it is a press fit in piston.

3) Remove and discard piston seal, boot, thrust screw "C" ring seal, end retainer "O" ring seal, end retainer lip seal and pin insulators.

Inspection

1) Clean all metal parts with isopropyl alcohol. Use clean dry compressed air to clean out and dry grooves and passages. Ensure caliper bore and component parts are free of any foreign material.

2) Inspect caliper bores for damage. Thrust screw bore must be smooth and free of pits. If piston is pitted, scored or chrome plating is worn off, replace piston adjuster assembly.

3) The adjuster can must be bottomed in piston to be properly seated and provide consistent brake function. If adjuster can is loose in piston, appears high in piston, is damaged or if brake adjustment is regularly too tight, too loose, or nonfunctioning, replace piston adjuster assembly.

NOTE: **Do not attempt to service adjuster at anytime. When service is necessary, replace piston adjuster assembly.**

4) Check adjuster operation by first assembling thrust screw into piston adjuster assembly, pulling 2 pieces apart by hand approximately 1/4" (6.35 mm), and then releasing them.

5) When pulling apart piston adjuster assembly and thrust screw, brass drive ring must remain stationary causing nut to rotate. When releasing piston adjuster assembly and thrust screw, nut must remain stationary with brass drive ring rotating. If components do not function properly, replace piston adjuster assembly.

6) Inspect all parts for damage and replace if necessary. Lightly sand or wire brush any rust or corrosion from caliper housing insulator bores.

Reassembly

1) Apply a coat of clean brake fluid to new caliper piston seal and install in cylinder bore. Ensure seal is not twisted and is seated fully in the groove. Install new

EAGLE PREMIER & FORD MOTOR CO.
SINGLE PISTON (Cont.)

dust boot by seating the flange squarely in outer groove of caliper bore.

2) Coat piston adjuster assembly with clean brake fluid, and install in cylinder bore. Spread dust boot over piston and seat in piston groove. Mount caliper in a vise. Fill piston adjuster assembly with clean brake fluid to bottom edge of thrust screw bore.

3) Coat a new thrust screw "O" ring seal with clean brake fluid and install in groove in thrust screw. Using 1/4" Allen wrench, install thrust screw by turning into piston adjuster assembly until top surface of thrust screw is flush with bottom of threads bore. Use care to avoid cuttting "O" ring seal.

4) Index thrust screw, so that notches on thrust screw and caliper housing are aligned. Install anti-rotation pin.

NOTE: **Thrust screw and operating shaft are not interchangeable from side-to-side because of ramp direction in ball packets. Pocket surface of operating shaft and thrust screw are stamped with proper letter (R or L), indicating part usage.**

5) Place a ball in each of three pockets of thrust screw, and apply a liberal amount of Silicone Dielectric Grease (D7AZ-19A331-A), on all components in parking brake mechanism.

6) Install operating shaft on balls. Install thrust bearing on operating shaft. Install new lip seal and "O" ring on end retainer. Coat "O" ring seal and lip seal with a light film of silicone grease. Install end retainer in caliper.

7) Hold operating shaft firmly seated against internal mechanism while installing end retainer to prevent mislocation of balls. If lip seal is pushed out of postition, reseat seal. Tighten end retainer to 75-95 ft. lbs. (101-103 N.m).

8) Install parking brake lever on keyed spline so lever arm points down and rearward, allowing parking brake cable to pass freely under axle. Tighten lever retaining screw to 16-22 ft. lbs. (22-29 N.m). Ensure parking brake lever rotates freely after tightening.

9) Arrange caliper in a vise and bottom piston with Piston Turning Tool (T75P-2588-B). Install new pin insulator in caliper housing. Ensure both insulator flanges straddle housing holes. Install caliper on vehicle.

TIGHTENING SPECIFICATIONS

Application	Ft. Lbs. (N.m)
Eagle Premier	
Caliper Hose	25 (34)
Caliper Mounting Pins	30 (41)
Wheel Stud Nuts	75 (102)
Ford Motor. Co.	
FWD Models	
Brake Hose-to-Caliper	35 (47)
Caliper Locating Pins	22 (29)
Hydraulic Tube Connections	14 (19)
Wheel Stud Nuts	93 (126)
RWD Models	
Brake Hose-to-Caliper	25 (34)
Brake Hose-to-Tube	14 (19)
Caliper Locating Pins	50 (68)
Splash Shield Nuts	12 (16)
Wheel Stud Nuts	93 (126)

DISC BRAKE ROTOR SPECIFICATIONS

Application	Disc Diameter In. (mm)	Lateral Runout In. (mm)	Parallelism In. (mm)	Original Thickness In. (mm)	Min. Refinish Thickness In. (mm)	Discard Thickness In. (mm)
Eagle Premier	10.433 (265)	.003 (.08)	.....	.866 (22.0)	.807 (20.5)	.....
Ford Motor Co.						
Front						
EXP & Lynx	9.25 (235.0)	.002 (.05)	.0004 (.010)	.945 (24.0)	.....	.882 (22.4)
Sable & Taurus	10.16 (258.0)	.003 (.08)	.0005 (.013)	.945 (24.0)	.....	.896 (22.75)
Tempo, Topaz & Escort	9.25 (235.0)	.003 (.08)	.0005 (.013)	.945 (24.0)	.....	.882 (22.4)
Crown Victoria, Grand Marquis & Town Car	11.08 (281.4)	.003 (.08)	.0005 (.013)	1.03 (26.2)	.....	.972 (24.7)
Continental	10.16 (2.58)	.002 (.05)	.004 (.010)	1.02 (26.0)	.....	.974 (24.75)
Mark VII, Mustang (5.0L) & Thunderbird 2.3L Turbo (Front)	10.91 (277.1)	.003 (.08)	.0005 (.013)	1.03 (26.2)	.....	.972 (24.7)
All Others	10.08 (256.0)	.003 (.08)	[1] .0005 (.013)	.870 (22.1)	.....	.810 (20.6)
Rear						
Continental & Mark VII	10.66 (270.8)	.004 (.10)	.0005 (.013)	.945 (24.0)	.....	.895 (22.7)
Thunderbird 2.3L Turbo	10.16 (258.1)	.003 (.08)	.0005 (.013)	.945 (24.0)	.....	.895 (22.7)

[1] – LTD and Marquis models parallelism specification is .0003" (.008 mm).

Disc Brake Systems
NOVA

DESCRIPTION

This brake system incorporates a dual master cylinder with diagonally split hydraulic circuit. Hydraulic pressure from master cylinder actuates single piston sliding calipers.

Power assist to master cylinder is provided by a single diaphragm vacuum booster. A dual proportioning valve, mounted to bulkhead, controls brake balance between front and rear brakes under heavy deceleration. Parking brake system is a hand operated mechanical linkage system.

ADJUSTMENTS

SERVICE BRAKES

Disc brakes are self-adjusting. Caliper piston seals are designed to retract pistons just enough to allow brake lining to lightly brush disc without any drag.

SERVICING

BLEEDING

See HYDRAULIC BRAKE BLEEDING in this section.

DISC BRAKE INSPECTION

If a squeaking noise occurs from front brakes while driving and braking, inspect disc brake pads. Rotor contacting pad wear indicator plate will cause a high pitched squealing sound.

REMOVAL & INSTALLATION

CALIPER & PADS

Removal & Installation

1) Remove 2/3 of the brake fluid from master cylinder. Raise and support vehicle. Remove front wheel. Reinstall 2 wheel nuts to retain rotor.

2) Remove 2 mounting bolts from mounting bracket. Remove caliper assembly and support caliper with a wire. Remove pads, wear indicator plates, anti-squeal shims and 4 support plates. Remove 2 anti-squeal springs. Check rotor thickness and runout. To install, reverse removal procedure. See Fig. 1.

OVERHAUL

CALIPER

Disassembly

1) Remove caliper. Remove union bolt and disconnect flexible hose. Use a container to catch brake fluid. Remove 2 mounting bolts and caliper. Remove 2

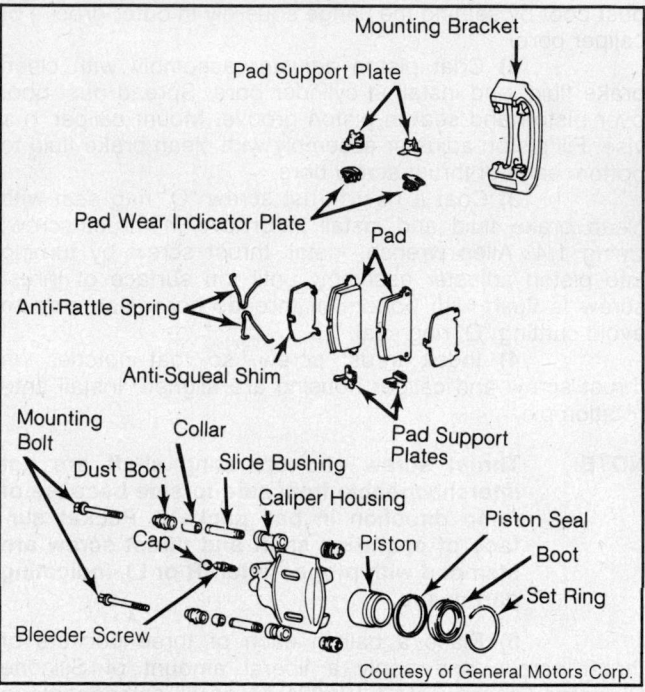

Fig. 1: Exploded View of Caliper Assembly

Courtesy of General Motors Corp.

caliper slide bushings, 4 dust boots, and 2 collars. Remove caliper boot set ring and boot.

2) Remove piston from caliper using clean shop towels to pad interior of caliper and remove piston by directing compressed air into caliper inlet hole. Using a seal pick, remove piston seal from caliper bore. Check all parts for wear or damage repair or replace as necessary.

Reassembly

1) Clean all parts. Use dry, filtered compressed air to dry parts and blow out all passages. Apply lithium grease to sliding bushing contact areas.

2) Install piston seal and piston in caliper bore. Install boot and set ring in caliper. Install collar and dust boot to caliper. Ensure boots are secured to each caliper groove. Install bushings into boots.

3) Ensure boots are secured firmly to each bushing groove. Install caliper and mounting bolts. Tighten mounting bolts. Install flexible hose with new gaskets and tighten union bolt. After installation of caliper, pump brake pedal firmly slowly to bring pads into contact with rotor. Bleed brakes.

TIGHTENING SPECIFICATIONS

Application	Ft. Lbs. (N.m)
Caliper	
Mounting Bolts	18 (25)
Mounting Bracket-to-Steering Knuckle	65 (88)
Flexible Hose	17 (23)

DISC BRAKE ROTOR SPECIFICATIONS

Application	Disc Diameter In. (mm)	Lateral Runout In. (mm)	Parallelism In. (mm)	Original Thickness In. (mm)	Min. Refinish Thickness In. (mm)	Discard Thickness In. (mm)
Nova	.....	.006 (.15)	.....	.531 (13.5)	.492 (12.5)	.492 (12.5)

BENDIX SINGLE ANCHOR AUTOMATIC ADJUSTER

**Chrysler Motors, Eagle Premier,
Ford Motor Co. (Except Continental
& Mark VII)**

DESCRIPTION

Units consists of a backing plate, 2 brake shoes, return springs, hold-down spring assemblies, self-adjusting components, and a wheel cylinder. Duo Servo Automatic adjuster consists of a cable (with spring hook and anchor fitting), cable guide, adjusting lever, lever pivot and adjusting screw (star).

AUTOMATIC ADJUSTER
Chrysler Motors

Adjuster screw thread is opposite that of other models; therefore, adjuster moves upward when brakes are applied. A cage and spring on adjuster cable absorbs secondary shoe movement, except when wear results in enough movement to cause adjuster to rotate. This feature reduces possibility of over-adjustment.

Eagle Premier

This Non-servo design brake uses an incremental adjuster that adjusts during braking whenever a wear gap appears sufficient to actuate the adjuster wheel. Brake adjustment occurs during forward and rearward braking.

Ford Motor Co.

On duo-servo design brakes the adjuster uses movement of rear (secondary) shoe during reverse brake application to turn brake adjusting screw. Screw is rotated a small amount to maintain proper lining-to-drum clearance.

Non-servo design brakes use an incremental adjuster that adjusts during braking whenever a wear gap appears sufficient to actuate the adjuster wheel. Brake adjustment occurs during forward and rearward braking.

ADJUSTMENTS

BRAKE SHOE ADJUSTMENT

This adjustment is made only after brake lining replacement or if brake applications are insufficient to actuate automatic adjuster.

Chrysler Motors

1) Adjust parking brake after service brake adjustment. Remove adjusting hole covers. On Horizon and Omni models, insert Adjuster (C-3784), or thin-bladed screwdriver into star wheel and rotate until road wheel turns with slight drag (locked on Horizon and Omni).

2) Back off star wheel (releasing adjuster lever if equipped) until wheels rotate freely with no drag. Back off 10 clicks on Horizon and Omni. On all models, adjustments must be equal on both wheels.

NOTE: On rear wheel drive models with Iso-Clamp rear suspension, bend rod to match angle of adjusting tool plus a 3/4 reverse bend at contact end. See Fig. 1.

Eagle Premier

With drum installed, rotate star adjuster thru access hole on backing plate to lock drum. Using a thin screw driver and brake spoon, push adjuster lever away revolution.

Fig. 1: Adjusting Rear Brake Shoe-to-Drum Clearance

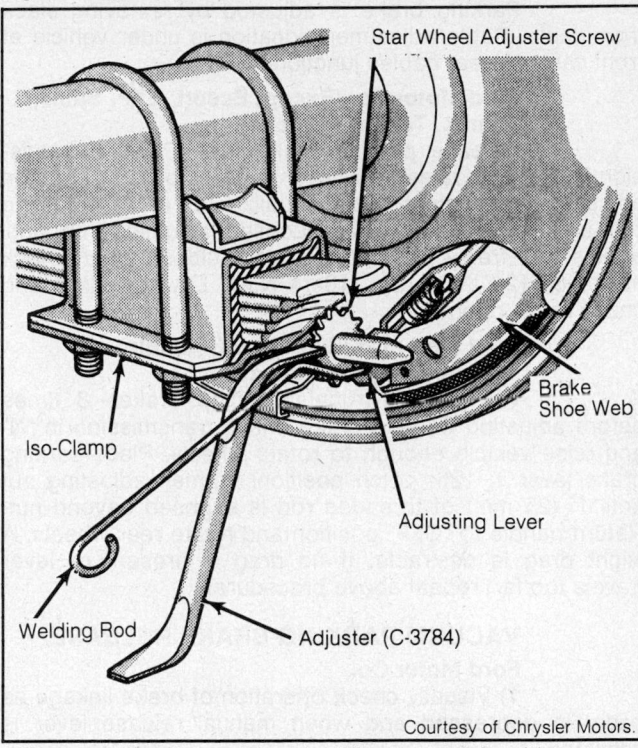

Courtesy of Chrysler Motors.

Adjustment shown on Chrysler Motors models with ISO-Clamp suspension.

from star wheel and back of star wheel one complete revolution.

Ford Motor Co.

1) On all models except Escort, EXP, Tempo and Topaz with 7" brakes, use a measuring tool to determine drum diameter and proper shoe diameter. Hold automatic adjusting lever out of engagement while rotating adjusting screw. Adjust brake shoes to fit gauge. Rotate gauge around shoe to ensure proper fit.

2) On Escort, EXP, Tempo and Topaz with 7" brakes, pivot adjuster quadrant until it meshes with knurled pin and is in 3rd or 4th notch of outboard end of quadrant. Install drum and wheel and adjust wheel bearings. See WHEEL BEARING ADJUSTMENT in SUSPENSION section.

3) On all models, complete adjustment by applying brakes several times while backing vehicle, with forward movement after each application. Use a minimum 50 lbs. (22 kg) pressure on non-power brakes and 25 lbs. (11 kg) on power brakes.

PARKING BRAKE ADJUSTMENT
Chrysler Motors

1) Ensure service brakes are properly adjusted. Back off parking brake cable and allow slack in cable. Clean and lubricate cable threads. Using Adjuster (C-3784) and a thin screwdriver inserted in brake adjusting hole to disengage adjusting lever, rotate star wheel to obtain light contact between brake shoe and drum.

2) Back off star wheel until no drag is felt. Adjust parking brake cable adjuster nut until a slight drag is felt while rotating rear wheels. Loosen adjusting nut until wheels just turn freely, then back off nut 2 full turns. Apply and release parking brake several times to make sure rear wheels do not drag.

Drum Brake Systems

BENDIX SINGLE ANCHOR AUTOMATIC ADJUSTER (Cont.)

Eagle Premier

Parking brake is adjusted by removing slack from cable. Cable adjustment location is under vehicle at front cable-to-rear cables junction.

Ford Motor Co. (Except Escort, EXP, Sable, Taurus, Tempo & Topaz)

Release parking brake fully. Place transmission in "N" and raise vehicle on axle type hoist. Tighten adjusting nut against cable equalizer or cable adjusting rod until rear brakes drag. Loosen adjusting nut until brakes turn freely, without drag. If equipped, tighten lock nut to 84-120 INCH lbs. (10-14 N.m). Lower vehicle and check brake operation.

Ford Motor Co. (Escort, EXP, Sable, Taurus, Tempo & Topaz)

With engine running, pump brakes 3 times before adjusting parking brake. Place transmission in "N" and raise vehicle enough to rotate wheels. Place parking brake lever in 12th notch position. Tighten adjusting nut until 1" (25 mm) of threaded rod is exposed beyond nut. Return handle to "OFF" position and rotate rear wheels. A slight drag is desirable. If no drag is present or lever travels too far, repeat above procedure.

VACUUM PARKING BRAKE RELEASE

Ford Motor Co.

1) Visually check operation of brake linkage as pedal is depressed and when manual release lever is activated.

CAUTION: Air pressure should never be applied to vacuum system as diaphragm in vacuum motor may be damaged.

2) Ensure a minimum of 10 in. Hg is available at all points where vacuum is applied. Start engine and let idle. Place transmission in "D" and observe that lever moves upward and parking brake releases. If it does not release, check for proper vacuum in system and replace components as necessary.

CLEANING & INSPECTION

NOTE: When servicing brake parts, do not create dust by grinding or sanding linings or using compressed air. Use water dampened shop towel to remove dirt and dust from brake parts during disassembly.

CLEANING

Clean all parts except linings and drums with brake cleaning solvent. To remove brake fluid contamination, clean all parts except brake linings with denatured alcohol. Contaminated brake linings must be replaced.

INSPECTION

1) Pull back wheel cylinder dust boots and check for evidence of leakage. If evidence of leakage is noted, cylinder should be disassembled, inspected and overhauled.

2) Polish brake support plate ledges with fine emery cloth and inspect for grooves that could restrict shoe movement. If grooves exist after polishing, support plate must be replaced.

3) Inspect lining wear pattern. If wear across width of lining is uneven, drums should be checked for distortion, shoes for correct positioning, and support plate for distortion.

4) Inspect all springs for evidence of overheating and fractures. Self-adjusting cables should be inspected for kinks, fraying, or elongation of eyelet. Inspect adjuster screws for freedom of rotation, and adjuster lever for wear and distortion. Replace all defective brake parts.

OVERHAUL

SHOE & LINING REPLACEMENT

Chrysler Motors (RWD)

1) Remove brake drums, releasing brake adjustment if necessary. Remove return springs, adjuster cable, overload spring, cable guide and anchor plate. Disengage adjusting lever from spring and remove by working it out from under spring. Remove spring from pivot. Remove shoe-to-shoe spring.

2) Disengage shoes from push rods (if equipped) and remove adjusting wheel assembly. Remove parking brake strut and anti-rattle spring. Remove brake shoe retainers, springs and nails. Disconnect parking brake cable and remove lever. Remove brake shoes.

3) Lubricate all brake shoe contact points and pivot end of parking brake lever. Insert brake lever into hole of secondary shoe from inner side of shoe web. Connect brake lever to cable. Slide secondary shoe against backing plate and anchor pin, while engaging shoe web with push rod (if equipped).

4) Slide parking brake strut behind hub and into lever slot. Install anti-rattle spring on strut. Spring tab must point up and rearward on outside of shoe web on 10" left brake and, point down and forward on inside of shoe web on 10" right brake.

5) Slide primary shoe into position, engaging shoe with push rod (if equipped) and strut. Install anchor plate and adjuster cable. Install primary shoe return spring. While holding cable guide in position on secondary shoe, install return spring through guide and into web. Place other end over anchor pin. Squeeze spring ends around anchor pin with pliers until parallel.

NOTE: Cable guide must remain flat and secondary spring must overlap primary spring.

6) Install adjusting assembly between shoes with star wheel next to secondary shoe. Install shoe-to-shoe spring. Coil must be forward and opposite adjuster lever on 11" brakes.

NOTE: Left star wheel is cadmium plated and stamped "L" on stud end; right star is Black and stamped "R" on stud end. Assemblies must be installed as indicated.

7) Install adjusting lever and spring over pivot pin. Lock lever in position by sliding it lightly rearward. Install shoe retaining nails, retainers and springs. Thread adjuster cable over guide and hook end of overload spring in lever. Install drums. Adjust and bleed brakes. Check for proper brake operation before moving vehicle.

NOTE: Cable eye must be tight against anchor and in a straight line with guide.

BENDIX SINGLE ANCHOR AUTOMATIC ADJUSTER (Cont.)

Fig. 2: Bendix Duo-Servo Brake Assembly

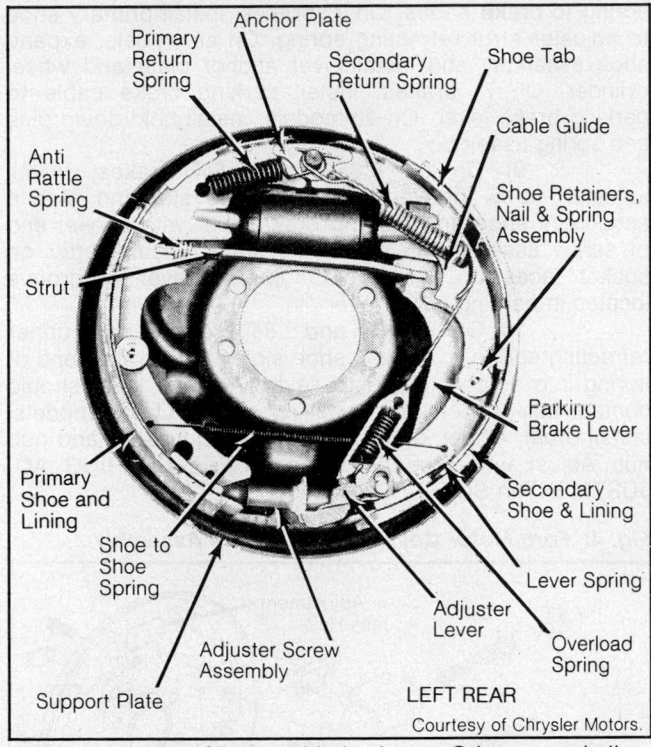

Courtesy of Chrysler Motors.

Chrysler Motors 10" assembly is shown. Others are similar.

Chrysler Motors (FWD)

1) Release brake adjustment. Remove grease cap, cotter pin, lock nut and washer. Remove brake drum and bearings. Remove parking brake cable, shoe anchor springs and hold-down springs. Spread shoes and remove adjuster assembly.

2) Remove brake shoes by raising parking brake lever, then pulling shoe away from support to remove spring tension and disengaging spring from support. Remove springs from brake shoes.

3) Install primary shoe return spring. Install primary shoe while engaging return spring end in support and shoe end under anchor plate. Install secondary shoe

Fig. 3: Chrysler Motors Non-Servo Brake Assembly

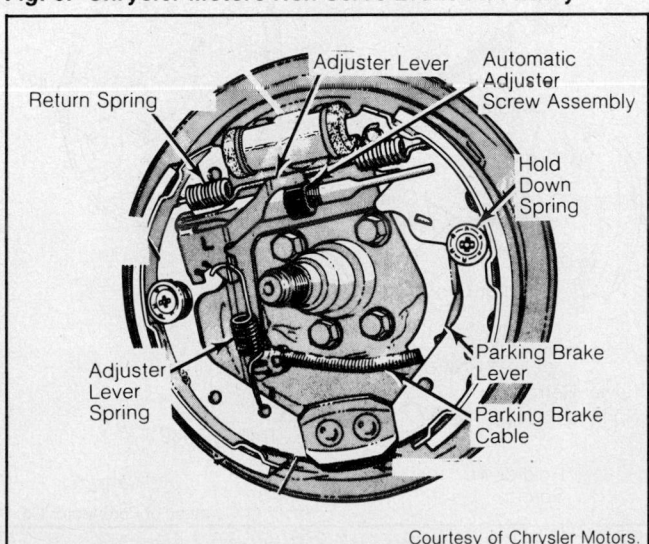

Courtesy of Chrysler Motors.

and spring in same manner. Spread shoes and install adjuster assembly with 2 stepped forks facing toward outboard side of shoes. Longer fork will be pointing to rear.

4) Install hold-down pins, springs and anchor springs. Compress parking brake cable housing spring to expose cable. Slide cable into parking brake lever. Position washer between parking brake cable housing spring and parking brake lever.

5) Install drum, bearing, washer, nut, cotter pin and grease cap. Adjust wheel bearing and bleed brakes. See WHEEL BEARING ADJUSTMENT in SUSPENSION section. Check for proper brake operation before moving vehicle.

Eagle Premier

1) Remove grease cap from hub. Remove cotter pin, nut lock and adjusting nut. Remove flat washer and outer bearing. Remove wheel, drum and hub assembly as a unit, being careful not to drag seal across spindle threads.

2) Remove upper and lower retracting spring. Remove hold-down spring and pins. Lift brake shoe and adjuster assembly off backing plate. Install wheel cylinder cup retainer. Remove parking brake cable from parking brake lever. Remove parking brake lever from rear shoe

3) Lubricate all brake shoe contact points, adjusting assembly, parking brake lever and lever pivot pin. Remove retaining clamp from wheel cylinder. Install parking brake lever on secondary shoe.

4) Install washer and new clip on parking brake lever pivot pin and crimp ends of clip. Install rear brake shoe to backing plate. Install hold down spring. Install adjuster screw and rear brake shoe making sure large notch on adjuster screw is fitted to brake shoe and small notch on adjusting screw is facing out.

5) Install adjuster lever to leading shoe adjuster lever pivot pin and fit adjuster lever into smallest of 2 notches on adjuster screw. Install upper spring. Center shoes on backing plate. Install brake drum and adjust.

Ford Motor Co. (Except Escort, EXP, Sable, Taurus, Tempo & Topaz)

1) Remove drum, releasing brake adjustment if necessary. Install clamp over wheel cylinder pistons. Remove shoe-to-anchor springs and unhook cable eye from anchor pin. Remove anchor pin plate.

2) Remove hold-down springs, shoes, adjusting screw, pivot nut, socket and automatic adjuster. Remove parking brake link spring and retainer. Disconnect parking brake cable from lever. After removing secondary shoe, disassemble parking brake lever from shoe by removing retaining clip and spring washer.

3) Assemble parking brake lever to secondary shoe and secure with spring washer and retaining clip. Lubricate brake shoe contact points. Position shoes on backing plate and install hold-down springs.

4) Install parking brake link, spring and retainer. Back off parking brake adjustment and connect cable to brake lever. Install anchor pin plate. Place cable eye over anchor pin with crimped side toward drum.

5) Install primary shoe anchor spring. Install cable guide on secondary shoe web with flanged hole fitted into hole in shoe web. Thread cable around anchor guide groove; NOT between guide and shoe web. Install secondary anchor spring. All parts should be flat on anchor pin.

Drum Brake Systems

BENDIX SINGLE ANCHOR AUTOMATIC ADJUSTER (Cont.)

6) Lubricate threads of adjusting screw and turn screw into pivot nut to limit of threads. Back off 1/2 turn and place socket on screw end. Install assembly between shoe ends with adjusting screw toothed wheel nearest secondary shoe.

7) Install cable hook in adjusting lever. Position hooked end of adjuster spring completely into large hole of primary shoe web. Connect loop end of spring to adjuster lever hole. Pull adjuster lever, cable and adjuster spring down and rearward, engaging pivot hook in large hole of secondary shoe web.

8) Ensure shoes are seated and centered on backing plate and that automatic adjuster is operating. Install drums and adjust and bleed brakes. Check for proper brake operation before moving vehicle.

Ford Motor Co. (Escort, EXP, Sable, Taurus, Tempo & Topaz)

1) Remove grease cap from hub. Remove cotter pin, nut lock and adjusting nut. Remove flat washer and outer bearing. Remove wheel, drum and hub assembly as a unit, being careful not to drag seal across spindle threads.

2) Remove hold-down spring and pins. Lift brake shoe and adjuster assembly off backing plate. Remove parking brake cable from parking brake lever. On 7" brakes remove lower retracting spring, then remove lower primary shoe retracting spring by rotating shoe over adjusting quadrant and disconnecting spring.

NOTE: If drum will not come off, insert a screwdriver through adjustment hole and apply side pressure to adjuster assembly pivot to release brake adjustment. On 8", 8.85" and 9.84" brakes it will be necessary to remove brake line-to-axle retention bracket to gain access to adjuster hole.

3) On 7" brakes remove secondary shoe-to-parking brake strut retracting spring by pivoting strut downward until it disengages from secondary shoe. On 8", 8.85" and 9.84" brakes, remove retracting springs from lower brake shoe attachment and upper shoe-to-adjuster lever.

4) On 7" brakes, disassemble adjuster by pulling quadrant away from knurled pin and rotating. Remove spring and slide quadrant out of slot. On all models, remove parking brake lever horseshoe retaining clip and spring washer. Lift lever off pin on brake shoe.

5) Apply a light coating of high temperature grease to contact points of brake shoes and backing plate and adjusting screw threads. On 7" brakes, install adjuster quadrant until it meshes with knurled pin in 3rd or 4th notch of outboard end of quadrant.

6) On 8", 8.85" and 9.84" brakes, install stainless steel washer over socket end of adjusting screw and install socket. Turn adjustng screw into adjusting pivot nut to limit of threads and back off 1/2 turn. On all models, assemble parking brake lever to secondary shoe. Install spring washer and new horseshoe clip. Crimp clip until lever is securely fastened.

7) On 8", 8.85" and 9.84" brakes, install parking brake cable to parking brake lever. On 7" brakes, install secondary shoe to parking brake strut retracting spring by attaching to slots in each part and pivoting strut to tension spring. Ensure spring end with hook parallel to centerline of coils is installed in hole in shoe web. Installed spring should be flat against shoe and parallel to strut.

8) On all models, attach lower shoe retracting spring to brake shoes. On 7" brakes, install primary shoe to adjuster strut retracting spring. On all models, expand shoe assembly and install over anchor plate and wheel cylinder. On 7" brakes, install parking brake cable to parking brake lever. On all models, install hold-down pins and spring assembly.

9) On 8", 8.85" and 9.84" brakes, install adjuster screw between primary shoe slot and slot in secondary shoe and parking brake lever with socket end of screw assembly in secondary shoe. Ensure letter on socket faces up. Assemble adjusting lever in groove located in parking brake lever pin.

10) On 8", 8.85" and 9.84" brakes, attach upper retracting spring to leading shoe slot. Stretch other end of spring into notch on adjuster lever. Adjuster lever should contact star wheel after installing spring. On all models, install drum, wheel, outer bearing, keyed washer and hub nut. Adjust wheel bearing. See WHEEL BEARING ADJUSTMENT in SUSPENSION section.

Fig. 4: Ford Motor Co. Non-Servo Brake Assembly

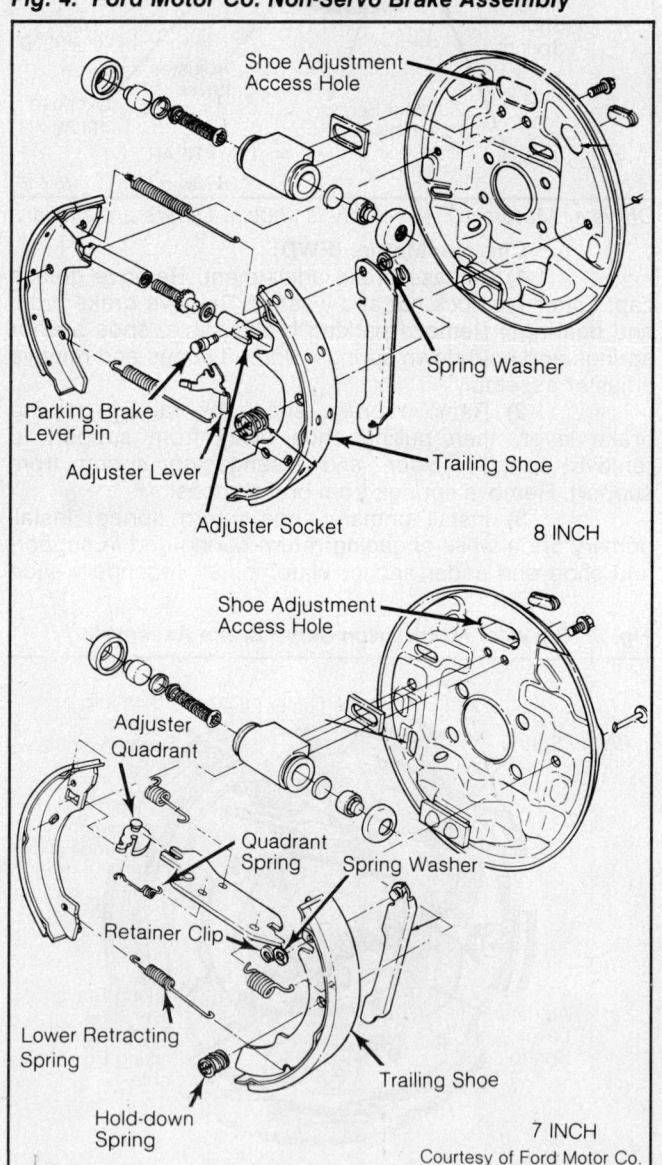

Courtesy of Ford Motor Co.

BENDIX SINGLE ANCHOR AUTOMATIC ADJUSTER (Cont.)

BLEEDING SYSTEM

See HYDRAULIC BRAKE BLEEDING in this section.

Application	Ft. Lbs. (N.m)
Eagle Premier	75 (102)
Chrysler Motors	
Diplomat, Fifth Avenue,	
Gran Fury	85 (115)
All Others	95 (129)
Ford Motor Co.	
Escort, EXP,	
Sable, Taurus,	
Tempo, Topaz	80-105 (109-143)
All Others	70-115 (96-155)

DRUM BRAKE SPECIFICATIONS

Application	Drum Diam. In. (mm)	Drum Width In. (mm)	Max. Drum Refinish Diam. In. (mm)	Wheel Cyl. Diam. In. (mm)	Master Cyl. Diam. In. (mm)
Eagle Premier	8.85 (224.8)	1.50 (38.1)	8.92 (226.5)	.940 (23.88)	.940 (23.88)
Chrysler Motors					
Aries, Horizon, Lancer, LeBaron, Omni, Reliant, Sundance, Shadow	7.87 (200.0)	.....	Stamped on Drum	.626 (15.90)	.827 (21.01)
Aries, Caravelle, Daytona, LeBaron, New Yorker, Reliant, 600	8.66 (220.0)	.....	Stamped on Drum	.562 (14.27)	.827 (21.01)
Diplomat, Fifth Avenue, Gran Fury Standard	10.00 (254.0)	2.50 (63.5)	10.06 (255.5)	.938 (23.8)	1.03 (26.1)
Heavy Duty [1]	11.00 (279.4)	2.50 (63.5)	11.06 (280.9)	.938 (23.8)	1.03 (26.1)
Ford Motor Co.					
Escort	7.00 (180.0)	1.26 (32.0)	7.06 (181.5)	.811 (20.59)	.827 (21.01)
Escort, EXP, Tempo, Topaz	8.00 (203.2)	1.34 (34.0)	8.06 (204.7)	.875 (22.23)	.827 (21.01)
Sable, Taurus Sedan	8.85 (225.0)	1.49 (38.0)	8.92 (226.5)	1.000 (25.4)	.875 (22.23)
Wagon	9.84 (250.0)	1.77 (45.0)	9.90 (251.5)	1.0 (25.4)	.875 (22.23)
Cougar, Thunderbird, Mustang Standard	9.00 (229.0)	1.75 (44.5)	9.06 (230.1)	.750 (19.05)	.827 (21.01)
Heavy Duty [1]	10.00 (254.0)	1.75 (44.5)	10.06 (255.5)	.750 (19.05)	.827 (21.01)
Crown Victoria, Grand Marquis, Town Car Standard	10.00 (254.0)	2.50 (63.5)	10.06 (255.5)	.938 (23.8)	1.00 (25.40)
Heavy Duty [1]	11.03 (280.2)	2.25 (57.2)	11.09 (281.7)	.938 (23.8)	1.00 (25.40)

[1] – Heavy Duty Models are Station Wagons, Police, Taxi and Trailer Tow.

Drum Brake Systems

GENERAL MOTORS AUTOMATIC ADJUSTER

Buick, Cadillac, Chevrolet (Exc. Corvette
& Nova), Oldsmobile, Pontiac

DESCRIPTION

General Motors automatic adjusting rear brakes are hydraulic single anchor and use Bendix-type shoes. Anchor pins for brake shoes are fixed to backing plate and are non-adjustable. Automatic system is made up of a link, actuating lever, pawl and pawl spring. Pawl spring is mounted on secondary brake shoe. System uses an override pivot plate and spring to protect against binding linkage.

NOTE: Some models use an adjuster pawl with a separate blade to contact star wheel. This system does not use an override spring.

OPERATION

Automatic adjusters operate only when brakes are applied as car is moving in reverse. The link, which holds top of actuating lever stationary, forces lever to pivot on secondary shoe. This pivoting action forces pawl downward against tooth on adjuster screw.

If lining-to-drum clearance is correct, the downward movement will stop before adjusting screw is turned. If clearance is too wide, secondary shoe will move outward. This allows pawl to move down enough to turn adjuster screw one notch. This brings lining-to-drum clearance back to correct specificatons.

If adjuster screw is frozen or clearance is too great, an override device will prevent adjuster movement. This will prevent binding of automatic adjuster linkage.

ADJUSTMENTS

BRAKE SHOE ADJUSTMENT

NOTE: Adjustment should only be required after relining or replacing shoes, or if length of adjusting screw is changed.

1) Raise vehicle and remove wheels and drums. Ensure parking brake cable and linkage, including

**Fig. 1: Adjusting Brake Shoe Clearance
(Through Backing Plate)**

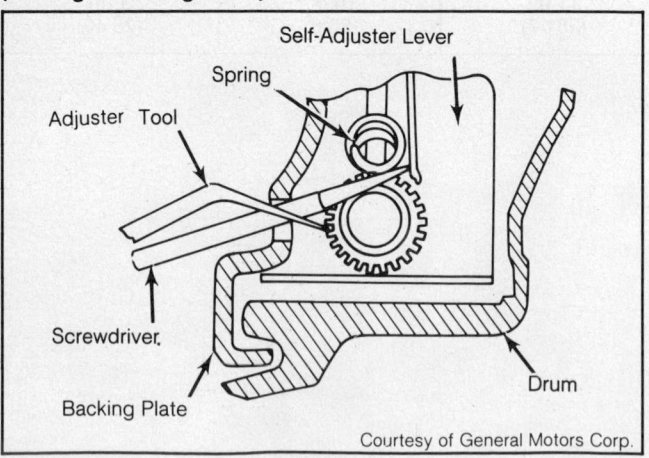

Courtesy of General Motors Corp.

levers on rear secondary shoes, are free. Measure brake drum inside diameter using inside caliper portion of Brake Drum Gauge (J-21177).

2) Adjust brake shoes to dimension obtained on outside caliper portion of Brake Drum Gauge (J-21177). Check brake fluid level in both master cylinder reservoirs. Add fluid if necessary. Adjust parking brake.

3) Install drums and wheel. Tighten wheel mounting nuts. Lower vehicle. Drive car alternately forward and backward, applying brakes moderately in each direction.

PARKING BRAKE ADJUSTMENT

NOTE: When rear drum brakes are serviced, parking brake linkage cable at equalizer must always be readjusted to prevent possible burn out of rear brakes.

Except "H" Body

1) Lubricate parking brake linkage at equalizer and cable stud. Ensure free movement of cables. Depress parking brake pedal or pull brake lever from fully released position. See PEDAL/LEVER ADJUSTMENT table. Raise rear wheel. Hold brake cable from turning and tighten equalizer nut one turn at a time.

2) Check for brake drag after each turn by turning wheel forward. When light drag is felt on both wheels, release parking brake. No drag should be present at either wheel.

PEDAL/LEVER ADJUSTMENT

Body Code	Ratchet Clicks
"A", "B", "C", "G" & "L"	3
"F"	2
"J" & "N"	5

"H" Body

1) Raise and support vehicle. Remove rear wheel and drums. Make sure stops on parking brake levers are against the edge of the shoe web. If parking brake cable is holding stops off edge of shoe web, loosen cable adjustment.

2) Measure drum inside diameter. Turn adjuster nut and adjust shoe and lining diameter to .05" (1.27 mm) less than drum inside diameter for each rear wheel. Install drums with at least 2 wheel nuts.

3) Adjust brake shoe-to-drum clearance. Apply and release service brake pedal 30 to 35 times until clicking noise from self adjusters stops on both side of vehicle.

4) Cycle brake system by fully applying parking brake with a pedal force of 100 lbs. (45 kg) and release. Apply and release parking brake 5 additional times as described above.

5) Check parking brake pedal assembly for full release by turning ignition switch to "ON" and observing brake warning light. Light should be off. If brake light is on and parking brake appears to be fully released, operate pedal release lever and pull downward on front parking brake cable to remove slack.

6) Remove drums. Adjust parking brake cable until a 1/8" (3.17 mm) drill can be inserted into space between shoe web and parking brake lever. Satisfactory adjustment is achieved when a 1/8" (3.17 mm) drill will fit into notch but a 1/4" (6.35 mm) drill will not.

GENERAL MOTORS AUTOMATIC ADJUSTER (Cont.)

7) Install brake drums and wheels. Lower car. Check operation of parking brake.

SERVICING

SHOE & LINING REPLACEMENT

NOTE: **Mark position of springs and star adjusters for reassembly reference.**

Removal

1) Release parking brake and loosen parking brake cable at equalizer. If necessary, back off brake adjustment before removing brake drums. Remove return springs. Remove brake shoe hold-down springs and cups. Lift up on parking brake actuator lever and remove actuator link. Remove actuator lever and return spring.

2) Separate brake shoes from wheel cylinder connecting links. Remove parking brake strut and spring. Disconnect parking brake cable. Remove brake shoes, spring and adjusting screw from backing plate. Detach spring and screw from brake shoes. Remove parking brake lever from secondary shoe.

Installation

1) Lubricate fulcrum end of parking brake lever and attach to secondary shoe. Connect adjusting screw spring, then place screw in position. Ensure star is aligned with adjusting hole. Lubricate surfaces where shoe and parking brake cable contact backing plate. Position shoes and insert into wheel cylinder links.

2) Connect cable to parking brake lever and install strut and spring between lever and primary shoe. Install actuator, actuator return spring and actuating link. Replace brake drums and wheels. Adjust parking brake and brake shoes. Check for proper operation of brakes before moving vehicle.

WHEEL CYLINDER REPLACEMENT

Two types of wheel cylinder retainers are used to hold wheel cylinder to backing plate. The first type uses a ring type retainer. *See Figs. 2 and 6.* The second type uses 2 retaining bolts. *See Figs. 3 and 5.*

Removal (Ring Type Retainer)

Remove dirt and foreign material from around wheel cylinder and pilot. Disconnect inlet tube line. Remove wheel cylinder retainer using 2 awls or pins of 1/8" diameter or less. Insert awls or pins into access slots between wheel cylinder pilot and retaining lock tabs. Bend both tabs away simultaneously until wheel cylinder is released.

Installation

To install, hold cylinder on backing plate by inserting a wood block between wheel cylinder and axle flange. Install a new retaining spring over wheel cylinder, lining up retainer tabs with cylinder tab grooves. Drive retainer into position using 1 1/8" socket and a 10" extension. Retainer is in position when tabs are snapped under retainer abutment.

Removal (Bolt Type Retainer)

Disconnect inlet tube line and remove 2 bolts holding wheel cylinder to backing plate. Remove wheel cylinder.

Installation

To install, place wheel cylinder in position and install bolts. Connect inlet tube line.

BLEEDING SYSTEM

See HYDRAULIC BRAKE BLEEDING in this section.

Fig. 2: Exploded View of Rear Direct Torque Type Drum Brake Assembly

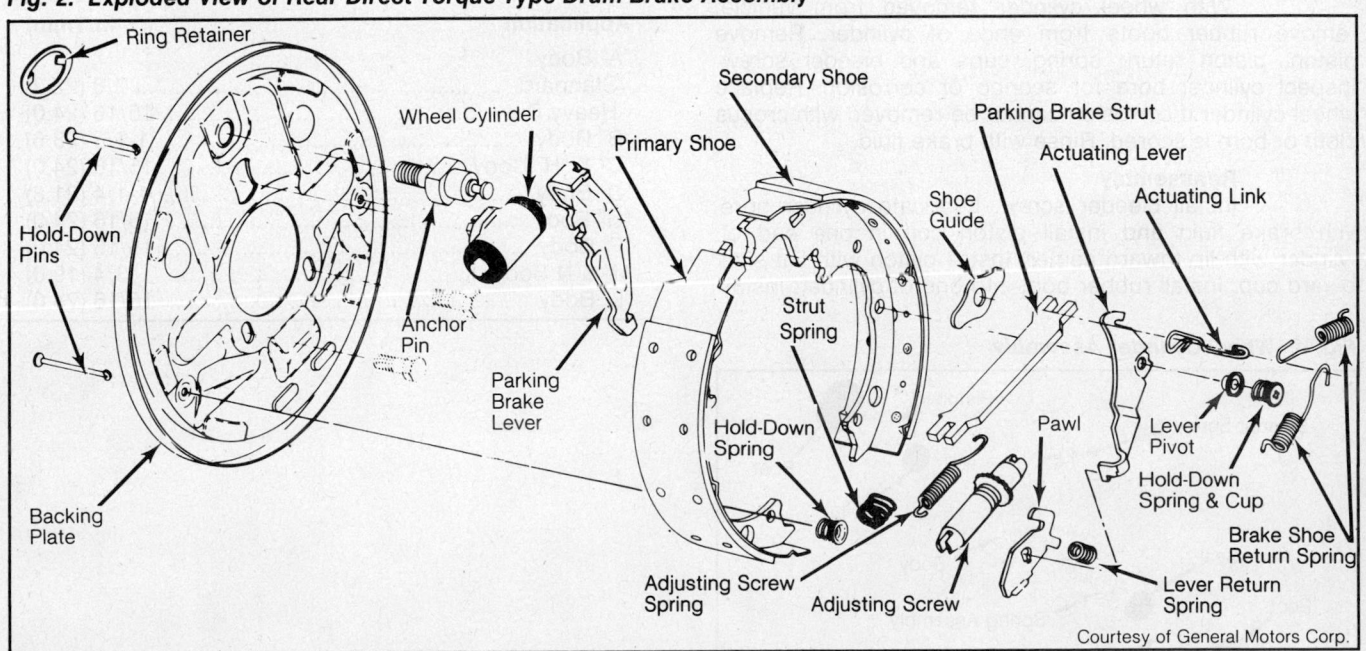

Courtesy of General Motors Corp.

Drum Brake Systems

GENERAL MOTORS AUTOMATIC ADJUSTER (Cont.)

Fig. 3: Exploded View of Conventional Type Rear Drum Brake Assembly

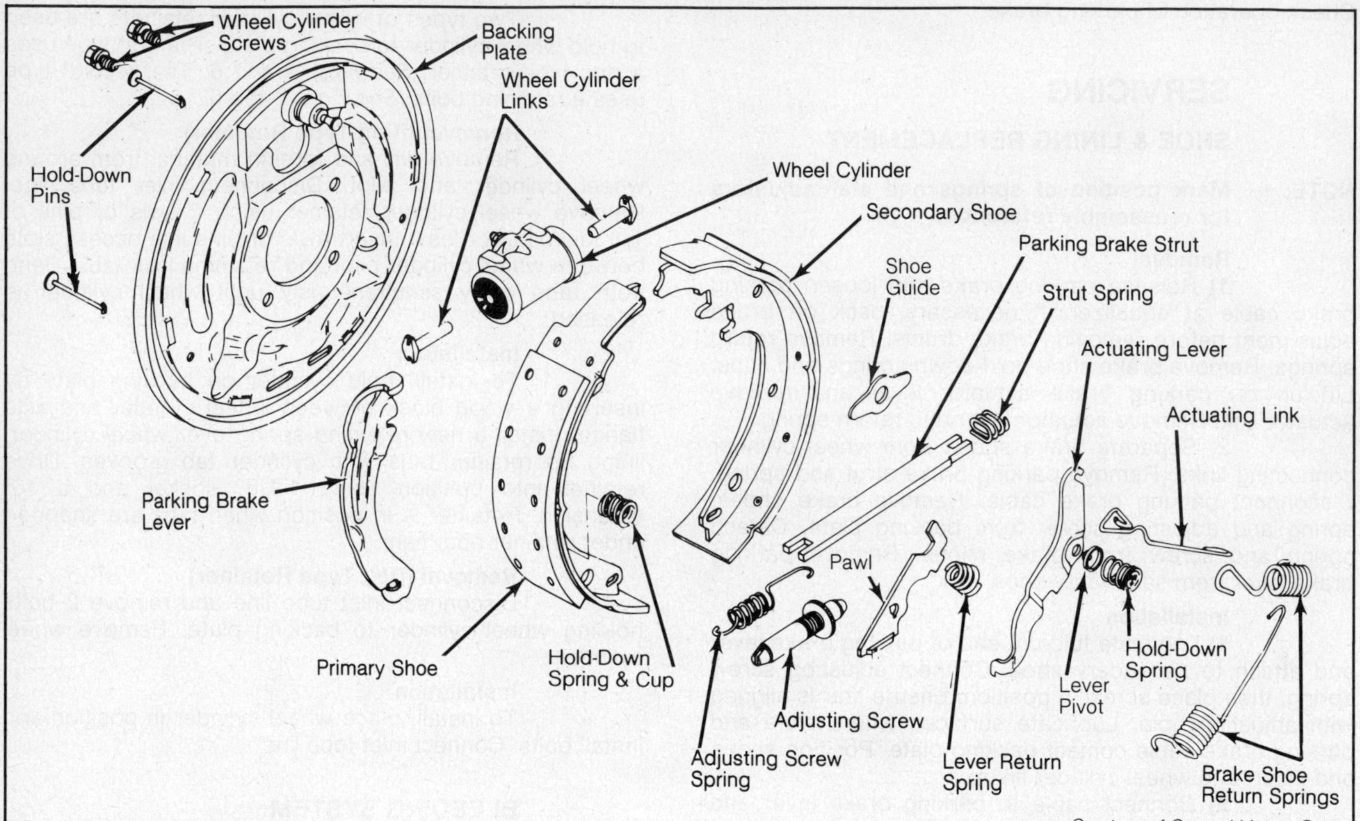

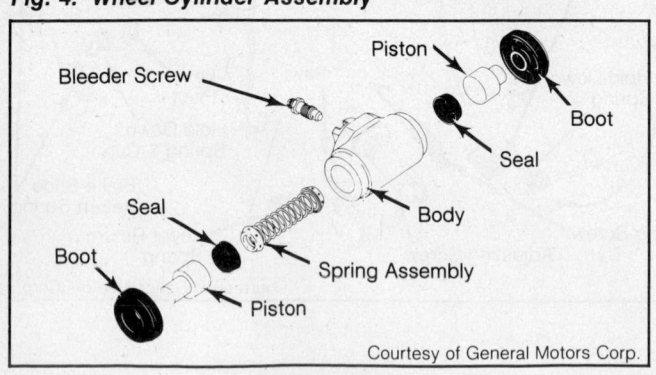

Courtesy of General Motors Corp.

OVERHAUL

WHEEL CYLINDER

Disassembly

With wheel cylinder removed from vehicle, remove rubber boots from ends of cylinder. Remove piston, piston return spring, cups and bleeder screw. Inspect cylinder bore for scoring or corrosion. Replace wheel cylinder if corrosion cannot be removed with crocus cloth or bore is scored. Rinse with brake fluid.

Reassembly

Install bleeder screw. Lubricate cylinder bore with brake fluid and install piston cup in one end of cylinder with lip toward center. Install piston with flat side toward cup. Install rubber boot into end of cylinder. Install spring and expander assembly into opposite end. Install remaining cup, piston and rubber boot.

MASTER CYLINDER DIAMETERS

Application	In. (mm)
"A" Body	
Standard	7/8 (22.2)
Heavy Duty	15/16 (24.0)
"B" Body	1-1/8 (28.6)
"C" & "H" Body	15/16 (24.0)
"D" Body	1-1/4 (31.8)
"G" Body	15/16 (24.0)
"F" Body	15/16 (24.0)
"J" & N Body	3/4 (19.0)
"L" Body	15/16 (24.0)

Fig. 4: Wheel Cylinder Assembly

Courtesy of General Motors Corp.

GENERAL MOTORS AUTOMATIC ADJUSTER (Cont.)

Fig. 5: Exploded View of Leading/Trailing Rear Drum Brake Assembly

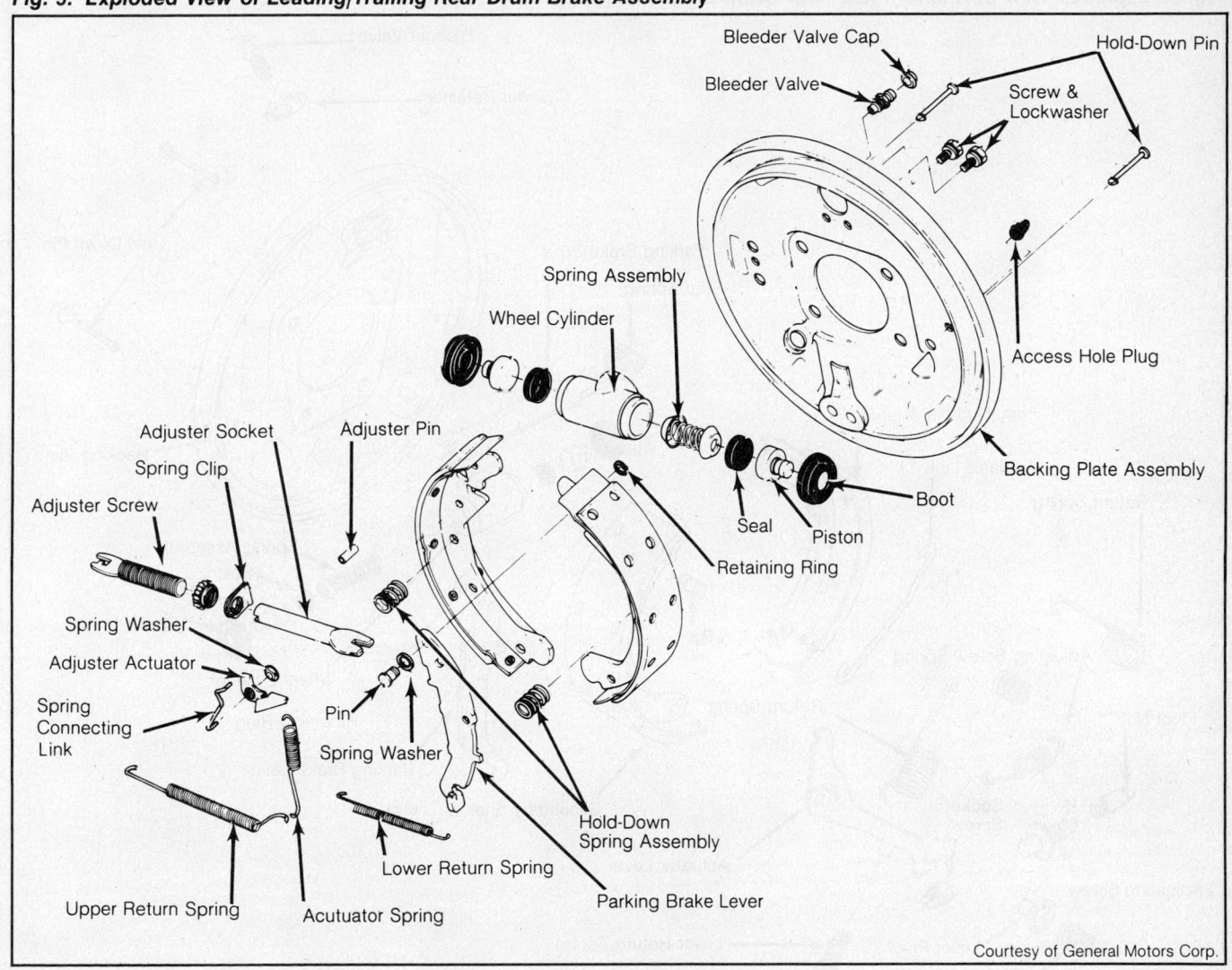

Courtesy of General Motors Corp.

WHEEL LUG NUT TIGHTENING SPECIFICATIONS

Application	Ft. Lbs. (N.m)
Buick	
Century Aluminum Wheels	90 (122)
All Others	80 (109)
Cadillac	100 (136)
Chevrolet	
Beretta & Corsica	100 (136)
Chevette	70 (95)
Camaro Aluminum Wheels	90 (122)
Caprice Wagon	100 (136)
All Others	80 (109)
Oldsmobile	
Cutlass Aluminum Wheels	90 (122)
88 Wagon & Ninety-Eight	100 (136)
All Others	80 (109)
Pontiac	
Aluminum Wheels	90 (122)
All Others	80 (109)

DRUM BRAKE SPECIFICATIONS

Application	Drum Diam. In.(mm)	Max. Drum Refinish Diam. In.(mm)
"A", "C" & "H"		
Body	8.860 (225.12)	8.920 (226.57)
"B", "F" & "G"		
Body		
w/9.5" Drum	9.500 (241.00)	9.560 (241.81)
w/11.0" Drum	11.000 (279.00)	11.060 (279.91)
"D" Body		
w/11.0" Drum	11.000 (279.00)	11.060 (279.91)
w/12.0" Drum	12.000 (304.80)	12.060 (306.32)
"J", "L" & "N"		
Body	7.879 (200.12)	7.899 (200.60)

Drum Brake Systems

GENERAL MOTORS AUTOMATIC ADJUSTER (Cont.)

Fig. 6: Exploded View of Anchor Plate Rear Drum Brake Assembly

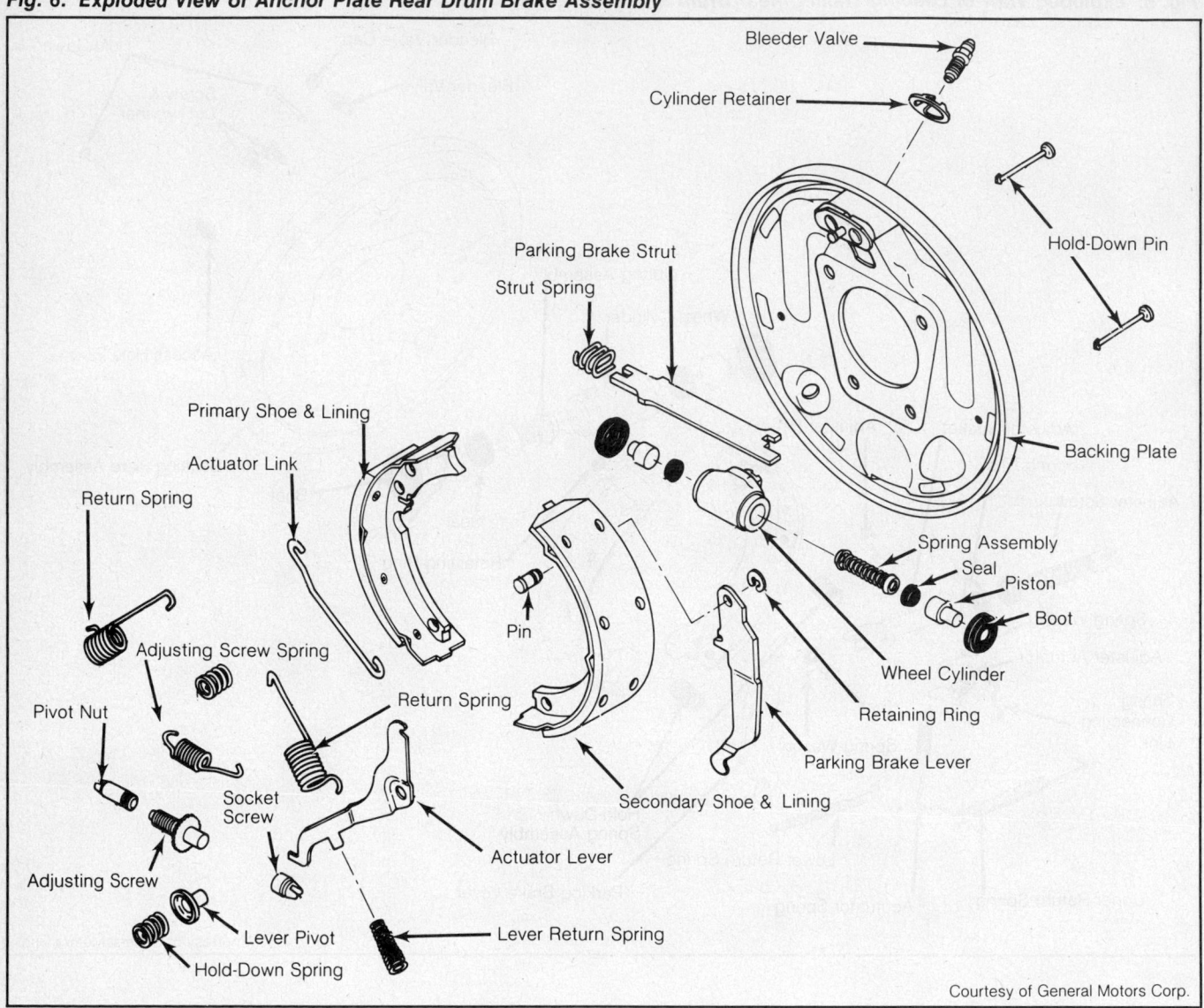

Courtesy of General Motors Corp.

WHEEL CYLINDER DIAMETERS

Application	In. (mm)
"A", "C" & "H" Body	
Standard	11/16 (17.5)
Police, Heavy Duty	3/4 (19.0)
Wagon	13/16 (20.6)
"B" Body	
Standard	3/4 (19.0)
Heavy Duty	15/16 (23.8)
Wagon	1 (25.4)
"D" Body	
Standard	1 (25.4)
Commercial Chassis	15/16 (23.8)
"F" & "G" Body	3/4 (19.0)
"J" & "N" Body	
Standard	5/8 (16.0)
Wagon	11/16 (17.5)
"L" Body	
Sedan	5/8 (16.0)
Coupe	3/4 (19.0)

BODY DESIGNATION CODES

Body Code	Model
"A"	Celebrity, Century, Cutlass Ciera, Cutlass Cruiser & 6000
"B"	Caprice, Custom Cruiser, Electric Wagon, LeSabre Wagon & Safari Wagon
"C"	Electra, Deville, Fleetwood & Ninety Eight
"D"	Brougham
"F"	Camaro & Firebird
"G"	Monte Carlo, Bonneville, Grand Prix, Cutlass Supreme & Regal GN
"H"	Bonneville, Delta 88 & LeSabre
"J"	Cavalier, Cimarron, Firenza, Skyhawk & Sunbird
"L"	Beretta & Corsica
"N"	Cutlass Calais, Grand Am & Skylark

Drum Brake Systems

NOVA

DESCRIPTION

This brake system incorporates use of a dual master cylinder with a diagonally split hydraulic circuit. Hydraulic pressure from master cylinder actuates drum brakes in rear.

Power assist to master cylinder is provided by a single diaphragm vacuum booster. A dual proportioning valve controls brake balance between front and rear brakes under heavy deceleration. Parking brake system is mechanical. It applies braking force to rear wheels by means of a hand operated mechanical linkage system.

ADJUSTMENTS

PEDAL HEIGHT

1) Check that pedal height is correct. *See Fig. 1.* Pedal height from floor should be 5.79-6.18" (147-157 mm). If necessary, adjust pedal height by removing instrument lower finish panel and air duct.

2) Loosen stoplight switch. Adjust pedal height by turning pedal push rod. Return stoplight switch until it lightly contacts pedal stopper. After adjusting pedal height, check and adjust pedal free play.

Fig. 1: Adjusting Brake Pedal Height

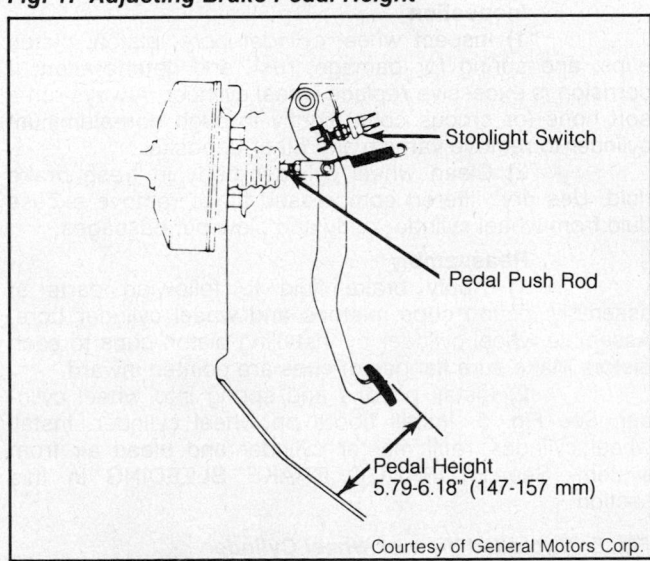

Stoplight Switch

Pedal Push Rod

Pedal Height 5.79-6.18" (147-157 mm)

Courtesy of General Motors Corp.

PEDAL FREEPLAY

1) To check pedal free play, stop engine and depress brake pedal several times until there is no more vacuum left in booster. Push in pedal until beginning of resistance is felt. Measure distance between beginning of free play and resistance. *See Fig. 2.* Pedal free play should be .12-.24" (3-6 mm).

NOTE: **The pedal free play is amount of stroke used before booster air valve is moved by pedal push rod.**

2) To adjust free play, turn pedal push rod. Start engine and confirm pedal free play exists. After adjusting pedal free play, check pedal height. Install air duct and instrument lower finish panel.

PEDAL RESERVE DISTANCE

To check that pedal reserve distance is correct, release parking brake. With engine running,

Fig. 2: Adjusting Brake Pedal Freeplay

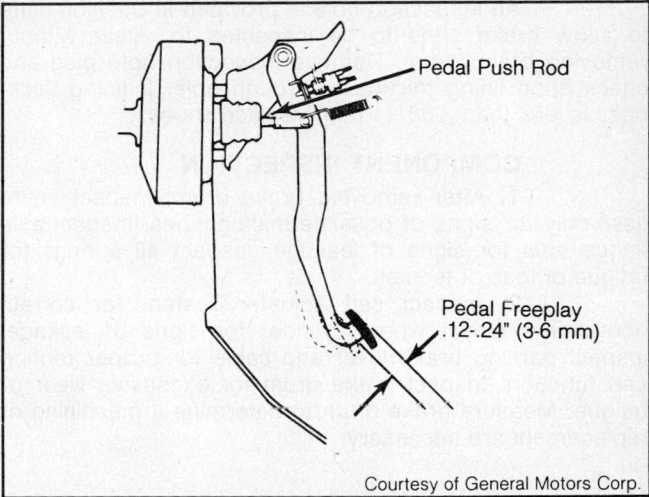

Pedal Push Rod

Pedal Freeplay .12-.24" (3-6 mm)

Courtesy of General Motors Corp.

depress pedal and measure pedal reserve distance. *See Fig. 3.* Distance from floor at 110 lbs. (50 kg) pressure should be more than 2.56" (65 mm). If incorrect, diagnose brake system. See TROUBLE SHOOTING at beginning of this section.

Fig. 3: Checking Pedal Reserve Distance

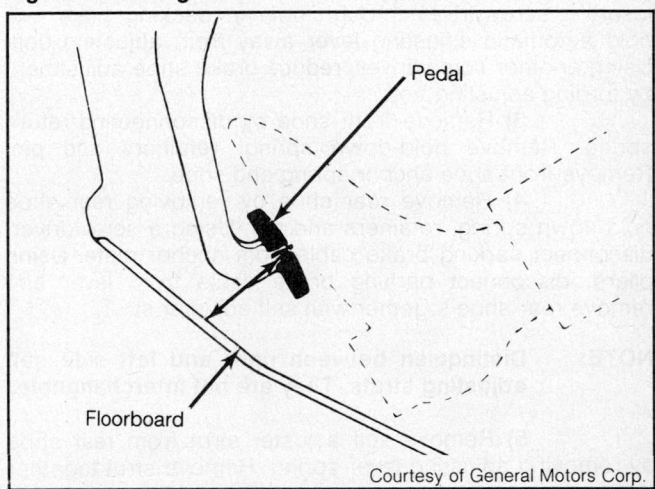

Pedal

Floorboard

Courtesy of General Motors Corp.

PARKING BRAKE

1) Check that parking brake lever travel is correct by pulling parking brake lever all the way up, and counting number of clicks. There should be 4 to 7 clicks. If necessary, adjust parking brake.

NOTE: **Before adjusting parking brake, make sure rear brake shoe clearance has been adjusted.**

2) To adjust, remove console box. Loosen lock nut and turn adjusting nut until travel is correct. Tighten lock nut and install console box.

SERVICING

BLEEDING

See HYDRAULIC BRAKE BLEEDING in this section.

Drum Brake Systems

NOVA (Cont.)

BRAKE SHOE INSPECTION

An inspection hole is provided in backing plate to allow brake shoe to be inspected for wear without removing brake drum. Remove inspection hole plug and check shoe lining thickness through hole. If lining thickness is less than .039" (1 mm), replace shoes.

COMPONENT INSPECTION

1) After removing brake drum, inspect entire assembly for signs of possible malfunctions. Inspect axle flange seal for signs of leakage. Inspect all springs for fatigue or loss of tension.

2) Inspect self adjuster system for correct operation. Inspect wheel cylinder for signs of leakage. Inspect parking brake lever and cable for proper routing and function. Inspect brake drum for excessive wear or fatigue. Measure brake drum to determine if machining or replacement are necessary.

REMOVAL & INSTALLATION

DRUM BRAKE ASSEMBLY

Removal

1) Raise and support vehicle. Mark relationship of wheel to axle. Remove rear wheel and drum.

2) If brake drum cannot be removed easily, insert a screwdriver through hole in backing plate and hold automatic adjusting lever away from adjusting bolt. Using another screwdriver, reduce brake shoe adjustment by turning adjusting bolt.

3) Remove front shoe by disconnecting return spring. Remove hold-down spring, retainers and pin. Remove front shoe anchor spring and shoe.

4) Remove rear shoe by removing rear shoe hold-down spring, retainers and pin. Using a screwdriver, disconnect parking brake cable from anchor plate. Using pliers, disconnect parking brake cable from lever and remove rear shoe together with self adjuster strut.

NOTE: **Distinquish between right and left side self adjusting struts. They are not interchangable.**

5) Remove self adjuster strut from rear shoe by removing adjusting lever spring. Remove strut together

with return spring. Remove parking brake lever and automatic adjusting lever from rear shoe using a screwdriver. Pry out "C" washer and remove shim and levers.

Installation

1) To install, reverse removal procedure. See Fig. 4. Before reassembly, measure brake drum inside diameter to ensure it complies with specification. If drum is larger than specification, it must be replaced.

2) Replace any parts that are damaged or discolored due to heat, stress or wear. Lubricate backing plate lube points. Inspect axle seal for leakage. Adjust brake shoes to obtain a very slight drag.

OVERHAUL

CAUTION: **DO NOT hone or resurface aluminum components if damaged, replacement is necessary.**

WHEEL CYLINDER

Disassembly

Remove following parts from wheel cylinder: boots, pistons, piston cups, spring, and bleeder screw. See Fig. 5.

Inspection

1) Inspect wheel cylinder bore, piston, piston cups, and spring for damage, rust, and deterioration. If corrision is excessive replace wheel cylinder. Always run a soft hone (or crocus colth) lightly through non-aluminum cylinder to remove varnish and other deposits.

2) Clean wheel cylinder body in fresh brake fluid. Use dry, filtered compressed air to remove excess fluid from wheel cylinder body and blow out passages.

Reassembly

1) Apply brake fluid to following parts at assembly: piston cups, pistons and wheel cylinder bore. Assemble wheel cylinder by installing piston cups to each piston. Make sure flanges of cups are pointed inward.

2) Install pistons and spring into wheel cylinder. See Fig. 5. Install boots on wheel cylinder. Install wheel cylinder, refill master cylinder and bleed air from system. See HYDRAULIC BRAKE BLEEDING in this section

Fig. 4: Exploded View of Rear Drum Assembly

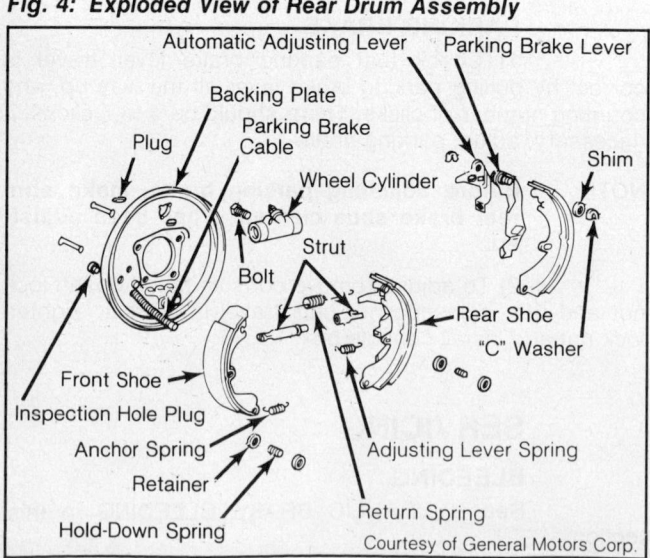

Courtesy of General Motors Corp.

Fig. 5: Exploded View of Wheel Cylinder

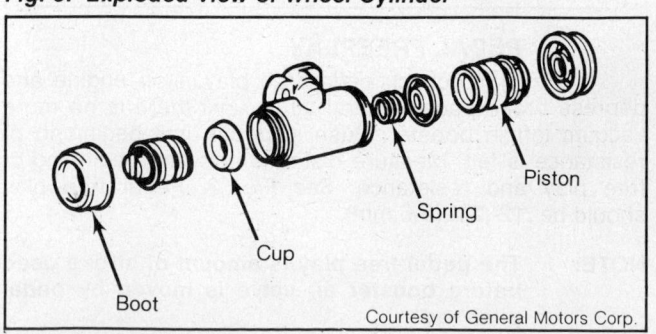

Courtesy of General Motors Corp.

TIGHTENING SPECIFICATIONS

Application	INCH Lbs. (N.m)
Parking Brake Lever-to-Body	108 (13)
Wheel Cylinder-to-Backing Plate	84 (10)
Brake Line	132 (15)

NOVA (Cont.)

DRUM BRAKE SPECIFICATIONS

Application	Drum Diam. In. (mm)	Drum Width In. (mm)	Max. Drum Refinish Diam. In. (mm)	Wheel Cyl. Diam. In. (mm)	Master Cyl. Diam. In. (mm)
Nova	7.874 (200.00)	.....	7.913 (201.00)	.....	.....

Master Cylinders

BENDIX/DELCO-MORAINE

**Chrysler Motors, Ford Motor Co.,
General Motors**

DESCRIPTION

All master cylinders are dual-piston, single-bore assemblies. When brake pedal is depressed master cylinder primary piston moves forward. Under normal conditions, combination of hydraulic pressure and force of primary piston spring move secondary piston forward at same time.

When pistons have moved forward, primary cups cover by-pass holes, hydraulic pressure is built up and transmitted to front and rear brake assemblies.

Some master cylinders have a residual pressure valve installed under tube seat insert in drum brake outlet. This valve keeps a small amount of pressure in drum brake systems and prevents air from entering system.

Many master cylinders are equipped with fluid level sensor switches and integral proportioning valves. The proportioning valves are designed to provide better front-to-rear braking balance. Many master cylinders also have a built-in quick take-up feature which allows a large quanity of brake fluid to remain in wheel cylinders for quicker braking action.

Fig. 1: Bench Bleeding Master Cylinder

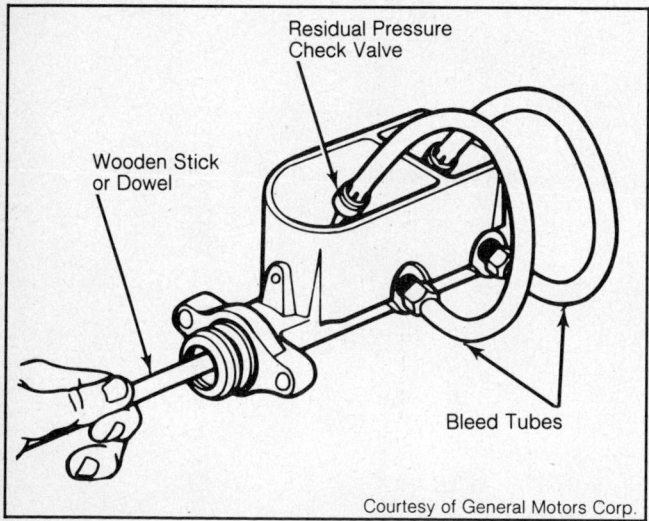

Residual Pressure Check Valve

Wooden Stick or Dowel

Bleed Tubes

Courtesy of General Motors Corp.

REMOVAL & INSTALLATION

MASTER CYLINDER

Removal

1) On power brake systems, disconnect brake fluid level indicator and brake warning switch leads (if equipped). Disconnect hydraulic brake lines. Remove master cylinder attaching nuts and remove master cylinder.

2) On manual brake systems, disconnect negative battery cable and warning switch lead (if equipped). Disconnect hydraulic brake lines. Remove push rod at brake pedal and remove stoplight switch (if equipped). Remove master cylinder attaching nuts and remove master cylinder.

Installation

1) Bleed master cylinder. To complete installation, reverse remainder of removal procedure. Bleed hydraulic brake system. See HYDRAULIC BRAKE BLEEDING in this section.

2) Check master cylinder compensating ports. Remove master cylinder cover and observe brake fluid. A slight surge or small spurt should appear in one or both reservoirs upon brake application. If no spurt appears, push rod may be improperly adjusted.

3) Adjust push rod at brake pedal, on manual brakes. Push rod should have a slight amount of play when brake pedal is released. On power brakes, see PUSH ROD ADJUSTMENT under POWER BRAKE UNITS in this section.

BENCH BLEEDING MASTER CYLINDER

NOTE: **Bleed tubes must have a residual pressure check valve installed to keep tubes from siphoning brake fluid.**

1) Clamp master cylinder in vise by mounting flange. Install bleed tubes in outlet ports. Fill reservoirs with clean brake fluid so that bleed tubes are below brake fluid level. *See Fig. 1.*

2) Slowly compress and release piston assemblies until bubbles no longer appear in brake fluid. Remove tubes and plug master cylinder outlets to keep fluid from draining.

OVERHAUL

MASTER CYLINDER

Disassembly

NOTE: **Do not remove plastic reservoir on Corvette master cylinder. Do not remove quick take-up valve on General Motors Quick Take-Up or Diagonal Split master cylinders, as it is not a serviceable item.**

1) Clean outside of master cylinder. Remove caps or cover/diaphram assembly. Remove brake fluid level indicator (if equipped). Pump and drain all brake fluid from master cylinder. Clamp master cylinder in vise by mounting flange. Remove plastic reservoir and grommets on 2-piece master cylinders.

2) Discard reservoir assembly used on Ford Motor Co. diagonal split master cylinder. Remove fluid control valve using a 12 mm socket on Ford Motor Co. diagonal split master cylinder. *See Fig. 3.*

3) Press primary and secondary piston inward until fully bottomed. Remove stop screw on Corvette master cylinder. Remove failure warning switch and combination piston assembly on Corvette master cylinder. *See Fig. 7.*

4) Remove proportioning valves, failure warning switch and failure warning switch piston assembly on General Motors diagonal split master cylinder. *See Fig. 5.* Remove push rod (if equipped).

5) Press primary piston inward and remove stop bolt (if equipped). Press primary piston inward and remove snap ring. Remove primary piston assembly. Apply compressed air to furthest back bleeder screw hole and remove secondary piston assembly.

BENDIX/DELCO-MORAINE (Cont.)

Fig. 2: *Typical Cast Iron Tandem Master Cylinder*

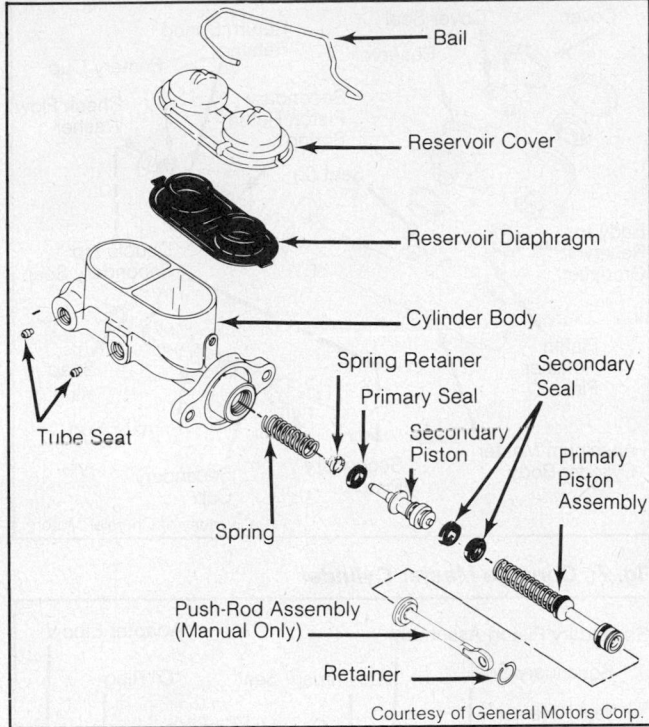

- Bail
- Reservoir Cover
- Reservoir Diaphragm
- Cylinder Body
- Spring Retainer
- Primary Seal
- Secondary Seal
- Secondary Piston
- Primary Piston Assembly
- Tube Seat
- Spring
- Push-Rod Assembly (Manual Only)
- Retainer

Courtesy of General Motors Corp.

Inspection

NOTE: **Do not wash combination piston assembly used on Corvette master cylinder as it is pre-lubricated with a special grease.**

1) Wash master cylinder body, bore and piston assemblies with denatured or isopropyl alcohol. Inspect piston assemblies and return springs. Replace pistons if they are scored galled, worn, cracked or broken. Replace springs if they are broken, bent, collapsed, distorted or fatigued.

2) Inspect tube seat inserts in outlet ports. Replace if they are cracked, scored, loose, cocked or worn. If removal kits are not available, replace by using spiral easy-out.

3) Remove check valve and spring from drum brake outlet (if equipped). Inspect cylinder bore for scoring, corrosion or wear. Aluminum master cylinders are anodized. Wear on the anodized surface, as evidenced by lighter areas, is normal.

4) Use crocus cloth to polish out light corrosion on cast iron master cylinders. Replace master cylinder if bore does not clean up using crocus cloth. Aluminum master cylinders may not be polished and must be replaced.

5) Inspect compensator and by-pass ports at bottom of reservoir. If they are plugged or dirty, clean them using brake cleaning solvent and compressed air only.

Reassembly

CAUTION: Do not install check valve in disc brake outlet, as this will cause disc brakes to lock up.

1) Install check valve and spring in drum brake outlet (if removed). Using a spare tubing nut, press tube

seat insert into place (if removed). Turn nut until tube seat insert bottoms. Remove nut and inspect outlet for burrs or shavings.

2) Coat bore of cylinder and piston assemblies with clean brake fluid. Install secondary and primary piston assemblies into bore. Press primary piston inward and install snap ring. Press primary piston inward and install stop bolt (if equipped). Install push rod (if equipped).

3) Install fluid control valve using a 12 mm socket on Ford Motor Co. diagonal split master cylinder.

Fig. 3 *Ford Motor Co. Diagonal Split Master Cylinder*

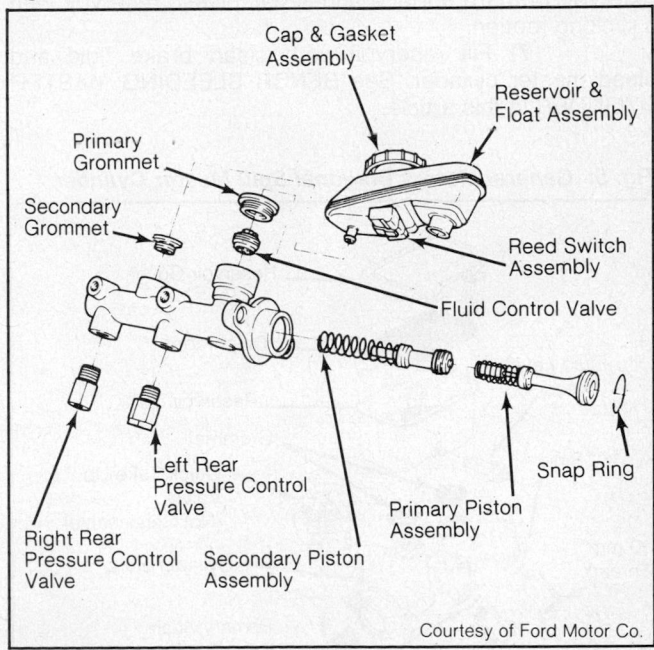

- Cap & Gasket Assembly
- Reservoir & Float Assembly
- Primary Grommet
- Secondary Grommet
- Reed Switch Assembly
- Fluid Control Valve
- Snap Ring
- Left Rear Pressure Control Valve
- Right Rear Pressure Control Valve
- Secondary Piston Assembly
- Primary Piston Assembly

Courtesy of Ford Motor Co.

Fig. 4: *General Motors Composite Master Cylinder*

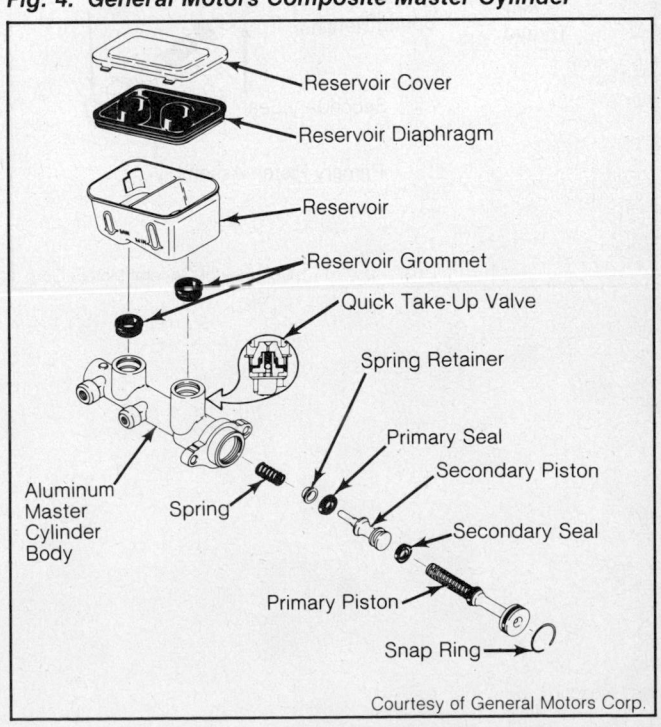

- Reservoir Cover
- Reservoir Diaphragm
- Reservoir
- Reservoir Grommet
- Quick Take-Up Valve
- Spring Retainer
- Primary Seal
- Secondary Piston
- Secondary Seal
- Aluminum Master Cylinder Body
- Spring
- Primary Piston
- Snap Ring

Courtesy of General Motors Corp.

Master Cylinders

BENDIX/DELCO-MORAINE (Cont.)

4) On Corvette models, press primary and secondary piston inward until fully bottomed and install stop screw into master cylinder. Install failure warning switch and combination piston on Corvette master cylinder.

5) Install proportioning valves, failure warning switch and switch piston assembly on General Motors diagonal split master cylinder.

6) On 2-piece master cylinders, lubricate grommets with clean brake fluid and install in master cylinder making sure that they are properly seated. Place reservoir on hard surface and install plastic reservoir with a rocking motion.

7) Fill reservoir with clean brake fluid and bleed master cylinder. See BENCH BLEEDING MASTER CYLINDER in this article.

Fig. 5: General Motors Diagonal Split Master Cylinder

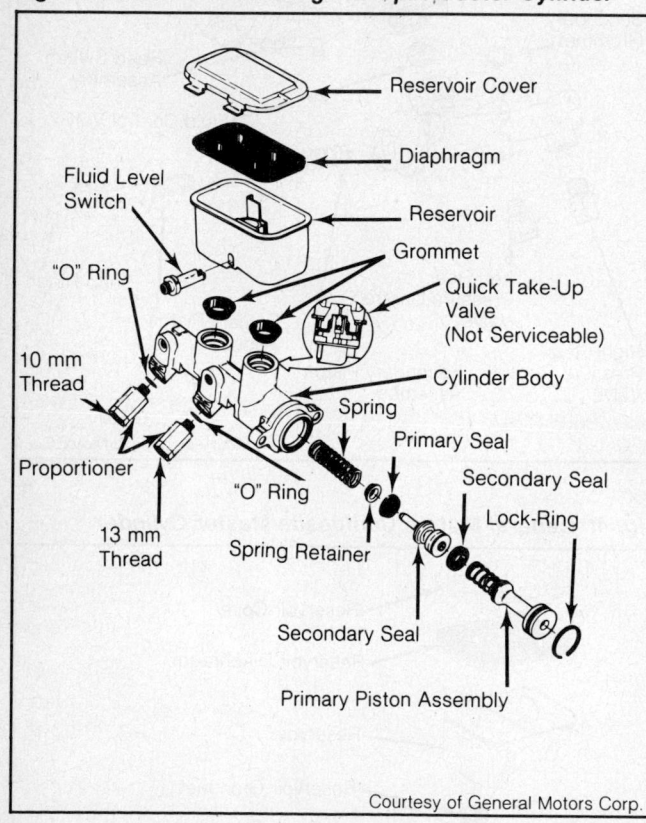

Courtesy of General Motors Corp.

Fig. 6: Chrysler Motors Composite Master Cylinder

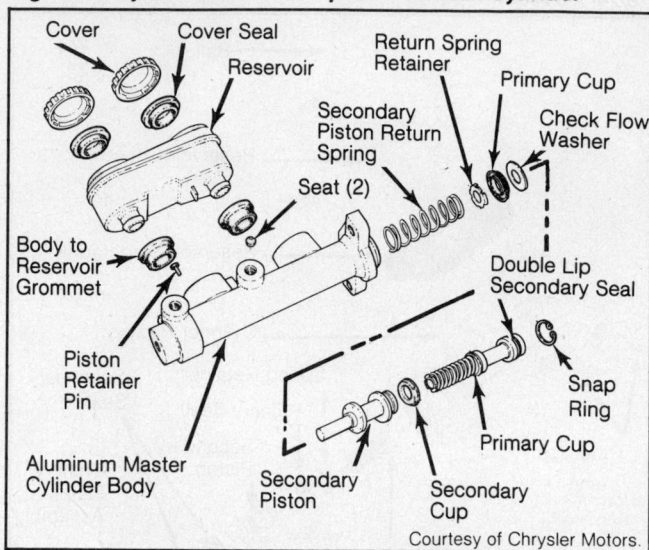

Courtesy of Chrysler Motors.

Fig. 7: Corvette Master Cylinder

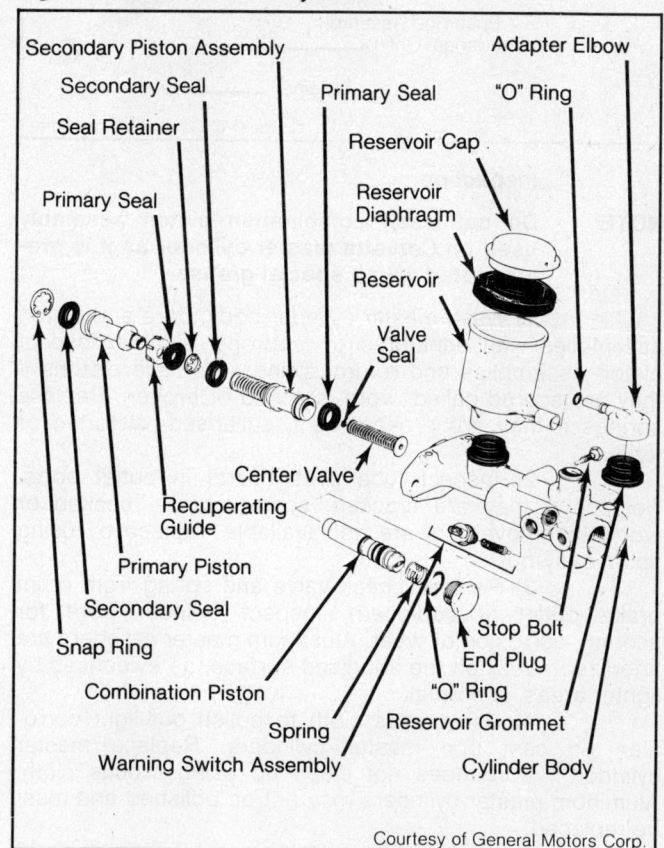

Courtesy of General Motors Corp.

Master Cylinders

BENDIX/DELCO-MORAINE (Cont.)

Fig. 8: General Motors Compact Master Cylinder

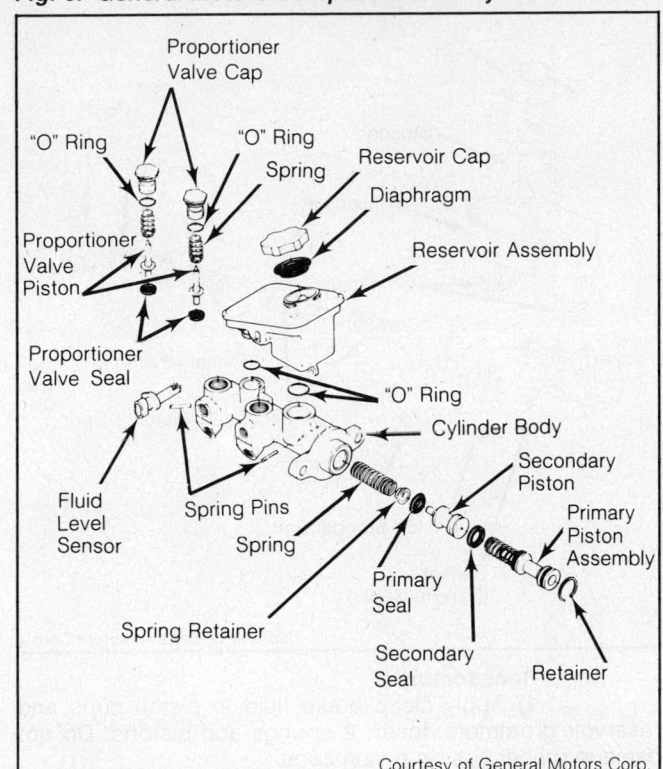

Courtesy of General Motors Corp.

TIGHTENING SPECIFICATIONS

Application	Ft. Lbs. (N.m)
Chrysler Motors	
Front Wheel Drive Models	
Master Cylinder-to-Power Unit	17-19 (23-26)
Brake Line-to-Master Cylinder	12-19 (16-26)
Rear Wheel Drive Models	
Master Cylinder-to-Power Unit	17-25 (23-34)
Brake Line-to-Master Cylinder	10-14 (14-19)
Ford Motor Co.	
Master Cylinder-to-Firewall	13-25 (18-34)
Master Cylinder-to-Power Unit	3-25 (18-34)
Brake Line-to-Master Cylinder	10-18 (14-24)
General Motors	
Master Cylinder-to-Firewall	22-30 (30-41)
Master Cylinder-to-Power Unit	
Cadillac (Exc. Cimarron)	20 (27)
Corvette	15 (20)
Oldsmobile	20 (27)
All Other Models	22-30 (30-41)
Brake Line-to-Master Cylinder	
Cadillac (Exc. Cimarron)	18 (24)
Corvette	13 (18)
Oldsmobile	18 (24)
All Other Models	10-15 (14-20)

Master Cylinder
NOVA

DESCRIPTION

The master cylinder consists of a cylinder housing, primary and secondary pistons, plastic reservoir, set screw, connecting grommet, strainer and reservoir cap. The unit is easily assembled and disassembled for repair. The unit is also equipped with a level warning switch which indicates when fluid level is low.

REMOVAL & INSTALLATION

MASTER CYLINDER

CAUTION: Do not allow brake fluid to contact painted surfaces.

Removal

Clean area around reservoir and brake lines on master cylinder. Disconnect level warning switch. Remove about 2/3 of brake fluid from master cylinder, using a syringe. Disconnect and plug brake lines. Remove 2 mounting nuts and lift off master cylinder.

Installation

1) Bleed air from unit before installation. Clean groove for master cylinder boot. Ensure "UP" mark on master cylinder boot is in correct postion. *See Fig. 1.*

Fig. 1: Positioning Master Cylinder Rear Boot

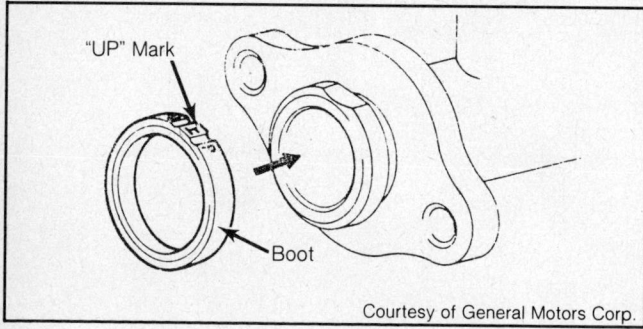

Courtesy of General Motors Corp.

2) Check and adjust rod length on master cylinder. Install new gasket and master cylinder on power booster. Tighten mounting nuts. Connect brake lines. Bleed brake system. See HYDRAULIC BRAKE BLEEDING in this section. Check for leaks.

OVERHAUL

MASTER CYLINDER

Disassembly

1) Remove cap and strainer from reservoir. Remove set screw and reservoir. Mount cylinder in vise by its mounting flange. Remove 2 grommets from master cylinder. *See Fig. 2.*

2) Compress piston and remove stopper bolt and gasket. Remove snap ring. Slowly release piston assembly. Pull piston assembly straight out. Note position of components for reassembly.

Inspection

Inspect cylinder body, reservoir, grommets, and piston assemblies for wear or corrosion. Replace all parts as necessary. Check inlet and return ports for obstructions. Use compressed air to clear if necessary.

Fig. 2: Exploded View of Nova Master Cylinder

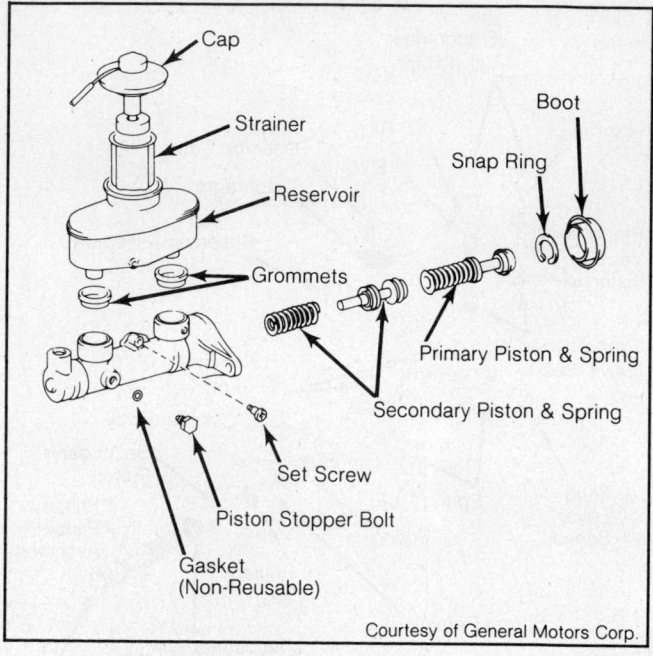

Courtesy of General Motors Corp.

Reassembly

1) Apply clean brake fluid to piston cups and reservoir grommets. Insert 2 springs and pistons. Do not damage rubber lips on piston cups.

2) Compress piston assemblies, install snap ring and piston stopper bolt and gasket. Install grommets. Push reservoir onto cylinder body.

3) Install set screw while pushing on reservoir. Tighten set screw to specification.

NOTE: **Set screw will not tighten down reservoir. There should be a small clearance between body and reservoir. See Fig. 3.**

Fig. 3: Reservoir & Set Screw Installation

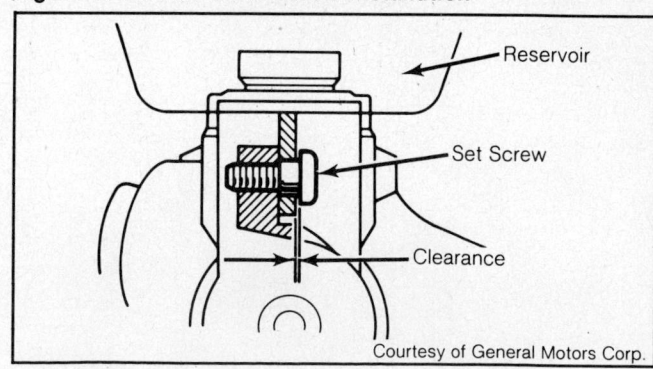

Courtesy of General Motors Corp.

TIGHTENING SPECIFICATIONS

Application	INCH Lbs. (N.m)
Brake Lines	132 (15)
Master Cylinder-to-Booster Nuts	108 (13)
Piston Stopper Bolt	88 (10)
Reservoir Set Screw	15.2 (1.7)

Section 10

WHEEL ALIGNMENT

CONTENTS

NOTE: ALSO SEE GENERAL INDEX

NOTE: ALSO SEE GENERAL INDEX

Wheel Alignment
TROUBLE SHOOTING

CONDITION	POSSIBLE CAUSE	CORRECTION
Premature Tire Wear	Improper tire inflation	Check tire pressure
	Front alignment out of tolerance	See ADJUSTMENTS in WHEEL ALIGNMENT
	Suspension components worn	See SUSPENSION
	Steering system components worn	See STEERING
	Improper standing height	See RIDING HEIGHT SPECIFICATIONS
	Uneven or sagging springs	See COIL SPRINGS in SUSPENSION
	Bent wheel	See WHEEL ALIGNMENT
	Improper torsion bar adjustment	See SUSPENSION
	Loose or worn wheel bearings	See WHEEL BEARING ADJ. in SUSPENSION
	Worn or defective shock absorbers	Replace shock absorbers
	Tires out of balance	Check tire balance
Pulls to One Side	Improper tire inflation	Check tire pressure
	Brake dragging	See BRAKES
	Mismatched tires	See WHEEL ALIGNMENT
	Broken or sagging spring	See SUSPENSION
	Broken torsion bar	See SUSPENSION
	Power steering valve not centered	See STEERING
	Front alignment out of tolerance	See ADJUSTMENTS in WHEEL ALIGNMENT
	Defective wheel bearing	See WHEEL BEARINGS in SUSPENSION
	Uneven sway bar links	See SUSPENSION
	Frame bent	Check for frame damage
	Steering system bushing worn	See STEERING
	Idler arm bushing too tight	See STEERING LINKAGE
Hard Steering	Idler arm bushing too tight	See STEERING LINKAGE
	Ball joint tight or seized	SEE BALL JOINT CHECKING in SUSPENSION
	Steering linkage too tight	See STEERING LINKAGE
	Power steering fluid low	Add proper amount of fluid
	Power steering drive belt loose	See STEERING
	Power steering pump defective	See STEERING
	Steering gear out of adjustment	See STEERING
	Incorrect wheel alignment	See WHEEL ALIGNMENT
	Damaged steering gear	See STEERING
	Damaged suspension	See SUSPENSION
	Bent steering knuckle or supports	See SUSPENSION
Vehicle "Wanders"	Strut rod or control arm bushing worn	See SUSPENSION
	Loose or worn wheel bearings	See WHEEL BEARINGS in SUSPENSION
	Improper tire inflation	Check tire pressure
	Stabilizer bar missing or defective	See SUSPENSION
	Wheel alignment out of tolerance	See Adjustment in WHEEL ALIGNMENT
	Broken spring	See SUSPENSION
	Defective shock absorbers	Replace shock absorbers
	Worn steering & suspension components	See SUSPENSION
Front End Shimmy	Tire out of balance/round	Check tire balance
	Excessive wheel runout	See WHEEL ALIGNMENT
	Insufficient or improper caster	See WHEEL ALIGNMENT
	Worn suspension or steering components	See SUSPENSION
	Defective shock absorbers	Replace shock absorbers
	Wheel bearings worn or loose	See WHEEL BEARING ADJ. in SUSPENSION
	Power steering reaction bracket loose	See STEERING
	Steering gear box (rack) mounting loose	See STEERING
	Steering gear adjustment loose	See STEERING
	Worn spherical joints	See SUSPENSION
Toe-In Not Adjustable	Lower control arm bent	See SUSPENSION
	Frame bent	Check frame for damage
Camber Not Adjustable	Control arm bent	See SUSPENSION
	Frame bent	Check frame for damage
	Hub & bearing not seated properly	See SUSPENSION

Wheel Alignment

WHEEL ALIGNMENT PROCEDURES

PRE-ALIGNMENT INSTRUCTIONS

NOTE: **For more information on wheel alignment theory and procedures, see Mitchell's Four Wheel Alignment manual.**

Before adjusting wheel alignment, check the following:

- Each axle uses tires of same construction and tread style, equal in tread wear and overall diameter. Verify that radial and axial runout is not excessive. Inflation should be at manufacturer's specifications.
- Steering linkage and suspension must not have excessive play. Check for wear in tie rod ends and ball joints. Springs must not be sagging. Control arm and strut rod bushings must not have excessive play. *See Fig. 1.*

Fig. 1: Checking Steering Linkage

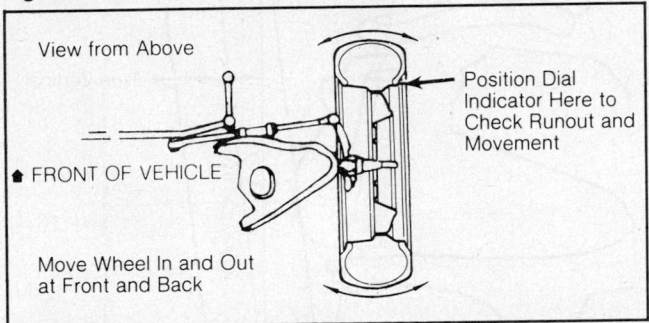

- Vehicle must be on level floor with full fuel tank, no passenger load, spare tire in place and no load in trunk. Bounce front and rear end of vehicle several times. Confirm vehicle is at normal riding height.
- Steering wheel must be centered with wheels in straight ahead position. If required, shorten one tie rod adjusting sleeve and lengthen opposite sleeve (equal amount of turns). *See Fig. 2.*
- Wheel bearings should have the correct preload and lug nuts must be tightened to manufacturer's specifications. Adjust camber, caster and toe-in using this sequence. Follow instructions of the alignment equipment manufacturer.

Fig. 2: Adjusting Tie Rod Sleeves (Top View)

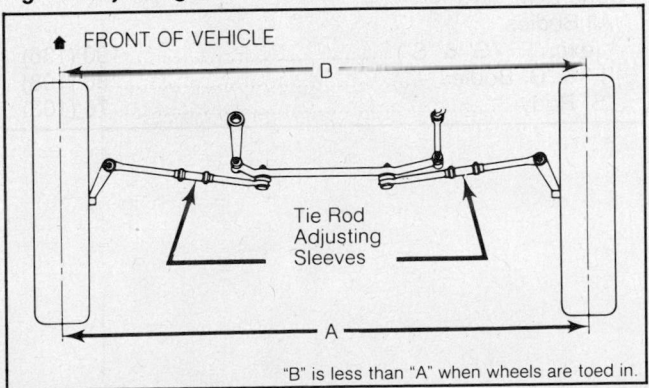

"B" is less than "A" when wheels are toed in.

CAMBER

1) Camber is the tilting of the wheel, outward at either top or bottom, as viewed from front of vehicle. *See Fig. 3.*

2) When wheels tilts outward at the top (from centerline of vehicle), camber is positve. When wheels tilt inward at top, camber is negative. Amount of tilt is measured in degrees from vertical.

Fig. 3: Determining Camber Angle

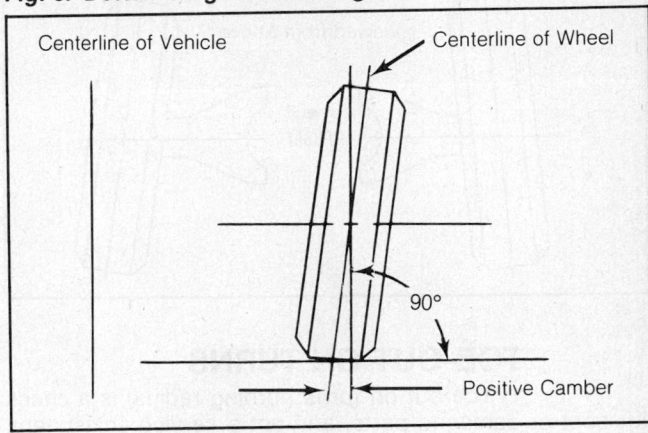

CASTER

1) Caster is the tilting of front steering axis either forward or backward from vertical, as viewed from the side of vehicle. *See Fig. 4.*

2) When axis is tilted backward from vertical, caster is positive. This creates a trailing action on front wheels. When axis is tilted forward, caster is negative, causing a leading action on front wheels.

Fig. 4: Determining Caster Angle

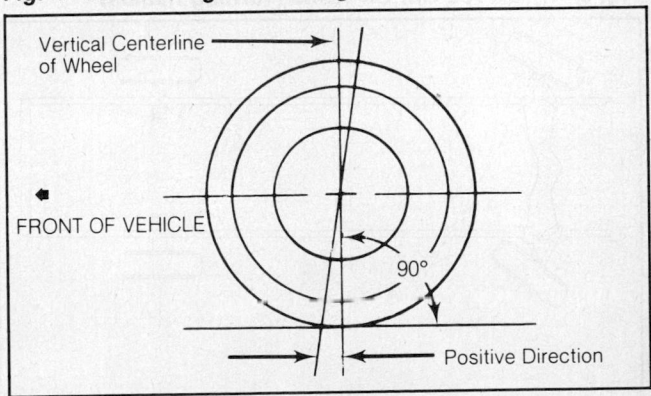

TOE-IN ADJUSTMENT

Toe-in is the width measured at the rear of the tires subtracted by the width measured at the front of the tires at about spindle height. A positive figure would indicate toe-in and a negative figure would indicate toe-out. If the distance between the front and rear of the tires is the same, toe measurement would be zero. To adjust:

1) Measure toe-in with front wheels in straight ahead position and steering wheel centered. To adjust toe-in, loosen clamps and turn adjusting sleeve or adjustable end on right and left tie rods. *See Figs. 2 and 5.*

WHEEL ALIGNMENT PROCEDURES (Cont.)

2) Turn equally and in opposite directions to maintain steering wheel in centered position. Face of tie rod end must be parallel with machined surface of steering rod end to prevent binding.

3) When tightening clamps, make certain that clamp bolts are positioned so there will be no interference with other parts throughout the entire travel of linkage.

Fig. 5: Wheel Toe-In

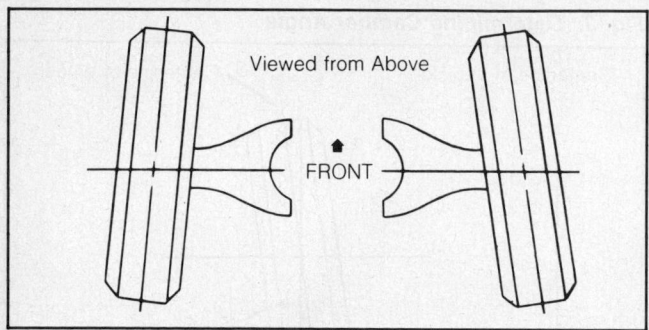

TOE-OUT ON TURNS

1) Toe-out on turns (turning radius) is a check for bent or damaged parts, and not a service adjustment. With caster, camber, and toe-in properly adjusted, check toe-out with weight of vehicle on wheels. *See Fig. 6.*

2) Use a full floating turntable under each wheel, repeating test with each wheel positioned for right and left turns. Incorrect toe-out generally indicates a bent steering arm. Replace arm, if necessary, and recheck wheel alignment.

CAUTION: Do not attempt to correct by straightening parts. Damaged parts must be replaced.

Fig. 6: Wheel Toe-Out On Turns (Turning Radius)

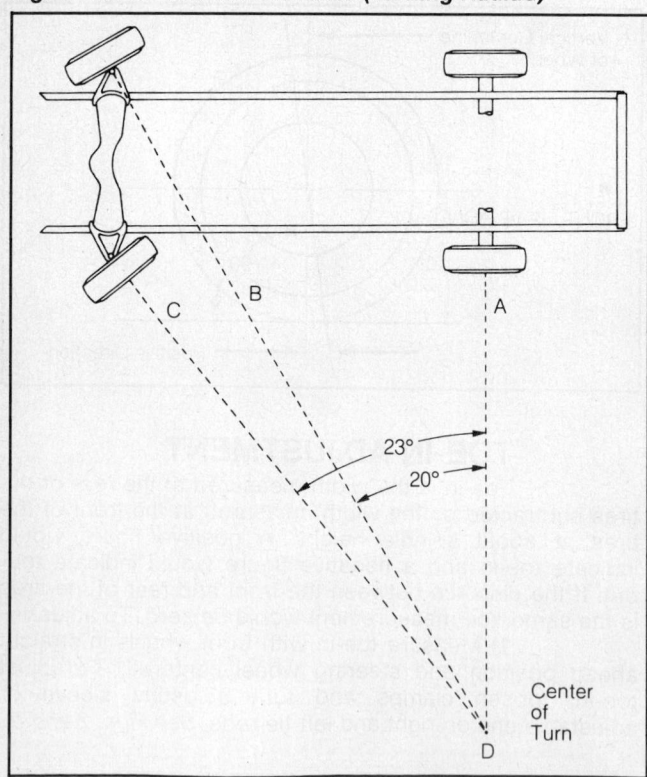

STEERING AXIS INCLINATION

1) Steering axis inclination is a check for bent or damaged parts, and not a service adjustment. Vehicle must be level and camber should be properly adjusted. *See Fig. 7.*

2) If camber cannot be brought within limits and steering axis inclination is correct, steering knuckle is bent. If camber and steering axis inclination are both incorrect by approximately the same amount, the upper and lower control arms are bent.

CAUTION: Do not attempt to correct by straightening parts. Damaged parts must be replaced.

Fig. 7: Checking Steering Axis Inclination

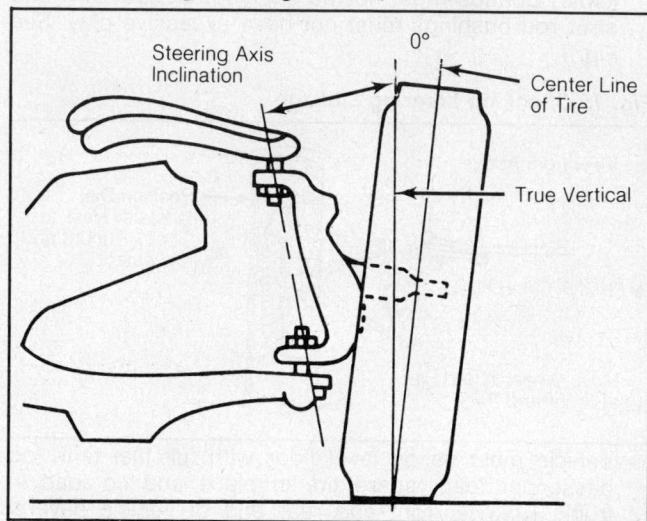

WHEEL LUG NUT TIGHTENING SPECIFICATIONS

Application	Ft. Lbs. (N.m)
Chrysler Motors	
All FWD Models	95 (129)
All RWD Models	85 (115)
Eagle	
Premier	75 (102)
Ford Motor Co.	
All Models	80-105 (108-142)
General Motors	
All Bodies	
(exc. "F", "G" & "S")	100 (136)
"F" & "G" Bodies	80 (108)
"S" Body	76 (103)

ALL MANUFACTURERS

PRE-MEASUREMENT PROCEDURE

Check tire pressure. Specifications can be found on door pillar, sidewall of tire, sun visor or in glove box. Trunk must be empty (except for spare tire and jack). Fuel tank should be full. Normalize springs by jouncing several times. Measure riding height at locations shown in *Fig. 1.*

Fig. 1: Riding Height Measuring Points (All Models)

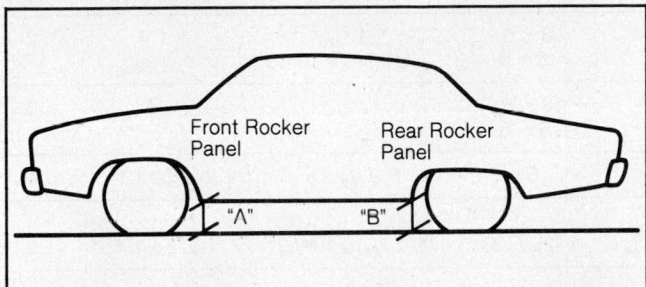

RIDING HEIGHT SPECIFICATIONS

Application	Front "A"	Rear "B"
Chrysler Motors		
Aries & Reliant	8.1"	7.0"
Caravelle & 600	9.9"	7.2"
Daytona		
Exc. Turbo Z	8.0"	7.2"
Turbo Z	8.3"	7.7"
Diplomat, Fifth Ave.,		
& Gran Fury	7.8"	7.2"
Dynasty & New Yorker	9.3"	8.4"
Horizon & Omni	8.4"	8.9"
Lancer, Le Baron		
& GTS	8.3"	7.3"
New Yorker Turbo	9.9"	7.2"
Shadow & Sundance	8.0"	6.8"
Eagle		
Premier	6.34"	5.65"
Ford Motor Co.		
Continental	7.1"	6.2"
Cougar &		
Thunderbird	8.0"	7.5"
Escort		
EXP	8.0"	8.1"
2-Door Hatchback	7.8"	7.5"
4-Door Hatchback	7.9"	7.7"
4-Door Wagon	7.9"	7.3"
LTD Crown Victoria		
4-Door Sedan	6.8"	6.1"
4-Door Wagon	7.2"	7.0"
Grand Marquis &		
Town Car	6.8"	6.1"
Mark VII	8.7"	8.2"
Mustang	7.6"	6.7"
Sable & Taurus	6.9"	6.1"
Tempo & Topaz	7.8"	7.5"

RIDING HEIGHT SPECIFICATIONS (Cont.)

Application	Front "A"	Rear "B"
General Motors		
"A" Body		
Celebrity & Century	9.9"	9.2"
Cutlass Ciera	8.4"	8.4"
Cutlass Cruiser	9.6"	9.9"
6000	9.0"	9.2"
"B" Body		
Caprice	10.5"	10.6"
Custom Cruiser	9.6"	9.9"
Electra Wagon	9.8"	10.2"
Le Sabre Wagon	10.4"	10.6"
Safari Wagon	10.4"	10.6"
"C" Body		
Electra	8.2"	7.8"
Deville & Fleetwood	8.9"	8.4"
Ninety Eight	8.8"	8.8"
"D" Body		
Brougham	9.2"	9.8"
"E" Body		
Eldorado	8.4"	8.4"
Riviera	7.5"	7.4"
Toronado	9.6"	9.6"
"F" Body		
Camaro	7.9"	7.8"
Firebird	7.2"	7.4"
"G" Body		
Cutlass Supreme		
Classic & Monte Carlo	9.8"	10.3"
Regal GN	9.8"	9.8"
"H" Body		
Bonneville	9.8"	9.8"
Delta 88	10.6"	10.6"
Le Sabre	10.3"	10.3"
"J" Body		
Cavalier		
Sedan	9.4"	9.3"
Wagon	9.7"	9.9"
Cimarron	9.4"	9.3"
Firenza	7.8"	7.6"
Skyhawk & Sunbird	9.5"	9.4"
"K" Body		
Seville	8.3"	8.4"
"L" Body		
Beretta & Corsica	9.0"	9.2"
"N" Body		
Cutlass Calais	8.7"	8.3"
Grand Am	8.7"	8.3"
Skylark	9.0"	9.1"
"P" Body		
Fiero	7.4"	7.3"
"S" Body		
Nova	7.7"	7.5"
"V" Body		
Allante	9.0"	9.5"
"W" Body		
Cutlass Supreme,		
Grand Prix & Regal	9.8"	9.8"
"Y" Body		
Corvette	7.5"	7.6"

Wheel Alignment

SPECIFICATIONS

WHEEL ALIGNMENT SPECIFICATIONS

MAKE & MODEL		ADJ. PROC.	CAMBER in DEGREES Fraction	CAMBER in DEGREES Decimal	CASTER in DEGREES Fraction	CASTER in DEGREES Decimal	LINE NO.
CHRYSLER MOTORS FWD Models (All Except Horizon, Omni & Wagon)	Front	1,2,4	$5/16 \pm 8/16$	$.3 \pm .5$	[1] $1\ 2/10$	[1] 1.2	1
	Rear	3	$-1/2 \pm 1/2$	$-.5 \pm .5$			
Horizon & Omni	Front	1,4	$5/16 \pm 8/16$	$.3 \pm .5$	[1] $1\ 4/10$	[1] 1.4	2
	Rear	3	$1/2 \pm 1/2$	$-.5 \pm .5$			
Wagon	Front	1,4	$5/16 \pm 8/16$	$.3 \pm .5$	[1] $1\ 9/10$	[1] .9	3
	Rear	3	$-1/2 \pm 1/2$	$-.5 \pm .5$			
RWD Models	Front	5,4	[2] $1/2 \pm 1/2$	[2] $-.5 \pm .5$	[3] $2\ 1/2 \pm 1$	[3] 2.50 ± 1	4
EAGLE Premier	Front	4	[6] $16/64 \pm 21/64$	[6] $.25 \pm .33$	[7] $1\ 5/64 \pm 1\ 48/64$	[7] 1.078 ± 1.750	5
FORD MOTOR CO. FWD Models Continental	Front	6,7	[4] $9/10 \pm 6/10$	[4] $.9 \pm .6$	[5] $4\ 8/10 \pm 8/10$	[5] $4.8 \pm .8$	6
	Rear	3	[6] $-1\ 3/10 \pm 7/10$	[6] $-1.3 \pm .7$			
Escort	Front	7	[6] L $1\ 2/10 \pm 3/4$ [6] R $13/32 \pm 27/32$	[6] L $1.20 \pm .75$ [6] R $-.41 \pm .85$	[7] $2\ 7/20 \pm 3/4$	[7] $2.35 \pm .75$	7
	Rear	8	[6] $28/64 \pm 57/64$	[6] $.44 \pm .85$			
Sable & Taurus (Sedan)	Front	7,9	L $16/32 \pm 19/32$ R $1/4 \pm 1/2$	L $.5 \pm .63$ R $.25 \pm .75$	$4\ 1/2 \pm 1\ 1/2$	4.5 ± 1.5	8
	Rear	4	$7/8 \pm 11/16$	$.88 \pm .69$			
Sable & Taurus (Wagon)	Front	6,9	$-1\ 9/10 \pm 1$	$-.9 \pm 1.0$	$4\ 5/16 \pm 1\ 8/16$	4.31 ± 1.5	9
Tempo & Topaz	Front	7	[6] L $1\ 13/32 \pm 24/32$ [6] R $31/32 \pm 24/32$	[6] L $1.41 \pm .75$ [6] R $.97 \pm .75$	[7] $2\ 13/32 \pm 24/32$	[7] $2.44 \pm .75$	10
	Rear	10	[6] $-10/64 \pm 48/64$	[6] $-.16 \pm .75$			
RWD Models Cougar & Thunderbird (Exc. Turbo Coupe)	Front	12,4	[8] $-13/20 \pm 15/20$	[8] $-.65 \pm .75$	[7] [8] $1\ 4/20 \pm 15/20$ 7	[7] [8] $1.20 \pm .75$	11
Thunderbird (Turbo Coupe)	Front	12,4	[9] $0 \pm 15/20$	[9] $0. \pm .75$	[7] [9] $1\ 7/20 \pm 15/20$	[7] [9] $1.35 \pm .75$	12
LTD Crown Victoria, Grand Marquis, Town Car & Wagon	Front	12,7	$-1/4 \pm 1/2$	$-.25 \pm .50$	[8] $4 \pm 3/4$	[8] $4 \pm .75$	13
Mark VII	Front	12,7	[9] $0 \pm 3/4$	[9] $0 \pm .75$	[7] [9] $1\ 1/2 \pm 1$	[7] [9] 1.5 ± 1	14
Mustang (Exc. 5.0L GT)	Front	12,7	[8] $-3/32 \pm 24/32$	[8] $-.10 \pm .75$	[7] [8] $1\ 11/64 \pm 48/64$	[7] [8] $1.17 \pm .75$	15
Mustang 5.0L GT	Front	12,7	[9] $3/64 \pm 3/4$	[9] $.15 \pm .75$	[7] [8] $1\ 11/32 \pm 24/32$	[7] [8] $1.35 \pm .75$	16

[1] – Left to right caster differential must not exceed $1\ 1/2°$ (1.5°).
[2] – Left to right camber differential must not exceed 1° (1.0°).
[3] – Left to right caster differential must not exceed $1\ 1/4°$ (1.25°).
[4] – Left to right camber differential must not exceed $7/10°$ (0.7°).
[5] – Left to right caster differential must not exceed $8/10°$ (0.8°).
[6] – Camber is factory set and cannot be adjusted.
[7] – Caster is factory set and cannot be adjusted.
[8] – Left side minus right side difference should be $0° \pm 3/4°$.
[9] – Left side minus right side difference should be $0° \pm 7/8°$.

SPECIFICATIONS (Cont.)

WHEEL ALIGNMENT SPECIFICATIONS (Cont.)

Line NO.	⋆ TOE-IN in INCHES Fraction	Decimal	⋆ TOE-IN in DEGREES Fraction	Decimal	TOE-OUT ON TURNS Inner	Outer	STEERING AXIS INCLINATION (SAI)
CHRYSLER MOTORS							
1	[10] $12/32 \pm 5/32$ [11] $0 \pm 5/16$	[10] $.375 \pm .156$ [11] $0 \pm .313$	[10] $1/10 \pm 1/10$ [11] $0 \pm 6/10$	[10] $.10 \pm .10$ [11] $0 \pm .6$	NS	NS	NS
2	[10] $12/32 \pm 5/32$ [12] $3/32 \pm 9/32$	[10] $.375 \pm .156$ [12] $.094 \pm .281$	[10] $1/10 \pm 1/10$ [12] $2/10 \pm 6/10$	[10] $.10 \pm .10$ [12] $.20 \pm .60$	NS	NS	NS
3	[10] $12/32 \pm 5/32$ [11] $0 \pm 5/16$	[10] $.375 \pm .156$ [11] $0 \pm .313$	[10] $1/10 \pm 1/10$ [11] $0 \pm 6/10$	[10] $.10 \pm .10$ [11] $0 \pm .6$	NS	NS	NS
4	[13] [14] $1/8 \pm 1/8$	[13] [14] $.125 \pm .125$	[13] [14] $1/8 \pm 1/8$	[13] [14] $.31 \pm .31$	20°	18°	8°
EAGLE							
5	$1/16 \pm 1/16$	$.063 \pm .063$	$1/8 \pm 1/8$	$.125 \pm .125$	NS	NS	NS
FORD MOTOR CO.							
6	NS	NS	[14] $-13/64 \pm 16/64$ [14] $-13/64 \pm 1/4$	[14] $-.20 \pm .25$ [14] $-.20 \pm .25$	20°	18.21°	NS
7	$-3/32 \pm 4/32$ [14] $3/16 \pm 3/16$	$-.100 \pm .125$ [14] $.180 \pm .180$	$-13/64 \pm 16/64$ [14] $23/64 \pm 23/64$	$-.20 \pm .25$ [14] $.360 \pm .360$	20°	18.2°	NS
8	$-6/64 \pm 7/64$ [14] $1/16 \pm 2/16$	$-.10 \pm .12$ [14] $.06 \pm .125$	$-13/64 \pm 16/64$ [14] $1/8 \pm 2/8$	$-.200 \pm .250$ [14] $.125 \pm .250$	20°	18.25°	NS
9	[14] $-3/32 \pm 4/32$	[14] $-.10 \pm .125$	[14] $-13/64 \pm 16/64$	[14] $-.200 \pm .250$	20°	18.25°	NS
10	[14] $-3/32 \pm 4/32$ [14] $0 \pm 11/64$	[14] $-.100 \pm .125$ [14] $0 \pm .170$	[14] $-13/64 \pm 16/64$ [14] $0 \pm 11/32$	[14] $-.200 \pm .250$ [14] $0 \pm .340$	20°	20°	NS
11	$3/16 \pm 2/16$	$.188 \pm .125$	$3/8 \pm 2/8$	$.375 \pm .250$	20°	19.73°	NS
12	$3/16 \pm 2/16$	$.188 \pm .125$	$3/8 \pm 2/8$	$.375 \pm .250$	20°	19.73°	NS
13	$1/16 \pm 2/16$	$.063 \pm .125$	$1/8 \pm 2/8$	$.125 \pm .250$	20°	18.51°	NS
14	$1/8 \pm 1/8$	$.125 \pm .125$	$1/4 \pm 1/4$	$.250 \pm .250$	20°	17.14°	NS
15	$3/16 \pm 2/16$	$.188 \pm .125$	$3/8 \pm 2/8$	$.375 \pm .250$	20°	19.84	NS
16	$3/16 \pm 2/16$	$.188 \pm .125$	$3/8 \pm 2/8$	$.375 \pm .250$	20°	19.84°	NS

⋆ – Any positive specification is expressed as Toe-In.
[10] – Preferred setting is $1/16" \pm 1/16"$ ($.063" \pm .063"$) or $1/10° \pm 1/10°$ ($.10° \pm .10°$).
[11] – Preferred setting (all exc. Horizon & Omni) is $0" \pm 1/8"$ ($0" \pm .125"$) or $0° \pm 1/4°$ ($0° \pm .25°$).
[12] – Preferred setting $3/32"$ ($.094"$) $13/64°$ ($0.2°$).
[13] – Preferred setting $1/8 \pm 1/16"$ ($.125" \pm .063"$) or $1/4° \pm 1/10°$ ($.25° \pm .10°$).
[14] – Total sum of left wheel plus right wheel.
NS – Information not available from manufacturer.

Wheel Alignment

SPECIFICATIONS (Cont.)

WHEEL ALIGNMENT SPECIFICATIONS

MAKE & MODEL		ADJ. PROC.	CAMBER in DEGREES Fraction	CAMBER in DEGREES Decimal	CASTER in DEGREES Fraction	CASTER in DEGREES Decimal	LINE NO.
GENERAL MOTORS							
FWD Models							
"A" Body	Front	7,13	[1] $0 \pm 1/2$	[1] $0 \pm .5$	[1] $1 \, 45/64 \pm 1$	[1] 1.7 ± 1	1
	Rear	3					
"E" Body	Front	7,13,14	$0 \pm 51/64$	$0 \pm .8$	[2] $2 \, 1/2 \pm 1$	[2] 2.5 ± 1	2
	Rear	3					
"H" Body	Front	7,14,15,16	$13/64 \pm 32/64$	$.2 \pm .5$	$3 \pm 1/2$	$3 \pm .5$	3
	Rear	15,17	$-19/64 \pm 32/64$	$-.3 \pm .5$			
"J" & "N" Body	Front	7	[1] $51/64 \pm 1$	[1] $.8 \pm 1$	[1] $1 \, 45/64 \pm 2 \, 32/64$	[1] 1.7 ± 2.5	4
"K" Body	Front	7,14,19	$0 \pm 1/2$	$0 \pm .5$	$2 \, 1/2 \pm 1/2$	$2.5 \pm .5$	5
	Rear	17					
"L" Body	Front	4,15	$51/64 \pm 32/64$	$.8 \pm .5$	[3] $1 \, 45/64 \pm 1$	[3] 1.7 ± 1	6
	Rear	3	[3][4] $-1/4 \pm 5/64$	[3][4] $-.25 \pm .08$			
"S" Body							
w/4A-GE Engine	Front	2,7	[5] $-1/4 \pm 3/4$	[5] $-.25 \pm .75$	[3] $3/4 \pm 3/4$	[3] $.75 \pm .75$	7
	Rear	20	[3][5] $-1/2 \pm 3/4$	[3][5] $-.50 \pm .75$			
w/4A-LC Engine	Front	2,7	[5] $-1/4 \pm 3/4$	[5] $-.25 \pm .75$	[3][5] $53/64 \pm 48/64$	[3][5] $.828 \pm .750$	
	Rear	20	[3] $-1/2 \pm 3/4$	[3] $-.50 \pm .75$			
"W" Body	Front	2,21	$45/64 \pm 32/64$	$.7 \pm .5$	[3] $2 \pm 1/2$	[3] $2 \pm .5$	8
	Rear	22,23	$25/64 \pm 32/64$	$.39 \pm .50$			
RWD Models							
"B" & "G" Body	Front	4,24	[2][6] $51/64 \pm 51/64$	[2][6] $.8 \pm .8$	[2][7] $2 \, 51/64 \pm 1$	[2][7] 2.8 ± 1	9
	Rear	25	[8] $0 \pm 3/64$	[8] $0 \pm .05$			
"C" Body	Front	7,14,15,16	L $-1/2 \pm 1/2$	L $-.5 \pm .5$	$2 \, 1/2 \pm 1/2$	$2.5 \pm .5$	10
			R $1/2 \pm 1/2$	R $.5 \pm .5$			
	Rear	15,17.	$-19/64 \pm 32/64$	$-.3 \pm .5$			
"D" Body	Front	4,24	$1/2 \pm 1/4$	$.50 \pm .25$	$3 \pm 1/2$	$3 \pm .5$	11
"F" Body	Front	28,15,26	[9] $19/64 \pm 32/64$	[9] $.3 \pm .5$	[2] $4 \, 45/64 \pm 32/64$	[2] $4.7 \pm .5$	12
"P" Body	Front	7,27	[10] $0 \pm 1/2$	[10] $0 \pm .5$	[11] $3 \pm 1/2$	[11] $3 \pm .5$	13
	Rear	4,13	$-1 \pm 1/2$	$-1 \pm .5$			
"Y" Body	Front	7,24	$51/64 \pm 32/64$	$.8 \pm .5$	$6 \pm 51/64$	$6 \pm .8$	14
	Rear	29	$0 \pm 1/2$	$0 \pm .5$			

[1] – Degrees per wheel.
[2] – Both sides equal within 1°.
[3] – Nonadjustable.
[4] – Beretta only. Nonadjustable.
[5] – Both sides equal within .5°.
[6] – On "B" body vehicles. Camber setting for "G" body vehicles is $32/64° \pm 51/64°$ ($.5° \pm .8°$).
[7] – On power steering equipped vehicles. Caster setting for vehicles with manual steering is $51/64° \pm 1°$ ($.8° \pm 1°$).
[8] – Although available, manufacture does not recommend the use of shims to correct alignment settings.
[9] – Both sides equal within .7°.
[10] – Preferred camber setting is 0°.
[11] – Preferred caster for manual steering equipped vehicles is 3°. Preferred caster setting for GT/Formula vehicles is 5°.

SPECIFICATIONS (Cont.)

WHEEL ALIGNMENT SPECIFICATIONS (Cont.)

Line NO.	* TOE-IN in INCHES Fraction	Decimal	* TOE-IN in DEGREES Fraction	Decimal	TOE-OUT ON TURNS Inner	Outer	STEERING AXIS INCLINATION (SAI)
GENERAL MOTORS							
1	[12] 0±3/32 [13] 0±3/32	[12] 0±.094 [13] 0±.094	[12] 0±13/64 [13] 0±13/64	[12] 0±.203 [13] 0±.203	NS	NS	NS
2	0±3/64 3/64±3/64	0±.047 .047±.047	0±3/32 3/32±3/32	0±.094 .1±.1	NS	NS	NS
3	[14] 0±3/32 [14] 3/64±3/32	[14] 0±.094 [14] .047±.094	[14] 0±13/64 [14] 3/32±13/64	[14] 0±.203 [14] .094±.203	NS	NS	NS
4	[12] 0±3/32	[12] 0±.094	[12] 0±13/64	[12] 0±.203	NS	NS	NS
5	[14] 0±3/32 [12] 3/64±3/64	[14] 0±.094 [12] .047±.047	[14] 0±13/64 [12] 3/32±3/32	[14] 0±.203 [12] .094±.094	NS	NS	NS
6	[14] 0±3/64 [15] 1/16±3/64	[14] 0±.047 [15] .063±.047	[14] 0±3/32 [15] 1/8±3/32	[14] 0±.094 [15] .125±.094	NS	NS	NS
7	[16] 3/64±3/64 2/64±3/64 [16] 3/64±3/64 5/32±3/64	[16] .047±.047 .031±.047 [16] .047±.047 .156±.047	3/32±3/32 5/64±3/32 3/32±3/32 5/64±3/32	.094±.094 .078±.094 .094±.094 .078±.094	NS NS	NS NS	NS NS
8	[12] 0±3/64 [14] -3/32±5/32	[12] 0±.047 [14] -.094±.156	[12] 0±3/32 [14] -13/64±19/64	[12] 0±.094 [14] -.203±.297	NS	NS	NS
9	[14] 3/64±3/64 [14] 0±3/64	[14] .047±.047 [14] 0±.047	[14] 3/32±3/32 [14] 0±3/32	[14] .094±.094 [14] 0±.094	NS	NS	NS
10	0±1/64 [14] 3/64±3/32	0±.016 [14] .047±.094	0±1/32 [14] 3/32±13/64	0±.031 [14] .094±.203	NS	NS	NS
11	[14] 1/16±1/8	[14] .063±.125	[14] 1/8±1/4	[14] .125±.250	NS	NS	NS
12	[12] 0±3/64	[12] 0±.047	[12] 0±3/32	[12] 0±.094	NS	NS	NS
13	[12] 5/32±3/32 [12] 5/64±3/64	[12] .156±.094 [12] .078±.047	[12] 19/64±13/64 [12] 5/32±3/32	[12] .297±.203 [12] .156±.094	NS	NS	NS
14	[12] 0±5/64 [14] 0±3/32	[12] 0±.078 [14] 0±.094	[12] 0±5/32 [14] 0±13/64	[12] 0±.156 [14] 0±.203	NS	NS	NS

* – Any postive specification is expressed as Toe-In.
[12] – Toe-In specification per wheel. Set each side separately.
[13] – Nonadjustable.
[14] – Total sum of left wheel plus right wheel.
[15] – Beretta only. Total toe should be between 0° and .4°.
[16] – Toe-In specification for front (in millimeters) is 1mm ±2mm.
NS – Information not available from manufacturer.

Wheel Alignment

ADJUSTMENT PROCEDURES — ALL MODELS

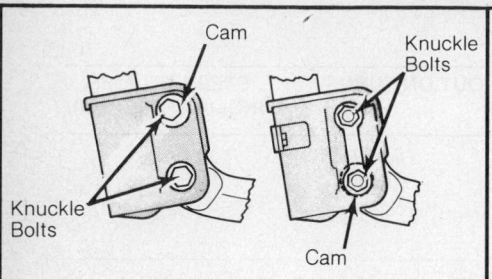

1 – Camber (Front)

Loosen cam and knuckle bolts. Rotate cam bolt to move top of wheel in or out to proper specifications. Tighten bolts to 45 ft. (65 N.m) plus 1/4 turn on "L" body, and 75 ft. lbs. (102 N.m) plus 1/4 turn on all others.

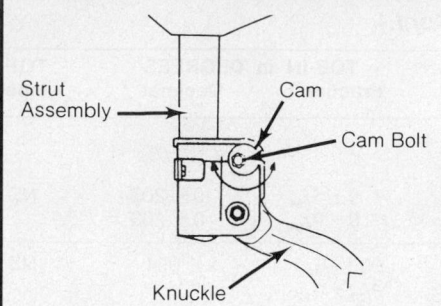

2 – Camber (Front)

Loosen upper and lower strut-to-knuckle nuts and bolts. Rotate cam to proper specification and tighten nuts to 140 ft. lbs. (190 N.m).

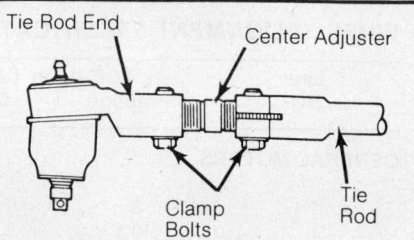

3 – Toe-In (Front)

Loosen tie rod clamp bolts. Adjust to specification by turning adjuster sleeves or center adjuster to proper specifications. On sleeve type adjusters, threaded end of bolts must face toward front of vehicle. Tighten clamp bolts to 41 ft. lbs. (55 N.m).

4 – Camber & Toe-In (Rear)

1) Check and record camber and toe angles. Remove both rear tires and brake drum assemblies. Loosen (do not remove) 4 bolts that mount spindle just enough to allow for installation of shims.
2) Arrange shims until proper specifications are met. Tighten spindle mounting bolts to 45 ft. lbs. (61 N.m).

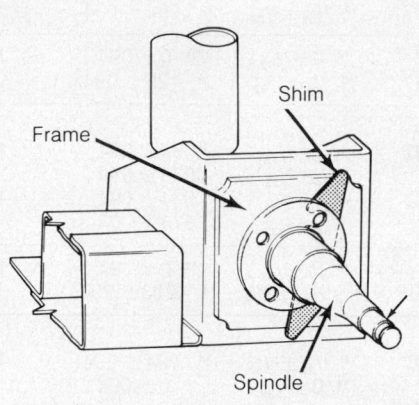

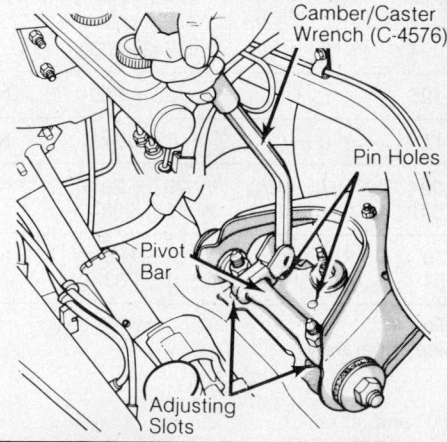

5 – Toe-In (Front & Rear)

Loosen jam nut on inner tie rod. Adjust toe to specification by turning inner tie rod. Do not twist boots (if equipped). Tighten nuts to 45 ft. lbs. (61 N.m).

6 – Camber & Caster (Front)

1) Determine initial camber and caster readings to confirm variance to specifications before loosening pivot bar bolts. Loosen nuts slightly while holding pivot bar (caster/camber bar).
2) Position claw of Camber/Caster Wrench (C-4576) on pivot bar and pin of tool into holes provided in tower or bracket. Move both ends of upper control arm in or out (in exact equal amounts) to adjust camber. Moving one end of the bar will change caster (and camber).
3) To preserve camber while adjusting caster, move each end of the upper control arm pivot bar (in exact equal amounts) in opposite directions. Tighten pivot bar bolts to 150 ft. lbs. (203 N.m).

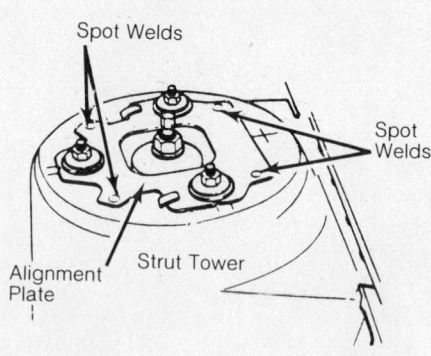

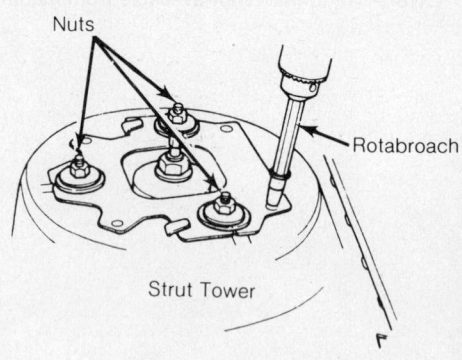

7 – Toe-In (Rear)

Loosen tie rod nut "B" and slide tie rod toward rear of vehicle to increase amount of negative toe. Loosen tie rod nut "A" and slide tie rod toward front of vehicle to increase amount of positive toe. Tighten rod nut "A" to 6-12 ft. lbs. (8-16 N.m), and tighten tie rod nut "B" to 35-50 ft. lbs. (47-68 N.m).

8 – Camber & Caster (Front)

1) Center punch 4 spot welds on alignment plates on upper strut tower. Loosen 3 strut attaching nuts. Using Rotobroach or equivalent, remove 4 spot welds.
2) Remove strut nuts and alignment plate. Clean burrs from tower and alignment plate. Install alignment plate and loosely install nuts. Make alignment adjustments for caster and camber. Tighten strut mount nuts to 20-30 ft. lbs. (27-41 N.m).
3) Drill (3) 1/8 inch holes through alignment plate and strut tower. Install (3) 1/8 x 1/4 inch grip range pop rivets.

Wheel Alignment

ADJUSTMENT PROCEDURES – ALL MODELS (Cont.)

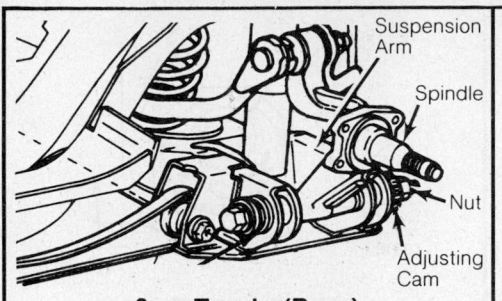

9 – Toe-In (Rear)
Loosen nut and bolt attaching spindle to lower suspension arm. Turn adjusting cam to obtain required alignment setting. While holding adjusting cam in position, tighten attaching nut to 60-86 ft. lbs. (81-115 N.m).

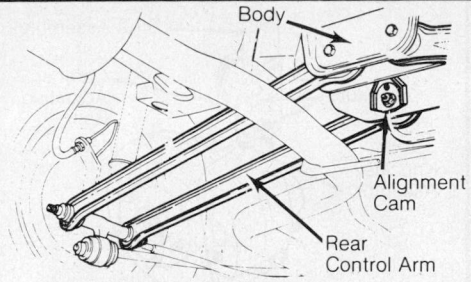

10 – Toe-In (Rear)
Adjust each wheel by loosening bolt attaching rear control arm to body and rotate alignment cam until the required alignment setting is obtained. Tighten control arm attaching bolt to 40-55 ft. lbs. (54-75 N.m).

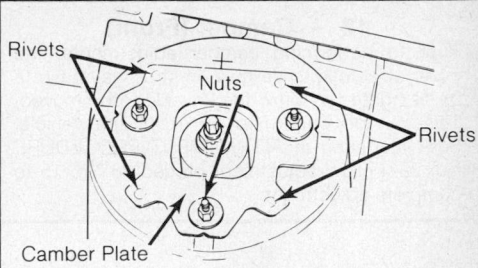

11 – Camber (Front)
Remove pop rivets on camber plate. Loosen 3 nuts holding strut mount to body apron. Move top of shock strut to obtain required camber angle. Tighten mounting nuts to 50-75 ft. lbs. (68-102 N.m).

12 – Camber & Caster (Front)
1) Check and record camber and caster readings. Insert 2 Caster/Camber Adjusters (T79P-3000-A) into frame holes and tighten nuts finger tight against inner shaft of upper arm. Tighten each nut one additional "hex flat" turn.
2) Loosen upper control arm inner shaft-to-frame attaching bolts to unload pressure. Firmly tap bolts to loosen lower assemblies and adjust camber and caster to specifications. Tighten upper arm inner shaft-to-frame bolts to 100-140 ft. lbs. (136-190 N.m).

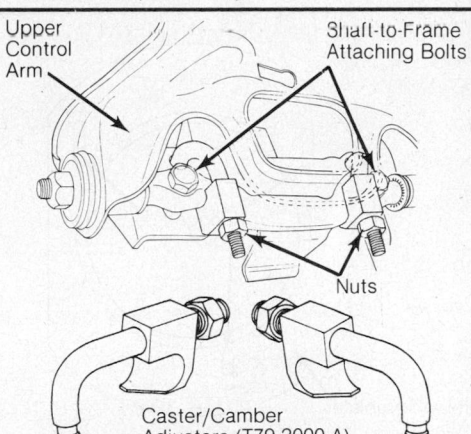

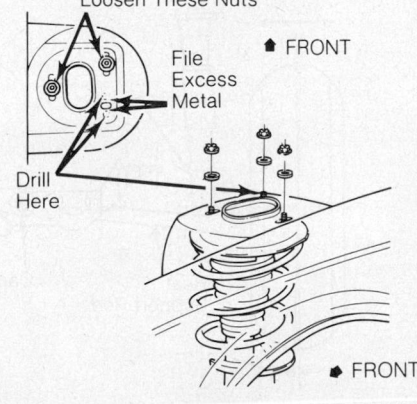

13 – Camber (Front)
Loosen both strut-to-knuckle nuts just enough to allow movement. Adjust camber to specification by moving top of wheel in or out. Tighten nuts to 140 ft. lbs. (190 N.m).

14 – Caster (Front)
1) Loosen (do not remove) one front outer nut and inner nut on top strut mounting tower. Remove remaining outer nut and washer over oval hole. Raise vehicle until outer strut stud has cleared hole.
2) With an 11/32" drill bit, drill one hole in front and one behind outer strut hole. File excess metal between holes to elongate front to rear. Reassemble strut and adjust caster angle to specifications. Tighten to 18 ft. lbs. (24 N.m).

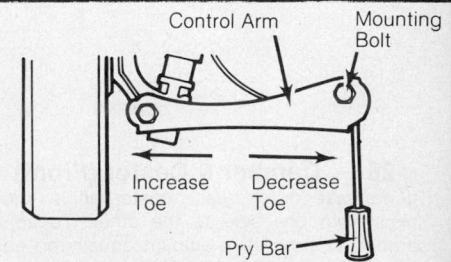

15 – Camber (Rear)
Loosen strut-to-knuckle mounting nuts. Install Camber Adjuster (J-29862) and adjust to proper specifications. Tighten nuts to 144 ft. lbs. (195 N.m).

16 – Camber (Front)
Loosen both strut-to-knuckle nuts. Install Camber Adjuster J-29862 and set camber to proper specification. Tighten nuts to 144 ft. lbs. (195 N.m).

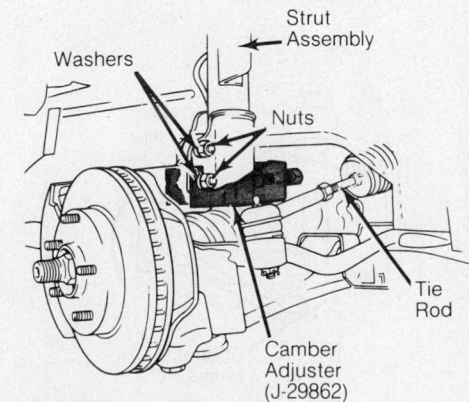

17 – Toe-In (Rear)
Loosen front and rear inside control arm mounting bolts. Pry between rear control arm mounting bolts and rear support assembly until proper toe settings are obtained. Tighten to 66 ft. lbs. (90 N.m).

Wheel Alignment

ADJUSTMENT PROCEDURES – ALL MODELS (Cont.)

18 – Camber (Front)

Prior to performing camber adjustments, the lower strut-to-knuckle hole on strut may have to be elongated to allow the knuckle to be moved. This can be performed on or off the vehicle. See illustration in ADJUSTMENT PROCEDURE No. 22. Follow adjustment procedure No. 15 to complete adjustment.

19 – Camber & Toe-In (Rear)

To correct a toe or camber problem, frame straightening equipment is preferred to be used to bring axle housing to proper specifications

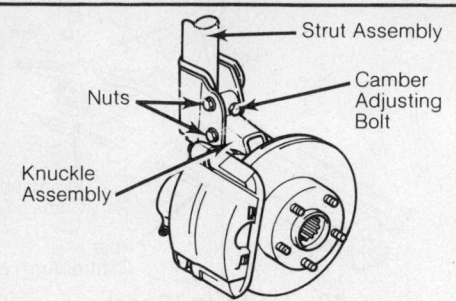

20 – Camber (Front)

Loosen both strut-to-knuckle nuts. Set camber to specification using camber adjusting bolt. Tighten strut nuts to 144 ft. lbs. (195 N.m) and adjusting bolt to 7 ft. lbs. (10 N.m).

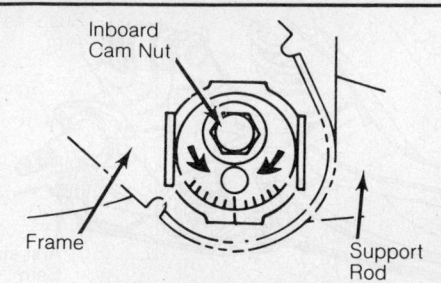

21 – Toe-In (Rear)

Loosen inboard cam nuts of rear support rod and turn each cam an equal amount in the opposite direction until proper toe specifications are obtained. Tighten nuts to 64 ft. lbs. (87 N.m).

22 – Camber (Front)

1) Remove strut cover and 3 strut mounting nuts. Lift front of vehicle just to the point where studs clear strut tower. Cover top of strut to catch metal filings. Use Template J-36892 and mark holes to be filed.

2) File holes no more than 5 mm in either direction. Reverse template and repeat procedure on opposite side. Set camber and tighten to 17 ft. lbs. (23 N.m).

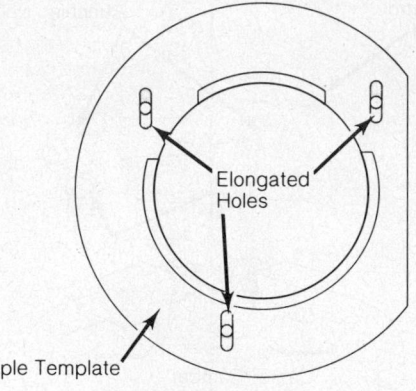

23 – Camber (Rear)

1) Remove rear auxiliary spring and strut assembly. See SUSPENSION section in this book.

2) File a lateral hole (oblong) on: lower strut-to-knuckle attaching hole, lower strut attaching hole and lower stabilizer bracket-to-strut attachng hole.

3) Install strut assembly and adjust camber to proper specifications. Tighten strut-to-knuckle nuts to 136 ft. lbs. (184 N.m).

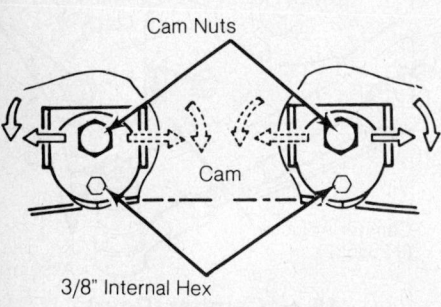

24 – Toe-In (Rear)

Loosen inboard cam nuts of rear support rod. Rotate cam to obtain proper toe specification. Tighten nuts to 140 ft. lbs. (190 N.m).

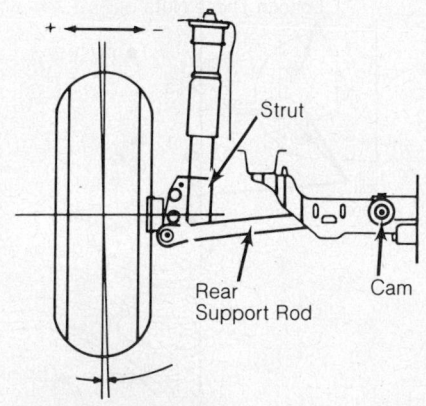

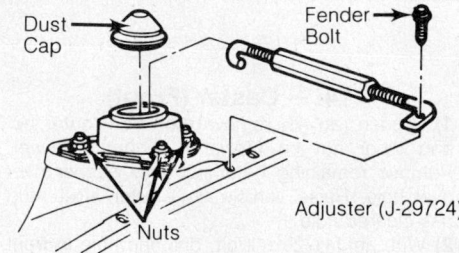

25 – Camber & Caster (Front)

To adjust camber and caster, remove dust cap and fender bolt from upper strut mount. Attach Adjuster (J-29724) with fender bolt to fender. Loosen 3 nuts attaching mount and adjust camber and caster angles to specifications. Tighten nuts to 21 ft. lbs. (28 N.m).

26 – Camber & Caster (Front)

To increase or decrease caster angle, move shims from one side to the other. To adjust camber, change shim amount equally on each side. Tighten to 63 ft. lbs. (85 N.m).

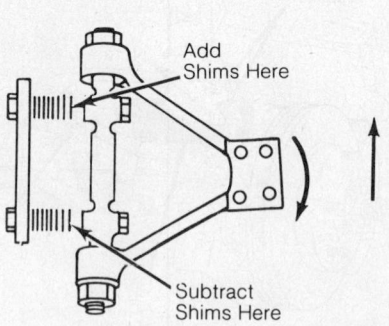

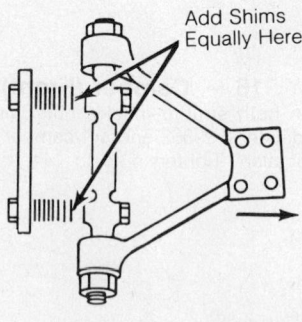

ADJUSTMENT PROCEDURES – ALL MODELS (Cont.)

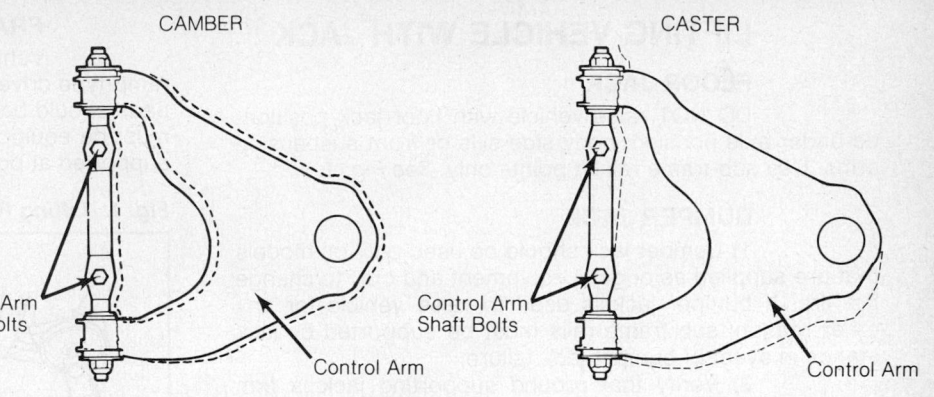

CAMBER

CASTER

27 – Camber & Caster (Front)
Loosen upper control arm shaft bolts. Tilt top of wheel in or out to adjust camber. Push control arm forward or backward to adjust caster. Tighten bolts to 52 ft. lbs. (70 N.m).

Control Arm Shaft Bolts

Control Arm

Control Arm Shaft Bolts

Control Arm

28 – Relay Rod Height Adjustment
1 Before adjusting camber, caster and toe, relay rod height must be checked and adjusted. To check height, clean both flats on bottom of relay rod. Install Relay Rod Adjustment Gauge (J-33093) on flat near Pitman arm.
2 Install socket onto head of front pivot bolt on left side lower control arm. Measure dimension "A" between flange of gauge and bottom of socket.
3 Transfer socket and adjustment gauge into position on idler arm end of relay rod. Loosen idler arm mounting bolts and position until dimension "B" matches dimension "A" within .04" (1 mm). All other alignment procedures can now be performed.

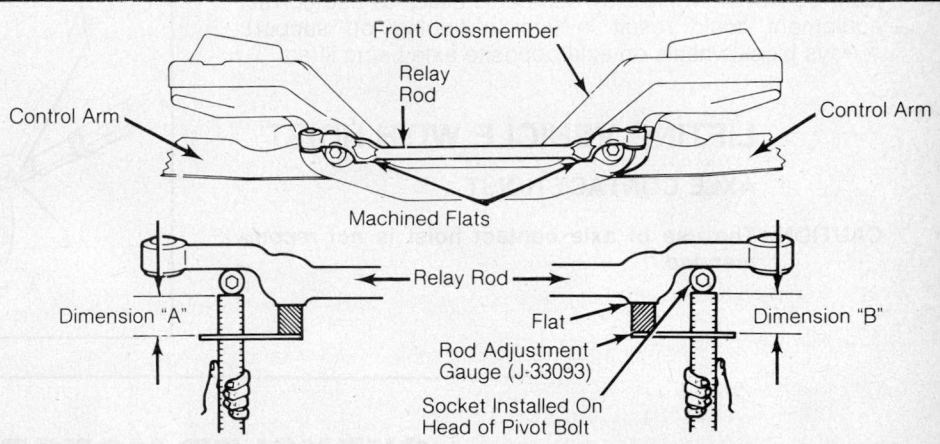

Front Crossmember

Relay Rod

Control Arm

Control Arm

Machined Flats

Relay Rod

Dimension "A"

Dimension "B"

Flat

Rod Adjustment Gauge (J-33093)

Socket Installed On Head of Pivot Bolt

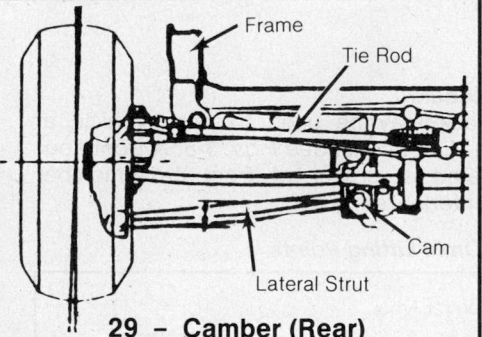

Frame

Tie Rod

Cam

Lateral Strut

29 – Camber (Rear)
Hold bolt head located at inner end of lateral strut. Loosen cam nut and rotate cam to obtain required specifications. Tighten cam nut to 25 ft. lbs. (34 N.m).

Jacking & Hoisting

EAGLE PREMIER

LIFTING VEHICLE WITH JACK

FLOOR JACK

DO NOT raise vehicle with floor jack positioned under axle housing, body side sills or front suspension arms. Use sub-frame rail lift points only. *See Fig. 1.*

BUMPER JACK

1) Bumper jack should be used only on models that are supplied as original equipment and only to change flat tire. If bumper jack is used to raise vehicle for any other reason, sub frame rails must be supported by jack stands in event of bumper jack failure.

2) Verify that ground supporting jack is firm and level. If vehicle is not supplied with a bumper type jack, do not lift vehicle by bumper. Failure to use correct equipment could result in vehicle tipping off support. Always block wheels on axle opposite axle being lifted.

LIFTING VEHICLE WITH HOIST

AXLE CONTACT HOIST

CAUTION: The use of axle contact hoist is not recommended.

FRAME CONTACT HOIST

Vehicle can be raised on swivelling arm or a ramp-type drive hoist. If swivelling arm hoist is used, lifting pads should be positioned evenly on subframe rails. Hoist must be equipped with proper adapters so vehicle will be supported at points marked. *See Fig. 1.*

Fig. 1: Lifting Points

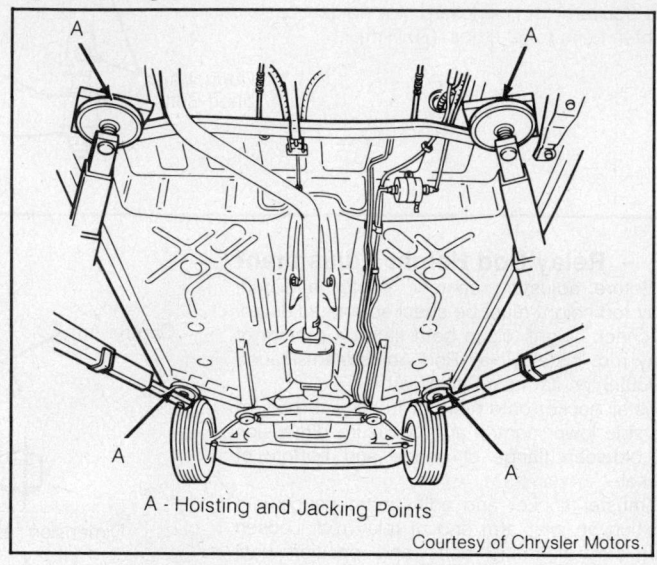

A - Hoisting and Jacking Points

Courtesy of Chrysler Motors.

CHRYSLER MOTORS

LIFTING VEHICLE WITH JACK

FLOOR JACK
RWD Models

Floor jack may be used under rear axle housing or front suspension lower control arms. DO NOT allow lifting plate fingers to contact axle cover plate when lifting from rear axle housing. Never use floor jack on any part of underbody.

CAUTION: DO NOT raise entire side of vehicle with floor jack midway between front and rear wheels or permanent body damage could result.

Fig. 2: RWD Vehicle Lifting Points

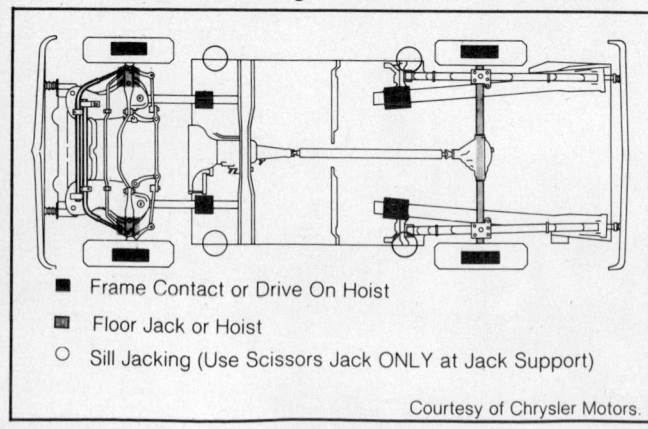

■ Frame Contact or Drive On Hoist

▨ Floor Jack or Hoist

○ Sill Jacking (Use Scissors Jack ONLY at Jack Support)

Courtesy of Chrysler Motors.

FWD Models

Floor jack may be used to raise vehicle at locations shown in illustrations. *See Figs. 3-8.* A front floor jack point is located at center of front crossmember (inboard) and at center of rear axle.

Fig. 3: Horizon & Omni Lifting Points

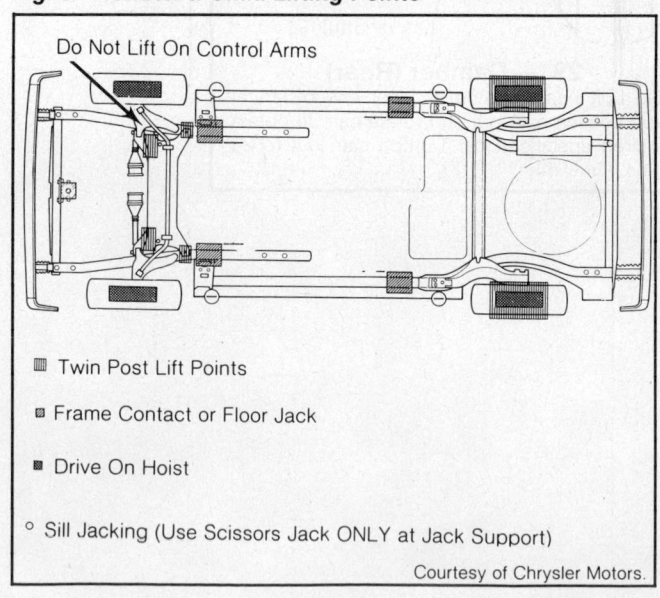

Do Not Lift On Control Arms

▥ Twin Post Lift Points

▨ Frame Contact or Floor Jack

■ Drive On Hoist

○ Sill Jacking (Use Scissors Jack ONLY at Jack Support)

Courtesy of Chrysler Motors.

CHRYSLER MOTORS (Cont.)

Fig. 4: Lifting Points for Aries, LeBaron & Reliant

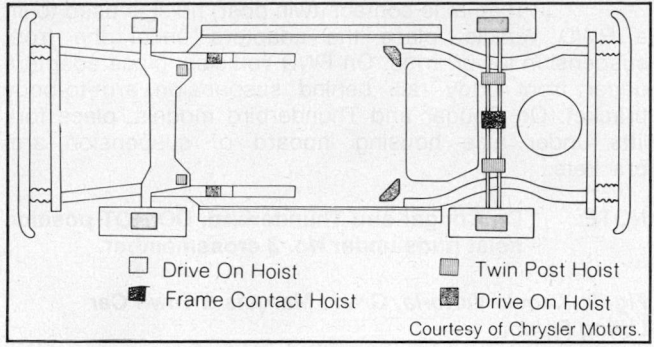

☐ Drive On Hoist   ▨ Twin Post Hoist
▧ Frame Contact Hoist   ▨ Drive On Hoist
Courtesy of Chrysler Motors.

Fig. 5: Lifting Points for Caravelle, New Yorker Turbo & 600

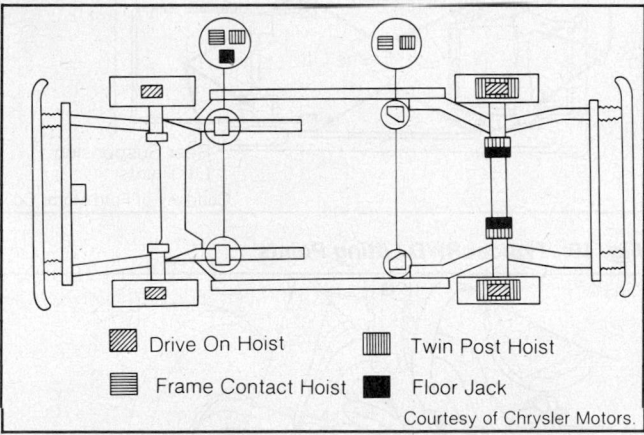

▨ Drive On Hoist   ▥ Twin Post Hoist
▤ Frame Contact Hoist   ■ Floor Jack
Courtesy of Chrysler Motors.

Fig. 6: Daytona, Shadow & Sundance Lifting Points

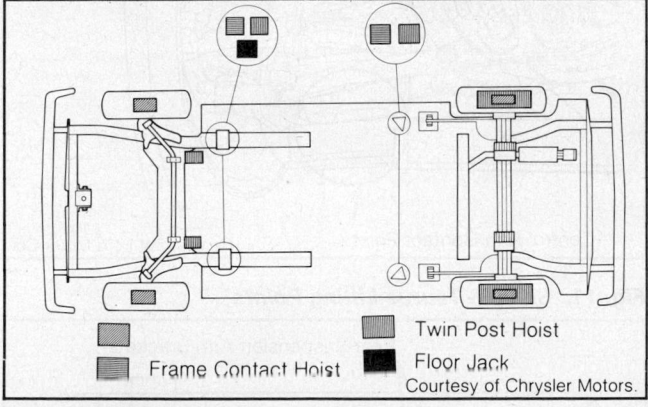

▥ Twin Post Hoist
▨ Frame Contact Hoist   ■ Floor Jack
Courtesy of Chrysler Motors.

Fig. 7: Lancer & LeBaron GTS Lifting Points

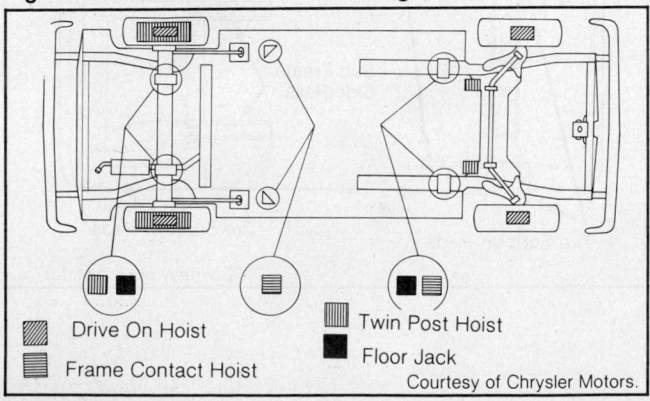

▨ Drive On Hoist   ▥ Twin Post Hoist
▤ Frame Contact Hoist   ■ Floor Jack
Courtesy of Chrysler Motors.

Fig. 8: Dynasty & New Yorker Lifting Points

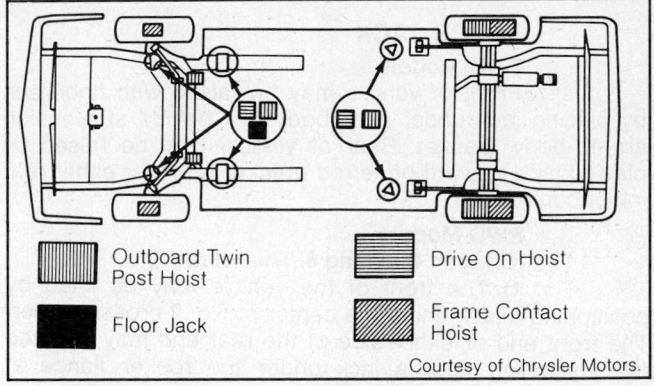

▥ Outboard Twin Post Hoist   ▤ Drive On Hoist
■ Floor Jack   ▧ Frame Contact Hoist
Courtesy of Chrysler Motors.

EMERGENCY JACKING

Scissor jack receptacles are located at body sills. DO NOT use floor jack at scissors jack locations. Ensure scissors jack flange is in contact with body sill and jack is engaged in body sill receptacle.

Ensure scissor jack engages with locator pin on body sills. Always block opposite wheels and jack on level surface.

LIFTING VEHICLE WITH HOIST

CAUTION: If removing rear axle, fuel tank, spare tire or lift gate on FWD vehicles and single post hoist is used, anchor vehicle to hoist. Place jack stands under vehicle or add weight on rear end of vehicle to prevent tipping when center of gravity changes.

FRAME CONTACT HOIST

Frame contact hoist must be equipped with proper adapters to support vehicle in correct locations. On rear wheel drive models, use adaptor plates to make firm contact with lower control arms and rear axle housing.

AXLE CONTACT HOIST

RWD Models

Hoist should contact lower control arms and rear axle housing.

FWD Models

Axle contact hoist may be used on points shown in illustrations. Do not pick up vehicle at front lower control arms or rear trailing arm suspension.

Jacking & Hoisting

FORD MOTOR CO.

LIFTING VEHICLE WITH JACK

FLOOR JACK

FWD Models

Front of vehicle may be raised with floor jack by placing jack under front body rail, behind suspension arm-to-body bracket. Rear of vehicle may be raised by placing jack forward of tie rod bracket or under either rear lower control arm.

RWD Models
(Cougar, Mustang & Thunderbird)

1) The front of the vehicle may be lifted by positioning a jack under the center of No. 2 crossmember. The front end or either side of the rear end may be lifted by positioning floor a jack under the rocker flange at contact points used for the jack originally supplied with the vehicle.

2) To lift both sides of rear at once, position floor jack under differential housing. Make sure that jack does not make contact with differential housing cover.

3) Position jack stands under rear axle housing between suspension arm brackets and differential housing. DO NOT place jack stands under suspension arm brackets.

NOTE: **On vehicles with air suspension, disconnect electrical power by removing negative battery cable or shutting off air suspension power switch located in trunk. Switch is located in trunk on left front side of inner panel.**

Crown Victoria, Grand Marquis, Mark VII & Town Car

1) Either front side of vehicle may be raised by jack contact at lower arm strut connection, on front crossmember or on side rail to which stabilizer is connected.

2) Front of vehicle may be raised by positioning jack under center of front crossmember. Care must be taken not to contact steering linkage or to compress stabilizer link insulators.

3) For rear of vehicle, position jack under rear axle housing between suspension arm brackets and differential housing. Do not place jack under suspension arm brackets.

BUMPER JACK

A bumper type jack may be used on Crown Victoria, Grand Marquis, Mark VII and Town Car models only. DO NOT raise other vehicles by the bumper at any time.

LIFTING VEHICLE WITH HOIST

CAUTION: **Follow hoist manufacturer's instructions. DO NOT allow hoist or adapters to contact suspension, exhaust or steering components.**

FRAME CONTACT HOIST

On frame contact hoists, adapters must be placed at 4 contact points. Position adapters so they are centered on contact area. All 4 contact points must contact adapters. On FWD vehicles, the rear contact points are forward of the tie rod body brackets.

AXLE CONTACT HOIST

If an axle contact (twin post) hoist is used to lift a RWD vehicle, place the adapters under the front suspension lower arms. On FWD vehicles, place adapters under front body rail, behind suspension arm-to-body bracket. On Cougar and Thunderbird models, place fork lifts under axle housing inboard of suspension arm brackets.

NOTE: **On Cougar and Thunderbird, DO NOT position hoist pads under No. 3 crossmember.**

Fig. 9: Crown Victoria, Grand Marquis & Town Car Lifting Points

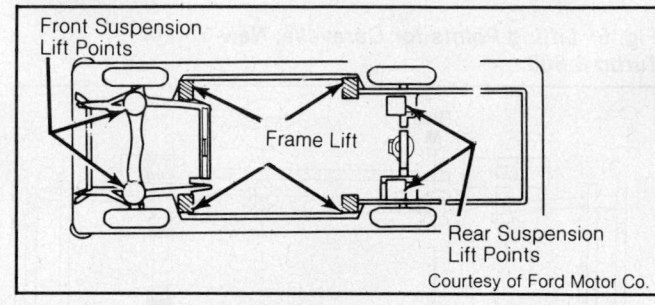

Courtesy of Ford Motor Co.

Fig. 10: Typical RWD Lifting Points

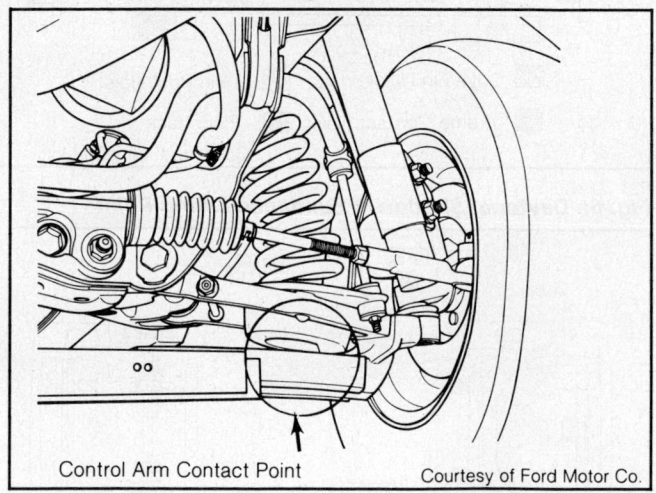

Control Arm Contact Point

Courtesy of Ford Motor Co.

Fig. 11: Sable & Taurus Lifting Points

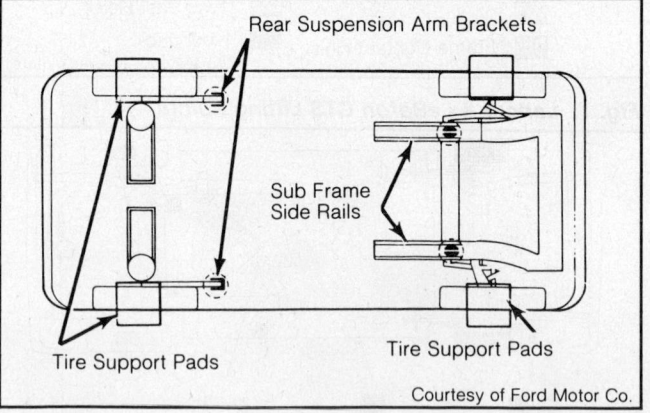

Courtesy of Ford Motor Co.

FORD MOTOR CO. (Cont.)

Fig. 12: Escort, Tempo & Topaz Lifting Points

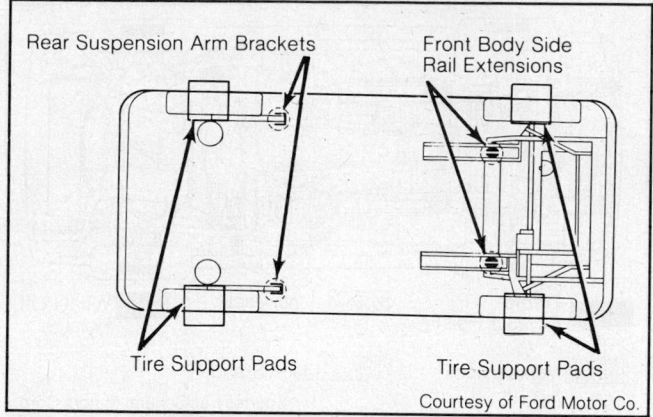

Rear Suspension Arm Brackets

Front Body Side Rail Extensions

Tire Support Pads

Tire Support Pads

Courtesy of Ford Motor Co.

GENERAL MOTORS

LIFTING VEHICLE WITH JACK

FLOOR JACK

FWD Models

When supporting vehicle with floor jack, the support should be placed at suspension lift points or frame lift points. Floor jacks may be placed under front crossmember on most models. *See Figs. 13-20.*

RWD Models

Floor jack may be used under rear axle or front suspension lower control arms while observing following precautions:

- Never use jack on any part of underbody.
- DO NOT raise entire vehicle at side rail, with jack midway between front and rear wheels, or permanent body damage may result.
- DO NOT allow lifting plate fingers to contact axle cover plate when lifting at rear axle housing.
- If vehicle is equipped with a stabilizer bar, DO NOT lift at rear axle housing. *See Figs. 13-20.*

BUMPER JACK

Bumper jack should be used only on models that are supplied as original equipment and only to change flat tire. If vehicle is not supplied with a bumper type jack, DO NOT lift vehicle by the bumper at any time.

HOISTING

Follow hoist manufacturers instructions. Do not allow hoist or adapters to contact suspension, exhaust or steering components. Frame contact must be made. Use adapters if necessary. Lift vehicle as shown in illustrations.

AXLE CONTACT HOIST

Hoist should contact lower control arms or front crossmember, and rear axle as shown in illustrations.

FRAME CONTACT HOIST

Hoist adapters must contact vehicle in specified areas. *See Figs. 13-20.* Adapters must be positioned to distribute load and support vehicle in a stable manner. DO NOT allow lift pads to contact exhaust system components.

Fig. 13: Lifting Points For "A" Bodies

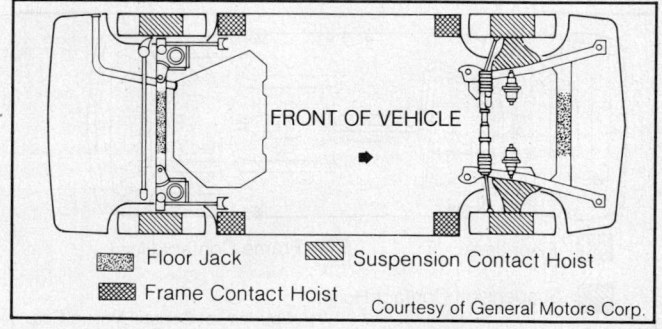

FRONT OF VEHICLE

Floor Jack   Suspension Contact Hoist

Frame Contact Hoist

Courtesy of General Motors Corp.

Fig. 14: Lifting Points For "B" & "G" Bodies

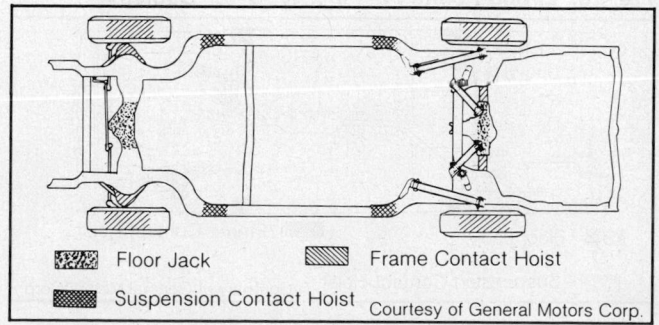

Floor Jack   Frame Contact Hoist

Suspension Contact Hoist

Courtesy of General Motors Corp.

Jacking & Hoisting

GENERAL MOTORS (Cont.)

Fig. 15: Lifting Points For "C", "H", "W" & "V" Bodies

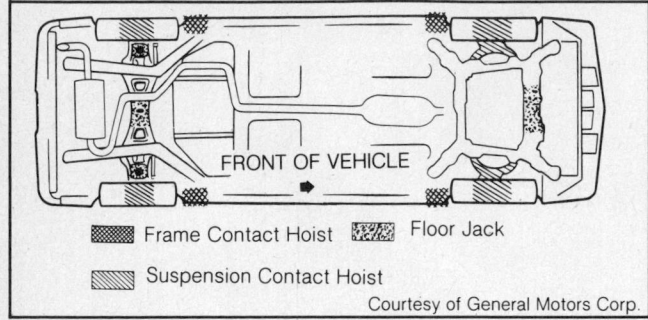

FRONT OF VEHICLE →

▨ Frame Contact Hoist   ▧ Floor Jack

▨ Suspension Contact Hoist

Courtesy of General Motors Corp.

Fig. 16: Lifting Points For "F" Bodies

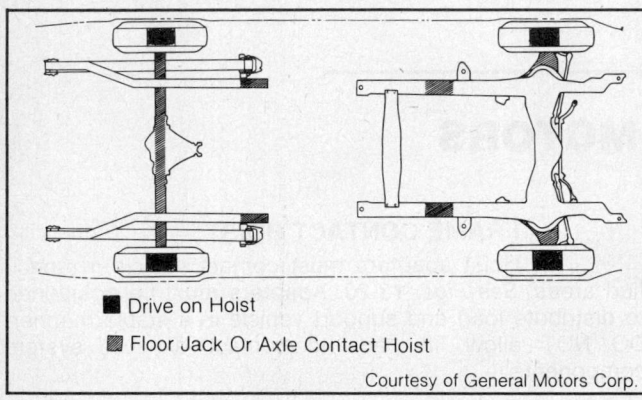

■ Drive on Hoist

▨ Floor Jack Or Axle Contact Hoist

Courtesy of General Motors Corp.

Fig. 17: Lifting Points For "E" & "K" Bodies

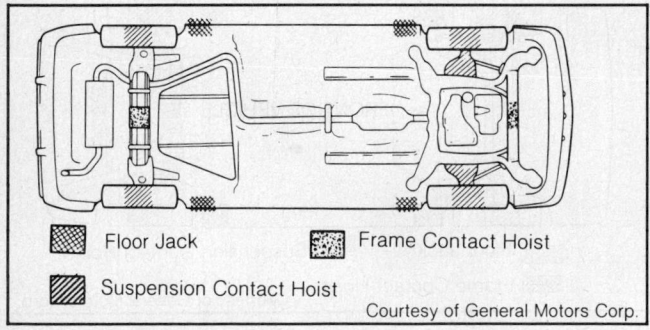

▨ Floor Jack   ▨ Frame Contact Hoist

▨ Suspension Contact Hoist

Courtesy of General Motors Corp.

Fig. 18: Lifting Points For "J", "N" & "L" Bodies

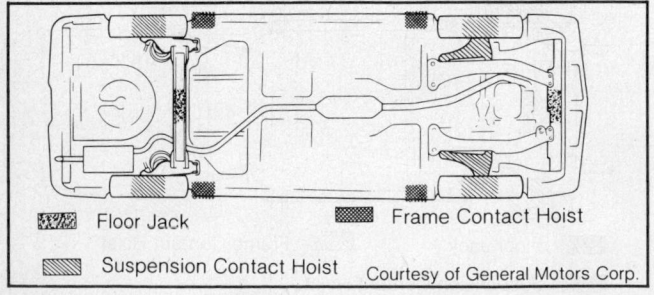

▨ Floor Jack   ▨ Frame Contact Hoist

▨ Suspension Contact Hoist   Courtesy of General Motors Corp.

Fig. 19: Lifting Points For "P" Body

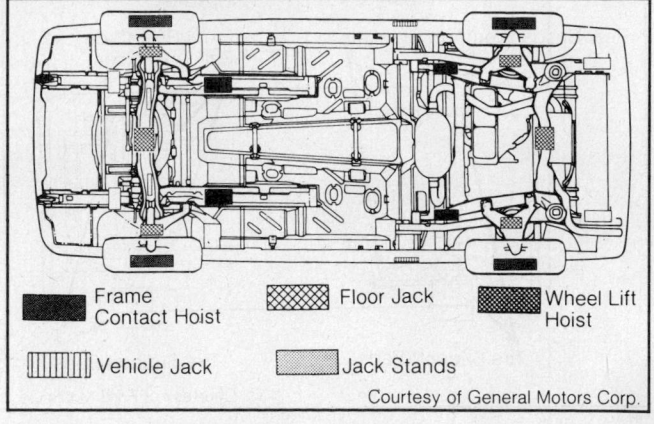

■ Frame Contact Hoist   ▨ Floor Jack   ▨ Wheel Lift Hoist

▥ Vehicle Jack   ▨ Jack Stands

Courtesy of General Motors Corp.

Fig. 20: Lifting Points For "S" Body

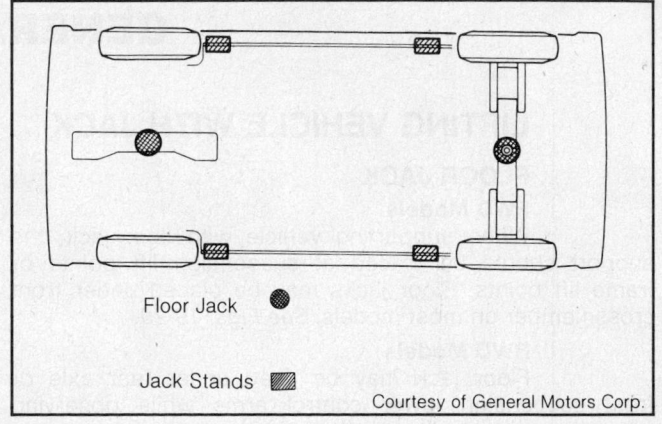

Floor Jack ●

Jack Stands ▨

Courtesy of General Motors Corp.

Section 11

SUSPENSION

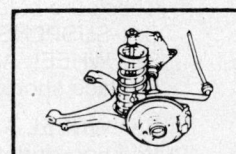

CONTENTS

NOTE: ALSO SEE GENERAL INDEX

Suspension
SUSPENSION TROUBLE SHOOTING

CONDITION	POSSIBLE CAUSE	CORRECTION
Front End Noise	Loose or worn wheel bearings	See Wheel Bearing Adjustment in SUSPENSION
	Worn shocks or shock mountings	Replace shocks or mountings.
	Worn struts or strut mountings	Replace struts or strut mountings
	Loose or worn lower control arm	See SUSPENSION
	Loose steering gear-to-frame bolts	See STEERING
	Worn control arm bushings	See SUSPENSION
	Ball joints not lubricated	Lubricate ball joints & see Ball Joint Checking in SUSPENSION
Front Wheel Shake, Shimmy or Vibration	Tires or wheels out of balance	Check tire balance
	Incorrect wheel alignment	See WHEEL ALIGNMENT
	Propeller shaft unbalanced	Check propeller shaft balance
	Loose or worn wheel bearings	See Wheel Bearing Adjustment in SUSPENSION
	Loose or worn tie rod ends	See SUSPENSION
	Worn upper ball joints	See Ball Joint Checking in SUSPENSION
	Worn shock absorbers	Replace shock absorbers
	Worn strut bushings	Replace strut bushings
Car Pulls to One Side	Mismatched or uneven tires	Check tire condition
	Broken or sagging springs	See SUSPENSION
	Loose or worn strut bushings	See SUSPENSION
	Improper wheel alignment	See WHEEL ALIGNMENT
	Improper rear axle alignment	Check rear axle alignment
	Power steering gear unbalanced	See STEERING
	Front brakes dragging	See BRAKES
Abnormal Tire Wear	Unbalanced tires	Check tire balance & rotation
	Sagging or broken springs	See SUSPENSION
	Incorrect front end alignment	See WHEEL ALIGNMENT
	Faulty shock absorbers	Replace shock absorbers
Scuffed Tires	Toe-In incorrect	See WHEEL ALIGNMENT
	Suspension arm bent or twisted	See appropriate SUSPENSION article
Springs Bottom or Sag	Bent or broken springs	See SUSPENSION
	Leaking or worn shock absorbers	Replace shock absorbers
"Dog" Tracking	Broken leaf spring	Replace leaf spring
	Bent rear axle housing	Check rear axle housing
	Frame misalignment	Check frame for damage
Spring Noises	Loose "U" Bolts	See SUSPENSION
	Loose or worn bushings	See SUSPENSION
	Worn or missing interliners	See SUSPENSION
Shock Absorber Noise	Loose shock mountings	Check & tighten mountings
	Worn bushings	Replace bushings
	Air in system	Bleed air from system
	Undercoating on shocks	Remove undercoating
Car Leans or Sways on Corners	Loose stabilizer bar	See SUSPENSION
	Faulty shocks or mountings	Replace shocks or mountings
	Broken or sagging springs	See SUSPENSION
Shock Absorbers Leaking	Worn seals or reservoir tube crimped	See SUSPENSION
Broken Springs	Loose "U" bolts	See SUSPENSION
	Inoperative shock absorbers	Replace shock absorbers

CHRYSLER MOTORS FWD MODELS

Aries, Caravelle, Daytona, Dynasty, New Yorker, Lancer, LeBaron, LeBaron GTS, Reliant, Shadow, Sundance, 600

DESCRIPTION

The front suspension is a MacPherson strut type. The bottom of the strut is bolted to top of steering knuckle. One bolt is formed to retain an eccentric cam for camber adjustment. Caster is fixed and has no adjustment.

ADJUSTMENTS

CAMBER & TOE-IN

See appropriate article in WHEEL ALIGNMENT section.

RIDING HEIGHT

See RIDING HEIGHT SPECIFICATIONS article in WHEEL ALIGNMENT section.

FRONT WHEEL BEARINGS

No lubrication or adjustment is necessary for permanently sealed front bearings. Replace hub nut and washer when removed, as they are not reuseable. Install a new bearing any time hub is removed from knuckle.

BALL JOINT CHECKING

Ball joints operate with no free play. Ball joint housing is pressed into control arm with ball joint stud retained in steering knuckle with a clamp bolt.

1) With vehicle on ground and wheels in straight-ahead position, grasp grease fitting and attempt to move fitting. No mechanical assistance or added force is needed to check joint. If ball joint is worn, fitting will move easily. If movement is noted, joint should be replaced.

2) Ball joints and control arm pivot bushings that are welded to control arms must be serviced by replacement of complete control arm assembly.

CAUTION: DO NOT raise vehicle by hoisting or jacking against the lower control arms.

REMOVAL & INSTALLATION

STABILIZER BAR

Removal

1) Raise and support vehicle. Remove stabilizer bar end bushing-to-control arm nuts, bolts and retainers. Detach stabilizer bar-to-crossmember nuts and bolts, and remove holding clamps. See Fig. 1.

2) Remove stabilizer bar from vehicle. Inspect for broken or distorted clamps and/or retainers. Replace components as needed. Inspect bushings for wear, deterioration or damage.

3) If inner (crossmember) bushing replacement is required, remove by opening split in bushing. Remove outer (control arm) bushing by cutting or hammering bushing from bar.

NOTE: On Dynasty and New Yorker, control arm bushings should be oriented as indicated on retainer. On all others, control arm bushing retainers are synmetrical and bend slightly upon installation.

Installation

1) Install new crossmember bushings on bar with curved surface up and split to front of vehicle. Lift bar into crossmember. Install clamps and bolts. Position retainers at control arms.

2) Insert bolts and install nuts. With lower control arms raised to design height, tighten all mounting bolts to specifications. Lower vehicle.

CAUTION: DO NOT attempt to modify any suspension or steering components by heating or bending.

LOWER CONTROL ARM, STUB STRUT BUSHING & PIVOT BUSHING

NOTE: On Dynasty and New Yorker, lower control arm can only be serviced as an assembly.

Removal

1) Raise and support vehicle. Remove front inner pivot through bolt. On all models except Dynasty and New Yorker, remove rear stub strut nut and retainer. On all models, detach ball joint-to-steering knuckle clamp bolt. Separate ball joint from steering knuckle.

CAUTION: DO NOT pull steering knuckle out from vehicle after releasing from ball joint, or inner CV joint can separate.

2) Remove stabilizer bar-to-control arm end bushing retainer nuts. Rotate control arm over sway bar. Remove rear stub strut retainer. Remove control arm pivot bolt. Lower control arm out of vehicle.

Pivot Bushing Replacement

1) Inspect control arm pivot bushing for distortion, wear, deterioration, or damage. If replacement of pivot bushing is necessary, position Control Arm Support (C-4700) between lower control arm flanges and around bushing to prevent control arm distortion.

2) Install a 1/2 x 2 1/2" bolt into bushing. With Receiving Cup (C-4699-2) on press base, position control arm inner flange against cup wall to support flange while receiving bushing. Remove bushing by pressing on bolt head.

3) To install pivot bushing, position Control Arm Support (C-4700) between control arm flanges. Install bushing inner sleeve and insulator into cavity of Receiver (C-4699-2).

4) Position assembly onto press base and align control arm to receive bushing. Position Installer (C-4699-1) to support control arm outer flange while receiving bushing. Press bushing into control arm until bushing flange seats against control arm.

Stub Strut Bushing Replacement

1) If stub strut bushing needs replacement, slide sleeve out of bushing and pry bushing from crossmember. To install stub strut bushing, position new bushing in crossmember.

2) Fabricate a bushing installer from a 1/2 x 7 1/2" bolt, 2 washers and a piece of 1.2" bar stock (2 x 4 1/2"). Press bushing into position.

Front Suspension

CHRYSLER MOTORS FWD MODELS (Cont.)

Installation

1) On all except Dynasty and New Yorker, install retainer on stub strut. On all models, position control arm over stabilizer bar. Install rear stub strut and front pivot into crossmember. Install front pivot bolt and assemble nut finger tight. On all except Dynasty and New Yorker, install stub strut retainer and assemble nut finger tight.

2) On all models, install ball joint stud into steering knuckle. Install clamp bolt and tighten to specifications. See TIGHTENING SPECIFICATIONS table. Position stabilizer bar end bushing retainer onto control arm. Install retainer bolts and tighten all to specifications.

CAUTION: The control arm pivot bolts must be tightened with suspension supporting vehicle at normal ride height.

3) Lower vehicle until suspension is supported at normal driving position and control arm is at design height. Tighten front pivot bolt and stub strut nut to specifications.

BALL JOINT

NOTE: **On some models, including Dynasty and New Yorker, ball joints are welded to lower control arm and are not serviceable.**

Removal

1) Raise and support vehicle. Remove wheels. Pry off dust seal. Position Receiving Cup (C-4699-2) to support lower control arm while receiving ball joint.

2) Install a 1 1/16" deep socket over stud and against joint upper housing. Use press to remove ball joint assembly from control arm.

Installation

1) Position new ball joint housing into control arm cavity. Position assembly in press with Installer (C-4699-1) supporting control arm. Align and press assembly until ball joint housing ledge stops against control arm cavity down flange.

2) Support ball joint housing with receiving cup. Position new seal over stud, against housing. With 1 1/2" socket, press seal onto joint housing until seal seat is against control arm.

3) During any service procedures where knuckle and drive shaft are separated, thoroughly clean seal and wear sleeve with solvent and relubricate both components. See FWD AXLE SHAFTS article in DRIVE AXLE & TRANSFER CASES section.

STEERING KNUCKLE

Removal

1) Remove cotter pin, nut lock and spring washer from hub. Loosen hub nut with vehicle on floor and brakes applied. Raise and support vehicle. Remove wheel. Remove hub nut. Ensure splined drive shaft is free to separate from hub spline by tapping hub out slightly with brass punch.

NOTE: **The hub and drive shaft are splined together through the steering knuckle/bearing assembly and retained by the hub nut.**

2) Remove tie rod end from knuckle steering arm with Remover (C-3894-A). Remove brake hose retaining clamp from strut damper. Remove ball joint stud clamp bolt and caliper mounting bolts. Remove caliper and hang with wire. Remove brake rotor.

3) Remove knuckle and cam bolts. Remove knuckle from strut damper and off of ball joint stud. Be sure drive shaft is supported during removal of knuckle to prevent separation of constant velocity joints.

Installation

1) Slide drive shaft through hub splines. Install hub with steering knuckle/bearing assembly onto lower control arm ball joint stud. Install ball joint-to-knuckle clamp bolt and tighten to specifications.

2) Position knuckle into strut. Install washer plate (if equipped), cam and knuckle bolts. Ensure cam bolt index mark is positioned properly for alignment reference.

3) Install tie rod end onto knuckle steering arm and tighten nut. Install new cotter pin. Install brake rotor. Install brake caliper assembly. Install caliper mounting bolts and tighten.

4) Attach brake hose retainer to strut damper and tighten. Install washer and tighten hub nut (with brakes applied). Install spring washer, nut lock and new cotter pin. Install wheel. Check and adjust front end alignment as necessary.

WHEEL BEARINGS, SEAL & HUB ASSEMBLY

Removal

1) Remove steering knuckle/bearing assembly and hub as previously described. Separate hub from bearing assembly with Hub/Bearing Remover/Installer (C-4811). To separate, back out 3 retainer screws from knuckle until hub is unseated from installed position.

2) Insert adapter screw into rear retainer screw threads. Place thrust button inside hub bore. Position Hub/Bearing Remover/Installer (C-4811) and install 2 screws firmly into tapped brake adapter extensions. Put nut and washer on adapter screw.

3) Tighten screw on the Hub/Bearing Remover/Installer (C-4811) to remove hub from bearing. If inner race remains on hub, use gear puller to remove it.

4) Remove Hub/Bearing Remover/Installer (C-4811) and attaching screws from knuckle. Remove 3 screws and bearing retainer. Carefully pry seal from machined recess in knuckle and discard seal. Clean recess. Press bearing out of knuckle with tool. Discard bearing.

NOTE: **Inspect hub surfaces for damage before installing new bearing. If damaged replace hub.**

Installation

1) Press new bearing into the knuckle with Bearing Remover/Installer (C-4811). Red seal on bearing faces outboard toward bearing retainer.

2) Install new seal and bearing retainer. Tighten retainer screws. Press hub into the knuckle/bearing assembly using the Bearing Remover/Installer (C-4811).

3) Position new seal in recess and drive into place with Installer (C-4698) and hammer. Lubricate full circumference of seal and wear sleeve with multipurpose grease.

CHRYSLER MOTORS FWD MODELS (Cont.)

4) If necessary, install wear sleeve in constant velocity joint housing using Installer (C-4698). Lubricate full circumference of seal and wear sleeve with grease. Install knuckle onto suspension.

STRUT DAMPER ASSEMBLY
Removal
Where reassembly procedure includes use of original strut and knuckle, mark outline of strut on knuckle on Lancer, LeBaron, Shadow and Sundance. On all others, mark cam adjusting bolt position for reassembly and alignment reference.

1) Raise and support vehicle. Remove wheel. Remove cam adjusting bolt, knuckle bolt, washer plate and brake hose-to-damper bracket retaining screw.

2) Remove strut damper-to-fender shield mounting nut washer assemblies. Remove strut damper and coil spring assembly from vehicle.

Disassembly
1) Compress coil spring with Spring Compressor (C-4838). On Horizon and Omni, ensure 4 coils on spring are compressed. On all others, compress 5 coils. Hold strut rod and remove strut rod nut. Remove retainers and bushings. Remove coil spring.

CAUTION: Do not grasp/damage strut rod seal surface or possible seal leakage can result.

2) Coil springs are rated separately for each side of vehicle depending on optional equipment and type of service. Mark coil spring to ensure it is installed on same side of vehicle.

Inspection
1) Inspect strut damper for fluid leakage, damage or excessive wear. A slight amount of fluid seepage is not unusual and does not affect performance. Replace strut only if a stream of fluid is found running down sides of strut.

2) Check strut damper mount assembly for severe deterioration of rubber isolator. Inspect retainers for cracks and distortion. Check bearings for binding. Ensure damper has no flat spots over its entire stroke. Replace all worn parts as necessary.

Reassembly
1) Install dust shield, isolator (if equipped), jounce bumper, spacer (as required) and spring seat onto top of spring. Install mount assembly, rebound retainer and rod nut.

NOTE: Be certain all verticle free play is gone between strut cartridge and strut housing before continuing reassembly.

Fig. 1: Exploded View of FWD Strut Damper Assembly

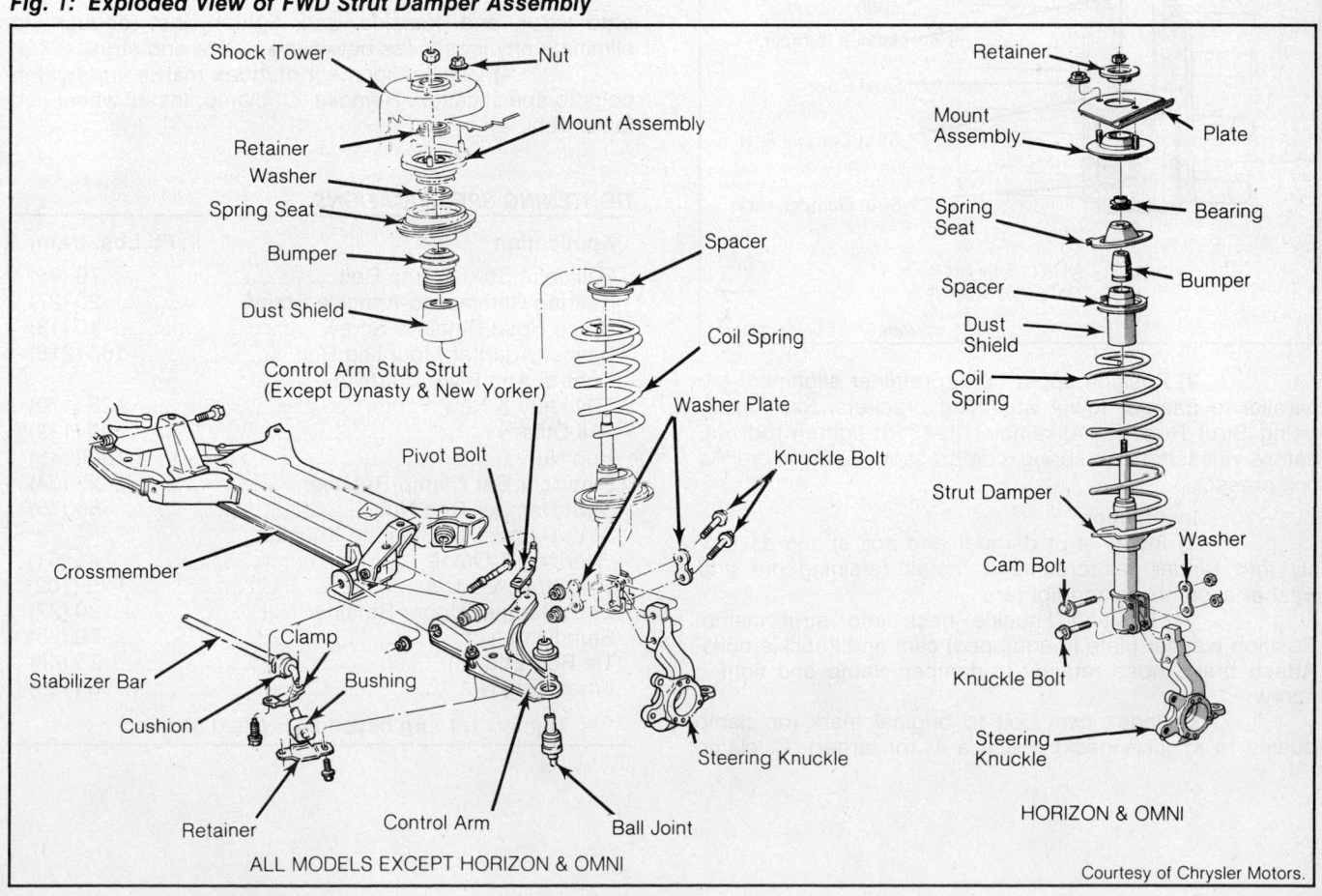

ALL MODELS EXCEPT HORIZON & OMNI

HORIZON & OMNI

Courtesy of Chrysler Motors.

Front Suspension

CHRYSLER MOTORS FWD MODELS (Cont.)

Fig. 2: Sectional View of Strut Damper Mount Assembly

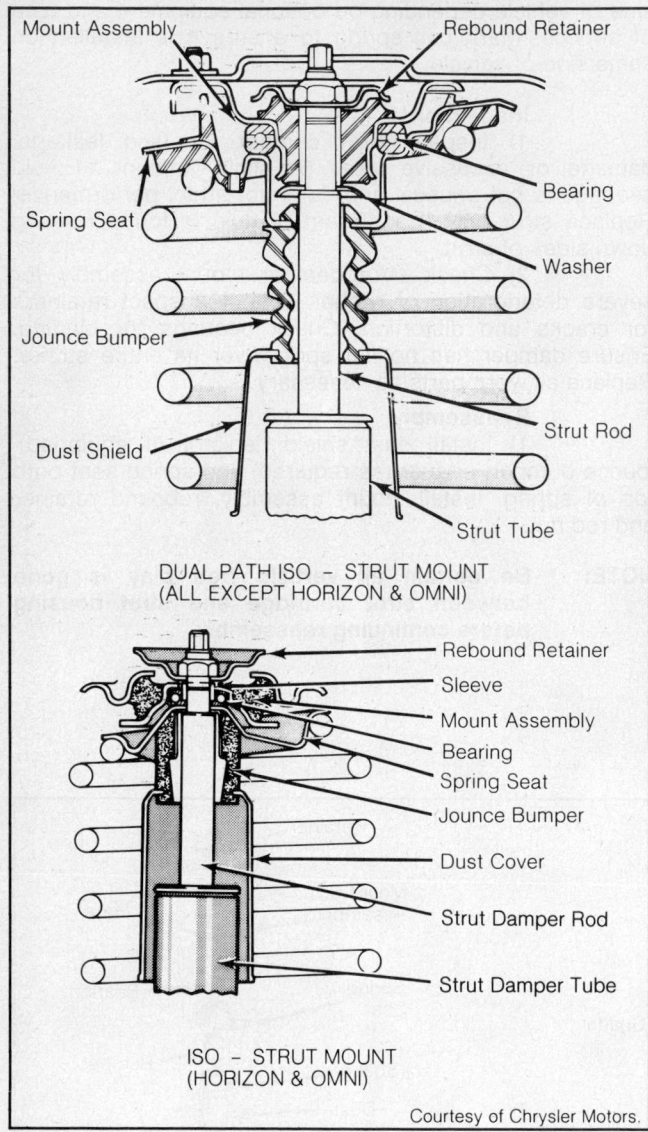

DUAL PATH ISO – STRUT MOUNT
(ALL EXCEPT HORIZON & OMNI)

ISO – STRUT MOUNT
(HORIZON & OMNI)

Courtesy of Chrysler Motors.

Fig. 3: Spring Seat & Retainer Position

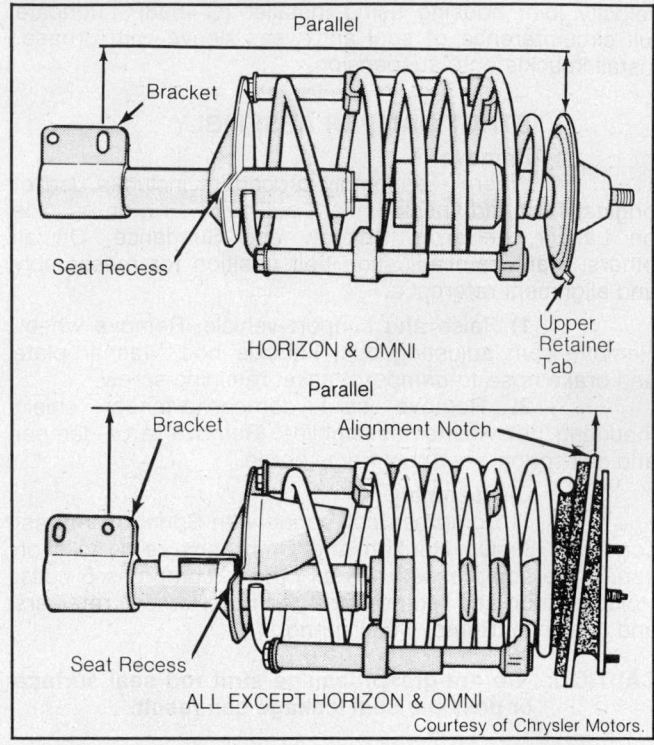

HORIZON & OMNI

ALL EXCEPT HORIZON & OMNI

Courtesy of Chrysler Motors.

2) Position upper spring retainer alignment tab parallel to damper lower attaching brackets. *See Fig. 3.* Using Strut Rod Nut Assembler (L-4558) tighten rod nut, before releasing the spring compressor. Remove spring compressor.

Installation

1) Install strut damper and coil spring assembly into fender reinforcement. Install retaining nut and washer assemblies and tighten.

2) Position knuckle neck into strut clamp. Position washer plate (if equipped) cam and knuckle bolts. Attach brake hose retainer-to-damper clamp and tighten screw.

3) Index cam bolt to original mark (or clamp outline to knuckle neck). Place a 4" (or larger) "C" clamp

onto strut and knuckle and tighten just enough to eliminate any looseness between knuckle and strut.

4) Check alignment of index marks and tighten bolts to specification. Remove "C" clamp. Install wheel and lower vehicle.

TIGHTENING SPECIFICATIONS

Application	Ft. Lbs. (N.m)
Ball Joint Stud Clamp Bolt	70 (95)
Bearing Retainer-to-Knuckle Screw	20 (27)
Brake Hose Retainer Screw	10 (13)
Caliper Adapter Mounting Bolt	160 (218)
Control Arm Pivot Bolt/Nut	
Dynasty & New Yorker	125 (170)
All Others	95 (129)
Hub Nut	180 (245)
Stabilizer Bar Clamp/Retainer	25 (34)
Strut Damper Rod Nut	55 (75)
Strut Damper-to-Steering Knuckle	
Horizon & Omni	[1] 45 (61)
All Other Models	[1] 75 (102)
Strut Damper Upper Retainer Nut	20 (27)
Stub Strut Nut	70 (95)
Tie Rod End Nut	35 (48)
Wheel Lug Nut	95 (129)

[1] – Tighten 1/4 turn beyond specified torque.

CHRYSLER MOTORS RWD MODELS

Diplomat, Fifth Avenue, Gran Fury

DESCRIPTION

All models use an independent torsion bar type suspension. Transverse torsion bars are mounted between outboard ends of lower control arms and forward portion of the suspension crossmember. Each torsion bar is anchored in the front crossmember opposite affected wheel. The stabilizer bar is mounted between both control arms and is bolted to the crossmember, adding a stabilizing effect to the front suspension system.

Height is controlled by the torsion bar anchor adjusting bolts, located on the front crossmember. The right torsion bar is adjusted by the left side and the left torsion bar is adjusted by the right side. Front height specifications must be correct to ensure proper wheel alignment, tire wear, satisfactory ride, and appearance.

ADJUSTMENTS

CASTER & CAMBER

See appropriate article in WHEEL ALIGNMENT section.

RIDING HEIGHT

See RIDING HEIGHT SPECIFICATIONS article in WHEEL ALIGNMENT section.

FRONT WHEEL BEARINGS

Under normal service, front wheel bearings should be inspected, lubricated and adjusted whenever front brakes are serviced or at least every 30,000 miles. For severe service use, check bearings at least every 9000 miles. Lubricate wheel bearings using only high temperature wheel bearing grease.

1) Raise vehicle. Remove tire and wheel. Remove caliper from rotor. Remove rotor assembly. Carefully drive out inner seal. Remove bearing with 3/4" diameter non-metallic rod.

2) Clean hub and bearings with solvent, mineral spirits or kerosene. Check bearing races for pitting, scoring or other damage. If races need replacement, drive bearing race out of hub with steel punch.

NOTE: **Replace inner and/or outer bearings and races as matched sets.**

3) Check bearing for signs of wear and/or damage. If bearings are okay, force grease between all rollers and case of bearing. Install bearing into rotor.

4) Using seal installer, position seal with lip facing inward, flush with end of hub. Clean spindle and apply light coat of grease. Install brake rotor assembly to spindle. Install outer bearing, thrust washer and adjusting nut.

5) While rotating brake rotor and hub assembly, tighten adjusting nut to 20-25 ft. lbs. (27-34 N.m). Stop rotation and back off adjusting nut 1/4 turn (90 degrees) to release preload. Finger tighten adjusting nut while rotating wheel. Position locking nut over adjusting nut. Install cotter pin and dust cover. Install wheel.

LOWER BALL JOINT CHECKING

1) Raise and support vehicle. Place jack stands under both lower control arms, as far outboard as possible. Ensure the stands DO NOT contact splash shield and upper control arms DO NOT contact the rebound bumpers.

2) With weight on control arms, place dial indicator and clamp assembly on lower control arm. Position plunger tip against steering knuckle arm and zero dial indicator.

3) Measure vertical travel of control arm by raising and lowering wheel with pry bar under center of tire. If control arm axial travel is more than .030" (.76 mm), replace ball joint.

UPPER BALL JOINT CHECKING

1) Raise and support vehicle with jack positioned under lower control arm. Tighten wheel bearing to remove wheel bearing play. Lower vehicle until wheel lightly contacts floor.

2) Hold wheel at top and bottom and apply force inward and outward. If any lateral movement at the ball joint between upper control arm and knuckle is noted, replace upper ball joint. Raise vehicle and adjust wheel bearings.

REMOVAL & INSTALLATION

STEERING KNUCKLE

Removal

1) Turn ignition off ("UNLOCKED" position). Raise front of vehicle. Place safety stands under lower control arms, as close as possible to wheels. DO NOT allow jack pads to contact brake splash shields.

NOTE: **DO NOT allow rubber rebound bumper to contact frame.**

2) Remove wheel assembly. Remove disc caliper mount bolts. Support and wire caliper out of way. Remove rotor assembly.

3) Remove brake splash shield. Loosen steering arm-to-knuckle bolts. Remove cotter pins from upper and lower ball joint nuts. Using Ball Joint Separator (C-3564A), separate steering knuckle from ball joints. Remove steering knuckle.

Installation

To install, reverse removal procedure. Tighten fittings to specifications. See TIGHTENING SPECIFICATIONS table. Adjust front wheel bearings. Install wheel and lower vehicle. Adjust front suspension height and front end alignment as necessary.

STEERING KNUCKLE ARM

Removal

1) Turn ignition off ("UNLOCKED" position). Raise front of vehicle. Place safety stands under lower control arms, as close as possible to wheels. DO NOT allow jack pads to contact brake splash shields.

NOTE: **DO NOT allow rubber rebound bumper to contact frame.**

Front Suspension

CHRYSLER MOTORS RWD MODELS (Cont.)

2) Remove wheel assembly. Remove disc caliper mount bolts. Support and wire caliper out of way. Remove rotor assembly. Remove brake splash shield. Unload torsion bars. Remove cotter pin from tie rod nut. Remove nut.

3) Using Ball Joint Separator (C-3564A), separate tie rod from steering knuckle arm. Separate lower ball joint from steering knuckle using separator. Remove 2 bolts and nuts attaching arm to steering knuckle. Remove steering knuckle arm.

Installation

To install, reverse removal procedure. Tighten fittings to specifications. See TIGHTENING SPECIFICATIONS table. Adjust front wheel bearings. Install wheel and lower vehicle. Adjust front suspension height and front end alignment as necessary.

LOWER BALL JOINT

Removal

1) Raise and support vehicle on frame hoist. Place jack stands under front frame. Remove front tire and wheel. Remove brake caliper and wire out of way. Remove hub and rotor. Remove brake splash shield. Disconnect shock absorber from lower shock absorber. Loosen torsion bar.

2) Remove cotter pin and nuts from upper and lower ball joints. Using Ball Joint Separator (C-3564-A), separate lower ball joint from steering knuckle. Using Adapter (C-4212) and hydraulic press, remove lower ball joint from control arm.

Installation

1) Using ball joint remover/installer, press new ball joint into lower control arm. Place new seal over ball joint. Using Seal Adapter (C-4039), press seal retainer down on joint housing until locked in position.

2) Insert ball joint stud into knuckle arm opening. Install stud retaining nut and tighten. Install cotter pin and lubricate ball joint.

3) Place load on torsion bar. Reassemble suspension and brake components. Lower vehicle. Adjust torsion bars for proper vehicle height. Check and adjust front end alignment as necessary.

UPPER BALL JOINT

Removal

1) Raise vehicle. Place jack stand under lower control arm, as close to wheel as possible. Ensure stand does not contact brake splash shield. Rubber rebound bumper must not contact frame.

CAUTION: Torsion bar will remain in loaded position.

2) Remove wheel. Remove cotter pin and nut from upper ball joint. Install Ball Joint Separator (C-3564-A) on lower ball joint stud, allowing tool to rest on knuckle arm.

CAUTION: DO NOT attempt to force stud out of knuckle using separator only.

3) Tighten tool securely to apply pressure to upper stud. Strike knuckle sharply with hammer to loosen stud. Disengage upper ball joint from knuckle.

4) Support knuckle and brake assembly to prevent damage to brake hose or lower ball joint. Using Socket (C-3560), remove upper ball joint.

Installation

1) Thread ball joint squarely into control arm as far as possible by hand. Ensure ball joint threads engage those of control arm correctly. Seals should always be replaced once they have been removed.

2) Thread ball joint into control arm until it bottoms on housing. Ensure ball joint is tightened to specifications. Using Seal Adapter (C-4039), press new seal over ball joint stud. Ensure seal is seated on ball joint housing.

Fig. 1: Exploded View of Chrysler Motors RWD Front Suspension

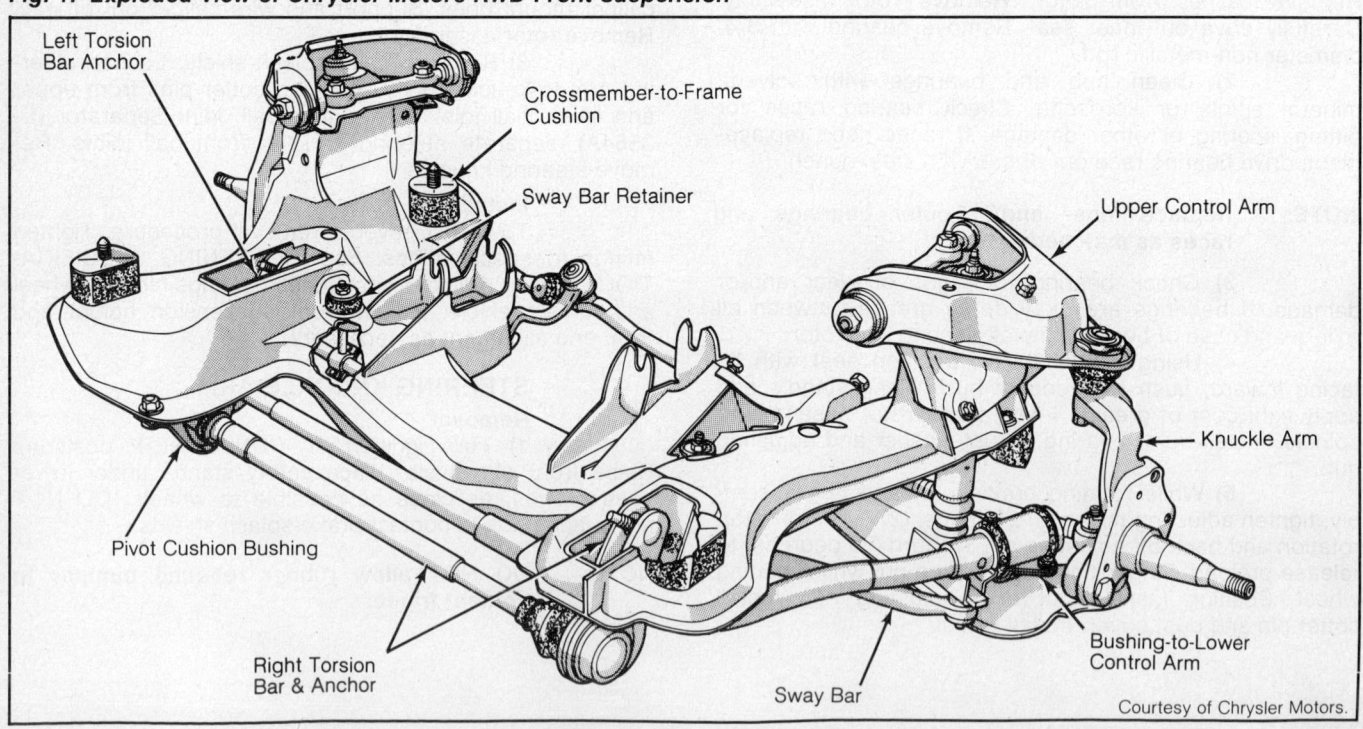

Left Torsion Bar Anchor

Crossmember-to-Frame Cushion

Sway Bar Retainer

Upper Control Arm

Knuckle Arm

Pivot Cushion Bushing

Right Torsion Bar & Anchor

Sway Bar

Bushing-to-Lower Control Arm

Courtesy of Chrysler Motors.

3) Position upper ball joint stud into steering knuckle. Install nut and tighten to specifications. Install and tighten lower ball joint stud nut into steering knuckle. Install cotter pins. Lubricate ball joint(s). Install brake components and wheel. Check and adjust front end alignment as necessary.

TORSION BAR, BUSHINGS & ANCHOR ASSEMBLY

Removal

1) Raise front of vehicle. Support vehicle so front suspension is in full rebound position. Release load on both torsion bars. Remove anchor adjusting bolt on torsion bar to be removed. Using a jack, raise lower control arm until clearance between crossmember ledge (at jounce bumper) and torsion bar end bushing is 2 7/8" (73 mm). *See Fig. 4.*

2) Support lower control arm at this design height (equal to 3 passenger position with vehicle on ground). This is necessary to align stabilizer bar and lower control arm attaching points for disassembly and reassembly.

3) Disconnect stabilizer bar from control arm. Remove 2 bolts attaching torsion bar end bushing to lower control arm. Remove 2 bolts attaching torsion bar pivot cushion bushing to crossmember. *See Fig. 2.* Remove torsion bar and anchor assembly from crossmember.

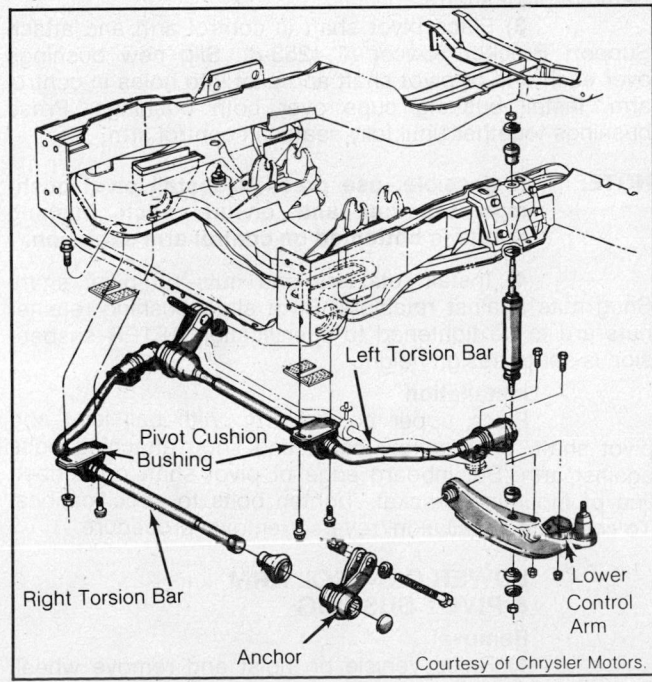

Fig. 2: Exploded View of Torsion Bar & Anchor Assembly

Courtesy of Chrysler Motors.

NOTE: Replacement torsion bars include the permanent pivot cushion bushing and replaceable torsion bar-to-lower control arm bushing. Check component condition to determine parts needing replacement.

Inspection

1) Check torsion bar pivot cushion bushing seals for cuts, tears or severe deterioration that may allow moisture under cushion. If corrosion is evident, replace torsion bar assembly.

2) Inspect torsion bar-to-lower control arm bushings for wear or damage and replace as necessary. Separate torsion bar from anchor. Remove all foreign matter from hex openings in anchors and from hex ends of torsion bar.

3) Check torsion bar adjusting bolt and swivel. Replace components if there is any sign of corrosion or other damage. Lubricate bolt and swivel.

Torsion Bar-to-Lower Control Arm Bushing Replacement

1) With torsion bar assembly removed from vehicle, clamp torsion bar-to-lower control arm bushing in soft-jawed vise with rivet head up (hex end of bar down).

2) Center punch rivet head. Drill rivet out enough to drive it from bushing with a 5/16" rod. If necessary, remove rivet head flange before driving rivet out. Use care not to enlarge 7/16" diameter hole in torsion bar bushing clamp.

3) Remove bushing from bar and discard. If necessary, clean any roughness under bushing with sandpaper to ease reassembly. Install new bushing by hand. Install new bushing retaining bolt and tighten to specifications.

Installation

1) Carefully slide torsion bar-to-anchor boot (balloon seal) over end of torsion bar with cupped end toward hex. Coat hex end of torsion bar with lubricant.

2) Install torsion bar hex end into anchor bracket. With torsion bar in a horizontal position, ensure ears of anchor bracket are positioned nearly straight up. *See Fig. 3.* Position swivel into anchor bracket ears.

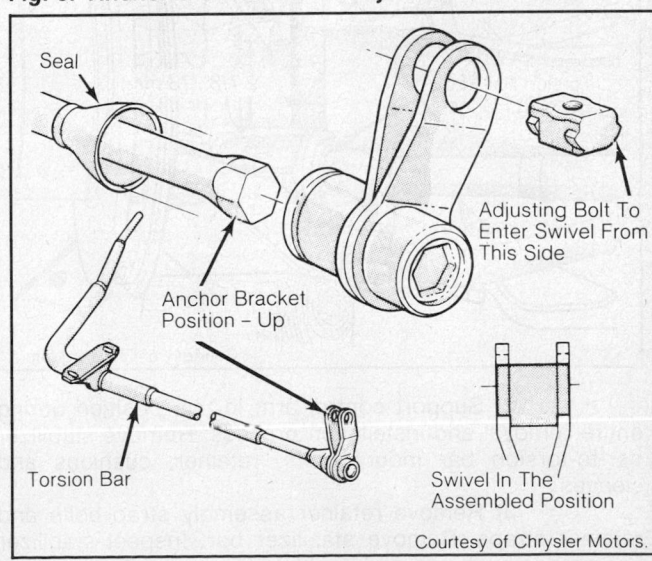

Fig. 3: Anchor & Swivel Assembly Installation Positions

Courtesy of Chrysler Motors.

3) Place bushing end of bar into position on top of lower control arm. Install anchor bracket assembly into crossmember anchor retainer. Install anchor adjusting bearing and bolt.

4) Attach pivot cushion bushing to crossmember with 2 bolt and washer assemblies (finger tight), leaving space for friction plates. Position lower control arms at design height. Install 2 bolt and washer assemblies attaching torsion bar bushing to lower control arm and tighten to specifications.

Front Suspension

CHRYSLER MOTORS RWD MODELS (Cont.)

NOTE: Ensure torsion bar anchor bracket is fully seated in crossmember.

5) Install friction plates between crossmember and pivot cushion with open end of slot to rear and bottomed out on mounting bolt. Tighten cushion bushing mount bolts to specifications. Position boot over anchor bracket.

6) Reinstall bolt through stabilizer bar, retainer cushions and sleeve. Load torsion bar. To complete installation, lower vehicle. Adjust ride height. Check and adjust front end alignment as necessary.

STABILIZER BAR

Removal

1) Raise and support vehicle with frame hoist. Release load on torsion bars. Raise lower control arm with jack until clearance between crossmember ledge (at jounce bumper) and torsion bar-to-lower control arm bushing is 2 7/8" (73 mm). See Fig. 4.

Fig. 4: Measuring Chrysler Motors RWD Front Suspension Design Height

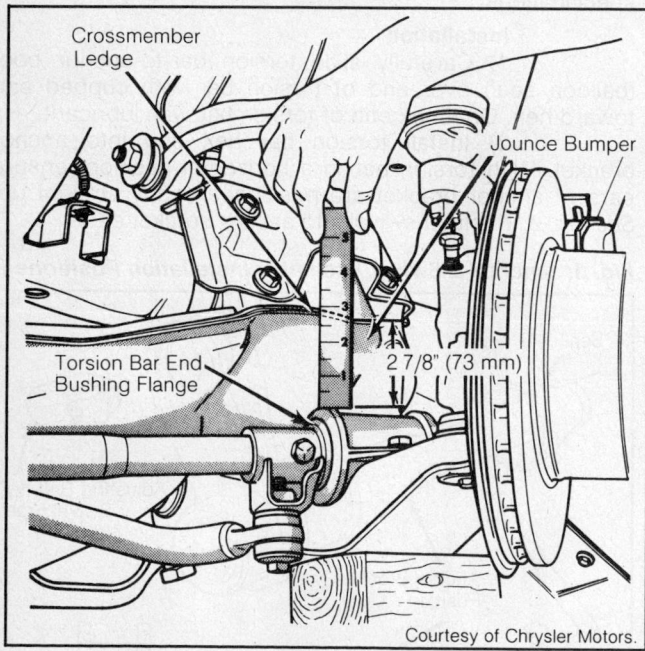

Crossmember Ledge

Jounce Bumper

Torsion Bar End Bushing Flange

2 7/8" (73 mm)

Courtesy of Chrysler Motors.

2) Support control arm in this position during entire removal and installation process. Remove stabilizer bar-to-torsion bar mount bolts, retainer, cushions and sleeves.

3) Remove retainer assembly strap bolts and retainer straps. Remove stabilizer bar. Inspect stabilizer bar rubber bushings and cushions for excessive wear or deterioration and replace parts as necessary.

Installation

1) Install new bolts through stabilizer bar retainer. Install cushions and sleeve. Attach torsion bar-to-lower control arm bushing. Tighten bolt to specifications.

2) Tighten stabilizer bar retainer and strap bolts to specifications. Load torsion bars. Lower vehicle and adjust vehicle height. Check and adjust front end alignment as necessary.

UPPER CONTROL ARM & PIVOT BUSHINGS

Removal

1) Place ignition switch in "UNLOCKED" and "OFF" position. Raise and support vehicle. Place jack pads under lower control arms near wheel without touching splash shield. Ensure rebound bumpers are not touching crossmember. Remove wheel and tire assembly. Remove brake caliper if necessary for clearance.

2) Remove cotter pin and nut from upper ball joint. Using Ball Joint Separator (C-3564-A), separate upper ball joint from steering knuckle. Support assembly to prevent damage to brake hose or lower ball joint. From under hood, remove engine splash shield to expose upper control arm pivot shaft.

3) Scribe a line on support bracket, along inboard edge of pivot shaft, for reassembly reference. Remove pivot shaft nut and bolts from upper control arm. Lift control arm away from support bracket and remove from vehicle.

Pivot Bushing Replacement

1) Place upper control arm in vise. Remove pivot shaft nuts and bushing retainers. Bolt Pivot Bushing Support (C-4253-1) to pivot shaft. Place Pivot Bushing Puller (C-4253-2) over end of pivot shaft and reinstall nut.

2) Snug puller bolts against arm. Turn bolts equally until bushing is free of arm. Remove tool and discard bushing. Repeat procedure for remaining bushing. Remove pivot shaft.

3) Place pivot shaft in control arm and attach Support Bracket Spacer (C-4253-8). Slip new bushings over each end of pivot shaft and pilot into holes in control arm. Install bushing cups over both bushings. Press bushings together until fully seated in control arm.

NOTE: If possible, use press to install pivot bushings together and ensure each bushing flange is bottomed on control arm extrusion.

4) Install retainers and nuts on pivot shaft. Snug nuts against retainers. Pivot shaft bushing retainer nuts are to be tightened to specification AFTER suspension is set to design height.

Installation

Place upper control arm, with ball joint and pivot shaft, on bracket. Install and snug attaching bolts against arm. Set inboard edge of pivot shaft on scribed line of mounting bracket. Tighten bolts to specifications. To complete installation, reverse removal procedure.

LOWER CONTROL ARM & PIVOT BUSHING

Removal

1) Raise vehicle on hoist and remove wheel. Disconnect lower ball joint as previously described. Remove shock absorber. Release load on both torsion bars.

NOTE: Release tension on both torsion bars even if only one control arm is being removed due to stabilizer bar reaction from opposite torsion bar.

Front Suspension

CHRYSLER MOTORS RWD MODELS (Cont.)

2) Raise lower control arm until clearance between crossmember ledge (at jounce bumper) and torsion bar-to-lower control arm bushing is 2 7/8" (73.0 mm). *See Fig. 4.* Support control arm at design height. Remove 2 bolts attaching torsion bar end bushing to lower control arm. Remove bushing pivot bolt and control arm.

Pivot Bushing Replacement

1) Place lower control arm in vise. Install Pivot Bushing Remover/Installer (C-4383) by placing support fixture between flanges of control arm and around bushing.

NOTE: Ensure proper fixture position to prevent control arm distortion during bushing removal.

2) Position cup over flanged bushing end with bolt through cup and bushing. Install pilot, thrust washer, plain washer and nut on through bolt. Press bushing out of lower control arm by holding bolt on cup end and turning nut on pilot end.

3) Discard old pivot bushing. Position flange end of new bushing into cup squarely and press bushing into control arm until bushing flange seats on arm.

Installation

1) Position lower control arm into crossmember flange. Install pivot bolt and flanged nut finger tight. Reinstall lower ball joint into steering knuckle as previously described.

2) Position control arm supported at design height. Install 2 bolts attaching torsion bar end bushing to lower control arm and tighten to specifications. Tighten lower control arm pivot bolt to specifications.

3) Install shock absorber stud through lower control arm. Install bushing retainer and nut. Tighten nut to specifications. Install brake rotor assembly and caliper. Reload torsion bar pressure. Install wheel. Lower vehicle and adjust suspension height and front end alignment as necessary.

TIGHTENING SPECIFICATIONS

Application	Ft. Lbs. (N.m)
Ball Joint-to-Control Arm Nut	100 (136)
Ball Joint-to-Upper Control Arm Nut	125 (169)
Disc Brake Caliper Adapter Bolt	110 (150)
Disc Brake Caliper Bolts	15 (20)
Idler Arm Bolt/Nut	70 (95)
Lower Control Arm Pivot Bolt	75 (102)
Pitman Arm Nut	175 (238)
Rebound Bumper Bolt	17 (23)
Shock Absorber	
Lower Mount Nut	35 (47)
Upper Mount Nut	25 (34)
Splash Shield Bolts	18 (24)
Stabilizer Bar	
Strap Nut	30 (41)
Cushion Bolt	50 (68)
Steering Knuckle	
Lower Bolt/Nut	160 (217)
Tie Rod End Nut	40 (54)
Torsion Bar Bushing	
Retaining Nut	50 (68)
Torsion Bar	
Pivot Cushion Retainer Nut/Bolt	85 (115)
Torsion Bar-to-Lower Control Arm	
Bushing Nut/Bolt	70 (95)
Upper Control Arm	
Pivot Bushing Nut	110 (150)
Pivot Shaft Bolts	150 (203)

	INCH Lbs. (N.m)
Stabilizer Bar	
Link Retainer Nut	97 (11)

Front Suspension

EAGLE PREMIER

DESCRIPTION

The independent strut design front suspension uses lower control arms which pivot from engine cradle. Lower control arms and engine cradle contain pivot bushings.

The upper end of strut is mounted to the body and lower end is mounted to the steering knuckle. The steering knuckle pivots on the lower control arm mounted ball joint. The steering knuckle is clamped to the ball joint stud.

Tie rods are connected to steering arms on the struts. The hub and bearing assembly are mounted to the knuckle and contains a replaceable bearing assembly.

ADJUSTMENTS

CASTER & CAMBER

See appropriate article in WHEEL ALIGNMENT section.

RIDING HEIGHT

See RIDING HEIGHT SPECIFICATIONS article in WHEEL ALIGNMENT section.

FRONT WHEEL BEARINGS

NOTE: The hub can be replaced without removing the bearing from the steering knuckle. Hub requires removal for bearing replacement on the steering knuckle.

Removal

1) Raise and support vehicle. Remove wheel. Remove brake caliper. DO NOT disconnect brake line. Using Hub Locking Bar (Rou. 604.01), hold hub and remove drive shaft nut.

2) Install Hub Puller (T.Av. 1050) on hub. Tighten bolt and push drive shaft from hub. Install slide hammer in hub puller. Using slide hammer and puller, remove hub and rotor.

3) Using hydraulic press, Adapter (Rou 15.01) and Bearing Puller (U-53P or U-536J), remove hub bearing race. To remove bearing located on the steering knuckle, remove bearing assembly retaining bolts. See Fig. 1.

Fig. 1: Steering Knuckle Bearing Assembly

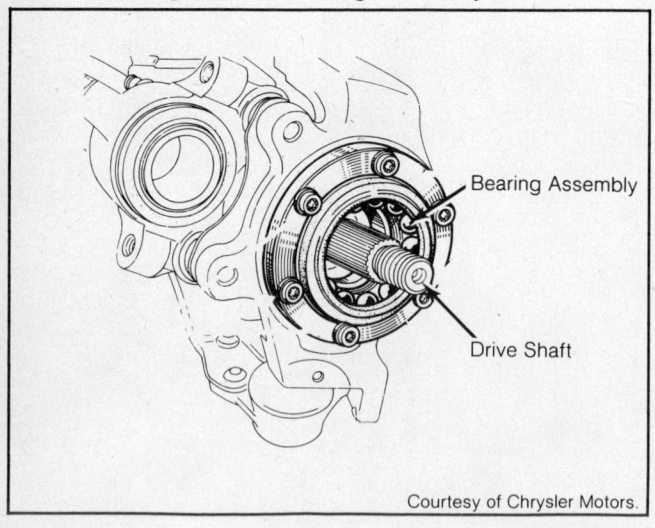

Courtesy of Chrysler Motors.

Installation

1) Remove plastic covers from outer edges and bore of new bearing assembly. Remove bearing races from new bearing. Pack bearing with grease supplied with bearing.

2) Press one bearing race on hub. Install remaining bearing race in bearing. Install bearing assembly on steering knuckle. Tighten bolts to specification.

3) Lubricate hub bearing race with EP type grease. Install hub on drive shaft and bearing assembly. Using soft-faced hammer, tap hub until 3-4 threads are visible on drive shaft.

4) Install drive shaft nut. Using hub locking bar, hold hub and tighten drive shaft nut to specification. See TIGHTENING SPECIFICATIONS table at end of article. Reverse removal procedures for remaining components. Tighten bolts to specification.

REMOVAL & INSTALLATION

LOWER BALL JOINT

Removal

1) Raise and support vehicle. Remove wheel. Place shop towel around drive shaft boot to prevent damage. Loosen stabilizer bar-to-frame retaining bolts. DO NOT remove bolts.

2) Remove stabilizer bar-to-control arm bracket retaining nuts. Remove bracket assembly. Install nuts back on bolts after bracket removal. The stabilizer bar mounting bracket bolts secure the lower ball joint to the control arm.

3) Move stabilizer bar from control arm. Remove ball joint-to-steering knuckle retaining bolt. Lower stabilizer bar. Loosen lower control arm retaining bolts. DO NOT remove bolts.

4) Lower control arm and remove plastic washer from ball joint. Remove ball joint retaining bolts. Tap upward on ball joint and remove from control arm.

Installation

1) Install ball joint and retaining bolts in control arm. DO NOT tighten bolts at this time. Install plastic washer on ball joint. Reverse removal procedures. Tighten bolts to specification.

2) Tighten ball joint and stabilizer bar retaining bolts to specification with vehicle at normal operating height.

STEERING KNUCKLE

NOTE: Hub and bearing are removed as an assembly during steering knuckle service.

Removal

1) Raise and support vehicle. Remove wheel. Place shop towel around drive shaft boot to prevent damage. Remove brake caliper. DO NOT disconnect brake line.

2) Using Hub Locking Bar (Rou. 604.01), hold hub and remove drive shaft nut. Install Hub Puller (T.Av. 1050) on hub. Tighten bolt and push drive shaft from hub.

3) Remove rotor-to-hub retaining bolts. Remove rotor from hub. Remove bearing assembly-to-steering knuckle retaining bolts. These bolts can be reached through hub access hole.

EAGLE PREMIER (Cont.)

4) Install rotor and Hub Puller (T.Av. 1050) on hub. Install slide hammer in hub puller. Using slide hammer and puller, remove hub and bearing assembly.

5) Remove ball joint-to-steering knuckle bolt. Disconnect ball joint from steering knuckle.

CAUTION: The strut-to-steering knuckle bolts are splined into the strut. Only the nuts can be turned. Following procedure must be followed to prevent damage to bolts and splines.

6) Loosen steering knuckle-to-strut retaining bolts. Position nuts at the end of the bolt. Using soft-faced hammer, tap on nut to loosen bolt splines. Remove nuts and retaining bolts. Remove steering knuckle.

Installation
Reverse removal procedures. Ensure ball joint-to-steering knuckle retaining bolt is seated on ball joint stud groove. Align splined strut bolts prior to installation. Tighten all retainers to specification.

Fig. 2: Exploded View of Front Suspension Components

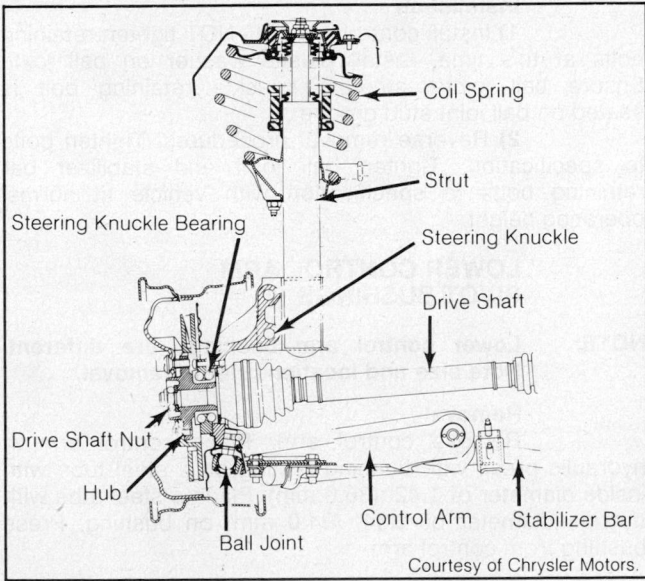

Coil Spring
Strut
Steering Knuckle Bearing
Steering Knuckle
Drive Shaft
Drive Shaft Nut
Hub
Ball Joint
Control Arm
Stabilizer Bar

Courtesy of Chrysler Motors.

STRUT DAMPER ASSEMBLY
Removal
1) Raise and support vehicle. Allow suspension to hang freely. Remove wheel. Remove tie rod-to-strut retaining nut. Using Joint Extractor (9T.Av. 476), separate tie rod end from strut.

2) Remove upper strut-to-body retaining bolts. DO NOT remove center nut of strut assembly.

CAUTION: DO NOT remove center nut of strut assembly. Coil spring is under excessive pressure. Removal may cause personal injury.

3) Ensure suspension is hanging free and no tension exists on suspension components. Loosen steering knuckle-to-strut retaining bolts. Position nuts at the end of the bolt. Using soft-faced hammer, tap on nut to loosen bolt splines. Remove nuts and retaining bolts.

4) Place shop towel around drive shaft boot to prevent damage. Move control arm downward and remove strut assembly.

Disassembly
1) Install lower plate from Spring Compressor (Sus. 1052.99) in a vise. The proper lower adapter plate from spring compressor is stamped with "R-21" on the flat side of the adapter.

2) Install proper lower adapter plate with shoulder downward into the lower plate. *See Fig. 4.* Install small adapter plates around lower area of strut assembly. Install strut assembly in lower plate. Ensure strut is properly seated.

3) Upper adapter plate will require modification to fit properly. Drill out proper holes to 7/16". *See Fig. 3.* Install upper adapter plate on strut. Align proper holes.

Fig. 3: Upper Adapter Plate Modification

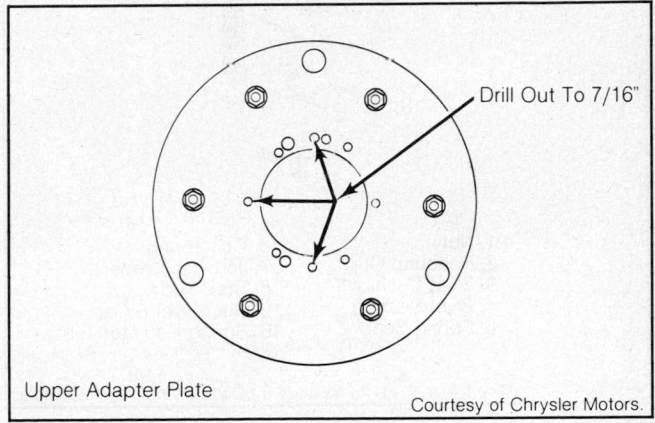

Drill Out To 7/16"
Upper Adapter Plate
Courtesy of Chrysler Motors.

Fig. 4: Compressing Strut Assembly Coil Spring

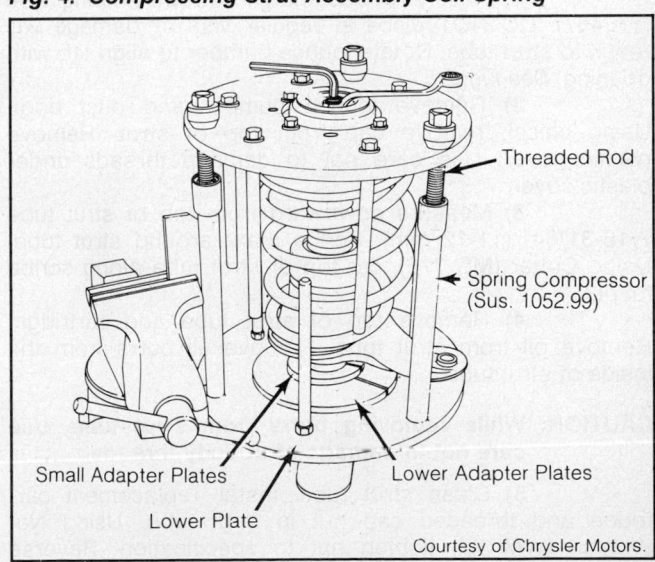

Threaded Rod
Spring Compressor (Sus. 1052.99)
Small Adapter Plates
Lower Adapter Plates
Lower Plate

Courtesy of Chrysler Motors.

4) Install sturt-to-upper plate retaining bolts. Install threaded rods into lower holes. Lubricate all threaded rods with oil. Slowly tighten threaded rods evenly to compress coil spring approximately 13/32".

5) Hold strut shaft and remove center nut from strut shaft. Evenly loosen threaded rods to release spring tension. Remove adapter plate and strut components. *See Fig. 5.*

NOTE: The strut internal piston rod assembly and fluid can be replaced using a service cartridge.

Front Suspension

EAGLE PREMIER (Cont.)

Fig. 5: Exploded View of Strut Assembly

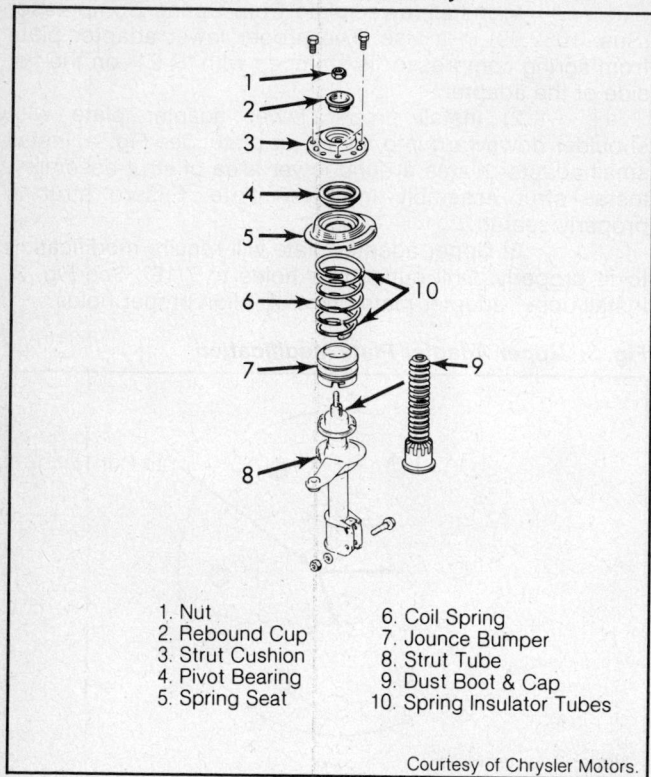

1. Nut
2. Rebound Cup
3. Strut Cushion
4. Pivot Bearing
5. Spring Seat
6. Coil Spring
7. Jounce Bumper
8. Strut Tube
9. Dust Boot & Cap
10. Spring Insulator Tubes

Courtesy of Chrysler Motors.

Strut Cartridge Replacement

1) Place strut assembly in Strut Clamping Vise (YA-457). DO NOT place in regular vise or damage will result to strut tube. Rotate jounce bumper to align tab with opening. *See Fig. 5.*

2) Remove jounce bumper and dust boot. Using chisel, remove cap from top of strut. Remove plastic cover. Use care not to damage threads under plastic cover.

3) Measure downward from top of strut tube 7/16-31/64" (11-12 mm). Scribe mark around strut tube. Using Cutter (MS 776), cut top of strut tube along scribe mark.

4) Remove top of strut tube and cartridge. Remove oil from strut tube. Remove all burrs from the inside of strut tube.

CAUTION: While removing burrs from strut tube, use care not to damage strut body threads.

5) Clean strut tube. Install replacement cartridge and threaded cap nut in strut tube. Using Nut Wrench (WM-S3), tighten nut to specification. Reverse removal procedures for remaining components.

Reassembly

1) Install strut assembly in spring compressor. Ensure spring ends are against spring stops. When compressing coil spring, guide strut shaft through upper strut mounting plate. Tighten threaded rods until approximately 15.7" (400 mm) exists between upper and lower adapter plates.

2) Tighten threaded rods until nut can be installed on strut shaft. Install rebound cup and new retaining nut. Tighten nut to specification. Remove spring compressor.

Installation

Install strut. Install upper retaining bolts. DO NOT tighten until strut is installed in steering knuckle. Reverse removal procedures. Tighten bolts to specificaton. Check and adjust toe-in.

LOWER CONTROL ARM

Removal

1) Raise and support vehicle. Remove wheel. Place shop towel around drive shaft boot to prevent damage. Loosen stabilizer bar-to-frame retaining bolts. DO NOT remove bolts.

2) Remove stabilizer bar-to-control arm bracket retaining nuts. Remove bracket assembly. Install nuts back on bolts after bracket removal. Stabilizer bar mounting bracket bolts secure the lower ball joint to the control arm.

3) Move stabilizer bar from control arm. Remove ball joint-to-steering knuckle retaining bolt. Remove control arm-to-cradle retaining bolts. Remove lower control arm. Remove plastic washer from ball joint.

Installation

1) Install control arm. DO NOT tighten retaining bolts at this time. Install plastic washer on ball joint. Ensure ball joint-to-steering knuckle retaining bolt is seated on ball joint stud groove.

2) Reverse removal procedures. Tighten bolts to specification. Tighten ball joint and stabilizer bar retaining bolts to specification with vehicle at normal operating height.

LOWER CONTROL ARM PIVOT BUSHINGS

NOTE: Lower control arm bushings are different. Note size and location prior to removal.

Removal

Remove control arm. Place control arm in hydraulic press with bushing resting on a steel tube with inside diameter of 1.42" (36.0 mm). Place a steel tube with outside diameter of 1.34" (34.0 mm) on bushing. Press bushing from control arm.

Installation

Reverse removal procedures. Press in bushings at small increments. Press bushings in control arm so that distance between the ends of the bushings is 7.48±.019" (189.9±.48 mm). The distance from end of bushing to the inner edge of control arm must be the same on both sides ±.197" (5.00 mm). *See Fig. 6.*

Fig. 6: Lower Control Arm Bushing Installation

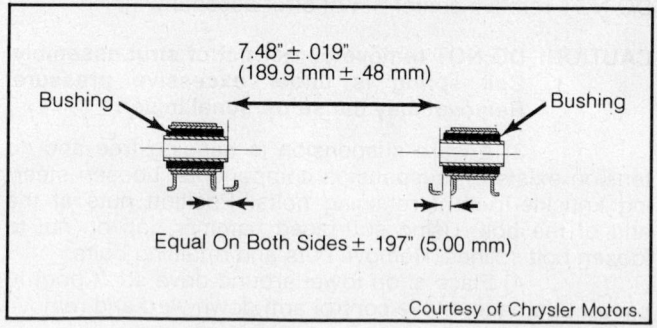

7.48"±.019"
(189.9 mm ±.48 mm)

Bushing   Bushing

Equal On Both Sides ±.197" (5.00 mm)

Courtesy of Chrysler Motors.

Front Suspension

EAGLE PREMIER (Cont.)

STABILIZER BAR

Removal

1) With vehicle at normal operating height, remove stabilizer bar-to-frame bolts and brackets. Remove stabilizer bar-to-control arm bracket retaining nuts. Remove bracket assembly.

2) Install nut back on bolts after bracket removal. The stabilizer bar mounting bracket bolts secure the lower ball joint to the control arm. This is done to prevent ball joint movement. Remove stabilizer bar.

Installation

Reverse removal procedures. Tighten ball joint and stabilizer bar retaining bolts to specification with vehicle at normal operating height.

TIGHTENING SPECIFICATIONS

Application	Ft. Lbs. (N.m)
Ball Joint-To-Knuckle Bolt	77 (104)
Bearing-To-Steering Knuckle Bolt	11 (15)
Control Arm Mount Bolt	[1] 103 (140)
Drive Axle Nut	181 (245)
Stabilizer Bar & Ball Joint Bolt	[1] 60 (81)
Stabilizer Bar-To-Frame Bolt	29 (39)
Strut Cap Nut	73 (99)
Strut Shaft Nut	52 (71)
Strut-To-Knuckle Nut	123 (167)
Tie Rod End Nut	35 (47)
Upper Strut Mount Bolt	17 (23)

[1] – Tighten with vehicle at normal operating height.

Front Suspension

FORD MOTOR CO. FWD MODELS

Escort, EXP, Sable, Taurus, Tempo, Topaz

NOTE: For information on Continental FWD, see FORD MOTOR CO. AIR SUSPENSION – CONTINENTAL article.

DESCRIPTION

The FWD front suspension is a MacPherson strut type with cast steering knuckles. Shock absorber strut assembly includes a rubber isolated top mount. *See Figs. 1 and 2.* The top of the strut assembly is bolted to the body side apron, with the bottom attached to the steering knuckle.

Fig. 1: Exploded View of Ford Motor Co. FWD MacPherson Strut Suspension (Sable & Taurus)

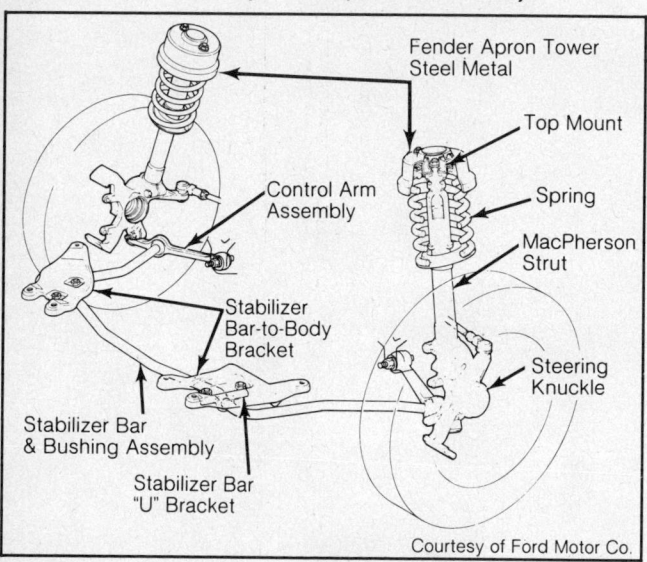

Courtesy of Ford Motor Co.

Fig. 2: Exploded View of Ford Motor Co. FWD MacPherson Strut Suspension (All Others)

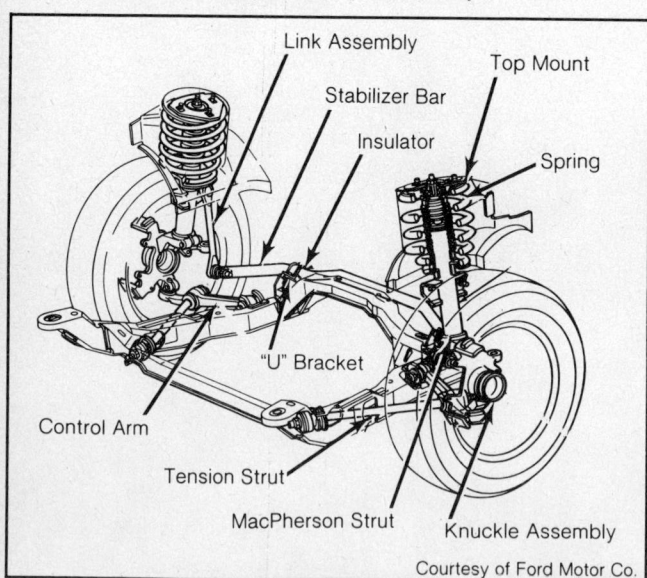

Courtesy of Ford Motor Co.

A pinch joint is designed into knuckle to retain ball joint stud. A forged control arm (lower) is attached to underbody side apron and steering knuckle. On Escort, EXP, Tempo and Topaz models, a stabilizer bar is connected to both control arms and secured to the crossmember. Taurus and Sable models feature tension struts connecting lower control arms to the subframe. A stabilizer bar is connected to the MacPherson struts by stabilizer links attached near the coil spring seats.

ADJUSTMENTS

CASTER & CAMBER

See appropriate article in WHEEL ALIGNMENT section.

RIDING HEIGHT

See RIDING HEIGHT SPECIFICATIONS article in WHEEL ALIGNMENT section.

FRONT WHEEL BEARINGS

Bearings are cartridge design and are pre-greased and sealed. They require no periodic maintenance or adjustment. If bearing is disassembled for any reason, it must be replaced as a unit. No individual service seals, rollers or races are available.

BALL JOINT CHECKING

Raise vehicle so that wheels fall to full down position. Grasp tire by top and bottom edge and move wheel assembly in and out. Any movement between lower end of knuckle and control arm indicates abnormal ball joint wear and requires replacement of lower control arm assembly.

CAUTION: When hoisting FWD vehicles, ensure hoist adapters are positioned properly. See appropriate JACKING & HOISTING article in WHEEL ALIGNMENT section.

REMOVAL & INSTALLATION

BALL JOINTS

Ball joints are not replaceable. Replace lower control arm and ball joints as an assembly.

STABILIZER BAR & INSULATORS

NOTE: When installing insulator bushings on stabilizer bar and in control arms, use only vegetable oil. Any mineral or petroleum based oil or brake fluid will deteriorate rubber bushings.

Removal (Except Sable & Taurus)

1) Raise vehicle on frame hoist. Remove stabilizer bar-to-control arm nuts and discard. Remove large dished washers from each control arm.

2) Remove stabilizer bar insulator "U" bracket bolts (discard) and "U" brackets. Remove stabilizer bar assembly. If stabilizer bar insulators are worn, remove by cutting away from bar.

Stabilizer Bar-To-Control Arm Insulator Replacement

1) Remove control arm inner pivot nut and bolt. Pull control arm down from underbody. If stabilizer bar is not already removed, pull control arm away from bar.

FORD MOTOR CO. FWD MODELS (Cont.)

2) Remove stabilizer bar-to-control arm insulator bushing spacer. Using "C" Clamp (T74P-3044-A1) and Adapter (T81P-5493-A), remove old insulator bushing from control arm. *See Fig. 3.*

Fig. 3: Removing Stabilizer Bar-To-Control Arm Insulator

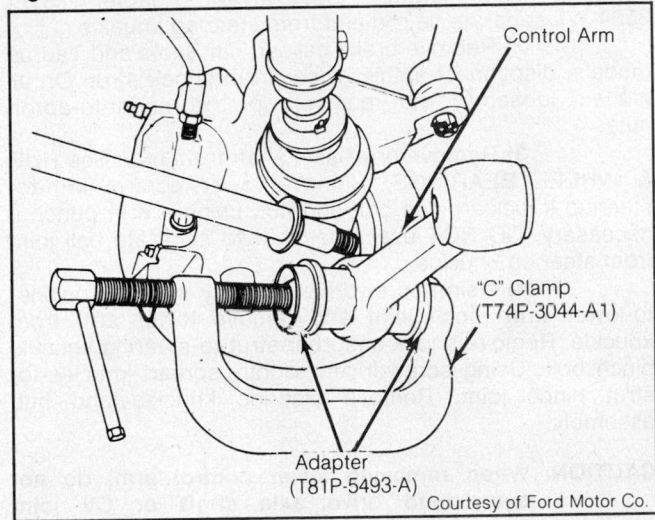

Courtesy of Ford Motor Co.

3) Coat new control arm insulator bushing and bushing bore with vegetable oil. Using "C" clamp and adapter, install bushing in control arm by slowly tightening "C" clamp until bushing pops into place.

Installation

1) Coat new stabilizer bar insulators and stabilizer bar with vegetable oil. Slide insulators onto stabilizer bar and position them in the proper locations. Ensure spacer is in place with washer end seated against machined shoulder of bar.

2) Clean stabilizer bar threads. Using new bolts, attach stabilizer bar and insulator "U" brackets to bracket assemblies. Hand start all 4 "U" bracket bolts. Tighten all bolts down halfway, then tighten to specifications.

3) Position control arm onto stabilizer bar. Ensure washer spacer is in place with washer end seated against bar machined shoulder. Position control arm to underbody.

4) Install new pivot nut and bolt. Install new nut and original dished washer (dished side away from bushing) on stabilizer bar. Lower vehicle.

Removal (Sable & Taurus)

1) Raise and support vehicle. Remove stabilizer bar-to-strut attaching nuts and discard. Remove nuts retaining steering gear to subframe, and move gear off subframe.

2) Place jack stands under subframe. Remove 2 rear subframe mounting bolts. *See Fig. 4.* Remove stabilizer bar "U" bracket bolts and lift out stabilizer bar. Remove insulators from bar and replace.

Installation

1) Clean stabilizer bar insulator mounting area. Lubricate insulators. Position new insulators on bar. Install "U" brackets on insulators. Install stabilizer bar on subframe.

2) Install new bolts on "U" brackets. Raise subframe and install new subframe-to-body attaching bolts. Continue installation in reverse order of removal procedure.

Fig. 4: Removing Stabilizer Bar (Sable & Taurus)

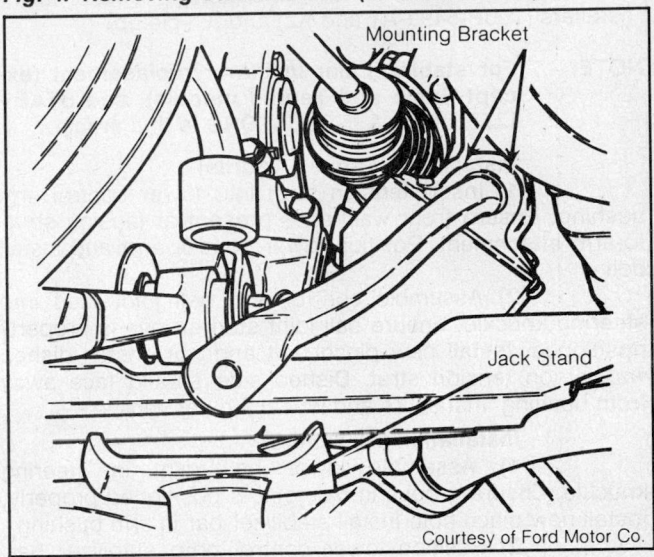

Courtesy of Ford Motor Co.

LOWER CONTROL ARM & BUSHINGS

CAUTION: When removing lower control arm, do not overextend drive axle shaft or CV joint components may separate.

Removal

1) Place ignition switch in the "unlocked" position. Raise and support vehicle. Remove wheels. On Taurus and Sable models, remove nut from tension strut. Pull off dished washer.

2) On all others, remove stabilizer bar-to-control arm nut and dished washer. Remove control arm inner pivot bushing nut and bolt. On all models, remove lower control arm ball joint pinch bolt. Do not damage seal bolt seal (if equipped).

3) Using screwdriver, slightly spread knuckle pinch joint and separate control arm from steering knuckle. A drift punch may be used to remove pinch bolt.

4) On Taurus and Sable, remove and discard lower control arm inner pivot bolt and nut. On all others, remove stabilizer bar bushing from arm bushing. On all models, remove lower control arm.

NOTE: The lower control arm inner pivot bushing can be replaced in the vehicle without removing arm from knuckle.

Lower Control Arm Inner Pivot Bushing Replacement

1) Using a sharp knife, cut away retaining lip of bushing before removal. Press bushing from control arm using "C" Clamp (T74P-3044-A1), Adapters (T86P-5493-A3 and T86P-5493-A2) on Sable and Taurus or Replacer (T81P-5493-B) on all others.

2) On all models, saturate new pivot bushing with vegetable oil (or equivalent) before installation. Using "C" clamp and adapter or replacer, install pivot bushing into control arm.

Tension Strut Insulator (Sable & Taurus)

Using Remover (T86P-5493-A5) and "C" Clamp (T74P-3044-A1), remove insulator. Apply vegetable oil to

Front Suspension

FORD MOTOR CO. FWD MODELS (Cont.)

new insulator before installation. Install insulator using Installers (T86P-5493-A1 and A2) and "C" clamp.

NOTE: For stabilizer bar insulator replacement (except Sable and Taurus models), see STABILIZER BAR & INSULATORS in this article.

Installation (Sable & Taurus)

1) Insert tension strut into lower control arm bushing. Ensure front washer is present at tension strut-to-arm attachment. Position lower control arm and install bolt.

2) Assemble control arm ball joint stud into steering knuckle. Ensure ball joint stud groove is properly positioned. Install new pinch bolt and nut. Install dished washer on tension strut. Dished side should face away from bushing. Install tire and wheel. Lower vehicle.

Installation (All Others)

1) Assemble lower ball joint in steering knuckle. Ensure groove in ball joint is positioned properly. Install new pinch bolt. Install stabilizer bar in arm bushing.

2) Position lower control onto stabilizer bar. Position lower control arm into inner underbody. Install stabilizer bar, dished washer and nut.

STABILIZER BAR-TO-CROSSMEMBER BRACKETS (EXCEPT SABLE & TAURUS)

Removal (Right-Hand Side)

Raise vehicle on frame hoist. Remove 2 bolts retaining stabilizer bar "U" brackets to front crossmember bracket assembly. Remove 3 bolts retaining bracket assembly to body. Remove bracket assembly from vehicle.

Installation

Install new bracket assembly using new bolts and nuts. Hand start all 3 long bolts. Starting with rear bolt first, tighten mounting bolts to specifications. Install stabilizer bar and "U" brackets to bracket assembly, using 2 new bolts. Tighten all bolts halfway, before tightening to specifications.

Removal (Left-Hand Side)

1) Raise vehicle on frame hoist. Remove the 2 stabilizer bar "U" bracket-to-front crossmember bracket bolts. With a block of wood as a cushion, place jack under transmission pan to support the weight of engine and transmission.

2) Remove nut and washer assembly retaining engine mount to bracket assembly. Remove 3 bolts retaining bracket assembly to body. Remove bracket assembly from vehicle.

Installation

1) Install new bracket assembly using new bolts and nuts. Hand start 3 long bolts. Starting with rear bolt, tighten bolts to specifications. Lower jack supporting engine and transmission.

NOTE: When lowering jack, ensure stud and locating tab on engine mount are in index slots on bracket assembly.

2) Tighten engine mount nut and washer assembly to specifications. Remove jack. Install stabilizer bar and "U" brackets into bracket assembly. Tighten bolts halfway, before tightening to specifications. Lower vehicle.

STEERING KNUCKLE

Removal

1) Turn ignition off, leaving switch in "unlocked" position. Raise vehicle on frame hoist. Remove wheel. Remove cotter pin and slotted nut from tie rod end stud. Using Tie Rod Remover (3290-C) and Adapter (T81P-3504-W), separate tie rod end from steering knuckle.

2) Remove brake caliper. On Sable and Taurus models, disconnect stabilizer bar from shock strut. On all models, loosen (do not remove) top strut mount-to-apron nuts.

3) Remove drive axle shaft from hub. See HUB & WHEEL BEARINGS. Remove lower control arm-to-steering knuckle pinch bolt and nut, using a drift punch if necessary. DO NOT use a hammer to separate ball joint from steering knuckle.

4) Using screwdriver, slightly spread knuckle-to-lower arm pinch joint and remove lower arm from knuckle. Remove shock absorber strut-to-steering knuckle pinch bolt. Using screwdriver, slightly spread knuckle-to-strut pinch joint. Remove steering knuckle and hub assembly.

CAUTION: When removing lower control arm, do not overextend drive axle shaft or CV joint components may separate.

Installation

To install, reverse removal procedure. Use new strut-to-knuckle pinch bolt, hub nut, tie rod end nut, and control arm-to-steering knuckle nut and bolt. Ensure ball stud groove is properly positioned.

HUB & WHEEL BEARINGS

Removal

1) Remove wheel cover. Remove hub retainer nut and washer by applying sufficient torque to break locking tabs. On Sable and Taurus models, retainer nut is crimped. On all models, discard nut. Raise vehicle on frame hoist. Remove front wheel.

2) Loosen brake caliper locating pins and rotate caliper off rotor. Do not remove caliper pins from caliper assembly. Lift caliper from rotor and hang with wire.

3) Pull rotor from hub. If difficult to remove, apply rust penetrant, and use a 3-jaw puller on rotor O.D. while pushing on hub center.

NOTE: If excessive force was needed for removal, check rotor for excessive lateral runout before installation and replace as necessary.

4) Disconnect the lower control arm and the tie rod from knuckle, but leave strut attached. Loosen top strut mount-to-apron nuts. Install Hub Remover/Installer (T81P-1104-C). Use Adapters (T83P-1104-BH1 and T86P-1104-A1) on Sable and Taurus models. Use Adapters (T81P-1104-A and T81P-1104-BH) on all other models. See Fig. 5.

5) Remove hub, bearing and knuckle assembly by pushing out CV joint outer shaft until it is free of assembly. Wire drive axle shaft to body to maintain level position. Support knuckle with wire. Remove strut bolt and slide hub and knuckle assembly off strut.

6) Remove support wire and place front hub and knuckle assembly on bench. Use Front Hub Puller

FORD MOTOR CO. FWD MODELS (Cont.)

Fig. 5: *Removing Drive Axle Shaft From Hub*

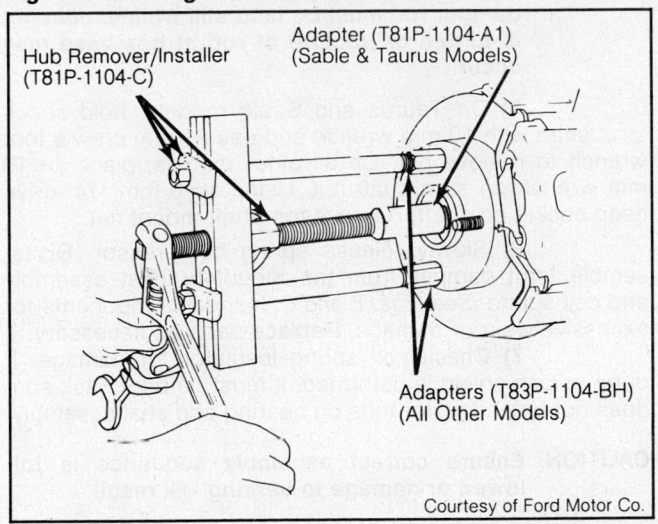

Courtesy of Ford Motor Co.

(D80L-1002-L) and Shaft Protector (D80L-625-1) to remove hub. *See Fig. 6.*

Fig. 6: *Removing Hub From Steering Knuckle*

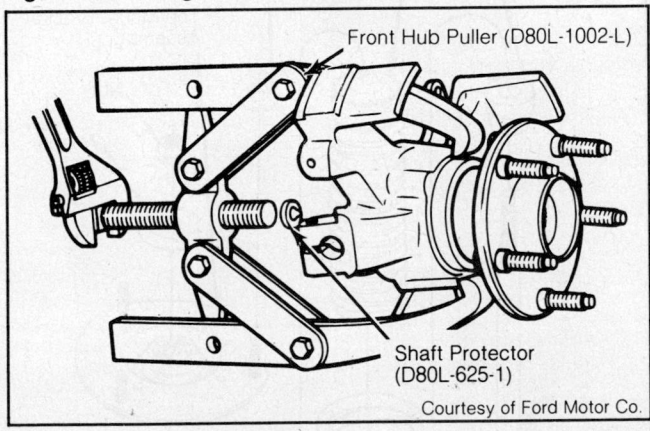

Courtesy of Ford Motor Co.

7) Remove and discard bearing snap ring from knuckle. Use Spacer (T86P-1104-A2) and Bearing Remover (T83P-1104-AH2) on Sable and Taurus models to press bearing out of knuckle. On all other models, use Bearing Remover (T83P-1104-AH2) and Spacer (T83P-1104-AH3). On all models, discard hub bearing. *See Fig. 7.*

Installation

1) Clean knuckle bearing bore and hub bearing journal. If hub bearing journal is scored or damaged, replace hub. Do not attempt to service hub. Place spacer, step side down, on press plate.

2) Position knuckle (outboard side down) on spacer. Position new bearing in bore on inboard side of knuckle. On Sable and Taurus models, place Spacer (T86P-1104-A2) in outboard side. On all others, use Spacer (T83P-1104-AH3). On Sable and Taurus, use Bearing Installer (T86P-1104-A3) to press bearing into knuckle. Use Bearing Installer (T83T-1104-AH1) on all other models. Press on outer race of bearing.

3) Ensure bearing seats against knuckle bore shoulder. Install new snap ring in knuckle groove. Place spacer on press plate with step side up. Position hub on spacer with studs facing down.

Fig. 7: *Pressing Cartridge Bearing Assembly From Steering Knuckle Bore*

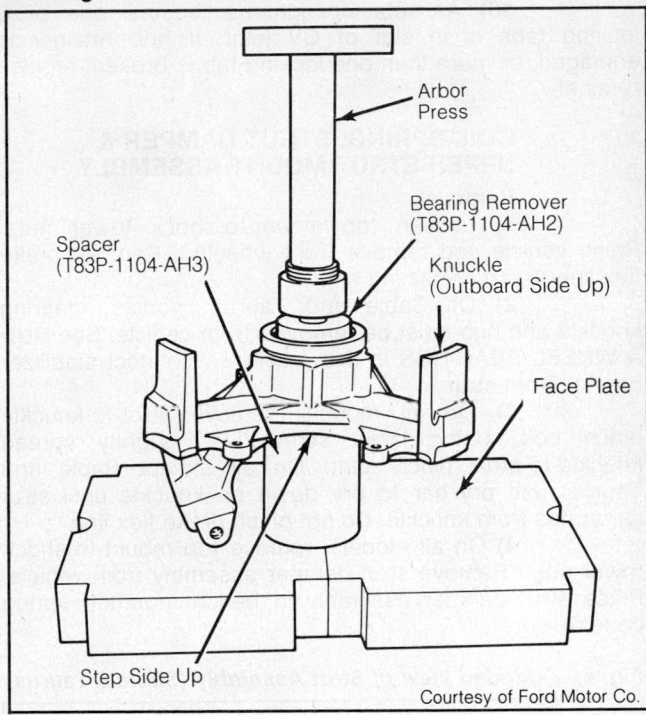

Courtesy of Ford Motor Co.

4) Position knuckle assembly (outboard side down) on hub barrel. On all except Sable and Taurus, place Bearing Installer (T83T-1104-AH1) on inner bearing race. Use Bearing Remover (T83P-1104-AH2) on Sable and Taurus models. On all models, press down on tool until bearing is fully seated onto hub. Ensure hub rotates freely in knuckle.

5) If removed, install new seal on outboard CV joint. Ensure seal flange faces outboard (toward bearing). Suspend hub and knuckle assembly on vehicle with wire. Attach strut assembly loosely to knuckle. Lubricate CV joint stub shaft splines with engine oil.

6) Insert shaft into hub splines, as far as possible, using hand pressure only. Check splines for proper engagement. Install brake rotor on hub. Using hub remover/installer and adapter tools, press hub and stub shaft together.

CAUTION: Do not use new hub retainer nut to draw drive axle shaft into hub.

7) Tighten hub installer tool to 120 ft. lbs. (163 N.m) to ensure hub is fully seated. Remove hub installer tool and adapters. Install washer with new retainer nut, and tighten finger tight.

8) Install front suspension components. Install brake caliper. Ensure outer brake shoe spring hook is seated under upper arm of knuckle. Install wheel. Lower vehicle and block wheels. Tighten wheel lug nuts. On Sable and Taurus, tighten hub nut.

CAUTION: Do not use impact wrench to tighten hub retainer nut. Do not move vehicle until hub nut is tightened and staked.

9) On all except Sable and Taurus models, use a 1 3/16" (30 mm) socket to tighten hub nut. During

Front Suspension

FORD MOTOR CO. FWD MODELS (Cont.)

installation, an audible click sound will indicate proper ratchet function of retainer.

10) As retainer tightens, ensure one of 3 locking tabs is in slot of CV joint. If hub retainer is damaged, or more than one locking tab is broken, replace retainer.

COIL SPRING, STRUT DAMPER & UPPER STRUT MOUNT ASSEMBLY

Removal

1) Loosen top mount-to-shock tower nuts. Raise vehicle and remove front wheel(s). Remove brake flex line-to-strut retaining bolt.

2) On Sable and Taurus models, steering knuckle and hub must be removed from vehicle. See HUB & WHEEL BEARINGS in this article. Disconnect stabilizer bar link from strut.

3) On all models, remove strut-to-knuckle pinch bolt. Using large screwdriver, slightly spread knuckle-to-strut pinch joint. On all except Sable and Taurus, use pry bar to pry down on knuckle until strut separates from knuckle. Do not pinch brake flex line.

4) On all models, remove top mount-to-shock tower nuts. Remove strut damper assembly from vehicle. Place strut damper assembly in bench mounted spring compressor.

CAUTION: On Taurus and Sable models shock strut damper rod must be held still while mount nut is turned or fracture of rod at hex base may occur.

5) On Taurus and Sable models, hold shock strut shaft with 10 mm wrench and use 21 mm crow's foot wrench to remove nut. On all other models, place an 18 mm wrench on strut shaft nut. Using an 8 mm 1/4" drive deep socket on shaft. Remove top shaft mount nut.

6) Slowly release spring compressor. Disassemble strut damper from top mount bracket assembly and coil spring. See Figs. 8 and 9. Inspect components for excessive wear or damage. Replace parts as necessary.

7) Check coil spring insulator for damage. If outer splash shield is deformed, it must be bent back so it does not touch locator tabs on bearing and seal assembly.

CAUTION: Ensure correct assembly sequence is followed or damage to bearing will result.

Fig. 8: Exploded View of Strut Assembly (Sable & Taurus)

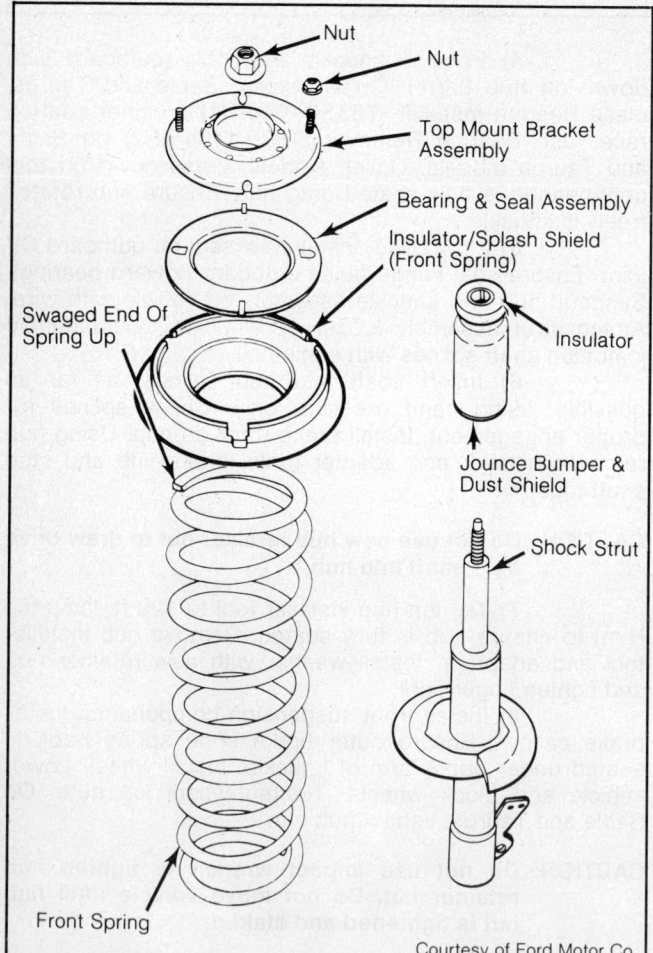

Courtesy of Ford Motor Co.

Fig. 9: Exploded View of Strut Assembly (All Others)

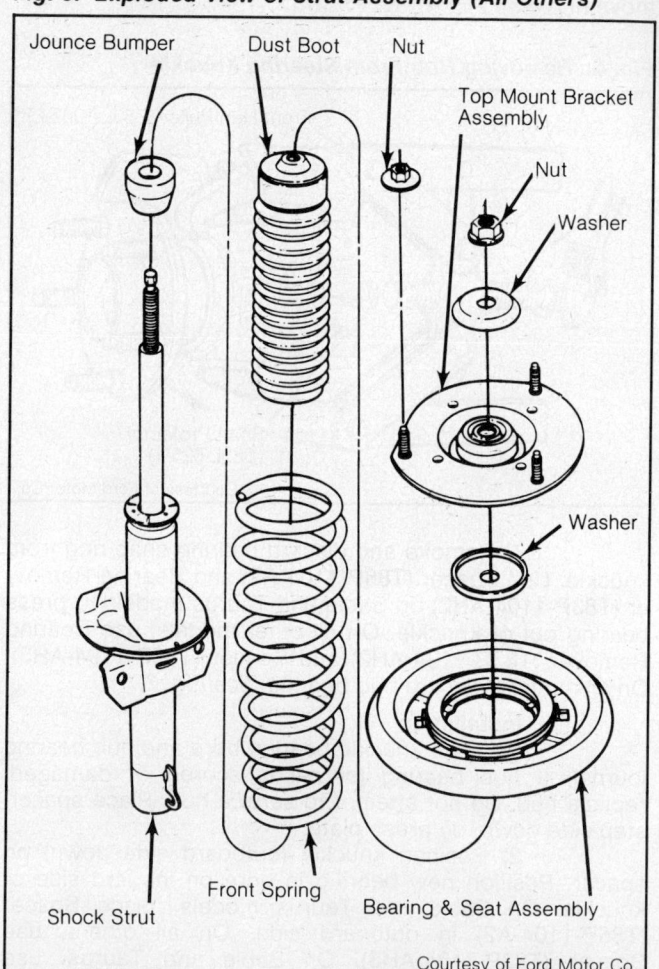

Courtesy of Ford Motor Co.

Installation

To complete installation, reverse removal procedures. When installing coil spring, ensure swaged end of spring is up and pigtail of spring is indexed in spring seat.

FORD MOTOR CO. FWD MODELS (Cont.)

TIGHTENING SPECIFICATIONS

Application	Ft. Lbs. (N.m)
Left-Hand Engine Mount-to-Crossmember Bracket Bolt	
Except Sable & Taurus	[1] 75-88 (102-119)
Hub Retainer Nut	180-200 (244-270)
Lower Control Arm-to-Body	
Inner Pivot Bushing Bolt	
Sable & Taurus	70-95 (95-129)
All Others	48-55 (65-75)
Lower Control Arm-to-Steering Knuckle Bolts	
Sable & Taurus	40-55 (54-75)
All Others	38-45 (52-61)
Stabilizer Bar (Except Sable & Taurus)	
Bushing-to-Control Arm Nut	98-115 (133-156)
Bracket-to-Crossmember Bracket Bolt	
Tempo & Topaz (Exc. GT)	59-68 (80-92)
GT & All Others	85-100 (115-135)
Crossmember Bracket-to-Body Bolt	47-55 (64-75)
Stabilizer Bar (Sable & Taurus)	
"U" Bracket Bolts	21-32 (28-44)
Link Nuts	35-48 (48-65)
Strut Damper	
Shaft-to-Top Mount Nut	35-50 (48-68)
Strut-to-Knuckle Pinch Bolt	70-95 (95-129)
Top Mount-to-Apron Nut	25-30 (34-41)
Subframe-to-Body Bolts	
Sable & Taurus	85-100 (115-136)
Tension Strut-to-Control Arm Nut	
Sable & Taurus	70-95 (95-129)
Tie Rod End-to-Steering Knuckle Nut	
Sable & Taurus	23-25 (31-34)
All Others	28-32 (37-44)
Wheel Lug Nut	80-105 (109-143)

[1] – Specification is for left front engine mount onto stabilizer bar crossmember bracket-to-body bolts.

Front Suspension

FORD MOTOR CO. ENCLOSED SPRING

Crown Victoria, Grand Marquis, Town Car

DESCRIPTION

Front suspension system is of the coil spring type. The coil springs are located between lower control arms and upper frame or front-end sheet metal. Upper or lower ball joints and lower control arm pivot bushings must be replaced with control arm as an assembly. Upper pivot bushings may be replaced individually. Side roll is controlled by stabilizer bar. Stabilizer bar ends are connected to lower control arms. Bar is mounted in rubber bushings held to frame side rails by clamps.

Fig. 1: Exploded Views of Ford Enclosed Spring Type Front Suspension Assembly

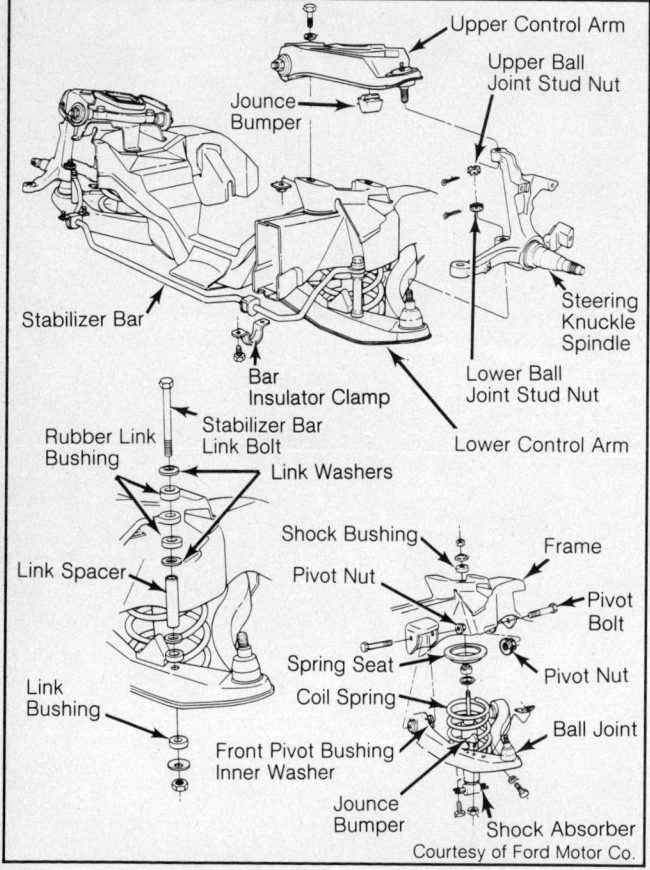

Courtesy of Ford Motor Co.

ADJUSTMENTS

CAMBER, CASTER & TOE-IN

See appropriate article in WHEEL ALIGNMENT section.

RIDING HEIGHT

See RIDING HEIGHT SPECIFICATIONS article in WHEEL ALIGNMENT section.

FRONT WHEEL BEARINGS

1) Raise vehicle. Remove grease cap from hub. Remove cotter pin and nut lock. Loosen adjusting nut 3 turns. Rock wheel assembly in and out to push brake pad away from rotor.

2) While rotating wheel, tighten adjusting nut to 17-25 ft. lbs. (23-34 N.m). Loosen nut 1/2 turn, then tighten to 10-12 INCH lbs. (1.1-1.7 N.m). Place nut lock on nut.

3) Ensure nut lock castellation aligns with hole in spindle. Install new cotter pin. Check for free wheel rotation. Install grease cap. Lower vehicle. Pump brake pedal before driving to restore normal pedal travel.

BALL JOINT CHECKING

Lower Ball Joint

1) With wheel bearings adjusted, support vehicle in normal driving position (ball joints loaded). Wipe grease fittings and checking surfaces clean. *See Fig. 2.*

2) Checking surface should project outside ball joint cover. If surface is inside cover, replace lower control arm assembly. *See Fig. 2.*

Fig. 2: Checking Lower Ball Joint For Worn Condition

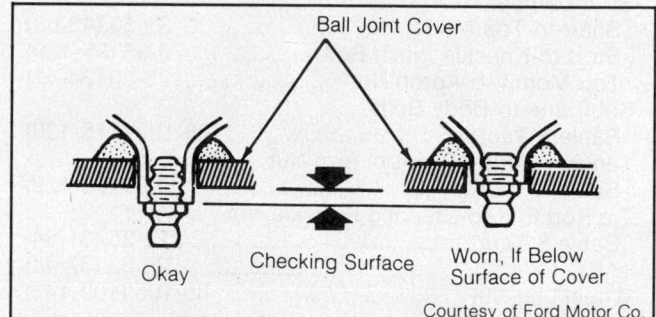

Courtesy of Ford Motor Co.

Upper Ball Joint

1) Ensure wheel bearings are adjusted and lower ball joints properly checked. Raise vehicle. Place floor jacks beneath lower control arms. Hold lower edge of tire and move wheel in and out.

2) While moving wheel, check for play between steering knuckle upper end and upper control arm. Movement indicates ball joint wear. Install new upper control arm assembly.

REMOVAL & INSTALLATION

UPPER & LOWER BALL JOINTS

Replace upper or lower ball joint with control arm as an assembly only. Do not install ball joint or other components in used control arm. See CONTROL ARM procedures in this article.

CAUTION: Gas-charged shock absorbers will extend unassisted during removal. Do not apply heat or flame to shock tube.

SHOCK ABSORBER

Removal

Remove nut, washer and bushing from shock absorber shaft upper end. Raise vehicle on hoist. Support

FORD MOTOR CO. ENCLOSED SPRING (Cont.)

with safety stands. Remove 2 self-tapping screws attaching shock to lower control arm. Remove shock.

Installation

1) Place washer and new rubber bushing on shock top stud. Position unit inside spring. Install 2 self-tapping screws and tighten to specifications.

2) Remove safety stands. Lower vehicle. Place new bushing and washer on top stud. Install and tighten nut to specifications.

NOTE: If threads in lower control arm become stripped or damaged, install new 5/16" x 18 lock nuts on lower shock mount screws.

STABILIZER BAR, LINK BUSHINGS & INSULATORS

Removal

1) Raise vehicle. Place jack stands under lower control arms. Remove nut, washer and insulator from each stabilizer bar link bolt. Remove remaining bolts, washers, insulators and spacers. Note locations for reassembly reference.

2) Detach stabilizer bar insulator clamp bolts. Remove clamps and bar assembly. Inspect rubber link bushings and bar insulators for wear, damage and/or deterioration.

3) If replacement is needed, install new stabilizer bar link bushing kit. If insulators need replacement, cut worn insulators from bar.

Installation

1) Assemble new cup washer and bushing on bolt. Insert bolt through stabilizer bar end (from top). Install new bushings, washers and spacer on link bolt. Install bolt through lower control arm. Install new bushing and cup washer. Install nut.

2) Coat inside of new rubber insulators with rubber lubricant. Slide insulators on stabilizer bar. Using new bolts, clamp bar to frame brackets. Remove supports. Lower vehicle.

COIL SPRING

CAUTION: Restraining devices for coil spring(s), are recommended for all coil spring related procedures.

Removal

1) Raise vehicle on hoist. Remove front wheel. Disconnect stabilizer bar link bolt from lower control arm. Remove shock absorber-to-lower control arm mounting screws.

2) Detach upper nut, washer and bushing and remove shock. Using separator, detach steering center link from pitman arm. Support vehicle with stands under jack pads. Lower hoist (but maintain working room).

3) Using a Spring Compressor (D78P-5310-A), tighten forcing nut until spring is compressed and is free in seat. Remove 2 lower control arm pivot bolts, nuts and washer. Detach lower arm from crossmember. Remove spring. *See Fig. 3.*

4) If installing new spring, note position of upper and lower spring ends to be sure correct installation is made. Loosen forcing nut to relieve spring tension. Remove compressor (if necessary).

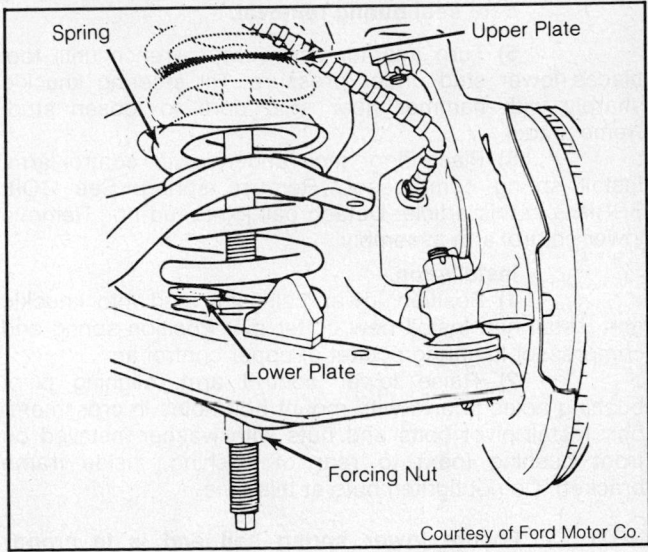

Fig. 3: Removing Coil Spring With Spring Compressor (D78P-5310-A)

Spring — Upper Plate — Lower Plate — Forcing Nut

Courtesy of Ford Motor Co.

Installation

To install coil spring, reverse removal procedures. Before compressing spring, ensure coil spring end is positioned properly. *See Fig. 4.* When installing lower front pivot bolt, ensure washer is placed on inside of front pivot bushing, next to rear of bushing, inside frame bracket.

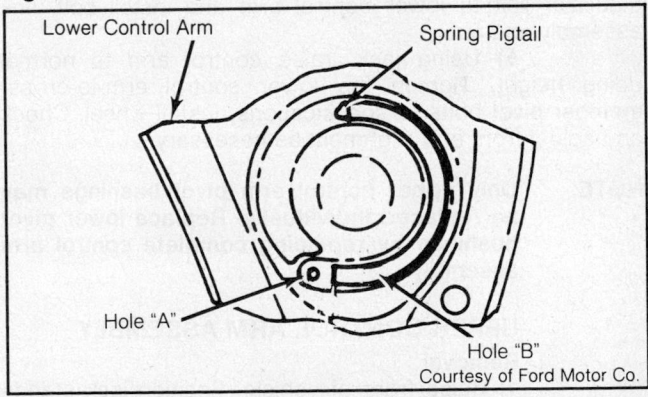

Fig. 4: Positioning Coil Spring on Lower Control Arm

Lower Control Arm — Spring Pigtail — Hole "A" — Hole "B"

Courtesy of Ford Motor Co.

End of spring must cover hole "B" but not cover hole "A".

LOWER CONTROL ARM ASSEMBLY

Removal

1) Raise vehicle. Place jack stands under both sides of frame, just behind lower control arms. Remove front wheel. Remove brake caliper, rotor and dust shield.

2) Remove jounce bumper and shock. Detach stabilizer bar link from lower arm. Using separator, pull steering center link off pitman arm.

3) Remove cotter pin from lower ball joint stud nut. Loosen stud nut one or 2 turns but do not remove at this time. Install Ball Joint Press (T57P-3006-B) between upper and lower joint studs (adapter screw on bottom).

4) Ensure ball joint press is firmly seated against both stud ends and not against stud nuts or upper stud cotter pin.

Front Suspension

FORD MOTOR CO. ENCLOSED SPRING (Cont.)

CAUTION: Do not loosen stud from steering knuckle with tool pressure only or damage ball joint boot seal during removal.

5) Turn adapter screw with wrench until tool places lower stud under pressure. Hit steering knuckle sharply with hammer near stud bore to loosen stud. Remove tool.

6) Place floor jack under lower control arm. Install spring compressor. Remove spring. See COIL SPRING in this article. Detach ball joint stud nut. Remove lower control arm assembly.

Installation

1) Position lower ball joint stud into knuckle and install nut. Install new cotter pin. Position spring and compressor in spring pocket of upper control arm.

2) Raise lower control arm, aligning pivot bushing holes in arm with mount bolt holes in crossmember. Install pivot bolts and nuts with washer installed on front bushing (next to rear of bushing, inside frame bracket). Do not tighten nuts at this time.

NOTE: Ensure lower spring coil end is in proper position on seat of lower control arm, between the 2 holes. See Fig. 4.

3) Remove spring compressor. Connect steering center link at pitman arm. Loosely install nut. Place idler arm and front wheels straight ahead to maintain front end alignment and prevent bushing damage.

4) Install center link-to-pitman arm nut. Install new cotter pin. Install shock absorber. Install jounce bumper. Install dust shield, rotor and caliper. Position stabilizer link to lower control arm and install bolt, link assembly and nut.

5) Using jack, raise control arm to normal riding height. Tighten the lower control arm-to-crossmember pivot bolts to specifications. Install wheel. Check and adjust front end alignment as necessary.

NOTE: Only upper control arm pivot bushings may be replaced individually. Replace lower pivot bushings by replacing complete control arm assembly.

UPPER CONTROL ARM ASSEMBLY

Removal

1) Raise front of vehicle. Position jack stands under both sides of frame, just behind lower control arms. Remove wheel. Remove upper ball joint stud cotter pin. Loosen stud nut one or 2 turns. Do not remove nut from stud at this time.

2) Install Ball Joint Press (T57P-3006-B) between upper and lower ball joint studs (adapter screw on top). Press must be firmly seated against both stud ends and not against stud nuts or lower stud cotter pin. Do not loosen stud from knuckle using tool pressure only.

3) Turn adapter screw with wrench until upper stud is under pressure. Using hammer, hit steering knuckle sharply near upper stud bore to loosen stud. Remove tool.

4) Place jack under lower control arm to support lower arm and spring assembly. Once upper arm is removed, damage to shock will be prevented. Remove upper control arm pivot bolts and ball joint stud nut. Remove upper arm assembly. If upper control arm is replaced, transfer jounce bumper from old arm.

Upper Control Arm

Pivot Bushing Replacement

1) With upper control arm removed, detach nuts and washers from ends of inner shaft. Use "C" Clamp (T74P-3044-A1) and Pivot Bushing Remover Adapters (T79P-3044-A2 and T75P-3044-A1) to remove bushings. Repeat procedure for other side.

NOTE: Front pivot bushing has larger diameter than rear.

2) Position shaft and new bushings in upper control arm. Ensure inner washer is installed on shaft (rear bushing only). Using "C" clamp and adapters, press bushings into upper control arm. Position inner shaft so serrated side contacts frame. See Fig. 5.

Fig. 5: Installing Upper Control Arm Inner Shaft

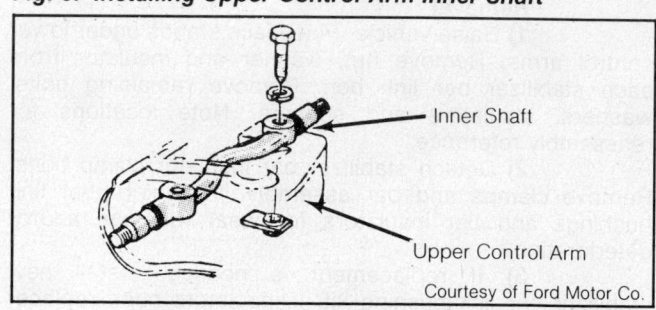

Inner Shaft

Upper Control Arm

Courtesy of Ford Motor Co.

3) Install 2 outer washers, with new nuts, on each end of inner shaft. Tighten nuts to specifications.

Installation

Position upper control arm assembly, on new shaft, to frame bracket. Install 2 attaching bolts and washers. Connect upper ball joint stud to knuckle. Install nut. Install new cotter pin and front wheel. Remove stands. Lower vehicle. Check and adjust front end alignment as necessary.

STEERING KNUCKLE

Removal

1) Raise vehicle. Place safety stands under both sides of frame, just behind lower arm. Remove wheel. Remove brake caliper, rotor and dust shield. Detach tie rod end from knuckle arm.

2) Remove cotter pins from both ball joint stud nuts. Loosen nuts one or 2 turns (do not remove nuts at this time). Position ball joint remover between upper and lower joint studs. Seat tool firmly on joint studs, not on stud nuts.

CAUTION: Restraining devices for coil spring(s), are recommended for all coil spring related procedures.

3) Turn tool with wrench until studs are under pressure. Using hammer, hit knuckle near stud bore to break joint stud loose. Do not loosen studs using tool pressure only. Position jack under lower arm, at lower ball joint area. Remove upper and lower ball joint stud nuts. Lower jack carefully. Remove knuckle.

Installation

To install, reverse removal procedure. Check and adjust front end alignment as necessary.

Front Suspension

FORD MOTOR CO. ENCLOSED SPRING (Cont.)

WHEEL BEARINGS

Removal

1) Raise and support vehicle. Remove front wheel. Remove caliper from knuckle and wire out of way. Remove grease cap from hub. Remove cotter pin, nut lock, adjusting nut and flat washer from spindle.

2) Remove outer bearing assembly. Pull hub and rotor off spindle. Remove seal. Remove inner bearing from hub.

3) Clean hub and bearings in solvent. Blow dry with compressed air. Do not spin bearings. Inspect bearings and races for scratches, pits, excessive wear or other damage. Replace worn bearings and races in matched sets.

4) If bearing race removal is necessary, pull races from rotor hub using bearing race remover and race puller.

Installation

1) Install inner or outer bearing race (if removed). Pack bearings with grease. Place inner bearing assembly into inner race. Apply grease to seal lips. Install seal.

2) Install hub and rotor assembly on knuckle spindle. Install outer bearing assembly and flat washer on spindle. Install nut. Adjust wheel bearings. Install caliper. Install wheel. Lower vehicle.

TIGHTENING SPECIFICATIONS

Application	Ft. Lbs. (N.m)
Ball Joint-to-Steering Knuckle	
Upper Mount Nut	60-90 (82-122)
Lower Mount Nut	80-120 (109-163)
Brake Dust Shield Bolt	10-15 (13-15)
Caliper Bolts	40-60 (54-82)
Center Link-to-Pitman Arm Nut	43-47 (58-64)
Jounce Bumper Nut	30-35 (40-48)
Lower Control Arm-to-Crossmember	
Pivot Bolt	100-140 (136-190)
Stabilizer Bar-to-Lower Control Arm	
Link Bolt/Nut	9-12 (12-16)
Stabilizer Bar-to-Frame Bracket	
Insulator Clamp Bolt	14-26 (19-35)
Shock Absorber	
Mount Screw [1]	12-18 (16-24)
Upper Mount Nut	22-30 (30-40)
Tie Rod Clamp Bolts	20-22 (27-30)
Upper Control Arm-to-Crossmember	
Pivot Bolt/Nut	100-140 (136-190)
Upper Control Arm	
Inner Shaft Mount Bolt	100-140 (136-190)
Wheel Lug Nut	80-105 (109-142)

[1] – The shock lower mount screws are self-tapping type. If threads in control arm are stripped, use 5/16" x 18 lock nuts on mount screws.

Front Suspension

FORD MOTOR CO. SINGLE ARM

Cougar, Mustang, Thunderbird

DESCRIPTION

Front suspension is a modified MacPherson strut design. The design uses a strut damper with coil spring located between lower control arm and a spring pocket in crossmember. All models use gas-pressurized hydraulic shock struts. A front stabilizer bar is also used. *See Fig. 1.*

The shock struts are non-serviceable and must be replaced as an assembly. The ball joints and lower control arm pivot bushings are not serviced separately and also must be replaced as an assembly.

Fig. 1: Exploded View of Ford Motor Co. Single Arm Front Suspension Assembly

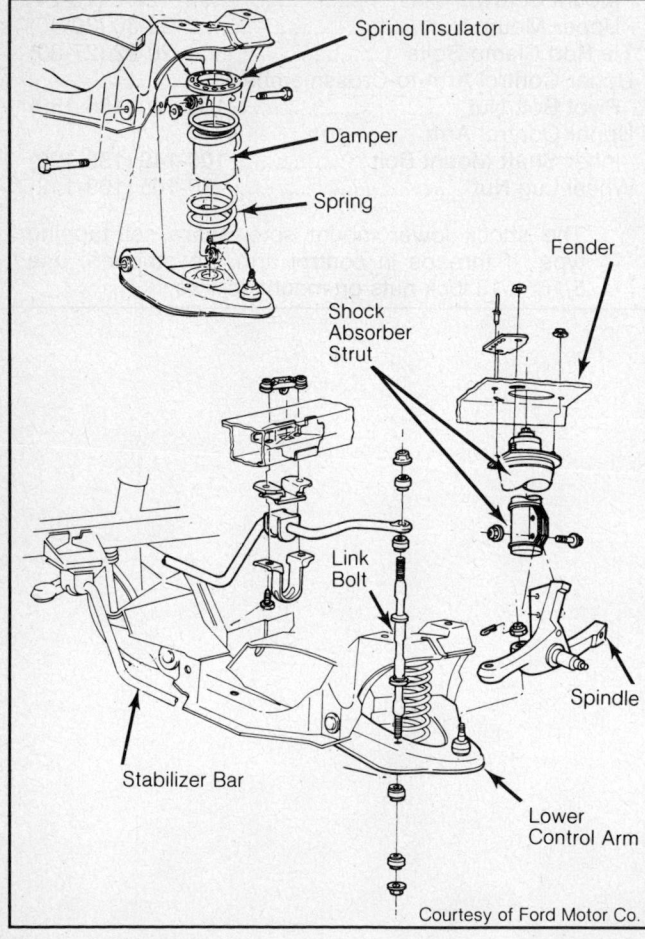

Courtesy of Ford Motor Co.

ADJUSTMENTS

CASTER & CAMBER

See appropriate article in WHEEL ALIGNMENT section.

RIDING HEIGHT

See RIDING HEIGHT SPECIFICATIONS article in WHEEL ALIGNMENT section.

FRONT WHEEL BEARINGS

1) Raise vehicle, and remove wheel cover and grease cap. Remove cotter pin and nut lock. Loosen adjusting nut 3 turns. Rock wheel, hub and rotor assembly in and out several times to push brake pads away from rotor.

2) Tighten adjusting nut to 17-25 ft. lbs. (23-34 N.m) while rotating wheel assembly. Loosen adjusting nut 1/2 turn, then retighten to 10-12 INCH lbs. (1.1-1.7 N.m).

3) Reinstall nut lock on adjusting nut and insert new cotter pin. Install grease cap and wheel cover. Lower vehicle. Before driving vehicle, pump brake pedal to restore normal brake pedal travel.

LOWER BALL JOINT CHECKING

1) Support vehicle in normal driving position with both ball joints loaded. On all models, clean dirt and grease from ball joint cover checking surface. *See Fig. 2.* Ensure checking surface projects beyond ball joint cover surface or ball joint must be replaced.

Fig. 2: Checking Lower Ball Joint Wear Indicator

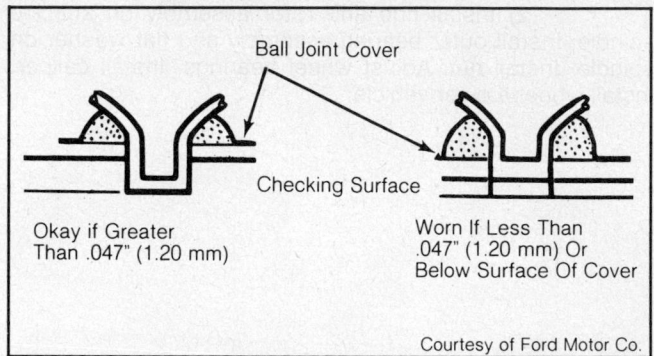

Courtesy of Ford Motor Co.

2) Ball joints are acceptable if wear indicator surface projects .047" (1.20 mm) or more beyond checking surface. Ball joint is worn if less than .047" projects beyond checking surface. Replace lower control arm and ball joint as an assembly.

REMOVAL & INSTALLATION

BALL JOINTS

Ball joints and lower control arm pivot bushings are not serviced separately and must be replaced with lower control arm as an assembly. See LOWER CONTROL ARM.

STABILIZER BAR, BUSHINGS & LINK INSULATORS

Removal

1) Raise and support vehicle on frame hoist. To disconnect stabilizer bar from each stabilizer link, remove nut, washer and rubber insulator from link bolt. If necessary, remove remaining insulators, washers and spacer.

2) Detach stabilizer insulator bushing attaching clamp bolts. Remove bar assembly. Detach adapter brackets from clamps. *See Fig. 1.*

FORD MOTOR CO. SINGLE ARM (Cont.)

3) Inspect stabilizer bar rubber link insulators and bar insulator bushings. Replace all worn or damaged components. If replacement is needed, cut worn insulator bushings from stabilizer bar with a sharp knife.

Installation

1) Lubricate rubber parts of stabilizer bar with rubber lubricant. Slide new insulator bushings onto stabilizer bar. Reinstall adapter brackets on clamps. *See Fig. 1.*

2) Using new nut and bolt, secure each end of stabilizer bar to link insulators on lower control arm. Ensure link insulator components are installed in proper order. *See Fig. 1.*

3) Using new bolts, mount attaching clamps, stabilizer bar and adapter brackets onto frame side rails. Lower vehicle.

COIL SPRING

Removal

1) Raise vehicle on frame hoist so control arms hang free. Remove tire and wheel assembly. Remove brake caliper and wire out of way. Remove tie rod end from steering knuckle arm. Disconnect stabilizer bar link from control arm.

2) If necessary, remove steering gear bolts. Position gear so control arm pivot bolt may be removed. Using Spring Compressor (T82P-5310-A), place tool upper plate into position in spring pocket cavity on crossmember.

NOTE: **When installing spring compressor components, ensure hooks on tool upper plate are facing center of vehicle.**

3) Install compression rod into lower arm spring pocket hole, through coil spring and into upper plate. Install lower plate, lower ball nut, thrust washer, bearing and forcing nut onto compression rod. Tighten forcing nut on tool until drag on nut is felt.

4) Remove control arm-to-crossmember pivot bolts and nuts. The compression tool forcing nut may have to be tightened or loosened for easier bolt removal. Loosen compression rod forcing nut until spring tension is relieved. Remove forcing nut. Remove compression rod, coil spring and spring insulator.

Installation

1) Position spring insulator on top of spring. Position spring into lower control arm spring pocket. Ensure spring end is positioned between 2 holes in lower arm spring pocket. *See Fig. 3.*

Fig. 3: Positioning Spring In Control Arm Spring Pocket

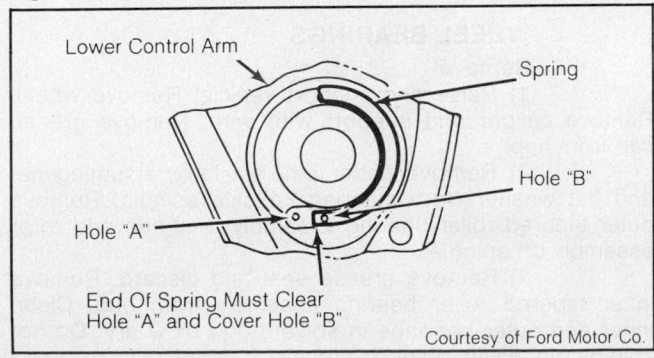

Lower Control Arm

Spring

Hole "B"

Hole "A"

End Of Spring Must Clear Hole "A" and Cover Hole "B"

Courtesy of Ford Motor Co.

2) Position spring into upper spring seat in crossmember. Insert compression rod through control arm and spring, then hook it to upper plate. Ensure upper plate is installed with hooks facing center of vehicle.

3) Install retaining spring compressor components. Tighten forcing nut. Position lower control arm into crossmember. Install new control arm pivot bolts and nuts finger tight. DO NOT tighten bolts and nuts at this time. Remove spring compressor.

4) Using a jack, raise control arm to normal riding height. Tighten control arm pivot bolts to specifications. Remove jack. Install steering gear-to-crossmember bolts and nuts (if removed).

5) Connect stabilizer bar link to control arm and tighten attaching nut. Install tie rod end into steering knuckle. Install new cotter pin. Install brake caliper and wheel. Lower vehicle.

LOWER CONTROL ARM

Removal

1) Raise vehicle on hoist so control arms hang free. Remove wheel. Remove brake caliper and hang out of work area with wire. Remove brake rotor and dust shield. Disconnect tie rod assembly from steering knuckle.

2) Remove steering gear bolts (if necessary) and position gear so that control arm pivot bolt may be removed. Disconnect stabilizer bar link from lower control arm.

3) Remove cotter pin from ball joint stud nut. Loosen ball joint nut one or 2 turns. Do not remove nut at this time. Tap steering knuckle boss sharply to relieve stud pressure. Install Spring Compressor (T82P-5310-A).

4) Tighten forcing nut on spring compressor until drag is felt on nut. Remove ball joint nut. Raise entire strut and steering knuckle assembly. Wire it out of the way to obtain more working room. Remove control arm-to-crossmember pivot bushing nuts and bolts.

5) Spring compressor forcing nut may have to be slightly loosened or tightened for easy bolt removal. Loosen compression rod forcing nut until spring tension is relieved. Remove forcing nut, lower control arm and coil spring.

NOTE: **Manufacturer recommends replacing all nuts and bolts, once removed.**

Installation

1) To install, reverse removal procedure. Ensure spring lower end is positioned between 2 holes in lower arm spring pocket. *See Fig. 3.*

2) Raise lower control arm to normal position before tightening attaching nuts. Tighten ball joint stud nut to specifications. After installation, check front end alignment and adjust if necessary.

STEERING KNUCKLE

Removal

1) Raise vehicle. Support with safety stands placed under both sides (at jacking pads, just behind lower control arms). Remove wheel. Remove brake caliper, rotor and dust shield. Remove stabilizer link from lower control arm.

2) Remove tie rod end from steering knuckle. Remove cotter pin from ball joint stud nut. Loosen nut one

Front Suspension

FORD MOTOR CO. SINGLE ARM (Cont.)

or 2 turns. Do not remove nut at this time. Tap steering knuckle sharply with hammer to relieve ball joint stud pressure.

CAUTION: Restraining devices for coil springs are recommended during all coil spring related removal procedures.

3) Place a jack under lower control arm. Compress spring and remove stud nut. Remove bolts attaching steering knuckle-to-shock strut. Compress shock strut until sufficient clearance is obtained, and remove steering knuckle.

Installation
1) Place steering knuckle on ball joint stud and install stud nut. Do not tighten nut at this time. Lower shock strut until attaching holes are in line with steering knuckle holes. Install 2 new bolts and nuts.

2) Tighten ball joint stud nut and install cotter pin. Do not back off nut to install cotter pin, tighten nut to align holes. Tighten shock strut-to-knuckle attaching nuts to specifications.

3) Lower and remove jack. Install remaining components in reverse order of removal procedure. Check front end alignment and adjust as necessary.

NOTE: Do not use impact wrench when replacing gas-pressurized front strut damper assembly. All strut damper and upper mount assemblies use metric fasteners.

STRUT DAMPER & UPPER MOUNT ASSEMBLY
Removal
1) Place ignition switch in "UNLOCKED" position. Raise vehicle by lower control arms until wheels are just off ground. From inside engine compartment, remove three 12 mm upper mount attaching bolts. DO NOT drive vehicle with these nuts removed.

2) Do not remove pop rivet holding camber plate in position. On Cougar and Thunderbird models, if upper mount is to be replaced, loosen 16 mm strut rod nut at this time. A screwdriver in the slot will hold rod still while removing nut.

3) On all models, raise vehicle and place safety stands under frame jacking pads, rearward of wheels. Remove wheel. Remove brake caliper and move out of way. Remove 2 lower nuts holding strut to steering knuckle, leaving bolts in place.

NOTE: Hold gas-pressurized struts firmly during removal of last steering knuckle-to-strut bolt since gas pressure will cause strut to fully extend when second bolt is removed.

4) Remove strut-to-knuckle mount bolts, push bracket free of knuckle. Lift strut up to compress rod and remove from steering knuckle. Pull down to remove strut from vehicle. Remove upper mount components and jounce bumper from strut if necessary. Inspect and replace components as needed.

5) On Cougar and Thunderbird models, upper mounts are a one-piece design and cannot be disassembled. On the Mustang, upper mounts consist of an assembly of several parts, which are to be assembled on the strut rod and body mounting bracket. See Fig. 4.

Fig. 4: Exploded View Of Upper Strut Mount Components

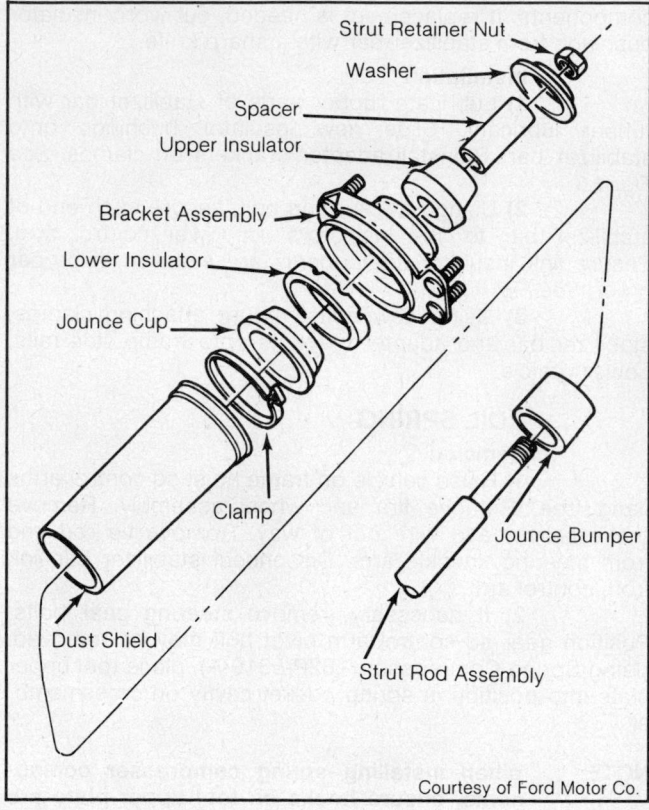

Strut Retainer Nut
Washer
Spacer
Upper Insulator
Bracket Assembly
Lower Insulator
Jounce Cup
Clamp
Dust Shield
Jounce Bumper
Strut Rod Assembly

Courtesy of Ford Motor Co.

NOTE: If a shock strut needs replacement, it is not necessary to replace both struts. Only strut in question should be replaced.

Installation
1) If removed, install upper mount and jounce bumper on strut. Position 3 upper mount studs into body mounting pad and camber plate. Start 3 new nuts, engaging as many threads as possible. Extend strut (if necessary) and position in steering knuckle. Install new lower mounting bolts and hand start nuts.

2) Remove suspension load from lower control arms. Tighten lower mount nuts. Raise control arms and tighten 3 strut-to-upper mount nuts (inside engine compartment) to specifications.

3) If necessary, tighten 16 mm strut rod nut. Install brake caliper. Install wheel. Remove safety stands and lower vehicle. Check and adjust front end alignment as needed.

WHEEL BEARINGS
Removal
1) Raise and support vehicle. Remove wheel. Remove caliper and support with wire. Remove grease cap from hub.

2) Remove cotter pin, nut lock, adjusting nut and flat washer from steering knuckle spindle. Remove outer tapered roller bearing assembly. Pull hub and rotor assembly off spindle.

3) Remove grease seal and discard. Remove inner tapered roller bearing assembly from hub. Clean inner and outer bearings in solvent and blow dry. Do not spin bearings with compressed air.

FORD MOTOR CO. SINGLE ARM (Cont.)

4) Inspect bearings and races for scratches, pits, excessive wear or other damage. Replace parts as necessary. If necessary, replace bearing and race as a set.

Installation

1) Install new outer bearing race in hub using bearing race installer or drift punch. Install new inner race using Bearing Race Installer (T73T-1202-B).

2) Thoroughly pack bearings with grease. Place inner bearing assembly in inner race. Apply a light film of grease to lips of new grease seal. Install seal using seal installer. Install hub and rotor assembly onto spindle.

3) Install outer bearing assembly and flat washer to steering knuckle spindle. Install adjusting nut finger tight. Adjust wheel bearings. See ADJUSTMENTS. Install brake caliper and wheel. Lower vehicle.

TIGHTENING SPECIFICATIONS

Application	Ft. Lbs. (N.m)
Ball Joint-to-Steering	
Knuckle Nut	100-120 (136-163)
Lower Control Arm-to-Crossmember	
Pivot Bolt/Nut	110-150 (150-203)
Stabilizer Bar	
Mount Clamp-to-Bracket Bolt	40-55 (54-74)
Link Bolt & Nut	12 (16)
Steering Gear-to-Crossmember	
Bolt	90-100 (122-136)
Strut Damper	
Strut-to-Upper Mount Nut	55-92 (75-125)
Strut-to-Knuckle Mount Nut	140-200 (190-271)
Upper Mount-to-Body Nut	50-70 (68-95)
Tie Rod	
End-to-Steering Knuckle Nut	35-47 (48-64)
Wheel Bearing Adjusting Nut	[1] 17-25 (23-34)
Wheel Lug Nut	80-105 (109-142)

[1] – Specification is for bearing seating only. Adjustment torque is 10-12 INCH lbs. (1.1-1.7 N.m).

Front Suspension

GENERAL MOTORS FWD
"A", "C", "H", "J", "L" & "N" BODIES

"A" Body: Celebrity, Century, Cutlass
   Ciera, 6000, 6000 LE
"C" Body: DeVille, Electra, Fleetwood,
   Ninety-Eight
"H" Body: Bonneville, Delta 88, LeSabre
"J" Body: Cavalier, Cimarron, Firenza,
   Skyhawk, Sunbird
"L" Body: Beretta, Corsica
"N" Body: Cutlass Calais, Grand Am,
   Skylark

DESCRIPTION

The MacPherson strut design front suspension uses lower control arms which pivot from engine cradle on "A", "C" and "H" bodies and from lower side rails on "J", "L" and "N" bodies. The cradle has isolation mounts to body. Lower control arms contain rubber pivot bushings.

The upper end of strut is isolated by a rubber mount containing a bearing for wheel turning. Lower end of steering knuckle pivots on the lower control arm mounted ball joint. The steering knuckle is clamped to the ball joint stud on all "A" bodies while it fits through tapered bore in the steering knuckle on all other models. Tie rods are connected to steering arms on the struts or to steering knuckle.

ADJUSTMENTS

CASTER & CAMBER

See appropriate article in WHEEL ALIGNMENT section.

RIDING HEIGHT

See RIDING HEIGHT SPECIFICATIONS article in WHEEL ALIGNMENT section.

FRONT WHEEL BEARINGS

Front bearings are pre-adjusted and lubricated requiring no routine maintenance or adjustment.

BALL JOINT CHECKING

Lower Ball Joint

Raise and support vehicle. Allow suspension to hang freely. Inspect ball joint seals for cracks or tears. Replace ball joint if seal is damaged. Grasp tire at top and bottom. Note horizontal movement while moving tire inward and outward. Replace ball joint if any horizontal movement exists.

REMOVAL & INSTALLATION

LOWER BALL JOINT

CAUTION: When servicing suspension, use Drive Axle Boot Seal Protector (J-33162) on inner Tri-Pot axle joint with silicone (Gray) boot. Boots made of Black thermo-plastic material require Boot Protector (J-34754). For outer double-offset joint, modify Boot Protector (J-34754) by removing 3 tabs on inside surface. DO NOT over extend inner Tri-Pot joint on drive axle or separation of internal parts may result.

Removal

1) Raise front of vehicle and support with jack stands under frame rails, behind front wheels or under engine cradle. Allow suspension to hang freely. Remove front wheel. Place drive axle boot seal protector on outer joint.

2) On all non-clamp type ball joint studs, remove cotter pin and nut from ball joint stud. Using Ball Joint Separator (J-36226) for "C" and "H" bodies or (J-29330) for all others, separate ball joint stud from steering knuckle.

3) On clamp (pinch) type ball joint studs, remove pinch bolt from ball joint stud. Separate ball joint from steering knuckle. Tap stud with mallet to loosen if necessary.

4) Drill out ball joint retaining rivets. Use care not to damage drive axle boots during rivet removal. Disconnect stabilizer bar from control arm. Lower the control arm. Remove ball joint from control arm.

NOTE: If insufficient clearance exists for ball joint removal, install Front Hub Spindle Remover (J-28733). Tighten front hub spindle remover until clearance is obtained to remove ball joint.

Installation

1) Install ball joint into lower control arm. Install retaining bolts. On "J" and "L" bodies, install ball joint retaining bolts facing upward. On all other bodies, install bolts facing downward.

2) Tighten ball joint retaining bolts to specification. See TIGHTENING SPECIFICATIONS table at end of article. Position steering knuckle over ball joint stud. On non-clamp type ball joint stud, install nut. Tighten to specification. Install new cotter pin.

CAUTION: Always install new pinch bolt and nut on "A" bodies whenever ball joint is separated from steering knuckle.

3) On clamp type ball joint stud, align notch in stud to allow pinch bolt to be installed. Install new pinch bolt and nut. Tighten to specification. Install stabilizer bar assembly. Tighten bolts to specification. Remove boot protectors. Install wheel and lower vehicle. Check wheel alignment.

STEERING KNUCKLE

Removal

1) Raise and support vehicle. Remove wheel. Install drive axle boot protectors. Disconnect stabilizer bar from control arm (if equipped). Remove hub assembly. See REMOVAL under HUB ASSEMBLY in this article.

CAUTION: DO NOT over extend drive axle CV joints or separation of internal parts may occur.

2) Disconnect tie rod from steering knuckle. Separate ball joint from steering knuckle. See REMOVAL under LOWER BALL JOINT in this article. On models equipped with anti-lock brake system, remove speed sensor mounting bracket.

3) On all models, scribe strut lower mount clamp outline on steering knuckle for camber alignment and reassembly reference. Remove strut-to-steering knuckle retaining bolts. Remove steering knuckle. See Figs. 1, 3 and 4.

GENERAL MOTORS FWD
"A", "C", "H", "J", "L" & "N" BODIES (Cont.)

Fig. 1: Exploded View of "C" & "H" Bodies Front Suspension Components

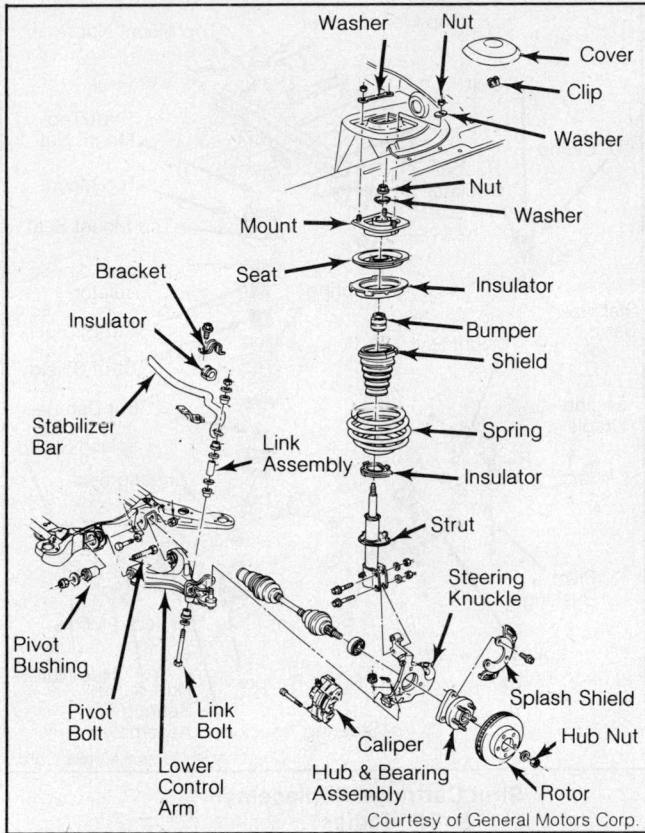

Courtesy of General Motors Corp.

Installation

1) Install new bearing seal (if removed). Loosely install steering knuckle to strut. Install steering knuckle onto ball joint. Tighten retaining nut or pinch bolt to specification. Always install new pinch bolt and nut.

2) Ensure axle boot protector is in place. Using floor jack, raise assembly to position steering knuckle holes in alignment with strut holes.

3) Align reference mark on strut lower mount clamp and steering knuckle. Install strut-to-steering knuckle retaining bolts. Tighten to specification.

4) Reverse removal procedure for remaining components. Install hub and bearing on steering knuckle. Lower vehicle and tighten hub nut.

5) On models with anti-lock brake system, loosely install bracket on steering knuckle. Bracket should be snug, but should be able to moved under hand pressure.

6) Measure gap with non-ferrous feeler gauge. Adjust speed sensor gap between tip of sensor and one tooth of sensor ring (on axle shaft) to .028" (.71 mm) by moving bracket. Tighten bracket mounting bolts and recheck gap.

HUB ASSEMBLY & SEAL
Removal

1) Raise and support vehicle. Allow suspension to hang freely. Remove wheels. Install drive axle shaft boot protectors.

2) Install drift punch into rotor and remove hub nut and washer. See Fig. 2. Remove disc brake caliper

without disconnecting brake line. Support caliper to prevent brake hose damage.

3) Scribe reference mark on hub and rotor for reassembly reference. Remove rotor. Using Front Hub Spindle Remover (J-28733), separate drive axle shaft from hub. Support drive axle out of the way.

4) Mark hub assembly-to-steering knuckle location. Remove hub assembly retaining bolts. Remove hub assembly.

5) Disconnect stabilizer bar from lower control arm. Separate lower ball joint. See REMOVAL under LOWER BALL JOINT in this article. Move drive axle from steering knuckle. Remove seal from steering knuckle.

NOTE: Factory seal is installed from engine side of steering knuckle on "A", "C" and "H" bodies. Service seal is installed from wheel side of steering knuckle.

Installation

1) Install new seal in steering knuckle. Lubricate seal lip with grease. Install "O" ring on hub assembly. See Fig. 2. Reverse removal procedures for remaining components. Use care not to damage seal during axle shaft and hub installation.

2) Align reference mark on hub and steering knuckle. Tighten bolts to specification. Align reference mark on hub and rotor. Install new nut on drive axle. Partially tighten nut to 74 ft. lbs. (101 N.m). Lower vehicle and tighten nut to specification.

Fig. 2: Exploded View Of Hub & Bearing Assembly

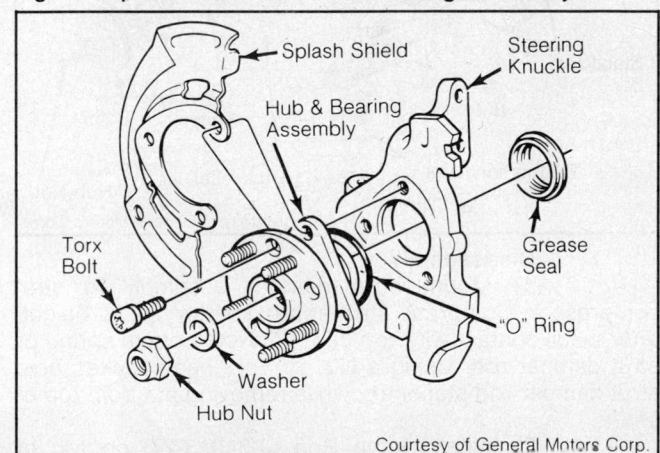

Courtesy of General Motors Corp.

STRUT DAMPER ASSEMBLY
Removal

1) Remove upper strut-to-body mount nuts. Raise and support vehicle. Allow suspension to hang freely. Remove wheel. Install drive axle shaft boot protectors.

2) On "J", "L" and "N" bodies, disconnect tie rod end from steering knuckle using Tie Rod Remover (J-24319). On models with anti-lock brake system, disconnect front sensors.

CAUTION: Support steering knuckle during strut removal to prevent tension from being applied to brake hose. DO NOT over extend drive axle shaft CV joints.

11-32

Front Suspension
GENERAL MOTORS FWD
"A", "C", "H", "J", "L" & "N" BODIES (Cont.)

3) On all models, remove brake line clip or bracket bolt. Scribe strut lower mount clamp outline on steering knuckle for camber alignment and reassembly reference.

4) Support steering knuckle to prevent over extending of drive axle shaft. Remove strut-to-steering knuckle retaining bolts. Remove strut assembly. DO NOT chip or scratch coil spring coating.

Fig. 3: Exploded View of "A" Body Front Suspension Components

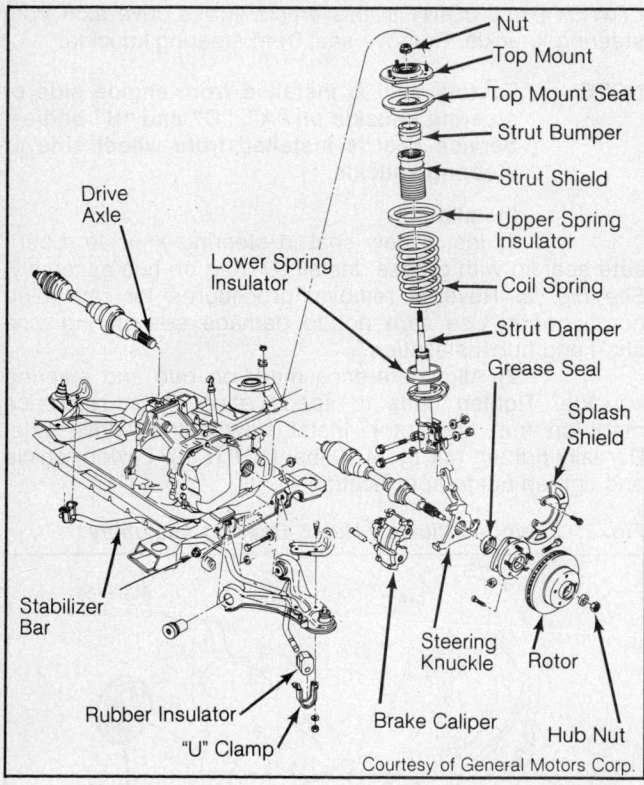

Courtesy of General Motors Corp.

Disassembly

1) Mount strut damper assembly in strut compressor. Compress strut approximately 1/2 its height, after initial contact with top cap. DO NOT bottom spring or strut damper rod. Using a No. 50 Torx head socket, hold strut damper rod stationary while removing nut from top of shaft.

2) Install Guide Rod (J-34013-27) on top of damper shaft. This is done to guide shaft straight down through bearing cap of upper mount assembly. Slowly loosen strut compressor screw while guiding damper from assembly. Continue to loosen screw until strut damper and spring can be removed.

NOTE: DO NOT chip or crack spring coating. Coil damage may occur if coating is damaged.

3) Remove, inspect and replace components as necessary. On "J" and "N" bodies only, internal piston rod assembly and fluid can be replaced using a service cartridge. Internal threads are located immediately below a cut line groove.

Fig. 4: Exploded View of "J", "L" & "N" Bodies Front Suspension Components

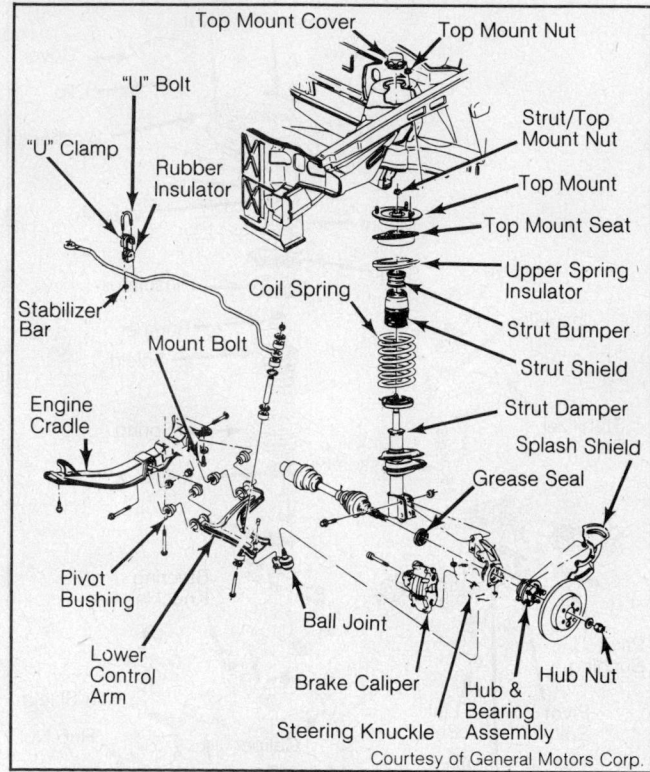

Courtesy of General Motors Corp.

Strut Cartridge Replacement ("J" & "N" Bodies)

1) Clamp strut in a vise. DO NOT over tighten. Locate cut line groove .79" (20 mm) below top of damper shoulder. Mislocation will result in thread damage. *See Fig. 5.*

2) Using Pipe Cutter (J-29800), cut around groove until reservoir tube is completely cut through. *See Fig. 5.* Remove end cap, cylinder and piston rod assembly. Remove strut from vise and drain fluid.

3) Using Flaring Cup (J-25589), deburr and flare cut edge of reservoir tube for service nut. Place strut in vise. Place flaring cup on open end of reservoir tube.

4) Strike flaring cup to remove any burrs. Remove flaring cup. Ensure that new service nut threads smoothly into reservoir tube. Install new strut cartridge into reservoir tube.

5) Rotate cartridge until it fully seats into base indentations. When fully seated the cartridge cannot easily be turned. *See Fig. 5.* Install nut into cartridge.

6) Using Nut Adapter (J-29778-A) and torque wrench, tighten nut to specification listed in repair kit with strut assembly in upright mounting position. Operate piston rod several times to ensure proper operation.

Reassembly

1) Reverse disassembly procedures. When installing bearing cap, ensure components are centered together and aligned properly. On "A" bodies, upper spring seat flat must be 10 degrees forward of center line of strut assembly spindle.

Front Suspension

11-33

GENERAL MOTORS FWD
"A", "C", "H", "J", "L" & "N" BODIES (Cont.)

Fig. 5: Replacing Damper Assembly Strut Cartridge

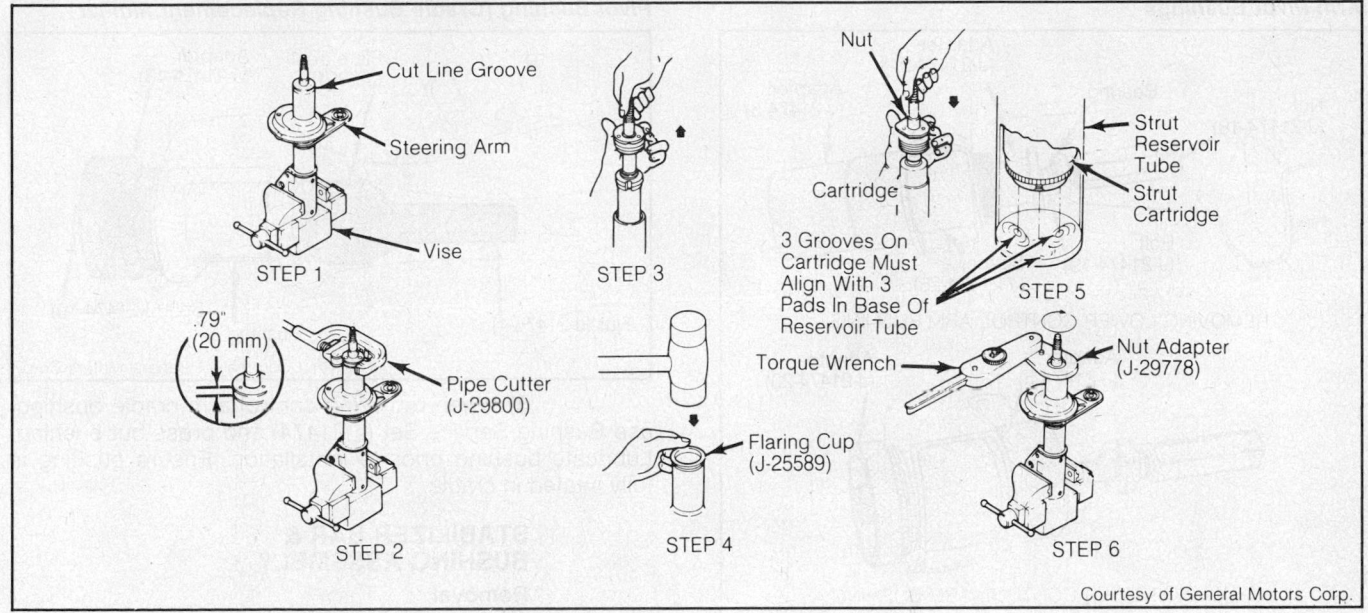

Courtesy of General Motors Corp.

2) On "C" bodies, upper spring seat flat must face outward 90 degrees from vehicle center line. On "H" bodies spring seat flat must face outward from vehicle center line.

3) On "J" and "N" bodies upper spring seat flat should be facing the center line of strut assembly spindle. On "L" bodies, ends of spring coil must be located 0-.39" (0-10 mm) from end of groove in upper insulator and .39-.59" (10-15 mm) from end of groove in lower insulator.

NOTE: **DO NOT scratch polished damper shaft surface. Hold shaft with Damper Rod Clamp (J-34013-20) to prevent it from receding into strut assembly during spring installation.**

4) Use guide rod to guide shaft through center of assembly during spring installation. Compress spring. Ensure damper rod does not bind on bearing cap.

5) Compress spring until nut can be installed on damper shaft. Remove guide rod and install damper shaft nut. Tighten nut to specification. Remove damper rod clamp (if used). Remove spring compressor.

CAUTION: **Vehicle front end alignment should be checked after strut installation.**

Installation
1) Before installation on "J", "L" and "N" bodies, strut may be modified to allow for camber adjustment during wheel alignment. File bottom mounting holes in strut outer flanges to enlarge holes until they match slots in inner flanges.

2) On all models, reverse removal procedure to install strut assembly. When installing strut assembly in steering knuckle, ensure scribe marks on steering knuckle are aligned with strut for proper lower adjusting cam bolt position. Upper spring seat flat must be aligned with lower strut-to-steering knuckle attachment.

3) On "J", "L" and "N" bodies, lower strut-to-steering knuckle mounting bolts must be installed with machined flats on bolt heads in horizontal position. Tighten bolts to specification.

LOWER CONTROL ARM
Removal
1) Raise and support vehicle. Allow suspension to hang freely. Remove wheel. Install boot protectors on inner and outer drive axle joints. Remove stabilizer bar from control arm.

2) Separate ball joint from lower control arm. See REMOVAL under LOWER BALL JOINT in this article. Remove control arm pivot bolts and control arm.

Installation
Reverse removal procedure. On pinch type ball joints install new bolt and nut. Tighten lower control arm pivot bolts with vehicle weight on control arms. On "J", "L" and "N" bodies tighten rear control arm bolts first, center bolts second and front bolts last. Check front end alignment.

CAUTION: **Lower control arm mounting bolts must be tightened to specification with vehicle weight on control arms.**

LOWER CONTROL ARM PIVOT BUSHINGS
Removal & Installation ("A", "J", "L" & "N" Bodies)
1) Remove lower control arm. See LOWER CONTROL ARM in this article. On "A" bodies, use Control Arm Bushing Service Set (J-21474-01) to press pivot bushing from control arm. *See Fig. 6.*

11-34

Front Suspension
GENERAL MOTORS FWD
"A", "C", "H", "J", "L" & "N" BODIES (Cont.)

Fig. 6: Replacing "A" Body Lower Control Arm Pivot Bushings

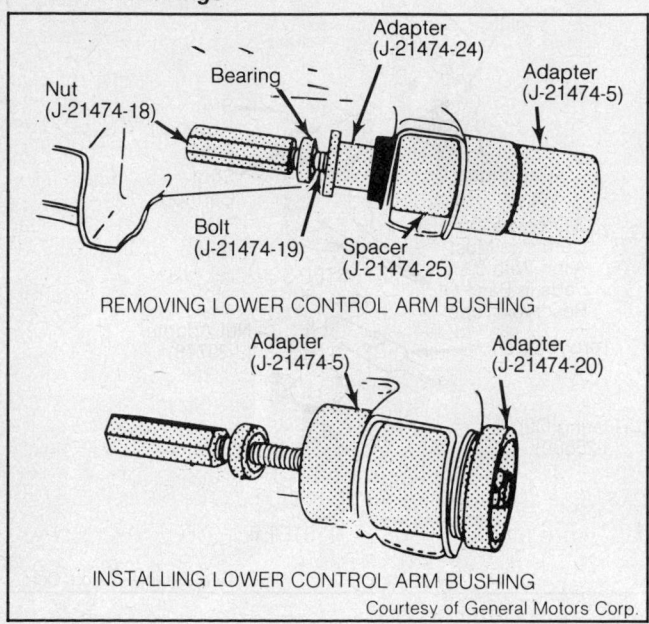

REMOVING LOWER CONTROL ARM BUSHING

INSTALLING LOWER CONTROL ARM BUSHING

Courtesy of General Motors Corp.

2) On "J", "L" and "N" bodies, use Control Arm Bushing Service Set (J-29792) to press pivot bushing from control arm. *See Fig. 7.* On all models, lubricate bushings prior to installation. Using control arm bushing service set, install bushings.

Fig. 7: Replacing "J", "L" & "N" Bodies Lower Control Arm Pivot Bushings

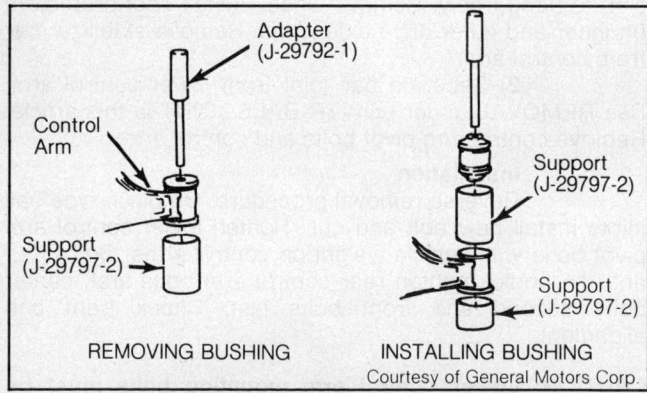

REMOVING BUSHING   INSTALLING BUSHING

Courtesy of General Motors Corp.

Cradle & Pivot Bushing Replacement ("C" & "H" Bodies)

1) Remove lower control arm. See LOWER CONTROL ARM in this article. Prior to control arm pivot bushing removal, tap down flare on lip of bushing using a hammer and punch.

2) Install Bushing Service Set (J-21474) and press out bushing. *See Fig. 8.* Lubricate new bushing prior to installation. Using bushing service set and Flare Tool (J-23915), install bushing. Tighten nut on flare tool to obtain a 45 degree flare.

Fig. 8: Replacing "C" & "H" Bodies Control Arm Pivot Bushing (Cradle Bushing Replacement Similar)

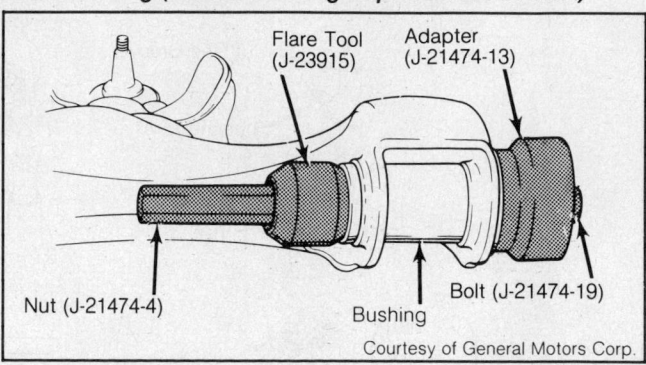

Courtesy of General Motors Corp.

3) When replacing control arm cradle bushing, use Bushing Service Set (J-21474) and press out bushing. Lubricate bushing prior to installation. Ensure bushing is fully seated in cradle.

STABILIZER BAR & BUSHING ASSEMBLY
Removal

1) Raise and support vehicle. Allow suspension to hang freely. Remove wheels. Disconnect stabilizer bar from lower control arms. Remove stabilizer bar mounting brackets on engine cradle or crossmember. On "A" bodies, remove stabilizer bar and insulators from vehicle.

2) On "J", "L" and "N" bodies, loosen, but do not remove, front engine cradle bolts. *See Fig. 4.* Remove rear and center engine cradle bolts. Lower engine cradle enough to remove stabilizer bar.

3) On "C" and "H" bodies, separate tie rod ends from steering knuckles. Disconnect exhaust pipe connecting exhaust manifold to catalytic converter. Disconnect air pipe to exhaust pipe (if equipped).

4) Turn right-hand strut assembly fully to the right. Slide stabilizer bar to the right over steering steering knuckle. Pull down on left side until stabilizer bar clears engine cradle.

5) On all models, inspect and replace all rubber bushings showing signs of wear, damage or deterioration.

Installation

1) Reverse removal procedures. During installation, loosely assemble all fasteners and ensure stabilizer bar is centered from side-to-side.

2) Ensure insulator bushing split area is toward front of vehicle on "C" and "H" bodies. On "J", "L" and "N" bodies, install stabilizer bar link bolt from the bottom. Tighten stabilizer bar insulator brackets with end of bar positioned 2.2" (55 mm) from bottom of engine cradle. Tighten bolts to specification.

Front Suspension

GENERAL MOTORS FWD
"A", "C", "H", "J", "L" & "N" BODIES (Cont.)

TIGHTENING SPECIFICATIONS ("A" BODIES)

Application	Ft. Lbs. (N.m)
Ball Joint-to-Control Arm Mount Bolt/Nut	50 (68)
Ball Joint-to-Steering Knuckle Pinch Bolt	33 (45)
Brake Caliper Mount Bolt	38 (52)
Control Arm-to-Crossmember Pivot Bolt	
Celebrity	66 (90)
All Others	61 (83)
Hub & Bearing Retainer Bolt	
With Heavy Duty Power Brakes	70 (95)
All Others	63 (85)
Hub-to-Drive Axle Nut	[1] 192 (260)
Stabilizer Bar	
Bar-to-Control Arm Clamp Nut	33 (45)
Bar-to-Crossmember Mount Bolt	41 (56)
Strut Damper Assembly	
Piston Rod Top Nut	65 (88)
Strut-to-Steering Knuckle Bolt	140 (190)
Strut-to-Upper Body Mount Nut	18 (24)
Tie Rod End-to-Steering	
Knuckle Mount Nut	[2] 30 (41)

[1] – Tighten to 74 ft. lbs. (101 N.m) during initial assembly. After installing wheels and lowering vehicle to ground, tighten nut to final torque.

[2] – May be tightened to 52 ft. lbs. (71 N.m) to align cotter pin hole.

TIGHTENING SPECIFICATIONS ("C" & "H" BODIES)

Application	Ft. Lbs. (N.m)
Ball Joint-to-Control Arm Bolt	50 (68)
Ball Joint-to-Steering Knuckle Nut	[1] 37 (51)
Brake Caliper Mount Bolt	38 (52)
Hub & Bearing Retainer Bolt	70 (95)
Hub-to-Drive Axle Nut	[2] 180 (245)
Control Arm-to-Crossmember Pivot Bolt	
Front	140 (190)
Rear	90 (122)
Stabilizer Bar	
Bar-to-Control Arm Clamp Nut	13 (18)
Bar-to-Crossmember Bolt	37 (51)
Strut Damper Assembly	
Piston Rod Top Nut	44 (60)
Strut-to-Steering Knuckle	
Mount Bolt (Upper)	144 (195)
Strut-to-Upper Body Mount Nut	18 (24)
Tie Rod End-to-Steering	
Knuckle Mount Nut	[3] 35 (47)

[1] – Tighten to 88 INCH Lbs. (10 N.m). Then turn additional 120 degrees (2 flats on nut) during which time final torque must be obtained.

[2] – Tighten to 74 ft. lbs. (101 N.m) during initial assembly. After installing wheels and lowering vehicle to ground, tighten nut to final torque.

[3] – May be tightened to 52 ft. lbs. (71 N.m) to align cotter pin hole.

TIGHTENING SPECIFICATIONS ("J", "L" & "N" BODIES)

Application	Ft. Lbs. (N.m)
Ball Joint-to-Control Arm Bolt	50 (68)
Ball Joint-to-Steering Knuckle Nut	
Beretta, Cimmaron, Corsica	55 (75)
All Others	45 (61)
Brake Caliper Mount Bolt	38 (52)
Hub & Bearing Retainer Bolt	70 (95)
Hub-to-Drive Axle Nut	
Beretta, Cavalier, Corsica	
Grand Am, Sunbird	[1] 192 (260)
All Others	[1] 185 (251)
Control Arm-to-Crossmember Pivot Bolt	63 (85)
Stabilizer Bar	
Bar-to-Control Arm Link Bolt	15 (20)
Bar-to-Crossmember Clamp Nut	18 (24)
Strut Damper Assembly	
Piston Rod Top Nut	
Beretta, Cavalier, Corsica	59 (80)
All Others	65 (88)
Strut-to-Steering Knuckle	
Mounting Bolt	133 (180)
Strut-to-Upper Body Mounting Nut	18 (24)
Tie Rod End-to-Steering Knuckle Nut	[2] 35 (47)

[1] – Tighten to 74 ft. lbs. (101 N.m) during initial assembly. After installing wheels and lowering vehicle to ground, tighten nut to final torque.

[2] – May be tightened to 52 ft. lbs. (71 N.m) to align cotter pin hole.

Front Suspension
GENERAL MOTORS FWD
"E", "K" & "V" BODIES

"E" Body: Eldorado, Toronado, Reatta, Riviera
"K" Body: Seville
"V" Body: Allanté

DESCRIPTION

All models use MacPherson strut-type front suspension. The frame has isolation mounts to the body. Rubber bushings are used for control arm pivots. The upper end of the strut is isolated by a rubber mount that contains a bearing to allow for wheel turning.

The lower end of the steering knuckle pivots on a ball joint riveted to the control arm. Control arm is the anchoring point for a stabilizer bar and tension strut.

Fig. 1: Exploded View of Front Suspension

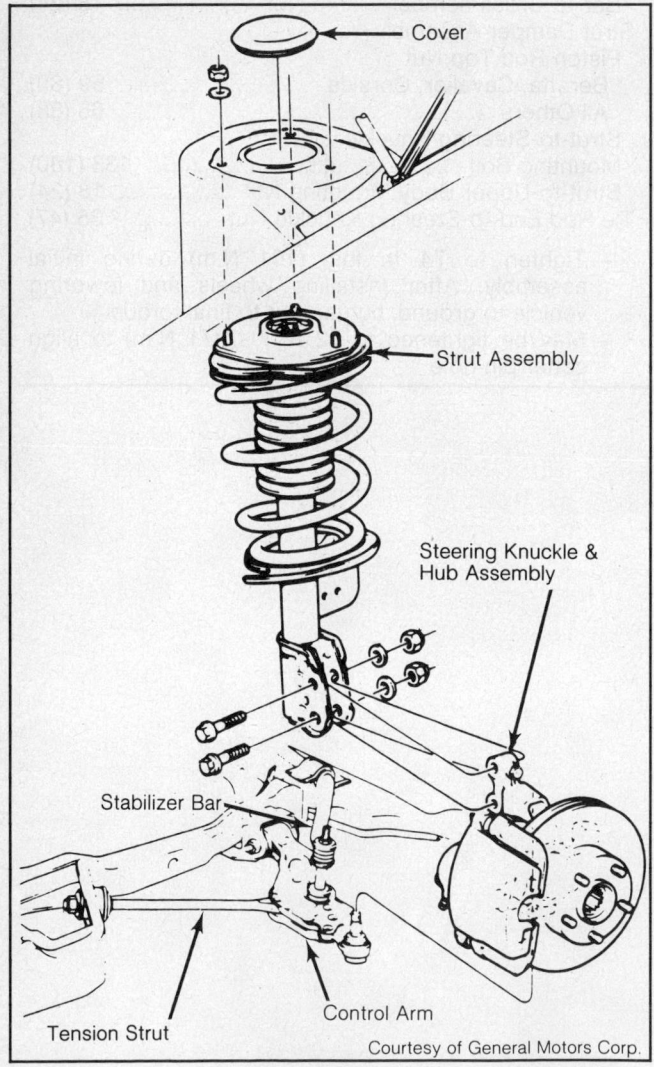

Cover
Strut Assembly
Steering Knuckle & Hub Assembly
Stabilizer Bar
Control Arm
Tension Strut

Courtesy of General Motors Corp.

ADJUSTMENTS

CASTER & CAMBER

See appropriate article in WHEEL ALIGNMENT section.

RIDING HEIGHT

See RIDING HEIGHT SPECIFICATIONS article in WHEEL ALIGNMENT section.

BALL JOINTS

Raise vehicle and support. Grab upper and lower portion of wheel and move up and down. Check for play in ball joint. If there is play, replace ball joint.

REMOVAL & INSTALLATION

NOTE: Before performing any service procedure that requires removing the strut from the steering knuckle, scribe mating marks on strut and knuckle for reassembly reference.

STABILIZER BAR & BUSHINGS
Removal & Installation

1) Raise and support vehicle. Place jack stands under cradle. Lower vehicle so weight of vehicle rests on jack stands and not on control arms.

2) Remove right wheel and tire assembly. Remove left and right insulators, retainers, spacers, and bolts. *See Fig. 2.* Remove left and right bracket bolts, brackets, and insulators.

3) Remove exhaust pipe from rear manifold and move pipe up. Lift out stabilizer bar. To install stabilizer bar, reverse removal procedure. Ensure stabilizer bar bracket insulator is installed with slit toward rear of vehicle.

Fig. 2: Exploded View of Stabilizer Bar Assembly

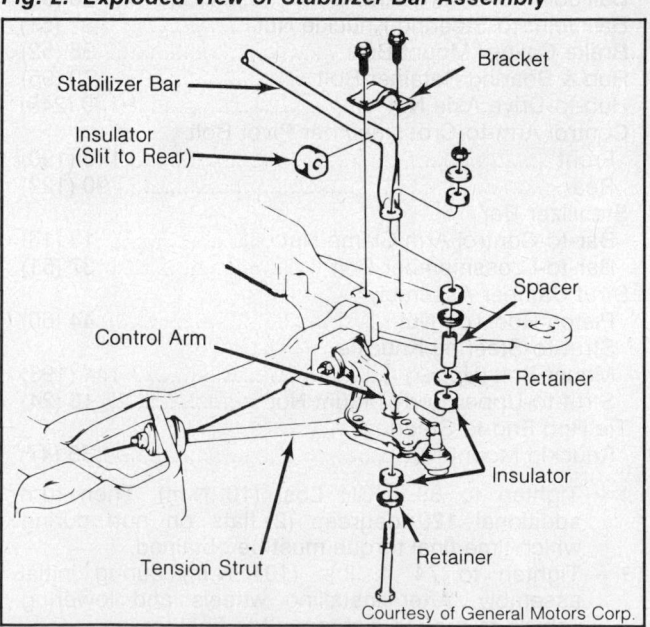

Stabilizer Bar
Bracket
Insulator (Slit to Rear)
Control Arm
Spacer
Retainer
Insulator
Tension Strut
Retainer

Courtesy of General Motors Corp.

STRUT ASSEMBLY
Removal

1) Remove nuts attaching top of strut to body. Raise and support vehicle. Place jack stands under cradle. Lower vehicle so weight of vehicle rests on jack stands and not on control arms. Remove wheel and tire assembly. Scribe knuckle and strut position.

CAUTION: Do not chip or scratch coating on front coil springs or premature failure may result. To prevent separation of internal components, do not overextend Tri-Pot joint on drive axle shaft.

2) Remove brake line bracket from strut. Remove strut-to-knuckle bolts and support knuckle with wire. Lift strut from vehicle.

Disassembly
1) Mount Strut Compressor (J-34013-A) in Holding Fixture (J-3289-20). Mount strut assembly in compressor. Lightly compress spring. Using a No. 50 or No. 55 Torx head socket, hold strut damper rod stationary while removing nut on top of shaft.

2) Install Guide Rod (J-34013-38) in top of damper rod to help guide shaft out of assembly. Slowly loosen compressor screw while guiding damper out of assembly. Continue to loosen screw until strut damper and spring can be removed. Remove, inspect and replace components as necessary.

Reassembly
1) Reassemble strut damper in reverse of disassembly procedure. *See Fig. 3.* Hold piston rod in extended position using Clamp (J-34013-20). Ensure flat on upper spring seat faces same direction as steering knuckle flange. During spring compression, use guide rod to guide shaft through exact center of bearing.

2) Compress spring until damper rod is visible through bearing cap. Do not compress spring any further. Install and tighten strut assembly top nut while holding piston rod.

Installation
Place strut assembly on vehicle and align mating marks. To complete installation, reverse removal procedure. Check front wheel alignment.

Fig. 3: Exploded View of Strut Assembly

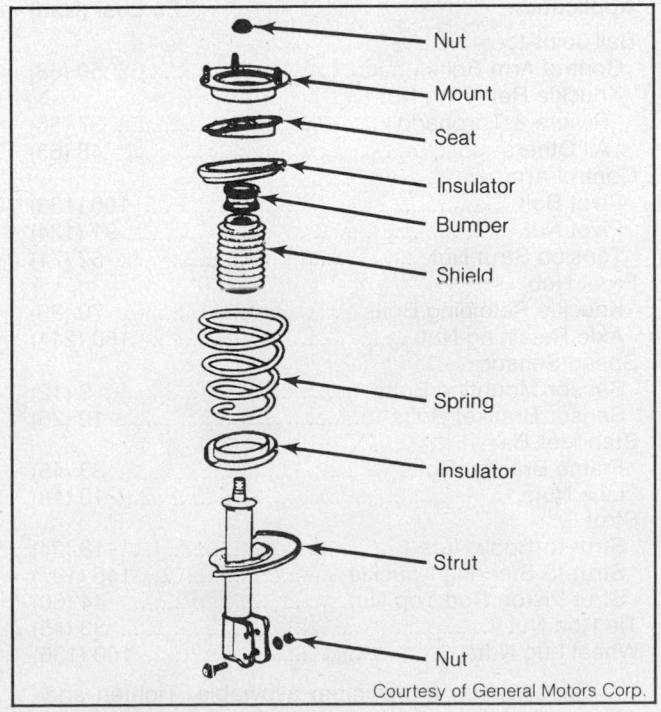

- Nut
- Mount
- Seat
- Insulator
- Bumper
- Shield
- Spring
- Insulator
- Strut
- Nut

Courtesy of General Motors Corp.

BALL JOINT
Removal
1) Raise vehicle on hoist. Place jack stands under cradle. Lower vehicle slightly so vehicle rests on jack stands and not on control arms. Remove wheel and tire assembly. Modify Boot Protector (J-34754) by cutting off 3 tabs on inside surface. Place drive axle boot seal protector on outer joint.

2) Remove stabilizer bar insulators, retainers, spacer and bolt. Disconnect ball joint from steering knuckle using Ball Joint Separator (J-35315). Drill out retaining rivets with a 1/4" drill bit and finish with a 1/2" drill bit. Remove ball joint.

NOTE: **If there is not enough clearance between ball joint and speed sensor ring on models equipped with anti-lock brake system, install Front Hub Spindle Remover (J-28733). Tighten remover until enough clearance is created to remove ball joint. See Fig. 3.**

Installation
New ball joint mounting bolts are installed from bottom of lower control arm. Install remaining components in reverse of removal procedure. Tighten ball joint-to-knuckle retaining nut. If necessary, tighten an additional 1/6 of a turn to allow for cotter pin installation.

STEERING KNUCKLE
Removal
1) Raise vehicle on hoist. Place jack stands under cradle. Lower vehicle slightly so vehicle rests on jack stands and not on control arms. Remove wheel and tire assembly. Modify Boot Protector (J-34754) by cutting off 3 tabs on inside surface and place drive axle boot seal protector on outer joint.

2) Separate tie rod end at knuckle. Remove hub and bearing assembly as described in this article. On models with anti-lock brake system, remove speed sensor bracket from steering knuckle. Remove ball joint from steering knuckle using Ball Joint Separator (J-35315). Remove strut-to-knuckle bolts. Lift out steering knuckle.

Installation
1) To install steering knuckle, reverse removal procedure. Tighten ball joint-to-knuckle retaining nut. If necessary, tighten an additional 1/6 of a turn to allow for cotter pin installation.

2) On models with anti-lock brake system, loosely install bracket on knuckle. Bracket should be snug, but should be able to move under hand pressure. Adjust sensor gap between tip of sensor and one tooth of sensor ring (on axle shaft) to .020" (.51 mm) by moving bracket. Tighten bracket mounting bolts and recheck gap.

NOTE: **If speed sensor is removed from mounting bracket, sensor body MUST be coated liberally with Anti-Corrosive Compound (1052856) at all points where sensor contacts mounting bracket.**

CONTROL ARM & PIVOT BUSHING
Removal
1) Raise vehicle on hoist. Place jack stands under cradle. Lower vehicle slightly so vehicle rests on jack stands and not on control arms. Remove wheel and tire assembly.

Front Suspension
GENERAL MOTORS FWD
"E", "K" & "V" BODIES (Cont.)

2) Modify Boot Protector (J-34754) by cutting off 3 tabs on inside surface and place drive axle boot seal protector on outer joint. Remove stabilizer bar insulators, retainers, spacer and bolt. Disconnect ball joint from steering knuckle using Ball Joint Separator (J-35315).

CAUTION: Do not overextend Tri-Pot joints on drive axle shafts or separation of internal components may occur.

3) Remove control arm tension strut front nut, retainer, and insulator. Remove control arm pivot bolt. Lift control arm out of vehicle.

Pivot Bushing Replacement

Replace bushing in control arm using hydraulic press and Bushing Remover/Installer Adapters (J-35561-1, 2 and 3). Lubricate new bushing with rubber lube before installation.

Installation

1) Install control arm on frame. Do not fully tighten pivot bolt. Install control arm tension strut front retainer, insulator, and nut. Do not tighten nut.

2) Place ball joint in steering knuckle. Install stabilizer bar insulators, retainers, spacer and bolt. Tighten ball joint-to-knuckle retaining nut. If necessary, tighten an additional 1/6 of a turn to allow for cotter pin installation.

3) Install wheel and tire assembly. Lower vehicle so weight of vehicle is supported by control arms. Tighten control arm pivot bolt and tension strut nut.

HUB & BEARING ASSEMBLY

Removal

1) Raise vehicle on hoist. Place jack stands under cradle. Lower vehicle slightly so vehicle rests on jack stands and not on control arms. Remove wheel and tire assembly.

2) Insert drift punch into rotor and remove hub nut and washer. Remove disc brake caliper and support bracket from steering knuckle. Without disconnecting brake line, wire caliper out of way.

3) Remove rotor. Separate drive axle shaft from hub using Front Hub Spindle Remover (J-28733). See Fig. 4. Remove hub and bearing retaining bolts. Lift hub and bearing assembly from vehicle.

Fig. 4: Removing Drive Axle Shaft From Front Hub

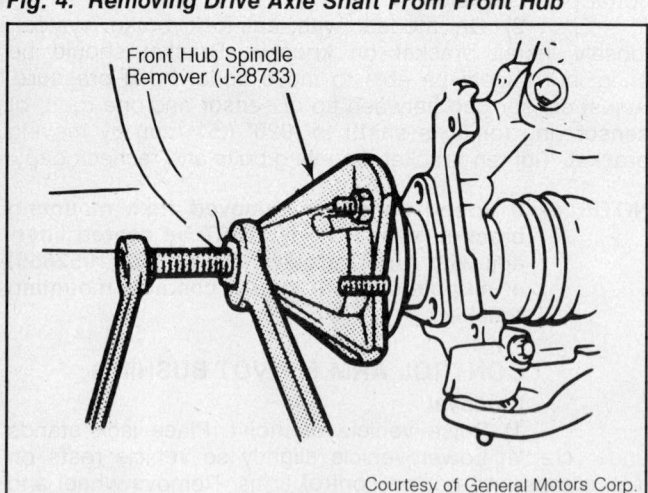

Front Hub Spindle Remover (J-28733)

Courtesy of General Motors Corp.

Knuckle Seal Replacement

If replacing seal, disconnect stabilizer bar from lower control arm. Disconnect tie rod from knuckle. Separate lower ball joint from knuckle. Remove drive shaft from knuckle. Remove seal. Install new seal.

Installation

1) Use new hub seal and "O" ring on reassembly. Lubricate lip of seal with wheel bearing grease. Install seal with Seal Installer (J-34657-A). See Fig. 5. Fill cavity between seal and bearing with wheel bearing grease. Install hub and bearing assembly. Install retaining nuts and tighten.

2) Install caliper support bracket with NEW mounting bolts. Install caliper and rotor. Install drift punch and partially tighten hub nut and washer. Install wheel and tire assembly. Lower vehicle to ground. Tighten hub nut to specification.

Fig. 5: Exploded View of Hub & Bearing Assembly

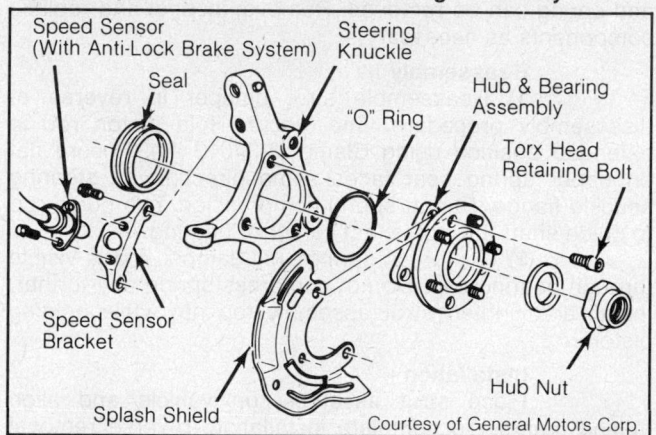

Speed Sensor (With Anti-Lock Brake System)
Seal
Steering Knuckle
"O" Ring
Hub & Bearing Assembly
Torx Head Retaining Bolt
Speed Sensor Bracket
Splash Shield
Hub Nut

Courtesy of General Motors Corp.

TIGHTENING SPECIFICATIONS

Application	Ft. Lbs. (N.m)
Ball Joint-to-	
Control Arm Bolts	50 (68)
Knuckle Retaining Nut [1]	
Riviera & Toronado	37 (50)
All Others	48 (65)
Control Arm	
Pivot Bolt	100 (136)
Pivot Nut	91 (124)
Tension Strut Nut	52 (71)
Front Hub	
Knuckle Retaining Bolts	70 (95)
Axle Retaining Nut	180 (244)
Speed Sensor	
Sensor Mounting Bolts	9 (12)
Sensor Bracket Bolts	19 (26)
Stabilizer Bar	
Frame Bracket Bolts	33 (45)
Link Nuts	13 (18)
Strut	
Strut-to-Body Nuts	18 (24)
Strut-to-Steering Knuckle	145 (197)
Strut Piston Rod Top Nut	44 (60)
Tie Rod Nut	33 (45)
Wheel Lug Nuts	100 (136)

[1] – Specification is minimum allowable. Tighten additional 1/6 of a turn to allow for cotter pin installation.

Front Suspension

GENERAL MOTORS FWD "W" BODY

Cutlass Supreme, Grand Prix, Regal

DESCRIPTION

The front suspension is a MacPherson strut type with stabilizer bar. The strut tube is welded to a stamped steel knuckle. Lower ball joints are riveted to the knuckles. The upper steering pivot point, the upper bearing, is placed below lower spring seat. Replacement strut cartridges can be installed from under the hood without removing strut.

ADJUSTMENTS

CASTER & CAMBER

See appropriate article in WHEEL ALIGNMENT section.

Fig. 1: Exploded View of "W" Body Front Suspension

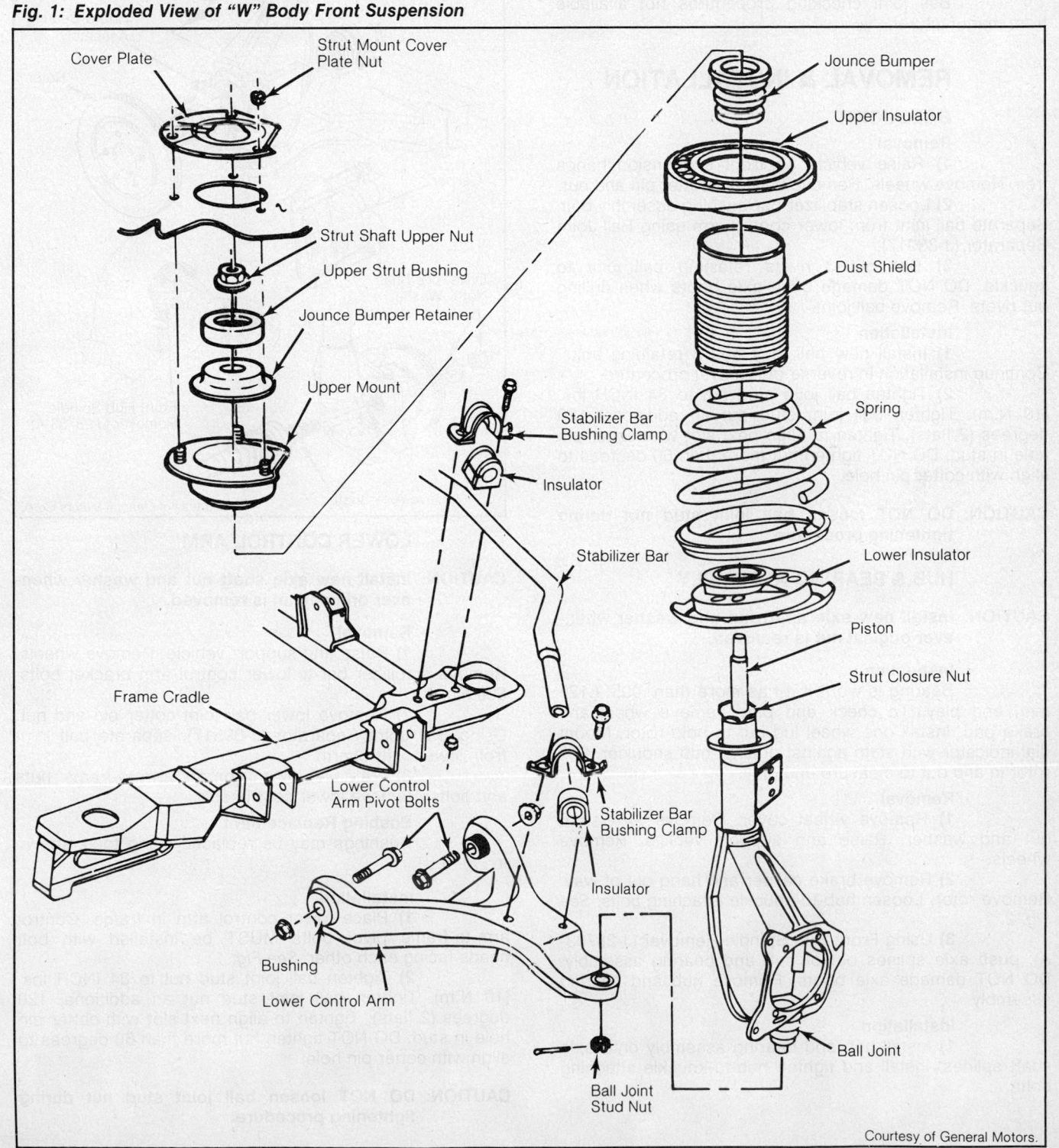

Courtesy of General Motors.

RIDING HEIGHT

See RIDING HEIGHT SPECIFICATIONS article in WHEEL ALIGNMENT section.

WHEEL BEARINGS

Wheel bearings are not adjustable. Tighten axle shaft nut to 184 ft. lbs. (250 N.m). Replace wheel bearing if end play is more than .005" (.127 mm).

BALL JOINT CHECKING

Ball joint checking procedures not available from manufacturer.

REMOVAL & INSTALLATION

BALL JOINT

Removal

1) Raise vehicle so front suspension hangs free. Remove wheels. Remove ball joint cotter pin and nut.

2) Loosen stabilizer bar bushing assembly bolt. Separate ball joint from lower control arm using Ball Joint Separator (J-35917).

3) Drill out 3 rivets retaining ball joint to knuckle. DO NOT damage drive axle boots when drilling out rivets. Remove ball joint.

Installation

1) Install new ball joint and 3 retaining bolts. Continue installation in reverse of removal procedure.

2) Tighten ball joint stud nut to 84 INCH lbs. (10 N.m). Tighten ball joint stud nut an additional 120 degrees (2 flats). Tighten to align next slot with cotter pin hole in stud. DO NOT tighten nut more than 60 degrees to align with cotter pin hole.

CAUTION: DO NOT loosen ball joint stud nut during tightening procedure.

HUB & BEARING ASSEMBLY

CAUTION: Install new axle shaft nut and washer whenever original nut is removed.

Inspection

Bearing is worn if it has more than .005" (.127 mm) end play. To check end play, remove wheel and brake pad. Install one wheel lug nut to hold rotor. Mount dial indicator with stem against against hub shoulder. Pull rotor in and out to measure end play.

Removal

1) Remove wheel cover. Remove axle shaft nut and washer. Raise and support vehicle. Remove wheels.

2) Remove brake caliper and hang out of way. Remove rotor. Loosen hub-to-knuckle attaching bolts. *See Fig. 2.*

3) Using Front Hub Spindle Remover (J-28733-A), push axle splines out of hub and bearing assembly. DO NOT damage axle boots. Remove hub and bearing assembly.

Installation

1) Install hub and bearing assembly onto axle shaft splines. Install and tighten hub-to-knuckle attaching bolts.

2) Install rotor and brake caliper. Lubricate caliper mounting bolt shaft with silicone grease. Install wheels. Lower vehicle.

3) Install NEW axle nut and washer and tighten to 184 ft. lbs. (250 N.m). Install wheel cover.

Fig. 2: Replacing Hub & Bearing Assembly

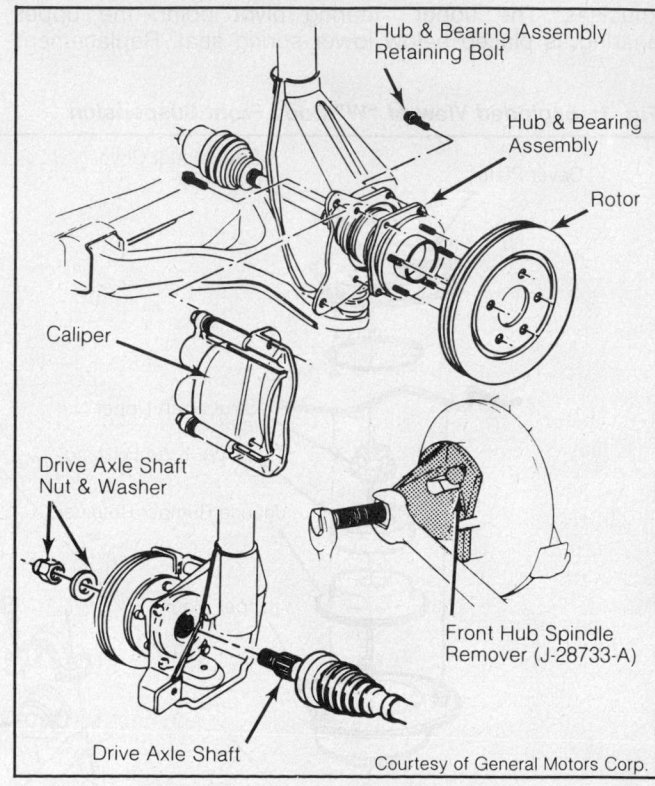

Hub & Bearing Assembly Retaining Bolt

Hub & Bearing Assembly

Rotor

Caliper

Drive Axle Shaft Nut & Washer

Front Hub Spindle Remover (J-28733-A)

Drive Axle Shaft

Courtesy of General Motors Corp.

LOWER CONTROL ARM

CAUTION: Install new axle shaft nut and washer whenever original nut is removed.

Removal

1) Raise and support vehicle. Remove wheels. Remove stabilizer bar-to-lower control arm bracket bolts. *See Fig. 1.*

2) Remove lower ball joint cotter pin and nut. Using Ball Joint Separator (J-39517), separate ball joint from lower control arm.

3) Remove lower control arm-to-frame nuts and bolts. Remove lower control arm.

Bushing Replacement

Bushings may be replaced using tools shown in *Fig. 3.*

Installation

1) Place lower control arm in frame. Control arm-to-frame pivot bolts MUST be installed with bolt heads facing each other. *See Fig. 1.*

2) Tighten ball joint stud nut to 84 INCH lbs. (10 N.m). Tighten ball joint stud nut an additional 120 degrees (2 flats). Tighten to align next slot with cotter pin hole in stud. DO NOT tighten nut more than 60 degrees to align with cotter pin hole.

CAUTION: DO NOT loosen ball joint stud nut during tightening procedure.

Fig. 3: Replacing Lower Control Arm Bushings

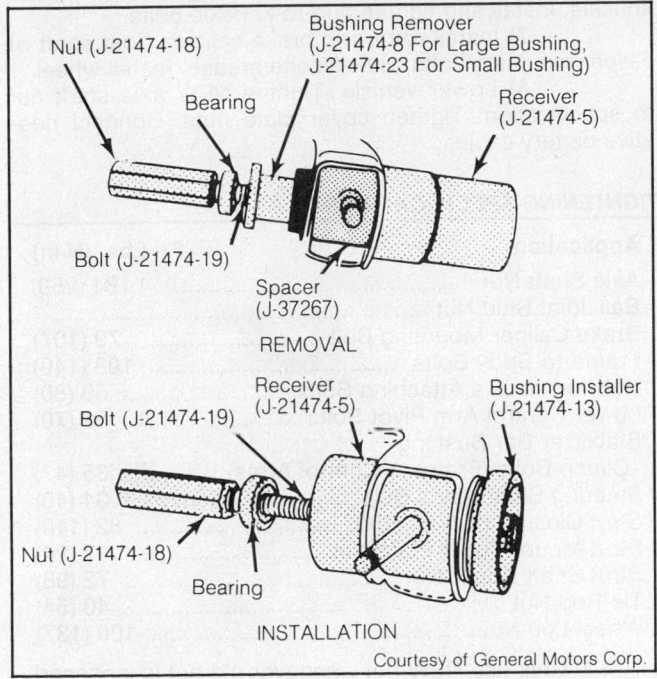

Courtesy of General Motors Corp.

3) Continue installation in reverse of removal procedure.

STABILIZER BAR & INSULATORS

Removal

1) Raise and support vehicle. Remove wheels. Slide steering shaft dust boot for access to pinch bolt. Remove pinch bolt from lower intermediate shaft.

2) Loosen all insulator clamp attaching nuts and bolts. Place jack stand under center of rear frame crossmember. Loosen 2 front frame-to-body bolts, 4 turns. Remove 2 rear frame-to-body bolts.

3) Lower rear of frame just enough to allow stabilizer bar removal. Remove insulators and clamps from control arms. Remove stabilizer bar.

Installation

1) Install stabilizer bar on vehicle. Coat insulators with rubber lubricant and install on bar.

2) Loosely install clamps at control arm and frame. Tighten all clamp fasterner.

3) Raise frame into position while guide steering shaft onto gear. Install rear frame-to-body bolts. Tighten all frame-to-body bolts to 103 ft. lbs. (140 N.m).

4) Install and tighten steering shaft pinch bolt. Continue installation in reverse of removal procedure.

STRUT CARTRIDGE

CAUTION: DO NOT remove cartridge unless weight of vehicle is on suspension.

Removal

1) Remove dust shield and strut mounting plate. *See Fig. 1.* Using No. 50 Torx bit and Strut Shaft Nut Remover (J-35669), remove upper strut nut. Pry out upper strut bushing.

2) To remove jounce bumper, place Strut Extension Rod (J-35668) on strut shaft. Compress shaft into cartridge. Remove rod and pull out jounce bumper.

3) Extend strut piston shaft with extension rod. Remove Strut Closure Nut with Strut Cap Nut Wrench (J-35671). *See Fig. 4.*

4) Lift out strut cartridge. Suction out oil from strut tube.

Fig. 4: Remove Strut Closure Nut

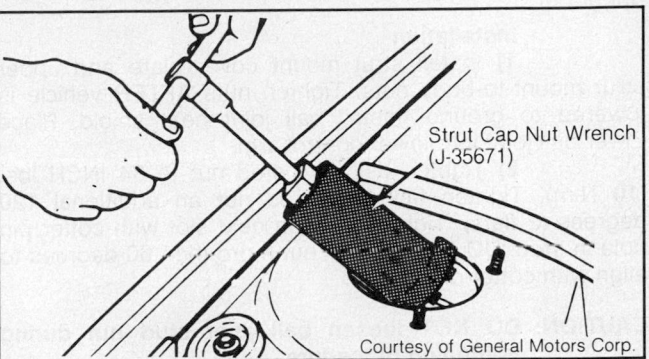

Courtesy of General Motors Corp.

Inspection

Clamp strut dampener upside down in vise. Stroke strut. If lag is noticed, gas filled cell has ruptured and cartridge should be replaced.

Installation

To install strut cartridge, reverse removal procedure. Tighten all fasteners to specification.

STRUT & KNUCKLE ASSEMBLY

CAUTION: Install new axle shaft nut and washer whenever original nut is removed. Springs are under high tension; do not remove strut shaft nut without compressing spring.

Removal

1) Disconnect negative battery cable. Scribe strut cover plate so it may be installed in original position. Loosen 3 cover plate nuts.

2) Raise and support vehicle. Remove wheels. Remove caliper from knuckle and hang out of way. Remove rotor. Remove hub-to-knuckle attaching bolts.

3) Using Front Hub Spindle Remover (J-28733-A), push axle splines out of hub and bearing assembly. *See Fig. 2.* DO NOT damage axle boots. Remove hub and bearing assembly.

4) Place drain pan below transaxle. Separate drive axle shaft from transaxle using a slide hammer and Axle Shaft Remover (J-33008). Lower drive axle shaft out of vehicle.

5) Remove tie rod-to-knuckle nut. Separate tie rod from knuckle using Tie Rod Remover (J-35917). Remove ball joint cotter pin and nut. Separate ball joint from lower control arm using Ball Joint Separator (J-35917).

6) Remove ball joint heat shield. Lower strut assembly out of vehicle.

Disassembly

1) Using spring compressor, compress spring enough to remove strut piston shaft nut with Strut Shaft Nut Remover (J-35669) and torx bit.

2) Relieve spring tension and lift out spring and other strut components. *See Fig. 1.* Use Strut Cap Nut Wrench (J-35671) to remove closure nut if cartridge is to be replaced.

Front Suspension
GENERAL MOTORS FWD "W" BODY (Cont.)

Reassembly

1) To reassemble strut, reverse disassembly procedure. Lower spring coil end must be visible between step and first retention tab of insulator.

2) Upper spring coil end must be between step and location mark on insulator. Align strut piston shaft using Strut Extension Rod (J-35668). Tighten strut shaft upper nut.

Installation

1) Install strut mount cover plate and upper strut mount-to-body nuts. Tighten nuts AFTER vehicle is lowered to ground. Install ball joint heat shield. Place lower ball joint into lower control arm.

2) Tighten ball joint stud nut to 84 INCH lbs. (10 N.m). Tighten ball joint stud nut an additional 120 degrees (2 flats). Tighten to align next slot with cotter pin hole in stud. DO NOT tighten nut more than 60 degrees to align with cotter pin hole.

CAUTION: DO NOT loosen ball joint stud nut during tightening procedure.

3) Install tie rod into steering knuckle. Tighten tie rod nut and install cotter pin.

4) Install drive axle shaft into opening in steering knuckle and into transaxle. Using frame cradle or lower control arm for leverage, seat drive axle shaft into transaxle. Use pry bar in groove provided on inner joint.

5) Ensure axle snap ring is seated by tapping on inner groove with a screwdriver. Grasp inner housing, NOT axle shaft, and pull outward. Axle will remain seated if snap ring is properly seated.

6) Install hub and bearing assembly into knuckle. Install and tighten hub-to-knuckle bolts.

7) Install rotor and brake caliper. Coat shaft of caliper mounting bolts with silicone grease. Install wheel.

8) Lower vehicle. Tighten NEW axle shaft nut to specification. Tighten cover plate nuts. Connect negative battery cable.

TIGHTENING SPECIFICATIONS

Application	Ft. Lbs. (N.m)
Axle Shaft Nut	[1] 184 (250)
Ball Joint Stud Nut	[2]
Brake Caliper Mounting Bolt	79 (107)
Frame-to-Body Bolts	103 (140)
Hub-to-Knuckle Attaching Bolts	59 (80)
Lower Control Arm Pivot Bolts	52 (70)
Stabilizer Bar Bushing Clamp Bolts (Frame & Control Arms)	35 (47)
Steering Shaft Pinch Bolt	34 (46)
Strut Closure Nut	82 (110)
Strut Mount Cover Plate Nut	17 (24)
Strut Shaft Upper Nut	72 (98)
Tie Rod Nut	40 (54)
Wheel Lug Nuts	100 (137)

[1] – Always use NEW nut whenever old nut is loosened or removed.
[2] – See text for procedure.

GENERAL MOTORS RWD
"B", "F" & "G" BODIES

"B" Body: Caprice, Custom Cruiser,
  Electra Wagon, LeSabre Wagon,
  Safari Wagon
"F" Body: Camaro, Firebird
"G" Body: Cutlass Supreme Classic,
  Monte Carlo, Regal GN

DESCRIPTION

The "B" and "G" bodies use independent front suspension. Each wheel attaches separately to frame by a steering knuckle, upper and lower control arm, and ball joint assembly.

Lower control arm inner ends connect to the frame with rubber pivot bushings and outer ends connect to steering knuckle with a ball joint. Upper control arm inner ends attach to pivot shaft, which bolts to frame. Upper control arm outer ends attach to steering knuckle with a ball joint.

The stabilizer bar controls suspension side roll. Coil springs, around shock absorbers, mount between each frame side rail or crossmember and lower control arm.

Camaro and Firebird use a steering knuckle, strut assembly, lower ball joint and lower control arm. Steering knuckles on Camaro and Firebird connect to the strut.

ADJUSTMENTS

CASTER & CAMBER

See appropriate article in WHEEL ALIGNMENT section.

RIDING HEIGHT

See RIDING HEIGHT ADJUSTMENTS and SPECIFICATIONS article in WHEEL ALIGNMENT section.

Fig. 1: Exploded View of "F" Body Vehicle Front Suspension Assembly

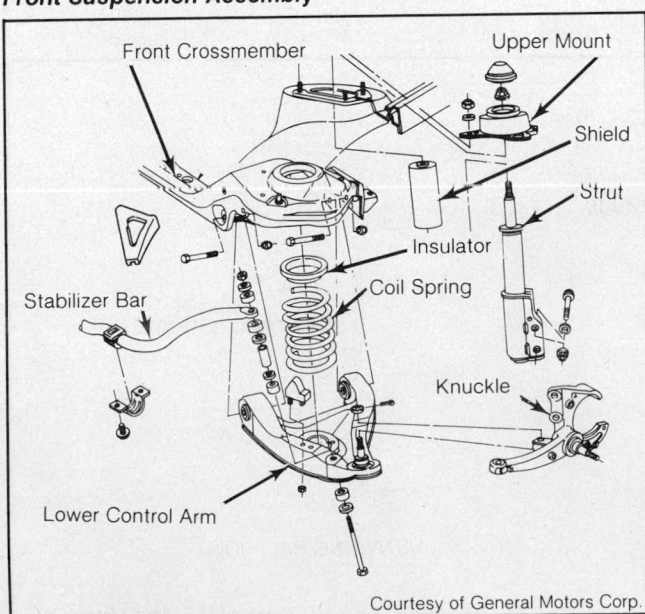

Courtesy of General Motors Corp.

FRONT WHEEL BEARINGS

1) Raise and support vehicle at lower control arms. Remove dust cap and cotter pin. Tighten spindle nut to 12 ft. lbs. (16 N.m), while spinning wheel forward by hand. Back off nut until just loose, then hand tighten.

2) Loosen or tighten nut, which ever is closest, until either hole in spindle lines up with a slot in the nut. Do not move nut more than 1/2 flat. Install new cotter pin.

3) Adjustment should provide .001-.005" (.03-.13 mm) end play. Install dust cap and lower vehicle.

Fig. 2: Exploded View of "B" & "G" Bodies Front Suspension Assembly

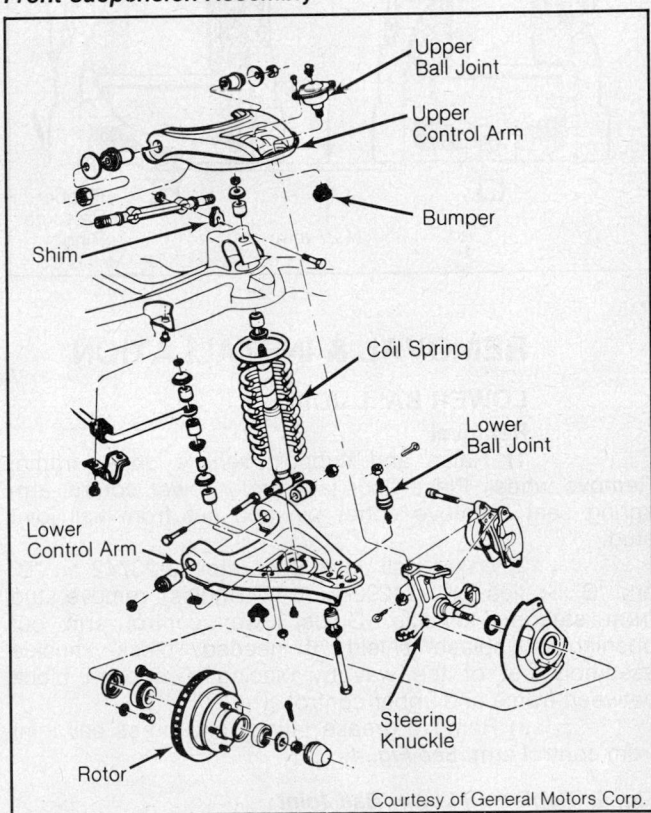

Courtesy of General Motors Corp.

BALL JOINT CHECKING

Upper Ball Joint (Exc."F" Body)

1) Raise vehicle and position jack stands under lower control arms near each ball joint. Upper control arm bumpers must not contact frame. Wheel bearings must be properly adjusted before checking ball joint.

2) Position dial indicator against lowest point of rim. Grasp wheel at top and bottom and move in and out. If gauge reads more than .125" (3.2 mm), replace ball joint.

Lower Ball Joint

1) Wheels must support vehicle to load ball joint. Check if ball joint grease fitting shoulder protrudes from ball joint cover.

2) If grease fitting shoulder is flush or inside cover, replace ball joint. See Fig. 3. Replace ball joint if boot is torn.

Front Suspension
GENERAL MOTORS RWD "B", "F" & "G" BODIES (Cont.)

Fig. 3: Checking Lower Ball Joint Wear Indicator

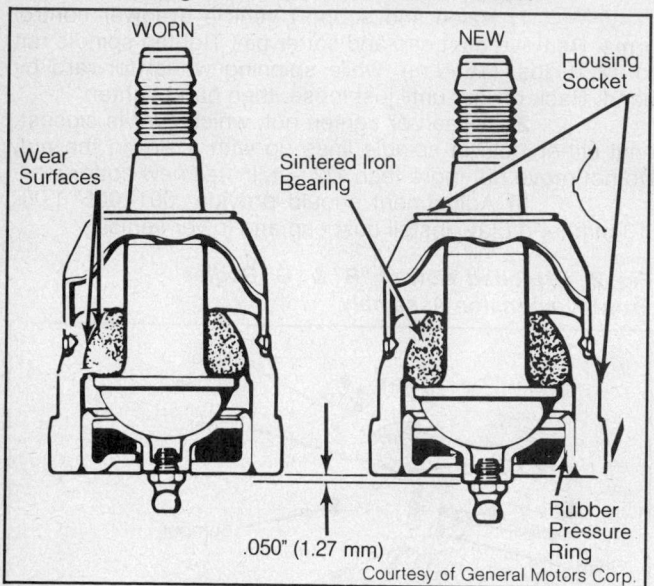

Courtesy of General Motors Corp.

REMOVAL & INSTALLATION

LOWER BALL JOINT

Removal

1) Raise and support vehicle under frame. Remove wheel. Place floor jack under lower control arm spring seat. Remove cotter pin and nut from ball joint stud.

2) Using Ball Joint Separator (J-23742 on "B" and "G" Bodies, or J-24292-A on "F" Bodies), remove stud from steering knuckle. Guide lower control arm out opening in splash shield. If needed, block knuckle assembly out of the way by placing a wooden block between frame and upper control arm.

3) Remove grease fittings and press ball joint from control arm. *See Fig. 4.*

Installation

To install, reverse removal procedure. Grease purge on seal must face inward. Tighten ball joint stud nut to specification. Check wheel alignment.

UPPER BALL JOINT

CAUTION: Floor jack or stand must remain under control arm during replacement to retain spring and control arm in position.

Removal ("B" & "G" Bodies)

1) Raise vehicle and support lower control arm near ball joint with floor stands. Remove wheel. Remove upper ball joint cotter pin and loosen nut. Install Ball Joint Separator (J-23742) between ball studs. Expand tool until stud breaks loose.

2) Remove separator and ball joint nut, and pull stud free from knuckle. Support knuckle assembly to prevent damage to brake hose. With the control arm raised, drill out top of rivet heads, using a 1/2" drill bit. Drill a 1/8" hole about 1/4" deep into remainder of rivet and drive out rivets with a punch. Remove ball joint.

Installation

1) Position new ball joint in control arm and install bolts that are supplied in the service kit. Tighten bolts to specification. Remove support from knuckle and install ball joint to steering knuckle. Tighten ball joint stud nut to specification and install cotter pin.

2) Do not loosen stud nut to insert cotter pin. Install and lubricate ball joint fitting until grease appears at seal. Install wheel and lower vehicle. Check wheel alignment.

COIL SPRING

Removal ("B" & "G" Bodies)

1) Raise vehicle support at frame side rails. Remove wheel. Disconnect shock absorber lower end and push up into spring. Install Floor Jack Adapter (J-23028) to floor jack and place into position supporting inner bushings.

Fig. 4: Replacing Lower Ball Joint

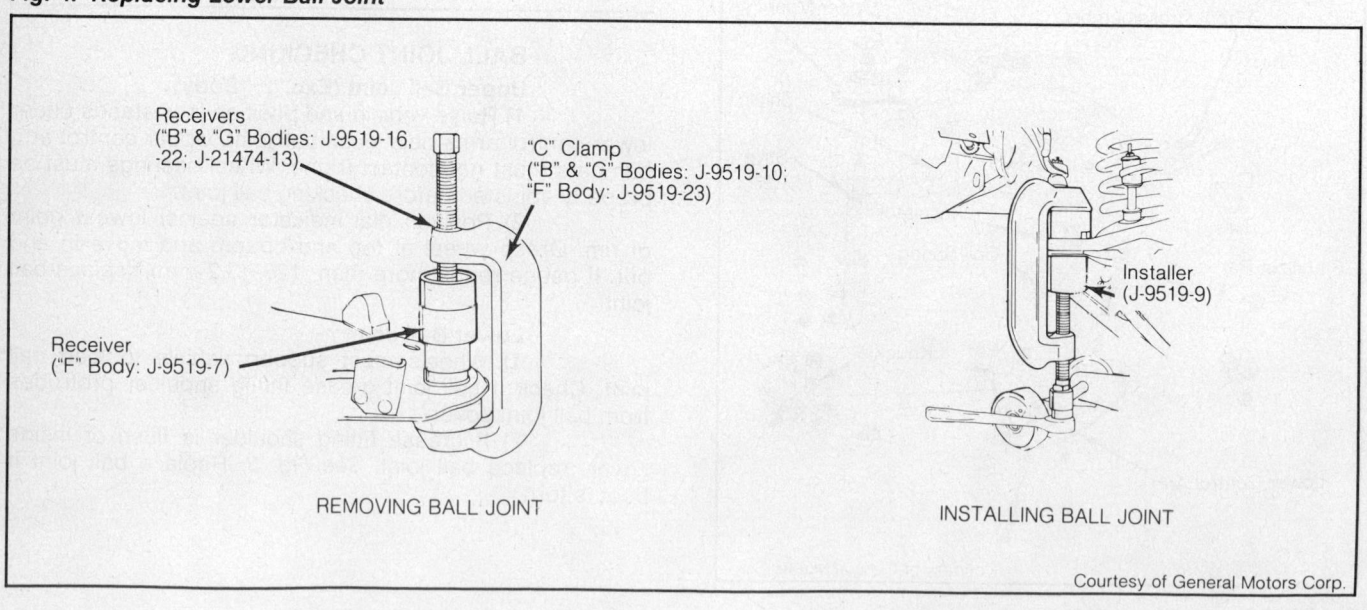

Courtesy of General Motors Corp.

GENERAL MOTORS RWD
"B", "F" & "G" BODIES (Cont.)

2) Disconnect stabilizer rod link from lower control arm. Raise jack to remove tension on lower control arm pivot bolts. Attach safety chain loosely around lower control arm and coil spring.

3) Remove pivot bolts and nuts (rear bolt first). Lower control arm slowly until spring is fully extended. Remove safety chain and spring.

NOTE: **Do not apply force on lower control arm and ball joint to remove spring. Proper maneuvering of spring will allow easy removal.**

Installation

To install, reverse removal procedure. *See Fig. 5.* When replacing front pivot bolt on lower control arm, bolt head MUST face forward. Rear pivot bolt may be installed either direction.

Fig. 5: Installing Coil Spring "B" & "G" Bodies

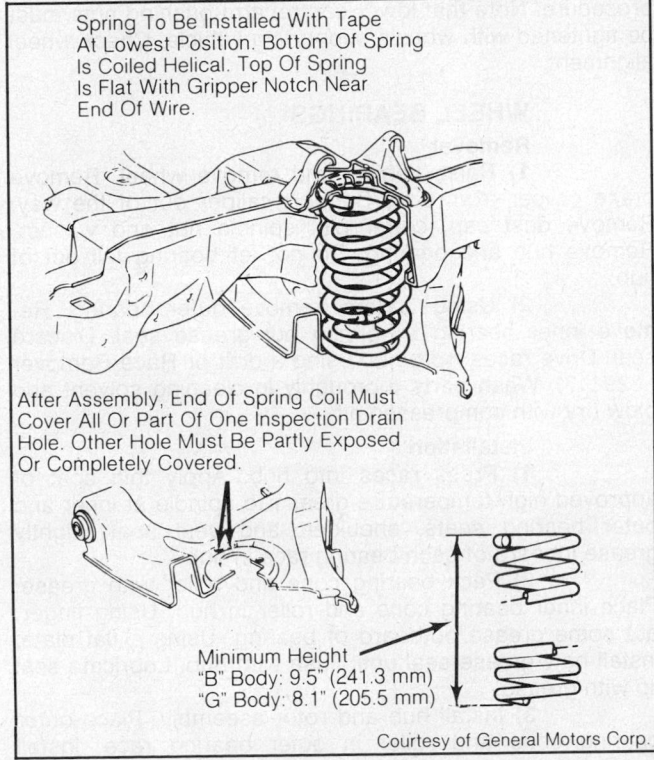

Spring To Be Installed With Tape At Lowest Position. Bottom Of Spring Is Coiled Helical. Top Of Spring Is Flat With Gripper Notch Near End Of Wire.

After Assembly, End Of Spring Coil Must Cover All Or Part Of One Inspection Drain Hole. Other Hole Must Be Partly Exposed Or Completely Covered.

Minimum Height
"B" Body: 9.5" (241.3 mm)
"G" Body: 8.1" (205.5 mm)

Courtesy of General Motors Corp.

Removal ("F" Body)

1) Raise vehicle and remove wheel. Remove stabilizer link and bushings at lower control arm. Remove pivot bolt nuts (do not remove bolts).

2) Install Floor Jack Adapter (J-23028) to floor jack and place into position supporting bushings. Install jack stand under outside frame rail on opposite side of vehicle.

3) Raise jack with adapter to remove both pivot bolts. Lower jack carefully. Remove spring and insulator. Tape insulator to spring.

Installation

To install, reverse removal procedure. Top of spring is coiled flat with gripper notch near end of wire. Spring must be turned so one inspection drain hole (in spring seat) is covered and second hole remains open.

STEERING KNUCKLE
Removal ("B" & "G" Bodies)

1) Raise and support vehicle at front lift points. Remove wheel, caliper, hub and rotor. Remove splash shield. Remove tie rod end from steering knuckle using Tie Rod Remover (J-24319-01).

2) Remove knuckle seal if knuckle is to be replaced. Remove lower ball joint cotter pin and nut. Using Ball Joint Separator (J-23742), break stud loose from knuckle. Place floor jack under lower control arm to keep coil spring in place.

3) Remove upper ball joint cotter pin and nut. Using Ball Joint Separator (J-23742), break stud loose from knuckle. Raise upper control arm to remove stud from knuckle. Raise knuckle from lower ball joint stud and remove knuckle.

Installation

To install knuckle, reverse removal procedure. Tighten ball stud nut, but do not loosen to insert cotter pin. Adjust front wheel bearings.

Removal ("F" Body)

1) Raise vehicle and remove wheel. Remove brake hose from strut. Remove caliper and support out of the way. Remove hub and rotor assembly.

2) Remove splash shield. Disconnect tie rod from knuckle. Support lower control arm. Disconnect ball joint from knuckle using Ball Joint Separator (J-24292-A). Remove 2 bolts attaching strut to knuckle and remove knuckle.

Installation

To install knuckle, reverse removal procedure. Adjust wheel bearings.

UPPER CONTROL ARM & BUSHINGS
Removal ("B" & "G" Bodies)

1) Note position of alignment shims for installation. Remove nuts from upper control arm pivot shaft. Raise vehicle and support lower control arms by placing safety stands between spring seats and ball joints.

2) Remove wheel. Separate ball joint from steering knuckle using Ball Joint Separator (J-23742). Support hub assembly to prevent damage to brake hose. Remove upper control arm.

Bushing Replacement

1) Remove pivot shaft nuts. Using "C" Clamp Fixture (J-22269-5, J-24770-2 and J-24770-3), press out and discard both bushings. To install bushings, place pivot shaft in control arm and push bushing over end of pivot shaft.

2) On "G" body vehicles, install both upper control arm bushings .50" (13.3 mm) from face of control arm to the bushing sleeve. Assemble nuts to ends of pivot shaft. Assemble using Adapter (J-24770-1). *See Fig. 6.*

Installation

To install upper control arm, reverse removal procedure. If bushings were replaced, fully tighten control arm pivot shaft end nuts AFTER vehicle is on ground. Check wheel alignment.

Front Suspension
GENERAL MOTORS RWD
"B", "F" & "G" BODIES (Cont.)

Fig. 6: Upper Control Arm Bushing Replacement on "G" Body Vehicles

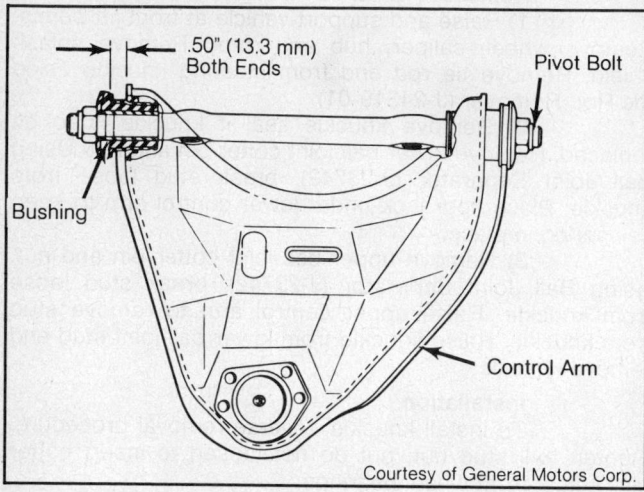

Courtesy of General Motors Corp.

LOWER CONTROL ARM & BUSHINGS

Removal

Remove coil spring. See COIL SPRING in this article. Separate ball joint from steering knuckle using Ball Joint Separator (J-23742 for "B" and "G" bodies, or J-24292A for "F" body). Support and remove lower control arm. Guide lower control arm out opening in splash shield.

Front Bushing Replacement

1) Using a blunt chisel, drive bushing flare down flush with bushing rubber. Press out bushing using the following tools:

- "B" Body – Control Arm Bushing "C" Clamp Fixture (J-21474-5, -8, -19; J-22323-1).
- "G" Body – Control Arm Bushing "C" Clamp Fixture (J-21474-5, -18, -19, -23; J-23737).

Fig. 7: Flaring Lower Control Arm Front Bushing

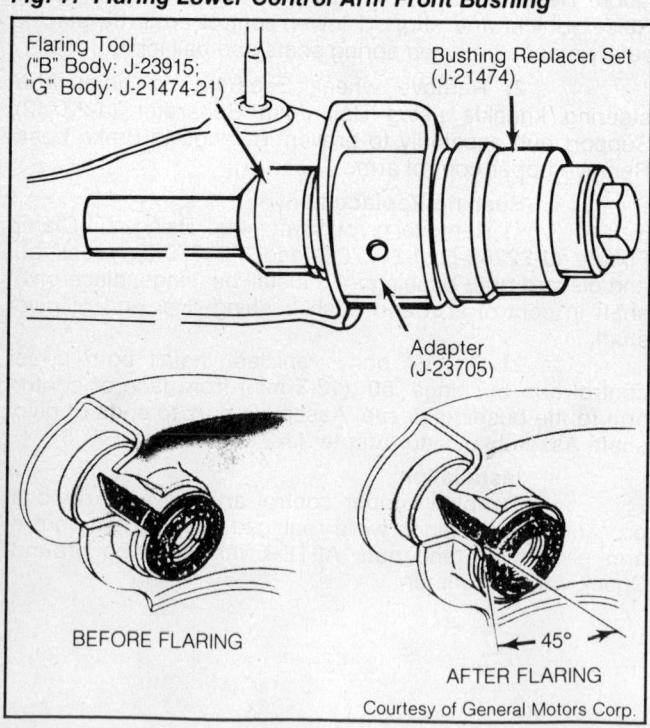

BEFORE FLARING

AFTER FLARING

Courtesy of General Motors Corp.

- "F" Body – Control Arm Bushing "C" Clamp Fixture (J-21474-5, -18, -19, -23; J-22899).

2) Using same tools, press new bushing in place. Front bushing must be flared after installation. *See Fig. 7.*

Rear Bushing Replacement

Replace bushing in control arm using following tools:

- "B" Body – "C" Clamp Fixture (J-21474-5, -8, -12, -18, -19).
- "G" Body • "C" Clamp Fixture (J-21474-5, -8, -18, -19; J-22899).
- "F" Body • "C" Clamp Fixture (J-21474-5, -18, -19, -23; J-22899).

Press in new bushing using same tools. Bushing should bottom against control arm.

Installation

To install lower control arm, reverse removal procedure. Note that lower control arm bushing nuts must be tightened with wheels supporting vehicle. Check wheel alignment.

WHEEL BEARINGS

Removal

1) Raise vehicle and remove wheel. Remove brake caliper from disc. Support caliper out of the way. Remove dust cap, cotter pin, spindle nut and washer. Remove hub and bearing. Do not let bearing fall out of hub.

2) Using fingers, remove outer bearing. Remove inner bearing by prying out grease seal. Discard seal. Drive races from hub using a drift or Race Remover (J-29117). Wash parts thoroughly in cleaning solvent and blow dry with compressed air.

Installation

1) Press races into hub. Apply thin coat of approved high temperature grease to spindle at inner and outer bearing seats, shoulder, and seal seat. Lightly grease inboard of each bearing race in hub.

2) Pack bearing cone and roller with grease. Place inner bearing cone and roller in hub. Using finger, put some grease outboard of bearing. Using a flat plate, install new grease seal until flush with hub. Lubricate seal lip with grease.

3) Install hub and rotor assembly. Place outer bearing cone and roller in outer bearing race. Install washer and nut. Install brake caliper. Adjust bearing preload. See FRONT WHEEL BEARING ADJUSTMENT in this article.

STABILIZER BAR

Removal

Raise vehicle and support with safety stands. Disconnect each stabilizer bar end linkage. Pull bolt from linkage and remove retainers, grommets and spacers. Remove bracket-to-body bolts. Remove stabilizer bar, bushings and brackets.

Installation

1) To install stabilizer bar, reverse removal procedure. On "B" and "G" bodies, install with stabilizer bar on right side of vehicle. On all vehicles, rubber bushings should be installed with slits facing forward.

GENERAL MOTORS RWD
"B", "F" & "G" BODIES (Cont.)

2) Stabilizer bar attaching bolts should be installed with bolt head facing down. On "F" body, hold end of stabilizer bar about 2" from bottom of side rail when tightening insulators. Tighten bracket bolts to specification.

TIGHTENING SPECIFICATIONS

Application	Ft. Lbs. (N.m)
Ball Joint Stud Nut [1]	
Lower	
"B" & "G" Body	83 (112)
"F" Body	78 (105)
Upper	
"B" & "G" Body	61 (83)
Lower Control Arm-to-Frame Bolts	
"B" Body	92 (125)
"F" Body	63 (85)
"G" Body	66 (90)
Strut-to-Steering Knuckle Bolts	
"F" Body	202 (275)
Stabilizer Shaft Bracket-to-Frame Nuts	
"F" Body	37 (50)
"B" & "G" Body	24 (33)
Stabilizer Shaft Link Nut	13 (18)
Upper Control Arm-to-Frame Bolts	
"B" Body	72 (98)
"G" Body	48 (65)
Upper Control Arm Bushing Nuts	
"B" & "G" Bodies	[2] 85 (115)

	INCH Lbs. (N.m)
Upper Ball Joint-to-Control Arm Bolts	96 (11)

[1] – Always advance nut to line up cotter pin slot; never loosen.

[2] – Tighten after wheels are on ground.

Front Suspension

CADILLAC BROUGHAM

DESCRIPTION

System is an independent spring type suspension, consisting of 2 upper and 2 lower control arm assemblies, coil springs, shock absorbers, a stabilizer bar, 2 integral steering arms, and knuckles. Suspension is designed to produce an anti-dive reaction during braking.

ADJUSTMENTS

CASTER & CAMBER

See appropriate article in WHEEL ALIGNMENT section.

RIDING HEIGHT

See RIDING HEIGHT SPECIFICATIONS article in WHEEL ALIGNMENT section.

FRONT WHEEL BEARINGS

Raise vehicle and support at lower control arm. Remove dust cap and cotter pin. Tighten spindle nut to 12 ft. lbs. (16 N.m) while rotating wheel by hand. Back off nut until just loose, then hand tighten until snug. Back off about 1/2 hex (1/12th turn) so cotter pin may be inserted. Adjustment should provide about .001-.005" (.03-.13 mm) end play. Install new cotter pin and dust cap. Lower vehicle.

BALL JOINT CHECKING

Upper Ball Joint

1) Ensure wheel bearings are properly adjusted. Raise vehicle. Position floor stands under lower control arm as near as possible to ball joint. Upper control arm bumpers must not contact frame.

2) Position dial indicator against lowest point of rim. Grasp front wheel at top and bottom and move in and out. Read gauge. If measurement is more than .13" (3.2 mm), replace ball joint.

Lower Ball Joint

1) Vehicle must be supported by wheels, so ball joints are properly loaded. Lower ball joint is inspected for wear by visual observation alone. Wear is indicated by the protrusion of the nipple into which grease fitting is threaded.

2) On new ball joints, this round nipple projects .050" (1.27 mm) beyond the surface of the ball joint cover. If fitting is flush or recessed, replace ball joint.

REMOVAL & INSTALLATION

UPPER BALL JOINT

Removal

1) Raise vehicle and remove wheel assembly. Remove caliper and support out of the way. Remove cotter pin from upper ball joint stud.

2) Loosen stud nut about one turn (do not remove). Install Ball Joint Separator (J-23742) and turn threaded end of tool until stud is free of steering knuckle.

NOTE: **Lower control arm must be supported so chassis spring cannot force arm down.**

3) Remove upper ball joint stud nut. Swing knuckle out of the way. Lift and support upper control arm with block of wood between frame and arm. Use a drill to remove heads of rivets. Use a punch to drive rivets out of control arm.

Installation

1) Install new ball joint in arm and attach with bolts (supplied in kit). Insert bolts from bottom of control arm. Stud cotter pin hole should run fore and aft.

2) Remove wood support from upper arm and clean tapered hole in steering knuckle. Attach ball joint to steering knuckle. Install caliper. Lubricate ball joint and install wheel assembly. Lower vehicle and check wheel alignment.

LOWER BALL JOINT

Removal

1) Raise vehicle and remove wheel assembly. Loosen stud nut one turn (do not remove). Using Ball Joint Separator (J-23742) between studs, turn threaded end of tool until stud is free of steering knuckle.

NOTE: **Lower control arm must be supported so chassis spring cannot force arm down.**

2) Remove lower stud nut. Pull outward on bottom of tire and at same time push wheel assembly upward to free knuckle from ball joint stud. Lift up on upper control arm, with knuckle and hub assembly attached, and place a block of wood between frame and upper arm.

3) Remove tie rod end from steering knuckle (if necessary). Place Ball Joint Remover/Installer (J-9519-03 and J-9519-7) over ball joint. Turn hex nut bolt until lower ball joint is pushed out of control arm.

Installation

1) Position ball joint in lower control arm with bleed vent in boot facing inward. Using remover/installer, turn down hex head bolt until joint is seated. Remove tool. Align stud cotter pin hole fore and aft.

2) Remove wood support from upper control arm. Inspect tapered hole in steering knuckle and clean. Connect lower joint stud to steering knuckle and install stud nut. Install new cotter pin.

NOTE: **Do not back off nut for cotter pin installation. Turn nut 1/6 turn maximum to install cotter pin.**

3) Lubricate ball joint. Install tie rod end (if removed). Install wheel assembly. Check wheel alignment.

UPPER CONTROL ARM

Removal

1) Raise vehicle and support at lower control arm. Remove wheel assembly. Separate upper arm ball joint stud from steering knuckle.

2) Remove nuts securing arm shaft to frame bracket and remove assembly. Mark shims for proper positioning upon reassembly.

Front Suspension

CADILLAC BROUGHAM (Cont.)

Fig. 1: Removing Upper Control Arm Bushing

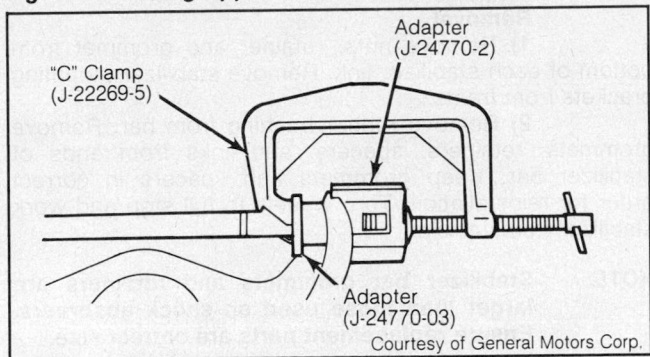

Courtesy of General Motors Corp.

Bushing Replacement

With upper control arm removed from vehicle, remove bushing nuts. Using Control Arm Bushing Replacer (J-22269-5, J-24770-2 and J-24770-3), remove bushings. *See Fig. 1.* Install bushings using Adapter (J-24770-1) and tools used for removal. *See Fig. 2.*

Fig. 2: Installing Upper Control Arm Bushing

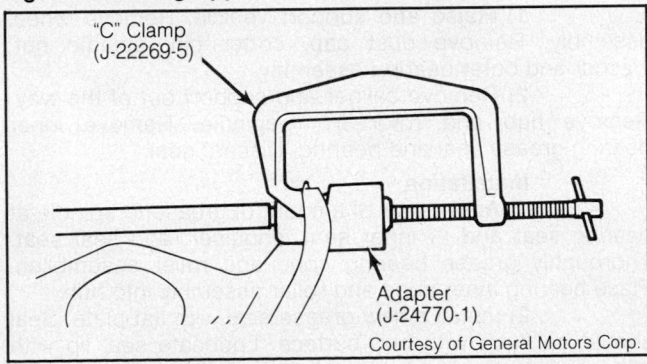

Courtesy of General Motors Corp.

Installation

1) Position new upper arm attaching bolts loosely in frame. Install control arm cross shaft on attaching bolts. Using a free running nut, instead of regular lock nut, tighten both nuts until serrated bolts are reseated.

2) Remove free running nuts. Install regular lock nuts. Install same number of shims to each bolt that was removed. Tighten mounting nuts. Tighten nut on thinner shim pack first for proper clamping force. Install wheel assembly and lower vehicle. Check wheel alignment.

LOWER CONTROL ARM & COIL SPRING

Removal

1) Raise vehicle. Remove shock absorber lower mounting bolts. Push shock up through control arm and into spring. Support vehicle so control arm hang free.

2) Place floor jack, with Adapter (J-23028-01) attached, into position so it cradles inner bushings of lower control arm. Adapter must be secured to jack. Remove stabilizer bar-to-lower control arm attaching bolts.

3) Raise jack to remove tension on lower arm pivot bolts. Install a safety chain around spring and through lower arm. Remove rear pivot bolt first, then remaining bolts and nuts.

4) Lower control arm by slowly lowering jack. When all compression is removed from spring, remove chain and spring. Do not use force to remove spring. Proper maneuvering of spring will allow it to be removed easily.

5) To remove lower control arm from steering knuckle, use Ball Joint Separator (J-23742). Remove lower control arm from vehicle.

Installation

Position the spring into frame so lower end of the coil covers all or part of one inspection hole in lower control arm. Second hole must be partially or completely uncovered. *See Fig. 3.* Reverse removal procedure to complete installation of lower control arm and spring.

Fig. 3: Coil Spring Positioning

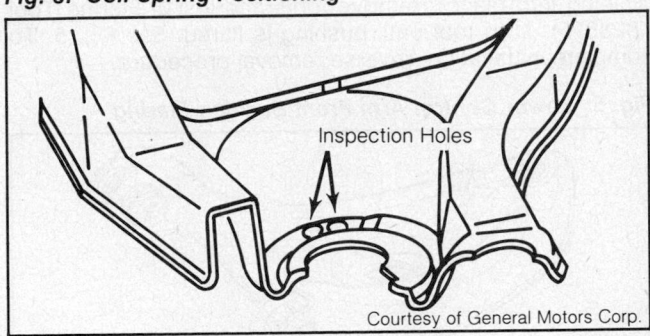

Inspection Holes

Courtesy of General Motors Corp.

LOWER CONTROL ARM REAR BUSHING

Removal

1) Raise vehicle. Support frame with jack stands so lower control arm hang free. Remove lower shock absorber mounting bolts. Push shock up through control arm into coil spring.

2) Position floor jack, with Adapter (J-23028-01) attached, under lower control arm so bushings seat in grooves of tool. Install safety chain around lower arm and through coil spring.

3) Remove lower arm rear pivot bolt first, then remaining bolts and nuts. If bolts hang up in lower control arm, release by using pry bar. Do not use a hammer. Lower control arm by slowly releasing jack.

4) Install Spacer (J-21474-12). *See Fig. 4.* Install remaining tools and turn hex bolt and nut until bushing is removed. Remove tools and discard bushing.

Fig. 4: Removing Lower Control Arm Bushing

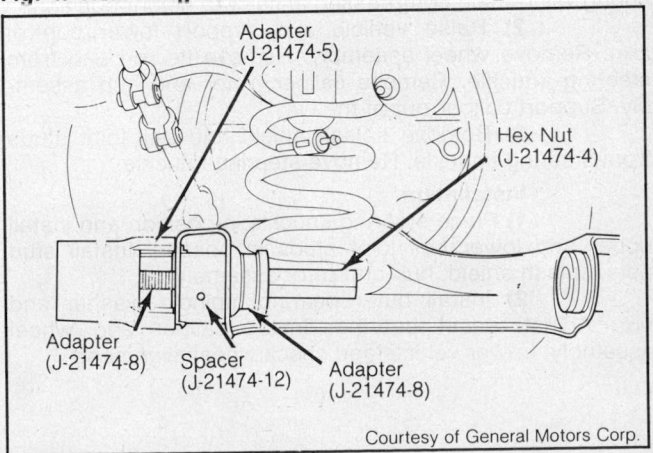

Courtesy of General Motors Corp.

Installation

Position new bushing and install correct tools. *See Fig. 4.* Turn hex bolt and nut until new bushing is seated. Reverse removal procedure to complete assembly.

LOWER CONTROL ARM FRONT BUSHING

Removal

Remove lower control arm as previously described. Remove bushing flare by tapping on edge with hammer. Install tools. *See Fig. 4.* Turn down on hex nut until bushing is removed.

Installation

Place installation tools in position. Press bushing into place. Remove tools and install Flaring Tool (J-23915). Turn tool until bushing is flared. *See Fig. 5.* To complete installation, reverse removal procedure.

Fig. 5: Lower Control Arm Front Bushing Flaring

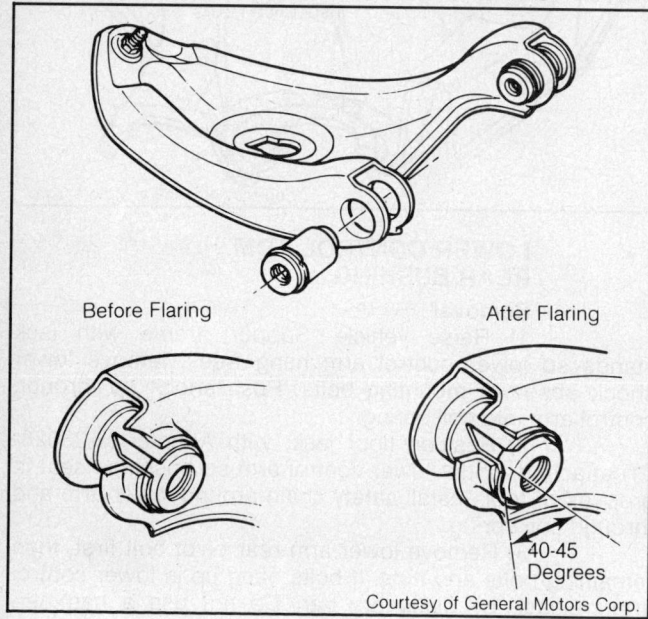

Before Flaring

After Flaring

40-45 Degrees

Courtesy of General Motors Corp.

STEERING KNUCKLE

Removal

1) If a frame hoist rather than twin post hoist is used to raise vehicle, support lower control arm so coil spring will remain compressed in its curb height position.

2) Raise vehicle and support lower control arm. Remove wheel assembly. Remove tie rod end from steering knuckle. Remove caliper, rotor and hub assembly. Support caliper out of the way.

3) Remove splash shield and ball joint studs from steering knuckle. Remove steering knuckle.

Installation

1) Place steering knuckle in position and install upper and lower ball joint studs in bosses. Install stud nuts, splash shield, hub and rotor assembly.

2) Install outer bearing, spindle washer and nut. Adjust wheel bearing. Install caliper and wheel assembly. Lower vehicle and check wheel alignment.

STABILIZER BAR

Removal

1) Remove nuts, retainer and grommet from bottom of each stabilizer link. Remove stabilizer mounting brackets from frame.

2) Remove rubber bushing from bar. Remove grommets, retainers, spacers, and links from ends of stabilizer bar. Keep grommets and spacers in correct order for reinstallation. Turn wheels to full stop and work stabilizer from vehicle.

NOTE: Stabilizer bar grommets and retainers are larger than those used on shock absorbers. Ensure replacement parts are correct size.

Installation

Position stabilizer bar under front frame side rails. Slide bushings into place with slit forward. Install mounting brackets over bushings and tighten bolts. To complete installation, reverse removal procedure.

WHEEL BEARINGS

Removal

1) Raise and support vehicle. Remove wheel assembly. Remove dust cap, cotter pin, spindle nut, washer and outer bearing assembly.

2) Remove caliper and support out of the way. Remove hub and rotor from spindle. Remove inner bearing grease seal and bearing. Discard seal.

Installation

1) Apply a small amount of grease to spindle at bearing seat and at inner seat, shoulder, and seal seat. Thoroughly grease bearing cone and roller assemblies. Place bearing inner cone and roller assembly into hub.

2) Install a new grease seal with flat plate. Seal should be flush with hub surface. Lubricate seal lip with thin coating of grease. Install hub and rotor assembly. Place outer cone and roller assembly in outer bearing cup.

3) Install washer and nut and finger tighten. Install caliper and wheel assembly. Install wheel mounting nuts finger tight. Adjust wheel bearings. See ADJUSTMENTS in this article. Install dust cap. Install wheel assembly and lower vehicle. Tighten nuts.

TIGHTENING SPECIFICATIONS

Application	Ft. Lbs. (N.m)
Lower Ball Joint-to-Knuckle Nuts	83 (112)
Lower Control Arm Bushing	
Bolts	114 (154)
Nuts	92 (125)
Shock Absorber Lower Bolts	20 (27)
Stabilizer Link Nuts	13 (18)
Stabilizer Bracket-to-Frame Bolts	24 (33)
Tie Rod Pivot-to-Knuckle Nuts	35 (47)
Upper Ball Joint-to-Knuckle Nuts	61 (83)
Upper Control Arm-to-Frame Nuts	72 (98)
Upper Ball Joint-to-Control Arm Nuts	20 (27)
Wheel Lug Nuts	100 (136)

Front Suspension

CORVETTE

DESCRIPTION

The independent front suspension is manufactured from a special high strength forged aluminum for the control arms and steering knuckles. A fiberglass monoleaf spring is mounted transversely below the control arms. Shock absorbers are secured to frame cradles and lower control arms.

Upper and lower control arm pivot shafts are mounted to the frame with adjusting shims between upper pivot shaft and crossmember for caster and camber adjustments. Tubular or solid stabilizer bar and offset spindles are used to provide better handling.

ADJUSTMENTS

CASTER, CAMBER & TOE-IN

See appropriate article in WHEEL ALIGNMENT section.

RIDING HEIGHT

See RIDING HEIGHT SPECIFICATIONS in WHEEL ALIGNMENT section.

FRONT WHEEL BEARINGS

Hub and wheel bearings are a sealed unit which require no adjustment.

BALL JOINT CHECKING

Upper Ball Joint

Raise and support vehicle with jack stands positioned under lower control arms near the ball joints. Position dial indicator with stem resting against the lowest point of the wheel. Grasp tire at top and bottom. Note reading while moving the wheel inward and outward. Replace ball joint if movement exceeds .125" (3.18 mm) or stud can be rotated with fingers when ball joint is removed.

Lower Ball Joint

Place car in normal operating position. Check that ball joint grease fitting shoulder does not protrude past ball joint housing cover. See Fig. 1. Replace ball joint if grease fitting is flush or below cover.

Fig. 1: Lower Ball Joint Wear Indicator

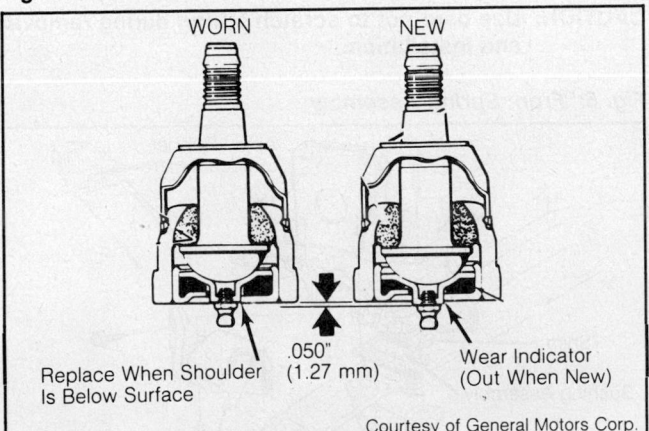

WORN   NEW

Replace When Shoulder Is Below Surface
.050" (1.27 mm)
Wear Indicator (Out When New)

Courtesy of General Motors Corp.

REMOVAL & INSTALLATION

UPPER BALL JOINT

Removal

1) Raise and support vehicle at lower control arms. Remove wheel. Remove ball joint stud cotter pin and nut. Install Ball Joint Separator (J-33436) between upper and lower ball joints with large end downward.

2) Expand separator to loosen ball joint from steering knuckle. Support steering knuckle and remove separator. Drill out rivet heads and remove. Remove ball joint.

Installation

Install ball joint in control arm. Install retaining bolts so that the nuts are positioned on top of the ball joint. Install ball joint into steering knuckle. Install new washer and nut. Tighten to specification. See TIGHTENING SPECIFICATIONS table at end of article. Install cotter pin from rear to front. Lubricate new ball joint. Check and adjust wheel alignment.

Fig. 2: Front Suspension Assembly

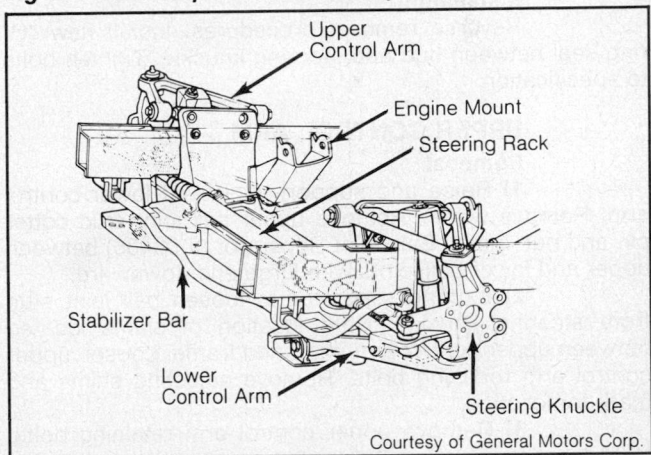

Upper Control Arm
Engine Mount
Steering Rack
Stabilizer Bar
Lower Control Arm
Steering Knuckle

Courtesy of General Motors Corp.

LOWER BALL JOINT

Removal

1) Raise and support vehicle at lower control arms. Remove wheel. Remove ball joint stud cotter pin and nut. Install Ball Joint Separator (J-33436) between upper and lower ball joints with large end upward.

2) Expand separator to loosen ball joint stud from steering knuckle. Support knuckle and remove separator. Using Ball Joint Extractor (J-9519-7) and Adapter (J-9519-10), remove lower ball joint from control arm.

Installation

1) Using Installer (J-9519-9) and Adapter (J-9515-10), install new ball joint in control arm. Install ball joint stud into steering knuckle. Install new washer and nut. Tighten nut to specification.

2) Install new cotter pin from rear to front. DO NOT loosen nut to align nut slot with stud hole. Install grease fitting so it is facing inward. Lubricate ball joint. Check and adjust wheel alignment.

Front Suspension

CORVETTE (Cont.)

STEERING KNUCKLE

Removal

1) Raise and support vehicle at lower control arm. Remove wheel, brake caliper, rotor and hub assembly. Disconnect brake sensor. Use care not to damage brake sensor wiring.

2) Disconnect tie rod from steering knuckle. Remove ball joint stud cotter pin and nut. Using Ball Joint Separator (J-33436-9), disconnect upper and lower ball joints from steering knuckle. Remove steering knuckle.

Installation

Reverse removal procedures. Tighten all retainers to specification. DO NOT loosen ball joint stud nut for cotter pin installation. Install new cotter pin from rear to front.

HUB & BEARING ASSEMBLY

Removal

Raise and support vehicle. Remove wheel, brake caliper and rotor. Remove hub and bearing assembly.

Installation

Reverse removal procedures. Install new "O" ring seal between hub and steering knuckle. Tighten bolts to specification.

UPPER CONTROL ARM

Removal

1) Raise and support vehicle at lower control arm. Remove wheel. Remove upper ball joint stud cotter pin and nut. Install Ball Joint Separator (J-33436) between upper and lower ball joints with large end downward.

2) Expand separator to loosen ball joint stud from steering knuckle. Note location of shims located between upper control arm shaft and frame. Loosen upper control arm retaining bolts. Remove adjusting shims and mark for location.

3) Remove upper control arm retaining bolts. Note location of washers located on retaining bolts. *See Fig. 3.* Remove upper control arm.

Installation

Reverse removal procedures. Ensure washers are properly positioned. *See Fig. 3.* Install shims in original location. Tighten bolts to specification. DO NOT loosen nut to align cotter pin slot. Install new cotter pin from rear to front. Check and adjust wheel alignment.

Fig. 3: Exploded View of Upper Control Arm

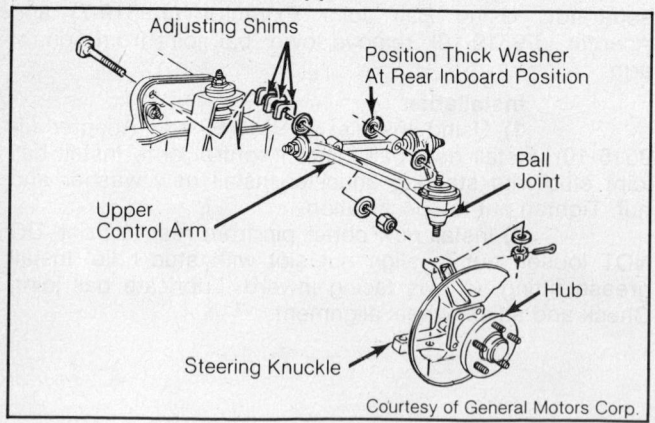

Adjusting Shims

Position Thick Washer At Rear Inboard Position

Ball Joint

Upper Control Arm

Hub

Steering Knuckle

Courtesy of General Motors Corp.

LOWER CONTROL ARM

Removal

1) Raise and support vehicle. Remove wheel. Remove spring protector. *See Fig. 5.* Using Spring Compressor (J-33432), compress spring. *See Fig. 4.* Remove shock absorber from control arm.

2) Using Ball Joint Separator (J-33436), disconnect lower ball joint from control arm. Remove lower control arm retaining bolts. Remove lower control arm.

Fig. 4: Compressing Front Spring

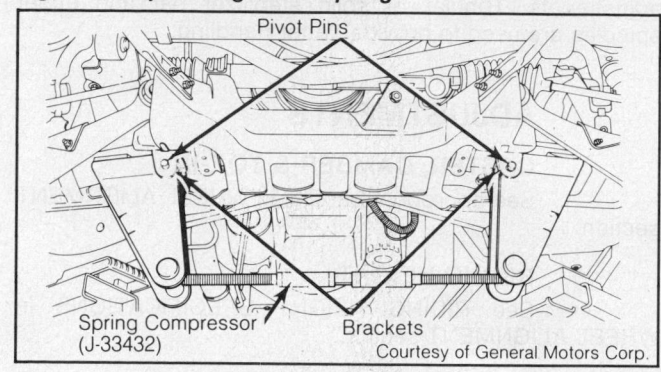

Pivot Pins

Spring Compressor (J-33432)

Brackets

Courtesy of General Motors Corp.

Installation

Reverse removal procedures. Maintain suspension in normal driving position while tightening lower control arm retaining bolts. Tighten bolts to specification. DO NOT loosen nut to align cotter pin slot. Install new cotter pin from rear to front.

TRANSVERSE SPRING

Removal

1) Raise and support vehicle. Remove wheels. Remove spring protectors. *See Fig. 5.* Remove spring retaining nuts. Install Spring Compressor (J-33432). *See Fig. 4.*

2) Using Ball Joint Separator (J-33436), disconnect lower ball joints from lower control arms. Compress spring compressor. Remove shock mounting bracket-to-lower control arm bolts. Remove stabilizer bar-to-lower control arm bolt. Release and remove spring compressor. Move lower control arms downward and remove spring. Mark spring shims for location.

CAUTION: Use care not to scratch spring during removal and installation.

Fig. 5: Front Spring Assembly

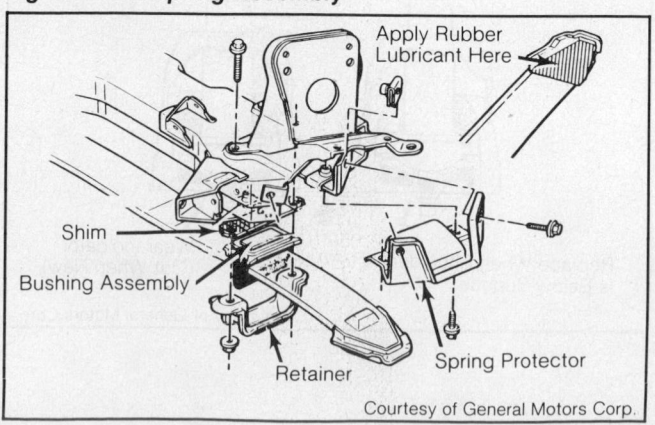

Apply Rubber Lubricant Here

Shim

Bushing Assembly

Retainer

Spring Protector

Courtesy of General Motors Corp.

CORVETTE (Cont.)

Installation

1) Reverse removal procedure. Apply rubber lubricant to the end of spring. *See Fig. 5.* Different number of shims must be installed according to spring color code. See SPRING SHIM REQUIREMENT table. Tighten retainers to specification.

    2) Install stabilizer bar using proper procedure. See INSTALLATION under STABILIZER BAR in this article. Check and adjust wheel alignment.

SPRING SHIM REQUIREMENT

Spring Color Code	Shims Required
Blue	0
Green	2
White	1

STABILIZER BAR

Removal

Disconnect stabilizer bar at lower control arm. Note direction of bolt. Disconnect stabilizer bar mounts at the frame. Remove stabilizer bar.

Installation

1) Loosely install stabilizer bar to frame. Press end bushings in stabilizer bar. Bushing should be positioned so that measurement from stabilizer bar to bushing flange is approximately 1/2".

    2) Install stabilizer bar-to-lower control arm bracket bolt so bolt head is toward the car frame. Tighten all bolts with suspension at "Z" trim height. *See Fig. 6.* The distance between lower inboard end and lowest inboard point on lower ball joint housing is the "Z" trim height. This height must be adjusted within .25" (6.4 mm) of specification. See "Z" TRIM HEIGHT SPECIFICATIONS table.

"Z" TRIM HEIGHT SPECIFICATIONS

Vin	Tire Size	Susp.	Height In. (mm)
YA00	P255-50VR16	STD	1.93 (49.2)
YA00	P255-50VR16	FE7	2.14 (54.6)
YA67	P255-50VR16	STD	2.31 (58.8)

Fig. 6: Determining "Z" Trim Height

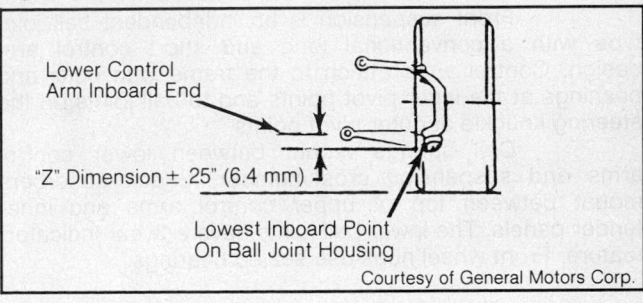

Lower Control Arm Inboard End

"Z" Dimension ± .25" (6.4 mm)

Lowest Inboard Point On Ball Joint Housing

Courtesy of General Motors Corp.

TIGHTENING SPECIFICATIONS

Application	Ft. Lbs. (N.m)
Ball Joint Stud Nut	
Lower	50 (68)
Upper	33 (45)
Control Arm Retaining Bolt	
Lower Control Arm	[1] 82 (111)
Upper Control Arm	37 (51)
Hub & Bearing Assembly Bolt	46 (62)
Shock Absorber Mounting Bolt	
Lower	19 (26)
Upper	19 (26)
Spring Mount Bolt	[1] 48 (65)
Spring Protector Bolt	18 (24)
Stabilizer Bar	
Link Bolt	[1] 35 (47)
Clamp-to-Frame Nut	[1] 40 (54)
Stabilizer Link-to-Lower	
Control Arm Bolt	22 (30)
Tie Rod Nut	32 (43)

[1] – Tighten with vehicle at normal operating height.

Front Suspension

FIERO

DESCRIPTION

Front suspension is an independent ball joint type with a conventional long and short control arm design. Control arms attach to the frame with bolts and bushings at the inner pivot points and to ball joints on the steering knuckle at outer pivot points.

Coil springs mount between lower control arms and suspension crossmember. Shock absorbers mount between top of upper control arms and inner fender panels. The lower ball joints have a "wear indicator" feature. Front wheel hubs use sealed bearings.

ADJUSTMENTS

CASTER & CAMBER

See appropriate article in WHEEL ALIGNMENT section.

RIDING HEIGHT

See RIDING HEIGHT ADJUSTMENTS article in WHEEL ALIGNMENT section.

FRONT WHEEL BEARINGS

Raise and support vehicle at lower control arms. Rotate wheel and check for bent rim. If bearings are noisy, spin wheels with engine (35 MPH maximum). If front wheel bearings are noisy, replace hub and bearing assembly.

BALL JOINT CHECKING

1) To determine if lower ball joints are worn, simply wipe off area around lower grease fitting and note position of grease fitting. If the tip of grease fitting is flush with bottom of ball joint housing, ball joint needs replacing.

2) To determine if upper ball joints are worn, raise vehicle. Position jack stands under lower control arms. Upper control arm bumper must not contact frame. Hold wheel assembly at top and bottom, move wheel in and out. If there is any movement in upper ball joint, wear is indicated. Replace ball joint.

REMOVAL & INSTALLATION

LOWER BALL JOINT

Removal

1) Raise and support vehicle on frame hoist. Remove wheel. Support lower control arm with jack to compress coil spring. Disconnect tie rod from steering knuckle. Remove cotter pin and lower ball joint stud nut.

2) Reinstall nut and tighten finger tight. Install Ball Joint Remover (J-26407) with cup end over upper joint stud nut. Ensure heavy flat washer is used between tool and upper stud nut.

3) Turn threaded end of remover until lower joint stud is free of knuckle. Remove tool and washer. Detach nut from stud. Remove ball joint from lower control arm. *See Fig. 2.* Clean and inspect tapered stud hole in steering knuckle. Replace knuckle if any wear condition is found. See STEERING KNUCKLE in this article.

Fig. 1: Exploded View of Front Suspension

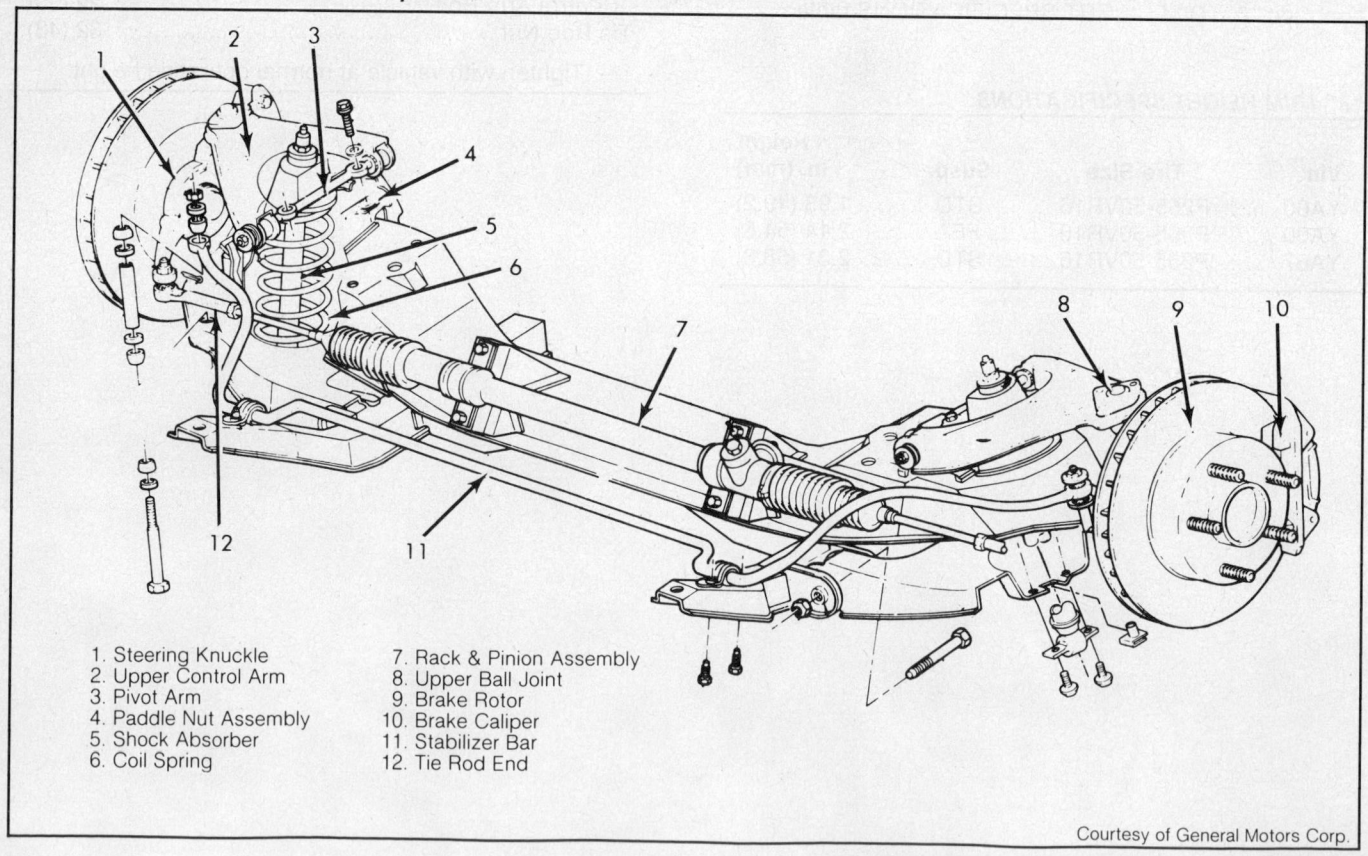

1. Steering Knuckle
2. Upper Control Arm
3. Pivot Arm
4. Paddle Nut Assembly
5. Shock Absorber
6. Coil Spring
7. Rack & Pinion Assembly
8. Upper Ball Joint
9. Brake Rotor
10. Brake Caliper
11. Stabilizer Bar
12. Tie Rod End

Courtesy of General Motors Corp.

FIERO (Cont.)

Installation

1) Install ball joint through lower control arm. *See Fig. 2.* Position stud into steering knuckle. With a used nut, draw ball joint into position and tighten nut to specification.

2) Remove and discard the used nut. Install a new special ball joint stud nut and tighten to specification. Remove jack. Install wheel and lower vehicle.

Fig. 2: Removing & Installing Ball Joint

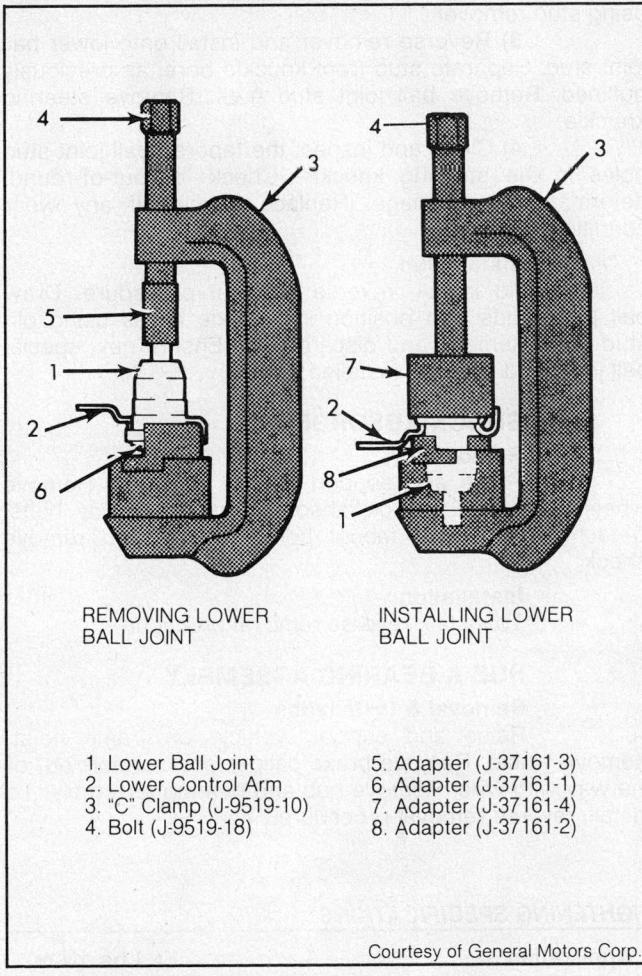

REMOVING LOWER
BALL JOINT

INSTALLING LOWER
BALL JOINT

1. Lower Ball Joint	5. Adapter (J-37161-3)
2. Lower Control Arm	6. Adapter (J-37161-1)
3. "C" Clamp (J-9519-10)	7. Adapter (J-37161-4)
4. Bolt (J-9519-18)	8. Adapter (J-37161-2)

Courtesy of General Motors Corp.

UPPER BALL JOINT

Removal

1) Raise and support vehicle on frame hoist. Remove wheel. Support lower control arm with jack to compress coil spring. Disconnect tie rod from steering knuckle. Remove upper ball joint stud nut. Partially reinstall stud nut.

2) Install Ball Joint Remover (J-26407) with cup end over lower ball stud nut. Turn threaded end of remover tool until upper ball stud is free of steering knuckle.

3) Remove ball joint remover. Detach nut from upper joint stud. Center punch 3 rivet heads retaining ball joint. Drill pilot holes. Drill rivet heads. Using a punch, remove rivets. Remove and discard ball joint. Clean and inspect tapered stud hole in steering knuckle and replace knuckle if any wear condition is found. See STEERING KNUCKLE in this article.

Installation

1) Install new bolts and nuts attaching ball joint to upper control arm. Insert upper control arm ball joint stud into knuckle. Install used stud nut and tighten to specification.

2) Remove and discard used stud nut. Install new special stud nut, tighten to specification. Only tighten stud nut to align cotter pin. Install wheel. Lower vehicle. Check and adjust front wheel alignment as necessary.

LOWER CONTROL ARM & COIL SPRING

CAUTION: The coil spring is under load and can cause injury if released too quickly. Ensure safety chain is installed and jack is lowered slowly.

Removal

1) Raise and support lower control arm with jack. Remove wheel. Disconnect shock absorber at lower control arm. Disconnect stabilizer bar link assembly from lower control arm. Detach tie rod end from steering knuckle.

2) Install safety chain through spring. Remove lower control arm pivot bolts. Slowly lower jack. Remove safety chain when spring tension is released. Remove spring and insulator. Disconnect lower ball joint from knuckle. See LOWER BALL JOINT in this article. Remove lower control arm.

Lower Control Arm Bushing Replacement

1) Install Bolt (J-21474-19) and Driver (J-21474-23) through lower control arm. *See Fig. 3.* Install small end of Bushing Receiver (J-21474-5) toward lower control arm. Install bearing and Sleeve (J-21474-18) on bolt.

2) Install spacer (J-37162-2) over lower control arm bushing. Tighten bolt until bushing is removed. *See Fig. 3.* To install bushing, place Bolt (J-21474-19), Spacer (J-37162-1) and new bushing through lower control arm.

3) Install Bushing Receiver (J-21474-5), Sleeve (J-21474-18) and bearing on bolt. Install Spacer (J-37162-2) in lower control arm. Tighten bolt until bushing is pressed into place. Remove tools.

Installation

1) Position lower control arm so lower ball joint starts in steering knuckle. Install ball joint nut and cotter pin. Position coil spring and insulator on lower control arm. Place safety chain through coil spring.

2) Using a jack, slowly raise lower control arm to compress coil spring. Align holes and install pivot bolts. DO NOT tighten pivot bolts at this time.

3) Remove safety chain. Install shock absorber. Install stabilizer bar. Install wheel. Lower vehicle. Tighten pivot bolts.

UPPER CONTROL ARM

NOTE: **When removing upper control arm, ensure all washer and shim locations and shim sizes are noted for reassembly reference.**

Removal

1) Raise and support vehicle with jack under lower control arm to support coil spring. Remove wheel. Remove bolt holding brake line clip to upper control arm. Disconnect tie rod from steering knuckle.

Front Suspension

FIERO (Cont.)

Fig. 3: Installing Lower Control Arm Bushings

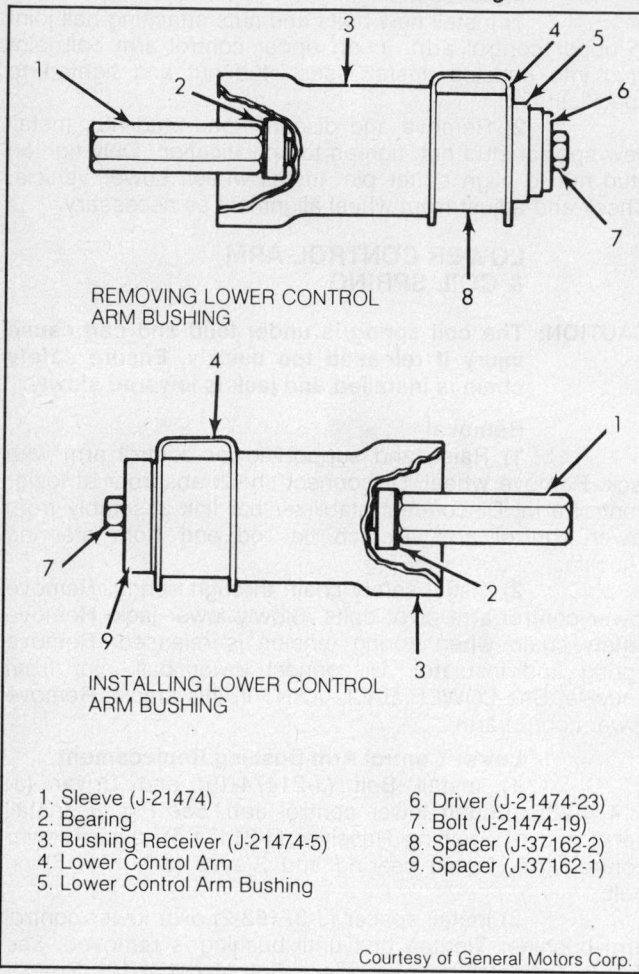

REMOVING LOWER CONTROL ARM BUSHING

INSTALLING LOWER CONTROL ARM BUSHING

1. Sleeve (J-21474)	6. Driver (J-21474-23)
2. Bearing	7. Bolt (J-21474-19)
3. Bushing Receiver (J-21474-5)	8. Spacer (J-37162-2)
4. Lower Control Arm	9. Spacer (J-37162-1)
5. Lower Control Arm Bushing	

Courtesy of General Motors Corp.

2) Using Ball Joint Remover (J-26407), separate upper ball joint from steering knuckle. Remove 2 bolts retaining upper control arm shaft to crossmember. Remove upper control arm.

Installation
To install, reverse removal procedure.

STABILIZER BAR
Removal
1) Mark stabilizer bar for reassembly purposes. Raise and support vehicle. Remove wheel assemblies. Disconnect tie rods from steering knuckle. Remove brake caliper, rotor and splash shield from left side. Wire brake caliper out of way. Remove stabilizer bar link assembly nuts and bolts from lower control arms. Note link assembly component locations for reassembly reference.

2) Detach stabilizer bar insulator bracket mount bolts. Remove brackets and bar from underbody. Move stabilizer bar to the left until right side clears frame rail. Inspect rubber link grommets and insulators for wear, damage or distortion. Replace components as necessary.

Installation
To install, reverse removal procedure. Slits in stabilizer bushings must face toward front of vehicle. Be certain that components are installed in the correct order or premature failure can result.

STEERING KNUCKLE
Removal
1) Raise and support vehicle. Place jack under lower control arm to compress coil spring. Remove wheel. Remove brake caliper and support out of the way with wire. Remove splash shield. Remove hub and bearing assembly.

2) Detach both ball joint stud nuts, and partially reinstall them. Remove tie rod end from knuckle arm bore. Separate upper joint stud from steering knuckle bore using stud remover.

3) Reverse remover and install onto lower ball joint stud. Separate stud from knuckle bore, as previously outlined. Remove ball joint stud nuts. Remove steering knuckle.

4) Clean and inspect the tapered ball joint stud holes in the steering knuckle. Check for out-of-round, deformation or damage. Replace knuckle if any wear condition is found.

Installation
To install, reverse removal procedure. Draw ball joint studs into position in knuckle bores using old stud nuts. Remove and discard nuts. Ensure new special ball joint stud nuts are installed.

SHOCK ABSORBER
Removal
Raise and support vehicle on hoist. Remove wheel. Detach 2 shock absorber upper mount bolts. Detach shock lower mount bolt and nut, and remove shock.

Installation
To install, reverse removal procedure.

HUB & BEARING ASSEMBLY
Removal & Installation
Raise and support vehicle on frame hoist. Remove wheel. Remove brake caliper and support out of the way with wire. Remove hub and bearing assembly. To install, reverse removal procedure.

TIGHTENING SPECIFICATIONS

Application	Ft. Lbs. (N.m)
Hub & Bearing Assembly Bolt	220 (299)
Lower Ball Joint Nut	[1] 26 (35)
Shock Absorber Lower Bolt	20 (27)
Stabilizer Bar Bushing Clamp Bolt	20 (27)
Stabilizer Bar Link Nut	12 (16)
Steering Gear-to-Crossmember Bolt	20 (27)
Tie Rod Nut	[1] 15 (20)
Upper Control Arm-to-Crossmember	[2] 37 (50)
Upper Control Arm Shaft-to-Crossmember Bolt	[3] 52 (71)
Upper Ball Joint Nut	30-40 (41-54)

	INCH Lbs. (N.m)
Shock Absorber Upper Nut	96 (11)

[1] – Tighten an additional 180 degrees.
[2] – Tighten an additional 270 degrees.
[3] – Tighten an additional 90 degrees.

Front Suspension

NOVA

DESCRIPTION

All models use independent, MacPherson strut front suspension with a single control arm. Camber is adjustable by turning an eccentric on the control arm lower bolt. The strut and strut support are isolated by a rubber mount. Models with 4A-GE engine are equipped with stabilizer bar.

ADJUSTMENTS

CASTER & CAMBER

See appropriate article in WHEEL ALIGNMENT section.

RIDING HEIGHT

See RIDING HEIGHT SPECIFICATIONS article in WHEEL ALIGNMENT section.

Fig. 1: Exploded View of Front Suspension & Strut Assembly

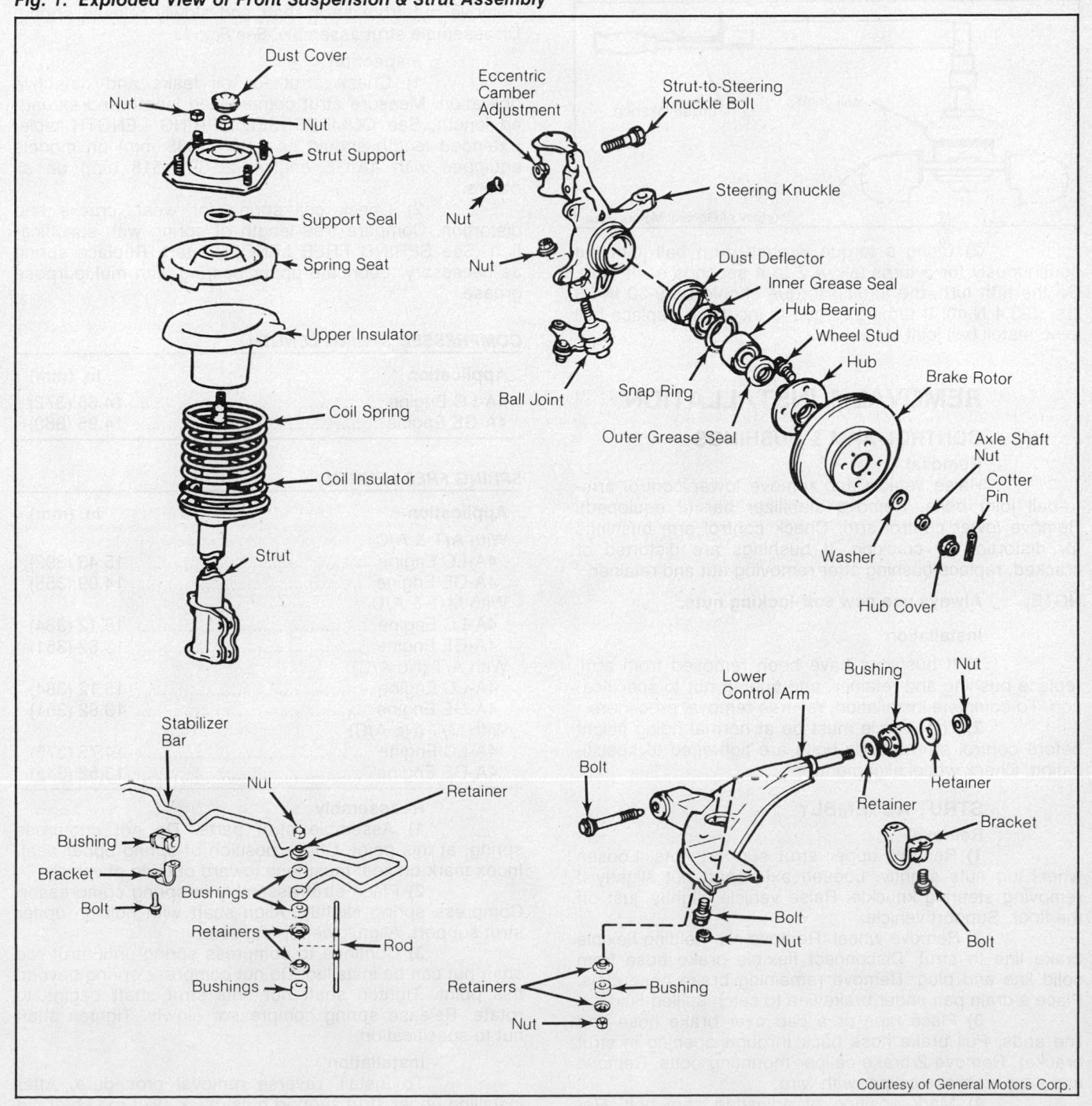

Courtesy of General Motors Corp.

Front Suspension

NOVA (Cont.)

WHEEL BEARINGS

Wheel bearings are not adjustable. Tighten axle shaft nut to 137 ft. lbs. (186 N.m).

BALL JOINT CHECKING

1) Remove ball joint from vehicle. See BALL JOINT REMOVAL & INSTALLATION in this article. Check for boot seal damage. Check for excessive wear or damage. Place ball joint in vise. See Fig. 2.

Fig. 2: Checking Ball Joint

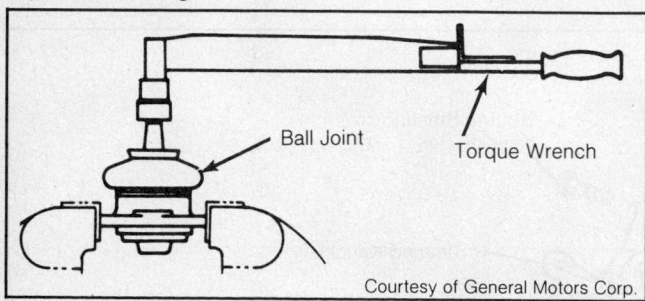

Courtesy of General Motors Corp.

2) Using a torque wrench, turn ball joint nut continuously for 5 turns (allow 2 to 4 seconds each turn). On the fifth turn, the turning torque should be 9-30 INCH lbs. (0-3.4 N.m). If turning torque is incorrect, replace ball joint. Install ball joint in vehicle.

REMOVAL & INSTALLATION

CONTROL ARM & BUSHINGS

Removal

Raise vehicle and remove lower control arm-to-ball joint bolts. Remove stabilizer bar (if equipped). Remove lower control arm. Check control arm bushings for distortion or cracking. If bushings are distorted or cracked, replace bushing after removing nut and retainer.

NOTE: Always use new self-locking nuts.

Installation

1) If bushings have been removed from arm, replace bushing and retainer, and tighten nut to specification. To complete installation, reverse removal procedure.

2) The vehicle must be at normal riding height before control arm-to-body bolts are tightened to specification. Check wheel alignment.

STRUT ASSEMBLY

Removal

1) Remove upper strut support nuts. Loosen wheel lug nuts slightly. Loosen axle shaft nut slightly if removing steering knuckle. Raise vehicle slightly, just off the floor. Support vehicle.

2) Remove wheel. Remove clip holding flexible brake line to strut. Disconnect flexible brake hose from solid line and plug. Remove remaining brake hose clips. Place a drain pan under brake line to catch spilled fluid.

3) Place tape or a cap over brake hose and line ends. Pull brake hose back through opening in strut bracket. Remove 2 brake caliper mounting bolts. Remove and support brake caliper with wire.

4) Mark position of adjusting cam bolt. Remove 2 strut-to-steering knuckle attaching bolts. Remove strut assembly. Remove camber adjusting cam from steering knuckle. Protect drive axle boot with cloth.

CAUTION: Strut spring is under high pressure. Do not remove the strut rod shaft nut before properly compressing spring.

Disassembly

1) Install strut into a spring compressor. Compress spring until tension on strut rod shaft nut is released.

2) Do not compress spring past this point. Remove nut from strut shaft and slowly release spring. Disassemble strut assembly. See Fig. 1.

Inspection

1) Check strut for oil leaks and defective operation. Measure strut compressed length and extended length. See COMPRESSED SPRING LENGTH table. Extended length should be 21.06" (535 mm) on models equipped with 4A-GE engine, 20.39" (518 mm) on all others.

2) Check coil spring for wear, cracks and distortion. Compare free length of spring with specification. See SPRING FREE LENGTH chart. Replace spring as necessary. Lubricate upper bearing with multipurpose grease.

COMPRESSED SPRING LENGTH

Application	In. (mm)
4A-LC Engine	14.65 (372)
4A-GE Engine	14.96 (380)

SPRING FREE LENGTH

Application	In. (mm)
With A/T & A/C	
4A-LC Engine	15.43 (392)
4A-GE Engine	14.09 (358)
With M/T & A/C	
4A-LC Engine	15.12 (384)
4A-GE Engine	13.82 (351)
With A/T (No A/C)	
4A-LC Engine	15.12 (384)
4A-GE Engine	13.82 (351)
With M/T (No A/C)	
4A-LC Engine	14.76 (375)
4A-GE Engine	13.58 (345)

Reassembly

1) Assemble strut parts. Do not compress spring, at this point. Check position of spring upper seat. Index mark on seat must face toward outside of vehicle.

2) Place strut assembly in spring compressor. Compress spring slightly. Align shaft with hole in upper strut support. Align lower spring seat.

3) Continue to compress spring until strut rod shaft nut can be installed. Do not compress spring beyond this point. Tighten shaft nut until strut shaft begins to rotate. Release spring compressor slowly. Tighten shaft nut to specification.

Installation

To install, reverse removal procedure. After installing upper strut support nuts, pack strut rod shaft nut area with grease and install dust covers. Tighten wheel

NOVA (Cont.)

lug nuts to specification. Check wheel alignment. Bleed air from brake system. See HYDRAULIC BRAKE BLEEDING article in BRAKE section.

BALL JOINT

Removal & Installation

Loosen wheel lug nuts slightly and raise vehicle. Remove wheel. Use Ball Joint Remover (J-35413) to separate joint from steering knuckle. Remove ball joint nuts and bolt. Discard self-locking nut. Remove ball joint. To install, reverse removal procedure.

STEERING KNUCKLE & WHEEL BEARINGS

NOTE: **DO NOT remove hub assembly unless absolutely necessary.**

Removal

1) Loosen wheel lug nuts and hub nut. Raise vehicle and remove wheel. Remove brake hose retaining clip at strut. Disconnect flexible brake hose from brake line.

2) Remove caliper mounting bolts and support caliper. Do not allow caliper to hang from brake line. Remove brake rotor. Remove drive axle nut. Using Puller J-25287, separate drive axle from hub assembly. *See Fig. 3.*

3) Remove tie rod cotter pin and nut. Using Puller (J-24319-01), separate tie rod end from steering knuckle. Remove bolts and nuts attaching ball joint to control arm. Scribe index mark on eccentric bolt (lower strut bolt). Remove strut-to-steering knuckle attaching bolts. Remove steering knuckle.

Fig. 3: Separating Axle Shaft From Hub Assembly

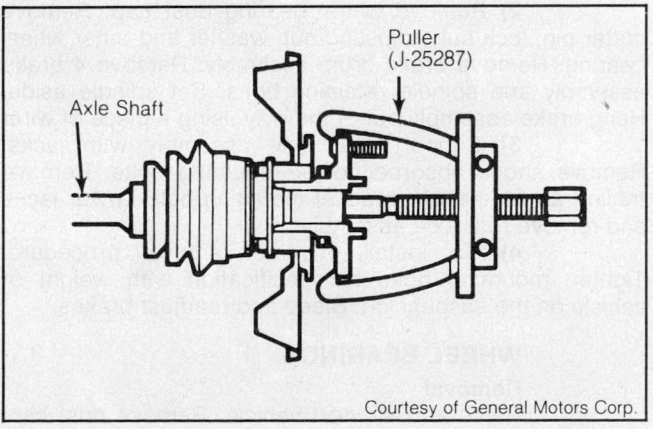

Puller
(J-25287)

Axle Shaft

Courtesy of General Motors Corp.

Disassembly

1) Mount steering knuckle in vise. Remove dust deflector. Remove inner grease seal with Seal Remover (J-26941). Remove inner bearing snap ring. Remove disc brake dust shield.

2) Separate hub from steering knuckle using Pullers (J-25287 and J-35378). Remove outer bearing race from hub using hub removers. Remove outer grease seal using seal remover. Use Bearing Remover/Installers (J-35399 and J-35379) to remove bearing assembly.

Reassembly

To reassemble, reverse disassembly procedures. Use Hub Bearing Installers (J-8092 and J-35411) to install hub bearing assembly. Use Seal Installer (J-35737) to install new inner and outer grease seals. Use Bearing Remover/Installer (J-35379) to install dust deflector ring.

Installation

To install, reverse removal procedure. Using old nut, install ball joint. Tighten nut to 14 ft. lbs. (19 N.m). Remove nut and discard. Install new nut and tighten to specification. Bleed brake system. See HYDRAULIC BRAKE BLEEDING article in BRAKE section. Check wheel alignment.

STABILIZER ARM

Removal & Installation

Raise front of vehicle and support. Disconnect stabilizer arm from lower control arm and body. Disconnect exhaust pipe from exhaust manifold. Remove stabilizer arm. To install, reverse removal procedure.

TIGHTENING SPECIFICATIONS

Application	Ft. Lbs. (N.m)
Axle Shaft Nut	137 (186)
Ball Joint-to-Control Arm Bolts	59 (80)
Ball Joint-to-Steering Knuckle Nut	82 (111)
Brake Line Flexible Hose	11 (15)
Caliper-to-Steering Knuckle Bolts	65 (88)
Exhaust Pipe-to-Exhaust Manifold Nuts	46 (63)
Lower Control Arm Bracket	64 (87)
Lower Control Arm Bushing	76 (103)
Lower Control Arm-to-Body Bolts	
Front	105 (142)
Rear	72 (98)
Stabilizer Arm-to-Body Bolts	14 (19)
Stabilizer Arm-to-Control Arm Bolts	13 (18)
Strut-to-Steering Knuckle Bolts	166 (226)
Tie Rod-to-Steering Knuckle Nut	36 (49)
Upper Strut Nut	34 (46)
Upper Strut-to-Body Nuts	13 (17)
Wheel Lug Nuts	76 (103)

Rear Suspension
CHRYSLER MOTORS FWD
HORIZON AMERICA & OMNI AMERICA

DESCRIPTION

Rear suspension is a semi-independent trailing arm type. Some models are equipped with an integral anti-sway bar. Spindles are attached to 2 trailing arms that extend rearward from mounting points on body.

Each arm is isolated from the body by rubber pivot bushings. A crossmember is welded between trailing arms, providing anti-sway stabilization for the rear suspension. Coil springs surrounding shock absorbers are used to dampen road variations.

Fig. 1: Rear Suspension Assembly

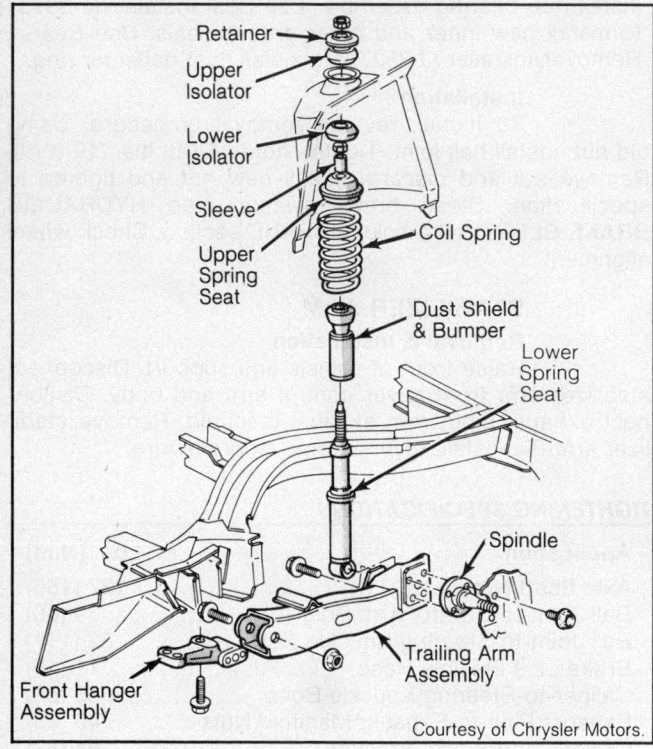

Courtesy of Chrysler Motors.

ADJUSTMENTS

CAMBER & TOE-IN

See appropriate article in the WHEEL ALIGNMENT section.

RIDING HEIGHT

See RIDING HEIGHT SPECIFICATIONS article in WHEEL ALIGNMENT section.

REAR WHEEL BEARINGS

1) Tighten spindle adjusting nut to 240-300 INCH lbs. (27-34 N.m), while rotating wheel. Back off adjusting nut to release bearing preload. Finger tighten adjusting nut. See Fig. 2.

2) Position lock nut, aligning one pair of slots in line with cotter pin hole. Install new cotter pin. Adjustment should provide .001-.003" (.03-.08 mm) end play. Clean and install grease cap.

REMOVAL & INSTALLATION

SHOCK ABSORBERS & COIL SPRINGS
Removal

Remove upper shock absorber mounting nut cap, located inside vehicle over rear wheelwell. On 2-door models, remove lower rear trim quarter panel. On all models, remove mounting nut, retainer and isolator. Raise and support vehicle. Remove bottom shock absorber mount bolt. Remove spring and shock absorber from trailing arm bracket.

Disassembly & Reassembly

1) Compress coil spring using Spring Compressor (C-4838). Hold flat on end of shock rod. Loosen retaining nut. Remove lower isolator, shock rod sleeve and upper spring seat. Remove shock absorber.

2) Remove jounce bumper and dust shield from shock rod. Remove lower spring seat. See Fig. 1. To reassemble shock assembly, reverse disassembly procedure. Make sure leveled surface on both spring seats are in position against ends of coil springs.

Installation

To install shock assembly, reverse removal procedure. When installing assembly in vehicle, leave lower shock absorber bolt loose. Tighten bolt after vehicle is resting on ground.

REAR AXLE ASSEMBLY
Removal & Installation

1) Raise and support vehicle. Remove wheels. Remove brake fittings and retaining clips that hold the flexible brake lines. Remove parking brake cable adjusting nut. Release both parking brake cables from the bracket. Pull parking brake cables through the bracket.

2) Remove wheel bearing dust cap. Remove cotter pin, lock nut, adjusting nut, washer and outer wheel bearing. Remove brake drum assembly. Remove 4 brake assembly and spindle retaining bolts. Set spindle aside. Hang brake assembly out of the way using a piece of wire.

3) Support rear axle assembly with jacks. Remove shock absorber lower mounting bolts. Remove trailing arm-to-hanger bracket mounting bolt. Lower jacks and remove rear axle assembly.

4) To install, reverse removal procedure. Tighten mounting bolts to specification with weight of vehicle on the suspension. Bleed and readjust brakes.

WHEEL BEARINGS
Removal

Raise and support vehicle. Remove dust cap, cotter pin, lock nut, adjusting nut and washer. Remove outer bearing. Slide drum off spindle. Carefully drive out inner seal and remove inner bearing inner race. Remove inner and outer bearing races with a non-metallic rod.

Installation

1) Seat new inner and outer bearing outer races against shoulder in hub. Force lubricant between all bearing rollers. Install inner bearing inner race and new seal. Position seal lip inward. Install seal flush with end of hub.

Rear Suspension
CHRYSLER MOTORS FWD
HORIZON AMERICA & OMNI AMERICA (Cont.)

Fig. 2: Exploded View of Wheel Bearings

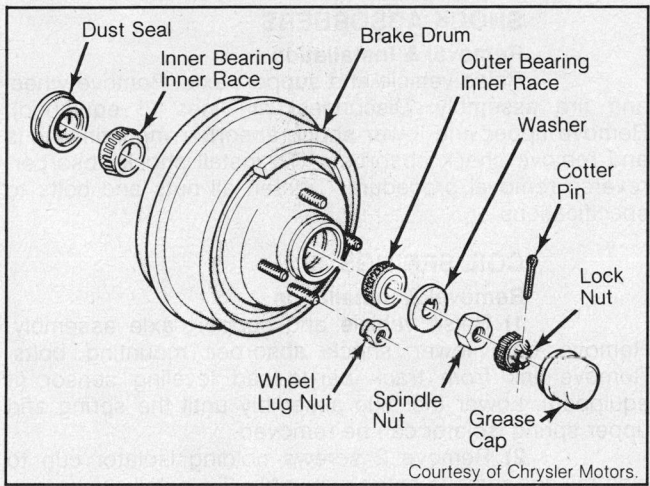

Courtesy of Chrysler Motors.

2) Install drum on spindle and install outer bearing, washer and adjusting nut. Adjust wheel bearings as previously described. Install lock nut and cotter pin. Install wheel and tire assembly and lower vehicle.

TIGHTENING SPECIFICATIONS

Application	Ft. Lbs. (N.m)
Shock Absorber	
Lower Bolt	40 (54)
Upper Nut	20 (27)
Spindle Retaining Bolts	45 (61)
Trailing Arm-to-Hanger Nuts	40 (54)
Wheel Lug Nuts	95 (129)

Rear Suspension
CHRYSLER MOTORS FWD
EXCEPT HORIZON AMERICA & OMNI AMERICA

Aries America, Caravelle, Daytona, Dynasty, Lancer, LeBaron, LeBaron GTS, New Yorker, Reliant America, Shadow, Sundance, 600

DESCRIPTION

Rear suspension is a trailing arm, solid type design. An integral tubular stabilizer bar is positioned inside the axle and is attached to the spindle mounting plates at either end of the axle channel. The trailing arms and coil spring seats are welded directly to the axle. The axle assembly is located fore and aft by blade-type trailing arms, attached to body mounted pivots. A track bar provides lateral stability. Coil springs and vertically-mounted shock absorbers complete the suspension assembly.

ADJUSTMENTS

CAMBER & TOE-IN

See appropriate article in WHEEL ALIGNMENT section.

RIDING HEIGHT

See RIDING HEIGHT SPECIFICATIONS article in WHEEL ALIGNMENT section.

REAR WHEEL BEARINGS

Tighten adjusting nut to 240-300 INCH lbs. (27-33 N.m) while rotating wheel. Stop rotation and back off adjusting nut 1/4 turn. Finger tighten adjusting nut while again rotating wheel. Position lock nut with slots in line with cotter pin hole. Install cotter pin.

REMOVAL & INSTALLATION

SHOCK ABSORBERS
Removal & Installation
Raise vehicle and support axle. Remove wheel and tire assembly. Disconnect air lines (if equipped). Remove upper and lower shock absorber mounting bolts and remove shock absorbers. To install shock absorber, reverse removal procedure. Tighten all nuts and bolts to specifications.

COIL SPRINGS
Removal & Installation
1) Raise vehicle and support axle assembly. Remove both lower shock absorber mounting bolts. Remove link from track bar-to-load leveling sensor (if equipped). Lower the axle assembly until the spring and upper spring isolator can be removed.
2) Remove 2 screws holding isolator cup to side rail and remove entire assembly. To install coil spring, reverse removal procedure. Tighten shock absorber nuts with weight of vehicle on spring.

NOTE: Do not stretch brake hoses when lowering axle assembly.

TRACK BAR, BRACE & BRACKET
Removal & Installation
1) Raise vehicle. Raise rear axle to curb height with jack stands. Disconnect load leveling system sensor link from track bar (if equipped). Remove track bar-to-axle through bolt and track bar-to-frame pivot bolt.
2) Remove track bar. Remove diagonal brace-to-underbody stud nut and brace. Remove 2 track bar bracket-to-frame bolts and remove bracket.

Fig. 1: Rear Suspension Assembly

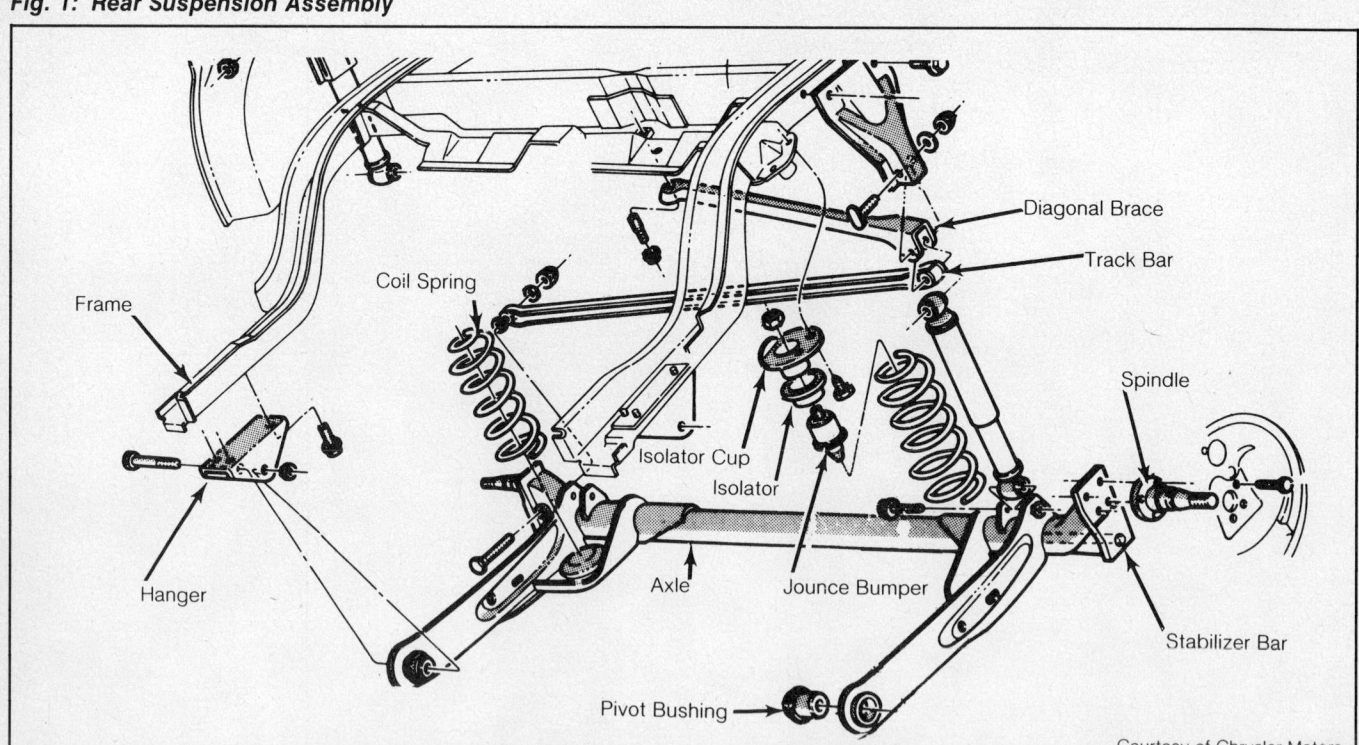

Courtesy of Chrysler Motors.

3) To install track bar and brace, reverse removal procedure. Tighten all bolts to specifications.

PIVOT BUSHING
Removal

1) Raise vehicle. Remove wheel and tire assembly. Remove brake hose mounting bracket bolt. Disconnect parking brake cable guide at the connector and from the front hanger bracket.

2) Disconnect load leveling system sensor link from the track bar (if equipped). Support rear axle assembly and remove lower shock absorber mounting bolts. Remove hanger bracket-to-frame side rail bolts.

Fig. 2: Removing Trailing Arm

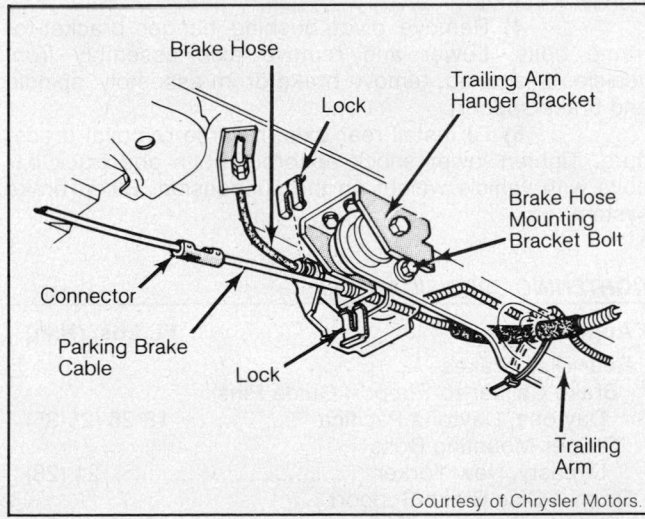

Courtesy of Chrysler Motors.

3) Lower axle assembly far enough to remove pivot bolt and hanger bracket. Position Bushing Remover (C-4702-7) over Support Cup (C-4366-1) and Press (C-4212).

4) Position assembly with support cup supporting trailing arm. Turn screw on press into remover and press bushing out. *See Fig. 3.*

Fig. 3: Removing Pivot Bushing

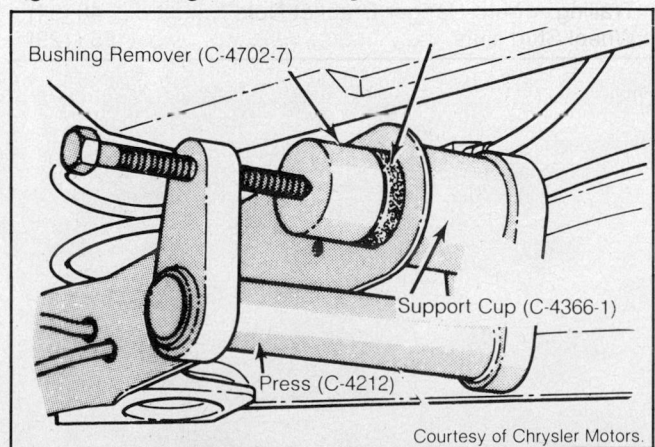

Courtesy of Chrysler Motors.

Installation

1) Align bushing to installer and arm cavity. *See Fig. 4.* Tap bushing slightly to hold position. Using Bushing Installer (C-4702-2), press bushing into trailing arm. *See Fig. 5.* Press in bushing to a depth of 5/8" (16 mm) as measured from the bushing flange to the trailing arm.

Fig. 4: Positioning Pivot Bushing

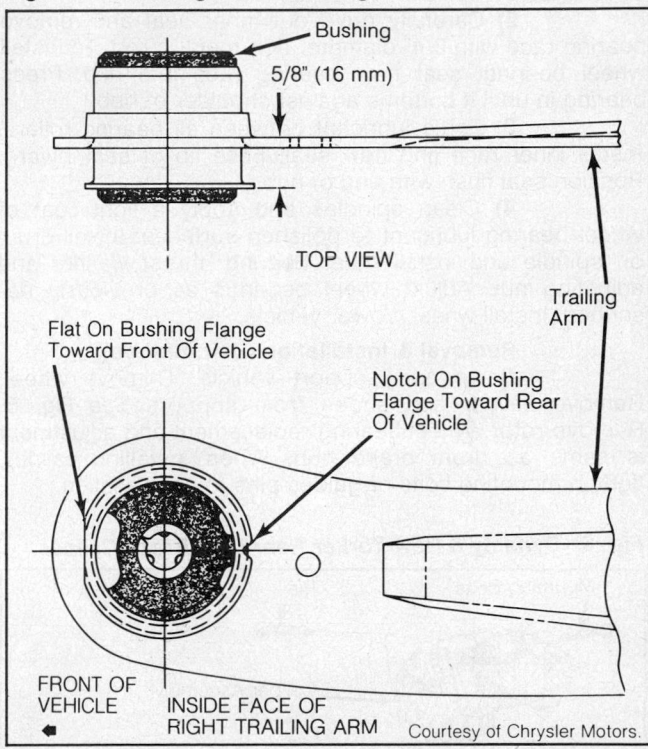

Courtesy of Chrysler Motors.

2) Position hanger bracket on pivot bushing and install bolt. Loosely install nut. Position hanger on frame. Install and tighten hanger bolts to specifications.

3) Install lower shock absorber mounting bolt, but DO NOT tighten yet. Install brake hose mounting bracket to trailing arm. Install and tighten retaining bolt. Install parking brake cable housing to the hanger bracket and cable to the connector.

4) Connect load leveling sensor link to the track bar (if equipped). Install wheel and tire. Lower vehicle and tighten pivot bolt nut and lower shock absorber bolt to specifications with vehicle weight on suspension.

Fig. 5: Installing Pivot Bushing

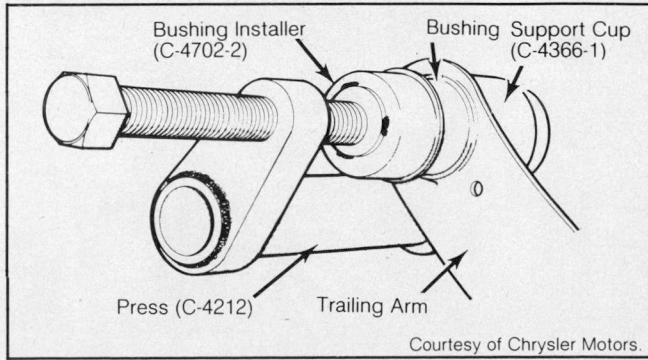

Courtesy of Chrysler Motors.

Tighten pivot nut with vehicle weight applied.

Rear Suspension
CHRYSLER MOTORS FWD
EXCEPT HORIZON AMERICA & OMNI AMERICA (Cont.)

WHEEL BEARINGS
Removal & Installation (Drum Brakes)

1) Raise and support vehicle. Remove wheel. Remove grease cap, cotter pin, nut lock and bearing adjusting nut. Remove thrust washer and outer bearing. Slide drum off spindle.

2) Carefully drive out inner seal and remove bearing race with 3/4" diameter non-metallic rod. To install wheel bearing, seat new bearing race into hub. Press bearing in until it bottoms against shoulder of hub.

3) Force lubricant between all bearing rollers. Install inner race and new seal. Face lip of seal inward. Position seal flush with end of hub.

4) Clean spindles and apply a light coat of wheel bearing lubricant to polished surfaces. Install drum on spindle and install outer bearing, thrust washer and adjusting nut. Adjust wheel bearings as previously described. Install wheel. Lower vehicle.

Removal & Installation (Disc Brakes)

Raise and support vehicle. Remove wheel. Remove caliper and shoes from support. See Fig. 6. Remove rotor. Wheel bearing replacement and adjustment is same as drum brake hub. When installing caliper, tighten mounting bolts or guides pins to specification.

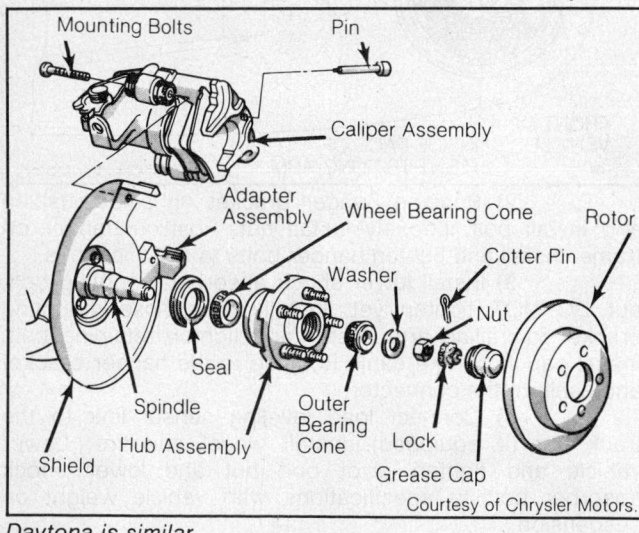

Fig. 6: Dynasty & New Yorker Rear Disc Brake Caliper

Mounting Bolts — Pin — Caliper Assembly — Adapter Assembly — Wheel Bearing Cone — Rotor — Cotter Pin — Washer — Nut — Lock — Seal — Spindle — Outer Bearing Cone — Grease Cap — Hub Assembly — Shield

Courtesy of Chrysler Motors.

Daytona is similar.

REAR AXLE ASSEMBLY
Removal & Installation

1) Raise vehicle and support axle with jack stands. Remove wheels. Separate parking brake cable at connector and detach. Separate brake tube assembly from brake hose at trailing arm support bracket and remove retaining clip.

2) Disconnect height sensor link from track bar, if equipped with automatic load leveling system. Remove lower shock absorber bolts and track bar-to-axle bolts.

3) Support track bar end with wire. Lower axle until spring and isolator assembly can be removed. Support pivot bushing end of trailing arms and axle beam with jack stands.

4) Remove pivot bushing hanger bracket-to-frame bolts. Lower and remove axle assembly from vehicle. If required, remove brake drum assembly, spindle and brake support.

5) To install rear axle, reverse removal procedure. Tighten lower shock absorber bolts and track bar bolts with vehicle weight on the suspension. Bleed brake system.

TIGHTENING SPECIFICATIONS

Application	Ft. Lbs. (N.m)
Rear Disc Brakes	
Brake Caliper-to-Support Guide Pins	
Daytona, Daytona Pacifica	18-26 (25-35)
Caliper Mounting Bolts	
Dynasty, New Yorker	21 (28)
Drum & Disc Brake Support	
Plate-to-Rear Axle Bolt	45-60 (61-81)
Lower Shock Absorber Bolts	45 (61)
Shock Absorber Mounting Nut	45 (61)
Track Bar	
Brace-to-Stud Nut	55 (75)
Mounting Bracket-to-Body Bolts	40 (54)
Track Bar-to-Axle Bolt	70 (95)
Track Bar-to-Mounting Bracket Bolt	55 (75)
Track Bar Brace-to-Stud Nut	55 (75)
Trailing Arm-to-Hanger Bracket Nuts	40 (54)
Wheel Stud Nuts	95 (129)

EAGLE PREMIER

DESCRIPTION

The rear axle and suspension consists of 2 trailing arms connected to a "V" shaped crossmember. Axle assembly is mounted to the body by the use of 2 anchor brackets which contain rubber bushings. An axle shaft is attached to the trailing arms.

Hub and bearings are mounted on axle shaft. Hub and bearings are non-serviceable and must be replaced as a complete unit.

Shock absorbers are mounted on each trailing arm and to the body. Use of the suspension torsion bars (front bar) and anti-sway torsion bars (rear bar) are used for providing suspension action for the rear axle.

Fig. 1: Rear Axle & Suspension Components

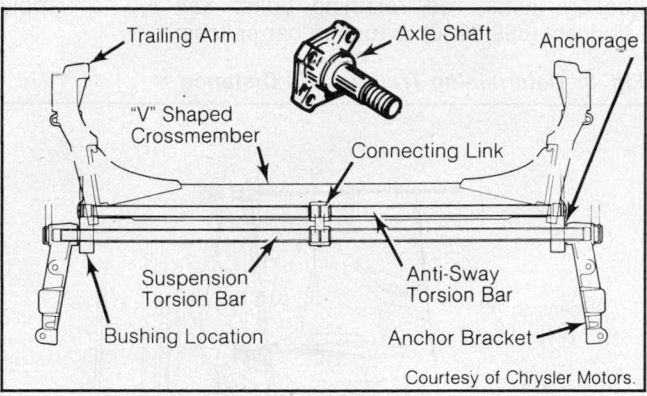

Courtesy of Chrysler Motors.

ADJUSTMENTS

REAR WHEEL BEARINGS

The hub and bearings are non-serviceable and must be replaced as a complete unit.

RIDING HEIGHT

See RIDING HEIGHT SPECIFICATIONS in WHEEL ALIGNMENT section. To check riding height, see RIDING HEIGHT in this article.

REMOVAL & INSTALLATION

REAR AXLE ASSEMBLY

CAUTION: Vehicle must not be raised under the "V" shaped channel on rear axle.

Removal

1) Torsion bars DO NOT require removal prior to rear axle removal. Raise and support vehicle. Remove wheels. Disconnect shock absorbers at rear axle.

2) Loosen emergency brake cable adjusting nuts to allow enough clearance for cable removal. Remove parking brake cables from adjusting bracket.

3) Disconnect brake hoses at rear axle. Support rear axle. Remove anchor bracket-to-body retaining bolts. Lower and remove rear axle.

Installation

Reverse removal procedures. Tighten bolts to specification. Bleed brake system. Adjust parking brake.

HUB & BEARING ASSEMBLY

Inspection

1) Raise and support vehicle. Remove wheel. Remove plastic cap from center of brake drum. Install dial indicator on brake drum with stem resting against end of axle shaft.

2) Move brake drum inward and note reading. Replace hub and bearing assembly if movement exceeds .001" (.03 mm).

Removal

1) Raise and support vehicle. Remove wheel. Remove brake drum-to-axle shaft retaining nuts (if equipped). Remove plastic cap from center of brake drum.

2) Remove brake drum. Remove axle shaft retaining nut. Using Hub Puller (T.Av. 1050), remove hub assembly from axle shaft.

Installation

Reverse removal procedures. Lightly oil axle shaft prior to hub installation. Install new axle shaft retaining nut. Tighten bolts to specification. Adjust brakes if necessary.

CAUTION: Always replace axle shaft retaining nut once removed.

AXLE SHAFT

Removal

Raise and support vehicle. Remove hub and bearing assembly. See HUB & BEARING ASSEMBLY in this article. Remove axle shaft-to-trailing arm retaining bolts. Remove brake backing plate-to-axle shaft retaining bolt. Remove axle shaft.

Installation

1) Install brake backing plate bolt finger tight. Coat axle shaft retaining bolts with Loctite prior to installation.

2) Using a criss-cross pattern, tighten axle shaft retaining bolts to specification, then tighten brake backing plate bolt. Reverse removal procedures. Use a new axle shaft nut. Tighten bolts to specification.

SHOCK ABSORBERS

Removal

1) Raise and support vehicle. Place jack under control arm below shock absorber lower mounting area. Raise jack to release tension on shock absorber.

2) Remove upper and lower shock absorber retaining bolts. Remove shock absorber.

Installation

Reverse removal procedures. Tighten bolts to specification.

TORSION BARS

NOTE: **The front torsion bar is referred to as the suspension bar and rear torsion bar as anti-sway bar.**

Removal

1) Raise and support vehicle. Remove wheels. Remove shock absorbers as previously described. Pry protective caps from the ends of suspension bars. Unscrew protective caps from end of anti-sway bars. See Fig. 1.

Rear Suspension

EAGLE PREMIER (Cont.)

2) Remove suspension and anti-sway bar retaining clips below protective cap area. Suspension bar mountings are marked "D" for initial positioning of suspension. *See Fig. 2.* Anti-sway bar must be marked prior to removal. This mark will be referred to as "E".

Fig. 2: Determining Torsion Bar Locations

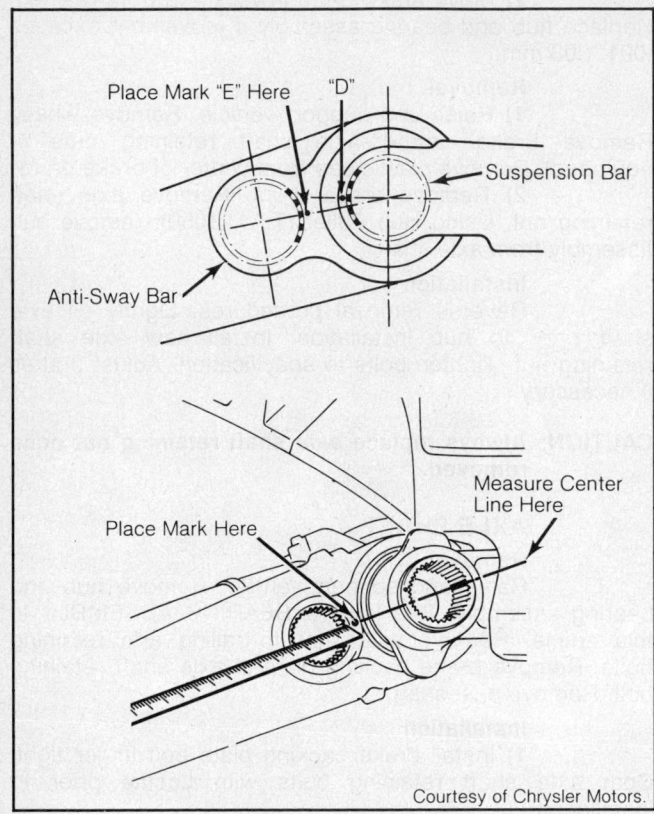

Place Mark "E" Here   "D"
Suspension Bar
Anti-Sway Bar
Place Mark Here
Measure Center Line Here

Courtesy of Chrysler Motors.

3) Place straightedge on center line of the 2 mounting holes. Scribe a mark at the bottom of a spline tooth on the anchorage. *See Fig. 2.* Note and record location of the DOTS located on the end of all torsion bars in relation to the "D" and "E" marks. *See Fig. 2.*

NOTE: Different DOT locations are determined by vehicle application. Location in relation to "D" and "E" marks may vary by application.

4) Install Slide Hammer (Emb. 880) in suspension bar. Remove suspension bars enough to disengage splines. Install slide hammer in anti-sway bars. Remove anti-sway bars from rear axle. Mark bars for location.

5) Place jack in the center of rear axle. Loosen the front anchor bracket-to-body retaining bolts approximately 4 turns and rear bolts approximately 10 turns. DO NOT remove bolts.

6) Lower jack, allowing the rear axle to drop approximately 1" (25 mm). Remove suspension bars. Mark bars for location.

CAUTION: Torsion bars must be installed in correct location. Left side may be identified by letter "G" and right side by letter "D" stamped in outside end of torsion bar. Install with DOT outward.

Installation

1) If bar is replaced, ensure correct bar is installed according to Part No. Install all bars with DOT area outward. Splined area must not be engaged with anchorage.

2) Ensure proper torsion bar is installed in correct location. Left side may be identified by letter "G" and right side by letter "D" stamped in outside end of torsion bar.

3) Raise jack and tighten anchor bracket-to-body retaining bolts to 68 ft. lbs. (92 N.m). Trailing arm distance must now be set. Adjust 2 Rods (Sus. Lm.02) to the dimension of 17 15/16" (456 mm). *See Fig. 3.*

4) Remove both shock absorbers. Install rods and Spacer (T.Ar. 1056) in place of shock absorber. Loosely install rod retaining bolts. *See Fig. 3.* Apply Lubricant (899 3630) to torsion bar splines.

Fig. 3: Determining Trailing Arm Distance

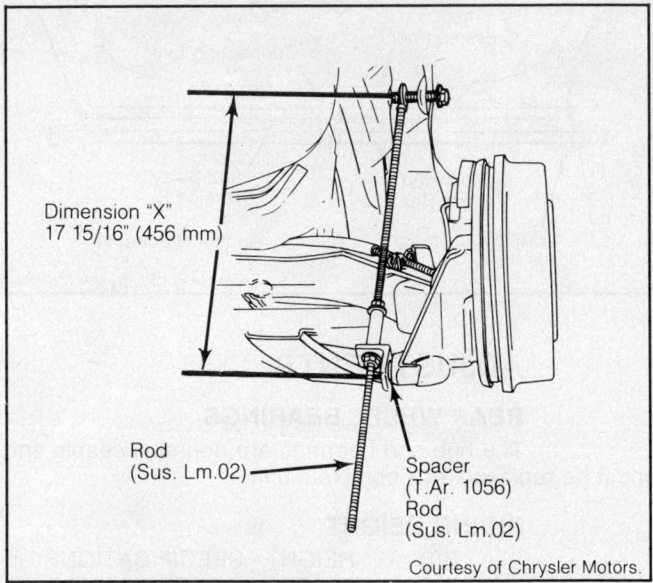

Dimension "X"
17 15/16" (456 mm)
Rod (Sus. Lm.02)
Spacer (T.Ar. 1056)
Rod (Sus. Lm.02)

Courtesy of Chrysler Motors.

5) Engage one of the anti-sway bars in original location. Ensure DOT is located in original location. Install connecting link on installed anti-sway bar.

6) Connecting link must be centered within "V" area of rear axle. Install remaining anti-sway bar into connecting link. Install one suspension bar and engage into connecting link.

7) Install remaining suspension bar. Ensure all bars are installed in original location. If dimension "X" on rod is correct and bars are installed in correct location, bars should slide easily into position.

8) Slight rotation of torsion bars may be required to align splines. All bars must be checked for correct centering. Using brass drift, tap suspension bar until outer end is 13/16" ± 1/16" (20.6 mm ± 1.6 mm) from outer edge of anchor bracket on both bars.

9) Tap anti-sway bar until outer end is 1/4" ± 1/16" (6.3 mm ± 1.6 mm) from outer edge of anchorage on both bars. Remove rods and install shock absorbers. Tighten bolts to specification.

10) Install torsion bar retaining clips. Reverse removal procedures for remaining components. Check riding height.

EAGLE PREMIER (Cont.)

ANCHOR BRACKET BUSHINGS

Removal

1) Remove rear axle. See REAR AXLE AS-SEMBLY in this article. Remove torsion bars. See TORSION BARS in this article. Using spacer and puller, pull anchor bracket from axle. *See Fig. 4.*

Fig. 4: Removing Anchor Bracket From Axle

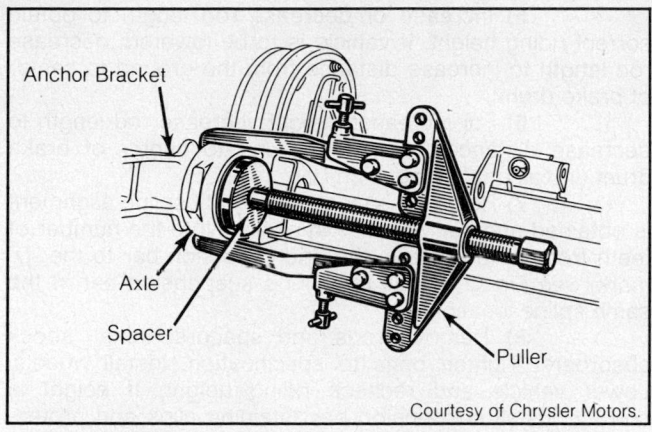

Courtesy of Chrysler Motors.

2) To remove bushing, weld a 26 mm nut on inside of bushing. Using press and Bearing Splitter (J-22912-01), press bushing from anchor backet.

Installation

1) Place bushing on rear axle. Using Bushing Installer (T.Ar. 1056), install bushing until it is even with outside of axle. *See Fig. 5.*

2) Install anchor bracket on axle. Anchor bracket must be properly positioned. Measure dimension

Fig. 5: Installing Anchor Bracket Bushing

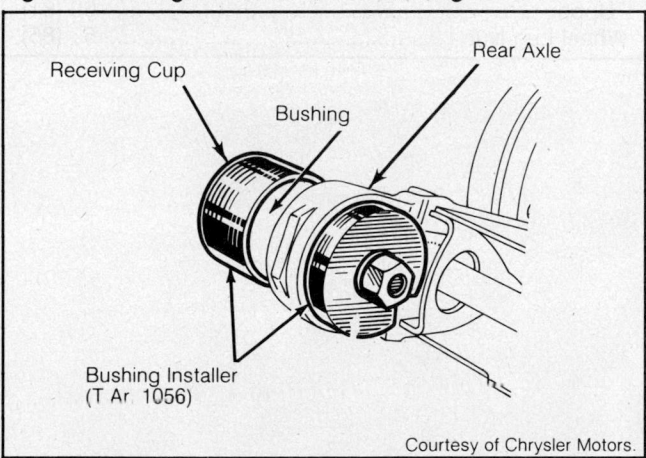

Courtesy of Chrysler Motors.

Fig. 6: Installing Anchor Bracket Bushing

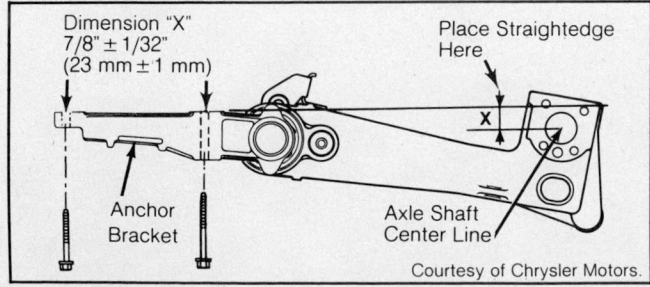

Courtesy of Chrysler Motors.

"X" by placing a straightedge across top of anchor bracket-to-body contact area. Place anchor bracket so that dimension "X" is 7/8" ± 1/32" (23 mm ± 1 mm). *See Fig. 6.*

3) Once correct dimension is obtained, using Bushing Installer (T.Ar. 1056), press anchor bracket on axle. *See Fig. 7.* Anchor bracket must be installed to correct dimension between center of bolt holes on each anchor bracket. *See Fig. 8.*

Fig. 7: Installing Anchor Bracket

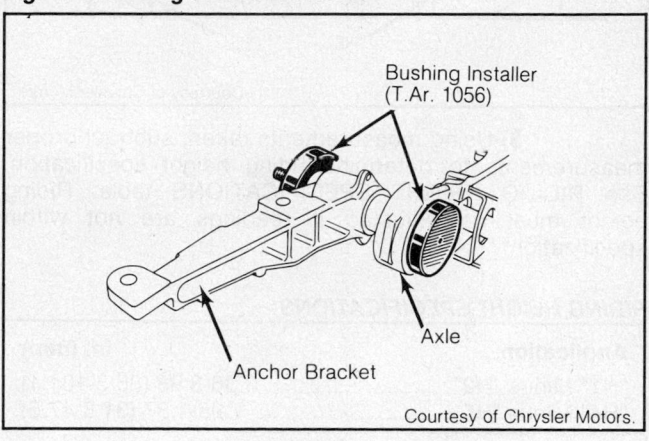

Courtesy of Chrysler Motors.

Fig. 8: Positioning Anchor Brackets

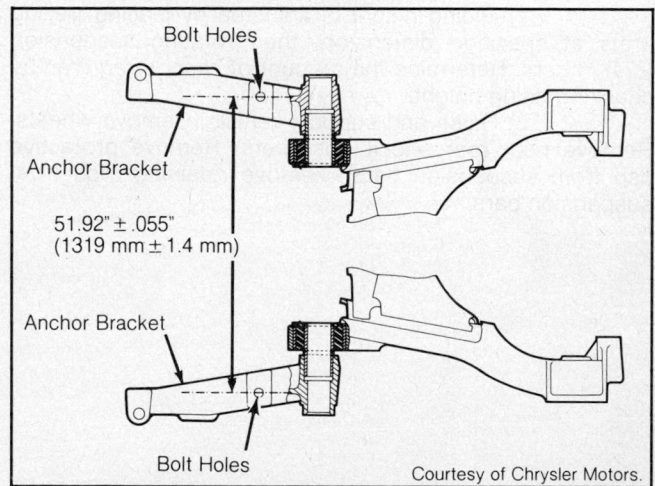

Courtesy of Chrysler Motors.

4) Reverse removal procedures for remaining components. Tighten bolts to specification. Check riding height.

RIDING HEIGHT

CHECKING RIDING HEIGHT

1) Ensure tire pressures are correct. Measurements are to be made with vehicle unloaded, full tank of gas and positioned on flat surface. Measure riding height at locations indicated. *See Fig. 9.*

2) Measurements "H1" and "H4" must be measured at wheel center line to the ground. Measurement "H2" is measured from engine cradle to the ground, while "H5" is taken between front torsion bar center line and the ground.

Rear Suspension

EAGLE PREMIER (Cont.)

Fig. 9: Measuring Riding Height

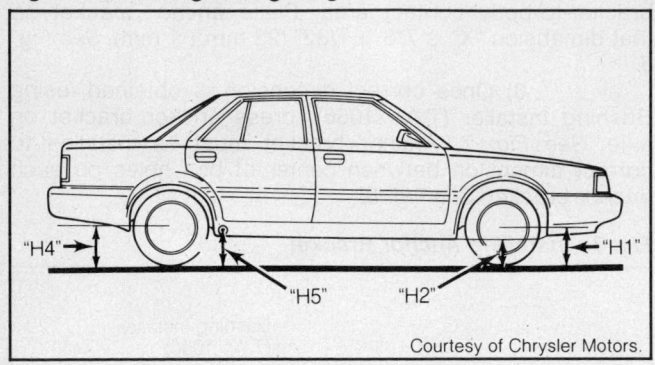

Courtesy of Chrysler Motors.

3) Using measurements taken, subtract proper measurements to determine riding height specification. See RIDING HEIGHT SPECIFICATIONS table. Riding height must be adjusted if readings are not within specification.

RIDING HEIGHT SPECIFICATIONS

Application	In. (mm)
"H1" Minus "H2"	3.36-3.98 (85.3-101.1)
"H4" Minus "H5"	1.25-1.87 (31.8-47.5)

ADJUSTING RIDING HEIGHT

1) Riding height is adjusted by placing trailing arms at specified dimension, then rotating suspension torsion bars. Determine the amount of change required by checking riding height.

2) Raise and support vehicle. Remove wheels. Remove both rear shock absorbers. Remove protective cap from suspension bars. Remove retaining clips from suspension bars.

3) Using Slide Hammer (Emb. 880), remove suspension bars enough to disengage splines. Trailing arm distance must now be set. Adjust 2 Rods (Sus. Lm.02) to the dimension of 17 15/16" (456 mm).

4) Install rods and Spacers (T.Ar. 1056) in place of shock absorber. Loosely install rod retaining bolts. *See Fig. 3.* Measure distance between center of rear brake drum and the ground.

5) Increase or decrease rod length to obtain correct riding height. If vehicle is to be lowered, decrease rod length to increase distance from the ground to center of brake drum.

6) For increased height, increase rod length to decrease distance from the ground to center of brake drum. Install one suspension bar.

7) Rotate suspension bar until spline alignment is obtained and bar will slide in easily. Note the number of teeth from drilled hole in the end of torsion bar to the "D" mark. *See Fig. 2.* Install remaining suspension bar in the same spline location.

8) Remove rods and spacers. Install shock absorbers. Tighten bolts to specification. Install wheels. Lower vehicle and recheck riding height. If height is correct, install suspension bar retaining clips and protective caps.

TIGHTENING SPECIFICATIONS

Application	Ft. Lbs. (N.m)
Anchor Bracket-To-Body Bolt	68 (92)
Axle Shaft Bolt	47 (64)
Axle Shaft Nut	123 (167)
Shock Absorber Bolt	
Lower	85 (115)
Upper	60 (81)
Wheel Lug Nut	63 (85)

FORD MOTOR CO. FWD — ESCORT & EXP

DESCRIPTION

These vehicles use a modified MacPherson strut independent rear suspension. Each side consists of a shock strut, lower control arm, tie rod, forged spindle and a coil spring mounted between the lower control arm and the body side rail.

The shock strut assembly is attached to the body side panel by a rubber insulated top mount assembly and nut. The lower end is bolted to the spindle. The lower control arm attaches to the underbody and the spindle. The tie rod attaches to the underbody and the spindle.

ADJUSTMENTS

WHEEL ALIGNMENT

See appropriate article in WHEEL ALIGNMENT section.

RIDING HEIGHT

See RIDING HEIGHT SPECIFICATIONS article in WHEEL ALIGNMENT section.

REAR WHEEL BEARINGS

1) Raise and support vehicle. Remove wheel and tire. Remove grease cap and cotter pin. Remove nut retainer. Retighten lock nut to 17-25 ft. lbs. (23-34 N.m) while rotating hub and drum assembly. Back off adjusting nut approximately 1/2 turn.

2) Retighten adjusting nut to 10-15 INCH lbs. (1-2 N.m). Position nut retainer so that slots are in line with cotter pin hole without rotating adjusting nut. Install dust cover. Install wheel and tire assembly.

REMOVAL & INSTALLATION

COIL SPRING

NOTE: **If a twin-post hoist is used, vehicle must be supported with jack stands placed under jack pads of underbody, forward of the tie rod bracket.**

Removal

Raise vehicle on hoist and place floor jack under lower control arm. Raise lower control arm to curb height. Remove tire and wheel. Remove nut, bolt, and washers retaining lower control arm to spindle. Slowly lower control arm with floor jack until spring can be removed.

Installation

1) Using new spring insulator, index insulator against tip of spring and press down until it snaps into place. *See Fig. 3.* Install spring in control arm, making sure it is properly seated in spring pocket. *See Fig. 2.*

2) Raise spring and control arm with floor jack. Position spring in pocket on underbody. Using new bolt, nut and washers, attach control arm to spindle. Head of bolt should face front of vehicle. Install tire and wheel. Remove floor jack and lower vehicle.

LOWER CONTROL ARM

NOTE: **If a twin-post hoist is used, floor jacks must be placed under lifting pads on underbody forward of tie rod body bracket. Lower rear hoist post out of way.**

Fig. 1: Rear Suspension Assembly

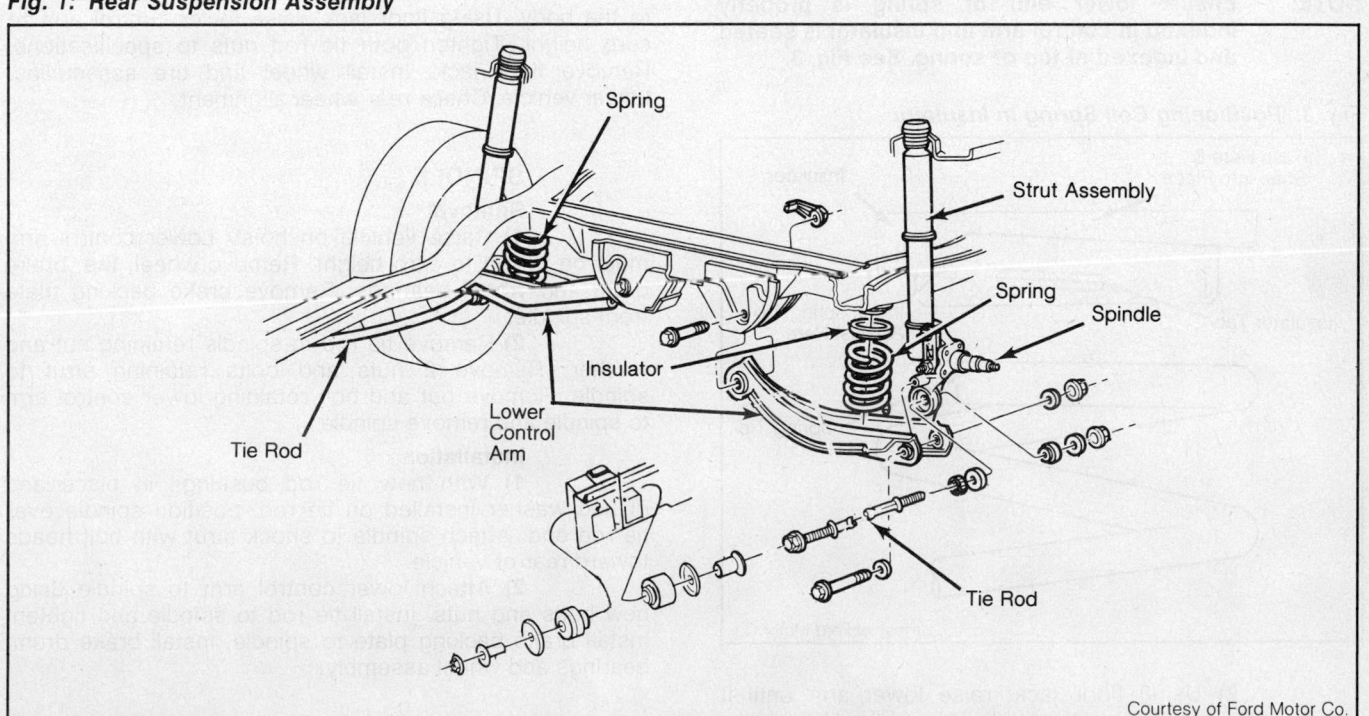

Courtesy of Ford Motor Co.

Rear Suspension

FORD MOTOR CO. FWD – ESCORT & EXP (Cont.)

Fig. 2: Index Location for Rear Spring

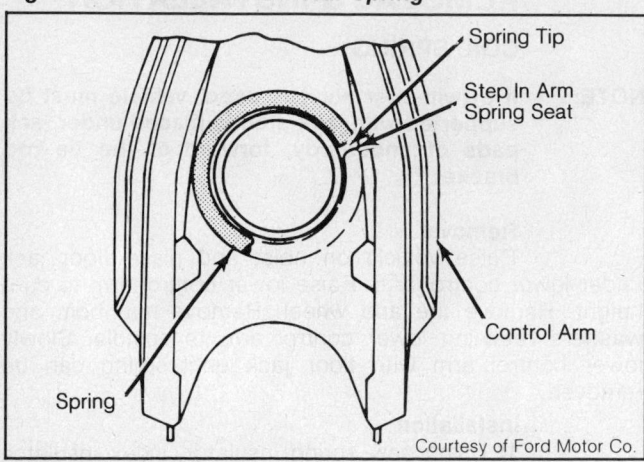

Courtesy of Ford Motor Co.

Removal

1) Raise vehicle on hoist. Remove tire and wheel. Place floor jack under lower control arm between spring and spindle end mounting.

NOTE: **Rear suspension should be at full rebound and shock strut fully extended.**

2) Remove nuts from control arm-to-body mounting bolt and control arm-to-spindle mounting bolt. Do not remove bolts at this time. Remove spindle end mounting bolt.

3) Slowly lower floor jack until spring and insulator can be removed. Remove bolt from body end and remove control arm.

Installation

1) Using new bolt and nut, attach lower control arm to body bracket. Do not tighten. Place spring in spring pocket in lower control arm.

NOTE: **Ensure lower end of spring is properly indexed in control arm and insulator is seated and indexed at top of spring. See Fig. 3.**

Fig. 3: Positioning Coil Spring in Insulator

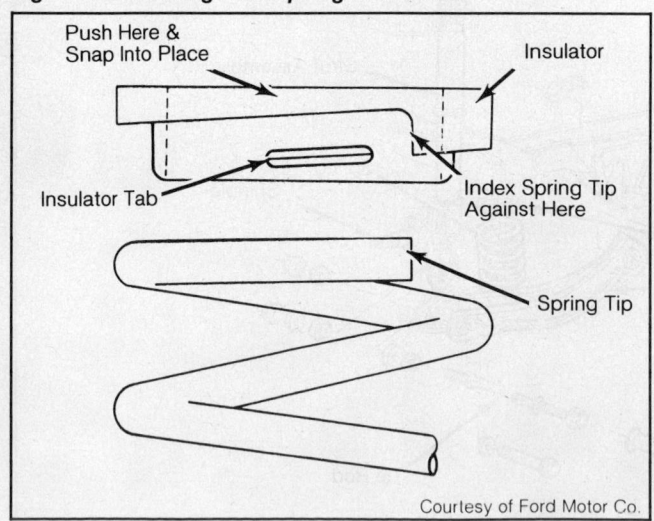

Courtesy of Ford Motor Co.

2) Using floor jack, raise lower arm until it comes in line with mounting hole in spindle. Using new bolt, nut and washer, attach lower arm to spindle. Do not tighten.

3) Using floor jack, raise lower arm to curb height. Tighten all bolts. Install tire and wheel. Remove jacks and lower vehicle.

TIE ROD & BUSHINGS
Removal

1) From inside vehicle, loosen, but do not remove shock top mount-to-body nut. Raise vehicle on hoist. Position floor jack under lower control arm. Remove wheel and tire assemblies. Remove parking brake cable attachment to body.

2) Remove nut retaining tie rod to spindle. Remove rear bushing and washer from tie rod. Remove forward nut retaining tie rod to the body. Remove nut washers and bolt attaching lower control arm to spindle. Move spindle outward and rearward far enough to remove tie rod.

3) Using 2 pry bars, pry tie rod rearward to separate inner sleeve from outer sleeve. Remove bushings, washers, and inner and outer sleeve from the body bracket.

Installation

1) Install new washer and bushing on rear of tie rod. Install outer sleeve (large inside diameter) on front end of tie rod. Insert front end of tie rod into body bracket. Install new bushing, washer, inner sleeve (small inside diameter) and nut. Do not tighten at this time.

NOTE: **Remove .3-.5" (8-13 mm) from length of small diameter sleeve before installation.**

2) Pull spindle outward and rearward far enough so that tie rod can be installed in spindle. Install new bushing, washer and nut. Do not tighten at this time. Attach lower control arm to the spindle using new bolt (with bolt head toward front of vehicle), washer and nut.

3) Install parking brake cable rear attachment to the body. Using floor jack, raise lower control arm to curb height. Tighten both tie rod nuts to specifications. Remove floor jack. Install wheel and tire assemblies. Lower vehicle. Check rear wheel alignment.

SPINDLE
Removal

1) Raise vehicle on hoist. Lower control arm must be raised to curb height. Remove wheel, tire, brake drum and wheel bearings. Remove brake backing plate from spindle.

2) Remove tie rod-to-spindle retaining nut and washer. Remove 2 nuts and bolts retaining strut to spindle. Remove nut and bolt retaining lower control arm to spindle and remove spindle.

Installation

1) With new tie rod bushings in place and dished washer installed on tie rod, position spindle over tie rod end. Attach spindle to shock strut with bolt heads toward rear of vehicle.

2) Attach lower control arm to spindle using new bolts and nuts. Install tie rod to spindle and tighten. Install brake backing plate to spindle. Install brake drum, bearings and wheel assembly.

FORD MOTOR CO. FWD — ESCORT & EXP (Cont.)

Fig. 4: Tie Rod Washer Installation

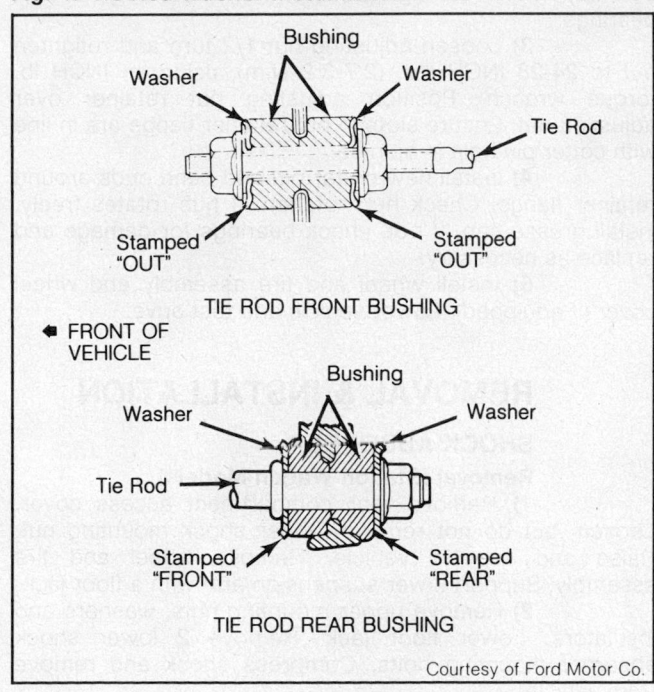

Courtesy of Ford Motor Co.

SHOCK ABSORBER STRUTS

Removal

1) Remove rear compartment access panels on 2-door models, or quarter trim panels on 4-door models. Loosen, but do not remove, top shock absorber attaching nut with a 43 mm deep Hex Drive Socket (T81P-18045-BH). Hold strut rod with an 8 mm deep socket and 1/4" Drive Handle (STMM-8) while loosening.

Fig. 5: Upper Shock Mounting Components

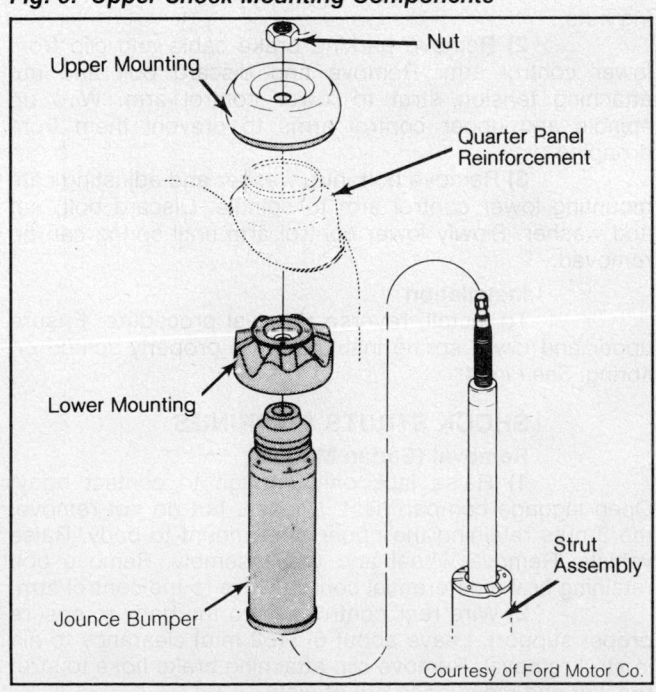

Courtesy of Ford Motor Co.

2) Raise vehicle on hoist and remove tire and wheel. Remove clip retaining flexible brake hose to rear shock and move hose aside.

NOTE: If a frame contact hoist is used, support lower control arm with floor jack. If twin-post hoist is used, support body with floor jacks placed on lifting pads forward of tie rod body bracket.

3) Loosen 2 bolts retaining shock to spindle. Do not remove bolts at this time. Remove top mounting nut, washer and rubber insulator. Remove 2 bottom mounting bolts and remove shock.

Installation

1) Extend shock absorber to maximum length. Install new lower washer and insulator assembly. Use tire lubricant to ease insertion into quarter panel shock tower.

2) Position upper part of shock shaft into shock tower opening in body and push slowly on lower part of shock until mounting holes are lined up with mounting holes in spindle.

3) Install, but do not tighten, new lower mounting bolts and nuts. Bolt heads should face to rear. Place new washer and upper insulator on upper shock shaft.

4) Using a 43 mm deep Hex Drive Socket (T81P-18045-BH), while holding strut shaft with an 8 mm deep socket, tighten upper shock nut. Tighten lower mounting bolts.

5) Install brake flex hose and retaining clip. Install wheel and tire assembly. Remove floor jacks and lower vehicle. Install quarter trim panels or rear access panels.

WHEEL BEARINGS

Removal

1) Raise vehicle. Remove wheel from hub and drum. Remove grease cap, cotter pin, nut retainer, adjusting nut and flat washer from spindle.

2) Pull hub and drum off spindle without dropping outer bearing assembly. Remove outer bearing assembly. Using Seal Remover (1175-AC), remove and discard grease seal. Remove inner bearing from hub.

Installation

1) If inner or outer bearing cups were removed, install new cups using Driver (T77F-1102-A and T77F-1217-A). Support drum on wood block to prevent damage.

2) Ensure spindle and bearing surfaces are clean. Thoroughly grease bearing. Install inner bearing and cone into inner cup. Apply light film of grease to lips of new seal. Install seal with Driver (T81P-1249-A).

3) Seat seal retainer flange. Apply light coat of grease to spindle shaft bearing surfaces. Install hub and drum assembly. Keep hub centered on spindle.

4) Install outer bearing assembly and flat washer on spindle. Install adjusting nut finger tight. Adjust bearings. Install grease cap. Install wheel and tire and lower vehicle.

TIGHTENING SPECIFICATIONS

Application	Ft. Lbs. (N.m)
Control Arm-to-Body Bolt	52-74 (70-100)
Control Arm-to-Spindle Bolt	70-96 (95-130)
Strut-to-Body Nut	35-55 (48-75)
Strut-to-Spindle Bolt	70-96 (95-130)
Tie Rod-to-Body Nut	52-74 (70-100)
Tie Rod-to-Spindle Nut	52-74 (70-100)

Rear Suspension

FORD MOTOR CO. FWD – SABLE & TAURUS

DESCRIPTION

Sable and Taurus sedan models utilize a MacPherson strut independent rear suspension. Each side consists of a strut assembly, 2 parallel control arms, tension strut, cast spindle and strut-mounted stabilizer bar.

Station wagon models use upper and lower control arms, shock absorber, 2-piece cast spindle, tension strut, control arm mounted stabilizer bar, and a coil spring mounted between the lower control arm and the body crossmember.

Fig. 1: Sedan Rear Suspension

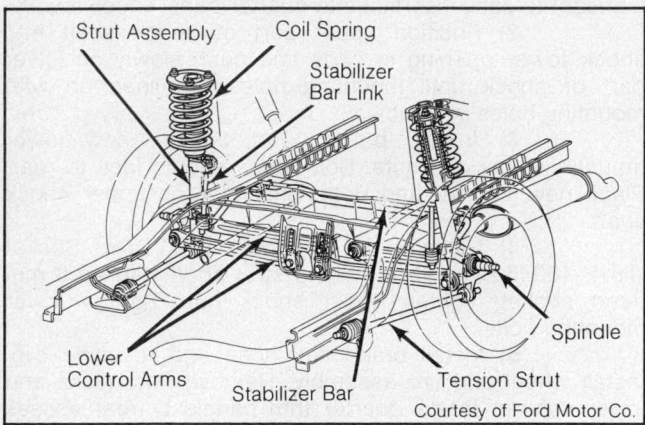

Courtesy of Ford Motor Co.

Fig. 2: Station Wagon Rear Suspension

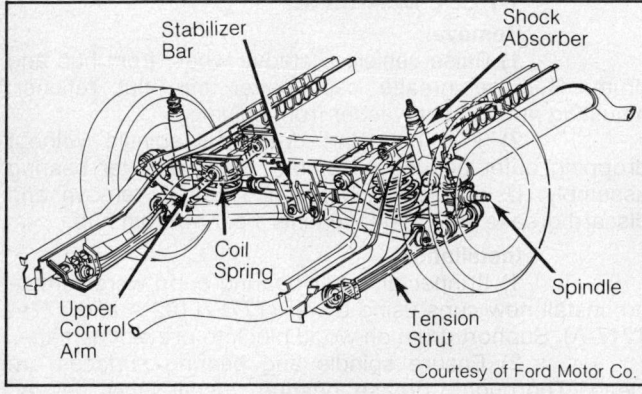

Courtesy of Ford Motor Co.

ADJUSTMENTS

RIDING HEIGHT

See RIDING HEIGHT SPECIFICATIONS article in WHEEL ALIGNMENT section.

TOE ADJUSTMENT

See appropriate article in WHEEL ALIGNMENT section.

REAR WHEEL BEARING

1) Raise vehicle until tire clears floor. Remove wheel cover or ornament and nut covers. If vehicle has styled steel or aluminum wheels, remove wheel and tire assembly. Remove grease cap from hub.

2) Remove cotter pin and nut retainer. Back off adjusting nut one full turn. Tighten nut to 17-25 ft. lbs. (23-

34 N.m), while rotating hub and drum assembly to seat bearings.

3) Loosen adjusting nut 1/2 turn and retighten nut to 24-28 INCH lbs. (2.7-3.2 N.m), using an INCH lb. torque wrench. Position adjusting nut retainer over adjusting nut. Ensure slots in nut retainer flange are in line with cotter pin hole in spindle.

4) Install new cotter pin and bend ends around retainer flange. Check hub rotation. If hub rotates freely, install grease cap. If not, check bearings for damage and replace as necessary.

5) Install wheel and tire assembly and wheel cover (if equipped). Lower vehicle and test drive.

REMOVAL & INSTALLATION

SHOCK ABSORBER

Removal (Station Wagon Models)

1) Remove rear compartment access cover. Loosen, but do not remove, upper shock mounting nut. Raise and support vehicle. Remove wheel and tire assembly. Support lower suspension arm with a floor jack.

2) Remove upper mounting nuts, washers and insulators. Lower floor jack. Remove 2 lower shock absorber mounting bolts. Compress shock and remove from vehicle.

Installation

To install, reverse removal procedure.

SPRINGS

Removal (Station Wagon Models)

1) Raise and support vehicle. Support lower control arm with a floor jack at normal riding height. Remove wheel and tire assemblies. Remove brake hose bracket. Remove stabilizer bar "U" bracket from lower control arm. Remove and discard shock absorber mounting nuts.

2) Remove parking brake cable and clip from lower control arm. Remove and discard bolt and nut attaching tension strut to lower control arm. Wire up spindle and upper control arms to prevent them from dropping.

3) Remove bolt, nut, washer and adjusting cam mounting lower control arm to spindle. Discard bolt, nut and washer. Slowly lower control arm until spring can be removed.

Installation

To install, reverse removal procedure. Ensure upper and lower spring insulators are properly seated on spring. *See Fig. 4.*

SHOCK STRUTS & SPRINGS

Removal (Sedan Models)

1) Raise jack only enough to contact body. Open luggage compartment. Loosen, but do not remove, the 3 nuts retaining the upper strut mount to body. Raise vehicle. Remove wheel and tire assembly. Remove bolt retaining brake differential control valve to the control arm.

2) Wire rear control arm to the body to ensure proper support. Leave about 6" (152 mm) clearance to aid in strut removal. Remove clip attaching brake hose to strut bracket and move hose out of way.

3) Remove stabilizer bar "U" bracket from body. Remove stabilizer bar link assembly from strut

Rear Suspension

FORD MOTOR CO. FWD — SABLE & TAURUS (Cont.)

mounting bracket (if equipped). Disconnect tension strut from spindle. Move spindle rearward enough to separate it from tension strut.

4) Remove pinch bolt retaining strut to spindle. Spread strut-to-spindle pinch joint (if necessary). Separate strut from spindle. From inside luggage compartment, remove 3 upper mount-to-body nuts and remove strut.

5) Mark insulator position to top mount for reassembly purposes. Compress spring with Spring Compressor (D85P-7178-A). With spring compressed, hold shaft and remove strut shaft-to-mount nut. Ensure spring is compressed to avoid fracture of shaft at base of hex. Remove spring, strut and mount from compressor.

Fig. 3: Strut, Spring & Upper Mount Components

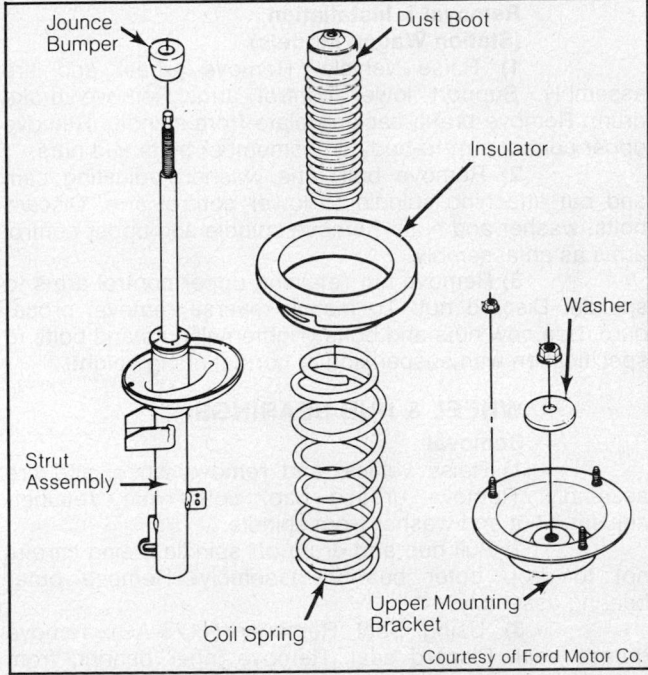

Courtesy of Ford Motor Co.

Installation

To install, reverse removal procedure. Ensure spring is properly located in the upper and lower spring seats. *See Fig. 4.* Tighten all nuts and bolts to specification.

Fig. 4: Spring Positioning in Spring Seats (Sedan Models)

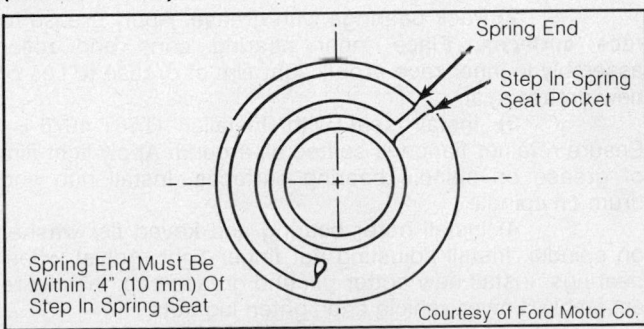

Courtesy of Ford Motor Co.

LOWER CONTROL ARM
Removal (Sedan Models)

Raise vehicle. Disconnect brake proportioning valve from left front arm. Disconnect parking brake cable from front control arm. Remove and discard control arm-to-spindle bolt, washer and nut. Remove and discard control arm-to-body bolt and nut. Remove control arm from vehicle.

Installation

To install, reverse removal procedure.

NOTE: **When installing new control arms, offset on arms must face up. Control arms are stamped "BOTTOM" on the lower edge. Flange edge of arm stamping must face front of vehicle on the right rear arm. Flange edge of arm must face rear of vehicle on all other arms.**

Removal (Station Wagon Models)

Raise and support vehicle at lifting pads. Remove wheel and tire assembly. Remove spring as previously described. Remove bolts and nuts mounting lower control arm to body and spindle. Remove lower control arm.

Installation

To install, reverse removal procedure. Install control arm-to-body bolt with head of bolt toward front of vehicle. Tighten mounting bolts and nuts to specification with vehicle at riding height.

UPPER CONTROL ARMS
Removal (Station Wagon Models)

1) Raise and support vehicle. Support lower control arm at curb height. *See Fig. 5.* Remove wheel and tire assemblies. Remove brake line bracket from body. Loosen, but do not remove, spindle-to-upper arm and lower arm mounting nuts.

2) Remove bolts and nuts mounting front and rear upper control arms to body brackets. Ensure spindle does not fall outward. Carefully tilt top of spindle outward, until ends of upper control arms are clear of the body bracket.

Fig. 5: Supporting Lower Control Arm

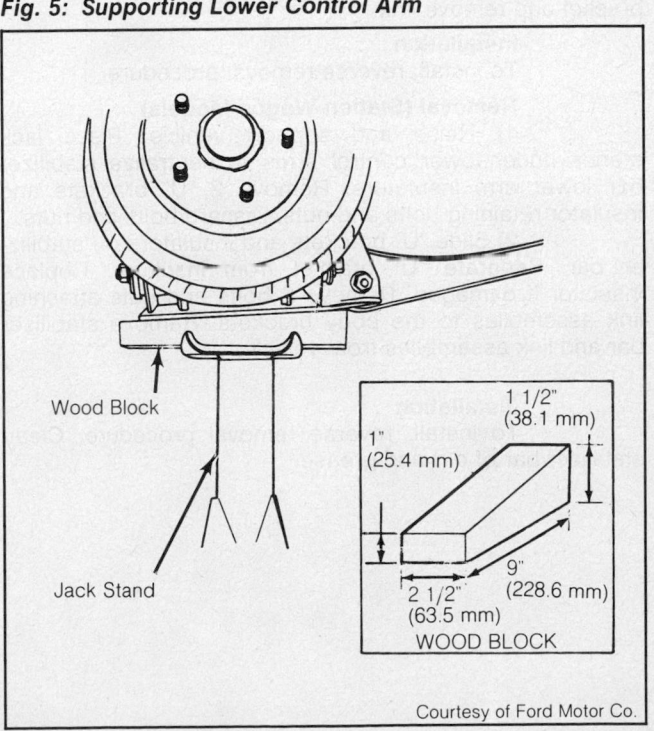

Courtesy of Ford Motor Co.

FORD MOTOR CO. FWD — SABLE & TAURUS (Cont.)

3) Wire spindle to the body in this position. Remove nut mounting upper control arms to spindle. Remove upper control arms from vehicle.

Installation
To install, reverse removal procedure.

TENSION STRUT
Removal & Installation
(Sedan Models)
1) Raise vehicle using lift pads located in front of rear wheels and rearward of front wheels. Loosen 3 upper strut nuts from inside luggage compartment. Remove tire and wheel assembly. Remove and discard tension strut-to-spindle and body nuts.

2) Move spindle rearward. Remove tension strut. To install, reverse removal procedure. Ensure rear bushing have indentations in them. Tighten bolts and nuts with vehicle at normal riding height.

Removal & Installation
(Station Wagon Models)
1) Raise and support vehicle. Support lower control arm at normal riding height. Remove wheel and tire assembly. Remove bolt and nut retaining tension strut to lower control arm. Remove bolt and nut retaining tension strut to body bracket. Remove tension strut assembly.

2) To install, reverse removal procedure. Install new mounting bolts and nuts. Tighten bolts and nuts to specification with vehicle at normal riding height. Perform rear wheel alignment.

STABILIZER BAR
Removal (Sedan Models)
Raise and support vehicle. Remove wheel and tire assemblies. Remove nut and insulator attaching stabilizer bar to end link assemblies. Remove 2 "U" brackets attaching stabilizer bar to the body. Remove stabilizer bar. Remove nut attaching link assembly to bracket and remove link.

Installation
To install, reverse removal procedure.

Removal (Station Wagon Models)
1) Raise and support vehicle. Place jack stands under lower control arms to neutralize stabilizer bar lower arm insulators. Remove 2 "U" brackets and insulator retaining bolts and nuts. Discard bolts and nuts.

2) Slide "U" brackets and insulators off stabilizer bar. Separate "U" bracket from insulator. Replace insulator if damaged. Remove 2 bolts and nuts attaching link assemblies to the body brackets. Remove stabilizer bar and link assemblies from vehicle.

Installation
To install, reverse removal procedure. Clean stabilizer bar of dirt and grease.

SPINDLE
Removal (Sedan Models)
1) Raise vehicle. Remove wheel and tire assembly. Remove brake drum. Remove bolt retaining brake flex hose bracket to strut. Remove 4 bolts retaining brake backing plate to spindle.

2) Remove brake backing plate from spindle and wire it out of way. Remove and discard control arm-to-spindle bolts, washers and nuts. Remove tension strut nut, bushing and washer. Discard nut. Remove pinch bolt retaining spindle to strut. Remove spindle.

Installation
To install, reverse removal procedure. Use new bolts and nuts.

Removal & Installation
(Station Wagon Models)
1) Raise vehicle. Remove wheel and tire assembly. Support lower control arm. Remove brake drum. Remove brake backing plate from spindle. Remove upper control arm-to-body crossmember bolts and nuts.

2) Remove bolt, one washer, adjusting cam and nut attaching spindle to lower control arm. Discard bolts, washer and nuts. Remove spindle and upper control arms as an assembly.

3) Remove nut retaining upper control arms to spindle. Discard nut. To install, reverse removal procedure. Use new nuts and bolts. Tighten all nuts and bolts to specification with suspension at normal riding height.

WHEEL & HUB BEARINGS
Removal
1) Raise vehicle and remove wheel and tire assembly. Remove grease cap, cotter pin, retainer, adjusting nut and washer from spindle.

2) Pull hub and drum off spindle, being careful not to drop outer bearing assembly. Remove outer bearing assembly.

3) Using Seal Remover (1175-AC), remove grease seal. Discard seal. Remove inner bearing from hub. Clean hub and spindle with clean cloth.

Installation
1) If bearing races were removed, install new inner and outer bearing races using Installer Set (T80T-4000-W, T77F-1217-B and T73F-1217-A). Support drum on wood block and ensure races are properly seated. DO NOT use cone and roller assembly to install races, as this will damage races.

2) Pack bearings with grease. Apply grease to race surfaces. Place inner bearing cone and roller assembly in inner race. Apply light film of grease to lips of new grease seal.

3) Install seal with Installer (T56T-4676-B). Ensure retainer flange is seated all around. Apply light film of grease on spindle bearing surfaces. Install hub and drum on spindle.

4) Install outer bearing and keyed flat washer on spindle. Install adjusting nut finger tight. Adjust wheel bearings. Install new cotter pin and grease cap. Install tire assembly. Lower vehicle and tighten lug nuts.

Rear Suspension

FORD MOTOR CO. FWD — SABLE & TAURUS (Cont.)

TIGHTENING SPECIFICATIONS

Application	Ft. Lbs. (N.m)
Lower Control Arm-to-Spindle Bolt	
Sedan	42-57 (57-78)
Station Wagon	60-86 (81-117)
Lower Control Arm-to-Body Bolt	
Sedan	45-65 (61-88)
Station Wagon	40-55 (54-75)
Lower Shock Absorber Nuts	13-20 (18-27)
Stabilizer Bar Link Bolt	
Station Wagon	40-55 (54-75)
Stabilizer Bar "U" Bracket-to-Body Bolt	
Sedan	25-37 (34-50)
Station Wagon	20-30 (27-41)
Strut Top Mount-to-Body Nut	19-26 (26-35)
Strut-to-Spindle Bolt	55-81 (75-110)
Strut-to-Top Mount Nut	35-50 (47-68)
Tension Strut Mounting Bolts	
Station Wagon	40-55 (54-75)
Tension Strut-to-Body Nut	
Sedan	52-74 (71-100)
Tension Strut-to-Spindle Nut	
Sedan	52-74 (71-100)
Upper Control Arm-to-Body Bolt	70-95 (95-129)
Upper Control Arm-to-	
Spindle Bolt	150-190 (203-257)
Upper Shock Absorber Nut	19-27 (26-37)
Wheel Lug Nuts	80-105 (108-142)

	INCH Lbs. (N.m)
Stabilizer Bar Link Bolt	
Sedan	72-144 (8-16)

Rear Suspension

FORD MOTOR CO. FWD – TEMPO & TOPAZ

DESCRIPTION

Tempo and Topaz utilize a MacPherson strut independent rear suspension. Each side consists of a gas pressurized shock absorber strut assembly, 2 parallel control arms, tie rod, forged spindle, shock bumper and dust shield.

Fig. 1: Independent Rear Suspension

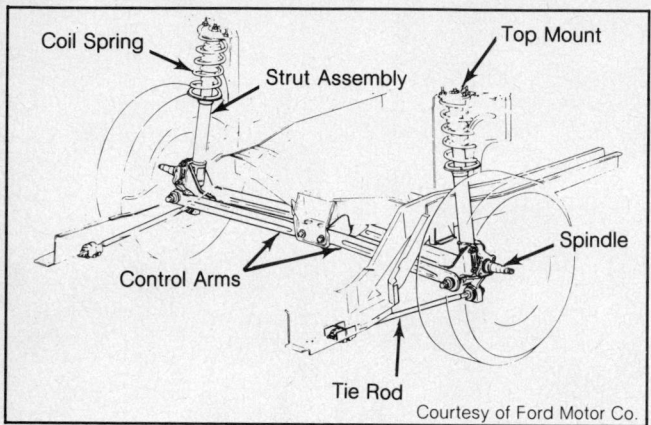

Courtesy of Ford Motor Co.

ADJUSTMENTS

WHEEL ALIGNMENT

See appropriate article in WHEEL ALIGNMENT section.

RIDING HEIGHT

See RIDING HEIGHT SECIFICATIONS article in WHEEL ALIGNMENT section.

REAR WHEEL BEARINGS

NOTE: **Wheel bearings on all wheel drive models are not adjustable.**

1) Raise vehicle until tire clears floor. Remove wheel cover or ornament and nut covers. If vehicle has styled steel or aluminum wheels, remove wheel and tire assembly. Remove grease cap from hub.

2) Remove cotter pin and nut retainer. Back off adjusting nut one turn. Tighten nut to 17-25 ft. lbs. (23-34 N.m) while rotating hub and drum assembly.

3) Loosen adjusting nut 1/2 turn and retighten nut to 10-15 INCH lb. (1.0-1.7 N.m) using an INCH lb. torque wrench. Position adjusting nut retainer over adjusting nut. Ensure slots in nut retainer flange are in line with cotter pin hole in spindle.

4) Install new cotter pin and bend ends around retainer flange. Check hub rotation. If hub rotates freely, install grease cap. If not, check bearings for damage and replace as necessary.

5) Install wheel and tire assembly, wheel cover, ornament and nut covers as required. Lower vehicle and test drive.

REMOVAL & INSTALLATION

SHOCK STRUT & SPRING

CAUTION: Struts are gas charged. DO NOT apply heat or flame to strut during removal.

Removal

1) Raise jack only enough to contact body. Open trunk lid. Loosen 2 nuts retaining the upper strut mount to body, but do not remove nuts. Raise vehicle. Remove wheel and tire assembly.

2) Place safety stand under control arm to support suspension. Remove bolt attaching brake hose bracket to strut and place it out of way. Do not stretch brake hose when removing strut, or damage to steel brake line may result.

3) Remove 2 bolts attaching bracket to spindle and remove bracket. Remove 2 bolts retaining strut to spindle. Remove 2 upper mount-to-body nuts and remove strut.

4) Compress spring with Spring Compressor (D83P-5310-A). With spring compressed, hold shaft and remove strut shaft-to-mount nut with spring compressed to avoid fracture of shaft at base of hex. Remove spring, strut and mount from compressor.

Installation

To install, reverse removal procedure. Ensure spring is properly located in the upper and lower spring seats. See Fig. 2. Position lower washer correctly. See Fig. 3. Tighten all nuts and bolts to specifications.

Fig. 2: Spring Positioning in Spring Seats

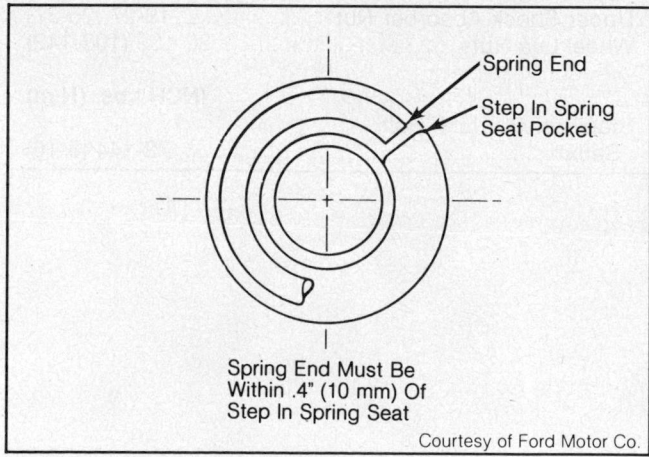

Courtesy of Ford Motor Co.

CONTROL ARMS

Removal

Raise vehicle. Remove and discard arm-to-spindle bolts and nuts. Remove and discard center mounting bolts and nuts. Remove arms from vehicle.

Installation

To install, reverse removal procedure. When installing new control arms, bushing with .39" (10 mm) hole is installed to center of vehicle and bushing with .48" (12 mm) hole is installed to spindle. Offset on arm must face up on right side of vehicle and down on left side. Flange edge of arm stamping must face rear of vehicle.

TIE ROD

Removal

1) Raise vehicle on a frame contact hoist using the lift pads located to the rear of the front wheels and the lift pads forward of the rear wheels. Raise hoist only enough to contact the body. From inside trunk, loosen, but do not remove, 2 strut top mount-to-body nuts.

2) Raise vehicle and place safety stand under suspension for support. Remove wheel and tire assembly.

FORD MOTOR CO. FWD — TEMPO & TOPAZ (Cont.)

Remove 2 top mount studs. Remove nut retaining tie rod to spindle. Remove nut retaining tie rod to body. Lower safety stand enough so that upper strut mount studs are out of holes in body. Move spindle rearward so that tie rod can be removed.

Installation

To install, reverse removal procedure. Note that front and rear tie rod bushings are different. Rear bushings have indentations in them. Replace washers and bushings if worn. Do not tighten 2 tie rod nuts until curb height has been obtained. Washers must be installed with dish facing away from bushings.

Fig. 3: Strut, Spring & Upper Mount Components

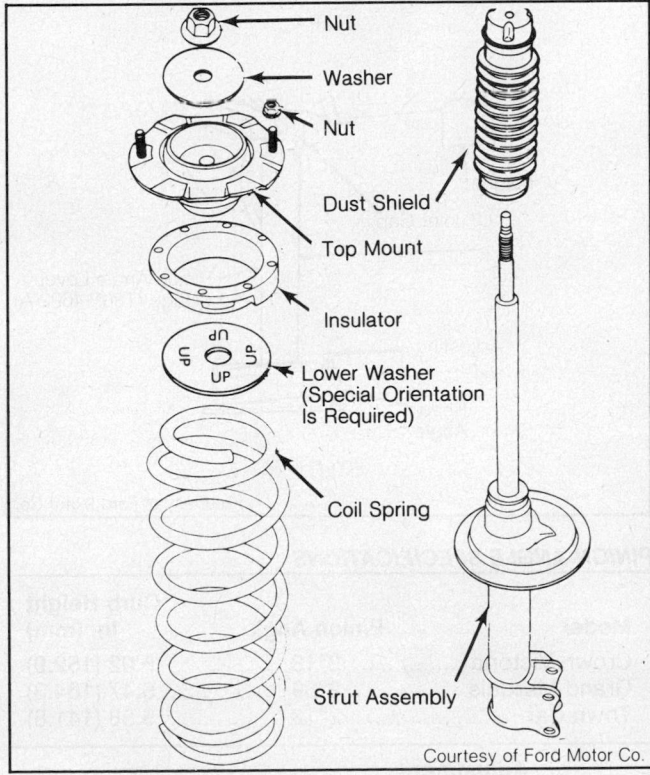

Nut
Washer
Nut
Dust Shield
Top Mount
Insulator
Lower Washer (Special Orientation Is Required)
Coil Spring
Strut Assembly

Courtesy of Ford Motor Co.

SPINDLE

NOTE: Note position of bolt head direction for reassembly reference.

Removal

1) Raise vehicle. Remove wheel and tire assembly. Remove brake drum. Remove bolt retaining brake flex hose bracket to strut. Remove 4 bolts retaining brake backing plate to spindle. Do not stretch brake hose or damage to metal brake line may result.

2) Remove brake backing plate from spindle and wire it out of way. Remove control arm to spindle bolt, washers and nut. Remove tie rod nut, bushing and washer. Remove 2 bolts retaining spindle to strut and remove spindle.

Installation

To install, reverse removal procedure. Use new nuts and bolts. Tighten all nuts and bolts to specification.

WHEEL & HUB BEARINGS

Removal (2WD)

1) Raise vehicle and remove wheel and tire assembly. Remove grease cap, cotter pin, retainer, adjusting nut and washer from spindle.

2) Pull hub and drum off spindle, being careful not to drop outer bearing assembly. Remove outer bearing assembly.

3) Using Remover (1175-AC), remove grease seal. Discard seal. Remove inner bearing from hub. Clean hub and spindle with clean cloth.

Installation

1) If bearing cups were removed, install new inner and outer bearing cups using Installer Set (T80T-4000-W, T77F-1202-A and T73T-1217-A). Support drum hub on wood block and ensure cups are properly seated. DO NOT use cone and roller assembly to install cups, as this will damage cups.

2) Pack bearings with grease. Apply grease to cup surfaces. Place inner bearing cone and roller assembly in inner cup. Apply light film of grease to lips of new grease seal.

3) Install seal with Installer (T81P-1249-A). Ensure retainer flange is seated all around. Apply light film of grease on spindle bearing surfaces. Install hub and drum on spindle.

4) Install outer bearing and keyed flat washer on spindle. Install adjusting nut finger tight. Adjust wheel bearings. Install new cotter pin and grease cap. Install tire assembly. Lower vehicle and tighten lug nuts.

Removal (All Wheel Drive)

1) Raise and support vehicle. Remove tire and wheel. Remove brake drum. Disconnect parking brake cable from brake backing plate. Disconnect brake line from wheel cylinder. Plug all openings. Remove outboard "U" joint straps.

2) Disconnect halfshaft and wire out of way. Disconnect control arm from spindle. Discard bolt, washer and nut. Disconnect tie rod. Discard nut. Remove and discard spindle-to-strut bolts.

3) Remove spindle assembly. Place spindle assembly in a vise. Remove cotter pin and nut from stub shaft. Using Puller (T77F-4220-B) and Protector (D80L-625-6), remove yoke from stub shaft. Remove stub shaft.

4) Remove snap ring. Remove backing plate from spindle. Using Adapter (T87P-7120-B), Handle (T80T-4000-W) and hydraulic press, remove bearing from spindle.

Installation

To install, reverse removal procedure. Use Step Plate Adapter (D80L-630-8) and handle to install bearing.

TIGHTENING SPECIFICATIONS

Application	Ft. Lbs. (N.m)
Control Arm-to-Body Bolt	30-40 (41-54)
Control Arm-to-Spindle Nut	60-80 (81-108)
Stabilizer "U" Bracket-to-Body Bolt	15-26 (20-35)
Strut Top Mount-to-Body Nut	20-30 (27-41)
Strut-to-Spindle Bolts	70-96 (95-130)
Strut-to-Top Mount Nut	35-50 (47-68)
Stub Shaft Nut	120-150 (163-204)
Tie Rod-to-Body Bolts	52-74 (71-100)
Tie Rod-to-Spindle Nut	52-74 (71-100)
"U" Joint Strap Bolt	15-17 (20-23)

FORD MOTOR CO. RWD — EXCEPT MARK VII

NOTE: For information on Mark VII, see FORD MOTOR CO. AIR SUSPENSION – MARK VII article in this section.

DESCRIPTION

The rear axle housing is suspended from frame by 2 upper control arms which control side-to-side movement, and 2 lower control arms which control front-to-rear movement. Each coil spring is mounted between an upper and lower seat. Shock absorbers are attached to upper spring seat, or upper shock tower on floorpan, and at lower shock brackets welded to axle tube.

Thunderbird models with 2.3L EFI Turbo and 5.0L with trailer towing package and Mustang models with handling suspension package, use 2 hydraulic axle dampers. These axle dampers are mounted rearward of axle, between axle bracket and frame, to control rotational forces during power applications.

ADJUSTMENTS

RIDING HEIGHT

See RIDING HEIGHT SPECIFICATIONS article in WHEEL ALIGNMENT section.

PINION ANGLE (CROWN VICTORIA, GRAND MARQUIS & TOWN CAR)

Checking

1) Vehicle must be at normal curb height. Curb height is measured vertically from top of axle housing tube to outboard edge of frame side rail. See Fig. 1.

Fig. 1: Measuring Curb Height (Crown Victoria, Grand Marquis & Town Car)

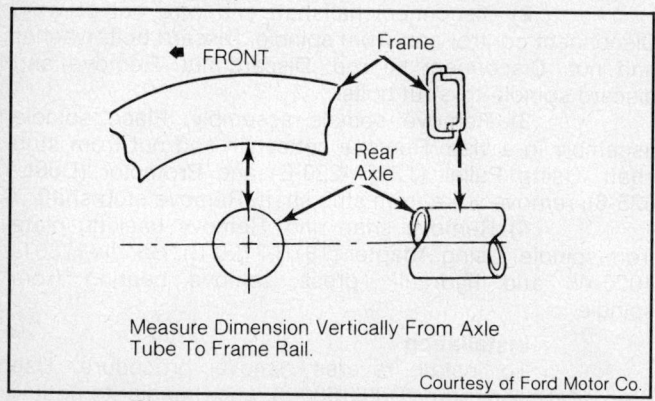

Measure Dimension Vertically From Axle Tube To Frame Rail.

Courtesy of Ford Motor Co.

2) Position "V" magnet of Pinion Angle Level Gauge (T86P-4602-A) on drive shaft. Make sure magnet is away from welds or balance weights. See Fig. 2.

3) From left side of vehicle, angle level gauge on magnet with adjusting screw to left. Adjust dial on tool until left hand edge of bubble is exactly on zero line.

4) Place angle level gauge on circular bearing cap of "U" joint with tool in same relative position as it was on drive shaft. See Fig. 2. Snap ring must be removed during reading.

5) Read position of bubble's left hand edge on scale to determine drive shaft angle. See PINION ANGLE SPECIFICATIONS table. If angle is not as specified, go to ADJUSTMENT.

Fig. 2: Measuring Pinion Angle

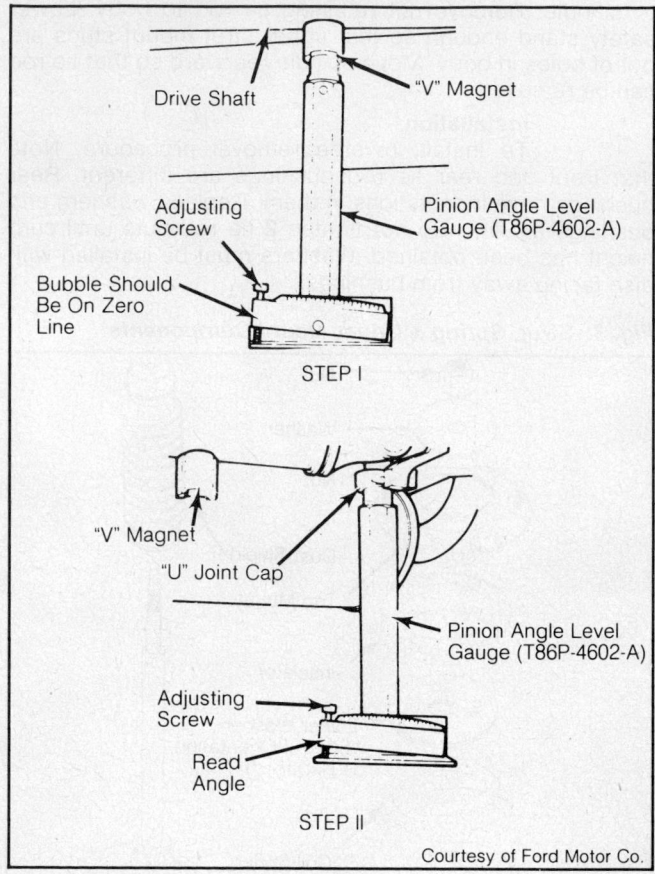

STEP I

STEP II

Courtesy of Ford Motor Co.

PINION ANGLE SPECIFICATIONS

Model	Pinion Angle	Curb Height In. (mm)
Crown Victoria	2°18′	6.02 (152.9)
Grand Marquis	2°59′	6.47 (164.3)
Town Car	2°18′	5.58 (141.8)

Adjustment

1) If pinion angle is not within specifications, install new upper control arm bushings equipped with adjustment cams. See REMOVAL & INSTALLATION in this article.

2) Eccentric cam in upper control arm can be rotated to change pinion angle. If cam is rusty, tap it with a drift to remove rust so cam will rotate. See Fig. 3.

Fig. 3: Adjusting Pinion Angle (Crown Victoria, Grand Marquis & Town Car)

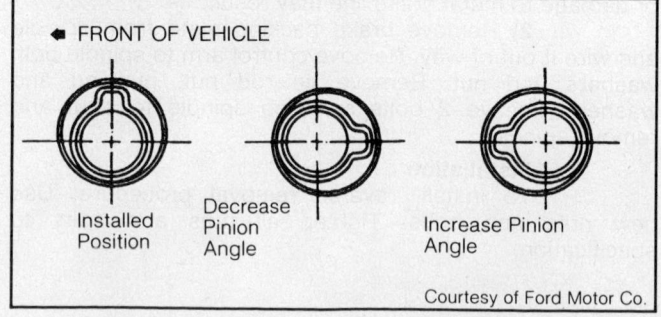

Courtesy of Ford Motor Co.

FORD MOTOR CO. RWD – EXCEPT MARK VII (Cont.)

REMOVAL & INSTALLATION

SHOCK ABSORBERS

CAUTION: All models, except police applications, are equipped with gas-pressurized shock absorbers. DO NOT apply heat or flame to the shock absorber.

Removal (Crown Victoria, Grand Marquis & Town Car)

1) Raise vehicle and support rear axle assembly. On models with a plastic dust tube, place an open end wrench on the hex stamped into the dust tube metal cap.

2) On models with metal dust tube, grasp the tube to prevent stud rotation and loosen the mounting nut. Remove mounting nut, washer and insulator from the stud on the upper side of the frame. Discard nut. New nut will should be used during installation.

3) Disconnect lower shock absorber mounting stud. Discard nut. Remove shock absorber.

Installation

1) Before installing shock absorber, place shock right side up (as installed in vehicle). Turn shock absorber upside down and fully compress it. Repeat procedure at least 3 times to get rid of any trapped air.

2) To install shock absorber, reverse removal procedure. Install new nuts on upper and lower attaching studs. Tighten mounting nuts to specification.

Fig. 4: Crown Victoria, Grand Marquis & Town Car Rear Suspension

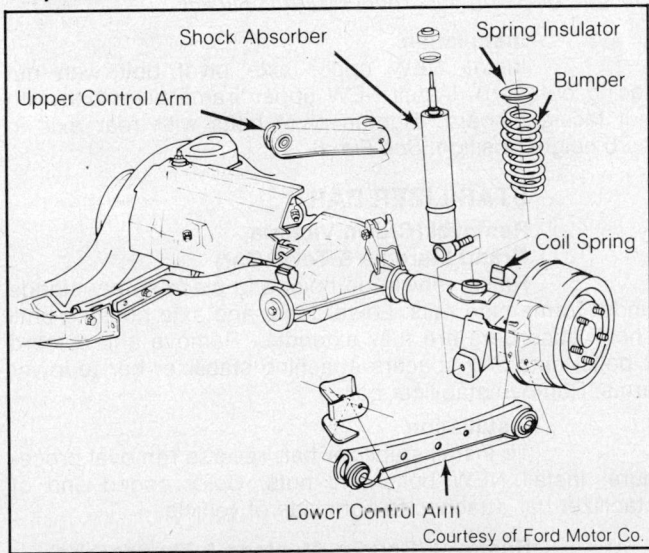

Courtesy of Ford Motor Co.

Removal (Cougar, Mustang & Thunderbird)

1) On all models except Mustang 3-door, open trunk to access upper shock absorber mounting stud. On Mustang 3-door models, open the rear hatch and remove the trim panel access door. On all models, remove the rubber cap (if equipped), mounting nut, washer and insulator from the shock absorber upper mounting stud.

2) Raise vehicle and support rear axle. On Cougar and Thunderbird models, remove the shock absorber cross bolt and nut from the lower shock bracket. On Mustang, remove the lower shock absorber bolt, washer and nut from the axle bracket. On all models, remove the shock absorber.

Installation

1) Before installing shock absorber, place shock right side up (as installed in vehicle). Turn shock absorber upside down and fully compress it. Repeat procedure at least 3 times to get rid of any trapped air.

2) To install shock, place inner washer and insulator on upper attaching stud. Place shock in upper mount. Align shock lower mounting eye to attachment.

3) On Mustang only, use a NEW load bearing washer between shock eye and axle bracket. Install a NEW Torx drive bolt through shock and axle.

4) Tighten lower mounting bolt while allowing self-wrenching nut to rotate freely so wrenching tab seats on outboard of axle bracket. DO NOT hold nut tab using any other method.

5) On Cougar, Mustang, Thunderbird, and Mustang with handling suspension, lower mounting bolt head must seat on inboard side of shock bracket. Install a new nut. Tighten lower shock cross bolt to specification.

6) On all models, lower vehicle. Install insulator, outer washer and NEW nut to upper shock stud. Tighten to specification.

COIL SPRINGS & INSULATORS

NOTE: If one spring must be replaced, replace both springs. Remove stabilizer bar (if equipped).

Removal (Crown Victoria, Grand Marquis & Town Car)

1) Place hoist under axle housing and raise vehicle. Place safety stands under frame side rails. Disconnect lower shock absorber mounts. Remove right side parking brake cable from the upper arm retainer.

2) Lower hoist and axle housing until coil springs are released. Remove springs and insulators from vehicle.

Installation

To install coil spring, reverse removal procedure. Ensure coil spring insulator is installed between upper end of spring and upper seat. Use NEW nuts on shock absorber mounting stud.

Removal (Cougar, Mustang & Thunderbird)

1) Raise vehicle and support body at rear crossmember. Lower hoist until shock absorbers are fully extended. Rear axle must be supported by stands. Place transmission jack under lower arm-to-axle pivot bolt.

2) Remove the bolt and nut. Lower transmission jack slowly to release spring load. Remove coil spring and insulator.

Installation

1) Place upper spring insulator on top of spring. Tape in place if necessary. Place lower spring insulator on lower arm. On Cougar and Thunderbird models, place internal damper into spring.

2) On all models, position coil spring on lower seat so that pigtail is at rear and pointing toward left side of vehicle. Slowly raise transmission jack until arm is in position.

3) Install NEW rear pivot bolt with nut facing out. Lower jack and raise axle to curb height. Tighten pivot bolt. Remove supports and lower vehicle.

LOWER CONTROL ARM

NOTE: If one lower control arm requires replacement, replace both lower arms.

Rear Suspension

FORD MOTOR CO. RWD — EXCEPT MARK VII (Cont.)

Removal (Crown Victoria, Grand Marquis & Town Car)

1) Remove stabilizer bar (if equipped). Raise vehicle on hoist and place safety stands under frame side rails. Lower hoist until shock absorbers are fully extended.

2) Support axle under differential pinion nose and under axle. Remove and discard pivot bolt from axle bracket. Disengage lower arm from bracket. Remove and discard pivot bolt from frame bracket and remove lower arm.

Installation

1) Position lower control arm in frame and in axle. Install NEW pivot bolts and nuts. Install bolts so heads face outboard.

2) Raise axle. Tighten pivot bolts to specification. Install stabilizer bar. Lower vehicle.

Removal (Cougar, Mustang & Thunderbird)

1) Remove stabilizer bar (if equipped). Raise vehicle and support at rear body crossmember. Support axle and lower hoist until shock absorbers are fully extended.

2) Place transmission jack under lower arm-to-axle pivot bolt and remove. Lower transmission jack slowly until coil spring can be removed. Remove lower control arm-to-frame pivot bolt and remove lower arm.

Installation

1) Position lower arm assembly into front arm bracket. Install NEW arm-to-frame pivot bolt and nut with nut facing outward. DO NOT tighten yet.

2) Install coil spring and raise axle. Install NEW lower pivot bolt and nut. Raise axle to curb height. Tighten upper and lower bolts to specification.

UPPER CONTROL ARM

NOTE: If one upper control arm requires replacement, replace both upper arms. To ensure safety, replace one arm at a time.

Removal (Crown Victoria, Grand Marquis & Town Car)

1) Raise vehicle and place safety stands under frame side rails. Support axle. Lower axle and support under differential pinion nose as well as under axle.

2) Disconnect parking brake cable from upper arm retainer. Remove and discard upper arm-to-axle housing bolt. Disconnect arm from housing. Remove and discard upper arm-to-frame bracket bolt, and remove upper arm.

Bushing Replacement

Upper control arm bushings may be replaced using special tool set. See Fig. 5.

Installation

Install NEW upper pivot bolt and self-locking nut with bolt facing front of vehicle. Install NEW lower pivot bolt and nut so nut faces inboard. Tighten all pivot bolts with axle in normal riding height position.

Removal (Cougar, Mustang & Thunderbird)

Raise vehicle on hoist and support at rear body crossmember. Remove upper arm-to-axle and upper arm-to-frame pivot bolts. Discard bolts and nuts. Remove upper arm.

Bushing Replacement

Bushing replacement is similar to Crown Victoria, Grand Marquis and Town Car. See Fig. 5.

Fig. 5: *Replacing Upper Control Arm Bushings on Crown Victoria, Grand Marquis & Town Car*

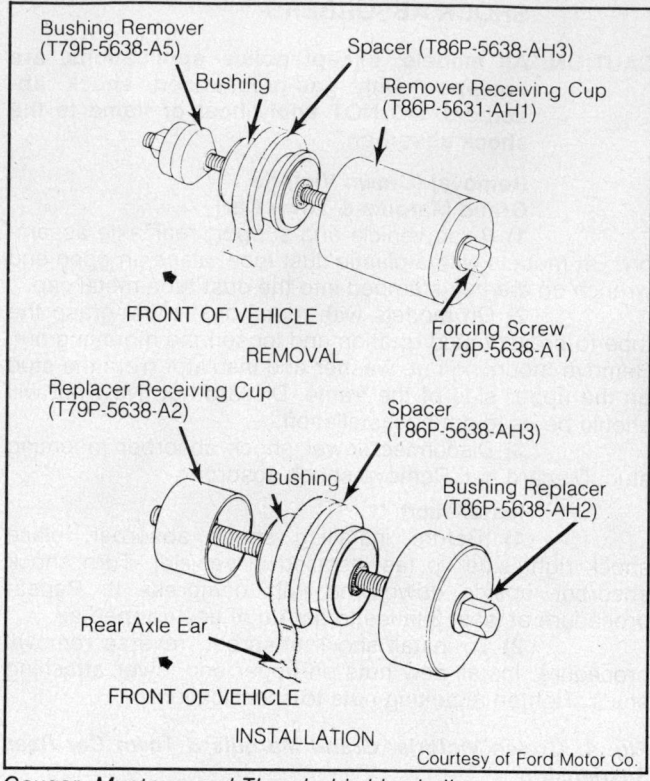

Courtesy of Ford Motor Co.

Cougar, Mustang and Thunderbird is similar.

Installation

Install NEW upper axle pivot bolt with nut facing outboard. Install NEW upper frame pivot bolt with nut facing inboard. Tighten pivot bolts with rear axle in curb height position. See Fig. 6.

STABILIZER BAR

Removal (Crown Victoria, Grand Marquis & Town Car)

Raise vehicle on hoist and place safety stands under frame side rails. Lower hoist and axle housing until shock absorbers are fully extended. Remove and discard 4 bolts, nuts and spacers attaching stabilizer bar to lower arms. Remove stabilizer bar.

Installation

To install stabilizer bar, reverse removal procedure. Install NEW bolts and nuts. Color coded end of stabilizer bar attaches to right side of vehicle.

Removal (Cougar, Mustang & Thunderbird)

Raise vehicle on hoist. Remove and discard 4 bolts attaching stabilizer bar to brackets in lower arms. Remove stabilizer bar.

Installation

To install stabilizer bar, reverse removal procedure. Install NEW bolts and stamped nuts. Color coded end attaches to right side of vehicle. Inspect for adequate clearance between stabilizer bar and lower arm.

Rear Suspension

FORD MOTOR CO. RWD — EXCEPT MARK VII (Cont.)

Fig. 6: Rear Suspension on Cougar, Thunderbird & Mustang With Handling Suspension

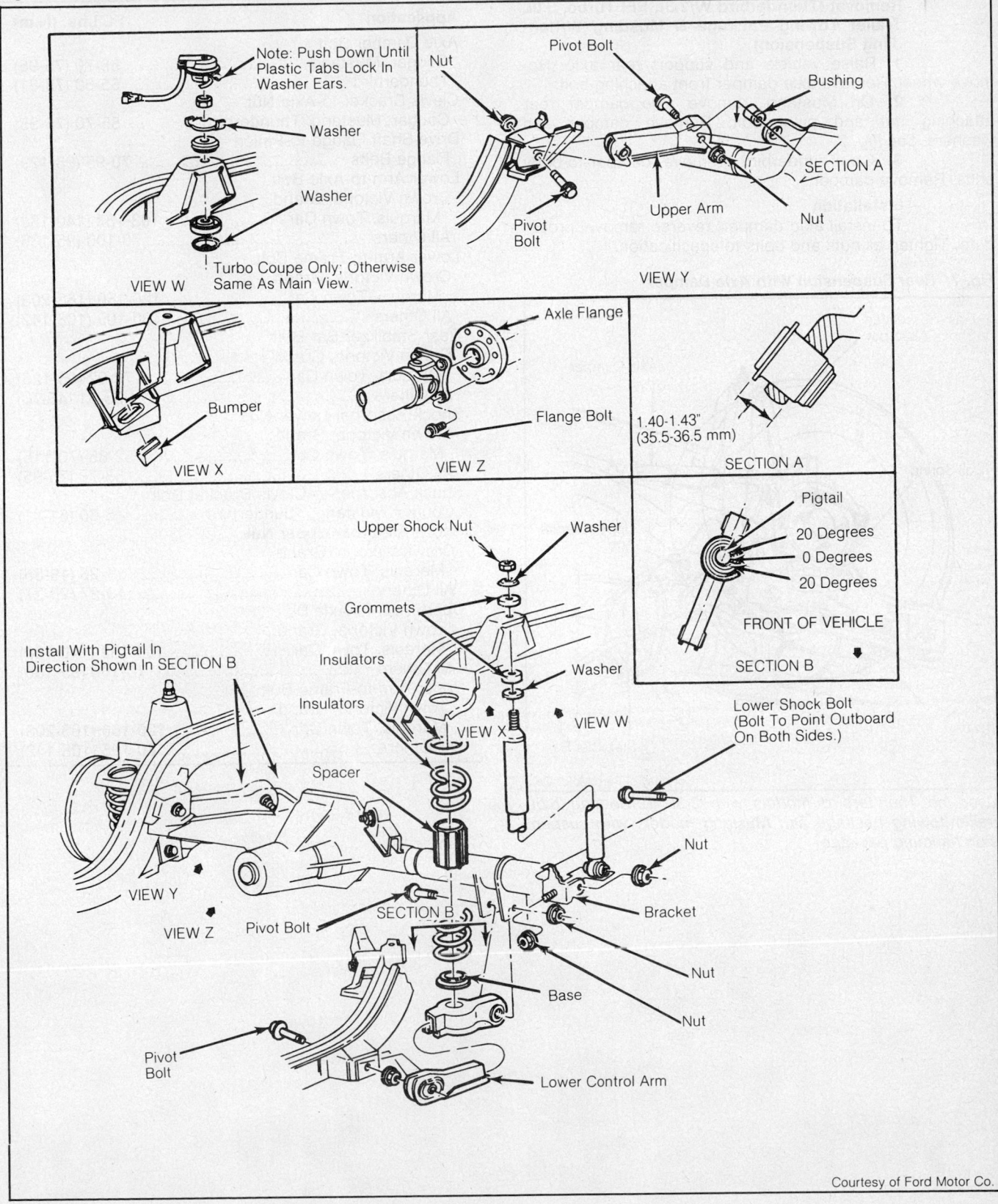

Courtesy of Ford Motor Co.

Standard Mustang suspension is similar.

Rear Suspension

FORD MOTOR CO. RWD — EXCEPT MARK VII (Cont.)

AXLE DAMPER

Removal (Thunderbird W/2.3L EFI Turbo, 5.0L Trailer Towing Package & Mustang W/Handling Suspension)

1) Raise vehicle and support rear axle. Remove wheel. Remove axle damper front attaching bolt.

2) On Mustang, remove axle damper rear attaching nut and pivot bolt. Remove damper and washers. *See Fig. 7.*

3) On Thunderbird, remove damper-to-body bolts. Remove damper.

Installation

To install axle damper, reverse removal procedure. Tighten all nuts and bolts to specification.

Fig. 7: Rear Suspension With Axle Damper

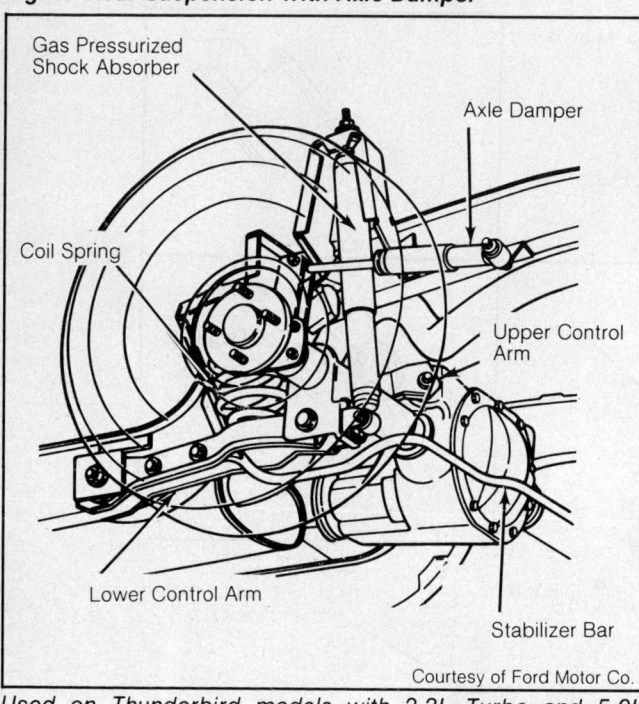

Gas Pressurized Shock Absorber

Axle Damper

Coil Spring

Upper Control Arm

Lower Control Arm

Stabilizer Bar

Courtesy of Ford Motor Co.

Used on Thunderbird models with 2.3L Turbo and 5.0L trailer towing package and Mustang models with suspension handling package.

TIGHTENING SPECIFICATIONS

Application	Ft. Lbs. (N.m)
Axle Damper Bolt	
Cougar, Mustang	55-70 (75-95)
Thunderbird	55-60 (75-81)
Clevis Bracket-to-Axle Nut	
Cougar, Mustang, Thunderbird	55-70 (75-95)
Drive Shaft Flange-to-Pinion	
Flange Bolts	70-95 (95-129)
Lower Arm-to-Axle Bolt	
Crown Victoria, Grand Marquis, Town Car	103-133 (140-180)
All Others	70-100 (95-136)
Lower Arm-to-Frame Bolt	
Crown Victoria, Grand Marquis, Town Car	120-150 (163-203)
All Others	80-105 (108-142)
Rear Stabilizer Bar Bolt	
Crown Victoria, Grand Marquis, Town Car	70-92 (95-125)
All Others	33-51 (45-70)
Shock Absorber Lower Nut	
Crown Victoria, Grand Marquis, Town Car	52-85 (70-115)
All Others	55-70 (75-95)
Shock Absorber-to-Clevis Bracket Bolt	
Cougar, Mustang, Thunderbird	45-60 (61-81)
Shock Absorber Upper Nut	
Crown Victoria, Grand Marquis, Town Car	14-26 (19-35)
All Others	19-27 (26-37)
Upper Arm-to-Axle Bolt	
Crown Victoria, Grand Marquis, Town Car	103-133 (140-180)
All Others	70-100 (95-136)
Upper Arm-to-Frame Bolt	
Crown Victoria, Grand Marquis, Town Car	120-150 (163-203)
All Others	80-105 (108-142)

Rear Suspension

GENERAL MOTORS FWD
"A", "J", "L" & "N" BODIES

"A" Body – Celebrity, Century, Ciera,
Cutlass Cruiser, 6000
"J" Body – Cavalier, Cimarron, Firenza,
Skyhawk, Sunbird
"L" Body – Beretta, Corsica
"N" Body – Calais, Grand Am, Skylark

NOTE: Following procedures DO NOT apply to vehicles equipped with electronic suspension systems.

DESCRIPTION

The "A" body rear suspension consists of a rear axle assembly, 2 coil springs, 2 shock absorbers and a track bar. Track bar on some models may contain an additional track bar brace.

Control arms, welded to the axle housing, provide axle-to-body mounting. Control arms and a non-serviceable track bar maintain proper body to axle relation during operation.

A non-serviceable stabilizer shaft is welded inside of the axle housing. Coil springs are retained between an underbody seat and a welded rear axle seat.

The "J", "L" and "N" body suspension consists of an axle and control arms. On "L" bodies, sedan models contain a twisting cross beam while coupe models may contain a tubular trailing arm.

Each suspension consists of 2 coil springs using upper spring insulators and lower compression bumpers. Axle assembly is mounted to the body through rubber control arm bushings. Optional stabilizer bar may be used on some models.

On all bodies, a single hub and bearing assembly is attached to the axle. Hub and bearing assembly are a complete unit and cannot be serviced individually.

Fig. 1: "A" Body Rear Suspension Assembly

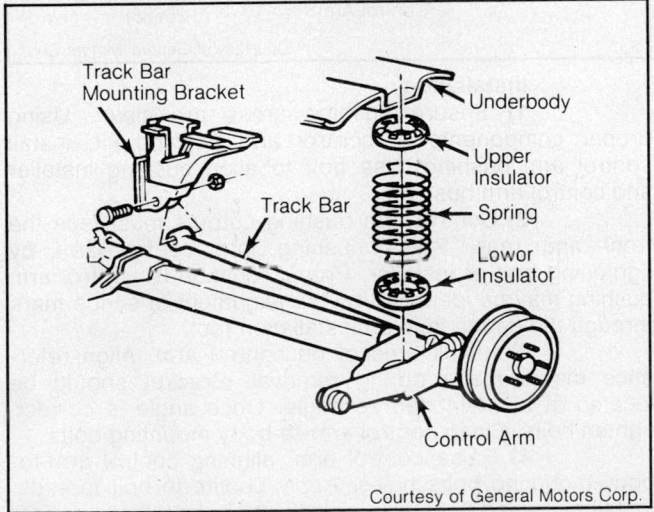

Track Bar
Mounting Bracket
Underbody
Upper Insulator
Track Bar
Spring
Lower Insulator
Control Arm

Courtesy of General Motors Corp.

ADJUSTMENTS

CAMBER & TOE-IN

See appropriate article in WHEEL ALIGNMENT section.

RIDING HEIGHT

See RIDING HEIGHT SPECIFICATIONS article in WHEEL ALIGNMENT section.

REMOVAL & INSTALLATION

SHOCK ABSORBERS

NOTE: DO NOT remove both shock absorbers at one time. Suspending rear axle at full length may damage brake lines and hoses.

Removal

Open deck lid and remove trim cover (if equipped). Remove upper shock retaining nut. Raise vehicle and support rear axle assembly. Remove lower retaining bolt and nut. Remove shock absorber.

Installation

1) Install shock absorber lower mounting bolt. Install nut finger tight only. Lower vehicle while guiding upper stud into body opening. Install upper nut finger tight only. Tighten lower mounting nut to specification.

2) Lower vehicle. Tighten upper nut to specification. Install trim cover (if equipped). On "L" bodies, trim cover must be installed with arrow on trim cover toward left side of vehicle.

COIL SPRINGS & INSULATORS

CAUTION: When removing rear coil springs, DO NOT use a twin-post type hoist. Swing arc tendency of axle caused when certain fasteners are removed may cause vehicle to fall.

Removal

1) Raise and support vehicle at rear control arms. Remove rear wheels. Remove brake line bracket retaining bolts. On models equipped with anti-lock brake systems, wheel speed sensor may need to be disconnected.

2) On all models, remove track bar-to-axle nut (if equipped). Remove lower shock absorber mounting bolts. Lower rear axle assembly. Carefully remove coil springs and insulators.

Installation

1) Prior to coil spring installation, it may be necessary to install upper insulators to the body using adhesive. This retains insulator in correct location during installation.

2) Install coil springs. On "A" bodies, coil springs must be positioned so leg of upper coil is parallel to the axle and must face outward within a specified distance. See Fig. 2.

3) On "J", "L" and "N" bodies, install coil springs with upper spring end positioned within .594" (15 mm) of spring stop located in spring seat. Raise axle. Install shock absorbers on rear axle. Loosely install retaining bolts.

4) Vehicle must be at normal operating height prior to tightening shock absorber retaining bolts. Install brake line brackets and wheels. Tighten to specification. Lower vehicle. Tighten shock absorber retaining bolts to specification.

11-84

Rear Suspension
GENERAL MOTORS FWD
"A", "J", "L" & "N" BODIES (Cont.)

Fig. 2: Coil Spring Installation on "A" Body

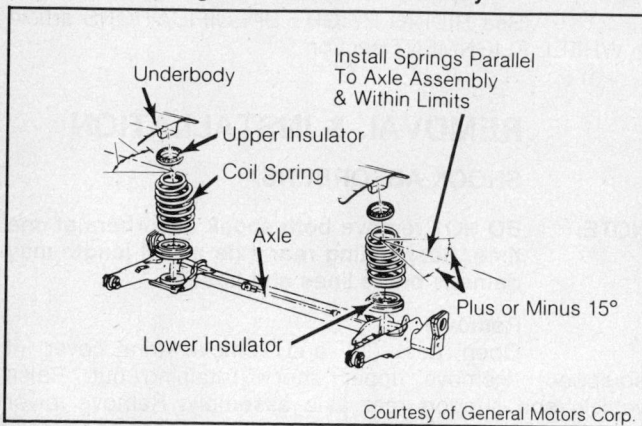

Underbody
Install Springs Parallel To Axle Assembly & Within Limits
Upper Insulator
Coil Spring
Axle
Lower Insulator
Plus or Minus 15°

Courtesy of General Motors Corp.

TRACK BAR ("A" BODY)

Removal

Raise vehicle and support rear axle. Remove bolts from brace to track bar (if equipped). Remove track bar bolts at body and axle assembly. Remove track bar.

Installation

Replace track bar if bushings are damaged. Install track bar on axle mount. DO NOT tighten bolt at this time. Install track bar on body mount. Install track bar brace (if equipped). Tighten bolts to specification.

STABILIZER BAR ("J", "L" & "N" BODY)

Removal

Raise and support vehicle. Remove stabilizer bar retaining bolts at axle and control arms. Remove brackets, insulators and stabilizer bar.

Fig. 3: "J", "N" & "L" Body Rear Suspension Assembly

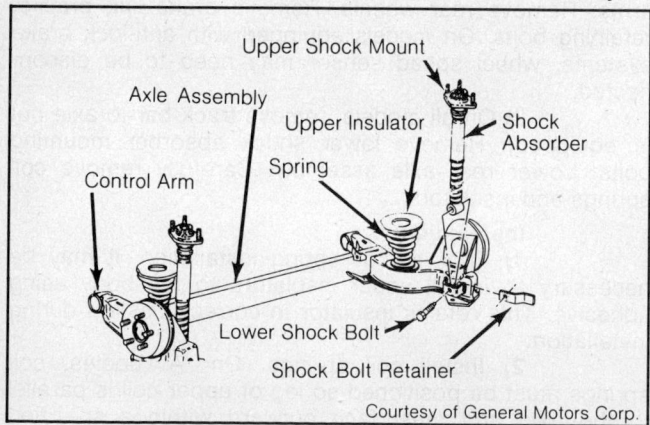

Upper Shock Mount
Axle Assembly
Upper Insulator
Shock Absorber
Control Arm
Spring
Lower Shock Bolt
Shock Bolt Retainer

Courtesy of General Motors Corp.

Installation

1) Replace damaged insulators. Install upper clamps, spacers and insulators on axle assembly. Install stabilizer bar in insulators. Loosely install lower clamps and nuts.

2) Install retaining bolts at control arms. Tighten to specification. Tighten remaining bolts on axle assembly to specification.

LOWER CONTROL ARM

Lower control arm is an integral part of axle assembly and cannot be replaced separately.

CONTROL ARM BUSHING REPLACEMENT

Removal ("A" Body)

1) Raise vehicle and support axle in front of coil spring seat. Remove wheels. When removing right control arm bushing, disconnect parking brake cable from hook guide. Remove parking brake cables from bracket for access to control arm bushing.

2) Remove brake line brackets. Remove shock absorber lower mounting bolt. Remove spring for access to control arm. Only one control arm bushing should be replaced at a time. On models equipped with anti-lock brake systems, wheel speed sensor may need to be disconnected.

3) On all models, remove control arm-to-body mounting bolt. Rotate control arm downward. Mark bracket location on control arm. Remove bracket from control arm. Control Arm Bushing Kit (J-28685) is used for bushing replacement.

4) Install bushing remover assembly on control arm bushing. See Fig. 4. Ensure components are aligned before tightening removal tool bolt. Tighten bolt until bushing is removed.

Fig. 4: Removing Control Arm Bushing On "A" Body

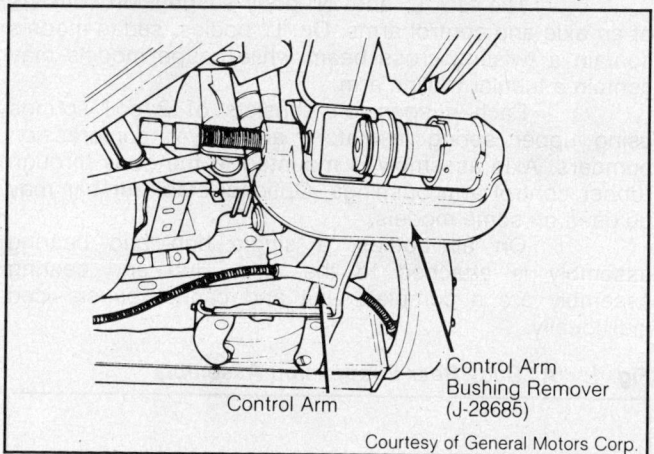

Control Arm
Control Arm Bushing Remover (J-28685)

Courtesy of General Motors Corp.

Installation

1) Ensure bushing areas are clean. Using proper components of control arm bushing kit, install control arm bushing. Use bolt to align bushing installer and control arm bushing.

2) Control arm bushing cutouts must face the front and rear. Press bushing into control arm by tightening bolt of installer. Proper location of control arm bushing may be identified by the alignment of scribe mark through the gauge hole on installation tool.

3) Install bracket on control arm. Align reference marks made during removal. Bracket should be located at a 40-44 degree angle. Once angle is correct, tighten bolts. Clean control arm-to-body mounting bolts.

4) Raise control arm, aligning control arm-to-body mounting bolts holes. Apply Loctite to bolt threads. Install bolts and tighten to specification. Install coil spring. Ensure coil spring is correctly installed. See INSTALLATION under COIL SPRING in this article.

5) Install shock absorber, brake line bracket and parking brake cables. Adjust parking brake cable. Connect wheel speed sensor (if equipped).

GENERAL MOTORS FWD
"A", "J", "L" & "N" BODIES (Cont.)

NOTE: Following procedure does not apply to the Beretta. Rear axle assembly must be removed for control arm bushing replacement on the Beretta.

Removal ("J", "L" & "N" Body)

1) Raise vehicle and support body. Remove wheels. On some models, when removing left control arm bushing, disconnect parking brake cable from hook guide. On all models, remove parking brake cables from bracket and move for access to control arm bushing.

2) Remove brake line brackets. Only one control arm bushing should be replaced at a time. Remove control arm-to-body mounting bolt. Note direction of bolt installation. Rotate control arm downward.

3) Control Arm Bushing Kit (J-29376) is used for bushing replacement. Install Receiver (J-29376-1) on control arm. Install bolt through Plate (J-29376-7) and receiver.

4) Install Remover (J-29376-6) and Nut (J-21474-18) on bolt. See Fig. 5. Ensure components are aligned. Tighten nut until control arm bushing is removed.

Fig. 5: Replacing "J", "L" & "N" Bodies Control Arm Bushing

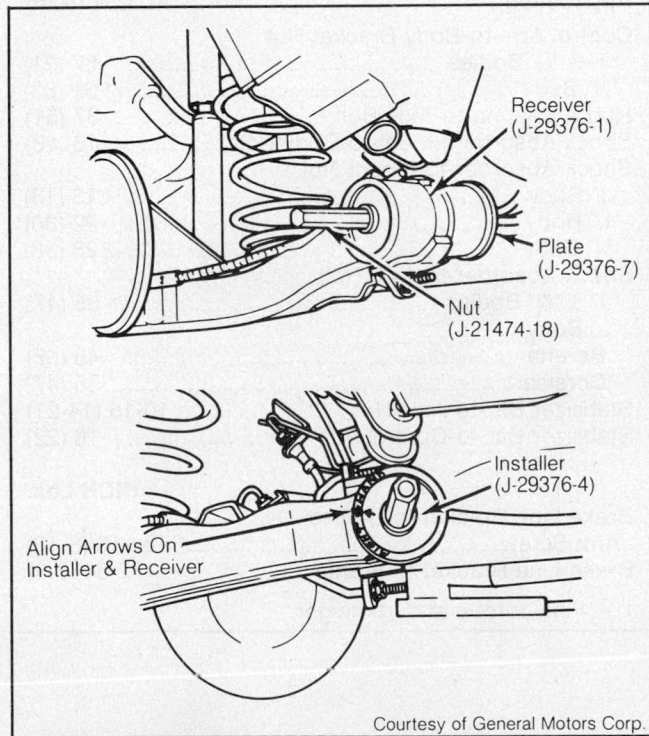

Courtesy of General Motors Corp.

Installation

1) Ensure bushing areas are clean. Install Receiver (J-29376-1) on control arm. Install bolt through Plate (J-29376-7) and receiver.

2) Install bushing on bolt and install in control arm. Align bushing installer arrow with receiver arrow. See Fig. 5. Install nut on bolt. Tighten nut to install bushing. Control arm bushing is properly located when end flange is even with control arm surface.

3) Rotate control arm upward until mounting bolts can be installed. Bolts must be installed from inboard side of control arm on some models. On all models, DO NOT tighten bolts at this time.

4) Install brake line and parking brake cables. Adjust parking brake cables. Install wheels. Support vehicle at curb height. Tighten control arm-to-body mounting bolts to specification.

Removal (Beretta)

Remove rear axle. See REAR AXLE in this article. Using hydraulic press, Bushing Remover (J-29376-6A) and Body/Receiver (J-29376-1), remove control arm bushings.

Installation

Ensure bushing areas are clean. Using hydraulic press, Bushing Installer (J-29376-4) and body/receiver, install control arm bushings. Install rear axle.

REAR AXLE

CAUTION: When removing rear axle, DO NOT use a twin-post type hoist. Swing arc tendency of axle caused when certain fasteners are removed may cause vehicle to fall.

Removal

1) Raise and support vehicle. Install support stand at front of vehicle. Place supports under control arms. Remove wheels and brake drums. Remove stabilizer bar or track bar (if equipped). See STABILIZER BAR or TRACK BAR in this article.

2) Disconnect parking brake cable. Remove brake lines from brackets on axle assembly. Remove shock absorber mountings from rear axle. Disconnect wheel speed sensor lead (if equipped).

3) On all models, remove coil springs and insulators. See COIL SPRINGS & INSULATORS in this article. While supporting rear axle, remove control arm-to-body mounting bolts. Note direction of bolt installation. Carefully lower rear axle from vehicle body.

Installation

1) Using transmission jack, install rear axle under vehicle. Install control arm-to-body mounting bolts. Bolts must be installed from the inboard side of control arm on some models. On all models, DO NOT tighten bolts at this time.

2) Install stabilizer bar or track bar (if equipped). Install brake lines, parking brake cable and coil springs. Ensure coil springs are properly positioned. See INSTALLATION under COIL SPRINGS & INSULATORS in this article.

3) If wheel speed sensor was removed from axle, air gap must be adjusted. Using non-ferrous feeler gauge, adjust wheel speed sensor air gap to .028" (.7 mm). Tighten retaining bolt to specification. Connect wheel speed sensor.

Fig. 6: Typical Hub & Bearing Assembly

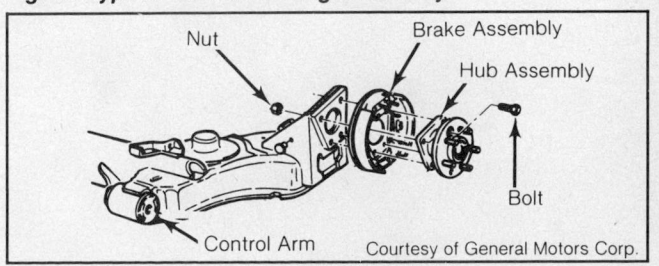

Courtesy of General Motors Corp.

Rear Suspension
GENERAL MOTORS FWD
"A", "J", "L" & "N" BODIES (Cont.)

4) On all models, install brake drums, shock absorbers and wheels. Bleed brake system. Place vehicle at curb height. Tighten control arm-to-body mounting bolts to specification.

HUB & BEARING ASSEMBLY

Inspection

1) Raise and support vehicle. Remove wheel. Free disc brake pads away from rotor or remove caliper. Remove brake drum (if equipped). Install 2 wheel nuts to secure rotor (if equipped).

2) Mount dial indicator with stem resting against hub. Push inward on rotor or hub. Adjust indicator to zero. Pull outward and note reading. Replace hub assembly if movement exceeds .005" (.12 mm).

Removal

Raise and support vehicle. Remove wheels and brake drum. Remove wheel speed sensor mounting bolt (if equipped). Support brake assembly. Remove hub retaining bolts. See Fig. 6. On some models, top rear retaining bolt will not clear brake shoe. Hub assembly must be loosened and top rear retaining bolt removed.

Installation

1) On models where top rear retaining bolt hits brake shoe, install retaining bolt in hub assembly prior to installation. On all models, install hub assembly on rear axle. Tighten retaining bolts to specification.

2) Install wheel speed sensor (if equipped). Using non-ferrous feeler gauge, adjust wheel speed sensor air gap to .028" (.71 mm). On all models, tighten retaining bolt to specification. Install brake drums and wheels.

TIGHTENING SPECIFICATIONS ("A" BODY)

Application	Ft. Lbs. (N.m)
Control Arm-to-Bracket Nut	78 (106)
Control Arm-to-Underbody Bolt	28 (38)
Hub & Bearing-to-Axle Bolt	47 (64)
Shock Absorber	
Lower End Nut	43 (58)
Upper End Nut	[1] 16 (22)
Track Bar-to-Axle Nut	44 (60)
Track Bar-to-Frame Nut	35 (47)
Track Bar Bracket-to-Body Bolt	34 (46)
Track Bar Bracket-to-Frame Bolt	45 (61)

	INCH Lbs.
Brake Line Bracket-to-Frame Screw	96 (11)
Wheel Speed Sensor Bolt	84 (9)

[1] – Final torque at curb height.

TIGHTENING SPECIFICATIONS ("J", "L" & "N" BODIES)

Application	Ft. Lbs.(N.m)
Control Arm-to-Body Bracket Nut	
"J" & "L" Bodies	[1] 67 (91)
"N" Body	[1] 61 (83)
Hub & Bearing-to-Axle Bolt	37 (51)
Shock Absorber Mount-to-Body Bolt	13 (18)
Shock Absorber-to-Mount Nut	
"J" Body	[1] 13 (18)
"L" Body	[1] 22 (30)
"N" Body	[1] 28 (38)
Shock Absorber-to-Axle Bolt	
"J" & "N" Bodies	35 (47)
"L" Body	
Beretta	43 (58)
Corsica	35 (47)
Stabilizer Bar-to-Axle Nut	10-15 (14-21)
Stabilizer Bar-to-Control Arm Nut	16 (22)

	INCH Lbs.
Brake Line Bracket-to-Control Arm Screw	72-110 (8-12)
Brake Line Bracket-to-Frame	72-84 (8-9)

[1] – Final torque at curb height.

Rear Suspension
GENERAL MOTORS FWD
"C", "E", "H" & "K" BODIES

"C" Body – DeVille, Electra, Fleetwood, Ninety-Eight
"E" Body – Eldorado, Reatta, Riviera, Toronado
"H" Body – Bonneville, Delta 88, LeSabre
"K" Body – Seville

DESCRIPTION

The "C" and "H" bodies use an independent rear suspension supported by 2 ball joints, lower control arms, coil springs, and non-serviceable struts. Air adjustable struts are standard on "C" body and optional on "H" body. Stabilizer bar is used to minimize body roll. Control arms are equipped with suspension adjustment links for toe adjustments.

The "E" and "K" bodies use an independent transverse mounted leaf spring rear suspension. Rear suspension components are mounted on a suspension crossmember assembly mounted to the body.

On all bodies, hub and bearing assembly is connected to the suspension system by the knuckle and struts. Hub and bearing assembly are a complete unit and cannot be serviced individually. Some models contain Electronic Level Control (ELC) for suspension operation depending on vehicle load.

Fig. 1: "C" & "H" Body Rear Suspension

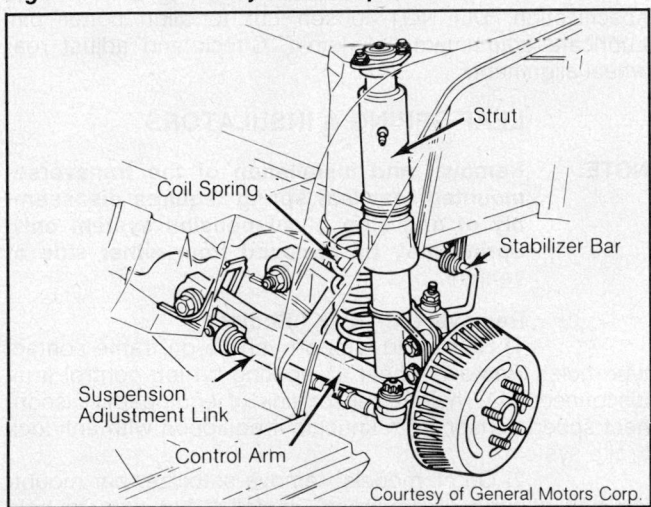

Courtesy of General Motors Corp.

Fig. 2: "E" & "K" Body Rear Suspension

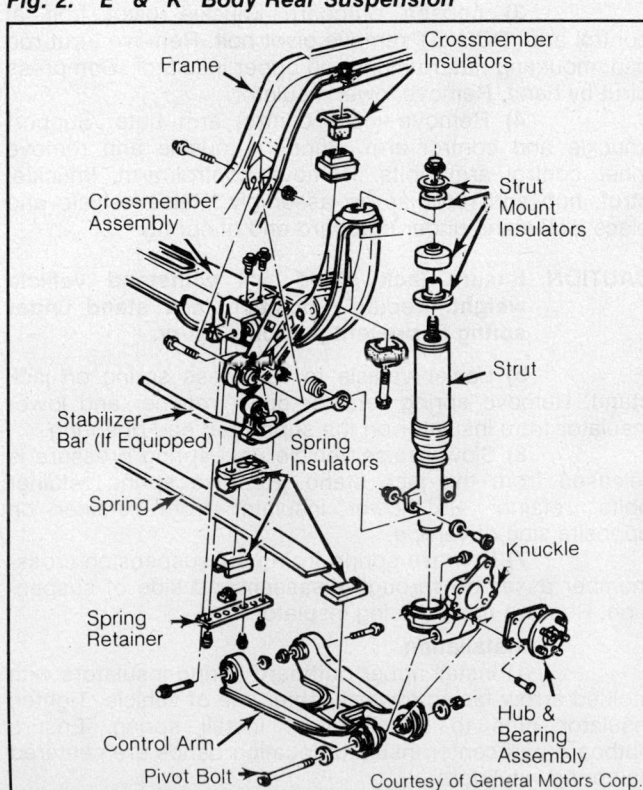

Courtesy of General Motors Corp.

ADJUSTMENTS

BALL JOINT INSPECTION
Lower Ball Joint ("C" & "H" Bodies)

1) On all models except DeVille or Fleetwood, inspect ball joint for looseness. Replace ball joint if looseness exists. On DeVille or Fleetwood models, position vehicle at normal operating height.

2) Check that ball joint grease fitting shoulder does not protrude past ball joint housing cover. *See Fig. 3.* Replace ball joint if grease fitting is flush or below cover.

Fig. 3: Ball Joint Wear Indicator

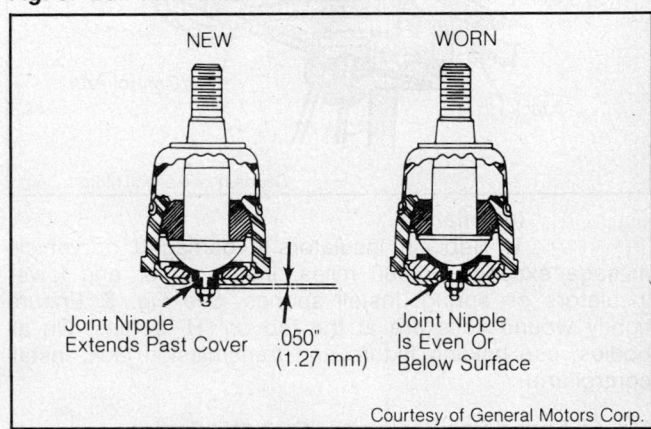

Courtesy of General Motors Corp.

ELECTRONIC LEVEL CONTROL
See ELECTRONIC SUSPENSIONS article in this section.

RIDING HEIGHT
See RIDING HEIGHT SPECIFICATIONS article in WHEEL ALIGNMENT section.

TOE-IN
See appropriate article in WHEEL ALIGNMENT section.

REMOVAL & INSTALLATION

COIL SPRINGS & INSULATORS
Removal ("C" & "H" Bodies)

1) Raise and support vehicle. Allow suspension to hang freely. Remove wheel. Remove ELC height sensor link on right control arm (if equipped). Remove

Rear Suspension
GENERAL MOTORS FWD
"C", "E", "H" & "K" BODIES (Cont.)

parking brake cable retaining clip at left control arm. Remove stabilizer bar from bracket.

2) Place chain around spring and through control arm for a safety precaution. Position Holding Fixture (J-23028-01) to cradle the control arm. *See Fig. 4.* Raise jack to remove tension from pivot bolts.

3) Remove rear pivot bolt from control arm. Carefully move jack to remove tension from front of control arm. Remove front pivot bolt. Slowly lower jack to allow control arm to pivot downward.

4) Once spring tension is relieved, remove safety chain, spring and insulators. DO NOT force control arm or ball joint to remove spring.

Fig. 4: Installing Control Arm Holding Fixture on "C" & "H" Bodies

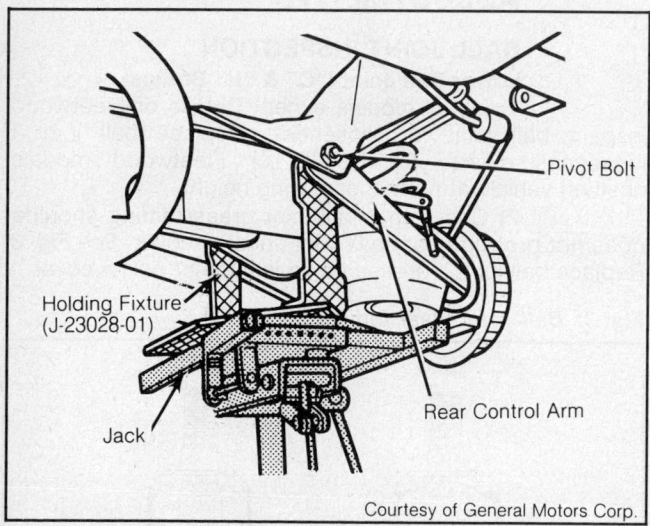

Courtesy of General Motors Corp.

Installation
1) Replace insulators if damaged or vehicle mileage exceeds 50,000 miles. Install upper and lower insulators on spring. Install springs. *See Fig. 5.* Ensure tightly wound coils are at the top on "H" bodies. On all bodies, use holding fixture and transmission jack, install control arm.

Fig. 5: Spring Positioning on "C" & "H" Bodies

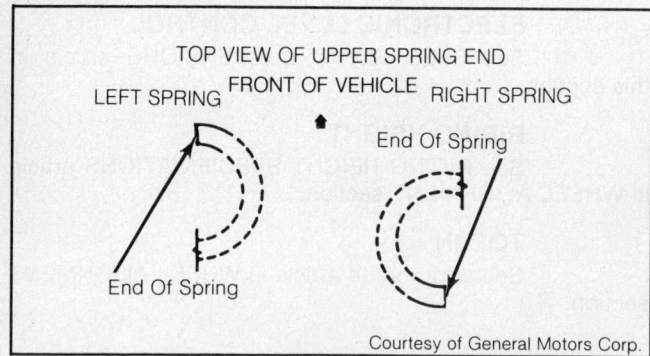

Courtesy of General Motors Corp.

2) Move jack and install front then rear pivot bolts. DO NOT tighten at this time. Install stabilizer bar to knuckle bracket. DO NOT tighten at this time.

3) Reverse removal procedures for remaining components. Tighten to specification. Lower vehicle to normal operating height. Tighten pivot nuts or bolts then stabilizer bar bolt to specification.

NOTE: Control arm pivot nuts, bolts and stabilizer bar must be tightened only in proper sequence with vehicle at normal operating height.

SUSPENSION ADJUSTMENT LINK
Removal ("C" & "H" Bodies)
Raise and support vehicle. Remove wheel. Remove cotter pin and nut. *See Fig. 1.* Using Puller (J-24319-01), separate link from knuckle. Remove retaining nut and washer from control arm. Remove adjustment link.

Installation
Reverse removal procedures. Bend lock tab over on retaining nut at control arm after tightening nut to specification. DO NOT loosen nut to align cotter pin. Lubricate adjustment link joints. Check and adjust rear wheel alignment.

LEAF SPRING & INSULATORS
NOTE: Removal and installation of the transverse-mounted rear leaf spring requires disassembly of one side of suspension system only. Spring may be removed from either side of vehicle.

Removal ("E" & "K" Bodies)
1) Raise and support vehicle on frame contact type hoist. Remove wheel. If working on left control arm, disconnect ELC height sensor link (if equipped). Disconnect speed sensor from knuckle if equipped with anti-lock brake system.

2) On all models, remove stabilizer bar mounting bolt at strut (if equipped). Install 2 lug nuts to hold rotor on hub. Remove brake caliper.

3) Loosen outboard knuckle pivot bolt at control arm. DO NOT remove pivot bolt. Remove strut rod cap, mounting nut, retainer and upper insulator. Compress strut by hand. Remove lower insulator.

4) Remove inner control arm nuts. Support knuckle and control arm. Support knuckle and remove inner control arm bolts. Remove control arm, knuckle, strut, hub and rotor as an assembly. Raise vehicle and place jack stand under outboard end of spring.

CAUTION: Ensure jack stand will withstand vehicle weight. Securely position jack stand under spring to prevent personal injury.

5) Lower vehicle to compress spring on jack stand. Remove spring retainer bolts, retainer and lower insulator from insulator on the supported end of spring.

6) Slowly raise vehicle until spring pressure is released from the jack stand. Remove spring retainer bolts, retainer and lower insulator from retainer on opposite side of vehicle.

7) Remove spring from rear suspension cross-member assembly through disassembled side of suspension. Remove upper spring insulators.

Installation
1) Install upper outboard spring insulators with molded arrow facing toward center line of vehicle. Tighten insulator nuts to specification. Install spring. Ensure outboard and center insulator locating bands are centered on spring insulators.

GENERAL MOTORS FWD
"C", "E", "H" & "K" BODIES (Cont.)

NOTE: **Improper positioning of spring correctly will result in reduced vehicle handling.**

2) Install lower insulator and spring retainer on side opposite disassembled portion of suspension system. Position jack stand under free end of spring. Slowly lower vehicle to compress spring so spring seats in suspension support.

3) Install lower insulator and spring retainer. Tighten to specification. Raise vehicle and remove jack stand. Install control arm assembly. Install inner control arm bolts and nuts. DO NOT tighten bolts at this time.

4) Install lower strut insulator. Position strut rod in suspension support assembly. Install upper strut insulator, retainer and nut. Tighten to specification. Reverse removal procedures for remaining components. Tighten bolts to specification. Check and adjust rear wheel alignment.

CONTROL ARM
Removal ("C" & "H" Bodies)
1) Raise and support vehicle. Remove wheel. Remove ELC height sensor link on right control arm (if equipped). Remove parking brake cable retaining clip. Separate suspension adjustment link from control arm. See SUSPENSION ADJUSTMENT LINK in this article.

2) Remove coil spring. See COIL SPRING & INSULATORS in this article. Separate ball joint from control arm. See step 3) under BALL JOINT in this article. Remove control arm retaining bolts. Remove control arm.

NOTE: **Control arm bushings are different sizes, requiring different combinations of removers/installers for replacement.**

Bushing Replacement
1) Install Spacer (J-22222-5 or J-33793-5), according to bushing size in control arm. Position Receiver Tube (J-25317-2) and Cap (J-29376-7) on outside of control arm. *See Fig. 6.* Ensure receiver tube does not contact bushing flange. Coat threaded portion of Bolt and Bearing (J-21474-19) with grease.

2) Install bolt through receiver, cap and bushing. Install Remover (J-22222-2 or J-28685-2) on bolt at inner side of control arm with small end contacting the bushing.

3) Place bearing on bolt and install Nut (J-21474-18). Tighten nut to remove bushing from control arm.

4) Install new bushing in control arm with flanged end facing outward. Install proper sized spacer on bushing. Position receiver tube and cap on inside of control arm.

5) Center receiver tube over hole. Coat threaded portion of bolt and bearing with grease. Install bolt through receiver, cap and bushing.

6) Place installer on bolt at outer side of control arm with large end contacting bushing flange. Place bearing on bolt and install nut. Bearing must be positioned between nut and installer. Tighten nut and draw bushing into control until bushing flange seats firmly against control arm.

Installation
Reverse removal procedures for control arm installation. Tighten pivot bolts or nuts, then tighten stabilizer bar bolts with vehicle at normal operating height.

Removal ("E" & "K" Bodies)
1) Raise and support vehicle. Remove wheel. If working on left control arm, disconnect ELC height sensor link (if equipped). Disconnect speed sensor from knuckle if equipped with anti-lock brake system. On all models, remove stabilizer bar mounting bolt at strut (if equipped).

2) Install 2 lug nuts to retain rotor. Remove caliper assembly. Loosen outer knuckle pivot bolt. DO NOT remove at this time. Remove strut rod cap, mounting nut, retainer and upper insulator.

3) Compress strut and remove lower insulator. Support knuckle and remove knuckle pivot bolt. Remove knuckle, strut, hub and rotor assembly from vehicle. Remove inner control arm bolts. Remove control arm.

NOTE: **Outer control arm bushings can be replaced without removing control arm. If inner control arm bolts are not disturbed, rear wheel alignment will not need to be checked after bushing replacement.**

Outer Control Arm Bushing Replacement
1) For on car service, perform steps 1) through 3) under REMOVAL of CONTROL ARM in this article.

Fig. 6: Removing & Installing Control Arm Bushings on "C" & "H" Bodies

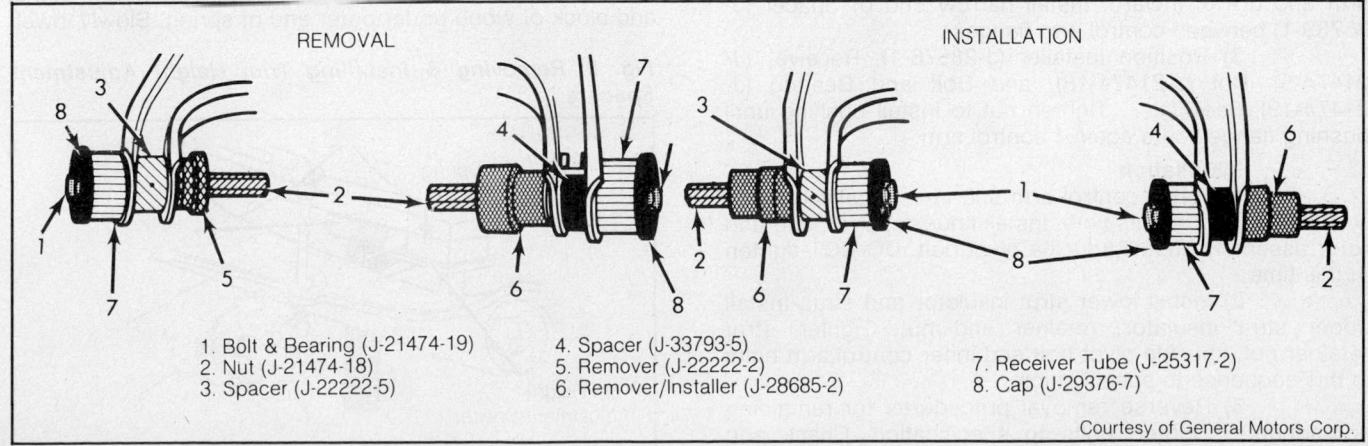

1. Bolt & Bearing (J-21474-19)
2. Nut (J-21474-18)
3. Spacer (J-22222-5)
4. Spacer (J-33793-5)
5. Remover (J-22222-2)
6. Remover/Installer (J-28685-2)
7. Receiver Tube (J-25317-2)
8. Cap (J-29376-7)

Rear Suspension
GENERAL MOTORS FWD
"C", "E", "H" & "K" BODIES (Cont.)

Fig. 7: Control Arm Bushing Removal & Installation on "E" & "K" Bodies

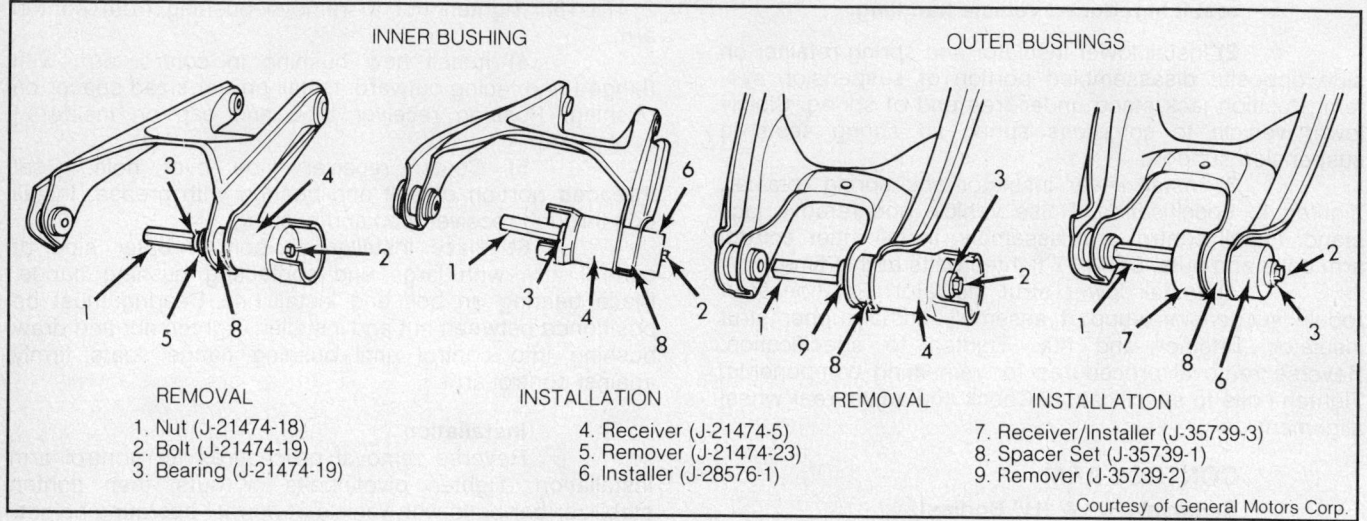

INNER BUSHING   OUTER BUSHINGS

REMOVAL
1. Nut (J-21474-18)
2. Bolt (J-21474-19)
3. Bearing (J-21474-19)

INSTALLATION
4. Receiver (J-21474-5)
5. Remover (J-21474-23)
6. Installer (J-28576-1)

REMOVAL

INSTALLATION
7. Receiver/Installer (J-35739-3)
8. Spacer Set (J-35739-1)
9. Remover (J-35739-2)

Courtesy of General Motors Corp.

Install Spacer (J-35739-1) between control arm flanges. Use wide spacer for outer bushing removal.

2) Coat threads of Bolt and Bearing (J-21474-19) with grease. Install Remover (J-35739-2), Receiver (J-21474-5), Nut (J-21474-18), and Bolt and Bearing (J-21474-19) on control arm. See Fig. 7. Tighten nut to remove bushing.

3) For installation, position new bushing on control arm. Install bushing from outside of control arm inward. Install wide end of spacer between control arm flanges.

4) Coat threads of bolt and bearing with grease. Place installer, receiver, nut, and bolt and bearing on control arm. See Fig. 7. Tighten nut until bushing flange seats against control arm.

Inner Control Arm Bushing
Replacement

1) To remove bushing, install Spacer (J-35739-1) between control arm flanges. Use narrow spacer for inner bushing removal. Coat threads of Bolt and Bearing (J-21474-19) with grease. Install Remover (J-21474-23), Receiver (J-21474-5), Nut (J-21474-18), and Bolt and Bearing (J-21474-19) in control arm. See Fig. 7. Tighten nut to remove bushing.

2) To install, position new bushing in control arm. Bushing must be installed from outside of control arm and drawn inward. Install narrow end of Spacer (J-35739-1) between control arm flanges.

3) Position Installer (J-28576-1), Receiver (J-21474-5), Nut (J-21474-18), and Bolt and Bearing (J-21474-19). See Fig. 7. Tighten nut to install bushing until bushing flange seats against control arm.

Installation

1) Install control arm and inner retaining bolts. DO NOT tighten at this time. Install knuckle, strut, hub and rotor assembly. Install knuckle pivot bolt. DO NOT tighten at this time.

2) Install lower strut insulator and strut. Install upper strut insulator, retainer and nut. Tighten strut retainer nut, knuckle pivot bolt and inner control arm bolts in this sequence to specification.

3) Reverse removal procedures for remaining components. Tighten bolts to specification. Check and adjust rear wheel alignment.

HUB & BEARING ASSEMBLY
Inspection

1) Raise and support vehicle. Remove wheel. Free disc brake pads away from rotor or remove caliper. Install 2 wheel nuts to secure rotor (if equipped).

2) Mount dial indicator with stem resting against hub. Push inward on rotor or hub. Adjust indicator to zero. Pull outward and note reading. Replace hub assembly if movement exceeds .005" (.12 mm).

Removal & Installation
("C" & "H" Bodies)

Raise and support vehicle. Remove wheel. Remove brake drum. Support brake backing plate assembly. Remove hub retaining bolts. Remove hub and bearing assembly. Reverse removal procedures for installation. Tighten bolts to specification.

Removal & Installation ("E" & "K" Bodies)

Raise and support vehicle. Remove wheel. Remove brake caliper. Remove rotor. Remove hub retaining bolts. Remove hub and bearing assembly. Reverse removal procedures for installation. Tighten bolts to specification.

TRIM HEIGHT ADJUSTMENT SPACER
Removal & Installation ("E" & "K" Bodies)

Raise and support vehicle. Place jack stand and block of wood under outer end of spring. Slowly lower

Fig. 8: Removing & Installing Trim Height Adjustment Spacers

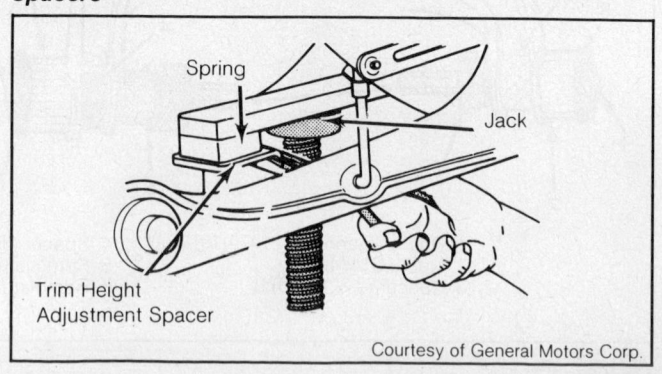

Spring

Jack

Trim Height
Adjustment Spacer

Courtesy of General Motors Corp.

Rear Suspension
GENERAL MOTORS FWD
"C", "E", "H" & "K" BODIES (Cont.)

vehicle until clearance between spring and spacer is approximately 3/8". *See Fig. 8.* Using pliers, remove and install spacer.

CAUTION: DO NOT allow spring to slip from jack. Spring is under pressure and may cause personal injury.

REAR SUSPENSION CROSSMEMBER

NOTE: **Crossmember may be removed without removing or disconnecting following components: spring, strut, control arm, knuckle, hub assembly, rotor, stabilizer bar assembly or ELC compressor. If spring is to be removed, remove spring prior to loosening any crossmember mounting bolts.**

Removal ("E" & "K" Bodies)
1) Raise vehicle on frame contact hoist. Remove wheels. Remove and support calipers. Remove necessary suspension components as required. Remove ELC height sensor connector and ELC compressor connector from body wiring harness (if equipped).

2) Remove ELC compressor air intake filter from body (if equipped). Remove intermediate parking brake cable from equalizer. Position cable clear of crossmember assembly. Remove brake crossover pipe retainer screws. Remove right rear brake hose retainer bolt and crossover pipe.

3) Support rear crossmember assembly with jack stands. Remove crossmember forward arm bolts, upper mounting bolts and lower insulators. *See Fig. 10.* Slowly raise vehicle. Ensure brake lines, hoses and calipers are not damaged when crossmember is lowered.

Crossmember Leading Arm Bushing Replacement
1) To remove, install Spacer (J-21474-25) between leading arm flanges. Coat threads of Bolt and Bearing (J-21474-19) with grease. Install Remover (J-21474-23), Receiver (J-21474-5), Nut (J-21474-18), and Bolt and Bearing (J-21474-19) in control arm. *See Fig. 9.* Tighten nut to remove bushing from leading arm.

2) To install, position new bushing in outside of leading arm. Position bushing with indentations positioned at the 12 and 6 o'clock position. *See Fig. 9.*

3) Install Spacer (J-21474-25) between leading arm flanges. Position Installer (J-35739-3), Receiver (J-21474-5), Nut (J-21474-18), and Bolt and Bearing (J-21474-19) on leading arm. *See Fig. 9.*

4) Tighten nut to install bushing into leading arm. Tighten nut until bushing flange seats against leading arm.

Installation
1) Place crossmember below vehicle on jack stands. Install upper crossmember insulators on crossmember assembly. Lower vehicle onto crossmember assembly. *See Fig. 10.* Align crossmember ensuring brake lines, hoses and calipers are not damaged.

2) Install crossmember forward arm bolts, nuts, washers, upper mounting bolts, and insulators. *See Fig. 10.* Reverse removal procedure for remaining components. Tighten bolts to specification.

NOTE: **Both forward arm bolts must be installed with nuts on right side of arm. The cup-shaped washer is used only on left forward arm.**

Fig. 10: Installing Crossmember Assembly on "E" & "K" Bodies

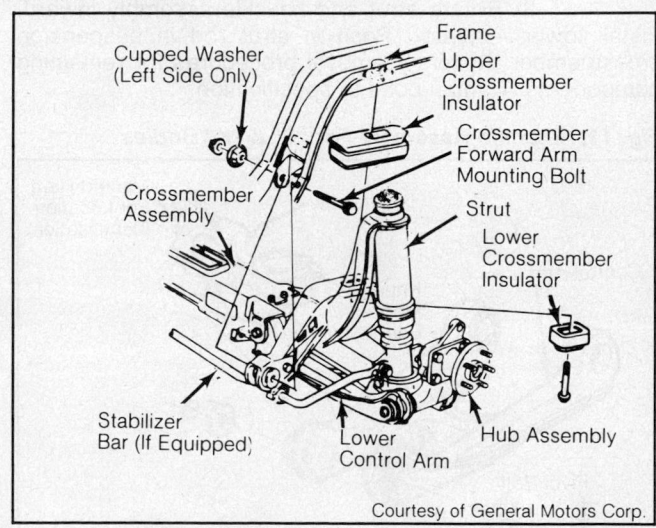

Courtesy of General Motors Corp.

KNUCKLE
Removal ("E" & "K" Bodies)
1) Raise vehicle on frame contact hoist. Remove wheel. When working on left control arm,

Fig. 9: Removing & Installing Crossmember Leading Arm Bushings on "E" & "K" Bodies

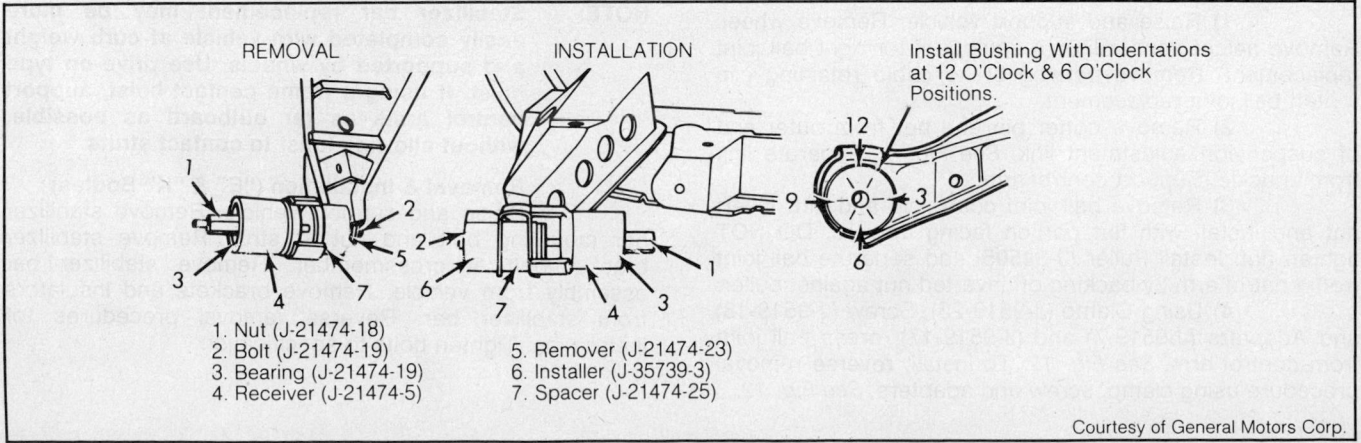

REMOVAL   INSTALLATION   Install Bushing With Indentations at 12 O'Clock & 6 O'Clock Positions.

1. Nut (J-21474-18)
2. Bolt (J-21474-19)
3. Bearing (J-21474-19)
4. Receiver (J-21474-5)
5. Remover (J-21474-23)
6. Installer (J-35739-3)
7. Spacer (J-21474-25)

Courtesy of General Motors Corp.

Rear Suspension
GENERAL MOTORS FWD
"C", "E", "H" & "K" BODIES (Cont.)

disconnect ELC height sensor link (if equipped). On vehicles equipped with anti-lock brake system, disconnect speed sensor from knuckle.

2) On all models, remove stabilizer bar mounting bolt at strut (if equipped). Remove and support caliper. Remove rotor. Remove hub and bearing assembly.

3) Loosen outboard knuckle pivot bolt. *See Fig. 11.* DO NOT remove at this time. Remove strut rod cap, mounting nut, retainer, and upper insulator. Compress strut and remove lower insulator.

4) Rotate strut and knuckle assembly outward. Remove knuckle pinch bolt. Remove strut from knuckle. Remove knuckle pivot bolt. Remove knuckle from control arm.

Installation

1) Knuckles are not interchangeable. Knuckles are marked with "L" for left side and "R" for right side on rear of knuckle. *See Fig. 11.* Install knuckle on control arm.

2) Install knuckle pivot bolt. DO NOT tighten at this time. Install strut in knuckle. Ensure strut is fully seated in knuckle, with strut tang bottomed in knuckle slot. Install knuckle pinch bolt. Tighten to specification.

3) Rotate strut and knuckle assembly inward. Install lower insulator. Position strut rod in suspension crossmember. Reverse removal procedures for remaining components. Tighten bolts to specification.

Fig. 11: Knuckle Assembly For "E" & "K" Bodies

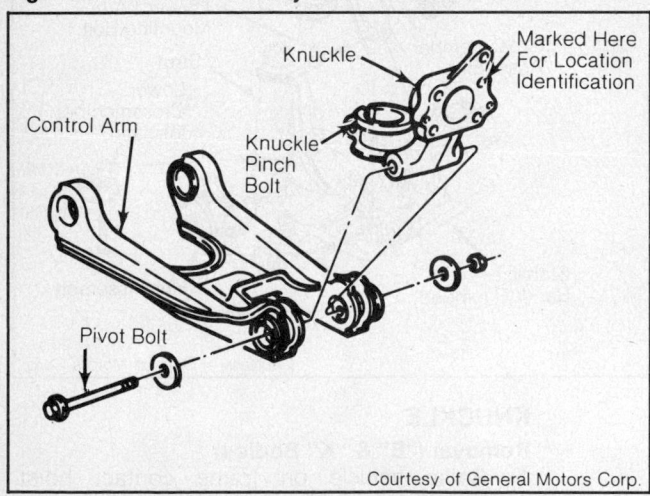

Control Arm
Knuckle
Marked Here For Location Identification
Knuckle Pinch Bolt
Pivot Bolt

Courtesy of General Motors Corp.

BALL JOINT

Removal & Installation ("C" & "H" Bodies)

1) Raise and support vehicle. Remove wheel. Remove height sensor link (if equipped) for right ball joint replacement. Remove parking brake cable retaining clip for left ball joint replacement.

2) Remove cotter pin and nut from outer end of suspension adjustment link. *See Fig. 1.* Separate link from knuckle. Support control arm.

3) Remove ball joint cotter pin and nut. Invert nut and install with flat portion facing upward. DO NOT tighten nut. Install Puller (J-34505) and separate ball joint from control arm by backing off inverted nut against puller.

4) Using Clamp (J-9519-23), Screw (J-9519-18) and Adapters (J-9519-7) and (J-9519-17), press ball joint from control arm. *See Fig. 12.* To install, reverse removal procedure using clamp, screw and adapters. *See Fig. 12.*

Fig. 12: Ball Joint Removal & Installation "C" & "H" Bodies

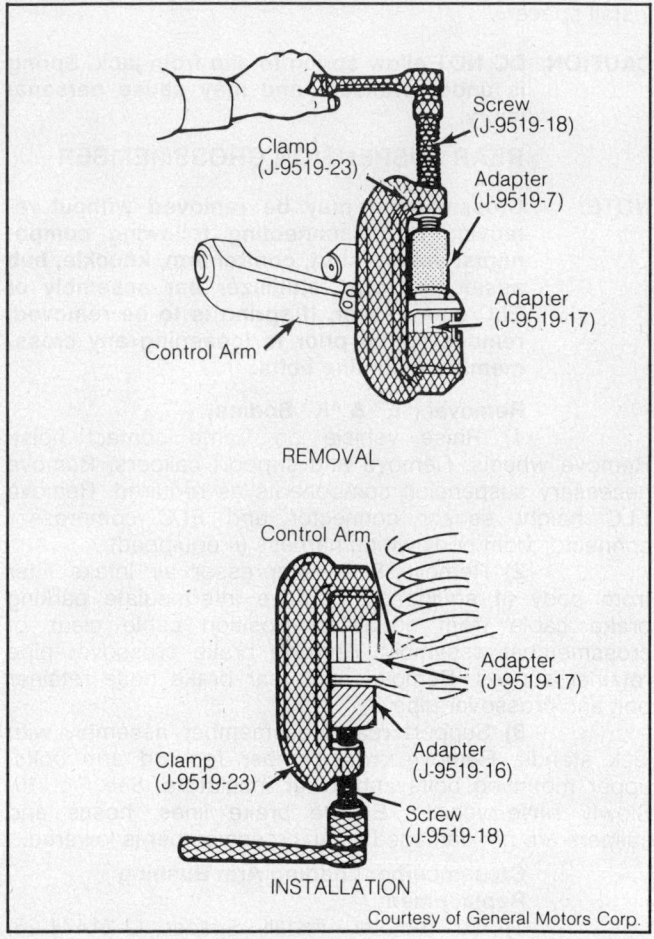

Clamp (J-9519-23)
Screw (J-9519-18)
Adapter (J-9519-7)
Adapter (J-9519-17)
Control Arm

REMOVAL

Control Arm
Adapter (J-9519-17)
Clamp (J-9519-23)
Adapter (J-9519-16)
Screw (J-9519-18)

INSTALLATION

Courtesy of General Motors Corp.

STABILIZER BAR

Removal ("C" & "H" Bodies)

Raise and support vehicle. Remove wheels. Remove nut, support bolt, retainer, and insulators retaining stabilizer bar to knuckle. Remove bushing clip bolt. Bend open end of bushing clip downward. Remove stabilizer and bushings. *See Fig. 13.*

Installation

Reverse removal procedures. Tighten bushing clip bolt with vehicle at normal operating height.

NOTE: **Stabilizer bar replacement may be more easily completed with vehicle at curb weight and supported by wheels. Use drive-on type hoist. If using a frame contact hoist, support control arms as far outboard as possible, without allowing hoist to contact struts.**

Removal & Installation ("E" & "K" Bodies)

Raise and support vehicle. Remove stabilizer bar mounting bolt and nut at strut. Remove stabilizer bracket bolt at crossmember. Remove stabilizer bar assembly from vehicle. Remove brackets and insulators from stabilizer bar. Reverse removal procedures for installation. Tighten bolts to specification.

Rear Suspension
GENERAL MOTORS FWD
"C", "E", "H" & "K" BODIES (Cont.)

Fig. 13: Exploded View of "C" & "H" Bodiy Stabilizer Bar

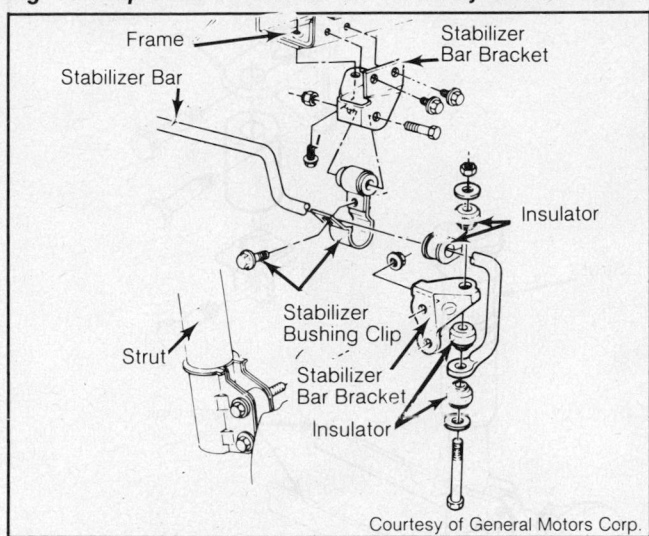

Courtesy of General Motors Corp.

STRUT ASSEMBLY

Removal ("C" & "H" Bodies)

1) Raise and support vehicle. Remove wheel and support control arm. Disconnect ELC air tube from strut (if equipped).

2) From inside trunk, remove upper strut mounting nuts. From under vehicle, remove lower strut bolts from knuckle and bracket. Remove strut. *See Fig. 14.*

Installation

Reverse removal procedures. Prior to lowering vehicle, lightly pressurize ELC system by grounding the Yellow wire of the compressor test lead located near ELC compressor in the engine compartment. Check and adjust rear wheel alignment.

Fig. 14: Exploded View of Strut For "C" & "H" Bodies

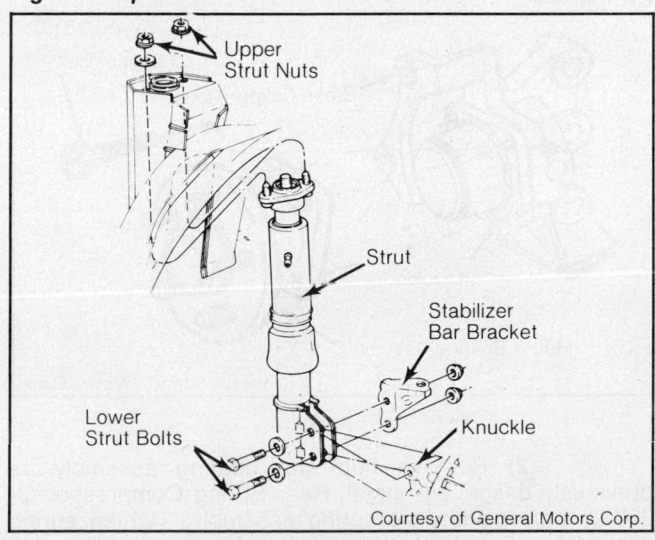

Courtesy of General Motors Corp.

Removal & Installation ("E" & "K" Bodies)

1) Raise and support vehicle on frame contact hoist. Remove wheel. On left strut replacement, disconnect ELC height sensor link (if equipped). Install 2 lug nuts to retain rotor on hub. Remove stabilizer bar mounting bolt at strut (if equipped). Remove and support caliper.

2) Loosen knuckle pivot bolt on outboard end of control arm. DO NOT remove pivot bolt. Remove strut rod cap, mounting nut, retainer, and upper insulator. Compress strut and remove lower insulator.

3) Rotate strut and knuckle assembly outward. Remove knuckle pinch bolt. *See Fig. 15.* Remove strut from knuckle. Reverse removal procedures for installation. Strut tang must be fully seated in knuckle slot. Tighten bolts to specification.

Fig. 15: Exploded View of Strut For "E" & "K" Bodies

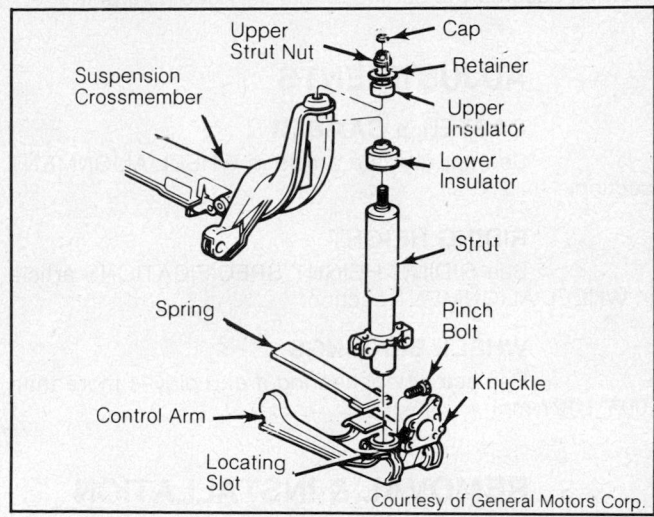

Courtesy of General Motors Corp.

TIGHTENING SPECIFICATIONS ("E" & "K" BODIES)

Application	Ft. Lbs. (N.m)
Caliper Mounting Bolt	83 (113)
Control Arm Bolt	66 (90)
Crossmember Forward Arm Bolt	66 (90)
Crossmember Upper Mount Bolt	66 (90)
Hub Mounting Bolt	52 (71)
Knuckle Pivot Bolt	40 (54)
Spring Insulator Nut	21 (29)
Spring Retainer Bolt	21 (29)
Stabilizer Mounting Bracket Bolt	43 (58)
Stabilizer-To-Strut Bolt	43 (58)
Upper Strut Nut	65 (88)

TIGHTENING SPECIFICATIONS ("C" & "H" BODIES)

Application	Ft. Lbs. (N.m)
Ball Joint Stud Nut	[1] 90 (122)
Control Arm Pivot Bolt	125 (170)
Control Arm Pivot Nut	85 (115)
Hub Mounting Bolt	52 (71)
Stabilizer Bushing Clip Bolt	37 (51)
Stabilizer Support Bolt	13 (18)
Strut-To-Knuckle Bolt	148 (201)
Strut-To-Upper Mount Nut	18 (24)
Suspension Adjusting Link Retaining Nut	63 (85)
Suspension Adjusting Link To-Knuckle Nut	37 (51)

[1] – Plus an additional 2/3 turn. Minimum torque must be 40 ft. lbs. (54 N.m).

Rear Suspension

GENERAL MOTORS FWD "W" BODY

Cutlass Supreme, Grand Prix, Regal

DESCRIPTION

The rear suspension features MacPherson struts coupled to a knuckle, trailing link, and front and rear lateral links. The suspension also includes a composite fiberglass mono-leaf transverse spring.

Rear wheel camber is adjustable through lower strut mounting bolts. Rear wheel toe may be adjusted with cams on the inner ends of rear lateral link. The hub and bearing assembly is sealed and is serviced as a unit.

ADJUSTMENTS

CASTER & CAMBER

See appropriate article in WHEEL ALIGNMENT section.

RIDING HEIGHT

See RIDING HEIGHT SPECIFICATIONS article in WHEEL ALIGNMENT section.

WHEEL BEARINGS

Replace wheel bearing if end play is more than .005" (.127 mm).

REMOVAL & INSTALLATION

AUXILIARY SPRING ASSEMBLY

Removal

1) Raise and support vehicle. Place jack stand under knuckle. Scribe mating line across strut and knuckle for reassembly reference.

2) Thread Auxiliary Spring Compressor (J-37098) through auxiliary spring assembly. *See Fig. 1.* Compress enough to hold for removal.

3) Remove auxiliary spring bolts and nuts from knuckle. Remove auxiliary spring.

Installation

To install auxiliary spring, reverse removal procedure. Use spring compressor to compress spring during installation.

HUB & BEARING ASSEMBLY

NOTE: Hub and bearing assembly is non-serviceable. Replace as an assembly.

Removal & Installation

1) Raise and support vehicle. Remove wheel. Remove brake caliper and support out of way. Remove brake rotor. REPLACE caliper mounting bolts if excessively corroded.

2) Remove hub and bearing retainer bolts. *See Fig. 2.* Remove hub and bearing assembly from knuckle. To install hub and bearing assembly, reverse removal procedure.

KNUCKLE ASSEMBLY

Removal

1) Raise and support vehicle. Remove wheel. Remove brake caliper and support out of way. Remove brake rotor. REPLACE caliper mounting bolts if excessively corroded.

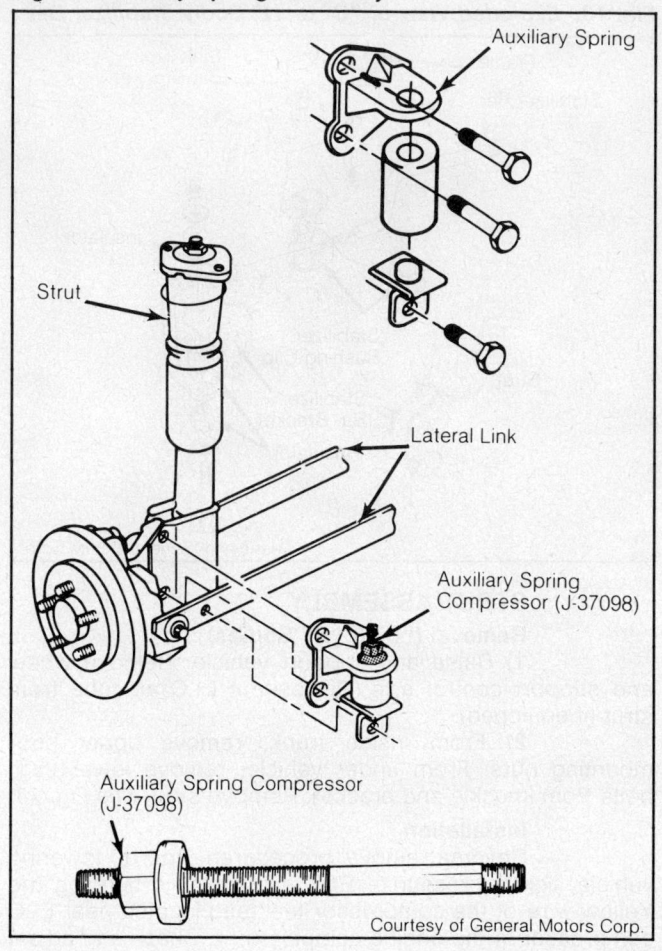

Fig. 1: Auxiliary Spring Assembly

Auxiliary Spring
Strut
Lateral Link
Auxiliary Spring Compressor (J-37098)
Auxiliary Spring Compressor (J-37098)
Courtesy of General Motors Corp.

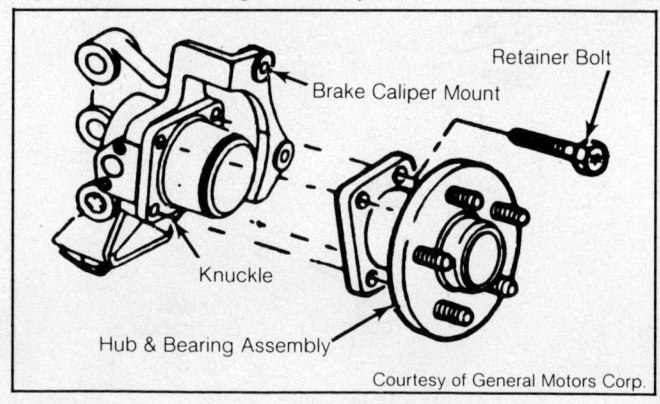

Fig. 2: Hub & Bearing Assembly

Retainer Bolt
Brake Caliper Mount
Knuckle
Hub & Bearing Assembly
Courtesy of General Motors Corp.

2) Remove hub and bearing assembly as previously described. Install Rear Spring Compressor (J-35778) onto transverse spring assembly. Tighten spring compressor to hold spring pressure. *See Fig. 3.*

3) Thread Auxiliary Spring Compressor (J-37098) into auxiliary spring to hold assembly. *See Fig. 1.* Separate trailing link from knuckle.

4) Scribe mating mark across strut and knuckle for reassembly reference. Disconnect front and rear lateral links from knuckle. *See Fig. 4.*

GENERAL MOTORS FWD "W" BODY (Cont.)

Fig. 3: Compressing Rear Spring

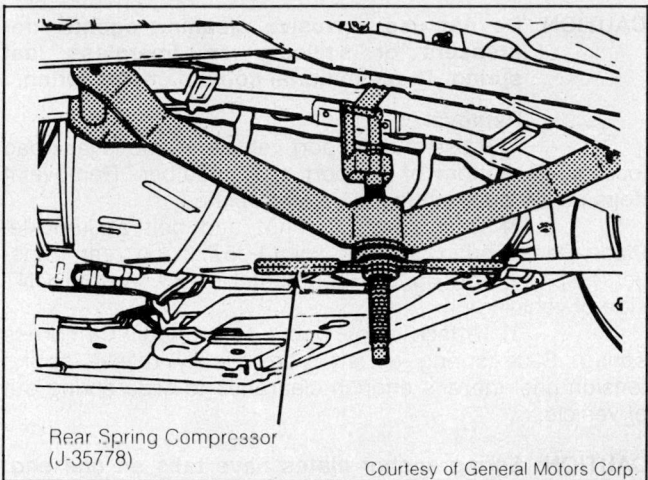

Rear Spring Compressor
(J-35778)

Courtesy of General Motors Corp.

5) Disconnect rear lateral link from auxiliary spring assembly. Remove strut-to-knuckle nuts and stabilizer bar bracket. Remove auxiliary spring and knuckle.

Installation
To install knuckle, reverse removal procedure. Be sure to align scribe marks on strut and knuckle.

REAR STRUT ASSEMBLY
Removal
1) Raise vehicle on hoist. Remove wheel. Thread Auxiliary Spring Compressor (J-37098) into auxiliary spring. *See Fig. 1.*

2) Remove brake caliper from knuckle and hang out of way. Remove brake rotor and brake hose bracket.

3) Scribe mating mark across knuckle and strut. Remove strut bolts at body and allow assembly to drop down. Remove stabilizer bar bracket by removing strut-to-knuckle nuts.

4) Remove strut-to-knuckle bolts. Lower strut assembly out of vehicle.

Installation
To install strut, reverse removal procedure.

STABILIZER BAR
Removal
1) Raise and support vehicle. Remove wheel. Scribe mating mark across knuckle and strut for reas-

Fig. 4: Exploded of "W" Body Rear Suspension

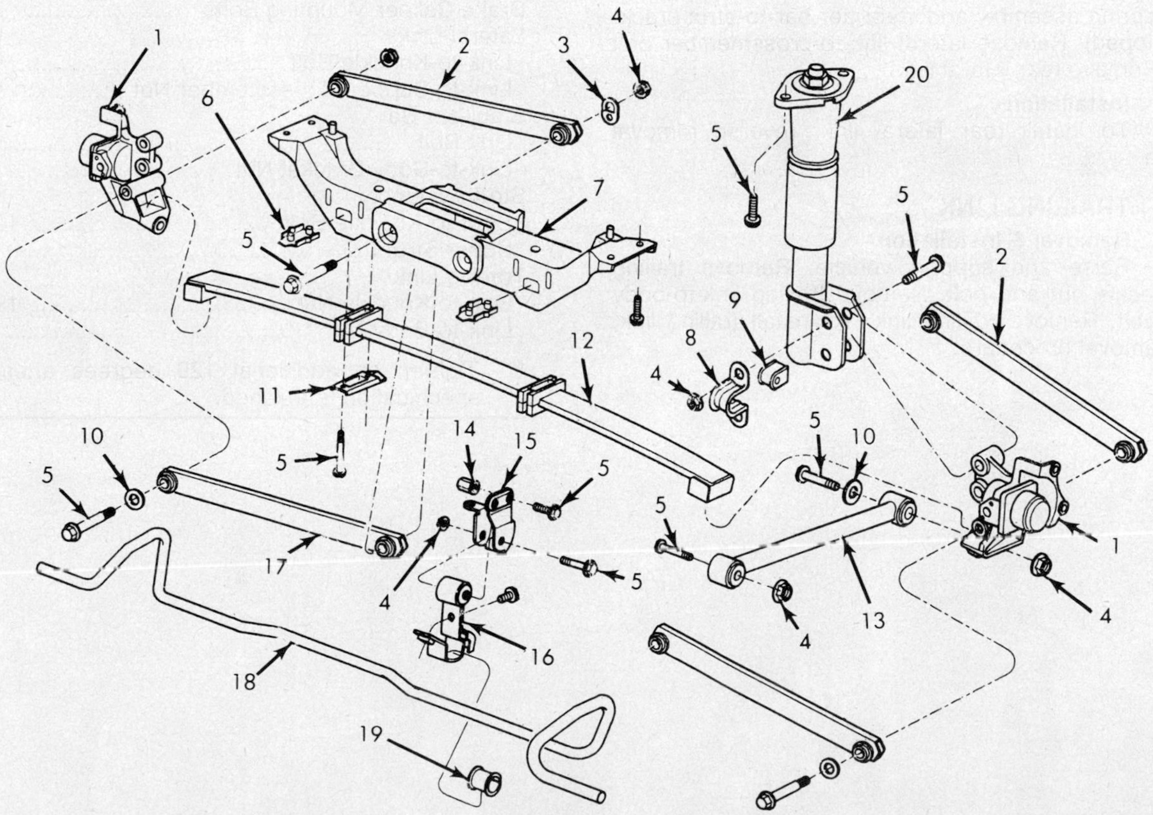

1. Knuckle Assembly	8. Rear Stabilizer Bar Bracket	15. Trailing Link Bracket
2. Rear Lateral Link	9. Stabilizer Bar Insulator	16. Rear Stabilizer Link
3. Lateral Link Adjusting Cam	10. Washer	17. Front Lateral Link
4. Nut	11. Spring Anchor Plate	18. Stabilizer Bar
5. Bolt	12. Rear Spring	19. Stabilizer Bar Insulator
6. Rear Spring Bracket Nut	13. Trailing Link	20. Strut Assembly
7. Support Crossmember	14. Trailing Link Bracket Nut	

Courtesy of General Motors Corp.

Rear Suspension

GENERAL MOTORS FWD "W" BODY (Cont.)

sembly reference. Remove left and right side stabilizer bar brackets. See Fig. 4.

2) Place jack stand under knuckle. Remove lower strut mounting bolts. Remove stabilizer bar.

Installation

To install stabilizer bar, reverse removal procedure.

LATERAL LINK (FRONT)

Removal

1) Raise and support vehicle. Remove wheel. Remove transverse spring. See TRANSVERSE SPRING ASSEMBLY.

2) Lower fuel tank for access to link. Remove lateral link-to-knuckle bolt. Remove lateral link-to-suspension crossmember nut and bolt. Remove front lateral link.

Installation

To install front lateral link, reverse removal procedure. Check wheel alignment after installation.

LATERAL LINK (REAR)

Removal

1) Raise and support vehicle. Remove wheel. Remove transverse spring. See TRANSVERSE SPRING ASSEMBLY in this article.

2) Support knuckle with jack stand. Remove rear lateral link-to-knuckle bolt and washer.

3) Remove strut-to-knuckle bolts and nuts, auxiliary spring assembly and stabilizer bar-to-strut bracket (if equipped). Remove lateral link-to-crossmember bolt and nut. Remove rear lateral link.

Installation

To install rear lateral link, reverse removal procedure.

TRAILING LINK

Removal & Installation

Raise and support vehicle. Remove trailing link-to-knuckle nut and bolt. Remove trailing link-to-body nut and bolt. Remove trailing link. To install trailing link, reverse removal procedure.

TRANSVERSE SPRING ASSEMBLY

CAUTION: Do not use corrosive cleaning agents, degreasers or solvents on fiberglass leaf spring. These material could damage spring.

Removal

1) Raise and support vehicle. Remove jack pad located on bottom of support crossmember. Remove 4 bolts on left and right spring anchor plates.

2) Remove trailing nut and bolt at knuckle. Place Rear Spring Compressor (J-35778) on rear transverse spring. See Fig. 3. Hang center shank from FRONT side of vehicle only.

3) Attach tool body to spring. Compress spring. Slide spring to left side. Slowly relieve spring tension until there is enough clearance to slide spring out of vehicle.

CAUTION: Spring anchor plates have tabs on one end. Tabs must be aligned with support crossmember to prevent fuel tank damage.

Installation

To install transverse spring assembly, reverse removal procedure.

TIGHTENING SPECIFICATIONS

Application	Ft. Lbs. (N.m)
Brake Caliper Mounting Bolts	79 (107)
Lateral Links	
Link-to-Knuckle Bolt	[1] 66 (90)
Link-to-Support Crossmember Nut	[1] 66 (90)
Stabilizer Bar	
Link Bolt	37 (50)
Link-to-Body Bracket Nut	18 (25)
Strut Assembly	
Strut-to-Knuckle Bolt	133 (180)
Upper Strut Bolts	34 (46)
Trailing Link	
Link-to-Knuckle Nut	192 (260)
Link-to-Body Nut	48 (65)

[1] – Tighten an additional 120 degrees after torque specification is reached.

GENERAL MOTORS RWD
"B", "D", "F" & "G" BODIES

"B" Body: Caprice, Custom Cruiser,
   Electra Wagon, Safari Wagon, LeSabre
   Wagon
"D" Body: Cadillac Brougham
"F" Body: Camaro, Firebird
"G" Body: Cutlass Supreme Classic,
   Monte Carlo, Regal GN

DESCRIPTION

Rear suspension is a 4-link type with coil springs, which are mounted between lower spring seats on the axle housing and upper spring seats in the frame. The axle housing is attached to the frame by 2 upper and 2 lower control arms. The control arms maintain a geometrical relationship between the axle housing and frame, to oppose torque reaction on acceleration and braking. Two shock absorbers are attached to the frame and axle housing. Camaro and Firebird models use an upper torque arm, 2 lower control arms and track bar to secure differential.

ADJUSTMENTS

CAMBER & TOE-IN

See appropriate article in WHEEL ALIGNMENT section.

RIDING HEIGHT

See RIDING HEIGHT SPECIFICATIONS article in WHEEL ALIGNMENT section.

REMOVAL & INSTALLATION

SHOCK ABSORBERS
Removal & Installation
(Camaro & Firebird)
1) Raise and support vehicle. Support rear axle assembly. From above, pull back carpeting and remove upper shock absorber mounting nut. Remove shock absorber lower mounting nut and remove shock absorber.

CAUTION: Support axle assembly before removing upper shock absorber mounting nut to avoid damage to brake lines, track bar and propeller shaft.

2) To install shock absorber, reverse removal procedure. Tighten mounting nuts to specification.

Removal (All Other Models)
1) Raise and support vehicle. Support rear axle assembly. Disconnect air line from shock absorber (if equipped). See Fig. 1.
2) Disconnect upper shock absorber mounting bolts. Use back-up wrench on upper shock absorber mounting nuts (if equipped). Disconnect lower mounting nut, using a back-up wrench to keep stud from turning.

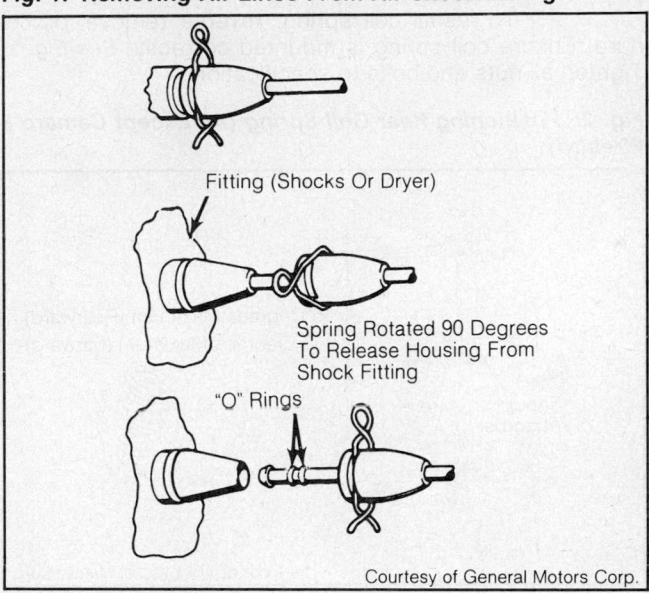

Fig. 1: Removing Air Lines From Air Shock Fitting

Fitting (Shocks Or Dryer)

Spring Rotated 90 Degrees
To Release Housing From
Shock Fitting

"O" Rings

Courtesy of General Motors Corp.

Installation
1) To install shock absorber, reverse removal procedure. If equipped with Electronic Level Control or Superlift Shocks, left air shock has 2 line connections while right shock only has one connection.

CAUTION: DO NOT allow vehicle weight to rest on air shock until it has been inflated to at least 10 psi.

2) Tighten mounting nuts to specification. Connect air line and add 10 psi (.7 kg/cm²) air pressure to prevent shock absorber damage (if equipped).
3) On Cadillac models with Electronic Level Control, turn ignition on and ground compressor test lead to active system and inflate shocks. Test lead is Green connector with Yellow wire located to left of brake booster.

COIL SPRINGS & INSULATORS

CAUTION: Manufacturers recommend removing and installing coil springs one side at a time.

Removal ("B" & "G" Bodies)
1) Turn off ignition so Electronic Level Control system (if equipped) will not activate. Raise vehicle and support axle housing with adjustable lifting device. Disconnect upper control arms at axle housing. Disconnect stabilizer bar (if equipped).
2) Remove brake hose support bolt at axle housing to allow axle to drop further. Remove shock absorber lower mounts. Lower axle enough to remove spring. Remove coil springs and insulators.

NOTE: Brake lines do not have to be disconnected to let axle drop. Do not lower axle to a point where brake line supports axle.

Rear Suspension
GENERAL MOTORS RWD
"B", "D", "F" & "G" BODIES (Cont.)

Installation

To install coil spring, reverse removal procedure. Ensure coil spring is mounted correctly. See Fig. 2. Tighten all nuts and bolts to specification.

Fig. 2: Positioning Rear Coil Spring (All Except Camaro & Firebird)

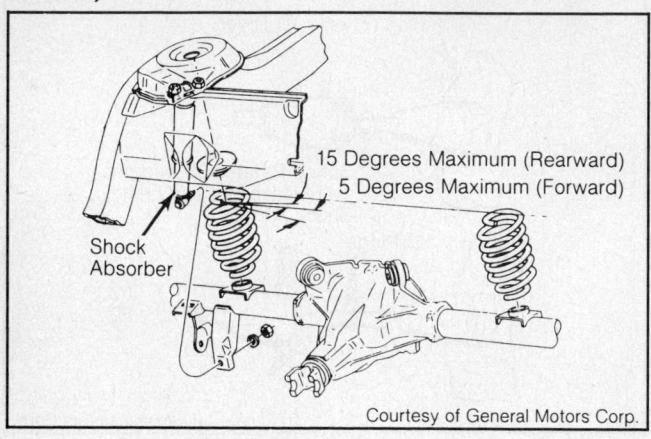

15 Degrees Maximum (Rearward)
5 Degrees Maximum (Forward)

Shock Absorber

Courtesy of General Motors Corp.

Removal (Cadillac)

1) Raise vehicle and support frame and rear axle. Remove shock absorbers as previously described. Remove stabilizer bar-to-lower control arm bolts, and remove stabilizer bar (if equipped).

2) Remove bolt securing junction block to top of rear axle. Disconnect brake lines from axle clips. Disconnect link from leveling sensor arm. Place jack stand under axle nose and remove lower control arm-to-axle bolts.

3) Disconnect propeller shaft from pinion flange. Support propeller shaft with wire. Remove jack stand from under axle nose. Remove upper arm pivot bolts at axle. Disconnect left side parking brake cable at equalizer. Disconnect cable at frame by removing clip and slide cable through hole.

4) Remove cable from clip at center of rear crossmember. Disconnect cable at connector located left of frame. Support rear frame rails. Lower axle enough to remove springs.

CAUTION: Do not let axle housing twist when lowered, as springs may snap from their seats and cause personal injury.

Fig. 3: Positioning Cadillac Rear Coil Springs

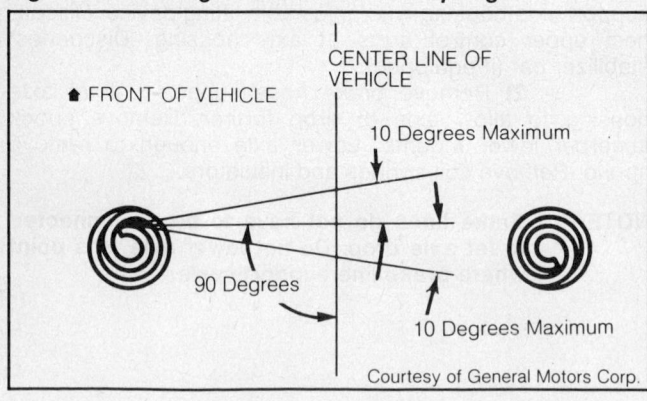

CENTER LINE OF VEHICLE

▲ FRONT OF VEHICLE

10 Degrees Maximum

90 Degrees

10 Degrees Maximum

Courtesy of General Motors Corp.

Installation

1) Tape upper rubber insulator to top of spring and position upper end of left rear spring coil toward left side rail. Position upper end of right rear spring coil toward right frame side rail. See Fig. 3.

2) Continue installation in reverse of removal procedure. Tighten all mounting nuts and bolts to specification. DO NOT tighten upper and lower control arms until vehicle is resting at normal standing height position.

Removal (Camaro & Firebird)

1) Raise and support vehicle. Support rear axle with adjustable lifting device. Remove track bar mounting bolt at axle assembly. Loosen track bar bolt at body brace.

2) Disconnect rear brake hose clip at underbody to allow axle drop. Remove both lower shock absorber attaching nuts. Remove drive shaft on 4-cylinder models. Lower rear axle and remove spring.

Installation

To install coil spring, reverse removal procedure. Manufacturer recommends using NEW track bar bolt if nylon patch in threads is damaged or will not hold correct torque.

Fig. 4: Typical Rear Coil Spring Suspension (Except Camaro & Firebird)

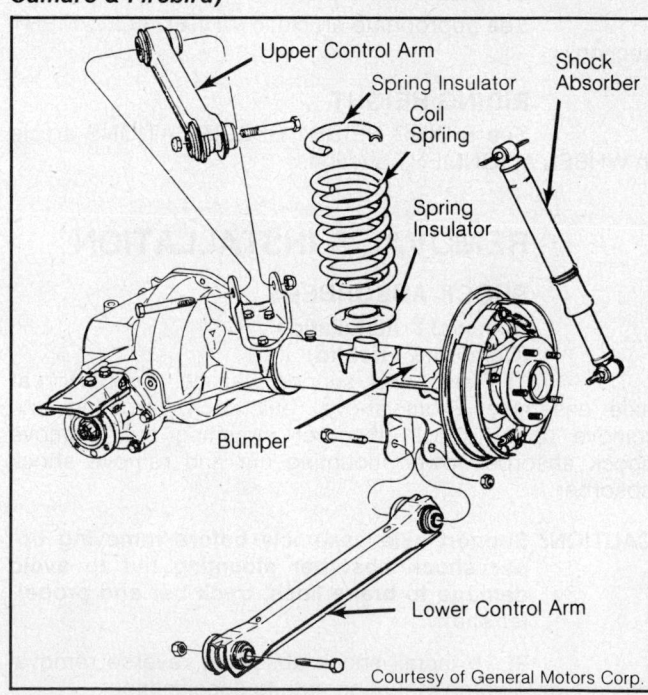

Upper Control Arm

Spring Insulator

Shock Absorber

Coil Spring

Spring Insulator

Bumper

Lower Control Arm

Courtesy of General Motors Corp.

UPPER CONTROL ARM

NOTE: **Remove and replace one control arm at a time to prevent rear axle from rolling or slipping. Bushings are not serviceable on Cadillac Brougham.**

Removal

1) Raise and support vehicle. If equipped with Electronic Level Control, remove height control sensor link-to-right upper control arm nut. Center overtravel lever.

GENERAL MOTORS RWD
"B", "D", "F" & "G" BODIES (Cont.)

2) Some vehicles may require disconnecting lower shock absorber mount to provide clearance for upper control arm removal. On all models, place jack stands under rear axle.

3) Unbolt control arm from upper and lower pivot bolt mounts. Remove control arm from vehicle.

Bushing Replacement
Except for Cadillac, bushings may be replaced using a press. *See Fig. 5.*

Installation
To install, reverse removal procedure. Tighten pivot bolts with vehicle on ground and at curb height. If equipped with Nylock or prevailing torque nuts, tighten nut, NOT bolt, to achieve accurate torque.

Fig. 5: Replacing Control Arm Bushings (Typical)

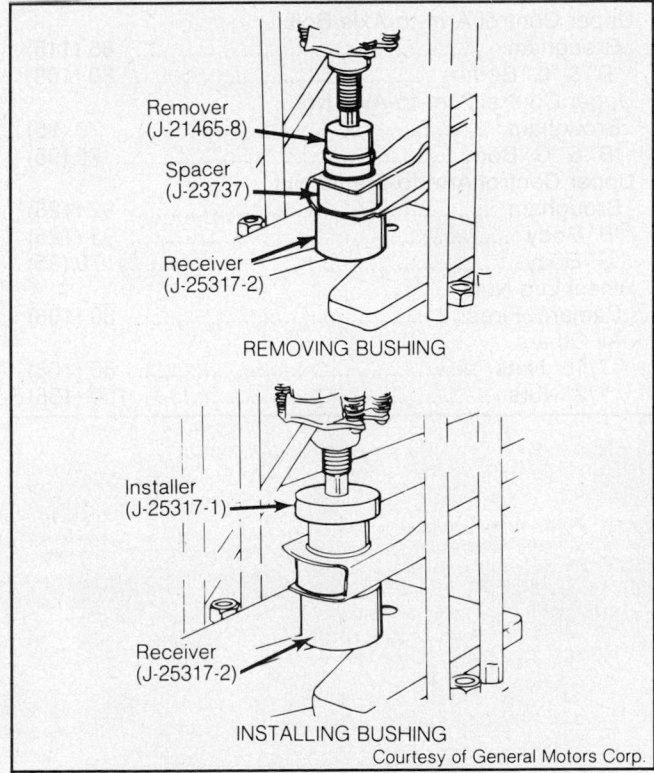

REMOVING BUSHING

INSTALLING BUSHING

Courtesy of General Motors Corp.

LOWER CONTROL ARM

NOTE: Remove and replace one control arm at a time to prevent rear axle from rolling or slipping.

Removal
Raise and support rear of vehicle. Support axle housing to relieve tension on control arm bolts. If equipped with stabilizer bar, disconnect bar at lower control arm. Remove lower control arm pivot bolt. Disconnect control arm from frame crossmember and remove control arm.

Bushing Relacement
Bushing replacement is similar to upper control arm. *See Fig. 5.*

Installation
To install, reverse removal procedure. Tighten pivot bolts with vehicle on ground and at curb height. If equipped with Nylock or prevailing torque nuts, tighten nut, NOT bolt, to achieve accurate torque.

Fig. 6: Camaro & Firebird Rear Suspension

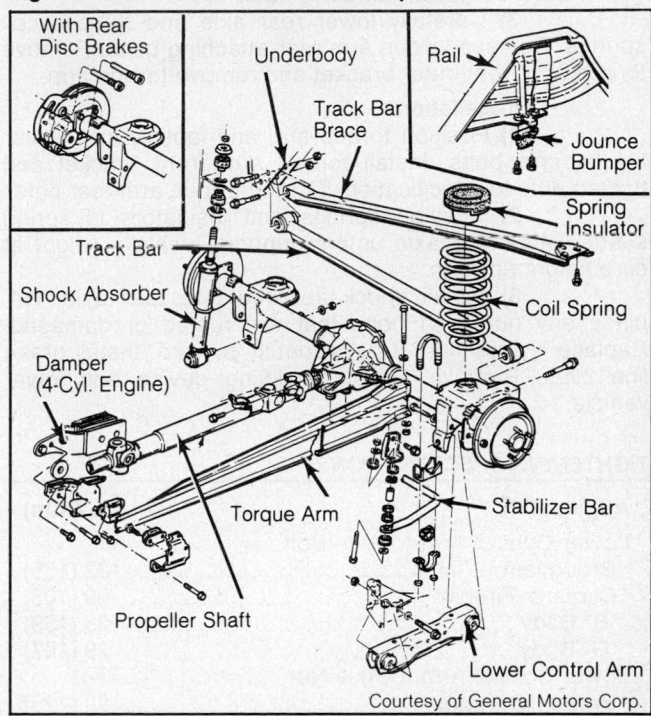

Courtesy of General Motors Corp.

TRACK BAR

Removal (Camaro & Firebird Models)
Raise vehicle. Support rear axle at curb height position. Remove track bar mounting bolt and nut at rear axle and body bracket. Remove 3 track bar-to-body mounting bolts. Remove track bar. *See Fig. 6.*

Installation
1) Thoroughly clean track bar-to-axle housing bolt and nut. Replace any nuts and bolts that are rusted or damaged. Replace Nylock nuts if nylon patch is worn.

2) Reinstall track bar mounting bolt at axle. Attach track bar to body bracket.

TRACK BAR BRACE

Removal (Camaro & Firebird)
Raise vehicle and support rear axle. Remove heat shield-to-track bar brace. Remove 3 track bar brace-to-body screws. Remove nut and bolt at body bracket and lift out track bar.

Installation
To install track bar, reverse removal procedure. Tighten 3 track bar brace-to-body screws before tightening nut and bolt. Tighten NUT at track bar brace, not bolt. Install heat shield and lower vehicle.

TORQUE ARM

CAUTION: Remove coil springs before removing torque arm to avoid rear axle twisting forward and damaging vehicle.

Rear Suspension
GENERAL MOTORS RWD
"B", "D", "F" & "G" BODIES (Cont.)

Removal (Camaro & Firebird Models)

1) Raise vehicle and support rear axle with adjustable lifting device. Remove track bar mounting bolt at axle assembly. Loosen track bar bolt at body brace.

2) Disconnect rear brake hose clips at underbody to allow more axle drop (if necessary). Remove both shock absorber lower attaching nuts.

3) Carefully lower rear axle and remove coil springs. Remove torque arm rear attaching bolts. Remove torque arm front outer bracket and remove torque arm.

Installation

1) Position torque arm and loosely install rear torque arm bolts. Install torque arm front bracket and tighten nuts to specification. Tighten torque arm rear nuts.

2) Position springs and insulators in spring seats. Raise rear axle until it supports vehicle weight at curb height position.

3) Install shock absorbers to rear axle. Replace any nuts and bolts that are rusted or damaged. Replace Nylock nuts if nylon patch is worn. Install brake line clips. Remove adjustable lifting device and lower vehicle.

TIGHTENING SPECIFICATIONS

Application	Ft. Lbs. (N.m)
Lower Control Arm-to-Axle Bolt	
Brougham	122 (165)
Camaro, Firebird	80 (108)
"B" Body	125 (169)
"G" Body	79 (107)
Lower Control Arm-to-Axle Nut	
Brougham	92 (125)
"B" Body	92 (125)
"G" Body	80 (108)
Lower Control Arm-to-Frame Bolt	
Brougham	89 (121)
Camaro, Firebird	80 (108)
Lower Control Arm-to-Frame Nut	
Brougham	92 (125)
"B" Body	92 (125)
"G" Body	70 (95)
Shock Absorber Nut (Lower Attachment)	
Camaro, Firebird	70 (95)
"B" Body	48 (65)
"G" Body	65 (88)
Shock Absorber Nut (Upper Attachment)	
Brougham	12 (16)
Camaro, Firebird	13 (18)
"B" & "G" Bodies	
Except Superlift Shocks	12 (16)
Superlift Shocks	20 (27)

TIGHTENING SPECIFICATIONS (Cont.)

Application	Ft. Lbs. (N.m)
Stabilizer Bar-to-Body Bracket Bolt	
Camaro, Firebird	16 (22)
"B" Body	52 (70)
Stabilizer Bar-to-Control Arm Bolt	
"G" Body	35 (47)
Stabilizer Bar-to-Control Arm Nut	
"B" & "G" Bodies	35 (47)
Stabilizer Bracket-to-Body Bolt	
Camaro, Firebird	35 (47)
Track Bar-to-Body Bracket Nut	78 (105)
Track Bar-to-Axle Bolt	59 (80)
Track Bar Brace-to-Body Brace Bracket	34 (46)
Torque Arm-to-Rear Axle Nut	100 (136)
Torque Arm-to-Outer Bracket Bolt	31 (42)
Upper Control Arm-to-Axle Bolt	
Brougham	85 (115)
"B" & "G" Bodies	80 (108)
Upper Control Arm-to-Axle Nut	
Brougham	70 (95)
"B" & "G" Body	70 (95)
Upper Control Arm-to-Frame Nut	
Brougham	92 (125)
"B" Body	92 (125)
"G" Body	70 (95)
Wheel Lug Nuts	
Camaro, Firebird	80 (108)
All Others	
7/16" Nuts	80 (108)
1/2" Nuts	100 (136)

CORVETTE

DESCRIPTION

Each wheel is mounted to a 5-link independent rear suspension, composed of a drive shaft, camber control knuckle support rod, upper and lower control arms and tie rod. A fiberglass transverse mounted spring is attached to the differential carrier beam. These components along with the aluminum knuckles, differential carrier beam and driveline support beam form the rear suspension.

ADJUSTMENTS

CAMBER & TOE-IN

See appropriate article in WHEEL ALIGNMENT section.

RIDING HEIGHT

See RIDING HEIGHT SPECIFICATIONS article in WHEEL ALIGNMENT section.

REAR WHEEL BEARINGS

Rear hub and wheel bearings are a sealed unit which require no adjustment.

REMOVAL & INSTALLATION

REAR HUB & WHEEL BEARINGS

Removal

Raise and support vehicle. Remove wheel and tire. Remove speed sensor. Use care not to damage speed sensor. Remove brake caliper and rotor. Disconnect transverse spring from knuckle. Using Torx Bit (J-34161), remove hub assembly mounting bolts. Remove cotter pin, spindle nut and washer. See Fig. 1. Remove hub assembly.

Installation

Replace spindle seal if necessary. Reverse removal procedures. Tighten bolts to specification. See TIGHTENING SPECIFICATIONS table at end of article. Check and adjust rear suspension alignment.

CAUTION: DO NOT move or rest vehicle on tires until spindle nut is tightened to specification.

Fig. 1: Rear Hub & Bearing

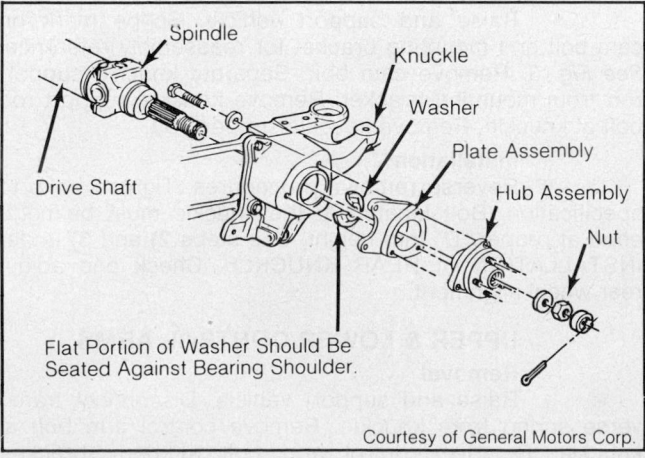

Courtesy of General Motors Corp.

REAR WHEEL SPINDLE

Removal

1) Raise and support vehicle. Remove wheel and tire. Remove speed sensor. Use care not to damage speed sensor. Remove brake caliper and rotor. Disconnect transverse spring from knuckle. See Fig. 2. Remove cotter pin, spindle nut and washer. See Fig. 1.

2) Remove drive shaft retaining straps at spindle yoke. Move knuckle outward and remove drive shaft from spindle yoke. Remove spindle.

Installation

Replace spindle seal if necessary. Reverse removal procedures. Tighten bolts to specification. See TIGHTENING SPECIFICATIONS table at end or article. Check and adjust rear suspension alignment.

REAR KNUCKLE

Removal & Installation

1) Raise and support vehicle. Remove wheel and tire. Remove speed sensor. Use care not to damage speed sensor. Remove brake caliper and rotor. Disconnect transverse spring from knuckle. See Fig. 2. Remove cotter pin, spindle nut and washer. See Fig. 1.

2) Using Torx Bit (J-34161), remove hub retaining bolts. Remove hub assembly. Disconnect stabilizer bar, tie rod end and shock absorber from knuckle. Disconnect knuckle support rod and upper and lower control arms from knuckle. See Figs. 3 and 4. Lower knuckle assembly and slide knuckle from spindle.

Fig. 2: Spring-to-Knuckle Components

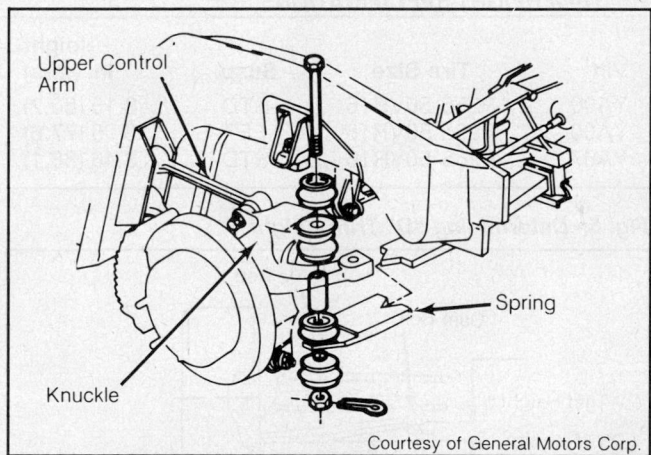

Courtesy of General Motors Corp.

Fig. 3: Knuckle Support Rod

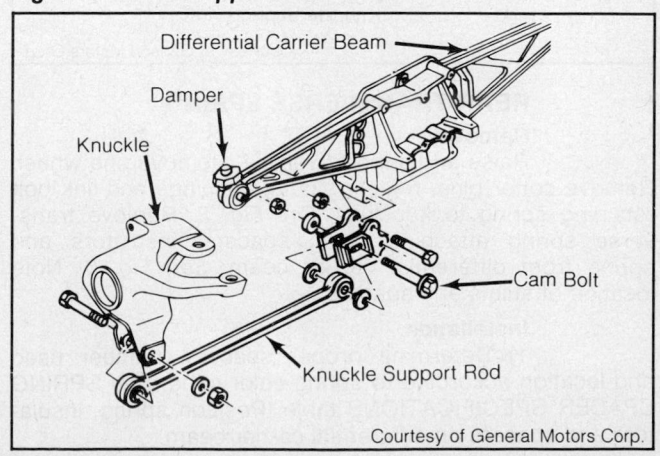

Courtesy of General Motors Corp.

Rear Suspension

CORVETTE (Cont.)

Fig. 4: Control Arm Assembly

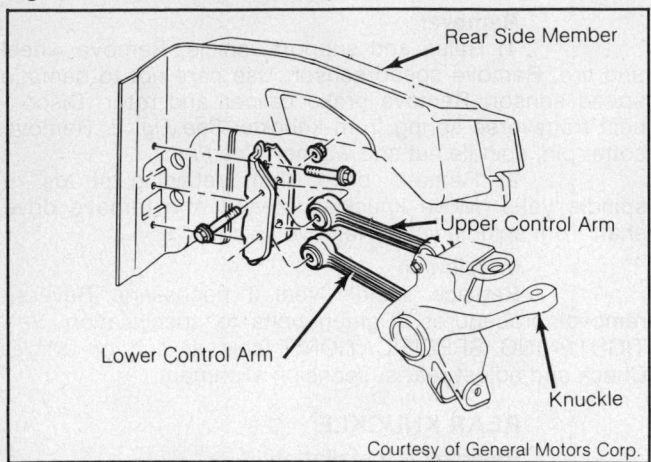

Courtesy of General Motors Corp.

Installation

1) Reverse removal procedures. Install new spindle seal. Tighten bolts to specification.

2) The knuckle support rod, upper and lower control arms and stabilizer bar retaining bolts must be tightened to specification with vehicle at proper "D" trim height. See Fig. 5. The distance between knuckle support rod inner and outer end is the "D" trim height.

3) This height must be adjusted within .25" (6.4 mm) of specification. See "D" TRIM HEIGHT SPECIFICATIONS table. Check and adjust rear wheel alignment.

"D" TRIM HEIGHT SPECIFICATIONS

Vin	Tire Size	Susp.	Height In. (mm)
YA00	P255-50VR16	STD	3.15 (80.2)
YA00	P255-50VR16	FE7	3.05 (77.6)
YA67	P255-50VR16	STD	3.46 (88.1)

Fig. 5: Determining "D" Trim Height

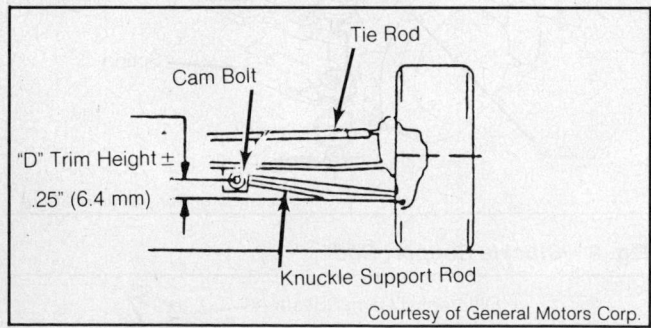

Courtesy of General Motors Corp.

REAR TRANSVERSE SPRING

Removal

Raise and support vehicle. Remove one wheel. Remove cotter pins, retaining nuts, bushings and link bolt retaining spring to knuckles. See Fig. 2. Remove transverse spring attaching bolts, spacers, insulators and spring from differential carrier beam. See Fig. 6. Note location of shims and spacers.

Installation

1) Determine proper spacers, number used and location according to spring color code. See SPRING SPACER SPECIFICATIONS table. Position spring, insulators and spacers on differential carrier beam.

2) Install retaining bolts. Tighten to specification. Install spring-to-knuckle retaining bolts. Tighten to specification. Install cotter pin.

SPRING SPACER SPECIFICATIONS

Spring Color Code	Spacer Part No.	No. Used	Spacer Location
Base Spring			
Yellow			
Or White	14044572	1	Above Spring
	14048950	1	Below Spring
	14044572	1	Below Spring
Green	14044572	1	Above Spring
	14048950	1	Above Spring
	14044572	1	Below Spring
Opt. Spring			
Yellow			
Or White	14084056	1	Above Spring
	14048950	2	Below Spring
Green	14084056	1	Above Spring
	14048950	1	Above Spring
	14048950	1	Below Spring
Convertible			
Yellow			
Or White	14044572	2	Above Spring
	14093185	1	Above Spring
	14084056	1	Below Spring

Fig. 6: Spring-to-Carrier Beam

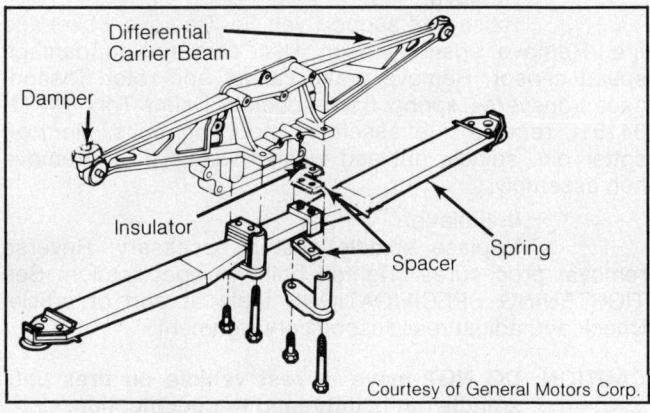

Courtesy of General Motors Corp.

KNUCKLE SUPPORT ROD

Removal

Raise and support vehicle. Scribe mark on cam bolt and mounting bracket for reassembly reference. See Fig. 3. Remove cam bolt. Separate knuckle support rod from mounting bracket. Remove knuckle support rod bolt at knuckle. Remove knuckle support rod.

Installation

Reverse removal procedures. Tighten bolts to specification. Bolt located at the knuckle must be tightened at proper "D" trim height. See steps 2) and 3) under INSTALLATION of REAR KNUCKLE. Check and adjust rear wheel alignment.

UPPER & LOWER CONTROL ARMS

Removal

Raise and support vehicle. Disconnect transverse spring from knuckle. Remove control arm bolt at knuckle. Remove control arm bolt at body bracket. Remove control arm. See Fig. 4.

CORVETTE (Cont.)

Installation

Reverse removal procedures for installation. Tighten all bolts to specification. The control arm bolts at the knuckle must be tightened at the proper "D" trim height. See steps **2)** and **3)** under INSTALLATION of REAR KNUCKLE.

REAR SHOCK ABSORBER

CAUTION: Shock absorbers may use oil and gas under high pressure. To avoid personal injury, due to explosion, do not apply heat or fire to shock absorbers.

Removal & Installation

Raise and support vehicle. Disconnect shock absorber at knuckle. Remove upper shock absorber retaining bolt. Remove shock absorber. Reverse removal procedures for installation. Tighten retaining nuts to specification.

REAR AXLE TIE ROD

Removal

Raise and support vehicle. Remove cotter pin and retaining nut from tie rod end at knuckle. Using Tie Rod Remover (J-24319-01), remove tie rod end from knuckle. Remove tie rod end from differential carrier beam. See Fig. 7.

Installation

Reverse removal procedures. Tighten bolts to specification. Check and adjust rear suspension alignment.

Fig. 7: Tie Rod Assembly

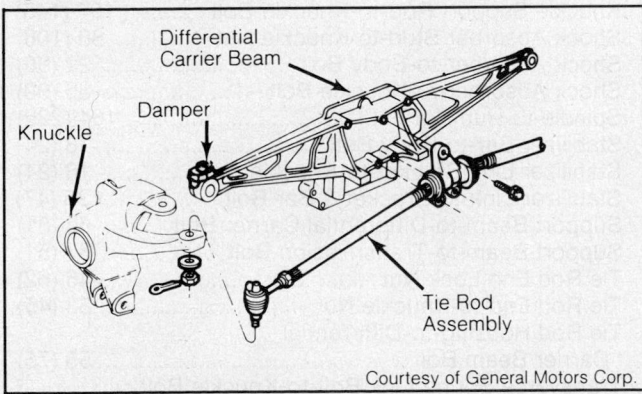

Courtesy of General Motors Corp.

STABILIZER BAR

Removal & Installation

Raise and support vehicle. Remove spare tire and carrier. Disconnect stabilizer bar from knuckles. Remove stabilizer bar bushing retainers, bushings and stabilizer bar from vehicle. See Fig. 8. Reverse removal procedures for installation. Tighten bolts to specification.

DRIVELINE SUPPORT

Removal

1) Raise and support vehicle. On convertible models, remove underbody braces. On all models, disconnect AIR pipe at the converter and AIR pipe clamps at exhaust pipe. Disconnect O$_2$ sensor lead.

2) On convertible models, remove exhaust hanger bolts at support. On all models, remove muffler hanger retaining bolts. Remove hanger bracket at convert-

Fig. 8: Rear Stabilizer Bar Assembly

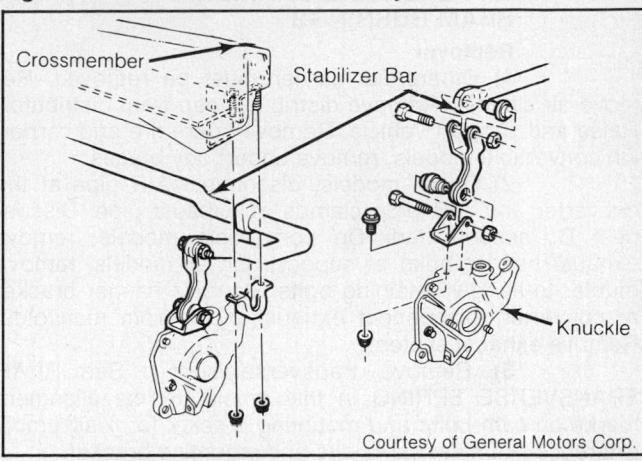

Courtesy of General Motors Corp.

er. Disconnect exhaust pipes from manifolds. Remove exhaust system.

3) Support transmission. Remove driveline support retaining bolts at differential carrier and transmission extension housing. Scribe mark on propeller shaft and axle yoke for reassembly reference. Remove propeller shaft. Pry between transmission and driveline support. Remove driveline support. See Fig. 9.

Installation

1) Reverse removal procedures. Align propeller shaft scribe marks. To ensure proper driveline alignment, a clearance of 1.52-2.02" (38.6-51.3 mm) must exist between top of support and the underbody.

2) A clearance of .85-1.35" (21.6-34.3 mm) must exist from the passenger's side of the support to the side wall. Measurements should be obtained directly above and to the right of propeller shaft front yoke. Apply sealant to mating surfaces of the transmission extension housing, differential carrier and support. Tighten bolts to specification.

NOTE: DO NOT overtighten driveline support to the transmission retaining bolts. Overtightening may cause transmission extension housing, bushing and seal damage, resulting in fluid leakage.

Fig. 9: Driveline Support Components

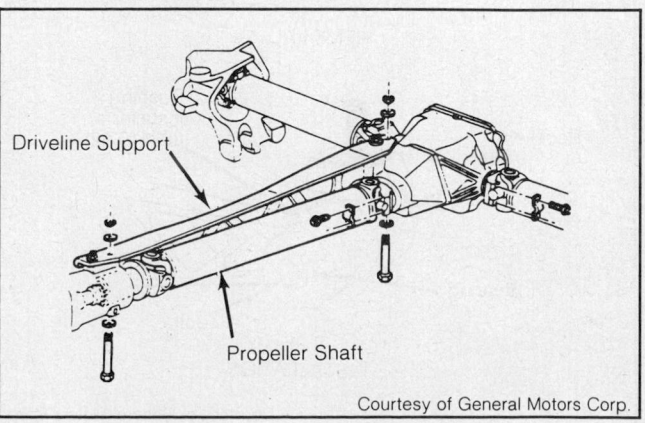

Courtesy of General Motors Corp.

DIFFERENTIAL CARRIER BEAM BUSHINGS

Removal

1) Differential carrier must be removed. Remove air cleaner. Remove distributor cap from distributor. Raise and support vehicle. Remove spare tire and carrier. On convertible models, remove underbody braces.

2) On all models, disconnect AIR pipe at the converter and AIR pipe clamps at exhaust pipe. Disconnect O_2 sensor lead. On convertible models, remove exhaust hanger bolts at support. On all models, remove muffler-to-hanger retaining bolts. Remove hanger bracket at converter. Disconnect exhaust pipes from manifolds. Remove exhaust system.

3) Remove transverse spring. See REAR TRANSVERSE SPRING in this article. Scribe alignment marks on cam bolts and mounting bracket for reassembly reference. Remove cam bolts and mounting bracket.

4) Disconnect tie rod ends at knuckles. Remove drive shafts from spindle yokes. Push wheel assemblies outward so drive shafts can be removed. Scribe mark on propeller shaft and axle yoke for reassembly reference. Disconnect propeller shaft and slide forward into transmission.

5) Support transmission. Remove differential carrier beam-to-frame retaining bolts. Remove driveline support retaining bolts at front of differential. Remove differential carrier assembly.

6) Install Receiver (J-34197-1), bolt, bearing and washer on flanged side of bushing (rear side). See Fig. 10. Install Bushing Remover (J-34197-3) over bolt until fully seated on front side of bushing. Install Long Nut (J-34197-5) on bolt. While holding long nut, tighten bolt until bushing is removed. See Fig. 10.

Fig. 10: Removing & Installing Differential Carrier Beam Bushings

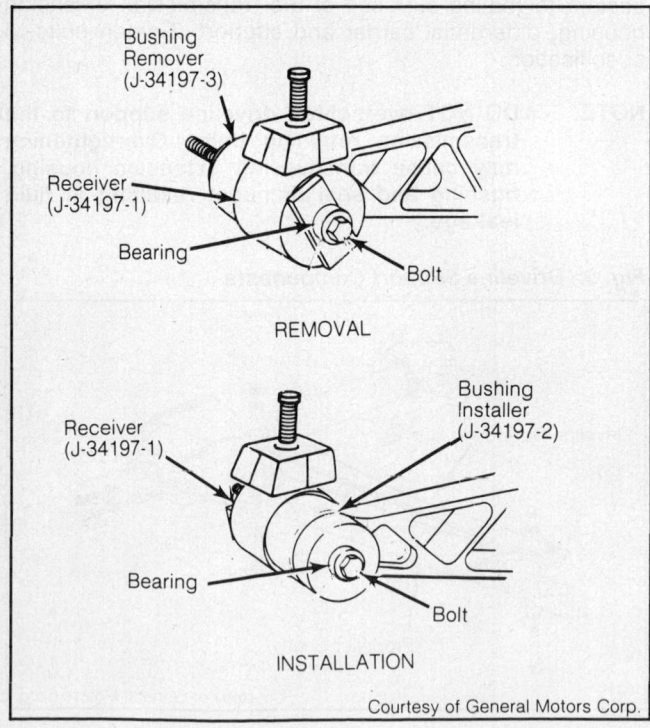

Courtesy of General Motors Corp.

Installation

1) Install bolt, bearing and washer on Bushing Installer (J-34197-2). Install assembly on flanged side of bushing. Install assembly on rear side of differential carrier beam. See Fig. 10.

2) Install Receiver (J-34197-1) on the bolt. Install Long Nut (J-34197-5) on bolt. While holding long nut, tighten bolt until bushing is even with differential carrier beam surface.

3) Reverse removal procedures for remaining components. Ensure scribe marks are aligned on propeller shaft. Check and adjust rear wheel alignment. Ensure proper clearance is maintained on driveline support. See INSTALLATION under DRIVELINE SUPPORT in this article. Tighten bolts to specification.

TIGHTENING SPECIFICATIONS

Application	Ft. Lbs. (N.m)
Cam Bolt-to-Support Rod	184 (250)
Control Rod-to-Body Bolt	63 (85)
Control Rod-to-Knuckle Bolt	[1] 140 (190)
Differential Carrier Beam-to-Body Bolt	100 (136)
Drive Shaft Retaining Straps-to-Side Gear Yoke Bolt	26 (35)
Drive Shaft Retaining Straps-to-Spindle Yoke Bolt	26 (35)
Hub-to-Knuckle Bolt	66 (90)
Jounce Bumper-to-Body Bolt	35 (47)
Knuckle Support Rod Bracket-to-Differential Carrier Bolt	60 (81)
Knuckle Support Rod-to-Knuckle Bolt	[1] 107 (145)
Shock Absorber Stud-to-Knuckle Nut	80 (108)
Shock Absorber-to-Body Bolt	22 (30)
Shock Absorber-to-Knuckle Bolt	66 (90)
Spindle-to-Hub Nut	164 (222)
Stabilizer Bar-to-Body Bolt	18 (24)
Stabilizer Link Bracket-to-Knuckle Bolt	18 (24)
Stabilizer Link-to-Bracket & Bar Bolt	[1] 35 (47)
Support Beam-to-Differential Carrier Bolt	60 (81)
Support Beam-to-Transmission Bolt	37 (51)
Tie Rod End Lock Nut	46 (62)
Tie Rod End-to-Knuckle Nut	33 (45)
Tie Rod Housing-to-Differential Carrier Beam Bolt	55 (75)
Transverse Spring Link Bolt-to-Knuckle Bolt	[2]
Transverse Spring-to-Differential Carrier Beam Bolt	37 (51)

[1] – Tighten with vehicle at proper "D" trim height.
[2] – Install nut to expose hole then insert cotter pin.

FIERO

DESCRIPTION

Rear suspension is MacPherson strut type. Strut lower end mounts to knuckle. Upper end mounts to body isolated through rubber bushings. Lateral control arm pivots on rubber bushings at engine cradle. A toe link rod, connecting knuckle to cradle, provides wheel alignment.

ADJUSTMENTS

CAMBER & TOE-IN

See appropriate article in WHEEL ALIGNMENT section.

RIDING HEIGHT

See RIDING HEIGHT SPECIFICATIONS article in WHEEL ALIGNMENT section.

REAR WHEEL BEARINGS

Rear wheel bearings are preadjusted and lubricated, requiring no routine maintenance or adjustment.

Fig. 1: Fiero Rear Suspension Assembly

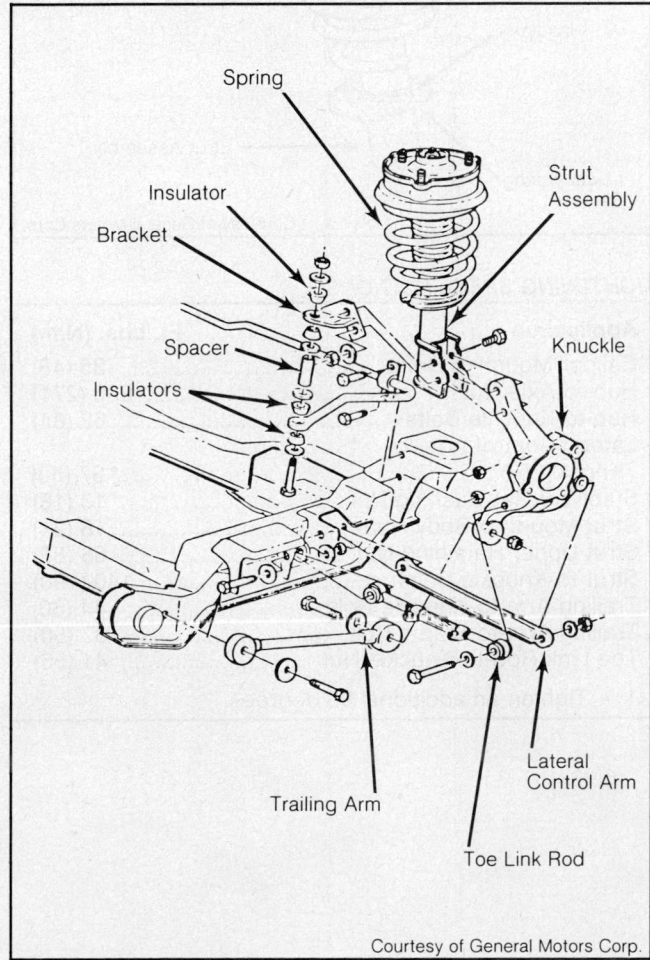

Spring

Insulator

Bracket

Spacer

Insulators

Strut Assembly

Knuckle

Trailing Arm

Lateral Control Arm

Toe Link Rod

Courtesy of General Motors Corp.

REMOVAL & INSTALLATION

HUB & BEARINGS
Removal

1) On vehicles with aluminum wheels, set parking brake and raise vehicle. Remove wheel and loosen hub nut. On vehicles with steel wheels, remove hub cap. Loosen hub nut. Raise vehicle and remove wheel.

2) On all vehicles, install Drive Axle Boot Protector (J-33162). Remove hub nut and discard. Remove brake caliper and rotor and wire out of work area. Remove hub and bearing attaching bolts, marking them for installation in their original locations. Ensure hub is loose in knuckle and use Hub Remover (J-28733-A) to remove hub assembly.

NOTE: **Do not move vehicle unless hub nut is tightened.**

Installation

1) If installing new bearing, replace knuckle seal using Installer (J-28671) and apply grease to seal and knuckle bore. Clean and inspect bearing mating surfaces and knuckle bore for dirt or scoring.

2) Install hub to axle and partially tighten (about 74 ft. lbs. or 100 N.m) new hub nut. To complete installation, reverse removal procedure. Tighten hub nut with wheels supporting vehicle.

KNUCKLE
Removal & Installation

1) Raise and support vehicle. Install Drive Axle Boot Protector (J-33162). Remove wheel and tire assembly. Remove and discard hub nut. Remove caliper and rotor. Wire caliper out of way. Disconnect trailing arm from knuckle.

2) Disconnect lateral control arm and strut from knuckle. Remove 2 strut-to-knuckle bolts. Remove knuckle. Remove hub and bearing from knuckle. To install, reverse removal procedure. Check wheel alignment.

MACPHERSON STRUT & COIL SPRING
Removal

1) Remove engine compartment cover. Remove 3 upper strut mounting nuts and washers. Loosen lug nuts. Raise vehicle and support rear control arm. Remove wheel and tire assemblies. Remove brake line clip. Install Axle Boot Protector (J-33162).

2) Scribe knuckle and strut for reinstallation. Remove 2 strut mounting nuts and bolts, noting their positions for reinstallation. Remove strut assembly and spacer plate. Install axle boot protector.

Disassembly

1) Place Clamp (J-34013-A) in Holding Fixture (J-3289-20). Place strut in Compressor Bottom Adapter (J-26584-89). Ensure locating pins engage. Place assembly in holding fixture. Rotate strut to align upper mount assembly lip with compressor support notch.

2) Insert Compressor Top Adapter (J-26584-450) on top spring seal. Position top adapter so that long stud is about 180 degrees from strut lower flange. *See Fig. 2.* Turn forcing screw clockwise until top support flange contacts Compressor Top Adapter (J-26584-450).

3) Place Compressor Top Adatper (J-26584-430) over spring seat. Reverse compressor screw to

Rear Suspension

FIERO (Cont.)

relieve spring tension. Remove top adapters, bottom adapter and strut.

Reassembly

1) With strut compressor clamped in vise, put strut in compressor bottom adapter. Ensure locating pins are engaged. Rotate strut until lower flange is opposite compressor screw. Seat spring on lower seat with smallest coil at lowest position and coil end about .55" (14 mm) from seat ridge.

2) Install dust shield, bumper, insulator, washer and upper seat. Position seat long stud about 180 degrees from strut mounting flange. *See Fig. 2.* Place Compresor Top Adapter (J-26584-450), over spring seat. Turn forcing screw until compressor top support contacts top adapters.

3) Install Strut Alignment Rod (J-26584-27) and thread hand tight onto strut damper shaft. Compress spring enough to install top nut. Do not over compress spring. Remove alignment rod and install strut upper mount, washer and nut. Relieve compressor tension and remove strut from compressor.

Installation

To install, reverse removal procedure. Align scribe marks on strut and knuckle. Replace nuts and bolts in the same order in which they were removed. Tighten nuts and bolts to specification.

Fig. 2: Strut Disassembly & Reassembly

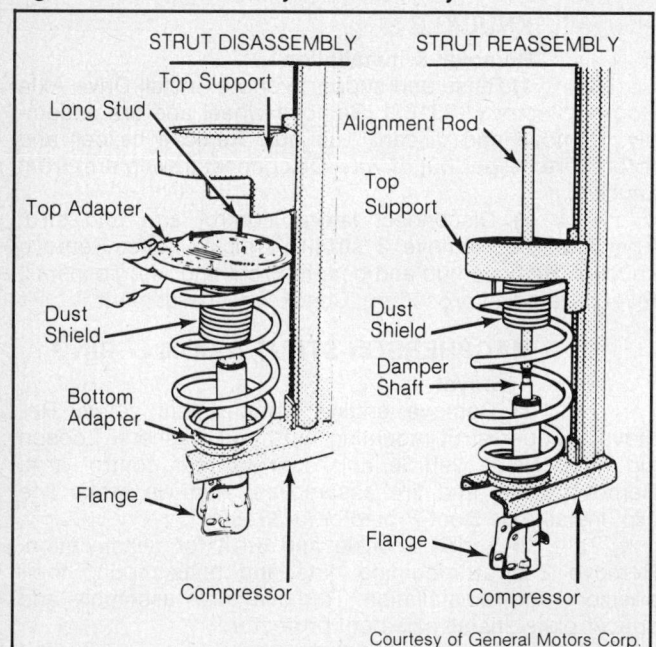

Courtesy of General Motors Corp.

Fig. 3: Exploded View of Strut Assembly

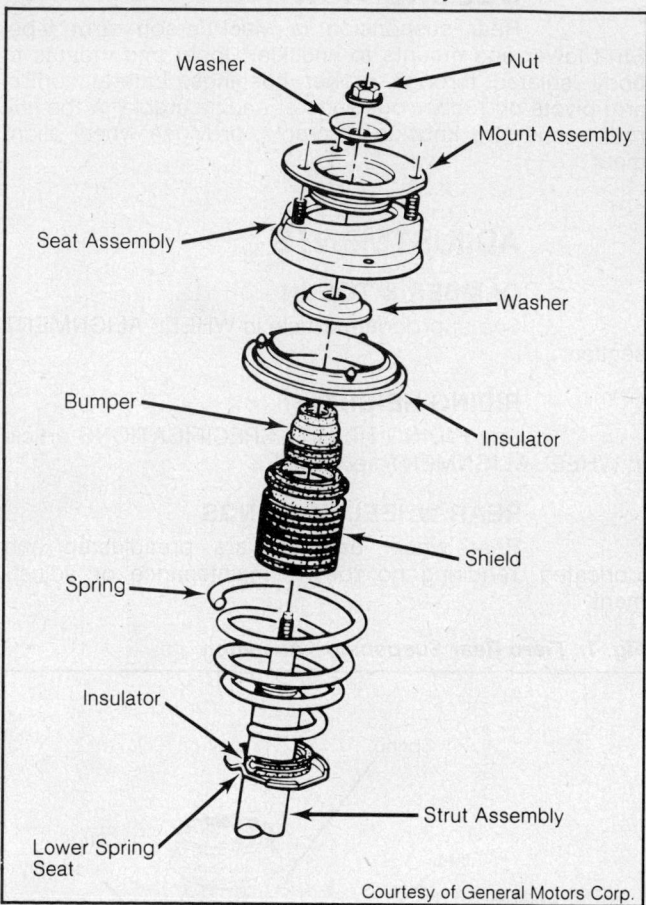

Courtesy of General Motors Corp.

TIGHTENING SPECIFICATIONS

Application	Ft. Lbs. (N.m)
Caliper Mounting Bolts	35 (48)
Hub-to-Axle Nut	200 (271)
Hub-to-Knuckle Bolts	62 (84)
Lateral Control Arm-to-Knuckle Bolt	[1] 37 (50)
Stabilizer Bar Bushing Nut	13 (18)
Strut Mount-to-Body Nuts	18 (24)
Strut Upper Retaining Nut	65 (88)
Strut-to-Knuckle Bolts	140 (190)
Trailing Arm-to-Knuckle Bolt	[1] 44 (60)
Trailing Arm-to-Frame Bolt	37 (50)
Toe Link Rod-to-Knuckle Nut	41 (56)

[1] – Tighten an additional 90 degrees.

DESCRIPTION

The rear suspension is a MacPherson strut independent type. Each side uses a coil spring mounted on a gas charged strut. Dual lower suspension arms, bearing and hub carrier along with a strut rod are also used on both sides. On models equipped with 4A-GE engine, a stabilizer bar helps eliminate vehicle sway.

ADJUSTMENTS

REAR WHEEL ALIGNMENT

See appropriate article in WHEEL ALIGNMENT section.

RIDING HEIGHT

See RIDING HEIGHT SPECIFICATIONS article in WHEEL ALIGNMENT section.

Fig. 1: Exploded View of Rear Suspension Assembly

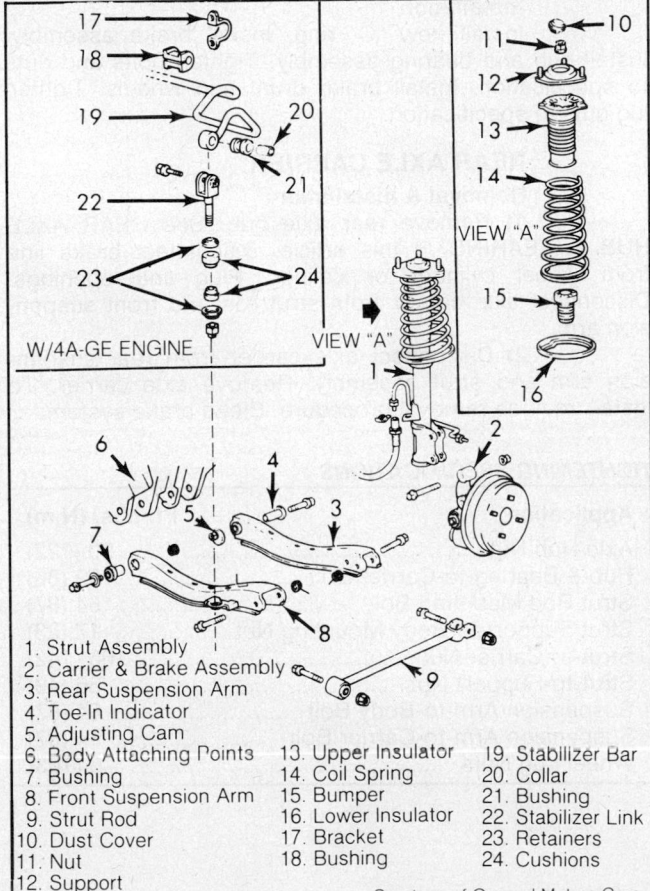

W/4A-GE ENGINE

VIEW "A"

1. Strut Assembly
2. Carrier & Brake Assembly
3. Rear Suspension Arm
4. Toe-In Indicator
5. Adjusting Cam
6. Body Attaching Points
7. Bushing
8. Front Suspension Arm
9. Strut Rod
10. Dust Cover
11. Nut
12. Support
13. Upper Insulator
14. Coil Spring
15. Bumper
16. Lower Insulator
17. Bracket
18. Bushing
19. Stabilizer Bar
20. Collar
21. Bushing
22. Stabilizer Link
23. Retainers
24. Cushions

Courtesy of General Motors Corp.

REMOVAL & INSTALLATION

STRUT & COIL SPRING

Removal

1) Remove quarter window garnish molding and back window panel. Remove rear wheel and tire assemblies. Disconnect brake line at flexible hose and plug line. Disconnect flexible hose from strut. Reconnect brake line to flexible hose to prevent excessive brake fluid loss.

2) Remove bolts holding strut-to-axle carrier. Remove suspension support-to-body nuts. Remove strut from vehicle.

Disassembly

Mount strut in Spring Compressor (J-34013). Compress strut spring until pressure on strut rod support nut is relieved. Remove the strut rod support nut. Slowly release tension from spring. Remove the suspension support, coil spring, insulator and bumper.

CAUTION: Strut is filled with high pressure gas. DO NOT disassemble the strut. If replacing the strut, drill a .079-.118" (2-3 mm) hole near the bottom of the strut to release the high pressure gas. Wear proper eye protection. DO NOT turn the piston rod in cylinder with the piston fully extended.

Reassembly

To assemble, reverse disassembly procedure. Ensure coil spring end is sitting in hollow. Ensure suspension support is aligned with lower strut bracket. *See Fig. 2.* Install new strut rod support nut and tighten to specification.

Installation

Disconnect brake line from the flexible hose. Install flexible hose on strut. Install brake line and bleed brakes. See HYDRAULIC BRAKE BLEEDING article in BRAKE section. To complete installation, reverse removal procedure. Check and adjust rear alignment as necessary.

Fig. 2: Aligning Suspension Support With Lower Strut Bracket

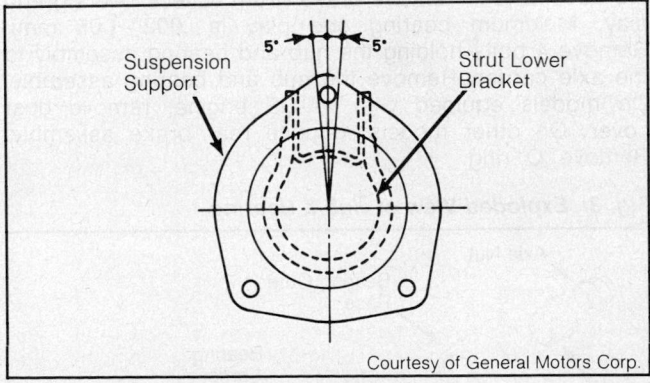

Suspension Support

5° 5°

Strut Lower Bracket

Courtesy of General Motors Corp.

REAR SUSPENSION ARM

Removal & Installation

1) Raise and support vehicle. Remove the bolt and nut holding the rear suspension arm to the axle carrier. Mark the cam plate for reassembly reference. Remove cam and bolt holding the rear suspension arm to the body and remove the suspension arm.

2) To install, reverse removal procedure. Tighten all nuts and bolts to specification. Lower vehicle before tightening control arm mounting bolts. Check and adjust rear wheel alignment as necessary.

FRONT SUSPENSION ARM

Removal & Installation

1) Raise and support vehicle. Disconnect stabilizer bar from front suspension arm (if equipped). Remove bolt and nut holding the front suspension arm to axle carrier. Remove bolt and nut holding front suspension arm to body. Remove the front suspension arm.

Rear Suspension

NOVA (Cont.)

2) To install, reverse removal procedure. Lower vehicle. Bounce vehicle to stabilize suspension. Tighten all nuts and bolts to specification. Check rear wheel alignment.

STRUT ROD

Removal

Raise vehicle. Remove nut and bolt holding strut rod to axle carrier. Remove nut and bolt holding strut rod to body. Remove the strut rod.

Installation

1) Connect strut rod to the body and tighten to specification. Connect the strut rod to axle carrier, but do not tighten mounting bolt.

2) Lower vehicle and bounce vehicle to stabilize the suspension. Tighten all nuts and bolts to specifications. Check and adjust rear wheel alignment as necessary.

STABILIZER BAR

Removal & Installation

1) Raise vehicle and suport. Remove tire and wheel. Disconnect stabilizer link from front suspension arm. Remove bolts retaining stabilizer bar to body.

2) Remove stabilizer bar from vehicle. Discard all stabilizer bolts and nuts. Use a sliding tee handle to remove collar (if necessary). Remove bushing by hand. To install, reverse removal procedure.

REAR AXLE HUB & BEARING

Removal

Raise and support vehicle. Remove wheel and tire assemblies. Remove brake drum. Check bearing end play. Maximum bearing end play is .002" (.05 mm). Remove 4 bolts holding the hub and bearing assembly to the axle carrier. Remove the hub and bearing assembly. On models equiped with 4A-GE engine, remove dust cover. On other models, remove rear brake assembly. Remove "O" ring.

Fig. 3: Exploded View of Hub & Bearing

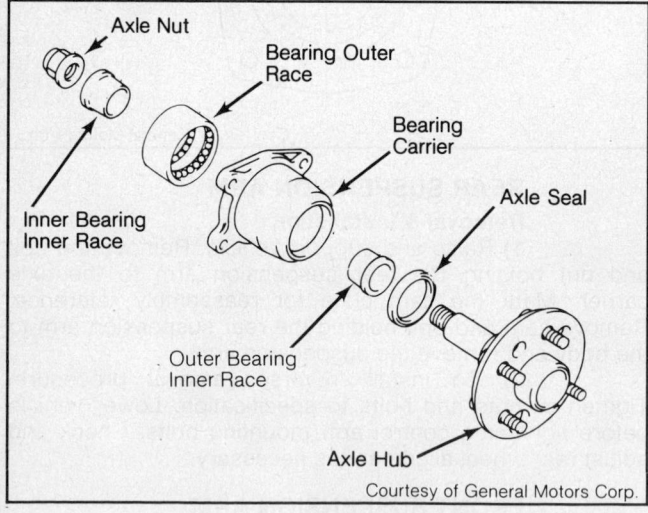

Courtesy of General Motors Corp.

Disassembly

1) Place hub and bearing assembly in a vise. Use jaw protectors to prevent damage to assembly. Remove hub nut. Using Puller (J-25287), remove bearing case from axle hub. Remove inner race, inner bearing and outer bearing.

2) Remove outer bearing inner race using a puller. Remove seal from axle hub. Press outer bearing race from the bearing case using the outer bearing inner race and Bearing Remover/Installer (J-35440).

NOTE: Always change complete bearing assembly whenever it is removed.

Reassembly

Lubricate outside of bearing outer race. Using Bearing Remover/Installer (J-35440), press new bearing outer race into bearing case. Lubricate and install new bearings and inner races into bearing case. Using Installer (J-35736), install new seal. Install bearing case on hub. Tighten nut to specification. Stake nut with a chisel.

Installation

Install new "O" ring. Install brake assembly. Install hub and bearing assembly. Tighten bolts and nuts to specification. Install brake drum and wheels. Tighten lug nuts to specification.

REAR AXLE CARRIER

Removal & Installation

1) Remove rear axle hub. See REAR AXLE HUB & BEARING in this article. Disconnect brake line from wheel cylinder or caliper. Plug line openings. Disconnect axle carrier from strut rod and front suspension arm.

2) Disconnect axle carrier from rear suspension arm and strut assembly. Removè axle carrier. To install, reverse removal procedure. Bleed brake system.

TIGHTENING SPECIFICATIONS

Application	Ft. Lbs. (N.m)
Axle Hub Nut	90 (122)
Hub & Bearing-to-Carrier Bolt	59 (80)
Strut Rod Mounting Bolt	64 (87)
Strut Support-to-Body Mounting Nut	17 (23)
Strut-to-Carrier Nut	105 (142)
Strut-to-Support Nut	36 (49)
Suspension Arm-to-Body Bolt	64 (87)
Suspension Arm-to-Carrier Bolt	64 (87)
Wheel Lug Nuts	76 (103)

CHRYSLER MOTORS REAR LEVEL CONTROL DYNASTY & NEW YORKER

NOTE: For Rear Level Control on New Yorker Turbo, see CHRYSLER MOTORS REAR LEVEL CONTROL ALL EXCEPT DYNASTY & NEW YORKER in this section.

DESCRIPTION & OPERATION

Rear level control system automatically adjusts rear height of vehicle, according to load. System consists of a compressor, control module, height sensor, air lines, relay, rear air shock absorbers, and air dryer.

As load is added or removed to rear of vehicle, height sensor, located on right rear shock absorber, sends a signal to the control module. Control module then opens ground circuit to compressor (to raise) or exhaust valve (to lower), located on compressor.

Height sensor signals control module when vehicle is at normal riding height. To prevent excess cycling between exhaust valve and compressor, control module has a 12-18 second delay between signal outputs. A residual of 10-22 psi (69-152 kPa) remains in system to improve ride under light load conditions.

TESTING

RESIDUAL AIR CHECK

1) Remove air line from air dryer and right rear shock absorber. Using 2 test pieces of nylon tubing, attach pressure gauge (0-300 psi) between shock absorber and air dryer. *See Fig. 1.*

2) A compression ball sleeve nut and sleeve for 3/16" tubing with ball sleeve connector and internal "T" fitting can be used as alternate way of attaching pressure gauge to system.

3) Cycle ignition off and on. Apply load of 300-325 lbs. (136-147 kg) to rear of vehicle. Compressor should operate and raise vehicle.

Fig. 1: Installing Pressure Gauge

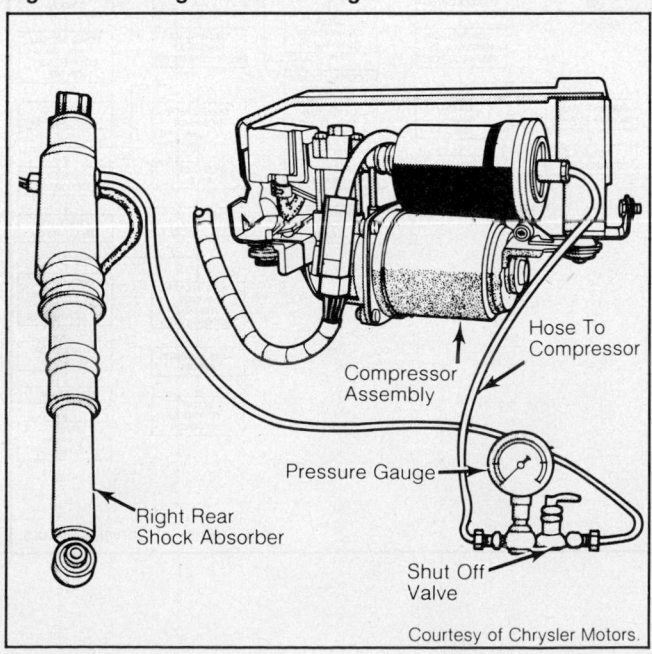

Compressor Assembly

Hose To Compressor

Pressure Gauge

Right Rear Shock Absorber

Shut Off Valve

Courtesy of Chrysler Motors.

4) When compressor stops operating, remove load. System should exhaust air. When no more air is exhausted, pressure gauge should read 10-22 psi (69-152 kPa). If pressure is not as specified, check for air leaks. If no air leak can be found, replace air dryer and retest.

LEAK CHECKS

1) Perform RESIDUAL AIR CHECK steps **1)**, **2)** and **3)** until pressure gauges reads 70-90 psi (483-621 kPa). DO NOT allow compressor to operate until it shuts down or exhaust valve will open resulting in leak down. This will indicate false air leak.

2) Unplug control module connector, located on right rear panel, inside luggage compartment. Remove load from vehicle. Vehicle should rise as load is removed. Turn ignition off. Observe pressure gauge reading for 15 minutes.

3) If system pressure drops or will not inflate more than 50 psi (345 kPa), check for leaks or pinched lines. Use a soapy solution to check for leaks. If system maintains pressure, see TROUBLE SHOOTING charts in this article.

COMPRESSOR PERFORMANCE TEST

1) Unplug compressor connector. Disconnect air line between air dryer and right shock absorber. Connect pressure gauge. See RESIDUAL AIR CHECK steps **1)** and **2)**. Connect an ammeter in series between Red wire terminal, at compressor, and 12-volt source. *See Fig. 2.*

2) Connect a jumper wire between Black wire terminal, at compressor, and known good ground. If current draw is more than 21 amps, replace compressor. If current draw is okay, disconnect wiring when system stabilizes at 120 psi (827 kPa).

3) If system leaks down below 90 psi (612 kPa) before it stabilizes or pressure is less than 110 psi (758 kPa) when it stabilizes, replace compressor. Do not allow system pressure to reach 220 psi (1517 kPa). If system reaches specified pressure, exhaust valve will open, allow air to escape. This can lead to false leak.

Fig. 2: Testing Compressor

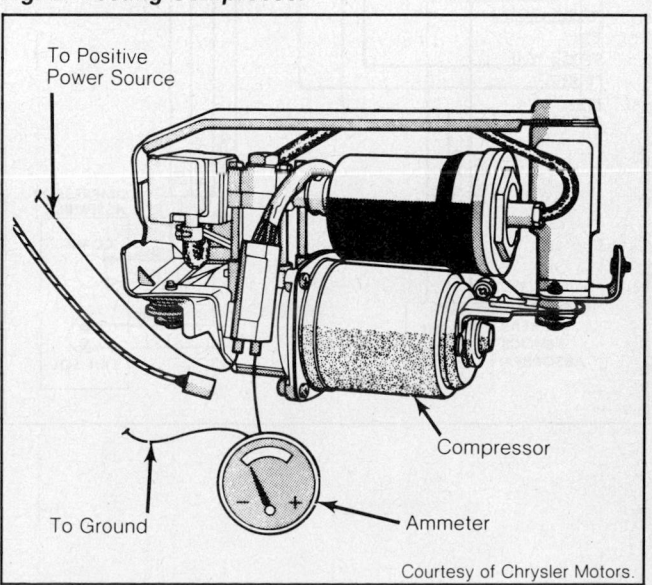

To Positive Power Source

Compressor

To Ground

Ammeter

Courtesy of Chrysler Motors.

Electronic Suspensions
CHRYSLER MOTORS REAR LEVEL CONTROL DYNASTY & NEW YORKER (Cont.)

REMOVAL & INSTALLATION

COMPRESSOR

Removal & Installation

1) Disconnect negative battery cable. Raise vehicle and support. Remove cover from compressor. Unplug electrical connectors from compressor.

2) Disconnect air line. Remove compressor from vehicle. Remove mounting bracket from compressor. To install, reverse removal procedure. Check system operation.

CONTROL MODULE & RELAY

Removal & Installation

Disconnect negative battery cable. Remove trim panel on right rear panel, inside luggage compartment. Unplug control module and relay connectors. Remove control module and relay. To install, reverse removal procedure. Check system operation.

RIGHT SHOCK ABSORBER & HEIGHT SENSOR

Removal & Installation

Disconnect negative battery cable. Raise vehicle and support. Remove right rear wheel and tire. Unplug height sensor connector, located on inside of frame rail. Disconnect air lines from shock absorber. Remove shock absorber. To install, reverse removal procedure.

TIGHTENING SPECIFICATIONS

Applications	Ft. Lbs. (N.m)
Lower Shock Absorber Nut	40 (54)
Upper Shock Absorber Nut	45 (61)

	INCH Lbs. (N.m)
Control Module Mounting Screws	19-29 (2-3)
Mounting Bracket-to-Compressor Screw	70 (8)
Mounting Bracket-to-Frame Rail Screw	70 (8)

Fig. 3: Electronic Height Control Wiring Diagram

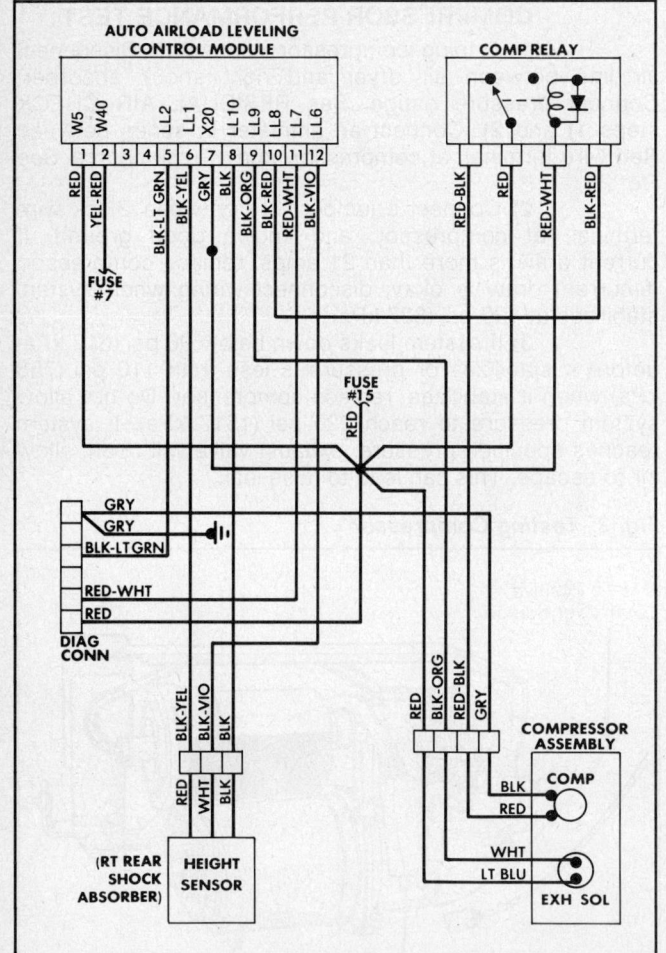

TROUBLE SHOOTING CHARTS

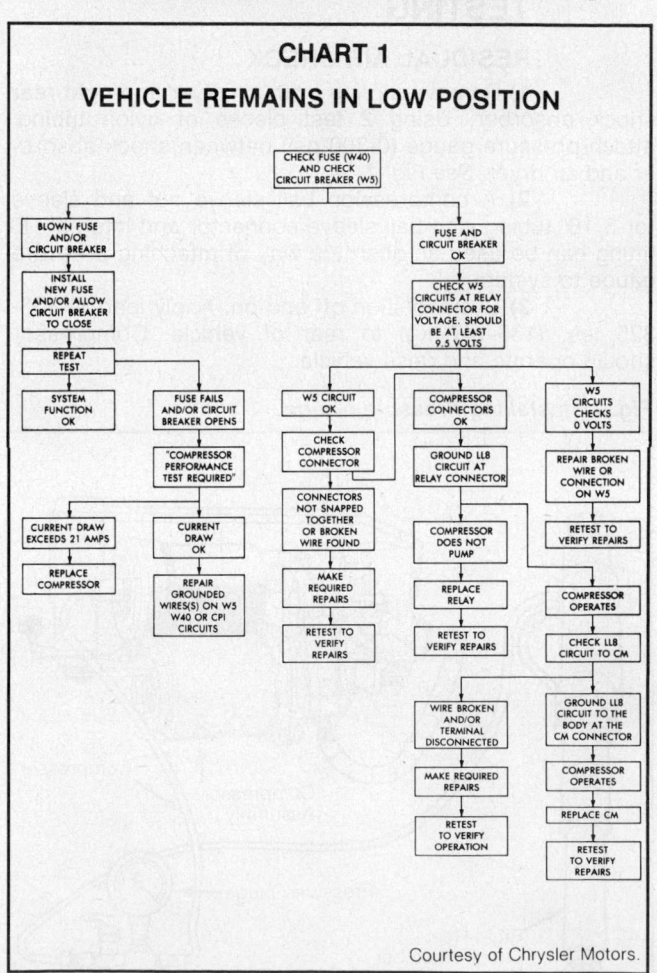

CHART 1

VEHICLE REMAINS IN LOW POSITION

Courtesy of Chrysler Motors.

CHRYSLER MOTORS REAR LEVEL CONTROL
DYNASTY & NEW YORKER (Cont.)

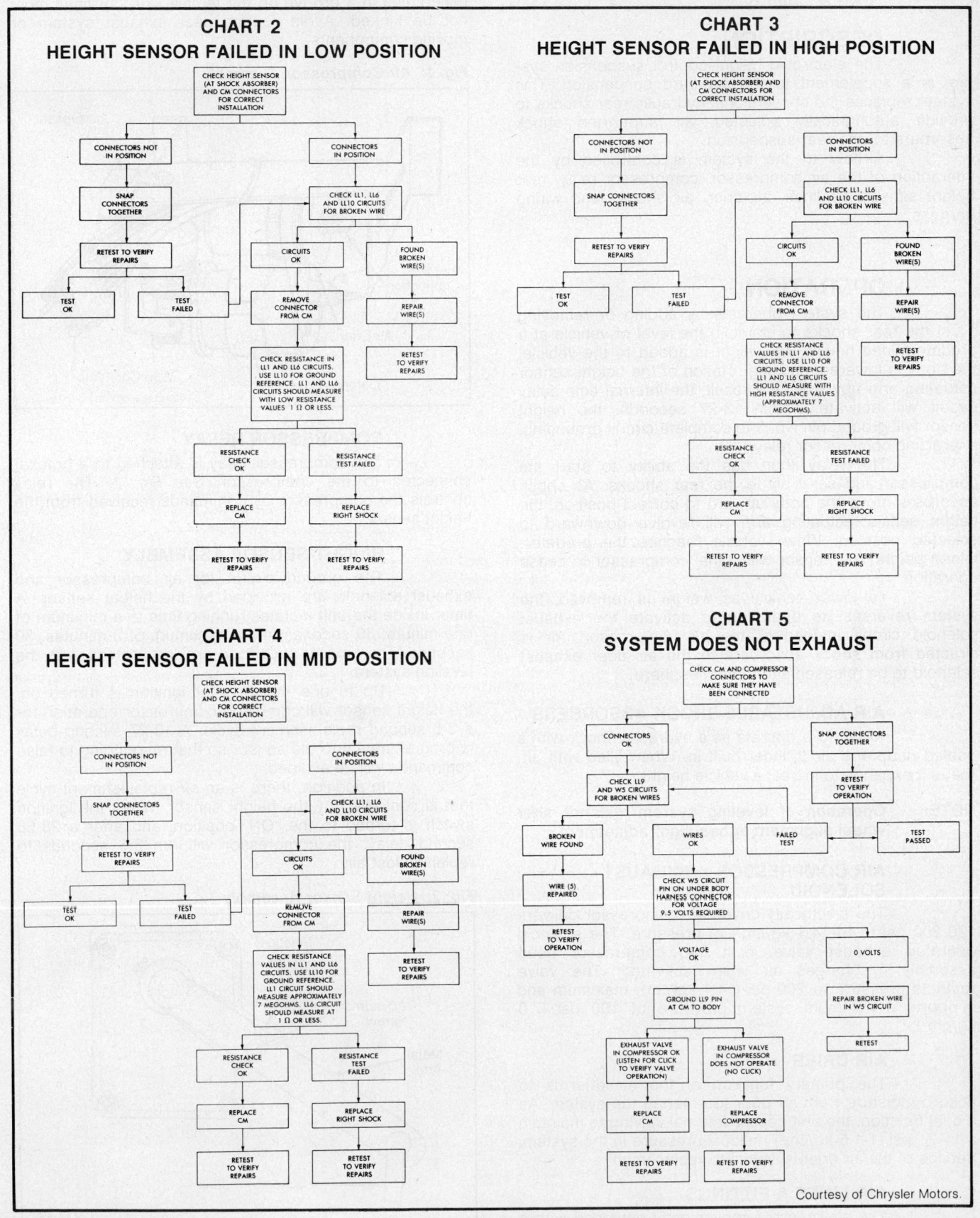

Courtesy of Chrysler Motors.

Electronic Suspensions

CHRYSLER MOTORS REAR LEVEL CONTROL
ALL EXCEPT DYNASTY & NEW YORKER

LeBaron, New Yorker Turbo,
Town & Country

DESCRIPTION

The electronic height control suspension system is a supplement to the standard suspension. This system replaces the conventional hydraulic rear shocks to provide automatically adjusted, air supported shock absorbers for the rear suspension.

Airflow to the system is controlled by the interaction of the air compressor, compressor relay, rear height sensor, air lines, air drier, air shocks and wiring harness.

OPERATION

The system operates by adding or removing air in the rear shocks to maintain the level of vehicle at a predetermined height. As weight is added to the vehicle, the body is lowered, causing rotation of the height sensor actuating arm upward. As a result, the internal time delay circuit will activate. Within 13-27 seconds, the height sensor will ground pin No. 3 to complete circuit grounding, energizing compressor relay.

The relay then has the ability to start the compressor and send air to the rear shocks. As shock absorbers move the body upward to correct position, the height sensor actuating arm will revolve downward to selected position. When vehicle reaches the predetermined height, the sensor will signal compressor to cease operation.

To lower vehicle as weight is removed, the system reverses its operation to activate the exhaust solenoid circuit instead of the air compressor. Air is directed from shock absorbers to the air drier exhaust solenoid to be released into the atmosphere.

AIR ADJUSTABLE SHOCK ABSORBERS

Air shocks operate as a hydraulic shock with a sealed neoprene air cylinder built in. When filled with air, the unit expands to increase vehicle height.

NOTE: Operation of leveling system will not alter wheel alignment or headlight adjustment.

AIR COMPRESSOR & EXHAUST SOLENOID

The electrically driven air compressor delivers 120-200 psi (8.44-14.1 kg/cm²) of pressure. The solenoid operated exhaust valve, built into compressor head assembly, discharges air when activated. The valve restricts pressure to 200 psi (14.1 kg/cm²) maximum and supports a minimum system pressure of 100 psi (7.0 kg/cm²).

AIR DRIER

The primary function of the air drier is to absorb moisture from air prior to entering the system. As a dual function, the unit applies internal valving to maintain a 14-21 psi (1-1.5 kg/cm²) residual pressure in the system. Service of the air drier is limited to replacement.

AIR LINES & FITTINGS

The air lines are conveniently equipped with a quick release on the male fittings. Double "O" rings are used for sealing and a spring retainer is used to lock the male fitting in a groove on the female side. Air lines must not be kinked. Avoid routing near exhaust system or moving components.

Fig. 1: Air Compressor Assembly

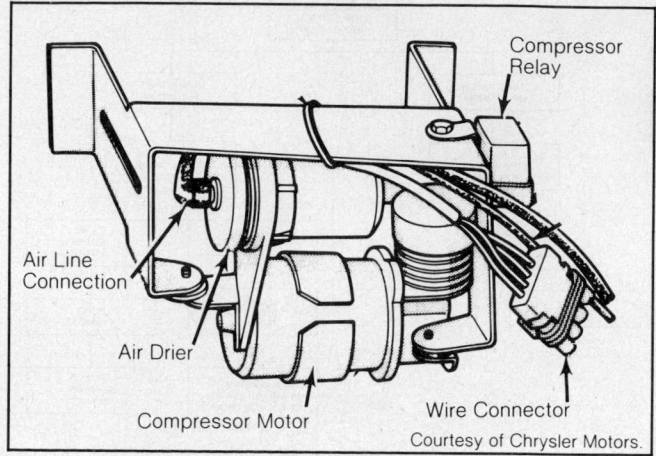

Courtesy of Chrysler Motors.

COMPRESSOR RELAY

The compressor relay is attached to a bracket connected to the compressor. See Fig. 1. The relay controls the compressor by commands received from the height sensor.

HEIGHT SENSOR ASSEMBLY

The ground circuit for air compressor and exhaust solenoid are provided by the height sensor. A timer inside the unit dictates running time to a minimum of one minute, 30 seconds and a maximum of 3 minutes, 30 seconds. The timer is built in to provide protection to the leveling system.

Up to one minute after ignition is turned on, the height sensor will command compressor operation for a 3-5 second replenishment cycle. A 13-27 second delay is programmed into the sensor so that responding to false commands will be avoided.

In addition, there is an air replenishment cycle that is controlled by the height sensor. When the ignition switch is turned to the "ON" position, and after a 28-56 second delay, the compressor will run 3-5 seconds to replenish lost air.

Fig. 2: Height Sensor Assembly

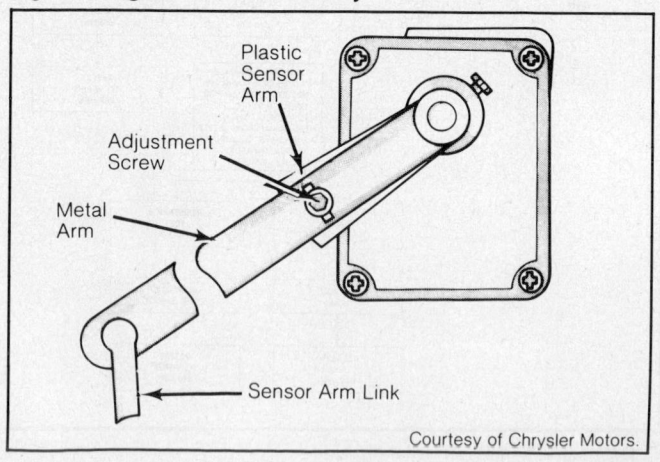

Courtesy of Chrysler Motors.

CHRYSLER MOTORS REAR LEVEL CONTROL
ALL EXCEPT DYNASTY & NEW YORKER (Cont.)

ADJUSTMENTS

CASTER & CAMBER

See appropriate article in WHEEL ALIGNMENT section.

HEIGHT OPERATIONAL CHECK

Cycle ignition switch from "OFF" to "ON" position. Raise vehicle and ensure height sensor is properly wired. Disconnect link from sensor arm and move up. After 13-27 seconds, shocks should start to inflate. After shocks are filled with air, move arm downward. There should be a 13-27 second delay before shocks begin to deflate.

HEIGHT ADJUSTMENT

1) On a level surface, turn ignition switch to the "ON" position. Load rear of vehicle with approximately 300 lbs. (136 kg) of weight. Vehicle should level out at 24-25 1/4" (610-641 mm). Which is measured from upper lip of rear wheel to level surface.

2) If adjustment is necessary, verify sensor arm link is attached securely. Loosen the plastic sensor arm adjusting screw. See Fig. 2. To increase vehicle curb height, adjust plastic sensor arm upward and tighten screw. Reverse procedure to lower vehicle height. Check for proper operation.

PRE-ALIGNMENT PROCEDURE

NOTE: Automatic Leveling System must be functioning correctly with system fully charged before wheel alignment adjustment is attempted.

1) Position vehicle on alignment rack and prepare equipment as necessary. With vehicle properly centered, turn ignition off and exit vehicle.

2) From outside vehicle, through driver's window, turn ignition switch to the "ON" position. With vehicle prepared for alignment adjustment, allow 2 minutes for settling.

3) Avoid any application of weight to vehicle while turning ignition off. Verify steering wheel is unlocked for caster sweep and proceed with alignment.

NOTE: If steering wheel cannot be unlocked with ignition off, disconnect negative battery cable and turn ignition on.

DIAGNOSIS & TESTING

COMPRESSOR PERFORMANCE TEST

1) Unplug compressor connector. Disconnect air line from "T" connector, located on frame rail. Connect an air pressure gauge in air line between compressor and "T" connector. See Fig. 3.

2) Connect an ammeter in series between Orange wire in compressor harness connector, and Dark Green wire in compressor connector. See Fig. 4. Connect an jumper wire between Black wire in compressor connector and a known good ground. Turn ignition on.

3) If current draw exceeds 14 amps, replace compressor. If current draw is okay, disconnect positive wire when pressure gauge reading stabilizes at 120 psi

(827 kPa). If air pressure leaks down to 90 psi (621 kPa) or output presure is less than 110 psi (758 kPa), replace compressor.

4) Do not allow compressor to build up pressure to 200 psi (1379 kPa). If pressure exceeds specification, exhaust valve will open after compressor turns off, resulting in a false leak.

Fig. 3: Pressure Gauge Test Connections

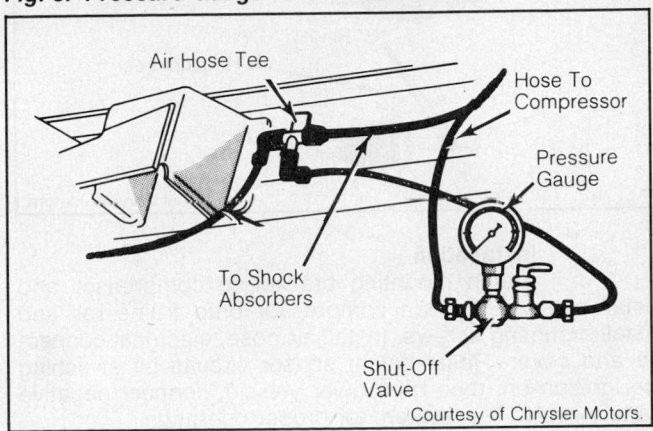

Courtesy of Chrysler Motors.

Fig. 4: Compressor Current Draw Test Connections

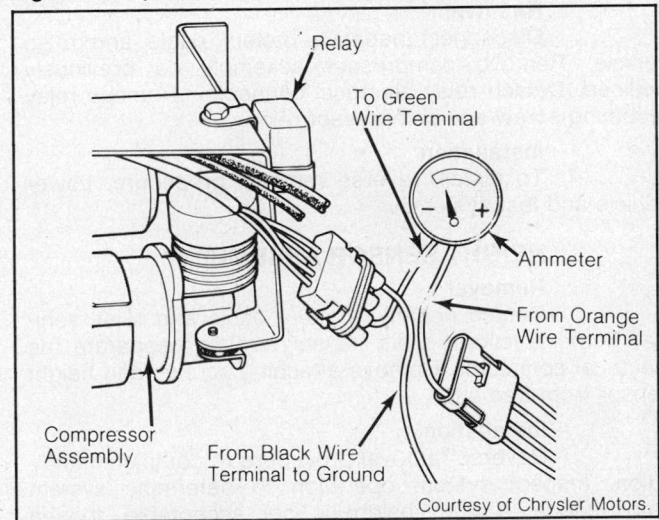

Courtesy of Chrysler Motors.

REMOVAL & INSTALLATION

AIR ADJUSTABLE SHOCK ABSORBERS

Air shock removal and installation is the same as hydraulic shock service procedure, except that air line removal is required. See Fig. 5. See CHRYSLER CORP. FWD REAR SUSPENSION article in this section.

COMPRESSOR ASSEMBLY

Removal

1) Detach negative battery cable. Raise vehicle to remove cover from compressor housing. Discharge system to remove electrical connections and air hoses.

2) Remove compressor mounting screws and separate compressor from vehicle. Remove mounting bracket by detaching screws and sliding assembly away from compressor.

Electronic Suspensions

CHRYSLER MOTORS REAR LEVEL CONTROL ALL EXCEPT DYNASTY & NEW YORKER (Cont.)

Fig. 5: Air Hose Fitting Removal & Installation.

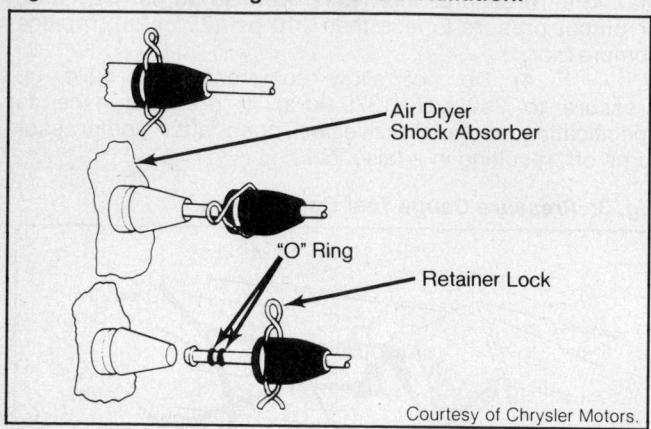

Courtesy of Chrysler Motors.

Installation

Attach mounting bracket to compressor and install screws. Position compressor onto frame rail and install mounting screws. Install air hose, electrical connector and cover. Reset height sensor circuits by switching the ignition on, then off. Lower vehicle, connect negative battery cable. Test system for proper operation.

COMPRESSOR RELAY

Removal

Disconnect negative battery cable and raise vehicle. Remove compressor assembly as previously outlined. Detach relay electrical connector. Remove relay mounting screw and compressor relay.

Installation

To install, reverse removal procedure. Lower vehicle and test system.

HEIGHT SENSOR ASSEMBLY

Removal

Detach negative battery cable and raise vehicle. Remove linkage from sensor arm and separate the electrical connector. Remove attaching screws and height sensor from frame rail.

Installation

Reverse removal procedure to complete installation. Inspect system operation to determine system performance. If curb height is not acceptable, loosen sensor lock nut and adjust plastic arm for correct height. Move plastic arm upward to increase height and downward to decrease height.

Fig. 6: Automatic Leveling System Electrical Diagram

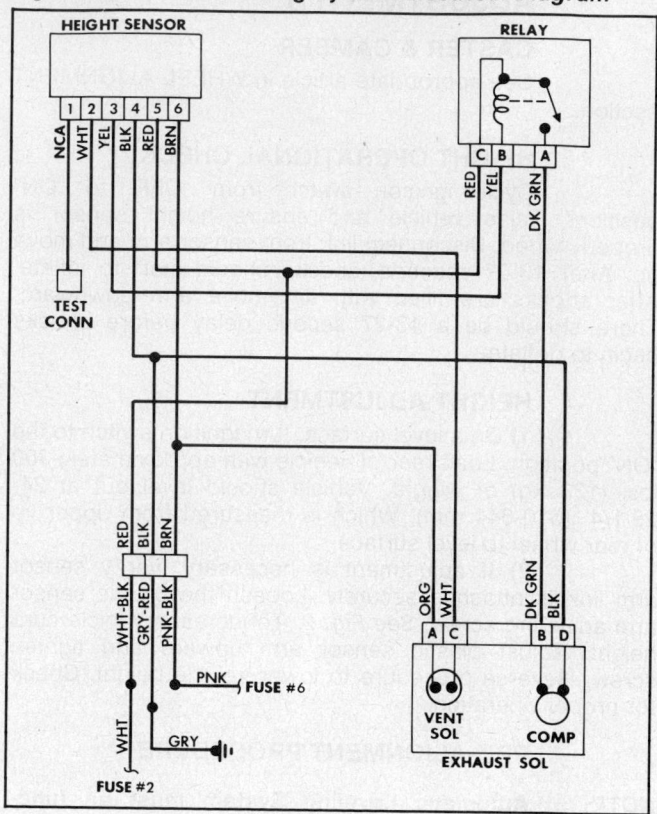

TIGHTENING SPECIFICATIONS

Application	Ft. Lbs. (N.m)
Lower Shock Mounting Bolts	45 (61)
Upper Shock Mounting Bolts	45 (61)

	INCH Lbs. (N.m)
Compressor-to-Frame Screws	70 (8)
Compressor Housing Cover Screws	70 (8)
Compresor Relay Retaining Screw	55 (6)
Height Sensor Linkage Screw	55 (6)
Height Sensor Mounting Screws	55 (6)

Electronic Suspensions
CHRYSLER MOTORS REAR LEVEL CONTROL
ALL EXCEPT DYNASTY & NEW YORKER (Cont.)

CHART 1
COMPRESSOR INOPERATIVE – CAR LOW

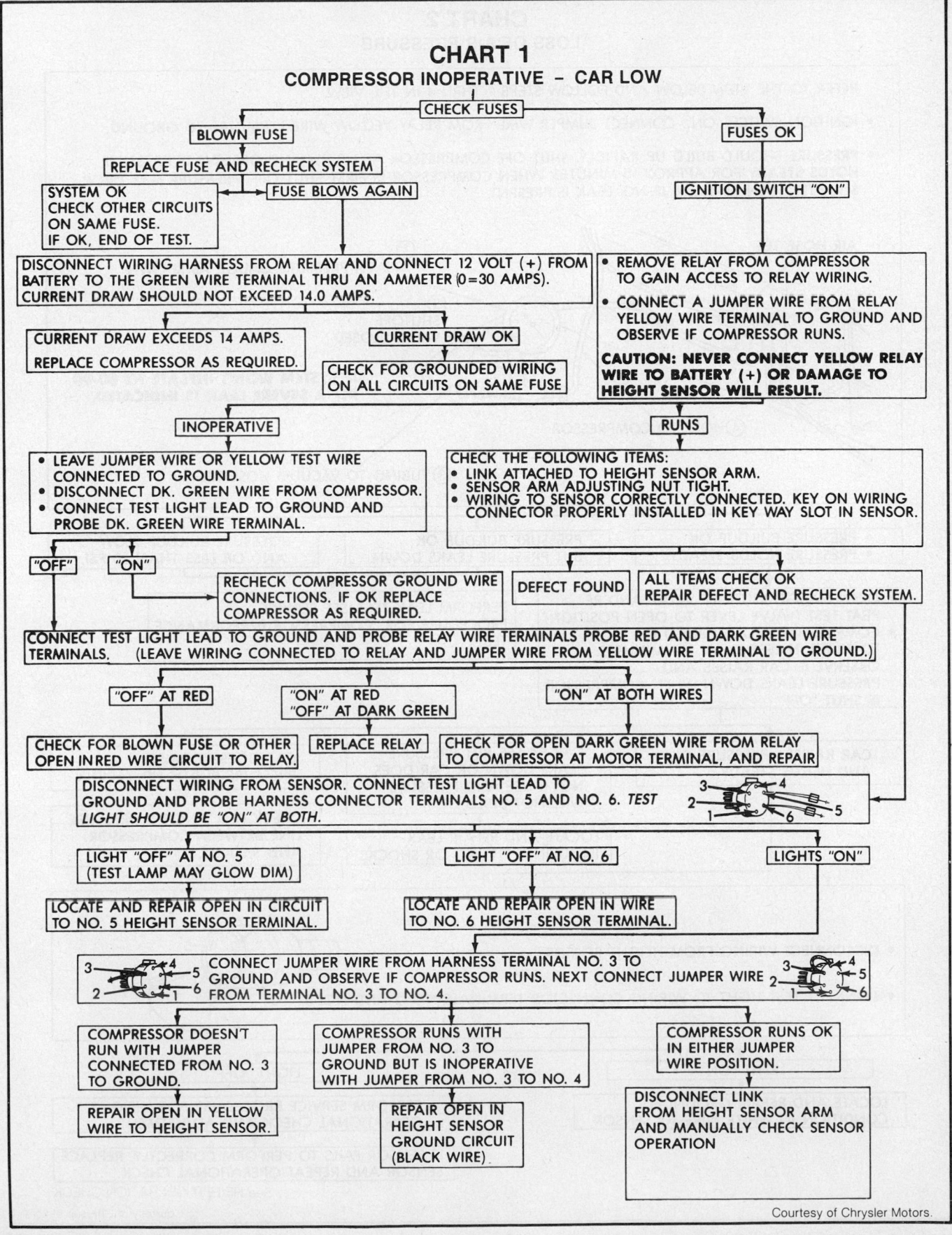

CHECK FUSES

BLOWN FUSE

REPLACE FUSE AND RECHECK SYSTEM

SYSTEM OK
CHECK OTHER CIRCUITS ON SAME FUSE. IF OK, END OF TEST.

FUSE BLOWS AGAIN

DISCONNECT WIRING HARNESS FROM RELAY AND CONNECT 12 VOLT (+) FROM BATTERY TO THE GREEN WIRE TERMINAL THRU AN AMMETER (0=30 AMPS). CURRENT DRAW SHOULD NOT EXCEED 14.0 AMPS.

CURRENT DRAW EXCEEDS 14 AMPS. REPLACE COMPRESSOR AS REQUIRED.

CURRENT DRAW OK

CHECK FOR GROUNDED WIRING ON ALL CIRCUITS ON SAME FUSE

FUSES OK

IGNITION SWITCH "ON"

- REMOVE RELAY FROM COMPRESSOR TO GAIN ACCESS TO RELAY WIRING.
- CONNECT A JUMPER WIRE FROM RELAY YELLOW WIRE TERMINAL TO GROUND AND OBSERVE IF COMPRESSOR RUNS.

CAUTION: NEVER CONNECT YELLOW RELAY WIRE TO BATTERY (+) OR DAMAGE TO HEIGHT SENSOR WILL RESULT.

INOPERATIVE

- LEAVE JUMPER WIRE OR YELLOW TEST WIRE CONNECTED TO GROUND.
- DISCONNECT DK. GREEN WIRE FROM COMPRESSOR.
- CONNECT TEST LIGHT LEAD TO GROUND AND PROBE DK. GREEN WIRE TERMINAL.

RUNS

CHECK THE FOLLOWING ITEMS:
- LINK ATTACHED TO HEIGHT SENSOR ARM.
- SENSOR ARM ADJUSTING NUT TIGHT.
- WIRING TO SENSOR CORRECTLY CONNECTED. KEY ON WIRING CONNECTOR PROPERLY INSTALLED IN KEY WAY SLOT IN SENSOR.

"OFF"   **"ON"**

RECHECK COMPRESSOR GROUND WIRE CONNECTIONS. IF OK REPLACE COMPRESSOR AS REQUIRED.

DEFECT FOUND

ALL ITEMS CHECK OK REPAIR DEFECT AND RECHECK SYSTEM.

CONNECT TEST LIGHT LEAD TO GROUND AND PROBE RELAY WIRE TERMINALS PROBE RED AND DARK GREEN WIRE TERMINALS. (LEAVE WIRING CONNECTED TO RELAY AND JUMPER WIRE FROM YELLOW WIRE TERMINAL TO GROUND.)

"OFF" AT RED

"ON" AT RED "OFF" AT DARK GREEN

"ON" AT BOTH WIRES

CHECK FOR BLOWN FUSE OR OTHER OPEN IN RED WIRE CIRCUIT TO RELAY.

REPLACE RELAY

CHECK FOR OPEN DARK GREEN WIRE FROM RELAY TO COMPRESSOR AT MOTOR TERMINAL, AND REPAIR

DISCONNECT WIRING FROM SENSOR. CONNECT TEST LIGHT LEAD TO GROUND AND PROBE HARNESS CONNECTOR TERMINALS NO. 5 AND NO. 6. *TEST LIGHT SHOULD BE "ON" AT BOTH.*

LIGHT "OFF" AT NO. 5 (TEST LAMP MAY GLOW DIM)

LIGHT "OFF" AT NO. 6

LIGHTS "ON"

LOCATE AND REPAIR OPEN IN CIRCUIT TO NO. 5 HEIGHT SENSOR TERMINAL.

LOCATE AND REPAIR OPEN IN WIRE TO NO. 6 HEIGHT SENSOR TERMINAL.

CONNECT JUMPER WIRE FROM HARNESS TERMINAL NO. 3 TO GROUND AND OBSERVE IF COMPRESSOR RUNS. NEXT CONNECT JUMPER WIRE FROM TERMINAL NO. 3 TO NO. 4.

COMPRESSOR DOESN'T RUN WITH JUMPER CONNECTED FROM NO. 3 TO GROUND.

COMPRESSOR RUNS WITH JUMPER FROM NO. 3 TO GROUND BUT IS INOPERATIVE WITH JUMPER FROM NO. 3 TO NO. 4.

COMPRESSOR RUNS OK IN EITHER JUMPER WIRE POSITION.

REPAIR OPEN IN YELLOW WIRE TO HEIGHT SENSOR.

REPAIR OPEN IN HEIGHT SENSOR GROUND CIRCUIT (BLACK WIRE).

DISCONNECT LINK FROM HEIGHT SENSOR ARM AND MANUALLY CHECK SENSOR OPERATION

Electronic Suspensions
CHRYSLER MOTORS REAR LEVEL CONTROL
ALL EXCEPT DYNASTY & NEW YORKER (Cont.)

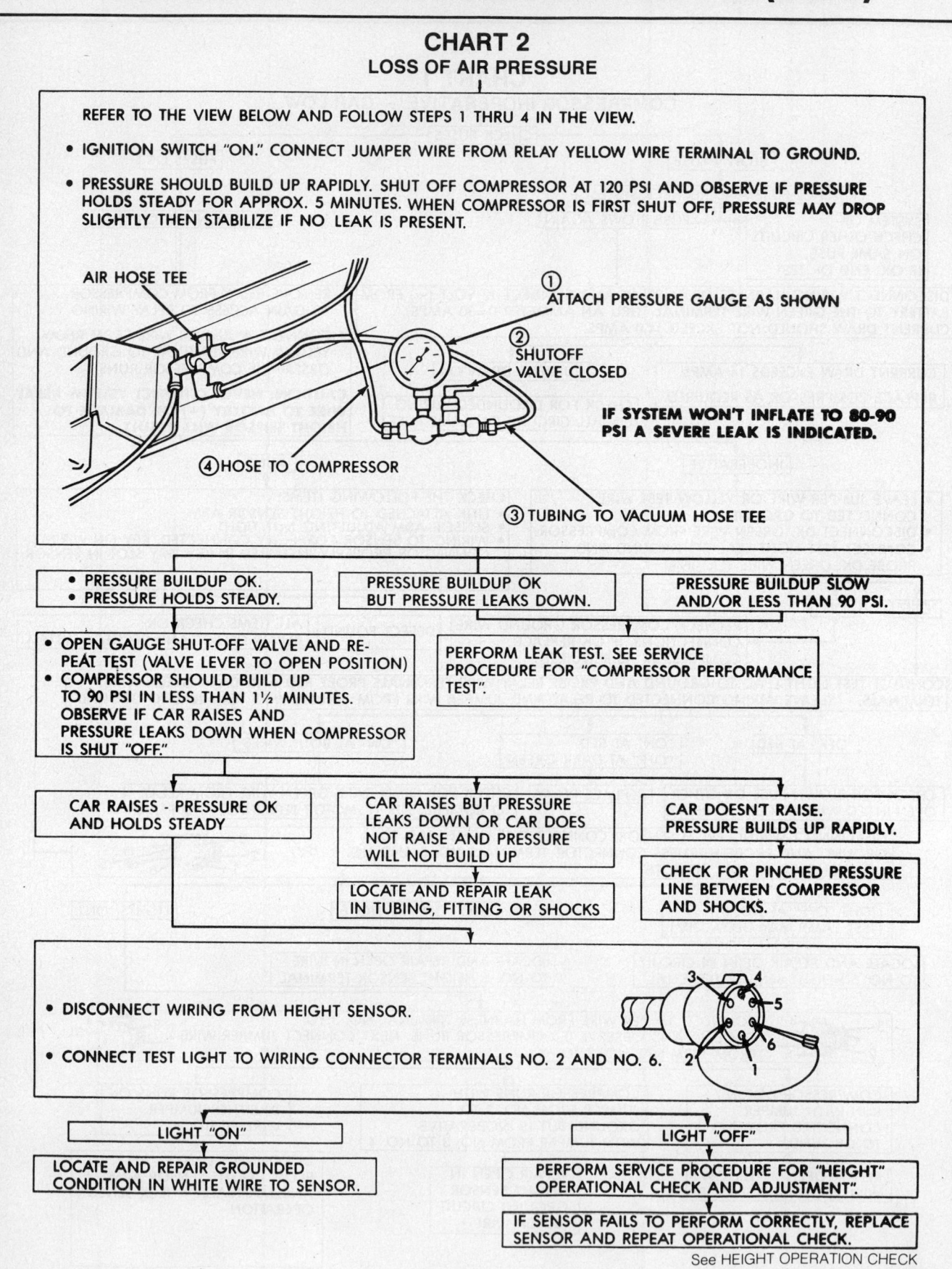

CHART 2
LOSS OF AIR PRESSURE

REFER TO THE VIEW BELOW AND FOLLOW STEPS 1 THRU 4 IN THE VIEW.

- IGNITION SWITCH "ON." CONNECT JUMPER WIRE FROM RELAY YELLOW WIRE TERMINAL TO GROUND.

- PRESSURE SHOULD BUILD UP RAPIDLY. SHUT OFF COMPRESSOR AT 120 PSI AND OBSERVE IF PRESSURE HOLDS STEADY FOR APPROX. 5 MINUTES. WHEN COMPRESSOR IS FIRST SHUT OFF, PRESSURE MAY DROP SLIGHTLY THEN STABILIZE IF NO LEAK IS PRESENT.

AIR HOSE TEE

① ATTACH PRESSURE GAUGE AS SHOWN

② SHUTOFF VALVE CLOSED

IF SYSTEM WON'T INFLATE TO 80-90 PSI A SEVERE LEAK IS INDICATED.

④ HOSE TO COMPRESSOR

③ TUBING TO VACUUM HOSE TEE

• PRESSURE BUILDUP OK. • PRESSURE HOLDS STEADY.	PRESSURE BUILDUP OK BUT PRESSURE LEAKS DOWN.	PRESSURE BUILDUP SLOW AND/OR LESS THAN 90 PSI.

- OPEN GAUGE SHUT-OFF VALVE AND RE-PEAT TEST (VALVE LEVER TO OPEN POSITION)
- COMPRESSOR SHOULD BUILD UP TO 90 PSI IN LESS THAN 1½ MINUTES. OBSERVE IF CAR RAISES AND PRESSURE LEAKS DOWN WHEN COMPRESSOR IS SHUT "OFF."

PERFORM LEAK TEST. SEE SERVICE PROCEDURE FOR "COMPRESSOR PERFORMANCE TEST".

CAR RAISES - PRESSURE OK AND HOLDS STEADY	CAR RAISES BUT PRESSURE LEAKS DOWN OR CAR DOES NOT RAISE AND PRESSURE WILL NOT BUILD UP	CAR DOESN'T RAISE. PRESSURE BUILDS UP RAPIDLY.

LOCATE AND REPAIR LEAK IN TUBING, FITTING OR SHOCKS

CHECK FOR PINCHED PRESSURE LINE BETWEEN COMPRESSOR AND SHOCKS.

- DISCONNECT WIRING FROM HEIGHT SENSOR.

- CONNECT TEST LIGHT TO WIRING CONNECTOR TERMINALS NO. 2 AND NO. 6.

LIGHT "ON"	LIGHT "OFF"
LOCATE AND REPAIR GROUNDED CONDITION IN WHITE WIRE TO SENSOR.	PERFORM SERVICE PROCEDURE FOR "HEIGHT" OPERATIONAL CHECK AND ADJUSTMENT".

IF SENSOR FAILS TO PERFORM CORRECTLY, REPLACE SENSOR AND REPEAT OPERATIONAL CHECK.

See HEIGHT OPERATION CHECK

Courtesy of Chrysler Motors.

Electronic Suspensions
CHRYSLER MOTORS REAR LEVEL CONTROL
ALL EXCEPT DYNASTY & NEW YORKER (Cont.)

CHART 3
CAR STAYS HIGH WITH LOAD REMOVED

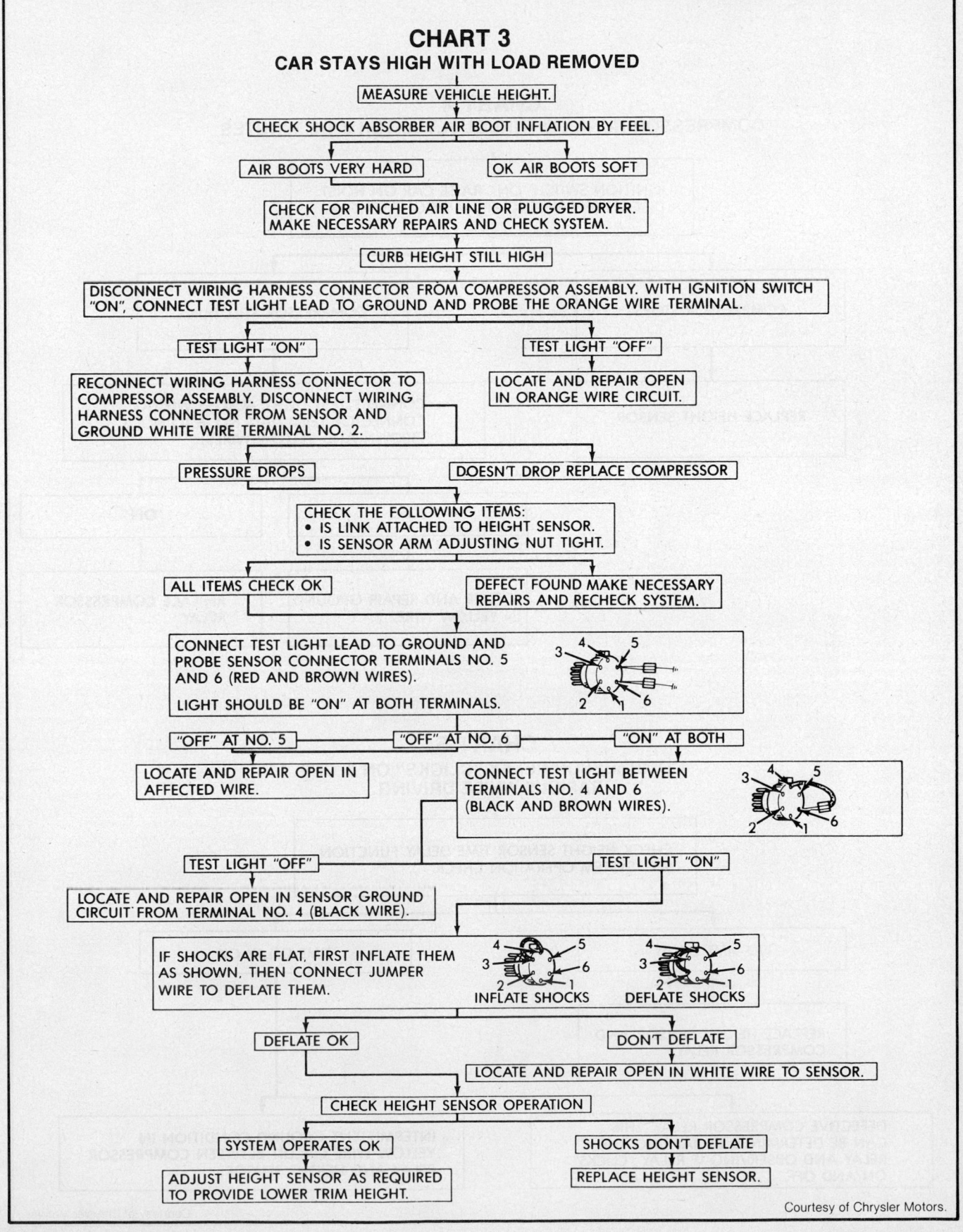

MEASURE VEHICLE HEIGHT.

CHECK SHOCK ABSORBER AIR BOOT INFLATION BY FEEL.

AIR BOOTS VERY HARD | OK AIR BOOTS SOFT

CHECK FOR PINCHED AIR LINE OR PLUGGED DRYER. MAKE NECESSARY REPAIRS AND CHECK SYSTEM.

CURB HEIGHT STILL HIGH

DISCONNECT WIRING HARNESS CONNECTOR FROM COMPRESSOR ASSEMBLY. WITH IGNITION SWITCH "ON", CONNECT TEST LIGHT LEAD TO GROUND AND PROBE THE ORANGE WIRE TERMINAL.

TEST LIGHT "ON" | TEST LIGHT "OFF"

RECONNECT WIRING HARNESS CONNECTOR TO COMPRESSOR ASSEMBLY. DISCONNECT WIRING HARNESS CONNECTOR FROM SENSOR AND GROUND WHITE WIRE TERMINAL NO. 2.

LOCATE AND REPAIR OPEN IN ORANGE WIRE CIRCUIT.

PRESSURE DROPS | DOESN'T DROP REPLACE COMPRESSOR

CHECK THE FOLLOWING ITEMS:
• IS LINK ATTACHED TO HEIGHT SENSOR.
• IS SENSOR ARM ADJUSTING NUT TIGHT.

ALL ITEMS CHECK OK | DEFECT FOUND MAKE NECESSARY REPAIRS AND RECHECK SYSTEM.

CONNECT TEST LIGHT LEAD TO GROUND AND PROBE SENSOR CONNECTOR TERMINALS NO. 5 AND 6 (RED AND BROWN WIRES).

LIGHT SHOULD BE "ON" AT BOTH TERMINALS.

"OFF" AT NO. 5 | "OFF" AT NO. 6 | "ON" AT BOTH

LOCATE AND REPAIR OPEN IN AFFECTED WIRE.

CONNECT TEST LIGHT BETWEEN TERMINALS NO. 4 AND 6 (BLACK AND BROWN WIRES).

TEST LIGHT "OFF" | TEST LIGHT "ON"

LOCATE AND REPAIR OPEN IN SENSOR GROUND CIRCUIT FROM TERMINAL NO. 4 (BLACK WIRE).

IF SHOCKS ARE FLAT, FIRST INFLATE THEM AS SHOWN, THEN CONNECT JUMPER WIRE TO DEFLATE THEM.

INFLATE SHOCKS | DEFLATE SHOCKS

DEFLATE OK | DON'T DEFLATE

LOCATE AND REPAIR OPEN IN WHITE WIRE TO SENSOR.

CHECK HEIGHT SENSOR OPERATION

SYSTEM OPERATES OK | SHOCKS DON'T DEFLATE

ADJUST HEIGHT SENSOR AS REQUIRED TO PROVIDE LOWER TRIM HEIGHT.

REPLACE HEIGHT SENSOR.

Courtesy of Chrysler Motors.

Electronic Suspensions
CHRYSLER MOTORS REAR LEVEL CONTROL
ALL EXCEPT DYNASTY & NEW YORKER (Cont.)

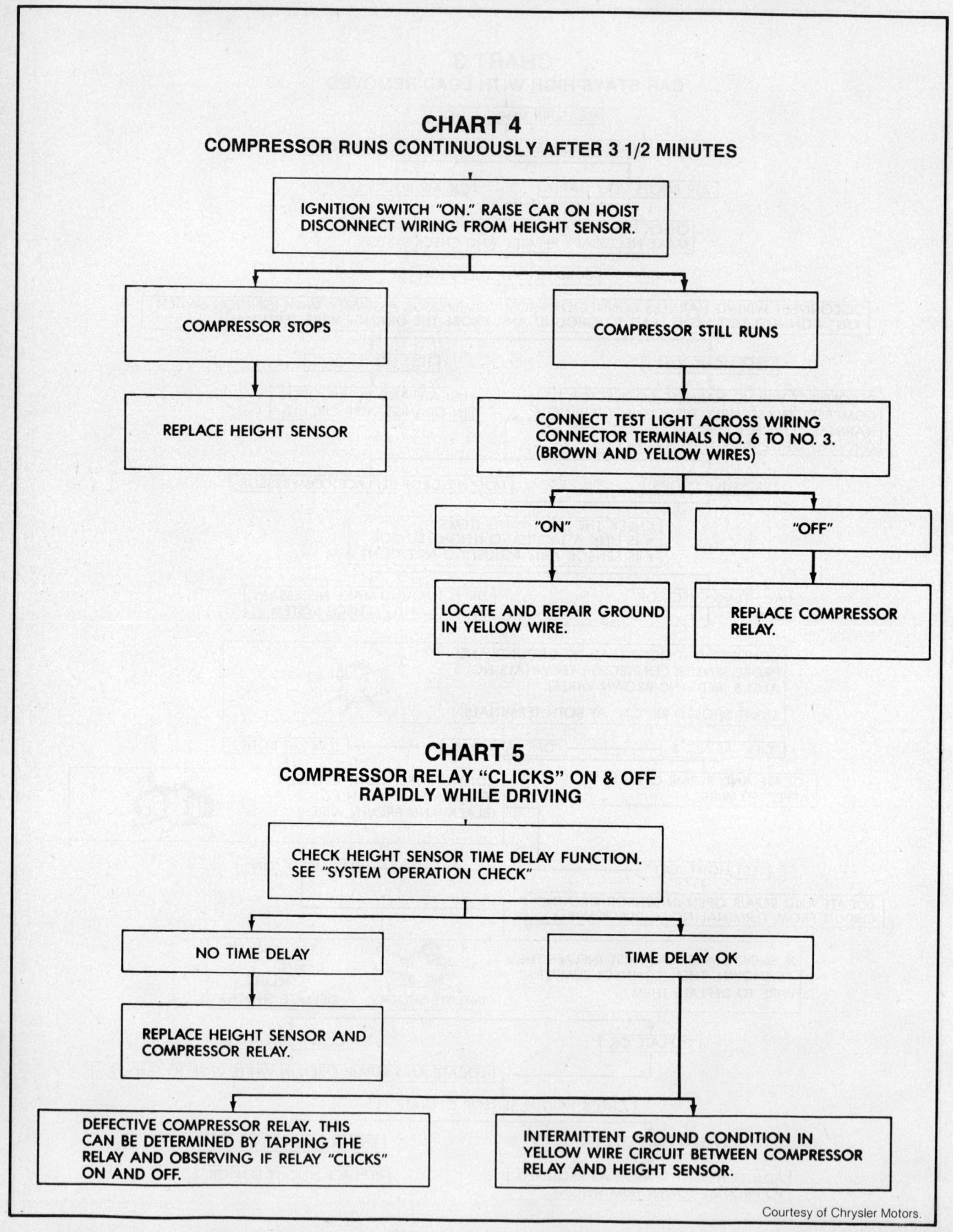

CHART 4
COMPRESSOR RUNS CONTINUOUSLY AFTER 3 1/2 MINUTES

IGNITION SWITCH "ON." RAISE CAR ON HOIST DISCONNECT WIRING FROM HEIGHT SENSOR.

COMPRESSOR STOPS → REPLACE HEIGHT SENSOR

COMPRESSOR STILL RUNS → CONNECT TEST LIGHT ACROSS WIRING CONNECTOR TERMINALS NO. 6 TO NO. 3. (BROWN AND YELLOW WIRES)

"ON" → LOCATE AND REPAIR GROUND IN YELLOW WIRE.

"OFF" → REPLACE COMPRESSOR RELAY.

CHART 5
COMPRESSOR RELAY "CLICKS" ON & OFF RAPIDLY WHILE DRIVING

CHECK HEIGHT SENSOR TIME DELAY FUNCTION. SEE "SYSTEM OPERATION CHECK"

NO TIME DELAY → REPLACE HEIGHT SENSOR AND COMPRESSOR RELAY.

TIME DELAY OK

DEFECTIVE COMPRESSOR RELAY. THIS CAN BE DETERMINED BY TAPPING THE RELAY AND OBSERVING IF RELAY "CLICKS" ON AND OFF.

INTERMITTENT GROUND CONDITION IN YELLOW WIRE CIRCUIT BETWEEN COMPRESSOR RELAY AND HEIGHT SENSOR.

Courtesy of Chrysler Motors.

Electronic Suspensions

FORD MOTOR CO. AIR SUSPENSION — CONTINENTAL

DESCRIPTION

The air suspension system combines air leveling and dual damping ride control in one system. Air leveling keeps the vehicle at the correct level under different load conditions. Dual damping ride control switches the shock absorbers between a soft and a firm ride.

OPERATION

SYSTEM OPERATION

Dual Dampening System

The dual dampening system automatically switches the MacPherson shock strut settings from soft to firm when driving conditions require it. The system monitors vehicle accelerations, decelerations, vertical (up-and-down) road wheel travel and steering wheel position as well as turning rates before responding to individual sensor inputs.

Road Undulation Function

The road undulation function uses the air suspension height sensors to measure road wheel vertical speed and travel (up-and-down travel). If a vertical wheel speed over a specified distance is above a predetermined level, the shocks are switched to a firm position. This function reduces sub-frame bottoming out on undulating road surfaces.

The function is used at vehicle speeds above 16 MPH. The control module will read unputs fom the height sensors every 4 milliseconds to determine if the rate of suspension travel changes is enough to require a firm shock setting.

The struts will remain in the firm position until the vehicle speed drops below 10 MPH and/or a rate of change in the suspension movement is below the control module's design limit.

Acceleration & Deceleration

Shock dampening is also switched to the firm position if the vehicle acceleration or decelertion values exceed predetermined limits. The acceleration signal provided by the EEC-IV module is a combination of the throttle position and/or engine vacuum level inputs to the EEC-IV control module.

The deceleration signal is provided by a pressure switch located in the brake hydraulic circuit. These 2 inputs improve the vehicle's pitch and drive characteristics during severe braking and heavy acceleration. Inputs are then combined with a vehicle speed parameter that will ignore the deceleration signal below vehicle speeds of 10 MPH.

The acceleration signal will also be ignored at vehicle speeds above 20 MPH to minimize harshness and maximize ride plushness.

Brake Pressure Switch & Vehicle Speed Input

The system uses a brake pressure switch and a vehicle speed input to signal the control module that the vehicle is in a braking maneuver mode of about .3g or greater.

When the brake pressure signal is activated above 10 MPH, the control module will switch the shocks to the firm position. If the brake pressure switch is deactivated and the vehicle speed is still above 10 MPH,

Fig. 1: Continental Air Suspension Components

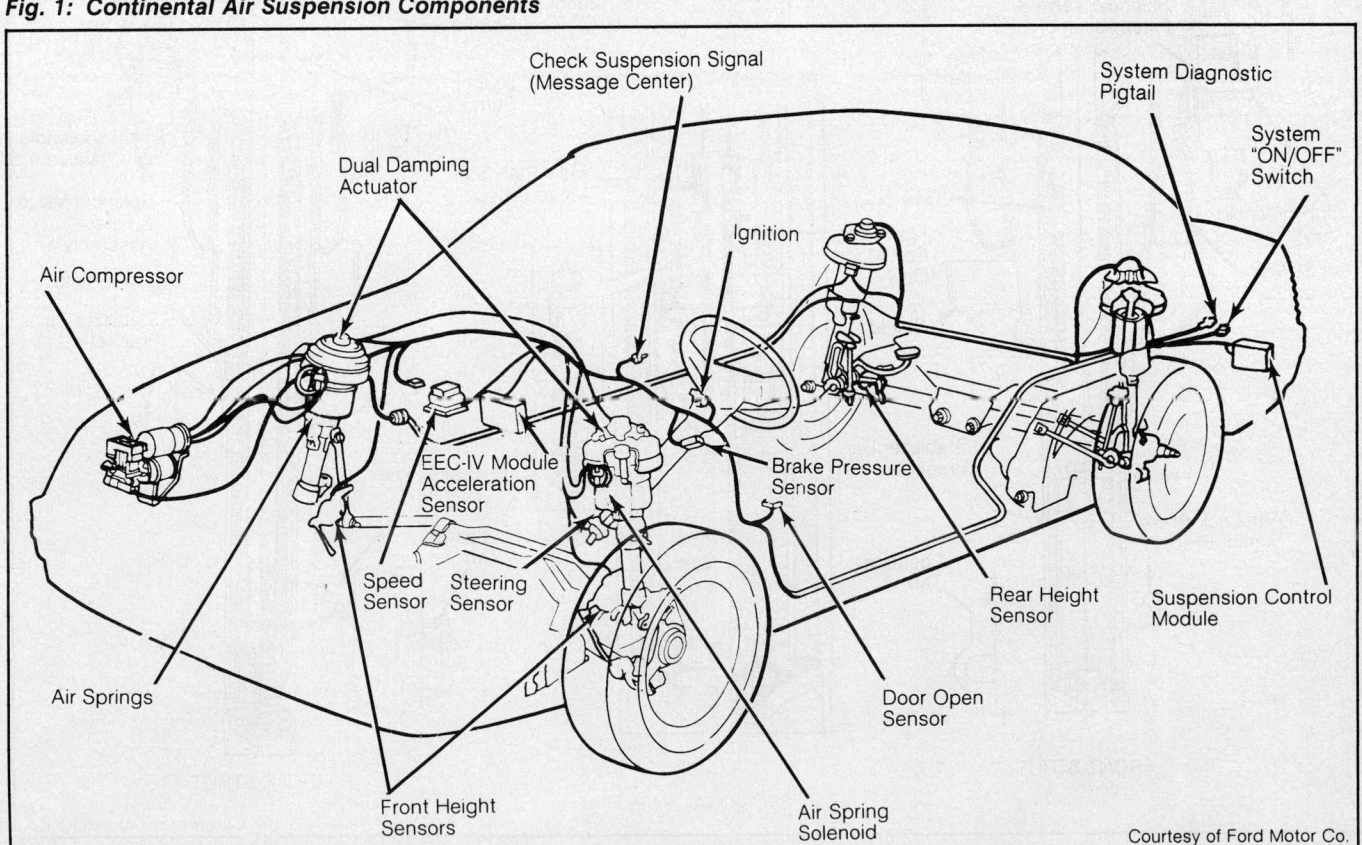

Courtesy of Ford Motor Co.

Electronic Suspensions

FORD MOTOR CO. AIR SUSPENSION – CONTINENTAL (Cont.)

the shocks will remain in the firm position an extra 1/2 second before switching back to the soft position.

If the brake pressure signal remains activated after the vehicle speed drops below 10 MPH, the shock struts will remain in the firm position for only 2.4 seconds. At one second after the vehicle speed drops below 10 MPH, the shock struts will be returned to the soft mode.

AIR COMPRESSOR

Air is supplied to the system by a single cylinder compressor mounted on the right fender apron. All airflow during compression or venting is directed through an integral dryer attached to the compressor. Air exhaustion is controlled by a vent solenoid on the compressor manifold.

The air springs are fed by 4 air lines attached to the compressor dryer. The dryer is a common pressure feed for all air lines. Air lines are color coded to identify to which spring they are attached.

AIR SPRING & STRUT ASSEMBLIES

Front and rear suspensions are equipped with MacPherson strut assemblies with integral air springs that incorporate 2-stage dampening mechanisms. A soft or firm ride (dual dampening) can be selected by changing piston orifice area with an externally mounted electronic rotary actuator. See Fig. 3.

The front struts are attached to the body through a precision ball bearing and rubber mount system. Ball bearings provide a smooth pivot point for the strut and wheel assembly.

Oversize rubber mountings provides impact and noise isolation on the top of the strut. See Fig. 2. Rear struts have a dual path mount which separates the strut and air spring mounting surfaces for maximum isolation.

Fig. 2: Continental Strut Assemblies

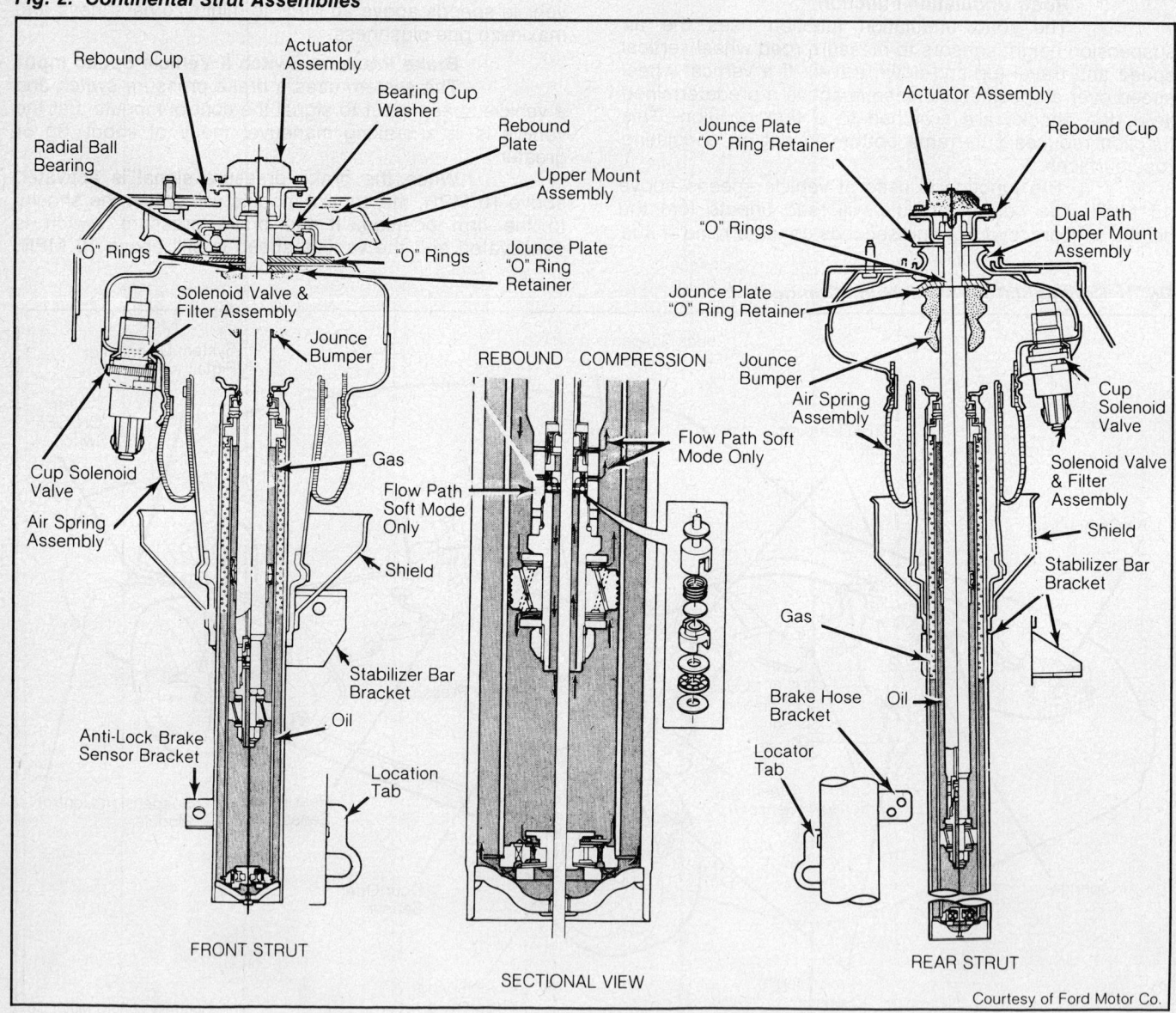

Courtesy of Ford Motor Co.

FORD MOTOR CO. AIR SUSPENSION – CONTINENTAL (Cont.)

Fig. 3: Electronic Rotary Actuator

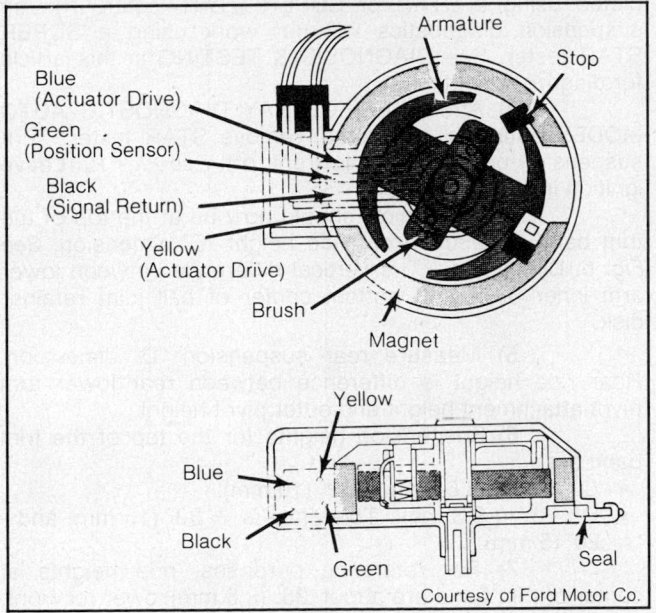

Courtesy of Ford Motor Co.

Fig. 4: Electronic Height Sensor

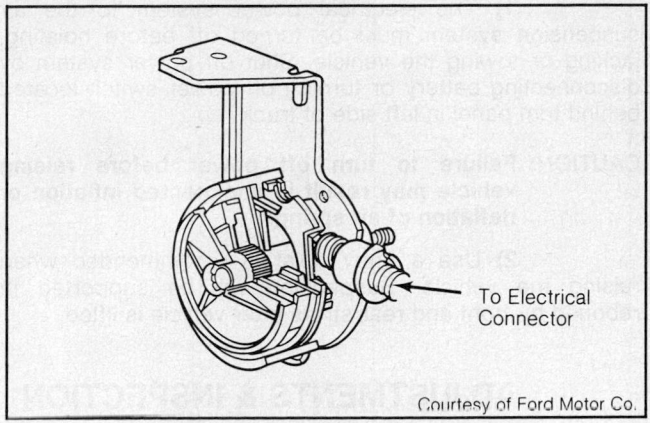

Courtesy of Ford Motor Co.

CONTROL MODULE

The control module is the electronic control center of the system. It receives signals from various sensors in the vehicle. The module uses sensor inputs to maintain desired ride height when vehicle is moving or stopped.

This is accomplished by opening or closing the air spring valves. The control module also operates the compressor through the compressor relay or opens the vent solenoids in response to signal inputs from height sensors.

The control module receives the following inputs:
- Vehicle speed.
- Steering wheel turning rotation.
- Engine vacuum level.
- Throttle position angle (supplied by EEC-IV system).
- Brake pressure sensor.
- Ignition switch position.
- Shock absorber damping position.
- Door switch position.
- Height sensor position.

ELECTRONIC HEIGHT SENSORS

The height sensors are a rotary style, Hall effect design that determines ride height. *See Fig. 4.* Sensors are located at the left front, right front and rear of the vehicle. Each sensor measures the difference between a set reference point and actual vehicle height so the control module can respond to variations in ride height.

In parking mode, additional height positions allow the control module to determine if an obstruction was found while parking the vehicle. In driving mode, road surface variations are sensed by checking road wheel vertical speed and vertical travel.

If average vertical speed and travel are above a predetermined level, the shocks are switched to the firm position. This reduces the chance of bottoming out the sub-frame when traveling over rough roads. Body rolls during long, high lateral (side) force turns are also neutralized to prevent unwanted leveling action at these times.

STEERING WHEEL INPUTS

Steering Wheel Sensor

An optical steering position sensor (photo-cell) is mounted on the steering column. *See Fig. 5.* The sensor is used to determine the straight-ahead position of the steering wheel. Once the control module determines this position, the module can measure the steering wheel turning angles and then calculate the lateral acceleration that results.

If calculated acceleration is less than predetermined values, the shock dampening is changed to the firm level of control. The input is not used until the vehicle speed is above about 20 MPH. When activated, the shocks will remain firm an additional 1/2 second after the vehicle's speed and/or steering wheel position drops below parameter levers.

Steering Wheel Turning Rate

The same steering column optical sensor also is used to calculate the rate at which the steering wheel is being turned. If the steering wheel is being turned faster than a predetermind rate, the shock dampening will be switched to the firm postion. This function is used for an accident avoidance type of maneuver.

Under these conditions, the action is fast but the actual movement and/or displacement of the steering wheel may not be enough to activate the steering position function. The steering rate function is not used until the vehicle's speed is more than 20 MPH. After the shocks are activated, they will remain in the firm mode for 1/2-3/4 of a second after the vehicle's speed and/or steering wheel rate drops below parameter levels.

Fig. 5: Steering Wheel Optical Sensor

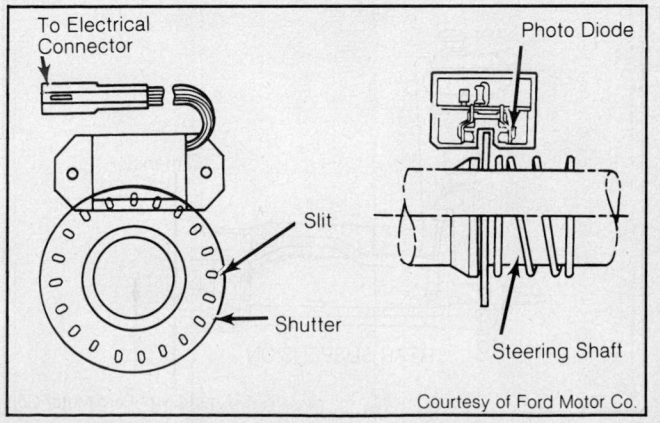

Courtesy of Ford Motor Co.

Electronic Suspensions

FORD MOTOR CO. AIR SUSPENSION – CONTINENTAL (Cont.)

JACKING & TOWING PRECAUTIONS

1) The electrical power system to the air suspension system must be turned off before hoisting, jacking or towing the vehicle. Shut off power system by disconnecting battery or turning off power switch located behind trim panel in left side of trunk.

CAUTION: Failure to turn off power before raising vehicle may result in unexpected inflation or deflation of air springs.

2) Use a body hoist is recommended when raising the vehicle. Suspension will be supported in rebound by front and rear struts after vehicle is lifted.

ADJUSTMENTS & INSPECTION

CASTER & CAMBER

See appropriate article in WHEEL ALIGNMENT section

RIDE HEIGHT ADJUSTMENT

NOTE: **Ride height must be checked and readjusted, if necessary, before wheel alignment is performed.**

Checking

1) Place vehicle on alignment rack. To ensure ride height is measured at a consistent point, height should only be measured after the "SERVICE BAY DIAGNOSTIC AUTO MODE" has been completed and STAR tester displays a code 12.

Fig. 6: Measuring Ride Height

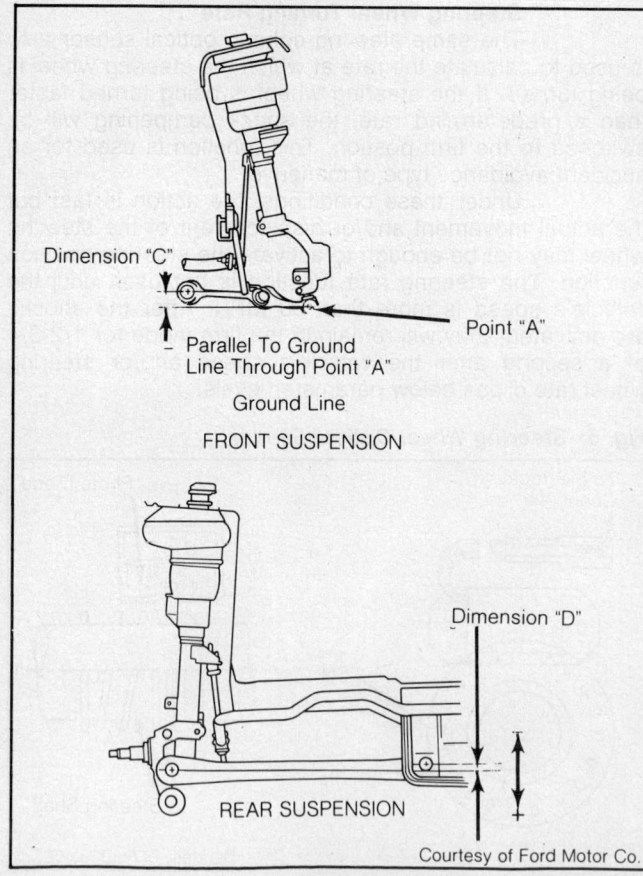

Courtesy of Ford Motor Co.

2) This diagnostic routine can only be completed using a STAR or SUPER STAR tester. The air suspension diagnostics will not work using a SUPER STAR tester. See DIAGNOSIS & TESTING in this article for diagnostic routine.

3) After "SERVICE BAY DIAGNOSTIC AUTO MODE" routine is completed, remove STAR tester. Turn suspension power switch in trunk off. See Fig. 10. Leave ignition in "RUN" position.

4) The vehicle should now be at the top of the trim band. Measure front ride height "C" dimension. See Fig. 6. Dimension "C" is vertical difference between lower arm inner pivot and bottom center of ball joint retainer disk.

5) Measure rear suspension "D" dimension. Rear ride height is difference between rear lower arm pivot attachment height and outer pivot height.

6) Suspension heights for the top of the trim band are:
- "C": 1.72" (43.6 mm) ± .39" (10 mm).
- "D": -.36" (-9.3 mm). Tolerance is + .39" (10 mm) and -.20" (5 mm).

7) For reference purposes, ride heights at center of trim band are about .35" (8.8 mm) lower for front, and .47" (12 mm) for rear than heights listed in step 6).

Front Ride Height Adjustment

1) Front ride height is adjusted by changing height sensor link. See FRONT RIDE HEIGHT SENSOR LINK DIMENSIONS table. See Fig. 7.

Fig. 7: Front Height Sensor Link

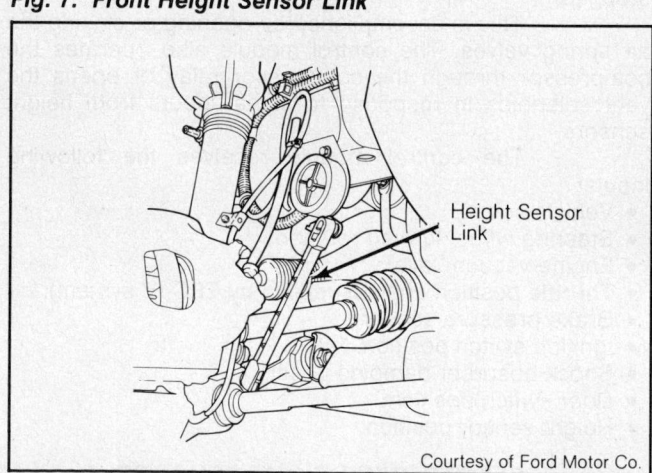

Courtesy of Ford Motor Co.

FRONT RIDE HIDE HEIGHT SENSOR LINK DIMENSIONS

Part No. [1] Left Front	[1] Part No. Right Front	Sensor Link	Front Ride Height [2] Change In. (mm)
CA	GA	+1 (Green)	+.24 (6)
BA	FA	-1 (Red)	-.24 (6)
JA	KA	Nominal (Blue)	0
DA	HA	+2 (Yellow)	+47 (12)
AA	EA	-2 (White)	-.47 (12)

[1] – All part numbers are preceeded by E80F-3C111-.
[2] – Ride height change is with respect to nominal link.

FORD MOTOR CO. AIR SUSPENSION – CONTINENTAL (Cont.)

2) When removing front link, carefully pry it off with a wide-bladed screwdriver. When installing link, support height sensor from behind to prevent sensor damage. Any front link change must be made with reference to the link that is to be removed.

NOTE: Any link change must be made with reference to link that is to be removed.

Rear Ride Height Adjustment

To adjust rear height sensor, loosen and reposition height sensor lever adjustment screw. Each notch on rear height sensor lever gives about .60" (15 mm) of ride height adjustment. See Fig. 8.

Fig. 8: Adjusting Rear Ride Height

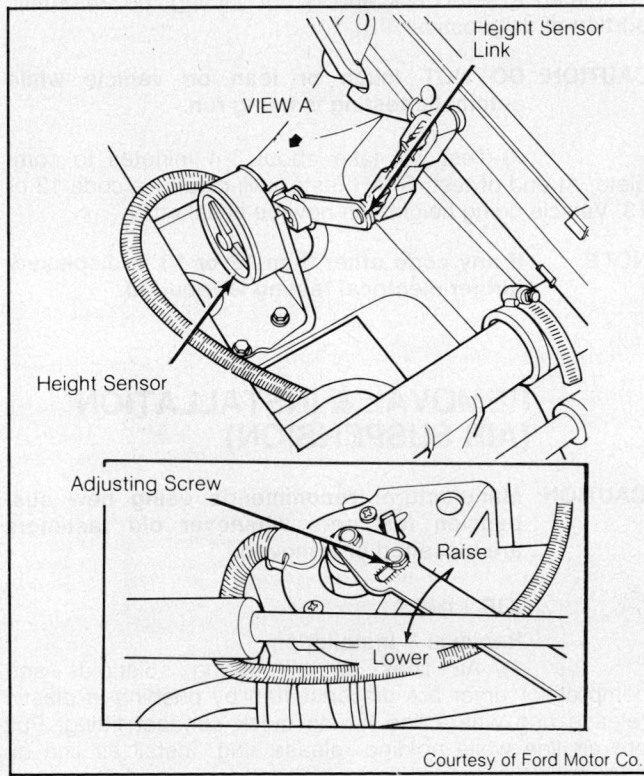

Courtesy of Ford Motor Co.

FRONT WHEEL BEARINGS

Front wheel bearings do not require periodic adjustments.

BALL JOINT CHECKING

1) Turn off air suspension switch located in left side of trunk. Raise and support vehicle until front wheels in fully extended position.

2) Move lower edge of tire in and out. Any movement at lower end of knuckle and lower control arm indicates ball joint wear. If any movement is seen, install new lower control arm assembly.

STRUT & SPRING ASSEMBLY
Inspection

1) The gas-filled hydraulic struts are nonadjustable and non-refillable and are serviced as assemblies. Before a strut is replaced because it is suspected to be defective, perform the following checks.

2) Check all tire pressures. Check the torque of all strut and suspension mounting bolts and nuts. Check strut for obvious external damage.

3) Check for fluid leakage by removing solenoid on top of strut. See AIR SPRING SOLENOID in REMOVAL & INSTALLATION (FRONT SUSPENSION) in this article. Check for oil film on solenoid or oil staurated oil filter. Replace strut if leaking.

Strut Noise Check

1) Bounce vehicle and try to isolate noise. Check spindle-to-fastener torque. Torque must exceed 55 ft. lbs. (75 N.m) on both rear strut lower mounting bolts. Front strut-to-knuckle torque must be greater than 70 ft. lbs. (95 N.m).

CAUTION: Strut lower mounting bolts contain a locking material in their threads. Bolt may appear to have correct torque but joint could be loose. Replace fasterner if equipped with locking material.

2) Check torque of strut upper mount-to-body nuts. Front torque must exceed 22 ft. lbs. (30 N.m). Rear torque must exceed 19 ft. lbs. (26 N.m).

3) Check torque of strut rod-to-mount nut. Torque must exceed 35 ft. lbs. (48 N.m). Rubber isolators must be in place.

4) Inspect connecting joints for damaged threads. Replace components as necessary. If noise is still present, remove strut and go to STRUT BENCH TEST.

Strut Bench Test

1) Struts should be fully extended when out of vehicle and not restrained. If a strut does not fully extend, it should be replaced. See Fig. 9.

Fig. 9: Measuring Strut Extended Length

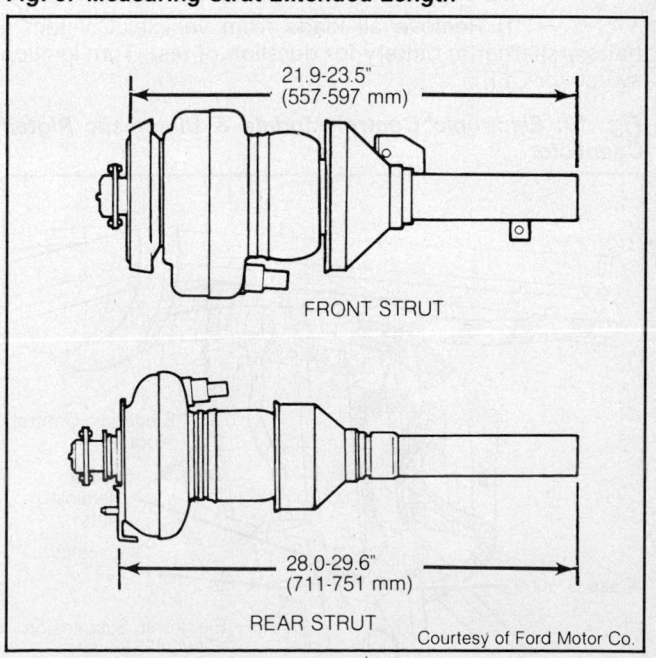

21.9-23.5" (557-597 mm)

FRONT STRUT

28.0-29.6" (711-751 mm)

REAR STRUT

Courtesy of Ford Motor Co.

2) With the strut in normal upright position, compress it. Allow strut to extend 3 times to purge pressure chamber or any trapped gas.

FORD MOTOR CO. AIR SUSPENSION – CONTINENTAL (Cont.)

3) Place shock absorber in vise. Hand stroke shock as fast as possible with as much travel as possible. Action should be smooth and uniform as possible on each stroke. Higher resistance on extension than on compression is normal.

4) Replace strut if any of the following conditions exist:
- A lag or skip at reversal of travel near mid-stroke when shock is properly primed and in installed position.
- Seizing.
- Noise other than faint "swish", such as clicking.
- Excessive fluid leakage.
- With rod fully extended, any side-to-side motion or rod in relation to outer can.

DIAGNOSIS & TESTING

CAUTION: Electrical testing for air suspenion system is not available.

TESTING PRECAUTIONS

1) Compressor relay, compressor vent solenoid and all air spring solenoids have internal diodes for noise suppression. Do not switch battery and ground feeds when testing components.

2) When charging the battery, the ignition switch MUST be in the "OFF" position if air suspension switch in trunk is "ON". If ignition switch is "ON", air compressor relay or motor may be damaged.

3) Use only a STAR or SUPER STAR II tester to diagnose system. A SUPER STAR tester will not work. Use an analog volt/ohmmeter (20,000 ohms per volt) to test circuits.

SERVICE BAY DIAGNOSTIC AUTO MODE

1) Remove all loads from vehicle. Connect a battery charger to battery for duration of test. Turn ignition switch to "OFF".

Fig. 10: Electronic Control Module & Diagnostic Pigtail Connector

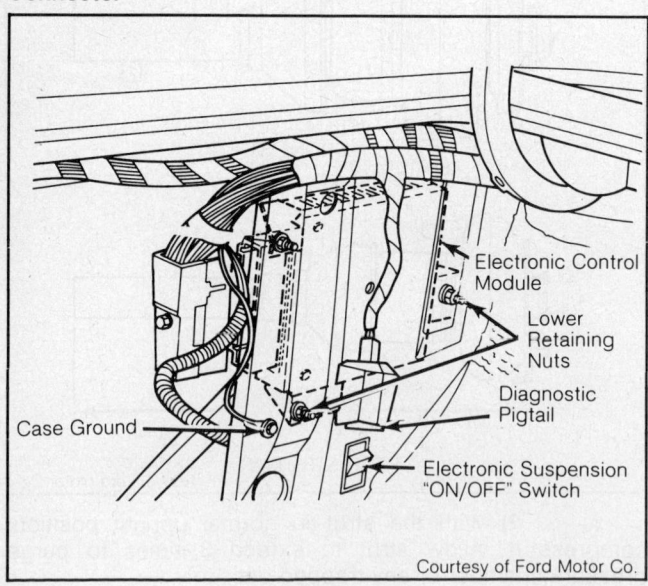

Electronic Control Module

Lower Retaining Nuts

Diagnostic Pigtail

Case Ground

Electronic Suspension "ON/OFF" Switch

Courtesy of Ford Motor Co.

2) Open trunk. Ensure air suspension switch is in the "ON" position. *See Fig. 10.*

3) Place the STAR test button in the "HOLD UP" position. Connect STAR tester to diagnostic pigtail next to control module. Control module is behind trim panel.

4) Turn air suspension "ON/OFF" switch "OFF", then back to "ON" position. Ensure all electrical accessories are off.

5) With brake pedal NOT depressed, turn the ignition switch to the "RUN" position. Wait 5 seconds and then depress STAR test button so it remains down in "TEST" position.

6) Within 20 seconds, STAR tester will display a code. If code 10 is displayed, air suspension module has completed a self-check and is conducting the automatic portion of diagnostics.

CAUTION: DO NOT touch or lean on vehicle while automatic testing is being run.

7) Test will take about 3-4 minutes to complete. At end of test, STAR tester will display a code 12 or 13. Vehicle riding height can now be checked.

NOTE: **If any code other than 12 or 13 is displayed, further electrical testing is required.**

REMOVAL & INSTALLATION (AIR SUSPENSION)

CAUTION: Manufacturer recommends using new suspension fasteners whenever old fasteners are loosened or removed.

AIR LINES
Removal & Installation

1) Air lines on air spring solenoids and compressor dryer are disconnected by pushing in plastic release ring where line meets quick connect fitting. Pull out air line while holding release ring. Install air line by pushing in tubing until flare on line is against release ring.

2) Quick connect fittings can be removed by disconnecting air line. Insert length of scrap air line into collet. *See Fig. 11.* Pull collet out by HAND. Remove "O" rings.

3) Clean "O" ring seat. Lightly coat "O" rings with silicone dielectric. Install new collet (prongs first) with finger pressure. Install release ring and line.

Repair
Service kits are available to repair damaged air lines. Sections of air line may be cut out and union installed. *See Fig. 11.*

FORD MOTOR CO. AIR SUSPENSION – CONTINENTAL (Cont.)

Fig. 11: Repairing Air Lines

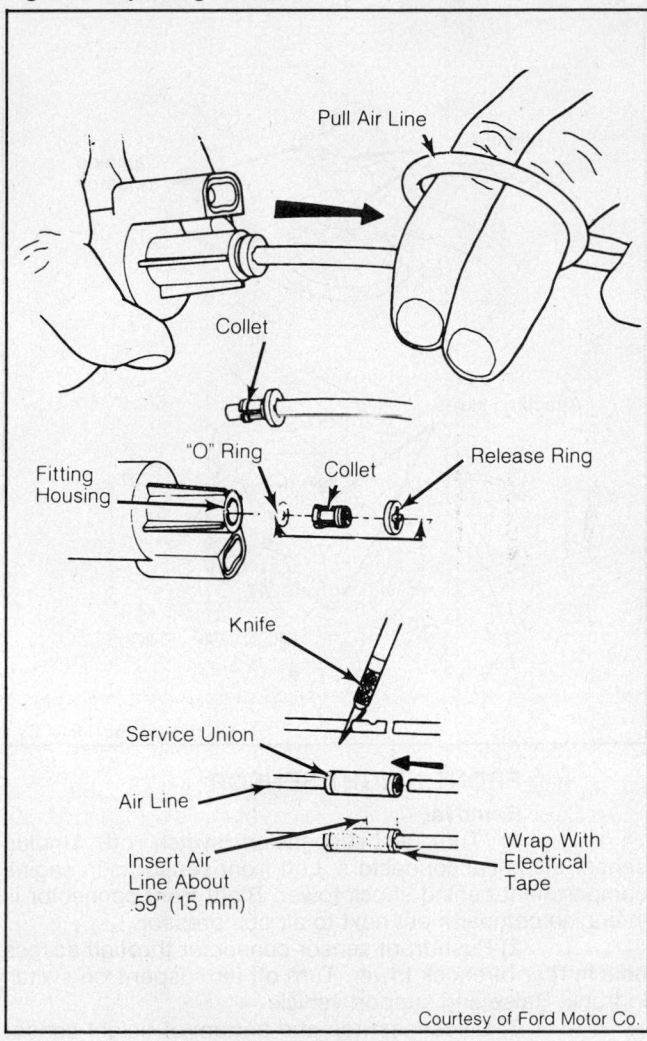

Pull Air Line

Collet

"O" Ring   Collet   Release Ring

Fitting Housing

Knife

Service Union

Air Line

Insert Air Line About .59" (15 mm)

Wrap With Electrical Tape

Courtesy of Ford Motor Co.

AIR SPRING SOLENOID

NOTE: If air spring solenoid is removed while air spring is installed in vehicle, a STAR tester is needed to deflate the spring.

Air Spring Deflation

1) Ensure air suspension switch is in "ON" position and ignition switch is turned "OFF". Install battery charger to prevent battery drain.

2) Open access door in trunk and and plug STAR tester into air suspension diagnostic pigtail. STAR test button must be in "HOLD" (up) position. Depress STAR test button to "TEST" position.

3) Control module will send spring fill selection codes to STAR tester. Codes will be displayed in scrolling manner. Codes descriptions are:
- 21 – Vent right front.
- 22 – Vent left front.
- 23 – Vent right rear.
- 24 – Compress right front.
- 25 – Compress left front.
- 26 – Compress right rear.
- 27 – Vent left rear.
- 28 – Compress left rear.

4) When deflating air springs, raise vehicle off ground. Each spring may be deflated or inflated by releasing the STAR test button while its code is displayed. For example, the left front air spring may be deflated by releasing the test button while code 22 is being displayed.

5) To stop a selected operation, depress STAR test button to TEST position. Spring codes will again begin scrolling. After the spring is deflated, turn air suspension switch off.

Removal

1) Remove wheel. Unplug electrical connector at solenoid valve. Disconnect air line by pressing in release ring at solenoid valve and pulling out line.

2) Remove solenoid clip. Rotate solenoid counterclockwise to first stop. Pull solenoid straight out slowly to second stop to bleed air from system. *See Fig. 12.*

CAUTION: Do not fully remove solenoid until air is bled from spring.

3) After air if fully bled from system, rotate solenoid counterclockwise to third stop, and remove from air spring. Inspect filter. Replace filter if it is oily. Very oily filter indicates a leaking air strut.

Fig. 12: Removing Air Spring Solenoid Valve

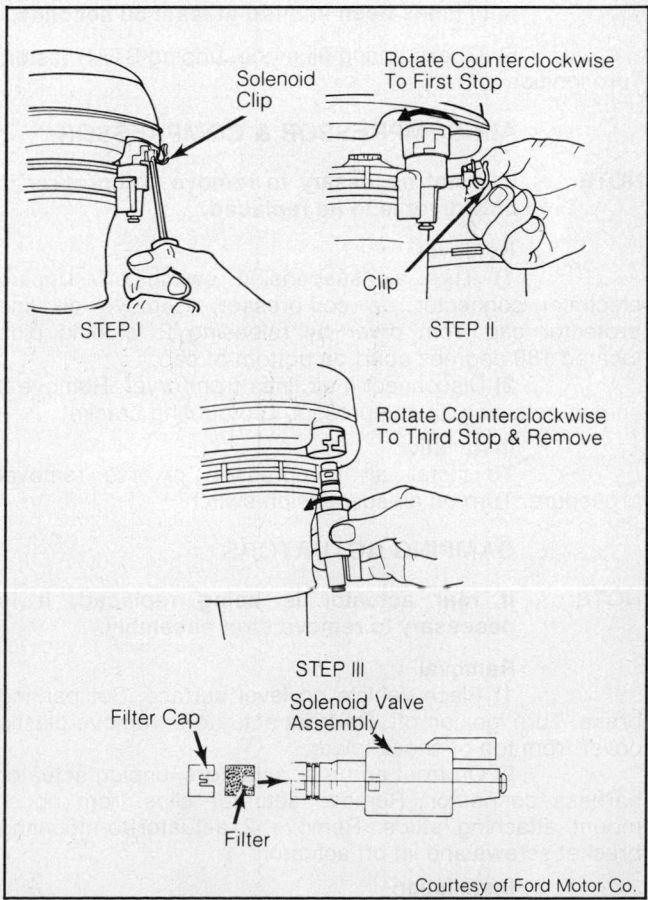

Solenoid Clip

Rotate Counterclockwise To First Stop

Clip

STEP I

STEP II

Rotate Counterclockwise To Third Stop & Remove

STEP III

Filter Cap

Solenoid Valve Assembly

Filter

Courtesy of Ford Motor Co.

Electronic Suspensions

FORD MOTOR CO. AIR SUSPENSION — CONTINENTAL (Cont.)

Installation

Replace solenoid "O" ring if defective. Lightly coat new "O" ring with silicone dielectric. To install solenoid valve, reverse removal procedure. Refill air springs.

Air Spring Refill

1) Ensure air suspension switch is in "ON" position. Turn ignition off. Install battery charger to reduce drain.

2) Plug STAR tester into control module diagnostic pigtail. Tester button should be in "HOLD" (up) position.

3) With brake pedal depressed, turn igntion switch to "RUN" position. Depress STAR tester button to "TEST" (down) position.

4) STAR tester will begin displaying spring fill codes again. Select the desired spring fill procedure by releasing the STAR button when desired code is displayed. For example, left front air spring may be inflated by releasing "TEST" button when code 25 is displayed.

5) As long as STAR tester button is released, desired operation (inflation or deflation) will continue. To stop an operation, depress STAR tester button to "TEST" position. Spring fill codes will scroll again.

CAUTION: DO NOT apply vehicle load to an air spring until it has been inflated at least 60 seconds.

6) To exit spring fill mode, unplug STAR tester. Turn ignition off.

AIR COMPRESSOR & COMPRESSOR

NOTE: **It is not necessary to remove compressor if only dryer is to be replaced.**

Removal

1) Turn air suspension switch off. Unplug electrical connector on compressor. Remove air line protector cap from dryer by releasing 2 latching pins located 180 degrees apart on bottom of cap.

2) Disconnect 4 air lines from dryer. Remove 3 screws retaining air compressor to mounting bracket.

Installation

To install air compressor, reverse removal procedure. Turn on air suspension switch.

DAMPING ACTUATORS

NOTE: **If rear actuator is being replaced, it is necessary to remove strut assembly.**

Removal

1) Place vehicle on level surface. Set parking brake. Turn ignition off. On front actuators, remove plastic cover from top of shock tower.

2) On front and rear actuators, unplug actuator harness connector. Remove actuator clips from upper mount attaching studs. Remove 2 actuator-to-mounting bracket screws and lift off actuator.

Installation

Ensure flats of actuator and shock absorber are aligned. See Fig. 13. Align actuator screw attaching holes with mounting bracket. With wheels straight ahead, wire leads should point inboard. Install and tighten attaching screws to 10-14 INCH lbs. (1.1-1.6 N.m).

Fig. 13: Installing Damping Actuator

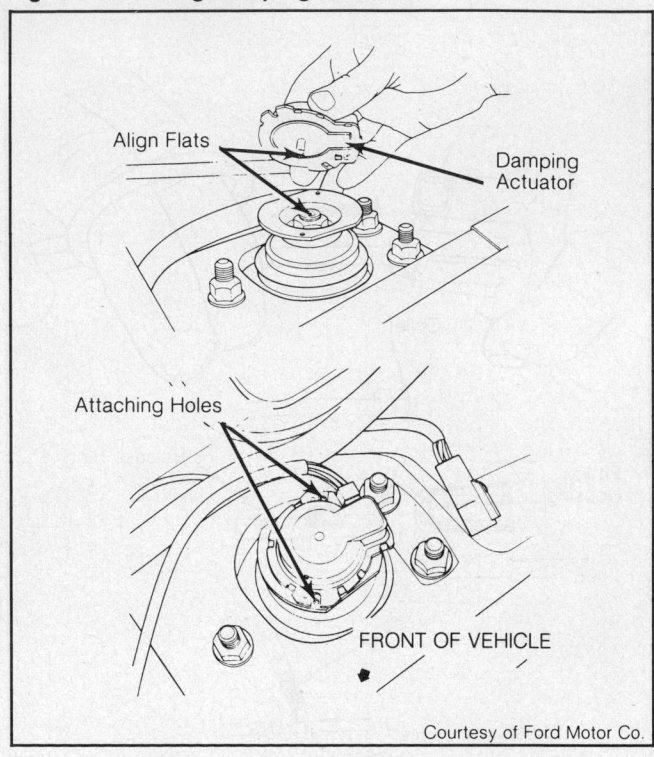

Align Flats — Damping Actuator — Attaching Holes — FRONT OF VEHICLE

Courtesy of Ford Motor Co.

FRONT HEIGHT SENSOR

Removal

1) Turn air suspension switch off. Unplug sensor electrical connectors. Left front sensor is in engine compartment behind shock tower. Right front connector is in engine compartment next to air compressor.

2) Push front sensor connector through access hole in rear of shock tower. Turn off air suspension switch in trunk. Raise and support vehicle.

3) Disconnect top and bottom of height sensor link from stud. See Fig. 14.

Fig. 14: Removing Height Sensor

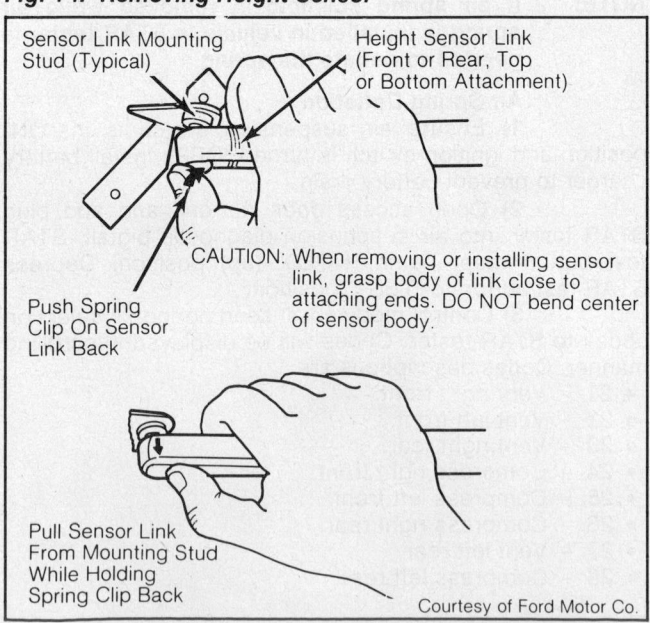

Sensor Link Mounting Stud (Typical) — Height Sensor Link (Front or Rear, Top or Bottom Attachment) — Push Spring Clip On Sensor Link Back

CAUTION: When removing or installing sensor link, grasp body of link close to attaching ends. DO NOT bend center of sensor body.

Pull Sensor Link From Mounting Stud While Holding Spring Clip Back

Courtesy of Ford Motor Co.

FORD MOTOR CO. AIR SUSPENSION – CONTINENTAL (Cont.)

4) Unplug anti-lock wire from bracket. Disconnect brake line from bracket. Remove attaching screws and remove sensor.

Installation
To install height sensor, reverse removal procedure. Turn on air suspension switch.

REAR HEIGHT SENSOR
Removal
1) Turn air suspension switch off. Unplug electrical connector in trunk in front of forward trim panel. Pull carpet back for access to sensor sealing grommet on floorpan.

2) Raise and support vehicle. Suspension must be at full rebound. Disconnect top and bottom end of height sensor link from attaching stud. *See Fig. 14.* Remove sensor attaching screws and lift off sensor.

Installation
To install height sensor, reverse removal procedure. Turn on air suspension switch.

STEERING SENSOR
Steering sensor is located at lower end of steering column. It may be replaced with steering column in or out of vehicle. Sensor and sensor rings are separate units. Sensor ring can only be removed by disassembling steering column.

Removal & Installation
1) Unplug sensor electrical connector from wiring harness. Remove sensor electrical connector from shift control cable bracket under instrument panel. *See Fig. 15.*

2) Remove 2 retaining screws and lift off sensor. To install sensor, reverse removal procedure.

Fig. 15: *Steering Sensor*

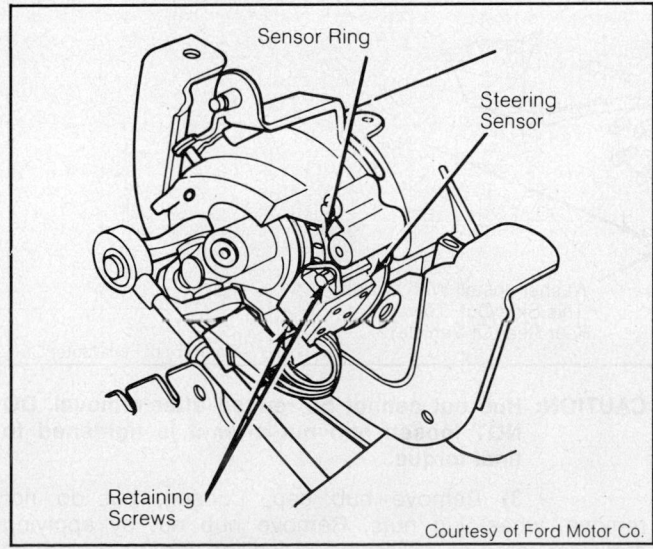

Sensor Ring

Steering Sensor

Retaining Screws

Courtesy of Ford Motor Co.

REMOVAL & INSTALLATION (FRONT SUSPENSION)

CAUTION: Manufacturer recommends using new suspension fasteners whenever old fasteners are loosened or removed.

BALL JOINTS
Ball joints are not replaceable. Replace lower control arm if ball joints are worn.

LOWER CONTROL ARM (FRONT)
Removal
1) Turn off air suspenion switch located in left side of trunk. Raise and support vehicle. Remove wheels.

2) Disconnect height sensor link from ball stud pin. Remove and discard nut from tension strut. A new nut should be used on reassembly. Remove dished washer. *See Fig. 17.*

3) Remove and discard lower control arm ball joint pinch bolt. Slightly spread knuckle pinch joint and separate control arm from steering knuckle. DO NOT damage bolt seal. DO NOT use a hammer to separate ball joint from knuckle.

4) Remove and discard lower control arm inner pivot bolt and nut. Remove lower control arm assembly from tension strut.

CAUTION: DO NOT allow drive axle shaft outboard halfshaft to move outward. CV joint may separate causing failure.

Inner Pivot Bushing & Tension Strut Insulator Replacement
1) Bushing and insulator may be replaced using "C" Frame And Clamp Assembly (T74P-3044-A1). Use correct adapters for removal and installation. *See Fig. 16.*

2) Place "C" frame in bench vise when replacing bushings. On inner pivot bushing, ensure bushing flange is at front of arm. Coat new insulator bushing with vegatable oil to ease installation. DO NOT use petroleum or mineral based oils.

Fig. 16: *Replacing Inner Pivot Bushing Or Tension Strut Insulator*

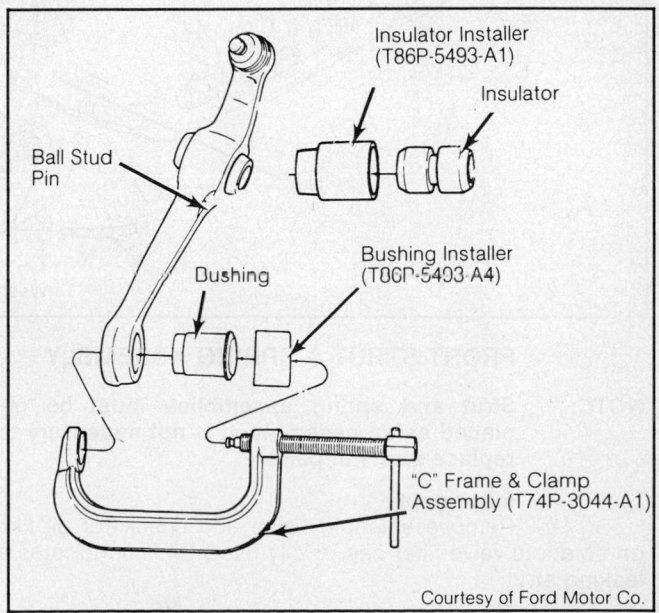

Ball Stud Pin

Insulator Installer (T86P-5493-A1)

Insulator

Dushing

Bushing Installer (T86P-5493-A4)

"C" Frame & Clamp Assembly (T74P-3044-A1)

Courtesy of Ford Motor Co.

Installation
To install lower control arm, reverse removal procedure. Always use NEW fasteners on lower control arm pivot and ball joint pinch bolts. Turn on air suspension switch.

FORD MOTOR CO. AIR SUSPENSION – CONTINENTAL (Cont.)

Fig. 17: *Front Suspension*

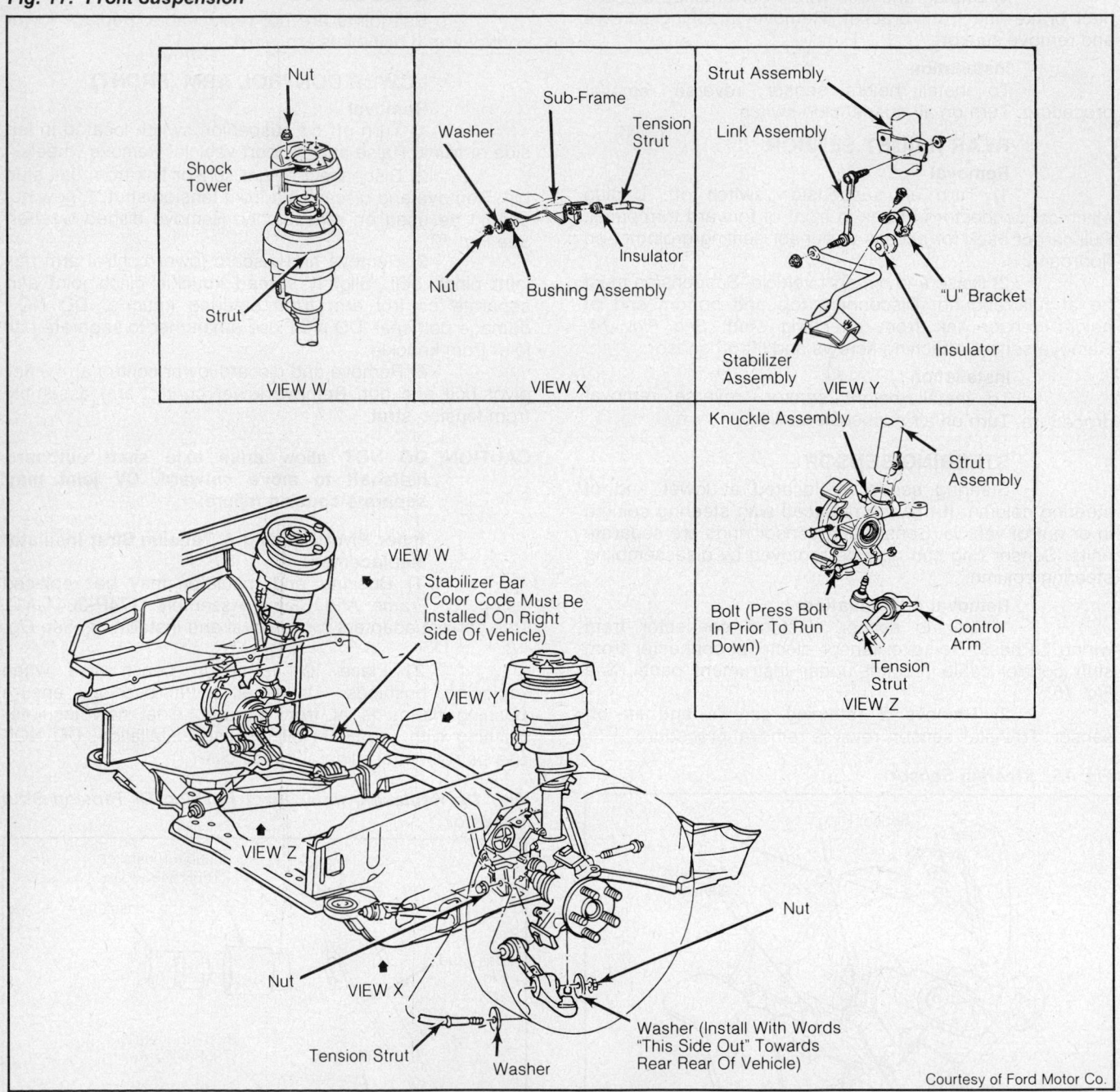

Courtesy of Ford Motor Co.

FRONT STRUT & SPRING ASSEMBLY

NOTE: Strut and spring assemblies must be replaced as an assembly. It is not necessary to replace struts in pairs.

Inspection

Remove solenoid valve and check for oil film on solenoid valve filter cap or oily filter. Oil film indicates a leaking strut.

Removal

1) Turn off air suspension switch in trunk. Turn ignition off and place steering column in unlocked position. Open hood.

2) Remove plastic cover from shock tower. Remove damping actuator as previously described.

CAUTION: Hub nut cannot be reused after removal. DO NOT loosen hub nut after it is tightened to final torque.

3) Remove hub cap. Loosen, but do not remove, wheel lug nuts. Remove hub nut by applying sufficient force to overcome prevailing torque feature of nut. DO NOT use an impact to remove nut.

4) DISCARD hub nut after removal. Remove hub nut washer. Loosen, but do not remove, 3 top mount-to-shock tower nuts. Raise and support vehicle. DO NOT support vehicle by lower control arm. Remove wheel.

5) Remove brake line bracket from strut assembly. Disconnect height sensor link from ball stud pin at lower control arm. Disconnect air line at solenoid valve.

FORD MOTOR CO. AIR SUSPENSION – CONTINENTAL (Cont.)

6) Unplug electrical connector at solenoid valve. Move brake caliper out of way. Separate tie rod end from steering knuckle. DISCARD tie rod end nut. A new nut should be installed on reassembly.

7) Remove stabilizer bar link nut. Separate link from strut.

8) Remove and DISCARD lower arm-to-steering knuckle pinch bolt and nut. Slightly spread knuckle-to-lower arm pinch joint. Separate lower arm from steering knuckle.

9) Press half-shaft from hub. *See Fig. 18*. Wire half-shaft so it supported in a level position. To prevent over extension of CV joint, do not allow half-shaft to move outward.

10) Remove shock strut-to-steering knuckle pinch bolt. Slightly spread knuckle-to-pinch strut joint and slip strut from knuckle. Remove 3 top mount-to-shock tower nuts. Remove strut assembly.

11) If air spring solenoid is to be replaced, remove solenoid clip. Rotate solenoid counterclockwise to first stop. Pull solenoid straight out slowly to second stop to bleed air from system.

12) DO NOT fully release solenoid until air is completely bled from air spring. After air is bled, rotate counterclockwise to third stop and remove solenoid from housing. Replace "O" ring if worn.

Fig. 18: Pressing Half-Shaft From Hub

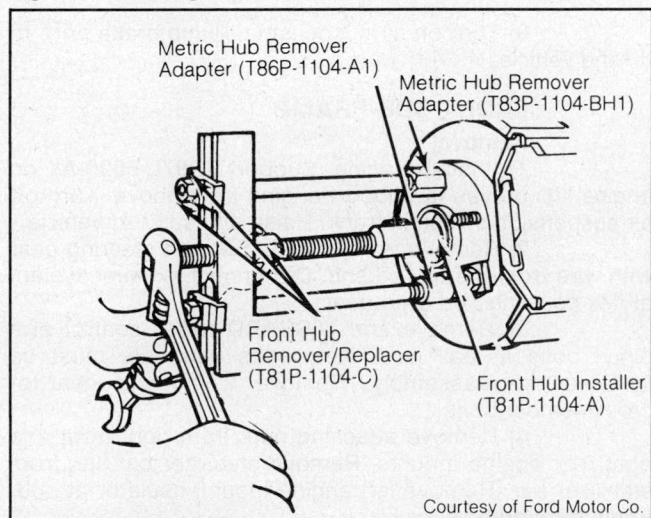

Metric Hub Remover
Adapter (T86P-1104-A1)

Metric Hub Remover
Adapter (T83P-1104-BH1)

Front Hub
Remover/Replacer
(T81P-1104-C)

Front Hub Installer
(T81P-1104-A)

Courtesy of Ford Motor Co.

Installation

1) To install strut and spring assembly, reverse removal procedure. Use NEW attaching hardware on following components:
- Shock strut-to-steering knuckle pinch bolt.
- Lower arm-to-steering knuckle bolt and nut.
- Stabilizer bar link nut.
- Tie rod end slotted nut.

2) Use a puller to install half-shaft into hub. DO NOT use new hub nut to pull half-shaft into hub.

CAUTION: DO NOT impact wrench to tighten hub nut. Use torque wrench and tighten by hand.

3) Fill air spring BEFORE lowering vehicle. See AIR SPRING REFILL under AIR SPRING SOLENOID in this article.

FRONT STABILIZER BAR, LINK & INSULATORS

NOTE: **Stabilizer bar link ball joints are not replaceable.**

Removal

1) Turn off air suspension switch in trunk. Raise and support vehicle. DO NOT support vehicle under front sub-frame. Remove and DISCARD stabilizer bar link-to-shock strut nut.

2) Remove sub-frame-to-steering gear nuts. Move gear off of sub-frame.

3) Place a set of jack stands under sub-frame. Lower vehicle on to jack stands. Remove and DISCARD 2 rear sub-frame bolts. New bolts must be used on reassembly.

4) Lower sub-frame to gain access to stabilizer bar mounting brackets. Remove stabilizer bar "U" bracket bolts. Remove stabilizer bar or insulators as required.

Installation

1) To install stabilizer bar and link, reverse removal procedure. If installing new stabilizer bar insulators, lubricate them to ease installation. DO NOT use petroleum or mineral based grease.

2) USE NEW "U" bracket bolts, sub-frame bolts and stabilizer bar link nut on reassembly. Turn on air suspension switch after vehicle is lowered.

UPPER MOUNT & BEARING ASSEMBLY (FRONT)

Removal

1) Remove front strut assembly as previously described. Bleed air spring in following manner.

2) Remove solenoid clip. Rotate solenoid counterclockwise to first stop. Pull solenoid straight out slowly to second stop to bleed air from system.

3) DO NOT fully release solenoid until air is completely bled from air spring. After air is bled, rotate counterclockwise to third stop and remove solenoid from housing. Replace "O" ring if worn.

4) Place actuator mounting bracket (rebound cup) loosely in vise by flats. Other end of strut should be resting on bench. Remove nut and rebound cup.

5) Remove upper nut mount and rebound assembly. Remove "O" ring retainer plate. Replace "O" ring if necessary.

Installation

To install mount assembly, reverse removal procedure. Fill air spring BEFORE lowering vehicle to ground. See AIR SPRING REFILL under AIR SPRING SOLENOID in this article.

STEERING KNUCKLE

Removal

1) Turn ignition to "OFF" position to unlock steering column.

CAUTION: Hub nut cannot be reused after removal. DO NOT loosen hub nut after it is tightened to final torque.

2) Remove hub cap. Loosen, but do not remove, wheel lug nuts. Remove hub nut by applying sufficient force to overcome prevailing torque feature of nut. DO NOT use an impact to remove nut.

FORD MOTOR CO. AIR SUSPENSION – CONTINENTAL (Cont.)

3) DISCARD hub nut after removal. Remove hub nut washer. Raise and support vehicle. DO NOT support vehicle by lower control arm. Remove wheel.

4) Remove and DISCARD tie rod end nut and cotter pin. New fastener must be installed on reassembly. Separate tie rod end from knuckle.

5) Remove stabilizer bar link from strut assembly. Discard nut.

6) Remove brake caliper. Wire caliper out of way. Remove brake rotor. Remove plastic cover from shock tower. LOOSEN, but do not remove, 3 top mounting nuts.

7) Remove and DISCARD lower arm-to-steering knuckle pinch bolt. Slightly spread knuckle to separate lower arm from knuckle. DO NOT use hammer to separate ball joint from knuckle. DO NOT damage ball joint boot.

8) Remove shock strut-to-knuckle pinch bolt. Slightly spread knuckle pinch joint. Press half-shaft from hub. *See Fig. 18.*

9) Wire half-shaft so it supported in a level position. To prevent over extension of CV joint, DO NOT allow half-shaft to move outward.

10) Remove rotor splash shield (if equipped). Remove knuckle from shock strut. If necessary, press hub from knuckle. *See Fig. 19.* Remove snap ring and press bearing from knuckle.

NOTE: A new bearing must be installed if original bearing is pressed out of knuckle.

Fig. 19: Removing Hub From Steering Knuckle

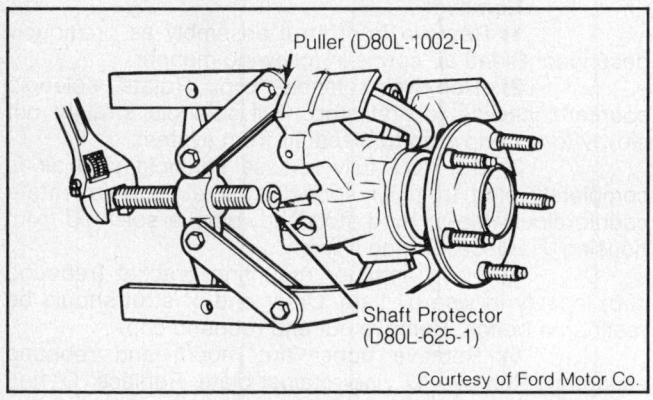

Courtesy of Ford Motor Co.

Installation

1) Install splash shield using new rivets. If removed, press NEW bearing into knuckle and install snap ring. Press hub into knuckle.

2) If necessary, replace seal on outboard CV joint. Install steering knuckle onto shock strut. Loosely install a NEW pinch bolt in knuckle to retain strut.

3) Install knuckle and strut on half-shaft. Install lower control arm to knuckle. Ensure ball stud groove is positioned correctly. Install a NEW nut and bolt. Tighten nut to specification. Tighten NEW strut-to-knuckle pinch bolt.

4) Install rotor and brake caliper. Coat caliper pins with silicone grease. Tighten caliper locating pins to specification.

5) With steering wheel in straight ahead position, place tie rod into knuckle. Install NEW slotted nut and tighten to specification. If needed, tighten tie rod nut slightly to align cotter pin holes. Install new cotter pin.

6) Install stabilizer bar link to strut. Install and tighten NEW nut to specification. Install wheels.

7) Lower vehicle. Install and tighten 3 top mount-to-apron nuts.

8) Use a puller to install half-shaft into hub. DO NOT use new hub nut to pull half-shaft into hub.

CAUTION: DO NOT impact wrench to tighten hub nut. Use torque wrench and tighten by hand.

9) Turn on air suspension. Pump brake prior to driving vehicle.

FRONT SUB-FRAME
Removal
1) Install Engine Support (D97L-6000-A) on engine lifting eyes to support engine from above. Turn off air suspension switch in trunk. Raise and support vehicle.

2) Remove front wheels. Support steering gear with wire from the tie rod end. Disconnect exhaust system at flex coupling and drop down.

3) Remove and DISCARD lower control arm pinch bolts at ball joint. New bolts and nuts must be installed on reassembly. Remove 2 steering gear-to-crossmember bolts.

4) Remove attaching nuts from right front and right rear engine mounts. Remove stabilizer bar link from stabilizer bar. Remove left engine mount insulator at sub-frame through bolt.

Fig. 20: Aligning Front Sub-Frame

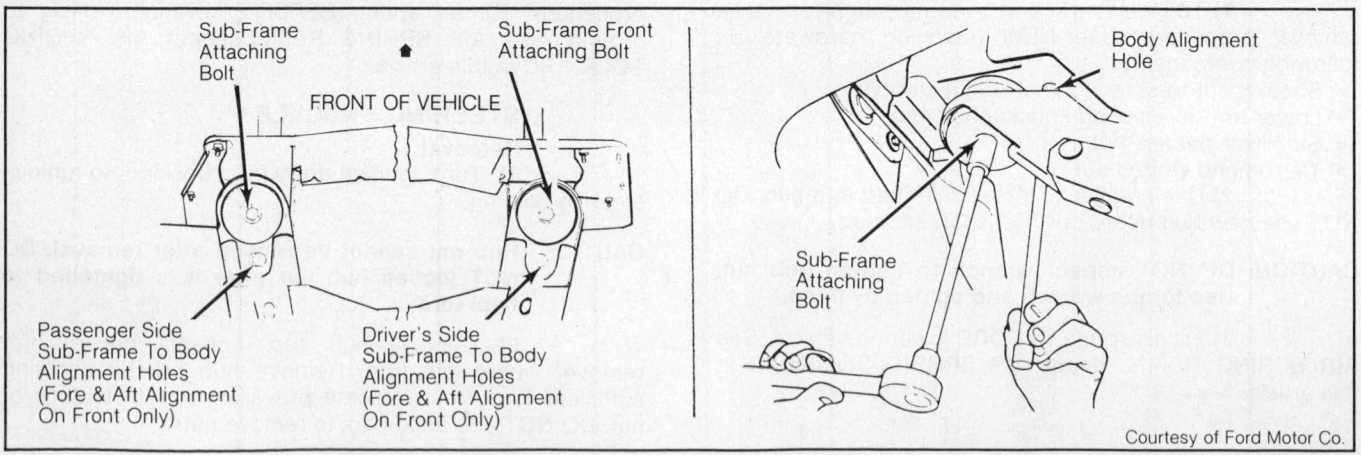

Courtesy of Ford Motor Co.

FORD MOTOR CO. AIR SUSPENSION – CONTINENTAL (Cont.)

5) Place jack stands at points where sub-frame meets body. Lower vehicle to jack stands. Remove 4 body mount attaching bolts. Raise vehicle enough to remove sub-frame.

Installation

1) Align sub-frame to body. Ensure all rubber mounts are in position. Install, but do not tighten, 4 sub-frame bolts.

2) Install a 3/4" O.D. pipe or similar tool into driver's side sub-frame and body alignment holes. *See Fig. 20.* Slightly tighten driver's side front body mount bolt.

3) Repeat step **2)** on right side (passenger) alignment holes. After verifying sub-frame is aligned, tighten mounting bolts to 65-85 ft. lbs. (90-115 N.m).

4) To complete installation, reverse removal procedure. Use NEW pinch bolt and nut at ball joint. Turn on air suspension switch after vehicle is lowered to ground.

REMOVAL & INSTALLATION (REAR SUSPENSION)

CAUTION: Manufacturer recommends using new suspension fasteners whenever old fasteners are loosened or removed.

REAR STRUT & SPRING ASSEMBLY

NOTE: Strut and spring assemblies must be replaced as an assembly. It is not necessary to replace in pairs.

Removal

1) Turn off air suspension switch in trunk. From inside trunk, unplug electrical connector for dual damping actuator. Loosen, but do not remove, 3 upper strut-to-body nuts.

2) Raise and support vehicle. Remove wheel. Disconnect air line from solenoid by pressing in release ring. Unplug electrical connector from solenoid valve.

3) Remove brake hose retainer at strut bracket. Disconnect parking brake cable from brake caliper. Remove all wire and parking brake cable retainers from lower control arm.

4) Disconnect height sensor link from ball stud pin on lower control arm. *See Fig. 21.* Remove caliper assembly from spindle and hang out of way.

Fig. 21: Rear Height Sensor Link

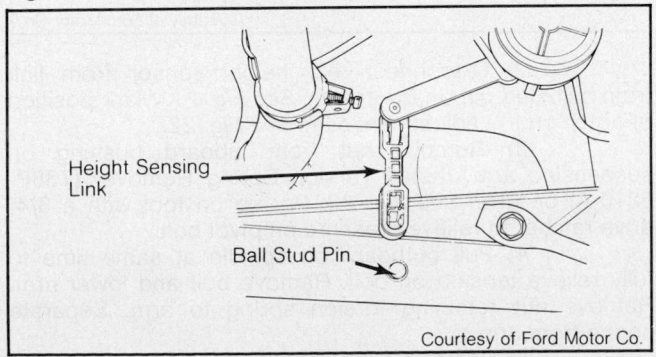

Height Sensing Link

Ball Stud Pin

Courtesy of Ford Motor Co.

5) Bleed air spring by removing solenoid clip. Rotate solenoid counterclockwise to first stop. *See Fig.12.* Pull solenoid straight out to second stop to bleed air.

6) After air is completely bled, rotate counterclockwise to third stop and remove solenoid from housing. Mark position of notch on toe adjustment cam. *See Fig. 22.*

Fig. 22: Rear Toe Adjustment Cam

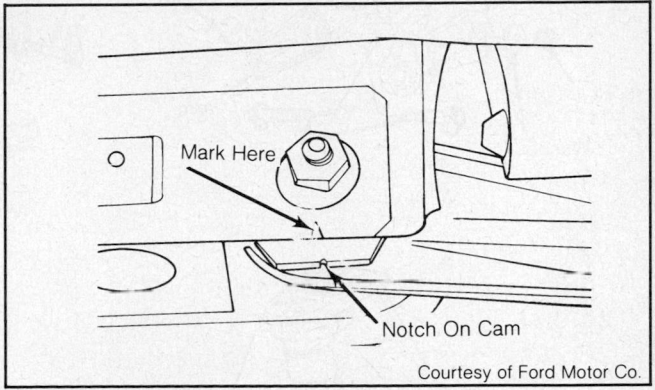

Mark Here

Notch On Cam

Courtesy of Ford Motor Co.

7) Remove nut from inboard bushing on suspension arm. Install Torsion Spring Remover (T88P-5310-A) on arm. Pry up on tool with a 3/4" drive ratchet to relieve pressure on pivot bolt. *See Fig. 23.*

8) Pull outboard on spindle at same time to fully relieve tension on bolt. Remove bolt and lower arm.

Fig. 23: Relieving Tension on Torsion Spring

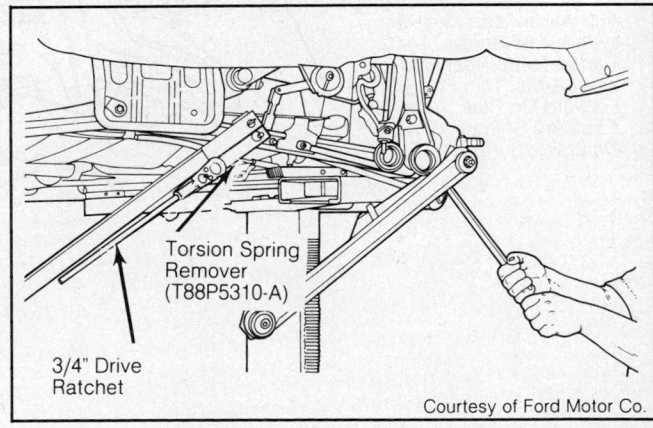

Torsion Spring Remover (T88P5310-A)

3/4" Drive Ratchet

Courtesy of Ford Motor Co.

9) Repeat steps **7)** and **8)** for opposite arm. Remove torsion spring from arms. Remove stabilizer "U" bracket from body. Remove nut, washer and insulator attaching stabilizer bar to link. Separate stabilizer bar from link.

10) Remove nut, washer and insulator that retain tension strut to rear spindle. Move spindle enough to separate it from tension strut.

11) Remove and DISCARD shock strut-to-spindle pinch bolt (if necessary) for removal. New pinch bolt and nut must be installed during reassembly if they are loosened or removed.

12) Separate spindle from strut and remove as an assembly with arms attached. From inside trunk, remove and DISCARD 3 upper mount-to-body nuts. Guide electric actuator wire through body opening.

Installation

To install shock strut, reverse removal procedure. Use NEW strut-to-spindle pinch bolt. Before tightening nut on inboard bushing of lower control arm, ensure toe alignment mark aligns with notch on cam. *See Fig. 22.* Adjust toe as necessary.

Fig. 24: Rear Suspension

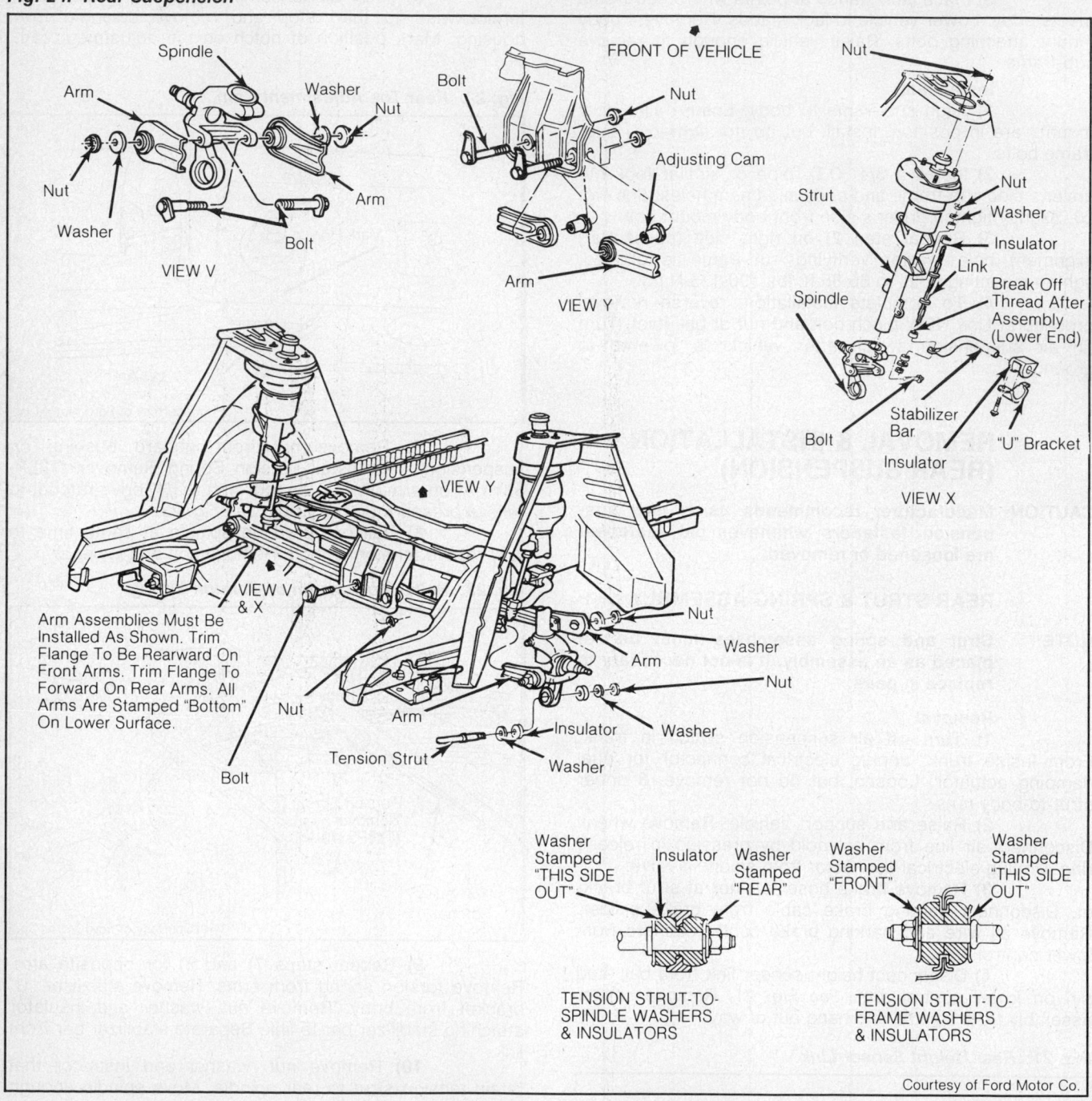

Arm Assemblies Must Be Installed As Shown. Trim Flange To Be Rearward On Front Arms. Trim Flange To Forward On Rear Arms. All Arms Are Stamped "Bottom" On Lower Surface.

TENSION STRUT-TO-SPINDLE WASHERS & INSULATORS

TENSION STRUT-TO-FRAME WASHERS & INSULATORS

Courtesy of Ford Motor Co.

CAUTION: Before lowering vehicle, fill air spring. See **AIR SPRING REFILL** under **AIR SPRING SOLENOID.**

LOWER CONTROL ARM (REAR)

NOTE: Control arm bushings are not serviceable. They are included with new control arm assembly.

Removal

1) Turn off air suspension switch in trunk. Raise and support vehicle. Remove all wire retainers and parking brake cable retainers from lower control arm.

2) Disconnect rear height sensor from link from ball stud pin on lower arm. See Fig. 21. Mark position of notch on toe adjustment cam. See Fig. 22.

3) Remove nut from inboard bushing on suspension arm. Install Torsion Spring Remover (T88P-5310-A) on arm. See Fig. 23. Pry up on tool with a 3/4" drive ratchet to relieve pressure on pivot bolt.

4) Pull outboard on spindle at same time to fully relieve tension on bolt. Remove bolt and lower arm. Remove nut retaining torsion spring to arm. Separate spring from arm.

5) Remove outboard attaching bolt at spindle. Repeat for other arm(s).

FORD MOTOR CO. AIR SUSPENSION – CONTINENTAL (Cont.)

Installation

1) When installing new control arms, offset must face up. Arms are stamped "BOTTOM" on lower edge. Rear control arm adjustment cams are installed from front of both arms. See Fig. 25.

Fig. 25: Rear Control Arm Adjustment Cams

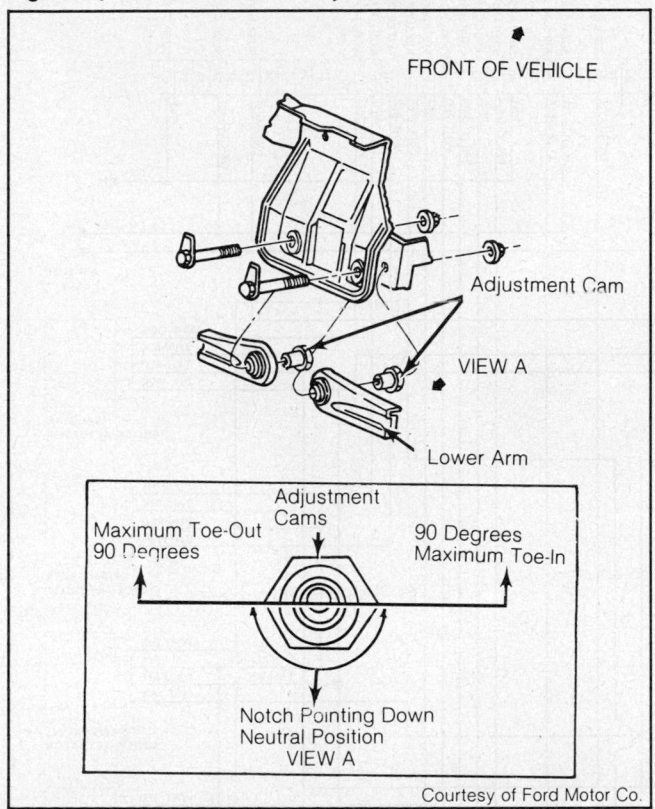

Courtesy of Ford Motor Co.

2) To complete installation, reverse removal procedure. Turn on air suspension switch after lowering vehicle to ground.

TENSION STRUT (REAR)
Removal

1) Turn off air suspension switch in trunk. Place vehicle on frame hoist. Raise hoist only enough to contact body.

2) From inside trunk, loosen but do not remove 3 upper shock strut-to-body nuts. Raise vehicle and remove wheels.

3) Remove and DISCARD tension strut-to-spindle nut. Remove and DISCARD tension strut-to-body. Move spindle rearward so tension strut can be removed.

Installation

1) Place new washers and bushings on both ends of tension strut. Front and rear bushings are different. Rear bushings have indentations in them. See Fig. 24.

2) Insert one end into body bracket. Install new bushing, washer and nut. DO NOT tighten at this time. Pull back on spindle enough so tension strut end can be installed in spindle.

3) Install new bushing, washer and nut. Ensure bushings are correctly installed. Tighten front and rear tension strut nuts. Support spindle with jack stand.

4) Remove 3 strut-to-body nuts. Install 3 NEW nuts and tighten to specification. Remove jack stand. Install wheel. Lower vehicle and turn on air suspension switch.

REAR SPINDLE
Removal

1) Turn off air suspension switch in trunk. From inside trunk, loosen, but do not remove, 3 upper strut-to-body nuts. Raise and support vehicle. DO NOT raise vehicle by tension strut.

2) Remove wheel. Remove brake hose retainer at strut bracket. Disconnect parking brake cable from brake caliper. Remove all wire and parking brake cable retainers from lower arm.

3) Disconnect height sensor link from ball stud pin on lower arm. See Fig. 21. Remove caliper assembly from spindle. Hang out of way with wire.

4) Remove rotor, hub, anchor plate, splash shield and brake adapter plate from spindle. Mark position of notch on toe adjustment cam. See Fig. 22.

5) Remove nut from inboard bushing on suspension arm. Install Torsion Spring Remover (T88P-5310-A) on arm. See Fig. 23. Pry up on tool with a 3/4" drive ratchet to relieve pressure on pivot bolt.

6) Pull outboard on spindle at same time to fully relieve tension on bolt. Remove bolt and lower arm.

7) Repeat steps 5) and 6) on opposite lower arm. Remove torsion springs from arms. Remove arms from spindle.

8) Remove and DISCARD shock strut-to-spindle pinch bolt. A new bolt must be installed on reassembly. Slightly spread spindle pinch joint so strut can be removed.

9) Remove nut, washer and insulator that retains tension strut to spindle. Slide tension strut from spindle. Remove spindle.

Installation

1) Install spindle on shock strut. Install a NEW shock strut-to-spindle pinch bolt. DO NOT tighten yet.

2) Position tension strut in spindle. Install insulator, washer and nut on tension strut. See Fig. 24. DO NOT tighten yet. Position spindle on lower arm. DO NOT tighten yet.

3) Install torsion spring on arms. Position inboard lower arm bushing in bracket using Torsion Spring Remover (T88P-5310-A). See Fig. 23. DO NOT tighten nut yet.

4) Set toe adjustment cam to alignment mark. See Fig. 22. Tighten ALL fasteners to specification.

5) Install brake adapter plate, splash shield, anchor plate and rotor hub on spindle. Before installing caliper on spindle, apply silicone dielectric lubricant to inside of slider pin boots and on slider pins.

6) Apply one drop of thread sealer to caliper pinch bolt threads. Install caliper. Hold slider pin while tightening pinch bolt.

7) Continue installation in reverse of removal procedure. Turn on air suspension switch after vehicle on the ground.

REAR STABILIZER BAR, LINK & INSULATORS
Removal

1) Turn off air suspension switch in trunk. Raise and support vehicle.

Electronic Suspensions

FORD MOTOR CO. AIR SUSPENSION – CONTINENTAL (Cont.)

Fig. 26: FWD Continental Electronic Suspension Wiring Diagram

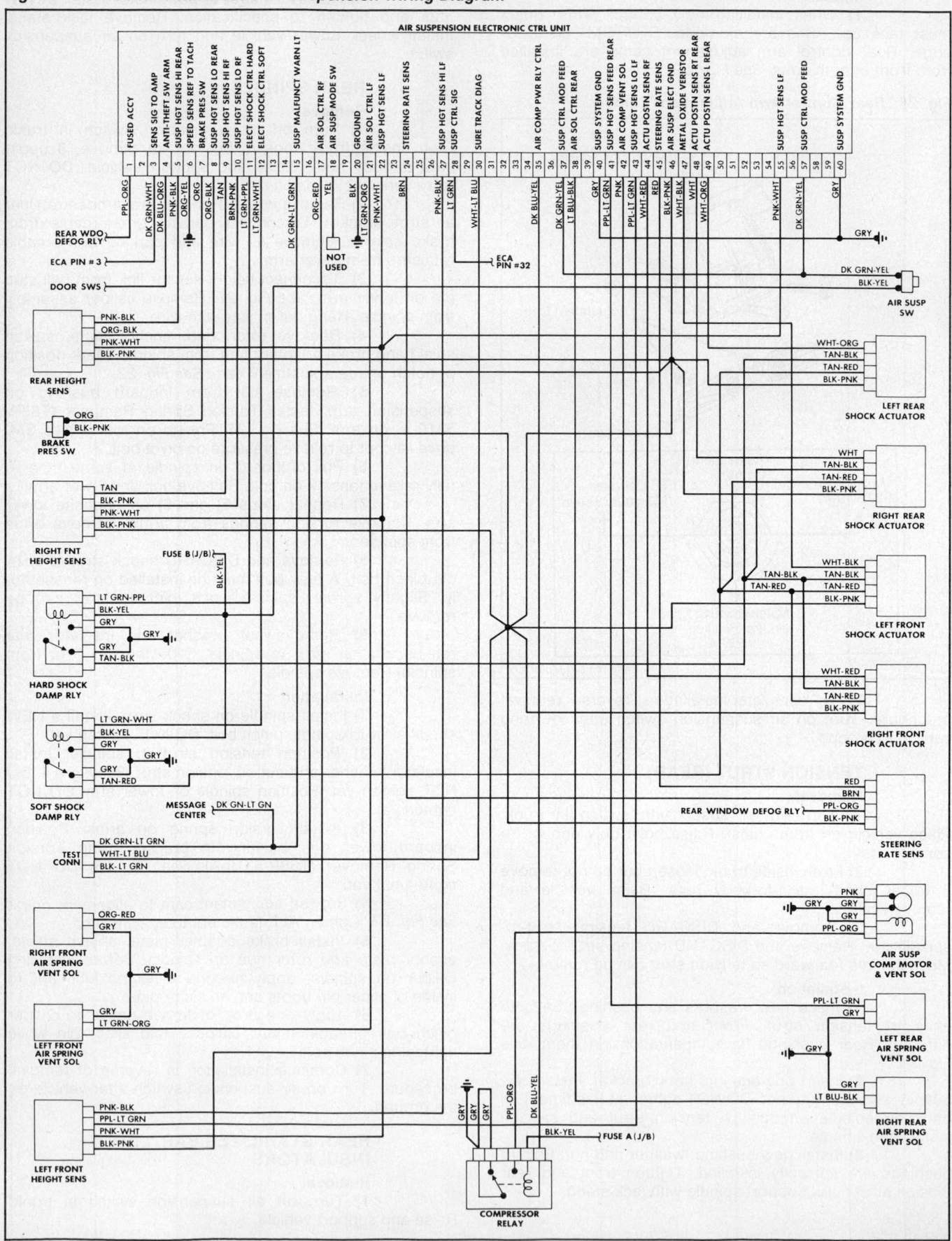

Electronic Suspensions

FORD MOTOR CO. AIR SUSPENSION – CONTINENTAL (Cont.)

2) Remove nuts, washers and insulators attaching stabilizer bar to right and left side links. DISCARD nuts. New nuts must be installed on reassembly.

NOTE: **Links have break-away threads at bottom for clearance purposes. Lower end of link rod will be rough.**

3) Remove and DISCARD "U" bracket bolts and stabilizer bar-to-body bolts. Remove stabilizer bar. Replace "U" bracket insulators if damaged or worn.

4) Remove nut, washer and insulator retaining link to shock strut bracket. DISCARD nut. It may be necessary to hold link nut while turning link with open end wrench at flats. Replace insulators if worn or damaged.

Installation

1) To install stabilizer bar, reverse removal procedure. When reusing old link, nut may be difficult to start. Align all parts as closely as possible before installing stabilizer bar.

2) If a new link is being installed, break off threads at cut after installing nut. Use NEW link-to-strut nut. Use NEW stabilizer bar-to-link nut. Use NEW stabilizer bar "U" bracket-to-body bolt.

TIGHTENING SPECIFICATIONS

Application	Ft. Lbs. (N.m)
Front Suspension	
Brake Caliper Locating Pins	18-25 (24-34)
Half-Shaft Hub Nut	180-200 (245-270)
Lower Control Arm-to-Frame Pivot Bolt	70-95 (95-129)
Lower Control Arm-to-Knuckle Nut	40-55 (54-75)
Stabilizer Bar-to-Stabilizer Bar Link Nut	35-48 (47-65)
Stabilizer Bar Link-to-Strut Nut	55-75 (75-101)
Strut-to-Knuckle Pinch Bolt	70-95 (95-129)
Strut-to-Top Mount Nut	35-50 (48-68)
Strut Top Mount-to-Shock Tower Nuts	22-32 (30-43)
Tension Strut Nut	70-95 (95-129)
Tie Rod End Nut	23-35 (31-47)
Rear Suspension	
Brake Caliper Pinch Bolt	[1] 30-35 (40-48)
Lower Control Arm-to-Body Nut	45-65 (62-88)
Lower Control Arm-to-Spindle Nut	42-57 (57-77)
Stabilizer Bar "U" Bracket-to-Body Bolt	25-37 (34-50)
Strut-to-Spindle Bolt	50-70 (68-95)
Strut Top Mount-to-Body Mount Nuts	19-26 (26-35)
Strut-to-Top Mount Nuts	35-50 (47-68)
Tension Strut-to-Body Nuts	52-74 (70-100)
Tension Strut-to-Spindle Nut	35-50 (48-68)

	INCH Lbs. (N.m)
Rear Suspension	
Stabilizer Bar Link-to-Strut Nut	72-144 (8-16)
Stabilizer Bar-to-Link Nut	72-144 (8-16)

[1] – Use one drop of thread sealer on caliper pinch bolts.

Electronic Suspensions

FORD MOTOR CO. AIR SUSPENSION — MARK VII

DESCRIPTION

The air suspension system is an air-operated, microprocessor controlled suspension system. This system replaces the conventional coil spring suspension and provides automatic front and rear load leveling. The 4 air springs, made of rubber and plastic, support the vehicle load at the front and rear wheels.

OPERATION

SYSTEM

Air suspension leveling system operates by adding or removing air in the springs to maintain level of vehicle at a predetermined front and rear suspension height. Suspension height is controlled by 3 height sensors (2 front and one rear).

Airflow to the entire system is controlled by the interaction of the air compressor, solenoids, height sensors and control module. Air solenoids are located on top of air springs. The air suspension is equipped with a self-diagnostic system. An air fill routine is preprogrammed into the control module memory. A warning light located in overhead console is used as a diagnostic aid and malfunction indicator.

CAUTION: Carefully read instructions to prevent damage to suspension system and possible personal injury due to automatic air filling procedure.

AIR COMPRESSOR

A single cylinder piston-type air compressor is mounted on left fender apron. Compressor is electrically operated and supplies air pressure to system. A regenerative type drier is attached to compressor manifold. All air flow during compression or venting passes through drier. A vent solenoid, located on compressor manifold, controls air exhaustion. Air compressor is replaced as a unit.

NOTE: The air compressor relay is on the left front shock tower.

CONTROL MODULE

A mirocomputer-based module controls the air compressor motor, vent solenoid and 4 air spring solenoids. The control module, located on left side of trunk, continuously monitors air suspension system through a pre-programmed test sequence. The system operates with ignition switch in both "OFF" and "RUN" positions.

DIAGNOSTIC SYSTEM

The air suspension system control module is equipped with an amber "CHECK SUSPENSION" warning light. The warning light is located in the overhead console.

Observation of warning light during normal operation with ignition on, can aid in detecting system problems. Warning light is lit by control module whenever a malfunction is noted in suspension system. Warning light is also used as a diagnostic aid during the preprogrammed test cycle.

HEIGHT SENSORS

The air suspension leveling system operates by adding or removing air to maintain vehicle (trim) height. Trim height is controlled by 3 height sensors. The height sensors are located at left and right front and one at rear. The sensors operate as follows:

As weight is added to vehicle, the body will settle under load. As vehicle lowers, height sensors shorten (low out-of-trim), sending a signal to control module which activates air compressor and opens air spring solenoid valves. When preset trim height is reached, air compressor and solenoid valves shut off.

Height sensors are attached to body and suspension arms, and will lengthen or shorten with suspension travel. When weight is removed, vehicle rises, which causes height sensors to lengthen (high out-of-trim). This sends a signal to the control module to open air compressor vent solenoid and air spring solenoid valves. As vehicle lowers, height sensors shorten, and when preset trim height is reached, air compressor vent and spring solenoid valves close.

Fig. 1: Exploded View of Ford Motor Co. Air Suspension System

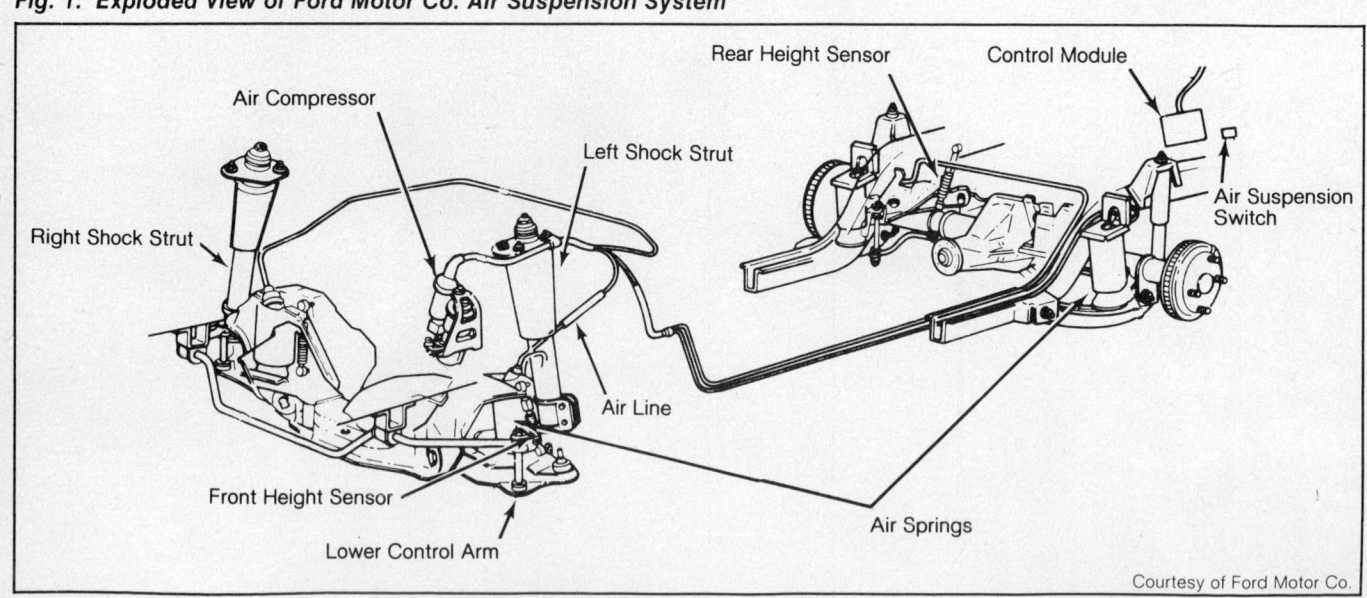

Courtesy of Ford Motor Co.

FORD MOTOR CO. AIR SUSPENSION – MARK VII (Cont.)

REPAIR PRECAUTIONS

Charging Or Jump Starting Battery

To prevent damage to air compressor relay or motor during battery charging, ignition switch must in "OFF" position if air suspension switch is on. Battery charger can be in use while diagnosing or testing system.

Jacking & Towing

The electrical power supply to the air suspension system must be shut off prior to hoisting, jacking or towing vehicle. Turn off air suspension switch located on left hand side of vehicle trunk or disconnect battery. *See Fig. 7.*

The following hoist restrictions must be observed: Use only a "body hoist". Lift vehicle using standard procedures and place jack stands at each corner as a safety precaution. If "body hoist" is not available, use standard hydraulic floor jack. Raise front of vehicle at No. 2 crossmember and place jack stands at front corners of body. For rear, use same procedure, but use rear jacking location.

ADJUSTMENTS

CASTER & CAMBER

See appropriate article in WHEEL ALIGNMENT section

RIDE HEIGHT ADJUSTMENT

NOTE: Pre-alignment procedure must be performed before alignment or ride height is checked so air suspension system will vent to trim. If vehicle is more than 20°F (6°C) colder or warmer than alignment area, time must be allowed for vehicle to match alignment area temperature.

Pre-Alignment Procedure

1) Drive onto alignment rack. Turn ignition off and exit vehicle. Level rack as necessary. Re-enter vehicle and turn ignition switch to the "RUN" position (DO NOT start).

2) Allow one minute for vehicle to level. Push trunk release, turn ignition off and exit vehicle. Allow 20 seconds for vehicle to vent to trim height (all doors closed).

3) Turn off air suspension system switch in trunk on left front side panel. *See Fig. 7.* Check for proper ride height. If necessary, adjust front ride height.

Adjusting Ride Height

1) Measure ride height at front and rear suspensions. *See Fig. 2.*

2) Adjust front ride height by moving front left and/or right lower sensor attaching stud.

3) There are 3 adjustment positions provided on bracket. Loosen attaching bolt and adjust as necessary. A one position change to sensor attachment point will result in 1/2" (12.7 mm) change, up or down. *See Fig. 3.*

4) Rear suspension ride height is adjusted by moving rear sensor attaching bracket up or down relative to right rear arm (slot adjustment is provided on bracket).

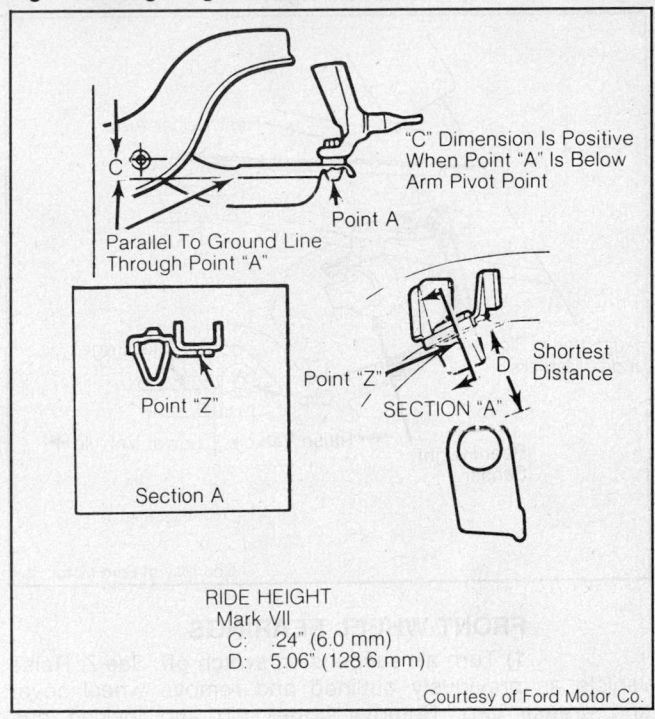

Fig. 2: Riding Height Check Points

"C" Dimension Is Positive When Point "A" Is Below Arm Pivot Point

Point A

Parallel To Ground Line Through Point "A"

Point "Z"

Section A

Point "Z"

SECTION "A"

Shortest Distance

RIDE HEIGHT
Mark VII
C: .24" (6.0 mm)
D: 5.06" (128.6 mm)

Courtesy of Ford Motor Co.

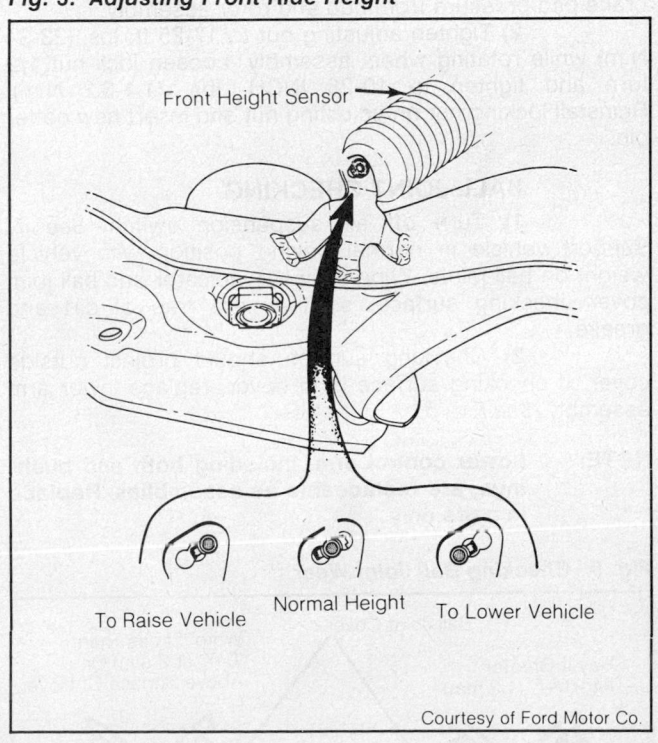

Fig. 3: Adjusting Front Ride Height

Front Height Sensor

To Raise Vehicle   Normal Height   To Lower Vehicle

Courtesy of Ford Motor Co.

5) Loosen attaching nut and adjust up or down as required. One index mark change to sensor attachment point will result in 1/4" (6.4 mm) change up or down. *See Fig. 4.*

FORD MOTOR CO. AIR SUSPENSION — MARK VII (Cont.)

Fig. 4: Adjusting Rear Ride Height

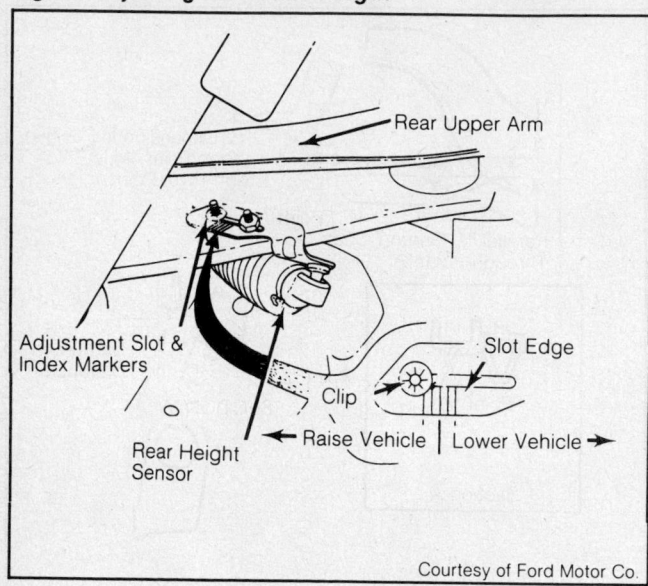

Rear Upper Arm

Adjustment Slot & Index Markers

Slot Edge

Clip

Rear Height Sensor

Raise Vehicle | Lower Vehicle →

Courtesy of Ford Motor Co.

FRONT WHEEL BEARINGS

1) Turn air suspension switch off. *See 7.* Raise vehicle as previously outlined and remove wheel cover and grease cap. Remove cotter pin and locking nut. Loosen adjusting nut 3 turns and rock wheel to relieve brake pad pressure from hub and rotor assembly.

2) Tighten adjusting nut to 17-25 ft. lbs. (23-34 N.m) while rotating wheel assembly. Loosen lock nut 1/2 turn and tighten to 10-28 INCH. lbs. (1.1-3.2 N.m). Reinstall locking nut on adjusting nut and insert new cotter pin.

BALL JOINT CHECKING

1) Turn off air suspension switch. *See 7.* Support vehicle in normal driving position with vehicle weight on ball joints. Wipe off wear indicator and ball joint cover checking surface, so they are free of dirt and grease.

2) Checking surface should project outside cover. If checking surface is in cover, replace lower arm assembly. *See Fig. 5.*

NOTE: Lower control arm, including both end bushings, are replaceable as assemblies. Replace in pairs only.

Fig. 5: Checking Ball Joint Wear

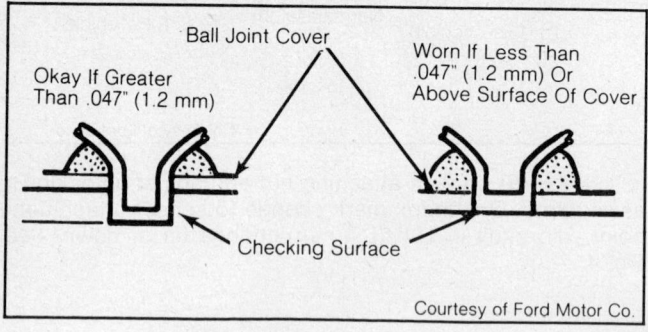

Ball Joint Cover

Okay If Greater Than .047" (1.2 mm)

Worn If Less Than .047" (1.2 mm) Or Above Surface Of Cover

Checking Surface

Courtesy of Ford Motor Co.

DIAGNOSIS & TESTING

TEST EQUIPMENT

The following test equipment is recommended to perform all tests on air suspension system. Do not attempt to test this system without proper equipment. Damage to vehicle components may result if improper equipment is used.
- Digital type volt/ohmmeters or an equivalent analog meter with 20,000 ohms per volt sensitivity.
- Fabricate a test light. Attach 2 test leads with pointed probes to a No. 194 bulb. Using any other bulb may damage air suspension system.
- 0-150 psi (0-70 kg/cm²) pressure gauge.

WARNING LIGHT

Main Functions

1) Warning light has 3 main functions. During normal operation with ignition in "RUN" position, a possible air suspension problem is indicated by a continuously glowing light.

2) During testing, the light cycles at about 2 blinks per second. This second function shows that control module diagnostic routine has been entered. Light will also blink test number that is being run during a test sequence.

3) The third function of the light is to show that the air spring fill routine in the module has been entered. During air spring fill routine, light will blink every 2 seconds.

Light Operation

1) On a vehicle operating normally, warning light will glow about one second and then go out when ignition is turned from "OFF" to "RUN" position. Light will NOT operate with ignition in "OFF" or "START" positions.

2) If light will not go out after turning ignition to "OFF" or "RUN" position, this is an indication of no battery power to control module.

3) Light can show height sensor or harness problem in following manner: light glows for about 1/2 second, goes out, and then glows continuously after 5-8 seconds when ignition is turned from "OFF" to "RUN" position.

4) System problem is indicated if light comes on and glows continuously at any time after 8 seconds when ignition is turned from "OFF" to "RUN".

5) If light comes on during an ignition "ON" cycle, it will glow continuously for that particular cycle. Any erratic light operation indicates a system malfunction.

SYSTEM LOGIC

The following describes how the air suspension system should work when all systems are operating properly.

Ignition In "OFF" Position

System operates for one hour after ignition is turned off. System is inoperable after one hour.

Ignition In "RUN" Position
(Less Than 45 Seconds)

System will raise front or rear of vehicle, if required. System will not lower vehicle.

Ignition In "RUN" Position
(More Than 45 Seconds)

1) If door(s) is open with brake off, system will raise vehicle, but will not lower vehicle until door(s) is

FORD MOTOR CO. AIR SUSPENSION — MARK VII (Cont.)

closed. If doors are closed and brake is off, system will raise or lower vehicle over a 45 second period.

2) If brake is applied and a door(s) is open, system will raise vehicle but not lower it. If brake is applied and doors are closed, system will NOT raise or lower vehicle. If rear of vehicle is in process of being raised, system will complete cycle.

General Operation

1) Vehicle will not be lowered if ANY door is open. System responds to signals from height sensors in following order: rear up, front up, rear down and front down.

2) With ignition in "RUN" position, warning light will come on for that ignition cycle if any up or down request from sensors is not carried out within 3 minutes. ONLY request that triggered light will be affected; all other up and down functions will operate normally.

3) Rear spring solenoids are operated together; front spring solenoids can operate independently.

Control module NEVER responds to front and rear signals at same time; front or rear height will be corrected separately.

4) Turning ignition from "RUN" to "OFF" clears all memory in module. Warning light may not immediately indicate a failure when ignition is turned to "RUN" position.

DIAGNOSTIC ROUTINE

How To Diagnose Air Suspension System

1) A quick system check can be made by following the QUICK TEST proceedure. If more detailed testing is required, go the Self-Test.

2) Follow all instructions in each step of the Self-Test. Self-Test will guide you to other tests (B through H) to repair the system.

QUICK TEST

All QUICK TEST measurements are made with air suspension switch "ON" amd the module unplugged.

Fig. 6: Quick Test

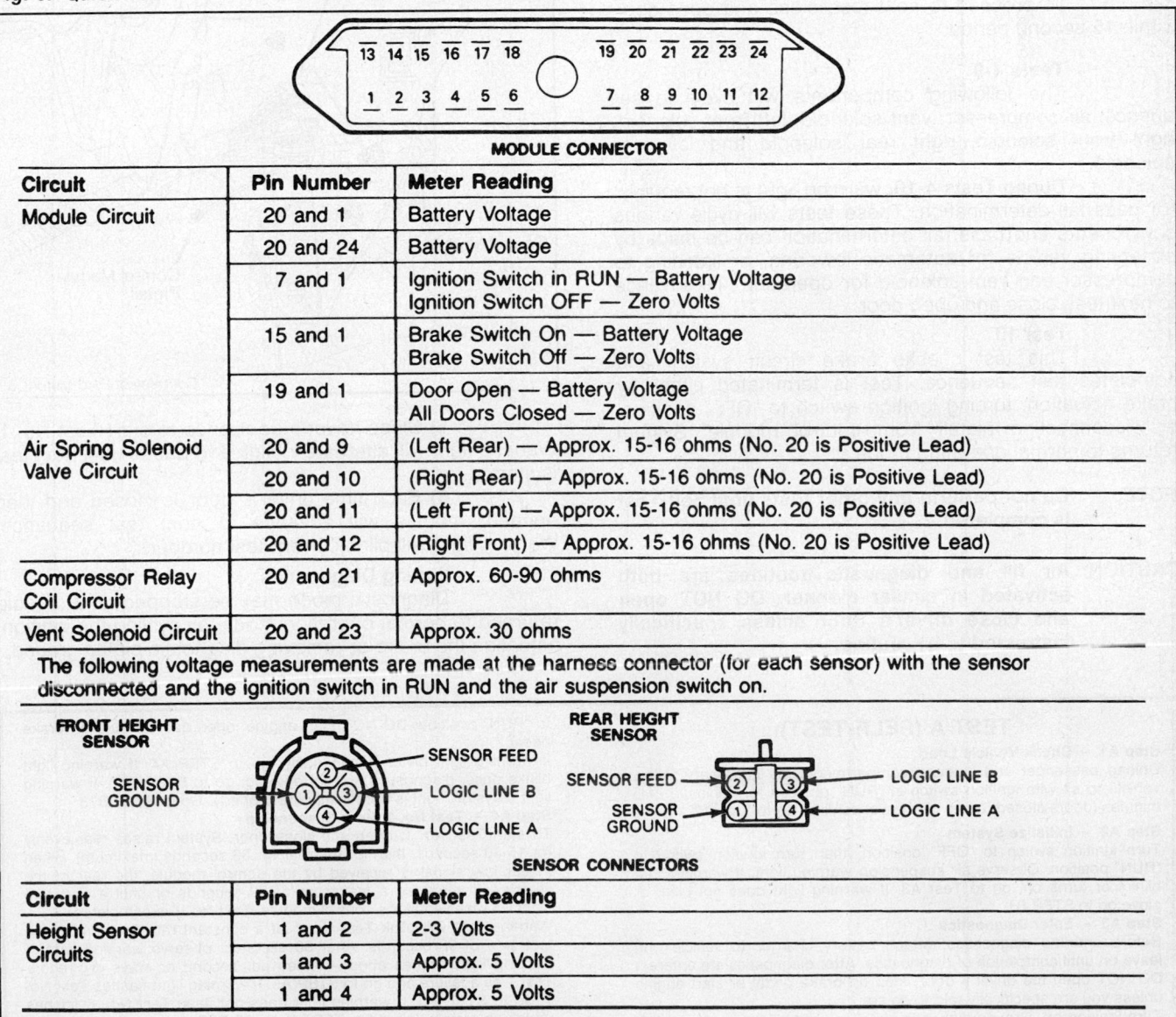

Circuit	Pin Number	Meter Reading
Module Circuit	20 and 1	Battery Voltage
	20 and 24	Battery Voltage
	7 and 1	Ignition Switch in RUN — Battery Voltage Ignition Switch OFF — Zero Volts
	15 and 1	Brake Switch On — Battery Voltage Brake Switch Off — Zero Volts
	19 and 1	Door Open — Battery Voltage All Doors Closed — Zero Volts
Air Spring Solenoid Valve Circuit	20 and 9	(Left Rear) — Approx. 15-16 ohms (No. 20 is Positive Lead)
	20 and 10	(Right Rear) — Approx. 15-16 ohms (No. 20 is Positive Lead)
	20 and 11	(Left Front) — Approx. 15-16 ohms (No. 20 is Positive Lead)
	20 and 12	(Right Front) — Approx. 15-16 ohms (No. 20 is Positive Lead)
Compressor Relay Coil Circuit	20 and 21	Approx. 60-90 ohms
Vent Solenoid Circuit	20 and 23	Approx. 30 ohms

The following voltage measurements are made at the harness connector (for each sensor) with the sensor disconnected and the ignition switch in RUN and the air suspension switch on.

Circuit	Pin Number	Meter Reading
Height Sensor Circuits	1 and 2	2-3 Volts
	1 and 3	Approx. 5 Volts
	1 and 4	Approx. 5 Volts

Courtesy of Ford Motor Co.

FORD MOTOR CO. AIR SUSPENSION – MARK VII (Cont.)

Air suspension switch MUST be "OFF" before unplugging module. Use a digital volt/ohmmeter or equivalent analog meter with 20,000 ohms per volt or greater sensitivity.

SELF-TEST (TEST A) EXPLANATION

The Self-Test (Test A) is a series of 10 individual tests which are conducted by the control module in a specific sequence.

During test sequence, warning light operation is an indication of system malfunction. Warning light will flash test number at constant rate during all tests.

Tests 1-3

These are complete cycles of suspension operation (raising and lowering; front first, then rear). Each successive transition from door closed to door open will cause control module to advance to next test.

During Tests 1-3, warning light will glow and remain on continuously if correct signal is not received within 30 seconds. If an illegal signal is received, warning light will flash rapidly. Either of these would indicate a failure. To repeat test, close and open door.

To proceed to next test, close and open door within 15-second period.

Tests 4-9

The following components will cycle in sequence: air compressor, vent solenoid, left front solenoid, right front solenoid, right rear solenoid and left rear solenoid.

During Tests 4-10, warning light is not required for pass/fail determination. These tests will cycle various components and pass/fail determination can be made by observing vehicle for automatic lowering, or listening to compressor and vent solenoid for operation. To advance to next test, close and open door.

Test 10

This test checks brake circuit system and completes test sequence. Test is terminated either by brake actuation, turning ignition switch to "OFF" position, or disconnecting pigtail from control module. System returns to normal operating mode.

NOTE: Do not perform any other tests until Self-Test is completed.

CAUTION: Air fill and diagnostic routines are both activated in similar manner. DO NOT open and close driver's door unless specifically instructed to by routine.

Entering Diagnostics

1) Turn on air suspension switch. Diagnostic pigtail located at rear of on/off switch in trunk must be ungrounded. See Fig. 7. Connect battery charger to battery to reduce drain.

2) Open driver's door with all other doors closed. Cycle ignition switch from "OFF" to "RUN" position, hold switch in "RUN" position for a minimum of 5 seconds. Turn ignition off.

3) Ground diagnostic pigtail on vehicle. Pigtail must remain grounded during diagnostic sequence.

4) Turn ignition switch to "RUN" position. Do not start vehicle. Warning light will blink continuously at a rate of about 1.8 blinks per second to indicate diagnostics routine has been entered.

Fig. 7: Location of Air Suspension Control Module & Switch

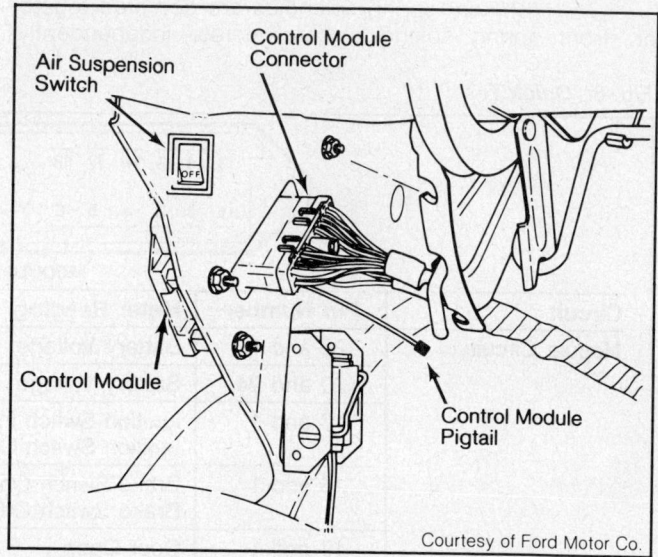

Air Suspension Switch

Control Module Connector

Control Module

Control Module Pigtail

Courtesy of Ford Motor Co.

5) Close driver's door once to start Test No. 1. Warning light will alternately blink and pause until next test is started.

6) Each time driver's door is closed and then opened, module will advance to next test sequence. Warning light will blink current test number.

Exiting Diagnostics

Diagnostic mode may be stopped, and module returned to normal operation mode, by cycling the ignition, actuating the brake or removing diagnostic pigtail ground.

TEST A (SELF-TEST)

Step A1 – Check Vehicle Load
Unload passenger and luggage compartments, as necessary. Allow vehicle to sit with ignition switch in "RUN" position for minimum of 5 minutes (doors closed, brake off). Level vehicle. Go to Step A2

Step A2 – Initialize System
Turn ignition switch to "OFF" position, then turn ignition switch to "RUN" position. Observe air suspension warning light. If warning light blinks or turns on, go to Test A3. If warning light does not blink or glow, go to STEP B1.

Step A3 – Enter Diagnostics
Before entering diagnostics, attach battery charger to vehicle and leave on until completion of diagnostics. After diagnostics are entered, DO NOT open the driver's door, step on brake pedal or start engine unless you are specifically told to do so.
Turn ignition off. Ground dianostic pigtail in trunk. Turn ignition switch

to "RUN" position; DO NOT start engine, open door or step on brake pedal.
If warning light blinks continuously, go to STEP A4. If warning light blinks once, diagnostics are not entered; go to STEP B10. If warning light stays on, light is not functioning properly. Go to STEP B13.

Step A4 – Test No. 1, Rear Suspension
To start Test No. 1, open and close door. System raises rear evenly for 15-30 seconds, then lowers rear for 30 seconds (maximum). When a rear low signal is received by the control module, the rear of the vehicle will raise for a maximum of 30 seconds or until a rear trim signal is received at the control module. Test No. 1 is completed.
Warning light will blink Test No. 1 at a constant rate for a maximum test time of 90 seconds. After 90 seconds, observe warning light. If warning light flashes about 4 times per second or stays on, record Test 1 as a failure and go to STEP A5. If warning light flashes Test No. 1, go to STEP A5. If warning light does not flash Test No. 1, flashes rapidly or remains on, go to TEST B, STEP B22. (Cont. on Next Page)

FORD MOTOR CO. AIR SUSPENSION — MARK VII (Cont.)

TEST A (Cont.)

Step A5 – Test 2, Right Front Suspension
To start test, open and close door once. If TEST NO. 1 failed, open and close door TWICE. System raises right front for 15-30 seconds, then lowers for 30 seconds (maximum). When right front low signal is received by control module, right front of vehicle will raise for maximum of 30 seconds or until right front trim signal is received by control module. Warning light will blink Test No. 2 at a constant rate for a maximum test time of 90 seconds.
After 90 seconds, observe warning light. If warning light flashes about 4 times per second or stays on, record Test No. 2 as a failure. Go to STEP A6. If warning light flashes Test No. 2, go to STEP A6

Step A6 – Test 3, Left Front Suspension
To start test, open and close door once. If Test No. 2 failed, open and close door TWICE. System raises left front for 15-30 seconds, then lowers for 30 seconds (maximum). When a vehicle high signal is received from left front sensor, left front of vehicle will raise for maximum of 30 seconds or until left front tim signal is received at control module. Warning light will blink Test No. 3 at a constant rate for a maximum test time of 90 seconds.
After 90 seconds, observe warning light. If warning light flashes about 4 times per second or stays on, record Test No. 3 as a failure. Go to STEP A7. If warning light flashes Test No. 3, system passed test. Go to STEP A7.

Step A7 – Test No. 4, Compressor
To start test, open and close door once. If Test No. 3 failed, open and close door TWICE. System cycles compressor on and off. Warning light will blink Test No. 4 continuously. Compressor will only cycle 50 times during test. Rear of vehicle may raise during test.
If compressor does not cycle, runs continuously or doesn't run, system failed test. Record Test No. 4 as a failure. Go to STEP A8. If compressor cycles, system passed test. Go to step A8.

Step A8 – Test 5, Vent Solenoid
To start test, open and close door. System cycles vent solenoid on and off. Solenoid is part of compressor assembly. Warning light will blink Test No. 5 continuously during test. If solenoid doesn't cycle, system failed test. Record Test No. 5 as a failure. Go to STEP A9 If solenoid cycles, system passed test. Go to STEP A9.

Step A9 – Test 6, Left Front Air Spring Solenoid
To start test, open and close door. Listen for air escaping from vent solenoid and for left front spring solenoid to cycle. Left front of vehicle will drop during test.
If spring solenoid doesn't cycle or air is not venting, system has failed test. Record Test No. 6 as a failure. Go to STEP A10. If spring solenoid cycles and air is escaping from vent solenoid, system passed test. Go to STEP A10.

Step A10 – Test 7, Right Front Air Spring Solenoid
To start test, open and close door. Listen for air escaping from vent solenoid and for right front spring solenoid to cycle. Right front of vehicle will drop during test.
If spring solenoid doesn't cycle or air is not venting, system has failed test. Record Test No. 7 as a failure. Go to STEP A11. If spring solenoid cyles and air is escaping from vent solenoid, system has passed test. Go to STEP A11.

Step A11 – Test 8, Right Rear Air Spring Solenoid
To start test, open and close door. Listen for air escaping from vent solenoid and for right rear spring solenoid to cycle. Right rear of vehicle will drop during test.
If spring solenoid doesn't cycle or air is not venting, system has failed test. Record Test No. 8 as a failure. Go to STEP A12. If spring solenoid cycles and air is venting, system has passed test. Go to STEP A12.

Step A12 – Test 9, Left Rear Air Spring Solenoid
To start test, open and close door. Listen for air escaping from vent solenoid and for left rear spring solenoid to cycle. Left rear of vehicle will drop during test.
If spring solenoid doesn't cycle or air is not venting, system has failed test. Record Test No. 9 as a failure. Go to step A13. If spring solenoid cycles and air is escaping, system has passed test. Go to STEP A13.

Step A13 – Test 10, Brake Circuit
To start test, open door. DO NOT close door. Sit in driver's seat and depress brake pedal. If warning light continues to blink, system has failed test. Go to TEST D, STEP B30. If warning light stops blinking, system has passed test. This completes diagnostic sequence. If system passed all Self-Tests, disconnect ground from pigtail.

Step A14 – Any Failures Recorded?
If any failures were recorded during Self-Test, go to STEP A15. If no failures were noted, system is working correctly. No further tests required.

Step A15
If warning light flashed rapidly for any of the first 3 tests, go to TEST C. If sensors okay, go to STEP A16.

Step A16
If warning light stayed on after completion of Test 1, check rear of vehicle. Go to TEST D. If light did not stay on, go to STEP A17.

Step A17
If warning light stayed on after completion of Test 2, go to Test E. If warning light did not stay on, go to STEP A18.

Step A18
If warning light stayed on after completion of Test 3, go to Test E. If light did not stay on, go to STEP A19.

Step A19
If left front solenoid cycled during TEST NO. 6, solenoid is okay. Go to STEP A20. If left front solenoid did NOT cycle during Test 6, go to TEST F.

STEP A20
If right front solenoid cycled during TEST NO. 7, solenoid is okay. go to STEP A21. If right front solenoid did not cycle during TEST 7, go to TEST E1.

Step A21
If right rear solenoids did NOT cycle or air did not escape from vent solenoid during Test 8, go to Test D. If solenoid did cycle, solenoid is okay. Go to **STEP A22**

If left rear solenoids did NOT cycle or air did NOT escape from vent solenoid during Test 9, go to TEST D. If solenoid did cycle, solenoid is okay.

TEST B (CANNOT ENTER, SEQUENCE OR EXIT DIAGNOSTIC TEST)

Step B1
Check air suspension warning light bulb, and replace if defective. Repeat Self-Test. If bulb is not defective, go to STEP B2.

Step B2 – Make Test Light
Make a test light out of a No. 194 bulb and 2 leads. Any other bulb WILL DAMAGE SYSTEM. Go to STEP B3.

Step B3 – Check Ignition Circuit
Check ignition circuit. Turn ignition and air suspension switch (in trunk) off. If warning light is off, go to STEP B4. If warning light stays on, repair short between battery to ignition in circuit No. 687. Circuit No. 687 is Gray/Yellow wire that ends at module pin No. 7. Turn air suspension switch on. Repeat Self-Test.

Step B4 – Check Ignition Circuit
Check ignition circuit using test light, connect one lead to ignition circuit No. 640 (Red/Yellow wire) at warning light and other lead to ground. Turn ignition switch to "RUN" position. If test light is on, go to STEP B6. If test light remains off, go to STEP B5.

Step B5 – Check Fuse
Check fuse in ignition circuit No. 640 (Red/Yellow wire on fuse panel). If fuse is okay, repair open in circuit No. 640. Repeat Self-Test. If fuse is blown, repair short in ignition circuit No. 640, and replace fuse. If second fuse fails, repeat Self-Test.

Step B6 – Check Ignition Circuit
Check ignition circuit. Using test light, connect one lead to pin No. 7 (circuit No. 687) of control module connector and other lead to ground. Turn ignition switch to "RUN" position.
If test light is on, go to STEP B7. If test light is off, repair short in ignition circuit No. 687. Turn air suspension switch on, and repeat Self-Test.

(Cont. on Next Page)

TEST B (Cont.)

Step B7 – Check Module Ground Circuit
Connect one test light lead to pin No. 7 (circuit No. 687) of control module connector. Turn ignition switch to "RUN" position. Connect other test light lead to pin No. 1 (circuit No. 430) of control module connector. Move lead on pin No. 1 of control module connector to pin No. 24 on control module connector.
If test light is on, go to STEP B8. If test light does NOT light, repair open in circuit No. 430 and repeat Self-Test.

Step B8 – Check Warning Light Circuit
Using volt/ohmmeter, connect negative test lead to ground. Connect positive lead to pin No. 21 (circuit No. 419) of control module connector. Turn ignition switch to "RUN" position.
If voltage is more than 5 volts, go to STEP B9. If voltage is 5 volts or less, repair short in warning light circuit No. 419 from control module connector to warning light connector. Turn air suspension switch on. and repeat Self-Test.

Step B9 – Check Battery Voltage
Connect negative lead to pin No. 24 (circuit No. 430) of control module connector and positive lead to pin No. 20 (circuit No. 418) of control module connector. Turn ignition switch to "RUN" position.
If voltage is less than 11 volts, check battery or faulty connection. Turn air suspension switch on and repeat Self-Test. If voltage is more than 11 volts, replace air suspension control module. Perform Self-Test.

Step B10
Check for proper ground at pigtail. If warning light blinks only once, go to STEP B11. If warning light blinks more than once, repeat Self-Test.

Step B11 – Test Light
If not already done, fabricate test light from a No. 194 light. Go to STEP B12.

STEP B12 – Check Pigtail
Using test light, connect one lead to pin No. 2 (circuit No. 606) of control module connector and other lead to pin No. 7 (circuit No. 687) of control module connector. Turn ignition to "RUN" position. Ground and then unground the diagnostic pigtail.
If test light is on, then off, pigtail circuit is good. Go to STEP B13. If test light is off, repair short in circuit No. 606 (White/Lt. Blue on module pin No. 2) and repeat Self-Test.

Step B13 – Checking System In Diagnostic Mode
Open and close door. If compressor starts running, go to STEP B20. If compressor is already running or does not start, go to STEP B14

Step B14 – Test Light
If not already done, fabricate test light from a No. 194 light. Go to STEP B15.

Step B15 – Checking Battery Circuit
Using test light, connect one lead to pin No. 20 (circuit No. 418) at control module connector and other lead to ground. If test light illuminates, go to STEP B21. If test light is off, go to STEP B16.

Step B16 – Check Fuse Link
Check battery circuit No. 175 (Black/Yellow wire) at on/off switch in trunk. If fuse link is good, go to STEP B17. If fuse link is blown, replace fuse link and repeat Self-Test.

Step B17
Check that air suspension switch is on. If on, go to STEP B18. If switch is off, turn air suspension switch on and repeat Self-Test.

Step B18 – Check Battery Circuit
Using test light, connect one lead to Black/Yellow wire (circuit No. 175) at air suspension switch pin No. 2 and the other lead to ground. If test light is on, go to STEP B19. If test light is off, repair short in battery circuit No. 175 from air suspension switch to battery and repeat Self-Test.

Step B19 – Checking On/Off Switch
Using test light, connect one lead to on/off switch pin No. 1 (circuit No. 418) of switch (control module side) and other lead to ground. If test light is on, repair short in battery from pin No. 1 to battery and repeat Self-Test. If test light is off, replace switch. Repeat Self-Test.

Step B20 – Check Warning Light Circuit
Unplug control module connector. If warning light is on, repair short in ground circuit No. 419 from control module connector to warning light. Plug in connector and repeat Self-Test. If warning light is off, go to STEP B21.

Step B21 – Checking Battery Voltage
Using volt/ohmmeter, connect negative lead to pin No. 24 (circuit No. 430) of control module connector and positive lead to pin No. 20 (circuit No. 418) of control module connector.
If voltage is less than 11 volts, check for low battery or faulty connections at battery and repeat Self-Test. If voltage is more than 11 volts, replace control module. Plug in connectors and repeat Self-Test.

Step B22 – Test Light
If not already done, fabricate test light from a No. 194 light. Go to STEP B23.

Step B23 – Checking Door Circuit
Using test light, connect one lead to pin No. 19 (circuit No. 24) at control module connector and other lead to ground. Close door.
If test light is on, repair short in circuit No. 24 or replace faulty door switch. Repeat Self-Test. If test light is off, go to STEP B24.

Step B24 – Checking Door Circuit
Open door. If test light comes on, circuit is good. Go to STEP B25. If test light is off, replace defective door switch or repair open or short circuit No. 24.

Step B25 – Checking Brake Circuit
Depress and release brake pedal. If rear brake lights operate properly, go to STEP B26. If brake lights do not operate properly, repair as necessary and repeat Self-Test.

Step B26 – Checking Compressor Circuit
Disconnect compressor relay connector. Perform STEPS A2-A4 of Self-Test. Observe warning light. If light flashes rapidly, flashes test number or stays on, go to STEP B27. If light does anything else, go to STEP B21.

Step B27 – Checking Compressor Circuit
DO NOT reconnect compressor relay connector. Using volt/ohmmeter, connect negative lead to ground and positive lead to pin No. 2 (circuit No. 417) on harness side of connector.
Measure resistance. If reading is greater than 1000 ohms, go to STEP B27. If reading less than 1000 ohms, repair short to ground on circuit No. 417 and repeat Self-Test.

Step B28 – Checking Compressor Current
Unplug compressor connector. Connect jumper wire (14 ga. minimum) between compressor connector (compressor side) pin No. 3 and a good ground. Using ammeter, (40 amps minimum) connect negative lead to pin No. 3 and positive lead to positive side of battery.
Measure amperage after compressor has run for 10 seconds. DO NOT allow compressor to run more than 60 seconds. If amperage is greater than 35 amps, replace compressor assembly and repeat Self-Test. If less than 35 amps, go to STEP B29.

Step B29 – Checking Compressor Voltage
Perform STEP B28, except measure battery voltage with compressor running. If more than 11 volts, replace control module. Plug in connectors and repeat Self-Test. If less than 11 volts, check battery and charge if necessary. Repeat Self-Test.

Step B30 – Test Light
If not already done, fabricate test light from a No. 194 light. Go to STEP B31.

Step B31 – Checking Brake Circuit
Depress and release brake pedal. If brake lights operate properly, go to STEP B32. If brake lights do not operate properly, repair as necessary and repeat Self-Test.

Step B32 – Checking Brake Circuit
Using test light, connect one lead to pin No. 15 (circuit No. 511) at control module connector and other lead to ground. Depress brake pedal. If test light is on, replace control module and repeat Self-Test. If light is off, repair short in brake circuit No. 511. and repeat Self-Test.

TEST C (SENSOR TESTS)

Step C1
If warning light flashed for all 3 tests, go to STEP C2. If not, go to STEP C11.

Step C2 – Checking Sensor Ground Circuit
Using test light, connect one lead to pin No. 1 (circuit No. 432) at left front sensor connector and connect other lead to the positive battery terminal. If test light is on, ground circuit is good. Go to STEP C5. If light is off, go to STEP C3.

Continued On Next Page

FORD MOTOR CO. AIR SUSPENSION — MARK VII (Cont.)

TEST C (Cont.)

Step C3 – Checking Sensor Ground Circuit
Using test light, connect one lead to pin No. 14 (circuit No. 432) at control module connector. DO NOT disconnect control module. Attach other lead to pin No. 20. If test light is on, repair open in ground circuit No. 432 and perform Self-Test. If light is off, go to STEP C4.

Step C4
Unplug control module connector. Check sensor ground pin No. 14, and control module ground pins No. 1 and No. 24 for corrosion or damage. If damage or corrosion is found, repair or clean pins and perform Self-Test. If pins are good, replace control module and perform Self-Test.

Step C5
Set volt/ohmmeter to read 3 volts DC. Connect negative lead to pin No. 14 (circuit No. 432) at control module connector. Connect positive lead to pin No. 4 (circuit No. 431) of control module connector. Turn ignition switch to "RUN" position.
If reading is less than one volt and steady, go to STEP C6. If readings are erratic or greater than one volt, but less than 5 volts, repair open in sensor power circuits No. 426 or No. 431, between control module and sensors. Perform Self-Test. If reading is more than 5 volts, replace control module and perform Self-Test.

Step C6 – Checking Left Front Sensor
Unplug harness at left front sensor and read volt/ohmmeter. If reading is less than one volt and steady, sensor is good. Go to STEP C7. If reading is erratic or more than one volt, replace left front sensor and perform Self-Test.

Step C7 – Checking Right Front Sensor
Do not reconnect left front sensor. Disconnect harness at right front sensor and read volt/ohmmeter. If reading is less than one volt and steady, sensor is good. Go to STEP C8. If reading is erratic or more than one volt, replace sensor and perform Self-Test.

Step C8 – Checking Rear Sensor
Do not reconnect left or right front sensor. Disconnect harness at rear sensor and read volt/ohmmeter. If reading is less than one volt and steady, sensor is good. Go to STEP C9. If reading is erratic or more than one volt, replace sensor. Reconnect all sensors (except rear) and perform Self-Test.

Step C9 – Checking Sensor Power Circuit
Do not reconnnect rear sensor. Disconnect control module. Using volt/ohmmeter, connect negative lead to pin No. 1 (circuit No. 430) of control module connector and positive lead to pin No. 3 (circuit No.426) at control module connector. Measure resistance.
If more than 1000 ohms, go to STEP C10). If less than 1000 ohms, repair short in circuit No. 426. Reconnect all sensors and control module. Perform Self-Test.

Step C10 – Checking Sensor Power Circuit
Move positive lead to pin No. 4 (circuit No. 431) at control module connector. Measure resistance. If more than 1000 ohms, replace control module and PERFORM Self-Test. If less than 1000 ohms, repair short to ground in circuit No. 431. Reconnect all sensors and control module and perform Self-Test.

Step C11
If warning light flashed rapidly on Test No. 1, go to STEP C12. If not, go to STEP C23.

Step C12 – Checking Sensor Ground Circuit
Turn air suspension switch off. Using volt/ohmmeter, connect positive lead to pin No. 1 (circuit No. 432) at rear sensor. Connect negative lead to ground. Measure resistance.
If more than 5 ohms, repair open in circuit No. 432 between control module connector and rear sensor. Perform Self-Test. If less than 5 ohms, go to STEP C13.

Step C13 – Checking Sensor Power Circuit
Turn air suspension switch on. Using volt/ohmmeter, connect negative test lead to pin No. 1 (circuit No. 432) at rear sensor connector and positive lead to pin No. 2 (circuit No. 426). Turn ignition switch to "RUN" position and read voltage.
If less than one volt and steady, repair open in circuit No. 426 from sensor to control module and Self-Test. If voltage is more than one volt or erratic, power circuit is good. Go to STEP C14.

Step C14 – Checking Rear Sensor "A" Circuit
Move positive lead to pin No. 4 (circuit No. 427) at rear sensor connector. Read voltage. If more than 1.5 volts, rear sensor circuit is good. Go to step C15. If less than 1.5 volts, go to STEP C15.

Step C15 – Checking Rear Sensor
Unplug rear sensor connector and read voltage. If more than 1.5 volts, replace rear sensor. Perform Self-Test. If less than 1.5 volts, go to STEP C16.

Step C16 – Checking Rear Sensor "A" Circuit
Do not connect rear sensor. Using a volt/ohmmeter, connect negative lead to pin No. 14 (circuit No. 432) and positive lead to pin No. 13 (circuit No. 427). Read voltage.
If more than 1.5 volts, repair open in circuit No. 427 between control module and sensor. Connect sensor lead and perform Self-Test. If less than 1.5 volts, go to STEP C17.

Step C17 – Checking Rear Sensor "A" Circuit
Unplug control module. Using volt/ohmmeter, connect negative lead to pin No. 1 (circuit No. 430) at control module connector and positive lead to pin No. 13 (circuit No. 427). Read resistance.
If more than 1000 ohms, replace control module unit. Connect rear sensor and perform Self-Test. If less than 1000 ohms, repair short to ground on circuit No. 427, between control module and rear sensor. Connect rear sensor and perform Self-Test.

Step C18 – Checking Rear Sensor "B" Circuit
Move postive lead to pin No. 3 (circuit No. 428) at rear sensor connector and read voltage. If more than 1.5 volts, rear sensor circuit is good. Go to STEP C19. If less than 1.5 volts, go to STEP C20.

Step C19 – Checking Control Module Damage
Repeat Self-Test, STEPS A2-A4. If warning light flashes rapidly, replace control module and perform Self-Test. If warning light is NOT flashing rapidly, perform Self-Test.

Step C20 – Checking Rear Sensor
Unplug rear sensor and read voltage. If more than 1.5 volts, replace rear sensor and perform Self-Test. If less than 1.5 volts, rear sensor is good. Go to STEP C21.

Step C21 – Checking Rear Sensor "B" Circuit
Do not connect rear sensor. Connect negative lead to pin No. 14 (circuit No. 432) at control module connector and positive lead to pin No. 18 (circuit No. 428) at module connector. Read voltage.
If more than 1.5 volts, repair short in circuit No. 428 between control module and sensor. Connect rear sensor and perform Self-Test. If less than 1.5 volts, go to STEP C22.

Step C22 – Checking Rear Sensor "B" Circuit
Unplug control module connector. Using volt/ohmmeter, connect negative lead to pin No. 1 (circuit No. 430) and positive lead to pin No. 18 (circuit No. 428). Read resistance.
If more than 1000 ohms, replace control module. Connect rear sensor and perform Self-Test. If less 1000 ohms, repair short in circuit No. 428 between control module and rear sensor. Connect control module and perform Self-Test.

Step C23
If warning light flashed rapidly during Self-Test, STEP A2, go to STEP C24. If not, go to STEP C35.

Step C24 – Checking Sensor Ground Circuit
Using test light, connect one lead to pin No. 1 (circuit No. 432) at right front sensor and other lead to positive side of battery.
If test light is on, sensor ground circuit is good. Go to STEP C25. If test light is off, repair short in circuit No. 432 between control module and right front sensor. Connect sensor and perform Self-Test.

Step C25 – Checking Sensor Power Circuit
Using volt/ohmmeter, connect negative lead to pin No. 1 (circuit No. 432) at right front sensor connector and positive lead to pin No. 2 (circuit No. 431) at right front sensor. Turn ignition switch to "RUN" position and read voltage.
If less than one volt and steady, repair open in circuit No. 431 from right front sensor to control module. Connect sensor and perform Self-Test. If voltage is more than one volt and erratic, sensor power is good. Go to STEP C26.

Step C26 – Checking Right Front Sensor "A" Circuit
Move positive lead to pin No. 4 (circuit No. 424) at right front sensor and read voltage. If more than 1.5 volts, right front sensor is good. Go to step C30. If less than 1.5 volts, go to STEP C27.

Step C27 – Checking Right Front Sensor
Unplug right front sensor and read voltage. If more than 1.5 volts, replace right front sensor and perform Self-Test. If less than 1.5 volts, right front sensor is good. Go to STEP C28.

Step C28 – Checking Right Front Sensor "A" Circuit
Do not connect right front sensor. Using volt/ohmmeter, connect negative lead to pin No. 14 (circuit No. 432) at control module connector and positive lead to pin No. 5 (circuit 424) at module connector. Read voltage.

(Cont. on Next Page)

11-144

Electronic Suspensions
FORD MOTOR CO. AIR SUSPENSION – MARK VII (Cont.)

TEST C (Cont.)

If more than 1.5 volts, repair short in sensor circuit No. 424 between control module and sensor. Connect sensor and perform Self-Test. If less than 1.5 volts, go to STEP C29.

Step C29 – Checking Right Front Sensor "A" Circuit
Do not connect control module. Using volt/ohmmeter, connect negative lead to pin No. 1 (circuit No. 430) at control module connector and positive lead to pin No. 5 (circuit No. 424) at control module connector. Read resistance.
If more than 1000 ohms, replace control module. Connect right front sensor and perform Self-Test. If less than 1000 ohms, repair short in circuit No. 424 between control module and right front sensor. Connect sensor and perform Self-Test.

Step C30 – Checking Right Front Sensor "B" Circuit
Move positive lead to right front sensor connector pin No. 3 (circuit No. 425) at right front sensor connector and read voltage. If more than 1.5 volts, replace right front sensor and go to STEP C31. If less than 1.5 volts, go to STEP C32.

Step C31 – Checking Control Module
Repeat Self-Test, STEPS A2-A5. If warning light flashes rapidly during test, replace control module. Perform Self-Test. If warning light is NOT flashing rapidly, perform Self-Test.

Step C32 – Checking Right Front Sensor
Unplug right front sensor and read voltage. If more than 1.5 volts, replace sensor and perform Self-Test. If less than 1.5 volts, go to STEP C33.

Step C33 – Checking Right Front Sensor "B" Circuit
Do not connect right front sensor. Using volt/ohmmeter, connect negative lead to pin No. 14 (circuit No. 432) at control module connector and positive lead to pin No. 16 (circuit No. 425) at control module connector. Read voltage.
If more than 1.5 volts, repair short in sensor B circuit No. 425 between control module and sensor. Connect sensor and perform Self-Test. If less than 1.5 volts, go to STEP C34.

Step C34 – Checking Right Front Sensor "B" Circuit
Unplug control module. Using volt/ohmmeter, connect negative lead to pin No. 1 (circuit No. 430) at control module connector and positive lead to pin No. 16 (circuit No. 425). Read resistance.
If more than 1000 ohms, replace control module. Reconnect sensor and perform Self-Test. If less than 1000 ohms, repair short in circuit No. 425 between control module and right front sensor. Perform Self-Test.

Step C35 – Checking Sensor Ground Circuit
Using test light, connect one lead to pin No. 1 (circuit No. 432) at left front sensor and other lead to positive battery terminal.
If test light is on, sensor ground is good. Go to STEP C36. If test light is off, repair short in circuit No. 432 between control module and left front sensor. Connect sensor and perform Self-Test.

Step C36 – Checking Sensor Power Circuit
Using volt/ohmmeter, connect negative lead to pin No. 1 (circuit No. 432) at left front sensor connector and positive lead to pin No. 2 (circuit No. 431) at left front sensor. Turn ignition switch to "RUN" position and read voltage.
If voltage is less than one volt, repair short in circuit No. 431 from left front sensor and control module. Connect sensor and perform Self-Test. If voltage is erratic or more than one volt, sensor circuit is good. Go to STEP C37.

Step C37 – Checking Left Front Sensor "A" Circuit
Move positive lead to pin No. 4 (circuit No. 422) at left front sensor connector and read voltage. If more than 1.5 volts or erratic, left front sensor is good. Go to STEP C41. If less than 1.5 volts, go to STEP C38.

Step C38 – Checking Left Front Sensor
Unplug left front sensor connector and read voltage. If more 1.5 volts, replace sensor. Perform Self-Test. If less than 1.5 volts, go to STEP C39.

Step C39 – Checking Left Front Sensor "A" Circuit
Do not connect left front sensor. Using volt/ohmmeter, connect negative lead to pin No. 14 (circuit No. 432) at control module connector and positive lead to pin No. 6 (circuit No. 422) at control module connector. Read voltage.
If more than 1.5 volts, repair short in circuit No. 422 between control module and sensor. Connect sensor and perform Self-Test. If voltage is less than 1.5 volts, go to STEP C40.

Step C40 – Checking Left Front Sensor "A" Circuit
Unplug control module. Using volt/ohmmeter, connect negative lead to pin No. 1 (circuit No. 430) at control module connector and positive lead to Pin No. 6 (circuit No. 422) at control module connector. Read resistance.
If more than 1000 ohms, replace control module. Connect left sensor and perform Self-Test. If less than 1000 ohms, repair short in circuit No. 422 between control module and left sensor. Connect left front sensor and perform Self-Test.

Step C41 – Checking Left Front Sensor "B" Circuit
Move positive lead to pin No. 3 (circuit No. 423) at left front sensor connector and read voltage. If more than 1.5 volts or erratic, replace sensor and go to STEP C42. If less than 1.5 volts, go to STEP C43.

Step C42 – Checking Control Module
Rerun Self-Test, STEPS A2-A4. If warning light flashes rapidly during TEST 3, replace control module and perform Self-Test. If warning light is not flashing rapidly during TEST 3, perform Self-Test.

Step C43 – Checking Left Front Sensor
Unplug left front sensor connector. Using volt/ohmmeter, check voltage. If more than 1.5 volts or erratic, install new left front sensor and perform Self-Test. If less than 1.5 volts, left front sensor is good. Go to STEP C44.

Step C44 – Checking Left Front Sensor "B" Circuit
Do not connect left front sensor. Using volt/ohmmeter, connect negative lead to pin No. 14 (circuit No. 432) at control module connector and positive lead to pin No. 17 (circuit No. 423). Read voltage.
If more than 1.5 volts, repair short in circuit No. 423 between control module and sensor. Connect sensor and perform Self-Test. If less than 1.5 volts, sensor is good. Go to STEP C45.

Step C45 – Checking Left Front Sensor "B" Circuit
Unplug control module. Using volt/ohmmeter, connect negative lead to pin No. 1 (circuit No. 430) at control module connector and positive lead to pin No. 17 (circuit No. 423) at control module connector. Read resistance.
If more than 1000 ohms, replace control module. Connect sensor and perform Self-Test. If less than 1000 ohms, repair short in circuit No. 423 between control module and sensor. Connect sensor and perform Self-Test.

TEST D (REAR SUSPENSION)

Step D1
If compressor did NOT cycle during Self-Test No. 4, go to TEST G. If compressor did cycle, go to STEP D2.

Step D2
If right rear solenoid did NOT cycle during test No. 8, go to STEP C12. If right rear solenoid did cycle, go to STEP D3.

Step D3
If left front solenoid did NOT cycle during test No. 9, go to STEP D23. If left front solenoid did cycle, go to STEP D4.

Step D4
If vent solenoid did NOT cycle during test No. 5, go to G. If vent solenoid did cycle, go to STEP D5).

Step D5 – Checking Compressor
Perform Self-Test STEPS A2 and A3. Disconnect all air lines at compressor. Plug 3 of the 4 air line fittings at compressor. Using a 0-150 psi (0-70 kg/cm²) pressure gauge, connect gauge to remaining open fitting on air compressor. Open and close door and observe pressure gauge.
If pressure is more than 120 psi (70 kg/cm²), compressor is good. Go to STEP D6. If pressure is less than 120 psi (70 kg/cm²), replace compressor. Connect all air lines and repeat Self-Test.

Step D6 – Checking Rear Sensor Connection
Check rear sensor, ball studs and bracket for secure mechanical connection. If all fittings are tight, go to STEP D7. If all fittings are not tight, tighten as necessary and repeat Self-Test.

(Cont. on Next Page)

FORD MOTOR CO. AIR SUSPENSION – MARK VII (Cont.)

TEST D (Cont.)

Step D7 – Checking Rear Air System
Disconnect air lines going to rear suspension at compressor. Repeat Self-Test STEPS A2 and A3. Open and close door and verify that air is escaping from air lines.
If air is escaping from both air lines, go to STEP D8. If air is not escaping from one rear air line, go to STEP D10. If air is not escaping from either air line because of no air in air springs, go to STEP D8.

Step D8
If vehicle failed Self-Test STEPS A2 and A3, go to STEP D9. If vehicle passed both tests, locate and repair air leaks in either spring or solenoid assembly.

Step D9
If rear of vehicle is at rebound (high), replace compressor assembly and repeat Self-Test. If vehicle is not at rebound, check all air lines and fittings. Repair air leaks and repeat Self-Test.

Step D10 – Checking Air Restrictions At Rear Solenoids
Connect air lines at compressor and remove air line from suspected rear solenoid. Open and close door and verify that air is escaping from suspected rear air spring.
If air is not escaping from rear solenoid air line, go to STEP D11. If air is escaping from solenoid, repair leak and repeat Self-Test.

Step D11
Check suspected air spring solenoid. If there are no air leaks, replace solenoid. Repeat Self-Test. If leaks are found, repair or replace as necessary and repeat Self-Test.

Step D12 – Cycle Right Rear Solenoid
Perform Self-Test STEPS A2 and A3. Open and close door until warning light blinks Test No. 8, then go to STEP D13.

Step D13 – Checking Right Rear Solenoid Circuit
Using test light, connect one lead to solenoid circuit No. 416 (Light Blue/Black wire) at right rear solenoid connector and other lead to battery circuit No. 175 (Black/Yellow wire) at right rear solenoid connector.
If test light is blinking, replace right rear solenoid solenoid and repeat Self-Test. If test light is on, go to STEP D21. If test light is off, go to STEP D14.

Step D14 – Checking Connector Polarity
Move test lead to pin No. 2 at right rear solenoid connector. Connect other test lead to ground. If test light is on, go to STEP D17. If test light is off, go to STEP D15.

Step D15 – Checking Connector Polarity
Connect test lead to pin No. 1 on right rear solenoid connector. Connect other lead to ground. If light is off, go to STEP D17. If light is on, repair crossed wires in solenoid connector and go to STEP D16.

Step D16 – Checking Battery Circuit
Move test lead connected to circuit No. 416 (Light Blue/Black wire) at right rear solenoid to ground. If test light is on battery circuit is good. Go to STEP D17. If light is off, repair short in circuit No. 175 (Black/Yellow wire) between right rear solenoid and fuse link. Repeat Self-Test.

Step D17 – Checking Control Module
Using test light, connect one lead to pin No. 10 (circuit No. 416) at control module connector and other to pin No. 20 (circuit No. 418) at control module connector. Do not disconnect control module connector.
If test light is blinking, repair short in circuit No. 416 between control module and right rear solenoid. Repeat Self-Test. If test light is off, go to STEP D18.

Step D18
If warning light is blinking Test No. 8, go to STEP D19. If light is off, go to STEP D12.

Step D19 – Checking Control Module Connector Pins
Disconnect control module connector and inspect pins. If pins are good. Go to STEP D20. If pins are bad, repair and repeat Self-Test.

Step D20 – Checking Right Rear Solenoid
Using volt/ohmmeter, connect negative lead to pin No. 1 at right rear solenoid connector and positive lead to pin No. 2 of right rear solenoid connector. Read resistance.
If more than 13 ohms, replace control module unit and repeat Self-Test. If less than 13 ohms, replace solenoid and control module unit. Repeat Self-Test.

Step D21
If warning light is blinking Test No. 8, go to STEP D22. If not, go to STEP D12.

Step D22 – Checking Right Rear Solenoid Circuit
Unplug control module connector. If test light is on, repair short in circuit No. 416 (Light Blue/Black wire) between control module and solenoid. Repeat Self-Test. If test light is off, replace control module and repeat Self-Test.

Step D23 – Cycle Left Rear Solenoid
Perform Self-Test STEPS A2 and A3. Open and close door until warning light blinks Test No. 9, go to STEP D24.

Step D24 – Checking Left Rear Solenoid Circuit
Using test light, connect one lead to circuit No. 429 (Pink/Light Green wire) at left rear solenoid connector and other lead to battery circuit No. 175 (Black/Yellow wire) at left rear solenoid connector.
If test light is blinking, replace solenoid and repeat Self-Test. If test light is off, go to STEP D25. If test light is on, go to STEP D32.

Step D25 – Checking Connector Polarity
Connect test lead to connector pin No. 2 at left rear solenoid. Connect other lead to ground. If test light is on, go to STEP D28. If test light is off, go to STEP D26.

Step D26
Check connector polarity. Connect test lead to pin No. 1 at left rear solenoid. Connect other lead to ground. If test light is off, go to STEP D28. If test light is on, repair crossed wires in solenoid connector and go to STEP D27.

Step D27 – Checking Battery Circuit
Move test lead connected to circuit No. 429 (Pink/Light Green wire) to ground. If test light is on, battery circuit is good. Go to STEP D28. If test light is off, repair short in circuit No. 418 (Dark Green/Yellow wire) between air suspension switch and right rear solenoid. Repeat Self-Test.

Step D28 – Checking Control Module
Using test light, connect one lead to pin No. 9 (circuit No. 429) at control module connector and other lead to pin No. 20 (circuit No. 418). Do not unplug control module connector. If test light is blinking, repair short in circuit No. 429 (Pink/Light Green wire) between control module and left rear solenoid. Repeat Self-Test. If test light is off, go to STEP D29.

Step D29
If warning light is blinking Test No. 9, go to STEP D30. If warning light is off, go to STEP D23.

Step D30 – Checking Control Module Connector Pins
If pins are good, go to STEP D31. If pins are bad, repair as necessary and repeat Self-Test.

Step D31 – Checking Left Rear Solenoid
Using volt/ohmmeter, connect negative lead to pin No. 1 at left rear solenoid connector. Connect positive lead to pin No. 2 at left rear solenoid connector. Read resistance.
If more than 13 ohms, replace control module unit and repeat Self-Test. If less than 13 ohms, replace solenoid and control module unit. Repeat Self-Test.

Step D32
If warning light is blinking Test No. 9, go to STEP D33. If warning light is off, go to STEP D23.

Step D33 – Checking Left Rear Solenoid Circuit
Unplug control module connector. If test light is on, repair short to circuit No. 429 between control module connector and left rear solenoid. Repeat Self-Test. If light is off, replace control module and repeat Self-Test.

(Cont. on Next Page)

Electronic Suspensions

FORD MOTOR CO. AIR SUSPENSION — MARK VII (Cont.)

TEST E (RIGHT FRONT)

Step E1
Did vehicle pass Self-Test No. 1. If so, go STEP E2. If not, go to TEST D.

Step E2
If right front solenoid passed Self-Test No. 7, go to STEP E3. If system did not pass, go to STEP E4. If system passes air but did not click, go to STEP E16.

Step E3 – Checking Right Front Sensor
Check sensor and ball studs for a tight mechanical connection. If connections are tight, go to STEP E6. If loose, tighten and repeat Self-Test.

Step E4 – Checking Right Front Solenoid Circuit
Perform Self-Test STEPS A2 and A3. Open and close door until warning light blinks Test No. 7. Using test light, connect one lead to circuit No. 414 (Orange/Red wire) at solenoid connector and other lead to battery circuit No. 175 (Light Green/Orange wire) at solenoid connector.
If test light blinks, system is good. Go to STEP E5. If test light is off, go to STEP E7. If test light is on, go to STEP E14.

Step E5 – Checking Restricted Right Front Air Line
Perform Self-Test STEPS A2 and A3. Right front of vehicle will drop during this test. Disconnect air lines at air spring solenoid. Open and close door twice and verify that air is escaping from spring solenoid line. If air is escaping, repair air line as necessary and repeat Self-Test. If air is not escaping, go to STEP E6.

Step E6 – Checking For Solenoid Or Air Spring Leaks
Connect air lines and perform Self-Test STEPS A2 and A3. Open and close door twice and verify that air is not leaking from air spring or solenoid. If air is not leaking, repair or replace air spring solenoid due to obstruction. If air is leaking, repair or replace leaky spring or solenoid. Repeat Self-Test.

Step E7 – Checking Connector Polarity
Connect test light to right front solenoid connector pin No. 2 and ground. If test light is on, go to STEP E10. If test light is off, go to STEP E8.

Step E8
Connect test light to the solenoid connector pin No. 1 and ground. If test light is off, go to STEP E10. If test light is on, repair crossed wires in solenoid connector and go to STEP E9.

Step E9 – Checking Battery Circuit
Move test lead from solenoid circuit No. 414 (Orange/Red wire) to ground. If test light is on, battery circuit is good. Go to STEP E10. If test light is off, repair short in battery circuit No. 175 (Light Green/Orange wire) between battery and solenoid. Repeat Self-Test.

Step E10 – Checking Control Module
Using test light, connect one lead to pin No. 12 at control module connector and other lead to pin No. 20. Do not unplug control module connector. If test light is blinking, repair short in circuit No. 414 (Orange/Red wire) between control module and right front solenoid. Repeat Self-Test. If test light is off, go to STEP E11.

Step E11
If warning light is blinking Test No. 7, go to STEP E12. If test light is not blinking, go to STEP E4.

Step E12 – Checking Control Module Unit
Unplug control module connector and inspect pins. If pins are good, go to STEP E13. If pins are bad, repair as necessary and repeat Self-Test.

Step E13 – Checking Right Front Solenoid
Unplug solenoid connector. Using volt/ohmmeter, connect negative test lead to pin No. 1 at solenoid connector and positive test lead to pin No. 2. Read resistance.
If more than 13 ohms, replace control module unit and repeat Self-Test. If less than 13 ohms, replace solenoid and control module unit and repeat Self-Test.

Step E14
If warning light is blinking, go to STEP E15. If warning light is not blinking, go to STEP E4.

Step E15
Unplug control module connector, leaving test light connected between circuits No. 414 and No. 175. If test light is on, repair short to ground in circuit No. 414 between control module connector and right front solenoid and repeat Self-Test. If test light is off, replace control module unit and repeat Self-Test.

Step E16
Unplug right front solenoid connector. Connect one test light lead to circuit No. 414 on harness side of connector. Connect other lead to battery circuit No. 175 on harness side of connector. If test light is on, repair short to ground in circuit No. 414 between control module connector and solenoid. Repeat Self-Test. If solenoid is off, replace solenoid. Repeat Self-Test.

TEST F (LEFT FRONT)

Step F1
If vehicle passed Self-Test STEP A1, go to STEP F2. If vehicle did not pass test, go to TEST D.

Step F2
If left front solenoid passed Self-Test STEP 6, go to STEP F3. If solenoid did not pass air, go to STEP F4. If solenoid passes air but does not click, go to STEP F16.

Step F3 – Checking Left Front Sensor
Check sensor and ball stud for tight mechanical connection. If loose, tighten sensor and repeat Self-Test. If sensor is good, go to STEP F6.

Step F4 – Checking Left Front Solenoid Circuit
Perform Self-Test STEPS A2 and A3. Open and close door until warning light blinks Test No. 6. Using test light, connect one lead to solenoid circuit No. 415 (Light Green/Orange wire) at left front solenoid connector and other lead to battery circuit No. 175 (Black/Yellow wire) at left front solenoid connector.
If test light is blinking, system is good. Go to STEP F5. If test light is off, go to STEP F7. If test light is on, go to STEP F14.

Step F5 – Checking for Restrictions In Left Front Air Line
Perform Self-Test STEPS A2 and A3. Left front of vehicle will drop during this test. Disconnect air lines at left front air spring solenoid. Open and close door 3 times and verify that air is escaping spring solenoid.
If air is escaping from solenoid, repair air lines as necessary. Reconnect air lines and repeat Self-Test. If air is not escaping, go to STEP F6.

Step F6 – Checking For Solenoid Or Air Spring Leaks
Connect air lines. Perform Self-Test STEPS A2 and A3. Open and close door 3 times and verify that air is not leaking from left front spring or solenoid.
If air is not leaking, repair or replace air spring solenoid due to obstruction. Repeat Self-Test. If air is leaking, repair or replace air spring or solenoid and repeat Self-Test.

Step F7 – Checking For Connector Polarity
Connect test light lead to pin No. 2 at left front solenoid connector. Connect other test lead to ground. If test light is on, go to STEP F10. If test light is off, go to STEP F8.

Step F8 – Checking For Connector Polarity
Connect test light lead to right front solenoid connector pin No. 1. Connect other test lead to ground. If test light is off, go to STEP F10. If test light is on, repair or service crossed wires at solenoid connector and go to STEP F9.

Step F9 – Checking Battery Circuit
Move test lead from left front solenoid circuit No. 415 (Light Green/Orange) to ground. If test light is on, battery circuit is good. Go to STEP F10. If light is off, repair short in circuit No. 175 (Black/Yellow) between the control module and solenoid. Repeat Self-Test.

Step F10 – Checking Control Module
Do not unplug control module connector. Using test light, connect one lead to pin No. 11 (circuit No. 415) at control module connector and the other lead to circuit pin No. 20 (circuit No. 418).
If test light is blinking, repair short in circuit No. 415 between control module and left front solenoid. Repeat Self-Test. If test light is off, go to STEP F11.

Step F11
If warning light is blinking Test No. 6, go to STEP F12. If warning light is not blinking, go to STEP F4.

Step F12
Check control module connector. Unplug control module connector and inspect pins. If pins are good, go to STEP F13. If pins are bad, repair as necessary and repeat Self-Test.

(Cont. on Next Page)

Electronic Suspensions

FORD MOTOR CO. AIR SUSPENSION – MARK VII (Cont.)

TEST F (Cont.)

Step F13

Check left front solenoid. Unplug left front solenoid connector. Using a volt/ohmmeter, connect negative lead to pin No. 1 at left front solenoid connector and positive lead to pin No. 2 at left front solenoid connector.

Read resistance. If more than 13 ohms, replace control module and repeat Self-Test. If less than 13 ohms, replace left front solenoid and control module. Repeat Self-Test.

Step F14

If warning light is blinking Test No. 6, go to STEP F15. If warning light is not blinking, go to STEP F4.

Step F15

Unplug control module connector and leave test light connected to circuits No. 415 and No. 175. If test light is on, repair short in circuit No. 415 between control module connector and left front solenoid. Repeat Self-Test. If test light is off, replace control module and repeat Self-Test.

Step F16

Unplug left front solenoid connector. Using test light, connect one lead to circuit No. 415 on harness side of connector and connect other lead to circuit No. 175 on harness side. If test light is on, repair short to ground in circuit No. 415 and repeat Self-Test. If test light is off, replace solenoid and repeat Self-Test.

TEST G (AIR SPRING FILL)

Step G1 – Checking Compressor Relay

Perform Self-Test STEPS A2 and A3. Open and close door until warning light blinks Test No. 4. Rear of vehicle may raise during this test. Compressor will cycle 50 times during Test 4 (about 3 minutes) then shut off and will not restart until Test No. 4 is reentered. If relay is cycling, go to STEP G2. If relay is not cycling, go to STEP G5.

Step G2 – Checking Compressor Circuit

Unplug compressor connector. Using test light, connect one lead to circuit No. 417 (Pink/Orange wire) at harness side of compressor connector. Connect other lead to ground.

If test light is blinking, compressor circuit is good. Go to STEP G3. If test light is on, replace compressor relay and perform Self-Test. If test light is off, go to STEP G4.

Step G3 – Checking Compressor Ground Circuit

Move ground lead of test light to circuit No. 430 (Gray wire) at harness side of compressor connector. If light is blinking, install new compressor and perform Self-Test. If test light is off, repair short in circuit No. 430 between compressor and battery. Perform Self-Test.

Step G4 – Checking Compressor Circuit

Plug in compressor connector and repeat STEP G1. Using test light, connect one lead to circuit No. 417 (Pink/Orange wire) at compressor relay. Connect other lead to ground.

If test light is blinking, repair short to ground in circuit No. 417 between compressor and compressor relay. Perform Self-Test. If test light is off, replace compressor relay and perform Self-Test.

Step G5 – Checking Compressor Relay Circuit

Using test light, connect one lead to compressor relay circuit No. 420 (Dark Blue/Yellow wire) at relay and connect other lead to positive side of battery. If test light blinks, module relay circuit is good. Go to STEP G6. If test light is on, go to STEP G8. If test light is off, go to STEP G9.

Step G6 – Checking Jumper Circuit

Using test light, connect one lead of jumper to pin No. 2 (circuit No. 175A) at compressor relay. Connect other lead to ground. If test light is on, replace compressor relay and perform Self-Test. If test light is off, go to STEP G7.

Step G7 – Checking Battery Circuit

Using test light, connect one lead to pin No. 3 (circuit No. 175) at compressor relay and other lead to ground. If test light is on, repair short in circuit No. 175A and perform Self-Test. If test light is off, repair short in circuit No. 175 between relay and battery. Perform Self-Test.

Step G8 – Checking Control Module Unit

Unplug control module connector. If test light is on, repair short to ground in circuit No. 420 (Dark Blue/Yellow wire) at compressor relay. Perform Self-Test. If test light is off, replace control module unit and perform Self-Test.

Step 9 – Checking Compressor Relay

Unplug compressor relay. Using volt/ohmmeter, connect negative lead to pin No. 2 at compressor relay connector. Connect other lead to pin No. 1 at compressor relay connector. Read resistance.

If more than 54 ohms, compressor relay is good. Go to STEP G10. If less than 54 ohms, replace compressor relay and perform Self-Test.

NOTE: This failure may have damaged control module.

Step G 10 – Checking Control Module

Perform STEP G1. Do not unplug control module connector. Using test light, connect one lead to pin No. 22 (circuit No. 420) at control module connector and the other lead to pin No. 20 (circuit No. 418).

If test light is blinking, repair short in circuit No. 420 between compressor relay and control module. Perform Self-Test. If test light is off, replace control module unit. Perform Self-Test.

TEST H (VENT SYSTEM)

Step H1 – Checking Vent Solenoid Circuit

Perform Self-Test STEPS A2 and A3. Open and close door until warning light blinks Test No. 5. Unplug air compressor connector. Using test light, connect one lead to pin No. 4 (circuit No. 421) at harness side of connector. Connect other lead to pin No. 1 (circuit No. 175) at harness side of connector.

If test light blinks, replace compressor assembly and perform Self-Test. If test light is off, go to STEP H3. If test light is on, go to STEP H2.

Step H2 – Checking Control Module

Unplug control module connector. If test light is on, repair short in vent solenoid circuit No. 421 (Pink wire) between compressor and control module. Perform Self-Test. If test light is off, replace control module and perform Self-Test.

Step H3 – Checking Battery Circuit

Move test light lead at vent solenoid circuit No. 421 (Pink wire) to ground. If test light is on, battery circuit is good. Go to STEP H4. If test light is off, repair short or open in circuit No. 175 between vent solenoid and battery. Perform Self-Test.

Step H4 – Checking Control Module

Do not unplug control module connector. Using test light, connect one lead to pin No. 23 (circuit No. 421) at control module connector and other lead to pin No. 20 (circuit No. 418).

If test light is blinking, repair open in circuit No. 421 between control module and compressor relay. If test light is off, go to STEP H5.

Step H5 – Checking Warning Light

If warning light blinks Test No. 5, go to STEP H6. If warning light did not blink Test No. 5, go to STEP H1

Step H6 – Checking Vent Solenoid

Unplug connector at compressor. Using volt/ohmmeter, connect negative lead to pin No. 4 at compressor assembly and positive lead to pin No. 1 at compressor assembly. Read resistance.

If more than 27 ohms, replace control module and perform Self-Test. If less than 27 ohms, replace compressor unit and control module. Perform Self-Test.

Electronic Suspensions

FORD MOTOR CO. AIR SUSPENSION — MARK VII (Cont.)

Fig. 8: Air Suspension Connector Identification

Component (Harness Number)	Harness Side Connector	Pin Number	Function	Circuit	Color	Gauge	Circuit End Point
Compressor (1) (14290)	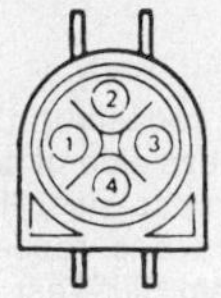	1	Solenoid Feed	175	BK/Y	14	Starter Relay
		2	Motor Feed	417	P/O	14	Compressor Relay
		3	Motor Ground	430	GY	14	Battery Ground Cable
		4	Solenoid Control	578	LB/PK	18	Module Pin No. 23
Spring Solenoid (4) (14290 LF/RF) (12614 LR/RR)		1	Control — LR	429	P/LG	18	Module Pin No. 9
			Control — RR	416	LB/BK	18	Module Pin No. 10
			Control — LF	415	LG/O	18	Module Pin No. 11
			Control — RF	414	O/R	18	Module Pin No. 12
		2	Feed	175	BK/Y	16	Starter Relay
Front Height Sensor (2) (14290)	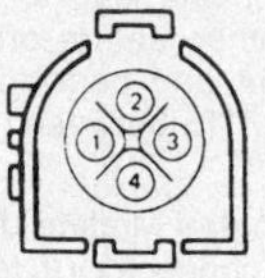	1	Ground	432	BK/PK	18	Module Pin No. 14
		2	Feed — LF (RF)	431	PK/W	18	Module Pin No. 4
		3	Logic Line B — RF	425	BR/PK	18	Module Pin No. 16
			Logic Line B — LF	423	P/LG	18	Module Pin No. 17
		4	Logic Line A — RF	424	T	18	Module Pin No. 5
			Logic Line A — LF	422	PK/BK	18	Module Pin No. 6
Rear Height Sensor (1) (12614)	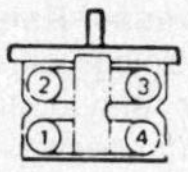	1	Ground	432	BK/PK	18	Module Pin No. 14
		2	Feed	426	R/BK	18	Module Pin No. 3
		3	Logic Line B	428	O/BK	18	Module Pin No. 18
		4	Logic Line A	427	PK/BK	18	Module Pin No. 13
Compressor Relay (1) (14290)	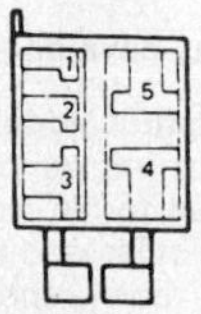	1	Control	420	DB/Y	18	Module Pin No. 22
		2	Feed (Coil)	175	BK/Y	18	Starter Relay
		3	Feed (Contacts)	175	BK/Y	12	Starter Relay
		4	Compressor Motor Feed	417	P/O	14	Compressor
		5	Compressor Motor Ground	430	GY	12	Battery Ground Cable
On/Off Switch (1) (12614)	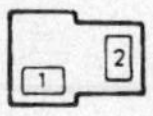	1	Feed to Module	418	DG/Y	14	Module Pin No. 20
		2	Feed to Switch	175	BK/Y	14	Starter Relay
Warning Lamp (1) (14A005)	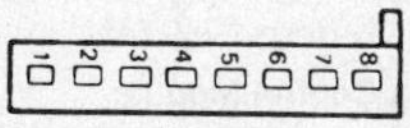	8	Control	419	DG/LG	20	Module Pin No. 21
		6	Feed	640	R/Y	20	Fuse Panel
Battery Ground Cable (14290)	—	—	System Ground	577	LG/RD	12	Module Pin No. 1 and 24
Diagnostic Pigtail	—	—	Access to System Diagnostics and Air Fill	606	W/LB	18	Module Pin No. 2
Ignition Switch (14401)	Branch of Existing Circuit	—	Ignition Sense	687	GY/Y	12	Module Pin No. 7
Stoplamp Switch (14A005)	Branch of Existing Circuit	—	Brake Sense	511	LG	18	Module Pin No. 15
Courtesy Lamp Door Switch (14488)	Branch of Existing Circuit	—	Door Sense	24	DB/O	20	Module Pin No. 19
Module (1) (12614)	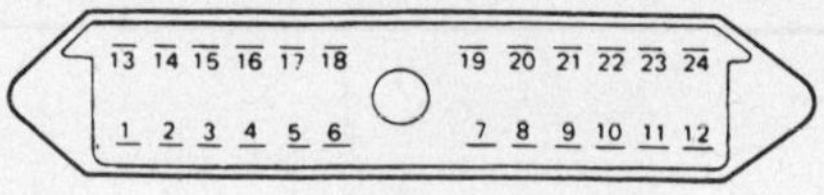						

Courtesy of Ford Motor Co.

FORD MOTOR CO. AIR SUSPENSION – MARK VII (Cont.)

Fig. 9: Air Suspension Wiring Diagram

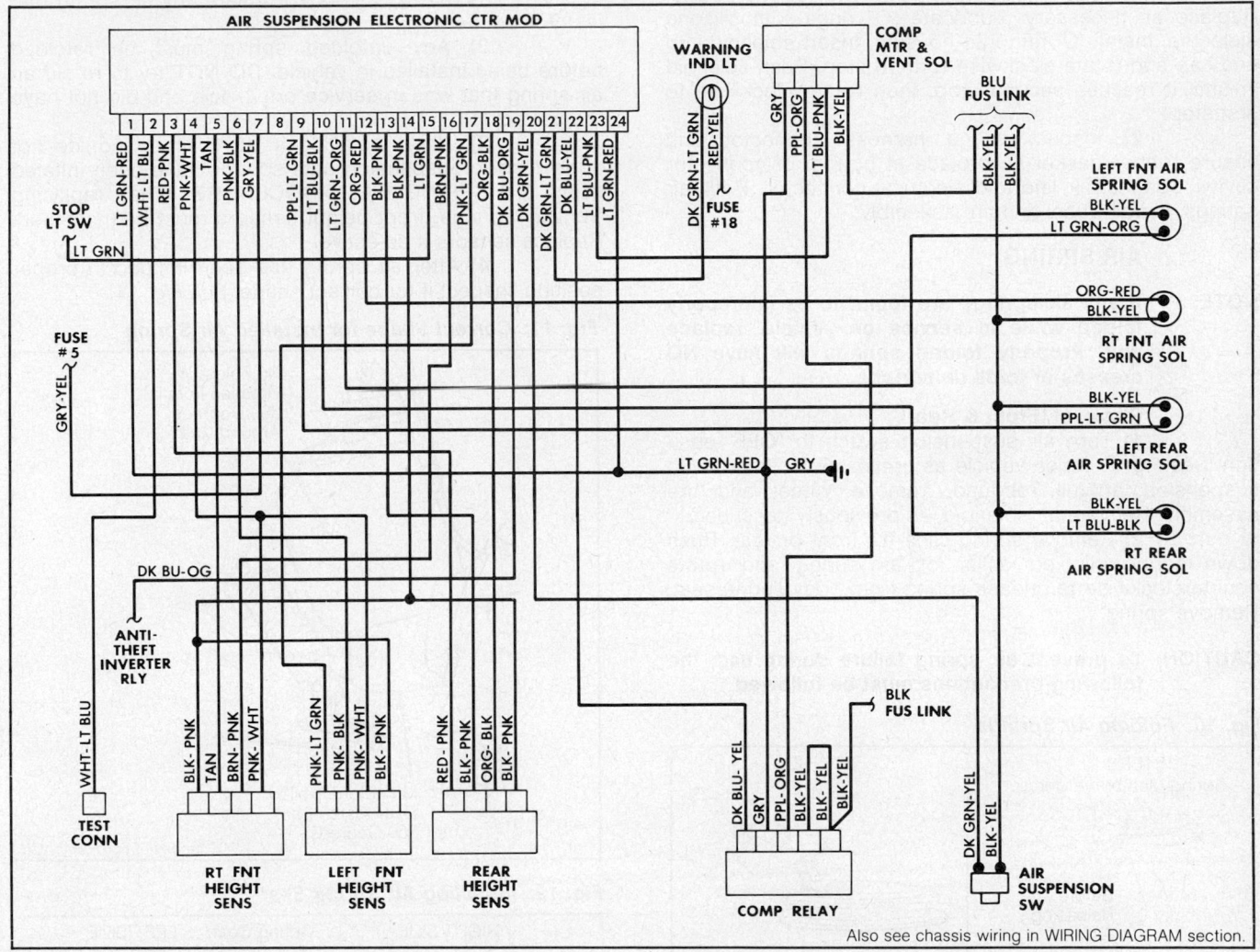

Also see chassis wiring in WIRING DIAGRAM section.

REMOVAL & INSTALLATION

AIR SPRING FILL PROCEDURE

NOTE: **This routine is used only to add air to front or rear air springs. Do not perform this routine unless a mechanical problem is verified as a cause of air loss (hole in spring, defective solenoid, etc.) and leak has been corrected.**

1) Raise vehicle as previously outlined. Do not apply a load to suspension. Disconnect ground from diagnostic pigtail and turn air suspension switch to "ON" position. See Fig. 7.

2) Install battery charger to reduce drain. Open driver's door. Turn ignition switch to "RUN" position. Hold in "RUN" position for 5 seconds, then turn ignition off.

3) Connect jumper lead between diagnostic pigtail and ground. Leave in grounded position during the entire test procedure. Apply brake pedal and turn ignition switch to "RUN" position. Leave driver's door open. Warning light will blink continuously every 2 seconds indicating spring fill sequence has been entered.

4) To fill rear springs, close and open door once. After 6 seconds, rear springs will fill for 60 seconds.

To fill front springs, close and open door twice. To fill front and rear springs, wait until rear springs are finished, then close and open door once.

5) After completion of air spring fill sequence, turn air suspension switch to "OFF" position. Inspect all air springs for proper inflation. Remove ground from pigtail. Any futher leveling will done automatically when vehicle is on the ground, if the air suspension is on.

AIR SPRING SOLENOID

NOTE: **Follow all cautions as previously outlined.**

Removal

1) Turn air suspension switch to "OFF" position. See Fig. 7. Raise vehicle as previously outlined. With suspension at full rebound, remove wheel and tire assembly. Unplug electrical connector. Remove air line.

2) The air spring solenoid has a 2-stage pressure relief fitting. First remove clip and rotate solenoid counterclockwise to first stop. Slowly pull solenoid straight out and release air out of air spring.

3) After air is fully bled from from air spring, rotate solenoid to third stop. Remove solenoid from spring. Remove "O" ring from solenoid housing.

FORD MOTOR CO. AIR SUSPENSION – MARK VII (Cont.)

Installation

1) Check "O" ring for cuts or abrasions. Replace as necessary. Lubricate "O" rings with silicone dielectric. Install "O" ring into housing. Insert solenoid into end cap and rotate clockwise to third stop. Push solenoid in until it reaches second stop, then rotate clockwise to first stop.

2) Inspect wiring harness connector and ensure rubber gasket is in place at bottom of connector cavity. Connect air line and electrical connector. Refill air springs. Install wheel and tire assembly.

AIR SPRING

NOTE: If any air springs are found to be improperly folded while in service on vehicle, replace unit. Properly folded springs will have NO creases or folds on surface.

Removal (Front & Rear)

1) Turn air suspension switch to "OFF" position. See Fig. 7. Raise vehicle as previously outlined. With suspension at full rebound, remove wheel and tire assembly. Remove air solenoid, as previously described.

2) Remove spring clips for front or rear. Push down spring clip on collar of air spring and rotate counterclockwise to release spring from body spring seat. Remove spring.

CAUTION: To prevent air spring failure during use, the following precautions must be followed.

Fig. 10: Folding Air Springs

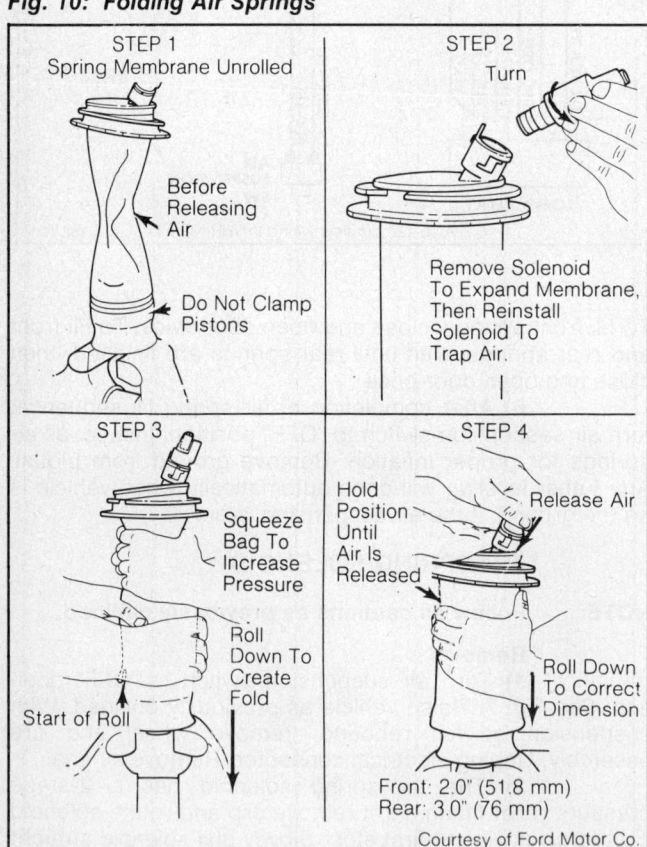

Courtesy of Ford Motor Co.

DO NOT try to refold air springs which were previously installed on vehicle and not folded correctly.

Installation Precautions

1) DO NOT install or inflate any air spring that is unfolded. See Fig. 10.

2) Any unfolded spring must be refolded before being installed in vehicle. DO NOT try to refold an air spring that was in service on vehicle and did not have the correct fold.

3) When installing a NEW air spring, do not apply load to suspension until springs have been inflated using AIR SPRING FILL PROCEDURE. When replacing front air springs, front height sensors must be inspected. Replace sensors if defective.

4) After air spring has been inflated in proper position, inspect it for correct shape. See Fig. 11.

Fig. 11: Correct Shape for Installed Air Spring

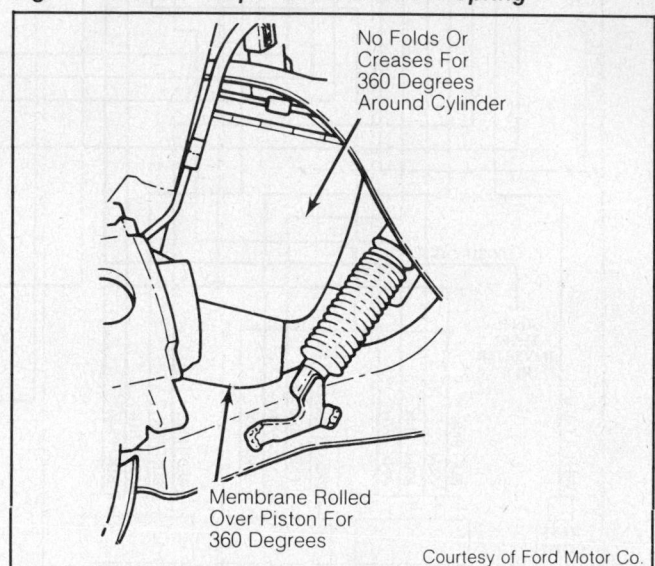

No Folds Or Creases For 360 Degrees Around Cylinder

Membrane Rolled Over Piston For 360 Degrees

Courtesy of Ford Motor Co.

Fig. 12: Installing Air Spring Seat

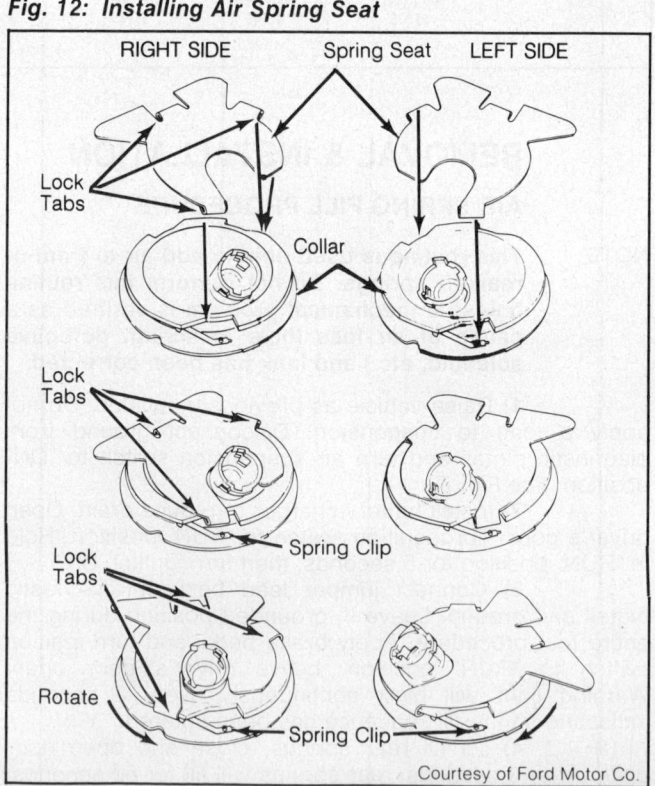

Courtesy of Ford Motor Co.

FORD MOTOR CO. AIR SUSPENSION — MARK VII (Cont.)

Installation

1) Install air spring solenoid as previously described. Ensure air spring seats are installed properly. *See Fig. 12.* Install air spring into body spring seat, being careful not to damage solenoid or electrical connections

2) Rotate air spring collar until spring snaps into place. Ensure collar is retained by 3 roll tabs on body spring seat. Attach air line and electrical connector to solenoid.

3) With suspension at full rebound and supported by shock absorbers, align and secure lower arm to spring attachment.

CAUTION: To prevent spring damage, do not allow vehicle suspension to compress before air springs are filled.

4) Replace wheel. Lower vehicle to 3" (76 mm) above floor. Refill springs as previously outlined.

Fig. 13: Repairing Air Lines

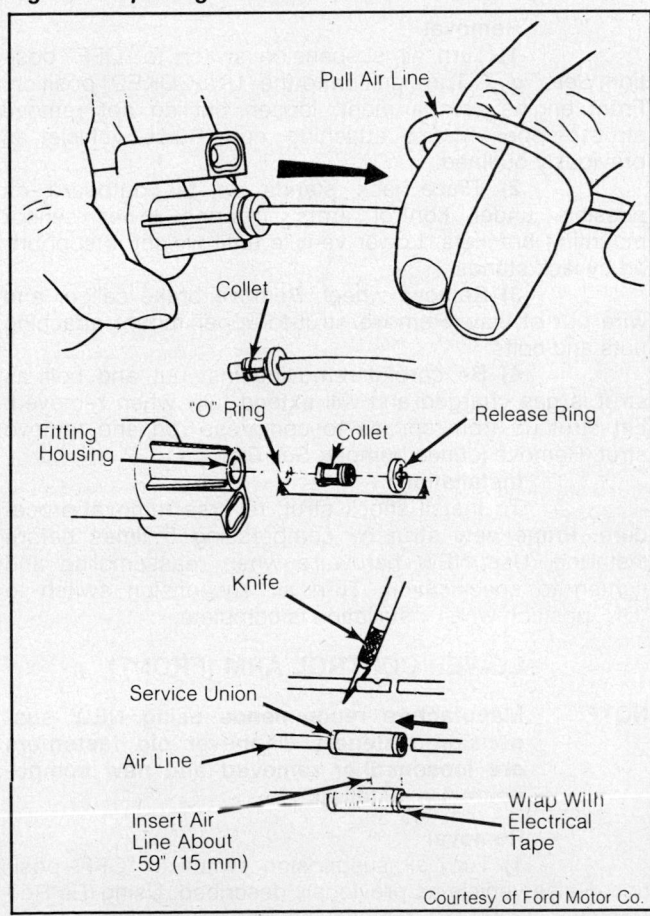

Pull Air Line

Collet

"O" Ring   Collet   Release Ring

Fitting Housing

Knife

Service Union

Air Line

Insert Air Line About .59" (15 mm)

Wrap With Electrical Tape

Courtesy of Ford Motor Co.

AIR LINES

Removal & Installation

1) Air lines on air spring solenoids and compressor dryer are disconnected by pushing in plastic release ring where line meets quick connect fitting. Pull out air line while holding release ring. Install air line by pushing in tubing until flare on line is against release ring.

2) Quick connect fittings can be removed by disconnecting air line. Insert length of scrap air line into collet. *See Fig. 13.* Pull collet out by HAND. Remove "O" rings.

3) Clean "O" ring seat. Lightly coat "O" rings with silicone dielectric. Install new collet (prongs first) with finger pressure. Install release ring and line.

Repair

Service kits are available to repair damaged air lines. Sections of air line may be cut out and union installed. *See Fig. 13.*

HEIGHT SENSOR

Removal (Front & Rear)

1) Turn suspension switch to "OFF" position. *See Fig. 7.* Unplug electrical connector located in engine compartment behind shock tower. Push connector through access hole in shock tower.

2) For rear sensor, electrical connector is located in the luggage compartment in front of forward trim panel. Pull luggage compartment carpet back for access to sensor sealing grommet located on floor pan.

3) Raise vehicle as previously outlined until suspension is at full rebound. Detach top and bottom of sensor from attaching studs by pushing spring clip on back of sensor ends.

4) Disconnect sensor wiring harness from plastic clips on shock tower and remove sensor. For rear sensor, push upward on sealing grommet to unseat sensor. Push sensor through floor pan hole into luggage compartment.

Installation

To install, reverse removal procedure. Turn air suspension switch to "ON" position after installation.

ELECTRONIC CONTROL MODULE

Removal & Installation

Turn air suspension and ignition switches to the "OFF" position. *See Fig. 7.* Remove left luggage compartment trim panel and disconnect harness connector. Remove 3 attaching nuts and remove unit. To install, reverse removal procedure.

COMPRESSOR RELAY

Removal & Installation

Unplug electrical connector. Remove relay retaining screw at left front shock tower. Remove relay. To install, reverse removal procedure.

AIR COMPRESSOR & DRIER ASSEMBLY

Removal

1) Turn air suspension switch to "OFF" position. *See Fig. 7.* Unplug electrical connection at compressor. Remove air line protector cap from drier by releasing 2 latching pins located at the bottom of cap, 180 degrees apart. Disconnect 4 air lines from drier. Remove 3 compressor bracket retaining screws and compressor.

2) To remove drier assembly, remove retainer clip and screw. Separate drier from head of compressor.

Installation

To install, reverse removal procedure. Replace "O" ring when installing new drier assembly.

UPPER MOUNT ASSEMBLY

NOTE: **Upper mounts use a one-piece design and cannot be disassembled. Manufacture recommends using NEW suspension fasteners whenever old fasteners are loosened or removed and new components are installed.**

FORD MOTOR CO. AIR SUSPENSION — MARK VII (Cont.)

Removal

1) Turn air suspension switch to "OFF" position. See Fig. 7. Turn ignition switch to the "UNLOCKED" position. From engine compartment, loosen but do not remove, 3 upper mount retaining nuts. Do not remove pop rivet holding camber plate. Loosen strut rod nut.

2) Raise vehicle as previously outlined. Place jack stands under lower control arms, as far outboard as possible. Be careful not to damage lower sensor bracket. Lower vehicle until weight is supported by lower control arms.

3) Remove wheel. Remove brake caliper and wire out of way. Remove upper and lower retaining nuts. Be careful removing last nut as gas pressurized strut will extend fully at this point. Lift strut up from spindle to compress rod, remove strut. Remove upper mount from strut. See Fig. 14.

Installation

1) Install new upper mount on strut and hand tighten NEW nut. Position upper mount studs and tighten nuts.

2) Compress strut and position onto spindle. Tighten NEW nuts and bolts to specification. To complete installation, reverse removal procedure. Turn air suspension switch to the "ON" position.

BALL JOINTS

Ball joints and lower suspension arm bushings are not serviced separately and must be replaced as an assembly.

STABILIZER BAR BUSHING & INSULATORS

NOTE: Manufacture recommends using NEW suspension fasteners whenever old fasterners are loosened or removed and new components are installed.

Removal (Front & Rear)

1) Turn air suspension switch to "OFF" position. See Fig. 7. Raise vehicle as previously outlined. Remove nut, washer and insulator from end of stabilizer bar link attaching bolts.

2) Remove remaining hardware. Remove adapter brackets and "U" clamps. Cut worn bushings from stabilizer bar. See Fig. 14.

Installation

To install bushing, reverse removal procedure. Lubricate bushings and insulators with silicone rubber lubricant. Use NEW nuts and bolt and tighten to specification.

SPINDLE ASSEMBLY

NOTE: Manufacture recommends using NEW suspension fasteners whenever old fasterners are loosened or removed and new components are installed.

Removal

1) Turn air suspension switch to "OFF" position. See Fig. 7. Raise vehicle as previously outlined. Remove wheel, brake caliper, rotor and dust shield. Remove stabilizer link from lower arm assembly. Using Tie Rod Remover (3290-D), remove tie rod end from spindle. Remove cotter pin from ball joint stud nut.

2) Loosen but do not remove nut. Tap spindle boss to relieve stud pressure. Place floor jack under lower control arm. Compress air spring and remove stud nut. Remove 2 bolts and nuts attaching spindle to shock strut. Compress shock strut until clearance is obtained. Remove spindle assembly. See Fig. 14.

Installation

1) Place spindle on ball joint stud. Install NEW stud nut, but do not tighten at this time. Lower shock strut until attaching holes are aligned with holes in spindle. Install 2 bolts and nuts.

2) Tighten ball joint stud nut and install cotter pin. To complete installation, reverse removal procedure.

SHOCK STRUT REPLACEMENT

NOTE: Manufacture recommends using NEW suspension fasteners whenever old fasterners are loosened or removed and new components are installed.

Removal

1) Turn air suspension switch to "OFF" position. See Fig. 7. Turn ignition to the "UNLOCKED" position. From engine compartment, loosen but do not remove strut-to-upper mount attaching nut. Raise vehicle as previously outlined.

2) Place jack stands as far outboard as possible under control arms, clearing lower sensor mounting brackets. Lower vehicle until weight is supported by jack stands.

3) Remove wheel. Remove brake caliper and wire out of way. Remove strut-to-upper mount attaching nuts and bolts.

4) Be careful removing last nut and bolt as strut is gas charged and will extend fully when removed. Lift strut up from spindle to compress rod and remove strut. Remove jounce bumper. See Fig. 7.

Installation

To install shock strut, reverse removal procedure. Prime new strut by compressing 5 times before installing. Use NEW hardware when reassembling and tighten to specification. Turn air suspension switch to "ON" position when installation is complete.

LOWER CONTROL ARM (FRONT)

NOTE: Manufacture recommends using NEW suspension fasteners whenever old fasterners are loosened or removed and new components are installed.

Removal

1) Turn air suspension switch to "OFF" position. Raise vehicle as previously described. Using Tie Rod Remover (3290-D), remove tie rod end from spindle assembly. If necessary, remove steering gear bolts. Position gear so that suspension arm bolt may be removed.

2) Disconnect lower stabilizer bar link. Disconnect lower end of height sensor from mounting stud. Mark for installation reference and remove sensor mounting screw and stud from lower arm bracket.

3) Loosen ball joint nut, but do not remove. Tap spindle boss to relieve pressure. Vent air spring. See AIR SPRING SOLENOID REMOVAL in this article. Reinstall solenoid.

FORD MOTOR CO. AIR SUSPENSION — MARK VII (Cont.)

Fig. 14: Exploded View of Front & Rear Suspension Components

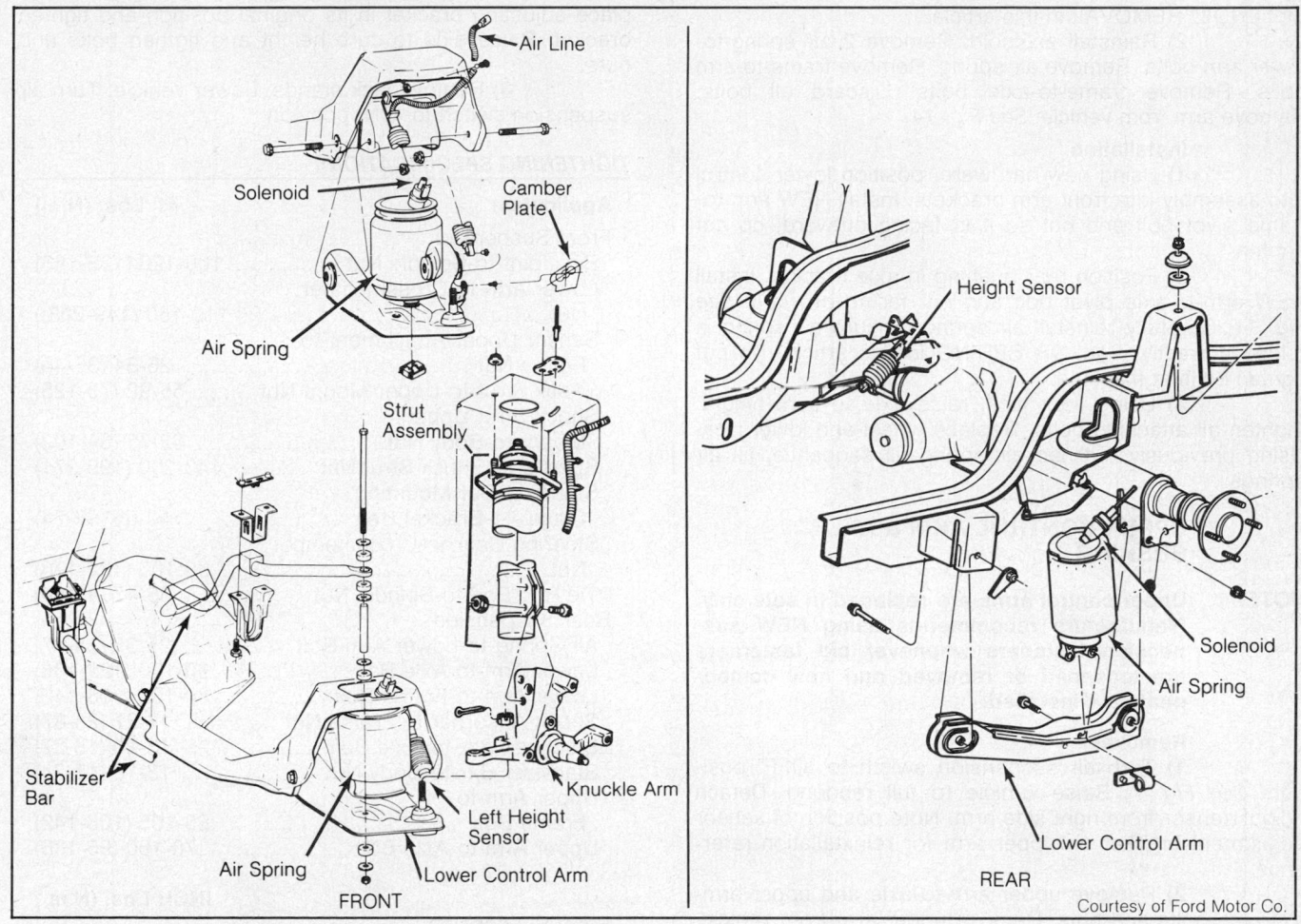

FRONT

REAR

Courtesy of Ford Motor Co.

4) Remove and discard air spring-to-lower arm fastener clip. Remove ball joint nut. Raise entire strut and spindle and wire out of way. Remove suspension arm-to-crossmember nuts and bolts. Remove arm from spindle. *See Fig. 14.*

Installation

1) Using new hardware, position arm into crossmember, but do not tighten. Attach ball joint to spindle, but do not tighten. Position air spring and install fastener.

2) Install sensor in original position. Connect lower end of sensor to lower mounting stud. Using floor jack, raise suspension arm to curb height. Tighten lower arm-to-crossmember nut. Tighten ball joint stud nut and install cotter pin. Remove floor jack.

3) If removed, install steering gear bolts. Position tie rod assembly into steering spindle. Tighten nut and install cotter pin. Connect stabilizer bar link to lower suspension and tighten nut.

4) Install wheel. Lower vehicle, but do not allow wheels to touch floor. Refill air springs as previously outlined. If necessary, check front wheel alignment.

REAR SHOCK ABSORBERS

CAUTION: Shocks are gas-pressurized and will extend when removed.

Removal

1) Turn air suspension switch to "OFF" position. Remove inside trim panels from luggage compartment. Loosen, but do not remove shock rod attaching nut. Raise vehicle as previously outlined. Place jack stands in position and lower vehicle until weight is supported by rear axle.

2) Remove upper attaching nut, washer and insulator. Remove right lower shock protective cover. Remove lower shock absorber cross bolt and nut. From beneath vehicle, compress shock absorber until clear from hole in upper shock tower.

Installation

To install rear shocks, reverse removal procedure. Prime new shocks by compressing 5 times before installation. Turn air suspension switch to "ON" position after installation is completed.

LOWER CONTROL ARM (REAR)

CAUTION: Replace lower control arm in sets only. Manufacture recommends using NEW suspension fasteners whenever old fasteners are loosened or removed and new components are installed.

Removal

1) Turn air suspension switch to "OFF" position. *See Fig. 7.* Raise vehicle until suspension is at full

FORD MOTOR CO. AIR SUSPENSION – MARK VII (Cont.)

rebound. Remove wheel. Vent air spring. See AIR SPRING SOLENOID REMOVAL in this article.

2) Reinstall solenoid. Remove 2 air spring-to-lower arm bolts. Remove air spring. Remove frame-to-arm bolts. Remove frame-to-axle bolts. Discard all bolts. Remove arm from vehicle. *See Fig. 14.*

Installation

1) Using new hardware, position lower control into assembly into front arm brackets. Install NEW arm-to-frame pivot bolt and nut so it is facing outward, do not tighten.

2) Position rear bushing in axle bracket. Install NEW arm-to-axle pivot bolt and nut facing outward. *See Fig. 14.* Carefully reinstall air spring. Ensure air spring is folded correctly. See AIR SPRING in this article. Do not tighten bolts at this time.

3) Using floor jack, raise axle to curb height. Tighten all attaching bolts. Replace wheel and lower jack. Using previously outlined air spring fill sequence, fill air springs.

UPPER CONTROL ARM & AXLE BUSHING

NOTE: Upper control arms are replaced in sets only. Manufacture recommends using NEW suspension fasteners whenever old fasterners are loosened or removed and new components are installed.

Removal

1) Turn air suspension switch to "OFF" position. *See Fig. 7.* Raise vehicle to full rebound. Detach height sensor from right side arm. Note position of sensor adjustment bracket on upper arm for reinstallation reference.

2) Remove upper arm-to-axle and upper arm-to-frame bolts and nuts. Remove upper arm from vehicle. If necessary, use Remover (T78P-5638-A) to replace axle bushings.

Installation

1) Place upper arm into frame and into axle. Install NEW bolts and nuts. Do not tighten yet.

2) When attaching right rear height sensor, place adjusting bracket in its original position and tighten bracket. Raise axle to curb height and tigthen bolts and nuts.

3) Remove jack stands. Lower vehicle. Turn air suspension switch to "ON" position.

TIGHTENING SPECIFICATIONS

Application	Ft. Lbs. (N.m)
Front Suspension	
Ball Joint-to-Spindle Nut	100-120 (136-163)
Lower Arm-to-Crossmember Nut	110-150 (149-203))
Sensor Upper Attachment-to-Frame Nut	26-34 (35-46)
Shock Strut-to-Upper Mount Nut	55-92 (75-125)
Shock Strut Upper Mount-to-Body Nut	62-75 (84-102)
Spindle-to-Shock Strut Nut	140-200 (190-271)
Stabilizer Bar Mounting Clamp-to-Bracket Bolt	40-55 (57-74)
Steering Gear-to-Crossmember Nut	90-100 (122-136)
Tie Rod End-to-Spindle Nut	35-47 (47-64)
Rear Suspension	
Air Spring-to-Lower Arm Bolt	25-35 (34-47)
Lower Arm-to-Axle Bolt	90-100 (122-136)
Lower Arm-to-Frame Bolt	80-105 (108-142)
Shock Absorber-to-Frame Nut	17-27 (23-37)
Stabilizer Bar-to-Axle Bolt	13-20 (18-27)
Stabilizer Bar-to-Body Nut	13-18 (18-24)
Upper Arm-to-Frame Bolt	80-105 (108-142)
Upper Arm-to-Axle Bolt	70-100 (95-136)

	INCH Lbs. (N.m)
Front Suspension	
Sensor Attachment-to-Lower Arm	96-144 (10-16)
Stabilizer Bar-to-Lower Arm Nut	108-144 (12-16)
Rear Suspension	
Sensor Lower Bracket-to-Arm Nut	84-120 (9-16)
Sensor Upper Bracket-to-Frame Bolt	110-150 (12-17)

Electronic Suspensions

FORD MOTOR CO. PROGRAMMED RIDE CONTROL

Thunderbird Turbo Coupe

DESCRIPTION

Programmed Ride Control (PRC) allows driver to select firm (sport) suspension or automatic ride control. System consists of a control switch, 4 actuators, brake sensor switch, speed sensor, steering sensor, PRC module, various relays and connecting wiring. *See Fig. 1.*

OPERATION

System is selected by a control switch, located on instrument panel. When driver selects "FIRM" position, control module will activate actuators on each shock to provide a firm (sport) ride. Green light on instrument panel will come on anytime system is in "FIRM" mode. When system is in "AUTO" mode, actuators are adjusted to provide a "soft" ride.

System will automatically switch to "firm" setting during heavy braking (brake system pressure above 400 psi), cornering (over .35g lateral acceleration) or acceleration (more than 90 percent of full throttle or above 83 MPH). This provides improved handling at high speeds. Green light will come on during this period. Light will flash to indicate system malfunction.

TESTING

TEST EQUIPMENT

To test system, Break-Out Box (014-00322) should be used. Fabricated tool must be used to assist in testing. *See Fig. 2.*

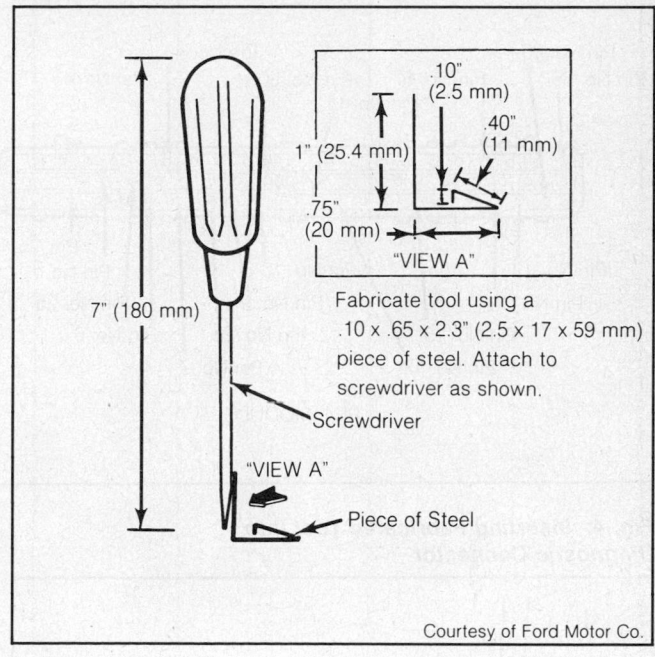

Fig. 2: Fabricated Tool Dimensions

Fabricate tool using a .10 x .65 x 2.3" (2.5 x 17 x 59 mm) piece of steel. Attach to screwdriver as shown.

Courtesy of Ford Motor Co.

Fig. 1: Exploded View of Programmed Ride Control Components

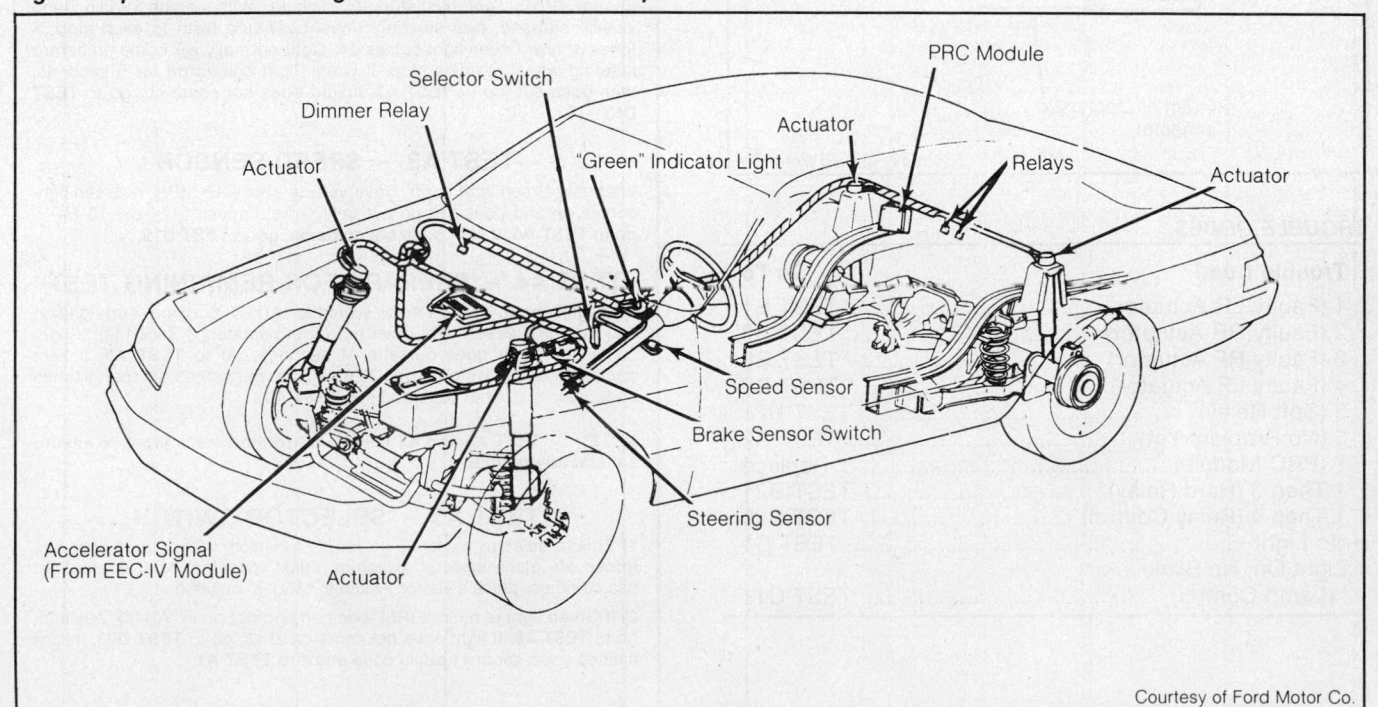

Courtesy of Ford Motor Co.

Electronic Suspensions

FORD MOTOR CO. PROGRAMMED RIDE CONTROL (Cont.)

Fig. 3: Testing Points

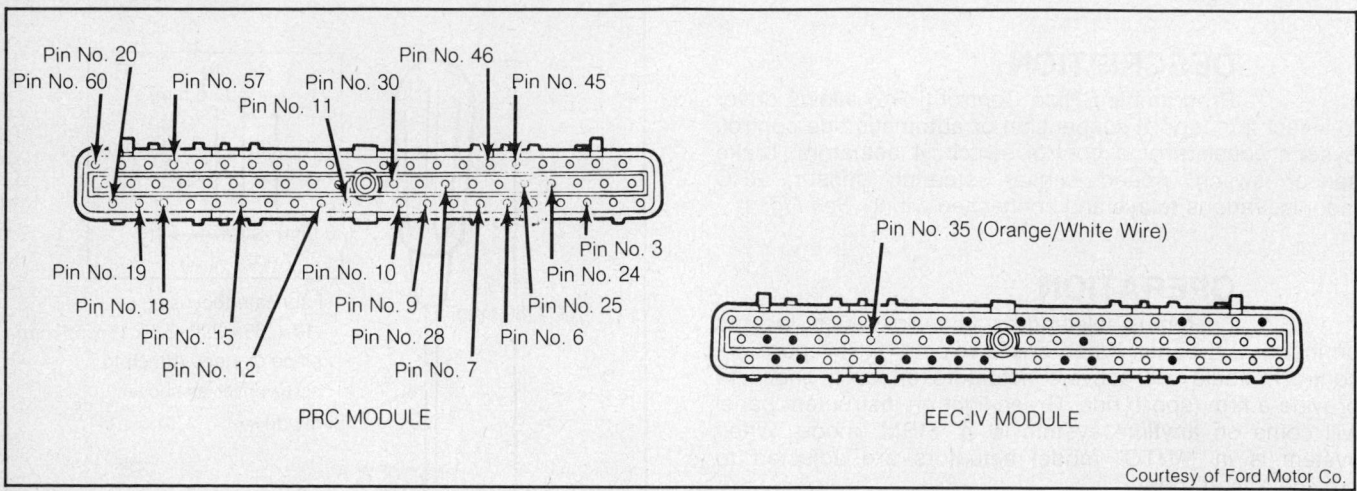

Courtesy of Ford Motor Co.

Fig. 4: Inserting Fabricated Tool Into Diagnostic Connector

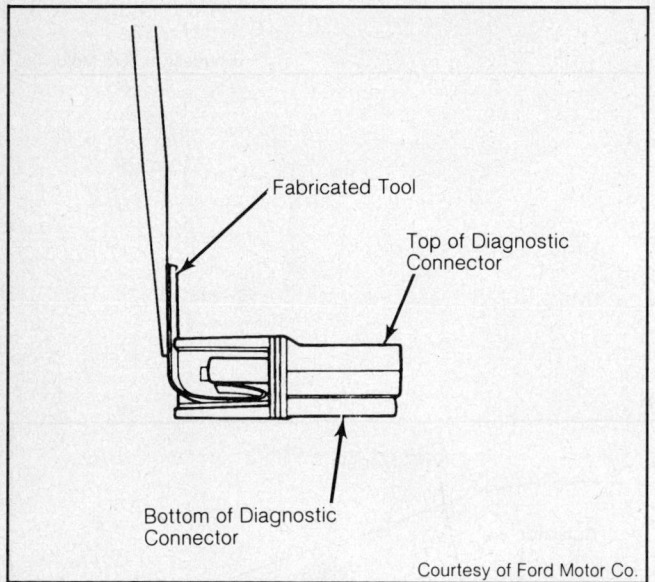

Courtesy of Ford Motor Co.

TROUBLE CODES

Trouble Code	Go To
1 (Faulty LR Actuator)	TEST B1
2 (Faulty RR Actuator)	TEST B8
3 (Faulty RF Actuator)	TEST B8
4 (Faulty LF Actuator)	TEST B8
5 (Soft Relay)	TEST B21
6 (No Problem Yet)	TEST A2
7 (PRC Module)	Replace
1 Then 3 (Hard Relay)	TEST B21
1 Then 4 (Relay Control)	TEST B25
No Light	TEST C1
Light On; No Blink (Lamp Control)	TEST C17

QUICK TEST

TEST A1 – ENTER DIAGNOSTIC

1) Turn ignition off. Ensure headlights and parking lights are off. Place selector switch in "AUTO" position. Remove ash tray from console. Insert fabricated tool in diagnostic connector. *See Fig. 4.* DO NOT move selector switch during test.

2) Start engine. Remove fabricated tool within 20 seconds after engine is started. Observe Green "FIRM" light on instrument panel. Number of times light blinks is trouble code. See TROUBLE CODE chart. Code will blink same codes, once every 9 seconds.

NOTE: Tests A2 and A3 may be repeated several times to ensure proper diagnosis. If ignition is turned off or selector switch is moved, proceed to TEST A4 or TEST A1.

TEST A2 – STEERING SENSOR

Ensure Green light has stopped blinking. With engine running and vehicle stopped, turn steering wheel back and forth to each stop, 3 times or until Green light comes on. Light normally will come on before steering wheel reaches stop. If Green light comes on for 5 seconds, then goes out, go to TEST A3. If light does not come on, go to TEST D13.

TEST A3 – SPEED SENSOR

Wait until Green light is off. Drive vehicle above 15 MPH. If Green light comes on and does not go out until vehicle speed is below 15 MPH, go to TEST A4. If light does not come on, go to TEST D19.

TEST A4 – PREPARE FOR REMAINING TEST

Turn ignition off. Turn selector switch to "AUTO" position. Turn ignition on. Wait until Green light goes out (approximately 4 seconds). If light comes on, then goes out after 4 seconds, go to TEST A5. If light comes on and stays on, go to TEST D6. If light comes on, then flashes code, record trouble code and see TEST A1.

NOTE: TEST A5 and A6 may be performed many times to ensure satisfactory results.

TEST A5 – SELECTOR SWITCH

1) Ensure selector switch is in "AUTO" position. After Green light has turned off, place selector switch in "FIRM" position. After Green light has come on, place selector switch in "AUTO" position.

2) If Green light is on in "FIRM" position and not on in "AUTO" position, go to TEST A6. If light does not come on at all, go to TEST D23. If light flashes code, record trouble code and see TEST A1.

FORD MOTOR CO. PROGRAMMED RIDE CONTROL (Cont.)

QUICK TEST (Cont.)

TEST A6 – BRAKE SENSOR

Ensure selector switch is in "AUTO" position. After light has turned off, depress brake pedal firmly until light comes on. After light goes on, release brake pedal. If light comes on as indicated, go to TEST A7. If light comes does not come on, go to TEST D27. If light flashes code, record trouble code and see TEST A1.

TEST A7 – ACCELERATOR SWITCH

1) Ensure selector switch is in "AUTO" position. After Green light has turned off, depress accelerator pedal to floor. Light should come on. Release accelerator pedal, light should turn off.

2) If Green light comes on and turns off as indicated, and TESTS A1 through TEST A7 have been performed, vehicle has passed QUICK TEST. If light did not come on, go to TEST D31. If light flashes code, record trouble code and see TEST A1.

ACTUATOR CONTROL CIRCUIT DIAGNOSIS

TEST B1 – CHECK ACTUATOR WIRING

Turn ignition off. Check all wiring and connectors for wear or damage. Repair or replace wiring as necessary. If no wear or damaged is found, go to TEST B2.

TEST B2 – UNPLUG PRC MODULE

Lower PRC module mounting panel. Module is located inside luggage compartment, on back of passenger side seat. Unplug 60-pin connector. Go to TEST B3.

TEST B3 – ENERGIZE HARD RELAY

Turn ignition on. Using a jumper wire, jump pin No. 11 to pin No. 60 on 60-pin connector for 1-2 seconds. Go to TEST B4.

TEST B4 – POSITION SWITCHES OPERATION

1) Using an ohmmeter, check resistance between the following pins: No. 46 and No. 19, No. 46 and No. 25, No. 46 and No. 7, and No. 46 and No. 10. If resistance is 1000 or more, switch is open. If resistance is less than 10 ohms, switch is closed.

2) If all switches are open, go to TEST B5. If all switches are closed, go to TEST B17. If switch is closed at pin No. 19, replace LR actuator and go to TEST B7. If switch is closed at pin No. 25, replace RR actuator and go to TEST B7.

3) If switch is closed at pin No. 7, replace RF actuator and go to TEST B7. If switch is closed at pin No. 10, replace LF actuator and go to TEST B7.

TEST B5 – ENERGIZE SOFT RELAY

Using a jumper wire, jump pins No. 12 and No. 60, on 60-pin connector for 1-2 seconds. Go to TEST B6.

TEST B6 – DO POSITION SWITCHES CLOSE?

1) Using an ohmmeter, check resistance between the following pins: No. 46 and No. 19, No. 46 and No. 25, No. 46 and No. 7, and No. 46 and No. 10. If resistance is 1000 or more, switch is open. If resistance is less than 10 ohms, switch is closed.

2) If all switches are closed, go to TEST B7. If all switches are open, go to TEST B17. If switch is closed at pin No. 19, replace LR actuator and go to TEST B7. If switch is closed at pin No. 25, replace RR actuator and go to TEST B7.

3) If switch is closed at pin No. 7, replace RF actuator and go to TEST B7. If switch is closed at pin No. 10, replace LF actuator and go to TEST B7.

TEST B7 – RECONNECT PRC MODULE CONNECTOR

Turn ignition off. Plug in 60-pin connector to PRC module connector. Go to TEST B8.

TEST B8 – CHECK ACTUATOR WIRING

Turn ignition off. Check all wiring and connectors for wear or damage. Repair or replace wiring as necessary. If no wear or damaged is found, go to TEST B9.

TEST B9 – ACTUATOR ROTATION TEST

Remove all problem actuator(s) from shock absorber(s). DO NOT unplug connectors. Turn ignition on and wait 5 seconds. Place selector switch in "AUTO" position. Record control tube position on bottom of actuator. Go to TEST B10.

TEST B10 – DO ACTUATORS ROTATE TO "FIRM" POSITION?

Place selector switch in "FIRM" position. Record control tube position on bottom of actuator. Did actuator move from position in TEST B9? If actuator rotated from "S" (soft) to "H" (hard), go to TEST B12. If actuator did not rotated, go to TEST B11. If actuator rotated from "H" to "S", circuits at actuator are reversed.

TEST B11 – DOES ACTUATOR ROTATE?

1) Turn ignition off. Unplug problem actuator and plug in at known go actuator. Turn ignition on. Place selector switch in "AUTO" position and check control tube position.

2) Place selector switch in "FIRM" position and check control tube position. If actuator does not move, replace actuator. If actuator does rotate, check wiring to actuator for short or open circuit.

TEST B12 – CHECKING ACTUATOR RESISTANCE

1) Unplug problem actuator connector. Using a small blade screwdriver, rotate control tube on problem actuator to "S" position. Using an ohmmeter, check resistance between Tan/Black wire and each of the following: Tan/Black on LF, White/Red on RF, White on RR and White/Orange on LR at connector terminals. Rotate control tube to "H" position.

2) If resistance is 1000 ohms or more, switch is open. If resistance is less than 10 ohms, switch is closed. If switch is closed in "S" position and open in "H" position, go to TEST B13. If switch is always open or always closed, replace actuator.

TEST B13 – CHECKING ACTUATOR FOR INTERNAL SHORT

Using small blade screwdriver, rotate control tube to "H" position. Using an ohmmeter, check for resistance between Tan/Black wire and Tan/Red wire terminals. If resistance is less than 10 ohms, replace actuator. If resistance is 1000 ohms or more, go to TEST B14.

TEST B14 – SIGNAL RETURN CIRCUIT

Measure resistance between the following wires and ground: LF actuator White/Black, RF actuator White/Red, RR actuator White, and LR actuator White/Orange. If resistance at any wire is 1000 ohms or more, check for open circuit in that wire. If resistance at all wires is less than 10 ohms, go to TEST B15.

TEST B15 – UNPLUG PRC MODULE

Turn ignition off. Lower PRC module mounting panel. Module is located inside luggage compartment, on back of passenger side seat. Unplug 60-pin connector. Go to TEST B16.

TEST B16 – SENSOR POSITION CIRCUIT

Check pin No. 46 at PRC module for damage. Check for continuity between pin No. 46 and Yellow/Black wire terminal at defective actuator. If there is no continuity, or pin is damage, repair as necessary. If there is continuity, go to TEST B37.

Electronic Suspensions

FORD MOTOR CO. PROGRAMMED RIDE CONTROL (Cont.)

ACTUATOR CONTROL CIRCUIT DIAGNOSIS (Cont.)

TEST B17 – RELAYS POWER CIRCUIT

Turn ignition off. Unplug soft and firm relay connectors. Turn ignition on. Check for voltage between Black/Orange (power) and Black (ground) wires at both relay connectors. If there is no voltage, go to **TEST B18**. If there is 12 volts, go to **TEST B19**.

TEST B18 – RELAYS POWER FEED

Using a voltmeter, check voltage between Black/Orange wire and ground at each relay connector. If there is voltage, check for open in Black wire circuit. If there is no voltage, check for blown fuse or open in Black/Orange wire circuit.

TEST B19 – RELAYS-TO-ACTUATOR CIRCUITS

Unplug RR actuator connector. Using an ohmmeter, check for continuity between each actuator and relays (Tan/Red and Tan/Black). If there is continuity in each wire, go to **TEST B20**. If there is no continuity in wire between each actuator and relays, repair defective wire.

TEST B20 – CROSSED RELAY CIRCUITS

Ensure Light Green/Purple and Tan/Black wire are in same connector. Light Green/White and Tan/Red wires should be in same connector. If wire locations are as specified, replace relay. If wire positions are not as specified, repair as necessary.

TEST B21 – UNPLUG PRC MODULE

Turn ignition off. Lower PRC module mounting panel. Module is located inside luggage compartment, on back of passenger side seat. Unplug 60-pin connector. Go to **TEST B22**.

TEST B22 – RELAY CONTROL CIRCUIT

1) Ensure Light Green/Purple wire is at PRC module pin No. 11. Light Green/White wire should be at pin No. 12. Turn ignition on. Check resistance between connector pins No. 11 and No. 60, and No. 12 and No. 60. If resistance is 1000 ohms or more at both circuits, replace PRC module.

2) If resistance at pin No. 11 is less than 10 ohms, check for fault in firm relay circuit. Go to **TEST B23**. If resistance at pin No. 12 is less than 10 ohms, check for fault in soft relay circuit. Go to **TEST B23**.

TEST B23 – UNPLUG FAULTY RELAY

Unplug faulty relay. Ensure wiring to relay is okay and wiring is not crossed. Repair wiring or reroute wiring as necessary. If wiring is okay, go to **TEST B24**.

TEST B24 – RETEST RELAY CONTROL CIRCUIT

Using an ohmmeter, check resistance between connector pins No. 11 and No. 60, and No. 12 and No. 60. If resistance at both points is 1000 ohms or more, replace faulty relay. If resistance is less than 10 ohms, check for short in wiring.

TEST B25 – UNPLUG PRC MODULE

Turn ignition off. Lower PRC module mounting panel. Module is located inside luggage compartment, on back of passenger side seat. Unplug 60-pin connector. Go to **TEST B26**.

TEST B26 – LIGHT CONTROL CIRCUIT

Turn ignition on. Using a jumper wire, jump pin No. 15 to No. 60 on 60-pin connector. Observe Green light on instrument panel. If Green light comes on, go to **TEST B27**. If light does not come on, check for faulty light control circuit. Go to **TEST B31**.

TEST B27 – ENERGIZE FIRM RELAY

Turn ignition on. Connect jumper wire between pins No. 11 and No. 60 for 1-2 seconds. Go to **TEST B28**.

TEST B28 – POSITION SWITCHES OPEN

1) Using an ohmmeter, check resistance between the following pins: No. 46 and No. 19, No. 25 and No. 46, No. 7 and No. 46, and No. 10 and No. 46. If resistance is 1000 ohms or more, switch is open.

2) If resistance is less than 10 ohms, switch is closed. If all switches are open, go to **TEST B29**. If switches are closed, fault in firm relay is indicated. Go to **TEST B34**.

TEST B29 – ENERGIZE SOFT RELAY

Using a jumper wire, jump pin No. 12 to pin No. 60 on 60-pin connector for 1-2 seconds. Go to **TEST B30**.

TEST B30 – POSITION SWITCHES CLOSE

1) Using an ohmmeter, check resistance between the following pins: No. 46 and No. 19, No. 25 and No. 46, No. 7 and No. 46, and No. 10 and No. 46. If resistance is 1000 ohms or more, switch is open.

2) If resistance is less than 10 ohms, switch is closed. If all switches are closed, replace PRC module. If switches are open, fault in soft relay is indicated. Go to **TEST B34**.

TEST B31 – DIMMER RELAY WIRING

Unplug dimmer relay. Dimmer relay is located inside glove compartment. Ensure wiring is not crossed or damaged. If wiring is okay, go to **TEST B32**.

TEST B32 – DIMMER RELAY POWER

Check for voltage between Purple/Orange wire (power) and Black wire (ground) at dimmer relay connector. If there is no voltage, repair or replace Purple/Orange wire between PRC module and dimmer relay. If there is voltage, go to **TEST B33**.

TEST B33 – DIMMER RELAY CONTROL CIRCUIT

Using an ohmmeter, check for continuity in Red/Black wire between dimmer relay and PRC module. If there is continuity, replace dimmer relay. If there is no continuity, repair or replace Red/Black wire.

TEST B34 – UNPLUG PROBLEM RELAY

Unplug problem relay. Ensure wire position is correct. Check for damage wires. Repair as necessary. If no problem can be found, go to **TEST B35**.

TEST B35 – COIL POWER FEED

Using a voltmeter, check for voltage between Purple/Orange wire at both relays. If there is no voltage at relays, repair or replace Purple/Orange wire between PRC module and relays. If there is voltage, go to **TEST B36**.

TEST B36 – DIMMER RELAY CONTROL CIRCUIT

Using an ohmmeter, check for continuity in Light Green/Purple wire between PRC module pin No. 11 and firm relay. Also check Light Green/White wire between PRC module pin No. 12 and soft relay. If there is continuity, replace relay. If there is no continuity, repair or replace wiring.

TEST B37 – ATTACH PROBLEM ACTUATOR

Attach problem actuator to shock absorber. Connect wiring and go to **TEST B38**.

TEST B38 – ENERGIZE FIRM RELAY

Turn ignition on. Connect jumper wire between pins No. 11 and No. 60 for 1-2 seconds. Go to **TEST B39**.

FORD MOTOR CO. PROGRAMMED RIDE CONTROL (Cont.)

ACTUATOR CONTROL CIRCUIT DIAGNOSIS (Cont.)

TEST B39 – POSITION SWITCHES OPEN

1) Using an ohmmeter, check resistance between the following pins: No. 46 and No. 14 on LR , No. 25 and No. 46 on RR, No. 7 and No. 46 on RF, and No. 10 and No. 46 on LF. If resistance is 1000 ohms or more, switch is open.

2) If resistance is less than 10 ohms, switch is closed. If any switch is open, go to **TEST B40**. If switch are close, replace actuator and shock absorber. Check for binding.

TEST B40 – ENERGIZE SOFT RELAY

Using a jumper wire, jump pin No. 12 to pin No. 60 on 60-pin connector for 1-2 seconds. Go to **TEST B41**.

TEST B41 – POSITION SWITCHES CLOSE

1) Using an ohmmeter, check resistance between the following pins: No. 46 and No. 19 on LR, No. 25 and No. 46 on RR, No. 7 and No. 46 on RF, and No. 10 and No. 46 on LF. If resistance is 1000 ohms or more, switch is open.

2) If resistance is less than 10 ohms, switch is closed. If any switch is closed, replace PRC module. If any switch are open, replace actuator and shock absorber. Check for binding.

FIRM RIDE INDICATOR LIGHT CIRCUIT DIAGNOSIS

TEST C1 – KEY ON SEQUENCE

Turn ignition off. Place selector switch in "FIRM" position. Shield Green light so it can be seen when it is on dim. Turn ignition on. If light does not come on, go to **TEST C2**. If light comes on dimly, go to **TEST C14**. If light comes on, go to **TEST D1**.

TEST C2 – UNPLUG PRC MODULE

Turn ignition off. Lower PRC module mounting panel. Module is located inside luggage compartment, on back of passenger side seat. Unplug 60-pin connector. Go to **TEST C3**.

TEST C3 – "FIRM" LIGHT OPERATION

Turn ignition on. Using a jumper wire, connect pin No. 15 on 60-pin connector to pin No. 60. Observe light. If light comes on, go to **TEST C4**. If light does not come on, go to **TEST C5**.

TEST C4 – PRC MODULE POWER CIRCUIT

Using a voltmeter, measure voltage between pin No. 57 (positive) and pin No. 60 (ground) on 60-pin connector. If there is no voltage, repair or replace Purple/Orange wire or 18-gauge fuse link between starter solenoid and PRC module pin No. 57. This circuit goes through 8-pin connector in RH kick panel. If there is 12 volts, replace PRC module.

TEST C5 – PRC MODULE GROUND CIRCUIT

Using an ohmmeter, check for continuity between pin No. 60 at 60-pin connector to ground. If there is no continuity, repair or replace Black wire between pin No. 60 and ground, located in luggage compartment. If there is continuity, go to **TEST C6**.

TEST C6 – DIMMER RELAY WIRING

Unplug dimmer relay. Dimmer relay is located inside glove box. Ensure wiring is okay and is properly routed. If wiring is okay, go to **TEST C7**.

TEST C7 – DIMMER RELAY POWER CIRCUIT

Using a voltmeter, check voltage between Purple/Orange wire (positive) and Black wire (ground) at dimmer relay. If there is 12 volts, go to **TEST C9**. If there is no voltage, go to **TEST C8**.

TEST C8 – DEFECTIVE CIRCUIT

Check voltage between Purple/Orange wire and body ground. If there is voltage, repair or replace Black wire between relay and body ground, located at instrument panel. If there is no voltage repair or replace Purple/Orange wire between relay and stater solenoid.

TEST C9 – DIMMER RELAY CONTROL CIRCUIT

Using an ohmmeter, check for continuity of Red/Black wire between dimmer relay and pin No. 15 at 60-pin connector. If there is no continuity, repair or replace Red/Black wire. If there is continuity, go to **TEST C10**.

TEST C10 – TEST LIGHT CIRCUITS

Plug dimmer relay connector back in. Unplug "FIRM" light connector from rear of tachometer. Go to **TEST C11**.

TEST C11 – LIGHT CONTROL CIRCUIT

1) Ensure headlights and parking lights are off. Using a jumper wire, jump pin No. 15 to pin No. 60 on 60-pin connector. Using a voltmeter, check voltage between Purple/Orange wire (positive) and Tan/Red wire (ground) at "FIRM" light connector. DO NOT use a test light.

2) If there is no voltage, go to **TEST C12**. If there is 12 volts, replace light bulb. Check for intermittent short in Tan/Red wire between light and dimmer relay.

TEST C12 – "FIRM" LIGHT POWER FEED

Using a voltmeter, measure voltage between Purple/Orange wire at light connector to body ground. If there is 12 volts, go to **TEST C13**. If there is no voltage, repair or replace Purple/Orange wire between starter solenoid and light connector.

TEST C13 – "FIRM" LIGHT GROUND CIRCUIT

Unplug dimmer relay connector. Using a ohmmeter, check Tan/Red wire for continuity between dimmer relay and "FIRM" light connector. If there is continuity, replace dimmer relay. If there is no continuity, repair or replace Tan/Red wire.

TEST C14 – ENSURE HEADLIGHTS ARE OFF

Ensure headlights are off. If headlights are on, turn headlights off. Go to **TEST A1**. If headlights are off, go to **TEST C15**.

TEST C15 – DIMMER RELAY WIRING

Turn ignition off. Unplug dimmer relay. Dimmer relay is located inside glove box. Ensure wiring is okay and is properly routed. If wiring is okay, go to **TEST C16**.

TEST C16 – HEADLIGHT SIGNAL TO DIMMER RELAY

Turn ignition on. Using a voltmeter, check voltage between Brown wire (positive) and Black wire (ground) at dimmer relay. If there is no voltage, replace dimmer relay. If there is 12 volts, repair or replace Brown wire between headlight switch and dimmer relay.

TEST C17 – DIMMER RELAY WIRING

Turn ignition off. Unplug dimmer relay. Dimmer relay is located inside glove box. Ensure wiring is okay and is properly routed. If wiring is okay, go to **TEST C18**.

TEST C18 – DIMMER RELAY CONTROL CIRCUIT

Place selector switch in "AUTO" position. Turn ignition on and wait 10 seconds. Using an ohmmeter, measure resistance between Red/Black wire and Black wire at dimmer relay connector. If resistance is more than 1000 ohms, replace dimmer relay. If resistance is 10 ohms or less, go to **TEST C19**.

Electronic Suspensions

FORD MOTOR CO. PROGRAMMED RIDE CONTROL (Cont.)

FIRM RIDE INDICATOR LIGHT CIRCUIT DIAGNOSIS (Cont.)

TEST C19 – UNPLUG PRC MODULE

Turn ignition off. Lower PRC module mounting panel. Module is located inside luggage compartment, on back of passenger side seat. Unplug 60-pin connector. Go to **TEST C20**.

TEST C20 – SHORT IN DIMMER RELAY CONTROL CIRCUIT

Ensure pin No. 15 (Red/Black wire) at PRC module is not damaged. Using an ohmmeter, check resistance between pin No. 15 and pin No. 60 at 60-pin connector. If resistance is more than 1000 ohms, replace PRC module. If resistance is 10 ohms or less, repair or replace Red/Black wire between dimmer relay and PRC module.

MODULE INPUT CIRCUIT DIAGNOSIS

TEST D1 – REPEAT ENTER DIAGNOSTIC MODE

Ensure fabricated tool is free of corrosion and is shaped properly. Repeat **TEST A1**. If second attempt is successful, continue **TEST A1**. If second attempt is not successful, go to **TEST D2**.

TEST D2 – SIGNAL RETURN CIRCUIT

Ensure wires at diagnostic connector are okay. Using an ohmmeter, check for continuity between Yellow/Black wire at diagnostic connector and ground. If there is no continuity, repair or replace Yellow/Black wire between connector and pin No. 46 at PRC module. If there is continuity, go to **TEST D3**.

TEST D3 – UNPLUG PRC MODULE

Turn ignition off. Lower PRC module mounting panel. Module is located inside luggage compartment, on back of passenger side seat. Unplug 60-pin connector. Go to **TEST D4**.

TEST D4 – SHORTED DIAGNOSTIC CIRCUIT

Ensure Gray/Red wire is at pin No. 30, on 60-pin connector, and is not damaged. Using an ohmmeter, check resistance between pin No. 30 and pin No. 60 on connector. If resistance is more than 1000 ohms, go to **TEST D5**. If resistance is less than 10 ohms, repair or replace shorted Gray/Red wire between 60-pin connector and diagnostic connector.

TEST D5 – OPEN DIAGNOSTIC CIRCUIT

Install fabricated tool in diagnostic connector. Check resistance between pin No. 30 and pin No. 46 at 60-pin connector. If resistance is less than 10 ohms, replace PRC module. If resistance is 1000 ohms or more, repair or replace Gray/Red wire between PRC module and diagnostic connector.

TEST D6 – CHECK SWITCH POSITION

Place selector switch in "FIRM" position. If Green light stays on, go to **TEST D7**. If Green light turns off, ensure wiring is correct. If so, replace selector switch.

TEST D7 – UNPLUG PRC MODULE

Turn ignition off. Place selector switch in "AUTO" position. Lower PRC module mounting panel. Module is located inside luggage compartment, on back of passenger side seat. Unplug 60-pin connector. Go to **TEST D8**.

TEST D8 – SHORTED BRAKE CIRCUIT

Ensure Orange/Light Green wire is at pin No. 9 on 60-pin connector and is not damaged. Using an ohmmeter, check resistance between pins No. 9 and No. 60 on connector. If resistance is more than 1000 ohms, go to **TEST D9**. If resistance is 10 ohms or less, repair or replace Orange/Light Green wire between brake sensor switch and PRC module.

TEST D9 – CLOSED BRAKE CIRCUIT

Using an ohmmeter, check resistance between pins No. 9 and No. 46. If resistance is more than 1000 ohms, go to **TEST D10**. If resistance is less than 10 ohms, replace brake sensor switch.

TEST D10 – CLOSED SELECT CIRCUIT

Ensure selector switch is in "AUTO" position. Ensure Brown/Light Green wire is at pin No. 18 and is not damaged. Using a voltmeter, measure voltage between pin No. 18 (positive) and pin No. 60 (ground). If there is no voltage, go to **TEST D11**. If there is 12 volts, replace selector switch.

TEST D11 – CLOSED THROTTLE POSITION SENSOR SIGNAL

Ensure Orange/White wire is at pin No. 28 and is not damaged. Using an ohmmeter, check resistance between pin No. 28 and pin No. 60 on connector. If resistance is 1000 ohms or more, replace PRC module. If resistance is less than 10 ohms, go to **TEST D12**.

TEST D12 – SHORTED THROTTLE POSITION SENSOR CIRCUIT

Turn ignition off. Unplug EEC-IV control module connector. Measure resistance between pin No. 28 and pin No. 60 on 60-pin connector. If resistance is 1000 ohms or more, check for defective throttle position sensor. If resistance is less than 10 ohms, repair or replace Orange/White wire between throttle position sensor and PRC module.

TEST D13 – UNPLUG PRC MODULE

Turn ignition off. Lower PRC module mounting panel. Module is located inside luggage compartment, on back of passenger side seat. Unplug 60-pin connector. Go to **TEST D14**.

TEST D14 – STEERING SENSOR CIRCUIT

Ensure Red/Yellow wire is at pin No. 45, Red/White wire at pin No. 24 and both wire are not damaged. Go to **TEST D15**.

TEST D15 – STEERING SENSOR SIGNALS

Using a jumper wire, jump pin No. 46 to pin No. 60 on 60-pin connector. Start engine. Using an analog ohmmeter, measure resistance between pins No. 45 and No. 60, and between pins No. 24 and No. 60. If ohmmeter does not swing for one or both circuits, go to **TEST D16**. If meter swings for both circuits, turn engine off. Replace PRC module.

TEST D16 – UNPLUG STEERING SENSOR

Turn ignition off. Unplug steering sensor connector. Steering sensor is located on lower portion of steering column. Using an ohmmeter, check continuity of Red/Yellow wire and Red/White wire between steering sensor and PRC module. If there is no continuity through either wire, repair or replace wire. If there is continuity, go to **TEST D17**.

TEST D17 – STEERING SENSOR CIRCUIT

Turn ignition on. Using a voltmeter, measure voltage between Purple/Orange wire (positive) and Yellow/Black wire (negative) at steering sensor connector. If there is no voltage, go to **TEST D18**. If there is 12 volts, replace steering sensor.

TEST D18 – STEERING SENSOR POWER CIRCUIT

Measure voltage between Purple/Orange wire (positive) and body ground. If there is 12 volts, repair or replace Yellow/Black wire between steering sensor and pin No. 46 on 60-pin connector. If there is no voltage, repair or replace Purple/Orange wire between steering sensor and pin No. 57 on 60-pin connector.

FORD MOTOR CO. PROGRAMMED RIDE CONTROL (Cont.)

MODULE INPUT CIRCUIT DIAGNOSIS (Cont.)

TEST D19 – UNPLUG PRC MODULE

Turn ignition off. Lower PRC module mounting panel. Module is located inside luggage compartment, on back of passenger side seat. Unplug 60-pin connector. Go to **TEST D20**.

TEST D20 – SPEED SENSOR SIGNAL

Ensure Dark Green/White wire is at pin No. 3, Orange/Yellow wire is at pin No. 6 on 60-pin connector, and both are not damaged. If wires are okay, go to **TEST D21**.

TEST D21 – SPEED SENSOR GROUND CIRCUIT

Using an ohmmeter, check for continuity between Dark Green/White wire at pin No. 3 and Black wire at pin No. 60 on 60-pin connector. If there is continuity, go to **TEST D22**. If there is no continuity, repair or replace Black wire between pin No. 60 and body ground.

TEST D22 – SPEED SENSOR TEST

1) Turn ignition on. Ensure speedometer displays all segments. If not, replace speedometer/odometer module. If all segments are displayed, drive vehicle and ensure odometer, tripminder and cruise control operate. Unplug speed sensor.

2) Using an ohmmeter, measure resistance between 2 wires at speed sensor connector. If resistance is less than 500 ohms, repair or replace Dark Green/White wire between speed sensor and pin No. 3 on 60-pin connector.

3) If resistance is 500 ohms or more, check resistance between speed sensor terminals. If resistance is not 200-230 ohms, replace speed sensor. If resistance is 200-230 ohms, check driven gear and retainer.

4) If okay, check drive gear, inside transmission. If drive gear is okay, check wiring to instrument cluster. If no problem can be found, replace PRC module.

TEST D23 – UNPLUG PRC MODULE

Turn ignition off. Lower PRC module mounting panel. Module is located inside luggage compartment, on back of passenger side seat. Unplug 60-pin connector. Go to **TEST D24**.

TEST D24 – "FIRM" SIGNAL

Ensure Brown/Light Green wire is at pin No. 18 on 60-pin connector and is not damaged. Turn ignition on. Place selector switch in "FIRM" position. Using a voltmeter, check voltage between Brown/Light Green wire at pin No. 18 and Black wire at pin No. 60 on 60-pin connector. If there is no voltage, go to **TEST D25**. If there is 12 volts, replace PRC module.

TEST D25 – UNPLUG SELECTOR SWITCH

Turn ignition off. Unplug selector switch. Ensure wiring to selector switch is not damaged. If okay, go to **TEST D26**.

TEST D26 – SELECTOR SWITCH POWER FEED

Turn ignition on. Using a voltmeter, measure voltage at Purple/Orange wire at selector switch. If there is no voltage, repair or replace wire between selector switch and PRC module. If there is 12 volts, replace selector switch.

TEST D27 – UNPLUG PRC MODULE

Turn ignition off. Lower PRC module mounting panel. Module is located inside luggage compartment, on back of passenger side seat. Unplug 60-pin connector. Go to **TEST D28**.

TEST D28 – CLOSED BRAKE SENSOR SWITCH

Ensure Orange/Light Green wire is located at pin No. 9 on 60-pin and is not damaged. Start engine. Depress brake pedal firmly to floor and hold. Using an ohmmeter, check resistance between Orange/Light Green wire at No. 9 and Black wire at pin No. 60 on 60-pin connector. If resistance is 1000 ohms or more, go to **TEST D29**. If resistance is less than 10 ohms, replace PRC module.

TEST D29 – UNPLUG BRAKE SENSOR SWITCH

Turn ignition off. Unplug brake sensor switch. Switch is located on proportioning valve. Ensure wiring is not damaged. If wiring is okay, go to **TEST D30**.

TEST D30 – BRAKE SENSOR SWITCH GROUND CIRCUIT

Using an ohmmeter, measure resistance between Yellow/Black wire at brake sensor switch connector and body ground. If resistance is 1000 ohms or more, repair or replace Yellow/Black wire between brake sensor switch and pin No. 28 on 60-pin connector. If resistance is less than 10 ohms, replace brake sensor switch.

TEST D31 – UNPLUG PRC MODULE

Turn ignition off. Lower PRC module mounting panel. Module is located inside luggage compartment, on back of passenger side seat. Unplug 60-pin connector. Go to **TEST D32**.

TEST D32 – CHECK PRC & EEC-IV MODULE CONNECTORS

Ensure Orange/White wire from pin No. 35 on EEC-IV module to pin No. 28 on PRC module 60-pin connector is not damaged. If okay, go to **TEST D33**.

TEST D33 – THROTTLE POSITION CIRCUIT

Using an ohmmeter, check continuity of Orange/White wire between pin No. 35 on EEC-IV module connector and pin No. 28 on PRC module 60-pin connector. If there is no continuity, repair or replace Orange/White wire. If there is continuity, replace PRC module.

REMOVAL & INSTALLATION

ACTUATORS

Removal (Front)

Park vehicle on level surface. Apply parking brake. Turn ignition off. Unplug actuator connector. Remove cover. Remove 2 actuator retaining screws. Remove actuator. Holding actuator bracket with pliers, remove shock absorber upper nut. Remove bracket.

NOTE: DO NOT raise vehicle with shock absorber nut removed.

Installation

To install, reverse removal procedure. Ensure flat sides on bracket are parallel with fender and are aligned with flat on shock absorber.

Removal (Rear)

1) Park vehicle on level surface. Apply parking brake. Turn ignition off. Remove side trim panel from luggage compartment. Unplug actuator connector.

2) Squeeze 2 actuator retaining tabs and remove actuator. Holding actuator bracket with pliers, remove shock absorber upper nut. Remove bracket. To install, reverse removal procedure.

BRAKE SENSOR SWITCH

Removal & Installation

Raise hood. Unplug connector from switch, located on brake control valve (proportioning valve). Remove brake sensor switch. To install, reverse removal procedure. Ensure "O" ring is installed on switch.

Electronic Suspensions

FORD MOTOR CO. PROGRAMMED RIDE CONTROL (Cont.)

SPEED SENSOR

Removal & Installation

Raise vehicle and support. Remove speed sensor retaining bolt from transmission. Remove speed sensor and driven gear. Unplug connector. Remove retainer and driven gear. To install, reverse removal procedure. Ensure "O" ring is properly seated.

STEERING SENSOR

Removal & Installation

1) Disconnect negative battery cable. Remove steering column from vehicle. See appropriate STEERING COLUMNS article. Squeeze end of plastic pin retaining steering sensor to steering column.

2) Wipe lower end of steering column shaft with a cloth. Ensure column is free of burrs. Remove steering sensor. To install, reverse removal procedure. Lubricate "O" ring with Grease (ESA-M1C45-A).

TIGHTENING SPECIFICATIONS

Application	Ft. Lbs. (N.m)
Upper Shock Nut	
Front	60-75 (82-102)
Rear	15-21 (20-29)
	INCH Lbs. (N.m)
Brake Sensor Switch	96-120 (10-14)

Fig. 5: Programmed Ride Control Wiring Diagram

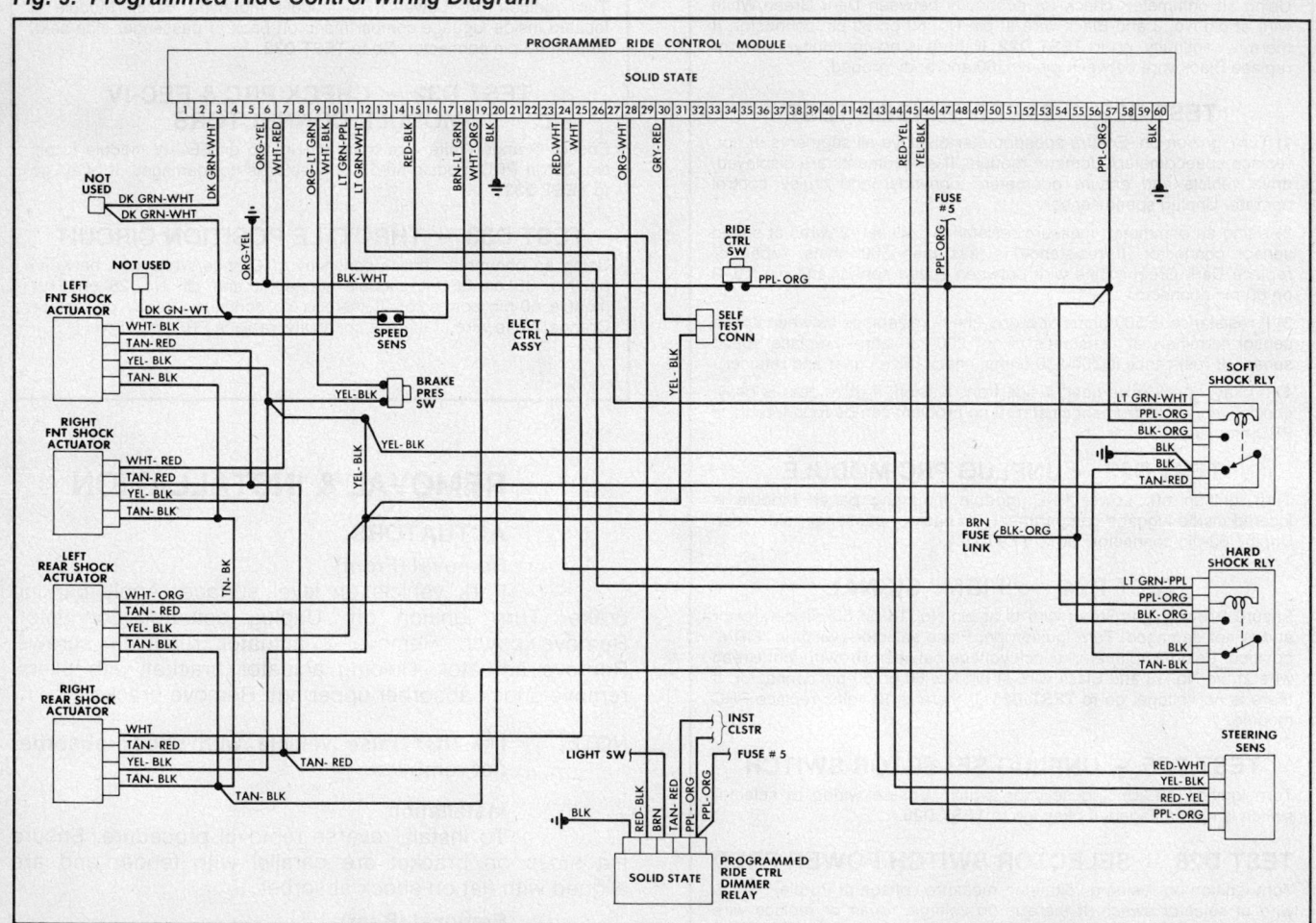

Electronic Suspensions

FORD MOTOR CO. REAR LEVEL CONTROL

Crown Victoria, Grand Marquis, Town Car

CAUTION: **DO NOT charge battery with ignition on. Damage to air compressor will occur.**

DESCRIPTION

The automatic leveling system is an air-operated, computer-controlled leveling system. Components are in addition to the standard rear suspension. Vehicle trim height (ride height) automatically adjusts to varying loads, with the aid of air shocks. The system consists of air-adjustable shocks, a compressor assembly, air drier with minimum retention valve, exhaust solenoid, compressor relay, rotary height sensor, microcomputer module, wiring and nylon tubing.

OPERATION

Air suspension leveling system operates by adding or removing air in the air shocks to maintain level of vehicle at a predetermined rear suspension height. The suspension height is controlled by a rotary height sensor. Airflow to the entire system is controlled by the interaction of the air compressor, vent solenoid, height sensor and microcomputer module.

AIR COMPRESSOR

A single cylinder piston-type air compressor is mounted on the left front wheelwell of all models. The compressor is electrically operated. A regenerative-type drier is attached to compressor manifold. The vent solenoid, located on compressor manifold, controls air expulsion. A minimum retention valve, located inside the air drier, maintains a minimum pressure in air shocks of 10-22 psi.

MICROCOMPUTER MODULE

The microcomputer module is mounted behind the right rear trim panel in the luggage compartment. It controls the compressor relay and vent solenoid. The microcomputer module also controls power and ground to the rotary sensor. The module provides a 7-13 second time delay before any circuit can be completed.

The microcomputer module monitors air suspension system through inputs from the height sensor and ignition circuits. It limits compressor run time to 2 minutes and exhaust solenoid time to one minute. This function is to limit continuous compressor operation in case of a severe system leak or a malfunctioning exhaust valve. The timer function is reset when ignition key is cycled to the "OFF" and "RUN" positions.

ROTARY HEIGHT SENSOR

Trim height is controlled by the rotary height sensor. The sensor is located at the center of rear crossmember above the center section of the axle.

The sensor operates as follows: as vehicle lowers, height sensor arm is rotated upward (low out-of-trim), sending 2 signals to microcomputer. After 7-13 seconds of continuous height sensor signal, the air compressor activates to send air to the shocks.

When pre-set trim height is reached, the air compressor shuts off. As weight is removed from the vehicle, the body will raise. The height sensor arm is

rotated downward (high out-of-trim). After sending a continuous 7-13 second signal to microcomputer, the vent solenoid is activated and allows air to escape. As vehicle lowers, height sensor rotates upward. When pre-set trim height is reached, vent solenoid valves close.

Fig. 1: Automatic Leveling Rear Suspension Components

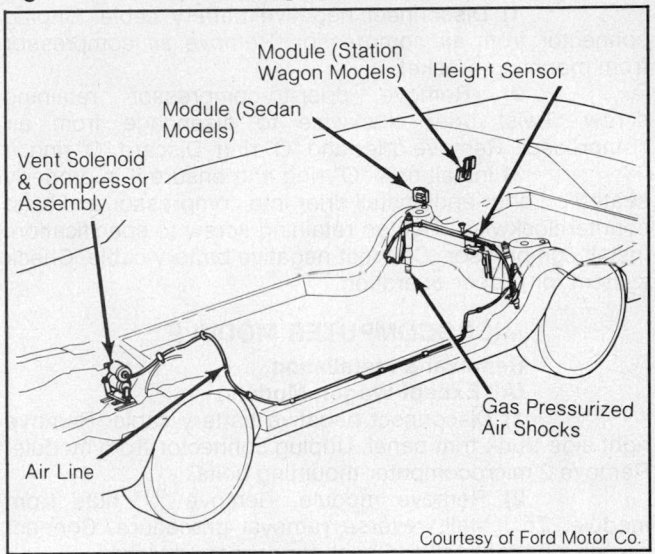

Courtesy of Ford Motor Co.

ADJUSTMENTS

RIDING HEIGHT

Raise and support vehicle. Loosen attaching nut at upper control arm. Move sensor attachment desired amount. There are 3 adjustment positions provided on the arm. One position change will provide .354" (9 mm) change. Lower vehicle and turn ignition on. Check ride height. *See Fig. 2.*

Fig. 2: Ride Height Adjustment

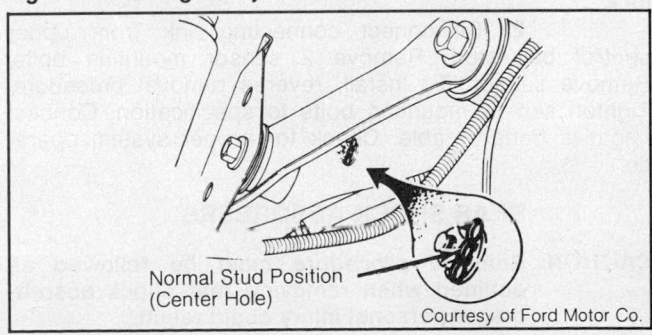

Normal Stud Position (Center Hole)

Courtesy of Ford Motor Co.

REMOVAL & INSTALLATION

AIR COMPRESSOR

NOTE: **During installation always reconnect negative battery cable last.**
Removal & Installation
1) Disconnect negative battery cable. Remove air line from drier by pushing in on retainer and pulling air line out. Unplug connector from air compressor.

Electronic Suspensions

FORD MOTOR CO. REAR LEVEL CONTROL (Cont.)

2) Remove air compressor. Remove mounting bracket. To install, reverse removal procedure. Reconnect negative battery cable. Check air lines for leakage. Check for proper system operation.

AIR DRIER
Removal & Installation
1) Disconnect negative battery cable. Unplug connector from air compressor. Remove air compressor from mounting bracket.

2) Remove drier-to-compressor retaining screw. Twist drier clockwise to disengage from air compressor. Remove drier and "O" ring. Discard "O" ring.

3) Install new "O" ring and ensure it is properly seated on drier end. Install drier into compressor and twist counterclockwise. Tighten retaining screw to specification. Install compressor. Connect negative battery cable. Check system for proper operation.

MICROCOMPUTER MODULE
Removal & Installation
(All Except Wagon Models)
1) Disconnect negative battery cable. Remove right side trunk trim panel. Unplug connector from module. Remove 2 microcomputer mounting bolts.

2) Remove module. Remove "U" nuts from module. To install, reverse removal procedure. Connect negative battery cable. Check for proper operation.

Removal & Installation (Wagon Models)
Disconect negative battery cable. Remove right rear spare tire cover or trim panel. Unplug connector from module. Remove module. To install, reverse removal procedure. Connect negative battery cable. Check for proper operation.

HEIGHT SENSOR
Removal & Installation
1) Disconnect battery ground cable. Unplug sensor connector, located on sensor mounting bracket under luggage compartment. Unlatch connecting link snap lock.

2) Disconnect connecting link from upper control ball stud. Remove 2 sensor mounting bolts. Remove sensor. To install, reverse removal procedure. Tighten sensor mounting bolts to specification. Connect negative battery cable. Check for proper system operation.

REAR SHOCK ABSORBERS

CAUTION: Removal procedure must be followed as outlined when removing rear shock absorbers, or personal injury could result.

NOTE: **Air shocks may be replaced separately. Replace only faulty shocks.**

Removal & Installation
1) Turn ignition off. Disconnect height sensor connector link. Raise vehicle. The vent solenoid will vent air while vehicle is on jack or hoist. Wait until air has stopped "hissing" before disconnecting air lines.

2) A residual pressure of 8-24 psi (55-165 kPa) will remain in air lines. Disconnect air lines by pushing in on retainer ring(s) and pulling out on line(s). Remove nut from upper shock retaining stud. Remove nut from lower shock stud. Remove shock absorber.

3) To install, reverse removal procedure. Tighten mounting nuts to specification. Ensure shock absorber rubber sleeve are marked and indexed properly.

TESTING

SYSTEM OPERATION CHECK

NOTE: **Always cycle ignition on and off before starting tests to ensure vent solenoid and compressor "on times" are reset.**

1) Set vehicle at curb height specification. Record ride height measurement. Briefly start and run engine. Apply a load of 300-350 lbs. (136-159 kg) to the rear of the vehicle. There should be a 7-13 second delay before the compressor turns on and rear of vehicle starts to rise.

2) Vehicle should rise to within 1/2" (13 mm) of ride height set in step **1)** by the time the compressor shuts off. If vehicle does not rise to within 1/2" (13 mm) of the unloaded specification, check trunk for overloading. If overloaded, remove load and retest.

3) Remove load applied in step **1)**. There should be a 7-13 second delay before vehicle starts to lower. Vehicle should lower to within 1/2" (13 mm) of ride height specification. If not, refer to DIAGNOSTIC TESTING in this article.

RESIDUAL PRESSURE CHECK
1) Remove the air line from the drier and attach it to one side of a pressure gauge. Connect the drier to the other side of the gauge using a short piece of nylon tubing. Cycle the ignition on and off.

2) Apply a load of 300-350 lbs. (136-159 kg) to the rear of vehicle to run the compressor and raise vehicle. Remove load and allow system to exhaust air pressure and lower vehicle.

3) When no more air is being exhausted, the gauge should read 8-24 psi (55-165 kPa). Remove pressure gauge and reconnect the system. Repeat steps **1)** and **2)** to ensure there is system air pressure in the shocks.

LEAK CHECK
1) Repeat steps **1)** and **2)** of RESIDUAL PRESSURE CHECK. Allow the system to fill until the gauge reads 70-100 psi (475-679 kPa). With load still applied, disconnect wiring harness connector from the microcomputer module and then remove the load.

2) Rear of vehicle should rise. Cycle ignition on and off. Observe system for leaks for about 15 minutes. If system will not inflate to more than 50 psi (339 kPa), a severe air leak is indicated. Check air line between compressor and shocks for damage.

3) Check all connections with soap/water solution. If pressure is stable, perform diagnostic test.

NOTE: **If compressor is allowed to run until maximum output pressure is reached, the vent solenoid valve will function as a relief valve. The leak-down after compressor shut-down will indicate a false air leak.**

4) Attach wire connector to module. Cycle ignition switch from "OFF" to "RUN" position. Allow air to exhaust and vehicle to lower. Remove pressure gauge

FORD MOTOR CO. REAR LEVEL CONTROL (Cont.)

Fig. 3: Harness Connector Chart

Wiring	Harness Side Connector	Pin Number	Function	Wire Harness			Circuit End Point
				Circuit	Color	Gauge	
Front Compressor and Vent Solenoid	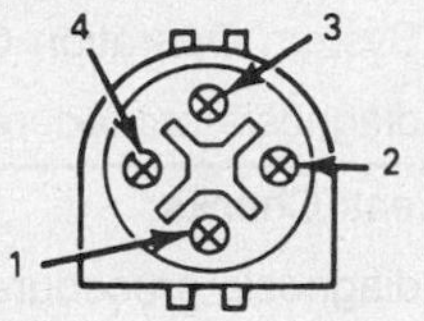	1	Solenoid Control	415	LG/O	14	Module Pin No. 9
		2	Motor Ground	57B	BK	12	Battery Ground Terminal
		3	Motor Feed	417	P/O	12	Compressor Relay
		4	Solenoid Feed	37F	Y	14	Starter Relay
Compressor Relay (1)	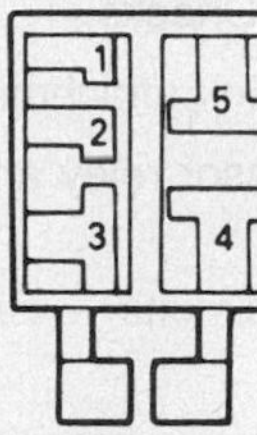	1	Control	420	DB/Y	18	Module Pin No. 8
		2	Feed (Coil)	298A	P/O	18	Compressor Relay
		3	Feed (Contacts)	37C	Y	12	Starter Relay
		4	Compressor Motor Feed	417	P/O	12	Compressor
		5	Compressor Motor Ground	57A	BK	12	Battery Ground Terminal
Front/Rear Harness Connector	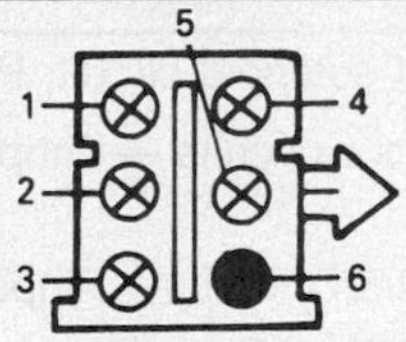	1	Control	420	DB/Y	18	Module Pin No. 8
		2	Ignition Sense	298A	P/O	18	Ignition Switch
		3	System Ground	57	BK	14	Battery Ground Terminal
		4	—	—	—	—	
		5	Module Power	37	Y	14	Module Pin No. 5
		6	Vent Solenoid Control	415	LG/O	14	Module Pin No. 9
Ignition Sense			Ignition Sense	298	P/O	18	Module Pin No. 4
				and	P/O	18	Compressor Relay
				298A			
Rear Height Sensor (1)	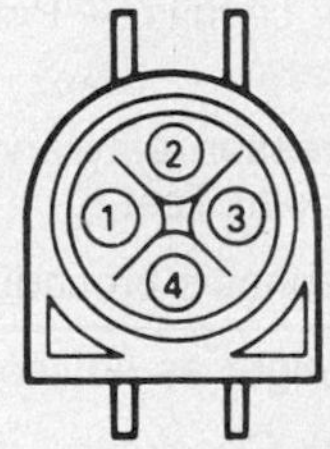	1	Logic Line B	428	O/BK	18	Module Pin No. 6
		2	Feed	431	PK/W	18	Module Pin No. 3
		3	Logic Line A	427	PK/BK	18	Module Pin No. 1
		4	Ground	430	GY	18	Module Pin No. 10
Module (1)			Diagnostic Monitor Lamp	693	O	18	Module Pin No. 7
				Wire Bundle			
							Control Module

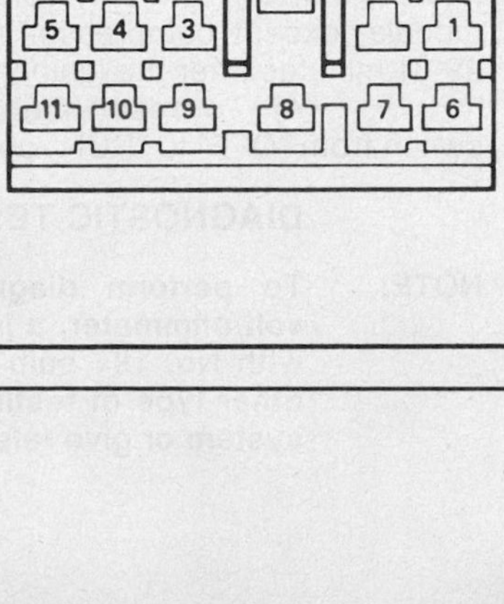

Electronic Suspensions

FORD MOTOR CO. REAR LEVEL CONTROL (Cont.)

Fig. 4: *Diagnosis Selection Chart*

SYMPTOM	ACTION TO TAKE
• System inoperative: compressor does not run. • Vehicle low or high: vehicle rises and lowers OK when load is added or removed, but normal trim height seems high or low.	• CHECK vehicle load. • CHECK trim height as outlined. • PERFORM System Operation Check. • PERFORM diagnosis procedure.
• Vehicle rises OK, but gradually leaks down. • Compressor cycles On and Off intermittently while driving.	• REFER to Leak Checks. • PERFORM diagnosis procedure. • PERFORM System Operation Check.
• Compressor runs continuously for two minutes with ignition switch in RUN. • Compressor turns Off after two minutes of accumulated operating time. **NOTE: Vehicle rear may or may not rise during either situation.**	• REFER to Leak Checks. • CHECK sensor link attachment. • CHECK compressor relay and motor circuit for short to ground. • CHECK sensor circuits — Pinpoint Tests G, H and J. • PERFORM diagnosis procedure.
• Vehicle high or will not lower with ignition switch ON or OFF.	• CHECK vent solenoid circuit, Pinpoint Test F. • CHECK sensor circuits — Pinpoint Tests G, H and J. • CHECK ignition circuit — Pinpoint Test D. • CHECK sensor link attachment and ball stud position. • PERFORM diagnosis procedure.
• Vehicle low or compressor does not run with ignition switch ON and a load applied.	• CHECK sensor link attachment. • CHECK ignition circuit — Pinpoint Test D. • CHECK sensor circuits — Pinpoint Tests G, H and J. • CHECK compressor relay and motor circuits — Pinpoint Test K. • PERFORM diagnosis procedure.
• Excessive bottoming in rear with load.	• CHECK trim height as outlined. • REFER to Leak Checks. • PERFORM System Operational Check.

Courtesy of Ford Motor Co.

from system and reconnect drier. Repeat steps **1)** and **2)** of RESIDUAL PRESSURE CHECK. Perform SYSTEM OPERATION CHECK.

MONITOR LIGHT OPERATION

1) Turning the ignition switch from "OFF" to "RUN" will cause monitor light to flash. The monitor light flashes once per second while compressor relay is on.

2) The light stays on while ignition is on and one or more of the following occur: height sensor wire connector is detached, an air line is removed, vent solenoid is on over one minute or compressor relay is on over 2 minutes.

3) Whenever an abnormal program run is detected, the microcomputer module suspends all controls

and the monitor light stays on. All system functions of the module, except compressor relay on, are energized for 29-31 minutes after the ignition is turned off.

4) To reset the system, cycle the ignition switch from "OFF" to "RUN" position.

DIAGNOSTIC TESTING

NOTE: **To perform diagnostic testing, an analog volt/ohmmeter, a jumper lead and a test light with No. 194 bulb must be used. Use of any other type of testing equipment may damage system or give false readings.**

FORD MOTOR CO. REAR LEVEL CONTROL (Cont.)

Fig. 5: Automatic Leveling System Testing Points

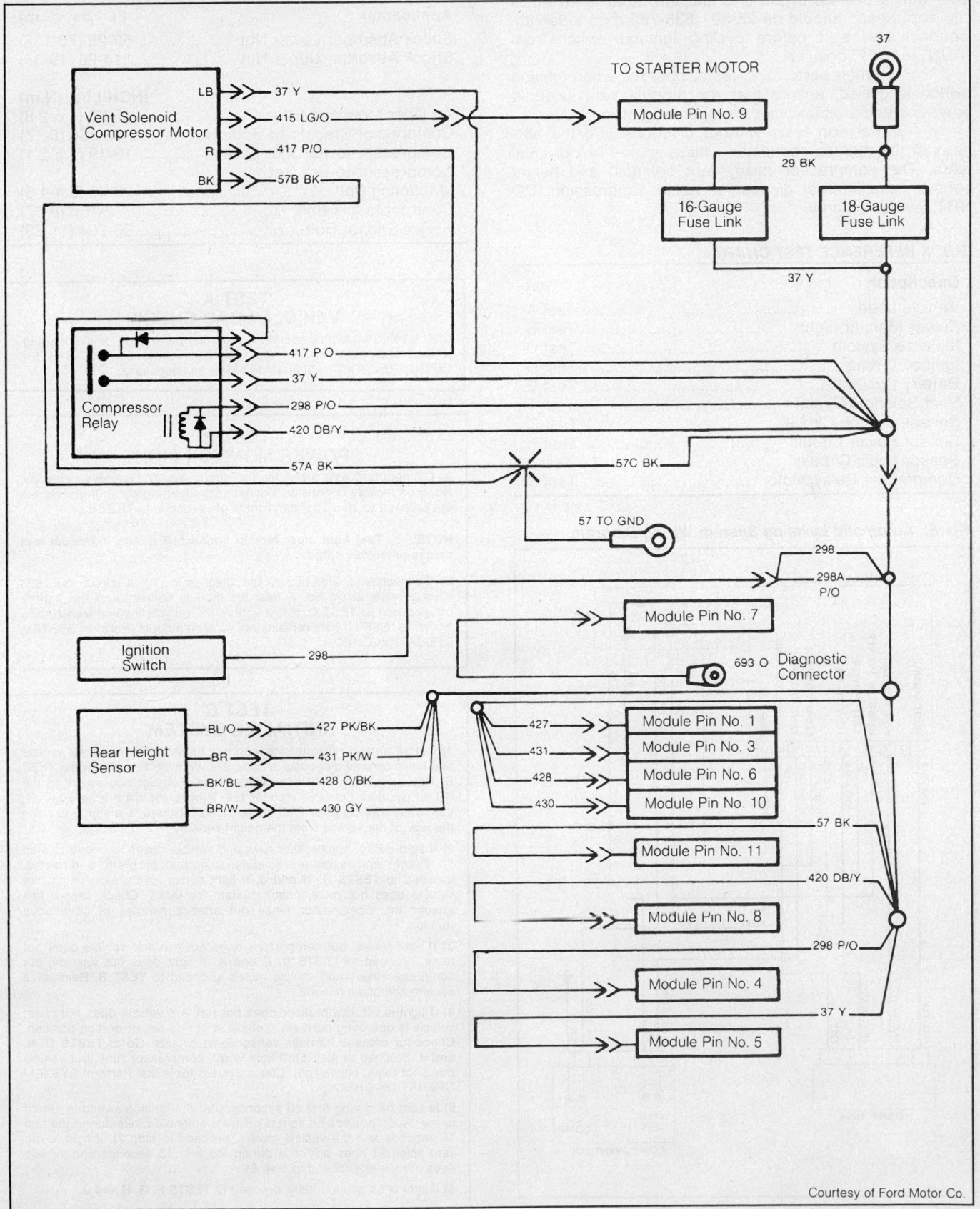

Courtesy of Ford Motor Co.

FORD MOTOR CO. REAR LEVEL CONTROL (Cont.)

Construct test light using a No. 194 bulb, one lead with a pointed probe end and the other lead with a clip end. Leads should be 25-30" (635-762 mm) in length. Connect test light before cycling ignition switch from "RUN" to "OFF" position.

When performing tests, observe when ignition switch is cycled, ensure that the module vent solenoid timer and compressor timer are operating properly.

Perform tests without disconnecting the harness at the module connector, unless stated in individual tests. The compressor relay, vent solenoid and height sensor have internal diodes for noise suppression. DO NOT reverse polarity.

QUICK REFERENCE TEST CHART

Description	Test
Vehicle Load	Test A
Power Monitor Light	Test B
Initialize System	Test C
Ignition Circuit	Test D
Battery Circuit	Test E
Vent Solenoid Circuit	Test F
Sensor Ground Circuit	Test G
Sensor Power Circuit	Test H
Sensor Logic Circuits	Test J
Compressor Relay/Motor	Test K

Fig. 6: Automatic Leveling System Wiring Diagram

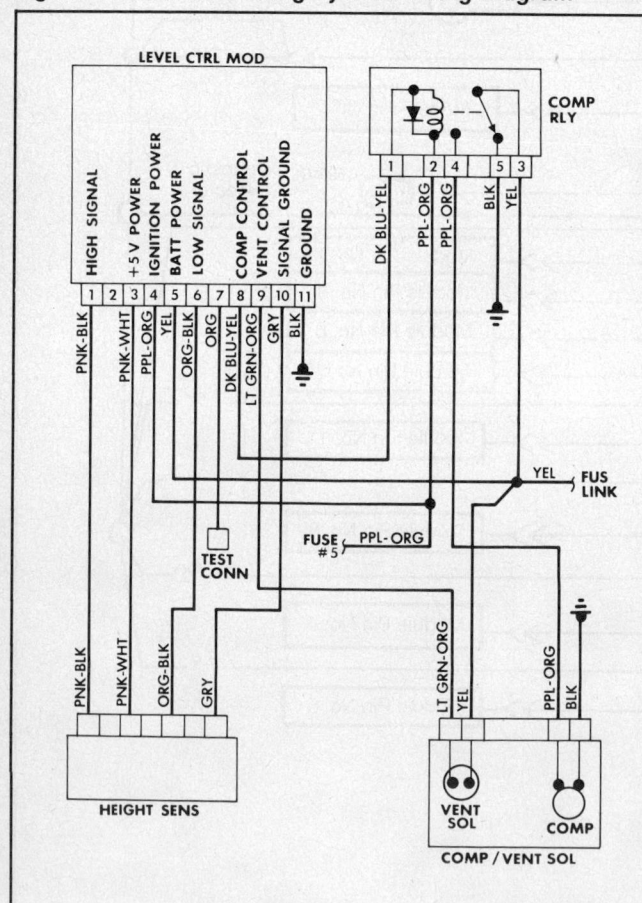

TIGHTENING SPECIFICATIONS

Application	Ft. Lbs. (N.m)
Shock Absorber Lower Nut	52-25 (70-115)
Shock Absorber Upper Nut	14-26 (19-35)

	INCH Lbs. (N.m)
Air Drier Mounting Screw	15-25 (1.6-2.8)
Compressor Bracket-to-Body Nut	72-156 (8-17)
Compressor-to-Air Drier Screw	13-19 (1.5-2.1)
Compressor-to-Bracket Mounting Bolt	30-40 (3.4-4.5)
Control Module Bolt	72-156 (8-17)
Height Sensor Bolt	96-204 (11-23)

TEST A
VEHICLE LOAD CHECK

Check vehicle passenger and luggage compartments for overloading. Unload as necessary. If ride height is okay, perform SYSTEM OPERATION CHECK. Adjust ride height as necessary.

TEST B
POWER MONITOR LIGHT

1) Connect test light probe lead to circuit No. 37 (Yellow wire) at pin No. 5 on module connector. Connect clip lead to ground. If test light is on, proceed to step **2)**. If test light is off, proceed to **TEST E**.

NOTE: Test light must remain connected during individual test unless otherwise noted.

2) Connect lead with clip to the diagnostic pigtail, circuit No. 693 (Orange wire) at pin No. 7, near the module connector. If test light is off, proceed to **TEST C**. If test light is on, recycle ignition switch from "RUN" to "OFF". If light remains on, replace module. Perform SYSTEM OPERATION CHECK.

TEST C
INITIALIZE SYSTEM

1) Before entering diagnostics, connect battery charger to the vehicle and leave on until diagnosis is complete. With ignition off, repeat **TEST B**. Review monitor light service functions. Turn ignition switch to the "RUN" position. Observe monitor test light. Light will normally be off, then start blinking after 7-13 second delay if there is a signal to raise the rear of the vehicle from the height sensor.

2) If light blinks, compressor runs and vehicle raises, proceed to step **5)**. If light comes on immediately, abnormal program is detected, proceed to **TESTS G, H and J**. If light blinks, compressor runs, but vehicle does not raise, check system for leaks. Check sensor link attachment. Compressor times out after 2 minutes of continuous running.

3) If light blinks, but compressor does not run and vehicle does not raise, proceed to **TESTS D, E and K**. If light does not turn on, but compressor runs and vehicle raises, proceed to **TEST B**. Reinitialize system and observe light.

4) If light is off, compressor does not run and vehicle does not raise, vehicle is operating normally. Vehicle is at ride height or high position. Check for crossed harness sensor logic circuits. Go to **TESTS G, H, and J**. Proceed to step **5)**. If light is off, compressor runs, but vehicle does not raise, check light. Check system for leaks. Perform SYSTEM OPERATION CHECK.

5) Is light off during first 60 seconds after the ignition switch is turned to the "RUN" position? If light is off, vent solenoid clicks during the first 15 seconds and the vehicle lowers, proceed to step **7)**. If light is off, vent solenoid does not click during the first 15 seconds and vehicle does not lower, proceed to step **8)**.

6) If light is on continuously, proceed to **TESTS F, G, H and J**.

FORD MOTOR CO. REAR LEVEL CONTROL (Cont.)

TEST C (Cont.)

7) Is light on after the first 60 seconds after the ignition switch is turned to the "RUN" position? If light is on, vent solenoid clicks within first 15 seconds and vehicle does/does not lower, this is normal operation. Vent solenoid timed out. Proceed to step **9)**.

8) If light is off, vent solenoid does not click within the first 15 seconds and vehicle does/does not lower, check test light. Vehicle may be in ride height position. Proceed to step **9)**.

9) Apply a 300 lb. (136 kg) load to the rear of the vehicle. Does light turn off within 15 seconds. If light turns off, vent time out function is okay. Remove load. Proceed to step **10)**. If light does not turn off after 15 seconds, check vent solenoid. Replace module. Turn ignition off. Perform SYSTEM OPERATION CHECK.

NOTE: Compressor may run after this time. Allow vehicle to vent and reach ride height position before proceeding to next step.

10) Disconnect air line at drier. Cycle ignition switch from "OFF" to "RUN" position. Apply a 300 lb. (136 kg) load to the rear of the vehicle. Does light turn on after 115-125 seconds and the compressor stop? If light turns on and compressor stops, compressor run timer is okay. Time begins when the compressor starts to run. Reconnect air line. Remove weight from rear of vehicle. Perform SYSTEM OPERATION CHECK.

NOTE: Light may turn off and air may escape when the line is removed.

11) If light does not turn on and compressor does not stop, replace module. Repeat step **10)**. Perform SYSTEM OPERATION CHECK.

TEST D
IGNITION CIRCUIT CHECK

1) Set voltmeter to the 12-volt scale. Connect negative lead to the module mounting screw. Connect positive lead to ignition power circuit No. 298 (Purple/Orange wire) at pin No. 4 on module connector. Turn ignition off and remove battery charger.

2) If there is zero volts, circuit from ignition sensor to module is okay. Proceed to step **3)**. If there is voltage, repair short to module on circuit No. 298 (Purple/Orange wire) between module connector and ignition switch. Repeat step **1)**.

3) Turn ignition on. Compressor may run and raise vehicle, or vent solenoid may operate and lower vehicle. If voltage is more than 10 volts, circuit between ignition switch and module is okay. Proceed to **TEST E**.

4) If voltage is less than 10 volts, repair open or short circuit to ground on circuit No. 298 (Purple/Orange wire). Check fuses. Repair low voltage condition due to faulty connection, open fuse or low battery. Repeat step **3)**. Perform SYSTEM OPERATION CHECK.

TEST E
BATTERY CIRCUIT CHECK

1) Turn ignition off. Remove battery charger. Set voltmeter to the 12-volt scale. Connect negative voltmeter lead to module mounting screw. Connect positive voltmeter lead to module power circuit No. 37 (Yellow wire) at pin No. 5 on module connector.

NOTE: With ignition off and 30-minute timer activated, solenoid may click and vehicle may or may not lower.

2) If voltage is more than 10 volts and steady, battery circuit to the module is okay. Perform **TEST B**. If voltage is less than 10 volts, repair low voltage condition due to faulty connection, low battery or fusible link at starter relay on circuit No. 37 (Yellow wire). Reconnect connectors as necessary. Repeat step **1)**.

TEST F
VENT SOLENOID SYSTEM CHECK

1) Check monitor light. Remove battery charger. Turn ignition switch to "OFF" position. If monitor light is off, test is okay. Go to step **2)**. If monitor light is on 55 seconds after ignition was turned off, vent time out is okay. Proceed to step **2)**.

2) Set voltmeter to the 12-volt scale. Connect negative voltmeter lead to module mounting screw. Connect positive lead to circuit No. 415 (Light Green/Orange wire) at pin No. 9 on module connector. If voltage reading is more than 8.5 volts and steady, circuit between vent solenoid and module is okay. Proceed to step **3)**. If voltage is less than 8.5 volts, check battery voltage. Proceed to step **3)**.

3) Remove positive lead from voltmeter and touch to a good ground. If vent solenoid clicks, vent solenoid and circuit No. 415 (Yellow wire) to module are okay. Reconnect test lead and proceed to step **4)**. If vent solenoid does not click, reconnect test lead and proceed to test **5)**.

4) Raise rear bumper with floor jack. Cycle ignition switch from "ON" to "OFF" position. If light is on after 55 seconds, vent times out is okay. Proceed to step **6)**. If light is off after 55 seconds, check sensor circuits. Replace module. Perform SYSTEM OPERATION CHECK.

5) Move positive voltmeter lead to solenoid feed circuit No. 37 (Yellow wire) at the compressor connector. Disregard monitor light. If voltage is more than 8.5 volts and steady, solenoid feed circuit from battery relay is okay. Proceed to step **6)**. If voltage is less than 8.5 volts and steady, repair low voltage condition, or open in feed circuit No. 37 (Yellow wire) from starter relay to the connector. Repeat step **5)**.

6) Move positive voltmeter lead to solenoid control unit circuit No. 415 at the compressor connector. Disregard the monitor light. If voltage reading is more than 8.5 volts, and steady, vent solenoid is okay. Proceed to step **7)**. If voltage is less than 8.5 volts, vent solenoid is inoperative. Replace compressor assembly. Repeat step **6)**.

7) Move voltmeter lead to control circuit No. 415 (Light Green/Orange wire) at pin No. 9 on module connector. Disregard monitor light. If voltage is less than 8.5 volts, repair open in control circuit No. 415 (Light Green/Orange wire) between module connector and compressor connector. Repeat step **7)**. If voltage is more than 8.5 volts, solenoid circuit is okay. Proceed to **TEST H**.

TEST G
SENSOR GROUND CIRCUIT CHECK

1) Cycle ignition switch from "ON" to "OFF" position. Remove battery charger. Unplug connector from module. Connect negative ohmmeter lead to module mounting screw. Connect positive lead to module pin No. 10. Disregard monitor light. If resistance is more than 2 ohms, record reading. Proceed to step **2)**. If reading is less than 2 ohms, sensor ground circuit through module is okay. Proceed to step **2)**.

2) Connect ohmmeter lead to circuit No. 431 (Pink/White wire) at pin No. 3 on module connector. Move negative ohmmeter lead to ground circuit No. 430 (Gray wire) at pin No. 10 on module connector. If resistance is more than 8 ohms, proceed to step **3)**. If resistance is less than 8 ohms, sensor circuit to ground is okay. Proceed to **TEST H**.

3) Disconnect rear harness sensor connector at underbody. On sedan models, push harness grommet up inside luggage compartment. On wagon models, use longer test leads. Move positive test lead of ohmmeter to ground circuit No. 430 (Gray wire) at the height sensor connector. If resistance is more than 2 ohms, repair open in sensor ground circuit No. 430 (Gray wire) between module connector and height sensor connector. Repeat step **3)**. If resistance is less than 2 ohms, proceed to step **4)**.

4) Move positive voltmeter lead to circuit No. 431 (Pink/White wire) at height sensor connector. Move negative lead to circuit No. 431 (Pink/White wire) at pin No. 3 on module connector. If resistance is more than 2 ohms, repair open in sensor circuit No. 431 between module connector and height sensor connector. Repeat step **4)**. If resistance is less than 2 ohms, circuit No. 431 is okay, proceed to step **5)**.

5) Move positive test lead to sensor circuit No. 431 (sensor side). Move negative test lead to sensor circuit No. 430. (sensor side). If resistance is more than 18 ohms, replace sensor. Perform SYSTEM OPERATION CHECK. If resistance is less than 18 ohms, proceed to step **6)**.

Electronic Suspensions

FORD MOTOR CO. REAR LEVEL CONTROL (Cont.)

TEST G (Cont.)

6) Reconnect all separated connectors. Perform procedure outlined in step 1). If resistance is less than 20 ohms, system is okay. If resistance is more than 20 ohms, replace module. Perform SYSTEM OPERATION CHECK.

TEST H
SENSOR POWER CIRCUIT CHECK

1) Connect module connector, if disconnected. Set voltmeter to 5-volt scale. Connect voltmeter negative lead to module mounting screw. Connect positive lead to sensor power circuit No. 431 (Pink/White wire) at pin No. 3 on module connector. Cycle igniton switch from "RUN" to "OFF" position. Disregard monitor light. Vent solenoid may click. Observe voltmeter.

NOTE: Voltage check must be completed within 30 minutes of cycling ignition switch, or voltage will return to zero.

2) If voltage is 5 volts and steady, module output power is okay. Proceed to step 3). If voltage is more than 5.3 volts, replace module. Repeat step 1). Perform SYSTEM OPERATION CHECK. If voltage is less than 4.7 volts, repeat step 1). If voltage is still less than 4.7 volts, replace module. Perform SYSTEM OPERATION CHECK.

3) Move positive test lead to sensor circuit No. 427 at pin No. 1 on module connector. Disregard monitor light. If voltage is more than 4.1 volts, module output power is okay. Proceed to step 5). If voltage is 1.3-4.1 volts, sensor is switching electrically from low-to-high or high-to-low. Add 300 lbs. (136 kg) to rear of vehicle and repeat step 3).

4) If voltage is less than 1.3 volts, but more than zero volts, module output power is okay. Proceed to step 5). If there is zero volts, recycle ignition switch to "RUN" and then to "OFF" position. Repeat step 3). If voltage is still zero volts, proceed to **TEST G.**

5) Move positive test lead to sensor circuit No. 428 at pin No. 6 on module connector. Disregard monitor light. If voltage is greater than 4.1 volts, or between zero and 1.3 volts, module power circuit is okay. Proceed to **TEST J.**

6) If voltage is 1.3-4.1 volts, add 300 lbs. (136 kg) to rear of vehicle. Repeat step 5). If there is zero volts, recycle ignition switch to "RUN" and then to "OFF" position. Repeat step 5). If voltage is still zero volts, proceed to **TEST G.**

TEST J
SENSOR LOGIC CIRCUIT CHECK

1) Connect module connector. Disconnect rear harness sensor connector at underbody. Turn ignition off. Set voltmeter to 5-volt scale. Connect negative test lead to the module mounting screw. Connect positive test lead to sensor circuit No. 427 at pin No. 1 on module connector. Disregard monitor light if connected. Test must be completed within 30 minutes. If not, recycle ignition switch to "RUN" and then "OFF" position to reset timer, as required.

2) If voltage is more than 4.3 volts, proceed to step 3). If voltage is less than 4.3 volts, recycle ignition switch to "RUN" and then to "OFF" position. Repeat step 1). Replace module. Perform SYSTEM OPERATION CHECK.

3) Move positive lead to sensor circuit No. 428 at pin No. 6 on module connector. If voltage is more than 4.3 volts, proceed to step 4). If voltage is less than 4.3 volts, recycle ignition switch from "RUN" to "OFF" position. Repeat step 3). Replace module. Perform SYSTEM OPERATION CHECK.

4) Move positive test lead to sensor circuit No. 428 (Orange/Black wire) at height sensor connector. If voltage is more than 4.3 volts, harness circuit is okay. If voltage is less than 4.3 volts, repair open in circuit No. 428, between module connector and height sensor connector. Repeat step 4).

5) Move positive test lead to sensor circuit No. 427 (Pink/Black wire) at height sensor connector. If voltage is more than 4.3 volts, harness circuit is okay. If voltage is less than 4.3 volts, repair open in circuit No. 427, between module connector and height sensor connector. Repeat step 5).

6) Disconnect module connector, move negative lead of ohmmeter to circuit No. 427 at pin No. 1 on module connector. Ohmmeter should read less than 2 ohms to indicate circuit No. 427 is okay. Perform

TEST J (Cont.)

SYSTEM OPERATION CHECK. If ohmmeter reads more than 2 ohms, circuit No. 427 and circuit No. 428 are crossed. Switch circuit leads at module or height sensor connector. Repeat step 6).

TEST K
COMPRESSOR RELAY MOTOR CHECK

1) Cycle ignition switch from "RUN" to "OFF" position. Set voltmeter to 12-volt scale. Disregard monitor light. Relay and/or vent relay may click. Place negative test lead to module mounting bolt. Connect positive test lead to circuit No. 420 (Dark Blue/Yellow wire) at pin 8 on module connector. If voltage is less than one volt, proceed to step 2). If voltage is more than one volt, repair short to module connector on circuits No. 298 (pin No. 4) and No. 420 (pin No. 8), between ignition switch relay and module connector. Repeat step 1).

2) Disconnect module harness from control module connector. Cycle ignition switch from "OFF" to "RUN" position. Connect positive test lead to circuit No. 420 (Dark Blue/Yellow wire) at pin No. 8 on module connector. If voltage is more than 8 volts, compressor relay control circuits No. 298 and No. 420 to the module are okay. Proceed to step 3). If voltage is less than 8 volts, repair low voltage condition due to faulty connection, relay, low battery or blown fuse on circuits No. 298 (Purple/Orange wire; pin No. 4) and 420 (Dark Blue/Yellow wire; pin No. 8). Repeat step 2).

3) Remove positive test lead from voltmeter and touch module mounting screw. Compressor relay should click. Touch test lead several times to ensure relay clicking can be heard. If compressor relay clicks, compressor relay coil is okay. Reconnect test lead to voltmeter. Proceed to step 4). If compressor relay does not click, replace relay. Repeat step 3). Perform SYSTEM OPERATION CHECK.

4) Check compressor motor. Repeat step 3). If compressor motor cycles, compressor and ground are okay. Reconnect test lead to voltmeter. Proceed to **TEST G.** If compressor does not cycle, reconnect test lead to voltmeter. Proceed to step 5).

5) Move test lead to circuit No. 37 (Yellow wire) at the harness side of the compressor relay connector. If voltage is more than 8 volts, battery feed circuit to the compressor relay is okay. Proceed to step 6). If voltage is less than 8 volts, repair open or short to ground on circuit No. 37, between battery and relay connector. Check fusible link and battery condition. Repeat step 5).

6) Connect jumper lead between circuit No. 420 (Dark Blue/Yellow wire) at pin No. 8 on module connector located in luggage compartment and a mounting screw. Relay should click. Compressor may cycle. If relay clicks, remove jumper wire from mounting screw. Proceed to step 7). If relay does not click, proceed to step 7).

7) Move positive test lead to compressor motor feed circuit No. 417 (Purple/Orange wire) at the harness side of the compressor motor connector. Touch the meter lead to the module mounting screw. Voltage reading should be more than 8 volts. Relay should click. Compressor may cycle. If voltage is more than 8 volts and relay clicks, remove jumper lead. Proceed to step 8). If voltage is less than 8 volts, and relay does not click, repair open or short to ground on circuit No. 417 (Purple/Orange wire) between relay and motor connector, or replace as necessary. Repeat step 7).

8) Touch test lead to module mounting screw. Compressor motor should cycle. If motor cycles, motor circuit is okay. Replace module. Perform SYSTEM OPERATION CHECK. If motor does not cycle, remove jumper lead from mounting screw. Proceed to step 9).

9) Disconnect compressor connector. Connect ohmmeter positive to feed circuit No. 417 (Purple/Orange wire) at motor connector. Connect negative lead to circuit No. 57 (Black wire) at motor connector. Ohmmeter reading should be less than 2 ohms. If ohmmeter reading is less than 2 ohms, compressor and circuit breaker are okay. Proceed to step 10). If reading is more than 2 ohms, replace compressor motor. Reconnect compressor and module connectors. Perform SYSTEM OPERATION CHECK.

10) Move negative test lead to motor ground circuit No. 57 (Black wire) at harness side of compressor connector. Move positive test lead to ground circuit No. 57 (Black wire) at pin No. 11 on module connector. Move positive test lead to body eyelet, ground circuit No. 57. Ohmmeter should indicate less than 2 ohms at both points.

11) If ohmmeter reading is less than 2 ohms, ground circuit is okay. Reconnect motor and module connectors. Perform SYSTEM OPERATION CHECK. If readings are not less than 2 ohms, repair open in circuit No. 57 (Black wire) between motor harness and ground and/or between module pin No. 11 and ground. Repeat step 10).

GENERAL MOTORS REAR LEVEL CONTROL

"A" Bodies: Celebrity, Century, Cutlass Ciera, Cutlass Cruiser, 6000
"B" Bodies: Custom Cruiser, Electra Wagon, LeSabre Wagon
"C" Bodies: Ninety-Eight, Electra, DeVille, Fleetwood
"D" Bodies: Brougham
"E" Bodies: Riviera, Eldorado, Toronado
"K" Bodies: Seville
"H" Bodies: Bonneville, Delta 88, LeSabre

DESCRIPTION

Rear level control is a leveling system that automatically adjusts rear height of vehicle with varying loads on rear suspension. System is activated when ignition is on and weight is added to or removed from vehicle.

Electronic Level Control (ELC) is made up of a compressor, air drier, exhaust solenoid, compressor relay, height sensor, air adjustable shock absorbers, pressure limiter, and connecting air lines.

Air drier contains a moisture absorbing chemical and also contains valving to maintain a minimum system pressure of 15-22 psi (1.0-1.5 kg/cm²) on DeVille and Fleetwood and 7-14 psi (.5-1 kg/cm²) on all other models. Pressure limiter valve prevents pressure at shocks from exceeding 64-74 psi (4.5-5.2 kg/cm²).

OPERATION

RAISING VEHICLE

When weight is added to vehicle, height sensor arm rotates upward. Rotating arm upward grounds compressor relay circuit. After a time delay of 8-14 seconds on "A" and "B" bodies, and Bonneville or 13-27 seconds on all others, grounding of compressor relay turns air compressor on, causing vehicle to rise.

As vehicle rises, height sensor rotates downward to curb height position. When vehicle is within 1" (25.4 mm) of curb height, height sensor opens ground circuit to compressor relay, turning compressor off.

LOWERING VEHICLE

When weight is removed from vehicle, height sensor arm rotates downward. After a time delay of 8-14 seconds on "A" and "B" bodies, and Bonneville or 13-27 seconds on all others, downward rotation of the arm grounds exhaust solenoid valve circuit. Energizing exhaust solenoid valve causes air to vent through air drier and out of exhaust solenoid valve.

As vehicle lowers, height sensor arm rotates upward to curb height position. When vehicle is within 1" (25.4 mm) of curb height, height sensor opens exhaust solenoid valve circuit, causing exhaust solenoid valve to close.

AIR REPLENISHMENT

In order to ensure the system is operating with at least minimum air pressure, the height sensor commands an air replenishment cycle each time the ignition is cycled on. An internal timer circuit is activated when ignition switch is turned to "ON" position. After a delay of 35-45 seconds, compressor turns on for 3-5 seconds to ensure residual system pressure.

If weight is added or removed from vehicle during 35-45 second delay, air replenishment cycle will be overridden and vehicle will raise or lower after normal time delay.

ADJUSTMENTS

HEIGHT SENSOR

To increase vehicle riding height, move plastic arm upward and tighten lock nut. To lower riding height, loosen lock nut and move plastic arm down and tighten lock nut. If adjustment cannot be made, check for proper sensor application. See Fig. 1.

Fig. 1: Height Sensor Adjustment

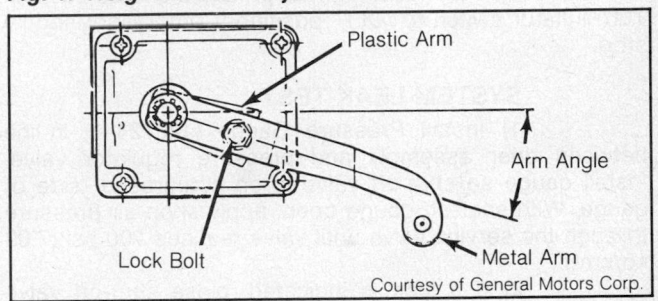

Courtesy of General Motors Corp.

RIDING HEIGHT

See RIDING HEIGHT SPECIFICATIONS article in WHEEL ALIGNMENT section.

TROUBLE SHOOTING

CAR LOADED, WILL NOT RISE

Leaks in air lines, fittings or shock absorbers. Pinched lines between compressor and shock absorbers. Defective height sensor. Compressor inoperative. Loose or damaged electrical connections to sensor or compressor.

CAR LOADED, RISES, THEN LEAKS DOWN

Severe leak in lines, fittings or shock absorbers.

CAR LOADED, RISES PARTIALLY

Height sensor out of adjustment. Compressor or wiring defective.

CAR RISES WHEN LOADED, LEAKS DOWN WHEN DRIVING

Defective drier or compressor. Pinched air lines or leaks in fittings or air lines.

CAR RIDES HIGH

Height sensor out of adjustment. Drier plugged or air lines pinched. Poor electrical connections.

GENERAL MOTORS REAR LEVEL CONTROL (Cont.)

SYSTEM TESTING

SYSTEM OPERATIONAL TEST

1) Unload vehicle. With ignition off, check riding height. Turn ignition on. Add 300-350 lbs. (136-159 kg) load to trunk. Compressor should start operating within 27 seconds. Vehicle should rise to within 3/4" (19 mm) of riding height.

2) Remove load from trunk. Exhaust should start within 27 seconds. Within 2 minutes, exhaust should stop and vehicle should be within 3/4" (19 mm) of riding height.

3) On Bonneville SSE, turn inflator switch to "ON" position. Switch is located in luggage compartment. Compressor should turn on and run continuously. Open valve on end of air hose. high air pressure should escape. Turn inflator switch to "OFF" position. Compressor should stop.

SYSTEM LEAK TEST

1) Install Pressure Gauge (J22124-A) in-line between drier assembly and pressure regulator valve. Install gauge so shut-off valve is on compressor side of gauge. With shut-off gauge open, apply shop air pressure through the service valve until valve reaches 100 psi (7.03 kg/cm²).

2) If a leak is indicated, close shut-off valve and continue to watch for a pressure drop. If pressure continues to drop, leak is external from the compressor. Leak test all connections. If pressure stops decreasing after shut-off valve is closed, leak is in the compressor assembly.

3) Check compressor for leaks. If pressure builds up rapidly, but vehicle does not raise, check for pinched air line or stuck or binding shocks.

COMPRESSOR PERFORMANCE TEST
Eldorado, Seville & Toronado

NOTE: Compressor can be check on or off vehicle.

1) Disconnect pressure line from dryer. Attach pressure gauge to dryer. Disconnect negative (Black) wire from compressor bracket. Install an ammeter between negative wire and compressor bracket. If testing on vehicle, ground ALDL terminal "K".

2) If testing off vehicle, apply 12 volts to compressor connector pin "B" and ground pin "D". With pressure gauge reading should be 100 psi (7.03 kg/cm²) minimum and ammeter reading should be 10 amps maximum.

3) Disconnect wiring and check compressor for leakdown. Replace compressor if readings are not as specified or internal leakdown is indicated.

All Others

1) Disconnect pressure line from drier and attach Air Pressure Gauge (J22124-A) to drier fitting. Disconnect wiring from compressor motor and exhaust solenoid terminals. *See Fig. 2.*

2) Connect 12-volt power supply to compressor through ammeter. Current draw must not exceed 14 amps. Allow pressure to reach 100 psi (7.03 kg/cm²) minimum and shut off compressor. Allow pressure to stabilize. Check for pressure leaks.

3) If compressor is allowed to run to maximum output pressure of 180 psi (12.7 kg/cm²), the solenoid

exhaust valve will act as a relief valve. This gives a false indication of system leakage. If compressor operates correctly, reconnect wiring and air lines. If compressor does not operate correctly, refer to TROUBLE SHOOTING in this article.

Fig. 2: Electronic Level Control (ELC) Compressor

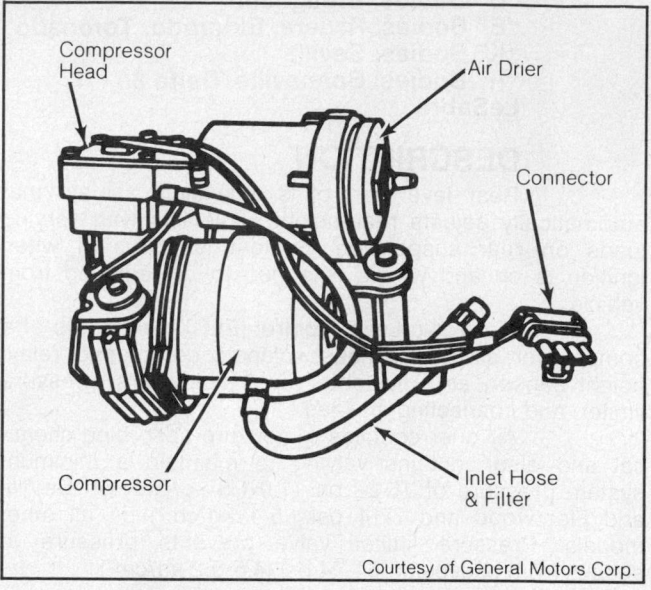

Courtesy of General Motors Corp.

HEIGHT SENSOR OPERATIONAL TEST
Eldorado, Seville & Toronado

1) Raise vehicle on hoist. Ensure all electrical connectors are properly mated. Cycle ignition off and on to reset sensor timing circuits. After a 35-45 second delay, compressor should run for 4 seconds. Disconnect height sensor link from control arm.

2) Move control arm upward. There should be a 13-27 second delay before compressor starts to run. As soon as struts start to fill, move control arm downward. After a 13-27 second delay, struts should start to deflate. Replace height sensor if it fails any of these tests.

All Others

1) Cycle ignition switch to the "ON" position. Raise vehicle on hoist. Ensure axle housing is supported as close to ride height specification as possible. Check all wiring for good connections. Disconnect link from height sensor arm.

2) Move sensor arm upward. After a 8-14 second delay on "A" and "B" bodies, and Bonneville or 13-27 second on all other models, the compressor should run and shock absorbers should start to inflate. As soon as shock absorber air boots fill, stop compressor by moving sensor arm down.

3) Move sensor arm below position where compressor stopped running. There should be a delay before shock absorbers start to deflate and vehicle lowers. Replace height sensor if it does not function correctly.

GENERAL MOTORS REAR LEVEL CONTROL (Cont.)

ELECTRICAL TESTING (DELTA 88 & NINETY-EIGHT)

ELC RELAY & COMPRESSOR MOTOR TEST

1) Ground ELC test lead connector, located near ELC compressor, with a fused jumper wire. If compressor runs, go to ACTUATOR ARM TEST. If compressor does not run, disconnect ELC relay connector and measure voltage from terminal "C" (Orange wire) to ground.

2) If voltage reads zero, check Orange wire and fuse No. 12 for an open. If voltage reads 12 volts, connect a fused jumper wire between terminals "C" (Orange wire) and "A" (Dark Green wire) of ELC relay connector. If compressor runs, replace ELC relay.

3) If compressor does not run with fused jumper still connected to ELC relay, unplug ELC compressor connector. Measure voltage between terminal "B" (Dark Green wire) at compressor connector and ground. If voltage reads zero, check Dark Green wire for an open.

4) If voltage reads 12 volts, measure voltage between terminals "B" (Dark Green wire) and "D" (Black wire) at ELC compressor connector. If voltage reads zero, check Black wire for an open. If voltage reads 12 volts, repair and/or replace ELC compressor assembly.

EXHAUST SOLENOID TEST

1) Unplug ELC height sensor connector. Ground terminal No. 2 (White wire) with a fused jumper wire. If exhaust solenoid clicks and air vents, go to ACTUATOR ARM TEST.

2) If exhaust solenoid does not click and air does not vent with fused jumper wire still connected at height sensor (from previous test), unplug ELC compressor connector. Measure voltage between terminal "A" (Orange wire) at compressor connector and ground.

3) If voltage reads zero, check Orange wire for an open. If voltage reads 12 volts, measure voltage between terminals "A" (Orange wire) and "C" (White wire) at ELC compressor connector. If voltage is now zero volts, check White wire for an open. If voltage reads 12 volts, replace exhaust solenoid.

ACTUATOR ARM TEST

Raise vehicle and ensure link is attached to actuator arm correctly and actuator arm is properly aligned.

ELC HEIGHT SENSOR TEST NO. 1

1) Unplug ELC connector. With ignition switch in the "ON" position, measure voltage between terminal No. 6 (Orange wire) and ground. If voltage reads 12 volts, go to HEIGHT SENSOR TEST NO. 2. If voltage does not read 12 volts, check and/or repair open in Orange wire. *See Fig. 3.*

2) With ignition switch in "RUN" position, measure voltage between terminals No. 6 (Orange wire) and No. 4 (Black wire). If voltage is 12 volts, go to HEIGHT SENSOR TEST NO. 2. If voltage does not read 12 volts, check and/or repair open to ground in Black wire.

Fig. 3: Height Sensor Harness Terminal Identification

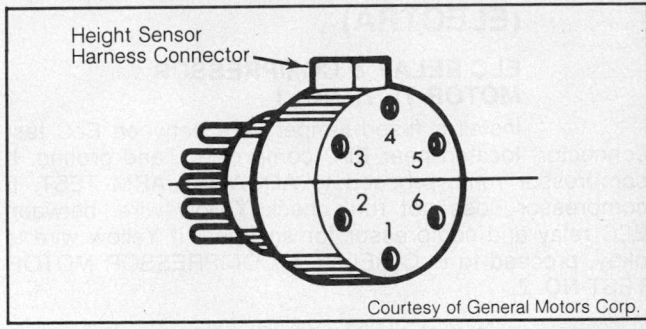

Courtesy of General Motors Corp.

NOTE: Dark Blue wire at terminal No. 5 splices into 2 different color wires. See appropriate wiring diagram when testing.

3) Measure voltage between terminal No. 5 (Dark Blue wire) and ground. If voltage reads 12 volts, go to HEIGHT SENSOR TEST NO. 2. If voltage does not read 12 volts, check and/or repair Dark Blue wire to terminal No. 5 for an open.

4) Measure voltage between terminal No. 3 (Yellow wire) and ground. If voltage reads 12 volts, go to HEIGHT SENSOR TEST NO. 2. If voltage does not read 12 volts, check and/or repair open in Yellow wire.

ELC HEIGHT SENSOR TEST NO. 2

1) Cycle ignition switch and place in "RUN" position. Raise vehicle and support rear axle housing at ride height. Disconnect link from actuator arm. Move actuator arm upward.

2) If compressor begins to run but shocks do not inflate after a 13-27 second delay, perform COMPRESSOR PERFORMANCE TEST and SYSTEM LEAK TEST. If compressor does not begin to run after a 13-27 second delay, replace ELC height sensor.

3) If compressor begins to run and shocks begin to inflate after a 13-27 second delay, slowly move actuator arm downward until compressor stops. If compressor does not stop, replace height sensor. If compressor does stop, continue to move actuator arm downward.

4) If the shocks do not start to deflate and vehicle does not begin to lower after a 13-27 second delay, replace the height sensor. If the shocks begin to deflate and the vehicle starts to lower after a 13-27 second delay, the ELC is okay.

EXHAUST SOLENOID SHORT TEST

1) Add 300 lbs. (136 kg) to luggage compartment. Disconnect ELC height sensor connector. Ground ELC test connector with a fused jumper. Allow compressor to run for 2 minutes.

2) If vehicle raises and maintains its height, replace ELC height sensor. If vehicle does not raise or raises and leaks down, check White wire for a short to ground.

3) If wire is found to have a short, repair it. If wire is okay, perform SYSTEM LEAK TEST and COMPRESSOR PERFORMANCE TEST.

Electronic Suspensions

GENERAL MOTORS REAR LEVEL CONTROL (Cont.)

ELECTRICAL TESTING (ELECTRA)

ELC RELAY & COMPRESSOR MOTOR TEST NO. 1

Install a fused jumper wire between ELC test connector, located near ELC compressor, and ground. If compressor runs, proceed to ACUATOR ARM TEST. If compressor does not run, check Yellow wire, between ELC relay and compressor for an open. If Yellow wire is okay, proceed to ELC RELAY & COMPRESSOR MOTOR TEST NO. 2.

ELC RELAY & COMPRESSOR MOTOR TEST NO. 2

Unplug ELC relay connector. Measure voltage at ELC connector between terminal "C" (Orange wire) and ground. If voltage reads 12 volts, proceed to ELC RELAY & COMPRESSOR MOTOR TEST NO. 3. If voltage does not read 12 volts, check Orange wire for an open.

ELC RELAY & COMPRESSOR MOTOR TEST NO. 3

Unplug ELC relay connector. Install a fused jumper wire at ELC connector between terminals "C" (Orange wire) and "A" (Dark Green wire). If compressor runs, replace ELC relay. If compressor does not run, leave fused jumper wire intact and proceed to ELC RELAY & COMPRESSOR MOTOR TEST NO. 4.

ELC RELAY & COMPRESSOR MOTOR TEST NO. 4

1) Unplug ELC compressor connector. Measure and note voltage at harness half of ELC compressor connector between terminal "B" (Dark Green wire) and ground. If voltage does not read 12 volts, check Dark Green wire for an open.

2) Measure voltage between terminals "B" (Dark Green wire) and "D" (Black wire). If voltage does not read 12 volts, check Black wire for an open. If both voltage checks show 12 volts, repair and/or replace compressor.

EXHAUST SOLENOID TEST NO. 1

1) Unplug ELC compressor connector. Install a fused jumper wire at ELC height sensor connector between terminal No. 2 (White wire) and ground. If exhaust solenoid clicks and air begins to vent, plug in connector and proceed to ACUATOR ARM TEST.

2) If exhaust solenoid does not click and air does not begin to vent, leave fused jumper wire intact and proceed to EXHAUST SOLENOID TEST NO. 2.

EXHAUST SOLENOID TEST NO. 2

1) Measure voltage at harness half of ELC compressor connector between terminal "A" (Orange wire) and ground. If voltage reads 12 volts, replace exhaust solenoid. If voltage does not read 12 volts, check Orange wire for an open.

2) Measure voltage between terminals "A" (Orange wire) and "C" (White wire). If voltage reads 12 volts, replace exhaust solenoid. If voltage does not read 12 volts, check White wire for an open.

ACTUATOR ARM TEST

Raise vehicle and ensure link is correctly attached and actuator arm is properly aligned.

ELC HEIGHT SENSOR TEST NO. 1

1) Unplug ELC height sensor connector. Turn ignition switch to "RUN" position. Measure voltage at ELC height sensor connector between terminal No. 6 (Orange wire) and ground. If voltage reads 12 volts, plug in connector and proceed to ELC HEIGHT SENSOR TEST NO. 2. If voltage does not read 12 volts, check Orange wire for an open.

2) Measure voltage between terminals No. 6 (Orange wire) and No. 4 (Black wire). If voltage reads 12 volts, plug in connector and proceed to ELC HEIGHT SENSOR TEST NO. 2. If voltage does not read 12 volts, check Black wire for an open to ground.

3) Measure voltage between terminal No. 5 (Dark Blue wire) and ground. If voltage reads 12 volts, plug in connector and proceed to ELC HEIGHT SENSOR TEST NO. 2. If voltage does not read 12 volts, check Dark Blue wire for an open.

4) Measure voltage between terminal No. 3 (Yellow wire) and ground. If voltage reads 12 volts, plug in connector and proceed to ELC HEIGHT SENSOR TEST NO. 2. If voltage does not read 12 volts, check Yellow wire for open.

ELC HEIGHT SENSOR TEST NO. 2

1) Cycle ignition switch and return to "RUN" position. Raise vehicle and support rear axle at ride height. Disconnect link from actuator arm. Move actuator arm upward.

2) If compressor does not begin to run after a 13-27 second delay, replace ELC height sensor. If shocks do not begin to inflate and vehicle does not begin to move upward after 13-27 seconds, perform SYSTEM LEAK TEST and COMPRESSOR PERFORMANCE TEST.

3) Slowly move arm downward until compressor stops. If compressor does not stop, replace height sensor. Continue to move actuator arm downward past the point where compressor stopped. If shocks do not begin to deflate and vehicle does not begin to lower after a 13-27 second delay, replace height sensor.

EXHAUST SOLENOID SHORT TEST

1) Add 300 lbs. (136 kg) to luggage compartment. Disconnect ELC height sensor connector and ground ELC test connector with a fused jumper wire. Allow compressor to run for 2 minutes.

2) If vehicle raises and maintains its height, replace height sensor. If vehicle does not rise or raises and leaks down, check White wire between ELC height sensor and compressor for a short to ground. If White wire is okay, perform SYSTEM LEAK TEST and COMPRESSOR PERFORMANCE TEST.

ELECTRICAL TESTING (RIVIERA)

ELC RELAY & COMPRESSOR MOTOR TEST NO. 1

1) With ignition switch in "RUN" position, connect a fused jumper wire at 5-pin connector located

GENERAL MOTORS REAR LEVEL CONTROL (Cont.)

under rear of vehicle at LR of crossmember, between terminal "B" (Yellow wire) and ground. If compressor begins to run and vehicle begins to level, proceed to ACTUATOR ARM TEST.

2) If compressor does not begin to run, check Yellow wire for an open. If Yellow wire (No. 321) is okay, proceed to ELC RELAY & COMPRESSOR MOTOR TEST NO. 2. If vehicle does not begin to level and dashboard indicator light does not come on, proceed to ELC RELAY & COMPRESSOR MOTOR TEST NO. 2.

ELC RELAY & COMPRESSOR MOTOR TEST NO. 2

Unplug ELC relay, located behind center of instrument panel. Turn ignition switch to "RUN" position. Measure voltage between ELC relay connector terminal No. 2 (Brown/White wire) and ground. If voltage reads 12 volts, proceed to ELC RELAY & COMPRESSOR MOTOR TEST NO. 3. If voltage does not read 12 volts, check Brown/White wire for an open.

ELC RELAY & COMPRESSOR MOTOR TEST NO. 3

1) Place ignition switch in "RUN" position. Unplug ELC relay connector. Install a fused jumper wire between terminals No. 2 (Brown/White wire) and No. 3 (Dark Green wire) on ELC relay connector.

2) If compressor does not begin to run, leave fused jumper wire installed and proceed to ELC RELAY & COMPRESSOR MOTOR TEST NO. 4. If vehicle begins to level and dashboard indicator light illuminates, replace ELC relay. If vehicle does not begin to level and light does not illuminate, check Dark Green wire (No. 322) for an open.

ELC RELAY & COMPRESSOR MOTOR TEST NO. 4

1) Unplug ELC compressor 4-pin connector, located below vehicle near right rear wheel. Turn ignition on. Measure voltage between terminal "B" (Dark Green) and ground on harness side. If voltage reads 12 volts, repair or replace compressor assembly. If voltage does not read 12 volts, check Dark Green wire for an open.

2) Measure voltage between terminal "B" (Dark Green wire) and terminal "D" (Black wire). If voltage reads 12 volts, repair or replace ELC compressor assembly. If voltage does not read 12 volts, check Black wire for an open.

EXHAUST SOLENOID TEST NO. 1

Unplug ELC height sensor connector. Install a fused jumper wire between ELC height sensor connector terminal No. 2 (White wire) and ground. If exhaust solenoid clicks and air vents, reconnect connector and proceed to ACTUATOR ARM TEST. If solenoid does not click and air does not vent, leave fused jumper wire installed. Proceed to EXHAUST SOLENOID TEST NO. 2.

EXHAUST SOLENOID TEST NO. 2

1) Unplug ELC compressor 4-pin connector, located under vehicle near right rear wheel. Measure voltage between terminal "C" (Orange/Black wire) and ground on harness side of connector. If voltage reads 12 volts, replace exhaust solenoid. If voltage does not read 12 volts, check Orange/Black wire for an open.

2) Measure voltage between terminals "C" (Orange/Black wire) and "A" (White wire). If voltage reads 12 volts, replace exhaust solenoid. If voltage does not read 12 volts, check White wire for an open.

ACTUATOR ARM TEST

Raise vehicle and ensure link is correctly attached and actuator arm is properly aligned.

ELC HEIGHT SENSOR TEST NO. 1

1) Unplug ELC height sensor connector. With ignition switch in "RUN" position, measure voltage between terminal No. 5 (Brown/White wire) and ground. If voltage reads 12 volts, reconnect connector and proceed to ELC HEIGHT SENSOR TEST NO. 2. If voltage does not read 12 volts, check Brown/White wire for an open.

2) Measure voltage between terminals No. 5 (Brown/White wire) and No. 4 (Black/White wire). If voltage reads 12 volts, plug in connector and proceed to ELC HEIGHT SENSOR TEST NO. 2. If voltage does not read 12 volts, check Black/White wire for an open.

3) Measure voltage between terminal No. 6 (Orange/Black wire) and ground. If voltage reads 12 volts, plug in connector and proceed to ELC HEIGHT SENSOR TEST NO. 2. If voltage does not read 12 volts, check Orange/Black wire for an open.

4) Measure voltage between terminal No. 3 (Yellow wire) and ground. If voltage reads 12 volts, plug in connector and proceed to ELC HEIGHT SENSOR TEST NO. 2. If voltage does not read 12 volts, check Yellow wire for an open.

ELC HEIGHT SENSOR TEST NO. 2

1) Cycle ignition switch. Raise vehicle and support rear axle at normal ride height. Disconnect actuator arm at height sensor and move upward slowly. If compressor does not begin to run after an 13-27 second delay, replace ELC height sensor.

2) If shocks do not begin to inflate and vehicle does not begin to rise after an 13-27 second delay, perform SYSTEM LEAK TEST and COMPRESSOR PERFORMANCE TEST.

3) Move actuator arm downward slowly until compressor stops. If compressor does not stop, replace ELC height sensor. Move actuator arm downward past the point where compressor stopped. If shocks do not begin to deflate and vehicle does not begin to lower after an 13-27 second delay, replace ELC height sensor.

EXHAUST SOLENOID SHORT TEST

1) Add 300 lbs. (136 kg) to luggage compartment. Unplug 5-pin connector, located under rear of vehicle near LR of crossmember. Ground terminal "B" (Yellow wire) with a fused jumper wire. Allow compressor to run for 2 minutes, then remove jumper wire.

2) If vehicle rises and maintains its height, replace height sensor. If vehicle does not rise and maintain its height or raises and leaks down, check White wire for a short to ground. If White wire is okay, perform SYSTEM LEAK TEST and COMPRESSOR PERFORMANCE TEST.

ELC RELAY SHORT TEST

Unplug 5-pin connector, located under rear of vehicle near LR of crossmember. If ELC compressor does

GENERAL MOTORS REAR LEVEL CONTROL (Cont.)

not run, replace ELC height sensor. If ELC compressor does run, check Yellow wire for short. If Yellow wire is okay, replace ELC relay.

ELECTRICAL TESTING (LESABRE)

ELC RELAY & COMPRESSOR MOTOR TEST NO. 1

Install a fused jumper wire between ELC test connector, located near ELC compressor, and ground. If compressor runs, perform ACTUATOR ARM TEST. If compressor does not run, check Yellow wire, between ELC height sensor and ELC relay for an open.

ELC RELAY & COMPRESSOR MOTOR TEST NO. 2

Unplug ELC relay connector. Measure voltage at ELC relay harness connector between terminal "C" (Orange wire) and ground. If voltage reads 12 volts, proceed to ELC RELAY & COMPRESSOR MOTOR TEST NO. 3. If voltage does not read 12 volts, check Orange wire for an open.

ELC RELAY & COMPRESSOR MOTOR TEST NO. 3

Unplug ELC relay connector. Install a fused jumper wire at ELC relay harness connector between terminals "C" (Orange wire) and "A" (Dark Green wire). If compressor runs, replace ELC relay. If compressor does not run, leave fused jumper wire installed and proceed to ELC RELAY & COMPRESSOR MOTOR TEST NO. 4.

ELC RELAY & COMPRESSOR MOTOR TEST NO. 4

1) Unplug ELC compressor connector. With fused jumper wire from previous test installed, measure voltage between terminal "B" (Dark Green wire) and ground. If voltage reads 12 volts, repair or replace ELC compressor assembly. If voltage does not read 12 volts, check Dark Green wire for an open.

2) Measure voltage between terminal "B" (Dark Green wire) and terminal "D" (Black wire). If voltage reads 12 volts, repair or replace ELC compressor assembly. If voltage does not read 12 volts, check Black wire for an open.

EXHAUST SOLENOID TEST NO. 1

Unplug ELC height sensor connector. Install a fused jumper wire at ELC height sensor connector between terminal No. 2 (White wire) and ground. If exhaust solenoid clicks and air begins to vent, plug in connector and proceed to ACTUATOR ARM TEST. If exhaust solenoid does not click and air does not begin to vent, leave fused jumper wire installed and proceed to EXHAUST SOLENOID TEST NO. 2.

EXHAUST SOLENOID TEST NO. 2

1) With fused jumper wire still installed from previous test, measure voltage at harness half of compressor connector between terminal "A" (Orange wire) and ground. If voltage reads 12 volts, replace exhaust solenoid. If voltage does not read 12 volts, check Orange wire for an open.

2) Measure voltage between terminals "A" (Orange wire) and "C" (White wire). If voltage reads 12 volts, replace exhaust solenoid. If voltage does not read 12 volts, check White wire for an open.

ACTUATOR ARM TEST

Raise vehicle and ensure link is correctly attached and actuator arm is properly aligned.

ELC HEIGHT SENSOR TEST NO. 1

1) Unplug ELC height sensor connector. Turn ignition switch to "RUN" position. Measure voltage at ELC height sensor connector between terminal No. 6 (Orange wire) and ground. If voltage reads 12 volts, plug in connector and proceed to ELC HEIGHT SENSOR TEST NO. 2. If voltage does not read 12 volts, check Orange wire for an open.

2) Measure voltage between terminals No. 6 (Orange wire) and No. 4 (Black wire). If voltage reads 12 volts, plug in connector and proceed to ELC HEIGHT SENSOR TEST NO. 2. If voltage does not read 12 volts, check Black wire for an open to ground.

3) Measure voltage between terminal No. 5 (Brown wire) and ground. If voltage reads 12 volts, plug in connector and proceed to ELC HEIGHT SENSOR TEST NO. 2. If voltage does not read 12 volts, check Brown wire for an open.

4) Measure voltage between terminal No. 3 (Yellow wire) and ground. If voltage reads 12 volts, plug in connector and proceed to ELC HEIGHT SENSOR TEST NO. 2. If voltage does not read 12 volts, check Yellow wire for an open.

ELC HEIGHT SENSOR TEST NO. 2

1) Ensure height sensor is connected. Raise vehicle and support rear axle at normal ride height. Disconnect link from actuator arm. Move actuator arm at ELC height sensor slowly upward.

2) If compressor does not run after a 13-27 second delay, replace ELC height sensor. If shocks do not begin to inflate and vehicle does not begin to rise after a 13-27 second delay, perform SYSTEM LEAK TEST and COMPRESSOR PERFORMANCE TEST.

3) Move actuator arm downward slowly until compressor stops. If compressor does not stop, replace ELC height sensor. Move actuator arm downward past the point where compressor stopped. If shocks do not begin to deflate and vehicle does not begin to lower after a 13-27 second delay, replace ELC height sensor.

EXHAUST SOLENOID SHORT TEST

Add 300 lbs. (136 kg) to luggage compartment. Disconnect ELC height sensor and ground ELC test lead with a fused jumper wire. Allow compressor to run for 2 minutes. If vehicle rises and maintains its height, replace ELC height sensor. If vehicle does not rise or rises and leaks down, check White wire between ELC height sensor and ELC compressor for a short to ground. If White wire is okay, perform SYSTEM LEAK TEST and COMPRESSOR PERFORMANCE TEST.

GENERAL MOTORS REAR LEVEL CONTROL (Cont.)

ELECTRICAL TESTING (TORONADO)

ELC RELAY & COMPRESSOR MOTOR TEST

1) With ignition switch in "RUN" position, install a fused jumper wire between ALDL connector terminal "K" (Yellow wire) and ground. If compressor runs, proceed to ACTUATOR ARM TEST.

2) If compressor does not run, disconnect ELC relay from interior relay center and measure voltage between terminal No. 2 (Pink/Black wire) and ground. If voltage does not read 12 volts, check Pink/Black wire and fuse No. 17 for an open.

3) If voltage does read 12 volts, install a fused jumper wire between terminals No. 2 (Pink/Black wire) and No. 3 (Dark Green wire) at interior relay center.

4) If compressor runs, replace ELC relay. If compressor does not run, leave fused jumper installed. Unplug ELC compressor connector. Measure voltage between terminal "B" (Dark Green wire) and ground at ELC compressor connector.

5) If voltage does not reads 12 volts, check Dark Green wire for an open. If voltage reads 12 volts, measure voltage between terminals "B" (Dark Green wire) and "D" (Black wire) at ELC compressor connector.

6) If voltage reads 12 volts, replace compressor assembly. If voltage does not read 12 volts, check Black wire for an open.

EXHAUST SOLENOID TEST

1) Install a fused jumper wire between terminal No. 2 (White wire) and ground at ELC height sensor connector. If exhaust solenoid clicks and air vents, proceed to ACTUATOR ARM TEST.

2) If exhaust solenoid does not click and air does not vent, unplug ELC height sensor connector. Leave fused jumper wire connected and measure voltage between terminal "C" (Orange/Black wire) of ELC height sensor connector and ground.

3) If voltage does not read 12 volts, check Orange/Black wire for an open. If voltage does read 12 volts, measure voltage between terminals "C" (Orange/Black wire) and "A" (White wire) of ELC compressor connector.

4) If voltage reads 12 volts, replace exhaust solenoid. If voltage does not read 12 volts, check White wire for an open.

ACTUATOR ARM TEST

Raise vehicle and ensure link is attached to actuator arm. If okay, proceed to ELC HEIGHT SENSOR TEST NO. 1.

ELC HEIGHT SENSOR TEST NO. 1

1) Unplug ELC height sensor connector. With ignition switch in "RUN" position, measure voltage between terminal No. 6 (Orange/Black wire) and ground. If voltage reads 12 volts, plug in connector and proceed to ELC HEIGHT SENSOR TEST NO. 2. If voltage does not read 12 volts, check Orange/Black wire for an open.

2) Measure voltage between terminals No. 6 (Orange/Black wire) and No. 4 (Black/White wire). If voltage reads 12 volts, plug in connector and proceed to ELC HEIGHT SENSOR TEST NO. 2. If voltage does not read 12 volts, check Black/White wire for an open to ground.

3) Measure voltage between terminal No. 5 (Brown/White wire) and ground. If voltage reads 12 volts, plug in connector and proceed to ELC HEIGHT SENSOR TEST NO. 2. If voltage does not read 12 volts, check Brown/White wire for an open.

4) Measure voltage between terminal No. 3 (Yellow wire) and ground. If voltage reads 12 volts, plug in connector and proceed to ELC HEIGHT SENSOR TEST NO. 2. If voltage does not read 12 volts, check Yellow wire for an open.

ELC HEIGHT SENSOR TEST NO. 2

1) Cycle ignition switch and place in "RUN" position. Raise vehicle and support rear axle at normal ride height. Disconnect link from actuator arm and slowly move it upward.

2) If compressor does not begin to run after a 13-27 second delay, replace ELC height sensor. If compressor begins to run but shocks do not begin to inflate after a 13-27 second delay, perform SYSTEM LEAK TEST and COMPRESSOR PERFORMANCE TEST.

3) Move actuator arm downward until compressor stops. If compressor does not stop, replace ELC height sensor. If compressor does stop, continue to move actuator arm downward past the point where compressor stopped.

4) If shocks do not begin to deflate and vehicle does not begin to lower after a 13-27 second delay, replace ELC height sensor. If shocks begin to deflate and vehicle does begin to lower after a 13-27 second delay, ELC height sensor is okay.

EXHAUST SOLENOID TEST

1) Add 300 lbs. (136 kg) to luggage compartment. Unplug ELC height sensor connector. Ground ALDL connector terminal "K" with a fused jumper wire. Allow compressor to run for 2 minutes.

2) If vehicle rises and holds its height after 2 minutes, replace ELC height sensor. If vehicle does not rise or rises and leaks off, check White wire for a short to ground. Repair White wire as necessary. If wire is okay, perform SYSTEM LEAK TEST and COMPRESSOR PERFORMANCE TEST.

ELECTRICAL TESTING (ELECTRA & LESABRE WAGONS)

SYSTEM VOLTAGE & GROUND TEST NO. 1

1) Unplug ELC compressor connector. Measure voltage between terminal "A" (Red wire) and ground at the harness connector. If voltage reads 12 volts, plug in connector and proceed to SYSTEM VOLTAGE & GROUND TEST NO. 2. If voltage does not read 12 volts, check Red wire (No. 2) and fusible link "K" for an open.

2) Measure voltage between terminals "A" (Red wire) and "D" (Black wire) of harness connector. If voltage reads 12 volts, plug in connector and proceed to SYSTEM VOLTAGE & GROUND TEST NO. 2. If voltage does not read 12 volts, check Black wire and ground point, located on left front fender, for an open.

Electronic Suspensions

GENERAL MOTORS REAR LEVEL CONTROL (Cont.)

NOTE: Fusible link "K" is located in ELC harness, behind alternator.

SYSTEM VOLTAGE & GROUND TEST NO. 2

1) Unplug ELC relay connector. Measure voltage between terminal "A" (Red wire) and ground at ELC relay harness connector. If voltage reads 12 volts, plug in connector and proceed to SYSTEM VOLTAGE & GROUND TEST NO. 3. If voltage does not read 12 volts, check Red wire and fusible link "K" for an open.

2) Measure voltage between terminal "B" (Red wire) and ground. If voltage reads 12 volts, plug in connector and proceed to SYSTEM VOLTAGE & GROUND TEST NO. 3. If voltage does not read 12 volts, check Red wire and fusible link "K" for an open.

SYSTEM VOLTAGE & GROUND TEST NO. 3

1) Unplug ELC height sensor connector. Turn ignition switch to "RUN" position. Measure voltage between terminal No. 6 (Red wire) and ground at the ELC height sensor harness connector. If voltage reads 12 volts, proceed to appropriate SYSTEM DIAGNOSIS CHART. If voltage does not read 12 volts, check Red wire for an open.

2) Measure voltage between terminals No. 6 (Red wire) and No. 4 (Black wire). If voltage reads 12 volts, proceed to appropriate SYSTEM DIAGNOSIS CHART. If voltage does not read 12 volts, check Black wire and ground point, located near LR shock absorber, for an open.

3) Measure voltage between terminal No. 5 (Brown wire) and ground. If voltage reads 12 volts, proceed to appropriate SYSTEM DIAGNOSIS CHART. If voltage does not read 12 volts, check Brown wire for an open.

4) Measure voltage between terminal No. 2 (White wire) and ground. If voltage reads 12 volts, proceed to appropriate SYSTEM DIAGNOSIS CHART. If voltage does not read 12 volts, check White wire for an open. If White wire is okay, replace vent solenoid.

5) Measure voltage between terminal No. 3 (Yellow wire) and ground. If voltage reads 12 volts, proceed to appropriate SYSTEM DIAGNOSIS CHART. If voltage does not read 12 volts, check Yellow wire for an open. If Yellow wire is okay, replace ELC relay.

COMPRESSOR MOTOR TEST

Unplug ELC relay connector. Install a fused jumper wire between terminals "A" (Red wire) and "D" (Dark Green wire) at ELC relay connector. If compressor runs, plug in connector and proceed to appropriate SYSTEM DIAGNOSIS CHART. If compressor does not run, check Dark Green wire for an open. If Dark Green wire is okay, repair or replace ELC compressor assembly.

ELC RELAY TEST

Unplug height sensor connector. Install a fused jumper wire between terminal No. 3 (Yellow wire) and ground. If compressor runs, proceed to appropriate SYSTEM DIAGNOSIS CHART. If compressor does not run, replace ELC relay.

VENT SOLENOID TEST

Unplug ELC height sensor connector. Install a fused jumper wire between terminal No. 2 (White wire) and ground. If solenoid clicks and air begins to vent, proceed to appropriate SYSTEM DIAGNOSIS CHART. If solenoid does not click and air does not begin to vent, replace ELC vent solenoid.

ACTUATOR ARM TEST

Raise vehicle and ensure link is correctly attached and actuator arm is properly aligned.

ELC HEIGHT SENSOR TEST

1) Cycle ignition switch. Raise vehicle and support rear axle at ride height position. Disconnect link from actuator arm. Move actuator arm upward. If compressor does not run after an 8-14 second delay, replace ELC height sensor. If shocks do not begin to inflate and vehicle does not begin to rise after an 8-14 second delay, perform SYSTEM LEAK TEST and COMPRESSOR PERFORMANCE TEST.

2) Move actuator arm slowly downward until compressor stops. If compressor does not stop, replace ELC height sensor. Continue to move arm downward past the point where compressor stopped. If shocks do not deflate and vehicle does not begin to lower after an 8-14 second delay, replace ELC height sensor.

ELC HEIGHT SENSOR SHORT TEST

Unplug ELC height sensor connector. If compressor begins to run, check Yellow wire between ELC height sensor and ELC relay for a short to ground. If Yellow wire is okay, proceed to ELC RELAY SHORT TEST. If system starts to vent, check White wire between ELC height sensor and ELC compressor for a short to ground.

ELC RELAY SHORT TEST

Unplug ELC relay connector. If compressor runs, check Dark Green wire between ELC relay and ELC compressor, and compressor for a short to voltage. If compressor does not run, replace compressor.

GENERAL MOTORS REAR LEVEL CONTROL (Cont.)

Fig. 4: Electra, Park Avenue, Delta 88, LeSabre & 98 ELC Electrical Diagram

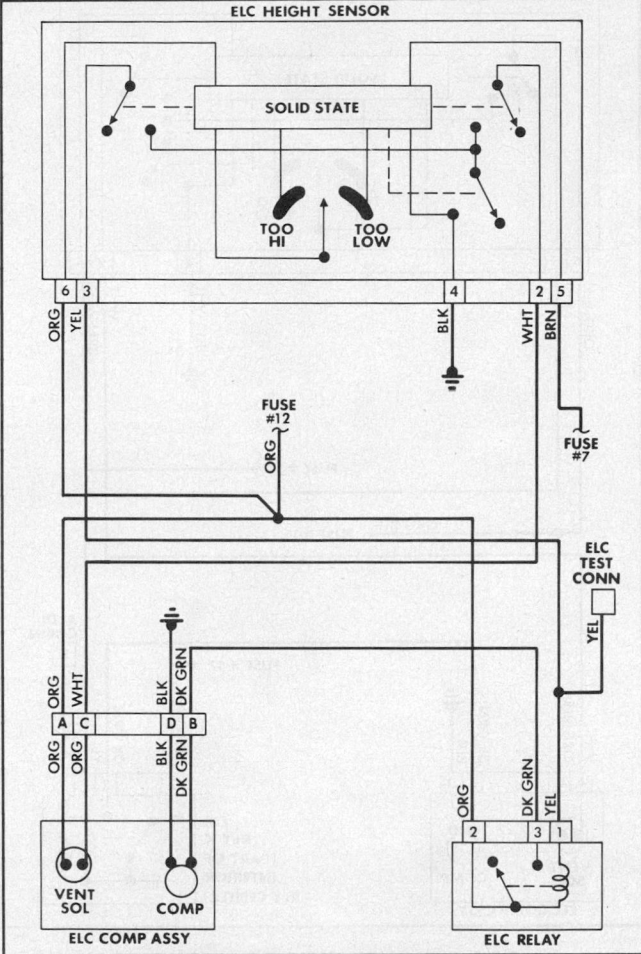

Fig. 5: Electra Estate Wagon & LeSabre Estate Wagon ELC Electrical Diagram

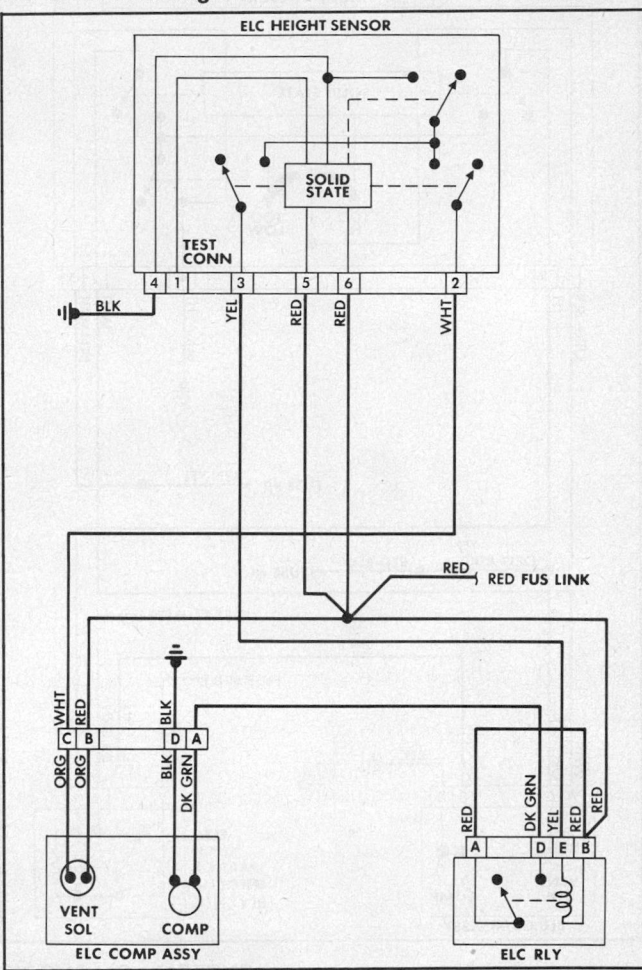

ELECTRICAL TESTING (CUSTOM CRUISER)

ELC RELAY & COMPRESSOR MOTOR TEST

1) With ignition switch in "RUN" position, unplug ELC height sensor connector and ground terminal No. 3 (Yellow wire) with a fused jumper wire. If compressor runs, plug in connector and proceed to ACTUATOR ARM TEST.

2) If compressor does not run, reconnect ELC height sensor and unplug ELC relay connector. Measure voltage between terminal "B" (Brown wire) and ground. If voltage reads zero volts, check Brown wire and A/C fuse for an open.

3) If voltage reads 12 volts, measure voltage between terminal "A" (Red wire) and ground at ELC relay connector. If voltage reads zero volts, check Red wire (No. 2) and fusible link "K" for an open.

4) If voltage reads 12 volts, connect a fused jumper wire between terminals "A" (Red wire) and "D" (Dark Green wire) of the ELC relay connector. If compressor runs, check Yellow wire for an open. If Yellow wire is okay, replace ELC relay.

5) If compressor does not run, leave fused jumper wire installed and measure voltage between terminal "B" and ground at unplugged ELC compressor

connector. If voltage reads zero volts, check Dark Green wire for an open.

6) If voltage reads 12 volts, measure voltage between terminals "B" (Dark Green wire) and "D" (Black wire) at ELC compressor connector. If voltage reads zero volts, check Black wire for an open. If voltage reads 12 volts, repair or replace ELC compressor.

EXHAUST SOLENOID TEST

1) Unplug ELC height sensor connector. Install a fused jumper wire between terminal No. 2 (White wire) and ground at ELC height sensor connector. If exhaust solenoid clicks and air begins to vent, proceed to ACTUATOR ARM TEST.

2) If exhaust solenoid does not click and air does not vent, leave fused jumper wire installed and measure voltage between terminals "A" (Red wire) and ground at unplugged ELC compressor connector. If voltage reads zero, check Red for an open.

3) If voltage reads 12 volts, measure voltage between terminal "A" (Red wire) and terminal "C" (White wire) at ELC compressor connector. If there is battery voltage, replace exhaust solenoid. If there is no voltage, check White wire for open.

ACTUATOR ARM TEST

Raise vehicle and ensure link is correctly attached to actuator and arm is properly aligned. If arm is

GENERAL MOTORS REAR LEVEL CONTROL (Cont.)

Fig. 6: *Riviera ELC Electrical Diagram*

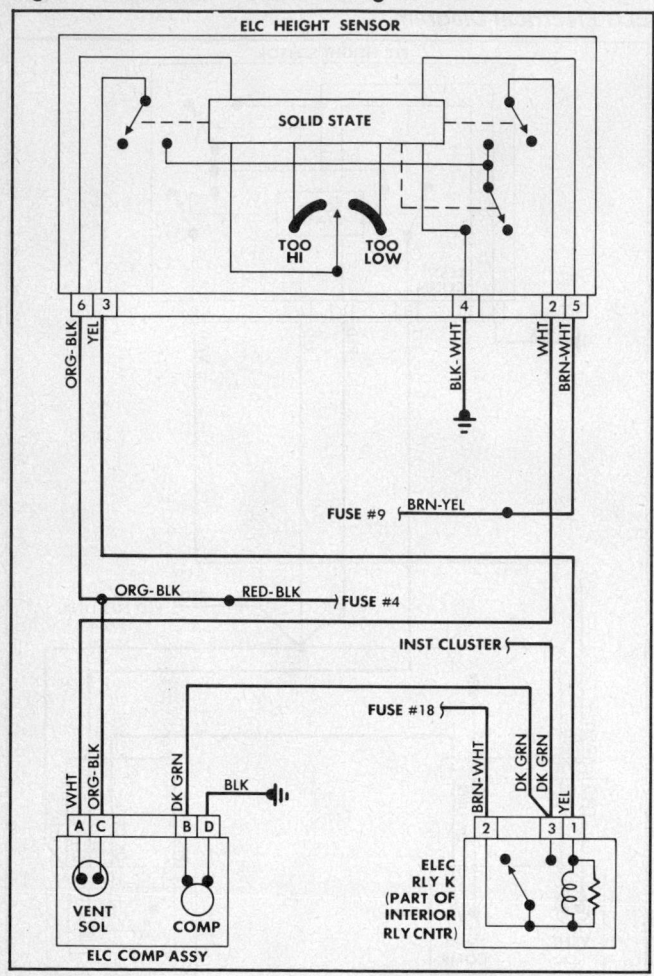

Fig. 7: *Toronado ELC Electrical Diagram*

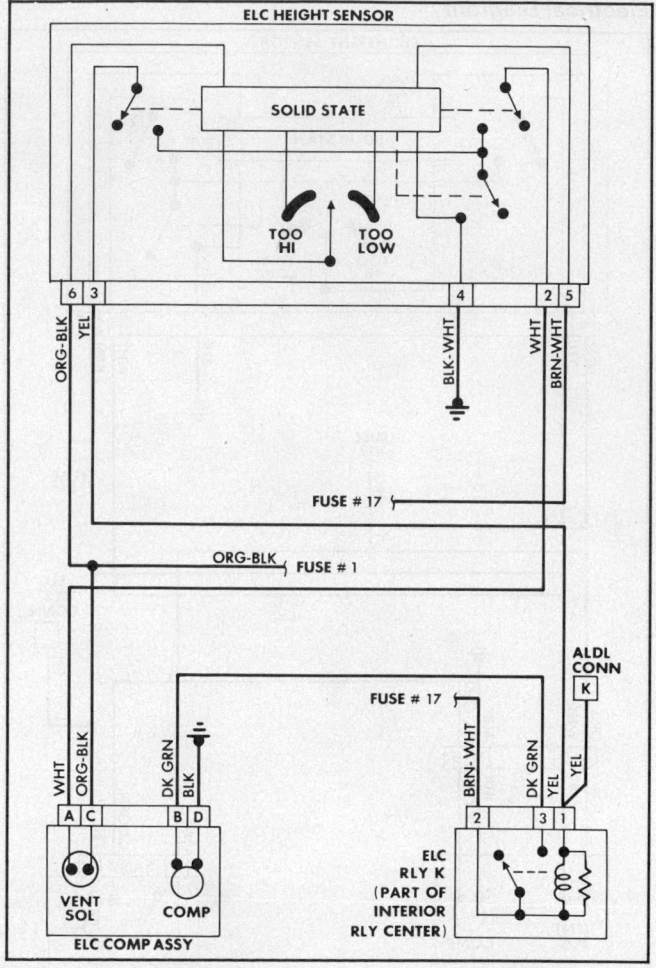

okay, proceed to appropriate SYSTEM DIAGNOSIS CHART.

ELC HEIGHT SENSOR TEST NO. 1

1) Unplug ELC height sensor connector. Turn ignition switch to "RUN" position. Measure voltage between terminal No. 6 (Red wire) on ELC height sensor connector and ground. If voltage reads 12 volts, plug in connector and proceed to ELC HEIGHT SENSOR TEST NO. 2. If voltage does not read 12 volts, check Red wire (No. 2) for an open.

2) Measure voltage between terminals No. 6 (Red wire) and No. 4 (Black wire). If voltage reads 12 volts, plug in connector and proceed to ELC HEIGHT SENSOR TEST NO. 2. If voltage does not read 12 volts, check Black wire (No. 151) for an open to ground.

3) Measure voltage between terminal No. 5 (Brown wire) and ground. If voltage reads 12 volts, plug in connector and proceed to ELC HEIGHT SENSOR TEST NO. 2. If voltage does not read 12 volts, check Brown wire for an open.

4) Measure voltage between terminal No. 3 (Yellow wire) and ground. If voltage reads 12 volts, plug in connector and proceed to ELC HEIGHT SENSOR TEST NO. 2. If voltage does not read 12 volts, check Yellow wire for an open.

ELC HEIGHT SENSOR TEST NO. 2

1) Cycle ignition switch and place in "RUN" position. Raise vehicle and support rear axle at normal riding height. Disconnect link from actuator arm and move arm slowly downward.

2) If compressor does not run after an 8-14 second delay, replace ELC height sensor. If compressor does runs and shocks begin to inflate after an 8-14 second delay, move actuator arm downward until compressor stops as vehicle begins to move upward.

3) If shocks do not begin to inflate and vehicle does not start to raise after an 8-14 second delay, perform SYSTEM LEAK TEST and COMPRESSOR PERFORMANCE TEST. If compressor does not stop, replace height sensor. If compressor does stop, continue to move arm downward past the point where compressor stopped.

4) If vehicle does not begin to lower and shocks do not begin to deflate after an 8-14 second delay, replace ELC height sensor. If shocks begin to deflate and vehicle begins to lower after an 8-15 second delay, ELC height sensor is okay.

EXHAUST SOLENOID TEST

1) Add 300 lbs. (136 kg) to luggage compartment. Unplug ELC height sensor connector and ground terminal No. 3 with a fused jumper wire. Allow compressor to run for 2 minutes.

GENERAL MOTORS REAR LEVEL CONTROL (Cont.)

*Fig. 8: Custom Cruiser Estate Wagon
ELC Electrical Diagram*

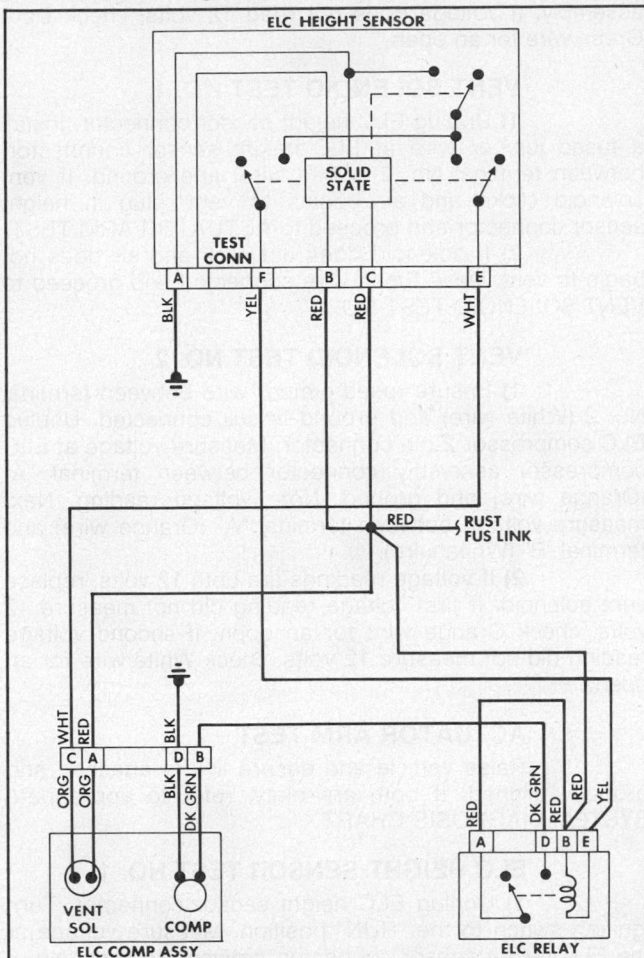

2) If vehicle rises and maintains its height, replace ELC height sensor. If vehicle rises or rises and leaks down, check White wire for a short to ground. If White wire is okay, perform SYSTEM LEAK TEST and COMPRESSOR PERFORMANCE TEST.

ELECTRICAL TESTING (CENTURY)

SYSTEM VOLTAGE & GROUND TEST NO. 1

Unplug ELC compressor connector. Measure voltage between ELC compressor connector terminal "A" (Orange wire) and ground. If voltage reads 12 volts, plug in connector and proceed to SYSTEM VOLTAGE & GROUND TEST NO. 3. If voltage does not read 12 volts, check Orange wire for an open.

SYSTEM VOLTAGE & GROUND TEST NO. 2

1) Unplug ELC relay connector. Measure voltage between terminal "A" (Orange wire) and ground. If voltage reads 12 volts, plug in ELC relay connector and proceed to SYSTEM VOLTAGE TEST NO. 3. If voltage does not read 12 volts, check Orange wire for an open.

2) Measure voltage at ELC relay connector between terminal "C" (Orange wire) and ground. If voltage reads 12 volts, plug in connector and proceed to SYSTEM VOLTAGE & GROUND TEST NO. 3. If voltage does not read 12 volts, check for an open in Orange wire.

SYSTEM VOLTAGE & GROUND TEST NO. 3

1) Unplug ELC height sensor connector. Turn ignition switch to "RUN" position. Measure voltage between terminal No. 6 (Orange wire) and ground. If voltage reads 12 volts, proceed to appropriate SYSTEM DIAGNOSIS CHART. If voltage does not read 12 volts, check Orange wire for an open.

2) Measure voltage between terminals No. 6 (Orange wire) and No. 4 (Black wire). If voltage reads 12 volts, refer to appropriate SYSTEM DIAGNOSIS CHART. If voltage does not read 12 volts, check Black wire and ground point, located at rear of vehicle, near ELC sensor bracket, for an open.

3) Measure voltage between terminal No. 5 (Pink wire) and ground. If voltage reads 12 volts, go to appropriate SYSTEM DIAGNOSIS CHART. If voltage does not read 12 volts, check Pink wire for an open.

4) Measure voltage between terminal No. 2 (White wire) and ground. If voltage reads 12 volts, refer to appropriate SYSTEM DIAGNOSIS CHART. If voltage does not read 12 volts, check White wire for an open. If White wire (No. 320) is okay, remove ELC compressor assembly and replace vent solenoid.

5) Measure voltage between terminal No. 3 (Yellow wire) and ground. If voltage reads 12 volts, go to appropriate SYSTEM DIAGNOSIS CHART. If voltage does not read 12 volts, check Yellow wire for an open. If Yellow wire is okay, replace ELC relay.

COMPRESSOR MOTOR TEST

1) Unplug ELC relay connector. Connect a fused jumper wire between terminals "A" (Orange wire) and "E" (Dark Green wire). If compressor begins to run, plug in relay connector and refer to appropriate SYSTEM DIAGNOSIS CHART.

2) If vehicle begins to level and indicator light comes on, check indicator bulb and Black wire from indicator light to ground point, located behind instrument panel, behind ash tray. If compressor does not run and fuse does not blow, check Dark Green wire and compressor ground for open.

3) If fuse blows, check Dark Green wire for a short to ground. If both wires are okay, repair or replace ELC compressor assembly

ELC RELAY TEST

Unplug ELC height sensor connector. Connect a fused jumper wire between Yellow wire terminal (No. 3) on ELC height sensor connector and ground. If compressor begins to run, plug in connector and refer to appropriate SYSTEM DIAGNOSIS CHART. If compressor does not run, replace ELC relay.

VENT SOLENOID TEST

1) Unplug ELC height sensor connector. Connect fused jumper wire at ELC height sensor connector, between terminal No. 2 (White wire) and ground. If solenoid clicks and air vents, plug in height sensor connector and refer to appropriate SYSTEM DIAGNOSIS CHART.

Electronic Suspensions

GENERAL MOTORS REAR LEVEL CONTROL (Cont.)

2) If solenoid does not click and air does not vent, remove ELC compressor and replace vent solenoid.

ACUATOR ARM TEST

Raise vehicle and ensure link is correctly attached to actuator arm. Also verify actuator arm is properly aligned.

ELC HEIGHT SENSOR TEST

1) Cycle ignition switch. Raise vehicle and support rear axle at ride height. Disconnect link from actuator arm. Move height sensor arm at ELC height sensor upward.

2) After an 8-14 second delay, compressor should run and shocks should inflate. If not, replace ELC height sensor. If shocks do not begin to inflate and vehicle does not begin to move upward after an 8-14 second delay, perform COMPRESSOR PERFORMANCE TEST and SYSTEM LEAK TEST.

3) Slowly move arm downward. If compressor does not stop, replace ELC height sensor. Continue to move arm downward, below the position where compressor stopped. If shocks do not begin to deflate and vehicle does not begin to lower after a delay of an 8-14 seconds, replace ELC height sensor.

ELECTRICAL TESTING (6000 & 6000 STE)

ELC RELAY & COMPRESSOR MOTOR TEST NO. 1

Install a fused jumper wire between terminal "E" (Yellow wire) and ground at ELC relay connector. If compressor runs, proceed to ACTUATOR ARM TEST. If compressor does not begin to run, proceed to ELC RELAY & COMPRESSOR MOTOR TEST NO. 2.

ELC RELAY & COMPRESSOR MOTOR TEST NO. 2

1) Unplug ELC relay connector. Measure voltage between terminal "A" (Orange wire) and ground at ELC relay connector. If voltage reads 12 volts, proceed to ELC RELAY & COMPRESSOR MOTOR TEST NO. 3.

2) If voltage does not read 12 volts, check Orange wire for an open. Measure voltage between terminal "B" (Orange wire) and ground. If voltage reads 12 volts, proceed to ELC RELAY & COMPRESSOR MOTOR TEST NO. 3. If voltage does not read 12 volts, check Orange wire for an open.

ELC RELAY & COMPRESSOR MOTOR TEST NO. 3

Install a fused jumper wire between terminals "A" (Orange wire) and "D" (Dark Green wire) of ELC relay connector. If compressor runs, replace ELC relay. If compressor does not run, proceed to ELC RELAY & COMPRESSOR MOTOR TEST NO. 4.

ELC RELAY & COMPRESSOR MOTOR TEST NO. 4

1) Ensure fused jumper is still connected between terminals "A" (Orange wire) and "D" (Dark Green wire) of ELC relay connector. Measure voltage at ELC compressor connector between terminal "C2" (Dark Green wire) and ground.

2) If voltage reads 12 volts, check Black wire to ground. If okay, repair or replace ELC compressor assembly. If voltage does not read 12 volts, check Dark Green wire for an open.

VENT SOLENOID TEST NO. 1

1) Unplug ELC height sensor connector. Install a fused jumper wire at ELC height sensor connnector, between terminal No. 2 (White wire) and ground. If vent solenoid clicks and air begins to vent, plug in height sensor connector and proceed to ACTUATOR ARM TEST.

2) If solenoid does not click and air does not begin to vent, leave fused wire connected and proceed to VENT SOLENOID TEST NO. 2.

VENT SOLENOID TEST NO. 2

1) Ensure fused jumper wire between terminal No. 2 (White wire) and ground is still connected. Unplug ELC compressor 2-pin connector. Measure voltage at ELC compressor assembly connector between terminal "A" (Orange wire) and ground. Note voltage reading. Next measure voltage between terminal "A" (Orange wire) and terminal "B" (White wire).

2) If voltage readings are both 12 volts, replace vent solenoid. If first voltage reading did not measure 12 volts, check Orange wire for an open. If second voltage reading did not measure 12 volts, check White wire for an open.

ACTUATOR ARM TEST

Raise vehicle and ensure link is attached and properly aligned. If both are okay, refer to appropriate SYSTEM DIAGNOSIS CHART.

ELC HEIGHT SENSOR TEST NO. 1

1) Unplug ELC height sensor connector. Turn ignition switch to the "RUN" position. Measure voltage at the ELC height sensor connector, between terminal No. 6 (Orange wire) and ground. If voltage reads 12 volts, reconnect connector and proceed to ELC HEIGHT SENSOR TEST NO. 2. If voltage does not read 12 volts, check Orange wire for an open.

2) Measure voltage between terminal No. 6 (Orange wire) and terminal No. 4 (Black wire). If voltage reads 12 volts, plug in connector and proceed to ELC HEIGHT SENSOR TEST NO. 2. If voltage does not read 12 volts, check Black wire for an open.

3) Measure voltage between terminal No. 5 (Pink wire) and ground. If voltage reads 12 volts, plug in connector and proceed to ELC HEIGHT SENSOR TEST NO. 2. If voltage does not read 12 volts, check Pink wire for an open.

4) Measure voltage between terminal No. 3 (Yellow wire) and ground. If voltage reads 12 volts, plug in connector and proceed to ELC HEIGHT SENSOR TEST NO. 2. If voltage does not read 12 volts, check Yellow wire for an open.

ELC HEIGHT SENSOR TEST NO. 2

1) Cycle ignition switch and return to the "RUN" position. Raise vehicle and support axle at ride height. Disconnect link from actuator arm.

2) Move actuator arm at ELC height sensor upward. If compressor does not run after an 8-14 second delay, replace ELC height sensor. If shocks do not begin to inflate and vehicle does not begin to raise after an 8-14

GENERAL MOTORS REAR LEVEL CONTROL (Cont.)

second delay, complete a COMPRESSOR PERFORMANCE TEST and a SYSTEM LEAK TEST.

3) Move actuator arm slowly downward until compressor stops. If compressor does not stop, replace ELC height sensor.

4) Continue to move actuator arm downward below position where compressor stopped. If shocks do not begin to deflate and vehicle does not begin to lower after an 8-14 second delay, replace ELC height sensor.

VENT SOLENOID SHORT TEST

1) Add 300 lbs. (136 kg) to luggage compartment. Disconnect height sensor connector and ground terminal No. 3 (Yellow wire) with a fused jumper wire. Allow compressor to run for 2 minutes. If vehicle rises and maintains its height, replace height sensor.

2) If vehicle does not rise or rises and leaks down, check White wire for a short to ground. If White wire is okay, perform COMPRESSOR PERFORMANCE TEST and SYSTEMS LEAK TEST.

ELECTRICAL TESTING (CUTLASS CRUISER & CUTLASS CIERA)

ELC RELAY & COMPRESSOR MOTOR TEST

1) Unplug ELC height sensor connector. Install a fused jumper wire between terminal No. 3 (Yellow wire) and ground. If compressor runs, reconnect ELC height sensor connector and proceed to ACTUATOR ARM TEST.

2) If compressor does not run, reconnect ELC height sensor. Disconnect ELC relay connector. Measure voltage between terminal "B" (Orange wire) and ground. If voltage reads zero volts, check for open in Orange wire and "COURTESY FUSE".

3) If voltage does read 12 volts, measure voltage between terminal "A" (Orange wire) and ground at ELC relay connector. If voltage does not read 12 volts, check Orange wire for an open. If voltage does read 12 volts, connect a fused jumper wire between terminals "A" (Orange wire) and "D" (Dark Green wire).

4) If compressor runs, check Yellow wire for an open. If Yellow wire is okay, replace ELC relay. If compressor does not run, unplug ELC compressor connector. Leave fused jumper wire intact and measure voltage between Dark Green wire and ground of ELC compressor connector. If voltage does not read 12 volts, check Dark Green wire for an open.

5) If voltage does read 12 volts, check Black wire and for an open. Repair or replace as necessary. If Black wire is okay and grounded good, repair or replace compressor assembly.

EXHAUST SOLENOID TEST

1) Unplug ELC height sensor connector. Ground terminal No. 2 (White wire) of ELC height sensor with a fused jumper wire. If exhaust solenoid clicks and air vents, proceed to ACTUATOR ARM TEST.

2) If exhaust solenoid does not click and air does not begin to vent, leave fused jumper wire in place at ELC height sensor. Unplug ELC compressor connector. Measure voltage between terminal "A" (Orange wire) and ground at the ELC compressor connector.

3) If voltage reads zero volts, check Orange wire for an open. If voltage reads 12 volts, measure voltage at compressor connector between terminals "A" (Orange wire) and "B" (White wire). If voltage reads zero volts, check White wire (No. 320) for an open. If voltage reads 12 volts, replace exhaust solenoid.

ACTUATOR ARM TEST

Raise vehicle and ensure link is correctly attached and actuator arm is properly aligned. If both are okay, refer to appropriate SYSTEM DIAGNOSIS CHART.

ELC HEIGHT SENSOR TEST NO. 1

1) Unplug ELC height sensor connector. Turn ignition switch to "RUN" position. Measure voltage between terminal No. 6 (Orange wire) and ground. If voltage reads 12 volts, plug in connector and proceed to ELC HEIGHT SENSOR TEST NO. 2. If voltage does not read 12 volts, check Orange wire for an open.

2) Measure voltage between terminals No. 6 (Orange wire) and No. 4 (Black wire). If voltage reads 12 volts, plug in connector and proceed to ELC HEIGHT SENSOR TEST NO. 2. If voltage does not read 12 volts, check Black wire for an open to ground.

3) Measure voltage between terminal No. 5 (Pink wire) and ground. If voltage reads 12 volts, plug in connector and go to ELC HEIGHT SENSOR TEST NO. 2. If voltage does not read 12 volts, check Pink wire for open.

4) Measure voltage between terminal No. 3 (Yellow wire) and ground. If voltage reads 12 volts, plug in connector and go to ELC HEIGHT SENSOR TEST NO. 2. If voltage does not read 12 volts, check Yellow wire for open.

ELC HEIGHT SENSOR TEST NO. 2

1) Cycle ignition switch and leave in "RUN" position. Raise and support rear axle at ride height. Disconnect link from actuator arm and move actuator arm upward. If compressor does not run after an 8-14 second delay, replace ELC height sensor.

2) If compressor does begin to run and shocks begin to inflate but vehicle does not rise after an 8-14 second delay, perform SYSTEM LEAK TEST and COMPRESSOR PERFORMANCE TEST.

3) If shocks inflate and vehicle rises after an 8-14 second delay, move actuator arm slowly downward until compressor stops. If compressor stops, continue to move arm downward. If compressor does not stop, replace height sensor.

4) If after continuing to move arm downward shocks start to deflate and vehicle begins to lower, ELC height sensor is okay. If shocks do not begin to deflate and vehicle does not begin to lower after an 8-14 second delay, replace ELC height sensor.

EXHAUST SOLENOID SHORT TEST

1) Add 300 lbs. (136 kg) to luggage compartment. Unplug ELC height sensor connector. Ground terminal No. 3 (Yellow wire) with a fused jumper wire. Allow compressor to run for 2 minutes.

2) If vehicle rises and maintains its height, replace height sensor. If vehicle does not rise or rises and leaks down, check White wire for a short to ground. If White wire is okay, perform SYSTEM LEAK TEST and COMPRESSOR PERFORMANCE TEST.

Electronic Suspensions

GENERAL MOTORS REAR LEVEL CONTROL (Cont.)

ELECTRICAL TESTING (BONNEVILLE & BONNEVILLE SSE)

ELC RELAY & COMPRESSOR MOTOR TEST NO. 1

Unplug ELC height sensor conmnector. Install a fused jumper wire between terminal No. 3 (Yellow wire) on ELC test connector and ground. If compressor runs, proceed to ACTUATOR ARM TEST. If compressor does not run, check Yellow wire for an open. If Yellow wire is okay, proceed to ELC RELAY & COMPRESSOR MOTOR TEST NO. 2.

ELC RELAY & COMPRESSOR MOTOR TEST NO. 2

1) Unplug ELC relay connector. Measure voltage between terminal No. 2 (Orange wire) and ground of ELC relay connector. If voltage reads 12 volts, proceed to ELC RELAY & COMPRESSOR MOTOR TEST NO. 3. If voltage does not read 12 volts, check Orange wire for an open.

2) Measure voltage between terminals No. 2 (Orange wire) and No. 1 (Yellow wire) on ELC relay connector. If voltage is 12 volts, proceed to ELC RELAY & COMPRESSOR MOTOR TEST NO. 3. If voltage is not 12 volts, check Yellow wire for open.

ELC RELAY & COMPRESSOR MOTOR TEST NO. 3

Unplug ELC relay connector. Install a fused jumper wire between terminals No. 2 (Orange wire) and No. 3 (Dark Green wire) at ELC relay connector. If compressor runs, replace ELC relay. If compressor does not run, leave fused jumper wire installed and proceed to ELC RELAY & COMPRESSOR MOTOR TEST NO. 4

ELC RELAY & COMPRESSOR MOTOR TEST NO. 4

Unplug ELC compressor connector. Measure voltage at harness half of ELC compressor connector between terminal "B" (Dark Green wire) and ground. If voltage reads 12 volts, ensure compressor is grounded properly. If so, repair or replace ELC compressor assembly. If voltage does not read 12 volts, check Dark Green wire for an open.

VENT SOLENOID TEST NO. 1

Unplug ELC height sensor connector. Install a fused jumper wire at ELC height sensor connector between terminal No. 2 (White wire) and ground. If vent solenoid clicks and air begins to vent, plug in connector and proceed to ACTUATOR ARM TEST. If vent solenoid does not click and air does not begin to vent, leave fused jumper wire connected and proceed to VENT SOLENOID TEST NO. 2.

VENT SOLENOID TEST NO. 2

1) Unplug ELC compressor connector. Measure voltage between terminal "A" (Orange wire) and ground on ELC compressor connector. If voltage reads 12 volts, replace vent solenoid. If voltage is not 12 volts, check Orange wire for open.

2) Measure voltage between terminals "A" (Orange wire) and "C" (White wire). If voltage reads 12 volts, replace vent solenoid. If voltage does not read 12 volts, check White wire for an open.

ACTUATOR ARM TEST

Raise vehicle and ensure link is correctly attached to actuator arm and actuator arm is properly positioned. If arm is okay, proceed to ELC HEIGHT SENSOR TEST NO. 1

ELC HEIGHT SENSOR TEST NO. 1

1) Unplug ELC height sensor connector. With ignition switch in "RUN" position, measure voltage between terminal No. 6 (Light Blue wire on SSE, Orange wire on all others) and ground. If voltage reads 12 volts, proceed to ELC HEIGHT SENSOR TEST NO. 2. If voltage does not read 12 volts, check Light Blue or Orange wire for open.

2) Measure voltage between terminals No. 6 and No. 4 (Black wire). If voltage reads 12 volts, plug in connector and proceed to ELC HEIGHT SENSOR TEST NO. 2. If voltage does not read 12 volts, check Black wire for an open.

3) Measure voltage between terminal No. 5 (Brown wire) and ground. If voltage reads 12 volts, plug in connector and proceed to ELC HEIGHT SENSOR TEST NO. 2. If voltage does not read 12 volts, check Brown wire for an open.

4) Measure voltage between terminal No. 3 (Yellow wire) and ground. If voltage reads 12 volts, plug in connector and proceed to ELC HEIGHT SENSOR TEST NO. 2. If voltage does not read 12 volts, check Yellow wire for an open.

ELC HEIGHT SENSOR TEST NO. 2

1) Cycle ignition switch and place in "RUN" position. Raise vehicle and support rear wheels at normal ride height. Disconnect link from actuator arm and slowly move arm upward.

2) If compressor does not begin to run after an 8-14 second delay, replace ELC height sensor. If shocks do not begin to inflate and vehicle does not begin to rise after an 8-14 second delay, perform SYSTEM LEAK TEST and COMPRESSOR PERFORMANCE TEST.

3) Slowly move arm downward. If compressor does not stop, replace ELC height sensor. Continue to move arm downward past the point where compressor stopped. If shocks do not begin to deflate and vehicle does not begin to lower after an 8-14 second delay, replace ELC height sensor.

VENT SOLENOID TEST

Add 300 lbs. (136 kg) load to rear of vehicle. Unplug ELC height sensor connector. Ground terminal No. 3 (Yellow wire) with aa fused jumper wire. If car rises and maintains height, replace ELC height sensor. If vehicle does not rise or leaks down, check White wire for short. If White wire is okay, see SYSTEM LEAK CHECK and COMPRESSOR PERFORMANCE TEST.

INFLATOR TIMER RELAY TEST NO. 1 (BONNEVILLE SSE)

1) Place a fused jumper wire between terminal "F" (White wire) and ground, on inflator timer relay connector. If compressor does not run, go to INFLATOR TIMER RELAY TEST NO. 2. Open air valve.

GENERAL MOTORS REAR LEVEL CONTROL (Cont.)

2) If high pressure air does not comes from air hose, leave jumper wire connected and go to INFLATOR TIMER RELAY TEST NO. 3. If compressor does not run and high air pressure does not escape from air hose, go to INFLATOR SWITCH TEST.

INFLATOR TIMER RELAY TEST NO. 2 (BONNEVILLE SSE)

1) Turn inflator switch off. Switch is located in luggage compartment. Measure voltage between terminal "D" (Orange wire) and ground on inflator timer relay connector. If voltage is not 12 volts, check Orange wire for open.

2) Measure voltage between terminal "E" (Yellow wire) and ground. If voltage is not 12 volts, check Yellow wire for open. Measure voltage between terminal "B" (Light Blue wire) and ground.

3) If volatge is not 12 volts, replace inflator timer relay. Measure voltage between terminals "D" (Orange wire) and "H" (Black wire). If voltage is not 12 volts, check Black wire for open. If 12 volts is measured at all test points, replace inflator timer relay.

INFLATOR TIMER RELAY TEST NO. 3 (BONNEVILLE SSE)

Measure voltage between terminal "C" (Dark Blue wire) and ground. Ensure jumper wire between terminal "F" (White wire) and ground is connected. If

voltage is 12 volts, go to INFLATOR SOLENOID VALVE TEST. If voltage is not 12 volts, replace inflator timer relay.

INFLATOR SWITCH TEST (BONNEVILLE SSE)

1) Ensure inflator switch connector is plugged in and turn on, and inflator timer relay connector is unplugged. Measure continuity between terminal "A" (White wire) and terminal "B" (Black wire). If there is no continuity, replace inflator switch.

2) If there is continuity, hold inflator switch in "OFF" position. Measure continuity between terminal "C" (Purple wire) and terminal "B" (Black wire). If there is no continuity, replace inflator switch. If there is continuity in both test, check for in White, Purple or Black wires.

INFLATOR SOLENOID VALVE TEST (BONNEVILLE SSE)

1) Unplug inflator solenoid valve connector. Connect a fused jumper wire between terminal "D" (Orange wire) and terminal "C" (Dark Blue wire) on inflator timer relay connector, with it plugged in. Measure voltage between Dark Blue wire on solenoid and ground.

2) If voltage is not 12 volts, check Dark Blue wire for open. Measure voltage between Dark Blue wire and Black wire at solenoid. If voltage is not 12 volts, check Black wire for open. If voltage at both test points is 12 volts, replace inflator solenoid valve.

Fig. 9: Century & Cutlass Ciera ELC Electrical Diagram

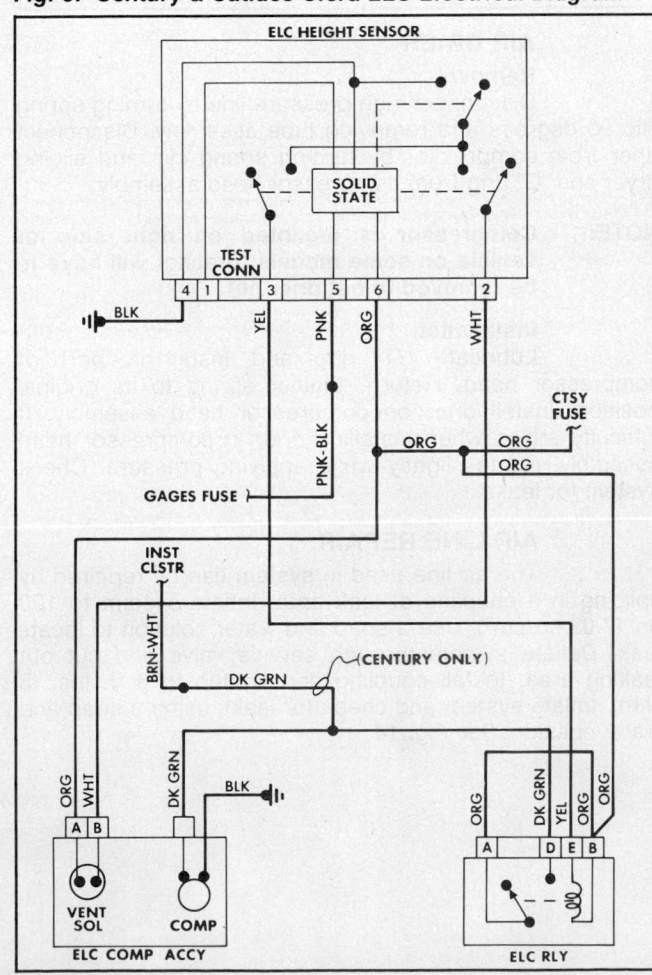

Fig. 10: 6000 ELC Electrical Diagram

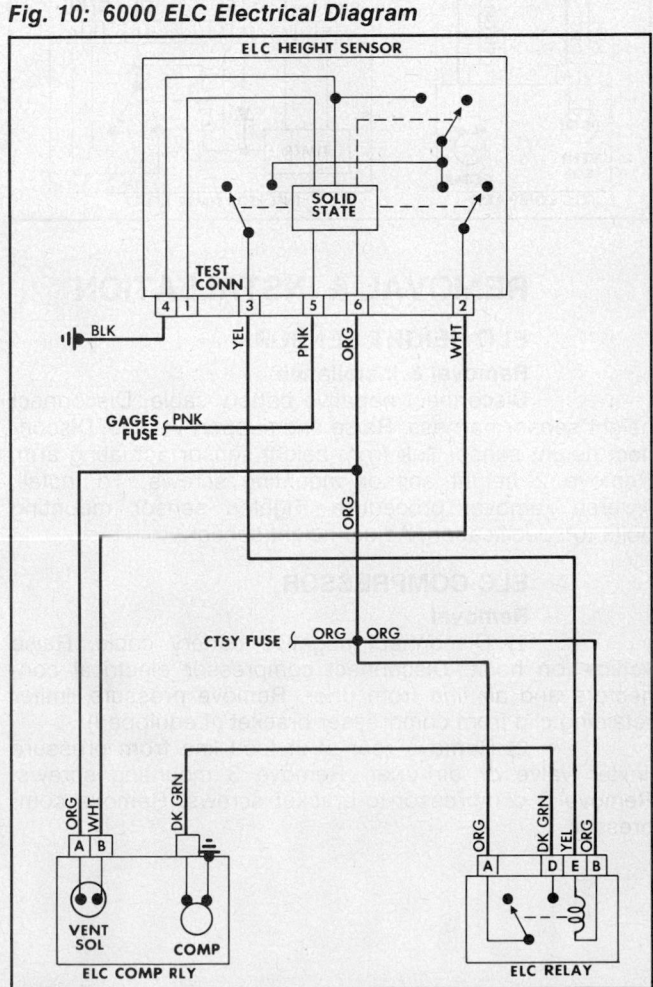

Electronic Suspensions

GENERAL MOTORS REAR LEVEL CONTROL (Cont.)

Fig. 11: 6000 STE ELC Electrical Diagram

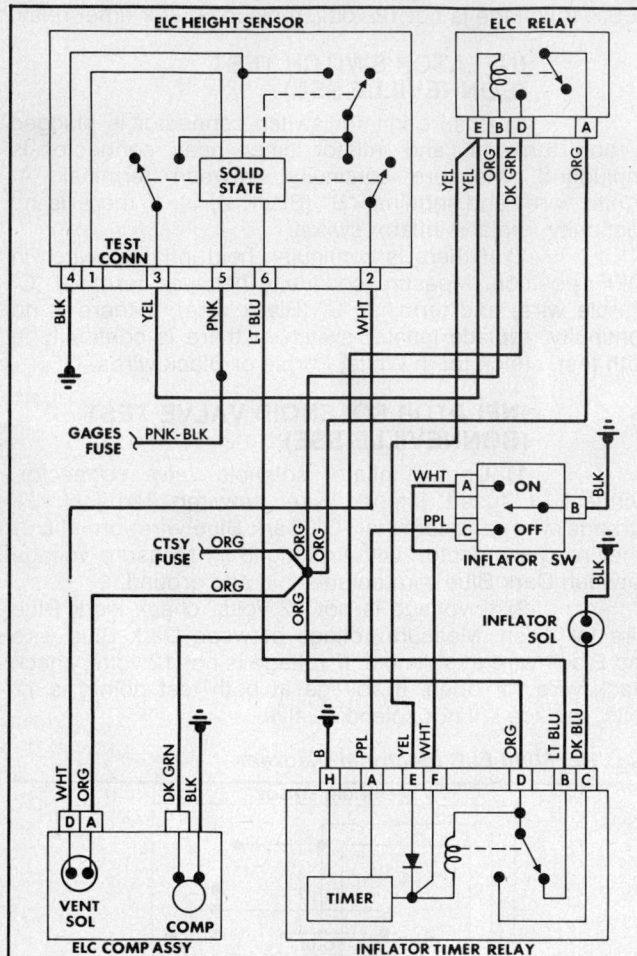

Installation

To install, reverse removal procedure. Turn ignition on and allow system to cycle. Check for leaks using soap and water solution. *See Fig. 12.*

Fig. 12: Compressor Leak Check

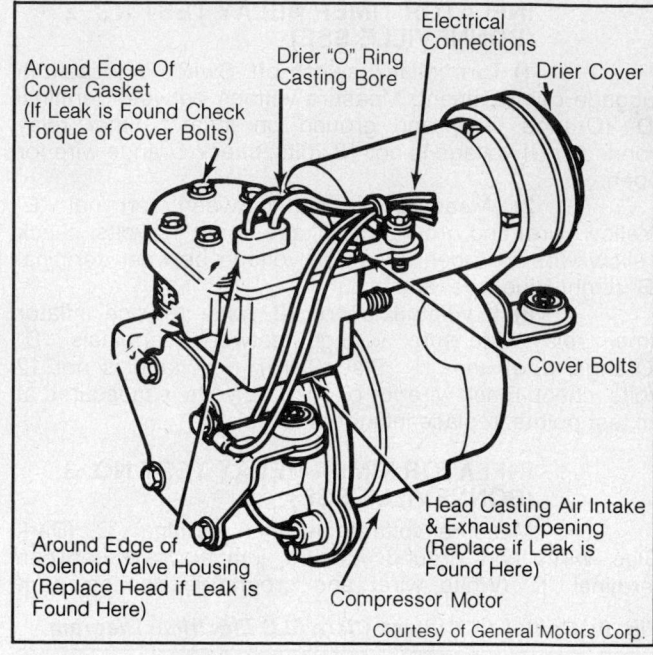

Courtesy of General Motors Corp.

REMOVAL & INSTALLATION

ELC HEIGHT SENSOR

Removal & Installation

Disconnect negative battery cable. Disconnect height sensor harness. Raise and support vehicle. Disconnect height sensor link from height sensor actuating arm. Remove 2 height sensor mounting screws. To install, reverse removal procedure. Tighten sensor mounting bolts to specification. Adjust height sensor.

ELC COMPRESSOR

Removal

1) Disconnect negative battery cable. Raise vehicle on hoist. Disconnect compressor electrical connectors and air line from drier. Remove pressure limiter retaining clip from compresser bracket (if equipped).

2) Remove rear strut feed line from pressure limiter valve or air drier. Remove 3 mounting screws. Remove 3 compressor-to-bracket screws. Remove compressor.

AIR DRIER

Removal

Disconnect high pressure line by turning spring clip 90 degrees and removing tube assembly. Disconnect drier from compressor by turning spring clip and sliding dryer and "O" ring from compressor head assembly.

NOTE: Compressor is mounted on right side of vehicle on some models. Bracket will have to be removed to get drier out.

Installation

Lubricate "O" ring and install in port of compressor head. Return retainer spring to its original position. Install drier on compressor head assembly. If difficulty arises when installing drier in compressor head assembly, rotate slightly while applying pressure. Check system for leaks.

AIR LINE REPAIR

The air line used in system can be repaired by splicing in a coupling at leak area. Inflate system to 100 psi (7.03 kg/cm²). Use a soap and water solution to locate leak. Deflate system through service valve and cut out leaking area. Install coupling and tighten to 6 ft. lbs. (8 N.m). Inflate system and check for leaks using a soap and water solution. *See Fig. 14.*

GENERAL MOTORS REAR LEVEL CONTROL (Cont.)

Fig. 13: DeVille & Fleetwood ELC Electrical Diagram

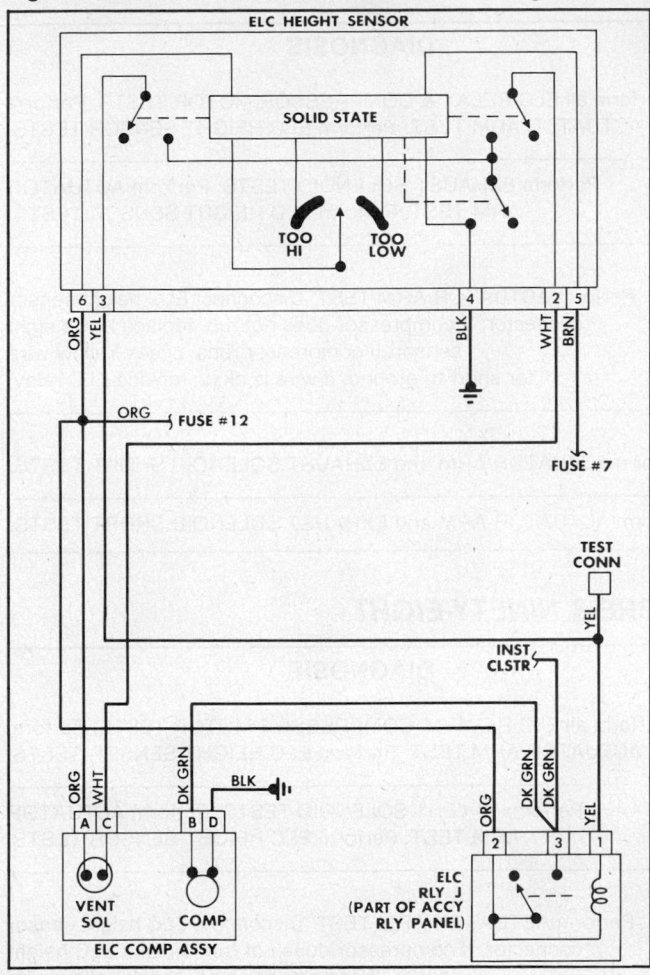

Fig. 15: Eldorado & Seville ELC Electrical Diagram

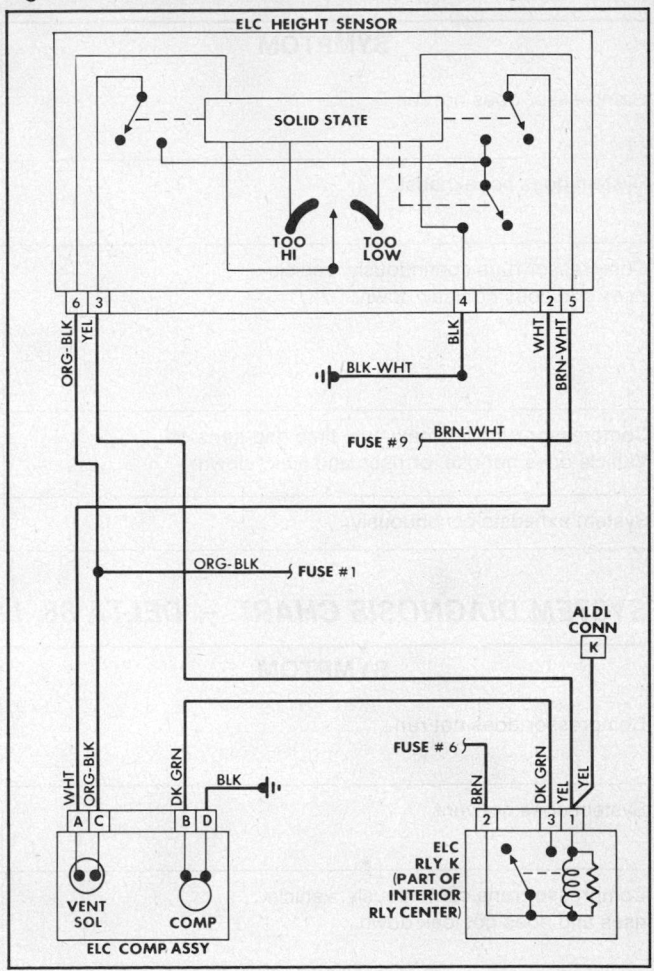

Fig. 14: Air Line Repair Coupling

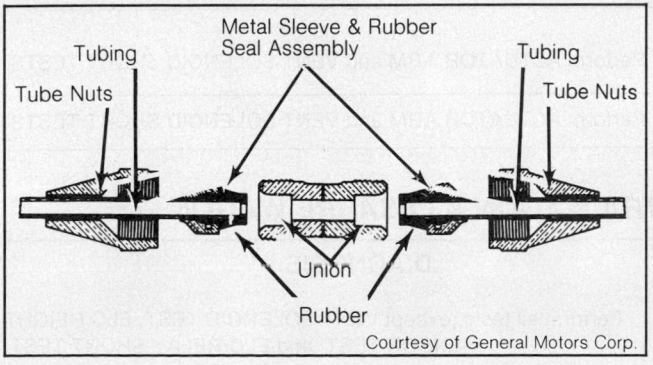

Courtesy of General Motors Corp.

TIGHTENING SPECIFICATIONS

Application	INCH Lbs. (N.m)
Compressor Bracket Mounting Screws	
"A", "C" & "H" Bodies	45 (5.1)
All Others	132 (15)
Compressor Head Bolts	36 (4.1)
Compressor Mounting Screws	
"A", "C" & "H" Bodies	45 (5.1)
All Others	35 (4.0)
Height Sensor Mounting Screws	
"A", "C" & "H" Bodies	62 (7)
Custom Cruiser	24 (2.7)
All Others	46 (5.2)

Electronic Suspensions
GENERAL MOTORS REAR LEVEL CONTROL (Cont.)

SYSTEM DIAGNOSIS CHART – CUTLASS CIERA & CUTLASS CRUISER

SYMPTOM	DIAGNOSIS
Compressor does not run.	Perform all ELC RELAY & COMPRESSOR MOTOR TESTS. Perform ACTUATOR ARM TEST. Perform ELC HEIGHT SENSOR TESTS.
System does not exhaust.	Perform EXHAUST SOLENOID TESTS. Perform ACTUATOR ARM TEST. Perform ELC HEIGHT SENSOR TESTS.
Compressor runs continuously, vehicle rises and does not leak down.	Perform ACTUATOR ARM TEST. Disconnect ELC height sensor connector. If compressor does not run, replace ELC height sensor. If compressor runs, check Yellow wire for short to ground. If wire is okay, replace ELC relay.
Compressor runs for maximum time and turns off. Vehicle does not rise, or rises and leaks down.	Perform ACTUATOR ARM and EXHAUST SOLENOID SHORT TESTS.
System exhausts continuously.	Perform ACTUATOR ARM and EXHAUST SOLENOID SHORT TESTS.

SYSTEM DIAGNOSIS CHART – DELTA 88, LESABRE & NINETY-EIGHT

SYMPTOM	DIAGNOSIS
Compressor does not run.	Perform all ELC RELAY & COMPRESSOR MOTOR TESTS. Perform ACTUATOR ARM TEST. Perform ELC HEIGHT SENSOR TESTS.
System does not vent.	Perform all VENT SOLENOID TESTS. Perform ACTUATOR ARM TEST. Perform ELC HEIGHT SENSOR TESTS.
Compressor runs continuously, vehicle rises and does not leak down.	Perform ACTUATOR ARM TEST. Disconnect ELC height sensor connector. If compressor does not run, replace ELC height sensor. If compressor runs, check Yellow wire for short to ground. If wire is okay, replace ELC relay.
Compressor runs for maximum time and turns off. Vehicle does not rise, or rises and leaks down.	Perform ACTUATOR ARM and VENT SOLENOID SHORT TESTS.
System vents continuously.	Perform ACTUATOR ARM and VENT SOLENOID SHORT TESTS.

SYSTEM DIAGNOSIS CHART – ELECTRA, ELECTRA WAGON & LESABRE WAGON

SYMPTOM	DIAGNOSIS
Compressor does not run.	Perform all tests, except VENT SOLENOID TEST, ELC HEIGHT SENSOR TEST, and ELC RELAY SHORT TEST.
System does not vent.	Perform SYSTEM VOLTAGE AND GROUND TESTS NO. 1 & NO. 3, VENT SOLENOID TEST, ACTUATOR ARM TEST, and ELC HEIGHT SENSOR TEST.
Compressor runs continuously.	Perform SYSTEM LEAK TEST, ACTUATOR ARM TEST, ELC HEIGHT SENSOR TEST, and ELC RELAY SHORT TEST.
System vents continuously.	Perform ACTUATOR ARM and ELC HEIGHT SENSOR TESTS.

GENERAL MOTORS REAR LEVEL CONTROL (Cont.)

SYSTEM DIAGNOSIS CHART – BONNEVILLE & 6000

SYMPTOM	DIAGNOSIS
Compressor does not run.	Perform all ELC RELAY & COMPRESSOR MOTOR TESTS. Perform ACTUATOR ARM TEST. Perform ELC HEIGHT SENSOR TESTS.
System does not exhaust.	Perform EXHAUST SOLENOID TESTS. Perform ACTUATOR ARM TEST. Perform ELC HEIGHT SENSOR TESTS.
Compressor runs continuously, vehicle rises and does not leak down.	Perform ACTUATOR ARM TEST. Disconnect ELC height sensor connector. If compressor does not run, replace ELC height sensor. If compressor runs, check Yellow wire for short to ground. If wire is okay, replace ELC relay.
Compressor runs for maximum time and turns off. Vehicle does not rise, or rises and leaks down.	Perform ACTUATOR ARM and EXHAUST SOLENOID SHORT TESTS.
System exhausts continuously.	Perform ACTUATOR ARM and EXHAUST SOLENOID SHORT TESTS.

SYSTEM DIAGNOSIS CHART – CENTURY

SYMPTOM	DIAGNOSIS
Compressor does not run and vehicle is leveling. Indicator light does not light.	Perform all tests except, VENT SOLENOID TEST.
Compressor does not run but vehicle is leveling. Indicator lights.	Check Dark Green wire and Black wire (to ground). If wire is okay, replace compressor.
Compressor runs, vehicle is leveling. Indicator does not light.	Check indicator bulb and associated wiring.
System does not vent.	Perform all tests except COMPRESSOR MOTOR & ELC RELAY.
Compressor runs continuously.	PERFORM ACTUATOR ARM TEST. Disconnect ELC height sensor. If compressor does not run, replace height sensor. If compressor runs, check Yellow wire for short to ground. If wire is okay, replace ELC relay.
System vents continuously.	Perform ACTUATOR ARM TEST. Disconnect ELC height sensor. If system does not vent, replace ELC height sensor. If system vents, check White wire for short to ground.

Electronic Suspensions
GENERAL MOTORS REAR LEVEL CONTROL (Cont.)
SYSTEM TESTING (ELDORADO, RIVIERA, SEVILLE & TORONADO)

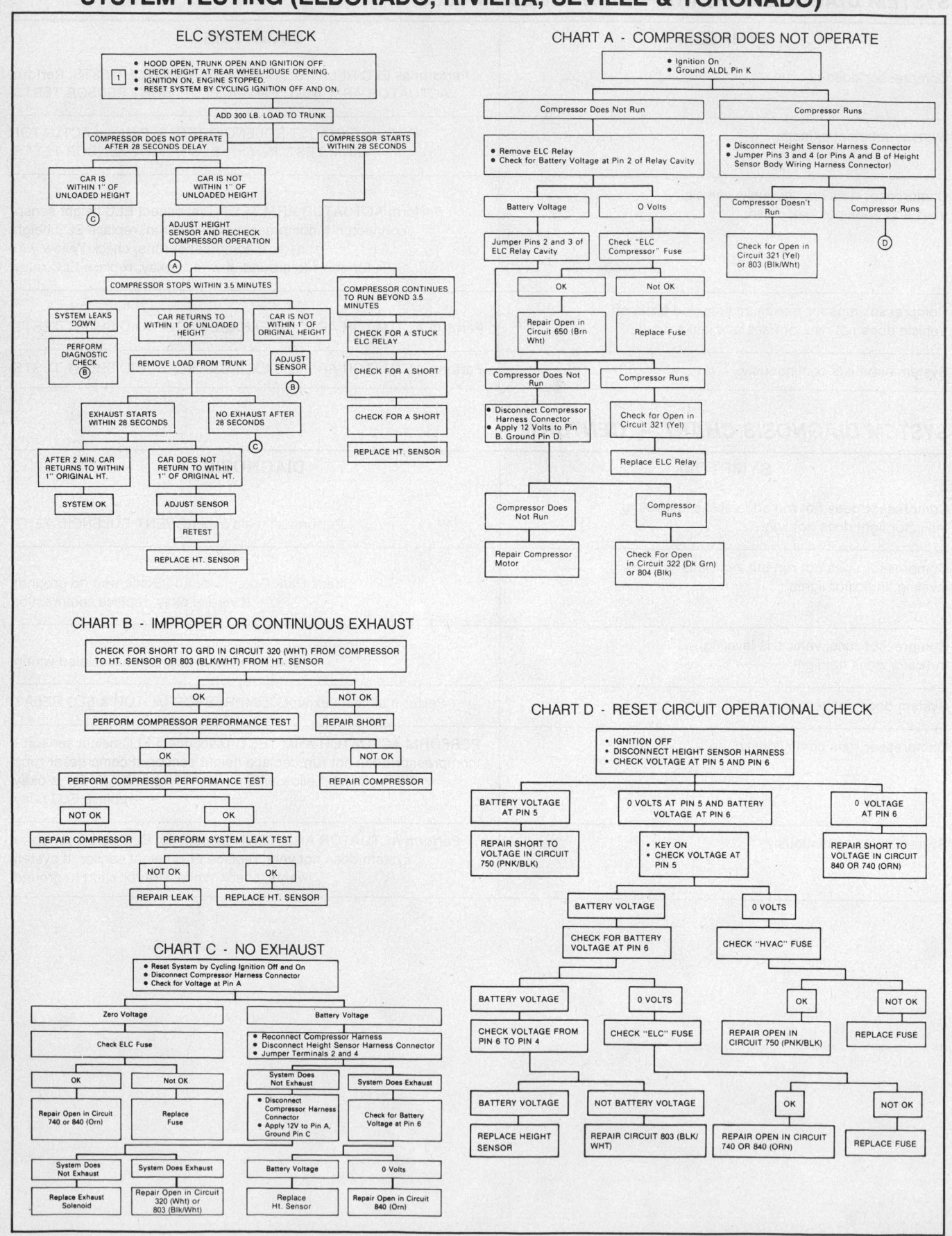

Section 12

STEERING

CONTENTS

NOTE: **ALSO SEE GENERAL INDEX**

Steering

STANDARD STEERING COLUMN TROUBLE SHOOTING

CONDITION	POSSIBLE CAUSE	CORRECTION
Noise in Steering	Coupling pulled apart	See STEERING COLUMNS
	Column not correctly aligned	See STEERING COLUMNS
	Broken lower joint	Replace joint
	Horn contact ring not lubricated	See STEERING COLUMNS
	Bearings not lubricated	See STEERING COLUMNS
	Bearing worn or broken	Replace bearing and lubricate
	Shaft snap ring not properly seated	Reseat or replace snap ring
	Plastic spherical joint not lubricated	See STEERING COLUMNS
	Shroud or housing loose	Tighten holding screws
	Lock plate retaining ring not seated	See STEERING COLUMNS
	Loose sight shield	Tighten holding screws
High Steering Shaft Effort	Column assembly misaligned	See STEERING COLUMNS
	Improperly installed dust shield	Adjust or replace
	Damaged upper or lower bearing	Replace bearings
	Tight steering universal joint	See STEERING COLUMNS
High Shift Effort	Column is out of alignment	See STEERING COLUMNS
	Improperly installed dust shield	Adjust or replace
	Seals or bearings not lubricated	See STEERING COLUMNS
	Mounting bracket screws too long	Replace with new shorter screws
	Burrs on shift tube	Remove burrs or replace tube
	Lower bowl bearing assembled wrong	See STEERING COLUMNS
	Shift tube bent or broken	Replace as necessary
	Improper adjustment of shift levers	See STEERING COLUMNS
Improper Trans. Shifting	Sheared shift tube joint	Replace as necessary
	Sheared lower shaft lever weld joint	Replace as necessary
	Improper shift lever adjustment	See STEERING COLUMNS
	Improper gate plate adjustment	See STEERING COLUMNS
Excess Play in Column	Instrument panel bracket bolts loose	Tighten bolts and check bracket
	Broken weld nut on jacket	See STEERING COLUMNS
	Instrument bracket capsule sheared	See STEERING COLUMNS
	Column bracket/jacket bolts loose	Tighten bolts and check bracket
Steering Locks in Gear	Release lever mechanism damaged	See STEERING COLUMNS

TILT STEERING COLUMN TROUBLE SHOOTING

CONDITION	POSSIBLE CAUSE	CORRECTION
Steering Wheel Loose	Excess clearance in support	Check and replace if necessary
	Excess clearance in housing/pivot pin	Check and replace if necessary
	Damaged anti-lash spring in spheres	See TILT STEERING COLUMNS
	Upper bearing not seated properly	See TILT STEERING COLUMNS
	Upper bearing inner race seal missing	Replace if necessary
	Improperly adjusted tilt/telescopic lock	See STEERING COLUMNS
	Loose support screws	Tighten and check bracket
	Bearing preload spring missing/broken	Replace spring
	Housing loose on jacket	Tighten and/or replace screws
Play in Column Mount	Loose support screws	Tighten and check bracket
	Loose shoes in housing	See TILT STEERING COLUMNS
	Loose tilt head pivot pins	See TILT STEERING COLUMNS
	Loose shoe lock pin in support	See TILT STEERING COLUMNS
Housing Scraping on Bowl	Bowl bent or out of round	See TILT STEERING COLUMNS
Wheel Will Not Lock	Shoe seized on its pivot pin	See TILT STEERING COLUMNS
	Shoe may have burrs/dirt in them	Clean or replace
	Shoe lock spring weak/broken	Replace if necessary

TILT STEERING COLUMN TROUBLE SHOOTING (Cont.)

CONDITION	POSSIBLE CAUSE	CORRECTION
Wheel Fails to Return	Pivot pins are bound up	Clean or replace
	Wheel tilt spring is damaged	See TILT STEERING COLUMNS
	Turn signal switch wires too tight	Loosen and check operation
Noise When Tilting	Upper tilt bumpers worn	Replace if necessary
	Tilt spring rubbing in housing	Adjust and check operation
Hard Steering	Incorrect tire pressure	Inflate to proper pressure
	Lack of lubricant in steering linkage	Service Steering, Suspension and Linkage
	Improper front end alignment	See FRONT ALIGNMENT
	Improper steering gear adjustment	See STEERING GEARS

MANUAL STEERING GEAR TROUBLE SHOOTING

CONDITION	POSSIBLE CAUSE	CORRECTION
Rattle or Chucking Noise in Rack and Pinion	Rack and pinion mounting bracket loose	Tighten all mounting bolts
	Lack of/or incorrect lubricant	See RACK & PINION STEERING
	Steering gear mounting bolts loose	Tighten all mounting bolts
Excessive Play	Front wheel bearing improperly adjusted	See FRONT SUSPENSION
	Loose or worn steering linkage	See STEERING LINKAGE
	Loose or worn steering gear shaft	See MANUAL STEERING GEARS
	Steering arm loose on gear shaft	See MANUAL STEERING GEARS
	Steering gear housing bolts loose	Tighten all mounting bolts
	Steering gear adjustment too loose	See MANUAL STEERING GEAR
	Steering arms loose on knuckles	Tighten and check steering linkage
	Rack and pinion mounting loose	Tighten all mounting bolts
	Rack and pinion out of adjustment	See adjustment in STEERING
	Tie rod end loose	Tighten and check steering linkage
	Excessive Pitman shaft-to-ball nut lash	See STEERING
Poor Returnability	Lack of lubricant in ball joint or linkage	Lubricate and service systems
	Binding in linkage or ball joints	See STEERING LINKAGE and SUSPENSION
	Improper front end alignment	See WHEEL ALIGNMENT
	Improper steering gear adjustment	See STEERING
	Improper tire pressure	Inflate to proper pressure
	Tie rod binding	See FRONT SUSPENSION
	Shaft seal rubbing shaft	See STEERING COLUMNS
Excessive Vertical Motion	Improper tire pressure	Inflate to proper pressure
	Tires, wheels or rotors out of balance	Balance tires then check wheels and rotors
	Worn or faulty shock absorbers	Check and replace if necessary
	Loose tie rod ends or steering	Tighten or replace if necessary
	Loose or worn wheel bearings	See SUSPENSION
Steering Pulls to One Side	Improper tire pressure	Inflate to proper pressure
	Front tires are different sizes	Rotate or replace if necessary
	Wheel bearings not adjusted properly	See FRONT SUSPENSION
	Bent or broken suspension components	See FRONT SUSPENSION
	Improper wheel alignment	See WHEEL ALIGNMENT
	Brakes dragging	See BRAKES
Instability	Low or uneven tire pressure	Inflate to proper pressure
	Loose or worn wheel bearings	See FRONT SUSPENSION
	Loose or worn idler arm bushing	See FRONT SUSPENSION
	Loose or worn strut bushings	See FRONT SUSPENSION
	Incorrect front wheel alignment	See WHEEL ALIGNMENT
	Steering gear not centered	See MANUAL STEERING GEARS
	Springs or shock absorbers defective	Check and replace if necessary
	Improper cross shaft	See MANUAL STEERING GEARS

Steering
POWER STEERING TROUBLE SHOOTING

CONDITION	POSSIBLE CAUSE	CORRECTION
Rattle or Chucking Noise in Steering	Pressure hoses touching engine parts	Adjust to proper clearance
	Loose Pitman shaft	Adjust or replace if necessary
	Tie rods ends or Pitman arm loose	Tighten and check system
	Rack and pinion mounts loose	Tighten all mounting bolts
	Free play in worm and piston assembly	See POWER STEERING GEARS
	Loose sector shaft or thrust bearing adjustment	See POWER STEERING GEARS
	Free play in pot coupling	See STEERING COLUMNS
	Worn shaft serrations	See STEERING COLUMNS
Growl in Steering Pump	Excessive pressure in hoses	Restricted hoses see POWER STEERING GEARS
	Scored pressure plates	See POWER STEERING GEARS
	Scored thrust plates or rotor	See POWER STEERING GEARS
	Extreme wear of cam ring	See POWER STEERING GEARS
Rattle in Steering Pump	Vanes not installed properly	See POWER STEERING PUMPS
	Vanes sticking in rotor slots	See POWER STEERING PUMPS
Swish Noise in Pump	Defective flow control valve	See POWER STEERING PUMPS
Groan in Steering Pump	Air in fluid	See POWER STEERING PUMPS
	Poor pressure hose connection	Tighten and check, replace if necessary
Squawk When Turning	Damper "O" ring on valve spool cut	See POWER STEERING PUMPS
Moan or Whine in Pump	Pump shaft bearing scored	Replace bearing and fluid
	Air in fluid or fluid level low	See POWER STEERING PUMPS
	Hose or column grounded	Check and replace if necessary
	Cover "O" ring missing or damaged	See POWER STEERING PUMPS
	Valve cover baffle missing or damaged	See POWER STEERING PUMPS
	Interference of components in pump	See POWER STEERING PUMPS
	Loose or poor bracket alignment	Correct or replace if necessary
Hissing When Parking	Internal leakage in steering gear	Check valve assembly first
Chirp in Steering Pump	Loose or worn power steering belt	Adjust or replace if neceesary
Buzzing When Not Steering	Noisy pump	See POWER STEERING PUMPS
	Free play in steering shaft bearing	See STEERING COLUMNS
	Bearing loose on shaft serrations	See STEERING COLUMNS
Clicking Noise in Pump	Pump slippers too long	See POWER STEERING PUMPS
	Broken slipper springs	See POWER STEERING PUMPS
	Excessive wear or nicked rotors	See POWER STEERING PUMPS
	Damaged cam contour	See POWER STEERING PUMPS
Poor Return of Wheel	Wheel rubbing against turn signal	See STEERING WHEEL SWITCHES
	Flange rubbing steering gear adjuster	See STEERING COLUMNS
	Tight or frozen steering shaft bearing	See STEERING COLUMNS
	Steering gear out of adjustment	See Adjustment in STEERING
	Sticking or plugged spool valve	See POWER STEERING PUMPS
	Improper front end alignment	See WHEEL ALIGNMENT
	Wheel bearings worn or loose	See FRONT SUSPENSION
	Ties rods or ball joints binding	Check and replace if necessary
	Intermediate shaft joints binding	See STEERING COLUMNS
	Kinked pressure hoses	Correct or replace if necessary
	Loose housing head spanner nut	See POWER STEERING GEARS
	Damaged valve lever	See POWER STEERING GEARS
	Sector shaft adjusted too tight	See ADJUSTMENTS in POWER STEERING GEARS
	Worm thrust bearing adjusted too tight	See ADJUSTMENTS in POWER STEERING GEARS
	Reaction ring sticking in cylinder	See POWER STEERING GEARS
	Reaction ring sticking in housing head	See POWER STEERING GEARS
	Steering pump internal leakage	See POWER STEERING PUMPS
	Steering gear-to-column misalignment	See STEERING COLUMNS
	Lack of lubrication in linkage	Service front suspension
	Lack of lubrication in ball joints	Service front suspension

POWER STEERING TROUBLE SHOOTING (Cont.)

CONDITION	POSSIBLE CAUSE	CORRECTION
Increased Effort When Turning Wheel Fast Foaming, Milky Power Steering Fluid, Low Fluid Level or Low Pressure	High internal pump leakage	See POWER STEERING PUMPS
	Power steering pump belt slipping	Adjust or replace if necessary
	Low fluid level	Check and fill to proper level
	Engine idle speed to low	Adjust to correct setting
	Air in pump fluid system	See POWER STEERING PUMPS
	Pump output low	See POWER STEERING PUMPS
	Steering gear malfunctioning	See POWER STEERING GEARS
Wheel Surges or Jerks	Low fluid level	Check and fill to proper level
	Loose fan belt	Adjust or replace if necessary
	Insufficient pump pressure	See POWER STEERING PUMPS
	Sticky flow control valve	See POWER STEERING PUMPS
	Linkage hitting oil pan at full turn	Replace bent components
Kick Back or Free Play	Air in pump fluid system	See POWER STEERING PUMPS
	Worn poppet valve in steering gear	See POWER STEERING GEARS
	Excessive over center lash	See POWER STEERING GEARS
	Thrust bearing out of adjustment	See POWER STEERING GEARS
	Free play in pot coupling	See POWER STEERING PUMPS
	Steering gear coupling loose on shaft	See POWER STEERING PUMPS
	Steering disc mounting bolts loose	Tighten or replace if necessary
	Coupling loose on worm shaft	Tighten or replace if necessary
	Improper sector shaft adjustment	See POWER STEERING GEARS
	Excessive worm piston side play	See POWER STEERING GEARS
	Damaged valve lever	See POWER STEERING GEARS
	Universal joint loose	Tighten or replace if necessary
	Defective rotary valve	See POWER STEERING GEARS
No Power When Parking	Sticking flow control valve	See POWER STEERING PUMPS
	Insufficient pump pressure output	See POWER STEERING PUMPS
	Excessive internal pump leakage	See POWER STEERING PUMPS
	Excessive internal gear leakage	See POWER STEERING PUMPS
	Flange rubs against gear adjust plug	See STEERING COLUMNS
	Loose pump belt	Adjust or replace if necessary
	Low fluid level	Check and add proper amount of fluid
	Engine idle too low	Adjust to correct setting
	Steering gear-to-column misaligned	See STEERING COLUMNS
No Power, Left Turns	Left turn reaction seal "O" ring worn	See POWER STEERING GEARS
	Left turn reaction seal damaged/missing	See POWER STEERING GEARS
	Cylinder head "O" ring damaged	See POWER STEERING PUMPS
No Power, Right Turns	Column pot coupling bottomed	See STEERING COLUMNS
	Right turn reaction seal "O" ring worn	See POWER STEERING GEARS
	Right turn reaction seal damaged	See POWER STEERING GEARS
	Internal leakage through piston end plug	See POWER STEERING GEARS
	Internal leakage through side plugs	See POWER STEERING GEARS
Lack of Effort in Turning	Left and/or right reaction seal worn	Replace, see POWER STEERING GEARS
	Left and/or right reaction oil passageway not drilled	Check housing and cylinder head
	Left and/or right reaction seal sticking in cylinder head	See POWER STEERING GEARS
Wanders to One Side	Front end alignment incorrect	See WHEEL ALIGNMENT
	Unbalanced steering gear valve	See POWER STEERING GEARS
Low Pressure Due to Steering Pump	Flow control valve stuck or inoperative	See POWER STEERING
	Pressure plate not flat against cam ring	See POWER STEERING PUMPS
	Extreme wear of cam ring	Replace and check adjustments
	Scored plate, thrust plate or rotor	See POWER STEERING PUMPS
	Vanes not installed properly	See POWER STEERING PUMPS
	Vanes sticking in rotor slots	See POWER STEERING PUMPS
	Cracked/broken thrust or pressure plate	See POWER STEERING PUMPS

CHRYSLER MOTORS

REMOVAL & INSTALLATION

PRECAUTION

Steering column must be lowered or removed for access to ignition switch on some vehicles. Steering wheel, directional signal and other components must be removed to gain access to lock cylinder retaining tab for lock cylinder removal.

HORN BUTTON

Removal & Installation

Disconnect battery ground cable. Remove steering wheel center pad assembly. Disconnect horn electrical connectors. Remove horn switch. To install, reverse removal procedure.

STEERING WHEEL

Removal & Installation

With center pad and horn electrical connectors disconnected, remove steering wheel nut and washer. Using Steering Wheel Puller (C-3428B), remove steering wheel. To install, reverse removal procedure.

Installation

To install steering wheel, reverse removal procedure.

Fig. 1: Horizon America & Omni America Steering Column Components

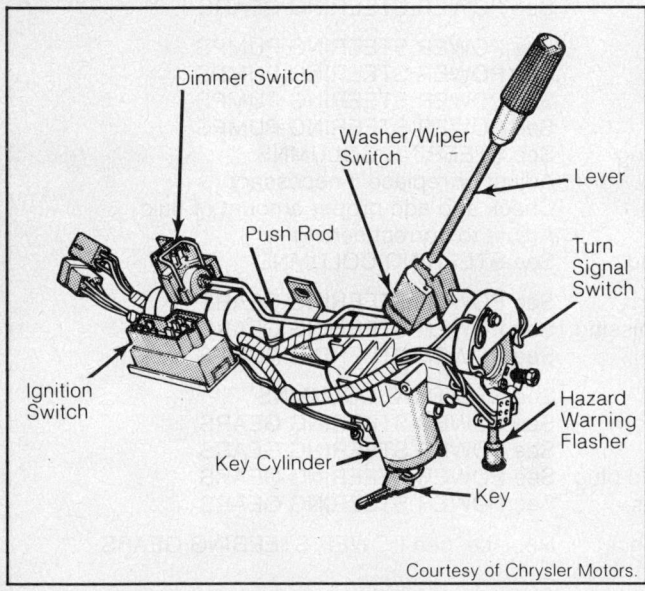

Courtesy of Chrysler Motors.

TURN SIGNAL SWITCH

Removal (Horizon America & Omni America)

Disconnect battery ground cable and steering column electrical connector. Remove steering wheel as previously described. Remove 4 lower column cover attaching screws. Remove lower column cover. Remove wiper/washer switch assembly. Remove wiring clip, turn signal switch retainer, and turn signal switch.

Installation

To install turn signal switch, reverse removal procedure.

Removal (All Others)

1) Disconnect battery ground cable. Remove horn pad and steering wheel. If equipped, remove insulation from below steering column. Remove lower instrument panel bezel. Loosen Allen screw on gearshift housing. Remove gearshift indicator.

2) If equipped with tilt column, position column at its mid-point. Remove 2 column-to-lower panel reinforcement nuts. Remove mounting bracket from steering column by removing 4 attaching bolts.

3) Pry out plastic buttons retaining wiring trough to column. Remove trough. Disconnect turn signal wiring harness. Wrap a piece of tape around connector to prevent snagging when removing switch.

4) On standard columns, place gearshift lever in full clockwise position. Remove screw holding turn signal switch pivot. Leave this assembly in its installed location. Remove 3 screws and bearing retainer fastening turn signal switch to upper bearing housing.

5) On tilt columns, remove plastic cover from lock plate. While depressing lock plate with Lock Plate Depressor (C-4156), pry retaining ring out of groove with screwdriver. The full load of upper bearing spring should not be relieved as retaining ring will turn too easily making removal more difficult.

6) On all models, remove lock plate, canceling cam, and cam spring. Place turn signal switch in right turn position. Remove hazard warning switch knob attaching screw. Remove 3 turn signal switch-to-steering column screws.

7) Remove turn signal/hazard warning switch by gently pulling switch up from column while straightening and guiding wires up through column opening.

Installation

1) On fixed columns, lightly lubricate turn signal switch pivot with grease. Wrap a piece of tape around connector to ensure smooth installation. Guide connector through opening in steering column. Carefully guide wires down through column.

2) Remove tape. Position turn signal switch and bearing retainer into position on upper bearing housing. Secure with 3 mounting screws. Place turn signal lever into switch pivot. Secure lever with screw through pivot.

3) On tilt columns, position turn signal switch in upper column housing. Place switch in right turn position. Secure with 3 mounting screws. Put link in position between turn signal switch and pivot. Secure link with screw.

4) On all models, install canceling cam, cam spring, and lock plate. Using Lock Plate Depressor (C-4156), depress lock plate. Install new retaining ring, hazard warning knob and plastic cover on lock plate.

5) Connect wiring harness connectors. Position wiring trough around wires. Mount wiring trough to column jacket with 4 plastic buttons.

6) On tilt column, secure mounting bracket to column with 4 bolts. Tighten bolts to 110 INCH lbs. (12 N.m). Position steering column into place in lower reinforcement, install nuts. Tighten nuts to 110 INCH lbs. (12 N.m).

7) On all models, place gearshift lever into "REVERSE" position. Position gearshift indicator at center of "REVERSE" position. Tighten Allen screw. Place column shift into "PARK" position.

CHRYSLER MOTORS (Cont.)

Fig. 2: Exploded View of Upper Steering Column (All Except Horizon America & Omni America)

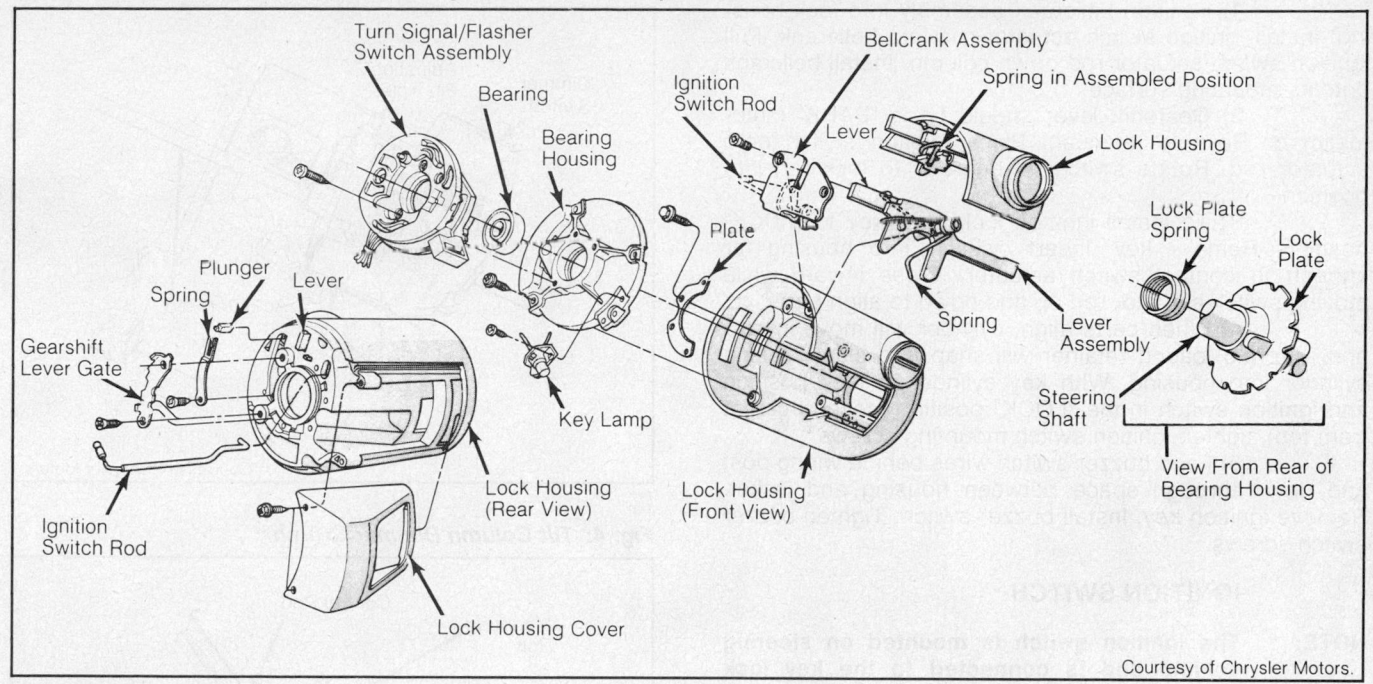

Courtesy of Chrysler Motors.

8) Install instrument panel bezels and insulation. Install steering wheel. Install horn pad. Connect battery ground cable. Ensure proper operation of turn signal, hazard warning, horn, and beam selector.

CRUISE CONTROL SWITCH
Removal
1) Disconnect battery ground cable. Remove lower steering column cover. On tilt column, drop column down, taking care not to damage gear indicator cable. Remove 4 screws attaching support bracket to column jacket. Remove wiring through.

2) On fixed column, unsnap 4 wiring trough plastic retainer clips. Remove wiring trough. Disconnect cruise control switch wiring harness connector.

3) On all models, remove wiper control knob from end of lever. Remove 2 screws attaching cruise control switch.

4) On tilt column, remove steering wheel. Attach flexible guide wire to lower end of cruise control switch harness. Pull wires up through lock housing between lock plate and side of housing. Disconnect guide wire. Remove switch.

5) On fixed column, remove 2 upper steering column lock housing cover retaining screws. Gently remove switch and harness from column, taking care to avoid damaging wires while pulling them through column.

Installation
1) On fixed column, insert harness connector through turn signal lever opening in column. Pull harness connector down and out lower end.

2) On tilt columns, insert harness wires through turn signal lever opening in column. Pull harness upward through upper housing. Attach guide wire to switch wiring harness. Pull wires gently downward through steering column opening between lock plate and side of housing.

3) On all models, reconnect wiring harness connector. Install 2 screws to attach cruise control switch to column. Push wiper control knob in place. To complete installation, reverse removal procedure.

LOCK CYLINDER
Removal (Horizon America & Omni America)
1) Disconnect battery ground cable. Remove steering wheel, both column covers, turn signal switch and wiper/washer switch.

2) Using a hacksaw blade, cut the upper 1/4" from key cylinder retainer pin boss. Using a drift punch, drive roll pin from housing. Remove key cylinder.

NOTE: **Removal and installation of lock cylinder must be done with key removed.**

Installation
Insert cylinder into housing. Ensure it engages lug on ignition switch driver. Install new roll pin.

Removal (All Others)
1) Remove turn signal switch, horn pad and key light ground wire. Remove ignition key light retaining screw. Lift key light assembly out of way.

2) Remove 4 bearing housing-to-lock housing screws. Remove snap ring, bearing housing, lock plate spring, and lock plate from steering shaft.

3) Place cylinder in "LOCK" position. Remove key. Remove buzzer switch retaining screw. Lift out buzzer switch. Remove 2 ignition switch attaching screws, rotate switch 90 degrees. Slide switch off actuating rod.

4) Remove 2 screws from dimmer switch. Disengage switch from actuator rod. Remove 2 screws from bellcrank. Slide bellcrank up into lock housing until it can be disconnected from ignition switch actuator rod.

5) Insert small screwdrivers into lock cylinder release slots. Push in to release spring loaded lock retainers. Pull lock cylinder out of housing bore.

CHRYSLER MOTORS (Cont.)

Installation

1) Position bellcrank assembly into lock housing. Install ignition switch actuator rod into bellcrank. Pull ignition switch actuator rod down column. Install bellcrank onto its mounting surface.

2) Gearshift lever should be in "PARK" (automatic) or Reverse (manual). Place ignition switch onto actuator rod. Rotate switch 90 degrees to lock rod into position.

3) To install ignition lock, turn key to "LOCK" position. Remove key. Insert cylinder into housing far enough to contact switch actuator. Press inward while moving switch actuator rod up and down to align parts.

4) When parts align, cylinder will move inward and a spring loaded retainer will snap into place locking cylinder into housing. With key cylinder in lock position and ignition switch in the "LOCK" position (second detent from top), tighten ignition switch mounting screws.

5) Feed buzzer switch wires behind wiring post and down through space between housing and jacket. Remove ignition key. Install buzzer switch. Tighten buzzer switch screws.

IGNITION SWITCH

NOTE: The ignition switch is mounted on steering column and is connected to the key lock assembly by a remote lock rod.

Removal

1) Disconnect battery ground cable. Disconnect ignition switch electrical connectors. Place lock cylinder in "LOCK" position. Remove key.

2) Remove screw and lift out buzzer/chime switch (if equipped). Remove 2 screws attaching ignition switch. Rotate switch 90 degrees and slide off actuating rod.

Installation

1) Fit actuator rod into slider by turning switch 90 degrees, inserting rod, and rotating back 90 degrees. Mount switch on column. Install, but do not tighten screws.

2) Position ignition switch with actuator rod at second detent from top. Push down lightly to remove lash in actuator rod. Finger tighten screws.

3) Install buzzer/chime switch (if equipped). Tighten screws. Install wiring connectors. Connect battery cable. Check switch for proper operation.

DIMMER SWITCH

Removal

Disconnect battery ground cable. Remove lower steering column cover. Disconnect dimmer switch electrical connector. Remove mounting nut and screw from switch. Disengage switch from push rod. Remove switch.

Installation

1) Firmly push rod into switch. Compressing switch, insert two 3/32" drill bit shanks through alignment holes.

2) Reposition upper end of push rod into pocket of washer/wiper switch. With a light rearward pressure on switch, install nut and screw. Remove drill bits.

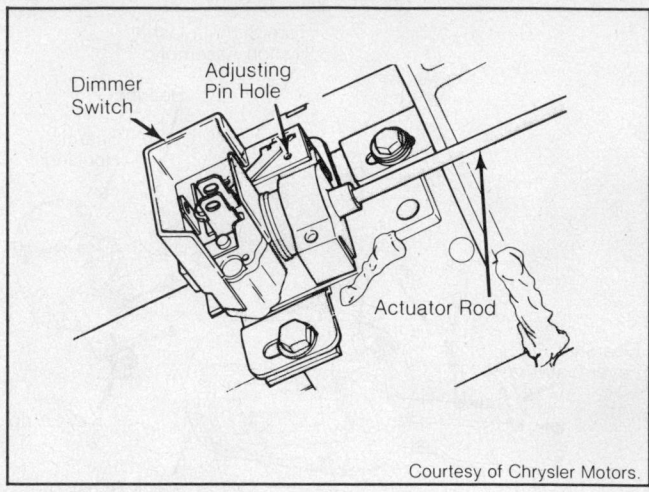

Fig. 3: Fixed Column Dimmer Switch

Courtesy of Chrysler Motors.

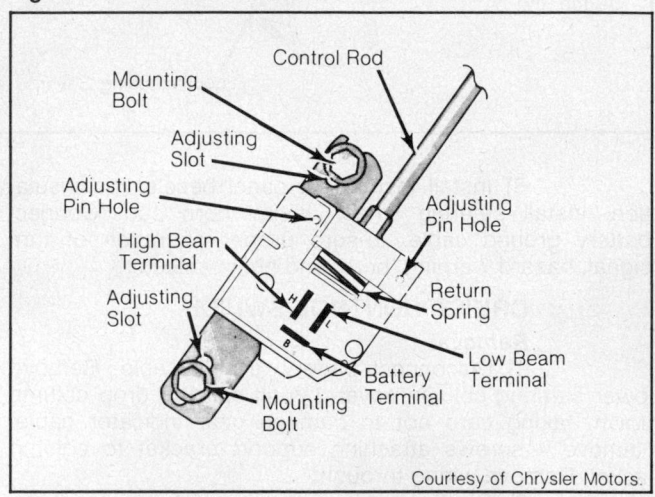

Fig. 4: Tilt Column Dimmer Switch

Courtesy of Chrysler Motors.

WINDSHIELD WIPER/WASHER SWITCH

Removal (Horizon America & Omni America)

1) Disconnect battery ground cable. Disconnect electrical switch from both washer/wiper switch and turn signal switch. Remove lower column cover. With fingers only, carefully lift out horn button.

2) Remove washer/wiper switch hider disc. Rotate ignition key to "OFF" position. Turn steering wheel so that access hole in hub area is at 9 o'clock position.

3) Using a flat-bladed screwdriver, loosen turn signal lever screw through access hole. Disengage dimmer push rod from washer/wiper switch. Unsnap wiring clip. Remove switch.

Installation

To install, reverse removal procedure taking care to properly position dimmer push rod in washer/wiper switch and to secure clip. Be sure to install washer/wiper switch hider disc.

Removal (All Others)

1) Disconnect battery ground cable. Remove steering wheel as previously described. Remove lower instrument panel bezel.

CHRYSLER MOTORS (Cont.)

2) On tilt columns, remove lock plate cover and lock plate). Remove gearshift indicator. Remove 2 nuts mounting column to lower panel reinforcement. Remove mounting bracket from steering column by removing 4 attaching bolts.

3) On all models, remove wiring trough from steering column by unsnapping 4 plastic retainer clips. Remove turn signal switch.

4) Remove 2 lock housing cover attaching screws. Remove cover. Gently pull wiper switch up from column while guiding wires up through column opening.

Installation
To install, reverse removal procedure.

TIGHTENING SPECIFICATIONS

Application	Ft. Lbs. (N.m)
Steering Wheel Retaining Nut	45 (61)

EAGLE PREMIER

REMOVAL & INSTALLATION

PRECAUTION

Steering column must be lowered or removed for access to ignition switch on some vehicles. Steering wheel, turn signal and other components must be removed to gain access to lock cylinder retaining tab for lock cylinder removal.

HORN BUTTON

Removal & Installation
Unsnap horn button from steering wheel. Unplug electrical connectors. Remove horn button. To install, reverse removal procedure.

STEERING WHEEL

Removal & Installation
Remove horn button. Note position of reference mark on end of steering shaft. Remove steering wheel nut. Slide steering wheel off shaft to remove. To install, reverse removal procedure, aligning reference marks.

TURN SIGNAL SWITCH

Removal
1) Turn signal switch is an integral part of headlight pod on left side of steering column. Disconnect battery ground cable. Remove 3 instrument panel lower cover retaining screws and lower cover.

2) Remove 6 headlight pod retaining screws from bottom and top of headlight pod. Remove wiring harness tie wraps from under steering column. Loosen steering column connector retaining nut.

3) Using a screwdriver, pry headlight pod connector from steering column connector. Push headlight switch pod connector out of channels in column connector.

Fig. 1: Exploded View of Eagle Premier Upper Steering Column Assembly

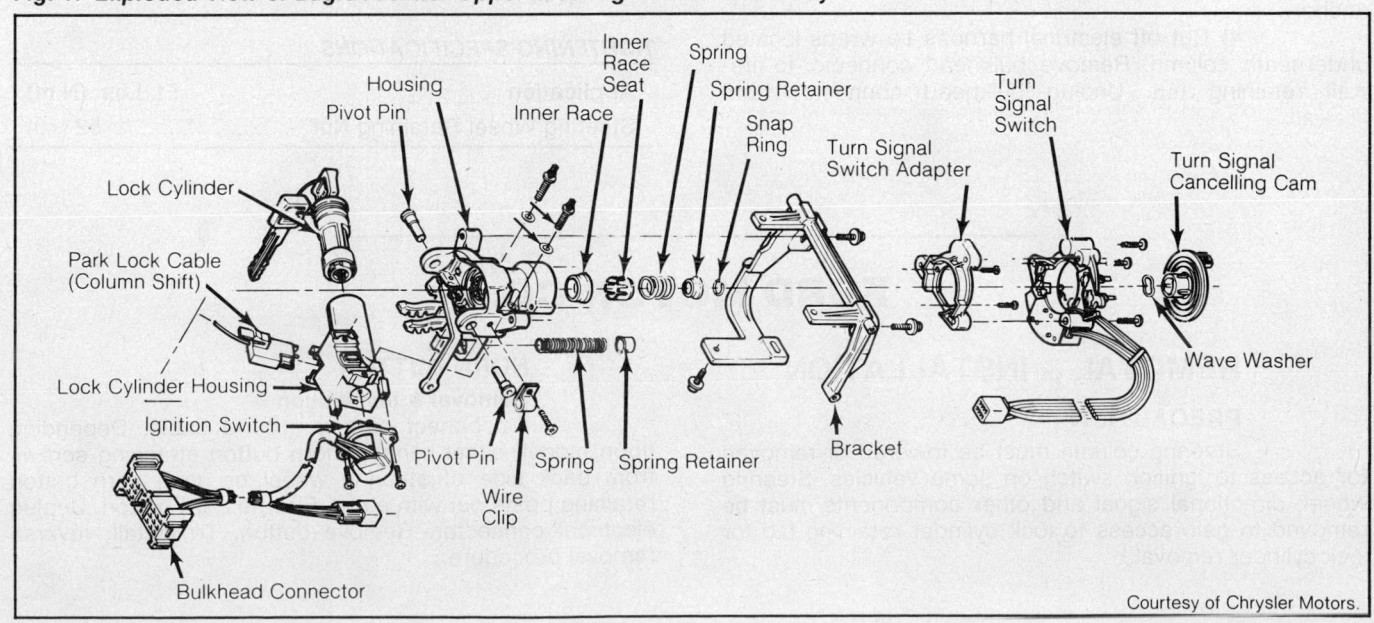

Courtesy of Chrysler Motors.

Tilt steering column is shown. Fixed steering column is similar.

EAGLE PREMIER (Cont.)

4) Pull headlight switch assembly from headlight switch pod. Carefully pull headlight switch wiring through housing to remove pod. Remove 2 Phillips screws inside pod, on steering column if necessary.

CRUISE CONTROL SWITCH

Removal & Installation

Unsnap horn button from steering wheel. Unplug electrical connectors. Remove horn button. Pry up on cover in steering wheel cross bar to remove cruise control switch. To install, reverse removal procedure.

LOCK CYLINDER

Removal

1) Remove steering wheel and turn signal switch as previously described. Remove heat/AC pod in same manner. Pry off ignition switch trim ring.

2) Remove screws retaining headlight pod housing and heat/AC pod housings. Pass headlight pod and heat/AC pod through openings in housings. Remove upper and lower steering column covers.

3) Insert ignition key in lock cylinder. Turn key to align key with groove in bottom of lock cylinder housing. Pressing in locking tab located in bottom of lock cylinder housing, pull out lock cylinder.

Installation

To install, reverse removal procedure.

IGNITION SWITCH

Removal

1) Disconnect battery ground cable. Remove instrument panel lower cover, steering wheel and turn signal switch as previously described. Remove heat/AC pod in same manner. Pry off ignition switch trim ring.

2) Remove screws retaining headlight pod housing and heat/AC pod housings. Pass headlight pod and heat/AC pod through openings in housings. Remove upper and lower steering column covers.

3) Remove 2 ignition switch retaining screws. Separate ignition switch from lock cylinder housing. Remove harness anchor retaining screw and harness anchor.

4) Cut off electrical harness tie wraps located underneath column. Remove bulkhead connector-to-firewall retaining nut. Unplug bulkhead connector from firewall.

5) Disconnect headlight pod and heat/AC pod connectors from ignition switch harness connector. Remove ignition switch and ignition switch harness.

Installation

1) Connect pod connectors to ignition switch connector from wire side of connector. Install bulkhead connector. Tighten bulkhead connector retaining nut.

2) Position ignition switch. Install and tighten screws. Secure harness with tie wraps. Install harness anchor. Install harness anchor screw.

3) Install upper and lower column covers. Pass pods through pod housings. Install and tighten pod housing attaching screws. Snap ignition switch trim ring in place.

4) Install pods into pod housings. Install pod retaining screws. Install instrument panel lower cover, steering wheel and turn signal switch as previously described.

5) To complete installation, reverse removal procedure. Check operation of ignition switch, headlight pod, heat/AC pod and lock cylinder. Reconnect battery cable.

DIMMER SWITCH

**Removal & Installation
(Eagle Premier)**

The dimmer switch is an integral part of headlight pod switch. Removal and installation is same as turn signal switch. See TURN SIGNAL SWITCH in this article.

WINDSHIELD WIPER/WASHER SWITCH

The windshield wiper/washer switch is an integral part of headlight pod switch. Removal and installation is same as turn signal switch. See TURN SIGNAL SWITCH in this article.

HEAT/AC SWITCH

Heat/AC switch is a pod switch, on right side of column, similar to headlight pod. Removal and installation is similar to the turn signal switch.

TIGHTENING SPECIFICATIONS

Application	Ft. Lbs. (N.m)
Steering Wheel Retaining Nut	52 (70)

FORD MOTOR CO.

REMOVAL & INSTALLATION

PRECAUTION

Steering column must be lowered or removed for access to ignition switch on some vehicles. Steering wheel, directional signal and other components must be removed to gain access to lock cylinder retaining tab for lock cylinder removal.

HORN BUTTON

Removal & Installation

Disconnect battery ground cable. Depending upon model, either remove horn button attaching screws from back side of steering wheel or push horn button retaining posts out with a rod. Elevate horn button. Unplug electrical connector. Remove button. To install, reverse removal procedure.

FORD MOTOR CO. (Cont.)

STEERING WHEEL

Removal & Installation
(Continental, Sable & Taurus)

Disconnect battery ground cable. Remove horn pad. Remove and discard steering wheel retaining bolt. Grasp steering wheel and pull off. DO NOT use steering wheel puller to remove steering wheel. To install, reverse removal procedure. Install and tighten new steering wheel retaining bolt.

Removal & Installation (All Others)

Disconnect battery ground cable. Remove steering wheel cover. Loosen steering wheel mounting bolt. Using Steering Wheel Remover (T67L-3600-A), remove steering wheel. Remove and discard steering wheel mounting bolt. To install, reverse removal procedure. Install and tighten new steering wheel mounting bolt.

Fig. 1: Exploded View of Steering Column Assembly (Modular Column)

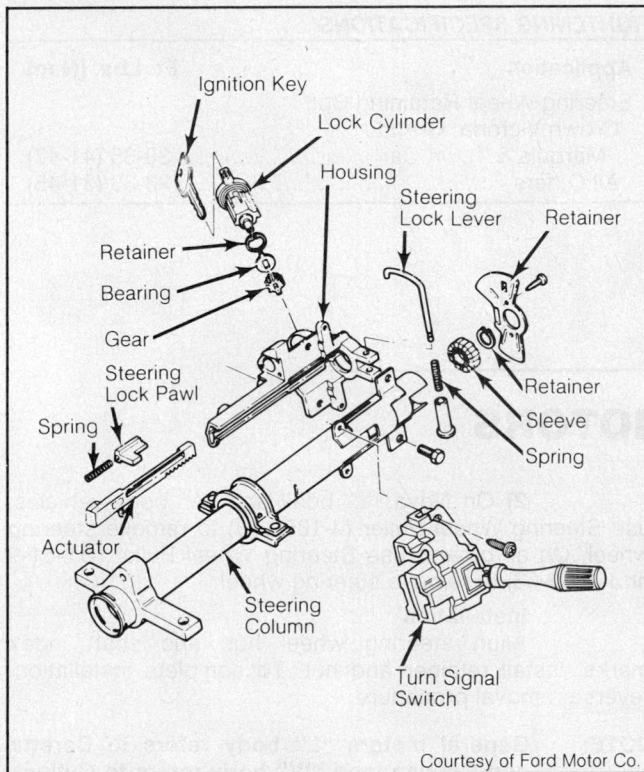

Courtesy of Ford Motor Co.

TURN SIGNAL SWITCH

Removal

NOTE: **On models equipped with tilt column, remove extension shroud by unsnapping shroud from retainer clip at 9 o'clock position.**

1) Disconnect battery ground cable. Remove upper and lower steering column shrouds. Remove switch lever by grasping and pulling it straight out.

2) Peel back foam switch cover from turn signal switch. Disconnect electrical connectors. Remove 2 screws attaching switch to the lock cylinder housing. Disengage switch from housing.

Installation

To install, reverse removal procedure.

Fig. 2: Exploded View of Steering Column Assembly (Except Modular Column)

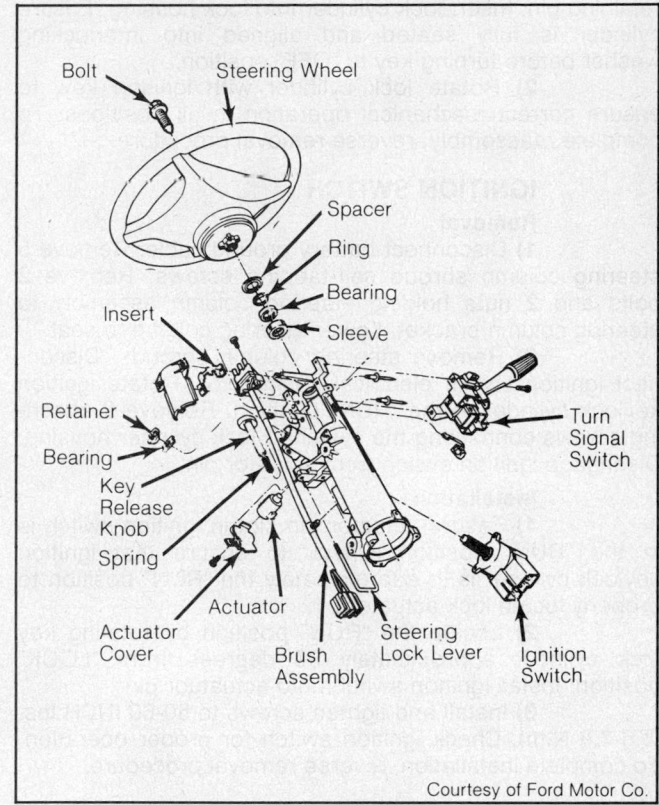

Courtesy of Ford Motor Co.

CRUISE CONTROL SWITCH

Removal

1) Remove steering wheel hub cover. Remove and discard steering wheel attaching bolt. Remove steering wheel as previously described.

2) Remove 6 screws attaching back cover to steering wheel. Separate control switch connector from terminal on back cover. Remove cruise control switch.

Installation

To install, reverse removal procedure. Ensure control switch harness is positioned properly in lower steering wheel spoke. Use a new steering wheel attaching bolt.

LOCK CYLINDER

NOTE: **For tilt steering column ONLY, remove upper extension shroud by unsnapping shroud from retainer clip at 9 o'clock position. On Tempo and Topaz, remove 2 shroud halves by removing 5 attaching screws. On Escort, Lnyx and EXP, remove lower shroud.**

Removal

1) Disconnect battery ground cable. Remove shrouds. Disconnect key warning buzzer electrical connector. Rotate ignition key lock cylinder to "ON" position.

2) Place a 1/8" drill bit, or pin into hole casting surrounding lock cylinder. Depress retaining pin while pulling out on lock cylinder to remove it from column.

FORD MOTOR CO. (Cont.)

Installation

1) Turn lock cylinder to "ON" position. Depress retaining pin. Insert lock cylinder into lock housing. Ensure cylinder is fully seated and aligned into interlocking washer before turning key to "OFF" position.

2) Rotate lock cylinder with ignition key, to ensure correct mechanical operation in all positions. To complete reassembly, reverse removal procedure.

IGNITION SWITCH

Removal

1) Disconnect battery ground cable. Remove 5 steering column shroud self-tapping screws. Remove 2 bolts and 2 nuts holding steering column assembly to steering column bracket. Lower steering column to seat.

2) Remove steering column shrouds. Disconnect ignition switch electrical connnector. Rotate ignition keylock cylinder to the "RUN" position. Remove 2 attaching screws connecting the switch to lock cylinder housing. Disengage ignition switch from actuator pin.

Installation

1) Ensure actuator pin slot in ignition switch is in the "RUN" position. Check to ensure that ignition keylock cylinder is in approximately the "RUN" position to properly locate lock actuator pin.

2) Locate the "RUN" position by rotating key lock cylinder approximately 90 degrees from "LOCK" position. Install ignition switch onto actuatuor pin.

3) Install and tighten screws to 50-60 INCH lbs. (5.6-7.9 N.m). Check ignition switch for proper operation. To complete installation, reverse removal procedure.

DIMMER SWITCH

NOTE: **Ford Motor Co. RWD vehicles use an automatic dimmer switch.**

Removal & Installation

On all models, the dimmer switch is an integral part of the turn signal switch. See TURN SIGNAL SWITCH in this article.

WINDSHIELD WIPER/ WASHER SWITCH

Removal & Installation

1) Disconnect battery ground cable. Remove upper and lower shrouds. On front wheel drive models, peel back foam switch cover, remove 2 screws holding switch. Remove switch.

2) On rear wheel drive models, remove 2 mounting screws, disconnect harness from switch. Remove switch. To install, reverse removal procedure.

TIGHTENING SPECIFICATIONS

Application	Ft. Lbs. (N.m)
Steering Wheel Retaining Bolt	
Crown Victoria, Grand	
Marquis & Town Car	30-35 (41-47)
All Others	23-33 (31-45)

GENERAL MOTORS

REMOVAL & INSTALLATION

PRECAUTION

Steering column must be lowered or removed for access to ignition switch on some vehicles. Steering wheel, directional signal and other components must be removed to gain access to lock cylinder retaining tab for lock cylinder removal.

HORN BUTTON

Removal & Installation (General Motors)

Disconnect battery ground cable. On models with sport wheel, lift off horn button, remove 3 screws and take off contact, insulator eyelet and spring. On all other models, remove screws from underside of wheel, partially lift off horn button. Unplug electrical connectors. Remove horn button. To install, reverse removal procedure.

STEERING WHEEL

Removal

1) Disconnect battery ground cable. Remove horn button. On models with tilt and telescoping columns, remove screws securing locking lever and flange to steering wheel hub. On all models, remove steering wheel nut. On Camaro & Firebird, use Steering Wheel Puller (J-2927) to remove steering wheel.

2) On Nova, "L" body and "W" body vehicles, use Steering Wheel Puller (J-1859-03) to remove steering wheel. On all others, use Steering Wheel Puller (BT-61-9 or J-1859-03) to remove steering wheel.

Installation

Align steering wheel hub and shaft index marks. Install retainer and nut. To complete installation, reverse removal procedure.

NOTE: **General motors "L" body refers to Beretta and Corsica, and "W" body refers to Cutlass Supreme, Grand Prix and Regal.**

TURN SIGNAL SWITCH

Removal ("L" & "W" Bodies)

1) Remove steering column from vehicle. See STEERING COLUMNS – SAGINAW in this section. Remove steering wheel nut retainer, lock nut and steering wheel. Remove cancelling cam, hazard switch knob retaining screw and hazard switch knob.

2) Remove column housing cover screw and column housing cover. Position turn signal switch to allow removal of 2 turn signal switch retaining screws.

3) Using Terminal Remover (J-35689-A), push buzzer switch terminals from turn signal switch connector (terminal "F" Light Green wire and terminal "G" Tan/Black wire). Remove turn signal switch.

GENERAL MOTORS (Cont.)

Fig. 1: Exploded View of Steering Column Assembly ("L" & "W" Body Vehicles)

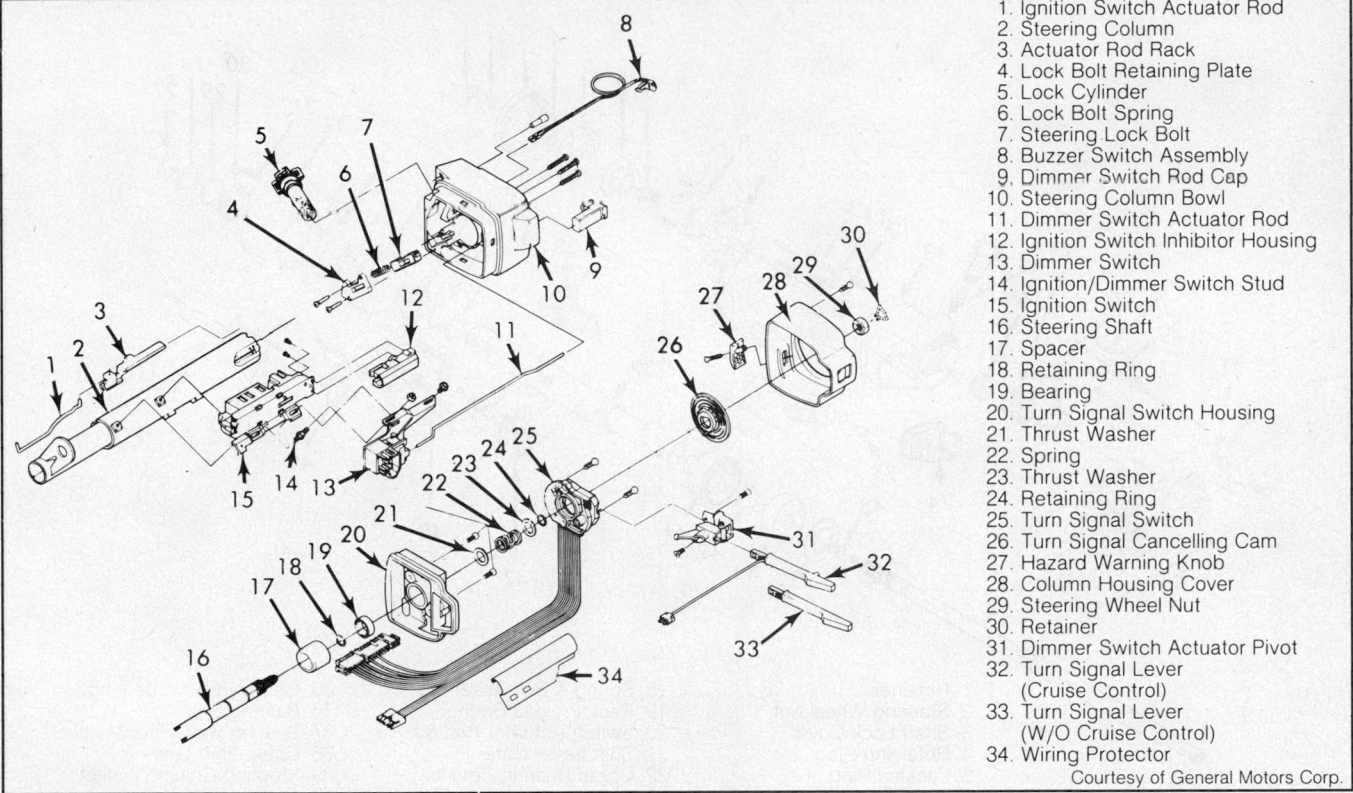

1. Ignition Switch Actuator Rod
2. Steering Column
3. Actuator Rod Rack
4. Lock Bolt Retaining Plate
5. Lock Cylinder
6. Lock Bolt Spring
7. Steering Lock Bolt
8. Buzzer Switch Assembly
9. Dimmer Switch Rod Cap
10. Steering Column Bowl
11. Dimmer Switch Actuator Rod
12. Ignition Switch Inhibitor Housing
13. Dimmer Switch
14. Ignition/Dimmer Switch Stud
15. Ignition Switch
16. Steering Shaft
17. Spacer
18. Retaining Ring
19. Bearing
20. Turn Signal Switch Housing
21. Thrust Washer
22. Spring
23. Thrust Washer
24. Retaining Ring
25. Turn Signal Switch
26. Turn Signal Cancelling Cam
27. Hazard Warning Knob
28. Column Housing Cover
29. Steering Wheel Nut
30. Retainer
31. Dimmer Switch Actuator Pivot
32. Turn Signal Lever
    (Cruise Control)
33. Turn Signal Lever
    (W/O Cruise Control)
34. Wiring Protector

Courtesy of General Motors Corp.

Installation

To install, reverse removal procedure.

Removal (All Except "L" & "W" Bodies)

1) Disconnect battery ground cable. Remove steering wheel, retaining ring, and shaft lock cover. Using Lock Plate Compressors (J-23653-4 and J-23653), remove lock plate. Remove cancelling cam assembly, upper bearing preload spring, and turn signal lever.

2) Push hazard switch in and unscrew knob. Remove actuator arm assembly and switch mounting screws, wrap a piece of tape around upper part of wires. Remove switch by pulling straight up.

Installation

To install, reverse removal procedure.

CRUISE CONTROL SWITCH

Removal & Installation ("L" & "W" Bodies)

1) Remove turn signal switch as previously described. Disconnect cruise control harness connector. Remove wiring protector.

2) Remove turn signal lever retaining screw. Remove turn signal lever and cruise control switch as a unit. To Install, reverse removal procedure.

Removal (All Except "L" & "W" Bodies)

1) With turn signal switch assembly removed, remove lower trim panel. Unplug switch harness connector. Connect 24" follower wire to end of switch harness connector. Disconnect turn signal lever from spring retainer.

2) Pull turn signal lever (cruise control lever) straight out of column. Remove lever and harness by pulling from column. Leave follower wire in column to guide new wire harness back into column.

Installation

Connect new harness to follower wire. Pull harness into column. Align key on turn signal lever with slot in turn signal switch. Push lever in until seated in spring retainer. To complete removal procedure.

LOCK CYLINDER

Removal ("L" & "W" Bodies)

1) Remove turn signal switch as previously described. Turn lock cylinder to "RUN" position. Remove turn signal switch housing screw.

2) Remove steering shaft and turn signal switch housing as an assembly. Using a screwdriver to lift buzzer switch tab, carefully pull on buzzer switch wires to remove switch from lock cylinder.

3) Place lock cylinder in "ACC" position. Remove lock cylinder retaining screw. Remove lock cylinder from steering column bowl.

Installation

1) Place lock cylinder in "ACC" position. Install lock cylinder in steering column bowl. Install and tighten screw to 22 INCH lbs. (2.5 N.m).

2) Turn lock cylinder to "RUN" position. Push buzzer switch into retaining bore until bottomed. Ensure plastic tab covers lock cylinder retaining screw.

3) Install steering shaft and turn signal switch housing as an assembly. Install and tighten turn signal switch housing screws to 88 INCH lbs. (10 N.m).

GENERAL MOTORS (Cont.)

Fig. 2: Exploded View of Steering Column Assembly (Except "L" & "W" Body Vehicles)

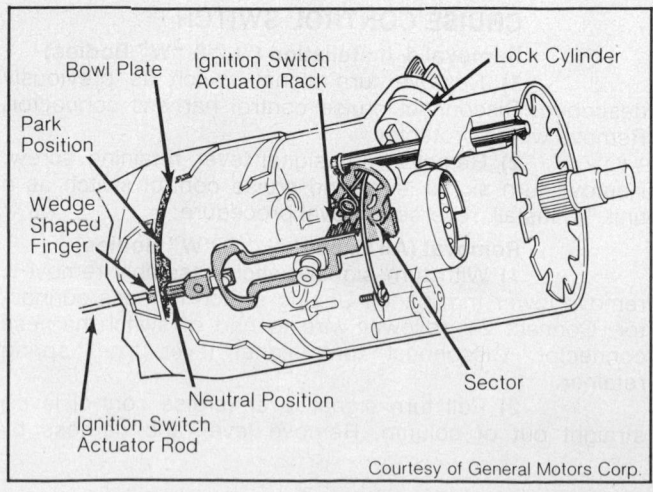

1. Retainer	18. Spring & Bolt Assembly	35. Gearshift Bowl Bearing
2. Steering Wheel Nut	19. Rack Preload Spring	36. Bearing Seat
3. Shaft Lock Cover	20. Switch Actuator Rod & Rack	37. Bearing Retaining Washer
4. Retaining Ring	21. Shift Lever Gate	38. Cable Shift Lever
5. Locking Ring	22. Upper Bearing Retainer	39. Steering Column Jacket
6. Turn Signal Cancelling Cam	23. Housing Adapter	40. Column Shift Tube
7. Upper Bearing Spring	24. Housing Cover	41. Column Jacket Bushing
8. Switch Actuator Arm	25. Switch Activator Pivot Pin	42. Steering Shaft Bearing
9. Turn Signal Switch	26. Switch Activator Pivot	43. Steering Shaft Seal
10. Buzer Switch	27. Wave Washer	44. Seal Retainng Washer
11. Buzzer Switch Retaining Clip	28. Bearing Retaining Washer	45. Retaining Ring
12. Thrust Washer	29. Bearing Seat	46. Steering Shaft
13. Steering Column Housing	30. Gearshift Bowl Bearing	47. Cable Mounting Bracket
14. Lock Cylinder	31. Shift Lever Spring	48. Ignition Switch
15. Switch Actuator Sector	32. Gearshift Lever Bowl	49. Dimmer Switch
16. Upper Bearing	33. Shift Lever Arm	50. Dimmer Actuator Rod
17. Bearing Retaining Bushing	34. Gearshift Bowl Shroud	51. Wiring Protector

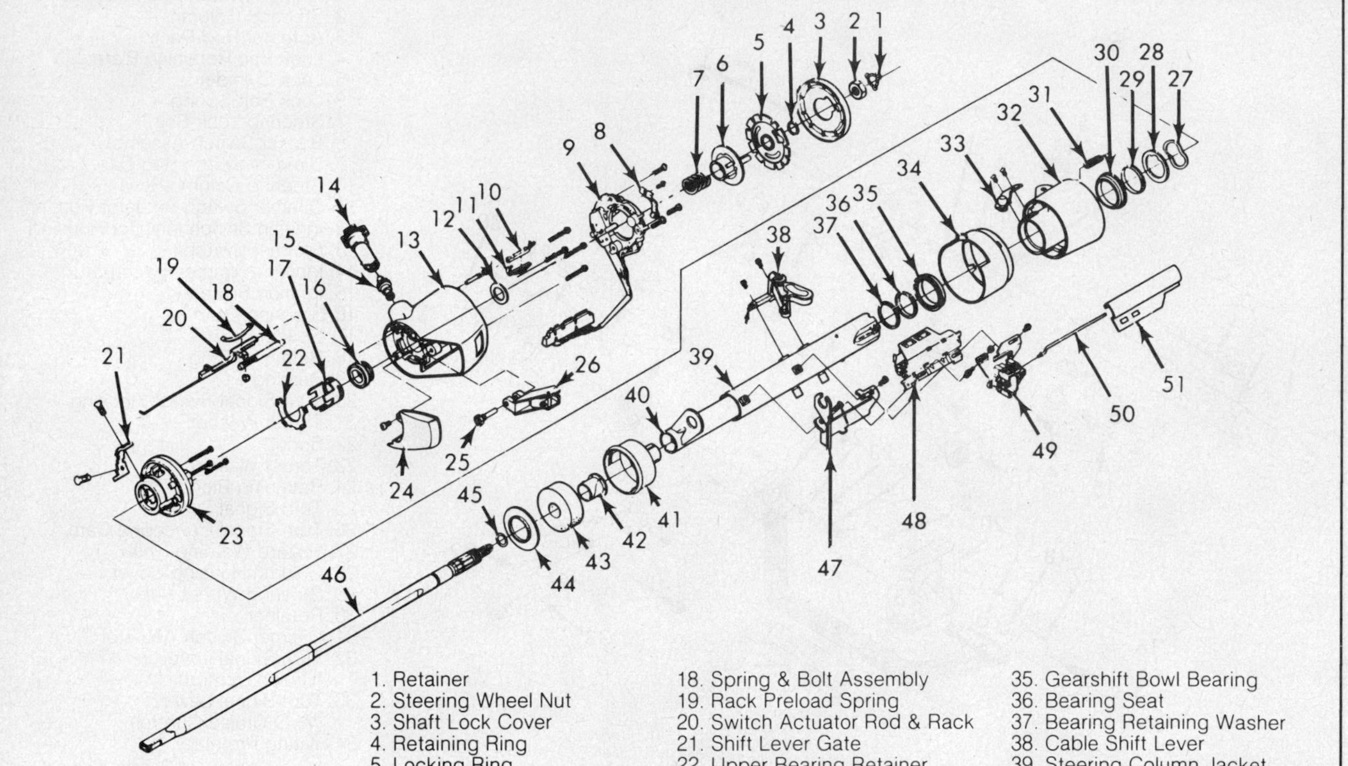

Courtesy of General Motors Corp.

4) Install turn signal switch and steering wheel as previously described. To complete installation, reverse removal procedure.

Removal (All Except "L" & "W" Bodies)

Remove turn signal switch as previously described. Turn lock cylinder to "ON" position. Remove key warning buzzer switch and lock cylinder attaching screw. Remove lock cylinder.

Installation

Turn lock cylinder to "STOP" position. Aligning lock cylinder in housing, install retaining screw. Turn lock cylinder to "ON" position. Install key warning buzzer switch. To complete installation, reverse removal procedure.

IGNITION SWITCH

Removal ("L" & "W" Bodies)

1) Remove lock cylinder as previously described. Loosen ignition switch and dimmer switch retaining nut and screw. Remove dimmer switch.

2) Remove dimmer switch actuating rod. Remove ignition switch and dimmer switch retaining stud.

Remove ignition switch. Remove lock bolt retaining plate attaching screws and lock bolt retaining plate.

Fig. 3: Lock Cylinder Mechanism (All Except "L" & "W" Body Vehicles)

Bowl Plate
Ignition Switch Actuator Rack
Lock Cylinder
Park Position
Wedge Shaped Finger
Sector
Neutral Position
Ignition Switch Actuator Rod

Courtesy of General Motors Corp.

GENERAL MOTORS (Cont.)

3) Remove ignition switch actuator rack and actuator. Remove steering shaft lock bolt and lock bolt spring.

Installation

1) Lubricate steering bolt and actuator rack teeth with lithium grease. Install lock bolt, spring, lock bolt retaining plate and lock bolt retaining plate screws.

2) Tighten lock bolt retaining plate screws to 27 INCH lbs. (2.5 N.m). Install switch actuator rack and switch actuator. Insert rack through opening in steering lock bolt until it rests on retaining plate.

3) Insert key in lock cylinder. Turn lock cylinder to "ACC" Position. Place lock cylinder in steering column bowl while holding rack against lock bolt retaining plate.

4) Install and tighten lock cylinder retaining screw to 27 INCH lbs. (2.5 N.m). Turn lock cylinder alternately from "ACC" position to "START" position to check operation.

5) The rack and lock bolt should extend and retract as key is turned. Install ignition switch so the slotted holes are centered over mounting holes. Install ignition switch retaining stud.

6) Tighten ignition switch mounting stud to 35 INCH lbs. (4 N.m). Install dimmer switch actuator rod, retaining nut, screw and rod cap. Turn lock to "RUN" position.

7) Push buzzer switch assembly into place until it is bottomed with plastic tab covering the lock retaining screw. Install steering shaft and turn signal housing as an assembly.

8) Install and tighten turn signal housing attaching screws to 88 INCH lbs. (10 N.m). Install turn signal switch, steering wheel and steering column as previously described.

Removal (All Except "L" & "W" Bodies)

1) Steering column must be lowered (removed on some models) to gain access to ignition switch. Steering wheel removal is not required. Place lock cylinder in "OFF" position.

2) If lock cylinder has already been removed, pull actuating rod up until it stops. Back off actuating rod 2 detents. Remove switch retaining screw and stud. Lift switch from column. Detach actuator rod.

Installation

1) Place lock cylinder in "OFF" position. Place switch in "OFF" position by moving selector to top of switch and then backing off 2 detents.

2) On fixed columns, fit actuator rod into slider hole. Install switch onto steering column. Tighten attaching stud and screw.

3) On tilt or telescope columns, install switch. Lightly push switch down on column to take up free play in actuator rod. Tighten attaching stud and screw. Connect wiring harness. Check operation of ignition switch.

DIMMER SWITCH

Removal & Installation ("L" & "W" Bodies)

Dimmer switch is mounted next to the ignition switch with the same mounting nut and screw. Refer to IGNITION SWITCH in this article.

Removal (All Except "L" & "W" Bodies)

1) Disconnect battery ground cable. Remove lower steering column cover. Remove 2 steering column-to-upper mounting bracket nuts.

2) Lower column. Remove nut and screw securing dimmer switch. Disconnect electrical connections. Remove switch.

Installation

1) Position switch on steering column and loosely install fasteners. Install electrical connectors. Insert one 3/32" drill through locating hole securing dimmer switch to connector body.

2) Connect actuator arm, slide dimmer switch up to remove lash. Tighten fasteners. Remove drill bit. Reverse removal procedure to complete installation.

WINDSHIELD WIPER/WASHER SWITCH

Removal ("L" & "W" Bodies)

Windshield wiper/washer switch is located on right side of instrument panel. See appropriate WIPER-/WASHER SYSTEMS article in ACCESORIES & EQUIPMENT section.

Removal & Installation (All Except "L" & "W" Bodies)

1) Remove turn signal switch as previously described. Remove ignition switch, dimmer switch, and lock cylinder.

2) Remove steering column housing attaching screws. Remove pivot pin, horn contact, bearing, and washer/wiper switch from column housing. To install, reverse removal procedure.

TIGHTENING SPECIFICATIONS

Application	Ft. Lbs. (N.m)
Steering Wheel Retaining Nut	30-35 (41-47)

Steering Columns

CHRYSLER MOTORS

Horizon America, Omni America

NOTE: For all other Chrysler Motors models, see SAGINAW STEERING COLUMNS in this section.

DESCRIPTION

Steering columns are designed to collapse upon impact. Steering shaft is a collapsible, 2-piece unit. Steering shaft sections are connected with "U" joints. Steering shaft connects to steering gear with a "U" joint.

CAUTION: Applying excessive pressure, or causing impact to mainshaft during service, may cause the column to collapse.

REMOVAL & INSTALLATION

STEERING COLUMN

Removal

1) Disconnect battery ground cable. Disconnect wiring harness connectors. Remove 4 column mounting screws.

2) Remove column upward and rearward to separate steering shaft upper coupling from lower coupling. DO NOT remove roll pin to remove steering column assembly.

3) To remove lower shaft, pull back carpet. Remove 2 silencer retaining nuts. Remove silencer. Remove 4 toe plate mounting screws.

4) Slide toe plate and seal off shaft. Drive out roll pin from steering gear side of "U" joint. Remove lower shaft toward passenger compartment.

Installation

To install, reverse removal procedure. Install new roll pin. Grease all sliding and wear surfaces. Do not crush break-away capsules when tightening.

OVERHAUL

STEERING COLUMN

Disassembly

1) Remove upper and lower steering column covers. Remove wiper/washer switch assembly. Remove wiring clip, turn signal switch retainer, and turn signal switch.

2) Unlock key cylinder. Shaft will turn 360 degrees. Remove upper snap ring. Slide steering shaft out through lower end of jacket. Remove "U" joint to service lower bearing. Remove turn signal switch.

3) Using a screwdriver, pry upper bearing from housing (if necessary). Remove inhibitor lever and spring retaining screw. Unhook ignition switch push rod from ignition switch.

4) Housing is serviced as a unit. Do not remove housing from jacket unless it is to be replaced. If necessary to remove housing from jacket, drive it off, or split housing with a hacksaw. If housing is removed, replace with a new one.

Fig. 1: Exploded View of Horizon America & Omni America Steering Column Assembly

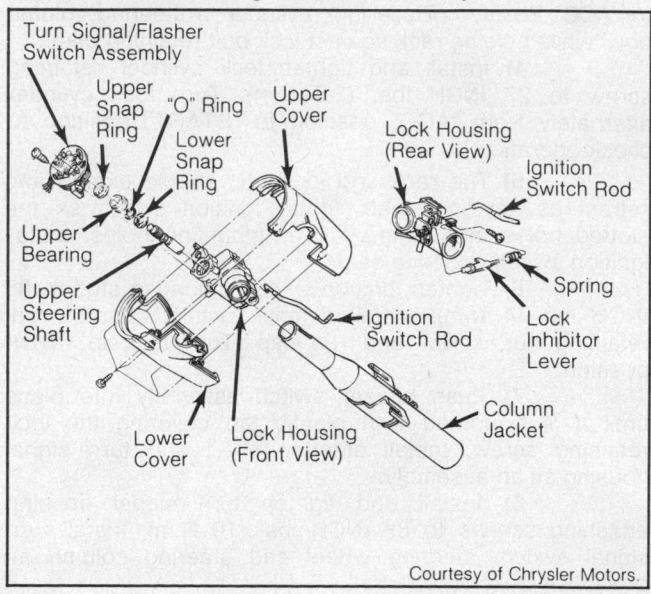

Courtesy of Chrysler Motors.

Reassembly

To reassemble, reverse disassembly procedure. Grease all sliding and wear surfaces. Check operation of all switches and lock cylinder mechanism after reassembly.

TIGHTENING SPECIFICATIONS

Application	Ft. Lbs. (N.m)
Steering Wheel Nut	45 (61)

Application	INCH Lbs. (N.m)
Column Clamp Bolt	105 (11)
Column Clamp Nut	105 (11)
Column Clamp Stud	20 (2)

EAGLE PREMIER

DESCRIPTION

Steering columns are column shift or floor shift type. Steering columns use an integral ignition lock switch. This lock secures steering wheel and shift linkage.

Columns have a 2-piece telescoping gear shift tube interconnected by plastic inserts and shear pins, and a 2-piece telescoping steering shaft with upper and lower sections connected by plastic collars and pins.

A mounting bracket connecting steering column and instrument panel allows column to slide forward on impact, but blocks rearward movement toward driver.

CAUTION: Columns must be handled with care to avoid stresses. Use only fasteners of same or equivalent part number if replacement is necessary. Improper fasteners or tightening could result in failure.

EAGLE PREMIER (Cont.)

REMOVAL & INSTALLATION

STEERING COLUMN

CAUTION: Applying excessive pressure, or causing impact to mainshaft during service, may cause column to collapse.

Removal

1) Disconnect battery ground cable. Remove instrument panel lower trim cover. Remove instrument panel support rod attaching bolts. Remove support rod.

2) Disconnect steering column harness connector. Remove bulkhead connector-to-firewall retaining screw. Disconnect bulkhead connector from firewall. See Fig. 1.

Fig. 1: Disconnecting Premier Steering Column & Bulkhead Connectors

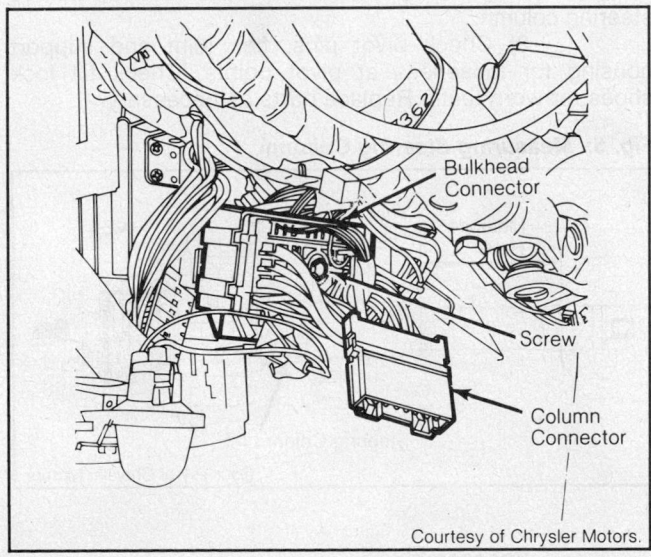

Courtesy of Chrysler Motors.

3) Using a screwdriver, pry shift cable end from shift tube arm. By compressing shift cable retainer tangs with pliers and pushing shift cable back into its mounting hole, move shift cable away from column.

4) Remove shift indicator bracket retaining screw. Remove shift indicator bracket. Lift shift indicator wire from shift column arm pin. See Fig. 2. Unsnap boot from steering column.

5) Slide upper part of 2-piece boot down to gain access to steering shaft-to-intermediate shaft "U" joint. Mark steering shaft-to-intermediate shaft "U" joint for reassembly reference.

6) Remove "U" joint clamp bolt. Remove package tray (if equipped). Remove steering column attaching bolts. Remove steering column by pulling down and toward passenger compartment.

Installation

1) Aligning marks made during removal, position steering shaft "U" joint on intermediate shaft. Position steering column under instrument panel.

2) Install and tighten steering column retaining nuts. Install boot, indicator wire, indicator bracket and shift cable in reverse order of removal. To complete installation, reverse removal procedure.

Fig. 2: Removing Shift Indicator Wire

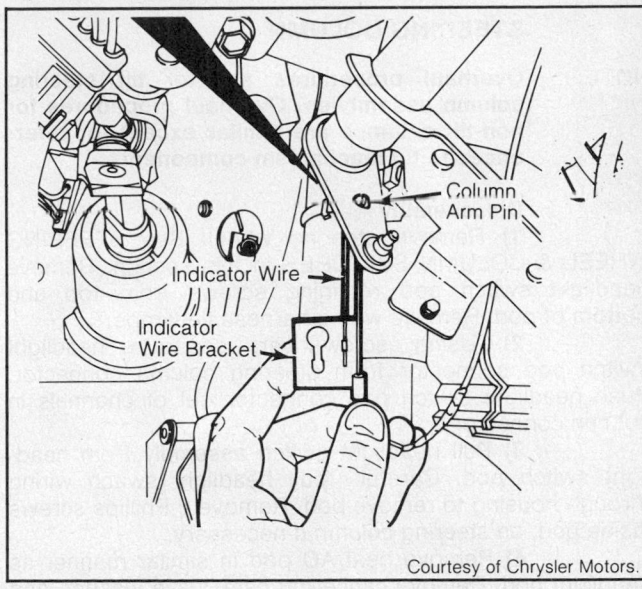

Courtesy of Chrysler Motors.

INTERMEDIATE STEERING SHAFT

Removal

1) Disconnect battery ground cable. Remove steering column as previously described. Unsnap boot flange from floorboard opening. Remove boot.

2) Mark intermediate shaft "U" joint-to-pinion shaft for reassembly reference. Remove "U" joint clamp bolt. Slide intermediate shaft from pinion shaft.

Installation

Aligning marks made during removal, install intermediate shaft on pinion shaft. To complete installation, reverse removal procedure.

Fig. 3: Shift Indicator & Bracket

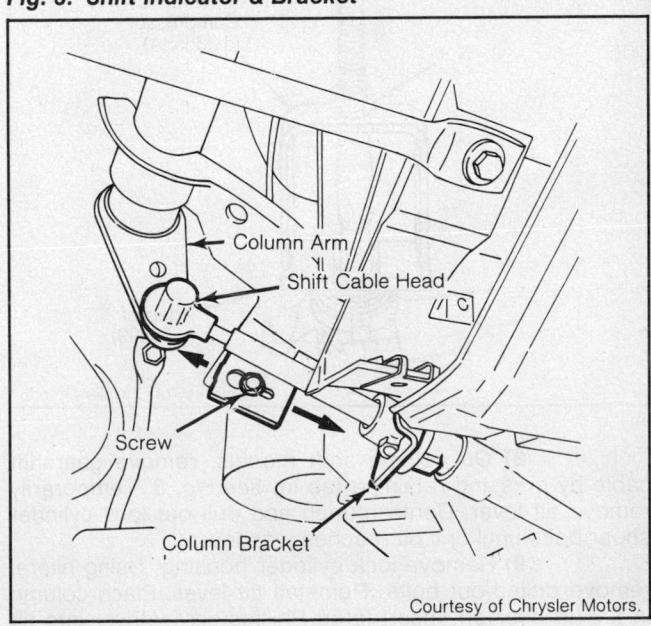

Courtesy of Chrysler Motors.

Steering Columns

EAGLE PREMIER (Cont.)

OVERHAUL

STEERING COLUMN

NOTE: Overhaul procedures are for tilt steering column assemblies. Overhaul procedures for non-tilt columns are similar except for references to tilt mechanism components.

Disassembly

1) Remove steering wheel. See STEERING WHEEL & COLUMN SWITCHES in this section. Remove headlight switch pod retaining screws from top and bottom of pod. Remove wiring harness tie wraps.

2) Using screwdriver, separate headlight switch pod connector from steering column connector. Push headlight switch pod connector out of channels in column connector.

3) Pull headlight switch assembly from headlight switch pod. Carefully pull headlight switch wiring through housing to remove pod. Remove 2 Phillips screws inside pod, on steering column if necessary.

4) Remove heat/AC pod in similar manner as headlight pod. Remove cancelling cam, wave washer, and turn signal switch screws. Remove turn signal switch. Remove shroud mounting screws. Remove shroud.

5) Remove ignition switch. Remove lock cylinder bezel. Insert ignition key into lock cylinder. Turn key to unmarked position. Pressing lock tab inward, remove lock cylinder from ignition switch.

6) Position Adapter (J-35899) on spring retainer. See Fig. 4. Thread Compressor (J-23653A) onto steering column shaft. Tighten spring compressor nut to compress bearing retainer spring.

7) Remove and discard snap ring. Loosen spring compressor nut. Remove spring compressor and adapter. Remove bearing retainer and spring.

Fig. 4: Removing Snap Ring & Bearing Retainer

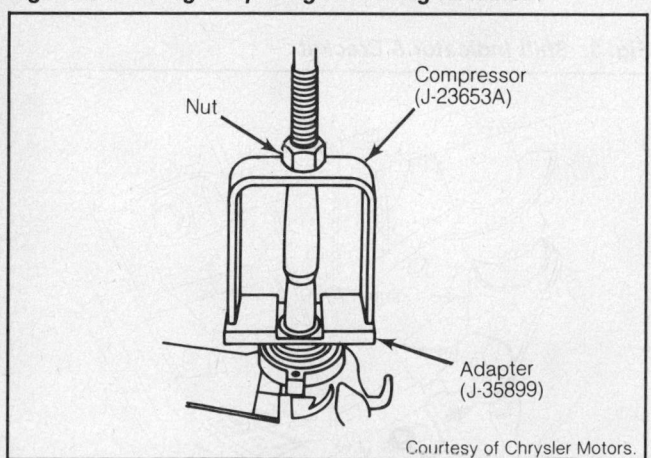

Courtesy of Chrysler Motors.

8) On column shift models, remove gearshift cable by pressing retaining tab in. See Fig. 8. Temporarily remove tilt lever. Center punch and drill out lock cylinder shear bolts until drill bit reaches washers.

9) Remove lock cylinder housing. Using pliers, remove drilled-out bolts. Reinstall tilt lever. Place column in full up position. Insert large Phillips screwdriver into tilt spring retainer recess.

10) Press retainer inward and turn it clockwise to remove retainer and spring. Place column in center position. Using Puller (J-21854-1), remove housing pivot pins. Move tilt lever to disengage lock shoes.

11) Slide housing off support. Pull steering shaft out toward support side of column. DO NOT strike shaft to remove. Remove support mounting screws.

12) Remove support from column. Rotate upper and lower steering column shaft to a 90 degree angle. Separate upper and lower steering shaft at flex joint.

Inspection

1) Column and housing bearings are not serviceable separately. If column or housing bearings are damaged or worn, replace column or housing as a unit.

2) Measure steering column if collapse of column is suspected. See Fig. 5. Measurement should be at least 3.54" (90 mm). If less than specification, replace steering column.

3) Check pivot pins, flex joint and support housing for looseness at pivot points. Check tilt lock shoes for worn teeth. Replace parts as necessary.

Fig. 5: Measuring Steering Column

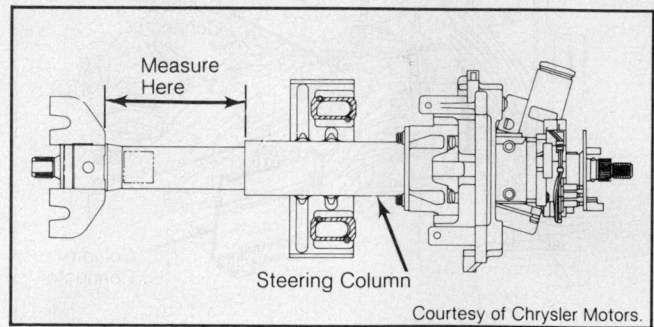

Courtesy of Chrysler Motors.

Reassembly

1) Lubricate column bearings. Install support on column. Install and tighten support-to-column attaching screws. Install centering spheres in upper and lower steering shafts. Connect upper and lower shafts.

2) Install snap ring to centering spheres. Slide steering shaft assembly into column from support side. Position housing over shaft and onto support.

3) Retract tilt lock shoes by pulling on tilt lever to align pivot pin holes. Insert pivot pins. Using hammer and drift, seat pivot pins. Using hammer and punch, stake each pivot pin in 2 places.

4) Install tilt spring in column. Place retainer on spring. Insert large Phillips screwdriver into retainer. Push retainer in and turn it counterclockwise to lock in position.

5) Place ignition lock cylinder housing on tilt housing. Install and tighten new shear bolts until heads break off. On column shift models, press tab to install shift cable in housing. See Fig. 8.

6) Slide race, seat and spring on steering shaft. Position Adapter (J-35899) on shaft. Thread Compressor (J-23653A) on shaft. See Fig. 4.

7) Tighten compressor nut to compress spring. Install snap ring into second groove of steering shaft. Loosen compressor nut. Remove compressor and adapter.

EAGLE PREMIER (Cont.)

Fig. 6: Exploded View of Premier Non-Tilt Steering Column Assembly

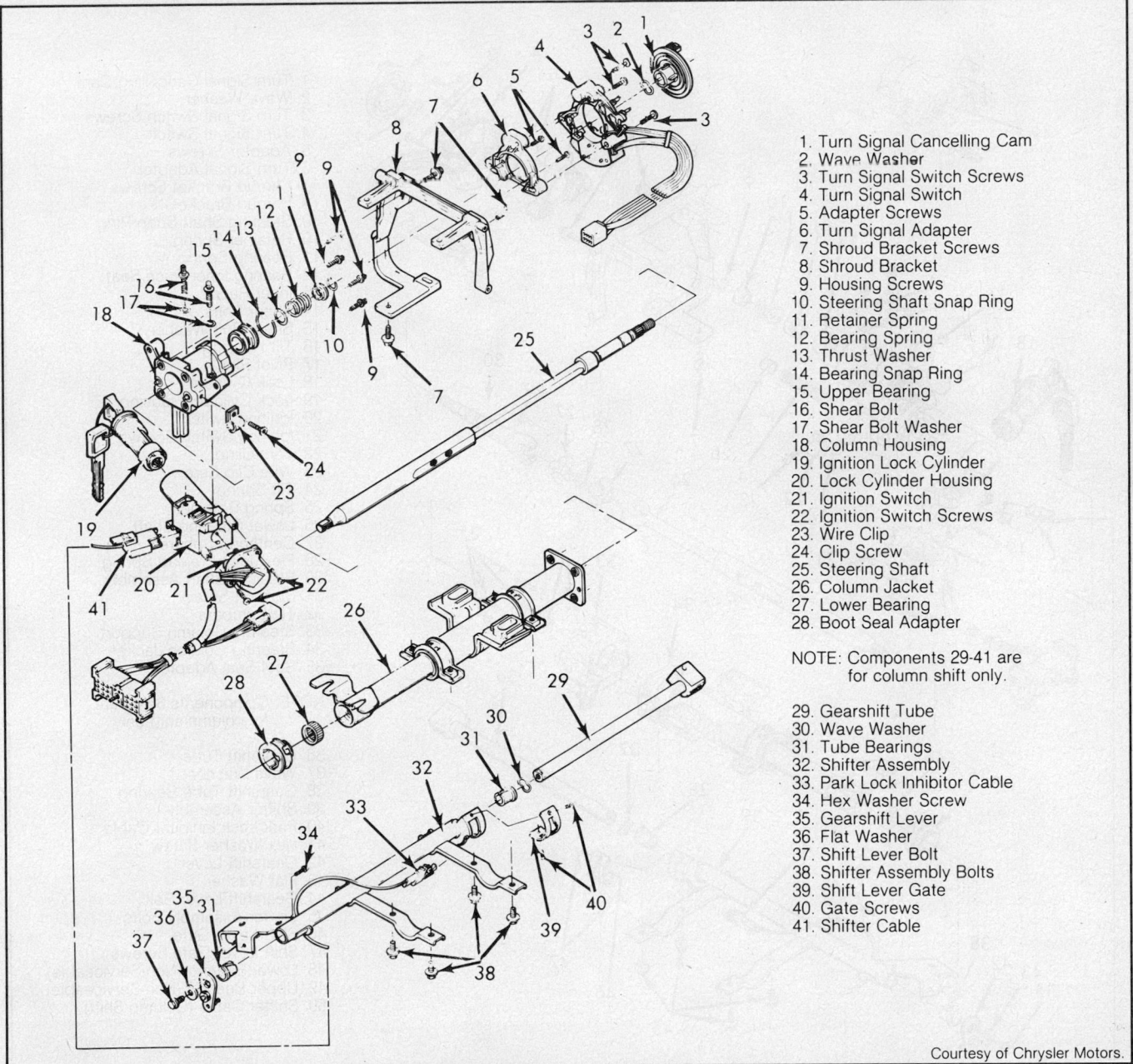

1. Turn Signal Cancelling Cam
2. Wave Washer
3. Turn Signal Switch Screws
4. Turn Signal Switch
5. Adapter Screws
6. Turn Signal Adapter
7. Shroud Bracket Screws
8. Shroud Bracket
9. Housing Screws
10. Steering Shaft Snap Ring
11. Retainer Spring
12. Bearing Spring
13. Thrust Washer
14. Bearing Snap Ring
15. Upper Bearing
16. Shear Bolt
17. Shear Bolt Washer
18. Column Housing
19. Ignition Lock Cylinder
20. Lock Cylinder Housing
21. Ignition Switch
22. Ignition Switch Screws
23. Wire Clip
24. Clip Screw
25. Steering Shaft
26. Column Jacket
27. Lower Bearing
28. Boot Seal Adapter

NOTE: Components 29-41 are for column shift only.

29. Gearshift Tube
30. Wave Washer
31. Tube Bearings
32. Shifter Assembly
33. Park Lock Inhibitor Cable
34. Hex Washer Screw
35. Gearshift Lever
36. Flat Washer
37. Shift Lever Bolt
38. Shifter Assembly Bolts
39. Shift Lever Gate
40. Gate Screws
41. Shifter Cable

Courtesy of Chrysler Motors.

8) Install shroud mounting bracket on column. Install turn signal switch adapter and turn signal switch. Install wave washer and cancelling cam.

9) With key in lock cylinder, turn key to unmarked position. Install lock cylinder into housing. Install ignition switch. Route headlight pod connector through housing and along bottom of column.

10) Push headlight pod into housing. Install and tighten headlight pod retaining screws. Install tie wraps to hold harness to column. Connect headlight pod connector to steering column connector.

11) Install steering column. See REMOVAL & INSTALLATION in this article. Install steering wheel. See STEERING WHEEL & COLUMN SWITCHES in this section.

12) Ensure proper operation of steering column, column shifter (if equipped), ignition switch and headlight pod switches.

EAGLE PREMIER (Cont.)

Fig. 7: Exploded View of Premier Tilt Steering Column Assembly

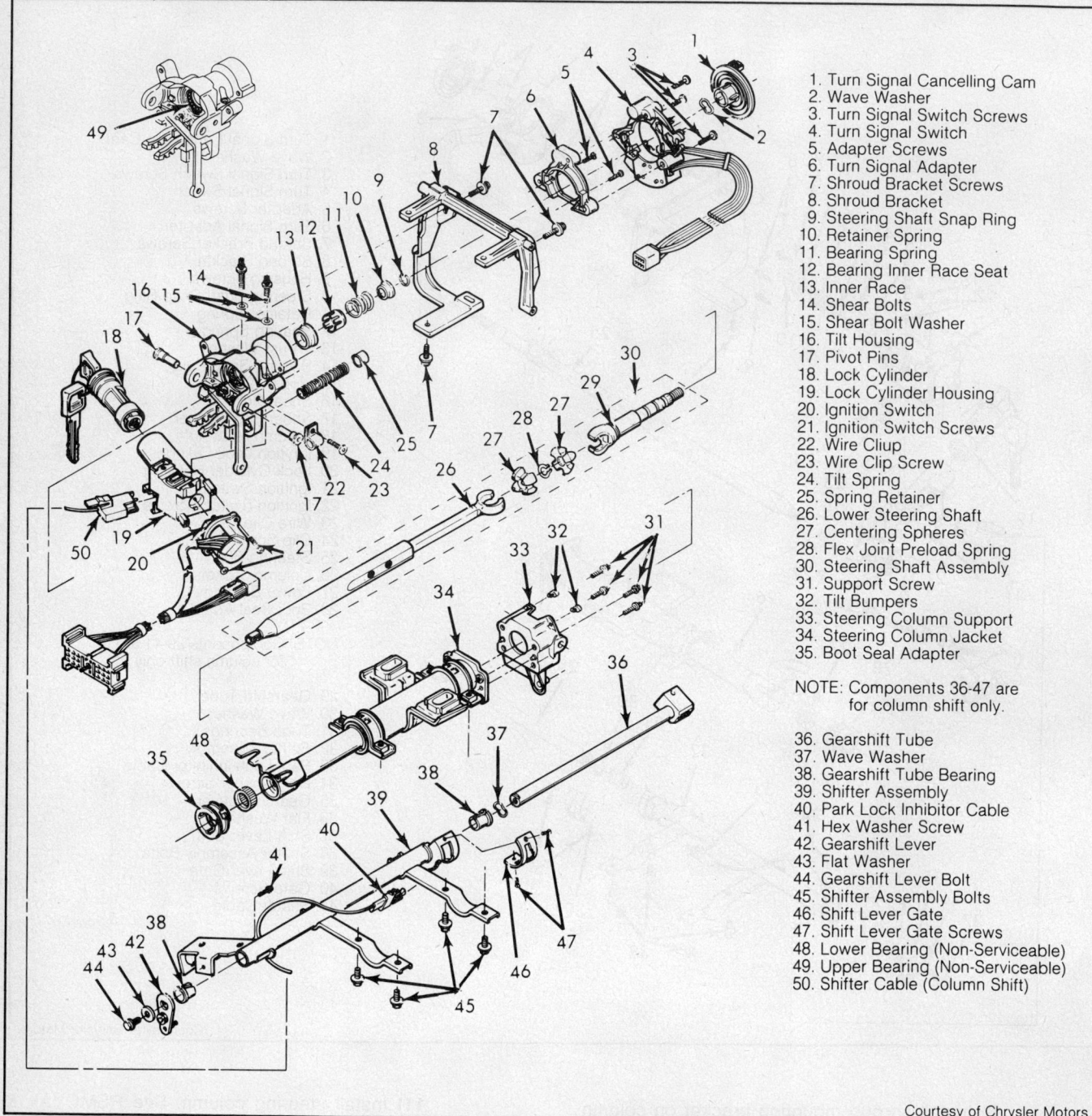

1. Turn Signal Cancelling Cam
2. Wave Washer
3. Turn Signal Switch Screws
4. Turn Signal Switch
5. Adapter Screws
6. Turn Signal Adapter
7. Shroud Bracket Screws
8. Shroud Bracket
9. Steering Shaft Snap Ring
10. Retainer Spring
11. Bearing Spring
12. Bearing Inner Race Seat
13. Inner Race
14. Shear Bolts
15. Shear Bolt Washer
16. Tilt Housing
17. Pivot Pins
18. Lock Cylinder
19. Lock Cylinder Housing
20. Ignition Switch
21. Ignition Switch Screws
22. Wire Cliup
23. Wire Clip Screw
24. Tilt Spring
25. Spring Retainer
26. Lower Steering Shaft
27. Centering Spheres
28. Flex Joint Preload Spring
30. Steering Shaft Assembly
31. Support Screw
32. Tilt Bumpers
33. Steering Column Support
34. Steering Column Jacket
35. Boot Seal Adapter

NOTE: Components 36-47 are for column shift only.

36. Gearshift Tube
37. Wave Washer
38. Gearshift Tube Bearing
39. Shifter Assembly
40. Park Lock Inhibitor Cable
41. Hex Washer Screw
42. Gearshift Lever
43. Flat Washer
44. Gearshift Lever Bolt
45. Shifter Assembly Bolts
46. Shift Lever Gate
47. Shift Lever Gate Screws
48. Lower Bearing (Non-Serviceable)
49. Upper Bearing (Non-Serviceable)
50. Shifter Cable (Column Shift)

Courtesy of Chrysler Motors.

EAGLE PREMIER (Cont.)

Fig. 8: Location of Shift Cable Tab

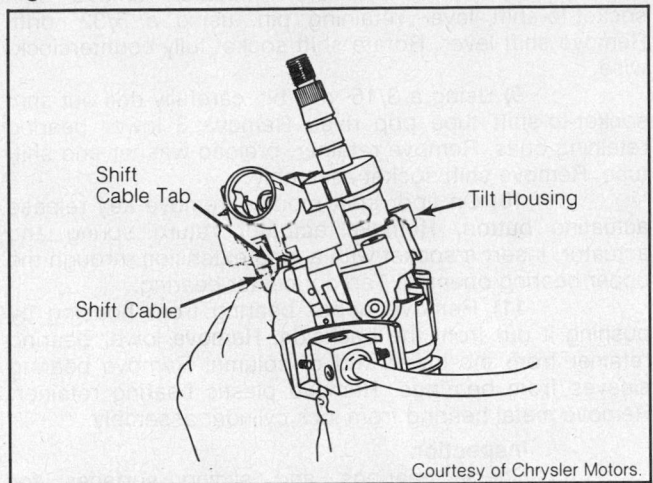

Shift Cable Tab
Tilt Housing
Shift Cable

Courtesy of Chrysler Motors.

TIGHTENING SPECIFICATIONS

Application	Ft. Lbs. (N.m)
Steering Column Mounting Bolts	33 (45)
Steering Column Mounting Nuts	33 (45)
Steering Wheel Nut	52 (70)
"U" Joint Clamp Bolt	30 (40)
	INCH Lbs. (N.m)
Tilt Support-to-Column Screws	36 (4)

FORD MOTOR CO. – EXCEPT MODULAR

**Continental, Escort, Sable,
Taurus, Tempo, Topaz**

DESCRIPTION

All models have a fixed column as standard equipment with a tilt steering column as an optional accessory. The turn signal, headlight dimmer, flash-to-pass, cornering light, hazard warning and wiper/washer switches are all incorporated in one multi-function switch body (combination switch).

REMOVAL & INSTALLATION

STEERING COLUMN

CAUTION: Applying excessive pressure, or causing impact to mainshaft during service, may cause the column to collapse.

Removal (Continental, Sable & Taurus)

1) Disconnect battery ground cable. Remove 2 lower steering column mounting screws. On tilt models, remove tilt release lever mounting screw.

2) Remove lock cylinder. Remove steering column cover mounting screws and covers. Remove horn pad and steering wheel. Refer to STEERING WHEEL & COLUMN SWITCHES in this section.

3) On column shift models, remove retaining screw to remove transmission shift indicator cable from lock cylinder. Remove cable from shift socket retaining hook.

4) On all models, disconnect column harness connectors. Remove combination switch. Remove 2 steering shaft-to-intermediate shaft "U" clamp nuts. Separate steering shaft from intermediate shaft.

5) On column shift models, carefully pry plastic shift cable terminal from selector lever with a screwdriver. Remove 2 shift cable bracket and cable assembly-to-lock cylinder retaining screws.

6) On all models, disconnect automatic parking brake release vacuum hose. On tilt models, remove tilt return spring. With steering column supported, remove 4 column-to-bracket mounting nuts.

7) Carefully lower steering column and pull toward passenger compartment to remove.

Installation

1) To install, reverse removal procedure. Tighten steering wheel and column mounting nuts to specification. Adjust gear shift indicator.

2) On models with ATX transaxle, place indicator and shifter in "D" for adjustments. On models with AXOD transaxle, place indicator and shifter in "OD" for adjustment. Check for proper operation.

Removal (Escort, Tempo & Topaz)

1) Disconnect negative battery cable. Remove 2 steering column-to-instrument panel mounting screws. Remove 2 speed control module mounting screws (if equipped). Remove 5 lower steering column shroud mounting screws. Loosen steering column retaining bolts and nuts.

2) Remove upper shroud. Disconnect all electrical connectors. Loosen steering column-to-intermediate shaft clamp. Remove bolt or nut. Remove steering column retaining bolts and nuts.

3) With steering column locked, carefully pry open steering column shaft in area of clamp on each side of bolt groove with steering column locked. Inspect column bracket clips for distortion. If clips are distorted, replace them with new ones.

Installation

To install, reverse removal procedure. Tighten steering shaft clamp nut and steering column mounting bolts and nuts to specifications.

INTERMEDIATE SHAFT

**Removal & Installation
(Continental, Sable & Taurus)**

Remove 2 intermediate shaft-to-steering column nut and retainer assemblies. Remove 3 primary boot

FORD MOTOR CO. – EXCEPT MODULAR (Cont.)

mounting nuts. Remove primary boot. Push secondary boot up to expose intermediate shaft. Remove intermediate shaft retaining bolt. Remove intermediate shaft. Remove secondary boot. To install, reverse removal procedure.

Removal & Installation (Escort, Tempo & Topaz)

Disconnect battery ground cable. Remove steering column. On models with power steering, remove steering column boot and seal assembly. On all models, remove and discard intermediate shaft-to-steering gear clamp. Remove seal. To install, reverse removal procedure. Install new clamp and seal.

OVERHAUL

STEERING COLUMN

NOTE: **Disconnect shift cable and bracket from steering column before removal.**

Disassembly (Continental, Sable & Taurus)

1) Remove key warning buzzer. Disengage speed control/horn brush wiring from lock cylinder by removing 2 wiring retainers from holes. Remove intermediate bracket Torx bolts. Remove intermediate bracket. Remove forward bracket from intermediate bracket.

2) On models with tilt column, loosen tilt release lever and cable. Position tilt lever in full open. Hold in position with vise grips. Remove position detent locator and bolt.

3) Turn ignition key to "RUN" position. Insert a 1/8" diameter wire pin through hole in trim cover under lock cylinder. Depress pin while pulling out lock cylinder to remove it from column.

4) If ignition key is lost or broken, drill out retaining pin with a 1/8" drill bit. Chisel ignition lock cylinder cap away from lock cylinder. Drill down key slot with 3/8" drill bit approximately 1 3/4" until lock breaks loose. Pull lock cylinder out. Clean drill shavings out of cylinder.

5) Remove ignition switch and mounting cover Torx bolts. Remove lock actuator cover bolt. Remove lock actuator assembly. Remove parking brake release vacuum switch (if equipped). Remove speed sensor (if equipped).

Fig. 1: Exploded View of Fabricated Tool

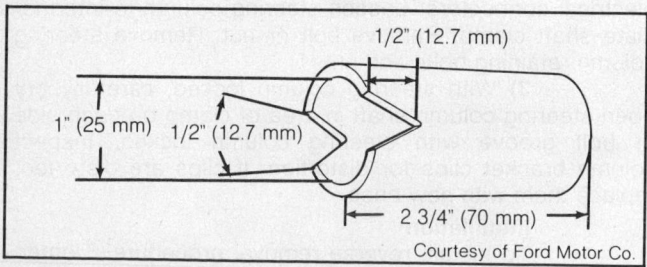

1/2" (12.7 mm)
1" (25 mm) 1/2" (12.7 mm)
2 3/4" (70 mm)

Courtesy of Ford Motor Co.

6) Remove switch actuator. Install fabricated tool and nut on steering shaft. *See Fig. 1.* Tighten steering wheel nut until spring pressure is released. Remove retaining pin fron shaft, using a 5/32" drift. Remove fabricated tool and nut.

7) Remove steering shaft retaining washer and upper alignment wedge. Slide steering shaft out of lock cylinder housing. Remove lower alignment wedge, washer and preload spring.

8) On column shift models, remove shift socket-to-shift lever retaining pin, using a 5/32" drift. Remove shift lever. Rotate shift socket fully counterclockwise.

9) Using a 3/16" drill bit, carefully drill out shift socket-to-shift tube pop rivet. Remove 3 lower bearing retaining bolts. Remove retainer, preload washer and shift tube. Remove shift socket assembly.

10) On floor shift models, remove key release actuating button. Remove actuator return spring and actuator. Insert a socket with a long extension through the upper bearing opening. Tap out center bearing.

11) Remove upper bearing from housing by pushing it out from the backside. Remove lower bearing retainer from the lower end of column. Remove bearing sleeves from bearings. Remove plastic bearing retainer. Remove metal bearing from lock cylinder assembly.

Inspection

Check bearings and sliding surfaces for smooth rotation. Check lock cylinder for scoring and smooth operation. Inspect "U" joints and pivot pins for looseness. Check that tilt mechanism locks securely in each detent position. Replace any worn or damaged parts.

Reassembly

To reassemble, reverse disassembly procedure. Grease all moving and sliding components. Check for proper operation. Install new seals, retaining clips and plastic bearing retainers.

Disassembly (Escort, Tempo & Topaz)

1) Remove upper bearing retainer plate, "C" clip and upper bearing. Remove lock cylinder housing from column. Remove ignition switch from lock cylinder.

2) Remove ignition lock cylinder, retainer and bearing. Drive out actuator gear from housing. Remove acuator. Remove key and rod from housing.

3) Loosen upper bearing retaining plate. Remove 2 locking cylinder-to-outer tube bolts. Remove retainer ring. Discard retainer. Remove lower bearing and sleeve.

4) Remove shaft through the top of outer tube assembly. Do not attempt to separate upper and lower shafts. Remove spring and upper bearing retainer plate.

CAUTION: **When removing pivot pins the tilt spring will remain under pressure. Care should be taken so spring does not expand rapidly.**

5) Remove "C" clip. Move tilt casting to upper position. Using Pivot Pin Remover (T70P-3D739-A), remove pivot pin, Lift tilt casing from column.

6) Remove tilt spring. From bottom of steering column, remove upper bearing, using drift. From top of column, remove lower bearing, using drift.

Inspection

Check bearings and sliding surfaces for smooth rotation. Check lock cylinder for scoring and smooth operation. Inspect "U" joints and pivot pins for looseness. Check that tilt mechanism locks securely in each detent position. Replace any worn or damaged parts.

Reassembly

To reassemble, reverse disassembly procedure. Grease all moving and sliding components. Check for proper operation. Install new seals, retaining clips and plastic bearing retainers.

FORD MOTOR CO. – EXCEPT MODULAR (Cont.)

Fig. 2: Exploded View of Continental, Sable & Taurus Steering Column

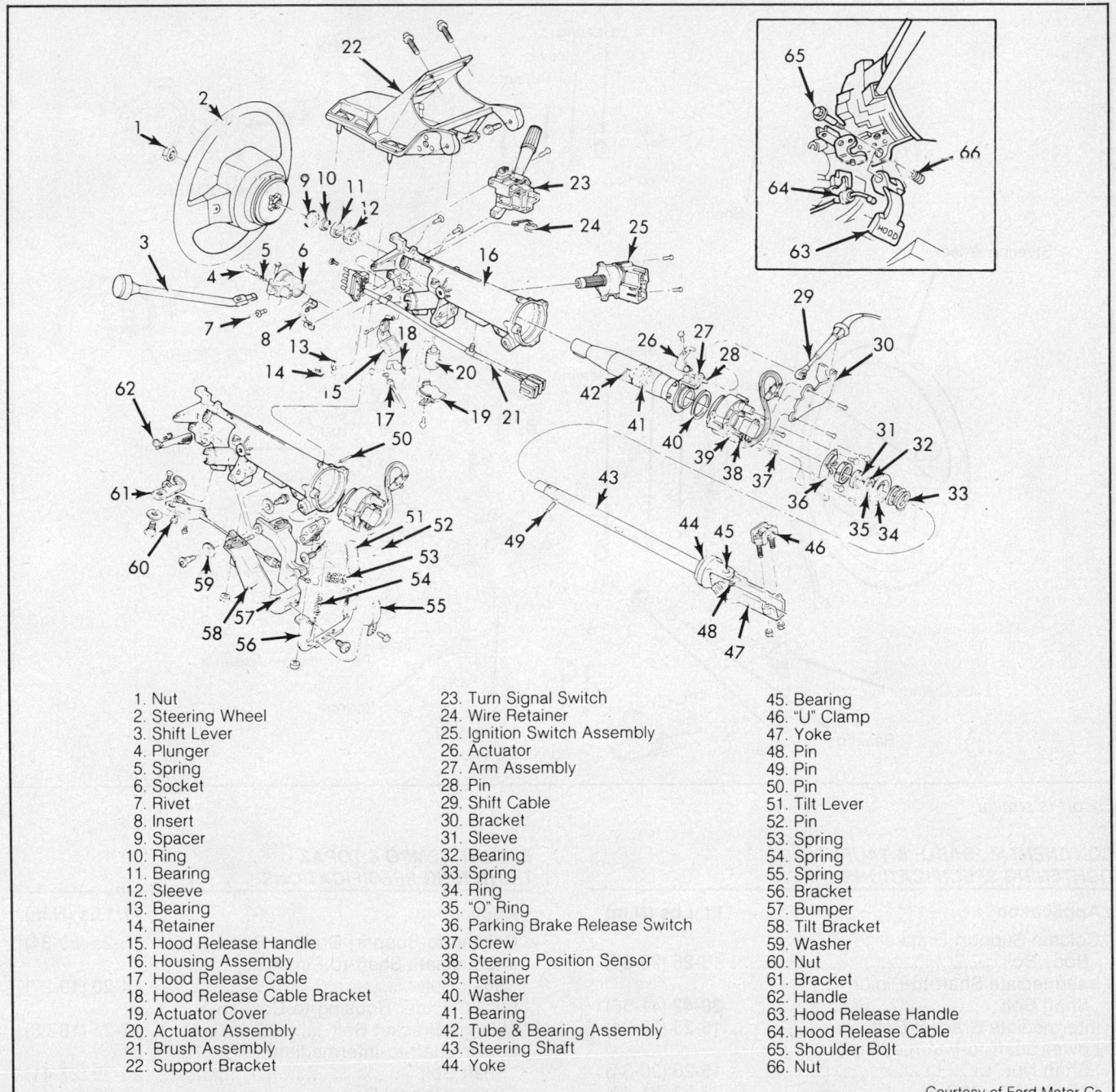

1. Nut	23. Turn Signal Switch	45. Bearing
2. Steering Wheel	24. Wire Retainer	46. "U" Clamp
3. Shift Lever	25. Ignition Switch Assembly	47. Yoke
4. Plunger	26. Actuator	48. Pin
5. Spring	27. Arm Assembly	49. Pin
6. Socket	28. Pin	50. Pin
7. Rivet	29. Shift Cable	51. Tilt Lever
8. Insert	30. Bracket	52. Pin
9. Spacer	31. Sleeve	53. Spring
10. Ring	32. Bearing	54. Spring
11. Bearing	33. Spring	55. Spring
12. Sleeve	34. Ring	56. Bracket
13. Bearing	35. "O" Ring	57. Bumper
14. Retainer	36. Parking Brake Release Switch	58. Tilt Bracket
15. Hood Release Handle	37. Screw	59. Washer
16. Housing Assembly	38. Steering Position Sensor	60. Nut
17. Hood Release Cable	39. Retainer	61. Bracket
18. Hood Release Cable Bracket	40. Washer	62. Handle
19. Actuator Cover	41. Bearing	63. Hood Release Handle
20. Actuator Assembly	42. Tube & Bearing Assembly	64. Hood Release Cable
21. Brush Assembly	43. Steering Shaft	65. Shoulder Bolt
22. Support Bracket	44. Yoke	66. Nut

Courtesy of Ford Motor Co.

Steering Columns

FORD MOTOR CO. — EXCEPT MODULAR (Cont.)

Fig. 3: Exploded View of Tempo & Topaz Steering Column

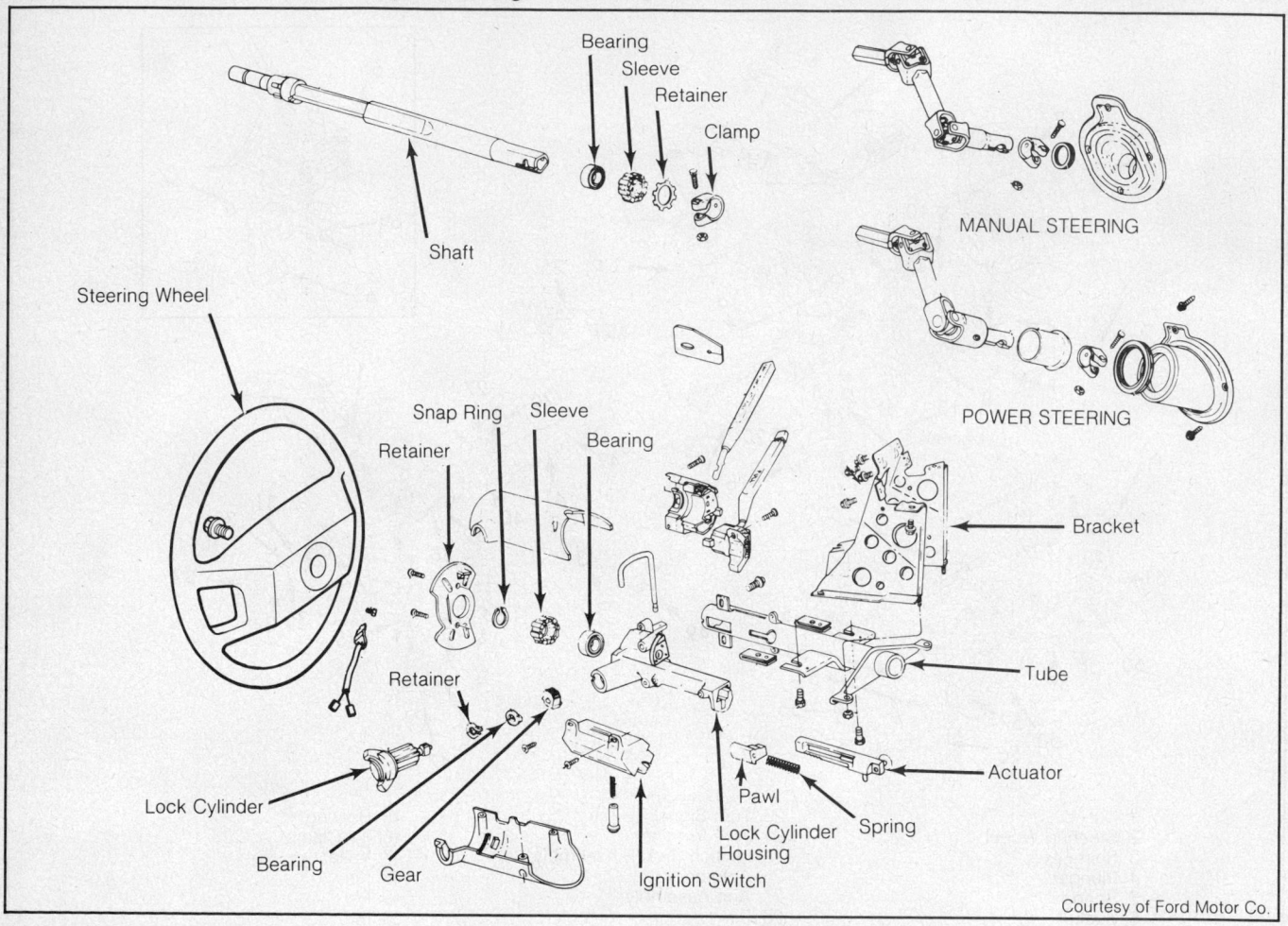

Courtesy of Ford Motor Co.

Escort is similar.

**CONTINENTAL, SABLE & TAURUS
TIGHTENING SPECIFICATIONS**

Application	Ft. Lbs (N.m)
Column Support Bracket-to-Body Bolt	15-25 (20-34)
Intermediate Shaft-to-Pinion Shaft Bolt	30-42 (41-56)
Intermediate Bracket Bolt	15-25 (20-34)
Lower Shaft-to-Intermediate Shaft Nut	15-25 (20-34)
Steering Wheel Bolt	23-33 (31-44)

**ESCORT, TEMPO & TOPAZ
TIGHTENING SPECIFICATIONS**

Application	Ft. Lbs (N.m)
Column-to-Support Bracket Bolts	15-25 (20-34)
Intermediate Shaft-to-Pinion Shaft Bolt	14-20 (19-27)
Lock Cylinder Housing-to-Column Flange Bracket Bolt	12-21 (16-28)
Lower Shaft-to-Intermediate Shaft Bolt	20-30 (27-41)
Steering Wheel Bolt	23-33 (31-44)

FORD MOTOR CO. MODULAR

**Cougar, Crown Victoria,
Grand Marquis, Mark VII, Mustang,
Thunderbird, Town Car**

DESCRIPTION

Modular steering columns are available in both fixed and tilt configurations. Automatic transmission models have a column shift mechanism. The modular design allows many of the same parts and procedures to be used on both standard and tilt columns.

The steering lock on tilt columns is cast with an integral pivot yoke. This yoke supports tilt housing and related components. Fixed column steering locks are cast without yoke and are machined to hold column upper bearing with a retaining ring and plate. All columns are impact absorbing to allow steering shaft and housing to collapse in the event of a collision.

FORD MOTOR CO. MODULAR (Cont.)

ADJUSTMENTS

SHIFT LEVER PLAY (COLUMN SHIFT)

1) Place selector lever in "PARK" position with lever fully engaged against "PARK" detent. Rotate lock cylinder to "LOCK" position. Remove key.

2) Disconnect battery ground cable. Remove instrument panel and steering column trim shrouds. Apply 36-60 INCH lb. (4-7 N.m) load to shift lever in downward direction, forcing lever against park detent stop.

3) Measure clearance between shift cane stop and lock actuator with feeler gauge. If clearance is less than .016" (.41 mm), spacer clip is okay. Reinstall trim shrouds. Reconnect battery cable.

4) If clearance is more than .016" (.41 mm), or if there is no clearance, replace spacer clip. Wedge a small screwdriver between spacer clip and shift tube.

5) Pry down on clip to remove it. Use a new spacer clip which is one size smaller than total feeler gauge thickness. Place ignition switch in "ON" position.

Fig. 1: Checking Shift Lever Play

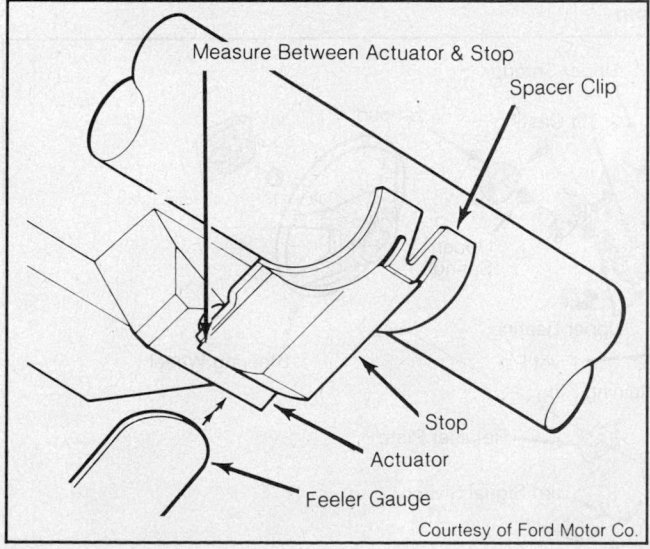

Measure Between Actuator & Stop

Spacer Clip

Stop

Actuator

Feeler Gauge

Courtesy of Ford Motor Co.

6) Install spacer clip onto shift tube over shift tube stop. Clip must be positioned so tab is located between stop and actuator.

7) Rotate ignition switch to "LOCK" position, then to "ON" position, and back to "LOCK" position. No binding should exist in switch and cylinder system.

8) If binding occurs, check for actuator boss hitting spacer. If binding persists, remove and resize clip. Replace clip if necessary. Reinstall instrument panel, column trim shrouds and battery cable.

REMOVAL & INSTALLATION

STEERING COLUMN

CAUTION: Applying excessive pressure, or causing impact to mainshaft during service, may cause the column to collapse.

Removal

1) Disconnect battery ground cable. On Lincoln Town Car, Crown Victoria, and Grand Marquis, remove upper steering shaft-to-lower steering shaft attaching bolt.

Disengage "U" joint stub shaft from column shaft by collapsing intermediate shaft assembly.

2) On Cougar, Mark VII, Mustang and Thunderbird, remove 2 flexible coupling-to-flange retaining nuts on steering input shaft. Disengage safety strap and bolt from flexible coupling.

3) On column shift models, disconnect transmission shift rod at selector lever. Using Grommet Remover (T67P-7341-A), remove shift linkage grommet. Remove steering wheel.

4) On all models, remove column trim shrouds, steering column cover and hood release mechanism. Disconnect all electrical connections to column switches. Loosen, but do not remove, 4 nuts attaching column to brake pedal support.

CAUTION: Do not lower steering column too far before disconnecting transmission shift indicator cable, or damage can result.

5) On automatic transmission models, lower column, reach behind column and instrument panel and lift shift indicator cable off cleat on indicator lever. Remove indicator cable clamp from column tube. Remove screws attaching dust boot to dash panel.

6) Remove 4 column-to-brake pedal support retaining nuts. Lower column to clear mounting bolts. Pull column out so "U" joint assembly passes through clearance opening in dash panel.

Installation

1) Insert column through opening in dash panel. Align and install 4 column-to-brake pedal support bolts. Install nuts loosely so column will hang with a clearance between column and instrument panel.

2) Loosely install shift indicator cable clamp to column outer tube. Reach behind column and attach indicator cable to shift lever by slipping cable loop over lever cleat. Tighten column-to-brake pedal support nuts.

3) Place shift lever in "DRIVE" position, against drive stop on insert plate. Rotate indicator bracket to midpoint on column outer tube. Continue to rotate clockwise or counterclockwise until pointer aligns with "D" mark. Tighten bracket retaining nut.

4) Connect column harness connectors. On Crown Victoria, Grand Marquis and Town Car, slide lower steering shaft assembly into column shaft. Tighten nut to specifications. Pry lower shaft up or down to achieve an 1/8" (3 mm) gap between metal couplings. Stone shield must be removed for access to coupling insulator.

5) On Cougar, Mark VII, Mustang and Thunderbird, engage safety strap and bolt assembly to flange on input shaft. Install and tighten 2 nuts securing column lower shaft and "U" joint assembly to flange on input shaft.

6) Position safety strap so no metal-to-metal contact exists after tightening nut. Pry steering shaft up or down to achieve a 1/8" (3 mm) gap between metal couplings. Using Shift Linkage Insulator Installer (T67P-7341-A), connect shift rod to shift lever on lower end of column.

7) On Crown Victoria, Grand Marquis and Town Car, raise vehicle and loosen adjustment nut on transmission shift rod. Move transmission selector lever to "DRIVE" position by rotating it towards the front (counterclockwise) of the vehicle until it stops.

8) Rotate lever back clockwise 2 detent positions. Ensure shift lever handle is in "DRIVE" position. Suspend an 8 lb. weight on shift selector to assure lever is

FORD MOTOR CO. MODULAR (Cont.)

firmly against drive detent. Tighten adjustment nut on shift rod. Lower vehicle.

9) On all models, engage dust boot to dash panel opening. Tighten screws. Attach trim shrouds. Install hood release mechanism and lower column cover. Install steering wheel. Connect battery ground cable. Check steering column operation.

OVERHAUL

CAUTION: Columns must be handled with care to avoid stresses. Use only fasteners of the same or equivalent part number if replacement is necessary. Improper fasteners or tightening could result in failure.

UPPER SHAFT BEARING

Disassembly

1) Remove steering wheel and column trim shrouds. On fixed columns, remove upper bearing retainer plate. Remove upper steering shaft-to-lower steering shaft retaining bolt.

2) Remove upper bearing-to-steering shaft retaining snap ring. Pull outward on steering shaft approximately 1/4". Insert 2 screwdrivers into slots of bearing bore. Gently pry bearing off steering shaft.

3) On tilt columns, remove conical coil spring and upper bearing plate. Remove upper bearing retaining "C" clip from shaft. Place tilt casting in upper postion to unload tilt spring. Using Pivot Pin Remover (T67P-3D739-B), remove pivot pins.

NOTE: **The tilt spring will exert an upward force. Use care when removing the pivot pins.**

4) Lift off tilt casting with 2 bearings, tilt release lever, and lock lever. Using drift, remove upper bearing, working from bottom side. If necessary, use drift to remove lower bearing by working from top side.

Reassembly (Fixed Column)

1) Use a punch to rough up area on steering shaft where upper bearing is to be installed. Install bearing and insulator onto shaft only as far as hand pressure will allow. DO NOT hammer on bearing.

Fig. 2: Exploded View of Ford Motor Co. Modular Steering Column

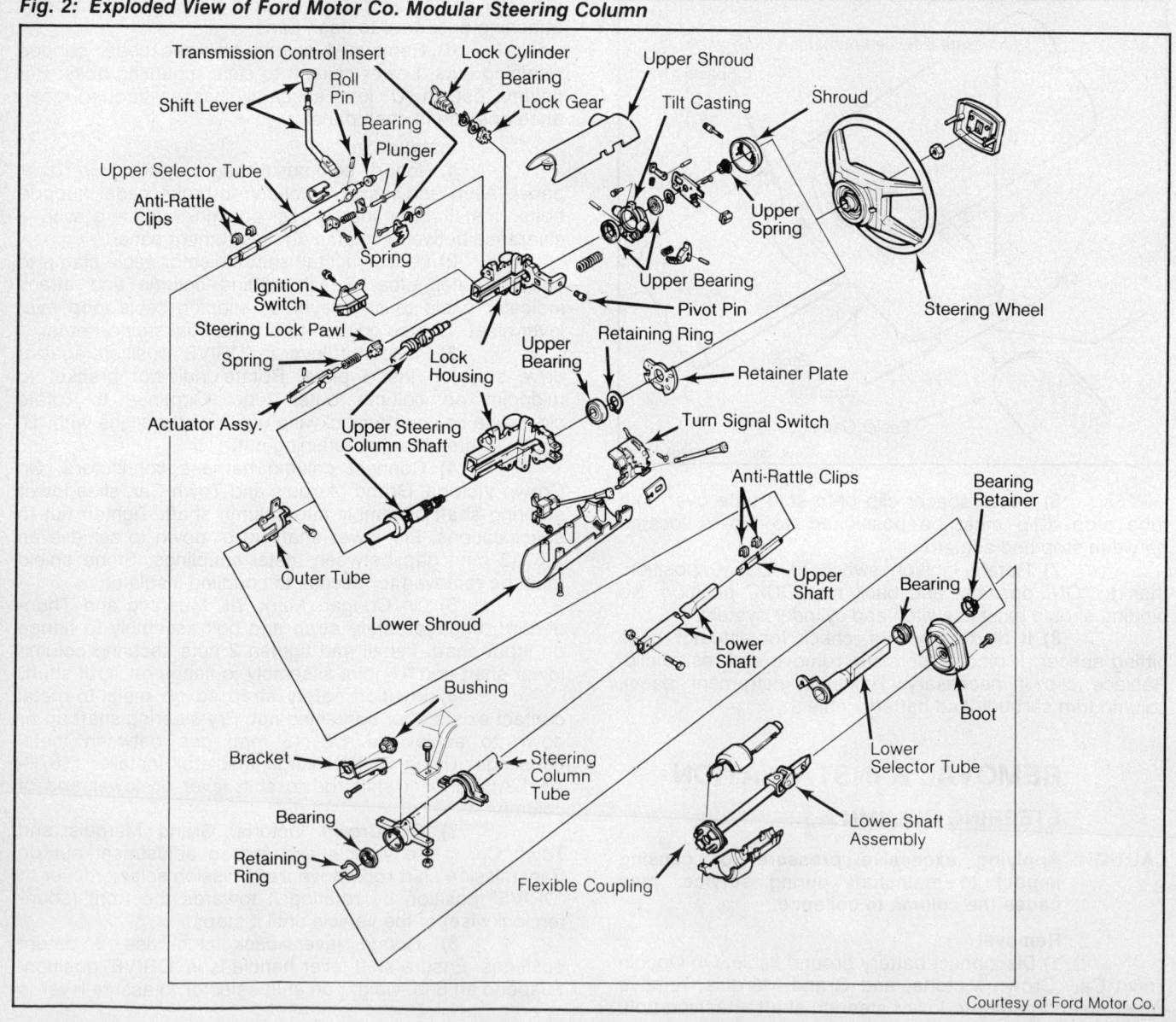

FORD MOTOR CO. MODULAR (Cont.)

2) Install section of 3/4" I.D. x 1-1/2" pipe over end of steering column upper shaft. Install the steering wheel attaching nut. Tighten steering wheel nut to seat bearing in housing. Remove nut and pipe.

3) Install snap ring into groove at top of steering column upper shaft. Install upper bearing retainer plate. Slide lower steering shaft into upper steering shaft.

4) Attach with bolt and nut. Tighten nut to specifications. Pry lower shaft up and down to achieve a 1/8" (3 mm) coupling insulator flatness. Reverse disassembly procedures to complete reassembly.

Reassembly (Tilt Column)

1) Press bearings into tilt casting, using care not to press on inner race during installation. Install tilt spring between upper and lower tilt castings.

2) Latch tilt release lever in upper position. Align 2 castings. Insert 2 new pivot pins. To complete reassembly, reverse disassembly procedure.

LOWER SHAFT BEARING

Disassembly

1) With steering column removed, remove upper bearing retainer ring. On column shift models, remove shift lever. Remove lock cylinder housing and steering shaft as an assembly.

2) For tilt columns, remove tilt casting and steering shaft as an assembly. On all models, remove lower bearing retainer ring. Remove lower steering shaft bearing and sleeve out of outer tube lower end.

Reassembly

On fixed columns, install steering shaft and lock cylinder housing. Grease and install lower shaft bearing and sleeve. Install bearing retainer ring. Install shift lever (if equipped). To complete reassembly, reverse disassembly procedure. Install steering column.

FLEXIBLE COUPLING

Disassembly & Reassembly

Remove lower steering shaft assembly. Drill out 2 rivets securing flexible coupling to lower shaft assembly. Separate flexible coupling from lower shaft assembly. To reassemble, reverse disassembly procedure.

SHIFT LEVER (COLUMN SHIFT)

Disassembly

1) Disconnect battery ground cable. Remove steering column. Remove 2 selector tube support bracket-to-steering column collar bolts. Remove wiper switch.

2) Remove upper bearing retainer plate screws. DO NOT remove plate. Remove selector shaft trim cover. Remove upper selector tube-to-shift lever roll pin. Remove lever.

3) Remove shift lever spring and plunger assembly from upper selector tube. Remove "C" clip retainer at upper end of selector tube assembly.

4) Using small drift and socket, push selector tube assembly out of bearing and washer located in lock cylinder housing and detent plate.

5) Mark upper and lower tubes for reassemble reference. Cut bearing lip off. Remove selector tube support bracket-to-steering column tube attaching bolts.

6) Remove selector indicator. Slide selector tube lower support bracket off of lower shaft. Remove metal spacer clip. Separate upper and lower tubes.

Inspection

Check bearings and sliding surfaces for smooth rotation. Check lock cylinder for scoring and smooth operation. Inspect "U" joints and pivot pins for looseness. Check that tilt mechanism locks securely in each detent position. Replace any worn or damaged parts. Bearing must be replaced if selector tube is removed.

Reassembly

1) Install lower selector tube support bracket with bushing on lower selector tube. Install 2 new anti-rattle clips in grooves on upper selector tube, with both clips facing in same direction.

2) Grease lower 6" of upper selector tube. Place lower selector tube in vise. Aligning marks made during disassembly, install upper tube on lower tube.

3) Install new bearing in detent plate. Align and attach lower support bracket to steering column. Install "C" clip retainer and washer. Install shift lever spring and plunger assembly.

4) Install plastic selector cover loosely on shift lever. Install new roll pin. Check shift lever assembly for smooth, rotational movement.

5) Grease selector lever, plunger, spring and detent plate. Install wiper switch. Install steering column. Check shift lever play. See ADJUSTMENTS in this article.

IGNITION SWITCH LOCK HOUSINGS

Disassembly (Gold Housing – Magnesium)

1) Remove lock cylinder assembly. Remove White plastic bearing retainer by inserting a screwdriver with a 90 degree bend between bearing retainer and bearing and prying upward. Note position of bearing retainer prior to removal.

2) Insert tip of a screwdriver into double "D" slot of bearing. Rotate screwdriver 90 degrees. Remove bearing. Remove lock drive gear. Carefully note relationship of lock drive gear to position of rack teeth.

Reassembly

1) Replace lock gear in housing by aligning last tooth of lock gear with last tooth of rack. Position bearing into lock cylinder housing. Insert tip of screwdriver into double "D" slot of bearing. Rotate screwdriver 90 degrees.

2) Press White plastic bearing retainer into lock housing. Ensure retainer is in original position. Line up flats of gear with flats of washer by pulling down on column lock actuator. Reinstall lock cylinder. Check for proper operation of ignition switch.

Disassembly (Silver Housing – Zinc)

Remove lock cylinder assembly. Remove snap ring and washer, and lock drive gear from lock cylinder housing. Note position of lock drive gear to position of rack teeth.

Reassembly

1) Replace lock gear in housing by aligning last tooth of lock gear with last tooth of rack. Install washer and snap ring. Line up flats of drive gear with flats of washer by pulling down on column lock actuator. Install lock cylinder and check for proper operation of ignition switch.

2) Check for proper start with shift lever in "PARK" and "NEUTRAL". Ensure start circuit cannot be actuated with shift lever in "DRIVE" or "REVERSE" positions. Ensure column locks when ignition switch is in "LOCK" position.

Steering Columns

FORD MOTOR CO. MODULAR (Cont.)

LOWER STEERING SHAFT

Disassembly

1) Remove stone shield. Remove bolt securing upper steering shaft to lower shaft assembly. Slide lower shaft out of upper steering shaft.

2) Remove bolt securing flexible coupling to steering gear pinion shaft. Slide lower shaft with flexible coupling assembly off pinion shaft.

Reassembly

1) Slide flexible coupling onto pinion shaft. Align "D" flat on coupling with "D" slot on pinion shaft. Secure flange-to-steering gear bolt. Tighten bolt to specifications.

2) Slide lower steering shaft into upper steering shaft. Position bolt head against concave side of column tube. Tighten nut to specifications.

3) Align flexible coupling so there is a 1/8" (3 mm) gap between metal couplings. Ensure flexible coupling does not make metal-to-metal contact on safety strap. Attach stone shield.

NOTE: See UPPER SHAFT BEARING in this article for tilt column procedures.

STEERING SHAFT ANTI-RATTLE CLIP

Disassembly

1) Remove steering column. See REMOVAL & INSTALLATION – STEERING COLUMN in this article. On fixed columns, remove shift tube, turn signal switch and washer/wiper switches. Remove upper steering shaft bearing and lock cylinder housing.

2) On tilt columns, remove tilt casting. On all models, remove steering shaft assembly from top of lock housing. Mark upper and lower steering shaft mating surface for reassembly reference.

3) Separate upper steering shaft from lower steering shaft. Remove and discard insulator clips.

Reassembly

1) Install new insulator clips on flats of steering column upper shaft. Install both clips facing same direction. Grease lower 6" of upper steering shaft.

2) Place lower steering shaft into a vise. Aligning marks made during disassembly, install upper shaft into lower shaft. Install upper bearing and retainer plate into lock cylinder housing.

3) Loosely fasten lock cylinder on steering column tube. Insert steering shaft into tube from top of tube. Install column outer tube to lock cylinder housing.

4) Tighten 2 lock housing-to-outer tube bolts. Install turn signal and washer/wiper switches. Install shift tube assembly. Install steering column.

TIGHTENING SPECIFICATIONS

Application	Ft. Lbs. (N.m)
Column-to-Brake Pedal Support	20-37 (28-50)
Coupling Flange-to-Steering Gear Bolt	20-30 (28-41)
Lock Housing-to-Column	12-20 (17-28)
Lower Support-to-Column Collar Bolt	15-22 (20-29)
Lower Column Shaft-to-Flange	20-37 (28-50)
Lower Column Shaft-to-Inter. Shaft	35-45 (48-61)
Steering Wheel Nut	30-35 (41-48)

NOVA

DESCRIPTION

The steering column is an impact absorbing type, designed to collapse in the event of a collision. Steering column attaches to pinion shaft with "U" joints.

REMOVAL & INSTALLATION

STEERING COLUMN

Removal & Installation

1) Remove steering wheel. See STEERING WHEEL & COLUMN SWITCHES in this section. Remove lower instrument panel trim. Remove air duct and lower column cover. Disconnect electrical connectors.

2) Remove 3 combination switch retaining screws and combination switch. Loosen hole cover boot retaining clamp. Remove "U" joint clamp bolt. Remove "U" joint from steering gear pinion shaft.

3) Remove lower column bracket mounting bolts. Remove upper column mounting bolts. Remove steering column. To install, reverse removal procedure.

OVERHAUL

STEERING COLUMN

Disassembly

1) Remove steering column. On tilt steering columns, remove tension springs, tilt lever, and adjusting nut and washer. Tilt lever has left hand threads. Remove lock bolt and tilt bracket.

2) On non-tilt steering columns, remove upper support. On all models, remove lower column support. Remove snap ring. Insert key into ignition switch to release steering lock.

3) Using a hammer and punch, tap out tapered-head bolt. Remove steering lock bracket bolts. Remove shaft. Remove thrust stopper snap ring. Using a screwdriver, remove upper bearing.

Inspection

Check bearings for damage, looseness and scoring. Check lock mechanism for smooth operation. Replace damaged or worn parts as necessary.

Fig. 1: Exploded View of Nova Steering Column

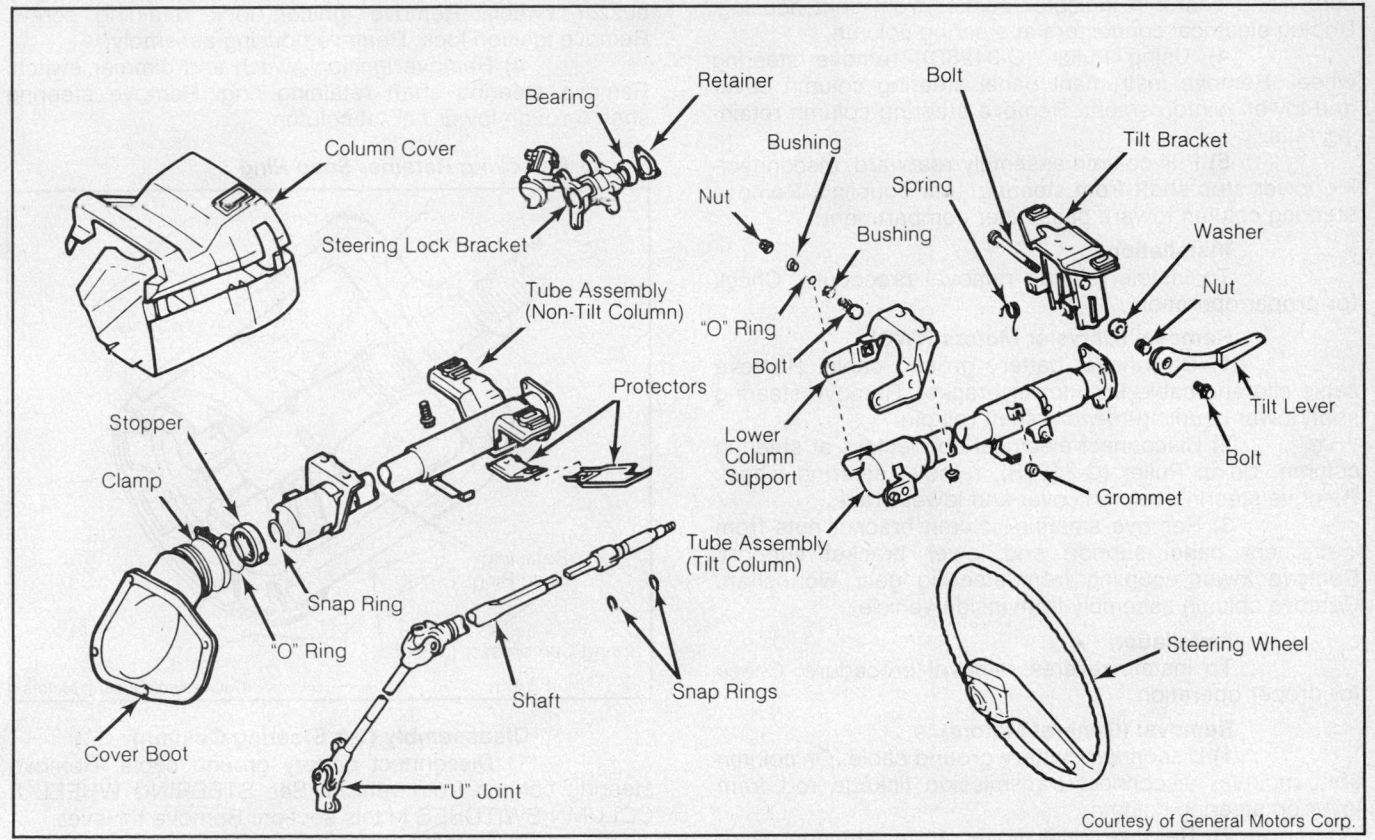

Courtesy of General Motors Corp.

Reassembly

Grease and install upper bearing. Lightly grease all moving parts. To complete reassembly, reverse disassembly procedure.

TIGHTENING SPECIFICATIONS

Application	Ft. Lbs. (N.m)
Upper & Lower Support Bolts	19 (26)
"U" Joint-to-Pinion Shaft Clamp Bolt	26 (35)

SAGINAW

Chrysler Motors: All Except Horizon America & Omni America;
General Motors: All Except Nova

DESCRIPTION

Steering columns are either floor shift or column shift. Construction and maintenance of both columns is the same except for addition of shift lever, tube and related components on column shift models. Column shift and floor shift steering columns are each available in 3 configurations: fixed column, tilt column and tilt/telescopic column.

Steering column design is basically the same for all columns with the main differences involving the addition of column shifters and tilt or tilt/telescopic mechanisms. Steering columns use an integral ignition lock switch. This lock secures the steering wheel and shift linkage (column shift).

Columns have a 2-piece telescoping gear shift tube (column shift), interconnected by plastic inserts and shear pins, and a 2-piece telescoping steering shaft with upper and lower sections connected by plastic collars and pins.

REMOVAL & INSTALLATION

STEERING COLUMN

Removal (Chrysler Motors FWD)

1) Disconnect battery ground cable. On column shift models, disconnect cable rod by prying rod out of grommet in shift lever. DO NOT remove roll pin.

2) If vehicle is equipped with speed control and manual transmission, use care not to damage clutch pedal speed control switch.

SAGINAW (Cont.)

3) Disconnect bezel. Remove indicator set screw and gearshift indicator pointer from shift housing. Unplug electrical connectors at steering column.

4) Using Puller (C-3428B), remove steering wheel. Remove instrument panel steering column cover and lower reinforcement. Remove steering column retaining nuts.

5) Pull column assembly rearward, disconnecting lower stub shaft from steering gear coupling. Remove steering column toward passenger compartment.

Installation

To install, reverse removal procedure. Check for proper operation.

Removal (Chrysler Motors RWD)

1) Disconnect battery ground cable. Remove cable clip and cable from lower bracket. Remove steering shaft lower coupling-to-wormshaft roll pin.

2) Disconnect electrical connectors at steering column. Using Puller (C-3428B), remove steering wheel. Remove steering column cover and lower brace.

3) Remove steering column bracket nuts from instrument panel support and lower bracket support. Remove lower coupling from steering gear wormshaft. Remove column assembly from inside vehicle.

Installation

To install, reverse removal procedure. Check for proper operation.

Removal (General Motors)

1) Disconnect battery ground cable. On column shift models, disconnect transmission linkage rod from lever on steering column.

2) Remove dust cover from steering shaft coupler at steering gear. Remove shaft coupler clamp bolt. Mark steering shaft coupler and steering gear shaft for reassembly reference.

3) Remove steering column floor plate mounting bolts. Remove lower trim panel. Unplug electrical connectors from steering column. Remove steering column bracket mounting nuts. Remove steering column.

Installation

To install, reverse removal procedure. Check for proper operation. Ensure there is at least 1/16" to 1/8" (1.6-3.2 mm) clearance between steering shaft and steering gear flanges.

OVERHAUL

STEERING COLUMN

Preparation

Steering column removal is not necessary if the lock plate cover, lockplate, steering shaft snap ring, canceling cam, turn signal switch, upper bearing preload spring or lock cylinder is to be serviced. For the remaining components, steering column must be removed. Disassembly procedure for the tilt/telescopic steering column is similar to the tilt steering column.

Disassembly (Non-Tilt Steering Column)

1) Disconnect battery ground cable. Remove steering column. Remove horn pad, steering wheel and combination switch. See STEERING WHEEL & COLUMN SWITCHES in this section.

2) Remove lock plate cover. Remove lock plate snap ring using Spring Compressor (J-23653). See Fig. 1. Remove lock plate, horn cam and spring.

3) Remove combination switch. Remove key buzzer switch. Remove ignition lock retaining screw. Remove ignition lock. Remove housing assembly.

4) Remove ignition switch and dimmer switch. Remove steering shaft retaining ring. Remove steering shaft through lower end of column.

Fig. 1: Removing Retainer Snap Ring

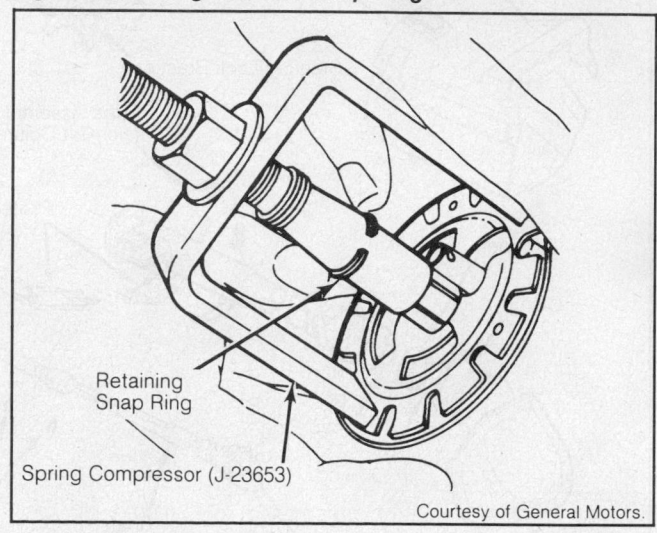

Retaining Snap Ring

Spring Compressor (J-23653)

Courtesy of General Motors.

Disassembly (Tilt Steering Column)

1) Disconnect battery ground cable. Remove steering column from vehicle. See STEERING WHEEL & COLUMN SWITCHES in this section. Remove tilt lever.

2) Remove hazard warning knob and ignition key light. Remove wiper switch knob. Remove wiper switch tube mounting screws. Remove wiper switch tube. Rotate shaft fully clockwise.

3) Remove shaft by pulling straight out on shaft. Carefully remove plastic cover from lock plate. Using Compressor (C-4156 for Chrysler Motors or J-23653 for General Motors), remove lock plate retaining ring from shaft. See Fig. 1.

4) Remove lock plate, cancelling cam and upper bearing spring. Remove turn signal switch and actuator arm. Place ignition lock cylinder in "LOCK" position.

5) Using a thin screwdriver, depress ignition lock cylinder tab retainer. See Fig. 2. Remove ignition lock cylinder. Remove housing cover from column.

Fig. 2: Removing Lock Cylinder

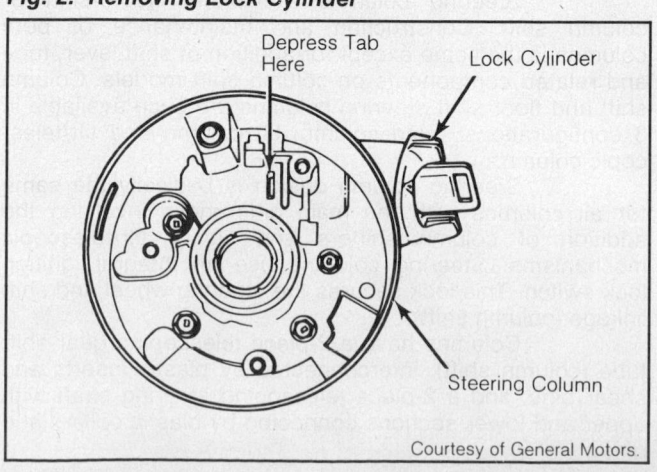

Depress Tab Here

Lock Cylinder

Steering Column

Courtesy of General Motors.

Fig. 3: Removing Tilt Spring

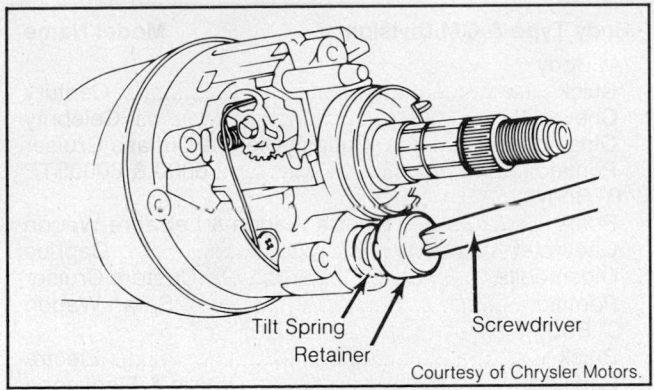

Tilt Spring Retainer

Screwdriver

Courtesy of Chrysler Motors.

6) Place column in fully up position. Remove tilt spring retainer and spring. *See Fig 3*. Remove dimmer switch. Remove steering shaft inner race seat and race. Remove ignition switch and back-up light switch.

7) Using Pivot Pin Remover (C-4016 for Chrysler Motors or J-21854-1 for General Motors), remove pivot pins. *See Fig. 4.* Pull tilt lever to unlock shoes. Remove housing. Remove actuator rods.

Fig. 4: Removing Pivot Pin

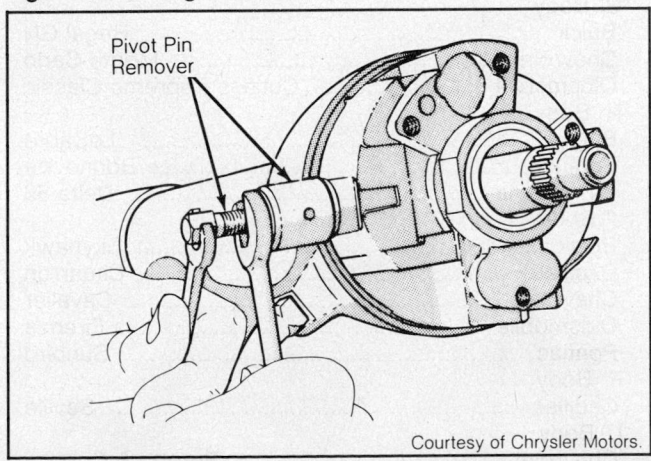

Pivot Pin Remover

Courtesy of Chrysler Motors.

8) Remove lower coupling roll pin. Remove steering shaft assembly from upper end. Remove support from lock plate. Remove shift tube retaining ring.

9) Remove thrust washer. Using screwdriver, disengage plastic shift tube from lower end of jacket. Using Puller (C-4120 for Chrysler Motors or J-23072 for General Motors), pull shift tube from bowl.

10) Inserting bushing on end of tool in shift tube, force bowl from shift tube. Remove shift tube through lower end. Remove jacket mounting plate and wave washer. Remove bowl from jacket.

Inspection (All Steering Columns)

1) Check for separation of the 2 break-away capsules. If capsules have moved more than 1/16" (1.6 mm), some column collapse may have occurred. Check for damaged steering shaft components.

2) Inspect jacket section of column for looseness, bends, collapsed mesh or bellows section. On General Motors models, check for mast jacket collapse by measuring for proper dimensions. *See Fig. 5.*

Fig. 5: General Motors Column Collapse Measurement

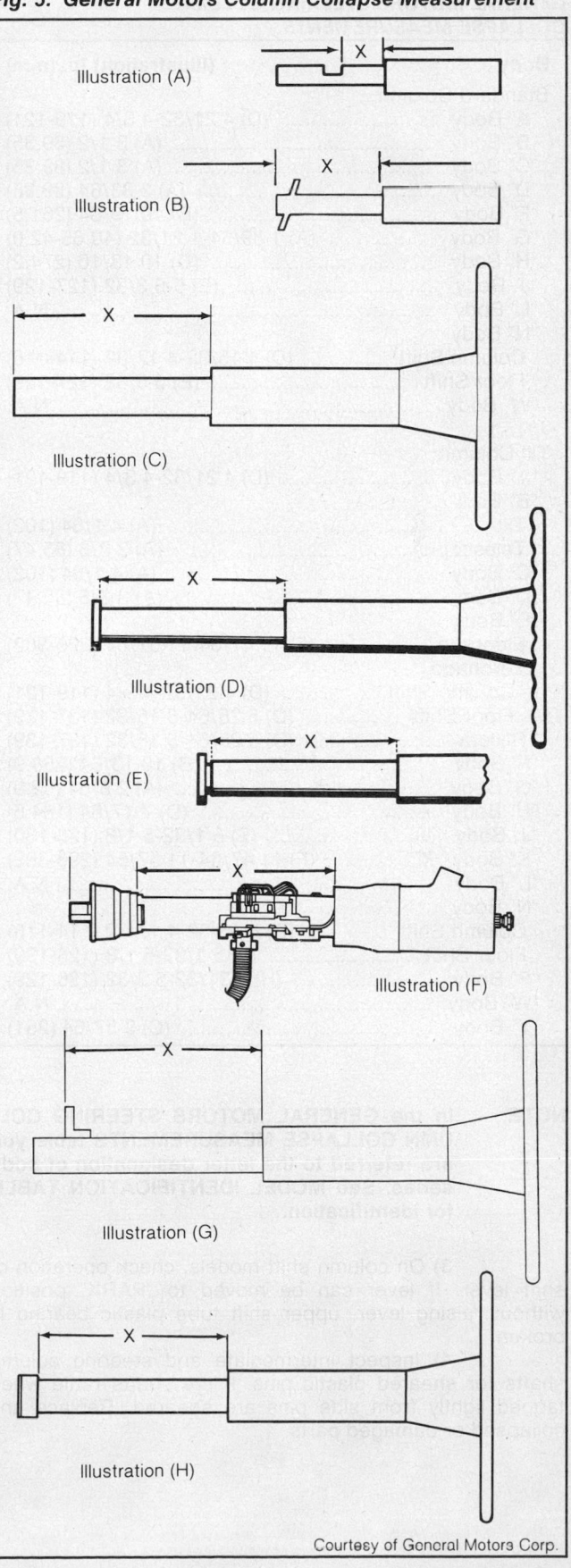

Illustration (A)

Illustration (B)

Illustration (C)

Illustration (D)

Illustration (E)

Illustration (F)

Illustration (G)

Illustration (H)

Courtesy of General Motors Corp.

SAGINAW (Cont.)

GENERAL MOTORS STEERING COLUMN COLLAPSE MEASUREMENTS

Body	(Illustration) In. (mm)
Standard Column	
"A" Body	(D) 4 21/32-4 3/4 (119-121)
"B" Body	(A) 3 1/2 (89.35)
"C" Body	(A) 3 1/2 (89.35)
"D" Body	(A) 3 33/64 (89.35)
"F" Body	(B) 10 19/64 (261.5)
"G" Body	(A) 1 39/64-1 21/32 (40.65-42.0)
"H" Body	(D) 10 13/16 (274.2)
"J" Body	(E) 5-5 3/32 (127-129)
"L" Body	N.A.
"N" Body	
Column Shift	(D) 4 15/32-4 17/32 (114-116)
Floor Shift	(E) 5 5/32 (127-129)
"W" Body	N.A.
Tilt Column	
"A" Body	(D) 4 21/32-4 3/4 (119-121)
"B" Body	
Tilt	(A) 4 1/64 (102)
Telescopic	(A) 3 3/8 (85.47)
"C" Body	(A) 4 1/64 (102)
"D" Body	(A) 3 3/8 (85.47)
"E" Body	
Eldorado	(F) 11 47/64-11 57/64 (298-302)
Toronado	
Column Shift	(D) 4 21/32-4 3/4 (119-121)
Floor Shift	(D) 5 25/64-5 15/32 (137-139)
Riviera	(D) 5 25/64-5 15/32 (137-139)
"F" Body	(B) 10 13/64 (258.9)
"G" Body	(A) 2 5/64 (52.9)
"H" Body	(D) 7 17/64 (184.6)
"J" Body	(E) 5 1/32-5 1/8 (128-130)
"K" Body	(F) 11 47/64-11 57/64 (298-302)
"L" Body	N.A.
"N" Body	
Column Shift	(D) 4 15/32-4 17/32 (114-116)
Floor Shift	(E) 5 1/32-5 1/8 (128-130)
"P" Body	(H) 4 31/32-5 3/32 (126-129)
"W" Body	N.A.
"Y" Body	(C) 9 57/64 (251)

NOTE: In the GENERAL MOTORS STEERING COLUMN COLLAPSE MEASUREMENTS table you are referred to the letter designation of body series. See MODEL IDENTIFICATION TABLE for identification.

3) On column shift models, check operation of shift lever. If lever can be moved to "PARK" position without raising lever, upper shift tube plastic bearing is broken.

4) Inspect intermediate and steering column shafts for sheared plastic pins. If the shafts rattle when tapped lightly from side pins are sheared. Replace any collapsed or damaged parts.

MODEL IDENTIFICATION TABLE

Body Type & GM Division	Model Name
"A" Body	
Buick	Century
Chevrolet	Celebrity
Oldsmobile	Cutlass Ciera & Cutlass Cruiser
Pontiac	6000 & 6000STE
"B" Body	
Buick	Electra Wagon & LeSabre Wagon
Chevrolet	Caprice
Oldsmobile	Custom Cruiser
Pontiac	Safari Wagon
"C" Body	
Buick	Electra
Cadillac	DeVille & Fleetwood
Oldsmobile	Ninety-Eight
"D" Body	
Cadillac	Brougham
"E" Body	
Buick	Riviera
Cadillac	Eldorado
Oldsmobile	Toronado
"F" Body	
Chevrolet	Camaro
Pontiac	Firebird
"G" Body	
Buick	Regal GN
Chevrolet	Monte Carlo
Oldsmobile	Cutlass Supreme Classic
"H" Body	
Buick	LeSabre
Pontiac	Bonneville
Oldsmobile	Delta 88
"J" Body	
Buick	Skyhawk
Cadillac	Cimarron
Chevrolet	Cavalier
Oldsmobile	Firenza
Pontiac	Sunbird
"K" Body	
Cadillac	Seville
"L" Body	
Chevrolet	Beretta & Corsica
"N" Body	
Buick	Skylark
Oldsmobile	Cutlass Calais
Pontiac	Grand Am
"P" Body	
Pontiac	Fiero
"W" Body	
Buick	Regal
Oldsmobile	Cutlass Supreme
Pontiac	Grand Prix
"Y" Body	
Chevrolet	Corvette

SAGINAW (Cont.)

Fig. 6: Exploded View of Chrysler Motors Column Shift Steering Column Housing

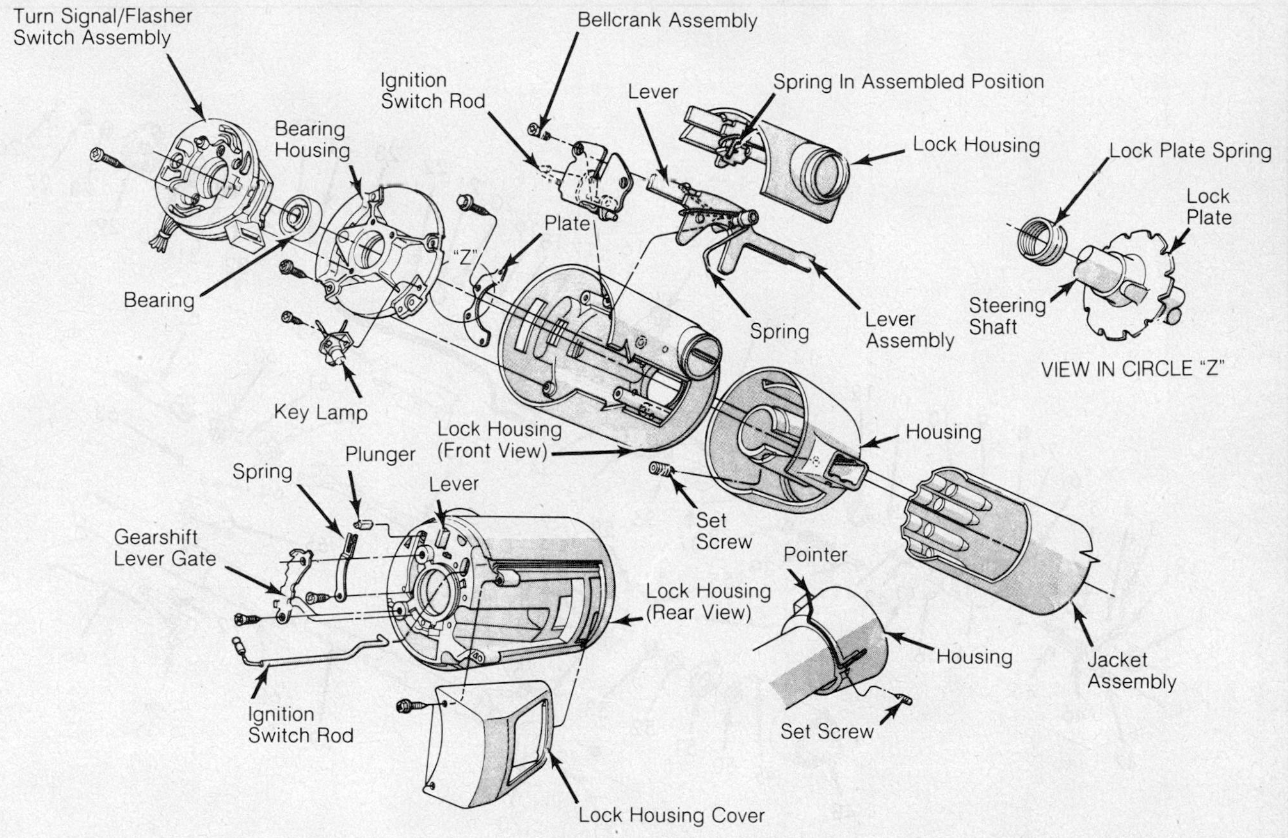

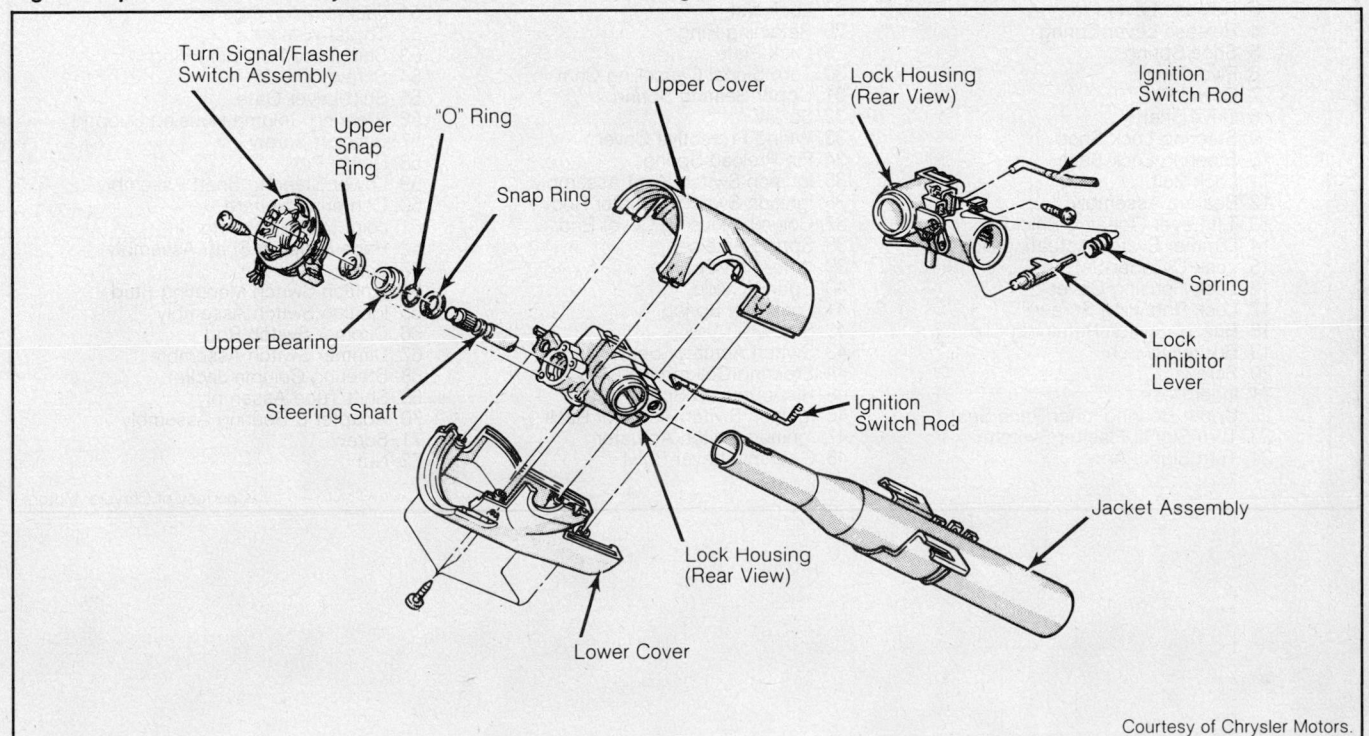

Turn Signal/Flasher Switch Assembly
Bellcrank Assembly
Ignition Switch Rod
Lever
Spring In Assembled Position
Bearing Housing
Lock Housing
Lock Plate Spring
Lock Plate
Plate
"Z"
Bearing
Steering Shaft
Spring
Lever Assembly
VIEW IN CIRCLE "Z"
Key Lamp
Lock Housing (Front View)
Housing
Plunger
Spring
Lever
Set Screw
Gearshift Lever Gate
Pointer
Lock Housing (Rear View)
Housing
Jacket Assembly
Ignition Switch Rod
Set Screw
Lock Housing Cover

Courtesy of Chrysler Motors.

Fig. 7: Exploded View of Chrysler Motors Floor Shift Steering Column Assembly

Turn Signal/Flasher Switch Assembly
Upper Cover
Lock Housing (Rear View)
Ignition Switch Rod
Upper Snap Ring
"O" Ring
Snap Ring
Spring
Upper Bearing
Lock Inhibitor Lever
Steering Shaft
Ignition Switch Rod
Jacket Assembly
Lock Housing (Rear View)
Lower Cover

Courtesy of Chrysler Motors.

Steering Columns
SAGINAW (Cont.)

**Fig. 8: Exploded View of Tilt Steering Column Assembly
(Chrysler Motors & All Except "L" & "W" Body General Motors Vehicles)**

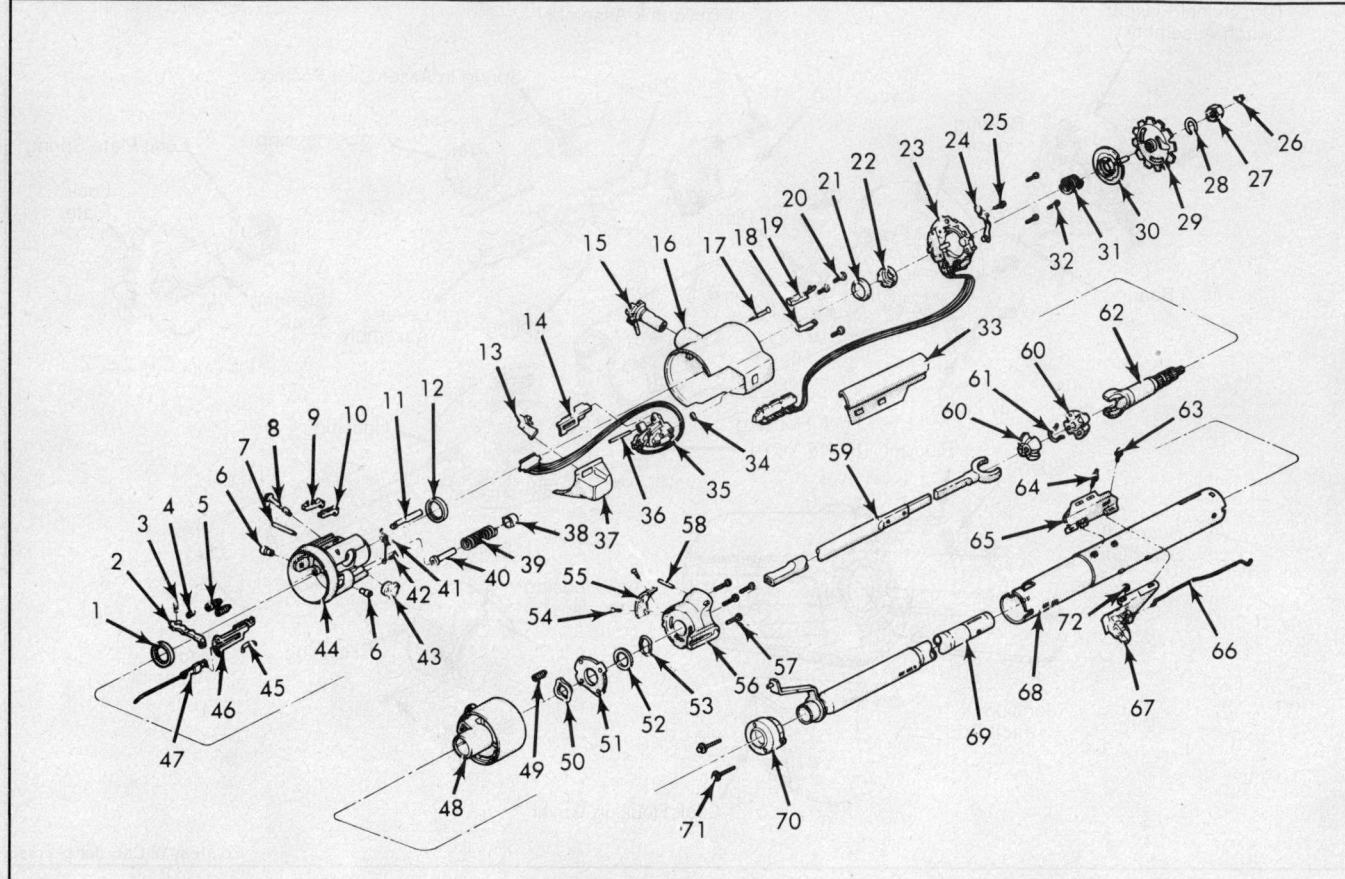

1. Bearing Assembly	25. Screw	49. Shift Lever Spring
2. Shoe Release Lever	26. Retainer	50. Wave Washer
3. Release Lever Pin	27. Lock Nut	51. Jacket Mounting Plate
4. Release Lever Spring	28. Retaining Ring	52. Thrust Washer
5. Shoe Spring	29. Lock Plate	53. Shift Tube Retaining Ring
6. Pivot Pin	30. Turn Signal Cancelling Cam	54. Screw
7. Dowel Pin	31. Upper Bearing Spring	55. Shift Lever Gate
8. Drive Shaft	32. Screw	56. Steering Column Housing Support
9. Steering Lock Shoe	33. Wiring Protective Cover	57. Support Screw
10. Steering Lock Shoe	34. Pin Preload Spring	58. Dowel Pin
11. Lock Bolt	35. Ignition Switch Pivot Assembly	59. Lower Steering Shaft Assembly
12. Bearing Assembly	36. Ignition Switch Actuator Rod	60. Centering Sphere
13. Tilt Lever Opening Shield	37. Column Housing Cover End	61. Joint Preload Spring
14. Dimmer Switch Actuating Rod	38. Spring Retainer	62. Race & Upper Shaft Assembly
15. Lock Cylinder Set	39. Wheel Tilt Spring	63. Screw
16. Lock Housing Cover	40. Spring Guide	64. Ignition Switch Mounting Stud
17. Lock Retaining Screw	41. Lock Bolt Spring	65. Ignition Switch Assembly
18. Buzzer Switch Retaining Clip	42. Screw	66. Dimmer Switch Rod
19. Buzzer Switch	43. Switch Actuator Sector	67. Dimmer Switch Assembly
20. Screw	44. Steering Column Housing	68. Steering Column Jacket
21. Inner Race	45. Rack Preload Spring	69. Shift Tube Assembly
22. Upper Bearing Inner Race Seat	46. Ignition Switch Actuator Rack	70. Adapter & Bearing Assembly
23. Turn Signal/Flasher Switch	47. Ignition Switch Actuator	71. Screw
24. Turn Signal Arm	48. Gearshift Lever Bowl	72. Nut

Courtesy of Chrysler Motors.

SAGINAW (Cont.)

Fig. 9: Exploded View of "L" & "W" Body General Motors Non-Tilt Steering Column Assembly

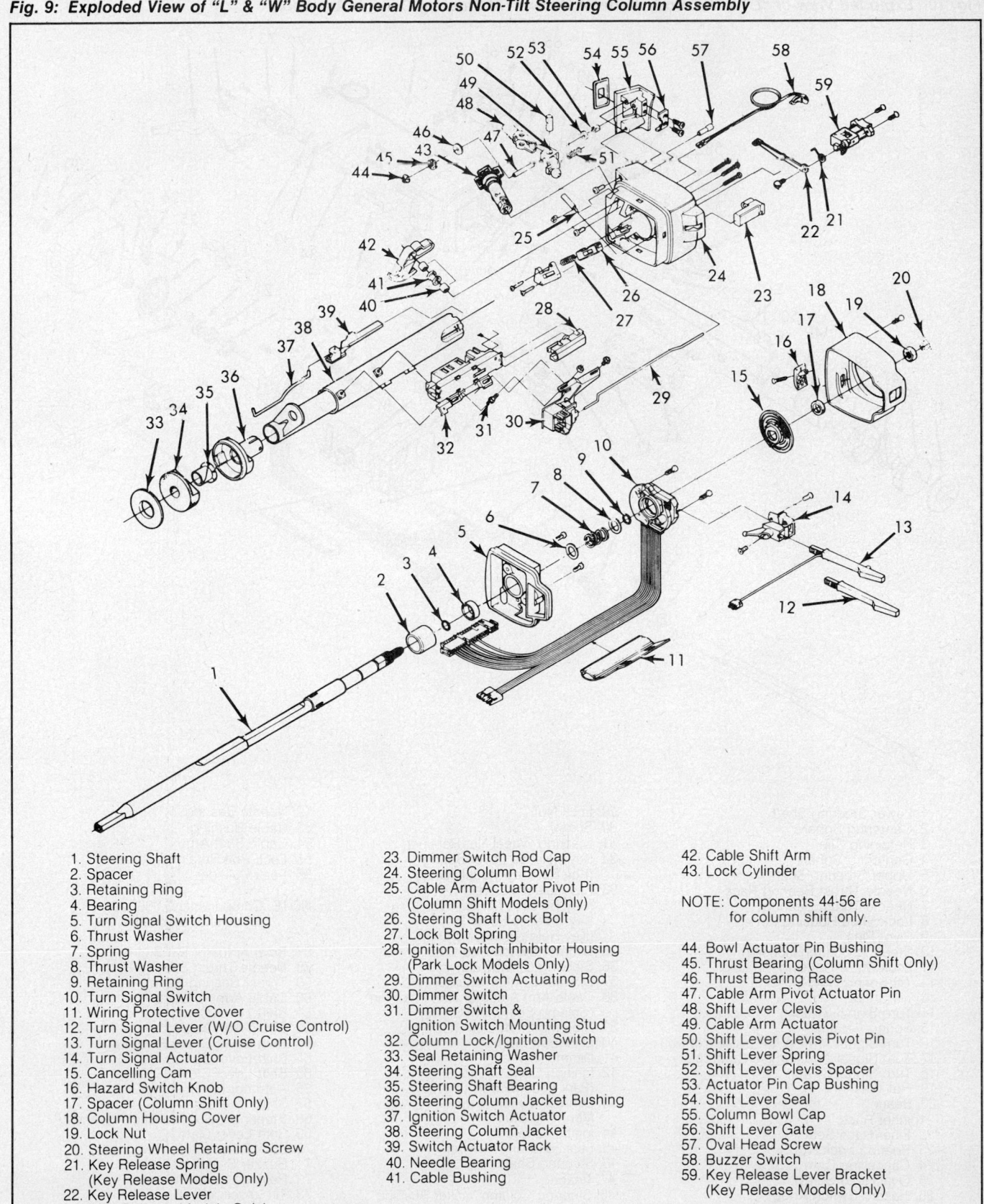

1. Steering Shaft
2. Spacer
3. Retaining Ring
4. Bearing
5. Turn Signal Switch Housing
6. Thrust Washer
7. Spring
8. Thrust Washer
9. Retaining Ring
10. Turn Signal Switch
11. Wiring Protective Cover
12. Turn Signal Lever (W/O Cruise Control)
13. Turn Signal Lever (Cruise Control)
14. Turn Signal Actuator
15. Cancelling Cam
16. Hazard Switch Knob
17. Spacer (Column Shift Only)
18. Column Housing Cover
19. Lock Nut
20. Steering Wheel Retaining Screw
21. Key Release Spring
    (Key Release Models Only)
22. Key Release Lever
    (Key Release Models Only)

23. Dimmer Switch Rod Cap
24. Steering Column Bowl
25. Cable Arm Actuator Pivot Pin
    (Column Shift Models Only)
26. Steering Shaft Lock Bolt
27. Lock Bolt Spring
28. Ignition Switch Inhibitor Housing
    (Park Lock Models Only)
29. Dimmer Switch Actuating Rod
30. Dimmer Switch
31. Dimmer Switch &
    Ignition Switch Mounting Stud
32. Column Lock/Ignition Switch
33. Seal Retaining Washer
34. Steering Shaft Seal
35. Steering Shaft Bearing
36. Steering Column Jacket Bushing
37. Ignition Switch Actuator
38. Steering Column Jacket
39. Switch Actuator Rack
40. Needle Bearing
41. Cable Bushing

42. Cable Shift Arm
43. Lock Cylinder

NOTE: Components 44-56 are
for column shift only.

44. Bowl Actuator Pin Bushing
45. Thrust Bearing (Column Shift Only)
46. Thrust Bearing Race
47. Cable Arm Pivot Actuator Pin
48. Shift Lever Clevis
49. Cable Arm Actuator
50. Shift Lever Clevis Pivot Pin
51. Shift Lever Spring
52. Shift Lever Clevis Spacer
53. Actuator Pin Cap Bushing
54. Shift Lever Seal
55. Column Bowl Cap
56. Shift Lever Gate
57. Oval Head Screw
58. Buzzer Switch
59. Key Release Lever Bracket
    (Key Release Models Only)

Steering Columns

SAGINAW (Cont.)

Fig. 10: Exploded View of "L" & "W" Body General Motors Tilt Steering Column Assembly

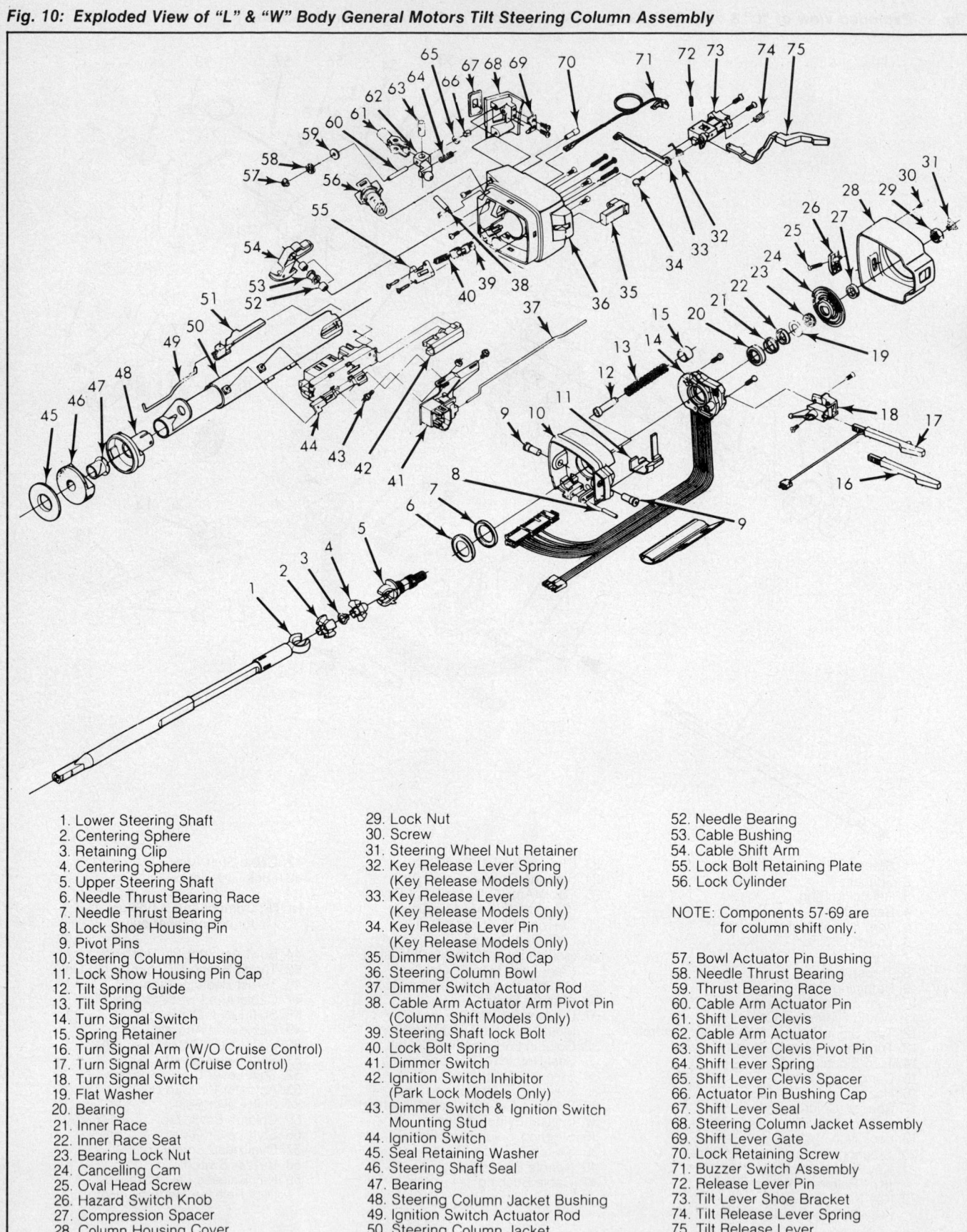

1. Lower Steering Shaft	29. Lock Nut	52. Needle Bearing
2. Centering Sphere	30. Screw	53. Cable Bushing
3. Retaining Clip	31. Steering Wheel Nut Retainer	54. Cable Shift Arm
4. Centering Sphere	32. Key Release Lever Spring	55. Lock Bolt Retaining Plate
5. Upper Steering Shaft	(Key Release Models Only)	56. Lock Cylinder
6. Needle Thrust Bearing Race	33. Key Release Lever	
7. Needle Thrust Bearing	(Key Release Models Only)	NOTE: Components 57-69 are
8. Lock Shoe Housing Pin	34. Key Release Lever Pin	for column shift only.
9. Pivot Pins	(Key Release Models Only)	
10. Steering Column Housing	35. Dimmer Switch Rod Cap	57. Bowl Actuator Pin Bushing
11. Lock Show Housing Pin Cap	36. Steering Column Bowl	58. Needle Thrust Bearing
12. Tilt Spring Guide	37. Dimmer Switch Actuator Rod	59. Thrust Bearing Race
13. Tilt Spring	38. Cable Arm Actuator Arm Pivot Pin	60. Cable Arm Actuator Pin
14. Turn Signal Switch	(Column Shift Models Only)	61. Shift Lever Clevis
15. Spring Retainer	39. Steering Shaft lock Bolt	62. Cable Arm Actuator
16. Turn Signal Arm (W/O Cruise Control)	40. Lock Bolt Spring	63. Shift Lever Clevis Pivot Pin
17. Turn Signal Arm (Cruise Control)	41. Dimmer Switch	64. Shift Lever Spring
18. Turn Signal Switch	42. Ignition Switch Inhibitor	65. Shift Lever Clevis Spacer
19. Flat Washer	(Park Lock Models Only)	66. Actuator Pin Bushing Cap
20. Bearing	43. Dimmer Switch & Ignition Switch	67. Shift Lever Seal
21. Inner Race	Mounting Stud	68. Steering Column Jacket Assembly
22. Inner Race Seat	44. Ignition Switch	69. Shift Lever Gate
23. Bearing Lock Nut	45. Seal Retaining Washer	70. Lock Retaining Screw
24. Cancelling Cam	46. Steering Shaft Seal	71. Buzzer Switch Assembly
25. Oval Head Screw	47. Bearing	72. Release Lever Pin
26. Hazard Switch Knob	48. Steering Column Jacket Bushing	73. Tilt Lever Shoe Bracket
27. Compression Spacer	49. Ignition Switch Actuator Rod	74. Tilt Release Lever Spring
28. Column Housing Cover	50. Steering Column Jacket	75. Tilt Release Lever
	51. Switch	

SAGINAW (Cont.)

Reassembly (All Steering Columns)

1) Install key release lever and spring into shroud. Install retainer plate. Using an arbor press, install bearings into housing (if removed). Using a .180" (4.5 mm) pin to align shoes, install lock shoe springs, lock shoes and shoe pin into housing. Relieve tension on release lever.

2) Install spring, release lever, and pin into bearing housing. Install drive shaft into housing. Lightly tap sector onto shaft, far enough to bottom on drive shaft. Install lock bolt.

3) Engage lock bolt with sector cam surface. Install rack and spring. Block tooth on rack should engage block tooth on sector. Install tilt release lever. Install lock bolt spring, and spring retaining screw. Tighten screw to 35 INCH lbs. (4 N.m).

4) On Chrysler Motors models, install shift lever spring in bowl by winding up with pliers and pushing in. On all models, slide bowl onto jacket. Position wave washer and mounting plate in place.

5) Work jacket mounting plate into notches in jacket by tipping jacket mounting plate toward bowl hub at 12 o'clock position and under jacket opening. Slide jacket mounting plate into notches in jacket.

6) Install shift tube into lower end of jacket. Align key in tube with keyway in bowl. Using Installer (C-4119 for Chrysler Motors or J-23073 for General Motors), pull shift tube into bowl. *See Fig. 11.* Do not tap on end of shift tube.

Fig. 11: Installing Shift Tube

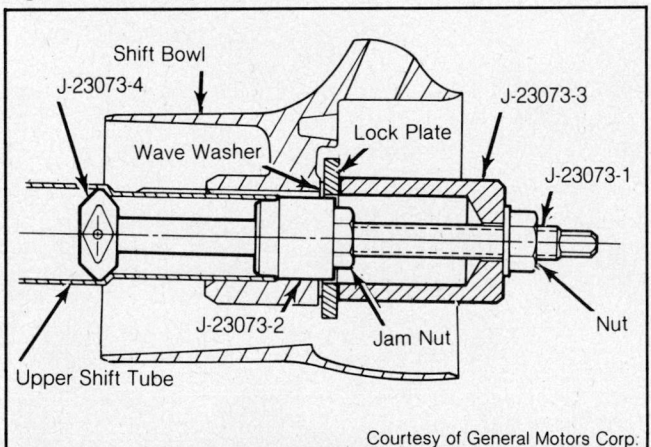

Courtesy of General Motors Corp.

7) Pulling up bowl to compress wave washer, install thrust washer and retaining ring. Slide dimmer switch actuator rod through hole in support. Aligning "U" in support with "U" notch in jacket, install support.

8) Insert 4 screws through support into lock plate. Tighten screws to 60 INCH lbs. (7 N.m). Drive lower bearing approximately 3/16" into tube. Slide ignition actuator rod between bowl and jacket.

9) Install centering spheres and anti-lash spring into upper steering shaft. Install lower steering shaft from same side of spheres that ends protrude. Ensure that master serration of upper shaft aligns with master serration of lower shaft.

10) Place shift bowl in "PARK" position. Holding lock shoes in disengaged position, install bearing housing over steering shaft until pivot pin holes align with holes in support. Ensure rack has engaged ignition switch actuator rod.

11) Install Pivot Pins. Use hand pressure to prevent damaging support pivot holes. Using small hammer and drift, tap in pins to complete installation. Place housing in the fully up position.

12) Install guide and peg onto support. Install tilt spring and spring retainer. Using a screwdriver turn retainer counterclockwise to engage. Install inner bearing race and seat. Install tilt lever opening shield in housing.

13) Remove tilt release lever. Install housing cover. Seat screw at 12 o'clock position. Install and tighten 3 screws to 100 INCH lbs. (11 N.m). Install buzzer/chime switch to spring clip with spring bowed away from switch on side opposite contact.

14) Push switch and spring into hole in cover with contacts toward lock cylinder. Install key light (if equipped). Install turn signal switch. Feed wires and connector through cover, bearing housing and shift bowl.

15) Install hazard warning knob. Install cancelling cam, cam spring and shaft lock plate. Using Compressor (C-4156 for Chrysler Motors or J-23653 for General Motors) to depress lock plate, install new retaining ring.

16) Reinstall tilt release lever and turn signal switch lever. Install upper shift lever. Drive in pivot pin. Position shaft lock cover over lock. Snap shaft lock cover into position by pressing on outer edges.

17) To install ignition lock, turn key to "LOCK" position. Remove key. Buzzer operating lever should retract into cylinder. Slide ignition switch to "LOCK" position (second detent from bottom).

18) Insert cylinder into housing far enough to contact drive shaft. Press inward while moving ignition switch actuator rod up and down to align parts. When properly aligned, cylinder will move in and spring loaded retainer will snap into place locking the cylinder into housing.

19) Push ignition switch lightly up column, toward lock housing, to remove lash in actuator rod. Tighten mounting screws to 35 INCH lbs. (4 N.m). Install wire protector. Seat actuator rod on dimmer switch.

Fig. 12: Aligning Dimmer Switch

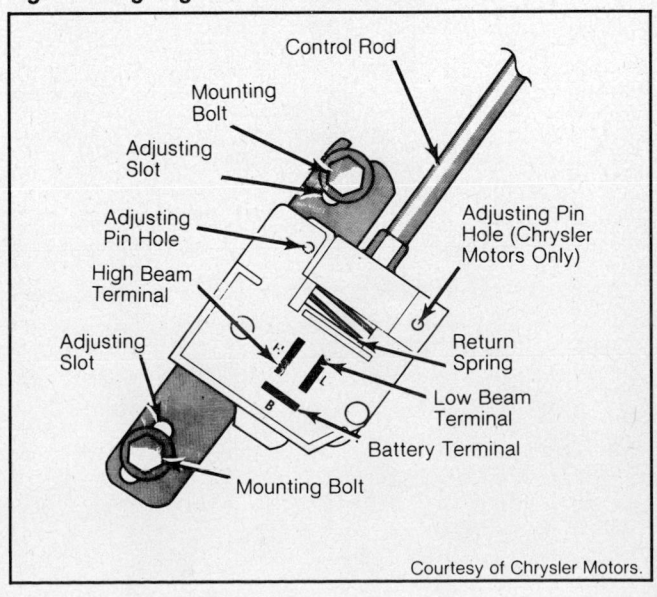

Courtesy of Chrysler Motors.

SAGINAW (Cont.)

20) On Chrysler Motors vehicles, depress dimmer switch until 2 3/32" drill bits can be inserted into alignment holes. *See Fig. 12.*

21) On General Motors vehicles, depress dimmer switch until one 3/32" drill bit can be inserted into alignment hole. *See Fig. 12.*

22) On all models, reposition upper end of actuator rod in pocket of washer/wiper switch. With light upward pressure on switch to remove lash, install and tighten 2 screws on switch. Remove drill bit(s).

23) Ensure that switch clicks as lever is lifted. Check for proper operation of ignition lock, wiper/washer switch, dimmer switch and steering mechanism.

CHRYSLER MOTORS TIGHTENING SPECIFICATIONS

Application	Ft. Lbs. (N.m)
Column Clamp Stud Nut	17 (23)
Flexible Coupling Nuts	17 (23)
Steering Wheel Nut	45 (61)

	INCH Lbs. (N.m)
Bracket-to-Column Nuts	20 (2)
Column Clamp Stud	110 (20)
Support Plate Bolts	60 (7)

GENERAL MOTORS TIGHTENING SPECIFICATIONS

Application	Ft. Lbs. (N.m)
Steering Wheel Nut	30 (41)
Bracket-to-Column Nuts	22 (30)
Bracket-to-Instrument Panel Stud Nuts	22 (30)
Flexible Coupling Nuts	20 (27)
Intermediate Shaft-to-Steering Shaft Bolt	35 (47)
Upper Intermediate Shaft-to-Steering Column	44 (60)
Lower Intermediate Shaft-to-Steering Gear Box	35 (47)

Manual Steering Gears

CHRYSLER MOTORS RACK & PINION

Aries, Horizon America, Omni America, Reliant

DESCRIPTION

Rotary motion of the pinion shaft is converted to transverse movement of the steering rack. Steering gear is connected to steering knuckles with tie rods. The steering gear is factory lubricated and sealed. The steering gear is not adjustable. Service is limited to replacement of tie rod ends and boots. Complete replacement is required in event of malfunction.

REMOVAL & INSTALLATION

STEERING GEAR

Removal

1) Raise and support vehicle. Remove front wheels. Remove cotter pins and castle nuts from tie rod ends. Using a puller, separate tie rod ends from knuckles.

2) Remove all 4 front suspension crossmember attaching bolts. Using transmission jack, lower crossmember. Drive out steering coupling roll pin.

3) Separate steering gear from steering shaft. Remove splash and boot seal shields. Remove bolts securing steering gear to front crossmember. Remove steering gear from crossmember

Installation

To install, reverse removal procedure. Install right rear crossmember bolt first. This aligns the cross-member. Tighten crossmember mounting bolts to 90 ft. lbs. (122 N.m). Check and adjust toe-in.

TIE ROD END

Removal

Remove castle nut and cotter pin. Using a puller, separate tie rod end from steering knuckle. Loosen jam nut. Remove outer tie rod ends from inner tie rods.

Installation

To install, reverse removal procedure. Check and adjust toe-in.

BOOT SEAL

Removal

With outer tie rod end removed, remove lock nut. Cut and discard inner boot clamp. Mark breather tube location for reassembly reference. Using small screwdriver, lift boot inner lip out of groove. Remove boot.

Installation

To install, reverse removal procedure. Use silicone lubricant on boot lips.

TIGHTENING SPECIFICATIONS

Application	Ft. Lbs. (N.m)
Crossmember-to-Frame Bolts	90 (122)
Tie Rod End-to-Knuckle Castle Nuts	38 (52)
Tie Rod End Lock Nuts	45-65 (60-90)
Steering Gear-to-Crossmember Bolts	21 (28)

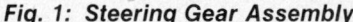

Fig. 1: Steering Gear Assembly

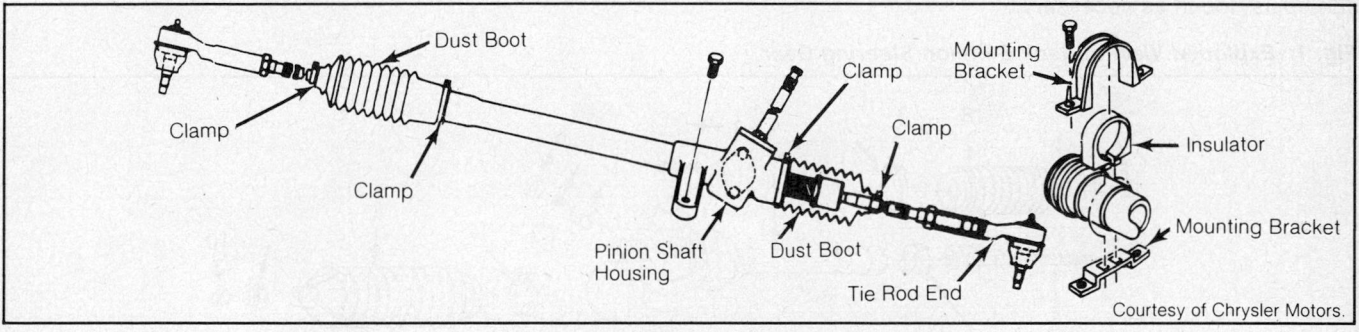

Courtesy of Chrysler Motors.

FORD MOTOR CO. RACK & PINION

Escort, Tempo, Topaz

DESCRIPTION

The steering system is rack and pinion type. Steering gear is connected to steering knuckles with tie rods. The input shaft connects to the steering shaft with double "U" joint intermediate shaft.

ADJUSTMENTS

RACK PRELOAD

Rack preload is adjusted during reassembly procedure. See OVERHAUL in this article.

REMOVAL & INSTALLATION

STEERING GEAR

Removal

1) Disconnect battery ground cable. Turn ignition switch to "RUN" position. Remove access panel from floorboard, below steering column. Remove intermediate shaft "U" joint bolts at pinion shaft.

2) Using a screwdriver, spread slots enough to loosen intermediate shaft at both ends. Intermediate shaft and pinion shaft can not be separated at this time.

3) Remove tie rod end cotter pins and castle nuts. Using a tie rod end puller, separate tie rod ends from steering knuckles. Turn right wheel to full left turn position.

4) Disconnect speedometer cable at transmission (automatic only). Disconnect secondary air tube at check valve. Remove exhaust system from exhaust manifold.

5) Remove steering gear mounting brackets and insulators. Turn steering wheel full left. Separate gear from intermediate shaft by having an assistant pull up on shaft from inside vehicle.

6) Carefully rotate gear forward and down to clear pinion shaft through floorboard opening. Ensure pinion shaft is in full left turn position.

7) Move gear through passenger side apron opening until left tie rod clears shift linkage. Lower gear left side. Remove steering gear. Do not rip boots.

Installation

To install, reverse removal procedure. Ensure flat on side mounting area is parallel to floorboard. Tighten left mounting bracket first to locate gear properly. Check and adjust toe-in as necessary.

OVERHAUL

DUST BOOT, TIE ROD & TIE ROD END

Disassembly

1) With steering gear removed, clean housing exterior. Mount housing in Holding Fixture (T57L-500-B). Loosen tie rod end lock nuts. Remove tie rod ends. Remove outer boot clamps.

2) Remove and discard inner boot clamps. Remove boot. Turn gear full right to expose rack teeth. Mount rack teeth in soft-jawed vise. Using pipe wrench on inner tie rod ball socket, remove and discard tie rod.

Inspection

Visually inspect rack end for corrosion or contamination. If either is present, overhaul or replace steering gear. See STEERING GEAR in OVERHAUL in this article.

Reassembly

1) Turn gear full right turn to expose rack teeth. Mount rack teeth in a soft-jawed vise. Install new tie rods. Tighten to specification. Remove assembly from vise. Supporting ball socket, stake socket to rack with a punch.

2) Center of punch should be approximately .6" (15 mm) away from rack end. *See Fig. 2.* Visually verify displacement of metal into rack slot.

3) Grease rack and rack teeth. Install boots and boot clamps. Ensure small diameter of boot is in the tie rod groove. Install lock nuts and tie rod ends.

Fig. 1: Exploded View of Rack & Pinion Steering Gear

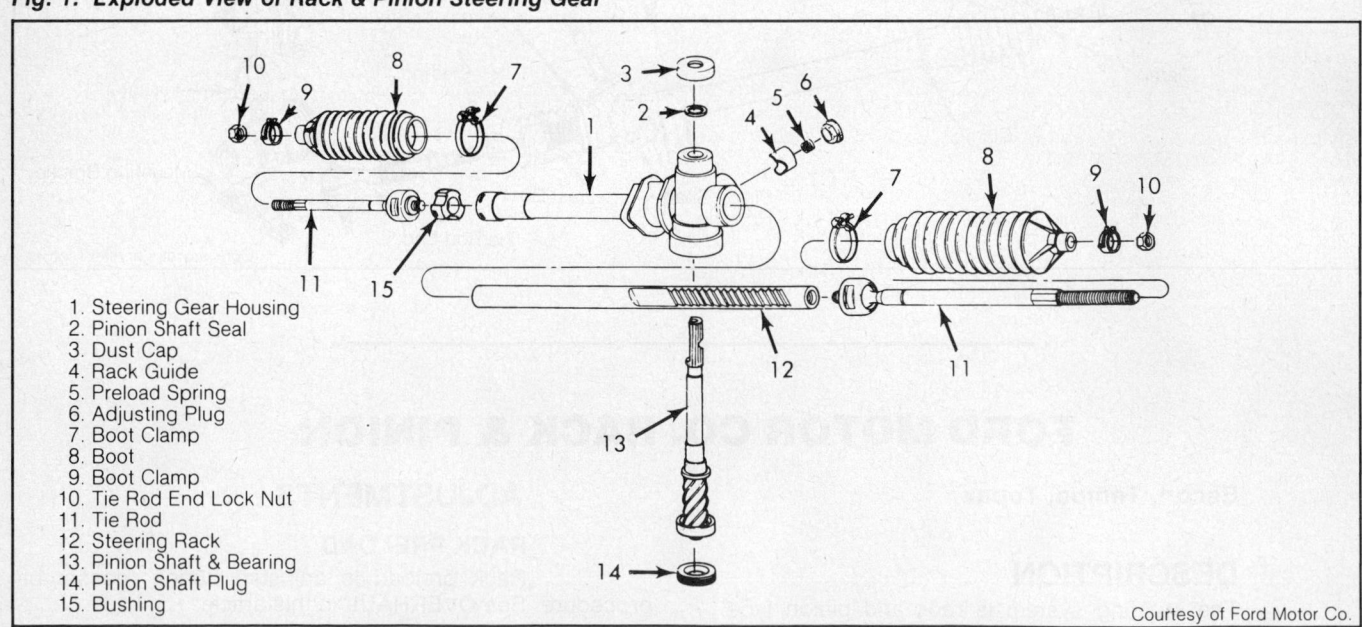

1. Steering Gear Housing
2. Pinion Shaft Seal
3. Dust Cap
4. Rack Guide
5. Preload Spring
6. Adjusting Plug
7. Boot Clamp
8. Boot
9. Boot Clamp
10. Tie Rod End Lock Nut
11. Tie Rod
12. Steering Rack
13. Pinion Shaft & Bearing
14. Pinion Shaft Plug
15. Bushing

Courtesy of Ford Motor Co.

FORD MOTOR CO. RACK & PINION (Cont.)

Fig. 2: Staking Service Tie Rods In Place

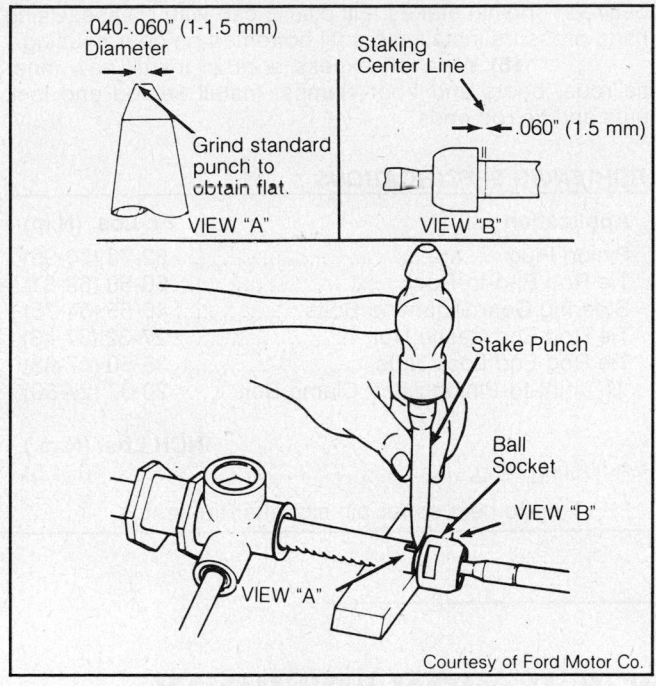

Courtesy of Ford Motor Co.

STEERING GEAR

NOTE: If pinion is removed, the entire gear must be disassembled for cleaning. The pinion plug threads must be retapped and cleaned.

Disassembly

1) With steering gear removed, remove tie rod ends, lock nuts, dust boots and tie rods as previously described. Mount rack assembly in Holding Fixture (T57L-500-B). Remove and discard pinion shaft plastic cap.

2) Turn pinion fully right. Using Plug Remover (T86P-3504-A), remove and discard pinion plug. With plug remover reversed, remove and discard adjusting plug.

3) Remove spring and rack guide bearing. Remove pinion and bearing assembly by pushing out through the pinion plug opening. Use plastic mallet if necessary.

4) Remove rack from pinion end of housing. Using screwdriver, carefully pry out pinion shaft seal. DO NOT damage housing. Discard seal.

Cleaning & Inspection

1) Using Plug Remover (T86P-3504-A), clean threads of adjusting plug and pinion plug bore. Wash all parts in mineral spirits. Air dry all parts.

2) Do not submerge plastic rack bushing in right end of housing. Inspect rack bushing for wear. Check pinion teeth and rack for corrosion, wear, straightness, cracks, scoring, pitting or breaks.

3) Inspect the lower pinion bearing for wear or roughness. If any of these conditions exist, replace the rack housing. Replace all other parts as necessary.

Reassembly

1) If rack bearing was not removed, go to step 4). If rack bearing was removed, align 3 slots of Rack Bushing Guide (T86P-3504-C2) over dimples in rack tube. Align extra slot over one of tube slots. *See Fig. 3.*

Fig. 3: Installing Rack Bushing To Housing

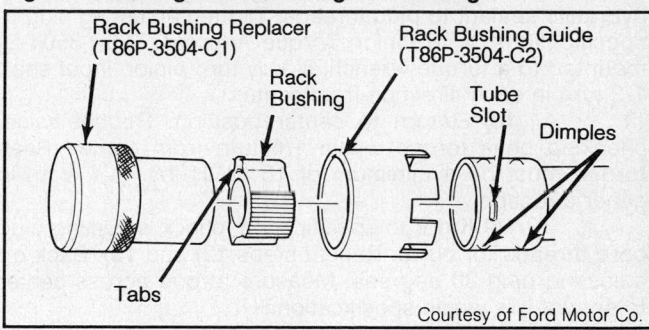

Courtesy of Ford Motor Co.

2) Lubricate new rack bushing outer diameter with steering gear grease. Insert new rack bushing into tool so tabs align with grooves in tool.

3) Using Rack Bushing Replacer (T86P-3504-C1) and hand pressure, push rack bushing into rack tube until tool bottoms. Remove rack bushing guide. Reapply hand pressure to rack bushing replacer to fully seat tabs in slots.

4) Fill rack teeth and cover rest of shaft with a light film of grease. Pack pinion shaft lower bearing and inboard of rack bushing with grease. Install rack into housing from left end.

5) Center the load slot in pinion bore. Coat all remaining sliding surfaces with grease. Pinion shaft teeth and bearing with grease. Install pinion shaft and bearing assembly from bottom through load slot in rack.

6) Install pinion shaft plug. Tighten to specification. Install, but do not tighten, left tie rod assembly to rack. Mount gear to Holding Fixture (T57L-500-B).

7) Hold pinion shaft flat in 9 o'clock position while pushing rack into housing. Jiggle rack to engage rack to pinion and to start rack in rack bushing. Push rack in all the way.

8) The pinion shaft flat should stop in the 6 o'clock position when the left ball joint contacts the housing. *See Fig. 4.* If flat is not in the 6 o'clock popsition, repeat step 7) until it is.

Fig. 4: Installing Rack To Housing

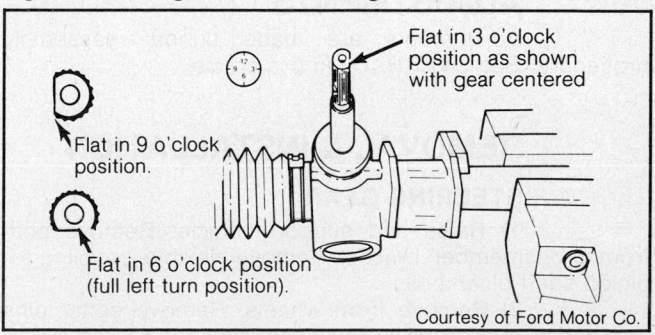

Courtesy of Ford Motor Co.

9) Install, but do not tighten, right tie rod to rack. Install rack guide, preload spring and adjusting plug. Tighten plug until most of play in rack is taken up.

10) Turn pinion lock-to-lock, counting number of turns necessary. Return pinion half the number of turns to center position. Pinion shaft flat should be at 3 o'clock position.

11) The pinion gear has only 4 teeth, so flat can only be in one of 4 positions, 90 degrees apart. If out of adjustment repeat step 7).

Manual Steering Gears

FORD MOTOR CO. RACK & PINION (Cont.)

12) Remove adjusting plug. Apply Loctite hydraulic sealant to plug threads. Tighten adjusting plug to specifications. With Pinion Torque Adapter (T86P-3504-B) mounted to a torque wrench, slowly turn pinion input shaft 1/2 turn in each direction from center.

13) Return to center position. Repeat twice, checking peak torque within 1/4 turn from center. Peak torque must be a minimum of 15 INCH lbs. (1.7 N.m) in either direction.

14) If not to specification, check adjusting plug bore threads for burrs. Repeat steps **12)** and **13)**. Back off adjusting plug 30 degrees. Measure torque across center to ensure it is within specification.

15) Stake adjusting plug in 3 places equally spaced apart. Each stake should be midway between original stakes. Pack the space above pinion shaft needle bearing 2/3 full of steering gear grease.

16) Coat new pinion shaft seal lip with grease. Using Pinion Cover Installer (T81P-3504-Y) and hand pressure, press seal in until flush with top of housing.

17) Stake pinion plug in 2 places midway between original stakes. Fill plastic cap with grease. Using hand pressure install cap until bottomed on gear housing.

18) Wipe off excess grease. Install new inner tie rods, boots and boot clamps. Install tie rod end lock nuts and tie rod ends.

TIGHTENING SPECIFICATIONS

Application	Ft. Lbs. (N.m)
Pinion Plug	52-73 (70-99)
Tie Rod End-to-Rack	50-60 (68-81)
Steering Gear Mounting Bolts	40-55 (54-75)
Tie Rod End Castle Nut	[1] 27-32 (37-43)
Tie Rod End Lock Nuts	35-50 (47-68)
"U" Joint-to-Pinion Shaft Clamp Bolt	20-37 (27-50)
	INCH Lbs. (N.m)
Adjusting Plug	40 (4.5)

[1] – Turn to next cotter pin slot after tightening.

GENERAL MOTORS RACK & PINION "P" BODY

Fiero

DESCRIPTION

Rotation of the pinion is transferred through pinion teeth which mesh with teeth on the rack to produce transverse motion necessary for steering purposes. Tie rod assemblies connect the unit to steering knuckles. Rack preload is adjustable. Tie rods contain a spring loaded inner ball joint, which permits both rocking and rotating movement.

ADJUSTMENTS

Adjustments are made during reassembly procedure. See OVERHAUL in this article.

REMOVAL & INSTALLATION

STEERING GEAR

1) Raise and support vehicle. Remove both front crossmember braces. Remove flexible coupling-to-pinion shaft pinch bolt.

2) Remove front wheels. Remove cotter pins and castle nuts from tie rod ends. Using a tie rod puller, separate tie rod ends from steering knuckles. Remove mounting brackets and steering damper. Remove steering gear.

Installation

To install, reverse removal procedure. Adjust toe-in.

TIE ROD END

Removal

Remove castle nut and cotter pin. Using a puller, separate tie rod end from steering knuckle. Loosen jam nut. Remove outer tie rod ends from inner tie rods.

Installation

To install, reverse removal procedure. Check and adjust toe-in.

STEERING DAMPER

Removal & Installation

Hold stud while removing nuts holding damper in place. Remove steering damper. To install, place damper assembly on rack studs. Install flat washers and nuts. Tighten nuts to specification.

DUST BOOT

Removal

1) Remove tie rod end. Cut and discard boot clamps. To remove left boot only, slide boot towards center of rack. Place a rubber band in outer boot groove. Slide boot off tie rod.

2) To remove right boot, remove damper assembly. Remove outer stud and boot support from rack assembly. Slide boot toward center of rack, place a rubber band in outer boot groove. Slide boot off tie rod.

Installation

1) To install left boot, place a rubber band in inner tie rod boot groove. Slide boot onto inner tie rod and housing assembly. Using Clamp Installer (J-22610), crimp new inner boot clamps in place. Remove rubber band. Engage boot to inner tie rod boot groove.

2) To install right boot, place a rubber band in inner tie rod boot groove. Slide boot over inner tie rod. Line up hole for shock damper. Install boot support and damper stud.

GENERAL MOTORS RACK & PINION "P" BODY (Cont.)

Fig. 1: Exploded View of Fiero Steering Gear Assembly

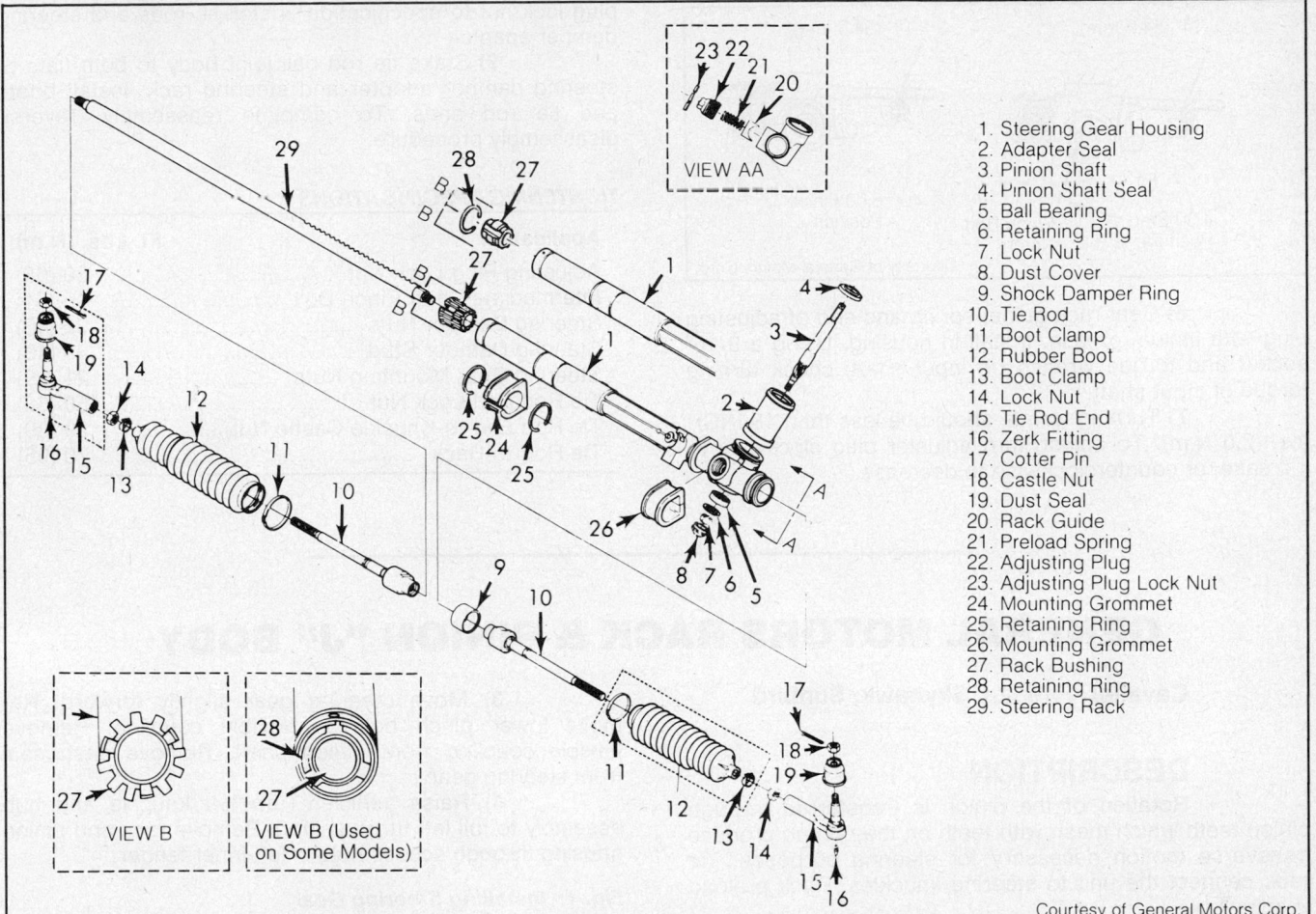

VIEW AA

1. Steering Gear Housing
2. Adapter Seal
3. Pinion Shaft
4. Pinion Shaft Seal
5. Ball Bearing
6. Retaining Ring
7. Lock Nut
8. Dust Cover
9. Shock Damper Ring
10. Tie Rod
11. Boot Clamp
12. Rubber Boot
13. Boot Clamp
14. Lock Nut
15. Tie Rod End
16. Zerk Fitting
17. Cotter Pin
18. Castle Nut
19. Dust Seal
20. Rack Guide
21. Preload Spring
22. Adjusting Plug
23. Adjusting Plug Lock Nut
24. Mounting Grommet
25. Retaining Ring
26. Mounting Grommet
27. Rack Bushing
28. Retaining Ring
29. Steering Rack

VIEW B

VIEW B (Used on Some Models)

Courtesy of General Motors Corp.

3) Tighten stud to specifications. Remove rubber band. Engage boot to tie rod boot groove. Install shock damper and tie rod ends. Adjust toe-in.

MOUNTING GROMMETS
Removal & Installation
Remove nuts and mounting straps holding gear assembly in place. Remove grommets. Split rubber grommets can be removed and installed without steering gear removal. Install grommets and mounting straps. Tighten mounting nuts to specifications.

OVERHAUL

STEERING GEAR
Disassembly
1) With rack removed from vehicle, remove outer tie rod ends and boots. Remove outer tie rod end while holding rack gear stationary to prevent internal rack damage.

2) Shock damper adapter will be removed with right tie rod. Mount steering gear on holding fixture. Remove adjusting plug lock nut. Remove adjusting plug, spring and rack guide.

3) Using Snap Ring Pliers (J-4245), remove pinion assembly retaining ring. Remove steering gear from holding fixture. Clamp pinion shaft in soft-jawed vise.

4) Tap housing around pinion shaft until pinion assembly separates from housing with adapter seal. With pinion shaft removed, slide rack out of housing.

5) Using an arbor press, remove roller bearing from pinion shaft housing. Using Snap Ring Pliers (J-4245), remove bushing retaining ring. Using a 3-fingered slide hammer, pull rack bushing from housing.

Reassembly
1) Using an arbor press and socket, press rack bushing into housing until fully seated. Install bushing retaining ring. Using Adapter (J-26269), press new roller bearing into place.

2) Ensure bearing is fully seated. Coat rack teeth with lithium based grease. Install rack into housing. Position rack so that 2.14" (54.3 mm) of gear extends from pinion shaft end of housing. See Fig. 2.

3) Insert pinion shaft assembly into housing with flat on pinion shaft in 4:30 o'clock position. Flat should be in 3:00 o'clock position, with gear teeth meshed and pinion completely engaged.

4) If flat side of pinion is more than 30 degrees from finished position, remove pinion. Rotate pinion one tooth. Reinstall pinion. See Fig. 2.

5) Install pinion shaft retaining ring. Ensure that clearance is .28" (7 mm) between snap ring tangs when installed. Fill pinion shaft retaining ring cavity with anhydrous grease.

Manual Steering Gears

GENERAL MOTORS RACK & PINION "P" BODY (Cont.)

Fig. 2: Pinion Shaft Installation Position

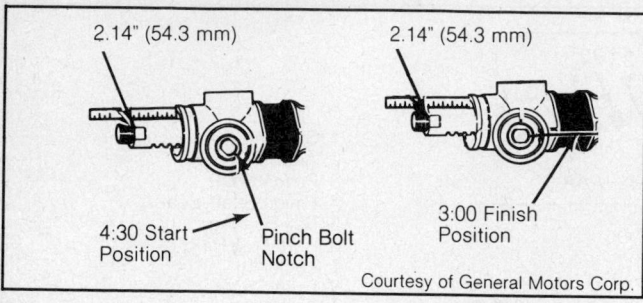

Courtesy of General Motors Corp.

6) Coat rack guide, spring and end of adjusting plug with lithium grease. Install in housing. Using a 9/16" socket and torque wrench on input shaft, check turning torque of input shaft.

7) Turning torque should be less than 18 INCH lbs. (2.0 N.m). To adjust, turn adjuster plug clockwise to increase, or counterclockwise to decrease.

8) When adjustment is correct, tighten adjuster plug lock nut to specification. Install tie rods and steering damper adapter.

9) Stake tie rod ball joint body to both flats of steering damper adapter and steering rack. Install boots and tie rod ends. To complete reassembly, reverse disassembly procedure.

TIGHTENING SPECIFICATIONS

Application	Ft. Lbs. (N.m)
Adjusting Plug Lock Nut	50 (68)
Intermediate Shaft Pinch Bolt	45 (61)
Steering Damper Nuts	32 (43)
Steering Damper Stud	35 (48)
Steering Gear Mounting Nuts	21 (29)
Tie Rod End Lock Nut	50 (68)
Tie Rod End-to-Knuckle Castle Nut	29 (39)
Tie Rod-to-Rack	70 (95)

GENERAL MOTORS RACK & PINION "J" BODY

Cavalier, Firenza, Skyhawk, Sunbird

DESCRIPTION

Rotation of the pinion is transferred through pinion teeth which mesh with teeth on the rack to produce transverse motion necessary for steering purposes. Tie rods connect the unit to steering knuckles. Rack preload is adjustable.

ADJUSTMENTS

RACK PRELOAD

1) Rack preload can can be done without removal of steering gear. Checking pinion preload is not necessary.

2) Raise front wheels. Center the steering wheel. Tighten adjusting plug to 72-132 INCH. lbs. (8-15 N.m). Back off adjusting plug 50 to 70 degrees.

3) Tighten lock nut to 50 ft. lbs. (68 N.m) while holding adjusting plug stationary. Check returnability of steering wheel to center after adjustment.

REMOVAL & INSTALLATION

RACK & PINION HOUSING

Removal

1) Remove driver's side sound insulator. Remove upper pinch bolt from flexible coupling. Raise and support vehicle. Remove front wheels. Remove tie rod end pinch bolts, cotter pins and castle nuts.

2) Using Tie Rod Remover (J-24319-01), remove tie rod from steering knuckle. Disconnect tie rod ends from steering knuckles. Lower car. Remove steering gear mounting brackets.

3) Move steering gear slightly forward. Remove lower pinch bolt on flexible coupling. Remove flexible coupling from pinion shaft. Remove dash seal from steering gear.

4) Raise vehicle. Turn left knuckle and hub assembly to full left turn position. Remove rack and pinion housing through access hole in left inner fender.

Fig. 1: Installing Steering Gear

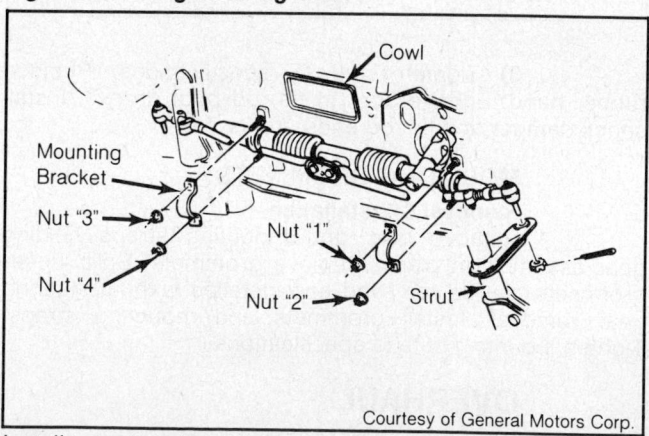

Courtesy of General Motors Corp.

Install mounting bracket nuts in order 1-4 as shown.

Installation

To install, reverse removal procedures. Install rack mounting nuts starting with the left upper, then left lower, right upper, and then right lower, as seen from drivers seat facing forward. See Fig. 1.

TIE ROD END

Removal & Installation

1) Loosen tie rod end pinch bolts. Remove tie rod end from tie rod.

GENERAL MOTORS RACK & PINION "J" BODY (Cont.)

Fig. 2: Exploded View of Steering Gear Assembly

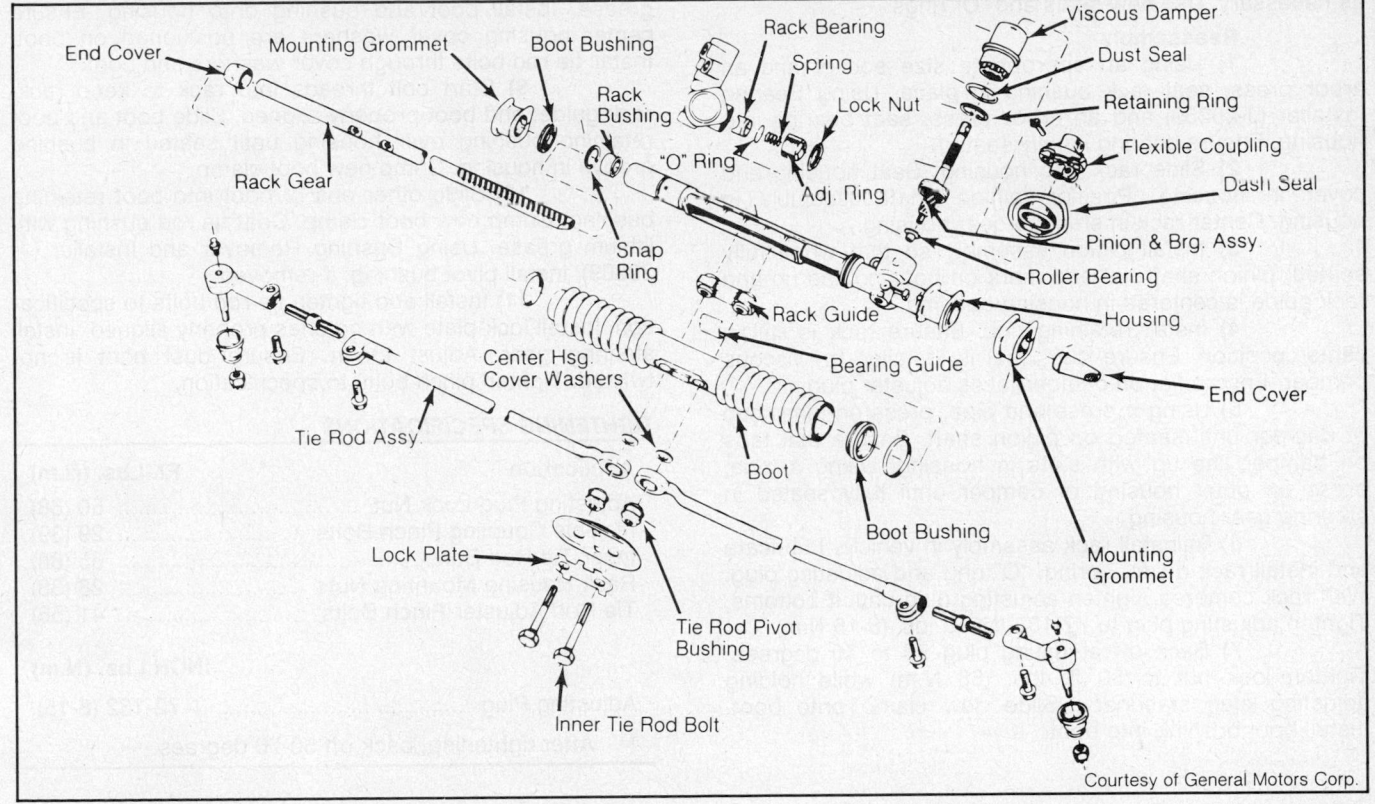

Courtesy of General Motors Corp.

2) To install, reverse removal procedure. Make toe-in adjustment by turning tie rod adjuster. Ensure dust boot is not twisted. Tighten pinch bolts to specification.

FLEXIBLE COUPLING
Removal & Installation
Loosen and remove pinch bolt. Remove steering coupling. To install, place flange and steering coupling onto stub shaft. Install and tighten pinch bolt to specification.

DASH SEAL
Removal & Installation
Lift upward and remove dash seal. To install, line up flat in dash seal with notch on housing. Ensure top of seal is flush or below top of housing.

OVERHAUL

STEERING GEAR
Disassembly
1) Mount steering gear in a soft-jawed vise. Loosen tie rod pinch bolts. Remove tie rod end and adjusting sleeve from tie rod. Note position of notches on lock plate and support plate.

2) Pry off lock plate. Remove tie rod bolts from support plate. Remove tie rods, making sure to reinstall bolt to keep dust boots and other parts aligned after removing first tie rod.

3) Using Bushing Remover and Installer (J-29809), remove inner tie rod pivot bushing, if required. Separate and remove right side mounting grommet. Left side need not be removed unless replacement is required.

4) Cut boot clamps and discard. For ease in dust boot removal, slide cylinder end of boot toward center of steering rack. Expose boot groove on cylinder.

5) Remove boot. Remove rack guide if necessary. Flattened cylindrical corners do not indicate part should be replaced. Remove housing end cover (if damaged). Thread inner tie rod bolt into rack.

6) Use rack as a slide hammer until housing end cover separates from housing. Remove inner tie rod bolt and remove rack from housing. Loosen adjusting plug lock nut.

7) Remove adjusting plug, spring, "O" ring and rack guide. Using a 3-finger puller on flange of viscous damper, remove damper. Replace dust seal if necessary.

8) Turn pinion shaft until rack guide is equal distance from both sides of housing opening (centered). Mark location of stub shaft flat on housing. Remove retaining ring from upper housing.

9) Clamp pinion shaft in soft jawed vise. Tap housing around stub shaft opening to remove pinion shaft from housing. Using an arbor press, press roller bearing from bottom of pinion shaft housing, out through top of housing.

10) Using Snap Ring Pliers (J-29823), remove internal retaining ring from right end of rack housing. Remove rack bushing, located behind retaining ring, using a slide hammer with a 3-finger puller attachment.

11) If slide hammer is not available, use a 2" x 15/16" pipe to carefully tap bushing out of housing from opposite end. Remove boot retaining bushing from pinion end of dust boot.

Inspection
Check all sliding surfaces for signs of wearing or scoring. Check boots for signs of dryness or cracking.

GENERAL MOTORS RACK & PINION "J" BODY (Cont.)

Inspect bearings for smooth rotation. Replace worn parts as necessary. Use new seals and "O" rings.

Reassembly

1) Using an appropriate size socket and an arbor press, seat rack bushing in place. Using Bearing Installer (J-26269) and an arbor press, seat bearing into housing. Ensure bearing is fully seated.

2) Slide rack into housing. Seat housing end cover in housing. Position pinion shaft assembly in housing. Center rack in steering gear housing.

3) Install pinion assembly so that when fully seated, pinion shaft flat and mark on housing line up and rack guide is centered in housing opening.

4) Install retaining ring. Ensure rack is still in center position. Ensure dust seal is installed on viscous damper. Ensure flat on damper faces adjuster plug.

5) Using a press and pipe, press on inner hub of damper until seated on pinion shaft. Ensure that tabs on damper line up with slots in housing. Using a pipe, press on outer housing of damper until fully seated in steering gear housing.

6) Reinstall rack assembly in vehicle. Lubricate and install rack guide, spring, "O" ring and adjusting plug. With rack centered, tighten adjusting plug until it bottoms. Tighten adjusting plug to 72-132 INCH. lbs. (8-15 N.m).

7) Back off adjusting plug 50 to 70 degrees. Tighten lock nut to 50 ft. lbs. (68 N.m) while holding adjusting plug stationary. Slide new clamp onto boot. Install boot bushing into boot.

8) Coat inner lip of boot bushing lightly with grease. Install boot and bushing onto housing. Ensure center housing cover washers are positioned on boot. Install tie rod bolts through cover washers and boot.

9) Start bolt threads into rack to keep rack, rack guide, and boot properly aligned. Slide boot and boot retaining bushing over housing until seated in bushing groove in housing. Crimp new boot clamp.

10) Slide other end of boot into boot retaining bushing. Crimp new boot clamp. Coat tie rod bushing with lithium grease. Using Bushing Remover and Installer (J-29809), install pivot bushing, if removed.

11) Install and tighten tie rod bolts to specification. Install lock plate with notches properly aligned. Install steering gear. Adjust toe-in. Ensure dust boot is not twisted. Tighten pinch bolts to specification.

TIGHTENING SPECIFICATIONS

Application	Ft. Lbs. (N.m)
Adjusting Plug Lock Nut	50 (68)
Flexible Coupling Pinch Bolts	29 (39)
Inner Tie Rod Bolts	65 (88)
Rack Housing Mounting Nuts	28 (38)
Tie Rod Adjuster Pinch Bolts	41 (56)

	INCH Lbs. (N.m)
Adjusting Plug	[1] 72-132 (8-15).

[1] - After tightening, back off 50-70 degrees.

NOVA RACK & PINION

DESCRIPTION

Pinion shaft rotation is transferred to steering rack through pinion teeth. This transfer of motion produces side-to-side movement necessary for steering purposes. Tie rod assemblies connect the unit to steering knuckles. Rack preload is adjustable. Tie rods contain a spring loaded inner ball joint, which permits both rocking and rotating movement.

ADJUSTMENTS

Adjustments are made during reassembly procedure. See OVERHAUL in this article.

REMOVAL & INSTALLATION

STEERING GEAR

Removal

1) Remove intermediate shaft cover. Remove intermediate shaft upper and lower coupling pinch bolts. Raise and support vehicle. Remove front wheels. Remove cotter pins and castle nuts from tie rod ends.

2) Using a tie rod end puller, separate tie rod ends from knuckles. Remove 4 steering gear mounting nuts and bolts. Remove steering gear through access hole.

Installation

To install, reverse removal procedure. Tighten nuts and bolts to specification. Adjust toe-in as necessary.

OVERHAUL

STEERING GEAR

Disassembly

1) Using steering gear brackets, clamp steering gear in a soft-jawed vise. Mark tie rod ends and tie rods for reassembly reference. Loosen tie rod end lock nut. Remove tie rod end and lock nut from tie rod.

2) Remove boot clamps and boots. Using a chisel, straighten the staked portion of the tab lock washers. Using Rack Holder and Tie Rod Remover (J-25423 and J-35414), separate tie rods from steering rack.

3) Remove and discard tab lock washers. Mark steering rack ends for reassembly reference. Using Lock Nut Wrench (J-35692), loosen and remove adjusting plug lock nut.

4) Using Adjusting Plug Wrench (J-25423), remove adjusting plug. Remove spring, rack guide and rack guide seat. Remove pinion shaft dust cover, lock nut, and pinion bearing adjusting screw with seal.

5) Pull pinion shaft with upper bearing from rack housing. Pull rack from rack housing. Using a gear puller, separate upper bearing from pinion shaft (if necessary).

NOVA RACK & PINION (Cont.)

Fig. 1: Exploded View of Nova Steering Gear Assembly

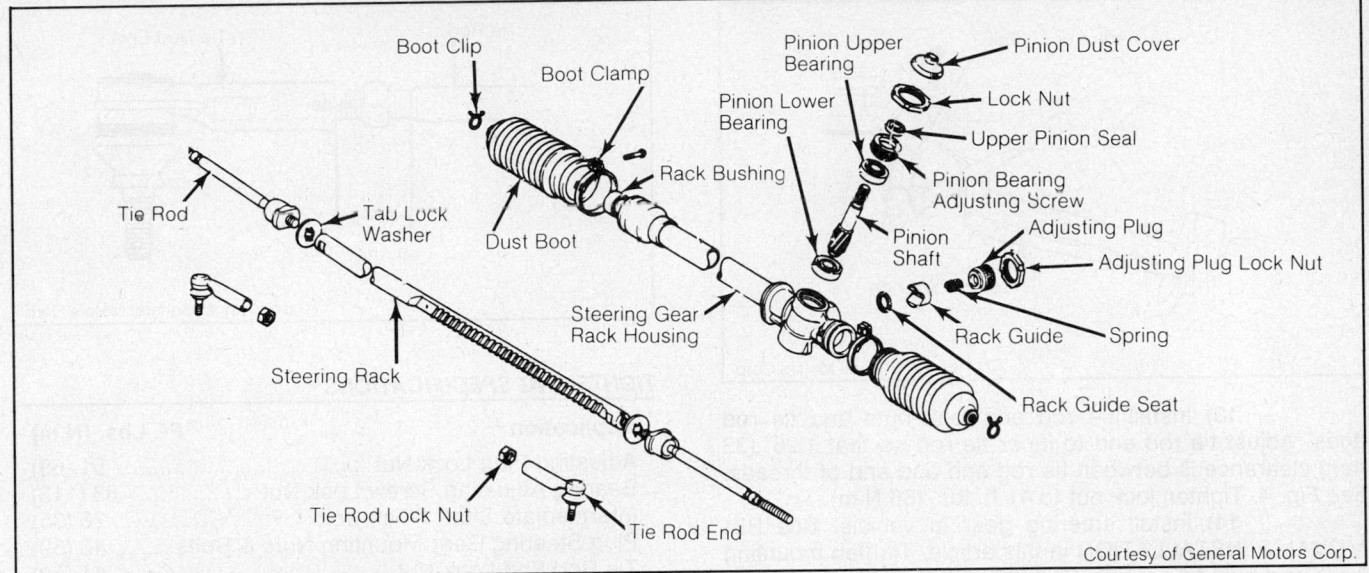

Courtesy of General Motors Corp.

6) Using Slide Hammer and Finger Attachment (J-6125-2B and J-35420), remove lower pinion bearing from rack housing (if necessary).

7) Using Bushing Puller (J-35420), remove rack bushing (if necessary). If replacing upper pinion seal, drive out old seal with a deep socket.

Cleaning & Inspection

1) Use only lint free rags or air to dry or wipe off parts. Never use a wire brush. If necessary, clean parts in mineral spirits only.

2) Inspect rack and pinion mating mating surfaces, seals and bearings for damage. Check rack for runout. Maximum runout should be less than .012" (.3 mm).

3) Inspect housing machined surfaces aand bore for excessive wear. Check tie rod end threads and ball joint. Replace worn parts as necessary.

Reassembly

1) Coat all sliding and rotating parts with lithium grease before reassembly. Using Bearing Driver (J-35682), drive new lower bearing into rack housing (if removed).

2) Using Bushing Driver (J-35421), install new rack bushing so that end of rack housing is flush with end of tool (if removed). Ensure air bleed holes are free and clear.

3) Using Seal Driver (J-35433), install upper pinion bearing seal so it protrudes approximately .02" (.5 mm) above adjusting screw (if removed).

4) With steering gear mounted in a soft-jawed vise, slide rack into rack housing. Using a press install upper pinion shaft bearing to pinion shaft (if removed).

5) With rack centered in housing, install pinion shaft until teeth are meshed and pinion shaft is fully seated. Coat threads of pinion bearing adjusting screw with sealer.

6) Using Pinion Bearing Adjusting Wrench (J-35416), install adjusting screw. Using Adapter (J-35422) and torque wrench, measure pinion turning torque. *See Fig. 2.*

Fig. 2: Adjusting Pinion Shaft Turning Torque

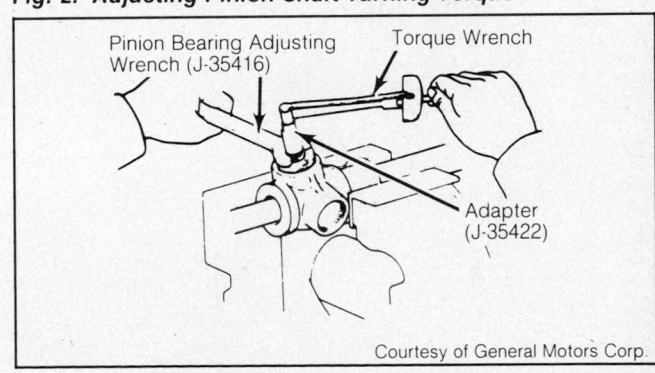

Courtesy of General Motors Corp.

7) Pinion shaft over center turning torque should be 3.2 INCH lbs. (.4 N.m). If not, adjust by turning adjusting screw. Loosen bearing adjusting screw until a turning torque of 2-2.9 INCH lbs. (.2-.3 N.m) is obtained.

8) Apply thread sealer to adjusting screw lock nut. Install and tighten lock nut to 83 ft. lbs. (113 N.m) while holding adjusting screw in position. Recheck turning torque. Adjust as necessary.

9) Lubricate and install rack guide seat, rack guide, spring and adjusting plug. Tighten adjusting plug to 18 ft. lbs. (25 N.m). Back off adjusting plug 25 degrees. Check pinion turning torque as before to obtain total rack preload torque.

10) Total rack preload should be 6.9-11.3 INCH lbs. (.8-1.3 N.m). If not, readjust as necessary. *See Fig. 3.* Coat adjusting plug lock nut with thread sealer. Using Lock Nut Adapter (J-35692), tighten lock nut to 51 ft. lbs. (69 N.m).

11) Install new tab lock washers to rack ends. Using Rack Holder and Torque Wrench Adapter (J-25423 and J-35418), install tie rods on steering rack. Tighten tie rods to 61 ft. lbs. (83 N.m)

12) Stake tab lock washers to flats of tie rod. Apply grease to inner surface of small end of boots. Install boots over tie rods onto rack housing. Ensure boots are not twisted. Install boot clamps.

Manual Steering Gears

NOVA RACK & PINION (Cont.)

Fig. 3: Adjusting Total Rack Preload

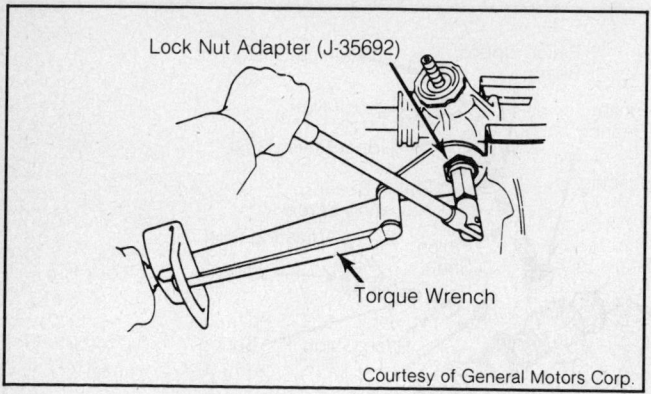

Courtesy of General Motors Corp.

Fig. 4: Adjusting Tie Rod End Length

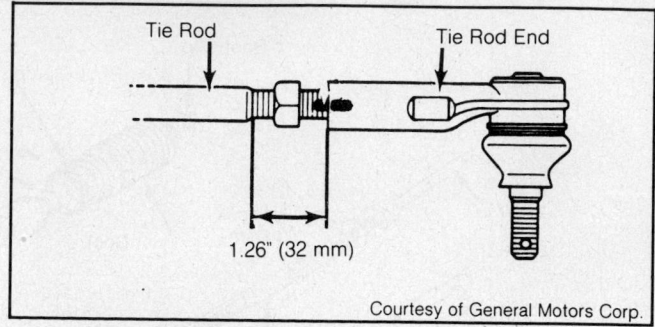

Courtesy of General Motors Corp.

13) Install tie rod end lock nuts and tie rod ends. Adjust tie rod end to inner tie rod so that 1.26" (32 mm) clearance is between tie rod end and end of threads. *See Fig. 4.* Tighten lock nut to 41 ft. lbs. (56 N.m).

14) Install steering gear in vehicle. See REMOVAL & INSTALLATION in this article. Tighten mounting bolts and nuts to specification. Adjust toe-in.

TIGHTENING SPECIFICATIONS

Application	Ft. Lbs. (N.m)
Adjusting Plug Lock Nut	51 (69)
Bearing Adjusting Screw Lock Nut	83 (113)
Intermediate Shaft Pinch Bolt	26 (35)
Plug Steering Gear Mounting Nuts & Bolts	43 (59)
Tie Rod End Lock Nut	41 (56)
Tie Rod End-to-Knuckle Castle Nut	36 (49)
Tie Rod-to-Rack	61 (83)
Wheel Lug Nuts	76 (103)

ALL MANUFACTURERS

LUBRICATION

SERVICE INTERVALS

On all models, check fluid level every 7500 miles. If vehicle is driven less than 12,000 miles a year, check fluid every 3000 miles.

CHECKING FLUID LEVEL

Chrysler Motors

Clean dirt and grease from filler cap area to avoid contaminating fluid. Check fluid level with engine stopped. Maintain fluid level at the "FULL" mark as indicated on dipstick.

Eagle Premier & General Motors

Clean filler cap and neck. Check fluid level with engine off and fluid at normal operating temperature. Fluid level must be between "FULL" and "ADD" marks on dipstick.

Ford Motor Co.

With engine running and fluid at normal operating temperature, cycle steering wheel from left to right several times. Turn engine off. Fluid level must be above full "COLD" mark on dipstick. Do not over fill system.

NOTE: **If fluid level becomes abnormally low, inspect power steering system for leaks. Refill pump using recommended fluid. Recheck after 500 miles to verify system condition.**

RECOMMENDED FLUID TYPE

Application	Fluid Type
Chrysler Motors	1 Mopar Power Steering Fluid P/N (431-8055)
Eagle Premier	Jeep/Eagle Power Steering Fluid P/N (8982-200-946)
General Motors	2 Power Steering Fluid P/N (1050017)
Ford Motor Co.	1 Power Steering Fluid P/N (ESW-M2C33-F)

1 – Do not use automatic transmission fluid.
2 – Dexron type automatic transmission fluid may be used in an emergency.

BLEEDING & REFILLING SYSTEM

(Except Ford Motor Co.)

1) Fill pump reservoir. Operate engine until power steering fluid reaches operating temperature. Stop engine. Recheck fluid level. Add fluid as necessary. Repeat procedure until fluid level stabilizes.

2) Raise and support vehicle so front wheels are off ground. Start engine. Turn steering wheel from side-to-side several times. Avoid hitting stops or holding wheel in full left or right position. Fluid level should remain visible.

3) Return wheels to center position. Operate engine for 2-3 minutes. Road test vehicle. Recheck fluid level. Fluid containing air will have a milky appearance. All air should be eliminated to obtain normal steering.

Ford Motor Co.

1) Fill pump reservoir. Operate engine until power steering fluid reaches operating temperature. Stop engine. Recheck fluid level. Add fluid as necessary. Repeat procedure until fluid level stabilizes.

2) Raise and support vehicle so front wheels are off ground. Start engine. Turn steering wheel from side-to-side several times. Avoid hitting stops or holding wheel in full left or right position. Fluid level should remain visible.

3) Return wheels to center position. Operate engine for 2-3 minutes. Road test vehicle. Recheck fluid level. Fluid containing air will have a milky appearance. All air should be eliminated to obtain normal steering.

NOTE: **Abnormal noise originating from the power steering system may be caused by air trapped in the system. Rotunda Vacuum Tester (021-00014) and the following procedure are designed to eliminate this condition.**

4) Carefully remove pump filler adapter and dipstick. Check and fill reservoir to "COLD" mark. Disconnect ignition coil lead. Raise front wheels off ground.

5) Crank engine while cycling steering wheel. DO NOT hold wheel on stops. Add fluid if necessary. Attach coil lead. Install evacuation tool onto reservoir.

6) Start engine. Apply 15 in. Hg on reservoir for approximately 3 minutes with engine idling. As air is purged from system, vacuum will decrease.

7) Maintain sufficient vacuum with vacuum source. Release vacuum. Check fluid level. Install filler adapter assembly and dipstick. Start engine.

8) Turn steering wheel from stop to stop while checking for leaks. If condition is severe, repeat procedure until all air is removed. Lower vehicle. Road test vehicle.

SERVICING

BELT TENSION

General Motors With Serpentine Belt

1) On General Motors vehicles with serpentine belts, belt tension is adjusted automaticly. Adjustment is not necessary. The belt tensioner moveable portion has indicator marks that align with marks on the non-moveable portion of tensioner.

2) When mark on moveable portion aligns with the "REPLACE BELT" mark, belt needs replacing. To install new belt, route new belt in same manner as old belt.

3) Turn tensioner as far towards "MIN. BELT" mark as possible. When new belt is around tensioner, release tensioner. Ensure mark on moveable portion of tensioner is between "MIN. BELT" mark and "NOM. BELT" mark. *See Fig. 1.*

All Others

1) Using a belt strand tension gauge, check tension of power steering belt. Refer to POWER STEERING BELT TENSION SPECIFICATIONS table.

2) To adjust belt tension, loosen power steering pump mounting bolts and adjusting bolt. Carefully pry pump until belt is to specification. See POWER STEERING BELT TENSION SPECIFICATIONS table. Tighten bolts.

ALL MANUFACTURERS (Cont.)

Fig. 1: General Motors Serpentine Belt Tensioner

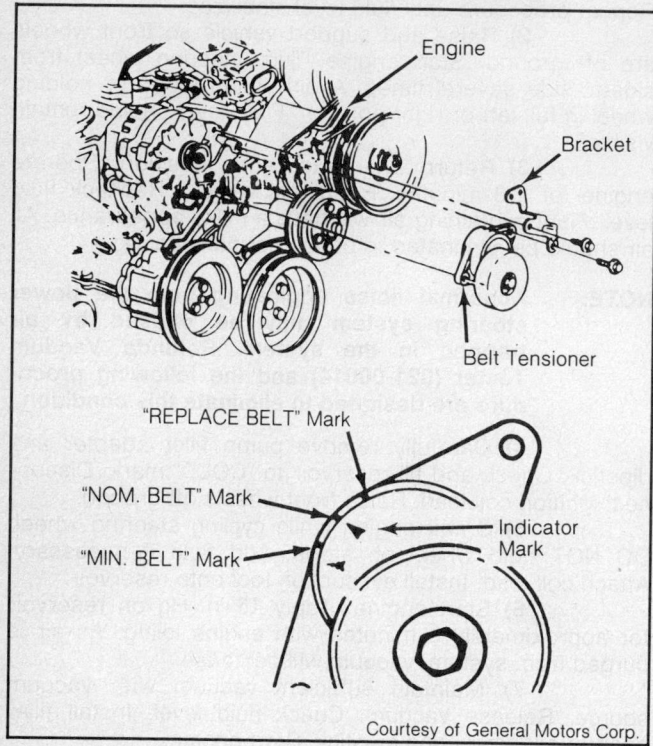

Courtesy of General Motors Corp.

POWER STEERING BELT TENSION SPECIFICATIONS

Application	New Belt Lbs. (Kg)	Used Belt Lbs. (Kg)
Chrysler Motors		
FWD	95 (43)	70 (32)
RWD		
W/Air Pump	120 (54)	60 (27)
W/O Air Pump	50 (23)	40 (18)
Eagle Premier	190 (86)	150 (68)
Ford Motor Co.		
1.9L	73 (33)	50 (23)
2.3L OHC	170 (77)	150 (68)
2.3L HSC	140 (63)	120 (54)
3.8L	170 (77)	150 (68)
5.0L	110 (50)	.....
H.D.	140 (63)	.....
2 Spd Belt	170 (77)	150 (68)
5.8L	170 (77)	150 (68)
General Motors		
1.6L		
SOHC	125 (57)	80 (36)
DOHC	175 (79)	115 (52)
2.0L	135 (61)	70 (32)
1.8L & 2.5L	165 (75)	100 (45)
2.8L, 3.0L, 3.1L		
3.8L, 4.1L & 4.5L	135 (61)	73 (33)
5.0L	125 (57)	75 (34)
5.7L	130 (59)	.....

TESTING

NOTE: Before testing power steering system, check fluid level, belt tension, pump pulley, tire pressure and engine idle speed.

AIR CONTROL VALVE
Chevrolet Nova
Start engine. Turn steering wheel right and left. Ensure engine RPM does not decrease more than 50 RPM. Pinch air hose shut. Turn steering wheel right and left. Ensure engine RPM decreases about 200 RPM. If engine RPM does not decrease about 200 RPM, replace air control valve.

PRESSURE TESTING
Chrysler Motors
1) Remove high pressure hose at steering pump and connect a spare hose to pump fitting. Connect opposite end of spare hose to Test Gauge (C-3309E). Connect pressure hose from valve side of steering gear to valve side of gauge. Valve must be installed on outlet side of gauge.

NOTE: Replacement fittings are required on Test Gauge (C-3309E) for adapting to "0" ring type hose tube ends.

2) With a thermometer in fluid reservoir, start engine and warm fluid to 160°F (72°C). Turning wheels from stop to stop will aid in warming fluid. DO NOT hold wheels against stop.

3) With engine at idle speed, gauge open, record maximum pressure while turning steering wheel from stop to stop. The minimum pressure at idle should read 80-125 psi (5.6-8.8 kg/cm²) on RWD models, and 30-50 psi (2.1-3.5 kg/cm²) on FWD models.

4) If pressure is less than specifications, steering system is not functioning properly. To determine which unit is faulty, momentarily close pressure gauge valve and note maximum pressure registered on gauge.

5) If pressure reads less than maximum pressure, 1200-1300 psi (87.7-91.4 kg/cm²) on RWD models, or 1000-1100 psi (70.3-77.3 kg/cm²) on FWD models, the pump is faulty and should be reconditioned.

6) If pressure reads low at step **3)**, but not at step **4)**, steering gear is at fault. When removing test equipment, ensure hose is installed in original position to avoid interference with engine or sheet metal.

Fig. 2: Typical Test Gauge Connections

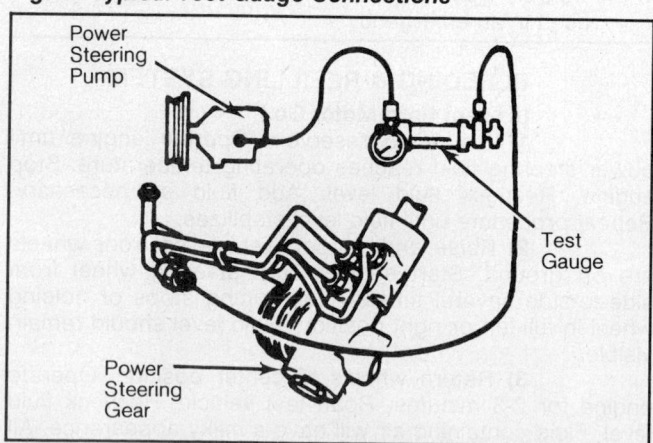

Eagle Premier & General Motors
1) Remove high pressure line from pump. Attach Adapter Fitting (J-5176-11 for General Motors or J-21567-5 for Eagle Premier) to pump.

ALL MANUFACTURERS (Cont.)

2) Using Pressure Gauge (J-5176-02 for General Motors or J-21567 for Eagle Premier) and Adapter (J-5176-12), connect gauge to hose.

3) Open valve fully. Run engine until fluid reaches normal operating temperature. Check fluid level. Add if necessary. With engine at operating temperature, pressure reading should be 80-125 psi (5.6-8.8 kg/cm²).

4) If pressure is more than 200 psi (14 kg/cm²), inspect system for restrictions or faulty poppet valve. Alternately close and then open gauge valve fully 3 times while recording highest pressure obtained.

CAUTION: Do not hold valve closed for more than 5 seconds as pump damage may result.

5) If recorded pressures are all within 50 psi (3.5 kg/cm²), pump performance is acceptable. If pressures are high and not within 50 psi (3.5 kg/cm²) of each other, flow control valve is sticking.

6) If pressures are constant and more than 100 psi (7.0 kg/cm²), but less than 1350 psi (94.9 kg/cm²), replace flow control valve. Retest pump pressure.

7) If pump meets specification, leave valve open. Turn steering wheel from stop to stop. Record and compare highest pressure with maximum pump pressure.

8) If pressure at both stops is not similar to maximum pressure, steering gear is leaking internally. Shut off engine, remove testing equipment, check fluid level, or make necessary repairs.

NOTE: **Alternative method of testing system pressure and measuring rate flow can be performed using Power Steering Analyzer (J-25323), using instructions with analyzer.**

NOTE: **When testing pump flow and pressure on Ford Motor Co. vehicles, use Rotunda Analyzer (014-00207). Check entire system for damage. Check pulley size and pump model for proper application.**

Ford Motor Co.

1) Reservoir must be kept full and at normal operating temperature during testing. Attach tester between pressure line and pump with gauge between pump and tester valve. Start engine and let idle for 2 minutes.

2) With engine idling and fluid hot, record pressure (with tester valve open) and flow. If flow is less than 1.5 gals. (5.68L) per minute, pump may require service. However, proceed with testing at this point.

3) If pressure is more than 150 psi (10.5 kg/cm²), check hoses for restrictions. Partially close tester valve. Allow pressure to increase to 740 psi (52 kg/cm²). Record flow. If flow is less than minimum, pump cam pack requires replacement. Proceed with testing.

4) Close and partially open tester valve 3 times. Tester valve must not remain closed over 5 seconds. Observe and record pressure each time valve is closed. If readings vary more than 50 psi (3.5 kg/cm²), flow control valve may be sticking.

5) If pressure is less than minimum specification, replace flow control valve. If pressure is more than maximum specification, remove flow control valve. Clean or replace flow control valve as necessary.

6) Increase engine speed to about 1500 RPM. Observe and record flow. If flow exceeds maximum free flow listed in chart, remove flow control valve. Clean or replace flow control valve as necessary.

7) Return engine to idle speed. Turn wheel from stop to stop. Observe and record flow at both stops. Pressure readings should be near maximum pressure specification listed in chart.

8) Flow should drop to less than .5 gals./min. (1.9 L/min.). If pressure fails to reach maximum or if flow does not drop to less than .5 gals./min. (1.9 L/min.), excessive internal leakage of steering gear is occurring.

9) With engine running, attach pull scale to rim of steering wheel. Measure pull required to turn wheel one complete revolution in each direction. Pull should be approximately 9 lbs. (2.25 kg) during turning.

ALL MANUFACTURERS (Cont.)

POWER STEERING PUMP TEST SPECIFICATIONS

Application	Pressure (psi)		Flow (gpm) [1]	
	Idle	Relief	Minimum	Maximum
Chrysler Motors				
FWD Models	30-50	1000-1100	.....	.....
RWD Models	80-125	1200-1300	.....	....
Eagle				
Premier	80-125	1100-1200	.....	.....
Ford Motor Co.				
1.9L All Models	150	750-1030	1.10	2.20
2.3L Tempo & Topaz	150	1100-1380	.95	2.20
2.3L Mustang & Thunderbird	150	850-1130	1.30	2.60
2.5L & 3.0L Sable & Taurus	150	1200-1480	.90	2.60
3.8L Continental	150	1300-1530	1.50	3.00
3.8L Cougar & Thunderbird				
With Handling Package	150	950-1230	1.40	2.60
Without Handling Package	150	950-1230	1.25	2.60
3.8L Sable & Taurus	150	1300-1530	.90	2.20
5.0L Crown Victoria & Grand Marquis				
Police	150	1100-1380	1.60	3.40
All Except Police	150	1100-1380	1.60	3.00
5.0L Cougar & Thunderbird	150	950-1230	1.40	2.60
5.0L Mustang				
Auto. Trans.	150	950-1230	1.40	2.60
Man. Trans.	150	950-1230	1.35	2.60
5.0L Mark VII				
LSC	150	1200-1480	1.60	3.00
Except LSC	150	1200-1480	1.60	2.60
5.0L Town Car	150	1100-1380	1.60	3.40
General Motors				
4.1L & 4.5L	80-125	1350-1450	1.32	3.10
5.0L	80-125	1000-1250	.....	.....
5.0L Commercial	80-100	1000-1250	.....	.....
All Other Engines (TC Series Pump)	80-125	1000-1250	.....	.....

[1] – Flow is measured in gallons per minute.

CHRYSLER MOTORS POWER RACK & PINION

FWD Models

DESCRIPTION

A rotary valve in the pinion assembly directs fluid to either side of the integral rack piston. Tie rods connect the steering gear to the steering knuckles. Loosely fitted pinion drive-tangs, will provide manual steering control in the event of a system malfunction.

LUBRICATION, TROUBLE SHOOTING & TESTING

See POWER STEERING GENERAL SERVICING & TROUBLE SHOOTING articles in this section.

REMOVAL & INSTALLATION

STEERING GEAR

Removal

1) Raise and support vehicle. Remove front wheels. Remove cotter pins and castle nuts from tie rod ends. Using a puller, separate tie rod ends from knuckles.

2) Remove all 4 front suspension crossmember attaching bolts. Using transmission jack, lower crossmember. Drive out steering coupling roll pin.

3) Separate steering gear from steering shaft. Remove splash and boot seal shields. Remove bolts securing steering gear to front crossmember. Remove steering gear from crossmember

Installation

To install, reverse removal procedure. Install right rear crossmember bolt first. This aligns the crossmember. Tighten crossmember mounting bolts to 90 ft. lbs. (122 N.m). Check and adjust toe-in.

TIE ROD END

Removal

Remove castle nut and cotter pin. Using a puller, separate tie rod end from steering knuckle. Loosen lock nut. Counting the number of turns necessary, remove tie rod ends from tie rods.

Installation

To install tie rod end, reverse removal procedure. Check and adjust toe-in.

TIE RODS

Removal

Separate tie rod end from steering knuckle as previously described. Remove lock nut, boot clamps and boots. Remove roll pin. Supporting flat side of rack with wrench, unscrew tie rod ball joint from rack.

Installation

To install tie rods, reverse removal procedure. Tighten ball joint. Install roll pin. Install tie rod ends as previously described.

OVERHAUL

STEERING GEAR

Disassembly

1) Loosen adjusting plug lock nut. Remove adjusting plug, spring and rack guide from housing.

Remove pinion seal retaining ring. Pry out upper pinion seal. Using Socket (C-4832), remove lower bearing cap.

2) Holding pinion shaft with Adapter (SP-3616) and a wrench, remove pinion shaft lock nut. Using Pinion Remover (L-4594-1-2-3) with Adapter (L-4594-8), remove pinion and valve assembly. Using Puller (C-4694), remove lower pinion seal.

3) Ensure pinion is fully engaged and rack is centered in housing. Mark position of pinion shaft, relative to housing. Using Pinion Shaft Puller and Adapter (L-4594-1-2-3 and L-4594-8), remove pinion shaft and valve assembly.

4) If valve body rings are to be replaced, remove them at this time. Remove bulkhead retaining ring with punch. *See Fig. 2.* Discard bulkhead retainer. Rotate retaining wire in clockwise direction with a punch until it can be grasped with pliers and pulled out.

Fig. 1: Exploded View of Bulkhead Assembly

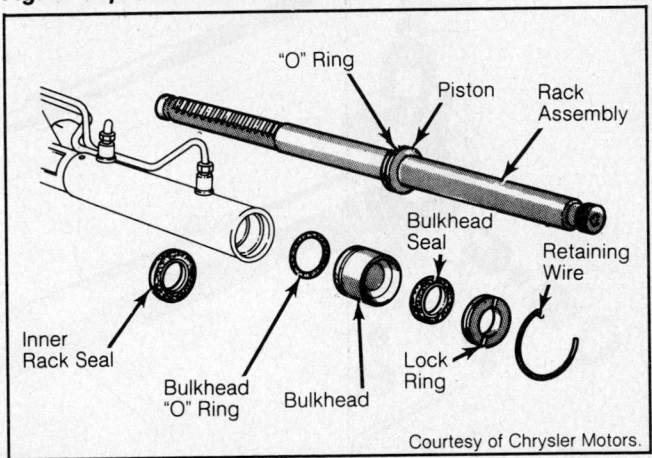

Courtesy of Chrysler Motors.

5) If the bulkhead, bulkhead seal or bulkhead "O" ring are being replaced, remove both hydraulic lines. Remove transfer tube Teflon gaskets. Plug hydraulic fittings to prevent contamination. Insert and rotate pinion shaft counterclockwise until bulkhead is forced out of housing.

6) Using Seal Remover (C-4665), remove bulkhead inner seal. Remove rack from steering gear housing. Remove and discard piston rings. Using drift or a small punch, carefully tap lower pinion bearing out of housing. Using Bushing Tool (C-4694), remove pinion bushing and seal.

Reassembly

1) Lubricate all new seals with power steering fluid. DO NOT use ATF. Using Seal Installer (C-4664), install pinion shaft lower seal. Align new pinion shaft lower bearing in hole. Place a socket on the bearing outer race.

2) Gently tap bearing into housing. Ensure bearing does not tilt during installation. Install bearing cap. Install new piston ring on rack. Slide seal over Seal Protector (C-4666) and onto rack assembly (seal lip toward piston). Install inner rack seal.

3) Remove seal protector. Seat the seal on the piston. Ensure seal lip is toward piston. Push plastic retainer onto rack and into seal. Ensure plastic insert is fully engaged with seal prior to installing rack in housing.

4) Lubricate rack teeth with lithium base grease. Install rack in housing. Tap with soft mallet to properly seat seal. Install plastic insert into inner seal.

Power Steering Gears

CHRYSLER MOTORS POWER RACK & PINION (Cont.)

Fig. 2: Exploded View of Power Steering Gear Assembly

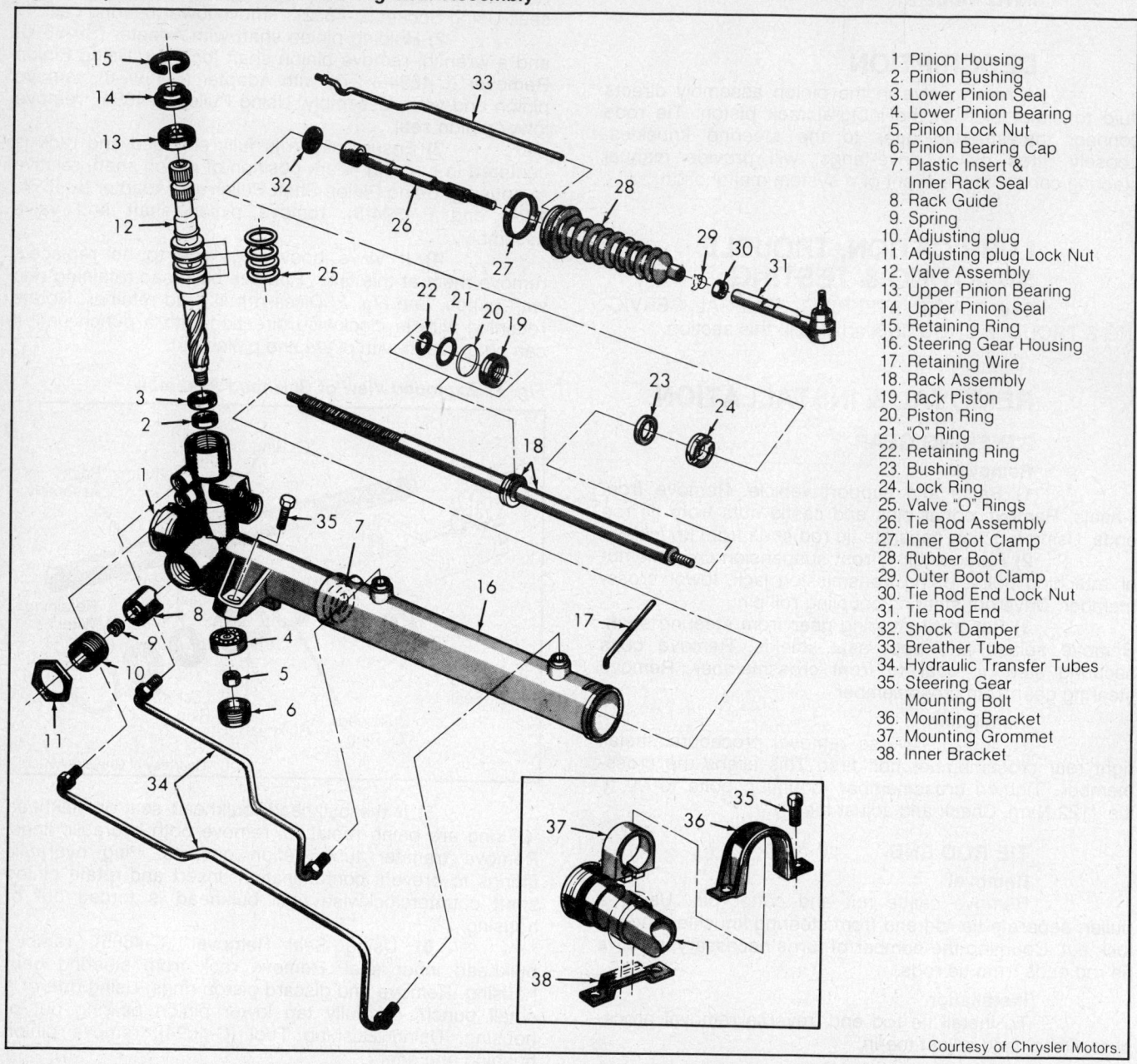

1. Pinion Housing
2. Pinion Bushing
3. Lower Pinion Seal
4. Lower Pinion Bearing
5. Pinion Lock Nut
6. Pinion Bearing Cap
7. Plastic Insert & Inner Rack Seal
8. Rack Guide
9. Spring
10. Adjusting plug
11. Adjusting plug Lock Nut
12. Valve Assembly
13. Upper Pinion Bearing
14. Upper Pinion Seal
15. Retaining Ring
16. Steering Gear Housing
17. Retaining Wire
18. Rack Assembly
19. Rack Piston
20. Piston Ring
21. "O" Ring
22. Retaining Ring
23. Bushing
24. Lock Ring
25. Valve "O" Rings
26. Tie Rod Assembly
27. Inner Boot Clamp
28. Rubber Boot
29. Outer Boot Clamp
30. Tie Rod End Lock Nut
31. Tie Rod End
32. Shock Damper
33. Breather Tube
34. Hydraulic Transfer Tubes
35. Steering Gear Mounting Bolt
36. Mounting Bracket
37. Mounting Grommet
38. Inner Bracket

Courtesy of Chrysler Motors.

Using Seal Installer (C-4669), install bulkhead outer oil seal.

5) Using Seal Protector (C-4670), install bulkhead assembly onto rack. Seat bulkhead assembly into steering gear housing. Install new retaining wire while rotating bulkhead assembly counterclockwise.

6) Insert Ring Expander (C-4791) into valve body rings. Position expander on valve body. Slide each ring off the expander and into their respective ring groove.

7) Using Valve Ring Protector (C-4789), install valve and pinion assembly into housing. Ensure rack is centered in housing and that previously scribed reference marks align. Holding pinion shaft with Adapter (SP-3616) and a wrench, tighten pinion shaft lock.

8) Using Seal Installer (C-4667), install pinion upper seal. *See Fig. 3.* Install retaining ring. Install rack guide, spring and adjusting plug. Tighten plug until it bottoms.

9) Back off adjusting plug 40-60 degrees. Holding adjusting plug stationary, tighten lock nut. Install new transfer tube Teflon gaskets (if removed). Install hydraulic transfer tubes (if removed). Install shock damper on rack.

10) Install tie rods. Tighten ball joints. Install roll pins. Install inner boot clamps, boots and outer boot clamps. Install tie rod ends as previously described.

CHRYSLER MOTORS POWER RACK & PINION (Cont.)

Fig. 3: Pinion Shaft Seal Installation

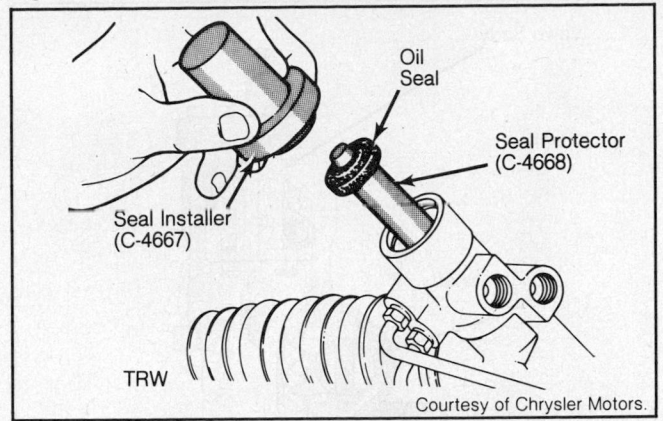

Oil Seal

Seal Protector (C-4668)

Seal Installer (C-4667)

TRW

Courtesy of Chrysler Motors.

TIGHTENING SPECIFICATIONS

Application	Ft. Lbs. (N.m)
Adjusting Plug Lock Nut	50 (68)
Pinion Bearing Cap	45 (61)
Pinion Shaft Lock Nut	26 (35)
Steering Gear Mounting Bolts	21 (28)
Tie Rod End-to-Knuckle Castle Nut	38 (52)
Tie Rod End Lock Nut	55 (75)
Tie Rod-to-Rack Ball Joint	70 (95)

CHRYSLER MOTORS POWER RECIRCULATING BALL

RWD Models

DESCRIPTION

The power steering gear consists of a gear housing, a geared sector shaft, and a geared power piston which is in constant mesh with the sector shaft and the worm shaft. The steering wheel is coupled to the worm shaft through a flexible joint and a pot type coupling.

OPERATION

Rotating the steering wheel causes the worm shaft to actuate the power piston through a series of recirculating balls. The steering valve is mounted above the steering gear and directs fluid through the system. Fluid is supplied to steering gear by an engine driven pump and is delivered through a high-pressure hose. Oil is returned to the pump reservoir through a low-pressure hose.

LUBRICATION, TROUBLE SHOOTING & TESTING

See POWER STEERING GENERAL SERVICING & TROUBLE SHOOTING articles in this section.

ADJUSTMENTS

SECTOR SHAFT PRELOAD

1) Disconnect center-link from pitman arm. Start engine and let idle. Turn steering wheel from lock to lock, counting revolutions. Turn steering wheel back to center position.

2) Loosen lock nut. Turn adjusting screw out until backlash is felt in pitman arm. Turn adjusting screw to obtain zero backlash. Tighten adjusting screw an additional 3/8 to 1/2 turn. Tighten lock nut.

VALVE BODY CENTERING

1) Loosen 2 valve body-to-housing screws. Retighten screws to 84 INCH lbs. (9 N.m) to prevent valve leakage during valve centering. Start engine. If unit is self-steering, tap valve up or down to correct. Turn steering wheel from lock to lock to purge air from system. Refill reservoir as required.

CAUTION: Do not turn steering wheel hard against locks. High pressure may blow out "O" rings.

2) With steering wheel centered, start and stop engine several times. Tap valve body up and down as required until there is no movement of steering wheel when engine is started or stopped. The valve is now centered. Tighten 2 valve body-to-housing attaching screws.

REMOVAL & INSTALLATION

STEERING GEAR

NOTE: It is recommended that steering column be completely detached from floor and instrument panel to prevent possible damage.

Removal

1) Disconnect battery ground cable. Remove steering column. See STEERING COLUMNS in this section. Disconnect hydraulic lines from steering gear.

2) Secure hydraulic lines above power steering pump to avoid loss of fluid. Mark pitman arm-to-sector shaft alignment for reassembly reference. Remove pitman arm retaining nut and lock washer.

3) Using Gear Puller (C-4150), separate pitman arm from sector shaft. Drop exhaust out of way. Remove starter heat shield. Remove 3 steering gear mounting bolts. Remove steering gear.

Power Steering Gears

CHRYSLER MOTORS POWER RECIRCULATING BALL (Cont.)

Fig. 1: Chrysler Motors Power Steering Gear Assembly

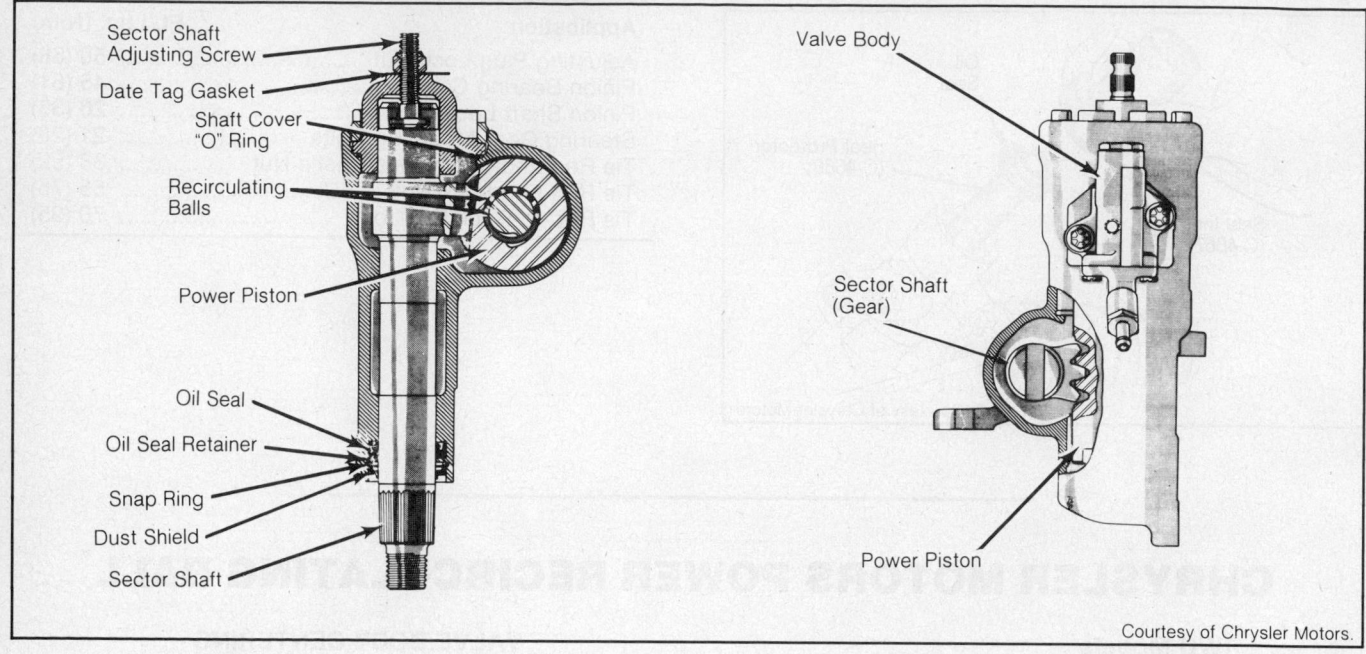

Sector Shaft Adjusting Screw
Date Tag Gasket
Shaft Cover "O" Ring
Recirculating Balls
Power Piston
Oil Seal
Oil Seal Retainer
Snap Ring
Dust Shield
Sector Shaft

Valve Body
Sector Shaft (Gear)
Power Piston

Courtesy of Chrysler Motors.

Installation

To install steering gear, reverse removal procedure. Center steering wheel. Rotate worm shaft by hand to center sector shaft. Align master serration on sector shaft with splines on steering arm.

ON-VEHICLE SERVICE

SECTOR SHAFT OIL SEAL

Removal

1) Remove pitman arm nut. Using Gear Puller (C-4150), separate pitman arm from sector shaft. Position Adapter (SP-3056) of Seal Tool (C-3350-A) over sector shaft. Thread nut onto sector shaft.

2) Maintain pressure on threaded adapter with nut. Screw adapter in until it engages metal portion of grease retainer. Place the 2 half-rings (SP-1932) of Seal Tool (C-3350-A) and retainer ring over both portions of seal tool.

3) Turn nut counterclockwise to remove retainer. Remove oil seal snap ring and seal back-up washer. Using Seal Tool (C-3350-A), remove grease retainer.

4) An alternate method of removing oil seal is as follows. Disconnect the pitman arm. Carefully pry grease seal out of housing. Remove oil seal retaining snap ring and seal retainer.

5) Place receptacle under gear. Start engine. Turn steering wheel to full left lock. Oil pressure will force seal out of steering gear housing.

Installation

1) Place new seal on flat surface (lip down). Lubricate inner lip with power steering fluid. Insert Seal Protector Sleeve (SP-1601) into the seal.

2) Position new seal on sector shaft (seal lip in). Place Adapter (SP-5148) against new seal. Slide adapter over shaft with seal lip toward housing.

3) Install nut on sector shaft. Tighten nut until shoulder of adapter contacts housing. Remove nut, adapter and protector. Install seal back-up washer and oil seal snap ring (identification mark out).

4) Fill housing with multipurpose grease. Position grease retainer in housing bore. Place short-step surface of Tool Adapter (SP-5148) against retainer.

5) Install nut on sector shaft. Tighten nut until shoulder of adapter contacts housing. With steering gear and wheels in straight-ahead position, install pitman arm and retaining nut.

WORM SHAFT OIL SEAL

Replacement

Remove steering column. Remove oil seal using Seal Remover (C-3638). Using Seal Installer (C-3650) and a soft-faced hammer, drive new oil seal in place (lip toward housing). Install and align steering column.

OVERHAUL

VALVE BODY

Disassembly

1) Disconnect hydraulic lines from valve body. Secure hydraulic lines above power steering pump to avoid loss of fluid. Remove 2 valve body-to-housing screws. Raise valve body. Disengage valve body from valve lever.

2) Remove 2 steering valve-to-control valve mounting screws. Separate the 2 sub-assemblies. Remove outlet, spring and piston from control valve body. Remove spool valve from steering valve body. See Fig. 2.

Inspection & Cleaning

1) Inspect spool valve for nicks and burrs. Use crocus cloth to clean up minor irregularities. DO NOT round-off any sharp edges on piston or spool valve.

2) Clean spool valve and piston in cleaning solvent. Blow-dry passages with compressed air. Lubricate pistons, valves and bores with power steering fluid. DO NOT use ATF.

Reassembly

1) Install spool valve in valve body. Ensure valve lever hole lines up with lever opening in valve body.

CHRYSLER MOTORS POWER RECIRCULATING BALL (Cont.)

Valve must move freely in bore. Install end plug (if removed) with a new gasket. Tighten to specification.

2) Install short spring, piston, long spring and outlet fitting to control valve. Tighten to specifications. Mount control valve body to steering valve body using new "O" rings. Tighten screws to specification.

3) Align spool valve lever hole with opening in valve body. Install valve body on housing. Ensure valve lever enters hole in spool and that keyed portion of valve body mates with keyway in housing. See VALVE BODY CENTERING.

STEERING GEAR
Disassembly
1) Clean exterior of gear housing. Drain housing. Mount housing in a vise. Remove valve body retaining screws, valve body and 3 "O" rings. Remove valve lever and spring. Carefully pry spherical head with screwdriver.

CAUTION: Do not collapse valve lever slotted end. This will damage bearing tolerances of spherical head.

2) Loosen sector shaft adjusting screw lock nut. Using Spanner Tool (C-3988), remove sector shaft cover spanner nut. Rotate worm shaft to position sector shaft teeth at center of piston travel. Using Power Train Wrench (C-3989), loosen steering power train retaining nut.

3) Compress power train parts by turning worm shaft to full left turn position. Remove power train retaining nut. While firmly compressing power train, pry on piston teeth with a flat-blade screwdriver, using sector shaft gear teeth as a fulcrum. Remove power train assembly.

NOTE: Cylinder head, center race and spacer assembly and housing head must be maintained in close contact with each other.

4) Place power train vertically in soft-jawed vise. Raise housing head until oil seal clears top of wormshaft. Position Arbor (C-3929) on top of wormshaft and into oil seal. Pull up on housing head until arbor is positioned in bearing. Remove housing head and arbor.

NOTE: If worm shaft seal is to be replaced, replace seal with housing head disassembled.

5) Remove large "O" ring from groove in housing head. Remove reaction seal from groove in face of housing head with compressed air directed into ferrule chamber. Remove reaction spring, reaction ring, worm balancing ring and spacer.

6) While holding worm shaft, turn nut until it releases from knurled section. Remove nut. Wire brush knurled sections to remove metal chips. Blow out nut and worm shaft to remove any metal particles.

7) Remove upper thrust bearing race and upper thrust bearing. Remove center bearing race. Remove lower thrust bearing and bearing race. Remove lower reaction ring and spring. Remove cylinder head.

8) Remove "O" rings from 2 outer grooves in cylinder head. Remove reaction "O" ring from groove in face of cylinder head by directing air pressure into oil hole between 2 "O" ring grooves.

9) Remove snap ring and seal. Test operation of worm shaft. Required torque to rotate wormshaft throughout its travel in or out of piston should not exceed 1.5 INCH lbs. (.17 N.m). Worm and piston are serviced as an assembly and should not be disassembled.

10) Test for excessive side play with piston held in vise (rack teeth up) and worm in its approximate center of travel. Vertical side play measured at a point 2.31" (58.7 mm) from piston flange should not exceed .008" (.20 mm) when end of worm is lifted with a force of 1 lb. (.45 kg).

Fig. 2: Exploded View of Valve Body Assembly

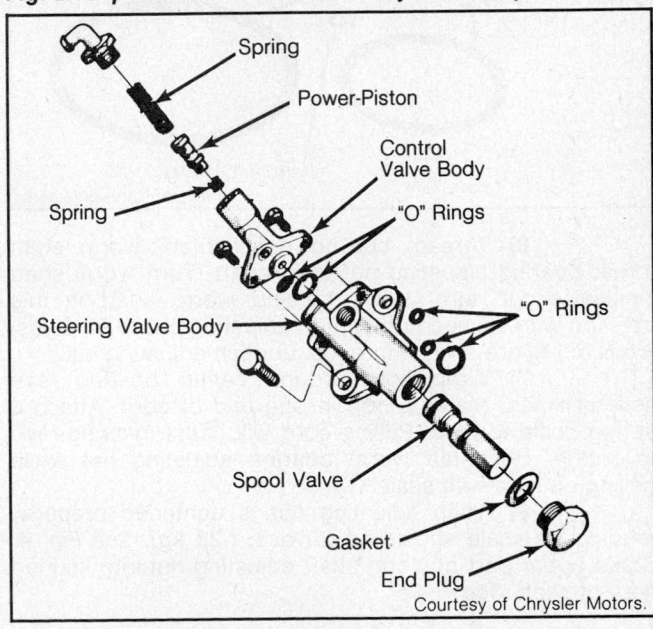

Spring
Power-Piston
Control Valve Body
"O" Rings
Spring
"O" Rings
Steering Valve Body
Spool Valve
Gasket
End Plug
Courtesy of Chrysler Motors.

Inspection & Reassembly
1) Inspect condition of Teflon seal ring. If replacement is necessary, install a new rectangular seal. Ensure seal is not twisted. Stretch Teflon ring as little as possible and slide ring into piston groove. Re-size Teflon ring by using a piston ring compressor.

2) Place piston assembly in vertical position (worm shaft up) in a soft-jawed vise. Inspect worm shaft Teflon seal for nicks and voids. To replace seal, cut with knife and remove. Replacement seal is split and should be installed using multipurpose grease to hold seal centered on shaft. Ensure end gap is closed.

3) Inspect cylinder head ferrule oil passages for obstructions and lands for burrs. Lubricate 2 large "O" rings. Install "O" rings in cylinder head grooves. Install lower reaction seal "O" ring in cylinder head groove. See Fig. 3.

4) Slide cylinder head assembly (ferrule up) onto worm shaft. Ensure gap on worm shaft seal ring is closed to avoid damaging ring as cylinder head moves against piston flange.

5) Lubricate all parts with power steering fluid. Install thick lower bearing race, lower thrust bearing and lower reaction spring (small hole over ferrule). Install lower reaction ring, flange up so ring protrudes through reaction spring and contacts reaction "O" ring in cylinder head. Install center bearing race, upper thrust bearing and thin upper thrust bearing race.

CHRYSLER MOTORS POWER RECIRCULATING BALL (Cont.)

Fig. 3: Cylinder Head Oil Seals

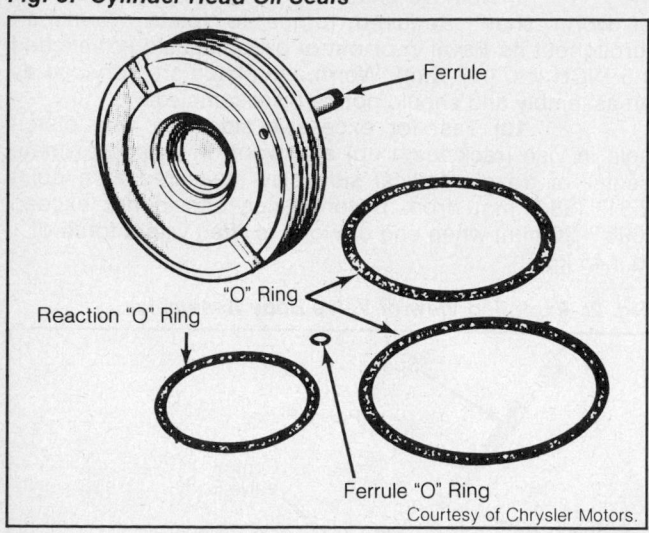

Courtesy of Chrysler Motors.

Fig. 5: Staking Adjusting Nut Onto Worm Shaft

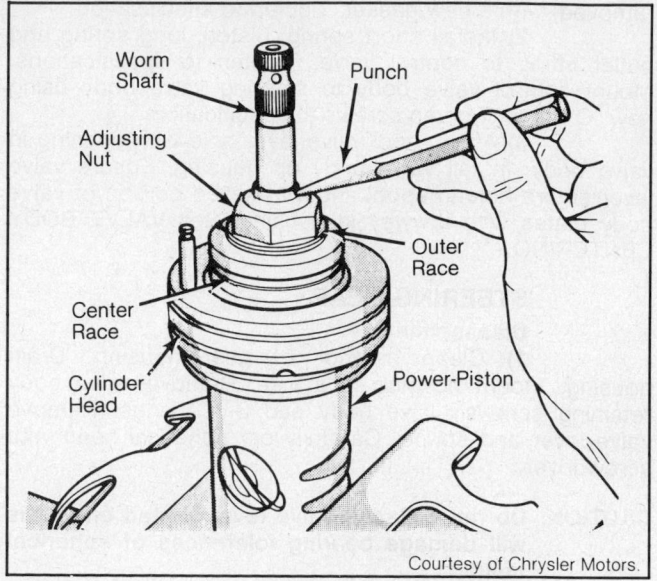

Courtesy of Chrysler Motors.

6) Thread, but do not tighten, worm shaft thrust bearing adjusting nut onto shaft. Turn worm shaft clockwise 1/2 turn. While holding worm shaft in this position with splined nut, tighten adjusting nut to 50 ft. lbs. (68 N.m.) to pre-stretch threads. Loosen adjusting nut.

7) Wrap cord around center bearing race several times. Make a loop in one end of cord. Attach a spring scale to loop. Pulling cord will cause bearing race to rotate. Retighten worm bearing adjusting nut while pulling on cord with scale.

8) When adjusting nut is tightened properly, reading on scale should be 20 ozs. (.28 kg). *See Fig. 4.* Stake upper part of worm shaft adjusting nut into knurled area of shaft. *See Fig. 5.*

Fig. 4: Measuring Center Bearing Preload

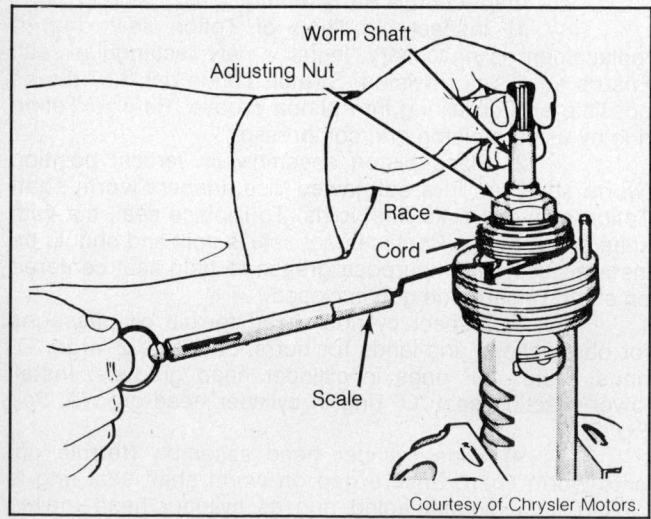

Courtesy of Chrysler Motors.

9) Check preload. If adjusting nut moved during staking operation, it can be corrected by striking nut with punch in direction required to correct setting. After testing for proper preload, stake nut in 3 more locations equally spaced around upper part of nut.

10) To test staking, apply 20 ft. lbs. (27 N.m) of torque in each direction. If nut does not move, staking operation is correctly completed. Position spacer assembly over center race. Dowel pin should engage slot in race and cylinder head ferrule should pass through slot in spacer.

11) Install upper reaction ring on center race and spacer with flange against spacer. Install upper reaction spring over reaction ring with cylinder head ferrule passing through hole in reaction spring. Install worm balancing ring (without flange) inside upper reaction ring.

12) Lubricate ferrule "O" ring with petroleum jelly. Install "O" ring in groove on cylinder head ferrule. If oil seal was removed from housing head, install new seal with lip facing bearing. Using Seal Driver (C-3650), drive seal into head until it bottoms on support.

13) Lubricate and install reaction seal in groove of housing head face with flat side of seal out. Install "O" ring in groove on housing head. Install the small "O" ring for the ferrule groove after upper reaction spring and spacer have been installed.

14) Slide housing head over worm shaft, carefully engaging cylinder head ferrule and "O" ring. Ensure reaction rings enter circular groove in housing head. Install power train in gear housing. If gear shaft needle bearings require replacement, turn adjusting screw clockwise until sector shaft becomes disengaged from cover.

15) Slide adjusting screw out of "T" slot in end of shaft. Do not remove sector shaft oil seal unless replacement is necessary. To remove seal, pry out grease retainer, remove oil seal snap ring and back-up washer. Pry out oil seal. Do not scratch seal bore.

16) Lubricate new seal with power steering fluid. Position seal with lip toward housing. Drive seal into housing. Install seal, back-up washer and snap ring (mark facing outward). Fill housing cavity with multipurpose grease. Position grease retainer on housing bore with metal side facing out.

17) Drive retainer into housing until shoulder of Driver Tool (SP-5148) contacts gear housing. Insert sector shaft and adjusting screw into cover. Using an Allen wrench, turn screw counterclockwise to pull shaft completely into cover. Install gasket, date tag and lock nut, but do not tighten. Install "O" ring in undercut shelf of cover.

CHRYSLER MOTORS POWER RECIRCULATING BALL (Cont.)

18) Lubricate power train bore of housing. Install power train. To keep reaction rings aligned in their grooves, keep worm turned fully counterclockwise. When installed in vehicle, piston teeth must face right side and valve lever hole in center race and spacer must face in upward direction.

19) Ensure cylinder head is bottomed on housing shoulder. Align valve lever hole in center bearing race with valve lever hole in gear housing. Install valve lever (double bearing end first) into center race and spacer through hole in gear housing. Engage center race and spacer.

20) Slots in valve lever must be parallel to worm shaft. Tap lightly on end of lever to seat lower pivot point in center race. Center lever by turning housing head. Install housing head tang washer so that it indexes with groove in housing. Install and tighten spanner nut.

21) Valve lever must remain centered in housing hole. Turn worm shaft until piston bottoms in both directions. Note action of lever. Valve lever must be centered in hole and snapped back to center position when worm shaft torque is relieved. Install valve lever spring (small end first).

22) Set power piston at center of travel. Install gear shaft and cover assembly with sector teeth indexed to rack piston teeth. Ensure cover "O" ring is installed correctly. Tighten cover spanner nut. Install valve body on housing. Ensure valve pivot lever enters hole in valve spool.

23) Ensure "O" ring seals are in place. Tighten valve mounting screws. If new worm shaft and piston assembly have been installed, master serration on power steering gear worm shaft spline must be machined to properly center steering shaft coupling.

24) To remove master serration, steering gear must be assembled and worm shaft centered in its travel. With steering gear in its normal upright position, use a file to remove one tooth of spline at the 12 o'clock position.

TIGHTENING SPECIFICATIONS

Application	Ft. Lbs. (N.m)
Control Valve Body-to-Steering Valve Bolt	17 (23)
Flexible Coupling Bolts	17 (23)
Housing Head Spanner Nut	200 (271)
Outlet Fitting-to-Valve	20 (27)
Pitman Arm Nut	175 (237)
Sector Shaft Adjusting Screw Lock Nut	28 (38)
Sector Shaft Cover Spanner Nut	150 (203)
Steering Column Clamp Stud Nut	17 (23)
Steering Gear Mounting Bolts	100 (136)
Steering Wheel Nut	45 (61)
Valve Body End Plug	50 (68)

	INCH Lbs. (N.m)
Steering Column Bracket-to-Column	20 (2)
Steering Column Clamp Stud	110 (12)
Steering Column Support Plate Bolts	60 (7)
Valve Body-to-Housing Attaching Bolts	108 (12)

FORD MOTOR CO.
INTEGRAL POWER RACK & PINION

All Except Continental, Crown Victoria, Grand Marquis & Town Car

DESCRIPTION

Two types of steering gears are used. A 2-piece TRW unit is used on the Escort, Tempo and Topaz. A one-piece Ford Motor Co. unit is used on all other models.

Steering gears are available in 3 ratios, a 20:1 or 18.4:1 variable ratio and a 15:1 constant ratio. The 15:1 constant ratio unit is used on Continental, Mark VII LSC, Mustang GT, Taurus, Thunderbird, and Sable. The 18.4:1 variable ratio unit is used on the Escort, Tempo and Topaz. The 20:1 variable ratio unit is used on all other rack and pinion models.

The 2 steering gear assemblies are basically the same except for dimensional differences in the rack teeth and valve assembly. Service procedures are the same for all steering gears.

OPERATION

A hydraulic-mechanical unit with an integral piston and rack provides power-assisted steering control. Internal valving directs pump flow and controls pressure to reduce steering effort. Units contain a rotary fluid control valve and a boost cylinder integral with gear rack.

LUBRICATION, TROUBLE SHOOTING & TESTING

See POWER STEERING GENERAL SERVICING and TROUBLE SHOOTING articles in this section.

ADJUSTMENTS

RACK PRELOAD & PINION SHAFT INITIAL TURNING TORQUE

(RWD Models)

1) Remove steering gear from vehicle. See REMOVAL & INSTALLATION in this article. Clean exterior of rack housing thoroughly. Mount steering gear to Holding Fixture (T57L-500-B).

2) Cover hydraulic ports. Drain fluid by rotating input shaft. Position Pinion Shaft Adapter (T74P-3504-R) and torque wrench on pinion shaft splines. Loosen adjusting plug lock nut.

3) With rack centered, tighten adjusting plug to 45 50 INCH lbs. Back off adjusting plug 45 degrees. Using

12-60

Power Steering Gears
FORD MOTOR CO.
INTEGRAL POWER RACK & PINION (Cont.)

an INCH lb. torque wrench and socket, check pinion shaft initial turning torque. *See Fig. 1.*

4) Initial turning torque should be 7-18 INCH lbs. (.8-2.0 N.m). While holding adjusting plug stationary, use Lock Nut Wrench (T78P-3504-H) to tighten lock nut to 44-66 ft. lbs. (60-89 N.m). If external lines were removed, replace them with new ones. Recheck pinion shaft torque.

Fig. 1: Adjusting Pinion Shaft Initial Turning Torque

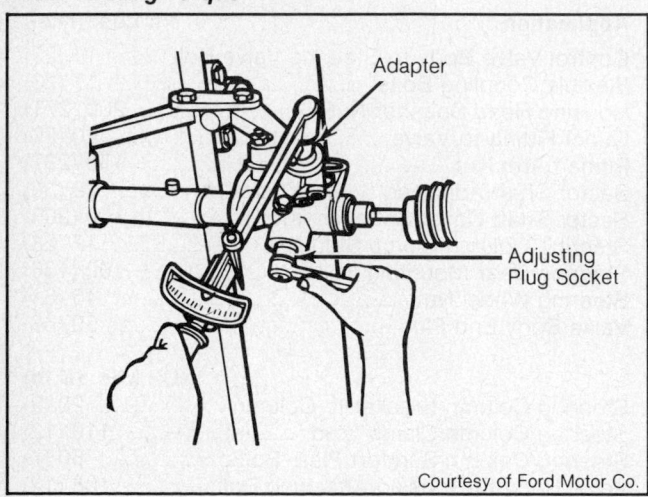

Courtesy of Ford Motor Co.

RACK PRELOAD
(FWD Models)

1) Rack preload adjustment is only required when the input shaft and valve assembly are removed. Do

Fig. 2: Adjusting Rack Preload

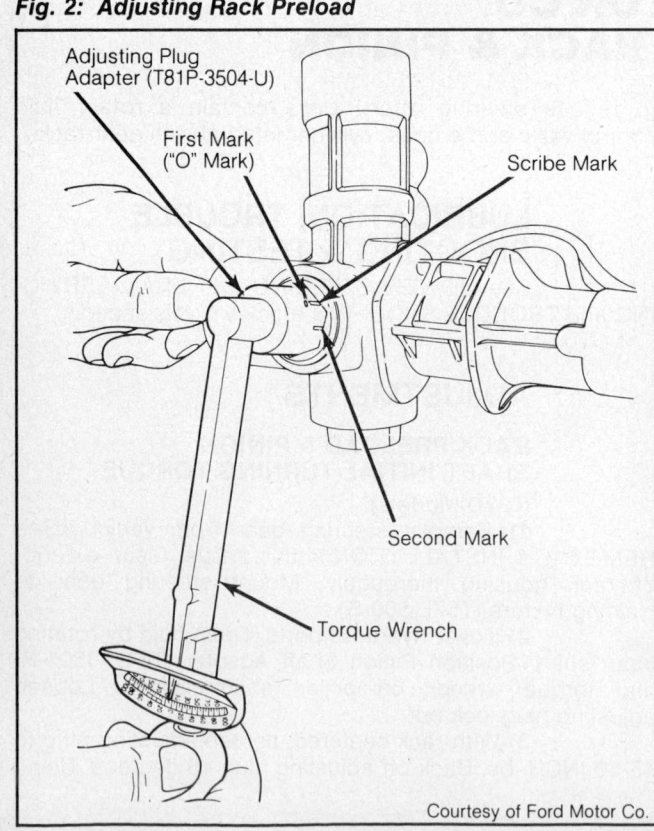

Courtesy of Ford Motor Co.

not remove external pressure tubes unless there is leakage or damage. If tubes are removed, replaced them with new ones.

2) Remove steering gear from vehicle. See REMOVAL & INSTALLATION in this article. Clean exterior of rack housing thoroughly. Remove hydraulic lines. Drain fluid out of openings. Mount gear in vise, near center of tube. Do not over tighten.

2) Loosen and remove adjusting plug lock nut. Back off plug one turn. Using Adjusting Plug Adapter (T81P-3504-U), tighten plug to 45 INCH lbs. (5 N.m).

3) Scribe gear housing in line with "O" mark on adjusting plug adapter. Back off plug so second mark on yoke plug adapter aligns with scribe mark on gear housing.

4) While holding adjusting plug stationary, use Adjusting Plug Lock Nut Wrench (T81P-3504-G) to tighten lock nut to 40-50 ft. lbs. (54-68 N.m). Refill steering gear with power steering fluid.

REMOVAL & INSTALLATION

STEERING GEAR
Removal (RWD)

1) Turn off air suspension switch located in luggage compartment. Disconnect battery ground cable. Turn ignition switch to "RUN" position. Raise and support vehicle. Position drain pan to catch fluid from steeering gear.

2) Remove flexible coupling-to-pinion shaft bolt. Remove cotter pins and castle nuts from tie rod ends. Using a tie rod end puller, separate, tie rod ends from steering knuckles.

3) Remove steering gear-to-crossmember bolts and nuts. Position gear forward to remove grommets. Disconnect and plug hydraulic lines to prevent contamination. Remove steering gear from vehicle.

Installation

1) Ensure rubber grommets are in position in gear housing. Position steering gear on crossmember. Loosely install mounting bolts. Install new plastic seals on hydraulic line fittings.

2) Install hydraulic lines. Line swivel is normal. Do not over tighten. Insert pinion shaft into flexible coupling. Tighten mounting bolts and nuts to specifications. Install tie rods to steering knuckles.

3) Tighten nuts to specification and install cotter pins. Lower vehicle. Install flexible coupling-to-pinion shaft bolt. Turn ignition switch to "OFF" position.

4) Connect battery ground cable. Turn air suspension switch to "ON" position. Fill power steering pump reservoir. Check fluid level. Add fluid as required.

5) Start engine. Cycle steering wheel from lock to lock. Inspect seals and hoses for leaks at maximum pressure. Check and adjust wheel alignment as required. See WHEEL ALIGNMENT section.

Removal (FWD)

1) Disconnect battery ground cable. Place ignition switch in "RUN" position. Remove access panel from floorboard (below steering column). Remove steering column boot retaining screws.

2) Slide boot up on intermediate shaft. Remove intermediate shaft-topinion shaft and intermediate shaft-to-steering shaft "U" joint clamp bolts. Spread slots

FORD MOTOR CO.
INTEGRAL POWER RACK & PINION (Cont.)

enough to loosen intermediate shaft at both ends. Do not separate shafts.

3) Separate pressure and return lines at intermediate connections. Drain fluid. Remove pressure switch. Disconnect exhaust secondary air tubes at check valve.

4) Disconnect exhaust system at exhaust manifold intermediate connections. Mark position of tie rod ends for reassembly reference. Remove cotter pins and castle nuts from tie rod ends.

5) Using Tie Rod Puller and Adapter (T00L-3290-C and T81P-3504-W), separate tie rods ends from knuckles. Remove left tie rod end on manual transmission models.

6) On automatic transmission models, disconnect speedometer and shift cable assembly at transmission. Remove vehicle speed sensor (if equipped). Turn steering wheel to full left turn position.

7) Remove steering gear mounting brackets and grommets. Drape cloth over apron opening edges to protect dust boots during gear removal.

8) Separate steering gear from intermediate shaft by pushing up on shaft with a bar from underneath, while pulling steering gear down.

9) Rotate gear forward and down to clear pinion shaft through floorboard opening. With steering gear in full left turn position, move gear through right side apron opening until left tie rod clears left apron opening.

10) Lower left side of gear. Remove gear from vehicle. Hydraulic lines should remain on gear unless they are leaking, or gear housing is being replaced.

Installation

1) Rotate pinion shaft to full left turn stop. Move right front wheel to full left turn position. Insert right end of steering gear through right fender apron opening until left tie rod clears left fender apron.

2) Raise and insert steering gear left side through apron opening. Rotate gear so pinion shaft enters floorboard opening. With an assistant guiding intermediate shaft from inside vehicle, insert pinion shaft into intermediate shaft coupling.

3) Tighten clamp bolts hand tight. Install grommets and brackets. Ensure flat in left mounting area is parallel to dash panel. Tighten brackets in sequence. Start by tightening driver's side upper bracket bolt half tight.

4) Tighten driver's side lower bolt to specification, followed by driver's side upper bolt to specification. Finally, tighten passenger's side upper and then lower bolts to specifications.

5) Attach tie rod ends to steering knuckles. Tighten nuts to minimum specified torque. Tighten further as necessary to align slots with cotter pin holes. Install cotter pins.

6) On automatic transmission models, connect transmission shift cable and speedometer cable. Install vehicle speed sensor (if equipped). Install exhaust system. Connect secondary air tube at check valve.

7) Connect hydraulic lines at steering gear intermediate connections. Install pressure switch (if equipped). Tighten flexible coupling-to-pinion shaft clamp bolt first. Tighten intermediate shaft-to-steering shaft clamp bolts.

8) Install steering boot to floorboard. Install access panel. Turn Ignition switch to "OFF" position.

Connect battery ground cable. Fill system with fluid. Check and adjust toe-in (if necessary). Tighten tie rod end lock nuts.

PINION SHAFT & SPOOL VALVE ASSEMBLY

Removal (FWD)

1) Set steering in straight ahead position. Lock steering column. Raise and support vehicle. Place drain pan under steering gear. Remove boot clamps. Slide boots outboard from gear housing.

2) Thoroughly drain fluid from boots. Remove pinion cap. Remove pinion nut. Lower vehicle. From inside vehicle, remove column boot from floorboard.

3) Place protective cover on floor of vehicle. Disconnect intermediate shaft from pinion shaft. It may be necessary to loosen steering column to separate intermediate shaft from pinion shaft.

4) Turn pinion shaft to center position so that "D" flat is in 3 o'clock position, and wheels are in straight-ahead position. Remove snap ring from gear housing.

5) Attach Pinion Shaft and Spool Valve Puller (T81P-3504-T) to pinion shaft. See Fig. 3. Remove pinion shaft and valve assembly slowly to minimize oil spillage.

6) Insert Lower Pinion Seal Remover Guide (T81P-3504-E) along with Lower Pinion Seal Remover (T78P-3504-E) into pinion housing, and tap tool to bottom. Expand tool inside housing. Using large pair of pliers, remove seal and tool.

Fig. 3: Removing Spool Valve Assembly on Ford Motor Co. FWD Models

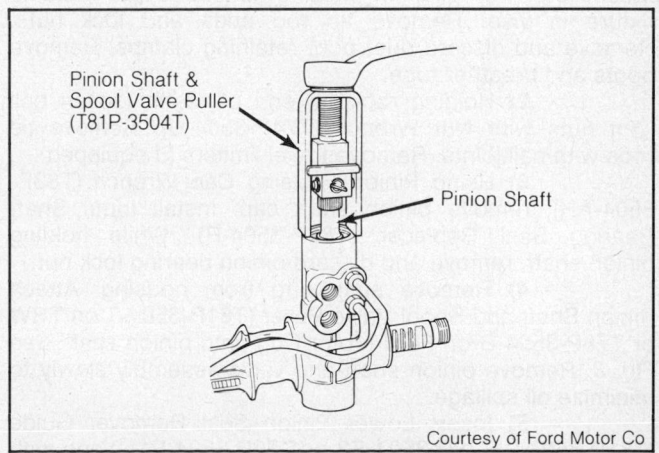

Pinion Shaft & Spool Valve Puller (T81P-3504T)

Pinion Shaft

Courtesy of Ford Motor Co

Installation

1) Apply power steering fluid to pinion oil seal. Place seal over Lower Pinion Seal Replacer (T84P-3504-F) with lip of seal toward tool. Install seal in valve bore, seating it against shoulder.

2) Remove input shaft seal and bearing from valve assembly. Wipe oil from pinion gear teeth. Lubricate pinion gear teeth with steering grease. Insert Sizer (T81P-3504-M3) into valve housing.

3) Position "D" flat on input shaft to right and vertical (3 o'clock). Insert valve assembly in bore. Raise and support vehicle. Using Input Shaft Bearing Replacer (T81P-3504-R) to turn input shaft, verify that pinion is centered by counting number turns from lock-to-lock.

12-62

Power Steering Gears
FORD MOTOR CO.
INTEGRAL POWER RACK & PINION (Cont.)

4) If unequal number of turns are required to turn from, lock-to-lock, remove valve assembly only far enough to move rack assembly one tooth at a time in either direction until it is equal.

5) Install input shaft bearing with wide face of case outward in valve bore. Seat with Input Shaft Bearing Seal Replacer (T81P-3504-R). Install Shaft Seal Protector (T81L-3504-P) over input shaft.

6) Apply a light film of grease to input shaft seal. Install seal with lip spring toward valve. Remove seal protector. Seat the seal until bottomed. Install snap ring in valve bore.

7) Reconnect intermediate shaft to pinion shaft. Tighten pinch bolts to specification. Tighten steering column bolts if column was loosened.

8) Install column boot to floorboard. Tighten screws to specification. With steering wheel locked, install new lock nut on pinion end of valve assembly.

9) Tighten lock nut to specification. Rack must be away from stops during this procedure. Install steering gear housing cap. Tighten cap to specification.

10) Install boots and boot clamps. Refill pump reservoir. Run engine. Cycle steering wheel from lock-to-lock several times. Recheck fluid level. Check for leaks.

OVERHAUL

STEERING GEAR
Disassembly
1) Thoroughly clean exterior of steering gear. Mount steering gear in holding fixture. Place holding fixture in vise. Remove tie rod ends and lock nuts. Remove and discard dust boot retaining clamps. Remove boots and breather tube.

2) Holding rack on end of teeth, loosen ball joint nuts with Nut Wrench (T74P-3504-U). Remove tie rods with ball joints. Remove travel limiters (if equipped).

3) Using Pinion Housing Cap Wrench (T83P-3504-AH), remove pinion shaft cap. Install Input Shaft Bearing Seal Replacer (T83P-3504-R). While holding pinion shaft, remove and discard pinion bearing lock nut.

4) Remove snap ring from housing. Attach Pinion Shaft and Spool Valve Puller (T81P-3504-T on TRW or T78P-3504-B on Ford Motor Co.) onto pinion shaft. See Fig. 3. Remove pinion shaft and valve assembly slowly to minimize oil spillage.

5) Insert Lower Pinion Seal Remover Guide (T81P-3504-E T78P-3504-E2 or D82P-3504-E1) along with Lower Pinion Seal Remover (T78P-3504-E) into pinion housing. Tap tool to bottom. Expand tool inside housing. Using large pair of pliers, remove seal and tool.

6) Remove rivet head with a sharp chisel. Using Roll Pin Remover (T78P-3504-N), push roll pin out of pivot bushing. Do not remove external hydraulic tubes.

Using Adjusting Plug Lock Nut Wrench (T81P-3504-G), remove adjusting plug lock nut.

7) Using Adjusting Plug Wrench (T81P-3504-U), remove adjusting plug, spring and rack guide. Remove "O" rings from spool valve by pushing them to one side and cutting with a knife. Do not scratch or nick valve sleeve corners or flats.

8) Using Seal Remover (T81P-3504-E), remove lower pinion shaft seal. Insert tool assembly in valve bore until it bottoms. Tap lightly with plastic hammer to seat.

9) Using Slide Hammer (T50T-100-A), pull tool and seal from valve bore. Discard pinion seal. Using Slide Hammer and Attachment (T58L-101-A), remove lower pinion shaft bearing.

10) On TRW units, inserting Lock Ring Tool (T77P-3504-A), engage end plate. Rotate tool clockwise until the lock ring retainer hole is visible. Rotate retainer clockwise until wire end is visible in slot. Remove retaining ring wire by leading wire out of slot while turning end plate counterclockwise.

11) On Ford Motor Co. units, remove snap ring Pull rack out of housing from right side, along with end plate and aluminum rack bushing.

12) If rack is difficult to remove, hand tighten a tie rod to rack gear. Place a slide hammer weight on tie rod. Install lock nut. Carefully remove rack. Using Expander (T78P-3504-J for Ford Motor Co. or T81P-3504-B for TRW), remove and discard inner rack oil seal.

13) Oil seal contains a nylon ring that may separate during removal. Ensure all parts of seal are removed from housing. Remove piston plastic seal ring from rack. Remove "O" ring.

14) Place tool in a vise Using Rack Oil Seal Remover (T81P-3504-B and Slide Hammer T50T-100-A for Ford Motor Co, or T78P-3504-L and Adapter T50T-100-A for TRW), remove seal. Remove "O" ring from rack bushing.

Fig. 4: Removing Pinion Bearing on TRW Steering Gears

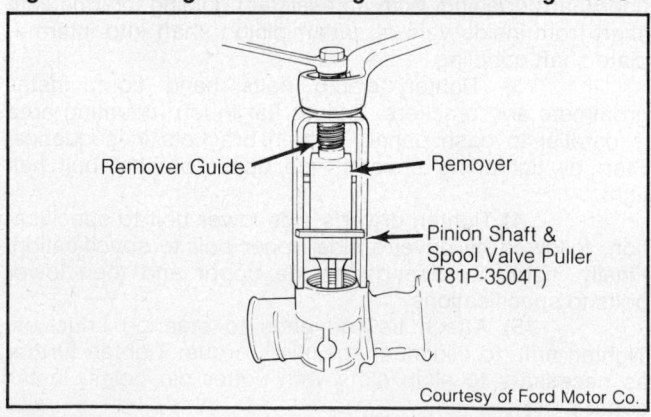

Courtesy of Ford Motor Co.

This removal tool used on TRW steering gears. Other gear tools are similar.

FORD MOTOR CO.
INTEGRAL POWER RACK & PINION (Cont.)

Fig. 5: Exploded View of Ford Motor Co. Steering Gear Assembly

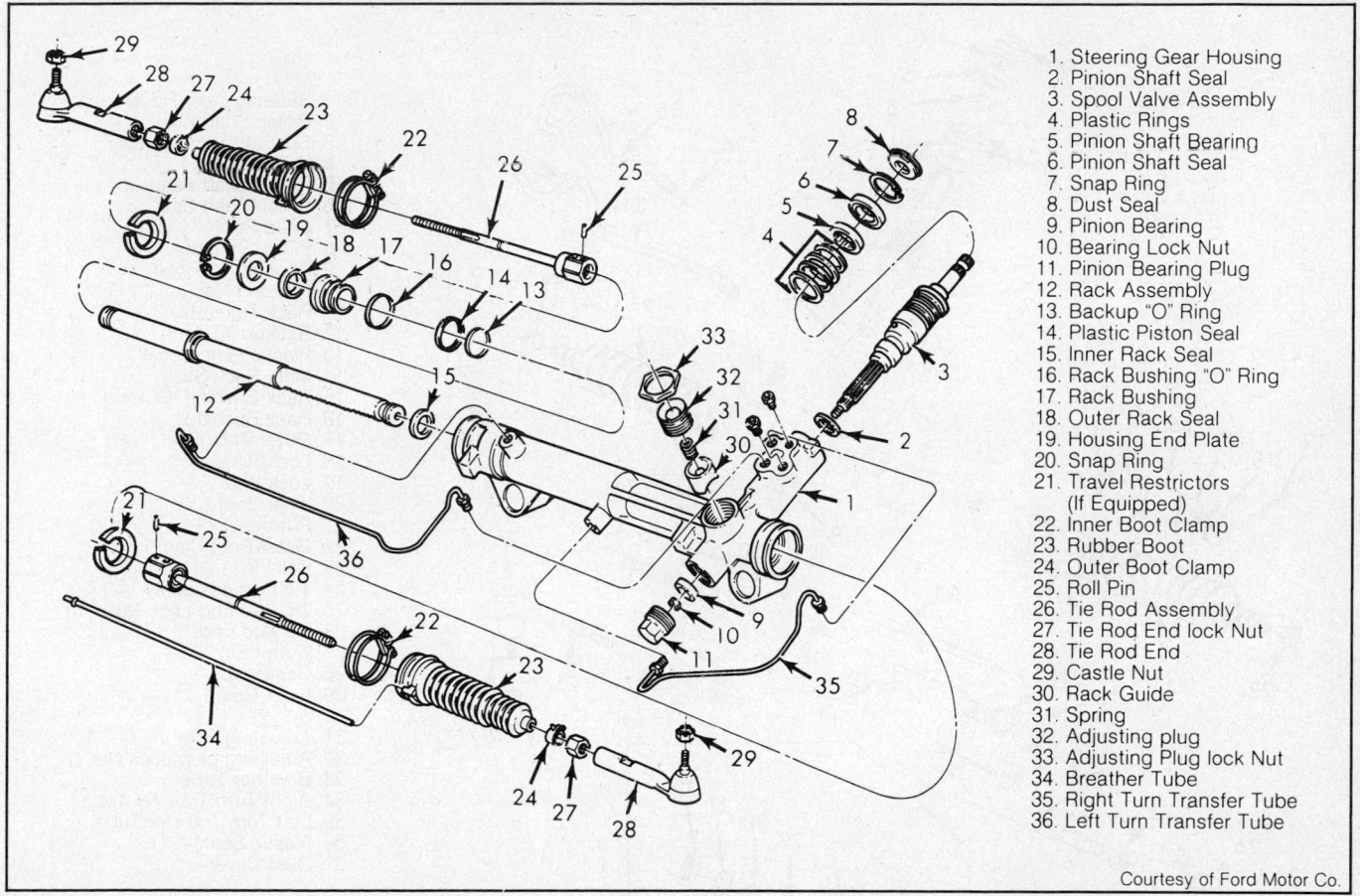

1. Steering Gear Housing
2. Pinion Shaft Seal
3. Spool Valve Assembly
4. Plastic Rings
5. Pinion Shaft Bearing
6. Pinion Shaft Seal
7. Snap Ring
8. Dust Seal
9. Pinion Bearing
10. Bearing Lock Nut
11. Pinion Bearing Plug
12. Rack Assembly
13. Backup "O" Ring
14. Plastic Piston Seal
15. Inner Rack Seal
16. Rack Bushing "O" Ring
17. Rack Bushing
18. Outer Rack Seal
19. Housing End Plate
20. Snap Ring
21. Travel Restrictors
    (If Equipped)
22. Inner Boot Clamp
23. Rubber Boot
24. Outer Boot Clamp
25. Roll Pin
26. Tie Rod Assembly
27. Tie Rod End lock Nut
28. Tie Rod End
29. Castle Nut
30. Rack Guide
31. Spring
32. Adjusting plug
33. Adjusting Plug lock Nut
34. Breather Tube
35. Right Turn Transfer Tube
36. Left Turn Transfer Tube

Courtesy of Ford Motor Co.

Reassembly

1) Insert rack bushing into Rack Bushing Holder (T81P-3504-D for TRW or T78P-3504-L for Ford Motor Co.), seal end first. On TRW units, insert Holder (T81P-3504-K) into right end of rack housing. Install inner rack seal onto Driver (T81P-3504-C).

2) Tap tool handle with a plastic hammer to seat seal. On all models, do not cock handle of tool. If tool binds in area of left turn pressure port, align flat on tool with pressure port.

3) On Ford Motor Co. units, paint a mark on center rack tooth for reassembly reference. On all models, install "O" ring into piston groove. Apply grease on rack teeth and rack bearing sliding surface.

4) Insert Holder (T81P-3504-K for TRW or T74P-3504-G for Ford Motor Co.) into right side of rack housing. Lubricate "O" ring and protective sleeve with power steering fluid. Using Protective Sleeve (D83P-3504-K for TRW or T85L-3504-B for Ford Motor Co.), install rack into housing.

5) Lead protector sleeve in through right side opening of rack housing. Carefully push rack in until protective sleeve protrudes from left end. Remove protector and sleeve from rack. Install left tie rod to prevent rack teeth from damaging inner oil seal.

6) Apply power steering fluid to outer rack oil seal. Install "O" ring onto shock damper. Install outer oil seal, nylon washer, and shock damper onto Seal Installer (T81P-3504-C for TRW or T74P-3504-F for Ford Motor Co.). Spring lip of seal must face inside of bushing.

7) Install Protective Sleeve (T81P-3504-N for TRW or T78P-3504-M for Ford Motor Co.) into right side rack housing opening. Lubricate sleeve and "O" ring with power steering fluid. Apply hand pressure to seat shock dampener. Remove protective sleeve.

8) Install end plate on rack. Position end plate against shock damper. Use Driver (T77P-3504-A for TRW or a 1 1/8" deep socket on Ford Motor Co.) to seat end plate if hand pressure will not.

9) On Ford Motor Co models, install retaining ring. Remove protective sleeve. On TRW models, turn lock ring with Holder (T77P-3504-A) until retainer hole is visible. Insert lock wire. Rotate retainer clockwise until wire is completely enclosed. Rotate an additional 180 degrees.

10) Using Bearing Installer (T78P-3504-G on Ford Motor Co. or T81P-3504-H on TRW), seat lower pinion shaft bearing against shoulder into pinion housing. Lubricate pinion oil seal with power steering fluid.

11) Using Seal Installer (T84P-3504-F on TRW or T78P-3504-F on Ford Motor Co.), install seal with lip of seal facing tool. Mount assembly in soft-jawed vise. Position mandrel tool over pinion shaft. Lubricate with power steering fluid.

12) Using Mandrel Kit (T81P-3504-M1, M2, M3, M4 on TRW or T75L-3517-A1, A2, A3, A4 on Ford Motor Co.), install 4 "O" rings in grooves of valve. Slide one ring over mandrel. Slide pusher tool over mandrel. By hand, force ring down ramp into fourth groove (closest to lock nut threads). *See Fig. 7.*

Power Steering Gears
FORD MOTOR CO.
INTEGRAL POWER RACK & PINION (Cont.)

Fig. 6: Exploded View of TRW Steering Gear Assembly

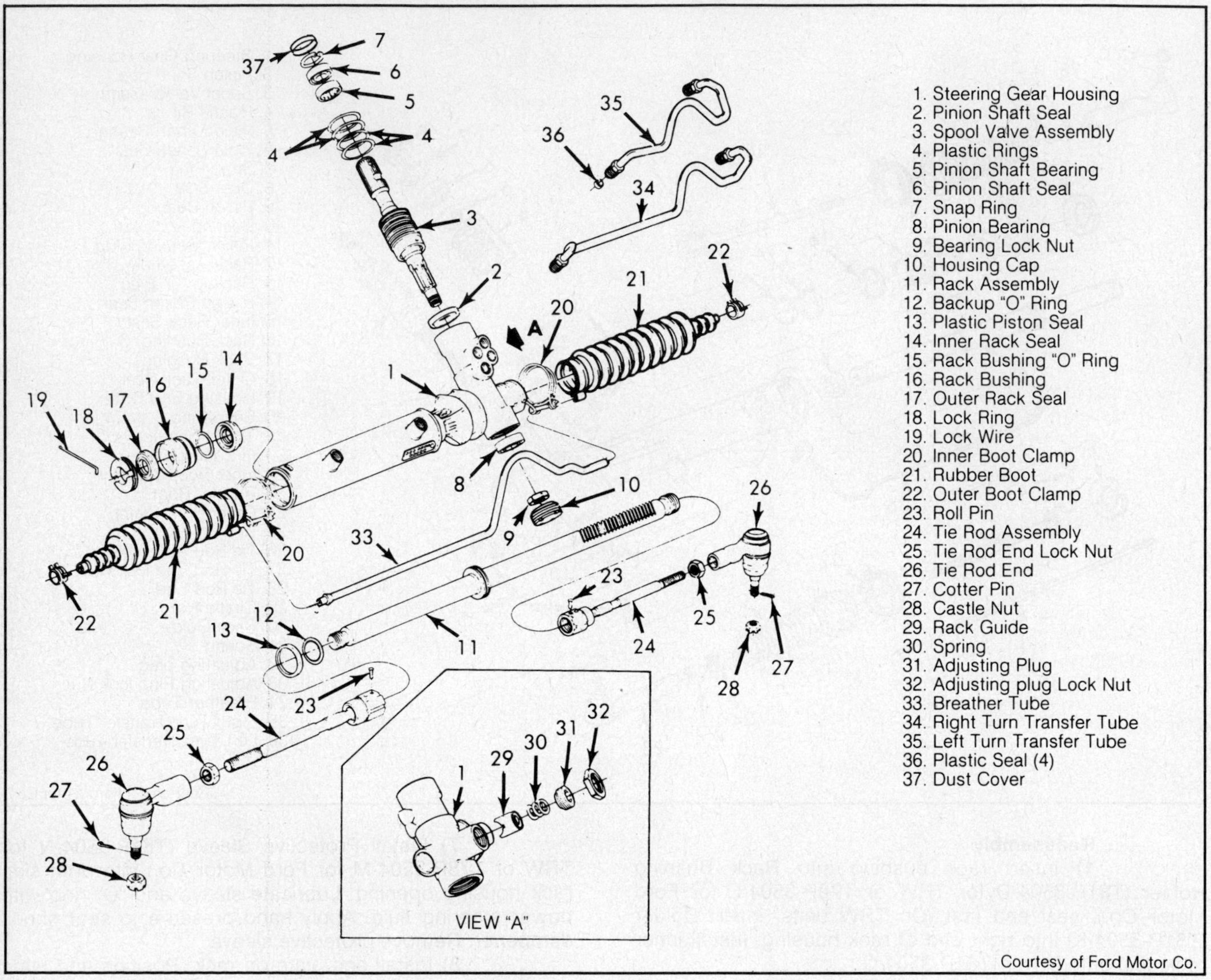

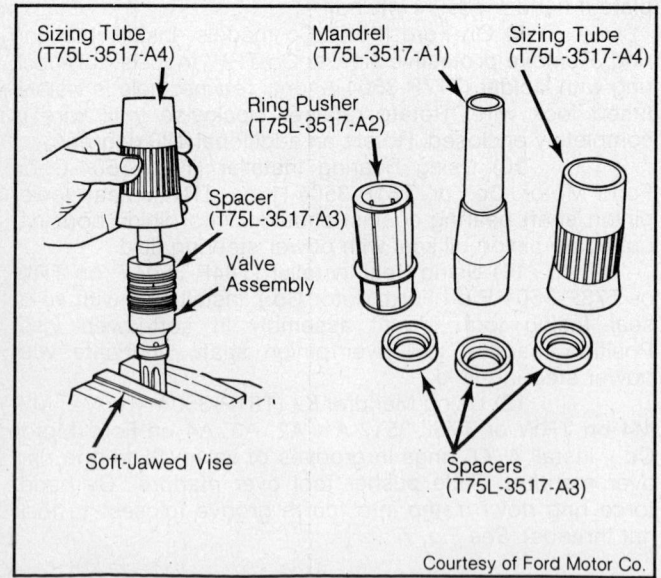

1. Steering Gear Housing
2. Pinion Shaft Seal
3. Spool Valve Assembly
4. Plastic Rings
5. Pinion Shaft Bearing
6. Pinion Shaft Seal
7. Snap Ring
8. Pinion Bearing
9. Bearing Lock Nut
10. Housing Cap
11. Rack Assembly
12. Backup "O" Ring
13. Plastic Piston Seal
14. Inner Rack Seal
15. Rack Bushing "O" Ring
16. Rack Bushing
17. Outer Rack Seal
18. Lock Ring
19. Lock Wire
20. Inner Boot Clamp
21. Rubber Boot
22. Outer Boot Clamp
23. Roll Pin
24. Tie Rod Assembly
25. Tie Rod End Lock Nut
26. Tie Rod End
27. Cotter Pin
28. Castle Nut
29. Rack Guide
30. Spring
31. Adjusting Plug
32. Adjusting plug Lock Nut
33. Breather Tube
34. Right Turn Transfer Tube
35. Left Turn Transfer Tube
36. Plastic Seal (4)
37. Dust Cover

VIEW "A"

Courtesy of Ford Motor Co.

Fig. 7: Installing "O" Rings on Spool Valve

Sizing Tube (T75L-3517-A4)
Mandrel (T75L-3517-A1)
Sizing Tube (T75L-3517-A4)
Ring Pusher (T75L-3517-A2)
Spacer (T75L-3517-A3)
Valve Assembly
Soft-Jawed Vise
Spacers (T75L-3517-A3)

Courtesy of Ford Motor Co.

13) Slide sizing tool over rings after installation. Insert spacers after installation of each ring. The last "O" ring will snap into outboard groove directly off "O" ring installer. Remove sizing tool. Ensure rings are not cut, and that they turn freely in grooves.

14) Using Installer (T78P-3504-C on Ford Motor Co. or T81P-3504-M3 on TRW), install valve assembly into housing. On Ford Motor Co. models, ensure right end of rack gear protrudes 1/4" (6 mm) more than left side. Align "D" flat of pinion shaft 180 degrees from center of dust cap hole.

15) On TRW models, ensure rack gear is centered. Align "D" flat facing 3 o'clock position. On all models, count number of turns from stop to stop to ensure rack gear is centered.

16) If number of turns is unequal, rotate pinion shaft one tooth in direction that required the least turns from center. Repeat until correct. Center rack gear. Install and tighten pinion shaft lock nut.

17) Using Seal Installer (T78P-3504-D on Ford Motor Co. or T81P-3504-R on TRW), seat pinion shaft dust seal. On all models, install pinion bearing dust cap.

FORD MOTOR CO.
INTEGRAL POWER RACK & PINION (Cont.)

Tighten dust cap to specification. Fill housing with gear lubricant.

18) Install rack guide, spring and adjusting plug. Set preload. Install lock nut. Hold one tie rod ball joint with an adjustable wrench while tightening other ball joint with Wrench (T74P-3504-U on Ford Motor Co. or T81P-3504-G on TRW). This tightens both tie rods at the same time.

19) Install new roll pins in ball joint by tapping lightly with plastic hammer. Apply lubricant to groove on tie rods where dust boots clamp. Install dust boots and breather tube. Install new boot clamps. Install lock nuts on tie rods.

20) Apply lubricant to tip of rod threads. Install tie rod ends. Install steering gear. Check and adjust toe-in as necessary. Tighten tie rod end lock nuts.

TIGHTENING SPECIFICATIONS

Application	Ft. Lbs. (N.m)
Flexible Coupling-to-Pinion Bolt	
Sable & Taurus	30-38 (41-51)
All Others	20-30 (27-41)
Hydraulic Fittings-to-Steering Gear	
Escort, Tempo & Topaz	20-25 (27-33)
All Others	15-25 (21-33)
Hydraulic Transfer Tubes	
Escort, Tempo & Topaz	15-21 (21-27)
All Others	22-28 (30-38)
Intermediate Shaft-to-Steering Shaft Nuts	
Escort, Tempo & Topaz	20-30 (27-41)
Sable & Taurus	15-25 (21-33)

TIGHTENING SPECIFICATIONS (Cont.)

Application	Ft. Lbs. (N.m)
All Others	35-45 (47-61)
Pinion Bearing Cap	
Escort, Tempo & Topaz	35-45 (48-61)
All Others	40-60 (54-81)
Pinion Bearing Cap Lock Nut	
Escort, Tempo & Topaz	20-35 (27-47)
All Others	30-40 (40-54)
Adjusting Plug Lock Nut	
Escort, Sable, Taurus, Tempo & Topaz	40-50 (54-68)
All Others	44-66 (60-89)
Steering Gear Mounting Bolts & Nuts	
Escort, Tempo & Topaz	55-70 (75-95)
Sable & Taurus	85-100 (115-135)
All Others	30-40 (40-54)
Tie Rod Ball Joint-to-Rack	
Escort, Tempo & Topaz	50-55 (68-75)
All Others	55-65 (75-88)
Tie Rod End Lock Nut	
Escort, Tempo & Topaz	[1] 42-50 (57-68)
All Others	35-50 (48-68)
Tie Rod End-to-Steering Knuckle	
Escort, Tempo & Topaz	[1] 27-32 (37-43)
All Others	35-47 (47-64)

	INCH Lbs. (N.m)
Adjusting Plug (All Models)	45 (5)

[1] - Tighten to specification and then to nearest cotter pin slot.

FORD MOTOR CO. INTEGRAL POWER STEERING

Crown Victoria, Grand Marquis, Town Car

DESCRIPTION

The system is a hydraulically assisted torsion bar type. The system incorporates a rotary valve, pinion shaft, torsion bar, worm shaft, one-piece rack piston, sector shaft and housing. The rotary valve is mounted on the input shaft and controls fluid pressure to each side of rack piston.

OPERATION

The control valve uses rotational position of the input shaft and valve sleeve to direct fluid flow. The valve is pinned to the worm, and the input shaft is connected to the worm through the torsion bar. In operation the valve and housing cylinder are always full of fluid, which dampens road shock.

LUBRICATION, TROUBLE SHOOTING & TESTING

See POWER STEERING GENERAL SERVICING & TROUBLE SHOOTING articles in this section.

ADJUSTMENTS

SECTOR SHAFT MESH LOAD

1) Disconnect pitman arm from sector shaft. Disconnect fluid return line at reservoir and cap line fitting. Place return line in container and cycle steering wheel to discharge fluid from gear.

2) Turn steering wheel to within 45 degrees of left stop. Using a INCH lb. torque wrench on steering wheel nut, measure rotational drag required to turn gear about 1/4 of a turn from the 45 degrees position.

3) Record reading. If vehicle is equipped with a tilt wheel, place wheel in center tilt position. Turn steering wheel to straight-ahead position. Measure torque in both directions. Reading should be 14-29 INCH lbs. (1.6-3.3 N.m).

FORD MOTOR CO. INTEGRAL POWER STEERING (Cont.)

Fig. 1: Exploded View of Ford Motor Co. Integral Power Steering Gear

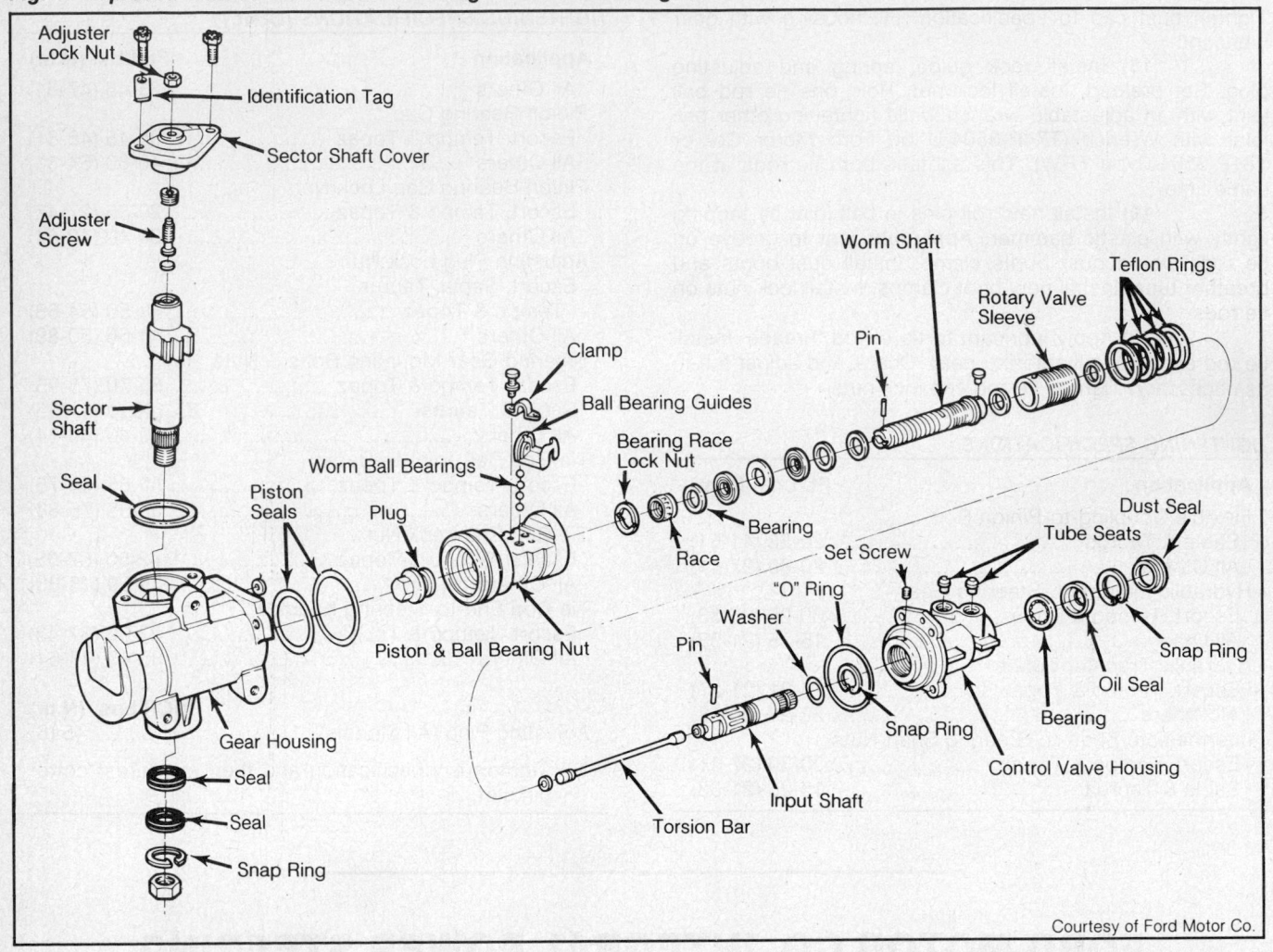

Courtesy of Ford Motor Co.

4) If adjustment is required, loosen adjuster screw lock nut. Turn screw to adjust sector mesh load. Set torque, measured rocking across center to a value of 14-20 INCH lbs. (1.6-2.3 N.m) greater than that measured 45 degrees from the right stop.

5) Tighten adjuster screw lock nut. Recheck rotational turning torque. Reconnect return line. Add fluid. Install pitman arm. Tighten nut to specification. Check and adjust power steering belt as necessary.

REMOVAL & INSTALLATION

STEERING GEAR

Removal

1) Remove stone shield. Disconnect hydraulic lines from gear. Mark hydraulic lines for reassembly reference. Plug lines and ports to prevent contamination.

2) Remove flexible coupling bolts. Raise and support vehicle. Remove sector shaft nut. Mark pitman arm and sector shaft for reassembly reference. Using Puller (T-64P-3590-F), remove pitman arm without damaging seals. Do not use a pickle fork.

3) Support steering gear. Remove gear attaching bolts. Remove flexible coupling clamp bolts. Separate gear from coupling. Remove gear from vehicle.

Installation

To install steering gear, reverse removal procedure. Tighten all bolts and nuts. Do not allow solvent to contact seals.

OVERHAUL

STEERING GEAR

Disassembly

1) Drain steering gear. and mount in a holding fixture. Remove lock nut and washer from adjusting screw. Turn input shaft to either stop. Turn back 1 5/8 turns to center gear. Indexing flat on pinion spline should be facing downward.

2) Remove sector shaft cover bolts. Tap lower end of sector shaft with a soft hammer. Lift cover and shaft from housing as an assembly. Discard "O" ring.

3) Turn sector shaft cover counterclockwise to remove cover from adjusting screw. Remove valve housing attaching bolts and identification tag. Lift valve housing from steering gear housing while holding piston to prevent it from rotating off worm shaft.

4) Remove and discard valve housing-to-gear "O" rings. Hold piston so ball bearing guide faces upward. Remove ball guide clamp screws and clamp.

FORD MOTOR CO. INTEGRAL POWER STEERING (Cont.)

5) Place finger over opening in ball bearing guide and turn piston so ball bearing guide faces over clean container. Allow guide tubes to drop into container. Rotate input shaft from stop to stop until all ball bearings fall into container. There should be a mimimum of 27 balls.

6) Remove valve assembly from piston. Ensure that all ball bearings have been removed. Install valve assembly in holding fixture. Loosen Allen head race nut lock screw from valve housing.

7) Using Adjuster/Lock Nut wrench and Spacer Valve Housing-to-Piston Holder (T66P-3553-B and T66P-3553-C), remove worm bearing race nut. Carefully slide pinion shaft, worm and valve assembly out of valve housing. *See Fig. 2.* Slightest cocking of spool may cause it to jam in housing and damage sleeve.

8) Remove snap ring from lower end of housing. Using Adapter and Impact Slide Hammer (T58L-101-A and T59L-100-B), remove and discard dust seal. Remove and discard pressure seal in same manner.

Fig. 2: Removing Worm Ball Bearing Race Nut

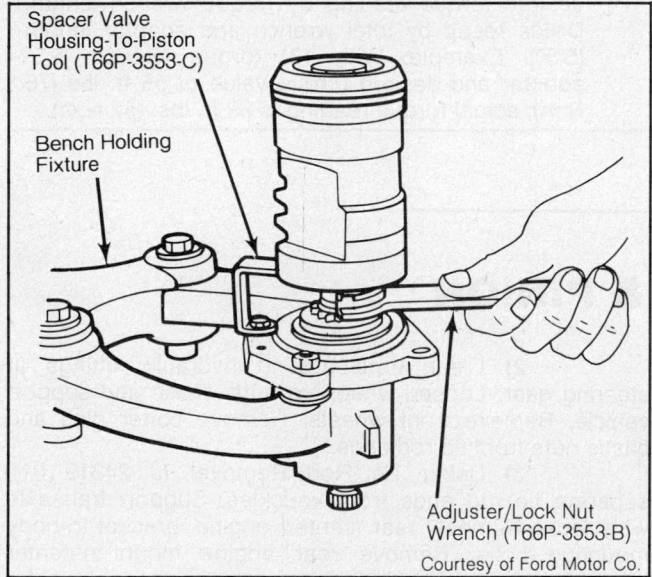

Spacer Valve Housing-To-Piston Tool (T66P-3553-C)

Bench Holding Fixture

Adjuster/Lock Nut Wrench (T66P-3553-B)

Courtesy of Ford Motor Co.

9) Using same adapter and impact slide hammer, remove and discard dust seal from rear of valve housing. Carefully insert Bearing Remover/Installer (T65P-3524-A2) in valve body assembly opposite oil seal. Gently tap bearing and seal out of housing. Discard seal.

10) If valve bore is damaged, remove inlet and outlet tube seats with Brass Tube Remover (T-74P-3504-2). Remove valve sleeve Teflon rings only if scratched or worn. Insert a knife blade under rings and cut them off. Avoid scratching valve sleeve. Remove plastic ring and "O" ring from piston and ball nut.

Reassembly

1) Install Mandrel (T75L-3517-A1) over sleeve. Slide one valve ring over mandrel. Slide Pusher (T75L-3517-A2) over mandrel. Rapidly push down on tool, forcing ring down ramp and into 4th groove of valve sleeve.

2) Repeat this procedure 3 more times, adding a Spacer (T75L-3517-A3), under mandrel each time. After installing 4 valve sleeve rings, apply gear lubricant to sleeve and rings. Install one spacer over input shaft as a pilot for installing sizing tube.

3) Slowly install Sizing Tube (T75L-3517-A4) over sleeve valve end of worm shaft onto valve sleeve rings. Ensure rings are not being bent over as tube is slid over them. Remove sizing tube. Check condition of rings. Rings must turn freely in grooves.

4) Coat new tube seats with petroleum jelly. Install new tube seals using Brass Tube Installer (T74P-3504-M). Coat bearing and seal surface of housing with petroleum jelly. Position bearing in housing. Press bearing with metal covered side facing out into position. Be sure bearing rotates freely.

5) Dip new oil seal in gear lube. Place seal in housing, metal side out. Drive seal into housing until outer edge does not quite clear snap ring groove. Place snap ring in housing. Drive snap ring in until it seats in groove.

6) With rubber side out, drive dust seal in position behind groove in input shaft. Lubricate seals and sector shaft bore. Place dust seal on Shaft Seal Installer (T77L-3576-A) so that raised lip of seal is toward tool.

7) Slide pressure seal on tool with flat of pressure seal against flat of dust seal. Carefully insert seals into sector shaft bore with tool until they clear snap ring groove. Do not bottom seals against bearing. Install snap ring.

8) Dip new "O" ring in gear lubricant. Install "O" ring on piston and ball nut. Install a new plastic ring on piston and ball nut. Do not stretch plastic ring any more than necessary. Mount valve housing in holding fixture, (flanged end up).

9) Lubricate valve sleeve rings. Install worm and valve in housing. Using Adjuster/Lock Nut Wrench and Spacer Valve Housing-to-Piston Holder (T66P-3553-B and T66P-3553-C), install and tighten race nut to 55-90 ft. lbs. (75-122 N.m). *See Fig. 2.*

10) Install Allen head race nut set screw through valve housing. Tighten set screw to 15-25 INCH lbs. (1.7-2.8 N.m). Place piston on bench, with ball bearing guide holes facing up. Insert worm shaft so first groove is aligned with hole nearest the center of the piston.

11) Place ball guides in piston. While turning worm shaft clockwise, (as viewed from input end of shaft), place a minimum of 27 ball bearings in ball bearing guide. If all ball bearings have not been fed into guide upon reaching right stop, rotate input shaft back and forth while installing remaining ball bearings. *See Fig. 3.*

NOTE: After all ball bearings have been installed, do not rotate input shaft more than 3 turns from right stop or ball bearings will fall out of circuit.

12) Secure guides in ball bearing nut with clamp. Tighten screws to 42-70 INCH lbs. (4.8-7.9 N.m). Apply petroleum jelly to seal on piston. Place new "O" ring on valve housing. Slide piston and valve into gear housing. Align oil passage in valve housing with passage in gear housing.

13) Position new "O" ring in gear housing oil passage. Install, but do not tighten, identification tag and attaching bolts. Rotate ball nut so teeth are parallel with sector teeth. Tighten valve housing bolts to specification. Install sector shaft cover "O" ring in gear housing. Turn input shaft to center piston.

14) Apply petroleum jelly to sector shaft journal. Position sector shaft and cover assembly in gear housing. Rotate input shaft one turn on either side of center. Install and tighten cover bolts to specification. Perform sector shaft adjustment as previously described.

FORD MOTOR CO. INTEGRAL POWER STEERING (Cont.)

Fig. 3: Installing Piston & Worm Shaft Ball Bearings

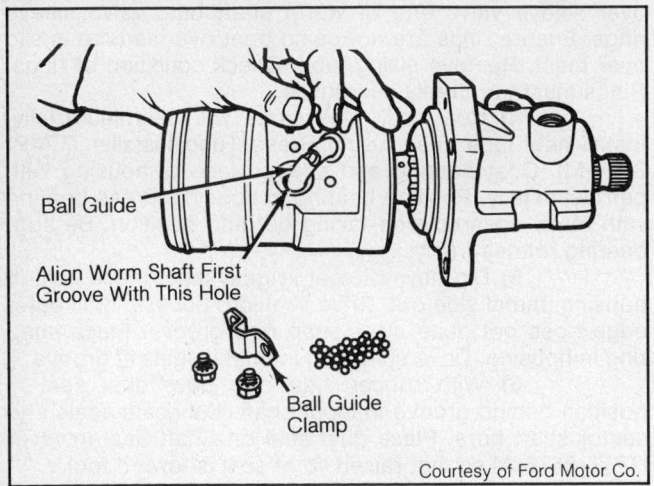

Ball Guide

Align Worm Shaft First
Groove With This Hole

Ball Guide
Clamp

Courtesy of Ford Motor Co.

TIGHTENING SPECIFICATIONS

Application	Ft. Lbs. (N.m)
Flexible Coupling Bolt	20-30 (27-41)
Piston End Cap	70-110 (95-149)
Pitman Arm Retaining Nut	200-250 (271-339)
Presure Line-to-Steering Gear	16-25 (22-34)
Return Line-to-Steering Gear	25-34 (34-46)
Sector Shaft Cover Bolts	55-70 (75-95)
Sector Shaft Adj. Screw Lock Nut	35-45 (47-61)
Steering Gear Mounting Bolts	50-65 (68-88)
Valve Housing Bolts	30-45 (41-61)
Worm Bearing Race Nut	[1] 55-90 (75-122)

	INCH Lbs. (N.m)
Ball Bearing Return Guide Clamp Screws	42-70 (4.8-7.9)
Hose Clamps	12-24 (1.4-2.7)
Race Nut Set Screw	15-25 (1.7-2.8)

[1] – To obtain proper torque reading when using Adjuster/Lock Nut Wrench (T66P-3553-B), multiply desired torque reading by torque wrench length. Divide result by total wrench and adapter length (5.5"). Example: With 13" torque wrench, 5.5" adapter and desired torque value of 55 ft. lbs (75 N.m), actual torque reading is 39 ft. lbs. (52 N.m).

NOVA RACK & PINION

DESCRIPTION

The steering system uses a rotary control valve which directs pressurized hydraulic fluid to either side of the rack piston. The piston is attached to the rack. The rack attaches to the steering knuckles with tie rods and tie rod ends. If the hydraulic assist fails, manual control is maintained, however, steering effort is increased.

LUBRICATION, TROUBLE SHOOTING & TESTING

See POWER STEERING GENERAL SERVICING & TROUBLE SHOOTING articles in this section.

ADJUSTMENTS

PINION TURNING TORQUE

Pinion turning torque adjustment is performed during reassembly procedure. See OVERHAUL in this article.

REMOVAL & INSTALLATION

STEERING GEAR

Removal

1) Remove intermediate steering shaft protector. Loosen upper and lower intermediate shaft pinch bolts. Remove intermediate shaft. Place drain pan below gear assembly.

2) Clean area around hydraulic fittings at steering gear. Loosen wheel lug nuts. Raise and support vehicle. Remove front wheels. Remove cotter pins and castle nuts from tie rod ends.

3) Using Tie Rod Remover (J 24319 01), separate tie rod ends from knuckles. Support transaxle with jack. Remove rear center engine bracket-to-body mounting bolts. Remove rear engine mount-to-center engine bracket nut and bolt.

4) Raise and lower rear of transaxle as necessary to gain access to steering gear mounting bolt and nuts. Disconnect hydraulic lines from steering gear. Remove 4 steering gear mounting bolts and nuts. Remove gear through access hole.

Installation

To install steering gear, reverse removal procedure. Add fluid and bleed system. Check toe-in.

TIE ROD END

Removal & Installation

1) Loosen tie rod pinch bolts. Using Tie Rod Remover (J 24319 01), remove tie rod from steering knuckle. Remove tie rod end from tie rod.

2) To install, reverse removal procedure. Make toe-in adjustment by turning tie rod adjuster. Ensure dust boot is not twisted. Tighten pinch bolts to 41 ft. lbs. (56 N.m).

NOVA RACK & PINION (Cont.)

Fig. 1: Exploded View of Nova Power Steering Gear Assembly

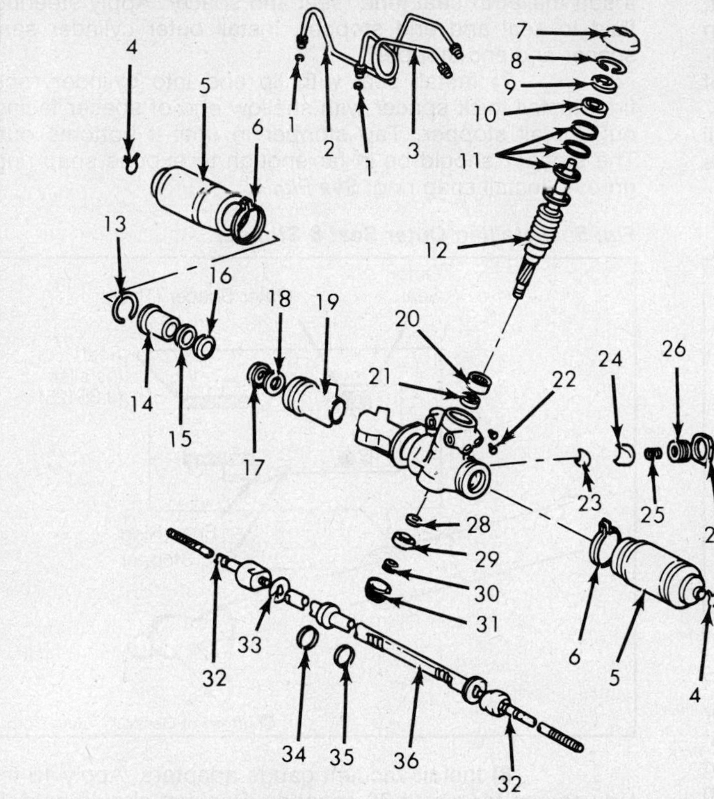

1. "O" Ring Seal
2. Right Turn Hydraulic Tube
3. Left Turn Hydraulic Tube
4. Boot Retaining Clip
5. Rubber Boot
6. Boot Retaining Clamp
7. Pinion Dust Cover
8. Snap Ring
9. Pinion Upper Seal
10. Pinion Upper Bearing
11. Control Valve Sealing Ring
12. Valve/Pinion Assembly
13. Snap Ring
14. Rack End Stopper
15. Outer Cylinder End Spacer (Thick)
16. Outer Cylinder End Seal
17. Inner Cylinder End Seal
18. Inner Cylinder End Spacer (Thin)
19. Rack Housing
20. Lower Pinion/Valve Bushing
21. Pinion/Valve Seal
22. Hydraulic Union Seat
23. Rack Guide Seat
24. Rack Guide
25. Spring
26. Adjusting Plug
27. Adjusting Plug Lock Nut
28. Valve/Pinion Lower Spacer
29. Valve/Pinion Lower Bearing
30. Valve/Pinion Lock Nut
31. Valve/Pinion Lower Cap
32. Tie Rod Ball Joint
33. Tab Lock Washer
34. "O" Ring
35. Piston Sealing Ring
36. Steering Rack

Courtesy of General Motors Corp.

OVERHAUL

RACK & PINION ASSEMBLY

Disassembly

1) Place steering gear in a soft-jawed vise. Remove pressure switch, tie rod ends, tie rod end lock nuts, boot clamps and boots. Using a chisel, bend back tab lock washer between tie rod and rack.

2) Using soft-jawed vise to hold rack flat section and a wrench to turn tie rod ball joint, remove tie rod from rack. Discard tab lock washer.

3) Disconnect right and left pipe assemblies between valve housing and rack housing. Using Lock Nut Wrench (J 35692 and J 35423), remove adjusting plug lock nut, cap, spring and rack guide. *See Fig. 1.*

4) Remove dust cover and snap ring. Using Pinion Shaft Holder (J 35428) and wrench, remove self locking nut from lower end of pinion gear. Remove pinion shaft assembly with upper bearing and oil seal.

5) Remove steering gear housing end stopper retaining snap ring. Carefully withdraw rack assembly with cylinder end stopper. Remove inner rack seal, spacer, piston and "O" ring seals from rack.

6) Using Bushing Remover (J 35420), remove inner bushing from valve housing. *See Fig. 2.* Using a brass drift, remove inner valve housing seal.

CLEANING & INSPECTION

NOTE: Always use lint free rags. Never use a wire brush. When necessary, mineral spirits can be used to clean parts. Carefully inspect mating surfaces, seals and bearings.

Fig. 2: Removing Inner Bushing

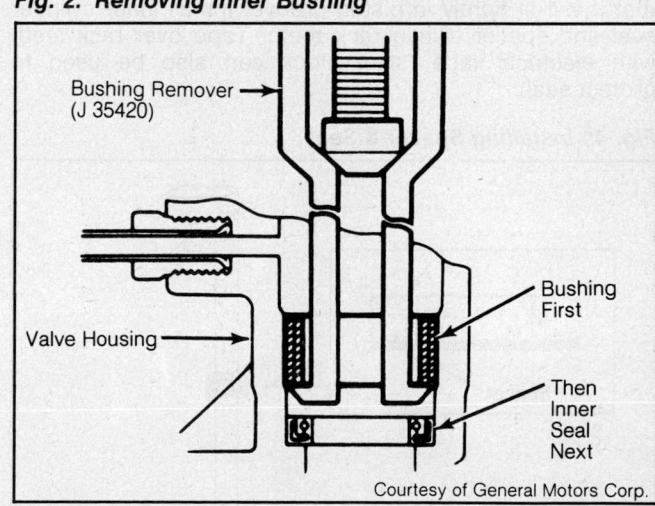

Courtesy of General Motors Corp.

1) Check rack for runout and tooth wear or damage. Maximum runout is .012" (.30 mm). If housing bore is scuffed, damaged cracked or porous, replace housing.

2) If valve assembly is defective, replace as a unit. Bearings can be serviced separately. Measure pinion bore inside diameter and valve assembly outside diameter. Subtract valve measurement from bore measurement to obtain oil clearance.

3) Standard clearance is .0002-.0047" (.005-.119 mm). Maximum clearance is .0049" (.125 mm). Check tie rod ball joints and tie rod ends for looseness. Replace any parts found defective.

Power Steering Gears

NOVA RACK & PINION (Cont.)

Reassembly

1) Using an arbor press and 24 mm socket, install inner seal to pinion housing lower end. Using an arbor press and Inner Bushing Installer and Adapter (J-35695 and J-8092), install inner bushing to a depth of 2.736" (69.5 mm).

2) If bushing is not pushed in far enough, it will interfere with the control valve and pinion. If bushing is pushed in too far, it will deform. *See Fig. 3.*

Fig. 3: Installing Inner Bushing

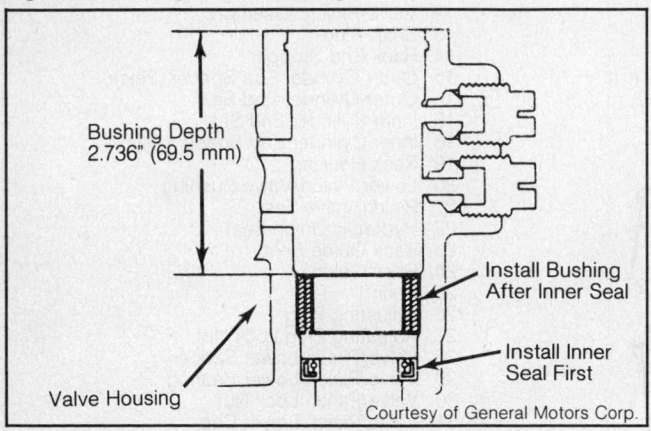

Bushing Depth 2.736" (69.5 mm)

Install Bushing After Inner Seal

Install Inner Seal First

Valve Housing

Courtesy of General Motors Corp.

3) Apply steering fluid to valve and inner bushing. Install control valve and pinion. Check to see that valve rotates smoothly. Remove valve. Apply steering fluid to rack piston and new "O" ring. Install new "O" ring on rack piston.

4) Using fingers, expand a new piston ring so that it will fit tightly in piston groove. Install inner cylinder seal and spacer. Clean rack teeth. Tape over rack teeth with electrical tape (shim stock can also be used to protect seal).

Fig. 4: Installing Spacer & Seal

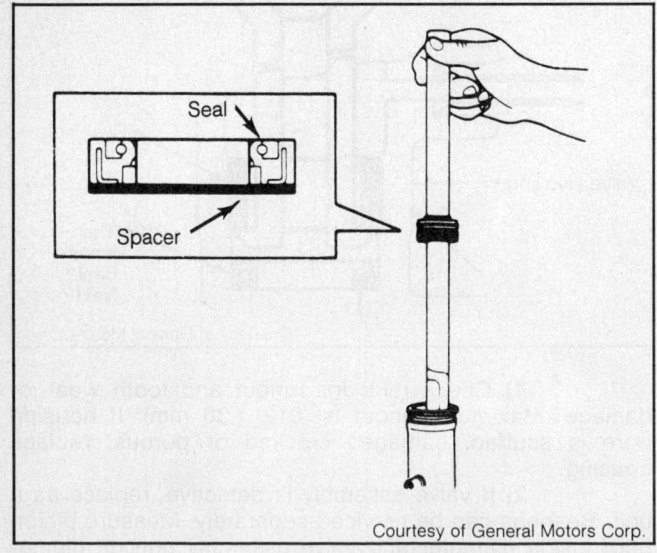

Seal

Spacer

Courtesy of General Motors Corp.

5) Apply steering fluid to housing bore and inner seal. *See Fig. 4.* Install inner cylinder seal and thin spacer onto rack with lip end of seal onto rack first. Install thin spacer. Carefully insert rack into cylinder.

6) With rack fully inserted, tap end of rack with a soft mallet to seat inner seal and spacer. Apply steering fluid to seal and end stopper. Install outer cylinder seal spacer and end stopper.

7) Install seal with lip end into cylinder rack first. Install thick spacer with shallow end of spacer facing out. Install stopper. Tap stopper in until it bottoms out. The stopper should be in far enough to expose snap ring groove. Install snap ring. *See Fig. 5.*

Fig. 5: Installing Outer Seal & Stopper

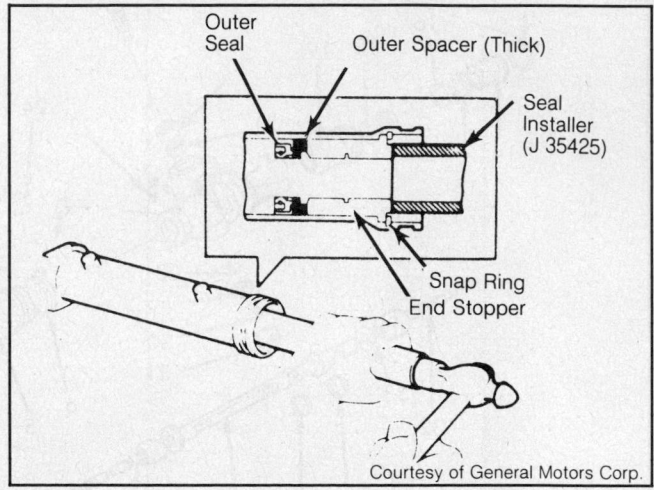

Outer Seal

Outer Spacer (Thick)

Seal Installer (J 35425)

Snap Ring End Stopper

Courtesy of General Motors Corp.

8) Install vacuum gauge adapters. Apply 16 In. Hg vacuum for about 30 seconds. Vacuum should hold. If vacuum does not hold, repeat steps **4)** through **7)**.

9) Install pinion/control valve into housing. Install upper pinion bearing. Apply steering fluid to seal. Install oil seal, snap ring and dust cover. Install spacer, lower bearing and new self-locking nut on pinion/valve shaft.

10) Using Pinion Shaft Holder (J 35428) and torque wrench, tighten lock nut to 43 ft. lbs. (59 N.m). Apply sealer to threads of lower cap. Tighten lower cap to 51 ft. lbs. (69 N.m). Stake housing to cap.

11) Install rack guide seat, rack guide and spring. Apply thread sealer to adjusting plug. Install adjusting plug. Install, but do not tighten, adjusting plug lock nut. Install tie rod tab lock washers on rack.

12) Install and tighten tie rods to 61 ft. lbs. (83 N.m). Stake tab lock washers. Make sure that air bleed holes in rack are clear. Install inner rack boots clamps and clips. Clips must be installed with loop facing away from boot.

13) Lube inside of boots. Install tie rod end lock nuts. Aligning marks made during disassembly, install tie rod ends. There should be approximately 2" (50 mm) of threads showing on tie rod, including lock nut.

14) Tighten lock nuts to 35 ft. lbs. (47 N.m). Install hydraulic tubes. Tighten to 18 ft. lbs. (25 N.m). Tighten adjusting plug to 18 ft. lbs. (25 N.m).

15) Back off adjusting plug 12 degrees. Using an INCH lb. torque wrench, rotate pinion rack back and forth a few times while checking turning torque required. Turning torque should be approximately 7-11 INCH lbs. (.8-1.3 N.m).

16) Readjust pinion if preload is incorrect. Install and tighten adjusting plug locking to 33 ft. lbs. (44 N.m). Apply sealer to threads. Install pressure switch.

SAGINAW CENTER-LINKED POWER RACK & PINION

Eagle: Premier;
General Motors
"J" Body: Cavalier, Cimarron,
Firenza, Skyhawk, Sunbird;
"L" Body: Beretta, Corsica;
"N" Body: Cutlass Calais, Grand Am,
Skylark

DESCRIPTION

The power rack and pinion steering system uses a rotary control valve to direct hydraulic fluid to either side of rack piston. Rack piston is integral with rack gear and converts hydraulic pressure to linear force. This force assists rack gear to move either left or right.

If hydraulic assist fails, an increase in steering effort can be expected. Manual control of steering is maintained. Power rack and pinion steering gear consists of an input pinion gear, steering rack gear, tube housing and a rotary valve assembly.

LUBRICATION, TROUBLE SHOOTING & TESTING

See POWER STEERING GENERAL SERVICING & TROUBLE SHOOTING articles in this section.

ADJUSTMENTS

RACK BEARING PRELOAD

1) Raise and support front of vehicle. Center steering wheel. Loosen adjusting plug lock nut. Turn adjusting plug clockwise until it bottoms in housing. Back off adjusting plug 50-70 degrees.

2) Tighten lock nut to specification while holding adjuster plug stationary. Check steering wheel movement for binding after adjustment.

REMOVAL & INSTALLATION

RACK & PINION ASSEMBLY

Removal (Cimarron)

Raise and support vehicle. Remove front wheels. Remove intermediate shaft lower connection. Disconnect both outer rods from steering knuckles. Remove line retainer and fluid lines. Remove 5 rack and pinion attaching bolts. Remove rack and pinion assembly by sliding out to side.

CAUTION: Failure to disconnect intermediate shaft from pinion shaft may cause damage to steering gear and/or intermediate shaft.

Installation

To install, reverse removal procedure. Tighten nuts and bolts to specifications.

Removal (Eagle Premier)

1) Remove instrument panel lower cover to gain access to steering shaft boot. Unsnap steering shaft boot flange from dash panel opening. Slide boot up intermediate shaft out of way.

2) Remove intermediate shaft-to-pinion "U" joint clamp bolt. Mark intermediate shaft and pinion shaft for reassembly reference. In the engine compartment, pry out splash shield retaining clips with a screwdriver.

3) Remove splash shield. Fold back the tabs on the tie rod center link lock plate. Loosen tie rod retaining bolts one or 2 turns. DO NOT remove bolts. Unsnap hydraulic lines from rubber mounting block.

4) Place a drain pan under vehicle. Disconnect hydraulic lines from steering gear. Remove front right mounting nut. Raise and support vehicle. Remove left front wheel. Remove cotter pins and castle nuts from knuckles.

5) Using a tie rod end puller, separate tie rod ends from struts. Remove 3 remaining steering gear mounting bolts. Remove steering gear with tie rods through access opening in left fender well.

6) Keep tie rods parallel to steering gear during removal. If necessary, Tape or tie wrap tie rods to steering gear to ease removal.

Installation

To install, reverse removal procedure. Replace hydraulic line "O" rings with new ones. Tighten nuts and bolts to specifications.

Removal (All Other Models)

1) Remove left side sound insulator. Remove upper pinch bolt from flexible coupling. Remove hydraulic line retainer. Raise and support vehicle. Remove front wheels. Using Puller (J 24319-01), separate tie rod ends from struts.

2) Lower vehicle. Remove mounting clamps. Remove hydraulic lines from steering gear. Move gear forward. Remove lower pinch bolt from flexible coupling. Remove coupling from pinion shaft.

3) Remove dash seal from rack assembly. Raise and support vehicle. Turn left knuckle and hub assembly to full left position. Remove rack and pinion assembly through access hole in left wheel opening.

Installation

If studs were removed with mounting clamps, reinstall studs. To install, reverse removal procedure. Tighten nuts and bolts to specifications.

TIE ROD END

Removal & Installation

Remove cotter pin and nut from tie rod end. Loosen tie rod end pinch bolt. Using tie rod end puller, separate tie rod end from strut. Counting number of turns for reassembly reference, unscrew tie rod end from adjuster. To install, reverse removal procedure.

OVERHAUL

INNER TIE ROD & INNER PIVOT BUSHING

Disassembly

Remove and discard lock plate from inner tie rod bolts. Remove tie rod bolts, one at a time, and slide tie rod out from under support plate. If both tie rods are to be removed, reinstall first tie rod bolt to keep boot and guides properly aligned before removing second bolt. Using Bushing Driver (J 29809), remove bushing from tie rod.

Power Steering Gears

SAGINAW CENTER-LINKED POWER RACK & PINION (Cont.)

Reassembly

Coat bushing with a light film of grease. Install bushing in tie rod using bushing driver. Ensure center housing cover washers are in place. Install tie rods one at a time. Tighten mounting bolts and secure bolts with lock plate tabs.

PINION SHAFT SEALS & UPPER BUSHING

Disassembly

Remove retaining ring from pinion shaft. Remove dust cap from lower end of pinion housing. Hold pinion shaft and remove pinion shaft lock nut. Using a press, ensure that threaded end of pinion is flush with lower bearing. Remove upper pinion bushing and seal with a punch.

CAUTION: Damage to pinion teeth will result if input shaft is not held when removing lock nut.

Reassembly

To install, reverse removal procedure. Use Seal Installer (J 29810) to install upper seal.

SPOOL VALVE RINGS & LOWER BEARING

Disassembly

Center rack gear. Mark location of pinion shaft flat on housing for reassembly reference. Press pinion at threaded end, until removal of valve and pinion assembly is possible. Note position of retaining ring. Remove retaining ring. Tap out lower bearing.

Reassembly

1) Press outer race of bearing in place. Ensure that bearing is not cocked in housing. Install retaining ring. Ensure beveled edge of retaining ring is facing same direction as when removed.

2) Soak new valve rings in hot water for 10 minutes before installation. Insert Ring Sizer (J 33057) over valve body for 10 minutes to resize rings.

3) Position Ring Sizer (J 33057) into pinion housing and install valve and pinion assembly. Center rack gear and install pinion. Ensure reference marks made at disassembly are aligned.

PINION SHAFT SEALS & UPPER BEARING

Removal

1) Remove rack and pinion assembly from vehicle. Remove adjuster plug lock nut, adjuster plug, spring and rack bearing with "O" ring. Remove retaining ring from bottom of housing.

3) Remove dust cover from housing. Holding pinion shaft stationary, remove lock nut from pinion. Pinion teeth will be damaged if pinion shaft is not held stationary.

3) Using a press, press on threaded end of pinion until it is flush with bearing assembly. Complete removal of valve and pinion is not required. Remove pinion shaft dust seal, pinion shaft seal and pinion shaft annulus bearing assembly from valve end of housing.

Installation

1) Bottom valve assembly into housing. Install lock nut to threaded end of pinion. Holding pinion shaft, tighten lock nut to specification. Install dust cover on housing.

2) Install pinion shaft annulus bearing on pinion shaft and slide into housing. Install Seal Protector (J 29810) on pinion shaft. Install pinion shaft dust seal and pinion shaft seal over protector and into housing.

3) Install retaining ring in groove in housing. Coat rack bearing, "O" ring, adjuster spring and adjuster plug with lithium base grease and install into housing. Adjust rack bearing preload. See RACK BEARING PRELOAD in ADJUSTMENTS in this article. To complete installation, reverse removal procedure.

RACK ASSEMBLY

Disassembly

1) Remove rack and pinion assembly from vehicle. Remove pinch bolt from flange and steering coupling. Remove steering coupling assembly. Remove dash seal from housing. Remove and discard lock plate from inner tie rod end bolts. Remove inner tie rod end bolts, support plate and inner tie rod end assemblies.

2) Remove hydraulic cylinder lines with "O" ring seals, starting at valve end of line. Separate and remove mounting grommet and boot clamps. Slide boot retaining bushing from rack and pinion boot. Slide boot, boot retaining bushing and housing retaining washers as an assembly from housing. Remove insert and rack guide from housing.

3) Loosen rack bearing adjusting plug lock nut. Remove adjuster plug from housing. Remove spring, rack bearing and "O" ring from housing. Remove retaining ring

Fig. 1: Rack & Pinion Housing Removal & Installation Procedure

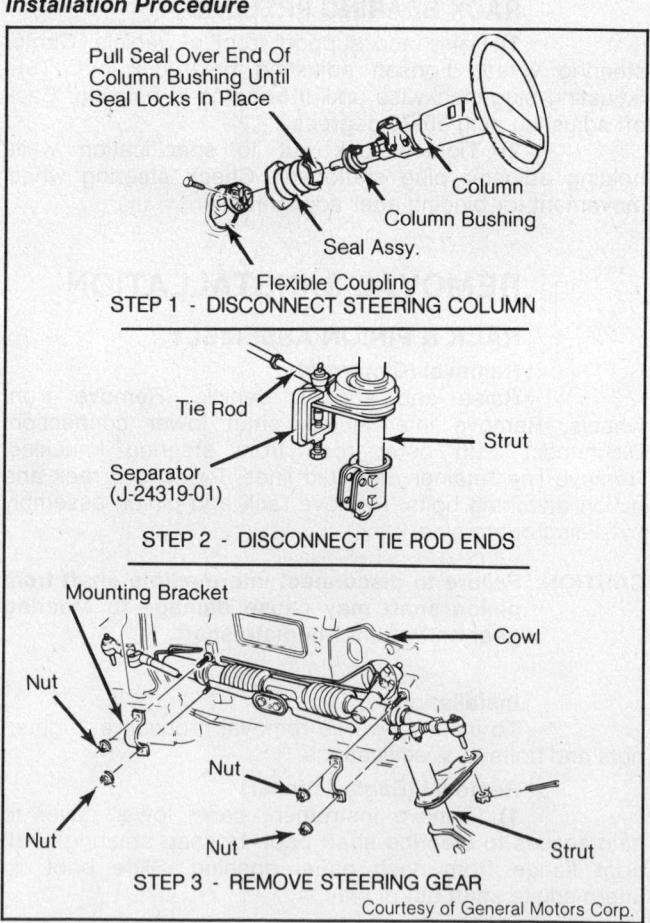

Pull Seal Over End Of Column Bushing Until Seal Locks In Place

Column
Column Bushing
Seal Assy.
Flexible Coupling

STEP 1 - DISCONNECT STEERING COLUMN

Tie Rod
Strut
Separator (J-24319-01)

STEP 2 - DISCONNECT TIE ROD ENDS

Mounting Bracket
Cowl
Nut
Nut
Nut
Nut
Strut

STEP 3 - REMOVE STEERING GEAR

Courtesy of General Motors Corp.

SAGINAW CENTER-LINKED POWER RACK & PINION (Cont.)

Fig. 2: Exploded View of Power Rack & Pinion Steering Gear

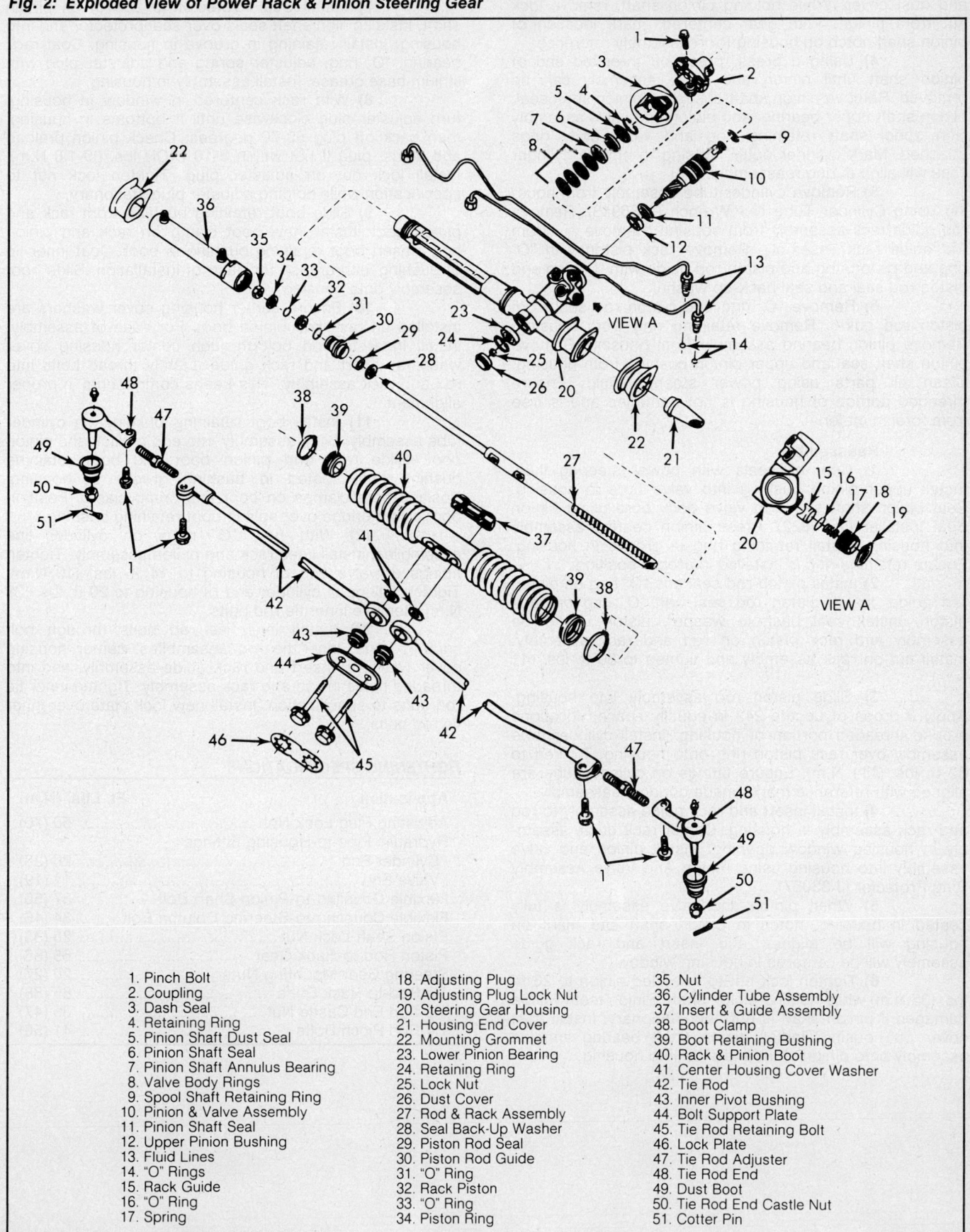

1. Pinch Bolt
2. Coupling
3. Dash Seal
4. Retaining Ring
5. Pinion Shaft Dust Seal
6. Pinion Shaft Seal
7. Pinion Shaft Annulus Bearing
8. Valve Body Rings
9. Spool Shaft Retaining Ring
10. Pinion & Valve Assembly
11. Pinion Shaft Seal
12. Upper Pinion Bushing
13. Fluid Lines
14. "O" Rings
15. Rack Guide
16. "O" Ring
17. Spring

18. Adjusting Plug
19. Adjusting Plug Lock Nut
20. Steering Gear Housing
21. Housing End Cover
22. Mounting Grommet
23. Lower Pinion Bearing
24. Retaining Ring
25. Lock Nut
26. Dust Cover
27. Rod & Rack Assembly
28. Seal Back-Up Washer
29. Piston Rod Seal
30. Piston Rod Guide
31. "O" Ring
32. Rack Piston
33. "O" Ring
34. Piston Ring

35. Nut
36. Cylinder Tube Assembly
37. Insert & Guide Assembly
38. Boot Clamp
39. Boot Retaining Bushing
40. Rack & Pinion Boot
41. Center Housing Cover Washer
42. Tie Rod
43. Inner Pivot Bushing
44. Bolt Support Plate
45. Tie Rod Retaining Bolt
46. Lock Plate
47. Tie Rod Adjuster
48. Tie Rod End
49. Dust Boot
50. Tie Rod End Castle Nut
51. Cotter Pin

Power Steering Gears

SAGINAW CENTER-LINKED POWER RACK & PINION (Cont.)

and dust cover. While holding pinion shaft, remove lock nut from pinion. With gear centered, mark location of pinion shaft notch on housing for reassembly reference.

4) Using a press, press on threaded end of pinion shaft until pinion and valve assembly can be removed. Remove pinion shaft dust seal, pinion shaft seal, pinion shaft upper bearing, and pinion and valve assembly with spool shaft retaining ring and valve body rings attached. Mark cylinder outer housing to ensure cylinder lines will align during reassembly.

5) Remove cylinder tube assembly from housing using Cylinder Tube Nut Wrench (J 36343). Remove rod guide rack assembly from housing. Remove nut from rod guide rack assembly. Remove rack piston with "O" ring and piston ring and piston rod guide with "O" ring and piston rod seal and seal back-up washer.

6) Remove "O" ring and piston rod seal from piston rod guide. Remove retaining ring from housing. Remove pinion bearing assembly from housing. Remove pinion shaft seal and upper pinion bushing from housing. Clean all parts using power steering fluid. Ensure threaded portion of housing is not damaged and is free from foreign material.

Reassembly

1) Coat all seals with power steering fluid. Install upper pinion bushing into valve bore in housing. Seat pinion shaft seal into valve body bore using Pinion Seal Installer (J 29822). Press pinion bearing assembly into housing. Install retaining ring in groove in housing. Ensure retaining ring is installed in proper position.

2) Install piston rod seal and "O" ring on piston rod guide. Install piston rod seal and "O" ring on rack piston. Install seal back-up washer, piston rod guide assembly and rack piston on rod and rack assembly. Install nut on rack assembly and tighten to 30 ft. lbs. (41 N.m).

3) Slide piston rod assembly into housing. Apply 3 drops of Loctite 242 in equally spaced locations around threaded portion of housing. Install cylinder tube assembly over rack piston ring onto housing. Tighten to 82 ft. lbs. (111 N.m). Ensure fittings on cylinder tube are aligned with reference marks made during disassembly.

4) Install insert and rack guide assembly to rod and rack assembly in housing. Center rack guide assembly in housing window opening. Install pinion and valve assembly into housing using Pinion And Valve Assembly Ring Protector (J 33057).

5) When pinion and valve assembly is fully seated in housing, notch in pinion shaft and mark on housing will be aligned and insert and rack guide assembly will be centered in housing window.

6) Tighten lock nut to threaded pinion to 26 ft. lbs. (35 N.m) while holding pinion shaft. Pinion teeth will be damaged if pinion shaft is not held stationary. Install dust cover on housing. Install pinion shaft bearing annulus assembly onto pinion shaft and slide into housing.

7) Install Seal Protector (J 29810) on pinion shaft. Install pinion shaft seals over seal protector and into housing. Install retaining in groove in housing. Coat rack bearing, "O" ring, adjuster spring and adjuster plug with lithium base grease. Install assembly in housing.

8) With rack centered in window in housing, turn adjuster plug clockwise until it bottoms in housing, then back off plug 50-70 degrees. Check pinion preload and adjust plug if not within 8-16 INCH lbs. (.9-1.8 N.m). Install lock nut on adjuster plug. Tighten lock nut to specification while holding adjuster plug stationary.

9) Slide boot retaining bushing from rack and pinion boot. Install new boot clamp on rack and pinion boot. Insert boot retaining bushing in boot. Coat inner lip of bushing with grease for ease of installation. Slide boot assembly onto housing.

10) Ensure center housing cover washers are installed on rack and pinion boot. For ease of assembly, install inner tie rod bolt through center housing cover washers, insert and rack guide. Lightly thread bolts into rod and rack assembly. This keeps components in proper alignment.

11) Install boot retaining bushing on cylinder tube assembly. Slide assembly into end of rack and pinion boot. Slide rack and pinion boot and boot retaining bushing until seated in bushing groove in housing. Position boot clamps on boot and crimp clamp. Position boot clamp bridge over split in boot retaining bushing.

12) With new "O" rings on cylinder line assemblies, install lines rack and pinion assembly. Tighten fittings at valve end of housing to 14 ft. lbs. (19 N.m). Tighten fittings at cylinder end of housing to 20 ft. lbs. (28 N.m). Remove inner tie rod bolts.

13) Install inner tie rod bolts through bolt support plate, inner tie rod assemblies, center housing cover washers, insert and rack guide assembly, and into threaded holes in rod and rack assembly. Tighten inner tie rod bolts to specification. Install new lock plate over inner tie rod bolts.

TIGHTENING SPECIFICATIONS

Application	Ft. Lbs. (N.m)
Adjusting Plug Lock Nut	50 (70)
Hydraulic Pipe-tp-Housing Fittings	
Cylinder End	20 (28)
Valve End	14 (19)
Flexible Coupling-to-Pinion Shaft Bolt	37 (50)
Flexible Coupling-to-Steering Column Bolt	34 (46)
Pinion Shaft Lock Nut	26 (35)
Piston Rod-to-Rack Gear	65 (88)
Steering Gear Mounting Nuts	20 (27)
Tie Rod-to-Rack Bolts	65 (88)
Tie Rod End Castle Nut	35 (47)
Tie Rod Pinch Bolts	41 (56)

Power Steering Gears

SAGINAW END-LINKED POWER RACK & PINION

"A" Body: Celebrity, Century,
Cutlass Ciera, 6000;
"E" Body: Eldorado, Riviera, Toronado;
"K" Body: Seville;
"W" Body: Cutlass, Grand Prix, Regal;
"Y" Body: Corvette

DESCRIPTION

The steering system has a rotary control valve which directs hydraulic fluid to either side of rack piston. The integral rack piston, attached to the rack, moves the rack piston left or right. In the event of a hydraulic failure, manual control is maintained. However, an increase in effort can be expected.

LUBRICATION, TROUBLE SHOOTING & TESTING

See POWER STEERING GENERAL SERVICING & TROUBLE SHOOTING articles in this section.

ADJUSTMENTS

PINION TURNING TORQUE

Pinion turning torque adjustment is performed during reassembly procedure. See OVERHAUL in this article.

REMOVAL & INSTALLATION

STEERING GEAR

Removal

1) Raise and support vehicle. Remove front wheels. Drain as much fluid as possible. Disconnect intermediate shaft-to-pinion shaft pinch bolt. Separate steering shaft from pinion shaft.

2) Remove cotter pins and castle nuts from steering knuckles, Using a tie rod end puller, separate tie rod ends from steering knuckles. Remove hydraulic lines.

3) Remove hydraulic lines. On Allanté models, remove pressure switch. On all models, remove steering gear mounting brackets. Remove steering gear from vehicle by sliding out to the side.

NOTE: On some models, removal of a stone shield, air management pipe bracket, electric fan or stabilizer bar may be required prior to removal of steering gear.

Installation

To install, reverse removal procedure. Refill with power steering fluid. Check and adjust toe-in as necessary.

TIE ROD ENDS

Removal & Installation

1) Remove cotter pins and castle nuts from tie rod ends. Loosen tie rod end lock nut. Using Tie Rod Puller (J-24319-01), separate tie rod end from steering knuckle.

2) Remove tie rod end from tie rod while recording number of turns required. To install tie rod end,

reverse removal procedure. Adjust toe-in. Ensure rubber boot is not twisted. Tighten lock nut to specifications.

RUBBER BOOTS

Removal & Installation

1) Remove tie rod end as previously described. Remove tie rod end lock nut. Cut off and discard boot clamps. Mark breather tube for reassembly reference (if equipped).

2) Remove breather tube. Slide tie rod end side of boot toward center of rack housing. Place a rubber band into outer boot seal groove. Remove boot.

Installation

1) Position new inner boot clamp. Aligning mark on breather tube, install breather tube (if equipped). Slide boot up onto housing. Install outer boot clamp. Using Banding Tool (J-22610), secure inner boot clamp.

2) Remove rubber band from boot seal groove. Ensure boot is not twisted. Install outer boot clamp. Install tie rod end. Check and adjust toe-in as necessary. Tighten tie rod end lock nut.

OVERHAUL

STEERING GEAR

Disassembly

1) Remove steering gear from vehicle as previously described. Place housing in holding fixture. Remove boots. Remove shock damper from tie rod ball joint. Slide shock damper back on rack.

2) Using a wrench on rack flat and ball joint, remove tie rod from rack. Remove retaining ring from upper end and dust cap from lower end of pinion housing. Holding splined end of pinion shaft with 11/16" 12-point socket, remove pinion lock nut.

3) Using a press, press on threaded end of pinion shaft until flush with ball bearing assembly. Remove pinion shaft dust seal and oil seal. If necessary, remove needle bearing and race from splined end of shaft.

4) Center the rack in steering gear housing. Mark pinion shaft flat and pinion housing for reassembly reference. Press on threaded end of pinion to remove valve and pinion assembly.

5) Carefully remove rings from spool valve body if replacement is necessary. If lower ball bearing requires replacement, note position of large lug and beveled side of retaining ring. Remove retaining ring.

6) Tap out bearing with soft drift. Remove upper pinion bushing and seal with a soft drift. Loosen adjusting plug lock nut. Remove adjusting plug, spring and rack guide. Using a punch in access hole, remove bulkhead retaining ring.

7) If only bulkhead "O" ring seal, bulkhead or rack seal are to be replaced, remove left cylinder hydraulic line. To prevent oil from leaking, plug port hole at cylinder using a plastic cap.

8) Temporarily install pinion shaft. Using an 11/16" 12-point socket, turn stub shaft. Place drain pan underneath steering gear. Move rack to right to force bulkhead out of housing.

9) Remove bulkhead assembly. Remove rack gear from housing. Remove both piston "O" rings. Insert Seal Remover (J-29738 or J-34987) into housing. Using a 12" drift, gently tap on seal until it is removed. Discard seal and "O" rings.

Power Steering Gears

SAGINAW END-LINKED POWER RACK & PINION (Cont.)

Fig. 1: Exploded View of Power Steering Gear

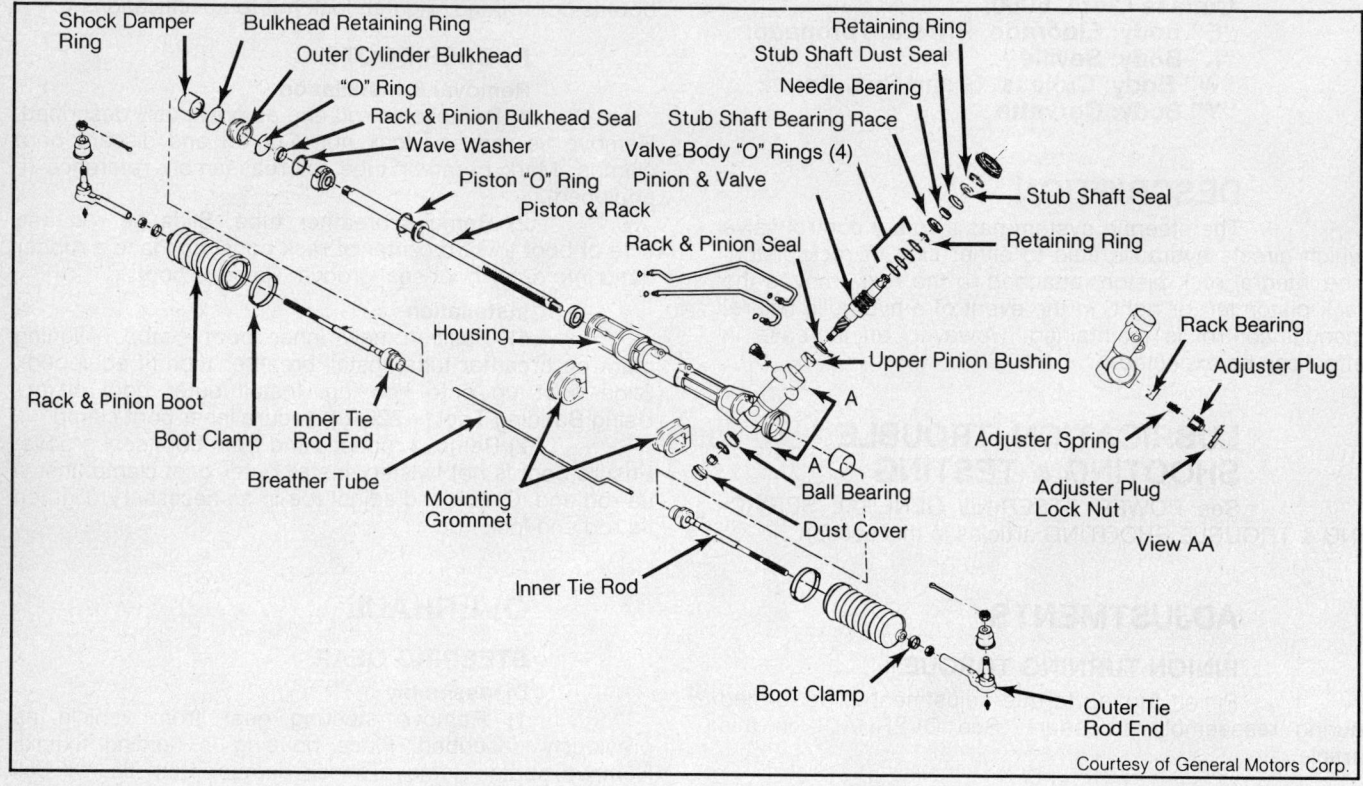

Courtesy of General Motors Corp.

Differences between models are limited to mounting hardware.

Reassembly

1) Carefully install new "O" rings onto piston. Wrap card stock around rack teeth. Apply power steering fluid onto seal lip. Slide seal with lip facing piston, onto card stock.

2) Ensure seal insert is fully engaged with seal before installation into rack housing. Apply power steering fluid completely around seal. Slide rack gear and seal in housing. Tap on rack gear with a rubber mallet to seat seal. Ensure seal is fully seated.

3) Use crocus cloth to remove burrs or sharp edges from retaining ring groove in housing. Reinstall parts using power steering fluid on all seals. Slip bullet Seal Protector (J-28478-A or J-29707) over end of rack. Install bulkhead.

4) Install bulkhead retaining ring. Ensure open end of retaining ring is approximately .50" (13 mm) from access hole. Retaining ring must be fully seated.

5) Using a socket, press on outer race of new ball bearing, being careful not to cock bearing during installation. Install retaining ring, properly locating beveled side. Install new upper pinion bushing.

6) Using Seal Installer (J-29822), seat seal. Ensure spring lip of seal is facing up. Carefully place new rings on valve body. Center rack in housing.

7) Using Protector (J-33057), install pinion and valve assembly so that shaft flat and mark on housing line up when assembly is seated. Tighten pinion lock nut to specification. Install lower dust cap.

8) Place Seal Protector (J-29810) over pinion shaft. Install seal and snap ring. Install shock damper on rack. Install tie rod until it bottoms on rack threads.

9) Using a wrench on rack gear flat and on tie rod ball joint, install and tighten tie rod assembly. Support rack and ball jointg. Stake ball joint to flat of rack. Inspect stake with a .010" (.25 mm) feeler gauge.

10) Gauge must not pass between rack gear and pivot bushing stake on either side. Slide shock damper onto ball joint. Apply lithium grease on contact surface of rack guide. Install rack guide, spring, and adjusting plug.

11) Turn adjusting plug in until it bottoms. Back off adjusting plug 50-70 degrees. Check pinion turning torque. Turning torque should be 19 INCH lbs. (2.2 N.m). Install adjusting plug lock nut. Holding adjusting plug stationary, tighten adjusting plug lock nut to specification.

TIGHTENING SPECIFICATIONS

Application	Ft. Lbs. (N.m)
Adjusting Plug Lock Nut	52-70 (70-95)
Intermediate Shaft Pinch Bolt	35 (47)
Pinion Shaft Lock Nut	26 (35)
Steering Gear Mounting Bolts & Nuts	24 (33)
Tie Rod Ball Joint-to-Rack	70 (95)
Tie Rod End Lock Nut	30-50 (41-68)
Tie Rod End-to-Knuckle Castle Nut	41 (56)

SAGINAW ROTARY VALVE

General Motors

DESCRIPTION

The Saginaw rotary valve integral power steering gear contains a control valve which directs hydraulic pressure to either side of the rack piston. The rack piston converts hydraulic pressure into mechanical torce. Power is transmitted to the mating pitman shaft teeth, through the pitman shaft to steering linkage.

A recirculating (rotary) ball system is incorporated in this type, with steel balls acting as rolling threads between the steering worm shaft and the rack piston. An adjusting plug provides the initial preload adjustment. As the worm shaft is turned right, the rack piston moves up inside the gear.

Turning the worm shaft left moves the rack piston down inside the gear. The rack piston teeth mesh with the sector shaft teeth, which is part of the pitman shaft. Rotation of the worm shaft turns the pitman shaft. Mechanical linkage from pitman arm to spindles complete the system.

LUBRICATION, TROUBLE SHOOTING & TESTING

See POWER STEERING GENERAL SERVICING & TROUBLE SHOOTING articles in this section.

ADJUSTMENTS

THRUST BEARING PRELOAD

NOTE: **The following adjustment procedures must be performed exactly as described and in sequence outlined. Failure to do so can result in damage to gear internal components and improper steering response. Always adjust worm bearing preload first; then adjust pitman shaft over-center turning torque.**

1) Using Spanner Wrench (J-7624), seat adjusting plug firmly in housing. Approximately 20 ft. lbs. (27 N.m) torque is required to seat adjusting plug. Index mark gear housing opposite one of the holes in adjusting plug.

2) Measure back (counterclockwise) 1/2" (13 mm) from index mark. Make another index mark on housing. Turn adjuster plug counterclockwise until hole in plug is aligned with second mark on housing.

3) While holding adjusting plug in position, install and tighten adjusting plug lock nut. Using an INCH lb. torque wrench and a 12-point deep socket, measure required torque to turn pinion shaft.

4) Take reading with beam of torque wrench at or near vertical position while turning pinion shaft at an even rate. Reading should be 4-10 INCH lbs. (.45-1.13 N.m).

5) If reading is not within specifications, adjusting plug may not be tightened properly or may have turned when lock nut was tightened, gear may be assembled incorrectly, or thrust bearings and races may be defective.

PITMAN SHAFT OVER-CENTER TURNING TORQUE

1) Rotate pinion shaft from stop to stop while counting total number of turns. Turn pinion shaft back 1/2 the total number of turns to center position. Flat on pinion shaft should face upward and be parallel with side cover.

2) Master spline on pitman shaft should be in line with adjusting screw. Back off preload adjustor until it stops. Turn adjuster in one full turn. Install an INCH lb. torque wrench and a 12-point socket on pinion shaft.

3) Place torque wrench in vertical position. Rotate torque wrench 45 degrees each side of center. Record the highest turning torque measured on or near center.

4) Adjust over-center turning torque by turning pitman shaft adjuster in until torque to turn pinion shaft is 6-10 INCH lbs. (0.7-1.1 N.m) more than previous reading. Preventing adjusting screw from turning, tighten adjusting screw lock nut to 20 ft. lbs. (27 N.m).

Fig. 1: Pitman Shaft Over-Center Adjustment

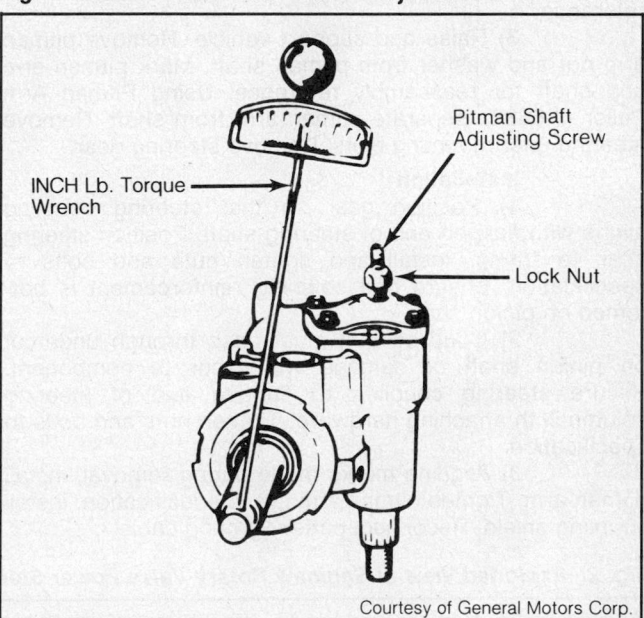

INCH Lb. Torque Wrench

Pitman Shaft Adjusting Screw

Lock Nut

Courtesy of General Motors Corp.

REMOVAL & INSTALATION

PITMAN SHAFT SEAL
Removal (In Vehicle)
1) Clean exposed end of pitman shaft and end of housing after removing pitman arm. Using Snap Ring Pliers (J-4245), remove seal retaining ring. Start engine and let idle. Turn wheels fully left to force seals and washer out.

2) Turn engine off. Inspect housing and shaft for imperfections. Small burrs inside housing may be removed with crocus cloth. Defects on the shaft require shaft replacement.

Installation
1) Lubricate new shaft seal with power steering fluid. Apply a single layer of tape to pitman arm shaft to avoid damaging seals.

Power Steering Gears

SAGINAW ROTARY VALVE (Cont.)

2) Using Seal Installer (J-6219), install single lip seal and back-up washer. Ensure there is clearance for remaining double lip seal, back-up washer, and retaining ring. Do not allow seal to bottom in end of counter bore.

3) Install double lip seal and back-up washer. Provide clearance for retaining ring when installing seal. Install retaining ring. Ensure retaining ring is properly seated.

STEERING GEAR

Removal

1) Disconnect battery ground cable. Remove coupling sheild (if equipped). Place wheels in straight-ahead position. Place drain pan under steering gear. Remove steering coupling-to-steering shaft flange nuts, lock washers and bolts.

2) Disconnect hydraulic hoses from gear. Secure hoses above pump level. Cap hose ends to prevent contamination. Mark flexible coupling and pinion shaft for reassembly reference. Remove flexible coupling-to-pinion shaft nuts, noting placement for installation reference.

3) Raise and support vehicle. Remove pitman arm nut and washer from pitman shaft. Mark pitman arm and shaft for reassembly reference. Using Pitman Arm Puller (J-6632), separate pitman arm from shaft. Remove steering gear mounting bolts. Remove steering gear.

Installation

1) Position gear so that steering coupling aligns with flanged end of steering shaft. Position steering gear to frame. Install and tighten nuts and bolts to specification. Ensure that coupling reinforcement is bottomed on pinion shaft.

2) Coupling bolt must pass through undercut on pinion shaft or damage will occur to component. Secure steering coupling to flanged end of steering column with attaching hardware. Tighten nuts and bolts to specification.

3) Aligning marks made during removal, install pitman arm. Tighten pitman arm nut to specification. Install coupling shield. Reconnect battery ground cable.

OVERHAUL

STEERING GEAR

Disassembly

1) Thoroughly clean gear exterior. Drain as much fluid as possible. Mount gear in soft-jawed vise with pitman shaft pointing down. Rotate gear housing end plug retaining ring until end of ring is over housing hole. Using a punch, unseat ring. Remove ring.

2) Using a 12-point socket, rotate stub shaft counterclockwise enough to force end plug from housing. Remove "O" ring seal. Holding pitman shaft adjusting screw with an Allen wrench, remove lock nut.

3) Remove side cover bolts. Remove pitman shaft adjusting screw from cover. Turn stub shaft until pitman shaft teeth are centered in housing. Tap end of pitman shaft with plastic hammer to remove it from housing.

4) Insert Ball Retainer (J-21552) into piston until it bottoms on worm shaft. Hold tool firmly against worm shaft while turning stub shaft counterclockwise to force piston from housing.

5) Remove rack piston and ball retainer from housing together. Remove adjusting plug lock nut. Using Spanner Tool (J-7624), remove adjusting plug. Remove valve body by pulling outward on splined end of pinion shaft.

6) Remove wormshaft lower thrust bearing and bearing races. Note position of races for reassembly reference. Clean end of housing thoroughly to prevent dirt from entering. Remove pitman arm shaft seal retaining ring using Snap Ring Pliers (J-4245).

7) Remove back-up washer. Insert a screwdriver between inner seal and housing shoulder to pry out seals. If inner seal is difficult to remove, it can be driven out from upper end of housing. It may be necessary to drive out bearing and seal together.

8) Remove needle bearing from housing bore using Bearing Remover (J-6278). Remove check valve from gear fluid line inlet. Care should be taken not to damage threads when prying on edge of housing.

Fig. 2: Exploded View of Saginaw Rotary Valve Power Steering Gear

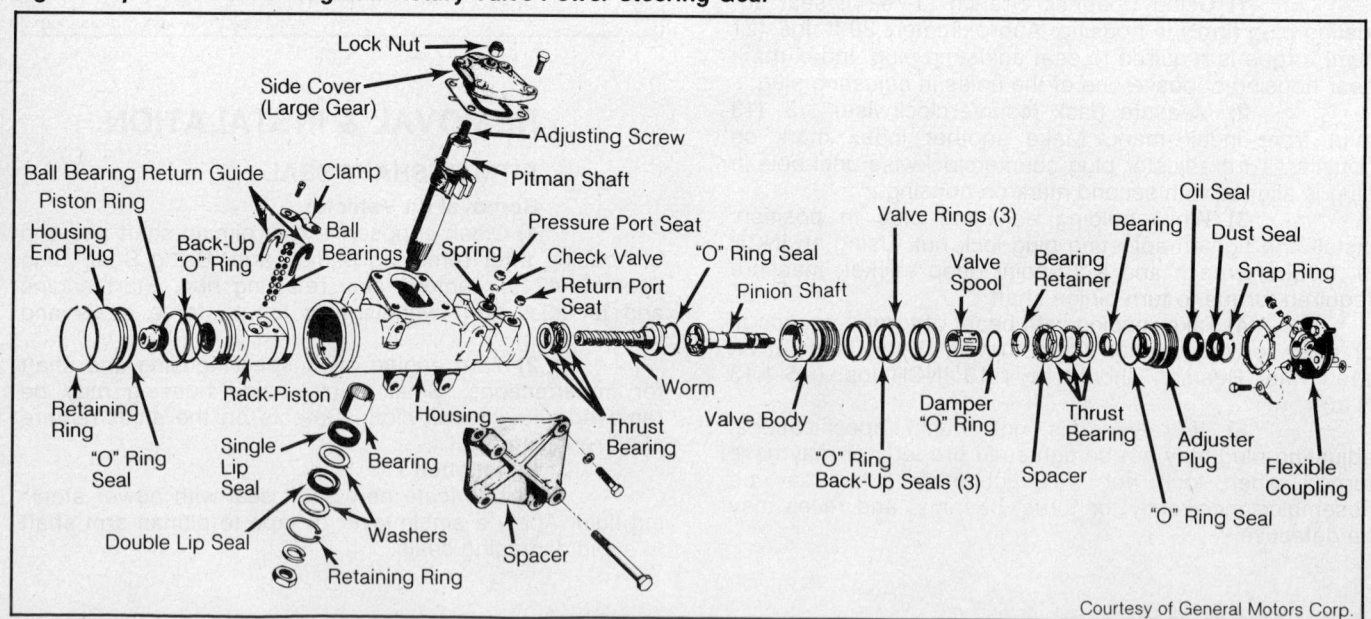

Courtesy of General Motors Corp.

SAGINAW ROTARY VALVE (Cont.)

9) Remove thrust bearing retainer and discard. Remove thrust bearing dust seal. Ensure that needle bearing bore is not damaged during removal process. Remove adjuster plug.

Fig. 3: Removing Thrust Bearing Retainer

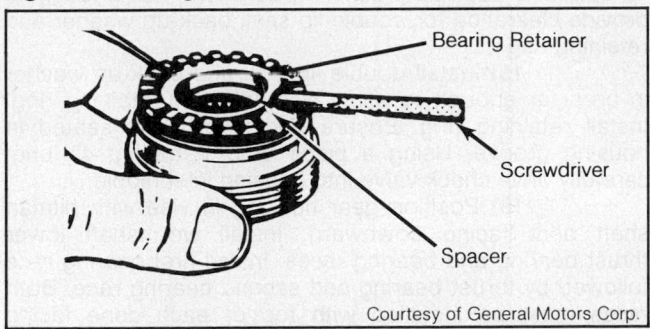

Courtesy of General Motors Corp.

10) Remove and discard "O" ring. Remove thrust bearing retainer. *See Fig. 3.* Remove small upper bearing race and thrust bearing spacer. Remove large upper bearing race and thrust bearing. Using an arbor press, remove needle bearing from adjusting plug.

NOTE: **Valve body has parts fitted to tolerances as close as .0004" (.010 mm). If replacement of any valve part other than seals or rings is necessary, replace complete valve body. Do not disassemble valve body unless absolutely necessary.**

11) Remove and discard valve body "O" ring and Teflon seals. Hold valve in both hands with pinion shaft pointing downward. Tap end of shaft lightly against workbench until shaft cap separates from valve body.

12) Do not pull shaft out too far or spool valve may become cocked in valve body. Pull outward on cap end of pinion shaft until it clears valve body by .25" (6.0 mm). Carefully disengage pinion shaft locating pin from spool valve locating hole. Remove pinion shaft.

Fig. 4: Valve Body & Pinion Shaft Assembly

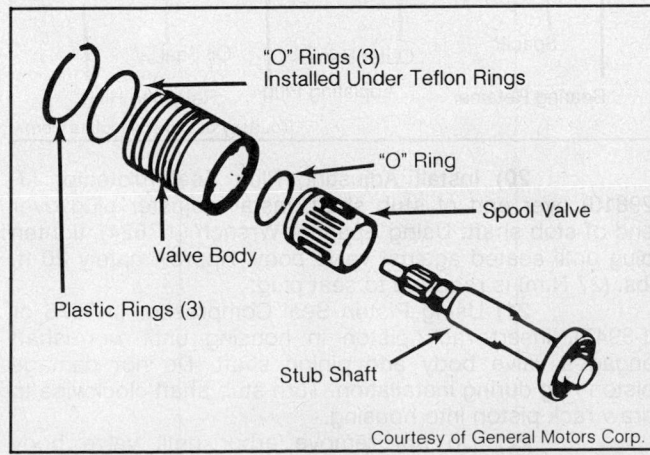

Courtesy of General Motors Corp.

13) Lubricate, and push spool valve out of steering column end of valve body while rotating valve. If valve becomes cocked, carefully realign valve and remove. Remove and discard damper "O" ring from spool valve. Remove 3 Teflon rings and back-up "O" rings (located under Teflon rings).

Fig. 5: Removing Pinion Shaft Assembly

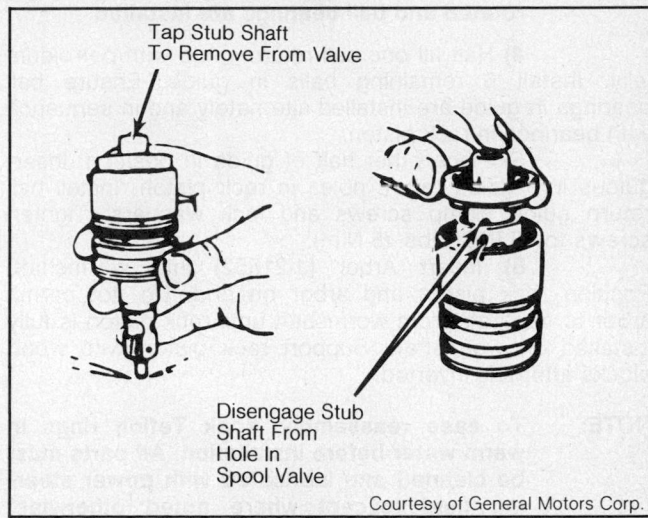

Courtesy of General Motors Corp.

14) Remove return guide clamp. Place on clean surface and remove ball return guides. Using Arbor Tool (J-21552), remove wormshaft and 24 ball bearings. Remove piston Teflon ring and "O" ring from rack piston.

Cleaning & Inspection

1) Clean housing with solvent. Clean and lubricate all internal components with power steering fluid. Inspect housing bore for scoring, scratching or other damage.

2) If housing bore is scored or damaged, replace steering gear housing. Inspect seals for signs of cracking or dryness. Replace all worn or damaged parts.

Fig. 6: Rack Piston & Wormshaft Assembly

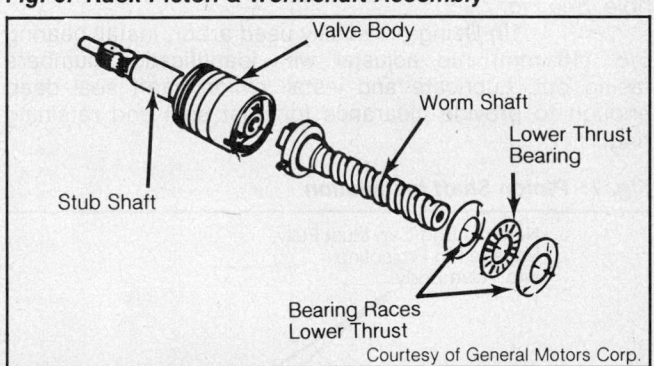

Courtesy of General Motors Corp.

Reassembly

NOTE: **When installing ball bearings, alternate between Black and Silver balls. Black balls are slightly smaller than Silver balls.**

1) Install "O" ring in rack piston groove. Do not allow "O" ring to become twisted during installation. Install piston Teflon ring over "O" ring. Install wormshaft completely into rack piston.

2) Alternately install one Black ball bearing followed by one Silver ball bearing. Install 18 ball bearings through return guide hole nearest rack piston ring.

3) To install ball bearings into circuit, rotate wormshaft counterclockwise (viewed from steering shaft end). Press downward after insertion of each ball bearing in order to provide room for each following ball bearing.

Power Steering Gears

SAGINAW ROTARY VALVE (Cont.)

4) Half fill one ball return guide with petroleum jelly. Install 6 remaining balls in guide. Ensure ball bearings in guide are installed alternately and in sequence with bearings in rack piston.

5) Place other half of guide in position. Insert guides into guide return holes in rack piston. Install ball return guide clamp screws and lock washers. Tighten screws to 48 INCH lbs. (5 N.m).

6) Insert Arbor (J-21552) into wormshaft. Position rack piston and arbor on end. Do not permit arbor to separate from wormshaft until rack piston is fully installed on wormshaft. Support rack piston with wood blocks after it is inverted.

NOTE: **To ease reassembly, soak Teflon rings in warm water before installation. All parts must be cleaned and lubricated with power steering fluid (except where noted otherwise) before reassembly.**

7) Install back-up "O" rings into valve grooves. Install Teflon rings over "O" rings. Do not cut rings during installation. Lubricate spool valve damper "O" ring with power steering fluid.

8) Install in spool valve groove. Lubricate spool valve and valve body with power steering fluid. Carefully insert spool valve into valve body. Insert spool valve through valve body until pinion shaft pin locating hole is visible from opposite end of valve body.

9) Spool valve should be flush with notched end of valve body. Install stub shaft into spool valve until stub shaft locating pin is aligned with spool valve locating hole. *See Fig. 7.*

10) Using previously used arbor, install bearing 5/8" (16 mm) into adjuster with identification numbers facing out. Lubricate and install pinion shaft seal deep enough to provide clearance for dust seal and retaining ring.

Fig. 7: Pinion Shaft Installation

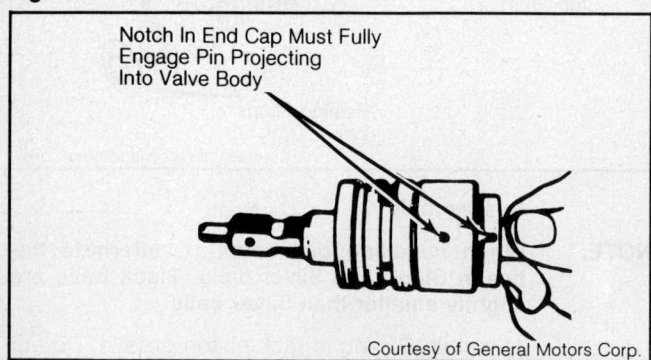

Notch In End Cap Must Fully Engage Pin Projecting Into Valve Body

Courtesy of General Motors Corp.

11) Lubricate dust seal with petroleum jelly. Install seal in adjusting plug with seal rubber face outward. Install retaining ring. Ensure retaining ring is properly seated. Lubricate "O" ring with petroleum jelly. Install "O" ring in groove of adjusting plug.

12) Install large upper bearing race, upper thrust bearing, small upper bearing race, thrust bearing spacer and bearing retainer into plug. Location of spacer notches are not important.

13) Using Bearing Installer Drift (J-8092) and Bearing Locator (J-2207), install bearing in housing until installer tool bottoms on housing and bearing is fully installed.

14) Using Seal Installer (J-21553), install single lip seal and back-up washer in bore only far enough to provide clearance for double lip seal, back-up washer and retaining ring.

15) Install double lip seal and back-up washer in bore far enough to allow clearance for retaining ring. Install retaining ring. Ensure ring is properly seated in housing groove. Using a piece of 3/8" tubing, 4" long, carefully drive check valve into housing inlet nipple.

16) Position gear housing in vise with pitman shaft bore facing downward. Install wormshaft lower thrust bearing and bearing races. Install first bearing race followed by thrust bearing and second bearing race. Both races must be installed with top of each cone facing bottom of gear housing.

17) Install pinion shaft-to-valve body "O" ring in valve body. Seat valve body against inner edge of shaft cap. Aligning narrow notch in valve body with pin in wormshaft, insert valve body into gear housing.

18) Seat valve body in housing. Do not press against pinion shaft to seat valve body. Pinion shaft and cap will separate from valve body and allow spool valve damper "O" ring to slip into valve body fluid grooves.

19) Using fingertips, seat valve body by pushing on outer diameter of body. Ensure Teflon rings do not bind inside housing. Valve body is correctly seated when all or most of fluid return hole in gear housing is visible.

Fig. 8: Adjusting Plug Assembly

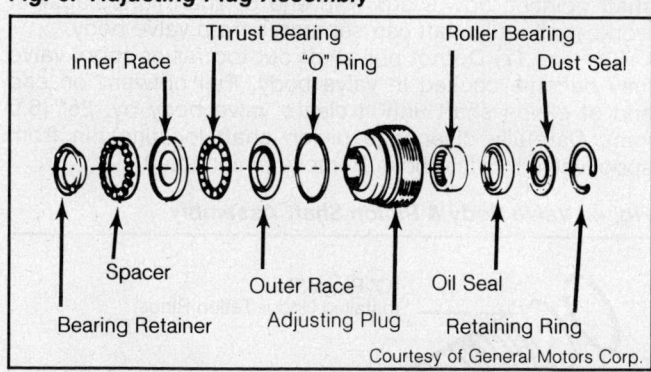

Inner Race | Thrust Bearing | "O" Ring | Roller Bearing | Dust Seal
Spacer | Outer Race | Oil Seal
Bearing Retainer | Adjusting Plug | Retaining Ring

Courtesy of General Motors Corp.

20) Install Adjusting Plug Seal Protector (J-29810) over end of stub shaft. Install adjuster plug over end of stub shaft. Using Spanner Wrench (J-7624), tighten plug until seated against valve body. Approximately 20 ft. lbs. (27 N.m) is required to seat plug.

21) Using Piston Seal Compressor (J-7576 or J-8947), insert rack piston in housing until wormshaft engages valve body and pinion shaft. Do not damage piston ring during installation. Turn stub shaft clockwise to draw rack piston into housing.

22) Do not remove arbor until valve body piston ring has entered housing bore. Turn stub shaft until rack piston center groove is aligned with center of pitman shaft bearing bore. Lubricate side cover gasket and install on side cover.

23) Ensure rubber seal in gasket is seated in side cover groove. Install side cover on pitman shaft by

SAGINAW ROTARY VALVE (Cont.)

threading cover onto adjusting screw until cover bottoms against pitman shaft.

24) Install pitman shaft so long center sector tooth meshes with rack piston center groove. Ensure side cover gasket is in place before installing side cover on housing. Install and tighten side cover bolts to 45 ft. lbs. (61 N.m).

25) Thread adjuster screw lock nut half way on adjuster screw. Prevent screw from turning with Allen wrench while installing nut. Install end plug in rack piston Tighten nut to 75 ft. lbs. (102 N.m). Lubricate and install housing end plug "O" ring on end plug.

26) Install and seat end plug in housing. If necessary, tap end of plug lightly with plastic mallet to seat properly. Install end plug retainer ring so ring end gap is not aligned with hole in side of gear housing. Tap lightly on plug to ensure ring is seated properly.

TIGHTENING SPECIFICATIONS

Application	Ft. Lbs. (N.m)
Flexible Coupling Pinch Bolt	30 (41)
Pitman Arm Retaining Nut	185 (251)
Pitman Shaft Adjuster Lock Nut	20 (27)
Steering Gear Mounting Bolts	80 (108)
Steering Gear Side Cover Bolts	45 (61)
Rack Piston Plug	75 (102)
Worm Adjusting Plug Lock Nut	80 (108)

¹ – Nut must be staked to shaft threads.

Electronic Power Steering Gear

FORD MOTOR CO. VARIABLE-ASSIST POWER STEERING

Continental

DESCRIPTION

Ford Motor Co. Variable-Assist Power Steering (VAPS) system consists of a microprocessor-based control module, power rack and pinion steering gear, actuator valve assembly, actuator valve assembly, connecting hoses and a power steering pump

OPERATION

The system uses a modified rotary valve in the steering gear with 2 separate hydraulic circuits (primary and secondary). During low-speed operation of the vehicle, pressurized fluid from the steering pump is directed to the primary circuit by the actuator valve.

As vehicle speed increases, the actuator valve gradually diverts fluid to the secondary circuit. Since the secondary circuit diverts fluid back to the pump, steering effort is increased due to less pressure in the steering gear. The actuator valve is a pressure-balanced variable orifice valve, controlled by a stepper motor-driven linear spool. The VAPS module computes inputs from a Vehicle Speed Sensor (VSS) to determine the output signal that will adjust the opening of the actuator valve.

The VAPS module is programmed to perform a self-diagnostic check every 16 milliseconds. If a fault is detected, the VAPS module will deactivate its outputs, allowing normal power steering function. The VAPS module is also programmed to perform a service diagnostic check if activated by a service technician.

A hydraulic-mechanical unit with an integral piston and rack provides power-assisted steering control. Internal valving directs pump flow and controls pressure to reduce steering effort. Units contain a rotary fluid control valve and a boost cylinder integral with steering gear rack.

ADJUSTMENTS

RACK PRELOAD

No adjustment procedure for rack preload is given by manufacturer. The only serviceable components on the steering gear are the boots, tie rods, actuator replacement and replacement of actuator bolts and seals. If steering gear is loose or damaged, replace with Short Rack Assembly (Part No. 3L547).

LUBRICATION, TROUBLE SHOOTING & TESTING

If steering effort is excessive at low speeds or if steering effort is low at all speeds, VAPS system is malfunctioning. For electronic variable-assist related testing procedures refer to VAPS TESTING in this article.

For all non-electronic variable-assist related lubrication, trouble shooting or testing procedures, see POWER STEERING GENERAL SERVICING and TROUBLE SHOOTING articles in this section.

VAPS TESTING

Testing can be done with a Rotunda Digital Volt-Ohmmeter (DVOM) (077-000001), Rotunda Inductive

Dwell Meter (059-00010), or equivalent. Diagnostic Connector (14489) is located in the engine compartment near the brake fluid reservoir and brake booster.

Fig. 1: VAPS Module Diagnostic Connector (14489)

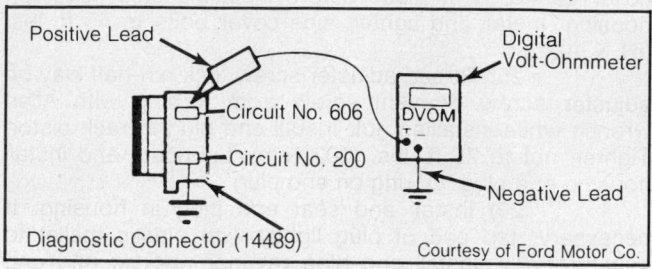

Courtesy of Ford Motor Co.

VAPS Module Test

1) Turn ignition switch to "OFF" position. Connect DVOM positive lead to circuit No. 606. Connect DVOM negative lead to vehicle ground. *See Fig. 1.* Position DVOM so it can be observed from inside vehicle. Start vehicle and let idle. Observe reading on DVOM.

2) DVOM reading should be between 11-14 volts. If voltage reading is correct, proceed to step **4)**. If voltage reading is incorrect, check VAPS fuse located in fuse panel below left side of instrument panel.

3) If fuse is good, proceed to ACTUATOR ELECTRICAL TEST NO. 2. If fuse is bad, replace fuse. Repeat steps **1)** and **2)**.

4) Turn engine off. Connect an analog voltmeter as in step **1)**. Start engine and let idle. Rotate steering wheel for approximately 90 seconds while noting any changes in steering effort.

5) Continue rotating steering wheel. After 90 seconds, steering effort should change and voltmeter will show a sweep pattern 4 times between battery voltage and zero volts.

6) If steering effort changes and there are 4 sweeps from battery voltage to zero volts, VAPS module is functioning properly. Proceed to VEHICLE TEST DRIVE.

7) If steering effort changes, but there are no sweeps from battery voltage to zero volts, or if there is no change in steering effort, but there are 6 sweeps from battery voltage to zero volts, proceed to ACTUATOR ELECTRICAL TEST NO. 2.

8) If there is no change in steering effort, but there are 4 sweeps from battery voltage to zero volts, proceed to ACTUATOR ELECTRICAL TEST NO. 1.

Vehicle Test Drive

1) Ensure VAPS system is connected. Drive vehicle up to 55 MPH. Note whether or not steering effort changes and if speedometer functions properly.

2) If steering effort increases as speed increases, decreases as speed decreases, and if speedometer functions properly, system is functioning properly.

3) If there is no change in steering effort, or if speedometer is not functioning properly, replace speedometer. See appropriate article in ACCESSORIES & EQUIPMENT section.

4) If there was no change in steering effort, but speedometer was functioning properly, proceed to SPEED SENSOR CIRCUIT TEST.

5) If steering effort is unequal for both right turns and left turns, replace steering gear. See STEERING GEAR REMOVAL & INSTALLATION in this article.

FORD MOTOR CO. VARIABLE-ASSIST POWER STEERING (Cont.)

Fig. 2: VAPS Module Harness Connector

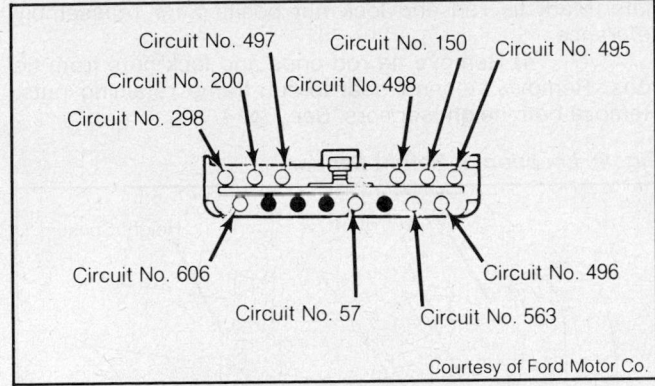

Circuit No. 497　Circuit No. 150　Circuit No. 495
Circuit No. 200　Circuit No.498
Circuit No. 298
Circuit No. 606　Circuit No. 496
Circuit No. 57　Circuit No. 563

Courtesy of Ford Motor Co.

Speed Sensor Circuit Test

1) Disconnect VAPS connector from module. Connect DVOM across circuits No. 150 and 563. *See Fig. 2.* Measure resistance.

2) If resistance is between 150-200 ohms, speed sensor is functioning properly. Replace VAPS module.

3) If resistance is less than 150 ohms, or greater than 200 ohms, proceed to ACTUATOR ELECTRICAL TEST NO. 1

Fig. 3: VAPS Actuator Connector

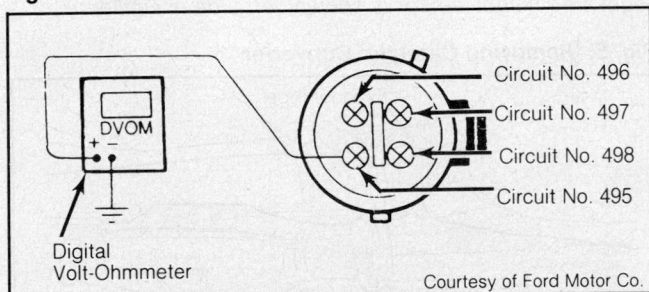

DVOM
+ −

Circuit No. 496
Circuit No. 497
Circuit No. 498
Circuit No. 495

Digital
Volt-Ohmmeter

Courtesy of Ford Motor Co.

Actuator Electrical Test No. 1

1) Turn ignition off. Disconnect actuator connector from harness connector. Connect DVOM leads to circuits No. 495 and 496 and then to circuits No. 497 and 498 on actuator side of connector. Note resistance values.

2) In both cases, resistance should be between 43 and 70 ohms. If resistance is less than 43 ohms or greater than 70 ohms, replace actuator. Repeat VAPS MODULE TEST.

3) If resistance was within specification, proceed to HARNESS VOLTAGE AT ACTUATOR CONNECTOR TEST

Harness Voltage At Actuator Connector Test

1) Verify that VAPS connector is connected to VAPS module. Disconnect actuator connector from VAPS harness connector. Turn ignition switch to "RUN" position.

2) Wait 5 seconds. On the harness side of connector, measure voltage between circuit No. 495 and vehicle ground. Repeat procedure for circuits No. 496, 497 and 498.

3) If all voltage readings are between 1.2-5.5 volts, voltages are correct, proceed to ACTUATOR MECHANICAL TEST

4) If any voltage reading is less than 1.2 volts or more than 5.5 volts, proceed to VAPS HARNESS & CONNECTORS TEST NO. 1

Actuator Mechanical Test

1) Turn ignition off. Remove actuator. See ACTUATOR REMOVAL & INSTALLATION in this article. Reconnect actuator connector to VAPS harness connector.

2) Attach positive lead of DVOM to diagnostic connector circuit No. 606. Connect negative lead to vehicle ground. Turn ignition switch to "ON" position.

3) The actuator will perform a 90 second effort change sequence diagnostic check. If actuator is functioning properly, valve will move through its 2 travel limits. This can be observed by watching the spring move.

4) If spring moves, actuator is functioning properly. Replace steering gear. See STEERING GEAR REMOVAL & INSTALLATION in this article. Repeat VAPS MODULE TEST.

5) If spring does not move, actuator is malfunctioning, replace actuator. See ACTUATOR REMOVAL & INSTALLATION in this article. Repeat VAPS MODULE TEST.

VAPS Harness & Connector Test No. 1

1) Turn ignition switch to "OFF" position. Connect positive lead of DVOM to VAPS module harness connector ground circuit No. 57. Connect DVOM negative lead to vehicle ground. *See Fig. 2.* Measure resistance.

2) If resistance is between 0-15 ohms, connect negative lead of DVOM to circuit No. 57 and positive lead to circuit No. 298. Note resistance. Leave negative lead on circuit No. 57. Move positive lead to all remaining circuits while noting resistance. Refer to VAPS MODULE HARNESS CONNECTOR RESISTANCE VALUES (IGNITION OFF) table for correct resistance values.

3) If values are within specification, proceed to VAPS HARNESS & CONNECTOR TEST NO. 2. If values are not within specification, repair harness. Repeat test.

VAPS MODULE HARNESS CONNECTOR RESISTANCE VALUES (IGNITION OFF)

Circuit No.	Function	Ohms
298	Power	6.2
200	Diagnostic	None
497	Actuator	26.4
498	Actuator	26.4
150	Speed Sensor	221
495	Actuator	26.4
606	Diagnostic	20
57	Ground	.1
563	Speed Sensor	14
496	Actuator	26.4

VAPS Harness & Connector Test No. 2

1) Turn ignition switch to "ON" position. Connect DVOM negative lead to circuit No. 57. *See Fig. 2.* Using the negative lead, measure voltage between circuit No. 57 and other circuits. Note voltage readings.

2) Refer to VAPS MODULE HARNESS CONNECTOR VOLTAGE VALUES (IGNITION ON) table for correct voltage values. If voltage readings are within specification, replace module. Repeat VAPS MODULE TEST. If values are not within specification, repair harness. Repeat test.

FORD MOTOR CO. VARIABLE-ASSIST POWER STEERING (Cont.)

VAPS MODULE HARNESS CONNECTOR
VOLTAGE VALUES (IGNITION ON)

Circuit No.	Function	Volts
298	Power	12
200	Diagnostic	4.7
497	Actuator	1.7
498	Actuator	1.7
150	Speed Sensor	None
495	Actuator	1.7
606	Diagnostic	20
57	Ground	...
563	Speed Sensor	None
496	Actuator	1.7

Actuator Electrical Test No. 2

1) Turn ignition switch to "OFF" position. Disconnect actuator connector from harness connector. See Fig. 3. Measure resistance between circuits No. 495 and 496, and between circuits No. 497 and 498 on actuator side of connector.

2) If resistance is 43-70 ohms, proceed to VAPS HARNESS & CONNECTOR TEST NO. 3. If resistance is less than 43 ohms or greater than 70 ohms, replace actuator. Repeat VAPS MODULE TEST.

VAPS Harness & Connector Test No. 3

1) Turn ignition off. Connect DVOM positive lead to circuit No. 57. Connect DVOM negative lead to vehicle ground. Measure resistance.

2) If resistance is 0-15 ohms, repeat VAPS HARNESS & CONNECTOR TESTS NO. 1 and NO. 2. If resistance is greater than 15 ohms, repair harness. Repeat test.

REMOVAL & INSTALLATION

ACTUATOR

Removal

Remove air inlet duct. Disconnect VAPS electrical connector from actuator. Disconnect pressure switch connector. Remove 2 actuator-to-steering gear attaching bolts. Lift actuator from steering gear.

Installation

Ensure the 2 seals between steering gear and actuator are in position. Align actuator on steering gear. Install and tighten 2 actuator-to-steering gear bolts to 20-25 ft. lbs. (28-33 N.m). Connect pressure switch and VAPS electrical connectors. Install air inlet duct.

STEERING GEAR

Removal

1) Remove primary steering column boot retainers. Remove intermediate shaft retaining bolts. Remove intermediate shaft. Refer to FORD MOTOR CO. (EXCEPT MODULAR) article in STEERING COLUMNS section.

2) Remove secondary steering column boot from inside passenger compartment. Raise vehicle on a twin post hoist. Remove front wheels. Support vehicle with 2 jack stands, just under rear edge of engine sub-frame, so sub-frame can be lowered.

3) Remove tie rod end cotter pins and castle nuts. Using Tie Rod Remover (TOOL-3290-D), separate tie

rod ends from steering knuckles. Loosen tie rod end lock nuts. Mark tie rod end lock nut position for reassembly reference.

4) Remove tie rod ends and lock nuts from tie rods. Remove steering gear-to-sub-frame retaining nuts. Remove both height sensors. See Fig. 4.

Fig. 4: Location of Height Sensor

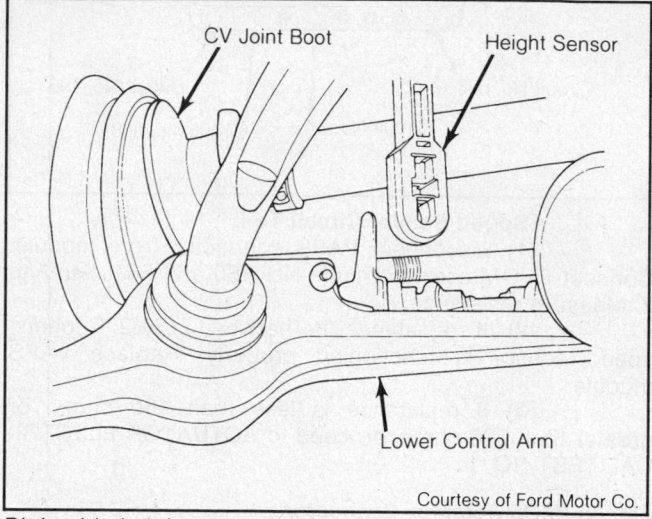

Courtesy of Ford Motor Co.

Right side height sensor is shown; left side is similar.

Fig. 5: Removing Catalytic Converter

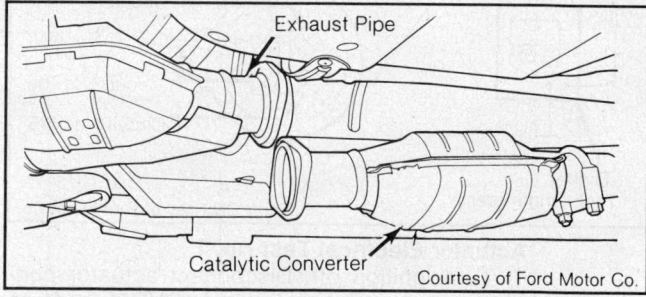

Courtesy of Ford Motor Co.

5) Remove rear sub-frame-to-body attaching bolts. Remove exhaust pipe-to-catalytic converter retaining bolts. See Fig. 5.

6) Lower twin post lift to allow approximately 4 inches of clearance between sub-frame and body. Remove heat shield retaining band. Fold heat shield down out of way. Disconnect VAPS electrical connector. See Fig. 6.

Fig. 6: Location of VAPS Actuator Connector

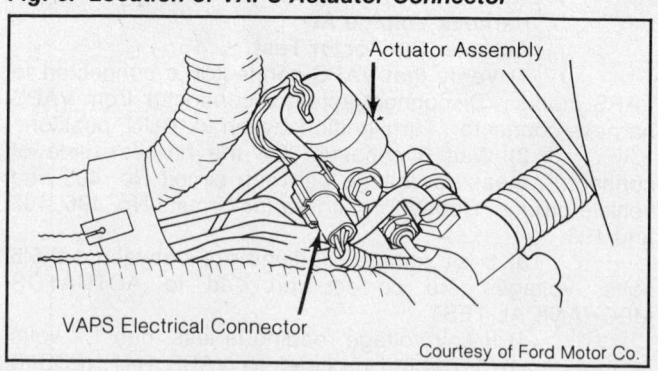

Courtesy of Ford Motor Co.

FORD MOTOR CO. VARIABLE-ASSIST POWER STEERING (Cont.)

Fig. 7: Location of Left Side Sway Bar Link

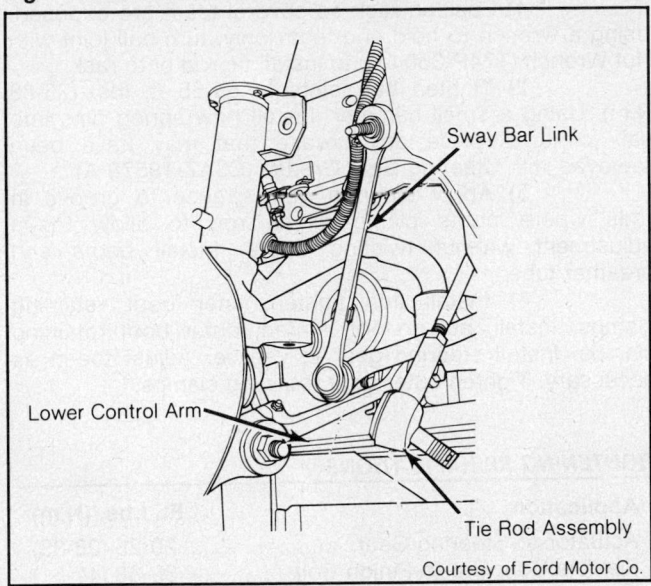

Courtesy of Ford Motor Co.

Fig. 8: View of Continental Hydraulic Line Routing

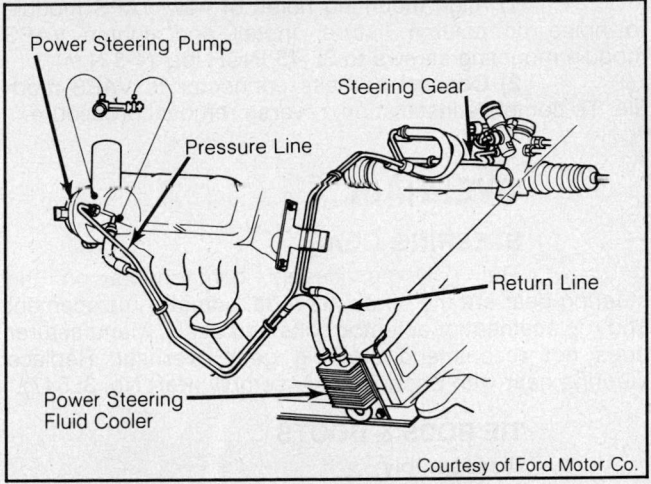

Courtesy of Ford Motor Co.

7) Rotate steering gear to clear bolts in subframe. Pull steering gear left to allow hydraulic line removal. Position drain pan under vehicle.

8) Remove hydraulic lines from steering gear. Remove left side sway bar link. *See Fig. 7.* Carefully remove steering gear through left wheel well opening.

Installation

1) Install new Ford Motor Co. specified "O" rings on hydraulic line fittings. Install steering gear retaining bolts in steering gear. Insert steering gear through left wheel well opening.

2) Install hydraulic lines to steering gear. Connect VAPS electrical connector. Position steering gear in sub-frame. Install tie rod end lock nuts and tie rod ends.

3) Install retaining band on heat shield. Attach tie rod ends on steering knuckles. Install and tighten NEW castle nut to minimum 35 ft. lbs. (47 N.m). Tighten castle nut further to align cotter pin slot. Install NEW cotter pins. Attach left side sway bar link.

4) Raise twin post hoist until sub-frame contacts body. Install sub-frame attaching bolts. Install and tighten steering gear-to-sub-frame retaining nuts to 85-100 ft. lbs. (115-135 N.m).

5) Install catalytic converter. Attach height sensors. Install wheels. Remove jack stands. Lower vehicle. Fill and bleed power steering system.

6) Install secondary steering column boot on steering gear from inside passenger compartment. Install primary steering column boot.

7) Attach intermediate steering column shaft. Refer to FORD MOTOR CO. (EXCEPT MODULAR) article in STEERING COLUMNS section. Align front end as necessary.

TIE ROD ENDS
Removal

1) Raise and support vehicle. Remove tie rod end cotter pins and castle nuts. Using Tie Rod Remover (TOOL-3290-D), separate tie rod ends from steering knuckles. Loosen tie rod end lock nuts.

2) Mark tie rod end lock nut position for reassembly reference. Remove tie rod ends and lock nuts from tie rods.

Installation

To install, reverse removal procedure. Install and tighten NEW castle nut to minimum 35 ft. lbs. (47 N.m). Tighten castle nut further to align cotter pin slot. Install NEW cotter pins. Adjust toe-in as necessary. Tighten tie rod end lock nut to 35-50 ft. lbs. (47-68 N.m).

VAPS MODULE
Removal

1) The VAPS module is located below instrument panel on the right side of steering column. Remove 4 lower instrument panel cover retaining screws from under steering column. Remove lower instrument panel cover.

2) Remove 3 sound insulation retaining push pins from instrument panel, under steering column. VAPS module should be visible to right of steering column.

3) Disconnect VAPS module harness connector from VAPS module. *See Fig. 9.* Remove 3 VAPS module fixture mounting screws. Remove VAPS module.

Fig. 9: Location of VAPS Module & Harness Connector

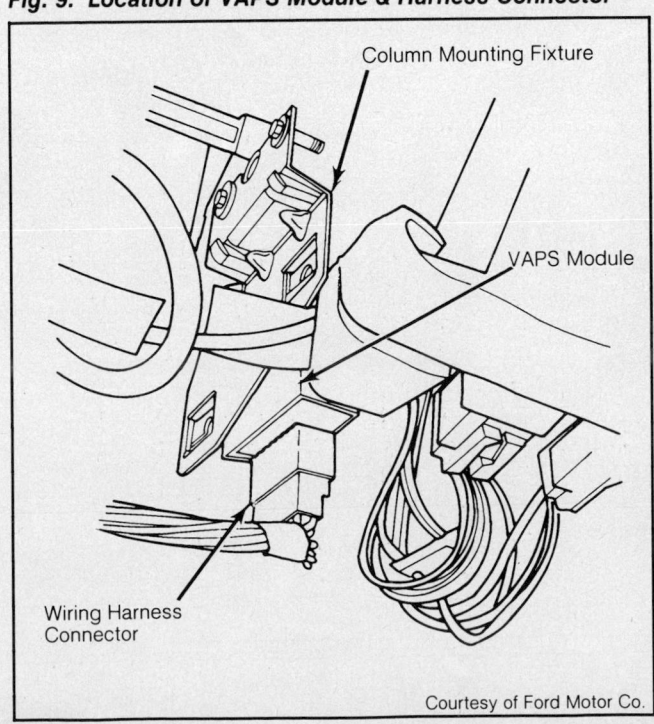

Courtesy of Ford Motor Co.

FORD MOTOR CO. VARIABLE-ASSIST POWER STEERING (Cont.)

Installation

1) Align mounting holes of new VAPS module to holes on column fixture. Install and tighten VAPS module mounting screws to 35-45 INCH lbs. (4-5 N.m).

2) Connect harness connector to VAPS module. To complete installation, reverse removal procedure.

OVERHAUL

STEERING GEAR

The only serviceable components on the steering gear are the boots, tie rods, actuator replacement and replacement of actuator bolts and seals. Manufacturer does not recommend steering gear overhaul. Replace steering gear with Short Rack Assembly (Part No. 3L547).

TIE RODS & BOOTS

Disassembly

1) With steering gear removed from vehicle, mount steering gear in Holding Fixture (T57L-500-B). It may be necessary to drill out the holes in the holding fixture with a 9/16" drill bit. Mount holding fixture in a vise.

2) Remove inner and outer boot retaining clamps. Remove boots with breather tube. Using Lock Nut Pin Remover (D81P-3504-N), remove spring pin from tie rod inner ball joint.

3) Position rack so several teeth are exposed. Using a wrench to hold end teeth only and turning ball joint with Nut Wrench (T74P-3504-U), separate tie rod from rack.

Cleaning & Inspection

Clean rack and housing bore of any foreign material. Check steering gear housing for cracks or leakage. If steering gear is damaged, replace with a new unit. Inspect boots for cracking or signs of dryness. Check clamps for damage or corrosion. Replace parts as necessary.

Reassembly

1) Position rack so several teeth are exposed. Using a wrench to hold end teeth only, turn ball joint with Nut Wrench (T74P-3504-U) to install tie rod onto rack.

2) Tighten ball joints to 55-65 ft. lbs. (75-88 N.m). Using a small hammer, install new spring pins into ball joints. Replace any grease that may have been removed with Steering Gear Grease (C3AZ-19578-A).

3) Apply steering gear grease to groove in rods where boots clamp to tie rod to allow toe-in adjustment without twisting boots. Install boots and breather tube.

4) Install and tighten inner boot retaining clamps. Install, but do not tighten, outer boot retaining clamps. Install steering gear in vehicle. Adjust toe-in as necessary. Tighten outer boot retaining clamps.

TIGHTENING SPECIFICATIONS

Application	Ft. Lbs. (N.m)
Actuator-to-Steering Gear	20-25 (28-33)
Flexible Coupling-to-Pinion Bolt	30-38 (41-51)
Hydraulic Fittings-to-Steering Gear	10-15 (14-21)
Hydraulic Transfer Tubes	22-28 (30-38)
Intermediate Shaft-to-Steering Shaft Nuts	15-25 (21-33)
Steering Gear-to-Sub-Frame Mounting Bolts & Nuts	85-100 (115-135)
Sub-Frame-to-Body Attaching Bolts	65-85 (90-115)
Tie Rod Ball Joint-to-Rack	55-65 (75-90)
Tie Rod End Lock Nut	35-50 (48-68)
Tie Rod End-to-Steering Knuckle	35-47 (48-64)

FORD MOTOR CO. MODEL C-II

All Models

DESCRIPTION

The C-II pump is a belt driven, 10-slipper pump which has an integral nylon reservoir. Spring loaded slippers within cam and rotor create the pumping action. A flow control relief valve maintains pump volume and pressure.

The pump design incorporates a swiveled pressure fitting. An identification tag attached to reservoir body indicates pump model. Use model code when requesting service parts, as slight differences in internal components do exist.

LUBRICATION, TROUBLE SHOOTING & TESTING

See POWER STEERING GENERAL SERVICING and TROUBLE SHOOTING articles in this section.

ADJUSTMENTS

PUMP BELT TENSION

See POWER STEERING GENERAL SERVICING article in this section.

REMOVAL & INSTALLATION

POWER STEERING PUMP

NOTE: Do not pry against reservoir to tighten belt. Pressure may crack reservoir.

Removal & Installation (RWD Models)

Drain reservoir by disconnecting fluid return line at reservoir. Disconnect pressure hose at pump. Remove mounting bracket retaining bolts. To install, reverse removal procedure. Adjust belt tension. Refill and bleed pump.

Removal & Installation (Escort & EXP)

1) Remove air cleaner, thermactor air pump and belt. Remove reservoir filler extension. Cover dipstick opening. On vehicles with EFI and remote reservoir, remove reservoir supply hose at pump.

2) Drain fluid. Cap opening. From under vehicle, loosen pump adjusting bolt. Remove pump-to-bracket mounting bolt. Disconnect return line.

3) Loosen adjusting and pivot bolts. Remove belt. Remove pump-to-bracket bolts. Remove pump by passing pulley through adjusting bracket opening.

4) Remove pressure hose from pump. To install pump, reverse removal procedure. Adjust belt tension. Refill and bleed pump.

Removal & Installation (Sable & Taurus With 2.5L Engine)

1) Disconnect battery ground cable. Using 1/2" drive hole provided, rotate tensioner pulley clockwise. Remove belt and power steering pulley. Disconnect and drain hydraulic lines. Using Hub Puller (T69L-10300-B), remove pulley from shaft.

2) Remove 3 pump-to-bracket retaining bolts. Remove pump. To install, reverse removal procedure. Using Steering Pump Pulley Installer (T65P-3A733-C), install pump pulley face flush with pump shaft within .10" (.25 mm). Adjust belt tension. Refill and bleed pump.

Removal & Installation (Sable & Taurus With 3.0L Engine)

1) Disconnect battery ground cable. Loosen idler pulley. Remove power steering belt. Remove pulley from hub. Remove return line from pump. Completely back off pressure line nut. Line will separate when pump is removed from bracket.

2) Remove pump mounting bolts. Remove pump. To install, reverse removal procedure. Adjust belt tension. Refill and bleed pump.

Fig. 1: Exploded View of Ford Motor Co. C-II Power Steering Pump

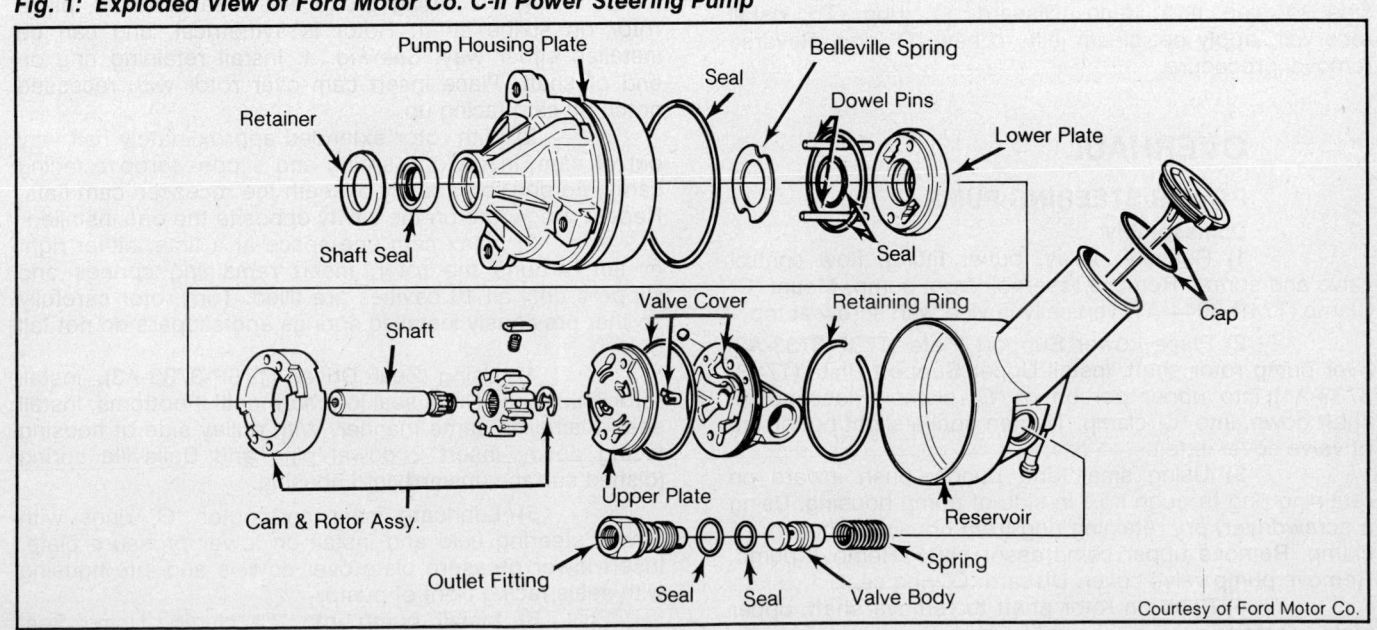

Courtesy of Ford Motor Co.

Power Steering Pumps

FORD MOTOR CO. MODEL C-II (Cont.)

Removal & Installation
(Tempo & Topaz)

1) Loosen alternator attaching and adjusting bolts. Remove alternator belt and radiator overflow tank. Loosen and remove power steering pump drive belt. Mark pulley location relative to hub. Remove pulley. Remove power steering fluid return line from pump.

2) Remove fluid pressure line nut, 3 pump mounting bolts and pump. Using Hub Puller (T71P-19703-B) and Shaft Protector (D80L-625-6), remove hub. To install pump, reverse removal procedure. Adjust belt tension. Refill and bleed pump.

POWER STEERING PUMP PULLEY

NOTE: On Escort and all RWD vehicles, pulley cannot be removed or installed with pump in vehicle.

Removal & Installation
(Escort & All RWD Models)

With pump removed from vehicle, drain as much fluid as possible through filler neck. Install Pulley Remover (T69L-10300-B) on pulley hub. Remove pulley. To install, reverse removal procedure. Using Pulley Installer (T65P-3A733-C), install pulley flush with shaft.

NOTE: When removing pulley, do not apply in and out pressure on pump shaft. Damage to internal thrust areas could result.

Removal & Installation
(All Other Models)

Remove radiator overflow tank. Mark pulley and hub position for reassembly reference. Remove pulley retaining bolts and pulley(s) from pump. To install pump, align pulley and hub. To complete installation, reverse removal procedure.

PUMP RESERVOIR

Removal & Installation

Place pump in vise. Remove outlet fitting, flow control valve and spring. Remove reservoir by twisting side to side and lifting. Discard "O" ring. To install reservoir, apply petroleum jelly to new "O" ring. Reverse removal procedure.

OVERHAUL

POWER STEERING PUMP

Disassembly

1) Remove pulley, outlet fitting, flow control valve and spring. Remove reservoir from pump. Mount "C" Clamp (T74P-3044-A1) vertically in vise with screw at top.

2) Place Lower Support Plate (T78P-3733-A2) over pump rotor shaft. Install Upper Support Plate (T78P-3733-A1) into upper portion of "C" clamp. Place pump, shaft down, into "C" clamp. Tighten until a slight bottoming of valve cover is felt.

3) Using small drift punch, push inward on retaining ring through hole in side of pump housing. Using a screwdriver, pry retaining ring from housing. Loosen "C" clamp. Remove upper compressor plate. Remove pump. Remove pump valve cover. Discard "O" ring seal.

4) Push on rotor shaft to remove shaft, upper plate, rotating group assembly and 2 dowel pins. To

remove cover plate and Belleville spring, slam pump housing on flat surface. Discard "O" rings. Pry rotor shaft seal and seal retainer from housing.

Fig. 2: Pump Positioned in "C" Clamp

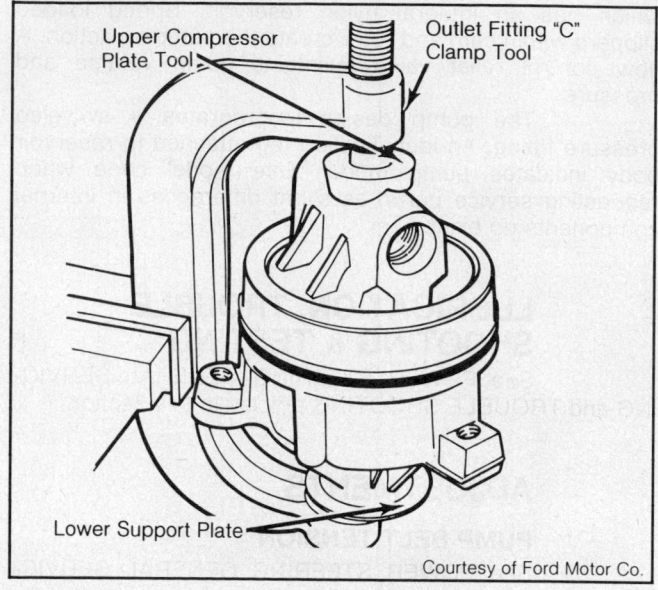

Upper Compressor Plate Tool

Outlet Fitting "C" Clamp Tool

Lower Support Plate

Courtesy of Ford Motor Co.

Fig. 3: Disassembled Pump

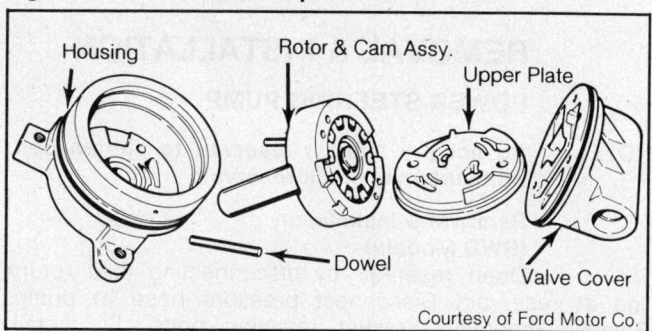

Housing

Rotor & Cam Assy.

Upper Plate

Dowel

Valve Cover

Courtesy of Ford Motor Co.

Reassembly

1) If rotating group was disassembled, place rotor on spline shaft. Rotor is symetrical, and can be installed either way. *See Fig. 4.* Install retaining ring on end of shaft. Place insert cam over rotor with recessed notch on cam facing up.

2) With rotor extended approximately half way out of cam, insert one spring and slipper (groove facing cam) into one rotor cavity beneath the recessed cam flats. Repeat procedure on the cavity opposite the one installed.

3) Index cam one space at a time, either right or left, around the rotor. Insert remaining springs and slippers until all 10 cavities are filled. Turn rotor carefully so that previously installed springs and slippers do not fall out.

4) Using Seal Driver (T78P-3733-A3), install rotor shaft seal. Drive seal into bore until it bottoms. Install seal retainer in same manner. With pulley side of housing facing down, insert 2 dowel pins and Belleville spring (dished surface upward) into housing.

5) Lubricate inner and outer "O" rings with power steering fluid and install on lower pressure plate. Insert lower pressure plate over dowels and into housing with seals facing front of pump.

6) Install pump into "C" clamp. Using Seal Driver (T78P-3733-A3), press lower plate lightly into

FORD MOTOR CO. MODEL C-II (Cont.)

housing until it bottoms. Install cam, rotor and slippers, and rotor shaft assembly over dowel pins and into housing. *See Fig. 4.*

Fig. 4: Assembling Cam & Rotating Assembly

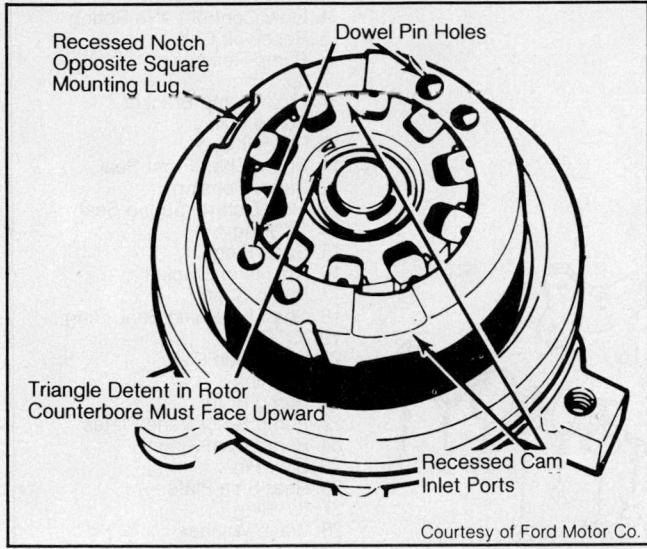

Recessed Notch Opposite Square Mounting Lug

Dowel Pin Holes

Triangle Detent in Rotor Counterbore Must Face Upward

Recessed Cam Inlet Ports

Courtesy of Ford Motor Co.

7) Place upper pressure plate over dowel pins with recess directly over recessed notch on cam insert and approximately 180 degrees opposite square mounting lug. *See Fig. 5.*

8) Lubricate and place new "O" ring on valve cover. If plastic baffle is loose in valve cover, apply petroleum jelly to baffle. Install baffle into position on valve cover.

9) Insert valve cover over dowel pins with outlet fitting hole directly in line with square mounting lug on housing. Place assembly in "C" clamp. Compress valve cover into pump housing. Install retaining ring with ends near access hole in housing.

Fig. 5: Upper Pressure Plate Installation

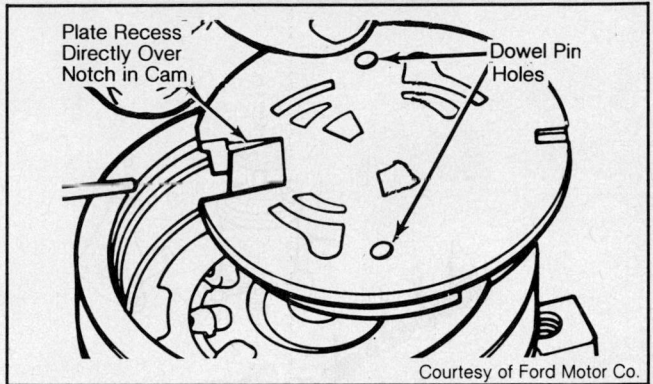

Plate Recess Directly Over Notch in Cam

Dowel Pin Holes

Dowel Pin Holes

Courtesy of Ford Motor Co.

10) Lubricate and install "O" ring on pump housing. Install reservoir. Install flow control valve and spring into valve cover. Use new "O" ring seals on outlet fitting and install into valve cover to specified torque.

CAUTION: If flow control valve is cocked, it may become stuck in valve cover. Do not force valve forward since chips may shear off and carry into valve bore.

11) Lubricate and place new "O" ring seals in the outlet fitting. Install outlet fitting into valve cover. Tighten outlet fitting to specification.

TIGHTENING SPECIFICATIONS

Application	Ft. Lbs. (N.m)
Brackets-to-Engine Bolts	30-45 (41-61)
Outlet Fitting	25-34 (34-46)
Pivot Bolt	30-45 (41-61)
Pump-to-Bracket	30-45 (41-61)
Pressure Hose Nut-to-Pump	10-15 (14-20)
Quick Connect Fitting	10-15 (14-20)

NOVA VANE PUMP

DESCRIPTION

The power steering pump is a belt-driven vane-type. Pump components include an engine-driven eccentric rotor with vane plates, an eccentric cam ring, and a flow control valve to regulate amount of oil flow and maximum oil pressure.

LUBRICATION, TROUBLE SHOOTING & TESTING

See POWER STEERING GENERAL SERVICING and TROUBLE SHOOTING articles in this section.

REMOVAL & INSTALLATION

POWER STEERING PUMP

Removal

Loosen pulley retaining nut. Remove drive belt. Disconnect hydraulic lines. Plug hydraulic lines. Elevate hydraulic lines to prevent fluid from draining. Drain fluid from pump. Disconnect air control valve hoses (if equipped). Remove pump retaining bolts. Remove pump.

Installation

To install, reverse removal procedure. Adjust drive belt tension. Bleed system.

Power Steering Pumps

NOVA VANE PUMP (Cont.)

Fig. 1: Exploded View of Nova Power Steering Pump Assembly

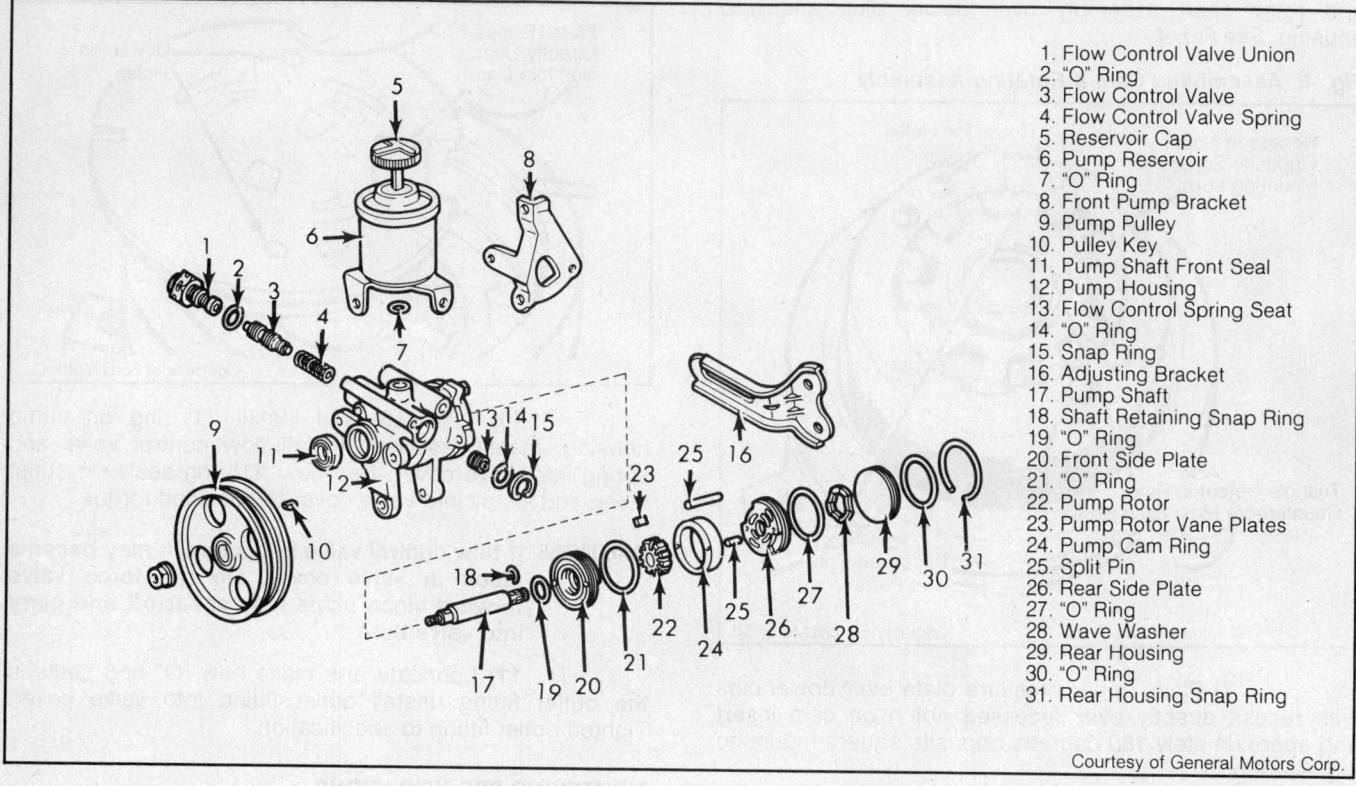

1. Flow Control Valve Union
2. "O" Ring
3. Flow Control Valve
4. Flow Control Valve Spring
5. Reservoir Cap
6. Pump Reservoir
7. "O" Ring
8. Front Pump Bracket
9. Pump Pulley
10. Pulley Key
11. Pump Shaft Front Seal
12. Pump Housing
13. Flow Control Spring Seat
14. "O" Ring
15. Snap Ring
16. Adjusting Bracket
17. Pump Shaft
18. Shaft Retaining Snap Ring
19. "O" Ring
20. Front Side Plate
21. "O" Ring
22. Pump Rotor
23. Pump Rotor Vane Plates
24. Pump Cam Ring
25. Split Pin
26. Rear Side Plate
27. "O" Ring
28. Wave Washer
29. Rear Housing
30. "O" Ring
31. Rear Housing Snap Ring

Courtesy of General Motors Corp.

OVERHAUL

POWER STEERING PUMP

Disassembly

1) Remove drive pulley. Place power steering pump in soft-jawed vise. Remove reservoir and bracket from pump. Remove "O" ring, pressure port union, flow control valve and spring.

2) Remove spring seat snap ring. Install a bolt into spring seat to remove seat. Mark front and rear housings for reassembly reference.

3) Remove rear housing. Remove rear side plate, vane plates and rotor shaft assembly. Disassemble rotor, shaft and front side plate.

Fig. 2: Checking Pump Housing Bushing-to-Rotor Shaft Clearance

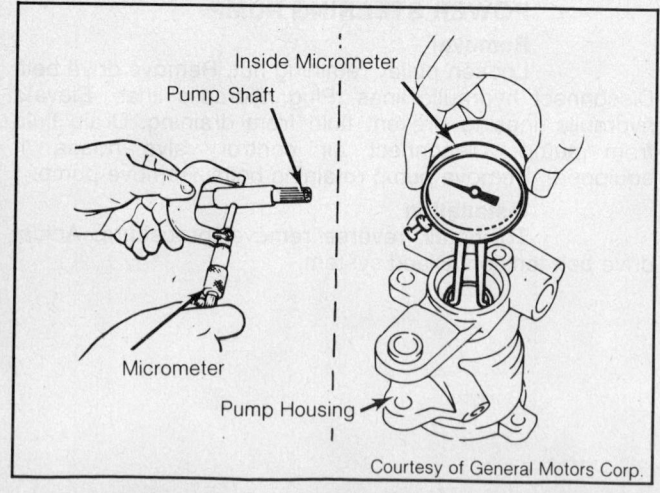

Courtesy of General Motors Corp.

Inspection

1) Check all parts for wear or damage. Replace parts as necessary. Check oil clearance between pump housing bushing and rotor shaft. *See Fig. 2.*

2) If difference is greater than .0028" (.07 mm), replace complete pump assembly. Discard all "O" rings. Always use new "O" rings for reassembly.

3) Measure difference between cam ring and rotor. Maximum difference should be .0024" (.06 mm). Replace cam ring with one that has same letter stamped on rotor (if necessary). *See Fig. 3.*

Fig. 3: Pump Rotor & Cam Ring Marks

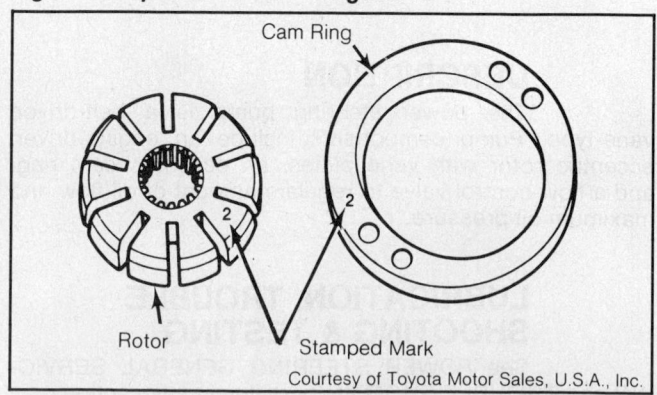

Courtesy of Toyota Motor Sales, U.S.A., Inc.

4) Check vane plates for wear or damage. Measure vane plates. Vane plate dimensions should be .590 x .319 x .070" (14.99 x 8.10 x 1.79 mm). *See Fig. 4.*

5) Using feeler gauge, measure clearance between vane plates and rotor groove. Maximum clearance between vane plate and rotor groove is .0011" (.028 mm). *See Fig. 5.*

NOVA VANE PUMP (Cont.)

6) Using compressed air, check flow control valve for leakage. Measure control valve spring length. Control valve spring length is 1.85-1.97" (47-50 mm).

Fig. 4: Measuring Vane Plates

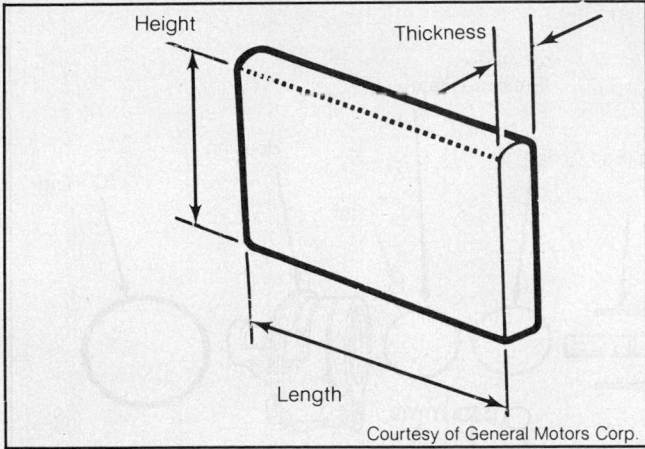

Courtesy of General Motors Corp.

Fig. 5: Measuring Vane Plate-to-Rotor Clearance

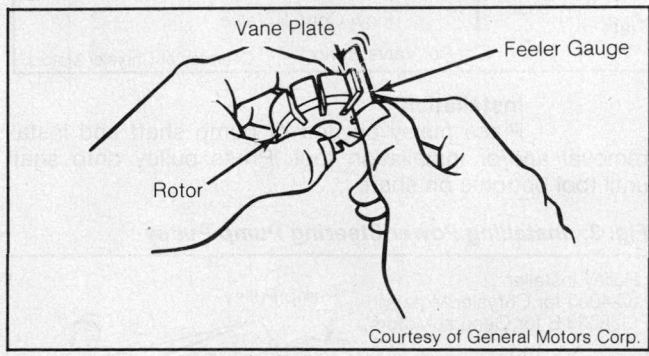

Courtesy of General Motors Corp.

Reassembly

1) Coat all sliding surfaces with ATF. Install "O" rings on front side plate. Position side plate on shaft. Place rotor (with mark facing up) onto shaft. *See Fig. 3.* Secure with snap ring.

2) Grease oil seal. Install long straight pin into front housing. Using plastic hammer, tap rotor shaft into front housing. Install pin.

3) Install cam ring with mark facing outward. Install vane plates with rounded end facing outward. Install new "O" ring to rear side plate. Install plate on cam ring. Align pin holes with pins.

4) Install wave washer and new "O" ring in rear housing. Using plastic mallet, tap rear housing into position. Install snap ring. Ensure rotor shaft turns smoothly.

5) Install pulley and pulley nut. Check rotating torque. Rotating torque should be less than 2.4 INCH lbs. (2.7 N.m). Install flow control spring seat, new "O" ring and snap ring.

6) Install spring, flow control valve, "O" rings and pressure port union. Tighten pressure port union. Install reservoir "O" ring, reservoir tank and bracket.

TIGHTENING SPECIFICATIONS

Application	Ft. Lbs. (N.m)
Flow Control Valve Union	51 (69)
Hydraulic Line Fittings	34 (47)
Pump Pully Nut	32 (43)
Pump Mounting Bolts	29 (39)

	INCH Lbs. (N.m)
Reservoir-to-Bracket Bolt	108 (13)

SAGINAW VANE WITH INTEGRAL RESERVOIR

Chrysler Motors, General Motors

DESCRIPTION

The Saginaw Vane power steering pump is a constant displacement, vane type pump with an integral fluid reservoir. A pressure hose and return line connect the pump to the steering gear.

Rectangular pumping vanes, carried by a shaft driven rotor, move the fluid from the intake to cam ring pressure cavities. As the rotor turns, the vanes pick up residual fluid. The rotor forces the fluid into a high pressure area.

Fluid is then forced into the cavities of the thrust plate through 2 crossover holes in the cam ring and pressure plate. The crossover holes empty into a high pressure area between the pressure plate and housing end cover.

When pressure exceeds set limits, the flow control pressure relief valve opens and allows fluid to return to the inlet side of the pump. Under normal conditions the pressure relief and flow control valves are closed.

LUBRICATION, TROUBLE SHOOTING & TESTING

See POWER STEERING GENERAL SERVICING and TROUBLE SHOOTING articles in this section.

REMOVAL & INSTALLATION

POWER STEERING PUMP

Removal

1) Place container under vehicle to catch drained fluids. Disconnect hoses at pump or steering gear. Plug fittings to prevent contamination. Loosen belt tension. Remove drive belt.

2) Remove pump mounting hardware and pump. Depending on engine and air conditioning configuration, it may be necessary to remove additional components in order to gain access to pump and mountings. On some models, power steering pump pulley may be removed to ease removal of pump.

SAGINAW VANE WITH INTEGRAL RESERVOIR (Cont.)

Fig. 1: Exploded View of Saginaw Vane Power Steering Pump

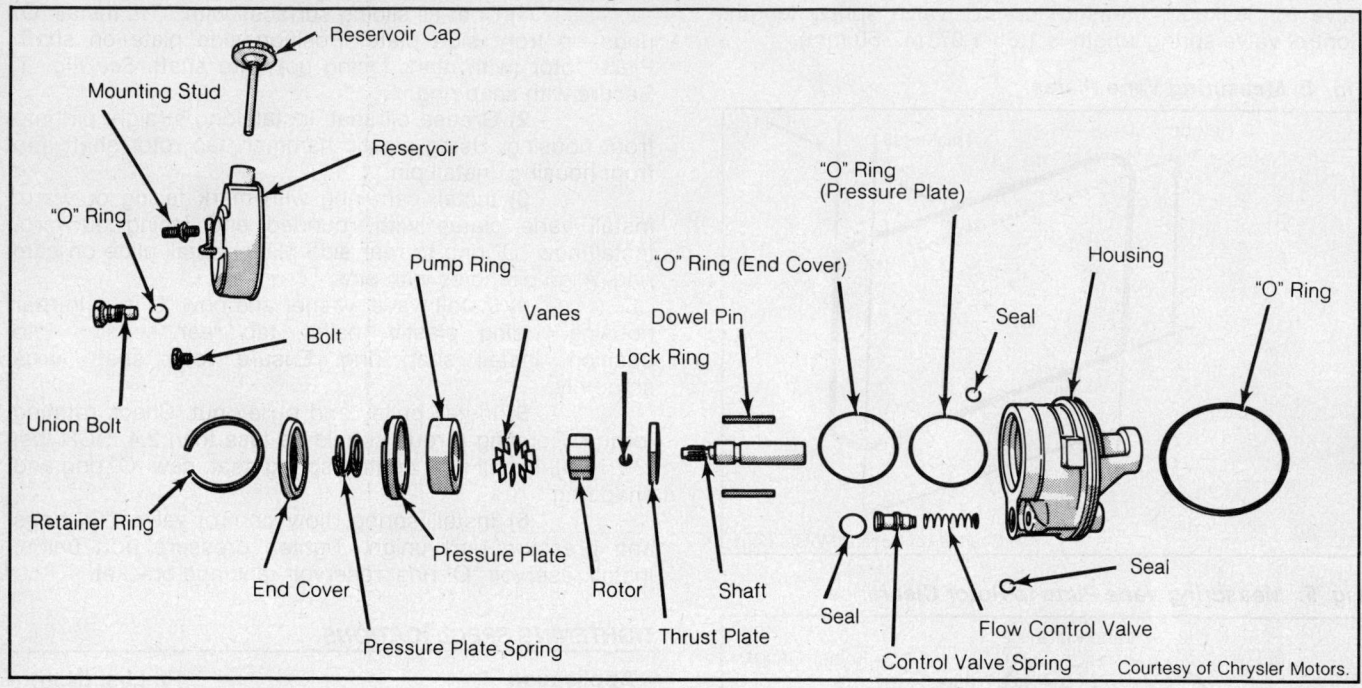

Courtesy of Chrysler Motors.

NOTE: It may be necessary to remove pump bracket with pump on some models. If bracket bolts extend into water jacket, catch coolant with drain pan.

Installation

To install power steering pump, reverse removal procedure.

POWER STEERING PUMP PULLEY

Removal

1) Pump pulley is a press fit on shaft and must be removed and installed with a puller. Do not hammer on puller, pulley or shaft. Damage to internal pump components may occur.

2) Clamp pump in vise at mounting bracket or front hub. Avoid clamping front hub too tightly with vise. With pulley removing tool aligned with shaft, remove pulley. See PUMP PULLEY SERVICE TOOLS for correct removal and installation tools.

Fig. 2: Removing Power Steering Pump Pulley

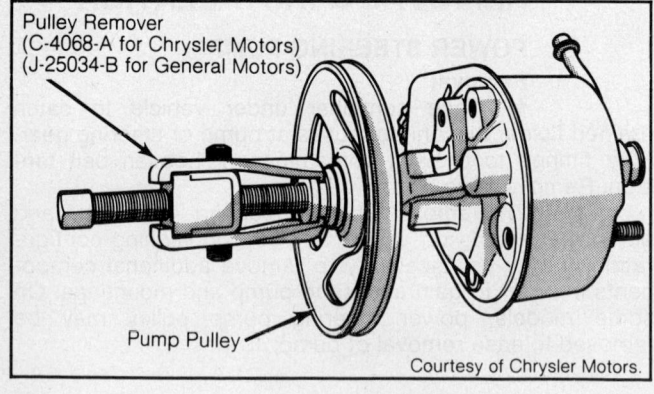

Courtesy of Chrysler Motors.

Installation

Place pulley on end of pump shaft and install removal and/or installation tool. Press pulley onto shaft until tool bottoms on shaft.

Fig. 3: Installing Power Steering Pump Pulley

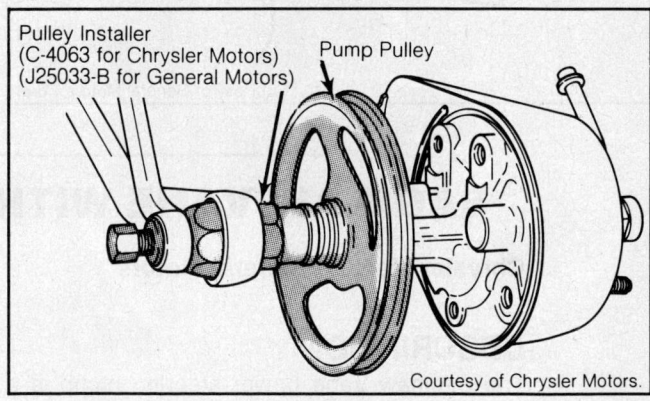

Courtesy of Chrysler Motors.

PUMP PULLEY SERVICE TOOLS

Application	Remover Tool No.	Installer Tool No.
Chrysler Motors	C-4068-A	C-4063
General Motors	J-25034-B	J-25033-B

DRIVE SHAFT SEAL

Removal & Installation

Remove power steering pump from vehicle. Remove pump pulley. Protect pump shaft with shim stock. Using a chisel, cut seal and remove. To install, coat shaft seal with power steering fluid. Using a 7/8" or 15/16" socket, drive new shaft seal in place until it bottoms on shoulder.

SAGINAW VANE WITH INTEGRAL RESERVOIR (Cont.)

RESERVOIR

Removal

1) Remove pump from vehicle. Drain fluid from pump. Mount pump in vise with pump shaft facing down. Do not allow vise jaws to contact reservoir.

2) Remove 2 reservoir-to-pump mounting studs at rear of pump. Remove pressure line outlet fitting. Using a soft mallet tap on filler neck of reservoir. Move reservoir back and forth until free of pump.

Installation

1) Use all NEW "O" rings. Lubricate and install pump housing "O" ring, 2 pump-to-reservoir stud "O" rings and outlet fitting "O" ring. Slide reservoir over pump. Ensure reservoir is seated properly.

2) Install pump-to-reservoir mounting studs. Torque to 26 ft. lbs. (35 N.m). Install outlet fitting. Torque to 55 ft. lbs (75 N.m). Install pump in vehicle. Adjust belt tension. Refill and bleed pump. Check for leaks.

OVERHAUL

CAUTION: When clamping pump in vise or mounting fixture, do not exert excessive force on front hub as housing may be distorted.

POWER STEERING PUMP

Disassembly

1) Remove pulley and key from shaft. Remove brackets from pump. Drain reservoir. Clean exterior of pump. Clamp pump in a soft-jawed vise, shaft down, between square boss and shaft housing.

2) Remove pressure fitting and "O" ring seal. Remove retaining studs. Rock filler tube back and forth gently to loosen. Work reservoir off pump body. Remove and discard all "O" rings.

3) Using a punch, tap end cover retaining ring until one end of ring is near hole in pump body. Insert punch in hole far enough to disengage ring from groove in pump bore. Pry ring out of pump body.

4) Tap end cover with plastic hammer to jar it loose. Spring located under cover should push it up. Remove pump body from vise. Place pump in an inverted position on a clean, flat surface.

5) Tap end of drive shaft with plastic hammer to loosen pressure plate, rotor, and thrust plate assembly from body. Lift pump body off rotor assembly.

6) Flow control valve and spring should slide out of bore. Remove and discard end plate and pressure plate "O" rings. Remove drive shaft oil seal.

7) Lift pressure plate and cam ring from rotor. Remove 10 vanes from slots. Clamp drive shaft in soft-jawed vise with rotor and thrust plate up.

8) Remove and discard rotor lock ring. Use care to avoid nicking rotor end face. Slide rotor and thrust plate off shaft. Remove shaft from vise.

NOTE: **Individual control valve parts are not available. Replace flow control valve as an assembly if worn or damaged. If pump is being overhauled because of contamination in system, valve can be disassembled for cleaning.**

Cleaning & Inspection

1) Clean all parts in solvent. Inspect flow control valve for wear or damage. Inspect seal bore in housing for burrs, nicks or scoring. Inspect fit of vanes in rotor. Vanes must slide freely into slots of rotor without binding.

2) Excessively loose vanes require replacement of rotor and/or vanes. Examine inner surface of cam ring for heavy scuff or chatter marks. Inspect flat surfaces of pressure and thrust plates for wear or scoring.

3) Light scoring can be removed by lapping on a flat surface. Inspect pump body drive shaft bushing for excessive wear. Replace pump body and bushing as an assembly if badly worn or scored. Replace any damaged or worn parts.

NOTE: **If pump is equipped with magnet, ensure all residue is cleaned from magnet.**

Reassembly

1) Lubricate all "O" ring seals and seal areas with power steering fluid. Place pump body on flat surface. Drive new pump shaft seal into bore with a 7/8" or 15/16" socket until seal bottoms on shoulder. Do not use excessive force as seal can be distorted.

2) Clamp pump body in vise with shaft down. Install end cover and pressure plate "O" rings in grooves in pump cavity. With drive shaft clamped, splined shaft up, install thrust plate on drive shaft with ported side up. *See Fig. 5.*

Fig. 5: Installing Thrust Plate

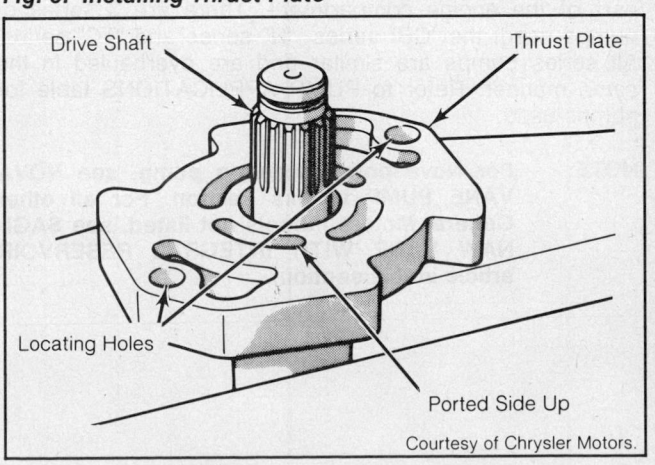

Courtesy of Chrysler Motors.

Fig. 4: Exploded View of Flow Control Valve

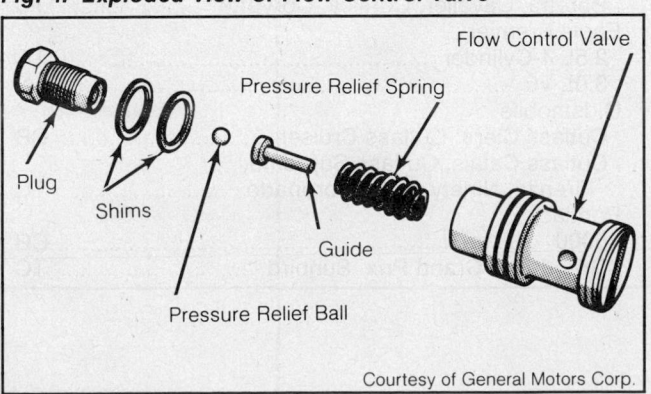

Courtesy of General Motors Corp.

Power Steering Pumps

SAGINAW VANE WITH INTEGRAL RESERVOIR (Cont.)

3) Slide rotor over splines with counterbore of rotor facing down. Install rotor lock ring. Insert both dowel pins in holes of pump cavity. Rotor must move freely on splines. Install pump shaft assembly in pump body, ensuring dowel pins are properly engaged in thrust plate.

4) Slide cam ring over rotor on dowel pins with arrow facing up. See Fig. 6. Install 10 vanes in rotor slots. Position pressure plate on dowel pins with plate spring groove facing upward. Place a 1 1/4" socket in groove of pressure plate. Seat entire assembly on "O" ring in pump cavity by pressing down with both thumbs.

Fig. 6: Installing Cam Ring

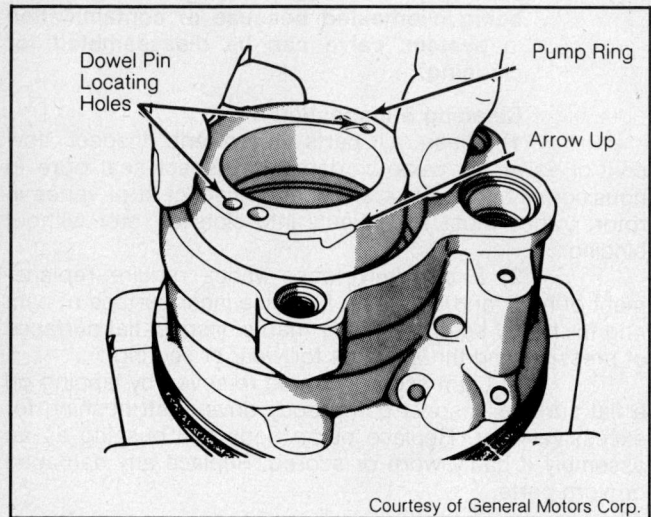

Courtesy of General Motors Corp.

5) Place spring in groove in pressure plate. Position end cover lip edge up over spring. Press end cover down below retaining ring groove with thumb. Install ring. Ensure ring is seated in groove. Take care to prevent cocking end cover in bore or distorting assembly.

6) Install flow control valve, if removed, in pump bore with spring and hex end of valve facing interior of bore. Using a punch, tap retainer ring end around groove until opening is opposite flow control valve bore. This is important for maximum retention of retainer ring.

7) Replace reservoir "O" ring seal, 2 mounting stud "O" ring seals and flow control valve "O" ring seal on pump body. Carefully position reservoir on pump body. Visually align mounting stud holes until studs can be started in threads.

8) Press reservoir down on pump to seat on pump body. Place new seal on pump union. Install union in flow control valve bore. Tighten mounting studs. Install pump pulley.

TIGHTENING SPECIFICATIONS

Application	Ft. Lbs. (N.m)
Flow Control Valve Fitting	55 (75)
High Pressure Line-to-Union	30 (41)
High Pressure Union	35 (47)
Mounting Bracket Bolts	30 (41)
Reservoir Mounting Bolt	26 (35)
	INCH Lbs. (N.m)
Flow Control Valve Plug	4 (.45)

SAGINAW VANE WITH REMOTE RESERVOIR

Eagle Premier
General Motors

DESCRIPTION

This pump uses a fluid reservoir separate from the pump. In some cases it is mounted to the top of the pump, connected by a tube. In others it is in a separate part of the engine compartment. There are 3 series of pumps used: the "CB" series, "N" series and "TC" series. All series pumps are similar and are overhauled in the same manner. Refer to PUMP APPLICATIONS table for pumps used.

NOTE: For Nova power steering pump, see NOVA VANE PUMP in this section. For all other General Motors models not listed, see SAGINAW VANE WITH INTEGRAL RESERVOIR article in this section.

PUMP APPLICATIONS

Make/Model	Pump Series
Buick	
Century	CB
Electra, Regal, Riviera,	
Skyhawk & Skylark	TC
Cadillac	
All Except Brougham	TC
Chevrolet	
Celebrity	CB
Beretta, Cavalier, Corsica, Corvette	TC
Eagle Premier	
2.5L 4-Cylinder	TC
3.0L V6	N
Oldsmobile	
Cutlass Ciera, Cutlass Cruiser	CB
Cutlass Calais, Cutlass Supreme,	
Firenza, Ninety-Eight, Toronado	TC
Pontiac	
6000	CB
Grand Am, Grand Prix, Sunbird	TC

SAGINAW VANE WITH REMOTE RESERVOIR (Cont.)

Fig. 1: Exploded View Of "CB" Series Power Steering Pump Components

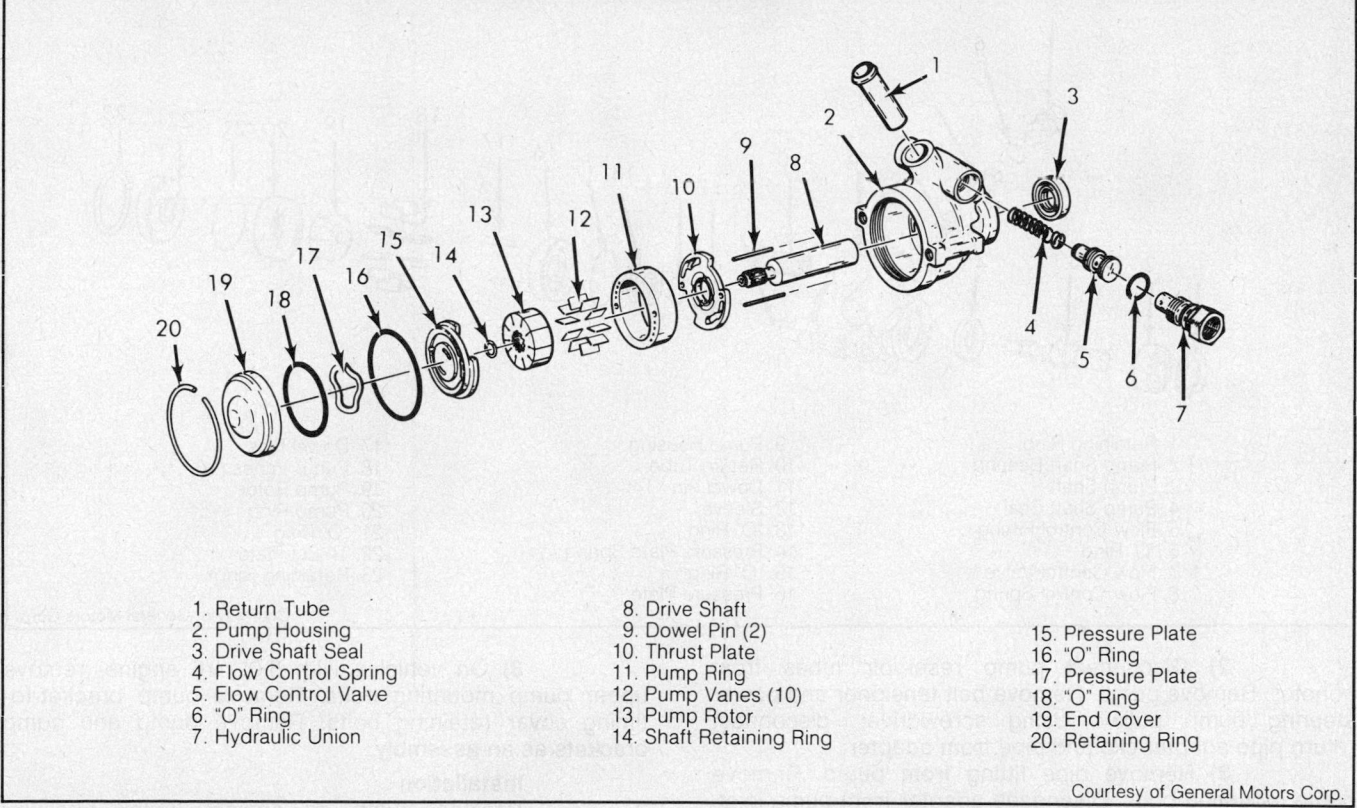

1. Return Tube
2. Pump Housing
3. Drive Shaft Seal
4. Flow Control Spring
5. Flow Control Valve
6. "O" Ring
7. Hydraulic Union

8. Drive Shaft
9. Dowel Pin (2)
10. Thrust Plate
11. Pump Ring
12. Pump Vanes (10)
13. Pump Rotor
14. Shaft Retaining Ring

15. Pressure Plate
16. "O" Ring
17. Pressure Plate
18. "O" Ring
19. End Cover
20. Retaining Ring

Courtesy of General Motors Corp.

OPERATION

Rectangular pumping vanes, carried by a shaft driven rotor, move fluid from intake to pressure cavities of the cam ring. As the rotor begins to rotate, centrifugal force throws the vanes against the inside surface of the cam ring to pick up residual oil, which is then forced into the high pressure area.

Oil is forced into cavities of the thrust plate and through 2 cross-over holes in the cam ring and pressure plate. This oil empties into the high pressure area between the pressure plate and housing end plate. Filling the high pressure area causes oil to flow under vanes in slots of rotor, forcing the vanes to follow the inside oval surface of cam ring. As the vanes rotate to the small area of cam ring, oil is forced out from between the vanes, creating high pressure.

LUBRICATION, TROUBLE SHOOTING & TESTING

For further information see POWER STEERING GENERAL SERVICING in this section.

REMOVAL & INSTALLATION

POWER STEERING PUMP

Removal (Allanté)

1) Remove pump reservoir to gain access to the pressure hose assembly and pump. Remove power steering pump cover and serpentine belt. Drain power steering fluid from reservoir. Remove reservoir mounting bolts.

Fig. 2: Exploded View Of "N" Series Power Steering Pump Components

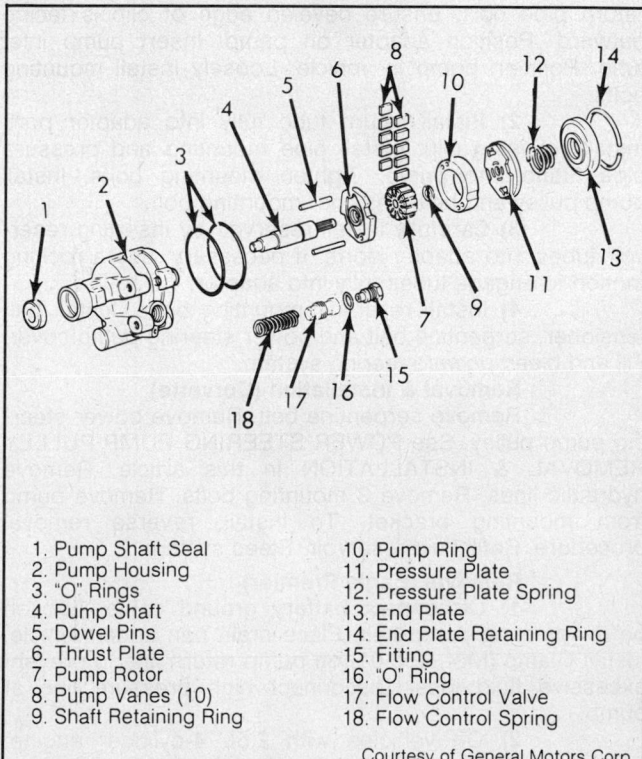

1. Pump Shaft Seal
2. Pump Housing
3. "O" Rings
4. Pump Shaft
5. Dowel Pins
6. Thrust Plate
7. Pump Rotor
8. Pump Vanes (10)
9. Shaft Retaining Ring

10. Pump Ring
11. Pressure Plate
12. Pressure Plate Spring
13. End Plate
14. End Plate Retaining Ring
15. Fitting
16. "O" Ring
17. Flow Control Valve
18. Flow Control Spring

Courtesy of General Motors Corp.

SAGINAW VANE WITH REMOTE RESERVOIR (Cont.)

Fig. 3: Exploded View Of "TC" Series Power Steering Pump Components

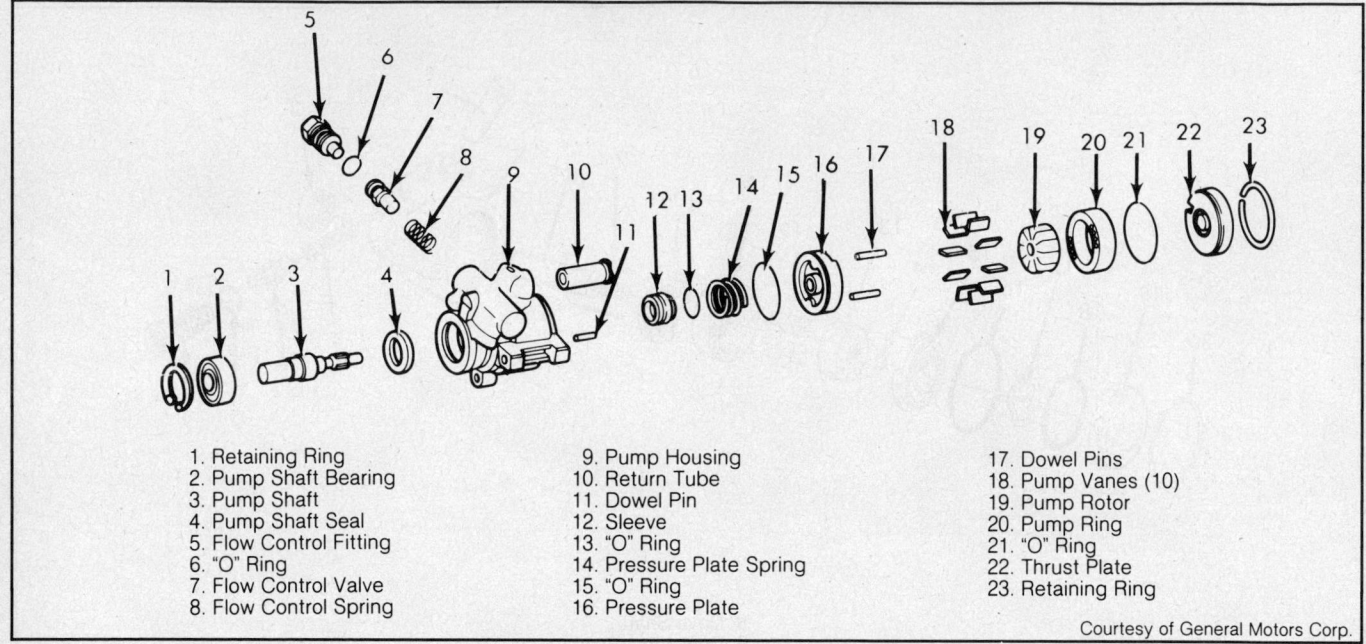

1. Retaining Ring
2. Pump Shaft Bearing
3. Pump Shaft
4. Pump Shaft Seal
5. Flow Control Fitting
6. "O" Ring
7. Flow Control Valve
8. Flow Control Spring
9. Pump Housing
10. Return Tube
11. Dowel Pin
12. Sleeve
13. "O" Ring
14. Pressure Plate Spring
15. "O" Ring
16. Pressure Plate
17. Dowel Pins
18. Pump Vanes (10)
19. Pump Rotor
20. Pump Ring
21. "O" Ring
22. Thrust Plate
23. Retaining Ring

Courtesy of General Motors Corp.

2) Disconnect pump reservoir tubes from adapter. Remove pump. Remove belt tensioner and power steering pump pulley. Using screwdriver, disconnect return pipe adapter clip and pipe from adapter.

3) Remove pipe fitting from pump. Remove pump mounting bolts. Disengage adapter from pump inlet. Ensure "O" ring is removed from pump inlet port.

Installation

1) Insert return pipe adapter clip on adapter at return pipe port. Ensure beveled edge of clip is facing outward. Position adapter on pump. Insert pump inlet tube. Position pump in vehicle. Loosely install mounting bolts.

2) Install return tube fully into adapter port. Install retaining clip. Install pipe mounting and pressure pipe fitting into pump. Tighten mounting bolts. Install pump pulley and belt tensioner mounting bolt.

3) Carefully install reservoir by inserting reservoir tubes into adapter ports. If necessary, use a rocking motion to engage tubes fully into adapter.

4) Install reservoir mounting bolts. Install belt tensioner, serpentine belt and power steering pump cover. Fill and bleed power steering system.

Removal & Installation (Corvette)

Remove serpentine belt. Remove power steering pump pulley. See POWER STEERING PUMP PULLEY REMOVAL & INSTALLATION in this article. Remove hydraulic lines. Remove 3 mounting bolts. Remove pump from mounting bracket. To install, reverse removal procedure. Refill fluid reservoir. Bleed system.

Removal (Eagle Premier)

1) Disconnect battery ground cable. Loosen power steering pump belt. Place drain pan under vehicle. Install Clamp (Mot. 453.01) on pump return line to prevent excessive fluid loss. Disconnect high pressure line at pump.

2) On vehicles with 2.5L 4-cylinder engine, remove upper pump mounting bolt and lower bracket retaining bolts. Remove pump.

3) On vehicles with 3.0L V6 engine, remove upper pump mounting bolts. Remove pump bracket-to-timing cover retaining bolts. Remove pump and pump brackets as an assembly.

Installation

Position pump on engine. Install retaining bolts. Install and adjust drive belt. Tighten mounting bolts. Connect hydraulic lines to pump. Remove Clamp (Mot. 453.01) from return line. Connect battery ground cable. Fill and bleed system as necessary.

Removal (Eldorado & Seville)

Remove power steering belt and power steering pump pulley. See POWER STEERING PUMP PULLEY REMOVAL & INSTALLATION in this article. Remove high pressure line fitting. Remove pump return hose. Remove 2 pump mounting bolts. Remove pump.

Installation

1) Position pump in vehicle. Install high pressure line fitting hand tight. Install and tighten pump mounting bolts to specification. Tighten high pressure fitting to specification.

2) Install pump return hose. Ensure that excess length of hose is positioned between tensioner bracket and generator brace and that hose is not in contact with tensioner pulley, belt or any moving part.

3) Install pump pulley and pump belt. Adjust belt tension. Refill reservoir. Bleed system.

**Removal & Installation
(Celebrity, Century, Cutlass Ciera,
Cutlass Cruiser & 6000 With 2.5L Engine)**

1) Raise and support vehicle. Remove right fender splash sheild. Remove upper mounting bolt and spacer. Remove lower mounting bolts and nuts. Remove belt.

2) Disconnect lines at pump. Remove rear bracket. Remove pump. To install, reverse removal procedure. Adjust belt tension. Refill reservoir. Bleed system.

SAGINAW VANE WITH REMOTE RESERVOIR (Cont.)

Removal & Installation
(Celebrity, Century, Cutlass Ciera, Cutlass Cruiser & 6000 With 2.8L Engine)

1) Disconnect battery ground cable. Remove blower motor. Drain radiator. Disconnect hoses from water pump and power steering pump.

2) Remove adjusting nut from plate. Remove front bracket stud and bolt. Remove pump and brackets. To install, reverse removal procedure. Adjust belt tension. Refill reservoir. Bleed system.

Removal (All Others)

1) Remove air cleaner assembly. Disconnect reservoir-to-pump hose from pump (if equipped). Disconnect pressure line from pump.

2) Remove clip securing pressure line to pump. Loosen adjusting bolt and pivot bolt. Remove belt. Remove pump-to-bracket bolts. Remove pump and pulley.

Installation

1) Install pump and pulley assembly into bracket. Loosely fasten pressure line to pump with clip. Do not connect pressure line at this time. Connect reservoir-to-pump hose to pump.

2) Add power steering fluid to reservoir. Observe pressure port at power steering pump. Connect pressure line to pump when fluid begins exiting pressure port.

3) Tighten clip securing pressure line to pump. Install and adjust power steering belt. Install air cleaner. Refill reservoir. Bleed steering system.

POWER STEERING PUMP PULLEY

Removal & Installation

Remove belt from pump. Remove pump as previously described (if necessary). Install Pulley Remover (J-25034-B or J29785-A) on pulley. Press pulley off shaft by holding body of tool with wrench and turning bolt into body of tool.

Installation

To install, use Pulley Installer (J-25033-B). Press pulley onto drive shaft until face of pulley hub is flush with pump drive shaft. Do not use arbor press to install pulley. Install pump on vehicle (if removed). Install belt onto pulley.

RETURN TUBE
Removal & Installation

1) Plug return tube to prevent chips from entering pump. Using a 9/16" 12 thread per inch tap, a 9/16" 12 thread per inch nut and five 5/8" washers, screw tap into tube, slide washers over end of tap and use the nut to draw tube out of pump body. See Fig. 4.

2) Using Loctite Solvent (75559) and Loctite Adhesive (290), coat end of the return tube. Using a press, press tube into housing until bottomed.

CONTROL VALVE ASSEMBLY

Removal & Installation

With pump removed from vehicle, unscrew flow control valve line fitting. Remove "O" ring, control valve assembly and flow control spring. See Fig. 5. To install reverse removal procedure. Tighten line fitting to specification.

Fig. 5: Control Valve Assembly Removal

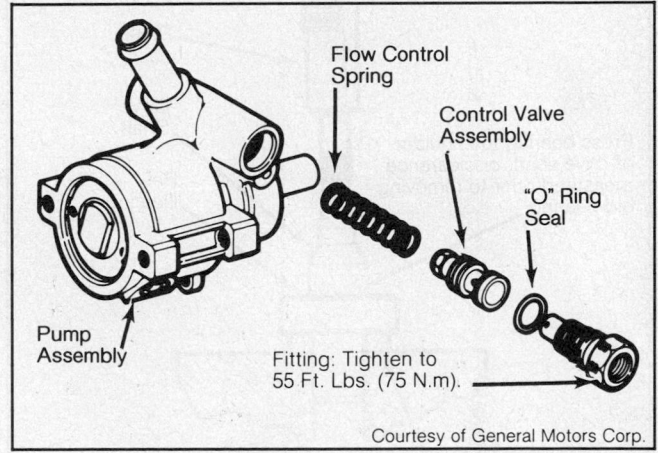

Courtesy of General Motors Corp.

DRIVE SHAFT & BALL BEARING ASSEMBLY

Removal

1) Remove pump from vehicle. See POWER STEERING PUMP REMOVAL & INSTALLATION in this

Fig. 6: Drive Shaft Bearing Removal

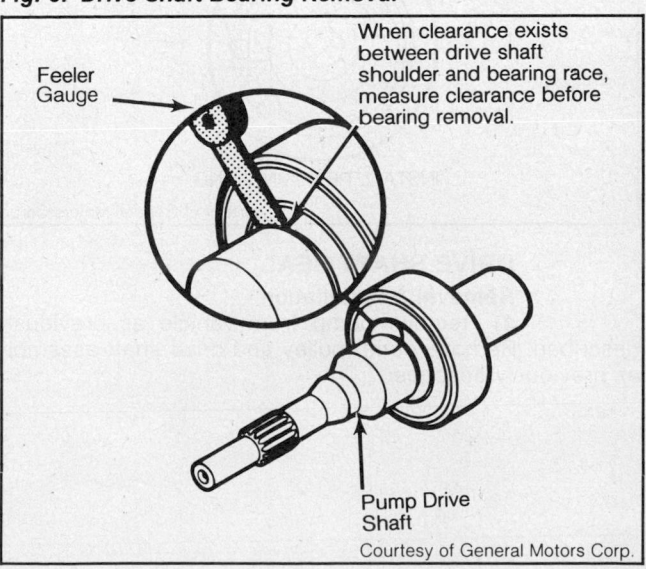

When clearance exists between drive shaft shoulder and bearing race, measure clearance before bearing removal.

Feeler Gauge

Pump Drive Shaft

Courtesy of General Motors Corp.

Fig. 4: Removal & Installation of Return Tube

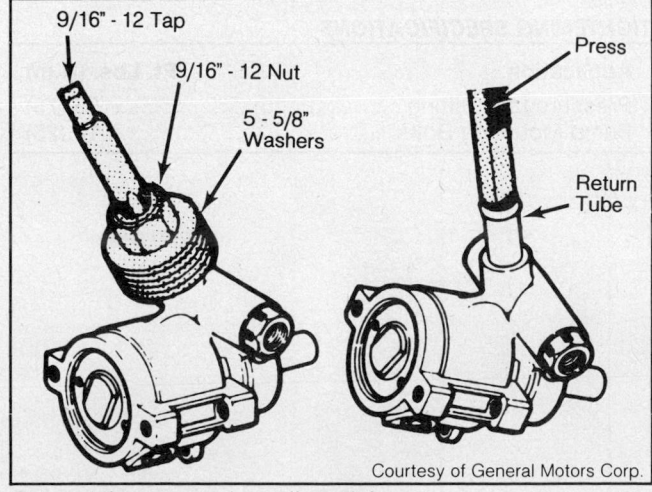

9/16" - 12 Tap
9/16" - 12 Nut
5 - 5/8" Washers
Press
Return Tube

Courtesy of General Motors Corp.

Return tube not used on all models.

Power Steering Pumps

SAGINAW VANE WITH REMOTE RESERVOIR (Cont.)

article. Remove pump pulley. See POWER STEERING PUMP PULLEY REMOVAL & INSTALLATION in this article.

2) Using snap ring pliers, remove retaining ring. Remove drive shaft and bearing assembly from housing. To remove bearing from shaft, support bearing inner race and press bearing off shaft. When clearance exists between drive shaft shoulder and bearing inner race, measure clearance before bearing removal and note. *See Fig. 6.*

Installation

To install, press bearing to shoulder of drive shaft or to clearance measured prior to disassembly. *See Fig. 7.* Slide assembly into housing while rotating drive shaft so shaft serations engage with rotor. Bottom bearing in housing. Install retaining ring with beveled side down. *See Fig. 7.*

Fig. 7: Bearing & Retaining Ring Installation

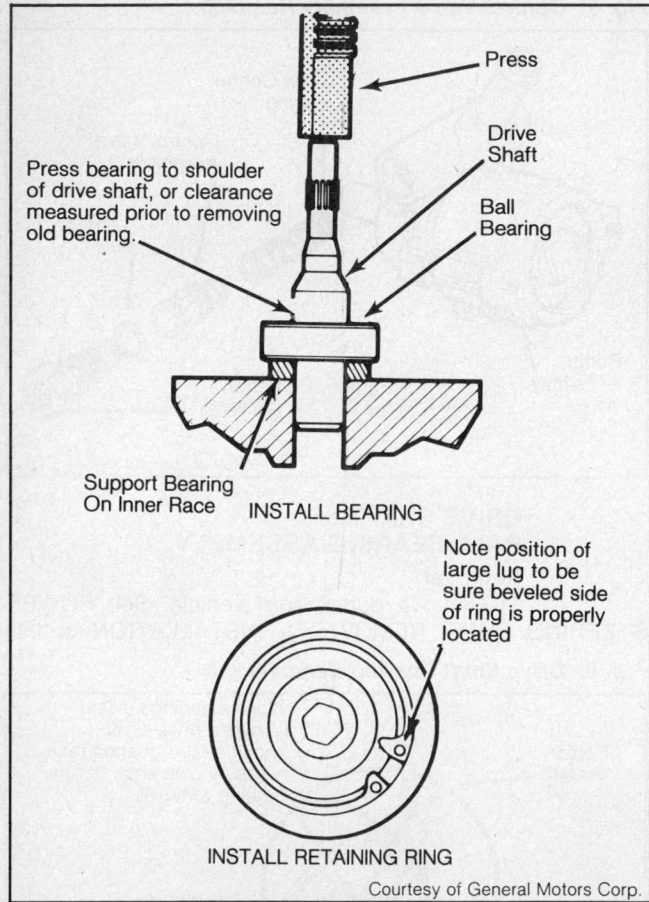

Courtesy of General Motors Corp.

DRIVE SHAFT SEAL

Removal & Installation

1) Remove pump from vehicle as previously described. Remove pump pulley and drive shaft assembly as previously described.

2) Using a screwdriver, pry old seal from housing. To install, use a suitable socket to drive oil seal into housing until bottomed. Install drive shaft, pump pulley and pump as previously described.

ROTATING GROUP

Removal

1) Remove pump from vehicle as previously described. Remove pump pulley and drive shaft assembly as previously described. Using a small punch in access hole, remove retaining ring.

2) Using a 5/8" piece of bar stock, press on pressure plate hub from drive shaft side of housing until thrust plate can be removed. Remove "O" ring seal from housing.

3) Remove pump rotor, rotor vanes, pump ring dowel pins, pump ring, pressure plate and pressure plate spring from housing. It may be necessary to use a press to remove pressure plate from pump cavity.

Installation

1) Lubricate and install new "O" ring seal into sleeve assembly. Insert small dowel pin into housing. Install pressure plate spring over sleeve assembly into housing. Lubricate and install new "O" ring seal onto pressure plate.

2) Mark top of pressure plate directly over dowel pin hole in plate. This will aid in aligning dowel pin. Install pressure plate in housing. Be sure dowel pin and hole in pressure plate properly engage.

3) Install 2 pump ring dowel pins in holes in pressure plate. Slide pump ring over these 2 pins. Be sure identification marks on pump ring are facing upward. Install rotor with counter bore side toward drive shaft end of housing. Add the 10 pump vanes.

4) Lubricate thrust plate "O" ring seal and install in housing. Install thrust plate in housing. Be sure that dimples in thrust plate line up with bolt holes in housing and that thrust plate engages pump ring dowel pins.

5) Using a press, press thrust plate in only far enough to get retaining ring in place. Install retaining ring with opening of ring centered with bolt hole in housing nearest to access hole.

6) Install pump pulley. Install pump in vehicle. Adjust belt tension, refill fluid reservoir. Bleed system.

TIGHTENING SPECIFICATIONS

Application	Ft. Lbs. (N.m)
Pressure Line Fitting	55 (75)
Pump Mounting Bolts	18 (25)

ALL MODELS

GENERAL INFORMATION

All steering component fasteners are made of special quality materials. Replacement fasteners must be of same material. Do not weld, heat or bend steering linkage to repair or straighten. Tighten all fasteners to specification.

When installing cotter pins, tighten nut to lower specified torque, then tighten nut to next slot that lines up with stud hole. Always use NEW cotter pins during reassembly. Hammering on ball studs may result in damage to threads. Ensure threads are clean and lightly lubricated prior to tightening.

REMOVAL & INSTALLATION

TIE RODS

Removal
(Rack & Pinion Steering Gear)

1) Raise and support vehicle. Remove cotter pins and castle nuts from tie rod ends. Using a puller, separate tie rod ends from steering knuckle. Remove tie rod end lock nuts. Mark position of tie rod end for reassembly reference.

2) Unscrew tie rod ends from tie rod. Remove outer boot clamps. Slide boots back out of way. Remove steering gear from vehicle (if necessary). See appropriate article in MANUAL STEERING GEAR or POWER STEERING GEAR in this section.

3) Bend back tab lock washers. Position rack to allow wrench to fit on end teeth. Holding rack, unscrew tie rod from rack by turning tie rod ball joint. Remove and discard tab lock washers.

Installation

1) Install new tab lock washers. Install tie rod. Tighten ball joint to specifications. Pull boots back, into position. Install outer boot clamps. Noting marks made during removal, install tie rod end lock nuts and tie rod ends.

2) Insert tie rod ends into steering knuckles. Install castle nuts and NEW cotter pins. Lower vehicle. Adjust toe-in. See WHEEL ALIGNMENT SPECIFICATIONS & PROCEDURES in WHEEL ALIGNMENT section. Tighten tie rod end lock nuts.

Removal
(Recirculating Ball Steering Gear)

1) Raise and support vehicle. Remove cotter pins and castle nuts from inner and outer tie rod ends. Using a puller, separate tie rod ends from steering knuckle and center link.

2) To remove tie rod ends from adjusting sleeve, loosen clamp bolts. Unscrew tie rod ends, noting number of turns necessary for reassembly reference.

Installation

1) If tie rod ends were removed, apply penetrating oil to clamps, tie rod threads and adjusting sleeve. Wipe threads clean. Lubricate threads with EP chassis lube. Install adjusting sleeve clamps.

2) Thread tie rod ends same number of turns required during removal. Ensure both ends are equal distance (within 3 threads) into sleeve.

3) Install tie rod assembly, castle nuts and NEW cotter pins. Properly position adjusting sleeve clamps. Lower vehicle. Adjust toe-in. See WHEEL ALIGN-MENT SPECIFICATIONS & PROCEDURES in WHEEL ALIGNMENT section. Tighten clamp bolts.

CENTER LINK

Removal & Installation

Raise and support vehicle. Remove cotter pins and castle nuts. Using a puller, separate inner tie rod ends, idler arm and pitman arm from center link. Remove center link from vehicle. Reverse removal procedure to install. Ensure idler arm stud seal is in place. Lower vehicle. Adjust toe-in.

IDLER ARM

Removal

1) Raise vehicle. Separate center link from idler arm. Remove 2 idler arm mounting bolts. If idler arm support is disconnected from frame for other work, wire support to idler arm to prevent rotation if equipped with a threaded bushing (G.M. Saginaw linkage types).

Fig. 1: Idler Arm positioning

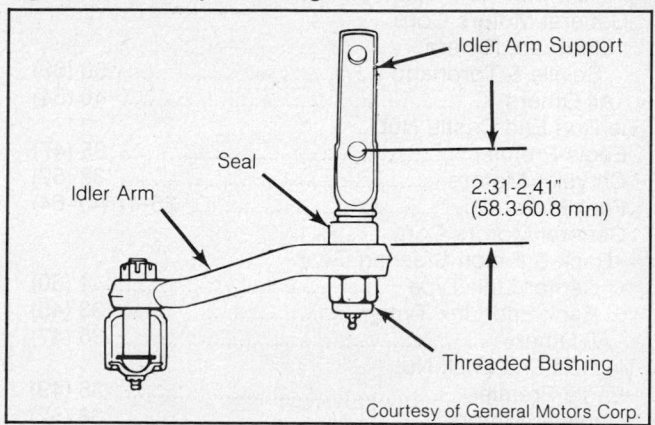

Courtesy of General Motors Corp.

2) Idler arm should be replaced when a vertical force of 25 lbs. (11 kg) is applied at center link end of idler arm, and vertical lash exceeds .13" (3.3 mm).

Installation

To install, reverse removal procedure. On General Motors models equipped with threaded bushing, thread idler arm support into bushing until the distance between the centerline of the lower mounting hole on the support and the upper face of the idler arm is 2.31-2.41" (58.3-60.8 mm). See Fig. 1. Idler arm must freely rotate 90 degrees in both directions from straight ahead.

PITMAN ARM

Removal & Installation

1) Raise and support vehicle. On Eldorado, Riviera, Seville and Toronado, disconnect steering gear from frame. On all models, mark pitman arm-to-steering shaft for reassembly reference.

2) Remove center link ball joint stud cotter pin and nut. Using a puller, separate center link from pitman arm. DO NOT hammer on end of puller.

3) Remove pitman arm retaining nut. Using a puller, separate pitman arm from steering gear. To install, reverse removal procedure. Tighten nuts to specification.

Steering Linkage

ALL MODELS (Cont.)

TIGHTENING SPECIFICATIONS

Application	Ft. Lbs. (N.m)
Idler Arm-to-Center Link Nut	
Chrysler Motors	40 (54)
Ford Motor Co.	60-70 (81-95)
General Motors Corp.	
Eldorado, Riviera,	
Seville & Toronado	61 (83)
All Others	40 (54)
Idler Arm-to-Frame	
Chrysler Motors	70 (95)
Ford Motor Co.	85-95 (115-129)
General Motors Corp.	
Camaro	60 (81)
Eldorado, Seville,	
Toronado & Riviera	40 (54)
All Others	61 (83)
Pitman Arm-to-Center Link Nut	
Chrysler Motors	40 (54)
Ford Motor Co.	43-47 (58-64)
General Motors Corp.	
Eldorado, Riviera,	
Seville & Toronado	50 (68)
All Others	40 (54)
Tie Rod End Castle Nut	
Eagle Premier	35 (47)
Chrysler Motors	38 (52)
Ford Motor Co.	35-47 (47-64)
General Motors Corp.	
Rack & Pinion Steering Gear	
Center-Link Type	44 (60)
Rack End-Link Type	33 (45)
All Others	35 (47)
Tie Rod End Lock Nut	
Eagle Premier	36 (49)
Chrysler Motors	38 (52)
Ford Motor Co.	35-50 (47-68)
General Motors Corp.	50 (68)
Tie Rod-to-Steering Rack	
Chrysler Motors	70 (95)
Eagle Premier	55 (75)
Ford Motor Co.	55-65 (75-88)
General Motors	
Center-Link Type	65 (88)
Rack End-Link Type	70 (95)

Section 13

TRANSMISSION SERVICING

CONTENTS

NOTE: ALSO SEE GENERAL INDEX.

IMPORTANT: For information on manual transmission removal and installation, see CLUTCHES section.

Transmission Applications

AUTOMATIC TRANSMISSIONS

MANUFACTURER & MODEL	TRANSMISSION MODEL
CHRYSLER MOTORS	
Aries America, Caravelle, Daytona, Dynasty, Horizon America, Lancer, LeBaron, LeBaron GTS, New Yorker, Omni America, Reliant America, Shadow, Sundance & 600 – 2.2L, 2.2L (Turbo) & 2.5L	Torqueflite A-413 Transaxle
Diplomat, Fifth Avenue & Gran Fury – 5.2L	Torqueflite A-904-LA
Eagle	
Premier – 2.5L	Model AR-4 4-Speed Electronic Transaxle
Premier – 3.0L	Model ZF 4HP 18 Transaxle
FORD MOTOR CO.	
Escort & EXP – 1.9L Tempo & Topaz – 2.3L	Ford Motor Co. 3-Speed ATX Transaxle
Cougar, Mustang & Thunderbird – 2.3L	Ford Motor Co. 4-Speed A4LD
Cougar & Thunderbird – 3.8L & 5.0L	Ford Motor Co. AOD
Mustang – 5.0L W/EFI Plus	Ford Motor Co. 4-Speed AOD
Mustang – 5.0L W/SEFI	Ford Motor Co. 4-Speed A4LD
Sable & Taurus – 2.5L & 3.8L	Ford Motor Co. 4-Speed AXOD Transaxle
Taurus – 3.0L	Ford Motor Co. 3-Speed ATX Transaxle
Continental – 3.8L	Ford Motor Co. 4-Speed AXOD
LTD Crown Victoria, Grand Marquis, Town Car & Mark VII – 5.0L & 5.8L (Police)	Ford Motor Co. 4-Speed AOD
GENERAL MOTORS	
BUICK Century – 2.5L & 2.8L Skyhawk – 2.0L Skylark – 2.5L & 3.0L CADILLAC – Cimarron – 2.8L CHEVROLET Beretta & Corsica – 2.0L & 2.8L Cavalier – 2.0L & 2.8L, Celebrity – 2.5L & 2.8L OLDSMOBILE Calais – 2.3L, 2.5L & 3.0L, Ciera – 2.5L & 2.8L Firenza – 2.0L & 2.0L (HO) PONTIAC Fiero – 2.5L & 2.8L Grand Am – 2.0L (Turbo), 2.3L & 2.5L Sunbird – 2.0L & 2.0L (Turbo), 6000 – 2.5L & 2.8L	Turbo Hydra-Matic 125C Transaxle
BUICK LeSabre & Electra Estate Wagon – 5.0L CADILLAC – Brougham – 5.0L CHEVROLET Caprice & Monte Carlo – 4.3L & 5.0L OLDSMOBILE – Custom Cruiser & Cutlass Supreme – 5.0L PONTIAC – Safari Wagon – 5.0L	Turbo Hydra-Matic 200-4R
CADILLAC – Brougham 5.0L (High Output)	Turbo Hydra-Matic 400

AUTOMATIC TRANSMISSIONS (Cont.)

MANUFACTURER & MODEL	TRANSMISSION MODEL
GENERAL MOTORS (Cont.)	
BUICK	
Century – 2.8L & 3.8L, Electra – 3.8L	
LeSabre, Riviera & Reatta – 3.8L	
Regal – 2.8L	
CADILLAC	
DeVille, Eldorado, Fleetwood & Seville – 4.5L	
CHEVROLET – Celebrity – 2.8L	
OLDSMOBILE	
Ciera – 2.8L & 3.8L, Delta 88 – 3.8L,	
Ninety-Eight & Toronado – 3.8L	
Cutlass – 2.8L	
PONTIAC	
Bonneville – 3.8L	
Grand Prix & 6000 – 2.8L	Turbo Hydra-Matic 440-T4 Transaxle
CHEVROLET	
Camaro – 2.8L, 5.0L & 5.7L	
Caprice – 4.3L, 5.0L & 5.7L (Police)	
Corvette – 5.7L	
Monte Carlo – 4.3L & 5.0L	
OLDSMOBILE – Custom Cruiser & Cutlass Supreme – 5.0L	
PONTIAC	
Firebird – 2.8L, 5.0L & 5.7L	
Safari Wagon – 5.0L	Turbo Hydra-Matic 700-R4
CHEVROLET	
Nova – 1.6L (Carbureted)	Toyota A131L 3-Speed Transaxle
Nova – 1.6L (DOHC, EFI)	Toyota A240E 4-Speed Transaxle

Transmission Application
MANUAL TRANSMISSIONS

MANUFACTURER & MODEL	TRANSMISSION MODEL
CHRYSLER MOTORS Aries America, Daytona, Horizon America, Lancer LeBaron, LeBaron GTS, Omni America, Reliant America Shadow, & Sundance – 2.2L, 2.2L (Turbo) & 2.5L	A-520, A-525 & A-555 5-Speed Transaxle
FORD MOTOR CO. Escort & EXP – 1.9L Tempo & Topaz – 2.3L Cougar & Thunderbird – 2.3L Turbo Mustang – 2.3L & 5.0L (EFI PLUS) Taurus – 3.0L	Ford Motor Co. 4 or 5-Speed MTX Transaxle T50D 5-Speed Overdrive T50D 5-Speed Overdrive Ford Motor Co. 5-Speed MTX Transaxle

GENERAL MOTORS
BUICK – Skyhawk – 2.0L
CHEVROLET
  Beretta & Corsica – 2.0L
  Cavalier – 2.0L
OLDSMOBILE
  Calais – 2.5L
  Firenza – 2.0L
PONTIAC
  Fiero – 2.8L
  Grand Am – 2.5L
  Sunbird – 2.0L
	Isuzu 76 MM 5-Speed Transaxle

CADILLAC – Cimarron – 2.8L
CHEVROLET
  Beretta & Corsica – 2.8L
  Cavalier & Celebrity – 2.8L
OLDSMOBILE
  Calais – 2.3L
  Cutlass Ciera & Cutlass – 2.8L
PONTIAC
  Fiero – 2.5L
  Grand Prix & 6000 – 2.8L
  Grand Am – 2.0L & 2.3L
  Sunbird – 2.0L Turbo
	Muncie 76 MM 5-Speed Transaxle

CHEVROLET – Camaro – 2.8L & 5.0L PONTIAC – Firebird – 2.8L & 5.0L	Borg-Warner 77 MM 5-Speed
CHEVROLET – Corvette – 5.7L	Doug Nash 83 MM 4-Speed W/Overdrive
CHEVROLET – Nova – 1.6L	Toyota C51 5-Speed Transaxle

Automatic Transmissions

OIL PAN GASKET IDENTIFICATION

Fig. 1: Chrysler Motors A-904-LA

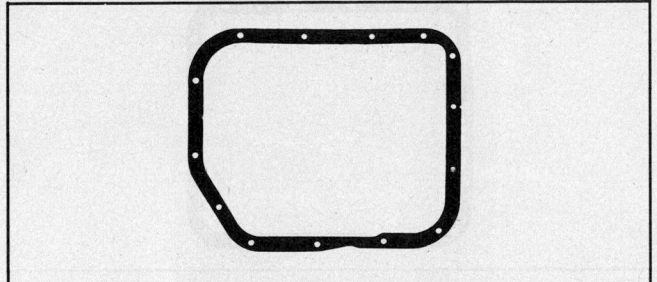

Fig. 2: Chrysler Motors A-413

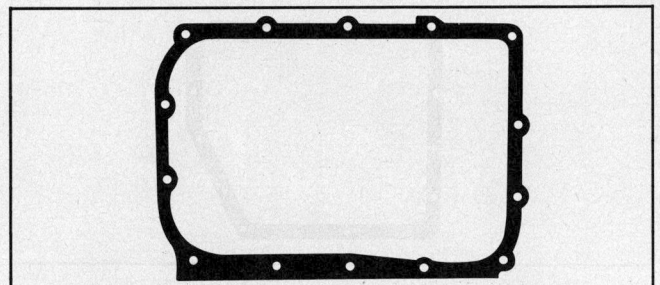

Fig. 3: Chrysler Motors A-727

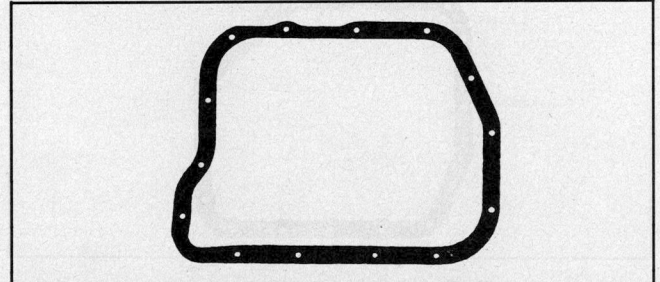

Fig. 4: Eagle Premier AR-4

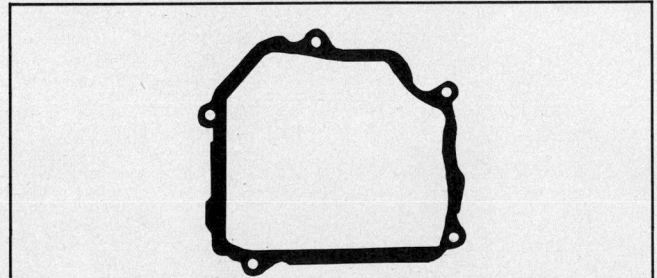

Fig. 5: Eagle Premier ZF 4HP 18

Fig. 6: Ford Motor Co. A4LD

Fig. 7: Ford Motor Co. AOD

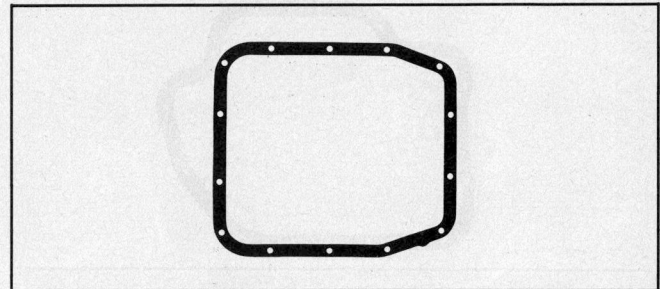

Fig. 8: Ford Motor Co. ATX

Fig. 9: Ford Motor Co. AXOD

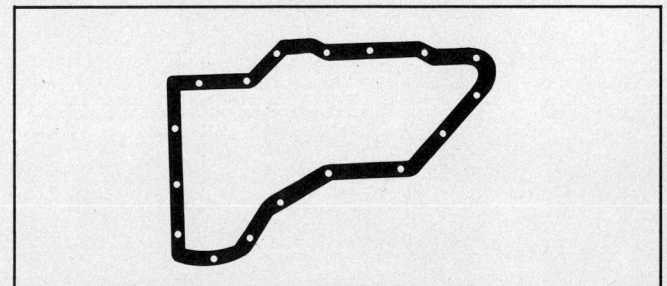

Fig. 10: General Motors Corp. THM 125C

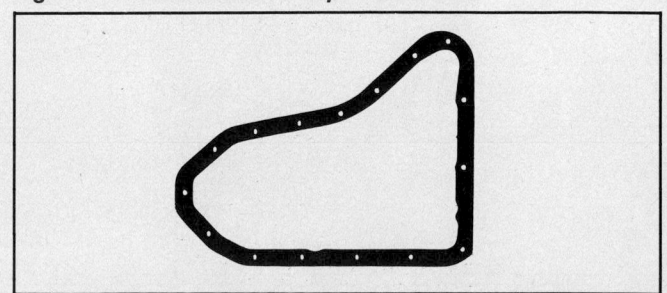

Automatic Transmissions

OIL PAN GASKET IDENTIFICATION (Cont.)

Fig. 11: General Motors THM 200-4R

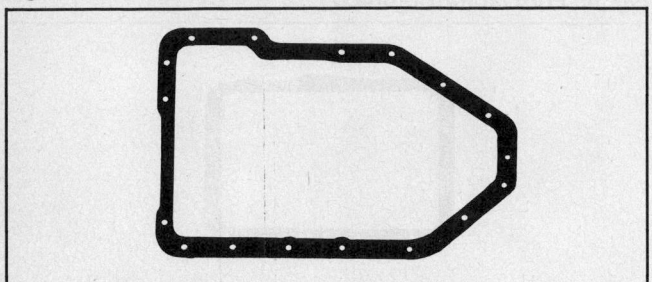

Fig. 12: General Motors THM 400

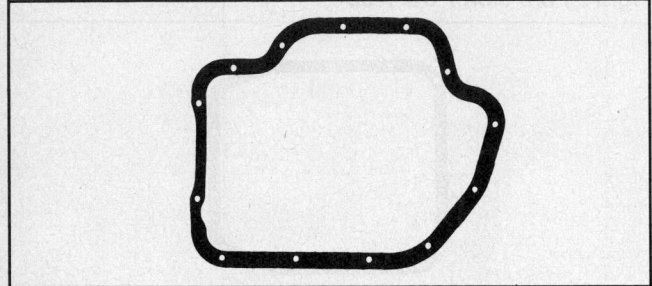

Fig. 13: General Motors THM 440-T4

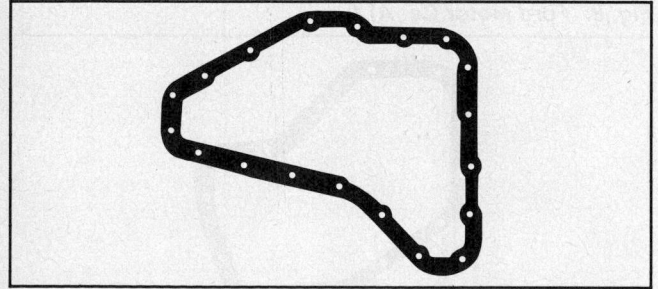

Fig. 14: General Motors THM 700-R4

Fig. 15: General Motors Nova A131L

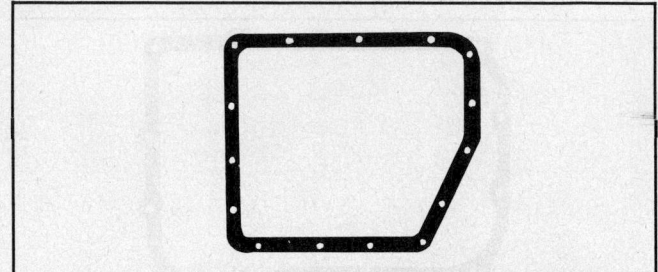

Fig. 16: General Motors Nova A240E

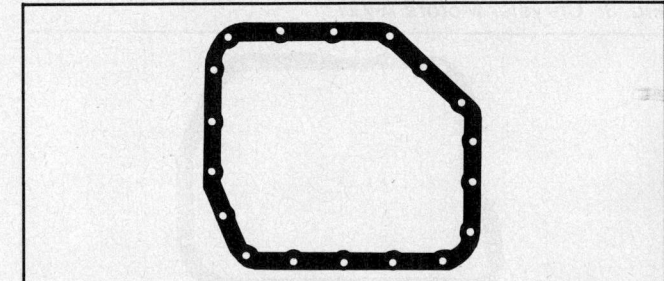

CHRYSLER MOTORS

LUBRICATION

SERVICE INTERVALS

Check fluid level every 6 months. Draining, refilling and band adjustments are not required under normal driving conditions. Under heavy duty (servere service) conditions, change fluid, replace filter, and adjust bands every 15,000 miles.

CHECKING FLUID LEVELS

RWD Models

1) With vehicle on level ground, apply parking brake. Start engine and run at curb idle. Shift gear selector through all positions, ending in Neutral.

2) Fluid level should be in crosshatch area on dipstick. Check condition of fluid for contamination.

FWD Models

1) With vehicle on level ground, apply parking brake, and run engine at curb idle for at least 60 seconds. Shift selector through all positons, ending in Park.

2) Fluid level should be in crosshatch area of dipstick marked "WARM" or "HOT", depending on fluid temperature. Check condition of fluid for contamination or burned smell. Do not overfill. Fully seat dipstick.

RECOMMENDED FLUID

Use only Dexron II ATF. Chrysler Motors does not recommend the use of any additives in transmissions.

FLUID CAPACITY

NOTE: **Transmission and converter assembly capacities given below are approximate. Correct fluid level should be determined by mark on dipstick.**

TRANSMISSION REFILL CAPACITIES

Application	Qts. (L)
A-904-LA (Lock-Up)	[1] 8.1 (7.7)
A-727 (Lock-Up)	8.4 (8.0)
A-413	[2] 9.0 (8.4)

[1] – Add .5 pts. (.2L) for non-lock-up converter or auxiliary oil coolers.
[2] – Add 1.4 pts. (.7L) for fleet models.

DRAINING & REFILLING

1) Loosen oil pan bolts at one corner. Tap pan to break it loose, allowing fluid to drain. Remove pan bolts and remove pan. Adjust rear band on RWD (if required).

2) Install a new filter and gasket (if equipped) on bottom of valve body and tighten screws. Clean pan.

3) On RWD models, install pan with new gasket. Make sure round magnet is over boss in right front corner of oil pan. On FWD models, install new pan, using RTV to form gasket.

4) On FWD models, add 4 qts. (3.8L) of ATF. On RWD models, add 2 qts. (1.9L) of ATF. Start engine and allow to idle for at least 2 minutes.

5) With engine at curb idle and parking brake applied, move shift selector lever through all positions, ending in "N" position ("P" on front wheel drive models). Add enough fluid to bring level to "ADD" mark on dipstick (1/8 below ADD on front wheel drive models).

6) Recheck fluid level after transmission has reached normal operating temperature. Do not overfill. Ensure dipstick is fully seated.

OIL PAN TIGHTENING SPECIFICATIONS

Transmission	INCH Lbs. (N.m)
FWD	165 (19)
RWD	150 (17)

ADJUSTMENTS

KICKDOWN BAND (FRONT)

NOTE: **Kickdown band adjusting screw is located on left side of transmission case above throttle linkage lever on rear wheel drive models, and on left side (top front) of transaxle case on front wheel drive models.**

1) Loosen adjusting screw lock nut, and back off 5 turns. After making sure adjusting screw turns freely in case, tighten screw to 72 INCH lbs. (8 N.m).

2) Back off screw 2 1/2 turns. Hold adjusting screw in this position and tighten lock nut to 35 ft. lbs. (47 N.m).

KICKDOWN BAND ADJUSTMENT

Application	Back Off Screw
FWD & RWD	2 1/2 Turns

LOW-REVERSE BAND (REAR)

Low-reverse band adjusting screw on FWD models is located on rear servo lever. It it not accessible unless valve body is removed. Transmission oil pan must be removed to provide access to band adjusting screw. Oil pan must also be removed on RWD models. *See Fig. 1.*

Fig. 1: Low-Reverse Band Adjustment Screw Location (RWD Models)

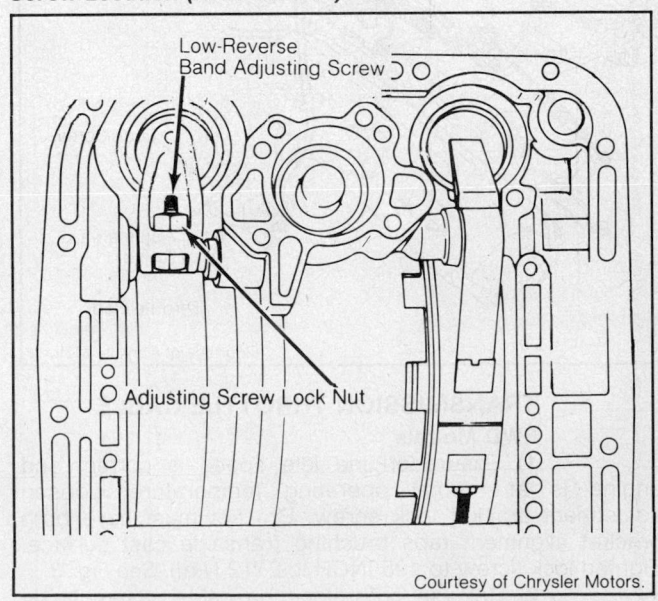

Courtesy of Chrysler Motors.

1) Drain transmission and remove oil pan. Loosen band adjusting screw lock nut about 5 turns. Ensure adjusting screw turns freely in case. On rear wheel drive models, tighten screw to 72 INCH lbs. (8 N.m). On front wheel drive models, tighten adjusting screw to 41 INCH lbs. (5 N.m).

2) On all models, back off adjusting screw specified number of turns given in LOW-REVERSE BAND ADJUSTMENT table. Hold in this position and tighten lock nut to 10 ft. lbs. (14 N.m) on FWD models and 30 ft. lbs. (41 N.m). Install oil pan and fill transmission with fluid.

LOW-REVERSE BAND ADJUSTMENT

Application	Back Off Screw
A-904-LA	4 Turns
A-727	2 Turns
A-413	3 1/2 Turns

TRANSMISSION THROTTLE ROD
RWD Models

1) Make sure carburetor is not on fast idle cam and idle speed is correctly set. Raise vehicle on hoist to make adjustment at transmission throttle lever. Loosen adjustable swivel lock screw. Swivel must be free to slide along flat end of throttle rod so that preload spring action is not restricted.

2) Hold transmission lever firmly forward against its internal stop, and tighten swivel lock screw. This completes throttle rod adjustment, as linkage backlash was automatically removed by the preload spring.

3) To check linkage freedom of operation, move throttle rod rearward, and release slowly. Ensure it returns to full forward position. See Fig. 2.

Fig. 2: Throttle Rod Adjustment Linkage For All RWD Models

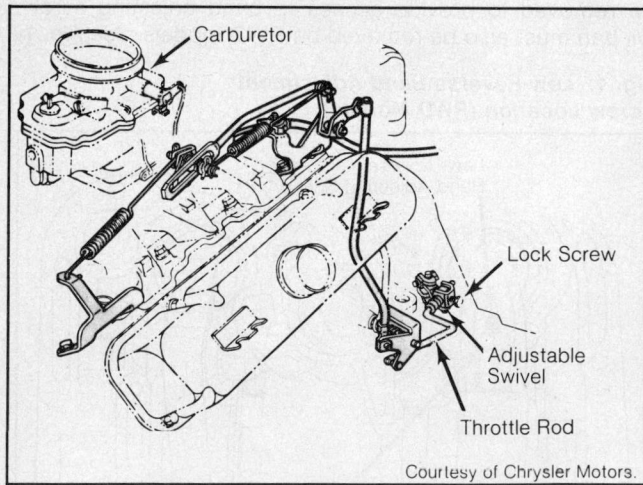

Courtesy of Chrysler Motors.

TRANSMISSION THROTTLE CABLE
FWD Models

1) Ensure engine idle speed is correct and engine is at normal operating temperature. Loosen adjustment bracket lock screw. Bracket must have both bracket alignment tabs touching transaxle cast surface. Tighten lock screw to 105 INCH lbs. (12 N.m). See Fig. 3.

2) Release cross-lock on cable assembly by pulling upward. To ensure correct adjustment, cable must be free to slide toward engine, against its stop, after cross-lock is released.

3) Move transaxle throttle control lever fully clockwise against its internal stop. Press cross-lock downward into locked position.

4) Move transaxle throttle lever counterclockwise. Slowly release it to ensure it will return to full clockwise position.

Fig. 3: Typical FWD Model Throttle Cable

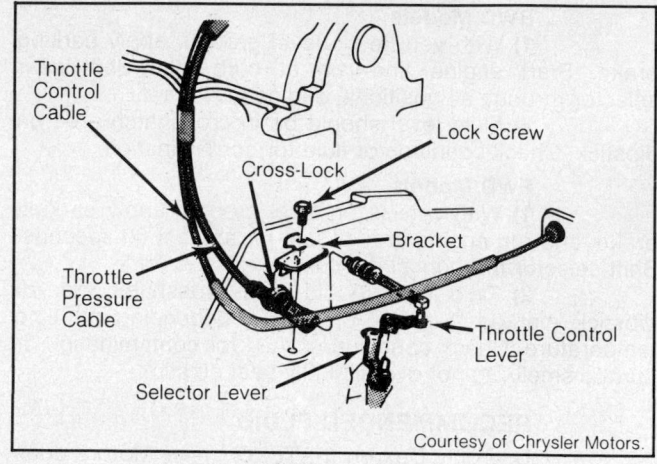

Courtesy of Chrysler Motors.

SHIFT LINKAGE
Column Shift (RWD Models)

1) Place shift selector in "P" position. Loosen adjustment swivel lock screw, making sure swivel block is free to turn on shift rod. Move shift lever on transmission all the way to rear detent position (Park). Tighten swivel lock screw to 90 INCH lbs. (10 N.m).

2) Check adjustment by moving shift selector. Detents for Drive and Neutral should be within limits of selector gate stops. Starter should operate only with selector in Park or Neutral. See Fig. 4.

Fig. 4: Column Shift Linkage For RWD Models

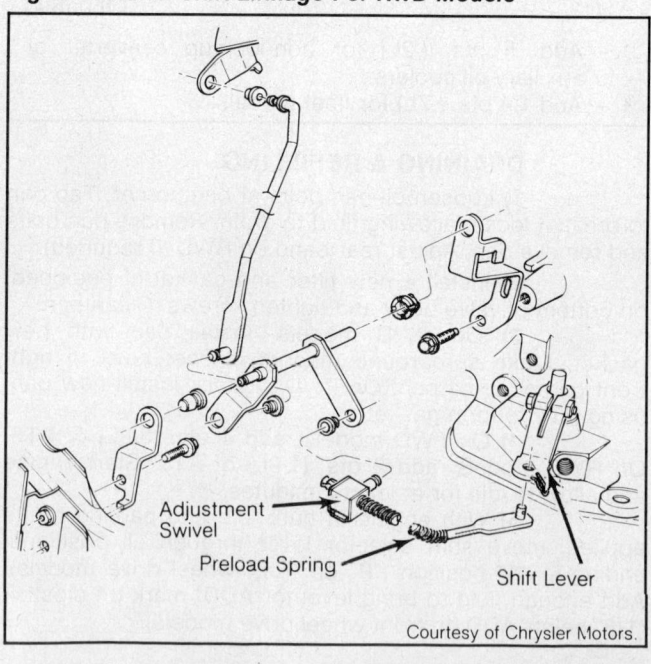

Courtesy of Chrysler Motors.

CHRYSLER MOTORS (Cont.)

CAUTION: On FWD and RWD models, replace old plastic grommets with new ones if necessary to remove linkage cable from lever. Use pliers to snap new grommet into lever and rod into grommet.

Console or Column Shift (FWD Models)

1) Place shift selector in "P" position. Loosen lock bolt on cable adjusting bracket on transaxle. *See Fig. 6.* On column shift models, ensure preload adjustment spring engages fork on transaxle bracket.

2) On all models, pull shift lever by hand all the way to front detent position (Park). Tighen lock screw to 100 INCH lbs. (11 N.m).

3) To check adjustment, gearshift lever should be within limits of hand lever gate stops when shifted through gear positions. Vehicle must only start in Park or Neutral.

Fig. 5: Floor Shift Linkage on FWD Models

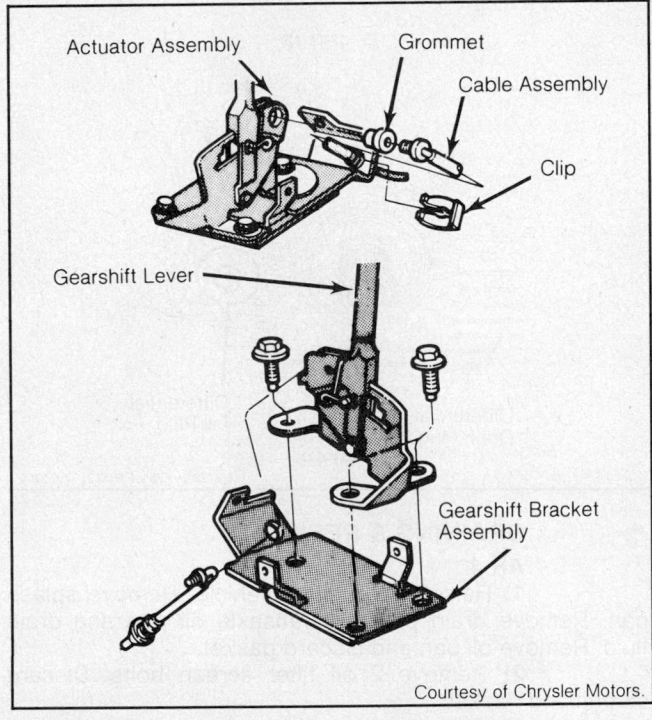

Courtesy of Chrysler Motors.

Fig. 6: Transmission Shift Lever on FWD Models

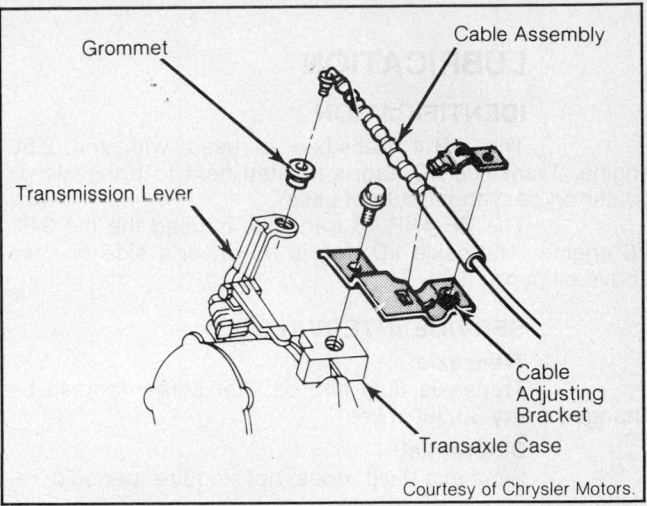

Courtesy of Chrysler Motors.

NEUTRAL SAFETY SWITCH

Combination neutral safety and back-up light switch is screwed into side of transmission case. Switch is nonadjustable. Switch may be tested for continuity using following method.

Testing

1) Center terminal of 3 terminal neutral safety and back-up light switch provides ground for starter solenoid circuit through shift lever in Park or Neutral positions only.

2) To test, remove wiring connector from switch and check for continuity between center pin of switch and case. Continuity should exist only when transmission is in Park or Neutral.

NOTE: Check shift linkage adjustment before replacing a switch that tests bad.

3) The back-up light switch circuit is through the 2 outside terminals of the switch. Continuity should exist between the 2 terminals only when transmission is in reverse. No continuity should exist from either terminal to case.

4) To replace, unscrew switch from case (some fluid will escape). Move shift selector lever to Park, and then to Neutral position. Check to see that switch operating fingers are centered in switch opening in case.

5) Install switch with new seal into case and tighten. Check transmission fluid level.

EAGLE

Premier

LUBRICATION

IDENTIFICATION

The AR-4 transaxle is used with the 2.5L engine. Transaxle I.D. tag is located next to transaxle oil cooler on passenger side of case.

The ZF 4HP 18 transaxle is used the the 3.0L V6 engine. Transaxle I.D. tag is on driver's side of case above oil pan.

SERVICE INTERVALS

Transaxle

Transaxle fluid and oil filter screen should be changed every 30,000 miles.

Differential

Synthetic fluid does not require periodic replacement.

CHECKING FLUID LEVELS

NOTE: Preferred method of checking fluid level is with transaxle cold. Fluid may also be checked with transaxle hot.

Transaxle

1) Place vehicle on level surface. Start and run engine at idle speed. Move shift lever through all gear positions ending in Park.

2) If transaxle is cold, fluid level should be at "FULL COLD" mark on dipstick. If transaxle is at normal operating temperature, fluid level should be at "FULL HOT" mark on other side of dipstick. About 1/4 quart is needed to increase level from "ADD" to "FULL" mark.

Differential

With vehicle on level surface, fluid level should be at bottom of fill plug hole. *See Fig. 1.*

RECOMMENDED FLUID

Transaxle

Use only Mercon type fluid.

Differential

Use SAE 75W-140 synthetic gear oil (Part No. 89982 200 945).

NOTE: Transaxle and differential are separate and require different lubricants.

FLUID CAPACITY

TRANSMISSION REFILL CAPACITY

Application	Dry Fill Qts. (L)	Overhaul Qts. (L)
Transaxle		
AR-4	2.8 (2.6)	7.4 (7.0)
ZF 4HP 18	5.6 (5.3)	2.8 (2.6)
Differential		
AR-4	.89 (.85)	
ZF 4HP 18	.73 (.70)	

Fig. 1: Differential Drain & Fill Plugs

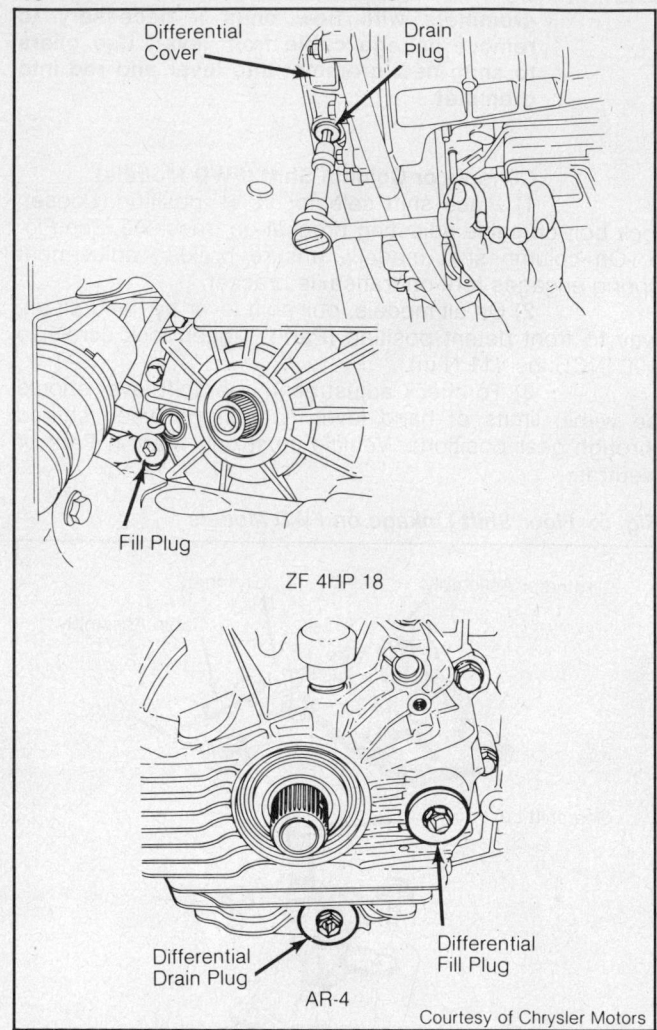

ZF 4HP 18

AR-4

Courtesy of Chrysler Motors

DRAINING & REFILLING

AR-4

1) Raise and support vehicle. Remove splash pan. Remove drain plug on transaxle oil pan and drain fluid. Remove oil pan and discard gasket.

2) Remove 2 oil filter screen bolts. Discard screen and gasket.

3) Use petroleum jelly to hold oil filter screen gasket in place. Install filter screen and tighten bolts to 46 INCH lbs. (5 N.m). Install oil pan with new gasket. Do not use any sealant.

NOTE: To prevent leaks, ensure all oil pan gasket hole spacers are in place before installation.

4) Use new seal ring on oil pan drain plug. Tighten drain plug to 177 INCH lbs. (20 N.m). Fill transaxle with ATF.

ZF 4HP 18

1) Raise and support vehicle. Remove splash shield. Loosen nut attaching dipstick tube to oil pan. Slide dipstick tube out to drain fluid.

2) Remove oil pan and discard gasket. Remove 10 oil filter screen cover bolts and remove cover. Remove oil filter screen and gasket.

EAGLE (Cont.)

3) Clean oil pan and magnet. Replace all parts using new gaskets and oil filter screen "O" ring. Ensure oil filter screen bolts are installed in correct position and tightened to correct torque. *See Fig. 2.* Fill transaxle with ATF.

NOTE: ZF 4HP 18 oil filter screen bolts are different lengths and must be replaced in original positions.

Fig. 2: ZF 4HP 18 Filter Screen Bolt Positions

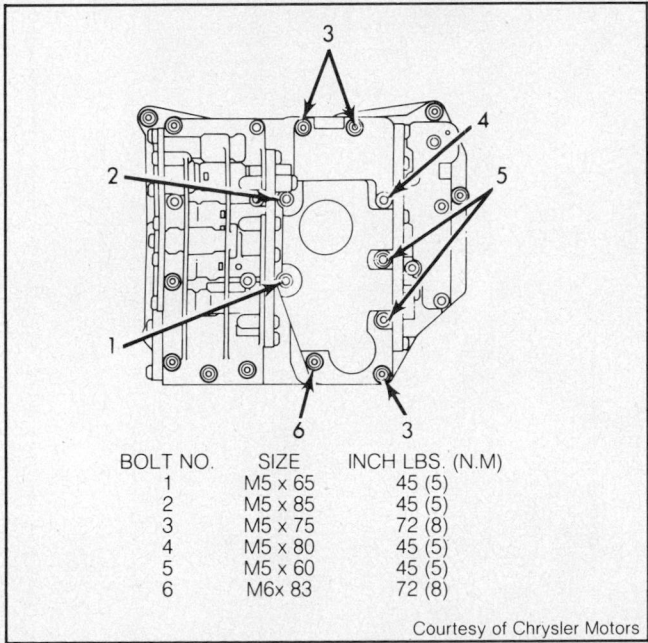

BOLT NO.	SIZE	INCH LBS. (N.M)
1	M5 x 65	45 (5)
2	M5 x 85	45 (5)
3	M5 x 75	72 (8)
4	M5 x 80	45 (5)
5	M5 x 60	45 (5)
6	M6x 83	72 (8)

Courtesy of Chrysler Motors

OIL PAN TIGHTENING SPECIFICATIONS

Application	INCH Lbs. (N.m)
AR-4	90 (10)
ZF 4HP 18	¹ 54 (6)

¹ – Specification for clamp nuts.

ADJUSTMENTS

THROTTLE VALVE CABLE

ZF 4HP 18

1) Loosen cable lock nuts and lift threaded shank out of engine bracket. *See Fig. 3.* Ensure throttle valve lever is in idle position.

2) Pull cable wire forward. Place a fabricated 1.55" (39.5 mm) gauge block between cable connector and cable end. Vernier calipers can be used to measure cable distance. *See Fig. 4.*

3) Pull cable shank rearward to detent position, but NOT to wide open throttle position. Detent position will have a definite feel, similiar to stop, when it is reached.

4) Hold shank at detent position and place it in engine bracket. Tighten lock nuts to lock shank in position. Remove gauge block. Detent position should be reached when cable travel is 1.52-1.59" (38.5-40.5 mm).

Fig. 3: ZF 4HP 18 Throttle Cable

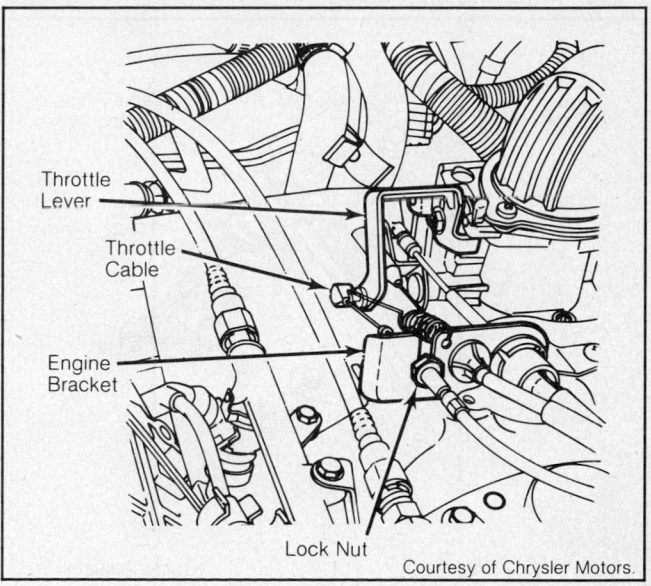

Courtesy of Chrysler Motors.

Fig. 4: Adjusting ZF 4HP 18 Throttle Cable

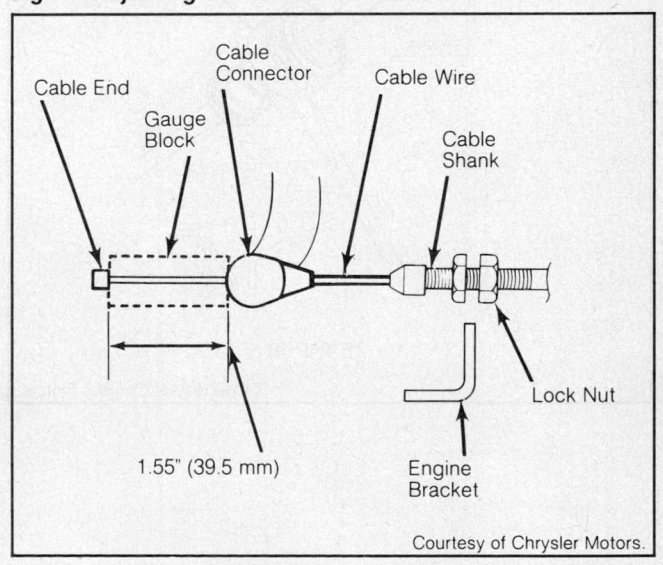

Courtesy of Chrysler Motors.

SHIFT CABLE

1) Shift transaxle into Park. Raise and support vehicle. Unlock shift cable by releasing clamp with screwdriver. *See Fig. 5.* Move clamp outward to release it.

2) Ensure tranaxle shift lever is in Park position and centered in Park detent (last rearward position). Lock shift cable by pressing adjuster clamp into position. Lower vehicle.

3) Turn ignition key to "LOCK" position. Shift lever should not be able to be moved out of Park. Turn ignition key to "ON." Engine should only start in Park and Neutral positions.

4) If engine starts in any other gear position, shift cable is out of adjustment or neutral safety switch is defective. Shift transaxle into Park. Ensure ignition key may return to "LOCK" position.

EAGLE (Cont.)

Fig. 5: Adjusting Shift Cable

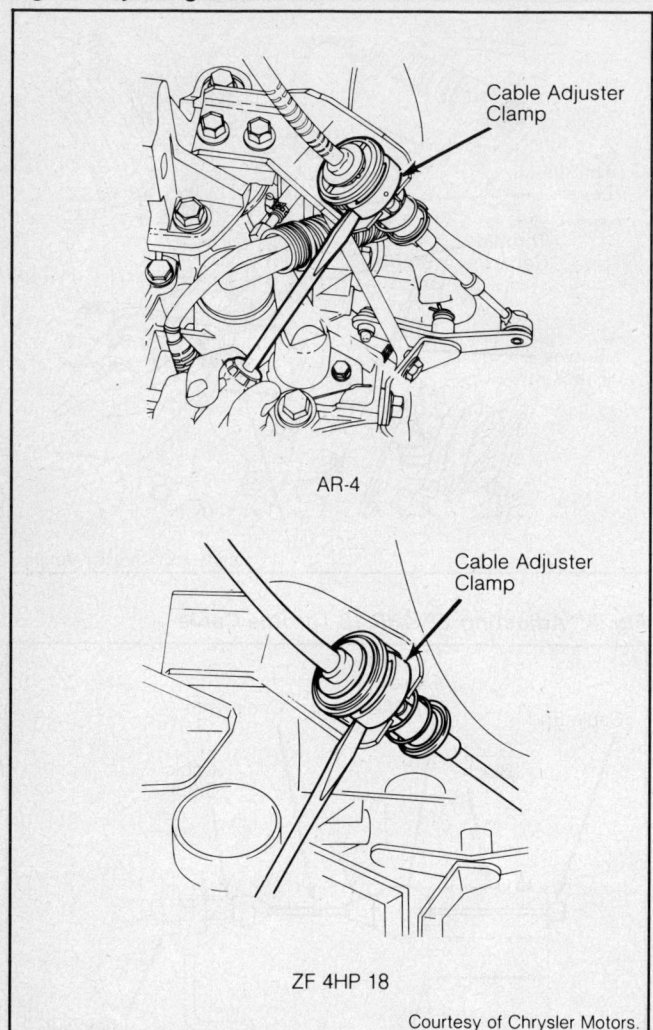

AR-4

ZF 4HP 18

Courtesy of Chrysler Motors.

NEUTRAL SAFETY SWITCH

Neutral safety switches for both transaxles are mounted on outside of case and are nonadjustable.

FORD MOTOR CO.

LUBRICATION

SERVICE INTERVALS

Check fluid level at every engine oil change. Fluid, filter changes and band adjustments are not required · under normal operation. Under heavy duty (severe service), change fluid and filter every 30 months or 30,000 miles. Adjust bands when fluid is changed.

CHECKING FLUID LEVEL

1) With transmission at normal operating temperature, place vehicle on level ground. Apply parking brake, and run engine at curb idle. Shift selector through all positions, ending in Park.

2) Fluid level should be in crosshatch area if checked at operating temperature. If transmission is at room temperature, fluid level should be between two dimples on bottom of dipstick.

3) Do not overfill. Check condition of fluid for contamination or burned smell. Fully reseat dipstick.

NOTE: AXOD transaxle can only have fluid level checked at normal operating temperature.

RECOMMENDED FLUID

For all 1988 models, Ford Motor Co. recommends using the new Mercon ATF in all automatic transmissions. Mercon is NOT recommended for power steering systems.

FLUID CAPACITY

NOTE: Transmission and converter assembly capacities given below are approximate. Correct fluid level should be determined by mark on dipstick, rather than by amount added.

TRANSMISSION REFILL CAPACITIES

Application	¹ Qts. (L)
AOD	12.3 (11.6)
ATX	8.3 (7.9)
AXOD	13.1 (12.5)
A4LD	9.5 (9.0)

¹ – Includes oil cooler (if equipped).

DRAINING & REFILLING

1) To drain torque converter on AOD transmission, remove lower engine dust cover. Rotate torque converter until drain plug is accessible. Remove plug and allow to drain.

2) On all models, loosen oil pan attaching bolts to drain fluid. Remove oil pan. On all except AOD transmissions, remove and clean filter screen. Reinstall filter screen using a new gasket. On AOD transmissions, discard used filter and gasket. Install new filter and gasket.

3) On AXOD transmission, ensure both "O" rings are changed if replacing filter. On all models, clean oil pan, and install pan with new gasket. Pour 3 qts. (2.8L) of fluid through filler tube. Check fluid level.

NOTE: Cooler and lines should be thoroughly flushed if transmission was removed for overhaul. Cooler Line Disconnecter (T82L-9500-AH) is necessary to remove cooler lines.

OIL PAN TIGHTENING SPECIFICATIONS

Transmission	INCH Lbs. (N.m)
AOD	72-124 (8-14)
ATX	144-204 (16-23)
AXOD	124-144 (14-16)
A4LD	96-124 (11-14)

FILTER SCREEN TIGHTENING SPECIFICATIONS

Transmission	INCH Lbs. (N.m)
AOD	80-97 (9-11)
ATX	80-108 (9-12)
A4LD	71-97 (8-11)

ADJUSTMENTS

INTERMEDIATE & OVERDRIVE BAND

A4LD

1) Clean all dirt from band adjusting screw area. Remove and discard adjusting screw lock nut. Install a new lock nut on adjusting screw, leaving lock nut loose.

2) Tighten band adjusting screw to 10 ft. lbs. (14 N.m). Back off adjusting screw EXACTLY 2 turns. Hold adjusting screw in this position and tighten lock nut to 40 ft. lbs. (54 N.m). *See Fig. 1.*

Fig. 1: Adjusting A4LD Bands

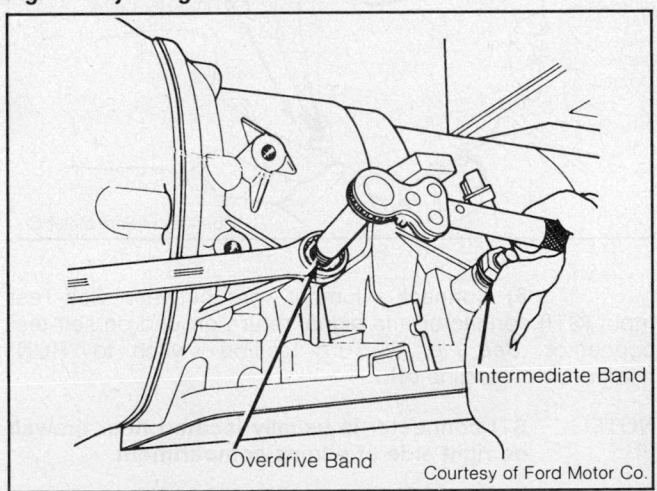

Intermediate Band

Overdrive Band

Courtesy of Ford Motor Co.

THROTTLE VALVE (T.V.) CONTROL

ATX (FWD)

1) On Escort, EXP, Tempo and Topaz with 2.3L or 1.9L CFI engines, verify vehicle has "learned idle." Set heater control lever to "FLOOR" position and heater fan to "OFF" position. Set parking brake. Start engine and run to normal operating temperature. Position wheels in straight ahead position. Place gear selector in Drive for one minute. Idle speed should decrease to setting defined on the engine emissions label.

FORD MOTOR CO. (Cont.)

2) Ensure parking brake and foot brake are applied during idle checking process. Depress and release accelerator to ensure idle returns to setting defined by engine emissions label. This confirms the processor has learned idle.

3) If idle speed does not return to proper setting, check for mechanical interference in accelerator and transaxle linkage. Vacuum leaks and misadjustment of throttle return control stop screw.

4) On 1.9L, 2.3L and 3.0L engines, engine must be at normal operating temperature and transaxle in Park.

5) Loosen bolt on sliding trunnion block at least one turn. Ensure block can slide freely on rod. *See Fig. 2.*

Fig. 2: Adjusting Throttle Valve Control on ATX Transaxle

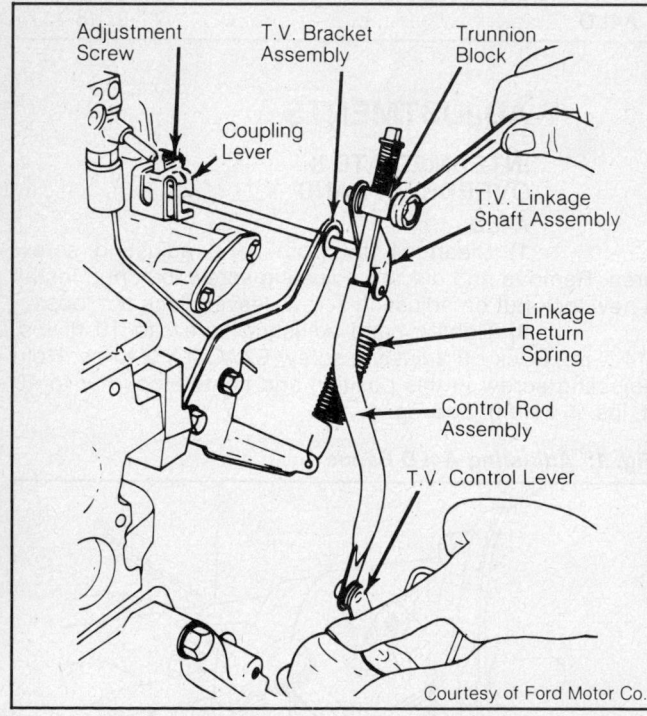

Courtesy of Ford Motor Co.

6) Connect a jumper wire between Self-Test Input (STI) connector and signal return ground on self-test connector. *See Fig. 3.* Turn ignition switch to "RUN" position, with engine off.

NOTE: STI connector is usually located near firewall on right side of engine compartment.

7) The ISC plunger will retract. When plunger is fully retracted after about 10 seconds, turn off key. Remove jumper wire.

8) Lightly pull up on transaxle T.V. control rod to ensure T.V. control lever is against its internal stop. Allow trunion to slide on rod to its natural position. While holding T.V. control lever, tighten trunnion block bolt.

NOTE: Carburetor linkage lever should also be readjusted if it is necessary to readjust idle speed by more than 50 RPM.

Fig. 3: Typical Location of Self-Test Connectors

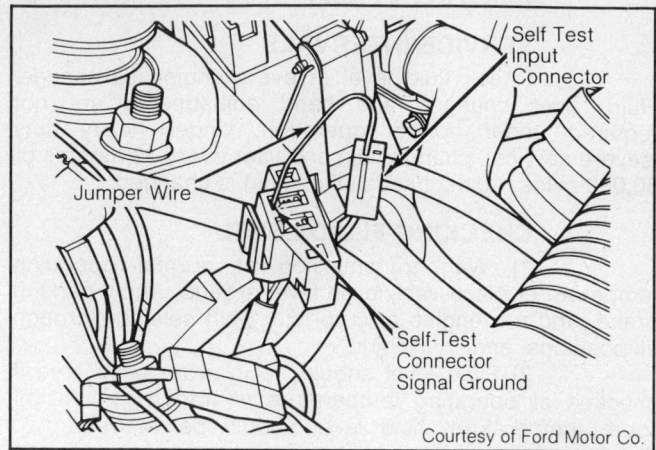

Courtesy of Ford Motor Co.

AOD (5.8L Police Special, Linkage Adjustment At Carburetor)

1) Engine must be at normal operating temperature. Remove air cleaner. Throttle lever must be resting on idle stop or throttle solenoid positioner stop. Place transmission selector lever in Neutral and set parking brake.

2) Back out linkage lever adjusting screw so screw end is flush with lever face. *See Fig. 4.* Turn in adjusting screw until a .005" (.127 mm) shim, or piece of writing paper fits snug between end of screw and throttle lever. Do not apply any load on lever while checking gap.

3) Turn in adjustment screw 3 turns. One turn minimum is permissible if screw travel is limited. If adjustment screw will not turn at least one turn or if it was not possible to obtain an initial gap as described in step **2)**, go to AOD (5.8L, POLICE SPECIAL, LINKAGE ADJUSTMENT AT TRANSMISSION).

Fig. 4: Typical Carburetor Throttle Linkage on 5.8L Police Special

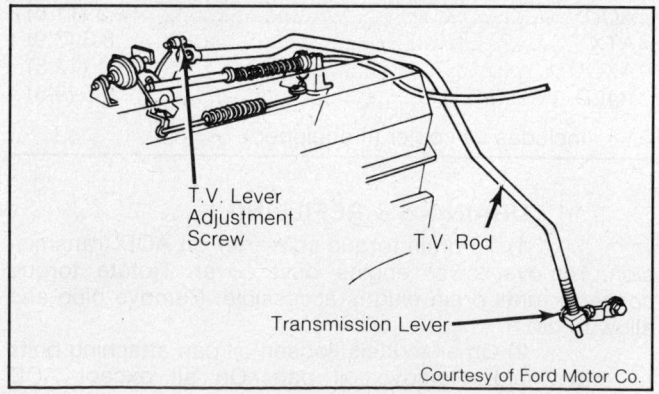

Courtesy of Ford Motor Co.

NOTE: Use transmission linkage adjustment for 5.8L if it was not possible to adjust T.V. linkage at carburetor. The following procedure must also be used if a NEW T.V. linkage rod is installed.

FORD MOTOR CO. (Cont.)

AOD (5.8L Police Special, Linkage Adjustment At Transmission)

1) Engine must be at normal operating temperature. Ensure engine is set at correct idle speed. Set carburetor at minimum idle stop. Place shift lever in Neutral and set parking brake.

2) Set linkage lever adjustment screw at approximately mid-range. If a new T.V. control linkage rod is being installed, connect linkage rod to carburetor.

3) Raise and support vehicle. Loosen bolt on sliding trunion block on T.V. control linkage rod. *See Fig. 4.* Push up on lower end of control rod to ensure control rod is against throttle lever.

4) Release force on rod. Rod must stay up. Push transmission T.V. control lever firmly against its internal stop. Tighten bolt on trunnion block.

5) Lower vehicle. Ensure throttle lever is still against minimum idle stop or throttle position solenoid stop. If not, repeat steps **2)** through **5)**.

AOD (Manual Locking T.V. Control Cable: 3.8L EFI Cougar & Thunderbird)

1) T.V. control pressure is checked and adjusted using a pressure gauge. Attach pressure gauge (0-60 psi) to T.V. port on right side of transmission. *See Fig. 5.* It may be necessary to use a 90 degree elbow to avoid contact with the exhaust system.

NOTE: Pressure gauge should have about 8 ft. of flexible hose attached so it may be read from passenger compartment.

Fig. 5: Checking T.V. Pressure (3.8L EFI, Thunderbird & Cougar)

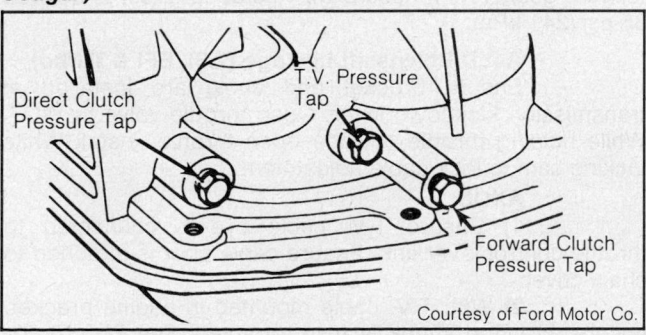

Courtesy of Ford Motor Co.

2) Insert Cable T.V. Gauge (T86L-70332-A) between crimped slug on end of cable and plastic cable fitting attached to throttle lever. *See Fig. 6.* Force crimped slug away from plastic fitting. Ensure T.V. gauge is pushed in as far as possible.

3) Engine and transmission must be at normal operating temperature. Set parking brake and place selector lever in Neutral. With gauge tool in place and engine idling in Neutral, T.V. pressure should be 30-40 psi (207-276 kPa).

NOTE: Do not check or set T.V. pressure in Park.

4) For best results, pressure should be as close to 33 psi (227 kPa) as possible. When shifted into forward gear, T.V. pressure will rise about 2 psi to desired 35 psi (241 kPa) pressure.

5) Pry up White toggle lever on cable adjuster located behind throttle body cable bracket. Adjuster

Fig. 6: Cougar & Thunderbird 3.8L Throttle Body

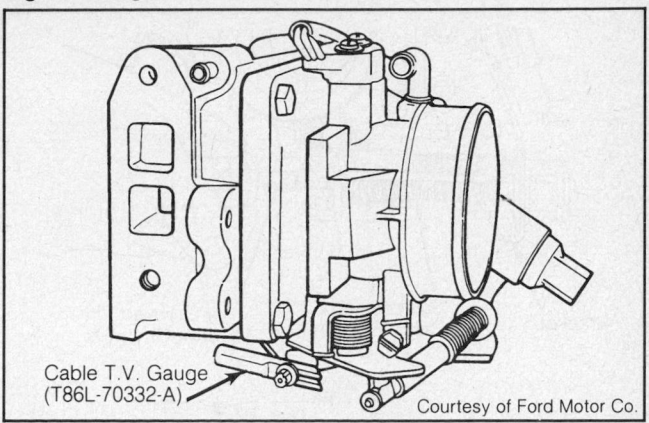

Cable T.V. Gauge (T86L-70332-A)

Courtesy of Ford Motor Co.

preload spring should cause adjusting slider to move away from throttle body and increase T.V. pressure.

6) Push on slide until T.V. pressure is 33 psi (227 kPa). *See Fig. 7.* While holding slider, lock toggle lever by pushing it down as far as it will go.

7) Remove gauge tool and allow cable to return to idle position. With engine idling and transmission in Neutral, T.V. pressure must be 0-4 psi (0-28 kPa).

8) If pressure is not 0-4 psi (0-28 kPa), reset pressure so it is less than 33 psi (227 kPa) but no less than 30 psi (207 kPa). Repeat steps **2)** through **7)**.

Fig. 7: Adjusting T.V. Pressure on 3.8L Cougar & Thunderbird

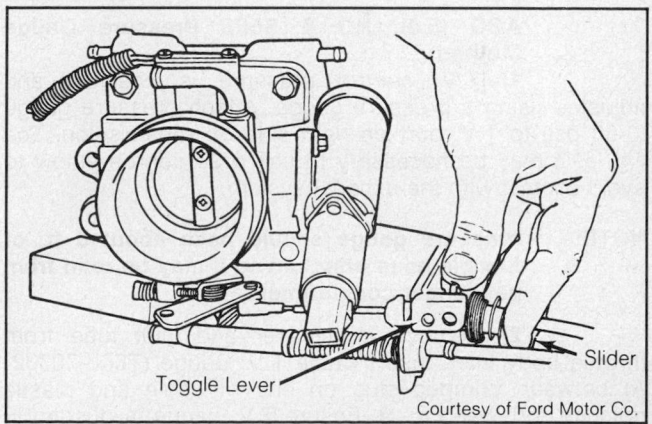

Toggle Lever

Slider

Courtesy of Ford Motor Co.

AOD (Self-Locking T.V. Control Cable: 5.0L HO & SEFI)

1) Remove air cleaner and inlet tube from throttle body inlet to expose throttle lever and cable assembly. Pry grooved pin on cable assembly out of grommet on throttle body lever. *See Fig. 8.* Push out White locking tab.

2) Ensure plastic block slides freely on notched rod. If not, White locking tab may not be pushed out far enough.

3) While holding throttle lever firmly against its idle stop, push grooved pin into grommet on throttle lever as far as it will go. DO NOT move throttle lever away from idle stop while pushing pin into grommet. Install air cleaner and inlet tube.

FORD MOTOR CO. (Cont.)

Fig. 8: Self-Locking T.V. Control Cable on 5.0L HO & SEFI

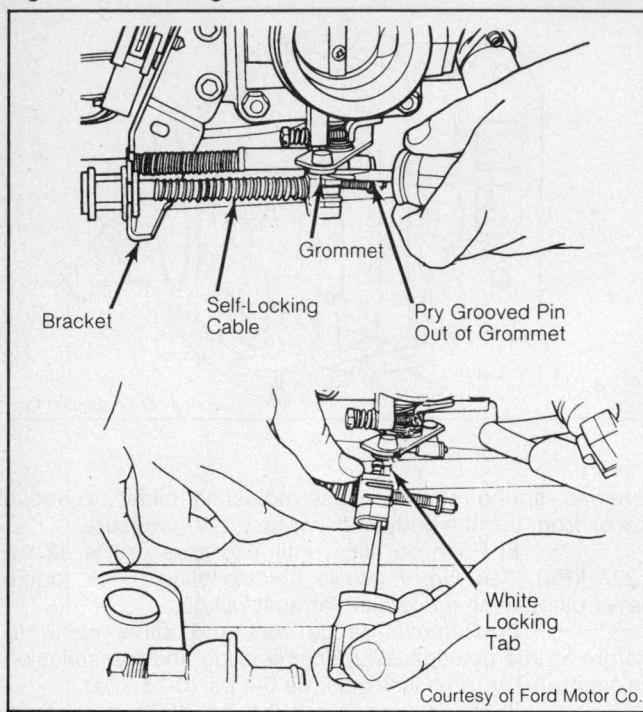

Bracket — Self-Locking Cable — Grommet — Pry Grooved Pin Out of Grommet — White Locking Tab

Courtesy of Ford Motor Co.

NOTE: **T.V. control linkage on AOD transmission with self-locking cable may also be adjusted with pressure gauge.**

AOD (5.0L HO & SEFI, Pressure Gauge Method)

1) T.V. control pressure is checked and adjusted using a pressure gauge. Attach pressure gauge (0-60 psi) to T.V. port on right side of transmission. See Fig. 5. It may be necessary to use a 90 degree elbow to avoid contact with the exhaust system.

NOTE: **Pressure gauge should have about 8 ft. of flexible hose attached so it may be read from passenger compartment.**

2) Remove air cleaner and inlet tube from throttle body inlet. Insert Cable T.V. Gauge (T86L-70332-A) between crimped slug on end of cable and plastic notched rod. See Fig. 9. Ensure T.V. gauge is pushed in as far as possible.

Fig. 9: Installing T.V. Gauge on 5.0L Throttle Cable

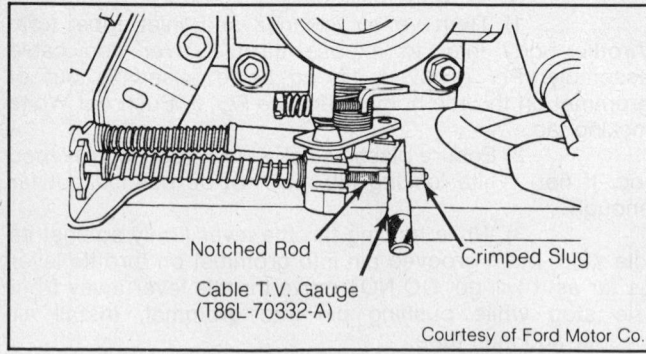

Notched Rod — Crimped Slug — Cable T.V. Gauge (T86L-70332-A)

Courtesy of Ford Motor Co.

3) Engine and transmission must be at normal operating temperature. Set parking brake and place selector lever in Neutral. With gauge tool in place and engine idling in Neutral, T.V. pressure should be 30-40 psi (207-276 kPa).

NOTE: **Do not check or set T.V. pressure in Park.**

4) If correct pressure is present, remove gauge tool. Allow engine to return to idle. With engine idling and transmission in Neutral, T.V. pressure must be 0-4 psi (0-28 kPa).

5) If pressures were not as specified in steps 3) and 4), readjust self-locking cable. See AOD (SELF-LOCKING T.V. CONTROL CABLE: 5.0L HO & SEFI).

6) Check T.V. pressure again. If pressure is still not correct, go to step 7).

7) Pry grooved pin out of grommet on throttle lever. Measure or mark location of plastic block on notched rod. Push out White locking tab. See Fig. 8.

8) Using mark or measurement on plastic block as reference, move plastic block towards throttle body to raise T.V. pressure. Move plastic block away from bracket to lower T.V. pressure. Push in White locking tab to secure block in position. Moving block one notch will change pressure about 2 psi.

9) Insert grooved pin into throttle body grommet. Ensure throttle lever is held firmly against idle stop while installing grooved pin. Check T.V. pressure using steps 2) through 4).

10) For best results, pressure should be as close to 33 psi (227 kPa) as possible with gauge tool installed and transmission in Neutral. When shifted into forward gear, T.V. pressure will rise about 2 psi to desired 35 psi (241 kPa).

A4LD Downshift Linkage (2.3L EFI & Turbo)

Ensure bracket and cable are installed at transmission kickdown lever. Open throttle valve to WOT. While holding throttle at wide open throttle, install White locking cam to lock cable adjustment.

AXOD

1) Ensure T.V. cable eye is connected to throttle control lever link. Ensure cable boot is attached to chain cover.

2) With T.V. cable mounted in engine bracket, ensure threaded shank is fully retracted. See Fig. 10. To retract shank, hold spring rest and wiggle top of threaded shank while pressing shank toward spring.

3) Attach end of T.V. cable to throttle body. Rotate throttle lever to wide open throttle position and release. Threaded shank must show movement or "ratchet" out of grip jaws. If no movement is observed, inspect T.V. cable system for broken or disconnected components and repeat procedure.

SHIFT LINKAGE (FWD)

ATX (Escort, EXP, Taurus, Tempo & Topaz)

1) Place gearshift lever in Drive. Gearshift lever must be held in rearward position during linkage adjustment.

2) Working at transaxle, loosen manual lever-to-control cable retaining nut. Move transaxle manual lever to Drive position (second detent from rear).

Fig. 10: Adjusting AXOD T.V. Cable

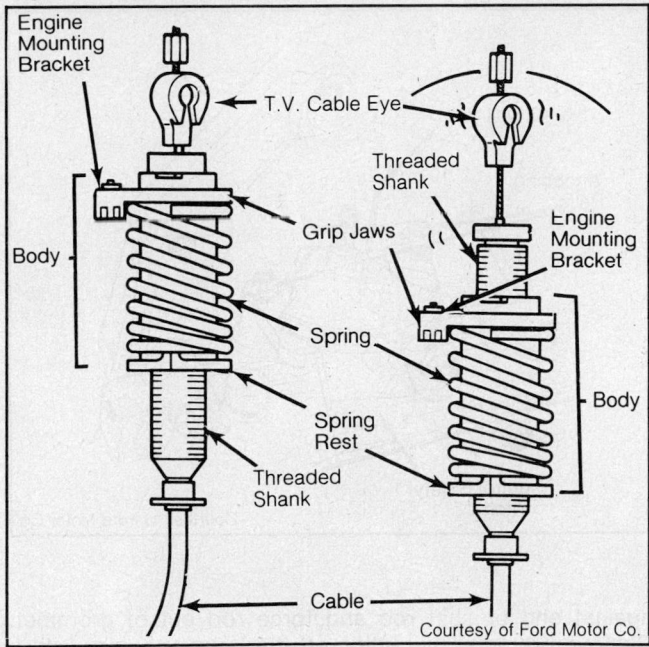

Courtesy of Ford Motor Co.

3) Tighten attaching nut to 16-27 ft. lbs. (12-20 N.m) on Taurus and 10-15 ft. lbs. (14-20 N.m) on all others. Ensure all gears engage correctly and vehicle only starts in Park or Neutral.

AXOD (Contintental, Sable & Taurus)

1) Place selector lever in "OVERDRIVE" position. Selector lever must be held in this position while adjusting linkage. Loosen manual lever-to-control cable retaining nut. *See Fig. 11.*

Fig. 11: AXOD Transaxle Shift Linkage

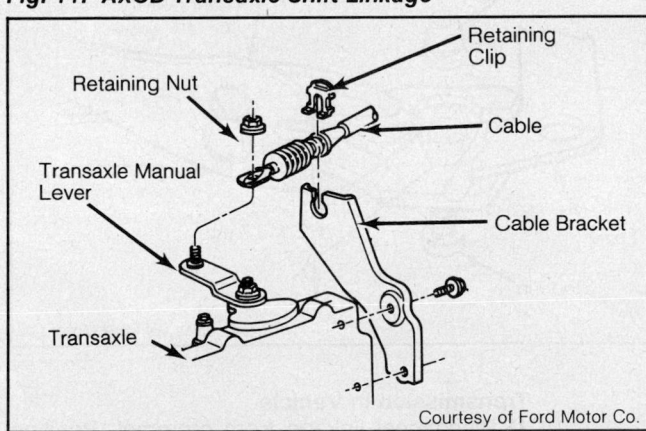

Courtesy of Ford Motor Co.

2) Move transaxle manual lever to "OVERDRIVE" position, second detent from most rearward position. Tighten attaching nut to 10-15 ft. lbs. (14-20 N.m). Check operation of transaxle in each gear position.

SHIFT LINKAGE (RWD)
Console (Floor) Shift

1) Move selector lever rearward against stop in Overdrive (AOD and A4LD). Ensure lever is tight against rearward drive/overdrive stop. Raise vehicle. Loosen manual lever-to-control cable (or rod) retaining nut.

2) Move transmission manual lever to Overdrive position (third detent from full counterclockwise). Hold selector in this position and tighten retaining nut. Check for normal operation in all selected positions. *See Fig. 12.*

Fig. 12: Typical Ford Motor Co. Console (Floor) Shift Linkage

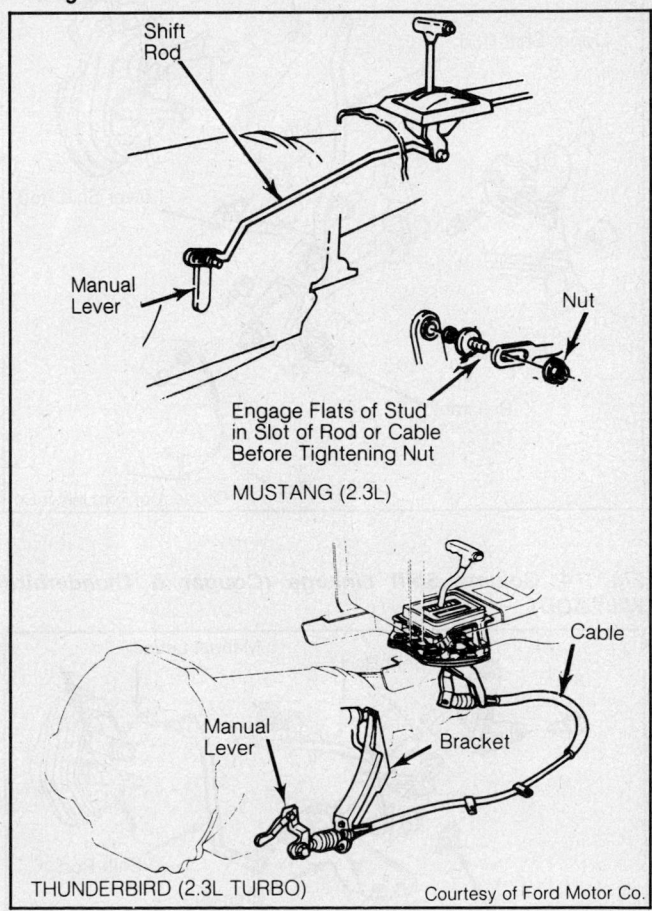

Courtesy of Ford Motor Co.

Column Shift

1) Place selector in Overdrive position. Make sure selector lever remains against stop by hanging an 8 lb. (3.6 kg) weight on selector lever.

2) Loosen shift rod adjusting bolt (or nut). Push manual transmission lever downward to lowest position (third detent from full counterclockwise position).

3) Ensure the slotted rod end has flats aligned with flats on mounting stud, (if equipped). Ensure selector lever has not moved from Overdrive. Tighten bolt (or nut) and check operation in all selector detent positions. *See Figs. 13 and 14.*

NEUTRAL SAFETY SWITCH
AOD & A4LD
Neutral safety switch is mounted on left side of tranmission and is not adjustable.

Automatic Transmission Servicing

FORD MOTOR CO. (Cont.)

ATX & AXOD

Loosen switch attaching bolts. With manual shaft in neutral detent, align switch using a No. 43 (.089") drill. *See Fig. 15.* Tighten bolts to 84-108 INCH lbs. (9-12 N.m).

Fig. 13: Column Shift Linkage (Crown Victoria, Grand Marquis & Town Car With AOD)

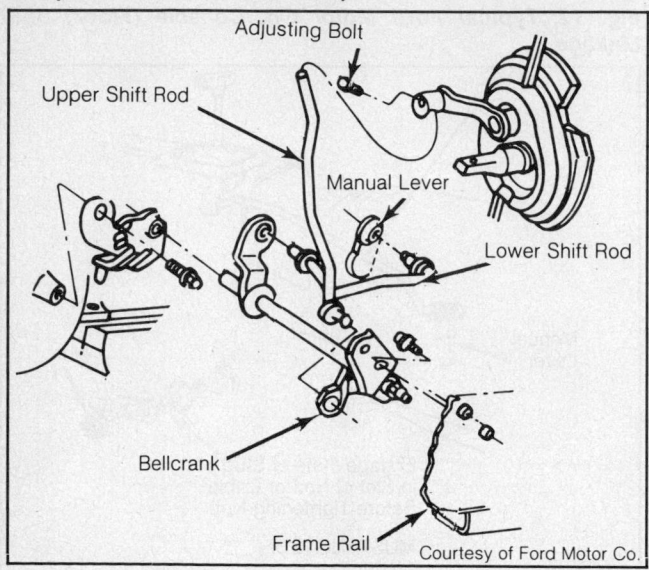

Courtesy of Ford Motor Co.

Fig. 14: Column Shift Linkage (Cougar & Thunderbird With AOD)

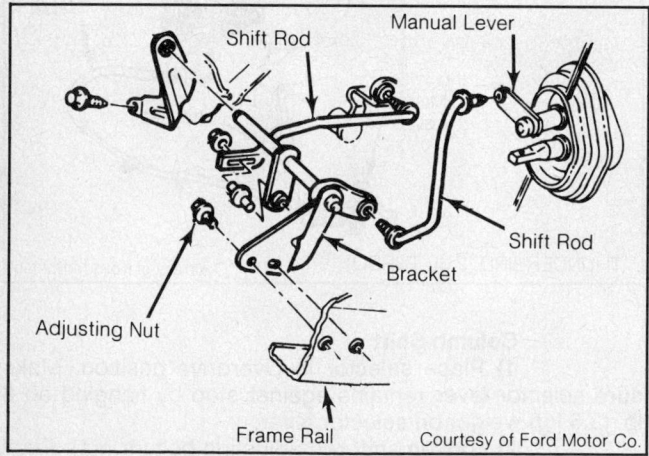

Courtesy of Ford Motor Co.

REMOVAL & INSTALLATION

RUBBER GROMMET

Shift linkage systems use an oil impregnated plastic grommet to connect various rods and levers. A new grommet MUST be installed each time any rod is disconnected from a grommet-type connector.

Transmission On Bench

1) Remover/Replacer (T67P-7341-A) is required to install grommet into shift lever and to install shift linkage rod into grommet.

2) Remove grommet by placing lower jaw of tool between shift lever and shift rod. Position stop pin

Fig. 15: Adjusting ATX & AXOD Neutral Safety Switch

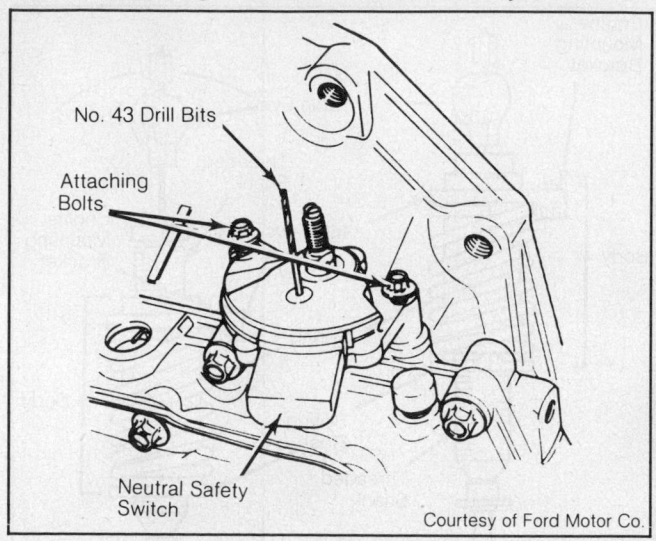

Courtesy of Ford Motor Co.

against end of shift rod and force rod out of grommet. Remove grommet by cutting off the large shoulder with a sharp knife.

3) Before installing new grommet, adjust stop pin to 1/2". Coat outside of grommet with lubricant. *See Fig. 16.* Place new grommet on stop pin and force it into lever hole.

4) Turn grommet several times to ensure proper seating. Squeeze rod into bushing until stopwasher seats against bushing.

Fig. 16: Replacing Shift Rod Grommets (On Bench)

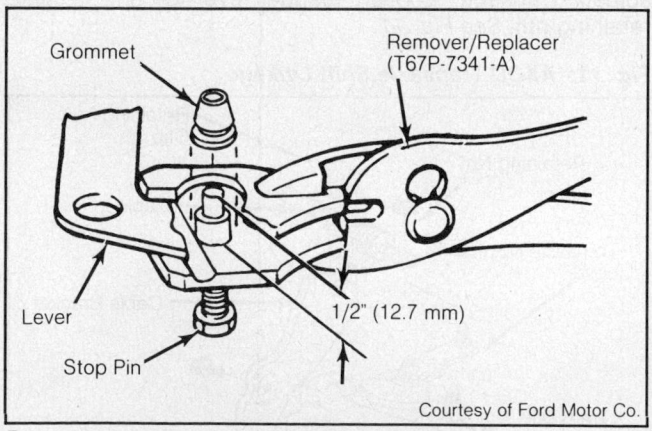

Courtesy of Ford Motor Co.

Transmission In Vehicle

1) Disconnect linkage from grommet. Position Grommet Remover (T84P-7341-A). Rotate screw in tool until grommet is forced out of lever.

2) Adjust stop on Grommet Replacer (T84P-7341-B) to 1/2". Coat outside of grommet with lubricant. Position grommet on lever. *See Fig. 17.*

3) Use replacer tool to force grommet into position. Ensure grommet is fully seated in lever. Connect linkage.

Fig. 17: Replacing Shift Rod Grommets (On Bench)

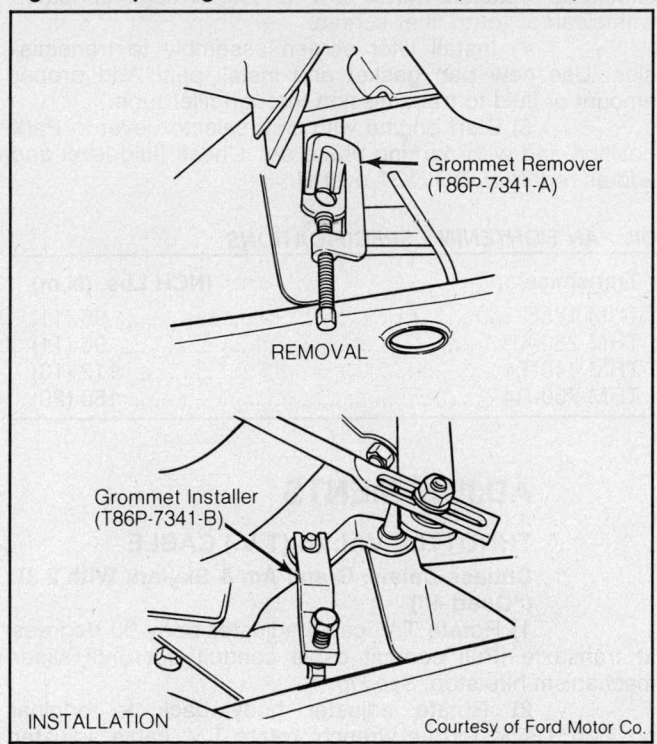

Grommet Remover
(T86P-7341-A)

REMOVAL

Grommet Installer
(T86P-7341-B)

INSTALLATION

Courtesy of Ford Motor Co.

Automatic Transmission Servicing

GENERAL MOTORS – EXCEPT NOVA

NOTE: For information on Nova, see GENERAL MOTORS – NOVA in this section.

LUBRICATION

SERVICE INTERVALS

Check fluid level at every oil change. Transmission fluid should be changed and filter replaced every 100,000 miles under normal operating conditions.

Under continuous extreme operating conditions (trailer towing, heavy city traffic with ambient temperature over 90°F/32°C or delivery service), fluid and filter should be changed every 15,000 miles.

CHECKING FLUID LEVEL

CAUTION: Do not overfill. One pint of fluid will raise level from "ADD 1 PT. OR .5L" to "FULL HOT" mark on dipstick with a hot transmission.

1) Warm transmission to normal operating temperature by at least 15 miles of highway driving. With engine at curb idle, move selector lever through all ranges, ending in Park.

2) Remove dipstick. Wipe dipstick clean and reinstall. Remove again and inspect level. Fluid level should check between "ADD 1 PT. OR .5L" and "FULL HOT" marks on dipstick.

CAUTION: If vehicle has been driven for extended period of time at high speed, in city traffic in hot weather, or if vehicle has been pulling a trailer, accurate fluid level cannot be checked until ATF has cooled about 30 minutes after vehicle has been parked.

RECOMMENDED FLUID

Use only Dexron II ATF.

FLUID CAPACITY

NOTE: Quantities listed are approximate. Correct fluid level should be determined by mark on dipstick rather than by amount added.

TRANSMISSION REFILL CAPACITIES

Application	Refill Qts. (L)	Total Qts. (L)
THM 125C	4.0 (6.2)	10 (9.5)
THM 200-4R	5.3 (5.0)	11 (10.4)
THM 440-T4	6.6 (6.2)	10 (9.5)
THM 700-R4	5.0 (4.7)	11.6 (11)

DRAINING & REFILLING

1) With vehicle raised and drain pan placed under transmission, remove front and side transmission oil pan bolts. Loosen rear pan bolts about 4 turns each.

2) Carefully pry pan loose with screwdriver, allowing fluid to drain. Remove remaining bolts and oil pan with gasket. Remove filter screen with "O" ring or seal. Clean pan and magnet.

3) Thoroughly clean pan and screen with solvent and dry with compressed air. Paper type filters should be replaced. Install new "O" ring or seal, lubricated with clean oil, onto filter screen.

4) Install filter screen assembly to transmission. Use new pan gasket and install pan. Add proper amount of fluid to transmission through filler tube.

5) Start engine with shift selector lever in Park position and with parking brake set. Check fluid level and add as required. DO NOT overfill.

OIL PAN TIGHTENING SPECIFICATIONS

Transmission	INCH Lbs. (N.m)
THM 125C	96 (11)
THM 200-4R	96 (11)
THM 440-T4	112 (13)
THM 700-R4	180 (20)

ADJUSTMENTS

THROTTLE VALVE (T.V.) CABLE

Cutlass Calais, Grand Am & Skylark With 2.3L ("Quad 4")

1) Rotate T.V. cable adjuster body 90 degrees at transaxle. Pull conduit cable conduit out until slider mechanism hits stop. See Fig. 1.

2) Rotate adjuster body back to original position. Using torque wrench, rotate T.V. cable adjuster until 85 INCH lbs. (N.m) is reached.

Fig. 1: 2.3L ("Quad 4") T.V. Cable

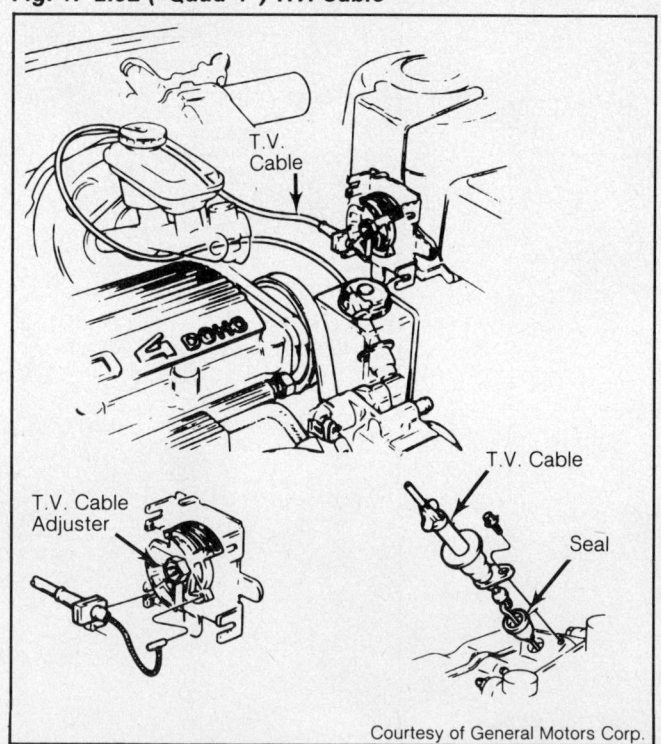

Courtesy of General Motors Corp.

Fiero & 6000

1) Check that T.V. cable is in full, nonadjusted position. Ensure T.V. cable operates smoothly and connected at transaxle.

2) Accelerator cable must be installed when adjusting T.V. cable. Rotate idler pulley (cam) clockwise

GENERAL MOTORS — EXCEPT NOVA (Cont.)

(Fiero) or counterclockwise (6000) to 65 INCH lbs. (7 N.m) to place cable in adjusted position. *See Fig. 2.*

Fig. 2: Fiero & 6000 T.V. Cable Adjustment

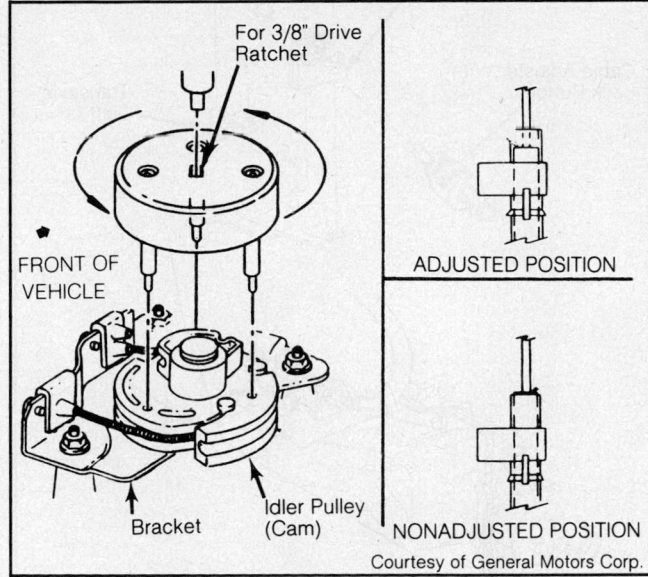

Courtesy of General Motors Corp.

All Other Models

1) Engine must be off. Depress metal lock tab on adjuster and hold it in depressed position. Adjuster is located at cable support bracket on engine.

2) Move slider until it stops against fitting. Release readjustment tab. *See Fig. 3.*

3) Rotate throttle lever to its full throttle position. Slider must move (ratch) toward lever when lever is rotated to its full throttle position. Check cable for sticking and binding.

Fig. 3: Self-Adjusting Throttle Valve Cable

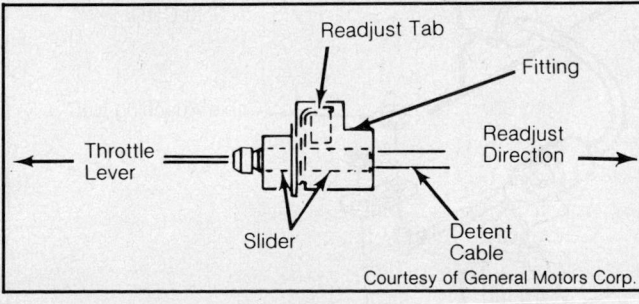

Courtesy of General Motors Corp.

4) On models equipped with THM 200-R4, road test vehicle. If delayed or only full throttle shifts occur, proceed in following manner. Remove transmission oil pan and inspect throttle lever and bracket assembly.

5) Ensure T.V. exhaust valve lifter rod is not distorted and binding in control valve assembly or spacer plate. T.V. exhaust check ball must move up and down as lifter moves. Lifter spring must hold lifter rod up against bottom of control valve assembly. Ensure correct throttle lever-to-cable link is used.

GEARSHIFT LINKAGE

1) Linkage should be adjusted so that engine cannot be started in any position except "P" or "N". If linkage is improperly adjusted, an internal leak could occur causing a clutch and/or band failure.

2) With selector lever in "P" position, parking pawl should engage rear/reaction internal gear lugs or output ring gear lugs. Pointer on indicator quadrant should line up properly with range indicators in all ranges.

Column Shift, Rod Type (RWD Models)

1) Position steering column shift lever in Neutral gate notch. Loosen swivel clamp screw and place transmission lever in Neutral. *See Fig. 4.*

2) Hold swivel clamp against equalizer lever. Tighten clamp screw without applying tension on either equalizer lever or selector rod. Ensure there is no tension on either equalizer lever or selector rod. *See Fig. 4.*

Fig. 4: Rod Type Column Shift Linkage

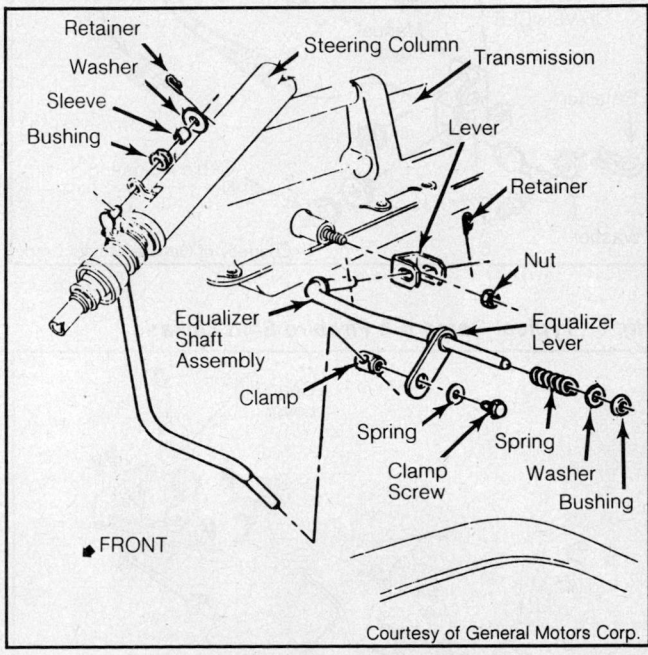

Courtesy of General Motors Corp.

Floor Shift, Cable Type (RWD Exc. Camaro, Corvette & Firebird)

1) Place shift lever in Park position. Raise and support vehicle. Ensure transmission is fully engaged in Park by rotating propeller shaft until parking pawl engages in transmission.

2) Loosen attaching nut in manual lever to allow pin to slide freely. With gearshift lever and transmission manual lever both in Park, tighten attaching nut. *See Fig. 5.*

Floor Shift, Cable Type (Camaro, Corvette & Firebird)

Place gearshift lever in Neutral position. Raise and support vehicle. Loosen cable attachment nut at transmission. *See Fig. 6.* Place transmission lever in Neutral position by moving clockwise to Park detent, then back (counterclockwise) 2 detents to Neutral. Tighten cable nut to 15 ft. lbs. (20 N.m).

NOTE: Lever must be held out of Park when tightening nut.

GENERAL MOTORS – EXCEPT NOVA (Cont.)

Fig. 5: Transmission Shift Cable (Floor Shift, Cable Type)

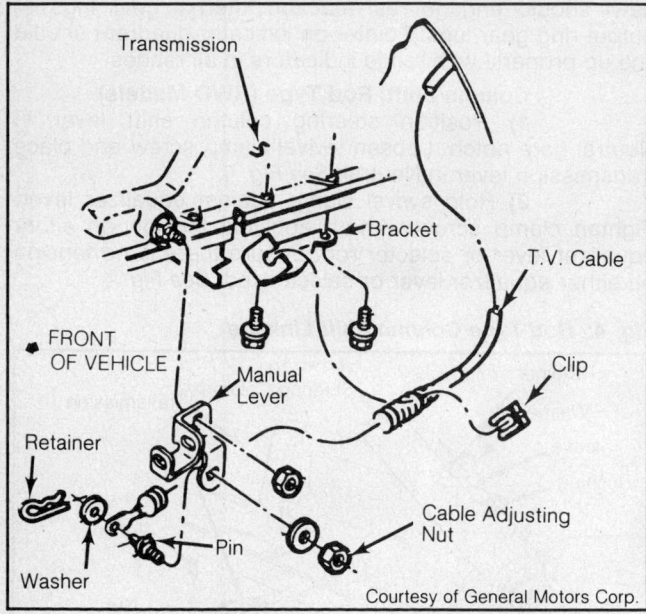

Courtesy of General Motors Corp.

Fig. 6: Typical Camaro & Firebird Shift Linkage

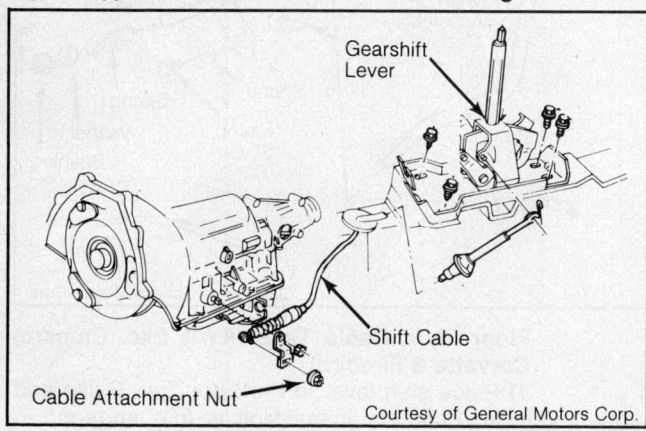

Courtesy of General Motors Corp.

Corvette is similar.

NOTE: **Self-adjusting shift cable is commonly used on A, C, H, N and W body styles.**

All Except Self-Adjusting Cable Type (FWD Models)

1) Place gearshift lever in Neutral position. Loosen cable attaching nut at transaxle shift lever. *See Fig. 8.*

2) Place transaxle lever in Neutral detent. Tighten cable attaching nut. Lever MUST be held out of Park when tightening nut. DO NOT use impact tools on nut.

NOTE: **Self-adjusting shift cable is commonly used on A, C, H, N and W body styles.**

Self-Adjusting Cable Type (FWD Models)

Place gearshift lever in Neutral. Lift up lock button on cable adjuster at transaxle mounting bracket. *See Fig. 7.* Place transaxle shift lever in Neutral detent. Push down on lock button.

Fig. 7: Self-Adjusting Cable For FWD Vehicles

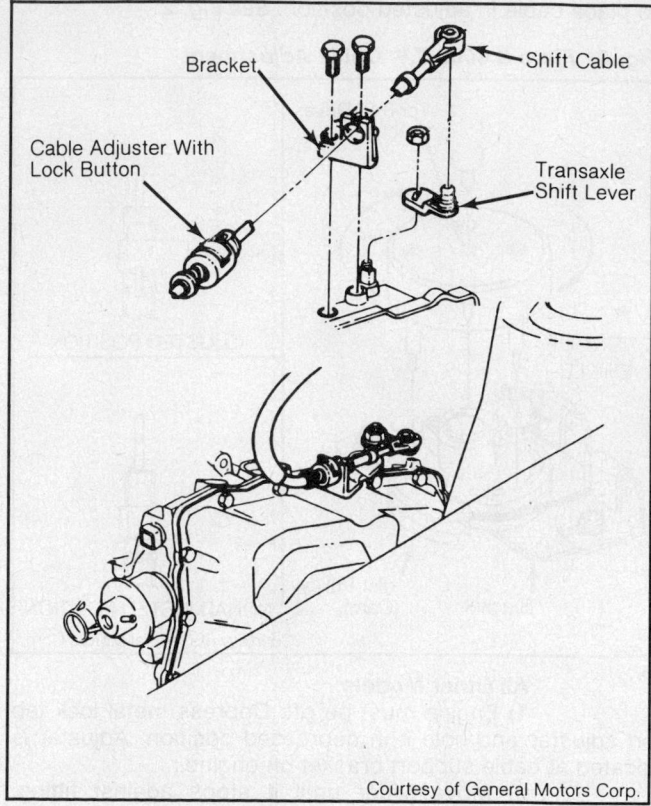

Courtesy of General Motors Corp.

Fig. 8: Typical Floor Shift Linkage (FWD Models)

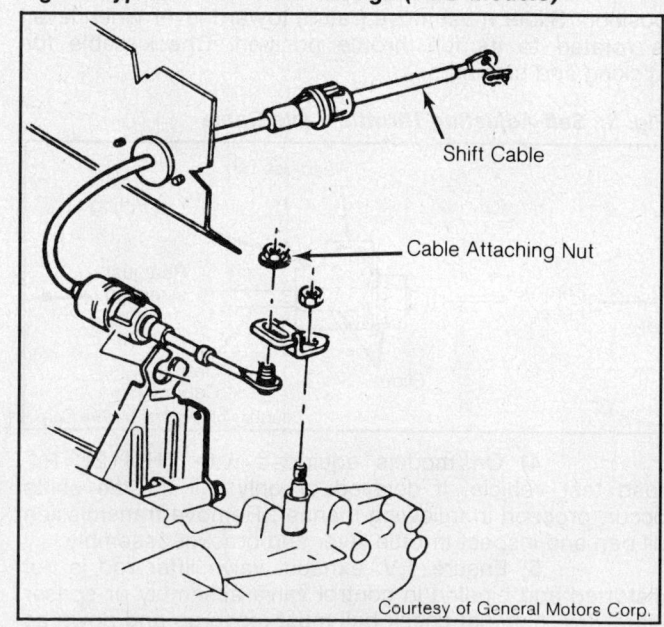

Courtesy of General Motors Corp.

PARK/LOCK CONTROL CABLE
Floor Shift Models

1) With shift lever in Park and key in "LOCK" position, gearshift lever should not be able to be moved to other gear positions. Ignition key should be removable from column.

Fig. 9: *Corvette Park/Lock Control Cable*

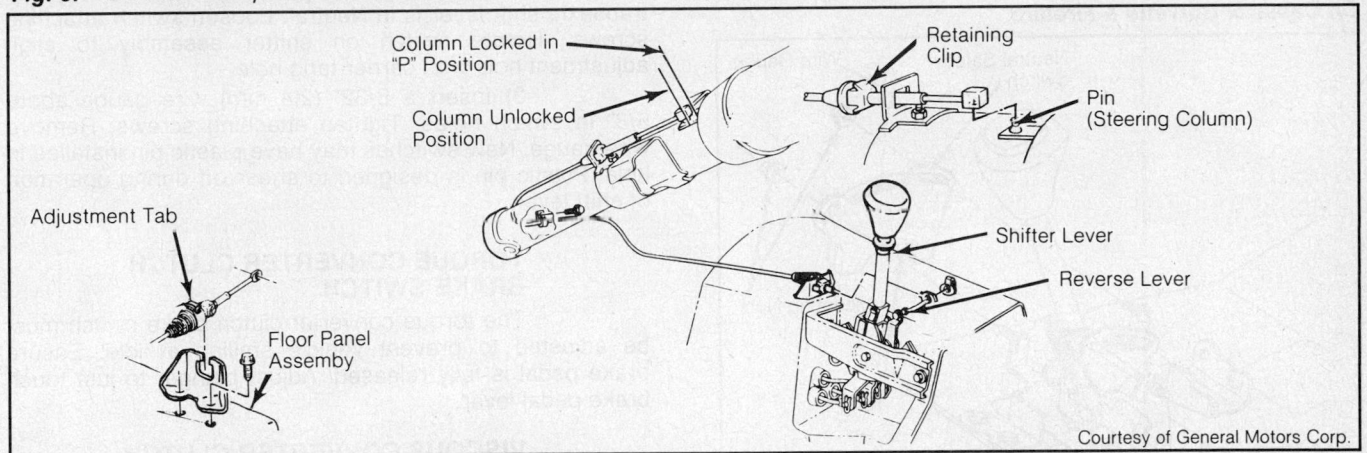

Courtesy of General Motors Corp.

2) With key in "RUN" position and gearshift lever in Neutral, ensure key cannot be turned to "LOCK" position. If system does not perform as described in steps **1)** and **2)**, go to step **3)** for adjustment procedure.

3) If key cannot be removed in Park, snap connector lock button to up position. Move cable connector nose rearward until key can be removed from ignition. *See Figs. 9, 10 and 11.* Snap lock button down.

Fig. 10: *Typical J & N Body Park/Lock Control Cable*

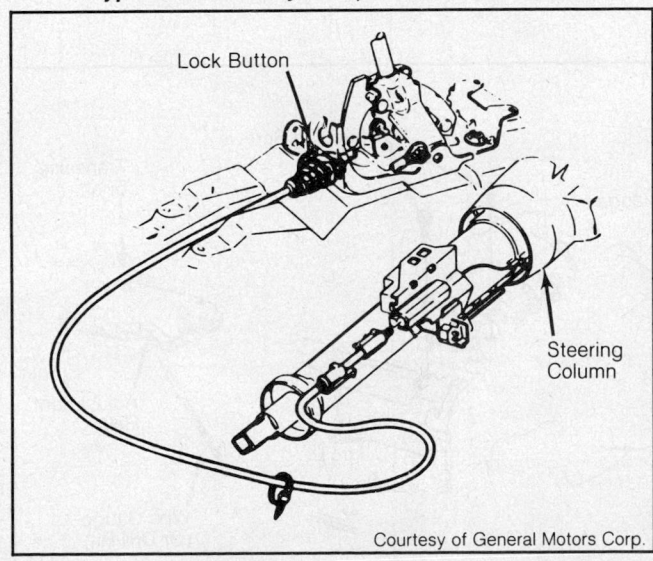

Courtesy of General Motors Corp.

NEUTRAL SAFETY SWITCH

RWD Models (Except Camaro, Corvette & Firebird)

Column shift models use a mechanical interference-type neutral start system. A wedge-shaped finger, attached to the ignition switch actuator rod, blocks movement of switch to "Start" position in all shift positions except "P" or "N".

RWD Models (Camaro, Corvette & Firebird)

1) Remove floor console cover. Place gearshift lever in Neutral. If old switch is being readjusted, go to step **2)**. If new switch is being installed, go to step **4)**.

2) Align tang on switch with tang slot on shift control. *See Fig. 12.* Loosen switch mounting nuts. Rotate

Fig. 11: *Typical A & W Body Park/Lock Control Cable*

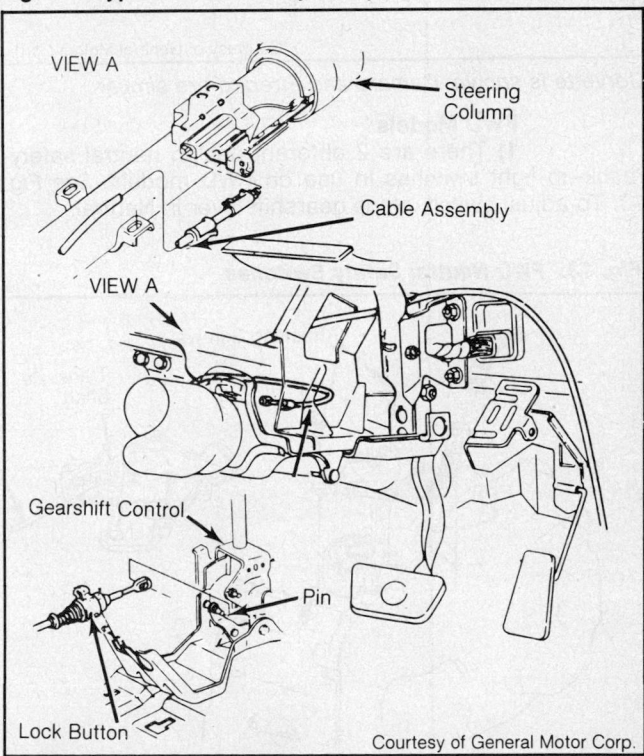

Courtesy of General Motor Corp.

switch to align service adjustment hole with carrier tang hole.

3) Insert a 3.32" (2.4 mm) wire gauge in adjustment hole in top of switch. Rotate switch until pin drops to depth of 19/32" (15 mm). Tighten mounting nuts. Vehicle should only start in Park or Neutral.

4) If new switch if being installed, insert switch tang in slot on shift control. Tighten mounting nuts.

5) If holes do not align with shift control, ensure gearshift lever is in Neutral. DO NOT rotate switch. Switch is pinned in Neutral.

NOTE: **If new switch has been rotated and pin broken during installation, use adjustment procedure in step 2).**

6) If holes align with shift control, move gearshift control lever out of Neutral to shear plastic pin.

GENERAL MOTORS – EXCEPT NOVA (Cont.)

Fig. 12: Adjusting Neutral Safety & Back-Up Light Switch On Camaro, Corvette & Firebird

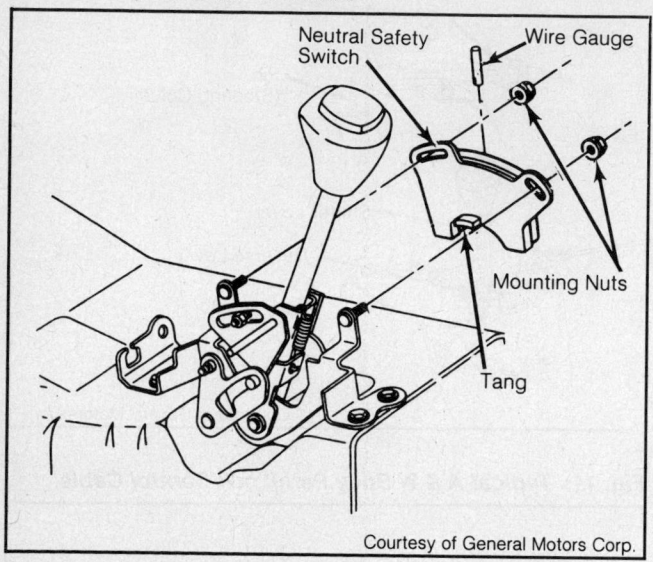

Courtesy of General Motors Corp.

Corvette is shown; Camaro and Firebird are similar.

FWD Models

1) There are 2 different design neutral safety-/back-up light switches in use on FWD models. *See Fig. 13.* To adjust switch, place gearshift lever in Neutral.

2) Ensure shift cable is adjusted correctly and transaxle shift lever is in Neutral. Loosen switch attaching screws. Rotate switch on shifter assembly to align adjustment hole with carrier tang hole.

3) Insert a 3/32" (2.4 mm) wire gauge about 5/8" in switch holes. Tighten attaching screws. Remove wire gauge. New switches may have plastic pin installed in hole. Plastic pin is designed to shear off during operation of shift lever.

TORQUE CONVERTER CLUTCH BRAKE SWITCH

The torque converter clutch brake switch must be adjusted to prevent vehicle stalling at idle. Ensure brake pedal is fully released. Adjust plunger to just touch brake pedal lever.

VISCOUS CONVERTER CLUTCH THERMISTOR SWITCH

Cadillac

The THM 440-T4 is equipped with a thermistor switch that senses the temperature of the transaxle fluid. This information is sent to the ECM for Viscous Converter Clutch (VCC) operation. The ECM will engage the VCC when fluid temperature is 200°F (93°C) or less, provided all other conditions have been met. If fluid temperature is higher than this, ECM will not allow VCC engagement until vehicle speed is about 36 MPH.

Fig. 13: FWD Neutral Safety Switches

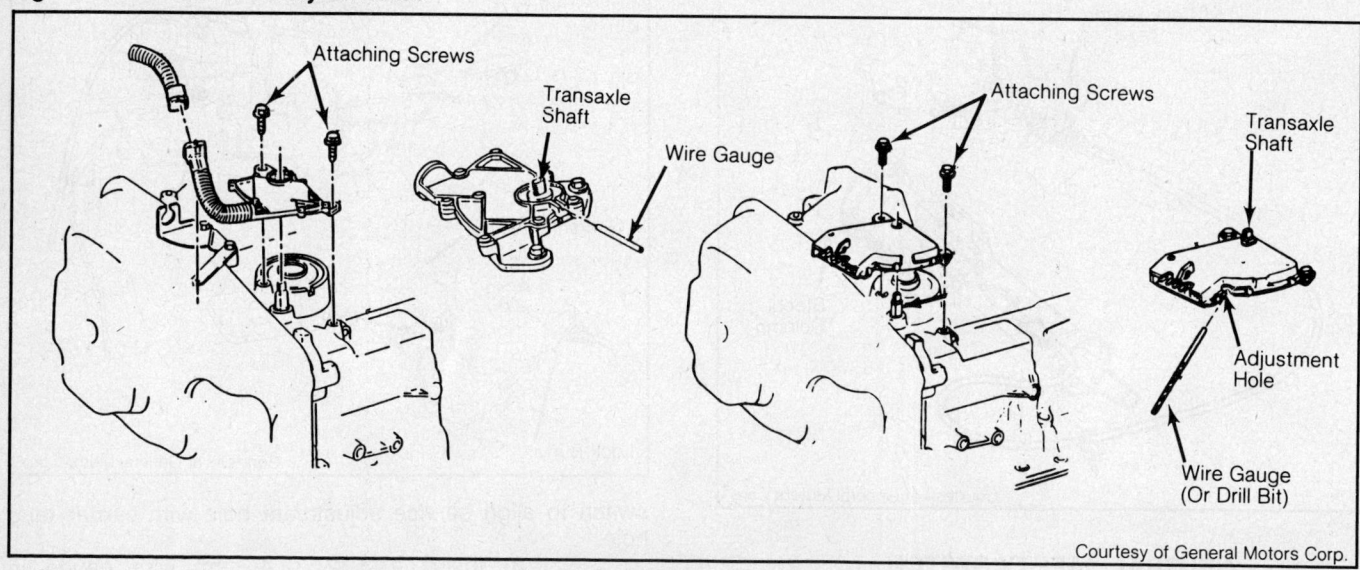

Courtesy of General Motors Corp.

GENERAL MOTORS — NOVA

LUBRICATION

SERVICE INTERVALS

Check transmission fluid every 15,000 miles. In severe conditions change transmission fluid and filter screen every 15,000 miles.

CHECKING FLUID LEVEL

Transaxle

Check transmission fluid level with engine idling. Shift each gear from "P" through "L" and back to "P". Fluid level should be within "COOL" or "HOT" ranges marked on dipstick. DO NOT overfill.

Differential

Differential is equipped with separate drain and fill plugs. See Fig. 1. Fluid should reach bottom of fill plug hole.

Fig. 1: Differential Drain & Fill Plugs

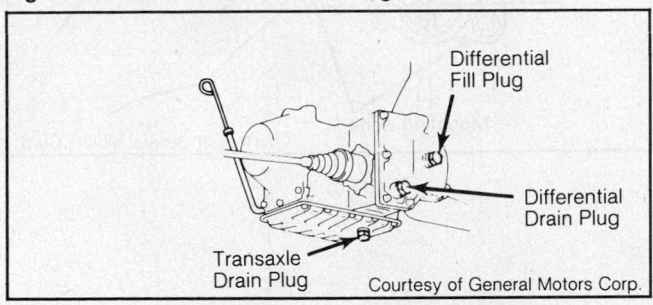

Courtesy of General Motors Corp.

RECOMMENDED FLUID

Use Dexron II ATF in transaxle and differential.

FLUID CAPACITY

TRANSMISSION REFILL CAPACITIES

Application	Refill Qts. (L)	Dry Fill Qts. (L)
Transaxle		
A131L	2.4 (2.3)	5.8 (5.5)
A240E [1]	3.3 (3.1)	7.2 (7.6)
Differential		1.5 (1.4)

[1] – Used with 16-valve engine.

DRAINING & REFILLING

Transaxle

1) Remove drain plug in pan in drain pan. Reinstall plug securely. If oil pan if being changed, remove oil pan. Clean pan and discard gasket.

2) Noting bolt length for reassembly, remove oil filter screen bolts. Remove filter screen and discard.

3) Install new filter screen. Ensure bolts are installed in original positions. See Fig. 2. Tighten oil strainer bolts to 84 INCH lbs. (10 N.m).

4) Install oil pan with new gasket. Tighten oil pan bolts to 43 INCH lbs. (4.9 N.m).

5) With engine off, add new fluid through dipstick tube. Start engine and shift into all gear positions.

6) With engine idling, check fluid level with transaxle in "Park" position. Add fluid up to "COOL" level on dipstick.

Fig. 2: Oil Screen Bolt Lengths

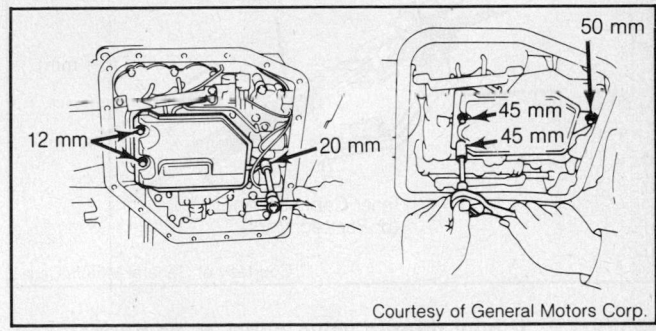

Courtesy of General Motors Corp.

Differential

Remove drain plug in differential carrier cover and drain fluid. See Fig. 1. Reinstall drain plug securely. Remove filler plug in side of carrier cover. Add new fluid (Dexron II) until it begins to run out of filler hole.

ADJUSTMENTS

FLOOR SHIFTER LINKAGE

1) Loosen swivel nut on shift lever at transaxle. See Fig. 3. Push manual lever fully toward right side of vehicle.

2) Return manual lever 2 notches to "Neutral" position. Set shift lever in "N" range. While holding lever lightly toward "R" range side, tighten swivel nut.

Fig. 3: Adjusting Transaxle Control Cable

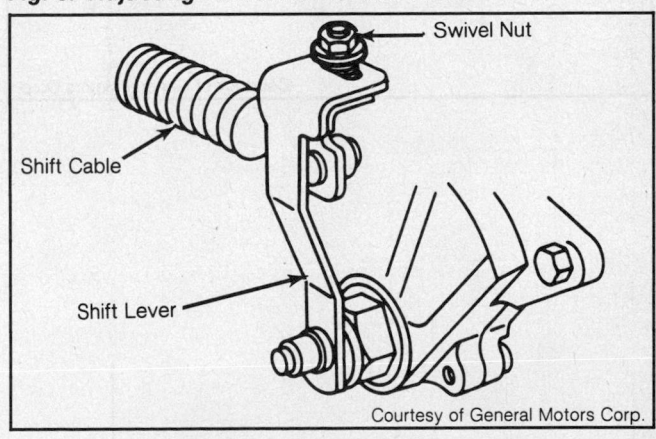

Courtesy of General Motors Corp.

THROTTLE CABLE

Adjustment

1) Depress accelerator pedal to floor and ensure throttle valve opens fully. If not, adjust accelerator link.

2) Fully depress accelerator. Loosen throttle cable adjusting nuts. See Fig. 4.

3) Adjust cable housing so distance between end of boot and stopper on cable is 0-.04" (0-1 mm). Tighten adjusting nuts. Recheck adjustment.

GENERAL MOTORS — NOVA (Cont.)

Fig. 4: Adjusting Nova Throttle Cable

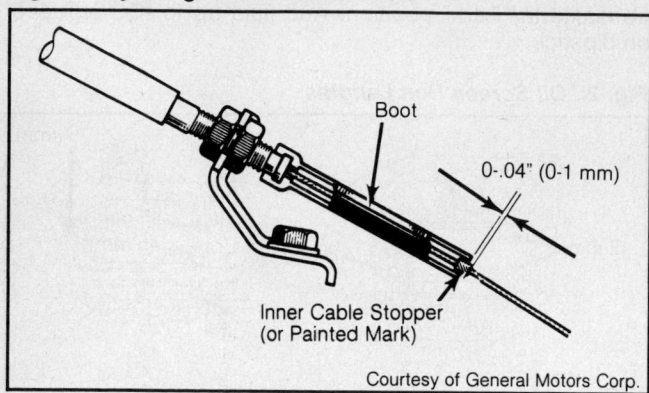

Courtesy of General Motors Corp.

NOTE: If new throttle valve cable is being installed, use the following procedure.

Replacement

1) If new throttle cable is being installed, a new stopper must be staked in position. Bend cable so it has about a 7.87" (200 mm) radius. *See Fig. 5.*

2) Pull inner cable lightly until a slight resistance is felt. Stake stopper .031-.059" (.8-1.5 mm) from end of outer cable.

Fig. 5: Staking Throttle Cable Stopper

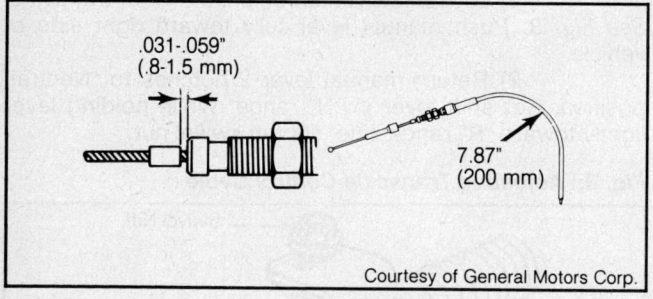

Courtesy of General Motors Corp.

NEUTRAL SAFETY SWITCH

1) Loosen neutral safety switch bolts at transaxle. Set shift selector lever in "N" range. Disconnect switch connector. *See Fig. 6.*

2) Connect an ohmmeter between terminals and adjust switch to the point where there is continuity between terminals. Tighten screws and plug in switch connector.

Fig. 6: Adjusting Neutral Safety Switch

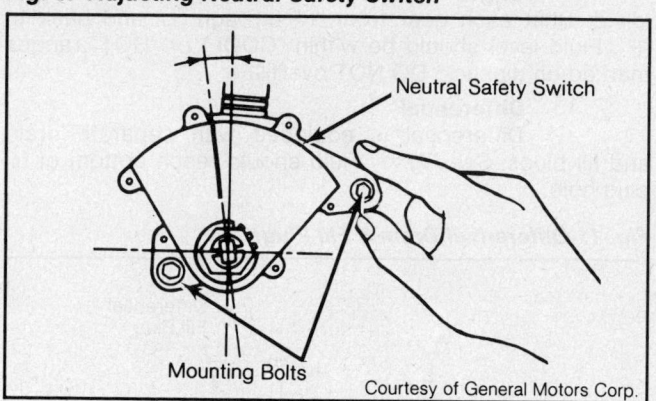

Courtesy of General Motors Corp.

CHRYSLER MOTORS

REMOVAL & INSTALLATION

TORQUEFLITE A-413 (FWD MODELS)
Removal

1) Disconnect negative battery cable. Disconnect throttle linkage and shift linkage from transaxle. Remove upper and lower oil cooling lines. Support engine from above. Remove upper bellhousing bolts. Remove axle hub cotter pins and castle nuts. Raise vehicle on a hoist.

2) Remove front wheels. Remove left splash shield. Remove speedometer cable from housing. Disconnect sway bar and remove pinch bolts at lower control arm ball joint. Pry control arm down to remove ball joint. Remove drive axle shafts from vehicle.

3) Remove torque converter dust cover. Mark torque converter and flexplate and remove flexplate bolts. Remove access plug (in right shield) to rotate engine. Unplug neutral safety switch connector on transaxle.

4) Remove engine mount bracket from front crossmember. Remove front mount through-bolt and bellhousing bolts. Position a jack under transaxle. Remove left engine mount. Remove starter and remaining bellhousing bolts. Lower transaxle on jack. Pry engine for clearance and remove transaxle from vehicle.

Installation

To install, reverse removal procedures. Adjust throttle cable and shift linkage as necessary. Fill transaxle and differential to correct level. See appropriate AUTOMATIC TRANSMISSION SERVICING article in this section.

TORQUEFLITE A-727 & A-904-LA (RWD MODELS)
Removal

1) Disconnect negative battery cable. Some models require exhaust system be dropped for clearance. Remove engine to transmission struts (if equipped). Remove cooler lines at transmission. Remove cooler line bracket, starter motor and torque converter cover. Loosen oil pan bolts, tap pan to break it loose allowing fluid to drain. Reinstall pan.

2) Mark converter and flex plate for installation reference. Using socket on crankshaft vibration damper bolt, rotate engine clockwise for converter attaching bolts for removal. Mark propeller shaft and yoke for installation reference. Remove propeller shaft.

3) Unplug neutral safety switch harness from transmission. Disconnect gearshift rod, torque shaft assembly and throttle rod lever from left side of transmission. Remove linkage at bellcrank from transmission (if equipped).

NOTE: Replace plastic grommets if linakge rods are disassembled.

4) Remove oil filler tube and speedometer cable. Support rear of engine with safety stand. Raise transmission slightly with jack to relieve load on mounts. Remove bolts securing transmission mount-to-crossmember and crossmember-to-frame. Remove crossmember.

5) Remove converter housing-to-engine attaching bolts. Pull transmission assembly back and remove from under vehicle.

NOTE: Attach a small "C" clamp to edge of converter housing to hold torque converter in place during transmission removal.

Installation

CAUTION: Flush oil cooler and cooler lines before replacing transmission.

1) To install, reverse removal procedures. Ensure converter fully engages pump inner rotor lugs. Surface of converter front cover lug should be at least 1/2" below front edge of transmission when converter is installed.

2) Attach small "C" clamp to converter housing. Inspect converter flex plate for distortion or cracks and replace if necessary. Coat converter hub hole in crankshaft with multipurpose grease.

NOTE: When flex plate replacement is necessary, ensure both transmission dowel pins are in engine block.

3) Place transmission and converter assembly on a jack. Rotate converter so mark on converter (made during removal) will align with mark on drive palte. Offset holes in drive plate are located next to 1/8" hole in inner circle of plate. A stamped "O" identifies offset hole in converter.

4) Place transmission in position rear of engine. Install and tighten all bolts. Adjust shift and throttle linkage. Refill transmission with DEXRON II ATF.

5) To complete installation, reverse removal procedure. Tighten bolts holding struts-to-transmission before tightening strut-to-engine bolts (if equipped).

TIGHTENING SPECIFICATIONS

Application	Ft. Lbs. (N.m)
Torqueflite A-413	
Ball Joint Bolt	70 (95)
Converter-to-Flex Plate Bolt	55 (74)
Drive Axle Shaft Hub Nut	180 (245)
Flex Plate-to-Crankshaft Bolts	70 (95)
Mount-to-Transaxle Bolt	40 (54)
Transaxle-to-Engine Bolt	70 (95)
Torqueflite A-727 & A-904-LA	
Converter-to-Flex Plate Bolt	23 (31)
Flex Plate-to-Crankshaft Bolts	55 (75)
Rear Mount-to-Transmission Bolt	50 (68)
Transmission-to-Engine Bolt	30 (41)

EAGLE

REMOVAL & INSTALLATION

AR-4

Removal (Premier W/2.5L)

1) Disconnect negative battery cable. Label for reassembly and unplug 6 connectors from Transmission Control Unit (TCU). TCU is on inner fender panel near washer bottle.

2) Clamp off and remove cooler lines from transaxle. Remove engine timing sensor from engine. Raise and support vehicle. Remove front wheels.

3) On bottom end of MacPherson strut there are 2 clamp bolts. Remove upper bolt and loosen lower bolt. Only turn lower strut NUT; bolt is splined and will not turn. Tilt steering knuckle outward. Remove splash shield. Drain transaxle fluid.

4) On inner end of drive axle shafts, punch out roll pins with a drift. Pull drive shafts out of differential. Remove tie straps and retainers securing transaxle wiring harness to vehicle body.

NOTE: **Do not remove transaxle sensors and wiring harnesses from transaxle.**

5) Remove starter and heat shield. Remove converter housing access plug. Remove flex plate-to-convert attaching bolts. Remove exhaust pipe-to-transaxle bolts.

6) Support transaxle with jack. Disconnect transaxle from rear mount and remove crossmember. Disconnect gearshift cable from transaxle. Remove shift cable bracket from transaxle.

7) Remove rear mount bracket from transaxle. Remove transaxle-to-engine bolts and lower transaxle out of vehicle.

Installation

1) To install transaxle, reverse removal procedure. Ensure transaxle-to-engine alignment dowel pins are installed in engine mating surface at 1 o'clock and 9 o'clock positions. Use Loctite No. 271 on converter mounting bolts. Ensure converter is aligned with flex plate trigger wheel.

2) Ensure transaxle output shaft "O" rings are in recess on shaft. *See Fig. 1.* Replace "O" rings if damaged.

Fig. 1: AR-4 Axle Shaft "O" Rings

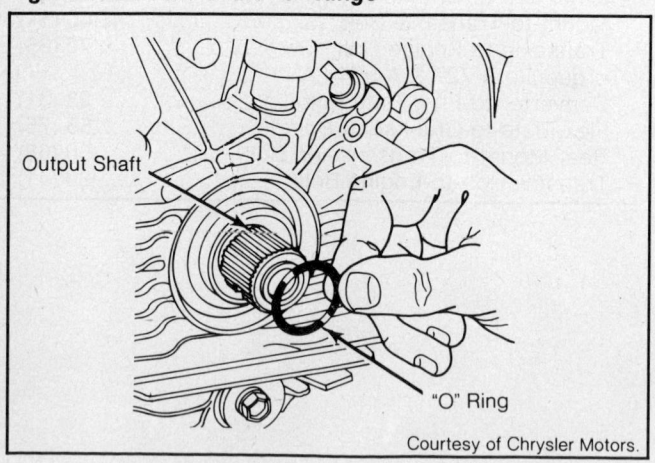

Output Shaft

"O" Ring

Courtesy of Chrysler Motors.

3) When installing inner ends of drive axle shafts in transaxle, ensure roll pin holes in axle shaft and

output shaft are aligned. Refill transaxle and differential. Adjust shift cable.

TIGHTENING SPECIFICATIONS (AR-4)

Application	Ft. Lbs. (N.m)
Converter-to-Flex Plate Bolts	25 (33)
Crossmember-to-Frame Bolts	31 (43)
Rear Mount-to-Crossmember Bolt	49 (67)
Steering Knuckle Clamp Bolts	148 (200)
Transaxle-to-Engine Bolts	55 (75)

ZF 4HP 18

Removal (Premier W/3.0L V6)

1) Disconnect negative battery cable. Raise and support vehicle. Remove front wheels.

2) On bottom end of MacPherson strut knuckle there are 2 clamp bolts. Remove upper bolt and loosen lower bolt. Only turn lower strut NUT; bolt is splined and will not turn. Tilt steering knuckle outward. Remove splash shield. Drain transaxle fluid.

3) Remove 2 converter housing covers. Remove flex plate-to-converter housing bolts. On inner end of drive axle shafts, punch out roll pins with a drift. Pull drive shafts out of differential.

4) Support transaxle with jack. Remove crossmember-to-side sill attaching nuts. Remove rear transaxle-to-crossmember mount bolt. Remove crossmember and mount.

5) Remove rear support mount from transaxle. Disconnect front exhaust pipe from manifolds. Disconnect catalytic converter from front pipe. Disconnect oxygen sensor wires. Remove exhaust pipe bracket bolts.

6) Loosen engine cradle bolts at side sill until there is about 1/2" between side sill and cradle. DO NOT remove side sill bolts.

7) Remove front exhaust pipe assembly. Remove starter. Disconnect shift cable from transaxle. Remove shift cable bracket from transaxle. After removing brace rod, replace bolt to hold neutral safety switch. Disconnect shift cable from bracket.

8) Remove engine timing sensor. Clamp off and remove cooler line hoses from transaxle. Unplug speedometer sensor harness. Remove engine-to-transaxle stud nuts and bolts. Lower transaxle out of vehicle.

Installation

1) To install transaxle, reverse removal procedure. Before installing transaxle, coat torque converter pilot hub with graphite grease.

2) Use Loctite No. 271 on converter mounting bolts. When installing inner ends of drive axle shafts in transaxle, ensure roll pin holes in axle shaft and output shaft are aligned. Refill transaxle and differential. Adjust shift cable and throttle valve cable.

TIGHTENING SPECIFICATIONS (ZF 4HP 18)

Application	Ft. Lbs.
Converter-to-Flex Plate Bolts	25 (33)
Engine-to-Transaxle	
Bolts	31 (43)
Stud Nuts	43 (31)
Engine Cradle Bolts	92 (125)
Rear Mount-to-Crossmember Bolt	49 (67)
Steering Knuckle Clamp Bolts	148 (200)

FORD MOTOR CO.

REMOVAL & INSTALLATION

AOD

Removal (Cougar, Crown Victoria, Grand Marquis, Mark VII, Mustang, Thunderbird & Town Car)

1) Raise and support vehicle. Drain transmission fluid (including converter). Remove converter access cover and adapter plate bolts from lower left side of converter housing. Remove 4 converter-to-flex plate nuts. Turn engine clockwise (as viewed from front) to gain access to nuts.

CAUTION: On belt driven overhead cam engines, NEVER turn engine counterclockwise (as viewed from front).

2) Mark position of yokes and remove propeller shaft. Install Seal Replacer (T74P-77052-A) in extension housing to prevent leakage. Disconnect and remove speedometer sensor from extension housing. Remove starter.

3) Remove rear mount-to-crossmember bolts and 2 crossmember-to-frame bolts. Remove 2 engine rear support-to-extension housing attaching bolts.

4) Disconnect T.V. linkage rod or cable from transmission. On Thunderbird and Cougar models, disconnect cable from bellcrank lever stud and remove self-tapping bolt from bellhousing bracket.

5) On all models, disconnect manual rod from transmission manual lever. Remove 2 bolts securing bellcrank bracket-to-converter housing. Disconnect neutral safety switch wires.

6) Position jack under transmission and raise it slightly. Remove engine support-to-crossmember bolts. Remove crossmember-to-frame bolts. Remove crossmember, insulator support and damper.

7) Disconnect and remove any interfering exhaust system hardware. Lower jack slightly to gain access to oil cooler lines. Disconnect oil cooler lines from transmission using Cooler Line Disconnector (T86P-77265-AH). Plug openings.

8) Remove lower converter-to-housing bolts. Remove transmission filler tube. Secure transmission to jack with a safety chain. Slide transmission to the rear and lower from vehicle.

Installation

1) To install transmission, reverse removal procedure. Ensure converter is fully seated in pump. Lubricate converter pilot with chassis grease. Align Orange balancing marks (if present) on converter and flex plate.

2) Align converter drive studs and drain plug with holes in flex plate. Readjust manual and downshift linkage.

3) Fill transmission with ATF to proper level. If any shift rods were disassembled, new plastic grommets must be installed. See appropriate AUTOMATIC TRANSMISSION SERVICING article in this section.

A4LD

Removal (Cougar, Mustang, Thunderbird & Town Car)

1) Raise and support vehicle. Drain transmission fluid (including converter). Remove converter access cover and adapter plate bolts from lower left side of converter housing. Remove 4 converter-to-flex plate nuts. Turn engine clockwise (as viewed from front) to gain access to nuts.

CAUTION: On belt driven overhead cam engines, NEVER turn engine counterclockwise (as viewed from front).

2) Mark position of yokes and remove propeller shaft. Install Seal Replacer (T74P-77052-A) in extension housing to prevent leakage. Disconnect and remove speedometer sensor from extension housing. Remove starter.

3) On Mustang models, disconnect shift rod at transmission manual lever. On Thunderbird models, disconnect shift cable from manual lever and retainer bracket on extension housing.

4) On all models, remove starter bolts and place starter out of way. Disconnect neutral safety switch and converter clutch harnesses. On Thunderbird models, disconnect the 3-4 shift solenoid. On all models, remove vacuum line from modulator.

5) Place jack under transmission and raise it slightly. Remove transmission rear support-to-crossmember bolts. Remove crossmember-to-frame bolts. Lower jack and allow transmission to hang.

6) Remove 2 upper transmission-to-engine bolts. Raise jack so it supports transmission. Disconnect oil cooler lines at transmission. Remove lower transmission-to-engine bolts.

7) Remove dipstick tube. Lower transmission from vehicle.

Installation

1) To install transmission, reverse removal procedure. Torque converter is properly installed when pilot hub is 7/16-9/16" (11-14 mm) from engine mating surface of converter housing.

2) Fill transmission with MERCON ATF. Adjust shift cable and throttle valve cable. See appropriate AUTOMATIC TRANSMISSION SERVICING article in this section.

TIGHTENING SPECIFICATIONS (AOD)

Application	Ft. Lbs. (N.m)
Converter-to-Flex Plate	20-34 (27-46)
Converter Drain Plug	8-28 (11-38)
Cooler Lines-to-Transmission	18-23 (24-31)
Crossmember-to-Side Support	70-100 (95-136)
Flex Plate-to-Crankshaft Bolts	
2.3L (OHC), 3.8L	56-64 (73-87)
5.0L, 5.8L	75-85 (102-115)
Transmission-to-Engine Bolts	40-50 (54-68)

TIGHTENING SPECIFICATIONS (A4LD)

Application	Ft. Lbs. (N.m)
Converter-to-Flex Plate Bolts	20-34 (27-46)
Crossmember-to-Frame	20-30 (27-41)
Flex Plate-to-Crankshaft Bolts	
2.3L (OHC), 3.8L	56-64 (76-87)
5.0L, 5.8L	75-85 (102-115)
Transmission-to-Engine Bolts	26-38 (38-51)

FORD MOTOR CO. (Cont.)

ATX
Removal
(Escort, EXP, Tempo & Topaz)

1) Disconnect negative battery cable. Remove air cleaner assembly. Disconnect wiring from neutral safety switch. Harness connector is near distributor. Disconnect throttle valve linkage and manual lever cable at transaxle.

2) Cover up timing window in converter housing to prevent contamination. Remove bolts retaining air injection system hoses (if equipped). Position valve and hoses away from tubing and master cylinder. Remove ground strap above engine mount (if equipped).

3) Remove coil and bracket assembly. Remove the 2 upper transaxle-to-engine attaching bolts. Raise and support vehicle. Remove wheels.

4) Remove control arm-to-steering knuckle attaching bolt and nut (at both ball joints) and discard. A NEW bolt and nut must be used during transalxe installation. Using pry bar, carefully separate control arms from steering knuckles.

CAUTION: Use care not to damage ball joint boot. Pry bar must not contact control arm. DO NOT use hammer on ball joints.

5) Remove bolts attaching stabilizer bar brackets to frame. Remove stabilizer bar-to-control arm nut and washer. Discard bolts and washer. Manufacturer recommends using NEW hardware on installation.

6) Pull stabilizer bar out of control arms. Remove bolts attaching brake hose routing clips to suspension strut brackets. Disconnect tie rod ends from steering knuckles.

7) Pry right side drive axle shaft out of transaxle using Halfshaft Remover (D83P-4026-A). See FWD AXLE SHAFTS in DRIVE AXLES section for removal procedure. Position shaft on transaxle housing.

8) Insert Differential Rotator (T81P-4026-A) into right side differential side gear. Drive left drive axle shaft from differential side gear. Pull drive axle shaft from transaxle and support out of way.

CAUTION: Do not let axle shaft hang unsupported. Damage to outboard CV joint may result.

9) Install Seal Plugs (T81P-1177-B) into differential seals to prevent spline misalignment. Remove starter. On throttle body equipped vehicles, remove 2 hose/bracket bolts on starter and one (1) bolt attached to converter. Disconnect hoses.

10) Remove transaxle support bracket. Remove torque converter housing dust cover. Remove flex plate-to-converter nuts. Position transmission jack under transaxle. Remove rear support bracket nuts. Remove nuts attaching left front insulator to body bracket. Remove bracket-to-body bolts and remove bracket.

11) Disconnect oil cooling lines at transaxle using Cooler Line Disconnector (T82L-9500-AH). Remove bolts attaching manual lever bracket to transaxle case. Support engine. Position transmission jack under transaxle and remove 4 remaining transaxle-to-engine bolts.

12) Insert screwdriver between flex plate and converter. Carefully move transaxle and converter away from engine. When converter studs are clear of flex plate, lower transaxle about 3". Disconnect speedometer cable and lower transaxle from vehicle.

NOTE: **If left-front insulator contacts body before converter studs clear flex plate, remove left-front insulator.**

Installation

1) To install transaxle, reverse removal procedure. ALWAYS replace snap ring on CV joint stub shaft.

2) To install drive axle shafts, carefully align splines on shaft with differential splines. Push CV joint until snap ring is felt to seat in groove in side gear.

3) Attach lower ball joint to steering knuckle, taking care not to damage or cut ball joint boot. Install NEW pinch bolt and NEW nut. DO NOT tighten bolt, tighten NUT to specification.

4) Fill transaxle with ATF. See AUTOMATIC TRANSMISSION SERVICING in this section.

Removal (Taurus)

1) Disconnect negative battery cable. Remove air cleaner assembly. Position engine control wiring assembly away from transaxle converter housing area. Disconnect throttle valve linkage and manual lever cable. Remove power steering hose brackets. Remove 2 upper transaxle-to-engine bolts.

2) Install Engine Lifting Bracket (D81L-6001-D) to right side rear area of cylinder with a M10 x 1.5 x 20 bolt. Install a second engine lifting bracket to left side front area of cylinder with same size bolt. Install 2 Engine Support Bars (D79P-6000-A).

NOTE: **An engine support bar can be fabricated from a length of 4" x 4" wood cut to approximately 57".**

3) Place one (1) engine support bar across vehicle in front of each shock tower. Place the other support bar between alternator and valve cover. Attach chains from each support bar to engine lifting brackets. Raise and support vehicle. Remove both wheels.

4) Remove catalytic converter inlet pipe. Disconnect engine exhaust air hose assembly. Remove each tie rod end from its spindle. Remove bolts and nuts attaching lower ball joints to struts. Separate and remove ball joints. Remove lower control arm from each spindle.

5) Remove stabilizer bar nuts and disconnect stabilizer bar. Remove nuts securing steering rack to subframe. Disconnect and remove auxiliary cooler from subframe. Position steering rack away from subframe and secure with wire. Remove right side front axle support and bearing assembly bolts.

6) Remove right side front drive axle shaft support and bearing assembly. Remove axle shaft assembly out of right side of transaxle. See DRIVE AXLES section for removal procedure.

7) Disengage left side halfshaft from differential side gear using Differential Rotator (T81P-4026-A). Pull halfshaft out of transaxle. Support and secure halfshaft. DO NOT allow halfshafts to hang unsupported.

8) Install Seal Plugs (T81P-1177-B) in transaxle to prevent spline misalignment. Remove front support insulator. Move left side front splash shield aside. Position bench or jack stands to support subframe after it is disconnected.

FORD MOTOR CO. (Cont.)

9) Lower vehicle to bench or jack stand. Block or support as needed. Remove subframe bolts and subframe.

10) Disconnect neutral safety switch wire assembly. Disconnect speedometer cable. Remove shift cable bracket bolts and bracket from transaxle. Disconnect oil cooler lines using Cooler Line Disconnector (T86P-77265-AA). Remove starter.

11) Remove dust cover from torque converter housing. Remove flex plate-to-converter nuts. Position transmission jack under transaxle and secure transaxle to jack. Remove remaining transaxle-to-engine bolts.

12) Insert a screwdriver between flex plate and torque converter. Carefully move transaxle and converter away from engine. When torque converter studs are clear of flex plate, lower transaxle and remove from vehicle.

Installation

1) To install transaxle, reverse removal procedure. Prior to installing drive axle shafts, replace snap ring on CV joint stub shaft.

2) To install halfshafts, carefully align splines on shaft with differential splines. See DRIVE AXLES in this section for installation procedure.

3) Attach lower ball joint to steering knuckle, taking care not to damage or cut ball joint boot. Install NEW BOLT and NEW NUT. DO NOT tighten bolt, tighten nut to specification.

4) Converter is correctly seated when pilot is 7/16-9/16" (11-14 mm) from engine mounting surface. Prevent converter from moving forward during installation.

5) Readjust T.V. linkage and manual linkage. Fill transaxle with ATF to proper level. See AUTOMATIC TRANSMISSION SERVICING in this section.

TIGHTENING SPECIFICATIONS (ATX)

Application	Ft. Lbs. (N.m)
Ball Joint Nut-to-Steering Knuckle Bolt	40-54 (54-74)
Converter-to-Flex Plate	23-39 (31-53)
Cooler Line Nut At Radiator & Transaxle	12-18 (16-24)
Cooler Line Push Connector At Transaxle	18-23 (24-31)
Flex Plate-to-Crankshaft	
1.9L, 2.3L, 2.5L	54-64 (73-87)
3.0L, 3.8L	54-64 (73-87)
Insulator Mount-to-Transaxle	25-33 (34-45)
Insulator-to-Bracket	55-70 (75-95)
Insulator Bracket-to-Frame	40-50 (54-68)
Tie Rod-to-Knuckle	[1] 23-35 (31-47)
Transaxle-to-Engine	25-33 (34-45)

[1] – Tighten to minimum torque; continue tightening to nearest cotter pin slot.

AXOD

NOTE: AXOD removal procedure for Sable and Taurus with 3.8L is not available from manufacturer.

Removal (Continental, Sable & Taurus)

1) Remove negative battery cable and air cleaner assembly. Remove shifter cable and bracket from transaxle. Disconnect neutral safety switch and bulkhead connector from rear of transaxle.

2) Remove T.V. cable from throttle body and transaxle. Remove through bolt from left motor mount strut. Remove upper transaxle-to-engine bolts. On Sable and Taurus, attach Engine Lifting Bracket (D81L-6001-D) to rear of left side cylinder head. Lifting bracket should already be installed on front of right side cylinder head.

3) On all models, attach Engine Support Bar (D79P-6000-A) across shock towers. Attach engine to support bar. Raise engine to take pressure off engine mounts.

4) Raise vehicle on hoist. Remove front wheels. Separate tie rod ends from spindles. Remove bolts and nuts securing ball joints. Remove lower ball joints.

5) Remove lower control arms from each spindle. Remove sway bar link-to-body bolts. Remove steering rack-to-subframe bolts.

6) Remove all subframe-to-engine mount bolts. Disconnect oxygen sensor lead. Remove exhaust system section under subframe and transaxle. Support subframe. Remove remaining subframe-to-body bolts and lower subframe.

7) Position transaxle jack under transaxle. Remove speedometer or vehicle speed sensor from transaxle. Remove transaxle-to-engine supports and transaxle mount. Remove starter and dust cover.

8) Remove 4 flex plate-to-torque converter nuts. Disconnect transaxle cooler lines. Pull CV joints from transaxle using a slide hammer with a CV Joint Puller (T86P-3514-A1) and Extension (T86P-3514-A2). See DRIVE AXLES section for removal procedure.

9) Remove remaining transaxle-to-engine bolts. Separate transaxle and lower out of vehicle.

Installation

To install transaxle, reverse removal procedure. Adjust T.V. cable and shift linkage. A NEW circlip MUST be used on drive axle inboard stub shaft before installation. Fill transaxle with ATF. See AUTOMATIC TRANSMISSION SERVICING in this section.

TIGHTENING SPECIFICATIONS (AXOD)

Application	Ft. Lbs. (N.m)
Ball Joint Nut-to-Steering Knuckle Bolt	37-44 (50-60)
Converter-to-Flex Plate	23-39 (31-53)
Cooler Line Nut At Radiator	12-18 (16-24)
Cooler Line Push Connector At Transaxle	18-23 (24-31)
Flex Plate-to-Crankshaft	
1.9L, 2.3L, 2.5L	54-64 (73-87)
3.0L, 3.8L	54-64 (73-87)
Insulator Mount-to-Transaxle	25-33 (34-45)
Insulator-to-Bracket	55-70 (75-95)
Insulator Bracket-to-Frame	40-50 (54-68)
Stabilizer-to-Control Arm	98-125 (133-169)
Tie Rod-to-Knuckle	[1] 23-35 (31-47)
Transaxle-to-Engine	41-50 (55-68)

[1] – Tighten to minimum torque; continue tightening to nearest cotter pin slot.

GENERAL MOTORS

NOTE: This article includes removal and installation procedures for Chevrolet Nova.

REMOVAL & INSTALLATION

THM 125C TRANSAXLES

Removal (All Models Except Fiero)

1) Disconnect negative battery cable. Remove air cleaner and T.V. cable from throttle lever and transaxle. Remove airflow meter and intake duct (if equipped). Remove shift linkage and wiring harness routing clips and straps.

2) On V6 models, remove exhaust crossover bolts at right side manifold, and left side exhaust manifold bolts at cylinder head. Raise and support manifold/crossover assembly.

3) On all models, remove filler tube and install Engine Holding Fixture (J-28467). Insert a 1/4" x 2" bolt in hole at front right motor mount to maintain driveline alignment.

4) Remove nut securing wiring harness to transaxle. Disconnect all external wiring connectors from transaxle. Disconnect manual shift linkage and remove from bracket. Remove top 2 transaxle-to-engine bolts and upper left transaxle bracket and mount.

5) Remove rubber hose from transaxle to vent pipe. Remove remaining upper engine-to-transaxle bolts. Raise and support vehicle and remove front wheels. Drain transaxle. Remove lower ball joints from control arms.

6) Install Axle Boot Protectors (J-34754). Remove and support axles. Refer to FWD AXLE SHAFTS article in DRIVE AXLES section for removal procedure. Remove transaxle mounting strut. Remove left stabilizer bar pin bolt and left stabilizer bar clamp nuts attaching left stabilizer bar to frame. Remove left frame support assembly.

7) On models equipped with 2.0L, remove header pipe at exhaust manifold. On models equipped with 2.8L, remove header pipe and front exhaust manifold. Disconnect speedometer cable and remove starter motor. Remove torque converter cover. Index mark torque converter to flex plate and remove converter mounting bolts.

8) Disconnect oil cooler lines. Remove transaxle-to-engine support bracket. Secure transaxle jack under transaxle and remove remaining engine-to-transaxle bolts. Slide transaxle away from engine and right axle shaft. Lower transaxle from vehicle.

Installation

To install, reverse removal procedure. Guide right axle shaft into transaxle when raising transaxle to engine. Adjust T.V. and shift cables after installation. Refill transaxle to proper fluid level. See AUTOMATIC TRANSMISSION SERVICING in this section.

Removal (Fiero)

1) Remove air cleaner and negative battery cable. Remove left and right side engine vent covers. Disconnect shift cable at lever and T.V. cable at transaxle and carburetor.

2) Disconnect neutral switch and all electrical connectors at transaxle. Disconnect speedometer electrical pick-up connector. Remove 5 upper transaxle bolts and wiring harness retainers. Remove cooler line support bracket.

3) Install Engine Support Fixture (J-28467-A) to support engine. Raise and support vehicle and remove rear wheels. Remove lateral control arm through bolts and disconnect trailing arms at knuckles.

CAUTION: Do not overextend Tri-Pot type joints in drive axle shafts. Overextending joint could result in separation of internal components.

4) Remove both axle drive shafts and properly support. Refer to FWD AXLE SHAFTS article in DRIVE AXLES section for removal procedure. Remove splash shields. Disconnect brake cables at calipers and remove brake control cable at frame.

5) Disconnect exhaust at manifold. Remove all nuts mounting both engine and transaxle mounts to cradle. Remove 2 front cradle retaining bolts and 2 rear cradle retaining nuts. Remove cradle from vehicle.

6) Remove starter and flexplate shield. Index mark flexplate to flywheel and remove 3 torque converter bolts. Disconnect transaxle oil cooler lines and secure a transaxle jack under transaxle. Remove remaining transaxle-to-engine bolts and lower transaxle from vehicle.

Installation

To install, reverse removal procedure. Adjust T.V. cable and shift cable after installation. Refill transaxle to proper level with fluid. See AUTOMATIC TRANSMISSION SERVICING in this section.

THM 440-T4 TRANSAXLES

Removal (All Models Except Celebrity, Century, Ciera & 6000)

1) Disconnect negative battery cable. On DeVille, Eldorado, Fleetwood and Seville, remove air cleaner, air injection crossover pipe, air management valve and exhaust crossover pipe. On all others, remove airflow meter.

2) Remove T.V. cable at throttle body and transaxle. Remove shift linkage and vacuum modulator line. Remove neutral safety switch, cruise control and vehicle speed sensor wiring. Remove 3 upper transaxle-to-engine mounting bolts.

3) Install Engine Support (J-28467) and raise engine to unload engine mounts. On Eldorado, Toronado and Seville, remove driveline damper and engine mount. On all vehicles, raise on a hoist and remove front wheels.

4) Remove both lower ball joints from steering knuckle. Install Axle Boot Protectors (J-34754). Using Drive Axle Remover (J-33008), remove drive axle shafts from transaxle. Refer to FWD AXLE SHAFTS article in DRIVE AXLES section for removal procedure. Secure drive axles out of way.

NOTE: If necessary, raise left side of engine 2" to remove left engine mount and left cradle attaching bolts. Ensure engine is lowered back to original position.

5) Remove stabilizer linkage at left side. Remove left splash shield, vacuum pump (if equipped), and disconnect all wiring and hoses. Remove all transaxle-to-cradle bolts. Remove engine-to-left cradle assembly mounting bolts. Support left cradle assembly. Remove right and left cradle attaching bolts and remove left cradle assembly.

GENERAL MOTORS (Cont.)

NOTE: Whenever cradle assembly is removed or lowered from vehicle, rack and pinion steering assembly must be disconnected from cradle. To prevent damage to intermediate shaft, steering assembly must be supported so it does not "hang" by intermediate shaft.

6) Disconnect oil cooler lines and remove dust cover. Index mark torque converter to flexplate and remove converter mounting bolts. Secure transaxle jack under transaxle. Remove remaining transaxle mounting bolts and remove from vehicle.

NOTE: Locate one bolt connecting transaxle-to-engine installed from opposite direction. On some models, a 3 FOOT socket extension placed through right wheelhousing will help remove this bolt.

Installation

To install, reverse removal procedure. Guide right axle shaft into transaxle when raising transaxle to engine. Adjust T.V. and shift cables. Refill transaxle to proper fluid level. See AUTOMATIC TRANSMISSION SERVICING in this section.

Removal (Celebrity, Century, Ciera & 6000)

1) Disconnect negative battery cable. Remove air cleaner, wiring and cable routing clips and straps. Remove bolt securing T.V. cable to transaxle. Install Engine Support (J-28467) and relieve weight from mounts.

2) Raise vehicle on a hoist. Drain transaxle fluid. Remove strut shock bracket bolts from transaxle. Remove oil cooler lines from strut bracket and transaxle.

3) On models equipped with THM 440-T4 transaxle, remove left front wheel. Disconnect left front lower ball joint from steering knuckle. Remove brake line bracket at strut. Remove stabilizer bolts from frame and control arm.

4) Remove transaxle-to-engine bolts leaving bolt near starter loosely installed. Remove speedometer cable at upper and lower couplings. Remove shifter linkage retaining clip, washer and bracket from transaxle.

5) Remove front and left sections of cradle. Install Axle Boot Protectors (J-34754). Position Axle Shaft Remover (J-33008) and Slide Hammer (J-2619-01) behind axle shaft cones and pull cones away from transaxle. Refer to FWD AXLE SHAFTS article in DRIVE AXLES section for removal procedure.

6) Rotate strut so axle shaft is out of way. Remove starter motor and converter shields. Index mark flexplate to torque converter and remove converter mounting bolts. Remove 2 transaxle extension bolts from engine-to-transaxle. Remove rear transaxle mount bracket. It may be necessary to raise transaxle to remove bracket.

7) Secure jack under transaxle. Remove 2 braces to right end of transaxle bolts. Remove remaining transaxle-to-engine bolt (located near starter). Slide transaxle from engine, toward driver's side. Lower transaxle from vehicle.

Installation

To install, reverse removal procedure. Guide right axle shaft into transaxle when raising transaxle to engine. Adjust T.V. cable and shift cable after installation. Refill transaxle to proper level with fluid. See AUTOMATIC TRANSMISSION SERVICING in this section.

THM 200-4R & THM 700-R4 TRANSMISSIONS

Removal (All Models)

1) Disconnect negative battery cable and remove air cleaner. Disconnect upper end of T.V. cable at throttle or carburetor linkage, and remove filler tube. Raise and support vehicle on a hoist. Index mark and remove propeller shaft.

2) On Corvette models, remove complete exhaust system and driveline beam. On Corvette convertible, remove upper and lower body braces. Camaro and Firebird, remove torque arm from rear suspension. On Cadillac, remove header pipe at exhaust manifold, catalytic converter, fuel line-to-transmission bracket and transmission-to-engine ground strap bolt.

3) Remove floor reinforcement (if equipped). Disconnect speedometer cable. Remove shifter linkage and electrical connectors. Remove flexplate cover. Index mark flexplate to torque converter and remove attaching bolts.

4) Remove catalytic converter support bracket and remove crossmember. Lower transmission slightly, disconnect oil cooler lines and remove T.V. cable hold down bolt.

5) Support engine with a screw jack and block of wood. Remove transmission-to-engine bolts. Pull transmission back enough to install Torque Converter Holder (J-21366). Lower transmission from vehicle.

Installation

1) To install transmission, reverse removal procedures. Observe index marks made during removal and align marks to original positions.

2) Test torque converter for freedom of rotation. Tighten flexplate bolts finger tight, then tighten to specifications. Adjust shift linkage and T.V. cable as necessary. Fill transmission to proper level with fluid. See AUTOMATIC TRANSMISSION SERVICING in this section.

TOYOTA A131L TRANSAXLE

Removal (Nova)

1) Disconnect negative battery cable and remove air intake tube. Disconnect neutral safety switch and all external electrical connectors leading to transaxle.

2) Disconnect thermostat housing and battery ground cable at transaxle. Disconnect T.V. cable from throttle linkage and remove from bracket. Remove upper mount-to-bracket bolt and 2 upper bellhousing bolts. Install Engine Support Fixture (J-28467) and relieve weight from mounts.

3) Raise and support vehicle. Drain transaxle and remove center, left and right splash shields. Disconnect shift control cable and remove from cable bracket. Disconnect oil cooler lines from bracket and disconnect oil cooler lines at transaxle.

4) Remove inspection cover, index mark flexplate to torque converter and remove converter bolts. Disconnect both lower control arms at ball joint connections. Remove both axle drive shafts at transaxle. Refer to FWD AXLE SHAFTS article in DRIVE AXLES section for removal procedure.

5) Remove starter motor bolts and remove 3 rear transaxle-to-engine bolts. Secure jack under transaxle and remove remaining transaxle-to-engine bolts. Remove transaxle from vehicle.

GENERAL MOTORS (Cont.)

Installation

1) To install transaxle, reverse removal procedures. Observe index marks made during removal and line-up in original positions.

2) Ensure that threaded pads on torque converter are flush with flexplate. Test torque converter for freedom of rotation. Tighten flexplate bolts finger tight, then tighten to specifications. Adjust shift linkage and T.V. cable as necessary. Fill transmission to proper level with fluid. See AUTOMATIC TRANSMISSION SERVICING in this section.

TOYOTA A240E TRANSAXLE
Removal

1) Disconnect negative battery cable and remove air cleaner. Disconnect neutral safety switch and all external electrical connectors leading to transaxle. Disconnect T.V. cable from throttle linkage and remove cable from bracket.

2) Remove thermostat housing and disconnect battery ground cable at transaxle housing. Raise vehicle and drain transaxle. Remove splash shields and disconnect shift control cable at bracket. Remove bracket.

3) Disconnect oil cooler hoses and remove front and rear engine mount bolts. Remove center mounting member. Disconnect oxygen sensor connector and remove front exhaust pipe.

4) Disconnect left and right drive axle shafts from transaxle. Refer to FWD AXLE SHAFTS article in DRIVE AXLES section for removal procedure. Remove left wheel and brake rotor assembly. Disconnect left steering knuckle from lower control arm and remove left drive axle shaft.

5) Remove starter motor and both stiffener plates at bellhousing. Remove dust cover, index mark flexplate to torque converter and remove converter bolts. Lower vehicle and install Engine Support Fixture (J-28467). Remove 3 rear engine mount bolts and raise vehicle. Remove transaxle-to-engine bolts and remove transaxle.

TIGHTENING SPECIFICATIONS

Application	Ft. Lbs. (N.m)
THM 125C & 440-T4	
Except Fiero	
Cooler Lines	16 (22)
Flexplate-to-Crankshaft	
2.0L	52 (70)
2.3L	[1] 30 (22)
2.5L	55 (75)
2.8L	35 (47)
4.3L & 5.0L	74 (100)
All Others	60 (81)
Front Cradle Assembly	
"J","L" & "N" Bodies	65 (88)
All Others	74 (100)
Torque Converter-to-Flexplate	
"J","L" & "N" Bodies	35 (47)
All Others	46 (62)
Transaxle-to-Engine	55 (75)
Transaxle-to-Mount Nuts	40 (54)
Fiero	
Cooler Lines	16 (22)
Engine Mount-to-Cradle	40 (54)
Flexplate-to-Crankshaft	
2.5L	55 (75)
2.8L	35 (47)
Front Cradle-to-Body	67 (90)
Rear Cradle-to-Body	76 (103)
Torque Converter-to-Flexplate	35 (47)
Transaxle-to-Engine	55 (75)
Transaxle Mount-to-Cradle	
Front	36 (49)
Rear	18 (24)
THM 200-4R & 700-R4	
Cooler Lines	16 (22)
Flexplate-to-Crankshaft	
2.8L	35 (47)
4.3L & 5.0L	74 (100)
All Others	60 (81)
Torque Converter-to-Flexplate	46 (62)
Transmission-to-Engine	35 (47)
Transmission-to-Mount	35 (47)
Toyota A131L & A240E	
Center Support-to-Body	29 (39)
Flexplate-to-Crankshaft	[1] 47 (64)
Mount-to-Center Support	29 (39)
Torque Converter-to-Flexplate	13 (18)
Transaxle-to-Engine (10 mm)	35 (47)
Transaxle-to-Engine (12 mm)	47 (64)

[1] – Rotate another 35 degrees.

CHRYSLER MOTORS

LUBRICATION

SERVICE INTERVALS

Check fluid level whenever other underhood services are performed. Under normal driving conditions, factory installed fluid will give satisfactory lubrication for the life of the vehicle. Under severe driving conditions, drain and refill at 15,000 mile intervals.

CHECKING FLUID LEVEL

1) Check lubricant level at filler plug hole on left side of transaxle (on rear end cover). Lubricant should be level with bottom of filler plug hole.

2) Fluid is drained by removing differential cover. Clean magnet. Use RTV sealant on differential cover.

RECOMMENDED FLUID

A-520, A-525 & A-555 Transaxles
Use SAE 5W-30 (SF) engine oil.

FLUID CAPACITY

NOTE: **A-525 transaxle model I.D. tag is attached to differential cover. A-520 and A-555 I.D. tag is attached to top of transaxle.**

TRANSAXLE REFILL CAPACITIES

Application	Pts. (L)
5-Speed	
A-525	4.4 (2.1)
A-520 & A-555	4.8 (2.3)

ADJUSTMENTS

SHIFT LINKAGE

Rod Operated Transaxles (Horizon & Omni)
1) Place transaxle in Neutral position. Working over left front fender, remove lock pin from transaxle selector shaft housing. *See Fig. 1.*

2) Reverse lock pin (long end down) and insert into same threaded hole while pushing selector shaft into selector housing. Hole in selector shaft will align with lock pin, allowing lock pin to be inserted in housing. Selector shaft will be locked in Neutral position.

3) Raise and support vehicle. Loosen clamp bolt that secures gearshift tube to gearshift connector. Ensure gearshift connector slides and turns freely in gearshift tube. *See Fig. 2.*

4) Position shifter mechanism connector assembly so isolator is contacting upstanding flange, and rib on isolator is aligned fore and aft with the hole in block-out bracket. Hold in this position while tightening clamp bolt on gearshift tube to 14 ft. lbs. (19 N.m). No force should be exerted on linkage during this operation.

5) Lower vehicle. Remove lock pin from selector shaft housing, and reinstall lock pin upside down (long end up) in selector shaft housing. Tighten lock pin to 105 INCH lbs. (12 N.m). Check for shift into 1st and Reverse. Check for block-out into Reverse.

Fig. 1: Removing Lock Pin From Transaxle Selector Shaft Housing

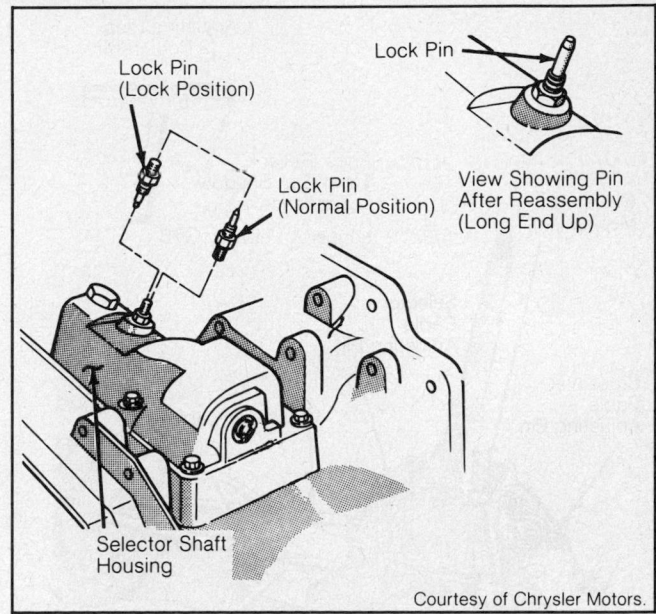

Courtesy of Chrysler Motors.

Fig. 2: Rod Operated Gearshift Linkage Adjustment

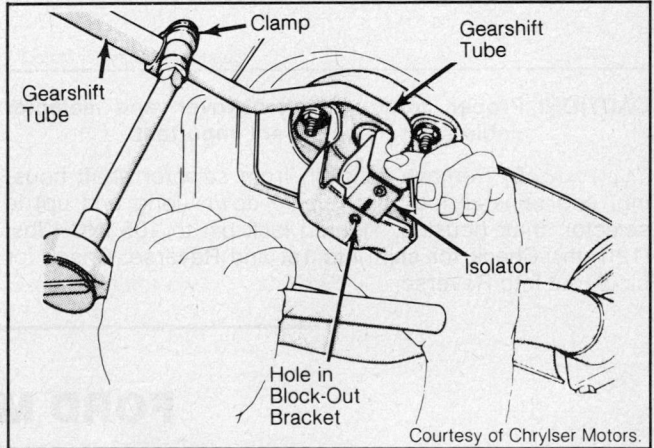

Courtesy of Chrylser Motors.

Cable Operated Transaxle (Except Daytona & LeBaron)
1) Place transaxle in Neutral position. Working over left front fender, remove lock pin from transaxle selector shaft housing. *See Fig. 1.*

2) Reverse lock pin (long end down) and insert into same threaded hole while pushing selector shaft into selector housing. Hole in selector shaft will align with lock pin, allowing lock pin to be inserted in housing. Selector shaft will be locked in Neutral position.

3) Remove gearshift knob, retaining nut and pull-up ring. Remove screws attaching center console and remove console. Fabricate 2 adjustment pins from 3/16" or 5/32" diameter rod, depending on model application. *See Fig. 3.*

4) Loosen crossover and selector cable adjustment screws. Allow both cables to center themselves in the adjustment slot. Install adjustment pins in gear shifter mechanism. Retighten cable adjustment set screws to 70 INCH. lbs. (8 N.m).

Manual Transmission Servicing

CHRYSLER MOTORS (Cont.)

Fig. 3: Cable Operated Gearshift Linkage Adjustments

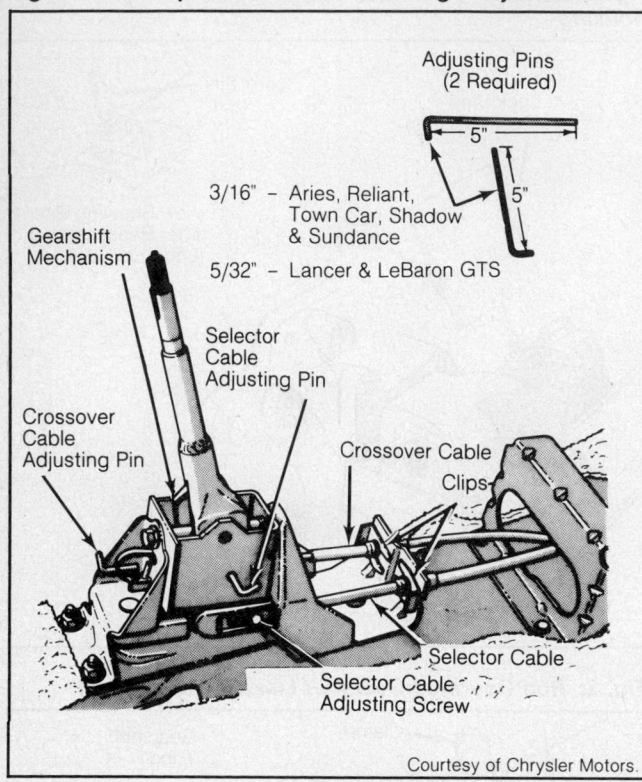

Courtesy of Chrysler Motors.

CAUTION: Proper torque on crossover and selector cable set screws is very important.

5) Remove lock pin from selector shaft housing, and reinstall lock pin upside down (long end up) in selector shaft housing. Tighten lock pin to 105 INCH lbs. (12 N.m). Check for shift into 1st and Reverse. Check for block-out into Reverse.

Cable Operated Transaxle (Daytona & LeBaron)

1) Follow procedure described in steps 1) and 2) in CABLE OPERATED TRANSAXLE (EXCEPT DAYTONA & LEBARON). Remove gearshift knob, retaining nut and pull-up ring. Remove center console.

2) An adjusting screw tool (left-hand threaded) is taped to shifter support bracket. Remove tool from bracket. Loosen crossover and selector cable adjustment screws.

3) Insert and tighten adjusting screw tool to 20 INCH lbs. (2 N.m). *See Fig. 4.* Retighten cable adjustment set screws to 70 INCH. lbs. (8 N.m).

4) Remove adjusting screw tool and fasten to support bracket. Follow procedure in step 5) of CABLE OPERATED TRANSAXLE (EXCEPT DAYTONA & LEBARON).

Fig. 4: Adjusting Gearshift Linkage (Daytona & LeBaron)

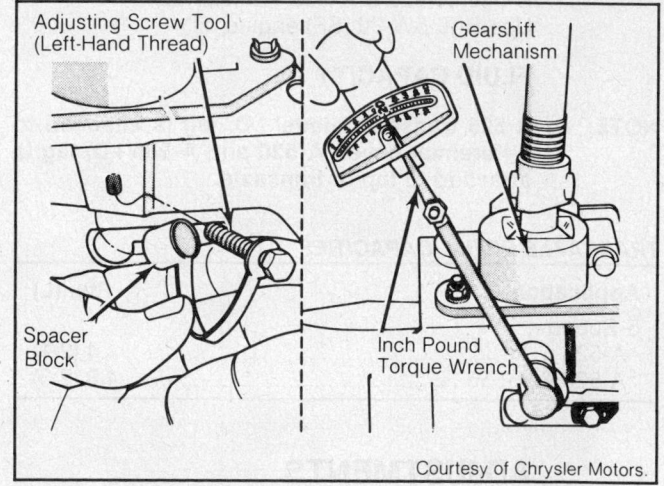

Courtesy of Chrysler Motors.

FORD MOTOR CO.

LUBRICATION

SERVICE INTERVALS

Check fluid level at 15 month/15,000 mile intervals. Draining and refilling are not required, except at time of overhaul or service.

CHECKING FLUID LEVEL

Check lubricant level at filler plug hole on side of transmission. Lubricant should be level with bottom of filler plug hole. Add lubricant as necessary to bring to correct level.

CAUTION: Drain and fill plugs for T50D are on right side of case. Do not remove reverse shift lever pin on left side of case.

RECOMMENDED FLUID

MTX Transaxle & T5OD
Use Type F or Mercon ATF.

FLUID CAPACITY

TRANSMISSION REFILL CAPACITIES

Application	Pts. (L)
MTX	
4 & 5-Speed	6.1 (2.9)
T5OD 5-Speed Overdrive	5.6 (2.6)

ADJUSTMENTS

SHIFT LINKAGE

No in-service adjustment of shift linkage is necessary.

GENERAL MOTORS

LUBRICATION

SERVICE INTERVALS

Check fluid level at 3 month/3000 mile intervals. Draining and refilling is not required, except at time of overhaul or service.

On Corvette, change fluid in overdrive unit every 30,000 miles. On Nova, change fluid in transaxle every 20,000 miles or 24 months.

CHECKING FLUID LEVEL

Camaro, Corvette & Firebird

Check lubricant level at filler plug hole on right side of transmission. Lubricant should be level with bottom of filler plug hole. Add lubricant as necessary to bring to correct level.

NOTE: **On Camaro and Firebird, DO NOT remove reverse shift lever pin on LEFT side of case.**

Isuzu & Muncie 5-Speed Transaxles

1) Vehicle should be on level surface. Transaxle fluid should be COLD when checking fluid. Fluid should be at "FULL" mark on dipstick. *See Fig. 1.* Drain plug is below dipstick tube.

2) On Fiero equipped with Isuzu transaxle, remove permanent magnet generator on driver's side of case. Fluid level should be between "L" and "H" marks on generator. *See Fig. 2.*

Fig. 1: Checking Fluid Level on Isuzu (Except Fiero) & Muncie 5-Speed Transaxles

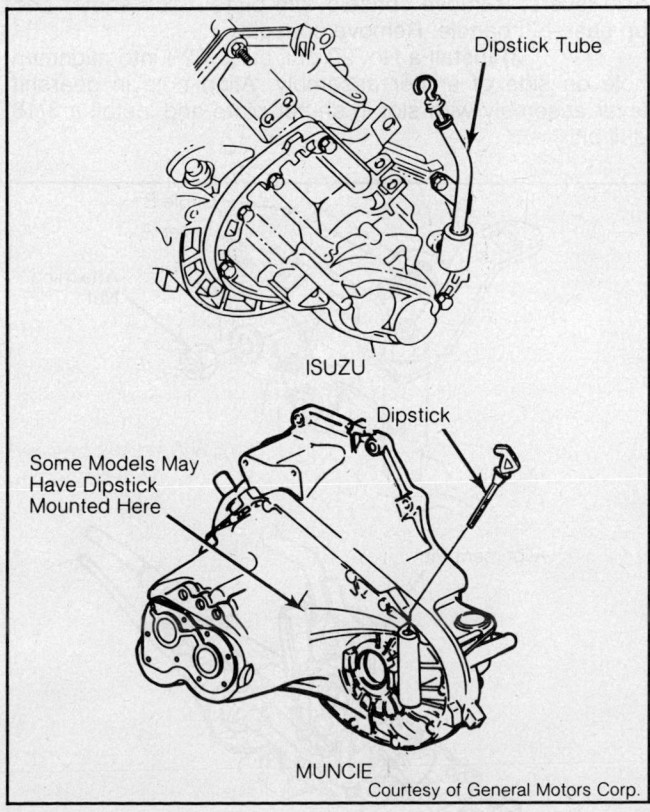

ISUZU

Some Models May Have Dipstick Mounted Here

Dipstick

MUNCIE
Courtesy of General Motors Corp.

Fig. 2: Checking Fluid Level on Isuzu (Fiero) 5-Speed Transaxle

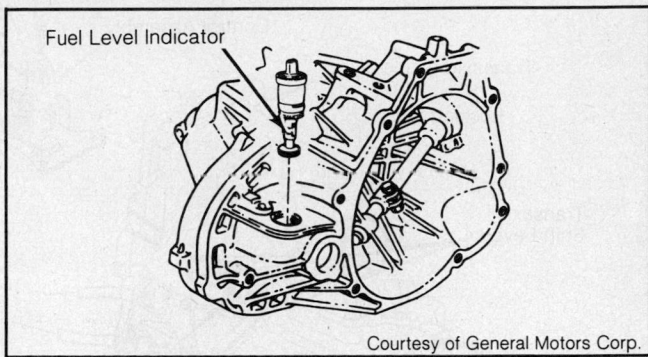

Fuel Level Indicator

Courtesy of General Motors Corp.

Toyota C51 5-Speed (Nova)
Ensure fluid level is bottom of fill plug hole. *See Fig. 3.*

Fig. 3: Toyota C51 Transaxle (Nova)

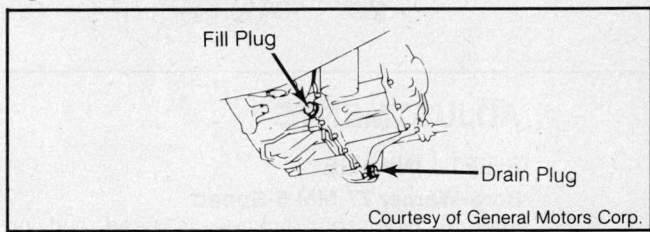

Fill Plug

Drain Plug

Courtesy of General Motors Corp.

RECOMMENDED FLUID

Borg-Warner 77 MM 5-Speed
Use Dexron II ATF.

Doug Nash 83 MM 4-Speed
Use SAE 80W-90 GL5 gear lubricant in transmission. Use Dexron II ATF in overdrive unit.

Isuzu & Muncie 76 MM 5-Speed Transaxle
Use Manual Transaxle Oil (Part No. 12345349).

Toyota C51 5-Speed Transaxle
Use SAE 75W-90 or 80W-90 GL-5 gear lubricant.

FLUID CAPACITY

TRANSMISSION REFILL CAPACITIES

Application	Pts. (L)
4-Speed	
Doug Nash 83 MM	[1]
Overdrive Unit	2.0 (1.0)
5-Speed	
Borg-Warner 77 MM	5.9 (2.8)
Toyota C51 Transaxle (Nova)	5.5 (2.6)
Isuzu 76 MM Transaxle	5.3 (2.5)
Muncie 76 MM Transaxle	
A & P Bodies	4.0 (1.9)
J, L, N & W Bodies	5.0 (2.1)

[1] – Fill to bottom of filler plug hole.

GENERAL MOTORS (Cont.)

Fig. 4: Isuzu 76 MM Transaxle Shift Cables (Except Fiero)

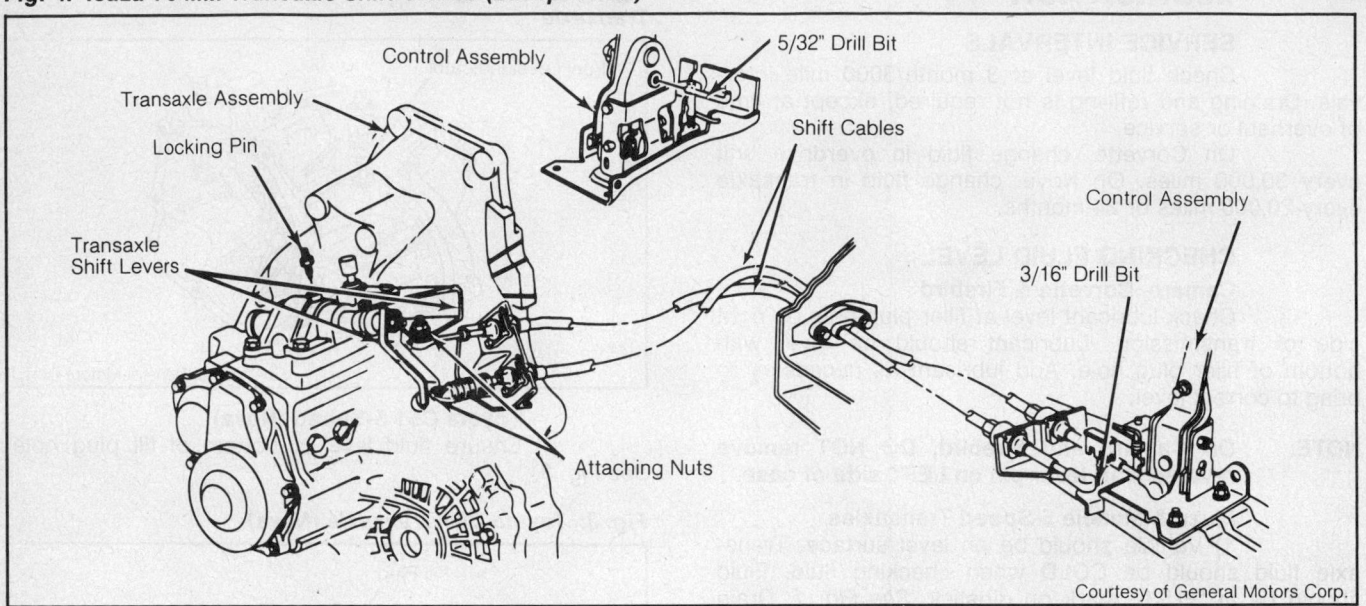

Courtesy of General Motors Corp.

ADJUSTMENTS

SHIFT LINKAGE

Borg-Warner 77 MM 5-Speed

Integral type shift linkage is used and no adjustment is necessary.

SHIFT CABLE

Toyota C51 5-Speed Transaxle (Nova)

Shift cables are fixed length. No adjustment is provided.

Isuzu 76 MM 5-Speed Transaxle (Except Fiero)

1) Disconnect negative battery cable. Shift transaxle into 3rd gear. Remove lock pin at transaxle. See Fig. 4. Install lock pin with tapered end down to lock transaxle into 3rd gear.

2) Loosen shift cable attaching nuts at transaxle levers. Remove console trim plate. Slide shifter boot up gearshift handle. Remove console.

3) Install a No. 22 drill bit (5/32") into alignment hole on side of shifter assembly. Align hole in gearshift lever assembly with slot in shifter plate and install a 3/16" drill bit.

Fig. 5: Isuzu 76 MM Transaxle Shift Cables (Fiero)

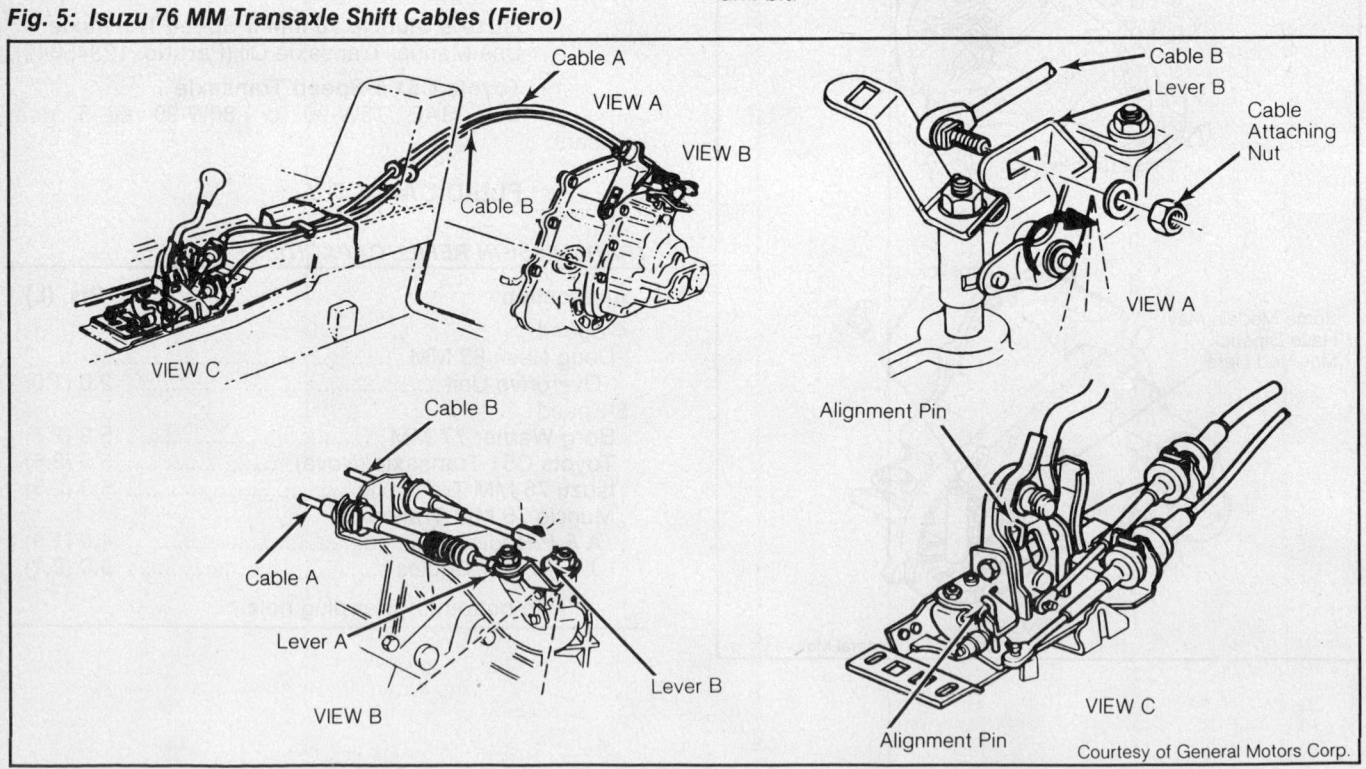

Courtesy of General Motors Corp.

GENERAL MOTORS (Cont.)

Fig. 6: Muncie 76 MM Transaxle Shift Cables (Except Fiero)

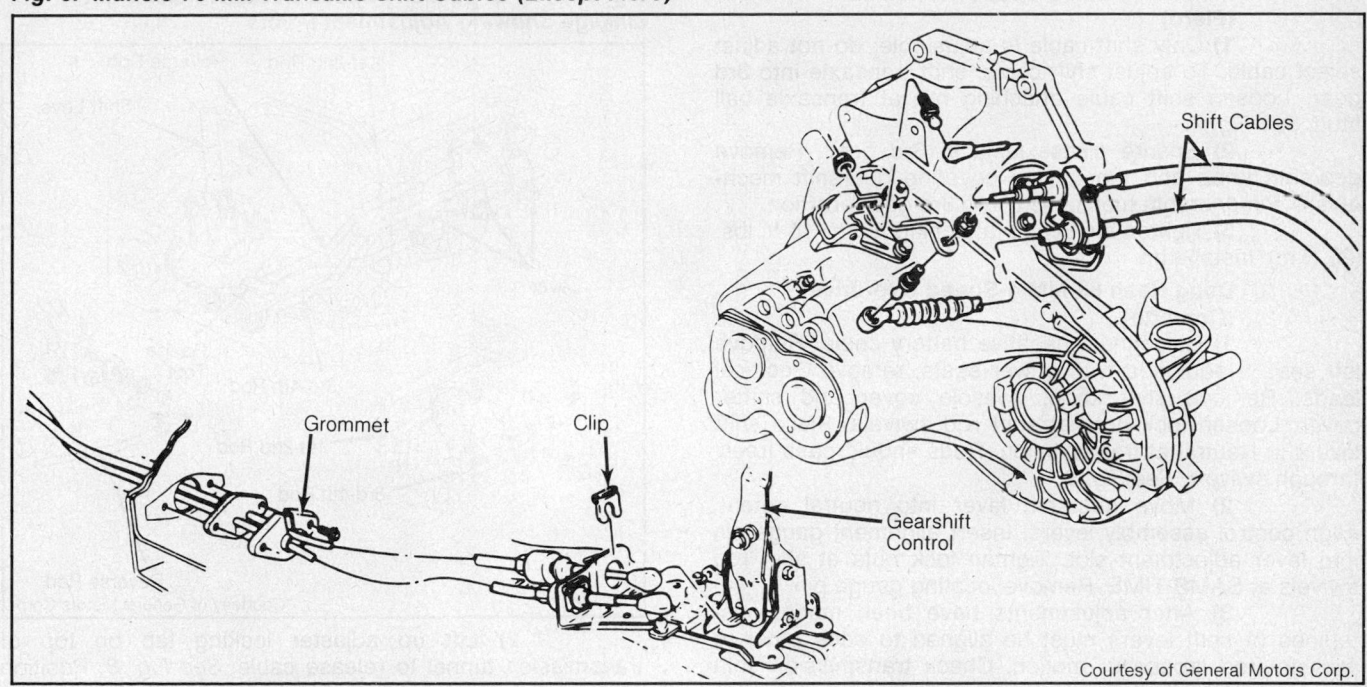

Courtesy of General Motors Corp.

4) Tighten cable attaching nuts at transaxle shift levers. Remove drill bits. Remove lock pin and install with tapered end up. Install console. Ensure transaxle shifts correctly.

Isuzu 76 MM 5-Speed Transaxle (Fiero)

1) Disconnect negative battery cable. Place transaxle in 1st gear. Loosen cable attaching nuts at transaxle shift levers. See Fig. 5.

2) Remove center console for access to gearshift lever mechanism. Holding gearshift lever against left hand stop in 1st gear, install alignment pins.

3) Remove free play from transaxle by rotating lever "B" in direction of arrow while tightening cable attachment nut to 20 ft. lbs. (27 N.m). DO NOT allow shift lever to move when tightening nut. See Fig. 5, View "A".

4) Tighten cable "A" attaching nut to 20 ft. lbs. (27 N.m). Lever "A" does not have to be rotated. Ensure reverse inhibit cam is against roller. Align if necessary.

5) Remove alignment pins. Install console. When moving gearshift lever from 1st to 2nd gear, or 2nd to 1st gear, cable "B" should not move.

Muncie 76 MM 5-Speed Transaxle (Except Fiero)

No adjustments are necessary for shift cables. See Fig. 6.

Fig. 7: Muncie 76 MM Transaxle Shift Cables (Fiero)

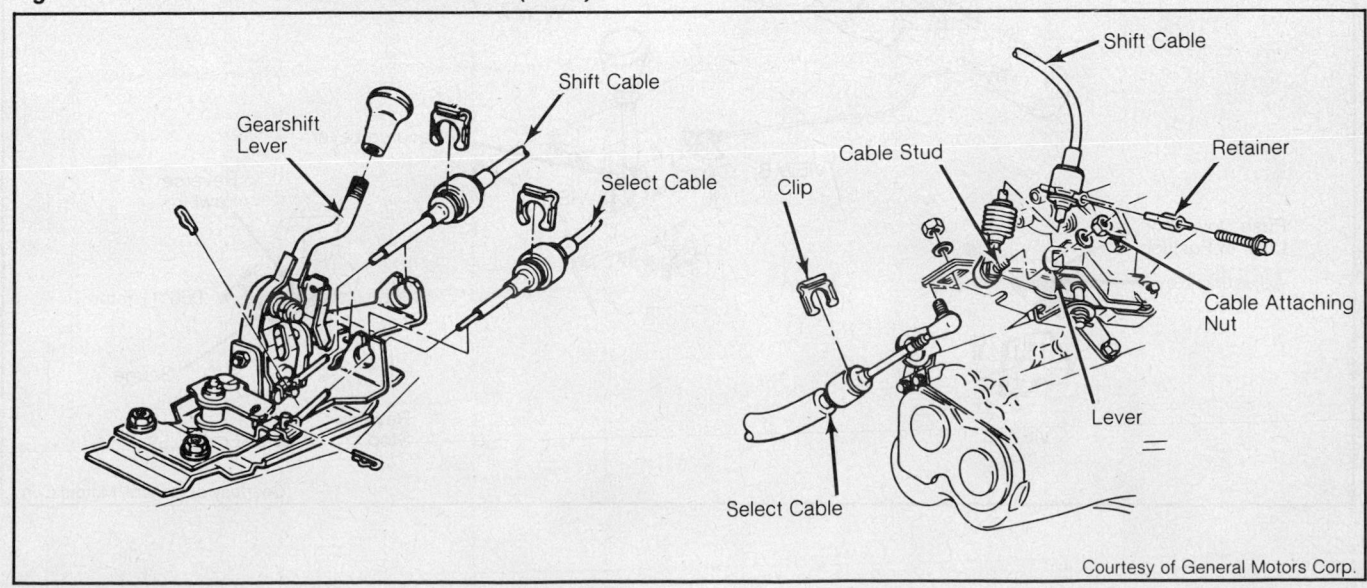

Courtesy of General Motors Corp.

Manual Transmission Servicing

GENERAL MOTORS (Cont.)

Muncie 76 MM 5-Speed Transaxle (Fiero)

1) Only shift cable is adjustable; do not adjust select cable. To adjust shift cable, shift transaxle into 3rd gear. Loosen shift cable attaching nut at transaxle ball stud. *See Fig. 7.*

2) Ensure transaxle is in 3rd gear. Remove gearshift knob and trim plates covering gearshift mechanism. Pin gearshift mechanism into 3rd gear position.

3) Tighten shift cable attaching nut to 18 ft. lbs. (25 N.m). Install trim.

Doug Nash 83 MM 4-Speed Overdrive (Corvette)

1) Disconnect negative battery cable. Remove left seat. If equipped with power seats, remove electrical leads. Remove shift knob, console cover and shifter cover. Loosen lock nuts at shift rod swivels. Place shift levers in Neutral at transmission. Rods should pass freely through swivels. *See Fig. 9.*

2) Move gearshift lever into neutral detent. Align control assembly levers. Insert alignment gauge pin into lever adjustment slot. Tighten lock nuts at shift rod swivels at SAME TIME. Remove locating gauge pin.

3) After adjustments have been made, centerlines of shift levers must be aligned to each other to provide free crossover motion. Check transmission shift operation. Readjust as necessary. Reinstall interior in vehicle.

PARK LOCK CABLE

Doug Nash 83 MM 4-Speed Overdrive (Corvette)

1) Disconnect negative battery cable. Remove left seat. If equipped with power seats, remove electrical leads. Remove shift knob, console cover and shifter cover.

Fig. 9: View of 83 MM 4-Speed Overdrive Gearshift Linkage Showing Adjustment Points

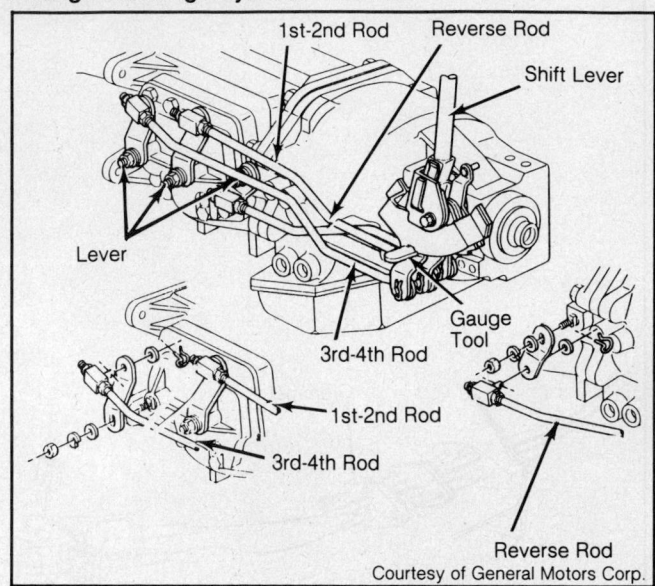

Courtesy of General Motors Corp.

2) Lift up adjuster locking tab on top of transmission tunnel to release cable. *See Fig. 8.* Position steering column lock lever in lock position. Shift transmission into Reverse gear.

3) Insert a .060" (1.5 mm) gauge against the lever stop, and pull reverse lever until reverse pawl contacts gauge. Push down on adjusting tab to set cable. Remove gauge and pull back on shifter lever. Check reverse pawl hits stop and locks shifter in reverse.

Fig. 8: Adjusting Corvette Park Lock Cable

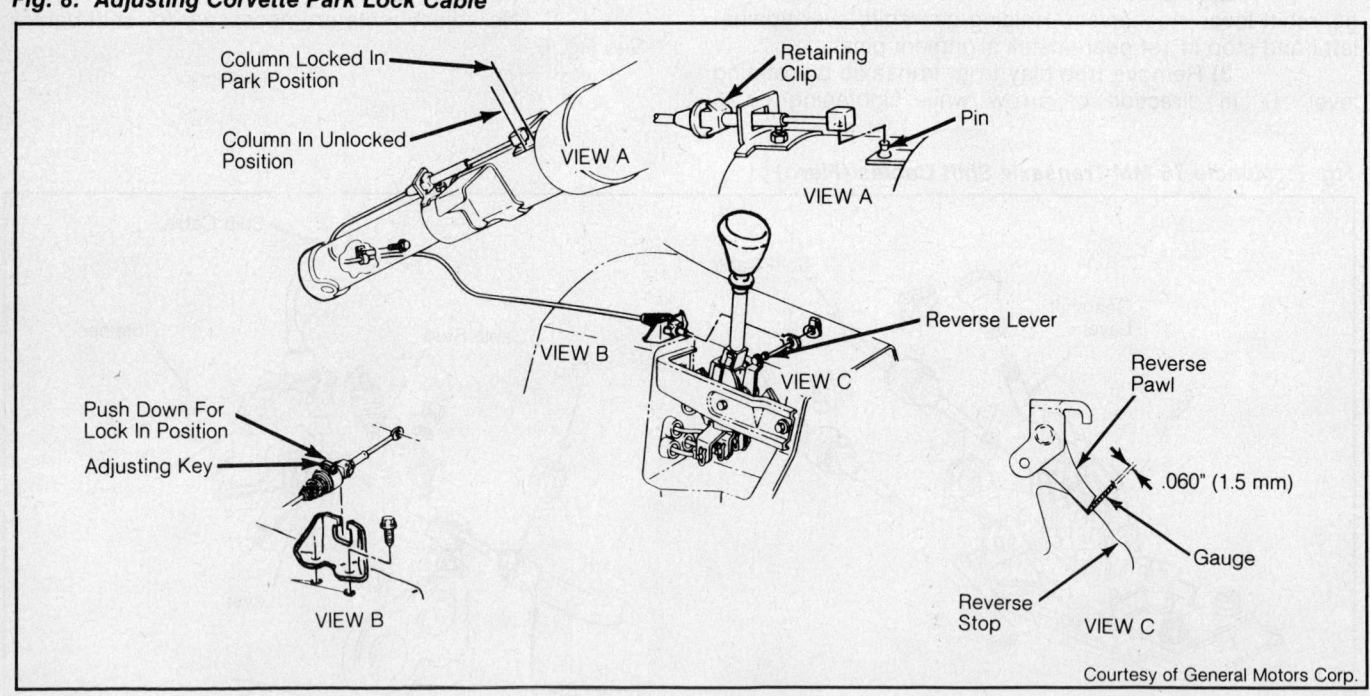

Courtesy of General Motors Corp.

LATEST CHANGES & CORRECTIONS

CONTENTS

Latest Changes & Corrections

FOR 1988 & EARLIER MODELS

NOTE: Latest Changes and Corrections represents a collection of last minute information that arrived too late to be included in the regular data. This section also consists of relevant technical service bulletins, and prior year information received since the last edition.

It may be useful to read through this section, find any changes or helpful information, and then go to the appropriate books and make the changes. Then, when working on a vehicle, the correct information will already be in the book and it won't be necessary to go through this section again.

ENGINES
SECTION 6

CHRYSLER MOTORS

▷1 *1986 & 1987 CHRYSLER MOTORS 2.2L & 2.5L ENGINE: REVISED VALVE GUIDE SERVICING* – In the 1986 and 1987 Chrysler 2.2L and 2.5L engine overhaul articles, a valve guide replacement procedure is described. On 1986 and later engines, the cylinder head should be REPLACED if the valve guides cannot be cleaned using an .031" (.81 mm) reamer. Please make this revision in the following publications.

DOMESTIC CARS, TUNE-UP, MECHANICAL, SERVICE & REPAIR manual and ENGINES, CLUTCH & DRIVE AXLE SERVICE & REPAIR SUPPLEMENT.
- 1986 – page 6-44.
- 1987 – page 6-47.

▷2 *1986 & 1987 CHRYSLER MOTORS 2.2L & 2.5L ENGINE: CAMSHAFT END PLAY* – In the 1986 and 1987 DOMESTIC CARS TUNE-UP, MECHANICAL, SERVICE & REPAIR manuals, camshaft maximum end play is listed as .006" (.15 mm). Correct end play should be .005-.013" (.13-.33 mm). Please make this revision in the following publications.

DOMESTIC CARS, TUNE-UP, MECHANICAL, SERVICE & REPAIR manual and ENGINES, CLUTCH & DRIVE AXLE SERVICE & REPAIR SUPPLEMENT.
- 1986 – page 6-44.
- 1987 – page 6-46.

▷3 *1986 & 1987 CHRYSLER MOTORS 2.2L & 2.5L ENGINE: BALANCE SHAFT CHAIN TENSION* – In 1986 and 1987 DOMESTIC CARS TUNE-UP, MECHANICAL, SERVICE & REPAIR manuals, add the following procedure for adjusting balance shaft chain tension.

1) Install chain tensioner with mounting bolts loose. Install Tension Gauge (C-4916) between tensioner and chain. Shim stock with thickness of .039" (.99 mm) and 2.57" (69.8 mm) long can be used in place of tension gauge.

2) Push tension gauge or shim stock and tensioner against chain. Apply firm pressure directly behind adjustment slot to tighten chain slack. Tighten top tensioner bolt, then bottom pivot bolt to specification with pressure applied.

3) Remove tension gauge or shim stock. Install chain guide. Ensure chain guide aligns with gear cover slot. Install guide retaining bolt. Tighten to specification.

▷4 *1986 & 1987 CHRYSLER MOTORS 2.2L & 2.5L ENGINE: CONNECTING ROD NUT TORQUE* – In 1986 and 1987 DOMESTIC CARS TUNE-UP, MECHANICAL, SERVICE & REPAIR manuals, connecting rod nut torque in the engine overhaul article is listed as 40 ft. lbs. (54 N.m). The torque should be 40 ft. lbs. (54 N.m) PLUS 1/4 TURN. Information should be revised in following publications.

DOMESTIC CARS, TUNE-UP, MECHANICAL, SERVICE & REPAIR manual and ENGINE, CLUTCH & DRIVE AXLE SERVICE & REPAIR SUPPLEMENT.
- 1986 – page 6-49.
- 1987 – page 6-52.

▷5 *1987 CHRYSLER MOTORS 2.2L & 2.5L ENGINE: BEARING CLEARANCES* – In 1987 DOMESTIC CARS TUNE-UP, MECHANICAL, SERVICE & REPAIR manual, bearing clearances on page 6-52 should be as follows:
Main Bearing Clearances
 Non-turbo – .0003-.0031" (.008-.079 mm).
 Turbo – .0004-.0023" (.010-.058 mm).
Rod Bearing Clearance
 Non-turbo – .0008-.0034" (.020-.086 mm).
 Turbo – .0008-.0031" (.020-.079 mm).
This information should also be changed on page 6-52 of the 1987 ENGINE, CLUTCH & DRIVE AXLE SERVICE & REPAIR SUPPLEMENT.

FORD MOTOR CO.

▷6 *1984-85 FORD MOTOR CO. 1.6L ENGINE: REVISED CYLINDER HEAD INSTALLATION PROCEDURE* – Please revise the engine overhaul article. Step **2)** of the cylinder head installation procedure should read as follows.

2) Turn camshaft until keyway is at 6 o'clock position. Turn crankshaft to position No. 1 piston at TDC. Install timing belt. DO NOT turn camshaft or crankshaft until after timing gears and belt are installed.
This procedure is found in the following publications.

DOMESTIC CARS, TUNE-UP, MECHANICAL, SERVICE & REPAIR manual and ENGINE, CLUTCH & DRIVE AXLE SERVICE & REPAIR SUPPLEMENT.
- Page 6-73 in 1984 and 1985.

▷7 *1986-87 FORD MOTOR CO. 1.9L ENGINE: REVISED CYLINDER HEAD INSTALLATION PROCEDURE* – Please revise the engine overhaul article. Step **2)** of the cylinder head installation procedure should be replaced with the following paragraph.

2) Turn camshaft until keyway is at 6 o'clock position. Turn crankshaft to position No. 1 piston at TDC. Install timing belt. DO NOT turn camshaft or crankshaft until after timing gears and belt are installed.
This procedure is found in the following publications:

DOMESTIC CARS, TUNE-UP, MECHANICAL, SERVICE & REPAIR manual and ENGINE, CLUTCH & DRIVE AXLE SERVICE & REPAIR SUPPLEMENT.
- 1986 – page 6-61.
- 1987 – page 6-64.

8 ▷ *1986-87 FORD MOTOR CO. 1.9L ENGINE: REVISED CONNECTING ROD JOURNAL SPECIFICATION* – The connecting rod journal diameter specification has been revised. The old specification of 1.854-1.862" (47.89-47.91 mm) should be changed to 1.7287-1.7279" (43.909-43.889 mm). This specification is found in the following publications.

DOMESTIC CARS, TUNE-UP, MECHANICAL, SERVICE & REPAIR and ENGINES, CLUTCH & DRIVE AXLE SERVICE & REPAIR SUPPLEMENT.
- 1986 – page 6-68.
- 1987 – page 6-71.

9 ▷ *1986 & 1987 FORD MOTOR CO. 1.9L ENGINE: CHECKING CYLINDER HEAD SQUISH HEIGHT* – On all 1.9L engines, the cylinder head-to-piston squish height must be checked BEFORE installing the cylinder head. The inspection procedure is included for the 1.9L engine on page 6-51 of the 1988 DOMESTIC CARS TUNE-UP, MECHANICAL SERVICE & REPAIR manual. The same inspection procedure must also be used on 1986 and 1987 engines.

GENERAL MOTORS

10 ▷ *1986 LATEST CHANGES & CORRECTIONS: MANUAL REVISION* – Item No. 44 in the 1986 DOMESTIC CARS TUNE-UP, MECHANICAL, SERVICE & REPAIR manual stated that cylinder head bolt specification on page 6-252 in 1985 manual was wrong. The specification in the 1985 manual is correct as stated: 125 ft. lbs. (170 N.m).

11 ▷ *1985-88 GENERAL MOTORS 2.5L ENGINE (6000, GRAND AM AND FIERO): CAMSHAFT LOBE LIFT* – Camshaft lobe lift specification has been revised for 1985-88 engines. Lobe lift should be .232" (5.8882 mm).

12 ▷ *1987 GENERAL MOTORS 2.5L ENGINE (VIN R & U): EXHAUST MANIFOLD TIGHTENING SEQUENCE* – On page 6-165 of the 1987 DOMESTIC CARS TUNE-UP, MECHANICAL SERVICE & REPAIR manual, the exhaust manifold tightening sequence is revised. Replace original *Fig. 2* with new *Fig. 2* which follows. This information should also be changed in the 1987 ENGINE, CLUTCH & DRIVE AXLE SERVICE & REPAIR SUPPLEMENT on page 6-165.

Fig. 2: Exhaust Manifold Tightening Sequence

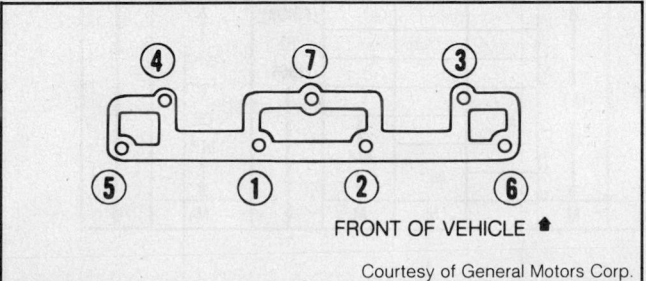

FRONT OF VEHICLE ⬆

Courtesy of General Motors Corp.

13 ▷ *1985-87 GENERAL MOTORS 3.8L ENGINE (VIN A, E, 3, 7, 9): CONNECTING ROD INSTALLATION* – On the left bank of cylinders, the chamfered end of the connecting rod cap should face the FRONT the engine. This information is printed incorrectly in *Fig. 6* of the engine overhaul article. The figure is located in the following publications:

DOMESTIC CARS TUNE-UP, MECHANICAL SERVICE & REPAIR manual and ENGINE, CLUTCH & DRIVE AXLE SERVICE & REPAIR SUPPLEMENT.
- 1985-86 – page 6-205.
- 1987 – page 6-197.

14 ▷ *1986-87 GENERAL MOTORS 4.1L ENGINE: CYLINDER HEAD TIGHTENING SPECIFICATION* – There is a revision to the 1986-87 engine overhaul article. A 3rd step should be added to the cylinder head tightening sequence listed in the tightening specification table. In the 3rd step, cylinder head bolts No. 1, 3 & 4 ONLY should be tightened to 90 ft. lbs. (120 N.m). This table is found in the following publications.

DOMESTIC CARS, TUNE-UP, MECHANICAL, SERVICE & REPAIR and ENGINES, CLUTCH & DRIVE AXLE SERVICE & REPAIR SUPPLEMENT.
- 1986 – page 6-220.
- 1987 – page 6-213.

STEERING SECTION 12

FORD MOTOR CO.

15 ▷ *1987 FORD INTEGRAL RACK & PINION STEERING GEAR: RACK YOKE PLUG PRELOAD* – On page 12-53 of the 1987 DOMESTIC CARS TUNE-UP, MECHANICAL SERVICE & REPAIR manual, please change step **2)** of the RACK YOKE PLUG PRELOAD adjustment to read as follows:

2) Position adapter and torque wrench on input shaft splines. Loosen yoke plug lock nut with a 3/4" drive socket wrench. With rack at center of travel, tighten yoke plug to 45-50 INCH lbs. (5.1-5.7 N.m). Back off yoke plug about 45 degrees, until initial torque to rotate input shaft is reached.

16 ▷ *1985-87 POWER STEERING GENERAL SERVICING: BELT TENSION* – Please revise the specifications in the power steering belt tension table as follows:

TENSION IN LBS. (Kg) USING STRAND TENSION GAUGE

Application	New Belt	Used Belt
American Motors		
"V" Belts	140 (63)	103 (47)
Serpentine Belts	190 (86)	150 (68)
Chrysler Motors		
FWD	95 (43)	70 (32)
RWD		
w/Air Pump	120 (54)	60 (27)
w/O Air Pump	50 (23)	40 (18)
Ford Motor Co.		
1.9L	73 (33)	50 (23)
2.3L OHC	170 (77)	150 (68)
2.3L HSC	140 (63)	120 (54)

Latest Changes & Corrections

FOR 1988 & EARLIER MODELS (Cont.)

TENSION IN LBS. (Kg) USING STRAND
TENSION GAUGE (Cont.)

Application	New Belt	Used Belt
Ford Motor Co. (Cont.)		
3.8L	170 (77)	150 (68)
5.0L	110 (50)	
H.D.	140 (63)	
2-Sp. Belt	170 (77)	150 (68)
5.8L	170 (77)	150 (68)
General Motors		
1.6L		
Chevrolet Nova	125 (57)	80 (36)
All Others	135 (61)	70 (32)
2.0L	135 (61)	70 (32)
1.8L & 2.5L	165 (75)	100 (45)
2.8L, 3.0L, 3.1L		
3.8L, 4.1L & 4.5L	135 (61)	73 (33)
5.0L	125 (57)	75 (34)
5.7L	130 (59)	

This table may be found in the following publications.
DOMESTIC CARS TUNE-UP, MECHANICAL SERVICE & REPAIR manual and ENGINE, CLUTCH & DRIVE AXLE SERVICE & REPAIR SUPPLEMENT

- 1985 – page 12-39.
- 1986 – page 12-49.
- 1987 – page 12-50.

TRANSMISSION SERVICING SECTION 13

FORD MOTOR CO.

17▷ *1964-88 FORD MOTOR CO. VEHICLES TRANSMISSION FLUID USAGE* – As of 1988, all Ford automatic transmissions use the new MERCON fluid. Use chart at bottom of page to determine correct fluid application.

GENERAL MOTORS

18▷ *1985-87 THM 440-T4: OIL FILTER SEAL* – Some THM 440-T4 transaxles use a seal assembly instead of an "O" ring at the transaxle oil filter. This seal assembly MUST BE replaced during a transmission filter service. Seal assembly can be removed using a seal puller.

Ford Motor Co. Automatic Transmission Fluid Usage Chart

Trans. Type / Model Year	JATCO for Courier	JATCO for Pass. Car	FMX	C3	C4	C5	C6	AOD	ATX	ZF	AXOD	A4LD	Other Auto. Trans.	MTX-I (4-Speed) and MTX-111 (5-Speed)	Std. Man. Trans.
1964															
1965															
1966															
1967															
1968															
1969													USE TYPE "F" FOR OTHER AUTO. TRANS. NOT LISTED HERE AND BUILT PRIOR TO 1964		STD. TRANS. LUB. ‡
1970															
1971					TYPE "F"		TYPE "F"								
1972															
1973															
1974	TYPE "F"		TYPE "F"	TYPE "F"											
1975															
1976															
1977		M*		TYPE "F"											
1978															
1979															
1980					M*										
1981				M*				M*						TYPE "F" OR M*	
1982						M*	M*								
1983				M*											
1984					M*		M*	M*							
1985									M*		M*				
1986										M*	M*				
1987															
1988				M	M	M		M	M			M			

M – MERCON.
* – Where asterisk is shown, existing DEXRON II inventory may be used. New purchases for this application must be MERCON.
‡ – Use MERCON in M50D manual transmissions in subfreezing temperatures to improve cold shift effort. The Borg-Warner T5 manual transmission can use MERCON. The Merkur XR4Ti transmission (Hummer 5-speed) uses fluid meeting Ford Specification ESD-M2175-A or E5RY-19C547-A.

GENERAL INDEX

CONTENTS

AUTOMOBILE MANUFACTURERS   Page

1988 Chrysler Motors Index

1988 Eagle Premier Index

1988 Ford Motor Co. Index

1988 Ford Motor Co. Index

1988 Ford Motor Co. Index

A

B

C

1988 General Motors Index

1988 General Motors Index

1988 General Motors Index

1988 General Motors Index

1988 General Motors Index

English-Metric Conversion Chart

CONVERSION FACTORS

Unit	To	Unit	Multiply By
LENGTH			
Millimeters		Inches	.03937
Inches		Millimeters	25.4
Meters		Feet	3.28084
Feet		Meters	.3048
Kilometers		Miles	.62137
Miles		Kilometers	1.60935
AREA			
Square Centimeters		Square Inches	.155
Square Inches		Square Centimeters	6.45159
VOLUME			
Cubic Centimeters		Cubic Inches	.06103
Cubic Inches		Cubic Centimeters	16.38703
Liters		Cubic Inches	61.025
Cubic Inches		Liters	.01639
Liters		Quarts	1.05672
Quarts		Liters	.94633
Liters		Pints	2.11344
Pints		Liters	.47317
Liters		Ounces	33.81497
Ounces		Liters	.02957

Unit	To	Unit	Multiply By
WEIGHT			
Grams		Ounces	.03527
Ounces		Grams	28.34953
Kilograms		Pounds	2.20462
Pounds		Kilograms	.45359
WORK			
Centimeter Kilograms		Inch Pounds	.8676
Inch Pounds		Centimeter Kilograms	1.15262
Meter Kilograms		Foot Pounds	7.23301
Foot Pounds		Newton Meters	1.3558
PRESSURE			
Kilograms/Sq. Centimeter		Pounds/Sq. Inch	14.22334
Pounds/Sq. Inch		Kilograms/Sq. Centimeter	.07031
Bar		Pounds/Sq. Inch	14.504
Pounds/Sq. Inch		Bar	.06895
Atmosphere		Pounds/Sq. Inch	14.696
Pounds/Sq. Inch		Atmosphere	.06805
TEMPERATURE			
Centigrade Degrees		Fahrenheit Degrees	$(C° \times 9/5) + 32$
Fahrenheit Degrees		Centigrade Degrees	$(F° - 32) \times 5/9$

Inches	Decimals	MM	Inches	Decimals	MM
1/64	.016	.397	33/64	.516	13.097
1/32	.031	.794	17/32	.531	13.494
3/64	.047	1.191	35/64	.547	13.891
1/16	.063	1.588	9/16	.563	14.288
5/64	.078	1.984	37/64	.578	14.684
3/32	.094	2.381	19/32	.594	15.081
7/64	.109	2.778	39/64	.609	15.478
1/8	.125	3.175	5/8	.625	15.875
9/64	.141	3.572	41/64	.641	16.272
5/32	.156	3.969	21/32	.656	16.669
11/64	.172	4.366	43/64	.672	17.066
3/16	.188	4.763	11/16	.687	17.463
13/64	.203	5.159	45/64	.703	17.859
7/32	.219	5.556	23/32	.719	18.256
15/64	.234	5.953	47/64	.734	18.653
1/4	.250	6.350	3/4	.750	19.050
17/64	.266	6.747	49/64	.766	19.447
9/32	.281	7.144	25/32	.781	19.844
19/64	.297	7.541	51/64	.797	20.241
5/16	3.13	7.938	13/16	.813	20.638
21/64	.328	8.334	53/64	.828	21.034
11/32	.344	8.731	27/32	.844	21.431
23/64	.359	9.128	55/64	.859	21.828
3/8	.375	9.525	7/8	.875	22.225
25/64	.391	9.922	57/64	.891	22.622
13/32	.406	10.319	29/32	.906	23.019
27/64	.422	10.716	59/64	.922	23.416
7/16	.438	11.113	15/16	.938	23.813
29/64	.453	11.509	61/64	.953	24.209
15/32	.469	11.906	31/32	.969	24.606
31/64	.484	12.303	63/64	.984	25.003
1/2	.500	12.700			

METRIC CONVERSIONS

Metric conversions are making life more difficult for the mechanic. In addition to doubling the number of tools required, metric-dimensioned nuts and bolts are used alongside English components in many new vehicles. The mechanic has to decide which tool to use, slowing down the job. The tool problem can be solved by trial and error, but some metric conversions aren't so simple.

Converting temperature, lengths or volumes requires a calculator and conversion charts, or else a very nimble mind. Conversion charts are only part of the answer though, because they don't help you "think" metric, or "visualize" what you are converting. The following examples are intended to help you "see" metric sizes:

LENGTH

Meters are the standard unit of length in the metric system. The smaller units are 10ths (decimeter), 100ths (centimeter), and 1000ths (millimeter) of a meter. These common examples might help you to visualize the metric units:

* A meter is slightly longer than a yard (about 40 inches).
* An aspirin tablet is about one centimeter across (.4 inches).
* A millimeter is about the thickness of a dime.

VOLUME

Cubic meters and centimeters are used to measure volume, just as we normally think of cubic feet and inches. Liquid volume measurements include the liter and milliliter, like the English quarts or ounces.

* One teaspoon is about 5 cubic centimeters.
* A liter is about one quart.
* A liter is about 61 cubic inches.

WEIGHT

The metric weight system is based on the gram, with the most common unit being the kilogram (1000 grams). Our comparable units are ounces and pounds:

* A kilogram is about 2.2 pounds.
* An ounce is about 28 grams.

TORQUE

Torque is somewhat complicated. The term describes the amount of effort exerted to turn something. A chosen unit of weight or force is applied to a lever of standard length. The resulting leverage is called torque. In our standard system, we use the weight of one pound applied to a lever a foot long–resulting in the unit called a foot-pound. A smaller unit is the inch-pound (the lever is one inch long). Metric units include the meter kilogram (lever one meter long with a kilogram of weight applied) and the Newton-meter (lever one meter long with force of one Newton applied). Some conversions are:

* A meter kilogram is about 7.2 foot pounds.
* A Newton-meter is about 1.4 foot pounds.
* A centimeter kilogram (cmkg) is equal to .9 inch pounds.

PRESSURE

Pressure is another complicated measurement. Pressure is described as a force or weight applied to a given area. Our common unit is pounds per square inch. Metric units can be expressed in several ways. One is the kilogram per square centimeter (kg/cm^2). Another unit of pressure is the Pascal (force of one Newton on an area of one square meter), which equals about 4 ounces on a square yard. Since this is a very small amount of pressure, we usually see the kiloPascal, or kPa (1000 Pascals). Another common automotive term for pressure is the bar (used by German manufacturers), which equals 10 Pascals. Thoroughly confused? Try the examples below:

* Atmospheric pressure at sea level is about 14.7 psi.
* Atmospheric pressure at sea level is about 1 bar.
* Atmospheric pressure at sea level is about 1 kg/cm^2.
* One pound per square inch is about 7 kPa.

Notes

Notes

Notes

Notes

Notes

Notes

Notes

Notes

Notes

Notes

Notes